A History
of Narrative Film

4

FOURTH EDITION

David A. Cook

EMORY UNIVERSITY

A History
of Narrative Film

W. W. NORTON & COMPANY • New York • London

W. W. Norton & Company has been independent since its founding in 1923, when William Warder Norton and Mary D. Herter Norton first published lectures delivered at the People's Institute, the adult education division of New York City's Cooper Union. The Nortons soon expanded their program beyond the Institute, publishing books by celebrated academics from America and abroad. By mid-century, the two major pillars of Norton's publishing program—trade books and college texts—were firmly established. In the 1950s, the Norton family transferred control of the company to its employees, and today—with a staff of four hundred and a comparable number of trade, college, and professional titles published each year—W. W. Norton & Company stands as the largest and oldest publishing house owned wholly by its employees.

The text of this book is composed in New Caledonia with the display set in Avenir.
Composition and layout by Binghamton Valley Composition
Digital art file manipulation by Jay's Publishers Services
Manufacturing by the Courier Companies—Westford Division

Editor: Peter Simon
Project editor: Thomas Foley
Production manager: Benjamin Reynolds
Manuscript editor: Carol Flechner
Editorial assistants: Rob Bellinger and Nicole Netherton
Book designer: Rubina Yeh

Library of Congress Cataloging-in-Publication Data
Cook, David A.
    A history of narrative film / David A. Cook.—4th ed.
        p. cm.
    Includes bibliographical references and index.
    ISBN 0-393-97868-0

    1. Motion pictures—History.   I. Title: Narrative film.   II. Title.
  PN1993.5.A1C65   2003
    791.43'09—dc22   2003061090
W. W. Norton & Company, Inc., 500 Fifth Avenue, New York, N.Y. 10110
www.wwnorton.com
W. W. Norton & Company Ltd., Castle House, 75 / 76 Wells Street, London W1T 3QT

2 3 4 5 6 7 8 9 0

For Diane,
always

Contents

3   D. W. Griffith and the Development of Narrative Form   51

4   German Cinema of the Weimar Period, 1919–1929   87

14 New Cinemas in Britain and the English-Speaking Commonwealth

15 European Renaissance: West

16   European Renaissance: East   605

17 The Former Soviet Union, 1945–Present

Preface

We spend much of our waking lives surrounded by moving photographic images. They have come to occupy such a central position in our experience that it is unusual to pass even a single day without encountering them for an extended period of time, through either film or television. In short, moving photographic images have become part of the total environment of modern industrial society. Both materially and psychologically, they have a shaping impact on our lives. And yet few people in our society have been taught to understand precisely how they work. Most of us, in fact, have extremely vague notions about how moving images are formed and how they are structured to create the multitude of messages sent out to us by the audiovisual media on an almost continuous basis. If we made an analogy with verbal language, we should be forced to consider ourselves barely literate—able to assimilate the language form without fully comprehending it. We would, of course, be appalled to find ourselves living in a culture whose general verbal literacy level corresponded to that of a three-year-old child. Most persons living in such a culture would, like small children, be easy prey to whoever could manipulate the language. They would be subject to the control of any minority that understood the language from the inside out and could therefore establish an authority of knowledge over them, just as verbally literate adults establish authority over children. Such a situation would be unthinkable in the modern industrial world, of course, and our own culture has made it a priority to educate its children in the institutions of human speech so that they can participate in the community of knowledge that verbal literacy sustains.

Imagine, though, that a new language form came into being at the turn of the twentieth century, an audiovisual language form that first took the shape of cinema and became in time the common currency of modern television. Imagine that because the making of statements in this language depended upon an expensive industrial process, only a handful of elite specialists were trained to use it. Imagine, too, that although public anxiety about the potentially corrupting influence of the new language was constant from its birth, it was *perceived* not as a language at all but as a medium of popular entertainment—that in this guise the language was gradually allowed to colonize us, as if it were the vernacular speech of some conquering foreign power. Finally, imagine waking up one day to discover that we had mistaken language for a mode of dreaming and in the process become massively illiterate in a primary language form, one that had not only surrounded us materially but that, as language forms tend to do, had invaded our minds as well. What would we do if that happened? We could choose to embrace our error and lapse into the anarchic mode of consciousness characteristic of preliterate societies, which might be fun but would most certainly be dangerous in an advanced industrial society. Or we could attempt to instruct ourselves in the language form from the ground up and from the inside out. We could try to learn as much of its history, technology, and aesthetics as possible. We could trace the evolution of its syntactic and semantic forms from their birth through their present stages of development, and try to forecast the shapes they might take in the future. We could, finally, bring the apparatus of sequential logic and critical analysis to bear on the seemingly random structures of the language in order to read them in new and meaningful ways.

This scenario conforms quite accurately, I believe, to our present situation in the modern world. The language of the moving photographic image has become so pervasive in our daily lives that we scarcely notice its presence. And yet it *does* surround us, sending us messages, taking positions, making statements, and constantly redefining our relationship to material reality. We can choose to live in ignorance of its operations and be manipulated by those who presently control it. Or we can teach ourselves to read it, to appreciate its very real and manifold truths, to recognize its equally real and manifold deceptions. As a lifelong student and teacher of language forms, both verbal and audiovisual, I believe that most intelligent and humane persons in our culture will opt for the latter. It is for them that I have written this book.

Preface to the Fourth Edition

The cinema has undergone two major changes in the eight years since the third edition of this book was published. The first is the hegemonic control by American distributors of virtually every film market in the world—the conscious and calculated effect of "globalization." The other is the fact that the majority of films produced in the United States and much of the developed world are previsualized, produced, and post-produced at least partially in the digital domain. In this edition, the dominance of American distributors is duly noted in the treatment of individual national cinemas, and the digitization of the filmmaking process is given a new chapter (21) of its own. This chapter argues that since the mid-1990s digital imaging technology has transformed the making of feature films in the industrialized West—and will soon transform their distribution and exhibition as well—in a way that redefines the very nature of cinema by bringing it closer to the condition of animation. I believe, in fact, that a shift has taken place in film aesthetics in which postproduction has acquired a status equal to production and in which cinema is no longer exclusively the art of the moving photographic image: the replication of the real is giving way to simulation through computer-generated imagery, or CGI.

Digital technology has clearly served to extend and solidify Hollywood's hegemony in the early years of the twenty-first century; it has also produced the potential (at least) to fracture it. A collateral effect of the cinema's digitization is the ability to produce feature-length films at relatively small expense using digital video (DV) cameras and desktop software editing programs like Final Cut Pro. Because these films begin and end as digital files, they can be transferred to DVD and/or distributed on the internet without the mediation of photographic film stock at any stage of the process. (Hollywood blockbusters can also be digitized, as they routinely are for transfer to DVD, but they are initially distributed as analog media—i.e., as 35mm prints for projection in brick-and-mortar theaters.) Thus, the reshaping of cinema as a digital form points in two directions at once: toward global market dominion by CGI-laden Hollywood spectacle, on the one hand, and toward the leveling, democratizing influence of independent DV features on the other. The anxiety with which the Hollywood majors currently view motion-picture file sharing on the internet relates as much to their fear of competition from independent producers as to their fear of copyright infringement and piracy.

In addition to its treatment of CGI, other new features of this edition include substantial sections on French and British cinema of the 1980s and 1990s, extensive material on recent filmmaking in New Zealand and Canada, and a new section on Dogme95. There are new discussions of the Japanese industry during the 1980s and 1990s and the rise of Bollywood cinema in India. Significant new material has also been added on the cinemas of the three Chinas, especially Hong Kong and Taiwan, as well as substantial new sections on Iranian cinema and New Korean Cinema, since these have become increasingly influential around the world.

Another notable change in this edition is its increased attention to exploitation genres. From the new discussion of Hammer Films in Chapter 14, through the new section on Italian exploitation in Chapter 15, to the new treatment of Japanese *roman porno* and horror in Chapter 18, the fourth edition acknowledges the economic and aesthetic importance of the low end of the cinematic scale. Not only is it often the case that a given industry's exploitation product subsidizes its art films, but exploitation films can have a permanent and lasting effect on film style—as in the pervasive influence of the Italian spaghetti Western, British and Italian gothic horror, and Hong Kong action genres.

Like art films, exploitation films have been recently saved from physical extinction by a remarkable byproduct of the digital revolution—the technology of DVD, which has done more to preserve the heritage of international cinema, high and low, than any medium that preceded it. Translated into digital files, films can be digitally manipulated to restore their original color or black-and-white imagery; their sound can be remixed; and missing elements from their negatives can be repaired. Played back (or projected) on a reasonably good system, restored and / or remastered films on DVD can look and sound better than they did in most theaters at the time of their release.

Thus, through DVD, digital technology has made this a particularly rich time for the study of film history. Ironically, and perhaps appropriately, this same technology portends the end of the photographic cinema in whose preservation it excels. The ability to generate photorealistic images directly in the computer displaces live-action photography as the only basic material of the cinema; conversely, live-action footage, when scanned into a computer and digitized, becomes just another set of pixels to be manipulated together with computer-generated ones. It is this circumstance that led Lev Manovich, in a 1997 article entitled "What Is Digital Cinema?" to predict that cinema would soon become "a particular case of animation which uses live action footage as one of its many elements."

But the more things change, the more they stay the same. The cinema is still fundamentally a narrative art whose major purpose is the telling of stories; and storytelling precedes every other form of organized human behavior except the burial of the dead. Its roots lie deep in our consciousness and preconsciousness, and its importance to us will not go away. Everyone acknowledges that the *Lord of the Rings* trilogy is great cinema, and director Peter Jackson is the first to admit that the films could never have existed without CGI. But, less obviously, neither could *Gladiator, Pearl Harbor, Moulin Rouge,* and dozens of similar films that, whatever their merits as art, possess powerful narrative arcs. These are films that use CGI to enhance and transform the narrative language of cinema while telling simple stories of valor and heroism, war and peace, love and loss—just like *Cabiria, The Birth of a Nation,* and *Broken Blossoms* did before them. We value those older films for the same reason that we should value the newer ones—for meeting difficult challenges of narrative expression at a time when the rules of their respective media were young. But we watch them today for another reason: they are still somehow relevant to our experience, either as we actually live it or as we imagine / desire it to be. CGI is finally just another way of telling stories, and that will probably not change much, however far the rules by which it operates may grow from the photochemical process we call "film."

Acknowledgments

The revision of this book for its fourth edition began with an invaluably helpful planning meeting in Santa Monica, California, in July 2001, in which Dana Polan of USC, Pete Simon of W. W. Norton & Company, and I discussed at length the strengths and weaknesses of the existing text and made decisions that would eventually cast it in new form. The revisions themselves were done between the fall of 2001 and the summer of 2003, and, as always, I incurred numerous intellectual debts in the process. Limits of time and space notwithstanding, I would like to thank the five reviewers of the third edition: Tom Stempel of Los Angeles City College; Christopher Sharrett of Seton Hall University; Catherine Lupton of the University of Surrey Roehampton; Richard Neupert of the University of Georgia; and Dana Polan. I also want to thank three Emory colleagues who read and corrected portions of the revised text: Wenli Wang of Emory's Goizueta School of Business, who gave me valuable insights into the cinema of mainland China; James Steffen of Emory's Institute for the Liberal Arts, who contributed information on Transcaucasian cinema and helped to regularize the spelling of Georgian and Armenian proper names; and Galina Aksenova, a Visiting Lecturer in Russian Culture, who shared with me her detailed knowledge of Soviet film history and contemporary Russian cinema. Thanks must also go to the several Film Studies graduate students who worked with me as research assistants during various stages of the revision process: Laurel Brooks, Tara Key, Irene Taylor, Matt Kiesner, and Aubry D'Arminio. Aubry's revision of the Selective Bibliography was extensive enough to earn her a byline as its coauthor (not forgetting that much of the groundwork was laid in the third edition by James Steffen and David Pratt). For helping to reconfigure the book's illustration program and preparing the online test files, I give special thanks to Evan Lieberman, whose status as both practicing filmmaker and academic film scholar make him uniquely suited to the task.

Nearly all of Chapter 21, "Hollywood Enters the Digital Domain," was written during a semester's sabbatical leave, for which I have to thank the Dean of Emory College, Robert A. Paul. That chapter was vetted at various points through several readers, the most important of whom was Evan Liebermann, who gave me professional advice about photographic versus digital color processes, and James True, an Atlanta-based graphics designer who fact-checked all of my descriptions of computer-graphics software against his own extensive knowledge of these systems.

The ability to screen 35mm films on campus in state-of-the-art facilities has been a valuable research tool for this revision. In that regard, I need to thank two successive deans of Emory College, Steve Sanderson and Robert Paul, for their sustained support of the Emory Cinematheque, a joint effort by the College and the Department of Film Studies begun in 1999 to provide the Atlanta community with programs of important international films throughout the academic year in a 35/70mm repertory cinema environment. For nurturing that environment and equipping it with state-of-the-art technology, thanks are due to Senior Associate Dean of the College Rosemary Magee. The richness of film culture at Emory has also been enhanced by the regular visits of archivist David Shepard, who hosts and programs our annual "Silent Heaven" series; our regular 35mm series of classical Japanese films with the Japanese Consulate; our annual 35mm series of recent and classical Indian films with the High Museum of Art and the Georgia-Indo American Chamber of Commerce; our yearly 35mm "Festival of New Italian Cinema" co-sponsored by Cine-città Studios-Rome; and our biannual film series with the Taipei Economic and Cultural Office in Atlanta, which in 2001 donated over 150 feature-film prints to Emory, representing the entire history of Taiwanese cinema.

As ever, I owe thanks to my colleagues in Emory's Department of Film Studies—Matthew Bernstein, Nina Martin, and Karla Oeler—for their many helpful comments on my work and for putting up with me while I produced it. I need also thank our departmental administrative assistant, Annie Hall (her real name), and secretary, Cecelia Shannon, not only for helping me with the revision's myriad clerical chores but for their unstinting kindness toward me in the process.

Finally, I want to thank my editor, Peter Simon at W. W. Norton & Company, whose generous, insightful collaboration has made working on this edition a highly rewarding experience. Among much else, I am indebted to his help (and that of his assistant, Rob Bellinger) in retooling the book's illustrations. Others at Norton I should thank are manuscript editor Carol Flechner and project editor Thom Foley, both of whom have done remarkable jobs in their various ways of ordering a complicated manuscript; Rubina Yeh, who redesigned the text for this edition; Debra Morton Hoyt, art director; Benjamin Reynolds, production manager; Marian Johnson, managing editor; and Nicole Netherton, editorial assistant during the first half of my work on the book.

A Note on Method

For reasons that will become apparent in the course of this book, I believe that the history of film as we have experienced it to date is the history of a narrative form. Many of the greatest films ever made were created by artists seeking to break the constraints of this form as it defined itself at different points in time, and there is much evidence to suggest that since the 1950s the cinema has been moving in an increasingly nonnarrative direction. But the fact remains that the language common to the international cinema from the last decade of the nineteenth century through the present has been narrative in both aspiration and structural form. For this reason, I have excluded documentary cinema, animated cinema, and the experimental avant-garde from consideration in this book except where they have influenced narrative form to a demonstrable and significant extent. This is not to suggest that any of these excluded forms is unimportant, but rather that each is important and distinctive enough to warrant a separate history of its own (several of which, in fact, already exist).

A Note on Dates, Titles, and Stills

Wherever possible, the date given for a film is the year of its theatrical release in its country of origin. Unless otherwise noted (as in the case of intermittent production or delayed release), the reader may assume a lapse of six months between the start of production and the date of release for features. This is important in correlating the history of film with the history of human events (for instance, many American films with the release date of 1942 went into production and were completed before the Japanese attack on Pearl Harbor on December 7, 1941).

As for titles of films in languages other than English, those in French, Italian, Spanish, Portuguese, and German are given in the original language, followed, in parentheses, by a literal English translation (and an alternate English-language release title, if one exists), followed by the date of release. After the initial reference, the original foreign-language title is used, except in the case of a film that is best known in the English-speaking world by its English title (for example, Jean-Luc Godard's *Breathless* [*À bout de souffle*, 1959]). For Scandinavian, Eastern European, Asian, and African languages the convention is reversed: the initial reference is given in English, followed by the original title in parentheses (a transliteration is supplied if the original title is in an alphabet other than our own). All subsequent references use the English title, unless the film is best known here by its foreign-language title (as in the case, for instance, of Akira Kurosawa's *Ikiru* [*Living/To Live*, 1952] and *Yojimbo* [*The Bodyguard*, 1961]). In the case of films for which the original foreign-language title was unavailable, only the English title is given.

The photographs used to illustrate the book represent a combination of production stills and frame enlargements. Since they are taken on the set by professional photographers, production stills yield a higher quality of reproduction; but since they are made initially for the purpose of publicity, they are sometimes "beautified" to the point of distortion. Frame enlargements, on the other hand, are blown up photographically from 16mm prints of the films themselves and, therefore, represent the actual images as composed and shot by the filmmakers. Their quality of reproduction is often lower than that of production stills since several extra steps of photographic transference are involved in printing them, but their correspondence with the film images is exact. Whenever shot sequences have been reproduced for discussion or when lengthy analysis accompanies an individual image or series of images, I have tried to use frame enlargements. When less analytical procedures are involved, I have used production stills. (Many films of the 1950s and most films of the 1960s, 1970s, 1980s, and 1990s were shot in some type of widescreen process, with aspect ratios varying from 2.55:1 to 1.85:1. For reasons of typography and design, some of the stills in this volume have been reproduced in the 1.33:1 aspect ratio of the Academy frame.) Although photographs can never replicate cinema, lacking as they do the essential component of motion, they can be made to represent it. Throughout the book, I have attempted to integrate the stills with the written text in a manner that will provide for maximum delivery of information. The reader is, therefore, encouraged to regard both photographic and verbal information as part of the same critical fabric, although neither, finally, can substitute for the audiovisual information contained in the films themselves.

The illustrations in this book were obtained from the Museum of Modern Art's Film Stills Archive with the following exceptions (and excluding frame enlargements supplied by the author):

The Academy of Motion Picture Arts and Sciences: 10.24.

The British Film Institute: 17.6, 17.7, 17.8, 17.9.

Forrest Ciesol of International Cinema Concepts: 17.18, 17.19, 17.20, 17.21, 17.22, 17.23, 17.24, 17.25, 17.28, 17.31, 17.32, 17.33, 17.34, 17.35, 17.36.

The Library of Congress: 1.11, 1.17, 2.1.

New Line Cinema: 15.69.

The New York Film Festival: 15.72.

New Yorker Films: 15.68.

Jerry Ohlinger's Movie Material Store: Insert illustrations for *Gone with the Wind, Kismet, 2001: A Space Odyssey.*

Superstock International, Inc.: Insert illustration for *She Wore a Yellow Ribbon.*

Unifilm: 19.12, 19.22, 19.31, 19.32.

Photofest: Insert illustration for *Toll of the Sea*

A History
of Narrative Film

Origins

Optical Principles

The beginning of film history is the end of something else: the successive stages of technological development throughout the nineteenth century whereby simple optical devices used for entertainment grew into sophisticated machines that could convincingly represent empirical reality in motion. Both toys and machines were dependent for their illusions upon interactive optical phenomena known as **persistence of vision** and the *phi phenomenon*. The former is a characteristic of human perception, known to the ancient Egyptians but first described scientifically by Peter Mark Roget in 1824, whereby the brain retains images cast upon the retina of the eye for approximately one-twentieth to one-fifth of a second beyond their actual removal from the field of vision. The latter, whose operation was discovered by the Gestalt psychologist Max Wertheimer in 1912, is the phenomenon that causes us to see the individual blades of a rotating fan as a unitary circular form or the different hues of a spinning color wheel as a single, homogeneous color. Together, persistence of vision and the phi phenomenon allow us to see a succession of static images as a single unbroken movement and permit the illusion of continuous motion upon which **cinematography** is based. Persistence of vision prevents us from seeing the dark space between the film frames by causing "flicker fusion" when the frequency with which the projection light is broken approaches fifty times per second; without this effect, our eyes would perceive the alternation of light and dark on the screen as each projected image succeeded the next, as, in fact, was the case in the earliest days of the movies, which became known colloquially as "flickers" or "flicks" for this very reason. The phi phenomenon, also known as the "stroboscopic effect," creates apparent movement from frame to frame at optimal projection speeds of 12 to 24 frames per second (fps). This much is known, but perceptual psychologists still understand very little about the neural and cognitive processes involved in the perception of motion.

The **frames** of a strip of film are a series of individual still photographs that the

1.1 The Thaumatrope.

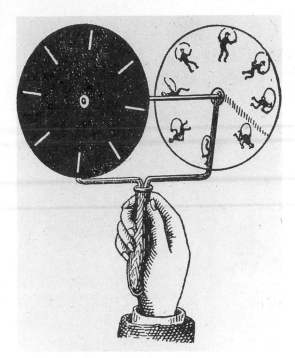

1.2 The Phenakistoscope.

motion-picture camera, as it was perfected by the Edison Laboratories in 1892 and as it exists today, imprints one at a time. The succession of frames recorded in the camera, when projected at the same or a similar speed, creates the illusion of continuous motion essential to the cinema. (Individual frames are actually held longer before the projector's lens than before the camera's, but the movement *between* frames is more rapid in projection, so that the speeds of both instruments remain synchronized.)

Illusion is the operative term here. Most motion-picture cameras today expose individual frames at the rate of twenty-four per second, with an exposure time of about one-forty-eighth of a second per frame (the other forty-eighth of a second allows time for the film to move from one exposure to the next). The illusion of continuous motion can be induced in our brains at rates as low as 12 fps, yet speeds have traditionally been set at about 16 fps for silent film and 24 for sound. On the film strip itself, these frames are separated by thin, unexposed frame lines, but in projection a rotating **shutter** opens and closes to obscure the intervals between frames and to permit each frame to be flashed upon the **screen** twice, thereby eliminating the flicker we would otherwise perceive by their movement. When we "watch" a film in a theater, we actually spend as much as 50 percent of the time in darkness, with the projector's shutter closed and nothing before us on the screen. Thus the continuity of movement and light that seems to be the most palpable quality of the cinema exists only in our brains, making

cinema the first communications medium to be based upon psychoperceptual illusions created by machines.[1] The second, of course, is television.

Persistence of vision and the phi phenomenon were exploited for the purpose of optical entertainment for many years before the invention of photography. A popular child's toy of the early nineteenth century was the Thaumatrope (from the Greek for "magical turning"), a paper disk with strings attached at opposite points on the perimeter so that it could be twirled between finger and thumb. A different image was imprinted on each face, and when the disk was spun the images seemed to merge into a single unified picture (a rider would mount a horse, a parrot enter its cage, etc.). Between 1832 and 1850,

---

1. It might be argued that photography and telephony are no less illusory. But when we look at a photograph, there *is* a materially real, light-encoded representation of reality before us, and when we use the telephone, there *is* a materially real human voice behind the electronic pulses transmitting it through the wire. When we watch a film in a theater, on the other hand, the movement we perceive on the screen does not exist materially on the screen but solely in our heads. The only empirically real movement in the "movies" is the motion of the film strip through the camera and projector. Television compounds this illusion by dematerializing the screen and relocating it *inside* our heads, so that neither movement nor screen is materially "there" before us.

and 1881 by the replacement of collodion wet plates with gelatine dry plates and by the introduction of "series photography" by the Anglo-American photographer Eadweard Muybridge (1830–1904).[3]

Series Photography

In 1872 Muybridge was hired by Leland Stanford (1824–1893), a former California governor and wealthy businessman, to prove that at some point in its gallop a racehorse lifts all four hooves off the ground (a convention of nineteenth-century graphic illustration required running horses to always be pictured with at least one foot on the ground). After several years of abortive experiments, Muybridge accomplished this in the summer of 1877 by setting up a battery of twelve electrically operated cameras (later studies used twenty-four) along a Sacramento racetrack and stretching wires across it that would trip the cameras' shutters. As a horse came down the track, its hooves tripped each shutter individually and

1.3 The Zoetrope.

hundreds of optical toys were manufactured that used rotating "phase drawings" of things in motion to produce a crude form of animation. Drawings representing successive phases of an action would be mounted on a disk or cylinder and rotated in conjunction with some type of shutter apparatus (usually a series of slots in the disk or cylinder itself) to produce the illusion of motion. Joseph Plateau's Phenakistoscope (from the Greek for "deceitful view"—1832) and George Horner's Zoetrope ("live turning"—1834) were among the most popular of these toys, which reached increasing stages of refinement as the century progressed. When still photography was invented by Louis Jacques-Mandé Daguerre (1789–1851) in 1839[2] and perfected throughout the next decade, it was a relatively simple step to replace the phase drawings in the motion-simulation devices with individually posed "phase photographs," as Plateau began to do in 1849. At this point, live action could be *simulated photographically*, but not *recorded spontaneously and simultaneously as it occurred*. This required the drastic reduction in photographic **exposure** time from fifteen minutes to one one-thousandth of a second that was achieved between 1876

2. The very first photographs were actually made by Daguerre's business associate Joseph Nicéphore Niepce (1765–1833) in 1826 using a camera obscura. This device, whose name literally means "dark room," was invented during the Renaissance and consisted of a sealed chamber or box with a tiny hole in one wall. The hole acted as a lens to focus light from the outside (and therefore the image of the objects before the hole) onto the opposite wall. This is the simple optical principle on which all photography is based. Niepce added the final step by fixing the image thus projected on a pewter plate covered with chemical emulsions. But the exposure time for Niepce's process was eight hours, and he died in 1833 without making further innovations. Daguerre's contribution was the introduction of silvered copper plates, which reduced the exposure time to fifteen minutes and made photography a practical reality. Daguerreotypy popularized photography throughout western Europe, but its prints were positive and therefore could not be reproduced. A rival process developed by the Englishman William Henry Fox Talbot (1800–1877) during the 1840s imprinted photographic images on negative paper stock coated with silver chloride, from which an infinite number of positive paper prints could be reproduced. Although his initial exposure time was three minutes, Talbot ultimately replaced his paper negatives with collodion film stock and by mid-century had reduced the exposure time to one-hundredth of a second, giving photography its modern form.

3. In her recent biography of Muybridge, which is also a cultural history of his times, Rebecca Solnit reveals that he was born Edward James Muggeridge, the son of a grain and coal merchant in Kingston-upon-Thames, and that he changed his name throughout his life to suit his occupation, arriving at the more elegant Eadweard Muybridge only after his reputation as an innovative photographer had been established. See Rebecca Solnit, *River of Shadows: Eadweard Muybridge and the Technological Wild West* (New York: Viking, 2003).

caused the cameras to photograph it in successive stages of motion during the gallop. Muybridge demonstrated his results in 1879 on a mechanism he called the zoopraxiscope. This special kind of "magic lantern"[4] projected colored, hand-drawn images that were based on these photographs and placed along the outer rim of a circular glass disk. Muybridge devoted the rest of his life to refining his process of series photography, but he was not "the man who invented moving pictures," as a recent biography proclaims. He recorded live action continuously for the first time in history, but he did so with a series of twelve or more cameras; until the separate functions of these machines

1.4 Muybridge's glass-plate series photographs.

could be incorporated into a single instrument, the cinema could not be born.

It was the French physiologist Étienne-Jules Marey (1830–1904) who recorded the first series photographs of live action in a single camera, which, as it happens, was also portable. Marey, a specialist in animal locomotion, invented the "chronophotographic gun" in 1882 in order to take series pictures of birds in flight. This instrument, a camera shaped like a rifle, took twelve instantaneous photographs of a movement per second and imprinted them on a rotating glass plate. A year later Marey switched from the cumbersome plates to paper roll film, which had the effect of introducing the film strip to cinematography. But, like most of his contemporaries, Marey was not interested in cinematography as such. In his view, he had invented a machine for the dissection of motion similar to Muybridge's apparatus but more flexible, and he never intended to project his results. (In 1892, however, after the idea of projection had gained currency, Marey did attempt to design a projector that used celluloid roll film on a continuous belt; he was unsuccessful.)

The next step was taken in 1887 in Newark, New Jersey, when an Episcopalian minister named Hannibal Goodwin (1822–1900) first used celluloid roll film as a base for light-sensitive **emulsions.** Goodwin's idea was

1.5 Marey's chronophotographic gun.

4. The optical, or magic, lantern was a simple projection device invented in the seventeenth century, consisting of a light source and a magnifying lens. It enjoyed great popularity as a projector of still transparencies (or slides) throughout the eighteenth and nineteenth centuries and became a major component in subsequent motion-picture projection. Prefiguring this invention in the 1870s was the introduction of slides with movable parts that could be manipulated by lever during projection.

appropriated by the American entrepreneur George East-man (1854–1932), who in 1889 began to mass-produce and market celluloid roll film on what would soon become an international scale.[5] Neither Goodwin nor Eastman was initially interested in motion pictures, but it was the introduction of a *plastic* recording medium (in the generic sense of both durable and flexible), coupled with the technical breakthroughs of Muybridge and Marey, that enabled the Edison Laboratories in West Orange, New Jersey, to invent the **Kinetograph,** the first true motion-picture camera.

Motion Pictures

Like his predecessors, Thomas Alva Edison (1847–1931) was not interested in cinematography in and of itself. Rather, he wished to provide a visual accompaniment for his vastly successful phonograph, and in June 1889 he assigned a young laboratory assistant named William Kennedy Laurie Dickson (1860–1935) to help him develop a motion-picture camera for that purpose. Edison, in fact, envisioned a kind of "coin-operated / entertainment machine" in which motion pictures made by the Kineto-graph would illustrate the sound from the phonograph.[6] This aspect of the Kinetograph's genesis is important for two reasons. In the first place, it shows that the idea of making motion pictures was never divorced from the idea

of recording sound. The movies were intended to talk from their inception, so that in some sense the silent cinema represents a thirty-year aberration from the medium's natural tendency toward a total representation of reality. More significant is the fact that the first viable motion-picture camera was invented as an accessory to a sound recording device and not for its own sake. The advent of the Kinetograph thus completes a pattern that has been emerging throughout this chapter and that should now be apparent: cinema was born as an independent medium only *after* the cinema machines had been evolved for other purposes. That is, the invention of the machines preceded any serious consideration of the cinema's possessing documentary or narrative potential; and this relationship has remained constant throughout the history of film because the cinema at its material base is a technological form—one in which technological innovation precedes the aesthetic impulse (i.e., no artist can express him- or herself in cinema in ways which would *exceed* the technological capabilities of the machines).

Dickson "invented" the first motion-picture camera in a brilliant synthesis of already existing principles and techniques that he had learned from studying the work of Muybridge, Marey, and others. After some ineffectual attempts to record photographic images microscopically on phonographlike cylinders, Dickson began to experiment with the use of celluloid roll film in a battery-driven camera[7] similar to Marey's chronophotographic gun, and he arrived at the Kinetograph in late 1891. The machine

---

5. This resulted in the first major patent infringement suit in film history, *Goodwin Film & Camera Company v. Eastman Kodak Company,* which was decided in Goodwin's favor in 1898 but for which claims litigation continued another sixteen years. (I am indebted to Dan Greenberg for pointing this out to me.) Celluloid, a derivative of the carbohydrate cellulose, was invented in 1869 by the printer John Wesley Hyatt (1837–1920) as a substitute for ivory in the manufacture of billiard balls, then in great demand. Celluloid was the first synthetic plastic to receive wide commercial use, and the range of products made from it by the turn of the century extended from false teeth to piano keys to industrial taps and valves (and, of course, motion-picture film and billiard balls). Celluloid's one drawback for all applications was its high flammability.

6. Perhaps Edison's most original invention, the phonograph was a combined product of certain principles of telegraphy (invented in 1839) and telephony (invented in 1876), although until very recently phonographic technology was mechanical rather than electrical. Edison discovered the technique of phonographic reproduction while attempting to design an automatic telegraph that would inscribe Morse code signals by needle onto continuously moving rolls of paper tape. In the process, he discovered the technology of voice and sound transcription, in which

sound waves are recorded as physical vibrations in the grooves of a revolving wax cylinder or disk and redeemed as sound by a vibrating stylus and diaphragm in the phonographic performance. Like the motion-picture camera, the phonograph was a mechanical rather than an electrical invention: its sound was amplified by a simple horn, its power provided by a hand-turned crank. Edison patented the phonograph on December 15, 1877, and he initially conceived of it as a dictating machine. But it was as a home-entertainment device that the phonograph enjoyed its first great success. (In fact, it was the so-called phonograph craze of 1878 that first brought Edison to international attention.) By the 1890s, however, sophisticated coin-operated phonographs had become extremely popular and lucrative, and it was in this context that Edison conceived of the Kinetograph camera and the coin-operated viewing device, which predated the projector by several years.

7. Edison's faith in electricity notwithstanding, hand-cranked cameras proved the most popular and efficient of the silent era since their operators could vary the speed of the film strip and rewind it at will to create such special effects as dissolves (the simultaneous fading out of one image and fading in of another). Hand-cranked cameras were also much lighter and more reliable than their counterparts.

1.6 W. K. L. Dickson (with violin) recording sound for an early Kinetophone experiment.

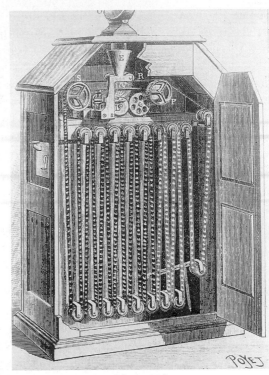

1.7 The Edison Kinetoscope.

incorporated what have come to be recognized as the two essentials of motion-picture camera and projector engineering: (1) a stop-motion device to insure the intermittent but regular motion of the film strip through the camera (at first at the rate of 40 fps, but ultimately at 16 and 24 fps for silent and sound film, respectively), and (2) a perforated celluloid film strip consisting of four **sprocket** holes on the bottom edge of each frame on a ¾-inch-wide strip (subsequently 1⅜ inches, the industry standard for 35mm still in use today).[8] The former, adapted by Dickson from the escapement mechanism of a watch, permits the unexposed film strip, in its rapid transit through the camera, to be stopped for a fraction of a second (usually twice the fps rate, to allow time for the movement of the film between frames—one thirty-second, one forty-eighth, etc.) before the lens while the shutter opens to *admit* light from the photographed object and expose the individual frames. In projection, the process is exactly reversed: each frame, now developed, is held intermittently before the projection lamp while the shutter opens to *emit* light through the lens and project the film image onto the screen. (In subsequent practice, the projection beam is broken once per frame by a rotating two-blade [for sound speed] or three-blade [for silent speed] shutter; this provides a shutter frequency of at least forty-eight "exposures" per second and eliminates the flicker effect through "flicker fusion.") Without a stop-motion device in both camera and projector, the film image would blur. The **synchronization** of film strip and shutter (which ensures the exact regu-

larity of this discontinuous movement) and the synchronization of the camera and projector are accomplished by means of the regular perforations in the film strip—inspired by the perforated paper of the Edison automatic telegraph—which is pulled through both machines by a system of clawed gears.

But Edison was not interested in projection. He mistakenly believed that the future of moving pictures lay in individual exhibition, so he commissioned Dickson to perfect the small viewing machine he had already designed for private use in the laboratory. The first moving pictures recorded in the Kinetograph were viewed by the public individually through the magnifing lens of a boxlike peep-show machine in which a continuous 40- to 50-foot film loop ran on spools between an electric lamp and a shutter. This device was dubbed the **Kinetoscope.** True to Edison's original intention, Dickson had attempted to design both viewer and camera so that sound and image could be

8. The original Kinetograph had a horizontal feed system, somewhat like that of 16mm cameras today. In October 1892, this was replaced by the now-standard vertical feed system, which employs a double set of sprocket holes, one on either side of the frame.

1.8 Peter Bacigalupi's Kinetoscope parlor, which opened in San Francisco in June 1894.

1.9 The "Black Maria."

synchronized and recorded simultaneously. But, in fact, accurate synchronization proved impossible, and the very few Kinetoscope films (called "Kinetophones") made with sound employed asynchronous musical accompaniment. Furthermore, when speculative emphasis shifted to projection a few years later, the reproduction of sound became doubly infeasible because there was as yet no means of amplifying it for a large audience. (It would remain so until amplification and recording technologies were invented in the Bell Laboratories early in the twentieth century.) Edison applied for patents on his new machines in 1891 but decided against paying the extra $150 to secure an international copyright, realizing that the Europeans had done so much of the essential mechanical invention of the apparatus that patent claims against them would not hold up. Soon after patents were granted in 1893, Edison began to market Kinetoscopes through several companies. The leading domestic sales agency, headed by Norman C. Raff and Frank R. Gammon, bought them from Edison for $200 apiece and sold them for $350 (as the novelty faded, the prices fell to roughly half these figures). The Edison Manufacturing Company went into the filmmaking business by establishing its own Kinetograph studio at West Orange, New Jersey.

On April 14, 1894, a Canadian entrepreneur named Andrew Holland opened the first Kinetoscope parlor in a converted shoe store at 1155 Broadway in New York City. Holland charged twenty-five cents per person for access to a row of five Edison peep-show viewers,[9] each

of which contained a single film loop shot with the Kinetograph, and he became the first man in history to make a living from the movies. Others followed his lead, and soon Kinetoscope parlors were opened across the country, all supplied with 50-foot shorts produced for them exclusively by the Edison Company's West Orange studio at the rate of $10 to $15 outright per print. This first motion-picture studio had been constructed by Dickson in 1893 for just over $600; it was an unusual edifice, to say the least. Called the "Black Maria" (after contemporary slang for what was later known as a "paddy wagon") because it was covered with protective tar-paper strips, Dickson's studio was a single room measuring about 25 by 30 feet. A section of its roof could be opened to admit the sunlight—then the cinema's only effective lighting source—and the whole building could be rotated on a circular track to follow the sun's course across the sky. Here, from 1893 to April 1895, Dickson was the producer, director, and cameraman for hundreds of brief films distributed by the Edison Company to the Kinetoscope parlors. (Both in the process of invention and pro-

9. In 1894, twenty-five cents was a skilled worker's hourly wage, so admission could also be had at the rate of five cents per standard single view (50 feet) or ten cents per fight film (150 feet). On recreation and entertainment patterns at the turn of the century, see Larry May, *Screening Out the Past: The Birth of Mass Culture and the Motion Picture Industry* (New York: Oxford University Press, 1980), pp. 3–42, and Garth S. Jowett, "The First Motion Picture Audiences," in *Film before Griffith*, ed. John L. Fell (Berkeley: University of California Press, 1983), pp. 196–206.

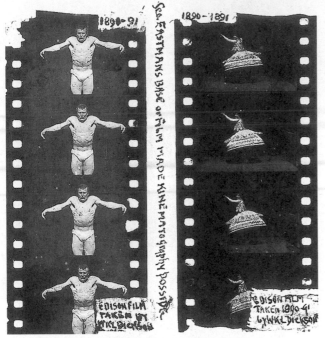

1.10 Original film strips of Strongman Sandow and the dancer Carmencita shot in the Black Maria, 1894. The handwriting and (inaccurate) dating are Dickson's. Full-scale reproduction.

recording quick vaudeville turns, **slapstick** comedy skits, and other kinds of brief performance. Some characteristic titles are *Chinese Laundry, The Gaiety Girls Dancing, Trained Bears, Blacksmith Scene, Dentist Scene, Bucking Broncos,* and *Highland Dance.* Taken together, the earliest Kinetoscope shorts preserve a series of standard theatrical routines whose only requisite content is motion. Structurally, the films are even cruder, consisting of continuous, unedited footage of what occurred before the lens of Dickson's stationary camera. This stasis was partially the result of technological limitations—especially the small enclosure of the Black Maria studio and the cumbersomeness of the Kinetograph, which resembled a small icebox in shape and size, and initially weighed over 500 pounds. But it was also the result of a natural ignorance of the ways in which the cinema machines might be used. The first impulse was simply to turn the camera on some interesting subject, staged or real, and let it run. So in terms of structure, the earliest films are simply brief recordings of entertaining or amusing subjects in which the camera was made to obey the laws of empirical reality. That is, it was treated as an unblinking human eye, and there was no concept of editing because reality cannot be edited by the human eye. At this point in the history of film, the camera was never permitted to record more than could be seen by a single individual standing in one fixed spot and focusing on a single event for a given length of time.

duction, Dickson worked closely with his assistant, William Heise, who was the camera operator on most early Edison films; Dickson left Edison in June 1895 to form the American Mutoscope and Biograph Company with three other partners [see p. 53].)

These first films seem extremely primitive today in both content and form. The 50-foot maximum format (approximately sixteen seconds at a speed of 40 fps; 60 at the later standard rate of 16) was not conducive to the construction of narratives, but was eminently suitable for

1.11 One of the most popular films made in the Black Maria, *Corbett and Courtney before the Kinetograph* (1894).

1.12 A contemporary drawing (c. 1894) of a motion picture being made in the Black Maria, showing the bulk and awkwardness of the Kinetograph.

Projection: Europe and America

Eadweard Muybridge's well-publicized presentations of his zoopraxiscope (in both Europe and America) during the 1880s did much to stimulate interest in perfecting the projection of a series of photographs. The basic requirements of projection engineering were (1) the enlargement of the images for simultaneous viewing by large groups and (2) a means of ensuring the regular but intermittent motion of the developed film strip as it passed between the projection lamp and the shutter (which would correspond with the discontinuous movement of the strip through the camera). The first requirement was easily and rapidly met by applying the principle of magic-lantern projection to film; the second proved more difficult but was eventually fulfilled by a variety of cams, shutters, and gears—and ultimately by the Maltese-cross system used in most projectors today. This system was perfected by the German film pioneer Oskar Messter (see pp. 87, 205). As indicated by the diagram, it has two basic parts: (A) a gear in the shape of a Maltese cross connected directly to the sprocket wheels that pull the film through the projector, and (B) a circular disk attached to the projector's drive mechanism, which carries a metal pin at its outer edge.

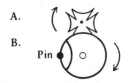

The disk rotates continuously, and the pin is located so that it enters one slot of the cross per cycle and propels it through a quarter of a revolution; but when the disk makes contact again with the edge of the cross itself, the gear is tightly locked until the pin rotates around to the next slot. This ensures the regular stop-and-go motion of the film strip through the projector.[1]

Many of the people credited with having perfected the first workable projectors through these means left no concrete proof of their endeavors. The English inventor William Friese-Greene (1855–1921) is supposed to have invented a combined camera and projector in 1887, but it never took or showed enough frames to create an effective illusion of movement. Similarly, a French scientist

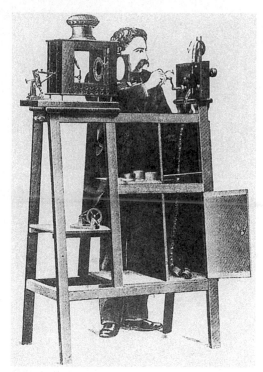

1.13 The Lumière Cinématographe in operation, c. 1895.

named Louis-Aimé-Augustin Le Prince (1841–1890) patented a camera-projector in 1888 and apparently did project moving pictures for French government officials at the Paris Opera in 1890, but he disappeared two months later and was never heard from again. It was actually the year 1895 that witnessed the most significant developments in projection technology, and these occurred almost simultaneously in every country in western Europe and in the United States. Ironically, the majority of projection devices brought forth in that year were modeled (quite legally and ethically, since there was no European copyright) upon the Kinetoscope, which the syndicate of Maguire and Baucus had marketed throughout Europe.

By far the most important of these devices was perfected by two brothers, Auguste and Louis Lumière (1862–1954 and 1864–1948, respectively), who operated a factory for the manufacture of photographic equipment in Lyons, France—and whose family name was, appropriately, the French word for "light." After a thorough

---

1. Today, the Maltese cross appears as the imprimatur of the AFL-CIO in the credits of every American film produced with union labor.

1.14 *L'Arrivée d'un train en gare* (Lumières, 1895).

1.15 A poster advertising an early Cinématographe projection, c. 1895.

study of the workings of the Edison machine, the Lumières invented an apparatus that could serve as camera, projector, and film printer and that was finally patented as the **Cinématographe,** thus coining the term that attaches to the medium of film to this day.[2] (It is generally acknowledged today that only the youngest Lumière, Louis, was responsible for the actual design and construction of the machine.) The Cinématographe was built to run at a speed of 16 fps and established the standard for silent film.[3] On March 22, 1895, the Lumière brothers projected their first film to a private audience in Paris. Many film historians designate *La Sortie des ouvriers de*

2. One distinct advantage of the Cinématographe was its portability. Whereas the Kinetograph was battery-driven and weighed several hundred pounds, the hand-cranked Lumière machine weighed just under sixteen. This and the Cinématographe's treble function as camera, projector, and printer freed it from the studio confinement of the Kinetograph and enabled Lumière cameramen to travel all over the world to film "local *actualités*."

3. Sixteen frames per second was the *intended* standard for silent films, but the speed was hardly universal. As Kevin Brownlow points out in "Silent Film: What Was the Right Speed?" (*Sight and Sound* 49, 3 [Summer 1980]: 164–67), exhibitors would frequently speed up or slow down projection to accommodate their schedules, and cameramen would overcrank or undercrank during shooting for a variety of reasons, including, most prominently, the absence of speed indicators from cameras until well into the 1920s. In practice, speeds among and even within silent films could vary by as much as 10 fps, from 14 to 24. (Indeed, several sequences in D. W. Griffith's *The Birth of a Nation* [1915] were so undercranked by Billy Bitzer that they could only be projected at 12 fps.) For practical purposes, then, 16 fps should be thought of as the average and not the uniform speed of silent film recording and projection. The motorization of cameras in the late 1920s made it possible for

l'usine Lumière (*Workers Leaving the Lumière Factory*) as the world's first moving picture;[4] certainly this was the first effective theatrical projection of a film made specifically for that purpose. On December 28, 1895, the Lumières rented a basement room in the Grand Café, on the Boulevard des Capucines in Paris, to project a program of about ten films for the first time to a paying audience. Some of the titles from that program were *L'Arrivée d'un train en gare* (*Arrival of a Train at a Station*), which dramatically marked the beginning of the cinema's long obsession with that particular icon of the Industrial Revolution;[5] *Déjeuner de bébé* (*Baby's Lunch*), a record of brother Auguste feeding his infant daughter; and *L'Arroseur arrosé* (*The Sprinkler Sprinkled*), a bit of slapstick in which a young boy steps on a hose, which then squirts a gardener in the face when he peers at the nozzle. *L'Arrivée* was a visual tour de force, and audiences are said to have dodged aside at the sight of the locomotive barreling toward them into the foreground on the screen.[6] Due to its relative lightness, the Cinématographe could be taken out of doors more easily than the Kinetograph, and for this reason the early Lumière films have a much higher **documentary** content than do Edison's (the Lumières called their films *"actualités,"* or documentary views).[7] Structurally, however, the earliest Lumière and Edison films are precisely the same—the camera and point of view are static (except when moved functionally, to reframe action) and the action continuous from beginning to end, as if editing "reality" was unthinkable to their makers.

Admission to the Lumière program was Fr 1 per customer, and the receipts for the first day totaled only Fr 35. But within a month the Cinématographe showings were earning an average of Fr 7,000 a week, and motion pictures had become, overnight, an extremely lucrative commercial enterprise. The most important aspect of the Cinématographe projections, however, was that they marked the end of the period of technological experimentation that had begun with Muybridge's series photography in 1872: the two machines upon which the cinema is founded had been perfected at last. In Germany, the Skladanowsky brothers, Max and Emil (1863–1939 and 1859–1945, respectively) developed almost simultaneously with the Lumières a projector for celluloid film strips called the "Bioskop" or Bioscope (a common term for many early cameras and projectors) and projected films of their own making in a public per-

formance at the Berlin Wintergarten on November 1, 1895. Projection reached England immediately thereafter, in 1896, when a manufacturer of scientific instruments named Robert W. Paul (1869–1943) patented the Theatrograph (later renamed the Animatograph), a projector based on the Kinetoscope[8]—although the Lumière Cinématographe was soon to capture both the British and the Continental markets.

Edison became aware of the vastly promising financial future of projection through the success of the Cinématographe at about the same time that Kinetoscope installations had reached saturation point in the United States (all told, just over nine hundred of them were sold), and he commissioned the invention of a projection device in the summer of 1895. In September of that year, however, Edison learned through Raff and Gammon that two aspiring inventors, C. Francis Jenkins (1867–1934) and Thomas Armat (1866–1948) had projected a program of Kinetograph shorts at the Cotton States Exposition in Atlanta, Georgia, with an electrically powered machine that incorporated a stop-motion mechanism superior to

---

sound speed to be internationally standardized at 24 fps. Since one reel of 35mm film contains just under 1,000 feet and runs about 60 feet per minute at 16 fps, a reel of silent film lasts approximately sixteen minutes; at sound speed, or 24 fps, film runs at the standard rate of 90 feet per minute, so that a reel lasts eleven minutes.

4. The oldest known print of *La Sortie des ouvriers*, dating from 1895, was discovered beneath the floorboards of a bank building in Perth, Australia, in October 1979. Twelve Lumière films were found in all, including three that previously had been unknown.

5. For a complete history of this relationship, see Lynne Kirby, *Parallel Tracks: The Railroad and the Silent Cinema* (Durham: Duke University Press, 1997).

6. It is difficult to imagine that the Lumières' educated, bourgeois audiences seriously expected a train to emerge from the screen and run them down. As Dai Vaughan points out, the story—real or invented—means "that the particular combination of visual signals present in that film had had no previous existence other than as signifying a real train pulling into a real station." ("Let There Be Lumière," in *Early Cinema: Space-Frame-Narrative*, ed. Thomas Elsaesser and Adam Barker [London: British Film Institute, 1990], p. 63.)

7. By the turn of the century, both firms were competing heatedly for both markets, Edison turning his attention to Lumière-like *actualités* on the American subcontinent and the Lumières shooting studio-bound domestic stage performances.

8. Birt Acres (1854–1918), Paul's former partner in the invention of England's first camera and the making of the first British films (*Oxford and Cambridge University Boat Race, The Derby, Rough Sea at*

anything then under patent.[9] Their projector also made use of a small but extremely important device employed earlier in the year by the Latham family (brothers Gray and Otway, along with their father Woodville). The Lathams, who had made money showing fight films with Edison's Kinetoscope, formed the Lambda Company to make motion pictures of prize fights and other sporting events, and then project these on the screen. Their contribution, the **Latham loop,** merits special consideration here.

One of the chief practical problems of early motion-picture production and exhibition was that of film breakage. At lengths of greater than 50 to 100 feet, the inertia of the take-up reel would frequently cause the film strip to tear or snap in the projector. Assisted by the engineer-inventors Enoch Rector and Eugene Augustin Lauste (see p. 207), the Lathams had discovered that by placing a small loop in the film strip just above and below the projection lens, and maintaining it with an extra set of sprockets, the stress could be redistributed in such a manner as to permit films of greater length in the magazine. This relatively simple technological innovation had far-reaching aesthetic consequences, since without it the cinema would have remained a medium whose basic form was the one-minute short subject. The Latham loop provides yet another example of the way in which technology and art are bound together in cinema. Here, as so often in film history, the meeting of a technological exigency created a new aesthetic dimension for the medium—the prospect of increased film length and the capacity for narrative it portends.

Edison was so impressed with the features of Armat's machine that he abandoned his own research project and bought the apparatus outright under a scandalous agreement whereby he would himself manufacture it and take full credit for its invention while Armat would be allowed a small plate on the back crediting him with "design." Edison dubbed the new machine the Vitascope and gave it its first public exhibition on April 23, 1896, at the popular Koster and Bial's Music Hall in New York City, where it received top billing as "Edison's greatest marvel." Some representative titles from the program of twelve short films included *Sea Waves, Butterfly Dance* (apparently the first color-tinted print), *The Barber Shop, A Boxing Bout, Venice—Showing Gondolas, Kaiser Wilhelm—Reviewing His Troops, Skirt Dance*, and *The Bar Room*. Like their predecessors, Edison's Vitascope films

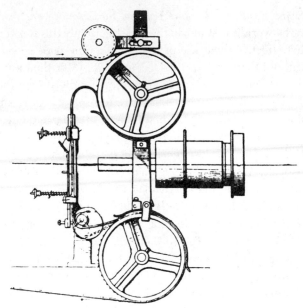

1.16 The Latham loop, as illustrated in the Armat patent application, 1901.

(some of which had originally been produced for the Kinetoscope, some of which had been illegally copied from the Lumières and the Birt Acres–Robert Paul collaboration) offered nothing more than unmediated glimpses of real action as it unfolded before the camera from a single point of view; but these rather crude "living pictures," as they were soon labeled, proved novel and engaging enough to satisfy the public's taste for several years to come. After all, the world had never seen their like before.

For example, a writer for *La Poste* commented on the Cinématographe projections of December 28, 1895: "The beauty of the invention resides in the novelty and ingenuity of the apparatus. When these apparatuses are made available to the public, everybody will be able to photograph those who are dear to them, no longer as static forms but with their movements, their actions, their

Dover—all 1895), demonstrated a projection device called the Kineopticon several months before Paul, but it was apparently never produced commercially. Acres also invented the first home movie camera, patented as the Birtac in 1898, which took 50-foot reels of 17.5mm film and would function as a projector by reversing its lens.

9. An improved version of the Phantoscope, developed by Jenkins and Armat in 1894. (The Kinetoscope, unlike the Kinetograph, ran continuously rather than intermittently.)

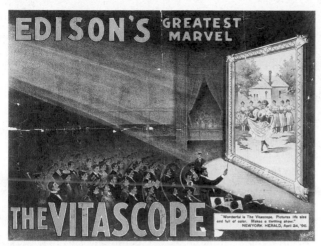

1.17 A poster and publicity sketches for an Edison Vitascope projection in a music hall, c. 1896.

familiar gestures, capturing the speech on their very lips. Then, death will no longer be absolute."[1] The original audiences for motion pictures did not perceive them as we do—as a succession of images linked together in a continuity of meaning—but rather as a series of discontinuous "animated photographs." Conditioned by lantern slide shows, comic strips, and other serial presentations of images, these audiences saw individual scenes as self-contained and did not infer meaning from one scene to the next. The shift in consciousness from films as animated photographs to films as continuous narratives began around the turn of the century.

The Vitascope and Cinématographe projections mark the culmination of the cinema's prehistory. By 1896, all the basic technological principles of film recording and projection had been discovered and incorporated into existing machines—which, with certain obvious exceptions like the introduction of light-sensitive sound, have remained essentially unchanged from that day to this. Thus, the history of cinema as an art form begins, for if our understanding of the machines was sophisticated, knowledge of how to use them was primitive indeed. In fact, the kind of documentary recording practiced by Edison and the Lumières was to become the mainstream tendency of the cinema until the turn of the century because there was as yet no notion that the camera might be used to tell a story—i.e., to *create* a **narrative** reality rather than simply *record* some real or staged event that occurred before its lens. It is true that during this period

films were able to grow in length to 1,000 feet, or approximately sixteen minutes, thanks to the Latham device, but they remained static in terms of form until their narrative dimension was discovered and articulated on the screen. Nevertheless, by the late 1890s cinema was already on its way toward becoming a mass medium with the then-unimaginable power to communicate without print or speech.

The Evolution of Narrative: Georges Méliès

During the 1890s, near the end of the decade, exhibitors often created multishot narratives that focused on such subjects as a fire rescue or the Spanish-American War. (Programs of unrelated, miscellaneous scenes also remained popular.) The showmen developed these stories by purchasing various one-shot films from production companies, then putting them in an order and delivering a narration, often combined with **sound effects** and lantern slides. Creative responsibility was thus divided between producer and exhibitor. By the turn of the century, however, producers were beginning to assume this editorial responsibility by making multishot films on their own. In the process, filmmakers assumed greater control over the narrative, allowing for greater specificity in the story line. In many respects, therefore, the producers began to resemble modern-day filmmakers. Such a development is most clearly apparent in the work of Georges Méliès (1861–1938), a professional magician who owned and operated the Théâtre Robert-Houdin in Paris. Méliès had been using magic-lantern projections in his conjuring acts for years, and when he attended the first Cinématographe programs in 1895 he immediately recognized the vast illusionist possibilities of the "living pictures." Accordingly, in early 1896 he attempted to buy a Cinématographe from the Lumières for Fr 10,000 but was promptly refused since the brothers recognized potential competition when they saw it. Méliès, however, who had also been a mechanic, an actor, an illustrator, a photographer, and a stage designer, was not easily discouraged.

1. *La Poste*, December 30, 1895, quoted in Georges Sadoul, *Louis Lumière* (Paris: Seghers, 1964), p. 119.

Several months later, he bought an Animatograph projector from the English inventor Robert W. Paul for Fr 1,000 and simply reversed its mechanical principle to design his own camera, which was constructed for him by the instrument maker Lucien Korsten.[2] By April 1896, Méliès was showing his own productions in his own theater. In time, he would become the cinema's first important narrative artist as well, but not before he had done some apprentice work in the manner of the Lumières and Edison by filming a series of *actualités*, comic episodes, and staged conjurer's tricks for projection in his theater.

According to Méliès's memoirs, one afternoon in the fall of 1896, while he was filming a Parisian street scene, his camera jammed in the process of recording an omnibus as it emerged from a tunnel. When he got the machine working again, a funeral hearse had replaced the omnibus, so that in projection the omnibus seemed to change into the hearse.[3] By this accident, Méliès came to recognize the possibilities for the manipulation of real time and real space inherent in the editing of exposed film. He had discovered that film need not obey the laws of empirical reality, as his predecessors had supposed, because film was in some sense a separate reality with structural laws of its own. Unfortunately, Méliès put his discovery to only limited use. Although he went on to make hundreds of delightful **narrative films,** his model for them was the narrative mode of the legitimate theater since it was what he knew best. That is, he conceived all of his films in terms of dramatic **scenes** played out from beginning to end rather than in terms of **shots,** or individual visual perspectives on a scene; the only editing, therefore, aside from that used in optical illusions of disappearance and conversion, occurs *between* scenes rather than *within* them. The scenes themselves are composed of single shots taken with a motionless camera from a fixed point of view, that of a theater spectator sitting in the orchestra center aisle with an excellent eye-level view of the action; and the actors move across the film frame from left to right and right to left as if it were the proscenium arch[4] of a stage. Normally, a viewer experiences no more narrative manipulation within a Méliès film than in watching a stage play of the same action; one sees a significant amount of stage illusion, of course, but changes in time and space coincide precisely with changes in scene, and the narrative point of view is rigidly static.

Méliès was nevertheless the cinema's first narrative artist. By adapting certain techniques of still photography, theater spectacle, and magic-lantern projection to the linear medium of the film strip, he innovated significant narrative devices like the **fade-in,** the **fade-out,** the overlapping, or **"lap," dissolve,** and **stop-motion photography.** To put his discoveries into effect, Méliès, in late 1896, organized the Star Film Company, and, by the spring of 1897, he had constructed a small production studio on the grounds of his house in the Paris suburb of Montreuil. The building measured 55 by 20 feet and was glass-enclosed like a greenhouse to admit maximum sunlight, the cinema's only effective lighting source until mercury-vapor lamps came into general use around 1907. Here Méliès produced, directed, photographed, and acted in some five hundred films[5] between 1897 and 1913, when, like so many other film pioneers, he was forced out of business by his competitors (principally Charles Pathé; see pp. 41–43) because he had lost touch with the rapid development of both the medium and the industry. Some representative early titles, in translation, are *The Cabinet of Mephistopheles* (1897), *Cinderella* (1899), and *The Man with the India-Rubber Head* (1901). These were short "trick films," by and large, whose impact

---

2. The machine was procured for Méliès by fellow magician David Devant (1868–1941), who then became the exclusive Star Film agent in England until 1900, when British sales were taken over by Charles Urban (1871–1942; see Chapter 7). Devant himself made several conjuring films and appeared in four for Paul, performing some of his most famous acts, which were also frequently reconstructed in film by Méliès.

3. According to Paul Hammond, in his authoritative study *Marvelous Méliès* (London: Gordon Fraser Gallery, 1974), Méliès's *Mes Mémoires* (originally published in the Italian journal *Cinema* [Rome, 1938]; rpt. in French in Maurice Bessy and G. M. Lo Duca, *Georges Méliès, mage* [Paris: Prisma, 1945]; 2nd ed. [Paris: J. J. Pauvert, 1961]) is notoriously unreliable and the incident may well be apocryphal (p. 34). But if the tale was fabricated, it at least suggests that Méliès was consciously aware of his own inventiveness.

4. In a theater, the part of the stage in front of the curtain (sometimes including the curtain). The proscenium provides a static framing device for the action on stage and marks the border between stage illusion and the real world.

5. Fewer than 140 of these survive today. Four hundred films were requisitioned by agents of the French army in 1917 and melted down to produce a chemical necessary in the manufacture of boot heels. When he went bankrupt in the summer of 1923, Méliès himself destroyed a batch of negatives and sold his own stock of prints by the kilo to a second hand film dealer.

1.18 The interior of Méliès's studio at Montreuil.

depended on a single special effect, usually accomplished through photographic double exposure or superimposition. Soon longer films, approximately one reel in length, began to appear—e.g., *A Trip to the Moon* (1902) and *The Palace of the Arabian Nights* (1905)—and by mid-decade Méliès was fully committed to narrative until the end of his career (e.g., *Twenty Thousand Leagues under the Sea* [1907], *The Conquest of the Pole* [1912]). Although he also made many films based on historical and contemporary events (*actualités reconstituées*, or "reconstructed newsreels," he called them—see, e.g., *The Dreyfus Affair* [1899], his first multiscene film), Méliès's most memorable productions concern the fantastic and bizarre and are acted out before lush, phantasmagoric backgrounds that he himself designed and painted. Many were released in color since at the height of his very substantial success Méliès employed twenty-one women at the studio of Madame Tuillier to hand-tint his films individually, frame by frame (a practice apparently initiated by Edison for the first Vitascope projection and continued with some regularity throughout the early silent period; for a thorough discussion of color processes, see pp. 214–21). Although Méliès went bankrupt in 1923 due to his ruin at the hands of Pathé Frères and other rivals, his films had immense popular appeal at the turn of the century. Indeed, by 1902 Star Film had become one of the world's largest suppliers of motion pictures, with offices in New York, London, Barcelona, and Berlin, and had nearly driven the Lumières out of production.

By far the most successful and influential film Méliès made at Montreuil was *Le Voyage dans la lune* (*A Trip to the Moon*). Produced in 1902, this film achieved international circulation within months of its completion, albeit through unethical distribution of "dupes" by rival concerns as much as through Méliès's own sales.[6] *Le Voyage dans la lune*, loosely adapted by Méliès from the Jules Verne novel of the same title, was 825 feet long (a little under fourteen minutes at the average silent speed of 16 fps), or three times the average length of the contemporary Edison and Lumière products (one of Méliès's achievements was increasing the standard length of fiction films). Utterly characteristic of both the strengths and weaknesses of Méliès's theatrical narrative mode, the film is composed of thirty separate scenes,[7] which he appropriately called "tableaux," all photographed from the same angle and connected by means of lap dissolves. The scenes are arranged in precise chronological sequence, as follows:

6. These were maverick times for the small but burgeoning film industry. The status of copyright had yet to be clearly established in the courts, and virtually no foreign films were copyrighted in United States before 1903 (although, when they were, copyright was *generally* respected in the United States because the threat of legal action was real). Despite massive distribution of "dupes" (a term referring to duplicate prints, usually made without the authorization of the picture's producer), however, *A Trip to the Moon* was so popular that Méliès made a fortune during its first year of distribution—a fact explained by the circumstance that films were not leased to exhibitors but sold to them outright until the advent of the first permanent theaters, the nickelodeons.

To prevent further piracy and to promote his films abroad, Méliès established an American branch of Star Film in New York in 1903 under the management of his older brother Gaston (1852–1915), who began to copyright Méliès "Star" films in mid-1903. Gaston founded his own production company and joined the Motion Picture Patents Company in 1908; between 1909 and 1913 he produced over 150 one-reel films—most of them Westerns and war "epics"—at the Star Film Ranch in San Antonio, Texas, and at Santa Paula, California, on the Pacific coast. Before going out of business in 1913, Gaston Méliès employed as directors both Wallace C. McCutcheon, the son of Biograph's Wallace McCutcheon (see p. 53), and Francis Ford, John Ford's eldest brother, who later convinced him to go into the motion picture business (see pp. 171, 259).

7. These are the "scenes" as listed by Méliès in the *Star Film Catalogue* of 1903. In fact, many are not separate scenes at all but successive episodes within the same *tableau*. Most circulating prints today contain only fifteen *tableaux*, corresponding to Star catalogue "scenes" 1–2, 3, 4, 5–6, 7, 8–9, 10–14, 15–17, 18–19, 20, 21, 22, 23, 24, and 25, as listed above. The missing episodes 26–30 represent a single concluding *tableau*.

1. The scientific congress at the Astronomic Club.
2. The planning of the trip itself.
3. The construction of the projectile in the factory.
4. The factory rooftop at night, with chimneys belching smoke in the background.
5. The boarding of the projectile by the astronomers.
6. The loading of the cannon (complete with female "Marines" in short pants and tights).
7. The firing of the cannon.
8. The flight of the projectile through space.
9. The landing in the eye of the moon (an action overlapped in the next shot).
10. The projectile landing, moonside, and the astronomers disembarking.
11. A view of the moon's topography.
12. The astronomers' dream (visions of the Pleiades and Zodiac signs).
13. A snowstorm on the moon.
14. The astronomers' descent into a crater.
15. A grotto of giant mushrooms in the interior of the moon.
16. Encounter with the moon creatures, or Selenites (acrobats from the Folies-Bergère).
17. The astronomers taken prisoner.
18. The astronomers brought before the King of the Moon and his Selenite army.
19. The astronomers' escape.
20. The Selenites' pursuit.
21. The astronomers' departure in the projectile.
22. The projectile falling vertically through space.
23. The projectile splashing into the sea.
24. The projectile at the bottom of the ocean.
25. The rescue and return to land.
26. The astronomers' triumphal return.
27. The decoration of the heroes.
28. Procession of "Marines."
29. The erection of the commemorative statue.
30. Public rejoicing.

The whole film very much resembles a photographed stage play, save for the inclusion of some of the optical tricks that were a Méliès trademark. Some of these, such as the disappearance of the Selenites in a puff of smoke when they are struck by the astronomers' umbrellas, were accomplished cinematically, through the use of stop-motion photography, but are not terribly important in terms of narrative. Many others, however, the product of nineteenth-century stage illusion pure and simple, serve to illustrate how very far Méliès really was from tapping the full narrative potential of the medium. The classic example of Méliès's lack of vision in this respect is that when he wished to show the astronomers' projectile crashing dramatically into the face of the moon, he moved the papier-mâché moon on a dolly into the lens of the camera rather than moving the camera into the moon—even though, as a practical matter, moving the camera would have been far simpler. Méliès, in fact, never moved his camera once in any of his more than five hundred films. Neither did he alternate the point of view within scenes or even between them by changing camera angles. His films were, as he once called them, "artificially arranged scenes," or "moving *tableaux*," and his camera functioned as the inert eye of a theater spectator from the beginning to the end of his career.

Viewed today, these early films are bound to seem primitive because cinema is for us a highly integrated narrative form. (In fact, "primitive cinema" is the term used by film historians—not in a pejorative sense—to describe the medium from the invention of its first machines to about 1910.) There is an increasing body of opinion, however, that their original audiences experienced these films very differently than we do—as a kind of performative spectacle, or "attraction," whose function was to *present* rather than to represent, to *show* rather than to narrate. Tom Gunning has called this phenomenon the "cinema of attractions" and suggests that it dominated the medium's first decade (1895–1906), after which the story film became dominant and the presentational mode went underground to become an important element of avant-garde cinema and certain narrative genres (e.g., the musical, science fiction).[8] In its earliest form, the cinema of attractions drew audiences to the technological display of its projection apparatus (the Vitascope was "Edison's greatest marvel," etc.) and, on screen, solicited their attention by "direct address"—i.e., the recurring look of the actors at the camera—or some other form of direct stimulation (stop-motion transformations, interpolated close-ups, phantom "rides," etc.). In this view, to look for narrative continuity in such early films—even such clearly plotted ones as *Le Voyage dans la lune*—is to miss the point that for filmmakers and audiences alike

---

8. Tom Gunning, "The Cinema of Attractions: Early Film, Its Spectator and the Avant-Garde," in Elsaesser and Barker, eds., *Early Cinema: Space-Frame-Narrative*, pp. 56–62.

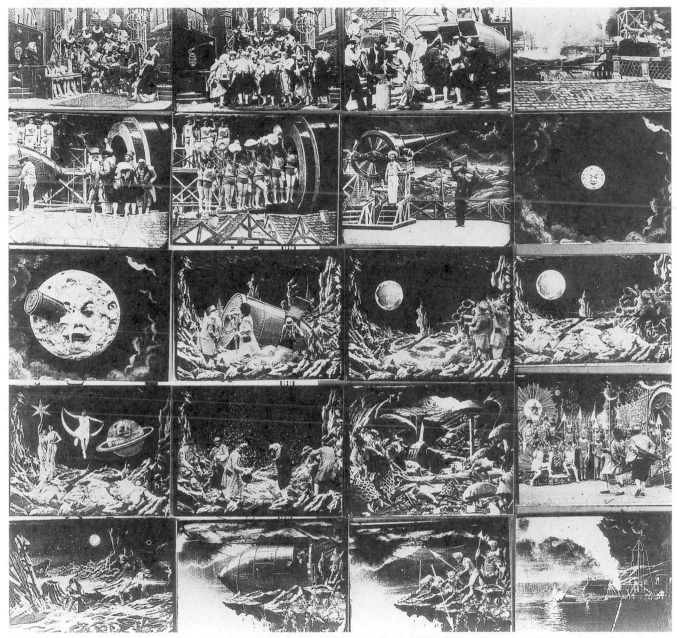

1.19 Frames from twelve of the original *tableaux* in *Le Voyage dans la lune* (Georges Méliès, 1902). Frames 1–2, 5–6, 8–9, 10–14, 11–12, and 18–19 represent separate episodes from the same *tableaux;* there are no perceptible splices between these frames in the film itself.

early cinema was conceived as a series of displays providing spectatorial pleasure through all of the objects, views, and events it could show, whether fictional or documentary, and whether in story form or not. This perspective has the distinct advantage of refusing to blame early cinema for what it was not—a stuttered and inarticulate version of what cinema would become during its so-called "classical" period, from the teens through the fifties, or what we regard as its even more advanced state today. On the other hand, when Gunning and others argue that it is wrong to see films like *Voyage* as "precursors of later narrative structures," they contradict the testimony of both the earliest and succeeding generations of filmmakers who claimed that this is *exactly* what these films were

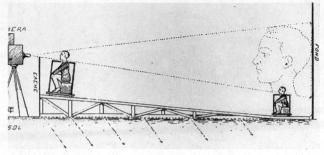

1.20 A drawing (c. 1896) illustrating the way in which Méliès simulated camera movement in his films.

to them—structures on which to found later narrative ideas and experiments.

Méliès discovered, if he did not exploit, the enormous potential inherent in the editing of exposed film, and through his influence on contemporary filmmakers he pointed the cinema well on its way toward becoming an essentially narrative rather than a documentary medium, as Edison and Lumière cameramen had originally conceived it. Furthermore, Méliès was an artist of unique and individual talent, and his films endure every bit as much for their distinctive imaginative power as for their contributions to cinematic form. He had stumbled into the narrative dimensions of the cinema very much as cinema had stumbled into being—arbitrarily, almost by accident—and he appropriated a conventional and unimaginative narrative model because it was what he knew best; yet those who came after him would understand. Charlie Chaplin called him "the alchemist of light," but D. W. Griffith, at the end of his own monumental career in 1932, put it best when he said of Méliès, "I owe him everything."[9]

Edwin S. Porter: Developing a Concept of Continuity Editing

Méliès ultimately lost his audience to the practitioners of a more sophisticated narrative style the origins of which are closely associated with the work of Edwin S. Porter (1870–1941). Porter had worked as a Vitascope projectionist in 1896, helping to set up the landmark Koster and Bial's projection of April 23, and he subsequently operated his own equipment in such mainline theaters as the Eden Musée in New York City. In 1900 Porter joined the Edison Manufacturing Company as a mechanic and in early 1901 became production head of its new skylight studio on East Twenty-first Street, where for the next few years he served as director/cameraman for much of the company's output. His first films were one-shot skits and *actualités*, such as *Kansas City Saloon Smashers* (1901) and *New York City in a Blizzard* (1902), and brief multiscene narratives based on political cartoons and contemporary events (*The Sampson-Schley Controversy*, 1901; *The Execution of Czolgosz*, 1901). Porter also filmed the extraordinary *Pan-American Exposition by Night* (1901), which used **time-lapse photography** to create a circular panorama of the illuminated fairgrounds, by modifying his camera to expose a single frame every ten seconds.

By 1901, Porter had encountered the films of Méliès and those of the two British pioneers George Albert Smith (1864–1959) and James Williamson (1855–1933). Smith, a portrait photographer, and Williamson, a lanternist, had constructed their own motion-picture cameras and, between 1896 and 1898, had begun to produce trick films featuring superimpositions (*The Corsican Brothers* [Smith, 1898]) and interpolated **close-ups** (*Grandma's Reading Glass* [Smith, 1900]; *The Big Swallow* [Williamson, 1901]). Smith would later develop the first commercially successful photographic color process (Kinemacolor, c. 1906–1908, with Charles Urban), while Williamson apparently experimented with intercutting between the interior and exterior of a building as early as 1901 in *Fire!*, a film that decisively influenced the structure and content of Porter's *Life of an American Fireman* (1903).[1] By 1902, both Smith and Williamson had built studios in their native Brighton and, with their associates, came to be known as members of the "Brighton school," although they did not really constitute the coherent movement that such a term implies. Some his-

9. The contemporary avant-garde also owes him a considerable debt. The American experimentalist Stan Brakhage (1933–2003), for example, has written, "I took my first senses of the individual frame life of a film from Méliès" (*Art Forum*, January 1973, p. 76). For a brilliant appreciation and revaluation of this aspect of Méliès's singular artistry, see Paul Hammond's *Marvelous Méliès*. See also the feature-length compilation film *Méliès et ses contemporains* (1983), prepared under the supervision of Franz Schmitt at the French State Film Archive in Bois d'Arcy.

1. See Martin Sopocy, *James Williamson: Studies and Documents of a Pioneer of the Film Narrative* (Cranbury, N.J.: Associated University Presses, 1998).

1.21 The editing sequence of the copyright version of Porter's *Life of an American Fireman* (1903): two frames per shot, excepting shot 5 (one frame), shot 6 (three frames), and shot 7 (not represented).

torians (notably Georges Sadoul, Kenneth Macgowan, and Barry Salt) have credited the Brighton school with making major contributions to narrative form between 1902 and 1908, which is difficult to prove given the low survival rate of the era's films. Yet it seems certain that Porter saw some of the earlier Brighton work since it was occasionally sold by Edison; and he may also have seen that of the Yorkshire-based filmmakers James Bamforth (*The Kiss in the Tunnel*, 1899), who produced films with the Riley brothers of Bradford under the banner of RAB (Riley and Bamforth), and Frank Mottershaw of the Sheffield Photo Co. (*A Daring Daylight Robbery*, 1903).[2] (The influence was mutual: several later Brighton productions were clearly influenced by the continuity editing of Porter's *The Great Train Robbery* [1903], as was the work of London filmmaker Cecil Hepworth [1874–1953], whose *Rescued by Rover* [1905] is considered to be one of the most skillfully edited narratives before Griffith.)[3]

Yet it may have been Porter's experience as a projectionist at the Eden Musée in the late 1890s that led him to the practice of continuity editing in the period from 1901 to 1903. As he moved from exhibition to production, Porter began to apply many of the editorial skills he had learned to filmmaking. He was also clearly influenced by Méliès's story films. Thus *Jack and the Beanstalk* (1902) shows a strong debt to Méliès's *Bluebeard* (1902). By his own admission, Porter was powerfully influenced by Méliès's *A Trip to the Moon* (1902), which he came to know well in the process of duplicating it for distribution (again, illegally) by Edison in October 1902. Years later, he claimed that it was the Méliès film that had given him the idea for "telling a story in continuity form," which resulted in *Life of an American Fireman*, produced in late 1902 and released in January 1903.[4] The subject of this film—the dramatic rescue of a woman and child from a burning building by firemen—was a popular one, having been featured in lantern slide shows and other films for years before. What was unusual was Porter's idea of combining **stock footage** from the Edison archive with staged scenes of the rescue to create a uniquely cinematic form: a fiction constructed from recordings of empirically real events (which is, of course, a good definition of cinema itself). About the sequencing of these events, however, there has been much controversy. On the basis of the standard print distributed by the Museum of Modern Art (MoMA) Department of Film, it was long thought that

in the final sequence of the film Porter intercut, or cut together, interior shots of a blazing room with exterior shots of a fireman climbing a ladder to rescue its occupants, creating a radically innovative effect—the illusion of separate but simultaneous and **parallel actions,** which was to become a basic structural element of cinematic narrative. But *Life of an American Fireman* was a lost film until 1944, when MoMA acquired a 35mm nitrate print from Pathé News, Inc. Although MoMA has never claimed that this print, known today as the "Cross-Cut Version," was the original, it conforms in principle to the editing continuity of the original as it has been described by American film historians from Terry Ramsaye (*A Million and One Nights* [1926]) through Lewis Jacobs (*The Rise of the American Film* [1939]) and beyond. Ramsaye's description was based either on memory or on Porter's own account of the film (more recently set forth by Budd Schulberg in *Variety*, May 9, 1979). Jacobs's description was based on a combination of Ramsaye's version, the Edison catalogue description, and a sequence of production stills made for copyright purposes by the Edison Company, which seem to suggest intercutting at the film's climax.

The Cross-Cut Version is 378 feet long (just over six minutes at the average silent speed of 16 fps) and consists of twenty separate[5] shots linked together by dissolves or straight cuts as follows:

---

2. Another film called *The Kiss in the Tunnel* was made by G. A. Smith several months before Bamforth's, and there were many more (e.g., Porter's own *What Happened in the Tunnel* [1903], made just before *The Great Train Robbery*). These "tunnel kiss" films were a variant of the then popular "phantom ride" films, wherein a camera mounted on the front of a locomotive would plunge viewers into the darkness of a tunnel and out into daylight again; when a shot of a couple kissing in a railway carriage was inserted into a phantom ride, exhibitors had a ready-made three-shot narrative. Sheffield Photo Co. (SPC) remade *A Daring Daylight Robbery* as *Daring Daylight Burglary* in 1904, and it, too, became a popular subtype of early narrative film.

3. See Charles Barr, "Before *Blackmail*: British Silent Cinema," in *The British Cinema Book*, ed. Robert Murphy, 2nd ed. (London: British Film Institute, 2001), pp. 11–19.

4. In a newspaper interview some years after *Life of an American Fireman,* Porter said: "From laboratory examination of some of the popular films of the French pioneer director, Georges Méliès—trick films like 'A Trip to the Moon'—I came to the conclusion that a picture telling a story in continuity form might draw the customers back to the theatres and set to work in this direction" (quoted in Charles Musser, "The Early Cinema of Edwin S. Porter," *Cinema Journal* 19, 1 [Fall 1979]: 25).

5. MoMA currently distributes the original or "Copyright Version," which contains only nine shots (see p. 21).

1. The fire chief asleep, dreaming of his wife and child, who appear in a circular vignette at the upper right-hand corner of the screen, later called the "dream balloon."

2. Close-up of a fire-alarm box and an anonymous hand pulling its lever (Porter's first close-up to be completely integrated with its narrative context). All other shots in the film are **long shots**.

3. Interior of the firemen's dormitory, with the men first asleep, then waking in response to the alarm—a slight temporal overlap from shot 2—dressing, and sliding down the pole.

4. Interior ground floor of the firehouse, actually an outdoor set, with the pole in the center upon which no one has yet appeared; workers harness the horses to the engines, and the firemen finally slide down the pole from above at the conclusion of the scene, as the engine races off to the right. There is a significant temporal overlap and redundancy of action between shots 3 and 4, clearly establishing narrative space and time.

5. Exterior of the firehouse as the doors are flung open and the engines charge out, overlapping the action of shot 4.

6. Suburban street scene: eight engines rush past the camera from right to left, passing a crowd of bystanders (stock footage apparently, since it's snowing in this scene but nowhere else in the film).

7. Street scene: four engines rush past the camera, which pans (moves horizontally on its vertical axis) dramatically to follow the fourth and comes to rest on the front of a burning house, where a fireman (Edison actor / producer James White) jumps from the vehicle.

8. Interior of the house: mother and child in an upstairs room filled with smoke.

9. Exterior of the house: the mother approaches an upstairs window and calls for help.

10. Interior: the woman collapses on a bed.

11. Exterior: a fireman enters the front door.

12. Interior: the same fireman runs into the room through a door at the right and breaks the window (which was open in shots 9 and 11, but closed in 8 and 10).

13. Exterior: firemen on the ground place a ladder against the broken window.

14. Interior: the fireman carries the woman to the ladder, which has appeared at the window.

15. Exterior: the fireman and the woman descend the ladder.

16. Interior: the fireman enters the window by the ladder and picks up the child.

17. Exterior: the woman becomes hysterical.

18. Interior: the fireman exits through the window with the child.

19. Exterior: the fireman descends the ladder with the child and reunites it with the mother.

20. Interior: firemen enter the room through the window to extinguish the fire with a hose.

By **crosscutting** (or, synonymously, **intercutting**) seven shots of an interior with six shots of an exterior to depict parallel actions occurring simultaneously, Porter seemed to have achieved—for the first time in motion-picture history—narrative omniscience over the linear flow of time, which the cinema of all arts can most credibly sustain. No other medium permits such a rapid alternation of multiple perspectives without destroying point of view. (There were precedents for parallel editing, or crosscutting, of course, in late nineteenth-century melodrama, fiction, magic-lantern projections, stereopticon slide shows, and newspaper comic strips.)

During the 1970s, however, another print of *Life of an American Fireman* came to light that is based on the paper print filed for copyright at the Library of Congress by the Edison Company in 1903. This so-called "Copyright Version" is 400 feet long and contains nine shots—the first seven as described above, and then the entire interior sequence (shots 8, 10, 12, 14, 16, 18, and 20 combined) followed by the entire exterior sequence (shots 9, 11, 13, 15, 17, and 19) without any intercutting between them. Intercutting these sequences, as the Cross-Cut Version does, creates the illusion of simultaneous actions occurring from simultaneously accessible points of view. The Copyright Version, which shows the entire rescue first from the inside and then from the outside, involves a returning to an early period of time, almost an "instant replay" from a new point of view. In fact, this use of temporal repetitions and overlapping action can be found in such comtemporaneous Porter films as *How They Do Things on the Bowery* (October 1902). Thanks primarily to the scholarship of Charles Musser, the Copyright Version was established as the original, and in the restored print circulated by MoMA since 1985, the two concluding scenes repeat the same rescue operation from interior and exterior points of view, depicting it as two completely autonomous actions.[6]

We know today that early filmmakers often overlapped events across their splices—as here and in the rocket landing in *A Trip to the Moon*—to establish spatial, temporal, and narrative relationships between shots. Yet, while this kind of overlapping continuity clearly defines spatial relationships, it leaves temporal ones underdeveloped and, to modern sensibilities, confused. Where, for example, in *Life of an American Fireman*, have the firemen *been* between the time they slide down the pole from their dormitory in shot 3 and appear on the pole on the ground floor in shot 4? Why, in *A Trip to the Moon*, does the rocket seem to land twice, once in shot 9 and again in shot 10? For a while, at least, these questions did not trouble contemporary audiences. Conditioned by lantern slide shows, stereopticon presentations, and even comic strips, they understood a sequence of motion-picture shots as a series of individual moving photographs, or "attractions," each of which was self-contained within its frame. If actions overlapped from shot to shot, it didn't matter since the temporal relationship between shots was assumed to be alinear—there was no assumption that time moved forward when **cutting** from one scene to the next. But spatial relationships in such pre-existing forms as slide shows were clear because their only medium *was* space. Motion added the dimension of time, and the major problem for early filmmakers would soon become the establishment of linear continuity from one shot to the next. Modern continuity editing, on which the classical Hollywood system was based (and which still predominates today), began when they realized that action could be made to seem continuous from shot to shot, and, conversely, that two or more shots could be made to express a single unit of meaning.

Porter himself moved toward this realization in *The Great Train Robbery* (December 1903), which exists in a single authoritative version and is widely acknowledged to be his finest achievement. Although its interior scenes were shot at the Edison studios in New York City and its exteriors near the Edison laboratory in Orange, New Jersey, *The Great Train Robbery* was simultaneously the cinema's first Western and, as Kenneth Macgowan has observed, the first film to exploit the violence of armed crime. The most significant thing about the film for us, however, is its editing continuity. Although *The Great Train Robbery* contains no intercutting *within* scenes, Porter cut *between* his scenes without dissolving or fading

and—most important—*without playing them out to the end*. In Méliès, and in early Porter for that matter, dramatic scenes are played out to their logical conclusion and new scenes are begun in the studied and gradual manner of nineteenth-century theater. There are no ellipses in the action of a continuous scene once it has begun, just as there would and could be none on the legitimate stage. But Porter saw that a filmmaker can in fact cut away from one scene before it is dramatically complete and simultaneously cut into another after it has already begun. This practice contains the rudiments of a truly cinematic narrative language because it posits that the basic signifying unit of film—the basic unit of cinematic meaning—is not the *scene*, as in Méliès, and not the continuous unedited film strip, as in the earliest Edison and Lumière shorts, but rather the *shot*, of which, as Griffith would later demonstrate, there may be a virtually limitless number within any given scene. In this respect, Porter anticipated the formulation of the classical Hollywood editing style.

Written, directed, photographed, and edited by Porter, *The Great Train Robbery* is 740 feet long (a little over twelve minutes at the average standard silent speed of 16 fps) and consists of fourteen separate nonoverlapping *shots*—not scenes—of actions, which are themselves dramatically incomplete. These are connected by straight cuts in the following **sequence**:

1. Interior of the railroad telegraph office: two bandits enter and bind and gag the operator while the moving train, visible through the office window, comes to a halt.
2. Railroad water tower: the other members of the gang board the train secretly as it takes on water.
3. Interior of the mail car with scenery rushing by through an open door; the bandits break in, kill a messenger, seize valuables from a strongbox, and leave.
4. Coal tender and interior of the locomotive cab: the bandits kill the fireman after a fierce struggle, throw his body off the train, and compel the engineer to stop.
5. Exterior shot of the train coming to a halt and the engineer uncoupling the locomotive.
6. Exterior shot of the train as the bandits force the pas-

6. Like so many other issues of early film history, this one is complicated by these factors: (1) producers sometimes filed prints for copyright with the scenes spliced together in the order in which they had been shot rather than as they were edited for final release, and (2) after 1910 the public demand for films became so great that distributors and pirates would frequently re-edit older film to conform with contemporary tastes and redistribute them as completely new productions.

1.22 The editing sequence of Porter's *The Great Train Robbery* (1903).

sengers to line up along the tracks and surrender their valuables; one passenger attempts to escape, runs directly into the camera lens, and is shot in the back.

7. The bandits board the engine and abscond with the loot.

8. The bandits stop the engine several miles up the track, get off, and run into the woods as the camera pans and tilts slightly to follow them.

9. The bandits scramble down the side of a hill and across a stream to mount their horses; the camera follows them in a sweeping horizontal panning shot.

10. Interior of the telegraph office: the operator's daughter arrives and unties her father, who then runs out to give the alarm.

11. Interior of a crowded dance hall: a "tenderfoot" is made to "dance," as six-guns are fired at his feet; the telegraph operator arrives and a posse is formed.

12. Shot of the mounted bandits dashing down the face of a hill with the posse in hot pursuit; both groups move rapidly toward the camera; one of the bandits is killed as they approach.

13. Shot of the remaining bandits examining the contents of the stolen mail pouches; the posse approaches stealthily from the background and kills them all in a final shoot-out.

14. Medium close-up (a shot showing its subject from the midsection up) of the leader of the bandits firing his revolver point blank into the camera (and, thus, the audience), a shot that, according to the Edison catalogue, "can be used to begin or end the picture."

In addition to cutting away from scenes (or shots) before they were dramatically concluded and avoiding temporal overlap, *The Great Train Robbery* contains other innovations. Although the interior sequences were shot in the conventional manner of Méliès, the camera placement in many of the exterior sequences was fresh and dynamic. Several shots, for example, were staged in depth: in shot 4 the camera looks down on the action in the engine cab from the coal tender as the train plunges through space, and in shot 6 an actor moves diagonally across the frame into the camera lens rather than horizontally across it— a major departure from the frontally composed, theatrical staging of Méliès. There is what seems to be an effective use of in-camera matting[7] in shot 1 (the moving train coming to a halt, seen through the telegraph office window) and shot 3 (the landscape rushing past the express car door), but is more likely double exposure or double printing. More significant, there are two authentic **panning shots**—a rather perfunctory tilt following the bandits as they dismount the engine in shot 8, and an impressively cinematic pan following the sweep of their flight through the woods in shot 9.[8] Finally, there is a suggestion of parallel editing reminiscent of the Cross-Cut Version of *Life of an American Fireman* when Porter cuts from the bandits' getaway back to the bound telegraph operator in shot 10.

Nevertheless, for all of its contributions to the medium, *The Great Train Robbery* was not an isolated breakthrough. As Charles Musser points out in *Before the Nickelodeon: Edwin S. Porter and the Edison Manufacturing Company, The Great Train Robbery* was well situated within the already popular subgenres of the chase and the railway travel film (a type of attraction popularized by Hale's Tours in which the audience was encouraged to assume the role of passengers on a moving train).[9] All of its interior scenes are photographed in the stagelike fashion of Méliès: the actors move from left to right or vice versa across the "proscenium" of the frame, and their gestures are exaggerated and stilted. Furthermore, Porter never uses more than one camera angle or position in any one setting, and, like those of Méliès, most of his shots are long shots showing the actors at full length. On the other hand, by building up a continuity of dramatic action out of thirteen separate shots, not counting the final close-up, Porter had shown that the narrative structure of cinema need not be that of *scenes* arranged according to the dicta of the legitimate stage, which must observe the unities of time and place, but could be that of shots arranged according to rules that film generates for itself. It remained for others to elaborate these rules, but Porter had hit upon the crucial fact that cinematic narrative depends not so much upon the *arrangement of objects or actors within a scene* (as does the theater and, to a large

---

7. Blacking out the window and door spaces on the first exposure and then double-exposing the film to imprint the projected sequence.

8. Panning was a relatively difficult operation before the introduction of the geared pan head for the camera tripod later in the decade. Charles Musser, however, points out that the technique had a long-established precedent in the photographic panoramas of the nineteenth century ("The Early Cinema of Edwin S. Porter," p. 17).

9. Charles Musser, *Before the Nickelodeon: Edwin S. Porter and the Edison Manufacturing Company* (Berkeley: University of California Press, 1991), pp. 259–65.

extent, still photography) as upon the *arrangement of shots in relation to one another*.

Contemporary audiences understood none of this, but they loved the dramatic excitement generated by Porter's editing and by what amounted at the time to his **"special effects,"** including bursts of hand-tinted orange-yellow smoke during the gunfights. So spectacular was the commercial success of *The Great Train Robbery* that the film was studied and imitated by filmmakers all over the world. It is frequently credited with establishing the realistic narrative, as opposed to Méliès-style fantasy, as the dominant cinematic form from Porter's day to our own and with temporarily standardizing the length of that form at a single reel—1,000 feet, or ten to sixteen minutes, depending on the speed of projection (as pointed out earlier in this chapter, films could grow in narrative sophistication only in proportion to their growth in length). Furthermore, *The Great Train Robbery* probably did more than any film made before 1912 to convince investors that the cinema was a moneymaking proposition, and it was directly instrumental in the spread of permanent movie theaters, popularly called **nickelodeons** or "store theaters," across the country.

More than fifty of Porter's subsequent films have survived. These display a richness of storytelling within the representational system that he had helped to establish. He continued to practice overlapping action in such conventional productions as *Uncle Tom's Cabin* (1903), a filmed play in fourteen "tableaux" linked together by descriptive intertitles (which he may have been the first to use), complete with painted backdrops and a cakewalk, and in the social-justice melodramas *The Ex-Convict* (1904) and *The Kleptomaniac* (1905), which are notable at least for their themes. Some of Porter's later work has modest technical interest—he matched camera angles from shot to shot in *Maniac Chase* (1904), employed dramatic, one-source lighting in *The Seven Ages* (1905), used panning shots in *The White Caps* (1905), and experimented with model animation in *Dream of a Rarebit Fiend* (1906) and *Teddy Bears* (1907), as well as animating the title sequences of a number of his other films (in fact, the titles of *How Jones Lost His Roll* [1905] are among the earliest extant examples of American animation).

But Porter could not adapt to the new methods of filmmaking and the emerging system of representation that developed in response to the rampant growth of the

1.23 The original "Nickelodeon," Pittsburgh, 1905.

nickelodeons, which by 1907 were drawing one million patrons per day. Their popularity had created a public demand for story films that forced the rationalization of production, which in his managerial capacity, at any rate, Porter initially encouraged. But as production became ever more hierarchical and rigorous, he left Edison to form his own production company. This eventually became the independent Rex Film, which he sold to Universal Film Manufacturing Company in 1912 to join Adolph Zukor as director-general of the Famous Players Film Company; there he supervised the entire output and directed conventionally successful adaptions of novels and plays as *The Prisoner of Zenda* (1913), *The Count of Monte Cristo* (1913), *Tess of the Storm Country* (1914), and *The Eternal City* (1914; filmed on location in Rome), until he left the business in 1916.[1] Like Méliès, Porter had a genius for constructing narratives that communicated with early audiences at a certain crucial point in

---

1. Always mechanically inclined, Porter spent a good deal of his time at Famous Players experimenting with sound recording, color and widescreen cinematography, and even 3-D projection. When he left, he bought enough shares in the Precision Machine Company to become its president. There he focused his energies on the manufacture of the Simplex projector, a product of his own invention, which became the industry standard of its era. Precision Machine merged with the International Projecting Company in 1925 and was wiped out by the crash of 1929, which Porter survived by another twelve years.

their developing relationship with the screen. The overlapping continuities of *How They Do Things on the Bowery* (1902) and *Life of an American Fireman* (1903), *The Kleptomaniac* (1905) and *Rescued from an Eagle's Nest* (1908) told their stories in ways their audiences could comfortably understand.

Ironically, it was the work of Porter as much as that of any other filmmaker that had created the nickelodeon boom. Before the rise of these nickelodeon theaters (1905–6), exhibition was carried out in a wide variety of sites: vaudeville theaters, summer parks, small specialized storefront theaters, lecture halls, churches, saloons, between acts of plays by repertory companies touring the nation's opera houses. With vaudeville theaters in the major cities paying the largest fees and giving the greatest visibility to motion pictures, fierce competition existed among such houses by the turn of the century. These theaters hired and advertised the name of the exhibition service as much as or more than the films ("The Cinématographe," "The Biograph," etc.). During the novelty period (1895–97), major exhibitors either made their own films (the Lumières' Cinématographe) or were closely affiliated with a production company (the Vitascope with the Edison Manufacturing Company). The exhibition service would supply the theater with an "operator" and a short (eight to fifteen minutes) program of films. At this point, then, the film industry functioned as a unit, with the producers leasing a complete film service of projector, projectionist, and shorts to the vaudeville houses as a self-contained "act." By 1897, this pattern changed as producers began to sell projectors and films outright to itinerant exhibitors, who would travel with their shows from one temporary location—theaters, fairgrounds, circuses, lyceums, and the like—to the next, as the novelty of their programs wore off. Itinerant exhibition separated that function from production for the first time and gave the exhibitor a large degree of control over early film form since he was responsible for arranging the one-shot films purchased from producers into coherent, crowd-pleasing programs. This process, which often involved the addition of narration, music, and sound effects, was effectively a form of editing, and the itinerant projectionists of 1897 to 1904 may be properly regarded as the first "authors" of motion pictures (some, like Porter, of course, became directors in the modern sense after the industry had stabilized in the first decade of the twentieth century).

Yet the practice of selling prints outright, which

encouraged itinerant exhibition, simultaneously discriminated against the owners of permanent sites and inhibited their future growth. In 1903, in response to this situation, Harry J. and Herbert Miles, operating between offices in New York and San Francisco, functioned as middlemen between producers and exhibitors, buying prints from the former and leasing them to the latter for 25 percent of the purchase price. Later, rental fees would be set according to production costs and admission returns per film, but the exchange system of distribution quickly caught on because it handsomely profited everyone concerned. The new film brokers, or "distributors," literally made fortunes by renting the same prints to different exhibitors over and over again; exhibitors found that they could vary their programs without financial risk and reduce overhead at the same time; and producers ultimately experienced a surge in demand so enormous that it forced the wholesale industrialization of production previously described. (For example, Robert C. Allen claims that between November 1906 and March 1907 producers increased their weekly output from 10,000 to 28,000 feet and still could not meet demand.)

The most immediate effect of the rapid formation and rise of the distribution sector was the "nickelodeon boom," in which the number of permanent theaters in the United States mushroomed from a mere handful in 1904 to between 8,000 and 10,000 by 1908. There had been such theaters in the United States since 1896, but few survived more than two or three years. Many had much briefer life spans. Thomas L. Tally opened his Electric Theater in Los Angeles in 1902 but closed it the following year to become a traveling exhibitor.[2] Storefront theaters did not become very profitable over the long term until the exchange system of distribution created an economic context for them and gave birth to the nickelodeons. Named for the original "Nickelodeon" (ersatz Greek for "nickel theater") that opened in Pittsburgh in 1905, these were makeshift exhibition sites lodged in converted storefronts that showed from ten minutes to sixty minutes worth of shorts for an admission price of five to ten cents, depending on the amenities, such as piano accompaniment and cushioned seats, and the location. Although they were originally associated with working-class audiences, nickelodeons appealed increasingly to

---

2. Musser to author, 4/14/88.

1.24 D. W. Griffith in Porter's *Rescued from an Eagle's Nest* (1908).

segments of the middle class as the decade wore on, becoming identified in the public mind with narrative; and their rapid spread across the country by the end of 1908 forced the standardization of film length at one reel, or 1,000 feet—about sixteen minutes at the average silent speed of 16 fps (see footnote, pp. 10–11)—to facilitate new economies of production, distribution, and exhibition.

This was the industrial system that Porter resisted and ultimately rejected. But before he left Edison in 1909, he did something that, by circumstance, was to prove immensely important to the history of cinema. His otherwise undistinguished melodrama *Rescued from an Eagle's Nest* (1908—see p. 53) provided a needy young actor named David Wark Griffith with his first leading role in films and marked the beginning of a career that was to last forty years and bring the embryonic narrative cinema to a high point of development.[3] Before he came to Porter, Griffith had tried his hand at almost everything, from hop picking to selling the *Encyclopaedia Britannica* door-

to-door, but he wanted most desperately to become a writer. A chain of rejected stories and failed plays led him inexorably to the Edison Corporation studios with a scenario based upon a work by the French playwright Victorien Sardou (1831–1908), *La Tosca*. This Porter flatly rejected as having too many scenes, but he offered Griffith a salary of $5 a day to appear in a film of his own, whose improbable story was based on a real event. In it, Griffith, who was more than a little ashamed to have accepted work as a film actor, played a heroic woodcutter who rescues his infant child from the mountain aerie of a large and vicious eagle, wrestling the bird to its death in the process. (Appropriately, the struggle was emblematic of Griffith's simplistic vision of human experience, which he depicted in his own films as one long, arduous battle between the forces of darkness and the forces of light.) When *Rescued from an Eagle's Nest* first appeared on the screen in early 1908, Porter had already abdicated his position of creative leadership in film, but the technology of cinema had long been born and the rudiments of its narrative language evolved. The cinema now awaited its first great narrative artist, who would refine that language, elaborate it, and ultimately transcend it.

---

3. The film was actually co-directed by J. Searle Dawley (?-1949). Following contemporary practice, Porter had hired Dawley in late 1907 as his collaborator. Dawley worked with him on scripts and directed the actors while Porter remained in charge of cinematography and editing, and ran the studio. As a former actor and playwright, Dawley had theatrical experience in staging that Porter lacked, while Porter possessed state-of-the-art skills in cinematography, and they worked together as a team until 1908, when Dawley was placed in charge of his own production unit. Even after Porter left Edison, Dawley stayed on, directing more than three hundred one-reelers for the company, until 1912, when he joined Porter at Famous Players as his executive assistant and creative consultant. There, he ultimately became a successful director of features, working with such stars as Mary Pickford and John Barrymore, until his retirement from the industry in the early 1920s. See Musser, *Before the Nickelodeon: Edwin S. Porter and the Edison Manufacturing Company.*

International Expansion, 1907–1918

The United States

THE EARLY INDUSTRIAL PRODUCTION PROCESS

By 1908 the cinema had risen from the status of a risky commercial venture to that of a permanent and full-scale, if not yet a major and respectable, industry. In that year, there were ten thousand nickelodeons and one hundred film exchanges operating in the United States, and they were supplied by about twenty "manufacturers" who churned out films at the rate of one to two one-reelers per director per week. A similar situation existed on the Continent and in Britain, and by the time Griffith entered the cinema, the studios or "factories" of the Western world could scarcely keep up with the public demand for new films. Furthermore, the novelty of the medium was such that almost anything the studios could produce, regardless of quality, was gobbled up by the international network of distribution and exchange. Although the introduction of mercury-vapor lamps encouraged several companies to construct indoor studios as early as 1903, films were generally shot out of doors in a single day on budgets of $200 to $500 and were rigorously limited to one reel of about 1,000 feet in length, with a running time of ten to sixteen minutes, depending on projection speed. Nearly all of the films were put together on an assembly-line basis following the stage-bound narrative conventions of Méliès and the overlapping continuities of Porter, with natural backgrounds and few, if any, retakes. Not surprisingly, industry emphasis on speed and quantity of production militated against creative experiment and demanded the detailed division of labor described by Lewis Jacobs in *The Rise of the American Film*:

> Action was divided into scenes, and these were photographed in consecutive order. The number of scenes was limited to seven or eight, each 100 to 150 feet long, in order to keep the story within the 1,000-foot length in which the raw film came. . . . Increased production necessitated more people and a division of duties to speed the output. By 1908 directing, acting, photo-

2.1 The exterior and interior of a typical nickelodeon, c. 1909.

graphing, writing, and laboratory work were separate crafts, all of equal status. Each worker regarded himself as a factory hand, lacking only a time-clock ritual for concrete evidence of his position. No one received any screen credit for the work he did, for, as the employers realized, a public reputation would mean higher wages. Besides, most of the directors, actors, and cameramen who had come to the movies were more or less ashamed of their connection with them; they stayed in their jobs because they needed work, and they gave little thought to the medium's possibilities or opportunities. Nearly everyone still regarded moviemaking as a shabby occupation.

Whatever the truth of this last point may have been, industrial conditions between 1907 and 1913 clearly motivated cost-efficient production practices and encouraged a trend toward centralization at the same time that they discouraged formal experiment except in the service of increased narrative clarity. As Janet Staiger has pointed out, the need to achieve continuous and regular production during this period led manufacturers to build factory-like studios and promote the use of scenario- and, ultimately, continuity-based scripts.[1] So from the nickelodeon boom to the advent of features, the main industrial tendency was toward centralization and standardization of production practice, and the uniform product was the one-reel film.

Nevertheless, financial competition among rival production companies was fierce and frequently lawless. Though Thomas Edison claimed ownership of essential patents for the motion-picture camera, many companies were using versions of his machines without paying royalties. Hundreds of suits and countersuits were filed by Edison and his competitors during this renegade period of rampant growth. At the other end of the industry, relationships between distributors and exhibitors became increasingly strained. Since copyright law for motion pictures was still being defined by the courts and legislatures and, in any case, most production companies did not bother to copyright their pictures, the majority of films were more or less in the public domain, and prints were often stolen, pirated, and illicitly duplicated, just as books had been before 1893. Theoretically, of course, what a production company made it owned, even if its product had been made with pirated equipment; but legal and professional standards for the film industry during this period of rapid international expansion were ill defined, and their enforcement was difficult.

None of this should surprise us since the same problems of ownership and duplication rights have arisen in our own day in connection with magnetic audio and video recording. The dispute over film patents and copyrights was perhaps more ruthless because it was conditioned by the mercenary social Darwinism of the Gilded Age,

---

1. See Janet Staiger, "The Hollywood Mode of Production to 1930," in David Bordwell, Janet Staiger, and Kristin Thompson, *The Classical Hollywood Cinema: Film Style and Mode of Production to 1960* (New York: Columbia University Press, 1985), pp. 123–27, 142–49. See also Charlie Keil, *Early American Cinema in Transition: Story, Style, and Filmmaking, 1907–1913* (Madison: University of Wisconsin Press, 2001).

which operated on the principle that might makes right. The period from 1880 to 1904 saw the rise of the great American "robber barons," and it is not in the least incongruous that Edison spies like Joseph McCay were engaged in industrial espionage against rival production companies during the same years that witnessed bloody strikebreaking by police, National Guardsmen, and Pinkertons all over the country as well as race riots and lynchings. As one might expect, it took a counterforce of considerable intensity to turn the young industry from the anarchic competitiveness of laissez-faire capitalism toward a more orderly pursuit of profit.

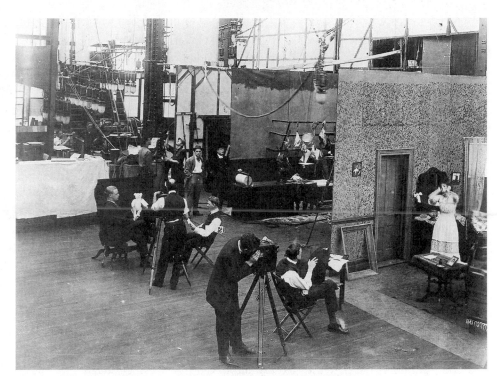

2.2 The interior of the Edison studio (c. 1912), showing the shooting of several separate films.

This counterforce was provided by attacks from what were to become the American cinema's two arch-antagonists: organized religion and the political Right. These institutions had tolerated "living pictures" so long as they promised to be a short-lived novelty, but when it became clear that the cinema was well on its way to becoming a major social and economic force in the nation, they took the offensive. In early 1907, for example, an editorial appeared in the conservative and influential *Chicago Tribune*, accusing the "Five Cent Theatre" of "ministering to the lowest passions of children" and being "wholly vicious." "Proper to suppress them at once," the editorial said. "They cannot be defended. They are hopelessly bad." The question basically was and is the ancient one, dating from Plato's *Republic*, of the state's right of censorship. But the fact that film is a mass medium of popular entertainment as well as an art form—and a medium that bypasses language to communicate directly with the senses through moving photographic images of the apparently real—makes the issue more complex than perhaps it has ever been in Western culture.[2] There was no complexity as far as the *Tribune* and its allies were concerned; between 1907 and 1909 it became obligatory in many parts of the country for ministers, businessmen, and politicians to inveigh against the movies as a corrupter of youth and a threat to public morality. Yet the issue at this point was perhaps less ideological than economic; in becoming a major entertainment industry overnight, the movies suddenly threatened the very substantial revenues of churches, saloons, and vaudeville theaters from coast to coast. The situation was not unlike the sudden emergence of television as a formidable rival to the movies in the late 1940s, for in both cases the older institutions sought to take social and economic sanctions against the newer ones and fell on their faces in the process. Like television, the movies came to stay, and no amount of mud-slinging or moralizing was going to change that fact.

THE MOTION PICTURE PATENTS COMPANY

Vilified by contemporary reformers and riven by internecine war, the most powerful American production companies banded together under joint Edison-Biograph

---

2. The superabundance of moving photographic images made possible by television and other video delivery systems in our own day further compounds the problem.

leadership in a protective trade association called the Motion Picture Patents Company, or the MPPC, on December 18, 1908.[3] To ensure their continued dominance of the market, Edison, Biograph, Vitagraph, Essanay, Kalem, Selig Polyscope, Lubin, Star Film, Pathé Frères, and Kleine Optical (the largest domestic distributor of foreign films) pooled the sixteen most significant U.S. patents for motion-picture technology and entered into an exclusive contract with Eastman-Kodak for the supply of raw **film stock.** The MPPC, also known simply as the "Trust" (which it was, Arthur Knight points out, "in the full Rooseveltian sense"), sought to control every segment of the industry through issuing licenses and assessing royalties therefrom. The use of its patents was granted only to licensed equipment manufacturers, and film stock could be sold only to licensed producers; licensed producers and importers were required to fix rental prices at a minimum level and set quotas for foreign footage to reduce competition; MPPC films could be sold only to licensed distributors, who could lease them only to licensed exhibitors; and only licensed exhibitors had the right to use MPPC projectors and rent company films. To this seemingly airtight system was added the General Film Company, which integrated the licensed distributors into a single corporate entity in 1910—the same year in which motion-picture attendance in the United States rose to 26 million persons a week.

Although it was clearly monopolistic in practice and intent, the MPPC helped to stabilize the American film industry during a period of unprecedented growth and change by standardizing exhibition practice, increasing the efficiency of distribution, and regularizing pricing in all three sectors. Furthermore, in the days when clarity of image and synchronization of camera and projector were still highly unreliable, Patents Company producers made the best films in the business because of their monopoly on the best equipment and film stock. MPPC films were generally static and unimaginative in narrative terms (Vitagraph and Biograph films were clear exceptions), but they guaranteed their viewers a degree of technical competence that few other manufacturers could match. For this reason, and because General Film could guarantee national distribution, many foreign distributors who were immune to the coercive machinery of the Patents Company did business with it willingly. Had things gone according to plan, the MPPC would have completely monopolized the film industry of the United

States and a large part of the Western world by 1911 or 1912. But the collusive nature of the Trust also provoked a reaction against it that ultimately destroyed it and gave the industry its modern form.

In a sense, the MPPC's ironclad efforts to eliminate competition merely fostered it. Almost from the outset, there was widespread resistance to the MPPC from independent distributors (numbering ten or more in early 1909) and exhibitors (estimated at 2,000 to 2,500); and in January 1909 they formed their own trade association, the Independent Film Protective Association—reorganized that fall as the National Independent Moving Picture Alliance—to provide financial and legal support against the Trust. A more effective and powerful anti-Trust organization was the Motion Picture Distributing and Sales Company, which began operations in May 1910, three weeks after the inception of General Film, and which eventually came to serve forty-seven exchanges in twenty-seven cities. For nearly two years, independents were able to present a united front through the Sales Company, which finally split into two rival camps in the spring of 1912: the Mutual Film-Supply Company, which distributed for the independent producers Thanhouser, Gaumont, American Film Manufacturing, Great Northern, Reliance, Eclair, Solax, Majestic, Lux, and Comet, at the rate of about twenty reels per week; and Universal Film Manufacturing Company, which distributed for New York Motion Picture Company, Independent Motion Picture Company (IMP), Powers, Rex, Champion, Republic, and Nestor. By imitating MPPC practices of combination and licensing, the early independents were able to compete effectively against the Trust: in the Trust's first three years, the independents netted about 40 percent of all American film business. Their product, the one-reel **short,** and their modes of operation were fundamentally the same. But the later independents, such as William Fox (1879–1952) of the Greater New York Film Rental Company, and Adolph Zukor (1873–1976) of the Famous Players Film Company, would revolutionize the industry by adopting the multiple-reel film as their basic product,

---

3. In the year prior, the Edison company had headed its own "trust," the Association of Edison Licensees, which Biograph resisted by forming an association with a group of foreign producers on the basis of its own patents. It was Biograph's ability to survive the Edison initiative that led to a pooling of their interests in late 1908 in the MPPC. (Charles Musser to author, 1/22/88.)

2.3 A typical advertisement by independent Carl Laemmle from the trade journal *Motion Picture World* attacking the Patents Company's monopoly on the industry.

to make or to distribute films of greater length. Until 1908, source material for most fiction films was freely borrowed from popular stage plays (themselves often adapted from popular novels), comic strips, and songs, which gave the audience a contemporary frame of reference for the action and contributed to narrative clarity. However, in 1908 a court ruling made motion pictures subject to the same copyright restrictions as other dramatic productions.[4] This encouraged filmmakers to turn to the classics, whose copyright lineage was often less clear than that of contemporary works, and to produce such anomalies as one-reel versions of fifteen Shakespearean plays, including *King Lear* (1909) and *The Tempest* (1911); five Dickens novels; three Wagner operas; and *The Scarlet Letter* (1909), *Vanity Fair* (1911), and *Ben Hur* (1907), although most production during this period featured more popular subjects. When films like J. Stuart Blackton's five-reel *The Life of Moses* (1909) and D. W. Griffith's two-reel *His Trust* (1911) were produced by Patents Company members (Vitagraph and Biograph respectively), they were released to exhibitors in serial fashion at the rate of one reel a week, which seriously damaged their continuity. In open revolt against this practice, many exhibitors began to hold up the first reel of a multireel film until they had received the others and could show them sequentially on the same bill—a procedure that ultimately forced the MPPC to release Griffith's second **two-reeler,** *Enoch Arden* (1911), as a single film.

THE ADVENT OF THE FEATURE FILM

The multiple-reel film—which came to be called a **feature,** in the vaudevillian sense of a headline attraction—had gained general acceptance in 1911 with the release of two European imports, *The Crusaders* (four reels) and *Dante's Inferno* (also known as *Inferno*, five reels).[5] But

a move that caused the MPPC to embrace the one-reeler with a vengeance and hastened its demise.

Film length had originally been standardized at one reel out of a conviction that the public had a negligible attention span and would not sit still for more. It is true, of course, that a majority of early filmgoers were untutored laborers, many of them non-English-speaking immigrants, lacking sophisticated verbal skills; but the processes of verbal and visual cognition are quite distinct from one another (recent scientific research, in fact, has demonstrated them to be functions of separate hemispheres of the brain). Furthermore, there are few things more compelling in human perceptual experience than the cinematic image in projection. Nevertheless, the entire MPPC system was geared toward the production of one-reelers, and its licensees were expressly forbidden

---

4. In *Harper & Brothers et al. v. Kalem Co. and Kleine Optical Co.*, filed April 6, 1908, the publisher successfully sued Kalem for producing a version of *Ben Hur* (1907) without compensating the copyright holder. See Charles Musser, *Before the Nickelodeon: Edwin S. Porter and the Edison Manufacturing Company* (Berkeley: University of California Press, 1991), pp. 420–21.

5. In vaudeville theater, *feature* referred to quality rather than length—i.e., the feature act was the best and most prominent on any given program—and Michael Quinn argues that this is the sense in which the term was initially understood in the distribution and exhibition sectors of the film industry as well ("Distribution, the Transient Audience, and

it was the smashing success of the four-reel French film *The Loves of Queen Elizabeth* (*Les Amours de la Reine Elizabeth* [Henri Desfontaines and Louis Mercanton, 1912]), starring the celebrated stage actress Sarah Bernhardt, that convinced the industry of the feature's commercial viability in America. Produced for the Histrionic Film Company, *Queen Elizabeth* was a laborious "filmed play" (for a discussion of such *films d'art*, see pp. 46–48), but it proved so profitable for importer Adolph Zukor that he was able to found the independent Famous Players production company with its returns (reportedly, $80,000 on an investment of $18,000, the amount he paid for the U.S. distribution rights).

Even more persuasive was the huge American success of the nine-reel Italian superspectacle *Quo vadis?* in the spring of 1913. Directed by Enrico Guazzoni (1876–1949) for the Cines Company, this film contained vast crowd scenes and lavish special effects that kept audiences entranced throughout its running time of more than two hours, and it proved to American producers beyond question that the future of cinema lay at least in part in the feature film. *Quo vadis?* also established another important precedent: it was shown exclusively in first-class legitimate theaters rather than nickelodeons (a policy that Griffith would later adopt for his features) and thus attracted a more prosperous and sophisticated audience than the American cinema had enjoyed at any time since its birth. The international success of *Quo vadis?* was so great that it permitted Italy to capture a large share of the world market until the outbreak of World War I, and the film was followed in early 1914 by a twelve-reel historical blockbuster, Giovanni Pastrone's (1883–1959) masterly *Cabiria*. In its liberal camera movement, elaborate **sets**, and skillfully constructed narrative, *Cabiria* anticipated the great epics of Griffith; in fact, Griffith probably saw the Italian films while he was working on *Judith of Bethulia* (1913) and *The Birth of a Nation* (1915), respectively.

A substantial portion of the filmgoing public had also been affected by the Italian spectacles, and soon a feature craze was sweeping the country and the industry, challenging the MPPC's conservative leadership and the very existence of its one- and two-reel films. At first, there were difficulties in distributing features since the exchanges associated with both the Patents Company and the independents were geared toward cheaply made one-reel shorts. Owing to their more elaborate production values, features had relatively higher negative costs, and

2.4 An "arty" advertisement for an early American feature, from a 1912 issue of the *New York Dramatic Mirror*.

were put at a disadvantage by a system that charged a uniform price per foot. By 1914, however, national feature distribution alliances were organized that correlated pricing with a film's negative cost and box-office receipts (among the first were Adolph Zukor and Jesse L. Lasky's Paramount, Warners' Features, and Lou Selznick's World Film Company), and these new exchanges demonstrated the economic advantage of multiple-reel films over shorts. Exhibitors quickly learned that features

the Transition to the Feature Film," *Cinema Journal* 40, 2 [Winter 2001]: 35–57]).

The oldest surviving American feature, a complete original nitrate print of which was discovered in 1996, is the five-reel *Richard III*, directed by James Keane, starring popular Shakespearean actor Frederick Warde, and produced in 1912 by the M. B. Dudley Amusement Company of New York City for $30,000. One of eight domestic features released that year (only two others of which survive in their entirety), *Richard III* was restored by the American Film Institute in 1996, complete with its original color tints and a new score by Ennio Morricone; it is available in this form on DVD from Kino Video.

could command higher admission prices and longer runs; single-title packages were also cheaper and easier to advertise than programs of multiple titles. On the manufacturing side, producers found that the higher expenditure for features was readily amortized by high-volume sales to distributors, who in turn were eager to share in the higher admission returns from the theaters. Soon the whole industry would reorganize itself around the economics of the multiple-reel film, and the effects of this restructuring gave motion pictures their characteristic modern form in almost every sense.

The feature film (arbitrarily defined in this era as any film of four or more reels) made motion pictures respectable for the middle class by providing a format analogous to that of the legitimate theater and suitable for the adaptation of middle-class novels and plays. The production companies of the century's first decade saw themselves as manufacturers of cheap entertainment for a generally uneducated mass public, and the MPPC had rigidly systematized this conception of filmmaking in its five-year domination of the industry. Audiences who aspired to more than short, simple action stories or comedies were unlikely to find it on the screen, so they stayed home and read or went to the theater instead, and their absence was felt by the small but growing number of filmmakers within the system—most notably D. W. Griffith—who were coming to regard their medium as a serious mode of expression. The advent of the feature, however, opened up the possibility of more complicated narratives and offered filmmakers a form commensurate with serious artistic endeavor. Features also placed a new premium on the quality of production as well as its quantity by demanding higher standards of verisimilitude. Longer films had to be made more slowly, with larger budgets and greater care than one- and two-reelers, and once the feature was popularly accepted, high technical standards and elaborate production values became a new focus of competition within the industry.

To accommodate the new films and their new audiences, a new kind of movie theater sprang up across the country, the first of which was the 3,300-seat Strand opened by Mitchell L. Marks in the heart of the Broadway theater district of Manhattan in 1914. No longer converted storefronts with sawdust floors and hard seats, the new theaters were the earliest of the big, comfortable, and elegantly appointed urban "dream palaces" that came to be controlled by the major Hollywood studios in the 1920s. The Strand, for example, featured a two-story gilt

2.5 "Dream palace" architecture in the 1920s: the auditoriums of the Ambassador Theater, St. Louis, and the Oriental Theater, Chicago.

and marble interior hung with tapestries and crystal chandeliers, plush pile carpeting, numerous lounges, a thirty-piece orchestra, and a monumental Wurlitzer organ—all for the respectably expensive admission price of twenty-five cents. Owing to their luxuriance, these houses required the regular showing of features to attract large audiences at premium prices, and by 1916 there were over 21,000 such new or remodeled film theaters in the country. Their arrival signaled the close of the nickelodeon era and the beginnings of the Hollywood studio system.

THE RISE OF THE STAR SYSTEM

The MPPC's attempt to monopolize the film industry through patents pooling and licensing was based on Edison's experience with the phonograph, and it failed to anticipate the unique volatility of the motion-picture market, especially the widespread resistance of the independents and the enormous potential of the feature film. Another issue that the Patents Company misjudged badly was the power of the marketing strategy that has come to be known as the "star system." Borrowed from the theater industry, this system involves the creation and management of publicity about key performers, or stars, to stimulate demand for their films. Initially, MPPC producers feared that using the real names of its actors, actresses, and directors in screen credits or advertisements would enable them to acquire a public following and demand higher salaries. Thus, for years the most popular of early performers were known to audiences only by the names of the characters they played (Mary Pickford was "Little Mary") or the companies in whose films they appeared (Florence Lawrence was "the Biograph girl"), even though producers were constantly deluged with requests for information about their leading players. In 1909, however, articles about personalities such as Ben Turpin, Pearl White, and Mary Pickford began to appear in trade journals; and in 1910, Carl Laemmle (1867–1939) of IMP lured Florence Lawrence away from Biograph and, through a series of media stunts, promoted her into national stardom.

Immediately after hiring Lawrence, Laemmle circulated anonymous press reports of her death, using her real name in public for the first time.[6] Then he undertook an extensive advertising campaign to denounce the story as a "black lie" spread by the Patents Company to conceal the fact that Miss Lawrence had come over to IMP; and,

2.6 A Laemmle advertisement in *Motion Picture World*.

as proof of her continued existence, Laemmle promised that King Baggott, IMP's leading man (also named publicly for the first time), would escort Miss Lawrence to St. Louis on the day that their first IMP picture together opened in that city. There was a near riot as what seemed to be half of St. Louis crowded into the train station to get a glimpse of the former Biograph girl's still earthly presence, and the star system was born. Laemmle's publicization of players like Florence Lawrence and King Baggott proved so successful that other independent pro-

6. In *Stardom: The Hollywood Phenomenon* (New York: Stein and Day, 1970), Alexander Walker maintains that Miss Lawrence had *already* been dismissed from Biograph for publicizing herself and had been blacklisted by all other licensed film companies when Laemmle hired her, which, if true, only serves to heighten the spectacular opportunism of the producer's coup.

ducers soon adopted star policies of their own. Even MPPC members began to use this kind of publicity, although never as flamboyantly as their rivals, and by 1911, Vitagraph, Lubin, and Kalem had all begun to publicize their performers. Biograph resisted this change the longest, and it was not until 1913 that it began to advertise the names of its actors and its chief director, D. W. Griffith, who would soon join the ranks of the independents in any case. The production companies now suddenly subjected their audiences to a publicity blitz of photographs, posters, postcards, and fan magazines featuring their favorite stars; and stardom rapidly began to acquire the mythic dimensions that would make it the basis of production policy in the American cinema for the next fifty years.

THE MOVE TO HOLLYWOOD

Those fifty years were spent almost exclusively in the Los Angeles suburb (originally a small industrial town) called Hollywood—the result of a mass migration of production companies from the East that occurred between 1907 and 1913. The reasons why a full-scale Eastern-based industry moved its entire operation to southern California during these years have never been completely clear, but the general contours of the phenomenon are obvious enough. In the wake of the nickelodeon boom, as exhibitors had begun to require as many as twenty to thirty new films per week, it became necessary to put production on a systematic year-round schedule. Since most shooting still occurred out of doors in available light, such schedules could not be maintained in the vicinities of New York and Chicago, where the industry had originally located itself to take advantage of trained theatrical labor pools; and, as early as 1907, producers such as Selig Polyscope began to dispatch production units in winter to warmer climates. It was soon clear that what producers required was a new industrial center—one with warm weather, a temperate climate, a variety of scenery, and other qualities (such as access to acting talent) essential to their highly unconventional form of manufacturing. Various companies experimented with location shooting in Jacksonville, Florida; San Antonio, Texas; Sante Fe, New Mexico; and even Cuba, but the ultimate site of the American film industry became Hollywood. It is generally thought that southern California's distance from the MPPC's headquarters in New York and proximity to the Mexican border made it an attractive sanctuary for inde-

2.7 Hollywood, c. 1915 and 1919.

pendents, but by 1911 MPPC members such as Selig, Kalem, Biograph, and Essanay had also established facilities there in response to the region's other attractions. These included the very type of climate required for year-round production (the U.S. Weather Bureau estimated that an average of 320 days per year were sunny and / or clear, so that even interiors could be shot outdoors if muslin sheets were placed overhead to soften the shadows) and a wide range of topography within a 50-mile radius of Hollywood, including mountains, valleys, lakes, islands, woodland, seacoast, and desert—the Mediterranean could be simulated on the Pacific coastline, and Griffith Park could stand in for the Alpine forests of central Europe. Other attractions were the status of Los Angeles as a professional theatrical center, the existence of a low tax base, and the presence of cheap and plentiful labor and land. This latter factor enabled the newly arrived production companies to buy up tens of thousands of acres of prime real estate on which to locate their studios, standing sets, and **back lots.** Between 1908 and 1912, many of the independents moved permanently to Hollywood, and several Patents Company members began to shoot films there on a seasonal basis. D. W. Griffith, for example, first took his Biograph crew west for the winter in 1910, and he con-

2.8 A Selig Polyscope Company stage, Hollywood, 1913. Note the compartmentalized sets and muslin sun diffusers overhead.

poration (to become Paramount Pictures, 1935), formed by a merger of Adolph Zukor's Famous Players Film Company, Jesse L. Lasky's Feature Play Company, and the Paramount distribution exchange in 1916; Universal Pictures, founded by Carl Laemmle in 1912 by merging IMP with Powers, Rex, Nestor, Champion, and Bison; Goldwyn Pictures, founded in 1916 by Samuel Goldfish (later Goldwyn) and Archibald Selwyn; Metro Pictures and Louis B. Mayer Productions, founded by Louis B. Mayer in 1915 and 1917, respectively; and the Fox Film Corporation (to become 20th Century–Fox, 1935), founded by William Fox in 1915. After World War I, these players were joined by Loew's, Inc. (parent cor-

tinued this practice until he left Biograph in 1913 to work in southern California year round with the independent Mutual Film Company.

THE NEW STUDIO CHIEFS AND INDUSTRY REALIGNMENT

By 1915, there were approximately 15,000 workers employed by the motion picture industry in Hollywood and over 60 percent of American production was centered there. In that same year, *Variety* reported that capital investment in American motion pictures—the business of artisanal craftsmen and fairground operators only a decade before—had exceeded $500 million. Owing to its poor business practices, the MPPC had been functionally inoperative since 1914 (it would be formally dissolved in 1918 as the result of an antitrust suit initiated by the Wilson administration in 1912). Thus, the most powerful companies in the new film capital were the independents, flush with cash from their conversion to feature production: the Famous Players–Lasky Cor-

poration of MGM, by merger of Metro, Goldwyn, and Mayer companies just cited, 1924), a national exhibition chain organized by Marcus Loew and Nicholas Schenck in 1919; First National Exhibitors Circuit, Inc. (after 1921, Associated First National Pictures, Inc.), a group of independent exhibitors that established its own production facilities at Burbank in 1922; Warner Bros. Pictures, incorporated by Harry, Albert ("Abe"), Sam, and Jack Warner in 1923 but active in the industry for at least a decade before; and Columbia Pictures, incorporated in 1924 by Harry and Jack Cohn. As their names indicate, these organizations were to become the backbone of the Hollywood studio system, and the men who controlled them shared several important common traits. For one thing, they were all independent exhibitors and distributors who had outwitted the Trust and clawed their way to the top through a genius for financial manipulation in the postnickelodeon feature boom, merging production companies, organizing national distribution networks, and ultimately acquiring vast theater chains. They saw their business as basically a retailing operation modeled on the practice of Woolworth's and Sears. (Or, as Marcus Loew, then board chairman of MGM, put it to a business group in the mid-1920s, "Chain-store methods in the movies are just like what you have in railroads, telephones, and automobiles.") And yet most of these men had been small tradesmen who had gambled on the movie business in the anarchic first decade of the cinema, hoping to turn a quick profit. From penny-arcade showmen and nickelodeon operators they became "manufacturers" of their own films, then producer-distributors, and finally Hollywood studio chiefs—the temporary custodians of the twentieth century's most influential and culturally significant art form. Not incidentally, these men were all first-generation Jewish immigrants, most of them with little formal education, from Eastern Europe, while the audience they served—which came to call them **"moguls,"** after the barbarian conquerors of the Indian Empire—was 90 percent Protestant and Catholic. This circumstance would become an issue during the 1920s, when the movies became a mass medium that was part of the life of every American citizen and when Hollywood became the chief purveyor of American culture to the world.[7]

The year 1914 was a crucial one for the American film industry. The feature film had by this time triumphed almost completely over the one- and two-reeler, or short, which survived only in the cartoon, newsreel, and serial installment (and, through the 1920s, as the vehicle for some of America's greatest comic talent, as will be seen in Chapter 6); and this development coincided with a general economic boom created by the outbreak of war in Europe. Profits soared along with costs, and the industry expanded rapidly in all directions, making and breaking fortunes in the process. Those companies—most notably Paramount—that had placed their faith in feature films became prosperous and powerful, while those that had cast their lot with the shorts were destroyed. The pioneers—Kalem, Star Film, General Film, Biograph, the Edison Company itself—were all wiped out by the new public hunger for feature films, and the MPPC dwindled to insignificance during the war years, finally succumbing in 1918 to the federal antitrust suit previously mentioned. Vitagraph, Lubin, Selig, and Essanay survived temporarily by merging as VLSE, and the independents Mutual, Reliance, and Keystone combined to form the short-lived but important Triangle Film Corporation, which simultaneously employed the talents of the American cinema's three top directors—D. W. Griffith, Thomas H. Ince, and Mack Sennett (whose careers will be explored in Chapters 3 and 6). Meanwhile, Paramount—and, to a lesser extent, Universal and Fox—had begun to produce features as never before. Jacobs estimates that by 1915 Paramount alone was releasing three to four features *per week* to some 5,000 theaters across the nation.

The vast new market for feature-length films produced far-reaching changes in both the structure and scale of the industry. As films quintupled in length, and star salaries and screen-rights payments increased dramatically, production costs rose from between $500 and $1,000 per film to between $12,000 and $20,000 and the figures would triple in the postwar years. Production profits were ensured during this period through promotion of the star system and through advertising on a grand scale to increase demand, but producers also sought some means of national distribution to multiply the return on their increasingly large investments. As usual, it was Adolph Zukor who led the way.

THE "BLOCK BOOKING" DISPUTE AND THE ACQUISITION OF THEATERS

In 1916, Zukor merged his Famous Players Company with the Paramount distribution exchange and twelve smaller companies to form the Famous Players–Lasky Corporation (later Paramount Pictures),[8] which briefly

---

7. For example, before his ouster as head of the corporation in 1931, William Fox personally approved every picture released by Fox Film: "No picture ever produced by the Fox Film Corporation was permitted to be viewed by the general public, until every title it contained had been approved and passed by me, and I don't remember a single picture ever made by the company that the titles contained therein were not corrected, edited, and rewritten by me" (quoted in *Upton Sinclair, Upton Sinclair Presents William Fox* [Los Angeles: Upton Sinclair, 1933], p. 5). Fox had quit school at the age of eleven in order to help support his family.

8. Paramount Pictures Corporation was founded as a feature distribution organization by W. W. Hodkinson (1881–1971) and other independent exhibitors on May 8, 1914. It financed and distributed the features of Zukor's Famous Players Film Company and Jesse L. Lasky's Feature Play Company (whose six-reel *The Squaw Man* [Cecil B. DeMille, 1914] was the first important feature made in Hollywood), among those of other producers, and in May 1916 Zukor and Lasky bought a controlling share of Paramount's stock. With Zukor as president, their Famous Players–Lasky Corporation was incorporated on June 19, 1916,

came to dominate the industry by inventing the practice of **block booking.** The block-booking system of distribution forced exhibitors to accept a production company's films in large groups, or "blocks," tied to several particularly desirable titles (usually prestigious star vehicles) in advance of production. This all-or-nothing distribution policy obviously favored the producer, who was provided with a constant outlet for his films regardless of their quality, and soon every production company in the business had adopted it. Within a year's time, however, the practice of block booking had led to such abuses that the nation's leading exhibitors rebelled against the Hollywood-based production companies in much the same way that independents like Zukor had only several years earlier rebelled against the Patents Company monopolists.

In 1917, executives of twenty-six of the largest first-run exhibition chains established the First National Exhibitors Circuit (known as Associated First National Pictures, Inc., after 1921), whose purpose was to challenge Paramount Famous Players–Lasky by producing and/or distributing its own features. It was an attempt to gain control over the means of film production and distribution, just as block booking represented an attempt on the part of producers to gain control over the means of distribution and exhibition. In short, both parties to the struggle, like Edison before them, recognized that whoever controlled distribution controlled the industry. Under the skillful management of W. W. Hodkinson, who had originally founded the Paramount exchange in 1914, First National was able to eliminate block booking temporarily by 1918 and to acquire sole distribution rights to the films of the industry's number-one star, Charlie Chaplin. In retaliation, Paramount Famous Players–Lasky in 1919 entered the theater business and bought up first-run houses and exhibition circuits all over the country. Zukor's campaign to acquire exhibition outlets was as aggressive and ruthless as the MPPC's war against the independent producers had been a decade before. His agents became known as "the wrecking crew" and "the dynamite gang" among independent theater owners from New England to Texas to Colorado, and by 1921 Paramount Famous Players–Lasky owned 303 theaters compared to First National's 639. Its war with First National—and, later, Loew's, Inc.—for control of distribution and exhibition extended well into the 1920s, culminating in Paramount's bankruptcy and First National's

absorption by Warner Bros. Before that occurred, however, First National had become a major power in its own right, and Fox, Goldwyn, and Universal had all joined Zukor in the race for theater acquisition.[9]

This race, which naturally required huge capital for real estate investment over and above normal production costs, was financed by the great Wall Street banking houses: Kuhn, Loeb, and Company were backing Paramount Famous Players–Lasky; the du Ponts and the Chase National Bank stood behind Goldwyn; Fox was supported by the John F. Dryden–Prudential insurance group and Universal by Shields and Company. Stock issues were floated for the production companies and listed on the New York Exchange for public investment, and trained financiers began to assume managerial positions within the industry to protect their own investments. The continuing involvement of American big business in motion pictures had begun, and, less than a decade after the demise of the storefront theater, the cinema had become a large-scale industry. By the arrival of sound in the late 1920s, it had become, by some accounts

---

but Paramount was kept as the company's trade name until 1927. From 1927 to 1930, the company was called Paramount Famous Lasky Corporation, and in 1930, it became the Paramount Publix Corporation. When the firm went bankrupt in 1933, Lasky (1880–1958) was forced out, and it was reorganized as Paramount Pictures, Inc. In 1966 it became a wholly owned subsidiary of Gulf and Western Industries, which in 1989 was reconfigured and renamed Paramount Communications, Inc., and in 1994 became a subsidiary of Viacom. In the text, I refer to Zukor's production-distribution-exhibition conglomerate of the 1910s and 1920s as Paramount Famous Players–Lasky (or simply Paramount, as it was commonly known during the 1920s), although each component was separately incorporated in a bid (ultimately unsuccessful, as will be seen in Chapter 11) to avoid antitrust suits.

9. Despite temporary victories, block booking persisted into later decades in one form or another until it was declared illegal as part of the Supreme Court's 1948 Paramount decision, as will be discussed in Chapters 8 and 11, and there is still a tendency for producer/distributors to coerce exhibitors (including, since the 1960s, television networks) into accepting their less desirable titles as part of package deals. In the mid-1970s, the film companies instituted the practice of "blind bidding," whereby first-run exhibitors are required to put up a lump-sum rental fee for a major film four to eight months in advance of its release (the revenues, in fact, are often used to finance the film's production). Like block booking, blind bidding insures a profitable rate of return for the producer/distributor regardless of a film's box-office success and leaves the exhibitor with a disproportionate burden of financial risk. In 1979, the National Association of Theater Owners (NATO), a trade organization representing 8,000 U.S. exhibitors, crafted an anti-blind-bidding bill for introduction in about thirty state legislatures; but it was not widely adopted, and the practice continues in most parts of the country.

(largely those of its own publicists—see footnote, p. 202), the fourth largest in the nation.

THE RISE OF HOLLYWOOD TO INTERNATIONAL DOMINANCE

Hollywood's rise to power was assured by the First World War, which temporarily eliminated the European competition (mainly French and Italian) and gave the United States dominion over the world film market for the next fifteen years (and even after, though the configuration of the market changed with the coming of sound). Before August 1914, the American film industry had been forced to compete on the open market with all of the major European industries and for some years had actually lagged behind those of Italy and France. Just prior to the war, however, France's market position had slipped, and Italy's world-famous spectacles were losing their audience to American competition. But in the United States, the arrival of the big-budget feature had resulted in a considerable rise in the standards of motion-picture production in the immediate prewar years, and the audience had been growing rapidly. In some sectors, the American film was even gaining respectability as an art form: serious books were written about it (for example, the poet Vachel Lindsay's *The Art of the Moving Picture* [1915] and the psychologist Hugo Münsterberg's *The Photoplay: A Psychological Study* [1916]), and newspapers established regular columns for "photoplay" reviews.

When war broke out on the Continent late in the summer of 1914, the European industries were virtually shut down since the same chemicals used in the production of celluloid were needed to manufacture gunpowder, but the American cinema prospered throughout the war in unchallenged economic and political security. Jacobs estimates that while in 1914 the United States produced just a little over one half of the world's motion pictures, by 1918 it was making nearly all of them. Thus, for four years America exercised complete control over the international market and set up a formidable worldwide distribution system, and between 1914 and 1918 the world at large, including Asia and Africa (but excepting the belligerent Germany), saw nothing but American films, if it saw films at all. In 1919, immediately following the Treaty of Versailles, 90 percent of all films screened in Europe were American, and the figure for South America was, and would remain for years, nearly 100 percent. During the 1920s, of course, the European figures would decline significantly as Germany and the Soviet Union became major powers in world cinema and as other nations attempted to shield their industries with protective laws. Nevertheless, World War I had placed the American film industry in a position of undisputed economic and artistic leadership—a position it would maintain until the coming of sound and in some respects forever after.

Expansion on the Continent

The German and Scandinavian film industries were still embryonic when war came to Europe in 1914,[1] and the British cinema, after taking an early lead through the work of the Brighton school (see pp. 18, 20), had failed to evolve industrially at all. But the industries of France and Italy had reached fairly advanced states of development in the first decade of the 1900s, and together they led the world cinema commercially and artistically until the American industry usurped them.

THE EMPIRE OF PATHÉ FRÈRES

From 1898 to 1904, the French cinema was dominated by Georges Méliès, whose stagebound fantasies became so widely popular that all other producers were forced to imitate his techniques in order to compete with him. This meant that trick photography and the static camera became key features of French films until about 1905. Nevertheless, Méliès's commercial influence began to decline in the latter half of the decade as his Star Film Company, basically a small-scale artisanal business, was driven into competition with the ruthless and monopolis-

---

1. An exception was Denmark's Nordisk Films Kompagni, founded in 1906 and still in existence (making it the world's oldest production company), which was well organized and actively competitive in the world market, largely due to the international popularity of its leading lady, Asta Nielsen (1882–1972), and the narrative prescience of such talented directors as Viggo Larsen (also company founder; 1880–1957), Robert Dinesen (1874–1940), August Blom (1869–1947), Urban Gad (1879–1947), and Benjamin Christensen (1879–1959). From 1911 to 1916, Nordisk led the world in feature production and is credited with having invented both the figure of the "vamp" and the sensationalistic "social problem" film. World War I irreparably damaged the company by causing the loss of its non-German markets, and most of Nordisk's key personnel went to work for other industries after 1919.

tic Pathé Frères, founded in 1896 by the former phonograph manufacturer Charles Pathé (1863–1957).

The French film historian Georges Sadoul has called Charles Pathé "the Napoleon of the cinema" because in just over a decade he created a vast industrial empire that gave France control of the international film market until the eve of the war. Financed by some of France's largest corporations, Pathé acquired the Lumière patents in 1902 and commissioned the design of an improved studio camera that soon dominated the market on both sides of the Atlantic (it has been estimated that, before 1918, 60 percent of all films were shot with a Pathé). Pathé also manufactured his own film stock and in 1902 established a vast production facility at Vincennes, where films were turned out on an assembly-line basis. The following year, he began to open foreign sales agencies, which rapidly developed into full-blown production companies—Hispano Film (1906), Pathé-Russe, Moscow (1907), Film d'Arte Italiano (1909), Pathé-Britannia, London (1909), and Pathé-America (1910)—and soon there were Pathé agents all over the world. (Indeed, Pathé Frères is credited with pioneering the film industries of Australia, Japan, India, and Brazil.) Pathé also acquired permanent exhibition sites in every part of Europe, building in 1906 the world's first luxury cinema in Paris (the Omnia-Pathé), and by 1908 the company dominated distribution on the Continent. Thus, while he did not totally eliminate his competition, Charles Pathé realized within the structure of a single organization what Edison was unable to achieve through the conglomerate MPPC (of which Pathé and Star formed the Continental wing)—a complete vertical monopoly over every aspect of the industry. In 1908 Pathé marketed twice as many films in the United States as all the American production companies put together, and by 1909 the same situation existed in Great Britain.[2]

With Pathé's profits fifty to one hundred times the cost of making its negatives, the company was able to become Méliès's distributor for several stormy years between 1911 and 1913, after which the "alchemist of light" abandoned his alchemy altogether. In 1923, Méliès was forced to sell his negatives for the chemical value of the celluloid (the reason that fewer than 140 of his 500 films survive—see note, p. 14), and in 1929 he was found operating a gift kiosk in a Paris Métro station[3]—like so many of the cinema's great pioneers, utterly forgotten. Happily, though, Méliès spent the remaining nine years of his life in the relative comfort of a rent-free apartment provided

2.9 Pathé's *La Passion* (Ferdinand Zecca and Lucien Nonguet, 1903).

by Mutuelle du Cinéma, a rest home for retired cinematographers, and had the satisfaction of seeing his achievements revaluated in the 1930s by the first real historians of the cinema.

The director-general of Pathé's huge studios at Vincennes was Ferdinand Zecca (1864–1947), a former music-hall singer whose canny instincts for what the public would pay to see contributed fundamentally to his employers' enormous financial success. Like Méliès, Zecca specialized in story films, and he was thoroughly conversant with the former magician's cinematic tricks. But in most of his productions Zecca broke away from the Méliès tradition of filmed theater by shooting out of doors and occasionally panning his camera to follow an action. His first films were realistic one-reel melodramas of the lower classes such as *L'Histoire d'un crime* (1901) and *Les victimes de l'alcoolisme* (1902—a five-minute version of Émile Zola's novel *L'Assommoir*), but he went on to become a master of many genres, including the historical romance, fantasy, farce, religious spectacle, and

---

2. For a history of the Pathé company in the United States as well as what he calls "a cultural history of our own cinema's nationalization" (in that Pathé competition focused the debate over what was "American" about American films at the very moment of cinema's institutionalization), see Richard Abel's *The Red Rooster Scare: Making Cinema American, 1900–1910* (Berkeley: University of California Press, 1999).

3. This story may also be apocryphal, deriving as it does from Méliès's now-discredited *Mes Mémoires* (originally published in the Italian journal *Cinema* [Rome, 1938]; rpt. in French in Maurice Bessy and G. M. Lo Duca, *Georges Méliès, mage* [Paris: Prisma, 1945]; 2nd ed. [Paris: J. J. Pauvert, 1961]).

2.10 Max Linder as Pathé's "Max."

the highly popular *actualité reconstituée*, or "reconstructed newsreel," innovated by Méliès. Furthermore, borrowing freely from the chase films of England's Brighton school, Zecca developed a uniquely Gallic version of the type—the *course comique* ("comic chase"), in which cutting for parallel action was combined with trick photography *à la Méliès* to achieve not suspense, but laughter. With titles like *Dix femmes pour un mari (Ten Wives for One Husband)*, *La Course à la perruque (The Pursuit of the Wig)*, *La Course aux tonneaux (The Pursuit of the Beer Barrels)*—all 1905—most of these films were shot in the streets of Paris and had a vitality and inventiveness that impressed the young Mack Sennett, among others, who found in them the model for his own Keystone Kops (see p. 172).

Zecca remained with Pathé until its dissolution in 1939[4] but never evolved beyond an intelligent synthesizer of the discoveries of others. Like his German counterpart Oskar Messter (see p. 87), he is best remembered as an authentic primitive who upgraded and varied the content of his nation's films and who worked toward the refinement of the medium generally, without making any unique personal contributions. Another Pathé talent was the comedian Max Linder (1883–1925), who became

world famous for his subtle impersonation of an elegant but disaster-prone man-about-town in prewar Paris. Linder wrote and directed most of his four hundred films and had a profound influence upon the work of Charlie Chaplin in the next decade (see pp. 172–76). Finally, it should be remarked that in 1910 Pathé inaugurated the first regular weekly newsreel, the *Pathé Gazette*, which acquired an international following in the years before the war.

LOUIS FEUILLADE AND THE RISE OF GAUMONT

Pathé's only serious rival on the Continent at this time was Gaumont Pictures, founded by the engineer-inventor Léon Gaumont (1864–1946) in 1895. Though never more than a quarter of the size of Pathé, Gaumont followed the same pattern of expansion, manufacturing its own equipment and mass-producing films under a supervising director (through 1906, Alice Guy [1875–1968], the cinema's first woman director; afterward, Louis Feuillade [1873–1925]). Like Pathé, Gaumont opened foreign offices and acquired theater chains, and for nearly a decade after their construction in 1905 its studios at La Villette were the largest in the world. From 1914 to 1920,[5] Gaumont was able to dominate the French cinema, largely through the popular success of Feuillade. Formerly a scriptwriter for Pathé, Feuillade had begun his career at Gaumont in 1906 by directing comic shorts and chase films in the manner of Zecca. He made hundreds of narrative films over the next few years and finally came into his own with the serial detective film *Fantômas*, shot in five episodes of four to six parts each between 1913 and 1914. This type of film had been originated by Victorin Jasset (1862–1913), an ex-sculptor directing for the Éclair

---

4. The company was revived in 1944—sans Charles Pathé, who had sold his interest in the business to Bernard Natan in 1929—as the Société Nouvelle Pathé-Cinéma, which today specializes mainly in distribution (see Charles Pathé, *De Pathé Frères à Pathé Cinéma* in *Premier Plan* 55 [Lyon: SERDOC, 1970]).

5. The outbreak of World War I in August 1914 temporarily paralyzed the French industry as general mobilization drained the studios of both personnel and equipment. Production by major companies resumed in 1915 but fell considerably below prewar levels, forcing the French to rely heavily on American films and ultimately to lose control of their own market.

2.11 *Fantômas* (Louis Feuillade, 1913–14): composition in depth.

2.12 *Les Vampires* (Louis Feuillade, 1915–16): density and depth.

company, in the *Nick Carter* series of 1908. Feuillade brought to the form a sense of plastic beauty and visual poetry that allowed his serials to achieve the status of art.

Fantômas was based on the popular serial novel by Pierre Souvestre and Marcel Allain about the adventures of the mysterious French supercriminal Fantômas, "Master of Terror," and the attempts of a ratiocinating police detective named Juve to track him down. The incredible exploits of Fantômas and his pursuer are all beautifully photographed on location in the streets, houses, sewers, and suburbs of prewar Paris and offer a strangely lyrical blend of naturalism and fantasy. Feuillade's other detective serials—the ten-episode *Les Vampires* (1915–16),[6] the twelve-episode *Judex* (1916), *La Nouvelle mission de Judex* (1917), *Tih Minh* (1918), and *Barabbas* (1919)— all manifest this same combination of mystery and the quotidian real, and their atmospheric beauty had a direct and continuing influence upon French film in the work of Jean Durand, Abel Gance, Jacques Feyder, and René Clair (see pp. 308–13).

Yet Feuillade was a conservative in terms of cinematic structure. As David Robinson has very aptly pointed out, Feuillade consistently rejected serially arranged shots (or **montage,** made famous by the Soviets, whose work will be explored in Chapter 5) in favor of *tableaux* elaborately composed in depth. This circumstance makes Feuillade not only a legitimate heir to Méliès, but the progenitor of **mise-en-scène**[7] (literally, "putting-in-the-scene") aesthetics, first articulated after World War II by the French film theorist André Bazin and the young critics of *Cahiers*

du cinéma (see pp. 441–43), which puts major emphasis on the creative use of movement and space *within* the shot rather than upon the relationship *between* shots, as does montage. At the height of his fame during World War I, Feuillade was recognized as a genius. Extremely successful with audiences all over the world, his serials were also admired by contemporary intellectuals—espe-

6. Recently restored by the Cinémathèque Française, with long-missing intertitles reinserted by Feuillade's grandson Jacques Champreux. See the feature-length documentary history *Mille et une Marguerites* (*A Thousand and One Daisies* [Pierre Phillipe, 1988]) made to celebrate Gaumont's ninetieth anniversary. The restored *Les Vampires* is available on DVD from Image Entertainment.

7. In theater, the arrangement of actors, scenery, and props in preparation for a performance. In cinema, that which occurs before the lens of the camera, as opposed to the effects created by editing.

cially the surrealists André Breton, Louis Aragon, and Guillaume Apollinaire, who saw in his skillful amalgamation of realistic detail, dense poetic imagery, and pure fantasy an analogue for their own attempts to "respiritualize" modern art. But because montage aesthetics dominated film theory from the era of Griffith and Eisenstein (see pp. 148–52) until the writings of Bazin began to appear in the late 1940s, Feuillade's reputation was in total eclipse from 1918 to this latter date, when the *Cahiers* critics (who would later become the *auteurs* ["authors," or directors with a personal style] of the French New Wave) finally recognized Feuillade as the first great *metteur-en-scène* (practitioner of *mise-en-scène* aesthetics), as seminal to their theory of film art as Griffith was to montage.

The success of Feuillade's serials led to widespread acceptance of the form throughout the world: *Fantômas* is the father of the American *Perils of Pauline* series (actually directed for Pathé by the French director Louis Gasnier), Britain's *Ultus*, Germany's *Homunculus*, and Italy's *Tigris*, all well received in their day. And their popularity allowed Gaumont to succeed Pathé as the most powerful French studio of the twentieth century's second decade, although by 1914 France's monopoly on the international market was doomed. In 1910 approximately 60 to 70 percent of all imported films in the West derived from French studios, making France's domination of world cinema as nearly complete as Hollywood's was to be. When the war began, however, France lost much of its market at a time when the rate of Hollywood production was multiplying almost monthly.

The Gaumont studio commanded the talents not only of Feuillade, but of his protégé Jean Durand (1882–1946), whose comedy series *Onésime, Calino* (originated by Romeo Bosetti, c. 1909), and *Zigoto*, made between 1907 and 1914 with his comic troupe Les Pouics, influenced the work of both Mack Sennett and René Clair (see pp. 171–72, 313–15). Gaumont also had under contract the former Alice Guy, Alice Guy Blaché[8] (*La Vie du Christ* [*The Life of Christ*, 1906]; *Fanfan la Tulipe* [*Fanfan the Tulip*, 1907]), and the cartoonist Émile Cohl (1857–1938), who applied the principle of stop-motion photography to the drawing board and became the father of modern **animation**. The practice of animating concrete objects by photographing them one frame at a time and changing their position between frames was popularized by the American director J. Stuart Blackton (1875–1941) in such Vitagraph films as *A Mid-Winter's Night*

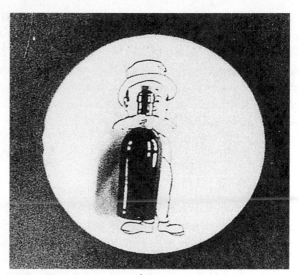

2.13 *Les Joyeux Microbes* (Émile Cohl, 1909).

Dream (1906) and *The Haunted Hotel* (1907) and was already known in France as *mouvement américain* when Cohl began to refine it near the end of the decade. In cartoons like the *Fantoche* series and *Les Joyeux Microbes* (*The Jolly Germs*, 1909), Cohl pioneered the frame-by-frame animation of line drawings, puppets, and natural objects, and also became the first director to combine

---

8. In 1907, Guy married Herbert Blaché (1882–1953), a Gaumont cameraman and, later, director. Alice and Herbert specialized in directing *phonoscènes*, shorts made to exploit Gaumont's Chronophone sound-on-disk system, and the couple came to the United States shortly after their marriage to help create a Chronophone franchise here. By 1909, Gaumont had built a studio in Flushing, New York, to produce English-language phonoscenes, but he abandoned the project in 1910, apparently under duress from Edison. At this point, Alice Guy formed her own production company, Solax, and rented the Flushing studio to make silent films that would be distributed by Gaumont. In 1912, she built her own production facility in Fort Lee, New Jersey, which made her the only woman to date who has owned her own film studio (although, if telefilm were included, Lucille Ball would figure here, too). Guy remained director-general of Solax until it was absorbed by Herbert's company, Blaché Features, in 1914. Together, they directed and produced features for a variety of independent distributors until Alice quit in 1920; Herbert directed through 1929, although the couple was divorced in 1922, when Alice returned to France with their two children. According to Alison McMahan's groundbreaking study *Alice Guy Blaché: Lost Visionary of the Cinema* (New York: Continuum, 2002), Guy pioneered a feminist mode of cinematic address by connecting diegetic and extradiegetic discourses in her comedies of cross-dressing and gender role reversal (pp. 207–9).

large-scale animation with live action. Finally, despite the French cinema's fall from international preeminence, Gaumont was able to establish a large production studio and exhibition circuit in England, called Gaumont-British, which remained under French control until 1922 and had a substantial impact on the development of British film (many of Alfred Hitchcock's first films, for example, were shot for Gaumont-British).[9]

THE SOCIÉTÉ FILM D'ART

The most influential phenomenon to occur in French cinema during the period of international expansion, however, came in the first decade of the twentieth century and was only remotely connected with a major production company (Pathé had partial control of the venture). This was the work of the Société Film d'Art, founded by the Parisian financiers Frères Lafitte in 1908 for the purpose of transferring to the screen prestigious stage plays starring famous performers. The idea was to attract the theatergoing middle class to the cinema by increasing its aesthetic and intellectual appeal—a revolutionary notion at a time in which the medium had only just emerged from the nickelodeon and the fairground tent.

The film historian Kenneth Macgowan has called Film d'Art "the first highbrow motion picture movement," and that description applies in both its positive and negative senses. On the one hand, the company used the best creative talent of the stage to mount its productions, commissioning original plays from members of the esteemed Académie Française and employing stars of the Comédie-Française to act in them. Leading composers wrote original scores for these plays, and eminent stage directors were contracted to direct them. From a literary and dramatic perspective, in fact, the credentials of Film d'Art were impeccable. From the standpoint of cinema, on the other hand, the Film d'Art productions were static if not regressive in their total embrace of the theatrical model.

For all their intellectual pedigree (and perhaps because of it), the lavishly staged productions of the Société Film d'Art were photographed plays; their directors made few concessions to the filmic medium, although, as Tom Gunning points out, some showed an awareness of the continuity of time and space that represents an advance over the discontinuous *tableaux* of Méliès.[1] Like a theater spectator in an orchestra seat, the camera occupied a central position with regard to the action and remained static

throughout, so that the film frame assumed the function of a proscenium arch. Most takes were long or medium-long shots, which permitted the players to appear at full length on the screen, just as they would on the stage. Each shot was made to correspond to an entire dramatic scene played out from beginning to end, although the acting itself was often notably restrained. Finally, as if to assure the spectators that they were indeed watching a "high-art film" (as one American distributor billed the product) and not just an ordinary "living picture," Film d'Art sets were constructed of papier-mâché and plaster, and the backgrounds were painted canvas; yet they frequently afforded the impressive staging in depth characteristic of many French films of this period.[2] As cinematic narratives, then, the Film d'Art productions were highly theatrical, but they were also self-contained dramatic wholes comprehensible to an audience in and of themselves. For several years they enjoyed an immense popular success and were imitated throughout the Western world.

The debut of the first Film d'Art production, *L'Assassinat du duc de Guise* (*The Assassination of the Duc de Guise*), took place in Paris on November 17, 1908, and it met with nearly universal acclaim. Directed by Charles Le Bargy and André Calmettes of the Comédie-Française, with an original script by Académicien Henri Lavedan and a score by Camille Saint-Saëns, *L'Assassinat du duc de Guise* was hailed by France's leading intellectual journals as a great cultural landmark; and one drama critic wrote that its premiere would prove as significant

9. Léon Gaumont retired in 1928, selling his distribution and theater chains to MGM. The production company became part of the Gaumont-Franco Film-Aubert consortium, which went bankrupt in the early 1930s, but the Gaumont name persists today in the Société Nouvelles des Établissements Gaumont, an international producer / distributor. Gaumont-British prospered independently under the stewardship of the producer Michael Balcon until he left in 1936 (see pp. 290–91), when it collapsed as a production / distribution firm. The exhibition chain was absorbed by the J. Arthur Rank Organization in the late 1940s, but newsreels continued to be made under the Gaumont-British logo until 1959.

1. Tom Gunning, *D. W. Griffith and the Origins of American Narrative Film* (Urbana: University of Illinois Press, 1991), pp. 173–74.

2. See Ben Brewster, "Deep Staging in French Films, 1900–1914," in *Early Cinema: Space-Frame-Narrative,* ed. Thomas Elsaesser and Adam Barker (London: British Film Institute, 1990), pp. 45–55, and Ben Brewster and Lea Jacobs, *Theatre to Cinema: Stage Pictorialism and the Early Feature Film* (New York: Oxford University Press, 1997).

to the history of film as the first public Cinématographe projection on December 28, 1895. In subsequent years, the Société Film d'Art filmed plays by Edmond Rostand, François Coppée, and Victorien Sardou, as well as versions of Dickens's novel *Oliver Twist*, *Madame Sans-Gêne* (a play by Sardou and Émile Moreau), and Goethe's novel *The Sorrows of Young Werther*, before the company was killed off by the introduction of sound. In its prime, however, the Société Film d'Art had so many imitators in France, Italy, Great Britain, Germany, Denmark, and ultimately the United States that it could scarcely compete with

2.14 *L'Assassinat du duc de Guise* (Charles Le Bargy and André Calmettes, for the Société Film d'Art, 1908).

them. France, for example, had not only the Société Cinématographique des Auteurs et Gens de Lettres, but the Série d'Art Pathé, Gaumont's Film Esthétique, Éclair's Association Cinématographique des Auteurs Dramatiques, and two independent companies, Film d'Auteurs and Théatro-Film.

For several years, the rage for lengthy adaptations of "classical" novels and plays—now known generically as *films d'art*—swept across western Europe, enshrouding the new medium of film in the literary orthodoxies of the past century. For a while it seemed as if everything written, sung, or danced (for filmed ballet and opera formed a large part of the *films d'art* corpus, too) in western Europe from the Renaissance to 1900 found its way into these stagebound and pretentious productions. Shakespeare, Goethe, Dumas *père* and *fils*, Hugo, Dickens, Balzac, Wagner, and Bulwer-Lytton, even the tragedies of Sophocles were all represented, side by side with the "modern classics" of contemporary authors like Anatole France and Henryk Sienkiewicz. Even Eastern Europe was affected: David Robinson maintains that the great

Russian vogue for historical costume films, which reached its aesthetic peak in Eisenstein's two-part *Ivan the Terrible* (1945–46), was born during this period, as was the Hungarian cinema's permanent fascination with literary subjects.

Although the *film d'art* vogue died out almost as rapidly as it had come into being, the movement's financial success had revealed a vast new audience that preferred serious, self-contained screen stories to comic chases and vaudeville acts, convincing producers all over the world to upgrade the content and narrative coherence of their films. Not surprisingly, when directors like Griffith and Feuillade began to cast serious stories into visually sophisticated form through montage on the one hand and *mise-en-scène* on the other, *film d'art* productions rapidly lost their audience, and the topsy-turvy state into which World War I threw the international market helped to accelerate the process.

Still, the *film d'art* movement had made the medium socially and intellectually respectable for the first time in its brief history and had heightened the respect of the

2.15 Sarah Bernhardt in *Les Amours de la reine Élisabeth* (Louis Mercanton, for Histrionic Films, 1912).

Finally, *film d'art* productions were directly responsiible for increasing the standard length of films from a single reel to four reels and more. As *films d'art* grew increasingly popular, they turned to ever weightier source material and grew proportionally in length. *L'Assassinat du duc de Guise* had been only 921 feet, or a little less than fifteen minutes long at standard silent speed. One of the last and most prestigious films d'art, Louis Mercanton's *Les Amours de la reine Élisabeth* (*The Loves of Queen Elizabeth*, 1912), ran four reels, or about fifty minutes. The story of how Adolph Zukor imported *Queen Elizabeth* into the United States and proved to the MPPC that Americans would sit through a film above a single reel in length (and pay a dollar each for the experience) has already been told. But it should be pointed out that the success of *film d'art* productions was also responsible for increasing film length in Great Britain, France, Italy, Germany, and Scandinavia, where the industries were less rigidly controlled than in the United States but equally conservative with regard to length. Thus, it fell to the *film d'art* movement to inaugurate the feature-length film in the West, though its advent had probably been inevitable since the invention of the Latham loop.

THE ITALIAN SUPERSPECTACLE

No country was more responsible for the rapid rise of the feature film than Italy, whose lavishly produced costume spectacles brought its cinema to international prominence in the years immediately preceding World War I. The Italian film industry may be said to have begun with the construction of the Cines studios in Rome, 1905–6, by the former inventor Filoteo Alberini (1865–1937). This firm gave the Italian cinema its first costume film,

a industry for itself. It also made a number of people— again, notably Griffith and Feuillade—aware of the necessity for developing a unique style of film acting that would eschew the broad gestures and facial grimaces of nineteenth-century theater in favor of a more subtle and restrained kind of playing. These contortions were important components of the grand theatrical style, appropriate and even necessary on a stage that is distant from its audience and fixed in space. In the cinema, however, a fixed distance between the figures on the screen and the audience cannot be maintained because spatial relationships are in a constant state of flux due to editing and camera movement. Furthermore, even in the most conservative of filmed plays—those photographed in long shot from a single camera angle and edited only between scenes—the figures in the *tableaux* appear much larger on the screen than they would on the legitimate stage, and the scrutiny of the camera lens is mercilessly accurate. For this reason, film acting has had to develop conventions of its own in recognition of the perverse thoroughness with which the camera records certain aspects of reality, and it might well be said that *film d'art* performances provided a model for these conventions.

La presa di Roma (*The Capture of Rome*, 1905), but devoted most of its first years to the production of short comedies in the French vein and modishly "decadent" melodramas starring the archetypal *femme fatale* Lyda Borelli (1884–1959—the model for America's own definitive vamp, Theda Bara [1890– 1955]). As major Italian financiers became increasingly interested in the film business, however, rival production companies began to proliferate. When Ambrosio Films of Turin released Luigi Maggi's (1867–1946) *Gli ultimi giorni di Pompeii* (*The Last Days of Pompeii*) in 1908, Cines once again turned its attention to his-

2.16 The chariot race from Enrico Guazzoni's *Quo vadis?* (1913).

torical themes, producing Mario Caserini's (1874–1920) feature-length *Catilina* and *Beatrice Cenci* in 1909, and his *Lucrezia Borgia* and *Messalina* in 1910. Concurrently, Pathé founded Film d'Arte Italiana in Milan to produce historical costume dramas on its own, and suddenly the boom was on.

The years 1909 through 1911 saw a flood of historical films with titles like *Giulio Cesare* (Julius Caesar [Giovanni Pastrone, 1909]), *La caduta di Troia* (*The Fall of Troy* [Pastrone, 1910]), and *Messalina* (Enrico Guazzoni, 1910); but 1913 witnessed the advent of the Italian super-spectacle in a ten-reel remake of Maggi's *Gli ultimi giorni di Pompeii*, directed by Mario Caserini for Ambrosio.[3] As Vernon Jarratt points out, however, this film is entitled to its designation as the first of the great **blockbusters** only by virtue of its length and its cast of 1,000 extras. It was actually the nine-reel *Quo vadis?*, directed by Enrico Guazzoni for Cines in 1912 and released in early 1913, that established the conventions of the superspectacle and captured the world market for the Italian cinema. Adapted from the novel by the Nobel laureate Henryk Sienkiewicz, *Quo vadis?* featured enormous three-dimensional sets designed by Guazzoni, crowd scenes with 5,000 extras, a real chariot race, a real fire representing the burning of

Rome, and a Coliseum full of real lions to devour the Christians. In terms of narrative, the film was a series of arranged scenes, but its spectacle properly made it an international hit, returning its producers twenty times their very substantial investment of 480,000 lire (about $48,000 in the currency of the period). So phenomenal was the success of *Quo vadis?* that the Cines technical staff was forced to work in twenty-four-hour shifts for some months to keep up with the worldwide demand for prints.

The successor to *Quo vadis?* was a film of even greater extravagance, grandeur, and distinction—the Italia Company's *Cabiria*, directed in 1914 by Giovanni Pastrone (under the name of Piero Fosco) and produced for the staggering sum of over 1 million lire (about $100,000 in the currency of the period). Pastrone wrote the script himself after twelve months of research in the Louvre and paid the famous Italian novelist Gabriele D'Annunzio 50,000 lire in gold to lend his name to it and to write the titles. Shot in Turin over a period of six months amid the

---

3. A rival version directed by the actor Enrico Vidali was produced in the same year by Ernesto Pasquali (1883–1919) for his own company, Pasquali Films, Turin.

2.17 Giovanni Pastrone's *Cabiria* (1914).

this process much more dynamically in *The Birth of a Nation* (1915) and *Intolerance* (1916), there is no question that Pastrone was the first director anywhere to attempt it on such a grand scale, and, for a while, slow tracking about a set became known in the industry as "*cabiria* movement." *Cabiria*'s other significant innovations were its systematic use of artificial (electrical) lighting to create dramatic effects, its use of careful and convincing process photography, its relatively restrained acting, and its painstaking reconstruction of period detail (subsequently a hallmark of Griffith's and Lubitsch's historical films).

Released on the eve of the war and overshadowed by the recent international triumph of the much less distinguished *Quo vadis?*, *Cabiria* was not the financial success for which its producers had hoped. Indeed, the Italian cinema's brief period of commercial and aesthetic dominance was abruptly ended by World War I, and the nation's subsequent descent into Fascism prevented a renaissance until after World War II. Nevertheless, it seems clear today that this last and greatest of the Italian superspectacles provided DeMille and Lubitsch with the model for their postwar historical spectacles and substantially influenced the narrative form of Griffith's epic masterworks. In fact, Griffith spoke of seeing both *Quo vadis?* and *Cabiria* while *The Birth of a Nation* was still in the planning stages, and there can be little doubt of their impact upon his development at a time when he was searching for an appropriate cinematic form into which to cast his epic vision of American history.[4]

most monumental and elaborate three-dimensional sets yet created for a motion picture, with exteriors filmed on location in Tunisia, Sicily, and the Alps, *Cabiria* is an epic saga of the Second Punic War between Rome and Carthage; it has been called by Vernon Jarratt "the dizziest peak of the Italian cinema." Its twelve reels develop a dramatically sophisticated narrative against a historical reconstruction of the entire struggle from the burning of the Roman fleet at Syracuse (accomplished through some of the best special effects to appear on the screen for the next twenty years) to Hannibal crossing the Alps and the sack of Carthage.

Spectacle aside, *Cabiria* contains some important innovations in film technique that may very well have influenced directors like Cecil B. DeMille and Ernst Lubitsch, as well as D. W. Griffith. The film is most notable for its use of extended, slow-moving **tracking** (or traveling) **shots,** which permitted the camera to roam about freely among the vast sets, moving in to isolate the characters in close-up and moving out again to reframe the shifting action. Pastrone and his innovative Spanish cameraman, Segundo de Chomón (1871–1929), improvised a dolly (which Pastrone patented) and a primitive crane to achieve these shots. Although Griffith was to use

---

4. By some accounts, Griffith is said to have purchased his own print of *Cabiria* and studied it intensively during the shooting of *The Birth of a Nation*.

D. W. Griffith and the Development of Narrative Form

3

The achievement of D. W. Griffith (1875–1948) is unprecedented in the history of Western art, much less Western film. In the brief span of six years, between directing his first one-reeler in 1908 and *The Birth of a Nation* in 1914, Griffith did more than any single individual to establish the narrative language of the cinema and turn an aesthetically inconsequential medium of entertainment into a fully articulated art form. He has been called, variously, and, for the most part, accurately, "the father of film technique," "the man who invented Hollywood," "the cinema's first great **auteur**," and "the Shakespeare of the screen." Yet in the many years since his most important work was completed, Griffith's stature as an artist has been the subject of continuous debate among film scholars, his critical reputation suffering more fluctuation than that of any other major figure in film history. The problem is that Griffith was essentially a paradox. He was unquestionably the seminal genius of the narrative cinema and its first great visionary artist, but he was also a provincial southern romantic with pretensions to high literary culture and a penchant for sentimentality and melodrama that would have embarrassed Dickens. Griffith was the film's first great technical master and its first legitimate poet, but he was also a muddleheaded racial bigot who quite literally saw all of human history in the black-and-white terms of nineteenth-century melodrama. In one sense, Griffith presents the paradox of a nineteenth-century man who founded a uniquely twentieth-century art form, and this tension between ages accounts for many disparities of taste and judgment that we find in his films today. But there is another contradiction in Griffith that is less easy to rationalize and that raises issues central to the nature of film art itself, and that is the very existence of such staggering cinematic genius side by side with the intellectual shallowness described above. Given the peculiar limitations of his vision, Griffith was never dishonest or hypocritical, but he was intellectually narrow to an alarming degree for a major artist in any medium.

3.1 D. W. Griffith during his Biograph years.

Formative Influences

David Wark Griffith, the seventh child of a Confederate Army colonel, Civil War hero, and local character, Jacob "Roaring Jake" Griffith, was born in a rural district of Kentucky near the Indiana border in 1875. Never affluent, the Griffiths had been impoverished by the Reconstruction, but they clung to the ideals of the past, and David Wark grew up steeped in the romantic mythology of the Old South, with its codes of honor, chivalry, and purity intact. This regionalism combined well with Griffith's penchant for the more popular Victorian poets and novelists to produce a set of naïvely romantic values that the young man was never to outgrow. When Jacob Griffith died in 1885,[1] Griffith's mother moved the family to Louisville, where she attempted, with scant success, to operate a boardinghouse, adding urban poverty to the list of formative influences upon her son. Like Dickens in similar circumstances (and there are more than a few resemblances between the two artists), Griffith was forced to quit public school and work to help support the family.

After a succession of menial jobs in Louisville, he became stagestruck and began to tour the Midwest with traveling stock companies. Griffith's acting career was probably less a matter of aptitude than of zeal and good looks (he was strikingly handsome and statuesque throughout his life), but between 1897 and 1905 he pursued this career from Minneapolis to New York to San Francisco by jumping freights, living in flophouses, and working his way to his next engagement at all manner of jobs, from shoveling ore to picking hops. From San Francisco, Griffith returned to the East in 1906 with a respectable part in the Nance O'Neill Company's production of *Elizabeth, the Queen of England*, after which he married the company's ingenue, Linda Arvidson (1884–1949), and began to write his own play, *A Fool and a Girl*, a serious melodrama derived from his recent experience of migratory workers in the California hop fields.

His acting career notwithstanding, Griffith's lifelong ambition had been to become a writer in the lofty and cultivated Victorian mode of his boyhood favorites. Unfortunately, he had little facility with language, and most of his literary productions were stilted and rhetorical. Miraculously, however, he sold his first play for $1,000 to the impresario James K. Hackett, who produced it in Washington, D.C., in the fall of 1907. *A Fool and a Girl* opened to hostile reviews and closed after two weeks, but Griffith was convinced of his talent and used his royalties to embark upon a new literary career. Within a year, he had managed to publish a handful of poems and short stories in mass-circulation middle-class magazines like *Collier's Weekly, Good Housekeeping*, and *Cosmopolitan*, and he had completed another play—a four-act epic drama of the American Revolution entitled *War*, based entirely on diaries and letters of the period that he found in the New York Public Library. Although much of its factual material was later incorporated into his film epic *America* (1924), *War* was never produced, and Griffith began to cast about again for steady employment.

It was under these circumstances in New York in late 1907 that he ran into Max Davidson, an old friend and acting colleague from Louisville, who advised him that a living might be made selling stories to the motion-picture companies that had suddenly sprung up in the city. Griffith was initially opposed to the idea, fearing that his literary reputation would be damaged by association with the vulgar new medium. He knew very little about the movies

---

1. Griffith always claimed that his father had died of complications from an improperly stitched Civil War wound; less romantic accounts suggest peritonitis.

at this time, but he held them in utter contempt. Nevertheless, he had to eat, and screen stories were then selling for around $5 apiece; so he tossed off an uncredited version of Victorien Sardou's play *La Tosca* under his stage name, Lawrence Griffith, and offered it to Edwin S. Porter at the Edison Company studios. Porter rejected the scenario on the grounds that it had too many scenes for a movie, but, impressed with the young man's looks, he offered Griffith the leading role in his current film, *Rescued from an Eagle's Nest*, at a salary of $5 per day. Griffith ruefully accepted. When the film was completed, Porter had no further use for the actor-scenarist, so Griffith approached the American Mutoscope and Biograph Company at 11 East Fourteenth Street with some of his screen stories.

The Beginning at Biograph

The American Mutoscope and Biograph Company had been founded in 1895 as the K.M.C.D. Syndicate, a partnership of E. B. Koopman, Henry Marvin, Herman Casler, and William Kennedy Laurie Dickson, the inventor of the Kinetograph and Kinetoscope. Alienated from the Edison Laboratory by a quarrel with the business manager, Dickson had combined with the others to perfect a motion-picture technology that would rival Edison's without infringing his patents. Dickson invented a portable peep-show device (the Mutoscope)[2] for the syndicate, and later a camera and projector (both called the Biograph), all of which legally circumvented Edison patents. Though American Biograph (the word "Mutoscope" was dropped shortly after Griffith was hired) joined the MPPC in late 1908, the firm for years provided Edison with his only significant American competition and employed several of the most talented persons in the business—including the man who was to become Griffith's personal **cinematographer**, G. W. "Billy" Bitzer (1872–1944).

In late 1907, however, the company was in serious trouble: it was $200,000 in debt to its bankers, and the public had begun to lose interest in its films. Furthermore, the health and energy of its director, Wallace McCutcheon, were flagging rapidly, and the company had fallen below its standard production rate of two one-reel films per week. The need to hire a new director was clear, but the handful of experienced motion-picture directors in the world at this time were all employed. Griffith, who was hired initially as an actor and story writer, was soon offered his first opportunity to direct by Biograph's general manager, Henry Marvin, on the basis of some perceptive remarks Griffith had made to Marvin's brother Arthur, the studio's other cameraman.

Characteristically, Griffith chose as the subject of his first film a melodramatic (and racist) tale of a child kidnapped by Gypsies and improbably rescued after shooting the rapids in an empty water cask. Called *The Adventures of Dollie*, it was *Rescued from an Eagle's Nest* without the eagle and one of a number of films in the then-popular genre of chases involving a lost or kidnapped child. Griffith shot the film in two days on location at Sound Beach, Connecticut, in June 1908, with a great deal of advice and moral support from Bitzer and from Arthur Marvin, who was the cameraman. Though the film was scarcely innovative, it was respectable enough to garner Griffith a $45-a-week director's contract with Biograph and a royalty of one mil (the equivalent of one-tenth of one cent) per foot on every print sold.[3] By the time *The Adventures of Dollie* was given its first screening in July, Griffith had already directed five more films and completed one begun by another director.

Innovation, 1908–1909: Interframe Narrative

In the five years that followed, Griffith directed over 450 one- and two-reelers for American Biograph, experi-

---

2. Rather than using a perforated film strip like the Kinetoscope, the Mutoscope mounted photographic impressions of individual film frames on cardboard cards and arranged them successively on a rotary wheel. When turned by a crank, the wheel would put the photographs in motion, flipping them rapidly one by one, to create "moving pictures" according to the same optical principles which govern the operation of camera and projector. Many Mutoscopes survive today in penny arcades and designated museums of Americana, official (the Smithsonian) and otherwise (Disneyland, Disney World). Due to the deterioration of so many early paper and nitrate prints, these Mutoscopes provide a rare opportunity to experience the images of primitive cinema at first hand.

3. William Johnson, however, correctly points out that *Dollie* contains an unusual high-angle shot of a field with action moving through it, as well as a shot in depth of a Gypsy wagon pulling away from the camera ("Early Griffith: A Wider View," *Film Quarterly* 29, 3 [Spring 1976]: 2–13). Neither of these would have been unprecedented in 1908, but they do suggest a more sophisticated concept of screen space than was common among filmmakers at the time.

menting with every narrative technique that he would later employ in *The Birth of a Nation* (1915) and *Intolerance* (1916) and that would pass into the conventional lexicon of the cinema. Yet Griffith seems to have been scarcely aware of his innovations, at least, in the process of making them. They were for him the unformulated results of practical problem-solving rather than of abstract theorizing, and his method of proceeding was always intuitive and empirical rather than formalistic. Unrestricted by narrative conventions since there were very few at the time, Griffith simply adopted for his Biograph films what worked best in the particular circumstances, according to the dynamics of the tale. If he had any methodology at all, it consisted in creating analogies between the conventions of stage narrative, which he knew implicitly from his long experience as an actor, and certain uniquely cinematic structural devices that he discovered as he went along. The narrative devices of the Victorian novels that Griffith had loved in his youth also provided models for his innovations. Ultimately, Griffith combined his own analogies between dramatic/novelistic modes and cinematic modes with those of others, like Porter and Pastrone, and molded them into the visual narrative language that we call generically "film." In the course of his career, in fact, Griffith effected a nearly complete translation of nineteenth-century narrative modes into cinematic terms, ensuring through the intensity, stature, and prestigiousness of his films that the cinema would remain a predominantly narrative form until some new technology or ideology was born to liberate it.

There is a prevailing sense among contemporary scholars that Griffith's role as an innovator has been overplayed and that in general "innovation was not simply a matter of a few daring filmmakers influencing each other," as Kristin Thompson has put it. Of the transition from primitive to classical cinema, which she brackets as 1907–17, she continues: "Individual innovations were certainly important, but people like Griffith and Maurice Tourneur changed production practices and filmic techniques in limited ways, governed by the overall production system." In light of the voluminous research assembled by Thompson and other contemporary film historians like Barry Salt, there can be no question that such a system was firmly in place by 1908, largely in response to the nickelodeon boom of 1906–8, and that film narrative had been systematically organized to accommodate the material conditions of production. My argument is simply that Griffith was prominent, in fact preeminent, in the transformation of the production system from its primitive to its classical mode. The historical record is clear, for example, that Griffith's Biograph films were enormously popular with contemporary audiences and widely imitated by other filmmakers, as were his day-to-day production practices. Nor can there be any doubt that in terms of social history the fame and infamy of *The Birth of a Nation* changed forever the way that motion pictures were regarded by everyone from shoe clerks to national politicians to Wall Street financiers. On the other hand, Griffith did not operate in a vacuum; a case in point would be the evolution of the **180-degree system.**

The concept of screen direction originated in the films of the early novelty period, when the frame was basically a proscenium containing action that audiences viewed as if from a theater seat. The direction of movement was maintained naturally in such films, as it would be on the stage. But the rise of multishot films in the late novelty period, especially chase films, demanded that screen direction be maintained consistently from one shot to the next so that—as one cameraman put it—the characters wouldn't "bump into themselves." (In a chase sequence, if all the characters don't move across the frame in the same direction from shot to shot, they will seem to run toward one another, rather than vice versa.) The method that evolved for maintaining screen direction is known today as the 180-degree system of shooting, which assumes that a scene's action will always progress along a straight line from the right to left or left to right of the frame. In feature films of the classical era, the axis of action (or center line, as it is also called) becomes the imaginary vector of movements, character positions, and glances in a scene; shooting and cutting a film so that the camera never crosses the line insures that the spectator will always be on the same side of the story action and, metaphorically speaking, the screen. Obviously, this 180-degree rule wasn't "invented" by any one person, but developed out of the trial-and-error experience of countless directors (including Griffith, who was grappling with problems of screen direction as late as 1909–10), cameramen, and editors, as well as rising audience expectations of continuity on the screen.[4]

---

4. In these matters, however, I am inclined to agree with Wagenknecht and Slide, who write in *The Films of D. W. Griffith* (New York: Crown, 1975) that "absolute priority . . . is of very little interest; what counts in art is not who did it first but who does it best" (p. 17).

Griffith's first movement toward classical narrative form involved the use of a "cut-in" in *The Greaser's Gauntlet* (1908), made four months after *The Adventures of Dollie*.[5] As part of the new seriousness he brought to his craft, Griffith wanted to heighten the emotional intensity of a scene in which a young woman has just saved a man from a lynch mob. To effect this, he cut from a **medium long shot** of the hanging tree to a much closer **full shot** of the same space, showing the two actors from head to toe as they exchange a token of friendship. By changing the position of his camera in midscene, Griffith enabled the audience to read the actors' emotions in their faces rather than having to infer them from broad gestures. In so doing, Griffith had not only broken up his scene into a number of shots (which Porter and others seem to have done occasionally before him), but had broken down the standard distance between the audience and the action. The cut from medium long to full shot also worked effectively to solve a major narrative problem by emphasizing the exchange of a small gift, and Griffith used this type of cut again and again in the next few months with very positive results.

Thus Griffith's first major innovation in the Biograph films of 1908–9 was to *alternate shots of different spatial lengths* (i.e., of different camera-to-subject distance), none of which was dramatically complete in itself, to create cinematic "sentences" within scenes. Later, he would cut long shots, full shots, **medium shots,** close shots, and close-ups together in order to render a single dramatic scene from multiple points of view—i.e., from multiple camera **setups.** In the process, Griffith came especially to learn the immense symbolic and psychological value of the close-up, unexpectedly interpolated between shots of other spatial lengths. Phenomenologically, the close-up has the effect of isolating a detail from its background and giving it greater dramatic emphasis by making it fill the frame. In subsequent Biograph films like *Ramona* (1911) and *The Battle of Elderbush Gulch* (1913), Griffith would also learn the importance of the **extreme long shot** in rendering panoramic or epic action sequences of the type essential to *The Birth of a Nation* and *Intolerance.*

Griffith's next narrative articulation was a logical extension of the first. In *After Many Years,* an October 1908 screen version of Tennyson's narrative poem *Enoch Arden,* Griffith resorted to parallel editing without benefit of a chase. Here, he interweaves the twin narratives of Annie Lee and her shipwrecked husband over a con-tinuum of eleven shots, suggesting the psychological burden and uncertainty of their separation. This kind of editing prefigures not only the **subjective camera** of F. W. Murnau and Karl Freund, but Sergei Eisenstein's "montage of attractions" (see pp. 103–05 and 122–25, respectively). Griffith would use it for the rest of his Biograph career in films like *A Corner in Wheat* (1909), where he cut from a shot of the wheat tycoon gorging himself at a sumptuous meal to a shot of poor sharecroppers standing in a breadline (an early form of associative montage as practiced later by the Soviets). In other films, he employed cutting to create what he called "objects of attention" when he cut from a character looking at something offscreen to a shot of what the character sees, either literally or figuratively, as he or she sees it. These have come to be known as "motivated point-of-view" shots, and, by placing the camera in the spatial position of the character, they induce a kind of optical subjectivity.[6] Griffith used a similar editing trope in other Biograph films to effect the **flashback,** or "switchback," as he termed it—a shot or sequence of shots that interrupts the narrative present and returns us momentarily to the past.

Now, however, the Biograph executives, who had opposed the production of *After Many Years* in the first place on the grounds that it had no action and no chase (and one of Griffith's many achievements was to upgrade the intellectual content of contemporary films), were vocally shocked by his experiment in intercutting the stories of Annie Lee and her husband, which violated every known canon of filmmaking in its disregard for the dramatic unities of time and space and for strict chronological sequence. Griffith's response to their criticism, as reported by Linda Arvidson Griffith, tells us a great deal about his attitude toward his new craft:

> When Mr. Griffith suggested a scene showing Annie Lee waiting for her husband's return to be followed by a scene

---

5. Griffith's first "cut-in" was formerly ascribed to *For Love of Gold* (1908), adapted from Jack London's "Just Meat," on the basis of an anecdote told by Linda Arvidson Griffith in *When the Movies Were Young* (New York: Dutton, 1925; rpt., New York: Dover, 1969) and repeated by Lewis Jacobs and others.

6. Motivated point-of-view cutting is the basis of the "eyeline match," which came into practice at approximately the same time: a shot of a character glancing offscreen is followed by a shot of the (obviously contiguous) space seen—not, however, from the character's point of view, but from the perspective of the first shot, i.e., the "objective" perspective of the audience. (See pp. 108–09.)

of Enoch cast away on a desert island, it was altogether too distracting.

"How can you tell a story jumping about like that? The people won't know what it's about."

"Well," said Mr. Griffith, "doesn't Dickens write that way?"

"Yes, but that's Dickens; that's novel writing; that's different."

"Oh, not so much, these are picture stories; not so different."

As Griffith saw it, films were narratives, or stories, that were told through the arrangement not of words, but of moving photographic images. Nevertheless, Biograph's managers felt Griffith had gone too far, and they closely watched the film's public reception. To their astonishment, *After Many Years* was hailed as a masterpiece, and, according to Lewis Jacobs, it was the first American film to be widely imported into foreign markets. In his first year as Biograph's director, in fact, Griffith's films had substantially, if anonymously, improved the company's fortunes, and the Biograph product was soon enjoying the kind of critical prestige normally reserved for successful stage plays.

Griffith's next step was even more radical, for it involved spatial and temporal fragmentation of the reality continuum to create the illusion of three parallel actions and, by using this fragmentation not just as a form of narrative shorthand but as the basis of his film's structure, to achieve a new kind of dramatic suspense. He had attempted intercutting among three parallel actions as early as his eighth film, *The Fatal Hour* (August 1908) but did not fully develop the technique until the June 1909 melodrama *The Lonely Villa*. This film was a remake of Pathé's 1908 melodrama *The Narrow Escape* (UK: *The Physician of the Castle*)—itself a reworking of Pathé's own *Terrible angoisse* (1906), adapted from Andre De Lorde's 1901 Grand Guignol play *Au téléphone*—which contains an elementary, ten-shot sequence of parallel editing among three spatial planes of action.[7] But, typically, it was Griffith who took this device to the next level, integrating the cinematic and the narrative to an unprecedented degree through the use of parallel editing across the entire length of a fifty-two-shot film. *The Lonely Villa* shows three actions occurring simultaneously: a band of robbers attempting to break into a suburban villa from without, a frightened woman and her children desper-

ately attempting to forestall the attack from within, and the husband rushing from town to rescue his family and drive away the robbers. In a logical extension of the technique he had employed in *After Many Years,* Griffith simply cut back and forth between one action and another, gradually increasing the tempo of alternation until all three actions converged in the dramatic climax of the tale. The effect of this crosscutting or intercutting among fifty-two separate shots was to transform the *dramatic* climax of his film into its *visual* or *cinematic* climax as well, so that the tale and the telling of the tale (i.e., the narrative technique) became the vehicles for one another—so that the medium, in effect, became the message. Several Pathé films from this period contain embryonic parallel editing, and certainly other filmmakers had experimented with the technique prior to 1909. But *The Lonely Villa* was probably the first dramatic film to employ the device as its basic structural principle across three separate spatial planes, and after its debut the practice of intercutting passed rapidly and permanently into the cinema's narrative lexicon.

So powerful was the impact of this film that its intercutting was widely imitated throughout the industry and came to be known generically as the "Griffith last-minute rescue." The term underscores an important element of this technique—its generation of suspense not simply through the rapid alternation of shots to portray simultaneous actions, but through the rapid alternation of shots of shorter and shorter duration—the paradigm for **accelerated montage** as later defined by Sergei Eisenstein (see Chapter 5). As Arthur Knight has noted, Griffith had discovered that the length of time a shot remained on the screen could create significant psychological tension in the audience—that the shorter the length of time a shot was held on the screen, the greater the tension it was capable of inducing. This is the chief principle of the intercut rescue sequences for which Griffith became world-famous, though of course this kind of editing is not restricted to the chase. It became, in fact, the structural foundation of the narrative cinema from *The Birth of a Nation* to the present. In the intercut rescues of the type that conclude *The Birth of a Nation* and *Intolerance*, for example, the alternating shots of the simultaneous actions

---

7. Tom Gunning, *D. W. Griffith and the Origins of the American Narrative Film: The Early Years at Biograph* (Urbana: University of Illinois Press, 1991), pp. 195–97.

3.2 Four shots of parallel action from the three-way rescue that concludes *The Lonely Villa* (1909): the besieged family and the husband rushing to the rescue. Missing are exterior shots of the robbers trying to break into the villa.

grow shorter and shorter as the dramatic climax mounts, until we end with the visual counterpart of a musical crescendo. In other words, the visual tempo of the cutting for simultaneous action parallels the dramatic tempo of the action photographed, so that content is perfectly embodied in form. Griffith's second major innovation, then, is the syntactical corollary of the first—to the alternation of shots of varying spatial lengths, he added the alternation of shots of varying *temporal lengths,* creating the basis for montage and the montage aesthetics that came to dominate the first fifty years of narrative cinema.

Once again, public approval of Griffith's innovations was resounding (although his name was still not associated with them because of Biograph's screen-credit policy and the industry's general tendency not to acknowledge directors), and he was offered his second contract with Biograph in August 1909. Though he still had misgivings about "working for the nickelodeons," as he called it, Griffith accepted the job and continued to pursue his vigorous experiments in film narrative.

Innovation, 1909–1911: Intraframe Narrative

The discoveries of 1908–9 (the alternation of shots of varying spatial and temporal lengths) had all been functions of editing, of the dynamic relationship *between* the clusters of frames we call shots (*inter*frame narrative), but Griffith soon showed himself equally concerned with what occurred *within* the frames and shots of his films (*intra*frame narrative). For one thing, he began to insist upon stories of high quality for his films, many of them derived from literary sources. To be sure, Griffith directed a fair number of chase films, melodramas, and potboilers during his tenure at Biograph, but he also adapted dramatic films from Shakespeare, Poe, Tennyson, Browning, Dickens, and Tolstoi, and some of his films, such as *A Corner in Wheat* (1909, adapted from two muckraking novels by Frank Norris), even had serious if simplistically treated contemporary social themes. By making the content of his films more serious, Griffith was attempting to dignify the medium of motion pictures itself. Another aspect of this concern was the care he took in selecting and directing his actors.

Griffith was in fact the first great actor's director.

Because he had been an actor himself and understood the psychology of the profession, he knew the value of careful rehearsals and rigidly imposed them upon his cast and crew, even though most other directors shot their films "cold." For their efforts, however, Griffith often paid his actors four times what they might receive at a rival studio, and by 1913 he had built his own stock company of ensemble players with such future luminaries as Mary Pickford and Lionel Barrymore (both soon to leave Griffith), Mae Marsh, Dorothy and Lillian Gish, Blanche Sweet, Henry B. Walthall, Bobby Harron, Donald Crisp, and Wallace Reid. Griffith also understood, as no director had before him, how immensely revealing the motion-picture camera is of exaggeration and artificiality in characterization, and he coached his performers for naturalness and subtlety of expression. Griffith's attention to detail extended even to his sets, whose design and construction he frequently supervised. To his employers, the care he lavished on his "nickelodeon" productions must at first have seemed a waste of time and money. Nevertheless, as early as 1909 audiences and critics alike were praising the "naturalness" and "authenticity" of films bearing the "AB" (American Biograph) trademark—as yet the only distinguishing mark of a Griffith production. Soon trade papers were writing enthusiastic articles on his motion pictures, and Biograph became the first studio to receive fan mail for individual films (Griffith's) rather than for individual stars.

Griffith's concern for the content of his films, however, went far beyond the care he bestowed upon his actors and sets. In late 1908, for example, in *A Drunkard's Reformation,* he had begun to experiment with expressive lighting by illuminating a scene with firelight. At a time when electric mercury-vapor lamps had recently been introduced for indoor shooting, this was a radical step because convention then dictated the flat and uniform illumination of every portion of the set. (Mercury-vapors were also well suited to the orthochromatic film stock used through most of the silent period since they produced a light concentrated in the blue-green part of the spectrum to which orthochromatic was most sensitive. On the other hand, mercury-vapors were incapable of directional lighting of the sort just described precisely because of their uniform diffusion.)[8] But the results of the effort were impressive, and Griffith went on to experiment with lighting more elaborately in a 1909 film version of Browning's dramatic poem *Pippa Passes* (the first film, incidentally, to be reviewed by the *New York Times*). The events

3.3 Lighting for dramatic effect in *Pippa Passes* (1909).

of this one-reeler take place in a single day, and the passage of time is effectively rendered by changes in directional lighting that simulate the movement of the sun across the sky. In Griffith's first all-California film, *The Threads of Destiny* (1910), interior scenes of an old Spanish mission were lit solely by the slanting rays of the sun as they came through a high window, illuminating some objects, like the pulpit, and leaving others in darkness. (This shaft of light later reappeared in *Intolerance* to illumine the "endlessly rocking" cradle of the transitional scenes.) Griffith went on to become a master of tonal or atmospheric illumination (dubbed "Rembrandt lighting" by Cecil B. DeMille's cameraman Alvin Wyckoff around 1915), which characterizes a given scene through patterns of highlight and shade. Moreover, although for financial reasons Griffith was forced to shoot most of his two great epics in direct sunlight, lighting for dramatic effect was soon established and elaborately refined by directors like Giovanni Pastrone in Italy, Ernst Lubitsch in Germany (and later the United States), and Cecil B. DeMille in the United States.

By far the most important of Griffith's contributions to intraframe narrative, however, were made after he began to move his company to southern California on a regular seasonal basis in early 1910. (Griffith was not the first filmmaker to locate in Hollywood: in the fall of 1907,

8. The Cooper-Hewitt mercury-vapor lamp was invented for industrial and commercial applications in 1901 and by 1907 was in general use for interior lighting in film studios. Mercury-vapors were electrically efficient and provided a soft, evenly diffused light over an entire set. (See pp. 321–22.)

the Selig Polyscope Company had built a small studio there.) Here, in films like *The Lonedale Operator* (1911) and *The Battle of Elderbush Gulch* (1913), he discovered the importance of camera movement and placement to the dramatic expressiveness of film. Before Griffith went to Hollywood, the camera had been largely static. There had been **panning** (horizontal) and **tilting** (vertical) movements in films like *The Great Train Robbery*, and Griffith had begun to experiment with narrative panning shots as early as 1908 (*The Call of the Wild*) and 1909 (*The Country Doctor*). But in 1910 most film narratives—even those of Griffith—were structured mainly through editing, whether the units edited together were scenes or shots. In California, Griffith became increasingly interested in structuring his films through intraframe as well as interframe movement. In the horizontal sweep of the panning shot, Griffith was able not only to follow the movement of his principals through any given scene, but to engage the audience in the total environment of his films. Moreover, in the tracking or traveling shot, in which the camera—and thus the audience—actively participates in the action by moving with it, Griffith brought a new kind of movement to the screen. In *The Lonedale Operator*, for example, in order to convey the breathless momentum of a locomotive speeding to the rescue of a young woman trapped by thieves, Griffith and Bitzer mounted their camera in the moving engine cab and crosscut between traveling shots of the engine plunging through the landscape and the desperate plight of the girl. In later years, Griffith and Bitzer would mount their camera in an automobile to follow moving action during the gathering of the Klan and the climactic riot sequence in *The Birth of a Nation*, and in the rescue sequence from the Modern story of *Intolerance*. (The Babylonian story of the latter film contains one of the longest and most elaborate tracking shots ever made. In order to move their camera from an extreme long shot of the mammoth set of Belshazzar's feast straight into a full shot of the action, Griffith and Bitzer built an elevator tower that rolled on rails and tracked it slowly forward in a single unbroken shot that lasts nearly sixty seconds onscreen.) With these additions to film language, the whole notion of the frame as a proscenium arch, pervasive since Méliès, began to break down, and by the time Griffith finished *The Birth of a Nation* in early 1915, it had nearly disappeared.

Griffith also discovered the dramatic expressiveness of camera placement during his early California years,

becoming one of the first directors to compose his shots in depth, with simultaneous action in background, middle ground, and foreground rather than on a single plane.[9] As early as 1910, he found that the perspective from which a shot was taken could be used to comment upon its content or to create dramatic emphasis for certain of its elements. A great deal can be said about a person's character metaphorically, for example, when he or she is photographed from a very low **camera angle** in a back-lit shot instead of a naturally lit head-on medium shot. The actor in a shot like this would seem to tower over the audience, and the lighting would create seemingly sinister shadows on the face. The reverse angle might be used to characterize someone who is helpless or weak, like Mae Marsh in the courtroom scene from the Modern story of *Intolerance*. Thus Griffith, who had already learned to create visual metaphors through associative editing (*After Many Years* and *A Corner in Wheat*), was now learning to create visual metaphors *within* the frame through camera placement. The logical extension of Griffith's metaphoric or symbolic style, seen at its height in *Intolerance* (1916) and *Broken Blossoms* (1919), occurs in the angular perspectives of German Expressionism and the subjective camera technique of F. W. Murnau and Karl Freund as described in Chapter 4.

Griffith created and used other technical innovations at Biograph that seem decidedly minor by comparison with his breakthroughs in editing and in camera movement and placement, but that are important nonetheless. For one thing, he perfected the dissolve and the fade, both very crude transitional devices derived from Méliès before Griffith rendered them more fluid. Since the 1920s, dissolves and fades have been synthetically processed in a machine called an **optical printer,** but in Griffith's time they were all accomplished in the camera. The scene that was to dissolve out was shot through a slowly closing lens **diaphragm;** then the film was stopped and rewound, and the scene that was to dissolve *in* was shot over the prior scene with the diaphragm slowly opening at the same speed. The fade-in and the fade-out, used by Griffith for the first time to begin and end film narratives, were accomplished by performing the same two processes separately. (Diaphragms, at this point, did not shut

---

9. Charles Musser points out that at this time the Vitagraph Company was much more oriented toward composing shots in depth than Griffith (Musser to author, 1/22/88).

3.4 An iris shot of Lillian Gish, from *The Birth of a Nation* (1915).

3.5 *The Musketeers of Pig Alley* (1912): Lillian and Dorothy Gish. Note the depth of the image.

down completely and left a small open circle in the center of the frame that cameramen had to eliminate by cupping their hands over the lenses.)[1] Griffith perfected the dissolve and the fade, like so many other devices he brought to general recognition, simply by exercising more care when using them than earlier directors had done. Indeed, aside from his cinematic genius, Griffith's greatest attribute as a filmmaker was his compulsion to take everything about the cinema seriously once he had cast his lot with it. Many of his "discoveries" were not discoveries at all, but simply the result of bestowing a degree of care on operations that earlier directors had performed in a slapdash manner.

Several innovations do belong solely to Griffith or to the Griffith-Bitzer collaboration. These include the flashback, the **iris shot,** the **mask,** the systematic use of the **split screen** and the **soft focus shot.** Like the dissolve and the fade, these devices were all essentially *graphic* embellishments, little used today except by way of allusion to the Griffith era; but we shall soon see how important they were in creating the rich visual texture of *The Birth of a Nation* at a time when they were uncommon.

Griffith's Drive for Increased Film Length

Griffith's apprenticeship, as his Biograph period is often called, reached its peak in 1911, when he was offered his

third contract at the extravagant salary of $75 a week plus royalties and when he finally changed his working name back from Lawrence to David Wark (D. W.) Griffith. The change signaled Griffith's increased pride in his work and his new conviction that motion pictures were a significant art form. The odd job he had taken three years earlier to keep from starving had finally become a career. As Griffith saw his one-reelers grow increasingly popular between 1911 and 1912, he opted for narratives of greater and greater complexity, like the tale of small-town hypocrisy, *The New York Hat* (1912), written by Anita Loos (1893–1981), and the contemporary street drama *The Musketeers of Pig Alley* (1912), shot on location in the streets of New York and often cited as a predecessor of Italian **neorealism.** Yet, by late 1911 Griffith had begun to chafe under the constraints of the one-reel (ten- to sixteen-minute) limit. He felt that he had exhausted the one-reel form and could continue his experiments in narrative only by increasing the length of his films. He also seems to have understood that for the cinema to achieve the status of an art it would have to evolve a form com-

1. David Bordwell and Kristin Thompson point out that in 1918 an automatic shutter device was introduced that permitted cinematographers to fully close down their shutter apertures with the camera running and achieve nearly flawless fades ("Toward a Scientific Film History?" *Quarterly Review of Film Studies* 10, 3 [Summer 1985]: 234). By facilitating in-camera fades and dissolves, the automatic shutter virtually eliminated the iris as a transitional device after 1919, although Griffith continued to use it well into the 1920s.

mensurate with that of other narrative arts, and that such a form would have to be an expansive one which could provide for the dynamic interplay of its own components. The idea of a serious novel, opera, or play that takes only ten or fifteen minutes to apprehend is ludicrous, and Griffith reasoned that the same was true of cinema.

Accordingly, against the wishes of his employers, Griffith decided to remake his successful one-reeler *After Many Years* (1908) as the two-reel *Enoch Arden* in late 1911. Griffith had attempted a two-reeler in 1910 (*His Trust*), but Biograph had titled each reel separately and released them both as separate films. After the completion of *Enoch Arden*, the studio tried to do the same thing by releasing the film in two parts, but the public, through the film's exhibitors, demanded the full version, and Biograph ultimately yielded. In an ironic turnabout the following year, Biograph actively encouraged Griffith to make two-reelers instead of the standard product in order to compete with an increase in two-reel films from domestic and European producers. This pleased Griffith well enough for a time, and in 1912 he made three two-reel films in California (in addition to many others), which prepared both him and his audience for his 1913 feature *Judith of Bethulia*.

The first of these two-reelers was *Man's Genesis* (remade the following year as *The Wars of the Primal Tribes*, or *Brute Force*), which the Biograph catalogue describes as "a psychological study founded upon the Darwinian theory of the Evolution of Man." While its allegorical account of intelligence triumphing over brute strength in prehistoric times is simplistic by contemporary standards, *Man's Genesis* was unique for its day.[2] In the same year, Griffith also made *The Massacre*, which Lewis Jacobs has called "America's first spectacle film." This two-reeler offered a historical reconstruction of a wagon-train massacre with overtones of Custer's last stand, and it presented Griffith with his greatest technical challenge to date. Nevertheless, its large-scale battle scenes look forward to those of *The Birth of a Nation* in their fluid editing continuity and their striking photographic composition, and Griffith had reason to expect that *The Massacre* would be hailed as a great achievement. Instead, it was barely noticed, for in the interim between the film's production and its release, *Queen Elizabeth* and other *films d'art* had come to America and touched off "feature fever" in a market once solely geared to shorts.

Except for its relative length, Griffith saw little to

3.6 *The Massacre* (1912).

admire in *Queen Elizabeth*, a filmed play that contained only twenty-three separate shots in its entire forty-eight-minute running time. (Griffith's one-reel *The Sands of Dee*, produced concurrently with *Queen Elizabeth*, used sixty-eight separate shots in less than ten minutes.) But he did not like being upstaged and immediately began production of his third important two-reeler of 1912, *The Mothering Heart*, a contemporary melodrama that Griffith hoped would be a masterpiece and whose extravagant budget was a source of deep concern to Biograph's president, J. J. Kennedy. Before the film was finished, however, Italy's spectacular *Quo vadis?* arrived in America, and *The Mothering Heart* fell into obscurity while audiences stood in line, naturally enough, to see the longest and most expensive motion picture ever made. Griffith was beside himself, for now he had been not only upstaged, but outclassed. *Quo vadis?* was scarcely innovative in terms of its narrative technique and today looks archaic next to Griffith's more sophisticated two-reelers, but it was the elaborate, big-budget feature that he had longed to make for the past two years. Now he was determined to best his new European rivals; he set to work frenetically upon a lavish new production that he vowed would clinch his title as supreme master of the cinema.

---

2. It later inspired Hal Roach's *One Million B.C.* (Hal Roach, Jr., 1940), for which Griffith served as technical advisor and probably directed some of the special effects. The Roach film was remade by Britain's Hammer Studios as *One Million Years B.C.* (Don Chaffey, 1966), with special effects by Ray Harryhausen.

Judith of Bethulia and the Move to Mutual

It is uncertain whether or not Griffith had actually seen *Quo vadis?* when he began shooting *Judith of Bethulia* in the secrecy of Chatsworth Park, California, in June 1913, but he had read enough about the film in the trade press to know that its essence was epic spectacle. Griffith's own film was based on a story from the Apocrypha about the Bethulian widow Judith, who feigned love for the Assyrian conqueror Holofernes in order to assassinate him and save her besieged city. The film was budgeted at $18,000, a very large sum for its day, but Griffith ended up spending more than twice that amount in his compulsive quest for dramatic authenticity and grandeur of scale. A substantial portion of the film's budget was spent rehearsing elaborate battle sequences on the 12-mile-square set at Chatsworth, which housed, among other wonders, a full-scale reconstruction of Bethulia. Griffith's penchant for accuracy of detail in costuming and production design accounted for another large chunk of the budget. But the most expensive aspect of the film was its length: Griffith shot enough film to make *Judith of Bethulia* a feature-length epic, editing it later into four reels.

This film represents the summation of Griffith's Bio-

3.7   *Judith of Bethulia* (1913).

graph career. Its complex story, like that of *Intolerance*, is divided into four contrapuntal movements and employs nearly every narrative device Griffith had discovered or perfected in his five years with the studio. Nevertheless, the economy of the film's narrative development is often quite remarkable given the sophistication of its technique. As spectacle, *Judith of Bethulia* moved beyond anything seen on the screen to date, with its mass scenes of sieges, open-field battles, and chariot charges; and yet, as in Griffith's later masterpieces, the personal drama of the protagonists is never lost amid the epic scale of the action. The film is also notable as a landmark in Griffith's problematic treatment of women. Judith uses her sexuality to liberate her people by decapitating Holofernes in an act of symbolic castration. But this phallic victory comes at the price of her own desire since Griffith revises the Apocrypha to explain that Judith has secretly fallen in love with the Assyrian before she kills him.[3] Whatever the case, *Judith of Bethulia* is clearly the most ambitious American film made before 1914. As Jacobs has remarked, "Even if Griffith had done nothing further than *Judith of Bethulia*, he would still be considered a sensitive and outstanding craftsman."

Griffith's employers at Biograph, however, were stunned at their director's extravagance and audacity, and they resolved to take action against him. When Griffith returned to New York with a six-reel assembly print of *Judith of Bethulia*, Biograph vice-president and general manager Henry Marvin informed him that he had been "promoted" to production chief of the studio, from which position he would supervise the work of other directors but not direct films or handle budgets himself. Moreover, caught up in the *film d'art* craze produced by *Queen Elizabeth*, Biograph had signed an ill-fated contract with the theatrical producers Marc Klaw and Abraham L. Erlanger to film their stage plays as five-reel features. The meaning of Griffith's new "promotion" was all too clear: he could stay at Biograph only if he would agree to supervise his former assistants in the mechanical reproduction of stage plays. This was impossible for him, and so he let

---

3. See the chapters on Griffith in Miriam Hansen's *Babel and Babylon: Spectatorship in American Silent Cinema* (Cambridge, Mass.: Harvard University Press, 1988) and Michael Rogin's *"Ronald Reagan, the Movie" and Other Episodes in Political Demonology* (Berkeley: University of California Press, 1987).

it be known among the independent producers that he was looking for a new job.

Because his Biograph shorts had come to epitomize successful film craftsmanship in the American industry, Griffith was almost immediately offered $50,000 a year by Adolph Zukor, but he turned it down because he rightly saw that Zukor's company would offer him no more creative freedom than Biograph had. More to his liking was the proposition of Harry E. Aitken (1870–1956), the president of a new film distributing company called Mutual, to come to work for his subsidiary firm of Reliance-Majestic as an independent producer-director at a salary of $52,000 per year. Aitken promised to let Griffith make two independent feature films a year in addition to the conventional program features he would be required to direct under his contract, and Griffith accepted the offer without hesitation. On December 3, 1913, Griffith announced his departure from Biograph in an advertisement in the *New York Dramatic Mirror* that modestly proclaimed him to be "Producer of all great Biograph successes, revolutionizing Motion Picture drama and founding the modern technique of the art." The advertisement went on to enumerate, with some exaggeration, his specific technical contributions to the form ("the large or close-up figures, distant views, . . . the 'switch-back,' sustained suspense, the 'fade out,' and restraint in expression") and to list 151 of his most important and successful Biograph films from *The Adventures of Dollie* through the still unreleased *Judith of Bethulia*. In this manner, Griffith publicly and legitimately laid claim to the hundreds of films he had directed for Biograph in almost complete anonymity between 1908 and 1913; but more important was the fact that the man who had once been so ashamed of working for the "living pictures" now proclaimed himself to be the founding father of the narrative cinema and its first great personal artist or, to borrow a term from contemporary criticism, its first great *auteur*.

Griffith took with him to Mutual / Reliance-Majestic most of the stock company of ensemble players he had built up during the years at Biograph, but his brilliant and invaluable cameraman, Billy Bitzer, at first refused to follow him on the grounds that there was more security in working for a Patents Company member than for an independent. After several months, however, Bitzer was finally persuaded to join Griffith as his director of photography. He was to stay with Griffith throughout his

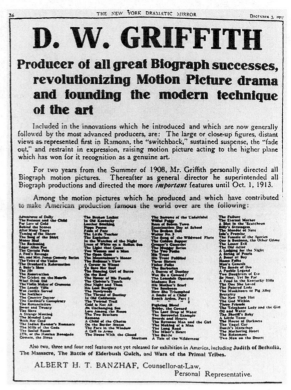

3.8 D. W. Griffith's advertisement for himself.

career and to work on at least twenty-four of the thirty-five feature films Griffith made between 1914 and 1931. With this, the Griffith company was once again complete and ready to embark upon the production of two of the most important and influential motion pictures ever made.[4]

---

4. After Griffith and his company left Biograph, the production company rapidly declined, and in 1915 it was liquidated. The more than 500 films that Griffith made from his first one-reeler *The Adventures of Dollie* (1908) through his final feature *The Struggle* (1931) are being catalogued and annotated by an international team of scholars in conjunction with a multiyear retrospective organized by the Pordenone Silent Film Festival under the rubric of "The Griffith Project." Under the editorship of Paolo Cherchi Usai, the multivolume catalogue, also entitled *The Griffith Project*, is being published by the British Film Institute; as of 2002, six volumes had appeared, representing all of the films through 1910. The primary source for filmographic information on the Biograph work for the Griffith Project is *D. W. Griffith and the Biograph Company*, compiled by Cooper C. Graham, Steven Higgins, Elaine Mancini, and Joao Luiz Viera (Metuchen, N.J.: Scarecrow Press, 1985).

3.9 Bitzer and Griffith examining rushes on the set of Mutual/ Reliance-Majestic's *The Avenging Conscience* (1914) shortly after their departure from Biograph.

The Birth of a Nation

PRODUCTION

Before he turned to his first independent project in late 1914, Griffith took his company to Hollywood and hurried through four minor program features[5] for Reliance-Majestic, one of which, a potboiler entitled *The Battle of the Sexes*, was shot in four days. Griffith nevertheless insisted that Mutual's president, Harry Aitken, promote each film with expensive advance publicity and rent a legitimate Broadway theater for its opening. Griffith had become so committed to cinema that even the reception of his potboilers was of serious concern to him. But he was still haunted by the success of the Italian superspectacles, and he sought everywhere for an epic subject that would enable him at last to rival them. He found it when one of his writers, Frank E. Woods, told him about a failed attempt to film a play entitled *The Clansman*. The play, adapted by southern-born clergyman Thomas E. Dixon, Jr., from his best-selling novel, was the story of a Confederate soldier's return to his ravaged home in South Carolina after the Civil War and his role there in organizing the Ku Klux Klan.[6] Both novel and play were decidedly mediocre as literature and openly racist in their depiction of the Reconstruction period as one in which renegade mulatto "carpetbaggers" and Negro thugs joined with unscrupulous white politicians to destroy the social fabric of the South. Yet this material had a natural

fascination for Griffith, whose romantic image of the South and the Civil War had stayed with him since childhood. In fact, some of his most spectacular Biograph films had dealt with incidents from the Civil War, and now he seized the opportunity to do a feature-length epic on the subject.

Aitken was induced to buy the screen rights to the story from Dixon for $10,000,[7] and Griffith and Woods collaborated on a loose scenario, supplementing *The Clansman* with material from another Dixon book, *The Leopard's Spots*, and with Griffith's own idealized vision of the South. When they were done, the story covered not only the Reconstruction period, but the years immediately preceding the Civil War and the war itself. The film was initially budgeted by Aitken at $40,000, or four times the usual rate for a conventional feature, but as Griffith became more and more obsessed with the project that figure grew until it nearly tripled. By the time the film was completed at a cost of $110,000, Griffith's entire personal fortune, including his weekly paychecks, had been pumped into the enterprise, along with the savings of many associates and friends.

Shooting began in total secrecy in late 1914, and, despite the rough scenario put together with Woods, Griffith worked wholly without a written script. Through six weeks of rehearsal and nine weeks of shooting—a remarkable schedule in an era when most features were cranked out in less than a month—Griffith carried around in his head every detail of the editing **continuity,** titles, settings, costumes, and props. So personal an undertaking was his Civil War epic that no one involved in the production but Griffith had any clear idea of what the film was about. The cast and crew were astonished at the number of camera

---

5. In recent years, one of these—*The Avenging Conscience* (1914), adapted from Poe's "The Tell-Tale Heart"—has been reappraised as an important avatar of surrealism.

6. Woods, who was also an editor of *Motion Picture News*, had worked briefly for the Kinemacolor Company (see Chapter 7), which in 1911 had commissioned William Haddock to shoot some experimental color footage of the play. According to Michael Pitts in *Hollywood and American History* (Jefferson, N.C.: McFarland & Co., 1984), Kinemacolor intended to use this footage to mount a feature-length adaptation of *The Clansman* that was subsequently abandoned but that became the source of Griffith's inspiration via Woods.

7. Dixon accepted a $2,500 down payment and later opted for a percentage of the film's profits rather than the $7,500 balance, whereby he became very rich.

setups he would demand for a single scene, and no one could imagine how the director intended to assemble into a single film the thousands of separate shots he was taking. As Lillian Gish wrote of the filming: "We were rarely assigned parts, and the younger members of the company always rehearsed for the older members when the story was being developed, as all the 'writing' was done by Griffith as he moved groups of characters around. . . . When the story was ready to go before the camera, the older players . . . came forward and acted the parts they had been watching us rehearse for them. . . . Very often we would play episodes without knowing the complete story. . . . Only Griffith knew the continuity of *The Birth of a Nation* in its final form." Griffith did indeed have a grand design for his film because he was quite consciously involved in creating "the greatest picture ever made." But this should not obscure the fact that he was a great *practical* genius whose finest effects were often improvised on the set to meet some specific requirement of the narrative or the shooting process.

Originally composed of over 1,544 separate shots—in an era in which the most sophisticated of foreign spectacles contained fewer than 100—*The Clansman* (as it was initially called) took Griffith some three months to edit and **score.** When the job was done, he had achieved on a vast scale the nearly total integration of every narrative technique he had ever used and, in collaboration with the composer Joseph Carl Breil[8] (1870–1926), had synthesized an orchestral score from the music of Grieg, Wagner, Tchaikovsky, Beethoven, Liszt, Rossini, Verdi, and American folk and period songs (e.g., "Dixie," "Marching through Georgia"), which dramatically paralleled the editing continuity of the film. He had also produced the longest (thirteen reels) and most expensive motion picture yet made in America, and because of its length the existing exchanges refused to distribute it. Griffith and Aitken were forced to form their own company, the Epoch Producing Corporation, to handle distribution of *The Clansman* amid widespread predictions that Griffith's "audacious monstrosity," as one MPPC member called it, would be a box-office disaster.[9] But within five years of its opening, Griffith's "monstrosity" would return more than $15 million.

The Clansman had its premiere on February 8, 1915, at Clune's auditorium in Los Angeles, and its first public opening on March 3, 1915, at the Liberty Theater in New York, where it was retitled *The Birth of a Nation* and ran for an unprecedented forty-eight consecutive weeks. At Aitken's insistence, it was the first film ever to command the $2 admission price of the legitimate theater, and its phenomenal popularity made it one of the top-grossing films of all time. By 1948, *The Birth of a Nation* had been seen in theaters by an estimated 150 million people all over the world and, according to trade legend, had grossed nearly $48 million, or more than any film made anywhere in the world up to that time.[1] From its very first screening in Los Angeles, the critics were unanimous in their praise of the film's technical brilliance. As the trade paper *Variety* remarked on March 12, 1915, "Daily newspapers pronounced it the last word in picture-making," and for a while it seemed that no critical hyperbole was too strong to describe Griffith's achievement. "Epoch-making" and "prestigious" were the terms most frequently applied to his film, and after a special White House screening (the first of its kind), President Woodrow Wilson, who was himself a professional historian, is reputed to have said, "It is like writing history with lightning."

---

8. Breil had composed scores for the American versions of *Queen Elizabeth* (1912) and *Cabiria* (1914), and he later collaborated with Griffith to score *Intolerance* (1916), *The White Rose* (1923), and *America* (1924). In 1930, Breil's original score was used to produce a considerably shortened sonorized version of *The Birth of a Nation* with full orchestral accompaniment.

9. The film was opened at first-class legitimate theaters in all of the major cities to garner publicity and $2 admissions (a marketing strategy later known as "road showing") and then distributed to small towns and cities on a "states' rights" basis. In this latter arrangement, regional distributors would buy the exclusive rights to control exhibition of the film in a given state or group of states, with Epoch receiving a percentage of the box-office grosses. In *D. W. Griffith: His Life and Work* (New York: Oxford University Press, 1972), Robert M. Henderson points out that Aitken's failure to set up an accurate accounting system for the states' rights returns (which he wrongly thought would be small) caused Mutual to lose millions of dollars in concealed profits to regional distributors. Operating as the states' rights distributor for Massachusetts, Louis B. Mayer alone made as much as $1 million in rake-offs from *The Birth of a Nation* (a fortune that would later enable him to become the driving force behind Metro-Goldwyn-Mayer) before the film was legally banned.

1. According to *Variety*'s Seventy-fourth Anniversary edition for January 9, 1980, the true figure is closer to $10 million. But the business practices described in the preceding note suggest that the actual grosses far exceeded those reported by regional distributors. For the same reason, it is impossible to know how many Americans actually saw *The Birth of Nation* in its original release, but *Boxoffice* magazine has estimated that the film had more admissions as a percentage of the total population than any other feature before or since.

But the film's extraordinary success was marred by controversy and scandal. Several weeks after the New York opening, Griffith yielded to pressure from the National Association for the Advancement of Colored People (NAACP, founded in 1908) and city officials to cut the film's most blatantly racist sequences. He grudgingly removed some 558 feet, reducing the total number of shots from 1,544 to 1,375. This excised material has never been recovered, but it apparently included scenes of white women being sexually attacked by renegade blacks as well as an epilogue suggesting that the solution to America's racial problems was the deportation of the Negroes to Africa. Despite this compromise by Griffith and President Wilson's endorsement, historians began to assail the director's distorted view of Reconstruction; and prominent citizens and community leaders such as the president of Harvard University, Jane Addams of Hull House, and the editors of progressive urban weeklies started to attack *The Birth of a Nation* for its racial bigotry and to demand its suppression. Oswald Garrison Villard, the editor of the *Nation*, called the film "improper, immoral, and injurious—a deliberate attempt to humiliate ten million American citizens and portray them as nothing but beasts," and the governor of Massachusetts had the film banned throughout the state after a race riot at its Boston premiere. Riots also occurred when the film opened in Chicago and Atlanta, where it was directly instrumental in the birth of the modern Ku Klux Klan. So extreme was the antagonism created by Griffith's epic that it was ultimately refused licenses for exhibition in Connecticut, Illinois, Kansas, Massachusetts, Minnesota, New Jersey, Wisconsin, and Ohio; and President Wilson was forced to retract his praise publicly and to suggest that the film had used its brilliant technique in the service of specious ends.[2]

Griffith was shocked and deeply injured by the unexpectedly hostile reaction to *The Birth of a Nation*. From his point of view, he had struggled for a full year against nearly insurmountable odds to bring forth what he considered to be not only "the greatest picture ever made," but a great epic of the American nation. The widespread public attacks upon his film seemed to him like attacks upon American civilization itself, and he struck back by publishing a pamphlet, *The Rise and Fall of Free Speech in America*, that vigorously defended *The Birth of a Nation* against censorship by attacking the practice itself, but that offered no answers to the specific charges of racism. The charges

were in fact unanswerable, for race was central to Griffith's interpretation of American history.

Epics are concerned with the origins of races, and the "nation" born out of Griffith's epic was quite clearly White America. It may be true, as a recent biographer has remarked, that Griffith's "racial bias was almost totally unconscious," but regional conditioning had so perverted his understanding of American history that his film became in many ways a pseudohistorical tract whose collective hero is the "Aryan" race (Griffith's term). In another sense, though, Griffith was simply confirming the stereotypes of his age, for *The Birth of a Nation* accurately incarnates the myth of Reconstruction propagated by politicians and historians alike in the late nineteenth and early twentieth centuries. The social economist and philosopher Thorstein Veblen remarked, after viewing the film in 1915, "Never before have I seen such concise misinformation"; but much of the misinformation contained in *The Birth of a Nation* belonged to an entire generation of Americans. If Griffith distorted history, then so did Woodrow Wilson in his five-volume *History of the American People* (1902), written while he was president of Princeton University, which in Volume V tells pretty much the same story as *The Birth of a Nation*, even to the point of spelling "negro" with a small "n"—a practice for which Griffith is still vilified.

In its monumental scale, in its concentration upon a crucial moment in American history, in its mixture of historical and invented characters, in its constant narrative movement between the epochal and the human, and, most significantly, in its chillingly accurate vision of an American society predicated on race, *The Birth of a Nation* is a profoundly *American* epic. We can and should fault Griffith for badly distorting the historical facts of Reconstruction, for unconscionably stereotyping the Afri-

---

2. A 1915 U.S. Supreme Court decision known as *Mutual Film Corporation v. Industrial Commission of Ohio,* or simply *Mutual v. Ohio,* handed down only weeks after the film's first public screening, held that the exhibition of motion pictures was "a business pure and simple, originated and conducted for profit, like other spectacles, not to be regarded . . . as part of the press of the country or as organs [*sic*] of public opinion" (*Banned Films: Movies, Censors and the First Amendment,* ed. Edward de Grazia and Roger K. Newman [New York: Bowker, 1982], p. 5). This ruling effectively denied First Amendment protection to motion pictures as a form of expression and left them legally vulnerable to censorship for the next thirty-seven years, until the Court reversed itself in *The Miracle* decision of 1952 (see "The Scrapping of the Production Code," pp. 428–29, in Chapter 12 of this volume).

**3.10 A classically structured Griffith battle
sequence from *The Birth of a Nation,* moving
from extreme long shot to long shot to
medium long shot to medium close shot:
Henry B. Walthall as Ben Cameron.**

can-American as either fool or brute, and for glorifying a
terrorist organization like the Klan, but we cannot deny
the forcefulness of his vision. Distasteful though it is,
Griffith's racism was shared implicitly by most white
southerners and many other Americans of his era.[3] The
difference is that they had neither the means, nor the
will, nor the genius to translate it into an epic film seen
around the world by millions. In that fact lies both Griffith's greatness and his shame.

STRUCTURE

The Birth of a Nation tells the story of the American Civil
War and its aftermath from a southern point of view,
treating, as an **intertitle** states, "the agony which the
South endured that a nation might be born." It is well to
remember that the events it depicts were recent history
to the audiences of 1915, only fifty years distant. Like
Griffith himself, many persons seeing the film in the year
of its release knew intimate details of the war from parents who had survived it, and the political and social divisions produced by the conflict still ran very deep.

The film begins with a prologue explaining that the
seeds of the tragedy were sown not by the South but by
the seventeenth-century New England traders who first
brought the slaves to America and who, ironically, Griffith
claims, were the ancestors of the nineteenth-century abo-
litionists. There follows a brief prewar interlude in which
two northern boys, both sons of the powerful abolitionist
senator Austin Stoneman (modeled on Thaddeus Stevens, Republican congressman from Pennsylvania and
leader of the radical Reconstructionists in the House
of Representatives), visit their former boarding-school
friends, the Cameron brothers, on the family's modest
plantation in Piedmont, South Carolina. During this idyll,
which is intended to show the grace and charm of southern culture as well as the general beneficence of plantation life, Phil Stoneman falls in love with the Cameron
daughter, Margaret, while young Ben Cameron discovers

---

3. On the pervasiveness and virulence of American racism during this
period, see Nell Irvin Painter, *Standing at Armageddon: The United
States, 1877–1919* (New York: Norton, 1987), Chapters 5 ("The White
Man's Burden," pp. 141–69) and 7 ("Race and Disenfranchisement,"
pp. 216–30), and Janet Staiger, "*The Birth of a Nation*: Reconsidering
Its Reception," in her *Interpreting Films: Studies in the Historical
Reception of American Cinema* (Princeton, N.J.: Princeton University
Press, 1992), pp. 139–53.

his ideal of feminine beauty in a daguerreotype of Phil's sister, Elsie. Immediately following the visit, civil war breaks out, and both the northern and southern brothers heed the call to arms of their respective governments.

The next portion of *The Birth of a Nation* deals with the war itself and is very nearly self-contained. It is this part of the film that most truly merits the description "epic," for it combines a sophisticated narration of historical events with spectacle on a colossal scale. From the moment the Piedmont regiment marches off gaily and naïvely to its first battle, to the assassination of President Lincoln at Ford's Theater, we are swept along on a narrative current so forceful and hypnotic that it is impossible even today to escape its attraction. The siege of Petersburg, the burning of Atlanta, and Sherman's march to the sea are all re-created in battle scenes whose intensity is still compelling, despite eight decades of technological refinement. Griffith and Bitzer composed these scenes after Mathew Brady's Civil War photographs and shot them from many different perspectives, combining extreme long shots of the battlefields with medium and close shots of bloody hand-to-hand fighting to evoke the chaotic violence of combat itself. Griffith increased the tension of these sequences by radically varying the duration of each shot and by cutting on contrary movements: at one point in the Battle of Petersburg, Griffith cuts from a group of Confederate soldiers charging across the screen from the left side of the frame to a band of Union soldiers charging across from the right, while a third cut shows their ferocious head-on collision on the field. For the burning-of-Atlanta sequence, Griffith used a diagonally split screen containing blazing buildings in the upper half and Sherman's relentlessly marching troops in the lower half, all illuminated by bursting shells and flames (according to Bitzer, the only artificially lit sequence in the film).

Griffith continues the personal story of the Stonemans and the Camerons against this panoramic overview of the Civil War. The families' two youngest sons die in each other's arms on the battlefield; and Ben Cameron, the "Little Colonel," is wounded and captured by federal troops after leading a daring charge against the Union lines at Petersburg. Meanwhile, in the South, a band of renegade Negro militiamen ransacks the Cameron homestead in Piedmont, leaving the family with little but their lives, and Atlanta is destroyed as Sherman marches to the sea. Griffith renders the devastating impact of this march

3.11 The surrender at Appomattox, an "historical facsimile" from *The Birth of a Nation:* Howard Gaye as Lee, Donald Crisp as Grant.

in a striking iris shot. A small iris at the upper left-hand corner of the frame gradually opens to disclose a sorrowful mother with her children gathered about her on a hillside. As the iris opens further, the source of the woman's misery is revealed to be Sherman's troops marching like columns of black ants through the valley below: cause and effect are thus dramatically and visually linked.[4]

Concurrently, in a Union military hospital in Washington, D.C., Ben Cameron finally meets Elsie Stoneman, who nurses him back to health in her capacity as a volunteer. Mrs. Cameron soon joins her son in the hospital when she learns that he is under a death sentence for guerrilla activities, and she successfully intercedes for his life with a reverently portrayed President Lincoln. Despite their sentimentality, the detailed composition in depth of these hospital scenes, whose actions in fore-

---

4. In his autobiography, *Billy Bitzer: His Story* (New York: Farrar, Straus and Giroux, 1973), Bitzer says that the mother and children were an actual family group that happened to stop along the hillside while the crew was setting up the Sherman's-march sequence below. Griffith ordered him to sneak up the hill and shoot them unawares. This shot was later combined with the long shot of the marching troops through matting to create the single iris-shot composition described above. As Bitzer comments, it was touches like this "that made *The Birth* so real and convincing to audiences accustomed to stilted acting and stock shots, especially in costume movies" (p. 108). It is worth noting here that the site of Griffith's famous battle scenes is now part of Forest Lawn Cemetery.

ground, middle ground, and background are autonomous, has long impressed critics with its verisimilitude. Equally authentic is the reconstruction of the Confederate surrender at Appomattox that follows — one of the several effective "historical facsimiles" that Griffith introduced from time to time into the narrative. As the war ends, the Camerons begin to rebuild their ravaged home, and Ben returns to Piedmont in a moving and understated homecoming scene.

In Washington, Phil and Elsie Stoneman attend a gala performance of *Our American Cousin* at Ford's Theater to celebrate the surrender of Lee, where they witness the assassination of President Lincoln.

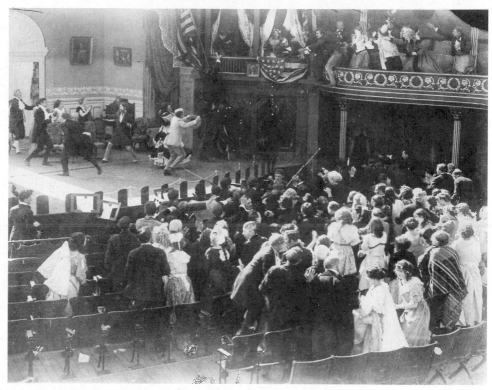

3.12 The assassination of Lincoln: Raoul Walsh as Booth, Joseph Henabery as Lincoln.

dent Lincoln. The assassination sequence is one of Griffith's great set pieces and provides an excellent example of his use of parallel editing to achieve tension in a scene. Running just over five minutes, the sequence is composed of fifty-five shots, some held for only a few seconds; it establishes dynamic *visual* relationships among Lincoln sitting in his theater box, John Wilkes Booth lurking outside, the president's bodyguard asleep at his post, the audience, Phil and Elsie, and the action of the play itself long before their *dramatic* relationship is energized by the assassination. One has only to imagine how a Porter or a Zecca might have handled this sequence in a single shot or perhaps several to understand the breadth of Griffith's achievement.

Lincoln's assassination, much lamented in the South, concludes the "War" section of *The Birth of a Nation* and inaugurates the most controversial part of the film—that dealing with Reconstruction. This section opens with the ascendancy of Senator Austin Stoneman to "the power behind the throne" after Lincoln's death. Determined, as a title informs us, to crush "the White South under the

heel of the Black South" (a phrase from Wilson's *History of the American People*, incidentally, and not an invention of Griffith's), Stoneman leads the radical Reconstructionists to victory in Congress and sends his fawning but secretly ambitious mulatto protégé, Silas Lynch, to Piedmont to administer a program of universal Negro suffrage there. Lynch and his lieutenants, however, organize the recently freed slaves into a mob and commit a series of outrages against the white community ranging from mere insult to bogus imprisonment and sexual assault.

Lynch subsequently becomes lieutenant governor of South Carolina and goes on to preside over a moronic all-Negro legislature that enacts statutes providing for the disenfranchisement of prominent whites and for interracial marriage. Although the state-legislature scene is speciously presented as a historical facsimile, it contains one of Griffith's most masterful uses of the **dissolve.** He opens it with a still photograph of the actual chambers and slowly dissolves to a replica of the hall swarming with raucous, gin-swilling Negro legislators. The sequence concludes with a revoltingly effective iris-in. After the leg-

3.13 Griffith's version of the South Carolina legislature.

islature has enacted its racial intermarriage bill, an iris begins to slowly close upon a group of Negroes on the assembly floor who are leering at something above them; then the iris moves like the lens of a telescope to reveal the object of this lustful attention: a group of frightened white women and children in the gallery.

While this travesty is enacted in the state capitol, back in Piedmont Ben Cameron decides that the "Black Empire" of Lynch and his cronies must be combated by an "Invisible Empire" of white southern knights, organized, as a title tells us, "in defense of their Aryan birthright." This is Griffith's account of the birth of the Ku Klux Klan, and it must be said that the account is not much different from that offered by academic historians of his era,[5] including Woodrow Wilson, who wrote in the fifth volume of his *History of the American People:*

> The white men of the South were aroused by the mere instinct of self-preservation to rid themselves, by fair means or foul, of the intolerable burden of governments sustained by the votes of ignorant negroes and conducted in the interest of adventurers. . . . They could act only by private combination, by private means, as a force outside the government, hostile to it, proscribed by it, of whom opposition and bitter resistance was expected, and expected with defiance.

Meanwhile, Austin Stoneman has come to Piedmont with his family to oversee the implementation of his policies. The senator has fallen ill in the interim, however, and becomes an easy dupe of the vicious Lynch and of Stoneman's own mulatto mistress, Lydia Brown. The

Elsie Stoneman–Ben Cameron and Phil Stoneman–Margaret Cameron romances start to blossom again in Piedmont but are cut short by the bitter residues of war. In one particularly striking scene, Phil proposes to Margaret, and Griffith intercuts the proposal with a flashback[6] to an earlier shot of her young brother lying dead on the field at Petersburg. Griffith once said, "You can photograph thought," and in this flashback sequence, and many others like it sprinkled throughout *The Birth of a Nation,* he demonstrated his point remarkably well. Finally, after another wave of indignities committed by blacks against whites, the terrorist reprisals of the Klan begin in earnest, and Elsie rejects Ben when she learns of his involvement with the organization.

At this point, the film takes an extremely nasty turn as young Flora Cameron, the family's darling, is attacked (but not actually raped) and driven to take her life by Gus, a "renegade negro" who wants to marry her. Gus chases Flora through a forest and up a cliff from which she plummets to her death rather than submit to his embraces, even as brother Ben races desperately to the rescue. Filmed amid the beautiful pine forests and foothills of Big Bear Lake, California, this sequence is perhaps the most skillfully edited three-way chase Griffith ever conceived. But, like a similar sequence in Ingmar Bergman's *The Virgin Spring* (1962; see p. 560), it is the most disturbing in the entire film, for there is no rational way for a viewer to defend against its wrenching images of racial violence and attempted violation. Here we see Griffith, like Eisenstein after him, a master of sensational manipulation, assaulting our sensibilities beyond the bounds of decency in order to drive home an ideological point. It is among the cinema's most compelling and horrifying sequences, as unforgettable—though by no means as for-

---

5. E.g., Columbia University's William A. Dunning, whose *Essays on the Civil War and Reconstruction and Related Topics* (rev. ed., 1904) and *Reconstruction, Political and Economic, 1865–1877* (1907), created the historical perspective popularized by Claude G. Bowers's *The Tragic Era: The Revolution after Lincoln* (1929). This widely read book blames the failure of Reconstruction on self-government by "simple blacks" who made "lustful assaults" on white women, concluding that it was "not until the original Klan began to ride that white women felt some sense of security" (pp. 307–8). See Scott Simmon, *The Films of D. W. Griffith* (Cambridge: Cambridge University Press, 1993), pp. 110–12, 133–34.

6. More accurately, in Bruce F. Kawin's term, a "mindscreen," or mental perspective (here, on the past) from the mind's eye of a character in the narrative—see his *Mindscreen: Bergman, Godard, and First-Person Film* (Princeton, N.J.: Princeton University Press, 1978).

3.14 **Gus (Walter Long) about to be lynched by the "Invisible Empire."**

3.15 **The torrential ride of the Klan.**

givable—as the Odessa steps massacre in Eisenstein's *Potemkin* (1925; see pp. 132–45) and the bullet-riddled death agony of Arthur Penn's protagonists in *Bonnie and Clyde* (1967; see pp. 848–50).

After Flora's death, Gus is tracked down by the Klan and summarily executed in a scene that is dramatically apposite but morally loathsome for the legitimacy it accords the practice of lynching. The body is dumped on the lieutenant governor's doorstep as a warning, and Lynch's reply is to call out the Negro militia for a roundup of suspected Klansmen. Old Dr. Cameron, head of the family, is arrested in the process but is ultimately rescued by two "faithful" black "souls," his daughter Margaret, and Phil Stoneman (now turned against his father) and taken to the sanctuary of a small woodland cabin. Meanwhile, Elsie Stoneman attempts to intercede with Lynch on Cameron's behalf only to find herself being forced into an interracial marriage with the vicious mulatto, who has become "drunk with power and wine" (Griffith's phrase) as the troops of his "Black Empire" run amok in the streets of Piedmont, arbitrarily assaulting and killing whites.

Now the film starts to build to its climax as the Lynch-Elsie sequence is intercut with the "Summoning of the Clans" sequence in which two hooded Klansmen, or "Night Hawks," ride through the countryside far and wide, spreading news of the Piedmont rampage and sounding the call to arms. As their wild ride progresses, Klansmen are drawn to the Night Hawks like tributaries

3.16 **Ben Cameron leads a charge of liberators in a rapid backward tracking shot.**

flowing into a central stream, until a vast army pours down the road to the rescue,[7] in the words of the poet and critic Vachel Lindsay, like "an Anglo-Saxon Niagara." Meanwhile, Negro militiamen have discovered the cabin containing Dr. Cameron, Margaret, and Phil, and have besieged it with every intention of murdering its occupants. Shots of this action are now intercut with shots of

---

7. As will be examined in Chapter 5, V. I. Pudovkin used a similar montage sequence for the climax of *Mother* (1926), in which individual workers flow together from the side streets and byways of St. Petersburg into a mighty revolutionary stream heading toward the factories.

3.17 The triumphal march: Margaret Cameron, Elsie Stoneman (Lillian Gish), and friends.

the torrential ride of the Klan, Negroes rioting in the streets of Piedmont, and what has become by this time Lynch's impending rape of Elsie Stoneman; so that we have a suspense-filled, multipronged "last-minute rescue" elaborately wrought of four simultaneous actions converging toward a climax. Griffith heightens the tension of his montage by decreasing the temporal length of each shot and increasing the tempo of physical movement as the sequence races toward its crescendo. When at last the Klan arrives in town to clear the streets, there follows an action sequence that rivals the battle scenes of the war section. Its dynamic continuity cutting and breathlessly moving camera caused Vachel Lindsay to describe this episode as "tossing wildly and rhythmically like the sea."

After Piedmont is secured and Elsie Stoneman rescued from Lynch, the Klan learns of the besieged cabin in the woods and begins its second ride. Though anticlimactic, this second rescue is more urgent than the first since the band of Negroes has almost succeeded in breaking into the little stronghold when the ride begins, and danger to the principals is imminent. After a flurry of intercutting in which the Negroes finally enter the house and actually grasp Margaret Cameron by her long tresses, the Klan arrives to disperse them and save the whites from violation and / or murder. There follows a parade of the Klan and the rescued parties through the streets of Piedmont, and a new election, easily dominated by the whites. Clearly the "Black Empire" has collapsed in the face of the "Invisible Empire," as an intertitle had predicted earlier, uniting the white North and white South

"in defense of their Aryan birthright." The two Cameron-Stoneman marriages take place, and the film concludes with a symbolic epilogue in which the God of War dissolves into the Prince of Peace and the final title proclaims, somewhat prematurely: *"Liberty and union, /* one and inseparable, / *now and forever!"*

IMPACT

It should be obvious by this point that, whatever it represents ideologically, *The Birth of a Nation* is a technical marvel. Griffith created it in the absence not only of firmly established narrative conventions, but of modern cinematic technology—what he might have accomplished with **widescreen** color cameras and **stereophonic sound** is beyond imagining.[8] And to have articulated these conventions and anticipated this technology in a film of epic proportions so early in the medium's history is a monumental achievement that no one can gainsay. Furthermore, in his symbolic use of objects in close-shot (inedible parched corn in the plate of a Confederate defender of Petersburg; a bird in the hands of the gentle "Little Colonel" during a rendezvous with Elsie Stoneman) and what might be called the "psychological" or "subjective" intercut (the image of Margaret Cameron's dead brother appearing during Phil Stoneman's proposal of marriage; flashbacks depicting recent Negro outrages in Piedmont as Ben Cameron narrates them to his family), Griffith moved the cinema in the direction of "symbolic realism," or the representation of reality that suggests a symbolic—i.e., a psychological or universal—meaning, which would find its fullest expression in the naturalism of Erich von Stroheim (see Chapter 5). Even without cutting, Griffith frequently manages to endow reality with symbolic significance. At the most rudimentary level, for example, Silas Lynch's cruelty to animals implies his capacity for evil, while Senator Stoneman's limp suggests his moral weakness and impotence. Griffith's approach to symbolic realism often degenerates into sentimentality, as when the "Little Colonel" and Elsie kiss the bird held in Ben's hand instead of each other, but his discovery and elaboration of the mode made possible the infinitely more sophisticated symbolic methods of Eisenstein and the school of Soviet montage, as will be seen in Chapter 5.

---

8. The film was in fact shot with a single camera—a $300 hand-cranked Pathé with two interchangeable lenses (a 2.52-inch and a wide-angle).

3.18 Sensationalistic posters, Peoria, Illinois, 1916.

Yet, precisely because of its remarkable emotional power, its tendency to incite and inflame rather than to persuade, *The Birth of a Nation* marked the emergence of film as a potent social and political force in the modern world. As Harry M. Geduld writes:

> It was the first film to be taken seriously as a political statement and it has never failed to be regarded seriously as a "sociological document." . . . People who had previously dismissed the movies as nothing more than a crude entertainment suddenly realized that they had become the century's most potent and provocative medium of expression: the mechanized age had produced mass communications, mass entertainment, and also the possibility of mass indoctrination.

The influence of *The Birth of a Nation* was not, of course, all benign. For one thing, it is a matter of historical record that the film's glowing portrait of the Ku Klux Klan was directly responsible for the modern revival and expansion of that organization, whose membership had reached 5 million by the time of World War II. Indeed, according to the Klan's current leaders, *The Birth of a Nation* was used as a key instrument of recruitment and indoctrination well into the 1960s. Less pernicious socially, but perhaps ultimately more destructive, was the enormous financial success of the film, which seemed to valorize Hollywood's taste for the emotional, sensational, and melodramatic as opposed to the rational, philosophical, and discursive at the very moment of its birth. As a supremely manipulative film, *The Birth of a Nation* showed the American industry how effectively and lucratively the movies could pander to public frustration, anxiety, and prejudice—a lesson that Hollywood has hardly ever forgotten in its more than ninety-year history. Thus, "the man who invented Hollywood" gave that institution not only its initial direction and its emotional tenor, but its first successful formula as well.

At the same time, *The Birth of a Nation* was so clearly a work of genius, however flawed, that it conferred great prestige upon the new medium of the feature film when it most needed it. The first film ever to be widely acclaimed as a great work of art and simultaneously reviled as a pernicious distortion of the truth, *The Birth of a Nation* is the cinema's seminal masterpiece, and its gparadox is the paradox of cinematic narrative itself. Whereas literary narrative tells invented tales through the deliberate manipulation of verbal signs that exist at a third remove from reality, film constructs its fictions through the deliberate manipulation of photographed reality itself, so that in cinema artifice and reality become quite literally indistinguishable. Perhaps the final comment on *The Birth of a Nation* and the whole narrative tradition it founded belongs to Woodrow Wilson, despite his subsequent retraction. It was, he said, "like writing history with lightning," and lightning is powerful, illuminating, even magical. But it is also unpredictable, potentially destructive, and highly imprecise.

Intolerance

PRODUCTION

More persons saw *The Birth of a Nation* in the first year of its release than had seen any single film in history. Attendance in the Greater New York area alone was over 825,000, and nationally the figure was close to 3 million. Griffith had achieved his goal of outdoing the Italian superspectacles on their own terms, and he was universally acknowledged to be the supreme master of the screen. But his victory was mixed with bitterness. Attacks on *The Birth of a Nation*'s content continued (indeed, they have never stopped), and the accusation that he was a bigot disturbed Griffith deeply. In *The Rise and Fall of Free Speech in America* (1915), his counterblast to the film's detractors, he had declared:

> The integrity of free speech and publication was not . . . attacked seriously in this country until the arrival of the *motion picture*, when this new art was seized by the powers of intolerance as an excuse for an assault on our liberties. . . . Intolerance is the root of all censorship. Intolerance martyred Joan of Arc. Intolerance smashed the first printing press. Intolerance invented Salem witchcraft.

Early in 1916, still stinging from charges of racism, Griffith determined to produce a massive cinematic polemic against these "powers of intolerance" as they had endangered civilization throughout human history. The resulting film, *Intolerance*, was not—as is sometimes claimed—Griffith's "liberal" atonement for his

"reactionary" Civil War epic, but rather a spirited defense of his right to have made it. Both films are cut from the same cloth, and their liabilities and assets are quite similar.

Just after *The Birth of a Nation* was released, Griffith had gone to work on a modest contemporary melodrama entitled *The Mother and the Law*. A relatively low-budget feature by its predecessor's standards, more on the scale of *The Battle of the Sexes* (1914) than *The Birth of a Nation*, it was based upon a recent case in which Pinkerton guards had killed nineteen workers during a strike at a chemical plant. *The Mother and the Law* had already been completed when Griffith conceived the idea of combining it with three other tales into an epic exposé of intolerance through the ages. One tale would be set in ancient Babylon during the invasion and conquest of Cyrus the Persian (538 B.C.), another during the St. Bartholomew's Day Massacre in sixteenth-century France (1572), and another in Judea during the crucifixion of Christ (we can guess which story Griffith saw as most closely paralleling his own recent martyrdom). This promised to be an expensive undertaking, but Griffith

3.19 The Babylonian set of *Intolerance* (1916) prepared for the Belshazzar's feast sequence and the lengthy tracking shot.

had been so elevated by the success of *The Birth of a Nation* that no project, however extravagant, could be denied him. He was now working for the Triangle Film Corporation, which his producer, Harry Aitken, had formed with Griffith, Mack Sennett, and Thomas H. Ince (see pp. 000–00) in late 1915, after he had been ousted from Mutual as the result of an internal power struggle. Triangle was not wealthy enough to produce Griffith's new epic, but Aitken incorporated the Wark Producing Corporation to finance the film, and investors fought one another for the privilege of betting on a second Griffith blockbuster.

It was well that they did, for with no standards left to exceed but his own, Griffith conceived of *Intolerance* on a scale so vast as to dwarf all of his previous work combined. Sparing no expense, financial or human, he threw up mammoth sets designed by the previously uncredited Walter Hall[9] for each of the four periods represented in the film, the most elaborate of which was a full-scale model of ancient Babylon covering more than 10 acres of land and standing some 300 feet above the ground. He hired sixty principal players and thousands of extras to people the film, and at one point the production's payroll alone exceeded $20,000 a day. Among his eight assistant directors (*The Birth of a Nation* had none) were four who would later have significant Hollywood careers of their own—Allan Dwan, Christy Cabanne, Tod Browning, and Erich von Stroheim. When the project was finally completed, Griffith had spent fourteen months and, it was claimed, nearly $2 million on it. *The Birth of a Nation*, by comparison, had been put together in seven months

for one-twentieth the sum. Indeed, a single banquet scene in the Babylonian section of *Intolerance* was purported to have cost more than $250,000 to film, or well over twice the entire budget of its predecessor.[1] This unprecedented extravagance caused alarm among Griffith's backers, and he was forced to plow back a substantial portion of his profits from *The Birth of a Nation* (from which he ultimately earned about $1 million) into *Intolerance* in order to keep the project afloat. If the film had been the popular success he expected, Griffith would have become one of the richest men in Hollywood. As it was, *Intolerance* produced heavy losses.

The **rough cut** of *Intolerance* ran for eight hours, and Griffith toyed with the notion of distributing the film at this length in two separate parts. Practicality got the better of him, however, and he cut the negative from 200,000 to 13,500 feet, approximately three and one-half hours. After the box-office failure of *Intolerance* became apparent, Griffith rashly cut into the negative and re-edited *The Mother and the Law* and *The Fall of Babylon* for release

3.20 The Babylonian set under construction, seen from behind.

9. Hall surfaced as the production designer of *Intolerance*, apparently his only film, with the publication of Karl Brown's *Adventures with D. W. Griffith* (New York: Farrar, Straus and Giroux, 1973). Brown was Bitzer's assistant and provides a lively and detailed account of the making of *The Birth of a Nation*, *Intolerance*, and other Griffith features. Hall was responsible for creating the film's superb central perspective system, but the Babylonian sets themselves were conceived during a 1915 visit to San Francisco by Griffith, Bitzer, and Brown to research conditions in the city jail and San Quentin prison for the Modern story. On the way back to Los Angeles, the three passed by the San Francisco Exposition, whose Asiatic architectural theme so impressed the director that he had Bitzer take matte shots of the Tower of Jewels for future use. Griffith may also have visited the Italian Pavilion and been reminded of the opulent sets of *Cabiria* (pp. 00–00); such, at least, is the premise of Paolo and Vittorio Taviani's *Good Morning, Babylon* (1987; p. 000), which chronicles the fates of several Italian immigrant masons brought down by Griffith from the Exposition to assist in the construction of the Babylonian sets. The sets also have sources, of course, in *Cabiria* itself and in several nineteenth-century religious paintings.

1. The actual cost of *Intolerance* is still a matter of dispute. Griffith's own papers (*D. W. Griffith Papers*) contain a statement to the effect that the negative cost of the film was exactly $385,906.77, with the lion's share going to set construction and salaries. According to another source, a Price, Waterhouse audit in 1916 set the negative cost at $485,000, a figure still forty times the budget of a conventional feature in that year. In *D. W. Griffith: an American Life* (New York: Simon and Schuster, 1984), Richard Schickel attributes the myth of *Intolerance*'s vast production costs to Griffith's publicists and to a *Scientific American* article of September 2, 1916, whose authors were given inflated financial information by the film's accountants. Whatever the case, it is possible that the *total* cost incurred by Wark Producing Corporation for *Intolerance*, inclusive of promotion, print duplication, and distribution fees, doubled or even tripled the negative cost.

as separate films to recoup his losses. Later, when he attempted to reconstruct the negative, nearly 2,000 feet had been permanently lost, so that today we can never see *Intolerance* in its original form, which, according to the custom of the day, also included tinting in blue, red, green, and sepia to achieve atmospheric effects (blue for melancholy and night, red for war and passion, green for the pastoral and for calm, and sepia for interiors; see "The Introduction of Color," below, pp. 000–000). Nevertheless, the version which has come down to us closely resembles the original in terms of its formal structure, and this is the most important aspect of the film from our standpoint.[2]

STRUCTURE

For *Intolerance*, Griffith conceived the revolutionary notion of crosscutting not only between parallel actions occurring simultaneously in separate spatial dimensions, as in his earlier films, but also between parallel actions occurring on separate temporal planes—those of the four stories. Thus, the plots of the four stories are interwoven like movements in a symphony until they converge in a crescendo at the film's climax. Before this quadruple climax, actions occurring in the separate historical periods are episodically self-contained and are drawn together by the recurrent transitional symbol of a mother rocking a

3.21 Transition: "Out of the cradle endlessly rocking . . ." Lillian Gish as The Woman Who Rocks the Cradle.

cradle, emblematic of human continuity. This image is illuminated by a shaft of sacred light and accompanied by Walt Whitman's line "Out of the cradle endlessly rocking. . . ." As the separate stories move toward their conclusions, however, Griffith largely abandons this transitional device and cuts back and forth directly between incomplete climactic actions in the process of unfolding on all four temporal planes. He told a contemporary interviewer: "[The] stories will begin like four currents looked at from a hilltop. At first the four currents will flow apart, slowly and quietly. But as they flow, they grow nearer and nearer together, and faster and faster, until in the end, in the last act, they mingle in one mighty river of expression." Although the Biblical and St. Bartholomew's Day plots are resolved before the more complicated Babylonian and Modern stories, for the better part of the film's last two reels Griffith involves us in three separate three-way rescues and a dramatically excoriating Crucifixion. In these passages, Christ's progress toward Calvary, the desperate ride of the "Mountain girl" across the Euphrates plain to warn Babylon of its impending destruction, the massacre of the French Huguenots, and the modern wife's race against time to save her innocent husband from execution are all rapidly intercut in shots of shorter and shorter duration to create what is even today among the most exciting and unusual climactic sequences in motion-picture history. As Iris Barry said of it, "History itself seems to pour like a cataract across the screen." Like *The Birth of a Nation*, *Intolerance* concludes with a symbolic montage in which prison walls dissolve into flowered meadows and a grim battle site becomes a field of frolicking children.

Contemporary audiences, who had only recently been exposed to the conventional, if striking, narrative intercutting of *The Birth of a Nation*, found this essentially metaphorical or symbolic intercutting difficult to understand—not surprisingly, for Griffith was cinematically years ahead his of time. He was already practicing in

---

2. In 1985, archivist / distributor Raymond Rohauer reconstructed *Intolerance* from Griffith's personal copy, complete with the original tinting and toning. To celebrate the film's seventieth anniversary, this print was shown on a 100-foot screen at the Avignon Film Festival in July 1986, accompanied by a new symphonic score composed by Antoine Duhamel and Pierre Jansen, and performed by the seventy-five-piece Orchestre de l'Île de France. This version, running 138 minutes at 20 fps, is currently available for rental in both 35- and 16mm from The Rohauer Collection of Alan Twyman Presents.

3.22 Christ on the road to Calvary: Howard Gaye.

of the longest and most elaborate tracking shots in the American cinema.

INFLUENCE AND DEFECTS

For sheer technical virtuosity and inventiveness, then, *Intolerance* must rank as Griffith's greatest film. Moreover, Griffith's handling of massive crowd and battle scenes, as well as more intimate personal ones, surpassed anything he had ever done before or would attempt again. For much of the twentieth century, however, it was customary to praise *Intolerance* far beyond its intrinsic worth because it had such a powerful influence upon the Soviet filmmakers who articulated

Intolerance the kind of abstract or "expressive" montage that Eisenstein and his Soviet colleagues would bring to perfection a decade later. Furthermore, the film contains the ultimate refinement of every narrative device Griffith had employed from *The Adventures of Dollie* through *The Birth of a Nation*. It uses revolutionary continuity editing, of course, but also huge close-ups, sweeping panoramas, assorted dissolves, irises, and masks (including a widescreen effect used for large battle sequences), dramatically expressive camera angles, and, finally, tracking movement that anticipates the elaborate maneuvers of F. W. Murnau and the German *Kammerspielfilm* (see Chapter 4, pp. 100–05) eight years later. For the climactic rescue in the Modern story, for example, Griffith mounted his camera in a moving automobile to follow a suspenseful chase between it and a train, just as he had done for the riot sequences in *The Birth of a Nation*. More important, Griffith built for *Intolerance* a huge elevator tower that rolled on rails to track the camera gradually from an extreme long shot of Babylon down into a full shot of actors on the set itself. The shot occurs several times in the film and is still one

and refined montage. It is also a relatively "safe" film to like compared to its volatile predecessor, and some critics have even tried (incorrectly) to make of it an apology for *The Birth of a Nation*. Yet, as an aesthetic experience

3.23 The St. Bartholomew's Day Massacre begins.

3.24 Griffith and Bitzer shooting the climactic chase in the Modern story: Mae Marsh (center) as The Dear One.

rather than a narrative structure, *Intolerance* is something of a white elephant. Its spectacular proportions are unwieldy, and its elaborate intercutting apparatus does not always work. There are moments of incoherence: the St. Bartholomew's Day story sometimes gets lost in the shuffle, and the precise sequence of events in the Babylonian episode occasionally becomes unclear. Worse, Griffith's case-pleading in both his images and his titles becomes nearly hysterical at times, and his expressed intention to show "how hatred and intolerance, through the ages, have battled against love and charity" is scarcely germane to either the Babylonian or the Modern sequences. Indeed, Griffith hardly seems to have known what he meant by the term "intolerance," except that he associated it with the bitter outcry against *The Birth of a Nation*. In the context of the film itself, "intolerance" is simply an omnibus word encapsulating any form of human evil; and evil, of course, has never been a difficult or an unpopular subject to attack.

Intolerance is, in fact, the most Manichean of Griffith's feature films: in portraying the melodramatic struggle of Good against Evil through the ages, Griffith allowed his sentimentality to become distinctly overripe. Indeed, there are so many pious, pompous titles in *Intolerance* that Iris Barry was led to describe the film as "an epic sermon." Ultimately, *Intolerance* is an erratic but brilliant film of undeniable importance whose decisive influence upon figures as diverse as Cecil B. DeMille, Sergei Eisenstein, V. I. Pudovkin, Fritz Lang, and Abel Gance is a matter of historical record. As a self-contained work of art, it is by turns ponderous, awe-inspiring, obsessive, and thrilling. The film historian Jay Leyda, in an essay written on the occasion of Griffith's death in 1948, called *Intolerance* "a towering compound of greatness and cheapness," but the filmmaker John Dorr put it more precisely: "*Intolerance* succeeded as a film of spectacle and as a film of narrative action, but not as a film of ideas."

For the audiences of 1916, which cared little for ideas in any event, *Intolerance* was simply too much—too big, too complicated, too serious, and too solemn. Ironically, the film's commercial failure was probably conditioned by its predecessor's enormous success. The millions who had been swept away by *The Birth of a Nation* expected Griffith's second epic to carry them off in the same tumultuous and inflammatory manner. Emotional appeal, however, was not one of *Intolerance*'s strong points, for Griffith had deliberately subordinated character development—hence, audience identification—to spectacle and historical process. Furthermore, the United States was preparing to enter the war in Europe when the film was released in September 1916, and a bellicose mood was sweeping the country. By a crushing historical irony, Griffith's rejoinder to the suppression of *The Birth of a Nation* was itself censured and suppressed in many American cities as a pacifist statement, despite the obvious enthusiasm of its battle scenes (many of them shot at night and illuminated by magnesium flares). Finally, after twenty-two weeks of distribution, the film was taken out of circulation, and in 1919 it was re-edited as two separate films, as previously described. This attempt by Griffith to salvage his enormous financial investment was only partially successful; he would continue to pay his debts on *Intolerance* until his death in 1948.[3]

---

3. The crumbling Babylonian set stood for years at the intersection of Sunset and Hollywood boulevards, becoming a familiar local landmark, because there was not enough money returned on *Intolerance* to have the structure torn down. It was finally removed by the WPA in the late 1930s.

3.25 Shot sequence from the "last-minute rescue" in the Modern story intercut with the Crucifixion: Bobby Harron as the Boy.

Griffith after *Intolerance*

The failure of *Intolerance* did not by any means end Griffith's career. It curtailed his independence as a producer and dampened his enthusiasm as a creator, but he went on to direct another twenty-six feature films between 1916 and 1931. Most critics see this period as one of marked decline in power. It is true that Griffith made no major narrative innovations after *Intolerance*, but it could reasonably be argued that there were very few left to make before the coming of sound. What seems to have happened is that Griffith lost touch with the prevailing tastes of the postwar era and, therefore, with the popular audience. Though the failure of *Intolerance* had convinced him of the necessity of catering to popular tastes, he experienced increasing difficulty in locating them after 1917. This was partially the result of rapid social change. Industrialization, modernization, and our involvement in World War I had caused an inversion of traditional American attitudes and values (see footnote, p. 169). The nineteenth-century virtues of morality, idealism, and purity, incarnated by the Cameron family in *The Birth of a Nation*, had given way to the pursuit of sensation and material wealth in the disillusioned postwar era. The verities of rural romanticism, so crucial to Griffith's prewar epics, were replaced by the sophistication, urbanity, and wit of filmmakers like Cecil B. DeMille and Ernst Lubitsch (see pp. 187–90), whose cynical amorality was all but incomprehensible to a director who had never permitted his lovers to so much as kiss on the screen. Griffith continued to make interesting films—he produced one masterpiece, *Broken Blossoms*—but most of his postwar features are either disappointingly conventional or hopelessly old-fashioned. In effect, the movies had entered the Jazz Age, while Griffith still lived in the afterglow of the nineteenth century.

A great artist's failures, however, are as interesting as his successes, and Griffith's are worth recording briefly here. Before *Intolerance* had even started to sink at the box office, Griffith was invited to England by the British government to make a propaganda picture in support of the war effort against Germany and to convince America to join it (which occurred shortly after Griffith's arrival). Initially conceived as an extended newsreel on the Somme offensive of April 1917 to be financed by Lord Beaverbrook's powerful War Office Cinematograph

Committee, *Hearts of the World* (1918) became instead a privately produced anti-German war epic shot on location in France and England that luridly depicted the effects of "Hunnish" occupation on a small French town. Recalling *The Birth of a Nation* in its battle scenes, *Hearts of the World* was enormously popular with domestic audiences during the war, although it lacked the focus and coherence of its predecessor. Griffith shot another film while he was in England—*The Great Love*, a morale booster designed to show "the regeneration of British society through its war activities," according to advance publicity. This feature, which hasn't survived, was produced by Adolph Zukor's Paramount-Artcraft Company,[4] which had agreed to become the American distributor for *Hearts of the World*. Before leaving for England, Griffith had signed a contract with Zukor to direct six films for his company and to oversee the production of several others—a wise decision since Triangle was about to be bankrupted through mismanagement and the depredations of rival production companies, Zukor's among them. Neither English film was a critical success; *Hearts of the World* seems especially crude today in its stereotyping of all German soldiers as beasts, although that, of course, was its avowed intention in the year it was made. Returning to Hollywood, Griffith directed five feature films for Zukor in rapid succession between 1917 and 1919—*True Heart Susie, A Romance of Happy Valley, The Greatest Thing in Life, The Girl Who Stayed at Home*, and *Scarlet Days* (his only feature-length Western, which also hasn't survived), all of them (except the last) dated, idyllic romances with little popular appeal. Next Griffith signed a contract to direct three quickie potboilers for First National in order to raise money for his newest project—the building of an independent studio on a large estate he had purchased near Mamaroneck, New York, where he hoped to become his own producer. According to one of Griffith's biographers, Robert M. Henderson, First National was interested only in the Griffith imprimatur and permitted him to leave the direction of these films to his assistants, which he apparently did. *The Greatest Question* (1919), a melodrama about spiritualism, and *The Idol Dancer* (1920; released 1922) and *The Love Flower* (1920), both exotic South Seas adventures, were

---

4. Part of Zukor's Paramount Famous Players–Lasky empire, founded in 1916, originally to distribute Mary Pickford's films.

of indifferent quality and did little to enhance the reputation of "the Master," as Griffith had recently been dubbed by the press. Between *The Greatest Question* and *The Idol Dancer*, however, Griffith independently produced *Broken Blossoms*, his last masterpiece and his first great commercial success since *The Birth of a Nation*.

Based on a story called "The Chink and the Child," from Thomas Burke's *Limehouse Nights* (1916), *Broken Blossoms* concerns a young waif of the London slums, brutally mistreated by her father, who finds brief sanctuary in the chaste love of a gentle young Chinese man.[5] When her father learns of the relationship, he beats the child to death with a whip handle; the boy then kills the father and commits suicide. Griffith shot this film entirely in the studio in eighteen days (with much prior rehearsal, however) on such a rigorously economical schedule that—according to Lillian Gish, who played the girl—there were no retakes and only 200 feet of printed stock were left unused (the normal ratio of footage printed to footage used in a commercial film was about 15 to 1 in 1919 and is 10 to 1 today). Yet *Broken Blossoms* shows no evidence of its hasty construction and is simultaneously Griffith's most richly evocative and tightly controlled film. Despite some overly sentimental touches (such as the wretched young girl's attempts to counterfeit a smile by propping up the corners of her mouth with her fingers), *Broken Blossoms* succeeds admirably as pathos and is probably the closest Griffith ever came to incarnating his Victorian sensibilities in an appropriate dramatic form. But more important than its dramatic structure is the film's dreamlike, atmospheric context—its mood-drenched *mise-en-scène*. Griffith derived the film's ambiance from a series of watercolors of London's Limehouse district, the city's Chinatown, by the English artist George Baker; but both photography and lighting in *Broken Blossoms* are distinctly Continental, probably because of the efforts of Billy Bitzer's recently acquired assistant, Hendrik Sartov,[6] a specialist in mood lighting and soft focus, or "impressionistic," photography. Griffith, Bitzer, and Sartov together created out of brooding London fogs, smoke-filled opium dens, and the petallike delicacy of the boy's rooms a *mise-en-scène* worthy of—and probably contributory to—the studio-produced *Kammerspielfilm* of the German cinema (as will be seen in Chapter 4).

For its release in May 1919, *Broken Blossoms* was tinted entirely in soft pastels and, to further enhance its

3.26 A wharf scene from the studio-produced *Broken Blossoms* (1919): Lillian Gish at the right of the frame.

visual lushness, projected onto a screen washed from above and below by rich pastel lights. Unpredictably, the film was a smashing commercial and critical success. Produced for the now modest sum of $90,000, it made nearly $1 million and was widely hailed as a masterpiece. One critic wrote that Griffith "had far exceeded the power of the written word," while others gave "the Master" a new title: "the Shakespeare of the screen." This praise was well deserved, for *Broken Blossoms* is Griffith's most highly

---

5. Griffith's sympathetic treatment of the Chinese boy in *Broken Blossoms*, during the height of anti-Oriental, "Yellow Peril" sensationalism in the United States, has troubled critics who prefer to see him as an unreconstructed and irredeemable racist. In fact, the historical record shows that Griffith took great pains in both the production and promotion of the film not to pander to the popular (and, by then, stereotypically Hollywood) image of the Oriental as inscrutable villain. Apparently, he was a man who at least could learn from his own mistakes.

6. Sartov was Lillian Gish's personal photographer and cameraman, brought into the production at her insistence, and Griffith quickly came to admire his work. In addition to assisting Bitzer on *Broken Blossoms* (1919), *Way Down East* (1920), and, with Arthur H. C. ("Hal") Sintzenich, *The White Rose* (1923), Sartov was the principal cinematographer for *Dream Street* (1921), *Orphans of the Storm* (1921, with Paul Allen), *One Exciting Night* (1922), *America* (1924, with Bitzer, Marcel Le Picard, and Sintzenich), and *Isn't Life Wonderful?* (1924, with Sintzenich). In 1924 Sartov followed Gish to MGM (where, for example, he photographed her in Victor Sjöström's *The Scarlet Letter* [1926]), and Griffith continued to work with some combination of Sintzenich, Harry Fischbeck, and Karl Struss in consultation with Bitzer, whose alcoholism and domestic problems left him increasingly unreliable. See Erik Barnouw, "The Sintzenich Diaries," *Quarterly Journal of the Library of Congress* 37, 3–4 (Summer–Fall 1980): 310–31.

integrated film as well as his most personal and poetic. There are indications that the chief appeal of *Broken Blossoms* to contemporary audiences was nostalgic. Whether or not Griffith understood this is unclear, but it is certain that the resounding accolades for his film convinced him more than ever before that he was a natural genius who could do no wrong on the screen.

Broken Blossoms was released through United Artists Corporation, the producing-distributing company that Griffith had formed with Charlie Chaplin, Mary Pickford, and Douglas Fairbanks in the spring of 1919, and the film's financial success made it possible for Griffith to equip his own studio at Mamaroneck as planned. His first project there was an adaptation of a creaky Victorian stage play of seduction and betrayal, *Way Down East*, the rights for which he paid $175,000. Once again Griffith was emotionally in tune with his material, and he produced an exciting and credible melodrama. Shot on location in New York, Connecticut, and Vermont, *Way Down East* (1920) possesses an unexpectedly cinematic vitality and concludes with a skillfully edited last-minute rescue equal to Griffith's best montage work of the teens. After an elaborate chase through a real blizzard, the heroine collapses on an ice floe moving rapidly downriver toward a steep falls (actually Niagara, cut into the sequence from stock shots). The hero emerges from the storm, leaps downstream from one floe to another, and finally rescues her on the very brink of the plunging falls in a sequence that most certainly influenced Pudovkin's ice-floe montage at the conclusion of *Mother* (1926; see pp. 158–59).

The audiences, if not the critics, were enthusiastic about *Way Down East* and made it Griffith's last great popular success. In fact, the film grossed $4.5 million, returning the largest profit of any Griffith film after *The Birth of a Nation*.[7]

Decline

Griffith took his share of the profits and plowed it back into his Mamaroneck studios. But he knew that the days of independent producing were rapidly drawing to a close, and there is evidence that with this knowledge he was driven to consider filmmaking more and more as a business activity and less and less as an art. His next several films confirmed this new preoccupation. *Dream Street* (1921) was a misbegotten effort to re-create the misty, poetic ambiance that had proved so lucrative with *Broken Blossoms*.[8] *Orphans of the Storm* (1921) was a spectacular attempt to capitalize on the new vogue for historical costume films created by Ernst Lubitsch's *Madame DuBarry* (English title: *Passion*, 1919) by setting a dated Victorian melodrama against the background of the French Revolution. The film was expensively produced at Mamaroneck and well received by the critics, but it lost so much money that it nearly terminated Griffith's dream of independence. In an effort to recoup his losses, he made two more potboilers—a haunted-house mystery entitled *One Exciting Night* (1922) and an old-fashioned piece of Deep South exoticism called *The*

3.27 The climatic rescue in *Way Down East* (1920): Lillian Gish, Richard Barthelmess.

7. Stung by unfavorable reviews, Griffith re-edited *Way Down East* thoughout its life in distribution, which concluded in a 1931 rerelease with a musical soundtrack, eventually reducing its length by about 25 percent. In 1984, MoMA produced a 163-minute restored version with the original intertitles, based on Griffith's several extant versions, the original cued score, and Griffith's own copyrighted shot sequence in the Library of Congress. Though it lacks five or six minutes of the release print, narrative gaps are bridged by stills and intertitles, and the MoMA restoration comes as close to Griffith's original conception of the film as we shall probably ever get. See Tom Gunning, "Rebirth of a Movie," *American Film* 10, 1 (October 1984): 18–19, 93, and Steve Vineburg, "The Restored *Way Down East*," *Film Quarterly* 39, 3 (Spring 1986): 54–57.

8. Nevertheless, Griffith was still experimenting technically: *Dream Street* contained several songs recorded (not very successfully) with an early sound-on-disk system (see pp. 205–06) and featured a prologue with Griffith himself speaking from the screen (not very audibly) on "the Evolution of the Motion Pictures."

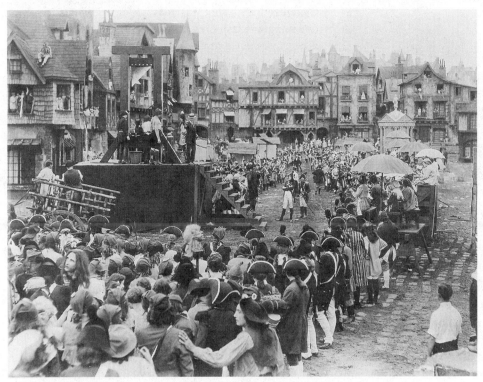

3.28 Griffith directing the guillotine scene in *Orphans of the Storm* 1921).

postwar inflation upon the German middle class. It is thought to have influenced both G. W. Pabst's *Die freudlose Gasse* (*The Joyless Street*; see p. 107), made in Ger-many the following year, and the neorealist cinema that sprang up in Italy after World War II (see pp. 531–55). Part of the film's uniqueness surely stemmed from the fact that before leaving the United States Griffith had secretly signed a contract to direct three fast films for Paramount Famous Players–Lasky in an attempt to stave off bankruptcy. He must have sensed that *Isn't Life Wonderful?* would be his last independent project.

Sadly, with the exception of his much maligned *The Struggle* (1931), it was. Zukor had just lost Cecil B. DeMille as his premier director, and he promptly hired Griffith for the job, which meant that for the first time since his early Biograph days Griffith was unable to choose his own material. The apathy this produced in him was very nearly fatal. At Paramount's Astoria, New York, studios he made two limp W. C. Fields vehicles, *Sally of the Sawdust* (1925) and *That Royle Girl* (1926), and a studio-contrived fantasy-spectacle, *The Sorrows of Satan* (1926), which had originally been intended for DeMille; but his direction of these unappealing projects was so pedestrian that his Paramount contract was not renewed when it expired in late 1926. At this point, Joseph Schenck (1878–1961), now president of United Artists, offered Griffith a job directing films for his independently owned Art Cinema Corporation in exchange for the voting rights to Griffith's United Artists stock (a swindle nearly as flagrant as Edison's theft of Thomas Armat's Vitagraph projector), but Griffith was foundering rapidly and was forced to accept.

White Rose* (1923). Both films were failures that served only to deepen Griffith's financial crisis.

Now Griffith began to dream of saving his company by duplicating the phenomenal success of *The Birth of a Nation*. He remembered *War*, the drama of the American Revolution that he had written years before he had ever seen a movie, and decided to produce an epic film on the subject. This costly attempt to remake *The Birth of a Nation* in other terms was called *America* (1924), and it succeeded admirably as spectacle. Its enormous battle scenes easily rival anything Griffith ever produced, but its dull textbook account of the Revolution and its heavy-handed patriotism made it a museum piece even in its own time. Like every film he had made since *The Love Flower*, except *Way Down East*, *America* lost money, and the Mamaroneck studios were doomed. Griffith was now facing extinction as a producer and simultaneously being squeezed for more films by his United Artists partners. Accordingly, in the summer of 1924 he traveled to Germany to make *Isn't Life Wonderful?*, his last film as an independent producer for United Artists. Based on contemporary events with exteriors shot entirely on location, the film is a semidocumentary account of the ravages of

For Art Cinema, Griffith made three undistinguished films—*Drums of Love* (1928), a medieval Italian melodrama based on the Paolo and Francesca legend; *The*

3.29 The last epic: *America* **(1924).**

Battle of the Sexes (1928–29), a humorless remake of his old Reliance-Majestic farce with a synchronized sound-on-film score; and *Lady of the Pavements* (1929), a romantic "women's picture," released in both silent and sound versions, that completely miscast the sexy Lupe Velez as an ingenue. Schenck was ready to fire Griffith (who, in addition to his other worries, had developed a drinking problem) when Griffith proposed that he direct a sound-film biography of Abraham Lincoln. The old *Birth of a Nation* mystique worked for Griffith one last time, and Schenck approved the project. The resulting film, *Abraham Lincoln* (1930), with a script by the American poet Stephen Vincent Benét, is a shadow of Griffith's great Civil War epic. The battle sequences and even the assassination look devitalized and grotesquely underbudgeted by comparison with analogous scenes in *The Birth of a Nation*; and, like most early sound films, *Abraham Lincoln* is visually wooden and static. But Griffith had turned in a respectable and intelligent performance in the most difficult years of the transition from silent pictures to sound, and he was rewarded for it. Several influential trade journals named him "Director of the Year," and the film itself was on most "Ten Best" lists for 1930.

Griffith now felt that he was one film away from complete rehabilitation, but he knew that he could never make that film for Schenck; so he quit Art Cinema and floated a bank loan of approximately $200,000 in order to produce what he hoped would be his first sound-era masterpiece—a version of Zola's *L'Assommoir* (*The Drunkard*) written by Anita Loos and entitled *The Struggle* (1931). It turned out, instead, to be his last film. Thinly

capitalized and shot for reasons of economy in semi-documentary fashion in and around New York City, *The Struggle* was an abject failure with both contemporary critics and the public. Like all Griffith films, it was visually impressive and had a sound track far above average quality for its time, but in terms of drama *The Struggle* was as archaic as "The Face on the Bar-Room Floor." The film was released in January 1932 and permanently withdrawn after a week of exhibition: audiences had walked out on its opening night, and the critics were mocking it, although some today regard it as a much better film than *Abraham Lincoln*. Sixteen years after *The Birth of a Nation*, "the Shakespeare of the screen" had become a figure of ridicule, and Griffith was forced to retire in humiliation from the industry that he, more than any single figure in its brief history, had helped to create. He lived out the remainder of his life in modest comfort on an annuity he had purchased for himself in more prosperous times, overseeing retrospective exhibitions of his greatest films and attending testimonial banquets in his honor. He died in Los Angeles in 1948, only five months after Sergei Eisenstein in Moscow, and was eulogized around the world as "the man who invented cinema." None were more moving in their praise than those who had for the previous sixteen years refused him employment.

The Importance of Griffith

Griffith remained until the end of his career the same paradoxical figure he had been at its beginning. To borrow Jay Leyda's terminology for *Intolerance*, the greatness and the cheapness of the man were inextricably mixed. By his own candid admission, Griffith derived most of his major narrative innovations from the techniques of nineteenth-century fiction and melodrama, but he also imbibed the simplistic world view of these two popular forms, to the everlasting detriment of his art. In his famous essay entitled "Dickens, Griffith, and the Film Today," Sergei Eisenstein pointed out that Griffith's constant resort to parallel editing was a function of his dualistic vision of human experience, in which an entire civil war or twenty centuries of human history were reducible to a melodramatic struggle between the forces of Good and Evil. As a dramatist, in fact, Griffith was less "the Shakespeare of the screen" than its Thomas Middleton.

But Griffith was also perhaps the greatest cinematic genius in history—the man who discovered (sometimes, admittedly, in the work of others), synthesized, and articulated the narrative language of film as it is practiced even today. In effect, the way he structured the cinema is the way most of us still perceive it.

His genius, however, was fundamentally innovative and intuitive, rather than critical or analytic. When the days of innovation ceased and intuition was no longer essential to the filmmaking process, Griffith was thrown back upon a world view that was hopelessly inappropriate to the postwar era and that had never been intellectually respectable, even in its own century. To compound the misfortune, the lionization of Griffith that followed *The Birth of a Nation* and continued well into the 1920s produced in him a kind of megalomania that permanently impaired his judgment. When Griffith began to think of himself as the prophet and philosopher of the film medium, he ceased to be its leading artist. And yet he achieved so much in so short a time with such limited means that to dwell upon the defects of his work or his character, however serious, is more than ungenerous. It is simply irrelevant, for the greatest of Griffith's achievements in a lifetime of achievement was that this fundamentally nineteenth-century man ultimately managed to transcend his defects of vision, judgment, and taste to become one of the great artists of the twentieth century.

German Cinema of the Weimar Period, 1919–1929

The Prewar Period

Prior to the First World War, the German cinema had reached a less advanced state of development than the cinemas of France, Italy, England, and the United States. Although the Skladanowsky brothers had unveiled their Bioskop projector in the Berlin Wintergarten in November 1895, almost simultaneously with the first Lumière Cinématographe projection, an indigenous German film industry had somehow failed to evolve in the fifteen years that followed. One reason for this seems to have been that in Germany, more than in the other nations of the West, the cinema became a cultural refuge for the illiterate, disenfranchised, and unemployed. Consequently, very few educated Germans took films or filmmaking seriously during these years, and most of the films shown in the early tent shows (*Wanderkinos*) and nickelodeons (*Ladenkinos*) were either imported from other countries or produced in Germany by fly-by-night showmen. Early German or Wilhelmine cinema (after Kaiser Wilhelm) was very much a "cinema of attractions" in Tom Gunning's sense; many domestic films were frankly pornographic, and few demonstrated a tendency toward narrative integration.

One notable exception was the work of Oskar Messter (1866–1943), an inventor who had been instrumental in perfecting the Maltese-cross movement for projection systems (see p. 9). In 1897, Messter established a small studio in the Berlin Friedrichstrasse and went on to produce hundreds of short entertainment films and *actualités* of a reasonably high caliber and some technical sophistication. He used close shots as early as 1903 and became one of the first directors anywhere in the world to light his sets artificially. Messter also experimented with synchronized sound, using the phonograph to produce *Tonbilder* ("sound images")—a type of prenarrative cinema featuring famous stars of cabaret and, ultimately, classical opera and ballet—which upgraded the content of early German film between 1904 and 1908. In 1909 he ventured into the production of feature films (*Grossfilme*) with *Andreas Hofer*, directed by Rudolf Biebrack (1866–

1938), and devoted his energies to that form almost entirely until 1917, when his company and most others in Germany came under the control of the new government-subsidized conglomerate Universum Film Aktiengesellschaft (UFA). One item of historical interest of Messter's features is that they provided the film debuts of performers like Henny Porten, Emil Jannings, Lil Dagover, and Conrad Veidt, who became major stars in the 1920s. Another is that they inaugurated two important forms of early German cinema—the melodrama (e.g., *Der Müller und sein Kind* [*The Miller and His Child*], *Im Glück vergessen* [*Forgotten in Happiness*], and *Tragödie eines Streiks* [*Tragedy of a Strike*], all starring Henny Porten and directed by Adolf Gärtner, 1911) and the social drama (e.g., *Heimgefunden* [*The Way Back Home*, 1910] and *Perlen bedeuten Tränen* [*Pearls Mean Tears*, 1911], directed by Adolf Gärtner and Curt Stark, respectively, both starring Henny Porten).

A more important development, however, began around 1910, when, in response to the great success of the French *film d'art* movement, directors, actors, and writers associated with the German theater began to take a serious interest in the cinema for the first time. In 1912 the first *Autorenfilm* ("famous author's film," and thus the German version of *film d'art*) was brought to the screen by the former stage director Max Mack (1884–1973). This predictably static adaptation of Paul Lindau's highly successful stage play *Der Andere* (*The Other*), about the split personality of a Berlin lawyer, starred the world-famous actor Albert Bassermann (1867–1952). The following year, the great stage director and producer Max Reinhardt (1873–1943) filmed versions of the plays *A Venetian Night* and *The Isle of the Dead*, and the poet-playwright Hugo von Hofmannsthal wrote the "dream-play" *Das fremde Mädchen* (*The Strange Girl*), the first serious German feature film to treat a purely supernatural theme. The influx of literary and theatrical people into German film had the effect of radically elevating its social status, but, as in France, the movement also retarded the development of true cinematic narrative by binding it tightly to the narrative conventions of the stage.

The first prewar German film to break with stage conventions was the Danish director Stellan Rye's production of *Der Student von Prag* (*The Student of Prague*) in 1913, shot by the pioneering lighting cameraman Guido Seeber (1879–1940) and starring a former Reinhardt actor, Paul

4.1 *Der Student von Prag* (Stellan Rye, 1913).

Wegener (1874–1948), in the title role. Based collectively on variants of the Faust legend in the work of E. T. A. Hoffmann, Edgar Allan Poe, and Oscar Wilde, the film concerns a young student who sells his mirror reflection, and thus his soul, to a sorcerer who in turn causes the image to become a murderous incarnation of the student's evil second self. Much of the film was shot on location in Prague, and it is distinguished by atmospheric lighting and many effective photographic illusions, as well as by Wegener's subtle performance in the double role of the student and the student's alter ego. The film's immediate impact, however, was felt more in terms of its content than its technical virtuosity, for, as Siegfried Kracauer has noted, *Der Student von Prag* introduced the morbid theme of "deep and fearful concern with the foundations of the self," which was to obsess the German cinema from 1913 to 1933, at which point it was taken over and anesthetized by the Nazis.[1] Moreover, as a tale of psychological horror in a specifically supernatural setting, *Der Student von Prag* prefigures the German Expressionist cinema, which began in earnest after the war; and, indeed, the film was itself remade in the Expressionist manner in 1926 by some of its original collaborators.

---

1. It should be pointed out, however (as Kracauer does not), that German literature had been preoccupied with the notion of the Doppelgänger ("double") since the Middle Ages (witness the Faust legends); and *Der Andere*, the first German feature film of any merit, had, of course, provided a treatment of the theme.

The War Years and the Influence of Scandinavia

In 1915, after the outbreak of war, Wegener and the scriptwriter Henrik Galeen (1882–1949; later to direct the 1926 version of *Der Student von Prag*) jointly directed another precursor of the Expressionist movement, *Der Golem* (*The Golem*), which was also set in Prague and photographed by Seeber. The film has not survived, but it too was remade after the war (by Wegener and Galeen in 1920), and we now know from the later version that it was based upon a Jewish legend in which a sixteenth-century rabbi brings to life a clay statue to guard his people against a pogrom. In the film, the giant statue is rediscovered in modern times, is infused with life, and becomes a raging monster that must be destroyed when the rabbi's daughter rejects him (cf. *Frankenstein* [USA, 1931]; *King Kong* [USA, 1933]). The pre-Expressionist theme of soullessness embodied in *Der Golem* appears in another German film of the era, the six-part serial *Homunculus*, directed by Otto Rippert in 1916. The most popular film of the war years, *Homunculus* deals with an artificially created being of great intellect and will that has no soul. Like the Golem, this "gnome" turns its energies to destruction when it discovers its synthetic origins, becoming a ruthless dictator that avenges itself upon the human race by means of war and mass murder.

Taken together, *Der Student von Prague, Der Golem*, and *Homunculus* provide a clear indication of the direction the German cinema was to take after the war, but they also indicate a relatively stepped-up pace of domestic production during the war itself. Between 1914 and 1919, Germany was cut off from its normally large supply of French, Italian, and American films. (Through 1915 only 10 percent of the films shown in Germany were produced there.) The only foreign productions it was able to import were those from neutral Sweden and Denmark, and consequently the Scandinavian and German industries grew very close during these years. Scandinavian films at this point were generally static and literary but often beautifully photographed by directors like Victor Sjöström and Mauritz Stiller; their visual clarity had a pronounced influence on postwar German cinema, which, with *film d'art* and the *Autorenfilm*, they helped to make intellectually respectable. Their popularity was also responsible for bringing a Danish production company—German Nordisk, a subsidiary of Nordisk Films Kompagni, A/S, founded by Ole Olsen in 1906, until it was absorbed by UFA—and a whole colony of Scandinavian film artists, including the famous Danish actress Asta Nielsen and the great Danish director Carl-Theodor Dreyer (see pp. 311–12), to Germany during World War I. (Astonishingly for a nation of 2.5 million people, in 1910 Nordisk was the world's second largest production company after Pathé-Frères. Its international success between 1910 and 1913 gave birth to a host of domestic rivals—e.g., Biorama, Fotorama, Kinografen—and briefly made the Danish cinema the most innovative in the world, developing new techniques in lighting, camera placement, and scenic design, as well as inaugurating a widely imitated genre—the "sensation film," or urban thriller. Set in the criminal underworld or its moral equivalent, this sort of film was calculated to deliver visceral thrills and had a deep impact on the cinema of German Expressionism and "street" realism, particularly the work of Fritz Lang.)

Sjöström (1879–1960), a Swede, and Stiller (1883–1928), born in Finland of Russian parents who moved to Sweden in 1904, were the founding fathers of the Scandinavian cinema. Both began directing in 1912 for Charles Magnusson's (1878–1948) recently formed Svenska Biografteatern company, which became Svensk Filmindustri in 1919 and by 1920 had subsidiaries all over the world, in part due to Sweden's neutrality during World War I. Between 1914 and 1920, both Sjöström and Stiller made many films that received international acclaim. A number of them, like Sjöström's *The Girl from the Marsh Croft* (*Tösen från Stormyrtorpet*, 1917) and *The Phantom Chariot* (*Körkarlen*, 1921), and Stiller's *Sir Arne's Treasure* (*Herr Arnes pengar*, 1919—influential of both Lang and Eisenstein) and *The Saga of Gösta Berling* (*Gösta Berlings saga*, 1924), were adapted from the work of the great Swedish novelist Selma Lagerlöf (1858–1940). The work of both directors has been described as stately, solemn, and static (terms that might be used to characterize the Scandinavian cinema generally until very recently), but Sjöström was the more ponderous of the two. Nevertheless, in his best dramas of pastoral life Sjöström managed, with an almost mystical force, to integrate the rugged Swedish landscape into the texture of his films—a feature noted and much admired by filmmakers in other countries. Stiller, who had a lighter touch, excelled at comedy, of which his *Erotikon* (1920), an acknowledged influence on Ernst Lubitsch, remains an impressive example. He must also be credited with introducing Greta Garbo (1905–1990) to the screen in *The Saga of Gösta Berling* and with helping to mold her early career. Both men went to Hollywood to work for MGM in the mid-1920s, where Sjöström (renamed Seastrom) made three neglected masterpieces—*He Who Gets Slapped* (1924), *The Scarlet Letter* (1926), and *The Wind* (1928)—and Stiller was reduced to directing star vehicles, only one of which (*Hotel Imperial*, 1926) remained completely his own work.

Sjöström returned to a life of semiretirement in Sweden in 1928, working occasionally as a director and an actor, and Stiller died in the same year, fatigued and disillusioned, some have said, by the Hollywood experience (see Chapter 6, p. 189). During the 1920s, the Swedish film industry, virtually monopolized by Magnusson's Svensk Filmindustri after 1919, fell into a period of stagnation from which it was not to emerge until the outbreak of World War II. The slump, during which Sweden produced only a handful of films for export, has been blamed primarily on competition from Hollywood, which, as in the cases of Sjöström, Stiller, Garbo, and actors such as Lars Hanson and Nils Asther, siphoned off its major talent to work in the American film industry; there were minor exceptions in the work of Gustaf Molander (1888–1973—*One Night* [*En natt*, 1931]; *Intermezzo*, 1936) and

Alf Sjöberg (1903–80—*The Strongest* [*Den starkaste*, 1929]; *Life at Stake* [*Med livet som insats*, 1939]).

The Founding of UFA

Nevertheless, there simply weren't enough Swedish and Danish motion pictures to fill the void created by the disappearance of other imported films from the German screen, and so the Germans renewed efforts to increase the quantity and quality of domestic production. The first major step was the establishment of the nationally subsidized film conglomerate Universum Film Aktiengesellschaft (UFA, commonly Ufa in German texts) by government decree in 1917. Aware of the depressed state of the domestic industry and also of the growing number of effective anti-German propaganda films emanating from the Allied countries, General Erich Ludendorff, commander in chief of the German army, on December 18, 1917, ordered the merger of the main German production companies, as well as exhibitors and distributors, into a single unit for the making and marketing of high-quality nationalistic films to enhance Germany's image at home and abroad. (The initial core of UFA was the Prussian War Ministry's film propaganda unit Bild und Film Amt, or Bufa, subsidized by a consortium of companies from the shipping, electrical, chemical, and banking industries under the leadership of Deutsche Bank director Emil Georg von Stauss.)[2] Huge new studios were built at Neubabelsberg, near Berlin, and UFA immediately set about the task of upgrading production, distribution, and exhibition by assembling a team of first-rate producers, directors, writers, and technicians. Perhaps the best comment on the organization's effectiveness in this regard is that, by the end of the war, German production facilities were ten times what they had been at the outset, the feature had been institutionalized as the dominant form, and the German film industry was ready to compete commercially with that of any other nation in the world. For a brief time during the 1920s, it became the only industry to successfully compete with Hollywood in foreign mar-

4.2 *The Phantom Chariot* **(Victor Sjöström, 1921).**

---

2. See Thomas Elsaesser, "Erich Pommer, 'Die UFA,' and Germany's Bid for a Studio System," in *Weimar Cinema and After: Germany's Historical Imaginary*, ed. Thomas Elsaesser (London: Routledge, 2000), pp. 106–42.

4.3 The UFA studios at Neubabelsberg

kets, including the American. When the war ended in a German defeat in November 1918, the government sold its shares in the company to the Deutsche Bank and to corporations like Krupp and I. G. Farben, and UFA was transformed into a private company whose capital base of 25 million marks made it the largest cartel in Germany. This caused little change in the studio's internal organization, which was fundamentally authoritarian, but its mission was altered slightly because of the compelling necessity of competing in a new international market.

It is often said that the German cinema as an art form was born with the founding of UFA, which was to become the greatest and largest single studio in Europe before World War II. The impression is often given that UFA monopolized German cinema during the 1920s and 1930s, or nearly so. But during the 1920s, at least, it functioned more as a distributor for smaller companies (Terra-Film AG, National Film A.G., Deulig Film, to name a few) than as a producer in its own right. One reason for the confusion is that, of the few films UFA did produce during the 1920s, nearly all became classics of the German cinema's so-called Golden Age.[3] As Kracauer points out, UFA was merely the instrument of the German cinema's birth, which was more directly linked to the *Aufbruch*—a wave of revolutionary intellectual excitement that swept over the whole of Germany in the wake of the war.

Germany's crushing defeat resulted in a complete rejection of the past by much of its intelligentsia and a new enthusiasm for the progressive, experimental, and avant-garde. A liberal democratic republic, culturally centered at Weimar, was established. Marxism became intellectually respectable for the first time in German history; **Expressionism**[4] became prominent in the arts; and in early 1919 the Council of People's Representatives abolished military censorship. In this creatively charged atmosphere, the last shreds of intellectual resistance to

the cinema disappeared, and Germany's radical young artists were ready to accept it as a new means of communicating with the masses. The new freedom of expression manifested itself most immediately in a series of well-mounted, independently produced pornographic films throughout 1919 (*Aufklärungsfilme*—"films of elucidation" or "films about the facts of life") with titles like *Prostitution, Vom Rande des Sumpfes (From the Verge of the Swamp), Verlorene Tochter (Lost Daughters), Hyänen der Lust (Hyenas of Lust), Aus eines Mannes Mädchenjahren (A Man's Girlhood),* and *Fräulein Mutter (Maiden Mother).* More direct in their appeal were the so-called *Sittenfilme,* or "films of sexual conduct," of which the

3. According to Eric Rhode in *A History of the Cinema from Its Origins to 1970* (New York: Hill & Wang, 1976), UFA produced only 12 of the 185 German features for 1926, 15 of 222 for 1927 (while distributing 105 of these), 16 of 224 for 1928 (distributing 18), and 13 of 183 for 1929 (distributing 68). Furthermore, as Julian Petley points out in *Capital and Culture: German Cinema, 1933–45* (London: British Film Institute, 1979), although it was small by Hollywood standards, UFA was "extremely large, powerful, and highly capitalized" compared to other German film companies, and it held a commanding position in an exceptionally fragmented industry (p. 32). Finally, in addition to its studios and distribution interests, the combine controlled the German assets of Nordisk Film (Denmark) and Sascha-Film (Austria), one hundred regional theaters, and the ten finest first-run houses in Berlin. The most complete and detailed account of UFA's history is Klaus Kreimeier's *The UFA Story: A History of Germany's Greatest Film Company, 1918–1945,* trans. Robert and Rita Kimber (New York: Hill & Wang, 1996).

4. Expressionism, a movement that began in German painting, music, architecture, and theater before the war in reaction to the pervasive naturalism of late nineteenth-century art, found a large public during the revolutionary *Aufbruch.* Unlike naturalism, which represented objective reality, Expressionism attempted to represent the artist's subjective feelings in response to objective reality. It employed a variety of nonnaturalistic techniques, including symbolism, abstraction, and perceptual distortion, to achieve this end. In its rejection of bourgeois codes of representation, Expressionism was one of the first recognizably modernist movements in the arts.

most famous was *Opium* (1919), a feature that showed the sexual degradation engendered by drug use. *Opium* played for months in major Berlin theaters. Like the Scandinavian sex films that glutted the world market in the late 1960s, the postwar German productions masqueraded as vehicles of sex education and social reform. Their only significant effect, however, was to stir up anti-Semitic sentiments against their supposedly Jewish producers and to cause the National Assembly of the recently established Weimar Republic to reinstitute state censorship through the Reich Film Act in May 1920. Significantly, it was this act which would later enable the Nazis to assert ideological control over the German cinema.

UFA's first peacetime productions were lavish costume dramas (*Kostümfilme*), initially made to compete with Italian spectacles like *Quo vadis?* and *Cabiria* (see pp. 49–50). Joe May's *Veritas vincit* (1918), an elephantine drama about the transmigration of souls through three different historical ages, probably established the conventions of the genre, but Ernst Lubitsch (1892–1947) was to become its master. Lubitsch had worked as an actor for Max Reinhardt and directed a popular series of short comedies before coming to UFA in 1918. In that year, he directed the Polish actress Pola Negri (1894–1987) in two lush costume films, *Die Augen der Mumie Ma* (*The Eyes of the Mummy Ma*) and *Carmen* (English title: *Gypsy Blood*), both of which were successful enough for Lubitsch and his producer, Paul Davidson, to attempt a third in 1919. This was *Madame DuBarry*

4.4 Pola Negri in *Madame DuBarry* (Ernst Lubitsch, 1919).

(English title: *Passion*), a story of the French Revolution, which became an international success and launched the famous series of historical pageants with which we associate the first part of Lubitsch's career. In rapid succession, Lubitsch directed *Anna Boleyn* (English title: *Deception*, 1920), *Das Weib des Pharao* (*The Loves of Pharaoh*, 1921), and *Sumurun* (*One Arabian Night*, 1921). These historical films—and Lubitsch directed many other types during his German period, including the brilliant feature-length comedies *Die Austernprinzessin* (*The Oyster Princess*, 1919), *Die Puppe* (*The Doll*, 1919), and *Die Bergkatze* (*The Wildcat*, 1921)—were distinguished technically by his dynamic handling of crowd scenes and his brilliant use of artificial lighting, both of which he seems to have learned from Reinhardt. Furthermore, he made innovative use of camera angles and rapid cutting, which impressed American critics like Lewis Jacobs as "revolutionary," though in fact the narrative syntax of American film was far advanced by this point. (Lubitsch emigrated to the United States in 1922, where he enriched the American cinema with his sophisticated comedies of wit, urbanity, and sexual innuendo; see p. 188.)

Nevertheless, Lubitsch's technical virtuosity was the first of its kind the German screen had witnessed, and this expertise, coupled with his painstakingly accurate rendition of period detail (called "historical realism" by contemporary critics) in film after film, made Lubitsch's spectacles among the most popular of the postwar years—not simply in Germany, but all over the world. Other UFA directors successfully used the Lubitsch formula, among them Dmitri Buchowetski in *Danton* (1921), *Othello* (1922), and *Sappho* (1922), and Richard Oswald in *Lady Hamilton* (1922) and *Lucrezia Borgia* (1922), all of which exploited the postwar mania for craftsmanlike reconstructions of the past. Yet there was more to the popularity of the German historical spectacles than a simple fascination with the past, for, as Kracauer has suggested, they tended to present history as a slave to individual passions and psychoses rather than as a process dependent upon a wide range of social and economic variables. Thus, the films of German "historical realism" are antihistorical in an important sense and romantic to the point of nihilism. Significantly, their popularity in Germany died out in 1924, the year that witnessed the rise of an unabashedly nihilistic **realism** in the triumph of the *Kammerspielfilm*, as will be discussed in a later section. Until this occurred, however, it was not the historical spectacle, but another type of film entirely that was to dominate the German cinema.

Das Kabinett des Dr. Caligari

In late 1918, a Czech poet, Hans Janowitz, and a young Austrian artist named Carl Mayer, who was later to become one of the most influential creative figures of the Weimar cinema, collaborated in writing a scenario based upon certain shared experiences of psychic phenomena and mysterious coincidence as well as a bizarre sex-slaying in Hamburg known personally to Janowitz. In it, a strange mountebank named Dr. Caligari comes to the north German town of Holstenwall with a traveling fair. His "act" consists of interrogating an apparently hypnotized somnambulist named Cesare, who can forecast the future. Shortly after their arrival, a series of brutal, inexplicable murders is committed in Holstenwall, which the young student Francis later discovers to be the work of Cesare, done at the evil Caligari's bidding. Francis gives the alarm and pursues Caligari into the countryside and finally to his refuge in a state insane asylum, where, it turns out, the showman is not an inmate, but the director. Papers found in his study indicate that the director had become obsessed with a homicidal eighteenth-century hypnotist named Caligari to the point of assuming his identity and causing one of his own patients (Cesare) to commit murders for him. Confronted with these proofs, the director goes mad and must be incarcerated in his own asylum. The script, entitled *Das Kabinett des Dr. Caligari*[5] (*The Cabinet of Dr. Caligari*)—a reference to the coffin-like box in which Cesare is kept by his master—was clearly antiauthoritarian if not subversive in its equation of power and madness.

Nevertheless, when Janowitz and Mayer submitted the scenario to Erich Pommer (1889–1966), chief executive of Decla-Bioskop (an independent production company that was to merge with UFA in 1921), it was immediately accepted. Whether Pommer grasped the script's radical nature is unclear, but he certainly saw in it an opportunity for upgrading the artistic content of his studio's films. The young Austrian director Fritz Lang was initially assigned to the project but was replaced by the more experienced Robert Wiene (1880–1938) so that Lang could direct the second part of Decla's successful

4.5 *Das Kabinett des Dr. Caligari* **(Robert Wiene, 1919): Caligari (Werner Krauss), Cesare (Conrad Veidt), and prey (Lil Dagover).**

4.6 *Caligari:* **Cesare carries his victim over the rooftops of Holstenwall.**

adventure series *Die Spinnen* (*The Spiders*, 1919–20). However, it was Lang who, against the authors' violent objections, convinced Pommer to add a *Rahmenhand-*

---

5. Originally *Das Cabinet des Dr. Caligari*, the title was officially "Germanized" in the 1930s to disguise its French derivation (a National Socialist policy). Many texts today prefer the original, but I have adopted the usage of Lotte H. Eisner from *The Haunted Screen* (Berkeley: University of California Press, 1969), *Murnau*, rev. and enl. ed. (Berkeley: University of California Press, 1973), *Fritz Lang* (New York: Oxford University Press, 1977), and other of her works.

lung (or framing story) to the film that inverted its meaning: Francis is made the narrator of the tale and introduced as a madman in an asylum that, we discover at the film's conclusion, is operated by the benevolent Dr. Caligari himself. Lang correctly thought that the reality frame would heighten the Expressionistic elements of the *mise-en-scène*, but it also transforms the body of the film from an antiauthoritarian fable into the recounting of a paranoid delusion, which ultimately justifies and glorifies the very authority it was intended to subvert. Still, in terms of its production design, *Das Kabinett des Dr. Caligari* became strikingly experimental under Wiene's direction.

Wiene hired three prominent Expressionist artists—Hermann Warm, Walter Röhrig, and Walter Reimann—to design and paint the sets for the film, which were to embody the tortured state of the narrator's psyche. Thus, the visual world of *Caligari* became a highly stylized one of exaggerated dimensions and deranged spatial relationships—an unnatural, sunless place in which buildings pile on top of one another at impossible angles, jagged chimneys reach insanely into the sky, and the very flesh of its inhabitants seems frozen under pounds of makeup. But the decision to use artificial backdrops was pragmatic as well as thematically appropriate since, in the economic recession that immediately followed the war, the film studios, like all other German industries, were allocated electric power on a quota basis. In a film like *Caligari* that required many dramatic lighting effects, it was cheaper and more convenient to simply paint light and shadow onto the scenery itself than to produce the effect electrically. (In fact, the Decla studio had nearly expended its power ration when *Caligari* was produced in late 1919—yet another instance of the way in which technological necessity can foster aesthetic innovation in the cinema.) On the other hand, there were several instances of stylized decor before *Caligari* that had nothing to do with technological imperatives. For example, *Thais* (1916, aka *Perfido incanto* [*Wicked Enchantment*]), directed by the Italian Futurist Anton Giulio Bragaglia, used a geometrically stylized set for its concluding scenes; Maurice Tourneur employed stylized scenery on painted backdrops in *The Blue Bird* (1918) and *Prunella* (1918); and Ernst Lubitsch used stylization to represent the world of dolls in a toy box in *Die Puppe* (*The Doll*, 1919). None of these films, however, was stylized in the truly Expressionist manner of *Caligari*, which probably derived more from the stagings of contemporary Expressionist theater than from any other source. Nevertheless, the angular distortion of the sets was clearly

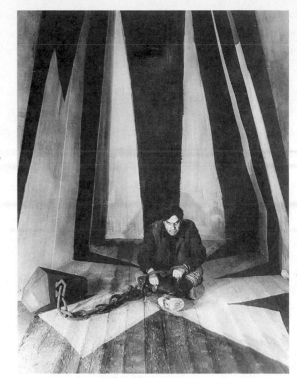

4.7 *Caligari:* a villager falsely imprisoned for Cesare's crimes.

intended by Wiene to provide an objective correlative for the narrator's insanity, and for this reason *Caligari* became the progenitor and exemplar of the German Expressionist cinema.

The classic study of this cinema, written by Lotte H. Eisner, is entitled *The Haunted Screen*, and the screen of German Expressionism was indeed a haunted one; but its terrors were those of morbid psychological states and troubled dreams rather than the more concrete horrors that Hollywood's Universal Studios was to offer in the 1930s (although Universal's horror films were the lineal descendants of Expressionism, created in many cases by the same artists, as will be seen in Chapter 8). The nightmarishly distorted decor of German Expressionist films and their creation of *Stimmung* ("mood") through shifting **chiaroscuro** lighting were *expressive* of the disturbed mental and emotional states they sought to portray. The setting for *Caligari* is warped and out of joint because the film itself, we learn at its conclusion, occurs largely in the twisted mind of its narrator. Thus, the creators of *Caligari* and its successors made a deliberate effort to portray subjective realities in objective terms, to render

4.8 *Caligari:* in a forest of the mind.

not simply narratives, but states of mind, moods, and atmosphere through the medium of the photographic image (a task more difficult than Expressionist representation in the other arts since there is, seemingly, nothing more objective than a photographic image but the object itself). German Expressionism, then, attempted to express interior realities through the means of exterior realities, or to treat subjective states in what was widely regarded at the time as a purely objective medium of representation. This was perhaps as radical an innovation for the cinema as Porter's elaboration of the shot since it added a nonnarrative and poetic dimension to what had been, even in the hands of Griffith, an almost wholly narrative medium.

In terms of narrative, however, *Caligari* was extremely conservative; its expressiveness was fundamentally a matter of decor and staging. We must remember that the years during which Germany was denied access to American films (1914–19) were precisely those in which Griffith made his most significant contributions to film langauge. Wiene practiced cinema in ignorance of the lessons of Griffith, and so the editing continuity of *Caligari* is essentially that of arranged scenes, though there is some rudimentary intercutting and some camera movement. In fact, the film is as stagy as any Méliès or Film d'Art production,

despite its wildly avant-garde design. *Caligari* imported Expressionism into the cinema but did not exploit it in cinematic terms and, as a *narrative* structure, did nothing to advance the medium. Thus, despite international acclaim when it was released in February 1920 (Lewis Jacobs has called it "the most widely discussed film of the time"), *Caligari* had little direct impact on the course of other national cinemas. Yet in terms of its set design, its psychological probing and thematic ambiguity, its sinister and morbid subject matter, and, above all, its attempt to render the internal and subjective through the external and objective, *Caligari* had an immense influence upon the German films that followed it.[6]

The production of *Caligari* marked the beginning of the German cinema's great decade. This era was to be characterized by films that, like *Caligari*, were completely studio-made and by intense admiration for the German studio product all over the world. The emphasis on studio production seems to have stemmed less from economic considerations, as it did in Hollywood, than from aesthetic ones. German directors found that they could exercise complete authority over every aspect of the filmmaking process when they worked in the controlled environment of the studio as they could not when they worked on location. As Arthur Knight has noted, these directors ultimately preferred to create their settings in the studio from the ground up rather than to discover them in reality at large; as a result, between 1919 and 1927 UFA became the largest and best-equipped studio in the Western world. During this period, there was no set so extravagant that it could not be constructed on the vast back lots of the UFA studio at Neubabelsberg, which offered some 40,000 square meters for exteriors alone. Mountains, forests, cities, and entire ages were all recreated with such astonishing fidelity that the critic Paul Rotha coined the term "studio constructivism" to characterize "that curious air of completeness, of finality, that surrounds each product of the German studios." The "realistic" *Kammerspielfilm* (see the following section) no less than the aggressively artificial Expressionist film, profited aesthetically from the large measure of control that studio production permitted a director, and the great cinema of the Weimar Republic could almost certainly not have existed without it.

---

6. On the cultural context, reception, and influence of *Caligari*, see Mike Budd, ed., *The Cabinet of Dr. Caligari: Texts, Contexts, Histories* (New Brunswick, N.J.: Rutgers University Press, 1990).

The Flowering of Expressionism

In any case, between 1919 and 1924 many successors to *Caligari* appeared upon the German screen. Most of these *Schauerfilme* (films of fantasy and terror) used horrific plots and Expressionist decor to embody the theme of the human soul in search of itself. Some representative titles are: F. W. Murnau's *Der Januskopf* (*Janus-Faced*, 1920—adapted from Robert Louis Stevenson's *Dr. Jekyll and Mr. Hyde*), Paul Wegener's remake of *Der Golem* (1920), Arthur Robison's *Schatten* (*Warning Shadows*, 1922), Robert Wiene's *Raskolnikov* (1923—a bizarrely stylized but utterly convincing version of Dostoevsky's *Crime and Punishment*), Paul Leni's *Das Wachsfiguren-kabinett* (*Waxworks,* 1924), and Henrik Galeen's remake of *Der Student von Prag* (1926). All of *Caligari*'s spiritual descendants were technically proficient and superbly designed, but two of them deserve special notice, both for their individual accomplishments and because their

4.10 *Raskolnikov* (Robert Wiene, 1923): art direction by Andrei Andreiev.

directors went on to become major figures in the cinema of the Western world. These are Fritz Lang's *Der müde Tod* (1921—literally, "The Weary Death," but usually entitled *Destiny* in English) and F. W. Murnau's *Nosferatu* (1922).

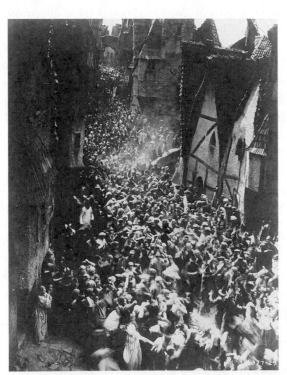

4.9 *Der Golem* (Paul Wegener, 1920): art direction by Hans Poelzig.

4.11 *Der müde Tod* (Fritz Lang, 1921): the bereaved lover (Lil Dagover) in the cemetery garden. Art direction by Robert Herlth, Walter Röhrig, and Hermann Warm.

4.12 *Der müde Tod:* **the Chinese episode.**

4.14 *Siegfried:* **the forest.**

FRITZ LANG

Fritz Lang (1890–1976) had already directed several feature films and serials (such as the recently reconstructed *Die Spinnen*)[7] when he and his wife, the scriptwriter Thea von Harbou (1888–1954), collaborated in the production of *Der müde Tod* for UFA. The film is a romantic allegory, set in the Middle Ages, about a girl whose lover is snatched away by Death himself. She seeks out this figure and demands her lover's return, but Death refuses and instead offers her three fantastic narratives in which lov-

ers attempt unsuccessfully to triumph over Death. These episodes are set in ninth-century Baghdad, in Renaissance Venice, and in a dreamlike, mystical China,[8] and in all of them the lovers are destroyed by cruel and insatiable tyrants. At the end of these exempla, Death tells the girl that only by offering her own life or that of another can she ensure the return of her lover. Later, in saving a baby from a burning hospital, she is killed, but she is reunited with her dead lover by Death in fulfillment of his pledge. Kracauer sees *Der müde Tod* as a manifestation of Germany's postwar obsession with doom and *Götterdämmerung*, the log-

4.13 *Siegfried* (Fritz Lang, 1923): **geometrical stylization of space. Art direction by Otto Hunte, Erich Kettelhut, and Karl Vollbrecht.**

7. Conceived by Lang as a Feuillade-like serial in four parts, only two were actually filmed—*Der goldene See* (*The Golden Lake*, 1919) and *Das Brillantenschiff* (*The Diamond Ship*, 1920), both photographed by Karl Freund. They have been restored by the film historian David Shepard as an adventure-melodrama (*Abenteurerfilm*) in two parts, with an organ score composed and performed by Gaylord Carter and are available on DVD from Image Entertainment, as is the Shepard restoration of *Der müde Tod*. The definitive study of Lang's career is Tom Gunning's *The Films of Fritz Lang: Allegories of Vision and Modernity* (London: British Film Institute 2000).

8. Douglas Fairbanks claimed that the Chinese episode of *Der müde Tod* inspired him to make *The Thief of Bagdad* (1924), which features similar cinematic sleight of hand.

ical culmination of the cultural pessimism of the late nineteenth century, as expressed in such works as Oswald Spengler's *The Decline of the West* (1918–22); and certainly the film's relationship to the major thematic concerns of Expressionism is clear. Lang added something new to the cinema, however, in his striking use of lighting to emphasize architectural line and space.

Lang had been trained as an architect, and he was to carry over his facility for stylized architectural composition as opposed to a purely graphic Expressionism into his other major films of the silent period. These were not intellectualized works in the manner of, say, *Caligari*, but they were all overwhelmingly impressive in terms of sheer plastic beauty and decorative design. *Dr. Mabuse, der Spieler* (*Dr. Mabuse, the Gambler*, 1922), for example, offers an Expressionistic treatment of a Caligariesque master criminal intent upon destroying the fabric of a postwar society whose rottenness clearly warrants it. In *Siegfried* (1922–24) and *Kriemhilds Rache* (*Kriemhild's Revenge*, 1923–24), Lang again exercised his penchant for legendary romance and compositional majesty in a mas-

sive retelling of the old Norse and Teutonic Nibelungen saga,[9] complete with studio-constructed mountains, forests, and a full-scale fire-breathing dragon.

Finally, in his last major silent film, *Metropolis* (1926; released 1927), Lang presented a terrifying if simplistic vision of a twenty-first-century totalitarian society whose futuristic architecture and technology were rendered brilliantly concrete through the process and model work of the special-effects photographer Eugen Schüfftan.[1] (Lang claimed that *Metropolis* was inspired by his first vision of the New York City skyline, from the deck of the SS *Deutschland* in October 1924, at night.) For *Metropolis* Schüfftan invented the trick-shot technique, still universally used and known today as the **Schüfftan process**, which works as follows: miniatures are reflected onto a glass with a magnifying mirrored surface, which is placed at a 45-degree angle relative to the camera lens. This surface is scraped away from the areas in which live action is to take place, leaving holes behind which the actual sets are constructed and lit to correspond with the lighting of the model. *Metropolis*, like all of Lang's Expressionist work, highlights the fact that the phenomenon was in many ways an art-film movement predicated upon special effects as well as decor and lighting. In this regard, German Expressionism stands at the beginning of a long line of films, extending into the digital era, whose ability to manipulate photographed reality in real time gives them their unique power.

4.15 The forest in *Siegfried* under construction at UFA-Neubabelsberg.

9. In Norse and Teutonic mythology, the Nibelungen are a race of dwarfs who possess a magic ring and a great hoard of gold. The *Nibelungenlied* ("song of the Nibelungen") is an anonymous thirteenth-century Middle High German epic in which Siegfried and Kriemhild, the archetypal Teutonic hero and heroine, become fatally involved with the Nibelungen and their treasure, bringing on cosmic chaos—the *Götterdämmerung*, or "Twilight of the Gods." The German Romantic composer Richard Wagner (1813–83) wrote a monumental tetralogy of music dramas based on the *Nibelungenlied*, but Lang's primary source was the original epic. (Lang had a particular dislike of Wagner's music, and he was outraged when UFA released shortened versions of *Siegfried* and *Kriemhilds Rache* abroad with Wagner scores.) Yet there is no denying that a Wagnerian mythic resonance inflects both of Lang's Nibelungen films. See David J. Levin, *Richard Wagner, Fritz Lang, and the Nibelungen: The Dramaturgy of Disavowal* (Princeton, N.J.: Princeton University Press, 1998).

1. Eugen Schüfftan (1893–1977) left Germany in 1932 after shooting only a few films and (as Eugene Shuftan) became a successful cinematographer, director, and technical advisor in England, France, and the United States.

4.16 An Expressionistic poster for Lang's *Metropolis* **(1926).**

4.17 *Metropolis:* **the quarters of the ruling class. Art direction by Hunte, Kettelhut, and Vollbrecht.**

4.18 The subterranean city of the robotlike workers.

4.19 The electric Moloch that powers Metropolis and that the workers serve.

Lang made two other silent films (*Spione* [*Spies*, 1928] and *Die Frau im Mond* [*The Woman in the Moon*, 1929]) before shooting his early sound masterpiece, *M* (see Chapter 9).[2] Many of his silent films were made for UFA and written by Thea von Harbou, who later became an ardent Nazi, and Lang himself was offered the leadership of the German film industry by the Nazi propaganda min-

2. Many of Lang's films have not been seen in their original versions in the United States. *Metropolis*, for example, was cut from seventeen to ten reels for its 1927 American release, and a full hour is missing from *Kriemhilds Rache*. However, since the 1970s the Munich Film Museum

4.20 Lang creating an "architecturalized" crowd. Lotte Eisner suggests that Lang's handling of crowd scenes was influenced by the practices of stage director Erwin Piscator (1893–1966).

ister, Joseph Goebbels, in early 1933 (*Metropolis* was Hitler's favorite film—for all the wrong reasons, of course). Half-Jewish and a political liberal, Lang refused the offer and fled Germany for Hollywood, where he became an important director of American sound films.

F. W. MURNAU AND THE *KAMMERSPIELFILM*

The second major figure to emerge from the Expressionist movement was F. W. (Friedrich Wilhelm) Murnau

(1888–1931), whose highly stylized vampire film *Nosferatu, eine Symphonie des Grauens* (*Nosferatu, a Symphony of Horrors*, 1922)[3] has become a classic of the **genre**. Trained as an art historian, Murnau became fascinated by the theater and began to write for films shortly after the war, collaborating with both Carl Mayer and Hans Janowitz. When he began to direct his own films, Murnau worked almost exclusively in the Expressionist vein, making films like *Der Bucklige und die Tänzerin* (*The Hunchback and the Dancer*, 1920—written by Mayer), *Der Januskopf* (*Janus-Faced*, 1920—written by Janowitz), and *Schloss Vogelöd* (*Castle Vogelod*, 1921—written by Mayer). It is *Nosferatu*, however, adapted loosely (and without credit) by Henrik Galeen from Bram Stoker's novel *Dracula* (1897), that represents the high point of Murnau's Expressionist period.

One of the remarkable things about *Nosferatu* is the apparent naturalness of its stylization, achieved, it should be noted, with a minimum of resources since the film was independently produced. Like the Scandinavian directors whose films flooded Germany during the war, Murnau had an affinity for landscapes, and he had most of *Nosferatu* shot on location in Central Europe by the great cinematographer Fritz Arno Wagner, whose specialty was a kind of low-contrast, realistic photography that exchanged stark black and white for a whole range of intermediate grays. While the film is essentially a thriller and is more than a bit creaky in terms of narrative structure, it nonetheless provides a succession of haunting

has been restoring Lang's German films along with other classics of the Weimar period. See John Gillett, "Munich's Cleaned Pictures," *Sight and Sound* 47, 1 (Winter 1977–78): 37–39. In 1985, synth-rock composer Giorgio Moroder (*Midnight Express* [Alan Parker, 1978]; *Flashdance* [Adrian Lyne, 1983]; *Top Gun* [Tony Scott, 1986]) bought the rights to *Metropolis* from the West German government and offered American audiences a $2 million color-tinted reconstruction, complete with lost footage, a contemporary "album-oriented" rock score, and subtitles based on a recently authenticated version of the Lang–von Harbou script. But even Moroder's revision did not follow Lang's original continuity. *Metropolis* was withdrawn by UFA shortly after its Berlin premiere on January 10, 1927, and cut to alter both its content and its length (the original version was estimated to have run 153 minutes at 24 fps). Apparently, three separate negatives were created as a result of this editing, one for the duping of German release prints, one for export prints, and one to be delivered to Paramount for distribution in the United States. Over time, as many as eight different "complete" versions of *Metropolis* were distributed worldwide. In 1986–87, after years of research, German archivist and historian Enno Patalas assembled a work print at the Munich Film Museum based on variant versions that used newly photographed intertitles derived from the original German

text. But since this version was also incomplete, in 1998 Martin Körber began a digital restoration project in collaboration with the postproduction house Alpha-Omega Film und Video GmbH: material from all extant source prints of the film was scanned into a computer and manipulated at 2K resolution, then scanned back out onto film. The resulting print thus experienced no loss of generation in the process because it was a digital rather than a photographic copy (see Chapter 21). For a detailed account of the history of the *Metropolis* negatives, the variant source prints, and the digital restoration process, visit the Alpha-Omega Web site at www.filmrestauration.de/index.html.

3. *Nosferatu* was remade under the same title by the brilliant German director Werner Herzog in 1978 (see Chapter 15). The original was recently reconstructed in its tinted version by the Munich Film Museum for accompaniment by Hans Erdmann's 1922 score, newly arranged by Berndt Heller. In 2000, American independent director E. Elias Merhige paid tribute to *Nosferatu* in *Shadow of the Vampire*, whose premise is that Murnau, in his eternal quest for perfection, cast a real vampire in the title role. Merhige's film offers an interesting, if not entirely accurate, portrait of the on-set dynamics of one of UFA's most famous productions.

4.21 *Nosferatu* (F. W. Murnau, 1922): Max Schreck as the vampire. Art direction by Albin Grau.

impressive today, perhaps, are the cinematic tricks that Murnau and Wagner used to create a supernatural atmosphere for the film. The forests surrounding Nosferatu's castle, for example, are made to seem ghostly through the use of **negative** footage, and the vampire's supernatural strength is rendered in terms of jerky accelerated action achieved through stop-motion photography, as discussed in Chapter 1. Nevertheless, *Nosferatu* as a whole remains one of the most ominous and expressive horror films ever made; as the Hungarian film critic Béla Balázs (see p. 636) wrote, "a chilly draft from doomsday" passes through its every scene.

visual images more authentically "expressive" of horror than those of *Caligari*. Whereas *Caligari*'s Expressionism was mainly graphic, *Nosferatu*'s is almost purely cinematic, relying upon camera angles, lighting, and editing rather than production design. Nosferatu, the vampire king, is frequently photographed from an extremely low angle which renders him gigantic and monstrously sinister on the screen (a device not lost upon Orson Welles, who would employ it obsessively throughout *Citizen Kane* eighteen years later; see Chapter 10). A number of these shots are lit so that the vampire's vast and angular shadow is cast across every object in the frame.[4] Many of the film's images are strikingly composed in depth, with action sharply in focus in the foreground, middle ground, and background simultaneously. This mode of composing the frame has the effect of integrating character and landscape, and much of *Nosferatu*'s "naturalness" derives from it. Composition in depth also produces some memorable expressive effects. Near the film's conclusion, its heroine, who is situated in the foreground of the frame, gazes through her window at a mass funeral procession for the vampire's victims, which is shot so that it seems to stretch away endlessly from the middle ground to infinity, suggesting the enormity of Nosferatu's crimes. Less

Murnau's next important film was made in the genre that superseded Expressionism—that of the *Kammerspiel* (literally, "intimate theater"), or "instinct," film. The scriptwriter Carl Mayer, of *Caligari* fame, was the founder and chief practitioner of this genre, which dealt realistically with the oppressiveness of contemporary lower-middle-class life and, by extension, with the irresistibility of fate in a disintegrating society. All of Mayer's scripts for the "instinct" films showed great compression of form and were specifically tailored to the technical requirements of cinema. They generally avoided the use of intertitles altogether and contained only a few characters, each of whom represented a destructive and uncontrollable impulse. Mayer began writing *Kammerspiel* scripts in the heyday of Expressionism, and there is no question that they contain Expressionist elements. Indeed, the whole realistic cinema that grew out of the *Kammerspielfilm* can be seen as both an extension of and a reaction against the Expressionist cinema in that it

---

4. A minor gaffe—vampires cast no shadow, as all horror buffs are well aware.

retained the morbid psychological themes of the earlier films but cast them in realistic form (and, furthermore, a realistic form that was the product of UFA studio shooting rather than documentary technique). The films made from Mayer's early *Kammerspiel* scripts are Leopold Jessner's melodrama *Hintertreppe* (*Backstairs*, 1921), and Lupu Pick's *Scherben* (*Shattered*, 1921) and *Sylvester* (1923); but it was *Der letzte Mann* (literally, "The Last Man," but usually entitled *The Last Laugh* in English), written by Mayer and directed by Murnau, which incarnated the type and inaugurated a new period of German realism in 1924.

Der letzte Mann, produced by Erich Pommer for UFA, is a distinguished film in every respect and an extremely important one in terms of the enormous influence it exercised, especially upon German and American cinema. The script by Mayer, the acting by Emil Jannings (1884–1950), and the production design by Walter Röhrig and Robert Herlth are all impressive; but it is the innovative use of camera movement that makes *Der letzte Mann* so important to the history of film, and this was achieved largely by Murnau and his cinematographer, Karl Freund.[5] It was Mayer who suggested that the camera be put into nearly continuous motion (the "unchained camera," he called it), and he specified its involvement in the action in his script. Freund, however, was responsible for the brilliant tactical maneuvering that permitted this movement, and Murnau, of course, directed it.

Like all *Kammerspielfilme*, *Der letzte Mann* has a fairly simple plot. It is also unrelievedly grim until the sudden appearance of a happy ending, which is emotionally satisfying in a primitive sort of way but wholly out of key with what has gone before. The film concerns an aging doorman (Jannings) in a fashionable Berlin hotel who loses his job and, more important, his resplendent uniform to a younger man. Within the lower-middle-class tenement where he lives with his daughter, the uniform has brought him prestige and dignity; its unexpected loss elicits a kind of furious ridicule from his neighbors that is chillingly sadistic. Demoted to the position of washroom attendant at the hotel and utterly humiliated in his own home, the old man begins to come apart. He becomes stoop-shouldered and slovenly overnight; he gets raging drunk at his daughter's wedding and experiences delusions of persecution; he even makes a desperate attempt to steal his uniform back out of a hotel locker. As the film nears its conclusion, we discover him crouched furtively against the wall of the hotel lavatory

4.22 Expressionistic set design: the porter's tenement.

like a trapped beast, terrified of the entire world outside himself and apparently as mad as Caligari. But no: the film's single title flashes on the screen to explain that whereas in the real world things would end at this point, the filmmakers have decided to take pity on the ex-doorman. There follows a farcical conclusion in which he inherits a vast sum of money by an outlandish coincidence and shows up in the hotel dining room to flaunt his wealth

5. Karl Freund (1890–1969) was director of photography for many of Germany's most distinguished silent films, including Murnau's *Januskopf* (1920), *Der letzte Mann* (1924), *Tartuffe* (1925), and *Faust* (1926); Lang's *Metropolis* (1926; with Günther Rittau); Walter Ruttmann's *Berlin, die Sinphonie der Grosßtadt* (*Berlin, the Symphony of a Great City*, 1927; supervision only); and E. A. Dupont's *Varieté* (*Variety*, 1925). He also worked with Reinhardt, Lubitsch, Wegener (*Der Golem*, 1920), and Dreyer (see Chapter 9, p. 373). With Fritz Arno Wagner (1894–1958: Murnau's *Nosferatu*, [1922], Lang's *Der müde Tod* [1921], *Spione* [1928], *M* [1931], and *Das Testament des Dr. Mabuse* [1933]; and Pabst's *Die Liebe der Jeanne Ney* [1927], *Westfront 1918* [1930], and *Kameradschaft* [1931]), Freund was one of the two great cinematographers of the Weimar period. After emigrating to Hollywood in 1930, he scored major successes both as a cinematographer (for Robert Florey's *Murders in the Rue Morgue* [1932], Tod Browning's *Dracula* [1931], George Cukor's *Camille* [1935], etc.) and as a director (*The Mummy* [1932], *Mad Love* [1935], etc.). He won an Academy Award for his cinematography on *The Good Earth* (Sidney Franklin, 1937), and continued to work as a DP for films (e.g., John Huston's *Key Largo* [1948]) well into the postwar era. In 1944, Freund founded the Photo Research Company, which developed, among other products, a direct-reading light meter, for which Freund received a Technical Achievement Award from the Academy in 1954. At about this time, he moved into television, becoming the head of cinematography at Desilu Productions, where he perfected the three-camera setup for *I Love Lucy* that became the industry standard for filming shows before live studio audiences.

before his former employers in a grandly vulgar but good-natured manner. It is thought that this contrived ending was tacked onto the film either to pander to the American audience's taste for such sentimental optimism or to parody it; no one is quite sure which. (The American cinema had finally begun to influence the German cinema by 1924 and was to have considerably more influence as the decade progressed.) But, whatever the case, the incongruity of the ending is the only notable flaw[6] in what is both cinematically and thematically a nearly perfect film.

Indeed, *Der letzte Mann* was the most technically innovative film to come out of Weimar cinema. Prior to it, most camera movement had been panning and tilting (see Chapter 1) wedded to a fixed tripod. With several significant exceptions (in the films of Griffith and the Italian film *Cabiria* [1914]), there had been little sustained *tracking* movement—i.e., movement in which the whole camera apparatus participates, either to follow another moving object or to isolate a static one by moving in close upon it. What is necessary to achieve this kind of fluidity is a *dolly*—a small wheeled cart on which to mount the camera during shooting and that may or may not use tracks (thus "tracking"). Today, the **boom** crane and a variety of sophisticated dollies (as well as Steadicams[7]) are available to permit such freedom, but these devices could only be improvised in 1924. (Murnau did, however, have access to motor-driven cameras, which allowed their operators to concentrate full attention on movement and focus.) Griffith, of course, had put his camera in the back of an automobile to follow the motion of the chase in *The Birth of a Nation* and *Intolerance*, and he had used an elevator tower that rolled on rails to track his machine into the gigantic set of Belshazzar's feast in *Intolerance*; other American directors had improvised dollies in order to follow the movement of actors within a scene without cutting; but *Der letzte Mann* was the first film in history to move its camera backward and forward, as well as up and down and from side to side, in scenes of substantial duration.[8]

These are scenes held for a single shot and kept alive almost solely through camera movement, rather than scenes built up out of a number of separate shots and kept alive through editing, as in the work of Griffith and Eisenstein. In the frequently cited opening sequence, for example, we ride via the camera down the hotel elevator, move through the bustling lobby, approach the revolving door (a major symbol of life's randomness in the film—a sort of existential roulette wheel), and come to focus on

the doorman on the sidewalk in what appears to be a single unbroken shot (there is actually a discrete cut in the middle of the track through the lobby). The film is replete with shots like this, and their accomplishment was by no means simple in the absence of modern cranes and dollies. For the shot just described, Freund mounted his camera on a bicycle in the descending elevator, rolled it out into the lobby, and tracked it several hundred feet to the revolving door. In other shots, the camera rode the ladder of a fire truck, anticipating the boom crane, and traveled on overhead cables. Indeed, Freund's camera seems to move almost continuously throughout *Der letzte Mann*, although there are actually many shots taken with the camera at full rest that provide an appropriate counterpoint for the others.

But of equal importance with the camera mobility achieved by Murnau and Freund was their use of the subjective camera—the technique whereby the camera lens becomes the eyes of a player in the film, usually the protagonist, so that the audience sees only what he or she sees and only from his or her angle of vision. Griffith's "objects of attention" intercut with facial close-ups are a rudimentary form of this technique: when he cuts from a character looking at something offscreen to a shot of what the character sees, either literally or figuratively, Griffith is practicing a kind of shorthand subjectivity. These "motivated point of view" shots, in combination with the eyeline match, were brought to a state of extreme refinement by the UFA director G. W. Pabst later in the 1920s. Few filmmakers before Murnau and Freund, however, had understood the full range of possibilities inherent in the subjective camera and the way it

---

6. Or, perhaps not. Bruce Kawin has suggested to me that this incongruity is calculated and highly effective—"a perfect early working example of deconstruction (by Mayer)." The porter, like the film and the studio that produced it, is saved in the end by a bequest from the rich American "A.G. Monney"—i.e., "Aktiengesellschaft [company] money" soon to flow into UFA's coffers as a result of the Parufamet deal (see pp. 122–23).

7. The trade name for a device which serves to stabilize the movement of hand-held cameras, introduced in 1976.

8. Orson Welles would create a similar sequence in *Citizen Kane* (1941) when he had Gregg Toland track his camera straight through the El Rancho nightclub sign and through a rain-drenched skylight down into the club below. Welles was also clearly influenced by Murnau's American film *Sunrise* (1927), whose nocturnal moving camera shots anticipate the opening sequence of *Kane*.

4.24 *Der letzte Mann:* **down and out.**

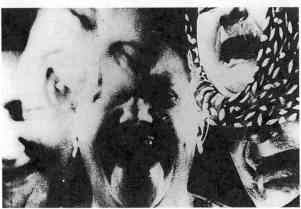

4.23 Subjective camera: the porter imagines ridicule during his drunken dream.

might be used to create multiple perspectives on a single narrative.[9]

The most famous subjective camera shot in *Der letzte Mann* occurs in the scene in which the doorman gets drunk in his apartment and sits down while the room seems to spin wildly about him. To render the character's point of view at this moment, Freund strapped a lightweight camera to his chest and stumbled drunkenly about the room. This is a fairly typical and straightforward use of the technique, but in *Der letzte Mann* the camera is subjective in another sense, too, a sense that demonstrates the roots of German realism in Expressionism. Quite frequently, in addition to assuming the position of the doorman's *physical eye*, the camera assumes the position of his *mind's eye* as well. During the same drunken scene, he feels acutely humiliated at the loss of his job and his prestigious uniform, and he later dreams himself to be the object of ridicule and scorn that he will in fact become on the following day, when his misfortune becomes known to all. At the height of his despair in the dream sequence, we see on the screen not the doorman (as with the "objective camera"), but a visual embodiment of what he *feels*—a long lap-dissolved montage of malicious laughing faces in close-up. Earlier, after he steals his old uniform and runs out of the hotel into the street, the doorman looks back at the building, which seems to tremble and sway as if about to fall and crush him. There is also a dream sequence, shot with distorting mirrors (in the manner of the Gance film *La Folie du Docteur Tube*), in which the porter imagines himself to be possessed of supernatural strength and bounces a large footlocker in the air like a balloon. We might say, then, that Murnau shows his Expressionist roots by using the subjective camera in a highly expressive way—to embody the morbid psychological state of his protagonist in terms of visual images. But there is more.

In scenes like these Murnau showed that he had grasped the concept that the camera was capable of first-person as well as third-person narration; that this first-person narration had both inner and outer modes; and,

9. Some who did are Abel Gance, whose Film d'Art short *La Folie du Docteur Tube* (1915) used distorting **mirror shots** throughout to suggest the hallucinatory effects of a drug (the producers refused to distribute the film, so it cannot have influenced *Der letzte Mann*), and Jacques Feyder, whose *Crainquebille* (1923) used several similar shots to evoke a character's disturbed mental state. The first film, however, whose narrative is entirely dependent upon the exploration of subjectivity is Germaine Dulac's *La Souriante Madame Beudet* (1923; see p. 304). (On the work of all three, see Chapter 9.)

finally, that a director could alternate between these several modes of narration at will to create multiple perspectives on a given subject. Thus, while *Der letzte Mann* is simple in terms of plot, it has an extremely elaborate structure in which the narrative point of view is in constant rotation between the third-person objective camera and the two modes of first-person subjective camera. This was an innovation at least as significant for cinematic narrative as, say, Griffith's construction of dramatic sequences from shots of varying temporal and spatial lengths. Like Griffith's innovations, both modes of subjective camera have now passed into the conventional lexicon of the cinema, but in 1924 they were virtually unprecedented, and the influence of *Der letzte Mann* upon contemporary cinema was immense. As *The Last Laugh*, it enjoyed worldwide success and had a greater effect upon Hollywood technique than any other single foreign film in history, in terms of both its fluidity and its titleless narration. As Murnau's biographer Lotte H. Eisner puts it, "It was the almost universal decision of Hollywood that this was the greatest picture ever made." Murnau was to leave Germany for a Hollywood career after completing two final superproductions for UFA (*Tartuffe* [1925] and *Faust* [1926]).

Hollywood was to be almost equally impressed in the following year with *Der letzte Mann*'s immediate successor, E. A. (Ewald André) Dupont's (1891–1956) *Varieté* (1925), also produced by Erich Pommer for UFA and photographed by Karl Freund. The film deals with a love triangle among trapeze artists (Emil Jannings, Lya De Putti, Warwick Ward) at the Berlin Wintergarten that ends in murder, and it contains camera movement even more breathlessly dynamic than that of *Der letzte Mann*. In almost documentary fashion, Freund's camera penetrates everywhere the human eye can go. It darts frenetically from face to face in a crowded room; it flies through the air with the acrobats, focusing subjectively on the swaying audience below; and at one point it seems to plummet to the floor of the Wintergarten as a performer falls to his death. Much of this movement is less functional than that of *Der letzte Mann* and gives the impression of having been contrived for its own sake. Moreover, the film is highly derivative of *Der letzte Mann* in terms of atmosphere and theme as well as technique. Nevertheless, as Lewis Jacobs writes, "*Variety* put American movie-goers into a white heat of enthusiasm over film art," and it insured the permanence of German influence

4.25 Decadence in *Varieté* (E. A. Dupont, 1925).

upon the Hollywood studios until the end of the silent era (which was soon matched by a tendency to "Americanize" the German film, as we shall see). For the German cinema, on the other hand, *Varieté* provided a bridge between the introspective *Kammerspiel* genre and a more objective kind of realism that was to emerge after 1924.

The Parufamet Agreement and the Migration to Hollywood

In 1924 the German mark had been stabilized and the spiral of postwar inflation halted by Germany's acceptance of the Dawes plan (named for the American financier Charles G. Dawes, who presided over an international committee set up to monitor Germany's war reparations payments). This provided for the long-term payment of reparations and admitted Germany back into the economic system of the Allies. The effect was to create in the German Republic a stabilized period of false confidence and even prosperity that lasted until the stock market crash of 1929. Ironically, however, the German film industry, which had survived rampant inflation, was seriously threatened by stabilization because the Dawes plan stipulated the curtailment of all exports. Thus, between 1924 and 1925 many independent production companies folded, and the surviving ones found it very difficult to borrow money from German banks. Sensing a chance to cripple its only European rival, Hollywood began to pour American films into Germany, founding its own distribution agencies and buying up theaters. By late 1925, UFA was on the brink of collapse due to external conditions and to the extravagance of its own recent productions, having lost over $8 million in the fiscal year just ended; at this point the American studios Paramount and MGM offered to subsidize UFA's huge debt to the Deutsche Bank by lending it $4 million at 7.5 percent interest in exchange for collaborative rights to UFA studios, theaters, and personnel—an arrangement that clearly worked in the American companies' favor.[1] The result was the foundation of the Parufamet (Paramount-UFA-Metro) Distribution Company in early 1926. Within a year, however, UFA was showing losses of $12 million and was forced to seek another loan, this time from the Prussian financier Dr. Alfred Hugenberg (1865–1951). Hugenberg, who had been a director of Krupp and was a leader of the right-wing German National party (Deutschnationalen Volkspartei, or DNVP), subsequently bought out the American companies and became chairman of the UFA board in March 1927.[2] Without fanfare, he established a nationalistic production policy that gave increasing prominence to Nazi party rallies in UFA newsreels and which finally permitted the Nazis to subvert the German film industry in 1933. While the republic survived, however, Hugenberg was content to wait.

The most immediate effect of the Parufamet Agreement was the migration of UFA film artists and technicians to Hollywood, where they worked for a variety of studios. Ernst Lubitsch had come to America in 1922 to direct *Rosita* for Mary Pickford, as had the world-famous UFA actress Pola Negri and her Russian-born director, Dmitri Buchowetski, shortly thereafter. They were joined in 1926–27 by the directors E. A. Dupont, Ludwig Berger, Lothar Mendes, Berthold Viertel, Paul Leni, F. W. Murnau, and Mihály Kertész (a Hungarian working for UFA, who became Michael Curtiz in America and went on to direct over one hundred films for Warner Bros. between 1927 and 1960, including the legendary *Casablanca* [1942]); the cinematographer Karl Freund; the performers Emil Jannings, Conrad Veidt (Cesare in *Caligari*), Greta Garbo (Swedish), and Lya De Putti (Hungarian); and the producer Erich Pommer and the scenarist Carl Mayer. This migration drained UFA of talent, although it was random and temporary. Many German technicians, actors, and minor directors settled in

4.26 *Caligari's* American children: the Universal horror films of the 1930s. Tod Browning's expressionistic *Dracula* (1931), photographed by Karl Freund.

Hollywood to pursue modestly successful careers. Karl Freund, for example, not only became one of the most able Hollywood cinematographers of the 1930s, but also

1. The loan was nearly made by Carl Laemmle's Universal in exchange for a mutual distribution contract and two of the five votes on the UFA board, but Paramount and MGM stepped in at the last minute with a better deal. See Kristin Thompson, *Exporting Entertainment: America in the World Film Market, 1907–34* (London: British Film Institute, 1985), pp. 106–11. (In the end, though, Universal did make a smaller loan to UFA—$275,000 in exchange for the right to distribute 50 of its films to German theaters.) See Thomas J. Saunders, *Hollywood in Berlin: American Cinema and Weimar Germany* (Berkeley: University of California Press, 1994). After Alfred Hugenberg took control of UFA's board, the $4-million loan was paid off by liquidating collateral real estate, and by 1928 Parufamet no longer distributed UFA products; the company was dissolved shortly after the coming of sound.

2. Hugenberg exercised complete control over UFA by personally owning a majority share of its stock; the rest of the company's capital was held by DNVP associates. The board was chosen from the most conservative representatives of German heavy industry and finance, including Louis Hager, Emil Strauss, Fritz Thyssen, and Heinrich von Schrötter, who also controlled vast newspaper publishing, advertising, and telecommunications interests.

directed a handful of superbly atmospheric horror thrillers for Universal and MGM (see footnote, p. 102) that conferred a substantial legacy of German Expressionism upon the Hollywood horror film as a sound-film genre. But the fate of the major German directors in Hollywood was similar to that of the Scandinavians Sjöström and Stiller.

To put it simply, Hollywood didn't want them to film the kinds of subjects that had made them great directors in their native industries. In effect, the American studios had bought a boatload of foreign talent that they literally didn't know how to employ. The major artists rapidly became bored with their dull assignments and returned to Germany (some only to return to America later as refugees from the Nazis). Only Lubitsch was able to adapt himself successfully to the complexity and vapidity of the Hollywood production process, and his American career proved much more significant than his German one. Murnau stayed on too, and it is conceivable that he might have brought his American career to greatness had his life not been cut short by an automobile accident in 1931. As it was, after he made the visually exquisite if saccharine *Sunrise* in 1927 (produced by Fox, written by Mayer, and shot by Karl Struss and Charles Rosher, but devoid of the thematic power of *Der letzte Mann*), the quality of Murnau's work declined. His last film, the independently produced South Seas tragedy *Tabu* (1931), was an aesthetic success, but the director died one week before it reached the screen.

G. W. Pabst and "Street" Realism

Another effect of the Dawes plan on the German film industry was less direct than the Parufamet agreement but more important to the general trend of domestic production. The period after 1924 produced, superficially at least, a return to social normalcy in Germany. As a consequence, the German cinema began to turn away from the morbid and mannered psychological themes of Expressionism and *Kammerspiel* and toward the kind of literal (but still studio-produced) realism exemplified by the "street films" (*Strassenfilme*) of the second half of the decade—G. W. Pabst's *Die freudlose Gasse* (*The Joyless Street*, 1925), Bruno Rahn's *Dirnentragödie* (*Tragedy of*

the Street, 1927), Joe May's *Asphalt* (1929), and Piel Jutzi's *Berlin—Alexanderplatz* (1930). Named for their prototype, Karl Grune's *Der Strasse* (*The Street*, 1923), these films all dealt realistically with the plight of ordinary people in the postwar period of inflation and incarnated the spirit of *die neue Sachlichkeit* ("the new objectivity"), which entered German society and art at every level during this time. Cynicism, resignation, disillusionment, and a desire to accept "life as it is" were the major characteristics of *die neue Sachlichkeit*, and these translated into a type of grim social realism in the street films.[3]

The undisputed master of the new realism was the Austrian-born director G. W. (Georg Wilhelm) Pabst (1885–1967). Trained in the theater, Pabst, a latecomer to the Weimar cinema, directed his first film, *Der Schatz* (*The Treasure*), rather perfunctorily in 1924. His next film, however, was *Die freudlose Gasse* (*The Joyless Street*, 1925), which achieved world recognition as a masterpiece of cinematic social realism. (In some countries recognition came in the form of censorship—England banned *Die freudlose Gasse*, and the prints seen in Italy, Austria, and France were substantially cut.) The film concerns the financial and spiritual ruin of the middle classes through inflation in postwar Vienna, focusing upon the lives of several destitute bourgeois families struggling to preserve their dignity and decency in the face of secret starvation. The misery of their existence is contrasted with the extravagant pleasure-seeking of the war profiteers. Daughters of the middle class—the most prominent played by the Scandinavian actresses Asta Nielsen

---

3. While the shift to social realism of some sort was fairly general in the German cinema at this point, two other more popular genres deserve mention. The *Kulturfilme* were feature-length escapist documentaries on esoteric subjects, expensively produced by UFA. With titles like *Wege zu Kraft und Schönheit* (*Ways to Health and Beauty*, 1925), these films became a German specialty on the international market and were a vast financial success for the studio. The other popular genre was an exclusively national phenomenon—the mountain films of Dr. Arnold Fanck (1889–1974), which exploited the Germanic predilection for heroic scenery and winter sports in vehicles like *Der Berg des Schicksals* (*Peak of Destiny*, 1924), *Der heilige Berg* (*The Holy Mountain*, 1927), and *Die weisse Hölle von Piz Palü* (*The White Hell of Pitz Palu*, 1929; codirected by Pabst). These were all fiction films, stunningly photographed on location by the best talent money could buy (the actress Leni Riefenstahl—see pp. 294–95—and Pabst were among Fanck's collaborators), which relied heavily upon spurious sentiment and inflated plots for their dramatic effect. Nevertheless, they enjoyed quite a cult among the German audience, and, according to Kracauer, their popularity was a harbinger of the heroic and irrational appeal of Nazism.

4.27 *Der Strasse* **(Karl Grune, 1923): the prototypical "street film."**

the discovery that the perceptual fragmentation created by editing within scenes could be effectively concealed for the purpose of narration by cutting a shot in the midst of a motion that is completed in the next shot.[4] The spectator's eye follows the character's movement and not the film's (not, that is, the cut itself), which renders the whole process of montage more fluid and comprehensible. Thus, a director who wished to cut smoothly from a full shot of an actor to a medium shot from the waist up might require the actor to begin some incidental movement or gesture in the full shot that could be completed in the medium shot after the

and Greta Garbo (in her German screen debut)—sell themselves into prostitution to save their families, while the wealthy amuse themselves at opulent black-market nightclubs where these girls must eventually come to be "bought." Yet there is no sentimentality or symbolism in the presentation. Pabst captures "life as it is" with a kind of photographic realism that completely rejects the subjective camera of Murnau and Freund (his cinematographers were Guido Seeber, Robert Lach, and the prolific documentarist Curt Oertel [1890–1960]). Like theirs, of course, Pabst's camera does move, but the essential dynamism of his films is generated through cutting and, more specifically, cutting on a character's movement.

Pabst was the first German director to be substantially influenced by Eisenstein's theory and practice of montage, which will be discussed in Chapter 5. In fact, prior to Pabst, the German cinema had evolved through its various phases as essentially a cinema of *mise-en-scène* rather than of montage since it had developed in isolation from the innovations of Griffith and his Russian successors. Pabst's own contribution to film technique was

cut—e.g., lighting a cigarette, answering a phone, or even rising from a chair. This kind of cutting (sometimes called "invisible editing" or **continuity editing**) became fundamental to the classical sound film, where it is often necessary to create visual bridges between shots corresponding to aural bridges on the soundtrack (for instance, a character may move from one shot into several others while speaking continuous dialogue, so that the visual sequence must be made to seem continuous as well). Ironically, by neutralizing the perceptual fragmentation inherent in narrative montage, Pabst actually increased its potential for use in any given sequence, and one hallmark of his later films is the large number of barely perceptible cuts he uses per scene.

Another hallmark is Pabst's increasing use of moti-

4. Barry Salt correctly points out that cutting on action was used by Ralph Ince (1887–1937) in films like *The Juggernaut* as early as 1915 (*Film Style and Technology: History and Analysis*, 2nd ed. [London: Starword, 1992], p. 138). But Pabst was the first director to structure entire films around the practice.

4.28 *Die neue Sachlichkeit: Die freudlose Gasse* (G. W. Pabst, 1925).

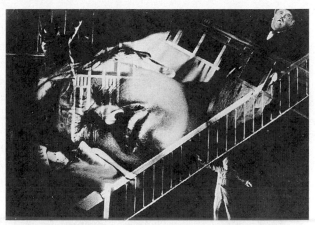

4.29 *Geheimnisse einer Seele* (G. W. Pabst, 1926): Freud on film.

vated point of view through the eyeline match and the shot-reverse-shot figure. In an eyeline match, the first shot shows a character looking at something offscreen (i.e., beyond the borders of the frame), while the second shot shows the object of his or her gaze, creating an illusion of spatial contiguity. Shot-reverse-shot is cutting back and forth between eyelines as two characters look offscreen at each other, and it would become the most prevalent continuity figure in the classical Hollywood cinema of the 1930s and 1940s.

Cutting on movement, in combination with motivated point of view in the eyeline match and the shot-reverse-shot figure, enabled Pabst to produce elaborate—but seemingly effortless—continuity structures. In *Die Liebe der Jeanne Ney* (*The Love of Jeanne Ney*, 1927), for example, one two-minute narrative sequence contains over forty fluid cuts representing—both subjectively and objectively—the perspectives of three separate characters as they move about a room during a heated argument. Pabst increasingly refined these techniques with each successive film, and it seems correct to say that, symbolically at least, he brought to its logical conclusion Edwin S. Porter's discovery that a scene may be broken down into more than one shot and that the shot is the basic signifying unit of the cinema.

Pabst's later films continue his involvement with social realism, although they are sometimes diluted by melodrama and fantasy, the inescapable legacy of Expressionism. *Geheimnisse einer Seele* (*Secrets of a Soul*, 1926), for example, a cinematic case history of an anxiety neurosis

(produced in collaboration with two disciples of Sigmund Freud [1856–1939], the founder of psychoanalysis—Dr. Hans Sachs and Dr. Karl Abraham—and shot by the brilliant team of Seeber, Lach, and Oertel), contains some of the most vivid dream sequences ever recorded on film. In *Die Liebe der Jeanne Ney* Pabst returned to the social arena to film the progress of a love affair caught up in the turmoil of the Russian Revolution and its aftermath. Photographed in semidocumentary fashion with natural lighting by Fritz Arno Wagner and Robert Lach, often using real locations, the film portrays postwar European society in the process of rapid disintegration; in it Pabst carried his sophisticated cutting techniques to new heights. Pabst's last two silent films,[5] *Die Büchse der Pandora* (*Pandora's Box*, 1929) and *Das Tagebuch einer Verlorenen* (*Diary of a Lost One*, 1929), both concern the lives of prostitutes (played in each case by the striking American actress Louise Brooks [1906–1985]) and the way in which their degraded roles relate to the general decadence of society. Pabst adapted himself readily to sound and became one of the foremost masters of the early sound film; his pacifist films *Westfront 1918* (1930) and *Kameradschaft* (*Comradeship*, 1931) are both among the most important works of the period. Indeed Pabst's career extended well into the 1950s, but his greatest work was done between 1924 and 1931—a time, ironically, when what has been called the Golden Age of German

---

5. Excluding the melodramatic "mountain film" *Die weisse Hölle von Piz Palü* (1929), which Pabst codirected with Arnold Fanck.

4.30 Pabst's *Die Büchse der Pandora* and *Das Tagebuch einer Verlorenen* (both 1929): Louise Brooks as an icon of Weimar decadence.

film was drawing to a close and the German cinema was about to begin its long decline.

Down and Out

In the past, it was fashionable to blame this decline upon the Nazis, who did indeed subvert UFA immediately after coming to power in 1933, turning the studio into a factory for the mass production of light entertainment and an instrument of propaganda for the state, under the direction of Joseph Goebbels. Recently, however, it has come to be recognized that the German cinema was dying of internal disorders long before the Nazi takeover, long before even the coming of sound. This is not to suggest that it was completely moribund by the end of the silent era. Far from it; for Germany produced three of the most distinguished early sound films made anywhere in the world: Josef von Sternberg's *Der blaue Engel* (*The Blue Angel*, 1930; see Chapter 8), Fritz Lang's *M* (1931), and Pabst's *Westfront 1918* (1930). Yet there is no doubt that the general quality of production declined sharply after 1924 and that the causes were deep-seated and manifold.

For one thing, it seems certain that the emphasis on studio production, so important to the aesthetic quality of the German cinema between 1919 and 1924, had proved stifling by the end of the silent period. The UFA style of architectural composition and pictorial lighting was becoming an end in itself, and the sheer extravagance of its productions had substantially diminished the studio's economic stability (Murnau's *Faust*, for example, was rumored to have overrun its costs by four times the budgeted amount). It is significant in this regard that the last two important films of the Weimar cinema were "montage documentaries" shot on location in and around Berlin. Walter Ruttmann's *Berlin: die Synphonie der Großstadt* (*Berlin: Symphony of a Great City*, 1927), based on an idea by Carl Mayer, employed the candid camera and rhythmic montage techniques of Dziga Vertov's "kino-eye" group (see Chapter 5) to create an abstract portrait of the city and its teeming life from dawn to midnight on a late spring day.[6] *Menschen am Sonntag* (*People on Sunday*, 1929), a semi-documentary account of two young couples on holiday at a lake outside Berlin, was the collaborative effort of several young men who would later become major directors of the sound era in America—Robert Siodmak, Fred Zinnemann, Edgar G. Ulmer, and Billy Wilder (Eugen Schüfftan, who would also emigrate to Hollywood, was the cinematographer). Like its wholly documentary predecessor, *Menschen am Sonntag* showed the marked influence of Vertov and Soviet montage.

It was the American influence, however, that proved most powerful, and many film historians have blamed the decline of Weimar cinema on the intrusion of Hollywood money and manners into Germany after the Parufamet agreement was signed. It is well known, for example, that Pabst was ordered by UFA executives to direct *Die Liebe der Jeanne Ney* in the "American style" and that the film barely survived the attempt. Indeed, the American style in Neubabelsberg proved even less successful than the UFA style in Hollywood. Other film scholars have argued that the German cinema was artistically impoverished by

---

6. Karl Freund cowrote the script of *Berlin* with Ruttmann and supervised the cinematography of Reimar Kuntze, Robert Baberske, and László Schäffer. Ruttmann cut it himself to parallel the rhythms of a score by the German Marxist composer Edmund Meisel, whose stirring revolutionary music for Eisenstein's *Potemkin* had helped to get that film banned in Germany. (Mayer dissociated himself from *Berlin* at this point, claiming that it had become too "formalistic"; on this aspect of the film see Matthew Bernstein, "Visual Style and Spatial Articulations in *Berlin, Symphony of a City* (1927)," *Journal of Film and Video* 36, 4 (Fall 1984): 5–12, 61). Ironically, Ruttmann (1897–1941) went on to become a leading documentarist of the Third Reich, assisting Leni Riefenstahl on *Olympiad* (1936) and directing the strident *Deutsche Panzer* (1940) to celebrate the victory over France.

4.31 *Berlin, die Symphonie einer Großstadt* (Walter Ruttmann, 1927).

the talent raids that Hollywood made upon UFA in 1926; certainly the loss of Murnau and so many of his associates was significantly detrimental to the studio. Finally, UFA was literally impoverished by American competition, both international and domestic, in the wake of the Dawes plan, so that it had to be bailed out by the political Right. It seems clear, however, that the most important reasons for Germany's decline as a major cinematic power run deeper than those put forth here already.

Lotte H. Eisner gets closer to the heart of the matter in the final chapter of *The Haunted Screen*, in which she suggests that the thematic legacy of Expressionism was tragedy and despair. Indeed, as Siegfried Kracauer shows time and time again in *From Caligari to Hitler*, the struggle for control of the self, which provided the great theme of the Weimar cinema, was always *lost* on the screen; and this had the effect of increasing the insecurity and thus

the authoritarian tendencies of the masses, which in the postwar era included large segments of the middle class brought low by inflation. Since the German form of government was republican and Germany was a conquered nation, however, this authoritarian impulse had no means of expression, and the collective mind of the society was paralyzed by its inability to articulate itself.[7] Thus, if Eisner and Kracauer are correct, the decline of the German cinema was due to multiple external factors underpinned by a nationwide inner paralysis which in some sense the German cinema, as an organ of German society, had helped to create. It was not the Nazis who destroyed the German cinema, then, but the cultural preconditions that permitted their rise to power; and even though UFA managed to produce a handful of truly distinguished films between 1929 and 1933, the vital spark of the German screen had been extinguished. Thanks to the virulence of the Nazi plague and the partitioning of Germany that followed World War II, it could not be rekindled until the generation of Germans born after the war came to artistic and political consciousness in the late 1960s. Since that time, the German cinema has become one of the most exciting and influential in all of Europe, and, in the work of such brilliant filmmakers as Werner Herzog, Rainer Werner Fassbinder, Wim Wenders, and Jean-Marie Straub, it stands once again on the very cutting edge of the international avant garde, as we shall see in Chapter 15.

---

7. The thesis of Kracauer's book, first published in 1947, was that Weimar cinema reflected a deep psychological conflict in the German people whose resolution led inevitably to Hitler's dictatorship. Widely accepted in the postwar era, this view was rejected by academic film historians a generation later as naïvely deterministic. Recently, however, a new appreciation of Kracauer's intellectual roots in Marxist historical materialism has led to renewed respect for his achievement. Today, as Mike Budd points out in *The Cabinet of Dr. Caligari: Texts, Contexts, Histories*, scholars of Weimar cinema tend to depend on Kracauer even when they disagree with him (p. 2). For an analytical introduction to the entire body of Kracauer's work, see Gertrud Koch, *Siegfried Kracauer: An Introduction*, trans. Jeremy Gaines (Princeton: Princeton University Press, 2000).

Soviet Silent Cinema and the Theory of Montage, 1917–1931

The Prerevolutionary Cinema

Before the Bolshevik (Communist) Revolution of October 1917, the film industry in Russia was mainly European. Agents of Lumière Frères, Pathé, Gaumont, and Danish Nordisk had established large distribution branches in several cities at the turn of the century, and the first native Russian studio (Drankov) was not founded until 1908. About 90 percent of all films shown in Russia between 1898 and the outbreak of World War I were imported. Between 1914 and 1916, this figure declined to 20 percent as the number of domestic film-producing firms more than doubled, from eighteen to forty-seven, in the absence of foreign competition. But most of these operations were thinly capitalized, and by mid-1917 there were only three major production companies in the entire country (Khanzhonkov, Ermoliev, and Thiemann & Reinhardt). Ninety percent of all filmmaking activity was concentrated in the major cities of Moscow and Petrograd.[1] All technical equipment and film stock were imported from Germany or France.

The film industry in Russia was small because the cinema had not yet become a popular form, as it had in the West. Unlike their German counterparts, the Russian working classes were too impoverished to attend the movies, and the ultraconservative ruling classes simply didn't care to.[2] Several artists from other media took an interest in the prerevolutionary cinema. In 1914, the **Futurist** poet Vladimir Maiakovski (1893–1930) and his colleagues made a unique avant-garde manifesto in film entitled *Drama in Futurist Cabaret No. 13 (Drama in kabare futuristov N13)*. Between 1915 and 1917,

---

1. The city's more Germanic name, St. Petersburg, had been changed to Petrograd when Russia entered the war against Germany in 1914. In 1924 it was renamed Leningrad by the Bolsheviks. The name St. Petersburg was restored in 1992, after the collapse of the Soviet Union.

2. For the middle-class perspective, such as it was, see Yuri Tsivian, *Early Cinema in Russia and Its Cultural Reception*, ed. Richard Taylor, trans. Alan Bodger (Chicago: University of Chicago Press, 1998).

the great stage director Vsevolod Meyerhold (1874–1940) adapted two famous literary works for the screen—Oscar Wilde's novel *The Picture of Dorian Gray* (*Portret Doriana Greia*, 1915) and Stanislaw Przybyszewski's *The Strong Man* (*Silnyi chelovek*, 1917)—both of which show a uniquely cinematic conception of *mise-en-scène*. By far the most impressive film of the period, and the last important one made before the October Revolution, was Iakov Protazanov's production of Lev Tolstoi's *Father Sergius* (*Otets Sergii*, 1918), whose acting, photography, and narrative construction surpassed anything made in Russia to date, although its editing is largely functional and prosaic.

With these few exceptions, prerevolutionary cinema was thought to be generally mediocre until Soviet archives were opened to the West in the late 1980s. It was discovered then that 286 of the 1,716 Russian films made from 1907 to 1917 had survived, revealing an unsuspected richness of subject matter and *mise-en-scène*, influenced—initially at least—by the French *film d'art* style.[3] Many adapt classic works of nineteenth-century Russian literature (notably Tolstoi, Turgenev, and Pushkin) and adhere to an aesthetic of immobility called the "Russian style," which combined the psychological pauses of the Moscow Art Theater with the poetic acting styles of early Danish and Italian cinema. The two major directors of the period were Iakov Protazanov (1881–1945) and Evgeni Bauer (1865–1917). Working mainly for the Ermoliev company, Protazanov made seventy-three films in every genre before the Revolution, only seven of which survive. These include four starring Ivan Mozhukhin (1890–1939), famous for his expressive acting style and, later, as the subject of the editing experiment that demonstrated the "Kuleshov effect" (see below)—*The Queen of Spades* (*Pikovaya dama*, 1916), *Satan Triumphant* (*Satana likuyushchili*, 1917), *Little Ellie* (*Malyutka Elli*, 1918), and *Father Sergius* (above). After the Revolution, Protazanov went briefly into exile in Paris and Berlin, but he returned in 1924 to make *Aelita*, the first Soviet science-fiction film, for the new Mezhrabpom-Russ studio in Moscow, where he continued to direct well into the sound era. (His last feature, *Nasreddin in Bukhara* [*Nasreddin v Bukhare*, 1943], was shot on location in Uzbekistan during World War II, when the Soviet film industry was evacuated to Central Asia.)

Bauer began working in the prerevolutionary cinema as a set designer and then directed eighty-two films between 1913 and 1917, most of which he also produced, scripted, and photographed. Of the twenty-six that survive, the earliest show the marked influence of Danish films (widely distributed in prerevolutionary Russia, as in prewar Germany) in terms of their lighting and framing. Bauer's most remarkable films—*Silent Witnesses* (*Nemye svideteli*, 1914), *Child of the Big City* (*Ditya bol'shogo goroda*, 1914), *After Death* (*Posle smerti*, 1915), and *A Life for a Life* (*Zhizn' za zhizn*, 1916)—tend to focus on the dramatic extremes of human emotion and contain bold scenic and lighting design as well as deep-space tracking shots, which Bauer conceived and executed himself. Bauer made all of his films for Khanzhonkov & Co., Ltd., in which he became a principal shareholder shortly before he died of pneumonia, contracted while shooting on location in the Crimea. Another prominent Khanzhonkov filmmaker was pioneer puppet animator Wladyslaw Starewicz (1882–1965—*The Ant and the Grasshopper*, 1912; *The Cameraman's Revenge*, 1912; *The Insect's Christmas*, 1913), who did remarkable experimental work for the Khanzhonkov studio, combining live action with animation through multiple exposure and montage, as well as directing about fifty features, before emigrating to Paris in 1919.

When Russia entered the war in 1914, foreign films could no longer be imported, and the tsarist government attempted to stimulate domestic production, especially of documentary and educational films, by creating a Military Film Section within the Skobelev Committee (an organization named for its chairman, which had originally been founded to assist veterans of the Russo-Japanese War) and giving it exclusive rights to film at the battlefront. The commercial film industry continued to make escapist entertainment, but the committee specifically encouraged the production of propaganda documentaries and features to stem growing discontent with the tsarist regime. This effort was not and could not have been successful because social conditions in Russia had become

---

3. Many of these are described in Paolo Cherchi Usai et al., *Silent Witnesses: Russian Films 1908–1919* (London: British Film Institute, 1989), a catalogue of the collection of prerevolutionary Russian films from 1908 to 1917 and of postrevolutionary, privately produced films from 1917 to 1919 as preserved in the Gosfilmofond RSSR archive. This catalogue was prepared to accompany a retrospective of prerevolutionary Russian cinema sponsored by the Associazione le Giornate del Cinema Muto at Pordenone, Italy, in 1989.

5.1 Early puppet animation: *The Cameraman's Revenge*
(Wladyslaw Starewicz, 1912).

so bad by the second year of the war that a revolution
was imminent. The armed forces, underfed and under-
equipped, had suffered heavy losses. There were shortages of food and fuel everywhere, and the civilian
population was completely demoralized.

The Origins of Soviet Cinema

In February 1917, the tsarist regime was replaced by a
provisional parliamentary government under Alexander
Kerenski (1881–1970), who unwisely attempted to continue Russia's involvement in the war. Kerenski's government immediately abolished film censorship and
reorganized the Skobelev Committee to produce anti-
tsarist propaganda. But only two films (*Nicholas II [Tsar
Nikolai II]* and *The Past Will Not Die [Proshloie ne
umryot]*) were made under this new dispensation, because
the provisional government was overthrown by the Bolsheviks, led by Vladimir Il'ich Lenin (1870–1924), in the
October Revolution of 1917. There followed the establishment of the Soviet government at Petrograd; a bitter
three-year civil war between the Red (pro-Communist)
and White (anti-Communist) factions of the Russian
army; an invasion by France, Britain, the USA, Japan, and
other World War I allies; a crippling foreign trade
embargo; and, finally, economic collapse and famine.[4] In
the midst of this chaos, the Bolshevik leaders looked to

film as a means of reunifying their shattered nation. As a
party of 200,000 that had assumed the leadership of 160
million people, most of them illiterate, scattered across
the single largest contiguous land mass in the world[5] and
speaking well over one hundred separate languages, the
Bolsheviks' most immediate task was one of communication and consolidation, and they saw film as the perfect
medium for this endeavor. Film, after all, speaks only one
language—one that doesn't require literacy to comprehend—and, through mass distribution, can communicate
the same ideas to millions of people at once. As Lenin
himself declared of the situation, "The cinema is for us
the most important of the arts."

Unfortunately, most producers and technicians of
the prerevolutionary commercial cinema were capitalists
openly hostile to the Bolshevik government (and vice
versa). They emigrated to Europe, taking their equipment
and film stock with them and, in the process, often wrecking the studios they left behind. No new equipment or film
stock (i.e., celluloid) could be imported into Russia
because of the foreign blockade, and massive power shortages severely restricted the use of what few resources
remained. Nevertheless, in the face of these obstacles, the
Soviet government scrapped the Skobelev Committee and
set up a special subsection on cinema (ultimately, the Cinema Committee) within the New People's Commissariat
of Education (Narodnyi kommissariat prosveshcheniia,
abbreviated Narkompros), whose head was the playwright
and literary critic Anatoli Lunacharski (1875–1933). In
August 1919 the Soviet film industry was nationalized and
placed under Narkompros. Headed by Lenin's wife,
Nadezhda Krupskaya (1869–1939), the Cinema Commit-

---

4. Warren Beatty's *Reds* (1981) offers an impressive account of these
events and of the revolutionary fervor that attended them. It is based
on the life of the American radical journalist John Reed (1887–1920),
who participated in the October Revolution and wrote of his experiences
in *Ten Days That Shook the World* (1919), a source for Eisenstein's
October (1928). (Reed's stirring reportage of the Mexican Revolution,
Insurgent Mexico [1913], later influenced Eisenstein's choice of subject
for *¡Que viva México!*, as will be seen in Chapter 9.) Reed was honored
in the Soviet Union as a founder of the Communist International, and
his ashes are buried beneath the Kremlin wall. Not to be outdone by
Hollywood, the Soviets filmed their own life of Reed in Sergei Bondarchuk's two-part epic *Red Bells* (*Red Bells: Mexico in Flames* [1982] and
Red Bells: I've Seen the Birth of the New World [1983]), a coproduction
with Mexico and Italy that met with faint praise outside of the USSR.

5. The USSR's area was 8,649,500 square miles, or 2.5 times that of
the United States.

tee founded a film school in Moscow to train actors and technicians for the cinema (another was established briefly at Petrograd): the VGIK (Vsesoyuznyi gosudarstveni institut kinematografii—All-Union State Institute of Cinematography) or Moscow Film School. This school was the first of its kind in the world, and it remained among the most widely imitated and respected until the Soviet Union's demise in late 1991. Its initial purpose was to train people in the production of *agitki*—newsreels edited for the purpose of agitation and propaganda, or "agitprop." Starting in 1918, these *agitki* toured Russia on specially equipped agit-trains and agit-steamers designed to export the Revolution from the urban centers to the provinces—an immense undertaking in a country containing one-sixth of the world's land mass and one-twelfth of its population.[6] Indeed, because of the severe shortage of film stock and the chaotic conditions of the new Soviet state, almost all films made during the years of the civil war (1918–20) were newsreels of this sort. Thus, at its birth, the Soviet cinema was a cinema of propaganda in documentary form. And its first major artist was, appropriately, the first great practitioner and theorist of the documentary form, Dziga Vertov.

Dziga Vertov and the Kino-Eye

Dziga Vertov (b. Denis Kaufman,[7] 1896–1954) was born in Białystok, Poland, then part of the Russian Empire. In 1918 he became an **editor** of newsreels for the Cinema Committee. Cameramen traveling about the country to record the progress of the Red Army in the civil war and the activities of the new government would send their footage back to Moscow, where it was edited into newsreels by Vertov and others. At first, Vertov was content to assemble the footage in a purely functional manner, but he gradually began to experiment with more expressive kinds of editing. By 1921, Vertov had made three feature-length compilation documentaries from his weekly newsreel footage: *Anniversary of the Revolution* (*Godovshchina revoliutsii*, 1919—the first Soviet feature film), *The Battle at Tsaritsyn* (*Srazheniie v Tsaritsyne*, 1920), and a thirteen-part *History of the Civil War* (*Istoriya grazhdanskoi voiny*, 1921). In all of them he experimented with subliminal cuts of one to two frames each, color tinting by hand, expressive titles,[8] and the dramatic reconstruction of documentary events.

The period immediately following the Revolution was one of extraordinary creative fervor in the arts. Since Ver-

5.2 A poster by Alexander Rodchenko for *Kino-glaz* (Dziga Vertov, 1924).

tov's early films were strongly pro-Soviet and he was one of few pro-Soviets making films, his experiments were actively encouraged by the Cinema Committee, and he began to gather about him a small band of committed

6. Ironically, after 1922 much of this activity was financed by box-office receipts from American films imported for the purpose by the Soviet Commissariat of Foreign Trade on the orders of Lunacharski and Lenin. In fact, between 1918 and 1931, over 1,700 American, German, and French films were distributed in the Soviet Union, as opposed to fewer than 700 domestic features.

7. *Dziga* is a Ukrainian word meaning "spinning top" or "restless, fidgety, bustling person." *Vertov* is derived from the Russian word *vertet* meaning "to turn, spin, rotate, or fidget." The pseudonym, adopted around 1915, suggests the sound of a hand-cranked movie camera; it is also, perhaps, Vertov's comment on the filmmaker's profession.

Vertov's brothers also earned places in film history. Boris Kaufman (1907–1980) was acclaimed as one of the world's great black-and-white cinematographers. He worked with Jean Vigo in France and with Elia Kazan (winning an Academy Award for *On the Waterfront* [1954]), Sidney Lumet, and other American directors. Mikhail Kaufman (1897–1980) began as Vertov's cinematographer but later produced a number of distinguished documentaries of his own.

8. Often gigantic abbreviated revolutionary slogans in capital letters that seemed to shout at the audience from the screen.

young documentarists who came to call themselves the *Kinoki* (from *kino-oki*—"cinema-eyes"). This group published a series of radical manifestos in the early 1920s denouncing conventional narrative cinema as "impotent" and demanding that it be replaced by a new cinema based on the "organization of camera-recorded documentary material" (Vertov). The key terms here are "camera-recorded" and "organization," for Vertov and his colleagues believed both in the absolute ability of the cinema apparatus to reproduce reality as it actually appears *and* in the necessity of editing to arrange this reality into an expressive and persuasive whole. This doctrine, called by Vertov **kino-glaz** ("cinema-eye"), contributed significantly to the montage aesthetics that as we shall see, came to dominate the Soviet silent cinema after 1924. But it also produced a number of stunning documentary achievements in its own right.

In 1922, Lenin ordered a fixed ratio (dubbed the "Leninist film proportion") to be established between Soviet information and entertainment films. The exact ratio was unspecified and in fact was never officially acknowledged, but Vertov militantly insisted that it should be four to one. Shortly thereafter, he launched a new series of consciously crafted newsreel-documentaries, collectively entitled *Kino-pravda* ("film-truth"), which were specifically designed to test his theories. The twenty-three *Kino-pravda* films Vertov made between 1922 and 1925

5.3 Vertov's experimental sound film *Enthusiasm: Symphony of the Don Basin* (1931).

employed a wide variety of experimental techniques, but none as startling as his first independently shot nonarchival feature, *Kino-glaz* (*The Movie-Eye* or *Cinema-Eye*, 1924), which used trick photography, animation, **microphotography,** multiple exposure, and "candid camera" techniques to create what one critic has called "an epic vision of actuality." Between 1925 and 1929 Vertov made three similar features—*Stride, Soviet!* (*Shagai, Soviet!*, 1926), *A Sixth of the World* (*Shestaia chast' mira*, 1926), and *Number Eleven* (*Odinnadtsatyi*, 1928)—but his most exhaustive essay in the "kino-eye" technique was his major work, *The Man with a Movie Camera* (*Chelovek s kinoapparatom*, 1929).

This film utilizes every resource of editing and camera manipulation known to silent cinema to create a portrait of "life caught unawares" on a typical day in Moscow from dawn to dusk. But *The Man with a Movie Camera* is less about Moscow than about cinema itself, for it constantly seeks to reveal the process of its own making. The film contains recurrent images of the cameramen, Vertov's brother Boris Kaufman, shooting it, Vertov's wife Elizaveta Svilova editing it, and people in a theater watching it. Point of view is manipulated to such an extent that it breaks down, and the camera's power to transform reality is flaunted in a continuous burst of cinematic pyrotechnics that include variable camera speeds, dissolves, split-screen effects, the use of prismatic lenses, multiple superimposition, animation, microphotography, and elaborately structured montage. In *The Man with a Movie Camera*, Vertov had progressed from documentarist to ciné-poet, creating a kind of metacinema, or self-reflexive cinema, that prefigures the work of the French New Wave (as will be explored in Chapter 13). To quote critic David Bordwell, "Long before the Marxist film theorists of *Cahiers du Cinéma* . . . called for a cinema which declares its sources in a context of production and consumption, Vertov was mounting a continuous *autocritique* of film-making."

Unlike most other serious filmmakers of his day, Vertov welcomed the coming of sound, seeing it as a means of augmenting the "cinema-eye" with the "radio-ear," and he continued to make films through the 1940s, including the experimental *Enthusiasm: Symphony of the Don Basin* (*Entuziazm: Simfoniia Donbassa*, 1931) and *Three Songs of Lenin* (*Tri pesni o Leninye*, 1934). Although his international influence throughout the 1930s on both the avant-garde and the conventional documentary was strong, by the late 1920s Vertov's switch from short films (which, packaged with commercial entertainment features, were seen by huge audiences in the USSR) to documentary features (which were attended by almost no one) earned him the reputation of a sponsored filmmaker who could not cover his costs and was spending too much of the government's money. In the 1930s, Vertov fell into disfavor with Stalin and was accused of **"formalist"** error—the sometimes deadly sin of exalting the aesthetic form of a work above its ideological content.[9] In the 1960s and 1970s, however, Vertov came to be regarded as a prophet of *cinéma vérité* (a term derived by translating *kino-pravda* into French) and the father of the new nonfiction film. Fittingly, the French New Wave director Jean-Luc Godard (b. 1930) and his political followers associated themselves with Vertov's work by naming their production cooperative after him: all of Godard's films between 1968 and 1973 were made collectively under the auspices of the Dziga-Vertov Group. More important, however, it is clear today that Vertov was a cofounder of the Soviet silent cinema, which gives him a major role in one of the greatest movements in the history of film.

Lev Kuleshov and the Kuleshov Workshop

The other recognized cofounder was Lev Kuleshov (1899–1970), one of the few prerevolutionary filmmakers to remain in Russia after 1917. Kuleshov began his career as a set designer at the Khanzhonkov studios for the director Evgeni Bauer (1865–1917) in 1916, at the age of seventeen, and actually completed Bauer's last feature, *For Luck* (*Za schast'en*, 1917), when the director was fatally injured while filming on location. During the civil war, he became a cameraman for the agit-trains and was active in establishing the VGIK in 1919. Like Vertov, Kuleshov was interested in the theory as well as the practice of cinema; he had published his first articles on the subject in the trade journal *Vestnik kinematografii* (*Cinema Herald*) in 1917. But Kuleshov's superiors at the film school lacked confidence in the zealous twenty year old's ability to work within an orthodox curriculum, and they permitted him to conduct his own study group outside the formal structure of the institute. This "Kuleshov Workshop" drew the most radical and innovative young students at the film school, Sergei Eisenstein and V. I.

Pudovkin among them, and concerned itself mainly with experiments in editing.

Because of the severe shortage of raw film stock and equipment that afflicted the Soviet Union in the immediate postrevolutionary period, the workshop's initial experiments involved the production of "films without celluloid." Kuleshov and his students would write scenarios, direct and act them out as if before cameras, and then—on paper—assemble the various "shots" into completed "films." Soon, however, Kuleshov had another subject and model for experimentation in the most sophisticatedly constructed film made to date—D. W. Griffith's *Intolerance* (1916).

Intolerance had been brought into Russia for commercial distribution in the year of its release,[1] but exhibitors had rejected it as incomprehensible. The film was shelved until after the Revolution, when the Bolshevik government arranged premiers in Petrograd (November 1918) and Moscow (May 1919) in recognition of its powerful "agitational" qualities. Lenin, impressed with what he took to be the proletarian sympathies of the Modern story, apparently ordered that it be shown throughout the Soviet Union—where, according to Iris Barry, it ran continuously for almost ten years. All available film stock was gathered up to be used in duplicating prints, and there are reports that Lenin actually cabled Griffith and offered him the directorship of the Soviet film industry, which Griffith supposedly declined only because of the opening of his new Mamaroneck studio. In any case, as the late Jay Leyda pointed out in his book *Kino*, a monumental history of the Russian and Soviet film, *Intolerance* went on to become the Soviet film industry's first great popular,

---

9. As distinct from "Formalism," a contemporaneous movement in literature that took the position that language has no inherent relationship with the reality it purports to signify.

1. According to Vance Kepley, Jr., it was imported by Jacques Robert Cibrario's film distribution firm Transatlantic ("*Intolerance* and the Soviets: A Historical Investigation," *Wide Angle* 3, 1 [Spring 1979]: 22–27). After the Revolution, this same Cibrario offered himself to the Cinema Committee as an international purchasing agent for urgently needed film equipment and stock. Between 1918 and 1921, he was given access to $1 million in prewar Russian bank deposits in New York City, where, by forging invoices and bills of lading, he embezzled most of it. In 1921, an indictment brought against him by the Soviets was dismissed because the United States did not recognize their government, and Cibrario fled to Europe, where his "profits" had been deposited in British, Dutch, and Italian banks. (A comic dramatization of this affair by Jim Hawkins, entitled *Thank You, Comrades*, was produced for the BBC and broadcast in the United States on PBS in 1978.)

political, and aesthetic success. To quote Leyda: "We know for certain of the popular success of *Intolerance*, and we know as certainly of the tremendous aesthetic and technical impetus given to *all* young Soviet film-makers by this and subsequently shown Griffith films. No Soviet film of importance made within the following ten years was to be completely outside *Intolerance*'s sphere of influence."

That influence was imbibed, elaborated, and disseminated largely through the Kuleshov Workshop, where prints of *Intolerance* (and, after the lifting of the blockade in 1920, *The Birth of a Nation*) were screened continuously until, according to legend, they fell apart. Kuleshov and his students spent months studying the precise manner in which Griffith had built up his complicated multiple narrative out of thousands of separate shots, until they had mastered the principle themselves. Then, they reassembled his sequences in hundreds of different combinations to test the ways in which an arrangement of shots produces meaning. As raw film stock began to dribble back into the Soviet Union between 1922 and 1923 as a result of a Soviet-German trade agreement and the success of Lenin's New Economic Policy (NEP), Kuleshov struck out on his own and carried the analysis of film structure far beyond anything that had gone before.

Though the form of Kuleshov's initial experiments was dictated by the relative scarcity of raw stock, his ultimate goal was to discover the general laws by which film communicates meaning to an audience—to discover, that is, the way in which film *signifies*. In his most famous experiment, as recounted by V. I. Pudovkin in *Film Technique and Film Acting*, Kuleshov took unedited footage of a completely expressionless face (that of the prerevolutionary matinee idol Ivan Mozhukhin, who had emigrated to Paris after the Revolution) and intercut it with shots of three highly motivated objects: a bowl of hot soup, a dead woman lying in a coffin, and a little girl playing with a teddy bear. When the film strips were shown to randomly selected audiences, they invariably responded as though the actor's face had accurately portrayed the emotion appropriate to the intercut object. As Pudovkin recalled: "The public raved about the acting of the artist. They pointed out the heavy pensiveness of his mood over the forgotten soup, were touched and moved by the deep sorrow with which he looked on the dead woman, and admired the light, happy smile with which he surveyed the girl at play. But we knew that in all three cases the face was exactly the same." Kuleshov concluded from these results, known today as the "Kuleshov effect,"[2] that the shot, or cinematic sign, has two distinct values: (1) that which it possesses in itself as a photographic image of reality and (2) that which it acquires when placed in relationship to other shots. In another experiment, Kuleshov cut together a shot of a smiling actor with a close-up of a revolver and a second shot of the same actor looking frightened. Audiences naturally interpreted the sequence as portraying cowardice, but when Kuleshov reversed the position of the two shots of the actor within the sequence, the opposite interpretation was made. He reasoned from this that the second value of the shot implicit in the Kuleshov effect, that which it acquires when juxtaposed with other shots, was infinitely more important in the generation of cinematic meaning than was the first. He concluded, that is, that meaning in cinema is a function of the celluloid strip, not of the *photographed reality*, and that it arises from the sequential arrangement of its parts. Griffith, of course, had practiced this principle instinctively in all of his major films, but Kuleshov was the first to give it a theoretical articulation and to suggest that it is the basis for the process of cinematic signification.

A further experiment involved the creation of "artificial landscapes" through "creative geography"—the juxtaposition of separate shots taken at separate places and times. In one of these, a shot of a man moving from right to left across the frame in one part of Moscow is cut together with a shot of a woman moving from left to right across the frame in another section of the city, while a third shot shows them suddenly meeting in yet another part of Moscow to shake hands. At the conclusion of this shot, the man points offscreen, and a fourth shot reveals the object of his attention to be the White House in Washington, D.C. The fifth and final shot of the sequence shows the two ascending the steps not of the White House, but of a well-known Moscow church. Kuleshov had thus created the cinematic illusion of spatial and temporal unity by cutting together five separate shots taken at five separate places and times. In yet another experiment, he synthesized the body of a woman out of shots of the face, torso, hands, and legs of several separate women.

---

2. Pudovkin later used this same effect in *Mother*.

5.4 *The Man with a Movie Camera* (Dziga Vertov, 1929).

What Kuleshov demonstrated in these and similar experiments was that in cinema "real" time and space are absolutely subordinate to the process of editing, or *montage*, as the Soviets came to call it, after the French verb *monter*, "to assemble." Furthermore, as Ron Levaco points out, Kuleshov had shown that the associational power of montage was not inherent in the edited film strip itself, but was the result of the viewer's *perception* of the edited film strip, which makes the montage process an act of consciousness for filmmaker and audience alike. Griffith, of course, had been the first to discover the profound psychological impact that editing could have upon an audience, and Soviet filmmakers had distilled many of their theoretical insights from his practice. But Kuleshov's theory of montage went beyond Griffith's editing in a manner described later by his former pupil Sergei Eisenstein: "Griffith's . . . close-ups create atmosphere, outline traits of character, alternate in dialogues of lead-

ing characters, and close-ups of the chaser and the chased speed up the tempo of the chase. But Griffith at all times remains on a level of representation and objectivity and nowhere does he try through the juxtaposition of shots to shape import and image." In other words, for Griffith, editing was primarily a narrative and representational mode. It generally served to advance a plot or tell a tale, and the "metaphorical" style of *Intolerance* was largely an aberration. As a result of their experiments, however— and, paradoxically, of their countless screenings of *Intolerance*—Kuleshov and his pupils conceived of montage as an expressive or symbolic process whereby logically or empirically dissimilar images could be linked together synthetically to produce metaphors (to produce, that is, nonliteral meaning). Building upon this fundamental notion, Eisenstein and Pudovkin, Kuleshov's two most brilliant students, went on to elaborate distinctly individual theories of montage in their own theoretical writings and films. But before this occurred, the Kuleshov Workshop had an opportunity to put its theories into practice.

By 1923, the workshop had secured enough equipment and film stock to begin work upon its first feature film—a parody of American detective thrillers entitled *The Extraordinary Adventures of Mr. West in the Land of the Bolsheviks* (*Neobychainye prikliucheniia Mistera Vesta v strane bolshevikov*, 1924), directed by Kuleshov. *Mr. West* was first and foremost a showcase for the workshop's newly acquired cinematic sophistication, but it was also a very intelligent and amusing satire on popular American misconceptions about the effects of the Bolshevik Revolution. The zany plot concerns an American YMCA president who journeys to Soviet Moscow on business, expecting it to be inhabited by brutes and criminals. Ironically, a street gang (composed of "counterrevolutionary degenerates") does latch on to him and proceeds to act out the kind of horror show that Mr. West has expected to see all along. Just as he is about to pay a sum of money to these extortionists, he is rescued by the state militia and shown the "real" Bolshevik Moscow. The film was an enormous success with Russian audiences, and it remains today a minor classic of silent comedy. The original Kuleshov group made one final feature together, a science-fiction mystery thriller called *The Death Ray* (*Luch smerti*, 1925), directed by Kuleshov and written by Pudovkin. *The Death Ray* was a technically dazzling but ultimately sterile attempt to synthesize material from several popular serials, including the American *Perils of Pauline* series and Feuillade's *Fantômas and Judex*, and it

5.5 *The Extraordinary Adventures of Mr. West in the Land of the Bolsheviks* (Lev Kuleshov, 1924).

came under attack from the Communist party leadership for not being sufficiently ideological.

The workshop broke up in 1925, apparently as a result of these attacks and because Kuleshov's leading actor-assistants got promoted to making their own films, but the following year Kuleshov went on to direct his most widely known film in the West. The feature, *By the Law* (*Dura lex / Po zakonu*, 1926), was sponsored by the newly centralized state cinema trust, Sovkino, which had been established in 1924 to control the film affairs of the entire Soviet Union through government financing.[3] Adapted from Jack London's short story "The Unexpected" with the collaboration of the Formalist critic Viktor Shklovsky (1893–1984), *By the Law* achieved an extraordinary blend of emotional intensity and geometrical stylization on the smallest budget ever allocated for a Soviet feature film. Set almost entirely in a one-room cabin in a desolate region of the Yukon during the winter, it tells the story of two people who are compelled by social conditioning to try, condemn, and execute a third person for the murder of two friends. There are no parallel lines of action and few changes of locale, but Kuleshov achieves an expansion of dramatic space through montage that is remarkable in a film of such narrowly defined scope and that probably influenced the style of Carl-Theodor Dreyer's *La Passion de Jeanne d'Arc* (1928; see pp. 311–

12) two years later. Indeed, the precision and economy of the film are such that one Soviet critic could write on its release, "*By the Law* was worked out in the spirit of an algebraic formula, seeking to obtain the maximum of effect with the minimum of effort." Unfortunately, the film was poorly received by most of the official critics, and Kuleshov's three subsequent silent features were unsuccessful. He made only one sound film of note, *The Great Consoler* (*Velikii uteshitel*, 1933), loosely based on some O. Henry short stories, which he may in fact have intended as an allegory of the plight of Soviet artists under Stalin. Like Vertov, Kuleshov was denounced for "formalist" error at the 1935 Congress of Film Workers and forced to recant much of his earlier work. He continued to make films until 1944, when he was rewarded for his party loyalty by appointment as head of the VGIK, where he taught and lectured until his death in 1970.

Though Kuleshov contributed a number of important films to his country's great cinema, it is as a theorist rather than a practitioner of cinema that he will be most prominently remembered. He was in fact the first practical theorist of the cinema, as Pudovkin recognized when he wrote, in an introduction to Kuleshov's theoretical study *Art of Cinema* in 1929,[4] "We make films—Kuleshov made cinematography." Ron Levaco estimates that more than half of the major Soviet directors since 1920—including Eisenstein, Pudovkin, Boris Barnet, Mikhail Kalatozov, and Sergei Parajanov (see Chapter 17)—had been his students at the Film School at one time or another. His legacy to them and to us is again best articulated by Pudovkin:

---

3. With greater administrative power and a much firmer financial base, Sovkino replaced Goskino, the state distribution monopoly created in 1922 by the Council of People's Commissars. Though Goskino (an acronym for Central State Photo-Cinema Enterprise, often translated as State Committee on Cinematography) lost its distribution authority, it continued to function as a production company until 1930. Sovkino was itself replaced by Soiuzkino (an acronym for All-Union Combine of Cinema-Photo Industries) at the beginning of the industrialization years in 1930, with Stalin's lieutenant Boris Shumiatski as its chairman (see p. 167). In 1963, Goskino was resurrected as the organ for state control of Soviet cinema and attached to the Council of Ministers, USSR. (See Chapter 17.)

4. Between 1917 and 1969, Kuleshov wrote eight books and over seventy essays on film theory and practice. Representative selections are contained in *Kuleshov on Film: Writings by Lev Kuleshov*, trans. and ed. Ronald Levaco (Berkeley: University of California Press, 1974). Technically, the first theorist of the cinema was the academic psychologist Hugo Münsterberg, who wrote *The Photoplay: A Psychological Study* in 1915 and published it in 1916.

All he said was this: "In every art there must be first a material, and secondly, a method of composing this material specifically adapted to this art. . . ." Kuleshov maintained that the material in filmwork consists of pieces of film, and that the method of composing is their joining together in a particular creatively conceived order. He maintained that film-art does not begin when the artists act and the various scenes are shot—this is only the preparation of the material. Film-art begins from the moment when the director begins to combine and join together the various pieces of film. By joining them in various combinations, in different orders, he obtains differing results.

The discovery and articulation of this notion was the enabling act of the Soviet silent cinema and the montage aesthetics upon which it was founded. But it would be wrong to assume, as so many past accounts have done, that the montage idea came solely from the Kuleshov Workshop, or the influence of *Intolerance*, or the economies imposed upon Soviet filmmakers by the scarcity of celluloid. The idea had in fact been very much alive in avant-garde art between 1910 and 1918. As David Bordwell has pointed out, this was the great period of Futurist and Formalist experimentation, and the notion of fragmentation and reassembly as a means of artistic construction was distinctly in the air. Furthermore, the analogies between montage structure and the Marxist historical dialectic are impressive, as we shall see in the works of Sergei Eisenstein.

Sergei Eisenstein

Sergei Mikhailovich Eisenstein (1898–1948) was, with D. W. Griffith, one of the two pioneering geniuses of the modern cinema. Yet, though their syntactical methods were similar and both worked on an epic historical scale, as artists the two men could hardly have been less alike. Griffith was a sentimentalist whose values were typically those of the Victorian middle class. His films were modernist in form, reactionary in feeling; they were seen by millions, and he made too many of them. Eisenstein, by contrast, was a contemporary Marxist intellectual whose vibrantly revolutionary films, while few in number and seen mainly by other intellectuals, left an indelible mark on history and cinema alike. Where Griffith was unschooled

5.6 Sergei Eisenstein seated on the tsar's throne in the Winter Palace during the shooting of *October* (1928).

and instinctive, Eisenstein was a modern Renaissance man whose exaggerated intellectualism and omnivorous knowledge astonished all who knew him. Though he completed only seven films in his twenty-three-year career, the impact of these films and of his theoretical writings on the film form itself has been greater than that of any other body of work in the history of the medium, save Griffith's. Griffith had discovered, in editing, the fundamental narrative structure of the cinema, but he and his followers had used it conservatively to tell nineteenth-century tales. Eisenstein formulated a self-consciously modernist theory of editing, allegedly based on the psychology of perception and the Marxist historical dialectic, which made it possible for the cinema to communicate on its own terms for the first time, without borrowing either matter or form from other media. And, like Griffith, Eisenstein gave the world a handful of films that will always rank among the highest aesthetic achievements of the cinema.

THE FORMATIVE YEARS

Eisenstein was born in Riga, Latvia, in 1898; his father was a well-to-do architect and city engineer. Despite early interests in art and the circus, Eisenstein was sent to the Institute of Civil Engineering in Petrograd, where he was a nineteen-year-old student when the tsarist regime began to crumble in February 1917. The institute immediately disbanded, Eisenstein's parents departed for western Europe, and Eisenstein joined the Red Army as an engineer. After a year of building bridges and fortifications during the civil war, he drifted back toward his natural impulses, working in 1919 as a poster artist on an agit-train and helping to stage amateur theatricals for army troops. Then, through a chance meeting with an old friend, he became first a set designer and then a director for the Moscow Proletkult[5] Theater. The Proletkult concept, with more than two hundred local branches, had been established during the Revolution for the purpose of "replacing the bourgeois culture of tsarist times with a purely proletarian one." When Eisenstein joined Moscow's Proletkult Theater in 1920, it was a virtual clearinghouse for avant-garde experiment and modernist ideas. The world-famous stage director Konstantin Stanislavski (1863–1938) lectured daily on "method" acting here, while the equally prominent director Vsevolod Meyerhold railed against Stanislavski's technique of realistic interpretation and called for an antitraditional theater—a stylized, nonverbal, and popular theater that would use pantomime, acrobatics, Meyerhold's own system of "bio-mechanics," and all the resources of circus spectacle and *commedia dell'arte*[6] to create "a machine for acting." Here too the Futurist poet and playwright Vladimir Maiakovski expounded his radical aesthetic doctrines, the actor-director Mikhail Chekhov lectured on Hindu philosophy and yoga, and weekly seminars were held on Marxism, Freudian psychology, and Pavlovian reflexology.[7]

Eisenstein fell first under the influence of Meyerhold, who had not worked in the cinema again after his two prerevolutionary films; but Eisenstein spoke of him as his "artistic father," much later, after Meyerhold had been discredited and denounced during the Stalin-era purge trials.[8] Meyerhold, for his part, claimed that "all Eisenstein's work had its origins in the laboratory where we once worked together as teacher and pupil." What Eisenstein learned from Meyerhold was, essentially, the possibility of mixing two ostensibly contradictory artistic approaches—that of rigorous systematization and spontaneous improvisation. Under Meyerhold's method for acting, which he called bio-mechanics, spontaneity was

systematically conditioned. According to Peter Wollen, the notion drew upon such varied sources as Pavlovian reflexology, Taylorism (the study of workers' physical movements, invented in America to increase production), the Italian *commedia dell'arte*, the philosophy of pragmatism articulated by William James, the acrobatic Douglas Fairbanks films, the German Romantic puppet theater, and the highly stylized Oriental theater. Eisenstein's encounter with bio-mechanics marked the beginning of his life-long theoretical concern with the psychological effects of the aesthetic experience: specifically, the question of what combination of aesthetic stimuli will produce what responses in the perceiver under what conditions.

Eisenstein's preoccupation with this phenomenon was encouraged by his friend and colleague at the Proletkult Theater, Sergei Iutkevich (1904–1985), who would become a prominent Soviet director during the sound era. It was Iutkevich who involved Eisenstein in designing sets for the Futurist Workshop Theater, run by an expatriate German baron named Foregger, where the use of parodic masks introduced him to the notion of **typage** so

---

5. An acronym for Proletarian Cultural and Educational Organizations. Founded in February 1917 as an independent organization for the production of proletarian culture (the necessary basis, in Bolshevik doctrine, for a socialist revolution), Proletkult became a Soviet government agency after October and was subordinated to the Commissariat of Education. Like many other revolutionary institutions, it was abolished during Stalin's consolidation of power in 1932.

6. A form of drama that originated in sixteenth-century Italy, *commedia dell'arte* employs standard characters (Pantaloon, Harlequin, Columbine), improvised dialogue, and clownish, often slapstick action based on a written script.

7. The science founded by the Nobel Prize-winning physiologist Ivan Pavlov (1849–1936) that interprets all behavior as consisting of simple and complex physiological reflexes.

8. In January 1938, the Meyerhold Theater in Moscow was liquidated for its director's refusal to follow the tenets of "socialist realism" (see p. 167). After publicly denouncing that doctrine at the All-Union Conference of Stage Directors in June 1939, Meyerhold was arrested, and his wife, the actress Zinaida Raikh, was found murdered in their flat. Meyerhold himself was executed in a Moscow prison on February 2, 1940. In spite of the very real danger to himself, Eisenstein remained faithful to Meyerhold, visiting his home frequently during 1938 and 1939, and, according to Edward Braun (*The Theatre of Meyerhold: Revolution on the Modern Stage* [New York: Drama Book Specialists, 1979]), Eisenstein saved Meyerhold's papers and notes by secreting them in the walls of his dacha.

important to his early films, and it was he who later introduced Eisenstein to the FEX group in Petrograd. The Factory of the Eccentric Actor, or FEX, was a Futurist theatrical movement run by Grigori Kozintsev and Leonid Trauberg (later to collaborate as director and scenarist on many important Soviet films of the 1920s and 1930s) that combined elements of the circus, cabaret, and music hall, as well as of American adventure and slapstick comedy films. Eisenstein's contact with the FEX group clearly influenced the form of his first stage production for the Proletkult in 1923, an adaptation of a work by the nineteenth-century dramatist Alexander Ostrovski (1823–1886) entitled *Enough Simplicity in Every Wise Man*, or simply *The Wise Man* (*Mudrets*). Eisenstein took the bare bones of the plot and organized them not into acts or scenes, but into a series of "attractions," as in a circus or cabaret. The stage, in fact, was laid out like a circus arena, with trapezes, tightropes, and parallel bars, and the audience was treated to a long procession of acrobatic acts, satirical sketches, "noise bands" reproducing the sounds of the "new industrial age," and, finally, firecrackers exploding beneath every seat in the house. At one point in the performance, Eisenstein even projected a short film (his first) parodying Dziga Vertov's *Kino-pravda* newsreel. (Appropriately, this film, entitled *Glumov's Diary*, is preserved in Vertov's *Kino-pravda* issue no. 16.)

Eisenstein called this assault on the audience's sensibility the "montage of attractions," and to elaborate the concept he published his first theoretical manifesto in Maiakovski's radical literary journal *Lef*[9] in 1923 (the same issue contained Vertov's first manifesto on the "kino-eye"). Eisenstein wrote that he had long sought a scientific "unit of measurement" for gauging the emotional effects of art and had found it at last in the "attraction":

> [A] roll on the kettledrums as much as Romeo's soliloquy, the cricket on the hearth no less than the cannon fired over the heads of the audience. For all, in their individual ways, bring us to a single idea—from their individual laws to their common quality of *attraction. The attraction . . . is every element that can be verified and mathematically calculated to produce certain emotional shocks.* [original emphasis]

Eisenstein said further that the montage of attractions ("units of impression combined into one whole") could be used to introduce "a new level of tension" into the aesthetic experience that would produce a theater "of such emotional saturation that the wrath of a man would be expressed by a backward somersault from a trapeze." Thus, before he ever attempted to make a serious film, Eisenstein had articulated a rudimentary theory of montage as a process whereby independent and arbitrary units of "attraction" or "impression" were assembled to produce a total emotional effect different from the sum of its parts. As Eisenstein came more and more under the influence of Freud and of Ivan Pavlov, discoverer of the conditioned reflex, he replaced the notion of "attractions" with that of shocks or stimuli, and, as Peter Wollen notes, this dovetailed neatly with his Marxist concern for the agitational aspects of his work.

Eisenstein's next effort for the Proletkult was a production of *Do You Hear, Moscow!* (*Slyshis', Moskva!*), Sergei Tretiakov's play about recent revolutionary events in Bavaria, which Eisenstein termed **"agit-Guignol."** Like *The Wise Man*, it had many cinematic elements, including a device for shifting the spectators' attention rapidly from one focal point on stage to another. As Yon Barna points out in his critical biography, *Eisenstein*, it was becoming apparent that Eisenstein had approached the limits of what he could achieve in the theater by cinematic means, and the cinema itself was exerting increasing appeal for him. In his last theatrical production for the Proletkult, however, Eisenstein went even further afield in his effort to produce a chain of aesthetic shock effects by staging Tretiakov's agitational play *Gas Masks* (*Protivogazy*) in the Moscow gasworks. The audience sat on benches amidst the machinery and the grand finale was the arrival of the actual night-shift workers to light their gas jets as the actors departed. The play was not a success because the actors were dwarfed by the machinery, but the failure convinced Eisenstein that the theatrical form—however stylized, modernized, or revolutionized—could no longer contain his developing

---

9. Published by a group calling itself LEF, an acronym for Left Front [of the Arts]. The LEF group opposed idealist conceptions of art as the product of bourgeois culture. Specifically, it rejected passive realism, subjectivism, and "psychologism" in art in favor of what Maiakovski called "social command," or "straightforward agitation which molds life and custom according to a plan." (See Dave Laing, ed., *Marxist Theory of Art* [Atlantic Highlands, N.J.: Humanities Press, 1978], pp. 30–34.) With Stalin's ascension in the late 1920s, LEF was dissolved, and its ideas were officially censured for "formalist" deviation.

notions of montage. As he had written in *Lef* in 1923, with characteristic overstatement: "The theater as an independent unit within a revolutionary framework . . . is out of the question. It is absurd to perfect a wooden plough; you must order a tractor."

FROM THEATER TO FILM

The "tractor" was ordered for Eisenstein by the Proletkult Theater when in early 1924 it decided to sponsor a series of eight films, to be collectively entitled *Toward the Dictatorship of the Proletariat* (*K diktature proletariata*), which would trace the rise of the Communist party from the late nineteenth century through 1917. One of the scripts was being written by Valeri Pletnyov, director of the Proletkult, and he invited Eisenstein to collaborate with him on the project, which ultimately became the Proletkult-Goskino production *Strike* (*Stachka*, 1924; released 1925), Eisenstein's directorial debut. *Strike* was intended as the fifth film in the series, but it was the first and only one to be made since, according to Eisenstein, it contained "the most mass action" and was therefore "the most significant." Between 1920 and 1924, Eisenstein had seen countless German Expressionist and American films in Moscow, including the major works of Griffith,[1] and had apprenticed himself for several weeks in March 1923 to his friend Esther Shub (1894–1959), the skillful *agitki* editor and, later, director of Goskino documentaries, when she was re-editing a print of Fritz Lang's two-part *Dr. Mabuse, der Spieler* (p. 98) for general release in Moscow as the single feature *Gilded Putrefaction* (*Pozolochennai gnil*).[2] He also attended the Kuleshov Workshop at the VGIK for three months in the winter of 1922–23. But, in fact, Eisenstein knew very little about the technical aspects of filmmaking when he began to work on *Strike*. Nevertheless, like Griffith, Eisenstein quickly apprenticed himself to the very best cinematographer at the Goskino studios, Eduard Tisse (1897–1961), and inaugurated a lifelong artistic collaboration whose importance is equaled only by the Griffith-Bitzer association. Yet even before he had learned how to use Goskino's technical equipment, Eisenstein undertook an exhaustive program of research into his subject from which he produced a minutely detailed scenario.

In it, Eisenstein conceived his film as a revolutionary assault upon the "bourgeois cinema"—i.e., the narrative cinema as practiced in the West thus far. To this end,

5.7 *Strike:* local criminals hired as strikebreakers emerge from hiding to receive instructions from the police.

though all sequences were shot against natural backgrounds, the strike of the title was itself made typical and representative rather than historical. Furthermore, Eisenstein abandoned the traditional individual hero for a collective one—his film's aggregate protagonist was the striking workers in their struggle against the brutal and oppressive factory system, and no single one of them was

1. Eisenstein later wrote that Griffith had played "a massive role in the development of montage in the Soviet film," concluding that "all that is best in the Soviet cinema has its origins in *Intolerance*" (quoted in Yon Barna, *Eisenstein* [Boston: Little, Brown, 1973], p. 74). Indeed, several scholars have recently argued that the Modern story of *Intolerance* provided the inspiration for Eisenstein's *Strike*.

2. Shub transformed the concluding battle between Mabuse and the police into a class-inspired street rebellion.

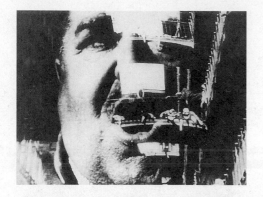

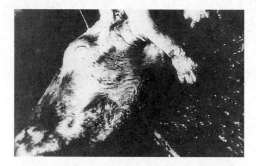

5.8 *Strike:* **the police chief (lap-dissolved with the workers' tenement) orders the final slaughter.**

shown to be more socially valuable or thematically significant than another. Finally, in an effort to forge an "unbreakable link" between the Marxist dialectic and cinematic form, Eisenstein planned the entire film as an extended montage of "attractions" or "shock stimuli" that would agitate the audience into identification with the striking workers. In the completed film, as in his theater productions, some of Eisenstein's "attractions" are mere tricks designed to seize the audience's attention in the most direct and forceful manner, but much of the time he was engaged in creating uniquely cinematic metaphors through the juxtaposition of two (or more) images to suggest a meaning different from and greater than what each image suggests separately. He was engaged, that is, in practicing the first stage of the highly complex and sophisticated montage process on which his greatest films are built.

Although it contains many grotesque and circuslike elements from Eisenstein's theater days, Strike evolves in a nonnarrative chronicle form that was clearly influenced by Vertov's doctrine of the "kino-eye" (though, to underscore the agitational aspect of his work, Eisenstein would later say, "I don't believe in the [kino]-eye; I believe in the [kino]-fist") and the editing experiments of Kuleshov. The film opens with a montage of smokestacks, industrial machinery, evil factory owners, and noble but horribly oppressed workers. We soon discover that the workers are planning a strike and that the management has hired *agents provocateurs* and informers to infiltrate their ranks. After a worker's suicide triggers the strike, the factory is temporarily shut down and the strikers enjoy the first leisure they have known in their lives—but only briefly, for their grievances are ignored by the owners, who finally resolve to break the strike by violent means. The police are enlisted to "interrogate" strike leaders and to stage provocations with the help of local criminals, but the workers refuse to be intimidated despite counterinsurgency and a general famine among them. Frustrated with intrigue, the police chief orders an armed invasion of the workers' apartments and the massacre of all strikers and their families. The famous concluding montage intercuts graphic footage of this atrocity with shots of cattle being slaughtered in an abattoir, and the film ends with a long shot of the ground before the apartment block littered with the bodies of hundreds of adults and children.

Strike was the first revolutionary mass film of the new Soviet state, and, although some critics accused it of formalism, its agitational impact upon the few who saw it was great (Eisenstein himself, with characteristic immodesty, proclaimed it "the October of the cinema").[3] More important, however, *Strike* inaugurated the classic period of Soviet silent cinema at a time when the silent cinemas of the West had nearly reached their peaks. In the United States by 1924, D. W. Griffith had already produced his greatest work, and Griffith, Erich von Stroheim, Robert Flaherty, Charlie Chaplin, and Buster Keaton were all at work on major films (*America, Greed, Moana, The Gold Rush,* and *Sherlock Jr.,* respectively). The German cinema was passing from Expressionism to the "new realism" with F. W. Murnau's *Der letzte Mann* (1924), and the careers of Murnau, Ernst Lubitsch, and Fritz Lang were flourishing. In France, the avant-garde cinema had reached its height with the films of Germaine Dulac, Louis Delluc, Jean Epstein, Marcel L'Herbier, Jacques Feyder, and René Clair (Clair's influential *Entr'acte* and Fernand Léger's famous *Ballet mécanique* both appeared in 1924). The Italian silent cinema had peaked with its series of prewar superspectacles and had declined long before 1924, but in Sweden the silent film was still enjoying the twilight of its great masters, Victor Sjöström (*The Phantom Chariot,* 1921) and Mauritz Stiller (*The Saga of Gösta Berling,* 1924). Thus, Soviet silent cinema was a latecomer compared to the silent cinemas of the West, in large part because of the socioeconomic chaos created by the 1917 Revolution and the civil war. But by 1924, though raw film stock and equipment were still in scant supply, the means of film distribution had once more been stabilized and all prerevolutionary cinema theaters (some 2,500 of them) had been reopened: the Soviet film industry was at last prepared to embark upon a period of creative growth.

THE PRODUCTION OF *BATTLESHIP POTEMKIN*

The year 1925 was the twentieth anniversary of the abortive 1905 Revolution against tsarism, and the Jubilee Committee decided to sponsor a series of films to commemorate it. On the basis of *Strike,* Eisenstein was selected to direct the keynote film, *Year 1905 (1905 God),* which was to provide a historical panorama of the entire uprising from the Russo-Japanese War in January to the crushing of the armed rebellion in Moscow in December. Eisenstein and Nina Agajanova-Shutko (1889–1974), a professional agitator who had actively participated in the 1905 revolt, collaborated on a hundred-page scenario covering dozens of events that had taken place in at least thirty separate locations from Moscow to Siberia to the Caucasus. Shooting began in Leningrad in June 1925, and bad weather prevented completion of this "northern" episode. Sticking to the shooting schedule, however, Eisenstein's company moved south for sunnier (and therefore better-lit) locations. Eisenstein took his crew first to Baku and then to the port of Odessa, on the Black Sea, where a short sequence of forty-two shots was to be made representing the mutiny of the tsarist battleship *Potemkin* and its bloody aftermath. When Eisenstein arrived in Odessa, however, he became obsessed with the cinematic possibilities of the vast flight of marble steps leading down to the city's harbor, where Cossacks had massacred citizens supporting the mutineers. Having failed to finish the earlier "northern" episodes, and facing a mid-December deadline for a completed film, he made the fateful decision to limit his treatment of the Revolution to this single representative episode.

Battleship Potemkin (*Bronenosets Potyomkin,* 1925), the film that emerged, has been called the most perfect and concise example of film structure in the history of the cinema. With *The Birth of a Nation* (1915) and *Citizen Kane* (1941), *Potemkin* is clearly one of the most important and influential films ever made, and its montage represents a quantum leap from the relatively simple juxtapositions of *Strike.* Indeed, Eisenstein created a completely new editing technique merely foreshadowed in his first film—one based upon psychological stimulation rather than narrative logic, which managed to communicate physical and emotional sensation directly to the audience. Furthermore, the film's revolutionary impact inaugurated a whole new school of filmmaking and brought international prestige to the young Soviet cinema at a time when it was sorely needed.

---

3. Though *Strike* was not exported for commercial distribution, the film's distinctiveness was recognized abroad when it won a major prize at the Exposition des Arts Décoratifs in Paris in 1925.

5.9 A revolutionary poster for *Battleship Potemkin* (Sergei Eisenstein, 1925), designed by Rodchenko.

Potemkin took ten weeks to shoot (the Odessa steps sequence was finished in seven days) and two weeks to edit, and, contrary to the prevailing mythology, its montage was *not* constructed according to some carefully pre-arranged and systematic plan. Eisenstein himself lent credence to this notion through his intricate structural analyses of the film in his later theoretical writings, but the truth is that, like *The Birth of a Nation* and *Citizen Kane, Potemkin* was less a matter of careful planning than an intense release of creative energy. The completed version of the film ran 86 minutes at silent speed (16 fps) and contained 1,346 shots—a remarkably high number when we consider that the released version of *The Birth of a Nation*, with a running time of 195 minutes, contained only 1,375 shots, or that the average American film of 1925 ran 90 minutes and contained approximately 600 shots. Clearly, the most important aspect of *Potemkin* is its editing, but it would be wrong to assume that Eisenstein's interest in montage caused him to neglect the pictorial or compositional aspects of his film. In fact, Eisenstein composed every single frame of *Potemkin* with a painter's eye for the distribution of light, mass, and geometric design (the triangle, circle, and diagonal intersection were his basic visual motifs).

Nevertheless, the film Eisenstein created from these beautifully composed frames was first and foremost a political film intended to possess the broadest possible audience appeal. Though *Potemkin* is hardly the "efficiently engineered political cartoon" that one contemporary critic has called it, the film *is* intensely manipulative

of audience response. Furthermore, though Eisenstein, like Griffith, was obsessed with the accuracy of historical detail in his work (to the extent of interviewing large numbers of survivors of the *Potemkin* mutiny and the Odessa massacre), he was also, like Griffith, wholly capable of distorting historical events to suit a specific set of ideological assumptions. Soviet "realism" was at its root a popular ideological cinema whose announced purpose was primarily agitational and didactic. It was, in other words, a cinema of political propaganda and indoctrination. That Eisenstein so often yielded to this tendency should not surprise us since he was at the time a committed Marxist whose filmmaking activity was completely subsidized by and dependent upon the state. Rather, it should surprise us that he so consistently and gloriously managed to transcend it.

THE STRUCTURE OF *POTEMKIN*

Like *Strike, Potemkin* is a drama of mass action with a collective hero, and it was shot entirely with nonactors against naturalistic backgrounds. (According to Eisenstein's theory of typage, actors were important not as individuals, but as "types"—elements within the composition of the frame that acquire meaning only through montage. He also used typage to represent general characteristics or types of people; the types are like masks since viewers will know what the actors are meant to embody when they see them.) Of its recognizably documentary surface Eisenstein would later write, "*Potemkin* looks like a chronicle or newsreel of an event, but it functions as a drama." Indeed, unlike its relatively formless predecessor, *Potemkin* is divided into five movements or acts whose structural symmetry is very nearly perfect.[4] The first act, entitled "Men and Maggots," begins with an image of natural turbulence as large waves break violently over an anonymous harbor jetty, creating a metaphor for the social tumult we are soon to witness aboard the battleship. A title quoting Lenin ("Revolution is the only lawful, equal, effectual war. It was in Russia that this war was

---

4. Tragically, *Potemkin* was Eisenstein's last silent film to be completed as he intended. He was forced to revise both *October* (*Ten Days That Shook the World*, 1928) and *Old and New* (original title: *The General Line*, 1929) as a result of political pressure.

declared and begun")[5] introduces us to a night of unrest aboard the *Potemkin* at sea, during which a petty officer beats a sleeping sailor in random anger, and Seaman Vakulinchuk (played by Alexander Antonov [1898–1962], one of the regular "types" from Eisenstein's stock company from the Proletkult Theater) urges his comrades to join their striking brothers on the shore and rise against tsarist oppression.

In the morning, the situation worsens as sailors on deck gather angrily around a maggot-ridden piece of meat intended for their consumption. Led by Vakulinchuk, they protest, "We have had enough of rotten meat," but the supercilious ship's surgeon, Dr. Smirnov, soon arrives to inspect the infested carrion through his pince-nez and, as the screen fills with a close-up of the swarming maggots, proclaims them to be "merely dead fly eggs that will wash off with salt water." Dispersed by senior officers, the outraged sailors go about their duties until the call for midday meal, which most refuse to eat. The ship's officers are furious, but their anger is purely institutional. The anger of the sailors, on the other hand, is deep and real, as we see from the scene that concludes this section of the film. A young sailor, washing dishes from the officers' mess, suddenly realizes that the plate in his hands bears the hypocritical inscription "Give us this day our daily bread." In a fit of rage that defies the laws of empirical time and space, he smashes this same plate against the table not once but *twice* in a four-second montage sequence that joins together nine separate but overlapping shots of the uncompleted action, ranging in length from one-quarter to three-quarters of a second, in order to emphasize the extreme violence of the sailor's response. By creating a cinematic metaphor for impotent fury erupting into violent action, this sequence leads us into *Potemkin*'s second movement, "Drama on the Quarterdeck."

This section opens with an assembly of officers and crew on the open quarterdeck of the battleship. Commander Golikov, the ship's captain, orders, "Those satisfied with the food . . . two paces forward," and only a handful of petty officers obey. Enraged, Golikov threatens the mass execution of all protesters and calls up the Marines to carry out punishment. Seaman Matiushenko breaks ranks and successfully rallies most of the men to the gun turret as the Marines arrive on deck, but several remain in the prow, where they are covered with a tarpaulin by officers in preparation for the firing squad. Group shots are juxtaposed with extreme close-ups as the

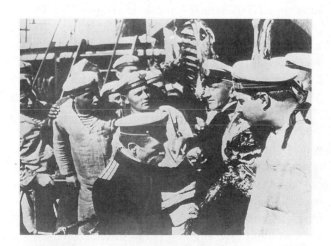

5.10 The rotting meat.

5. According to Steven P. Hill ("The Strange Case of the Vanishing Epigraphs," in *The Battleship Potemkin: The Greatest Film Ever Made*, ed. Herbert Marshall [New York: Avon, 1978], pp. 74–86), the film's original epigraph was derived from Leon Trotski's widely read, and contextually more appropriate, history of the 1905 Revolution: "The spirit of insurrection hovered over the Russian land. Some enormous and mysterious process was taking place in countless hearts. The individual was dissolving in the mass, and the mass was dissolving in the outburst." These words were replaced by Lenin's in all circulating prints of *Potemkin* sometime after Trotski's fall from grace in 1927. Hill provides a detailed analysis of the various available prints of the film and concludes that, while none is entirely complete with regard to intertitles, the MoMA print used by David Mayer for his shot-by-shot presentation (*Sergei M. Eisenstein's "Potemkin": A Shot-by-Shot Presentation* [New York: Grossman, 1972]) and for my discussion has the greatest visual and structural fidelity to the original negative.

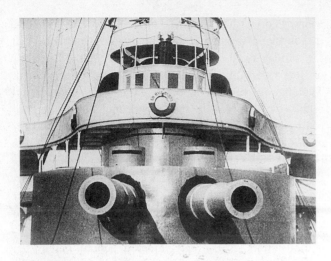

5.11 Tsarist might: the firing squad.

situation becomes increasingly tense: the sailors massed around the gun turret are anxious about their comrades, the officers become nervous about their own safety, and the Marines show signs of reluctance to carry out their orders. The ship's priest, a white-bearded Russian Ortho-dox monk, appears from below, pompously praying for the condemned as the order is given to fire. The squad hesitates, and the priest begins to count off the seconds by tapping his palm with a crucifix. In a much-quoted sequence, Eisenstein intercuts a close shot of this action with another of a junior officer nervously stroking the hilt of his sword, suggesting the unholy alliance that existed between Church and State in tsarist Russia.

The sailors under the tarpaulin fall to their knees in terror, and a second order is given to fire. Suddenly Vak-ulinchuk cries out from the gun turret: "Brothers! Do you realize who you are shooting?" The rifles waver, and one after another the Marines lower their arms. It is important to note that although the incidents that occur between the mustering of the Marines and their refusal to fire on their shipmates would take only a few seconds in empirical real-ity, they last nearly three full minutes on the screen. Like Griffith and those who came after him, Eisenstein fre-quently used editing to compress time for the sake of nar-rative economy, but here and in the fourth section of *Potemkin,* "The Odessa Steps," he employs editing to *expand* time in order to create certain aesthetic and emo-tional effects. In "Drama on the Quarterdeck," by render-ing the events just described into fifty-seven separate shots of varying temporal and spatial lengths, Eisenstein draws out the Marines' moment of decision for what seems an eternity, generating maximum psychological tension in the audience and achieving a highly expressive effect. After the firing squad has balked, the senior officer (played by Grigori Alexandrov) continues to scream the order to shoot, but it is too late: the mutiny has begun.

The quarterdeck is suddenly swarming with confusion. Sailors attack the officers and beat them to their knees. The melee spreads rapidly through the entire ship, as one by one the symbols of tsarist tyranny are chased down and killed by the crew. The old priest is knocked through a hatchway, and his fallen crucifix sticks upright in the wood of the deck like the instrument of oppression to which it has been recently compared. The ship's surgeon is dragged from his hiding place and thrown overboard, raising an eddy of white foam on the dark surface of the ocean. Eisenstein cuts abruptly to a close-up of white maggots swarming on a dark field of meat and follows it with another of the surgeon's pince-nez dangling pathet-ically from the riggings where he has gone over, remind-ing us of the gross moral indifference that produced the mutiny. The bloodshed on deck continues until finally the cry goes up: "Comrades! The ship is in our hands!" But in another part of the ship a brutal senior officer has cor-nered Vakulinchuk, leader of the rebellion, and shot him in the head. As the sailor topples from the yardarm, he is caught in a cradle of ropes and hangs suspended above the water as though crucified. Vakulinchuk's body is care-fully recovered and given a martyr's funeral by his com-rades. That evening a launch bearing the dead hero's corpse and attended by an honor guard of seamen steams slowly toward the port of Odessa. There, in a tent at the

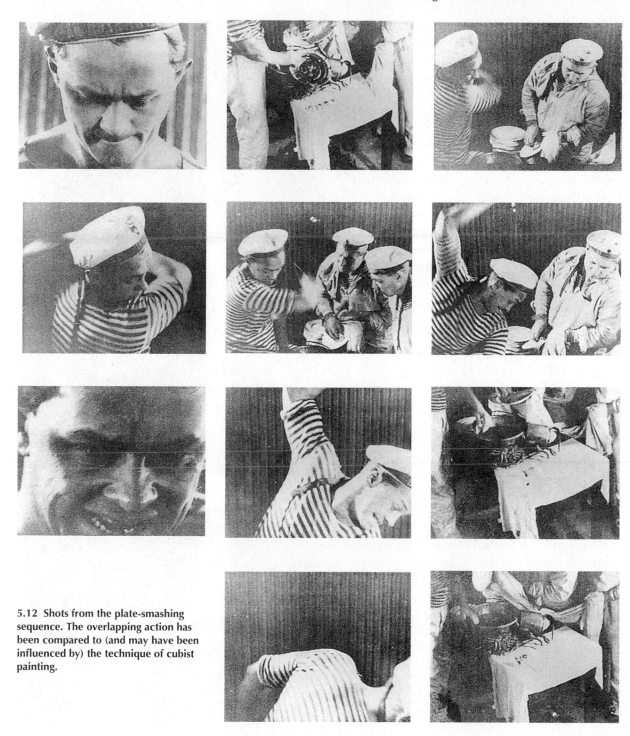

5.12 Shots from the plate-smashing sequence. The overlapping action has been compared to (and may have been influenced by) the technique of cubist painting.

end of the quay, Vakulinchuk's remains come to lie in
state, an inspirational symbol of the revolution for which
he perished. A mood of somber calm prevails as night
descends on both the harbor and the bier.

This mood is sustained through the famous "fog montage" that opens the third section of the film, "An Appeal
from the Dead." In it, Eisenstein joins together a sequence
of shots depicting various aspects of the harbor just before
daybreak—sailing vessels and steamships at anchor, a
gull-covered buoy, dockside cranes, Vakulinchuk's tent
outlined against the sky—each of which grows progressively lighter as the sun rises and gradually disperses the
thick Odessa fog. By the end of this lyrical sequence,
dawn has fully broken, and the harbor resumes its normal
waking activity. Now the tent begins to attract attention.
At first only a handful of Odessa's citizens come to pay
homage to the fallen hero, but as the day grows lighter a
large procession of mourners starts to descend the steps
to the quay and file past the bier. Soon the crowd has
grown into a vast, classless multitude that surges excitedly
toward the quay from all quarters of the city.

At this point, Eisenstein begins to intercut extreme
close-ups of individual mourners with long shots of the
masses as they stream endlessly across the breakwater
and swarm about the tent, the tempo of the cutting
increasing with the anger of the crowd as agitators begin
to harangue it. Suddenly, to a student's cry of "Down with
the executioners!" a supercilious bourgeois responds,
"Down with the Jews!" Heads turn in unison; a paroxysm
of violent emotion grips the crowd, and the bourgeois is
beaten to the ground. In Odessa, the masses continue to
surge convulsively across and under a huge stone viaduct
toward the quay, where raised fists now bristle into the
sky in a show of solidarity. A delegation of workers from
the shore arrives on the quarterdeck of the battleship to
assure the mutineers of their support. As one of the delegates proclaims his mission from the bridge of the ship,
a large flag is raised on the mainmast, to the jubilant
cheers of both the sailors and the masses assembled on
the quay. (In the original release prints of *Potemkin*, this
revolutionary flag was actually hand-tinted bright red at
the end of the film.)

The fourth section of *Potemkin*, "The Odessa Steps,"
is constructed around what is probably the single greatest and most influential montage sequence in the history
of the cinema—that depicting the massacre of the
Odessa citizens by tsarist troops on the stone steps lead-

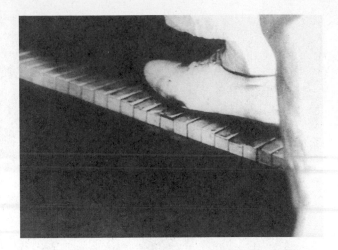

5.13 Mutiny: crushing the symbols of oppression.

ing down to the harbor. This was the incident that had gripped Eisenstein's imagination from the outset of the production, for he saw it as a virtual paradigm of tsarist treachery, brutality, and oppression. Part Four begins on the same joyful note of solidarity with which Part Three concluded, as dozens of yawls sail out to the battleship from Odessa, laden with food and supplies for the mutineers. Townspeople are massed along the quay, shouting encouragement to the men on the ship and cheering on the yawls. Close-ups reveal individuals in the crowd who will later figure prominently in the mass action of the massacre—a white-bloused woman with dark bobbed hair, accompanied by a bearded man in black; a well-dressed elderly woman wearing pince-nez, with her arm about a schoolgirl; an ardent young student in wire-rimmed glasses.

As they approach the *Potemkin* at anchor, the yawls are seen as photographed from a launch moving with them across the bay. One by one, the sailboats overtake the camera and glide past it toward the battleship, where cheering sailors greet the boatmen and help the gift-bearing civilians on board. On shore, the inhabitants of Odessa watch this fraternal encounter from the harbor steps and signal their enthusiastic support by waving. On the deck of the battleship, civilians and sailors embrace. The townspeople on the steps continue to wave and cheer en masse, and Eisenstein again cuts to close shots of individual members of the crowd. We see the old woman in pince-nez once more, an elegantly attired lady with an open white parasol, a legless child—premonitory of the horror soon to come—who scoots along the steps with one hand and hails the ship with the other, a young mother directing her son's attention toward the anchored ship and urging him to wave, two children held up above the crowd by adult hands to get a better view.

Then, a single, sinister title—"Suddenly"—and a chilling close shot of a row of jackbooted feet stepping in perfect unison onto the first flight of stone stairs. The dark bobbed hair of the woman in white (played by Alexandrov's wife, Olga Ivanova) fills the screen from one edge of the frame to the other and jerks backward so violently that the image is blurred by the motion. Through a series of **jump cuts** that abruptly eliminates the forward return, she yanks her head back again and again in utter horror at what she sees—which, however, Eisenstein doesn't permit the audience to see yet. The cripple leaps wildly on his hands down the steep balustrades that flank the steps,

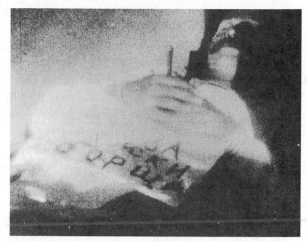

5.14 Vakulinchuk on his bier. The hand-lettered sign reads: "For a spoonful of soup."

and the lady with the open parasol dashes madly into the camera, filling the entire screen with its white, beribboned fabric. Eisenstein pulls back to a long shot from below of townspeople scrambling pell-mell down the vast sweep of the stairs, and then reverses the angle to show the object of their terror from above: at the top of the stairs, a line of white-jacketed troops carrying rifles with fixed bayonets has started its murderous descent. Another long shot from below of townspeople pouring down the stairs, and the slaughter begins.

Eisenstein cuts to close shots of knees buckling, of bodies falling through the air and sprawling across the steps in heaps. Now a second line of troops has appeared and begun its descent, and the camera starts to track laterally down the side of the steps with the escaping civilians. When the militiamen fire downward into the fleeing mass, the small boy we have seen earlier on the quay falls wounded. His mother screams in horror as he is trampled by the stampeding crowd: her face and then her eyes in extreme close-up fill the screen. She gathers his body into her arms to march up the corpse-littered steps against both the downward flight of the masses and the inexorable advance of the troops. Meanwhile, the woman in pince-nez, who has sought refuge with several others behind a parapet, decides to appeal to the troops. Now two groups are moving up the death-strewn stairs in opposition to the troops—the enraged mother with her dead son, screaming at the troops in anguish, and the woman in pince-nez and her followers, who attempt to supplicate them. The camera moves up the steps with both groups, and the troops move rhythmically and irresistibly down. The mother with the child stops on a landing so close to the bristling rifles of the troops that their shadows fall upon her. There is a pause as she madly entreats the soldiers to help her son. Instead they fire, she falls with her son, and the troops sweep calmly over their bodies. At the bottom of the steps, more horror: saber-slashing Cossack horsemen appear from nowhere and charge into the crowd as it reaches the quay, cutting off the only line of escape. On the steps, volley after volley is fired into the crowd, and the long line of troops continues its implacable, orderly descent, in complete contrast to the chaotic flight of the masses below.

Now Eisenstein begins the tour de force of his sequence, cutting to yet another young mother as she pushes her baby's carriage hurriedly across a landing in advance of the firing troops. Fleeing civilians rush past her, jolting the carriage, which she is clearly afraid to push down the next steep flight of steps. Above her, the troops march relentlessly on. Trapped between them and the steps, she hesitates and screams. We see a line of jack-boots in close shot slowly descend the stairs and then a line of rifles against the sky erupting into smoke. The mother's head sways back in close-up; another close shot shows the wheels of the baby carriage teetering on the edge of the steps. The mother's white-gloved hands clutch the silver buckle of her belt, while on the quay below we see people being trampled, slashed, and beaten indiscriminately by Cossacks. Now a close-up returns us to the mother as blood begins to drip over her gloves and belt. Her body starts to sway forward and sink slowly off-screen. Behind her, the baby in the carriage reaches into the air; before her, the troops continue their measured cadence down the stairs. Slowly, the mother sways back against the carriage and pushes it offscreen. From a lower level of the steps, the woman in pince-nez screams in horror as the rear wheels of the carriage roll over the edge of the landing and the steps. Now, through a series of quick cuts, we see the carriage bounce its way unevenly down the stairs past the dead and wounded, slowly at first, then with gathering speed. The camera moves with it from the side, as Eisenstein intercuts its fatal progress with medium shots from above of the baby jostling violently inside and with close reaction shots of the horror-stricken woman in pince-nez and the student with wire-rimmed glasses. On the steps above the carriage, we see a line of soldiers from the waist down firing their bayoneted rifles into a heap of supplicating wounded. Below, the student screams as the carriage fairly leaps across the steps, then suddenly tilts and flips end over end.[6]

The wrenching "agit-Guignol" of the massacre ends as it began, with a series of violent jump cuts. On the quay below, we see a ferocious young Cossack slash his saber down again and again in a series of four discontinuous close shots—some no longer than a few frames apiece—that eliminate his backward strokes and intensify the shocking violence of his action. Then Eisenstein cuts to the object of this murderous assault in the final shot of the massacre sequence—a close-up of the elderly woman in pince-nez beneath whose shattered glasses blood spurts from a slashed and blinded eye.

In the harbor, the muzzles of the *Potemkin*'s two huge turret guns swing slowly into the camera. A title informs us: "The brutal military power answered by the guns of the battleship. . . ." Onshore, the decorative stone sculpture of the Odessa Theater, headquarters of the tsarist generals, stands silhouetted against the sky. White smoke erupts from the *Potemkin*'s battle cannon, and Eisenstein cuts again to the sculptured parapet of the theater. Then, from several angles, we see the ornamental iron gate and heavy stone columns of the theater burst asunder and topple in a billowing cloud of debris and smoke. Finally, in a brief but justly famous three-shot montage sequence, a sculptured stone lion rises from his sleep and roars, symbolizing the outrage of the Russian people at the atrocity just committed on the steps and their awakening anger against the regime that perpetrated it. The shots, of course, are of three separate stone lions posed in three separate positions and actually located near Yalta, far from Odessa, but by joining them together in the manner of Kuleshov's "creative geography" to create the illusion of a continuous action impossible in empirical reality, Eisenstein generates a cinematic metaphor for rage much more

---

6. This part of the Odessa-steps sequence is clumsily recreated in Brian De Palma's American gangster film *The Untouchables* (1987), in the context of a shoot-out on the steps of a train station; in this case, the baby—but not the film—survives.

5.15 The gathering on the quay. Accelerated intercutting of extreme long shots and close-ups produces agitational frenzy on the screen, but compositional continuity is preserved in the geometrical motifs that dominate the individual shots—here, as throughout the film, the circle, the triangle, and the diagonal intersection.

5.16 **Shot sequence from the Odessa-steps massacre (continues through page 145).**

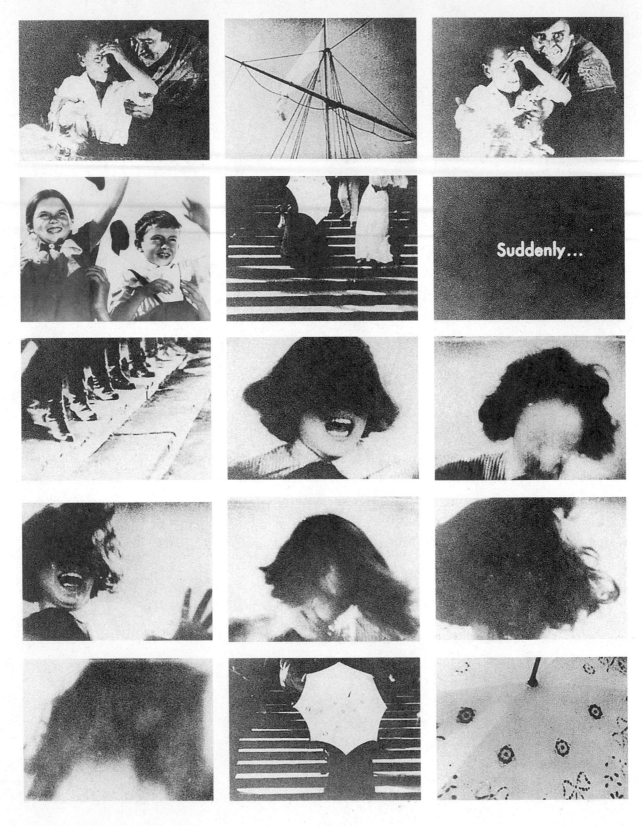

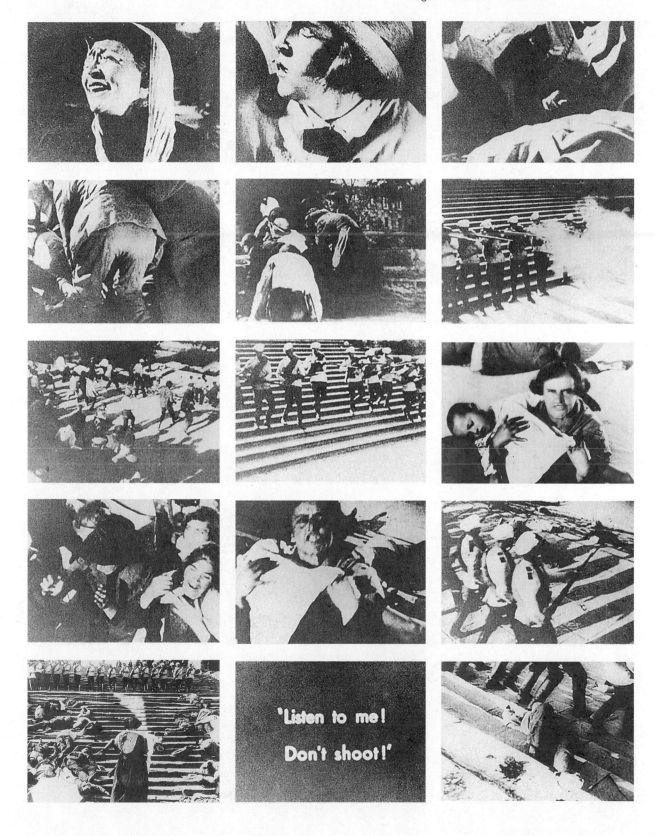

forcefully and economically than he could have done in a straightforward narrative sequence.[7]

Eisenstein created another cinematic metaphor in the timing of the massacre sequence itself. Even though the rate of the cutting in this sequence is terrifically accelerated (the average shot length is fifty-two frames, or just over two seconds, as opposed to eighty-eight frames, or nearly four seconds, for the rest of the film), it takes much longer for the massacre to occur on the screen than it would take in actuality. This is because Eisenstein wished to suggest a *psychological* duration for the horrible event that far exceeded its precise chronological duration. As Arthur Knight writes, "Eisenstein realized that for the people trapped on the steps these would be the most terrifying (and, for many, the final) moments of their lives." By drawing out, through the montage process, the time it would normally take for the militiamen and their victims to reach the bottom of the stairs, Eisenstein manages to suggest destruction of a much greater magnitude than we actually witness on the screen, just as at the end of Part One he had suggested the black rage of the oppressed seamen by drawing out the time it takes the sailor to smash the officer's plate.

Part Five of *Potemkin*, "Meeting the Squadron," is both literally and aesthetically anticlimactic after the dynamic, emotionally draining Odessa-steps sequence. It begins with a contentious shipboard meeting in which the citizens of Odessa urge the sailors to land and join forces with the army in rebellion against the tsar. But it is learned that the Admiralty squadron has been sent out against the *Potemkin*, and the sailors vote unanimously to face it at sea. Here Eisenstein cuts to the empty deck of the battleship some time later, and a title tells us: "A night of anxiety begins." Now a montage of sixty-eight shots evokes the calm that precedes the storm. From a variety of camera angles we see the ship at anchor in the moonlight, the watch moving slowly about the deck, a searchlight directed on the water, the motionless needles of the pressure gauges in the engine room, and sailors sleeping fitfully belowdecks. Meanwhile, the squadron creeps up stealthily in the darkness. At last, a seaman with a telescope spots the squadron on the horizon and sounds the alarm. Agitated sailors leap from their berths and assume

7. This was Eisenstein's interpretation, at any rate. The sequence could equally be read to signify the rigid reflex of the imperial regime in the face of the uprising or as a blatantly Pavlovian incitement to fury in the agitprop vein since Eisenstein's montage frequently allowed for more ambiguity of meaning than he claimed. In this particular case, however, the stone lions have a historically specific frame of reference that makes their meaning unmistakable: they are taken from the Lion Steps of the Palace Museum of Alupka, a Crimean city on the Black Sea, which was designated as a "Monument to the Victims of the Civil War" by the Bolsheviks in 1921. (See Victor and Jennifer Louis, *The Complete Guide to the Soviet Union* [New York: St. Martin's, 1991], pp. 665–66.)

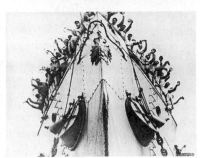

across a brief expanse of sea, and the intent faces of sailors peer forth from the gun turrets in a painfully drawn-out agony of suspense. Suddenly, one of them smiles, and a title exclaims, "Brothers!" The faces of elated seamen crowd the screen. The *Potemkin*'s deserted quarterdeck begins to swarm with cheering, laughing sailors. The ship's cannons are lowered as the tsarist ships, their decks packed with friendly, cap-waving sailors, steam past within a thousand yards. A title reads: "Over the heads of the tsarist admirals roared a brotherly cheer. . . ." Without a shot being fired, the *Potemkin* is allowed to pass unmolested through the ranks of the fleet. Caps fly in the air, and shots from all angles show the jubilant mutineers crowding the decks of their ship. The flag, not tinted red, flutters victoriously above them, and from the waterline we see the *Potemkin*'s giant prow steam straight into the camera and seemingly break through the frame in enormous close-up as it carries its crew to safety and freedom.

their battle stations. The cannons are loaded with heavy shells. A title appears—"Full speed ahead"—and yet another breathless montage sequence begins.

At an ever-increasing tempo Eisenstein intercuts close shots of the churning pistons, rotating camshafts, and plunging piston heads of the powerful ship's engines with Matiushenko giving orders from the bridge, the ship's funnels belching smoke, the *Potemkin* itself cutting rapidly through the waves, and the port cannons seeking the range of the squadron, which has begun to mass on the horizon. As the *Potemkin* draws closer and closer to the squadron, Eisenstein increases the tension by accelerating the cutting rate to fever pitch. Suddenly the sequence is augmented by shots of two large battleships bearing down on the *Potemkin*. The *Potemkin*'s cannon swing slowly toward them as they steam into firing range. From the bridge, Matiushenko orders the semaphorist to run up the signal "Don't fight—join us." Billowing signal flags are now injected into the sequence, as the fleet remains mute, drawing ever nearer. The *Potemkin*'s gigantic cannon stretch diagonally across the screen, outlined against the sky; the gunners await their signal.

Now the *Potemkin* swings the muzzles of its huge cannon directly into the camera, filling the entire screen. The cannon of the fleet ships are raised menacingly toward those of the *Potemkin*. On the mast, the mutineers' flag is whipped by the wind. Cannon confront each other

Potemkin was given a gala public opening in Moscow on January 18, 1926, but its run on the screen lasted only a few weeks, and it was replaced by more commercially slanted entertainment films. Rival filmmakers claimed that *Potemkin* was a glorified documentary, inaccessible to the average audience. But when Soviet embassies in Paris and Berlin showed the film to left-wing opinion makers at invitational screenings, its word-of-mouth reputation soared. In the spring of 1926, the German Marxist composer Edmund Meisel worked closely with Eisenstein to prepare a stirring revolutionary score for *Potemkin* (a collaboration that Eisenstein later described as his "first work in the sound film") that made the film's agitational appeal very nearly irresistible. *Potemkin* was shown commercially in Germany for several weeks but was officially banned in many other European countries, where it was nevertheless shown underground to small audiences of leftists and intellectuals, and its fame spread rapidly throughout the Western world. The film's triumphs abroad (at its Berlin screening the great stage director Max Reinhardt, whose styles of lighting had so influenced German Expressionism, observed, "After viewing *Potem-*

kin, I am willing to admit that the stage will have to give way to the cinema") earned Eisenstein the temporary favor of Soviet officials. Critical attacks on *Potemkin* ceased, and the film was revived for second-run showings in the Soviet Union, where it became quite popular.[8] As Eisenstein later wrote, "I awoke one morning and found myself famous."

EISENSTEIN'S THEORY OF DIALECTICAL MONTAGE

Part of Eisenstein's growing fame was as a theorist of film as well as a practitioner. The body of his writings on the medium—later collected into two volumes, *The Film Sense* (1942) and *The Film Form* (1948)—had been steadily accumulating since 1923, and after the resounding international success of *Potemkin*, he began to articulate his most important contribution to film theory—his notion of dialectical montage. To summarize briefly, Eisenstein saw film editing, or montage, as a process that operated according to the Marxist dialectic. This dialectic is a way of looking at human history and experience as a perpetual conflict in which a force (*thesis*) collides with a counterforce (*antithesis*) to produce from their collision a wholly new phenomenon (*synthesis*) that is not the sum of the two forces, but something greater than and different from them both. The process may be diagrammed thus:

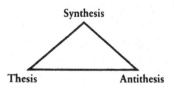

The synthesis emerging from the thesis-antithesis conflict will ultimately become the thesis of a new dialectic, which will in turn generate a new synthesis, and so on until the end of historical time. Eisenstein maintained that in film editing the shot, or "montage cell," is a thesis that when placed into juxtaposition with another shot of opposing visual content—its antithesis—produces a synthesis (a synthetic idea or impression) that in turn becomes the thesis of a new dialectic as the montage sequence continues.[9] This visual opposition between shots may be a conflict of linear directions, planes, volumes, lighting, etc., and need not extend to the dramatic content of the shot. Thus, Eisenstein defined montage as a series of ideas or

impressions that arises from "the collision of independent shots," and in a characteristically industrial metaphor he compared its process to "the series of explosions of an internal combustion engine, driving forward its automobile or tractor." Another of Eisenstein's favorite analogies was linguistic: just as the individual words in a sentence depend for their meaning upon the words that surround them, so the individual shots in a montage sequence acquire meaning from their interaction with the other shots in the sequence.

The underlying cognitive assumption of this theory is that the viewers of a film perceive the shots in a montage sequence not *sequentially*, or one at a time, but rather *simultaneously*, as if one were continuously superimposed upon another. That is, they respond not to an incremental or additive process in which each shot is modified by the ones that precede it ($ABC \neq A+B+C$), but to a *gestalt*—a totality or a whole that is different from and greater than the sum of its parts ($ABC = x$). This is so because shots A, B, and C can be strictly said to follow one another only on the film strip; when the film strip is projected, however, the viewer's mind puts the shots together in a manner analogous to photographic superimposition. Thus, at the end of the Odessa-steps section of *Potemkin*, when we are shown three consecutive shots of a stone lion sleeping, a stone lion awakening, and a stone lion rising, we see the sequence not as a combination of its parts, but as something quite different—a single unbroken movement with a specifically ideological signification.

---

8. The official attendance figures indicate this, at least. But they may have been exaggerated by the authorities, who had a stake in demonstrating to the rest of the world that there was a large Soviet audience for Soviet films. See the casebook of contemporary reviews and documents, *The Battleship Potemkin: The Greatest Film Ever Made*, ed. Herbert Marshall, which reminds us, among other things, that Eisenstein's film inspired a Soviet opera (1937), a Polish ballet (1967), a poem by Brecht, and otherwise influenced numerous novels, plays, and paintings of its day (not to mention a whole generation of American wartime musicals with production numbers staged on the quarterdecks of battleships). In 1986, *Potemkin* was revived for a multicity European tour with the original Edmund Meisel score performed by the Netherlands' Brabants Orchestra.

9. In a very important sense, as Eisenstein realized, the dialectic can also be used to describe the psychoperceptual process of cinema itself: in projection, two (or more) independent still photographs on a film strip collide to produce something different from and greater than them both—the illusion of continuous motion.

Although Griffith's two great epics and Kuleshov's experiments in editing clearly stand behind these notions, Eisenstein developed many of them from his study of the psychology of perception; and to illustrate the process of dialectical montage, he would frequently use the example of the Japanese pictograph or ideogram. In Japanese character-writing, completely new concepts are formed by combining the symbols for two separate older ones. Moreover, the new concept is never merely the sum of its parts and is invariably an abstraction that could not be represented graphically on its own terms. For example, the symbol for *dog* plus the symbol for *mouth* create an ideogram meaning not "dog's mouth," as one might expect, but "bark." Similarly,

$$\text{child} + \text{mouth} = \text{scream}$$
$$\text{bird} + \text{mouth} = \text{sing}$$
$$\text{knife} + \text{heart} = \text{sorrow}$$
$$\text{water} + \text{eye} = \text{weep}$$
$$\text{door} + \text{ear} = \text{listen}$$

Thus, in every case the combination of two distinct signs for concrete objects produces a single sign for some intangible or abstraction. What Eisenstein was attempting to suggest by these examples was the way in which film, whose signs are moving photographic images and therefore *wholly* tangible, can communicate conceptual abstractions on a par with other language forms.

Eisenstein conceived that whole films, as well as autonomous sequences within them, could be constructed according to the dialectic. In theoretical essays like "A Dialectical Approach to Film Form" (1929) and "The Structure of the Film" (1939), he wrote lengthy postfactum analyses of the dialectical structure of *Potemkin*. Eisenstein claimed that each part or act of *Potemkin* was broken into two equal halves by a "caesura," a term (borrowed from poetry and music) denoting a strong medial pause in the action, and that the film as a whole was similarly divided by the harbor-mist sequence that begins the third act. The dialectical pattern of each act (and of the film itself) was one of mounting tension followed by a resolution or exploding of tension, which together produced a synthesis that became the thesis of the next act. Eisenstein diagrammed the structure of Acts II through V as follows:

II. Scene with the tarpaulin ⟶ mutiny
III. Mourning for Vakulinchuk ⟶ angry demonstration
IV. Lyrical fraternization ⟶ shooting
V. Anxiously awaiting the fleet ⟶ triumph

Finally, Eisenstein outlined the ideological dialectic of sequences within acts. At the outset of the Odessa steps massacre, for example, he perceives the following dialectical structure:

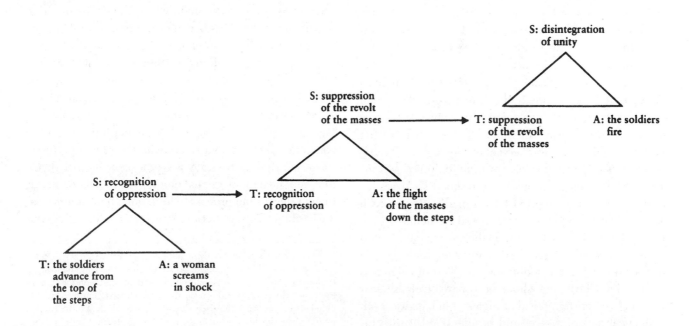

At this point, the dialectical conflict on the steps becomes directional. The orderly descent of the rows of militiamen opposes the pell-mell flight of the disordered masses in terms of tempo and volume, but both together oppose the movement of the individual supplicants and the lone mother and child who are simultaneously ascending. The young mother stopped still on the landing with her baby opposes the movement of all four groups, and later her rapidly descending baby carriage adds a new dimension of motion to the sequence, which might be diagrammed as follows:

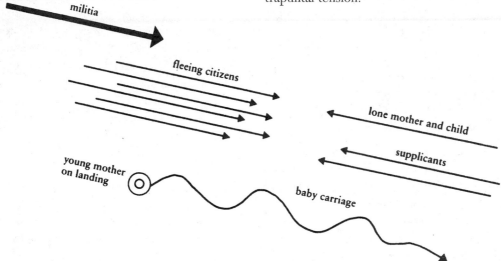

As the sequence ends at the bottom of the steps, the young Cossack savagely swinging his saber collides with the bloodied face of the woman in pince-nez to produce the synthesis: rage. Then, the guns of the *Potemkin* collide with the generals' headquarters to produce the ultimate synthesis: collective action.

In other articles Eisenstein attempted to distinguish five separate types or "methods" of montage, all of which may be used simultaneously within any given sequence: (1) the metric, (2) the rhythmic, (3) the tonal, (4) the overtonal, and (5) the intellectual or ideological. "Metric montage" is concerned solely with the tempo of the cutting, regardless of the content of the shots. The basis for editing is thus the temporal length or duration of each shot, and these lengths are determined by the imposition of a regular metrical pattern upon the cutting rate. A good example of accelerating metric montage would be the Griffith intercut chase sequence, in which the climax is reached by alternating shots of progressively shorter duration.[1] (Eisenstein felt that metric montage was both mechanical and primitive, and he identified it with his

major Soviet rival, V. I. Pudovkin.) "Rhythmic montage" Eisenstein described as an elaboration of metric montage in which the cutting rate is based upon the rhythm of movement *within* the shots as well as upon predetermined metrical demands. This rhythm may be used either to reinforce the metric tempo of the sequence or to counterpoint it. As an example of the latter, Eisenstein cites the Odessa steps sequence from *Potemkin*, in which the steady rhythm of the soldiers' feet as they descend the stairs within the frame is made to violate regularly the metric tempo of the cutting, creating contrapuntal tension.

"Tonal montage," Eisenstein claimed, represents a stage beyond the rhythmic in which the dominant emotional *tone* of the shots becomes the basis for editing. As an example of tonal montage, Eisenstein cites the fog sequence at the beginning of the third act of *Potemkin*. Here, the basic tonal dominant of the shots is the quality of their light ("haze" and "luminosity"), which all the other plastic elements of the shots subserve. Tonal montage, then, has to do with neither the cutting rate nor the content of the shots, but rather with their texture. "Overtonal montage" is basically a synthesis of metric, rhythmic, and tonal montage that emerges in projection rather than in the editing process (where only the "undertones" are visible). This is not really a distinct category, but

---

1. As Griffith wrote of his own method in 1925: "The action must quicken to a height in a minor climax, then slow down and build again to the next climax, which should be faster than the second and on to the major climax, where the pace should be fastest. Through the big moments of the story, the pace should be like the beat of an excited pulse." ("Pace in the Movies," *Liberty*, April 18, 1925.)

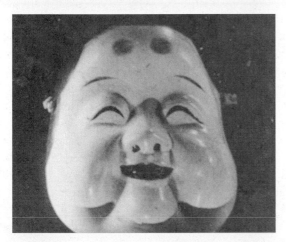

5.18 Intellectual montage: Kerenski and the peacock in *October*.

5.17 Final frames from the "gods" sequence in *October* (Sergei Eisenstein, 1928).

another way of looking at montage based upon the totality of stimuli.

"Intellectual or ideological montage" was the type that most fascinated Eisenstein in both his theory and his practice. All of the preceding montage methods are concerned with inducing emotional and/or physiological reactions in the audience through a sophisticated form of behavioristic stimulation. But Eisenstein also conceived that montage was capable of expressing abstract ideas by creating *conceptual* relationships among shots of opposing visual content. The intercutting of the massacre of the workers with the slaughter of an ox at the end of *Strike* and the intercutting of the priest tapping his crucifix with the ship's officer tapping his sword in the second act of *Potemkin* are simple manifestations of intellectual montage. But the most sophisticated use of this metaphorical technique occurs in Eisenstein's third film, *October* (*Oktiabr*; alternatively titled *Ten Days That Shook the World*, 1928), a magnificent failed attempt to recount the events of the Bolshevik Revolution in terms of pure intellectual cinema. Eisenstein himself cited the "gods" sequence of this film, omitted from most American prints, as a prime example of the method. In it, he offers a montage of various religious icons, beginning with a baroque statue of Christ and concluding with a hideous primitive idol, to debunk the traditional concept of God. As Eisenstein pointed out later: "These pieces were assembled in accordance with a descending intellectual

5.19 Heroic metaphor and documentary realism in *October*.

scale—pulling back the concept of God to its origins, forcing the spectator to perceive this 'progress' intellectually." A more complex example of intellectual montage in *October* is the famous sequence depicting the rise to power of Alexander Kerenski, head of the coalition or provisional government that preceded the Bolshevik Revolution. Eisenstein presents successive shots of Kerenski solemnly climbing the Baroque marble staircase of the Winter Palace and intercuts them with grandiose titles announcing his ascent through the ranks of the government ("Minister of the Army," "And the Navy," "Generalissimo," "Dictator") and with shots of military flunkies bowing and scraping before him on the landings. At one point, Kerenski passes beneath a statue of Victory that seems about to place a crown of laurels on his head. Then, as he reaches the top of the stairs and stands before the doorway to his office, Eisenstein cuts from his highly polished military boots to his gloved hands, and finally to a

mechanical peacock spreading its tail in prideful splendor. The whole sequence is meant to suggest the inflated vanity, monumental pride, and dictatorial ambition of Kerenski and his government.

All of Eisenstein's thinking on montage worked toward the establishment of a uniquely cinematic language based upon psychological association and stimulation that had little or nothing to do with narrative logic. Deriving from his lifelong study of the dynamics of aesthetic perception, this language, which Eisenstein chose to call "dialectical montage," operated according to a precise manipulation of audience psychology on both the emotional and cerebral levels of experience. Later critics, notably followers of the French film theorist André Bazin, have claimed that dialectical montage is too manipulative, even "totalitarian," in its selective ordering of the viewer's reponse. Their objection is largely philosophical, for they believe that the analytical fragmentation of a filmed event through montage, as in the Odessa-steps sequence, destroys "the reality of space" (Bazin) that provides the necessary relationship between the cinematic image and the real world. They believe, in other words, that dialectical montage substitutes artificial and contrived spatial relationships for natural ones. And yet it is precisely its lack of dependence upon "real" or "natural" spatial relationships that renders dialectical montage a symbolic and metaphoric—and, therefore, a *poetic*—language rather than a narrative one. As Paul Seydor points out in an essay intended to be highly critical of Eisenstein: "Eisenstein's early cinema is quintessentially a cinema of (though not necessarily for) the mind. Space and movement are not literally seen, that is, are not on the screen; they exist only in the viewer's imagination, his eye serving to register the details with which his mind will make the 'proper' points." Whether or not such a process is ideologically appropriate is a moot point when it works as well aesthetically as it does, say, in *Potemkin*. But, for Eisenstein and for others, it didn't always work, and his third film provides a measure of its limitations.

OCTOBER (*TEN DAYS THAT SHOOK THE WORLD*, 1928): A LABORATORY FOR INTELLECTUAL MONTAGE

In the spring of 1927, Eisenstein was commissioned by the Central Committee of the Communist party and Sovkino to make a film commemorating the tenth anniversary of the Bolshevik Revolution. Using hundreds of personal memoirs and interviews, newsreel and newspaper accounts, and John Reed's book *Ten Days That Shook the World* (the title by which a heavily edited version of the film was known in the United States and Great Britain), Eisenstein and his coscenarist, Grigori Alexandrov (1903–1984),[2] wrote a detailed shooting script, entitled *October*, which initially covered the history of the entire Revolution. But, as with *Potemkin*, Eisenstein ultimately narrowed his scope to focus on a few representative episodes—the events in Petrograd (now St. Petersburg; at the time of filming, Leningrad) from February to October 1917. Vast resources, including the Soviet army and navy, were placed at Eisenstein's disposal, and life in the city was completely disrupted during the six months of shooting as mass battles like the storming and bombardment of the Winter Palace were restaged with casts of tens of thousands. When editing was completed in

November 1927, the film ran approximately 13,000 feet, or just under three hours, with a carefully integrated score composed by Edmund Meisel. But during its production Leon Trotski (1879–1940), who as commissar of war had played an enormously important role in the Revolution and civil war, was expelled from the Politburo (executive committee) of the Communist party and forced into exile by Iosif Stalin (1879–1953),[3] and Eisenstein was compelled to cut *October* by several thousand feet[4] in order to eliminate all references to the ousted leader. (For the same reason, Reed's book was banned in the Soviet Union from late 1927 until after Stalin's death in 1953.) When this truncated version[5] was finally released to the public in March 1928, it was poorly received. Audiences could not understand its abstract intellectual montage, and party critics attacked it bitterly for "formalist excess"—a charge that publicly announced the widening rift between Eisenstein's aesthetics and the new Stalinist establishment. (Eisenstein was hardly alone in this: during the key years of Stalin's rise, 1927 and 1928, half of the 135 films produced by the Soviet industry were suppressed—13 permanently so—and over one-third restricted to limited audiences.)

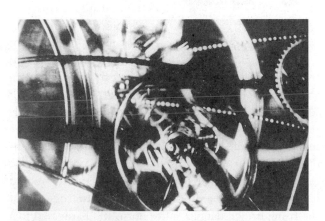

5.20 Synecdoche and symbol in *October*: wheels spinning, a broken statue.

2. For an account of Alexandrov's own career as a director in the 1930s and 1940s, see Norman Swallow, "Alexandrov," *Sight and Sound* 48, 4 (Autumn 1979): 246–49.

3. Born Iosif Vissarionovich Jugashvili in Gori, Georgia, Stalin was one of Lenin's several lieutenants before, during, and after 1917. He adopted his pseudonym—Russian for "man of steel"—shortly after being named by Lenin to the Bolshevik Central Committee in 1912. He played an important, if not crucial, role in the October Revolution and afterward became general secretary of the Central Committee of the Communist party. Lenin was preparing to remove Stalin from this post for abuse of power when he suffered the series of strokes that led to his death in 1924. Thereafter, Stalin outmaneuvered his opponents (chiefly Trotski, Grigory E. Zinoviev [1883–1936], and Nikolai I. Bukharin [1888–1938]—all of whom he later had executed) to become virtual dictator of the Soviet Union from 1928 to 1953. See Alex De Jonge, *Stalin and the Shaping of the Soviet Union* (New York: Morrow, 1986).

4. Estimates range from 1,000 feet or about eleven minutes (Ephraim Katz, *The Film Encyclopedia*, 2nd ed. [New York: HarperCollins, 1994], p. 413) to 4,000 feet (Barna, *Eisenstein*, p. 123). Eisenstein himself was vague, but remarks he made while editing the film indicate that about one-third of what he shot is missing.

5. The version released as *Ten Days That Shook the World* in Britain and North America was even further shortened through the elimination or abridgment of key montage sequences. For the fiftieth-anniversary celebration of the Revolution in 1967, Grigori Alexandrov reconstructed the original version of *October* on the basis of Eisenstein's notes, with a new score by Dmitri Shostakovich. The reconstruction contains over 3,200 shots, counting the intertitles.

5.21 The faces of the Soviet people: typage in _October_.

part to symbolize the whole—is verywhere apparent: rifles waving in the air tell us that the army has joined the Bolshevik cause; the hands of bureaucrats frantically clicking their telephone receivers indicate that the Kerenski government has lost control.

Countless other rhetorical devices are used by Eisenstein to maximize the film's ideological effect, from complicated interframe symbolism (as when the history of religion is condensed into a series of shots proceeding from the most "civilized" of icons to the most primitive and barbarous) to simple cinematic trickery (as when a statue of Tsar Alexander III, demolished earlier in the film to represent the success of the Revolution, is magically reassembled through reverse projection to represent the monarchists' vain hopes of returning to power). In a much-discussed sequence, Eisenstein uses the agonizingly slow raising of a drawbridge to suggest that the city of Petrograd has been split asunder by the Revolution. From one side of the rising bridge dangles a live horse still harnessed to a cart, from the other the flaxen hair of a dead girl, shot during a demonstration, and this hair for a long time spans the crevice between the two halves before falling into the breach. In narrative terms, the drawbridge has been raised by the police in order to cut off retreating workers from their quarters, but Eisenstein turns the event into a poetic metaphor by lingering on the slowly widening gulf between the two sides and by drawing out the moment of their separation far beyond the time it would naturally take in reality. As in the plate-smashing sequence and the Odessa-steps massacre of _Potemkin_, Eisenstein here expands time to represent the psychological duration of an event as opposed to its chronological duration.

Yon Barna has called _October_ "an experimental film of immense proportions," and indeed it was, for Eisenstein used it as a laboratory in which to test his theories of intellectual montage upon an actual audience. In _October_, Eisenstein employed intellectual montage on the order of the stone-lion sequence in _Potemkin_ to comment upon each and every aspect of the Revolution depicted in the narrative portion of the film. Thus, Kerenski is compared to a peacock and his militia to tin soldiers and empty wineglasses through the insertion of shots from outside the dramatic context of the film. Similarly, the treacherous pleading of the Mensheviks at the Second Congress of Soviets is intercut with shots of soft female hands stroking harps, and the union of the Motorcycle Battalion with the congress is juxtaposed with shots of abstractly spinning bicycle wheels, in association with the entrance of the new delegates. (Eisenstein wrote of this sequence in _The Film Form_, "In this way the large-scale emotional content of the event was transformed into actual dynamics.") At one point, Eisenstein suggests the stolid emptiness of the tsarist regime through a series of still shots of elaborate ornamental façades and heavily beribboned military tunics. Synecdoche—the use of a

In its publicly released form _October_ does appear to

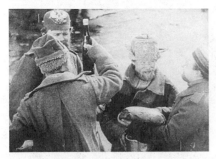

5.22 *October:* fraternization between Russian and German soldiers at the front.

5.23 Lenin addresses his supporters at various points in *October.*

be, as its critics charged, excessively formalistic—concerned more with the intricacies of its own cinematic mechanisms than with its revolutionary content. Furthermore—and, by Eisenstein's own standards, most damning of all—the film's intellectual montage does not always work. There is sometimes a disturbing disparity between the idea Eisenstein seeks to communicate and its technical expression. Eisenstein wrote in 1929: "The hieroglyphic language of the cinema is capable of expressing any concept, any idea of class, any political or tactical slogan, without recourse to the help of a rather suspect dramatic or psychological past."[6] And yet a cinema of pure intellectual abstraction, excepting certain specialized forms of animation, can never really exist since cinematic statements can be made only through the juxtaposition of concrete images. Eisenstein's notion, of course, was that concrete images properly arranged can *suggest* abstract ones, and this is true. But all available evidence indicates that the technique of intellectual montage will work only when it is firmly grounded in some specific narrative or dramatic context. When intellectual montage usurps its narrative context, as it often does in *October,* it tends to create a class of nonreferential symbols that have meaning neither as abstractions nor as objects.

EISENSTEIN AFTER *OCTOBER*

Eisenstein's next film was a continuation of a project begun just prior to the commissioning of *October.* Initially entitled *The General Line (General'naiia liniia)*—i.e., the "general line" or policy of the Communist party—and renamed *Old and New (Staroe i novoie,* 1929) when Stalinist bureaucrats disavowed it, and the film was conceived by Eisenstein as a lyrical hymn of praise, in semidocumentary form, to the collectivization of Soviet agriculture. It tells the didactic tale of the evolution of a typical Russian peasant village from backwardness and

6. An index of how firmly Eisenstein believed this statement is that between 1927 and 1928 he seriously considered making a film of Marx's massive socioeconomic dissection of capitalism, *Das Kapital* (1867), which he hoped would raise intellectual montage "into the realm of philosophy." (Quoted in Barna, *Eisenstein,* p. 126.) After reading James Joyce's *Ulysses* (which he called "the Bible of the new cinema") in February 1928, Eisenstein also came to believe that intellectual montage could be practiced in literature: "Indeed," he wrote, "in the linguistic kitchen of literature Joyce occupies himself with the same thing I rave about in relation to laboratory researches on cinema language." (Sergei Eisenstein, *Immoral Memories: An Autobiography,* trans. Herbert Marshall [Boston: Houghton Mifflin, 1983], p. 213.) The following year in Paris, Eisenstein would spend hours talking with Joyce about adapting *Ulysses* to the screen—a hopeful but unlikely prospect, since the writer by this time was nearly blind.

poverty to prosperity through the establishment of a collective farm. For the first time, Eisenstein told his story through a central character, Marfa Lapkina, a simple peasant woman (played in the film, according to Eisenstein's theory of typage, by a real peasant) who becomes a devoted supporter of the cooperative effort and is instrumental in its ultimate success. Like all Eisenstein films, *Old and New* was carefully researched and shot mainly on location, and, as with *October*, Eisenstein used it as a laboratory for experiment—this time not with "intellectual" but with "overtonal" montage, and much more successfully than before. According to this technique, which Eisenstein also called "polyphonic montage" and "the filmic fourth dimension," a film is assembled through the harmonic orchestration of tonal dominants—i.e., through what André Bazin would later term *mise-en-scène* as opposed to wholly analytic editing, as we will see in Chapter 13. Unlike the intellectual montage of *October*, all the shots in this method arise naturally out of the dramatic context of the film, and they are carefully composed in depth within the frame to orchestrate the "thematic major" and "thematic minor" keys.

Eisenstein's analogy, of course, was with the composition of symphonic music. As he wrote of *Old and New* in *The Film Form*, "The whole intricate, rhythmic and *sensual* nuance scheme of the combined pieces (of certain sequences) is conducted almost exclusively according to a line of work on the 'psychophysiological' vibrations

5.25 Overtonal montage: old and new.

of each piece." Famous sequences include Marfa's first encounter with a mechanized cream separator, the arrival and mating of the village bull, and the final "dance" of the tractors; but Eisenstein's cutting throughout the film is the most sophisticated and subtle he was ever to achieve. In fact, many critics have come to regard it as his most beautiful silent film. Sounding like one of his Italian neorealist successors, Eisenstein wrote that his purpose in *Old and New* was "to exalt the pathos of everyday existence." And indeed the film's extraordinary lyrical quality—its feeling for sky, sun, and soil, and for humanity itself—works in tandem with its superb visual form to create a kind of "total cinema" that Eisenstein was never to attain again. However, when the film was completed in the spring of 1929, Soviet officials were dissatisfied, and Eisenstein was forced to shoot another ending at Stalin's command. Despite this adjustment and much popular acclaim, *Old and New* was bitterly denounced by

5.24 **The ultimate typage: Marfa Lapkina as Marfa Lapkina in Eisenstein's *Old and New* (1929).**

5.28 Marfa's vision of fertility: a cow decked with bridal flowers on her way to mate with a bull.

5.26 Hostile kulaks, superstitious peasants.

party critics, who dissociated themselves from its politics and again raised the old charge of formalism.[7] This reaction portended serious trouble for Eisenstein, but in 1929 he stood at the height of his international fame, and the party could not afford to overlook the prestige he was bringing to the Soviet Union from all parts of the globe.

5.27 Marfa transformed by the operation of the cream separator.

With *Old and New*, Eisenstein had taken the silent film form about as far as it would go, just as six years earlier he had reached the outer limits of the legitimate stage and "fallen into the cinema." Now, at the peak of his artistic powers, he stood on the very brink of the sound film, in whose aesthetic prospect he had become almost insatiably interested. Sadly, for the next decade Eisenstein's contributions to the art of the sound film were to be almost solely theoretical, for this great architect of the Soviet silent cinema was not permitted to complete another motion picture until *Alexander Nevski* in 1938. A political tragicomedy, Stalin's "Great Turn," was about to be enacted in the Soviet Union, which would make it impossible for Eisenstein to practice cinema in his own country for nearly nine years. For the moment, however, Eisenstein was an internationally acclaimed master with several huge successes to his credit, and many persons throughout the West looked to him as the supreme arbiter of cinematic form. Accordingly, in August 1929, at the age of thirty-one, Eisenstein was sent by Soiuzkino together with scenarist Alexandrov and cinematographer Tisse to study the cinemas of western Europe and espe-

7. Between 1928, when production of *Old and New* began on the basis of a revised 1926 script, and the film's release in October 1929, Soviet agrarian policy was radically transformed by Stalin. At the fourteenth party congress in December 1927, collectivization of the peasantry was conceived as a distant and voluntary goal, but in November 1929 Stalin announced a "Great Turn" in the party line on agriculture toward forced collectivization. In December, he established the "liquidation of kulaks [wealthy peasants] as a class" as state policy and embarked on the campaign of mass murder described below (see footnote, p. 163). See James Goodwin, *Eisenstein, Cinema, and History* (Urbana: University of Illinois Press, 1993), pp. 98–102.

cially the United States, where for much of 1930 he was to work on several abortive projects for Paramount[8] before journeying to Mexico to shoot his remarkable unfinished epic *¡Que viva México!* (1931–32). Eisenstein's American sojourn marked his first practical encounter with the new technology of sound recording and the beginning of a series of tragic complications that would plague him until his early death in 1948; these will be examined in Chapter 9.

Vsevolod Pudovkin

Vsevolod I. Pudovkin (1893–1953), the second great director of the Soviet silent cinema, had been trained as a chemist, but he decided to renounce his profession and become a filmmaker after seeing D. W. Griffith's *Intolerance* in Moscow in 1920. He joined the Moscow Film School and spent two years as a member of the Kuleshov Workshop, where he participated in the famous editing experiments described earlier in this chapter and was directly involved in the production of *The Extraordinary Adventures of Mr. West in the Land of the Bolsheviks* (1924) and *The Death Ray* (1925). Pudovkin's first full-length film was a documentary on Pavlovian reflexology entitled *The Mechanics of the Brain* (*Mekhanika golovnogo mozga*, 1926), in which he successfully used editing principles discovered by Kuleshov as a pedagogical device to explain conditioning theory to an unsophisticated audience. At about the same time, Pudovkin shot *Chess Fever* (*Shakhmatnaia goriachka*, 1925; codirected with Nikolai Shpikovski), a two-reel comedy in the manner of Mack Sennett's Keystone films (see pp. 171–72), but constructed according to Kuleshovian principles (woven into the plot is footage of the chess champion José Capablanca obtained by one of Pudovkin's cameramen posing as a newsreel photographer). Both films were photographed by Anatoli Golovnia (1900–1982), who was to become Pudovkin's constant collaborator from 1925 to 1950, and both were popular with domestic audiences, but it was Pudovkin's first dramatic feature film, *Mother* (*Mat*, 1926), that thrust him into the international limelight as Eisenstein's closest Soviet rival.

Loosely adapted by Pudovkin and the scenarist Nathan Zarkhi (another frequent collaborator) from Maxim Gorki's novel of the same title,[9] and photographed by Golovnia, *Mother* is set during the time of the 1905 Revolution. It

tells the story of a politically oppressed woman married to a brutal (and brutalized) drunkard who works with their son, Pavel, in a factory. The family leads a life of abject poverty, and to finance his drinking the father joins the ranks of the Black Hundreds, a counterrevolutionary goon squad in the pay of the tsarist government. During a violent confrontation between striking workers and the Black Hundreds in the factory yard, the father discovers that Pavel is one of the strikers. They fight, and the father is accidentally killed by one of Pavel's friends. Later, the police come to Pavel's home searching for weapons, and the mother, in her naïveté, betrays her son, believing that he will be exonerated. Instead, Pavel is arrested and sentenced to prison in a rigged trial; the mother is first anguished and then radically politicized by this experience of tsarist tyranny. She maintains close contact with Pavel's friends and later helps him to escape from jail. At the conclusion of the film, they meet again, on May Day, at the head of a workers' demonstration. A regiment of Cossacks attacks the demonstrators, and mother and son die heroically confronting tsarist tyranny.

Mother enjoyed an immediate international success similar to that of *Potemkin*, and for some of the same reasons.[1] It is a beautifully proportioned film, carefully photographed by Golovnia and brilliantly edited by

---

8. Notably, *Sutter's Gold*, based on Blaise Cendrars's Futurist novel *L'Or* (1925) about John Augustus Sutter, the German immigrant who started the California gold rush and built an empire on this wealth, but who ultimately became a Communist, for which Eisenstein wrote a script showing "the paradise of primitive, patriarchal California, destroyed by the lust for gold," and a Marxist treatment of Theodore Dreiser's *An American Tragedy* (1926), both of which were rejected as being too critical of American society. *An American Tragedy* was finally made at Paramount by Josef von Sternberg in 1931 with a new script (as we will see in Chapter 8) and made again by the same studio twenty years later as *A Place in the Sun* (George Stevens, 1951—see Chapter 12) from yet a third script. Eisenstein's *Sutter's Gold* treatment was revised by William Faulkner for Howard Hawks in 1934; both Faulkner and Hawks then abandoned the project, which was ultimately produced by Universal in 1936, with James Cruze directing. Ironically, the same year saw a Nazi version of Sutter, *Der Kaiser von Kalifornien* (The *Kaiser of California*, Tobis, 1936), directed by and starring the Austrian filmmaker Luis Trenker, which portrayed Sutter as a visionary German nationalist who heroically rejects "degenerate" American capitalism.

9. The German playwright Bertolt Brecht (1898–1956) dramatized the novel for the stage in 1932; his highly stylized adaptation (which includes songs) provides an interesting contrast to Pudovkin's film.

1. In a poll of 117 film critics from 26 countries to choose the 12 best films of all time at the 1958 Brussels World's Fair, *Potemkin* ranked first and *Mother* eighth.

Pudovkin. Its action proceeds rhythmically through four symmetrical parts, and its montage effects are masterfully controlled. Yet *Mother* is in many ways a quieter, less spectacular film than its predecessor. Though it is essentially a political parable dealing with violent action, it eschews the epic proportions of *Potemkin* to concentrate on the human drama played out against the backdrop of a great historical moment. Eisenstein's film was about that moment itself, Pudovkin's about the people caught up in it. This is the pattern that appeared throughout Pudovkin's silent films and that above all others made them more popular with the Soviet masses than Eisenstein's. Whereas Eisenstein was the grand master of the mass epic, Pudovkin's approach to filmmaking was more personal. As the French critic Léon Moussinac would later write, "A film of Eisenstein's resembles a scream, one of Pudovkin a song." Pudovkin had learned from Griffith to contrast scenes of mass action with the more intimate drama of the "little people" whose lives are transfigured by it. Though he subscribed in part to current theories of typage, Pudovkin had also learned from Griffith the importance of emotionally credible film acting, and he coaxed magnificent performances from his two leading players, Vera Baranovskaia (1885–1935) as the mother and Nikolai Batalov (1898–1937) as the son. Their presence alone imbues the film with a kind of emotional lyricism completely alien to Eisenstein's work, with the sole exception of parts of *Old and New*.

But despite the more direct emotional appeal of his film, Pudovkin's montage was every bit as sophisticated as that of Eisenstein, from whom he and all Soviet filmmakers had learned a great deal (Pudovkin always said that the second major film experience of his life, after *Intolerance*, was *Potemkin*). Some of the great montage sequences from *Mother* include that in which the mourning mother keeps vigil over her husband's corpse while water drips slowly into a bucket beside her; Pavel's lyrical fantasy of escape from prison, in which images of spring coming to the land are intercut with his smiling face; and Pavel's actual escape from prison over the ice floes, which eventually modulates into the concluding massacre. The sequence on the ice derives from Griffith's *Way Down East* (1920) rather than from Gorki's novel, but Pudovkin reveals the heritage of the Kuleshov Workshop by making the montage metaphorically as well as narratively functional. As the sequence begins, ice cakes floating downriver are intercut with workers marching toward the factory and their heroic confrontation with the troops. As the river becomes more and more clogged with ice, the ranks of the workers swell, until they overflow the curbs of the street. The narrative function of the ice floes becomes apparent when we see that the river runs past the prison and will provide Pavel with the medium for his escape. He joins the marchers on the opposite bank by leaping across the floes like the hero at the climax of *Way Down East*, but the metaphorical function of the sequence reasserts itself as the floes smash suddenly and violently into the piers of a stone bridge—the very bridge upon which moments later the workers will clash head-on with the troops. The complex montage of the massacre itself, second only to the Odessa-steps sequence of *Potemkin* in conveying the plight of individuals caught up in violent action, provides an emotionally gripping, revolutionary climax to an intensely affecting film.

From the foregoing account it should be clear that Pudovkin's montage, even at its most symbolic, usually serves some narrative purpose. Unlike Eisenstein, Pudovkin rarely engaged in intellectual abstraction. He had good theoretical reasons for this, believing that the process of montage operated differently from the way Eisenstein conceived it. For Pudovkin, the key process of montage was not collision, but **linkage.** As he wrote in the introduction to the German edition of his book *Film Technique and Film Acting* (1926; trans. Ivor Montagu, London, 1950): "The expression that the film is 'shot' is entirely false, and should disappear from the language. The film is not *shot*, but *built*, built up from the separate strips of celluloid that are its raw material." Thus, Pudovkin chose an architectonic model for film structure and Eisenstein a dialectical one, though in practice both frequently mixed effects.[2] Ultimately, however, the argument between Eisenstein and Pudovkin was less about the formal aspects of montage than about the psychology of the viewer, with Eisenstein believing that cinematic meaning is generated through the cognitive collision of frames within the viewer's mind and Pudovkin that it is generated through the cognitive linkage of frames. The opposition between these two points of view has never

---

2. For a sustained analysis of the influence of the classical Hollywood style ("maintaining narrative linearity . . . [and] . . . establishing a scenographic space that assures spectator orientation from one shot to the next") on Pudovkin's theory and practice, see Vance Kepley, Jr., "Pudovkin and the Classical Hollywood Tradition," *Wide Angle* 7, 3 (Fall 1985): 53–61.

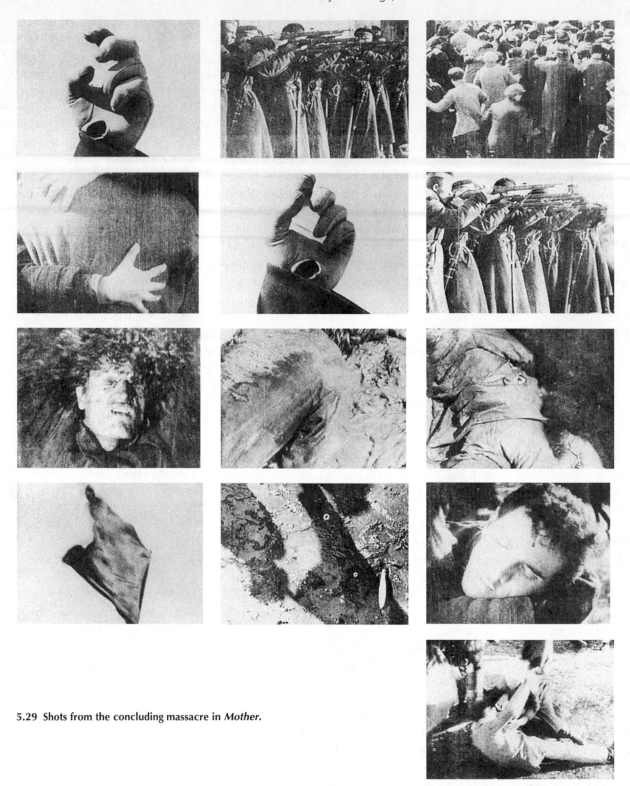

5.29 Shots from the concluding massacre in *Mother.*

been resolved, and it will not be until we know a good deal more about the processes of perception involved in watching films. By August 1928, however, confronted with the imminent introduction of sound, Eisenstein and Pudovkin had managed to resolve their aesthetic differences sufficiently to issue a joint manifesto (with Grigori Alexandrov) endorsing the use of asynchronous, or contrapuntal, sound as opposed to lip-synchronized dialogue, or synchronous sound, which they correctly saw as a threat to the art of montage as practiced in the silent film.

Pudovkin's next film, like Eisenstein's *October*, was commissioned by the Central Committee to commemorate the tenth anniversary of the Bolshevik Revolution. It was entitled *The End of St. Petersburg (Koniets Sankt-Peterburga*, 1927), and, as he had done in *Mother*, Pudovkin once again chose to focus upon the personal drama of individuals caught up in the Revolution. The first half of the film tells the story of a peasant boy who comes to the tsarist capital, St. Petersburg, on the eve of World War I to find employment. Because he is politically unenlightened, the boy takes work as a strikebreaker and informer. When he later comes to understand the plight of the workers under capitalism, however, he attacks his employer in a frenzy and is tossed into jail, from which he is conscripted into the army when war is declared. Then the focus of the film shifts to the war itself and to the Revolution as experienced by the young soldier. The second part of *The End of St. Petersburg*, covering the years 1915 to 1917, often resembles Eisenstein's work in its use of expressive montage to communicate the historic impact of great events. But in Pudovkin's films the human element is always intertwined with the epic and symbolic. He uses montage brilliantly throughout this section to contrast the profiteering of the capitalists with the human misery caused by war. As he had done in *Mother*, Pudovkin also makes use of expressive camera angles in the manner of Griffith. When the boy comes to St. Petersburg for the first time, the camera observes him from an extremely high angle, so that he seems dwarfed by the great buildings and monuments of the city. But when he returns as a Bolshevik soldier at the conclusion of the film to storm the Winter Palace, the angles are effectively reversed. *The End of St. Petersburg*, which unlike Eisenstein's film, was completed and released on schedule, was successful in the Soviet Union and was hailed as a masterpiece abroad. Many critics today consider it superior to Eisenstein's film as an analysis of the Revolution,

5.30 A bombastic tsarist orator addressing a mindless crowd in *The End of St. Petersburg* (Vsevolod Pudovkin, 1927).

although *October* is such a singular and eccentric work that it is difficult to compare them.

Pudovkin's last great silent film, *Heir to Genghis Khan (Potomok Chingis-Khana*, 1928; aka *Storm over Asia)*, continued the narrative pattern, begun in *Mother*, in which a politically naïve person is galvanized into radical action by tsarist tyranny. But *Heir to Genghis Khan* is set in Soviet Central Asia in 1920, and its protagonist is a

Mongol trapper who is exploited not by Russians, but by the foreign armies of intervention that fought against the Red Army in Asia during the civil war.[3] As this most exciting of Pudovkin film opens, the young Mongol Bair attacks an English fur trader who has badly cheated him and flees to join the Soviet partisans in the north. The British army of intervention eventually tracks him down, shoots him, and leaves him gravely wounded; but a colonel finds an amulet among Bair's belongings that declares him to be a direct descendant of Genghis Khan. The British nurse Bair back to health and set him up as a puppet ruler over Buryat Mongolia. The Mongol accepts his role at first but ultimately realizes that he is being used to oppress his own people, and he turns against the British with a fury that assumes nearly cosmic proportions as the film concludes: like Samson, Bair literally pulls the British headquarters down upon the heads of his captors; then he leaps on a pony and gathers an impossibly vast horde of Mongol horsemen, who ride in wave after wave after wave against the British oppressors, becoming finally an apocalyptic windstorm that hurls the interventionists helplessly about and literally blows them from the face of the land.

This magnificent symbolic conclusion initially contained hundreds of shots (some prints derived from the German version shorten it to twenty-seven) and was roundly attacked by literal-minded critics who considered it unrealistic—which, of course, it was meant to be—and insufficiently ideological. Critics also found fault with the luxuriant pictorial beauty of the film, shot on location by Golovnia, which they thought indulgently formalistic. *Heir to Genghis Khan* was a great popular success, and foreign audiences were much taken with its technical virtuosity; but Pudovkin had been shaken by the bitterness of official Soviet criticism, and his next film, an attempt to put his theory of contrapuntal sound into practice, was a failure. Entitled *A Simple Case* (*Prostoi sluchai*, 1932), it was a very subjective love story told in impressionistic bits and pieces that seems much closer to Eisenstein's theories than to Pudovkin's own earlier films. *A Simple Case* was released briefly, after much reworking, in a silent print only, and Pudovkin was publicly charged with formalism, signaling again that the great experimental period of Soviet art was drawing to a close. Though Pudovkin managed to weather the storm of criticism that was about to engulf the great montage artists of the Soviet cinema—he went on to make several respected sound

films (*Deserter* [*Dezertir*, 1933]; *Suvorov* [codirected with Mikhail Doller, 1941])—he would never again achieve the stature of his three silent masterpieces, owing to the constant interference of party bureaucrats.[4]

Alexander Dovzhenko

The third major artist of the Soviet silent film, and perhaps the most unconventional, was Alexander Dovzhenko (1894–1956). The son of Ukrainian peasants, Dovzhenko had been a teacher, a diplomat, a political cartoonist, and a painter before joining the Odessa Studios in 1926 at the age of thirty-two. Like Griffith, he knew little about cinema when he began his career in it ("I very rarely saw films," Dovzhenko wrote of his former life), and his first three productions for Odessa were highly derivative of the American slapstick comedies then popular with Soviet audiences. But in 1928 he made a film that revealed a remarkable depth of poetic feeling and that was so technically unconventional that officials of the Ukrainian Film Trust asked Eisenstein and Pudovkin to preview it in order to certify its coherence. The film was *Zvenigora*, a boldly stylized series of tales about a hunt for an ancient Scythian treasure. The tales are set at four different stages of Ukrainian history, enabling Dovzhenko to contrast the region's past and present and to formulate a contemporary political allegory; Eisenstein and Pudovkin immediately recognized its importance. Eisenstein wrote later that its striking blend of fantasy, reality, and "profoundly national poetic invention" was reminiscent of the work of the Russian writer Nikolai Gogol (1809–1852). Dovzhenko himself called the film "a catalogue of my creative possibilities," and indeed it was, for in its bold stylization of narrative form, its emotional lyricism, and its passion-

---

3. Political pressure from foreign ministries made it necessary to label the British "White Russians" in many exported versions of the film, but they remain unmistakably British.

4. The party loyalist Doller, for example—who had assisted him brilliantly on *Mother*—was assigned by Mosfilm to collaborate with Pudovkin on several occasions (*Victory* [*Pobeda*, 1938], *Minin and Pozharski* [*Minin i Pozharski*, 1939], *Suvorov*) to insure his adherence to "socialist realism," as were Sergei Iutkevich and Alexander Ptushko (*Three Encounters* [*Tri vstrechi*, 1948]) and Dmitri Vasiliev (*Zhukovski*, 1951) in later films. According to Yon Barna, Herbert Marshall, and others, Pyotr Pavlenko and Dmitri Vasiliev were appointed to "assist" Eisenstein on *Alexander Nevsky* (1938) for similar reasons.

5.31 The absurd horror of war in *Arsenal* (Alexander Dovzhenko, 1929).

ate sensitivity to Ukrainian life, *Zvenigora* prefigured *Arsenal* (1929) and *Earth* (*Zemlia*, 1930), the two great silent masterpieces to come.

Arsenal is an epic film poem about the effects of revolution and civil war upon the Ukraine. Beginning with the world war and ending in a violent strike by workers at a munitions factory in Kiev, the film does not so much tell a story as create an extended visual metaphor for revolution, encompassing the nightmarish horrors of war, the miseries of economic oppression, and, finally, the ineradicable spirit of freedom in the hearts of the Ukrainian people. Structurally, *Arsenal* provides a synoptic view of the Bolshevik Revolution in the Ukraine through a series of imagistic vignettes in which history, caricature, folklore, allegory, and myth are combined. In the beautifully composed frames of cameraman Danylo Demutsky (1893–1954), people not only live and die, but horses talk, portraits come to life, and, at the end of the film, the protagonist himself bares his breast to volley after volley of reactionary bullets and miraculously continues to stand, a symbol of the irrepressible revolutionary spirit. Of the film's highly symbolic, nonnarrative organization, Eisenstein remarked that it was the prime example in cinema of a "liberation of the whole action from the definition of time and space." Indeed, the official critics experienced some difficulty with *Arsenal*, and yet, accord-

ing to Jay Leyda, the public seemed to accept the film almost intuitively upon its own terms.

Dovzhenko's next film, *Earth* (*Zemlia*, 1930), is universally acknowledged to be his masterpiece. Though its scant plot concerns a commonplace manifestation of the class struggle, the film is essentially a non-narrative hymn to the continuity of life and death in Dovzhenko's beloved Ukraine. Unfolding with a slow, natural rhythm, like the processes of life itself, *Earth* tells the simple story of the tension between a family of well-to-do landowning peasants (kulaks) and the young peasants of a collective farm in a small Ukrainian village.[5] When the kulaks refuse to sell their vast land holdings to the collective, Vasyl, the village chairman, commandeers the property, buys a new tractor, and turns the collective into a thriving enterprise. One evening, after making love to his betrothed, Vasyl is shot dead on the way home by the kulaks' deranged son. In his grief, Vasyl's father sends away the village priest

---

5. Kulaks were identified as class enemies, or "rural capitalists," by Stalin in 1929, and "dekulakization" became part of his brutal collectivization campaign begun the following year, in which millions of wealthy peasants were arrested, deported, and/or executed, and their property expropriated by the state. The remaining peasants were then forced onto collective farms or left to starve to death in the artificially created famine of 1932–33. Starvation was particularly brutal in the Ukraine, where some historians believe it was used to eradicate local nationalism. In

5.33 *Earth:* Vasyl dances by moonlight.

5.32 *Earth* (Alexander Dovzhenko, 1930): visual poetry.

and demands a "modern" funeral for his son "with new songs about new life," and the film concludes with an ecstatic funeral celebration for the young man, after which rain begins to descend upon the crops. Lewis Jacobs has accurately described *Earth* as "a luminous contribution to the realm of lyric cinema." It is a rare film of mysterious beauty that perpetually transcends its contemporary political context to exalt the everlasting fecundity of the soil and the inevitable cyclic recurrence of birth, life, love, and death. The film begins with an old man joyfully biting into an apple as he dies and concludes with the mystically sensuous funeral procession, during which Vasyl's fiancée rips her clothes from her body in grief, his mother goes into labor with her last child, and warm rain falls to replenish the earth.

The central sequence of *Earth* follows the plenteous harvest and is dominated by what Dovzhenko called a "biological, pantheistic conception." Young couples lie in ecstasy under the moonlit summer's night, the hands of the boys on the girls' breasts. Vasyl and his fiancée are among them. They part, and, alone on the dusty road, Vasyl breaks spontaneously into a dance celebrating his deep spiritual joy in life and love. Suddenly, in the middle of a slow-motion pirouette, he falls dead, pierced by the bullet of his hidden assassin. But what would be tragedy in the work of other directors becomes jubilant affirmation in Dovzhenko, for Vasyl has died at the moment of his young life's most perfect self-expression, and life will continue to renew itself as ever before. Ivor Montagu has written: "Dovzhenko's films are crammed with deaths.... But no death in Dovzhenko was ever futile.... The sum of his films instead is beauty and glory. He is saying to the widow: 'Glory in your children,' and to the childless widow: 'Glory in all the children of man.' "

Though it was later twice voted among the twelve greatest films of all time by panels of international film experts, when first released *Earth* was poorly received by the Soviet critics, who denounced it as "defeatist," "coun-

The Harvest of Sorrow: Soviet Collectivization and the Terror-Famine (New York: Oxford University Press, 1986), Robert Conquest estimates that 14.5 million Ukrainian citizens died in the process of collectivization and the subsequent famine.

terrevolutionary," and, in one case, "fascistic." Dovzhenko's domestic reputation, like those of Eisenstein and Pudovkin, was about to enter a period of political eclipse. After a self-imposed hiatus of nearly two years, Dovzhenko readily adapted his talents to the new demands of the sound film (*Ivan* [1932]; *Aerograd* [1935]; *Shchors* [1939]), but increasing pressure to conform to the party line made it impossible for him to reach the lyric heights of *Arsenal* and *Earth* ever again, even though for the rest of his life he courageously continued to try.

Other Soviet Filmmakers

Before examining the reasons for the dramatic decline of the Soviet cinema in the 1930s and the selective suppression of some of its major artists, it is necessary to mention several other filmmakers who played an important role in the great decade of experiment that followed the Revolution. Most notable, perhaps, was the team of Grigori Kozintsev (1905–1973) and Leonid Trauberg (1902–1990), who had founded FEX, the Factory of the Eccentric Actor, in 1921. Kozintsev and Trauberg together produced a number of ebullient, wildly experimental shorts like *The Adventures of Oktiabrina* (*Pokhozhdeniia Oktiabrini*, 1924) before turning to an extremely successful expressionistic adaptation of Gogol's *The Overcoat (Shinel)* in 1926. Their masterpiece, however, magnificently scored by the great modernist composer Dmitri Shostakovich, was *New Babylon* (*Novyi Vavilon*, 1929), a highly stylized drama of the rise and fall of the Paris Commune,[6] set in a luxurious Parisian department store. (The Kozintsev-Trauberg collaboration would continue through the celebrated "Maxim Trilogy" of 1935–39 [see p. 297] and end with *Plain People* [*Prostie liudi*, 1946], which was banned for a decade by the Central Committee of the Communist party as a "false and mistaken" film; Kozintsev subsequently produced several important literary adaptations, and Trauberg turned to screenwriting.) Trauberg's younger brother, Ilia (1905–1948), after working as an assistant to Eisenstein on *October*, made a remarkable feature debut with *The Blue Express (Goluboi ekspress*, 1929), an exciting adventure film set in the Far East that also functions as a political allegory of China's movement toward Communism.

Boris Barnet (1902–1965), a pupil of Kuleshov,

directed several impressive comedies of contemporary manners in the late silent era, among them *Girl with the Hatbox* (*Devuska s korobkoi*, 1927), a gently satiric tale of everyday life in Moscow under the New Economic Policy. Two prerevolutionary directors reemerged to make significant films during this period. Iakov Protazanov (1881–1945) created a science-fiction fantasy entitled *Aelita* (1924), which is notable as the only Soviet film ever designed completely in the **Constructivist** style. Its sets notwithstanding, Aelita was basically an exotic and expensively produced entertainment, and the film was attacked for "commercialism" by many party critics. Protazanov went on to regain his position as the country's top box-office director with a series of comedies starring Igor Ilinski. The former Protazanov actress Olga Preobrazhenskaia (1881–1971) directed a somber and poetic evocation of traditional Russian peasant life, *Women of Riazan (Baby Riazanski*, 1927). *Bed and Sofa (Tretia meshchanskaia*, 1927), directed by Abram Room (1894–1976) and designed by Eisenstein's friend Sergei Iutkevich, was a realistic love story about a ménage à trois caused by the housing shortage. Iutkevich himself, who had helped to form the FEX and was to become an important figure in the sound film, produced two lively features at the end of the silent era, *Lace (Kruzheva*, 1928) and *The Black Sail (Chernyi parus*, 1929). Three other directors who were to become major figures in the Soviet sound film began their careers during this period: Friedrich Ermler (1898–1967) of Leningrad, with socially critical realistic dramas like *Fragment of an Empire (Oblomok imperii*, 1929); Mikhail Kalatozov (1903–1973) of Georgia, with *Salt for Svanetia (Sol Svanetii*, 1930); and Mark Donskoi (1901–1981) of Moscow, with *In the Big City (V bol'shom gorode*, 1928).

Finally, some mention must be made of the documen-

---

6. After the siege of Paris, which ended the Franco-Prussian war of 1870–71, many of the inhabitants of the city rebelled against the government of the Third Republic and established their own council of municipal self-government, called the Commune of Paris. Ostensibly socialist, the Commune governed for two months, until it was brutally suppressed by the French army. Karl Marx hailed the Paris Commune as the first great revolt of the proletariat against the bourgeoisie, and in Marxist-Leninist dogma the Commune is thought to have prefigured the Bolshevik Revolution of 1917. *New Babylon* was revived with its original score at the 1976 Paris Film Festival, performed by Marius Constant's Ars Nova ensemble. Subsequent performances took place in London, New York, and San Francisco in 1982 and 1983.

5.36 *Fragment of an Empire* (Friedrich Ermler, 1929).

5.34 and 5.35 Iakov Protazanov's *Aelita* (1924).

taries of the Ukrainian director Viktor Turin (1895–1945) and those of Eisenstein's friend and teacher Esther Shub. Turin's *Turksib* (1929), a dynamic feature-length account of the building of the Turkistan-Siberian Railway, won international acclaim and influenced the development of the British documentary tradition, but his other films are uneven. The work of Shub is broader, more substantial, and more consistent. From her early experience as a Goskino editor she perfected the **compilation film**, a documentary form that mixes together existing newsreel footage from other films, and her remarkable sense of rhythm and tempo in cutting allowed her to create several brilliant feature-length chronicles of Russia's revolutionary past. Her greatest achievements are *The Fall of the Romanov Dynasty* (*Padenie dinastii Romanovykh*, 1927) and *The Great Road* (*Velikii put*, 1927), made to commemorate the tenth anniversary of the February and October revolutions. Together with her next film, *The Russia of Nicholas II and Lev Tolstoi* (*Rossiya Nikolaia*

5.37 *The Fall of the Romanov Dynasty* **(Esther Shub, 1927).**

II i Lev Tolstoi, 1928), these compilations form an epic trilogy of three decades of Russian and Soviet history, from 1897 to 1927.

Socialist Realism and the Decline of Soviet Cinema

The fate of the Revolution was also the fate of the Soviet cinema, whose decline coincided with the coming of sound but was not directly attributable to it. Some Soviet directors, of course, had difficulty adjusting to the new technology of sound, but on the whole its arrival was greeted enthusiastically as a means of expanding the medium's artistic potential. Dziga Vertov had eagerly anticipated the introduction of sound since the mid-1920s; in August 1928 Eisenstein, Pudovkin, and Alexandrov published a manifesto collectively endorsing the creative use of sound in motion pictures; and Eisenstein, Alexandrov, and Tisse journeyed to western Europe and America in 1929 and 1930, where they were able to investigate developments in the sound film at firsthand. The truth seems to be that the Golden Age of Soviet cinema, like that of German cinema, came to an end as much for political reasons as for technological ones.

At the fifteenth Communist party congress in 1927, Iosif Stalin, who had been the general secretary of the Central Committee since 1922, succeeded in outmaneuvering his opponents to become dictator of the Soviet Union for the next twenty-six years. Unlike his predecessors, Lenin (died 1924) and Trotski (exiled 1929), Stalin

and many of the men who surrounded him were insular, provincial, and highly intolerant of the arts—especially of the avant-garde experiments of the past decade. As a ruthlessly practical politician, Stalin recognized the enormous importance of film as a means of mass communication, but whereas Lenin had said, "The cinema is for us the most important of the arts," Stalin was more blunt: "The cinema," he wrote, "is the greatest medium of mass agitation. The task is to take it into our hands." And this is precisely what happened.

At the sixteenth party congress in 1928, Stalin demanded greater state control of the arts in order to make them both more accessible and more relevant to the masses. In 1929, Stalin removed Sovkino from Anatoli Lunacharski's authority in the Commissariat of Education (Lunacharski resigning as commissar shortly thereafter) and placed it under the direct control of the Supreme Council of the National Economy. Reorganized as "Soiuzkino" (an acronym for All-Union Combine of Cinema-Photo Industries) in 1930, the film trust was turned over to the doctrinaire bureaucrat Boris V. Shumiatski, who openly discouraged all manner of "formalism," symbolism, and montage experiment in favor of didactic plots and, ultimately, blatant propaganda. In 1933, Soiuzkino was itself reorganized as the main Administration of the Cinema-Photo Industry with Shumiatski as central manager. In 1936, Shumiatski was also made head of the Motion-Picture Section of the Committee on Art Affairs, which gave him near-dictatorial control of the Soviet film industry until he was purged in 1938. (On his sworn enmity with Eisenstein, see Chapter 9, pp. 297–300.) Where Lunacharski had suggested, Shumiatski decreed, and as the Soviet leadership grew more and more authoritarian, the arts were pushed increasingly toward the narrow ideological perspective known as **socialist realism**.

This was a prosaic and heavy-handed brand of didacticism that idealized the Soviet experience in order to inspire the masses with the glories of life under Lenin and, especially, Stalin. The guiding principle was that individual creativity should be subordinated to the political aims of the state and that the present should be interpreted in the light of the future predicted by the current party line. Socialist realism was officially defined as the "artistic method whose basic principle is the truthful, historically concrete depiction of reality in its revolutionary development, and whose most important task is the Communist education of the masses." It was, in other words, an artistic method that demanded the "socialization" of Soviet art as a propaganda medium for Communist party policy. Since that policy shifted with expediency, the doctrine could only be contextually defined. In general, however, socialist realism involved an extreme literal-mindedness that eschewed the "symbolic" and "psychological" for simple narratives centering on representative Soviet heroes (and, rarely, heroines). (During the 1930s and 1940s, it was often true that these heroes physically resembled Stalin.) When socialist realism was declared the official style of all Soviet art at the first Congress of the Soviet Writers Union in 1934, the genius of the Soviet cinema was devastated since anything unique, personal, or formally experimental was explicitly forbidden to appear upon the screen.

In 1933, immediately following the de facto imposition of socialist realism, Soviet film production fell to its lowest level in a decade; only 53 features were completed, as compared with 119 the year before. Shumiatski blamed the transition to sound, but confusion and fear in the studios were equally responsible. Tragically, if characteristically, it was the founders of Soviet cinema who were most injured by this reactionary decree. Eisenstein, Pudovkin, Dovzhenko, Kuleshov, and Vertov were all variously denounced and, in some cases, publicly humiliated for their past "formalist aberrations." They continued to work under the burden of official disfavor for the rest of their lives, their visions and their methods straitjacketed by Stalinist paranoia from that time forth. With the sole exception of Eisenstein, none of them produced work in the sound era equal to their greatest silent films because (as the Nazis would discover almost simultaneously with the Stalinists) art shackled by ideology ceases to be art and becomes something else. Great art may sometimes be ideological, as *Potemkin*, *Mother*, and *Arsenal* clearly illustrate, but ideology in the service of itself alone can never be great art. Stalinism continued to cripple the Soviet film industry long after the death of its namesake on March 5, 1953. In fact, with varying degrees of intensity, Soviet cinema remained in its repressive grip until the advent of glasnost in 1985–86, and socialist realism was not categorically rejected as the official style of Soviet film art until a unanimous vote by the membership of the Filmmakers Union in June 1990 (see Chapter 17).

Hollywood in the Twenties

By the end of World War I, the American film industry had assumed the structure it would retain for the next forty years. The independent producers, led by Adolph Zukor, William Fox, and Carl Laemmle, had triumphed over the monopolistic Motion Picture Patents Company to become vertically integrated monopolies themselves, controlling their own theater chains and distributorships. With the refinement of the feature film, motion-picture audiences became increasingly middle-class, and exotic "atmospheric" theaters that could seat up to 3,000 patrons spread to cities small and large across the country. Thanks to increased film length, monetary inflation, and the monumental salaries newly commanded by stars, production budgets rose by as much as ten times their prewar level, and the movies became a major national industry in the span of several years. Filmmaking practices and narrative formulas were standardized to facilitate mass production, and Wall Street began to invest heavily in the industry for both economic and political gain (i.e., it was in the material interest of the wealthy and the powerful to have the new mass medium of the movies—and later of radio—under their control). New money, new power, and the "new morality"[1] of the postwar Jazz Age all combined to make Hollywood in the 1920s the modern Babylon of popular lore.

The industry giants at the beginning of the 1920s, known collectively as the "Big Three," were Zukor's Famous Players–Lasky Corporation, which had acquired Para-

---

1. The mood of postwar America was one of bitterness, disillusionment, and cynicism not unlike that of the post-Watergate era, but intensified by the deaths of 500,000 Americans during the "Spanish flu" epidemic of 1918-19. The "new morality" was an adjunct of this mood. It rejected the "old morality" of Victorian idealism for a fashionable materialism that emphasized wealth, sensation, and sexual freedom. The "new morality" encouraged the widespread use of drugs (mainly nicotine and alcohol; in Hollywood, cocaine), female liberation (women won the vote in 1920), and sexual promiscuity. Its spread was facilitated by the decade's relative economic prosperity and by simultaneous revolutions in communications (mass distribution of films; the booming of network radio) and transportation (mass marketing of the private automobile; the beginnings of commercial aviation). Politically, however, the period was characterized by violent strikebreaking, anti-Bolshevism, and right-wing reaction.

6.1 A typical "atmospheric" theater interior of the 1920s, with Moorish decor and cloud machine.

6.3 The formation of United Artists, 1919: Fairbanks, Griffith, Pickford, and Chaplin.

mount Pictures as its distribution and exhibition wing in 1916 and was commonly known as Paramount; Loew's, Inc., the national theater chain owned by Marcus Loew that had moved into production with the acquisition of Metro Pictures in 1920; and First National (after 1921, Associated First National), the company founded in 1917 by twenty-six of the nation's largest exhibitors to combat the practice of block booking (invented by Zukor) by

6.2 A drawing of the auditorium of the Roxy Theater—"the Cathedral of the Motion Picture"—in New York City, c. 1927.

financing its own productions (see pp. 39–40). United Artists was formed in 1919 by the era's four most prominent film artists—D. W. Griffith, Charlie Chaplin, Mary Pickford, and Douglas Fairbanks—in order to produce and distribute their own films, and it was a major force in the industry until the advent of sound (and became so again, in the 1970s). Metro-Goldwyn-Mayer emerged as a powerful new studio combine in 1924 through the merger of Metro Pictures, Goldwyn Pictures, and Louis B. Mayer Productions under the auspices of Loew's, Inc. Hollywood's second string in the 1920s, the "Little Five," consisted of the Fox Film Corporation; Producers Distributing Corporation (PDC); Film Booking Office (FBO); Carl Laemmle's Universal Pictures; and Warner Bros. Pictures, which would force the industry to convert to sound by introducing the Vitaphone process in 1926 and would absorb First National in the process. Below these were about thirty thinly capitalized minor studios, of which only Columbia, Republic, and Monogram survived the coming of sound.[2]

2. Some sense of the studios' economic strength during the decade is provided by the following figures. In 1923, Famous Players–Lasky, First National, Loew's, Fox, and Universal each released between 46 and 63 features apiece; Warner Bros. and United Artists released 11 each; and all of the other companies combined released 123 (including 26 by the American branch of the Pathé exchange, mainly Hal Roach and Mack Sennett comedies). Simultaneously, the "Big Three" were moving to eliminate competition by extending distribution internationally and purchasing first-run theaters in major urban markets, foreign and domestic. Famous Players-Lasky arrived on the top of the heap in 1926 when it acquired First National's most profitable theater chains, notably the Balaban & Katz circuit in Chicago. The coming of sound, of course, would change all of these relationships radically.

Thomas Ince, Mack Sennett, and the Studio System of Production

It was in the 1920s that the studios became great factories for the large-scale production of mass commercial entertainment, and this was mainly due to the example of Thomas Harper Ince (1882–1924) in the previous decade. Like Griffith, Ince had begun his career as an actor-director at American Biograph in 1910 and ultimately established his own studio, Inceville, in the Santa Ynez Canyon near Hollywood in 1912. Here Ince directed over a hundred films, ranging in length from two to five reels, before turning exclusively to production in late 1913. Between 1914 and 1918, he built Inceville into the first recognizably modern Hollywood studio, complete with five self-contained shooting stages; his mode of production became the prototype for the highly organized studio system that was to dominate the American film industry for the next forty years. Ince's practice was to set up a number of production units on his lot, each headed by a director. Writers, working in close collaboration with both Ince and the directors, would prepare detailed shooting scripts (also known as continuities or scenarios) in which the entire production was laid out shot by shot. Ince would then approve the script, and the film would go into production according to a strict timetable. When the shooting was finished, Ince would supervise the editing and retain authority over the final cut.[3] This kind of filmmaking was very much the opposite of Griffith's mode of improvisation, but it represented the wave of the American cinema's heavily capitalized future, and it helps to explain why Griffith was not to be a part of that future for very long. Still, Ince was like Griffith in his genius for visualizing narrative, and most of his productions—the vast majority of them action-packed Westerns—tended to be well-paced, tightly constructed features that bore the strong stamp of his personality.

Ince and Griffith actually became business partners for several years with Mack Sennett in the ill-fated Triangle Film Corporation, founded by Harry Aitken after he left Mutual in 1915. In conception, this organization was sound: each of the three directors was to supervise the production of films of the type that had made him

popular and famous—action films and Westerns for Ince, two-reel slapstick comedies for Sennett, melodrama and spectacle for Griffith. In practice Triangle failed after three years due to miscalculation of the public's taste and misguided attempts to bring stars of the legitimate stage to the screen. When the failure occurred, Ince built himself a large new studio at Culver City (which would become the physical plant of MGM some ten years later) and continued to produce features there until his death in 1924. In the course of his career, Ince had introduced the detailed scenario, or continuity script, to the filmmaking process and pioneered the studio system of production. He had also given many talented actors and directors their first important opportunities to work in film: William S. Hart, Sessue Hayakawa, Billie Burke, Frank Borzage, Henry King, Lloyd Ingraham, Fred Niblo, Rowland V. Lee, Lambert Hillyer, and Francis Ford all trained at Inceville. Finally, as a director Ince had contributed to the cinema a number of tautly constructed feature films in several genres, such as *The Battle of Gettysburg* (1913), *The Typhoon* (1914), *The Coward* (1915), *Hell's Hinges* (1916), *The Aryan* (1916), *Civilization* (1916), *The Patriot (1916), The Beggar of Cawnpore (1917), Human Wreckage (1923), and Anna Christie* (1923), which are for the most part models of fast-paced and economical narrative form. As John Ford remarked, "Ince had a great influence on films, for he tried to make them move."

Another architect of the American studio system, and the founder of silent screen comedy, was Ince's and Griffith's partner in the Triangle Film Corporation, Mack Sennett (1880–1960). Sennett had worked as an actor in many of Griffith's Biograph films and set himself consciously to study the director's methods. He too

---

3. For an economic analysis of the Ince system and the central role of the continuity script as a blueprint for shot assembly and quality/cost-control, see Janet Staiger, "Dividing Labor for Production Control: Thomas Ince and the Rise of the Studio System," *Cinema Journal* 18, 2 (Spring 1979): 16–25, and "The Central Producer System: Centralized Management after 1914," in David Bordwell, Janet Staiger, and Kristin Thompson, *The Classical Hollywood Cinema: Film Style and Mode of Production to 1960* (New York: Columbia University Press, 1985), pp. 128–141. Ince had two brothers who were also in the film business, John (1879–1947), who was a not terribly successful actor-director, and Ralph (1887–1937), who began his directing career in 1912, working nonstop first at Inceville and, after the coming of sound until his death in an auto accident, at Warner Bros.' UK studio in Teddington, near London, where he is credited with "discovering" the young Australian actor Errol Flynn (1909–1959).

6.4 Keystone mayhem in an unidentified Sennett film.

began to direct films for Biograph in 1910 but was given very little creative freedom. So in September 1912 Sennett founded the Keystone Film Company in Fort Lee, New Jersey, with the financial backing of Adam Kessel, Jr., and Charles O. Baumann, the owners of the New York Motion Picture Company, and within the month he had moved his company to the old Bison studios in Hollywood. Here, between 1913 and 1935, he produced thousands of one- and two-reel films and hundreds of features that created a new screen genre—the silent slapstick comedy—that was to become the single most vital American mode of the 1920s. Influenced by circus, vaudeville, burlesque, pantomime, the comic strip, and the chase films of the French actor Max Linder, Sennett's Keystone comedies posited a surreal and anarchic universe where the logic of narrative and character was subordinated to purely visual humor of a violent but fantastically harmless nature. It is a world of inspired mayhem—of pie-throwing, cliff-hanging, auto-chasing, and, preeminently, blowing things up. The slam-bang comic effect of these films depended upon rapid-fire editing and the "last-minute rescue" as learned from Griffith, and also upon Sennett's own incredibly accurate sense of pace. He had a genius for timing movement, both the frenetic physical activity that filled the frames of his films and the breathless editing rhythms that propelled them forward at breakneck speed. Sennett's films often parodied the conventions of other films, especially those of Griffith (e.g., *Teddy at the Throttle*, 1916), or satirized

contemporary America's worship of the machine (*Wife and Auto Trouble*, 1916). Just as often, they would develop a single improvised sight gag involving the Keystone Kops or the Sennett Bathing Beauties into a riotous series of visual puns whose only logic was associative editing (*The Masquerader*, 1914; *The Surf Girl*, 1916).

In the first two years at Keystone, Sennett directed most of his films himself, but after 1914 he adopted the Inceville model and began to function exclusively as a production chief in close association with his directors, actors, and writers. Unlike Ince, however, Sennett preferred simple story ideas to detailed shooting scripts, and he always left room in his films for madcap improvisation. The number of great comedians and directors who began their careers at Keystone is quite amazing. Sennett discovered and produced the first films of Charlie Chaplin, Harry Langdon, Fatty Arbuckle, Mabel Normand, Ben Turpin, Gloria Swanson, Carole Lombard, Wallace Beery, Marie Dressler, and W. C. Fields. He also provided the training ground for some of the most distinguished directors of comedy in the American cinema: Chaplin and Keaton, of course, but also Malcolm St. Clair, George Stevens, Roy Del Ruth, and Frank Capra. Furthermore, the enormous international popularity of Sennett's Keystone comedies contributed substantially to America's commercial dominance of world cinema in the years following World War I. Sennett's realization that the cinema was uniquely suited to acrobatic visual humor established a genre that in the 1920s would become perhaps the most widely admired and vital in the history of American film. Many serious critics, at least, regard it as such. And yet Sennett's conception of comedy was wed to the *silent* screen. Purely visual humor loses a great deal to the logic of language and naturalistic sound; and when silence ceased to be an essential component of the cinema experience, the genre that Sennett had founded vanished from the screen. Sennett himself continued to make films after the conversion to sound, but by 1935 Keystone was bankrupt, and its founder did not produce another film before his death in 1960.

Charlie Chaplin

Sennett's most important and influential protégé was Charlie Chaplin (1889–1977). Chaplin, the son of impov-

6.5 The final shot of Chaplin in *The Tramp* (Charles Chaplin, 1915).

the six-reel feature *Tillie's Punctured Romance* (Mack Sennett, 1914) at Keystone, progressively refining the character of the sad little clown in oversized shoes, baggy pants, and an undersized coat and derby.

But Chaplin's gifts were meant for a more subtle style of comedy than the frenetic rhythms of the Keystone films allowed, so in 1915 he signed a contract with Essanay to make fourteen two-reel shorts for the then-enormous sum of $1,250 a week. He directed these and all of his subsequent films himself, based on his experiences at Keystone, evolving his brilliant characterization of the little tramp, totally at odds with the world about him, through the exquisite art of mime. Chaplin's best Essanay films were *The Tramp, Work, The Bank,* and *A Night at the Show* (all 1915), and they made him so popular that in the following year he was able to command a star salary of $10,000 a week plus a signatory bonus of $150,000 in a contract for twelve films with Mutual, of which the greatest are *The Floorwalker* (1916), *The Fireman* (1916), *One A.M.* (1916), *The Pawnshop* (1916), *The Rink* (1916), *Easy Street* (1917),

erished British music hall entertainers, had spent his childhood on stage. Like Charles Dickens and D. W. Griffith, both of whom he greatly resembled, Chaplin's vision of the world was colored by a youth of economic deprivation, and he felt deeply sympathetic toward the underprivileged all of his life. Chaplin was already a performer on an American vaudeville tour when he was engaged by Keystone Film in 1913 for $150 a week. In his first film for Sennett, *Making a Living* (1914), he played a typical English dandy, but by his second, *Mabel's Strange Predicament* (1914), he had already begun to develop the character and costume of "the little tramp," which would make him world-famous and become a kind of universal cinematic symbol for our common humanity. Chaplin made thirty-four shorts and

6.6 *The Immigrant* (Charles Chaplin, 1917): arriving at Ellis Island.

6.7 Chaplin makes a meal of a boot in *The Gold Rush* (Charles Chaplin, 1925).

The Immigrant (1917), and *The Adventurer* (1917). These two-reelers were produced with infinite care and constitute twelve nearly perfect masterpieces of mime. They also made Chaplin internationally famous and first showed his great gift for social satire—a satire of the very poor against the very rich, of the weak against the powerful, that endeared him to the former but not to the latter, especially during the Depression. In *The Immigrant*, for example, one of the most memorable sequences is predicated upon the hypocrisy of American attitudes toward immigration and upon the brutality of the immigration authorities themselves. As Charlie's ship arrives at Ellis Island, he looks up with hope and pride at the Statue of Liberty. Then a title announcing "The Land of Liberty" is followed by a shot of the New York port police forcibly herding together a large number of immigrant families for processing like so many cattle. In the next shot, Charlie casts another glance at the Statue of Liberty—this one suspicious, even disdainful.

By June 1917 Chaplin had gained such star power that he was offered a $1 million contract with First National to produce eight films for the company, regardless of length. This deal enabled him to establish his own studios, where he made all of his films from 1918 until he left the country in 1952. His cameraman for all of these productions was Rollie Totheroh (1891–1967), whom he had first met in 1915 at Essanay. Most of Chaplin's First National films were painstakingly crafted two- and three-reelers, like *A Dog's Life* (1918), *Shoulder Arms* (1918), *The Idle Class* (1921), and *Pay Day* (1922), which continued the vein of social criticism begun at Mutual. But Chaplin's most successful effort for First National was the first feature-length film he directed, *The Kid* (1921). This was an

autobiographical comedy/drama about the tramp's commitment to an impoverished little boy of the slums that combined pathos with tender humor and became an international hit, earning over $2.5 million for its producers in the year of its release and making its child lead, the five-year-old Jackie Coogan, a star. Chaplin's last film under the First National contract was the four-reel feature *The Pilgrim* (1923), a social satire in which an escaped prisoner (Chaplin) is mistaken for a minister by the venal parishioners of a small Texas town, with hilarious results. The film is a brilliant comic assault on religious hypocrisy, and it may well have contributed to the venomous personal attacks launched against Chaplin by religious groups a few years later.

After he had fulfilled his obligation to First National, Chaplin was free to release his films through United Artists. His first United Artists film was the much-admired *A Woman of Paris* (1923), a sophisticated "drama of fate" whose subtle suggestiveness influenced filmmakers as diverse as Ernst Lubitsch and René Clair (see pp. 188–90 and 311–12). Chaplin appeared only briefly as a porter in *A Woman of Paris*, which, like all of his films after 1923, was a full-length feature, but in his comic epic *The Gold Rush* (1925) he returned to the central figure of the little tramp. Set against the Klondike gold rush of 1898, this film manages to make high comedy out of hardship, starvation, and greed as three prospectors fight it out for the rights to a claim. In the subtlety of its characterization, the brilliance of its mime, and its blending of comic and tragic themes, *The Gold Rush* is Chaplin's most characteristic work. It is as popular today as it was in 1925, and it remained his personal favorite. *The Circus* (1928), in which the tramp attempts to become a professional clown, is a beautifully constructed silent film released during the conversion to sound. In honor of it, Chaplin was given a special award at the first Academy Awards ceremony in 1929 for "versatility and genius in writing, acting, directing, and producing." During the filming of *The Circus*, however, Chaplin was involved in a divorce suit brought by his second wife, and he became the target of a vicious campaign of personal abuse on the part of religious and "moralist" groups, which nearly drove him to suicide. It was the first of many clashes between Chaplin and the established order in America.

Characteristically, Chaplin's first two sound films were produced with musical scores (written by Chaplin) and sound effects but little spoken dialogue: it was his way of extending the great art of silent mime into the era of sound.[4] *City Lights* (1931) is a sentimental but effective film in which the unemployed tramp falls in love with a blind flower girl and goes through a series of misadventures, including robbery and a jail term, in order to raise money for the operation that can restore her sight. Chaplin called the film "a comedy romance in pantomime," and it is, but *City Lights* is also a muted piece of social criticism in which the cause of the poor is defended against that of the rich. If there were any remaining doubts about the nature of Chaplin's social attitudes, they were dispelled by *Modern Times* (1936), a film about the dehumanization of the common working man in a world run for the wealthy by machines. In it, Chaplin plays a factory worker who is fired when he suffers a nervous (but hilarious) breakdown on the assembly line, moves through a variety of other jobs, and ends up unemployed but undefeated.[5] The film's satire on industrialization and inequity in the "modern times" of the Great Depression earned it little popularity among the powerful in the United States, where in some quarters it was called "Red propaganda," or in Germany and Italy, where it was banned. But *Modern Times* was enormously successful in the rest of Europe, and it remains today one of Chaplin's funniest, best structured, and most socially committed works.

In *The Great Dictator* (1940) Chaplin produced his first full talkie and one of the first anti-Nazi films to come out of Hollywood. A satire on European dictatorships, the film chronicles the rule of Adenoid Hynkel, dictator of Tomania, as he persecutes the Jews and plunges Europe

6.8 *Modern Times* **(Charles Chaplin, 1936).**

into yet another war. Chaplin played the dual role of Hynkel and an amnesiac Jewish barber who is Hynkel's double. Released some eighteen months before Pearl Harbor, the film was not well received by the critics: many thought its politics too serious, others found them not serious enough. Still, *The Great Dictator* was a commercial hit owing to its maker's continuing popularity as a star. During the war, however, Chaplin gave a series of openly political speeches in support of the Soviet Union,

4. Since *A Woman of Paris*, Chaplin had taken active interest in the musical accompaniment for his silent films, and he went on to compose the scores for all seven of his sound features, plus the silent compilation film *The Chaplin Review* (1959). The legend of Chaplin's "heroic" resistance to sound seems to have been largely self-propagated. *City Lights*, e.g., meticulously shot over a three-year period (December 1927–January 1931), contains numerous visual cues for sound effects, and *Modern Times*, in production even longer (September 1933–January 1936), mounts a sophisticated critique of the dialogue film by having all of its audible speech issue from machines (phonographs, PA systems, etc.).

5. According to David A. Hounshell in *From the American System to Mass Production, 1800–1932* (Baltimore: Johns Hopkins University Press, 1984, pp. 319–20), the assembly line in *Modern Times* was based on Henry Ford's Model T "factory belt" system—the result of a VIP tour Chaplin had been given by Ford of his Highland Park plant in 1923. The film itself, however, which Chaplin had originally wanted to call *The Masses*, was inspired by René Clair's 1931 feature *À Nous la liberté* (see p. 313).

which made him a prime candidate for the postwar black-list (which will be discussed in Chapter 11). Worse, he became ensnared in a notorious paternity suit by a former "protégée" (Joan Barry) and was put on federal trial in 1944 for violating the Mann Act.[6] Not unreasonably, Chaplin's next film, originally suggested to him by Orson Welles, was the dark and cynical *Monsieur Verdoux* (1947), "a comedy of murder" based upon the exploits of the infamous French mass-murderer Landru. In it, a Parisian bank clerk (Chaplin) loses his job and takes up the practice of marrying and then murdering rich, middle-aged women in order to support his invalid wife and small son. He is caught, and while awaiting execution Verdoux states the film's theme concisely in an argument with a fellow prisoner: "Wars, conflict, it's all business. One murder makes a villain; millions a hero. Numbers sanctify." The film was bitterly attacked in the United States, where it was released on the eve of the hysterical anti-Communist witch-hunts of the Cold War era; it was withdrawn from circulation after six weeks but had great success in France. The relationship between Chaplin and his American audiences had grown increasingly strained since the disappearance of the little tramp and the emergence of the liberal social critic, but resentment of Chaplin went back at least as far as the moralistic campaigns of the 1920s. Some of this animosity was generated by Chaplin's retention of British citizenship since coming to the United States and his inconsistency in paying his federal income tax.

In his last American film, *Limelight* (1952), Chaplin returned to the London music halls of his childhood to tell the bittersweet tale of an aging performer who triumphs over his own declining power and imminent death by curing a young ballet dancer of paralysis and starting her on her career. The film is long (two and a half hours), slow, and cinematically archaic, but it is one of Chaplin's finest testaments to that dignity and decency of human nature that he felt the twentieth century had done so much to destroy. In September 1952, Chaplin and his family were granted six-month exit visas to attend a royal premiere of *Limelight* in London. On the first day at sea, Chaplin received news by radio that the U.S. attorney general had rescinded his re-entry permit, subject to his appearance before an Immigration and Naturalization Service board of inquiry to answer charges of political and moral turpitude. In this manner, the highest-paid and most popular star in the history of American film

was forcibly ushered from his adopted country. Chaplin chose to take up residence in his homeland and, later, in Switzerland.

Five years later he responded to the U.S. Justice Department with *A King in New York* (1957). This strained political parable, independently produced in England, is about a European head of state who, while visiting the United States, is ruined by the malicious charges of the House Un-American Activities Committee, as Chaplin himself had been. *Limelight* had been subjected to an American Legion picketing campaign that forced the major theater chains to withdraw it after several weeks of distribution, and, given the prevailing climate, *A King in New York* could not be distributed in the United States at all. The former was rereleased in this country in 1972 and promptly won an Academy Award for the year's Best Original Score. (In that same year, Chaplin received an Honorary Academy Award "for the incalculable effect he has had on making motion pictures, the art form of this century.") *A King in New York* had its first American release in 1976, to generally unenthusiastic reviews. The film is understandably bitter and indifferently directed, but it does contain some fine satire on life in America during the 1950s.

Chaplin's last film was a limp bedroom farce, *The Countess from Hong Kong* (1966), starring Marlon Brando and Sophia Loren. The film is misconceived in terms of both script and direction, and it underscores the fact that Chaplin's greatest genius was as an actor and a mime. His sight gags turned on brilliantly conceived and executed camera blocking, and so long as his little tramp character stood at the center of his films, they were masterworks of comedy and pathos. When the tramp disappeared, the limitations of Chaplin's directorial ability became increasingly apparent. During the 1920s, however, the image of the little tramp became a worldwide symbol for the general excellence of the American cinema, and Chaplin himself will always remain one of its most important and distinguished directors.[7]

---

6. Chaplin was ultimately acquitted of these charges, which had been clandestinely encouraged by the FBI, which had kept the filmmaker under continuous surveillance since 1922.

7. Chaplin's status as a director has grown in light of the materials assembled by film historians Kevin Brownlow and David Gill for their

Buster Keaton

It's useful to compare Chaplin's cinema with that of his fellow filmmaker and comic genius Buster Keaton (1895–1966). Like Chaplin, Keaton had been raised in vaudeville by his parents; he made his first stage appearance with them at the age of three. From earliest youth, he was involved in solving complicated problems of *mise-en-scène* for the family act, and his later skill in direction may be traced to this experience. Though his reputation was eclipsed by Chaplin's throughout the 1920s, it seems clear today that Keaton was Chaplin's equal as both an actor and a director. When the family act broke up in 1917, the twenty-one-year-old Keaton was already a star. He was offered a contract to appear in the Shuberts' popular *Passing Show* of 1917; but he decided to enter the movies instead by going to work as a supporting player at Joseph M. Schenck's Comique Film Corporation, formed in the spring of 1917 to produce the films of Roscoe "Fatty" Arbuckle for release through Paramount. Here Keaton made fifteen two-reel shorts with Arbuckle—from *The Butcher Boy* in 1917 to *The Garage* in 1919—in which the quality and sophistication of the studio's product increased notably in both form and substance.

In late 1919, Schenck formed Buster Keaton Productions to produce two-reel comedy shorts starring Keaton and acquired the former Chaplin studios for the purpose. Schenck handled all of the financing but gave Keaton complete creative freedom in writing and directing at a salary of $1,000 per week plus 25 percent of the profits. The resulting nineteen shorts, made between 1920 and 1923 and released through Metro and First National, represent, with Chaplin's Mutual films, the high point of American slapstick comedy.[8] The best of them are films like *One Week* (1920), *The Goat* (1921), *Playhouse* (1921), *The Boat* (1921), *Cops* (1922), and *The Balloonatic* (1923), whose complexity of structure and fine visual sense make them unique among slapstick shorts. Keaton always maintained that comedy must be funny without being ridiculous, and for this reason he took great pains to make his films credible in dramatic as well as comic terms. Unlike Sennett and his many imitators, much of Keaton's excellence as a filmmaker stemmed from a strict adherence to the dramatic logic of his narratives and the use of gags that progress in a geometrical pattern grounded in character and plot. Keaton's first feature was the seven-reel *The Saphead*, directed by Herbert Blaché (1882–1953) for Metro late in 1920. This rather limp adaptation of an 1887 comedy about a family of Wall Street brokers was important to Keaton's development since it gave him his first opportunity to create a continuous dramatic characterization in film. By 1923, two-reelers were becoming increasingly unprofitable to produce due to the public's mania for features, and Schenck[9] changed the Keaton studio's production output from eight shorts to two independent features per year, to be distributed by Metro/

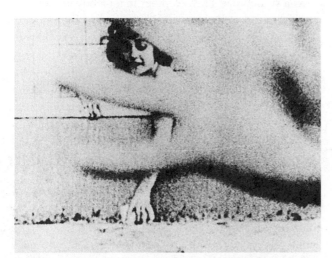

6.9 *One Week* (Buster Keaton, 1920): a hand blocks the lens for privacy.

three-hour Thames Television series *The Unknown Chaplin* (1983). Working with Chaplin's widow Oona and silent-film collector Raymond Rohauer, Brownlow and Gill recovered from Chaplin's private archive and other sources some 300,000 feet of film never before seen by the public, including rushes and out takes from the Mutual two-reelers *The Circus, City Lights,* and *Modern Times*, plus home movies, camera tests, and two complete shorts, *How to Make Movies* (1918) and *The Professor* (1922). The footage reveals Chaplin to have been a fanatical perfectionist who "rehearsed" on film, shooting and printing literally hundreds of takes until he got a particular sequence right or rejected it. He never intended the public to see these "rough drafts" of his work, but they document a hitherto unsuspected concern for technical precision.

8. Sixteen of these were nominally co-directed by Sennett veteran Eddie Cline (1892–1961) and two by Malcolm St. Clair (1897–1952).

9. By this time, Schenck and Keaton were brothers-in-law, the latter having married Natalie Talmadge (1898–1969) in 1921. Schenck had married the actress Norma Talmadge (1897–1957) in 1917 and promoted both her and her sister Constance (1900–1973) to stardom by the mid-1920s. Natalie seems to have been the least talented of the three Talmadge sisters, although she costarred admirably with Keaton in three of his silent features. They were divorced in 1932.

6.10 **Perfect timing: part of a trajectory gag from** *Cops.*

MGM, but over which the filmmaker was to retain complete artistic control. Keaton's salary was raised to star level ($2,500 per week plus 25 percent of the profits), and he entered the period of his greatest creativity.

It has been said that after 1923 Keaton was as important as any director practicing in Hollywood, and so strong was his creative personality that this is true even of the films that do not bear his name on the direction credits. His first independent feature for Keaton Productions, *The Three Ages* (1923), was a sparkling parody of Griffith's *Intolerance* directed by Keaton in collaboration with Eddie Cline (1892–1961) that depicted the trials of courtship through the ages by intercutting stories from three separate historical periods: the Stone Age, ancient Rome, and contemporary America. Though its *mise-en-*

scène is not as elaborate or its narrative as tightly integrated as those of his subsequent films, *The Three Ages* is a successful comedy whose hilarious conclusion introduced a classic Keaton device—the "trajectory" gag, in which the perfect timing of acting, directing, and editing propels the Keaton character through an extended series of dramatically connected sight gags ending in the denouement of a sequence or of an entire film. At the conclusion of the modern sequence of *The Three Ages*, for example, Keaton in long shot leaps from the fire escape of a six-story building toward an adjacent building, misses the ledge, and falls. A second long shot shows him falling through two canvas window awnings and catching hold of a third. In the next shot, Keaton uses the awning for ballast as he grabs hold of a drainpipe that comes loose in his arms. Another long shot shows him, still holding the pipe, pivoting into an open window two stories down. We cut here to a medium shot of the interior of a firehouse dormitory, with Keaton hurtling through the window, catching hold of the firemen's pole, and sliding down it. In the next shot, he arrives at the ground floor below and leaps onto the back of a fire engine about to answer an alarm. The final shot of the sequence shows Keaton arriving at a burning building and recognizing it as the police station from which he has just escaped as a wanted man. He slips quietly away, thus completing the trajectory.

Keaton's second independent feature, *Our Hospitality* (1923), represents a tremendous advance over *The Three Ages* and is one of his greatest films. Directed by Keaton in collaboration with Jack Blystone (1892–1938), it concerns a young man's involvement in a bloody family feud in the American South in the early days of the railroad. The film is a nearly perfect example of Keaton's ability to create serious narrative situations and then cause the gags to grow naturally out of them. It is also a film of great pictorial beauty that makes significant use of the **long take,** or **sequence shot,** composed in depth with dramatic action in the foreground, middle ground, and background of the frame. As always, Keaton's editing is fluid and perfectly timed, but unlike Griffith and his followers (Henry King, King Vidor, Rowland V. Lee, Frank Borzage), he does not exploit the montage effect for its own sake. And, as in many of Keaton's later films, **location shooting** (on Lake Tahoe) and close attention to the details of period costume and setting give *Our Hospitality* a realistic surface that both involves us in the narrative and lends credibility to the action.

Sherlock Jr. (1924), directed and edited solely by Keaton, is perhaps his most extraordinary feature-length work. In it, Keaton plays a projectionist in a neighborhood theater who is accused of theft by his girlfriend's father. Later, he falls asleep at work, while a ghostly image of himself leaves the projection booth, walks through the auditorium below, and enters the screen to become a part of the action, which has been transformed into the real-life drama of the framing story. At first, Keaton is thrown out of the frame by the villain. As he scrambles back into it, the scene changes through a cut and he is suddenly standing in front of a door. As he reaches to open it, the scene changes again and he finds himself in a garden. As he tries to sit down on a garden bench, there is a cut to a crowded street scene and Keaton tumbles into a stream of rushing traffic. This routine goes on for nearly three minutes before leading us into a more continuous dream narrative in which Keaton becomes "Sherlock Jr." and clears himself of all false charges, finally waking to his girlfriend's embrace in the projection room. The film is full of breathtakingly complicated (and dangerous) trajectory gags, but the sequence that depicts a real person trapped inside a movie is in many ways a comment on the process of film editing itself; the French avant-garde director René Clair called attention to its surrealistic aspects as early as 1925, when he compared *Sherlock Jr.* to Luigi Pirandello's play *Six Characters in Search of an Author* (1921),[1] and Woody Allen (see p. 410) has demonstrated the continuity of its influence as recently as *The Purple Rose of Cairo* (1985).

Keaton's next film, *The Navigator* (1924), directed in collaboration with Donald Crisp (1880–1974), was another virtuoso piece of sustained comic narrative. In it, Rollo Treadway (Keaton), a useless millionaire who can't even shave himself, and his scatterbrained fiancée are set adrift on an ocean liner by foreign spies. Alone, "these beautiful spoiled brats—the most helpless people in the world," as Keaton called them in a contemporary newspaper interview, must chart their survival through some hilarious adventures at sea. Unlike Chaplin, Keaton did not play the same character over and over again, but the narrative situation in which his characters find themselves was always pretty much the same: a vulnerable but plucky human hero, as in *The Navigator*, is confronted with some vast and seemingly insurmountable problem, usually involving objects and machines rather than other humans. It is a classical absurdist situation, and the comic effect arises from the hero's spirited but futile attempts to surmount the insurmountable, at which he ultimately—and for totally arbitrary reasons—somehow succeeds. Remarkably, Keaton never once repeated a narrative formula in his entire career.

Seven Chances (1925), directed by Keaton and adapted from an old David Belasco[2] farce, concerns a young man who stands to inherit a fortune if he can marry within twenty-four hours. The news is made public, and Keaton soon finds himself being pursued through the southern California hills by hundreds of rampaging prospective brides. The chase ends in one of Keaton's most striking and dangerous trajectories as he is forced to run down the sheer face of a hill dodging a landslide of 1,500 papier-mâché boulders that range in

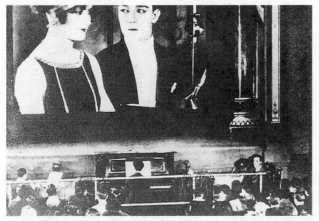

6.11 Keaton projects himself onto the screen within the screen in *Sherlock Jr.* **(Buster Keaton, 1924).**

1. In fact, Keaton's films were widely admired among European avant-gardists of the era, dadaists, surrealists, and absurdists alike. His work was known not only to Pirandello (1867–1936), but to Eugène Ionesco (1912–1994), Federico García Lorca (1899–1936—who wrote the short surrealist farce *El paseo de Buster Keaton* [*Buster Keaton Takes a Walk*] in 1930), and Samuel Beckett (1906–1989, who is said to have written *Waiting for Godot* (1952) with Keaton in mind and who later cast him in the leading role of his original screenplay *Film* (directed by Alan Schneider, 1965). Keaton's films also seem to have inspired both of the Luis Buñuel–Salvador Dalí collaborations, *Un Chien andalou* (1929) and *L'Âge d'or* (1930).

2. David Belasco (1854–1931) was an extremely successful writer, director, and producer of spectacular stage melodrama at the turn of the century. Griffith may have borrowed certain styles of lighting and decor from Belasco's *mise-en-scène* since he was well aware of them from his own career in the theater.

diameter from 1 to 8 feet. Once the sequence was set up, the rest was left to chance and to Keaton's great improvisatory talent as both director and performer: the conclusion of *Seven Chances* remains one of the most stunning of any slapstick comedy, and it clearly provided the inspiration for the opening of Steven Spielberg's *Raiders of the Lost Ark* (1981). Keaton's next two films were somewhat gag-impoverished, perhaps because he had lost the team of writers who had been collaborating with him since the days of the shorts—Clyde Bruckman, Jean Havez, and Joseph Mitchell. *Go West* (1925), a parody of the popular Western genre, misfires through uncharacteristic sentimentality and disunity, while *The Battling Butler* (1926) is a tale of a spoiled rich boy who pretends to be a boxing champion in order to impress his girlfriend. The latter film concludes with an unaccountably brutal fight sequence that reminds us that Keaton's comedy, like Chaplin's, could occasionally turn bitter, melancholy, and surprisingly unpleasant.

In 1927, Keaton returned to the top of his form with *The General*, which he directed in collaboration with his former scriptwriter Clyde Bruckman for release by United Artists, of which Joseph Schenck had become president in 1926. Although it was poorly received by Keaton's contemporaries, many critics today regard this film as his masterpiece, and Walter Kerr has linked it with Chaplin's *The Gold Rush* (1925) as one of the two great comic epics of the cinema. Based on a real incident from the American Civil War in which Union undercover agents hijacked a Southern locomotive,[3] *The General* achieved a nearly perfect integration of dramatic action and comedy. Keaton plays Johnny Gray, a civilian railroad engineer during the war who has been unjustly accused of cowardice. His locomotive, the *General*, and his fiancée are seized by Union spies and driven northward. Johnny singlehandedly pursues the train into the heart of enemy territory, recaptures it along with his fiancée, and speeds back to the South with what seems to be the entire Union army in hot pursuit. At Rock River, he burns a railroad bridge behind him and precipitates a spectacular comic catastrophe, as a Union locomotive hurtles onto the bridge, causing its collapse, and plunges 30 feet into the river, creating a huge geyser of smoke and steam. In sheer pictorial beauty *The General* surpasses even *Our Hospitality* (1923). Shot on location in the forests of Oregon, its battle scenes are lit and composed, like those of *The Birth of a Nation*, to resemble the Civil War photographs of Mathew Brady. But Keaton achieves a more authentic re-

6.12 **Keaton examines a mortar in** *The General* **(Buster Keaton, 1927).**

3. Walt Disney Productions made an adventure film based on the same incident, entitled *The Great Locomotive Chase* (Francis D. Lyon, 1956). The Keaton film was reworked once, by MGM, as *A Southern Yankee* (S. Sylvan Simon, 1948), with Red Skelton in the Keaton role. Ironically, both later films were commercial hits, while *The General* was a dismal box-office failure, actually losing money for Schenck and UA.

6.13 The collapse of the railroad bridge in *The General*.

creation of the era than either Griffith or John Huston twenty-five years later in *The Red Badge of Courage* (1951) through the impeccable verisimilitude of his costumes and sets. As for comedy, the timing and structure of *The General*'s trajectories have never been equaled. The film seems to validate the statement by his biographer that Keaton "could perform miracles as easily as he breathed."

Keaton made only two more independent features—both distributed at a loss by United Artists—before his studio was acquired by the MGM conglomerate. *College*, co-directed with James W. Horne (1880–1942), has Keaton as a contemporary college student, a bookworm who aspires to the hand of the most popular girl in school by constantly attempting to prove his nonexistent athletic prowess. The film is conventionally structured and photographed (perhaps because of the interference of the studio's new business manager), but it is as crammed full of energetic gags and trajectories as any Keaton short. *Steamboat Bill Jr.* (1928), the last film Keaton produced himself, was one of his finest. The plot is classic Keaton: an effeminate youth returns from college to his burly father's Mississippi riverboat and falls in love with the daughter of his father's rival, wreaking havoc on both families. The film concludes with a spectacularly realized cyclone that blows away the whole town, a sequence that contains Keaton's most dangerous stunt: in the midst of

the storm, an entire house front collapses on him, but he is saved by virtue of standing precisely at the point of a window opening in the façade, the frame clearing his head and body by inches on either side. As Keaton remarked to an interviewer, "It's a one-take scene. . . . You don't do those things twice." Co-directed with Charles F. Reisner (1887–1962), *Steamboat Bill Jr.* is one of Keaton's most technically polished films, full of fluid camera movement and striking composition in depth as well as the perfectly edited cyclone sequence. Once again, however, the public failed to respond, and the picture lost money.

In 1928, Keaton allowed his company to be absorbed by MGM with the promise that Joseph Schenck's brother Nicholas, the newly installed president of Loew's, Inc., would allow him to continue his creative mode of production. There was little hope that the promise would or could be kept within the factory-like system of the world's largest studio, and Keaton soon found his team of directors, writers, and technicians dispersed to work on other MGM projects. Keaton himself was cast in a film about a bumbling Hearst newsreel cameraman trying to win the hand of another Hearst employee (Hearst owned large shares of MGM stock, and his papers could be counted on for good reviews). The improbable result was *The Cameraman* (1928), Keaton's last great film, co-directed with Edward Sedgwick (1892–1953), which has been described as "a newsreel by Buster Keaton of a newsreel by Buster Keaton." In many ways, *The Cameraman* is as self-reflexive as *Sherlock Jr.*, mixing documentary footage of real events with footage of dramatically staged events and at some points integrating the two completely—as when Keaton and his sweetheart are showered with confetti in a New York tickertape parade and the camera pulls back to reveal the world-famous aviator Charles Lindbergh, who had made the first transatlantic flight the year before, seated in the car behind them. Keaton's last silent fea-

6.14 Two shots from the cyclone sequence in _Steamboat Bill Jr._ (Charles F. Reisner, 1928).

(e.g., _Doughboys_ [Edward Sedgwick, 1930]; _Sidewalks of New York_ [Jules White, 1931]; _The Passionate Plumber_ [Edward Sedgwick, 1932]; _What! No Beer?_ [Edward Sedgwick, 1933]), however bad, were quite successful at the box office, and no one at MGM, from Schenck through Irving Thalberg through Mayer, _wanted_ to fire him. But Keaton could simply not adapt himself to working within the restrictive environment of the studio system, and his unhappiness manifested itself in heavy drinking. His increasingly erratic behavior and long absences from the set caused costly production slowdowns, and Mayer finally decided to fire him on February 2, 1933, less for personal reasons (although he loathed Keaton as he loathed all artists) than for corporate ones.[5] Simultaneously, his personal life fell apart, and though he played small parts in numerous talkies (most prominently, Billy Wilder's _Sunset Boulevard_ [1950] and Chaplin's _Limelight_ [1952]) and appeared occasionally on television, his career as a filmmaker effectively ended in 1929. It seems clear today that of the two great silent clowns, Chaplin and Keaton, Keaton had the stronger sense of narrative structure and _mise-en-scène_. His films as a director were often more formally beautiful than Chaplin's, and Keaton's technical genius for setting up and filming his strenuously elaborate gags, and the reckless physical courage with which he performed them, were extraordinary. (Keaton never used a stunt man in his films, although he did employ an Olympic champion to pole vault for him in _College._) Yet, like Chaplin, Keaton was a magnificently subtle actor. His "great stone face" was actually capable of suggesting a vast range of emotion, and there was very little that he could not express with his body. Like Chaplin, Keaton knew that great comedy always exists close to the brink of tragedy, but sentimentality does not play an important part in Keaton's work, as it does in Chaplin's. For both artists, comedy was a strange blend of logic and fantasy in which the impossible was made to seem real. But Keaton seems to have best understood how dreamlike and surreal is the process of film itself.

ture, _Spite Marriage_ (Edward Sedgwick, 1929), was a great popular success, even though it was released at the height of the public's new mania for sound. It contained a great many subtle gag routines growing out of the situation in which a lowly pants-presser marries a beautiful actress, but the film was not the equal of its predecessors and showed signs of interference by MGM executives.[4]

There is no question that Keaton's talent could have survived and even profited from the conversion to sound, but in 1933, after appearing in seven witless talking features for MGM, he was fired from the studio by vice president and general manager Louis B. Mayer. Keaton always insisted that he had been dismissed because of a personal insult to Mayer; but, according to his most recent biographer, Tom Dardis, the situation was more complex. The evidence shows that Keaton's sound films

---

4. Like _The General_, Keaton's last two silent features were remade by MGM as Red Skelton vehicles—_Spite Marriage_ as _I Dood it_ (Vincente Minnelli, 1943) and _The Cameraman_ as _Watch the Birdie_ (Jack Donohue, 1950). Keaton was an uncredited gag writer on all three.

5. After 1937, MGM employed Keaton sporadically as an uncredited gag-writer for Red Skelton and the Marx Brothers for $200 to $300 a week. He also served as technical advisor for Paramount's specious and unfunny "biopic" _The Buster Keaton Story_ (Sidney Sheldon, 1957), which cast Donald O'Connor in the title role.

Harold Lloyd and Others

Another important architect of silent comedy was Harold Lloyd (1893–1971). Lloyd was working as an extra for Universal Pictures in 1914 when he met Hal Roach, Sr. (1892–1992), who was to become Sennett's only major rival in the production of comic shorts in the 1920s. Roach had just established his own production company on the basis of a $3,000 inheritance, and he hired Lloyd as a comic at $3 per week. Between 1915 and 1917 Lloyd played tramp figures called "Lonesome Luke" and "Willie Work" that were highly imitative of Chaplin's tramp. But in a 1917 two-reeler entitled *Over the Fence* he discovered for the first time his very own comic persona—the earnest, mild-mannered boy next door with his horn-rimmed glasses. Over the next decade Lloyd developed this character into an archetype of American "normalcy" and niceness. Like all Americans, "Harold" was eager to succeed and could become quite aggressive in competition, but beneath it all there was a sound core of decency and innocence.

When he began to do feature work in the 1920s, Lloyd specialized in the "comedy of thrills"—a bizarre variant of Keystone mayhem in which the protagonist placed himself in real physical danger to elicit shocks of laughter from the audience. Lloyd's most famous film of this sort was *Safety Last* (directed by Fred Newmeyer and Sam Taylor, 1923), in which he scales the sheer face of a twelve-story building, apparently without safety devices, and ends up hanging more than a hundred feet above the rushing traffic, suspended from the hands of a large clock. Other important Lloyd features were *Grandma's Boy* (Fred Newmeyer, 1922), *Dr. Jack* (Fred Newmeyer, 1922), *Why Worry?* (Fred Newmeyer and Sam Taylor, 1923), *Girl Shy* (Newmeyer and Taylor, 1924), and *The Freshman* (Newmeyer and Taylor, 1925). By the mid-1920s, Lloyd had become more popular with American audiences in box-office terms alone than either Chaplin or Keaton. But, as with so many of the great silent clowns, his highly kinetic brand of humor did not survive the coming of sound, although he managed to make four sound films (including Preston Sturges's *The Sin of Harold Diddlebock* [1947])[6] before retiring in 1952. Lloyd's comic genius had neither the intellectual depth of Keaton's nor the emotional depth of Chaplin's. But as a slam-bang, razzle-dazzle acrobat Lloyd had no peers, and, as Walter Kerr has put it, his comedy of pure sensation made a whole generation of Americans feel good about themselves.

Two other popular Hal Roach comedians were Stan Laurel (1890–1965) and Oliver Hardy (1892–1957). Laurel was an Englishman who had first come to America in the same vaudeville troupe as Chaplin and had become a minor comic star for a variety of studios in the teens. Hardy was a native of Georgia who made his living as a singer and bit player until he was signed to a long-term acting contract by Roach in 1926. Laurel was signed shortly afterward, and in 1927 the two were teamed together in a two-reeler called *Putting the Pants on Philip* (Clyde Bruckman, 1927), initiating a comic partnership that lasted another twenty-five years. Between 1927 and 1929, Laurel and Hardy made twenty-seven silent shorts for Roach, including the minor classics *You're Darn Tootin'* (Edgar Kennedy, 1928), *Two Tars* (James Parrot, 1928), *Liberty* (Leo McCarey, 1929), *Wrong Again* (Leo McCarey, 1929), *Big Business* (James Horne, 1929), *Men of War* (Lewis Foster, 1929), *Bacon Grabbers* (Lewis Foster, 1929), and *The Hoosegow* (James Parrott, 1929); and they became the first important comic team in the history of film.

6.15 Harold Lloyd in *Safety Last* (Fred Newmeyer and Sam Taylor, 1923).

---

6. Released by United Artists at eighty-nine minutes; recut and reissued by RKO in 1950 as *Mad Wednesday* at seventy-seven minutes. See Tom Dardis, *Harold Lloyd: The Man on the Clock* (New York: Viking, 1983), pp. 263–84.

Since Laurel and Hardy had both been trained for the stage, they made an easy transition to sound, and as a consequence of two-reel talkies like *Hog Wild* (Parrott, 1930), *Another Fine Mess* (Parrott, 1930), *Laughing Gravy* (Horne, 1931), *Helpmates* (Parrott, 1931), *The Music Box* (Parrott, 1932), *Scram* (Raymond McCarey, 1932), *Busy Bodies* (Lloyd French, 1933), and *Them Thar Hills* (Charles Rogers, 1934), the team became extremely popular in the 1930s. They also survived the inevitable conversion from shorts to features in *Pardon Us* (Parrott, 1931), *Pack Up Your Troubles* (George Marshall and Raymond McCarey, 1932), *Fra Diavolo* (Hal Roach and Charles Rogers, 1933), *Sons of the Desert* (William A. Seiter, 1933), *Babes in Toyland* (Gus Meins and Charles Rogers, 1934), *Our Relations* (Harry Lachman, 1936), *Way Out West* (Horne, 1937), *Blockheads* (John G. Blystone, 1938), and *A Chump at Oxford* (Alfred Goulding, 1940). Though they frequently worked with such fine directors as George Stevens and Leo McCarey, Laurel was the guiding genius of the team. He wrote many of their scripts and produced some of their major films of the 1930s. The careers of Laurel and Hardy effectively ended after 1940, when they stopped working for Roach and were absorbed into the megalithic studio system. At Fox and MGM they were unable to shape their own material, and the features that they made after 1940 were weak attempts to recycle the great humor of their heyday.

Like Harold Lloyd's comedy, that of Laurel and Hardy was in the visually violent tradition of Keystone and usually ended in some form of anarchic destruction. Unlike the randomly organized Sennett shorts, however, Laurel and Hardy films always had a kind of structural logic whereby a single misbegotten incident would be progressively multiplied toward some catastrophic infinity. As characters, both comedians were simply overgrown children whose naked aggression and vengefulness was mirrored in the middle-class world about them. And the physical contrast they presented on the screen was undeniably funny. Laurel, the weak, whimpering, and barely coordinated little fool, and Hardy, the inept, self-important, and grossly inflated bully, offered a comic version of bourgeois stupidity that Flaubert might have admired.

Two other silent comics deserve mention here, although, like Laurel and Hardy, both are decidedly minor by comparison with Chaplin, Keaton, and Lloyd. Harry Langdon (1884–1944) came to work for Mack Sen-

6.16 Harry Langdon in *The Strong Man* (Frank Capra, 1926).

nett from vaudeville in 1924. In numerous shorts at Keystone between 1924 and 1926 he developed the haunting character of a middle-aged, baby-faced innocent whose pathetic naïveté was somewhat reminiscent of Chaplin without Chaplin's dignity. Langdon rose briefly to stardom in a series of three popular features made between 1926 and 1928—*Tramp, Tramp, Tramp* (Harry Edwards, 1926), *The Strong Man* (Frank Capra, 1926), and *Long Pants* (Frank Capra, 1927). Since the first of these films was written and the latter two were directed by Frank Capra, it has been suggested that he alone was responsible for the appeal of Langdon's whimsical comic presence. But Langdon was a brilliant pantomimist in his own right, and there was something uncanny in his infantile foolishness that belonged exclusively to the character he first created at Keystone. Nevertheless, Langdon's own features as a director, *Three's a Crowd* (1927), *The Chaser* (1928), and *Heart Trouble* (1928), were not as successful as the Capra films, and his stardom did not survive the coming of sound, although he continued to work as a character actor until his death.

Roscoe "Fatty" Arbuckle (1887–1933), tipping the scales at 270 pounds, also began at Keystone, where he worked successfully with Chaplin from 1914 to 1916 and became Sennett's principal star after Chaplin's departure for Essanay. Arbuckle's comic appeal rested almost solely upon the broad base of his fatness, his childishness, and a certain Sennettesque flair for mayhem. But his popularity was second only to Chaplin's during the brief course

6.17 Fatty Arbuckle in a Sennett short.

of his career. In 1917, Joseph M. Schenck founded the Comique Film Corporation to produce Arbuckle's work, and Arbuckle gave his friend Buster Keaton his first job in films there as a supporting player. In the earliest Arbuckle-Keaton collaborations, the latter was clearly the foil, but by 1919 Keaton had totally usurped Arbuckle as a comic talent. Arbuckle was still extremely popular and made eight successful features for Paramount between 1919 and 1921, when his career ended in a catastrophic scandal that rocked the movie industry and changed the course of Hollywood history.

Hollywood Scandals and the Creation of the MPPDA

Since the earliest days of the nickelodeon, moralists and reformers had agitated against the corrupting nature of the movies and their effects upon American youth, much as similar groups are concerned about the effects of television in our own era. Powerful pressure groups, often working through religious organizations, had been formed to protect American audiences from the display of morally pernicious materials on the screen. Though differently motivated, the storm of well-organized protest that greeted *The Birth of a Nation* in 1915 and caused its suppression in twelve states is a good example of how effective such pressure groups could be. But World War I, the coming of Prohibition, and increasing middle-class patronage of the movies had alleviated some of this ten-

sion; and after the war, the content of American films became increasingly sophisticated and risqué, reflecting the "new morality" of the Jazz Era—a compound of materialism, cynicism, and sexual license. The sentimental conventions of Griffithian melodrama were abandoned by all but a few as films suddenly began to depict and even glorify adultery, divorce, drinking, and drug taking. Simultaneously, the Hollywood of Babylonian legend was born of the impossibly extravagant production budgets and star salaries that mushroomed in the late teens—the Hollywood of baronial mansions, orgiastic parties, sexual promiscuity, and multiple divorce that has fascinated the American tabloid press from that day to our own. For a while, the stars were worshiped by the public from afar as a kind of new American royalty, a race of beautiful demigods basking in the sun-drenched splendors of Beverly Hills. But it transpired that many of the stars were human after all, some quite scandalously so, and producers soon sought to play down the publicity given to their private lives, properly fearing a moralistic backlash against the amorality of their life styles, which frequently involved the abuse of drugs, alcohol, and sex.

These fears were realized with a vengeance in September 1921, when Fatty Arbuckle was charged with the rape and murder of a young starlet named Virginia Rappe in the aftermath of a Labor Day weekend drinking party at a hotel suite in San Francisco. Arbuckle was indicted for manslaughter and stood trial three times before he was finally acquitted for lack of evidence in 1923. Miss Rappe had a history of peritonitis and had apparently died of a ruptured bladder aggravated by alcohol, but there were widespread allegations in the press that Arbuckle had raped her with a champagne bottle and crushed her beneath his great weight. Tabloids across the country portrayed him as a perverted beast, and the public outcry became so violent during this period that his pictures had to be withdrawn from circulation. To appease the moralists, Paramount fired Arbuckle, who was permanently barred from working in the industry again, even after he was exonerated by the courts. But Hollywood had more to account for than Fatty's indiscretions. During Arbuckle's second trial in February 1922, the chief director of Famous Players–Lasky and current president of the Screen Directors Guild, William Desmond Taylor (1877–1922), was found murdered in his Beverly Hills apartment. It seems that he had been conducting simultaneous affairs with the actress Mary Miles Minter (1902–

1984) and the popular Keystone comedienne Mabel Normand (1894–1930), who had been the last person to see him alive. Hungry for more scandal, the tabloid press implicated both women in the murder, though they were manifestly innocent, and destroyed their careers in the process. Within a year, Wallace Reid (1891–1923), a handsome actor who was a prototype of the clean-living American male, died of a drug overdose and was revealed to have been a long-term narcotics addict. These three scandals, as well as many smaller ones that were unearthed by the sensational press, produced a storm of public outrage against the depravity of Hollywood that was unprecedented in the film industry's brief history. Editorial denunciations by respectable publications like *Good Housekeeping* became commonplace; ministers and priests across the nation forbade their parishioners to go to the movies; women's clubs and reform groups demanded a mass boycott; and, by early 1922, thirty-six states and the federal government were considering the enactment of censorship laws. (The 1915 U.S. Supreme Court decision *Mutual v. Ohio* had placed motion pictures in a class with circuses "and all other shows and spectacles"; they were not protected against censorship by the First Amendment until the Court's *Miracle* decision of 1952—see Chapters 3, footnote p. 66, and 12, p. 428.) The threat was rendered even more serious by a steep decline in film attendance in 1922, a result less of the scandals than of two new sources of competition for Americans' leisure time—the radio, which began commercial **broadcasting** in 1922, and the family automobile, which became available through installment credit loans at about the same time. In brief, 1922 was the dawning of the age of mass communications and mass consumption in America, and Hollywood, whose chief business was both, found itself in the embarrassing position of having deeply offended its audience.

Following the example of major-league baseball, which had recently whitewashed a national bribery scandal (see John Sayles's *Eight Men Out* [1988]) by appointing a conservative federal judge to oversee its operations, the frightened Hollywood producers formed a self-regulatory trade organization, the Motion Picture Producers and Distributors of America (MPPDA) in March 1922, amid much publicity, and hired President Warren G. Harding's postmaster general, Will Hays (1879–1954), for $150,000 a year to head it. Hays was an ultraconservative Republican, Mason, Kiwanian, Rotarian, and Presbyterian elder

from Indiana, and his presence made the film industry's gesture of self-censorship convincing to the public and the government alike. Initially, the Hays Office, as the MPPDA[7] came to be called for the next twenty-three years, was a public-relations and lobbying organization that engaged in little real censorship, although it did help producers to compile a blacklist of 117 stars who were banned from the industry because of unfavorable publicity about their personal lives. There was a gently chiding "Purity Code," known facetiously as the "Don'ts and Be Carefuls," and producers were required to submit summaries of their screenplays to the Hays Office for approval. But the only "censorship" consisted of informal advising according to the principle of "compensating values" whereby, to paraphrase Arthur Knight, vice could be flaunted for six reels so long as virtue triumphed in the seventh. The main task of the Hays Office in the 1920s was to stave off the threat of government censorship by mollifying pressure groups, managing news, deflecting scandal, and generally discouraging close scrutiny of the industry. In the early 1930s, when sound helped to produce a new wave of excess in American films and touched off another round of national protest concerning the way in which the sounds of violence and vulgar language were exploited by early sound producers, the Hays Office became the medium for a very rigid form of censorship indeed, as administrator of the Draconian "Production Code." But in the 1920s it merely provided whitewash for overly enthusiastic manifestations of the "new morality" and helped producers subvert the careers of stars whose personal lives might make them too controversial. Today, it is clear that Hays himself was one of the more crooked members of the corrupt Harding administration, but he was an undeniably effective figurehead for the MPPDA who lent Hollywood a much-needed aura of respectability, sobriety, and moral rectitude at a time when its "sinfulness" had become a major national issue.

---

7. Hays was succeeded as "movie tsar" by U.S. Chamber of Commerce president Eric A. Johnston (1896–1962) in 1945, when the organization's name was changed to the Motion Picture Association of America (MPAA). Johnston was ultimately replaced by Jack Valenti (b. 1921) in 1966, and the Production Code was scrapped in favor of a ratings system instituted in 1968 (see pp. 428–29); like Hays, both successors have had close ties with the White House. Hays's crucial role in the creation and administration of the MPPDA during the 1920s is chronicled in *The Will Hays Papers, Part I: December 1921–March 1929*, ed. Douglas Gomery, a forty-three-reel microfilm publication with printed guide (Frederick, Md.: University Publications of America, 1987).

(Hays was also an effective lobbyist for the industry in Washington, where he helped to minimize federal taxes and forestall antitrust litigation.)

Cecil B. DeMille

The most successful and flamboyant representative of the "new morality" in all of its manifestations was Cecil B. DeMille (1881–1959).[8] A virtual incarnation of the values of Hollywood in the 1920s, DeMille had an uncanny ability to anticipate the tastes of his audiences and give them what they wanted before they knew they wanted it. He began his career by directing *The Squaw Man* (1914), the first feature-length Western ever made in Hollywood, for Jesse Lasky's Feature Play Company. The film was a great popular and critical success, and DeMille followed it with a series of Western features (*The Virginian*, 1914; *Call of the North*, 1914) and stage adaptations (*Carmen*, 1915) that made him famous. Like Griffith, DeMille had apprenticed in the melodramatic theatrical tradition of David Belasco, and these early films were striking for their expressive "Rembrandt" or "Lasky" lighting and vivid *mise-en-scène*. During the war, DeMille made a group of stirringly patriotic films—*Joan the Woman* (1917); *The Little American* (1917); *Till I Come Back to You* (1918)—and then shifted gears to pursue the postwar obsession with extramarital sex among the leisure class.

6.18 "Rembrandt" or "Lasky" lighting in Cecil B. DeMille's *The Woman God Forgot* (1917).

In a series of sophisticated comedies of manners aimed directly at Hollywood's new middle-class audience—*Old Wives for New* (1918), *Don't Change Your Husband* (1919), *Male and Female* (1919), *Why Change Your Wife?* (1920), *Forbidden Fruit* (1921), *The Affairs of Anatol* (1921), *Fool's Paradise* (1921), *Adam's Rib* (1922), and *Saturday Night* (1922)—DeMille made the bathtub a mystic shrine of beauty and the act of disrobing a fine art, as "modern" marriages collapsed under the pressure of luxuriant hedonism. These films did not simply embody the values of the "new morality"; they also legitimized them and made them fashionable.

When the Hays Office was established, DeMille embraced the "compensating values" formula and made it uniquely his own in *The Ten Commandments* (1923), a sex- and violence-drenched religious spectacle that made him internationally famous. Costing over $1.5 million to produce, with Biblical sequences in two-color Technicolor (generally lost today—see pp. 217–18), this film became one of the most profitable motion pictures of the era, and it offers a good example of the way in which the Hays Office worked to permit the lurid depiction of "sin" so long as it was shown to be ultimately punished. This successful formula for religious spectacle became a DeMille trademark, and he used it time and again throughout his career—in *King of Kings* (1927), *The Sign of the Cross* (1932), *Samson and Delilah* (1949), and finally in his last film, *The Ten Commandments* (1956), a full-color widescreen remake of the prototype. But DeMille excelled at other forms of spectacle as well: historical (*Cleopatra*, 1934; *The Crusades*, 1935; *The Buccaneer*, 1938), Western (*The Plainsman*, 1938; *Union Pacific*, 1939), and circus (*The Greatest Show on Earth*, 1952). With the exception of a brief venture into independent production between 1925 and 1929, DeMille worked all of his life for some incarnation of Paramount—first the Lasky Feature Play Company, then Famous Players–Lasky, and finally Paramount itself after 1930. A frequent collaborator was the scenarist Jesse Lasky, Jr. (1910–1988—*Union Pacific, Samson and Delilah*), son of the studio's cofounder, and in the sound era DeMille became closely identified with the Paramount "style" as described in Chapter 8. A few of his films, such as *Male*

---

8. DeMille had been a stage actor for about ten years before he got into motion pictures. Professionally, he always spelled his name "DeMille" but used the family spelling of "de Mille" in private.

6.19 *The Ten Commandments* (Cecil B. DeMille, 1923).

and Female (1919) and *Union Pacific* (1939), are classics of their genres, but on the whole DeMille was a great showman, rather than a great director, who incarnated the values of Hollywood in the 1920s throughout his career. He was extravagant, flamboyant, and vulgar, but he possessed a remarkable instinct for the dualistic sensibilities (some would simply say "hypocrisy") of his middle-class American audiences, who paid by the millions for over fifty years to sit through his kinetic spectacles of sex, torture, murder, and violence so long as some pious moral could be drawn from them at the end.

The "Continental Touch": Lubitsch and Others

Another director of sophisticated erotica during the 1920s, but a filmmaker of much greater taste and refinement than DeMille, was Ernst Lubitsch. Lubitsch, a German Jew, was the genius of the lavish postwar *Kostümfilm* at UFA (see pp. 92–93) and had come to Hollywood in late 1922 with the scenarist Hanns Kräly (1885–1950) to direct Mary Pickford in *Rosita* (1923). Once there, he embarked upon a series of stylish sex comedies that made him famous for his subtle visual wit. In films like *The Marriage Circle* (1924), *Three Women* (1924), *Forbidden Paradise* (1924), *Kiss Me Again* (1925), *Lady Windermere's Fan* (1925), *So This Is Paris* (1926), and *The Student Prince* (1927), Lubitsch pioneered the functional use of decor to avoid titles and became a master of sexual

innuendo. Soon all Hollywood spoke of the "Lubitsch touch"—the use of symbolic detail, such as a meaningful glance or gesture, or the closing of a bedroom door, to suggest sexual activity that could not have been depicted with impunity upon the screen. In sum, Lubitsch brought a touch of Continental elegance and irony to Hollywood in the 1920s that was widely imitated by other directors. He went on to become an important innovator of the early sound film with *The Love Parade* (1929), *Monte Carlo* (1930), and *The Smiling Lieutenant* (1931), and by 1935 he had become production chief of Paramount. As a French critic of the day wrote of Lubitsch, "He set about bringing to the Americans the European comedy in all its charm, decadence, and frivolity."

There were other Europeans in Hollywood during the 1920s, most of them Germans who had come to work for the American film industry as a result of the Parufamet Agreement of 1926. Between 1926 and 1927, Hollywood saw the arrival of the UFA directors F. W. Murnau (*Sunrise*, 1927;[9] *4 Devils*, 1928; *Tabu*, 1931), Paul Leni (*The Cat and the Canary*, 1927, which pioneered the popular "comedy-mystery" genre; *The Last Warning*, 1929), Lothar Mendes (*A Night of Mystery*, 1927), Ludwig Berger (*The Sins of the Fathers*, 1928), Dmitri Buchowetski (*Crown of Lies*, 1926), Mihály Kertész (*Noah's Ark*, 1928), and Alexander Korda (*The Private Life of Helen of Troy*, 1927); the UFA cinematographer Karl Freund; the UFA performers Emil Jannings, Conrad Veidt, Werner Krauss, Pola Negri, Greta Garbo, and Lya De Putti; and the UFA producer Erich Pommer and scenarist Carl Mayer. The Hungarian director Paul Fejos (born Pál Fejös, 1897–1963) made *The Last Moment* (1927) and the experimentally naturalistic *Lonesome* (1928) for Universal before returning to Europe in 1930; the Frenchman Jacques Feyder (1885–1948) directed some mediocre melodramas for MGM (*The Kiss*, 1928; *Daybreak*, 1931;

---

9. *Sunrise* was an extraordinary film produced by William Fox but made almost entirely by UFA personnel. It featured a scenario by Carl Mayer from Hermann Sudermann's novella *Journey to Tilset*, photography by Charles Rosher and Karl Struss, production design by Rochus Gliese, Edgar G. Ulmer, and Alfred Metscher, and, of course, direction by Murnau. In its balletically moving camera shots and complex lighting effects—techniques first learned by Rosher at UFA as a consultant on Murnau's *Faust* (1926)—*Sunrise* influenced Hollywood production techniques even more than *Der letzte Mann* (Murnau, 1924); and it won 1927–28 Academy Awards for Best Actress (to Janet Gaynor), Cinematography, and Artistic Quality of production.

6.20 *Heksen (Witchcraft through the Ages* [Benjamin Christensen, 1921]).

6.22 *The Scarlet Letter* (Victor "Seastrom," 1926): Lillian Gish as Hester Prynne.

Song of India, 1931); and the Dane Benjamin Christensen (1879–1959), famous for his Swedish film *Heksen* (1921— shown in a heavily edited English-language version as *Witchcraft through the Ages*),[1] directed a fine series of melodramas for MGM (*The Devil's Circus*, 1926; *Mockery*, 1927) and comedy-mysteries for First National (*The Haunted House*, 1928; *Seven Footprints of Satan*, 1929). The great Swedish directors Victor Sjöström and Mauritz

Stiller (see pp. 89–90) were both imported in the mid-1920s by MGM, where Sjöström—renamed Seastrom— produced three neglected masterpieces—*He Who Gets Slapped* (1924), *The Scarlet Letter* (1926), and *The Wind* (1928)—and Stiller was reduced to directing star vehicles, although his atmospheric *Hotel Imperial* (1926) remains a distinguished film. Sjöström returned to a life of semi-retirement in Sweden in 1928, and Stiller died in the same year, fatigued and disappointed by the Hollywood experience.

The fate of most foreign directors in Hollywood during the 1920s was similar to that of the Swedes. The American industry had imported them to lend Continental elegance and class to the standard studio product, but it had in fact refused to let them tamper with the nature of the product itself; and so, bitterly disillusioned, most went home. Of the directors, only Lubitsch and the Hungarian-born Mihály Kertész (Michael Curtiz) stayed on to adapt themselves to the Hollywood production system. Murnau stayed too but was killed in an auto accident in 1931, before he had achieved his promise. Yet the European,

6.21 **The enormous crane constructed by Universal for Paul Fejos's art-deco musical *Broadway* (1929), shot in both silent and sound versions.**

---

1. Usually spelled *Häxan* in American texts and not shown in the United States until 1929, the film is a unique blend of historical documentary and fiction—alternately macabre, erotic, and realistic—which deeply influenced Continental surrealists such as Luis Buñuel. *Heksen* was the most expensive film produced in Scandinavia to date, and a restored and tinted print of the original exists today in the Royal Danish Film Museum.

and especially the Germanic, presence in Hollywood during the 1920s influenced the American cinema far more deeply than a purely descriptive account might suggest. The Germans taught American filmmakers at first hand the Expressionistic use of lighting and camera that had helped to produce their native cinema's greatest works. Some, like Freund, made long, successful careers in Hollywood and soon, in the early years of sound, were joined by their distinguished countrymen Max Reinhardt, Fritz Lang, Max Ophüls, Detlef Sierck (Douglas Sirk), Curt and Robert Siodmak, William Dieterle, Billy Wilder, Edgar G. Ulmer, Eugen Schüfftan (Eugene Schuftan), Theodor Sparkuhl, Hans (John) Brahm, Otto Preminger, and Fred Zinnemann, after the collapse of the Weimar Republic. All told, the Germanic influence upon Hollywood camera style, lighting, and decor was a permanent, if understated, one, and it contributed substantially to the visual texture of American cinema in the sound era before the advent of widescreen.

In the American Grain

Despite the sophisticated cinema of the "new morality" and all of the European incursions just discussed, there was still a homegrown American tradition of sentimental melodrama and rural romance based upon the uncomplicated narrative montage of Griffith's prewar films. Griffith had established this tradition in his Biograph shorts and continued it well into the 1920s in features like *True Heart Susie* (1919), *A Romance of Happy Valley* (1919), *The Love Flower* (1920), *Way Down East* (1920), *The White Rose* (1923), and *Sally of the Sawdust* (1925). Other practitioners were Henry King ([1888–1982] *The White Sister*, 1923; *Stella Dallas*, 1925; *The Winning of Barbara Worth*, 1926), whose narrative montage in *Tol'able David* (1921) was much admired and analyzed by V. I. Pudovkin; King Vidor ([1894–1982] *The Jack-Knife Man*, 1919; *Happiness*, 1923; *The Big Parade*, 1925); William Wellman ([1896–1975] *The Vagabond Trail*, 1923; *Beggars of Life*, 1927); Clarence Brown ([1890–1987] *Smouldering Fires*, 1924; *The Goose Woman*, 1925); Rowland V. Lee ([1891–1975] *Alice Adams*, 1923; *Doomsday*, 1925); Allan Dwan ([1885–1981] *Robin Hood*, 1922; *The Iron Mask*, 1927); and Frank Borzage ([1893–1962] *Humoresque*, 1920; *Seventh Heaven*, 1927).

Side by side with the Griffith tradition, which was extinguished by the coming of sound, there grew up two native genres—the Western and the action spectacle. The Western had been a major component of the American cinema since Edwin S. Porter's *The Great Train Robbery* in 1903, and Thomas Ince had become a master of the tough, realistic Western as exemplified in the films of William S. Hart in the teens (*Hell's Hinges* [Ince, 1916]; *The Aryan* [Ince, 1916]; *The Narrow Trail* [Lambert Hillyer, 1917]). But it wasn't until the 1920s that the Western came into its own as a unique feature genre; as David Robinson suggests, this may well have been a function of collective public nostalgia for the lost frontier. When Porter made the first Western in 1903, the American West was still an authentic borderland between civilization and the wilderness. By the mid-1920s, America had become an urbanized, industrialized mass society predicated upon mass consumption, mass communications, and rapid transportation; and the Edenic potential of the frontier had been permanently circumscribed by a mushrooming corporate economy. So it was during the 1920s that the classical form of the Western genre was codified and given its first epic expression in films like King Baggott's *Tumbleweeds* (1925), James Cruze's *The Covered Wagon* and *The Pony Express* (1925), and John Ford's *The Iron Horse* (1924).

The adventure spectacle was largely the province of a single performer, Douglas Fairbanks (1883–1939), whose star personality so influenced the character of his films that he deserves to be called an *auteur*. Fairbanks began his career at Griffith's Triangle Company, where he starred in comedies like *Manhattan Madness* (Allan Dwan, 1916), *Reaching for the Moon* (John Emerson, 1917), and *The Mollycoddle* (Victor Fleming, 1920), which debunked contemporary manners and parodied current film genres and fads. In these films, most of them written by Anita Loos, Fairbanks played an all-American boy—boisterous, optimistic, and athletic—who detested weakness, insincerity, and social regimentation in any form. After Fairbanks became a superstar and helped form United Artists, he cast himself as the protagonist in a series of lavish costume-adventure spectacles, including *The Mark of Zorro* (Fred Niblo, 1920), *The Three Musketeers* (Fred Niblo, 1921), *Robin Hood* (Allan Dwan, 1922), *The Thief of Bagdad* (Raoul Walsh, 1924), *Don Q, Son of Zorro* (Donald Crisp, 1925), *The Black Pirate* (Albert Parker, 1926), *The Gaucho* (F. Richard Jones, 1927), and *The Iron Mask* (Allan Dwan,

6.23 *The Thief of Bagdad* **(Raoul Walsh, 1924), produced and written by Douglas Fairbanks for United Artists.**

6.24 *Nanook of the North* **(Robert Flaherty, 1922).**

1929). In these extravagant seriocomic "swashbucklers," the very first of their kind, Fairbanks displayed the full gamut of his energetic athleticism to contemporary audiences, thrilling them with a nearly continuous succession of breathtaking stunts. Fairbanks's physical agility was his major virtue as a performer, and he was forced into retirement in 1934 under the twin pressures of sound and advancing age. But during his meteoric ascent to stardom he had initiated a perennially popular genre (witness, among recent incarnations, Richard Lester's *The Three Musketeers*, 1974; *The Four Musketeers*, 1975; *Royal Flash*, 1975; and *The Return of the Musketeers*, 1989; John Milius's *The Wind and the Lion*, 1975; John Huston's *The Man Who Would Be King*, 1976; Roman Polanski's *Pirates*, 1986; Kevin Reynold's *Robin Hood: Prince of Thieves*, 1991; Stephen Herek's *The Three Musketeers*, 1993; and Michael Caton-Jones's *Rob Roy*, 1995), and he incarnated for millions of Americans Hollywood's obsession with physical culture and glamour.

A third genre, which might be called the "narrative documentary," was founded in the 1920s by the American explorer and amateur cameraman Robert Flaherty

(1884–1951). Flaherty was originally a mineralogist in the Canadian Arctic who had surveyed the Belcher Islands in 1917 and became interested in the harsh lives of the Eskimo who populated them. In 1920, sponsored by the fur company Revillon Frères, Flaherty returned to the islands to live with an Eskimo family and make a film about the daily lives of its members. After sixteen months he returned to the United States with the footage and edited it into the seventy-five-minute feature documentary *Nanook of the North* (1922), which was distributed internationally by Pathé with great commercial and critical success. One source of *Nanook*'s popularity was its exoticism: it represented the first sustained encounter between the civilized world and the Eskimo, outside of professional ethnographic circles. But *Nanook* was also unique in using the editing syntax of narrative film to portray a documentary reality. Flaherty had shot close-ups, **reverse angles,** tilts, and pans on location to be intercut later with the rest of his footage, and he had assumed a third-person point of view toward his subject throughout the film. He had also directed the Eskimos in enacting or re-enacting certain scenes before the camera to accord with a loosely constructed story line that was true to the spirit, if not the letter, of their lives.

The American industry was so impressed with *Nanook*'s high audience appeal and low cost (about $55,000) that Jesse L. Lasky of Paramount commissioned Flaherty to make another such film anywhere in the world

6.25 **The Hollywood boom: the castle set for Douglas Fairbanks's extravagant 1922 production of** *Robin Hood* **(directed by Allan Dwan), made six years after Griffith's** *Intolerance,* **at twice the cost.**

6.26 **The interior of the castle set.**

on a subject of his choice.[2] The result was *Moana* (1926), an idyllic documentary of life on the South Seas island of Samoa photographed over a period of twenty months, which Herman G. Weinberg described in a contemporary review as an "intensely lyrical poem on the theme of the last paradise." Its beauty was enhanced by the recently introduced Eastman **panchromatic stock,** which was sensitive to the entire visible spectrum, as opposed to the then-standard **orthochromatic stock** (on which *Nanook* had been shot), which was relatively insensitive to yellows and reds (see pp. 321–22). Flaherty also used a high percentage of telephoto-lens shots in *Moana,* which became a hallmark of his later camera style. Once again, Flaherty had edited his film as a narrative and had reconstructed reality instead of simply recording it. The film was attacked by anthropologists as poetic fantasy (which it was) rather than an accurate representation of Samoan life, and it was acclaimed by critics on precisely the same grounds. But audiences stayed away this time, despite Paramount's crude attempt to bill the film as "The Love Life of a South Sea Siren."

Flaherty was next commissioned by MGM to collaborate with W. S. Van Dyke (1889–1943) on the production of *White Shadows in the South Seas* (1929), a dramatic feature based on a popular book by Flaherty's friend Frederick O'Brien to be shot on location in Tahiti, but he quit the project in revulsion at its commercialism.

A subsequent collaboration with F. W. Murnau on the independently produced *Tabu* (1931), a narrative about the lives of Tahitian pearl divers, proved more successful, but Flaherty became disillusioned with Murnau's melodramatic approach to the material and withdrew from the film after supervising its photography.[3] At this point in his career, thoroughly disgusted with the Hollywood studio system, Flaherty emigrated to England, where he exercised a decisive influence upon John Grierson and the British social-documentary movement of the 1930s, contributing both *Industrial Britain* (1932, edited by Grierson) and the lyrical *Man of Aran*

2. The popular interest in primitive peoples stimulated by *Nanook* led Paramount to commission two other important films, Merian C. Cooper and Ernest B. Schoedsack's *Grass* (1925) and *Chang* (1927). The former was a documentary about the arduous seasonal migration of some 50,000 Bakhtīarī tribesmen over the Zardeh Kuh mountains from Persia (now Iran) into Turkey in search of grasslands for their herds; the latter, a dramatized documentary about villagers struggling to survive in the jungles of Siam (now Thailand). Both films exhibit a taste for exotic fiction epitomized in Cooper and Schoedsack's classic thriller *King Kong* (1933).

3. Originally to have been a Technicolor silent, *Tabu* was released in black and white with a postsynchronized score owing to the financial collapse of its original backer, Colorart Studio, and the industry's conversion to sound during its production. Flaherty shared script and production credits with Murnau and the photography credit with Floyd Crosby (1899–1985), who won an Academy Award for his debut effort and went on to collaborate on important documentaries with Pare Lorentz and Joris Ivens. On Flaherty's specific contributions to the film, see Mark J. Langer, "*Tabu*: The Making of a Film," *Cinema Journal* 24, 3 (Spring 1985): 43–64.

(1934),[4] which continued his experiments with long-focus lenses. He also directed the Indian location scenes for Zoltan Korda's *The Elephant Boy* (1937), based on Kipling's famous *Jungle Book* story "Toomai of the Elephants." Flaherty was far too personal and individual an artist to ever work again in Hollywood, but he did return to the United States in later life to make two more powerful films for nontheatrical release—*The Land* (1942), produced for the U.S. Department of Agriculture under the auspices of another documentarist, Pare Lorentz (1905–1992), and *Louisiana Story* (1948), produced for Standard Oil of New Jersey—both among the finest achievements in documentary narrative.

Despite the presence of so much individual talent in Hollywood in the 1920s, most American films were produced according to formula. Soaring production costs throughout the decade forced the studios toward a rigid standardization of product. Whereas Griffith had spent just over $100,000 to produce *The Birth of a Nation* in 1914, MGM spent more than $4.5 million to produce *Ben Hur* (Fred Niblo, 1925) only ten years later. In fact, Benjamin Hampton estimates that there was a 1,500 percent across-the-board increase in the cost of feature production during this period, which meant that the pressure to make films according to tried-and-true formulas was extreme. Experimenting with public taste (never very advanced) for the sake of art could result in a crippling capital loss, and it was during the 1920s that "Play It Safe" became the enduring First Commandment and Golden Rule of the American film industry. Consequently, of the more than 5,000 American features produced between 1920 and 1929, only a handful made contributions either to the "literature" of world cinema or to the evolution of narrative form; and most of these, as we have seen, were in the realm of slapstick comedy. But there was a towering exception to this general law in the work of a single man—the enigmatic, distasteful, and finally tragic figure of Erich von Stroheim (1885–1957).

Erich von Stroheim

Von Stroheim was born Erich Oswald Stroheim in Vienna, the son of a Jewish merchant from Silesia, and emigrated to the United States some time between 1906 and 1909. Little is known of his early life here, but he eventually came to Hollywood, where he affixed the "von" to his

6.27 Erich von Stroheim as "The Man You Love to Hate" in Griffith's *Hearts of the World* (1918).

surname and propagated the myth that he was descended from the Austrian aristocracy and had been a cavalry officer in his youth. As Erich von Stroheim, he first went to work as an extra and developed a great admiration for Griffith after a brief appearance in *The Birth of a Nation* (1915).[5] He subsequently became an assistant to Griffith on *Intolerance* (1916) and, between 1915 and 1917, to

---

4. The subject of *Aran* (1979), a documentary by the French filmmaker George Combe. Flaherty's film, edited to seventy-six minutes from thirty-seven hours of original negative, provoked a storm of ideological controversy about the nature and function of documentary cinema when it was attacked by leftist critics for romanticizing the harsh lives of the Aran islanders. Socially committed writers charged it with perpetuating the fascist paradigm of the "noble savage," a misreading encouraged by Mussolini's awarding *Man of Aran* the Gold Cup at the 1934 Venice Film Festival. See William T. Murphy, *Robert Flaherty: A Guide to References and Resources* (Boston: G. K. Hall, 1978), pp. 70–75, and Paul Rotha, *Robert J. Flaherty: A Biography*, ed. Jay Ruby (Philadelphia: University of Pennsylvania Press, 1983), pp. 139–60.

5. Von Stroheim often claimed to have appeared in blackface in the film, but he is only identifiable as the white man who falls off the roof during the guerrilla raid on Piedmont.

Triangle Company directors John Emerson (1878–1956), Allan Dwan (1885–1981), and George Fitzmaurice (1885–1940). In 1918, von Stroheim served as assistant director and military advisor on Griffith's World War I epic *Hearts of the World,* in which he also played his first feature role as a brutal Prussian officer—the kind of role that later made him famous to American audiences as "The Man You Love to Hate."[6]

Von Stroheim was given his first chance to direct by Carl Laemmle of Universal Pictures, who permitted him to adapt his original screenplay, *The Pinnacle,* as *Blind Husbands* in 1919. The film concerns the seduction of a naïve American wife by a cynical Prussian officer (played by von Stroheim) at a resort in the Austrian Alps, and it was among the very first American postwar films to deal with sex in a sophisticated way. Despite its rather conventional plot, *Blind Husbands* is full of subtle psychological insights and visual wit, and it was a tremendous popular success.[7] Von Stroheim's next two films repeated the pattern of *Blind Husbands* with something like obsessiveness: each concerns a sexual triangle in which an American wife in Europe is seduced by an army officer, and each is rendered with unsparing documentary and psychological realism. Moreover, the three films among them brought together the production team with which von Stroheim was to work for most of his career—the cameramen Ben Reynolds and William Daniels, and the performers Gibson Gowland, Sam De Grasse, Mae Busch, and Maude George. There are no surviving prints of *The Devil's Passkey,* which was made for Universal in 1919 and released in 1920, but it ran to the amazing length of twelve full reels (well over two hours) and forecast von Stroheim's desire to expand the narrative cinema to a form commensurate with that of the great realistic novels of the nineteenth century. Based on the evidence of contemporary reviews, it contained some spectacular tinting and toning effects, including a rhythmic montage sequence involving alternating colors. *The Devil's Passkey* was also the last film that the director was ever permitted to finish as he had planned.

To complete his trilogy of adultery (although, according to the formula of the day, the act of adultery itself was never shown to be consummated), von Stroheim made *Foolish Wives* (1922), which most critics consider to be his first great film. This sordid and satiric tale of a lecherous Russian "count" (von Stroheim), who makes his living on the Riviera by bilking rich American tourists,

was initially conceived by Laemmle as the perfect von Stroheim vehicle, and shooting began in July 1920. To augment its realism, von Stroheim constructed an elaborate full-scale reproduction of the main square of Monte Carlo on the Universal backlot, with hotels, cafés, and casinos represented in minute detail. Furthermore, von Stroheim insisted that the exteriors for these sets be constructed at an isolated location on the Monterey Peninsula, 300 miles from the studio, where the California coast most resembles the Mediterranean. Originally budgeted at $250,000, the costs of *Foolish Wives* began to soar toward $750,000, and the Universal publicity department seized upon the opportunity to promote it as the most expensive motion picture ever made. (E.g., a Universal advertisement in *Moving Picture Weekly* in October 1920 showed von Stroheim's Russian count wielding a whip above the logo "He's going to make you hate him! Even if it takes a million dollars of our money to do it!") Finally completed in June 1921 at $1,124,500, the film ran twenty-four[8] reels (approximately 315 minutes, or five and one-quarter hours), much of it handcolored by Gustav Brock, and von Stroheim planned to release it in two parts, as Lang's *Dr. Mabuse, der Spieler* had been released that year in Europe. But the Universal production manager, Irving Thalberg (1899–1936), ordered it cut to fourteen reels (210 minutes) by studio editor Arthur Ripley (1897–1961) for its New York premiere in January 1922 and changed many of its titles to read less candidly than its director intended—this, partially in response to the Hollywood scandals of late 1921.

---

6. The title of a feature-length documentary on von Stroheim's life and work, directed by Patrick Montgomery and written by Richard Koszarski, is *The Man You Loved to Hate* (1979). Koszarski's critical biography of the same title (*The Man You Loved to Hate: Erich von Stroheim and Hollywood* [New York: Oxford University Press, 1983]) points out that while von Stroheim was never one of Griffith's closest assistants, he grasped the significance of Griffith's achievement better than any of his contemporaries and modeled his own career on it. Von Stroheim later wrote of his mentor, "He was the man who had put beauty and poetry into a cheap and tawdry form of amusement."

7. *Blind Husbands,* which Richard Koszarski calls "the most impressive and significant debut in Hollywood history" before *Citizen Kane* (1941), no longer exists in its original form. Universal cut into the negative in 1924 to eliminate nineteen minutes of running time for a streamlined reissue, and all surviving prints derive from this or subsequently scaled-down versions (*The Man You Loved to Hate: Erich von Stroheim and Hollywood,* p. 45).

8. Von Stroheim alternately claimed thirty and thirty-two, but the running time of 315 minutes agrees with all sources.

6.28 The casino, the hotel, and the Café de Paris in Monte Carlo reconstructed to scale on the Universal back lot in the San Fernando Valley for *Foolish Wives* (Erich von Stroheim, 1922).

Norris's novel, like Zola's *L'Assommoir* (1877), was a model of the nineteenth-century **naturalist** convention by which some hereditary flaw or character trait brings its protagonists to ruin through a steady process of degeneration. The title character of *McTeague* is a young man with a family heritage of brutality who sets up as a dentist in San Francisco and eventually marries Trina Sieppe, the daughter of lower-middle-class German immigrants. Trina wins $5,000 in a lottery and becomes a monster of avarice in her attempts to retain the entire sum without spending a penny. McTeague loses his job through trusting a rival, and the couple sinks lower and lower in the socio-economic scale until they are reduced to a state of total degradation. McTeague begins to drink; finally, his hereditary brutishness asserts itself and he murders Trina

Foolish Wives was cut still further for general release to ten reels, but even in its mutilated version[9] it remains a brilliant, brutal film, full of studied vignettes of postwar European decadence and rich psychological characterization. Thanks to Universal's publicity campaign, *Foolish Wives* was a *succès de scandale*, but thanks to its huge budget, the film produced a loss of $255,200. Nevertheless, its reception had established von Stroheim as an industry giant, very nearly on a par with Griffith, and his next film for Universal was *Merry-Go-Round* (1922), the beginning of another erotic trilogy, set this time in prewar Austria during the decline of the Hapsburg Empire. Midway through the shooting, in October, Thalberg removed the director from the film because of his lavish and expensive attention to detail (including the construction of a full-scale model of the Prater, Vienna's mammoth amusement park) and replaced him with Rupert Julian (1889–1943), terminating von Stroheim's association with Universal. But his celebrity as both an actor and a director was such that within a month he had negotiated a three-film contract with Goldwyn Pictures, the first of which was to be the realization of a long-cherished project—an adaptation of Frank Norris's naturalistic American novel *McTeague* (1899).[1]

9. The negative of the ten-reel version, which von Stroheim described widely in the press as "only the skeleton of my dead child," was recut by Universal to eight reels in 1928 for a general reissue with music and sound effects. The narrative was completely restructured and most of the titles rewritten to change the names and identities of the characters. This is the version distributed by MoMA and most other archives today. The only other surviving version is an eleven-reel composite prepared by Arthur Lennig for the American Film Institute from the 1928 reissue and several European versions derived from 1922 export prints. This latter is probably as close as we shall ever come to the original *Foolish Wives*.

On the reception of *Foolish Wives*—which *Variety* called a "leering insult to Americans in general, and American womanhood in particular" and *Moving Picture World* a "Darwinian Phantasy of Bad Manners and Sneers"—see Janet Staiger, "'The Handmaiden of Villainy': Methods and Problems in Studying the Historical Reception of a Film," *Wide Angle* 8, 1 (Winter 1986): 19–27.

1. *McTeague* had been adapted once before as the five-reel *Life's Whirlpool* (1916) by the director Barry O'Neil. The film has not survived, but on the basis of contemporary reviews and production stills, Richard Koszarski suggests that von Stroheim may have been influenced by its stark visual quality (*The Man You Loved to Hate: Erich von Stroheim and Hollywood*, p. 117).

for her gold. The novel ends in Death Valley, where the fugitive McTeague encounters his rival, Marcus, and beats him to death with a pistol butt. But McTeague, too, is doomed, for in the process of his struggle with Marcus he has become handcuffed to the corpse. This grim tale was unlikely raw material for Hollywood commercial entertainment, but it was von Stroheim's intention to translate the novel, as a totality, into cinematic terms and to render its naturalism photographically meaningful.[2]

The film was shot by Ben Reynolds and William Daniels entirely on location in the streets and rooming houses of San Francisco,[3] in Death Valley, and in the northern California hills, on the basis of von Stroheim's own script. The process took nine months and cost over half a million dollars—three times the amount originally budgeted but all of it approved in stages by Goldwyn executives. After von Stroheim had personally edited the film in early 1924, he presented Goldwyn with a forty-two-reel work print running over nine hours (an alternative account has forty-five reels at nine and one-half hours). He was asked to reduce it to a reasonable length for commercial distribution in two parts. This twenty-two reel, five-hour version was completed in March but was still too long for Goldwyn, so von Stroheim shipped the film to his friend, the Metro director Rex Ingram (1892–1950), for further reduction. Collaborating with the editor Grant Whytock, who had worked with von Stroheim on *The Devil's Pass-key*, Ingram broke the film into two halves, eliminating some of the subplots. This eighteen-reel print, which Ingram and von Stroheim considered the absolute minimum to which the film could be cut without destroying its continuity, ran approximately four hours and was intended for release in two parts. In the meantime, however, Goldwyn Pictures had merged with Metro Pictures and Louis B. Mayer Productions to become MGM, and Mayer replaced Goldwyn as executive in charge of production. Among Mayer's first acts as studio chief was to turn von Stroheim's epic over to his new assistant and the director's old adversary, Irving Thalberg, for further editing. The film was eventually cut to ten reels by an MGM title writer, Joseph Farnham, who had read neither the novel nor the shooting script, and the excised footage was destroyed. Retitled *Greed* (1924), this mutilated version of the film was the only one ever publicly seen, and it opened to modest critical acclaim, despite its incoherence, and actually made a profit of a quarter million dollars.[4]

6.29 *Greed:* **Prologue, 1908. McTeague (Gibson Gowland) as a car-boy in the Big Dipper gold mine in the northern California hills. Note the composition-in-depth.**

At one-fourth of its original length, *Greed* is a fragmentary masterpiece with vast gaps in continuity bridged by lengthy and often ludicrous titles, but it is a masterpiece nonetheless. Because von Stroheim was an original master of the long take and built up his most powerful effects *within* shots rather than editing between them,

2. In fact, von Stroheim undertook several significant adaptations of the text and added a thirty-page prologue to his script showing the environmental and hereditary origins of McTeague's degeneration in his harsh youth in a gold-mining camp, his father's death through alcoholism, and his mercenary apprenticeship to a traveling dentist. These scenes, occupying close to an hour of screen time, were shot on location in and around the Big Dipper Mine in northern California—the actual site of the character's youth in the novel—which von Stroheim had specially restored for the purpose. (Von Stroheim's script for *Greed* was published by Simon and Schuster in 1972.)

3. Since the novel was set in the 1890s, von Stroheim went to great lengths to re-create the look of the city before it was destroyed by the 1906 earthquake and fire. But as Richard Koszarski points out, the costumes, street traffic, and calendar events were all deliberately updated to coincide with the period 1908–22, making the film "a bizarre amalgam of Norris's events jammed into the chronology of von Stroheim's life in America" (*The Man You Love to Hate: Erich von Stroheim and Hollywood*, p. 129).

4. In 1972, von Stroheim's close friend, the film critic Herman G. Weinberg, published *The Complete "Greed" of Erich von Stroheim* (New York: Dutton), using 348 still photographs left to him by the director, together with fifty-two production stills. Weinberg has performed the same valuable service for *The Wedding March* (1974) and the other films in the von Stroheim canon in *Stroheim: A Pictorial Record of His Nine Films* (New York: Dover, 1975).

6.30 Ten years later: McTeague with a patient in his "dental parlours" on Polk Street, San Francisco (seen through the bay windows).

6.32 Saturday dinner at the Sieppes' (cut from the released version). Far right: McTeague's friend Marcus Schouler (Jean Hersholt) and Marcus's cousin, Trina Sieppe (Zasu Pitts), with whom McTeague will soon become infatuated.

many of the film's greatest sequences have survived intact. Even as it stands, *Greed* is overwhelming in its psychological intensity, for von Stroheim used strikingly clear deep-focus photography and a documentary-like *mise-en-scène* to totally immerse us in the reality of the film. His camera moves very little, and, in a manner forecasting the work of Michelangelo Antonioni (whose films will be studied in Chapter 15), the narrative proceeds through a gradual accretion of detail in which the time

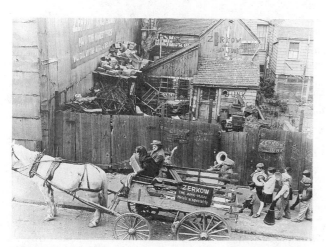

6.31 Zerkow and Maria set out in the junk wagon to bury their dead child. Like the deranged McTeague, Zwerkow will later murder his wife because of his lust for gold. Note the density and depth of the frame.

and space of the characters in the film become our own. Palpably real photographic objects—a caged canary, a funeral cortège, a huge gold tooth, cuts of meat—acquire symbolic value through composition in depth rather than expressive montage or the Griffithian intercut close-up. Finally, despite *Greed*'s structural disunity and its unpleasant subject matter, the atmospheric density of the film holds us from beginning to end. *Greed* is not a "realistic" film, as, for example, G. W. Pabst's *Die freudlose Gasse* strives to be, but rather a "naturalistic" one in the literary sense of the term. In its uncompromising depiction of degradation and despair, it raises reality to the level of symbol and asks profound questions about the nature of human experience.

Von Stroheim, who had mortgaged his home and his car to support himself during the editing of *Greed* (he was paid only for direction), disowned the film and refused to see it after it was released.[5] Incredibly, he was hired back by MGM in 1925 and given a free hand in adapting the Franz Lehár operetta *The Merry Widow* (1925), although he was forced to use the stars John Gilbert and Mae Murray against his will. By reducing the

5. Von Stroheim finally saw what was left of his epic in 1950, at the instigation of Henri Langlois of the Cinémathèque Française. Immediately afterward he commented: "This was like an exhumation for me. In a tiny coffin I found a lot of dust, a terrible smell, a little backbone and shoulder-bone."

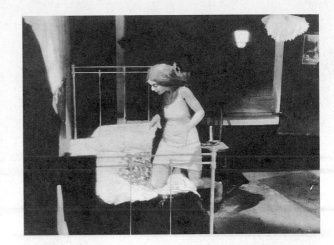

6.33 McTeague contemplates a gigantic golden molar, a birthday gift from Trina, meant to hang in his window to advertise his trade. Like other objects and/or symbols of gold in the film, it was tinted gold-yellow by the Handschiegl stencil process in the original release print to emphasize the obsessive nature of greed.

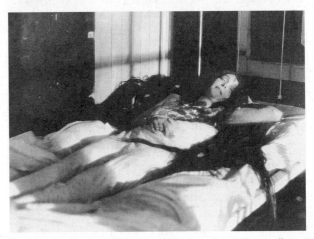

operetta to less than one-half of the film's running time and adding his own material, von Stroheim was able to turn this purely commercial venture into the second film in his darkly satiric trilogy on the corruption of the Viennese aristocracy. Although technically set in an imaginary Ruritanian kingdom named Monteblanco, *The Merry Widow* clearly reflects the decadence of the Hapsburg Empire at the turn of the century and reveals the rotten-

6.35 A sequence cut from the released version: Trina madly worshiping her lottery winnings, converted now to gold coin.

6.34 Meticulous *mise-en-scène:* McTeague and Trina's wedding feast, an orgy of feeding.

ness and perversion concealed beneath its elegant façade. The studio deleted a few scenes from the release print due to their explicit sexual content, but *The Merry Widow* came closer to realizing its director's intentions than any film he had made since *The Devil's Passkey* in 1919. Stencil-colored by the Handschiegl process, with a concluding two-minute Technicolor sequence shot by Ray Rennahan, it was an international success, both critically and commercially, and it made a fortune for MGM.

At this point in his career, von Stroheim left MGM for good in a bitter dispute over financial and creative differences to make a film of his choice for Pat Powers's independent Celebrity Pictures. The result was *The Wedding March* (1928), von Stroheim's last great film and the concluding section of his trilogy on the decadence of

6.36 Von Stroheim, with the cinematographer Ben Reynolds, directing the final scenes of *Greed* in Death Valley during the summer of 1923. The other cameramen on the film were William H. Daniels and Ernest B. Schoedsack.

6.37 Marcus alone in the desert, in desperate pursuit of McTeague.

imperial Austria. It tells the bitterly sardonic tale of a forced marriage between an impoverished Viennese nobleman (von Stroheim) and the crippled daughter of a wealthy industrialist; and it is among the most visually extravagant films ever made. *The Wedding March* was also to have finally realized von Stroheim's perennial desire to make a long film in two parts, whose form would approximate that of the great nineteenth-century novels. Shooting began in June 1926, and *Part I* was completed as von Stroheim had intended (except that he had

replaced cinematographers Henry Thorpe and Bill McGann with Hal Mohr, who would himself resign and be replaced by Roy Klaffki). But midway through the filming of *Part II,* in January 1927, he was removed from the project by Paramount, to whom Powers had been forced to sell his option when von Stroheim overran his original budget of $750,000 by $400,000. Paramount turned the footage over to Josef von Sternberg (see pp. 255–59) to edit into a single film. Between them, von Stroheim and von Sternberg were able to put together a

6.38 From the final frames of *Greed:* McTeague bludgeons Marcus with his revolver, sealing his destiny—to die like a beast in the wild.

6.39 Crown Prince Mirko of Monteblanco (John Gilbert) and his party prepare for an evening of mirth in *The Merry Widow* (Erich von Stroheim, 1925).

6.40 The wedding in *The Wedding March* (1928): Erich von Stroheim, Zasu Pitts.

version of *The Wedding March* that corresponded roughly to the original *Part I* and concluded with the wedding of the protagonists in St. Stephen's Cathedral (shot in Technicolor by Ray Rennahan). But Vice President for Production Jesse Lasky rejected this version and had it recut by studio editor Julian Johnson into what eventually became a twelve-reel release print. The film was scheduled for a January 1928 premiere but was temporarily shelved due to the advent of sound while studio executives decided to add a synchronized score by J. S. Zamecnik and Louis De Francesco. This version was finally released in October 1928 to dismal reviews and box-office failure. Paramount editors then combined footage from *Parts I* and *II* into a hodgepodge entitled *The Honeymoon*, which was released in Europe in 1929 and subsequently disowned by von Stroheim. Just before his death in 1957, the director recut the first part of the film to conform more closely to his original intention, and there is now preserved in the archives of the Cinémathèque Française von Stroheim's own 16mm sound-on-film reconstruction of this most lavish and erotic masterpiece of *mise-en-scène*.

After the *Wedding March* debacle, as after *Greed*, von Stroheim's reputation among Hollywood producers was not good, but his singular talent was indisputable. In 1928, he was commissioned by Joseph Kennedy (then an independent producer) to write and direct a star vehicle for Gloria Swanson (1899–1983), who had quit Paramount in 1926 to produce her own films for release through United Artists. The two-part script, which was

approved by the Hays Office and originally called *The Swamp*, can only be described as bizarre. In the European episode, Prince Wolfram, betrothed to the queen of the small Bavarian state of Cobourg-Nassau, falls in love with a young convent girl named Kitty Kelly (Swanson) and later abducts her to his apartments in the royal palace. They are caught by his fiancée, Queen Regina, who whips Kelly from the palace with a riding crop and has Wolfram imprisoned. Meanwhile, after an abortive suicide attempt, Kelly finds she has been summoned to German East Africa, where her guardian aunt lies dying in Dar-es-Salaam. *Part II* begins when Kelly arrives in Africa to discover that her aunt is the owner of a run-down brothel. Penniless, the old woman has arranged for her niece to marry "the richest guy in Africa," an aged, degenerate planter named Jan, which in a delirium of disgust Kelly does. Eight months later, Kelly has transformed the seedy whorehouse into the classy "Poto-Poto" bordello and installed herself as its reigning queen. Subsequently, Jan dies of syphilis; and Prince Wolfram arrives by steamer from Germany, where Queen Regina has also died. He ultimately convinces Kelly to return with him to Cobourg-Nassau, where they are married and she is coronated "Queen Kelly," institutionalizing the regal spirit she has carried within her all along—but also suggesting the continuity of depravity between "civilized" Europe and "barbaric" Africa.

Working with cinematographers Gordon Pollock and Paul Ivano, von Stroheim had shot more than half of this fantastic film, including some harrowing African sequences, when he was removed from the project at Swanson's insistence in January 1929. Increasingly fearful of censorship of the African scenes and morally outraged at what she later called "Mr. von Stroheim's apocalyptic vision of hell on earth," Swanson authorized Kennedy to find another director to salvage the project, but this ultimately proved impossible owing to the industry's wholesale conversion to "talkies" and other factors. (Among those who tried and failed in this salvage operation over the next few years were Paul Stein, Edmund Goulding, Richard Boleslavsky, Sam Wood, and Delmer Daves.) Finally, in November 1931, Swanson—who had invested about $800,000 in the production so far—tacked an abrupt conclusion onto the European episode showing Kelly's suicide attempt (shot by Gregg Toland) to have been successful, added an orchestral score by Adolf Tandler, and released the film in Europe the following year as "an original von Stroheim," where it was widely hailed but little seen. Like the mutilated *Greed* and *The Honeymoon*, this remnant was disowned by von Stroheim, but a recent reconstruction has restored *Queen Kelly* as the director originally shot it, although it remains, of course, incomplete.

Von Stroheim had shot ten reels of a projected thirty in precise dramatic sequence when the film was canceled. Eight reels constituted the European episode; the other two contained scenes set in Dar-es-Salaam. Miss Swanson used only the European footage in her "released version," whose most famous apparition is in Billy Wilder's self-reflexive black comedy *Sunset Boulevard* (1950) where a clip of it is projected for the faded silent star Norma Desmond (Swanson) by her has-been director/husband Max von Mayerling (von Stroheim). But two edited reels containing nearly all of the African footage were discovered in 1965, and in 1978 Donald Krim of Kino International began negotiating for the rights to the entire film. Finally, in collaboration with Dennis Doros, Krim put together a ninety-six-minute restoration print of *Queen Kelly* that was premiered at the Los Angeles County Museum of Art in February 1985. Working from detailed production notes and von Stroheim's final shooting script, Doros assembled this version from sixty-six minutes of the Swanson 1932 European release (eliminating the tacked-on ending), twenty-two minutes of the African reels, and an additional ten minutes of outtakes and stills from archives all over the world to bridge continuity gaps. The 1985 reconstruction also includes new titles by Doros and remixes Adolf Tandler's original score. All told, it suggests that, if completed as planned, *Queen Kelly* might well have been von Stroheim's greatest film.

The cancellation of *Queen Kelly* was a professional disaster for von Stroheim. It seemed to confirm his vastly inflated reputation for excess and perversity in the eyes of all Hollywood, and the conversion to sound became a pretext on the part of his many enemies for squeezing him out of the industry. He was reduced to writing screenplays (*Tempest*, 1927; *East of the Setting Sun*, 1929) and acting in other people's films (*The Great Gabbo* [James Cruze, 1929]; *Three Faces East* [Roy Del Ruth, 1930]; *As You Desire Me* [George Fitzmaurice, 1932]) to make a living. Yet, after an abortive attempt to remake *Blind Husbands* for Universal in sound and (two-color) Technicolor between 1930 and 1931, von Stroheim was given his last chance to direct by Winfield Sheehan,

an executive for the Fox Film Corporation, who signed him to adapt an unproduced Dawn Powell play, *Walking Down Broadway*, in late 1931. Though this story of two small-town girls rooming together in contemporary New York City was conceived as a modest program picture[6] by Fox, von Stroheim lavished infinite care upon its visual texture, working in close collaboration with the cinematographer James Wong Howe (1899–1976). After several delays, shooting started on September 2, 1932, and *Walking Down Broadway* was completed in an exemplary manner forty-eight days later for the budgeted amount of $300,000, but in the process it seems to have become a study of morbid psychology with crypto-lesbian undertones. When Fox vice president Sol Wurtzel saw the film, he was outraged and halted its release. Von Stroheim was fired, the script rewritten, and the film turned over to several directors, including Alan Crosland, Raoul Walsh, Sidney Lanfield, Edwin Burke, and Alfred Werker, to be reshot. The revised version, containing about one-half of the original, was released in March 1933 as *Hello, Sister!* without von Stroheim's name appearing on the credits. Fired by Universal, MGM, Paramount, United Artists, and Fox in turn, von Stroheim's reputation as a filmmaker was completely destroyed, and he was never permitted to direct again. He worked for a while as a dialogue writer at MGM, much as Keaton was forced to do, before turning completely to acting. Between 1934 and 1955, von Stroheim appeared in some fifty-two films for other directors and gave many distinguished performances (for instance, in Jean Renoir's *La Grande illusion* [1937] and Billy Wilder's *Sunset Boulevard* [1950]). He made a fair living at this profession, wrote several novels, and was still a celebrity when he died in France in 1957.

Simultaneously a romanticist, a determinist, and a cynic, Erich von Stroheim was Hollywood's last great independent director and its last great personal *auteur*. For most of his films he was his own scenarist, art director, costume designer, editor, assistant cameraman, and star. His obsessive realism became a Hollywood legend, and yet realism for von Stroheim was always a means toward the end of symbolic naturalism—a mode practiced by late-nineteenth-century novelists like Zola, Maupassant, Crane, and Norris, in which the accumulation of

---

6. A cheaply produced second feature—the bottom half of a double bill (also called a "B film"), although the budget of $300,000 was very generous for this type of film.

surface detail ultimately leads us beneath the surface of things to some deeper human meaning. To this end as well, von Stroheim rejected Griffithian montage in favor of the long take, or sequence shot, composed in depth from a relatively static camera—shots that have the naturalistic effect of linking characters with their environment. In his classic essay "The Evolution of the Language of the Cinema," André Bazin has described von Stroheim as "the creator of the virtually continuous cinematic story, tending to the permanent integration of the whole space. . . . He has one simple rule for direction. Take a close look at the world, keep doing so, and in the end it will lay bare for you all its cruelty and its ugliness." But if von Stroheim was a naturalist, he was also, often simultaneously, an ironic fantasist. His fascination with sexual perversion is a case in point. He did not use it to titillate, as DeMille might have done, or even to display his worldliness, as might have been expected of Lubitsch. Like Luis Buñuel after him (as we will see in Chapter 15), von Stroheim used sexual pathology as a metaphor for a more pervasive cultural decadence that was his major philosophical concern. The corruption of the European aristocracy, the corruptibility of the American bourgeoisie, and the degradation of the masses are the recurrent themes of von Stroheim's major work. They bespeak a profound cultural pessimism born of late-nineteenth-century Europe—the bitter dregs of a failed idealism—which is balanced in the films themselves by an obvious sympathy for the individual humans caught up in the self-destructive impulses of the race.

"Self-destructive" is an adjective that many persons have applied to von Stroheim himself, and it is true that he was in some sense a victim of his own temperament and his own myth. But he was also a casualty of Hollywood's transformation from a speculative entrepreneurial enterprise into a vertically and horizontally integrated big business, and his beleaguered career as a director from 1918 to 1932 is a virtual paradigm of that transformation. What happened to von Stroheim in Hollywood during the 1920s was the same thing that happened to Griffith, Chaplin, and Keaton, those three other great independent producer-directors of the American silent film. When von Stroheim and Griffith first began to make feature films in southern California in the teens, there was no established procedure for producing them since they were an unprecedented commodity. As things evolved at the time, some individual or group of individuals with investment capital—a Harry Aitken or a Carl Laemmle,

for example—would provide the financial backing, and Griffith and von Stroheim would "produce" their own films in the most literal sense of the term. Script writing, casting, locations, set design, art direction, and the general logistics of shooting the film, in addition to the shooting and editing itself, were all directorial responsibilities; and this assured a high degree of personal artistic freedom for the individual director. As American film production grew into what its promoters claimed to be the nation's fourth largest industry[7] between 1919 and 1927, this system of independent production yielded first to the privately owned studio (Triangle Films, Keaton Productions, Chaplin Productions) and finally to the monopolistic industrial combines of Paramount, Fox, Associated–First National, and MGM. By 1927, the studio filmmaking process had been standardized under the supervisory production system pioneered by Thomas Ince and Mack Sennett a decade before, and there was little place within the system for such an individual and eccentric talent as a von Stroheim or a Keaton or a Griffith.

The coming of sound was to clinch the matter. The studios had to borrow huge sums of money to pay for the conversion on the very eve of the Great Depression, which spurred them to increase the efficiency of their production process by totally effacing the concept of the personal director and replacing it with the concept of the executive producer, modeled on MGM's Irving Thalberg, the man who had done such injury to *Foolish Wives* and *Greed*. Thus, the coming of sound meant a great deal more for the American cinema than the transformation

---

7. This "fourth largest industry" claim, long accepted as gospel by film historians (and, apparently, for at least a decade by the U.S. Chamber of Commerce), has recently been challenged by Douglas Gomery. In "Hollywood, the National Recovery Administration, and the Question of Monopoly Power" (*Journal of the University Film Association* 31, 2 [Spring 1979]: 49; reprinted with commentary in *The American Movie Industry: The Business of Motion Pictures*, ed. Gorham Kindem [Carbondale: Southern Illinois University Press, 1982], pp. 205–14), he maintains that on the basis of total sales for 1933, the industry ranked somewhere between the thirty-seventh and forty-fifth so that it could hardly have been the fourth largest a decade before. Gomery believes that the industry began circulating this specious claim to power during the 1920s as a form of self-advertisement and, perhaps, intimidation of government regulatory agencies. This may be so, but in terms of its *social* as opposed to its economic influence—in terms of the sheer number of persons deeply and permanently affected by its values—the American film industry was surely among the most powerful since the Industrial Revolution. Only radio and television would exceed its power as a medium of mass persuasion and social control.

of those dreamlike, hallucinatory demigods of the silent screen into mere mortals with accents, drawls, and lisps—more even than the regressive inertia temporarily caused by the early technology of recording sound. It meant the transformation of a wildcat business run largely by filmmakers fascinated with the process of film itself into a large-scale technological industry controlled by corporate managers who exercised supreme authority over all artistic variables in order to maximize profits. Like so many other aspects of modern American life—including mass communications, mass consumption, and rapid transit—gigantic corporate capitalism was born of the 1920s. That decade was the only time in the history of American film that so much talent has ever been allowed to display itself so extravagantly and magnificently, and then been so ruthlessly destroyed.

The Coming of Sound and Color, 1926–1935

Sound-on-Disc

After the invention of the cinema itself, the most important event in film history was the introduction of sound. In fact, the idea of combining motion pictures with some type of synchronized sound had been present since their inception. Thomas Edison originally commissioned the invention of the Kinetograph with the notion of providing a visual accompaniment for his phonograph, and W. K. L. Dickson had actually achieved a rough synchronization of the two machines as early as 1889. Many other inventors, such as Georges Demeny and Auguste Baron in France and William Friese-Greene in England, experimented with devices for coupling sound and image before the turn of the century. At the Paris World Exposition of 1900 three separate systems that synchronized phonograph recordings with projected film strips were exhibited: the Phonorama of L. A. Berthon, C. F. Dussaud, and G. F. Jaubert; Léon Gaumont's Chronophone; and the Phono-Cinéma Théâtre of Clément-Maurice Gratioulet and Henri Lioret, which offered minute-long performances by great stars of the theater, opera, and ballet. In Germany, Oskar Messter began to produce short synchronized sound films as novelty items in 1903, and by 1908 he was supplying exhibitors with recorded musical scores for nearly all of his productions. In Britain, Gaumont's Chronophone proved popular, as did Cecil Hepworth's system, Vivaphone; and in the United States the Edison Corporation achieved modest technical success with two phonofilm systems—Cinephonograph and **Kinetophone.**

All of these early systems relied on the phonograph to reproduce the sound component of the filmed performance. The earlier ones used wax cylinders and the later ones discs, but all had three difficulties in common: synchronizing the sound recording with the filmed event, amplifying the sound for presentation to a large audience, and reconciling the brevity of the cylinder and disc formats with the standard length of motion pictures. The first problem was partially solved by using a number of regulatory devices intended to ensure an exact correspondence of sound and image, but these were usually imperfect in operation. If the phonograph stylus skipped a groove in performance, for example, or if the film strip broke in the projector, regaining synchronization was nearly impossible. The problem of amplification was generally dealt with by concealing a battery of single-horn speakers behind the screen, although experiments with compressed-air speakers of the sort used today began around 1910. The third problem was the most difficult to solve. By 1905, the length of the standard narrative film had far exceeded the four-minute playing time of the phonograph cylinder and the five-minute time of the 12-inch disc. The introduction of automatic changers and multiple phonographs did not resolve the difficulty since changing records frequently caused a loss of synchronization, and the use of oversized discs only resulted in poor sound quality. In the years before the First World War, as the standard length of films grew even longer and their interframe structure more complex, experimental interest in the imperfect phonofilm sound systems died out. They remained extant through the war mainly as a means of making short novelty films in single takes.

But the imperfection of the phonofilm systems did not leave the motion pictures soundless. In fact, the "silent" cinema was rarely that. Sound effects provided by individual performers or by sound-effect machines like the Allefex and Kinematophone were a standard feature of films after 1908, and live music had been a part of the cinema since its beginnings. A pianist had accompanied the first commercial motion-picture exhibition, the Lumière Cinématographe program at the Grand Café, Paris, December 28, 1895, and Méliès personally provided piano accompaniment for the Paris debut of *Le Voyage dans la lune* in 1902. Pianists were employed in most storefront theaters and nickelodeons in the first decade of the twentieth century to improvise music to fit the scenes. As the standard film length increased from one reel (about 1,000 feet, or 16 minutes at the average silent speed of 16 fps) to six to ten reels (90 to 160 minutes) between 1905 and 1914, film narratives grew increasingly sophisticated; and, according to Harry M. Geduld, the practice of musicians playing intermittently during film programs gave way to continuous musical accompaniment in which the nature of each scene determined the kind of music played with it.[1]

During this period, the nickelodeons and storefronts began to be replaced by "dream palaces" that could seat thousands of movie goers and accommodate hundred-piece orchestras or, at the very least, a mighty Wurlitzer organ that could produce a wide range of orchestral effects. By the time the feature film had become the dominant cinematic form in the West, many producers were commissioning original scores for their class-A productions; and during the 1920s all features, regardless of quality, were accompanied by cue sheets suggesting appropriate musical selections to be played at designated points in the film. The first original piece of film music was composed in 1907 by Camille Saint-Saëns for the Société Film d'Art's *L'Assassinat du duc de Guise* (1908). Other memorable and distinguished scores of the "silent" era were Joseph Carl Breil's scores for Griffith's *The Birth of a Nation* (1915) and *Intolerance* (1916), Victor Schertzinger's score for Thomas H. Ince's *Civilization* (1916), Hugo Riesenfeld's score for James Cruze's *The Covered Wagon* (1925) and F. W. Murnau's *Sunrise* (1927), Louis F. Gottschalk's scores for Griffith's *Broken Blossoms* (1919) and *Orphans of the Storm* (1921), Mortimer Wilson's score for Douglas Fairbanks's *The Thief of Bagdad* (1923), William Frederick Peters's score for Griffith's *Way Down East* (1920), Erno Rapee's score for John Ford's *The Iron Horse* (1924), and Leo Kempenski's score for Erich von Stroheim's *Greed* (1924). In Europe, Edmund Meisel wrote brilliant revolutionary scores for Eisenstein's *Potemkin* (1925) and *October* (1928), and Gottfried Huppertz composed for Fritz Lang's *Siegfried* (1923) and *Metropolis* (1926). Other European composers who scored films during the 1920s include George Antheil, Erik Satie, Darius Milhaud, Arthur Honegger, Jacques Ibert, Jean Sibelius, Roger Désormière, Paul Hindemith, and Dmitri Shostakovich.

Sound-on-Film

The notion that sound could complement and vivify the experience of cinema, then, came of age with the cinema itself. But since only a handful of exhibitors in major cities

---

1. For an excellent anthology of scholarly essays on early sound practice, see *The Sounds of Early Cinema*, ed. Richard Abel and Rick Altman (Bloomington: Indiana University Press, 2001). See also James Lastra, *Sound Technology and the American Cinema: Perception, Representation, Modernity* (New York: Columbia University Press, 2000).

could afford full-scale orchestras or even Wurlitzer organs, the search for an inexpensive and effective means of recording sound for films continued during and after the war, when experimental emphasis shifted from sound-on-disc to sound-on-film systems. It was reasoned at this point that the massive problems of synchronization encountered in the disc systems could be solved by recording the sound on the same strip of film as the images. The potential for recording sound photographically, or optically, by converting sound waves into patterns of light and shade, had been understood a decade before the invention of the Kineto-graph, but the first successful attempt to record sound directly on a film strip, side by side with the image track, was made by Eugene Augustin Lauste, a former mechanical assistant to W. K. L. Dickson, in 1910, on the basis of a 1907 British patent for converting sound-modulated light beams into electrical impulses by means of a photoconductive selenium cell. Though he could find no significant financial backing for his system, which he called Photocinematophone, Lauste's experiments were to become the basis for RCA Photophone, one of the two major sound-on-film systems adopted by Hollywood in the early sound era. Another pioneer of sound-on-film technology was the Polish American inventor Joseph T. Tykociner, who had experimented with a sound-modulated gas flame as a light source as early as 1896, but the first workable sound-on-film, or optical sound, systems were not perfected until after the war.

In 1919, three German inventors—Josef Engl, Joseph Massole, and Hans Vogt—patented the Tri-Ergon (literally, "the work of three") process, a sound-on-film system that used a photoelectric cell to convert sound waves into electric impulses and electric impulses into light waves that were then recorded photographically on the edge of the film strip. Built onto their projector was a "reader," composed of an incandescent light and another photoelectric cell, which retranslated the patterns of light and shade back into sound waves as the film strip passed through the projector, insuring perfect synchronization of sound and image. The Tri-Ergon process also incorporated a flywheel mechanism on a sprocket that prevented variations in film speed as the strip passed through the projector—a device necessary to maintain the continuous reproduction of sound without distortion. This flywheel was heavily protected by international patents, so that between 1920 and 1927 all other manufacturers of optical sound equipment had to either pay royalties to Tri-Ergon,

infringe the patent, or market an inferior product. Tri-Ergon, whose technology was later employed throughout Germany, eventually sold its American rights to William Fox of Fox Film Corporation in 1927 (a sale ruled illegal by the U.S. Supreme Court in 1935) and its Continental rights to UFA, which in 1928 sold them to Tonbild Syndicate, A.G., merged as Tobis-Klangfilm in 1929.

In 1923 an American inventor who had been active in the development of radio broadcasting, Dr. Lee de Forest (1873–1961), patented (independently of the German inventors) a sound-on-film system, very similar to the Tri-Ergon process, that also decisively solved the problem of amplification. In 1907, to improve radio reception, de Forest had patented the Audion 3-Electrode Amplifier Tube, or triode, a vacuum tube that amplified the sound it received electronically and drove it into a speaker. The **audion** tube became essential to the technology of all sound systems requiring amplification—radio, public address, sound film, and, ultimately, high-fidelity recording and television—because it is to sound reproduction what the lens is to projection; that is, it enables its message or signal to reach large numbers of people simultaneously.[2] de Forest became preoccupied with the development of "talking pictures" in 1919, when he realized that incorporating his audion tube into an optical sound-on-film process would provide more amplification than was possible with any other system of the period. By 1922, de Forest had worked enough of the bugs out of his system to test it commercially, and in November of that year he founded the De Forest Phonofilm Company to produce a series of short sound films in cooperation with Dr. Hugo Riesenfeld, a composer of silent-film scores.

Working at the Norma Talmadge Studios in New York City, de Forest made several one- and two-reel phono-films each week, and their success was such that by the middle of 1924 some thirty-four theaters in the East had been wired to show them and another fifty were in the process of being wired elsewhere in the United States, in Britain, and in Canada. The content of de Forest's films was varied, but they all somehow exploited sound. They included set pieces from grand opera, instrumental performances by famous musicians, popular vaudeville acts,

---

2. De Forest sold the telephone rights to his audion patents to AT&T in 1913, enabling it to open the first coast-to-coast long-distance circuits in 1915, using vacuum-tube reamplifiers, or repeaters. He sold the radio rights to the same company in 1914.

scenes from current plays, speeches by prominent persons such as President Calvin Coolidge, Senator Robert La Follette, and George Bernard Shaw, and even an original narrative from time to time. (It is also possible that de Forest used the phonofilm process to provide full-length recordings of Riesenfeld's scores for James Cruze's *The Covered Wagon* in 1924 and Fritz Lang's *Siegfried* in 1925, but the historical record on this point is unclear.) Although de Forest experienced some popular success with the more than one thousand short sound films he made in New York between 1923 and 1927, his attempts to interest Hollywood producers in the phonofilm process proved fruitless, because they did not want to spend the money required to convert their entire system of production and exhibition. As early as 1923, he had offered it to moguls like Carl Laemmle of Universal and Adolph Zukor of Paramount, only to be ignored. The studio chiefs tended to regard "talking pictures" as an expensive novelty that had no future beyond causing financial ruin for its backers, and not a single Hollywood executive showed the slightest interest in phonofilm until the phenomenal success of a rival sound-on-disc system called Vitaphone forced them to reassess their options in 1926.

Vitaphone

Vitaphone was a sophisticated sound-on-disc system employing multiple 33⅓ rpm discs developed at great expense by Western Electric and Bell Telephone Laboratories, a subsidiary firm of American Telephone and Telegraph Corporation (AT&T), in blithe ignorance of (or at least indifference to) Hollywood's antipathy toward sound. When representatives of Western Electric attempted to market the system to the major studios in 1925, they were politely refused. But the financially venturesome and, at the time, emphatically minor Warner Bros. Pictures decided to take a chance on sound. Warner Bros. was not on the verge of bankruptcy, as is frequently claimed. In fact, it had embarked upon an aggressively expansionist campaign against its larger competitors and was having temporary cash-flow problems. The studio's executives conceived the acquisition of sound as an offensive rather than a defensive maneuver. So, in April 1926, Warner Bros., with the financial assistance of the Wall Street banking group Goldman Sachs,[3] established the Vitaphone

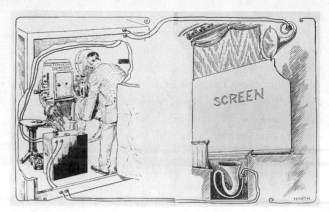

7.1 **The Western Electric Vitaphone projection system.**

Corporation, formally leased the sound-system from Western Electric, and for $800,000 secured the exclusive right to sublease it to other studios. There was at first no question of making "talking pictures." Warner Bros.' notion was that Vitaphone could be used to provide synchronized musical accompaniment for all Warner Bros. films, enhancing their appeal to the second- and third-run theaters that had no orchestras. An official statement prepared for Vitaphone underscored the Warners' appeal to smaller exhibitors: "The invention will make it possible for every performance in a motion picture theater to have a full orchestral accompaniment to the picture regardless of the size of the house." Having cast its lot with Vitaphone, Warner Bros. decided to promote it on a spectacular scale at a total cost of over $3 million. For its world premier at the "Refrigerated[4] Warner Theater" at Broadway and Fifty-

3. Waddill Catchings, head of the Goldman Sachs investment division, arranged for the studio to underwrite a $4.2 million note issue to finance Vitaphone. Catchings subsequently became a Warner board member and facilitated the acquisition of the Stanley theater chain and the First National studio and exchanges in late 1928.

4. Although it could be enormously expensive, costing up to $40,000 per theater, air-conditioning of some sort had become a standard feature of most American picture palaces during the 1920s, and installations proceeded (with a brief pause for World War II) until by 1950 three-quarters of all domestic theaters were cooled. Initiated by the Chicago chain of Balaban & Katz in a borrowing from the meat-packing industry of about 1917, fan-coiled air-cooling systems provided a major attraction for large first-run theaters during the summer months and ultimately transformed summer into the film industry's major season. As Douglas Gomery points out, "Few Americans ever experienced air-conditioning during the 1930s and 1940s outside a movie house" ("Movie-Going during Hollywood's Golden Age," *North Dakota Quarterly* 51, 3 [Summer 1983]: 40).

7.2 **An actual Vitaphone projection in progress.**

7.3 **A billboard in New York City, 1926.**

second Street in New York City on August 6, 1926, Warner Bros. presented *Don Juan* (Alan Crosland, 1926), the latest and most lavish John Barrymore costume drama, with an elaborate recorded orchestral score performed by the New York Philharmonic. The feature was preceded by a one-hour, $1 million program of sound shorts, featuring the stars of the Metropolitan Opera and the New York Philharmonic Orchestra, which was itself preceded by a brief filmed speech by Will Hays, president of the MPPDA, announcing "the beginning of a new era in music and motion pictures."

Again, it was as a revolutionary way of providing synchronized musical accompaniment for "silent" films that Vitaphone was initially promoted, and its debut as such was enormously successful. The first Vitaphone program ran eight weeks in New York, where it was seen by more than a half-million people, who paid nearly $800,000. It went on to have record-breaking runs in Chicago, Los Angeles, Boston, Detroit, St. Louis, and many European cities. The critics were unanimous in their praise of the Vitaphone system, describing it as "uncanny in its excellence," "impossible to imagine," and "the eighth wonder of the world." Of Hays's filmed speech before the program, Professor of Physics Michael Pupin of Columbia University remarked, "No closer approach to resurrection has ever been made by science." Nevertheless, the future of Vitaphone was still uncertain in late 1926. No one could determine at this point whether its warm public and critical reception was the result of a passing fancy or a legitimate interest in sound films. But, as Harry M. Geduld writes, "Warners had too much at stake to accept the idea that Vitaphone might be an ephemeral novelty—

while the rest of the film industry had too much at stake to entertain the notion that it might not."

The rest of the film industry had a very good reason for hoping that the enthusiasm for Vitaphone would pass. It was understood among studio chiefs that a full-scale conversion to sound would cost an incalculable amount of money and perhaps even bring the industry to financial collapse. New sound studios would have to be built and costly recording equipment installed. Thousands of cinema theaters across the country, many of them now owned by the studios, would have to be wired for sound and perhaps wired twice due to the incompatibility of competing systems. (In 1927 the installation of Vitaphone equipment alone could cost as much as $25,000 per theater.) Each studio would suddenly have a huge backlog of silent films representing millions of dollars in capital investment, and the industry's vast overseas market would be decimated if easily translated intertitles gave way to spoken dialogue. The star system, which sustained the American studios and helped to sell their product all over the world, would also be thrown into disarray when actors and actresses trained solely in the art of mime suddenly had to start speaking dialogue. Finally, as *Variety*, the industry trade paper, asked, "What would happen to the class theatres with expensive orchestras and stage shows, if any jerk-water movie joint was able to give its patrons gorgeous feasts of music via the screen?" In short, conversion to sound threatened the entire economic structure of the American (and, therefore, the Western) film industry, and the industry had every reason to resist it. But by the beginning of 1927, Vitaphone's popular success could not be ignored, and in February of that year executives of the Big Three—Loew's (MGM); Famous Players–Lasky, soon to become Paramount; and First

7.4 *Variety* proclaims the arrival of a new era in film.

National—and the largest of the Little Five—Universal and Producers Distributing Corporation (PDC)—signed an accord (known somewhat confusingly as the "Big Five Agreement") to adopt a uniform sound system if and when conversion became necessary; it was this agreement that ultimately led to the promotion of rival systems and the eventual triumph of sound-on-film over sound-on-disc.

For the time being, however, Vitaphone was still the best system on the market, and, buoyed by the success of the *Don Juan* program, Warners announced that all of its silent films for 1927 would be produced with synchronized musical accompaniment. It also announced plans to buy one major theater in every large American city and wire it for sound. By April 1927, the Vitaphone Corporation had completed 150 installations, an average of 12 per week. In the same month, Warners completed construction of the first sound studio in the world, where, a month later, production began on the picture that would

insure the triumph of the sound film and determine its future direction: Alan Crosland's *The Jazz Singer* (1927). Although Warners had been recording synchronized scores for its pictures and providing with them programs of sound shorts since August 1926, *The Jazz Singer* was to be the start of the studio's regular production of Vitaphone features for distribution to Vitaphone theaters. It was planned as a prestigious production ("Warner Brothers' Supreme Triumph," said the publicity posters), and the popular vaudeville star Al Jolson (1886–1950) was hired for $20,000 to play the lead.

The Jazz Singer, adapted from a successful Broadway play that had originally starred George Jessel (1898–1981), told the sentimental story of the son of a Jewish cantor who undergoes an anguished conflict between his religion, his family, and his career as a music-hall singer.[5] Like previous Vitaphone productions, it was conceived as a silent picture with a synchronized orchestral score, some Jewish cantorial music, and seven popular songs performed by Jolson. It was conceived, that is, as a "singing" rather than a "talking" picture, and all dialogue was to be provided by interpolated titles (intertitles). But, during the shooting of two musical sequences, Jolson ad-libbed some dialogue on the set, which Warners shrewdly permitted to remain in the finished film. At one point near the beginning of the picture, Jolson speaks to his audience in the middle of a nightclub act and delivers his famous "Wait-a-minute. . . . Wait-a-minute. . . . You ain't heard nothin' yet!" Later in the film, as he sits at a piano in his mother's parlor, he has a sentimental exchange with her that lasts several minutes, between verses of "Blue Skies." This was the only spoken dialogue in the film, yet its impact was sensational. Audiences had heard synchronized speech before, but only on formally contrived and easily anticipated occasions, such as the speech that preceded *Don Juan.* Suddenly, though, here was Jolson not only singing and dancing but speaking informally and spontaneously to other persons in the film as someone might do in reality. The effect was not so much of *hearing* Jolson speak as of *overhearing* him speak, and it thrilled audiences bored with the conventions of silent cinema and increasingly indifferent to the canned performances

---

5. *The Jazz Singer* has been twice remade as a theatrical film—once in 1952, with Michael Curtiz directing Danny Thomas in the Jolson role, and again in 1980, with Richard Fleischer directing Neil Diamond. There have also been several television versions.

7.5 A contemporary poster for *The Jazz Singer* (Alan Crosland, 1927).

of the Vitaphone shorts. Thus, we say that the "talkies" were born with *The Jazz Singer* not because it was the first feature-length film to employ synchronized dialogue,

7.6 Al Jolson in *The Jazz Singer*.

but because it was the first to employ it in a realistic and seemingly undeliberate way.

The combination of Jolson, Vitaphone, and synchronized dialogue made *The Jazz Singer* an international success from the date of its premiere on October 6, 1927, eventually earning over $3.5 million. By the end of 1927, it was playing to huge crowds in cities all over the world, and Warner Bros. was already starting to recoup its massive investment in the Vitaphone system. Most important, the film's success had convinced the other Hollywood studios that sound was here to stay in the form of "talking" pictures, and in accordance with the Big Five Agreement they began a series of maneuvers to acquire sound-recording equipment of their own.

Fox Movietone

Another organization that hastened the conversion to sound was the Fox Film Corporation, like Warner Bros. a minor studio at the time. In 1927 its president, William Fox, secretly acquired the American rights to the Tri-Ergon sound-on-film process, including the flywheel mechanism, for $50,000. A year earlier he had bought the rights to an American sound-on-film system from Theodore W. Case and Earl I. Sponable; this system was similar in many respects to de Forest's phonofilm and had, in fact, been based on it as the unintended result of a de Forest–Case collaboration between 1922 and 1925. Neither knowing nor caring about the latter,[6] Fox formed the Fox-Case Corporation in July 1926 to make short sound films with the system and exhibit them in his theaters under the name of Fox Movietone. Fox-Case experimented with Movietone for nearly a year before presenting its first program in New York City on January 21, 1927 (some six months after the premier of Vitaphone), a short series of canned performances by a Spanish cabaret singer, followed by the silent feature *What Price Glory?* (Raoul Walsh, 1926). Several **newsreels** followed (of marching West Point cadets [April 30]; of Charles A. Lindbergh's fabled takeoff for Paris [May 20]), as well as an ambitious program on May 25, 1927, of three short performance films, including a brief dialogue sketch by comedian Chic Sale entitled "They're Coming to Get

---

6. De Forest's suit against Fox for patent infringement helped to cause the mogul's downfall a decade later.

Me," followed by the feature film *Seventh Heaven* (Frank Borzage, 1927), with a synchronized orchestral score by Erno Rapee.

But it was the fifth Movietone program, offered on June 14, 1927, some four months before the opening of *The Jazz Singer*, that received international acclaim and convinced Fox of the value of the "talkies." On a bill with a conventional silent feature, Fox presented Movietone shorts of Lindbergh's reception at the White House by President Coolidge and of a speech by Italian dictator Benito Mussolini. These shorts of famous personalities speaking directly and clearly from the screen electrified the audience, and popular reaction to them was so favorable that Fox and his newsreel producer Courtland Smith established the Fox Movietone News that autumn in response to it. This was the first regular sound newsreel series, and its success was phenomenal. Within the year, Fox Movietone was sending camera crews around the world to interview everyone from George Bernard Shaw to the pope, and delivering three to four newsreels to Fox theaters per week.

When he inaugurated the Movietone News, Fox was certain that sound was on its way in, so he negotiated a reciprocal contract between Fox-Case and Vitaphone in which each corporation licensed the other to use its sound systems, studios, technicians, and theaters. This had the effect of covering both Fox and Warners if one sound system won out over the other, and of combining their resources to ensure survival in the face of any rival system that might be promoted by their competitors. As it turned out, though, most of the competition came over to their side. Financially, 1927 had been a very bad year for every Hollywood studio but Warners, and 1928 was already looking worse. Movie audiences had been dwindling since 1926, when the public apparently began to tire of Hollywood's retrograde production formulas and its heavily promoted stars. In addition, the ready availability of the automobile and the radio to the average American family since the early 1920s had created considerable competition for the silent cinema, much as television would challenge the sound film in the late 1940s and 1950s. In 1927, only sound films had been able to regularly attract large audiences, and, according to the film historian Richard Griffith, by the spring of the next year the worst sound film would outdraw the best silent picture in any given community in the country.

The Process of Conversion

By 1928, then, the American public had clearly chosen sound, and the studios could only acquiesce or be damned. The signatories of the Big Five Agreement and their peers were at this point able to choose among several competing optical systems. While still marketing Vitaphone, Western Electric had developed a sophisticated sound-on-film process similar to that of Pedersen and Poulsen[7] that was ready for diffusion through its nontelephone subsidiary, Electrical Research Products, Incorporated (ERPI); Fox stood ready to market Movietone (though he currently lacked the financial muscle to back it up); and Radio Corporation of America (RCA) was offering a newly perfected General Electric system called Photophone. RCA general manager David Sarnoff came very close to winning over Paramount and Loew's, but in the end ERPI's John Otterson was able to offer the studios a better deal, and on May 11, 1928, Paramount, Loew's, First National, and United Artists all signed licensing agreements with Western Electric; Universal, Columbia, Tiffany-Stahl, Hal Roach Comedies, and Christie Comedies soon followed. Sarnoff's reaction was to create his own vertically integrated major to exploit the Photophone process, acquiring Joseph P. Kennedy's production-distribution syndicate Film Booking Office (FBO), Pathé (which had itself just taken over PDC), and the Keith-Albee-Orpheum chain of two hundred downtown vaudeville theaters. This combine was merged as Radio-Keith-Orpheum (RKO), and by the summer of 1928 every studio in Hollywood, willingly or not, had somehow prepared itself for the conversion to sound.

Warner Bros., however, continued to lead the way. Having produced the first "part-talkie"—*The Jazz Singer*—it went on to produce the first "100 percent all-talkie"—*Lights of New York* (Bryan Foy, 1928), a clumsily plotted tale of two small-town barbers who come to the city to seek their fortunes and become dangerously

---

7. A rival optical process developed by the Danish engineers P. O. Pedersen and Valdemar Poulsen in 1923 used an oscillograph to modulate light in recording and a selenium cell in reproduction, apparently to obviate the Tri-Ergon patents. This process was marketed as Tonfilm in Germany and was licensed by Gaumont in France and British Acoustic, Ltd., in England.

7.7 The first all-dialogue film: Warner Bros.' *Lights of New York* (Bryan Foy, 1928). Enormously popular, it returned its producers' $75,000 investment more than fourteen times.

involved with a gang of bootleggers. *Lights of New York* ran only fifty-seven minutes and was awkwardly directed, but twenty-two of its twenty-four sequences contained recorded dialogue, making it the first film in history to rely entirely upon the spoken word to sustain its narrative. The enormous popular success of *Lights of New York* demonstrated to Hollywood that all-dialogue films not only could be made, but could draw huge audiences as well. In fact, the talkies (or "audible photoplays," as the trade press called them) were drawing so well by the end of 1928 that it was clear to all that the silent cinema was dead. This was an unexpected blow to the film industry since it had been assumed by nearly everyone in Hollywood that sound and silent pictures would be able to coexist, for a while at least. Now, suddenly, Hollywood became aware that the public would no longer pay to see silent films.

The upshot was a nearly total conversion to sound by the end of 1929 that radically changed the structure of the film industry and revolutionized the practice of cinema all over the world. In that year, fully three-fourths of all films made in Hollywood were released with some kind of prerecorded sound. *Film Daily Yearbook* for 1929 lists the production of 335 all-dialogue features, 95 features with a mixture of dialogue and subtitles, and 75 features with musical scores and sound effects. The films in the last two categories were silent pictures to which some sound had hastily been added to satisfy public demand, a common way of salvaging expensively pro-

duced silent features during the year of transition. Hollywood also released 175 straight silent features in 1929 for exhibition in those provincial theaters that had not yet been wired for sound (an operation costing between $8,500 and $20,000, depending on the seating capacity and the sound process); but by the end of the year, almost every American theater of any size had installed sound equipment. In fact, the number of theaters wired for sound increased more than fifty times between December 31, 1927, and December 31, 1929. As Alexander Walker writes, "There has never been such a lightning retooling of an entire industry—even wartime emergencies were slower. . . ." Yet, the transition was orderly and well planned, with the Academy of Motion Picture Arts and Sciences functioning as a clearinghouse for information and a general industry resource. Starting in May 1928, it organized intensive educational seminars for studio personnel and set up special committees to help the studios solve technical problems and handle contractual disputes with equipment manufacturers.

The cost of the conversion, however, was staggering, requiring that the studios borrow huge sums of money from Wall Street. In July 1929, Fox's general manager, Winfield Sheehan, estimated that Hollywood had invested more than $50 million in the changeover. The final figure would be in excess of $300 million—nearly four times the market valuation of the entire industry for fiscal year 1928.[8] Much of this capital was lent to the studios by the two corporate giants of the era, the Morgan and the Rockefeller groups, which also controlled Western Electric and RCA, thus strengthening the alliance between Hollywood and Wall Street that had begun in the early 1920s and that exists ever more visibly today. As Arthur Knight remarks, representatives of the financiers were soon sitting on the boards of the motion picture companies, making policy decisions and giving power to sound engineers imported from the broadcasting and telephone industries who knew nothing about film.

Nevertheless, the prodigious borrowing of 1928–29 was offset by the prodigious profits of the same year.

---

8. This estimate is from Alexander Walker's well-researched *The Shattered Silents: How the Talkies Came to Stay,* and it includes the costs of wiring theaters as well as converting production. Other estimates vary, and the true figure will probably never be known owing to the untrustworthy, if creative, accounting procedures of the day.

Weekly attendance shot up from 60 million in 1927 to 90 million in 1930, with an increase in box office receipts of 50 percent. After a deficit of over $1 million in 1927 owing to its heavy investment in Vitaphone, Warner Bros. reported profits of over $2 million for 1928 and over $17 million for 1929, enabling the production company to gain control of five hundred exhibition outlets by buying the Stanley theater chain and First National (one of the Big Three with which, two years earlier, Warners had been in such unequal competition) to become for over a decade one of the most powerful studios in Hollywood. By 1929, Fox's profits had soared high enough for the company to build itself a new $10-million all-sound studio (Movietone City, in the Los Angeles suburb of Westwood) and for Fox himself to pay $50 million for a controlling interest in Loew's, Inc., which owned MGM, and another $20 million for a 45-percent share of Gaumont-British, England's largest producer/distributor/exhibitor.[9] In the same year, Paramount, with its international distribution network and vast Publix theater chain, acquired one-half of the newly formed Columbia Broadcasting System (CBS) and proposed a merger with Warner Bros. If things had continued on course, "Paramount-Vitaphone" and "Fox-Loew's" would have divided the entertainment industries of the English-speaking world between them, but the Justice Department of the Hoover administration intervened to prevent these combinations. Most of the other studios' profits doubled between 1928 and 1930 due to the public's mania for the talkies, and it is probably true that the introduction of sound, more than any other factor, enabled Hollywood to survive the Great Depression, which began with the stock market crash of October 1929.[1] As Kenneth Macgowan comments: "If the producers had waited till late October 1929—as they might well have done except for the daring of Warner Brothers and Fox— sound would have been impossible for ten more years, and receiverships [bankruptcy] would have come quite some time before 1932."

When the Depression finally did hit Hollywood in 1932, the silent cinema was a distant memory. All sound equipment had been standardized by international agreement in 1930. Sound-on-film—Fox Movietone and RCA Photophone in the United States, Tobis-Klangfilm's Tri-Ergon process on the Continent—had won out over sound-on-disc because of the superior quality of reproduction in the former and the manifold problems of synchronization posed by the latter. Sound-on-film had also proved the most flexible system for recording on location, as the naturalistic sound track of Fox's *In Old Arizona* (Raoul Walsh, 1928), the first all-talkie shot outdoors, had demonstrated. The immense profits Warners had reaped from Vitaphone enabled it to switch systems in its studios and theaters without risk. And in 1935, after nine years of litigation, Dr. Lee de Forest, who had spent $200,000 of his own funds developing the sound-on-film system that Hollywood eventually adopted but who had lacked the resources to promote it, was finally awarded the sum of $100,000 for patent infringement by the Fox-Case and Vitaphone Corporations. Even with the compensation, de Forest had to borrow money to pay his legal fees, but he had at least won the right to call himself the inventor of the process that changed forever the aesthetic configuration of the cinema.

The Introduction of Color

The so-called "natural" or photographic color processes became institutionalized at approximately the same time as sound, although, like sound, color had been a component of the film experience for a long time. Hand tinting

---

9. This bid on Fox's part to control the largest production companies and major theater chains in the United States and England, respectively, as well as to control all of the West's sound-on-film patents through Movietone, was nothing less than an attempt to consolidate the film industries of both countries under his personal command; and for several months, the "Fox-Loew's Corporation" became the largest motion picture company on earth. This extraordinarily ambitious and avaricious plan collapsed about Fox's ears within a year of its implementation when the Justice Department of the newly elected Hoover administration (notoriously chummy with Louis B. Mayer, who stood to lose a fortune in the Fox-Loew's deal) ordered Fox to divest himself of the Loew's stock. The stock market crashed simultaneously, killing the Gaumont-British deal and forcing Fox to sell his shares in Loew's at a $30-million loss. In 1931, Fox was ousted from his company by a coalition of executives and stockholders, and he finally declared bankruptcy in 1936. His legal entanglements continued until 1941, when he was sentenced to a year in prison for attempting to bribe a federal judge at his bankruptcy hearing. After serving six months of the term in 1943, he retired to live reasonably well on the several sound film patents he had managed to retain through the court battles of the 1930s. Fox's apologia for this incredible career is contained in *Upton Sinclair Presents William Fox* (Los Angeles: Upton Sinclair, 1933).

1. Some characteristic studio profits for fiscal year 1929 were Warner Bros., $17,271,805; Fox, $9,469,050; Paramount, $15,544,544; and MGM, $11,756,956.

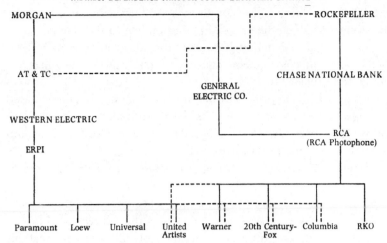

INDIRECT DEPENDENCE THROUGH SOUND EQUIPMENT CONTROL

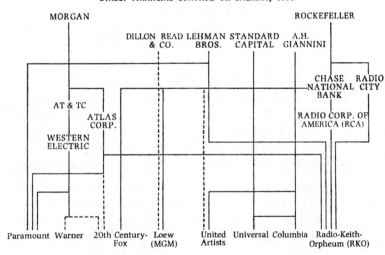

DIRECT FINANCIAL CONTROL OR BACKING, 1936

7.8 Charts showing direct and indirect financial control of the American sound film (and thus of the American film industry) during the 1930s. (From F. D. Klingender and Stuart Legg, *Money behind the Screen* [London, 1937]). Reprinted by permission of Lawrence & Wishart Ltd.) A critique of Klingender and Legg's analysis is contained in Janet Wasko, *Movies and Money: Financing the American Film Industry* (Norwood, N.J.: Ablex, 1982), ch. 3, "The Introduction of Sound and Financial Control (1927–1939)," pp. 47–102.

had been widely practiced during the primitive period, when films were short enough to make it commercially viable. Méliès, for example, employed twenty-one women at Montreuil to hand-tint his most spectacular films frame by frame, and Edison regularly tinted portions of his films (e.g., the bursts of gunsmoke in Porter's *The Great Train Robbery* [1903]). In 1905, as the length of films and the number of prints required by exhibitors increased, Charles Pathé invented the Pathécolor stencil process (renamed Pathéchrome in 1929) to mechanize the application of color. Frame-by-frame stencils were cut by pantograph to correspond to those areas to be tinted in any one of six standard colors. After a stencil had been made for the whole length of film, it was placed into contact with the print to be

colored and run at high speed (60 feet per minute) through a staining machine, a process repeated for each set of stencils and dyes to be applied. By 1910, Pathé Frères employed over four hundred women in its stenciling operation at the Vincennes factory (Gaumont had adopted a similar system in 1905), and the process was used in Europe well into the 1930s. In the United States, another form of stenciling was patented in 1916 by the St. Louis engraver Max Handschiegl and cinematographer Alvin Wyckoff of the Famous Players–Lasky Corporation laboratory. Popularly known as the Handschiegl process (and later as the Wyckoff-DeMille process), it employed the principles of three-color lithography to machine-tint such big-budget studio productions as

Cecil B. DeMille's *Joan, the Woman* (1917), Erich von Stroheim's *Greed* (1924) and *The Merry Widow* (1925), Rupert Julian's *Phantom of the Opera* (1925), and King Vidor's *The Big Parade* (1925).

As film became a major international industry during the 1920s, however, the need to mass-produce prints led to the development of tinting and toning, both mechanized nonphotographic color processes. Tinting, the most commonly used, involved immersing black-and-white positive stock in a bath of dye, whose color was varied according to the mood and/or setting of a given scene. (Theoretically, at least—In practice, the colors were often chosen arbitrarily from a range of exotically trade-named dyes, including Verdante, Azure, Nocturne, Purplehaze, Fleur de lis, Amaranth, Inferno, Argent, Rose doree, Firelight, Peachblow, and Sunshine.) Toning affected only the black-silver portion of the image; it was accomplished by chemically treating the silver to convert it into a dye composed of colored silver salts. Whereas tinting produced a uniform color throughout, toning colored only the darker area of the frame, leaving the lighter parts white. With care, the two processes could be used in combination to produce more elaborate effects, such as an orange-tinted sunset in a blue-toned sky; and by the early 1920s 80 to 90 percent of all American films used some form of tinting or toning for at least some scenes.[2] But the colors provided by both were notably artificial, and the coming of sound presented new problems because the dyes used in tinting and toning interfered with the sound track by absorbing too much light. Eastman Kodak responded quickly in 1929 by introducing Sonochrome, a black-and-white positive stock available on a range of sixteen tinted bases corresponding to the standard dyes used in tinting. But by this time developments in the field of color cinematography had overtaken the quest for color.[3]

The principles on which color photography is based were first proposed by the Scottish physicist James Clerk Maxwell (1831–1879) in 1855 and demonstrated by him at the Royal Institution in London in 1861. At this time, it was known that light comprises a spectrum of different wavelengths that are perceived as different colors as they are absorbed and reflected by natural objects. What Maxwell discovered was that all natural colors in this spectrum are composed of different combinations of three primary colors—red, green, and blue—which, when mixed together equally, produce white. Color, it followed, could be produced either by adding together various measures of the primary colors or by subtracting various measures from white light. These two methods, the additive and the subtractive, are the ones that have been used to produce color photographically in film.

The first process to employ these principles in motion-picture photography successfully was Charles Urban's two-color sequential additive system Kinemacolor. It was based on the work of Brighton filmmaker G. A. Smith, who in 1906 had discovered that by fusing two primary colors, red and green, through persistence of vision, he could obtain a range of colors nearly equivalent to those produced by three.[4] The American entrepreneur Charles

---

2. Mordanting, or dye fixing, was a variant of toning in which the silver was replaced by an uncolored silver salt (the mordant) and then by a pigmented salt, whose intensity could be varied from one portion of the scene to the next. When tinting and toning (or mordanting) were combined, the operation was tricky and needed manual supervision. Because toning conventionally preceded tinting, tints could sometimes render tones instable. To address this problem both Eastman Kodak and Pathé, the two largest manufacturers of raw film stock at the time, produced special stocks designed to ensure the uniform stability and distribution of dyes on the emulsion. In 1926, for example, Pathé offered nine different stocks for use in tinting. See Paolo Cherchi Usai, "The Color of Nitrate," in *Silent Film*, ed. Richard Abel (New Brunswick, N.J.: Rutgers University Press, 1996), pp. 21–30, and "The Way of All Flesh Tones," in Paolo Cherchi Usai, *Silent Cinema: An Introduction* (London: British Film Institute, 2000), pp. 21–43.

3. Tinting and toning continued to be used for expressive effect well into the sound era and are occasionally used for the same end today. In the 1930s and 1940s, Westerns were often filmed on sepia-tinted stock to evoke old photographs, and several important films of the period—e.g., *The Rains Came* (Clarence Brown, 1939), *Of Mice and Men* (Lewis Milestone, 1939), *Ziegfield Girl* (Robert Z. Leonard, 1941), *Tortilla Flat* (Victor Fleming, 1942)—employed sepia toning for the same purpose. David O. Selznick used green tinting for the storm sequence of *Portrait of Jennie* (William Dieterle, 1948), and RKO's *Mighty Joe Young* (Ernest B. Schoedsack, 1949) was tinted red for a fire sequence and amber for the sentimental conclusion. Postwar science-fiction films had occasional recourse to tinting (e.g., bluish pink for the Mars sequence of *Rocketship XM* [Kurt Neumann, 1950], green for the lost world in *The Lost Continent* [Samuel Newfield, 1951]), as have such major directors as Alfred Hitchcock (the orange-red gun blast into the audience in *Spellbound* [1945]; the red suffusions indicating psychological disorder in *Marnie* [1965]) and Sergei Parajanov (*Shadows of Forgotten Ancestors* [1964] makes extensive use of both tinting and toning).

4. The claim that two colors could transmit the full spectrum contradicts classical color theory. Nevertheless, the CBS field-sequential color television system first broadcast in 1951 operated on the same principle.

Urban (1867–1942) bought the patent rights and demonstrated the system publicly as Kinemacolor before the Royal Society of Arts on December 9, 1908. Urban and Smith began commercial operations shortly thereafter, forming the Natural Color Kinematograph Company to produce and distribute Kinemacolor films. At first, these were shown on an occasional basis in London, Nottingham, and Blackpool, but by April 1911 Urban had begun showing complete programs of Kinemacolor *actualitiés*, such as the coronation of George V, at the Scala in London. Kinemacolor's most spectacular production and greatest commercial success was the two-and-one-half hour *Durbar at Dèlhi* (1912), shot on location in India by Urban and a crew of twenty-three cameramen. By 1913, Kinemacolor films were being shown regularly in thirteen countries, including the United States, where Kinemacolor of America was incorporated in 1910; and Urban had camera crews all over the world shooting and releasing new films at the rate of two to three per week.

Yet by 1915, Kinemacolor was all but defunct, a victim of patent litigation brought on by the rival Bioschemes, Ltd.; as a result, Smith's patent was revoked in April 1914. Other difficulties affecting Kinemacolor were the rising popularity of dramatic features at a time when the company was militantly committed to the factual film, and technological problems inherent in the system itself, among which were color fringing in moving objects and the poor registration of blues. But Urban had demonstrated that a lucrative market existed worldwide for color films, and, as Gorham Kindem points out, no color process seems to have rivaled the early commercial success of Kinemacolor until Technicolor began to market its two-color subtractive process in the 1920s.

Still, other systems were constantly being developed and tested, including such three-color additive systems as Gaumont's Chronochrome (patented 1912), which used a three-lens camera and projector, and such two-color nonsequential additive systems as Cinechrome (1914) and British Raycol (1929). In the two-color nonsequential additive systems, a single camera lens was fitted with a system of prisms that split the light beam in two, creating two pairs of red and green exposures simultaneously, which would be superimposed in projection. Ultimately, however, additive systems proved too complicated, costly, and imprecise[5] to bring color wholesale into the cinema. The first entirely successful motion-picture color system was two-strip subtractive Technicolor.

The Technicolor Corporation was formed in 1915 in Boston by Dr. Herbert T. Kalmus (1881–1963), Dr. Daniel F. Comstock, and W. Burton Wescott[6] as an offshoot of their successful industrial consulting firm, to exploit a two-color additive process in which a prismatic beam-splitter produced separate red and green exposures in-camera and superimposed them in projection. The company produced only one film in this process, *The Gulf Between* (Irvin Willat, 1917); its failure led Kalmus to abandon the additive system for a subtractive one. His goal was to have both color components printed in register on positive film stock and eliminate the superimposition of images in projection (and thus special projectors). The new system, patented in 1922, used a beam-splitting camera to produce two separate negatives that were printed separately as positives on specially thin-based Kodak stock. These were then chemically treated to remove the silver and form transparent "relief images" of exposed gelatin, dyed red-orange on one print and green on the other. Finally, the two relief prints were cemented base to base for projection through an ordinary projector.

The industry was so excited by this innovation that Loew's, Inc., offered to produce Technicolor's first film in the process, *The Toll of the Sea* (Chester Franklin, 1922), which was supervised by Joseph M. Schenck and released through Metro Film Company by Nicholas Schenck. The film was a great success, grossing more than $250,000 (of which Technicolor received approximately $165,000), and it demonstrated the commercial viability of subtractive Technicolor in no uncertain terms. Although its cost was inordinately high (Technicolor had to charge twenty cents per foot for release prints), this "cemented positive" process worked well enough to be used for color sequences in several major productions of 1923–24, including Paramount's *The Ten Command-*

---

5. All additive systems suffered from a loss of illumination in projection, with as much as 70 percent of the light being absorbed by the color filters, causing registration difficulties. In addition, systems like Kinemacolor and Chronochrome, which involve high-speed shooting and projection, used more film stock and required more rapid print replacement than black-and-white. Finally, the special projection equipment required by additive systems at a time when the exhibition sector was becoming increasingly powerful and conservative militated against their use.

6. Kalmus and Comstock were alumni of the Massachusetts Institute of Technology who had returned to teach there after earning Ph.D.s abroad, and many of the company's early employees were MIT students. As Kalmus was later to acknowledge, MIT is the "Tech" in Technicolor.

ments (Cecil B. DeMille, 1923), First National's *Cytherea* (George Fitzmaurice, 1924), and MGM's *The Merry Widow* (Erich von Stroheim, 1925), and for such complete features as Jesse L. Lasky's *Wanderer of the Wasteland* (Irvin Willat, 1924) and Douglas Fairbanks's *The Black Pirate* (Albert Parker, 1926).

In 1928, however, Technicolor introduced an improved two-color process in which the two relief prints became *matrices* for the transfer of dyes to a third and final print. Specifically, when the matrix prints were brought into contact with a blank, gelatin-coated film, the dyes were transferred in exact registration through a process known as *imbibition,* which became the basis for the Technicolor process from 1928 through the 1970s. Imbibition dye-transfer eliminated the use of a "cemented positive" and made it possible to mass-produce release prints from the matrices, which could simply be redyed between successive transfers.

The innovation of Technicolor's second subtractive system, of course, coincided with the coming of sound, and this circumstance helped to create a boomlet for the process. For one thing, as noted earlier, dyes used in the nonphotographic tinting and toning processes so popular during the 1920s were rendered obsolete by sound because they interfered with the optical sound track. Although this problem was addressed by Eastman Kodak's introduction of Sonochrome in 1929, it gave Technicolor an open field during the most crucial year of the conversion. For another thing, many early sound films were musicals, a genre whose fantastic, spectacular nature was particularly suited to color representation.[7] In fact, Technicolor's new process was first used for sequences in *Broadway Melody* (Harry Beaumont, 1929) and *The Desert Song* (Roy Del Ruth, 1929), and the first all-Technicolor sound films were Warner Bros.' *On with the Show* (Alan Crosland, 1929) and *Gold Diggers of Broadway* (Roy Del Ruth, 1929)—both smashing box-office hits, the latter grossing over $3.5 million.

In 1930, Technicolor was under contract for thirty-six features, some of the most lavishly produced in that year, including *Whoopee!* (Thorton Freeland), *The Vagabond King* (Ludwig Berger), *No, No, Nanette* (Clarence Badger), *Rio Rita* (Luther Reed), *Paramount on Parade* (Dorothy Arzner and Otto Brower), and *Rogue Song* (Lionel Barrymore). Yet by 1932 the production of Technicolor films had nearly ceased. The sudden rush to color failed because audiences grew increasingly dissatisfied

with the poor registration of the two-color process, in which flesh tones could vary from pink to orange (according to Technicolor, a phenomenon resulting from misuse of the process by untrained studio cameramen) and also because the process itself was expensive, adding as much as 30 percent (or $100,000 to $300,000 in Depression currency) to the production costs of the average feature and raising distribution costs from three to five cents a foot over black and white. By contrast, recent improvements (c. 1925) in Eastman's panchromatic stock had made it sensitive to a wider range of tones than ever before and lowered its price; and in 1928 incandescent, or tungsten, lighting had been established as the relatively inexpensive norm (as opposed to the **arc lighting** required by Technicolor) for use with it. Thus, black and white became the standard medium for the sound film through the early 1950s, when less expensive color and lighting systems were devised.

In 1932, however, Technicolor perfected the three-color system whose predictability and accuracy was to give it a virtual monopoly over the production of color in motion pictures for the next twenty years. The camera employed a prismatic beam-splitter behind the lens to expose three separate black-and-white negatives running through two gates at right angles to one another (see Figure 7.9). The gate on the left contained a "bipack" of two negatives, the one in front dyed red-orange so that it absorbed the blue light and filtered the red light through to the one behind it. The gate on the right contained a single negative sensitive to green. Each of these "color separation" negatives would be developed as matrices for the same imbibition dye-transfer process used previously by Technicolor's two-color systems, resulting in a single three-color release print. (A blank silver negative containing the optical soundtrack was combined with the matrices during the imbibition stage, and Technicolor sometimes used a black fourth matrix to achieve a subtler range of colors, as was the case with *Gone with the Wind* [Victor Fleming, 1939].)

The three-color system was technically superior to any

---

7. According to Gorham Kindem in "Hollywood's Conversion to Color," fourteen of seventeen full-color features and twenty-three of thirty-four black-and-white features with color sequences released in 1929 and 1930 were musicals (*The American Movie Industry: The Business of Motion Pictures,* ed. Gorham Kindem [Carbondale, Ill.: Southern Illinois University Press, 1982], p. 156).

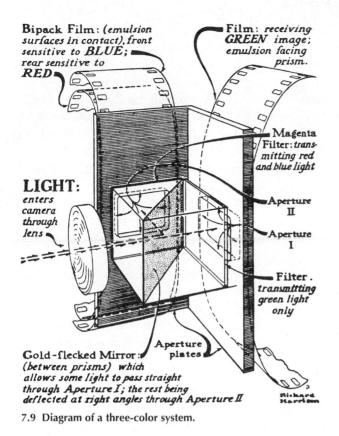

Bipack Film: *(emulsion surfaces in contact), front sensitive to BLUE; rear sensitive to RED*

Film: *receiving* GREEN *image; emulsion facing prism.*

Magenta Filter: *transmitting red and blue light*

LIGHT:
enters camera through lens

Aperture II

Aperture I

Filter. *transmitting green light only*

Richard Harrison

Gold-flecked Mirror: *(between prisms) which allows some light to pass straight through Aperture I; the rest being deflected at right angles through Aperture II*

Aperture plates

7.9 Diagram of a three-color system.

yet produced, but still it had its drawbacks. The "three-strip" cameras, which cost $30,000 apiece to manufacture, were large and heavy, complicating location shooting, and the process of exposing three black-and-white negatives simultaneously required a great deal of light, which further increased production costs. Furthermore, as David Bordwell has pointed out, because the 1929–1931 two-strip boom had resulted in so many unqualified cinematographers using the process, Technicolor standardized three-strip filming procedures and exerted a large measure of control over production:

> To make a Technicolor film, a producer had to rent the cameras, hire a Technicolor cameraman (eventually to be called a "camera optical engineer"), use Technicolor make-up, and have the film processed and printed by Technicolor. The producer would also have to accept a "color consultant" who would advise what color schemes to use on sets, costumes, and make up. . . . Only trained crews could operate the camera, and the production's cinematographer had to work closely with the Technicolor cameraman. (*The Classical Hollywood Cinema*, p. 354)

For all of these reasons, plus the general decline in film attendance caused by the Depression, producers were a good deal more conservative about adopting three-color Technicolor than its predecessors. Technicolor, for similar reasons, did not want to venture into production on its own, so it offered the process initially to the small independents Walt Disney and Pioneer Films (operated by Merian C. Cooper and John Whitney); and Disney became the first to use it in his "Silly Symphony" cartoon *Flowers and Trees* (1932) and *The Three Little Pigs* (1933), which were so successful—both winning Oscars and *Pigs* grossing over $750,000—that Disney contracted with Technicolor for a whole series of films and ultimately adopted the process for all of his studio's productions. (Disney actually negotiated a three-year exclusive contract for use of Technicolor in the field of animation in 1933, but it was subsequently revised to one year in order to accommodate demand from the majors.)[8]

The first live-action film in three-color Technicolor was Pioneer Films' *La Cucaracha* (1934), a thinly plotted two-reel short focusing on the romantic passions of two cantina dancers. The film was basically an extended test of the process under conditions of live production, and it impressed the industry so favorably that it won the 1934 Academy Award for the best Comedy Short Subject. Buoyed by this success, Pioneer ventured the first three-color feature, an eighty-three-minute version of Thackeray's classic Victorian novel *Vanity Fair* (1847–48), entitled *Becky Sharp* (Rouben Mamoulian, 1935).[9] At first, audiences rushed to see the $1 million costume film, but after a few weeks interest peaked, and the release ended in commercial failure. Undaunted, Kalmus organized a British subsidiary, Technicolor, Ltd., which in 1936 produced England's first Technicolor feature, the race-track melodrama *Wings of the Morning* (Harold

---

8. Disney retained exclusive rights to three-color Technicolor until the spring of 1935, while the other animators were allowed to use only the two-color process. See Richard Neupert, "A Studio Built of Bricks: Disney and Technicolor," *Film Reader 6: Investigations in Film History and Technology* (1985): 33–40.

9. Technicolor produced a total of 448 prints of the film, of which none has survived. Ironically, until it was restored by the UCLA Film Archives in 1984, *Becky Sharp* could only be seen in an inferior two-color Cinecolor version and in an edited-for-television black-and-white print. The Archives next plan to restore *Toll of the Sea*, the first two-color subtractive feature, from the original negative. For details, see Robert Gitt and Richard Dayton, "Restoring *Becky Sharp*," *American Cinematographer* 65, 10 (November 1984): 99–106.

Schuster). In Hollywood, the majors began to test the waters cautiously—20th Century–Fox with a rendition of the classic Indian saga *Ramona* (Henry King, 1936) and Paramount with *Trail of the Lonesome Pine* (Henry Hathaway, 1936), the first Technicolor film shot entirely on location. But it was David O. Selznick's newly formed independent company Selznick International that proved the commercial viability of Technicolor feature production once and for all with the star-studded hits *The Garden of Allah* (Richard Boleslavsky, 1936; with Charles Boyer and Marlene Dietrich), *Nothing Sacred* (William Wellman, 1937; with Fredric March and Carole Lombard), and *A Star Is Born* (William Wellman, 1937; Fredric March and Janet Gaynor), the first and last of which were honored with Special Academy Awards for their color cinematography (to the team of W. Howard Greene and Harold Rosson). Selznick scored again in 1938 with *The Adventures of Tom Sawyer* (Norman Taurog), and by this time nearly the whole industry had climbed on the bandwagon—MGM with *Sweethearts* (W. S. Van Dyke, 1938; first Academy Award in newly created Color Cinematography classification to Oliver Marsh); Paramount with *Ebb Tide* (James Hogan, 1937), *Vogues of 1938* (Irving Cummings, 1938), *Men with Wings* (William Wellman, 1938), and *Her Jungle Love* (George Archainbaud, 1938); 20th Century–Fox with *Kentucky* (David Butler, 1938); Samuel Goldwyn Productions with the lavish musical review *The Goldwyn Follies* (George Marshall, 1938); London Films (Alexander Korda) with *Drums* (Zoltan Korda, 1938) and *The Divorce of Lady X* (Tim Whelan, 1938), and, most prominently, Walt Disney with *Snow White and the Seven Dwarfs* (1937), the first full-length animated feature, and Warner Bros. with *The Adventures of Robin Hood* (Michael Curtiz and William Keighley, 1938), a film whose aesthetic use of the Technicolor system earned it three Academy Awards.

By the end of the year, Technicolor had twenty-five features in production, and on the books for the banner year of 1939–40 were Fox's The *Little Princess* (Walter Lang, 1939) and *Drums along the Mohawk* (John Ford, 1939), Warner Bros.' *Dodge City* (Michael Curtiz, 1939) and *The Privates Lives of Elizabeth and Essex* (Michael Curtiz, 1939), two Disney features—*Fantasia* (1940) and *Pinocchio* (1940)—and the era's quintessential blockbusters, MGM's *The Wizard of Oz* (Victor Fleming, 1939) and David O. Selznick's *Gone with the Wind* (Vic-

tor Fleming, 1939). Though not technically a full-length color film since it began and ended in sepia, *The Wizard of Oz* sustained its illusion of fantasy through the most imaginative and sophisticated use of Technicolor yet (amply assisted by the stunning art direction of Cedric Gibbons and William A. Horning). *Gone with the Wind*, on the other hand, was the first film to be shot using Technicolor's new, faster, fine-grained stock—a major technical breakthrough in that it cut lighting levels by 50 percent, bringing them closer to those used for monochrome. This in turn provided for the use of smaller, directional units for facial lighting, improved color rendition (especially in the green part of the spectrum), and increased depth of field. Appropriately, when *Gone with the Wind* swept the Academy Awards for 1939, Ray Rennahan and Ernest Haller shared the Oscar for its cinematography and William Cameron Menzies received a special plaque for his "outstanding achievement in the use of color for the enhancement of dramatic mood" in the film.

During the 1940s, the improved three-color system received greater use in such major productions as *Blood and Sand* (Rouben Mamoulian, 1941), *The Black Swan* (Henry King, 1942), *Henry V* (Laurence Olivier, 1944), *Leave Her to Heaven* (John M. Stahl, 1945), *The Yearling* (Clarence Brown, 1946), *Forever Amber* (Otto Preminger, 1947), and *Black Narcissus* (Michael Powell and Emeric Pressburger, 1947), but it was still limited by its expense and the Technicolor Corporation's virtual monopoly of the field. The former was improved somewhat in 1941 by the introduction of Technicolor Monopack, a multilayered film stock based on Eastman Kodachrome. Monopack produced a direct color positive from exposure in a conventional camera, which was then printed through red, green, and blue filters as separate matrices for the Technicolor dye-transfer process. The new stock proved valuable for location shooting since it eliminated the bulky three-strip camera, and it was first used for aerial sequences (*Dive Bomber* [1941] and *Captain of the Clouds* [1942, both Michael Curtiz]) and exteriors (*The Forest Rangers* [George Marshall, 1942]; *Lassie Come Home* [Fred M. Wilcox, 1943]). By 1944, Monopack had been improved to the point that it could be used to shoot entire features (e.g., *Thunderhead—Son of Flicka* [Louis King, 1945]), and Kalmus seriously considered abandoning the three-strip process in favor of it. But the postwar film attendance boom escalated the demand for Technicolor services and prevented any wholesale conversion until the 1950s, when the rival Eastmancolor system—cheaper, faster, but less stable—rendered the three-strip Technicolor camera obsolete, as we will see in Chapter 12.

Problems of Early Sound Recording

It is important to note that the introduction of sound is analogous in almost every respect to the invention of the cinema itself. In each case, the technological principles upon which the invention was based had been known for decades prior to their combination into a workable apparatus. In each case, the apparatus was developed and exploited for the purposes of novelty and commerce without a thought to aesthetic ends (early "movies" are comparable to early "talkies" in that both initially exploited their most novel feature at the expense of proportion and common sense). Finally, there was a long delay between the introduction of the sophisticated machine and the sophisticated artistic use of it.

The aesthetic and technical problems caused by the introduction of sound to the cinema were immense, and, if the transition was orderly from a corporate perspective, inside the studio sound stages there was confusion often bordering on chaos. For one thing, there were initially three competing systems (Western Electric Vitaphone, Fox Movietone, and RCA Photophone), none of which was compatible with the others, and equipment for all three was being so constantly modified and redesigned that it was sometimes obsolete before being uncrated.

The most serious problems involved sound recording in production (there was no postrecording yet), but there were also less spectacular difficulties at the exhibition sites. The initial deployment in 1928 of RCA Photophone, the optical sound system that was to become the industry standard, provides a good example of these. For one thing, RCA's original theater speakers were of the 12-inch cone type, nondirectional and barely adequate for speech greproduction. By early 1929 RCA was forced to add 5-foot horns to its speakers to improve their directional quality. These "directional baffles" were used with modest success in Photophone-wired theaters until a cross-licensing agreement in 1930 permitted RCA to install

7.10 On an unidentified Vitaphone set, 1927. Note the camera booth and microphone.

the superior horn-type speakers originally patented by Western Electric for its Vitaphone system. These speakers were highly directional and concentrated sound energy on the audience rather than diffusing it throughout the auditorium, and they eventually were adopted industry-wide.

Another immediate problem lay in projection. Before 1928, projection depended on the regular but intermittent motion of the film strip as it passed frame by frame between the lamp and shutter and the lens. To ensure fidelity of reproduction, however, the optically recorded sound track had to move with constant linear velocity across the photoelectric sound head. And, since in all optical systems the image track and the sound track were separated by only twenty frames, intermittent motion

7.11 A Vitaphone camera in its soundproof booth.

would be transferred to the sound head, causing audio distortion. RCA met the problems first with a mechanical "compensator" and then with a series of filters, which were not perfected and adopted as the industry standard until 1930. A further difficulty for exhibitors during the early transitional period was the necessity of maintaining both sound-on-disc and sound-on-film reproduction equipment until a uniform industry standard was chosen. As late as 1931, studios were still releasing films in both formats to accommodate theaters owned by sound-on-disk interests.

More important, as it has become almost axiomatic to say, the movies ceased to move when they began to talk, because between 1928 and 1931 they virtually regressed to their infancy in terms of editing and camera movement. In large part this was because the early microphones that were used to record sound had two substantial defects. First, they had a very limited range, so that to be heard on the sound track at all actors were forced to speak directly into them. This had the regressive effect of rendering actors motionless within the frame while they delivered their lines, and led to some remarkable exercises in concealing microphones on the set in flowerpots, ship's lanterns, and clumps of sagebrush. The second major defect of the microphones was, paradoxically, that within their limited range they were highly sensitive and omnidirectional—they picked up and recorded *every sound* made within their range on the set. This characteristic not only created problems in sound engineering, but rendered the camera almost totally inert: in order to avoid distortion in the synchronized sound track, all cameras were motorized to run at a standard speed (24 fps) in 1929. This meant, for one thing, that cameras could no longer be undercranked or overcranked by their operators to achieve expressive effects. But motorization also caused cameras to make a noisy, whirring clatter that would inevitably be picked up by the microphones. To prevent this, early sound cameras and their operators were at first enclosed in soundproof glass-paneled booths, 6 feet on a side, ironically dubbed "iceboxes" because they were so hot and stuffy. This practice literally imprisoned the camera, since it could neither tilt nor track (although it could pan as much as 30 degrees on its tripod), which helps to account for the static nature of so many early sound films. At their worst, these resembled the "filmed thea-

ter" of Méliès and *film d'art* far more than they resembled their immediate silent predecessors.

In fact, sound recording briefly rendered the cinema even *more* static than the filmed plays of its first decade because actors had to keep within range of both a static microphone *and* a static camera. Not only was the frame or camera itself rendered motionless, but the actors had to remain motionless *within* the frame (that is, within a given camera setup) if they were to have their voices picked up by the crude recording equipment. In filmed plays like *Queen Elizabeth* (1912) the actors, at least, could move around on the set, even though the cameras didn't move at all, but now they too were rendered immobile.

Another production problem was studio lighting. The carbon arc lamps that had provided principle lighting during the 1920s produced a humming noise and could not be used when recording synchronized dialogue. In 1930, muting circuits were selectively introduced in the arcs, but most studios had by then converted to **tungsten incandescent** lamps as their principle lighting source. These were less intense than arcs and had their own liabilities—as, for example, the sheer numbers required to light for two or three cameras at once, as was often the case in the early sound period when multiple shots would be made of the same scene to avoid editing the sound track in postproduction. Arcs continued to be used selectively throughout this era—providing, e.g., the main lighting source for Technicolor production—and tungsten incandescent and arc lamps remain the principle sources of film lighting today.

The impact of sound recording on film editing was probably the single most important factor in causing the regression of the transitional era. In the silent film, editing was unrestricted by content: dialogue was scarcely ever spoken word by word, and intertitles could either encapsulate it or eliminate it altogether to facilitate the montage structure of a given sequence. In the early sound film, editing—like camera movement, placement, and lighting—was subordinated absolutely to the technology of recording dialogue and became purely functional rather than expressive. In sound-on-disk films, scenes were initially made to play for nearly ten minutes in order for dialogue to be recorded continuously on 16-inch disks. Editing these scenes was out of the question, of course, until the technology of rerecording was perfected in the early 1930s, although if multiple cameras

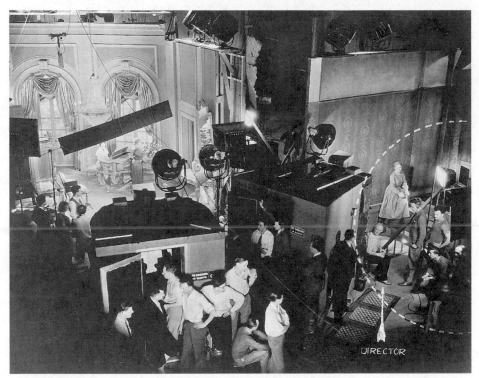

7.12 On the set of *Lummox* **(Herbert Brenon, 1930). Before the advent of post synchronization, any sounds to be heard simultaneously in the finished film had to be recorded simultaneously on the set. Here, a mother (right) listens to her daughter (left) singing in the room next door, which required that the two scenes be photographed and recorded at the same time.**

of Griffith, the montage structure of Eisenstein, and the fluid, expressive camera movement introduced by Murnau and Freund—all were effectively, if temporarily, eliminated by the clumsy technology of early sound recording. They were replaced by a series of talking photographs taken from the same angle at medium range and varied only when the talking stopped. Ironically, Edison's original conception of the film as a sequence of moving pictures to accompany and illustrate sound recordings was fully realized in the first few years of the sound era.

To make matters worse, the studios were so anxious to exploit the novelty of sound and amortize their borrowings that they turned to scripts (called "proper-

were used to shoot the same scene some variety could be added to the image track.[1] (It was also possible, if not very practical, to vary "shots" by alternating lenses of different focal length within the same camera setup.) Sound-on-film systems also militated against editing at first because of the necessary displacement between image and sound track in optical systems, in which the sound runs twenty frames in advance of its corresponding image.[2] This initially made it impossible to edit a composite optical print without eliminating portions of the relevant sound. In both sound-on-disk and sound-on-film systems, therefore, most early editing was largely *transitional*—a device for changing linearly from one scene to the next, rather than a mode for expressing multiple points of view—since, in general, cuts could only be made (as the camera could only be moved) when no sound was being recorded synchronously on the set. Crosscutting between actors speaking to one another, close-ups intercut with shots of other spatial lengths, the editing syntax

1. David Bordwell points out that multiple-camera shooting became the dominant studio practice from 1929 to 1931, as filmmakers strove to retain the option of cutting. The resultant editing structures, however, were "repetitive, even routine" (David Bordwell, Kristin Thompson, and Janet Staiger, *The Classical Hollywood Cinema: Film Style and Mode of Production to 1960* [New York: Columbia University Press, 1985], ch. 23, "The Introduction of Sound," p. 305).

2. Since it is mechanically impossible for the lens and the sound head of a projector to be located in the same place, there must be a displacement between image and sound track on composite sound-on-film exhibition prints. In 35mm filming, the sound track runs twenty frames in advance of the corresponding image track, making it impossible to edit a composite print without eliminating portions of the relevant sound. (In many of today's magnetic recording systems the sound runs *behind* the image, and the separation varies a great deal from one format to the other.) From a production standpoint, this problem was resolved by the introduction and refinement of postsynchronization, or dubbing, between 1929 and 1932. But to keep very early dialogue scenes from lapsing into inertia, the same sequence was frequently filmed simultaneously by as many as four cameras and later intercut. In this way, the images could be varied while the sound track remained constant, but the method was prohibitively expensive.

ties") that emphasized and even exaggerated the cinema's new inertia. Many producers assumed that the sound film would provide a perfect medium for photographing stage hits with their original casts and bringing them to a mass audience; between 1929 and 1931 much of the American cinema became "canned theater" in which Broadway plays and musicals were transferred from stage to screen verbatim with little or no adaptation. The impulse to record stage performances live on film at the beginning of the sound era was the same as that which had motivated the *film d'art* craze of 1908–12, and its failure was no less emphatic. The public rapidly tired of these "100 percent all-talking" productions (or "teacup dramas," as they were sometimes called), but they had the lasting effect of bringing Broadway players and directors to Hollywood on a more or less permanent basis.[3] Similarly, the urgent necessity for dialogue scripts revolutionized the profession of screenwriting and caused the studios to import literary talent from the East in the form of editors and critics, playwrights and novelists, many of whom stayed on to make lasting contributions to the quality and sophistication of American sound films.[4]

Actors with stage experience were especially valuable during the early sound era because directors could no longer shout out instructions on the set as they had done before and therefore needed players who could work on their own through long dialogue takes. They also needed players with good voices and clear articulation, which meant that stage actors, and film actors with stage experience,[5] rapidly replaced many silent stars who spoke with heavy foreign accents (like Emil Jannings, Pola Negri, Vilma Banky, and Lya De Putti) or whose voices somehow did not match their screen images (like Norma Talmadge, Colleen Moore, Corinne Griffith, and John Gilbert[6]). Other silent stars, such as Greta Garbo, Gary Cooper, and Janet Gaynor, were able to make the transition with the aid of voice specialists and diction coaches from the theater world. The advent of sound caused other new arrivals in Hollywood. Sound technicians from the broadcasting and telephone industries who had no understanding of filmmaking suddenly appeared on the studio sets endowed with tremendous authority to determine camera and microphone placement. Arthur Knight writes of their brief but dictatorial rule: "[The] experts, concerned with nothing beyond the sound quality of the pictures they worked on, continually simplified their problems by insisting that scenes be played in corners, minimizing long-shots for the more readily controllable close-up. In no time at all the techniques, the artistry that directors had acquired through years of silent films were cast aside and forgotten in the shadow of the microphone."

The Theoretical Debate over Sound

Indeed, so great a threat to the cinema as a creative form did sound recording seem at the outset that many direc-

---

3. Among the Broadway players who came to stay were George Arliss, Helen Hayes, Humphrey Bogart, Fredric March, Leslie Howard, Clark Gable, Sylvia Sidney, Fred Astaire, Paul Muni, Spencer Tracy, and Katharine Hepburn. The directors included Richard Boleslavsky, George Cukor, and Rouben Mamoulian. For a brief period in 1928, it even seemed as though the migration might be reversed and that the film industry might shift its production base back to New York City in order to be close to Broadway talent (it took nearly four days to cross the country by train in this era; only the super rich could afford to fly) and to the sophisticated audio technology of the recording and broadcasting industries. By mid summer of that year, Paramount, MGM, First National, and Warners had all set up soundstages in New York, but after a brief flurry of filmmaking activity there, economies of scale brought the conversion back home to Hollywood. See Alexander Walker, *The Shattered Silents*, pp. 90–106.

4. Among the more prominent—Herman Mankiewicz, Robert Benchley, P. G. Wodehouse, Donald Ogden Stewart, Dorothy Parker, Samson Raphaelson, S. J. Perelman, S. N. Behrman, Charles Lederer, Ben Hecht, Charles MacArthur, George S. Kaufman, Maxwell Anderson, James M. Cain, Dashiell Hammett, F. Scott Fitzgerald, William Faulkner, and Nathanael West.

5. These included Ronald Colman; Claudette Colbert; William Powell; Ethel, John, and Lionel Barrymore; George Bancroft; Herbert Marshall; Marie Dressler; Clive Brook; Boris Karloff; and Charles Laughton. British actors like Colman, Brook, Marshall, and Laughton were particularly valued in Hollywood for their low-pitched, well-modulated voices, which registered with near perfection on the sound track.

6. A recent biography by Gilbert's daughter, Leatrice Gilbert Fountain, maintains that her father's early sound-film appearances were mechanically sabotaged during the recording process by MGM executive Louis B. Mayer, who apparently hated every artist in his employ (*Dark Star*, with John R. Maxim [New York: St. Martin's, 1985]). This may indeed be true, but there is significant evidence to suggest that audiences conditioned by the silents did not *want* their favorite screen idols to talk at all and were inevitably disappointed when voices made them merely human.

tors and theorists of film violently opposed its arrival. They were appalled that the cinema, which was currently in its most advanced state of articulation, might be permanently retarded by the public's passing fancy for a crude novelty. Paul Rotha spoke for this group in 1930:

> No power of speech is comparable to the descriptive value of photographs. The attempted combination of speech and pictures is the direct opposition of two separate mediums, which appeal in two utterly different ways. . . . [A] silent visual film is capable of achieving a more dramatic, lasting, and powerful effect on an audience by its singleness of appeal than a dialogue film. . . . Immediately a voice begins to speak in a cinema, the sound apparatus takes precedence over the camera, thereby doing violence to natural instincts.

Others, like Eisenstein and Pudovkin, perceived the threat posed by sound but also recognized its potential for adding a new dimension to the medium. In "Sound and Image," a manifesto published on August 5, 1928, Eisenstein, Pudovkin, and Alexandrov correctly predicted:

> The sound film is a two-edged sword, and it is very probable that its users will follow the path of least resistance, that is, they will attempt simply to satisfy the public's curiosity. First we shall see commercial exploitation of the merchandise which is easiest to manufacture and sell: the talkie, the film in which the recorded word coincides most exactly and realistically with the movement of lips on the screen, in which the public enjoys the illusion that it is really listening to an actor, an automobile horn, a musical instrument, etc.
>
> This first period of sensationalism will not prejudice the new art's development, but there will be a second period—a terrible period. With the decline of the first exploration of practical possibilities, people will try to substitute dramas taken from "good literature" and will make other attempts to have theater invade the screen.
>
> Used in this way, sound will destroy the art of montage.

Then, they offered an antidote to the situation:

> Only the use of sound as counterpoint to visual montage offers new possibilities of developing and perfecting montage. The first experiments with sound must be directed toward its "noncoincidence" with visual images. Only this method can produce the feeling we seek, the feeling which, with time, will lead to creation of a new orchestral counterpoint of image-vision and image-sound.

Finally, they pointed out that the sound film provided one distinct technical advantage over the silent cinema:

> The new technical discovery is not a chance factor in the history of cinema but is a natural way out for the cinema's avant-garde, thanks to which filmmakers can escape from a large number of dead ends which probably had no exit.
>
> The title, despite innumerable attempts to incorporate it into the movement or images of a film, is the first such dead end.
>
> The second is the explanatory hodgepodge which overloads the composition of scenes and slows the film's rhythm. . . .
>
> Sound, treated as a new element of montage (and as an element independent of the visual image), will inevitably introduce a new, extremely effective means of expressing and resolving the complex problems which we have not been able to solve so far. It is impossible to find the necessary solutions if we have only visual elements with which to work.

Eisenstein, especially, spoke from a long and generally negative experience of trying to integrate his titles with his images. Titles were a definite liability to the silent cinema since they interfered with the flow of its narratives and the rhythms of its montage. It is often pointed out, for example, that one of the last great films of the silent era, Carl-Theodor Dreyer's *La Passion de Jeanne d'Arc* (1928), was seriously flawed by the insertion of dialogue titles at crucial positions within the narrative and would have profited immensely from a recorded sound track. By eliminating the necessity for titles, the sound film had liberated the cinema from its thirty-year bondage to the printed word and provided it with a narrative dimension that need not interefere with the visual dynamics of montage. The task now was not to reshackle the medium to the spoken word of the talkie.

Another European cinematic formalist had similar feelings about sound. The young French director René Clair (born René-Lucien Chomette, 1898–1981) wrote in 1929 that he was opposed to the "100 percent talkie" but could see distinct possibilities for the creative use of sound in films (a potential that he would later realize in 1931 with his own films *Le Million* and *À Nous la liberté*): "The talking film is not everything. There is also the sound film—on which the last hopes of the advocates of the silent film are pinned. They count on the sound film to ward off the danger represented by the advent of talkies. . . . [If] *imitation* of real noises seems limited and disappointing, it is possible that an *interpretation* of noises may have more of a future in it [original emphasis]." Clair reserved special praise for the early MGM musical *The Broadway Melody* (Harry Beaumont, 1929) as a film that used its sound track with great intelligence. He particularly admired a sequence in which the noise of a door being slammed and a car driving off are heard on the sound track but not illustrated on the image track, which contains only a close-up of the heroine's anguished face witnessing the departure. In another sequence the heroine is on the verge of tears, and as her face disappears in a fade-out we hear a single sob from the blackened screen. Clair concludes from this: "In these two instances the sound, at an opportune moment, has replaced the shot. It is by this economy of means that the sound film will most probably secure original effects."

What the three Soviet filmmakers and Clair had all realized was that sound recording posed a threat to the cinema *only* if the microphone became as slavishly subservient to the spoken word, or to "naturalistic" sound, as the early camera had been to empirical reality in its unwillingness to disrupt the natural continuity of time and space. So they denounced **synchronous** or *"naturalistic"* sound, whereby the audience *hears* exactly what it sees on the screen as it sees it and sees exactly what it hears on the sound track as it hears it, as a noncreative form of recording that threatened the formal achievement of the silent cinema. And they advocated instead the use of **asynchronous** or **contrapuntal** sound— sound that would counterpoint the images that accompanied it for expressive effect in the same way that conflicting shots in a silent montage sequence counterpointed one another. That is, they endorsed sound recording as an extension and expansion of montage, in which noise, dialogue, and music were all to be used in counterpoint to visual images like individual shots in a montage sequence. As Pudovkin wrote, "Sound and human speech should be used by the director not as literal accompaniment, but to amplify and enrich the visual image on the screen."

The controversy between the advocates of synchronous versus asynchronous sound became the great theoretical debate of the early sound era, and it was precisely analogous to that which we may imagine to have occurred in the first decade of film itself. The question became whether the sound track, like the early camera, should simply record reality "naturalistically" or whether it should create a synthetic reality of its own. Practically speaking, the question was whether sound should be synchronized with the images to produce "naturalistic" or *literal* sound, or whether it should be placed in creative conflict with the image track. Because of the large middle ground between these two positions, there was clearly an either/or fallacy involved in the debate: in fact, the best cinema mixes both practices, as all the pioneers of creative sound recording were to discover. But for the first several years, at least, it seemed that the future of the sound film lay in one direction or the other.

From 1928 to 1931, the main emphasis had been on obtaining high-quality sound in production, with little thought given to the possibility of modifying the sound track after it had been recorded. The idea that sound as originally produced on the set was the necessary end product of the recording process had several sources. One was that the model for early sound recording was live radio broadcasting, where sound was produced for spontaneous transmission. Since many of the audio technicians who flooded the gates of Hollywood in the early years of the transition came directly from the broadcast industry, they brought their practices and preconceptions with them intact. A deeper reason lay in the conservatism of the American producers, who believed that an absolute pairing of sound and image was necessary to avoid confusing their literal-minded audiences. They felt that to separate sound and image—even to the small extent of recording naturalistic sound but not visualizing it (for example, having a door slam offscreen, as in *The Broadway Melody*)—would disorient audience perception, just as their predecessors had thirty years earlier been loath to fragment the visual reality continuum. So for several years both practice and ideology in the American studios dictated that sound and image be recorded simultaneously, with the result that everything heard on the sound track would be seen on the screen and vice versa. Thus the huge number of "100 percent talkies" (films like *Lights of New York*) that were little more than illustrated radio plays. On the other side of the issue were the cinematic formalists, like Eisenstein, Pudovkin, and Clair, who saw contrapuntal sound as the only way to use the new technique—sound in which music, choruses, sound effects, and perhaps a bare minimum of dialogue would be used to counterpoint and comment upon the visuals. The controversy was ultimately resolved through the discovery of a process known as **postsynchronization,** or

dubbing, which permitted synchronous and asynchronous sound to be used together consistently and simultaneously within the same film.

The Adjustment to Sound

Postsynchronization was first used by the American director King Vidor (1894–1982) for his first talking picture, *Hallelujah!* (1929), which is also generally regarded as the first major film of the sound era. *Hallelujah!* was shot on location in and around Memphis, Tennessee, with an all-black cast, and its final sequence depicts a wild chase through an Arkansas swamp. Vidor shot the entire sequence silent with a continuously moving camera, and then later in the studio he added to it a sound track containing naturalistic noises of the pursuit—breaking branches, screeching birds, heavy breathing, etc.—all of which had been separately recorded.[7] Given the crudity of early sound-recording equipment, this was a technically brilliant achievement. But since the sound track was physically separate from the image track though printed beside it on the same strip of film,[8] the potential for postdubbing sound had existed in the sound-on-film systems from the time of their invention. Lewis Jacobs explains: "The detachment of sound and its reproduction in a film are made possible by the mechanical nature of the recording apparatus and the editing process. Microphone and camera are independent instruments, recording what is seen and heard either together simultaneously or separately at different times." Vidor, however, was the first to realize this and to realize simultaneously that sound could create a psychological impact quite independent of the images. Another American director, Lewis Milestone (1895–1980), used postdubbing for the battlefield sequences of his great pacifist film *All Quiet on the Western Front* in 1930, shooting them with a mobile silent camera on location and dubbing in the battle sounds later.[9] In 1931, Milestone was able to keep his camera constantly in motion during the fast-talking dialogue comedy *The Front Page*, adapted from the stage play by Ben Hecht and Charles MacArthur. Ernst Lubitsch also used dubbing in his first sound films, the dynamic musicals *The Love Parade* (1929) and *Monte Carlo* (1930), as did René Clair in *Sous les toits du Paris* (1930). These films and others like them (for example, Edward Sutherland's *The Saturday Night Kid*

7.13 On the set of Paramount's *The Love Parade* (Ernst Lubitsch, 1929).

[1929], Victor Fleming's *The Virginian* [1929], Paul Sloane's *Hearts in Dixie* [1929], and William Wellman's *Chinatown Nights* [1929]) demonstrate a gradual shift in emphasis from production recording to rerecording during the period 1929–31, with increased importance finally being given to the latter.

In all of the cases just cited, sound was recorded and manipulated on a single track, but Rouben Mamoulian (1897–1987), a Broadway stage director, introduced a new element into sound recording when he used two sep-

7. This was in part the result of a happy accident: Vidor's sound truck failed to show up when the crew arrived in Memphis, so he started to shoot the movie silent out of necessity and simply continued the practice when he realized how liberating it was. The postdubbing process itself was extremely difficult, and Vidor's editor is said to have suffered a nervous breakdown in the midst of it.

8. But see footnote on displacement, p. 228.

9. Winner of the 1929/30 Academy Awards for Best Picture and Director, this classic antiwar film was cut by 25 minutes for general release but archivally restored to its original 130-minute running time in the 1980s and is available in this form today on videocassette.

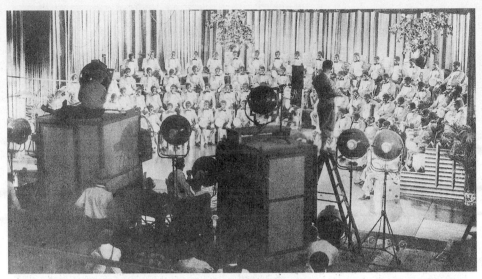

7.14 On the set of Warner Bros.' *Mammy* (Michael Curtiz, 1930). The camera is still enclosed, but the microphone is suspended from an improvised boom.

arate microphones to record overlapping dialogue in a single scene of *Applause* (1929) and mixed them together on the sound track. Earlier sound tracks had consisted of a single channel, which meant that there was no way to isolate one type of sound from another. Everybody on the set spoke into the same microphone, and there could be no background music or sound effects while dialogue was being delivered unless these were provided off-camera simultaneously as the lines were spoken. By introducing two microphones and mixing the sound from each, Mamoulian opened up the possibility of multiple-channel recording and postrecording, which would permit the precise manipulation of all sounds on the track—a possibility realized for four-channel recording as early as 1932. Two years later, in *City Streets* (1931), Mamoulian introduced the first sound "flashback," as snatches of dialogue spoken earlier in the film recur on the sound track accompanied by a close-up of the heroine, suggesting the process of memory.

In general practice, however, one type of sound or the other dominated the sound track through 1932—i.e., there was either dialogue or music on the track, but rarely both together unless they had been recorded simultaneously on the set, as in fact they sometimes were (e.g., Josef von Sternberg's *Der blaue Engel* [1930]). By 1933, however, technology had been introduced to mix separately recorded tracks for background music, sound

effects, and synchronized dialogue without audible distortion at the dubbing stage, and by the late 1930s it was possible in the RCA system to record music on multiple channels. By 1935, according to veteran sound editor James G. Stewart, the supervising dubbing mixer on a production often occupied a position equal to that of the film editor. The subsequent introduction of elaborate dialogue equalizers to alter level and frequency, and of compression and noise-suppression technology, further refined the dubbing process. By the late 1930s, postsynchronization, or rerecording, originated as a means of adding sound effects to moving camera sequences, had become a process for the production of the entire release track. Today, the practice is nearly universal for theatrically released features, and it is not uncommon for as much as 90 percent of the dialogue in these films to be rerecorded in postproduction. With the introduction of magnetic sound in the late 1950s, any number of separate channels could be rerecorded onto a single track or stereophonically rerecorded onto as many as six tracks, and it was not uncommon for widescreen epics in the 1950s and 1960s to use as many as fifty channels for mass scenes. In the 1970s, sound quality was further enhanced through the adoption of a wireless eight-track recording system that used radio microphones and, near the end of the decade, nonmagnetic stereo-optical Dolby surround sound for playback in exhibition. Today, most film sound is recorded and reproduced digitally through one of three proprietary systems—Dolby's SR.D (Dolby Digital), Universal's DTS (Digital Theater Systems), or Sony's SDDS (Sony Dynamic Digital Sound); see Chapter 21.

The practice of postsynchronization was a prime force in liberating the sound-film camera from its glass-paneled booth and the sound film generally from the single-minded notion that everything seen on the screen must be heard on the sound track, and vice versa. In its infancy, sound recording had bound film to the laws of empirical reality more securely than ever before, but postsynchronization reintroduced the plastic, manipulative element. From the experience of dubbing, directors gradually came to understand that the most "cinematic" sound track was neither wholly synchronous nor asynchronous but a composite of many different types of sound, all of which were under their control—perhaps even more so than the visuals since sound could be synthetically produced. Arthur Knight writes: "Each sound could be independently distorted, muffled, exaggerated or eliminated at will. The director could shoot his scene with a silent camera and dub in the sound later. He could reinforce dialogue passages with music, combine them with noises or bury them under other, post-synchronized sounds. . . . Post-synchronization became the first point of departure in the development of a new art."

Other developments that helped to liberate the sound film from its initial stasis were more purely technological. Most such problems had been resolved by 1933 through various combinations of practical necessity, ingenuity, and technological refinement. By 1931, for example, both sound-on-disk and multiple-camera filming had been abandoned, and all studios had removed their cameras from the "iceboxes" and converted to the use of **blimps**. These were lightweight, soundproof housings that encased the cameras to muffle the clatter of their motors and enabled them to record synchronous sound outside of the booth. Within several years, smaller, quieter, self-insulating cameras were produced, eliminating the need for external soundproofing altogether. Blimping permitted studios to return to the free use of arc lamps, although most continued to employ tungsten units throughout the 1930s for "soft light" effects. Tracking was again made possible by the introduction of a wide range of boom cranes, camera supports, and steerable dollies between 1931 and 1933 (forecast as early as 1929 when directors like Alfred Hitchcock [*Blackmail*] and Rouben Mamoulian [*Applause*] had moved their cameras by putting their booths on wheels). Microphones, too, became increasingly mobile as a variety of microphone booms were developed from 1930 onward. These long radial arms suspended the mike just above the set and out of the frame, allowing it to follow the movements of the actors and rendering the stationary, clumsily concealed microphones of the early years obsolete. Microphones also became more directional throughout the decade—better able to "hear" at one frequency or in one direction only—and

7.15 A "blimped" camera shooting a dialogue scene whose sound is recorded by an off-frame boom microphone. (The film is Warner Bros. First National's *Lilies of the Field* [Alexander Korda, 1930], with Corinne Griffith and Ralph Forbes; behind the camera are Lee Garmes, the cinematographer [left], and William Goetz, the producer [right].)

track-noise suppression techniques came into use as early as 1931.

During the same years, technology was introduced that greatly facilitated the editing process. The sound Moviola first became available in 1930 and went through several stages of evolution during the decade. Adapted from the silent film-editing machine of the same name, the sound Moviola consisted of contiguous picture and sound heads that could be operated separately or locked together to run in synchronization. Optical sound film was pulled through the machine by a continuously moving sprocket drive, as in a projector, but could be stopped and moved across either head by hand. In 1932, the system known as "rubber numbering" or "edge numbering" was introduced to insure the precise synchronization of sound and image track in the cutting process itself. Machine-coded footage numbers were stamped on the outer edges of the image and sound track for each shot so that both tracks could be edited autonomously and resynchronized as empirically measured units. (With modifications for wide-gauge film and multitrack stereo sound, both the Moviola and coded numbering system are still used in studio editing today.)

As Barry Salt points out, it was only in the middle 1930s that the technical innovations of 1929 to 1932 began to have their full effect. Even then, some aspects of the recording process were not fully understood, and optical systems were still of two separate types: variable density and variable area. In the former, the density of the sound track varies longitudinally from opaque to transparent along the length of the film strip; in the latter, there is no gradation of variants but a binary modulation of two densities, complete opacity and complete transparency, over the width (or area) of the track. The variable-density format, first used by Fox Movietone in 1927, was superior in dialogue reproduction, while variable area, introduced by RCA Photophone in 1928, was superior in musical reproduction, owing to its higher output and greater frequency range. From 1928 to 1935, variable area suffered from volumetric distortion at the high and low extremes of voice frequency, and it was assumed by RCA engineers to be a nonlinear system since variable density was presumably linear. Not until these technicians experimented with transferring the variable area sound track for Rouben Mamoulian's *Becky Sharp* (1935) to variable density did they discover that the opposite was true. Thus, optical sound had been in use in the industry for over eight years before its fundamental nature was understood. When this finally occurred, RCA engineers were able to design a compressor for variable area recording that eliminated distortion in dialogue, and this was put into use in the dubbing stage in 1936. In 1937 RCA began to manufacture compressors to be used in original recording equipment on the set, and after 1938 compressors were used in all variable area recording. The format's superior volume and frequency range then made it preferable to variable density for all types of sound, and by 1945 the latter format had been gradually phased out. Although most motion-picture and television sound today is *recorded* magnetically (a technology introduced in 1958–59), the sound tracks for composite release prints in both media are always optical variable area.

The Sound Film and the American Studio System

New Genres and Old

Sound radically changed the configuration of the Western cinema. In the United States, it gave rise to important new genres and a system of production that determined the character of American films for more than twenty years. The most significant of the new genres was the musical film, whose development parallels that of the sound film. Photographed versions of Broadway musicals were among the first sound films ever made, and *The Jazz Singer* (1927), of course, was one of them. At first, these movie musicals were little more than filmed theater, but within a few years the form had grown enough in cinematic sophistication to become the major genre of 1930s cinema. This was largely the work of two men—Busby Berkeley (1895–1976) and Fred Astaire (1899–1987).

A dance director from the New York stage, Berkeley came to Hollywood to work for Samuel Goldwyn in 1930, but his genius was not revealed until he moved to Warner Bros. in 1933. There, as dance director for musicals like *42nd Street* (Lloyd Bacon, 1933), *Gold Diggers of 1933* (Mervyn LeRoy, 1933), *Footlight Parade* (Lloyd Bacon, 1933), *Dames* (Ray Enright, 1934), *Gold Diggers of 1935* (Busby Berkeley, 1935), *In Caliente* (Busby Berkeley, 1935), and *Gold Diggers of 1937* (Lloyd Bacon, 1937), most of which starred some combination of Dick Powell, Joan Blondell, and Ruby Keeler, he developed a flamboyant visual style that turned the production numbers of pedestrian backstage romances into surreal fantasies for the eye. Based upon the use of swooping aerial photography (or "crane choreography"[1]), kaleidoscopic lenses, highly expressive camera movement, and sophisticated montage techniques, Berkeley's production numbers come closer to an experimental cinema of abstract impressionism than to anything in the traditional narrative film.

---

1. Aerial photography accomplished by means of a large boom crane.

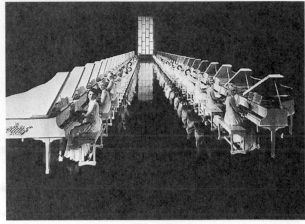

8.3 *Gold Diggers of 1935* (Busby Berkeley, 1935). Warner Bros.

8.1 **Busby Berkeley's choreography:** *Gold Diggers of 1933* (Mervyn LeRoy, 1933). Warner Bros.

Fred Astaire, by contrast, achieved a much greater integration of music and dance with narrative in the series of RKO musicals in which he played opposite Ginger Rogers between 1933 (*Flying Down to Rio*, Thornton Freeland) and 1939 (*The Story of Vernon and Irene Castle*, H. C. Potter). Beginning as a performer, Astaire left an extremely successful stage career to work in films, and he went on to direct and choreograph his dance sequences in *The Gay Divorcee* (Mark Sandrich, 1934), *Roberta* (William Seiter, 1935), *Top Hat* (Mark Sandrich, 1935), *Swing Time* (George Stevens, 1936), *Follow the Fleet* (Mark Sandrich, 1936), *A Damsel in Distress* (George Stevens, 1937), *Shall We Dance* (Mark Sandrich, 1937), and *Carefree* (Mark Sandrich, 1938), developing a sophisticated but highly functional camera style in which the camera itself became a partner in the dance through cutting and movement designed to preserve its physical integrity. Furthermore, Astaire's RKO musicals contributed significantly to the development of creative recording techniques through their rhythmic pairing of sound and image.[2]

Another contribution to sound-film genres was made by Walt Disney (1901–1966), whose Silly Symphony series, begun in 1929 with *The Skeleton Dance*, pioneered what

8.2 **Berkeley choreography:** *Dames* (Ray Enright, 1934). Warner Bros.

2. Although he was the chief creative force behind all of his dance sequences, Astaire often worked with a "dance director" or "choreographer" who received official billing in the credits. His closest collaborator in this regard was Hermes Pan (1910–1990), the choreographer for seventeen of Astaire's thirty-one musicals, including all of his RKO films.

the experimental *Fantasia* (1940), which attempted a total fusion of animated visuals and classical orchestral scores.

At the other end of the spectrum, the new realism permitted by sound bred a cycle of tersely directed urban gangster films that exploited armed violence[3] and tough vernacular speech in a context of social alienation. There were a handful of silent antecedents in the work of Lewis Milestone (*The Racket*, 1928) and Josef von Sternberg (*Underworld*, 1927), but sound films like Mervyn LeRoy's *Little Caesar* (1930), William Wellman's *The Public Enemy* (1931), and Howard Hawks's *Scarface* (1932) forged a new generic tradition. In 1933–34, however, the brutal violence of these films provoked a public outcry that caused producers to shift emphasis from the gang-

8.4 Fred Astaire and Ginger Rogers in a dance sequence from *Top Hat* (Mark Sandrich, 1934). RKO.

might be called the "animated musical," or the musical cartoon. Unhampered by the restrictions of early sound filming procedures, Disney could combine sound and image in an expressive manner impossible for his peers in the live-action narrative cinema and nevertheless achieve perfect frame-by-frame synchronization (today, the precise coordination of sound and image in animation is still called "Mickey Mousing"). The success of his first musical cartoon, *Steamboat Willie* (1928), which introduced Mickey Mouse to the world, and his Silly Symphony shorts, in which all of the action is set to music and which culminated in 1933 with the immensely popular all-color hit *The Three Little Pigs*, led Disney to produce three extraordinary animated color features before World War II—*Snow White and the Seven Dwarfs* (1937), *Pinocchio* (1940), and

ster as "tragic hero," to borrow Robert Warshow's phrase, to the gangster as social victim.[4] This produced a cycle of prison films (such as Lloyd Bacon's *San Quentin*, 1937) and socially oriented crime films (among them William Wyler's *Dead End*, 1937; Fritz Lang's *You Only Live Once*, 1937; Lloyd Bacon's *Marked Woman*, 1937; Michael

---

3. A recurrent motif in the Depression-era gangster film was the sound of the recently invented Thompson submachine gun.

4. A similar sort of critical outrage was vented against the violence of *Bonnie and Clyde* in 1967 (as we will see in Chapter 20), but that may have been because its protagonists represented social revolutionaries, rather than gangsters, to its audience. In any case, one reason for Hollywood's obsession with gangsters during the Depression may well have been organized crime's entry into the film industry in the early 1930s. According to Eugene Rosow in *Born to Lose: The Gangster Film in*

8.5 Mickey Mouse in *Steamboat Willie* (Walt Disney, 1928).

Curtiz's *Angels with Dirty Faces*, 1938; and Raoul Walsh's *The Roaring Twenties*, 1939) later in the decade.

Another tough-talking, realistic film cycle that emerged from the early sound years was that of the newspaper picture. Comprising films like *The Front Page* (Lewis Milestone, 1931), *Five Star Final* (Mervyn LeRoy, 1931), *Scandal Sheet* (John Cromwell, 1931), and *Platinum Blonde* (Frank Capra, 1931), the cycle was immensely popular during the 1930s and important for helping to refine the technique of the dialogue film. While many newspaper films were made according to formula (*Front Page Woman* [Michael Curtiz, 1935]; *Libeled Lady* [Jack

Conway, 1936]), the cycle produced several comic masterpieces (such as Howard Hawks's *His Girl Friday*, 1940—a remake of *The Front Page* with the gender roles switched) and influenced the content of many more, including Orson Welles's *Citizen Kane* (1941), whose central figure is a newspaper magnate.

The historical biography, or **biopic,** was another important sound genre. The vogue began in 1933 with the international triumph of Alexander Korda's *The Private Life of Henry VIII*, the first British film to achieve success in the United States. *Henry VIII* had its origins in the lavish *Kostümfilme* pioneered by Ernst Lubitsch in postwar Germany, but there can be no question that the addition of sound enhanced the historical verisimilitude of the genre so enormously as to transform it. Perhaps the popularity in the 1930s of films about the private lives of famous persons stemmed from the impact of the first Fox Movietone newsreels (c. 1927), in which audiences heard the actual voices of prominent celebrities. In any case, between 1934 and 1940, historical biographies became staple products of every major American and British studio; and films like *Voltaire* (John Adolfi, 1933), *Queen Christina* (Rouben Mamoulian, 1933), *Viva Villa!* (Howard Hawks and Jack Conway, 1934), *House of Rothschild* (Alfred Werker, 1934), *Catherine the Great* (Paul Czinner, 1934), *Cardinal Richelieu* (Rowland V. Lee, 1935), *Rembrandt* (Alexander Korda, 1936), *Lloyd's of London* (Henry King, 1936), *Marie Antoinette* (W. S. Van Dyke, 1938), *The Private Lives of Elizabeth and Essex* (Michael

8.6 *The Public Enemy* (William Wellman, 1931): Mae Clarke, James Cagney. Warner Bros.

America (New York: Oxford University Press, 1978) and other sources, gangsters began loan-sharking to the studios following the Wall Street crash. Harry Cohn, e.g., wrested control of Columbia Pictures from his brother Jack in 1932 with mob money borrowed through Johnny Roselli, and William Fox turned to similar sources in his unsuccessful bid to regain control of his own company in 1933. At the same time, the MPPDA was hiring gangsters as strikebreakers against the Hollywood unions, and the Chicago mob was infiltrating the International Alliance of Theatrical Stage Employees and Moving Picture Operators (IATSE), which represented both stagehands and projectionists. By 1935, the racketeers George Browne and Willy Bioff had taken control of IATSE and begun to extort protection money from the Big Five in the sum of $50,000 per studio per year. In exchange, IATSE kept the wage demands of its members low and provided "safety" in the majors' theaters. In *The Hollywood Studio System* ([New York: St. Martin's, 1986], p. 88), Douglas Gomery estimates that over $1 million changed hands this way before the racket was exposed at the decade's end. Bioff, Browne, and five of their associates were convicted of racketeering and went to jail, as did 20th Century–Fox board chairman Joseph Schenck (briefly—for tax evasion in the transfer of payoff funds), who was the Big Five's corporate bagman.

Curtiz, 1939), and William Dieterle's *The Story of Louis Pasteur* (1936), *The Life of Emile Zola* (1937), *Juarez* (1939), and *Dr. Ehrlich's Magic Bullet* (1940) were very successful on the international market.

In addition to creating new genres, sound permanently changed some older ones. Perhaps the most vital of silent genres, slapstick comedy, was replaced in the 1930s by the anarchic dialogue comedies of the Marx Brothers (*The Cocoanuts* [Robert Florey and Joseph Santley, 1929]; *Animal Crackers* [Victor Heerman, 1930]; *Monkey Business* [Norman Z. McLeod, 1931]; *Horse Feathers* [Norman Z. McLeod, 1932]; *Duck Soup*, [Leo McCarey, 1933]; *A Night at the Opera* [Sam Wood, 1935]; *A Day at the Races* [Sam Wood, 1937]) and W. C. Fields (*The Golf Specialist* [Monte Brice, 1930]; *The Dentist* [Leslie Pierce, 1932]; *Million Dollar Legs* [Eddie Cline, 1932]; *The Fatal Glass of Beer* [Clyde Bruckman, 1933]; *Six of a Kind* [Leo McCarey, 1934]; *The Man on the Flying Trapeze* [Clyde Bruckman, 1935]; *You Can't Cheat an Honest Man* [George Marshall, 1939]; *The Bank Dick* [Eddie Cline, 1940]), and the **screwball comedies** of such directors as Frank Capra (*Platinum Blonde*, 1931; *Lady for a Day*, 1933; *It Happened One Night*, 1934; *Mr. Deeds Goes to Town*, 1936; *You Can't Take It with You*, 1938) and Howard Hawks (*Twentieth Century*, 1934; *Bringing Up Baby*, 1938; *His Girl Friday*, 1940). The screwball comedy was a film type characterized by wisecracking dialogue, furious pacing, and a certain element of visual burlesque carried over from the silent slapstick days. The focus of the action

8.7 Dialogue comedy: the Marx Brothers in *Horse Feathers* (Norman Z. McLeod, 1931). Paramount.

was usually a couple in a bizarre predicament. Some other memorable screwball comedies of the decade were: *Private Lives* (Sidney Franklin, 1931) and *Design for Living* (Ernst Lubitsch, 1933), both adapted from plays by Noël Coward; *The Good Fairy* (William Wyler, 1935); *My Man Godfrey* (Gregory La Cava, 1936); *Theodora Goes Wild* (Richard Boleslavsky, 1936); *Nothing Sacred* (William Wellman, 1937); *Easy Living* (Mitchell Leisen, 1937); *The Awful Truth* (Leo McCarey, 1937); and *Midnight* (Mitchell Leisen, 1939).

In the 1940s, screwball comedy provided a precedent for the darker social satire of the writer-director Preston Sturges (1898–1959), who between 1940 and 1944 produced eight films, mainly for Paramount, that are recognized today as important and highly original contributions to the American comic tradition. The objects of Sturges's satire, however, were much more serious than the frivolous rich of the screwball comedy: American politics (*The Great McGinty*, 1940), American materialism and avarice (*Christmas in July*, 1941; *The Palm Beach Story*, 1942), American sexual attitudes (*The Lady Eve*, 1940), American small-town life (*The Miracle of Morgan's Creek*, 1944; *Hail the Conquering Hero*, 1944), and American cinema (*Sullivan's Travels*, 1941). At a time when Hollywood was unabashedly extolling the virtues of American society for the purposes of war propaganda (see Chapter 11), Sturges's films offered audiences a vision of a corrupt, ridiculous, but often vital people whose chief flaw was a profound lack of self-knowledge.

The careers of Mack Sennett, Harold Lloyd, Harry Langdon, and Buster Keaton all declined rapidly with the coming of sound, and even Chaplin's two features of the 1930s, *City Lights* (1931) and *Modern Times* (1936), were basically silent films with synchronized sound tracks. Some silent comedians, such as Laurel and Hardy, survived by creating a unique blend of slapstick and dialogue, but purely visual comedy was necessarily destroyed by sound, except insofar as it found a new home in the animated sound cartoon. Another important silent genre, the Western, went underground in the early years of sound, when it existed largely as a "B" form, only to emerge at the end of the 1930s with renewed vitality and realism in John Ford's *Stagecoach* (1939). From 1939 to 1950, however, the Western would experience a renaissance. Finally, sound provided a new impetus for films of mystery and detection like *The Thin Man* (W. S. Van Dyke, 1934) and its sequels, and for the horror-fantasy genre. Traditionally rooted in the silent cinema of German Expressionism, this latter genre was greatly enhanced by sound, which not only permitted the addition of eerie effects but restored the dimension of literary dialogue present in so many of the original sources. In fact, Hollywood's three great horror classics—*Dracula* (Tod Browning, 1931), *Frankenstein* (James Whale, 1931), and *The Mummy* (Karl Freund, 1932)—were all early sound films.

Studio Politics and the Production Code

It is impossible to comprehend the American film during the 1930s without understanding the mechanisms of the Hollywood studio system. The great studios were founded in the era before World War I, when the Motion Picture Patents Company was destroyed and the independents moved to assume monopolistic control over film production, distribution, and exhibition. Through a series of complicated business maneuvers, both legal and illegal, they succeeded, and by the end of the war the studios were on the brink of becoming the vast industrial empires of popular mythology. In the period of economic growth that followed the war, Wall Street began to invest heavily in the studios for both financial and political reasons. It was clear, in the first place, that motion pictures were on their way to becoming a major industry; it was equally clear during these years of the "Red Scare" that the movies were a medium of mass persuasion and propaganda

par excellence. For Hollywood films to extol the virtues of corporate capitalism and "the American way of life" was to erect an impenetrable barrier against Bolshevism.[5] This perception encouraged Wall Street to invest massive sums in the Hollywood studios immediately following the war. The capital of Adolph Zukor's Famous Players–Lasky (soon to become Paramount) alone rose from $10 million to $20 million in two years, and every important studio received large corporate loans from American big business.

Lewis Jacobs describes the inevitable results: "New men from Wall Street, educated in finance, became the overseers of the motion picture business. Characteristic of the new managerial figures were two directors of a new and powerful company, Loew's: W. C. Durant, at that time also head of General Motors Corporation, and Harvey Gibson, president of the Liberty National Bank." Naturally enough, the leadership of these men left its permanent imprint upon the process of production. As David Robinson puts it, "The bureaucrats and accountants, eager to overcome the unpredictable and intractable element in the creation of films, began to codify certain principles of commercial production that still prevail in the industry: the attempt to exploit proven success with formula pictures and cycles of any particular genre which temporarily sells, at the expense of other and perhaps unorthodox product; the quest for predictable sales values—star names, best-selling success titles, costly and showy production values—which have little to do with art." Films came to be made according to the most efficient production method American industry had ever devised—the standardized assembly-line technique. The

5. On the whole, the decade from the end of World War I in 1919 to the stock-market crash of 1929, which began the Great Depression, was one of the least liberal in America history. In the early 1920s, America's business leaders were panicked by the success of the Bolshevik Revolution in Russia and by the attempted organization of labor at home. Woodrow Wilson's attorney general, A. Mitchell Palmer (1872–1936), played upon these fears by declaring the country to be in the grip of a Communist conspiracy, much as Senator Joseph McCarthy would do thirty years later. In January 1920 he authorized the infamous "Palmer Raids," in which over five thousand persons—most of them labor organizers—in thirty-three American cities were rounded up and held without trial for alleged "revolutionary activities." (J. Edgar Hoover [1895–1972] was Palmer's chief organizer for these raids, out of which the FBI was born several years later, with Hoover as director.) Many were imprisoned for long periods of time; great numbers of those who were not native-born were deported; Palmer became a national hero and a

serious contender for the 1920 Democratic presidential nomination (he lost to James M. Cox). This latter fact provides some indication of the temper of the times: the country was in a nasty, insular mood, and aliens of all sorts were regarded with hostility. Patriotism became a façade for racism of murderous intensity. Immigrants, blacks, and Jews were openly persecuted for not being "100 percent American," and the Ku Klux Klan's membership grew so rapidly that by 1925 the organization had nearly attained the status of a third political party. Organized crime also grew, thanks to the Eighteenth Amendment (1918) and the Volstead Act (1921), providing for federal enforcement of Prohibition. During the 1920s the average weekly film attendance increased from 40 million to 90 million Americans per week, making the cinema a mass medium on a par with network radio and the tabloid press (or with television today). It was therefore essential to the maintenance of the status quo that the ideological content of films be as carefully controlled as the ideological content of other mass media.

producer's role as supervisor became enormously important in this process, while the director's role declined, and by the time sound was introduced filmmaking in America had become a fairly conventionalized and predictable operation.

It was to become even more so through the intervention of the Hays Office and the Catholic Church in 1934. The Hollywood scandals of 1921–22 (see pp. 185–87) had alerted many civic-minded persons to the power of the movies to influence social attitudes and behavior; and, when the first data on movie attendance in the United States were systematically gathered in 1922, it was discovered that some 40 million tickets were sold every week. By the end of the decade, the figure had more than doubled to 90 million, among whom there were an estimated 40 million minors, including 17 million children under the age of fourteen. As with television during the 1960s, the rapid spread of the medium and its easy accessibility to children was cause for national alarm, and—just as with television—there was a widespread public demand for research. In 1928, William H. Short, executive director of a newly formed "procensorship" body called the Motion Picture Research Council, solicited a large grant ($200,000 or about $1 million in current value) from the Payne Fund, a private philanthropic foundation, to conduct a nationwide study of the influence of motion pictures on children by a group of university psychologists, sociologists, and education specialists. The result was a series of twelve specific investigations, known as the Payne Fund studies, undertaken by nationally known researchers over the period 1929 to 1932. The project's conclusions, published in eleven volumes between 1933 and 1935, were popularly summarized by the journalist Henry James Forman in his 1933 volume *Our Movie Made Children*—a title that came to characterize the whole generation of Americans who grew up during the Depression, came of age in World War II, and became the first national audience for network television in their middle years. The Payne Fund findings confirmed the worst—the movies did seem to bring new ideas to children; did influence interpretations of the world and day-to-day conduct; did present moral standards, particularly with regard to sexual behavior, different from those of many adults. The media effects that researchers today take for granted, in fact, were shocking new knowledge to an America that had just begun to enter the media age.

Concurrent with these studies, the coming of sound had produced a wave of grim, often violent, screen realism and yet another public outcry against the "immorality" of Hollywood films. This time the reaction was organized by the American bishops of the Roman Catholic Church, who—armed with the Payne Fund volumes, Forman's *Our Movie Made Children*, and, apparently, a mandate from the Vatican itself—set up the Legion of Decency to fight for better and more "moral" motion pictures. In April of 1934, with the support of both Protestant and Jewish organizations, the Legion called for a nationwide boycott of movies considered indecent by the Catholic Church. The studios, having lost millions of dollars in 1933 as the delayed effects of the Depression finally caught up with the box office, were intimidated into imposing self-censorship before it was too late. In 1927, a Motion Picture Production Code had been drafted by the MPPDA based on the "Don'ts and Be Carefuls" formula of the immediate postscandal years (see pp. 185–87), and in 1930 the Hays Office had adopted a more formal but still voluntary Code to Maintain Social and Community Values. Now Hays was authorized to create the Production Code Administration (PCA) and to appoint a prominent Catholic layman, Joseph I. Breen, to head it. Under Breen's auspices, Father Daniel A. Lord, a Jesuit priest, and Martin Quigley, a Catholic publisher, coauthored the Draconian Production Code whose provisions would dictate the content of American motion pictures, without exception, for the next twenty years.[6]

In a pendulum swing away from the excesses of the "new morality" of the Jazz Era, the Production Code was awesomely repressive, prohibiting the showing or mentioning of almost everything germane to the situation of normal human adults. It forbade depicting "scenes of passion" in all but the most puerile terms, and it required that the sanctity of the institution of marriage and the home be upheld at all times (married couples, however, were never to be shown sharing a bed). Adultery, illicit sex, seduction, or rape could never be more than suggested, and then only if it was absolutely essential to the plot and severely punished at the end (a favorite means was death from accident or disease). Also prohibited were the use of profanity (a term extended to include "vulgar"

---

6. The code was completely revised to eliminate its censorship provisions in 1966, but it had become basically unenforceable by the mid-1950s (see pp. 428–29).

expressions like *cripes, guts,* and *nuts*) and racial epithets; any implication of prostitution, miscegenation, sexual aberration, or drug addiction; nudity of all sorts; sexually suggestive dances or costumes; "excessive and lustful kissing"; and excessive drinking. It was forbidden to ridicule or criticize any aspect of any religious faith, to show cruelty to animals or children, or to represent surgical operations, especially childbirth, "in fact or in silhouette."

But the code's most labyrinthine strictures were reserved for the depiction of crime. It was forbidden to show the details of a crime, or to display machine guns, submachine guns, or other illegal weapons, or to discuss weapons at all in dialogue scenes. It was further required that law-enforcement officers never be shown dying at the hands of criminals and that all criminal activities within a given film were shown to be punished. Under no circumstances could a crime be shown to be justified. Suicide and murder were to be avoided unless absolutely necessary to the plot, and the suggestion of excessive brutality or wholesale slaughter of any kind was absolutely prohibited. The antiviolence strictures of the code seem positively civil in this age of the cinema of cruelty, but the code as a whole was obviously restrictive and repressive. From 1934 until the mid-1950s it rigidly dictated the content of American films and in a very real sense kept them from becoming as serious as they might have, and, perhaps, should have, been.

Under the administrative provisions, no studio belonging to the MPPDA was to distribute or release any film without a certificate of approval signed by Breen, as director of the PCA, and bearing the PCA's seal. Failure to comply would cause a fine of $25,000 to be levied by the MPPDA against the offending company (the fine was never imposed, but it proved an effective sanction for over twenty years). The process whereby this certification was obtained was a long and sometimes humiliating one for filmmakers. Raymond Moley has outlined its major stages:

1. A preliminary conference between Breen or other members of the staff of the PCA and the producer, to consider the basic story before the screen adaptation is written or purchased; at this point the plot as a whole is discussed in its relation to the code.
2. Careful scrutiny of the script submitted by the producing company.
3. Scenario conference with writers and others to effect necessary changes in the script.

4. Approval in writing by Breen of the script for production.
5. Continued conferences during production, so that any change made in the script as well as all lyrics, costumes, and sets may be observed and passed upon.
6. Preview of separate sequences during the course of production, whenever the producer is in doubt about their conformity with the code; this is done upon the request of the producer.
7. Preview of the completed picture in the PCA viewing theater by the same two staff members who worked on the script and by a third staff member who comes to the picture with a fresh mind.
8. After deletion of scenes, dialogue, etc., which violate the code, issue of its certificate of approval by the Production Code Administration.

The reasons that the moguls were willing not merely to accept, but to institutionalize what was clearly a system of de facto censorship and prior restraint were several—all of them ultimately related to staying in business. For one thing, obviously, the economic threat of a boycott during the worst years of the Depression was real, and an industry dependent upon pleasing a mass audience several times a week must deliver to that audience what it thinks, at least, the audience wants. For another thing, producers found that they could turn the code to work decisively in favor of more efficient production. By rigidly prescribing and proscribing the kinds of behavior that could be shown or described on the screen, the code could be used as a kind of scriptwriter's blueprint. A love story, for example, could only move in one direction (toward marriage), adultery and crime could only have one conclusion (disease and/or horrible death), dialogue in all situations had well-defined parameters, and so forth. The code, in other words, provided a framework for the construction of screenplays and enabled studios to streamline what had always been (and still is) the thorniest and yet most formative task in the production process—the creation of filmable continuity scripts. Finally, we should remember that the Depression was a time of open political anti-Semitism in the United States, with Henry Ford's *Dearborn Independent* editorials, Father Coughlin's network radio show, and lesser demogogues inveighing against the economic treachery of the Jews every week. If Will Hays alone couldn't reassure the moguls' Christian audience of their decency, perhaps a code of ethics dictated by the Catholic bishops could.

The Structure of the Studio System

The most significant force shaping the American sound film, however, was economic. In 1928, the studios had greatly increased their debt to Wall Street by borrowing vast sums of capital for the conversion to sound (see business chart, p. 215). Wall Street was happy to oblige since the novelty of sound had nearly doubled weekly admission figures over the previous year. By 1930, a series of mergers and realignments had concentrated 95 percent of all American film production in the hands of eight studios, five "majors" and three "minors." The major studios were organized as vertically integrated corporations, controlling the means not only of production, but of distribution and exhibition (or consumption) as well, through their ownership of film exchanges and theater chains. Distribution was conducted at a national and an international level: since about 1925, foreign rentals had accounted for half of all American feature revenues and would continue to do so for the next two decades. Exhibition was controlled through the majors' ownership of 2,600 first-run theaters, that 16 percent of the national total which generated 75 percent of the revenue. (The majors had divided the country into thirty markets, each subdivided into zones whose theaters were classified as first-run, second-run, and subsequent-run; clearances of fourteen to forty-two days were required before a film could move to the next zone, enabling the Big Five to wring maximum profit from each release.) Despite the national mania—actively stimulated by studio publicity and marketing departments—for the "Hollywood of the Stars," production throughout the 1930s and 1940s consumed only 5 percent of total corporate assets, with another 1 percent accounted for distribution. With 94 percent of total investment going to the exhibition sector, as Douglas Gomery has pointed out, the five majors during the studio era can best be characterized as "diversified theater chains, producing features, shorts, cartoons, and newsreels to fill their houses."

These studios were, in order of relative economic importance, Metro-Goldwyn-Mayer, Paramount, Warner Bros., 20th Century–Fox, and RKO. The minor studios—which owned no theaters[7] and were dependent upon the majors for first-run exhibition outlets—were Universal, Columbia, and United Artists.

As David Robinson points out, the nearly total domination of the studios by Wall Street had far-reaching consequences for the organization of the American film industry and for the character of the American film in the period between the introduction of sound and the Second World War, especially when the Depression finally took effect in Hollywood:

> Depression in the industry, which reached its peak in 1933, when a third of the nation's cinemas were closed down, only served to tighten the financiers' control over the organisation of film production. There was even less place for imponderables. Emphasis was laid upon achieving the highest possible standards in those aspects of film-making which could be controlled: quality of equipment, techniques, photography, staging and costuming. Every step was taken to eliminate those unpredictable elements which are of the nature of art.[8]

Charles Higham describes how these results were achieved at Warner Bros., perhaps the most typical American studio of the era:

---

7. United Artists had initiated its own theater circuit in 1926 but sought participation with the majors (mainly Loew's and Paramount) to minimize its risk. The company owned first-run houses outright only in Detroit, Chicago, and Los Angeles, and it agreed to halt theater expansion during the 1930s in exchange for distribution agreements with the Big Five. In 1936, UA severed corporate ties with its theater operations, which nevertheless retained the corporate name; today, United Artist Communications, Inc., is the country's largest theater circuit, with 2,398 screens reported as of 1993.

8. The source of this information is F. D. Klingender and Stuart Legg, *Money behind the Screen* (London: Lawrence and Wishart, 1937). Discussing the impact of Wall Street control in *Movie-Made America: A Cultural History of American Movies* (New York: Random House, 1976; rev. and updated ed., 1994), Robert Sklar suggests that it makes much less difference who *owns* a movie company (or eight of them) than who operates it. He argues that although four of the eight Hollywood studios (Paramount, 20th Century–Fox, RKO, and Universal) experienced major changes in management during the 1930s, the character of American filmmaking did not significantly change since all of the studio managers, old and new—if not the studio owners—were entertainment-industry veterans intimately familiar with their product and its consumers. But it also seems likely, as David Robinson implies (in *The History of World Cinema* [New York: Stein and Day, 1973; 2nd ed., 1981]), that financial concentration brought with it a much more relentless emphasis on economies of scale than the industry had experienced in its first three decades, resulting in an unprecedented standardization of production and a high-quality product.

The writers [of whom as many as twenty would frequently work on a single script] . . . unquestionably occupied first place: they set the entire tone of the pictures of the time. The scripts were prepared in detail, even down to specific compositions of the shots, and the writers were almost invariably present on the sets during the shooting. Once a producer had approved a finished screenplay, he cast the stars of the picture. The director was called in, and in rare instances helped with casting of minor roles or changes in the writing. For economic reasons, he had orders to rehearse his players, then only use one take for a scene. The producer or studio manager selected the art directors, the composers, the cameramen, the cutters. These were seldom the choice of the directors, and all conformed to studio style.

Between 1930 and 1945, the Hollywood studios mass-produced some 7,500 feature films in which every stage of production from conception to exhibition was carefully controlled. These films took their styles and values as much from the studios that made them as from the individual artists involved in their production, and so it is important to understand how these studios were composed.

MGM

MGM was the biggest, most prosperous, and most prolific of American studios in the 1930s. At mid-decade, it was producing an average of one feature per week, which, as John Baxter notes, was the largest output of any studio in the history of the cinema. Its parent firm, Loew's, Inc., ruled from New York by Nicholas Schenck (1881–1969), provided MGM with a large national exhibition outlet,[9] and its close affiliation with the Chase National Bank gave the studio access to nearly unlimited capital. There was no film so big that MGM couldn't produce it, no talent so large that MGM couldn't buy it. The studio had under contract some of the greatest film talent of the 1930s— the directors Frank Borzage, Clarence Brown, King Vidor, George Cukor, Sidney Franklin, W. S. Van Dyke, Jack Conway, Sam Wood, and Victor Fleming; the cinematographers Karl Freund, William Daniels, George Folsey, and Harold Rosson; the art director Cedric Gibbons; and, finally, a cast of stars unparalleled in Hollywood history ("More stars than there are in Heaven," as the MGM publicity slogan had it)—Greta Garbo, Jean Harlow, Norma Shearer, Joan Crawford, Margaret Sullavan, Myrna Loy, Clark Gable, Spencer Tracy, Robert Montgomery, the Barrymores, Marie Dressler, Wallace Beery, William Powell, James Stewart, Robert Taylor, Nelson Eddy, Jeanette MacDonald, Judy Garland, and Mickey Rooney. MGM was run during this period (and until his ouster in 1951) by its vice president in charge of production, Louis B. Mayer (1885–1957), a ruthless businessman with little concern for art, or even entertainment, except insofar as it could be merchandised; but the studio's canny young production manager, Irving Thalberg, was able to maintain a consistently high level of achievement in MGM films until his early death. Mayer's son-in-law, David O. Selznick (1902–1965), who was hired from RKO to assist Thalberg in 1933, also acquired the reputation of an artistic producer, and between them the two men produced some of the most prestigious MGM films of the decade.

The predominant visual style of these films was characterized by **high-key lighting**[1] and opulent production design (the one employed to reveal the other), and their cultural values were the typically American middle-class ones of optimism, materialism, and romantic escapism. MGM's major genres in the 1930s were the melodrama, the musical, and the prestigious literary or theatrical adaptation; some of its most characteristic films were *Anna Christie* (Clarence Brown, 1930); Grand Hotel (Edmund Goulding, 1932); *Dinner at Eight* (George Cukor, 1933); *Queen Christina* (Rouben Mamoulian, 1933); *Viva Villa!* (Jack Conway, 1934); *Mutiny on the Bounty* (Frank Lloyd, 1935); the Marx Brothers' *A Night at the Opera* (1935) and *A Day at the Races* (1937), both directed by Sam Wood; *David Copperfield* (George Cukor,

---

9. Actually, MGM's theater chain was the smallest of the Big Five, a circumstance that helped it to maintain profits when attendance dropped off during the worst years of the Depression. See Gomery, *The Hollywood Studio System*, pp. 6–23.

1. Studio cinematographers had evolved a "three-point" lighting system by the early 1930s that involved the use of a **key light,** a **fill light,** and a **backlight** for each major character in a scene. The key light was the primary source of illumination, usually placed diagonally to the front of the subject, with the fill light to its side and the backlight to the rear. The fill light and backlight were used to supplement and balance the key light, whose tonal dominant could range from high to low. Both could also be used to create special lighting effects—e.g., the backlighting often found in Welles (see *Citizen Kane* [1941]; *Macbeth* [1948]) and *film noir* (see *The Big Combo* [1955]), or "source" lighting effects in similar films (see *Call Northside 777* [1948] and *The Blue Dahlia* [1946]). With contemporary variation, three-point lighting is still widely practiced in the industry today.

8.8 A ballroom scene from *Marie Antoinette* (W. S. Van Dyke, 1938), illustrating the MGM style of high-key lighting and elaborate production design.

has the depth or force of personal artistic vision, but both are opulent, epic, and spectacularly entertaining products of the studio system at its most efficient, spinning out beautifully crafted fairy tales for children and adults alike. (In 1973 MGM ceased to exist as a studio, although it remained marginally involved in the production of theatrical films through investment and resumed distribution in 1979; it acquired United Artists from Transamerica Corporation in 1981 and became MGM/UA Entertainment Company in 1983. This was sold to Turner Broadcasting in 1985 and resold to Las Vegas financier Kirk Kerkorian in 1986; in 1990 MGM/UA was absorbed by Pathé Communications, Inc., and renamed MGM-Pathé Communications, but in 1992 it was bought by the French bank Crédit Lyonnais and renamed Metro-Goldwyn-Mayer, Inc., its financial future still uncertain; see p. 249.)

1935); *Anna Karenina* (Clarence Brown, 1935); *Romeo and Juliet* (George Cukor, 1936); *San Francisco* (W. S. Van Dyke, 1936); *Libeled Lady* (Jack Conway, 1936); *Rose Marie* (W. S. Van Dyke, 1936); *The Great Ziegfeld* (Robert Z. Leonard, 1936); *Camille* (George Cukor, 1937); *The Good Earth* (Sidney Franklin, 1937); *Captains Courageous* (Victor Fleming, 1937); *Boys Town* (Norman Taurog, 1938); *Too Hot to Handle* (Jack Conway, 1938); *The Citadel* (King Vidor, 1938); *Marie Antoinette* (W. S. Van Dyke, 1938); *Goodbye, Mr. Chips* (Sam Wood, 1939); and *Broadway Melody of 1940* (Norman Taurog, 1940).

MGM also produced some of the most popular low-budget cycles of the decade, including the Andy Hardy, Tarzan, Dr. Kildare, and "Thin Man" series, as well as a few controversial and/or technically innovative productions like King Vidor's *Hallelujah!* (1929) and Fritz Lang's *Fury* (1936). Yet the studio's ambience and attitudes during the 1930s are best summed up by its two super-productions of 1939, *The Wizard of Oz* and *Gone with the Wind* (actually a Selznick International production released and partially financed by MGM; see p. 250), both nominally directed by Victor Fleming. Neither film

PARAMOUNT

If MGM was the most "American" of the American studios, Paramount was the most "European." Many of Paramount's directors, craftsmen, and technicians had come to it directly from Germany via the Parufamet agreement of 1926, and the UFA influence on the Paramount style was substantial. For this reason, Paramount made the most sophisticated and visually ornate films of the 1930s. The studio's German art director, Hans Dreier, and its German cinematographer, Theodor Sparkuhl (1891–1945), as well as his American colleagues Victor Milner (1893–1972) and Karl Struss (1891–1981), created for its films a baroque pictorial style that was counterpointed by their subtle content. As John Baxter remarks, "Paramount's was the cinema of half-light and suggestion; witty, intelligent, faintly corrupt." The studio was controlled throughout the 1930s (and for some twenty years thereafter) by its founder, Adolph Zukor and, after 1936, its president, Barney Balaban (1887–1971). Through its formation of the 1,200-house Publix theater chain in 1925–26, Paramount owned the largest motion-picture circuit in the world; this forced the company into receivership during the worst years of the Depression but brought it record profits in the 1940s, when World War II drove public demand for movie entertainment to an all-time high (see pp. 372–74). Lacking MGM's Depression-era financial stability, Paramount nevertheless made almost as many films. And, because it was less tightly organized at the level of production than its rivals, these films often bore the personal imprint of their directors more than the standard 1930s studio product.[2]

Cecil B. DeMille (see pp. 187–88) continued to turn out the lavish sex-and-violence-soaked spectacles that had made him the star talent of Famous Players–Lasky in the silent era. His most profitable films for Paramount in the 1930s were *The Sign of the Cross* (1932), *Cleopatra* (1934), *The Crusades* (1935), *The Plainsman* (1937), *The Buccaneer* (1938), and *Union Pacific* (1939). At the other extreme were the films of the urbane Ernst Lubitsch (see pp. 92, 188–90), innovator of the UFA *Kostümfilme* and the silent comedy of manners, who had come to America in 1922 and stayed on to become Paramount's most prestigious director of the 1930s. (He was also in charge of production from 1935 to 1936—the only director ever to be given complete creative authority over the output of a major studio.)

In the sound era, Lubitsch specialized in musical comedy, light opera, and, once again, the comedy of manners. His major films of the decade were *The Love Parade* (1930), *Monte Carlo* (1930), *The Smiling Lieutenant* (1931), *One Hour with You* (1932), *Trouble in Paradise* (1932), *Design for Living* (1933), *The Merry Widow* (1934), *Angel* (1937), *Bluebeard's Eighth Wife* (1938) and *Ninotchka* (1939), to all of which he lent a distinctly European lightness of touch and a vaguely decadent charm.[3] Equally decadent but far more bizarre were the Paramount films of Josef von Sternberg, all of which cast his protégée Marlene Dietrich (1901–1992) as the archetypal *femme fatale* in some impossibly exotic setting: *Morocco* (1930), *Dishonored* (1931), *Shanghai Express* (1932), *Blond Venus* (1932), *The Scarlet Empress* (1934), and *The Devil Is a Woman* (1935). In these virtually (and deliberately) content-less films, von Sternberg achieved a degree of visual elegance that has led one critic to describe them as "poems in fur and smoke." Paramount was also the producer of the mannered, technically innovative films of the Armenian-born director Rouben Mamoulian, including *Applause* (1929), *City Streets* (1931), *Dr. Jekyll and Mr. Hyde* (1932), *Love Me Tonight* (1932), *Song of Songs* (1933), and *High, Wide, and Handsome* (1937).

Other notable Paramount directors of the 1930s were Mitchell Leisen (1898–1972), whose stylish films *Death Takes a Holiday* (1934), *Hands Across the Table* (1935), *Easy Living* (1937), and *Midnight* (1939) are much admired today for their sense of visual design; Henry

8.9 "Erotic-historical baroque": Cecil B. DeMille's *The Sign of the Cross* (1932). Fredric March, Claudette Colbert. Paramount.

2. Unlike the other majors, Paramount did not have an executive continuously in charge of production until 1936, when William LeBaron (1883–1958) assumed the role. In 1938, LeBaron was replaced by Y. Frank Freeman who remained Paramount's vice president in charge of production until 1959.

3. The last two were produced for MGM; Lubitsch's Paramount contract permitted him to direct one outside film per year, but he left the studio after eleven years in 1938 and began to freelance, producing *The Shop around the Corner* (1940) for MGM, *That Uncertain Feeling* (1941, a remake of his 1925 *Kiss Me Again*) for UA, and *To Be or Not to Be* (1942—a sophisticated and, at the time, controversial black comedy focused on the Nazi invasion of Poland, starring Carole Lombard and Jack Benny, and remade in 1983 as a vehicle for Anne Bancroft and Mel Brooks, Alan Johnson directing) for Alexander Korda–UA. Lubitsch finally signed a three-year producer-director contract with 20th Century–Fox, where he made *Heaven Can Wait* (1943, his first film in color), *Cluny Brown* (1946), and two films completed by Otto Preminger, owing to his failing health, *A Royal Scandal* (1945) and *That Lady in Ermine* (1948). Lubitsch died of a heart attack at the age of fifty-five during production of the latter on November 30, 1947.

8.10 Paramount's Continental touch: Ernst Lubitsch's *Design for Living* (1933). Miriam Hopkins, Fredric March, Gary Cooper.

Hathaway (1898–1985), who demonstrated a high degree of technical polish in such handsome productions as *Lives of a Bengal Lancer* and *Peter Ibbetson* (both 1935); and Dorothy Arzner (1900–1979), one of the industry's few women directors (*Working Girls*, 1931; *Christopher Strong*, 1933; *Nana*, 1934; *Craig's Wife*, 1936; *The Bride Wore Red*, 1937; *Dance, Girl, Dance*, 1940), who was famous for her editing skills. Finally, the best and most anarchic of the Marx Brothers' comedies, *The Cocoanuts* (Robert Florey and Joseph Santley, 1929), *Animal Crackers* (Victor Heerman, 1930), *Monkey Business* (Norman Z. McLeod, 1931), *Horse Feathers* (Norman Z. McLeod, 1931), and *Duck Soup* (Leo McCarey, 1933) were made for Paramount, as were the 1930s films of W. C. Fields (1879–1946) and Mae West (1892–1980). Major Paramount stars of the decade were George Raft, Ray Milland, Fredric March, Claudette Colbert, Miriam Hopkins, Herbert Marshall, Sylvia Sidney, Gary Cooper, Cary Grant, Kay Francis, Bing Crosby, Dorothy Lamour, Fred MacMurray, and Carole Lombard. In the early 1940s, the Bing Crosby–Bob Hope "Road" pictures (*Road to Singapore* [Victor Schertzinger, 1940], *Road to Zanzibar* [Victor Schertzinger, 1941], *Road to Morocco* [David Butler, 1942], etc.) brought Paramount the highest grosses of any series of the studio era. (As a subsidiary of Gulf and Western Industries from 1966 to 1989, of Paramount Communications, Inc. [a renamed and reconfigured Gulf and Western], from 1989 to 1994, and of Viacom-owned

Paramount thereafter, Paramount Pictures remains today a major producer of theatrical films and television series; see pp. 858–59.)

WARNER BROS.

In the cultural hierarchy of American studios in the 1930s, Warner Bros. fell below the sophisticated Paramount and the respectably middle-class MGM. It was in fact the studio of the working class, specializing in low-life melodramas and musicals with a Depression setting throughout the decade. Conditioned by its origins as a minor studio, Warner Bros. imposed a strict code of production efficiency on its directors, technicians, and stars alike. Directors were expected to produce at least five features a year. Actors and actresses were hired at low salaries and held to them long after they had become stars. Sometimes, when a film was being prepared for distribution, Warners' editors were required to cut single frames from every shot simply to tighten the film's structure and increase its speed. (The process was salutary: Warners' editor-in-chief, Ralph Dawson, won three Academy Awards for the studio during the 1930s.) Finally, the Warners cinematographers, Hal Mohr, Ernest Haller, Tony Gaudio, and Sol Polito, were required to adopt a style of flat, low-key lighting in order to obscure the spareness of the studio's economical sets.

This emphasis on maximum economy of means, enforced by executives like Hal B. Wallis (1899–1986), Henry Blanke (1901–1981), and the ruthlessly pragmatic Jack L. Warner,[4] produced a group of films that were models of fast-paced, disciplined narrative construction. Warners in the 1930s was preeminently the home of the gangster cycle (*Little Caesar* [Mervyn LeRoy, 1930]; *The Public Enemy* [William Wellman, 1931]) and the Busby Berkeley backstage musical (*42nd Street* [1933]; the *Gold Diggers* series); but it also undertook some major works of social realism like William Wellman's *Wild Boys of the Road* (1933), Mervyn LeRoy's *I Am a Fugitive from a Chain Gang* (1932), and Michael Curtiz's *Black Fury* (1935). Warners was also responsible (and rather

---

4. Of all the majors, only Warners was family-run: Jack (1892–1978) was in charge of production; Albert ("Abe," 1884–1967) supervised distribution; and Harry (1881–1958), as president, managed the entire system. Samuel Warner (1888–1927), who reputedly had convinced his brothers to convert to sound, died of a cerebral hemorrhage one day before the premiere of *The Jazz Singer*.

8.11 **Warner Bros. realism: Paul Muni in** *I Am a Fugitive from a Chain Gang* **(Mervyn LeRoy, 1932).**

courageously so) for the first American anti-Nazi film, Anatole Litvak's *Confessions of a Nazi Spy* (1939), as well as for a series of prestigious biographical films directed by the former UFA actor William Dieterle (1893–1972) which included *The Story of Louis Pasteur* (1936), *White Angel* (1936—a biography of Florence Nightingale), *The Life of Emile Zola* (1937), *Juarez* (1939), and *Dr. Erhlich's Magic Bullet* (1940). Dieterle also directed a marvelously expressionistic and, for Warners, utterly uncharacteristic version of *A Midsum-*

8.12 **Warner Bros. fantasy:** *A Midsummer Night's Dream* **(Max Reinhardt and William Dieterle, 1935). Titania (Anita Louise) and the Indian Prince (Kenneth Anger).**

mer Night's Dream in collaboration with the great German stage director Max Reinhardt in 1935. Other top directors at Warners in the 1930s were Michael Curtiz, the Hungarian filmmaker who had worked for UFA in the 1920s, and Mervyn LeRoy (1900–1987). Given the studio's rigid organization and tight production schedule, neither Dieterle, Curtiz, nor LeRoy was able to pursue a personal vision in his Warners films, but all three proved themselves to be remarkably versatile professional filmmakers who could function as master craftsmen within a system that militated strongly against creative freedom. Warners was also distinguished in the 1930s for its art directors, Anton Grot and Robert Haas, and its two great composers, Erich Wolfgang Korngold and Max Steiner, both of whom joined the studio in 1935. Among the major Warners stars of the period were Bette Davis, Barbara Stanwyck, Paul Muni, James Cagney, Humphrey Bogart, Pat O'Brien, Edward G. Robinson, and Errol Flynn—players who seemed to embody the tough vernacular pragmatism of the studio's films themselves. (Warner Bros. prospers today as the film and television production division of Warner Communications, Inc. [WCI]; it also has close ties to Orion Pictures and The Ladd Company; in 1989 WCI merged with Time, Inc. to become Time Warner; see pp. 858–59.)

20th CENTURY–FOX

20th Century–Fox was born of financial difficulties, and yet it would become, after MGM and Paramount, the most profitable studio of its era. In March 1935, the U.S. Supreme Court ruled against William Fox in his all-or-nothing attempt to retain complete control of the U.S. patent rights to the Tri-Ergon sound-on-film process which was the basis for the Fox Movietone system. Had Fox won, he would have been due incalculable sums in damages from every producer of sound films in the country and would have come very close to his dream of monopolizing the entire American film industry. As it was, he lost his personal fortune of $100 million as a result of corporate bankruptcy proceedings and was ousted as president of Fox Film Corporation by Sidney Kent, who arranged a merger with Joseph M. Schenck's Twentieth Century Pictures in late 1935, forming 20th Century–Fox and securing Twentieth Century executive producer Darryl F. Zanuck (1902–1979) as the new company's vice president in charge of production.[5] (Fox was forced out of his company in 1931; he didn't declare bankruptcy until 1936.) Zanuck, who reigned as production chief through 1956, replaced Fox's lieutenant Winfield Sheehan (1883–1945). Despite William Fox's depredations, 20th Century–Fox was heir to the Movietone City complex in Los Angeles and newsreel studios in New York; extensive theater chains in the United States (National Theater), England (Gaumont British Pictures), Australia (the Hoyts Circuit), New Zealand, and South Africa; and 147 film exchanges serving every country on earth but the Soviet Union.

The studio's films of the 1930s acquired a reputation for hard, glossy surfaces produced through careful budgeting and production control. Fox's major director at this time was John Ford, although he also worked sporadically for other studios. Ford's most important films for Fox during the period were *Dr. Bull* (1933), *Judge Priest* (1934), and *Steamboat 'round the Bend* (1935)—all three starring the popular vaudeville wit Will Rogers; *The Prisoner of Shark Island* (1935), *Young Mr. Lincoln* (1939), *Drums along the Mohawk* (1939), *The Grapes of Wrath* (1940), and *How Green Was My Valley* (1941). Fox also specialized in musicals like Henry King's *Alexander's Ragtime Band* (1938), American period nostalgia like the same director's *State Fair* (1933) and *In Old Chicago* (1938), and such popular B-film series as the Charlie Chan mysteries, starring Warner Oland and then Sidney Toler in the title role, but its fortunes in the 1930s were also built in large part upon the films of its popular child star Shirley Temple,[6] which included *Stand Up and Cheer* (Hamilton McFadden, 1934), *Curly Top* (Irving Cummings, 1935), *Captain January* (David Butler, 1935), *The Littlest Rebel* (David Butler, 1935), *The Little Colonel* (David Butler, 1935), *Wee Willie Winkie* (John Ford, 1937), *Heidi* (Allan Dwan, 1937), *Rebecca of Sunnybrook Farm* (Allan Dwan, 1938), and *The Blue Bird* (Walter Lang, 1940). Other Fox stars of the 1930s were Tyrone Power, Charles Boyer, Alice Faye, Don Ameche, Warner Baxter, Henry Fonda, Loretta Young, and Janet Gaynor. The studio's major cinematographers were Bert Glennon and Arthur Miller, and its music director was the brilliant arranger Alfred Newman. Finally, Fox was noted for having the best special-effects department of all the major studios—a reputation borne out by the disaster sequences of *Dante's Inferno* (Harry Lachman, 1935) and *The Rains Came* (Clarence Brown, 1939)—as well as pro-

8.13 The gloss of Fox: Lionel Barrymore and Shirley Temple in *The Little Colonel* (David Butler, 1935).

ducing the most Technicolor features through 1949. (20th Century–Fox remains today an important producer of film and television; with Walt Disney Productions, it is the only major Hollywood studio not under the control of a corporate conglomerate, although it was acquired by Texas oilman Marvin Davis in 1981, who sold a controlling interest to media baron Rupert Murdoch in 1985. See p. 859).

RKO

The smallest of the majors was RKO, which remained financially unstable through the 1930s and 1940s, and was sold in 1955 to General Teleradio, Inc., a subsidiary of the General Tire and Rubber Company, which wanted access to its film library for broadcast use. (RKO ceased production entirely in 1957, and its studio facilities

---

5. Kent died of a heart attack in 1941, and Schenck, who was board chairman, went to jail for tax evasion in the same year (after serving four months, he returned to the Fox board but remained in the background of the industry until forming the Magna Corporation with Michael Todd in 1953). As its new president in 1942, 20th Century-Fox selected Spyros Skouras (1893–1971), then head of Fox Metropolitan Theaters, who served until he was ousted by Zanuck following the *Cleopatra* debacle of 1963 (see Chapter 12).

6. She had so endeared herself to the American public by 1937 that Louis B. Mayer offered Clark Gable and Jean Harlow to 20th Century–Fox in exchange for the child star, whom he wanted to play the lead in *The Wizard of Oz.* Negotiations were terminated by Miss Harlow's sudden death in 1937, and Judy Garland was cast in the role.

were sold to Desilu Television Productions; today, as RKO General, it holds broadcasting and cable television franchises for its parent firm, GTR, and produces an occasional feature.) RKO was ruled by eight successive regimes from 1929 to 1952 (the last being that of millionaire Howard Hughes [1905–1976], who is credited with wrecking it), and it was the most volatile and risk-taking of all studios of the era; the decade of the 1930s, however, was its most stable period—probably because the corporation was in receivership from 1933 to 1939 and placed under the administration of a federal district court.[7] In 1934, RKO became the home of the Fred Astaire–Ginger Rogers musical with the success of their first film together, *Flying Down to Rio* (Thornton C. Freeland, 1933), in which they had second billing. From 1934 to 1939, the studio made eight Astaire-Rogers vehicles under the auspices of its innovative young producer Pandro S. Berman (1905–1996) and star directors like Mark Sandrich (1900–1945) and George Stevens (1904–1975). Films like *The Gay Divorcee* (Sandrich, 1934), *Top Hat* (Sandrich, 1935), and *Swing Time* (Stevens, 1936) made the Astaire-Rogers team one of the most popular box-office attractions in America and gave RKO a reputation for stylishness and sophistication throughout the decade, although it produced its share of B-films for the second half of double bills.

The studio also had a penchant for literary adaptations like *Little Women* (George Cukor, 1933), *Of Human Bondage* (John Cromwell, 1934), and *The Hunchback of Notre Dame* (William Dieterle, 1938). John Ford directed three such films for RKO in the 1930s: adaptations of two plays—Maxwell Anderson's *Mary of Scotland* (1936) and Sean O'Casey's *The Plough and the Stars* (1936)—and a masterly, expressive rendition of Liam O'Flaherty's novel *The Informer* (1935), which some historians regard as the first recognizably modern sound film in its symbolic, non-literal use of the medium. RKO's most extraordinary production of the decade and one of its most successful was the monster thriller *King Kong* (Merian C. Cooper and Ernest B. Schoedsack, 1933), whose brilliant stop-motion photography and special effects by Willis O'Brien (1886–1962) are still a marvel of technical achievement. The studio's major star during this period was Katharine Hepburn (b. 1907), who made fourteen films for RKO between 1932 and 1938, including *A Bill of Divorcement* (George Cukor, 1932), *Little Women* (Cukor, 1933), *Mary of Scotland* (John Ford, 1936), *A Woman Rebels* (Mark

8.14 RKO's spectacular *King Kong* (Merian C. Cooper and Ernest B. Schoedsack, 1933).

Sandrich, 1936), *Stage Door* (Gregory La Cava, 1937), and the classic screwball comedy *Bringing Up Baby* (Howard Hawks, 1938). RKO's art director from 1930 to 1943 was the distinguished Van Nest Polglase (1898–1968), whose genius was equally responsible for the stylish elegance of the Astaire-Rogers musicals and the murky expressiveness of Ford's *The Informer* and *Mary of Scotland*. In addition to its own films, RKO also released independent productions for Samuel Goldwyn and David O. Selznick, and it became the distributor for Walt Disney's animated features and shorts with the release of *Snow White and the Seven Dwarfs* in Christmas week, 1937.[8] The studio ended the decade with bravado by signing the *enfant terrible* of broadcasting, Orson Welles, to a highly publicized six-film contract in 1939,

---

7. In 1931, RKO had embarked upon an expansionary campaign by acquiring Pathé Exchange, Inc. This gave it new studio space in Culver City, a newsreel service (Pathé News), and an international distribution network, but left it badly overextended. Then, in 1932, it opened the 6,200-seat Radio City Music Hall, part of whose lease required RKO to move its corporate headquarters to Rockefeller Center, the most expensive piece of real estate in the country. By January 1933, the company had defaulted on more than $3.5 million in loans and was placed under the authority of the court. (The distinct styles of RKO's eight successive management teams are recounted in Betty Lasky's closely researched *RKO: The Biggest Little Major of Them All* [Englewood Cliffs, N.J.: Prentice Hall, 1984].)

8. Rereleased for the seventh time in 1987 to commemorate its fiftieth anniversary, *Snow White* was a phenomenon in its own day and has become one of the most profitable films in history, earning the equivalent of $325 million worldwide. Its original release was accompanied

the first product of which was *Citizen Kane* (1941; see pp. 328–44).

THE MINORS

Universal Pictures, which remained under the control of its founder, Carl Laemmle, until 1936, had been a leading studio in the 1920s, producing for such talents as Erich von Stroheim, Lon Chaney, and Rudolph Valentino, but by the 1930s the company had slipped into a minor position. Unlike the Big Five, it had failed to acquire a chain of downtown first-run theaters and was forced to concentrate its production and distribution efforts on subsequent-run houses in suburban and rural areas.[9] It produced a number of prestigious films during the decade, including Lewis Milestone's *All Quiet on the Western Front* (1930), James Whale's *Showboat* (1936), and George Marshall's *Destry Rides Again* (1939), and it achieved some commercial success with the popular melodramas of John M. Stahl (1886–1950—*Back Street*, 1932; *Imitation of Life*, 1934; and *Magnificent Obsession*, 1935), but its standard product was the low-budget feature designed for double bills. Nevertheless, Universal did manage to distinguish itself in the horror-fantasy genre during the 1930s, drawing upon the UFA tradition of Expressionism and the talents of the directors James Whale (1889–1957) and Tod Browning (1882–1962), and the former UFA cameraman Karl Freund.

Tod Browning's *Dracula*, broodingly photographed by Freund, began the Universal horror cycle in 1931, and it was continued by James Whale's powerful and chilling version of *Frankenstein* in the same year. Whale, an Englishman of great sophistication with a fine feeling for Gothic atmosphere, became Universal's star director of the 1930s on the basis of his elegantly mounted horror films. He went on to direct *The Old Dark House* (1932), *The Invisible Man* (1933), and the oddly baroque *Bride of Frankenstein* (1935) for the studio before turning to other genres. Other important Universal horror films of the 1930s were Robert Florey's Caligariesque *Murders in the Rue Morgue* (1932), photographed by Freund; Karl Freund's evocative thriller *The Mummy* (1932); Edgar G. Ulmer's bizarre essay in Expressionist mayhem, *The Black Cat* (1934); Stuart Walker's *Werewolf of London* (1935); and Lambert Hillyer's *The Invisible Ray* (1935) and *Dracula's Daughter* (1936). The latter concluded the cycle of serious horror films begun with *Dracula* in 1931. A sec-

8.15 Universal horrors: *Dracula* (Tod Browning, 1931): Bela Lugosi, Dwight Frye. *Frankenstein* (James Whale, 1931): Boris Karloff.

ond cycle was begun at Universal in 1939 with *Son of Frankenstein*, stylishly directed by Rowland V. Lee, and George Waggner's atmospheric *The Wolf Man* (1941). These were worthy successors to the Whale series, but the films of the second cycle quickly lapsed into imitation

by multiple marketing tie-ins with sheet music, toys, and books, plus an original sound track recorded on RCA Victor 10-inch 78s. As the first American animated feature, *Snow White* represented an enormous risk for Disney, who had spent the equivalent of $32 million ($1,488,000 in 1937 currency) and three years to produce it. Nearly 750 artists were employed to draw the 2 million drawings that make up the film—which was known in the industry as "Disney's Folly" until it returned its investment five times over in 1938.

9. Universal did, however, maintain an international distribution network and had considerable success releasing its Westerns in Europe.

and self-parody with titles like *The Invisible Man Returns* (1940), *The Mummy's Hand* (1940), *The Ghost of Frankenstein* (1942), and *Frankenstein Meets the Wolf Man* (1943). When the first horror cycle ended, Universal discovered the teenage singing star Deanna Durbin and featured her in a series of musical comedies made by the producer-director team of Joe Pasternak and Henry Koster (*Three Smart Girls*, 1936; *Mad about Music*, 1938; *Three Smart Girls Grow Up*, 1939; *Spring Parade*, 1940) that kept the studio from bankruptcy until the second horror cycle began to pay off. Other stars under contract to Universal during the 1930s included, appropriately, Boris Karloff, Bela Lugosi, and Lon Chaney, Jr.; and, in the early 1940s W. C. Fields (*The Bank Dick*, 1940; *My Little Chickadee*, 1940; *Never Give a Sucker an Even Break*, 1941—all directed by Edward Cline), Abbott and Costello (*Buck Privates*, 1941; *In the Navy*, 1941; *Hold That Ghost*, 1941; *Keep 'Em Flying*, 1941; *Ride 'Em Cowboy*, 1942—all directed by Arthur Lubin), and Basil Rathbone and Nigel Bruce, stars of the twelve-film "modern" Sherlock Holmes cycle[1] (e.g., *Sherlock Holmes Faces Death*, 1943; *The Scarlet Claw*, 1944), most of them produced and directed by Roy William Neill. (As a subsidiary of the entertainment conglomerate MCA, Universal became Hollywood's leading studio during the 1970s and 1980s, producing more theatrical films and prime-time television series than anyone else in industry; in 1990 it was acquired by Matsushita Electrical Industrial Corporation of Japan; see p. 860.)

Columbia Pictures was the brainchild of a single man, Harry Cohn (1891–1958), who founded the corporation in 1924 with his brother Jack (1889–1956) and Joe Brandt (all three former employees of Carl Laemmle), and who ruled over it absolutely from 1932 until his death. Columbia owned no theater circuits but maintained a successful international distribution network under the management of Jack Cohn, which enabled it to sustain continuous profits during the Depression and finally to double its assets during the postwar boom. Columbia's staple product during the studio era was the low-budget cofeature, mainly Westerns and long-run series films adapted from other media (e.g., the twenty-eight-film "Blondie" series, 1938–51, based on the Chic Young comic strip). But Cohn had a policy of hiring, for single pictures, stars who were temporarily disaffected from their regular studios, and he managed to produce a number of first-class films at low overhead in this manner, including

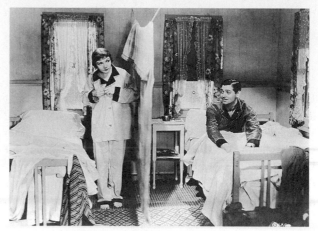

8.16 Columbia's "sleeper" *It Happened One Night* (Frank Capra, 1934): Claudette Colbert, Clark Gable.

George Cukor's *Holiday* (1938); Rouben Mamoulian's *Golden Boy* (1939); and Howard Hawks's *Twentieth Century* (1934), *Only Angels Have Wings* (1939), and *His Girl Friday* (1940). The studio's star director was Frank Capra (1897–1991), whose New Deal and screwball comedies written by Robert Riskin (1897–1955) were largely responsible for keeping Columbia solvent during the 1930s. The prototype of the form was the enormously successful *It Happened One Night* (1934), written by Riskin and starring Clark Gable (on loan from MGM) and Claudette Colbert (on loan from Paramount). This romantic comedy concerns the adventures of a runaway heiress and a newspaperman who discovers her identity and finally marries her. The film is full of witty, fast-talking dialogue, ingenious gags, and incredible twists of plot that established a new style in Hollywood comedy for the rest of the decade. Other Capra-Riskin films— the social comedies *Mr. Deeds Goes to Town* (1936) and *You Can't Take It with You* (1938), the more serious *Mr. Smith Goes to Washington* (1939), and the utopian fantasy *Lost Horizon* (1937)—possess the same qualities of refreshing informality mixed with New Deal optimism and populism, constituting what one critic has called

---

1. As opposed to the two Fox big-budget period films, *The Hound of the Baskervilles* (Sidney Lanfield, 1939) and *The Adventures of Sherlock Holmes* (Alfred Werker, 1939), both produced by Darryl F. Zanuck and starring Rathbone and Bruce, which initiated American sound-film adaptations of the Conan Doyle stories. There were, of course, countless silent versions on both sides of the Atlantic and numerous sound films from England, Germany, and Czechoslovakia.

"fantasies of good will." Other Columbia assets were the gifted comedienne Jean Arthur and the opera star Grace Moore, whose popular series of musicals—*One Night of Love* (Victor Schertzinger, 1934), *Love Me Forever* (Schertzinger, 1935), and *I'll Take Romance* (Edward H. Griffith, 1937)—put it well on its way to becoming a major studio in the 1940s and 1950s, when, through its Screen Gems division (established 1952), Columbia became the first Hollywood studio to produce programming for the new medium of television. (As a subsidiary of the Coca-Cola Company from 1982 to 1989, Columbia Pictures Industries, Inc., was a financially powerful producer of theatrical films and television; in 1987, it merged with TriStar to become Columbia Pictures Entertainment and was acquired by Sony Corp. in 1989; it was renamed Sony Pictures Entertainment in 1991; see Chapter 20.)

United Artists was not, strictly speaking, a studio at all, but a distributor for the films of independent producers. It had been founded by Charlie Chaplin, Mary Pickford, Douglas Fairbanks, and D. W. Griffith in 1919 to distribute their own films, and in the 1930s it handled the independent productions of Samuel Goldwyn, David O. Selznick, Walter Wanger, Hal Roach, and the Hungarian-born British producer-director Alexander Korda, among others. United Artists was unique in that it owned no production facilities and no exhibition chains, so production and distribution of its films were negotiated on an individual basis. Because United Artists had no studio and no stars, it did not fare well financially during this period of Hollywood's massive corporate growth, but by the same token the absence of a huge overhead enabled it to survive, if not always to prosper, during hard times. Its most important releases of the 1930s were Chaplin's *City Lights* (1931) and *Modern Times* (1936), King Vidor's *Street Scene* (1931) and *Our Daily Bread* (1934), Lewis Milestone's *The Front Page* (1931), Howard Hawks's *Scarface* (1932), René Clair's *The Ghost Goes West* (1936), William Cameron Menzies's *Things to Come* (1936), and Alexander Korda's *The Private Life of Henry VIII* (1933), *Rembrandt* (1936), and *Elephant Boy* (1937)[2]—the last five all products of a long-term contract with Korda's London Films production company. United Artists also had a distribution contract with Samuel Goldwyn, who released through the company, as an independent producer, *Stella Dallas* (King Vidor, 1937), *Dead End* (William Wyler, 1937), and *Wuthering Heights* (William Wyler, 1939), among other films.

Throughout the studio era, UA relied upon the Big Five for access to first-run theaters; this was generally not a problem during the reign (1924–35) of board chairman—and, from 1926, president—Joseph M. Schenck, since his brother Nicholas was concurrently president of Loew's, Inc., and helped him to negotiate bookings with the majors, including, of course, MGM. But when Joseph left to head up the newly formed 20th Century–Fox in 1935, UA was left without an ally among the Big Five, and its fortunes declined rapidly as producers turned away from it one by one (Goldwyn and Wanger in 1941, Korda in 1942, Selznick in 1945). For these reasons, UA became the only Hollywood studio that did not profit from the postwar boom, although it was revitalized after 1951, when it was acquired by the entertainment lawyers Arthur B. Krim and Robert S. Benjamin. The company absorbed the B-film studio Eagle-Lion and was revitalized by the production of several major hits [*The African Queen*, 1951; *High Noon*, 1952]. During the 1950s, UA supported a large roster of independent producers and began television distribution operations in 1957; it subsequently acquired long-term distribution contracts with the Mirisch Corporation and Eon Productions, the Albert R. Broccoli–Harry Saltzman partnership that produced the James Bond series of the 1960s and 1970s [Harry Saltzman sold his share in Eon to UA in 1974; see footnote, p. 415]. As a subsidiary of the Transamerica Corporation from 1967 to 1981, UA produced the commercial hits *Rocky* [1976] and *Rocky II* [1979] and such critically esteemed films as *One Flew over the Cuckoo's Nest* [1975], *Annie Hall* [1977], and *The French Lieutenant's Woman* [1981] but was brought to its knees through the financial debacle of *Heaven's Gate* [1980; see p. 859]. In 1981 it was bought by MGM, which merged with it to form MGM/UA Entertainment Company in 1983, and went on to produce the popular *Rocky III* [1982] and *IV* [1985] and *Poltergeist* [1982] and *Poltergeist II* [1985] before it was bought by Turner Broadcasting in 1985; Turner resold the company to Kirk Kerkorian in 1986, and it was acquired by Pathé Communications in 1990; renamed MGM-Pathé, this company was taken over by Crédit Lyonnais in 1992, renamed Metro-Goldwyn-Mayer, Inc., and the last vestiges of United Artists removed.)

---

2. Codirected by Zoltan Korda and Robert Flaherty.

There were a handful of independent producers in Hollywood during the heyday of the studio system, most of whom released their films through United Artists or RKO. The two most influential were Samuel Goldwyn of Samuel Goldwyn Productions and David O. Selznick of Selznick International Pictures. As Samuel Goldfish, Goldwyn had founded the Goldwyn Pictures Corporation with the brothers Edgar and Archibald Selwyn in December 1916, combining the first and last syllables of their respective names into the famous surname that Goldfish legally took as his own in 1918. In 1923, shortly before the merger that created Metro-Goldwyn-Mayer (and that simultaneously dealt him out of the new corporation), Goldwyn formed Samuel Goldwyn Productions, a completely independent company, and went on to become one of the most prestigious producers of the 1930s and 1940s. The logo "Samuel Goldwyn Presents" became synonymous with high-quality family entertainment during these years and served to introduce much new talent to the industry. Although he produced the films of many important directors (e.g., King Vidor, John Ford), Goldwyn's most fruitful association was with William Wyler, who provided him with some of his biggest hits (*Dodsworth*, 1936; *Dead End*, 1937; *Wuthering Heights*, 1939; *The Little Foxes*, 1941; *The Best Years of Our Lives*, 1946). David O. Selznick left MGM to found Selznick International Pictures in 1936 and became the very type of creative independent producer that so many filmmakers enmeshed in the cogs and gears of the studio system longed to be. His motto "In a tradition of quality," Selznick produced a series of lavish but tasteful films whose meticulous attention to detail borders on the obsessive: William Wellman's *A Star Is Born* (1937) and *Nothing Sacred* (1937); Alfred Hitchcock's *Rebecca* (1940), *Spellbound* (1945), and *The Paradine Case* (1948); John Cromwell's *Since You Went Away* (1944); King Vidor's *Duel in the Sun* (1946); William Dieterle's *Portrait of Jennie* (1948); and, as coproducer with Alexander Korda, Carol Reed's *The Third Man* (1949). Although like Goldwyn he released mainly through UA and RKO, Selznick's most famous film, *Gone with the Wind* (1939), was produced for MGM so that he could cast MGM contract star Clark Gable in the role of Rhett Butler.

The studio system of production could exist only as long as the majors maintained their monopolistic control of the means of exhibition.[3] Without a guaranteed weekly audience, films would have to be made and sold on terms other than the system allowed. In July 1938, in *The United States v. Paramount Pictures*, the federal government began litigation against the five major studios for combining and conspiring to restrain trade unreasonably and to monopolize the production, distribution, and exhibition of motion pictures. The three minors were charged with combining and conspiring with the majors for the same purpose. When war seemed imminent in 1940, a consent decree was issued, permitting the studios to retain their exhibition chains, with minor restrictions, but the case was reactivated in 1945 and concluded in May 1948, when the U.S. Supreme Court ruled that the vertical integration of the majors violated federal antitrust laws and ordered the five companies to divest themselves of their theaters over a five-year period (see pp. 372–73). The divestiture order, known as the "Paramount decrees" or "consent decrees," destroyed the studio system by eliminating the guaranteed distribution and guaranteed weekly audience, which were its mainstay.

"POVERTY ROW"

Below even the minor studios were the "B-studios." These came into existence in the 1930s as the result of a uniquely American movie phenomenon: the double bill. When the novelty of sound had worn off and the Depression had set in, audiences began to stay away from the movies. From 90 million admissions a week in 1930, the figure dropped to 60 million by 1932. By midsummer of 1935, 5,000 of the 16,000 movie theaters in the United States were closed. To combat this situation Hollywood invented the double bill, which offered two features, a cartoon, and a newsreel for the price of a single admission. By 1935, 85 percent of all American theaters were offering double bills, and from 1935 to around 1950 American audiences expected three-hours-plus worth of entertainment every time they went to the movies. The B-studios

---

3. As previously stated, the Big Five actually owned only 16 percent of the nation's theaters, but that 16 percent comprised more than 70 percent of the first-run houses in the ninety-two largest cities. This de facto monopoly on first-run theaters guaranteed the majors bookings for all new productions and ensured that their features would capture 75 percent of all box-office revenues during the studio era, with another 20 percent going to the minors. Today, without that guarantee, filmmaking in the United States has become a much greater speculative risk than it was during the years of the studio system.

were created by the rental system that the major studios devised for double features. Whereas the producer/distributor and the exhibitor would split the box-office receipts for the main feature, or the A-film (usually 60/40 or 80/20), the **B-film** was rented to the exhibitor at a flat rate. This meant that there was very little financial risk involved in producing B-films (since distribution was guaranteed), but that there was also very little profit in it since the film would never make more money than the fixed rate allowed. For this reason the major studios initially had scant interest in producing B-features (although the minors produced them in quantity, and the Big Five started operating B-units around 1935), and so in the early 1930s about a dozen small companies sprang up in Hollywood for the specific purpose of producing cheap, hour-long genre films for the bottom half of double bills.

Collectively known as "the B-Hive," or "Poverty Row," these studios operated on an extremely thin profit margin with very little capital. A B-feature might cost $75,000 to $80,000 to produce and make a profit of $10,000 to $15,000 nationwide; but the average budget and profit figures were $20,000 and $3,000 to $4,000, respectively. Shooting schedules ranged from seven to fourteen days, depending on the material, and were rigidly followed: to keep a cast and crew on tap for a single day beyond the scheduled completion date would often destroy the small profit margin. The most important B-studios were Republic Pictures, Monogram Productions, Grand National Films, and—in the 1940s—Producers Releasing Corporation (PRC) and Eagle-Lion Films. At their peak, each studio produced forty to fifty films per year, much of which was trash. But the B-studios also provided the training ground for many a director who went on to better things (in the 1930s, for example, Christy Cabanne, Richard Thorpe, and Charles Vidor; in the 1940s, Edward Dmytryk, Laslo Benedek, Anthony Mann, Budd Boetticher, Ida Lupino, Jacques Tourneur, and Phil Karlson), and they produced a number of extraordinary films in their own right (for example, Edgar G. Ulmer's *Detour*, 1946; Ben Hecht's *Spectre of the Rose*, 1946; Orson Welles's *Macbeth*, 1948; Allan Dwan's *The Sands of Iwo Jima*, 1949; and Joseph H. Lewis's *Gun Crazy*, 1949). In the wake of the postwar boom, Herbert J. Yates's Republic even became successful enough to produce such A-films as Frank Borzage's *Moonrise* (1948), Lewis Milestone's *The Red Pony* (1949), Fritz Lang's *House by the River* (1950), and Nicholas Ray's *Johnny Guitar* (1954), and to distribute John Ford's Argossy productions, *Rio Grande* (1950), *The Quiet Man* (1952), and *The Sun Shines Bright* (1953), although this extravagance eventually contributed to its bankruptcy in 1958.

When the major studios were divested of their theater chains between 1948 and 1953, the double bill was no longer profitable. The B-studios folded, and the B-film found a new home in the form of the television series. Only Monogram survived: in the form of Allied Artists (incorporated 1952), it went on to produce such successful features as *Friendly Persuasion* (William Wyler, 1956) and *Love in the Afternoon* (Billy Wilder, 1957). Allied continued to produce films occasionally during the 1960s and 1970s (*Cabaret*, 1972; *Papillon*, 1973; *The Man Who Would Be King*, 1975), until it was sold to the television company Lorimar Productions in 1980.

ETHNIC CINEMA

Another source of independently produced, low-budget films during the 1930s was ethnic cinema—movies aimed at a small but specific market category as distinguished by race or religion, usually featuring all-ethnic casts and distributed on a states' rights basis.[4] Like the B's of Poverty Row, ethnic films were shot quickly and cheaply, but they often lacked the technical competence associated with even the most lowly studio environment. Inferior lighting, sound recording, and editing—as well as poor scripting and acting—combined to produce films whose appeal lay not in narrative pleasure, but ethnicity. In its sometimes bizarrely nonclassical construction, ethnic cinema can be understood as an alternative mode of film practice, but it was also movie making on a shoestring for audiences too marginalized to demand more.

The largest component in this subcategory was black cinema, often called "race cinema," which had begun during the 1910s in response to the outrageous stereotyping of African Americans in mainstream cinema, most prominently *The Birth of a Nation* (1915). By 1918, eight independent companies had produced race movies with

---

4. In the states' rights system, regional distributors paid a flat fee to producers for limited exclusive rights to exhibit a film within a given state or group of states, with the distributor absorbing the cost of release prints and promotion. Though fees to producers ranged as high as $50,000, the distributor was guaranteed a small but predictable profit through exclusivity. States' rights production quality was moot since neither distribution nor exhibition depended on it.

all-black casts, and in the next three decades over 150 companies would be created for the same purpose. But, as Richard Grupenhoff points out, only 75 percent of these would produce one or more films, and only 33 percent would be completely black-owned.[5] (The profit margin for such productions was slim, since the market was limited not only by its size, but by its lack of access to exhibition—theaters in the North and Midwest were segregated, and all-black theaters in the South were usually owned by whites.) Two such companies were the Lincoln Motion Picture Company, which was founded by the brothers George and Noble Johnson in Los Angeles in 1916 to produce two-reelers like *The Realization of a Negro's Ambition* (1916), and the Colored Players Corporation of Philadelphia, which produced several influential features during the 1920s, including the legendary *Scar of Shame* (1927), a melodrama focused on the class and color caste system of the black middle class.

The most consistent all-black production companies of the 1920s and 1930s, however, were those owned and operated by Oscar Micheaux (1884–1951),[6] the black film pioneer who between 1918 and 1948 produced, directed, edited, and distributed (often personally, striking his own deals with exhibitors) about forty feature films to African-American audiences across the nation. Only ten of these —one silent (*Body and Soul*, 1924; starring Paul Robeson) and nine sound films—have survived, but all had racial themes and some treated provocative subjects like lynching (*Within Our Gates*, 1920), the Ku Klux Klan (*The Symbol of the Unconquered*, 1921), "passing for white" (*Deceit*, 1923), separatism versus assimilation (*Birthright*, 1924; remade 1938), and interracial marriage (*Veiled Aristocrats*, 1931). On the other hand, many of Micheaux's films were frankly exploitative action (*A Daughter of the Congo*, 1930; *Harlem after Midnight*, 1935) and crime films (*Ten Minutes to Live*, 1932; *Underworld*, 1936; *Lying Lips*, 1940), and all were made with scant attention to Hollywood's stylistic norms. Scenes were shot unrehearsed on location (often business offices or Harlem nightclubs hooked for the free publicity) in single takes and used regardless of quality; narrative gaps were padded with canned cabaret routines and outtakes. Micheaux's early sound films are so clumsy that in one of them (*The Girl from Chicago*, 1932) his voice can be heard on the sound track directing the actors. But Micheaux, whose own budgets rarely exceeded $15,000, had been formative in the development of a race-film market that by the coming of sound extended to over 600 theaters and had begun to attract the attention of the major studios. Furthermore, even though his own output comprised only fifteen of about seventy-five independent black features produced during the 1930s, Micheaux decisively influenced several generations of African-American filmmakers, a fact acknowledged by the Directors Guild of America when it gave him its Fiftieth Anniversary "Golden Jubilee Award" in 1986.

Hollywood's attempt to co-opt the race-film market with all-black musicals like MGM's *Hallelujah!* and Fox's *Hearts in Dixie* (both 1929) and such later black-cast productions as United Artists' *The Emperor Jones* (1933) and Warners' *Green Pastures* (1936) fizzled, leaving the field to Micheaux and a number of mixed-race independents, of which Ralph Cooper's all-black Million Dollar Pictures and Richard Kahn's Hollywood Productions were the most financially successful. Both had access to Poverty Row studio facilities and distribution channels, and, together with International Road Shows and Harlem-based Paragon Pictures, they specialized in making black versions of popular studio genre films—crime (*Dark Manhattan*, 1937; *Mystery in Swing*, 1939), musicals (*Harlem Is Heaven/Harlem Rhapsody*, 1932; *The Duke Is Tops*, 1938—Lena Horne's debut, rereleased as *The Bronze Venus*, 1943; *Broken Strings*, 1940), Westerns (*Harlem on the Prairie*, 1937; *The Bronze Buckaroo*, 1938; *Harlem Rides the Range*, 1939), and horror (*Louisiana/ Voodoo Drums*, 1933; *The Devil's Daughter*, 1939; *Son of Ingagi*, 1940). Many of these films were written by Spencer Williams (1893–1969), a unique director/actor/writer best remembered today for his role as Andy in the *Amos 'n' Andy* television series of 1951–53. During the 1940s, Williams teamed with Jewish entrepreneur Alfred Sack of Sack Amusement Enterprises, Dallas, to produce a series of nine all-black features from his own screenplays, which included religious films (*The Blood of Jesus*, 1941; *Go Down Death*, 1944), dramas (*Marchin' On*, 1943; *The Girl in Room 20*, 1946), and comedies (*Dirty Gertie from*

5. Richard Grupenhoff, "The Rediscovery of Oscar Micheaux, Black Film Pioneer," *Journal of Film and Video* 40, 1 (Winter 1988): 43.

6. Micheaux's companies were the Micheaux Book and Film Company (founded 1918), the Micheaux Pictures Corporation, and the Micheaux Film Corporation. Micheaux was also a prolific novelist who adapted some of his films (e.g., *The Homesteader*, 1919; *The Millionaire*, 1927) from his own work.

8.17 Paul Robeson in the United Artists adaptation of Eugene O'Neill's play *The Emperor Jones* (Dudley Murphy, 1933).

8.18 Yiddish Talking Pictures' *Uncle Moses* (Sidney M. Goldin, 1932): Maurice Schwartz, as a wealthy sweatshop owner, in the title role.

Harlem U.S.A., 1946; *Juke Joint*, 1947). As black films grew closer to mainstream Hollywood product in both content and form by the early 1940s, the concept of the race film as an entirely separate mode began to disappear, preparing the way for post–World War II black independent production on a scale previously inconceivable.

A second important type of ethnic filmmaking during the 1930s was Yiddish cinema.[7] Beginning in tsarist Russia as an offshoot of Yiddish theater, Yiddish film came to America on the eve of World War I, with the New York Yiddish stage (especially the plays of Jacob Gordin) providing much of its material. After the war, Yiddish cinema was carried forward by sporadic production in the newly created states of Poland, Austria, and the Soviet Union, adapting the work of Jewish novelists like Sholom Aleichem and Isaac Babel. All of these films were silent with Yiddish-language intertitles, but the coming of sound created a boom that resulted in the production of nearly three hundred Yiddish films worldwide over the next decade, about fifty of them in the United States.

The first Yiddish talkie, *Ad Mosay* (*Until When*; released as *The Eternal Prayer*, 1929), was directed by Sidney M. Goldin (1880–1937), known as the "grandfather of Yiddish cinema" owing to his production of such Jewish independent three-reel features as *The Sorrows of Israel, Bleeding Hearts*, and *The Black 107* (all 1913). The "father" of Yiddish cinema would have to be Joseph Seiden, the owner of New York's first sound-equipment rental company, who brought Goldin together with sev-

eral theater owners to form Judea Pictures Corporation in late 1929. Judea's first features, *Mayn Yiddishe Mame* (*My Jewish Mama*) and *Eybike Naronim* (*Eternal Fools*), both directed by Goldin in 1930, were followed by a series of shorts featuring the best-known choirs and cantors of the day (the "cantorial short" became a popular form of early Yiddish sound film) and a compilation of such material entitled *The Voice of Israel* (1931). Another popular form was the Yiddish compilation film, pioneered by director/editor George Roland in *Joseph in the Land of Egypt* and *Yidishe Tokhter* (*Jewish Daughter*), both 1933, which combined footage from silent foreign features with Yiddish sound narration. As the demand for Yiddish films grew, Goldin left Judea to direct for a number of other New York producers, making *Zayn Vaybs Lubovnik* (*His Wife's Lover*, 1931) for High Art, *Uncle Moses* (1932) for Yiddish Talking Pictures, and finally *Dem Khazns Zundl* (*The Cantor's Son*, 1937) for Eron.

---

7. Yiddish is a Germanic language with heavy borrowings from Hebrew and Slavic that is written in Hebrew characters. As the vernacular of Eastern European Jewish communities before World War II and emigrant communities all over the world, it was once spoken by 12 million people.

8.20 Edgar G. Ulmer's *Green Fields* (1937): Helen Beverly, Michael Goldstein, Herschel Bernardi.

8.19 Joseph Green's Polish Yiddish features: *Yiddle with the Fiddle* (codirected with Jan Nowina-Przybylski, 1936): Molly Picon in the title role; and *The Dybbuk* (Michal Waszynski, 1937): Lili Liliana as Leah, a young woman possessed by the spirit of a dead student.

Meanwhile, Seiden had formed another company, Jewish Talking Pictures, to produce such features as *Der Yidishe Kinig Lir* (*The Jewish King Lear* [Harry Thomashefsky, 1935]) and *Ikh Vil Zayn a Mame* (*I Want to Be a Mama* [George Roland, 1937]), and producer-director Henry Lynn had entered the field with *Der Yidishe Foter* (*The Jewish Father*, 1934), *Bar Mitzve* (1935), and *Vu Iz Mayn Kind?* (*Where Is My Child?*, 1937).

To varying degrees, these American Yiddish talkies were characterized by the same poor direction and technical ineptitude that afflicted race films—and for the same reasons. In 1936, however, the Polish-born producer Joseph Green went to Warsaw with the express purpose of making high-quality films for the Yiddish market. There he co-directed four films that became nodal points for the so-called Golden Age of Yiddish Cinema, 1936–40. Rich in Jewish theater, art, and culture, Poland was the ideal context for this revival, which produced many excellent films and several international hits, including Green's own *Yidl mitn Fidl* (*Yiddle with the Fiddle* [co-directed with Jan Nowina-Przybylski, 1936], *Dir Dibek* (*The Dybbuk* [Michal Waszynski, 1937]), and

A Brivele der Mamen (*A Letter to Mama* [Joseph Green and Leon Trystan, 1938]). Yiddish cinema in Poland reached its apex in the eighteen months before the Nazi invasion of September 1939, during which time fully eight of the twenty-three Yiddish films that opened in New York had been made in Warsaw. Influenced by the success of Joseph Green's Polish films, producer Roman Rebush brought the Golden Age to America by adapting Peretz Hirschbein's classic Yiddish play of life in the shtetl (Jewish ghetto), *Grine Felder* (*Green Fields*, 1937). Under the direction of Hollywood veteran Edgar G. Ulmer, *Green Fields* became a commercial hit not only with Yiddish-speaking audiences, but with the public at large (like many Yiddish films, it was subtitled in English), and Rebush followed it with another film based on the Eastern European Jewish experience—*Der Zingendiker Shmid* (*The Singing Blacksmith*, 1938)—adapted from a Yiddish play by David Pinski and directed by Ulmer. Afterward, Ulmer struck out on his own, directing two more Yiddish features—the expressionistic *Di Klyatshe* (*The Dobbin*; released in English as *The Light Ahead*, 1939) and the low-budget comedy *Amerikaner Shadkhn* (*American Matchmaker*, 1940).[8] The Yiddish "quality"

8. During the late 1930s, Ulmer made his living as a freelance ethnic director. In addition to his four films in Yiddish (which, although he was a Czech-born Jew, he never fully learned to speak), Ulmer made two Ukrainian films (*Natalka Poltavka*, 1937, and *Zaporozhets zu Dunayem*

8.21 Leo Fuchs (left) as the *American Matchmaker* (1940), Ulmer's last Yiddish film.

cycle ended with *Mirele Efros* (Josef Berne, 1939), *Tevye der Milkhier* (*Tevye the Milkman* [Maurice Schwartz, 1939]), and *Der Vilner Shtot Khazn* (*The Vilna Cantor*; released as *Overture to Glory* [Max Nosseck, 1940]), all adapted from Yiddish literature. Joseph Seiden continued to produce low-budget Yiddish movies for the next two years, and a handful of Yiddish films were made in the postwar era, but the audience for Yiddish cinema by then had largely vanished—in the United States through assimilation and in Europe through destruction in the Holocaust.

Major Figures of the Studio Era

The period 1930 to 1939 saw the production of some five thousand feature films in the United States and was, in many ways, a Golden Age for the American cinema. Despite the rigors and impersonality of the Hollywood production system, at least four directors working in America in the 1930s emerged as major figures of the sound film. They were Josef von Sternberg, John Ford, Howard Hawks, and Alfred Hitchcock.

JOSEF VON STERNBERG

Born Jonas Stern in Vienna, Josef von Sternberg (1894–1969) began his career in the United States during World

War I as a maker of training and indoctrination films for the Army Signal Corps. He spent his apprenticeship as a technical assistant, scenarist, and cameraman for a variety of filmmakers in America and England before directing his first film, the independently produced *The Salvation Hunters*, in 1925. Constructed according to the principles of the German *Kammerspielfilm* and strongly influenced by the psychological naturalism of von Stroheim, whose *The Wedding March* (1928) he would later re-edit for Paramount, this highly symbolic tale of low life on the San Pedro mudflats was shot on location in three weeks for the extremely small sum of $4,500. Distributed by UA, *The Salvation Hunters* established von Sternberg as an important new director in Hollywood.

In 1927, after several failed attempts at films for Charlie Chaplin (*The Sea Gull*, 1926) and MGM (*The Exquisite Sinner*, 1926), von Sternberg went to work for Paramount, where he made *Underworld* (1927), generally considered to be the first modern gangster film, although its realism was tempered by the lush visual poetry which would soon become a von Sternberg trademark. Based on a contemporary story idea by Ben Hecht,[9] this sumptuously photographed film was an immediate international success and had a great influence on European directors, especially Jacques Prévert, Marcel Carné, and Julien Duvivier (whose work will be explored in Chapter 9) in its treatment of the gangster as modern antihero. *Underworld* was so popular that it made von Sternberg and everyone connected with it world-famous. In 1928, after directing Emil Jannings in an immensely successful melodrama of the Russian Revolution entitled *The Last Command*, von Sternberg returned to *Kam-*

[*Cossacks in Exile*, 1938]), one all-black feature (*Moon over Harlem*, 1939), and a series of three shorts for the National Tuberculosis Association featuring African Americans (*Let My People Live*, 1938), Mexican Americans (*Cloud in the Sky*, 1939), and Native American Navajos (*Another to Conquer*, 1940).

9. Ben Hecht (1894–1964) was a journalist and playwright who collaborated with Charles MacArthur (1895–1956) on some of the best Hollywood screenplays of the 1930s, including an adaptation of their own popular stage play *The Front Page* (1931); *Scarface* (1932, Hecht solo); *Twentieth Century* (1934); *Soak the Rich* (1936); *Nothing Sacred* (1937, Hecht solo); and *Wuthering Heights* (1939). In the 1940s, Hecht worked on his own for Hitchcock (*Spellbound*, 1945; *Notorious*, 1946) and for numerous other directors into the 1950s and 1960s. (Howard Hawks collaborated on the *Underworld* script with Hecht but did not receive screen credit.)

8.22 Marlene Dietrich as Lola-Lola in Josef von Sternberg's *Der blaue Engel* (1930).

merspielfilm with *The Docks of New York*. This brooding tale of an encounter between a ship's stoker and a prostitute along the New York waterfront is renowned as a masterpiece of pictorial composition. The film was produced entirely in the studio, and its visually complex *mise-en-scène* creates a dreamlike atmosphere, reminiscent of Griffith's *Broken Blossoms* (1919), which was resurrected a decade later in Carné and Prévert's *Quai des brûmes* (*Port of Shadows*, 1938).

Von Sternberg made the transition to sound with the realistic gangster/prison drama *Thunderbolt* in 1929, and in that year he was summoned to Germany by Erich Pommer to direct, for UFA, Emil Jannings's first talking picture, a version of Heinrich Mann's novel *Professor Unrat* (1905); it became the first real classic of the sound film, *Der blaue Engel* (*The Blue Angel*, 1930). Adapted from the novel by von Sternberg, *Der blaue Engel* is a powerful film on the theme of sexual domination in which a middle-aged bourgeois teacher, played by Jannings, becomes enslaved to a sensual cabaret singer named Lola-Lola. The singer was played by Marlene Dietrich, a stage and film actress under contract to UFA whom von Sternberg chose for the part and subsequently brought to stardom in America. *Der blaue Engel* is striking for its creative use of sound and its impressive re-creation of the sleazy atmosphere of cabaret life; it owed a great deal in this regard to the *Kammerspiel* tradition. But it is also the film in which von Sternberg first began his career-long struggle with the problem of "dead space," that is, the space that separates the camera from its subject and the

subject from its background. (Initially, as in *Der blaue Engel*, he attempted to occupy this space with a variety of streamers, nets, posters, veils, and even cardboard cutouts hanging from the ceiling above the stage,[1] but in his later films he realized that only by thickening the air with camera filters, diffusers, and gauzes could he achieve the gradations of light necessary to fill the screen as he wished.) Though Dr. Alfred Hugenberg, the right-wing head of UFA, denounced the film as an attack on the German bourgeoisie (which it was), *Der blaue Engel* was an instant international success.

In 1930, von Sternberg returned with Dietrich to the United States to begin the series of six films for Paramount that were to make her one of Hollywood's most glamorous and sought-after stars and simultaneously to wreck his career. The first of these was the successful *Morocco* (1930), the story of a romance between a European cabaret singer and a Foreign Legionnaire in Mogador, North Africa, written by Jules Furthman (1888–1966). Photographed by Lee Garmes and designed by Hans Dreier, *Morocco* presents Dietrich in all of her seductive, androgynous charm, and was one of the most innovative of early American sound films. Upon its release, Sergei Eisenstein, then visiting Hollywood, sent von Sternberg a telegram stating: "Of all your great works, *Morocco* is the most beautiful." After making a sardonic and not particularly inspired spy thriller, *Dishonored* (1931), set in prewar Vienna, von Sternberg directed a low-budget version of Theodore Dreiser's novel *An American Tragedy* (1931), a project originally meant for Eisenstein but abandoned when studio executives found his treatment too "political." Characteristically, von Sternberg turned Dreiser's great work of social criticism into a tale of erotic obsession, much to the disgust of the author.[2] By this time, von Sternberg's reputation had grown so large that his name was appearing on theater marquees with the

---

1. Cinematographer Günther Rittau (1893–1971) was able to give these images (as well as those of Dietrich's face) a diffusely luminous quality without sacrificing depth of field through the use of a "Rosher bulls-eye"—a customized soft-focus lens given to him by the American cinematographer Charles Rosher (1885–1974) during the latter's term as consultant on UFA's *Faust* (Murnau, 1926).

2. Paramount produced yet another version in 1951 as *A Place in the Sun*, with George Stevens directing. Though this film is closer to the tragedy of entrapment contained in the novel, its lush romanticism (for which it won six Academy Awards) would probably have pleased Dreiser (1871–1945) even less than von Sternberg's eroticism.

titles of his films—a rare practice in the United States at that time—and he was frequently ranked with Eisenstein as one of the foremost directors of the era.

With *Shanghai Express* (1932), written by Furthman, von Sternberg entered his richest period of creativity. Herman G. Weinberg has called this film "high cinema-baroque," and it is certainly one of the most visually evocative that the director ever made. It concerns the interactions of a group of passengers on an express train running from Peking to Shanghai that is hijacked by a rebellious warlord, and it focuses on a glamorous pros-titute, Shanghai Lily (Dietrich), and her former lover, a glacial British army officer played by Clive Brook. Essentially a melodrama of deception and desire, *Shang-hai Express* is a film in which decor becomes a theme in itself. From the hypnotic chiaroscuro photography of Lee Garmes, the incredibly exotic costumes of Travis Banton, and the lavish production design of Hans Dreier, von Sternberg created a mythological China where "dead space" is virtually absent. The tour-de-force opening sequence in which the train leaves the chaotic, flag-draped Peking station, the poetic encounters between Dietrich and Brook on the observation deck of the express, and the long lateral tracking shots down the latticed corridors of the cars themselves—all con-structed in the studio—achieve a visual saturation rare outside of German Expressionism and the later work of Eisenstein.

Von Sternberg's next Dietrich vehicle was the bizarre *Blonde Venus* (1932), another stylistically striking film with a weak narrative concerning the broken life of yet

8.24 Dietrich in von Sternberg's *Blonde Venus* (1932).

8.25 *Shanghai Express:* Dietrich, Warner Oland, Clive Brook.

8.23 "High cinema-baroque": Anna May Wong and Dietrich in von Sternberg's *Shanghai Express* (1932).

8.26 Von Sternberg's *The Scarlet Empress* (1934): Dietrich as Catherine the Great, with John Lodge.

another beautiful cabaret singer. (Dietrich's "Hot Voo-doo" production number in this film may well contain the most outrageous variation upon the "beauty and the beast" metaphor in the history of modern culture: she comes onstage as a snarling gorilla and strips off the costume slowly, piece by piece, to reveal her own blonde loveliness and another costume of feathers and sequins beneath.) Then followed a fantastic and beautiful film "based on episodes from the private diaries of Catherine the Great," *The Scarlet Empress* (1934). This film re-created eighteenth-century Russia with as much poetic license as *Shanghai Express* had re-created contemporary China, and yet was visually more sumptuous than the original could have ever been. With grotesque statues and gargoyles by the Swiss sculptor Peter Ballbusch, Byzan-tinesque icons and portraits by the German painter Rich-ard Kollorsz, impossibly magnificent costumes by Travis Banton, and perhaps the most lavish production design ever undertaken by Hans Dreier, *The Scarlet Empress* apotheosized Dietrich as the ultimate symbol of sexual domination and degradation. The operatic grandeur and massive scale of the film are thought to have influenced Eisenstein's stylized design for *Ivan the Terrible, Parts I* (1945) and *II* (1946). Enormously expensive to produce, *The Scarlet Empress* failed at the box office (predictably so in a year whose smash hit was Frank Capra's populist fantasy *It Happened One Night*), and its director's favored status at Paramount was abruptly ended. Von Sternberg's final film with Dietrich for the studio and the one that

virtually ended his career was *The Devil Is a Woman* (1935), based on the novel *La femme et le pantin* (*Woman and Puppet*, 1898) by the decadent French romanticist Pierre Louÿs.[3] It tells the now familiar Sternbergian tale of a middle-aged man—this time an aristocratic member of the Spanish Civil Guard at the turn of the century—who is dominated and humiliated by a temptress. Thought by many critics to be among the most beautiful films ever made, *The Devil Is a Woman* is the only film for which von Sternberg took credit for cinematography (with Lucien Ballard), although he had supervised the photography and lighting of all his other films. In it, he achieved the ultimate in his attempt to make the two-dimensional cinema frame three-dimensional by filling dead space with decor and subtle gradations of light.

Sadly, *The Devil Is a Woman* was suppressed by Paramount shortly after its release due to protests by the Spanish government that it insulted the Spanish armed forces; it was not resurrected until after World War II. Simultaneously, the sympathetic B. P. Schulberg (1892–1957) left his post as production manager of Paramount to go to work for Columbia and was replaced by Ernst Lubitsch, who had a deep personal and cultural antipathy toward von Sternberg. This was the end for the director. Destroyed by his refusal to compromise with the studio system and by his own profligate style, his contract was canceled, and von Sternberg and Dietrich went their separate ways. Following a wretched term at Columbia during which he directed a limp modern version of Dos-toevsky's *Crime and Punishment* (1935) and a silly Grace Moore vehicle entitled *The King Steps Out* (1936), both gorgeously photographed by Ballard, von Sternberg went to London to direct an epic version of Robert Graves's novel *I, Claudius* for Alexander Korda. This star-crossed production failed financially and aesthetically at midpoint and was never completed, though the surviving footage, preserved in the BBC television documentary *The Epic That Never Was* (1966), confirms von Sternberg's pho-tographic genius. Returning to America, von Sternberg directed a low-grade police thriller for MGM entitled *Sergeant Madden* (1939) and the independently pro-

---

3. Also the source for the opera *Conchita* (1911) by Riccardo Zandonai, the operetta *Frasquita* (1922) by Franz Lehár, and two other films—Julien-Duvivier's *La femme et le pantin* (English title: *A Woman Like Satan*, 1958) and Luis Buñuel's *Cet obscur objet du désir* (*That Obscure Object of Desire*, 1977).

duced *Shanghai Gesture* (1941), a baroque attempt to evoke the stylish eroticism of the Paramount-Dietrich cycle in 1940s terms. After a graceful documentary short on American cultural values for the Office of War Information (see pp. 368–70) called *The Town* (1944), several abortive projects in the late 1940s, and an unhappy two-picture contract with RKO that produced *Jet Pilot* (1951; released 1957, with sequences reshot by Jules Furthman and Howard Hughes) and *Macao* (1952, with retakes directed by Nicholas Ray), von Sternberg ended his career with the Japanese-American coproduction *The Saga of Anatahan* (1953). This unusual film, the only one over which the director had total artistic control, tells the story of the tensions between twelve Japanese sailors shipwrecked on an isolated Pacific jungle island and a man and his mistress—an Asian variant of the typical Sternbergian seductress—who already inhabit the atoll. Produced, directed, photographed, designed, written, and narrated by von Sternberg alone, *The Saga of Anatahan* was shot in black and white, in a lush artificial jungle constructed on a soundstage in Kyoto. It is utterly appropriate that the last film by this master of cinematic artifice should have been made in a studio, when real jungles were available not far away.

The British documentarist John Grierson objected to one of von Sternberg's more visually extravagant productions by remarking in a contemporary review, "When a director dies, he becomes a photographer." (Von Sternberg *was*, in fact, a photographer, having begun as a cameraman and having maintained his membership in the prestigious American Society of Cinematographers throughout his career.) Von Sternberg would have considered this a compliment because, for him, the image was the only true medium of cinematic art. Strongly influenced by graphic art, his greatest films constituted a kind of painting with light. It is fruitless to maintain that his plots are trivial or frivolous because von Sternberg was not attempting to create a narrative cinema. In fact, he had little but contempt for the American tradition of narrative film as exemplified by the work of Griffith, Ince, and DeMille. On the contrary, von Sternberg's great achievement was to create *within* the American narrative cinema a cinema of mood and atmosphere based upon European styles of camera composition and lighting and his own eccentric vision of human passion and desire. It was a cinema of exoticism, eroticism, and, ultimately, cultural decadence, but one of astounding sensuous beauty that is unique in the history of film and modern art.

JOHN FORD

Like von Sternberg, John Ford (b. Sean Aloysius O'Feeney, 1895–1973) began his career in the silent film, but beyond that similarity it would be difficult to imagine two more different directors. Whereas von Sternberg had contempt for American narrative cinema and for American values, Ford was a staunch proponent of both. Whereas von Sternberg contributed to the cinema a handful of exotic and eccentric masterworks between 1927 and 1935, Ford directed over 125 films, most of them popular and commercial products of the studio system, in a career that extended from 1917 to 1970.

John Ford first came to Hollywood in 1914 to work as a prop man for his older brother, Francis (1881–1953), a **contract director** at Universal. From 1917 to 1921, as Jack Ford, he was employed by Universal as a director of low-budget Westerns and adventure dramas, including twenty-five films with the former silent star Harry Carey (1878–1947), only one of which—*Straight Shooting* (1917)—survives. In 1922 he went to work for Fox, winning fame as a stylist with *The Iron Horse* (1924), a feature-length epic on the building of the first transcontinental railroad that became a smash hit, and a sweeping drama of the Dakota land rush entitled *Three Bad Men* (1926), which did not. In 1927, deeply impressed by the Fox-produced *Sunrise*, Ford fell under the influence of F. W. Murnau and made a series of films—*Mother Machree, Four Sons, Hangman's House* (all 1928)—replete with expressive decor, stylized lighting effects, and elaborate moving camera shots in imitation of the German director. Murnau's realist-Expressionist influence is also evident in Ford's first talking features, *The Black Watch* (1929),[4] which has been described by one critic as a "neo-Wagnerian music-

---

4. Fox, of course, was instrumental in the innovation of sound, and Ford directed both the studio's first dramatic talkie (*Napoleon's Barber* [1928], a three-reeler that has been lost) and its first on-screen song (in *Mother Machree*). *Mother Machree* and *Four Sons* both were released with music and synchronized sound effects. *The Black Watch*, which was Fox's top-grossing film of 1929, was remade by the studio in 1954 in CinemaScope as *King of the Khyber Rifles* (Henry King).

drama," but Ford's first major sound film was the lost *Men without Women* (1930), a submarine drama in which one man must die to save the rest of the crew. For this film, Ford used a real submarine and submerged his camera underwater in a glass box, among other innovative techniques. It also marked the beginning of Ford's long and fruitful collaboration with the scenarist Dudley Nichols[5] and the cameraman Joseph August (1890–1947) on many a successful project. Other notable Ford films of the early sound era were his version of Sinclair Lewis's novel *Arrowsmith* (1931), a critical and commercial hit produced by Samuel Goldwyn for UA; the Murnauesque *Air Mail* (1932), made for Universal and photographed by the frequent Murnau collaborator Karl Freund; his Fox "Americana" trilogy starring the famous humorist Will Rogers (1879–1935), *Dr. Bull* (1933), *Judge Priest* (1934), and *Steamboat 'round the Bend* (1935); and an RKO desert adventure called *The Lost Patrol* (1934). But he was not regarded as a major figure until *The Informer*, his first great critical success, cheaply and quickly produced for RKO in 1935. Adapted by Nichols from the 1925 novel by Liam O'Flaherty and ingeniously, if frugally, designed by Van Nest Polglase, it tells the symbol-laden story of an ignorant hulk of a man

who betrays a fellow member of the Irish Republican Army to the British for money during the Irish Rebellion of 1922 and is psychologically tormented by his act until the IRA finally kills him in retribution. The film was photographed by Joseph August in a brooding manner reminiscent of classical German Expressionism and the *Kammerspielfilm*, and much use was made of subjective camera techniques to portray the informer's tortured state of mind, as when a crumpled "wanted" poster for the friend he has betrayed appears to pursue him down a foggy Dublin street like his own guilty conscience. Though it looks somewhat less impressive today, *The Informer* became one of the most highly regarded films of the decade, winning unanimously the New York Film Critics' Award for Best Film of the Year and four awards from the Academy of Motion Picture Arts and Sciences— Best Direction, Ford; Best Actor, Victor McLaglen in the title role; Best Writing (i.e., Screenplay), Dudley Nichols; Best Score, Max Steiner. (Nichols refused his Oscar, becoming the first person ever to do so, and both Nichols and Ford boycotted the Awards cermony of 1936 to show their solidarity with the various Screen Guilds then involved in labor disputes with Academy producers.)[6]

---

5. Dudley Nichols (1895–1960) was another important scriptwriter of the 1930s and 1940s, working not only with Ford but also with Howard Hawks (*Bringing Up Baby*, 1938; *Air Force*, 1943); Fritz Lang (*Man Hunt*, 1941; *Scarlet Street*, 1945); and Jean Renoir (*Swamp Water*, 1941; *This Land Is Mine*, 1943).

6. The Academy of Motion Picture Arts and Sciences (AMPAS) was founded in 1927 by Louis B. Mayer and other film industry leaders— including Cecil B. DeMille, Douglas Fairbanks, and Mary Pickford, in their roles as producers—with the expressed purpose of advancing the educational, cultural, and technical standards of American movies. Its real, and, ultimately, unsuccessful, purpose was to combat trade unionism among the growing ranks of directors, technicians, and performers who were pressing for higher wages and better working conditions as filmmaking became one of the nation's largest industries. In 1937, in the wake of considerable negative publicity, the Academy officially removed itself from the arena of labor relations and concentrated in earnest on its annual awards for professional achievement and on technical research, helping to achieve within a decade the industry-wide standardization of everything from script format, to back projection, to the official shade of white in black-and-white panchromatic film (see David Bordwell, Janet Staiger, and Kristin Thompson, *The Classical Hollywood Cinema: Film Style and Mode of Production to 1960* (New York: Columbia University Press, 1985), pp. 258–61). The Academy's membership (originally 36, now over 5,000) is drawn from prominent individuals in every branch of the industry, and its chief function is, and

always has been, the annual presentation of "Oscars" (Academy Awards) for distinguished film achievement in the previous year. In actual practice, the correlation between Academy Awards and cinematic excellence is not at all precise. For one thing, the winning of Oscars involves a great deal more than prestige since they inevitably increase the earning power of the films and performers that receive them. Each year, expensive campaigns are mounted by studios and other financial backers to "lobby" Academy members for votes that can be translated into profit in the marketplace. (For a detailed account of Universal Pictures' $300,000 promotion to impress Academy members with the merits of *The Deer Hunter* [Michael Cimino, 1978], see *Advertising Age*, April 16, 1979, pp. 1, 80.) Furthermore, Hollywood is a closed and really rather small community, many of whose members have known one another for a long time. The Academy's judgment is often colored by personal sentiment, both positive and negative, and there is always the implicit bias that what is good for the community in material terms (financially successful films and film careers) is good in critical terms as well. In short, it would be a mistake to assume that Academy Awards invariably signal excellence in films or performances. In fact, the awards are probably best regarded as a company town's certification of the company product, and in this regard they do at least provide some indication of Hollywood's ever-changing image of itself as fabricator of American dreams. In addition to giving its annual awards, the Academy also maintains a large collection of printed matter relating to film, and an extensive film archive with screening facilities open to the public in Hollywood; retrospectives are common.

8.27 Aftermath of *The Hurricane* (John Ford, 1937): storm by James Basevi, sets by Richard Day and Alex Golitzen.

imprisoned for unwittingly treating Lincoln's assassin. RKO's *Mary of Scotland* (1936) was an intelligent political tragedy adapted by Nichols from the Maxwell Anderson play, but the same studio's *The Plough and the Stars* (1936) was an awkward version of the Sean O'Casey play about the Easter Rising of 1916, when a small group of IRA troops seized control of Dublin and held off the huge British garrison for twenty-four hours. Ford's most unusual film of the period, and certainly his most commercially successful, was *The Hurricane* (1937),[7] a Samuel Goldwyn–UA production that concerned the sadistic imprisonment of a South Seas islander by a brutal European governor and concluded with a spectacularly realized tropical storm.[8]

After this success, Ford was given projects with a more social and historical orientation than his action films had possessed. Fox's *The Prisoner of Shark Island* (1936) told the true story of the fate of Dr. Samuel Mudd, who was

The year 1939, however, witnessed the release of three of Ford's finest films. In *Stagecoach*, produced by Walter Wanger for UA, Ford returned to the Western for the first time in thirteen years and produced a film that was to revitalize the genre, largely in his own hands, for another twenty. Written by Dudley Nichols and photographed by Bert Glennon, this tale of a dangerous coach ride through hostile Indian territory by a group of misfits from every level of frontier society embodies what was to become a classical Fordian theme—the convolutions of human character under the pressure of extreme stress. Its stark and awesome setting in Monument Valley, Arizona—a location

8.28 *Stagecoach* (John Ford, 1939).

7. Remade, disastrously, under the same title by Jan Troell in 1979.

8. This sequence was created by the special-effects expert James Basevi (1890–1962), with the assistance of Stuart Heisler. Basevi, who worked with Ford as art director on seven subsequent films, was renowned in the 1930s for his disaster sequences, including (in collaboration with Arnold Gillespie) the famous earthquake in MGM's *San Francisco* (W. S. Van Dyke, 1936).

to which Ford would return time and time again—creates a symbolic landscape of the individual alone in an alien environment. The film was a great popular and critical success, receiving awards from both the New York Film Critics and the Academy of Motion Picture Arts and Sciences (it also made John Wayne [1907–1979] a star). At Fox again, Ford made *Young Mr. Lincoln*, whose formal qualities have been much admired in recent years; the film was a somber rendition of an original screenplay by Lamar Trotti and succeeded in raising the story of Lincoln's early career as a small-town lawyer to the level of national myth. Ford's final film of 1939, *Drums along the Mohawk*, dealt with yet another aspect of the American past. His first work in color, the film is a visually striking re-creation of the American revolutionary era in New York State that was shot on location in the forests of Utah's Wasatch Mountain.[9]

Ford's new burst of creative energy continued into the 1940s with *The Grapes of Wrath* (1940), perhaps the most important Hollywood film of the Depression era. Adapted by Nunnally Johnson (1897–1977) from the John Steinbeck novel, it concerns a family of dispossessed farmers migrating to California across the dust bowl of the Southwest during the Depression. Although the film sentimentalizes the suffering of the Joad family, it is notable for the stark documentary texture of its exteriors, achieved through the beautifully restrained camerawork of the cinematographer Gregg Toland. Like *The Informer* and *Stagecoach, The Grapes of Wrath* was recognized as a distinguished film by both the New York Film Critics and the American Academy (although Ford himself never particularly liked it). After lukewarm adaptations of Eugene O'Neill's play *The Long Voyage Home* (1940, Walter Wanger–UA—Ford's only non-Fox film until the postwar period)[1] and Erskine Caldwell's novel *Tobacco Road* (1940), Ford directed his last commercial film before World War II, *How Green Was My Valley* (1941), adapted from the novel by Richard Llewellyn. This romantic and nostalgic film, for which an elaborate Welsh village was constructed on the 20th Century–Fox back lot, deals with the disintegration of a Welsh mining family and the communal society in which it lives at the turn of the century; in the year of *Citizen Kane*, it won five Academy Awards.[2]

During the war, Ford joined the navy and made documentaries for the Office of Strategic Services (OSS),

8.29 The Welsh mining village in *How Green Was My Valley* (John Ford, 1941).

including the famous *Battle of Midway* (1942, theatrically released by Fox), which he photographed himself from a water tower during the Japanese air attack, winning the Purple Heart (he was wounded in his left arm) and an Academy Award for Best Documentary in the process. Ford became chief of the Field Photographic Services of the OSS (which later became the CIA), supervising the production of such restricted and/or classified films as *How to Operate behind Enemy Lines, How to Interrogate Enemy Prisoners, Living off the Land, Nazi Industrial Manpower, Inside Tibet*, etc., as well as filmed reports on battle conditions, Allied defenses, bombing raids, and landings. In addition to *The Battle of Midway*, Ford personally codirected *December 7th* (1943) with cinematographer Gregg Toland, which went unreleased in its original eighty-five-minute version, but whose thirty-five-

---

9. Original plans to shoot on location in the Mohawk Valley had to be scrapped when it was learned that industrialization had completely destroyed the landscape.

1. *The Long Voyage Home*, was, however, distinguished by Toland's deep-focus cinematography and was the first film before *Citizen Kane* (1941—also shot by Toland) in which composition in depth appears as a consistent visual style (see p. 321).

2. Best Picture, Best Director, Best Supporting Actor (Donald Crisp, as the father), Best Cinematography—Black-and-White (Arthur Miller), Best Art Direction—Black-and-White (Richard Day, Nathan Juran, and Thomas Little).

minute recut won the 1943 Academy Award—Ford's fourth Oscar—for Best Documentary.[3]

Ford's first postwar film, *They Were Expendable* (1945, MGM), was a moving tribute to the unstinting courage and discipline of the men with whom he had served. Exquisitely photographed by Joseph August, it tells the story of the sailors who pioneered the use of the PT boat during the American evacuation of the Philippines, and it is one of Ford's most intensely personal films. His next film, *My Darling Clementine* (1946, Fox), is among the most classically beautiful Westerns ever made. It concerns the events leading up to the legendary gunfight between the Earp brothers, here assisted by Doc Holliday, and the Clanton family at the OK Corral in Tombstone, Arizona; and it contains scenes of frontier communal life (like the lyrical dedication ceremony of Tombstone's first church) that are among Ford's most visually poetic creations.

In March 1946, like several other major Hollywood directors, Ford formed his own production company, Argosy Pictures Corporation, with the producer Merian C. Cooper ([1894–1973] *Grass*, 1925; *Chang*, 1927; *King Kong*, 1933; *The Last Days of Pompeii*, 1935; etc.).[4] Its first film was the final Ford-Nichols collaboration—a version of Graham Greene's 1940 novel *The Power and the Glory* entitled *The Fugitive* (1947), coproduced by the distinguished Mexican director Emilio Fernández (1904–1986) and photographed by his cameraman Gabriel Figueroa (1907–1997), which in both theme and technique was reminiscent of *The Informer*. Like its predecessor, *The Fugitive* lost money, and Ford shot a series of brilliantly mythic Westerns on location in Monument Valley to recoup his losses, including the so-called Cavalry trilogy—Fort *Apache* (1948), which inaugurated Ford's long association with the screenwriter Frank S. Nugent,[5] *She Wore a Yellow Ribbon* (1949), and *Rio Grande* (1950)—and *Wagon Master* (1950). These, together with his final Argossy films—*The Quiet Man* (1952), a nostalgic paean to Irish village life shot on location at the Feeney family homestead in Connemara, and *The Sun Shines Bright* (1953), a picaresque remake of *Judge Priest*, which was the director's favorite film—stand today among Ford's finest achievements.[6]

After Argossy was dissolved, Ford returned to working for the studios and produced some extraordinary films—the African adventure *Mogambo* (1953, MGM), a remake of Victor Fleming's *Red Dust* (1932); *The Long Gray Line* (1955, Columbia), a biography of West Point athletic trainer Marty Maher and Ford's first film in Cinema-Scope; and, pre-eminently, the epic questing/captivity narrative *The Searchers* (1956, Warners), widely regarded today as one of the greatest Westerns ever made. There

---

3. For a detailed account of Ford's obsession with the military and his own military career, see Andrew Sinclair's biography *John Ford* (New York: Dial/James Wade, 1979); for a more intimate portrait, see his grandson Dan Ford's *Pappy: The Life of John Ford* (Englewood Cliffs, N.J.: Prentice-Hall, 1979); and on the OSS films themselves, see Tag Gallagher, *John Ford: The Man and His Films* (Berkeley: University of California Press, 1986).

4. In the euphoric atmosphere of the postwar boom, amid speculation that the federal courts were going to break up the studio system's monopoly, a number of important filmmakers attempted to achieve independence (and, less nobly, to exploit capital-gains loopholes in the Revenue Act of 1945) by forming their own companies—among them Frank Capra, William Wyler, and George Stevens (Liberty Films, 1945–47); Fritz Lang (Diana Productions, 1945–47); Alfred Hitchcock (Transatlantic Pictures, 1946–48); and Howard Hawks (Monterey Productions, 1946–47; Winchester Pictures Corporation, 1950–52). Like Argossy, they proved no match for the majors, even after the divestiture ordered by the Paramount decrees of 1948, although by the late 1950s independent production had come into its own (see pp. 425–27).

5. Frank S. Nugent (1908–1966), a former newspaper critic and script doctor, collaborated with Ford on ten subsequent films, including *Three Godfathers* (1949), *She Wore a Yellow Ribbon* (1949), *Wagon-master* (1950), *The Quiet Man* (1952), *Mister Roberts* (1955—a troubled production only nominally directed by Ford), *The Searchers* (1956), *The Rising of the Moon* (1957), *The Last Hurrah* (1958), *Two Rode Together* (1961), and *Donovan's Reef* (1963). Nugent also worked occasionally for other directors—never with the same degree of success—on films with Fordian themes, e.g., Stuart Heisler (*Tulsa*, 1948), Otto Preminger (*Angel Face*, 1953), Raoul Walsh (*The Tall Men*, 1955), and Phil Karlson (*They Rode West*, 1954; *Gunman's Walk*, 1958).

6. Although *The Quiet Man* was Ford's biggest box-office hit to date, grossing nearly $4 million on an investment less than half the size, and won Oscars both for direction and color cinematography (to Winton C. Hoch), its success was not enough to prevent Argossy's dissolution in 1953. In its seven-year existence, it had produced eight Ford films (the seven noted, plus the Western comedy-drama *Three Godfathers* [1949], which is dedicated to Harry Carey and stars his son), and *Mighty Joe Young* (Ernest B. Schoedsack, 1949), a revamping of *King Kong* with Academy Award–winning special effects by Willis O'Brien and Ray Harryhausen.

8.30 A communal celebration in _My Darling Clementine_ (John Ford, 1946): Cathy Downs, Henry Fonda.

Warners), a trilogy of Irish tales shot on location and performed by the Abbey Theatre Players; the London police procedural _Gideon's Day_ (1958, Columbia British);[7] _The Last Hurrah_ (1958, Columbia), a film of Boston politics adapted from the best-selling novel by Edwin O'Conner; a disjointed Civil War epic called _The Horse Soldiers_ (1959, the Mirisch Corporation–UA), based on an actual Union cavalry raid into the deep South in 1863; _Sergeant Rutledge_ (1960, Warners), a courtroom drama about a black cavalryman on trial for the rape and murder of a white woman, narrated in flashback and shot in Expressionistic color by Bert Glennon; _Two Rode Together_ (1961, Columbia), a sort of pessimistic inversion of _The Searchers_ about the ransoming of some white captives from the Comanches. In his later life, Ford had clearly lost interest in certain formal aspects of his art, and, until recently, the period 1962 to 1965 was viewed as one of continuing decline. Several critics now maintain, however, that Ford's last work was his greatest and approaches the sublime. This could certainly be argued of the elegiac, meditative Westerns _The Man Who Shot Liberty Valence_ (1962) and _Cheyenne Autumn_ (1964), although the apparent excesses of _Donovan's Reef_ (1963) and _Seven Women_ (1965) make them more difficult to see in this light.

Sometimes racist (the Indians in his Westerns are either bloodthirsty devils or noble savages—but always, with the notable exception of _Cheyenne Autumn_, formidable opponents), frequently sentimental, and always culturally conservative, John Ford was nevertheless a great American director. His accommodation with the studio system did not prevent him from making films of great technical virtuosity and strong personal vision that are admired for their classicism all over the world.[8] In his Westerns, he created a coherent mythology of the American past that brings him close to Griffith—for both men, in fact, history was the embodiment of moral rather than

were other interesting, if increasingly uneven, films—_The Wings of Eagles_ (1957, MGM), an oddly incohesive biography of Ford's friend Spig Wead, a World War I flying ace who became a Hollywood screenwriter after being paralyzed by an accident; _The Rising of the Moon_ (1957,

8.31 _The Horse Soldiers_ (John Ford, 1959): John Wayne. Compositions like this one influenced Japanese director Akira Kurosawa (see pp. 834–42).

---

7. A film whose expressive use of color we have been denied by Columbia's decision to release the film (retitled _Gideon of Scotland Yard_) in black-and-white rather than go to the expense of striking color prints. See Tag Gallager, _John Ford: The Man and His Films_ pp. 358–63, on the Technicolor version.

8. Among the filmmakers who have acknowledged Ford's influence are Sergei Eisenstein, V. I. Pudovkin, Orson Welles, Frank Capra, Howard Hawks, Ingmar Bergman, Mark Donskoi, Akira Kurosawa, Elia Kazan, Douglas Sirk, Samuel Fuller, Budd Boetticher, Lindsay Anderson, Jean-Marie Straub, Peter Bogdanovich, John Milius, Bertrand Tavernier, and Peter Weir.

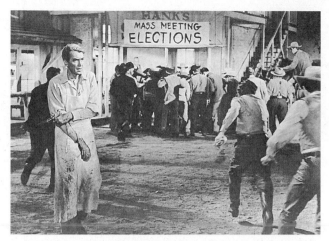

8.32 *The Man Who Shot Liberty Valance* **(John Ford, 1962): James Stewart as Ransom Stoddard.**

empirical truth, and their visions of the past do not often conform to fact. Historical inaccuracy notwithstanding, all of Ford's major films sustain a worldview based upon his admiration for the traditional values of community life—for honor, loyalty, discipline, and, finally, courage—and it is a worldview as consistent and compelling as any the cinema has to offer.

HOWARD HAWKS

Another important director who dealt with typically American themes was Howard Hawks (1896–1977). Less

a stylist than either von Sternberg or Ford, Hawks characteristically concerned himself with the construction of tough, functional narratives that embodied his personal ethic of professionalism, quiet courage, and self-respect. He directed forty-three features,[9] contributing major films to every popular American genre, during a career that spanned nearly half a century.

Hawks had been an aviator in World War I before entering the cinema in 1919 as a prop man for the Mary Pickford Company. Between 1920 and 1925, he rose to editor, scriptwriter, and, finally, assistant director, before leaving to work as a contract director for the Fox Film Corporation. He made seven silent films at Fox, one of which, *A Girl in Every Port* (1928), was modestly successful in France, but Hawks's career did not begin in earnest until the arrival of sound, when he began to work independently of long-term studio contracts. His first all-talking picture was First National's *The Dawn Patrol* (1930), a grim World War I drama about the awesome death toll among air-force flyers, which featured some splendid aerial photography. After a fine prison picture for Columbia, *The Criminal Code* (1931), and a motor-racing drama for Warners, *The Crowd Roars* (1932), Hawks directed his most important work of the early 1930s—the classic gangster film *Scarface*, produced by Howard Hughes for UA. Loosely based by screenwriter Ben Hecht upon the career of Al Capone and superbly photographed by Lee Garmes (1898–1978), this violent, cynical film portrays the rise and fall of a Chicago mobster named Tony Camonte whose gang is like a dynasty of murderous Renaissance princes.[1] *Scarface*, the greatest of the 1930s gangster films, marked the beginning of the brilliant Hecht-Hawks collaboration that was to continue throughout the decade. (They had, of course, worked earlier together on the script of von Sternberg's 1927 gang-

8.33 *Cheyenne Autumn* **(John Ford, 1964).**

9. Forty-six and one-fifth, if we count Hawks's three uncredited features—*The Prize Fighter and the Lady* (W. S. Van Dyke, 1933), *The Outlaw* (Howard Hughes, 1941), and *The Thing* (Christian Nyby, 1951)—plus "The Ransom of Red Chief," contribution to the five-part *O. Henry's Full House* (1952).

1. Hughes, who was very proud of the film, withdrew it from circulation several years later; it did not become available again until three years after his death, in 1979, when his Summa Corporation sold the rights to Universal (before that date, *Scarface* could be seen only in bootleg prints). Four years later, the studio produced an ultraviolent remake, directed by Brian De Palma, which set the story among Cuban drug smugglers in contemporary Miami.

ster film *Underworld*, which Garmes also photographed and whose visual texture is very similar to that of *Scarface*.)

The title card of *Scarface* claims that it is based on a novel by Armitage Trail, but there is little resemblance between the book and the film beyond their titles and their source of inspiration: Capone. The film, Hawks's favorite, was shot in 1930 but not released for two years, while Hughes fought with the Hays Office (MPPDA) over cuts. The film was finally released in 1932, but only after some scenes were expurgated, a moralistic conclusion and several inserts added, and the title changed to *Scarface, Shame of a Nation*. Nevertheless, *Scarface* became a *cause célèbre* among those forces agitating for the imposition of the Production Code because of its violence and supposed amorality.

Hawks's next important project was *Viva Villa!* (1934), a distinguished MGM biopic written by Hecht and Hawks but completed by Jack Conway owing to the interference of Louis B. Mayer. But the subsequent Hecht-Hawks collaboration for Columbia, *Twentieth Century* (1934), was a smashing success. It tells the story of a tyrannical Broadway producer (John Barrymore) who spends the entire film, much of which takes place aboard the Twentieth Century Limited Express from Chicago to New York, attempting to cajole his estranged actress-wife (Carole Lombard) into appearing in his next show. With its rapid-fire dialogue and fast-paced editing, *Twentieth Century* became the prototype of the screwball comedies of the later 1930s and 1940s. Perhaps Hawks's most distinguished film of the 1930s was *The Road to Glory* (1936),[2] which ranks with Lewis Milestone's *All Quiet on the Western Front* (1930) and Stanley Kubrick's *Paths of Glory* (1957) and *Full Metal Jacket* (1987) as one of the American cinema's strongest antiwar statements. The film, produced by Darryl F. Zanuck for Fox, was the product of an unusual combination of talents. Directed by Hawks, written by William Faulkner and Joel Sayre (with the uncredited assistance of Hawks and Nunnally Johnson), photographed by Gregg Toland, and superbly acted by Fredric March and Warner Baxter, it tells a searing tale of the horrors of trench warfare during World War I and ultimately suggests that professionalism, comradeship, and devotion to duty are the only forces that will sustain men in such a brutally hostile environment.

A similar theme pervades *Only Angels Have Wings* (1939, Columbia), which Hawks wrote with Jules Furthman on the basis of his own experience as a flyer during World War I. Thought to be his most beautiful aviation film, this tale of a small commercial airline pioneering the delivery of airmail in Latin America is a classical Hawksian parable of the necessity of professionalism and esprit de corps in the face of daily peril and death. Hawks enlarged his contribution to the screwball comedy with the anarchic *Bringing Up Baby* (1938, RKO), which provided the model for Peter Bogdanovich's rather pallid *What's Up, Doc?* (1972, Warners), and *Ball of Fire* (1941, RKO).[3] He also successfully remade Lewis Milestone's *The Front Page* (1931) as *His Girl Friday* (1940, Columbia), replete with fast-paced overlapping dialogue, before returning to more serious themes in the quietly patriotic biography of America's greatest World War I hero, *Sergeant York* (1941), which, like his next three films, was produced for Warners.

During World War II, Hawks made the tough combat drama *Air Force* (1943), photographed with documentary-like realism by James Wong Howe, and the hard-boiled romantic melodrama *To Have and Have Not* (1944), adapted from an Ernest Hemingway novel by William Faulkner and Jules Furthman and teaming Humphrey Bogart for the first time with Lauren Bacall (in her screen debut). The couple also starred in Hawks's bizarre and atmospheric **film noir** *The Big Sleep* (1946), whose plot is so convoluted that even the director and his screenwriters (Faulkner, Furthman, and Leigh Brackett, working from the Raymond Chandler novel) claimed that they didn't understand it. Hawks's last serious film of the 1940s was the epic Western *Red River* (1948), which sets the psychological duel between a man (John Wayne) and his adopted son (Montgomery Clift) against the sweeping

2. Not to be confused with his 1926 directorial debut, which has the same title but a completely different subject. *The Road to Glory* (1936) was closely modeled on the French antiwar film *Les Croix de bois* (Wooden Crosses [Raymond Bernard, 1932]), which Fox had bought for its battle footage. Bruce Kawin informs me that there is a great deal of Bernard footage in the Hawks film, and that there are many sequences for which Hawks shot new material to match something in Bernard. Kawin also says that in matters of characterization and plot the original script of *The Road to Glory* was much closer to *Wooden Crosses* than the final film. For more, see Bruce F. Kawin, *Faulkner and Film* (New York: Ungar, 1977), pp. 88–95.

3. Remade by Hawks, not very happily, as the Danny Kaye–Virginia Mayo musical comedy *A Song Is Born* (1948, Goldwyn–RKO). Other remakes from Hawks include Lloyd Bacon's *Indianapolis Speedway*, (1939, from *The Crowd Roars*, with footage from same) and Michael Winner's soporific *The Big Sleep* (1975). On Hawks's unrealized film projects, see Todd McCarthy, "Phantom Hawks," *Film Comment* 18, 5 (September–October 1982): 63–76.

8.34 *Bringing Up Baby* (Howard Hawks, 1938): Cary Grant, Katharine Hepburn.

8.35 *To Have and Have Not* (Howard Hawks, 1944): Lauren Bacall, Humphrey Bogart.

backdrop of the first cattle drive from Texas to Kansas in 1865.[4] Hawks returned to comedy with three films for Fox: *I Was a Male War Bride* (1948) and *Monkey Business* (1952), which endeavored to resurrect the screwball genre, and the robust Technicolor musical *Gentlemen Prefer Blondes* (1953). In *The Big Sky* (1953), he

produced a modestly successful Western from a Dudley Nichols script,[5] and he continued to make films sporadically throughout the 1950s and 1960s. Most of these were disappointing in the light of his achievements of the 1930s and 1940s (for example, *Land of the Pharaohs* [1955]; *Man's Favorite Sport* [1964]; *Red Line 7000* [1965]; *Rio Lobo* [1970—his last film]), but several, such as the African adventure-comedy *Hatari!* (1962) and the Westerns *Rio Bravo* (1959) and *El Dorado* (1967), still contain the vital spark of hard-hitting, fast-paced Hawksian narrative.

Like one of his own heroes, Howard Hawks was a versatile professional who distinguished himself in every

---

4. Red River was Hawks's first and only film for his independent company Monterey Productions. Budgeted at $2 million, it was shot on location in 1947 and bankrupted Monterey by running $800,000 over cost. The film could not be released until 1948 because of injunctions threatened by the Teamster's Union, which represented Arizona cowhands owed $20,000 in back pay by Monterey when it went broke; by Pathé Film Laboratory, which had not been paid for processing; and by Howard Hughes, who claimed that Hawks had plagiarized the ending from his 1941 film, *The Outlaw*. When *Red River* was finally distributed in 1948, the ending had been re-edited (by Hughes! in order to placate him) and a voice-over narration added to shorten the running time by seven and one-half minutes to just under two hours. When United Artists rereleased the film several years later, it struck new prints from Hawks's original negative, which contained the unedited version of the ending and handwritten narration (from the pages of the book, *Early Tales of Texas*). When UA realized its error, Hawks advised them for legal reasons to reissue not his original but the Hughes-authorized release print, which was the only version available to the public until UA released the 132-minute Hawks version on video in 1987 through

CBS / Fox. See Gerald Mast, *Howard Hawks: Storyteller* (New York: Oxford University Press, 1982), pp. 337–46, for details.

5. One of two films produced by Hawks's second independent company, Winchester Pictures Corporation, for distribution by RKO. The other was the paradigmatic science-fiction film, *The Thing* (1951), nominally directed by Christian Nyby (1913–1993—Hawks's brilliant editor on *To Have and Have Not, The Big Sleep, Red River*, and *The Big Sky*), but clearly bearing the stylistic influence of Hawks. (*The Thing* was remade—horribly—by John Carpenter in 1982.) Hawks was also the uncredited director of Howard Hughes's production of *The Outlaw* (1941; released 1943). Though tame by contemporary standards, this notorious "sex-Western" challenged the MPPDA by including a rape scene and prominent footage of star Jane Russell's cleavage. After minor cuts and a protracted legal battle, *The Outlaw* was granted the PCA Seal of Approval but was withheld by Hughes for two years while he mounted a salacious, not to say sexist, advertising campaign for it, fetishizing Ms. Russell's breasts.

268 The Sound Film and the American Studio System

major American film genre and virtually inaugurated several of them. Having begun his career as a screenwriter, he worked on the script of almost every film he ever made. Hawks was not primarily a visual stylist—he generally composed his scenes into the eye-level medium shots[6] favored by the studios and worked within the frame as much as possible, avoiding both spectacular montage effects and self-conscious camera movement. As for lighting, he left it to his cameramen, who were among the most distinguished Hollywood has ever known: Gregg Toland, Lee Garmes, James Wong Howe, Tony Gaudio, Ernest Haller, Russell Harlan, and Sid Hickox. But Hawks was a great visual storyteller with an urbane wit and a nearly existential concern with the condition of men in extreme situations. His films are frequently characterized as "masculine," and there is no question that his heroes prize the company only of women who, like the characters played by Lauren Bacall, seem to share the code by which these men live. But it is probably more accurate to call his films simply "American," in the sense expressed by the French film archivist Henri Langlois: "He [Hawks] is the embodiment of modern man. It is striking how his cinema anticipates his time. An American he certainly is, no less than a Griffith or a Vidor, but the spirit and physical structure of his work is born from contemporary America and enables us to better and more fully identify with it, both in admiration and criticism."

ALFRED HITCHCOCK

The fourth major figure of the American sound film in this period was an Englishman trained within the British studio system, Alfred Hitchcock (1899–1980). Like Ford and Hawks, he was a brilliant craftsman; like von Sternberg, a subtle stylist. He spent most of his career working in a single genre—the suspense thriller—but his mastery of film form transformed and finally transcended it. Indeed, Andrew Sarris has called him the only contemporary director whose style unites the divergent classical traditions of Murnau (camera movement and *mise-en-scène*) and Eisenstein (montage). In the past two decades, moreover, Hitchcock has arrested the attention of critics and theorists of every imaginable hue, from conservative Roman Catholicism to radical poststructuralist feminism.

After receiving his formal education from the Jesuits at St. Ignatius College and working as a draftsman in the advertising department of a telegraph company, Hitchcock joined the London branch of Famous Players–Lasky at Islington as a title writer in 1921. He became a scriptwriter, set designer, and finally, assistant director; and when producer Michael Balcon bought the Islington studio to form Gainsborough Pictures in 1924, Hitchcock joined the company as a contract director. Because of a reciprocal agreement between Balcon and Erich Pommer of UFA, Hitchcock's first two features were made in German studios,[7] where he fell under the spell of Expressionism and *Kammerspielfilme*; this influence was to last throughout his silent period and linger on considerably beyond it. Appropriately, his first major success, *The Lodger* (subtitled *A Story of the London Fog*, 1926; released 1927),[8] was in the genre that he was to make so uniquely his own. This Expressionistic suspense thriller, based on Marie Belloc-Lowndes's sensational Jack the Ripper novel of the same title, earned Hitchcock a high reputation at the age of twenty-seven; and it already contained one of his most memorable effects: the pacing feet of a suspected murderer on the floor above shot through a 1-inch-thick plate-glass ceiling from the perspective of a family group seated below. The young director made six more silent films (two for Gainsborough—*Downhill*, 1927, and *Easy Virtue*, 1927; four for British International Pictures—*The Ring*, 1927; *The Farmer's Wife*, 1927, released 1928; *Champagne*, 1928; *The Manxman*, 1928, released 1929) before returning to the genre again in his—and Britain's—first talkie.

Blackmail (1929) was initially made as a silent film but reshot and partially dubbed as a sound film (the voice of the heroine, played by a Polish actress, had to be dubbed by the English actress Joan Barry) with some RCA Pho-

---

6. As Gerald Mast points out, this would be at the eye-level of a sitting onlooker, which is not so conventional after all since such shots establish a casual intimacy between characters and audience by aligning the camera's perspective with that of the spectator.

7. The melodramas *The Pleasure Garden* (1925; released 1927) and *The Mountain Eagle* (1925; lost film), both made for Emelka Studios–Munich and released in 1927. Shortly before producing these, Hitchcock had worked at UFA as art director on Gainsborough's *The Blackguard* (Graham Cutts, 1925). Here, Murnau was simultaneously shooting *The Last Laugh*, and the German director gave Hitchcock some pointers on the use of forced perspective that he immediately applied to his own work. See Donald Spoto, *The Dark Side of Genius: The Life of Alfred Hitchcock* (Boston: Little, Brown, 1983), pp. 77–104.

8. *The Lodger* was the first film in which Hitchcock made a brief walk-on appearance, an in-joke and, later, publicity ploy that would characterize all of his subsequent features, except *The Wrong Man* (1957), which he personally introduces in a brief prologue. In addition to being trademarks, however, these appearances offered a legitimate way for him to "sign" his work.

tophone equipment hastily imported from America by British International Pictures (BIP) president John Maxwell. It is one of the best films of its era, notable for its fluid camera style and its expressive use of both naturalistic and nonnaturalistic sound. Adapted from a popular play by Charles Bennett, the plot concerns a woman who is being blackmailed for the murder of an attempted rapist, and Hitchcock used the new medium of sound to inaugurate his characteristic theme of the nightmarish amid the commonplace. At one point, for example, the heroine's subjective feelings of guilt are conveyed by the seemingly endless clanging of a shop bell; later the word "knife," recalling the murder weapon, emerges from a harmless conversation to haunt her long after the conversation itself has become an indistinct murmur on the sound track. Hitchcock's freedom to achieve such creative effects arose from the necessity of postsynchronizing scenes that had already been shot silent. For the same reason, the action sequences of *Blackmail*, especially those of the first and last reels, manifest a fluidity quite remarkable for an early sound film. And *Blackmail* concludes with what would become a characteristic Hitchcock motif: a spectacularly realized chase through famous settings—in this case, the pursuit of the blackmailer by police across the dome of the British Museum.

After directing portions of a BIP musical review entitled *Elstree Calling* (1930) and an uninspired version of Sean O'Casey's *Juno and the Paycock* (1930), Hitchcock returned to the thriller form with *Murder* (1930; adapted by Alma Reville[9] from a play by Helen Simpson and Clemence Dane) and again proved himself an innovator in the creative use of sound. This story of a famous actor who,

8.37 The British Museum chase from the conclusion of *Blackmail*.

convinced of a condemned girl's innocence, solves a murder to prove it, contains the first improvised dialogue sequence, the first use of the sound track to convey a character's stream of consciousness (while a thirty-piece orchestra plays the Prelude to Wagner's *Tristan und Isolde*, supposedly issuing from the radio, offscreen), and many other experiments with nonnaturalistic sound, including a 360-degree pan while dialogue is spoken. Hitchcock was by now regarded as Britain's most important director. After three more BIP films of varying quality—an adaptation of John Galsworthy's talky social melodrama *The Skin Game* (1931); the parodic thriller *Number Seventeen* (1931; released 1932), which concludes with an ingenious train chase–collision sequence assembled from stock footage and model shots; *Rich and Strange* (1932), an episodic romantic comedy structured around a recently married couple's world cruise—and the independently produced *Waltzes from Vienna* (1933), a quite good musical about the Strauss family, he signed a five-film contract with Gaumont-British, where Michael Balcon had become production chief in 1931, and launched the series of thrillers that was to make him internationally famous. The first was *The Man Who Knew Too Much* (1934). This complicated and darkly Expressionistic film, the only one that Hitchcock ever remade, concerns a

8.36 Hitchcock on the set of *Blackmail* (1929), attempting to record Anny Ondra's voice. Note the camera enclosed in the soundproof booth.

9. Hitchcock's wife, Alma Reville (1899–1982), provided screenplays, adaptations, or continuities for many of his films from 1927 to 1950. She began her career as an editor at Famous Players–Lasky, Islington, where she met Hitchcock in 1923. They were married in 1926, and she became his lifetime collaborator, advisor, and companion. Their only child, Patricia (b. 1928), was an occasional actress who appeared in small roles in two of her father's films, *Strangers on a Train* (1951) and *Psycho* (1960).

8.38 *The Man Who Knew Too Much* (Alfred Hitchcock, 1934): the scream that prevents a murder in the Royal Albert Hall.

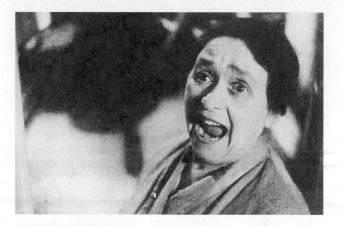

8.39 The famous sound match from *The 39 Steps* (1935).

couple on holiday in St. Moritz who learn of a plot to assassinate a visiting statesman in London. Their daughter is kidnapped by the assassins (led by Peter Lorre, who had become internationally famous as the child murderer in Fritz Lang's *M* [1931], in his first English-speaking role), and the couple must simultaneously recover their child and foil the murder plot without telling the police. The film is a classic Hitchcockian parable of horror asserting itself in the midst of the ordinary and innocent. Its famous set pieces include the concert in the Royal Albert Hall (shot by using the Schüfftan process), where the assassination is aborted by the mother's scream, and the gun battle in the East End, with which the film concludes.

Hitchcock's next film, *The 39 Steps* (1935), freely adapted from the John Buchan novel, is among his finest achievements. Suspenseful but light of touch, it deals with yet another classical Hitchcock situation—that of an innocent man who must prove his innocence while being simultaneously pursued by both villains and police. In *The 39 Steps*, a female secret-service agent is mysteriously murdered in the apartment of Richard Hannay (Robert Donat), who flees London to the north by train and arrives in Scotland. There, he inadvertently walks into the hands of the villain himself, escapes, and then walks into the hands of the police. After a series of further misadventures, he finds himself being pursued across the Scottish moors by both groups while handcuffed to a pretty young teacher (Madeleine Carroll) who believes him a murderer. This exciting chase, with its superb ensemble playing by Donat and Carroll, eventually ends in London, where all secrets are revealed and all problems resolved. Witty, fast-paced, and technically brilliant, *The 39 Steps* is narrative filmmaking at its very best.[1] It

---

1. *The 39 Steps* has been remade twice—first by Ralph Thomas in 1959, then by Don Sharp in 1978. Neither production (both are British) even approaches the stature of the original.

8.40 The master shot for the dinner table scene in Hitchcock's *Sabotage* (1936), followed by the shot sequence of the murder. Sylvia Sidney, Oskar Homolka.

also contains some classic examples of audiovisual montage, as when the scream of Hannay's cleaning lady on discovering the secret agent's corpse becomes the shriek of the whistle on the locomotive of the train carrying Hannay to Scotland.

Hitchcock's next film was a curious version of a play by Campbell Dixon, based on Somerset Maugham's "Ashenden" adventure stories, entitled *Secret Agent* (1936). It concerns a famous writer (John Gielgud) who works as a British agent to track down and kill a German spy in Switzerland during World War I, and its calculated moral ambiguity left many viewers confused, as did its remarkable successor, *Sabotage* (1936). This film, Hitchcock's grimmest prior to *Psycho* (1960), was, confusingly enough, a contemporary version of Joseph Conrad's novel *The Secret Agent* (1907), in which Verloc, the owner of a small London cinema, works secretly for a group of anarchists bent on destroying the city. *Sabotage* contains some of Hitchcock's most masterful sequences. The film's high point occurs when Verloc sends his wife's young brother out to plant a time bomb without the boy's knowledge. The child is waylaid through circumstance at almost every point in his journey—here a crowd, there a puppet show. As the time for detonation grows closer and closer, he boards an omnibus, and Hitchcock's montage becomes increasingly complex until at last the tension is released in a spectacular audience-alienation effect: the bomb explodes, and the boy and his fellow passengers are blown to bits. Later, Mrs. Verloc learns of the death and her husband's responsibility for it, and she murders him at the dinner table with a carving knife. The editing of the dinner scene that immediately precedes this act is among the most powerful and restrained in all of Hitchcock's work: Mrs. Verloc's mounting determination to kill her husband is gradually shown to coincide with his own desire to die for his crime.[2] In addition to such sophisticated montage effects, *Sabotoge* is full of references to the cinema and cinematic spectating owing to Verloc's role as theater manager (in the novel, he is a dealer in pornographic literature!): for example, Verloc himself loathes murder films but books them anyway to pander to his audience; Mrs. Verloc's decision to kill her husband is catalyzed by the apparition of a Disney cartoon in which a robin is shot though the breast with an arrow by another bird while the sound track intones "Who Killed Cock Robin?"; and so forth.

After a light double-chase film entitled *Young and Innocent* (1937), which contained a 145-foot tracking movement from a long shot into a close-up of a character's eye, Hitchcock made *The Lady Vanishes* (1938), the last of his British thrillers.[3] This was a stylish film of espionage and intrigue in Central Europe, set largely aboard a train. It revealed the same deftness as *The 39 Steps* and was a clear parable of England's blindness to the Nazi threat.

At this point in his career, having brought international prestige to the British film industry, Hitchcock decided to come to Hollywood. Certainly, America's economic bounty and Europe's uncertain political future were factors in this move, but it was unquestionably motivated by aesthetic considerations as well. The British economy and the domestic film industry were shrinking (see pp. 290–91) while Hitchcock's artistic ambitions were soaring; and by the end of the Depression, the Hollywood studios had become what UFA had been during the 1920s (almost literally since they were employing small armies of former UFA personnel [see pp. 105–107])—the center of big-budget film art in the West. He made one more British film, a melodramatic adaptation of Daphne du Maurier's gothic thriller *Jamaica Inn* (1939) for Erich Pommer and Charles Laughton's Mayfair Productions, and began a seven-year contract with David O. Selznick by adapting another du Maurier novel for the film *Rebecca* (1940).[4] The stately rhythms of this highly polished film marked a change of pace for Hitchcock, who now had the vast technical resources of the American studios at his disposal. Despite (or, perhaps, *because* of) Selznick's now notorious interference with the project, *Rebecca* was recognized by Academy Award nominations in every major category of achievement, winning two—Best Picture and Best Black-and-White Cinematography (to George Barnes). Hitchcock's second American film was a tour de force of anti-isolationist propaganda (the war had been going on in Europe for several months when production

---

2. See the shot sequence on pages 271–72.

3. Remade in 1978, with a script by George Axelrod and direction by Anthony Page.

4. Disliked by Hitchcock, du Maurier, and most critics to this day, *Jamaica Inn* was nevertheless extremely popular with British audiences and rereleased twice, in 1944 and 1948. Only three films were made for Selznick International under Hitchcock's contract (*Rebecca*, 1940; *Spellbound*, 1945; and *The Paradine Case*, 1947), but Selznick himself profited handsomely by hiring Hitchcock out to other producers and studios (Walter Wanger, RKO, Universal, and 20th Century–Fox) between 1940 and 1944—a period during which Selznick International was in liquidation for tax purposes.

8.41 *Rebecca* (1940), Hitchcock's first American film: Judith Anderson, Joan Fontaine, and "Rebecca."

began) cast in the mold of his very best British thrillers, *Foreign Correspondent* (1940), which was also nominated for several major Oscars. Produced by Walter Wanger for UA, it was loosely based on the memoirs of Vincent Sheehan and contained several elaborate effects, including a spectacular seaplane crash, created by production designer William Cameron Menzies (1896–1957) and cinematographer Joseph Valentine (1900–1949).

His next two films were for RKO—a fine, if uncharacteristic, screwball comedy entitled *Mr. and Mrs. Smith* (1941), commissioned for the talented comedienne Carole Lombard (1908–1942), who died in a plane crash shortly thereafter, and the tense psychological thriller *Suspicion* (1941), a film of considerable intelligence and his first with Cary Grant (1904–1986). In *Suspicion*, Grant plays a ne'er-do-well fortune hunter who marries a wealthy—and, clearly, sexually repressed—Joan Fontaine (in her first appearance since *Rebecca*); and she gradually comes to suspect him of plotting to murder her

for her money. Though set convincingly in the English countryside, the film was shot entirely on a soundstage by Harry Stradling (1902–1970); and it is both sinister and psychologically subtle—qualities not significantly damaged by the studio-mandated ending in which Fontaine's fears are shown to be the product of neurotic delusion (which, in a way, is more sinister yet). In a perfect example of Hollywood's institutional/ideological sexism,[5] RKO ordered this ending so as not to blemish Grant's image as a star persona.

Hitchcock then returned to the subject of espionage with *Saboteur* (1942), a spectacular double-chase film that includes newsreel footage of an actual act of sabotage (the burning of the SS *Normandie*) and concludes with a mad pursuit at the top of the Statue of Liberty. In 1943 Hitchcock made what he considered his best American film, *Shadow of a Doubt*, a restrained tale of a psychotic murderer's visit to relatives in the small California town of Santa Rosa, where he is perceived to be normal. Produced by Jack H. Skirball for Universal, the film is distinguished by Joseph Valentine's subtle camera work, superb performances by the entire cast—especially Teresa Wright as the devoted niece and Joseph Cotten as the charming, menacing, and finally lethal "Uncle Charlie"—and Thornton Wilder's intelligent screenplay, resonating perversely of *Our Town*, written five years before. The sound track employs overlapping dialogue mixes of the type used by Orson Welles in *Citizen Kane* (1941) and *The Magnificent Ambersons* (1942; see pp. 344–46), but it is ultimately the visual texture of the film, with its intricate psychological doublings, that makes *Shadow of a Doubt* one of Hitchcock's three or four undisputed masterworks. Hitchcock turned to the war itself with *Life-boat* (1944), an allegory of the world conflict in which a group of people representing a wide cultural and political spectrum are trapped together in a lifeboat after a Nazi U-boat attack. Based on a story by John Steinbeck, the film was shot in a studio tank at 20th Century–Fox and is constructed mainly of close shots.

Hitchcock's first postwar film was the psychological thriller *Spellbound* (1945), in which the head psychiatrist of an asylum comes to believe that he is in reality a murderous amnesiac. Expensively produced by Selznick

5. The 1987 television remake of *Suspicion*, directed by the British filmmaker Andrew Grieve and starring Jane Curtin in the Joan Fontaine role, rectifies the sexism but keeps the equivocal ending.

International, this movie was cluttered with Freudian symbols and contained many spectacular technical effects, including a dream sequence designed by the artist Salvador Dalí and the American cinema's first partially electronic score (for which composer Miklós Rózsa won an Academy Award). *Notorious* (1946), a tale of atomic espionage by Nazis set in Rio de Janeiro, was equally well produced and directed by Hitchcock at RKO. Its elegant black-and-white photography by Ted Tetzlaff (1903–1995) was an aesthetic triumph. There are several splendid sequences in the film, but the most stunning involves a swooping crane shot that begins at the top of a ballroom staircase and proceeds through a whole series of chambers before finally coming to rest in close-up on a key held in the heroine's hand. *Notorious* was an enormous popular success, not least because of the erotic frisson generated between stars Cary Grant and Ingrid Bergman during a prolonged kissing sequence.

After directing a technically dazzling but ponderous courtroom melodrama called *The Paradine Case* (1947), from a disjointed screenplay by Selznick, Hitchcock made two films for his own production company, Transatlantic Pictures. He had formed this company in 1946 with the British theater-chain owner Sidney Bernstein (1899–1993), a friend and advisor who had long admired the director's work.[6] Hitchcock's first Transatlantic film was also his first film in color—the boldly experimental *Rope* (1948). It was adapted from a play by Patrick Hamilton (based upon the infamous Leopold-Loeb case of 1924) in which two young intellectuals murder a friend in order

8.42 The murderers confronted in Hitchcock's *Rope* (1948): James Stewart, John Dall, Farley Granger; the miniature skyline.

to prove their Nietzschean superiority to conventional morality,[7] conceal his corpse in a living-room chest, and then stage a dinner party around it for his relatives. The film was shot by Joseph Valentine (in facilities rented from Warner Bros.) within the confines of a single large penthouse set in ten-minute takes with a continuously moving camera, for which Hitchcock developed tracking shots of extraordinary complexity.[8] The few cuts were concealed by invisible editing and confined to reel changes, and there were no time lapses in the narrative, so the running time of the film and dramatic time of the

6. A life-long film enthusiast, Bernstein began his career as a small distributor and went on to become a leading figure in British film culture. He founded the London Film Society (where he first met Hitchcock) in 1924, the Granada theater chain in 1930, and the Granada television group in 1954. During World War II, Bernstein served as film advisor to the British Ministry of Information and was chief of the Film Section of Supreme Headquarters, Allied Expeditionary Forces. It was in this latter capacity that he commissioned Hitchcock to make a compilation film on the Nazi concentration camps at the end of the war, with the purpose of showing the German people the specific nature of their leaders' crimes. This uncompromising hour-long documentary was suppressed by the military command as too volatile, but a copy was discovered in the Imperial War Museum in 1983, where it is preserved today as Film F3080—see Elizabeth Sussex, "The Fate of F3080," *Sight and Sound* 53, 2 (Spring 1984): 92–97. (In 1944, Hitchcock had made two short films celebrating the French Resistance—*Bon Voyage* and *Aventure Malgache*—at Bernstein's behest; both were shelved, but copies survived at the British Film Institute, and both are available today on videocassette from Milestone.) Bernstein was made a baron in 1969.

For more, see Caroline Moorehead, *Sidney Bernstein: A Biography* (London: Cape, 1984).

7. Friedrich Wilhelm Nietzsche (1844–1900) was a German philosopher who emphasized the will to power as the driving force of all organisms, individual and social. The posthumous debasement of his thought by right-wing German ideologues created the myth of the superman—the notion that certain people could *will* themselves out of normal moral categories and commit with impunity acts that would ordinarily be regarded as crimes (mass murder, say, or other forms of barbarism). The first articulation of this ideology in Hitchcock is offered quite explicitly by the Nazi U-boat commander in *Lifeboat*, so much so that some critics wrongly accused Hitchcock of embracing it.

8. There are actually eleven takes in the completed film, averaging about seven-and-a-half minutes each, and over 150 different camera movements. The piano music Hitchcock chose for *Rope*'s credit sequence, later played by one of the murderers during the dinner party, is Francis Poulenc's *Mouvement perpétuel n. 1*.

action coincide, and the film appears to have been shot as a single continuous take. The camera's costar in *Rope* was the set's arduously constructed background—an exact miniature replica of some 35 miles of New York skyline lighted by 8,000 tiny incandescent bulbs and 200 neon signs, each wired separately, which marked time by gradually representing the coming of twilight and nightfall to a vault of spun-glass clouds. Yet *Rope* was a critical and popular failure because the ten-minute take didn't work to sustain dramatic tension as Hitchcock had intended and because of its unpleasant subject matter.

The second and last Transatlantic production, *Under Capricorn* (1949), was also shot in color, by Jack Cardiff (b. 1914), at Elstree Studios, London. This costume film set in nineteenth-century Australia continued Hitchcock's experiments with the long take in several sequences of extraordinary beauty, but it ultimately failed to cohere as a narrative and was poorly received. Similar difficulties afflicted *Stage Fright* (1950), a Warner Bros. production shot in London, much admired today for its subtle interplay of cinematic and theatrical illusion and the fluid camerawork of Wilkie Cooper (1911–2000). Actively seeking now to produce a commercial hit, Hitchcock entered his second major period with *Strangers on a Train* (1951, Warners), based on a Patricia Highsmith novel with a screenplay by Raymond Chandler and Czenzi Ormonde. This psychological thriller concerns a murder pact jokingly made between two young men, Bruno and Guy, who meet on a train, each agreeing to kill someone who stands in the other's way. Bruno, a psychotic, unexpectedly fulfills the pact by murdering Guy's troublesome wife and then expects Guy to murder his (Bruno's) father. Horrified and consumed with guilt, Guy refuses to carry out his end of the deal, and Bruno attempts to frame him for the murder already committed. Photographed on location by Robert Burks (1910–1968), who with a single exception became Hitchcock's constant collaborator from 1951 until Burks's death in 1968, this film contains some of Hitchcock's most psychologically subtle characterizations (especially in Robert Walker's Bruno) and concludes with a spectacular fight between Bruno and Guy on a merry-go-round that careens out of control and collapses. As Hitchcock had anticipated, *Strangers on a Train* was an enormous popular success, and he made two more films for Warners. *I Confess* (1952), shot on location in the city of Quebec, concerns a priest who hears the confession of a murderer and is then accused of committing

8.43 The film frame as window frame, and the audience/ photographer as voyeur: Hitchcock's *Rear Window* (1954).

the murder himself. *Dial M for Murder* (1954) was an ingenious adaptation of a stage play filmed in color and 3-D[9] but released "flat" when the vogue for the process had died away (see pp. 389–92). In addition to eliciting a superb performance from Grace Kelly (1929–1982), Hitchcock made the film a model of narrative economy and staging in depth.

Hitchcock's next four films were made in color for Paramount. In *Rear Window* (1954) he restricted his scope of action even more rigidly than he had done in either *Lifeboat* or *Rope*. The entire film is shot from a camera confined within the apartment of a professional photographer, L. B. Jeffries, who is recovering from a broken leg, and during most of the film the camera records what he sees through his rear window. To pass the time, the photographer begins to spy on his neighbors through his telescopic lenses and gradually forms the conviction that one of them has murdered his wife, dismembered the corpse, and buried it in the courtyard garden. Jeffries's subsequent attempts to prove the murder endanger his fiancée's life (and, finally, his own), while—like the audience itself—he can only sit and watch from a perspective limited by the sequencing of his neighbors' windows and the power of his lens. *Rear Window* is a disturbing and

9. A desperate attempt to compete with the burgeoning popularity of television, 3-D, or "Natural Vision," was a cumbersome stereoscopic process for producing three-dimensional moving pictures that enjoyed a brief vogue between 1953 and 1954. Only sixty-nine films were made in 3-D during this period, and some, like *Dial M for Murder*, had to be released "flat" because of audience disenchantment with the process.

8.44 *Rear Window:* "We've become a race of peeping Toms . . ." James Stewart, Grace Kelly, Thelma Ritter.

profoundly modern film: its theme of the moral complicity of the voyeur (and, by extension, the film spectator) in what he watches anticipates both Antonioni's *Blowup* (1966; see pp. 537–38) and Francis Ford Coppola's *The Conversation* (1973; see p. 861), to say nothing of Hitchcock's own *Psycho* (1960).

In 1955 (the year he became a naturalized American citizen), Hitchcock directed *To Catch a Thief*, a stylish comedy thriller about a cat burglar, shot on location on the French Riviera in Paramount's new widescreen process, VistaVision. As we might expect, he became one of the first directors to use the wide screen effectively for pictorial and dramatic composition, and all of his subsequent films, with the exception of *The Wrong Man*, were shot in widescreen ratios. *The Trouble with Harry* (1955), which inaugurated his brilliant nine-year collaboration with composer Bernard Herrmann (1911–1975), used VistaVision to capture the autumn splendor of the Vermont woods as a background to a sophisticated[1] and witty black comedy about a corpse that refuses to stay buried because someone keeps digging it up. In the same year, Hitchcock remade *The Man Who Knew Too Much* as a big-budget commercial entertainment, featuring a lush Bernard Herrmann score and sequences shot on location in Morocco and London. Though updated and modernized, the second version reprises the Albert Hall sequence of the original on a vast scale, with Herrmann conducting the one hundred-piece London Symphony Orchestra in Arthur Benjamin's "Storm Cloud Cantata" in six-track stereophonic sound. One of its director's favorites and a great box-office success, the film is gorgeously photographed in VistaVision; even today we scarcely notice Hitchcock's experiments with the oblique 360-degree editing continuities he would later use so stunningly in *Vertigo*. As if to expiate his extravagance, Hitchcock next made a stark semidocumentary of false arrest and imprisonment, *The Wrong Man* (1957), his last Warners film, shot on location in black and white in New York City.

In 1958 Hitchcock directed *Vertigo*, shot on location in San Francisco in VistaVision, which many critics consider his greatest and most visually poetic film. Cast in the form of a detective thriller, *Vertigo* is actually a tale of romantic obsession brilliantly adapted by Alec Coppel and Samuel Taylor from the novel *D'Entre les Morts (From Amongst the Dead)*, by Pierre Boileau and Thomas Narcejac, the authors of *Les Diaboliques* (see p. 000). Scottie (James Stewart), a former police detective, has acquired a pathological fear of heights (acrophobia, or vertigo) by accidentally causing a fellow officer to fall to his death from a rooftop—facts conveyed by an extraordinary twenty-five-shot montage sequence in the film's first ninety seconds. He quits the force because of this debility but reluctantly accepts a job from a wealthy acquaintance named Gavin Elster to follow his wife, Madeleine (Kim Novak), who believes herself to be a reincarnation of her Spanish great grandmother, Carlotta Valdez—a much-abused woman who died insane, by her own hand. In the process of trailing Madeleine through the precipitous streets of San Francisco and saving her from an apparent suicide attempt near the Golden Gate Bridge, Scottie falls in love with her. She dies—or seems to—by throwing herself off the bell tower of an old Spanish mission, in part because Scottie's vertigo prevents him from stopping her. After an inquest ascribing her death to his negligence, Scottie plunges into madness, but is subsequently cured.

Later, still deeply bereaved, he discovers a shopgirl, named Judy, who bears a striking physical resemblance to Madeleine, although she is coarse and common whereas Madeleine was a romantic idol, and he spends the rest of the film obsessively trying to re-create the image of the

---

1. Too much so for the mass audience, apparently—*The Trouble with Harry* became the only Hitchcock film of the decade to actually *lose* money at the box office. On Herrmann's collaboration, see Royal S. Brown, "Herrmann, Hitchcock, and the Music of the Irrational," *Cinema Journal* 21, 2 (Spring 1982): 14–49.

8.45 *Vertigo* (Alfred Hitchcock, 1958): James Stewart and Kim Novak as Scottie and Madeleine.

8.46 The bell-tower staircase in *Vertigo:* Scottie's disequilibrium (and ours).

dead woman in the living one. The two women are actually the same woman who has acted as a foil in an audacious murder plot of Elster's—a fact that Hitchcock reveals to the audience (but not to Scottie) two-thirds of the way through the film, destroying suspense in order to concentrate our attention on mood and ambience. The poignancy of Scottie's situation (and also of Judy's, since she has fallen in love with him during her masquerade) is that the closer he comes to making Judy over as Madeleine, the farther he moves from both since Madeleine wasn't real in the first place but rather—like an actress in a film—someone playing a made-up part. The logic of this awful double bind produces *Vertigo*'s harrowing, inevitable conclusion in which Scottie, having at last re-created Madeleine perfectly in Judy, realizes that they have been the same person all along. Then, his vertigo finally cured, he literally drags her to the top of the bell tower where Madeleine "died," and Judy-Madeleine falls accidentally to her—this time, very real—death. No brief description can really do justice to the intricate structure of this remarkable film, whose theme of love transcending death resonates through such mainstays of Western narrative art as William Shakespeare's *Romeo and Juliet*, Emily Brontë's *Wuthering Heights*, and Richard Wagner's *Tristan und Isolde*. Bernard Herrmann's haunting score sustains this resonance, alternating passages of discordant contrary movement with lush orchestral leitmotifs based on Wagner's opera, especially the *Liebestod* ("love-death") aria of its conclusion.

Visually and aurally, *Vertigo* is constructed as a series of descending spirals, as Scottie is drawn irrevocably deeper into the spiritual vortex created by his romantic longing for Madeleine, whose very inaccessibility is her most fatal attraction. His vertigo—the image and emblem of this longing—is transferred to the audience at various points through dizzying reverse-tracking/forward-zoom shots, elaborately executed by Hitchcock's special-effects team, as Scottie peers into chasms from precarious heights (a city street from a rooftop, the bottom of the bell tower from its staircase, etc.). Madeleine's unattainability is conveyed—as when Scottie first glimpses her at Ernie's Restaurant—through oblique 360-degree cutting, which, by violating the rules of classical Hollywood editing, creates for her a narrative space that doesn't (or, at least, shouldn't) exist. Such "vortical" editing, combined with Burks's subtly tracking subjective camera and the film's highly stylized use of color, are strategies whereby we become so completely identified with Scottie's perspective that his vision of Madeleine—i.e., his psychological entrapment by a manufactured romantic goddess—becomes our own.

But after Judy's revelation of the murder plot, our perceptual path diverges from Scottie's, and his delusion, which we can no longer share, appears to us increasingly pathetic, hopeless, and doomed. The critic Robin Wood, who wrote the first serious English-language study of Hitchcock's art (*Hitchcock's Films*, 1965), has recently remarked that the last third of *Vertigo* is "among the most disturbing and painful experiences the cinema has to offer," and this is unquestionably true. Because we have shared the failure of Scottie's romantic aspirations so thoroughly in the body of the film, its horrible recurrence at *Vertigo*'s conclusion defies all of our narrative expectations. We are robbed not merely of a Hollywood-style happy ending, but also of the cathartic satisfaction of classical tragedy. When *Vertigo* ends, all the pain and death has meant nothing: in ending, the film suggests that its whole torturous process is about to start again. By consistently revealing the vulnerability of its male protagonist and the spurious nature of its heroine, and in refusing (emotionally, at any rate—like the closed circle of a descending spiral) to end, *Vertigo* suggests not only the fraudulence of romantic love, but of the whole Hollywood narrative tradition that underwrites it. At a deeper level, however, it suggests a more difficult truth: that the ultimate consequence of romantic idealism—of aspiring beyond the possible—is, successively, neurosis, psychosis, and perversion, or, more specifically, necrophilia.

Vertigo[2] was not successful with either the critics or the public, and it is not difficult to see why in a year in which Josh Logan's *Sayonara* and *South Pacific* were among the country's top-grossing films. Hitchcock always claimed dismay at this negative response and blamed it privately on Stewart's age and Novak's inexperience (both crucial attributes of their characters in the film, of course). This was not only mean-spirited, but dishonest: Hitchcock surely understood the risk he took in making such a nihilistic and radically experimental film for the American mass market. (Scriptwriter Samuel Taylor: "Hitchcock knew exactly what he wanted to do in this film, exactly what he wanted to say, and how it should be seen and told. I gave him the characters and the dialogue he needed and developed the story, but it was from first frame to last his film. There was no moment when he wasn't there. And anyone who saw him during the making of the film could see, as I did, that he felt it very deeply indeed.")

Whatever the case, Hitchcock was determined that his next film should be a great popular success, and he produced exactly that in *North by Northwest* (1959), a return to the witty double-chase mode of *The 39 Steps* (1935),

8.47 Cary Grant pursued by a crop duster in Hitchcock's *North by Northwest* (1959).

which at times it seems intended to parody. Stylishly scripted by Ernest Lehman (b. 1920) and shot by Burks in VistaVision for MGM, this film of a New York advertising man pursued across America by both government authorities and nuclear spies contains some classic Hitchcock sequences, most notably the (literally) cliff-hanging conclusion on Mount Rushmore and the superbly constructed machine-gun attack on the hero by a crop duster in the middle of an Indiana cornfield. It also employs a sophisticated manipulation of Freudian symbols, especially those of the Oedipal fantasy, and a stunning Ber-

2. Until recently, *Vertigo* was a "lost" film in that it was part of a group including *Rope, Rear Window, The Trouble with Harry,* and *The Man Who Knew Too Much* (1956) to which Hitchcock owned the rights and that, for financial reasons, he kept out of circulation during the last years of his life. In 1983, all five were rereleased theatrically in their original ratios (thought not, of course, in the case of *Harry, The Man Who Knew Too Much,* and *Vertigo,* in the now obsolete VistaVision process) by Universal Classics, which proved a great intellectual boon for Hitchcock scholarship and an economic one for MCA since all did handsomely at the box office.

nard Herrmann score to create a totality of effect wholly satisfying to the senses, emotions, and intellect. Or, as Hitchcock confessed to Lehman at one point during the shooting: "Ernie, do you realize what we're doing in this picture? The audience is like a giant organ that you and I are playing. At one moment we play *this* note on them and get *this* reaction, and then we play *that* chord and they react *that* way. And someday we won't even have to make a movie—there'll be electrodes implanted in their brains, and we'll just press different buttons and they'll go 'ooooh' and 'aaaah' and we'll frighten them, and make them laugh. Won't that be wonderful?"

That was to be *Psycho* (1960), adapted by Joseph Stefano from the novel by Robert Bloch,[3] Hitchcock's coldest, blackest, and most brilliant Hollywood film. Hitchcock produced *Psycho* for $800,000, using his own television crew at Revue Studios, the television branch of Universal Pictures. Shot for Paramount in black and white by John L. Russell, *Psycho* is at once the fulfillment of *Vertigo*'s necrophilic longing and a savage revenge on that film's critics. Before one-third of the film is over, the beautiful and sexually provocative heroine (Janet Leigh [b. 1927]), who is on the run from the police for having stolen $40,000 from her boss, is slashed to death in a motel shower in a harrowing forty-five-second montage sequence that many critics think rivals the Odessa Steps sequence of Eisenstein's *Potemkin*.

Psycho is an outrageously manipulative film and is thus, like *Potemkin*, a stunningly successful experiment in audience stimulation and response. Hitchcock's precisely planned knife-murder sequence is in fact a masterful vindication of the Kuleshov-Eisenstein school of montage: in a series of eighty-seven rapidly alternating fragmentary shots, we seem to witness a horribly violent and brutal murder on the screen, and yet only once do we see an image of the knife penetrating flesh, and that image is completely bloodless.[4] A second murder is so perfectly and unpredictably timed that it delivers a large perceptual shock, even after many viewings. Time and again, Hitchcock uses his camera and his montage to deceive the audience by leading it up cinematic blind alleys and strewing the screen with visual red herrings. He also offers the most morbid narrative of his career— the knife murderer is Norman Bates (Anthony Perkins [1932–1992]), a psychotic mama's boy who lives in a gothic house with the rotting corpse of his mother, some twelve years dead by his own hand (or so we are told at the end by the police psychiatrist). Many critics in 1960 were revolted by *Psycho* and appalled at its cynicism, but today its technical brilliance places it among the most important of postwar American films, and its blackness and bleakness look decidedly modern.[5] (Probably

8.48 Archetypal horror: Norman Bates (Anthony Perkins) stands before his mother's house in *Psycho* (Alfred Hitchcock, 1960).

3. Bloch's novel was based on the real-life case of Ed Gein, a Wisconsin mass murderer whose killing spree also inspired Tobe Hooper's *The Texas Chainsaw Massacre* (1974) and, very loosely, Jonathan Wacks's *Ed and His Dead Mother* (1993).

4. The sequence is perfectly complemented by the shrieking staccato violins of Bernard Herrmann's edgy score. Hitchcock had wanted to use only naturalistic sound effects for the murder, but Herrmann, felicitously, talked him out of it—an impressive example of artistic collaboration in a professional relationship that lasted from *The Trouble with Harry* (1955) through *Marnie* (1964). Two other Hitchcock collaborators of the late period deserve special mention here: Henry Bumstead, art director for *The Man Who Knew Too Much* (shared credit with Hal Pereira), *Vertigo* (shared credit with Pereira), *Topaz*, and *Family Plot*; and the graphic designer Saul Bass (1920–1996), who did the striking title designs for *Vertigo*, *North by Northwest*, and *Psycho*, as well as the storyboard for *Psycho*'s shower sequence.

5. There have, of course, been several sequels, and, for better or worse, the Norman Bates character has become something of a cult figure. *Psycho II* (Richard Franklin, 1983) has Norman released from a mental asylum some twenty years after his crimes to become a victim himself. *Psycho III* (Anthony Perkins, 1986) is an 1980s-style gore-fest that nevertheless demonstrates an intelligent grasp of Hitchcockean mood and theme, as well as reprising some set pieces from his other films, while *Psycho IV: The Beginning* (Mick Garris, 1990; written by Joseph Stefano) takes us back to the source of Norman's psychosis via a radio talk show. Perkins plays Bates in all three sequels.

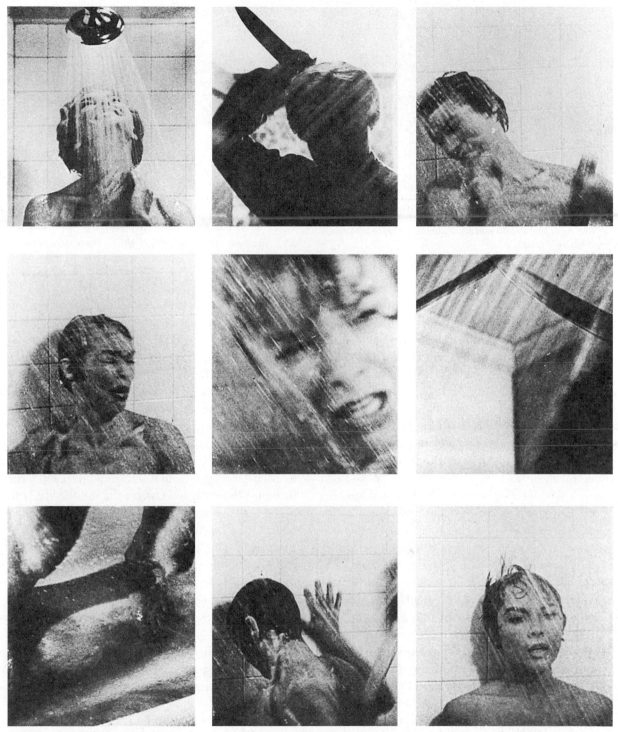

8.49 *Psycho:* shots from the shower sequence. Janet Leigh, Anthony Perkins.

8.50 A shot from the second murder sequence in *Psycho:* Martin Balsam, Anthony Perkins.

8.51 *The Birds* (Alfred Hitchcock, 1963). The attack on the school.

because it was the second highest-grossing film of 1960—after William Wyler's lumbering religious epic *Ben Hur*—*Psycho* did win Academy Award nominations for direction and black-and-white cinematography; it received neither but went on to earn over $11 million in its initial run.)

By the late 1940s, Hitchcock had become a major client of the talent agency MCA (formerly Music Corporation of America) and formed a close relationship with its president, Lew Wasserman (1913–2002), that would influence much of his later career. In 1955, Wasserman packaged a deal for Hitchcock to produce and lend his name to a program of weekly half-hour telefilms for CBS, which from 1955 to 1960 became one of the highest-rated shows in television history. Hitchcock personally directed only twenty episodes, but the programs, and especially his droll introductions to them, made Hitchcock a national figure. They also made him rich: by exchanging his rights to the series, plus *Psycho*, in 1962 for 150,000 shares of MCA stock, he became the third largest shareholder in the conglomerate, which gave him considerable freedom to produce his own films. No other director in America could have produced *Vertigo* as a big-budget feature with major stars in 1958 or received an Academy Award nomination for a film as dark and cheaply made as *Psycho* in 1960. As with virtually every other aspect of his life, Hitchcock used his television career to further his all-consuming, solitary passion to make films.[6]

After becoming one of the three largest shareholders

in MCA, Hitchcock produced all of his films for Universal. The first of these, *The Birds* (1963), was nearly three years in preparation and at the time of its release seemed to many an exercise in pure technique. Adapted by Evan Hunter from a Daphne du Maurier short story, it concerns a savage assault by the millions of birds in the vicinity of Bodega Bay, California, upon the human population of the area. The special effects (consisting of 371 trick shots) by Hitchcock and Ub Iwerks (1901–1971), one of Disney's greatest animators, are remarkable, as is the menacing electronic sound track produced and recorded by Remi Gassmann and Oskar Sala. But the film is slowly paced until the bird attacks begin en masse, and it has an oddly formal quality. Today, critics are inclined to see *The Birds* as forming the third part of a trilogy with *Vertigo* and *Psycho*, which posits a world gone speechless and numb through the dislocation of human feeling. Although the bird attacks on the town are spectacularly rendered through classically structured montage, the overall mood of the film is no less stark than that of *The Wrong Man*. (Its art director Robert Boyle has said that the film's overall design was inspired by Edvard Munch's *The Scream*—"the sense of bleakness and madness in a kind of wilderness expressing an inner state.")

The Birds, Hitchcock's most expensive film, was also one of his most successful, and he went on to cast its star,

6. See John McCarty and Brian Kelleher, *Alfred Hitchcock Presents: An Illustrated Guide to the Ten-Year Television Career of the Master of Suspense* (New York: St. Martin's, 1985).

8.52 The end of the world as we know it: Rod Taylor prepares to leave his home with his mother, lover, and sister (Jessica Tandy, Tippie Hedren, and Veronica Cartwright, right to left) at the conclusion of *The Birds*.

Tippi Hedren (b. 1935), in his last important work, *Marnie* (1964), based by Jay Presson Allen on the novel by Winston Graham. Like *Vertigo*, it is a film of obsession in which a man falls in love with a severely neurotic woman (here, an incorrigible kleptomaniac) and attempts to cure her. While it was much maligned for the visible artificiality of the process photography and painted backdrops of some of its scenes (whose stylization may, in fact, have been intentional), *Marnie* contains sequences of hallucinatory beauty worthy of Hitchcock's finest work, and it belongs, at the very least, to that category designated by François Truffaut as "greatest flawed films." *Marnie*, however, failed miserably at the box office, and it became Hitchcock's last film with the three most important collaborators of his late period—cinematographer Robert Burks and editor George Tomasini, both of whom died shortly after *Marnie* was completed, and composer Bernard Herrmann, whose score was blamed by Universal for *Marnie*'s unpopularity and whom Hitchcock stupidly fired.

He next made two Cold War espionage films—*Torn Curtain* (1966), based on an original screenplay by Brian Moore, and *Topaz* (1969), adapted by Samuel Taylor from Leon Uris's best-selling novel—which showed progressive indifference, if not decline. *Frenzy* (1971), however, deftly scripted by Anthony Shaffer from Arthur La Bern's novel *Goodbye Piccadilly, Farewell Leicester Square*, marked a strong comeback by combining the excitement of the British double-chase films with the psychological introspection, kinetic violence, and technical virtuosity of *Psycho*. Shot on location in London by Gil Taylor, this film concerns a sexual psychopath who strangles women with neckties; although it is profoundly misogynistic and contains a strangulation scene that borders on the pornographic (and for which it was duly rated "R"), *Frenzy* became one of the most popular films of 1972.

With *Family Plot* (1976), adapted by Ernest Lehman from a Victor Canning novel, Hitchcock returned to black humor in a bizarre tale of kidnapping, phony spiritualism, and murder that contained distinct overtones of *The Man Who Knew Too Much* (the 1956 version) and *North by Northwest*. He was working on the screenplay of *The Short Night*, an espionage thriller based on the real-life case of the British double agent George Blake, when he died at his home in Beverly Hills on April 29, 1980.

Owing to his rigorous preproduction practices, in which each film was conceptualized, storyboarded, and planned logistically from beginning to end in advance of shooting, Hitchcock exercised an unusual degree of control over the fifty-three features he made between 1925 and 1976, even when he was working for such a megalomaniac as David Selznick. (After leaving Selznick International in 1947, he functioned as his own producer no matter who was financing and releasing his films.) Yet the tendency to see him as merely a brilliant technician, long

8.53 *Frenzy* (Alfred Hitchcock, 1971; released 1972): Jon Finch as a man falsely accused of serial killings.

the prevailing critical trend, gave way in the 1970s to a more judicious assessment of him as both a formalist and moralist, a status acknowledged by the American Film Institute's presentation to him of its Life Achievement Award in 1979. Today, Hitchcock is understood to be one of the leading figures in film history, the peer of Griffith, Eisenstein, Renoir, and Welles.

About his commitment to style there can be no question—during the 1930s, he was one of the few directors to use Eisensteinian montage in an era of primarily functional editing; his mastery of the long take and the moving camera has been apparent since the 1940s; and his achievements in widescreen composition in the 1950s are of major historical importance for the contemporary film. Beyond form, however, there is Hitchcock the moralist and fatalist who created an image of the modern world in which the perilous and the monstrous lurk within the most ordinary circumstances of everyday life. It is a world that shares much with the work of Franz Kafka and comprehends what Hannah Arendt termed "the banality of evil." It is also a world in which, as Robin Wood has noted, there erupts from time to time "an animus against women and specifically against the female body," every bit as real as Griffith's racism. Hitchcock's designation as "the master of suspense" was a public-relations gambit based on the popular misperception of his work. His greatest films—*Sabotage, Shadow of a Doubt, Vertigo, Psycho, The Birds*—have little or none of that quality. Hitchcock

did not so much work in a genre as create one—the "Hitchcock film"—that has been endlessly imitated but never surpassed.[7] He was an original whose life was his art and who succeeded, perhaps more than any other artist of the century, in making his own fears, obsessions, and fantasies part of our collective psyche.

GEORGE CUKOR, WILLIAM WYLER, AND FRANK CAPRA

Three other directors of historical importance emerged from Hollywood in the 1930s, although their work was less substantial and cohesive than that of the four major figures discussed in this chapter.

George Cukor (1899–1983) originally came to Hollywood from Broadway as a dialogue director, working with both Lewis Milestone and Ernst Lubitsch before directing his first important film, *A Bill of Divorcement*, starring Katharine Hepburn and John Barrymore, in 1932. With a series of stylish comedies and sophisticated literary adaptations, he established himself as one of the foremost craftsmen of the American cinema. Cukor had a flair for elegant decor and witty dialogue, and a facility for directing female stars that has typed him as a "women's director," but his talent was really more versatile than the term implies. Cukor worked exclusively under contract to MGM in the 1930s and 1940s but began to freelance in the postwar era.

Among his most important films are *Dinner at Eight* (1933), *Little Women* (1933), *David Copperfield* (1935), *Camille* (1936), *Holiday* (1938), *The Women* (1939), *The Philadelphia Story* (1940), *Gaslight* (1944),[8] *Adam's Rib* (1949), *Born Yesterday* (1950), *The Marrying Kind* (1951), *Pat and Mike* (1952), *It Should Happen to You* (1954), *A Star Is Born* (1954),[9] *Bhowani Junction* (1956),

7. For the record, *North by Northwest* inspired the James Bond cycle, *Psycho* the slasher cycle, *The Birds* the disaster film, all of which are still very much with us; *Vertigo* has been remade time and time again (and not just by Brian De Palma); *Shadow of a Doubt* stands firmly behind *Blue Velvet* (David Lynch, 1986); and so on.

8. A remake of the 1940 British version of Patrick Hamilton's play directed by Thorold Dickinson. MGM purchased the rights to the British film and withdrew it from circulation in the United States in order to produce its own version.

9. *A Star Is Born*, Cukor's first film in Technicolor, CinemaScope, and stereophonic sound, was made for Warner Bros. at a cost of $5 million; it originally ran 181 minutes, but was cut to 140 for distribution, against Cukor's wishes. In 1983, it was restored to its original form by Ronald

Les Girls (1957), and *My Fair Lady* (1964), which earned him a long-deserved Oscar for direction. These are all handsome, graceful productions that feature brilliant performances by some of the most talented actors and actresses in the American cinema, many of whom he guided to awards: John Barrymore, Jean Harlow, Marie Dressler, Greta Garbo, Katharine Hepburn, Cary Grant, Norma Shearer, Joan Crawford, Rosalind Russell, James Stewart, Ingrid Bergman, Charles Boyer, Judy Holliday, Spencer Tracy, Judy Garland, Jack Lemmon, James Mason, and Audrey Hepburn. Cukor's work reveals no strong personal vision, but it is remarkably consistent in its intelligence, sensitivity, and taste. In 1981, he received the prestigious D. W. Griffith Award from the Directors Guild of America and, with *Rich and Famous*, became the oldest director ever to make a major studio film; in 1982, the film won the Golden Lion at Venice.

William Wyler (1902–1981) was another fine American filmmaker. He began his career by directing B-Westerns and shorts for his uncle, Carl Laemmle, at Universal Pictures. In 1935 he went to work for Samuel Goldwyn and earned a reputation as an accomplished adaptor of other people's work—most notably Lillian Hellman's play *The Children's Hour*, which Wyler filmed as *These Three* in 1936 and remade under its original title in 1962; Sidney

8.55 Wyler's adaptation of *The Little Foxes* (1941), photographed by Toland. Note the depth of the image and how the action occurs on several planes at once. Herbert Marshall, Bette Davis.

Kingsley's play *Dead End*, with a screenplay by Hellman (1937); and Hellman's play *The Little Foxes* (1941). He also directed adaptations of novels—*Dodsworth* (1936), *Wuthering Heights* (1939), *Mrs. Miniver* (1942, MGM), and *The Heiress* (1949, Paramount—from Henry James's *Washington Square*)—and other plays (*Jezebel*, 1938, and *The Letter*, 1940, both for Warners). His collaborator for much of this period was the brilliant cinematographer Gregg Toland, who experimented with deep-focus photography in Wyler films like *Wuthering Heights* and *The Little Foxes* before he used the process so magnificently in Orson Welles's *Citizen Kane* (1941; see pp. 328–44). Wyler's *The Best Years of Our Lives* (1946), his last film for Goldwyn, was hailed as a masterpiece in the year of its release and swept the Academy Awards (as *Mrs. Miniver* had done four years before), although it is really a rather conventional, if intensely felt, drama of the problems of servicemen attempting to adjust to postwar American life. The inflated reputation brought him by

8.54 William Wyler's version of *Wuthering Heights* (1939), shot by Gregg Toland on the moors of the San Fernando Valley: Merle Oberon and Laurence Olivier as Cathy and Heathcliff.

Haver, head of the Film Department of the Los Angeles County Museum. (See Ronald Hauer, "A Star Is Born Again," *American Film* 8, 9 (July–August 1983): 28–33, 59.) Cukor's film was a remake of an earlier version directed by William Wellman for David O. Selznick in 1937, which was itself inspired by Cukor's *What Price Hollywood?* (1932). There was another remake in 1976, directed by Frank Pierson, set in the context of high-rolling rock music, rather than motion-picture stardom.

his wartime films led Wyler to pursue ever more inflated projects in the 1950s, culminating in the widescreen blockbusters *The Big Country* (1958, UA) and *Ben Hur* (1959, MGM), which set an all-time record by receiving eleven major Oscars. Nevertheless, he continued to produce interesting work during this period, much of it for Paramount, including his tough, cynical action film *Detective Story* (1951), his adaptations of Dreiser's turn-of-the-century novel *Sister Carrie* (*Carrie*, 1952) and Joseph Hayes's tense contemporary drama *The Desperate Hours* (1955), the delightful romantic comedy *Roman Holiday* (1953), and the unconventional (for the 1950s) *Friendly Persuasion* (1956, Allied Artists), the story of an Indiana Quaker family trying to maintain its pacifism in the midst of the Civil War. In the 1960s, Wyler staged something of a critical comeback with a powerful adaptation of John Fowles's novel *The Collector* (1965), but *Funny Girl* (1968) and *The Liberation of L. B. Jones* (1969) did little to confirm his renewed reputation. Nevertheless, in 1975 Wyler was selected for the American Film Institute's Life Achievement Award in recognition of his past contributions.

Frank Capra (1897–1991) was a Sicilian who emigrated with his family to Los Angeles in 1903, where he ultimately earned a degree in chemical engineering from the California Institute of Technology. Unable to find employment in that field, he went to work as a gag writer for Hal Roach, Mack Sennett, and finally Harry Langdon, for whom he wrote the hit *Tramp, Tramp, Tramp* (1926) and directed *The Strong Man* (1926) and *Long Pants* (1927). When this collaboration ended in creative differences, Capra went to work for Harry Cohn at Columbia Pictures, where he made the studio's first talking feature (*The Donovan Affair*, 1929) and a popular series of armed-forces adventure films with the team of Jack Holt and Ralph Graves (*Submarine*, 1928; *Flight*, 1930; *Dirigible*, 1931). In 1931, Capra made his first film with screenwriter Robert Riskin (the Jean Harlow vehicle *Platinum Blonde*) and began the collaboration that would produce the great Columbia screwball comedies *Lady for a Day* (1933), *It Happened One Night* (1934), *Mr. Deeds Goes to Town* (1936), *You Can't Take It with You* (1938), and *Mr. Smith Goes to Washington* (1939), as well as the sumptuous utopian fantasy *Lost Horizon* (1937).[1] Capra won the Academy Award for direction three times with this series, and he ended the decade as one of the most sought-

8.56 Jimmy Stewart in *Mr. Smith Goes to Washington* (1939), a Capra "fantasy of good will."

after filmmakers in Hollywood. Such was his clout that he and Riskin were able to form an independent company (Frank Capra Productions) to produce and distribute their next film, the antifascist parable *Meet John Doe* (1941), which was a failure and ended their relationship.

During World War II, Capra was inducted into the army and quickly became head of the Morale Branch's newly formed film unit. Here, with the backing of Army Chief of Staff General George C. Marshall, Capra became producer-director of the extraordinary documentary series *Why We Fight* (see p. 369). Originally commissioned to indoctrinate servicemen, this seven-film series was ultimately shown to general audiences in theaters around the country at President Roosevelt's behest, so powerful was it as an instrument of mass persuasion

---

1. Originally 132 minutes but later cut to 108, *Lost Horizon* was recently restored as a joint venture of the American Film Institute and the UCLA Pacific Archives, with permanently lost footage replaced by voice-over dialogue and stills. The film was remade (ill-advisedly) as a musical, with direction by Charles Jarrott and songs by Burt Bacharach, in 1973.

8.57 *It's a Wonderful Life* (Frank Capra, 1946): Jimmy Stewart and H. B. Warner as George Bailey and Mr. Gower, the pharmacist he saves from criminal disgrace.

8.58 Back from the future: George returns to Bedford Falls with Zu-Zu's petals in *It's a Wonderful Life:* **Ward Bond (as Bert the cop), Jimmy Stewart.**

(Capra won his fourth Oscar for *Prelude to War*, 1942, the series' first installment). Only months after the war, Capra attempted independence again by forming Liberty Films with George Stevens and William Wyler. Capra made only two Liberty films before the company was sold to Paramount in 1947, *It's a Wonderful Life* (1946)[2] and *State of the Union* (1948), both of which failed at the box office. After two Bing Crosby films (*Riding High*, 1950, and *Here Comes the Groom*, 1951) made to fulfill his part of the Liberty deal with Paramount, Capra went into semi-retirement, emerging to direct the Frank Sinatra vehicle *A Hole in the Head* (1959) and *Pocket Full of Miracles* (1961), a remake of *Lady for a Day*. After he published his best-selling autobiography, *The Name above the Title*, in 1971, Capra became something of a cult figure but made no more films. His influence, however, has been acknowledged across so wide a range of directors as John Ford, Ermanno Olmi, Milos Forman, Satyajit Ray, and Yasujiro Ozu, and he received the American Film Institute's Life Achievement Award in 1982. During the 1930s, Capra had achieved a degree of autonomy and

recognition unprecedented within the American studio system, and it may be that the failure of his own company after the war embittered him to the filmmaking establishment. Whatever the case, he made only one great film after his triumphs of the Depression years, *It's a Wonderful Life*, and that is a work that, for all of its apparent buoyancy, suggests some extremely dark possibilities for postwar American life.

The coming of sound threatened to destroy the international market that film had enjoyed since Méliès by introducing the language barrier between national industries. During the first few years of sound, Frenchmen would hiss and boo the dialogue in German films, and vice versa; the British and Americans found each other's accents incomprehensible; and there was the problem of regional dialects within a single nation. To overcome this barrier,

---

2. Remade as the telefilm *It Happened One Christmas* (Donald Wrye, 1977), with a gender change (Marlo Thomas for Jimmy Stewart) and considerably less darkness.

films were for several years shot in different language versions at the time of production. This expensive practice was soon abandoned when a whole new branch of the industry was evolved for the dubbing and subtitling of films for foreign markets. The American industry, long accustomed to international dominion, was able to maintain its control of the world market by virtue of its vast capital and, for a while at least, its wholesale ownership of the major patents for sound equipment.[3] But because of the economic domination of the American studios themselves by the country's largest corporate interests, the American cinema of the 1930s had a specifically ideological orientation, which the Production Code incarnated.

The central tenets of the code were that the Depression, if it existed at all, had little impact on most people's lives; that there was no crime in the streets or corruption in government; that the authority of the police and the military were absolute; that religion and the nuclear family were sacred, coextensive institutions; and, finally, that most Americans in the 1930s lived in cottages behind white picket fences on peaceful streets in Anytown, U.S.A. By regulating the "moral" content of American films, the Breen Code was regulating their social content as well, so that what purported to be a blueprint for "cleaning up the movies" was actually an instrument of social control in a period of economic chaos. Thus, however great its aesthetic achievements—and they are clearly manifold—the American cinema of the 1930s consistently concealed the *reality* of the Depression and, later, of the war in Europe from the American people. This is a matter not of opinion, but of historical record: with several notable exceptions (e.g., Warner Bros.' *I Am a Fugitive from a Chain Gang*, Mervyn LeRoy, 1932; United Artists' *Our Daily Bread*, King Vidor, 1934), Hollywood did not seriously confront the social misery caused by the Depression until the release of Fox's *The Grapes of Wrath* (John Ford) in 1940; the first Hollywood film to acknowledge the Nazi threat in Europe, Warner

Bros.' *Confessions of a Nazi Spy* (Anatole Litvak), did not appear until 1939.[4] So perhaps the final comment on Hollywood in the 1930s should be this: Sound had been added to the cinema as the result of a bitter economic struggle between competing American production companies; the technology of sound recording had first been perfected by American engineers; and the creative use of sound had been pioneered almost exclusively by American filmmakers. Yet, with regard to the social, sexual, and political dimensions of human experience, the American sound film throughout the 1930s remained quite effectively "silent."

---

3. In Hollywood, foreign-language versions of English-language features could be made for under 30 percent of the original budget, and in early 1930, Paramount built a vast studio at Joinville in the suburbs of Paris to mass-produce films in five separate languages. Within months the other Hollywood majors had joined Paramount, and Joinville—already christened "Babel-sur-Seine"—became a movie factory that operated twenty-four hours a day to produce films in as many as fifteen languages (including Romanian, Lithuanian, Egyptian, and Greek), often in less than two weeks per feature. The quality of the Joinville product was predictably low, although many promising young directors like Marc Allégret and Claude Autant-Lara (see Chapter 13) were trained there. By the end of 1931, the technique of dubbing had been sufficiently improved to provide an inexpensive alternative to multilingual production, the latter practice was abandoned, and Paramount converted the Joinville studios into a dubbing center for all of Europe. Dubbing (and, less frequently, subtitling) is still practiced for foreign-release versions throughout the world today.

4. One reason for the latter was that studio executives did not wish to antagonize Axis or neutral countries where their corporations had major markets and/or holdings. Incredibly, a faction within the Hays Office in 1939 demanded that the script of *Confessions of a Nazi Spy* acknowledge Hitler's "unchallenged political and social achievements" and eliminate its "unfair" references to the recent dismemberment of Czechoslovakia (see Clayton R. Koppes and Gregory D. Black, *Hollywood Goes to War: How Politics, Profits, and Propaganda Shaped World War II Movies* [New York: Free Press, 1987], pp. 28–30). The Warners forged ahead, less for political reasons than for personal ones: their chief salesman in Germany, Joe Kaufman, had been beaten to death by Nazi thugs in a Berlin alleyway in 1936, and Jack Warner would never forget it. (See Colin Shindler, *Hollywood Goes to War: Films and American Society, 1939–1952* [London: Routledge and Keegan Paul, 1979], pp. 8–9.)

Europe in the Thirties

The International Diffusion of Sound

Having successfully created large new markets for their sound recording technologies at home, Western Electric and RCA were anxious to do the same abroad, and this motive went hand in glove with the desire of American studios to extend their control of the international film industry into the sound era. Accordingly, the Big Five began to export sound films in late 1928, and ERPI (Electrical Research Products, Incorporated—Western Electric's aggressive marketing agent) and RCA began installing their equipment in first-run European theaters at the same time. British exhibitors converted most rapidly, with 22 percent wired in 1929 and 63 percent by the end of 1932.

German and French exhibitors converted more slowly, largely because in 1928 a German cartel had been formed to stem the invasion of American sound equipment. Backed by German, Dutch, and Swiss capital, Tobis (the Tonbild Syndikat, AG) had acquired the European rights to the Tri-Ergon sound-on-film system and began to wire German theaters for its use. At the same time, Germany's two largest electrical manufacturers, Siemens & Halske, AG, and Allgemeine Elektrizitätsgesellschaft (AEG), formed the Klangfilm Syndicate to exploit a competing system mutually developed by the corporations on the basis of Kuchenmeister, Pederson-Poulsen, and Messter patents. After several months of feuding with each other over European markets, Tobis and Klangfilm merged in March 1929 to combat the threat of American domination of the sound film. With capital assets of over $100 million and venture capital provided by the Dutch bank Oyens and Sons, Tobis-Klangfilm quickly concluded cross-licensing agreements with the British and French Photophone Company and British Talking Pictures, Ltd., giving it production, distribution, and manufacturing branches in every country in Europe.

Almost immediately, Tobis-Klangfilm began to enter suits against Western Electric and ERPI, and their licensees, for patent infringement in all of its territories, and won final injunctions in Germany, Holland, Czechoslovakia, Hungary, Switzerland, and Austria. As American foreign grosses plummeted by 75 percent, the Hollywood monopolists agreed to boycott the markets in dispute. Simultaneously, in July 1929, the General Electric Corporation (which held a controlling interest in RCA) acquired part interest in AEG and nudged Tobis-Klangfilm into a cooperative releasing agreement with RKO. To avoid a self-destructive patent war, ERPI (i.e., Western Electric), RCA, and Tobis-Klangfilm convened the German-American Film Conference in Paris on June 19, 1930. Their purpose was to carve up among themselves a world market for sound film equipment conservatively valued at $250 million. A final agreement signed on July 22, 1930, divided the world into four territories: Tobis-Klangfilm was given exclusive rights to Central Europe and Scandinavia; ERPI and RCA got the United States, Canada, Australia, New Zealand, India, and the Soviet Union; the United Kingdom was split between them, 25 percent going to Tobis-Klangfilm and 75 percent to ERPI and RCA; and the rest of the world was open territory. The three giants also agreed to pool all of their patents, exchange technical information, and drop all pending litigation. This informal cartel never really held together, and its terms were renegotiated several times before it collapsed in 1939 in the face of war in Europe. Nevertheless, Tobis-Klangfilm succeeded in fending off the American bid for world domination and produced, in conjunction with other factors, a marked decline in Hollywood's influence in Europe.

Britain

Due to the rapidity with which its theaters were wired and the (relative) lack of a language barrier, however, the United Kingdom became Hollywood's first major foreign market for sound films. The British cinema had always been a stepchild of the American industry, and during the 1920s it had almost ceased to exist. But in 1927 Parliament passed the Cinematograph Film Act, setting strict quotas on the number of foreign films that could be shown in the country; this had the effect of stimulating domestic production and investment. The British film industry doubled in size from 1927 to 1928, and the number of features it produced rose from 20 to 128. The expansion continued well into the 1930s, enabling the British

9.1 The original "biopic." Alexander Korda's *The Private Life of Henry VIII* (1933): Charles Laughton's performance as the gluttonous monarch made him internationally famous.

to compete with Hollywood not merely nationally, but—for the first time in its history—internationally, on a modest scale. Many of the films produced by the new boom were "quota quickies"—the British equivalent of the low-budget American B-film—but some were distinguished undertakings by serious producers such as Alexander Korda (b. Sándor Kellner, 1893–1956) and Michael Balcon (1896–1977).

The producer-director Korda and his two younger brothers, the director Zoltan (1895–1961) and the art director Vincent (1897–1979), were Hungarians who settled in England and founded London Film Productions there

9.2 London Films' spectacular *The Thief of Bagdad* (Ludwig Berger, Michael Powell, and Tim Whelan, 1940): Sabu and the genie's foot. The film won American Academy Awards for art direction, color cinematography, and special effects.

9.3 *The Jungle Book* (Zoltan Korda, 1942), produced by Alexander Korda for London Films in Hollywood: Sabu, as Mowgli the Wolf Boy, converses with Kaa the Python.

in the early 1930s. They collaborated on many outstanding costume spectacles, including *The Private Life of Henry VIII* (Alexander Korda, 1933), *Rembrandt* (Alexander Korda, 1936), *Elephant Boy* (Robert Flaherty and Zoltan Korda, 1937), *The Four Feathers* (Zoltan Korda, 1939), *The Thief of Bagdad* (Ludwig Berger, Michael Powell, Tim Whelan, 1940), and *The Jungle Book* (Zoltan Korda, 1942), which did much to establish Great Britain's position in the international market.

Michael Balcon was successively director of production for the most important and discriminating British studios of the era: Gainsborough (which he founded in 1924), Gaumont-British (where he produced for Hitchcock), Ealing Studios, and the Rank Organization. This was the era in British cinema that witnessed the flowering of Hitchcock's thrillers, the literate period films of Anthony Asquith (1902–1968—*A Cottage on Dartmoor*, 1930; *Tell England*, 1931), the Jessie Matthews musicals of Victor Saville (1895–1979—*Evergreen*, 1934; *First a Girl*, 1935; *It's Love Again*, 1936), and the excellent documentaries produced by John Grierson (1898–1972) and his socially "committed" British documentary movement (see p. 481) for the Empire Marketing Board (EMB— e.g., *Drifters* [Grierson, 1929]; *Upstream* [Arthur Elton, 1931]; *Industrial Britain* [Robert Flaherty, 1933]) and the General Post Office (GPO—e.g., *Coal Face* [Alberto Cavalcanti, 1935]; *Song of Ceylon* [Basil Wright, 1934]; *Night Mail* [Wright and Harry Watt, 1936]). By 1937, the British industry had the second largest annual output in the world (225 features), and British films were competing

strongly with American films on an international scale. Yet British producers were also deeply in debt, and the following year witnessed many bankruptcies and studio closings. In 1938, fewer than one hundred features were made and fewer still were released, a reflection of Europe's uncertain political future and the troubled world economy.

Germany

The German industry entered the sound era from a position of relative strength due to its ownership of the Tobis-Klangfilm recording patents, although the Weimar Republic was already on the brink of collapse. As in the United States, the first German sound films were unremarkable popular musicals, and the trend toward escapist entertainment grew as the nation sank ever more deeply into economic and political trouble. Yet some very important and distinguished films came out of the early sound period in Germany.

Perhaps the most significant and influential work of Germany's early sound period was Fritz Lang's *M* (1930), with a script by Thea von Harbou (Lang's wife) based on the famous Düsseldorf child-murders. In *M*, Peter Lorre (1904–1964) plays a psychotic murderer of little girls in a large German city who is ultimately tracked down not by the police, but by members of the local underworld. Through cutting, Lang establishes a clear parallel between the two groups. Lorre is brilliant as the tortured psychopath who wants desperately to stop killing but is constantly overpowered by his uncontrollable compulsion, and *M* is very much in the gloomy tradition of *Kammerspiel*. Studio-produced and highly stylized in its realism, the film contains no musical score, but is distinguished by its expressive use of nonnaturalistic sound such as the recurring theme from Grieg's *Peer Gynt Suite*, which the murderer whistles offscreen before committing his crimes. Not the least amazing thing about *M* is the way it deals with a revolting subject in a subtle and tasteful manner. Lang achieves this primarily through editing and the fluid camera style of Fritz Arno Wagner. Near the beginning of the film, for example, Lorre entices a little girl with a balloon; Lang cuts to shots of the girl's worried mother waiting for her return in an apartment; then he cuts to a shot of the balloon floating out and away from a small forest thicket to become entangled in some utility

9.4 Peter Lorre in *M* (Fritz Lang, 1930).

Das Testament des Dr. Mabuse (*The Last Will of Dr. Mabuse*, 1932), also sumptuously photographed by Wagner, the arch-tyrant directs his league of world crime from a lunatic asylum. Lang later claimed to have modeled Mabuse on Hitler and to have put Nazi slogans into the mouths of his criminal minions. This claim may be the result of hindsight, but the Nazis apparently recognized something of themselves in the film and banned it when they came to power in 1933. After bluntly refusing Joseph Goebbels offer of an important post with UFA, Lang escaped to France four months later (leaving behind his wife, a devout Nazi), where in 1934 he adapted Ferenc Molnár's play *Liliom* to the screen for Fox-Europa.

He later emigrated to the United States, where he made two brilliant films before the war. *Fury* (1936), shot at MGM, is a compelling indictment of mob violence that probes as deeply into the complex relationship between will and fate as had Lang's German films. *You Only Live Once* (1937), produced by Walter Wanger for UA, is another powerful tale of injustice and destiny: a young ex-convict is falsely accused of murder and sentenced to death; with his wife's help he escapes from prison hours before his execution, and together the two flee across America until they are hunted down and killed at a roadblock on the Canadian border. Expressionist in atmosphere, composition, and lighting, *You Only Live Once* became the model for Joseph Lewis's *Gun Crazy* (1950) and Arthur Penn's *Bonnie and Clyde* (1967; see pp. 848–50). The couple's desperate flight through nocturnal America has a tragic, brooding character that both later films preserve. Lang directed another twenty-one films in the United States for a variety of studios between 1938 and 1956, but only his *film noir* masterpiece *The Big Heat* (1953, Columbia), achieved the quality and depth of his greatest work. The majority of these were formulaic but always visually interesting genre films— Westerns (*The Return of Frank James* [1940]; *Western Union* [1941]; *Rancho Notorious* [1952]); espionage thrillers (*Man Hunt* [1941]; *Ministry of Fear* [1945]; *Cloak and Dagger* [1946]); melodramas (*Clash by Night* [1952]; *Human Desire* [1954]—many of which have long been considered classics of their type.

But Lang's other American films have been significantly revaluated in recent years by Tom Gunning and others, who tend to locate their meaning thematically, but also in the details of their *mise-en-scène*. Gunning, for example, proposes a typology that groups *You Only Live*

wires, and we know that the child has been murdered. At another point, to establish the identity between the bosses of the local underworld and the police, Lang contrives to have the chief of police complete a gesture begun by the chief of thieves in the previous shot. This persistent equation of authority with criminality, and a brooding sense of destiny, make *M* as much about the crisis of German society at the time it was made as about child-murder.

Lang's next film was a sequel to his popular silent thriller about the master criminal Dr. Mabuse, *Dr. Mabuse, der Spieler* (*Dr. Mabuse, the Gambler*, 1922). In

Once, Fury, and *You and Me* (1938) as a social trilogy; links four paradigmatic 1940s *film noirs* as works about "framed desire" for "imaginary women" (*The Woman in the Window* [1944], *Scarlet Street* [1945], *Secret Beyond the Door* [1948], and *The House by the River* [1950]; and sees four 1950s crime thrillers as exposés of social corruption (*The Blue Gardenia* [1953], *The Big Heat* [1953], *While the City Sleeps* [1955], and *Beyond a Reasonable Doubt* [1956]).[1] In 1958, Lang returned to Germany to make an exotic two-part costume epic based on a 1920 screenplay by Thea von Harbou, *Der Tiger von Eschnapur* (*The Tiger of Eshnapur*) and *Das indische Grabual* (*The Indian Tomb*), both released in 1959. These were poorly received, as was his last effort, *Die Tausend Augen des Dr. Mabuse* (*The Thousand Eyes of Dr. Mabuse,* 1961), an updated pastiche of his Mabuse films. Subsequently, Lang retired and remains much honored around the world. He died in 1976.

The German film industry that Lang had left was con-

trolled from 1933 to 1945 by Goebbels, who spent considerable energy banning undesirable and "unhealthy" films like *Kameradschaft* and *M* as *entartete Kunst,* or "degenerate art." Working through the Reich Film Chamber (Reichsfilmkammer, established July 1933), under the authority of the Reich Cinema Law (Reichslichtspielgesetz, enacted February 1934), Goebbels mounted a rigorous campaign to rid the industry of its many Jews, but he saw no reason to nationalize the German cinema until well into the war, in 1942. Like the Soviet leaders, Goebbels regarded film as the century's most important communications medium,[2] but unlike them he was not much concerned with agitprop. Under his regime, Goebbels encouraged German films to remain well made but primarily escapist since he wished the populace entertained rather than enlightened. The Nazis were in fact quite skilled at manipulating the symbols of popular culture to objectify their ideals—see, for example, the musical comedies *Viktor und Viktoria* (Reinhold Schünzel, 1933) and *Amphytrion* (Schünzel, 1935).[3] Of the 1,100 to 1,300 features produced under Nazi rule, perhaps less than 25 percent contained overt propaganda. Propaganda as such was confined to newsreels and *Staatsauftragsfilme*—films conceived and financed by the state. These included bio-

9.5 Nazi cinema: Werner Krauss in *Jud Süss* (Veit Harlan, 1940).

1. See "PART IV: Fritz Lang's America—the Social Trilogy," "PART V: Framing Desire," and "PART VI: The 50s Exposés and Lang's Last Testament," in Tom Gunning, *The Films of Fritz Lang: Allegories of Vision and Modernity* (London: British Film Institute, 2000), pp. 203–480.

2. Goebbels, in a speech of February 9, 1934: "We are convinced that in general film is one of the most modern and far-reaching methods of influencing the masses. A regime thus must not allow film to go its own way." (Quoted in David Weinberg, "Approaches to the Study of Film in the Third Reich: A Critical Appraisal," *Journal of Contemporary History* 19 [1984]: 105.)

3. For years there were only two books in English dealing with Nazi cinema—David Stewart Hull's *Film in the Third Reich: A Study of the German Cinema, 1933–1945* (Berkeley: University of California Press, 1969) and Erwin Leiser's *Nazi Cinema,* trans. G. Mander and D. Wilson (New York: Macmillan, 1974). Within the past few years, however, there has been a boomlet in literature on the subject, ranging from the semipopular—e.g., Cinzia Romani's *Tainted Goddesses: Female Stars of the Third Reich,* trans. Robert Connolly (New York: Sarpedon, 1992)—to the scholarly—most exhaustively, Eric Rentschler's *The Ministry of Illusion: Nazi Cinema and Its Afterlife* (Cambridge, Mass.: Harvard University Press, 1996). Other scholarly books include Linda Schulte-Sasse's *Entertaining the Third Reich: Illusions of Wholeness in Nazi Cinema* (Durham: Duke University Press, 1996), Jo Fox's *Filming Women in the Third Reich* (New York: Berg, 2000), and Sabine Hake's *Popular Cinema of the Third Reich* (Austin: University of Texas Press, 2001).

9.6 A camera crew shooting *Triumph des Willens* (Leni Riefenstahl, 1935) at the 1934 Nazi party rally in Nuremberg.

9.7 Leni Riefenstahl's (and Adolf Hitler's) *Triumph des Willens*.

graphical and historical films of the heroic national past like *Bismarck* (Wolfgang Liebeneiner, 1940), *Der grosse König* (*Frederick the Great*, Veit Harlan, 1942), and *Kolberg* (Harlan, 1945)—the latter two in Agfacolor; dramatic films directly adulatory of the Nazi party, like *S. A. Mann Brandt* (Franz Seitz, 1933), *Hitlerjunge Quex* (Hans Steinhoff, 1933), and *Hans Westmar* (Franz Wenzler, 1933); and, finally, scurrilous racial propaganda films like the infamous *Jud Süss* (*Jew Süss*, Veit Harlan, 1940) and *Der ewige Jude* (*The Eternal Jew*, Fritz Hippler, 1940), as well as such anti-Semitic, anti-British hybrids as *Die Rothschilds Aktien von Waterloo* (*The Rothschilds' Share in Waterloo*, Erich Waschneck, 1940; rereleased 1941).[4]

The only great films to emerge from Nazi Germany were two propaganda "documentaries," both personally commissioned by Hitler for the Nazi party. The first, *Triumph des Willens* (*Triumph of the Will*, 1935), is a film of nearly mythic dimensions. Assigned to the direction of Leni Riefenstahl (b. 1902) at Hitler's insistence, *Triumph* portrays the 1934 Nazi party rally at Nuremberg as a quasi-religious, mystical experience. Working with virtually limitless financial resources, thirty cameras and a crew of 120 persons, and her own utter ideological commitment, Riefenstahl shot the film in six days with the

active cooperation of party leaders. She later wrote, "The preparations for the party congress were made in concert with the preparations for the camera work," but recent studies document that the entire congress was *staged* for her cameras by Hitler's architect Albert Speer and that nothing was left to chance.

It took her eight months to edit the footage, some of it shot after the fact to cover mistakes and continuity gaps, into a powerfully persuasive and visually beautiful piece of propaganda. Hitler is depicted as the new messiah descending from the clouds in his airplane to succor his people (the titles for this sequence were written and designed by Walter Ruttmann, who had been given the original commission on the film). Once on earth, he is greeted by the awakening city of Nuremberg and begins a god-like procession to the Kongresshalle (Congress Hall), where the impassioned rhetoric of his followers rings through the chamber. The rest is all pseudo-Wagnerian music composed by her career-long collaborator Herbert Windt, monumental Nazi architecture, mass rallies, and torchlight parades choreographed for Riefenstahl's camera. The Führer himself speaks at several points in the pageant but never more forcefully than at its emotional conclusion, where the Nazi ideal of *Blut und Boden* ("blood and soil") is invoked against the backdrop of a gigantic swastika, while SA men (Brown Shirts) in a

---

4. On Nazi and Soviet propaganda films during this era, see Richard Taylor, *Film Propaganda: Soviet Russia and Nazi Germany* (London: Taurus, 1998), and Nicholas Reeves, *The Power of Film Propaganda: Myth or Reality?* (London: Cassell, 1999).

9.8 *Olympische Spiele 1936* (Leni Riefenstahl, 1938).

super-imposed low-angle shot seem to march into distant clouds.

Triumph of the Will was effective enough to be banned in Britain, the United States, and Canada, and to become a model for film propaganda among the Allies during the coming war. Hitler was so impressed that he commissioned Riefenstahl to make a spectacular film of the 1936 Berlin Olympics. Again, unlimited resources were placed at her disposal, and her team of cameramen shot 1.5 million feet of film, which took her eighteen months to edit. The completed motion picture was released in two parts as *Olympische Spiele 1936* (*Olympiad/Olympia*) in 1938 with a dynamic score by Windt, and it stands even today as a great testament to athletic achievement, a forerunner of Kon Ichikawa's *Tokyo Olympiad* (1965) and the omnibus film of the 1972 Munich Olympics, *Visions of Eight* (Juri Ozerov, Mai Zetterling, Arthur Penn, Michael Pfleghar, Kon Ichikawa, Milos Forman, Claude Lelouch, and John Schlesinger, 1973). Riefenstahl's innovative use of slow-motion photography and telephoto lenses created images of compelling kinetic beauty, but, like *Triumph of the Will*, the film is steeped in the Nazi mystique that makes a cult of sheer physical prowess. Beyond these two powerful and disturbing films, the Nazi cinema produced few films of note, probably because most of the major filmmakers of the Weimar period had been either deported to prison camps or forced into exile.

One exception among the exiles was G. W. Pabst. Like so many of his colleagues, Pabst emigrated to Hollywood when the Nazis came to power in 1933, and he made one film, *A Modern Hero* (1934), for Warner Bros. This mildly anticapitalist melodrama was a commercial failure, effectively ending Pabst's American career, and he moved with his family to Paris, where he made a series of indifferent films for the French industry (e.g., *Mademoiselle Docteur*, 1937). Just before Germany invaded Poland in September 1939, Pabst announced his intention to re-emigrate to the United States and become a citizen, but he then crossed the Swiss border into Austria where he spent the rest of his life. Pabst would always claim that he was trapped inside the Reich by the war, yet he made three features for the Nazis, two of which, *Komödianten* (*Comedians*, 1941) and *Paracelsus* (1943), survive. These are not propaganda films as such (although Pabst may have contributed to such propaganda "documentaries" as *Feldzug em Polen* [*Campaign in Poland*, 1939]), but ideological epics of "German genius." After the war, Pabst made the anti-Nazi films *Der Prozess* (*The Trial*, 1949), a study of pogroms in nineteenth-century Hungary that won the Golden Lion at Venice; *Der letzte Akt* (*The Last Act/The Last Ten Days*, 1955–about Hitler in the bunker); and *Es geschah am 20. Juli* (*Jackboot Mutiny*, 1955), on the 1944 generals' plot to assassinate Hitler. None of this, however, could remove the moral stain of Pabst's return to the Greater German Reich to make films for Goebbels, and he did not work for the last ten years of his life.

Italy

Sound came slowly to the Italian cinema because competition from the American and German industries during the 1920s had already pushed it to the brink of collapse. By 1925, from a peak of 150 features in 1919, annual production had fallen to 15 films, most of which were coproductions with other nations. In an effort to combat the "foreign invasion" and revive the failing domestic industry, the entrepreneur Stefano Pittaluga (1887–1931) founded the Società Anonima Stefano Pittaluga (SASP) in 1926. SASP absorbed the major Italian studios (Cines, Italia, Palatina) into a private monopoly with government sanction. (An earlier attempt at private combination, L'Unione Cinematografica Italiana [UCI, founded 1919], had recently gone bankrupt and provided the core for Pittaluga's company.) In 1927, Fascist dictator Benito Mussolini (1883–1945) granted the SASP exclusive distribution rights to the documentaries and newsreels produced by L'Unione Cinematografica Educative (whose acronym, LUCE, is Italian for "light"), representing the first major collaboration between the commercial film industry and the Fascist state. It was an SASP subsidiary, Cines-Pittaluga, that produced Italy's first talkie—Gennaro Righelli's *La canzone dell'amore* (*The Song of Love*, 1930); it ultimately provided the basis for the Ente Nazionale Industrie Cinematografiche (ENIC), the distribution and exhibition agency through which the Fascists controlled the Italian industry after 1935 (see p. 356).

The earliest Italian sound films were notably undistinguished, with the exception of Alessandro Blasetti's *Terra madre* (*Mother Earth*, 1931) and *Resurrectio* (*Resurrection*, 1931) and Mario Camerini's *Figaro e la sua gran giornata* (*Figaro and His Big Day*, 1931) and *Gli uomini, che mascalzoni!* (*What Rascals Men Are!*, 1932), the latter starring the future neorealist director Vittorio De Sica. (Ironically, Camerini's *Rotaie* [*Rails*], shot and edited as a silent film in 1929 but released in 1931 with music and sound effects, was the Italian sound film's first great popular and critical success.) The introduction of sound, however, did draw Mussolini's attention to the enormous propaganda value of film, and his regime successfully manipulated the Italian industry through the decade by encouraging its expansion and controlling film content. The specific tactics will be discussed in Chapter 11, but, in general, economic incentives and subsidies caused production to rise annually until it reached 87 features by 1939. As in Nazi Germany, strict Fascist censorship dictated the production of Hollywood-style genre films—mainly romantic comedies (known as *telefono bianco* or "white telephone" films, owing to their glamorous studio sets) and family melodramas plus a modicum of nationalist propaganda centered on "heroic" themes from the past (for example, Blasetti's *1860* [1934]; Luis Trenker's German-Italian coproduction *Condottieri* [1937]; Carmine Gallone's *Scipione l'africano* [*Scipio Africanus*, 1937]) and the Fascist movement itself (Giovacchino Forzano's *Camicia nera* [*Black Shirt*, 1933]; Blasetti's *Vecchia guardia* [*The Old Guard*, 1934]).[5]

The Soviet Union

Sound was also slow in coming to the Soviet Union. Although the Soviet engineers P. G. Tager and A. F. Shorin had designed optical systems (variable density and vari-

able area, respectively) as early as 1926–27, neither was workable until 1929, and only Tager's was adopted by the industry. (The first Soviet sound films, such as Yuli Raizman's [1903–1994] *The Earth Thirsts* [*Zemlia zhazhde*, 1930], were recorded with German equipment.) It is often argued that the Soviets' late start enabled them to profit from the mistakes of their Western counterparts, and it is true, for example, that the Soviet studios never had to struggle with sound-on-disc, which was already obsolete by the time they started sound production. But it is also true that the earliest Soviet transitional films were technically inferior to those of the West and clearly suffered from their makers' lack of instruction and experience.

There were exceptions, of course—Kuleshov's *The Great Consoler* (*Velikii uteshitel*, 1933), Vertov's *Enthusiasm* (*Entuziazm*, 1931, suppressed) and *Three Songs of Lenin* (*Tri pesni o Leninye*, 1934), Pudovkin's *A Simple Case* (*Prostoi sluchai*, 1932—released silent due to Communist party intervention) and *Deserter* (*Dezertir*, 1933), and Dovzhenko's *Ivan* (1932). Moreover, it was Soviet directors like Vertov who pioneered the sound documentary and sound montage. Nevertheless, sound and silent cinema continued to coexist for nearly six years, the last Soviet silent production being released in 1936, the same year as the first Soviet color film. (Indeed, the majority of Soviet theaters were not wired for sound until 1938.)

Sound arrived in the Soviet Union, as it had in Germany, during a period of political reaction. The first of the great purges, in which millions of Soviet citizens as well as government functionaries were imprisoned or executed, began in the late 1920s. Fear and xenophobia were rife, and, again as in Germany, the Soviet cinema became increasingly escapist as the government became increasingly repressive. The bold revolutionary experiments of the past decade were dead. They were replaced by Hollywood-influenced musicals like Grigori Alexandrov's *The Jolly Fellows/Jazz Comedy* (*Veselye rebiata*, 1934); historical spectacles like Vladimir Petrov's *Peter the Great, Parts I and II* (*Petr Pervyi*, 1937–38); and biog-

5. Recent work touching on the cinema of Italian Fascism includes Simonetta Falasca-Zamponi, *Fascist Spectacle: The Aesthetics of Power in Mussolini's Italy* (Berkeley: University of California Press, 1997); Ruth Ben-Ghiat, *Fascist Modernities: Italy, 1922–1945* (Berkeley: University of California Press, 2001); and Jacqueline Reich and Piero Garofalo, eds., *Re-viewing Fascism: Italian Cinema, 1922–1943* (Bloomington: Indiana University Press, 2002).

raphies of revolutionary heroes, like the Vasilievs' *Chapaev* (1934)[6] and Dovzhenko's *Shchors* (1939), putatively evocative of Stalin. Related to the latter genre were dramatic reconstructions of revolutionary events in the stolid style of socialist realism, such as Mikhail Romm's *Lenin in October* (*Lenin v oktiabre*, 1937) and *Lenin in 1918* (*Lenin v 1918 godu*, 1939).

Perhaps the most vital Soviet films of this period were two trilogies. The first, directed by Grigori Kozintsev and Leonid Trauberg, created a "synthetic biography" of a typical young party worker during the revolutionary period in *The Youth of Maxim* (*Yunost Maksima*, 1935), *The Return of Maxim* (*Vozvrashchenie Maksima*, 1937), and *The Vyborg Side* (*Vyborgskaia storona*, 1939). All three films were shot by the brilliant cinematographer Andrei Moskvin (1901–1961), who would later work closely with Eisenstein. Mark Donskoi contributed a robust adaptation of the three-volume autobiography of the Soviet writer Maxim Gorki (1868–1936)—*The Childhood of Maxim Gorki* (*Detstvo Gorkogo*, 1938), *My Apprenticeship* (*V Liudiakh*, 1939), and *My Universities* (*Moi universitety*, 1940).

During most of this period, the man who might have returned the Soviet cinema to its former glory remained inactive. Sergei Eisenstein had returned to Moscow from his American sojourn badly discouraged. All of his Paramount projects had been abortive, so in late 1930 he had signed a contract with the Mexican Film Trust, a corporation formed by the American novelist Upton Sinclair (1878–1968)[7] and other investors to produce an Eisenstein film in Mexico. Eisenstein had long been interested in Mexico as both a cultural and a revolutionary phenomenon, and he later wrote that the film he had envisioned would have been "four novels framed by prologue and epilogue, unified in conception and spirit, creating its entity." Provisionally entitled *Que viva México!*, the film would have been an attempt to encapsulate revolutionary Mexican history and evoke the spirit of the culture and the land. Eisenstein (working with Alexandrov and Eduard Tisse) had shot all of the film's sections except the last by 1932, when, as the climax of a series of misunderstandings, Sinclair abruptly ordered him to abandon the project, claiming correctly that Eisenstein had far exceeded his budget. All of the footage was in Hollywood for processing, and it was never sent back to Eisenstein. Although Sinclair had promised to ship the negative to Moscow for Eisenstein to edit into a feature

film, he eventually turned it over to the independent producer Sol Lesser (1890–1980). Lesser cut parts of one episode into a silent melodrama of revenge entitled *Thunder over Mexico* (1933), with a recorded orchestral score by Hugo Riesenfeld. Parts of the epilogue, also edited by Lesser, were released in 1934 as *Death Day*. Both films were critical and commercial failures, and there was a heated controversy among American artists and intellectuals over the question of who was to blame. The rest of the footage ultimately found its way into various documentaries about the making of the film, and into the archives of MoMA in New York. From what is left of it, we can surmise that *Que viva México!* might have been Eisenstein's greatest film and the ultimate vindication of his theories of montage. Its dismemberment disturbed Eisenstein deeply, and it remains, with von Stroheim's *Greed* (1924; see Chapter 6) and Welles's *The Magnificent Ambersons* (1942; see Chapter 10), one of the great lost masterworks of the cinema.[8]

In Moscow again, Eisenstein conceived a number of projects, but they were systematically thwarted by Boris Shumiatski, the head of the Soviet film industry, who with full official sanction began a campaign to discredit Eisenstein and reduce his influence within the Soviet cinema. The Stalin government believed that Eisenstein had grown too independent during his American tour and that he set a dangerous example for other Soviet artists. Also, Shumiatski hated Eisenstein personally, not an uncommon response to the director's eccentric personality and irreverent sense of humor. In 1935 Eisenstein was publicly insulted at the Congress of Party Film Workers and

---

6. Sergei (1900–1959) and Georgi (1899–1946) Vasiliev were unrelated filmmakers who met as students of Eisenstein at the VGIK. As "the Vasiliev brothers," they collaborated closely on the direction of six features between 1930 and 1943.

7. Sinclair was an internationally prominent socialist writer and a friend of the Bolshevik Revolution. Like Lenin, he believed that film was the most powerful medium of ideological persuasion in modern times, and he saw in the Eisenstein venture a chance to produce a sort of Latin American *Potemkin*.

8. In 1973 the Soviet state film archive Gosfilmofond negotiated a deal with MoMA and the Sinclair estate to secure copies of all extant footage of Eisenstein's Mexican film. In August 1979, Sovexport released an "official" restoration of *Que viva México!* by Grigori Alexandrov, Eisenstein's assistant on the production, who claimed to possess Eisenstein's original cutting schedule. Reviews were unenthusiastic, but the Alexandrov reconstruction is as close as we are ever likely to come to the film Eisenstein intended.

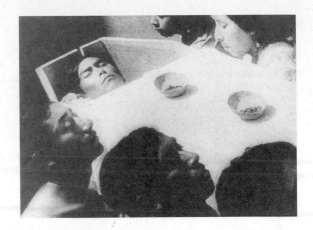

9.9 Stills from Eisenstein's aborted epic *Que viva México!* (1930–32, uncompleted and unreleased).

attacked in the official press. He was also offered projects by Shumiatski that he seemed likely to reject, but the most flagrant abuse committed against him was the suppression of what would have been his first sound film, *Bezhin Meadow* (*Bezhin lug*), which had been approved for production in 1935.

Starting from a short story by the nineteenth-century writer Ivan Turgenev, Eisenstein planned to dramatize the real-life tragedy of a contemporary kulak who killed his son (Pavlik Morozov) for turning informer and for supporting collectivization. Shooting began in the spring of 1935 but was interrupted in September, when Eisenstein fell ill with smallpox. Upon Eisenstein's return to the set, Shumiatski demanded major revisions in the

9.10 Stills from Eisenstein's suppressed *Bezhin Meadow* (1935, uncompleted and unreleased).

9.11 *Alexander Nevski:* Teutonic barbarism in the captured city of Pskov.

script to force it in the direction of socialist realism. Eisenstein undertook these, in collaboration with Isaac Babel, and he had nearly completed the film when he fell ill again. This time, Shumiatski halted production and published a harsh attack on Eisenstein in *Pravda*; the director himself was forced to publicly recant the film and confess to ideological errors that, in fact, had little to do with its content. This act of self-abasement apparently satisfied the party bureaucrats: a year later, after Shumiatski was deposed and killed, Eisenstein was entrusted with the production of a big-budget historical film of major political importance, *Alexander Nevski* (1938).

On what many observers felt was the eve of a Nazi invasion, Eisenstein was chosen to make a film about how the great Slavic hero Prince Alexander Nevski of Novgorod had rallied the Russian people to repel an invading force of Teutonic Knights in the thirteenth century. It was Eisenstein's first sound film and the consummate realization of his theories of contrapuntal sound. According to Georges Sadoul, Eisenstein conceived the entire film as an opera in which Sergei Prokofiev's brilliant score would alternately complement and conflict with the film's visual rhythms. And these rhythms are among the most beautiful the director ever achieved. Every shot in *Alexander Nevski* is painstakingly composed in terms of the plastic arrangement of space, mass, and light within the frame. The Teutonic Knights, for example, always appear in strictly geometrical formations, while the Russian ranks are asymmetrical, suggesting the monolithic rigidity of the Germans as contrasted with the vital but disorganized Russians. Eisenstein closely supervised the details of the production, including costume design and makeup,[9] and one of his most striking conceptions was the battle dress of the German invaders. Clearly influenced by the sinister headgear of the Ku Klux Klansmen in *The Birth of a Nation*, Eisenstein costumed his Teutonic Knights throughout the film in menacing steel helmets with tiny slits for eyeholes, so that their faces were not visible, unlike those of the Russians. The barbaric military regalia that adorned these helmets, the symbol of the cross on the Knights' white tunics and capes (cleverly positioned to resemble armbands with swastikas), and the atrocities committed upon the people of Pskov in the second reel all serve to identify clearly the Teutons with the Nazis.

The film's most impressive sequence is the famous Battle on the Ice on frozen Lake Peipus in northwest Russia, actually shot in the outskirts of Moscow in midsummer with artificial snow and ice. Here the decisive battle between the Teutons and the Russian defenders is rendered in a spectacular audiovisual montage complete with **swish pans** and a jolting, rough-and-tumble camera style that would not be seen again until the early days of the French New Wave. (The Battle on the Ice in *Nevski*

greatly influenced the staging of the Battle of Agincourt in Laurence Olivier's *Henry V* [1944], a film with similar nationalistic/patriotic motives.) Eisenstein appropriately called *Alexander Nevski* "a fugue on the theme of patriotism." Despite the objections of some foreign critics to its operatic structure, the film was an enormous critical and popular success in many Western countries as well as in the Soviet Union, where it temporarily restored Eisenstein to his position of esteem within the Soviet cinema. (He received both the Order of Lenin and the Stalin Prize for it in 1939 and 1941, respectively.)

Alexander Nevski was discreetly withdrawn from domestic distribution in the wake of the Nazi-Soviet Non-aggression Pact of 1939, but it was revived with a great display of patriotism after Hitler's treacherous invasion of Russia in 1941. In the meantime, Eisenstein wrote the scenario for *The Great Ferghana Canal* (with Pyotr Pavlenko, his coscenarist on *Nevski*), which he envisioned as "a triptych about the struggle for water" in the Central Asian desert spanning three stages of history from antiquity to the present. The project was approved, and Eisenstein had begun location shooting in Uzbekistan, when— for reasons still unknown—it was abruptly canceled. Shortly thereafter, however, he was invited to stage Wagner's opera *Die Walküre* at the Bolshoi Theater to commemorate a state visit by the Nazi propaganda minister, Joseph Goebbels, "in the mutual interests of German and Russian culture." Eisenstein accepted and produced a remarkable version of the massive Teutonic music drama in which he attempted, as he later wrote, to achieve "a fusion between the elements of Wagner's score and the wash of colors on the stage" through lighting. The psychologist of perception was still very much alive in Eisenstein, but he had advanced from reflexology to synesthesia.[1] And just as he had used the Proletkult Theater as a testing ground for his developing theories of montage, he used his 1940 production of Wagner's opera as a laboratory for his new ideas on the dramatic interplay

---

9. According to Jay Leyda and Zina Voynow in *Eisenstein at Work* (New York: Pantheon/Museum of Modern Art, 1982), this careful planning permitted much of the actual shooting to be done by Eisenstein's assistant director, Dmitri Vasiliev (unrelated to "the Vasiliev brothers"); they also maintain that *Nevsky* was released with a reel missing, which has never been recovered.

1. The use of one mode of sensory stimulation to produce responses in other senses.

9.12 *Alexander Nevski:* the Battle on the Ice is joined.

9.13 Eisenstein's *Ivan the Terrible, Part I* (1945): the coronation of Ivan Vasilievich as tsar of Moscow, autocrat of all the Russias, in the Ouspensky Cathedral, January 16, 1547. Nikolai Cherkasov as Ivan.

9.15 Retired to a provincial palace, the grief-stricken Ivan is petitioned to return to Moscow by his people.

of sound, space, and color, so important to his last two films.

Some time in 1940, Eisenstein conceived the notion of making an epic film trilogy about the life of Tsar Ivan IV, known in Russian as *grozny* ("awesome," "terrible"), the Nevski-like figure who had first unified much of Russia in the sixteenth century. This project was to be the consummation of all his theory and practice, and Eisenstein spent two full years studying his subject. Production began simultaneously on all three films at the Alma-Ata studios in Central Asia in 1943.[2] Instead of a shooting

9.14 Ivan in his study with an ambassador to England.

script, Eisenstein used a series of his own sketches as his scenario. *Ivan the Terrible (Ivan Grozny), Part I* was completed and released in early 1945, and it immediately won the Stalin Prize for artistic achievement. *Part II, The Boyars' Plot (Boyarskii zagovor)*, completed in Moscow between 1945 and 1946, was previewed in August 1946 and promptly banned by the Party Central Committee for "ignorance in the presentation of historical fact." (Eisenstein had apparently been too critical of the *oprichniki*, Ivan's political police, for Stalin's paranoid taste.) When this happened, Eisenstein was in the hospital recovering from a heart attack, and the four completed reels of *Part III* were surreptitiously confiscated and destroyed. In February 1947, Eisenstein bargained personally with Stalin for alterations that would permit *Part*

2. Soviet motion-picture studios and equipment factories near the invasion front were evacuated eastward with their personnel after June 1941. Mosfilm, Lenfilm, and the VGIK were relocated to Alma-Ata in the Kazakh Republic, whose modest facilities (actually, the former Palace of Culture) could accommodate only one set at a time. The interiors for Ivan's three parts were shot there in 1943 and 1944 from dusk to dawn, when electricity could be safely diverted from wartime industries. Exteriors for *Part I* and some of *Part II* were also shot at Alma-Ata; but the Soviet production system resumed its normal configuration after the Allied victory in May 1945.

9.16 *Ivan the Terrible, Part II* (1946): in the pompous throne-room of King Sigismond of Poland, the conspirators against the tsar learn of his return to Moscow.

II's distribution, but he never regained his health sufficiently to make them. (The film was suppressed until 1958, five years after Stalin's death.) Eisenstein wrote his memoirs, dreamed of adapting *War and Peace*, and died at the age of fifty, on February 11, 1948, only a few months before the death of D. W. Griffith.

His last bequest to the cinema was a two-part film of incomparable formal beauty of which he wrote, "The grandeur of our theme necessitated a grandiose design." *Ivan the Terrible, Parts I* and *II*, is quintessentially a

9.17 In Moscow, Pimen, archbishop of Novgorod, plots with Euphrosinia to murder Ivan and place her weak-minded son Vladimir on the throne.

film whose meaning is its design. The montage aesthetics of the great silent films are subordinated here, like all other plastic elements, to elaborate compositions within the frame photographed by Tisse (exteriors) and Moskvin (interiors) in which even the actors become part of the decor (much as they were part of the montage patterns of the silent films). Eisenstein demanded highly expressive and even contorted performances from his actors—especially from Nikolai Cherkasov (1903–1966), in the role of Ivan (he had also played Nevski)—and achieved a *mise-en-scène* whose hieratic stylization is deliberately reminiscent of the work of the sixteenth-century painter El Greco. Like *Alexander Nevski, Ivan the Terrible* is an operatic film with a magnificent Prokofiev score employed contrapuntally throughout. Furthermore, in his quest for synesthesia and total sensory saturation, Eisenstein even used a red–tinted color sequence (his first—made with Agfacolor stock captured from the Germans) in *Part II* to create a certain emotional tonality for the wild dance of the *oprichniki*.

Ivan the Terrible may seem a strange ending to a career that began with *Strike* and *Potemkin*. It is heavy, ornate, and static where they are light and fast. But, ultimately, all of Eisenstein's films are cut from the same cloth. His devotion to pictorial beauty, his fascination with the psychology of perception, and his epic aspirations pervade everything he undertook. If Eisenstein turned from agitprop to grand opera in his later years, it was perhaps because, after nearly two decades of bitter experience under the Stalin regime, he no longer believed in any cause beyond the nobility and necessity of art.

France

AVANT-GARDE IMPRESSIONISM, 1921–1929

Next to America's, the film industry with the most prominent national image in the 1930s was that of France. After World War I, Paris had become the center of an international avant-garde encompassing cubism, **surrealism,** dadaism, and futurism, and many intellectuals involved with these movements had become intensely interested in the possibilities of film to embody dream states and to express modernist conceptions of time and space. The most prominent among them was the young author and editor Louis Delluc (1890–1924), who founded the journal *Cinéma* and became, long before Eisenstein, the first aesthetic theorist of the film. Delluc's practical mission was the founding of a truly French national cinema that would be authentically cinematic. To this end, he rejected much of French cinema as it had evolved before the war—especially the theatrical abuses of *film d'art*—and turned instead to the models of Sweden (Sjöström and Stiller), America (Chaplin, Ince, and Griffith), and Germany (Expressionism and *Kammerspiel*). Delluc began to write original scenarios and gathered about him a group of young filmmakers who became known as the French "impressionist" school,[3] or the "first avant-garde"—Germaine Dulac, Jean Epstein, Marcel L'Herbier, and Abel Gance—although, as Richard Abel points out, "narrative avant-garde" would be a better term, since all of them worked at the periphery of the French commercial industry making features. Delluc himself directed a handful of important films, including *Fièvre* (*Fever*, 1921) and *La Femme de nulle part* (*The Woman from Nowhere*, 1922), both of which are reminiscent of *Kammerspiel* in their concern with creating atmosphere and preserving the unities of time and place.

Germaine Dulac (1882–1942), one of cinema's first female artists, directed Delluc's first scenario *La Fête espagnole* (*The Spanish Festival*, 1920) and went on to become an important figure in the avant-garde and documentary cinema. Her most significant impressionist films were short, forty-minute features: *La Souriante Madame Beudet* (*The Smiling Madame Beudet*, 1923), an intimate psychological portrait of middle-class marriage in a drab provincial setting adapted from the play by avant-gardists André Obey and Denys Amiel, and *La Coquille et le clergyman* (*The Seashell and the Clergyman*, 1928), a surrealist exposition of sexual repression from a scenario by Antonin Artaud. *La Souriante Madame Beudet* employs a minimal storyline as an armature for the subjective camera, which is used to convey the interiority not only of its main character, but of others as well (and predates the subjective camera of Murnau's *Der letzte Mann* by at least a year). As Sandy Flitterman-Lewis points out, more than half the film is devoted to a form of cinematic internal monologue, which conveys an enormous range of internal states, from ideas and memories through fantasy and hallucination.[4] *The Seashell and the Clergyman* is arguably the first surrealist feature, con-

9.18 Surrealism in *La Coquille et le clergyman* (Germaine Dulac, 1928).

structed entirely on dream logic and the materialization of unconscious processes, which links it more closely with the "second" avant-garde than with impressionism (see pp. 308–13).

Jean Epstein (1897–1953), like Delluc, began his career in film as a theorist but contributed a major work to the impressionist cinema in 1923 with *Coeur fidèle* (*Faithful Heart*), the story of a working-class love triangle in Marseilles with a fine feeling for landscape and atmosphere that is nevertheless boldly experimental in form. Yet according to the film historian Georges Sadoul, this film, for all its sophisticated use of the moving camera and rapid cutting, incarnates the quality of *populisme*, which may be seen in French films as early as the Lumière shorts[5] and which was the major legacy of impressionism to the French cinema—a fascination with

3. Unrelated to the late nineteenth-century movement in painting known as French Impressionism. See Eugene C. McCreary, "Louis Delluc, Film Theorist, Critic, and Prophet," *Cinema Journal* 16, 1 (Fall 1976): 14–35.

4. Sandy Flitterman-Lewis to author, 10/25/92. I am indebted to Flitterman-Lewis for my entire discussion of Dulac, whose art is most fully delineated in her *To Desire Differently: Feminism and the French Cinema* (Urbana: University of Illinois Press, 1990).

5. Later (and, predominantly, Marxist) French critics, however, have found little populisme in the Lumière films. Vincent Pinel writes of

ordinary people and settings, with dramas of the working class, and with outdoor shooting in natural settings such as seaports, fairgrounds, and bistros. Epstein's later *La Chute de la maison Usher* (*The Fall of the House of Usher*, 1928) used a variety of brilliant technical effects to create for this Edgar Allan Poe tale what Henri Langlois called "the cinematic equivalent of Debussy," while his *Finis terrae* (1929), shot on location at Land's End in Brittany, was an avant-garde forecast of neorealism.

The most faithful follower of Delluc's theories was Marcel L'Herbier (1890–1979), who had been a prominent symbolist poet before turning to filmmaking in 1917. The most cerebral member of the impressionist group, L'Herbier was concerned largely with abstract form and with the use of visual effects to express inner states. His *L'Homme du large* (*The Big Man*, 1920) was an adaptation of a short story by the nineteenth-century realist Honoré de Balzac shot on location on the southern coast of Brittany, whose frames were composed to resemble Impressionist paintings. The visual texture of *Eldorado* (1921), a melodrama of Spanish lowlife set in a cabaret, recalls the paintings of Claude Monet and virtually synthesizes early avant-garde technique, while *Don Juan et Faust* (*Don Juan and Faust*, 1923) used cubism to the same end. L'Herbier's most extravagant impressionist film, *L'Inhumaine* (*The Inhuman Woman*, 1924), with a score by Darius Milhaud and sets by the cubist painter Fernand Léger and Robert Mallet-Stevens, was an essay in visual abstraction thinly disguised as science fiction; it ends with an apocalyptic montage sequence designed

to synthesize movement, music, sound, and color.[6] But *L'Argent* (1929)—a spectacular updating of Zola's 1891 novel about stock-market manipulation during the Second Empire (c. 1868)—is widely regarded today as L'Herbier's greatest film. In it, he employed antitraditional camera and editing strategies to create a destabilized narrative space within a series of immense, streamlined studio sets designed by André Barsacq and Lazare Meerson, providing both an image and a critique of unbridled capitalism on the brink of the Great Depression.

Abel Gance (1889–1981), like Erich von Stroheim, was one of the great maverick talents of the cinema, and his affiliation with the impressionists was fleeting at best. Born into a bourgeois family, Gance had been a poet, an actor, and a scriptwriter before forming his own production company in 1911. Despite some impressive experimental work, including the Caligariesque *La Folie du Docteur Tube* (*Dr. Tube's Mania*, 1915), Gance did not achieve fame until the success of his beautifully photographed[7] melodramas, *Mater Dolorosa* (1917) and *La Dixième Symphonie* (*The Tenth Symphony*, 1918; restored from an original tinted print in 1986 by the Ciné-

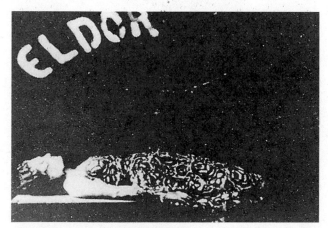

9.19 *Eldorado* (Marcel L'Herbier, 1921).

them, for example: "The image which these 'views' give of appearances (by the choice of subjects more than by a bias caused by any deliberate rhetoric or deformation) is the image that the dominant class at the end of the century seeks to give of the world and itself. An image of self-satisfaction, a clear conscience, a quiet certainty, and values posited (or imposed) as universal and eternal. Lumière's films praise in their way—and admirably—the virtues of Work, Family, and Fatherland. Which after all is surely a normal effect of the historical situation" ("Louis Lumière," in *Anthologies du cinéma*, No. 78 [Paris, 1974], p. 447).

6. Like American films of the era, most French films were tinted and/or toned in a variety of colors during the 1920s, often with spectacular psychological effect (see Chapter 7, on tinting and toning). Most of the color in these films, like their original musical arrangements and special scores, has been lost, as has the singular impact of those few films that were exhibited exclusively in black and white (e.g., Dreyer's *La Passion de Jeanne d'Arc*, 1928; Epstein's *La Chute de la maison Usher*, 1928). See Kevin Brownlow, "The Glory That Was France," *Sight and Sound* 56, 3 (Summer 1987): 204–9, on the two-part British National Film Theatre season celebrating French cinema of the 1920s (January-April 1987). See also Maureen Turim, "French Melodrama: Theory of a Specific History," *Theater Journal* 39 (Spring 1989), 307–27.

7. The cinematographer for most of Gance's silent features was Léonce-Henri Burel (1892–1977), a pioneering genius of a cameraman who also did distinguished work for Jacques Feyder and Jean Renoir, and ended his career by collaborating with Robert Bresson on his greatest films from 1951 to 1963.

9.20 Polyvision triptych from *Napoléon vu par Abel Gance* (1927).

mathèque Française). Then he struck out on his own to pursue a dual obsession with technical innovation and epic form. Deeply influenced by *Intolerance*, Gance practiced complex metaphorical intercutting in his symbolic antiwar narrative *J'accuse!* (*I Accuse!*, 1919),[8] and then contributed the extraordinary modern epic *La Roue* (*The Wheel*, 1922–23) to the impressionist movement.

Written, directed, and edited by Gance, *La Roue* was shot almost entirely on location, from the railway yards at Nice to the Alps at St. Gervaise, and took nearly three years to complete. It tells the tragic story of an engine driver and his son who are both in love with the same woman—their adopted daughter and sister, respectively—

and deliberately resonates with the myths of Oedipus, Sisyphus, Prometheus, and Christ. Like von Stroheim's *Greed* (1924), the film was intended for release in a nine-hour version but was cut by Gance at the request of its producer (Charles Pathé) to two and a half hours. *La Roue* also attracted the intense admiration of Griffith, to whom Gance had shown *J'accuse!* during a visit to the United States in 1921. *La Roue*, whose editing clearly owes much to the contact with Griffith, was originally thirty-two reels long and divided into a prologue and

---

8. Remade by Gance as a sound film in 1937.

three parts; Gance cut the general-release version to fourteen, and rereleases have reduced it even further. Even in the shortened version, Gance's intercutting approaches Eisenstein's in its sophistication and metaphorical power, and its atmospheric evocation of life in the railway yards is close to the spirit of the nineteenth-century epic naturalist Émile Zola. Monumental, technically dazzling, hyperromantic, and frequently tasteless, *La Roue* influenced a whole generation of French avant-garde filmmakers, including Fernand Léger and Jean Cocteau, and its editing was widely studied in the Soviet film schools during the 1920s.

Gance's next film, *Napoléon vu par Abel Gance: première époque: Bonaparte* (*Napoleon as Seen by Abel Gance: First Part: Bonaparte*, 1927), was produced by the Société Génerale des Films and financed largely by Russian émigré funds. It stands today with *Intolerance* (1916) and *Greed* (1924) as one of the great eccentric masterpieces of the silent cinema. Twenty-eight reels in its original version but reduced to eight by subsequent distributors, *Napoléon* required four years to produce and was only the first part of a projected six-part film of the life of Bonaparte (strikingly played by Albert Dieudonné) that was never completed. As it stands, it covers his youth, the revolution, and the opening of the Italian campaign, and there is scarcely a passage in the film that does not make use of some innovative and original device. From beginning to end, Gance assaulted his audience with the entire arsenal of silent-screen techniques, and the effect is impressive. As in *La Roue*, he used sophisticated metaphorical intercutting to inundate the viewer with significant images, many of them lasting only a few frames; and at times he superimposed as many as sixteen simultaneous images on the screen. At several points in *Napoléon*, Gance also used a widescreen process called Polyvision,[9] which expanded the frame to three times its normal width, but the most original achievement of *Napoléon* was the astonishing fluidity of its camera work.

The recent manufacture in France of lightweight, portable cameras (specifically, the Debrie Photociné Sept) made possible many extraordinary subjective camera shots and traveling shots that went far beyond the pioneering work of Murnau and Freund in *Der letzte Mann* (1924) and that would not be seen again until the advent of the handheld 35mm sound camera some twenty-five years later. In the Corsican sequence, for example, the camera was strapped to the back of a galloping horse to shoot the landscape as it would have been seen by the rider. Later, encased in a waterproof box, the camera was hurled from a steep cliff into the Mediterranean to approximate the impressions of Napoleon as he dived. To film the tumultuous Paris Convention, Gance mounted the camera on a huge pendulum to convey the radical swaying back and forth between Girondist and Jacobin factions, and he intercut this shot with one of Napoleon's boat on its way to France pitching to and fro in a storm at sea. Finally, in scenes from the siege of Toulon, a small camera was even mounted in a football and tossed into the air to simulate the perspective of a cannonball.

The Polyvision process, conceived by Gance specifically for *Napoléon* and designed by camera pioneer André Debrie, anticipated the modern Cinerama process in that it employed a triptych, or three-panel screen, to show three standard 35mm images side by side. Gance used the process in two distinct ways. Often he would supplement the primary image on the middle screen with complementary and/or contrapuntal images on either side to achieve a kind of lateral montage within the frame. At several points during the Italian campaign, for instance, huge close-ups of Bonaparte's head or of a symbolic eagle dominate the middle screen while marching troops of the Grande Armée stream across the side panels. (This widescreen triptych effect was not again used successfully until Michael Wadleigh's documentary *Woodstock* in 1970; see p. 855.) At other times, Gance used Polyvision more naturalistically to explode the screen into a single vast panoramic image for mass scenes, as during the Italian campaign and the Convention. This image was photographed by three identical Parvo-Debrie cameras mounted one on top of the other in an arc and synchronized to run concurrently by means of a flexible motor shaft. Like so many other elements of *Napoléon*, Polyvision was twenty-five years ahead of its time (and, by his own admission, it inspired Professor Henri Chrétien, the father of modern widescreen processes, to perfect the **anamorphic lens** in 1941; see pp. 392–95).

Gance made nothing comparable to *Napoléon* for the

rest of his career,[1] although he constantly returned to it, adding stereophonic sound for Arthur Honegger's original score, some dialogue scenes, and, as late as 1971, re-editing it in a four-hour version with new footage as *Bonaparte et la révolution*. Yet audiences in only eight European cities saw *Napoléon* in its original form, which, of course, included a full range of tints and tones, with the triptych screen becoming an enormous blue, white, and red tricolor at the film's stirring conclusion. It was cut to less than one-third of its length for overseas distribution, and there was no definitive print of the original silent film until a Herculean task of restoration was performed by the British filmmaker and film historian Kevin Brownlow (b. 1938) in 1979. A seventeen-reel reconstruction by the Cinémathèque Française excited the passionate admiration of the young *cinéastes* of the French New Wave when it was shown in Paris in the late 1950s and contributed substantially to a resurrection of Gance's critical reputation. But Brownlow's full-triptych reconstruction runs twenty-eight reels, or six hours at 20 fps, although approximately one-half hour of the original footage is still missing. It was premiered at the Telluride (Colorado) Film Festival in September 1979—with Gance present, in honor of his ninetieth birthday[2]—demonstrating with finality what Brownlow has maintained all along: "The visual resources of the cinema have never been stretched further than in *Napoléon vu par Abel Gance*. The picture is an encyclopedia of cinematic effects—a pyrotechnic display of what the silent film was capable of in the hands of a genius."

THE "SECOND" AVANT-GARDE

Louis Delluc died of tuberculosis in 1924, and the French impressionist film entered a period of decadent formalism shortly thereafter; but, in the rise of serious French film criticism and the *ciné-club* (film society) movement, Delluc's influence survived him and the school he founded. By the mid-1920s, film reviews had become a standard feature of almost every newspaper published in France. Professional film writers like Léon Moussinac (1890–1964) were establishing a tradition of cinema studies in France that was to make that country the home of the most advanced and subtle thinking on film from 1925 through the present. As Georges Sadoul has written: "This group of men [sic] was the first in Europe to assert the stature of the film as an art—the equal (or even the superior) of music, literature and the theatre—and to obtain recognition for it as such. With the creation of independent film criticism they gave body and substance to their claim. . . . Henceforward the cinema became a subject of dinner-table conversation like the novel or the play, and there emerged a group among the intellectual elite for whom it was a major artistic preoccupation." The *ciné-club* movement was founded by Delluc, Moussinac, Germaine Dulac, and Ricciotto Canudo (1879–1923) in Paris, where it achieved great success and spread rapidly to the provinces. Some *ciné-clubs* ultimately became specialized film theaters, where a knowledgeable public could see serious films unavailable to it in conventional cinemas. Since French commercial film production reached a new low point during the 1920s, both finan-

---

1. Some critics would argue that Gance's *Un Grand amour de Beethoven* (1936), recently restored by Images Archives, represents a contribution to the aesthetics of the sound film comparable *in kind*, if not degree, to that of *Napoléon* to silent cinema.

2. In Telluride, Gance announced plans for another film epic, to be entitled *Christopher Columbus*. "Right now the cinema is dead," he said; "*Columbus* will bring it back to life" (*Variety*, September 18, 1979, p. 28). On the general difficulty of seeing Gance films in the United States, see William M. Drew, "Abel Gance: Prometheus Bound," *Take One* 6, 8 (July 1978): 30–32, 45. Brownlow's reconstruction, produced by the British Film Institute and Images Archives in association with Thames Television, was distributed theatrically in the United States by Francis Ford Coppola's Zoetrope Studios with an orchestral score by Carmine Coppola and tinted triptych sequences for projection at 24 fps. In the summer of 1983, an even more complete version was shown by Brownlow in Paris and deposited with the Cinémathèque Française as the definitive print (to date). A full account of Brownlow's twenty-year struggle to restore *Napoléon* is contained in Kevin Brownlow, "Abel Gance's Epic *Napoléon* Returns from Exile," *American Film* 6, 1 (January-February 1981): 28–31, 68–72; and *Napoleon: Abel Gance's Classic Film* (New York: Knopf, 1983). See also James Welsh and Steven Kramer, *Abel Gance* (Boston: Twayne, 1978), which contains previously unpublished material from the *Columbus* script; William K. Everson, "The Many Lives of 'Napoleon,'" *Film Comment* 17, 1 (January–February 1981): 21–23; Peter Pappas, "The Superimposition of Vision: Napoleon and the Meaning of Fascist Art," *Cinéaste* 11, 2 (Spring 1986): 4–13; Sean French, "The *Napoleon* Phenomenon," *Sight and Sound* 51, 2 (Spring 1982): 93–96; Richard Abel, "Charge and Counter-Charge: Coherence and Incoherence in Gance's *Napoléon*," *Film Quarterly* 35, 3 (Spring 1982): 2–14; and Norman King, *Abel Gance: A Politics of Spectacle* (London: British Film Institute, 1984). Films on Gance include Nelly Kaplan's *Abel Gance: hier et demain* (Abel Gance: Yesterday and Tomorrow [1963, 28m.]); Kevin Brownlow's *Abel Gance: The Charm of Dynamite* (1968, 56m.); and Kaplan's *Abel Gance et son Napoléon* (Abel Gance and His Napoléon [1984]).

cially and aesthetically, it was largely these specialized theaters and *ciné-clubs* that kept the creative tradition of French cinema alive and that ushered it into the sound era by enabling a second wave of French avant-garde filmmakers to find an audience.

The "second" avant-garde had its roots in the literary and artistic movements of dadaism and surrealism. Like the impressionists, the members of these later groups represented the first generation to "think spontaneously in animated images," as Émile Vuillermoz put it in a contemporary review of Gance's *La Roue*. Unlike the impressionists, however, they wished to create a pure cinema of visual sensation completely divorced from conventional narrative—or, as they put it in their manifestos, to make films without subjects. The first to attempt this was an American photographer living in Paris, Man Ray (1890–1976), whose brief *Le Retour à la raison* (*Return to Reason*, 1923) offered its audience a kaleidoscopic succession of barely discernible images. A year later the cubist painter Fernand Léger and his American technical collaborator Dudley Murphy produced *Ballet mécanique*, in which isolated objects, pieces of machinery, posters, and newspaper headlines were animated into a rhythmic ballet of plastic forms. The most famous of the early avant-garde films was indisputedly René Clair's *Entr'acte* (1924), made to be shown at the intermission of Francis Picabia's dadaist ballet *Relâche* (*Performance Suspended*). With a score by Erik Satie, who also wrote the music for the ballet, *Entr'acte* was a logically meaningless succession of outrageous images, many derived from the tradition of the Pathé/Gaumont *course comique* and the serials of Feuillade (see pp. 43–46). Clair's *Paris qui dort* (English title: *The Crazy Ray*, 1924) was an irreverent but lyrical nonstory of a mad scientist who invents an invisible ray to immobilize all of Paris except for six persons who eventually take up residence in the Eiffel Tower. Clair went on to become a major figure in the sound film, as did the Spanish-born director Luis Buñuel (1900–1983), whose *Un Chien andalou* (*An Andalusian Dog*, 1929) represents the avant-garde at its most mature, most surreal, and most Freudian.

Written in collaboration with the surrealist painter Salvador Dalí (1904–1989), *Un Chien andalou* provides a seemingly incoherent stream of brutal, erotic images from the unconscious that Buñuel called "a despairing, passionate call to murder." In the course of the film, we witness in close-up a woman's eyeball being slashed in two

9.21 Part of a film loop from *Ballet mécanique* (Fernand Léger, 1924) in which a woman seems to endlessly climb a flight of stairs.

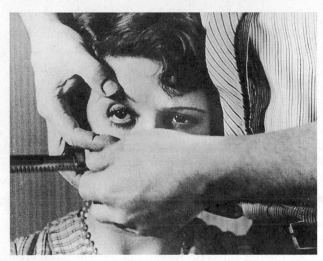

9.22 *Un Chien andalou* (Luis Buñuel, 1929).

with a razor, a man in full harness pulling two grand pianos upon which are draped the rotting carcasses of two donkeys, swarms of ants crawling from a hole in a man's palm, and a whole succession of gratuitous murders, severed limbs, and symbolic sexual transformations. Designed to create a series of violent antagonisms within the viewer through shock, titillation, and repulsion, the film nevertheless has a formal logic based on deconstruction of continuity and association of images through graphic match.[3] *Un Chien andalou* is the prototype of film surrealism, yet Buñuel later added a recorded score comprising popular contemporary tangoes and the *Liebestod* from Wagner's opera *Tristan und Isolde*, as if to suggest that *Un Chien andalou* was as much about the collapse of European culture between the wars as a subterranean voyage through the recesses of the unconscious mind. A subsequent Buñuel-Dalí collaboration in the early sound period produced *L'Âge d'or* (*The Golden Age*, 1930), a film no less surreal than its predecessor but one whose attacks upon religion and the established social order were so violent as to excite the wrath of the French Fascists, who ultimately succeeded in having it banned. Buñuel made no more overtly surrealist films after *L'Âge d'or*, but the surrealistic strain remained strong in his films throughout his career (see pp. 572–78).

One of the most remarkable works of the new avant-garde was Dmitri Kirsanoff's *Ménilmontant* (1924), which employed elaborate montage effects nearly a year before the release of Eisenstein's *Strike* and *Potemkin*. Kirsanoff

(1899–1957), a Russian émigré who apparently knew nothing of the montage experiments of Kuleshov, Pudovkin, and Eisenstein, was deeply influenced by Gance's cutting of *La Roue* (the Soviets also later acknowledged a debt to Gance, as did Akira Kurosawa). *Ménilmontant* clearly anticipates the rapid metaphorical cutting of Kirsanoff's Soviet counterparts in many ways. The film itself tells the story of two young women from the country whose lives are ruined by the brutal murder of their parents. The women come to the Parisian suburb of Ménilmontant, where one drifts into prostitution, and the remainder of the film recounts their sordid existence there. Some scholars see Kirsanoff's film as a precursor of Italian neorealism (which will be discussed in Chapter 11) in its sensitive use of on-location photography and natural settings.

The poet and playwright Jean Cocteau (1889–1963) turned to the avant-garde cinema for the first time as the director of *Le Sang d'un poète* (*Blood of a Poet*, 1930), a collage of intensely personal poetic symbols that attempts to evoke the sacrificial nature of art. By the end of the decade, however, the avant-garde had taken an abrupt turn away from introspection toward social commitment. Abstract films continued to be made by artists such as Man Ray (*Les Mystères du château du Dé* [*The Mysteries of the Chateau of the Dice*, 1929]) and Jean Grémillon (*Tour au large* [1927]), but the main tendency after 1927 was toward documentary cinema.

Influenced by the screening of the officially banned films of Vertov, Eisenstein, and Pudovkin in the *ciné-clubs*, French avant-garde *cinéastes* turned from abstractionism to the poetry of everyday life in a group of films that anticipated both the British documentary school of John Grierson and Italian neorealism. As early as 1926, the Brazilian-born filmmaker Alberto Cavalcanti (1897–1982), later to become a major figure in the British documentary and narrative cinemas (*Coal Face*, 1936; *Dead of Night*, 1945), directed *Rien que les heures*, a composite chronicle of a day in the life of a modern city (which happens, in this case, to be Paris) which may well have influenced Ruttmann's *Berlin, die Symphonie einer Grosstadt* (1927; see p. 110). Georges Lacombe (1902–1990), in *La Zone* (1928), offered a moving account of the lives

---

3. A logic pointed out to me by Richard Allen of the Cinema Studies Department, New York University.

of ragpickers in the shantytowns of Paris, while the first film of Marcel Carné (1909–1996), *Nogent, Eldorado du dimanche* (*Nogent, Sunday's Eldorado*, 1929), was a short documentary about Sundays at a popular working-class resort on the Marne.

During this same period, Jean Painlevé (1902–1989) began to produce the series of beautiful nature films that culminated in *L'Hippocampe* (1934), a poetic documentary on the life cycle of the seahorse. A bit later, Luis Buñuel combined surrealism with social commitment in the powerful and subversive *Las Hurdes* (English title: *Land without Bread*, 1932), which depicts the degradation, misery, and ignorance of the denizens of Spain's poorest district in the coolly ironic tones of a conventional travelogue. But the indisputable masterpiece of the French avant-garde documentary movement was the first film of Jean Vigo, *À propos de Nice* (1929). Vigo used the "cinema-eye" techniques of Dziga Vertov—whose brother Boris Kaufman was Vigo's cameraman—to create a lyrical but angry polemic against bourgeois decadence in a fashionable resort town. Vigo and Kaufman followed with *Taris* (1931), a formally subversive sound short on the championship swimmer Jean Taris that begins as an instructional documentary and ends as a dreamlike fantasy on weightlessness and water.

The general bleakness of the French commercial cinema during this period of widespread independent experimentation was illuminated here and there by the films of Jacques Feyder, René Clair, and Carl-Theodor Dreyer. Feyder (b. Jacques Frédérix, in Brussels, 1885–1948) was a Belgian who made dozens of French commercial films before establishing his reputation with *L'Atlantide* (1921), an opulent tale of the lost continent of Atlantis with exteriors shot in the Sahara desert. His critical and popular success continued through *Crainquebille* (1922), a semi-impressionistic version of the novel by Anatole France, which was much admired by Griffith, and a highly praised adaptation of Zola's *Thérèse Raquin* (1929), which has not survived. But when his gently satiric sound film *Les Nouveaux messieurs* (*The New Gentlemen*, 1929) was unfairly banned for impugning "the dignity of Parliament and its ministers," Feyder left France temporarily for Hollywood, where he spent four years working on melodramas (among them two Garbo films: *The Kiss* [1930] and the German-language version of Clarence Brown's *Anna Christie* [1932]).

René Clair had turned from the avant-garde to the commercial cinema in 1925 but did not achieve artistic success until he made the delightful *Un Chapeau de paille d'Italie* (*An Italian Straw Hat*, 1927) and *Les Deux timides* (*Two Timid Souls*, 1928), which transformed popular nineteenth-century farces by Eugène Labiche into highly cinematic comic chase films in the manner of Mack Sennett and Jean Durand. Clair's art director for the remarkable series of films from *Un Chapeau de paille d'Italie* (1927) through *Quatorze Juillet* (1932) was the brilliant Lazare Meerson (1900–1938), who more than any other single individual helped to create the style of "poetic realism" (see below). In his studio-built street scenes for Clair and, later, for Feyder (*Le Grand jeu* [1934]; *Pension mimosas* [1935]; *La Kermesse héroïque* [1935]), Meerson turned away from Expressionism, impressionism, and naturalism to create an ambiance described by Georges Sadoul as "simultaneously realistic and poetic." In addition to being one of the greatest designers in the history of European cinema, Meerson also trained a group of young assistants who became important figures in their own right (most notably, Alexandre Trauner, [1906–1993]—*Quai des brumes*, 1938; *Hôtel du nord*, 1938; *Le Jour se lève*, 1939; *Les Visiteurs de soir*, 1942; *Les Enfants du paradis*, 1945; *Othello*, 1952]), and his influence was felt well into the 1960s.

Carl-Theodor Dreyer (1889–1968) is an important director, the major body of whose work lies outside the mainstream of film history. Like that of Robert Bresson (see pp. 434–36) and Yasujiro Ozu (see pp. 745–47), Dreyer's art has been called religious and his style "transcendental" because of its simplicity and austerity.[4] Originally a journalist and a scriptwriter for Danish Nordisk, Dreyer began by making films in direct imitation of Griffith (such as *Blade af Satans bog* [*Leaves from Satan's Book*, 1921]). But by the late 1920s he was making films of such an extraordinary character as to defy classification.

The Danish director made his late silent masterpiece *La Passion de Jeanne d'Arc* (*The Passion of Joan of Arc*, 1928) for the Société Générale des Films (SGF) in Paris between 1927 and 1928. This austere and anguished film, which condenses the trial, torture, and execution of St. Joan (Maria Falconetti, 1892–1946) into a single tension-charged twenty-four-hour period, was based on actual

---

4. See Paul Schrader, *Transcendental Style in Film: Ozu, Bresson, Dreyer* (Berkeley: University of California Press, 1972).

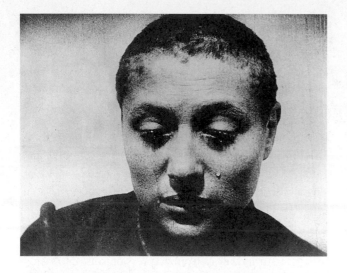

9.23 Maria Falconetti in *La Passion de Jeanne d'Arc* (Carl-Theodor Dreyer, 1928).

also a radical formal experiment whose strategy, as David Bordwell points out, is to subvert the classical stylistic relationships between narrative logic and cinematic space in order to construct a formal space for the sacred (that of Joan) untouched by the space of the profane (that of her inquisitors).

Dreyer also made his first sound film in France, the hauntingly atmospheric *Vampyr* (1932), shot on location in the village of Courtempierre by Maté. Designed, like *La Passion*, by Hermann Warm (who had also designed the sets for *Caligari*, *Der müde Tod*, and other Expressionist works), *Vampyr* seems less distinctly Gallic than *La Passion*, perhaps because its sound track was post-recorded in Berlin.

Because of the physical confinement he imposed on his dramas, Dreyer has sometimes been accused of theatricality (*Du skal aere din hustru* [*Master of the House*, 1925], for example, was shot entirely in a small four-room house). But, typically, Dreyer's subject is deep human emotion, frequently suffering, and his ability to evoke spiritual intensity through concentration and confinement was perhaps his greatest gift as a film artist. Dreyer's work is characterized by extraordinarily complex camera movement and luminous photography (often by great cinematographers like Rudolph Maté, Karl Freund, and Gunnar Fischer), expressive decor, antitraditional editing, and a totally radical construction of narrative space. His painstaking production procedures and his fierce artistic integrity led him to make only fourteen films in a career that spanned forty-five years. The most significant are

trial records and shot in sequence, largely in extreme close-ups against stark white backgrounds, to enhance its psychological realism. To the same end, Dreyer and his chief cameraman, Rudolph Maté (1898–1964), chose to photograph the film on newly available low-contrast panchromatic stock, and the actors and actresses were forbidden to wear make up. Dreyer had intended to make *La Passion de Jeanne d'Arc* a sound film, but he abandoned the notion for lack of equipment, so the film remains the last great classic of the international silent screen. Jean Cocteau wrote of it: "*Potemkin* imitated a documentary and threw us into confusion. *La Passion de Jeanne d'Arc* seems like an historical document from an era in which the cinema didn't exist," and yet the film is

9.24 *Ordet* (Carl-Theodor Dreyer, 1954).

Mikaël (1924), *Du skal aere din hustru* (1925), *La Passion de Jeanne d'Arc* (1928), *Vampyr* (1932), *Vredens dag* (*Day of Wrath*, 1943), *Ordet* (*The Word*, 1954), and his last film, *Gertrud* (1964). When he died in 1968, Dreyer was preparing to make a historical film on the life of Jesus from his own original screenplay.[5]

SOUND, 1929–1934

The coming of sound spelled the end for the French experimental avant-garde cinema. Production costs soared with the introduction of sound because France, unlike the United States and Germany, possessed no patents for the new process. Thus, the French studios were at the mercy of Western Electric and Tobis-Klangfilm, both of which exacted crippling sums for the rights to use their sound equipment. But the success of American and German sound films in France was such that financiers were eager to invest in the foreign patent rights. Hollywood and Tobis attempted to plunder the French industry further by establishing huge production facilities in the suburbs of Paris. Paramount built a vast plant at Joinville, but the quality of its mass-produced multilingual films fell to such a low level that the facility eventually became a dubbing studio for American-made films. The Tobis operation in Epinay was a much more respectable affair; its very first production was a motion picture praised around the world as the first artistic triumph of the sound film: René Clair's *Sous les toits de Paris* (*Under the Roofs of Paris*, 1930).

As with several other French directors making the transition to sound, Clair's involvement with the avant-garde of the 1920s had predisposed him to experiment with the new process. *Sous les toits de Paris* was a brisk musical comedy about ordinary people set in a delightfully designed Parisian *faubourg* (residential district); it used a bare minimum of dialogue and vindicated Clair's own theoretical defense of asynchronous or contrapuntal sound. Advertised as "the most beautiful film ever made," *Sous les toits de Paris* was an international triumph, and its stunning integration of sound with sophisticated visuals earned Clair a somewhat inflated reputation as a master of the sound film. His next Tobis film was another ebullient musical comedy, *Le Million* (*The Million*, 1931), which employed a whole range of nonnaturalistic effects on the sound track and a wild chase through an opera house to create what many historians feel is the best

European musical comedy of the period between the wars.

With *À nous la liberté* (*Liberty Is Ours*, 1931), Clair turned to the more serious themes of industrialization and economic depression, still, however, using the musical-comedy form. Based loosely on the life of Charles Pathé (see pp. 41–43), the film tells the story of an escaped convict who becomes a fabulously wealthy industrialist. He is subsequently discovered and blackmailed by a prison buddy, but in the utopian conclusion he gives up his role as a captain of industry to become a happy vagabond. The buoyant wit of this film, its great visual precision, and its brilliant use of asynchronous sound have made it a classic. But it is also notable for its humanistic indictment of mechanized modern industry, which Clair, through parallel editing, consistently equates with the experience of imprisonment. *À nous la liberté* has many similarities with Chaplin's *Modern Times* (1935; see p. 175)—so many, in fact, that Tobis pressed Clair to sue Chaplin for copyright infringement after the latter film's release. Clair declined, saying that he could only be honored to have inspired so great a filmmaker as Chaplin.

Clair's next film for Tobis, another Parisian musical entitled *Quatorze Juillet* (*The Fourteenth of July*, 1932), was less successful aesthetically than his earlier films; the old formula was beginning to wear thin. Clair changed modes with *Le Dernier milliardaire* (*The Last Multimillionaire*, 1934), a satire on dictatorship that was begun for Tobis but completed for Pathé when Goebbels, head of the German film industry since 1933, terminated the project.[6] The film was not up to Clair's best work, but it was maliciously defamed by France's increasingly powerful right-wing press upon its release. Deeply disturbed by this reaction, Clair accepted a contract to direct *The Ghost Goes West* (1935), a fantasy-satire about an American millionaire who buys a haunted Scottish castle and takes it home with him, for Alexander Korda in London. After this project and the independently produced musical comedy *Break the News* (1937), Clair returned briefly

---

5. The definitive work on Dreyer in English is David Bordwell's superbly crafted *The Films of Carl-Theodor Dreyer* (Berkeley: University of California Press, 1981).

6. All films made for Tobis at Épinay were shot in French and German versions, which gave a dual nationalistic edge to the studio's productions as France and Germany, for the second time in a generation, veered toward war.

9.26 The pillow fight in *Zéro de conduite* (Jean Vigo, 1933).

9.25 The bleakly futuristic assembly line in *À nous la liberté* (René Clair, 1931), and the open road of possibility with which the film concludes.

to France where he began shooting *Air pur*, a film about the urban poor, in Nice. Production was halted in 1939 by the outbreak of war, and Clair went west, to Hollywood, where he worked on a series of fantasy-comedies (*I Married a Witch*, 1942; *It Happened Tomorrow*, 1943) until the end of World War II, when he returned to France.[7]

Another important figure of the early sound film in France, although his total output amounts to little over three hours of viewing time, was Jean Vigo (1905–1934). The son of a famous anarchist who was jailed and probably murdered by the French government during World War I, Vigo spent his youth as an orphan in a series of wretched boarding schools. He later became an assistant cameraman and met one of Dziga Vertov's brothers, the cameraman Boris Kaufman, with whom he made his first feature: the forty-five-minute masterpiece *Zéro de con-*

duite (*Zero for Conduct*, 1933). This much admired film concerns the revolt of the boys of a rundown provincial boarding school against their petty, mean-spirited teachers; it is autobiographical in its anarchic spirit and many of its specific details. The film is simultaneously lyrical, surrealistic, comical, and profoundly serious. Important sequences include the balletic, slow-motion pillow fight during the dormitory rebellion in which feathers swirl about the room like snowflakes in a blizzard; the official visit of the schools inspector—a dwarf wearing a top hat; and the final assault on the courtyard, in which the boys stand on the school roof and bombard dignitaries at a pompous assembly with rubbish. *Zéro de conduite* was remarkably scored by Maurice Jaubert (1900–1940). A symphonic composer who began writing film music in 1929 (for *Le Petit chaperon rouge* [Alberto Cavalcanti]), Jaubert created a musical analogue for *Zéro*'s visual fantasy by having his score for it played and recorded back-

7. Clair's later films—*Le Silence est d'or* (English title: *Man about Town*, 1947); *La Beauté du diable* (*Beauty and the Devil*, 1950); *Les Belles-de-nuit* (*Beauties of the Night*, 1952); *Les Grandes manoeuvres* (English title: *Summer Maneuvers*, 1955—his first color film); *Porte des Lilas* (*Gates of Paris*, 1957); *Tout l'or du monde* (1961); *Les Fêtes galantes* (1965)—rarely approach the brilliance of his early work, and their prevailing mood is melancholy. In the late 1950s, Clair was attacked by the young critics of *Cahiers du cinéma*—unfairly it would now seem—as a paragon of the studio-based "scenarist" tradition against which they were in revolt (see Chapter 13). This circumstance, combined with the poor reception of his last two features, led Clair to retire from directing and devote himself to creative writing (three novels, several short stories) and criticism (*Cinéma d'hier, cinéma d'aujourd'hui*, 1970). During his active career, 1923–65, Clair either wrote or collaborated in writing the screenplay of every film he made.

ward. In rerecording, he invented a process whereby the notes were in the right order but their emission reversed—an effect at once eerie and playful.

By pitting the free and rebellious spirit of the children against the bourgeois repressiveness of the adults, Vigo was sounding a classical anarchist theme, and French authorities acknowledged this by banning *Zéro de conduite* from public viewing until the Liberation in 1944. This intensely personal film, with its subtle blend of poetry, fantasy, and realism, has had a great impact upon succeeding generations of directors, especially that of French New Wave filmmakers such as François Truffaut. Truffaut's *Les Quatre cents coups* (*The Four Hundred Blows*, 1959) and the British director Lindsay Anderson's *If. . . .* (1968), for example, both owe a great deal to it in terms of structure, style, and theme.

Vigo's next film, and his last, *L'Atalante* (1934), was another unique masterpiece sensuously photographed by Kaufman. Based upon a commissioned script about the life of two young newlyweds aboard a river barge, it was planned as an eighty-nine–minute commercial feature; Vigo turned it into a powerful lyric poem about life and love. By blending realistic details of life on the barge, and of the bleak industrial landscape through which it passes, with surreal fantasy and bizarre exaggeration of character, Vigo created a film that both revived the tradition of *populisme* from the 1920s and announced the "poetic realism" of the brief but glorious era of French cinema that was about to begin. Georges Sadoul speaks correctly of "the astonishing quality of poetry [*L'Atalante*] engenders from a world superficially ordinary and drab." Poetry meant little to the film's distributors, however, who cut and re-edited *L'Atalante* as *Le Chaland qui passe* (*The Passing Barge*) in order to exploit a popular song by that title that was added to the sound track as its theme, mutilating Maurice Jaubert's vibrant score in the process. Vigo died of tuberculosis complicated by heart disease on the day of the film's premiere in Paris; he was twenty-nine. In a tragically brief career he had made two great films whose influence on future generations would be immense, and there can be no question that the French cinema lost one of its geniuses when he died.

POETIC REALISM, 1934–1940

The character of French production during the 1920s had been artisanal and craftlike—a large number of small stu-

9.27 The newlyweds in Vigo's *L'Atalante* (1934).

dios leased their facilities to independent companies, often formed to produce single films—while the French exhibition system was, on the whole, familial and independent. This arrangement had lent itself readily to experimentation, encouraging the great work of the narrative avant-garde previously discussed; but it left producers and exhibitors alike vulnerable to the highly organized distribution networks of the Americans and the Germans. In the face of this threat, the French industry regrouped itself into two mammoth consortia formed around the former giants of the 1910s: Pathé and Gaumont. In February 1929, producer Bernard Natan (born Natan Taneuzapf) bought a controlling interest in Pathé-Cinema, Pathé-Consortium, and the Lutetia cinema chain to form a huge production/distribution/exhibition conglomerate called Pathé-Natan. The same summer, Franco-Film consortium bought the Aubert cinema chain and was itself absorbed a year later by Gaumont, with the backing of the Swiss electrical industry, to form Gaumont-Franco-Film-Aubert (GFFA). It seemed briefly that the French industry had reconstituted its pre-World War I glory and approached the condition of the American industry circa 1921. The appearance was false; within five years both companies were bankrupted through mismanagement and fraud.

Except for the work of Clair and Vigo, the French cinema of the early sound era had not been in good health either aesthetically or financially, and in 1934—the year of Clair's departure for England and Vigo's death—the industry experienced a major economic crisis. In that year, because of worldwide depression and internal mismanagement, domestic production fell off significantly, Gaumont and Pathé collapsed, and the end of French cinema was widely prophesied. Instead, the French cinema entered its period of greatest creative growth. The fall of the studio combines necessitated a return to the system of independent production that had prevailed before the coming of sound, at a time when sound itself had stimulated an unprecedented demand for French-language films on French themes. The figures tell the tale: between 1928 and 1938, French production nearly doubled, from 66 to 122 features annually; box-office receipts increased to the point that the French audience was considered second in strength only to the American and far ahead of those of the USSR, the United Kingdom, and Germany; by 1937–38 the French cinema had become the most critically acclaimed in the world, winning prizes and leading export markets in every industrial country, including the United States.

The predominant style of this period (1934–40) has been characterized by Georges Sadoul as "poetic realism"—a blend of lyricism and realism that derives from "the influence of literary naturalism and Zola, certain traditions of Zecca, Feuillade, and Delluc, certain lessons also from René Clair and Jean Vigo." Poetic realism seems to have had two phases—one born of the optimism created by the Popular Front movement[8] of 1935–37, the other a product of the despair created by the movement's failure and the realization that Fascism in some form was at hand. The same directors and scriptwriters contributed films to both phases.

Among the first practitioners of poetic realism was Jacques Feyder, who had returned to France from self-imposed exile in the United States in 1934, as if to compensate for the loss of Vigo and Clair. Feyder made his most important films of the period in collaboration with the art director Lazare Meerson and Charles Spaak (1903–1975), the screenwriter who, with Jacques Prévert (1900–1977), contributed most to the development of poetic realism. Together, Feyder and Spaak produced *Le Grand jeu* (*The Great Game*, 1934), a brooding melodrama of life in the Foreign Legion; *Pension mimosas* (1935), a grim, naturalistic drama of gambling in high society and low that provided the foundation for poetic realism as practiced later by Feyder's assistant Marcel Carné; and the beautiful costume film *La Kermesse héroïque* (English title: *Carnival in Flanders*, 1935), set in sixteenth-century Flanders, with a *mise-en-scène* based

9.28 *La Kermesse héroïque* **(Jacques Feyder, 1935).**

on the paintings of the great Flemish masters. This elaborate period farce won numerous international awards but was banned by Goebbels after the Nazi invasion because it dealt humorously with the subject of collaboration with the enemy.

During this same period, Spaak also wrote successfully for Julien Duvivier (1896–1967), a prolific director of commercial films who did his best work under the influence of poetic realism. Together, Duvivier and Spaak produced *La Bandera* (English title: *Escape from Yesterday*, 1935), the story of a criminal seeking refuge in the Foreign Legion, and *La Belle équipe* (English title: *They*

---

8. In 1934, the coalition of Radicals and Socialists that had taken control of the Chamber of Deputies in 1932 was in serious jeopardy. By that year, right-wing agitation, much of it overtly Fascist, had become so violent that there was a threat of civil war. As an emergency measure, all of the parties of the Left, including the Communists, banded together into a "Popular Front" in 1935 and reasserted their control of the country and the government by delivering the premiership to the Socialist leader Léon Blum early in 1936. This alliance was never very sound, but it was effective until 1937, when the Blum government was overthrown by a coalition of rightist and centrist parties. With Hitler arming his legions just across the Rhine, many Frenchmen saw the collapse of the Popular Front as a sign that Fascism was inevitable.

Were Five, 1936), in which five unemployed Parisian workers make a cooperative effort to open a restaurant on the banks of the Marne. Both films starred Jean Gabin (1904–1976), who later became the archetype of the doomed modern hero in Duvivier's internationally successful *Pépé le Moko* (1937). Written by Henri Jeanson (and influenced by Howard Hawks's 1932 film *Scarface* and other American gangster films), *Pépé le Moko* is about a Parisian gangster (Gabin) hiding out with his gang in the Casbah in Algiers while the police wait outside for the move that will betray him. The love of a woman draws Pépé out of his sanctuary, and he is gunned down by the police. As a genre film, *Pépé le Moko* can compete with the very best of the Hollywood gangster cycle,[9] but in its muted violence and fatalism it is highly representative of the pessimistic side of poetic realism.

The greatest exponent of this darker aspect of poetic realism was the young Marcel Carné, who had made the avant-garde documentary *Nogent, Eldorado du dimanche* in 1930 and had begun his career in the sound film as an assistant to Feyder. Carné's great collaborator was the surrealist poet Jacques Prévert, with whom he produced a series of films in the late 1930s that incarnate the romantic pessimism of the French cinema in the latter part of its great creative decade. Influenced by the films of von Sternberg and the German tradition of *Kammerspiel*, *Quai des brumes* (*Port of Shadows*, 1938) deals with a deserter from the colonial army (Jean Gabin) who finds himself trapped in the port of Le Havre. Like Pépé le Moko, he becomes involved with the underworld and is doomed to die through his love for a woman. Photographed entirely in the studio by Eugen Schüfftan, with art direction by Alexandre Trauner and music by Maurice Jaubert, *Quai des brumes* is an ominously gloomy film. It exudes such a pervasive sense of fatality that a spokesman for the collaborationist Vichy government later declared, "If we have lost the war, it is because of *Quai des brumes*. . . ." (Carné replied that the barometer shouldn't be blamed for the storm.) In the Carné-Prévert film *Le Jour se lève* (*Daybreak*, 1939), released just before the war, a man (Gabin) commits murder and locks himself in an attic room to await the inevitable police assault at dawn. Through the night (in what is perhaps the most structurally perfect flashback ever filmed) he remembers the love affair that led to his crime, and at daybreak he commits suicide. Simultaneously metaphysical and realistic, *Le Jour se lève* exploits the metaphor of a decent

9.29 *Quai des brumes* **(Marcel Carné, 1938): Jean Gabin, Michèle Morgan.**

man irreversibly trapped by fate more persuasively and powerfully than any other French film of the period, and it had enormous influence abroad during the war, even though it was banned in Nazi-occupied Europe.

During the Occupation, the Carné-Prévert association produced two of the most spectacular films ever made in France. *Les Visiteurs du soir* (English title: *The Devil's Envoys*, 1942), an adaptation of a medieval legend about a failed attempt by the devil to intervene in a human love affair, provided a stunning re-creation of fifteenth-century France. (Carné and Prévert intended the devil in the film to represent Hitler, but the allusions were necessarily so indirect as to be unrecognizable.) *Les Enfants du paradis* (*Children of Paradise*,[1] 1945), more than three

---

9. *Pépé le Moko* was remade twice in Hollywood—first as the romantic thriller *Algiers* (John Cromwell, 1938), then as the musical *Casbah* (John Berry, 1948).

1. A reference to theatergoers who can afford only the cheapest seats in the theater, those at the very top, known in theatrical slang as "Paradise," or "the gods."

hours long, evoked the world of the nineteenth-century theater. Inspired by the great French novelists of that era, the film explores the classic theme of the relationship between life and art, and, more specifically, between reality, cinema, and theater, in the context of a complicated love affair between a beautiful woman and a famous professional mime. Elaborate, intelligent, superbly acted, and beautifully mounted, *Les Enfants du paradis* has become a classic of the French cinema. It is clearly Carné and Prévert's masterpiece, and though they collaborated several times more after the war, they never again produced a work equal to this one.

Some mention must also be made of the films of Marcel Pagnol (1895–1974), the famous playwright who built his own studio in the south of France in order to transfer his stage plays to film. An outspoken advocate of "canned theater" who saw film primarily as an actor's medium, Pagnol produced a series of robust and vigorous comedies that probably did much to establish the reputation of French cinema in English-speaking countries. His trilogy of life among the ordinary people of Marseilles—*Marius* (directed by Alexander Korda, 1931), *Fanny* (directed by Marc Allégret, 1932), and *César* (directed by Pagnol, 1936)—and the delightful farce *La Femme du boulanger* (*The Baker's Wife*, directed by Pagnol, 1938), also set in Marseilles, are flavored by a kind of populist realism (or *populisme*) that brings them very close to the mainstream of poetic realism in its more optimistic days.

Another French filmmaker with roots firmly in the theater was the actor and playwright Sacha Guitry (1885–1957), who, even more than Pagnol, saw film as essentially a means of preserving his own stage plays and performances. Guitry's most important cinematic achievement was the feature *Le Roman d'un tricheur* (*The Story of a Cheat*, 1936), in which he used a voice-over commentary by the protagonist (Guitry himself) to describe the action on the screen, which occurred wholly in pantomime.

JEAN RENOIR

By far the greatest and most influential director to emerge from French poetic realism was Jean Renoir (1894–1979). Son of the Impressionist painter Pierre-Auguste Renoir (1841–1919),[2] he began his career in cinema with an uneven series of eight silent films, including a brilliant adaptation of Zola's novel *Nana* (1926), inspired by von Stroheim's *Foolish Wives* (1922);[3] *La Petite marchande*

d'allumettes (1927), a modern-dress version of Hans Christian Andersen's fairy tale *The Little Match Girl*; and *Tire-au-flanc* (1928), a farce that compares well with Clair's *Un Chapeau de paille d'Italie*, combining slapstick, satire, and poetic fantasy. Renoir's other silent films were strictly commercial vehicles, and it was not until the coming of sound that he began to distinguish himself as an artist. His first sound film was *On purge bébé* (*Purging the Baby*, 1931), adapted from a play by Georges Feydeau and starring Renoir's frequent collaborator during this period, Michel Simon (1895–1975). This relatively trivial domestic comedy was nevertheless a great commercial success and permitted Renoir to make his first important sound film, *La Chienne* (*The Bitch*, 1932), a year later. This melodrama of a middle-class bank clerk and Sunday painter (Simon) who has an affair with a prostitute and later kills her for deceiving him owed much to the example of von Sternberg's *Der blaue Engel* (1929; see p. 256), and it achieved a degree of social realism in evoking its milieu, which exceeded even that of its German predecessor.

After the suspenseful detective film *La Nuit de carrefour* (*Night at the Crossroads*, 1932), adapted from a work by Georges Simenon, and the lightweight comedy *Chotard et cie* (*Chotard and Company*, 1932), Renoir once again returned to the theme of *La Chienne*, pitting the bourgeois life against the anarchic values of a tramp in *Boudu sauvé des eaux* (*Boudu Saved from Drowning*, 1932).[4] In this film, a respectable Parisian bookdealer saves a seedy vagabond, Boudu (Michel Simon), from drowning in the Seine and insists that he move in with him. After seducing both the wife and mistress of his benefactor, and generally wreaking havoc on the household, Boudu leaves happily to resume his wanderings. Produced independently with complete creative freedom, *Boudu*, like *La Chienne*, was a commercial failure. Renoir's next film was a fine adaptation of Flaubert's

---

2. Renoir is also the uncle of the cinematographer Claude Renoir (1914–1993) and the brother of the actor Pierre Renoir (1885–1952), with both of whom he worked frequently in the 1930s.

3. In *The Man You Loved to Hate: Erich von Stroheim and Hollywood* (New York: Oxford University Press, 1983), Richard Koszarski maintains that the rabbit-hunting sequence in *La Règle du jeu* (1939) is an homage to the pigeon-shooting episode of *Foolish Wives*.

4. *La Chienne* was remade in the United States by Fritz Lang as *Scarlet Street* (1945); *Boudu* was remade by Paul Mazursky as *Down and Out in Beverly Hills* (1986).

9.30 A shot in depth from Renoir's *La Nuit de carrefour* (1932).

9.32 Experimenting with depth in *Toni* (Jean Renoir, 1935).

Madame Bovary (1934) in which he attempted to translate the novel's symbolic substructure into cinematic terms. Originally more than three and a half hours long, but cut to two hours by its distributors, *Madame Bovary* was another commercial failure; fortunately, Renoir was given a chance in the following year to undertake a much-cherished project by producer Marcel Pagnol. This was *Toni* (1935), a story of Italian immigrant workers in the quarries of southern France. Shot entirely on location and making extensive use of nonactors, *Toni* harks back to Soviet realism and is a forerunner of Italian neorealism (see Chapters 5 and 11).

After this attempt to make a film, in Renoir's words,

9.31 Depth perspective in *Madame Bovary* (1934): Valentine Tessier.

"as close as possible to a documentary," Renoir entered into his only collaboration with the scriptwriter Jacques Prévert; the resulting film marks a major turning point in his work. Shot during the great electoral triumphs of the Popular Front in 1935, *Le Crime de Monsieur Lange* (*The Crime of Monsieur Lange*, 1935) is in many ways a political parable of the need for collective action in the face of capitalist corruption. The employees of a publishing house form a cooperative to run the business when they learn of the accidental death of their lecherous and exploitative boss. The co-op experiences great success until the boss unexpectedly returns to claim his business. One of the workers, a writer of Wild West serials named M. Lange (his name is a pun on the French *l'ange*, "angel"), shoots him and flees the country for freedom. Shot largely on a single set representing the courtyard of a Parisian working-class tenement, *Le Crime de Monsieur Lange* announced the new spirit of social commitment that would pervade Renoir's work through his last prewar films. The strength of this commitment was demonstrated in *La Vie est à nous* (*Life Is Ours / People of France*, 1936), an election propaganda film for the French Communist party that mixes newsreel footage with dramatic episodes to show the necessity of presenting a united front against Fascism. Financed solely by public subscription, the film was banned from French commercial theaters but enjoyed a lively underground reputation in the *ciné-clubs* and specialist theaters. It was thought to have been destroyed during the war, but a copy came to light in 1969, and *La Vie est à nous*, appro-

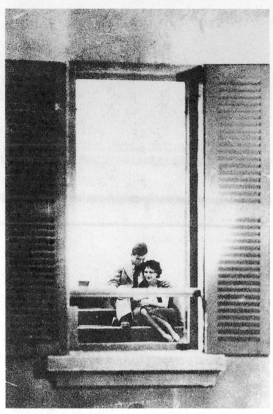

9.33 *Le Crime de Monsieur Lange* (Jean Renoir, 1935) emphasizing depth.

1936 was a somewhat inconclusive version of Maxim Gorki's play *The Lower Depths* (*Les Bas-fonds*, 1936), written by Renoir and Charles Spaak, set not in late nineteenth-century Russia but in some unidentified time and place.

Renoir's next film, *La Grande illusion* (*The Grand Illusion*, 1937), also written in collaboration with Spaak, has proved to be an enduring masterpiece. It portrays European civilization on the brink of cultural collapse and pleads for the primacy of human relationships over national and class antagonisms, simultaneously asserting the utter futility of war and the necessity of international solidarity to combat this most destructive and degrading "grand illusion" of the human race. One winter during World War I, three downed French pilots—an aristocrat (Pierre Fresnay), a mechanic (Jean Gabin), and a Jewish banker (Marcel Dalio)—are captured by the Germans and subsequently transferred to a series of prison camps—each one a microcosm of European society— and finally to the impregnable fortress of Wintersborn, commanded by the sympathetic Prussian aristocrat von Rauffenstein (Erich von Stroheim). Boieldieu, the French aristocrat, and von Rauffenstein become friends because they are of the same caste, and they pursue a long intellectual dialogue on the role of their dwindling class in European society. Despite the cultural barrier between Boieldieu and his two compatriots, he has earlier assisted

priately, had its first commercial success in France during the height of the student-worker rebellion of the late 1960s.

Renoir's next two films were literary adaptations. *Une Partie de campagne* (*A Day in the Country*) was a version of a Maupassant short story shot in 1936 but not edited and released until 1946. Just forty minutes long, *Une Partie* is the bittersweet tale of an 1880 Parisian bourgeois who takes his wife, his daughter, and her fiancé to the country for a Sunday outing. At a restaurant on the banks of the Marne they meet two men who take the women for a short boat ride up the river. In the process, the daughter falls in love with one of them. They embrace briefly but realize that they must return to their separate worlds. The pictorial quality of the film—its unique feeling for landscape and nature—is reminiscent of the paintings of Renoir's father and his fellow Impressionists Manet, Monet, and Degas. Renoir's other adaptation of

9.34 *La Grande illusion* (Jean Renoir, 1937): Brother aristocrats Boieldieu (Pierre Fresnay) and von Rauffenstein (Erich von Stroheim). Note the potted geranium between them, a small symbol of hope in the arid environment of the prison camp.

9.35 An alliance of the working class and the bourgeoisie in *La Grande illusion*: Maréchal (Jean Gabin) and Rosenthal (Marcel Dalio) plan their escape.

them in digging a tunnel under a prison wall in the dead of winter—the whole film takes place in this season—because it is his duty as an officer to help them escape. Equally trapped by his officer's code, von Rauffenstein must later shoot Boieldieu during an escape attempt at Wintersborn in which he willingly plays the decoy. Boieldieu dies painfully in von Rauffenstein's quarters, and the German commander, in a gesture of remorse, snips the flower from his much-cherished geranium plant. Both men have been victims of a rigid code of behavior that has left them no option but mutual destruction despite their friendship; Renoir suggests that the old ruling class of Europe is doomed for precisely the same reasons (which are also the same reasons for the "grand illusion" of war). The future of Europe seems to lie with the Jew, Rosenthal, and the mechanic, Maréchal—representatives of the bourgeoisie and working class, respectively—who have escaped together over the castle wall. After a grueling trek across Germany during which they argue continuously and nearly desert one another, Rosenthal and Maréchal finally cross the border to Switzerland, and freedom, as a result of their cooperation.

This extraordinarily rich and humane film contains magnificent ensemble playing by all of its leading actors as well as the best performance of von Stroheim's career, perhaps because he played a character whose demeanor and doomed idealism so closely resembled his own. But the most striking aspect of *La Grand illusion* is Renoir's

use of the long take, or sequence shot—unedited shots made from a single camera set up that generally (but not always) constitute entire dramatic sequences within a film. Dramatic tension in such shots is created through *composition in depth*, or the simultaneous arrangement of dramatically significant action and objects on several spatial planes within the frame. Composition in depth is essentially an attempt to make the two-dimensional space of the cinema screen three-dimensional, and it can be achieved only through what is known as **deep-focus** photography—a mode of filming in which the foreground, middle ground, and background of a shot are simultaneously in sharp focus. Technically, deep-focus photography is the achievement of a nearly perfect **depth of field** (the range of distances within which objects will be in sharp focus) within the frame; it should not be confused with *depth of focus*, a term used in describing the relationship in a camera between the lens and the surface of the film. Aesthetically, deep-focus photography provides a way of incorporating close shot, medium shot, and long shot within a single frame, and of linking character with background. It also *appears* to reproduce the field of vision of the human eye, although the eye does not possess extreme depth of field but, rather, is able to so rapidly alter focus within a depth perspective that we are never aware of the discontinuity.

The earliest film stock—and that used by nearly all commercial filmmakers until 1927—was *orthochromatic*. It possessed an extraordinary capacity for deep focus, or depth of field, in that it was relatively "fast," or sensitive to light, enabling cameramen to use small lens apertures[5] that kept both the foreground and background of their shots in focus (see, for example, the still from Griffith's *Musketeers of Pig Alley*, 1912, Figure 3.5). To attain its full depth of field, orthochromatic stock requires a strong, penetrating source of light to strike the negative through the narrow aperture of the lens—the sun during the cinema's first decade, mercury-vapor lamps during its second, and finally carbon arc lamps during its third. But

---

5. The lens aperture is the iris-like diaphragm at the optical center of the lens, a point midway between the front and rear elements. Varying the diameter of this opening, which is measured in **"f-stops"** (e.g., f-1, f-1.4, f-2, f-2.8, f-4, f-5.6, f-8, f-11, f-16, f-22, f-32, f-45, f-64—the larger the number, the smaller the aperture), determines the amount of light that the lens will transmit to the emulsion surface of the film and, therefore, in conjunction with shutter speed, determines the visual quality of the image imprinted on the negative stock.

orthochromatic was limited by its insensitivity to the red and yellow areas of the spectrum and required special filters to register them. In 1927, concurrent with the arrival of sound, orthochromatic was replaced as the industry standard by *panchromatic* stock, a film sensitive to all parts of the spectrum from blue to red but initially "slower" than the earlier film.[6] Simultaneously, the carbon arc lamps, which sputtered and popped noisily in operation, were replaced by incandescent, or tungsten, lighting, which was soundless. The new incandescent light, however, was softer and less penetrating than the light provided by the arc lamps, so cameramen were forced to widen their lens apertures and decrease the depth of field of the image. Thus, early panchromatic focus was relatively shallow; the backgrounds of close shots were diffused, and a face in close-up would tend to become detached from its environment. With a few notable exceptions (such as James Wong Howe's photography for *Transatlantic* and *Viva Villa!* in 1933, and Hal Mohr's for *Tess of the Storm Country* in 1932),[7] this "soft" style of photography characterized the sound film until 1940, when technical innovations in lenses, film stock, and lighting, and the creative genius of Orson Welles and Gregg Toland, restored the cinema's physical capacity for deep focus, as we will see in Chapter 10.

Despite underdeveloped technology, however, Renoir was the first major director of the sound film to compose his shots in depth, even though the depth was achieved artificially by constantly adjusting the focus of his camera to follow dramatic action within a given take. He had experimented with this technique in many of his early sound films, most successfully in *Toni* (1934), but *La Grande illusion* was his first film based consistently on the principle of the long take, or sequence shot. Generally, Renoir's films include realistic and dramatically significant background and middle ground activity in every sequence shot. Actors range about the set transacting their business while the camera shifts its focus from one plane of depth to another and back again. Significant off-frame action is often followed with a moving camera, characteristically through a series of pans within a single continuous shot. The scene of Boieldieu's death in *La Grande illusion*, for example, is rendered through three evocative panning shots. "Von Rauffenstein has just finished a bedside conversation with the dying Frenchman in which both have agreed that their caste is doomed to

extinction." In the next shot, we see that von Rauffenstein has risen from his chair and walked off-frame left to his liquor cabinet; there he takes a drink before walking off-frame right in response to a call from Boieldieu's nurse. At the cut, the camera pans right with von Rauffenstein as he moves back toward the bedside, where Boieldieu has just expired, and it continues to follow his gloved hand as he reaches down to gently close the dead man's eyes. In the sequence's final shot, von Rauffenstein enters from frame-right and walks toward a row of leaded windows, on the sill of which sits his prized geranium—a fragile thing of beauty that he has nurtured within the desolate environs of Wintersborn even as he has attempted to preserve a shred of aristocratic civility in the midst of modern warfare. Following his movement, the camera dollies into a medium-close shot of the German officer at the window as he looks out briefly on the falling snow, and it continues moving into a close-up of the geranium's single bloom as von Rauffenstein cuts it off with a pair of scissors, leaving the deflowered plant to stand alone at the center of the frame. After a fade to black, Renoir makes the transition to his next scene with yet another pan: his camera moves slowly over the snowy German countryside in long shot to discover Rosenthal and Maréchal, dressed in dirty civilian clothes, hiding in a ditch at the end of the pan. *La Grande illusion* is composed almost completely of such moving sequence shots, but Renoir and his cinematographer, Christian Matras (1900–1988), never permit them to become flashy or self-conscious.

In the year of its release, *La Grande illusion* won both

---

6. Eastman Kodak had introduced panchromatic stock in 1913 for use in such experimental color processes as Charles Urban's Kinemacolor and Léon Gaumont's Chronochrome, but the company's marketing campaign didn't begin until 1925, when the film's price was lowered and its speed increased. By 1928, panchromatic had been adopted as the standard stock of the sound era, just as the dominant stock of the silent period had been orthochromatic.

7. In Charles Higham's *Hollywood Cameramen: Sources of Light* (Bloomington: Indiana University Press, 1970), Howe claims that for William K. Howard's *Transatlantic*, "I used wide angles, deep focus throughout, long before *Kane*. Eighty percent of the picture was shot with a twenty-five millimeter lens. . . . I carried focus from five feet back to twenty, thirty feet" (p. 84). Other uses of wide-angle lenses in early sound films are discussed in David Bordwell, "Deep-focus Cinematography," Chapter 27 of David Bordwell, Kristin Staiger, and Janet Thompson, *The Classical Hollywood Cinema: Film Style and Mode of Production to 1960* (New York: Columbia University Press, 1985), pp. 341–52.

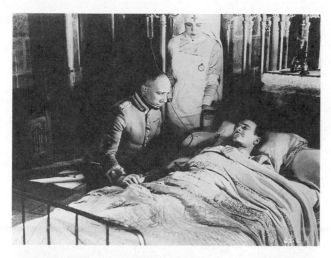

9.37 Depth: Renoir's _La Marseillaise_ (1937).

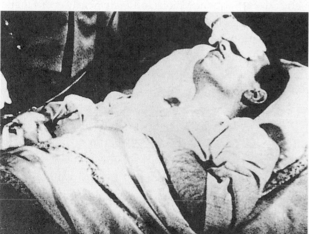

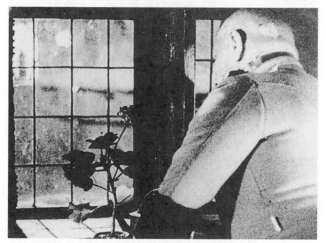

9.36 Stills from the sequence shots of Boieldieu's death.

the New York Critics Award for the Best Foreign Language Film and a special prize at the prestigious Venice Film Festival, even though it was banned from commercial exhibition in both Italy and Germany. In 1957, together with _Potemkin_ and _Mother, La Grande illusion_ was voted one of the twelve greatest films of all time at the Brussels World's Fair.

Renoir's next project was _La Marseillaise_ (1937), a semidocumentary reconstruction of some major episodes from the French Revolution, financed by the trade unions and flavored with the politics of the Popular Front. Next came _La Bête humaine_ (_The Human Beast_, 1938), an adaptation of Zola's naturalistic novel about an alcoholic railroad engineer (played by Jean Gabin) cast in modern terms.[8] Renoir's final French film of the period was his greatest masterpiece and one of the great works of the cinema, _La Règle du jeu_ (_The Rules of the Game_, 1939). Like _La Grande illusion_, it is about a culture teetering on the brink of collapse, but it is a much more complicated film in both attitude and technique.

Informed by the gracious rhythms of Mozart, Johann Strauss, and Chopin, and patterned on the classical French theater of Marivaux and Beaumarchais,[9] _La Règle du jeu_ is an elegant tragicomedy of manners whose intricate plot defies easy summarization. Briefly, the young aviator

8. Fritz Lang directed another adaptation of Zola's novel in 1954, under the title _Human Desire_.

9. Renoir, in fact, conceived of the film as an updated version of the comedy _Les Caprices de Marianne_ by the Romantic poet and playwright Alfred de Musset (1810–1857).

9.38 *La Règle du jeu* (Jean Renoir, 1939): Christine de la Chesnaye (Nora Gregor) questions her maid, Lisette (Paulette Dubost) about her own marriage.

André Jurieu, who has just completed a daring transatlantic flight, is in love with Christine, the wife of a wealthy Jewish landowner, the Marquis Robert de la Chesnaye (Marcel Dalio). La Chesnaye organizes a large weekend hunting party at his country estate, La Colinière, to which he invites Jurieu, Octave (a mutual friend of Jurieu and Christine, played by Renoir), and his own mistress. After a day of hunting in which hundreds of rabbits and birds are slaughtered and maimed, we are treated to a series of love intrigues among the *haute bourgeoisie* abovestairs and among the servants belowstairs—who, in their snobbery, insincerity, and pride, are the precise mirror images of their masters. The major characteristic of these intrigues is that not a single one is serious, and Jurieu has broken an important "rule of the game" by sincerely declaring his love for Christine in the most public way imaginable—in a radio broadcast from Orly Airport just after his transatlantic flight. Later, during an evening fête featuring extravagant theatrical entertainment and a fancy-dress ball, a jealous gamekeeper attempts to shoot his wife's suspected lover (a local poacher) in a comic chase through the ballroom reminiscent of a Marx Brothers film. Finally, the gamekeeper decides that Octave, not the poacher, is the lover, and he shoots Jurieu to death on the veranda, mistaking him for Octave and Christine for his wife. A model of civilized restraint, the marquis takes immediate command of the situation, apologizes to his guests for the "regrettable accident," and takes all appropriate steps to restore equilibrium to the world of La Colinière.

Witty, elegant, and profoundly pessimistic, *La Règle du jeu* is ultimately concerned with social breakdown and cultural decadence at a particularly critical moment in European history. Renoir presents us with a world in which feeling has been replaced by manners and all that remains of civilized values is their external form—a form that will itself soon crumble. Society has become a vast collective lie, and those, like Jurieu, who break its "rules" by telling the truth, come to no good. *La Règle du jeu* has the moral and intellectual depth of a great novel, but it is also a brilliant piece of filmmaking. Renoir had never used the long take and deep focus to such striking dramatic effect. Sequence shots dominate nearly every major scene, and the camera moves continuously to follow significant action within the frame. Fluid, graceful, and exquisitely precise are terms that describe Renoir's camera style in *La Règle du jeu*. He resorts to expressive montage only once in the entire film—appropriately, to render the mindless organized violence of the hunt.

Renoir expected *La Règle du jeu* to be controversial, but he could hardly have anticipated the extremity of the reaction. The film provoked a political riot at its Paris premiere, was cut and re-edited by its distributor from 113 to 80 minutes, and was finally banned in late 1939 by French military censors as "demoralizing." The Nazis banned it during the Occupation, and Allied bombing destroyed the original negative in 1942. Happily, the integral version of *La Règle du jeu*, minus one short scene, was reconstructed under Renoir's supervision by two French film producers in 1956 and has enjoyed a prestigious international reputation ever since. In 1962 and 1972, an international poll of film critics ranked it among the ten greatest films ever made.

In the summer of 1939, Renoir accepted an invitation to teach at the Centro Sperimentale in Rome (Italy's national film school) and to direct there a version of Puccini's opera *Tosca*, with a screenplay by Luchino Visconti (see pp. 358–59).[1] The film was begun by Renoir's crew but completed by others, notably the director and coscenarist Carl Koch, because Italy joined Hitler's war

---

1. The invitation, sent through diplomatic channels, came from Mussolini himself, who greatly admired Renoir as a filmmaker despite his politics (Il Duce was said to own a private copy of *La Grande illusion*,

9.39 Shots from the hunting sequence in *La Règle du jeu*.

against France on June 10, 1940, and Renoir, who was on the Nazis' extermination list because of his leftist politics, was forced to emigrate to the United States. Here he went to work for a variety of studios, filming in rapid succession *Swamp Water* (1941)—a sort of commercial, American *Toni* shot on location in the swamps of Georgia—and two war propaganda films—*This Land Is Mine* (1943) and *Salute to France* (1944). Renoir's most distinguished American film was *The Southerner*, made in 1945 for United Artists. This austere, semidocumentary account of the lives of poor white farmers in the Deep South was shot on location with complete creative freedom; more than any other of Renoir's American films, it harks back to the poetic realism of the 1930s. With *The Diary of a Chambermaid* (1946), Renoir returned to French sources (Octave Mirbeau's novel, which Luis Buñuel would also film, in 1964), but moved away from

the realism of his greatest period. Independently produced and shot entirely in the studio, this film about the decadence of French bourgeois society in the late nineteenth century resembled *La Règle du jeu* in theme but lacked the great depth of the earlier work, and it was universally condemned in Europe, where Renoir's prewar reputation had declined. His last American film was *The Woman on the Beach* (1947), a tale of romantic obsession in a wild coastal setting. The film failed commercially

although it was officially banned by his Fascist government). Renoir accepted the invitation at the behest of the French government, which was anxious to preserve Italy's neutrality in the "phony war" with Germany, which began on September 3, 1939, and ended on May 10, 1940, when SS Panzer divisions smashed through the Maginot Line. On Renoir's reception in the United States, see Alexander Sesonske, "Discovering America: Jean Renoir: 1941," *Sight and Sound 50*, 4 (Autumn 1981): 256–61.

and aesthetically in large part because RKO re-edited it no fewer than three times.

At this point Renoir became increasingly interested in theater and spectacle, as they contrasted with his earlier "realistic" style. He left Hollywood to make *The River* (1951), a British coproduction, on the banks of the Ganges River. This beautiful film—Renoir's first in color—was strikingly photographed by the director's nephew, Claude Renoir, and is about the response of a fourteen-year-old British girl to India. Renoir next went to Italy to make *Le Carrosse d'or* (*The Golden Coach*, 1952), about a *commedia dell'arte* theater troupe in eighteenth-century Peru; this color film attempted to explore the relationships among film, theater, and reality. Renoir appropriately abandoned composition in depth and the moving camera for *La Carrosse d'or* in favor of a more theatrical *mise-en-scène* using long takes from a relatively stationary camera.

In 1954 Renoir returned to his native land for the first time since the war and began his last important series of French films. *French Cancan* (1954) is set in Montmartre in the late 1890s of Renoir's childhood and tells the story of the impresario who founded the famous Moulin Rouge theater. Its brilliant use of color in motion evokes the paintings of the Impressionists but goes beyond them, reaching its height in the spectacular twenty-minute cancan dance with which the film concludes. *Elena et les hommes* (English title: *Paris Does Strange Things*, 1957),[2] a romantic costume drama set during the Franco-Prussian War, showed signs that Renoir's creative power was waning; his next two films seemed to many to confirm this. *Le Testament du Dr. Cordelier* (1959) is a modern adaptation of Robert Louis Stevenson's *Dr. Jekyll and Mr. Hyde* shot in black and white for French television. *Le Déjeuner sur l'herbe* (*Picnic on the Grass*, 1959) is Renoir's summary exploration of the world of instinct and nature, whose visual texture is closer to that of French Impressionist painting than anything Renoir had ever filmed. In his final feature film, *Le Caporal épinglé* (*The Elusive Corporal*, 1962), Renoir returned to the subject of prisoners of war with a lightweight comedy about the multiple escape attempts of a French corporal from a German prison camp during World War II. Renoir's filmmaking career ended in 1969 with a series of short plays for French television entitled *Le Petit théâtre de Jean Renoir* (*The Little Theater of Jean Renoir*, 1969). Later, Renoir retired to southern California, where he wrote plays, a biography of his father, seven novels, and, finally, his own memoirs.

Jean Renoir, indisputably one of the great masters of world cinema, resolutely refused to be compromised by his own success. In a career that spanned forty-six years of cinema, he never ceased to experiment and explore, to consistently renew his creative vitality by striking out in new directions. *La Règle du jeu* (1939) is as different from *La Carrosse d'or* (1952) as both are from *Toni* (1934) and *The Southerner* (1945), and yet all four of these films are masterworks on their own terms. Renoir was also the pioneer of composition in depth in the sound film, and, according to André Bazin, he became the father of a new aesthetic: "He alone in his searchings as director prior to *La Règle du jeu* . . . forced himself to look back beyond the resources provided by montage and so uncovered the secret of film form that would permit everything to be said without chopping the world up into little fragments, that would reveal the hidden meanings in people and things without disturbing the unity natural to them." Renoir's influence on Orson Welles, who brought the technique of composition in depth to its ultimate perfection in *Citizen Kane*, is well known,[3] and his impact on Italian neorealism was strong. His technical genius notwithstanding, Renoir was perhaps the most humanistic of all of Western cinema's major figures. He wrote: "I'm not a director—I'm a story-teller. . . . The only thing I bring to this illogical, irresponsible, and cruel universe is my love." An artist of strong and uniquely personal vision, Jean Renoir also represents the flowering of the period of poetic realism (1934–40), when French films were generally regarded as the most important and sophisticated in the world.

---

2. Distributed by Warner Bros., this Americanized version was dubbed, cut from 98 to 86 minutes, and given a different beginning and ending than Renoir intended, to romanticize the persona of Ingrid Bergman in its title role. Critically attacked for incoherence, the film was disowned by Renoir, but a restored version is currently available in the United States from Interama, Inc., in New York City.

3. Welles wrote a moving eulogy when Renoir died on February 12, 1979, at his home in Beverly Hills, after a long illness. It appeared in the *Los Angeles Times* on February 18, 1979.

Orson Welles and the Modern Sound Film

At the very moment that France was being occupied by the Nazis and the rest of Europe was engulfed in war, a young American director made a film that was to transform the cinema substantially. In 1939 Orson Welles (1915–85) was brought to Hollywood by the financially troubled RKO Pictures under an unprecedented six-film contract that gave him complete control over every aspect of production.[1] At twenty-four, Welles's experience in radio and theater was vast. From 1933 to 1937 he directed and acted in numerous Broadway and off-Broadway plays, including a production of *Macbeth* with a voodoo setting and an anti-Fascist *Julius Caesar* set in contemporary Italy; in 1937, with John Houseman (1902–1988), he founded the famous Mercury Theatre company; and between 1938 and 1940 he wrote, directed, and starred in the weekly radio series *Mercury Theatre on the Air*, whose pseudodocumentary broadcast based on H. G. Wells's *War of the Worlds* caused a nationwide panic on Halloween night in 1938.

Welles had made several short films in connection with his theatrical productions (such as *Too Much Johnson*, 1938), but he had never been on a **soundstage** in his life. His first feature film was to have been an adaptation of Joseph Conrad's *Heart of Darkness*, filmed with a subjective camera from the point of view of the narrator (who is also a participant in the action), but this project was abandoned indefinitely due to technical problems, cost overruns, and other difficulties, including the outbreak of war in Europe and the internment of its female lead, the German actress Dita Parlo.[2] Next, Welles

1. According to Frank Brady in *Citizen Welles: A Biography of Orson Welles* (New York: Scribner's, 1989), the original RKO contract, signed on July 22, 1939, was actually a two-film deal that gave Welles a remarkable degree of control over production on the set but also gave the studio the right of preproduction story refusal and postproduction "consultation" on the release print (pp. 199–200). The exaggeration of the contract's terms was probably the work of RKO's publicity department.

2. Dita Parlo (1906–1971) was working in the French film industry when the war began (she had played featured roles in Vigo's *L'Atalante* [1934] and Renoir's *La Grande illusion* [1937], among other films); military officials had her arrested as an alien and, ultimately, deported to Germany. For a full account of the *Heart of Darkness* project and its termination, see Robert L. Carringer's *The Making of Citizen Kane*, (Berkeley: University of California Press, 1985), ch. 1.

undertook to film a script written by himself and Herman J. Mankiewicz (1898–1953) about the life and personality of a great American entrepreneur. Originally entitled simply *American*, the Welles-Mankiewicz scenario ultimately became the shooting script for *Citizen Kane* (1941), the now-legendary cryptobiography of America's most powerful press lord, William Randolph Hearst (1863–1951).

Citizen Kane

PRODUCTION

Welles claimed that his only preparation for directing *Citizen Kane* was to watch John Ford's *Stagecoach* (1939) forty times. Ford's influence on the film is pronounced, but it is equally clear that Welles was steeped in the major European traditions, especially those of German Expressionism and the *Kammerspielfilm*[3] and French poetic realism. If *Kane*'s narrative economy owes much to the example of Ford, its visual texture is heavily indebted to the chiaroscuro lighting of Lang, the fluid camera of Murnau, the baroque *mise-en-scène* of von Sternberg, and the deep-focus realism of Renoir. Credit is also due Welles's remarkably talented collaborators—Mankiewicz; the Mercury Theatre players; the composer Bernard Herrmann; the editor Robert Wise; and the unit art director, Perry Ferguson.[4]

But Welles's greatest single technical asset in the film-ing of *Kane* was his brilliant director of photography, Gregg Toland (1904–1948). Toland had earned a distinguished reputation as a cinematographer in Hollywood in the 1930s and had experimented with deep-focus photography and ceilinged sets in his three most recent films, *Wuthering Heights* (William Wyler, 1939), for which he had won an Academy Award, *The Grapes of Wrath* (John Ford, 1940), and *The Long Voyage Home* (John Ford, 1940). Welles (or Mankiewicz) had conceived *Kane* as a film structured largely in flashback as characters recall their acquaintance with the great man (played by Welles himself) after his death, and he wanted the narrative to flow poetically from image to image in a manner analogous to the process of human memory. Thus, Welles used straight cuts largely for shock effect and made the most of his narrative transitions through lingering, in-camera lap dissolves. More important, Welles planned to construct the film as a series of long takes, or sequence shots, scrupulously composed in-depth to eliminate the necessity for narrative cutting within major dramatic scenes.

To accomplish this, Toland perfected for Welles a method of deep-focus photography capable of achieving an unprecedented depth of field. As explained in Chapter 9, the "soft" style of photography favored by the studios during the 1930s was characterized by diffused lighting and relatively shallow focus—a product of the wider lens apertures required for filming in incandescent light. By the end of the decade, technical improvements in film stocks and lighting permitted greater depth of field, but most studio cinematographers were conservative and continued to practice the "soft" style. Toland, however, was a bold experimenter whose work in-depth—espe-

10.1 Welles directing Toland and Dorothy Comingore in an opera sequence near the end of the principal photography. (Welles had broken his ankle running down the stairs in pursuit of "Boss" Jim Gettys in the scene depicted in 10.23.)

3. As John Russell Taylor has observed, "*Citizen Kane* may be the best American film ever made; but it just might be also the best German film ever made." (Quoted in *German Film Directors in Hollywood: Catalogue of an Exhibit of the Goethe Institutes of North America* [San Francisco: Goethe Institute, 1978], p. 5.) To make the question of influence even richer, Howard Hawks claimed in a 1976 interview that Welles modeled *Kane* on his own *His Girl Friday* (1940) and had told him so in 1941 (Bruce F. Kawin, "Introduction: *No Man Alone*," in *To Have and Have Not*, ed. Bruce F. Kawin (Madison: University of Wisconsin Press, 1980), p. 41.

4. As administrative head of the RKO art department, Van Nest Polglase received official screen credit for this function, with Ferguson listed as "Associate," but the latter was art director in fact. This practice reflected the bureaucratic hierarchy of the studio system, whereby department heads were contractually entitled to screen credits (and, therefore, to awards) for work performed by their subordinates.

cially in *The Long Voyage Home*—had earned him a reputation for the kind of flamboyant originality prized by Welles in his Mercury Theatre productions. Toland's self-styled "pan focus" photography for *Kane* was a synthesis of many techniques he had used before. It employed the newly available Eastman Super XX film stock (an ultra-fast film with a very high sensitivity to light—four times faster, in fact, than its standard Super X, without a notable increase in grain) in combination with a 24mm **wide-angle lens** whose aperture was stopped down to f-8 or less—a radical reduction in its size (see footnote, p. 321). The scenes were lit by the high-intensity arc lamps recently introduced for Technicolor production, and the lenses were coated with a clear plastic substance (magnesium fluoride) to reduce glare. Finally, Toland used the Mitchell Camera Corporation's self-blimped BNC, a relatively small and portable camera first used professionally in *Wuthering Heights*, which greatly increased the operator's freedom and range of movement.[5] With these tools, Toland was able to achieve something very close to "universal" focus within the frames of *Citizen Kane*, and Welles was able to distribute dramatic action across a depth perspective unlike anything ever used in a sound film. Since the early 1960s, improvements in lenses, lighting, and film emulsions have greatly simplified deep-focus photography, but the technical principles remain much the same. Welles's use of the deep-focus sequence shot in *Kane* demonstrated a mastery of composition in depth. Like Renoir, he used the deep-focus format functionally, to develop scenes without resorting to montage, but he also used it expressively—as Eisenstein had used montage—to create metaphors for things that the cinema cannot represent directly on the screen.

At the height of his arrogance and power, for example, Kane often looms like a giant in the foreground of the frame, dwarfing other characters in the middle ground and background, and towering over the audience, often from a low camera angle. Later, Kane's self-absorbed alienation from the world and everyone in it is conveyed by the growing distance that separates him from all other characters within the frame. In these instances, Welles's use of depth perspective involves an expressive distortion of space that creates a metaphor for something in Kane's psychology. At other times, Welles uses deep focus both to achieve narrative economy and to echelon characters dramatically within the frame. Early in the film, a brilliant deep-focus sequence shot encapsulates the story of Kane's lost childhood. We see the front room of a board-

10.2 The aging Kane with his second wife, Susan Alexander (Dorothy Comingore), at Xanadu. The depth perspective that separates them suggests an unbreachable gap. (From Susan's narrative.)

inghouse in which Charlie Kane's mother signs the agreement that will permit her son to be taken to the East and later inherit a fortune. In exchanging her son's childhood for an adult life of fantastic wealth, she is selling him, and she knows it. Welles set the shot up like this: In the foreground of the frame, Mrs. Kane and Mr. Thatcher, whose bank is the executor of the estate, sign the agreement. The middle ground is occupied by Charlie's weak-willed father, whose vacillation about the agreement is rendered visible as he paces back and forth between foreground and background. In the back of the room is a window through which, in the extreme background of the frame, we see Charlie playing unsuspectingly in the snow with his sled and shouting, "The Union forever!" while in the foreground of the same shot, he is being indentured to his own future. Thus, in a single shot, Welles is able to communicate a large amount of narrative and thematic information that would require many shots in a conventionally edited scene.

Kane is a film of much fluid intraframe movement. The sequence just described, for instance, actually begins with

---

5. Additionally, a new fine-grain stock for producing release prints had been introduced in 1939. It virtually eliminated graininess in print generation and preserved image depth in films like *The Long Voyage Home* and *Kane*.

10.3 Depth as fate: Mrs. Kane (Agnes Moorehead) and Thatcher (George Coulouris); Mr. Kane (Harry Shannon); Charlie (Buddy Swan) outside, framed by the window. (From Thatcher's narrative.)

a medium long shot of Charlie at play in the snow through the open window of the boardinghouse; then the camera pulls back rapidly to reveal the other characters and elements in the composition. But there are three virtuoso moving camera shots in the film, each of which is a tour de force of fluidity and continuity. In the first, from a shot of a poster announcing the appearance of Kane's second wife, Susan, at the El Rancho nightclub, the camera cranes up vertically to the club's flashing neon sign, then tracks horizontally *through* it and down onto the rain-spattered glass of a skylight. The movement continues after a quick dissolve (made invisible by flashing lightning and distracting thunder), as the camera descends to a medium shot of Susan Alexander Kane and a newsman talking together at a table in the club's interior. In another shot, midway through the film, the camera cranes up vertically from a long shot of Susan singing on the stage of the Chicago Municipal Opera House to a catwalk some four stories above it, where a stagehand makes a vulgar but richly deserved gesture of contempt for her performance. Finally, there is the long swooping **crane shot** that concludes the film, as the camera tracks slowly across the vast collection of artifacts that Kane has amassed in a lifetime of collecting, coming to rest on the object of the search for "Rosebud" that gives the film its narrative impulse or motive.

Other remarkable aspects of this wholly remarkable film are its expressive chiaroscuro lighting[6] and frequent use of extreme low-angle photography in connection with the figure of Kane. The latter necessitated many muslin ceilinged sets, which had been used in Hollywood before, especially in the work of Toland, but never so consistently and effectively to suggest a sense of claustration and enclosure. (Filmmakers have conventionally left their interior sets roofless, first to admit the sunlight and later to facilitate artificial lighting and the free movement of the boom crane and microphone.) Finally, and most significantly, attention must be called to *Kane*'s innovative use of sound.

Welles's experience in radio served him well in recording the sound track for *Kane*. He invented for his few montage sequences a technique he called the "lightning mix," in which shots were rapidly linked together not by the narrative logic of their images, but by the continuity of the sound track. Kane's growth from child to adult is conveyed in a matter of seconds: a shot of his guardian giving him a sled and wishing him "a Merry Christmas" is cut together with a shot of the same man some fifteen years later, as he completes the sentence—"and a Happy New Year"—again addressing Kane, but in a different dramatic context. Another lightning mix conveys the entire progress of Kane's campaign for governor of New York State in four brief shots. First we see Kane listening to Susan Alexander sing (wretchedly) at the piano in the parlor of her boardinghouse. This dissolves into another shot of the two in the same relative positions in a much more elegantly appointed parlor, that of an apartment in which Kane has obviously set her up. At the end of Susan's performance, Kane claps, and the shot is dovetailed with another of a friend addressing a small street rally in Kane's behalf. The applause, which has been continuous on the sound track since the parlor shot, grows louder and multiplies in response to the speaker's words: "I am speaking for Charles Foster Kane, the fighting liberal . . . who entered upon this campaign with one purpose only—." Welles cut finally to a long shot of Kane himself addressing a huge political rally at Madison Square Garden and completing the sentence as the camera begins to track toward the speaker's platform: "—to point out and make public the dishonesty, the downright vil-

---

6. There are two major lighting styles in Kane—the sharp, high-contrast "daylight" style associated with Kane's youth and rise to power, and the dark, expressionistic "low-light" style, which characterizes his corruption and decline.

10.4 Jed Leland (Joseph Cotton) confronts Kane after the lost election. The low camera angle and expressive lighting create a sense of menace and tension. Note that the camera shoots into the ceiling. (From Leland's narrative.)

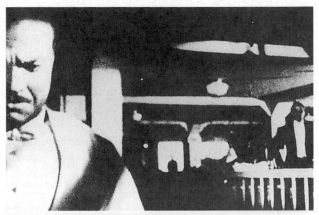

10.6 Kane finishing Leland's review: visual and aural depth combined. (From Leland's narrative.)

lainy of Boss Jim Gettys' political machine." The address continues, and the narrative resumes a more conventional form.

Another device introduced by Welles in *Kane* was the overlapping sound montage in which—as in reality—people speak not one after another (as they do on the stage), but virtually all at once so that part of what is said is lost. Overlapping dialogue between major players in a film had been used as early as 1931 by Lewis Milestone in *The Front Page*, but it had not been used to produce a sense of realistic collective conversation as it was in *Kane*. A good example in the film (and there is an example

10.5 Kane alone, after wrecking Susan's bedroom. The extreme low camera angle and sinister backlighting characterize an alienated, destructive (and, finally, self-destructive) personality. Again, note the ceiling. (From Raymond's narrative.)

in almost every major sequence) occurs in the screening room after the projection of the "News on the March" newsreel. So many persons are speaking on the track simultaneously that one has the distinct sense of having accidentally stumbled into the aftermath of a board meeting. Welles continued to use this technique in his later films, and it has influenced many other filmmakers—both his contemporaries, like Carol Reed, and more recent directors, like Robert Altman, who has been so firmly committed to overlapping sound montage that unknowledgeable critics once complained about the "poor quality" of his sound tracks.

A final example of Welles's subtle refinement of sound occurs in one of his best deep-focus setups. Kane, in a newsroom, is seated at a typewriter in the extreme foreground of the frame, finishing a bad review of Susan Alexander Kane's Chicago opera debut that his ex-friend Jed Leland has written. Correspondingly, we hear the tapping of the typewriter keys on the "foreground" of the sound track. From a door in the background of the frame, Leland emerges—barely recognizable, so great is the distance—and begins to walk slowly toward Kane. As he moves from the background to the foreground of the frame, Leland's footsteps move from the "background" to the "foreground" of the sound track—from being initially inaudible to having nearly an equal volume with the keys. Similarly, in the Chicago Opera House shot, as the camera dollies up from the stage to the catwalk, Susan's voice grows ever more distant on the track, creating once more a precise correspondence of visual and aural "space."

10.7 Reality frame: the opening shots of *Citizen Kane*. The camera pans up from the "No Trespassing" sign and slowly dissolves to the crested gate and then into Xanadu.

10.8 Reality frame: as Kane dies, the glass globe drops from his hand and shatters.

10.9 Reality frame: the nurse, shot as through broken glass.

STRUCTURE

The formal organization of *Citizen Kane* is extraordinary. Like a Jorge Luis Borges story, it begins with the death of its subject. Through an elaborate series of lap-dissolved stills, we are led from a No Trespassing sign on a chain-link fence farther and farther into the forbidding Kane estate of Xanadu, as if by the tracking movement of a camera, until at last we approach a lighted window high in a Gothic tower. The light is suddenly extinguished, and Welles dissolves to the interior of the room, where Charles Foster Kane dies in state, clutching a small glass globe that contains a swirling snow scene and whispering "Rosebud"—the wordo that motivates the film and echoes through it until the final frames. Kane drops the globe in dying; it rolls down the steps and breaks in close-up. Through the distorting lens of the convex broken glass (actually, a wide-angle lens focused through a diminishing glass), we watch a nurse enter the room from a door in the background in long shot; she walks to the foreground in close-shot, folds Kane's arms, and pulls the covers up to his chest. After a fade to a medium shot of Kane's body silhouetted against the window, we suddenly cut to a logo projected obliquely on a screen, and the sound track booms the title "News on the March!"—introducing a sophisticated parody of a *March of Time* newsreel[7] on

Kane's life and death. Welles is thus able to give a brief and coherent, if unsequential, overview of the major events in Kane's life before they become jumbled like the pieces of a jigsaw puzzle in the succeeding narratives.

In a sense, the newsreel is *Citizen Kane* itself in miniature. Like the larger film, it begins with Kane's death (or his funeral), covers the same events in a similar overlapping, chronological manner, and ends with the mystery of Kane's character unresolved. We learn from the newsreel that Kane, hated and loved by millions of Americans, was an enormously controversial figure whose vast wealth was inherited by fluke: a supposedly worthless deed left to his mother in payment for a boardinghouse room gave

7. *The March of Time* was a popular series of skillfully (some would say slickly) produced film news journals released monthly in the the United States between 1935 and 1951. Each issue was twenty minutes long and, generally, focused on a single subject. Since these films were usually shown as preludes to features, *Citizen Kane*'s original audiences might well have watched an authentic *March of Time* newsreel just before seeing the parodic "News on the March" in *Kane*. *The March of Time* series was politically conservative, reflecting the editorial policies of its financial backer, Time-Life, Inc., and of Time-Life's director, Henry R. Luce (1898–1967). Time-Life succeeded the Hearst empire, which was badly crippled by the Depression, to become a major shaper of public opinion during the 1930s, 1940s, and 1950s. The identification in *Citizen Kane* of Rawlston's news organization with the Luce press is entirely deliberate since it extends the Kane/Hearst analogy.

10.10 *News on the March:* logo.

10.11 *News on the March:* Teddy Roosevelt and Charles Foster Kane.

10.12 *News on the March:* Kane in exile at Xanadu, shot candidly by a hidden cameraman.

him sole ownership of the priceless Colorado Lode. We learn that in an earlier period of American history, near the turn of the century, Kane's wealth and the influence of his newspapers were incalculable. We learn that he was married twice—first to a president's niece, then to Susan Alexander, "singer," for whom he built the Chicago Municipal Opera House and Xanadu. We learn that Kane's promising and apparently nonstop political career was destroyed during a campaign for the governorship of the state of New York by a "love-nest" scandal involving Susan Alexander. We learn finally that Kane's newspaper empire was crippled by the Depression and that he subsequently exiled himself to the solitude of Xanadu, where, after many years of seclusion, he died in 1941. The newsreel ends, and the camera discovers a dimly and expressionistically lit projection room, where the contemporary media journalists (successors of the Kane/Hearst empire and identified with the Luce press) who produced the film discuss it. Rawlston, the executive in charge, thinks

it needs an "angle" that will somehow explain the paradoxical figure of Kane. Someone seizes upon the man's dying words, the film's release is postponed, and a journalist named Thompson (played by William Alland) is sent out to interview all of Kane's intimate acquaintances to discover the meaning of "Rosebud" and, it is hoped, of Kane himself.

The rest of the film is contained in a series of five narratives—told in flashback by each of the people Thompson talks to—and a balancing epilogue of sorts. The narratives overlap with each other and with the "News on the March" newsreel at certain points so that some of the events in Kane's life are presented from several different points of view within the total film. From the screening room, a shock cut takes us to a poster on a brick wall, suddenly illuminated by lightning, which announces the El Rancho nightclub appearance of the second Mrs. Kane. Through the elaborate craning movement previously described, we are brought into the interior of the club, where a drunk and hostile Susan Alexander Kane

10.13 Reality frame: a startling change of camera angle at the newsreel's conclusion takes us out of the film within the film and places us unexpectedly in a projection room.

10.14 Reality frame: Thompson (William Alland) is dispatched to find "Rosebud—dead or alive . . ."

10.15 Thatcher's narrative: Thatcher meets young Charles for the first time outside his mother's boardinghouse.

10.16 Thatcher's narrative: some twenty years later, Thatcher takes the Kane papers into receivership. Bernstein (Everett Sloane) is in the foreground of the frame.

(Dorothy Comingore) refuses to talk to Thompson. He can get no information from the headwaiter either, and the screen then fades out and into a daytime sequence at the Walter P. Thatcher Memorial Library. (Thatcher, we come to understand later in the sequence, was Kane's guardian and executor of the Colorado Lode estate.) Here, Thompson is grudgingly given access to Thatcher's memoirs, and, as the journalist reads the words "I first encountered Mr. Kane in 1871 . . . ," the screen dissolves from a close-up of Thatcher's longhand to a lyrical shot

of a boy playing with a sled in front of Mrs. Kane's boardinghouse, somewhere in Colorado, during a snowstorm.

In the long deep-focus shot described above, Mrs. Kane (Agnes Moorehead) signs the papers that make Thatcher's bank the boy's guardian and certify his inheritance. Outside, young Kane is told of his imminent departure for the East; he pushes Thatcher (George Coulouris) into the snow with his sled. We dissolve to a medium shot of the sled, some time later, covered with drifting snow, and then into the "Merry Christmas—Happy New Year" lightning mix, which places us in New York City many years later on the occasion of Kane's twenty-first birthday.[8] We learn that of all the holdings in "the world's sixth largest private fortune," which Kane is about to inherit, only the financially failing daily newspaper, the *New York Inquirer*, interests him because he thinks "it would be fun to run a newspaper." Next, in a brief but potent montage sequence, we see Thatcher increasingly outraged by the *Inquirer*'s populist, muckraking (and anti-Republican) headlines, until he finally confronts Kane in the *Inquirer* office. Their antipathy for one another—both ideological and personal—is apparent, and Thatcher warns Kane of financial disaster. As if to confirm this prophecy, the following sequence, composed

10.17 Bernstein's narrative: youthful exuberance. Leland, Kane, and Bernstein on their first day at the *Inquirer*. (Production still from a scene that doesn't appear in the finished film.)

---

8. An apparent inconsistency in the continuity script since seconds earlier in Colorado we have heard Thatcher tell Mrs. Kane that the fortune is "to be administered by the bank in trust for your son . . . until he reaches his twenty-fifth birthday."

10.18 Bernstein's narrative: youthful idealism. Kane proposes his "Declaration of Principles."

10.19 Bernstein's narrative: depth as character. The banquet for the former *Chronicle* staff. Twin ice sculptures of Bernstein and Leland in the extreme foreground frame the real Bernstein and Leland in the middle foreground; the former *Chronicle* men stretch away from them toward the extreme background; Kane stands in the middle distance bantering with Bernstein. The shot renders in compositional terms what Leland will moments later suggest to Bernstein verbally—that Kane will become increasingly distanced from his old friends and his liberal ideals by the intervention of all the new men from the *Chronicle*.

in depth, shows Kane, much older, signing his now vast but bankrupt newspaper chain over to Thatcher in the midst of the Depression, and here Thatcher's narrative ends.

Thompson next visits Mr. Bernstein (Everett Sloane), once Kane's general manager and right-hand man, now the aging chairman of the board of the Kane Corporation. Bernstein's narrative begins by recalling in flashback the first day at the *Inquirer* office, when he, Kane, and Kane's old college buddy Jedediah Leland (Joseph Cotten) arrived to claim the paper in what was clearly to be a lark for all three young men. But the playfulness is mitigated a few scenes later when, in the presence of Bernstein and Leland, Kane composes a "Declaration of Principles" for his first front page.[9] Leland asks to keep the manuscript, comparing it facetiously to the Declaration of Independence. In this sequence, the twenty-one-year-old Kane is revealed to be the romantic idealist of the crusading populist headlines so repugnant to Thatcher, and Leland's admiration for him is unqualified. In the next sequence, Kane, Leland, and Bernstein are seen reflected in the window of the *New York Chronicle* Building, gazing at a photograph of the *Chronicle*'s top-flight staff, which, they admit, has made it the most successful newspaper in the city. The camera moves in close upon the picture and then back out to reveal the group, suddenly animated and sitting for another photograph six years later—this time to commemorate their joining the staff of the *Inquirer* en masse. A raucous banquet

10.20 Bernstein's narrative: chorus girls enliven the celebration as Leland worries about the future.

10.21 Leland's narrative: the breakfast-table sequence. (How Leland could recount these intimate details without having been present at the table is never made clear, and his ability to do so verbatim constitutes one of several violations of dramatic point of view in the film. The cinematic logic of the narratives is so perfect, however, that we scarcely notice.) Like so many others, this sequence begins and ends with the four-part in-camera dissolves used throughout the film to evoke the process of memory: first the background of a scene fades out while that of a new scene fades in, then the foreground figures fade out and the new ones fade in. This is accomplished by dimming the light banks in sections on the first set, and bringing them up in the same sequence on the second, then superimposing them photographically.

sequence follows in which the dining table is photographed in extreme depth, with ice sculptures of Leland and Bernstein in the foreground at one end, Kane in the background at the other, and the new staff members occupying the space in between. During the revelry, Leland expresses to Bernstein his concern that these new men, so fresh from the *Chronicle* and its policies, will change Kane, and the scene dissolves into another one of Bernstein and Leland uncrating boxes of sculpture that Kane has been collecting on a European tour. It is revealed by Bernstein that Kane may also be "collecting" something (or someone) else. A dissolve brings us to the interior of the *Inquirer* office some time later, on the day of Kane's return from Europe. The staff attempts to present him with an engraved loving cup, and he awkwardly leaves them a notice announcing his engagement to Miss Emily Monroe Norton, the niece of the president of the United States. The staff watches from the windows of the *Inquirer* Building as Kane and his fiancée drive off in a carriage; and the second narrative draws to a close with Bernstein speculating to Thompson that maybe "Rosebud" was "something he lost."

Thompson next pays a visit to Leland, who has become a somewhat senile (but still intelligent) old man confined to a nursing home. Indeed, the dissolves into the Leland narrative flashback are among the most lingering in the whole film, as if to suggest the sluggishness of his memory; and not a little of the film's impact derives from this flashback technique of narration, which permits us to see all of the major characters in youth and age almost simultaneously. Like those of the other characters, Leland's narrative is chronological but not continuous. Initially, he relates the story of Kane's first marriage in a sequence that convincingly compresses the relationship's slow decline into a series of brief breakfast-table conversations linked by swish pans and overlapping sound—that is, a lightning mix. Next, in a much longer flashback, Leland describes Kane's first meeting with Susan Alexander and Kane's subsequent political ruin at the hands of his opponent, "Boss" Jim Gettys (and as a result of his own stubborn, egomaniacal refusal to withdraw from the race). Of particular note is the scene in which Leland confronts Kane after he has lost the election. The entire sequence is shot in depth from an extremely low angle (the camera was actually placed in a hole in the floor to make the shot), so that Kane looms above both Leland and the audience, a grotesque, inflated parody of the politically powerful

10.22 Leland's narrative: candidate Kane addresses a huge rally in Madison Square Garden on the eve of what should be a smashing victory over his opponent, Jim Gettys.

10.23 Leland's narrative: from the staircase of the apartment, Kane rains empty threats on Gettys (Ray Collins) in a low-angle, deep-focus shot.

10.24 Leland's narrative: after his election defeat Kane still looms large, in a low-angle, deep-focus shot.

lengthy vertical craning shot from Susan performing abjectly on the stage to the stagehand holding his nose occurs here, as does Leland's long, deep-focus walk from the back of the *Chicago Inquirer* newsroom to the extreme foreground of the frame, where an embittered Kane finishes Leland's bad review of the performance and summarily fires him.

Here Leland's narrative ends, and Thompson returns once more to the El Rancho nightclub. Again the camera travels up from the poster of Susan Alexander, cranes through the sign, and dissolves through the skylight to a medium close shot of Thompson and Susan sitting at a table. Susan, who has finally agreed to talk, begins her story with a flashback to a session with her voice coach, Signor Matisti, that occurred shortly after her marriage to Kane. Susan, Matisti, and a pianist occupy the foreground of a deep-focus shot of a large, expensively decorated room. Susan's voice is so bad that Matisti refuses to continue the lesson, but at this point Kane emerges from a door in the back of the room and walks toward the group, becoming larger and larger as he moves toward the lens. When he reaches the foreground, he browbeats both Matisti and Susan into continuing the humiliating session, until a dissolve brings us to the second version of Susan's singing debut at the Chicago Municipal Opera House. We have already seen her performance from Leland's point of view in his narrative, and now we see virtually the same events from Susan's perspective as she looks out into the vast and terrifying void of the audience, invisible beyond the

figure he has so desperately tried (and failed) to become. Drunk, and disillusioned with his idol, Leland insists that he be transferred to the Chicago office, and Kane reluctantly consents. The final section of Leland's narrative concerns Kane's marriage to Susan Alexander and her singing debut at the opera house he has built for her. The

10.25 Leland's narrative: Susan Alexander's debut as a singer, from Leland's optical perspective.

10.26 Susan's narrative: the debut from her own optical point of view.

footlights. Her aria begins, and as she attempts to fill the huge theater with her frail voice,[1] Welles intercuts subjective shots of Matisti frantically coaching her with audience reaction shots (contempt, boredom, disbelief) and close-ups of an aging Kane peering grimly toward the stage. When the performance ends with very light applause, Kane claps loudly, as if to fill the hall with his solitary accolade. A dissolve brings us to Kane and Susan the morning after in a Chicago apartment, where Susan shrilly denounces Leland for his bad review—actually completed by Kane. We learn that Kane has fired Leland and sent him a check for $25,000, which Leland has returned along with the pompously idealist "Decla-

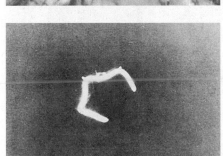
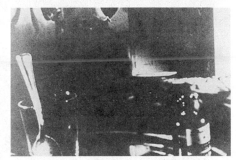

10.27 Susan's narrative: shots from the montage showing her rapid rise to stardom through media hype, her collapse, and the half-empty glass of poison after her suicide attempt.

ration of Principles" that Kane had printed in his first issue of the *New York Inquirer* years before. We also learn that Susan's singing career has been imposed upon her by Kane, who insists that it continue.

There follows a rapid montage of dissolves, overlaid on the sound track by Susan's voice, in which *Inquirer* headlines from cities around the country acclaiming Susan Alexander's meteoric rise to stardom are lap-dissolved alternately with shots of flashing call lights, Susan onstage, Matisti in the prompter's box, and Susan receiving flowers at an ever-increasing rate until a klieg light suddenly fizzles and goes out, cutting off Susan's voice and leaving us in total darkness. Moments later, we slowly fade in on a deep-focus shot of a darkened room: in the extreme foreground is a near-empty glass of liquid and a spoon (this particular foreground object is reproduced not through deep focus, but an in-camera matte shot); in the middle ground Susan tosses in bed, breathing heavily; in the background a door flies open and Kane bursts into the room, barely foiling her suicide attempt. Susan is treated by a discreet doctor, and Kane promises that she needn't sing again.

Now we fade to Xanadu, sometime later, where the

final portion of Susan's narrative takes place. Here, in deep-focus shots that grotesquely distance them from one another across the breadth of a palatial chamber, Kane and Susan pursue a series of conversations that show them to be utterly at odds. Kane has become a cynical domestic tyrant and Susan a virtual prisoner of the estate; she passes the time endlessly working and reworking jigsaw puzzles—a metaphor for the mystery of identity in the film. Against Susan's will, Kane arranges a spectacularly extravagant weekend "picnic" in the Everglades, where the two break openly and he slaps her. The next day at Xanadu, Susan announces to Kane that she is leaving him for good; he begs her to stay, but, realizing

1. In 1973, at a symposium at the George Eastman House in Rochester, New York, Bernard Herrmann pointed out that Susan (or, rather, the singer dubbing her voice) actually could sing, but only modestly. The high tessitura overture to *Salammbô*, the fake opera Herrmann composed for her debut, was purposely designed to exceed the capacity of her voice and create "that terror-in-the-quicksand feeling" of a singer hopelessly out of her depth at the very outset of a long performance. (Quoted in *Sound and the Cinema: The Coming of Sound to American Film*, ed. Evan William Cameron [Pleasantville, N.Y.: Redgrave, 1980], p. 128).

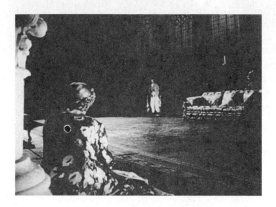

10.28 Susan's narrative: working puzzles interminably at Xanadu, increasingly estranged from Kane.

some mechanized madman, smashing furniture, mirrors, cosmetic jars, and all manner of trinkets and bric-a-brac until his hand finally comes to rest on the glass globe with the snow scene that we first saw at his death in the beginning of the film and later saw in Susan's apartment when they met. We hear Kane whisper "Rosebud!" and watch him shuffle slowly out of Susan's demolished room, past a gauntlet of staring servants and guests, and down a huge hall of mirrors as Raymond's narrative concludes.

Now Thompson and Raymond move down the central staircase into the great hall of Xanadu, where we see in long shot that a multitude of reporters, photographers, and workmen have assembled in a mass effort to catalogue and liquidate Kane's huge collection of objects. The camera pulls back to follow the two men as they pass through the hall, discovering as it does so newspeople photographing both the treasures and trash of the Kane collection —Renaissance sculpture, Kane's

Kane's nearly constitutional inability to return love, she refuses and walks out the door. Susan concludes her narrative by advising Thompson to talk to Raymond, the butler, who "knows where all the bodies are buried," when he visits Xanadu. The camera moves back and up, dissolves through the skylight, and pulls back through the El Rancho sign, reversing the movement of its entry.

Dissolves bring us to the gate of Xanadu and then to the interior for Raymond's brief narrative, which begins where Susan's ended. It opens not with a dissolve, but with a shocking straight cut from Raymond (Paul Stewart) and Thompson on the stairs to a close shot of a shrieking cockatoo, behind which we see Susan in the middle ground emerging from the same door she has begun to walk through (from the other side) at the end of her own narrative as she leaves Kane and Xanadu. Raymond's flashback then depicts the violent tantrum Kane throws as she departs: he staggers about Susan's bedroom like

mother's pot-bellied stove, Oriental statuary, the loving cup presented to Kane by the *Inquirer* staff on his return from Europe, priceless paintings, a myriad of jigsaw puzzles, etc. Thompson's colleagues ask him whether he has discovered the meaning of "Rosebud." He replies that he hasn't and that, in any case, he no longer believes in the quest: "I don't think any word can explain a man's life. No, I guess 'Rosebud' is just a piece in a jigsaw puzzle, a missing piece."

Thompson and the others leave to catch the train back to New York, and a lap dissolve brings us to an aerial view of the hall, with the camera shooting down over the vast collection that stretches away into the distance. Another lap dissolve brings the camera a little closer to the collection as it begins to track slowly over the entire mass of crates, statues, boxes, and belongings—the ruins and relics of Kane's loveless life—that, from our aerial perspective, resemble nothing so much as the pieces of a jigsaw

10.29 Susan's narrative: in the Everglades, a bloated, domineering Kane as he appears to Susan after slapping her.

10.32 Raymond's narrative: Kane, berserk, destroying Susan's room.

10.30 Susan's narrative, conclusion: in her bedroom at Xanadu, Kane pleads with Susan to stay, but she refuses.

10.33 Reality frame: Thompson and Raymond in the great hall.

10.31 Raymond's narrative: Raymond (Paul Stewart) watches a now totally isolated Kane vanish as he stands in the doorway to Susan's room just after she has left him.

10.34 Reality frame: a high-angle shot of the newspeople preparing to leave Xanadu; Thompson (slightly right of center) admits that his quest has failed.

10.35 Reality frame: an extreme high-angle shot of the hall, replicating a news photographer's point of view.

10.36 Reality frame: a still from the long, slow track of Kane's vast collection of "things."

puzzle. The shot continues for some time until the camera reaches the humble possessions of Mrs. Kane and dollies down gracefully into an eye-level shot of her things. We see a man grab a sled and, in the next shot, throw it into a furnace at Raymond's command. We dissolve to a close-up of the burning sled and can read on it the word "Rosebud" just before the letters melt away in flames. A dissolve brings us to an exterior long shot of Xanadu at night, as we first encountered it, with smoke billowing from its chimneys. The camera tilts up to follow the smoke, dissolves to the chain-link fence surrounding the estate, and pans down slowly to the No Trespassing sign with which the film began.

Thus, *Citizen Kane* concludes with the mystery of its central figure unresolved. The identity of "Rosebud"

is clearly inadequate to account for the terrible emptiness at the heart of Kane, and of America, and is meant to be. Its power as a symbol of lost love and innocence lies in its very insufficiency, for the "missing piece" of the jigsaw puzzle of Kane's life, the "something he lost," turns out to be an inanimate object, and a regressive one at that. In its barrenness, "Rosebud" becomes a perfect symbol of Kane's inability to relate to people in human terms, or to love, and the ultimate emblem of his futile attempt to fill the void in himself with objects. In the film's two-hour running time we have seen Kane from seven separate perspectives—those of the newsreel, the five narrators, and the concluding reprise—and we probably have come to know more about the circumstances of his life than the man would have known himself. We know what he did and how he lived and died, but we can never know what he *meant*—perhaps, Welles seems to suggest, because, like "Rosebud," he was ultimately meaningless, or perhaps because reality itself is ambiguous and unreliable. In any case, it is the quest for meaning rather than its ultimate conclusion that makes *Citizen Kane* such a rich and important film.

INFLUENCE

In the year of its release, *Citizen Kane* was a radically experimental film—fully twenty years ahead of its time—and was widely recognized as such by American critics. But it failed at the box office less because of its experimental nature than because of an aura of fear in Hollywood created by attacks on Welles and RKO in the Hearst press. Hearst was still living, and his vassals attempted to suppress what they correctly took to be an unflattering portrait of their master. Though they were unsuccessful in preventing the film's release, the adverse publicity made it difficult for Kane to get bookings and advertising.[2] As a result, the film did poorly outside of New York City and was withdrawn from circulation until the mid-1950s, when it played the **art house** circuit and began to acquire a more sophisticated audience. Since then, *Kane* has been voted the "Best Film of All Time" in five successive international polls (Brussels, 1958; *Sight and*

---

2. For the fullest account of *Kane*'s postproduction and release, see Carringer, Chapter 5.

10.37 Reality frame: the burning sled in Xanadu's incinerator.

10.39 Economy of means: the matte used for the exterior of Xanadu, painted for RKO by Mario Larrinaga.

10.38 Reality frame: "Rosebud."

Sound, 1962, 1972, 1982, 1992), and there is every indication that its critical reputation continues to grow.

The influence of *Citizen Kane* upon the cinema has been enormous and nearly universal. The film's impact did not begin to be felt until after the war, when its use of low-key lighting and wide-angle lenses to achieve greater depth of field influenced the visual style of American *film noir* and its flashback narrative technique began to be imitated in more conventional films like Robert Siodmak's *The Killers* (1946). There were also imitations of *Kane*'s structure and/or theme: George Cukor's *Keeper of the Flame* (1942), Max Ophüls's *Caught* (1949), and, after the art-house revival, José Ferrer's *The Great Man* (1957). Directors like Britain's Carol Reed (*Odd Man Out*, 1947; *The Third Man*, 1949; *Outcast of the Islands*, 1952—all highly Wellesian films) absorbed much of the film's visual and aural textures; and, according to François Truffaut, the young French *cinéastes* who would later form the New Wave found in *Kane*'s 1946 Paris premiere the ultimate justification of their reverence for American cinema.

Kane's most important and pervasive influence, however, did not begin to be felt until the mid-1950s, after the advent of the widescreen processes, when European critics—notably Bazin—discovered in it (and, less emphatically, in Renoir's films) the model for a new film aesthetic based not upon montage, but upon the "long take," or sequence shot. The primary concern of the long-take aesthetic is not the *sequencing of images*, as in montage, but the *disposition of space within the frame*, or *mise-en-scène*. Welles is today regarded for all practical purposes as the founder and master of this aesthetic (in the same way that Eisenstein is regarded as the founder and master of montage), though its lineage can be traced as far back as Louis Feuillade. Finally, *Kane* was the first recognizably modern sound film; and it stood in the same relationship to its medium in 1941 as did *The Birth of a Nation* in 1914 and *Potemkin* in 1925—that is, it was an achievement in the development of narrative form, years in advance of its time, that significantly influenced most of the important films that followed it. Through deep-focus photography, *Kane* attempts to technically reproduce the actual field of vision of the human eye in order to structure our visual perception of screen space by means of composition in depth. Through its innovative use of sound, it attempts to reproduce the actual aural experience of the human ear and then to manipulate our aural perception of screen space by distorting and qualifying this experience. And in both respects, though the technology is not the same, *Kane* brilliantly anticipates the contemporary cinema of widescreen photography and stereophonic sound.

Contrary to popular belief, *Kane* was anything but a financially extravagant production. The entire film—cavernous ceilinged sets and all—was made for \$839,727,[3] with a remarkable economy of means: for many scenes Welles and Ferguson converted standing sets from other RKO pictures, and, in the Everglades sequence, they actually used jungle footage from *Son of Kong* (1933), complete with animated bats. Nevertheless, the financial failure of the film stigmatized Welles as a loser in Hollywood, and he was never again permitted to have total control of an industry production.[4]

10.40 *The Magnificent Ambersons* (Orson Welles, 1942): the Amberson family circle in the 1890s, with the mansion in the background and the pampered young George Amberson Minafer in the foreground center.

10.41 Eugene Morgan (Joseph Cotton), inventor of horseless carriages, who knows implicitly that automobiles will "change men's minds."

Welles after *Kane*

Welles's second film, *The Magnificent Ambersons* (1942), is one of the great lost masterworks of the cinema. Like von Stroheim's *Greed* (1924) and Eisenstein's *Que viva México!* (1930–32), *The Magnificent Ambersons* was taken out of its director's hands and radically recut to satisfy the exigencies of the new wartime economy as perceived by the Bureau of Motion Picture Affairs (see pp. 368 and 371). While Welles was in Brazil shooting footage for a semidocumentary entitled *It's All True*, cosponsored by RKO and the State Department, RKO cut *The Magnificent Ambersons* from 132 to 88 minutes and provided it with a totally incongruous happy ending shot by the film's production manager, Freddie Fleck.[5]

3. This figure includes postproduction costs. Only about 7 percent of it, or \$59,207, went to the construction of *Kane*'s record number of 116 sets. By contrast, the many fewer sets of *The Magnificent Ambersons* cost \$137,265, or about 13.5 percent of that film's total budget of \$1,013,760.

4. Welles's notoriously difficult personality also figured in his alienation from (and of) the American film industry.

5. In addition, one scene was reshot by the editor, Robert Wise, and another by Mercury Theatre business manager Jack Moss. For years it was thought that the forty-five minutes of cut footage might exist somewhere in the vaults of Paramount Pictures, which had bought portions of the RKO feature library in 1958, but in *The Magnificent Ambersons: A Reconstruction* (Berkeley: University of California Press, 1993), Robert Carringer maintains that RKO burned the negative trims and outtakes for lack of storage space—a relatively common practice at the time. There is still the possibility that an original preview print might surface someday, but in its absence Carringer provides a textual edition

10.42 The Amberson ball, "the last of the great, long-remembered dances that everybody talked about": Eugene Morgan and Isabel Amberson (Dolores Costello).

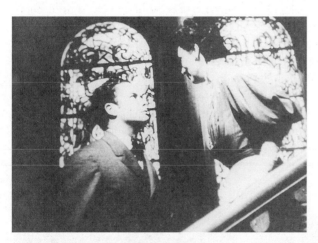

10.43 A grown George Amberson Minafer (Tim Holt) confronts his spinster aunt (Agnes Moorehead) on the main staircase of the Amberson mansion, an emblem of splendor and the central dramatic locus of the film.

10.44 A Morgan Motors "Invincible" rides into a Currier and Ives landscape self-consciously framed by a Griffith-like iris.

10.45 In a classical Wellesian dissolve, Fanny grieves for her brother's death as townspeople comment on its significance.

10.46 George is enjoined by his bachelor uncle Jack (Ray Collins) in deep focus.

10.47 Shortly before his death, old Major Amberson stares into the fire and remembers things past: "The sun. It must be the sun."

Flawed though it is, *The Magnificent Ambersons* remains a great and powerful film. Adapted by Welles from Booth Tarkington's novel, it parallels the turn-of-the-century decline of a proud and wealthy provincial family with the rise of the modern industrial city of Indianapolis. It is an unabashedly nostalgic film whose *mise-en-scène* is carefully calculated to create a sense of longing for the past. Although he was no Gregg Toland, cinematographer Stanley Cortez's high-contrast lighting and deep-focus photography of the interior of the Amberson mansion produced some of the most beautiful sequence shots ever to appear on the American screen. Like *Citizen Kane*, the film is constructed largely of long takes, with much spectacular tracking movement of the camera, and Welles's revolutionary use of the lightning mix and sound montage exceeds even his own earlier work. Though the 88-minute version that has survived can only hint at the epic sweep of the original, *The Magnificent Ambersons* as it stands today is a masterpiece of mood, decor, and composition in depth. It is also a remarkably intelligent and prophetic film that suggests (in 1942, and in a story set in 1905) that the quality of American life will ultimately be destroyed by the automobile and urbanization.

The Magnificent Ambersons, distributed on a double bill with a Lupe Velez comedy, was a commercial disaster. So was *Journey into Fear* (1942; released 1943), a stylish adaptation of an Eric Ambler espionage novel set in the Middle East, starring Welles and the Mercury Players, and co-directed by Welles (uncredited) and Norman Foster (1900–1976). With his third box-office failure behind him, Welles was recalled from Brazil and removed from *It's All True*, which was never completed; the Mercury Players were given forty-eight hours to clear off the RKO lot. Originally entitled *Pan-American*, *It's All True* was to have been a four-part anthology feature shot on location in the United States, Mexico, and Brazil with the purpose of promoting hemispheric cooperation as part of Franklin Delano Roosevelt's anti-Nazi "Good Neighbor" policy. (Behind the venture was Nelson Rockefeller, then coordinator of Inter-American Affairs and a major RKO stockholder; in neither role did he lack self-interest—see footnote, p. 368.) The project was terminated for various financial and political reasons, and much of the film's negative, including a Technicolor carnival sequence shot in Rio, dumped into Santa

10.48 A Wellesian low-angle shot from *Journey into Fear* (Orson Welles and Norman Foster, 1943): Joseph Cotton.

of *The Magnificent Ambersons*, using the March 12, 1942, cutting continuity to indicate what was excised from the original version of the release print, what scenes were reordered, and what new footage was shot by others and integrated into the film while Welles was in Brazil.

10.49 *The Lady from Shanghai* (Orson Welles, 1947; released 1948): the fantastic love scene before the aquarium tanks. Welles as Michael O'Hara, Rita Hayworth as Elsa Bannister.

10.51A Lost in the fun house.

10.50 *The Lady from Shanghai:* Elsa in Chinatown.

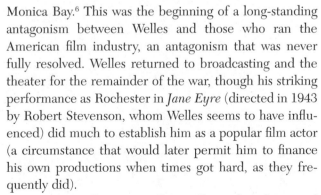

10.51B O'Hara plunges toward the hall of mirrors.

Monica Bay.[6] This was the beginning of a long-standing antagonism between Welles and those who ran the American film industry, an antagonism that was never fully resolved. Welles returned to broadcasting and the theater for the remainder of the war, though his striking performance as Rochester in *Jane Eyre* (directed in 1943 by Robert Stevenson, whom Welles seems to have influenced) did much to establish him as a popular film actor (a circumstance that would later permit him to finance his own productions when times got hard, as they frequently did).

In 1945, Welles returned to Hollywood to direct and star in *The Stranger* (1946) for the newly formed International Pictures, but was required to adhere closely to an existing script and a pre-arranged editing schedule. Welles submitted to the condition, and the resulting film

6. In 1985, eighteen to twenty hours of Welles's Brazilian footage, including three Technicolor sequences, were found in an old RKO vault by Paramount Pictures executive Fred Chandler (Paramount having bought Desilu Studios, which had earlier acquired RKO's production facilities). This was used to produce a twenty-two-minute documentary on the film's central sequence, "Four Men in a Raft," which debuted at the Venice Film Festival in 1986 and attracted considerable attention. (In the same year, a Brazilian docudrama, *Nem tudo é verdade* [*Not Everything Is True*, directed by Rogério Sganzerla] recounted the film's troubled production history from a Latino perspective.) Over the next six years, an international team of production artists, archivists, and scholars led by Los Angeles-based filmmaker Myron Meisel put together a ninety-minute documentary feature on the making of *It's All True* that premiered at the New York Film Festival in 1993. At the film's core are reconstructed versions of "Four Men in a Raft" and Technicolor sequences from two other segments—"The Story of the Samba" and "My Friend Bonito"—which show an extraordinary film artist working at the height of his creative powers.

10.52 A studio publicity still, followed by frames from the final shoot-out in *The Lady from Shanghai:* O'Hara; Elsa; and her husband, Arthur Bannister (Everett Sloane).

is an intentional, if preposterous, self-parody about the tracking down of a Nazi war criminal (Welles) who is, somehow, posing as a master at a New England prep school and is married to the headmaster's daughter (Loretta Young). Technically, the film is fairly conventional, and Welles regarded it as his worst. Nevertheless, nationally distributed by RKO, its commercial success helped him to land a job at Columbia directing his brilliant and exotic essay in *film noir, The Lady from Shanghai* (1947; released 1948), which starred Welles and his second wife, Rita Hayworth (1918–1987). This bizarre film of corruption, murder, and betrayal is cast in the form of a thriller, but its theme is the moral anarchy of the postwar world. Though its intricate, rambling plot is almost impossible to follow,[7] cinematically the film is one of Welles's finest achievements: the haunting sequence shots of the assignation between Welles and Hayworth in the San Francisco Aquarium, the perfectly cut chase in the Chinese theater, and, most of all, the montage of the two-way shootout in the hall of mirrors that concludes the film have become textbook examples of Welles's genius. Because of the obscurity of its narrative, *The Lady from Shanghai* was a financial failure, and Welles

became persona non grata in Hollywood for nearly a decade.

In order to continue making films, he was forced to exile himself to Europe, but before he left, he turned out a final Mercury Theatre production—a nightmarishly Expressionistic version of *Macbeth* (1948) shot in twenty-three days on papier-mâché and cardboard sets for the B-studio Republic Pictures. More Welles than Shakespeare, with Welles playing Macbeth, the film still manages to convey an atmosphere of brooding evil and to create a convincing portrait of a man driven by ambition beyond the bounds of the moral universe (a characteristic theme of both Shakespeare and Welles) in a culture that has only just emerged from barbarism. Originally 112 minutes long, *Macbeth* was cut to 86 minutes by its producers after Welles had left for Europe, and the sound track—in which the actors spoke with Scottish

---

7. A fact abetted by Harry Cohn, president of Columbia Pictures, who held up the film's release by a year (it was originally completed in 1946) while it was re-edited, redubbed, and rescored under Welles's supervision.

10.53 *Macbeth* (Orson Welles, 1948): "The Three"—Druidic sorceresses who control Macbeth's destiny.

10.54 Iconographic violence: Lady Macbeth (Jeanette Nolan) tormented by blood-guilt.

burrs for verisimilitude—was rerecorded to "Americanize" the accents. This recut, redubbed version was the only one known in the United States until 1979, when a UCLA archivist discovered the original among the university's collection of NTA Film Services (Republic's distributor) nitrate prints. In 1980, *Macbeth* was restored to its original form through a joint endeavor of UCLA and the Folger Shakespeare Library, complete with the Scottish-accented sound track and an eight-minute overture by the film's composer, Jacques Ibert. Among the most startling discoveries within the missing footage was a ten-minute-long take of continuous dramatic action, probably the first ever attempted in a theatrical film (Hitchcock's *Rope* went into production a few months after Welles's film was completed).

In moving to Europe, Welles lost the great technical and financial resources of the Hollywood studios, but he gained much in creative freedom. As a result, his European films tend to be technically imperfect and imaginatively unrestrained. The first of these was another Shakespeare adaptation, *Othello* (1952), with Welles in the title role; the film was made over a period of four years, from 1948 to 1952, while Welles financed the production by acting in other people's films. With interiors shot all over Europe and exteriors shot in the ancient citadel at Mogador, Morocco, *Othello* is a film of light and openness—of wind, sun, and sea—as opposed to the brooding darkness of *Macbeth* and *The Lady from Shanghai*. Continuously recast, reshot, recut, and redubbed,

10.55 Macbeth prepares for his climatic battle with Macduff.

10.56 The Moor prepares to murder his bride.

10.57 From the conclusion of the lengthy tracking shot that opens *Touch of Evil* (Orson Welles, 1958): Charlton Heston, Janet Leigh.

10.58 Welles as Hank Quinlan in *Touch of Evil.*

Othello nevertheless won the Grand Prix at the Cannes Film Festival when it was finally completed in 1952.[8] (Welles bequeathed the rights to *Othello* to his daughter Beatrice Welles-Smith, and in 1989 she embarked on a $500,000 restoration project with Chicago-based filmmakers Michael Dawson and Arne Saks. The restored *Othello*, based on Welles's original nitrate negative, was released to mark its fortieth anniversary in 1992; the original dialogue track was remixed with newly created sound effects and a digital rerecording of the original score.)

Welles's next film, *Mr. Arkadin* (British title: *Confidential Report*, 1955), a failed attempt to remake *Citizen Kane* in European terms, was shot on an extremely low budget during an eight-month period in Spain, Germany, and France. On the French Riviera, a down-at-the-heels adventurer named Van Stratten is hired by the mysterious European business tycoon Gregory Arkadin (based on the real-life war profiteer Miles Krueger, and played by Welles) to piece together the details of his buried past. Van Stratten's Kafkaesque quest takes him all over Europe as he interviews the people who possess the secrets of Arkadin's past life, only to discover at the end of the film that he is the finger man in a murder plot whereby the tycoon is systematically destroying all who can reveal his criminal past as soon as they are identified. Poorly acted, written, and recorded, with Welles himself dubbing in the voices of most of the other characters, *Mr. Arkadin* is an ambitious and intermittently brilliant failure.

No such difficulties attend *Touch of Evil* (1958), for which Welles returned to Hollywood for the first time

in ten years. Universal, still a minor studio, had signed Welles and Charlton Heston to play the leads in what was to be a conventional police melodrama, and Heston insisted that Welles also direct. Welles accepted the job and was permitted to rewrite the script, turning it into a nightmarish parable of the abuse of power in a dark and sinister world. Shot against the garish background of Venice, California, *Touch of Evil* is another study of a man like Kane, Macbeth, and Arkadin, whose obsession with control causes him to transgress the laws of the moral universe. Hank Quinlan (Welles), a police captain in a seamy Mexican-American border town, has spent thirty years framing murder suspects about whose guilt he had "a hunch" in order to ensure their conviction. He ultimately runs afoul of an honest Mexican narcotics agent (Heston) who exposes his practices and indirectly causes his death. The grotesque, inflated, and yet somehow sympathetic Quinlan is superbly played by Welles as a man whose once strong character has been utterly corrupted by an obsession.

As a director, Welles demanded the impossible from the cinematographer Russell Metty (who also shot *The Stranger*) and got it. The film opens with a continuous moving crane shot (unfortunately obscured in the release print by the credits), which begins with a close-up of a time bomb and ends with the explosion of the device in a car nearly two and a half minutes later, making it one of the longest unbroken tracking shots attempted before

---

8. Actually, it shared the prize with Renato Castellani's comedy *Due soldi di speranza* (*Two Pennyworth of Hope*, 1952).

the advent of the Steadicam. Later, Metty was required to track his camera from the exterior of a building through a lobby and into a crowded elevator, and then ride up five floors to shoot Heston greeting the occupants as the doors slide open from within. There is also significant use of deep-focus photography and sound montage for the first time since *The Lady from Shanghai* (1947). Like Welles's previous films, *Touch of Evil* was shot in high-contrast black and white. Ignored in every country but France (where it won the Cannes Grand Prix) in the year of its release, *Touch of Evil* is today considered a Welles masterpiece whose technical brilliance and thematic depth bring it close to the stature of *Kane*. When it was released, the film was cut from 108 to 95 minutes under the supervision of Universal postproduction head Ernest Nims to make its editing continuity easier for contemporary audiences to follow.[9] In 1976, the deleted footage was restored by Universal, and a version closer to Welles's original was released for distribution in 16mm and, subsequently, on video cassette. But a complete restoration did not occur until 1998, when producer Rick Schmidlin located a 58-page memo that Welles had sent to Universal executives after seeing the studio's cut in 1958, detailing changes he wanted them to make in the release print. Schmidlin recruited Academy Award–winning editor and sound designer Walter Murch (*Apocalypse Now* [1979]; *The English Patient* [1996]) to re-edit the film as specified in Welles's memo and remaster the sound track. This version, which entails about fifty editorial changes and removes the credits from the opening sequence shot, was released by Universal theatrically in 1998 and on DVD in 2000.

But the film's financial failure in 1958 confirmed Welles's status as a pariah in Hollywood; he returned to Europe, where French producers offered him an opportunity to direct a film based on a major literary work of his choice. He selected Kafka's novel *The Trial*, published in 1925. Despite budgeting problems, *The Trial* (1962) became the only one of his films since *Kane* over which Welles exercised total control. His customary visual complexity notwithstanding, the results are disappointing. Shot in black and white in the streets of Zagreb, Croatia (then Yugoslavia), and in the fantastic Gare d'Orsay in Paris, the film finally fails to evoke the antiseptic modern hell of Kafka's novel, perhaps because of some disparity between the world views of the two artists.

Welles's next European film and his last completed

10.59 *The Trial* **(Orson Welles, 1962): Anthony Perkins as "K."**

feature, *Chimes at Midnight* (British title: *Falstaff*, 1966), is widely regarded as a masterpiece. Returning to an idea that he had first tried in his 1938 Theater Guild production *Five Kings*, Welles assembled all the Falstaff parts from *Henry IV, Parts I* and *II, The Merry Wives of Windsor*, and *Henry V*, and linked them together with a narration from Holinshed's *Chronicles* (the medieval source of Shakespeare's history plays) to create a portrait of the character as his privileged friendship with Prince Hal passes gradually from affection to bitterness, disillusionment, and decay. Like *Citizen Kane*, it is a film about decline and loss, and like *The Magnificent Ambersons*, it is full of nostalgia for a vanished past; but it is as much the work of an older man as *Kane* and *The Magnificent Ambersons* are the work of a younger one. Shot in Spain (for financial reasons) over a period of several years, *Chimes at Midnight* is superbly photographed and acted, with Welles at his best in the title role. Its moving crane shots have been widely praised, and the lengthy montage sequence depicting the Battle of Shrewsbury has been favorably compared to Eisenstein's Odessa

9. As Nims would later remark: "He [Welles] was ahead of his time. He was making those *quick* cuts—in the middle of a scene you cut to another scene and then come back and finish the scene and then cut to the last half of the other scene" (quoted in Barbara Leaming, *Orson Welles: A Biography* [New York: Viking, 1985], p. 428). Specifically, Nims recut the film's first five reels to conform to conventional continuity practice, deleted certain auditory shock effects Welles had devised for the sound track, and added several inserts shot by Universal contract director Harry Keller (1913–1987; *The Face in the Mirror*, 1958). See John Belton, "A New Map of the Labyrinth: The Unretouched *Touch of Evil*," *Movietone News*, no. 47 (January 21, 1976): 1–9, and no. 48 (February 29, 1976): 23.

10.60 Welles as Falstaff in *Chimes at Midnight* (Orson Welles, 1966).

10.61 *Chimes at Midnight:* from the Battle of Shrewsbury sequence.

Steps sequence in *Potemkin* (1925) and the Battle on the Ice in *Alexander Nevski* (1938). Yet *Chimes at Midnight* is anything but technically extravagant. It is rather a quiet, elegiac, and dignified film whose restrained style and austere black-and-white photography correspond perfectly with its sober themes of human frailty, mortality, and decay.

It is no longer possible—as it was, perhaps, even several years ago—to speak of Orson Welles as a director important for a single, if monumental and awe-inspiring, film. Welles produced five masterpieces—*Citizen Kane, The Magnificent Ambersons, The Lady from Shanghai, Touch of Evil,* and *Chimes at Midnight*—and his Shakespearean films, extravagant and eccentric as they sometimes are, represent major contributions to the genre. In *Citizen Kane* he gave us the first modern sound film and effectively pioneered the aesthetic of the long take, or composition in depth. All of his films of the 1940s significantly anticipated the contemporary cinema of widescreen photography and stereophonic sound. But technological wizardry notwithstanding, Welles produced a body of work that deserves to be ranked with the great narrative art of our century. Welles was a traditional moralist whose major themes were characteristically those of classical Western literature: the corrupting nature of ambition; the disparity between social and psychological reality; the destructive power of self-delusion, appetite, and obsession; and the importance of a sense of the past. Confirming these thematic concerns was his intermittent work from 1955 until his

death in 1985 on a version of *Don Quixote* set in modern times (a more or less complete work print of which is currently being restored by Welles's companion and collaborator Oja Kodar). Stylistically, however, Welles was always an innovator and a radical experimenter—an authentic American Expressionist with a decidedly baroque sense of form who has profoundly influenced the course of Western cinema.

In his latter years, he made several attempts to become an active part of that cinema again, in collaboration with Kodar, as his principal scriptwriter and actress, and the cinematographer Gary Graver, most notably in the still unreleased *The Other Side of the Wind*. This three-hour color film, which Welles described as "96-percent finished" in 1979, stars John Huston as a Welles-like director contemplating his career in flashback at the end of his life. In a tribute presented to him by the American Film Institute in 1975, Welles showed some provocative footage from it in an unsuccessful attempt to raise money for its completion. Between 1978 and 1985, he worked on *The Dreamers*, a romantic adventure story based upon two of Isak Dinesen's *Gothic Tales*, but only a few scenes of it were actually shot.

When he died, Welles was working on a long-cherished project—his own adaptation of *King Lear* in video, with himself in the title role and Kodar as Cordelia—which also remained unfinished. Welles's death on October 10, 1985, was mourned around the world, appropriately, as the passing of a twentieth-century American genius. It is difficult to know who or what to blame for the wasteful attenuation of his later career, and it is probably better not to try. But surely Welles would have appreciated the irony in the fact that only his death would make a whole generation of Americans aware that its favorite public fat man and talk-show raconteur was the single most important architect of the modern film. As Jean-Luc Godard observed of him at the height of the French New Wave, "Everyone will always owe him everything."[1]

1. Quoted in Michel Ciment, "Les Enfants terrible," *American Film* (December 1984): 42. Welles made several important films of less-than-feature length as well. *The Immortal Story* (*Histoire immortelle*, 1968), based on a novella by Isak Dinesen, was written and directed by Welles for France's nationalized television company, ORTF. Running fifty-eight minutes, it was Welles's first film in color and stars Welles, Jeanne Moreau, and Fernando Rey. *The Deep* (also called *Dead Calm* or *Dead Reckoning*) was written and directed by Welles, and was shot by Gary Graver off the Dalmatian coast of Yugoslavia between 1967 and 1969. Based on the novel *Dead Calm* by Charles Williams, the film stars Welles, Jeanne Moreau, Laurence Harvey, Oja Kodar, and Michael Bryant. There is a plot summary of *The Deep*, based on an early version of the script, in James Naremore's *The Magic World of Orson Welles*, rev. ed. (Dallas: SMU Press, 1989); *The Deep* was completed but remains unreleased because of continuity gaps resulting from the death of Harvey in 1973 and the undubbed part of Moreau. In 1969 Welles shot an abridged color version of *The Merchant of Venice* in Trogir, Croatia (then Yugoslavia), and Asolo, Italy, which was completed, edited, scored, and mixed, but remains unreleased due to the theft of two of its reels; Kodar is currently at work on a reconstruction. Finally—and most significantly—Welles wrote and co-directed with the French documentarist François Reichenbach *F for Fake* (1975; released in France as *Vérités et mensonges*, 1973), a hybrid documentary about the dynamic of fakery. It focuses on the famous art forger Elmyr de Hory; his biographer (and the fraudulent pseudobiographer of Howard Hughes), Clifford Irving; and Welles himself, who, as director of the film, is the chief illusionist among them. According to William Johnson in his *Film Quarterly* review of *F for Fake* (Summer 1976), the film provides a "commentary on the ontology of the film medium" and that medium's "specious realism." In 1978 the documentary *Filming Othello* (also known as *The Making of Othello*) was produced for West German television by Klaus and Juergen Hellwig; it featured interviews with the cast and crew of the 1952 Mercury Films Production and narrated footage of the original film—all of it directed by Welles.

Wartime and Postwar Cinema: Italy and the United States, 1940–1951

The Effects of War

World War II left the national cinemas of Western Europe in a state of economic, physical, and psychological paralysis. Cinema is an industry, and industries are dependent for their survival upon the stability of the economic systems in which they function. The Nazis had destroyed the shaky prewar economy of Europe and set up another in its place. That in turn was destroyed by the Allied victory in the spring of 1945. Until the Marshall Plan for the economic rehabilitation of Europe began to take effect in 1948–49, national industries of all types found it impossible to resume production on a large scale. Furthermore, the physical devastation wreaked upon the European film industries by the war was immense. In England, air raids destroyed 330 film theaters, or close to 25 percent of the total number. Germany lost nearly 60 percent of its film-production facilities in the firebombing of Berlin. And in France, which had managed to maintain fairly high standards of film production during the German Occupation, the industry was reduced to a state of chaos by Allied bombardment of Paris and street fighting during the liberation of the city in August 1944. In all of Europe, only the Italian film industry was left with its production facilities reasonably intact, a result of Italy's early surrender and the unique circumstances of its liberation.

More devastating to the cinema than either economic instability or physical destruction of facilities, however, was the state of psychological and moral collapse in which Europe found itself immediately following the Nazi surrender. It is estimated that World War II killed over 48 million people in Europe and created more than 21 million refugees. Whole urban districts, with nearly their entire civilian populations, had been wiped out in minutes by firebombing and the artifacts of centuries-old civilizations reduced to rubble. Indeed, at least 35 percent of all permanent dwellings in Western Europe were destroyed by the war. Liberation was joyful when it came, but the experience of Nazi barbarism left a dark imprint on the European consciousness; and the revelation of the true extent of Nazi atrocities in the occupied territories was nothing less than shattering. In one large province of the Soviet Union, for example, 40 percent of the inhabitants had been deported to death camps, and Poland had lost 25 percent of its entire population to the camps. The German-born sociologist and philosopher Theodor Adorno, himself a refugee from Hitler, was moved to state that there could be "no poetry after Auschwitz,"[1] and indeed, for a while there could not. The human spirit rekindles quickly, however—too quickly, some have felt, given the magnitude of this particular horror. Economies, on the other hand, most frequently do not, and until the benefits of the Marshall Plan began to be felt, the European national cinemas, except for that of Italy, were unable to approach anything like their prewar levels of production.[2] In Italy, the revitalization of the national cinema was set in motion even before the war had ended.

Italy

THE ITALIAN CINEMA BEFORE NEOREALISM

When the Fascists, under Benito Mussolini, seized power in 1922, Italian cinema had already fallen far from the position of international leadership it held during the early silent period (see Chapter 2). Epic spectacles like Enrico Guazzoni's world-famous *Quo vadis?* (1913) and Giovanni Pastrone's *Cabiria* (1914) were a thing of the past; and by the time sound arrived in 1930, Italian studios were producing only a handful of features per year, the majority of which were either American-style romantic comedies—*telefono bianco* ("white telephone") films— and family melodramas (see Chapter 9). But the Fascists, aware of cinema's immense potential for propaganda, were committed to reviving the Italian industry and putting it in the service of the state.

A former Marxist, Mussolini was particularly impressed by the Soviet achievement in blending film and politics (he even paraphrased Lenin in calling cinema *"l'arma più forte"*—"the strongest weapon" of the age), and he sought to reorganize the Italian industry along Soviet lines (see Chapter 5). In 1924 Mussolini founded L'Unione Cinematografica Educativa (LUCE), a state film service to produce documentaries and newsreels about his regime for the purpose of "civil and national educa-

tion." Then, gradually but deliberately, he cultivated financial relations with the private sector, culminating in the creation of the Ente Nazionale Industrie Cinematografiche (ENIC) in 1935 as a centralized bureaucracy to control the distribution and exhibition of all films within the Fascist state. The following year, Mussolini ordered the establishment of a national film school (unprecedented outside of the Soviet Union), the Centro Sperimentale della Cinematografia, and authorized the construction of the vast **Cinecittà** studios in Rome, whose size and technical facilities rivaled those of UFA-Neubabelsberg, with 16 soundstages, 600,000 square meters for exteriors, and corridor upon corridor of dressing rooms.[3] To emphasize the importance of film to his regime, Mussolini personally inaugurated the facility in 1937—on April 21, the mythical date of the founding of Rome—and within a year Cinecittà had released more than 80 films, doubling the rate of Italian film production.

Meanwhile, the Centro Sperimentale, under the direction of the filmmaker Luigi Chiarini (1900–1975), a covert Marxist, had attracted such promising students as Roberto Rossellini, Luigi Zampa, Pietro Germi, Giuseppe De Santis, and Michelangelo Antonioni—all to become major directors of the postwar cinema—and had begun to publish its own theoretical journal, *Bianco e nero (Black and White),* which remains Italy's premier academic film journal to this day. A rival periodical called *Cinema* was soon founded under the editorship of Vittorio Mussolini, son of Il Duce. *Cinema* published translations of the major theoretical writings of Eisenstein, Pudovkin, and Balázs (see Chapters 5 and 16), as well as contributions from native talents like the young Luchino Visconti. Finally, to further upgrade and increase pro-

---

1. The streamlined mass-extermination complex built by the Nazis in eastern Poland, where over 1 million people died in two years.

2. In the United States, by contrast, 1946 was the most profitable year in the history of Hollywood before 1973. Box-office receipts exceeded $1.7 billion, no small part of which derived from the exhibition of American films in Europe (people *will* have movies—in the worst of times probably more than in the best). In fact, it is arguable that the regeneration of the European national cinemas was substantially and deliberately retarded by a massive influx of American films in the immediate postwar period. However, the superior craftsmanship of Hollywood productions may have inspired the European cinemas to new levels of technical competence when their renewal finally began.

3. Both the Centro Sperimentale and Cinecittà are in operation today. After the VGIK in Moscow (founded 1919), the Centro is the oldest state film school in the world; and Cinecittà, its wartime bombing damage repaired, is still the largest studio in Europe.

duction Mussolini attempted to establish a wholly protected industry by imposing strict import quotas on foreign films; and when Italy entered the war in 1940, he banned American films altogether. (Previously, he had contented himself with rather childishly maligning American films through "imperial edict." In 1933, for example, Italian audiences had been forbidden to laugh at the Marx Brothers in *Duck Soup,* but the film itself was not banned.) During the first year of the war, Italian production reached the all-time high of eighty-six films per annum.

The cinema subsidized by Mussolini and his Fascist state was an enormous popular success. As Ted Perry has written, "The fifteen years from the coming of sound to the end of Mussolini's reign provided . . . an entertainment industry that rivaled Hollywood in the charm and sophistication of its narratives, its acting and direction." According to James Hay, moreover, the films produced by this industry helped form Italy's first truly national *cultura popolare* (see *Popular Film Culture in Fascist Italy: The Passing of the Rex* [Bloomington: Indiana University Press, 1987]). This cinema's most salient artistic feature was the style neorealist film critic and director Giuseppe De Santis (1917–1997) designated as **calligraphism**—a sort of decorative, pictorial formalism that manifested itself in meticulously photographed adaptations of late-nineteenth-century and early-twentieth-century fiction. Among the more prominent works of calligraphism were Luigi Chiarini's adaptation of *Via delle Cinque Lune* (*Five Moons Street,* 1941), a story by the Neapolitan realist Matilde Serao; Mario Soldati's (1906–

11.1 Calligraphism: Renato Castellani's *Un colpo di pistola* (1942). Fosco Giachetti, Massimo Serato.

1999) *Piccolo mondo antico* (*Little Old-Fashioned World,* 1941), a nineteenth-century tale of passion adapted from the novel by Antonio Fogazzaro; Renato Castellani's *Un colpo di pistola* (*A Pistol Shot,* 1942), a version of Pushkin's 1831 short story *The Shot;* and Alberto Lattuada's *Giacomo l'idealista* (*Jacob, the Idealist,* 1943), based on a turn-of-the-century melodrama by the Lombard novelist Emilio De Marchi. In many ways the antithesis of neorealism, calligraphism nevertheless provided a training ground for the scriptwriters, technicians, performers, and other creative personnel associated with it. So, too—ironically—did the Fascist propaganda documentary of the period.

Francesco De Robertis (1902–1959), as head of the film section of the naval ministry, was responsible for several semidocumentary feature films that anticipated neorealism in their use of nonprofessional actors, on-location shooting, and a photographic style similar to that of contemporary newsreels. In *Uomini sul fondo* (*Men on the Bottom*; English title: *S.O.S. Submarine*), which he directed as his first feature in 1941, De Robertis re-created the undersea rescue of a disabled Italian submarine so authentically that critics all over the country took note. In the same year, he supervised the production of *La nave bianca* (*The White Ship*), which realistically reconstructed life aboard an Italian hospital ship by combining staged scenes with actual footage and gave Roberto Rossellini (1906–1977) his first job directing a feature film. The influence of De Robertis was mainly technical, however, for he was a devout Fascist whose world view was in no way compatible with the liberal humanism that neorealism came to espouse. (Yet Rossellini went on to make two more films under his tutelage—*Un pilota ritorna* [*A Pilot Returns,* 1942; scripted in part by Antonioni and Vittorio Mussolini] and *L'uomo dalla croce* [*The Man of the Cross,* 1943]—which, together with *La nave bianca,* form a sort of Fascist trilogy.)[4]

---

4. The best explanation of this "collaboration" with the Fascist regime is advanced by Peter Brunette in his critical biography, *Roberto Rossellini* (New York: Oxford University Press, 1987), where he attributes it to the director's *trasformismo*—"that particularly Roman talent, honed by centuries of constantly changing power relationships, for knowing which way the wind is blowing, for being able to shift loyalties quickly in order to survive" (p. 37). Rossellini and his contemporaries had adapted to Italian Fascism as a prevailing system of government—the only one that most had known since youth—but all this changed when Mussolini was deposed and the Nazis occupied Rome.

More attuned to neorealism conceptually was the middle-class comedy of manners as practiced by Alessandro Blasetti (1900–1987) in *Quattro passi fra le nuvole* (*Four Steps in the Clouds*, 1942) and Vittorio De Sica in *I bambini ci guardano* (*The Children Are Watching Us*, 1942). Although both films are elaborations of an older genre perfected by Mario Camerini (1895–1981) in the 1930s, and are slightly flawed by sentimentality, they are notable for their studied social observation and their realistic scripts by the Marxist screenwriter Cesare Zavattini (1902–1989), who was shortly to become to neorealism what Carl Mayer had been to the *Kammerspielfilm*—its chief ideological spokesman and major scenarist.[5]

THE FOUNDATIONS OF NEOREALISM

Zavattini was the theoretical founder of neorealism. In 1942 he called for a new kind of Italian film—one that would abolish contrived plots, do away with professional actors, and take to the streets for its material in order to establish direct contact with contemporary social reality. Plot was inauthentic, according to Zavattini, because it imposed an artificial structure on "everyday life," and professional actors simply compounded the falsehood since "to want one person to play another implies the calculated plot." It was precisely the dignity and sacredness of the everyday life of ordinary people, so alien to the heroic ideal of Fascism, that Zavattini demanded that the new realism capture. As he was to write later of the emergence of neorealism: "The reality buried under the myths slowly reflowered. The cinema began its creation of the world. Here was a tree; here, an old man; here, a house; here, a man eating, a man sleeping, a man crying. . . . The cinema . . . should accept, unconditionally, what is contemporary. *Today, today, today.*"

In early 1943, Umberto Barbaro (1902–1959), an influential critic and lecturer at the Centro Sperimentale, published an article that attacked the reactionary conventions of the Italian film and invoked the term "neorealism" to refer to what was lacking. Barbaro's specific allusion was to French poetic realism—the 1930s cinema of Renoir, Carné, Duvivier, and Clair—but the term was soon picked up by Giuseppe De Santis and other progressive critics at *Bianco e nero and Cinema* to designate the revolutionary agitation for a popular and realistic national cinema that was soon to sweep the Italian film schools, cinema clubs, and critical journals. The influences

on the young men demanding a "new realism" were many and varied. For one thing, most of them were clandestine Marxists in addition to being professionally trained film critics, and the "realism" they wished to renew was quite specifically the Soviet expressive realism of Eisenstein, Pudovkin, and Dovzhenko. This influence was less technical than ideological, however, and the stylistic resemblances between Italian neorealism and Soviet expressive realism, although they do exist, are slight.

A more direct and practical influence on the neorealist movement was French poetic realism, which had achieved international preeminence by 1939. In addition to being technically brilliant, the films of poetic realism espoused a kind of socialist humanism that Italians found at least as appealing as the strident Soviet Marxism. *Toni* (1934), Jean Renoir's drama of immigrant Italian laborers shot on location in the south of France with nonprofessional actors, provided an important structural model. Furthermore, several major directors of the neorealist cinema actually served their apprenticeships under French filmmakers. Luchino Visconti (1906–1976), for example, had been an assistant on Renoir's *Une partie de campagne* (1936; released 1946) as well as a scriptwriter for the version of *La Tosca* (1940) begun by Renoir and completed by Carl Koch (see pp. 324–25); and Michelangelo Antonioni (see pp. 535–39) had worked as an assistant to Marcel Carné on *Les Visiteurs du soir* (1942). Most significant of all, perhaps, is the fact that the cinema of poetic realism represented aesthetic and intellectual freedom to young Italian artists trapped in the hothouse atmosphere of the Fascist studios. Many, like Rossellini, had begun their careers as government loyalists but turned bitterly against the regime as they were forced to make compromise after compromise to Fascist policy and public taste. In fact, as Roy Armes has suggested, by straitjacketing Italy's film artists Fascism probably contributed to the rise of neorealism more than did any other single historical force.

Indeed, Italian Fascism had always contained the seeds of its own destruction, and in 1943 political and historical events conspired to liberate the forces of neorealism from

---

5. Zavattini continued to write screenplays long after neorealism's decline (for example, *Un cuore semplice* [*A Simple Heart*—from Flaubert, directed by Giorgio Ferrara, 1978]; *Ligabue* [directed by Salvatore Nocita, 1978]; and *La verit-a-a-a-à* [*The Tru-u-u-u-th*, 1982, directed by Zavattini at age eighty]).

the journal pages. The Allies invaded Sicily in July, and Mussolini was turned out of office by his own party. An armistice was then signed with the Allies, whose forces landed on the mainland and began their sweep up the peninsula. To add to the confusion, the new Italian government, under Marshal Badoglio, declared war on Germany, while in the north of Italy Mussolini was installed as the head of a Nazi puppet state called the Salo Republic. Partisan fighting erupted everywhere, the Nazis occupied Rome, and the Allied movement northward was slowed. Rome did not fall until June 1944, and even then it took another year of heavy fighting to effect the Germans' unconditional surrender. But in the midst of this chaos, Fascist control of the Italian film studios relaxed somewhat, and the armistice of 1943 had no sooner been signed than neorealism was heralded by the release of Luchino Visconti's grim tale of passion and murder in modern Italy, *Ossessione* (*Obsession*).

Ossessione was based (without permission) on the luridly poetic thriller *The Postman Always Rings Twice* by the American novelist James M. Cain; it could not be shown outside of Italy until 1976 because it infringed the author's copyright.[6] The novel is a violent tale of sexual obsession and corruption in which a young drifter contracts an affair with the sensual wife of the owner of a roadside cafe. Together they murder the husband for his insurance money, but they are later trapped in their own deceptions. Visconti retained the melodramatic plot and brutal characters but transferred the setting to the contemporary Italian countryside near Ferrara, whose

bleakness, provinciality, and poverty he captured with great fidelity. In 1948, the coscenarist (with Giuseppe De Santis) of *Ossessione*, Antonio Pietrangeli, offered this description of the film's visual texture: "Ferrara, its squares, its gray and deserted streets; Ancona and its San Ciriaco Fair; the Po and its sandy banks; a landscape streaked with a rubble of cars and men along the network of highways. Against this backdrop are silhouetted the wandering merchants, mechanics, prostitutes and inn boys . . . beset by violent proletarian love affairs, primitive anger, and the sins that the flesh is heir to."

Clearly, the technical virtuosity of *Ossessione* would have made it an important film under any circumstances, but coming as it did upon the heels of the neorealist manifestos of Zavattini and Barbaro, it seemed to validate their notion that a new Italian cinema was about to be born—one that would take its cameras out of the studios and into the streets and countryside to probe the lives of ordinary men and women in relation to their environment. Thus, *Ossessione* can be said to have provided the blueprint for neorealism. It anticipated some of the movement's themes and styles (popular setting, realistic treatment, social content), though lacking the neorealist political commitment and historical perspective. But, unfortunately, political and economic circumstances intervened to make the film less immediately influential than it might have been. The Fascist censors still controlled the industry, and though they had originally approved the project, they were shocked at the harsh portrait of Italian provincial life Visconti had painted. Their response was to ban the film and subsequently release it in a version cut to less than half its original length. Visconti reconstructed *Ossessione* after the war, but even then the film could not be shown abroad due to its copyright violation; for this reason, the first Italian neorealist film to reach the other countries of the West was Roberto Rossellini's *Roma, città aperta* (*Rome, Open City*, 1945).

11.2 *Ossessione* **(Luchino Visconti, 1943): Giovanna (Clara Calamai) in her kitchen.**

6. It was Renoir who brought *The Postman Always Rings Twice* to Visconti's attention and gave him a French typescript of the book during the shooting of *Une Partie de campagne* in 1936. Appropriately, the American version of Cain's novel, directed by Tay Garnett in 1946, is one of the great classics of *film noir*, a type of film discussed later in this chapter. There is also a 1937 French version directed by Pierre Chenal entitled *Le dernier tournant*, but Visconti had not seen it at the time he directed *Ossessione*. A second American version of the novel was directed by Bob Rafelson in 1981.

NEOREALISM: MAJOR FIGURES AND FILMS

A remarkable film of Italian resistance and Nazi reprisal, *Roma, città aperta*, was based upon events that had occurred in Rome in the winter of 1943–44, when the Germans declared that the city was "open."[7] It tells the story of a Communist underground leader who brings death to himself and his friends in a vain but heroic attempt to outlast a Gestapo manhunt. The film was planned in the midst of the Nazi occupation by Rossellini and his associates (Sergio Amidei, Anna Magnani, Aldo Fabrizi, and Federico Fellini—several of whom were actively involved in the Resistance at the time). Shooting began only weeks after Rome's liberation. Because Cinecittà had been damaged by Allied bombing, only two studio sets were used in the entire film, and the rest was shot on location in the streets of Rome, where the events it dramatized had actually taken place. In the interest of speed, Rossellini shot *Roma, città aperta* silent and dubbed in the actors' voices after it was edited. Moreover, because his film stock was of relatively low quality (Rossellini having bought it piecemeal from street photographers and spliced it onto motion-picture reels), the finished film had the look of a contemporary newsreel. Indeed, many who saw *Roma, città aperta* when it was first released in 1945 thought that they were watching a record of actual events unfolding before the cameras and were astonished that Rossellini could have been per-

mitted to reveal so much of Nazi brutality with the Germans still in Rome. They were equally amazed at the intelligence, integrity, and technical ingenuity of the film because, as far as international audiences were aware, these qualities had been absent from the Italian cinema since 1922, when the Fascists came to power.

For all of these reasons, and because it has an appealing melodramatic plot line, *Roma, città aperta* enjoyed immense success in almost every country in the Western world. In the United States alone its distributors grossed over half a million dollars, and in Italy it was the most profitable film since the outbreak of the war. Furthermore, *Roma, città aperta* won major prizes in a number of international film festivals, including the Grand Prix at Cannes in 1946, and critical acclaim for it was very nearly universal. The American critic James Agee, for example, was so awed by the film that he publicly refused to review it. Only in Italy was *Roma, città aperta* coldly received by the established critics, and this was less for aesthetic reasons than for ideological and political ones. It is true, of course, that the film has a number of structural flaws and that these relate at least as much to Rossellini's limitations as a director as to the difficult conditions under which it was made; but in spite of these defects, *Roma, città aperta* is one of those watershed films, like *The Birth of a Nation, Das Kabinett des Dr. Caligari, Potemkin,* and *Citizen Kane,* that changed the course of Western cinema. Rossellini's film became the paradigm for Italian neorealism and set the standard for everything that succeeded it—in its achievement of a documentary surface through on-location shooting and postsynchronization of sound,[8] its mixture of professional performers (Magnani and Fabrizi) and nonprofessionals, its references to contemporary national experience (or at least very recent national history), its social commitment and humanistic point of view, and, above all, what Penelope Houston has called its "driving urge" to rehabilitate the national reputation. It could be argued that its primacy is the result of a historical accident, given the suppression of *Ossessione,* but that primacy itself is indisputable.

11.3 *Roma, città aperta* (Roberto Rossellini, 1945): Pina (Anna Magnani) murdered by the SS.

7. An "open city" is one that is not to be fought through or bombed, according to international rules of war. But in this case, the Nazis' declaration was grimly ironic since they themselves had imposed brutal martial law on Rome during their occupation of the city.

8. Postsynchronization, or dubbing, has been standard Italian practice since the war.

Rossellini's next two films confirmed his mastery of the neorealist mode and extended his commitment to his country's recent past. *Paisà* (*Paisan*, 1946), like its predecessor, was written by Rossellini, Amidei, and Fellini. It recounts six unrelated episodes in the liberation of Italy, from the American landing in Sicily in 1943 to the Nazi evacuation of the Po Valley in 1945, and was shot on location all over the country: in Sicily, Naples, Rome, Florence, and the Po delta. Unlike *Roma, città aperta*, *Paisà* was a costly venture (in fact, the most expensive Italian film of 1946). Nevertheless, Rossellini once again combined professional and nonprofessional actors— using an American black man who was not an actor to play a GI, along with people from the district in which the director happened to be shooting—and he improvised part of his script to create what James Agee called in a contemporary review of *Paisà* "the illusion of the present tense." Like *Roma, città aperta*, the film contains flaws of structure, but in its authentic representation of common people caught up in the madness and horror of war, *Paisà* validates the broadly humanistic world view of neorealism and confirms the effectiveness of its improvisatory techniques.[9]

Rossellini's next film, the final one in what is often called his "war trilogy," was *Germania, anno zero* (*Germany, Year Zero*, 1947). Shot on location in bombed-out Berlin and acted entirely by nonprofessionals, the film is an attempt to probe the social roots of Fascism through the contrived story of a young German boy corrupted by Nazism who murders his bedridden father and commits suicide in the wake of the German defeat. It is generally agreed that *Germania, anno zero* represents a personal failure for Rossellini (who, in addition to directing, wrote the script), but its specifically neorealistic elements have been widely praised. For example, the long, nearly wordless concluding sequence in which the boy wanders through a gutted Berlin toward his personal *Götterdämmerung* is frequently cited as one of the glories of Italian neorealist cinema. In the end, however, that cinema proved nontransplantable in alien soil, and the relative failure of *Germania, anno zero*—both commercially and critically—foreshadowed the larger failure of the neorealist movement to transcend its specific social and historical contexts. Rossellini did not attempt another film in the neorealist vein, but he outlasted the movement to become a major figure in world cinema.[1]

---

9. Seeing *Paisà* for the first time had a formative influence on numerous future directors, including Ermanno Olmi, Paolo and Vittorio Taviani, and Gillo Pontecorvo, by their own accounts (see Chapter 15). It was also the experience that convinced Ingrid Bergman (1915–1982), then at the height of her popularity in Hollywood, to make a film with Rossellini—an impulse that resulted in an international scandal when she left her husband and young daughter to marry the director and bear him three children. The couple was subjected to a well-coordinated hate campaign in the United States, and Bergman was blacklisted by Hollywood until the late 1950s. Bergman starred in five much-maligned features for the Italian director, from *Stromboli* (1949) through *La Paura* (*Fear*, 1954–55).

1. Rossellini's major films after 1947 were *Il miracolo* (*The Miracle*, 1948; released in the United States in 1950 and banned in New York State for "sacrilege," the film was exonerated in a landmark U.S. Supreme Court decision in 1952 that extended First Amendment protection to motion pictures as a form of expression, for the first time in history); *Stromboli, terra di Dio* (*Stromboli, Land of God;* released in the United States as *Stromboli,* with twenty minutes cut by the distributor, RKO); *Francesco, giullare di Dio* (*Francis, God's Jester;* released in America as *The Flowers of St. Francis,* 1950); *Europa '51* (1952); *Viaggio in Italia* (*Voyage to Italy;* released in the United States as *Strangers,* 1953); the influential semidocumentary *India* (1958); *Il generale della Rovere* (*General della Rovere,* 1959; starring Vittorio De Sica); *Viva l'Italia!* (1960, an epic of the Risorgimento); *Vanina Vanini* (*The Betrayer,* 1961); *La prise de pouvoir par Louis XIV* (*The Rise of Louis XIV,* 1966; made for French television, ORTF, but theatrically distributed abroad); *Atti degli apostoli* (*Acts of the Apostles,* 1969; made for Italian television, RAI, ORTF, and TVE, Madrid); *Socrate* (*Socrates,* 1970, made for RAI, ORTF, and TVE); *Agostino d'Ippona* (*St. Augustine of Hippo,* 1972; made for RAI); *Blaise Pascal* (1972; made for RAI); *L'Età di Cosimo de'Medici* (*The Age of the Medici,* 1972; RAI); *Cartesius* (*Descartes,* 1974; RAI, ORTF); and *Il Messia* (*The Messiah,* 1975; independently produced for television). When he died on June 3, 1977, Rossellini was planning a biopic of Karl Marx, for which he had just completed the script. In his films of the 1950s, Rossellini had become a master of the long take and the Pancinor zoom lens (which he invented and operated himself), and he exercised an enormous influence on the young directors of the French New Wave and *cinéma vérité* movements (see Chapter 13), which was appropriate, given his own reverence for the French masters of the 1930s. His later docudramas for RAI and ORTF helped to break down the barriers between cinema and television—he was, in fact, the first major film director to take the new medium seriously. Furthermore, as Andrew Sarris has remarked, Rossellini's biographical films are the most impressive in the history of the cinema. But despite the director's claim of neutrality, his vision of history was highly deterministic because he always believed in a given human nature that did not change according to historical era. For this reason, his historical films are still the subject of intense critical and ideological controversy. The definitive study of Rossellini's work—a staggering eighty-four hours of screen time in a forty-year career—is Peter Brunette's exhaustively researched *Roberto Rossellini*.

11.4 Three episodes from Rossellini's *Paisà* (1946): Sicily, Naples, the Po Valley.

The second major director of the Italian neorealist movement, and one who worked within it until its demise in the 1950s, was Vittorio De Sica (1901–1974). A matinee idol during the "white telephone" era of the 1930s, De Sica began his directing career near the end of that decade with a number of conventional middle-class comedies, at least one of which (*I bambini ci guardano*, 1942) anticipates the neorealist concern with social problems. This film began De Sica's collaboration and lifelong friendship with the scriptwriter and theoretician of neorealism Cesare Zavattini. Though De Sica's sensibility was essentially comic, he apparently fell under the influence of Zavattini's ideas sometime during the war, for in 1946 the two men began a series of films concentrating on the urban problems of postwar Italy.

Sciuscià (*Shoeshine*, 1946), shot in three months under primitive conditions, is a bleak tale of the corruption of innocence in Nazi-occupied Rome. Two young shoeshine boys who are best friends become involved in a black-market deal in an effort to buy a horse. They are caught and sent to prison, where one inadvertently betrays the other and is later killed by him in revenge. Like *Roma, città aperta*, *Sciuscià* was not well received in Italy but proved highly successful in the United States, where it won a special Academy Award in 1947.[2] De Sica's next film with Zavattini, *Ladri di biciclette* (*Bicycle Thieves/The Bicycle Thief*, 1948), received even greater international acclaim and is thought by some critics to be the most important film of the postwar era. In it, a family man who has been out of work for almost two years (unemployment in postwar Italy had reached 22 percent by 1948) finds a job as a municipal bill poster, for which he must provide his own transportation. He pawns the family's sheets in order to buy a bicycle, which is stolen his first day out. For the rest of the film he and his little boy search in vain for the thief; near the conclusion the man is driven to steal a bicycle himself but is caught in the act. Shot on location in Rome with nonactors in the leading roles (the protagonist was played by a factory worker brilliantly coached by De

2. The award was for "an Italian production of superlative quality made under adverse circumstances," which the next year the Academy Board of Governors turned into an award for Best Foreign Language Film, a category that still exists.

11.5 De Sica's *Ladri di biciclette* (1948): Antonio (Lamberto Maggiorani) with his son (Enzo Staiola).

11.6 *La terra trema* (Luchino Visconti, 1948).

Sica), *Ladri di biciclette* was an international success, winning among other honors the 1949 Academy Award for Best Foreign Language Film, and its rambling narrative form was widely imitated by other directors. As was recognized at the time, the film actually has meaning on several different planes: it is a powerful social document firmly committed to the reality it portrays, a poignant story of the relationship between a father and his son, and a modern parable of alienated man in a hostile and dehumanized environment. De Sica and Zavattini were to collaborate on two more neorealist endeavors, mixing social protest with fantasy in *Miracolo a Milano* (*Miracle in Milan*, 1951) in the manner of Clair's *Le Million* and *À Nous la liberté* (both 1931), and giving neorealism its final masterpiece in *Umberto D.* (1952). But before we examine the decline of the movement, it is necessary to mention a film that will probably prove to be the single most enduring legacy of neorealism to world cinema, though its own neorealist traits are of a paradoxical nature: Luchino Visconti's *La terra trema* (*The Earth Trembles*, 1948).

La terra trema was the first part (*L'episodio del mare* [*The Sea Episode*]) of a never-completed trilogy Visconti had planned on the economic problems of fishing, mining, and agriculture in postwar Sicily. It was the first film he had directed since the Fascist assault on *Ossessione* (in the interim, he had worked for the Resistance and directed theater in Rome), and it was shot entirely on location in the Sicilian fishing village of Aci Trezza without a script and with a cast of nonprofessionals recruited from the local populace. Initially financed by the Italian Communist party but modestly subsidized later by a commercial company, *La terra trema* was adapted by Visonti from a novel by the nineteenth-century realist Giovanni Verga (*I malavoglia* [*The House by the Medlar Tree*, 1881]) that relates the story of the downfall of a proud family of peasant fishermen through economic exploitation by wholesalers and market men. By transferring the tale from 1881 to 1947 and giving it a Marxist interpretation, and by shooting the film on location with nonactors, Visconti was clearly working within the neorealist conventions he had helped to establish in *Ossessione*.

But despite its neorealist attributes, *La terra trema* is not a purely neorealist film because Visconti was a paradoxical artist whose work always hovers somewhere between realism and aestheticism—some would say between realism and decadence. For one thing, though much of the Sicilian dialogue was improvised on the spot, every other aspect of the film was elaborately planned in advance and carefully controlled in the production process itself. *La terra trema*'s formal structure is masterful, and most of its shots are so sumptuously composed and photographed by the veteran cinematographer G. R. Aldo (Aldo Graziati, 1902–1953) that Orson Welles (perhaps in a fit of professional jealousy) once remarked that Visconti was the only director in the history of the cinema to photograph starving peasants like fashion models in *Vogue*. But realism in cinema (and in any art form) is a style, not an ideology, and it is an error to equate it with ugliness or desolation. Rather, in his sweeping, stately camera movements, his rhythmic editing, and above all the beautiful and elaborate composition of his shots, Visconti achieves for his peasant tragedy a visual grandeur that is not at all at odds with its social polemic, but that lends it an almost mythic resonance. One critic has called the style of *La terra trema* "a kind of operatic **cinéma vérité**," and the tension between visual lushness and social realism that this term suggests characterizes all of Visconti's work from *Ossessione* (1943) to the posthumously released *L'innocente* (*The Innocent*, 1979). It has frequently been remarked that this tension was the product of ambiguities within the artist himself—an aristocrat by birth, a Marxist by philosophy, and a director of grand opera and theater several months out of each year by choice. Nonetheless, it is important to recognize that in the course of his career Visconti proved himself to be one of the world's greatest film directors, and that *La terra trema* is one of his most significant works.

Like *Ossessione*, *La terra trema* unfortunately had little immediate impact upon contemporary cinema. Running over two and a half hours and spoken in a dialect all but incomprehensible to mainland Italians, the film was a commercial disaster on the domestic market and suffered the same fate as its predecessor under Fascism: it was drastically cut and dubbed into Italian for rerelease. *La terra trema* was exported only to France, where a voice-over narration completely destroyed its ideological content but where the film critic and theorist André Bazin saw it and communicated its importance to the generation of young film enthusiasts from whose ranks would soon be drawn the directors of the French New Wave. Visconti himself temporarily abandoned the cinema once more for the theater, returning in 1951 to direct Anna Magnani in *Bellissima*, a melodrama with few roots in neorealism, and to begin thereby a new phase of his career.[3]

If the relationship of *La terra trema* to neorealism is problematic, it is because Visconti as an artist was never comfortable working within the confines of a single perspective or cinematic mode, and informed all of his work with a uniquely personal vision, whether he was adapting American pulp fiction, Giovanni Verga, or Thomas Mann. But other Italian directors of the postwar period identified more closely with the new movement, and the years 1946 to 1949 witnessed a number of neorealist films by relatively minor figures who nevertheless deserve mention. Inspired by the successes of Rossellini and De Sica, the Italian partisan organization (ANPI) produced two films between 1946 and 1947, both collectively written,[4]

3. Visconti continued to produce eccentric, operatic masterpieces after his neorealist phase. The most significant of these are elaborate historical dramas—*Senso* (1954), set among the Venetian aristocracy during the Risorgimento; *La caduta degli dei* (*Götterdämmerung*; English title: *The Damned*, 1969), a lurid, epic parable of the Nazis' corruption of the German bourgeoisie; *Ludwig* (1973), a fantastic biography of Ludwig II (1845–1886), the mad king of Bavaria, which was released, badly cut from 257 to 189 minutes, then restored to its original length at Venice in 1980; and literary adaptations—*Le notti bianche* (*White Nights*, 1957; from the novella by Dostoevsky); *Il gattopardo* (*The Leopard*, 1962; from the novel by Giuseppe Tomasi di Lampedusa; released dubbed and horribly cut from 205 to 160 minutes, then restored to its original length in 1983); *Lo straniero* (*The Stranger*, 1969; from the novel by Albert Camus); and *Morte a Venezia* (*Death in Venice*, 1971; from the novella by Thomas Mann). *Rocco e i suoi fratelli* (*Rocco and His Brothers*, 1960) was conceived by Visconti as a sequel to *La terra trema*; it is a loosely structured epic about the migration of a peasant family from southern Italy to the industrial north. *Vaghe stelle dell'Orsa . . .* (*Beautiful Stars of the Ursa . . .* [English title: *Sandra*, 1965]) is a Sartrean drama, loosely based on the Electra myth, of a contemporary Italian family's decline. Most of these films were shot in color by Giuseppe Rotunno (b. 1923), Visconti's close collaborator and one of the world's great cinematographers, or, after 1969, by Pasqualino De Santis. Other important Visconti collaborators were the editors Mario Serandrei and Ruggero Mastroianni, the scriptwriters Enrico Medioli and Suso Cecchi D'Amico, and the composer Nino Rota (1911–1979). In the last twenty years of his career, Visconti became increasingly famous for his expressive use of color and decor. His final films—*Gruppo di famiglia in un interno* (*Conversation Piece*, 1975; from the novel by Mario Praz) and *L'innocente* (1979; from the novel by Gabriele D'Annunzio) were released posthumously. See Donald Lyons, "Visconti's Magnificent Obsession," *Film Comment* 15, 2 (March–April 1979): 9–13, and James McCourt, "*The Innocent*: Visconti's Last Fresco," 15, 2 (March–April 1979): 14–16. See also Monica Stirling's critical biography *A Screen of Time: A Study of Luchino Visconti* (New York: Harcourt Brace Jovanovich, 1979); Gaia Servadio's *Luchino Visconti: A Biography* (New York: Watts, 1983); Luciano de Giusti's *I Film di Luchino Visconti* (Rome: Gremese, 1985); and Elaine Mancini's *Luchino Visconti: A Guide to References and Resources* (Boston: G. K. Hall, 1986).

4. Although Giuseppe De Santis, Michelangelo Antonioni, Umberto Barbaro, Cesare Zavattini, and others contributed, the principal author of both film scripts was the Marxist intellectual Carlo Lizzani (b. 1922).

which examined the war and its aftermath from the point of view of the partisan Left. Aldo Vergano's *Il sole sorge ancora* (*The Sun Rises Again*, 1946) tells of the formation of the Resistance in Lombardy through the adventures of a young Italian soldier who has deserted in order to join it; Giuseppe De Santis's *Caccia tragica* (*The Tragic Hunt/Pursuit*, 1947) shows the continuation of the partisan spirit after the liberation, as the members of a collective farm pursue and capture a gang of thieves that has robbed them. Alberto Lattuada (b. 1914), a practitioner of calligraphism in the early 1940s, made three films between 1946 and 1949 that, while unmistakably commercial, are essentially neorealist in method and theme. His *Il bandito* (*The Bandit*, 1946) is the story of a former Italian prisoner of war who cannot find a place for himself in the corrupt society of postwar Turin and turns in desperation to a life of crime. In *Senza pietà* (*Without Pity*, 1948), written by Federico Fellini and Tullio Pinelli, with Luigi Comencini (b. 1916),[5] two lovers, both displaced persons, are corrupted by their involvement in black-market activities in Livorno. Lattuada's final film with neorealist affinities was *Il mulino del Po* (*The Mill on the Po*, 1948), also written by Fellini and Pinelli, which uses the events of a farm-workers' strike in the Po Valley in 1876 to depict the plight of contemporary agricultural workers.

At the other end of the country, Pietro Germi (1914–1974) traveled to Sicily to direct the neorealist *In nome della legge* (*In the Name of the Law*, 1948), which explores the pervasive influence of the Mafia upon contemporary Sicilian life, and *Il cammino della speranza* (*The Road to Hope*, 1950), which dramatizes the hardships of postwar emigrants from the poverty-stricken island as they struggled across the length of Italy on their way to France. In the same period, the former critic Giuseppe De Santis directed two noteworthy neorealist films on agrarian themes. His *Riso amaro* (*Bitter Rice*, 1948) initially concerns the economic exploitation of itinerant female rice workers in the Po Valley but degenerates rapidly into the sensational melodrama and eroticism that brought international fame to its two leading performers, Silvana Mangano and Vittorio Gassman, and that some believe marked the beginning of neorealism's ultimate decline into commercialism.[6] De Santis's *Non c'e pace tra gli ulivi* (*No Peace among the Olives*, 1949) is less ideologically equivocal in its tale of a young soldier who returns from the war to find both his girlfriend and his farm stolen by a powerful provincial bourgeois and who must take the

11.7 Giuseppe De Santis's *Riso amaro* (1948): Silvana Mangano (third from left).

law into his own hands to regain them. Finally, a list of minor neorealist works should not omit the comedies of Luigi Zampa (1905–1991—*Vivere in pace* [*Living in Peace*, 1947]), Renato Castellani (1913–1985—*Sotto il sole di Roma* [*Under the Roman Sun*, 1947]), and Luciano Emmer (b. 1918—*Domenica d'agosto* [*Sunday in August*, 1949]), all of which borrowed the production techniques of the movement without adopting its themes. Like *Riso amaro*, these works in their lack of serious social commitment foreshadowed the collapse of neorealism into the slick sensationalism of the 1950s. But before that collapse occurred, neorealism produced its last masterpiece through the next collaboration of Vittorio De Sica and Cesare Zavattini in *Umberto D.* (1952).

Umberto D. probably comes as close to realizing Zavattini's ideal of a pure cinema of everyday life as any film the neorealist movement produced. It has no plot but is structured around a series of loosely connected incidents

---

5. Comencini is now a highly respected director within the Italian commercial cinema (e.g., *L'ingorgo* [*Bottleneck*, 1979]; *Cuore* [*Heart*, 1985]; *La storia* [*History*, 1986]; *Un ragazzo di Calabria* [*A Boy from Calabria*, 1987]; *La Bohème* [1988]; etc.).

6. *Riso amaro*, described by one Italian critic as a "neorealist colossal," employed a huge cast and crew and took seventy-five days to shoot on location and another two months to edit. A potent brew of sex, violence, and anti-Americanism—and the only neorealist film to succeed commercially in the domestic market—it was meticulously choreographed by De Santis, who used elaborate dolly and crane mechanisms to move his cameras flamboyantly over the rice fields.

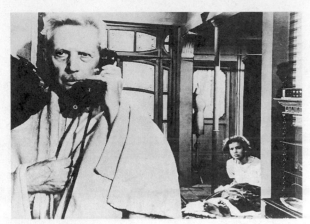

11.8 *Umberto D.* (Vittorio De Sica, 1952): Carlo Battisti.

in the title character's life. Although most of these incidents are generated by a single circumstance (Umberto D. is poor and can't pay his rent), the film begins and ends *in medias res* because it is about a condition rather than about a series of events. Filmed on location in Rome with an entirely nonprofessional cast, *Umberto D.* offers a portrait of an old-age pensioner attempting to eke out a meager existence for himself and his dog in a furnished room, while retaining a modicum of personal dignity. The fragile equilibrium Umberto has managed to maintain between mere want and degrading poverty is destroyed when his callous landlady, in an effort to drive him out, demands that he pay his back rent in a lump sum. Umberto sells what few possessions he has, attempts to borrow money from ex-colleagues (he is apparently a retired civil servant), and even tries to beg, but finds it impossible to raise the amount he needs. Finally, after the landlady has publicly humiliated him by letting his room to prostitutes and has all but thrown him out into the street, Umberto resolves to commit suicide. He ultimately fails, however, because he can't bring himself to abandon his dog. The conclusion leaves the two alive together, but with no place to go and no prospects for the future.

Obviously, a film about a downtrodden old man and his dog is prone to be sentimental by its very nature, and *Umberto D.* does not avoid this pitfall (no neorealist film about victimized people ever did). But most of the emotion the film contains is honest enough because De Sica and Zavattini do not attempt to make their protagonist

seem better or nobler than he is. Umberto can be thoroughly disagreeable, and he is in most respects an average person. Roy Armes suggests that as a character he is Chaplinesque (and De Sica admired Chaplin extravagantly)— a little man adrift in an alien environment that continually threatens him. It is true, of course, that *Umberto D.* is a closely observed social document that comments on the hypocrisy, cruelty, and indifference of bourgeois society toward its own aged members, but as in the earlier De Sica–Zavattini collaborations, an examination of emotional relationships lies at the center of the film. In *Sciuscià* the crucial relationship was that between the two young shoeshine boys; in *Ladri di biciclette*, between the father and son. In *Umberto D.*, however, the only significant relationship is that of the protagonist and his dog, as if to imply that relationships between human beings have become increasingly difficult or even impossible in our emotionally attenuated modern society. Others have found *Umberto D.* less pessimistic than this comment suggests, but it seems clear that its commercial failure was a direct result of the grim view it took of contemporary life.[7] In the year of its release, in fact, some Italian politicians, notably Giulio Andreotti (see below), attempted to prohibit the film's exportation on the grounds that it presented a falsely gloomy picture of Italian society.

---

7. As if to validate his own pessimistic premise, De Sica's career declined after this film, although he continued to work closely with Zavattini until almost the end. With *Stazione Termini* (*Station Terminus*, 1953), produced for David O. Selznick and released cut and re-edited in the United States as *Indiscretion of an American Wife* (1954), De Sica entered a long period of commercial compromise dominated by romantic melodrama (*L'oro di Napoli* [*The Gold of Naples*, 1954]; *Amanti* [*A Place for Lovers*, 1968]) and slick sex comedies (*Ieri, oggi, domani* [*Yesterday, Today, and Tomorrow*, 1963]; *Matrimonio all'Italiana* [*Marriage Italian Style*, 1964]; *Caccia alla volpe* [*After the Fox*, 1966]; *Sette volte donna* [*Woman Times Seven*, 1967]), with an occasional recurrence to neorealist modes and themes (*Il tetto* [*The Roof*, 1956]—regarded by many critics as "the last neorealist film"; *La ciociara* [*Two Women*, 1960], adapted from the novel by Alberto Moravia; *Un mondo nuovo* [*A New World*, 1966], an essay in *nouvelle vague* styles and social concerns shot on location in Paris). The beautiful and poignant *Il giardino dei Finzi-Contini* (*The Garden of the Finzi-Continis*, 1971) helped to reestablish his critical reputation and reaffirm his essentially tragic vision of human experience, as did the posthumously released *Una breva vacanza* (*A Brief Vacation*, 1974), his last collaboration with Zavattini, and *Il viaggio* (*The Voyage*), adapted from the Luigi Pirandello novel, but De Sica was clearly an artist in eclipse before his death in 1974.

THE DECLINE OF NEOREALISM

Neorealism in Zavattini's ideal sense ("the ideal film would be ninety minutes of the life of a man to whom nothing happens") probably never existed. In practice, it was a cinema of poverty and pessimism firmly rooted in the immediate postwar period. When times changed and economic conditions began to improve, neorealism lost first its ideological basis, then its subject matter. As Penelope Houston puts it, neorealism was a revolutionary cinema in a nonrevolutionary society, and certainly the movement could never have outlasted the prosperity and affluence of the 1950s. But even if Italy had remained unchanged from *Roma, città aperta* to *Umberto D.*, the neorealist cinema would have failed for other reasons. In the first place, for all of its collectivist aspirations, neorealism had never been a popular cinema in Italy and was dependent for its survival upon foreign markets—especially the United States. The Italian film industry experienced a major crisis in 1949 due to the wholesale importation of American films (the sociologist George Huaco has found that only 10 percent of the feature films exhibited in Italy in December of that year were Italian, while 71 percent were American). The government then passed the protective Andreotti Law, named for Giulio Andreotti,[8] the undersecretary of public entertainment. *La legge Andreotti* taxed imported films and required theaters to show Italian films for eighty days of the year, thus tripling domestic distribution. It also established the Direzione Generale del Spettacolo, which was empowered to grant government-subsidized production loans to scripts submitted for prior approval that were found "suitable" and to ban from both domestic screening and exportation films deemed inimical to the "best interests of Italy." The Andreotti Law, then, placed the Italian film industry under state control, and when the government became openly hostile to neorealism in the early 1950s, backing for projects dried up altogether. Since Italy joined the North Atlantic Treaty Organization (NATO) in March 1949, some have speculated that the Andreotti Law was enacted with the implicit purpose of slowly strangling neorealism, whose ideological orientation was Marxist. This is quite possible, given the general stupidity of governments in their relations with the arts, but it also seems clear that neorealism had burned itself out internally before the Andreotti Law had any significant effect on production.

In their desire to achieve "the illusion of the present tense" which James Agee had noted in Rossellini's *Paisà*, the neorealist directors frequently ignored the narrative elements of their films or treated them as irrelevant, causing the plots to degenerate into stereotypes. The same concentration on methodology also resulted in the lapses into sentimentality that led the British critic Raymond Durgnat to label neorealist films the "male weepies," as opposed to the "female weepies" of Hollywood melodramatists like Vincent Sherman, Irving Rapper, and Daniel Mann. To all of this it might first be replied that the neorealists were interested not so much in constructing narratives as in reconstructing the atmosphere and ambiance of a contemporary reality, something they achieved admirably. And, as André Bazin suggests in his essay on neorealism called "An Aesthetic of Reality," it is not at all unrespectable or even unusual for an innovative movement in cinema to dissipate its creative energies in a brief span of time. Innovation in an art form whose medium is photographic reproduction and whose influence literally travels with the speed of light is bound to be short-lived (as innovation, that is) and to produce its own reaction rapidly. But the real vindication of the neorealist movement has been its influence on the international cinema, which has been enormous.

THE IMPACT OF NEOREALISM

Neorealism completely revitalized Italian film so that today it has become one of the major creative forces in world cinema. Not only did neorealism itself produce masterpieces and become the temporary medium for great directors like Rossellini and Visconti, but it provided training for two men currently thought to be among the international cinema's greatest artists—Federico Fellini (1920–1993), who worked extensively as a scriptwriter on neorealist films (*Roma, città aperta*; *Paisà*; *Senza pietà*; etc.), and Michelangelo Antonioni (b. 1912), who was writing criticism for *Cinema* and directing documentaries during the same period (e.g., *Gente del Po* [People of the Po, 1943; 1947], etc.). In their films of the 1950s, especially Fellini's *I vitelloni* (1953) and Antonioni's *Le amiche*

---

8. This is the same Giulio Andreotti (b. 1919) who later became prime minister and in 2002 was given a twenty-four-year sentence for complicity in the 1979 Mafia killing of a journalist who supposedly had damaging information about him during his term in office.

(1955), both directors may be said to have continued the neorealist mode by turning it inward so that the object of attention becomes not society, but the human self. This element of what might be called introspective neorealism largely disappeared from their work in the 1960s, but it is not farfetched to see in their mature images of modern alienation and disorder vestiges of the bombed-out, fragmented neorealist landscapes of the late 1940s. Indeed, Penelope Houston suggests that the strength of the Italian cinema lies precisely in its *inability* to escape the neorealist heritage, so that even the generation of filmmakers that succeeded that of Fellini and Antonioni felt compelled to confront and come to terms with the neorealist tradition (see Chapter 15).

Neorealism was the first postwar cinema to liberate filmmaking from the artificial confines of the studio and, by extension, from the Hollywood-originated studio system. On-location shooting, the use of nonprofessional actors, and improvisation of script, which have all become a part (though not always a large part) of conventional filmmaking today, were techniques almost unknown to the narrative sound film before neorealism. The movement's influence on the French New Wave directors in this regard is a matter of record, but its impact on the American cinema has been generally ignored: in the postwar work of American directors as diverse as Nicholas Ray (*They Live by Night*, 1948), Elia Kazan (*Boomerang!*, 1947), Jules Dassin (*The Naked City*, 1948), Joseph Losey (*The Lawless*, 1950), Robert Rossen (*Body and Soul*, 1947), and Edward Dmytryk (*Crossfire*, 1947), substantial elements of neorealism can be found, including a political commitment to the left.[9] Finally, several scholars have pointed out the profound influence of neorealism on filmmakers in countries that lacked strong national cinemas of their own. Michael Cacoyannis (b. 1922—*Zorba the Greek*, 1964) in Greece; Luis García Berlanga (b. 1921—*Las pirañas*, 1967) and Juan Antonio Bardem (b. 1922—*Muerte de un ciclista*, 1955) in Spain; and Satyajit Ray (1921–1992—the Apu trilogy: *Pather panchali*, 1955; *Aparajito*, 1956; *Apu sansar*, 1958) in India have all testified to the enormous influence of neorealism upon their work (see Chapters 15, 16, and 18). Indeed, Ray has claimed that a single viewing of De Sica's *Ladri di biciclette* in London in 1950 led him to film his trilogy according to neorealist methods. It is clear that neorealism was a great deal more than a localized national phenomenon; its formative influence extended well beyond the Italian

cinema. There can be no question today that, whatever its limitations of vision and form, Italian neorealism was one of the great innovative movements in the history of the cinema, whose importance and impact are comparable in degree to that of Soviet silent realism or the French New Wave, between which it most appropriately mediates.

The United States

HOLLYWOOD AT WAR

Like Italian cinema, American film had been moving toward a heightened kind of realism in the early 1940s when the war interrupted and Hollywood was pressed into the service of the federal government. On December 18, 1941, immediately following the attack on Pearl Harbor and America's declaration of war upon Japan, President Franklin D. Roosevelt established a Bureau of Motion Picture Affairs (BMPA) within the Office of War Information (OWI) to mobilize the studios for the national defense effort. Hollywood responded by creating the War Activities Committee, comprising studio executives, distributors, exhibitors, actors, and labor-union officials, to coordinate American filmmaking activity with the propaganda and morale-boosting programs of the government.[1] The government suggested six thematic categories for

---

9. It is no coincidence that all of these American directors except Ray were targeted in the anticommunist witch-hunt of the late 1940s and 1950s (described in the second part of this chapter). Other American filmmakers influenced by neorealism include the director Henry Hathaway (*13 Rue Madeleine*, 1946; *Kiss of Death*, 1947; *Call Northside 777*, 1948), the producer-director Stanley Kramer (b. 1913—*Home of the Brave* [Mark Robson, 1949]; *The Men* [Fred Zinnemann, 1950]), and screenwriter Paddy Chayefsky (1923–1981—*Marty* [1955]; *The Bachelor Party* [1957]; *Middle of the Night* [1959]—all directed by Delbert Mann); see Chapter 12.

1. Hollywood's cooperation with the war effort was encouraged considerably by the Selective Service System's 1942 ruling that the movies were an "essential industry" whose equipment and materials were subject to price controls and whose personnel could not be drafted. In addition, the Justice Department temporarily backed off of its antitrust suit against the studios and did not resume the case until August 1944, with the war in Europe very nearly won. A final reason that Hollywood was only too glad to cooperate with the government was that it lost 33 percent to 50 percent of its traditional revenues as markets in Europe and the Far East closed one by one due to the war. Through the Office of the Coordinator of Inter-American Affairs, however, the State Department proposed to help the industry exploit the South and Central American markets to offset losses (see p. 346).

Hollywood films that would be consonant with its war-aims information campaign but that would not preclude conventional entertainment values. As listed by Lewis Jacobs, these were: (1) The Issues of the War: what we are fighting for, the American way of life; (2) The Nature of the Enemy: his ideology, his objectives, his methods; (3) The "United Nations": i.e., our allies in arms; (4) The Production Front: supplying the materials for victory; (5) The Home Front: civilian responsibility; and (6) The Fighting Forces: our armed services, our allies, and our associates. Hollywood complied at first by producing a raft of fatuous, superpatriotic melodramas of the battlefield and home front that glorified a kind of warfare that had never existed in the history of the human race, much less in the current upheaval. With titles like *Salute to Courage, Dangerously They Live, Captain of the Clouds, To the Shores of Tripoli, United We Stand, The Devil with Hitler,* and *Blondie for Victory,* these unsophisticated films disappeared rapidly from the American screen when Hollywood and the general public were confronted with an infinitely more authentic version of the war, contained in newsreels from the battlefronts and government-produced information films.

From 1941 to 1945, the War Department, the Army Pictorial Services, the Army Educational Program, the American Armed Forces (AAF) First Motion Picture Unit, the Signal Corps of the combined services, the U.S. Navy, the U.S. Marine Corps, and the Overseas Branch of the OWI were involved in the production of documentary films designed to explain and justify the war to the servicemen fighting it and the civilian populace actively supporting it. Major Hollywood directors like Frank Capra, John Huston, John Ford, George Stevens, and William Wyler had been recruited into the armed forces, together with professional documentarists like Willard Van Dyke (1906–1986) and Irving Lerner (1909–1976), to operate these programs, and the films they produced collectively are among the most outstanding documentaries in the history of the form. The seven films of the *"Why We Fight"* series produced by Frank Capra, for example—*Prelude to War* (Frank Capra, 1942), *The Nazis Strike* (Capra and Anatole Litvak, 1942), *Divide and Conquer* (Capra and Litvak, 1943), *The Battle of Britain* (Capra and Litvak, 1943), *The Battle of Russia* (Litvak, 1943), *The Battle of China* (Capra and Litvak, 1943), *War Comes to America* (Litvak, 1944)—were documentaries edited from stock footage that persuasively and unromantically explained the

11.9 *The Nazis Strike* **(Frank Capra and Anatole Litvak, 1942) and** *Divide and Conquer* **(Capra and Litvak, 1943).**

necessity of America's involvement in the war. Other information films, like Wyler's *Memphis Belle* (1944) and *Thunderbolt* (1945), Ford's *The Battle of Midway* (1942) and *December 7th* (1943; co-directed and photographed by Gregg Toland), and Huston's *Report from the Aleutians* (1943) and *The Battle of San Pietro* (1944),[2] were shot on

2. The third film in Huston's war trilogy, *Let There Be Light* (1946), was shelved by the U.S. War Department as "unsuitable" for public viewing. Finally released in 1980, the 58-minute documentary is in fact an intensely moving account of the recuperation of shell-shocked soldiers in an army psychiatric hospital. It was apparently suppressed to maintain the heroic "warrior" mythology of the nation's World War II experience. See Scott Hammen, "At War with the Army," *Film Comment* 16, 2 (March–April 1980): 19–23.

11.10 *The Battle of San Pietro* (John Huston, 1944).

11.11 *The Hitler Gang* (John Farrow, 1944): Robert Watson as the Führer.

location in every theater of operations in the war and constitute masterly pieces of reporting. The characteristic feature of these films was their sobriety. War was shown to be a brutal, unglamorous, and murderous business that was pursued out of utter necessity and that had nothing to do with the Yankee Doodle Dandy heroics of Hollywood. Vast numbers of Americans saw these documentaries at home and overseas, and there can be little doubt that they did much to upgrade the realism and honesty with which Hollywood approached the war.

The years 1943 and 1944 witnessed many films whose presentation of the war and attendant themes was much more convincing than that of their predecessors. Whereas earlier films had caricatured Fascists as either cowardly buffoons or stock villains, other films of the period—e.g., Frank Capra's *Meet John Doe* (1943), Fritz Lang's *Ministry of Fear* (1944), and Alfred Hitchcock's semiallegorical *Lifeboat* (1944)—portrayed the dangers of Fascism abroad and on the home front with a sophisticated understanding of the ruthlessness, intelligence, and actual power of the enemy.[3] Another group of films provided a more realistic treatment than heretofore of "our allies in arms," attempting with varying degrees of success to show what life was like inside the occupied countries and to promote a bond of sympathy with them. Frank Tuttle's *Hostages* (1943), Irving Pichel's *The Moon Is Down* (1943), Jean Renoir's *This Land Is Mine* (1943), Fritz Lang's *Hangmen Also Die* (1943), Lewis Milestone's *Edge of Darkness* (1943), and Tay Garnett's *The Cross of Lorraine* (1943) offered fairly convincing representations

of oppression and resistance in Nazi-occupied Europe (specifically in Norway, Czechoslovakia, Hungary, and France). Other films, like Lewis Milestone's *The North Star* (1943), Gregory Ratoff's *Song of Russia* (1943), Jacques Tourneur's *Days of Glory* (1944), and Michael Curtiz's *Mission to Moscow* (1943), attempted to promote goodwill between America and its incongruous new ally, the Soviet Union—in the case of *Mission to Moscow,* by trying to rationalize Stalin's purge trials of the 1930s. (It is one of the most bitter ironies of recent American history that many of the people who worked on these *government-authorized* propaganda films were subjected to vicious accusations of disloyalty and treason during the late 1940s and early 1950s; see pp. 380–84.)

Perhaps the most telling index of the documentary influence on American cinema during the war years was the increasing number of serious-minded and realistic combat films that portrayed the war very much as it must have seemed to the men who were fighting it. Indeed, one of the reasons that Hollywood outgrew its post-Pearl Harbor romanticism so quickly was a massive GI reaction against the patent phoniness of the early war films, but by 1944 the true horror and anguish of warfare devoid of flag-waving jingoism was being brought home to Americans in films like Tay Garnett's *Bataan* (1943) and Lewis Seiler's

---

3. A handful of intelligent anti-Fascist films were made between 1940 and Pearl Harbor: for instance, Alfred Hitchcock's *Foreign Correspondent* (1940), Frank Borzage's *The Mortal Storm* (1940), and John Cromwell's *So Ends Our Night* (1941).

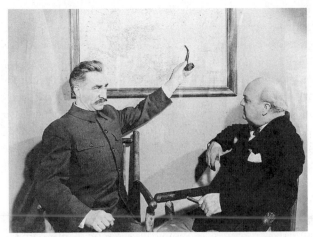

11.12 Stalin (Manart Kippen) and Churchill (Dudley Field Malone) in the film version of Ambassador Joseph E. Davies's memoir, *Mission to Moscow* (Michael Curtiz, 1943).

11.13 The realities of war: Lewis Milestone's *A Walk in the Sun* (1945): Dana Andrews.

Guadalcanal Diary (1944). Lewis Jacobs notes another significant category of late combat films, such as Lloyd Bacon's *Action in the North Atlantic* (1943), Delmer Daves's *Destination Tokyo* (1943), Zoltan Korda's *Sahara* (1943), Lewis Milestone's *A Walk in the Sun* (1945), Raoul Walsh's *Objective, Burma!* (1945), John Ford's *They Were Expendable* (1945), and William Wellman's *The Story of GI Joe* (1945), in which the battle action becomes a vehicle for a more personal kind of cinema—one concerned with "the deep emotional crisis and individual agony of the average Joe, anxiously examining his own conscience." In their focus on the individual American in conflict with himself, these productions anticipate the searching, introspective, and ultimately disillusioned films of the immediate postwar period, in which the democratic ideals for which so many Americans fought and died are brought into serious question.[4]

In 1945, however, with the end of the war clearly in sight, Hollywood was more concerned with empirical victory than metaphysical defeat and had already begun its search for buoyant postwar subject matter. War themes were jettisoned for lighter material that would coincide with the momentary mood of public euphoria, and for a brief season on the American screen, following the Japanese surrender on August 14, 1945, it was as if the war had never taken place at all.[5] But the war had not been unkind to Hollywood, even though it had lost its foreign markets and had devoted nearly one-third of its production between 1941 and 1945 to the war effort (according

to Lewis Jacobs, more than 500 of the 1,700 films made during this period were directly concerned with Fascism and war). Hollywood had even complied with the government's discomfiting request to reduce the length of A-films on double bills to economize on theater lighting—a measure that caused at least one catastrophe for the international cinema when RKO cut Orson Welles's second masterpiece, *The Magnificent Ambersons* (1942), by forty-five minutes and made it the first half of a double bill with the comedy *Mexican Spitfire Sees a Ghost* (see Chapter 10). Nevertheless, Hollywood enjoyed the most profitable four-year period in its history during the war, with weekly attendance estimated at 90 million persons (nearly five times the current figure), despite the restric-

4. Two other categories of American wartime cinema were films of women coping on the home front, such as *Tender Comrade* (Edward Dmytryk, 1943) and *Since You Went Away* (John Cromwell, 1944), and morale-boosting "service musicals," which featured radio and film celebrities and "bevies of beautiful girls" in service settings, epitomized by *Hollywood Canteen* (Delmer Daves, 1944).

5. Box-office figures tell the tale. In fiscal year 1941–42, six of the twenty-one top-grossing films had had some connection with the war. In 1942–43, 1943–44, 1944–45, 1945–46, and 1946–47, the ratio rose and fell as follows: thirteen of twenty-four, twelve of twenty-five, six of thirty-four, two of thirty-six, and one (*The Best Years of Our Lives*) of twenty-six. So strong, in fact, was the national revulsion against the war and all things military that the AAF film unit suppressed many of its own late productions, of which *Let There Be Light* (see footnote p. 369) is the classic case.

tions imposed upon it by the government and its own errors of judgment about what the public wanted to see. For one thing, all of its combat films were (and, with few exceptions, still are) produced with the "technical assistance" of the armed forces, which can be worth up to 50 percent of a motion picture's budget in free production values.[6] For another, the government had cleverly levied a special war tax on theater tickets in 1942, so that going to the movies during the war years took on the character of a patriotic act. Full employment and unprecedented prosperity after a decade of economic depression also helped to keep attendance high. (In most industrial centers the theaters stayed open twenty-four hours a day to accommodate shift workers.) But most important of all in determining Hollywood's high wartime profits was the perennial therapeutic function that films assume in periods of social stress. It is almost literally true that, since the inception of the medium, the worst of times for human history have been the best of times for the cinema, even bad cinema, because there is no fantasy realm within our waking experience that renders its make-believe so inescapably and ineluctably real.

THE POSTWAR BOOM

For all of these reasons, Hollywood came through the war years with its powerful studio production system and time-tested film genres pretty much intact, making the American the only major national cinema in the West to preserve a direct continuity of tradition with its past after 1945. In Europe—even in Italy—national cinemas had to be entirely rebuilt, which in most cases involved a beneficial process of rejuvenation and a subsequent influx of new talent and ideas. But Hollywood had experienced the war as the most stable and lucrative four years in its history with a mere change of pace, and the industry gave every indication that it intended to march into the postwar period in the same way that it had marched out of the Depression—by avoiding the depiction of any of the unpleasant realities of American life. In 1946 there was much cause for confidence. Victory had opened vast, unchallenged markets in the war-torn countries of Western Europe and Southeast Asia, and Hollywood had already resumed its economic domination of international cinema because only America was in a material position to provide high-quality films to a world hungry for diversion. Moreover, the domestic audience had reached its highest peak ever, at an estimated 100 million per week (two-thirds of the population), and the yearly box-office receipts of $1.75 billion broke all previous records.[7] Thus, by the end of 1946 it seemed that Hollywood's most lucrative path lay in maintaining the prewar status quo; but no sooner had the industry charted this course than serious obstacles began to appear.

An eight-month studio union strike in 1945 combined with spiraling postwar inflation led to a 25 percent pay increase for studio personnel in the following year.[8] Moreover, Hollywood's chief overseas market, Great Britain, from which it drew one-quarter to one-third of its net income, levied a 75 percent protective tax on all foreign

---

6. For the purpose of public relations, the American military establishment has traditionally cooperated in helping Hollywood to produce films that glorify the armed forces. The military can help production companies by providing them with free historical and technical research and, at cost, heavy equipment and armaments, large casts of uniformed extras, and authentic locations for shooting. (It is rumored, for example, that the maneuvers required of the combined services in restaging the 1944 Allied invasion of Normandy for 20th Century–Fox's *The Longest Day* [Ken Annakin and Bernhard Wicki, 1962] were more complicated than those of the actual event and were worth well over $1 million to the studio.) That this relationship, probably a necessity in wartime, can become corrupt was demonstrated by the 1972 CBS television documentary "The Selling of the Pentagon." Today, the office of the Assistant Secretary of Defense for Public Affairs receives approximately two hundred requests for production assistance a year. After reviewing a film's script for "authenticity"—which to the Pentagon means portraying the services in a favorable light—the office decides whether military help should be offered. In general, films like *The Right Stuff* (Philip Kaufman, 1983) and *Top Gun* (Tony Scott, 1986) receive it, while films like *Platoon* (Oliver Stone, 1986) and *Full Metal Jacket* (Stanley Kubrick, 1987) do not. It should be noted, though, that an equally close relationship existed between the military establishments and national cinemas of certain Communist countries, where the relationship was mediated by the state rather than by mutual self-interest. Sergei Bondarchuk's eight-hour adaptation of Tolstoi's *War and Peace* (1965–67), e.g., involved the entire Red Army in restaging the Battle of Borodino, as Eisenstein and Pudovkin had used the Soviet armed forces in their epics of the Revolution, and as World War II is frequently refought in grand scale on Soviet soil—most recently in Elem Klimov's award-winning *Come and See* (1985)—with the Red Army taking both sides.

7. The 1946 profits of the majors—$39 million at Paramount; $25 million at Fox; $22 million at Warners'; $18 million at Loew's; and $12 million at RKO—were not approached again in real dollars until the 1970s.

8. Many of those active in the strike fell victim to the witch-hunt of the late 1940s and early 1950s (see pp. 380–84).

film profits, and this reduced the American industry's annual British revenue from $68 million in 1946 to under $17 million in 1947. Other Commonwealth countries and European nations followed suit (Italy, for example, with the Andreotti Law), and even though in some cases Hollywood was able to retaliate successfully with boycotts, the damage was significant. With the end of the War Production Board's price controls in August 1946, the industry's major suppliers of raw film stock, Eastman and du Pont, raised their prices, by 18 and 13 percent, respectively, adding over $2.5 million in annual costs for the studios. Most disastrous of all from a financial standpoint, however, was the adjudication of the antitrust suit begun by the federal government against the five major and three minor studios in 1938, resulting in the "Paramount decrees" or "consent decrees" of May 1948—court orders that forced the companies to divest themselves of their lucrative exhibition circuits according to a mutually agreed-upon schedule over the next five years.[9] Most immediately, divestiture meant the end of block booking and of the automatic box–office receipts that this practice had created; ultimately, it meant the end of the powerful studio system that had been the shaping force of the American film industry for thirty years. Hollywood was faced with the task of restructuring its entire production and delivery system in the midst of the most severe financial crisis it had experienced since the coming of sound. Even worse was to follow, but at the beginning of 1948 things were bad enough: in the major studios unemployment had risen by 25 percent; the independent companies Rainbow, Liberty, and Eagle-Lion[1] had failed completely; and Warner Bros. was preparing for a temporary shutdown. As early as 1947, radical economizing had begun. Production budgets were cut by as much as 50 percent, and expensive projects like costume films, extravagant spectacles, and grade-A musicals were abandoned altogether. Only months after the American film industry's banner year of 1946, Hollywood people were starting to ask themselves how the bubble had burst, unaware that their bad luck had only just begun.

But for a while, at least, the urgent necessity to cut back on production costs had a vitalizing and invigorating effect upon the American cinema. As Charles Higham and Joel Greenberg point out, efficiency became the order of the day. The industry's perpetual obsession with lavish production values temporarily gave way to a new concern for high-quality scripts and preplanning at every stage of the shooting process to avoid expensive retakes.

For the first time in Hollywood's history, studios gave high priority to projects that could be shot on location with small casts and crews, and the content of films thus took on a greater social and psychological realism than ever before. The influence of the wartime documentary tradition and of Italian neorealism, which had earned a high reputation among American filmmakers by 1947, had a great deal to do with this sudden rejection of escapist subject matter, but much of the credit must go to the cultural impact of the war itself upon the American people.

After the elation of victory had passed, a mood of disillusionment and cynicism came over America that had at least as much to do with the nation's image of itself as with the distant horror of the war. The federal government's wartime propaganda machine, of which Hollywood was the most essential component, had created an image of an ideal America of white picket fences, cozy bungalows, and patiently loyal families and sweethearts[2]— a pure, democratic society in which Jews, blacks, Italians, Irish, Poles, and WASP farm boys could all live and work together, just as they had done in the ethnically balanced patrol squads of so many wartime combat films. This America, of course, had never existed, but a nation engaged in a global war of survival had an overwhelming need to believe that it did. When the war ended and the troops returned home, however, people began to discover that the basic goodness and decency of American society

---

9. The Supreme Court found that the majors, with the collusion of the minors, had exercised a clear monopoly over motion-picture production, distribution, and exhibition from 1934 through 1947, and in 1948 it forced the Big Five to spin off either their distribution or exhibition channels. They naturally chose to retain the distribution function, where control over product resides, enabling them to set clearance and minimum admission prices and to limit the supply of features at the exhibitors' expense.

1. Eagle-Lion's product was distributed by United Artists from 1949 to 1951, when its studio space (formerly that of the Producers Releasing Corporation) was auctioned off and its film rights acquired by United Artists. During that period, it produced the influential *films noirs* of Anthony Mann (e.g., *T-Men* and *Raw Deal*, 1948; *The Black Book*, 1949).

2. In fact, according to John Costello in *Virtue under Fire: How World War II Changed Our Social and Sexual Attitudes* (Boston: Little, Brown, 1986), by the third year of our involvement in the war, the juvenile crime rate in the United States had doubled, the divorce rate had soared, and infidelity was the order of the day. Since 1941, teenage prostitution had risen 70 percent, and major cities like New York had to set up special Wayward Minors courts to process the arrests.

11.14 Coming home: William Wyler's *The Best Years of Our Lives* (1946). Dana Andrews.

was more difficult to find than, for example, John Cromwell's slickly directed domestic fantasy *Since You Went Away* (1944) had made it appear—more difficult even than William Wyler's relatively sophisticated *The Best Years of Our Lives* (1946), which dealt with the successful attempts of three returned combat veterans to reintegrate themselves into civilian life, made it seem. Less difficult to locate in postwar America were social inequities and racial prejudices in every part of the country, profiteering in big business, and corruption in state and local government. What is more, many of our "boys"—especially those who had been maimed in defense of their country—came home to discover that they couldn't get jobs, obtain loans, or even resume their education. The film critic and director Paul Schrader has suggested that postwar disillusionment was in many ways a delayed reaction to the 1930s and to the socioeconomic imbalances that had helped to cause the Depression. Whatever the reasons, when the euphoria of victory had passed, America suddenly found itself in worse shape internally than Hollywood or any other element of American society would have dared to suggest during the war. The war was over now, however, and as a result of its self-imposed economies Hollywood had become increasingly dependent upon the talents of individual writers and directors—people whose vision of things was frequently less sanguine than what the studio system, under normal circumstances, would permit them to express. But circumstances were not normal for either the industry or the nation, and soon

manifestations of America's social malaise began to appear on screens all over the country.

Postwar Genres in the United States

"SOCIAL CONSCIOUSNESS" FILMS AND SEMIDOCUMENTARY MELODRAMAS

The Hollywood films generated by postwar disenchantment with American life were of several basic types.[3] The least complex were those that dealt melioristically with contemporary social problems and their resolution. Often called "social consciousness," or "problem," pictures, these films enjoyed a tremendous vogue in the late 1940s (in 1947, for example, nearly one-third of the films produced in Hollywood had a "problem" content of some sort) and concerned themselves with such subjects as racism, political corruption, and other inequities within our social institutions. In this category, Edward Dmytryk's *Crossfire* (1947), a tersely directed melodrama of murderous anti-Semitism in postwar America, is outstanding for both its thematic candor and its cinematic excellence. Elia Kazan's *Gentleman's Agreement* (1947) provides a much less honest treatment of the same theme, and his *Pinky* (1949), the sentimental tale of a young black woman who tries to pass for white, is even less credible. Nevertheless, 1949

---

3. Traditional genres of film did not fare at all poorly in postwar Hollywood. On the contrary, the late 1940s produced major films in every genre except comedy (assuming Chaplin's *Monsieur Verdoux*, 1947, and the films of Preston Sturges to be in a class by themselves), including conventional melodrama (Max Ophüls's *The Reckless Moment* [1949]); fantasy (Frank Capra's *It's a Wonderful Life* [1946] and William Dieterle's *Portrait of Jennie* [1949]); horror (Val Lewton's RKO cycle [1942–46, see p. 250]; Robert Florey's *The Beast with Five Fingers* [1946]); suspense (Hitchcock's *Notorious* [1946]); adventure (Vincent Sherman's *The Adventures of Don Juan* [1948] and Henry King's *Captain from Castile* [1947]); the Western (John Ford's *My Darling Clementine* [1946], King Vidor's *Duel in the Sun* [1946], Howard Hawks's *Red River* [1948], William Wellman's *Yellow Sky* [1948]); the musical (Vincente Minnelli's *The Pirate* [1948]; Gene Kelly's *On the Town* [1949]); and what were known in studio parlance as "women's pictures" (see footnote p. 379)—romantic melodramas designed to appeal to female audiences and constructed around a popular female star (Edmund Goulding's *The Razor's Edge* [1946, Gene Tierney], Curtis Bernhardt's *A Stolen Life* [1946, Bette Davis], Jean Negulesco's *Humoresque* [1946, Joan Crawford], and Max Ophüls's *Letter from an Unknown Woman* [1948, Joan Fontaine] and *Caught* [1949, Barbara Bel Geddes]).

was a good year for films on racial intolerance. Mark Robson's *Home of the Brave* (1949; produced by Stanley Kramer), sympathetically portraying the psychiatric odyssey of a black veteran, initiated what has come to be known as the "Negro cycle" of that year, which included Clarence Brown's restrained and dignified version of William Faulkner's *Intruder in the Dust*, shot on location in Oxford, Mississippi, as well as Alfred Werker's *Lost Boundaries* (produced by the documentarist Louis De Rochemont), which was based on the true story of an ostensibly "white" man's shattering discovery of his black parentage. The latter was also shot on location (in Maine and New Hampshire) with a largely nonprofessional cast. This same technique was practiced in the "problem" cycle's most elaborate exposé of political corruption, Robert Rossen's adaptation of Robert Penn Warren's novel *All the King's Men* (1949), a portrait of an authentic American demagogue based upon the career of Louisiana governor Huey Long. Other social-consciousness films dealt realistically for the first time in Hollywood history with the problems of alcoholism (Billy Wilder's *The Lost Weekend*, 1945; Stuart Heisler's *Smash-Up*, 1947), mental illness (Anatole Litvak's *The Snake Pit*, 1948), juvenile delinquency (Nicholas Ray's *Knock on Any Door*, 1949), prison injustice (Jules Dassin's *Brute Force*, 1947) war profiteering (Irving Reis's *All My Sons*, 1948; from the play by Arthur Miller), and the rehabilitation of paraplegic veterans (Fred Zinnemann's *The Men*, 1950; also produced by Kramer). Moreover, although they can scarcely be described as problem pictures, there were several other films of the postwar era that employed various forms of social corrup-

11.16 *The Set-Up* (Robert Wise, 1949): Robert Ryan, down for the count.

tion as metaphors for more serious disorders in the cosmos and in the human soul. Robert Rossen's *Body and Soul* (1947; written by Abraham Polonsky (1910–1999)[4] and Robert Wise's *The Set-Up* (1949), for example, both used corruption in the prize-fighting business and the brutality of the "sport" itself to suggest something about the nature of human evil; while Polonsky's own poetically directed *Force of Evil* (1948) used the numbers racket in New York City to create a paradigm of capitalism collapsing internally from its own rottenness.

Closely related to the problem pictures was a series of semidocumentary crime melodramas that frequently had social overtones. These films were usually based on true criminal cases and shot on location with as many of the original participants in the cast as it was feasible to assemble. The first was Henry Hathaway's *The House on 92nd Street* (1945), a dramatic re-enactment of an authentic case of domestic espionage based entirely on FBI files and produced for 20th Century–Fox by Louis De Rochemont (1899–1978), creator of *The March of Time* newsreels (1935–51). De Rochemont followed this film with three other semidocumentary productions, which gave Fox clear leadership in the field: Hathaway's *13 Rue Madeleine*

11.15 *The Lost Weekend* (Billy Wilder, 1945): Ray Milland.

---

4. Remade, badly, in 1981, with an all-black cast under the direction of George Bowers.

(1946), a re-creation of OSS[5] activity in Montreal during the war; Elia Kazan's critically acclaimed *Boomerang!* (1947), based on the true story of a state's attorney who faced the wrath of an entire Connecticut town to clear an accused man of murder; and Hathaway's *Kiss of Death* (1947), an unglamorized account of criminals and cops in New York City's underworld. The outstanding commercial success of these films produced many others using the same formula of a fictionalized story based on fact and shot on location with nonprofessional actors; Jules Dassin's *The Naked City* (1948), William Keighley's *The Street with No Name* (1948), and Anthony Mann's T-Men (1948) are among the best of these. In *The Naked City*, conceived and produced by Mark Hellinger, Dassin used a conventional crime melodrama as the vehicle for an uncompromisingly naturalistic portrait of the brutal and impersonal modern city; much of this film was shot by cinematographer William Daniels (1895–1970) in *cinéma vérité* fashion with hidden cameras. After 1948, the semidocumentary melodrama largely degenerated into stereotype, and most critics consider that the final collaboration of Hathaway and De Rochemont, *Call Northside 777* (1948), based on the true case of a Chicago reporter (played by James Stewart) who attempted to clear a Polish American of a murder charge, was the last important film of its type. Nevertheless, the influence of these motion pictures continued well into the 1950s, as the documentary surfaces of fiction films like John Huston's *The Asphalt Jungle* (1950), Elia Kazan's *On the Waterfront* (1954), and Alfred Hitchcock's *The Wrong Man* (1957) attest.

FILM NOIR

For a while, both the problem pictures and the semidocumentary crime thrillers made it seem that Italian neorealism had found a home in an uneasy, if affluent, America. The critic James Agee wrote in 1947, "One of the best things that is happening in Hollywood is the tendency to move out of the place—to base fictional pictures on fact and, more importantly, to shoot them not in painted studio sets but in actual places." But another variety of postwar American film, one that depended on the controlled environment of the studio as well as upon real locations for its depiction of the seamy underside of American life, soon appeared. This was *film noir* (literally, "black film"), discovered and named by French critics in 1946 when, seeing American motion pictures for the first time since 1940, they perceived a strange new mood of cyni-

11.17 The prototypical *film noir: Double Indemnity* (Billy Wilder, 1944). Barbara Stanwyck, Fred MacMurray, Edward G. Robinson.

cism, darkness, and despair in certain crime films and melodramas. They derived the term from the "Serie Noire" detective novels then popular in France, many of which were translations of works by members of the "hard-boiled" school of American crime writers—Dashiell Hammett, Raymond Chandler, and James M. Cain (later joined by Horace McCoy, Mickey Spillane, and Jim Thompson)—

---

5. The abbreviation for Office of Strategic Services, the American intelligence operation during World War II. The OSS provided the model and much of the personnel for the Central Intelligence Agency (CIA), which was established in 1947. *13 Rue Madeleine* was a paragon of cost-cutting semidocumentary technique, taking a total of seventy-five days on location, and not one day in the studio, to complete. Like other films of the type, its story material was drawn from contemporary documents and newspaper accounts, which were virtually cost-free.

whose books were also frequently adapted in *films noir*. Like the novels, these films were characterized by a downbeat atmosphere and graphic violence, and they carried postwar American pessimism to the point of nihilism by assuming the absolute and irredeemable corruption of society and of everyone in it. Billy Wilder's corrosive *Double Indemnity* (1944), which startled Hollywood in the year of its release and was almost banned by the Hays Office, may be regarded as the prototype for *film noir*, although some critics trace the origins back to such tough but considerably less cynical films as *High Sierra* (Raoul Walsh, 1943), *This Gun for Hire* (Frank Tuttle, 1942), *The Maltese Falcon* (John Huston, 1941; adapted from Hammett), and *Stranger on the Third Floor* (Boris Ingster, 1940).[6] Adapted by Wilder and Raymond Chandler from a James M. Cain novel, *Double Indemnity* is the sordid story of a Los Angeles insurance agent (Fred MacMurray) seduced by a client's wife (Barbara Stanwyck) into murdering her husband for his death benefits; it has been called "a film without a single trace of pity or love."

Indeed, these are qualities notably absent from all *films noir*, as perhaps they seemed absent from the postwar America that produced them. Like *Double Indemnity*, these films thrived upon the unvarnished depiction of greed, lust, and cruelty because their basic theme was the depth of human depravity and the utterly unheroic nature of human beings—lessons that were hardly taught but certainly re-emphasized by the unique horrors of World

11.18 *The Blue Dahlia* (George Marshall, 1946): Alan Ladd, Veronica Lake.

War II. Most of the dark films of the late 1940s take the form of crime melodramas because (as Dostoevsky and Dickens knew) the mechanisms of crime and criminal detection provide a perfect metaphor for corruption that cuts across conventional moral categories. These films are often set in southern California—the topographical paradigm for a society in which the gap between expectation and reality is resolved through mass delusion. The protagonists are frequently unsympathetic antiheroes who pursue their base designs or simply drift aimlessly through sinister night worlds of the urban American jungle,[7] but

---

6. It is possible, as Paul Schrader has argued ("Notes on *Film Noir*," *Film Comment* 8, 1, (Spring 1972; rpt. in *Film Noir Reader*, ed. Alain Silver and James Ursani [New York: Limelight 1996], pp. 53–63.), that *film noir* would have evolved naturally out of the late 1930s and early 1940s had the war not intervened. But it also seems likely that the antiheroic vision of *film noir* was generated specifically in response to the actual horrors of the war and the multiple hypocrisies of postwar American society.

7. And they are antiheroes in the most extreme sense of the term: murderous *femmes fatales* (*Double Indemnity*; Edgar G. Ulmer's perverse "quickie" classic *Detour* [1945]; Tay Garnett's *The Postman Always Rings Twice* [1946]; John Cromwell's *Dead Reckoning* [1947]; Orson Welles's darkly brilliant *The Lady from Shanghai* [1948]); down-at-the-heels and/or paranoid private eyes (Edward Dmytryk's *Murder, My Sweet* [1945]; George Marshall's *The Blue Dahlia* [1946]; Jacques Tourneur's *Out of the Past* [1947]); fugitive criminals (Robert Siodmak's *The Killers* [1946], *Cry of the City* [1948], and *Criss Cross* [1949]; Delmer Daves's *Dark Passage* [1947]; Nicholas Ray's *They Live by Night* [1949]; Joseph H. Lewis's quintessential fugitive couple film *Gun Crazy* [also known as *Deadly Is the Female*, 1950]); ruthless con men, blackmailers, and racketeers (Anthony Mann's *Desperate* [1947], *Railroaded* [1947], and *Raw Deal* [1948]; John Farrow's *The Big Clock* [1948]; Jules Das-

sin's *Night and the City* [1950]); psychopathic killers and/or mental patients (John Brahm's *The Locket* [1947]; Rudolph Maté's *The Dark Past* [1948]; Raoul Walsh's apocalyptic *White Heat* [1949]); corrupt, victimized, or simply neurotic cops (Otto Preminger's *Laura* [1944] and *Where the Sidewalk Ends* [1950]; Rudolph Maté's *D.O.A.* [1949]; Fritz Lang's *The Big Heat* [1953]); and, into the 1950s, assorted punks, madmen, mobsters, and degenerates (John Huston's *The Asphalt Jungle* [1950]; Nicholas Ray's *In a Lonely Place* [1950] and *On Dangerous Ground* [1952]; Samuel Fuller's *Pickup on South Street* [1953]; Joseph H. Lewis's *The Big Combo* [1955]; Robert Aldrich's *noir* masterpiece *Kiss Me Deadly* [1955]). Significantly, many of *film noir*'s male protagonists are cynical, war-weary combat veterans—sometimes afflicted with amnesia or other psychological disabilities—and many of the women are wives, fiancées, and sweethearts who have betrayed their men with other lovers during the war. Furthermore, many stars of *film noir* (such as Dick Powell, Barbara Stanwyck, Fred MacMurray, John Garfield, Lana Turner, Alan Ladd, Joan Bennett, Deanna Durbin, Robert Cummings, Van Johnson, Robert Young, and Tyrone Power) were playing totally unsympathetic characters for the first time in their careers—playing, that is, against their established box-office images, which added yet another touch of eeriness to the form.

11.19 *The Big Heat* (Fritz Lang, 1953): Glenn Ford.

they are just as often decent people caught in traps laid for them by a corrupt social order. In this latter sense, *film noir* was very much a "cinema of moral anxiety" of the sort practiced at various times in postwar Eastern Europe, most recently in Poland at the height of the Solidarity movement—i.e., a cinema about the conditions of life forced upon honest people in a mendacious, self-deluding society.

The moral instability of this world was translated into a visual style by the great *noir* cinematographers John Alton, Nicholas Musuraca, John F. Seitz, Lee Garmes, Tony Gaudio, Sol Polito, Ernest Haller, Lucien Ballard, and James Wong Howe. These technicians rendered moral ambiguity palpably real through what has been called antitraditional cinematography. The style included the pervasive use of wide-angle lenses, permitting greater depth of field but causing expressive distortion in close-ups; low-key lighting and night-for-night shooting (that is, actually shooting night scenes at night rather than in bright daylight with dark filters), both of which create harsh contrasts between the light and dark areas of the frame, with dark predominating, to parallel the moral chaos of the world; and angular, unnatural compositions. If all of this seems reminiscent of the artificial studio technique of German Expressionism, it should, because—like the Universal horror cycle of the 1930s—*film noir* was created to a large extent by German and Eastern European expatriates, many of whom had received their basic training at UFA in the 1920s and early 1930s. The *noir* directors Fritz Lang, Robert Siodmak, Billy Wilder, Otto

Preminger, John Brahm, Anatole Litvak, Max Ophüls, William Dieterle, Douglas Sirk, Edgar G. Ulmer, and Curtis Bernhardt; the director-cinematographer Rudolph Maté; the cinematographers Karl Freund and John Alton; and the composers Franz Waxman and Max Steiner had all been associated with or influenced by the UFA studio style.

Nevertheless, given its subject matter, *film noir* could scarcely escape the general realistic tendency of the postwar cinema, and *noir* directors frequently shot exteriors on location. Such wartime innovations as smaller camera dollies and portable power packs, higher speed lenses and more sensitive, fine-grain film stocks simplified the logistics of location shooting and helped to create for *film noir* a nearly homogeneous visual style.[8] For this reason, it has become fashionable to speak of *film noir* as a type (some believe it is a genre) of "romantic" or "expressive" realism; but its heritage includes such a wide range of cultural forces—German Expressionism and horror, American gangster films of the 1930s, Sternbergian exoticism and decadence, the poetic realism of Carné and Duvivier, the hard-boiled tradition of American fiction, the 1940s popularization of Freud, postwar American disillusionment (especially a sense of sexual betrayal among returning GIs) and the wave of cinematic realism it engendered, Cold War paranoia, and of course, *Citizen Kane*—that it seems better to characterize it as a cycle rather than to delimit its boundaries too rigidly.

Furthermore, as several critics have suggested, *film noir* describes a period as well as a style or a genre, for darkness and cynicism invaded *all* genres in the late-1940s cinema, not simply that of the crime thriller and melodrama. Raymond Durgnat points out that films as disparate as John M. Stahl's bizarre romance *Leave Her to Heaven* (1945), King Vidor's epic Western *Duel in the*

---

8. As Alain Silver and Elizabeth Ward point out in *Film Noir: An Encyclopedic Reference to the American Style* rev. exp. ed. (Woodstock, N.Y.: Overlook, 1992), in a random selection of productions—*The Big Clock* (Paramount), *Cry of the City* (20th Century–Fox), *Strangers on a Train* (Warner's), *People against O'Hara* (MGM), *Out of the Past* (RKO), *Criss Cross* (Universal), and *Dead Reckoning* (Columbia)—six different directors and seven different cinematographers, of great and small technical reputations (John F. Seitz, Lloyd Ahern, Robert Burks, John Alton, Nicholas Musuraca, Franz Planer, Leo Tover), working at seven different studios, completed seven ostensibly unrelated motion pictures with one cohesive visual style.

11.20 The image of postwar angst: *In a Lonely Place* (Nicholas Ray, 1950). Gloria Grahame, Humphrey Bogart.

11.21 *The Big Combo* (Joseph H. Lewis, 1955).

Sun (1946), and Frank Capra's *It's a Wonderful Life* (1946) have distinctly *noir* elements, and there was a whole series of late-1940s melodramas that may be said to range from off-black to gray (*films gris*), the models for which were Hitchcock's *Rebecca* (1940) and George Cukor's *Gaslight* (1944),[9] not to mention the atmospheric low-budget horror cycle of RKO producer Val Lewton (1904–1951)—*Cat People, I Walked with a Zombie,* and *The Leopard Man* (Jacques Tourneur, 1942, 1943, and 1943); *The Seventh Victim* and *The Ghost Ship* (both Mark Robson, 1943); *The Curse of the Cat People* (Gunther von Fritsch and Robert Wise, 1944); *Isle of the Dead* (Mark Robson, 1945); *The Body Snatcher* (Robert Wise, 1945); and *Bedlam* (Mark Robson, 1946). In the end, perhaps the most categorical thing we can say about *film noir* is that both thematically and stylistically it represents a unique and highly creative countertradition in the American cinema, derived from eclectic sources and motivated by the pervasive existential cynicism of the postwar era. With several significant exceptions (for example, Mervyn LeRoy's *I Am a Fugitive from a Chain Gang* [1932] and Fritz Lang's *You*

Only Live Once [1937]) most American films of the prewar Depression era—and most American films, for that matter—had been optimistic, affirmative, and generally supportive of the status quo. We have seen, however, that postwar America produced, with the problem picture and the semidocumentary melodrama, a cinema of disillusionment and searching that rejected the epic heroics and callow idealism of World War II films—but one that always suggested that the inequities of American society could be resolved through good faith and work. Yet *film noir* showed all human values to be seriously embattled, if not ultimately corrupt, and sneered at the prospects for change (perhaps, as some suggest, because the atomic future was too frightening to contemplate). Never before had the American cinema handed down such extreme indictments of Ameri-

---

9. Closely related to the *noir* cycle and concurrent with it, these gothic romances frequently had period settings and were produced by almost every studio in Hollywood between 1940 and 1952. Like the contemporary melodramas known as "women's pictures" (see footnote, p. 374), they were intended primarily for female audiences, and their appearance during the 1940s was the result of a widespread impression among studio executives that women made up a majority of the filmgoing public. This may have been true for a short time during World War II, but, as Leo A. Handel pointed out in *Hollywood Looks at Its Audience: A Report of Film Audience Research* (Urbana: University of Illinois Press, 1950), it was not at all the case before and after, when the sexes were almost evenly distributed in the national market. Representative gothic titles are *Rebecca* (1940), *Gaslight* (1944), *Experiment Perilous* (Jacques Tourneur, 1944), *Hangover Square* (John Brahm, 1945), *Dragonwyck* (Joseph L. Mankiewicz, 1946), *So Evil My Love* (Lewis Allen, 1948), *Sleep, My Love* (Douglas Sirk, 1948), and *My Cousin Rachel* (Henry Koster, 1952).

can society or any other, and it would not do so again until the late 1960s, when the indictments would be mitigated by libertarian idealism. However briefly, then, *film noir* held up a dark mirror to postwar America and reflected its moral anarchy.[1] Not surprisingly, a number of important and powerful Americans did not like what they saw.

THE WITCH-HUNT AND THE BLACKLIST

Our Cold War with the Soviet Union began officially in July 1947, when Stalin refused to accept the Marshall Plan for the Soviet Union or any of its satellites; but, of course, Soviet-American tensions, although briefly relaxed during the alliance to defeat Hitler, had been mounting ever since the Bolshevik Revolution. Among other things, this meant that in the public mind the menace of Nazi agents and fifth columnists was replaced by the menace of Communist spies and "fellow travelers," doubly sinister since they looked just like everyone else and didn't speak with an accent. Furthermore, what David Caute has called "the myth of the Vital Secret"—the inflated notion that members of the American Communist party were feverishly conducting atomic espionage on behalf of the Soviet Union—was widespread during this era and would result in the conviction of Alger Hiss (1948), the rise and fall of Senator Joseph R. McCarthy (1950–54), and the execu-

tions of Julius and Ethel Rosenberg (1953). Politically, the country was in the throes of an anti-New Deal backlash that had been building since the tumultuous 1930s, and Hollywood, as a signal beneficiary of FDR's economic and social policies,[2] became the target for a squalid inquisition that brought shame and/or ruin to hundreds of key industry personnel.

In the spring of 1947 the House Committee on Un-American Activities (commonly—and pejoratively—known as HUAC), which had been inactive since the hot war ended, decided to undertake a full-scale investigation of what its chairman, J. Parnell Thomas (R–N.J.), called "communism in motion pictures." As John Howard Lawson, one of the victims of this investigation, later wrote, the charge that American films contained "communist propaganda" in the late 1940s or at any other time was wholly laughable because the American film industry was one of the most conservative elements in the country. There were, however, recent films of predominantly liberal sentiment, such as the problem pictures and the semidocumentary melodramas, and there were the apolitical *films noir*, which did not take a very sanguine view of life under any system of government. There were also all of those pro-Russian films made at the OWI's behest during the war, when the Soviet Union had been America's ally (a HUAC subcommittee report would later claim that "some of the most flagrant Communist propaganda

---

1. The revival of the genre in the Watergate era (*The Long Goodbye* [Robert Altman, 1973]; *The Outfit* [John Flynn, 1974]; *Chinatown* [Roman Polanski, 1974]; *Farewell, My Lovely* [Dick Richards, 1975; a remake of Dmytryk's 1945 *Murder, My Sweet]; Night Moves* [Arthur Penn, 1975]; *The Nickel Ride* [Robert Mulligan, 1975]; *Hustle* [Robert Aldrich, 1975]; *Taxi Driver* [Martin Scorsese, 1976]) and during the morally bankrupt presidency of Ronald Reagan (*Body Heat* [Lawrence Kasdan, 1981]; Bob Rafelson's remake of *The Postman Always Rings Twice* [1981]; *Blade Runner* [Ridley Scott, 1982]; *Breathless* [Jim McBride, 1983]; *Against All Odds* [Taylor Hackford, 1984; a remake of Tourneur's *Out of the Past*]; *Blood Simple* [Joel and Ethan Coen, 1984]; *Body Double* [Brian De Palma, 1984]; *Jagged Edge* [Richard Marquand, 1985]; *Angel Heart* [Alan Parker, 1986]; *Blue Velvet* [David Lynch, 1986]; *No Mercy* [Richard Pearce, 1987]; *Black Widow* [Bob Rafelson, 1987]; *Tough Guys Don't Dance* [Norman Mailer, 1987]; *Manhunter* [Michael Mann, 1987]; *No Way Out* [Roger Donaldson, 1987; a remake of *The Big Clock*]; *The Big Easy* [Jim McBride, 1987]; *Fatal Attraction* [Adrian Lyne, 1987]; *Best Seller* [John Flynn, 1987]; *Deadly Illusion* [William Tannen, 1987]; *House of Games* [David Mamet, 1987]; *Someone to Watch over Me* [Ridley Scott, 1987]; *Slow Burn* [Matthew Chapman, 1987; Showtime]; *Lady Beware* [Karen Arthur, 1987]; *Suspect*

[Peter Yates, 1987]; *The Stepfather* [Joseph Rubin, 1987]; *Positive I.D.* [Andy Anderson, 1987]; *Laguna Heat* [Simon Langton, 1987; HBO]; *Julia and Julia* [Peter Del Monte, 1987]; *Slamdance* [Wayne Wang, 1987]; *The Killing Time* [Rick King, 1987]; *Dead of Winter* [Arthur Penn, 1987]; *Masquerade* [Bob Swaim, 1988]; *The House on Carroll Street* [Peter Yates, 1988]; *D.O.A.* [Rocky Morton, 1988; a remake of the Rudolph Maté original, also remade in Australia as *Color Me Dead*, 1969]) suggests a continuing relationship among *film noir*, political malaise, and social disintegration.

2. In addition to the perks mentioned in the footnote on p. 368, Roosevelt had exempted motion pictures from war censorship in 1941 and, together with other information media, from licensing as a condition of sale or distribution in 1942—effectively, if temporarily, granting films First Amendment protection under the Constitution. Furthermore, as Richard Maltby points out in "Made for Each Other: The Melodrama of Hollywood and the House Committee on Un-American Activities, 1947," by doing so, FDR's administration had provided the film industry with an unprecedented degree of social and political status. (See *Cinema, Politics and Society in America*, ed. Philip Davies and Brian Neve [New York: St. Martin's, 1981], pp. 76–96.)

films were produced as a result of White House pressure" during the war and that Roosevelt's National Labor Relations Board had infiltrated Communists into the industry). But most damaging of all, because there was at least factual substance to the charge, a number of famous Hollywood directors, screenwriters, and actors had joined the Communist party or contributed funds to its activities during the Depression, when it had seemed to offer a viable alternative to starving under capitalism. Some had merely supported causes, such as relief for refugees from Franco's Spain, that also were supported by Communists. It was among these people, most of whom had dropped their Communist party affiliation years before, that HUAC was able to do the most damage.

In September 1947 the tragicomedy began as the committee subpoenaed 41 witnesses, 19 of whom declared their intention to be "unfriendly"—i.e., to refuse to answer questions about their political beliefs. When the hearings began on October 20, the so-called friendly witnesses— among them the producers Jack L. Warner and Louis B. Mayer; the writers Ayn Rand and Morrie Ryskind; the actors Adolphe Menjou, Robert Taylor, Robert Montgomery, George Murphy, Ronald Reagan, and Gary Cooper; the directors Leo McCarey and Sam Wood; and producer-director Walt Disney—were called first. They proved their patriotism by naming people whom they identified as leftists, and generally telling the congressmen what they wanted to hear ("Hollywood," claimed the right-winger Menjou, "is one of the main centers of Communist activity in America"; Disney testified that the Screen Cartoonists Guild was Communist-dominated and had tried to take over his studio). Of the 19 unfriendly witnesses, 11 were summoned to the witness stand the following week for questioning about their alleged Communist party membership[3]—the German émigré playwright Bertolt Brecht; the screen writers Alvah Bessie, Lester Cole, Ring Lardner, Jr., John Howard Lawson, Albert Maltz, Samuel Ornitz, Adrian Scott, and Dalton Trumbo; and the directors Herbert Biberman and Edward Dmytryk. Hollywood liberals, including John Huston, William Wyler, Gene Kelly, Danny Kaye, Humphrey Bogart, and Lauren Bacall, responded by forming the Committee for the First Amendment (CFA) to fight for the constitutional rights of the "accused witnesses"—a contradiction in the terms of jurisprudence, if there ever was one—but opposition fal-

11.22 Subpoenaed filmmakers leaving the HUAC hearing room in October 1947; ten would soon go to jail for contempt of Congress. Left to right: (front row) Lewis Milestone, Dalton Trumbo, John Howard Lawson, and attorney Bartley Crum; (center row) Gordon Kahn, Irving Pichel, Edward Dmytryk, and Robert Rossen; (back row) Waldo Salt, Richard Collins, Howard Koch, Albert Maltz, Herbert Biberman, Lester Cole, Ring Lardner, Jr., and attorney Martin Popper.

tered when the now-famous Hollywood Ten listed above (less Brecht, who temporized before the committee and fled the country several days later) defied HUAC by refusing to testify and were subsequently given prison sentences of six months to a year for contempt of Congress.[4]

---

3. There was about this more than a whiff of anti-Semitism, since thirteen of the nineteen were Jewish and a number of congressmen were on record as believing that America had been duped into supporting the wrong side in World War II by a "Jewish-Bolshevist" (read "anti-Nazi") conspiracy in Hollywood—a ridiculous, not to say criminally stupid, attitude given the moguls' unwillingness to offend even Hitler himself before our entry into the war (see footnote, p. 288).

4. Since the hearings were not a court of law, "unfriendly" witnesses were not allowed to be accompanied by their lawyers or to cross-examine other witnesses, nor was documented evidence required of their accusers. The Ten tried to read prepared statements, but only Maltz was permitted to do so. When questioned about their own political activities and beliefs—and those of their friends and casual acquaintances—they refused to answer (Ring Lardner, Jr., quipped: "I could answer that question, but I would hate myself in the morning"), invoking their rights under the First and Fifth Amendments to the U.S. Constitution. The Ten were cited for contempt by the House in November and indicted by a federal grand jury the following month. Blacklisted and unemployed, they spent the next few years raising funds for their

The committee's action was scandalous, but its meaning was crystal clear: HUAC wished to purge Hollywood and, if possible, the entire country of any and all liberal tendencies by creating and then exploiting anticommunist hysteria. The threat of state censorship loomed, and panic broke out in the nation's most image-conscious industry, which was already plagued by antitrust actions, unemployment, and rapidly declining profits.

On November 24, 1947, the same day that the House of Representatives by a nearly unanimous vote approved HUAC's contempt citations for the Ten, Hollywood closed ranks against some of the most talented artists it had ever known. The 50 members of the Motion Picture Association of America (MPAA; MPPDA before 1945) and the Association of Motion Picture Producers[5] (representing the industry's most powerful executives, including Eric Johnston, Nicholas M. Schenck, Harry Cohn, Joseph M. Schenck, Walter Wanger, Samuel Goldwyn, Henry Ginsberg, Albert Warner, Louis B. Mayer, Dore Schary, Spyros Skouras, and William Goetz) produced the Waldorf Statement censuring the behavior of the Ten, firing them, and refusing to re-employ any one of them "until such time as he is acquitted or has purged himself of contempt and declares under oath that he is not a Communist." The statement continued by spelling out future industry policy: "We will not knowingly employ a Communist or member of any party or group which advocates the overthrow of the government of the United States by force or by illegal or unconstitutional methods." This was the beginning of the infamous practice of blacklisting, which brought to an end one of the most creative periods in the history of American film and made Hollywood a wasteland of vapidity, complacency, and cowardice for well over a decade. From 1948 to 1951, there was a lull of sorts as the production community drew a cautionary lesson from the fate of the Ten and allowed the Committee for the First Amendment to disintegrate, with Bogart and Bacall, for example, publicly calling their participation a "mistake."[6] The once-liberal Screen Actors Guild (SAG), under the new leadership of Ronald Reagan, required that its members take a loyalty oath and in the following year openly condoned the blacklist. But in March 1951 HUAC, now chaired by John S. Wood (D–Ga.), began a new onslaught by subpoenaing 45 unfriendly witnesses, who were called upon very specifically to name names and inform on former colleagues. By the end of the sec-

ond round of hearings—which were televised, adding to their *frisson*—110 men and women had testified, 58 of them confessing past party membership and collectively providing the committee with the names of 212 alleged fellow travelers. Those who refused to inform were put under tremendous pressure to "come clean"—a process of self-abasement that involved denouncing one's friends (especially if they had already been denounced by previous witnesses), confessing one's own guilt by association, and groveling not only before HUAC, but before a host of self-appointed Grand Inquisitors and "clearance" agencies in the private sector, such as the American Legion and American Business Consultants, editors of the scurrilous public blacklists *Counterattack* and *Red Channels*.

Some refused to cringe, and at the end of the process in 1951 (which was resumed when Senator Pat McCarran's Internal Security Subcommittee reopened the hearings in 1952, subpoenaing Judy Holliday, Burl Ives, and others), 324 persons had been fired by the studios and were no longer permitted to work in the American

---

appeals and other costs (this included lecture tours and the production of a polemical twenty-minute short called *The Hollywood Ten*, 1948). The appellate process was exhausted in April 1950, when the Supreme Court denied *certiorari*, and in June all ten went to federal prison—two of them for six months and eight for a year—along with the chairman of the committee, who had, in the interim, been convicted of mishandling public funds. See Larry Ceplair and Steven Englund, *The Inquisition in Hollywood: Politics in the Film Community, 1930–1960* (Garden City, N.Y.: Doubleday, 1980; rpt. Berkeley: University of California Press, 1983); Victor S. Navasky, *Naming Names* (New York: Viking, 1980); also *Hollywood on Trial* (Tristram Powell, 1973), a feature-length documentary on the hearings produced by the BBC.

5. The business and public-relations component of the MPAA, now the Association of Motion Picture and Television Producers (AMPTP). Among other functions, the AMPTP negotiates labor contracts for its members and maintains Central Casting Corporation as a means of supplying extras.

6. The format for Bogart's recantation was an article he wrote for the March 1948 issue of *Photoplay* magazine entitled "I'm No Communist," in which he admitted being a "dope." The title is resonant of many such public confessions of the era—for example, John Garfield's self-abasing "I Was a Sucker for a Left Hook," which was to have appeared in a fall 1951 issue of *Look* magazine shortly before his death, and Edward G. Robinson's wretched "How the Reds Made a Sucker Out of Me," ghost-written for him by the professional Red-hunter and Hearst columnist George Sokolsky, which was published in the *American Legion Magazine* in October 1952.

film industry.[7] Among them were some of the most talented directors, writers, and actors of the postwar cinema: Joseph Losey (*The Lawless*, 1950), Michael Gordon (*Another Part of the Forest*, 1947), Jules Dassin (*The Naked City*, 1948), Abraham Polonsky (*Force of Evil*, 1948), and Herbert Biberman (*The Master Race*, 1944); also Carl Foreman, Donald Ogden Stewart, Albert Maltz, Guy Endore, Dorothy Parker, Lillian Hellman, Gordon Kahn, Howard Koch, Sidney Buchman, Ring Lardner, Jr., John Howard Lawson, Dalton Trumbo, Lester Cole, Samuel Ornitz, Adrian Scott, and Waldo Salt; Gale Sondergaard, Karen Morley, Dorothy Comingore, Lee Grant, Sam Jaffe, Lionel Stander, Zero Mostel, Anne Revere, Larry Parks, Paul Muni, John Garfield, Jeff Corey, Will Geer, Howard Da Silva, and many others.

Some of the writers were able to make a living by selling their scripts on the black market under the names of real people, or "fronts."[8] (The 1956 Academy Award for the Best Original Screenplay, for example, went to a mysterious "Mr. Robert Rich" for Irving Rapper's *The Brave One*. The Oscar could not be picked up at the time because Rich was actually Dalton Trumbo; four years later, tensions had relaxed to the point that Trumbo could receive screen credit in his own name—for Otto Preminger's *Exodus* and Stanley Kubrick's *Spartacus*, both 1960.) But the highly visible actors and directors were doomed to unemployment (Muni) or exile (Losey and Dassin went to Europe). Some lost their lives: Philip Loeb, one of the stars of the popular television series *The Goldbergs*, committed suicide; the screen actors John Garfield, Canada Lee, J. Edward Bromberg, and Mady Christians died as a result of the stress they were subjected to. Hundreds of other film people were maligned by HUAC but managed to survive under the cloud of either marginal blacklisting (e.g., Lewis Milestone, Fredric March, José Ferrer, Edward G. Robinson) or their own collaboration with the investigating body (e.g., Elia Kazan, Richard Collins, Harold Hecht, Clifford Odets, Isobel Lennart, Bernard Schoenfeld, Lee J. Cobb, Lucille Ball, Sterling Hayden, Lloyd Bridges, Frank Tuttle, Budd Schulberg, and, ultimately, Edward Dmytryk and Robert Rossen). Several commentators have suggested that for members of the latter group the moral catastrophe of informing proved as destructive as the practical effects of being blacklisted, but materially, at least, quite the reverse was true. While the victims of the blacklist lost their jobs, their families, and even their lives, most of the informers prospered. Ball,

Cobb, Schulberg, and Kazan, for example, were all rewarded with stunning career success in the 1950s, Kazan winning an Academy Award for directing a paean to informing in *On the Waterfront* (1954)—which, not coincidentally, was written by Schulberg, starred Cobb, and was also named Best Film of the Year by the Academy, the New York Critics Society, and the National Board of Review. At the same time, Lester Cole was working in a warehouse, Sidney Buchman operated a parking garage, and Alvah Bessie was a stagehand at a nightclub; others struggled to support their families as maître d's, appliance repairmen, and outside salesmen.

The practice of blacklisting in the American film industry continued well into the 1950s, and its impact was felt throughout the 1960s.[9] Abraham Polonsky, for example, was not able to direct again in Hollywood until 1969, when his *Tell Them Willie Boy Is Here* appeared—twenty-one years after *Force of Evil*. But as damaging to the American cinema as the loss of individual talent was the pervasive mood of fear, distrust, and self-loathing that settled over Hollywood in the wake of the hearings. Everyone was scared of the government and of everyone else, and the industry tacitly imposed a form of self-censorship more repressive and sterile than anything HUAC could have devised. As early as 1948, William Wyler speculated that a modestly progressive film like his own *The Best Years of*

---

7. The Waldorf Statement also admitted the risk of "creating an atmosphere of fear" and "hurting innocent people," but the hard-line implications of the policy were clear, and many observers felt that the film executives had been pressured into adopting it by their conservative Wall Street financiers, who had approximately $60 million invested in the industry at the time. Ed Sullivan, for example, remarked of the Waldorf Statement, "Wall Street jiggled the strings, that's all" (quoted in Andrew Dowdy, *The Films of the Fifties: The American State of Mind* [New York: Morrow, 1973], p. 20). The blacklist extended also to radio, television, Broadway, and even folksinging and provincial theater.

8. As in *The Front* (Martin Ritt, 1976), a film about television blacklisting made by a formerly blacklisted writer, director, and producer, with Woody Allen in the title role. The first Hollywood film to deal openly with the blacklist was Sydney Pollack's *The Way We Were* (1973), which was nevertheless heavily cut for general release.

9. In the American theater, blacklisting continued until the late 1950s. In radio and television, it did not end until the mid-1960s. The effect of blacklisting on the content of American motion pictures, as charted by Dorothy B. Jones, shows the following shift: 28 percent of all Hollywood films dealt with "social themes or psychological problems" in 1947; the percentage declined to only 9.2 percent in 1954. See Jones, "Communism and the Movies: A Study of Film Content," in John Cogley, *Report on Blacklisting*, 2 vols. (New York: Fund for the Republic, 1956), I, pp. 196–233.

Our Lives (1946) could not be made in America again, adding, "In a few months we won't be able to have a heavy who is an American." Wyler was right. No one in Hollywood was willing to take the slightest chance on anybody or anything; the industry had had its fill of trouble and wanted no more of it. Safety, caution, and respectability were the watchwords of the studio chiefs, and controversial or even serious subject matter was avoided at all costs. Thus, vitiated, frightened, and drained of creative vitality, Hollywood experienced in miniature what the whole of American society was to experience during the McCarthy-era witch-hunts—intellectual stagnation and moral paralysis.

THE ARRIVAL OF TELEVISION

Finally, as if the devastating impact of the hearings was not enough to sink Hollywood's already foundering ship, a new entertainment medium suddenly emerged that threatened to do the job all by itself. This, of course, was **television**—a system for transmitting moving images based on the process of electronic image analysis and synthesis[1] patented by the independent inventor Philo T. Farnsworth in 1930. RCA, which had been moving toward the development of just such a system for several years through the work of the Russian scientist Vladimir K. Zworykin, attempted first to buy and then to pre-empt Farnsworth's patents through litigation. But in 1939 the courts gave legal priority to Farnsworth, and in September RCA licensed his patents for a period of ten years for $1 million—the first and only time in its history that the corporation was forced to pay royalties rather than collect them. Formally introduced to the public at the 1939 New York World's Fair, television was a smashing success, and RCA began marketing receivers in the same year for regularly scheduled daily broadcasts (about fifteen hours per week) via its NBC subsidiary. CBS began telecasting in the following year, and in July 1941 the FCC set format standards for black-and-white transmission and authorized the full operation of commercial television. Wartime restrictions soon put a halt to the manufacture of television transmission equipment and receivers, and the networks were forced to curtail their telecasts sharply. When the war ended, however, they resumed regular daily telecasting, and the production of transmitters and receivers burgeoned. By 1949 there were 1 million TV sets in use in the United States, and the television broadcasting

11.23 As the 1950s begin, America's dream palaces succumb to television.

industry had begun in earnest. Only two years later, there were ten times that many sets in use, and by 1959 the number had risen to 50 million. In 1946, when two-thirds of the total population of the country went to the movies weekly, attendance had been guaranteed by the nearly complete lack of alternate sources of audiovisual entertainment. Now that lack was met with a vengeance.

At first, Hollywood attempted to enter the television business by applying for station licenses in major markets and by innovating large-screen television in its theater circuits (HBO-like subscription programming for in-house viewing was also tested). But the studios were outmaneuvered politically by the dominant radio networks, and NBC, CBS, and ABC moved directly into television broadcasting with the blessing of an FCC that looked askance at the movie monopolists' recent conviction in the Paramount case; in this context, moreover, theater/subscription television simply could not compete with the

---

1. In this process, simply put, the image to be transmitted is broken down into 210,000 "bits" of discrete audiovisual information, or "picture elements," by a camera tube; these are broadcast as FM electronic signals to video receivers, where they are resynthesized as images by picture tubes (see footnote, p. 387). William Lafferty points out, however, that in very broad terms, "the technical development of television paralleled that of motion pictures, although displaced by almost fifty years." See Lafferty, "Chapter II: Film and Television," in *Film and the Arts in Symbiosis: A Resource Guide*, ed. Gary R. Edgerton (New York: Greenwood, 1988).

"free" programming provided by the networks.[2] When it became clear that film and television were in direct competition for the same audience, the members of the MPAA adopted a bunker mentality and until 1956 refused to sell or lease their product for broadcast—a strategy that in the long run may have hurt the industry financially more than either direct competition from television itself or the Paramount decrees. Furthermore, many studios contractually restrained their stars from appearing on television, which simply stimulated the new medium to develop star personalities on its own, and by 1949 the American film industry was seriously threatened by television. In that year, attendance dropped to 70 million, from 90 million in 1948, and it continued to decline in direct proportion to the number of television sets in use. In the first quarter of 1949, only twenty-two features, or half the normal number, were in production in Hollywood, and by the end of the year the major studios were ordering large layoffs and salary reductions, star contracts were being permitted to lapse, and all over the country the great movie palaces had begun to close their doors. In the wake of three years of unprecedented bad luck, a spiritual torpor descended upon Hollywood (some critics have speculated that the most manic of the late *film noirs* are unconscious reflections of this malaise). From the pinnacle of its creative and commercial power in 1946–47, the American cinema, assisted by labor disputes, antitrust actions, political investigations, and television, had been brought very low indeed, and in 1949 many people took it for granted that Hollywood could never recover its losses. But those who predicted the demise of Hollywood overlooked the American film industry's quintessential feature: its nearly protean capacity for adaptation. Though Hollywood was never to recover its immediate postwar status or to recapture its once vast audiences from television, in the decade of the 1950s it adapted, counterattacked, and—as always (to date, at least)—survived.

---

2. Paramount did, however, acquire a controlling share of the short-lived Dumont network (1945–55); and United Paramount Theaters, the 1,424-screen exhibition chain Paramount was forced to spin off in 1949 by the consent decrees, was merged with ABC from 1952 until 1978, when the broadcaster sold it to Plitt Theaters, Inc.

Color Technologies: A Brief Overview

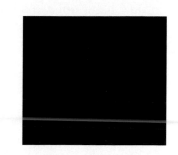

FOR EXTENSIVE DISCUSSIONS OF THE DEVELOPMENT OF COLOR FILM TECHNOLOGIES, SEE PAGES 214–221 AND 905–909.

Hand Coloring and Stencil Coloring

The earliest color in the cinema—used initially to create depth by making characters stand out from their monochrome backgrounds—was applied directly to positive film stock by hand. The first hand-colored films were probably Edison's *Butterfly Dance* (1895) and Robert W. Paul's *The Miracle* (1886), but it was Georges Méliès who rationalized the process by employing twenty-one young women at Madame Tuillier's workshop near Montreuil to hand-tint his prints. **1** Each frame was colored individually by workers who were responsible for a single tint; color was supplied by transparent aniline dyes (aniline is an organic synthetic substance that is highly toxic) diluted with water and alcohol. Together with several similar studios (Mademoiselle Rouillon's, Madame Vallouy's, and

1 Frames from two of Georges Méliès's hand-tinted films: *Le Chaudron infernal* (*The Infernal Cauldron*, 1903) and *Le Voyage à travers l'impossible* (*The Impossible Voyage*, 1904).

A. M. Fornelio's), Madame Tuillier supplied color to the entire French industry and employed about two hundred workers during her peak years. **2**

At the turn of the century, the laborious process of hand coloring was improved somewhat by the introduction of powerful magnifying lenses and extrafine sable brushes, but it still cost 50 percent more to produce a color print than a black-and-white one, and it was only viable at a time when films averaged about 50 feet (or 400m) in length and were released in limited quantities. Hand tinting was used selectively in some movies, such as Edwin S. Porter's *The Great Train Robbery* (1903), for sensational effect. **3**

In 1905, as the length of films and exhibitor demand both increased, Charles Pathé introduced the Pathécolor stencil process (renamed Pathéchrome in 1929), which

2 A contemporary photograph of hand-coloring operations at Madame Tuillier's workshop.

3 A frame from the conclusion of Edwin S. Porter's *The Great Train Robbery* (1903).

mechanized the application of color to positive prints. In it, frame-by-frame stencils were cut by pantograph, one shot at a time, to correspond to those areas to be tinted in any one of six standard colors. By 1910, Pathé had over four hundred women working in stenciling operations at its Vincennes plant, and the process was used in Europe well into the 1930s. **4** **5** **6** Another form of stenciling, based on the principles of three-color lithography, was patented in the United States by engraver Max Handschiegl and cinematographer Alvin Wyckoff in 1916 for the mechanized tinting of features at Famous Players–Lasky.

4 These frames from *The Golden Beetle* (Ferdinand Zecca, 1907) demonstrate the remarkable precision of the Pathécolor stencil process. Cinematography by Segundo de Chomón.

5 A frame from *King Lear* (Gerolamo Lo Savio, 1910), a production of Film d'Arte Italiana: Pathécolor stencil.

6 *Cyrano De Bergerac* (Augusto Genina, 1922; released 1925) represents the high-water mark of the Pathécolor stencil process. The film reputedly took nearly three years to color.

Chemical Tinting and Toning

The uniform coloring of film stock, or tinting, entered the cinema gradually between 1900 and 1908, as did toning, a technique for coloring only part of an image by subtracting silver halide (salts) from the emulsion sur- face of the film. Whereas tinting produced a uniform color throughout the frame, **7** **8** **9** toning colored only the halftones and shadows. From 1908 to 1925 tint- ing and toning became standard industry practice, so that fully 85 percent of total production contained some form of them. Tinting, toning, and hand coloring or stencil

7 *Nero, or the Fall of Rome* (1909), a one-reel epic showing early use of chemical tint-ing: Nero's vision of the burning city is uniformly colored in reddish burnt sienna.

8 A delicate shade of red, tending toward magenta, was used to tint disaster sequences in Mario Caserini's ten-reel super-spectacle *Gli ultimi giorni di Pompeii* (*The Last Days of Pompeii*, 1913).

coloring were sometimes used in combination to broaden the filmmakers' spectrum of creative options. **10** In general, however, producers followed a fairly conventional tinting code in which red was associated with "danger, fire, and love" (as one German colorist's manual had it); blue with the sea, rain, and darkness; green with nature; and sepia with interiors. Beyond that, color was often randomly applied to increase a scene's sensory appeal, with little or no attention paid to its context. Not surprisingly, given his many other innovations, D. W. Griffith made more elaborate use of tinting and toning than any of his peers. **11** **12** **13**

Hand coloring, stencil coloring, and tinting/toning were all means of artificially adding color to black-and-

9 An aquamarine tint suffuses an enchanted undersea chamber in *The Thief of Bagdad* (Raoul Walsh, 1924). Cinematography by Arthur Edeson.

10 Tinting combined with toning in *The Bells* (James Young, 1926). Lionel Barrymore is bathed in a ghastly green tint, with the snowflakes on his fur coat, buttons of his inner jacket, and highlights on his face and hair toned white; the highlights on the chest of drawers, vases, and flowers next to him are also toned white. Cinematography by L. William O'Connell.

white prints. But there had been early attempts to develop a "natural" or photographic color system in which color could be captured on negative stock as it occurs in nature. There, color is a function of the properties of light, whose spectrum of different wavelengths generates all colors through different combinations of the three primary ones—red, green, and blue. When mixed together equally, the primary colors produce white light, so that color can be created either by adding various measures of red, green, and blue, or by subtracting them from white light. Both additive and subtractive methods have been used to produce color photographically in film.

11 Two tinted frames from D. W. Griffith's *The Birth of a Nation* (1915): the sepia-tinted interior of the Cameron mansion evokes the "Old South"; a frame from the burning-of-Atlanta sequence is tinted an infernal red. Cinematography by Billy Bitzer.

12 Four frames from Griffith's *Intolerance* (1916): the attack on Babylon, uniformly tinted ocher yellow; the siege of the city, beginning in the glow of sunset; the siege, continuing into the night, accompanied by hellish flames of war and some yellowish hand-colored smoke; an interior from the Modern story evoking documentary photography. Cinematography by Billy Bitzer and Karl Brown.

13 Mood tints in *Broken Blossoms* (1919). A nocturnal shade of blue characterizes Limehouse at night; Cheng Huan (Richard Barthelmess) and Lucy Burrows (Lillian Gish) are bathed in rose pastel, suggesting the tenderness and fragility of their relationship. Cinematography by Billy Bitzer, Karl Brown, and Hendrik Sartov.

Photographic Color Systems: Technicolor

The earliest photographic color systems were additive—Charles Urban's two-color Kinemacolor (1909–15), Gaumont's three-color Chronochrome (1912–13), William V. D. Kelley's Prizmacolor (1917–18), and Herbert Kalmus's two-color Technicolor Process No. 1 (1915–17). All of these additive systems tended toward poor registration in projection, and several involved high-speed shooting and projection, which doubled the price of raw stock. Looking for a better color system, in 1922 Kalmus patented Technicolor Process No. 2, a two-color subtractive system that used a beam-splitting camera to produce two separate negatives that were printed separately as positives (or "relief prints") on extra-thin Kodak stock and cemented together base-to-base for projection. **14** **15** **16** This expensive but commercially viable process was improved in 1928 by Technicolor Process No. 3, in which the two relief prints

14 The box-office success of *Toll of the Sea* (Chester M. Franklin, 1922), the first feature shot in two-strip, two-color subtractive Technicolor (Process No. 2), demonstrated the commercial viability of the "cemented positive" process. Cinematography by J. A. Ball.

15 This frame from *The Phantom of the Opera* (Rupert Julian, 1925; rereleased 1929), whose spectacular Bal Masque sequence was shot by Virgil Miller, Charles Van Enger, and Milton Bridenbecker in Technicolor (Process No. 2), illustrates the color bias created by two-strip Technicolor's reliance on red and green to derive all other colors of the spectrum.

became matrices for the transfer of dyes to a third and final print through a chemical process known as imbibition, which became the basis for the Technicolor system in its various manifestations through the 1970s. Imbibition dye transfer made possible the mass production of release prints.

Technicolor's second subtractive system enjoyed a brief boom between 1929 and 1931. Since the system coin-cided with the coming of sound, producers had to look for an alternative to chemical tinting/toning because of its potential to interfere with optical sound tracks. Thus many early musicals have production numbers filmed in Technicolor Process No. 3. But the system had several drawbacks, the most important one being that it added 30 percent to overall production costs. Furthermore, like

16 *The Black Pirate* (Albert Parker, 1926), filmed entirely in Technicolor (Process No. 2) by Henry Sharp.

17 *The Garden of Allah* (Richard Boleslawski, 1936), shot in Technicolor's three-strip three-color system (Process No. 4) by W. Howard Greene and Hal Rosson, who won a special Academy Award for its cine-matography.

all two-color systems, it had poor registration of (Caucasian) flesh tones, which tended to print as deep pink or orange. So in 1932, Kalmus unveiled Technicolor Process No. 4, the three-color system that would virtually monopolize the production of color in film for the next twenty years. **17** **18** **19**

Three-strip Technicolor was the most accurate and stable system of photographic color reproduction in the history of film, and until cinema entered the digital realm, there would be nothing to match it. Until the mid-1950s, this system allowed the Technicolor Corporation to monopolize color film production in the United States

18 *Nothing Sacred* (William Wellman, 1937). Technicolor (Process No. 4) cinematography by W. Howard Greene.

and much of the world by requiring producers to rent its proprietary three-strip cameras, to hire Technicolor cameramen and "color consultants," and to use Technicolor makeup and Technicolor lab processing. In 1941, to reduce its costs to producers and to facilitate location shooting, Technicolor introduced Monopack—a multilayered negative stock based on Eastman Kodachrome that produced a direct color positive from exposure in a conventional 35 mm camera; this positive was then printed through red, green, and blue filters to create the color-separation matrices necessary for the Technicolor dye-transfer process. Monopack thus eliminated the bulky and expensive three-strip camera, but the laboratory fees remained constant. **20** **21**

19 *Gone with the Wind* (Victor Fleming, 1939), shot on fine-grain Technicolor stock by Ernest Haller and Ray Rennahan, assisted by Lee Garmes, Joseph Ruttenberg, and Wilfred Cline. Academy Award for Best Color Cinematography.

20 *Black Narcissus* (Michael Powell, 1947), shot by Jack Cardiff, Britain's leading Technicolor cinematographer. Academy Award for Best Color Cinematography.

21 *She Wore a Yellow Ribbon* (John Ford, 1949), Ford's second color feature, shot by Winton C. Hoch, demonstrated the range of Technicolor Monopack for both exteriors and interiors. Academy Award for Best Color Cinematography.

Photographic Color Systems: Eastmancolor

Concurrent with the arrival of three-strip Technicolor in Hollywood, a rival system was developed in Europe for use by the German industry—Agfacolor, a process invented by the Agfa Corporation in 1936 for 16mm applications; it employed a multilayered negative stock composed of photographic emulsions sensitive to red, green, and blue bonded together in a single roll of film. Modified for feature production, this "integral tripack" negative formed three color images simultaneously when exposed in a standard 35mm camera and, after development through a process know as dye-coupling, was printed onto a multi-layered positive stock for release; unlike Technicolor Monopack, specialized processing facilities were not required to produce Agfacolor prints. The first features shot in Agfacolor were the Nazi-inspired epics (*Die goldene Stadt* (*The Golden City* [Veit Harlan, 1940]), *Immensee* (*Immense* [Veit Harlan, 1943]), *Baron Munchhausen* (Josef von Báky, 1945), and *Kolberg* (Veit Harlan, 1945); and Sergei Eisenstein used captured Agfacolor stock to film the experimental color sequences of *Ivan the Terrible, Part II* (1945–46). **22** After the war and the release of Agfa's patents, integral tripack and dye-coupling became the technical basis for many single-strip color systems, including Sovcolor in the Soviet Union, Fujicolor in Japan, and Eastmancolor in the United States. This latter process was to replace Technicolor as the industry standard when it

22 *Ivan the Terrible, Part II* (Sergei Eisenstein, 1945–46) was shot by Eduard Tisse on Agfacolor stock liberated from German studios in Prague. Agfacolor became the model for Eastmancolor and other integral tripack systems.

23 *2001: A Space Odyssey* (Stanley Kubrick, 1968), shot in Metrocolor—a variant of Eastmancolor named after the releasing studio, MGM—by Geoffrey Unsworth; additional photography by John Alcott. British Academy Award for Best Cinematography.

incorporated "automatic color masking"—a principle already used successfully in Kodacolor film for still photography to compensate for dye deficiencies and to increase clarity and brilliance. [23] Requiring neither specialized cameras nor processing, Eastmancolor made color production the cost equivalent of black and white so that by 1979, 96 percent of all American features were being shot in color. Unfortunately, the colors produced by dye-coupling proved to be much less stable than those produced by imbibition, and films shot in Eastmancolor were subject to serious color fading—a problem insoluble until the era of digital color correction. [24] [25]

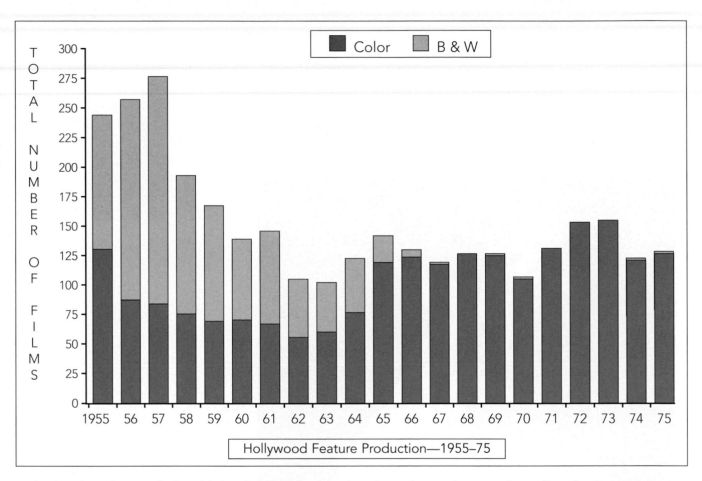

TOTAL NUMBER OF FILMS

Color   B & W

Hollywood Feature Production—1955–75

This chart shows the ratio of color to black-and-white cinematography in the production of American feature films after the introduction of Eastmancolor, the cost-effective single-strip process that replaced three-strip Technicolor as the industry standard. The dip in color production between 1956 and 1965 is due to the fact that television sales became a major source of revenue for Hollywood during that time and television was then broadcast almost exclusively in black and white. Producers could cut their costs and make their films more attractive to the television market by filming in black and white, which lost nothing in the translation from one medium to the other.

24 *Kismet* (Vincente Minnelli, 1955), shot in Eastmancolor and CinemaScope by Joseph Ruttenberg.

25 *Kwaidan* (Masaki Kobayashi, 1964). The Japanese were among the first to use Eastmancolor expressionistically. Cinematography by Yoshio Miyajima.

Desaturation through Forced Development and Flashing/Fogging

During the 1970s Eastman introduced several new color negative stocks that had high contrast, finer grain, and increased color saturation (brightness and luminance), qualities that work together to produce sharp, clean images.

But cinematographers who wanted darker images responded by desaturating them in two distinct ways. Some, like Gordon Willis (*The Godfather* [Francis Ford Coppola, 1972], *The Godfather, Part II* [Coppola, 1974]), "pushed" their negative in development to increase its speed and achieve a darker look. This process, known as "forced development," can also be observed in the work of director of photography Michael Chapman, who pushed night-rated film for *Taxi Driver* (Martin Scorsese, 1976) **26** and *Invasion of the Body Snatchers* (Philip Kaufman,

1978), **27** and Néstor Almendros, who did the same for *Days of Heaven* (1978) and whose exteriors were shot primarily in what director Terrence Malick called "the magic hour," the twenty to twenty-five minutes of light left after the sun has set. **28**

A similar laboratory procedure known as "flashing" or "fogging" was used by several other cinematographers during the 1970s. It involved exposing the negative briefly to white light in a printer before or after exposure to increase its speed and desaturate the color. The DP most closely associate with flashing in the 1970s was Vilmos Zsigmond, who used it to tone down the brilliant greens of the north Georgia mountains in *Deliverance* (John Boorman, 1972) **29** and to lend an old-fashioned, faded

26 Shooting *Taxi Driver* (Martin Scorsese, 1976), director of photography Michael Chapman "pushed" the night-rated Technicolor stock in development to capture the neon-lit night world so important to the movie's style and themes.

27 *Invasion of the Body Snatchers* (Philip Kaufman, 1978), another example of Chapman's "pushing" Technicolor stock in development.

quality (modeled on the paintings of Andrew Wyeth) to the images of *McCabe & Mrs. Miller* (Robert Altman, 1971) **30** and *Heaven's Gate* (Michael Cimino, 1980), for which he flashed both the negative and the print. **31** Haskell Wexler flashed nearly the entire negative of the Woody Guthrie biopic *Bound for Glory* (Hal Ashby, 1976) and used heavy lens diffusion to achieve a softening of shadows and pasteling of colors that evoke the atmosphere of the Oklahoma dust bowl during the Great Depression. **32**

28 *Days of Heaven* (Terrence Malick, 1978). Cinematography by Néstor Almendros; additional photography by Haskell Wexler.

29 *Deliverance* (John Boorman, 1972). Cinematography by Vilmos Zsigmond.

30 *McCabe & Mrs. Miller* (Robert Altman, 1971). Cinematography by Vilmos Zsigmond.

Nondigital Bleach-Bypass/Silver-Retention Processes

In the mid-1990s a variety of proprietary photochemical processes known as silver-retention, bleach-bypass, or skip-bleach processes served to produce darker, thicker negatives, which increased film grain, desaturated color, and rendered blacker blacks. This was the look that director David Fincher and DP Darius Khondji wanted for *Seven* (also known as *Se7en*, 1995), which was processed using a DeLuxe silver-retention process called CCE to create a dark, gloomy, menacing look. **33** Tim Burton and DP Emmanuel Lubezki chose the same CCE process for the horror fantasy *Sleepy Hollow* (1999) but with a different end: to evoke the black-and-white cinematography of Mario Bava's *Black Sunday* (*La Maschera del demonio*, 1960) in a gothic mise-en-scène recalling Hammer's lurid Eastmancolor horror films of the same period. **34** Bleach-bypass technology was used to represent the washed-out quality of light on a planet with three suns in *Pitch Black* (David Twohy, 2000), **35** to lend a raw, dusty immediacy to the Mexican sequences of *Traffic* (Steven Soderbergh, 2000), **36** and to create a sense of

33 *Seven* (also known as *Se7en*; David Fincher, 1995). Cinematography by Darius Khondji.

34 *Sleepy Hollow* (Tim Burton, 1999). Cinematography by Emmanuel Lubezki.

35 *Pitch Black* (David Twohy, 2000). Cinematography by David Eggby.

spiritual dryness in the theological horror film *Lost Souls* (Janusz Kaminski, 2000). **37** A unique approach to color manipulation was taken by director Josef Rusnak in *The Thirteenth Floor* (1999) **38** for sequences set in Los Angeles circa 1937. The film was shot on color stock and the negative processed to create both color and black-and-white interpositives from which a percentage of each (60 percent color, 40 percent black and white) was extracted and combined in the final printing to create a sort of "black and white in color."

36 *Traffic* (Steven Soderbergh, 2000). Cinematography by Peter Andrews.

37 *Lost Souls* (Janusz Kaminski, 2000). Cinematography by Mauro Fiore.

38 *The Thirteenth Floor* (Josef Rusnak, 1999). Cinematography by Wedigo von Schultzendorff.

Digital Manipulation of Color: Color Correction, Color Timing, and the Digital Intermediate Process

The digital intermediate process, also known as digital film mastering, refers to the process of scanning and color correcting an entire feature film in the computer. Kodak's Cinesite Digital Imaging became the first Hollywood-based facility to perform such a scan when it digitized approximately 100 minutes of *Pleasantville* (Gary Ross, 1998), **39** using a Philips Spirit DataCine scanner to achieve the selective desaturation of its color images, many of which were registered as black and white (the interpenetration of black-and-white with color imagery was central to the story con-

cept). Once that work had been done, the digital files were recorded directly onto 35mm color intermediate film to create a master for release prints. (This is the same technology that was once used to "colorize" black-and-white films and is now used to digitally restore older color films whose brilliance and color balance have been lost to fading.) Speaking of his experience with the digital intermediate process, *Pleasantville* DP John Lindley remarked, "There is a new player in town who can affect contrast, brightness and all the things that the cinematographer normally controls."

In the same vein, director Vincent Ward combined the digital intermediate process with new, image-based animation software to create the "Painted World" sequences of *What Dreams May Come* (1998), combining live actors with digitally created sets modeled on the style and actual works of nineteenth-century painters. **40** But the first digitally mastered film to attract wide-

39 *Pleasantville* (Gary Ross, 1998). Cinematography by John Lindley.

40 The "Painted World" of *What Dreams May Come* (Vincent Ward, 1998). Cinematography by Eduardo Serra.

spread attention was Joel and Ethan Coen's *O Brother, Where Art Thou?* (2000), for which the brothers wanted the look of old hand-tinted postcards—"a dry, dusty Delta look with golden sunsets," according to DP Roger Deakins. Furthermore, because the film was shot on location in Mississippi during the summer, Deakins faced the same problem of lush green foliage that Zsigmond had encountered on *Deliverance* twenty-eight years earlier. After considering several bleach-bypass processes, the Coens and Deakins decided to time the film digitally at Cinesite, toning down the greens and moderating overall saturation. **41** In the same year, *Mission to Mars* (Brian De Palma, 2000) and *Red Planet* (Anthony Hoffman, 2000) both used digital color correction to produce the reddish-orange glow of the Mars surface. **42** As of late 2003, some twenty-five U.S. theatrical features had been treated to the digital intermediate process—

mainly at Cinesite, Technique, and Efilm (a joint venture of Panavision and Deluxe Labs), although other laboratory and postproduction facilities were entering the field—to the point that, according to DP Newton Thomas Sigel (*Three Kings* [David O. Russell, 1999]; *Confessions of a Dangerous Mind* [George Clooney, 2002]), "the difference between film output through a traditional process and through a digital intermediate is almost indistinguishable." Interestingly, the effect that Clooney and Sigel wanted to achieve for *Confessions* through digital mastering was "a 21st Century version of hand-colored photography, where the actual color and relationship of the color to the objects wasn't necessarily real or naturalistic." This is a pretty fair definition of the digital intermediate process itself, reminding us that the more things change in the history of cinema, the more they stay the same.

41 *O Brother, Where Art Thou?* (Joel and Ethan Coen, 2000). Cinematography by Roger Deakins.

42 *Red Planet* (Anthony Hoffman, 2000). Cinematography by Peter Suschitzky.

Hollywood, 1952–1965

Much that characterized Hollywood between 1952 and 1965 can be understood as a response to anticommunist hysteria and the blacklist on the one hand and to the advent of television and economic divestiture on the other. In the name of combating communism, films directly critical of American institutions, such as the "problem pictures" and semidocumentary melodramas so popular in the immediate postwar years, could no longer be made. Instead, Westerns, musical comedies, lengthy costume epics, and other traditional genre fare—sanitized and shorn of explicit political and social referents—became the order of the day. Such films dominated the domestic market of the era both because their subject matter was uncontroversial and because their spectacular nature was suited to the new screen formats, which the studios had embraced to do battle with television and, simultaneously, to make their product more attractive to their former subsidiaries, the newly independent first-run exhibitors.

The Conversion to Color

Television threatened Hollywood with a new technology, and Hollywood fought back in kind by isolating and exploiting the technological advantages that film possessed over television. The cinema had two such advantages in the early 1950s, both of them associated with spectacle—the vast size of its images and the capacity to produce them in color.[1] (Soon, the capacity for stereophonic sound would be added to the list.) It was the

---

1. There was also—and still is—the question of image resolution. The television, or video, image is produced by (1) electronically breaking down the televised subject into 210,000 discrete picture elements, or "bits," and (2) transmitting or recording these bits as 525 (U.S. standards) or 625 (European standards) successive horizontal lines, at rates consistent with persistence of vision—thirty times per second by U.S. standards, twenty-five by European. The resolution of a video image is the product of the number of horizontal lines scanned for each complete picture and the number of successive pictures produced per second. (These pictures are called "frames," as in film, although they are *not* individual photographic =cells since they never exist as

competition with television that resulted in Hollywood's rapid conversion from black-and-white to color production between 1952 and 1955. In 1947 only 12 percent of American feature films were made in color; by 1954 the figure had risen to over 50 percent.[2]

The changeover was made possible by the breakup of Technicolor's de facto monopoly over color technology and aesthetics. The Justice Department had filed an antitrust suit against Technicolor and its supplier, Eastman Kodak in 1947 for monopolization of color cinematography. Even though yearly Technicolor production did not increase dramatically—from under twenty films in the early 1940s to over fifty in 1948—and rival processes such as Cinecolor and Trucolor were in general use, the company was judged to exercise a monopoly by virtue of its authoritarian control of the three-color process. In 1950, a federal consent decree ordered the corporation to set aside a certain number of its three-strip cameras for use by independent producers and minor studios on a first-come, first-served basis. But it was another event of that year, commercial introduction of a viable single-strip color process in Eastmancolor, that finally brought Technicolor's effective monopoly to an end.

First used experimentally in 1949, Eastmancolor was based on the German Agfacolor process invented for 16mm use by the Agfa Corporation in 1936. Like Technicolor Monopack, Agfacolor used a multilayered film stock, but the layers were composed of photographic emulsions sensitive to red, green, and blue bonded together in a single roll. This "integral tripack" negative formed three color images simultaneously and, after development through a process known as dye-coupling,[3] was printed onto a multilayered positive film for release. First used commercially in 1940, the process briefly became a jewel in the crown of Nazi cinema when it was used in such spectacular productions as *Die goldene Stadt* (*The Golden City*, Veit Harlan, 1942), *Immensee* (*Immense*, Veit Harlan, 1943), *Münchhausen* (Josef von Báky, 1945), and *Kolberg* (Veit Harlan, 1945; rereleased 1966). Eisenstein used Agfacolor stock captured from the studios of liberated Prague to film the color sequences of *Ivan the Terrible, Part II* (1945–46), and it became the technical basis for the Sovcolor system officially adopted by the Soviet industry during the 1950s (Sergei Yutkevich's *Othello* [1956] was the first major Sovcolor feature). After the war and the release of Agfa's patents, Agfacolor principles were also used in a number of Western systems, most notably Anscocolor, which had wide currency in Hollywood from 1953 to 1955 and appeared in such popular productions as *The Wild North* (Andrew Marton, 1953), *Kiss Me Kate* (George Sidney, 1953), *Seven Brides for Seven Brothers* (Stanley Donen, 1954), *The Student Prince* (Richard Thorpe, 1954), and *Brigadoon* (Vincente Minnelli, 1954). But it was Kodak's subtle refinement of integral tripack that permitted Eastmancolor to replace Technicolor as the dominant color system of the West (just as Fujicolor, another Agfa-based system introduced in 1955 in Japan, would replace it in the East).

Unlike Agfacolor, Sovcolor, or Anscocolor, Eastmancolor incorporated "automatic color masking," a principle already used successfully in Kodacolor still photography to enhance the clarity and brilliance of the final print. Eastmancolor was thus able to offer the industry a low-cost negative tripack stock capable of excellent color contrast, which could be shot through a conventional single-lens camera and processed in a conventional laboratory, just like black and white. When it was discovered simultaneously that imbibition printing did not yield enough resolution for the new anamorphic widescreen processes (see pp. 392–95), Technicolor's fate was sealed. In 1952, Kodak received an Academy Award for Eastmancolor (Scientific or Technical Award, Class I), and within two years the Technicolor three-strip camera and special processing service was rendered obsolete. (Technicolor cameras were used for the last time in the production of *Foxfire* [Joseph Pevney, 1955], but Technicolor continued its imbibition printing activities—sub-

---

complete images at any given moment.) When the promise of high-definition television (HDTV)—which scans more than 1,000 lines per frame and has a widescreen aspect ratio—is fulfilled, virtually every advantage that film once possessed over video will be lost.

2. Ironically, color production declined to about 25 percent of the total between 1955 and 1958, when Hollywood began to sell recent features to television, an important second market for its theatrical films. At this point, using black-and-white film became an effective way to cut production costs (at least for the television market) since almost all television broadcasts of the day were in black and white. But as American television converted to full-color broadcasting between 1965 and 1970, color films became an attraction for both the theatrical *and* the television market, causing Hollywood color production to increase dramatically until it reached 94 percent of the total by 1970.

3. The globules of dye in the different emulsion layers are coupled to silver grains, and their dyes are released during development of those grains.

sequently improved for use with widescreen—until 1975, using Eastmancolor negatives to produce its matrices.) Though the system has since come to be known by the trade names of the studios who pay to use it (Warnercolor, Metrocolor, Pathécolor) or the labs that do the processing (Movielab, Technicolor, Deluxe), it was Kodak Eastmancolor which inaugurated and sustained the full-color age with integral tripack and dye-coupler printing, and by 1975 even the Technicolor Corporation had converted to a printing process similar to Eastman's.[4] Since the 1950s, color has become an infinitely more subtle medium than black and white (which does *not* mean that black-and-white originals have anything to gain aesthetically from computerized colorization), and color cinematography has today reached an unparalleled degree of sophistication. By 1979, 96 percent of all American feature films were being made in color.

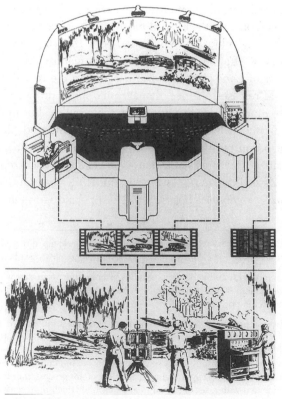

12.1 A schematic diagram of the multiple-camera Cinerama photography and projection process. Reprinted with permission of the University of California Press from *The Quarterly of Film, Radio, and Television*, 12, no. 2 (Winter 1956): 126.

Widescreen[5] and 3-D

MULTIPLE-CAMERA/PROJECTOR WIDESCREEN: CINERAMA

In a simultaneous attempt to exploit the *size* of the screen image, Hollywood began to experiment with new optical systems that lent greater width and depth to the image. The earliest of the new formats was a multiple-camera/projector widescreen process called **Cinerama,** introduced in September 1952, that was similar to the Polyvision process Abel Gance had used in *Napoléon* (1927) some twenty-five years before (see Chapter 9) and that was originally devised as a battle simulator for gunnery training during World War II by the inventor Fred Waller (1886–1954). In Cinerama, three synchronized 35mm cameras linked together in an arc would simultaneously record a wide-field image, which three similarly linked projectors would later cast upon a vast wraparound screen (actually a three-screen triptych). The projected image was thus three times as wide as the standard 35mm image; it was also nearly twice as tall because of two extra sprocket holes (six instead of four) per frame on the film strip.[6] The seams between the three images were concealed by a slight overlapping of

4. The problem with the Eastman-based systems, unforeseen at the time of their introduction and not manifest until a decade afterward, is that dye-coupling produces color much less stable (i.e., more subject to fading) than Technicolor's older imbibition process. (Ironically, the only Technicolor imbibition printing plant in operation in the world today is in the People's Republic of China.) While all color prints are subject to fading, most color films and negatives made in dye-coupler processes—that is, most American films made between 1955 and the present—are in imminent danger of extinction, and preserving them is the number-one problem facing film archivists today.

5. Several scholars (e.g., Bruce F. Kawin in *How Movies Work* [New York: Macmillan, 1987]) use the term "widescreen" to refer specifically to flat (i.e., nonprocessed) film formats with aspect ratios of 1.66:1 (European standard) or 1.85:1 (American standard), which are achieved by either masking 35mm film or using one of several wide-film systems. Here and throughout the book, I use the term more broadly to denote *all* formats that give a screen image wider than the Academy ratio of 1.33:1, whether processed or not. (See pp. 392–93.)

6. The Cinerama aspect ratio varied from 3:1 to 2.6:1; it covered a visual field that extended 146 degrees horizontally and 55 degrees vertically, approximating the cone of human sight (180 degrees horizontally and 90 degrees vertically). Furthermore, Cinerama was originally shot and projected at 26 fps to achieve crisper resolution and heighten the illusion of actuality.

the camera lenses and by floating metal combs in the projectors, a technique that never proved wholly satisfactory. Nevertheless, the Cinerama image was six times the standard size, and its curvilinear shape added the phenomenon of peripheral vision to the screen. Cinerama also surrounded its audience with seven-track stereophonic sound, recorded magnetically rather than optically on a separate strip of 35mm film, which permitted a directional use of sound appropriate to its sprawling image. All of these factors combined to create an illusion of depth and spectator involvement that was thrilling to audiences accustomed to the flat, rectilinear screen of decades past, and for a time Cinerama became immensely popular.

But the process was cumbersome and very expensive for both filmmaker and exhibitor, and therefore for the paying public. Only theaters in large cities could afford to install the complicated projection equipment and the huge three-panel screens (the installation cost $75,000), and so it was as a costly urban novelty that Cinerama enjoyed its initial success. Accordingly, it offered its audiences circuses rather than narrative. Films like *This Is Cinerama* (1952),[7] *Cinerama Holiday* (1955), *The Seven Wonders of the World* (1956), *Search for Paradise* (1957), *Cinerama South Seas Adventure* (1958), and *Windjammer* (1958—shot in a rival process called Cinemiracle, which had been bought out by the Cinerama Corporation) featured a succession of wild rides, extravagant spectacles, and exotic travelogues, but no stories. The first story films made in Cinerama, *How the West Was Won* (1962) and *The Wonderful World of the Brothers Grimm* (1962), proved that the multiple-camera process was simply too clumsy and costly for the production of conventional narratives.[8] *How the West Was Won*, for example, required the services of three directors (John Ford, Henry Hathaway, and George Marshall) and four cinematographers; it cost the then-staggering sum of $14 million to shoot.

In 1963, driven by economic necessity, Cinerama appropriated a single-lens wide-film widescreen system (Ultra Panavision 70) for its next film, *It's a Mad, Mad, Mad, Mad World* (1963), and finally adopted its own wide-film system, Super Cinerama, which, combined with a special elliptical projection lens, allowed it to keep and fill its deeply curved screen. Given its great expense and peculiar technology, multiple-camera Cinerama

never really had a chance of becoming a widely used process. At the height of its popularity, only a hundred cities all over the world were equipped to show Cinerama films. But the astounding success of Cinerama in the early 1950s was the catalyst that started the widescreen revolution and brought audiences back into the theaters again in large numbers for the first time since 1946. For this reason alone, Cinerama holds a special place in the history of film.

DEPTH: STEREOSCOPIC 3-D

Hollywood's next experiment with new optical formats was considerably less successful, although, like Cinerama, it was initially quite popular. Stereoscopic 3-D had precedents in the cinema's earliest days, when such pioneers as William Friese-Greene and the Lumières experimented with anaglyphic systems. In these, two strips of film, one tinted red and the other blue-green, were projected simultaneously for an audience wearing glasses with red and blue-green filtered lenses. The effect was stereoscopic synthesis in monochrome,[9] and experiments with anaglyphic 3-D continued into the 1920s, when Harry K. Fairall produced the first feature film, *The Power of Love* (1922), in the process. In the late 1930s, MGM released a series of anaglyphic shorts produced by Pete Smith under the title of "Audioscopiks," but in the meantime Edwin Land had developed polarized filters that permitted the production of full-color 3-D images. Polarized features using lenses developed concurrently by Zeiss Ikon, A. G., were produced in Italy in 1936 (*Nozze vagabone* [*Beggar's Wedding*]) and Germany in

---

7. Coproduced by Merian C. Cooper, with a prologue directed by Ernest B. Schoedsack—the creators of *King Kong* twenty years before.

8. In fact, to simplify logistics, portions of both films were shot with a single-camera 65mm system whose negative was optically divided into three 35mm positive prints for Cinerama projection.

9. In stereoscopy, as in reality, depth perception is a function of binocular vision: because our eyes function separately and are spaced apart, each has a slightly different perspective on the same image; the brain resolves the two images into a single one with a depth dimension. Stereoscopy depends upon photographic mimicry of this process: the viewer is presented with a set of paired images, each of which represents the angle of vision of the left or the right eye and is accessible to that eye only (e.g., through anaglyphasis, or polarization), so that the brain is forced to process the two images as a single three-dimensional one, even though both are flat.

12.2 A contemporary advertisement for *Kiss Me Kate* (George Sidney, 1953), giving a fanciful impression of 3-D illusion: Howard Keel and Kathryn Grayson. MGM.

1937 (*Zum Greifen Nah [You Can Nearly Touch It]*) and 1939 (*Sech Madel Rollen in Wochenend [Six Girls Drive into the Weekend]*), and the Chrysler Corporation presented a polarized 3-D short in Technicolor at the New York World's Fair in 1939 (also the site of "the Perisphere," Fred Waller's first multiple-camera/projector demonstration), but the war postponed further exploitation of the process.

In November 1952, however, the independent producer Arch Oboler (1909–1987) introduced a polarized

3-D process called Natural Vision, which had been invented by a team of opticians and camera engineers, in the Anscocolor feature *Bwana Devil*. In Natural Vision, two interlocked cameras whose lenses were positioned to approximate the distance between the human eyes recorded a scene on two separate negatives. In the theater, when the two positive prints were projected simultaneously onto the screen from the same angles as the camera lenses, spectators wearing disposable glasses with polarized lenses perceived them as a single three-dimensional image. Roundly trashed by reviewers, *Bwana Devil* nevertheless became a phenomenal box-office hit, and the studios were so impressed that most of them rushed into 3-D production, using either Natural Vision or some other stereoscopic process. As Arthur Knight points out, the great appeal of Natural Vision for Hollywood was that it required no large-scale conversion of existing equipment, as did Cinerama, but only the addition of a twin-lens Natural Vision camera. Similarly, the cost of projector installation to exhibitors was less than $2,000, a bargain compared with Cinerama's $75,000. The second Natural Vision feature, Warner Bros.' *House of Wax* (André De Toth, 1953; rereleased in 1971), featuring six-track stereophonic sound, was a critical as well as a popular success, returning $5.5 million on an investment of $680,000, and the race to produce "depthies," as the trade press was now calling them, became a stampede.

Between 1953 and 1954 Hollywood produced sixty-nine features in 3-D, mostly action films that could exploit the depth illusion—Westerns like *The Charge at Feather River* (Gordon Douglas, 1953) and *Taza, Son of Cochise* (Douglas Sirk, 1954), science-fiction films like *It Came from Outer Space* (Jack Arnold, 1953), and horror films like *Creature from the Black Lagoon* (Jack Arnold, 1954.)[1]

12.3 A 1953 audience wearing 3-D glasses.

1. *Creature from the Black Lagoon* was the first 3-D feature exhibited in a single-strip process with the two stereoscopic layers stacked one above the other in alternating frames. Such systems vastly simplified the projection of stereoscopic films and received considerable attention in the waning days of the 3-D craze. Today, all commercially viable systems rely on stacked imagery and single-projector polarization, whether they employ one or two cameras in the production process. Some mention should be made here of the Soviet lenticular stereoscopic system, known as Stereokino, perfected by S. P. Ivanov during the 1940s. This system, introduced to the public in the feature *Robinson Crusoe* (1946) and still used today, employs an intricately ribbed glass screen to reflect the left and right stereoscopic images into the corresponding eye of the viewer, and it requires no glasses.

The craze for stereoscopic 3-D reached its peak in June 1953, when Warners announced that two of its upcoming superproductions, *A Star Is Born* and *East of Eden*, would be shot in Natural Vision. In fact, the only (relatively) big-budget films made in 3-D turned out to be the independently produced *Hondo* (John Farrow, 1953; distributed by Warners'), Columbia's *Miss Sadie Thompson* (Curtis Bernhardt, 1953), MGM's *Kiss Me Kate* (George Sidney, 1953), and Warners' *Dial M for Murder* (Hitchcock, 1954), the latter two nationally released flat[2] in 1954 because the popularity of the process had taken a nosedive and Natural Vision suddenly had become, in the Hollywood phrase, box-office poison.

Stereoscopic 3-D died in that year for a number of reasons. One was that producers found it difficult to make serious narrative films in such a gimmicky process, although Hitchcock's work, as usual, was an exception. Most of the 3-D films of 1953–54 were blatant attempts to exploit the illusion of stereoscopic depth by having animals leap and people hurl objects into the Natural Vision camera lens. Another problem was that the illusion of depth created by 3-D was not particularly authentic or satisfying because the planes of depth within the image were highly stratified. Things appeared not in the round, as they do in a hologram,[3] but as a series of stratified two-dimensional planes. In fact, deep-focus widescreen photography is actually capable of producing a greater illusion of depth than stereoscopic 3-D. Also, people disliked wearing the polarized glasses necessary to achieve the 3-D effect; many complained of eyestrain and headaches. But the biggest single factor in 3-D's demise was probably the sweeping nationwide success in the fall of 1953 of a self-proclaimed rival, the anamorphic widescreen process patented by 20th Century–Fox as CinemaScope (see pp. 392–95). Though nonstereoscopic, this process exploited depth through peripheral vision and advertised itself to 3-D's disadvantage as "The Modern Miracle You See Without Glasses."

Attempts to revive 3-D in the last three decades have met with varying degrees of success. Arch Oboler's *The Bubble* (1966; rereleased as *Fantastic Invasion of Planet Earth*, 1976) was a commercial failure, but the 1969 softcore pornographic feature *The Stewardesses* (Alf Silliman) grossed $26 million and sparked an X-rated 3-D miniboom, culminating in *Andy Warhol's Frankenstein* (Paul Morrissey, 1974). Then, in the summer of 1981, the unexpected success of the independently produced West-ern *Comin' at Ya!* (Ferdinando Baldi) demonstrated the continuing popularity of 3-D with general audiences and led to the production of several mainstream Hollywood features in the process (*Friday the 13th, Part III*, Steve Miner; *Jaws* 3-D, Joe Alves—both 1983), whose commercial success proved that stereoscopic 3-D could once again sustain a pattern of wide general release. At about the same time, vintage 3-D films from the 1950s began to be broadcast over the air on commercial television. Today, the notion of an authentically three-dimensional cinema continues to fascinate filmmakers and audiences alike, as Hollywood's recent experiments with holographic photography and such nonstereoscopic 3-D processes as Showscan and Omnimax make clear. Furthermore, stereoscopic 3-D achieved a landmark of sorts with the production of *Wings of Courage* (Jean-Jacques Annaud, 1995)—the first feature in the giant-screen IMAX 3-D process, using cordless liquid-crystal glasses whose lenses are synchronized with the shutters of the dual-filmstrip projector by infrared signal.

THE ANAMORPHIC WIDESCREEN PROCESSES

The new optical format that came to stay during the war with television was **CinemaScope,** which arrived in September 1953 with 20th Century–Fox's biblical epic *The Robe* (Henry Koster). This system was based on the "Hypergonar" anamorphic distorting lens invented by Dr. Henri Chrétien (1879–1956) and first used in film as early as 1928 (in Claude Autant-Lara's *Pour construire un feu* [*Origins of Fire*]; released 1930). In it, a wide-field image is "squeezed" laterally by a cylindrical lens with a compression ratio of 2:1 onto conventional 35mm film stock and redeemed as a widescreen image by a compensating lens in projection. The conventional **aspect ratio** of the cinema screen (the ratio of width to height), known as the **Academy aperture,** had been standardized at 4:3, or 1.33:1, in 1932 by the Academy of Motion Picture Arts and Sciences.[4] CinemaScope offered a radically new ratio

---

2. Both have subsequently been rereleased in 3-D several times.

3. An image produced through holography—a process of photography that uses lasers to create perfect three-dimensional facsimiles of objects photographed.

4. This was done to achieve a uniform international standard for the gauge of sound film, although in practice most films had conformed to

12.4 When "unsqueezed" in projection, this close shot of Marilyn Monroe in Fox's CinemaScope production of *How to Marry a Millionaire* (Jean Negulesco, 1953) reveals distortion and lots of wasted space.

of 2.55:1 (approximately 8:3), subsequently reduced to 2.35:1, which gave the screen image a broadly oblong shape like that of Cinerama and similarly enhanced peripheral vision when used in combination with a curved screen. The process also featured four-track stereophonic sound recorded magnetically on the film strip, and it was aggressively marketed by Fox as a cost-effective alternative to both 3-D and Cinerama. CinemaScope had the distinct advantage of requiring no special cameras, film stock, or projectors, only special lenses, a metallized wide screen, and a four-track magnetic stereophonic sound system available in a package costing between $15,000 and $25,000, depending on the size of the theater (the price dropped considerably in July 1954 when Fox made the stereo equipment optional). Its initial disadvantages were a loss of picture brightness since standard projectors were designed to illuminate less than half the screen area required for widescreen (Fox's reflective Miracle Mirror screen helped to compensate for this loss by directing light into the useful seating area of the theater), and problems of geometrical distortion inherent in the early lenses manufactured by Bausch & Lomb. Because these were curved outward to extend their peripheries, objects in close-up appeared disproportionately large and horizon-

tal lines seemed to run the wrong way at the edges of the frame; distortion was also common in lateral movement across the frame and in tracking shots. Finally textures could become grainy and colors indistinct through the blowing-up process: the early **Scope** image was often described as fuzzy. Nevertheless, CinemaScope brought the widescreen revolution to the everyday world of functional filmmaking because, unlike Cinerama and 3-D, it was cheap, flexible, and simple enough to be used on a regular basis in the commercial cinema.

Most important, the public adored it. *The Robe* was an indifferent DeMille-like spectacle, but its box-office receipts of over $17 million in the year of its release made it the third most lucrative production in the history of American film, after *The Birth of a Nation* (1915) and *Gone with the Wind* (1939). Within the next few months, the anamorphic process took Hollywood by storm as Fox agreed to sell its CinemaScope lenses and conversion kits to rival production companies. At first, Fox president Spyros Skouras insisted that all CinemaScope productions be shot in full color and with four-track stereo, but he soon relaxed these conditions in order to accommodate smaller producers and exhibitors who could not afford to convert their sound systems.

By the end of 1953, every major studio in Hollywood except Paramount had been licensed to make CinemaScope films, 75 full-color anamorphic features were in production, and 5,000 theater installations had been performed. A year later the latter figure had tripled, and by 1957 CinemaScope had virtually saturated the market, with 84.5 percent of all U.S. and Canadian theaters (17,644 of 20,971) converted to the process. Indeed, the widescreen look had become so popular that films still shot in the old ratio of 1.33:1 were cropped for exhibition—that is, their tops and bottoms were masked in projection and the image was cast over a wider area of the screen, which was ultimately standardized at 1.85:1 in the United States and 1.66:1 in Europe. (This unfortunate practice forced directors working in the old format or, later, in VistaVision to compose shots "loose," so that action would be kept away from the top and bottom of

the 4:3 ratio since the early 1890s, when Edison standardized the width of theatrical film at 35mm. The Academy aperture is the aperture plate dimension 0.864 inches by 0.63 inches in printer and projector that produces the Academy ratio on-screen. The camera uses a full-screen aperture of 0.98 inches by 0.735 inches in order to create the largest possible negative for printing.

the frame. Many directors today, acutely aware that their widescreen films will eventually appear on television screens whose shape was modeled on the Academy frame, attempt to keep significant action in the midframe, "TV-safe," or "safe-action," area, which imposes similar artistic constraints.)[5] In the next few years, a great many problems with the CinemaScope system were solved. The aspect ratio was reduced from 2.55:1 to 2.35:1, which gave the image more visual density in projection,[6] and the anamorphic lenses were consistently improved to give a sharper and clearer screen image.

In 1960, Robert E. Gottschalk invented the variable prismatic **Panavision** lens, which offered a nearly distortion-free definition of image to anamorphic films, and Panavision gradually replaced CinemaScope as the leading anamorphic system. Today it is practically the only process used in 35mm widescreen cinematography.[7] By the mid-1950s, the conversion to anamorphic widescreen films in America was nearly total, and the process spread rapidly to other parts of the world as foreign audiences found themselves suddenly confronted by a bewildering array of "scopes." In 1956 alone, France introduced Franscope and Dyaliscope, Italy contributed Ultrascope and Colorscope, Sweden Agascope, the USSR Sovscope, and Japan Tohoscope, Daieiscope, and Nikkatsuscope; all were variations of the CinemaScope system.

There was a single holdout in Hollywood, however. Paramount had refused to adopt an anamorphic process on the advice of its technicians, who said that the squeezing and blowing-up process would debase the visual quality of the image. They also thought that the ribbonlike CinemaScope image was too long and narrow to permit good composition. Accordingly, in April 1954 in *White Christmas* (Michael Curtiz), Paramount introduced its own widescreen system called **Vista Vision.** This was a unique nonanamorphic process in which 35mm film stock was run through the camera horizontally rather than vertically to produce a double-frame negative (eight sprocket holes per frame) twice as wide as the conventional 35mm frame, and slightly taller. The negative was then optically rotated 90 degrees in the printing process so that the positive prints could run vertically on any projector. (Vista Vision films were occasionally shown full-frame on horizontal transport projectors—as, for example, at the system's premiere at Radio City Music Hall, where *White Christmas* appeared on a giant 55-by-30-foot screen—but the normal practice was to reduce the image in printing to standard 35mm stock, increasing not its size but its density.) The Vista Vision aspect ratio was variable from 1.33:1 to 1.96:1 and could, therefore, accommodate any theater, but Paramount recommended projection in the "golden

---

5. The shape of the American television screen, standardized by the FCC in 1939, was and is modeled on the Academy frame so that all widescreen films lose image space when shown on TV or released on videotape or videodisc, often as much as 50 percent. To restore lost visual information, video technicians commonly employ a process known as "panning and scanning" that follows significant dramatic action back and forth across the width of the frame, in effect redirecting the film and creating camera movement that wasn't originally there. (At first, scanning was performed optically with a telecine converter; today, it is done electronically by a flying-spot scanner that scans each frame line by line for translation as a video image.) Worse, in scenes where side-to-side action or dialogue occurs too rapidly for scanning to follow, technicians resort to cutting from one side of the frame to the other as if they were separate shots. In either case, the original composition and structure of the image is badly compromised. Furthermore, title and credit sequences of anamorphic films are usually shown squeezed on television, so that their printed matter will remain within the borders of the screen. Add to this the fact that a film's light levels, color balance, and sound values all must be adjusted for the conditions of electronic transmission and in-home viewing, and you will have a good sense of how different the experience of watching a film in video format can be from a theatrical screening. In this light, in fact, the threat of colorization becomes one more step in the long-term process of the degrading of

the filmic image in the name of "enhancing" it for television. See John Belton, "Pan and Scan Scandals," *Perfect Vision* 1, 3 (Indian Summer 1987): 40–49.

6. The immediate reason for the change was to provide space on the film strip for a combined magnetic and optical sound track in response to exhibitor demand. In the original CinemaScope system, stereophonic sound was recorded on four magnetic tracks running on either side of the perforations, which were reduced in size to accommodate them. In July 1954, under pressure to lower installation costs, Fox agreed to make its features available in a choice of four-track magnetic, single-track magnetic, or single-track optical sound, which, of course, meant striking three separate prints per film. By 1956, however, only 4,609 of the 17,591 CinemaScope theaters in America had converted to magnetic sound. So in June of that year, Fox announced that it would release all future product with both magnetic *and* optical tracks, requiring a 10 percent reduction in picture area per print.

7. Panavision's success stemmed from its resolving many of Cinema-Scope's optical problems. For one thing, its images are better illuminated because the system uses a smaller picture area (the Academy aperture) for its squeeze and reduces its aspect ratio to 2.25:1. Furthermore, Panavision eliminated CinemaScope's wide-angle distortion almost entirely through the use of highly curved spherical lenses.

ratio" of 1.85:1 to achieve a modified widescreen effect. The enhanced picture resolution and clarity produced by Vista Vision's larger negative was immediately apparent to audiences, and exhibitors liked the system because it required no modification of existing equipment. Vista Vision films were released in Perspecta sound, an audio process that used a single optical track for playback through a conventional single speaker but that could be combined with a Perspecta Sound Integrator to produce a simulated stereo effect through three horns. The Perspecta Sound Integrator and speakers cost less than half the price of Fox's four-track stereo, and the process was a highly effective marketing tool for Paramount among exhibitors. (In fact, it was competition from Vista Vision and Perspecta sound that initially caused Fox to make CinemaScope prints available in both magnetic and optical versions.) Paramount continued to use the Vista Vision process throughout the decade. In 1961, following the release of *One-Eyed Jacks* (Marlon Brando), the studio converted to the perfected Panavision anamorphic process for financial reasons, but Vista Vision is still used extensively today in optical special-effects work.

THE NONANAMORPHIC, OR WIDE-FILM, WIDESCREEN PROCESSES

As theater screens grew increasingly large in response to public demand (many measuring three to four times their original size), one of the reasons for Paramount's dissatisfaction with CinemaScope became apparent. The anamorphic image cast on a 60-by-30-foot screen lost clarity and brightness because its visual information was distributed across too large a field through the magnification process. The only technical answer to this problem was to increase the actual width of the film stock itself so that it would correspond to the wide field of the camera lens. Then the visual information from the photographic field and the visual information recorded on the negative film stock would be approximately proportional in scale, and the positive print would reproduce the density of the photographic field in projection. But the introduction of wide-gauge film would require special wide-gauge projectors, and the studios were loath to force another expensive conversion upon the exhibitors, with whom relations had become increasingly strained since the Paramount decrees of 1948 (see Chapter 11). One way to meet the problem was to shoot a wide-film negative and

reduce it photographically to 35mm for projection, which would increase the visual density of the image without altering its shape. This was the method used most often by Vista Vision and Fox's experimental wide-film process, CinemaScope 55.[8]

Nevertheless, in 1955 a 70mm wide-film process was introduced to selected American theaters in a film version of the 1943 Rodgers and Hammerstein Broadway hit *Oklahoma!* (Fred Zinnemann), independently produced by Michael Todd (1909–1958). The process, called Todd-AO, was developed by the American Optical Company and designed to compete not only with CinemaScope, but with Cinerama as well since its wide-gauge film and wide-angle lenses offered the wraparound visual coverage of that process without resorting to its multiple cameras and projectors. Designed for running at 30 fps to enhance its resolution, Todd-AO proved to be a beautifully precise optical system, and *Oklahoma!*, which also featured six-track stereophonic sound, was a huge financial success. (The Todd-AO negative was 65mm; the projection print was 70mm, with the extra 5mm carrying the six magnetic sound tracks, plus a seventh for audio control.) Todd produced two more blockbusters using the process—the elephantine *Around the World in 80 Days* (Michael Anderson, 1956)[9] and the spectacularly garish *South Pacific* (Joshua Logan, 1958)—then died in a plane crash in 1958. Fox purchased the rights to the system at that time and produced eight films in Todd-AO thereafter, including the multimillion-dollar *Cleopatra* (1963) and *The Sound of Music* (1965).

Other wide-film systems developed simultaneously with Todd-AO were Super Panavision (aka Panavision 70), which used an unsqueezed 65mm negative for projection in either a 35mm or 70mm format, and Ultra Panavision 70 (originally called MGM Camera 65 when introduced in 1956), which combined anamorphic and wide-gauge

---

8. Introduced in 1955 and used in only two productions (*Carousel* [Henry King, 1956] and *The King and I* [Walter Lang, 1956]), CinemaScope 55 was an anamorphic system that used a 55mm negative for striking 35mm prints. The squeeze ratio was the same as for standard CinemaScope, 2:1, but reducing the image size increased grain and definition, rendering a vastly improved picture in projection.

9. Todd had *Oklahoma!* and *Around the World in 80 Days* shot simultaneously in both 65mm Todd-AO and 35mm CinemaScope, using dual camera setups. He took this unusual step to insure that 35mm anamorphic prints of the films would be available to the many theaters that had not yet converted to 70mm projection.

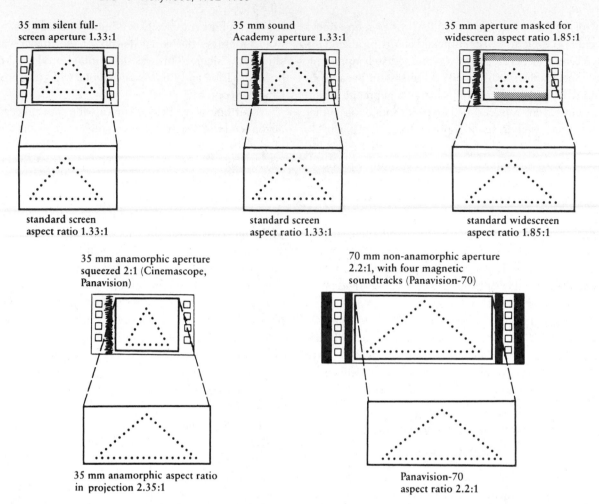

35 mm silent full-screen aperture 1.33:1

35 mm sound Academy aperture 1.33:1

35 mm aperture masked for widescreen aspect ratio 1.85:1

standard screen aspect ratio 1.33:1

standard screen aspect ratio 1.33:1

standard widescreen aspect ratio 1.85:1

35 mm anamorphic aperture squeezed 2:1 (Cinemascope, Panavision)

70 mm non-anamorphic aperture 2.2:1, with four magnetic soundtracks (Panavision-70)

35 mm anamorphic aspect ratio in projection 2.35:1

Panavision-70 aspect ratio 2.2:1

12.5 A schematic diagram of standard film gauges and screen aspect ratios for silent, sound, and widescreen cinema. Please note that, with the exception of 12.7, all of the widescreen stills in this chapter have been cropped for publication. This practice will be duly noted in subsequent chapters, where it occurs.

principles to squeeze a wide-field image onto 65mm stock (the squeeze ratio was only 1.25:1; but since the picture area was already 2.25:1, the 70mm anamorphic positive projected an image with the enormous aspect ratio of 2.75:1, which was perfect for epic spectacle but probably not much else—MGM's gargantuan *Mutiny on the Bounty* [1962], e.g., used this process). All of these other wide-film systems, however, were subject to the same limitations as Todd's process. Wide-film cameras are bulky (at least twice the normal size) and difficult to move, especially since wide-angle lenses are subject to distortion in panning. And, like Cinerama, the wide-film processes are very expensive to use; film stock, shooting, processing, exhibition (often at a higher than normal frames-per-second rate)—everything—costs about twice as much as it would in a conventional 35mm film. For these reasons, the wide-film systems and Cinerama in the 1960s were used almost solely for spectacular productions like *Spartacus* (Stanley Kubrick, 1960), *El Cid* (Anthony Mann, 1961), *Lawrence of Arabia* and *Doctor Zhivago* (David Lean, 1965), *Grand Prix* (John Frankenheimer, 1966), and *2001: A Space Odyssey* (Stanley Kubrick, 1968), which could be "road-shown"—toured from city to city for exclusive engagements at inflated admission prices to recoup high production costs. For general release, such films were usually reduced to 35mm prints for anamorphic projection. Wide-film systems continue to provide the most optically flawless widescreen image, but today it is rare for films to be shot in a 65mm negative because of the expense. Instead, the vast majority of widescreen films—which is to say the vast majority of films—are either made in an anamorphic process or shot in 35mm and blown up to 70mm prints for special showing through such processes as Super Technirama 70.

An important footnote to the coming of the widescreen processes is that it produced a nearly total conversion from optical to magnetic sound recording (though sound was still played back optically in exhibition). As already noted, most early widescreen films—whatever their process—were accompanied by multiple-track stereophonic sound recorded magnetically either on a separate strip (Cinerama) or on the film strip itself (CinemaScope, Todd-AO, etc.). Multiple-track stereo not only inundated the audience with realistic sound and enhanced the illusion of depth, but allowed early widescreen filmmakers to use sound *directionally* by having dialogue and naturalistic effects emanate from that portion of the huge screen appropriate to the image at a given moment. Thus, stereophonic sound permitted a director to differentiate aurally what was often undifferentiated visually within the vast space of the early widescreen frame. As we have seen, most theaters outside of large cities could not afford the conversion to stereophonic speaker systems in the 1950s, and even today many still use optical playback equipment only. But after the widescreen revolution, magnetic sound became the preferred means of recording and mixing in all segments of the industry because of its flexibility, its accuracy, and the compactness of its equipment. By the late 1970s, the use of a wireless eight-track recording system that employs miniature radio microphones and the **Dolby** noise reduction system (see Chapter 20) for playback in exhibition was increasingly common.

ADJUSTING TO WIDESCREEN

The advent of the widescreen processes in many ways parallels the introduction of sound. Once again, a financially troubled industry gambled on a novelty long implicit in the medium, and once again the novelty produced a technological and aesthetic revolution that changed the narrative form of the cinema. Like sound, widescreen photography presented many difficulties to filmmakers used to an older mode of production. Close-

ups were suddenly problematic, given the vast size of widescreen images and the tendency of early anamorphic lenses to distort them. Even undistorted, on a 60-foot screen close-ups frequently appeared ludicrous, menacing, or both, which made critics wonder whether intimate scenes would be possible in the widescreen medium at all. Montage became problematic for the same reason: the perceptual disorientation produced by the rapid intercutting of widescreen images was less exciting than simply confusing. Focal shifts and tracking shots were similarly subject to distortion. Finally, composition and lighting for the widescreen image were difficult for directors and camera operators accustomed to the 4:3 rectangle of the Academy frame. Because early anamorphic lenses had short focal lengths (and, therefore, shallow depth of field), for example, deep focus composition was initially out of the question. There was, moreover, the purely practical problem of how to fill and balance all that newly available space. For these reasons, many felt that the widescreen processes would destroy the cinema as an art form, and it is true that, like the first sound films, the first widescreen films were static and theatrical, with a heavy-handed emphasis on spectacle.

But as widescreen filmmaking practices and optics were refined throughout the 1950s and into the 1960s, it became apparent that many of the initial assumptions about the limitations of widescreen were false. With certain stylistic modifications, close-ups and montage were not only possible, but more effective in widescreen than in the old format; intimate scenes *could* be played with total authenticity in widescreen; and the cinema did *not* ultimately succumb to circus spectacle as a result of its new shape and size. For one thing, a director using widescreen could bring his characters into a tight close-up without eliminating the background and middleground of the shot, as often happened in Academy ratio close-ups of the 1930s and 1940s. He could also have two or even three speaking characters in close-up, with ample space between their faces, instead of having to cut back and forth from one to the other or to squeeze them together artificially within the narrow borders of the Academy frame. Furthermore, with the introduction of distortion-free variable-focus Panavision lenses in the early 1960s, it became clear that widescreen could greatly enhance the image's capacity for depth (and thus for spectator involvement) as well as width, due to increased peripheral vision. Whereas early widescreen pioneers like Otto

12.6 Widescreen potential: dialogue in close-up without cutting in *The Wild Bunch* (Sam Peckinpah, 1969, Panavision). William Holden, Ernest Borgnine.

12.7 Using widescreen to link character and environment: *Rebel without a cause* (Nicholas Ray, 1955) and *Wild River* (Elia Kazan, 1960). James Dean; Jo Van Fleet. CinemaScope.

Preminger (*River of No Return*, 1954), Elia Kazan (*East of Eden*, 1955), and Nicholas Ray (*Rebel without a Cause*, 1955) had been able to exploit compositional depth only by pushing against the limits of their technology (by using big, brightly lit sets or by shooting out of doors in direct sunlight, for example, which enabled them to stop down their lens apertures), by the mid-1960s, for all practical purposes, the deep-focus capacity that Welles and Toland had labored so hard to attain in *Citizen Kane* (1941) had suddenly become available to any director who possessed the imagination to use it. Finally, for a variety of reasons, widescreen encouraged the use of longer-than-average takes, and it seems clear today that the widescreen processes created the functional grounds for a new film aesthetic based upon composition in width and depth, or *mise-en-scène*, rather than upon montage.

In this new aesthetic, which might be called the long-take, or *mise-en-scène*, aesthetic, the major emphasis would shift from editing to shooting since a long take composed in width and depth is capable of containing a long shot, medium shot, and close-up, action and reaction, within a single frame without resorting to fragmentation of the image. At least one veteran Hollywood director recognized this as early as 1955. In an interview with the British film journal *Sight and Sound*, Henry King said: "This lens [the anamorphic] enables the director . . . for the first time to show on the screen cause and effect in the same shot, whereas before we used to have to *cut* from cause to effect in a story" (my italics). Obviously, film narratives would continue to be assembled through the editing process, but the primary unit of narration would no longer be the dialectical shot (or "montage cell," in Eisenstein's phrase) but the long take or sequence shot composed in width and depth and/or constantly moving

to reframe significant dramatic action. Theorists of the long-take aesthetic like André Bazin and his follower Charles Barr would later maintain (in *Cahiers du cinéma* and the British journal *Movie*, respectively) that the long take preserves the integrity of time and space by linking foreground, middle ground, and background within the same shot, whereas montage destroys it. The close-up is a case in point (ironically, since early critics thought widescreen incapable of close-ups). In montage, the figure in close-up is divorced from its background by virtue of both focal limitations and the rapidity with which images flash upon the screen. In the long-take close-up, the figure in close-up is temporally and spatially linked with its environment by virtue of the shot's *mise-en-scène*, and for Bazin and Barr, at least, this constitutes a more authentic mode of representation than the dissociated close-up of montage.

According to the long-take theorists, montage evolved over time because it was the first technologically feasible way to structure film, or to give it "speech." But in the 1950s and 1960s, they argued, the technology of cutting was usurped by the technology of shooting, so that the radical fragmentation of montage could be replaced by the organization of complex images within the frame. This is certainly true to the extent that the widescreen image, composed in depth, is capable of containing much more visual information than the old Academy frame, and its greater visual density makes it the perfect medium for rendering detail, texture, and atmosphere in relation to character. Finally, both Bazin and Barr insisted that the width and depth perspective created by the widescreen long take offers the viewer a "democratic" and "creative" alternative to the manipulative process of montage. Though shot composition can guide his or her seeing to some extent, they reasoned, the viewer of a long take can choose which details or actions to concentrate upon within a given shot,[1] rather than have them pointed out to him or her by close-ups or be drawn to some inexorable conclusion through a montage sequence like Eisenstein's massacre on the Odessa steps. Although montage was the traditional aesthetic of the cinema, extending from Griffith through Eisenstein to the classical Hollywood paradigm of the studio years, Bazin and his followers were able to construct a historical countertradition for the long-take aesthetic stretching back to Feuillade and including the "integral style" of von Stroheim and Murnau, the deep-focus "realism" of Renoir and Welles, and the postwar neorealism of Rossellini and De Sica. According to this version of film history, Welles began the revolution in favor of the long take with *Citizen Kane* in 1941, and the arrival of widescreen technology in the early 1950s assured its permanent success. As a corrective to the influence of Soviet-style montage and three decades of classical Hollywood continuity editing, the Bazinian view was healthy, if impressionistic (overlooking, e.g., the integration of montage and *mise-en-scène* in *both* Griffith and Welles). But in any case, it took the widescreen aesthetic yet another decade to evolve, and the years 1953–60, like the years 1928–35, witnessed much experimental blundering before the major artists of the new form of cinema could emerge.

THE WIDESCREEN "BLOCKBUSTER"

In Hollywood, the emergence of a widescreen aesthetic was delayed by the sudden proliferation of a venerable film type known as the "blockbuster,"[2] newly renovated to exploit the physical novelty of the big screen. These inflated multimillion-dollar productions were the widescreen counterparts of the "100 percent all-talking, all-singing, all-dancing" films of the early sound period— lavish and excessively lengthy superspectacles in the DeMille tradition, every element of which was made to subserve sheer visual magnitude. The blockbuster craze started in 1956 when King Vidor's *War and Peace* (Vista Vision; 3 hours, 28 minutes), Michael Anderson's *Around*

12.8 The "democratic" perspective of widescreen, preserving the integrity of real time and space: *Bad Day at Black Rock* (John Sturges, 1955, CinemaScope). Spencer Tracy.

1. The classical example of this laissez-faire composition for the long-take theorists was the raft sequence in Preminger's *River of No Return* (1954), described here by V. F. Perkins: "As Harry . . . lifts Kay from the raft, she drops the bundle which contains most of her 'things' into the water. Kay's gradual loss of the physical tokens of her way of life has great symbolic significance. But Preminger is not overimpressed. The bundle simply floats away offscreen while Harry brings Kay ashore. It would be wrong to describe this as understatement. The symbolism is in the event, not in the visual pattern, so the director presents the action clearly and leaves the interpretation to the spectator." (*Film as Film: Understanding and Judging Movies* [Baltimore: Penguin, 1972], p. 80.)

2. A term traditionally used in Hollywood to designate any large-scale, big-budget production. *Intolerance* (1916) and *Gone with the Wind* (1939) were both called "blockbusters" in their day. The term now means a film that earns more than $100 million.

12.9 A shot from the chariot race in the blockbuster *Ben-Hur* (William Wyler, 1959, MGM Camera 65): Charlton Heston.

12.10 *Lawrence of Arabia* (David Lean, 1962, Super Panavision; restored and rereleased, 1989): exploiting the new width and depth for spectacle. Peter O'Toole.

the World in 80 Days (Todd-AO; 2 hours, 58 minutes), and C. B. DeMille's remake of his own *The Ten Commandments* (VistaVision; 3 hours, 39 minutes) were all released simultaneously in wide-film widescreen processes and full stereophonic sound. Because the production costs for blockbusters were abnormally high, the films had to have a correspondingly high box-office gross simply to break even, and this factor, combined with their artistic unwieldiness, would ultimately destroy them. But for a while they reigned supreme. *Around the World in 80 Days*, for example, which cost $6 million to produce, grossed over $22 million in the year of its release, and *The Ten Commandments*, which cost $13.5 million, grossed nearly $43 million.

Other major blockbusters of the era were Joshua Logan's *South Pacific* (1958— Todd-AO; 3 hours), William Wyler's *Ben-Hur* (1959—

MGM Camera 65; 3 hours, 37 minutes), Stanley Kubrick's *Spartacus* (1960—Super Technirama 70; 3 hours, 16 minutes), Otto Preminger's *Exodus* (1960— Super Panavision; 3 hours, 33 minutes), Anthony Mann's

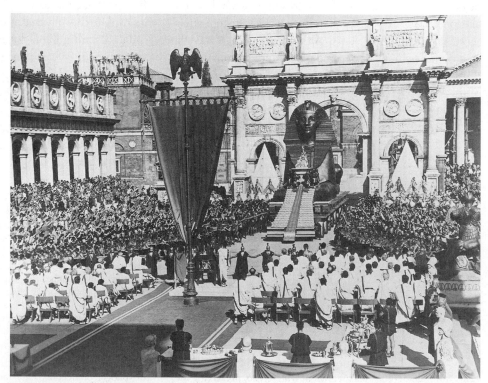

12.11 A scene from *Cleopatra* (Joseph L. Mankiewicz, 1963, Todd-AO), the blockbuster that nearly sank 20th Century–Fox.

El Cid (1961—Super Technirama 70; 3 hours, 6 minutes), Lewis Milestone's *Mutiny on the Bounty* (1962—Ultra Panavision; 3 hours, 5 minutes), and David Lean's *Lawrence of Arabia* (1962—Super Panavision; 3 hours, 42 minutes—rereleased in 1989 in its original 70mm format, restored and recut by Lean, at 3 hours, 36 minutes). By the early 1960s, production budgets for blockbusters had grown so large through inflation that most were produced abroad in Italy (by Dino De Laurentiis at Rome's Cinecittà studios), Spain (at Samuel Bronston's vast studio complex on the outskirts of Madrid), and Yugoslavia (at the Zagreb studios) to cut costs. Even so, many—such as *El Cid*, *Mutiny on the Bounty*, and Nicholas Ray's *55 Days at Peking* (1963—Super Technirama 70)—went down to ruin at the box office, alerting producers to the fact that the blockbuster trend had exhausted itself with the public. But the film that demonstrated this most graphically was Joseph L. Mankiewicz's disastrous *Cleopatra* (1963—Todd-AO; 4 hours, 3 minutes), which took four years and $40 million to produce, nearly wrecking 20th Century–Fox. This film had returned only half of its negative costs by 1964 and did not break even until its sale to network television in 1966. Other blockbusters have been made since, including the fantastically successful *The Sound of Music* (Robert Wise, 1965) and *Dr. Zhivago* (David Lean, 1965), but few were able to recover their production costs before sale to television, and producers turned away from the blockbuster policy until it was revived, with substantial modifications, in the mid-seventies.

12.12 Composition for widescreen: *Wild River* (Elia Kazan, **1960, CinemaScope) and** *Exodus* (Otto Preminger, 1960, Super **Panavision). Both films were conventional narratives distinguished by their creative use of the widescreen frame.**

AMERICAN DIRECTORS IN THE EARLY WIDESCREEN AGE

Some American films that are notable for their early innovative use of widescreen are Otto Preminger's *River of No Return* (1954), *Carmen Jones* (1954), *Bonjour Tristesse* (1958), and *Exodus* (1960; Panavision 70); George Cukor's *A Star Is Born* (1954) and *Bhowani Junction* (1956), William Wellman's *Track of the Cat* (1954); John Sturges's *Bad Day at Black Rock* (1995); Elia Kazan's *East of Eden* (1955) and *Wild River* (1960); Nicholas Ray's *Rebel without a Cause* (1955), *The True Story of Jesse James* (1957), *Bitter Victory* (1958), and *Party Girl* (1958); Douglas Sirk's *Magnificent Obsession* (1954), *All That Heaven Allows* (1955), *Written on the Wind* (1956), *Battle Hymn* (1956), and *The Tarnished Angels* (1958);

Robert Aldrich's *Vera Cruz* (1954) and *The Angry Hills* (1959); John Huston's *Heaven Knows, Mr. Allison* (1957), *The Barbarian and the Geisha* (1958), and *The Roots of Heaven* (1958); Bud Boetticher's *Ride Lonesome* (1959) and *Commanche Station* (1960); Anthony Mann's *The Man from Laramie* (1955), *The Last Frontier* (1955), *Man of the West* (1958), and *El Cid* (1961; Super Technirama 70); Stanley Donen's *Seven Brides for Seven Brothers* (1954) and *It's Always Fair Weather* (1955); Vincente Minnelli's *Brigadoon* (1954), *Kismet* (1955), *The Cobweb* (1955), *Lust for Life* (1956), *Some Came Running* (1959), and *Home from the Hill* (1960); Samuel Fuller's *Hell and High Water* (1954) and *China Gate* (1957); Richard Quine's *My Sister Eileen* (1955) and *Strangers When We*

Meet (1960); Richard Fleischer's *20,000 Leagues under the Sea* (1954), *The Girl on the Red Velvet Swing* (1955), *Violent Saturday* (1955), *Bandido* (1956), *The Vikings* (1958), and *Barrabas* (1962; Technirama 70); and Sam Peckinpah's *Ride the High Country* (1962). Nearly all of these films were shot in CinemaScope or Panavision, and some are obviously less important in themselves than for their purely formal achievements but most of their directors were major talents who made other significant films during the 1950s and early 1960s. As usual, Hitchcock was different: his work in Vista Vision—*To Catch a Thief* (1955), *The Trouble with Harry* (1955), *The Man Who Knew Too Much* (1956), *Vertigo* (1958), and *North by Northwest* (1959)—formed a category unto itself, with *Vertigo* standing as the single greatest film of the 1950s and perhaps of the entire postwar American cinema.

In addition to pioneering widescreen composition, Otto Preminger (1906–1986), who had made his first film in Vienna in 1932 and emigrated to Hollywood in 1936, made major contributions to the social history of American film by breaking both the Production Code (with *The Moon Is Blue* [1953], a sex farce; *The Man with the Golden Arm* [1955], a film about narcotics addiction; and *Anatomy of a Murder* [1959], a courtroom drama about rape) and the blacklist (by giving Dalton Trumbo screen credit for writing the script for *Exodus*, 1960). Moreover, his haunting *film noir* of 1945, *Laura*, and the semidocumentary *Where the Sidewalk Ends* (1950) are minor classics of their respective genres. Preminger continued his contributions to widescreen in the political thriller *Advise and Consent* (1962), which also contains one of Hollywood's first treatments of a homosexual theme; *The Cardinal* (1963); *In Harm's Way* (1965); and *Bunny Lake Is Missing* (1965); but much of his later work (e.g., *Hurry Sundown*, 1967; *Tell Me That You Love Me, Junie Moon*, 1970; and *Rosebud*, 1975) was disappointing.

Stage director Elia Kazan (b. 1909) gave the 1950s three of its most persuasive and characteristic films: *A Streetcar Named Desire* (1951; adapted by Tennessee Williams from his own play), *Viva Zapata!* (1952; from an original story and screenplay by John Steinbeck), and *On the Waterfront* (1954; from an original story and screenplay by Budd Schulberg), all starring Marlon Brando (b. 1924). Much of Kazan's work of the era was shaped in one form or another by his friendly testimony before HUAC in 1952, in the course of which he denounced former colleagues at New York's radical Group Theater as Communists. *Viva Zapata!* he described to the committee as an "anticommunist picture," despite its focus on a revolutionary hero; his next film, *Man on a Tightrope* (1953), was in fact a trenchantly anticommunist thriller set in postwar Czechoslovakia; and *On the Waterfront* used labor racketeering as a metaphor for Communist espionage to build an unequivocal case for the morality of informing. The enormous critical and commercial success of the latter enabled Kazan to form his own company, Newtown Productions, for which he made his next three films. *Baby Doll* (1956) was a potboiler based on two of Tennessee Williams's one-act plays, but *A Face in the Crowd* (1957, also scripted by Schulberg from his own story) proved to be a prescient indictment of the abuses of celebrity power within the television industry, and *Splendor in the Grass* (1961) was a well-received version of William Inge's play about the traumas of adolescent sexuality. In addition to his motion-picture career, Kazan was also a successful Broadway theater director from the late 1940s through 1964, when he turned his attention to novel-writing, interrupted occasionally by personal films such as *America America* (1963) and *The Arrangement* (1969), both adapted from his own writings. Kazan's last film was an unsatisfying version of F. Scott Fitzgerald's *The Last Tycoon* (1976), scripted by Harold Pinter.

In his films of the 1950s, especially *Rebel without a Cause* (1955), Nicholas Ray (born Raymond Nicholas Kienzle, 1911–1979) provided a definitive statement of the spiritual and emotional ills that beset America during the period. Initially identified with *film gris* (*Knock on Any Door*, 1949) and *film noir* (*They Live by Night*, 1947, released 1949; *In a Lonely Place*, 1950; *On Dangerous Ground*, 1951), Ray simultaneously became a cult figure in Europe and one of the highest paid directors in Hollywood until his career collapsed beneath the weight of two commercially unsuccessful blockbusters, *King of Kings* (1961) and *55 Days at Peking* (1963). In later life, he taught filmmaking at Harpur College and collaborated with his students on a number of experimental projects combining film and video. Ray is also the focus of the one-hour documentary *I'm a Stranger Here Myself* (David Helpern, Jr., 1975) and the feature-length *Lightning over Water* (1980), a painfully personal film that he made in collaboration with the brilliant German director Wim Wenders on the subject of his own lingering death from cancer.

12.13 Alienated youth: *Rebel without a cause* (Nicholas Ray, 1955, CinemaScope). Jim Backus, James Dean, Ann Doran.

Douglas Sirk (b. Detlef Sierck, Denmark, 1900–1987) proved himself a master stylist of color in *Magnificent Obsession* (1954), *All That Heaven Allows* (1956), *Written on the Wind* (1957), *Interlude* (1957), and *Imitation of Life* (1959)—a series of visually stunning melodramas that are classics of their type. Before retiring in 1959 from filmmaking, Sirk also contributed several impressive widescreen action films (*Sign of the Pagan*, 1954; *Captain Lightfoot*, 1955; *Battle Hymn*, 1957) as well as the moving antiwar film *A Time to Love and a Time to Die* (1958), adapted from the novel by Erich Maria Remarque. He spent the remainder of his life in Germany, directing stage plays and teaching at the Munich Academy of Film and Television.

Robert Aldrich (1918–1983) emerged at this time as America's most powerful practitioner of post-1940s *film noir* in *Kiss Me Deadly* (1955; adapted from Mickey Spillane), a masterpiece of the form whose commercial success led Aldrich to establish his own production company, Associates and Aldrich, for which he directed twelve films in the next seventeen years. Aldrich had begun his directing career in television, and his first big-budget film had been the boisterous widescreen Western *Vera Cruz* (1954), shot on location in Mexico and a clear antecedent of Sam Peckinpah's *The Wild Bunch* (1969). During the 1950s, he earned a distinguished reputation for such award-winning films as *The Big Knife* (1955;

adapted from Clifford Odets; Silver Prize, Venice), *Autumn Leaves* (1956; Silver Bear, Berlin), and *Attack* (1956; Italian Critics Award, Venice), although he also directed a number of indifferent features under contract to various studios (e.g., *The Angry Hills*, 1959; *The Last Sunset*, 1961; *Sodom and Gomorrah*, 1963). During the 1960s, however, Aldrich became a major figure with the sardonic *noir* hits *What Ever Happened to Baby Jane?* (1962) and *Hush . . . Hush, Sweet Charlotte* (1964) and the violent World War II commando epic *The Dirty Dozen* (1967), which became the year's highest-grossing film ($18.2 million) and enabled him to purchase his own studio. Always a maverick, he produced three controversial and unpopular films at Aldrich Studios—*The Killing of Sister George* (1968), *Too Late the Hero* (1970), and *The Grissom Gang* (1971)—before its failure forced him to return to contract directing. In his later years, Aldrich made such intelligent films as *Ulzana's Raid* (1972), *Emperor of the North* (1973), *The Longest Yard* (1974), *Hustle* (1975), and *Twilight's Last Gleaming* (1977); he served two distinguished terms as president of the Directors Guild of America between 1975 and 1979 and directed several unsuccessful comedies (*The Frisco Kid*, 1979; *. . . All the Marbles*, 1981) before his death in 1983.

Other filmmakers associated with adult themes during the 1950s were John Huston (1906–1987), Budd Boetticher (1916–2001), and Anthony Mann (1906–1967). Originally an actor and a screenwriter, Huston had become famous as a director during the 1940s through his classic detective film *The Maltese Falcon* (1941) and his classic adventure film *The Treasure of the Sierra Madre* (1948), both of which have proved highly influential (*Falcon*, e.g., of *film noir* and *Sierra Madre* of such important later works as Peckinpah's *The Wild Bunch*). After directing *Key Largo* (1948), a moody adaptation of Maxwell Anderson's play, and *We Were Strangers* (1949), a controversial drama about revolutionary activity in 1930s Cuba starring the soon-to-be-blacklisted John Garfield, Huston began the 1950s with a surge of creative energy in the naturalistic *film noir The Asphalt Jungle* (1950), a documentary-like adaptation of Stephen Crane's *The Red Badge of Courage* (1951), and the award-winning *The African Queen* (1952), his first theatrical film in color. For the rest of the decade, Huston displayed his talents for both parody (*Beat the Devil*, 1954) and imaginative literary adaptation (*Moulin Rouge*,

1953; *Moby Dick*, 1956; *Heaven Knows, Mr. Allison*, 1957; *The Roots of Heaven*, 1958). In the 1960s, he turned increasingly to original material in such films as *The Misfits* (1961; screenplay by Arthur Miller) and *Freud* (1962; screenplay by Wolfgang Reinhardt and Charles Kaufman). Nevertheless, the written word remained a major source of Huston's inspiration in his later career, whether it derived from popular fiction (*The List of Adrian Messenger*, 1963; *Casino Royale*, 1967; *The Kremlin Letter*, 1970; *The Mackintosh Man*, 1973; *Phobia*, 1980), literature (*The Bible*, 1966; *Reflections in a Golden Eye*, 1967; *The Man Who Would Be King*, 1975; *Wise Blood*, 1980; *Under the Volcano*, 1984), or something in between (*The Night of the Iguana*, 1964; *A Walk with Love and Death*, 1969; *Fat City*, 1972; *Victory*, 1981; *Annie*, 1982; *Prizzi's Honor*, 1985). When he died of emphysema in December 1987, Huston had become a prominent spokesman for the Directors Guild of America against the practice of "colorization" (of which *The Maltese Falcon* was an early victim) and had just completed a sublime adaptation of James Joyce's short story *The Dead* (1987), scripted by his son, Tony, and starring his daughter, Angelica.

Boetticher and Mann were the architects of the modern adult Western during the 1950s, but both were also notable for other kinds of films. Boetticher, for example, was a professional bullfighter, whose films on the subject—*The Bullfighter and the Lady* (1951; produced by John Wayne for Republic Pictures; released at 87 minutes in a version edited by John Ford, and restored to its original 124-minute running time by UCLA archivist Bob Gitt in 1987), *The Magnificent Matador* (1965), and *Arruza* (1971; an epic documentary on the great Mexican matador Carlos Arruza, which took Boetticher a decade to complete)—are much admired. Mann, on the

other hand, began his career as a specialist in such gritty, low-budget *films noirs* as *Desperate* (1947), *Railroaded* (1947), *Raw Deal* (1948), and *T-Men* (1948) for B-studios like Eagle-Lion, but by the early 1960s had become an acknowledged master of the widescreen epic in *El Cid* (1961) and *The Fall of the Roman Empire* (1964).

Stanley Donen (b. 1924) and Vincente Minnelli (1903–1986) were also closely associated with a single genre during the 1950s (the musical), but Donen later dealt successfully in suspense (*Charade*, 1963; *Arabesque*, 1966) and romantic comedy (*Two for the Road*, 1967; *Bedazzled*, 1967), and Minnelli was able to turn a number of literary potboilers into the gorgeously stylized widescreen melodramas *The Cobweb* (1955), *Lust for Life* (1956), *Some Came Running* (1959), *Home from the Hill* (1960), *Two Weeks in Another Town* (1962), and *The Sandpiper* (1965). Their later work is discussed below.

Other American directors whose work is anchored mainly in the decade of the 1950s but extended well beyond it are the Austrian-born Fred Zinnemann (1907–1997)—*The Men*, 1950; *High Noon*, 1952; *A Mem-*

12.14 Epic scale in Anthony Mann's *El Cid* (1961, Super Technirama 70).

ber of the Wedding, 1953; *From Here to Eternity*, 1953; *Oklahoma!*, 1955; *A Hatful of Rain*, 1957; *The Nun's Story*, 1959; *The Sundowners*, 1960; *Behold a Pale Horse*, 1964; *A Man for All Seasons*, 1966; *Julia*, 1977; *Five Days One Summer*, 1982); Robert Rossen (1908–1966—*Body and Soul*, 1947; *All the King's Men*, 1949; *The Brave Bulls*, 1951; *Alexander the Great*, 1956; *Island in the Sun*, 1957; *They Came to Cordura*, 1959; *The Hustler*, 1961; *Lillith*, 1964); and the important action directors Don Siegel (1912–1991—*Riot in Cell Block 11*, 1954; *Invasion of the Body Snatchers*, 1956; *Baby Face Nelson*, 1957; *The Line-Up*, 1958; *The Killers*, 1964; *Madigan*, 1968; *The Beguiled*, 1970; *Dirty Harry*, 1972; *Charley Varrick*, 1973; *The Shootist*, 1976; *Escape from Alcatraz*, 1979); and the more primitive Samuel Fuller (1911–1997). The latter two have become cult figures in the past several decades, but Fuller has contributed more to the American cinema in terms of his vital creative energy and unique personal style. *The Steel Helmet* (1950), for example, is simply the best domestic feature about the Korean War, while *Pickup on South Street* (1953; winner of a Bronze medal at that year's Venice Festival), contains the fullest exposition of 1950s-style anticommunist paranoia of any American film. *Shock Corridor* (1963) and *The Naked Kiss* (1965) are forceful treatments of contemporary social pathology and corrupted human nature. Working throughout the 1950s, 1960s, and 1970s in such action genres as war film (*Fixed Bayonets*, 1951; *Hell and High Water*, 1954; *China Gate*, 1957; *Verboten!*, 1959; *The Big Red One*, 1979), crime films (*House of Bamboo*, 1955; *The Crimson Kimono*, 1959; *Underworld U.S.A.*, 1961; *Dead Pigeon on Beethoven Street*, 1972; *Les voleurs de la nuit* [*Thieves after Dark*], 1984); and Westerns (*I Shot Jesse James*, 1949; *The Baron of Arizona*, 1950; *Run of the Arrow*, 1957; *Forty Guns*, 1957; *Merrill's Marauders*, 1962), Fuller has produced a major body of work characterized by violent metaphor and raw emotional power.

Veteran director Raoul Walsh (1887–1980) was an *original* widescreen and blockbuster pioneer, having directed *The Big Trail* in Fox's 70mm Grandeur process in 1930 and the most visually spectacular entertainment of the 1920s in *The Thief of Bagdad* (1924). During the 1950s Walsh did his last major work, primarily as a widescreen action director in such films as *Battle Cry* (1955), *The Tall Men* (1955), and *Band of Angels* (1957). George Stevens (1904–1975), another studio veteran of the 1930s and 1940s, also made important films during the 1950s.

Although sententiousness sometimes got the better of his scripts, *Shane* (1953), *Giant* (1956), and *A Place in the Sun* (1951), his melodramatic rendition of Theodore Dreiser's novel *An American Tragedy* (1925), are all films that American cinema would be the poorer without. Sententiousness was also a problem in the films directed during this period by Stanley Kramer (1913–2001), which tended to be visually limp and heavily laden with social commentary. Still, a few Kramer films, like *The Defiant Ones* (1958), *Inherit the Wind* (1960), *Judgment at Nuremberg* (1961), and the later *Ship of Fools* (1965) and *Oklahoma Crude* (1973), are notable despite their flaws. A similarly erratic producer-director was Richard Brooks (1912–1992), who specialized in literary adaptations for which he wrote the scripts himself. His successes (*The Blackboard Jungle*, 1954; *Cat on a Hot Tin Roof*, 1959; *Elmer Gantry*, 1961; *Sweet Bird of Youth*, 1962; *The Professionals*, 1966; *In Cold Blood*, 1967; *Bite the Bullet*, 1975; *Wrong Is Right*, 1982) balance his failures (*Something of Value*, 1957; *The Brothers Karamazov*, 1958; *Lord Jim*, 1964; *Looking for Mr. Goodbar*, 1977; *Fever Pitch*, 1985) pretty evenly.

Finally, after the Hollywood witch-hunts had destroyed their American careers, Jules Dassin (b. 1911—*Brute Force*, 1947; *The Naked City*, 1948; *Thieves' Highway*, 1949) and Joseph Losey (1909–1984)—*The Boy with Green Hair*, 1948; *The Lawless*, 1950; *The Prowler*, 1951) became important figures abroad. Dassin, influenced by Lang, originally specialized in *film noir*, and his last American production was the urban *noir* classic *Night and the*

12.15 Interracial fraternity: *The Defiant Ones* **(Stanley Kramer, 1958). Sidney Poitier, Tony Curtis.**

2.16 Sex: *Cat on a Hot Tin Roof* **(Richard Brooks, 1959). Paul Newman, Elizabeth Taylor.**

City (1950) shot on location in London for Fox. In France during the 1950s and 1960s, he turned increasingly to popular "caper" films and comedies like *Rififi* (*Du Rififi chez les hommes*, 1955), *Never on Sunday* (1960), and *Topkapi* (1964); but he has also produced such serious films as *He Who Must Die* (*Celui qui doit mourir*, 1956), based on *The Greek Passion* by Nikos Kazantzakis, a modern version of *Phaedra* (1961), an all-black version of John Ford's *The Informer* entitled *Up Tight* (1969), and *A Dream of Passion* (1978), a contemporary meditation on the Medea legend shot in Greece. Like Dassin, Losey had been associated with the socially committed *film noir*, but in exile in England he tended to become a stylish and somewhat strained student of contemporary alienation, often collaborating with British playwright Harold Pinter on his screenplays (e.g., *The Servant*, 1964; *Accident*, 1967; *The Go-Between*, 1971). (Losey's more recent work is discussed in Chapter 14.)

1950s Genres

Despite the balanced work of many fine craftsmen, Hollywood's mania for producing films on a vast scale in the 1950s affected even the conventional dramatic feature. For one thing, the standard feature length rose from ninety minutes to an average of three hours before stabilizing at a more manageable two hours in the mid-1960s. Moreover, there was a tendency on the part of the studios to package every class-A production as a splashy, big-budget spectacle whether or not this format suited the material. Thus, from 1955 to 1965 most traditional American genres experienced an inflation of production values that destroyed their original forms and caused them to be re-created in new ones.

THE MUSICAL

The Hollywood musical had reached an exquisitely high point of sophistication and color at the turn of the decade under the auspices of the MGM producer Arthur Freed (1894–1973), who in the middle to late 1940s assembled a stellar production unit featuring the talented directors Vincente Minnelli (*Meet Me in St. Louis*, 1944; *Yolanda and the Thief*, 1945) and Stanley Donen; the choreographer-directors Charles Walters (1911–1982) and Gene Kelly (1912–1996); and such gifted performers as Kelly himself, Fred Astaire, Judy Garland, June Allyson, and Cyd Charisse. Over the next decade, this team produced some thirty medium-budget musicals, among them the extraordinary *The Pirate* (Minnelli, 1948), *Easter Parade* (Walters, 1948), *On the Town* (Kelly/Donen, 1949), *An American in Paris* (Minnelli, 1951), *Singin' in the Rain* (Kelly/Donen, 1952), *Brigadoon* (Minnelli, 1954), *It's Always Fair Weather* (Kelly/Donen, 1955), and *Invitation to the Dance* (Kelly, 1956), as well as more lavish efforts like *The Band Wagon* (Minnelli, 1953), *Kismet* (Minnelli, 1955), *Silk Stockings* (Rouben Mamoulian, 1957), and *Gigi* (Minnelli, 1958). As a professional lyricist himself, Freed believed that musical production numbers should be integrated with a film's dialogue and plot, rather than stand alone as intermezzos. In theory, this meant that the songs and dances should serve to advance the narrative, but in practice it produced the unrealistic convention of a character's bursting into song at the slightest dramatic provocation. The first such "integrated" musical was probably *The Wizard of Oz* (1939), for which Freed was the associate producer, but by the time of *On the Town* integration had become the state of the art, and the practice was continued throughout the 1950s and 1960s. By 1955, however, the musical genre contracted a fifteen-year case of elephantiasis, as well as a compulsion

12.17 *Singin' in the Rain* **(Gene Kelly and Stanley Donen, 1952): Gene Kelly.**

to abandon original scripts in favor of adapting successful stage plays, often concurrently running hits. Such Broadway vehicles as *Oklahoma!* (Fred Zimmermann, 1955), *Guys and Dolls* (Joseph L. Mankiewicz, 1955), *The King and I* (Walter Lang, 1956), *South Pacific* (Joshua Logan, 1958), *West Side Story* (Robert Wise, 1962), *The Music Man* (Morton da Costa, 1962), *Gypsy* (Mervyn LeRoy, 1963), and *My Fair Lady* (George Cukor, 1964) proved successful with the public, although many of them employed stars who could neither sing nor dance (the voices of professional singers were frequently dubbed in and professional dancers stood in for the production numbers), and many were directed by men who had never filmed a musical before. This tendency peaked with the release of 20th Century–Fox's astoundingly popular film *The Sound of Music* (Robert Wise, 1965), the ultimate big-budget supermusical, which grossed more money ($79 million in domestic rentals) than any American film produced before the era of *The Godfather* (Francis Ford Coppola, 1972), *Jaws* (Steven Spielberg, 1975), and *Star Wars* (George Lucas, 1977). *The Sound of Music* (subsequently known in the industry as *"The Sound of Money"* and to the readers of critic Pauline Kael as *"The Sound of Mucus"*) was a glossily

professional adaptation of a Rodgers and Hammerstein stage musical based on the true story of the Trapp family singers and their heroic escape from Nazi-occupied Austria. The production, shot on location in Salzburg, was one of Hollywood's last great escapist confections—a sort of conflation of *The Bells of St. Mary's*, *The Wizard of Oz*, and *Gone with the Wind*. The huge success of this film gave rise to a host of multimillion-dollar descendants—*Camelot* (Joshua Logan, 1967), *Star!* (Robert Wise, 1968), *Dr. Doolittle* (Richard Fleischer, 1967), *Goodbye, Mr. Chips* (Herbert Ross, 1969), *Oliver!* (Carol Reed, 1968), *Hello, Dolly!* (Gene Kelly, 1969)—all of which lost money, glutted the public on musicals, and virtually killed the form of the genre as it had evolved since the 1930s by blowing it out of all proportion. Bob Fosse's (1927–87) intelligent, socially conscious, and masterfully crafted film version of the stage success *Cabaret* (1972) signaled a resurrection of the genre in a form more appropriate to the 1970s—one that featured increased realism, serious subject matter, a resegregation of musical numbers and plot, and renewed emphasis on the authentic musical talent of its stars. Fosse's *All That Jazz* (1979), Milos Forman's *Hair* (1979), Luis Valdez's *Zoot Suit* (1981), and Herbert Ross's *Pennies from Heaven* (1981) seemed to confirm that resurrection at the decade's turn, although such MTV-inspired musicals of the mid-1980s as *Flashdance* (Adrian Lyne, 1983) and *Footloose* (Herbert Ross, 1984) raised some doubts about its longevity (see Chapter 20).

COMEDY

Comedy was another genre that suffered seriously from widescreen inflation and the generally depressed social ambiance of the McCarthy–Cold War era, although there were clear exceptions in such small gems as Vincente Minnelli's *Father of the Bride* (1950) and *Father's Little Dividend* (1951). The big-budget widescreen comedy was represented by films like *How to Marry a Millionaire* (Jean Negulesco, 1953), *The Long, Long Trailer* (Vincente Minnelli, 1954), *High Society* (Charles Walters, 1956—a widescreen color remake, with music by Cole Porter, of George Cukor's 1940 *Philadelphia Story*), and *A Hole in the Head* (Frank Capra, 1959). The strong point of film comedies like these was less verbal or visual wit than excellent production values. This was, after all, the major strategic element in Hollywood's war on television, and for a while the strategy worked, although the new medium continued to woo both audiences and comedians away from the cinema as the decade progressed. Bob Hope (b. 1903—*Son of Paleface*, Frank Tashlin, 1952; *Casanova's Big Night*, Norman Z. McLeod, 1954) and Danny Kaye (1913–1987—*The Court Jester*, Norman Panama, 1956; *Merry Andrew*, Michael Kidd, 1958), whose film careers had begun in the decade past, were both popular in class-A productions throughout the 1950s,[3] as was the slapstick team of Dean Martin (1917–1995) and Jerry Lewis (b. 1926), who had succeeded Abbott and Costello. Martin and Lewis made seventeen films together between 1949 and 1956, the best among them *At War with the Army* (Hal Walker, 1951), *Sailor Beware* (Walker, 1952), *Jumping Jacks* (Norman Taurog, 1952), *The Stooge* (Taurog, 1953), *Scared Stiff* (George Marshall, 1953), *Living It Up* (Taurog, 1954), *You're Never Too Young* (Taurog, 1955), *Artists and Models* (Frank Tashlin, 1955), and *Pardners* (Taurog, 1956). When the team split up after *Hollywood or Bust* (Tashlin, 1956), Martin began a successful career as an actor and television entertainer, while Lewis went on to become a major comic star by himself in such films as *The Delicate Delinquent* (Don McGuire, 1957), *Rock-a-Bye Baby* (Tashlin, 1958), and *The Geisha Boy* (Tashlin, 1958), ultimately directing (and often writing and producing) his own films in the 1960s—e.g., *The Bellboy* (1960), *The Errand Boy* (1961), *The Nutty Professor* (1963), *The Patsy* (1964), and *The Family Jewels* (1965). Today he still directs an occasional film (*Hardly Working*, 1981; *Cracking Up*, also known as *Smorgasbord*, 1983). Technically

innovative (e.g., he pioneered video-assist technology for his 1960s productions), Lewis is regarded by the French as a major *auteur*, but his idiotic comic persona has not found much favor with American critics.

Much more sophisticated than Lewis, and certainly as brilliant as Hope and Kaye, were the era's two major comediennes: Judy Holliday (1922–1965—*Born Yesterday*, George Cukor, 1950; *It Should Happen to You*, George Cukor, 1954; *Phffft*, Mark Robson, 1954; *The Solid Gold Cadillac*, Richard Quine, 1956; *Full of Life*, Richard Quine, 1957; *Bells Are Ringing*, Vincente Minnelli, 1960) and Marilyn Monroe (1926–1962—*Gentlemen Prefer Blondes*, Howard Hawks, 1953; *How to Marry a Millionaire*, 1953; *The Seven Year Itch*, Billy Wilder, 1955; *Some Like It Hot*, Billy Wilder, 1959). Both appeared in a number of witty, adult comedies before early deaths (Monroe was an apparent suicide; Holliday died of cancer) cut short their careers. These films were succeeded by the sanitized sexiness of the expensively produced Rock Hudson/Doris Day battle-of-the-sexes cycle, beginning in 1959 with *Pillow Talk* (Michael Gordon), and continuing to *Lover Come Back* (Delbert Mann, 1961) and *Send Me No Flowers* (Norman Jewison, 1964). These films and others that imitated them[4] were in turn succeeded by a cycle of cynical, big-budget sex comedies concerned with the strategies of seduction (David Swift's *Under the Yum-Yum Tree*, 1963; Richard Quine's *Sex and the Single Girl*, 1964, and *How to Murder Your Wife*, 1965; Gene Kelly's *A Guide for the Married Man*, 1967; Fielder Cook's *How to Save a Marriage* [*And Ruin Your Life*], 1968) which reflected, sometimes rather perversely, the "sexual revolution" of the late

12.18 *Scared Stiff* (George Marshall, 1953): Jerry Lewis, Lizabeth Scott, Dean Martin.

---

3. Between 1941 and 1953, Hope ranked consistently among Hollywood's top ten box-office attractions; during the 1980s, he continued to occupy superstar status, ranking in popularity with the likes of Clint Eastwood and Barbra Streisand. In fact, Hope may well be the longest continuously popular entertainer in the history of mass communications, and, with an estate valued at nearly $1 billion, he is certainly the richest.

4. The formula was to cast the stubbornly virginal Day against a rapacious and sexy leading man—Hudson in the originals, Cary Grant in *That Touch of Mink* (Delbert Mann, 1962). James Garner in *Move Over, Darling* (Michael Gordon, 1963), and *The Thrill of it All* (Norman Jewison, 1963), and Rod Taylor in *Do Not Disturb* (Ralph Levy, 1965); Tony Randall or Gig Young were frequently involved as an alternative love interest (for Day). Although *Pillow Talk* catalyzed this astonishingly dishonest cycle, its progenitor was probably the more intelligent and urbane *Teacher's Pet* (George Seaton, 1958), written by Fay and Michael Kanin, where Day is pitted against no less a power than Clark Gable in one of his last major roles.

12.19 *Born Yesterday* (George Cukor, 1950): Broderick Crawford, Judy Holliday.

1960s.[5] Related to the amoral cynicism of this cycle was what might best be called the "corporate comedy" of films like *Cash McCall* (Joseph Pevney, 1959) and *The Wheeler Dealers* (Arthur Hiller, 1963), which dealt openly and humorously with business fraud and prefigured the morass of corporate and governmental deceit underlying the Watergate and "Koreagate" scandals of the 1970s. The elegant, big-budget comedies of Blake Edwards (b. 1922—*The Pink Panther*, 1964; *A Shot in the Dark*, 1964; *The Great Race*, 1965; *The Party*, 1968) relied on sight gags to provide a lighter kind of humor, as did his later films in the Pink Panther series (*The Return of the Pink Panther*, 1975; *The Pink Panther Strikes Again*, 1976; *The Revenge of the Pink Panther*, 1978; *The Trail of the Pink Panther*, 1982, etc.); but by the 1980s, with such films as *"10"* (1979), *S.O.B.* (1981), *Victor/Victoria* (1982), *The Man Who Loved Women* (1983), *Micki & Maude* (1984), *That's Life!* (1986), and *Skin Deep* (1989), Edwards had indisputably become a major practitioner of social satire.

The dark genius of American comedy during this period was the German émigré director Billy Wilder (1906–2002), whose *Double Indemnity* (1944) had been one of the prototypes for *film noir*. Wilder carried this strain into the 1950s with the relentlessly cynical *Ace in the Hole* (also known as *The Big Carnival*, 1951), which

portrayed the media circus created by a corrupt reporter around a New Mexico mining disaster and won an international prize at Venice, but he began increasingly to specialize in *comédie noir*. In *Sunset Boulevard* (1950) he served up the decadence of Hollywood, old and new, in a tale of a bitterly symbiotic relationship between an aging silent-film star and a fortune-hunting young writer. *Stalag 17* (1953) was a perverse satire on heroism set in a German POW camp during World War II; *The Seven Year Itch* (1955) was a send-up of American sexual mores and advertising practices; *Witness for the Prosecution* (1958) was a sardonic courtroom thriller derived from a play by Agatha Christie; and *Some Like It Hot* (1959) was a torrid, fast-paced sex farce set amid gangster wars and an "all-girl" band during Prohibition. Wilder also enriched the decade with a pair of sparkling romantic comedies, *Sabrina* (1954) and *Love in the Afternoon* (1957), as well as his inventive, underrated account of Charles Lindbergh's transatlantic crossing, *The Spirit of St. Louis* (1957). He entered the 1960s with *The Apartment* (1960), a film about the battle of the sexes made in dark parody of the Hudson/Day cycle, which won numerous critical accolades and awards, including Oscars for Best Film and Best Direction. *One, Two, Three* (1961) satirized the Cold War and American corporate imperialism, and in *Irma La Douce* (1963) and *Kiss Me, Stupid* (1964) Wilder brought the cynical sex comedy *à la* Lubitsch into contemporary American film. In *The Fortune Cookie* (1966), he did a comic turn on *Ace in the Hole*, as an ambulance-chasing lawyer presses a phony damage claim against a professional football team and the city of Cleveland and nearly wins; and by the end of the decade he was spoofing the most revered of Victorian detectives in *The Private Life of Sherlock Holmes* (1969). In the 1970s, Wilder directed, among other films, a contemporary version of Lewis Milestone's *The Front Page* (1974) and an elegant reworking of the *Sunset Boulevard* theme in *Fedora* (1979). He also produced the farces *Avanti!* (1972) and *Buddy Buddy* (1982), about which there are considerably mixed opinions. Wilder has always coauthored his own screenplays, in close collaboration with such professional scriptwriters as Charles Brackett, Raymond Chandler,

---

5. The attitudes underlying these later films were marvelously satirized at the decade's conclusion in Paul Mazursky's *Bob & Carol & Ted & Alice* (1969) and earnestly, if joylessly, dissected in Mike Nichols's *Carnal Knowledge* (1970). See Chapter 20.

12.20 *Sunset Boulevard* (Billy Wilder, 1950): Gloria Swanson.

12.21 *Love and Death* (Woody Allen, 1975): Woody Allen with the Grim Reaper.

George Axelrod, and, since 1959, I.A.L. Diamond (Wilder began his film career as a scriptwriter for UFA). Through the influence of Wilder and others (for instance, Stanley Kubrick in *Dr. Strangelove*, 1963, a radical masterpiece far in advance of its time), American comedy became increasingly sophisticated through the 1950s and 1960s, until it emerged in the 1970s as a wholly adult genre. Films like *M°A°S°H* (Robert Altman, 1970), and the work of comic *auteurs* like Woody Allen (b. Allen Konigsberg, 1935—*Take the Money and Run*, 1969; *Bananas*, 1971; *Play It Again Sam*, 1972; *Everything You Always Wanted to Know about Sex, but Were Afraid to Ask*, 1972; *Sleeper*, 1973; *Love and Death*, 1975), and Mel Brooks (b. Melvin Kaminsky, 1927—*The Producers*, 1968; *Blazing Saddles*, 1973; *Young Frankenstein*, 1974; *Silent Movie*, 1976; *High Anxiety*, 1977; *History of the World Part I*, 1981; *Space Balls*, 1987; *Life Stinks*, 1991) all bear testimony to the increasing maturity of American film comedy—much of it undertaken in parody of other traditional genres. Allen, especially, has emerged as an important and extremely intelligent filmmaker, moving from the broad social satire of his earlier works to the pointed social commentary of *Annie Hall* (1977),

Manhattan (1979), and the remarkable pseudodocumentary *Zelig* (1983), whose special photographic effects were brilliantly rendered by Gordon Willis, Allen's regular cinematographer from 1977 through 1985. All of Allen's work is filmically literate, and he has produced self-reflexive meditations on the film experience ranging from the narcissistic *Stardust Memories* (1980) to the ingenious *The Purple Rose of Cairo* (1985), which deconstructs the psychology of spectatorship in the manner of Keaton's *Sherlock Jr.* (1924). *A Midsummer Night's Sex Comedy* (1982) has its roots in Shakespeare's *A Midsummer Night's Dream* and Max Reinhardt's 1935 Warner Bros. film of it, but also, less obviously, in Bergman (*Smiles of a Summer Night*, 1955) and Renoir (*Une partie de campagne*, 1936; *La règle du jeu*, 1939), while *Broadway Danny Rose* (1984) has been seen by some critics as a recapitulation and inversion of Francis Ford Coppola's *The Godfather* (1972). Allen's most mature films to date are *Hannah and Her Sisters* (1986), a seriocomic narrative of adult relationships set among Manhattan's upper-middle class, and *Radio Days* (1987), a personal memoir structured around a nostalgic history of America's first broadcast medium. Although it is generally agreed that he has been less successful with straight dramatic material, notably in *Interiors* (1978), *September* (1987), *Another Woman* (1988), and *Alice* (1991), there can be no question of Allen's seriousness of purpose and genuine cinematic talent, as *Crimes and Misdemeanors* (1989), *Husbands and Wives* (1992), *Manhattan Murder Mystery* (1993), and *Bullets over Broadway* (1994) confirm.

THE WESTERN

The genre that seems to have best survived the wide-screen inflation of the 1950s and 1960s is the Western, where the landscape provides a naturally important element, although Westerns, too, experienced some major changes in attitude and theme corresponding to changes in American society. The heroic, idealized, epic Western of John Ford and his imitators remained popular in the 1950s but was gradually replaced by what was called the "adult Western." This genre, whose prototypes were *The Gunfighter* (Henry King, 1950) and *High Noon* (Fred Zinnemann, 1952), concentrated on the psychological or moral conflicts of the individual protagonist in relation to his society, rather than creating the poetic archetypes of order characteristic of Ford. The directors Delmer Daves ([1904–1977]—*Jubal*, 1956; *3:10 to Yuma*, 1957; *Cowboy*, 1958) and John Sturges ([1911–1992]—*Gunfight at the O.K. Corral*, 1957; *Last Train from Gun Hill*, 1958) both contributed to the new psychological style during this period, but the foremost director of adult Westerns in the 1950s was Anthony Mann, who made eleven such films between 1950 and 1960, five of them in close collaboration with the actor James Stewart (for example, *Winchester '73*, 1950). Mann's Westerns tended to be more intensely psychological and violent than those of his peers, and he was among the first to discover that the topography of the genre was uniquely suited to the wide-screen format. In films like *Bend of the River* (1952), *The Naked Spur* (1953), *The Far Country* (1955), *The Man*

12.22 *Gunfight at the O.K. Corral* **(John Sturges, 1957).**

from Laramie (1955), *The Last Frontier* (1955), *The Tin Star* (1957), and *Man of the West* (1958), Mann carried the genre permanently into the realm of adult entertainment and created an austere visual style that, according to Andrew Sarris, closely resembles that of Michelangelo Antonioni.

Mann's successor was Budd Boetticher, who directed a series of adult Westerns in collaboration with producer Harry Joe Brown and actor Randolph Scott for Ranown Productions in the late 1950s. In such films as *Seven Men from Now* (1956), *Decision at Sundown* (1957), *The Tall T* (1957), *Buchanan Rides Alone* (1958), *Ride Lonesome* (1959), and *Comanche Station* (1960), Boetticher forged elemental and even allegorical dramas of ethical heroism in which men alone are forced to make moral choices in a moral vacuum. The Fordian tradition of the epic romance was carried on, of course, by Ford himself in *Wagonmaster* (1950), *Rio Grande* (1950), and, preeminently, *The Searchers*, (1956—see Chapter 8), and by the makers of such "big" widescreen Westerns as *Shane* (George Stevens, 1953)—a film shot in the old ratio and disastrously blown up for widescreen exhibition; *The Big Country* (William Wyler, 1958); *The Alamo* (John Wayne, 1960); *How the West Was Won* (John Ford, Henry Hathaway, George Marshall, 1962—Cinerama); and the inflated, big-budget Westerns of Andrew V. McLaglen (*McLintock!*, 1963; *Shenandoah*, 1965; *The Rare Breed*, 1966). It was the Mann-Boetticher tradition that won out in the 1960s, as the early films of Sam Peckinpah (*The Deadly Companions*, 1961; *Ride the High Country*, 1962) clearly demonstrate. But the new-style Westerns were soon deeply influenced by another tradition, the Japanese samurai film, with its heavy emphasis on honor, fatality, and violence (see Chapter 18).

This influence was first demonstrated in John Sturges's violent and popular *The Magnificent Seven* (1960), a version of Akira Kurosawa's *The Seven Samurai* (1954) set in the American West. In both films, seven hardened warriors (gunmen in Sturges) are inexplicably driven to risk their lives to defend the inhabitants of a small rural village from bandits. *The Magnificent Seven* was a popular success and sparked an international trend toward samurai imitations that ultimately produced the "spaghetti Western"—violent films of the American West starring American actors that were shot in Italy or Yugoslavia by Italian filmmakers. The master craftsman of the spaghetti Western was Sergio Leone (1921–1989), whose *A Fistful of Dollars*—a direct,

12.23 Eastern Western: from the showdown that concludes *Yojimbo* (Akira Kurosawa, 1961). Toshiro Mifune.

almost shot-for-shot copy of Kurosawa's *Yojimbo* (1961), itself reputedly a version of Boetticher's *Buchanan Rides Alone*—started the cycle in 1964. Leone, who turned out to have talent of his own, followed up with *For a Few Dollars More* (1965), *The Good, the Bad, and the Ugly* (1966), and finally, *Once upon a Time in the West* (1967)—a bold, brilliant parody of all the mythic/romantic themes of the traditional American Western.[6] The films of Leone and his many imitators tended to be stylish, colorful, and excessively bloody—the latter achieved through the practice of graphically depicting, for the first time on the screen, impact and exit wounds produced by bullets. For this reason mainly, one fears, the spaghetti Westerns were enormously successful in the United States and produced a number of American-made imitations (e.g., Ted Post's gratuitously brutal *Hang 'Em High*, 1968). They also played a major role in conditioning American audiences to the new levels of violence that were to emerge at the end of the decade in the non-Western gangster film *Bonnie and Clyde* (Arthur Penn, 1967) and in Sam Peckinpah's apocalyptic *The Wild Bunch* (1969; see Chapter 20). The latter work probably did more to demythologize the American West than any single film of its era, but the process had been going on since Anthony Mann's *The Naked Spur* (1953).

Mann, Boetticher, Sturges (in *The Magnificent Seven*), the Italians, and Peckinpah evolved a Western tradition counter to that of Ford—one that was antiheroic and realistic. One important index of this change was a complete reversal of the genre's attitude toward Native Amer-

icans. The hostile savages of the 1930s, 1940s, and most of the 1950s were suddenly presented as a race of gentle, intelligent people upon whom the U.S. military establishment had committed genocide. Two films of the period, Ralph Nelson's *Soldier Blue* (1970) and Arthur Penn's *Little Big Man* (1971), graphically depicted the massacre of defenseless Indians by U.S. Cavalry troops (the analogy with the My Lai massacre in both films was inescapable and deliberate). Good "classical" Westerns continued to be made in the 1960s by such Fordian craftsmen as Henry Hathaway (*The Sons of Katie Elder*, 1965; *True Grit*, 1969) and by maverick individualists like Howard Hawks (*Rio Bravo*, 1959; *El Dorado*, 1967), but the prevailing trend was toward graphic realism (*Will Penny* [Tom Gries, 1967]; *Monte Walsh* [William Fraker, 1970]) or parody (*Cat Ballou* [Elliot Silverstein, 1965]; *Waterhole #3* [William Graham, 1967]; *Butch Cassidy and the Sundance Kid* [George Roy Hill, 1969]). From *Fort Apache* (John Ford, 1948) and *Red River* (Howard Hawks, 1948) to *Soldier Blue* (Ralph Nelson, 1970) and *The Wild Bunch* (Sam Peckinpah, 1969), the external form of the American Western did not significantly change. The Ford and Nelson films, for example, have the same subject, the same landscape, and very nearly the same plot; and *The Wild Bunch* duplicates many of the mythic elements of *Red River* without parody. It is the way in which these elements are viewed by American filmmakers and their audiences that has changed. That change is profound, but it has more to do with alterations in the way America perceives itself and its past than with the evolution of a film genre.

THE GANGSTER FILM AND THE ANTICOMMUNIST FILM

The gangster film, which had been replaced by the domestic-espionage film during the war, re-emerged in

---

6. *The Good, the Bad, and the Ugly* and *Once upon a Time in the West* were both shortened by their American distributors—the first from 180 to 148 minutes, the second from 168 to 144 minutes—to allow for more screenings per day, causing obvious damage to them. The initial appeal of the spaghetti Westerns involved a combination of Clint Eastwood's persona as "The Man with No Name," Leone's dynamic montage, and the innovative musical scores of Ennio Morricone (b. 1928—also the composer for Gillo Pontecorvo's *Battle of Algiers* [1965] and *Queimada!* [1968], and, more recently, Bernardo Bertolucci's *1900* [1976], Terrence Malick's *Days of Heaven* [1978], and all of Leone's films).

the late 1940s under the influence of *film noir*. At that time, "dark" crime films like *The Killers* (Robert Siodmak, 1946), *Kiss of Death* (Henry Hathaway, 1947), *I Walk Alone* (Byron Haskin, 1947), *The Naked City* (Jules Dassin, 1948), *Force of Evil* (Abraham Polonsky, 1948), *They Live by Night* (Nicholas Ray, 1949), *White Heat* (Raoul Walsh, 1949), *Gun Crazy* (Joseph H. Lewis, 1950), *Kiss Tomorrow Goodbye* (Gordon Douglas, 1950), and *Where the Sidewalk Ends* (Otto Preminger, 1950) tended to concentrate on the individual criminal in his relationship to the underworld. In the paranoid 1950s, the emphasis shifted from the individual wrongdoer to the existence of a nationwide criminal conspiracy, commonly known as "the syndicate," which was responsible for many of America's social ills—murder, gambling, prostitution, narcotics, and labor racketeering. Since Prohibition, American gangster films have been firmly rooted in the reality of American crime, and—paranoia notwithstanding—that such a criminal conspiracy did exist and that it was closely connected with the Sicilian secret society known as the Mafia was demonstrated by the findings of the Senate Special Committee to Investigate Organized Crime, headed by Senator Estes Kefauver, in 1951. Based on the revelations of the Kefauver committee, *The Enforcer* (also called *Murder, Inc.*; Bretaigne Windust, 1951) was the first film to posit such an organization on the screen, but it became the major component in *The Big Heat* (Fritz Lang, 1953), *On the Waterfront* (Elia Kazan, 1954), *New York Confidential* (Russell Rouse, 1954), *The Big Combo* (Joseph Lewis, 1955), *The Phoenix City Story* (Phil Karlson, 1955), *The Brothers Rico* (Phil Karlson, 1957), *The Garment Jungle* (Vincent Sherman, 1957), *Murder, Inc.* (Stuart Rosenberg, 1960), *Underworld U.S.A.* (Samuel Fuller, 1960), and many other gangster films of the decade. The syndicate cycle experienced a decade-long hiatus in the 1960s—except for Martin Ritt's *The Brotherhood* (1968)—only to reemerge with unprecedentedly graphic violence in the blood-soaked 1970s with *The Godfather*, and *The Godfather, Part II* (Francis Ford Coppola, 1972 and 1974), *The Valachi Papers* (Terence Young, 1972), *The French Connection* (William Friedkin, 1971) and *The French Connection II* (John Frankenheimer, 1975), and *Honor Thy Father* (Paul Wendkos, 1971; released 1973).

Another type of gangster film, the biography of the Prohibition and/or Depression criminal, was initiated by Don Siegel's *Baby Face Nelson* (1957). Films in this cycle—*The Bonnie Parker Story* (William Witney, 1958), *Machine Gun Kelly* (Roger Corman, 1958), *Al Capone* (Richard Wilson, 1959), *The Rise and Fall of Legs Diamond* (Budd Boetticher, 1960), *Mad Dog Coll* (Burt Balaban, 1961), *Portrait of a Mobster* (about Dutch Schultz; Joseph Pevney, 1961)—tended to rely on period reconstruction, and their apotheosis came in the late 1960s with Arthur Penn's *Bonnie and Clyde* (1967), Roger Corman's *The St. Valentine's Day Massacre* (1967) and *Bloody Mama* (1969), and John Milius's *Dillinger* (1973).

Two interesting subtypes of the gangster film that appeared in the 1950s were the "caper" film and the "anti-Red" action thriller. The caper film, which began with John Huston's *The Asphalt Jungle* (1950), concentrates on the mechanics of pulling off a big heist and is still a very popular type. It is sometimes deadly serious, sometimes light and witty. Subsequent manifestations both in America and abroad include *Rififi* (Jules Dassin, 1955), *The Killing* (Stanley Kubrick, 1956), *Odds against Tomorrow* (Robert Wise, 1959), *Seven Thieves* (Henry Hathaway, 1960), *Big Deal on Madonna Street* (Mario Monicelli, 1960), *The League of Gentlemen* (Basil Dearden, 1960), *Topkapi* (Jules Dassin, 1964), *Grand Slam* (Giuliano Montaldo, 1967), and *They Came to Rob Las Vegas* (Antonio Isasi, 1968). The anti-Red action film was a localized, primitive type endemic to the early 1950s and exemplified by Robert Stevenson's *I Married a Communist* (also known as *The Woman on Pier 13*, 1950), Gordon Douglas's *I Was a Communist for the FBI* (1951),[7] Edward Ludwig's *Big Jim McLain* (1953), and Samuel Fuller's more morally ambiguous *Pickup on South Street* (1953). In this type, the criminal figure is a Communist spy and the syndicate is the "international Communist conspiracy," but the traditional iconography of the gangster film is maintained.

The Communist-as-gangster film was part of a larger cycle of more than fifty anticommunist films produced by nearly every studio in Hollywood between 1948 and 1955 (the exceptions were Disney and Universal-International) in ritual self-abasement before HUAC and the minions

---

7. *I Was a Communist for the FBI* was adapted from a memoir by real-life infiltrator Matt Cvetic, which was also dramatized as a radio serial in 1951.

of Senator Joseph McCarthy.[8] Many of these, such as *The Iron Curtain* (William Wellman, 1948), *Walk a Crooked Mile* (Gordon Douglas, 1948), *The Red Menace* (R. G. Springsteen, 1949), *The Whip Hand* (William Cameron Menzies, 1951), *Diplomatic Courier* (Henry Hathaway, 1952), *The Thief* (Russell Rouse, 1952), *The Atomic City* (Jerry Hopper, 1952), *Walk East on Beacon* (Alfred L. Werker, 1952), and *A Bullet for Joey* (Lewis Allen, 1955), had their roots in the World War II espionage film (see Chapter 11) and simply substituted villainous Reds for villainous Nazis. Others were set inside the Iron Curtain and focused on innocent individuals attempting to get out (e.g., *The Red Danube* [George Sidney, 1949] *The Steel Fist* [Wesley Barry, 1952], *Assignment—Paris* [Robert Parrish, 1952], *Man on a Tightrope* [Elia Kazan, 1953], *Never Let Me Go* [Delmer Daves, 1953]), while still others posed as domestic melodramas (*Shack Out on 101* [Edward Dein, 1955]), semidocumentaries (*Red Snow* [Boris L. Petroff and Harry S. Franklin, 1952]; *Invasion USA* [Alfred E. Green, 1952]), science fiction (*Red Planet Mars* [Harry Horner, 1952]; *Project Moonbase* [Richard Talmadge, 1953]), combat films (*Prisoner of War* [Andrew Marton, 1954]), Westerns (*California Conquest* [Lew Landers, 1952]), or even South Seas adventures (*Savage Drums* [William Berke, 1951]). But the ultimate anticommunist film was indisputably *My Son John* (1952), written, produced, and directed for Paramount by the talented Leo McCarey (1898–1969), one of the great comic filmmakers of the 1930s (*Duck Soup*, 1933; *Ruggles of Red Gap*, 1935; *The Awful Truth*, 1937), who had

apparently lost his sense of humor. A feverish blend of anti-intellectualism, oedipal obsession, and pseudo-Christian piety, *My Son John* stars the brilliant young actor Robert Walker (1918–1951) in his last role[9] as a State Department Red whose treachery stops just short of parricide. So impassioned and viscerally engaging is this film that it deserves to be ranked with *The Birth of a Nation* and *Triumph of the Will* among the cinema's definitive works of authoritarian propaganda, and, like them, it has remained controversial since the day of its release.

The anticommunist cycle coincided almost precisely with the period between the first HUAC Hollywood hearings and the U.S. Senate's censure of Joseph McCarthy, but a trickle of films continued—*The River Changes* (Owen Crump, 1956), *The Girl in the Kremlin* (Russell Birdwell, 1957), *The Fearmakers* (Jacques Tourneur, 1958)—through the end of the decade when the last Communist-as-gangster film appeared in *The FBI Story* (Mervyn LeRoy, 1959), which also dealt with Prohibition/Depression gangsters and Nazi spies. The central impulse of the anticommunist film was preserved in the James Bond espionage thrillers of the 1960s, which were adapted from the novels of British writer Ian Fleming and produced by Albert R. Broccoli and Harry Saltzman's London-based Eon Productions for distribution by United Artists. These immensely popular films and their imitators in effect usurped the gangster genre between 1962 and 1969 by positing criminal conspiracy on a worldwide scale and offering violent gangsterism on the part

---

8. Joseph McCarthy (1908–1957), junior Republican senator from Wisconsin from 1948 through 1956, was the most successful and infamous exploiter of the anticommunist hysteria churned up by HUAC and the atomic-spy syndrome (see Chapter 11). On February 9, 1950, in Wheeling, West Virginia, McCarthy began a political reign of terror that would last more than four years by accusing the State Department of selling out China to the Communists and harboring 205 known Communist party members among its senior staff. He went on to accuse countless U.S. civil servants and private citizens of treason on the basis of half-truths and innuendo, mobilizing a rising tide of anti-intellectualism and class suspicion that focused on WASPish establishment figures (like Secretary of State Dean Acheson) and their educated urban Jewish counterparts. As chairman of the Senate Subcommittee on Investigations from 1953 to 1955, McCarthy conducted sensational public witch-hunts and proved himself to be a skilled manipulator of mass opinion, especially through the new medium of television. Appropriately, it was television that brought him down, first through a negative profile on Edward

R. Murrow's *See It Now* in March 1954 and then, in April and May, through the televised Army-McCarthy hearings, where McCarthy's mendacity and fraudulence were revealed at last to the nation. On December 2, 1954, his conduct was officially censured by an overwhelming majority of his fellow senators, and though he served out his term, McCarthy's political career was over from that point on. McCarthyism itself, however, lived on, and in its paranoid style and bullying tactics gave the 1950s and part of the 1960s their dominant mood. See Emile de Antonio's film on the McCarthy hearings, *Point of Order!* (1964).

9. Walker, who had recently suffered a series of nervous breakdowns and been hospitalized in the Menninger Clinic, died during the filming of *My Son John* following the administration of a sedative by a doctor. Since the conclusion had not yet been shot, McCarey was forced to piece one together from out takes from Walker's previous film, Hitchcock's *Strangers on a Train* (1951).

of both the conspirators and the superhero ("licensed to kill") sent to stop them. Fleming's work was probably brought to the attention of Broccoli and Saltzman by an article that appeared in *Life* magazine on March 17, 1961, naming *From Russia with Love* as one of President Kennedy's ten favorite books (the ninth, in fact—just ahead of Stendhal's *The Red and the Black*). The president didn't live to see the movie, whose American premiere was in April 1964, but Eon's sexy, gadget-ridden James Bond series became one of the most successful in motion-picture history, earning nine Academy Award nominations and over $500 million in rentals from 1962 through 1985. The Bond films of the 1960s—*Dr. No, From Russia with Love,* and *Thunderball* (Terence Young; 1962, 1963, 1965), *Goldfinger* (Guy Hamilton, 1964), *You Only Live Twice* (Lewis Gilbert, 1967), and *On Her Majesty's Secret Service* (Peter Hunt, 1969)—greatly influenced the decade's popular culture, spawning imitative television series like *The Man from U.N.C.L.E.* (1964–68), *Secret Agent* (1965–66), *I Spy* (1965–68), and *Mission: Impossible* (1966–73), and such theatrical clones as the two Charles Vine films (*Second Best Secret Agent in the Whole Wide World* [also known as *Licensed to Kill*, Lindsay Shonteff, 1965] and *Where Bullets Fly* [John Gilling, 1966]), the two Derek Flint films (*Our Man Flint* [Daniel Mann, 1966] and *In Like Flint* [Gordon Douglas, 1967]), and the Matt Helm series (*The Silencers* [Phil Karlson, 1966]; *Murderer's Row* [Henry Levin, 1966]; *The Ambushers* [Henry Levin, 1967]; *The Wrecking Crew* [Phil Karlson, 1968]), whose formula of gangster-as-international-conspirator versus gangster-as-government-agent, however playful, sank the espionage thriller into a state of moral confusion from which it never emerged.[1]

In the late 1950s and early 1960s, the young directors of the French New Wave borrowed heavily from the conventions of the American gangster film in works like *Breathless* (Jean-Luc Godard, 1960) and *Shoot the Piano Player* (François Truffaut, 1960), but the genre remained dormant in America itself until 1967, when Arthur Penn's *Bonnie and Clyde* revitalized it for the 1970s. Penn's film, very much a product of the rebellious spirit of the late 1960s, owed a great deal stylistically to the example of the French New Wave, but *Bonnie and Clyde* also restored the gangster to his traditional position as tragic hero and unified the genre by borrowing motifs from three great crime films of the past—Fritz Lang's *You Only Live Once*

(1937), Nicholas Ray's *They Live by Night* (1949), and Joseph Lewis's *Gun Crazy* (1950). Since *Bonnie and Clyde*, the gangster film, like the Western has re-entered the mainstream of American cinema as the vehicle for serious artistic and social expression (e.g., *The Godfather* and *The Godfather Part II*) that it was during the 1930s.

SCIENCE FICTION

Another interesting development of the 1950s was the emergence of the science-fiction film as a distinct genre. There had been films of science fantasy long before World War II. One of the first important narrative films, Georges Méliès' *Le Voyage dans la lune* (1902), fits the description, as do Fritz Lang's *Metropolis* (1926) and *Die Frau im Mond* (*The Woman in the Moon*, 1929). But with the exception of William Cameron Menzies's futuristic fantasy *Things to Come* (1936) and Lothar Mendes's *The Man Who Could Work Miracles* (1937)—both based on works by H. G. Wells—science fiction before World War II concentrated on individual conflicts rather than global ones. With the war and the threat of nuclear holocaust came a widespread recognition that science and technology were in a position to affect the destiny of the entire

---

1. The first five James Bond films starred the Scottish-born actor Sean Connery, and he became closely identified in the public mind with the series. But he grew tired of the role and refused it for *On Her Majesty's Secret Service,* which offered the Australian actor George Lazenby in the part with scant popular success. The first Eon production of the 1970s, *Diamonds Are Forever* (Guy Hamilton, 1971), brought Connery back, but no one was really happy with the arrangement. After *Live and Let Die* (Hamilton, 1973), Saltzman sold his share in Eon to UA; from then until 1985—in *The Man with the Golden Gun* (Hamilton, 1975); *The Spy Who Loved Me* (Lewis Gilbert, 1977); *Moonraker* (Gilbert, 1979); *For Your Eyes Only* (John Glen, 1981); *Octopussy* (Glen, 1983); and *A View to a Kill* (Glen, 1985)—Bond was played by the urbane Roger Moore, who had achieved fame as Simon Templar in the Bond-like British TV series *The Saint*. In 1987, the fifteenth Eon production, *The Living Daylights* (Glen), introduced a new Bond in the person of Timothy Dalton, who also played the role in *License to Kill* (John Glen, 1989). Dissatisfied with the performance of the Dalton films, Eon cast Pierce Brosnan as Bond for a four-film series beginning with *Golden-Eye* (Martin Campbell, 1995). Two Bond films have been made outside of the Eon-UA umbrella—*Casino Royale* (John Huston, 1967), adapted from the only Fleming novel (his first) not originally optioned by Broccoli and Saltzman, and *Never Say Never Again* (Irvin Kershner, 1983), a virtual remake of *Thunderball,* produced by Jack Schwartzman for Warner Bros, which brought Connery back as an older, heavier, but still effective James Bond.

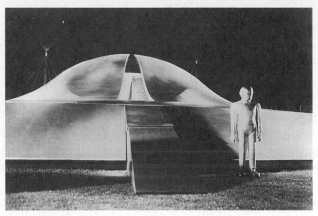

12.24 *The Day the Earth Stood Still* (Robert Wise, 1951): a flying saucer lands in Washington, D.C.

12.25 Visions of a catastrophic future: *When Worlds Collide* (Rudolph Maté, 1951).

human race, and shortly after, the modern science-fiction film, with its emphasis on global catastrophe and space travel, began to take shape. The first important example of the form was *Destination Moon* (Irving Pichel, 1950), which was followed rapidly by *Rocketship X-M* (Kurt Neumann, 1950), *Five* (Arch Oboler, 1951), *The Thing* (also known as *The Thing from Another World*; Christian Nyby, 1951), *The Day the Earth Stood Still* (Robert Wise, 1951), *When Worlds Collide* (Rudolph Maté, 1951), *The Man from Planet X* (Edgar G. Ulmer, 1951), *Flight to Mars* (Lesley Selander, 1951), *Invaders from Mars* (William Cameron Menzies, 1953), *War of the Worlds* (Byron Haskin, 1953), *This Island Earth* (Joseph Newman, 1955), *Forbidden Planet* (Fred Wilcox, 1956), and *Invasion of the Body Snatchers* (Don Siegel, 1956).[2] All of these films were well produced on budgets of widely varying scale, and the element common to most was some form of world-threatening crisis produced by nuclear war or alien invasion (and, in the Siegel film, an invasion that threatens not destruction, but conversion)—with obvious political implications.

In fact, with their constant warnings against infiltration and invasion, the paranoid politics of the Cold War permeated the science-fiction boom of the 1950s almost as thoroughly as state-of-the-art special effects, which reached a new plateau in the early years of the decade with the films of producer George Pal (1908–1980) and special effects director Ray Harryhausen (b. 1920). Pal, a native-born Hungarian whose brilliant matte work

won Special Effects Oscars for *Destination Moon*, *When Worlds Collide*, and *War of the Worlds*, had begun his career as a UFA set designer and became a puppet animator in Hollywood during the war (e.g., Paramount's *Puppetoons* series, 1943–44); after his successes of the

2. *Rocketship X-M* was rushed into production several months after *Destination Moon* but was actually released two months before it, having many fewer special effects. *Invasion of the Body Snatchers* was remade twice—first by Philip Kaufman in 1978, with appearances by its original director, Don Siegel, and star, Kevin McCarthy, and then by Abel Ferrara as *Body Snatchers* in 1994. *The Thing* was remade by John Carpenter as a high-tech eighties-style gore fest in 1982; *Strange Invaders* (Michael Laughlin, 1983) contains significant elements of *The Day the Earth Stood Still*; and *Invaders from Mars* was remade by Tobe Hooper in 1986.

12.26 *Invasion of the Body Snatchers* (Don Siegel, 1956): Dana Wynter and Kevin McCarthy pursued by pod people.

early 1950s, Pal went on to produce and direct such fantasy films as *Tom Thumb* (1958; Academy Award for Special Effects), *The Time Machine* (1960; Academy Award for Special Effects), *Atlantis, the Lost Continent* (1961), *The Wonderful World of the Brothers Grimm* (co-directed with Henry Levin, 1962; Cinerama), and *The Seven Faces of Dr. Lao* (1964). Harryhausen was a protégé of special-effects pioneer Willis O'Brien (1886–1962; *The Lost World*, 1925; *King Kong* and *Son of Kong*, 1933; *The Last Days of Pompeii*, 1935; *Mighty Joe Young*, 1949; etc.),[3] who specialized in a three-dimensional, stop-motion process that enabled him to combine animated models with live action. Patented in 1957 as Dynamation, versions of the technique were used in some of the best of the monster films as well as in the more elaborate Sinbad series (e.g. *The Seventh Voyage of Sinbad* [Nathan Juran, 1958], *The Golden Voyage of Sinbad* [Gordon Hessler, 1974]; *Sinbad and the Eye of the Tiger* [Sam Wanamaker, 1977]; adaptations from Swift (*The 3 Worlds of Gulliver* [Jack Sher, 1960]), Verne (*Mysterious Island* [Cy Endfield, 1961]), and Wells (*First Men in the Moon*, [Nathan Juran, 1964]); the prehistoric adventure epic *One Million Years B.C.* (Don Chaffey, 1966), and the

mythological fantasies *Jason and the Argonauts* (Don Chaffey, 1963) and *Clash of the Titans* (Desmond Davis, 1981).

All of the decade's science-fiction films contained an element of dread, but *The Thing*, which concerned the coming to Earth of a dangerous creature from another galaxy, started a phenomenally popular cycle of films about monsters and mutations produced by nuclear radiation or materialized from outer space that dominated the genre for the next ten years. Science-fiction purists argue that the monster films of the 1950s were less science fiction than horror, but the line between the two categories is sometimes difficult to draw. The films of the Universal horror cycle of the 1930s (*Dracula, Frankenstein*, etc.—see Chapter 8) and the imaginative widescreen color remakes of them produced by England's Hammer Films in the late 1950s and the 1960s, for example, are clearly distinguishable in iconography and theme from science-fiction classics like *Invasion of the Body Snatchers* and *Forbidden Planet*. Here science fiction seems to be concerned with the catastrophic impact of technology on civilization—an impact that means the end of evolution—while horror focuses upon the potential evil within the human heart. But monster films pose the specifically modern (that is, postwar) problem of how human evil and technology *combine* to threaten the existence of the race, and therefore they seem to straddle the generic fence between science fiction and horror.[4]

Some of the early monster films were carefully produced by the majors, like RKO's *The Thing*, Warner Bros.' *The Beast from 20,000 Fathoms* (Eugene Lourie, 1953; effects by Harryhausen), and the same studio's *Them!* (Gordon Douglas, 1954). Other monster films of

---

3. O'Brien worked into the 1950s and early 1960s, contributing special effects to the monster films *The Black Scorpion* (Edward Ludwig, 1957) and *The Giant Behemoth* (Eugène Lourié, 1959), a remake of *The Lost World* (Irwin Allen, 1960), and *It's a Mad Mad Mad Mad World* (Stanley Kramer, 1963; Cinerama). He also wrote the story for *The Beast of Hollow Mountain* (Edward Nassour, 1956), a combination Western–science-fiction thriller shot on location in Mexico.

4. Of course, works of fiction as far back as Mary Shelley's novel *Frankenstein* (1818) have contemplated this problem, but it was not until the discovery of nuclear fission and its "practical" applications that technology and malevolence could *literally* combine to destroy the species.

12.27 *The Beast from 20,000 Fathoms* (Eugène Lourié, 1953).

12.29 *It Came from Outer Space* (Jack Arnold, 1953, 3-D)—and Steven Spielberg must have watched it over and over again.

the 1950s—e.g. Columbia's *It Came from beneath the Sea* (Robert Gordon, 1955) and *20 Million Miles to Earth* (Nathan Juran, 1957), both with effects by Harryhausen: Fox's *Kronos* and *The Fly* (both Kurt Neumann; 1957, 1958); and Paramount's *The Colossus of New York* (Eugène Lourié, 1958) and *The Blob* (Irvin S. Yeaworth, 1958)[5]—relied heavily on their special effects. By mid-decade, monster films had largely become the province of exploitation producers, but there were clear exceptions in the inventive work of Jack Arnold (1916–1992), most of it for Universal-International, who directed *It Came from Outer Space* (1953; 3-D), a major source for Steven Spielberg's *E.T. The Extra-Terrestrial*

(1982); *Creature from the Black Lagoon* (1954; 3-D) and its sequel, *Revenge of the Creature* (1955; 3-D), the last film released in the 1950s version of 3-D (the final entry in the "Gill Man" cycle was *The Creature Walks among Us*, 1956, directed by Arnold's protégé John Sherwood); *Tarantula* (1955), one of the best of the insect mutation thrillers; *The Incredible Shrinking Man* (1957), a film that cleverly inverts the premise of the monster/mutant cycle, (ineptly parodied by Joel Schumacher in *The Incredible Shrinking Woman* twenty-four years later; *Monster on the Campus* (1958); and *The Space Children* (1958), one of the era's first antinuclear science-fiction films.[6]

The Japanese, recent witnesses to nuclear horror themselves, entered the atomic-monster field with a well-crafted series of films directed by Inoshiro Honda (b.

12.28 *Them!* (Gordon Douglas, 1954): an avatar of *Aliens* (James Cameron, 1986)—see still 20.46.

---

5. *The Fly* was strikingly remade for Fox by the Canadian director David Cronenberg in 1986. The original version had generated two sequels, both Fox productions: *Return of the Fly* (Edward Bernds, 1959) and *Curse of the Fly* (Don Sharp, 1965). *The Blob* was remade for TriStar in 1988, with high-tech special effects and direction by Chuck Russell.

6. Arnold, who began his career as a documentarist for the U.S. State Department, directed successful films in other genres during this period, including *film gris* (*The Tattered Dress, Man In the Shadow*, both 1957) and comedy (*The Lady Takes a Flyer*, 1958; *The Mouse That Roared*, 1959; *Bachelor in Paradise*, 1961). He occasionally coproduced and coscripted his own work (e.g., *Tarantula*, 1955) as well as that of colleagues (e.g., *The Monolith Monsters*, John Sherwood, 1957). See Dana M. Reemes, *Directed by Jack Arnold* (Jefferson, N.C.: McFarland, 1988).

12.30 Making a lot with a little: Jack Arnold's *The Incredible Shrinking Man* (1957). Grant Williams.

1911) for Toho Studios with effects by Eiji Tsuburaya (1901–1970), beginning with *Godzilla, King of the Monsters* (*Gojira*, 1954; English-language version, Terrell O. Morse, 1956) and continuing through such widescreen color epics as *Rodan* (1956), *Varan the Unbelievable* (1958; rereleased 1962), *The Mysterians* (1957), *Battle in Outer Space* (1959), *Mothra* (1961), *Gorath* (1962), *Atragon* (1963), and, with increasing silliness, *King Kong vs. Godzilla* (1962), *Godzilla vs. the Thing* (1964), *Ghidra, the Three-Headed Monster* (1964), *Frankenstein Conquers the World* (1965), *Monster Zero* (also known as *Invasion of the Astro-Monster*, 1965), *War of the Gargantuas* (1966), *King Kong Escapes* (1967), and the cycle's *Götterdammerung, Destroy All Monsters* (1968). Typically, American distributors enhanced the box-office appeal of these imports by peppering them with extraneous footage of American actors like Raymond Burr, Russ Tamblyn, or Nick Adams, with the result that their plots, never a strong point, became virtually incoherent. But during the 1950s, at least, their imaginative special effects and model work made the Japanese monster films very popular with audiences all over the world.

Most of the American low-budget science-fiction quickies of the 1950s were made by Allied Artists (AA) or American International Pictures (AIP), the successors to the B-film studios of the 1930s and 1940s.[7] AA

---

7. The popularity of the form was such, however, that virtually every film-releasing organization in the country, from the largest studio to the sleaziest distributor, was involved. Fox contributed several interesting CinemaScope entries shot in black and white by Karl Struss (*She Devil* [Kurt Neumann, 1957]; *The Alligator People* [Roy Del Ruth, 1959]); Paramount offered the exploitationally entitled but intriguing *I Married a Monster from Outer Space* (Gene Fowler, Jr., 1958); MGM handled *Fiend without a Face* (Arthur Crabtree, 1958) and *The First Man Into Space* (also known as *Satellite of Blood* [Robert Day, 1959]); Columbia contributed *The Creature with the Atom Brain* (Edward L. Cahn, 1955), *The Gamma People* (John Gilling, 1956), *The Mole People* (Virgil Vogel, 1956) and *The Deadly Mantis* (Nathan Juran, 1957)—these two written and produced by the former Mercury Theatre actor William Alland (who played the reporter Thompson in *Kane* and was also the producer of Universal-International's popular Creature series)—*The Giant Claw* (Fred F. Sears, 1957), *The Night the World Exploded* (Sears, 1957), *The 27th Day* (William Asher, 1957), and *The Electronic Monster* (Montgomery Tully, 1960); Universal-International was responsible for *The 4D Man* (Irvin S. Yeaworth, 1959), and *The Leech Woman* (Edward Dein, 1960); United Artists fronted *The Magnetic Monster* (Curt Siodmak, 1953), *Gog* (Herbert L. Strock, 1954; 3-D), *The Monster that Challenged the World* (Arnold Laven, 1957), *It! The Terror from beyond Space* (Edward L. Cahn, 1958), *(It Fell from) The Flame Barrier* (Paul Landers, 1958), and *Invisible Invaders* (Edward L. Cahn, 1958); the minuscule Astor Films inflicted *Robot Monster* (Phil Tucker, 1953; 3-D—allegedly made for $502.25), *Cat Woman of the Moon* (Arthur Hilton, 1953), its remake, *Missile to the Moon* (Richard Cunha, 1959), and *She Demons* (Cunha, 1958); Distributor's Corporation of America (DCA) had the fortune to distribute the works of Edward D. Wood (1922–1978), widely considered to have been the worst director of all time (*Glen or Glenda?*, 1953; *Jail Bait*, 1954; *Bride of the Monster*, 1956; *Plan 9 from Outer Space*, 1959; *Night of the Ghouls*, unreleased—see Tim Burton's 1994 biopic *Ed Wood*), as well as *Monster from Green Hell* (Kenneth Crane, 1958), the British imports *The Cosmic Monster* (Gilbert Gunn, 1958) and *The Crawling Eye* (Quentin Lawrence, 1958); finally, regional pickup distribution accounted for the release of such films as *Fire Maidens from Outer Space* (Cy Roth, 1956), *Giant from the Unknown* (Richard Cunha, 1958), *The Brain from Planet Arous* (Nathan Hertz [Juran], 1958), *The Hideous Sun Demon* (Robert Clarke, Thomas Boutross, and Gianbatista Cassarino, 1959), *The Giant Gila Monster* (Ray Kellogg, 1959), *The Killer Shrews* (Ray Kellogg, 1959), *The Beast of Yucca Flat* (Coleman Francis, 1961) and *The Slime People* (Robert Hutton, 1963).

was in fact a reincarnation of Monogram Productions, which had changed its corporate name in 1952. The studio struggled through much of the 1950s and 1960s, producing a handful of good science-fiction entries—notably, *Invasion of the Body Snatchers*, *The Giant Behemoth* (Eugène Lourié 1959; effects by Willis O'Brien), and Britain's *Day of the Triffids* (Steve Sekely, 1963)—but surviving mainly on such cheapies as *Target Earth* (Sherman A. Rose, 1954), *The Indestructible Man* (Jack Pollexfen, 1956), *The Attack of the Crab Monsters* and *Not of This Earth*[8] (both Roger Corman, 1956), *From Hell It Came* (Dan Milner, 1957), *Attack of the 50 Ft. Woman* (Nathan Hertz [Juran], 1958), *The Cosmic Man* (Herbert Greene, 1958), *Frankenstein 1970* (Howard W. Koch, 1958), *The Atomic Submarine* (Spencer G. Bennet, 1959), and *The Wasp Woman* (Roger Corman, 1959), plus an occasional essay in widescreen and color (*World without End* [Edward Bernds, 1956]; *Queen of Outer Space* [Bernds, 1958]).[9]

The ultimate exploitation producer of the era, however, was AIP, founded by James H. Nicholson and Samuel Z. Arkoff as American Releasing Corporation (ARC) in 1954, with working capital of $3,000. Nicholson and Arkoff were able to build an empire from these humble beginnings by tapping into a market that mainstream producers were ignoring—the children of the baby boom and their teenaged precursors. With the exception of late afternoons and Saturday mornings, television programming of the 1950s was targeted at adults, and so was Hollywood's widescreen Eastmancolor counterprogramming. The majors welcomed box-office spillover from the kids and were always happy to have produced a family hit, but only Disney among them was actually producing films *for* children, and for younger ones, parents in tow, at that.[1] But AIP discovered a market of kids alone, kids who were ready to pay good money for the cheapest kind of audiovisual thrills, as long as their cultural values weren't offended.

During the 1950s AIP produced its share of bargain-basement Westerns, crime thrillers, and teenage exposés, but its real profit center was the monster film, the more sensational and lurid the better. Like its B-studio predecessors, AIP initially rented its features to exhibitors at a flat rate, which meant that they usually wound up at the bottom half of double bills, but by 1956 Nicholson and Arkoff had arrived at the successful for-

mula of packaging their films as already-paired double bills, which enabled them both to better control the market and to double their rentals. The idea was so successful that other exploitation producers copied it, with the result that nearly all of the low-budget films described in this section were seen by their original audiences as parts of a two-film program, yoked with their mates through dual promotion and publicity. AIP was set up as a constellation of five independent producers, among whom were the producer-directors Bert I. Gordon (b. 1922) and Roger Corman (b. 1926). Gordon, who sometimes wrote his own scripts, specialized in low-budget special effects that he produced himself through extensive use of rear-screen projection and mattes, often quite successfully. His insect-mutation film (giant grasshoppers) *Beginning of the End* (1957) was distributed by Republic, but his next five films—*The Cyclops* (1957); *The Amazing Colossal Man* (1957); its sequel, *War of the Colossal Beast* (1958); *Attack of the*

---

8. *Not of This Earth* was remade in 1988 by Corman's Concorde Pictures, with direction by Jim Wynorski.

9. The fortunes of Allied Artists (AA) turned up in 1965 with its release of the popular Elvis Presley vehicle *Tickle Me* (Norman Taurog, 1965), but in 1967 it sold its studio and, under the leadership of Emanuel L. Wolf, briefly became a releasing company for foreign films—notably *A Man and a Woman* (Claude Lelouch, 1966), *Belle de jour* (Luis Buñuel, 1968), and *The Story of O* (Just Jaeckin, 1975)—before returning to production in the 1970s, financing such successful films as *Cabaret* (Bob Fosse, 1972), *Papillon* (Franklin J. Schaffner, 1973), *The Man Who Would Be King* (John Huston, 1975), and *Conduct Unbecoming* (Michael Anderson, 1975). An attempt at diversification failed in 1979, and AA and its library of 450 films were sold to Lorimar Productions the following year (see Chapter 20).

1. The Disney studios actually produced one of the science-fiction classics of the decade, albeit a specialized one: *20,000 Leagues under the Sea* (Richard Fleischer, 1954), with elaborate special effects by Ralph Hammeras. This $4-million CinemaScope version of Jules Verne's 1870 novel, first adapted by Georges Méliès in 1907, was a remake of Universal's 1916 silent spectacular (directed by Stuart Paton, with effects by the father of underwater photography, John Ernest Williamson), and its popular success led to a cycle of Verne adaptations over the next decade, including *From the Earth to the Moon* (Byron Haskin, 1958), *Journey to the Center of the Earth* (Henry Levin, 1959), *Master of the World* (William Witney, 1961), *Mysterious Island* (Cy Endfield, 1961; effects by Harryhausen), and *Around the World under the Sea* (Andrew Marton, 1966).

12.31 Bargain-basement spectacle: Bert I. Gordon's *The Amazing Colossal Man* (1957).

Puppet People (1958); and *The Spider* (1958)—were all big money makers for AIP.[2]

Corman, a much more important figure, initially specialized in monster/horror quickies, some of which—e.g., *Monster from the Ocean Floor* (1954), *The Day the World Ended* (1956), *It Conquered the World* (1956), *The Undead* (1957), *The Viking Women and the Sea Ser-*

12.32 AIP's *I Was a Teenage Werewolf* (Gene Fowler, Jr., 1957): Whit Bissell, Vladimir Sokoloff, Michael Landon (as the werewolf). Earlier in the decade, Fowler had been an editor for Fritz Lang.

pent (1957), *The She Gods of Shark Reef* (1959), and *The Wasp Woman* (1959)—were reputedly produced in less than three days. But he also produced the much-admired black-humor trilogy *A Bucket of Blood* (1959), *The Little Shop of Horrors* (1960),[3] and *Creature from the Haunted Sea* (1960)—the latter two for his own company, Filmgroup—and when AIP decided to make its films in CinemaScope and color, Corman was given the first such assignment, *The Fall of the House of Usher* (1960), adapted from Edgar Allan Poe by the novelist Richard Matheson and budgeted at a princely $350,000. This film was both a critical and commercial success, becoming the first AIP release since 1956 to play by itself (in most theaters) and the first ever to rent on a percentage basis in the manner of a standard mainstream feature. It was followed by a series of increasingly successful Poe films, scripted by some combination of Matheson, Charles Beaumont, and Robert Towne, and produced and directed by Corman: *The Pit and the Pendulum* (1961), *The Premature Burial* (1962), *Tales of Terror* (1962; an anthology of three Poe stories woven together in the manner of the British classic *Dead of Night* [1945]), *The Raven* (1963), *The Haunted Palace* (1963; "inspired" by Poe's poem but actually adapted

---

2. AIP continued to grind out 1950s-style monster fare until 1963, when it struck a new vein with *Beach Party* (William Asher, 1963), which established a successful formula that was reworked in such near-clones as *Bikini Beach* (Asher, 1964), *Muscle Beach Party* (Asher, 1964), *Pajama Party* (Don Weis, 1964), *Beach Blanket Bingo* (Asher, 1965), *Dr. Goldfoot and the Bikini Machine* (Norman Taurog, 1965), *How to Stuff a Wild Bikini* (Asher, 1965), and *Ski Party* (Alan Rafkin, 1965). Teenage exploitation films, or "teenpix," had been launched by Columbia's *Rock around the Clock* (Fred F. Sears), starring Bill Haley and the Comets, in 1956 and immediately cloned at AIP by Edward L. Cahn (*Shake, Rattle, and Rock*, 1957) and Roger Corman (*Rock All Night*, 1957); these were followed by a host of other rock 'n' roll-themed cheapies like *Rock, Pretty Baby* (Richard Bartlett, 1957), *Rock, Rock, Rock!* (Will Price, 1957), and *Don't Knock the Rock* (Fred F. Sears, 1957). In the same year, AIP gene-spliced the teenpic with the monster film in a remarkably successful cycle produced by Herman Cohen—*I Was a Teenage Werewolf* (Gene Fowler, Jr.), *I Was a Teenage Frankenstein* (Herbert L. Strock), *Blood of Dracula* (Strock), and in later years *How to Make a Monster* (Strock, 1958) and *Konga* (aka *I was a Teenage Gorilla*, John Lemont, 1961). (Other contributions came from James Marquette [*Teenage Monster*, also known as *Meteor Monster*, 1957], Roger Corman [*Teenage Caveman*, 1958], Tom Graeff [*Teenagers from Outer Space*, 1959], and Jerry Warren [*Teenage Zombies*, 1960].)

3. Adapted by Howard Ashman and Alan Menken as a successful Broadway musical and a 1986 film directed by Frank Oz.

from an H. P. Lovecraft story), *The Masque of the Red Death* (1964), and *The Tomb of Ligeia* (1965), the last two featuring extraordinary cinematography by future director Nicolas Roeg (see Chapter 14).[4] In between, Corman was churning out box-office fodder like *The Last Woman on Earth* (1960), *Ski Troop Attack* (1960), *The Tower of London* (1962), *The Young Racers* (1963), and *The Secret Invasion* (1964), in addition to a chilling portrayal of lynch-mob violence in *The Intruder* (1962), the now-legendary *The Terror* (1963—a film shot in two days on the dismantled sets of *The Raven*, which combined the acting talents of Boris Karloff and Jack Nicholson with the directorial skills of Corman, Francis Coppola, and Monte Hellman,[5] and *X—The Man with X-Ray Eyes* (1963), an intelligent moral allegory of *seeing* in the form of medical science fiction. Corman demonstrated his continued prescience by producing two visually imaginative films that helped to shape the "youth cult" boom of the late 1960s, *The Wild Angels* (1966), a graphically violent, *cinéma vérité*–style biker epic that became the American entry in the Venice Film Festival for that year, and *The Trip* (1967), a guided tour through an LSD experience, both starring Peter Fonda. Corman also made two excellent medium-budget gangster films (having already produced two striking low-budget ones in *Machine Gun Kelly* and *I Mobster*, both 1958)—*The St. Valentine's Day Massacre* (1967, Fox), whose ballistic Grand Guignol forecasts that of *Bonnie and Clyde* (Arthur Penn, 1967) later in the year, and *Bloody Mama* (1969), an account of the brutal Ma Barker family made to cash in on *Bonnie and Clyde*'s phenomenal popularity. In 1970, Corman left AIP to form New World Pictures, which over the next decade was to become the largest independent producer/distributor in the United States.

Here, as at AIP, Corman was able to back a number of talented but unknown young directors in their first features. In fact, Francis Ford Coppola (*Dementia 13*, 1963), Peter Bogdanovich (*Targets*, 1968),[6] Jonathan Demme (*Caged Heat*, 1974; *Crazy Mama*, 1975), Joe Dante (*Hollywood Boulevard*, with Allan Arkush, 1976; *Piranha*, 1978), and Ron Howard (*Grand Theft Auto*, 1977) all debuted in Corman productions, and Martin Scorsese made his first Hollywood film for Corman (*Boxcar Bertha*, 1972—a sequel to *Bloody Mama*). Furthermore, during the 1970s New World Pictures became the American distributor for some of the decade's most important foreign films, including *Cries and Whispers* (Ingmar Bergman, 1972), *The Harder They Come* (Perry Henzell, 1973), *Fantastic Planet* (Rene Laloux, 1974), *Amarcord* (Federico Fellini, 1974), *The Story of Adèle H.* (François Truffaut, 1975), *The Lost Honor of Katharina Blum* (Volker Schlöndorff and Margarethe von Trotta, 1975), *Lumière* (Jeanne Moreau, 1977), *Small Change* (Truffaut, 1977), *Dersu Uzala* (Akira Kurosawa, 1978), *Autumn Sonata* (Bergman, 1980), *The Tin Drum* (Schlöndorff, 1980), *Mon Oncle d'Amerique* (Alain Resnais, 1980), and *Breaker Morant* (Bruce Beresford, 1980). Although he did not personally direct a film between 1971 (*Von Richthofen and Brown*, UA) and 1990 (*Frankenstein Unbound*, Warners), Corman continued to exert an important influence on the American cinema as a producer through New World (*Death Race 2000* [Paul Bartel, 1975]; *Saint Jack* [Peter Bogdanovich, 1979]; *Humanoids from the Deep* [Barbara Peeters, 1980]; *Battle beyond the Stars* [Jimmy T. Murakami, 1980]; *Love Letters* [Amy Jones, 1981]; *Galaxy of Terror* [B. D. Clark, 1981]), until he sold it in 1983 to form Concorde Pictures with his wife, Julie (first productions: *Streetwalkin'* [Joan Freeman, 1985]; *Big Bad Mama II* [Jim Wynorski, 1987]); *Stripped to Kill* [Katt Shea Ruben, 1987]; *The Terror Within* [Thierry Notz, 1989]; *Overexposed* [Larry Brand, 1990]; *Carnosaur* [Adam Simon, 1993], etc.). New World continued to produce such Cormanesque films as *Children of the Corn* (Fritz Kiersch,

---

4. To the AIP Poe cycle should be added *War Gods of the Deep* (Jacques Tourneur, 1965) because it was technically based on the poem "The Doomed City" and the short story "A Descent into the Maelstrom." Produced by Daniel Haller, the film owed nothing to Corman except that it was inspired by the success of his Poe films.

5. Old habits die hard—in 1987, Corman produced two films, *Big Bad Mama II* (Jim Wynorski, 1987) and *Daddy's Boys* (Joe Minion, 1988) simultaneously in twenty-two days and on the same set.

6. *Targets* is an excellent example of the kind of synergy Corman could create among his young collaborators at AIP. The film began when Corman approached Bogdanovich with the proposition that he make a Boris Karloff film by combining new footage of the actor (who still owed Corman two days under contract from *The Terror*) with footage from *The Terror*. Bogdanovich quickly produced a remarkable script that told concurrent stories of an aging horror star and a young Charles Whitman–style mass murderer whose fates converge in a drive-in theater at the film's conclusion. *Targets* was produced for $130,000 and sold to Paramount, which released it with a brief prologue entitled "Why Gun Control?" in the wake of the Robert Kennedy assassination in June 1968. It has deservedly become a cult classic and remains, with *The Last Picture Show* (1972), Bogdanovich's best film.

1984), *The Philadelphia Experiment* (Stewart Raffill, 1984), and *Reform School Girls* (Tom DeSimone, 1986) until its demise in 1987.

In the 1960s and early 1970s, science fiction too became more mainstream, if frequently less exciting. In the United States[7] a series of medium- to high-budget films replaced the exploitation quickies in productions like *The Time Machine* (George Pal, 1960), *The Day Mars Invaded Earth* (Maury Dexter, 1963), *Robinson Crusoe on Mars* (Byron Haskin, 1964; effects by Pal), *The Day the Earth Cracked* (Andrew Marton, 1965), *Fantastic Voyage* (Richard Fleischer, 1966), *Planet of the Apes* (Franklin Schaffner, 1968),[8] *The Omega Man* (Boris Sagal, 1971—a remake of the Corman-produced *The Last Man on Earth* [Sidney Salkow and Ubaldo Ragona, 1964], itself a version of Richard Matheson's postnuclear vampire novel *I Am Legend*), and *The Andromeda Strain* (Robert Wise, 1971). From England came a number of inventive, well-crafted features, including *Gorgo* (Eugène Lourié, 1961), *The Day the Earth Caught Fire* (Val Guest, 1961), *The Day of the Triffids* (Steve Sekely, 1963; adapted from the novel by John Wyndham), and *The Earth Dies Screaming* (Terence Fisher, 1964). England was also the setting for Wolf Rilla's eerie *Village of the Damned* (1960), adapted from John Wyndham's novel about alien children, *The Midwich Cukoos*, and it begat sequels in *Children of the Damned* (Anton M. Leader, 1965) and the more portentous *The Damned* (also known as *These Are the Damned* [Joseph Losey, 1961]; released in the United Kingdom, 1963; in the United States, 1965). Finally, Britain produced *Five Million Years to Earth* (also known as *Quatermass and the Pit* [Roy Ward Baker, 1968]), the third film in Hammer's Quatermass series based on the popular BBC-TV serial written by Nigel Kneale, the first two having been *The Creeping Unknown* (also known as *The Quatermass Experiment* [Val Guest, 1956]) and *Enemy from Space* (also known as *Quatermass II* [Guest, 1957]).

In fact, that science fiction had become a fully respectable genre by the mid-1960s was demonstrated by the number of serious filmmakers who had begun to work in it. These included Joseph Losey, Jean-Luc Godard (*Alphaville*, 1965), François Truffaut (*Fahrenheit 451*, 1966), Elio Petri (*The Tenth Victim*, 1965), Alain Resnais (*Je t'aime, je t'aime*, 1968), and, of course, Stanley Kubrick, who apotheosized the science-fiction film in *2001: A Space Odyssey*, with its multimillion-dollar special effects by

Douglas Trumbull and its deeply metaphysical theme (see Chapter 20). In the 1970s, American science fiction proved to be a dreary affair (e.g., the four *Planet of the Apes* sequels; *The Omega Man* [Boris Sagal, 1971]; *Westworld* [Michael Crichton, 1973]; *Soylent Green* [Richard Fleischer, 1973]; *Rollerball* [Norman Jewison, 1975]; *Logan's Run* [Michael Anderson, 1976]). However, there were notable exceptions, such as Joseph Sargent's *Colossus: The Forbin Project* (also known as *The Forbin Project, Colossus 1980*, 1970), George Lucas's *THX 1138* (1971), Douglas Trumbull's *Silent Running* (1972), John Boorman's *Zardoz* (1974), and Nicholas Roeg's *The Man Who Fell to Earth* (1976), and finally George Lucas's phenomenally successful *Star Wars* in 1977. This film combined sophisticated computerized effects (created by John Dykstra), Dolby stereo sound, and a fantasy-adventure plot containing folkloric elements to create a new breed of American science fiction perpetuated in the sequels *The Empire Strikes Back* (Irvin Kershner, 1980) and *The Return of the Jedi* (Richard Marquand, 1983), as well as in Steven Spielberg's *Close Encounters of the Third Kind* (1977; effects by Dykstra and Trumbull) and *E.T. The Extra-terrestrial* (1982), and the *Star Trek* series (*Star Trek: The Motion Picture* [Robert Wise, 1979; effects by Trumbull]; *Star Trek II: The Wrath of Khan* [Nicholas Meyer, 1982]; *Star Trek III: The Search for Spock* [Leonard Nimoy, 1984]; *Star Trek IV: The Voyage Home* [Nimoy, 1986]); *Star Trek V: The Final Frontier* [William Shatner,

---

7. Although most of the science-fiction films of the era came from American and British producers, a strong and serious tradition for it was evolving in the countries of Eastern Europe, including Czechoslovakia (*Krakatit* [Otakar Vávra, 1951; adapted from Karel Capek]; *The Fabulous World of Jules Verne* [also known as *An Invention of Destruction*, Karel Zeman, 1957; animated]; *Man from the First Century* [Oldřich Lipský, 1962], *Ikarie XB1* [Jindrich Polák, 1963]; *The Lost Face* [Pavel Hobl, 1965]; *The End of August at the Hotel Ozone* [Jan Schmidt, 1965; 1967]; *1, Justice* [Zbyněk Brynych, 1968]); Poland (*The First Spaceship on Venus* [Kurt Maetzig, 1959; 1963]); Yugoslavia (*War* [Veljko Bulajić, 1960]); and the Soviet Union (*Planet of Storms* [Pavel Klushantsev, 1962; adapted from Stanislaw Lem's *Planet of Death*] and *The Amphibious Man* [Y. Kasancki, 1963]). See Chapters 16 and 17.

8. Loosely adapted from Pierre Boulle's novel, this popular blend of science fiction and satire inspired four sequels—*Beneath the Planet of the Apes* (Ted Post, 1970), *Escape from the Planet of the Apes* (Don Taylor, 1971), *Conquest of the Planet of the Apes* (J. Lee Thompson, 1972), and *Battle for the Planet of the Apes* (J. Lee Thompson, 1973), as well as a short-lived television series.

1989]; *Star Trek VI: The Undiscovered Country* [Nicholas Meyer, 1991]). Among the many, many imitators of the *Star Wars* formula, *The Last Starfighter* (Nick Castle, 1984) stands out for its imaginative integration of live action with special effects generated entirely by computer.[9] During the 1980s, this emphasis on high-tech special effects and sound continued in science-fiction films, which, successful or not, often had a more serious edge, including Peter Hyams's *Outland* (1981) and *2010* (1984—the inevitably doomed sequel to *2001*), Ridley Scott's *Alien* (1979) and *Blade Runner* (1982; effects by Trumbull), Douglas Trumbull's *Brainstorm* (1983), John Carpenter's *Starman* (1984), David Lynch's *Dune* (1984), Wolfgang Petersen's *Enemy Mine* (1985), Tobe Hooper's *Lifeforce* (1985; effects by Dykstra), Ron Howard's *Cocoon* (1985), Terry Gilliam's *Brazil* (1985), James Cameron's *The Terminator* (1984), *Aliens* (1986), and *The Abyss* (1989), Rene Laloux's *Light Years* (1987), John McTiernan's *Predator* (1987), and Paul Verhoeven's *RoboCop* (1987) and *Total Recall* (1990).

Distinct subgenres of science fiction that emerged during the decade were the pornographic (*Flesh Gordon* [Michael Benveniste and Howard Ziehm, 1973], *Cafe Flesh* [Rinse Dream, 1982]); the parodic/satiric (*Time after Time* [Nicholas Meyer, 1979], *Flash Gordon* [Mike Hodges, 1980], *Time Bandits* [Terry Gilliam, 1981]. *The Adventures of Buckaroo Banzai across the Eighth Dimension* [W. D. Richter, 1983], *Spaceballs* [Mel Brooks, 1987]); and the punk (*Liquid Sky* [Slava Tsukerman, 1982], *Vortex* [Scott B and Beth B, 1982], *Repo Man* [Alex Cox, 1984], *The Brother from Another Planet* [John Sayles, 1984], *Night of the Comet* [Thom Eberhardt, 1984]. *UFOria* [John Binder, 1986]). In the years surrounding the Reagan administration's deployment of intermediate-range missiles in Western Europe, there was a rash of films dealing with the *immediate* effects of a nuclear war—rather than life in some postnuclear future, whose treatment extends from Arch Oboler's *Five* (1951) through George Miller's *Mad Max* series, 1978–85 (see Chapter 14). These films, all originally made for television, were *The Day After* (Nicholas Meyer, 1983), *Testament* (Lynne Littman, 1983), *Threads* (Mick Jackson, 1984), *Special Bulletin* (Edward Zwick, 1983), and *Countdown to Looking Glass* (Fred Barzyk, 1984). Other science-fiction subtypes include the witty if sometimes juvenile Superman cycle—*Superman The Movie* (Richard Donner, 1978); *Superman II* (Richard Lester, 1980;

1981); *Superman III* (Lester, 1983; and *Superman IV: The Quest for Peace* (Sidney J. Furie, 1987), as well as the unique and occasionally loathsome science-fiction/horror films of the Canadian director David Cronenberg—*They Came from Within* (1975); *Rabid* (1976); *The Brood* (1978); *Scanners* (1979); *Videodrome* (1982); *The Dead Zone* (1983); *The Fly* (1986); *Dead Ringers* (1988); and science-fiction films involving "medical" research (*Coma* [Michael Crichton, 1978]; *Re-Animator* [Stuart Gordon, 1985]), gene splicing (*Parts: The Clonus Horror* [Robert Fiveson, 1979]; *The Kindred* [Stephen Carpenter and Jeffrey Obrow, 1987]), and the cloning of DNA (*Jurassic Park* [Steven Spielberg, 1993]; *Species* [Roger Donaldson, 1995]).

THE "SMALL FILM": AMERICAN KAMMERSPIEL

The final generic development of the American 1950s was the brief appearance of the "small film," a low-budget black-and-white film shot in the Academy frame format with television techniques and concerned with the everyday lives of ordinary people. Clearly influenced by Italian neorealism, these films were independently produced, shot largely on location, and usually adapted from original teleplays for live drama by writers like Rod Serling, Paddy Chayefsky, and Reginald Rose. The first small film was *Marty* (Delbert Mann, 1955), based on a downbeat Chayefsky teleplay about the life of a shy, unattractive butcher in New York City. It was produced by the independent Hecht-Lancaster organization (see p. 426) and was an unprecedented critical success, winning both the Grand Prix at Cannes and the American Academy Award for Best Actor (to Ernest Borgnine) in the year of its release. *Marty* was also a great commercial success, and this encouraged the production of other small films adapted from teleplays. Rod Serling's tense drama about the viciousness of corporate power struggles, *Patterns of Power*, was adapted by Fielder Cook as *Patterns* (1956), while Hecht-Lancaster attempted to repeat the success of *Marty* in *The Bachelor Party* (1957), written by Cha-

---

9. Whereas the effects for *Star Wars* were computer-assisted, those for *The Last Starfighter* were entirely digitalized, an important distinction. (See Chapter 21.)

12.33 The "small film." *Marty* **(Delbert Mann, 1955). Ernest Borgnine.**

yefsky and directed by Delbert Mann. Rose's *12 Angry Men* (Sidney Lumet, 1957), Serling's *Requiem for a Heavyweight* (Ralph Nelson, 1962), and Chayefsky's *The Catered Affair* (Richard Brooks, 1956) and *Middle of the Night* (Delbert Mann, 1959) were all adapted for the screen as "small films," but as live drama began to disappear from television in the late 1950s, to be replaced by weekly filmed series, the small-film movement vanished, too. The barrier between cinema and television had been broken by the small film, however, and the relationship was to remain an open one, so that ultimately the two media learned to co-exist and even to subsist upon one another. By the late 1950s, for instance, the major studios were devoting a substantial percentage of their production facilities to the filming of weekly television series modeled on the B-pictures of the 1930s and 1940s. And by the mid-1960s some of the American cinema's most important new directors—John Frankenheimer, Irvin Kershner, Sidney Lumet, and Sam Peckinpah, to name a few—had begun their careers in studio television production.

Independent Production and the Decline of the Studio System

As this account of the small film suggests, independent production outside of the studio was on the rise in the 1950s. Four of the decade's most brilliant American films—*Kiss Me Deadly* (Robert Aldrich, 1955; Parklane Productions), *The Night of the Hunter* (Charles Laughton, 1955; Paul Gregory Productions—the actor's only film as a director), *The Sweet Smell of Success* (Alexander Mackendrick, 1957; Hecht-Hill-Lancaster), and *Paths of Glory* (Stanley Kubrick, 1957; Harris-Kubrick Productions)—were independently produced, all of them for United Artists release, as were seven of the films given the Academy Award for Best Picture between 1954 and 1962. Stanley Kramer started his independent production activities as early as 1948, producing *Home of the Brave* (Mark Robson, 1949), *Champion* (Mark Robson, 1949), *The Men* (Fred Zinnemann, 1950), and *High Noon* (Fred Zinnemann, 1952) on modest budgets in rapid succession. While Kramer's status as a director is equivocal, his production record is distinguished; it also includes a film version of Arthur Miller's play *Death of a Salesman* (Laslo Benedek, 1952), *The Member of the Wedding* (Fred Zinnemann, 1953), and *The Wild One* (Laslo Benedek, 1954). United Artists, which distributed most of Kramer's films, found that its liabilities of the 1930s and 1940s became assets during the 1950s and 1960s. Having no expensive production facilities to maintain in an era of ever-increasing location shooting, and no theater circuits to lose to the consent decrees, United Artists had become the most important independent producer in Hollywood by 1956. In this capacity, it distributed some of the era's landmark films, including Fred Zinnemann's anti-McCarthy Western *High Noon* (1952), Chaplin's controversial *Limelight* (1952), the first film in Natural Vision (Oboler's *Bwana Devil*, 1953), Otto Preminger's code-breaking *The Moon Is Blue* (1953) and *The Man with the Golden Arm* (1955), most of the "small films" mentioned above, and such road-shown widescreen blockbusters as *Around the World in 80 Days* (Michael Anderson, 1956) and *Exodus* (Preminger, 1960). United Artists also produced much of John

Huston's major work during the period—*The African Queen* (1952), *Moulin Rouge* (1953), *Beat the Devil* (1954), and *The Misfits* (1961), as well as the early films of Stanley Kubrick (*Killer's Kiss*, 1955; *The Killing*, 1956; *Paths of Glory*, 1957). The Hecht-Lancaster Company (Hecht-Hill-Lancaster after 1956), organized in 1947 by producer Harold Hecht and actor Burt Lancaster, was another successful independent. From the early 1950s, it specialized in sophisticated action films starring Lancaster, such as *The Crimson Pirate* (Robert Siodmak, 1952), *Apache* (Robert Aldrich, 1954), *Vera Cruz* (Robert Aldrich, 1954), *The Kentuckian* (Burt Lancaster, 1955), and *Trapeze* (Carol Reed, 1956), although it also produced a number of important "small films." Other notable independent production companies born in the 1950s, all of which released through United Artists, were the Walter Mirisch Corporation, Seven-Arts, and actor Kirk Douglas's Bryna Productions. By 1958, in fact, 65 percent of Hollywood's motion pictures were made by independents, as the focus of production shifted away from the studios to the production unit itself.

No account of independent production in the 1950s would be complete without mentioning two distinct phenomena at the high and low ends of the exploitation scale. As the search for new formats in the war with television intensified in 1959–60, several filmmakers introduced Aroma-Rama and Smell-O-Vision, systems designed to let theater audiences smell what they saw on screen. Aroma-Rama pumped its scents through a theater's existing air-conditioning system and removed them (not entirely successfully) with electronic air filters. Smell-O-Vision (also known as Scentovision) used individual atomizers strategically positioned between the rows of seats. Only one feature was made with each process—Aroma-Rama's *Behind the Great Wall*, a documentary on China that premiered at the Mayfair Theater in New York City on December 2, 1959, and Smell-O-Vision's *Scent of Mystery*, produced by Mike Todd, Jr., and premiered at the Cinestage Theater in Chicago on January 12, 1960 (the latter was rereleased, odorless, the same year as *Holiday in Spain*). Like 3-D earlier in the decade, neither system survived its novelty period, although, when working properly, both could create an impressive olfactory illusion. (The Baltimore-based producer-director John Waters revived the idea for *Polyester* [1981], providing theater patrons with Odorama

scratch-and-sniff cards keyed to numbers flashed onscreen.)

Closer to Waters's own sensibility in the late 1950s was the independent producer-director William Castle (see Waters's "Whatever Happened to Showmanship?" *American Film* 9, 3 [December 1983]: 55–58). Castle (1914–1977) evinced a genius for cheap but effective exploitation gimmicks that were often more engaging than the films they were employed to market. For *Macabre* (1958), for example, a $90,000 uncredited remake of Clouzot's *Diabolique* (1955), he insured the life of every theater patron for $1,000 with Lloyd's of London against death from fright; *The House on Haunted Hill* (1959) boasted a "process" called Emergo, which was actually a 12-foot plastic skeleton that would zoom over the audience on a wire at a certain point in the film; *The Tingler* (1959) was "shot" in Percepto, which meant that a seat in each theater row was wired with an electric buzzer that would cause the spectator to "tingle" when the monster supposedly got loose in the theater—an unconsciously Brechtian moment, when the projector "breaks" and, from the dark screen, a character, Vincent Price, speaks directly to the audience of its peril; *Thirteen Ghosts* (1960) offered Illusion-O, which permitted audiences to see infrared superimpositions of ghostly images by using special glasses; *Homicidal* (1961), a shameless rip-off of *Psycho* (1960), had a "Fright Break" of two minutes before its horrific conclusion, during which patrons could have their admissions refunded if they were willing to stand in "Coward's Corner" first; finally, Castle shot two separate endings for *Mr. Sardonicus* (1961) so that viewers could vote on the fate of the villainous title character in a "Punishment Poll" near the film's conclusion. Castle went on to produce and direct such gimmick-free shockers as *Strait-Jacket* (1964), which handily cast Joan Crawford in the role of an ax-murderer, *I Saw What You Did* (1965), *Let's Kill Uncle* (1966), and *Project X* (1968), and to produce the almost entirely respectable *Rosemary's Baby* (Roman Polanski, 1968); but he is best remembered for his successful practice of participatory cinema, albeit of the dime-store variety, long before the advent of *The Rocky Horror Picture Show* (Jim Sharman, 1975) and its brethren.

The old studio production system remained in operation throughout the 1950s, but continued to crumble under the combined threats of political pressure, television, rising independent production, and, perhaps most serious, loss of the exhibition chains. By mid-decade, steadily increasing monetary inflation could be added to this catalogue of woes, and all of these forces spelled the beginning of the end for Hollywood as it had been structured since the 1920s. From the peak year of 1946, when American theaters had averaged nearly 100 million admissions per week, film attendance dropped to 46 million in 1955. Production fell from nearly 500 features per year throughout the 1930s to 383 in 1950, to 254 in 1955. Decca Records absorbed Universal Pictures in 1952 and was absorbed in turn by the huge entertainment conglomerate MCA between 1959 and 1962.[1] RKO ceased production entirely in 1957 (although the famous name survives in RKO General, the broadcast ownership division of the General Tire and Rubber Company). American film production and audience attendance both continued to decline while production costs soared until, by 1966, 30 percent of all films made in the United States were independently produced, and 50 percent of all American films were "runaway" productions—that is, films shot on location in foreign countries (usually Italy, Yugoslavia, or Spain) to economize on sets and labor (nonunion and therefore cheaper). In other words, by the mid-1960s, 80 percent of all American films were made outside the once ironclad studio system. Moreover, as discussed in the next chapters, the foreign industries had recovered from the war by the late 1950s and for the first time were offering Hollywood vigorous commercial competition. Stiff postwar import duties on nondomestic productions had severely restricted Hollywood's most profitable European markets—especially England, Italy, and France—while American demand for foreign films had been growing steadily since the divestiture order of 1948 first permitted U.S. exhibitors to show what they chose rather than what the studios had chosen for them. In fact, between 1958 and 1968, the number of foreign films in distribution in the United States would actually exceed the number of domestic productions, often by a ratio of two (and sometimes, three) to one.

As the studio system declined throughout the 1950s, so too did the star system with which it had been intimately linked for over thirty years. As studios were forced to cut back on production due to the inroads of television, inflation, and other blights, expensive promotional campaigns were abandoned and star contracts went from long-term to short-term and finally to simple profit-sharing options on individual films. This practice began as early as 1949, when *Variety* reported that Warner Bros. and Paramount had negotiated profit-sharing deals for as high as 33 percent with John Garfield, Danny Kaye, Milton Berle, Bob Hope, and Bing Crosby. But the historic catalyst for the shift occurred in 1950, when Lew Wasserman of MCA negotiated a 50 percent share of Universal's *Winchester '73* for Jimmy Stewart, earning him $600,000 when the film became a popular success. Obviously, deals like these made the stars increasingly independent of the studios, and some, like Burt Lancaster and Kirk Douglas, even formed their own production companies. There were American stars in the 1950s, to be sure, and many whose careers had begun under the studio system—among them, Lancaster, Douglas, James Stewart, Cary Grant, Henry Fonda, John Wayne, Rock Hudson, Tony Curtis, Charlton Heston, Montgomery Clift, Robert Mitchum, William Holden, Frank Sinatra, Yul Brynner, Glenn Ford, Gregory Peck, Gary Cooper, Ava Gardner, Jean Simmons, Grace Kelly, Audrey Hepburn, Susan Hayward, Gina Lollobrigida, Sophia Loren, Deborah Kerr, Debbie Reynolds, Elizabeth Taylor, Kim Novak, Doris Day, and—quintessentially—Marilyn Monroe, Marlon Brando, and James Dean. But they worked more independently of the system than had earlier stars, and, to quote Alexander Walker, the 1950s in general were the transitional period "from studios who owned stars to stars who owned pictures."

---

1. Music Corporation of America (MCA) was founded in 1924 by Dr. Jules Stein (1896–1981) as a booking agency for dance bands in Chicago. MCA moved to Hollywood in 1936 and became a major talent-broker there under the aggressive leadership of Stein's protégé Lew Wasserman (b. 1913), who became corporate president in 1946 and still serves as chairman of the board. Wasserman's genius lay in engineering deals for his clients. By the early 1950s MCA had become one of the most powerful forces in the industry, controlling 1,400 top entertainers and moving into the new field of television production through its Revue subsidiary. In July 1952, Ronald Reagan, then president of the Screen Actors Guild, granted MCA a seven-year waiver of the guild's prohibition against agents acting simultaneously as producers, giving the company an enormous competitive edge over its rivals and creating a clear conflict of interest for the duration. Meanwhile, MCA continued to grow, acquiring Decca Records and Universal Pictures between 1959 and 1962, when the Justice Department finally forced the divestiture of its agency business. Called the "star-spangled octopus," or simply the Octopus, by its critics, MCA remains one of Hollywood's most powerful conglomerates.

The Scrapping of the Production Code

A final important development of the 1950s in America was the breaking of the Production Code and the achievement of an unprecedented freedom of expression for the cinema. Ever since a U.S. Supreme Court decision of 1915 (*Mutual v. Ohio*), the movies had not been considered a part of the press, whose freedom is guaranteed by the First Amendment to the Constitution. For this reason, six states and hundreds of local communities had film censorship boards, and of course, through the Production Code, Hollywood had imposed an extreme form of censorship upon itself. But this situation changed in 1952, after the state of New York attempted to prevent the exhibition of the Italian film *II miracolo* (*The Miracle* [Roberto Rossellini, 1948; written by Federico Fellini, Tullio Pinelli, and Rossellini himself]) on the grounds that it committed "sacrilege." Producer-distributor Joseph Burstyn took the case to the U.S. Supreme Court, which ruled in May 1952 that movies were "a significant medium for communication of ideas" and were, therefore, protected against the charge of sacrilege by both the First and Fourteenth Amendments. Subsequent court rulings between 1952 and 1958 clarified the *Miracle* decision, and by the early 1960s films were guaranteed full freedom of expression.[2]

While these legal battles were in progress, the Pro-

duction Code was being challenged from within by the influx of "unapproved" foreign films and, especially, by the rise of independent production. Since the studios no longer owned America's theaters, they could no longer force them to accept their product exclusively. Shrewdly realizing this, director Otto Preminger openly challenged the code by producing two films for United Artists with sensational (for that era) content—*The Moon Is Blue* (1953), which used the forbidden word *virgin*, and *The Man with the Golden Arm* (1955), in which Frank Sinatra portrayed a heroin addict. As Preminger had anticipated, both films were denied the Production Code's Seal of Approval, and both were released independently to great commercial success. It didn't take long for the studios to find out which way the wind was blowing: Elia Kazan's *Baby Doll*, released by Warner Bros. in 1956 to a storm of protest, was the first motion picture of a major American studio ever to be publicly condemned by the Legion of Decency, the Catholic organization responsible for instituting the Production Code in the first place. The financial success of these three films sounded the death knell for the legion's influence in Hollywood, and the Production Code was scrapped altogether in the 1960s in favor of a **ratings** system administered by the Motion Picture Association of America (MPAA), which does not proscribe the content of films, but rather classifies them as appropriate for certain segments of the public, according to age.

Instituted in 1968 and revised in 1972 and 1984, the MPAA ratings system uses the following five classifications for films: G (general audience); PG (parental guidance suggested for children under seventeen); PG-13 (parental guidance suggested for children under thirteen); R (restricted to persons seventeen or older unless accompanied by an adult); and NC-17 (no children under seventeen admitted; formerly X). Many people believe that the ratings system has contributed significantly to the decline of high-quality films in the G and PG range and to the sharp increase in exploitative sex and violence in

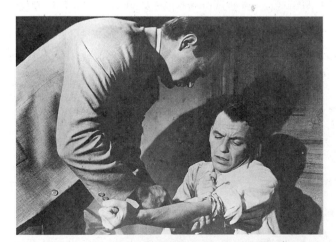

12.34 Breaking the Production Code: Frank Sinatra shooting dope in *The Man with the Golden Arm* (Otto Preminger, 1955).

2. This trend is currently being reversed in federal and state court cases dealing with obscenity. The U.S. Supreme Court ruling of 1973, which left the definition of obscenity to elusive "community standards," confused the whole issue of film and freedom of speech since the Court did not specify what it meant by "community." Thus, films like Just Jaeckin's *Histoire d'O* (*The Story of O*, 1975)—the softest of soft-core erotica—have been successfully prosecuted in cities like Detroit on the grounds that they are offensive to the "community."

the R and NC-17 classifications. Like the concept of "Family Viewing Time" on network television, it would seem that a system designed to protect children from debasing entertainment has served to debase the entertainment of both children and adults.

In about 1955, human sexuality began to be overtly depicted on the American screen for the first time since the code's imposition some twenty years before, and, more generally, a fascination with veiled (and increasingly unveiled) eroticism came to pervade American films in the late 1950s and early 1960s. This, more than any other single factor, accounts for the vast popularity of the *Pillow Talk* cycle, the seven adaptations from the exotic plays of Tennessee Williams, and such sexy imports as *And God Created Woman* (*Et Dieu créa la femme* [Roger Vadim, 1956]; 1957), *The Lovers* (*Les Amants* [Louis Malle, 1958; 1959]), and *La dolce vita* (Federico Fellini, 1960) during this period.

Other taboos were broken, too, as a new realism of content entered the American cinema after a long period of repression. Social problems like juvenile delinquency (*Rebel without a Cause*, 1955; *Blackboard Jungle*, 1955), alcoholism, drug addiction, and even race were suddenly fair game for filmmakers working both inside and outside the studios.[3] Crime began to be treated less moralistically and melodramatically so that it became possible by the end of the decade to sympathize with criminals as human beings, though they did not become wholly admirable ones until Arthur Penn's *Bonnie and Clyde* (1967). The next cultural taboo the American cinema was to overcome (simultaneously with Italy and preceded slightly by Japan) was the convention against the graphic, excessive, and/or poetic depiction of brutality and violence. This, however, could not occur until President Kennedy and his alleged assassin had been gunned down in Dallas in 1963 before running movie cameras and, for much of the decade that followed, the war in Vietnam had been brought nightly into American living rooms by television.

---

3. Important films on these themes made outside of the system during the 1960s include the *cinéma vérité* work of Shirley Clarke (1925–1997)—*The Connection* (1961), which deals with drug addiction; *The Cool World* (1964), focusing on the lives of young blacks in the ghetto; and *Portrait of Jason* (1967), an extended monologue by a black homosexual prostitute—and the improvisational dramas of John Cassavetes (1929–1989) on race (*Shadows*, 1961) and middle-class malaise (*Faces*, 1968; *Husbands*, 1970). Clarke moved on to video, but Cassavetes continued to make films (*Minnie and Moskowitz*, 1971; *A Woman under the Influence*, 1974; *The Killing of a Chinese Bookie*, 1976, 1978; *Opening Night*, 1978; *Gloria*, 1980; *Love Streams*, 1983; *Big Trouble*, 1984) in collaboration with his wife, the brilliant actress Gena Rowlands (b. 1934). See Raymond Carney, *American Dreaming: The Films of John Cassavetes and the American Experience* (Berkeley: University of California Press, 1985).

The French New Wave and Its Native Context

The Occupation and Postwar Cinema

During the German Occupation of France, from 1940 to 1944—when Feyder, Renoir, Duvivier, and Clair were all in exile—a new generation of French directors emerged, most of whom had worked as scriptwriters or assistants under the major figures of poetic realism in the 1930s.[1] Claude Autant-Lara (1901–2000), who had worked as a designer for Marcel L'Herbier and as an assistant to Clair, directed a number of sophisticated period films during the Occupation, including *Le Mariage de Chiffon* (1942), *Lettres d'amour* (1942), and the satirical *Douce* (1943). Autant-Lara's critical reputation rests most firmly, however, upon a series of stylish literary adaptations written by Jean Aurenche (1904–1992) and Pierre Bost (1901–1975) that he made in the postwar era—especially *Le Diable au corps* (*The Devil in the Flesh*, 1947; from the Raymond Radiguet novel),[2] *L'Auberge rouge* (*The Red Inn*, 1951; from Aurenche), *Le Blé en herbe* (*The Ripening Seed*, 1954; from Colette), *Le Rouge et le noir* (*The Red and the Black*, 1954; from Stendhal), and *Le Joueur* (*The Gambler*, 1958; from Dostoevsky). Writing as a team, Aurenche and Bost became specialists in tightly scripted films; they also worked

---

1. Perhaps the most important film event of the Occupation was the founding of the Institut des Hautes Études Cinématographiques (IDHEC) by Marcel L'Herbier in 1943. This government-subsidized film school today offers professional training in every aspect of film production as well as in history and aesthetics. It provides certification for persons wishing to enter the French film industry, and its high standards have attracted students from all over the world. See André Bazin, *French Cinema of the Occupation and Resistance: The Birth of a Critical Esthetic*, trans. Stanley Hochman (New York: Ungar, 1981); see also Evelyn Ehrlich, *Cinema of Paradox: French Filmmaking under the German Occupation* (New York: Columbia University Press, 1985), and Edward Lowry, *The Filmology Movement and Film Study in France* (Ann Arbor, Mich.: UMI Research Press, 1985).

2. Remade in separate versions by the Australian director Scott Murray in 1985 and the Italian director Marco Bellocchio in 1986.

13.1 *Jeux interdits* (René Clément, 1952): Brigitte Fossey, Georges Poujouly.

13.2 *La Belle et la bête* (Jean Cocteau and René Clément, 1946): Josette Day, Jean Marais.

closely with the director René Clément (1913–1996), whose first film had been a neorealistic account of the activities of the French Resistance, *La Bataille du rail* (*The Battle of the Rails*, 1946).

Clément also co-directed *La Belle et la bête* (*Beauty and the Beast*, 1946) with playwright Jean Cocteau and made the suspenseful anti-Nazi thriller *Les Maudits* (*The Damned*, 1947). But his two greatest films of the postwar era, both written by Aurenche and Bost, were the poetic antiwar drama *Jeux interdits* (*Forbidden Games*, 1952) and a strikingly evocative adaptation of Zola's *L'Assommoir* entitled *Gervaise* (1956). These films won multiple international awards, as did Clément's comic masterpiece *Monsieur Ripois* (*The Knave of Hearts*), shot in England in 1954. Afterward Clément turned to big-budget international coproductions like *Is Paris Burning?* (1966) and *Rider on the Rain* (1969), most of them distinctly mediocre.[3]

Jean Grémillon (1902–1959), who had made important films in the silent era (*Un Tour au large*, 1927; *Maldone*, 1928), produced his greatest work during the Occupation—*Lumière d'été* (1943), a Renoiresque portrait of the decadent French ruling classes written by Jacques Prévert, and *Le Ciel est à vous* (English title: *The Woman Who Dared*, 1944), a beautiful film about a provincial woman who breaks the world record for long-distance flying with the help of her husband and the people of her town. After the war, Grémillon turned to the documentary but continued to exercise great influence upon French cinema as president of the Cinémathèque Française (see p. 441).

Jean Cocteau (1889–1963), who had confined himself to writing scripts during the Occupation (for Jean Delannoy's modernized version of the Tristan and Isolde legend, *L'Éternel retour* [*The Eternal Return*, 1943]; for Robert Bresson's *Les Dames du Bois de Boulogne* [*The Ladies of the Bois de Boulogne*, 1945]; see p. 434), returned to filmmaking in the postwar years. Perhaps more than any other figure, he incarnated the literary tendency of French cinema during this period. In 1946 he wrote and co-directed (with Clément) an enchantingly beautiful version of the Flemish fairy tale *La Belle et la bête* (*Beauty and the Beast*) in a visual style based upon the paintings of Vermeer; it stands today as perhaps the greatest example of the cinema of the fantastic in the history of film.[4] Next, Cocteau directed two film versions of his own plays, the satirical *Ruy Blas* (1947) and *Les Parents terribles* (English title: *The Storm Within*, 1948), a domestic tragicomedy set within the confines of a single room. With *Orphée* (1950), a modern version of the

---

3. Like Autant-Lara, Clément continued to contribute traditional narrative films to the French cinema well into the 1980s. So, too, did Jean Delannoy (e.g., *Bernadette*, 1988), also discussed on this page.

4. *Beauty and the Beast* was remade in 1979 by the Slovak surrealist Juraj Herz (b. 1934), mixing French and Middle European folk traditions (see Chapter 16). American versions include a United Artist B-film directed by Edward Cahn (1963), a 1976 telefilm directed by Fielder Cook, and Disney's award-winning animated feature of 1991 (Gary Trousdale, Kirk Wise). On Cocteau himself, see Edgardo Cozarinsky's film *Jean Cocteau—Autoportrait d'un inconnu* (*Jean Cocteau—Portrait of an Unknown Man*, 1984).

Orpheus legend, Cocteau returned to the surreal, psychomythic regions of *Le Sang d'un poète* (*Blood of a Poet*, 1930) to create his most brilliant film. He adapted his play *Les Enfants terribles* (*The Terrible Children*, directed by Jean-Pierre Melville) for the screen in 1950 and gave the cinema his final artistic statement in *Le Testament d'Orphée* (*The Testament of Orpheus*, 1959), a surrealistic fable that is replete with personal symbols and that attempts to suggest the relationships among poetry, myth, death, and the unconscious.

Jacques Becker (1906–1960) is another figure who emerged during the Occupation and came to prominence in the postwar years. As assistant to Renoir from 1931 to 1939, Becker tended to direct films that cut across the traditional class barriers of French society. *Goupi Mains Rouge* (English title: *It Happened at the Inn*, 1943) is a realistic portrait of peasant life; *Falbalas* (English title: *Paris Frills*, 1945) is a drama set in the Parisian fashion houses; *Antoine et Antoinette* (1947) is a tale of young love in a working-class milieu; *Rendez-vous de juillet* (1949) offers a sympathetic study of the attitudes and ambitions of postwar youth; and *Édouard et Caroline* (1951) examines young married life in high society. But Becker's masterpiece is unquestionably *Casque d'or* (*Golden Helmet/Golden Marie*, 1952), a visually sumptuous tale of doomed love set in turn-of-the-century Paris and written by Becker himself. Cast in the form of a period gangster film and based upon historical fact, *Casque d'or* is a work of great formal beauty whose visual texture evokes the films of Feuillade and engravings from la belle époque. *Touchez pas au grisbi* (English title: *Honor among Thieves*, 1954), adapted from an Albert Simonin novel, is a sophisticated tale of rivalry between contemporary Montmartre gangs; it started the vogue for gangster films and thrillers that typified French cinema in the late 1950s (for instance, the American émigré Jules Dassin's *Rififi*, 1955). After making three commissioned films of uneven quality, Becker directed his final masterpiece, *Le Trou* (*The Hole/The Night Watch*, 1960), shortly before his death in 1960. Like Bresson's *Un Condamné à mort s'est échappé* (*A Man Escaped*, 1956; see pp. 435), this film, set entirely in a prison cell where five men plot an ill-fated escape, is a restrained exploration of loyalty, freedom, and human dignity.[5]

Another important director whose career began during the Occupation was Henri-Georges Clouzot (1907–1977), a former scriptwriter for E. A. Dupont and Anatole Litvak at UFA. Clouzot's first feature was unre-

13.3 *Casque d'or* (Jacques Becker, 1952): Simone Signoret (in the title role) and friends.

markable, but his second, *Le Corbeau* (*The Raven*, 1943), established him as the chief progenitor of French *film noir*. This darkly pessimistic tale of a town destroyed by poison-pen letters is a masterpiece of psychological suspense, but because it was produced by the Nazi-owned Continental Corporation and seemed to be anti-French (although it was actually misanthropic), both Clouzot and his coscenarist, Louis Chavance (1907–1979), were accused of collaboration and briefly suspended from the French film industry after the Liberation. Clouzot, in fact, was apolitical, but his films typically dealt with the brutal, the sordid, and the neurotic, and his entire career was marked by an aura of scandal. His first postwar film, *Quai des orfèvres* (English title: *Jenny Lamour*, 1947) was a violent thriller that transcended its genre by creating Hitchcockian suspense. In *Manon* (1949), Clouzot modernized the Abbé Prévost's eighteenth-century classic, *Manon Lescaut*, setting it in the post-Liberation context of the Paris black market and the illegal emigration of Jews to Palestine. And with *Le Salaire de la peur* (*The Wages of Fear*, 1953),[6] Clouzot achieved a masterpiece of unrelenting horror and alienation in a film about a group of down-and-out European expatriates trapped in a miserable South American town who are driven by

5. Becker's son Jean emerged as an important figure in the 1980s with *L'Eté meurtrier* (*One Deadly Summer*, 1983), a superior adaptation of Sébastien Japrisot's suspense thriller, scripted by the author.

6. Remade by the American director William Friedkin in 1977 as *Sorcerer*, *The Wages of Fear* was cut for its American release from 148 to 105 minutes; the missing footage was restored in a 1991 rerelease.

13.4 *Le Salaire de la peur* (Henri-Georges Clouzot, 1953): Charles Vanel.

plage (*Riptide/Such a Pretty Little Beach*, 1948), and *Manèges* (English title: *The Cheats*, 1950), all written by Jacques Sigurd (1920–1987). The former lawyer André Cayatte (1909–1989) was another popular director of dark films in the late 1940s. But his major claim to significance rests upon his four "judicial" films scripted by Charles Spaak—*Justice est faite* (*Justice Is Done*, 1950), *Nous sommes tous des assassins* (*We Are All Murderers*, 1952), *Avant le déluge* (*Before the Deluge*, 1953), and *Le Dossier noir* (*The Black File*, 1955)—a series of scathing attacks upon the French legal system.[8] The same period witnessed the best work of Jacqueline Audry (1908–1977), who collaborated closely with her husband, the scriptwriter Pierre Laroche (1902–1962), to produce tasteful adaptations of work by Sartre (*Huis clos* [*No Exit*, 1954]) and Colette (*Mitsou*, 1956).

ROBERT BRESSON AND JACQUES TATI

Clearly, except for *film noir*, the prevailing mode of postwar French cinema was literary adaptation, which caused French films to become increasingly verbal and theatrical. It was against this tendency—identified as "the tradition of quality" ("*la tradition de la qualité*") by François Truffaut and the other critics writing in *Cahiers du cinéma*—that the New Wave reacted in the late 1950s and 1960s. In fact, the war had not produced a break with cinematic traditions in France as it had in Italy and other European nations, except for the innovative work of Robert Bresson and Jacques Tati.

Robert Bresson (1907–1999), a former scriptwriter, was the more important of the two. His two Occupation films—*Les Anges du péché* (*The Angels of Sin*, 1943), written with the playwright Jean Giraudoux, and *Les Dames du Bois de Boulogne* (*The Ladies of the Bois de Boulogne*, 1945), freely adapted by Bresson and Jean Cocteau from a story by the eighteenth-century writer Denis Diderot—established Bresson as a serious and disciplined artist within the "scenarist," or literary, tradition of French cinema. But in *Le Journal d'un curé de campagne* (*The Diary of a Country Priest*, 1950), adapted

despair and greed to undertake the suicidal mission of hauling nitroglycerine for an American oil firm.

Always a meticulous and professional craftsman in the French studio tradition, Clouzot became increasingly erratic as the 1950s progressed. The film that confirmed his international reputation, *Les Diaboliques* (*Diabolique*, 1955), is a brilliantly manipulative exercise in horrific suspense involving a complicated murder plot in a boarding school. Like Hitchcock's *Vertigo*, it was adapted from a novel by Pierre Boileau and Thomas Narcejac. Similarly, *Le Mystère Picasso* (*The Picasso Mystery*, 1956) is an ingenious 75-minute study of Picasso at work shot in desaturated color and CinemaScope. But *Les Espions* (*The Spies*, 1957), set in a psychiatric clinic, is a failed attempt to combine the bitter naturalism of his earlier films with surrealistic fantasy. *La Vérité* (*The Truth*, 1960) is a professional but glib film cast in the form of a murder trial and narrated in flashbacks. A projected film on the destructive effects of jealousy, *L'Enfer* (1964), was scrapped because of Clouzot's ill health,[7] and he was able to complete only a single feature before his death in 1977—the controversial and somewhat experimental *La Prisonnière* (*The Prisoner*, 1968), which returns to the perverse and pathological mode of *Le Corbeau* to examine the dynamics of sexual degradation.

Mining the same dark vein as Clouzot in the postwar period was Yves Allégret (1907–1987), brother and former assistant to the veteran director Marc Allégret (1900–1973), who became something of a specialist in *film noir* with *Dédée d'Anvers* (*Dedee*, 1947), *Une Si jolie petite*

---

7. *L'Enfer* was finally made, from Clouzot's original script, by Claude Chabrol in 1993.

8. Cayatte made *La Raison d'état* (*Reasons of State*) in 1978, a polemical film on the corrupt practices of the French government in its arms sales to terrorists.

13.5 *Le Journal d'un curé de campagne* (Robert Bresson, 1950): Claude Laydu, Nicole Maurey.

from the novel by Georges Bernanos, Bresson displayed a highly personalized style whose psychological realism is predicated upon an absolute austerity of acting, dialogue, and *mise-en-scène*. All of Bresson's later films display this austerity and precision of style, which has led some critics to call him a classicist, although he preferred to be thought of as a realist practicing close to the borderline of abstraction. His masterpiece, *Un Condamné à mort s'est échappé* (*A Man Escaped*, 1956), concerns the arrest, escape, and recapture of a young Resistance fighter during the Occupation, and it takes place almost entirely in the condemned man's cell. Most of Bresson's subsequent films—*Pickpocket* (1959), *Le Procés de Jeanne d'Arc* (*The Trial of Joan of Arc*, 1961, which, like Dreyer's film, is based upon the actual trial records), *Au hasard Balthasar* (1966), *Mouchette* (1967), *Un Femme douce* (*A Gentle Creature*, 1969), and *Quatre nuits d'un rêveur* (*Four Nights of a Dreamer*, 1971, an adaptation of Dostoevsky's novella *White Nights*)—were derived from literary sources and dealt with humanist themes. Others are more pessimistic. *Lancelot du lac* (*Lancelot of the Lake*, 1976) offers a dark, ascetic vision of a Camelot that has outlived its own ideals. In *Le Diable probablement* (*The Devil Probably*, 1977), it is contemporary society that has outlived its ideals and its promise. *L'Argent* (1983), based on a short story by Tolstoi, is a film devoid of all psychology; it is about a man's irreversible descent into crime and degradation and shared the Cannes Grand Prix for Best Direction with Andrei Tarkovsky's *Nostalghia* in the year of its release. All of Bresson's films are painstakingly

crafted attempts to bring to life the spiritual dilemmas of the race through the moral struggles of individuals, which makes Bresson a kind of contemporary Carl-Theodor Dreyer. And, indeed, André Bazin often suggested that Bresson, more than any practicing director, had succeeded in fusing the values of the silent cinema with those of sound.

Jacques Tati (b. Jacques Tatischeff, 1908–1982), a former music-hall entertainer and pantomimist, became one of the international cinema's great comic talents in the postwar era, rivaling such masters of the silent film as Max Linder, Charlie Chaplin, and Buster Keaton. In his first feature, *Jour de fête* (*Big Day/The Village Fair*, 1949), which took him several years to complete, Tati plays a French postman who is seduced by a documentary into employing sophisticated American postal-service technology in his small village, with disastrous results. As in all of Tati's films, the humor, which is largely visual, is achieved through scrupulous planning and brilliant mime.[9] In *Les Vacances de M. Hulot* (*Mr. Hulot's Holiday*, 1953), Tati created a new comic character, Mr. Hulot, a vague, wacky, middle-class Frenchman who goes to spend his holiday at a seaside resort in Brittany. Hulot's misadventures there are represented to us as a series of meticulously worked-out sight gags, in which things simply "happen" to the character with no particular logic or cause. With *Mon oncle* (*My Uncle*, 1958), his first film in color, Tati turned to the more serious vein of satire. Here, Hulot's traditional and somewhat archaic lifestyle in an old quarter of Paris is contrasted to the antiseptic and mechanistic environment of his brother-in-law, Arpel, who lives in an ultramodern house in the city's new suburban wasteland and works as an executive in a plastics factory. The humanistic impact of the satire is not unlike that of Clair's *À nous la liberté* (1931) or Chaplin's *Modern Times* (1936), although its appeal is totally unsentimental.

9. *Jour de fête*, which took prizes at both Venice and Cannes, was originally shot in a three-color additive lenticular process patented as Thomsoncolor that proved to be undevelopable in postproduction. Fortunately, Tati had simultaneously shot a black-and-white backup version of the film, and this was ultimately cut together as the release print. Had it been released as intended, *Jour de fête* would have been one of the first French features in color. In 1987, it was discovered that the original 15,000-foot color negative had been preserved by Tati's daughter, the film editor Sophie Tatischeff (whose credits include her father's *Trafic* and *Parade*), and it has since been restored at the Eurocitel labs in Joinville. (Interestingly, the restoration cost approximately $517,000, whereas the original was produced for $36,000.)

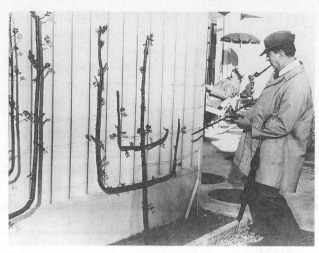

13.6 Jacques Tati as Monsieur Hulot in *Mon oncle* (Jacques Tati, 1958).

Tati's next film, *Playtime* (1967), took him three years to complete and was shot in color and 70mm Panavision with five-track stereophonic sound. Using the full resources of the widescreen format to create spectator involvement, Tati offers in *Playtime* a series of quietly humorous vignettes about a group of American tourists who come to see the "real" Paris and end up experiencing a space-age city of steel, glass, chrome, and plastic. Widely regarded today as a modernist masterpiece, it is not a film of belly laughs, but of sustained, intelligent humor, and it clearly represents Tati's finest achievement. But *Playtime* was a multimillion-dollar commercial failure,[1] and since he had financed it himself, the director was nearly bankrupted. To recoup his losses, Tati made *Trafic* (*Traffic*, 1971), a minor Hulot film that comments upon the auto mania of modern industrial society. His last work was *Parade* (1974), a children's film made for Swedish television that featured Tati performing pantomimes at a circus show. After this, he developed the scenario for another Hulot film to be called *Confusion* but was unable to find backing for it. A painstaking craftsman who planned every detail of his films far in advance of production, Tati made only five features in his entire career. Nevertheless, he was a master cinematic humorist, whose concept of comedy was almost purely visual, and he deserves to be ranked with the greatest of the silent comedians for the breadth of his humanity and the restrained brilliance of his comic achievement.

MAX OPHÜLS

Another major figure working in French cinema in the 1950s, and one who had a profound influence on the New Wave generation that succeeded him, was Max Ophüls (b. Max Oppenheimer, 1902–1957). Ophüls was a German Jew who had directed films for UFA between 1930 and Hitler's rise to power in 1933 (*Die verkaufte Braut* [*The Bartered Bride*, 1932]; *Liebelei* [1933]). For the next seven years he made films in Italy, the Netherlands, and France, where he ultimately became a citizen in 1938. Ophüls was forced to flee to Hollywood when France fell to the Nazis in 1940, and after four years of anonymity, he was finally able to make a series of stylish melodramas for Paramount: *The Exile* (1947), *Letter from an Unknown Woman* (1948), *Caught* (1949), and *The Reckless Moment* (1949), which are among his very best films. Returning to France in 1949, Ophüls entered the period of his greatest creativity, making four elegant, masterful films in succession between 1950 and 1955—*La Ronde, Le Plaisir, Madame de . . .* , and *Lola Montès*. Ophüls had always worked within the studio system, so that the subject matter of his films—often light and operetta-like—was never as important to him as visual style. And it is for their dazzling *mise-en-scène* that Ophüls's last four films, all photographed by the great French cameraman Christian Matras (1903–1977), are most remarkable.

La Ronde (1950) is an adaptation of an Arthur Schnitzler play set in turn-of-the-century Vienna. Its ten separate episodes posit that love is a perpetual roundabout in which one partner is regularly exchanged for another until the pattern comes full circle, like the movements of a waltz, only to begin again. This unbroken circle of affairs is presided over by a master of ceremonies who manipulates and comments on the behavior of the characters, becoming a surrogate for Ophüls himself. *Le Plaisir* (English title: *House of Pleasure*, 1952) is derived from three Maupassant stories, linked by a narrator; they illustrate the theme that pleasure may be easy to come by but happiness is not. Like all of Ophüls's work, the film is marked by meticulous

---

1. In an effort to salvage the film, Tati reduced it from 155 to 108 minutes for European distribution; for distribution in the United States in 1972, *Playtime* was further reduced to 93 minutes and released in a 35mm monaural format.

13.7 *Le Plaisir* (Max Ophüls, 1952): **Simone Simon.**

attention to period detail and by an incessantly moving camera. In one famous sequence, the camera circles the exterior of a brothel time and time again, never entering the set but peering voyeuristically through windows at significant dramatic action taking place within. In *Madame de . . .* (English title: *The Earrings of Madame de . . .*, 1953), also set at the turn of the century, Ophüls constructs yet another circular narrative that rotates around a central axis of vanity, frivolity, and lust. Here, the passage of a pair of earrings from a husband to his wife to the husband's mistress to the wife's lover and finally back to the husband again constitutes a single perfect revolution in the roundabout of infidelity. The characters are ultimately shallow because everything in *Madame de . . .* is subordinate to its aesthetic design. As if to mirror the movement of the waltzes on the sound track, the camera whirls and pirouettes continuously to follow the film's principals through its glittering period decor, suggesting that life is itself a kind of waltz in which all of us are caught up while the music plays.

Lola Montès (1955) is generally considered to be Ophüls's masterpiece, the consummation of his life's work. Conceived by its producers as a big-budget superspectacle in Eastmancolor and CinemaScope with an international cast of stars, it was based on the scandalous life of a mediocre nineteenth-century dancer who became the mistress of the composer Franz Liszt and, during the revolutions of 1848, of Ludwig I, deposed king of Bavaria. She finally ended as a circus performer selling kisses to earn her keep. Ophüls cared nothing for the subject, remarking of Lola herself, "Her role is roughly the same as that of our pair of earrings in *Madame de. . . .*" That is, he merely used her story to create a dazzling exercise in visual style, and *Lola Montès* became one of the most intricate, opulent, and elaborate films to appear on the French screen since Abel Gance's *Napoléon* (1927). Ironically, Ophüls was initially opposed to the use of CinemaScope, but his sense of visual patterning was such that he turned *Lola Montès* into a stunning exhibition of composition for the widescreen frame. He frequently broke the horizontal space of the screen with vertical dominants and framed shots through arches, columns, and drapery. He learned to compose close-ups by balancing both sides of the frame, and at other times— as during the circus scenes—he would fill the entire CinemaScope frame with significant dramatic action. The film begins and ends within the circus tent, where the ringmaster introduces Lola's act by recalling the circumstances of her past life, which is then represented on the screen in a series of achronological flashbacks. Ophüls uses color nonnaturalistically throughout the film, especially in these flashback sequences, where each is tinted according to its prevailing emotional tone. Finally, the camera seems never to stop its circular tracking around some invisible axis, in or out of the tent, making the circularity of things seen on the screen a metaphor for life itself. As Andrew Sarris has remarked, "With Ophüls it is movement itself that is emphasized rather than its terminal points of rest."

As with *Intolerance* (1916) and *Citizen Kane* (1941), the narrative technique of *Lola Montès* was so unconventional that audiences stayed away from it. In response, its producers, the Gamma Company, first cut the film from 140 to 110 minutes, and finally re-edited the story in chronological sequence for release in a 90-minute version. Still, the film's commercial failure was so complete that Gamma was eventually bankrupted by it,

13.8 *Lola Montès* (Max Ophüls, 1955): Martine Carol.

Influence of the Fifties Documentary Movement and Independent Production

and it seems likely that Ophüls's death from a rheumatic heart condition in 1957 was hastened by the mutilation of his masterpiece. In 1969, however, the original version was reconstructed and rereleased, to great critical acclaim.

The key to Ophüls's style is his mastery of the long take and, especially, of the continuously moving camera. Ophüls was also a genius at composition within the frame, and the influence upon him of both German Expressionism and French pictorial Impressionism was profound. In his passion for decor and his obsession with the sensuous surfaces of reality, Ophüls most closely resembles Josef von Sternberg. In his cynicism and worldly wit, he is close to Ernst Lubitsch. That his films are devoid of content—a charge frequently leveled against both von Sternberg and Lubitsch—is quite true, if we mean by the term *verbal* or *conceptual* substance. But as the New Wave generation was to argue and to demonstrate time and again, the substance of cinema is *audiovisual*, not verbal, and it exists on a level of discourse—like that of the circular tracking shots in *Lola Montès*—where perception and conceptualization become one.

By 1955, French commercial cinema was approaching stagnation because many filmmakers who had emerged during the Occupation were firmly ensconced within the studio system or working on big-budget spectacles and international coproductions. The cinematic individualism of Bresson and Tati, and also of Cocteau, offered the succeeding generation of French directors examples of how film could be used as a medium of personal expression; and Ophüls had forecast the possibility of a purely audiovisual language for the screen. But the major stylistic influences upon this next generation of filmmakers came from the French documentary movement of the 1950s, which was their training ground, and from the films of independent directors working outside the studio system of production.

The documentary movement can be said to have begun in 1946 with Georges Rouquier's *Farrebique*, a lyrical feature-length documentary about peasant life on a farm through the four seasons.[2] Jean Grémillon (*Le Six juin à l'aube* [*The Sixth of June at Dawn*, 1945]) and Roger Leenhardt (*Les Dernières vacances* [*The Last Holiday*, 1947]) both made countless short documentaries throughout the 1950s on art and on the lives of great men. But the master of French documentary cinema during

---

2. Thirty-seven years later Rouquier produced, with funds from the U.S. National Endowment for the Humanities, a sequel, *Biquefarre* (1983), which focuses on the new generation of the same farming community.

this period was Georges Franju (1912–1987), a totally original filmmaker who was deeply influenced by German Expressionism and has often been called a surrealist.

Franju had been working in cinema since 1937, when he made a 16mm amateur film with Henri Langlois. However, his first major film was *Le Sang des bêtes* (*The Blood of the Beasts*, 1949), a brutally graphic documentary short about the daily activity of a slaughterhouse in a quiet Parisian suburb, whose butchery was made deliberately resonant of the horrors of the Nazi death camps. *En Passant par la Lorraine* (*Passing by Lorraine*, 1950) depicted the steel mills of that peaceful region as furnaces consuming the lives of the men who worked them. In *Hôtel des invalides*, possibly his finest film, Franju turned an ostensibly objective account of the French War Museum into a devastating antiwar statement by exposing the human suffering that underlies the myths of heroism and glory enshrined by that institution. Other important Franju shorts were *Le Grand Méliès* (1952) and *Monsieur et Madame Curie* (1953), documentary tributes to the great pioneers of modern cinema and modern science, respectively. In 1958 Franju directed his first feature, *La Tête contre les murs* (English title: *The Keepers*), a half-documentary, half-surrealistic account of a sane man who is committed to a French lunatic asylum; the film is often cited as a forerunner of the New Wave. The grisly horror film *Les Yeux sans visage* (*Eyes without a Face*, 1959; released—cut and dubbed—in the United States as *The Horror Chamber of Dr. Faustus*) concerns a mad doctor who kidnaps young girls in a futile effort to transplant

13.10 *Nuit et brouillard* **(Alain Resnais, 1955).**

their faces onto the head of his own disfigured daughter. His *Pleins feux sur l'assassin* (*Spotlight on the Murderer*, 1961) is an atmospheric thriller adapted from a novel by Boileau and Narcejac. Franju's next two films were adaptations from François Mauriac: *Thérèse Desqueyroux* (1962) and *Judex* (1963), an *hommage* to Louis Feuillade's twelve-part serial of 1916. Franju made only five other features—*Thomas l'imposteur* (*Thomas the Imposter*, 1965), *Les Rideaux blancs* (*The White Curtains*, 1966), *Marcel Allain* (1966), *La Faute de l'Abbé Mouret* (*The Sin of Abbé Mouret*, 1970), and *L'Homme sans visage* (*Man without a Face*, 1974)—all but one of them intensely poetic visualizations of literary works, which have little in common with the style of the New Wave that his own documentaries helped to create.

Alain Resnais (b. 1922), whose first feature, *Hiroshima, mon amour* (1959), became the clarion call of the New Wave, was another important figure in the French documentary movement. He made documentary shorts for the first eleven years of his career, beginning with a series of films about art—*Van Gogh* (1948), *Gauguin* (1950), *Guernica* (1950)—and progressing to *Nuit et brouillard* (*Night and Fog*, 1955), a profoundly disturbing meditation on the horrors of the Nazi death camps and on the way time and memory affect our perception of them, written by Jean Cayrol[3] with an original score by

13.9 *Les Yeux sans visage* **(Georges Franju, 1959): Edith Scob.**

3. Cayrol (b. 1911) is a French novelist and scriptwriter who was himself deported to the camps. The title and controlling metaphor of Resnais's film was borrowed from *Poèms de la nuit et du brouillard*, a volume of poetry on the experience that Cayrol published in 1945. He later wrote the script of Resnais's masterpiece *Muriel* (1963).

Hanns Eisler. *Toute la memoire du monde* (*The Memory of the World*, 1956), a study of the books "imprisoned" in the French National Library, has a similar temporal theme, as do most of Resnais's features.

Other figures associated with the documentary short in the 1950s were Chris Marker (see p. 471), an original and highly personal filmmaker who would later organize the radical cooperative, La Société pour le Lancement des Oeuvres Nouvelles (SLON), for the production of *Loin du Vietnam* (1967) and similar polemical work; the ethnographic filmmaker Jean Rouch (see pp. 471–72), who became the apostle of *cinéma vérité* in the 1960s (he invented the term by translating Dziga Vertov's *Kino-pravda* into French for his coproduction, with the sociologist Edgar Morin, *Chronique d'un été* [*Chronicle of a Summer*, 1961]); Frédéric Rossif (1922–1990), who specialized in compilation films (*Mourir à Madrid* [*To Die in Madrid*, 1962]); and Agnès Varda (b. 1928), a former photographer whose first feature, the influential *La Pointe-Courte* (1955), is discussed below (see also p. 464).

The example of independent production outside of the traditional studio system was another important influence upon the emergent New Wave generation. Jean-Pierre Melville (b. Jean-Pierre Grumbach, 1917–1973) was a vastly significant figure in this regard. A lover of cinema from an early age, Melville founded his own production company in 1945. His first feature, *Le Silence de la mer* (*The Silence of the Sea*, 1947), earned him the admiration of Cocteau, who commissioned him to direct *Les Enfants terribles* in 1949. The commercial success of *Quand tu liras cette lettre* (*When You Read This Letter*, 1952) allowed Melville to purchase his own studio and move into totally independent production. The result was the much-admired gangster film *Bob le flambeur* (1955), a highly personalized work whose production methods—location shooting, small crew, use of unknown actors (all borrowed, of course, from neorealism)—became the model for New Wave filmmakers. Melville's work itself became increasingly commercial after he directed *Léon Morin, prêtre* (*Léon Morin, Priest*, 1961), a star vehicle for Jean-Paul Belmondo, but his fascination with the iconography of the American gangster film and the underworld of urban crime caused him to produce a trilogy of popular gangster films in the 1960s that are among the most admired in the genre—*Le Doulos* (*The Finger Man*, 1962), *Le deuxième souffle* (*Second Breath*, 1965), and *Le Samouraï* (*The Samurai*, 1967).

Another independent production that foretold the

13.11 *Le Doulos* (Jean-Pierre Melville, 1962): Jean-Paul Belmondo.

New Wave—and that some critics have called its first manifestation—is Agnès Varda's *La Pointe-Courte* (1955). This film about the dissolution and reconstruction of a marriage set against the backdrop of a small fishing village was produced by a collective of crew and actors. It was edited by Alain Resnais and is considered to be a direct antecedent of his own *Hiroshima, mon amour* (1959). The drama of the husband and wife is highly stylized and "literary," but the day-to-day life of the village is presented in semidocumentary form. (Varda apparently got the idea of using two counterposed structures from reading the first French translation of Faulkner's *The Wild Palms* in 1953.)[4]

It was the early films of Roger Vadim (1928–2000), however, that contributed most to the economic development of the New Wave. The spectacular commercial success of his independently produced first feature, *Et Dieu créa la femme* (*And God Created Woman*, 1956), demonstrated to the stagnant French film industry that young directors and new themes could attract large audiences. A visually sumptuous production in widescreen and color, *Et Dieu créa la femme* was a sensitive examination of the vagaries of amoral youth set against the luxurious background of St. Tropez. It starred Vadim's wife,

---

4. See Bruce Kawin, *Faulkner and Film* (New York: Ungar, 1977), pp. 146–49. According to Kawin, Varda, Resnais, and Chris Marker—all friends—were part of "the Left Bank group" of the New Wave, as distinct from "the *Cahiers* group." The former drew much of their inspiration from modernist literature, whereas the latter were more exclusively devoted to film as film.

13.12 *Et Dieu créa la femme* (Roger Vadim, 1956): Jean-Louis Trintignant, Brigitte Bardot.

Brigitte Bardot, and featured a number of explicit love scenes, which made it an international hit. In subsequent films, such as *Les Liaisons dangereuses (Dangerous Liaisons*, 1959), *Et Mourir de plaisir* (English title: *Blood and Roses*, 1960), *La Ronde* (English title: *Circle of Love*, 1964—a remake of the Ophüls film), *Barbarella* (1968), and *Pretty Maids All in a Row* (United States, 1971), Vadim's commercialism and exploitativeness increased, but he remained an impeccable craftsman and elegant stylist of the widescreen color film.[5] Moreover, it was Vadim, more than any other single figure in the French cinema, who opened the doors of the industry to his generation of filmmakers and provided the economic justification for the New Wave.

Theory: Astruc, Bazin, and *Cahiers du Cinéma*

The theoretical justification for the New Wave cinema came from another source: the film critic Alexandre Astruc (b. 1923), who published a highly influential article in *L'Ecran française* (no. 144) in March 1948 on the concept of the **caméra-stylo,** which would permit the cinema "to become a means of expression as supple and subtle as that of written language" and would therefore accord filmmakers the status of authors, or *auteurs*. Astruc's notion was to break away from the tyranny of narrative in order to evolve a new form of audiovisual language. He wrote: "The fundamental problem of the cinema is how to express thought. The creation of this language has preoccupied all the theoreticians and writers in the history of cinema, from Eisenstein down to the scriptwriters and adaptors of the sound cinema." Like Bazin, Astruc questioned the values of classical montage and was an apostle of the long take, as exemplified in the work of Murnau. Astruc later became a professional director after apprenticing himself to Marc Allégret (1900–1973), but his own films (*Le Rideau cramoisi* [*The Crimson Curtain*; English title: *End of Desire*, 1952] and *Une Vie* [*A Life*, 1958]) do not attempt to realize the ideal of the *caméra-stylo*. Following the example of German Expressionism, Astruc's films tend to be highly stylized elaborations of visual imagery that make excessive use of mannered compositions and camera angles.

Astruc was succeeded as a theorist by the vastly influential journal **Cahiers du cinéma** (literally, "cinema notebooks"), founded in 1951 by André Bazin (1918–1958) and Jacques Doniol-Valcroze (1920–1989), which gathered about it a group of young critics—François Truffaut, Jean-Luc Godard, Claude Chabrol, Jacques Rivette, and Eric Rohmer—who were to become the major directors of the **New Wave.** These young men were **cinéphiles,** or "film lovers." They had grown up in the postwar years watching great American films of the past and present decades (many available for the first time only when the German Occupation ended) as well as classical French films at the amazing **Cinémathèque Française** in Paris, the magnificent film archive and public theater founded in 1936 by Georges Franju and Henri Langlois to promote cinema study and cinema culture in France and throughout the world. During the Occupation, Langlois kept the enterprise in operation secretly at

---

5. Vadim's adaptation of *Les Liaisons dangereuses* modernized Choderlos de Laclos's controversial 1786 novel, setting it in contemporary Paris and Deauville. In 1988, a period version was filmed in France by the British director Stephen Frears (in the same year Vadim himself remade *And God Created Woman* in the United States with Rebecca De Mornay in the Bardot role); and in 1989 Milos Forman directed a French-American version entitled *Valmont*.

great personal risk, and afterward, through André Malraux, minister of culture, he obtained a large government subsidy for it. Today the Cinémathèque is the largest public film archive in the world, housing over 50,000 films, three theaters, and a museum in the Palais de Chaillot devoted entirely to film history.[6] It was Langlois who preserved the works of Griffith, Keaton, Gance, Vigo, and Renoir for the postwar generation of *cinéphiles* and introduced them to the then-unrecognized genius of directors like Ingmar Bergman and the great Japanese masters Akira Kurosawa and Yasujiro Ozu (see Chapters 15 and 18). Under Langlois's tutelage, these young men came to love film and desperately wanted to become filmmakers themselves, but they found the French commercial cinema inaccessible to them because of the powerful influence exerted by the trade unions. Since they knew more about film than any other generation in history, based on the experience of actual viewing, they became critics and theorists instead.

The *Cahiers* critics had two basic principles. The first, deriving from Bazin, was a rejection of montage aesthetics in favor of *mise-en-scène*, the long take, and composition in depth. *Mise-en-scène*, the "placing-in-the-scene," is probably best defined as the creation of mood and ambience, though it more literally means the structuring of the film through camera placement and movement, blocking of action, direction of actors, etc.—in other words, everything that takes place on the set prior to the editing process. Integral to the concept of *mise-en-scène* is the notion that film should be not merely an intellectual or rational experience, but an emotional and psychological one as well. The second tenet of the *Cahiers* critics, derived from Astruc, was the idea of personal authorship that François Truffaut expressed in a 1954 essay entitled "Une certaine tendance du cinéma français" ("A Certain Tendency in French Cinema") as *la politique des auteurs*. This "policy of authors," christened "the *auteur* theory" by the American critic Andrew Sarris, states that film should ideally be a medium of personal artistic expression and that the best films are therefore those that most clearly bear their maker's "signature"—the stamp of his or her individual personality, controlling obsessions, and cardinal themes. The implicit assumption was that with each successive film an *auteur* grows increasingly proficient and mature of vision, an assumption that is not always borne out by fact.

Truffaut's essay, which appeared in *Cahiers du cinéma* (no. 31) for January 1954, began by attacking the postwar "tradition of quality"—that is, the commercial scenarist tradition of Aurenche and Bost, Spaak, and directors such as Clair, Clément, Clouzot, Autant-Lara, Cayatte, and Yves Allégret, with its heavy emphasis on plot and dialogue. The key figure in this literary/theatrical cinema was the scriptwriter, the director being merely "the gentleman who added the pictures." To these "*littérateurs*" and their "*cinéma de papa*," Truffaut counterposed "*un cinéma d'auteurs*" in the work of such French writer-directors as Gance, Vigo, Renoir, Cocteau, Becker, Bresson, and Ophüls, and of numerous American directors—both major and minor—who had somehow managed to make personal statements despite the restrictions imposed upon them by the studio system. Some of the American choices—Welles, Hitchcock, Hawks, Lang, Ford, Nicholas Ray, and Anthony Mann, all masters of *mise-en-scène*—made perfect sense. Others—Jerry Lewis, Otto Preminger, Roger Corman—were based less on the quality of their films than on evidence of their personal directorial control. And the unquestioning allegiance that the *Cahiers* group gave to the figures in its pantheon made many skeptics wonder whether one form of iron-clad dogmatism had not simply been exchanged for another. But for all its deficiencies (and a proneness to fanaticism and cultism seems to be a major one), the *auteur* theory does offer a valuable schematic model for interpreting the filmmaking process and goes some way toward solving a very basic methodological problem of film criticism: that is, to whom or what does one attribute cinematic creation? Furthermore, the *Cahiers* critics were able to partially vindicate the *auteur* theory by becoming filmmakers themselves and practicing it.

The New Wave's challenge to the "tradition of quality" was economic as well as aesthetic. Under the system that prevailed from 1953 to 1959, government aid was awarded to productions by the Centre National de la

---

6. Although a warehouse fire in 1980 destroyed some 7,000 of its French titles, the Cinémathèque today has access to the State Film Archive (les Archives du Film, Centre National de la Cinématographie) at Bois-d'Arcy where, since 1977, the government has mandated the deposit of one print of every new French release. See Richard Roud, *A Passion for Films: Henri Langlois and the Cinémathèque Française* (New York: Viking, 1983), Michel Ciment, "The Legacy of Langlois," *American Film* 12, 3 (December 1988): 17–19, and Glenn Myrent and Georges P. Langlois, *Henri Langlois: First Citizen of Cinema*, trans. Lisa Nesselson (New York: Twayne, 1995).

Cinématographie (CNC, founded 1946) on the basis of reputation, so potential directors needed an established record of success, and very few new people could hope to enter the industry. But in 1959, the laws relating to aid for film productions were changed to allow first films to be funded by the state on the basis of a submitted script alone, enabling hundreds of new filmmakers to become their own producers and creating the economic context for the New Wave. Moreover, the international commercial success of films like *Les Quatre cents coups* (see below), which was produced for $75,000 and brought $500,000 for its American distribution rights alone, dramatically increased the number of private producers willing to finance new work. Thus, for a while at least, until the failures mounted, Truffaut's concept of *un cinéma d'auteurs* was realized in France by placing the control of the conception of a film in the same hands that controlled the actual production.

The New Wave: First Films

The first films of this "new wave" (*nouvelle vague*)[7] of French directors were independently produced dramatic shorts, many of them shot in 16mm and subsequently blown up for 35mm exhibition. Jacques Rivette's *Le Coup du berger* (*Fool's Mate*, 1956), François Truffaut's *Les Mistons* (*The Mischief-Makers*, 1957), and Jean-Luc Godard's *Tous les garçons s'appellent Patrick* (*All Boys Are Named Patrick*, 1957) all fall into this category. But the first feature-length success of the New Wave is generally acknowledged to have been Claude Chabrol's first film, *Le Beau Serge* (*The Handsome Serge/Bitter Reunion*, 1958), though Varda's *La Pointe-Courte* preceded it by three years. While still a *Cahiers* critic, Chabrol (b. 1930) shot *Le Beau Serge*, about the rehabilitation of a village drunkard, on location with funds provided by a small inheritance. The success of *Le Beau Serge* enabled Chabrol to follow it with *Les Cousins* (*The Cousins*, 1959), an ironic study of sexual intrigue and murder set against the backdrop of Parisian student life. The influence of Hitchcock became increasingly apparent in *À Double tour* (English title: *Leda/Web of Passion*, 1959), a highly stylized tale of pathological murder, and the darkly satiric *Les Bonnes femmes* (*The Good Women*, 1960), a film about the lives (and, in one case, the death) of Parisian shopgirls; its huge commercial failure caused

13.13 Jean-Pierre Léaud in *Les Quatres cents coups* (François Truffaut, 1959), the first Antoine Doinel film.

Chabrol to turn for a while from the New Wave mode to more conventional thrillers like *Landru* (English title: *Bluebeard*, 1962) and *Le Scandale* (English title: *The Champagne Murders*, 1966).

Nevertheless, 1959 was the *annus mirabilis* for the New Wave because in that year three of the major figures of the movement released their first features. François Truffaut's *Les Quatre cents coups* (*The 400 Blows*), made for $75,000 with a loan from his father-in-law when the director was twenty-seven years old, is a lyrical but wholly unsentimental account of an adolescent delinquent, shot on location in Paris. Dedicated to the memory of André Bazin (who died on the second day of shooting) and photographed in Dyaliscope (a French version of Cinema-Scope) by the talented New Wave cinematographer Henri Decaë (1915–1987), the film is consciously evocative of Vigo's *Zéro de conduite* (1933). It won the prize for Best Direction at Cannes in the year of its release, as well as the New York Film Critics award for Best Foreign Language Film in 1959.[8] (In the same year, the highly coveted

---

7. The term was apparently first applied to the phenomenon by critic François Giroud of *L'Express* and traveled almost immediately to the United States, where the movement was sometimes facetiously referred to as the "new vague," owing to the perceived difficulty of its films.

8. The title derives from the French expression *"Faire les quatre-cents coups,"* meaning to get oneself into a lot of trouble by "raising hell," so to speak. Originally 94 minutes, *Les Quatre cents coups* was re-edited by Truffaut to 101 minutes for the Annecy Film Festival tribute to him in 1967; for the same event, he reduced *Les Mistons* from 26 to 17 minutes.

Cannes Golden Palm award went to the work of another unpracticed, unconventional French director, Marcel Camus's *Orphée noir* [*Black Orpheus*, 1958]). It was also the first film in Truffaut's Antoine Doinel series, a kind of continuing cinematic autobiography starring Jean-Pierre Léaud (b. 1944), an actor who physically resembles Truffaut. The series includes *Antoine et Colette* (a contribution to an international compilation film entitled *L'Amour à vingt ans* [*Love at Twenty*, 1962]), *Baisers volés* (*Stolen Kisses*, 1968), *Domicile conjugal* (*Bed & Board*, 1970), and *L'Amour en fuite* (*Love on the Run*, 1979).

More remarkable in structure and theme was Alain Resnais's first feature, *Hiroshima, mon amour* (1959), which, like *Nuit et brouillard*, examines the relationship between time and memory in the context of a terrible atrocity. With a brilliant script by the novelist Marguerite Duras (who was to become an important director herself in the 1970s) and cinematography by Sacha Vierny (1919–2001), the film concerns a love affair between a French actress working in Hiroshima and a Japanese architect, in the course of which both recall their memories of the past war in Asia and Europe. Resnais maintains the counterpoint between present and past by continuously shifting narrative modes from objective to subjective and, in several extraordinary sequences, by combining dramatic footage of the couple making love with documentary footage of the aftermath of the Hiroshima blast. *Hiroshima, mon amour*, like *Les Quatre cents coups*, was a great commercial success and conferred further prestige upon the New Wave by winning the New York Film Critics award for Best Foreign Language Film in 1960.

The third important New Wave film of 1959, Jean-Luc Godard's *À bout de souffle* (*Breathless*), was in many ways the most characteristic and influential film of the movement. *Breathless*, which was written by Godard after a story by Truffaut and shot by cinematographer Raoul Coutard (b. 1924) in four weeks for less than $90,000,[9] is dedicated to Monogram Pictures, one of the larger American B-film studios of the 1930s and 1940s, which were famous for their ability to turn out tightly paced films on short shooting schedules and poverty-line budgets. This was precisely the ideal of the New Wave (or, at least, of its dominant *Cahiers* branch), but instead of making cheap films in order to make a quick profit, the New Wave directors made cheap films in order to be able to make films at all since their productions were necessarily inde-

13.14 Belmondo in *À bout de souffle*.

pendent of the industry. (Happily, many of the first New Wave films, including *Breathless*, made a great deal of money, which temporarily insured the future of the movement.) Modeled on the American gangster film in a simultaneous spirit of parody and *hommage*, *Breathless* is about an amoral young thug on the run who is finally betrayed to the police by his American girlfriend (deliberate shades of *Pépé le Moko*, 1937, and *Quai des brumes*, 1938), and it contains virtually every major technical characteristic of the New Wave film. These include use of shaky, **handheld** 35mm camera **shots,**[1] location shoot-

9. *Breathless* was filmed on location in Paris and Marseilles from August 17 to September 15, 1959, and released on March 16, 1960. Truffaut wrote the original story in 1955–56, and his name also appears as scriptwriter in the credits. This was a ploy to gain financial backing for *Breathless* since *Les Quatre cents coups* had just won the Grand prix de la mise-en-scène at Cannes (the scenario was actually written by Godard alone). *Breathless* was remade in 1983 by independent director Jim McBride, with a new script by McBride and L.M. Kit Carson set in contemporary Los Angeles.

1. For the tracking shots of *Breathless*, e.g., Godard pushed Coutard around in a wheelchair.

ing, natural lighting, improvised plot and dialogue, and **direct sound** recording on location with portable tape machines that were electronically synchronized with the camera.

But the most important technical characteristic of the New Wave film was its jagged, elliptical style of editing, which employed a high percentage of jump cuts within and mismatches between scenes in order to destroy the spatial and temporal continuity of the viewing experience. As *Breathless* begins, for example, we witness the following sequence of events: Michel, the young hood, steals a car in Paris with the help of his French mistress and speeds out into the countryside alone; he passes at high speed several other vehicles on his side of the road; he briefly contemplates picking up two female hitchhikers; and, to occupy the time, he talks to himself and to the audience about a variety of subjects. Next, he passes a large truck at a road construction site and suddenly finds himself pursued by two motorcycle cops; he pulls off the road into a small wooded area and pretends to be having car trouble. One cop passes him by, the second spots him and pulls into the wood. At this point, Michel reaches into the car, grabs a revolver, and guns down the cop. He then flees across an open field and hitchhikes back to Paris. In a conventional commercial film of the day— French, American, British, or Italian—this sequence would have been rendered in many separate shots fully depicting each of the actions. In *Breathless*, the whole sequence is conveyed in only several brief shots: alternating close-ups of Michel and his mistress on a Paris street; a quick take of the car theft at eye level; medium-close shots, taken from the passenger's seat, of Michel driving the car; medium-long shots, which pass away rapidly through the windshield, of the road and later the hitchhikers; a shot of the motorcycle cops appearing in the rearview mirror, followed by one of Michel pulling off the road and opening the hood of his car as the cop discovers him; an extreme close-up of the revolver, followed by a medium-long shot of the murder; a long shot of Michel running across a field; and a medium shot of him arriving in Paris as a passenger in the backseat of an unidentified car. Later in the film, Godard begins many scenes with a huge disorienting close-up and only later cuts, or pulls his camera back, to reveal the context of the action—which completely reversed conventional practice of the day.

Most radical of all, however, was Godard's use of the jump cut, in which a section of a single continuous shot is eliminated and then what remains is spliced together, creating a completely nonnaturalistic ellipsis in the action and calling attention to the director's power to manipulate all aspects of his medium. This radical elimination of transitional scenes (of what Hollywood calls **establishing shots**—medium or long shots of exteriors that indicate changes in dramatic space), and even of continuity *within* the shot itself, was thought extremely confusing when Godard and his peers first practiced it on a large scale, and yet it is no more than a logical extension of the discoveries of Méliès, Porter, and Griffith that cinematic narrative is by its nature *dis*continuous or, as Eisenstein discovered, that spatial and temporal continuity in the cinema resides not on the screen but in the viewer's mind as it makes the connections that the images on the screen, by their arrangement, suggest. In the conventional continuity, or "invisible," editing style of classical Hollywood cinema, orderly narrative transitions were felt to be crucial. As late as 1958, Orson Welles was forced by Universal to shoot additional establishing scenes for his *Touch of Evil* so that his fast-paced editing would not confuse contemporary audiences. Today, elliptical editing and the jump cut have passed into our conventional cinematic lexicon so pervasively that it is not unusual to find them in abundance in any television series. But in 1959 elliptical editing was thought radically innovative, and it became paramount among the stylistic conventions associated with the New Wave.

The New Wave: Origins of Style

These conventions, like all film conventions, sprang from two sources—theoretical conviction and material circumstances (not necessarily in that order). The material circumstances were these: the young directors of the New Wave were the first *film*-educated generation of filmmakers in history. They approached the cinema from the experience of having viewed almost the whole of its history at Langlois's Cinémathèque Française and from having written about it theoretically and critically in *Cahiers du cinéma* for nearly a decade. When they finally came to practice cinema, they knew more about the medium as an art form and less about the practical aspects of production than anyone who had ever made films before them. Consequently, they made many mistakes that their low budgets and tight shooting schedules would not permit them to correct. Like the Soviet filmmakers during the film-stock shortage that followed the 1917 Revolution, the New Wave directors could not afford to retake shots, so they relied on elliptical editing to conceal technical defects on the screen. Jump cuts, for example, were a means not only of creating perceptual dislocation in the audience, but also of restoring botched scenes by excising some actor's or cameraman's blunder from the middle of a take. But there were sound theoretical reasons for the stylistic conventions of the New Wave as well as budgetary ones. If location shooting with handheld cameras was inexpensive, it was also totally at odds with the fluid, studio-bound cinematography of the contemporary commercial film. If jagged editing and jump-cutting were useful in concealing defective footage, they also eliminated the smooth transitions that permit an audience to forget that it is watching a film—that is, a consciously crafted product of human imagination rather than some "found" reality.

The psychological effect of these conventions—and they must be considered calculated effects by the directors as well as functions of economic necessity—is to establish aesthetic distance between the audience and the film. New Wave films constantly remind us that we are watching a film, and *not* the reality that a film inevitably resembles, by calling attention to their "filmicness"—that is, to their artificially created nature. The abrupt and, above all, obvious manipulation of our perception in these films, through the use of the jump cut, hand held cameras, and so forth, jolts us out of our conventional involvement with the narrative and our traditional identification with the characters, who are often less recognizable as characters than as actors playing characters. This is because New Wave cinema is, in a sense, *self-reflexive cinema*, or *metacinema*—film about the process and nature of film itself. According to the New Wave *cinéastes* (loosely, film artists), the conventional cinema had too faithfully and for too long reproduced our normal way of seeing things through its studiously unobtrusive techniques. The invisible editing and imperturbably smooth camera styles of the commercial cinema of the 1930s, 1940s, 1950s, and much of the 1960s were designed to draw the spectator's attention away from the fact that he or she was watching a consciously crafted artifact. But the disruptive editing and camera styles of the New Wave say to us constantly, "Look, there's a film being made right before your eyes," and to emphasize the point a director or his technical crew will sometimes appear just inside the frame of a narrative sequence, as if by accident, to remind us that whenever we watch a film a handful of artists are controlling the process immediately beyond the borders of the frame.

The theoretical position of the New Wave filmmakers is therefore that film must constantly call attention to the process of its own making and to the medium's own unique language—thus, the unparalleled cinematic *éclat*, or explosiveness, of the New Wave, its emphasis upon "magical" cinematic tricks like the jump cut, the iris-in and iris-out, decelerated and accelerated motion, and optically violent camera movement—all devices of which film and no other medium is capable. In this sense, the New Wave represents a return to Méliès and his conspicuously cinematic brand of conjuring. It envisions film as a special kind of magic that requires of its viewers a uniquely cinematic way of seeing in order to comprehend. On the other hand, the New Wave reaches back equally to Lumière because its most characteristic techniques are essentially documentary in practice. In fact, *cinéma vérité*, the chief documentary mode of the 1960s and 1970s, constitutes an application of New Wave shooting and recording practices to real events rather than staged ones. Furthermore, Jean-Luc Godard, the most innovative and radical director to emerge from the New Wave, has virtually rejected narrative cinema in favor of cinematic "essays" on ideology and social praxis. New Wave cinema is aware of this paradox because it is aware of its history and conscious of the mediating position it holds between the narrative and documentary traditions of Western film. The allusions to and "quotations" from films of the past (sometimes called *hommages*) with which New Wave films are replete are no mere mannerisms, but rather testaments to the critical-historical cinematic consciousness out of which the movement grew.

Major New Wave Figures

The critical and commercial success of the New Wave in 1959 was so great that between 1960 and 1962 over one hundred new French directors were able to find funding for their first features—an extraordinary thing in an industry formerly so conservative. In some cases, the director of a commercial hit, like Godard or Truffaut, would produce for a less fortunate friend. In many others, a French commercial studio would produce, hoping to come up with a smash hit like *Breathless* on a B-film budget. In fact, the climate of creative and commercial enthusiasm during these two years was such that virtually anyone with the will to do so could obtain financial backing to make a low-budget film, though many who turned to directing lacked either the talent or the discipline to bring their projects to a successful conclusion. The commercial failures of the less talented began en masse in 1962, and by 1964 the studios had been so badly disappointed by well-intentioned amateurs that production money for first features was more difficult to raise than it had been in the 1950s. By this time, the New Wave as a collective phenomenon was over, and the French film industry had resumed its conventionally rigid contours. But French cinema continued to be dominated creatively by the handful of young *cinéastes* who had initiated the movement and who emerged from it as distinctly major figures—François Truffaut, Jean-Luc Godard, Alain Resnais, Claude Chabrol—and by a small group of sophisticated but less spectacular talents, such as Louis Malle, Eric Rohmer, Jacques Demy, Jacques Rivette, and Agnès Varda.

FRANÇOIS TRUFFAUT

François Truffaut (1932–1984), the most commercially successful of the post–New Wave group, was able to maintain his independence by forming his own production company, Les Films du Carrosse (1957), named in *hommage* to Renoir's *Le Carrosse d'or* (1952). His major cinematic influences were the American B-film, *film noir*, and the work of Alfred Hitchcock and Jean Renoir. He followed *Les Quatre cents coups* (1959) with what he called "a respectful tribute to the Hollywood B-film," *Tirez sur le pianiste* (*Shoot the Piano Player*, 1960) based on an American gangster thriller (*Down There*) by the novelist David Goodis. The film concerns Charlie, a timid honky-tonk piano player in a sleazy Parisian bar who, we learn in a series of extended flashbacks, was once the great concert pianist Edouard Saroyan. He and his girlfriend, Lena, become involved with two gangsters who are after his younger brother, and the couple is forced to flee the city when Charlie accidentally kills his employer

in self-defense. The film ends with a shoot-out between the brothers and the gangsters at a farmhouse in the snow, in which Lena is killed. Criticized on its release for its radical shifts in mood from comedy to melodrama to tragedy, and for the manipulativeness of its disjointed narrative style, *Shoot the Piano Player* was nevertheless Truffaut's *Breathless*—a quintessentially New Wave film replete with bizarre visual puns, allusions to other films, a mixture or "explosion" of genres, and all the self-reflexive anticonventions of the movement. Like *Les Quatre cent coups*, it was stunningly photographed by the innovative New Wave cinematographer Raoul Coutard in Dyaliscope.

Truffaut's third feature, *Jules et Jim* (1961), stands as a tribute to the influence of Renoir and the French lyrical tradition.[2] As in Renoir's work, the basic themes of *Jules et Jim* are friendship and the impossibility of achieving true freedom in love (or, as Truffaut himself put it, "monogamy is impossible, but anything else is worse"). Adapted from a novel by Henri-Pierre Roché, this beautiful and sensitive film concerns two close friends—one French, the other Austrian—who fall in love with the same woman (Catherine), are separated by World War I, and afterward attempt to live together in a ménage à trois. Intellectually sound, the situation proves emotionally impossible for all three, and at the end of the film Catherine drowns herself with Jim, leaving Jules to cremate and bury them. The film is striking in its re-creation of the period through natural settings and in the remarkable performances of its principals—especially Jeanne Moreau[3] as the manic, enigmatic Catherine. While it appropriately avoids the self-conscious pyrotechnics of *Shoot the Piano Player, Jules et Jim* is gorgeously composed and photographed in Franscope, yet another version of CinemaScope, by Raoul Coutard and sustains its emotional lyricism through the unconventional use of telephoto zooms, slow motion, freeze frames, anamor-

---

2. Truffaut has said that *Jules et Jim* was also influenced by Edgar G. Ulmer's B-Western *The Naked Dawn* (1956); it, too, concerns the psychological and emotional vagaries of a sexual triangle.

3. Moreau (b. 1928) became a director in her own right, making an impressive debut with the semiautobiographical *Lumière* (1977), a film about four independent and interdependent women and the dynamics of stardom. It was followed by *L'Adolescente* (*The Adolescent*, 1979), which deals with a young girl's passage from childhood to adolescence. Her *Lillian Gish* (1984) is an affectionate documentary portrait of the venerable actress.

13.15 The triad in Truffaut's *Jules et Jim* (1961): Jeanne Moreau, Henri Serre, Oskar Werner.

phic distortion (of World War I combat footage), and even a helicopter shot. After directing *Antoine et Colette*, also shot by Coutard in Franscope, for the anthology film *L'Amour à vingt ans* (1962), Truffaut produced in collaboration with this inventive cinematographer a restrained and sympathetic study of middle-aged adultery, *Le Peau douce* (*The Soft Skin*, 1964), which was marred by an overly melodramatic ending. His erratic adaptation of Ray Bradbury's *Fahrenheit* 451 (1966), Truffaut's first film in color and English, is generally regarded as a failure because it played down traditional science-fiction themes. But its portrait of a near-future society of emotionless, hedonistic people mindlessly tripped out on big-screen color television seems more than prophetic today, and Nicolas Roeg's cinematography is first-rate.

In 1967, Truffaut published a book-length interview with Alfred Hitchcock in which he demonstrated his reverence for the American director by comparing him not only to Griffith, Hawks, and Ford, but to Kafka, Dostoevsky, and Poe. Appropriately enough, Truffaut's next two features were conceived as direct tributes to the Hitchcock thriller. *La Mariée était en noir* (*The Bride Wore Black*, 1967), photographed by Coutard, is a suspenseful tale of vengeance in which a woman (Jeanne Moreau) relentlessly tracks down and kills the five men responsible for the accidental shooting of her husband on their wedding day. Adapted from a novel by William Irish—the author of the novel on which the film *Rear Window* (Hitchcock, 1954) is based—and with a musical

score by a frequent Hitchcock collaborator, Bernard Herrmann, Truffaut's film contains a dense pattern of allusions to specific Hitchcock films, uses Hitchcockian plot construction, and is intensely manipulative of audience expectations in order to generate suspense. *La Sirène du Mississippi* (*Mississippi Mermaid*, 1969), also adapted from a William Irish novel and shot in Dyaliscope by Denys Clerval, is dedicated to Jean Renoir and contains many allusions to his films (especially in its "open" ending, which is a visual *hommage* to the conclusion of *La Grande illusion*, 1937). But in terms of style and construction, this minor thriller about the degradation of an honest man by a *femme fatale* is pure Hitchcock.

Between *La Mariée était en noir* and *La Sirène du Mississippi*, Truffaut made his second Antoine Doinel feature, *Baisers volés* (*Stolen Kisses*, 1968), handsomely photographed by Clerval, a tender and affectionate portrait of Antoine's coming to adult consciousness through a series of affairs and, finally, his engagement to Christine (Claude Jade). *Domicile conjugal* (*Bed & Board*, 1970), the third feature in the Doinel series, examines the first few years of Antoine and Christine's marriage, its deterioration under the pressure of an affair, and its ultimate, uneasy reconstitution. The film is light and humorous, and its comedy is quite successful, but like *Jules et Jim* it also raises some serious questions about the institution of marriage and its alternatives. Truffaut concluded the Doinel series, begun with *Les Quatre cents coups* twenty years before, with *L'Amour en fuite* (*Love on the Run*,

1979), which begins with Antoine's uncontested divorce from Christine and proceeds through his chance encounters with figures from his past.

For *L'Enfant sauvage* (*The Wild Child*, 1969), based upon the true account of a "wolf-boy" captured in the forests of central France in 1806, Truffaut both directed and played the part of Dr. Itard, the eighteenth-century rationalist who undertakes the painstakingly slow education of the wild child. Set in its period and shot in quasidocumentary style by the award-winning cinematographer Néstor Almendros,[4] *The Wild Child* allowed Truffaut to explore more

13.16 The set within the set of Truffaut's *La Nuit américaine* (1973).

intensively those themes of confinement versus freedom, and social conditioning versus nature, which he had first broached in *Les Quatre cents coups*. *Les Deux Anglaises et le continent* (*Two English Girls*, 1971), adapted from another novel by Henri-Pierre Roché and set at the turn of the century, inevitably evokes comparison with *Jules et Jim*, of which it contains many deliberate echoes. The story of a young Frenchman's love for two English sisters, it was Truffaut's most visually sensuous work to date. Its sumptuous re-creation of la belle époque is conveyed in shots composed after Impressionist paintings of the period, and its use of color was the most subtle Truffaut had achieved so far.

Une Belle fille comme moi (*Such a Gorgeous Kid Like Me*, 1972) is a sardonic portrayal of a murderous nymphomaniac that failed, on the whole, to break new ground. But *La Nuit américaine* (*Day for Night*, 1973) provided the ultimate in self-reflexive cinema: a film starring Jean-Pierre Léaud (the Truffaut figure in the Antoine Doinel series) and directed by Truffaut, about the making of a film starring Léaud and directed by Truffaut. **Day for night** (or *la nuit américaine*) is the technical term for shooting night scenes in daylight through a filter; by

choosing it as his title Truffaut intended to evoke the entire arsenal of cinematic tricks of which it is merely typical. Dedicated to Dorothy and Lillian Gish, the great Griffith actresses, the whole film is predicated upon cinematic illusion, and in this respect it recalls Fellini's *8½* (1963) and Bergman's *Persona* (1966). It is difficult from the outset to tell whether a scene is occurring in the film or in the film *within* the film because the cast and crew live so closely together that there is little distinction between their work and their personal lives. The film is funny, affectionate, and strangely disquieting in its gradual revelation that the same people making the film within the film are simultaneously making *Day for Night* and that confusion between illusion and reality is the very essence of the cinema.

---

4. Almendros, a native of Cuba, won the American Academy Award for Cinematography in 1978 for *Days of Heaven* (Terrence Malick). He worked closely with Truffaut on all the director's subsequent films except *Une Belle fille comme moi* (1972), *La Nuit américaine* (1973), and *L'Argent de poche* (1976)—all shot by Pierre-William Glenn—and *La Femme d'à côté* (1981), which was shot by William Lubtchantsky. Almendros also collaborates regularly with Eric Rohmer and Barbet Schroeder (see p. 462).

Day for Night was in many ways a consummation for Truffaut. It combined the stylistic influence of American realism with that of French lyricism and drew together his dual thematic obsessions with autobiography and psychology in a hymn of praise to the cinema—an art form to which he was passionately devoted for his entire life. It answered the question posed by its own director-character—"Are films more important than life?"—with an emphatic "Yes!"

Truffaut's next project was *L'Histoire d'Adèle H.* (*The Story of Adèle H.*, 1975).[5] Based upon the diary of Victor Hugo's youngest daughter, this subtle and powerful film is about the psychology of a woman in the grip of a romantic obsession. Adèle's romantic fascination with a young English lieutenant leads her to follow him all over the world until she finally goes mad in Barbados and must spend the last forty years of her life in an asylum. The film begins like a conventional romantic melodrama, but as it progresses we are drawn into the increasingly demented world of the heroine with an impact that is both shocking and hauntingly beautiful. In *The Story of Adèle H.*, Truffaut demonstrates a total mastery of the new cinematic language that he helped to create and triumphantly confirms his status as one of the most important film artists of our time. His films of the late 1970s include the comedies *L'Argent de poche* (*Small Change*, 1976) and *L'Homme qui amait les femmes* (*The Man Who Loved Women*, 1977); *La Chambre verte* (*The Green Room*, 1978), based on several short stories by Henry James; and *Le Dernier métro* (*The Last Metro*, 1980), a fascinating account of life in a small Paris theater under the Nazi Occupation—inspired by the autobiography of the stage and film actor Jean Marais (1913–1998)—which became his biggest box-office success. In 1979, Truffaut was honored with an extraordinary twenty-year retrospective by the American Film Institute and the Los Angeles County Museum of Art; but many critics feared he was becoming the kind of mainstream establishment director he had begun his career by attacking. His last two films, however, marked a modest return to the familiar terrain of obsessive romance (*La Femme d'à côté* [*The Woman Next Door*, 1981]) and the Hitchcockian comic thriller *Vivement dimanche!* (*Finally Sunday!*, 1983; American release title *Confidentially Yours*).[6] On October 21, 1984, François Truffaut died of a brain tumor; he was fifty-two years old.

JEAN-LUC GODARD

Jean-Luc Godard (b. 1930) is the most prolific and stylistically radical of all the directors who came to prominence during the New Wave. He has made over forty feature films since *Breathless* (1960), working closely with Raoul Coutard as his director of photography on most of them, and he is among the most influential figures in world cinema today. Unlike Truffaut, Godard is a militantly intellectual and ideologically committed filmmaker whose films almost always involve some form of *autocritique* or interrogation of cinema itself. In a certain sense, they collectively constitute a *theory* of cinema because, better than any of his peers, Godard understood the essential impulse of the New Wave: "The whole New Wave," he wrote in *Cahiers*, "can be defined, in part, by its new relationship to fiction and reality." Godard's films have consistently tested this relationship by rejecting narrative in favor of praxis, the working out of social or political theory within the cinematic process. Since the early 1960s, his films have become increasingly dialectical and rhetorical in structure, and Godard himself calls them "critical essays." Most of these "essays" are personal to the point of being idiosyncratic, and Godard has maintained his independence by producing them quickly and cheaply. His films are therefore not as carefully crafted as those of Truffaut and his other peers, and they frequently appear to be less finished films than unvarnished journals about the making of a film, full of technical blunders and undigested facts. And, unlike his peers, Godard is still in the business of breaking every known cinematic convention—even the more recent conventions established by the New Wave itself—in a ceaseless attempt to expand the medium's form and pursue its potential for artistic, intellectual, and political self-expression.

Several of Godard's early films were characteristic New Wave tributes to the American cinema. *À bout de*

---

5. For the scores of this film and his next three, Truffaut used the music of the great French film composer Maurice Jaubert (1900–1940), who had contributed so much to the success of poetic realism (see Chapter 9).

6. *Vivement Truffaut* is the title of a documentary tribute to Truffaut assembled by Claude de Givray for the 1985 Cannes Film Festival; *Finally Truffaut* is a film-by-film guide to the director's work by his friend Don Allen (New York: Beaufort, 1985).

souffle (*Breathless*, 1960) was modeled on the B-film gangster thriller. *Une Femme est une femme* (*A Woman Is a Woman*, 1961), described by Godard as "a neorealist musical—that is, a contradiction in terms," was a studio-produced tribute to the American musical comedy, made in Franscope and color. *Le Petit soldat* (*The Little Soldier*, 1960), made between these two films, was banned by the French government for three years because it commented on the Algerian War. Like *Breathless*, it has the form of a gangster film and turns on the theme of betrayal; but its protagonist belongs to a fascist terrorist organization fighting the Algerian liberation front in Geneva, and the film graphically depicts the use of torture by both sides. Both *Le Petit soldat* and *Une Femme est une femme* starred Godard's sensuously beautiful first wife, Anna Karina, and his fourth film seemed intended as a kind of portrait of her. *Vivre sa vie* (*My Life to Live*, 1962), a study of a woman who chooses to be a prostitute, is constructed in the form of a twelve-part sociological tract on the problem of prostitution, complete with statistics and pseudo-clinical jargon.

With *Les Carabiniers* (*The Soldiers/The Riflemen*, 1963), an adaptation of Beniamino Joppolo's play *I carabinieri*, cowritten by Roberto Rossellini, Godard created a fable about the nature of war in a style that is both a parody of and an *hommage* to the early documentary style of Lumière. The film, whose narrative line is often fragmented to the point of breaking down, achieves an almost

13.18 and 13.19 An hommage to Lumière (top) and image and reality merge (bottom) in Godard's *Les Carabiniers* (1963).

13.17 *Une Femme est une femme* (Jean-Luc Godard, 1961): Anna Karina, Jean-Paul Belmondo.

Brechtian detachment from its subject and is clearly among Godard's most important works. It is the first of his "critical essays," for, as one critic has said, *Les Carabiniers* is less a war movie than "a series of propositions about war." *Le Mépris* (*Contempt*, 1963), based upon Alberto Moravia's novel *A Ghost at Noon*, was Godard's sixth feature. It was an international coproduction starring Jack Palance and Brigitte Bardot shot in widescreen and color, and like Truffaut's *Day for Night* it concerns the making of a movie. This film within the film is a version of Homer's *Odyssey* being shot in Rome by Fritz Lang, who plays himself. The narrative portion of *Le Mépris*, which concerns the dissolution of the scriptwriter's marriage, is less important than Godard's use of the self-reflexive conceit.

13.20 *Le Mépris* (Jean-Luc Godard, 1963): images of image making. Jack Palance, Brigitte Bardot, Michel Piccoli.

Godard had disputes with the producers of *Le Mépris* over the editing and scoring of the film, and for his seventh feature he formed his own production company, Anouchka Films. *Bande à part* (*Band of Outsiders*, 1964) is based upon an American pulp thriller and constitutes Godard's first return to the gangster genre since *Breathless*. It deals with a burglary attempt by three Parisian students—two men and a woman—that ends in tragic farce when one of the would-be criminals is killed. The narrative is filmed straightforwardly, but our experience of it is strangely distanced through a running commentary spoken by Godard in which he summarizes the plot for latecomers, tells us what the characters are thinking, makes observations upon the drab suburban setting, or simply reads newspaper headlines. In *Une Femme mariée* (*A Married Woman*, 1964), ironically subtitled "Fragments of a Film Shot in 1964," Godard mixed a wide range of narrative and documentary styles to create a sociological study of woman's role in modern culture. The film portrays twenty-four hours in the life of a married woman who is having an affair, and its visual texture is quite complex: straightforward narration is broken up by three highly stylized scenes of lovemaking, seven *cinéma vérité*–type interviews with the people around the protagonist, a typically Godardian dissertation on advertising for women's underwear, and a clip from Resnais's *Nuit et brouillard* (1955), which two of the characters watch in a theater.

In *Alphaville* (1965) Godard used the form of the science-fiction thriller to create a parable about the alienating

13.21 Allusion (to *Jules et Jim*) and to pulp violence in Godard's *Bande à part* (1964)—a film, the credits tell us, by "Jean-Luc/ Cinema/Godard": Sami Frey, Anna Karina, Claude Brasseur.

effects of technology. At some time in the future, private eye Lemmy Caution (played by the pop-thriller star Eddie Constantine [1917–1993]) travels through intergalactic space from the Outer Countries to the city of Alphaville, where his mission is to destroy Dr. von Braun. Von Braun is the inventor and operator of Alpha-60, the computer that runs the desensitized, lobotomized society of Alphaville. Caution succeeds in destroying both the doctor and his invention, and he escapes the crumbling Alphaville with von Braun's daughter. Originally entitled *Tarzan vs. IBM*, *Alphaville* is one of Godard's most sustained and disciplined performances. He makes brilliant use of contemporary Paris to evoke the future, which serves to remind us that the world of Alphaville is already upon us.

In *Pierrot le fou* (*Crazy Pete*, 1965), Godard returned

to the disjointed and self-reflexive narrative style of *Les Carabiniers* and to the generic model of the gangster film: a man (Jean-Paul Belmondo) and a woman (Anna Karina) run away from a Parisian gang to live an idyllic, desert-islandlike existence in the south of France until a series of betrayals causes their horribly violent, if apparently accidental, deaths.[7] Scriptless and virtually plotless, the film comes close to realizing the Godardian ideal of "a film where there has been no writing, no editing, and no sound mixing." *Masculin/féminin* (1965) marks a definitive turning away from narrative. Like *Vivre sa vie* and *Une Femme mariée*, it is a film of sociological inquiry hung upon a slender plot, but here the plot is almost irrelevant to the inquiry. The film is concerned with illustrating fifteen distinct problems of the younger generation, the "children of Marx and Coca-Cola," members of which are interviewed and interview one another in

13.22 Lyricism in *Pierrot le fou* (Jean-Luc Godard, 1965): Anna Karina.

cinéma vérité fashion. Godard shows that their idealism is belied by the world of cynical sex and violence that surrounds them. Since *Masculin/féminin*, Godard's films have become increasingly ideological and, in some cases, structurally random. As he wrote in 1966: "Cinema is capitalism in its purest form. . . . There is only one solution, and that is to turn one's back on the American cinema." The ironic result of this logic was *Made in U.S.A.* (1966).

Though it is loosely based on a detective thriller, *Made in U.S.A.* has no narrative thread at all and is a film intent upon destroying virtually every illusion of which cinema—especially traditional American cinema—is capable. Ostensibly a remake of Hawks's *The Big Sleep* (1946) with Karina in the Bogart role, the film is so self-reflexive as to have no content: characters speak to the audience, explaining their behavior and commenting on the triviality of the plot, the dialogue is nonsensical and sometimes deliberately rendered inaudible on the sound track. The film's meaning lies at its periphery, in its comment upon political violence, the viciousness and stupidity of the Right, the sentimentality and fecklessness of the Left. *Deux ou trois choses que je sais d'elle* (*Two or Three Things I Know about Her*, 1966) is a collage of images and interviews centering around a Parisian housewife who has turned to casual prostitution in order to keep herself in middle-class luxury. The film is a radical indictment of capitalist technocracy in the West, which, Godard holds, makes prostitutes of us all through its system of economic constraints. So, too, is *La Chinoise* (1967), subtitled *A Film in the Making*, which depicts five students who set up a Maoist cell and fail, each in his or her separate way, to achieve cultural revolution. Godard also contributed a long, single-take monologue to the collective polemic *Loin du Vietnam* (*Far from Vietnam*) produced by SLON in 1967.

But Godard's most savage attack upon the values of Western capitalist society is *Weekend* (1967), a film that begins as a recognizable, if violent, narrative and ends as an apocalyptic vision of the collapse of civilization in the

7. The idea for *Pierrot le fou* was almost certainly implanted by David Newman and Robert Benton's screenplay for *Bonnie and Clyde* (Arthur Penn, 1967), which had been submitted for consideration to Truffaut and then passed on to Godard in mid-1965. Godard actually wanted to direct the American script, but only if he could begin shooting immediately—a condition unacceptable to the producers.

13.23 Godard's *La Chinoise* (1967): Anne Wiazemsky about to be napalmed by the Esso (now Exxon) tiger.

West. A young bourgeois couple set out to visit the woman's mother in Normandy in order to borrow some money from her. They become trapped in a monumental weekend traffic jam, which Godard renders in a single slow lateral tracking shot lasting fully 4 minutes on the screen. Gradually, we pass from a real landscape into a symbolic one in which the highway is littered with burning automobiles and the bloodied, mutilated bodies of crash victims. From this point on, the film is dominated by images of mindless slaughter and mayhem from which the thin veneer of civilization has been stripped away. When the couple reach the mother's house and are refused the money, they hack her to pieces and steal it.[8] As they return to Paris, they are overtaken by a band of Maoist renegades armed with submachine guns, who have turned to cannibalism—the mirror image of capitalism, for Godard—to survive. The husband is killed, and his wife joins the group in eating him. *Weekend* is a harsh and brutal film that uses vivid color photography and tight dramatic construction to drive home the point that Western civilization is merely a façade elaborated by technology concealing a hard core of bestiality.

After *Weekend* and the political turmoil of May 1968,[9] Godard attempted to abandon narrative altogether, considering it a bourgeois form. *Le Gai savoir* (1968) is a rambling cinematic essay on language as an instrument of social conditioning and control, based on the philosophical assumptions of structural linguistics. All of Godard's films between 1968 and 1973 were produced by the Dziga-Vertov Group (actually an uneasy creative partnership between Godard and the ideologist Jean-Pierre Gorin), and Godard came to make increasing use of the arsenal of agitational techniques employed by the Soviet revolutionary cinema of 1924–28. *Un Film comme*

13.24 Capitalist apocalypse: Godard's *Weekend* (1967), alternately subtitled "A Film Lost in the Cosmos" and "A Film Found on the Scrap Heap." Jean Yanne, Mireille Darc.

8. Godard remarked to interviewers that his films after *Pierrot* might seem to have a lot of blood in them, but it was really a lot of "red." During this period, *Cahiers du cinéma* became politicized along Marxist-Leninist lines—alienating all members of its founding group but Godard, who was militantly committed to this political position. The journal also fell deeply under the influence of Bertolt Brecht's radical theories of theater.

9. French society was thrown into an unexpected political crisis in May 1968. Early in the month a series of rallies by student radicals on university campuses in Paris mushroomed into civil disorder. The immediate catalyst for the demonstrations was the firing of Henri Langlois as director of the Cinémathèque Française by the Gaullist minister of culture André Malraux, but the rallies were also related to the recent success of the North Vietnamese Tet offensive in Vietnam and the political upheavals it had produced in the United States and all over the world. By the middle of May, the disturbance had spread beyond Paris to universities in other cities and to unionized workers, some 10 million of whom participated in a series of strikes that paralyzed the country. On May 30, however, President Charles de Gaulle (1890–1970) managed to turn the workers against the students by appealing for law and order on national television and calling for new national elections to be held on June 23. On that day, faced with a choice between what the president called "de Gaulle and anarchy," the French people chose the former; but the "events of May" 1968 left many thoughtful Frenchmen in doubt about the legitimacy of their government and continue to haunt those who lived through them.

les autres (*A Film Like Any Other*, 1968), for example, is a 16mm record of an elementary political discussion that takes place among several people lying in tall grass, none of whom is clearly distinguishable. Godard makes a point of its randomness by suggesting that a coin be tossed to determine which one of its several reels is screened first. *One Plus One* (*Sympathy for the Devil*, 1968) is a film of seemingly unrelated fragments: a Bolivian revolutionary hiding out in a London men's room, the Rolling Stones rehearsing the song "Sympathy for the Devil," black-power militants plotting revolution in a junkyard, a television interview with a lobotomized fairy godmother called Eve Democracy, a man reading *Mein Kampf* in a Soho porno shop, etc.

At one point in *One Plus One* a character remarks: "There is only one way to be an intellectual revolutionary, and that is to give up being an intellectual." Some critics believe that Godard followed the logic of this statement to the point of nihilism. All of his films for the now defunct Dziga-Vertov Group—*British Sounds* (*See You at Mao*, 1969), *Pravda* (1969), *Le Vent d'est* (*Wind from the East*, 1969), *Luttes en Italie* (*Struggles in Italy*, 1969), *Vladimir et Rosa* (1970), *Tout va bien* (1972),[1] and *Letter to Jane* (1972)—show Godard concerned with the nature and function of ideology, regardless of its medium. Although his later work demonstrates a renewed interest in narrative, it has been suggested that Godard's cinematic "essays" are not films in the conventional sense at all, but a form of narrative embattled with discourse. Nevertheless, Godard's impact on contemporary cinema generally, as distinct from his importance to the French New Wave, has been immense. His most discernible influence in the 1970s and 1980s was upon the materialist cinema of Jean-Marie Straub and Danièle Huillet, the omnibus films of Hans-Jürgen Syberberg (for both, see Chapter 15), and the award-winning minimalist work of Belgian filmmaker Chantal Akerman (b. 1950), creator of *Jeanne Dielman, 23 quai de Commerce, 1080 Bruxelles* (1977), *Les Rendez-vous d'Anna* (1978), *Toute une nuit* (*All Night Long*, 1982), *Les Années 80* (*The Golden Eighties*, 1983), and *Nuit et jour* (*Night and Day*, 1991). But Godard made a whole generation question the accepted conventions of filmmaking, remaining all the while a solitary and independent figure.

After ending his association with Gorin in 1973, Godard experimented with a combination of film and **videotape** that permitted him to superimpose two or

13.25 Combining video and film in*Numéro deux* (Jean-Luc Godard, 1975).

more images on the screen simultaneously. In film/tapes like *Numéro deux* (*Number Two*, 1975), *Comment ça va?* (*How Goes It?*, 1975), *La Communication* (1976), *Ici et ailleurs* (*Here and There*, 1970; 1976), and *Six fois deux* (*Six Times Two*, 1976),[2] he pioneered a new means of interrogating the cinematic image by offering two contradictory perspectives on "reality" at once. In 1980, Godard produced his first theatrical feature in nearly eight years. Technically evocative of his films of the late 1960s, *Sauve qui peut (la vie)* (*Every Man for Himself/ Slow Motion*) is an essay on the metaphysics of survival shot on location in Switzerland, that paradigm of Western capitalist survivorship, that characteristically constructs a sustained analogy between sexual degradation and economic exploitation. Godard, who now lives in Switzerland himself, has continued to make features, renewing his extraordinary collaboration with Raoul Coutard in *Passion* (1982), *Prénom Carmen* (*First Name: Carmen*, 1983), and the controversial *Je vous salue Marie* (*Hail, Mary*,

---

1. The uncharacteristic two-year hiatus in Godard's normally breakneck production schedule was occasioned by a nearly fatal motorcycle accident in June 1971. Although Godard intended the title *Tout va bien* (*All's Well*) as an ironic comment on bourgeois complacency, it also signified his literal well-being in having fully recovered from his injuries. See James Roy MacBean, "Godard and the Dziga-Vertov Group: Film and Dialectics," *Film Quarterly* 26, 1 (Fall 1972): 30–43.

2. The last two were made in collaboration with Anne-Marie Miéville. Of *Numéro deux*, Godard said he was remaking *Breathless*, so the title has the ironic force in French of "*Breathless II*."

1984), a modern retelling of the immaculate conception that affronted much of the Catholic world. In 1987, Godard—who once said that "one could make a good film in twenty seconds"—began directing jeans commercials for the designers Marithé and François Girbaud (M.F.G.) in exchange for the foreign distribution of his French telefilm *Grandeur et décadence d'un petit commerce de cinéma* (1986)—confirming for himself, no doubt, his 1967 declaration that "cinema is capitalism in its purest form." Some of Godard's more recent features are *Détective* (1985), *King Lear* (1987)—a remarkable contemporary "approach" to the play with Burgess Meredith in the title role and Molly Ringwald as Cordelia (and Peter Sellars as Shakespeare)—*Soigne ta droite* (*Keep Up Your Right*, 1987), *Nouvelle vague* (1990), *Allemagne neuf zéro* (*Germany Year Nine Zero*, 1991, in which Eddie Constantine reprises the role of Lemmy Caution from *Alphaville*), *Hélas pour moi* (*Woe Is Me*, 1993), and *JLG/JLG* (1994). His feature-length video program *Histoire(s) du cinéma* (1989–98), which first toured the United States in 1993, creates a montage of images from painting, photography, film, and video to "present some possible stories in the history of cinema" in a characteristically flamboyant way. *For Ever Mozart* (1996), in which a French theater troupe attempts to stage a play during the siege of Sarajevo, received widespread critical acclaim for its meditation on the possibility of art in time of war, as did the atypically elegiac *Éloge de l'amour* (*In Praise of Love*, 2001), which was shot entirely on digital video and transferred to 35mm.

ALAIN RESNAIS

Alain Resnais (b. 1922) is identified with the New Wave because his first major successes, *Hiroshima, mon amour* (1959) and *L'Année dernière à Marienbad* (*Last Year at Marienbad*, 1961), both appeared during its height. But Resnais is a generation older than the *Cahiers* group, and he began his film career not as a critic but as an editor and director of short films in the scenarist tradition. Unlike several of his New Wave counterparts, he prefers to work from an original script, usually one written especially for the screen by a major novelist like Jean Cayrol, Marguerite Duras, Alain Robbe-Grillet, or Jorge Semprún. He also works slowly and plans his films meticulously in advance of production, in close collaboration with his writers and technicians, believing that film is

13.26 *L'Année dernière à Marienbad* (Alain Resnais, 1961): human geometry.

basically a collective art. Yet Resnais is an avant-garde intellectual who has been strongly influenced by the philosophy of Henri Bergson.[3] And because his major theme is the effect of time on human memory and the relationship between memory and politics, he communicates by exploding the conventional boundaries of narrative form. His almost Proustian fascination with time and memory leads Resnais to create remarkable structures for his films, in which past, present, and future are perceived upon the same spatial and temporal plane, and in which objectivity and subjectivity are never clearly distinguishable.

In *L'Année dernière à Marienbad* (1961), written by French experimental novelist Alain Robbe-Grillet, a man, X, meets a woman, A, at a baroque chateau that seems to be a resort for the very rich and that may or may not be Marienbad (a spa in Czechoslovakia). He claims to have met her, or a woman like her, with a man, M, who was perhaps her husband, "last year at Marienbad." She denies this, and their debate, which is a debate about the nature of reality itself, recurs endlessly through the film as labyrinthine images of past, present, and future framed in Dyaliscope by cinematographer Sacha Vierny seem to merge in the same visual continuum of highly stylized tracking shots (a Resnais trademark) and frozen geomet-

---

3. Bergson (1859–1941) was a French philosopher whose theories of time and "creative evolution" have had considerable impact upon twentieth-century thought.

ric compositions. X and A seem to have had or to be having or to desire to have an affair; the end is A's death at the hands of her husband. Whether the film represents an attempt to re-create the process of memory in the mind of X, a long interior monologue on the part of A, or an exercise in sheer visual abstractionism, is impossible to say. But, like Bergson's philosophy, the film is clearly concerned with mental process rather than narrative—or perhaps with redefining mental process *as* narrative. As Resnais remarked, *Marienbad* represents "an attempt, still crude and primitive, to approach the complexity of thought and its mechanisms." The film won the prestigious Golden Lion at the Venice Film Festival in 1961 and is one of the few authentically modernist works in cinema.

In *Muriel, ou le temps d'un retour* (English title: *Muriel*, 1963), written by Jean Cayrol, author of the commentary for *Nuit et brouillard* (1955), Resnais returned to the material world for a film about a mother and her stepson haunted by the past. The mother must confront her lover of twenty-two years past, who arrives for a visit accompanied by his most recent mistress, and the stepson is tormented by the memory of Muriel, a young Algerian girl whom he and a friend tortured and killed during the recently concluded French-Algerian War. In terms of content, *Muriel* is a brilliant political film and, although government censors did not recognize it at the time, perhaps the most damning of all films about the Algerian situation as it affected France. But in its remarkably complex montage of nearly a thousand shots, Sacha Vierny's luminous color cinematography, the innovative sound recording of Antoine Bonfanti, and a score featuring the music of avant-garde composer Hans Werner Henze, *Muriel* approaches the cinema of pure association and is clearly Resnais's greatest work.

With *La Guerre est finie* (*The War Is Over*, 1966), written by the Spanish novelist Jorge Semprún, Resnais entered the arena of political commitment. More conventional in narrative structure and more realistic than his other features, this film still manages to suggest the overlapping of memory and imagination, and the relationship that necessarily exists between an individual's past and present and his or her identity. *La Guerre est finie* concerns three days in the life of a middle-aged revolutionary named Diego (Yves Montand) who, some thirty years after the Spanish Civil War, still works for the overthrow of the Franco regime. Diego has come to Paris

13.27 Resnais's *La Guerre est finie* (1966): Yves Montand.

to plan strategy and see his mistress, but he also has a chance affair there with a radical young student. His sense of identity is called into question by her revolutionary friends, who challenge Diego's methods and his commitment to the struggles of the past. As he recrosses the border into Spain at the end of the film, he imagines his arrest by Spanish secret police, but through a slow dissolve we see that his mistress is on her way to save him, suggesting the possibility of a new beginning.

After contributing to the 1967 anthology *Loin de Vietnam*, Resnais produced *Je t'aime, je t'aime* (*I Love You, I Love You*, 1968), a science-fiction film, written by Jacques Sternberg and with a score by Krzysztof Penderecki, about a man, projected into the past after an unsuccessful suicide attempt, who becomes lost within the structure of time itself. With Chris Marker's short *La Jetée* (1962) and Stanley Kubrick's *2001: A Space Odyssey* (1968)— which also included some music composed by Penderecki—*Je t'aime, je t'aime* was one of the most provocative science-fiction films of the decade. However, its elliptical narrative structure and densely poetic dialogue prevented it from reaching a large audience, and its commercial failure was at least partially responsible for a six-year hiatus in Resnais's career.

During the 1960s, Resnais's films, like Godard's, became increasingly unfashionable and unconventional as he pursued the logic of his own artistic development at the cost of financial gain. If Godard's films became critical essays on ideological praxis, Resnais's had always been philosophical investigations into the workings of the human mind, and this meant the loss of popular audiences after his initial success with *Hiroshima, mon amour*. As a result, Resnais was unable to direct for five years after 1968 for lack of financial backing. But in 1975 his *Stavisky* was released to both critical acclaim and commercial success. Written by Jorge Semprún and starring Jean-Paul Belmondo in the paradoxical title role, *Stavisky* is a political period film about a colossal financial scandal that toppled the French government in 1934. With a melodic score by Stephen Sondheim, it was shot by Sacha Vierny to evoke the two-color Technicolor process of the early 1930s, and it became Resnais's most popular film to date. *Providence* (1977), scripted by David Mercer, which takes place entirely within the mind of a dying novelist, won a New York Film Critics Award for John Gielgud as Best Actor. Resnais himself won a unanimous Special Jury Prize at Cannes in 1980 for *Mon oncle d'Amérique* (*My American Uncle*), a narrative of interpersonal relationships poisoned by ambition, based upon the behaviorist theories of the French biologist Henri Laborit, who appears in his laboratory at several points during the film to offer short discourses on the science of "aggressiology." In the 1980s, Resnais sustained this metaphor of sociological observation in *La Vie est un roman* (*Life Is a Novel*; British title: *Life Is a Bed of Roses*, 1983), which superimposes three historically distinct stories—each narrated according to contemporaneous cinematic styles—on the quotidian proceedings of an educational conference; *L'Amour à mort* (1984), a film about the archaeology of knowledge set in the southern French Protestant town of Uzès and structured around the avant-garde compositions of Hans Werner Henze; and *Mélo* (1986), an extraordinary real-time adaptation of a 1929 boulevard melodrama by the forgotten playwright Henry Berstein, which had already been filmed five times before. Like *Mon oncle d'Amérique*, all of these last three films were scripted by Jean Gruault, who had worked extensively with Truffaut; none has yet been distributed in the United States, nor has the five-hour *Smoking/No Smoking* (1993), a deliberately incredible version of Alan Ayckbourn's series of plays on indeterminancy, *Intimate Exchanges*, adapted by Resnais as two contiguous films. In 1997 the director scored a popular hit with *On connaît la chanson* (*Same Old Song*), a tribute to TV writer Dennis Potter (1935–1994), in which the actors deliver their dialogue as lip-synched songs in the style of Potter's "Pennies from Heaven" and "The Singing Detective."

Frequently accused of coldness and abstractionism, Resnais is a serious, committed filmmaker whose technical mastery of his medium has enabled him to create a handful of films of great visual beauty and intellectual depth that rank among the masterworks of French cinema. When asked, in a recent interview, about the filmmakers who had most influenced him, Resnais mentioned Griffith, Pudovkin, and Eisenstein. He also spoke of the Czech-born British director Karel Reisz (see Chapter 14) as his "real teacher" through Reisz's book *The Technique of Film Editing*.[4] In other words, Resnais clearly sees his work as growing out of the tradition of classical montage. And in his fascination with the manipulation of the space-time continuum, Resnais serves to remind us that montage aesthetics are still alive and well in a film culture that looks to *mise-en-scène* as a kind of cinematic god.

CLAUDE CHABROL

Claude Chabrol (b. 1930), who had been forced to make a series of commercial thrillers after the financial failure of *Les Bonnes femmes* in 1960, returned to the top of his form with *Les Biches* (*The Does*, 1968), a subtle, visually exquisite study of lesbian sexual obsession and domination set in St. Tropez in winter. *Les Biches* marked the beginning of his long collaboration with the cinematographer Jean Rabier (b. 1927), formerly the camera operator for Henri Decaë, who had shot Chabrol's earliest films. Like Resnais, Chabrol believes that filmmaking is a collective enterprise, and since *Les Biches* he has had a team of collaborators who work with him on every film. These include, in addition to Rabier, his coscenarist, Paul Gégauff; his art director, Guy Littaye; his editor, Jacques Gaillard; and his leading actress (and wife), Stéphane Audran.

Chabrol achieved absolute mastery of his medium with *La Femme infidèle* (*The Unfaithful Wife*, 1968)—an investigation into the violent consequences of adultery in a typical French bourgeois family—which owes much technically to Hitchcock. Like Truffaut, Chabrol (with Eric Rohmer) wrote a book on Hitchcock; in fact, Cha-

---

4. Appropriately, the second edition of Reisz's authoritative manual, cowritten with Gavin Millar (London: The Focal Press, 1968), includes a lengthy analysis of *L'Année dernière à Marienbad*.

13.28 *Les Biches* (Claude Chabrol, 1968): Stéphane Audran, Jacqueline Sassard.

brol has been stylistically influenced by the American director more than any other figure of the New Wave generation. One critic sees the whole body of Chabrol's work as an extended *hommage* to Hitchcock. But while Chabrol frequently employs Hitchcockian structures and metaphors (such as the simultaneous tracking out and zooming in that occurs near the end of *Vertigo* [1958] and in the final shot of *La Femme infidèle*), he has a theme that is very much his own—the impact of a crime of passion on a small but intimate network of human relationships, such as those that exist within a middle-class family, a love triangle, or even a small community. Chabrol dissects the psychological complexities of these relationships with clinical precision; yet in his mature films this ironic detachment from his material never seems indifferent or cold and at its best can evoke feelings of compassion devoid of sentimentality. Perhaps it is Fritz Lang and his deterministically plotted cinema of destiny (*M*, 1931; *Fury*, 1936; *The Big Heat*, 1953), rather than Hitchcock, whom Chabrol most resembles in this respect.

Que la bête meure (*Killer/The Beast Must Die*, 1969) is an ironic revenge tragedy about a man who relentlessly tracks down the driver of an automobile that has killed his young son in a hit-and-run accident and comes to love the murderer's son in the process. Chabrol continued to probe the violence and bestiality that lie just beneath the surface of everyday life in *Le Boucher* (*The Butcher*, 1969), which one Parisian critic hailed as the best French film since the Liberation and which is clearly among the best two or three works to emerge from the immediate post–New Wave period. Told with a remarkable economy and purity of cinematic style, *Le Boucher* is essentially a love story set in a small French village in which one of the lovers is a sexual psychopath given to murdering young women and mutilating their bodies. This "butcher," however, is made the most sympathetic character in the entire film, and the compassionate psychological study of his relationship with a young schoolteacher, who loves him even as she becomes increasingly convinced of his guilt, represents a high point in contemporary French cinema.

Since *Le Boucher*, Chabrol has directed approximately one film a year. *La Rupture* (*The Break-Up*, 1970); *Juste avant la nuit* (*Just before Nightfall*, 1971); *La Décade prodigieuse* (*Ten Days' Wonder*, 1972); *Les Noces rouges* (*Blood Wedding*, 1973); *La Banc de la désolation/De Grey*, two hour-long telefilms based on Henry James stories (1973); *Nada* (English title: *The Nada Gang*) and *Une Parti de plaisir* (*A Piece of Pleasure*, both 1974) and *Les Innocents aux mains sales* (English title: *Dirty Hands*, 1974); *Les Magiciens* (*The Magicians*) and *Folies bour-*

13.29 Chabrol's *Le Boucher* (1969): Stéphane Audran, Jean Yanne.

geoises (*Bourgeois Madness*), both 1975; *Alice, ou la dernière fugue* (*Alice, or the Last Escapade*) and *Les Liens de sang* (*Blood Relatives*), both 1977; and *Violette Nozière* (English title: *Violette*, 1978), a macabre film of parricide based on the true story of an eighteen-year-old girl (brilliantly portrayed by Isabelle Huppert) who poisoned her parents in 1933, e.g., were his contributions of the 1970s.

Like Truffaut, Godard, and Resnais, Chabrol is a major figure in contemporary French cinema, although his films of the 1980s have been uneven. *Le Cheval d'orgueil* (*Horse of Pride*, 1980), for example, was a successful exposition of pre–World War I French country life, but *Les Fantômes du Chapelier* (*The Hatter's Ghosts*, 1982) was a clumsy version of a Georges Simenon novel. *Le Sang des autres* (*The Blood of Others*, 1984), a Simone de Beauvoir adaptation set in occupied Paris, was well received but two subsequent *film noirs*—*Poulet au vinaigre* (1985) and its sequel, *Inspecteur Lavardin* (1986)—were not. In 1987, however, Chabrol returned to form by all measures with the psychological thrillers *Masques* (*Masks*) and *Le Cri du hibou* (*The Cry of the Owl*), while *Une Affaire des femmes* (*Women's Affair*, 1988) won international acclaim for its serious treatment of the last woman to receive capital punishment in France—a provincial housewife tried as an abortionist and sent to the guillotine by the Vichy government in 1943, which government fell under his documentary lens several years later in *L'Oeil de Vichy* (*The Eye of Vichy* [1993]). More recently, *Dr. M* (aka *Club Extinction*, 1990) was an updating of Fritz Lang's "Dr. Mabuse" series, based on Norbert Jacques's original novel; *Madame Bovary* (1991) was a reverential adaptation of Flaubert's classic, with Isabelle Huppert in the title role; and *L'Enfer* (*Hell*, 1993), adapted from an unrealized script by Henri-Georges Clouzot (see p. 433), was a return to the Hitchcockian thriller of sexual obsession. For the rest of the decade, Chabrol continued to produce socially insightful thrillers, most of them, starring Huppert and/or Sandrine Bonnaire. *La Cérémonie* (1995) featured them both (they shared the Best Actress award at Venice for their ensemble performance as housemaid and local postal clerk, respectively) and was widely admired for its observant analysis of class conflict in the provinces, while *Rien ne va plus* (English title: *The Swindle*, 1997)—Chabrol's fiftieth film—starred Huppert as a small-time con artist who becomes involved in a big-time caper and double

cross. In *Au Coeur du mensonge* (English title: *The Lying Heart*, 1999), Chabrol returned to the subject matter of *Le Boucher* for an examination of the impact of a child murder, as investigated by a female police inspector (Bonnaire), on the insular society of a small town on the coast of Brittany. *Merci pour le chocolat* (*Thanks for the Chocolate*, 2000) is another crime thriller, set in the corporate world of a large Swiss chocolate company controlled by a female CEO (Huppert).

LOUIS MALLE

Louis Malle (1932–1995), a former assistant to Bresson and the celebrated underwater filmmaker Jacques-Yves Cousteau (with whom he co-directed *Le Monde du silence* [*The Silent World*, 1955]), began his career as a director two years before the debuts of Godard and Truffaut with the taut suspense thriller *Ascenseur pour l'échafaud* (*Frantic/Elevator to the Gallows*, 1957), and earned an international reputation the following year with *Les Amants* (*The Lovers*, 1958). This lyrical film about a brief love affair between a bored socialite and a young student for whom she leaves her husband was beautifully photographed by Henri Decaë and produced with Malle's own funds. *Zazie dans le métro* (1960) was an anarchic adaptation of Raymond Queneau's novel about a foulmouthed ten-year-old girl who comes to visit her uncle in Paris and wreaks havoc everywhere she goes. The film is a technically exciting attempt to find visual equivalents

13.30 Jeanne Moreau in *Les Amants* (Louis Malle, 1958).

for Queneau's neo-Joycean puns through the use of trick shots, superimposition, variable camera speeds, jump cuts, and multiple allusions to other books and films (especially Resnais's *Hiroshima, mon amour*, Fellini's *La dolce vita*, and Malle's own *Les Amants*). Malle continued his experiments in narrative form in *Vie privée* (*Private Life*, 1961), a film about a young provincial girl's rise to stardom based loosely on the experience of its own star, Brigitte Bardot.

But *Le Feu follet* (*The Fire Within/Will o' the Wisp*, 1963), adapted by the director from a novel by Drieu La Rochelle, with a piano score by Erik Satie, is regarded as Malle's masterpiece of the 1960s. It depicts the last forty-eight hours in the life of an alcoholic playboy who is relentlessly driven to suicide by his disgust at the world around him. Many critics feel that the film's mood of psychological intensity and Malle's sureness of touch in sustaining it bring *Le Feu follet* close to the best work of Bresson. As a change of pace from the brooding atmosphere of *Le Feu follet*, Malle attempted a romantic spectacle in *Viva Maria* (1965), set at the turn of the century and shot in Panavision by Henri Decaë, in which Jeanne Moreau and Brigitte Bardot, as traveling entertainers, invent the striptease and foment a revolution in the imaginary South American republic of San Miguel. In *Le Voleur* (*The Thief*, 1967), Malle used a period setting to create a portrait of a wealthy young bourgeois driven to burglary by his hatred of society. His "William Wilson" episode (based on a Poe story) in the anthology film *Histoires extraordinaires* (*Spirits of the Dead*, 1968) hauntingly examines the phenomenon of the *doppelgänger*, or "double."

After contributing to the 1967 collective film *Loin du Vietnam*, Malle journeyed to the East to film the feature-length *Calcutta* (1969), part of his brilliant six-hour documentary essay *Phantom India* (1970), for French television. This film, which has also been shown theatrically, offers a marvelously complex vision of the paradoxical subcontinent that has always so fascinated and puzzled the West. Using his own consciousness as a sounding board, Malle ultimately fails to penetrate the Indian mystery, ostensibly by refusing to interpret it through Western eyes. In 1971, Malle produced a masterpiece equal to *Le Feu follet* in the remarkable *Le Souffle au coeur* (*Murmur of the Heart*), a delicate and irresistibly funny tale of casual incest among the bourgeoisie of Dijon in 1954—the time of the fall of Dien

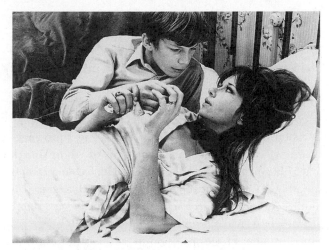

13.31 Mother and son in Malle's *Le Souffle au coeur* (1971): Benoît Ferreux, Lea Massari.

Bien Phu, Vietnam. Scripted by Malle and sumptuously photographed by Decaë, this film offers an amiable, intelligent, and perversely humorous portrait of middle-class French family life in the postwar era, as well as a sensitive study of the sexual and social agonies of adolescence. Malle's next film, *Lacombe, Lucien* (1974), received international acclaim for its subtle portrayal of a seventeen-year-old peasant boy who joins the French Gestapo during the Occupation for no particular reason and is subsequently torn between destroying and protecting a Jewish family with whose daughter he has fallen in love. With *Black Moon* (1975), photographed by the Swedish cinematographer Sven Nykvist (a frequent collaborator of Ingmar Bergman; see Chapter 15), Malle moved from realism to symbolism in a film that the Paris newspaper *L'Express* described as existing "at the crossroads of fantasy and science fiction." In 1978, Malle directed *Pretty Baby* in the United States. Shot entirely on location in New Orleans by Nykvist, this controversial film deals with a love affair between an eccentric photographer and a child prostitute in a turn-of-the-century Storyville brothel. In 1980 Malle turned northward to direct *Atlantic City*, an ironic drama of small-time hoods that shared the Venice Golden Lion that year with John Cassavetes's *Gloria*. Malle's subsequent American films include the brilliant tour-de-force conversation piece *My Dinner with Andre* (1981) and the documentary panorama of recent immigrant experience *And the Pursuit of Happiness* (1986), as well as the less successful *Crackers*

(1984), a remake of Mario Monicelli's 1956 caper classic *Big Deal on Madonna Street*, and *Alamo Bay* (1985), a fictionalized account of conflict between Vietnamese immigrants and American fishermen on the Gulf coast of Texas. In 1987, Malle returned triumphantly to France to make the quasiautobiographical *Au revoir les enfants* (*Good-bye, Children*), a chronicle of a friendship between a Catholic and a Jewish boy set in a provincial boarding school during the last months of World War II, and *Milou en mai* (*May Fools*, 1990), which counterpoints the May 1968 student rebellion in Paris with a bourgeois family gathering in the countryside. *Damage* (1992), adapted by David Hare from Josephine Hart's novel, is a film of ruinous erotic obsession set in the context of British politics; its depiction of psychological unravelment within a rigidly class-bound system stands as one of Malle's finest achievements. With *Vanya on 42nd Street* (1994), Malle returned to the subject of *My Dinner with Andre*, filming New York theater director Andre Gregory's experimental production of Chekhov's *Uncle Vanya* in the then-derelict New Amsterdam Theater. He died of cancer in November 1995.

Malle, unquestionably an important filmmaker, is frequently accused of eclecticism because of his wide range of subjects and styles. Pauline Kael has pointed out that had he chosen a single theme and stuck with it—as Chabrol has done, say, since 1968—Malle would have been acclaimed as a major figure long ago. But Malle's intellectual restlessness and his remarkable ability to present material from simultaneously opposing points of view have led some critics to dismiss him as an elegant stylist with little substance at the core. *Le Feu follet, Phantom India, Le Souffle au coeur, Lacombe, Lucien, Atlantic City, My Dinner with Andre*, and *Au revoir les enfants* offer ample proof that only the first part of this proposition is true.

ERIC ROHMER AND JACQUES RIVETTE

The former *Cahiers* critic Eric Rohmer (b. Jean-Marie Maurice Schérer, 1920) began to blossom as a director in the late 1960s. His first feature, *Le Signe du lion* (*The Sign of Leo*, 1959), received virtually no notice in the year of its release, but between 1962 and 1963 Rohmer made the first two of his six "Moral Tales," or "*Contes moraux*," whose basic theme is the antagonism that exists between

personal identity and sexual temptation, or between the spiritual and passional sides of human nature.[5]

La Boulangère de Monceau (*The Baker of Monceau*, 1962) and *La Carrière de Suzanne* (*Suzanne's Vocation*, 1963) were both shorts shot in 16mm and produced by Barbet Schroeder,[6] who produced the entire series. *Ma Nuit chez Maud* (*My Night at Maud's*, 1967), *La Collectionneuse* (*The Collector*, 1968), *Le Genou de Claire* (*Claire's Knee*, 1969), and *L'Amour, l'apres midi* (English title: *Chloe in the Afternoon*, 1972) are the 35mm features that complete the *Contes moraux*, providing four more variations on Rohmer's single theme and inaugurating his long-term collaboration with the cinematographer Nestór Almendros. Abstract, intellectual, supremely ironic, these inquiries into the nature of human passion are constructed with all the precision of Cartesian logic, and they have been hailed internationally as components of a philosophical masterpiece. Subsequently, Rohmer made a beautiful, ambiguous version of Heinrich von Kleist's *Die Marquis von O.* (*The Marquise of O.*, 1975) which continues his metaphysical probing of human sexuality in the story of a young noblewoman who awakes one day to find herself inexplicably pregnant. With *Perceval le Gallois* (English title: *Perceval*, 1978), he successfully attempted to evoke the consciousness of the Middle Ages in his own adaptation of a twelfth-century poem by Chrétien de Troyes set in the time of King Arthur. In its stylized sets, artificial scenery, and deliberately foreshortened perspective, *Perceval* captures the mimetic sensibility of both medieval literature and painting; it demands of its viewers a quite extraordinary revision of narrative expectations.

Perhaps because of his late start, Rohmer is one of the few original New Wave figures still consistently producing major work. During the 1980s he contributed yet another extraordinary contemporary cycle entitled "Comedies and Proverbs," achieving in *La Femme de l'aviateur* (*The Aviator's Wife*, 1981), *Le Beau marriage* (*The Perfect Mar-*

---

5. Rohmer wrote the "*Contes moraux*" as short stories in the late 1950s before filming them. They have been published in English as *Six Moral Tales*, trans. Sabine d'Estrée (New York: Viking, 1980).

6. Schroeder (b. 1941) became an important director in his own right in the 1970s with *More* (1969); *The Valley Obscured by Clouds* (1972); the feature documentary *Idi Amin Dada* (*General Idi Amin*, 1974); *Maîtresse* (*Mistress*, 1976); and *Koko, le gorilla qui parle* (*Koko the Talking Gorilla*, 1978). After a final French project (*Tricheurs*, 1983), Schroeder came to Hollywood, where he has directed a series of unusual mainstream films—e.g., *Barfly* (1987), *Reversal of Fortune* (1990), *Single White Female* (1992), and *Kiss of Death* (1995).

riage, 1982), *Pauline à la plage* (*Pauline at the Beach*, 1983), *Les Nuits de la pleine lune* (*Full Moon in Paris*, 1984), *Le Rayon vert* (*Summer*, 1986), and *L'Ami de mon amie* (*My Girlfriend's Boyfriend*, 1987) a formal beauty and classical precision unequaled even in his previous work. Like his *Quatre aventures de Reinette et Mirabelle* (*Four Adventures of Reinette and Mirabelle*, 1987), several of these were shot in 16mm and blown up for 35mm theatrical exhibition, as in the earliest days of the New Wave. Rohmer's cycle of four seasonal films dealing with the power of myth—*Conte de printemps* (1990), *Conte d'hiver* (1992), *Conte d'été* (1996), and *Conte d'automne* (1998)—was followed by *L'Anglaise et le duc* (English title: *The Lady and the Duke*, 2001), based on the memoirs of a Scottish gentlewoman stranded in Paris during the Great Terror of 1792, whose precincts are simulated digitally from contemporary-looking paintings and panoramas.

Jacques Rivette (b. 1928), another *Cahiers* critic, and former assistant to both Renoir and Becker, also directed a handful of important films in the 1960s that show a marked predilection for literature and the theater. *Paris nous appartient* (*Paris Belongs to Us*, 1960) concerns the members of a Parisian acting troupe who are rehearsing a version of Shakespeare's *Pericles*, and who, through a series of coincidences and insinuations, come to believe themselves enmeshed in a Fascist conspiracy to destroy the world. At the end of the film, this "conspiracy" turns out to be the invention of a paranoid American novelist, but the confusion has caused two deaths and wrecked the lives of everyone involved. Rivette shot *Paris nous appartient* on a day-to-day basis between 1957 and 1959 with money for film stock borrowed from Truffaut and a camera borrowed from Chabrol. (Appropriately, the "film" that the Doinel family goes to see at the Gaumont-Palace in *Les Quatre cents coups* is *Paris nous appartient*, although it was in fact still in the process of production.) None of the cast or crew was paid until after the film's release, at which time the *Cahiers* group issued a joint statement concerning its crucial importance to *la politique des auteurs*. Rivette's film, they wrote, was "primarily the fruit of an astonishing persistence over several years to bring to the screen a personal vision of the world as rich and diverse *as if expressed by any other means*" (italics added).

Rivette's second feature, *La Religieuse* (*The Nun*, 1965), was based upon Denis Diderot's eighteenth-cen-

13.32 *Le Religieuse* (Jacques Rivette, 1965): Anna Karina as the novice Suzanne Simonin.

tury novel about a woman driven to prostitution and suicide through the hypocrisy of religious orders. This bleak film acquired something of a sensational reputation due to its suppression in France, but its sober camera style and rather conventional narrative structure lend it a seriousness that no amount of scandal can belie. Rivette's third film is his greatest to date, and it, too, reveals his literary tastes. *L'Amour fou* (*Crazy Love*, 1968) is a four-hour study of the slow disintegration of a marriage set against the filming of a television production of Racine's tragedy *Andromaque*, in which the protagonist of the film plays the lead. Cold, austere, and agonizingly slow, *L'Amour fou* provides Rivette with a laboratory in which to explore questions about the nature of film and stage illusion, as Renoir did in *Le Carrosse d'or* (1952). During the 1970s, Rivette made six features—*Out One* (1971), which exists only as a thirteen-hour workprint; *Out One: Spectre* (1972), a four-and-one-half-hour abridgment, or "spectre," of *Out One*; *Céline et Julie vont en bateau* (*Celine and Julie Go Boating*, 1974); *Duelle* (1976); *Noroît* (1977); and *Merry Go Round* (1978)—but only *Céline et Julie* and *Duelle* have been distributed outside of France.[7] The 1980s saw Rivette continuing to elaborate the mysteries of identity in such vaguely surrealistic films as *Le Pont du nord* (*North Bridge*, 1981) and *L'Amour par terre* (*Love on Earth*, 1984), culminating, oddly, in his most accessible film so far, *Hurlevent* (*Wuthering Heights*, 1985), a straightforward adaptation of the Emily Brontë novel that shifts the setting from nineteenth-century Yorkshire to the early 1930s in Brittany, and *La Belle noiseuse* (1991), a four-hour adaptation from Balzac that became a commercial hit in France. Because of his obscurity and artistic integrity, Rivette had little commercial success with his films before the 1990s, but in that decade his work took a more popular turn. Following his six-hour life of *Joan of Arc*, *Jeanne la Pucelle* (*Joan the Maid*, 1994), Rivette made the epic musical *Haut bas fragile* (*Up Down Fragile*, 1995), the psychological murder mystery *Secret défense* (English title: *Top Secret*, 1998), and *Va savoir* (*Who Knows?*), a romantic comedy about a theater troupe staging a Pirandello play in contemporary Paris.

AGNÈS VARDA, JACQUES DEMY, AND OTHERS

Agnès Varda (b. 1928), whose *La Pointe-Courte* (1955) had been something of a New Wave landmark, continued to write and direct fine films in the 1960s. Her second feature, *Cléo de cinq à sept* (*Cléo from 5 to 7*, 1962), photographed by Jean Rabier, depicts exactly 90 minutes (the running time of the film) in the life of a young pop singer who is waiting for a lab report that will tell her

13.34 Varda's *Le Bonheur* (1965): François (Jean-Claude Drouot) and his mistress Emilie (Marie-France Boyer).

whether or not she has cancer. *Le Bonheur* (*Happiness*, 1965) is a strangely detached film about a happily married family man whose affair with another woman causes his wife to commit suicide and who proceeds to lead a happy existence with his mistress after his wife's death. The film is highly decorative but ambiguous in terms of psychological and moral considerations. In *Les Créatures* (*The Animals*, 1966), Varda examined the relationship between fantasy and reality in the mind of a writer who talks to animals and cannot distinguish real people from the characters in his novels. Varda also contributed to the collective *Loin du Vietnam* (1967), and in 1969 she came to America to make the improvisational feature *Lions Love*.

During the 1970s Varda directed the semidocumentary *Daguerréotypes* (1976; French release, 1979), a feature-length study of the rue Daguerre in Paris, where she had lived for many years, and *L'Une chante, l'autre pas* (*One Sings, the Other Doesn't*, 1977), a fifteen-year chronicle of two women friends pursuing totally different lifestyles. In the United States once more, Varda made a pair of films that commented on each other—*Murs murs* (*Walls Walls*, 1981), a documentary study of Los Angeles wall murals, and *Documenteur: An Emotion Picture*

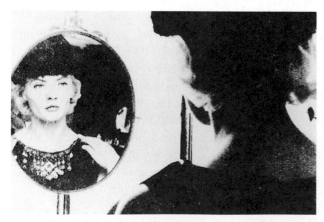

13.33 *Cléo de cinq à sept* (Agnès Varda, 1962): Corinne Marchand.

---

7. *Duelle* and its companion piece, *Sérial* (1976), a deliberate exercise in mystification directed by Rivette's scenarist Eduardo de Gregorio, were featured together at the 1976 New York Film Festival and later released commercially on the east and west coasts. De Gregorio went on to better things in *La Mémoire courte* (*Short Memory*, 1979) and *Céline et Julie*, which was released in the United States in 1982.

(1981), a 16mm mood piece about a secretary working on the production of *Murs murs* while taking care of her young son (Varda's own). In *Sans toit ni loi* (*Without a Roof and beyond the Law*; English title: *Vagabond*, 1985), Varda produced a Bressonian film about an aimlessly drifting teenage girl and the people she meets before her wretched death from exposure. More recently, Varda made a diptych of features on the British actress Jane Birkin, who, since marrying the director Jacques Doillon, has become a French movie star—*Jane B. par Agnès V.* and *Kung Fu Master* (the title of a particularly obsessive video game), both in 1987. Throughout 1990, Varda collaborated with her dying husband, the director Jacques Demy, to produce a filmic autobiography/biography of his youth. The resulting *Jacquot de Nantes* (1991) covers Demy's life through 1949, at which point his lifelong infatuation with cinema began to fulfill itself as a career. As a pendant, Varda directed *Les Demoiselles ont eu vingt-cinq ans* (*The Young Girls Turn 25*, 1992) a witty documentary tribute to Demy's *Les Demoiselles de Rochefort* (1996). After another documentary about her late husband (*L'Universe de Jacques Demy*, 1995) and an affectionate Arabian Nights–style parable about film history (*Les Cent et une nuits de Simon Cinema*, 1995), Varda made the self-reflexive documentary feature *Les*

Glaneurs et les glaneuses (*The Gleaners and I*, 2000), which examines the social, cultural, and political implications of scavenging even as it contemplates her own mortality.

Demy himself (1931–1990) became a specialist during the 1960s in colorful, bittersweet melodramas reminiscent of poetic realism and the work of Max Ophüls. His *Lola* (1961), which is dedicated to Ophüls and owes much to the fluid camera work of Raoul Coutard, is a gay, lighthearted film about love, set in Nantes and similar in style to *La Ronde*. It has been called "a musical without songs or dances," and it earned Demy an international reputation. *Les Parapluies de Cherbourg* (*The Umbrellas of Cherbourg*, 1964) is an actual musical about a romance between a shop girl and a service-station attendant in which the dialogue is sung, as in an opera; it is also notable for the vivid decor of designer Bernard Evein (b. 1929) and the riotous color cinematography of Jean Rabier. *Les Demoiselles de Rochefort* (*The Young Girls of Rochefort*, 1966) is a lively *hommage* to the Hollywood musical directed in collaboration with Gene Kelly. After the American-made *Model Shop* (1968), Demy's work declined into such frivolity as *L'Événement le plus important depuis que l'homme a marché sur la lune* (*The Most Important Event since Man Walked on the Moon*, 1973)— a film about a pregnant man—and the Japanese-French coproduction *Lady Oscar* (1979), a period romance set during the French Revolution and based on a popular comic strip. In 1982, Demy returned successfully to his all-singing formula with *Une Chambre en ville* (*A Room in Town*), his first French-language film in over eight years, but *Parking* (1985), a pop-musical remake of Cocteau's 1950 *Orphée*, was generally thought to be a failure, as were his final features, *La Table tournante* (1987) and *Trois places pour le 26* (1988).

After the Wave

Other noteworthy French filmmakers since the New Wave who have distinct ties with it are Philippe de Broca (b. 1933), a former assistant to Chabrol and Truffaut, who has become a skilled director of sophisticated comedy and satire (*Cartouche*, 1961; *L'Homme de Rio* [*That Man from Rio*, 1964]; *Le Roi de coeur* [*King of Hearts*, 1966]; *Tendre poulet* [*Dear Detective*, 1977]; *On a volé la cuisse de Jupiter* [*Someone Has Stolen Jupiter's Thigh*, 1980];

13.35 *Les Demoiselles de Rochefort* (Jacques Demy, 1966): Catherine Deneuve, Gene Kelly, Françoise Dorléac.

13.36 *L'Homme de Rio* (Philippe de Broca, 1964): Jean-Paul Belmondo spoofs James Bond.

L'Africain [*The African*, 1983]; *La Gitane* [*The Gypsy*, 1986]; *Chouans!* [1988]; and *Les Clés du Paradis* [*The Keys to Paradise*, 1991]).[8] During the 1990s, de Broca did most of his work for French television. Also Pierre Étaix (b. 1928), a former circus clown and gag writer for Jacques Tati, directed a number of excellent comic films (*Le Soupirant* [*The Suitor*, 1962] and *Yoyo* [1965]) in the tradition of Max Linder and Buster Keaton; Étaix starred in all of his own films but stopped directing features in 1971. The former actor Jean-Pierre Mocky (b. 1929) became a fine and prolific director of iconoclastic comedy in films like *Les Snobs* (1961), *Les Vierges* (*The Virgins*, 1963), and, more recently, *Litan* (1982), *À Mort l'arbitre* (*Kill the Referee*, 1984), *Le Pactole* (*The Boodle*, 1985), *La Machine à découdre* (*The Unsewing Machine*, 1986), *Agent Trouble* (*Trouble Agent*, 1987), and *Les Saisons du plaisir* (*The Seasons of Pleasure*, 1988). His later films— e.g., *Il gèle en Enfer* (*A Day in Hell*, 1989), *Ville à vendre* (*City for Sale*, 1992), and *Noir comme le souvenir* (*Black for Remembrance*, 1996)—are notable for their edgy black humor. Alain Robbe-Grillet (b. 1922), the major practitioner of the French *nouveau roman*[9] and the scriptwriter for Resnais's *L'Année dernière à Marienbad*, turned to directing in the 1960s and 1970s with *L'Homme qui ment* (*He Who Lies*, 1968), followed by *Le Jeu avec le feu* (*Playing with Fire*, 1975) and *La Belle captive* (*The Beautiful Prisoner*, 1983). His last film was *Un Bruit qui rend fou* (English title: *The Blue Villa*, 1995), set in a brothel on an isolated Greek island. His films are all nar-

ratives about the mental process of constructing narratives, and he makes no distinction between them and his novels, calling both *ciné romans* (film novels). In 1973, Jean Eustache (1938–1981) contributed perhaps the last authentically New Wave film in *La Maman et la putain* (*The Mother and the Whore*). This provocative 220-minute assault on the intellect and senses focuses on the disillusionment of the generation that produced the political upheaval of May 1968, and it won the Special Jury Prize at Cannes in the year of its release. Unfortunately, Eustache was unable to sustain his success through *Mes petites amoureuses* (*My Little Sweethearts*, 1976) and several later works, and he committed suicide in the wake of a disabling accident in 1981.

Alain Jessua (b. 1932) produced several important films during the 1960s, including the remarkable *La Vie à l'envers* (*Life Upside Down*, 1964), a subjective portrait of the inception of madness, and *Jeu de massacre* (*The Killing Game*, 1967), in which the protagonist becomes so obsessed with the heroes of his favorite comic strip that he can no longer distinguish fantasy from reality. Later, Jessua directed *Traitement de choc* (*Shock Treatment*, 1974), a horror film by genre but thematically a parable of capitalist exploitation of the underdeveloped nations (Portuguese workers are murdered so that their blood may be given to a rich Frenchman undergoing an exotic medical treatment). *Les Chiens* (*The Dogs*, 1979) is a parable of the violence of modern life, focusing on the increased use of guard dogs for self-protection by citizens of contemporary France. Jessua continued in this vein with the medical science-fiction film *Paradis pour tous* (*Paradise for All*, 1982); *Frankenstein 90* (1984), a comic version of the classic with a cybernetics genius replacing the doctor; and the *noir* thriller *En toute innocence* (*No Harm Intended*, 1988). He has only made one

---

8. In 1984, de Broca directed the dual cinema/television superproduction *Louisiane* (*Louisiana*), distributed as both a three-hour theatrical feature and a six-hour video miniseries.

9. Literally, the "new novel"—an influential form of avant-garde fiction practiced in France in the 1950s and 1960s by such writers as Robbe-Grillet, Marguerite Duras (now a filmmaker herself), Nathalie Sarraute, and Michel Butor. Formally influenced by the cinema, the *nouveau roman* was antihumanist in its concentration on the objective, even clinical, description of material phenomena at the expense of character, motivation, and plot. The *nouveau roman* was often "metafictional" in that it created narrative metaphors for the process of its own writing (see Robbe-Grillet's *Dans le labyrinth* [*In the Labyrinth*, 1959]).

film since—*Les coleurs du Diable* (*Devil's Colors*, 1997)—a retelling of the Faust legend in the form of a psychological thriller. The single New Wave feature by Jacques Rozier (b. 1926), *Adieu Philippine* (1962), has acquired the reputation of a minor masterpiece, although it is really something less than that: an engagingly improvised narrative about a Parisian youth in the 1960s filmed in *cinéma vérite* fashion, which contains a hilarious parody of French television. Rozier's only other significant feature, *Du Côté d'Oroët* (1973), is a hyperrealistic film about the experience of three girls on holiday in Brittany; but his confusing comeback film, *Maine-Océan* (*Maine-Ocean Express*, 1986), seemed to confirm the decadence of New Wave–style auteurism. Against all odds, Rozier's next feature, *Fifi Martingale* (2001), struck a popular nerve in its satire on the pretensions and paranoia of a Parisian theater director. The Greek-born director Constantine Costa-Gavras (b. 1933), formerly associated with conventional thrillers, developed into a masterful director of political films in the 1970s with Z (1969) and *L'Aveu* (*The Confession*, 1970), both shot by Raoul Coutard; *État de siège* (*State of Siege*, 1973), *Section spéciale* (*Special Section*, 1975), *Clair de femme* (*Womanlight*, 1979), all starring Yves Montand; and, for the American producers Edward and Mildred Lewis (Universal), *Missing* (1981). Some of Costa-Gavras's later films, such as *Hanna K.* (1983) and *Conseil de famille* (*Family Council*, 1986), suffered from weak scripts or, like *Betrayed* (1988) and *The Music Box* (1989), from excessive polemics. But *Mad City* (1997) was an intelligent thriller about the symbiosis between crime and media coverage, and *Amen* (2001) was an intense and deeply serious film examining Pope Pius XII's complicitous silence during the Holocaust.

Much interesting work whose origins are traceable to the New Wave appeared during the 1970s in the French-speaking Swiss cinema. The director Alain Tanner's first feature, *Charles mort ou vif* (*Charles Dead or Alive*, 1969), was a characteristic product of the 1960s in which a middle-aged businessman drops out of bourgeois society, goes to live with some young intellectuals, and is subsequently committed to an asylum by his family. Tanner (b. 1929) had worked at the British Film Institute and for BBC television in London from 1955 to 1958, and he was deeply influenced by the British Free Cinema movement (see Chapter 14) and its New Left ideology. His *La Salamandre* (*The Salamander*, 1971) and *Le Milieu du monde* (*The Middle of the World*, 1974), both concerned with day-to-day existence in modern industrial society, have been compared to the best work of Rohmer, while his *Le Retour d'Afrique* (*Return to Africa*, 1974) is as experimental and politically committed as anything attempted by Godard. With the critical success of *Jonas qui aura 25 ans en l'an 2000* (*Jonah Who Will Be 25 in the Year 2000*, 1976), Tanner was proclaimed a major European filmmaker—a status confirmed by his harrowing dissection of Swiss society in *Messidor* (1979) and his wry portrait of Ireland in *Light Years Away* (1981), which won the prize for Best Direction at Cannes. In the 1980s Tanner continued his exploration of people living on the social and psychological periphery of the modern urban wasteland with *Dans la ville blanche* (*In the White City*, 1983), set in Lisbon; *No Man's Land* (1985), set on the Franco-Swiss border; and *La Vallée fantôme* (*The Ghost Valley*, 1987), set in an Italo-American neighborhood in Brooklyn. In recent collaborations with the writer/actress Myriam Mézières—*A Flame in My Heart* (1987) and *Le Journal de Lady M* (*The Diary of Lady M*, 1992)—Tanner has attempted to explore the dynamics of female sexual pleasure, as he puts it, "from inside a woman's head." Recent Tanner films include *Requiem* (1998), a dramatic tribute to the Portuguese writer Fernando Pessoa, and *Jonas et Lila, à demain* (*Jonas and Lila, Till Tomorrow*, 1999), a whimsical sequel to his landmark 1976 film in which Jonah has indeed reached the age of twenty-five, graduated from film school, and married his African girlfriend.

Other Swiss directors with a marked personal style are

13.37 Costa-Gavras's award-winning Z (1969), based on a right-wing assassination plot in contemporary Greece.

Jean-Louis Roy—*Black-Out*, 1970; Claude Goretta (b. 1929)—*L'Invitation* (*The Invitation*, 1972), *Pas si méchant que ça* (*Not as Wicked as That/The Wonderful Crook*, 1975), *La Dentellière* (*The Lacemaker*, 1977), *Les Chemins de l'exil* (*The Roads of Exile*, 1978), *La Provinciale* (*The Girl from Lorraine*, 1980), *La Mort de Mario Ricci* (*The Death of Mario Ricci*, 1983), *Si le soleil ne revenait pas* (*If the Sun Never Returns*, 1987); Michel Soutter (1932–1991)—*L'Escapade* (*The Escapade*, 1973), *Repérages* (English title: *Location Hunting*, 1978), *L'Amour des femmes* (*Women's Love*, 1981), *Signé Renart* (*Signed Renart*, 1987); and Yves Yersin (b. 1942)—*Les Petites fugues* (*The Little Escapes*, 1979). Like Tanner, these four French-speaking directors were part of Groupe Cinq (Group Five), a band of young *cinéastes* who came together in 1968 in Geneva to make films in coproduction with Swiss television. At the same time, the country's leading Swiss-German director emerged in Daniel Schmid (*Nacht oder Nie* [*Tonight or Never*, 1972]; *La Paloma* [1974]; *Violanta* [1978]; *Hécate* [1982]; *Il Bacio di Tosca* [*Tosca's Kiss*, 1984]; *Jenatsch* [1987]). By the late 1980s, Switzerland was producing more than twenty features a year, most with some form of government subsidy.

The work of the French director Claude Lelouch (b. 1937) is more controversial than that of the filmmakers discussed above because of its blatant appeal to a mass audience. Lelouch uses all the modern narrative techniques of his New Wave counterparts, and he is an *auteur* in the most comprehensive sense of the term in that he produces, directs, writes, photographs, and edits all of his own films (such as *Un Homme et une femme* [*A Man and a Woman*, 1966]; *Vivre pour vivre* [*Live for Life*, 1967]). But while these films are visually engaging, they lack emotional depth and have the quality of extended television commercials. There are exceptions in the ingenious comedy-thriller *Cat and Mouse* (1978) and the picaresque *À Nous deux* (*Us Two/An Adventure for Two*, 1979), but the work of Lelouch during the 1980s and 1990s (*Les Uns et les autres* [*The Ins and the Outs*, 1981]; *Édith et Marcel* [1983]; *Vive la vie!* [*Long Live Life!*, 1984]; *Partir revenir* [*Departure, Return*, 1985]; *Un Homme et une femme vingt ans déjà* [*A Man and a Woman: 20 Years Later*, 1986]; *Attention bandits!* [*Warning, Bandits*, 1987]; *La Belle histoire* [1991] seemed to confirm his essential vacuity. Yet in 1995, Lelouch produced a remarkable variation on Victor Hugo's *Les Misérables* (1995), which uses the novel as a gloss on an act of heroism and resistance by a Jean Valjean–like character during the Nazi Occupation.

Another French director whose films have been largely unaffected by the New Wave but whose recent work has become prominent is Claude Sautet (1924–2000). After graduating from IDHEC in 1950 and working as an assistant to both Georges Franju and Jacques Becker, Sautet began his career as a director with a series of *Rififi*-style thrillers (*Classe tous risques* [English title: *The Big Risk*, 1960]; *L'Arme à gauché* [English title: *Guns for the Dictator*, 1965]). During the 1970s, he began to collaborate with the scriptwriter Jean-Loup Dabadie and became an astute observer of French bourgeois society, famous for his direction of ensemble playing. Sautet's *Les Choses de la vie* (*The Things of Life*, 1970), *Max et les ferrailleurs* (*Max and the Junkmen*, 1971), *César et Rosalie* (*Cesar and Rosalie*, 1972), *Vincent, François, Paul, et les autres* (*Vincent, François, Paul, and the Others*, 1974), *Mado* (1976), *Une Histoire simple* (*A Simple Story*, 1978), *Un Mauvais fils* (*A Bad Son*, 1980), *Garçon!* (1983), *Quelques jours avec moi* (*A Few Days with Me*, 1988), and *Un Coeur en hiver* (*A Heart in Winter*, 1991) all deal with middle-class people trapped at midlife by the patterns of their own routines, and the films have been much admired for their sympathetic understanding of a class that it has become almost obligatory for contemporary European directors to malign. After providing the script for an American remake of *Les Choses de la vie* (*Intersection* [Mark Rydell, 1994]), Sautet made a final film before his death from cancer in July 2000—*Nelly et Monsieur Arnaud* (1995), a moving analysis of bourgeois repression and failed relationships that encapsulated his major themes and won several French Academy of Cinema Awards (Césars).

Another important French filmmaker not of the New Wave but decisively influenced by it is Bertrand Tavernier (b. 1941). Originally a film critic and learned *cinéphile*, Tavernier in many ways represents a reconciliation between the post-New Wave generation of directors and the "tradition of quality" so roundly attacked by the *Cahiers* school. His favorite screenplay collaborator, for example, is Jean Aurenche, who, with Pierre Bost, had been the prime target of Truffaut's vilification in "A Certain Tendency in French Cinema" in 1954. In fact, Tavernier chose Aurenche and Bost as the scriptwriters for his first feature, *L'Horloger de Saint Paul* (*The Clockmaker*, 1974), an adaptation of a Simenon murder mystery with a metaphysical twist, which is dedicated to another great screenwriter of "quality," Jacques Prévert. Since that time, Tavernier has produced films covering an extraordinary range of material, all of them characterized by a combination of New Wave-style cinematic éclat and classically tight narrative construction. *Que la fête commence* (*Let Joy Reign Supreme*, 1975) is an ironic tale of palace intrigue set in the court of Louis XVI; *Le Juge et l'assassin* (*The Judge and the Assassin*, 1976) coolly dissects the symbiotic relationship between a nineteenth-century judge and a serial killer; *Des Enfants gâtés* (*Spoiled Children*, 1977) chronicles a filmmaker's May-September romance as well as his various aesthetic and political commitments; *La Mort en direct/Deathwatch* (1979), Tavernier's first film in English, presents an Orwellian vision of a future world in which the pornography of sex has been replaced by that of death; and *Une Semaine de vacances* (*A Week's Vacation*, 1980) is about a young French schoolmistress's search for identity; like *L'Horloger de Saint Paul*, it is set in his native city of Lyons. Tavernier's two most important films to date are clearly *Coup de torchon* (*Clean Slate/Pop.1280*, 1981) and *Un Dimanche à la campagne* (*A Sunday in the Country*, 1984), the former a delicious black comedy of adultery and murder adapted from a Jim Thompson novel and set in a French colonial town in West Africa in 1938, and the latter, based on a novella by Pierre Bost, a lyrical account of a day in the life of an aging Impressionist painter who receives a visit from his grown-up children at his country home in the late summer of 1912. Sublimely photographed in widescreen by his new collaborator Bruno de Keyzer, *Un Dimanche à la campagne* won Tavernier the Best Director prize at Cannes in the year of its release. These films—together with his documentary on the American South, *Mississippi Blues* (codirected with Robert Parrish); *Round Midnight* (1986), a superbly crafted feature about the friendship that develops between a young French jazz devotee and an aging American jazz musician in Paris; and *La Passion Béatrice* (*The Passion of Beatrice*, 1987), a dark and violent period piece set in the fourteenth century during the Hundred Years' War—have insured Tavernier's position as the most respected French filmmaker of his generation, and later work, in multiple genres—like the antiwar film *La vie et rien d'autre* (*Life and Nothing But*, 1989), the family melodrama *Daddy Nostalgie* (1990), and the swashbuckling adventure *La fille de d'Artagnan* (English title: *The

Return of the Musketeers*, 1994)—has confirmed it. Since directing the controversial police procedural *L.627* (1992), which focuses on the everyday life of a drug-squad cop, Tavernier has concentrated on films with contemporary social themes. For example, *L'Appât* (*The Bait*, 1995) is about the consequences of economically motivated urban crime, while *Ça commence aujourd'hui* (*It All Starts Today*, 1999) offers an uncompromisingly grim picture of provincial life in the north of France. Even the World War I epic *Capitaine Conan* (1996) has contemporary resonance in its attempt to distinguish between war crimes and the crime of war itself. In this regard, *Laissez-passer* (2002) offered a revisionist account of filmmaking under the Occupation that disturbed many French intellectuals. Although Tavernier's goal was to rehabilitate the postwar "tradition of quality" reviled by the *Cahiers* critics in the 1950s, to some the film seemed like an apologia for collaboration. (*Laissez-passer*, which means something like "Let it go" or "Let's move on," starred several veterans of the scenarist tradition—Jean Aurenche, Pierre Bost, Charles Spaak (see Chapter 9)—playing characters very much like themselves.) In addition to his work in features, Tavernier has made a number of brilliant documentaries that reflect a similar, inherently conservative perspective—e.g., *La guerre sans nom* (also known as *The Undeclared War*, 1992) is about the French debacle in Algeria; and *De l'autre côté du périphe* (*On the Other Side of the Tracks*, 1998) provides an insider's view of a Parisian housing project, most of whose residents are North African immigrants. As a producer, he has also given many younger *cinéastes* their first opportunities to direct, and as president of the French directors guild, La Société des Réalisateurs de Films, Tavernier has become a major force within the leadership of the domestic industry.

Other prominent post–New Wave directors are Maurice Pialat (1925–2003), Bertrand Blier (b. 1939), Alain Corneau (b. 1943), Claude Miller (b. 1942), Diane Kurys (b. 1948) and André Téchiné (b. 1943). Pialat was a much acclaimed television director when he started making a series of powerful, emotionally confrontational features with *L'Enfance nue* in 1969, which concerns the problems of an unwanted child; then came *Nous ne vieillirons pas ensemble* (*We Won't Grow Old Together*, 1972), which deals with the breaking up of a love affair, and *La Gueule ouverte* (*The Mouth Agape*, 1974), which many consider to be his masterpiece, about a woman's losing battle with cancer. The uncompromising nature of Pialat's material and his contentious methods of working with actors kept the quantity of his output relatively low, but in films like *Passe ton bac d'abord* (1979), a chronicle of teenage life in a provincial town, *Loulou* (1980), a violent tale of working-class sexual passions, and *À nous amours* (1983), a disturbing film on the dissolution of bourgeois family life, Pialat achieved an intensity of vision unrivaled in the French cinema. Since then, he has made a metaphysical detective thriller, *Police* (1985), an extraordinary adaptation of Georges Bernanos's 1926 novel *Sous le soleil de Satan* (*Under the Sun of Satan*, 1987), and the thoughtful biopic *Van Gogh* (1991). Pialat continued his wry dissection of the family in *Le Garçu* (1995), in which a four-year-old boy is passed around among several families as a result of his parents' separation.

After several false starts in the 1960s (e.g., *Hitler, connais pas*, 1963), Bertrand Blier found his metier in anarchic sexual comedy, often featuring the seduction of adults by children (*Les Valseuses* [English title: *Going Places*, 1974] and *Préparez vos mouchoirs* [*Get Out Your Handkerchiefs*, 1977]); incest (*Beau-père*, 1981); and, of course, the classical ménage à trois (*La Femme de mon pôte* [*My Best Friend's Girl*, 1983] and *Tenue de soirée* [*Evening Dress*, 1986]). Blier's other vein is the Buñuelian allegory of *Buffet froid* (*Cold Cuts*, 1979) and *Notre histoire* (*Our Story/Separate Rooms*, 1984). Blier's later films are the intricately structured comedies of adultery *Trop belle pour toi* (*Too Beautiful for You*, 1989), *Merci la vie* (*Thanks to Life*, 1991), and *Un deux trois soleil* (1993). Several of Blier's more recent films focus on the film industry itself—e.g., *Les Acteurs* (*The Actors*, 2000)—but *Mon homme* (*My Man*, 1998) returned French sexual mores to center stage in its treatment of a successful prostitute who, unaccountably, decides she needs a pimp. Deeply influenced by American cinema,[1] especially the crime thriller, Alain Corneau appropriated the ever popular *"policier"* genre (see below) as a vehicle for social criticism in such sober and deliberately paced films as *France société anonyme* (*France, S.A.*, 1974), *Police Python 357* (1976), *La Menace* (1977), *Série noire* (1979), and *Les Choix des armes* (*Choice of Weapons*, 1981), turning briefly to the colonial epic *Fort Saganne* (1984—reputedly the most expensive film made in France to date) before resuming his engagement with the urban underworld in *Le Môme* (*The Kid*, 1986). Less typically, Corneau directed *Tous les matins du monde* (1991), an unusual costume melodrama set at Versailles and focusing on the lives of Louis XIV's court musicians (Corneau was himself originally a jazz musician). After this big-budget heritage film, Corneau worked on a smaller scale in crime films like *Le Cousin* (*The Cousin*, 1997) until he made *Le Prince du Pacifique* (*The Prince of the Pacific*, 2000), a comic riff on colonialist epics set on the island of Tahiti in 1914. Claude Miller, a former assistant to both Truffaut and Godard, has produced a small body of high-quality films that have won him an international critical following; Miller's best works—*La Meilleure façon de marcher* (*The Best Way to Walk*, 1976), *Dites-lui que je l'aime* (U.S. title: *This Sweet Sickness*, 1977), *Garde à vue* (U.S. title: *The Grilling*, 1981—remade by Stephen Hopkins as *Under Suspicion* [2000]), *Mortelle randonnée* (*Deadly Circuit*, 1983), and *L'Effrontée* (*The Hussy*, 1985)—deal persuasively with the theme of obsession and are clearly influenced by the style of American *film noir*. In 1989, Miller directed *La Petite voleuse* (*The Little Thief*), a lively homage to Truffaut based on a script by him and longtime collaborator Claude de Givray, which was followed by *L'Accompagnatrice* (*The Accompanist*, 1992), a grim drama of "making it" in Vichy France. More recently, Miller directed the surreal comedy *La Chamber des magiciennes* (U.S. title: *Of Women and Magic*, 2000) and several relatively dark psychological studies in *Le Sourire* (*The Smile*, 1994), *La Classe de neige* (U.S. title: *Class Trip*, 1998), and *Betty Fisher et autres histories* (*Betty Fisher and Other Stories*, 2001)—the latter based on Ruth Rendell's novel *The Tree of Hands*. The films of Diane Kurys, on the other hand, have all been vaguely autobiographical and yet charmingly eclectic—*Diabolo menthe* [*Peppermint Soda*, 1979] is about the quotidian lives of teenage sisters, 1963–64, following their parents' divorce; *Cocktail Molotov* (1980) concerns her own participation in the "events of May" 1968; *Coup de foudre* (also known as *Entre nous*, 1983) deals with the friendship of two young women in the period 1952–53, and is modeled on the experience of her parents; and so on, leading finally to her much acclaimed English-language film *Un Homme amoureux* (*A Man in Love*, 1987) and

---

1. Always popular with French audiences and filmmakers alike, American movies climbed from 27 to 37 percent of total box-office returns between 1976 and 1986, making France the largest export market for the U.S. film industry after Canada and Japan. Today they hover at around 50 percent.

13.38 *Diabolo menthe* (Diane Kurys, 1979): how it feels to be a teenager.

C'est la vie (1990), which backtracks to the era of *Diabolo menthe* and the moment of the parents' separation; in 1994, Kurys directed *À la folie* (also known as *6 days, 6 Nights*), about a ménage à trois in which two sisters share the same man, and in 1999 *Les Enfants du siècle* (*Children of the Century*) concentrating on the troubled relationship between protofeminist novelist George Sand and the romantic poet Alfred de Musset in the early 1830s. Originally a *Cahiers* critic, André Téchiné directed some of the French cinema's greatest actresses in award-winning performances once he entered the industry with *Souvenirs d'en France* (also known as *French Provincial*, 1974), which starred Jeanne Moreau as a social-climbing laundress, and *Barocco* (1976), a stylized crime drama starring Isabelle Adjani. Téchiné's breakthrough film was *Les Soeurs Brontë* (1979), a psychobiography of the three famous Victorian sisters—creative, repressed, and ultimately dysfunctional—played by Marie-France Pisier (Charlotte), Isabelle Adjani (Emily), and Isabelle Huppert (Anne). Many of Téchiné's later films involved collaborations with Catherine Deneuve—*Hôtel des Amériques* (1981), *Le Lieu du crime* (*Scene of the Crime*, 1986), *Ma Saison préférée* (*My Favorite Season*, 1993), and *Les Voleurs* (1996)—and Juliette Binoche—*Rendez-vous* (1985) and *Alice et Martin* (1998)—and tended to deal with dark, romantic themes often spiked by violence. Téchiné's greatest film may be *Les Roseaux sauvages* (*Wild Reeds*, (1994), a coming-of-age drama set in Provence during the Algerian War that won multiple domestic and international awards; it was produced as part of a historic collaboration between French film and television that has since become a model for the entire industry.[2]

In the field of documentary cinema, Chris Marker (b. Christian François Bouche-Villeneuve, 1921) has produced a number of brilliant film essays (*Cuba sí*, 1961; *Le Joli mai*, 1963; *Le Mystère Koumiko*, 1965) as well as the Bergsonian science-fiction short *La Jetée* (1962), composed almost entirely of still photographs. Marker is a close associate of Resnais and the chief organizer of SLON, the film cooperative that produced *Loin de Vietnam* (1967) and several other political documentaries of the era. In 1977, Marker made the striking four-hour compilation film *Le Fond de l'air est rouge* (literally, *The Essence of the Air Is Red*), a documentary on the state of radical politics in France in the mid-1970s. Later, he produced *Sans soleil* (*Sunless*, 1983), a remarkable meditation on obsession and repetition that won a British Film Institute award, *A.K.* (1985), a documentary portrait of Akira Kurosawa at work on *Ran* (see Chapter 18), and *Le Tombeau d'Alexandre* (also known as *The Last Bolshevik*, 1993), a study of the Soviet filmmaker Alexander Medvedkin (1900–1989). Marker also directed *Une journée d'Andrei Arsenevitch* (*One Day in the Life of André Arsenevitch*, 1999), a documentary on the death and art of another great Russian director, Andrei Tarkovksy (1932–1986). Ever the innovator, Marker has recently experimented with multimedia installations (e.g., *Silent Movie*, 1995) and the internet. His feature film *Level Five* (1997) represents the experience of a computer-game designer using the internet to research the Battle of Okinawa in the latter days of World War II; the resulting collage of hyperlinked images causes her to reflect on the relationship between history and memory in her own life. Appropriately, Marker has been working for the last decade on an autobiographical CD-ROM entitled *Immemory*. The work of the *cinéma vérité* documentarist Jean Rouch (b. 1917—*Chronique d'un été* [*Chronicle of a Summer*,

2. Téchiné's film was part of a unique collaboration between the French national arts television channel La Sept/Arte and the film studio IMA Production in which nine directors were invited to make a feature film dealing with his or her own adolescence for a series entitled *Tous les garçons et les filles de leur âge*. Three of these autobiographical films later won awards at Cannes—André Téchiné's *Les Roseaux sauvage* (*Wild Reeds*, 1994), Cédric Kahn's *Trop de bonheur* (*Too Much Happiness*, 1994), and Olivier Assayas's *L'Eau froide* (*Cold Water*, 1994). Cofunding arrangements between French film and television have since become an industry mainstay.

13.39 Citizens of Paris in *Le Joli mai* (Chris Marker, 1963).

13.40 *Le Chagrin et la pitié* (Marcel Ophüls, 1971): Hitler admiring the Eiffel Tower after his troops have occupied Paris.

1961] and *La Punition* [*Punishment*, 1963]) and that of Mario Ruspoli (1925–1986—*Les Inconnus de la terre* [*The Unknown of the Earth*, 1961]) had wide influence during the 1960s on both the documentary (in the films of the Americans D. A. Pennebaker, Albert and David Maysles, and Frederick Wiseman) and the narrative cinema (in the work of Rozier, Godard, and Tanner, and in countless individual French, Swiss, Italian, West German, British, and American films). In the 1970s, Rouch continued to produce distinguished ethnographic films, focusing mainly on black African culture (*Funérailles à Bongo: Le Vieil Anaï; 1849–1971* [*Funeral in Bongo: Old Anaï*, 1849–1971, 1979]), but later he turned to such unusual features as *Brise-glace* (*Icebreaker*, co-directed with Titte Törnroth and Raoul Ruiz, 1988), *Enigma* (1988), and *Cantate pour deux généraux* (*Cantata for Two Generals*, 1990—about a Haitian voodoo ritual). Rouch returned in later films—*Madame L'Eau* (*Madame Water*, 1993) and *Moi fatigué debout, moi couché* (*I am Tired of Standing, I Lie Down*, 1997)—to sub-Saharan Africa.

The most prominent French documentarist, however, is Marcel Ophüls (b. 1927), the son of the great postwar director Max Ophüls. Marcel Ophüls's masterpiece is the four-and-a-half-hour *Le Chagrin et la pitié* (*The Sorrow and the Pity*, 1971), a shattering documentary that mixes newsreel footage with contemporary interviews in an attempt to assess the impact of the Nazi Occupation on the provincial city of Clermont-Ferrand and, by extension, on the whole of France. The verdict is that, except

for the systematic murder of Jews and of those non-Jews who openly opposed the Nazis, business went on very much as usual during the Occupation, largely because the Nazis obtained the cooperation of most of the French bourgeoisie and because the existence of a large, efficiently coordinated Resistance movement was a myth propagated after the war. Originally made for Swiss and West German television companies, *Le Chagrin et la pitié* was not shown on French television (ORTF), a state monopoly, until 1981, but as a theatrical release in France and abroad it received much attention. Ophüls's more recent films are *A Sense of Loss* (1974), which chronicles the plight of Northern Ireland, and *The Memory of Justice* (1976), a remarkable documentary meditation on collective guilt that counterposes the question of the Nazi death camps and the Nuremberg war-crimes trials with that of French atrocities in Algeria and American atrocities in Vietnam. The difficulties of trying to get the latter distributed against the wishes of myriad political censors and special interest groups led Ophüls to give up filmmaking for over a decade and to turn to writing instead. In 1987, however, he renewed his filmic confrontation with history in *Hôtel Terminus: Klaus Barbie, His Life and Times*. Released at 267 minutes in 1988, this film was shot on three continents and concluded with the unrepentant Nazi's widely publicized trial. Since then, Ophüls has made feature-length documentaries on the fall of East Germany (*November Days*, 1992) and twentieth-century wartime journalism (*Veillées d'armes* [also known as *The Troubles We've Seen*], 1994), the first two parts of which focus on the siege of Sarajevo. Ophüls's documentary influence can be seen most clearly in the work of his friend Claude Lanzmann (b. 1925), whose astonishing nine-and-a-half-hour meditation on the Holocaust, *Shoah* (1985—from the Hebrew word for annihilation), was assembled from 350 hours of interviews and took ten years to produce. *Shoah* was actually the second film of a trilogy exploring modern Jewish experience, whose first part was *Pourquoi Israel?* (*Why Israel?*, 1972) and whose third installment was *Tsahal* (1994), dealing with the role of the military in Israeli society. Lanzmann continued to probe the phenomenon of the death camps in *Un Vivant qui passe* (*A Visitor from the Living*, 1999), an extended interview with a Red Cross official who inspected both Theresienstadt and Auschwitz, and gave them a seal of approval, and *Sobibor, 14 octobre 1943, 16 heures* (*Sobibor, Oct. 14, 1943, 4 P.M.*, 2001), an account, based on survivor interviews, of the only successful revolt of camp inmates against the SS.

French Cinema in the 1980s and 1990s

The 1980s and 1990s witnessed the rise of several popular French film genres that have been influential abroad. The "heritage film" was a big-budget historical costume drama resonant of the postwar "tradition of quality," sometimes adapted from literature, that often privileged pictorialism and the visual arts. Examples are Claude Berri's (b. 1934) *Jean de Florette* (1986), *Manon des sources* (*Manon of the Springs*, 1986), and *Germinal* (1993), the first two derived from novels by Marcel Pagnol and the last from a novel by Émile Zola; Bruno Nuytten's (b. 1945) *Camille Claudel* (1988), a biography of the mistress and most brilliant protégée of the sculptor Auguste Rodin; Régis Wargnier's *Indochine* (1992), a romance set against the epic backdrop of French colonial imperialism in Vietnam; Patrice Chéreau's (b. 1944) *La Reine Margot* (*Queen Margot*, 1994), a violent and sexually explicit epic of the events surrounding the St. Bartholomew's Day Massacre (which also inspired one of the stories in Griffith's *Intolerance* [1916]; see below), adapted from a novel by Alexandre Dumas *père*; Jean-Paul Rappeneau's (b. 1932) *Le*

Hussard sur le toit (*The Horseman on the Roof*, 1995), based on Jean Giono's novel of post-Napoleonic Austria; and Patrice Leconte's (b. 1947) *Ridicule* (1996), a tale of intrigue in the court of Louis XIV, and *La Veuve de Saint-Pierre* (*The Widow of Saint-Pierre*, 2000), an ironic romantic melodrama set on a remote island off the coast of Nova Scotia in 1849. Heritage productions are particularly apt to attract government subvention, consecrating, as they implicitly do, several different manifestations of French culture at once (e.g., French literature, history, art, and cinema—see above).

Another popular film type of the era was known as *"cinéma du look"*—youth-oriented films with high production values and a flashy visual style ("le look") that often involved intertextual allusion, especially to the *mise-en-scène* of French poetic realism (1934–40), and imagery borrowed from contemporary popular media. These films often featured eclectic sound tracks that were a pastiche of classical and popular music. *Cinéma du look* was inaugurated by Jean-Jacques Beineix (b. 1946) with the frenetic *film noir Diva* (1981) and extended through his *La Lune dans le caniveau* (*Moon in the Gutter*, 1983) and *37°2 le matin* (also known as *Betty Blue*, 1986). Luc Besson (b. 1959) was another early practitioner of *cinéma du look*. The commercial success of his hyperkinetic thrillers *Subway* (1985), *Le Grand bleu* (*The Big Blue*, 1988), and *Nikita* (also known as *Le Femme Nikita*, 1990), led him to production contracts with Columbia Pictures, the fruits of which were the brooding, desultory *Léon* (also known as *The Professional*, 1994) and the $90-million science-fiction blockbuster *Le Cinquième élément* (*The Fifth Element*, 1997), whose computer-generated imagery (produced by Digital Domain) represented a landmark in the field of digital effects; the film lost about $30 million at the box office and sent Besson back to France where he next directed the distinctively weird biopic *Jeanne d'Arc* (also known as *The Messenger: The Story of Joan of Arc*, 1999). A third director associated with the neo-Baroque of *cinéma du look* was Leos Carax (b. Alex Dupont, 1960), whose trilogy *Boy Meets Girl*, (1984), *Mauvais sang* (*Bad Blood*, 1986), and *Les Amants du Pont-Neuf* (*Lovers on the Bridge*, 1991) represent the style as at its most experimental. The latter film especially offers an exuberant vision of cinema as a riotous feast for the senses in its virtually plotless account of homeless, star-crossed lovers who seal their fate on the Pont-Neuf in Paris; it contains specific allusions to Vigo's *L'Atalante*

13.41 *Diva* (Jean-Jacques Beineix, 1981): Frederic Andréi, Thuy An Luu. The template for *"cinema du look,"* this film about a young man whose obsession with a black opera diva entangles him in a murder plot was broadly influential for its postmodern attitude and style.

and evocative cinematography (by Darius Khondji) notwithstanding, this fourth installment in the *Alien* franchise lost $22 million against its $70 million investment, proving with some finality that *cinéma du look* did not travel well. Back in Paris, however, Jeunet produced the hit romantic comedy *Le Fabuleux Destin d'Amélie Poulain* (also known as *Amélie*, [2001]), whose whimsical vision of life in the Montmartre district demonstrated a continuing flair for fantasy minus the usual darkness.

(1934) and Carné's *Hôtel du Nord* (1938) as well as to a host of New Wave precursors. (*Les Amants*, which took three years to complete, became the most expensive film produced in the country to date, when Carax built a full-scale replica of the bridge and its surroundings in the south of France—very much as the great art director Alexandre Trauner created elaborate studio-constructed cityscapes for the most prominent poetic realist films.) The promise of *cinéma du look* continues in Carax's remarkable expressionist fairy tale *Pola X* (1999), shot on location in Normandy and adapted from Herman Melville's *Pierre, or the Ambiguities* (for whose title the film is an acronym). A fourth figure whose early work can be categorized as *cinéma du look* is Jean-Pierre Jeunet (b. 1953), whose nightmarish farce *Delicatessen* (co-directed with Marc Caro, 1991) is a visually ornate inversion of the type of populist comedy practiced by René Clair in the early 1930s (e.g., *Le Million* [1931]), in which the friendly neighborhood butcher is a cannibal. Originally working in animation, Jeunet and Caro next developed a grotesque, cartoonlike *mise-en-scène* for their dystopic adult fantasy *La Cité des enfants perdus* (*The City of Lost Children*, 1995), whose commercial success was such that Jeunet was invited to Hollywood by 20th Century–Fox to direct *Alien Resurrection* (1997), for which Caro served as design supervisor. Its surrealistic production design

Other popular French genres are the *"film policier"* or *"polar,"* and the *banlieue* film. The *polar,* whose origins reach back to the work of Henri-Georges Clouzot and Jean-Pierre Melville (and, beyond that, to the French obsession with Hitchcock) are Hollywood-inspired crime thrillers that tend to focus on police procedures and criminal detection, some of the best of which are Jean-Pierre Melville's *Un Flic* (*A Cop*, 1972), Jacques Deray's *Flic Story* (*Cop Story*, 1975), Alain Corneau's *Police Python 357* (1976) and *Série noire* (1979), Maurice Pialat's *Police* (1985), Claude Chabrol's *Le Cri du hibou* (*The Cry of the Owl*, 1987), Patrice Leconte's *Monsieur Hire* (1989), and Bertrand Tavernier's *L. 627* (1992). *Polars* were especially viable during the 1980s, when about 25 percent of domestic production was devoted to them. *Banlieue* films are a more recent form, focusing on neighborhoods and subcultures at the outskirts of large cities, usually working-class and often of North African, or Maghrebi, origin. (In this respect, they are closely related to *cinéma beur*—in which *beur* is a play on the French word *arabe*—films made by and for second-generation North African immigrants, focusing on their socioeconomic conditions and ethnicity—e.g., Karim Dridi's *Bye-Bye* [1995].) A recent example of the *banlieue* film is Mathieu Kassovitz's *La Haine* (*Hate*, 1995), winner of the Best Director Award at Cannes, which took a stark, black-and-white snapshot of the Pari-

13.42 *Jeanne d'Arc* (also known as *The Messenger: The Story of Joan of Arc* [Luc Besson, 1999]): former fashion model Milla Jovovich in the title role on the field of battle. This film combined the stylistic panache of *cinéma du look* with the detailed historical re-creations of the heritage genre.

sian racial underclass in all of its alienation, hopelessness, and casual brutality.

It must finally be noted that French cinema during the 1990s was characterized by the emergence of what has been called the "New New Wave," whose directors are engaged with contemporary social issues that the original *nouvelle vague* more or less avoided in its preoccupation with form and style. Moreover, in sharp contrast to the calculated artificiality of *cinéma du look*, the New New

Wave employs distinctive social and geographical settings and a naturalistic acting style that favors nonprofessional performers. Many of its filmmakers are women, highlighting the fact that during the 1980s and 1990s France had a higher percentage of practicing women directors than any other national cinema. For example, films by Catherine Breillat (b. 1948—*Parfait Amour!* [*Perfect Love*, 1996]; *Romance* [1999]; *À ma souer!* [*To My Sister*, 2001]), Claire Denis (b. 1948—*Beau travail* [*Good Work*, 1999; loosely adapted from Melville's *Billy Budd*]; *Trouble Every Day* [2001]), and Virginie Despentes and Coralie Trinh Thi (*Baise-moi* [*Rape Me*, 2000]) explore new territory in the realm of sexuality and gender roles, often with graphic realism. Most New New Wave directors de-emphasize plot and strive for an openness of structure; furthermore, they are nonideological and draw most of their social consciousness from personal experience of contemporary life. For example, Cédric Klapisch's (b. 1961) *Chacun cherche son chat* (English title: *When the Cat's Away*, 1996) is a comedy about daily life of thirty-something Parisians whose neighborhood is undergoing gentrification, while his *Un Air de famille* (English title: *Family Resemblances*, 1997) is a black comedy of dysfunctional family life. In *Métisse* (also known as *Café au Lait*, 1993), Mathieu Kassovitz (b. 1967) practiced for *La*

13.43 *Pola X* (Leos Carax, 1999): Pierre (Guillaume Depardieu) literally blows his cousin's (Laurent Lucas) brains out near the end of the film, whose title is an acronym for the French title of the source novel, Melville's *Pierre; ou, Les ambiguïtés.*

13.44 *La Cite des enfants perdue* (Jean-Pierre Jeunet, 1995): Ron Perlman, near the conclusion of the film, guides his rowboat through an expressionistically mined harbor.

Haine (see above) with a comedy about multicultural romance set in an ethnically diverse district of Paris, whereas his controversial *Assassins* (1997) was aimed squarely at the relationship between television violence and actual murder, and seemed to prepare him for *Les Rivières pourpres* (*Crimson Rivers*, 2000), a cerebral if gruesome *polar* that dissects the social fabric of a provincial university town. Another New New Wave director is Arnaud Desplechin (b. 1960), whose work spans several genres—horror (*La Sentinelle* [1992]), satiric comedy (*Comment je me suis disputé . . . ma vie sexuelle* [*My Sex Life, or How I Got into an Argument*, 1996]), and costume drama (*Esther Kahn* [2000])—but all rests on a foundation of acute social observation. Other filmmakers notable for their sharp commentary on France's urban social milieu are Christian Vincent (*La Discrète* [1990]; *La Séparation* [1994]; *Sauve-moi* [*Save Me*, 2001]) and Benoît Jacquot (b. 1947—*La Fille seule* [*A Single Girl*, 1995]; *L'École de la chair* [*The School of Flesh*, 1998]), both of whom tend to focus on contemporary sexual mores. Dealing with similar social concerns in northern industrial settings are several filmmakers whose work centers on the working class and is stylistically indebted to British directors like Ken Loach and Mike Leigh (see Chapter 14). For example, Erick Zonca's debut feature *La Vie rêvée des anges* (*The Dreamlife of Angels*, 1998) examines the dilemma of untrained jobless women in a bleak factory town; similarly, Julie Lopes-Curval's *Bord*

de mer (2002), which won the Camera d'Or for best first film at Cannes, is about the daily lives of assembly-line workers in a small Atlantic seaside community. The most prominent director working this vein, ever, is clearly Bruno Dumont, whose first film, *La Vie de Jésus* (1997), treats alienation and gang violence among young men in an economically depressed rural town. Dumont's second feature, *L'Humanité* (1999), which won multiple awards at Cannes, is set in the same town (Bailleul, near Flanders) and achieves an odd transcendence in recounting the investigation by a simple police inspector of the brutal murder of an eleven-year-old girl.

Two other directors associated with the New New Wave but more eclectic in their styles are Olivier Assayas (b. 1955) and François Ozon (b. 1967). A former *Cahiers* critic and television screenwriter, Assayas debuted with *L'Eau froide* (*Cold Water*, 1994), an impressively observed story of thwarted teenage love. Next he contributed *Irma Vep*, a dark comedy about a failed director's attempt to remake Feuillade's popular serial *Les Vampires* (1915), richly layered with filmic allusions, whose subtext is the imperiled status of French cinema in the face of globalization. After the international success of *Irma Vep* and the tragic romance *Fin août, début septembre* (*Late August, Early September*, 1999), Assayas delivered a mainstream but highly stylized heritage film in *Les Destinées sentimentales*, (2000); this three-hour adaptation of Jacques Chardonne's multivolume epic novel on the rise and fall of a great mercantile family from the early 1900s through the end of World War II was heavily indebted to Luchino Visconti's *The Leopard* (1963) for its opulent production design. Ozon began his career as a director of shorts, producing as his first feature an outrageous satire on bourgeois family life called *Sitcom* (1998), whose graphic depiction of sex and violence made him controversial overnight. His casually brutal *Les Amants criminel* (*Criminal Lovers*, 1999) proceeded from a long line of fugitive

13.45 *Romance* (Catherine Breillat, 1999): Caroline Ducey (Marie) is dominated by François Berléand (Robert), one of her many lovers in a film that examines the varieties of human sexual experience from the perspective of a woman.

couple movies (e.g., Terrence Malick's *Badlands* [1973] and Oliver Stone's *Natural Born Killers* [1994]), but veered off into Grimm's fairy-tale territory in midcourse, confounding critics with its tonal shifts and generic hybridity. Yet *Sous le sable* (*Under the Sand*, 2000) demonstrated remarkable artistic restraint in its *Vertigo*-like drama of a middle-aged woman (Charlotte Rampling in an astonishing performance) who refuses to acknowledge her beloved husband's death and continues to communicate with him (apparently) beyond the grave. Moving from the terrain of

13.46 *La Vie rêvée des anges* (Erick Zonca, 1998): Isa (Élodie Bouchez) is fired from her garment-factory job in Lille. Bouchez and her costar, Natacha Régnier, shared the Best Actress Award at Cannes in 1998 for their performances in this film.

Hitchcock into that of Fassbinder, Ozon adapted a four-act play by the German director, *Gouttes d'eau sur pierres brûlantes* (*Water Drops on Burning Rocks*, 2000), as a hilarious comedy of sexual manners.

At the beginning of the twenty-first century, France had one of the most productive film industries in the world, both in absolute terms (it typically places third or fourth, after India, the United States, and sometimes the United Kingdom) and relative to the size of its population of 61 million; it produces around 180 features per year, as much as one-third of them by first- and second-time directors. (Italy and Spain, with nearly the same populations, produce 80 to 100.) What made this possible was an inordinately high level of government protectionism that is rationalized by a concept known as *l'exception culturelle française*, or the French cultural exception, which holds that cultural products are not merchandise subject to the same rules of free exchange as commodity goods. In other words, French-language film and television, as well as books and music, are entitled to protection against stronger competitors like the United States in order to maintain the cultural distinctiveness of French society. (The "cultural exception" policy dates from 1993, when, at French insistence, the European Union successfully excluded cultural products from GATT.) To this end, the state heavily subsidizes production via the *avance sur recettes*, an advance from the government on all French films funded by a ticket tax and investment from French television companies that are mandated to devote 40 percent of their programming to domestic films. During the 1990s, 60 percent of all French films were at least partially financed by television, although most were released theatrically. By far the most important player here is the national pay-television company Canal Plus, currently owned by Vivendi Universal, which options for broadcast 90 percent of all French films and invests more than $150 million annually in production—about one-third of total investment, making it the single largest underwriter of French cinema (and causing it a chronic operating loss of more than $300 million per year). This system of protection and subsidy has not only given France one of the largest film industries in the world, but it has made it the only European nation in which foreign films (overwhelming American) represent less than half of the domestic market. There is intense, ever-present competition from Hollywood, and Ameri-

13.47 *L'Humanité* (Bruno Dumont, 1999): Emmauel Shottéas Pharaon De Winter, The Bailleul police inspector tries to tend his own garden but is drawn ever deeper into the mystery of a murdered eleven-year-old girl.

13.48 *Les Destinées sentimentales* (Olivier Assayas, 2000): the Barnery family's porcelain factory around the time of World War I. As with other heritage films, this one contains scrupulously detailed period costumes and sets.

can blockbusters are extremely popular with French audiences, who remain the most avid cinemagoers in all of Europe. Yet, as a legacy of the New Wave—itself part of a rich and distinguished national film heritage extending all the way back to Méliès—filmmaking in France is still regarded as more art than industry, and *auteurism,* as a matter of practice rather than theory, still reigns supreme. In fact, virtually all French directors still write or collaborate in the writing of their own screenplays, just as did the *cinéastes* of the *nouvelle vague.*

The Significance of the New Wave

The impact of the French New Wave upon world cinema would be difficult to overestimate. The movement can be credited with almost singlehandedly revitalizing the stagnant British and American cinemas during the 1960s, and it produced similar chain reactions in Italy, West Germany, Eastern Europe, and indeed around the world. To suggest that the New Wave was a monolithic phenomenon is sim-

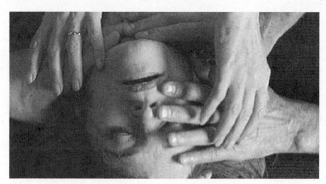

13.49 *Sous la sable* (François Ozon, 2000): Marie (Charlotte Rampling) imagines the tender caresses of husband, who is missing and presumed dead but keeps appearing to her both in dreams and broad daylight.

plistic. Varda, Resnais, Marker, and Malle, for example, evolved from a completely different context than did Truffaut, Godard, Chabrol, Rivette, and Rohmer. The former had begun their filmmaking careers as assistants and editors within the established industry; the latter had begun theirs as theorists and critics in total revolt against the industrial system.[3] And all of them, of course, went their separate artistic ways in the later 1960s and 1970s. But two common notions bound them together and made their films vastly important to the evolution of narrative cinema. First, they believed that film was an art form that could provide an artist with a medium of personal expression as rich, as varied, and as sensitive as any other. This assumption is implicit in the concept of personal authorship, or *la politique des auteurs*, according to which film directors are not simply analogous to writers of novels, but are literally capable of "writing novels" in the audiovisual language of film. Second, they shared the belief that the narrative conventions they had inherited from the 1930s and 1940s were insufficient to achieve these ends, that in fact many of these conventions prevented the audiovisual language of film from approaching its full range of expression. So they broke the old conventions and established new ones in the process, elaborating an audiovisual language that could express a whole gamut of internal and external states. This is implicit in the notion of *mise-en-scène*, according to which a film should not be simply a succession of meaningful images telling a story, but an all-engrossing, mind- and sense-engaging experience. The number of major filmmakers who emerged from the New Wave and who are still in the process of making ever greater and more influential features is astounding. But even more astounding is the impact that these new ideas about audiovisual language and its operations have had and continue to have upon the international cinema at large. By calling into question the very form and process of narrative cinema, the filmmakers of the New Wave insured that the cinema could never again rely upon the easy narrative assumptions of its first fifty years.

---

3. Rivette alone among the *Cahiers* group had received some practical training as an assistant director to Renoir and Becker in the early 1950s.

New Cinemas in Britain and the English-Speaking Commonwealth

Great Britain

POSTWAR BRITISH CINEMA AND ITS CONTEXT

While the French were experiencing the New Wave, the British were enjoying a film renaissance of their own. Before World War II, Britain had produced a vastly important contribution to documentary cinema in the government-funded work of John Grierson (see Chapter 9) and his protégés Alberto Cavalcanti (1897–1982)—*Coalface*, 1935; Paul Rotha (1907–1984)—*Shipyard* and *The Face of Britain*, both 1935; Basil Wright (1907–1987)—the four-part *Song of Ceylon*, 1934, and *Children at School*, 1937); Arthur Elton (b. 1906) and Edgar Anstey (1907–1987)—*Housing Problems*, 1937; Stuart Legg (b. 1910)—*BBC—The Voice of Britain*, 1935; Harry Watt (1906–1987)—*Night Mail*, co-directed with Wright, 1936, and *The North Sea*, 1938; and Humphrey Jennings (1907–1950)—*Spring Offensive*, 1939. All of these directors had trained under Grierson in 1933 at the General Post Office (GPO) Film Unit, which had succeeded the Empire Marketing Board (EMB) Film Unit. It was renamed the Crown Film Unit in 1940 and became part of the Ministry of Information (MOI).

During the war, the Crown Film Unit moved toward a blending of narrative and documentary form in such films as Watt's *London Can Take It* (1940) and *Target for Tonight* (1941); Jennings's *Heart of Britain* (1941), *Words for Battle* (1941), *Listen to Britain* (1941), and *Fires Were Started* (1943); and Pat Jackson's *Western Approaches* (1944; Technicolor). Meanwhile the commercial industry produced quasi-documentary features praising the armed forces—the navy, in *In Which We Serve* (Noël Coward, 1942); the army, in *The Way Ahead* (Carol Reed, 1944); the air force, in *The Way to the Stars* (Anthony Asquith, 1945); and the home front, in *Next of Kin* (Thorold Dickinson, 1942), *Went the Day Well?* (Alberto Cavalcanti, 1942), and *Millions Like Us* (Frank Launder and Sidney Gilliat, 1943). Since the innovations of the Brighton school at the turn of the century, however, Britain had produced little significant narrative cinema, outside of the work of Alfred Hitchcock; the films directed or produced by Alexander Korda (1893–1956)—*The Private Life of Henry VIII*, 1933; *Rembrandt*, 1936; *Things to Come*, directed by William Cameron Menzies, 1936; *The Thief of Bagdad*, co-directed by Tim Whelan, Ludwig Berger, and Michael Powell, 1940; *The Jungle Book*, directed by Zoltan Korda, 1942; and adaptations from the stage by Anthony Asquith (1902–1968), such as *Pygmalion*, co-directed with Leslie Howard, 1938. This surge of energy during the 1930s briefly freed the British industry from its perennial domination by Hollywood, but by the end of the decade most British commercial production was geared toward making second features to accompany American films on double bills.

During and after World War II, however, a traditional staple of native British cinema—literary adaptation—experienced a sharp upswing. Two lavish Technicolor productions—Gabriel Pascal's version of George Bernard Shaw's *Caesar and Cleopatra* (1945) and Alexander Korda's

14.2 Pip confronts Magwitch in David Lean's adaptation of Dickens's *Great Expectations* (1946): John Mills, Finlay Currie.

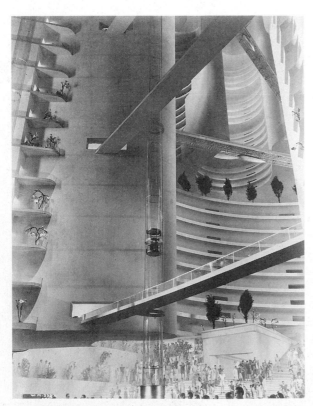

14.1 Part of the futuristic "Everytown" set in *Things to Come* (William Cameron Menzies, 1936).

adaptation of Oscar Wilde's *An Ideal Husband* (1947)—proved to be expensive failures. But the actor-director Laurence Olivier (1907–1989) offered distinguished adaptations of three plays by Shakespeare—*Henry V* (1944; Technicolor); *Hamlet* (1948), the first British production ever to receive an American Academy Award as Best Film; and *Richard III* (1955; Technicolor and VistaVision). And David Lean (1908–1991), after adapting several plays of Noël Coward (*Blithe Spirit* [1945] and *Brief Encounter* [1945], among them), produced two carefully crafted, atmospheric adaptations of Charles Dickens's works, *Great Expectations* (1946) and *Oliver Twist* (1947), both models of their form. Anthony Asquith's stylish adaptations of Terence Rattigan's plays *While the Sun Shines* (1947), *The Winslow Boy* (1948), and *The Browning Version* (1951), and of Oscar Wilde's play *The Importance of Being Earnest* (1952; Technicolor), were matched by a brilliant expressionistic version of Alexander Pushkin's story *The Queen of Spades* (1949), directed by Thorold Dickinson (1903–1984). Carol Reed (1906–1976) directed *Odd Man Out* (1946), *The Fallen Idol* (1948), and *The Third Man* (1949), the latter two adapted from stories by Graham Greene, and *Outcast of the Islands* (1951; adapted from Joseph Conrad's novel). These finely wrought dramatic narratives were resonant at their best of French poetic realism and the films of Orson Welles. *The Red Shoes* (1948) and *The Tales of Hoffmann* (1951), the extravagant ballet spectaculars made by Michael Powell (1905–1990) and Emeric Press-

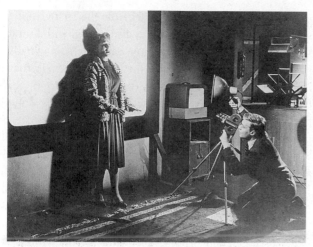

14.3 Maligned masterpiece: Michael Powell's *Peeping Tom* (1959). Anna Massey, Carl Boehm.

burger (1903–1988) also appeared during this period. So, too, did the best work of the twin Boulting brothers, John (1913–1985) and Roy (b. 1913), who alternated as producer and director on such fine postwar films as *Brighton Rock* (1947; adapted from the Graham Greene novel), *The Magic Box* (1951; the story of William Friese-Greene, the putative inventor of the first British cinema machines), *Lucky Jim* (1957; adapted from the Kingsley Amis novel), and *I'm All Right, Jack* (1959).

Among the most important British films of the postwar era was a series of intelligent and witty comedies made for Michael Balcon's family-run Ealing Studios. These films were directed by Charles Crichton (1910–1999)—*Hue and Cry*, 1947; *The Lavender Hill Mob*, 1951; *The*

14.4 *The Red Shoes* (Michael Powell and Emeric Pressburger, 1948): Moira Shearer, Robert Helpmann, Léonide Massine.

Titfield Thunderbolt, 1953; by Alexander Mackendrick (1912–1993)—*Whisky Galore* (American title, *Tight Little Island*), 1949; *The Man in the White Suit*, 1951; *The Ladykillers*, 1955; by Henry Cornelius (1913–1958)—*Passport to Pimlico*, 1948; *Genevieve*, 1953; and by Robert Hamer (1911–1963)—*Kind Hearts and Coronets*, 1949; *Father Brown*, 1954. The splendid work of the actor Alec Guinness (1914–2000) in a number of these films made him an international star. The omnibus film *Dead of Night* (1945), co-directed by Alberto Cavalcanti, Robert Hamer, Charles Crichton, and Basil Dearden, is also a landmark of British postwar cinema because of its convincing *mise-en-scène* and circular narrative structure.

By the mid-1950s, British cinema had began to decline into cliché, and Britain was once again in danger of becoming a Hollywood colony. A notable exception was the well-made, tightly budgeted genre films being turned out by Hammer Films. This was a small independent production company founded in 1947 by James Carreras (1910–1990) and Anthony Hinds, who in 1951 had built soundstages on the grounds of a large country-estate house at Bray, near London.[1] Between 1954 and 1968, the Bray Studios produced a series of science-fiction, crime, and horror films whose combination of violence, carnality, and visceral thrills made them very popular at home and abroad. Success came first with a trio of black-and-white alien-invasion films derived from a popular BBC television series written by Nigel Kneale, *The Quatermass Experiment* (1953), a sort of precursor to the Fox Network's *The X-Files* series, which first aired forty years later in 1993: *The Quatermass Xperiment* (U.S. title: *The Creeping Unknown* [Val Guest, 1955]), *X the Unknown* (Leslie Norman, 1956; an imitation rather than a direct sequel), and *Quatermass II* (U.S. title: *Enemy from Space* [Val Guest, 1957]) were all shot in black-and-white and considered so gruesome that British censors gave them a "Certificate X" so that they would be off-limits to children.[2] Following this trend, Hammer broke into the gothic/horror market with *The Curse of Frankenstein*

---

1. The origin of the production company was a distribution company called Exclusive Films, founded in 1935, which James Carreras and Anthony Hinds had taken over from their fathers, Enrique Carreras and Will Hinds, a former actor whose stage name was Will Hammer—thus, Hammer Films. Some of the early Hammer horrors bore a "Hammer Films/Exclusive Films Release" logo.

2. Ever canny in the ways of exploitation, Carreras and Hinds changed the title of the first Quatermass film to *The Quatermass Xperiment*, once the "Certificate X" had been issued to it.

14.5 *Kind Hearts and Coronets* **(Robert Hamer, 1949): Alec Guinness surrounds Valerie Hobson with six of his eight incarnations in Ealing Studios' most famous comedy.**

14.6 **Alberto Cavalcanti's "The Ventriloquist's Dummy" episode in** *Dead of Night* **(Cavalcanti, Hamer, Crichton, and Dearden, 1945): Michael Redgrave, with John McGuire as Hugo the dummy.**

(1957), a widescreen Eastmancolor version of Mary Shelley's classic, whose shocks were quite literally visceral since the *mise-en-scène* was strewn with organs and dismembered body parts. Produced for little more than $100,000 (£65,000), the film grossed well over $4 million (£2 million), half of it in the American market—unprecedented for a postwar British film of any sort. *The Curse of Frankenstein* was quickly followed by *Dracula* (U.S. title: *The Horror of Dracula* [Terence Fisher, 1958]), and the two films together set the mold for what came to be known as "Hammer horror"—full-color, widescreen var-

iants of Universal's horror classics from the 1930s, replete with violence, sex, and gore, but also graced with literate scripts (often written by Jimmy Sangster), imaginative art direction (usually by production designer Bernard Robinson) and cinematography (by DP—director of photography—Jack Asher), as well as professionally honed performances by Hammer's two male leads, Peter Cushing (1913–1994) and Christopher Lee (b. 1922), both Shakespearean-trained actors who were usually cast as antagonists. The director most closely associated with Hammer horror was Terence Fisher (1904–1980), who in rapid succession made colorful versions of *The Mummy* (1959), *The Hound of the Baskervilles* (1959), *The Two Faces of Dr. Jekyll* (1960), *The Curse of the Werewolf* (1961), *The Phantom of the Opera* (1962), as well as sequels to most of them (e.g., *The Revenge of Frankenstein* [1958], *The Brides of Dracula* [1960]).[3] Over the next decade, Hammer produced five more Frankenstein sequels, six Dracula sequels, and nine other vampire films, together with two more Jekyll-and-Hyde films, and three mummy sequels. Predictably, British mainstream critics hated Hammer films, seeing them as prurient and sadistic, but nearly all of them were profitable. The Hammer formula was so successful in the United States, in fact, that it was imitated at AIP by Roger Corman, whose

---

3. Other directors who helped to make Hammer a trademark for well-made, sensational horror were Val Guest (b. 1911)—"Quatermass" films above, *The Abominable Snowman of the Himalayas* (1957); John Gilling (1910–1985)—*The Reptile* (1966), *The Plague of the Zombies* (1967), *The Mummy's Shroud* (1967); Roy Ward Baker (b. 1916)—*Quatermass and the Pit* (1967), *The Vampire Lovers* (1970), *The Scars of Dracula* (1970); Freddie Francis (b. 1917)—*Nightmare* (1963), *The Evil of Frankenstein* (1964), *Dracula Has Risen from the Grave* (1968); Seth Holt (1923–1971)—*Scream of Fear* (1961), *The Nanny* (1965), *Blood from the Mummy's Tomb* (1971); and Peter Sasdy—*Taste the Blood of Dracula* (1970), *Countess Dracula* (1970), *Hands of the Ripper* (1971). Some critics have argued that, far from being an aberration, Hammer proved the point that horror was a uniquely British genre. In *A Heritage of Horror: The English Gothic Cinema, 1946–1972* (New York: Avon, 1973), p. 9, e.g., David Pirie wrote that horror "remains the only staple cinematic myth which Britain can claim as its own and which relates to it in the same way as the western relates to America." See also Bruce Lanier Wright, *Nightwalkers: Gothic Horror Movies, the Modern Era* (Dallas: Taylor, 1995); Jack Hunter, ed., *House of Horrors: The Compete Hammer Films Story*, 2nd rev. ed. (London: Creation, 1996); Andy Boot, *Fragments of Fear: An Illustrated History of British Horror Films* (London: Creation, 1996); Bruce Sachs and Russell Wall, *Greasepaint and Gore: The Hammer Monsters of Roy Ashton* (Sheffield, Eng.: Tomahawk, 1998); Jonathan Rigby, *English Gothic: A Century of Horror Cinema* (London: Reynolds & Hearn, 2000); and Steven Chibnall and Julian Petley, eds., *British Horror Cinema* (London: Routledge, 2002).

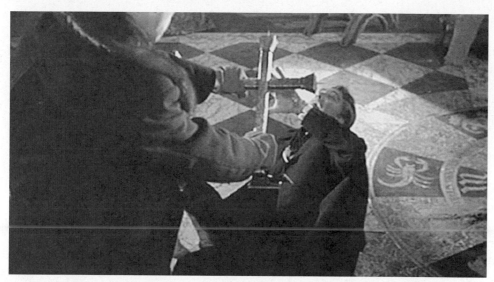

14.7 *Dracula* (U.S. title: *The Horror of Dracula* [Terence Fisher, 1958]): Peter Cushing, Christopher Lee. Hammer Films' literate and imaginative version of Bram Stoker's 1898 novel inspired a renaissance of the horror genre in England, Italy, and the United States.

stylized Edgar Allan Poe adaptations of the early 1960s (e.g., *House of Usher* [1960]; see Chapter 12) were inspired by it. Hammer also had a decisive influence on the Italian horror film, which can be clearly seen in the work of Riccardo Freda and Mario Bava (see Chapter 15). Furthermore, a subgenre of the Hammer horror film, the film of terror inspired by *Psycho*—of which the studio made ten, starting with the lurid prototype *Scream of Fear* (Seth Holt, 1960) and continuing through *Crescendo* (Alan Gibson, 1970), all scripted by Sangster—had an impact on the homegrown Italian *giallo* (see Chapter 15). After 1966, Hammer's fortunes began to decline because its formulas were getting tired and excess wasn't what it used to be, but not before it had demonstrated decisively the commercial viability of British films in the postwar world (in recognition of which the studio received the Queen's Award for Industry in 1968).

THE FREE CINEMA MOVEMENT

As early as 1947, the Oxford University film journal *Sequence* (1947–52), edited by the future directors Lindsay Anderson (1923–1994) and Karel Reisz (b. Czechoslovakia, 1926), had attacked the controlling assumption of British cinema: "The British commercial cinema has been a bourgeois rather than a revolutionary growth; and

it is not a middle-class trait to examine oneself with the strictest objectivity, or to be able to represent higher or lower levels of society with sympathy and respect."

Anderson and Reisz went on to act upon their beliefs in 1954 and 1955 by organizing the **Free Cinema** movement, which, like Italian neorealism, celebrated, as a manifesto put it, "the importance of the individual and . . . the significance of the everyday." Like the French New Wave, the Free Cinema movement was dedicated to the belief that film should be a medium of personal expression for the filmmaker, who should be socially committed to illuminating the problems of contemporary life.

In practice, Free Cinema meant the production of short, low-budget documentaries like Anderson's *O Dreamland* (1954), a satirical assault on the spiritual emptiness of working-class life, set in an amusement park, and Reisz's and Tony Richardson's *Momma Don't Allow* (1956), a study of postwar youth in the environment of a London jazz club. Between February 1956 and March 1959, the Free Cinema movement presented a series of six programs at the National Film Theater that featured most prominently *O Dreamland; Momma Don't Allow; Every Day Except Christmas* (1959), Anderson's study of Covent Garden flower and vegetable vendors; *We Are the Lambeth Boys* (1958), Reisz's portrait of a South London youth club; and a number of recent Continental films: Georges Franju's *Le Sang des bêtes* (1949); Alain Tanner and Claude Goretta's *Nice Time* (1957, shot in Piccadilly Circus); François Truffaut's *Les Mistons* (1957); Roman Polanski's *Two Men and a Wardrobe* (*Dwaj ludzie z szafą*, 1958); and Claude Chabrol's *Le Beau Serge* (1958) (see chapters 13 and 16).

At the time that the Free Cinema movement emerged, a revolution was under way in British theater and literature in which liberal working-class values emanating from the East End of London and the provinces were overturning the established bourgeois tradition of the preceding decades. John Osborne's antiestablishment diatribe *Look Back in Anger* rocked the world of traditional culture when it was staged at the Royal Court Theatre in May 1956 by calling into question the whole class structure of British society and assailing the moral bankruptcy of the welfare state.[4] The following years witnessed the appearance of a new group of young, antiestablishment, working-class novelists such as David Storey, John Braine, Alan Sillitoe, and Shelagh Delaney, who treated similar themes in a style that can be accurately characterized as "social realism." By 1959—significantly, the year that the French New Wave won a great number of the prizes at Cannes—the time was ripe for the overthrow of the class-bound British feature cinema in favor of working-class social realism.

In that year, the industry itself produced two films that announced the revolution: Jack Clayton's (1921–1995) adaptation of John Braine's novel *Room at the Top* and Tony Richardson's adaptation of *Look Back in Anger*, scripted by the author. Both films were big-budget commercial productions with well-known stars that nevertheless dealt seriously with the disillusionment and frustration of the British working classes, and both were international hits. *Look Back in Anger* was so successful, in fact, that Richardson (1928–1991) and Osborne (b. 1929) were able to form, with the financial backing of producer Harry Saltzman (later responsible for the slick James Bond series), their own production company, the

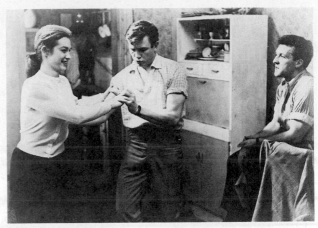

14.9 *Saturday Night and Sunday Morning* (Karel Reisz, 1960): Shirley Anne Field, Albert Finney, Norman Rossington.

short-lived but influential Woodfall Films (1959–63). In Woodfall's first feature, coproduced with Holly Films, Richardson collaborated with Osborne again to adapt his second play, *The Entertainer* (1960). It starred Laurence Olivier as the seedy music-hall comedian Archie Rice and was partially shot on location in Blackpool. Woodfall's first completely independent production, Karel Reisz's *Saturday Night and Sunday Morning* (1960), a version of the Alan Sillitoe novel, was shot on location in Nottingham with unknown actors for a budget of under $300,000, or less than one-third of the standard feature allocation. But it recovered this figure in the first two weeks of its London run alone and went on to become the biggest international success the British film industry had known since the 1930s.

BRITISH "NEW CINEMA," OR SOCIAL REALISM

Saturday Night and Sunday Morning became the prototype for what may be fairly labeled British "New Cinema," a social-realist film movement whose themes were borrowed from Italian neorealism and whose techniques were modeled upon the Free Cinema documentary of the late 1950s and the films of the French New

14.8 *Look Back in Anger* (Tony Richardson, 1959): Richard Burton, Mary Ure.

---

4. Since World War II, Britain has had one of the highest degrees of state ownership and one of the most comprehensive welfare systems in Western Europe.

14.10 John Schlesinger's *Billy Liar* (1963): Billy (Tom Courtenay) daydreams of military glory.

Like the French New Wave, British New Cinema reached its peak around 1963 and then rapidly declined as a movement while its directors went their separate ways. During the mid-1960s, in fact, a reaction to the bleakness of social realism set in, and the depressing images of the industrial Midlands were replaced by those of "swinging London" in big-budget widescreen color productions like *Alfie* (Lewis Gilbert, 1966), *Smashing Time* (Desmond Davis, 1967), and *Joanna* (Michael Sarne, 1968), all of which, however, did have working-class protagonists. Nevertheless, Lindsay Anderson continued to pursue anti-establishment themes in *if . . .* (1968), a brilliant film about the nature of individualism and authority cast in the form

Wave.[5] The New Cinema movement's films were generally set in the industrial Midlands and shot on location in black and white against the gloomiest backgrounds their makers could find. The films featured unknown young actors, and their protagonists were typically rebellious working-class youths like Richardson/Osborne's Jimmy Porter or Reisz/Sillitoe's Arthur Seaton—youths who were contemptuous of the spiritual torpor that had been induced in their parents and friends by the welfare state and by mass communications, as exemplified by the BBC. The films' heroes spend a good deal of their time in pubs, drinking and brawling, and use a tough vernacular speech until then unheard in British cinema. Major New Cinema productions include Tony Richardson's *A Taste of Honey* (Woodfall, 1961; script by Shelagh Delaney) and *The Loneliness of the Long Distance Runner* (Woodfall, 1962; adapted from a Sillitoe novel); John Schlesinger's *A Kind of Loving* (1962) and *Billy Liar* (1963); Lindsay Anderson's *This Sporting Life* (produced by Reisz, 1963); Canadian-born Sidney J. Furie's *The Leather Boys* (1963); and Karel Reisz's *Morgan: A Suitable Case for Treatment* (1966).

of a surrealist satire on the British public school system. One of the 1960s' most important films, *if. . . .* can be favorably compared with Vigo's *Zéro de conduite* (1933), to which it contains several explicit allusions; it established Anderson as the most influential figure to emerge from the New Cinema movement. In Anderson's powerful *O Lucky Man!* (1973), whose mock-poetic title refers back to his first film, *O Dreamland* (1953), the protagonist of *if. . . .* continues his education through the various levels of corruption in London society, only to be totally corrupted himself at the end of the process—by being "discovered" by the director Lindsay Anderson to star in a motion picture entitled *O Lucky Man!* The film *Britannia Hospital* (1982) continued Anderson's dissection of the contemporary British psyche in an unsparing

5. Another film of 1960 that forecast social realism was *The Angry s-Silence*, coproduced by Bryan Forbes and Richard Attenborough and directed by Guy Green. Shot on location in the Midlands, the film deals with the manipulation of an industrial strike by communist agitators, and though it shares many formal characteristics with *Saturday Night and Sunday Morning*, *The Angry Silence* is as politically equivocal as was Elia Kazan's *On the Waterfront*, which probably inspired it.

14.11 Anarchic violence at the conclusion of *if . . . .* (Lindsay Anderson, 1968).

absurdist satire on labor strikes, racial tensions, and the misuse of the National Health Service by doctors and patients alike. More recently, he directed *The Whales of August* (1987), a delicate mood piece adapted by David Berry from his own 1981 play, about two elderly sisters (played in the film by Bette Davis and Lillian Gish) living out their last years in a family home on the coast of Maine.

After an impressive start in *Saturday Night and Sunday Morning*, the work of Karel Reisz generally declined during the 1960s (e.g., *Isadora*, 1968), with the exception of *Morgan* (1966; also known as *Morgan: A Suitable Case for Treatment*), a subtle and painfully funny film about mental breakdown. But Reisz's intelligent, American-made *The Gambler* (1975) signaled renewed vigor. His second American feature, *Who'll Stop the Rain?* (1978), a corrosive adaptation of Robert Stone's best-selling allegorical thriller *Dog Soldiers*, about heroin smuggling during the Vietnam War, marked his return to prominence. His version of John Fowles's complex "Victorian" novel *The French Lieutenant's Woman* (1981), scripted by Harold Pinter and strikingly photographed by Freddie Francis, was a triumph of the filmmaker's art. More recently, Reisz has directed *Sweet Dreams* (1985), an intelligent biography of country singer Patsy Cline, who was killed in a plane crash at the height of her success, and *Everybody Wins* (1990), from an original screenplay by Arthur Miller (his first since *The Misfits* in 1961). Wherever Reisz's far-ranging aesthetic sensibilities lead him next, it should be noted that his important book, *The Technique of Film Editing*, has greatly influenced such major film artists as Alain Resnais.

The same general falling-off was seen in the work of Tony Richardson, who, after a series of three excellent working-class films and the flamboyant period comedy *Tom Jones* (1963; adapted from Henry Fielding's novel), abandoned social commitment for big-time commercial cinema. Since then, most of his films, like the American-made *The Loved One* (1965), have been failures. But a filmmaker of substantial verve is still perceptible in *The Charge of the Light Brigade* (1968), *Ned Kelly* (1970), and *Joseph Andrews* (1977), another Fielding adaptation. Later, Richardson worked in the United States to produce *The Border* (1981), a tale of passion and intrigue on the Mexican-American border, *The Hotel New Hampshire* (1984), an adaptation of John Irving's rambling chronicle of an eccentric American family, and *Blue Sky* (1991; released 1994), a drama about the mentally unstable wife of an army captain, for which Jessica Lange won the 1995 Academy Award for Best Actress.

John Schlesinger (1926–2003), who began his career as a BBC documentarist, has been much more successful artistically than either Reisz or Richardson. He made his first feature, *A Kind of Loving*, in 1962. After *Billy Liar* (1963), he achieved great commercial success with *Darling* (1965), a modish examination of upper-class decadence filmed *à la nouvelle vague*, for which Julie Christie won the 1965 Academy Award for Best Actress (the film also won for Best Costume Design [Julie Harris] and Best Screenplay [Frederic Raphael]). Schlesinger's best film of the decade, however, was *Far From the Madding Crowd* (1967), shot on location in Dorset and Wiltshire by Nicolas Roeg with exceptional painterly skill. This big-budget ($4 million) adaptation of a novel first published by Thomas Hardy in 1876 is astonishingly faithful both to the artistic vision of its source and the cinematic spirit of its times. With *Midnight Cowboy* (1969) and throughout the 1970s, Schlesinger continued to specialize in stylish and intelligent films—*Sunday, Bloody Sunday* (1971), *The Day of the Locust* (1975; from the novel by Nathanael West), *Marathon Man* (1976), and *Yanks* (1979). After a failed attempt at social satire in *Honky Tonk Freeway* (1980), he redeemed himself with the BBC telefilm *An Englishman Abroad* (1983), based on an incident from the life of Cold War defector and spy Guy Burgess, and the American-produced real-life espionage film *The Falcon and the Snowman* (1984), both of which ponder the moral implications of treason. Many critics felt that Schlesinger's violent voodoo-cult thriller *The Believers*

14.12 *Sunday Bloody Sunday* (John Schlesinger, 1971): Glenda Jackson, Murray Head.

14.13 The demonic (?) children of Bly in Jack Clayton's *The Innocents* (1961).

(1986) was an exercise in needless mystification, but *Madame Sousatzka* (1988), a leisurely narrative focused on a middle-aged piano teacher and her circle, was much admired, as were the ambiguous American thriller *Pacific Heights* (1990) and the British espionage films *A Question of Attribution* (1991) and *The Innocent* (1993). Schlesinger has mainly directed for television since then, enjoying considerable success with TV movies like the satiric *Cold Comfort Farm* (1995), which was so popular with British audiences that it was released theatrically in the United States.

Jack Clayton, whose *Room at the Top* (1959) is often credited with having begun British social realism, turned away from the movement in his second feature, *The Innocents* (1961), a beautiful, terrifying, and appropriately ambiguous visualization of Henry James's novel *The Turn of the Screw*. But Clayton continued to make distinctly individual films such as *The Pumpkin Eater* (1964; script by Harold Pinter) and *Our Mother's House* (1967). Clayton's career as a director was nearly ended by the commercial and critical failure of his opulent, Hollywood-produced version of F. Scott Fitzgerald's *The Great Gatsby* (1974) but resumed with his skillful adaptations of Ray Bradbury's horror novel *Something Wicked This Way Comes* (1982) and Brian Moore's *The Lonely Passion of Judith Hearne* (1987). More recently, Clayton directed features for British television (e.g., *Memento Mori*, 1992).

Other important British filmmakers of the 1960s were

Bryan Forbes (b. 1926) and Basil Dearden (1911–1971).[6] Forbes made many features—*Whistle Down the Wind* (1961), *The L-Shaped Room* (1963), *Seance on a Wet Afternoon* (1964), *King Rat* (1965), *The Wrong Box* (1966), *The Whisperers* (1967), *Deadfall* (1967), and *The Raging Moon* (1970)—that demonstrate a remarkably subtle sense of atmosphere and *mise-en-scène*. He continued to work sporadically in the 1970s and 1980s, producing the satiric science-fiction/horror hybrid *The Stepford Wives* (1975), now a minor classic, and a charming musical version of "Cinderella" in *The Slipper and the Rose* (1976), shot on location in Austria. The more traditional Dearden, whose archetypal British police thriller *The Blue Lamp* (1949) won numerous awards and made Dirk Bogarde a star, also directed *Sapphire* (1959), *The League of Gentlemen* (1960), *The Mind Benders* (1963), and *Khartoum* (1966). Also of interest is the work of Ronald Neame (b. 1911)—*The Horse's Mouth* (1958), *Tunes of Glory* (1960), *The Prime of Miss Jean Brodie*

---

6. Dearden's son, James (b. 1949), also directs. His first feature was the psychological thriller *The Cold Room* (1984), and he has since directed *Pascali's Island* (1988) and *A Kiss before Dying* (1991).

(1969).[7] During the same years, the television director Peter Watkins (b. 1935) made two brilliant pseudodocumentary films for the BBC—*Culloden* (1964), a historical re-creation of the bloody suppression of the 1746 Jacobite rebellion, and *The War Game* (1965), a projection of what would happen to Britain in the aftermath of a nuclear attack. The BBC refused to broadcast *The War Game*, and it was banned from television internationally for the next twenty years.[8] Watkins's first theatrical feature, *Privilege* (1967), offered a strikingly original vision of England as a totalitarian state but could not be compared with his television work. His more sophisticated *Punishment Park* (1971) depicted a fascist America in the wake of the Vietnam War. And his *Edvard Munch* (1974, 1976) used documentary techniques to dramatize the life, milieu, and creative agonies of the Norwegian Expressionist painter.[9] After a decade of making docudramas in Sweden and Denmark (e.g., *Fallan* [*The Trap*, 1975]; *Aftenlandet* [*Evening Land*, 1977]), Watkins produced his fourteen-and-one-half-hour "Film for Peace," *The Journey* (1987), an epic documentary on the arms race and the threat of nuclear holocaust. Shot between 1984 and 1986 in sixteen countries on five continents and in eight separate languages, *The Journey* was the result of an extraordinary international fund-raising effort begun in 1981. Watkins's most recent work is the six-hour-long semi-documentary *La Commune (Paris, 1871)*, released in 2001; it offers a CNN-like account of the creation and violent suppression of the proto-Marxist Paris Commune following the French defeat in the Franco-Prussian War of 1870. The British stage director Peter Brook (b. 1925) made several fine films during the 1960s, including versions of William Golding's novel *Lord of the Flies* (1962), of Peter Weiss's drama *Marat/Sade* (1966), and of Shakespeare's *King Lear* (1969; released 1971), as well as *Tell Me Lies* (1967), a bitter and incisive polemic against American involvement in Vietnam. Brook subsequently has produced *Meetings with Remarkable Men* (1979); an odd three-cast version of Bizet's *Carmen* (*La Tragédie de Carmen*, 1983), adapted from his own Paris stage hit; and *The Mahabharata* (1989), a lengthy version of the great Hindu epic whose interpolation, the *Bhagavadgita*, is "the Song of God." Also notable was a film directed by Kevin Brownlow (b. 1938) and Andrew Mollo (b. 1930), the independently produced *It Happened Here* (1964; released 1966), a "documentary" reconstruction of an imagined German occupation of England during World War II.[1]

British cinema was further enhanced in the 1960s and 1970s by the presence of two American expatriates,

---

7. The films made in the 1970s and 1980s by both Forbes and Neame, the majority for American studios, were uneven but demonstrated skilled craftsmanship. Forbes made *The Stepford Wives* (1975), *The Slipper and the Rose—Story of Cinderella* (1976), *International Velvet* (1978), *Sunday Lovers* (1980), *Better Late Than Never* (1983), and *The Naked Face* (1984); Neame directed *Scrooge* (1970; a musical based on Dickens's *A Christmas Carol*), *The Poseidon Adventure* (1972), *The Odessa File* (1974), *Meteor* (1978), *Hopscotch* (1980), *First Monday in October* (1981), and *Foreign Body* (1986).

8. After months of debate, the BBC did permit the film to be released theatrically in 1966; it won the American Academy Award for Best Documentary Feature. The BBC finally televised *The War Game* on July 31, 1985, as part of a week's programs commemorating the fortieth anniversary of the destruction of Hiroshima (the film had originally been scheduled to commemorate the twentieth).

9. Originally produced for Norwegian television, *Edvard Munch* was first telecast in Sweden and Norway in November 1974 with a running time of 210 minutes; the theatrical version distributed in the United States in 1976 was cut to 167 minutes.

1. Since that time, Brownlow and Mollo have made only one other film together, *Winstanley* (1975), another "imaginary documentary" based on David Caute's novel about the seventeenth-century English Digger movement. Brownlow, of course, is also a prominent film historian whose numerous books (e.g., *The Parade's Gone By*, 1968), reconstructions (e.g., Abel Gance's 1927 epic *Napoléon*—see Chapter 9), and compilation films (e.g., *The Unknown Chaplin*, 1985—see Chapter 6) have greatly enhanced our understanding of the silent era. But unlike *It Happened Here*, which was personally financed by the filmmakers and took seven years to complete, *Winstanley* was subsidized by the British Film Institute (BFI) Production Board. Since the mid-1960s, this institution has made limited funds available to independent filmmakers such as Don Levy (b. 1932—*Herostratus*, 1967); American-born Stephen Dwoskin (b. 1939—*Central Bazaar*, 1976); David Gladwell (*Requiem for a Village*, 1974); Peter Smith (*A Private Enterprise*, 1974); and Nick Broomfield and Joan Churchill (*Juvenile Liaison*, 1975). The first truly impressive work made with BFI support was Bill Douglas's (1937–1991) autobiographical trilogy *My Childhood* (1972), *My Ain Folk* (1974), and *My Way Home* (1978) that some critics feel was the greatest achievement of British cinema in the 1970s. (See p. 000, n. 00.) The first feature-length BFI production was Richard Woolley's metaphysical murder mystery *Brothers and Sisters* (1980); but the most ambitious BFI project by far (also funded in part by the private national broadcasting network Channel Four) was Peter Greenaway's strikingly original *The Draughtsman's Contract* (1982). Other recent productions funded in whole or part by the BFI include *Doll's Eve* (Jan Worth, 1983), *Ascendancy* (Edward Bennett, 1983), *1919* (Hugh Brody, 1984), and *The Terence Davies Trilogy* (Terence Davies, 1984).

Joseph Losey (1909–1984) and Richard Lester (b. 1932). Losey, who became a British citizen after being hounded out of Hollywood during the McCarthy era, produced some of the most significant British films of the decade in collaboration with absurdist playwright Harold Pinter (b. 1930). These included *The Servant* (1963); *Accident* (1967); and *The Go-Between* (1971), adapted from the novel by L. P. Hartley. A subtle stylist whose major themes are the destructiveness of the erotic impulse and the corrupting nature of technocracy, Losey also produced such important work as *Eva* (also known as *Eve*, 1962), a decadent melodrama about a phony novelist's attraction toward an archetypal *femme fatale*, shot on location in Rome and Venice by two of the world's then-greatest cinematographers (Henri Decaë and Gianni Di Venanzo), and the remarkable antiwar drama *King and Country* (1964), set in the trenches of World War I, which features superb performances by two iconic actors of British New Cinema, Tom Courtenay and Dirk Bogarde. Losey's films of the 1970s were *The Assassination of Trotsky* (1972); a version of Henrik Ibsen's *A Doll's House* (1973); *The*

Romantic Englishwoman (1975), an elegant and witty film about modern marriage scripted by the playwright Tom Stoppard; *Mr. Klein* (1976), a study of anti-Semitism in Occupied France; a version of Mozart's opera *Don Giovanni* (1979), shot on location in northern Italy; and *Les Routes du sud* (*Roads of the South*, 1979), an intimate portrait of a father-son relationship set in rural France that contains autobiographical elements. The director's final works were the visually riveting *La Truite* (*The Trout*, 1982), based on an existential novel by Roger Vailland, and *Steaming* (1985), an adaptation of Nell Dunn's ebulliently feminist stage play.

Richard Lester directed several award-winning shorts, notably *The Running, Jumping, and Standing Still Film* (1960)[2] and *The Mouse on the Moon* (1963; a sequel to Jack Arnold's *The Mouse That Roared*, 1959), before he came to fame and fortune through his two Beatles films, *A Hard Day's Night* (1964) and *Help!* (1965), which employ the full cinematic arsenal of the New Wave—telephoto zooms and swoops, flashbacks, jump cuts, and every conceivable device of narrative displacement—to create a dazzling new kind of audiovisual comedy. His subsequent films—*The Knack* (1965), *How I Won the War* (1967), *Petulia* (1968), and *The Bed Sitting Room* (1969)—use the same techniques to more serious dramatic purpose, often with less success, though *Petulia*'s disjointed narrative style works perfectly to embody the psychological disintegration of its principal characters. During the 1970s, Lester directed the highly successful swashbucklers *The Three Musketeers* (1973), *The Four Musketeers* (1975), and *Royal Flash* (1975); the historical romance *Robin and Marian* (1976); an adaptation of the Broadway comedy *The Ritz* (1977); the comic Western "prequel" *Butch and Sundance: The Early Days* (1979); and *Cuba* (1979), a political thriller set in the last days of the Batista regime. His films in the 1980s included two entries in the *Superman* cycle, *Superman II* (1980) and

14.14 *The Servant* **(Joseph Losey, 1963): Dirk Bogarde, James Fox.**

2. Featured in this Lester short were the Goons—Peter Sellers, Spike Milligan, and Harry Secombe—stars of the long-running BBC radio hit *The Goon Show*, which paved the way for the upsurge of brilliant British comedies in the 1950s and 1960s. Some examples are Frank Launder's "St. Trinian's" series, with Alastair Sim (*The Belles of St. Trinian's*, 1954; *Blue Murder at St. Trinian's*, 1957; *The Pure Hell of St. Trinian's*, 1960); *The Wrong Arm of the Law* (Cliff Owen, 1962) and *Heavens Above* (Roy Boulting, 1963), both starring Sellers; *Bedazzled* (Stanley Donen, 1967), featuring Peter Cook and Dudley Moore, etc., right up through Monty Python, who very clearly inherited the Goons' mantle.

14.15 An archetypal image of the 1960s: the Beatles in *A Hard Day's Night* (Richard Lester, 1964).

Superman III (1983), the caper farce *Finders Keepers* (1984), and the final installment of his Musketeers trilogy, *The Return of the Musketeers* (1989), which combines the casts of the two earlier films. *Get Back* (1991) was a fairly straightforward documentary on Paul McCartney's worldwide tour of that year.

THE END OF SOCIAL REALISM AND BEYOND

In the late 1960s, with the decline of social realism and the increasing influence of American investment in the now lucrative British cinema (90 percent by 1968), the distinctly national flavor of British films was lost. Many American directors (such as Billy Wilder, Richard Fleischer, Sidney Lumet, Delbert Mann, Stanley Donen, George Stevens, Otto Preminger, Anthony Mann, Richard Brooks, William Wyler, Fred Zinnemann, John Huston, and Stanley Kubrick) came to work in British studios during these years, as did such major Continental figures as Roman Polanski (*Repulsion*, 1965; *Cul-de-sac*, 1966); François Truffaut (*Fahrenheit 451*, 1966); and Michelangelo Antonioni (*Blow-Up*, 1966). Furthermore, the British-based directors Richardson, Lester, and Schlesinger—as well as David Lean (*The Bridge on the River Kwai*, 1957; *Lawrence of Arabia*, 1962; *Dr. Zhivago*, 1965; *Ryan's Daughter*, 1970)[3] and Carol Reed (*The Agony and the Ecstasy*, 1965; *Oliver!*, 1968; *Flap*, 1970)— all began to make films within the American industry.

And Reisz (*Isadora*, 1968) and Forbes (*The Madwoman of Chaillot*, 1969) both became involved in big-budget international coproductions.

Nevertheless, in the late 1960s a new, more visually oriented generation of British directors began to appear. Some, like Clive Donner (b. 1926)—*The Caretaker* (1964), *Here We Go round the Mulberry Bush* (1967), *Rogue Male* (1976), *To Catch a King* (1984), *Stealing Heaven* (1988)—and Hungarian-born Peter Medak (b. 1937)—*Negatives* (1968), *A Day in the Death of Joe Egg* (1970), *The Ruling Class* (1972), *The Changeling* (1980), *The Men's Club* (1986), *The Krays* (1990), *Romeo Is Bleeding* (1993)—produced a handful of interesting films before going heavily commercial. Others, such as the former television directors Alan Bridges (b. 1927)—*The Hireling* (1973), *The Return of the Soldier* (1982), *The Shooting Party* (1984)—and Ken Loach (b. 1936)—*Poor Cow* (1967), *Kes* (1969), *Family Life* (1972), *Black Jack* (1979), *The Gamekeeper* (1980)—sacrificed popularity to integrity, with the austerely analytical work of Loach proving especially influential.

Loach, who is often labeled a social realist, worked only sporadically during the 1980s (as did many left-wing critics of Thatcherism) but experienced a genuine renewal in the 1990s, first with the documentary-like political thriller *Hidden Agenda* (1990). This film, which is set against the backdrop of war-torn Northern Ireland, won the 1990 Jury Prize at Cannes, and it was followed by *Riff Raff* (1991) and *Raining Stones* (1993), both of them more humorous treatments of working-class strife, which also won awards at Cannes (the 1991 International Critics Prize and the 1993 Jury Prize, respectively). Loach's social commitment remained on dramatic display through the end of the century—*Ladybird Ladybird* (1994) is a docudrama about a single mother's battle with the British social-service system to retain custody of her children; *Land and Freedom* (1995) concerns the internal divisions among Loyalist freedom fighters during the Spanish Civil War; and *Carla's Song* (1996) is a love story set in the context of the Nicaraguan revolution. Later Loach films have dealt with the life of a recovering alcoholic in working-class Glasgow (*My Name Is Joe* [1998]),

---

3. Lean returned to directing after an absence of fourteen years with his beautifully restrained adaptation of E. M. Forster's *A Passsage to India* (1984), which he wrote and edited himself.

a janitors' strike in contemporary Los Angeles (*Bread and Roses* [2000]), and the social dislocation produced by the privatization of British Rail (*The Navigators* [2001]).

Perhaps the most significant directors of this generation, however, managed to combine both impulses in films that were commercially viable and at the same time formally significant. Peter Yates (b. 1929), a director known for his ability to combine action with an intelligent exploration of character, has worked in America since the success of *Bullitt* in 1968 (producing, e.g., such fine films as *The Friends of Eddie Coyle* [1973] and *Breaking Away* [1979], and such uneven ones as *The Deep* [1977], *Eyewitness* [1981], and *Krull* [1983]), but he returned to British themes with *The Dresser* (1984), a film about the last performance of an aging provincial actor, and to international ones in the politically controversial *Eleni* (1985), based on Nicholas Gage's true account of his search for the men who killed his mother during the Greek civil war. Recent Yates successes have been thrillers like *Suspect* (1987), *The House on Carroll Street* (1988), and *Year of the Comet* (1992). In 1995, Yates and his son Toby co-directed *The Run of the Country*, a tale of star-crossed young lovers whose families are at odds across Ireland's north-south divide, shot on location in County Cavan.

John Boorman (b. 1933) also scored his first successes in the United States with *Point Blank* (1967), *Hell in the Pacific* (1969), and *Deliverance* (1972), returning briefly to England to make *Leo the Last* (1970), a contemporary revolutionary allegory for which he won the Director's Prize at Cannes. Shooting on location in Ireland, he confirmed his taste for esoteric subjects in the mythical science-fiction epic *Zardoz* (1974), which he also wrote and produced, and, in the United States once more, the disappointing *Exorcist II—The Heretic* (1977). Next,

however, Boorman produced an authentically British masterpiece, *Excalibur* (1981), also shot in Ireland, an intellectually and visually powerful retelling of the Arthurian legend from the mystical perspective of Merlin. This ambitious project was followed by his most exotic work, *The Emerald Forest* (1985), which concerns the young son of an American engineer (played by Boorman's own son, Charley) raised by a primitive Amazonian tribe and the murderous clash of cultures that ensues when his father attempts to "rescue" him. In an unpredictable change of pace, Boorman delighted 1987 audiences with *Hope and Glory*, a richly detailed account of English middle-class family life during World War II that was derived from his own childhood experience. *Where the Heart Is* (1990) was notably less successful in its examination of homelessness in New York City, but *Beyond Rangoon* (1995) delivers a good deal more in its startling address of contemporary Burmese politics. Boorman won the Director's Prize at Cannes a second time for *The General* (1998), a biographical portrait of the flamboyant Irish gangster and folk hero Martin Cahill (superbly played by Brendan Gleeson) and the events leading up to

14.16 John Boorman's *Excalibur* (1981): Sir Lancelot (Nicholas Clay) swears allegiance to King Arthur (Nigel Terry).

his 1994 assassination by the IRA in front of his Dublin home, which he also wrote and produced; the film was shot in anamorphic widescreen and color by Irish cinematographer Seamus Deasy but printed on high-contrast black-and-white release stock. (This same technique was used three years later by British cinematographer Roger Deakins for the Coen brothers' *The Man Who Wasn't There* [2001].) In 2001, Boorman wrote, produced, and directed a finely nuanced adaptation of John Le Carré's satiric espionage thriller *The Tailor of Panama*, which is set amid the political intrigue surrounding the American takeover of the Panama Canal in late 1989.

The two most original British directors of the 1970s were undeniably Ken Russell and Nicolas Roeg. Russell (b. 1927) first attracted attention in the mid-1960s with a series of fictionalized biographies of composers, dancers, and poets flamboyantly directed for BBC-TV. International recognition came with his lavish theatrical adaptation of D. H. Lawrence's *Women in Love* (1969). This was followed by a series of controversial features— *The Music Lovers* (1971); *The Devils* (1971; adapted from John Whiting's play of the same title and Aldous Huxley's *The Devils of Loudun*); *The Boy Friend* (1972); *Savage Messiah* (1972); *Mahler* (1974); *Tommy* (1975, a version of the popular rock opera by The Who); *Lisztomania* (1975); *Valentino* (1977); and *Altered States* (1981)— which oscillated between the outrageously vulgar and the outrageously brilliant. Russell directed opera exclusively from 1982 through 1984 (including a spectacular updated version of Puccini's *Madama Butterfly* at the Spoleto Festival in Charleston, South Carolina, in 1983), before returning to features with *Gothic* (1987), an account of the stormy June night in 1816 at Lord Byron's villa in Switzerland which inspired both Dr. Polidori's *The Vampyre* and Mary Shelley's *Frankenstein*. Russell portrays the evening as a descent into orgiastic, drug-induced horror in which—as in all of his best work—the line between reality and fantasy is not simply blurred, but destroyed. The same atmosphere characterizes his rigorous adaptation of Oscar Wilde's banned *symboliste* drama *Salome* (1892), entitled *Salome's Last Dance* (1988). The film was brilliantly conceived by Russell in the form of a private, homoerotic performance staged for the author in a London brothel on the eve of his fateful arrest for sodomy. Equally inspired are *The Lair of the White Worm* (1988), a hilarious send-up of British class values, kinky sex, and 1960s Hammer horror films, freely adapted by Russell

14.17 David Bowie as *The Man Who Fell to Earth* (Nicolas Roeg, 1976).

from Bram Stoker's last novel (1905), and a lushly romantic adaptation of *The Rainbow* (1989), Lawrence's novelistic "prequel" to *Women in Love*. *Whore* (1991) was less successful in its first-person account of the life of a London streetwalker as manically depicted by Theresa Russell. Since that time, Russell has mainly directed for television, where his talent for making the most of small budgets is keenly appreciated.

Less flamboyant than Russell, but quite as unique, Nicolas Roeg (b. 1928) began his career as a cinematographer for Lester, Schlesinger, Truffaut, and others before co-directing *Performance* (1968; released 1970) with Donald Cammell.[4] Like his other films of the decade—*Walkabout* (1971); *Don't Look Now* (1973); *The Man Who Fell to Earth* (1976); and *Bad Timing* (1979)— it was cut by distributors to make it more accessible to the public and exists in several versions. Often experimental in form, Roeg's beautiful and enigmatic films go far beyond narrative to immerse the viewer in a fluent stream of audiovisual images whose most legitimate meaning is their psychological affect. His subsequent films, however—*Eureka* (1983), *Insignificance* (1985), *Castaway* (1986), *Track 29* (1988), *The Witches* (1990)— have taken slightly more conventional narrative forms. An example of Roeg's recent work is *Two Deaths* (1996), a

---

4. Cammell has directed only two other features—*The Demon Seed* (1977) and *White of the Eye* (1987)—both thrillers of unusual interest.

psychological drama set at a dinner party in Bucharest on the night that Romania's Communist dictator, Nicolae Ceausescu, was deposed in a bloody coup.

After Russell and Roeg, the most influential British director of the past decade has probably been Ridley Scott (b. 1937), a former set designer and television-commercial director whose first feature, *The Duellists* (1977), adapted from a short story by Joseph Conrad, won high praise at Cannes in the year of its release. Scott's next film was the smash hit *Alien* (1979), made for 20th Century–Fox in the United States and hailed as a minor

14.18 *Alien* **(Ridley Scott, 1979): John Hurt finds an egg chamber in the hull of a derelict ship. Production design based on drawings by H. R. Giger.**

masterpiece of science fiction and visceral horror. He mixed science fiction and *film noir* with the same effectiveness in the technically dazzling *Blade Runner* (1982), based on Philip K. Dick's 1968 genre classic *Do Androids Dream of Electric Sheep?*, but his British-produced fantasy *Legend* (1985) was a critical failure and for its 1986 release in the United States was cut by twenty minutes.[5] Nevertheless, Scott's stylish thriller *Someone to Watch over Me* (1987) was among the most successful entries in the *film noir* cycle of the late 1980s, and *Black Rain* (1989) was a complex fusion of American police thriller and Japanese *yakuza* film shot on location in Osaka that commented reflexively on the growing influence of the Japanese in U.S. corporate life. Scott began the 1990s by producing an artistically successful but socially ambiguous essay in pop feminism in *Thelma & Louise* (1991) and an epic box-office disaster in *1492: Conquest of Paradise* (1992), one of two films made to commemorate the five-hundredth anniversary of Columbus's discovery of America (the other was John Glen's *Christopher Columbus: The Discovery*). Neither *White Squall* (1996), a boys' adventure story with a tragic twist, nor *G.I. Jane* (1997), a fictionalized account of the first woman to receive combat training as a Navy SEAL, were sufficiently successful to redeem the failure of *1492*, which lost $40 million. But

Gladiator (2000) was a huge commercial and critical success, grossing $188 million against its $103 million budget, and winning four Academy Awards, including Best Picture; it was also a landmark in the history of digital effects and put Scott in the vanguard of directors like Steven Spielberg, Paul Verhoeven, and Michael Bay, who regularly integrate live action with computer-generated imagery (see Chapter 21). Scott's *Hannibal* (2001), a sequel to Jonathan Demme's *Silence of the Lambs* (1991), adapted from Thomas Harris's controversial novel (the third in his Red Dragon series), was a deliberate exercise in theatrical Grand Guignol, but *Black Hawk Down* (2001) had the immediacy of a *cinéma-vérité* newscast in recounting an American recovery mission gone wrong in Mogadishu, Somalia, during the UN's intervention in that nation's bloody civil war. Although his work sometimes lacks narrative cohesion, on a purely visual (and visceral)

---

5. The European version of *Legend* runs 109 minutes and has music by Jerry Goldsmith; the 89-minute American version has an electronic score by Tangerine Dream. In 2002, Universal Pictures released both versions on DVD with a commentary track by Scott and a host of supplemental materials. The European version is enhanced by 5 minutes of never-before-seen footage so that it now officially becomes Scott's "director's cut."

14.19 Ridley Scott's futuristic *film noir Blade Runner* (1982), an American release.

14.20 Harrison Ford stalks rebellious replicants in Los Angeles, c. 2020.

level Scott remains one of the most engaging filmmakers working in the Anglo-American industry today.

Scott is one of several directors who came to work in the American industry in the late 1970s from British "new wave" television advertising and documentary. The most consistently successful has been Alan Parker (b. 1944), whose first feature, *Bugsy Malone* (1976), a musical spoof of gangster films using an all-child cast, was followed by the harrowing *Midnight Express* (1978), which won Academy Awards for its screenplay (Oliver Stone) and score (Giorgio Morode). Parker's other work has been equally original—*Fame* (1980), *Shoot the Moon* (1982), *Pink Floyd—The Wall* (1982), *Birdy* (1984), the controversial *noir* shocker *Angel Heart* (1987), which he also scripted, and the equally controversial *Mississippi Burning* (1988), based on a 1964 FBI investigation into the murders of three civil rights workers in the deep South. More recently Parker has directed *Come See the Paradise* (1990), a powerful drama based on the U.S. government's internment of Japanese Americans during World War II, and *The Commitments* (1991), a dazzling film about the fortunes of a 1990s Dublin working-class band that plays 1960s-style soul music. After *The Road to Wellville* (1994), based on a comic novel about the real-life holistic health spa established by Dr. John Harvey Kellogg, the creator of Corn Flakes, Parker scored a solid box-office and critical hit with *Evita* (1996), a lavish musical biography of Argentine folk hero Eva Perón, adapted from Andrew Lloyd Webber's stage hit, written and produced by Parker, and photographed by the masterful Iranian-born cinematographer Darius Khondji (b. 1955). Parker's adaptation of *Angela's Ashes* (1999), Frank McCourt's Pulitzer Prize–winning memoir of growing up poor in Limerick, Ireland, was considerably grimmer and lost money accordingly.

The prolific Michael Apted (b. 1941) began as a director of documentaries for BBC television and started making features for David Puttnam's Goldcrest Company in the mid-1970s (see below). He scored his first American success with *Coal Miner's Daughter* (1980), a strikingly intelligent and socially aware biography of country singer Loretta Lynn, for which Sissy Spacek won the Academy Award for Best Actress. The film was also a box-office hit, earning nearly $79 million, and Apted followed it with *Gorky Park* (1983), a version of Martin Cruz Smith's bestselling police thriller set in pre-glasnost Moscow (for which location shooting in Helsinki provided a credible replica). Many of Apted's later features took a similar form—i.e., that of the carefully observed commercial thriller; *Firstborn* (1984), *Class Action* (1991), *Thunderheart* (1992), *Blink* (1994), *Extreme Measures* (1996), *Enigma* (2001), and *Enough* (2002) all fit this description. He has also made successful comedies (*Continental Divide* [1981], *Critical Condition* [1987]) and such prestige productions as *Gorillas in the Mist* (1988), the life story of the murdered anthropologist Dian Fossey, and *Nell*, (1994), a drama about the socialization of a "wild child" found living in primitive conditions in the North Carolina backwoods. But Apted's commitment to documentary form and ethnographic method is long and deep:

in 1963 with *Seven Up* he began a series of films about the lives, thoughts, and attitudes of fourteen seven-year-olds from all strata of London society, with the idea of reassembling them for continuing interviews every seven years. So far, he has completed *Seven Plus Seven* (1970) *21 Up* (1977), *28 Up* (1984), *35 Up* (1991), and *42 Up* (1998), and the project continues. (Starting in 1991, he became the executive producer for *7-Up in America*, which has so far extended to *14 Up in America* [1998].)

Adrian Lyne (b. 1941), like Alan Parker, began his career directing television commercials and in his first features adopted the style of music video, so that *Foxes* (1980) and *Flashdance* (1982) looked as if they might have been made for MTV. He developed a reputation for stylish eroticism in the wake of *9½ Weeks* (1986), which was released in both R-rated and unrated versions. In the same vein, Lyne produced *Fatal Attraction* (1987), which became the third highest-grossing film of the year with its stylish, high-energy tale of a weekend fling gone wrong. (Like *9½ Weeks*, *Fatal Attraction* was released in two versions—one with a happy ending tacked on after principal photography to satisfy the desire of preview audiences, and the other with the original, downbeat ending for release on video.) The success of Lyne's erotic thrillers led him toward projects that exploited sexual content (*Indecent Proposal* [1993]) but also toward films that treated sexuality in a mature and serious way, such as *Lolita* (1997), his admirable adaptation of Vladimir Nabokov's novel of pedophilic desire, and *Unfaithful* (2002), a contemporary film of adultery inspired by Claude Chabrol's *La Femmme infidèle* (1969). But Lyne's most important work to date is unquestionably *Jacob's Ladder* (1989), in which a troubled Vietnam War veteran (brilliantly portrayed by Tim Robbins) tries to come to terms with a nightmarish, but seemingly irretrievable, battlefield memory. The film is masterfully directed in a way that combines acute social observation with arresting visuals and supernatural horror.

Tony Scott (b. 1944), Ridley's younger brother, entered features with the stylishly erotic vampire film *The Hunger* (1983), which proved his ability to manufacture slick, attention-getting images. Tony then teamed up with blockbuster producers Don Simpson and Jerry Bruckheimer to make what became the highest-grossing film of 1986 and the second of 1987, *Top Gun* and *Beverly Hills Cop II*, respectively. After *Top Gun*, it was difficult for Scott to break out of the military mold, and some of

his most successful features have either reworked the plot elements of that film in other terms (e.g., *Days of Thunder* [1990], where the naval air-station flight school becomes the NASCAR driving circuit) or had similar military settings and themes (*Crimson Tide* [1995], *Enemy of the State* [1998]). Scott continued to work with Bruckheimer after Simpson died in 1996, and he has moved increasingly into the role of executive producer himself (e.g., of *The Hunger* TV series) via his own company, Scott Free Productions.

Another source of vitality in British cinema has been the work of the multitalented comedy team Monty Python (essentially, the performers John Cleese, Michael Palin, Eric Idle, and Graham Chapman; writer-director Terry Jones [b. 1942]; and American-born animator-director Terry Gilliam [b. 1940]). Their first film, *And Now for Something Completely Different* (Gilliam and Ian McNaughton, 1979) was merely a collection of sketches derived from their popular BBC-TV series *Monty Python's Flying Circus*, but *Monty Python and the Holy Grail* (Jones and Gilliam, 1975) was a wholly original parody of the Arthurian romance that also managed to convey the look and feel of the Middle Ages in a convincing way. The same was true of Gilliam's version of Lewis Carroll's *Jabberwocky* (1977) and, in Biblical terms, of Jones's irreverent and controversial *Monty Python's Life of Brian* (1979), which was the first production of the independent company Handmade Films. Handmade, whose chairman was ex-Beatle George Harrison (1943–2001), was later responsible for Gilliam's *Time Bandits* (1981), a bizarre fantasy in which six dwarfs romp through history, and such other comic work as *The Missionary* (Richard Loncraine, 1982), *Bullshot* (Dick Clement, 1983), and *A Private Function* (Malcolm Mowbray, 1984), as well as more serious films like John Mackenzie's *The Long Good Friday* (1980; distribution only), Mai Zetterling's *Scrubbers* (1984), and Neil Jordan's *Mona Lisa* (1986). The Python group itself was featured in the omnibus *Monty Python's The Meaning of Life* (Terry Jones, 1983), and Terry Gilliam went on to direct for Handmade the darkly brilliant *Brazil* (1985), which posits an alternately absurd and terrifying distopia in Britain's near future, for Columbia the phantasmagorical *The Adventures of Baron Munchausen* (1989), a dazzling if somewhat empty display of pyrotechnics rumored to have cost over $50 million (but whose actual costs were probably closer to $40 million), and, for TriStar, a seriocomic

14.21 *Monty Python's Life of Brian* (Terry Jones, 1979). Graham Chapman as Brian, fleeing the Romans and about to land on the head of Michael Palin in a Judean marketplace.

14.22 Britain as nightmare state: Terry Gilliam's *Brazil* (1985). Jonathan Pryce.

return to the grail legend in *The Fisher King* (1991). Gilliam's *Twelve Monkeys* (1995) was a convoluted, feature-length remake of Chris Marker's short, poetic film about time travel, *La Jetée* (1962), while *Fear and Loathing in Las Vegas* (1998), adapted Hunter Thompson's hallucinogenic paean to psychotropic drugs and "gonzo journalism" as if it were one long, nightmarish acid trip.

In the realm of the narrative avant-garde, several British filmmakers became prominent during the 1980s, most notably Peter Greenaway (b. 1943), whose early structural films (*A Walk through H,* 1978; *Vertical Features Remake,* 1978) and the three-hour absurdist fantasia *The Falls* (1981) won the support of the British Film Institute (BFI) and Channel 4 for his enigmatic medium-budget

feature *The Draughtsman's Contract* (1982). Set in an English country house in 1694, this densely allusive work about the relationships among artists, patrons, and spectators is cast in the form of a metaphysical murder mystery. In 1984, Greenaway, whose regular cinematographer was Sacha Vierny (1919–2001), directed a pair of documentaries profiling American avant-garde composers (*Modern American Composers I* and *II*). He returned to feature work with the uncompromisingly intellectual *A Zed and Two Noughts* (1985), or "Z-O-O," which is about twin zoologists who become obsessed with the process of postmortem decay, various aspects of which they record using time-lapse photography, the display of which comprises a significant portion of the film. Since that time, Greenaway has alternated between more accessible and (in a narrative sense) conventional films like *The Belly of an Architect* (1987), *Drowning by Numbers* (1988), and *The Cook, the Thief, His Wife, and Her Lover* (1989), and works of a more nonlinear, painterly form—e.g., *Prospero's Books* (1991), a version of Shakespeare's *The Tempest*, and *The Pillow Book* (1996), which takes the form of erotic poetry literally "written on the body." In these more experimental films, Greenaway has increasingly made use of electronic paintbox programs to integrate his photographic material with new layers of digital imagery.

The former painter and set designer for Ken Russell (*Savage Messiah; The Devils*), Derek Jarman (1942–1994) burst upon the avant-garde scene with *Sebastiane* (1976), a profane, homoerotic account of the famous saint and martyr that was performed in Latin, with English subtitles and a Brian Eno score. *Jubilee* (1977) offered a vision of anarchic social breakdown to mark both the royal Jubilee and Britain's "Summer of Punk." Jarman's version of Shakespeare's *The Tempest* (1979), shot in the fire-gutted ruins of a Warwickshire estate, was an overwhelming critical success. The same was true of his richly imagined biography *Caravaggio* (1986), which re-created Renaissance Italy on the London docks to project the life of the influential painter (1573–1610) who, among his other achievements, is said to have invented chiaroscuro lighting. *The Last of England* (1987) is a bleak comedy about life in the ruins of empire inventively shot in Super 8mm. But Jarman's *War Requiem* (1988) is a stunning visualization of Benjamin Britten's oratorio made for the BBC on the (relatively) enormous budget of $1.2 million. Jarman completed four more extraordinary films—*The Garden* (1990), *Edward II* (1991; adapted from the tragedy by Christopher Marlowe), *Wittgenstein* (1993), and *Blue* (1993)—before dying of AIDS in 1994.

Much of the work discussed above was financed, in various combinations, by the producer David Puttnam (b. 1941), the British film and television investment company Goldcrest, and the independent television network Channel 4. Puttnam produced early films by Ken Russell, Alan Parker, Michael Apted, Ridley Scott, and Adrian Lyne before producing an international hit, the Oscar-winning *Chariots of Fire* (Hugh Hudson, 1981). Subsequently, he produced Bill Forsyth's Scottish-American comedy *Local Hero* (1982), the Irish-based *Cal* (Pat O'Connor, 1984), and, for his Enigma Company, *The Killing Fields* (Roland Joffe, 1984) and *The Mission* (Roland Joffe, 1986). Both of the latter films received American Academy Awards for Chris Menges's cinematography, and *The Mission* also won the Golden Palm at Cannes; they brought Puttnam to the attention of Columbia Pictures Industries, Inc., where he served a brief term as chairman from 1986 to 1987 before returning to England. Most of these films also were backed by Goldcrest, as were the films in Puttnam's *First Love* series—e.g., Gavin Millar's *Secrets* (1984), which premiered on Channel 4. In addition, Goldcrest funded in whole or part such notable non-Puttnam productions as Richard Attenborough's *Gandhi* (1982), which swept

the Oscars for the year of its release; Marek Kanievska's *Another Country* (1984); Julien Temple's *Absolute Beginners* (1986); and Attenborough's *Cry Freedom* (1987).[6]

Launched in 1980 to provide alternative programming, Channel 4 has become the fourth largest national television network in Britain, after the two BBC services and the advertiser-supported Independent Television (ITV). Unlike the other networks, however, Channel 4 produces no programs of its own but commissions production companies for original work. In this way, it provided funding for such important low- and medium-budget features as Jerzy Skolimowski's *Moonlighting* (1981; see Chapter 16); Peter Greenaway's *The Draughtsman's Contract* (1982); Neil Jordan's *Angel* (Ireland; 1982); Richard Eyre's *The Ploughman's Lunch* (1983); Michael Radford's *Another Time, Another Place* (1983); David Hare's *Wetherby* (1985); Chris Bernard's *Letter to Brezhnev* (1985); Stephen Frears's *My Beautiful Laundrette* (1985); Mike Newell's *Dance with a Stranger* (1985); James Ivory and Ishmail Merchant's *Heat and Dust* (1983), *Room with a View* (1986), and *Maurice* (1987); Peter Ormrod's *Eat the Peach* (Ireland; 1987); and Alex Cox's *Sid and Nancy* (1986), giving the lie to Alison Pearson's axiom that "the British make great television and lousy films" by combining the best attributes of both. Channel 4 coproduced as well some non-British films like Gregory Nava's *El Norte* (1983), Wim Wenders's *Paris, Texas* (1984), Andrei Tarkovsky's *The Sacrifice* (1986), and Mrinal Sen's *Genesis* (1986). In the late 1980s, Channel 4 was the single largest producer of independent features in England and a major force in the cultural life of the nation, functioning on a par with West Germany's ZDF and Italy's RAI.

Like the French New Wave, from which it partially sprang, the British social-realist cinema disappeared along with the social context that had motivated it. But

6. The commercial failure of several recent Goldcrest-financed films—Puttnam's *The Mission, Absolute Beginners,* and *Revolution* (Hugh Hudson, 1986)—has forced the company to concentrate mainly on distribution and sales. Hemdale Films, a tiny firm when it was founded in 1967, has moved to fill the vacuum in creative production by buying the American rights to major British independent films like *Defence of the Realm* (David Drury, 1985) and *In the Belly of an Architect* (Greenaway, 1987), and financing such unconventional American work as *The Terminator* (James Cameron, 1984), *At Close Range* (James Foley, 1986), and *Salvador* (Oliver Stone, 1986). Hemdale also provided one-third of the financing ($7 million) for Bernardo Bertolucci's *The Last Emperor* (1987).

14.23 Alex Cox's *Sid and Nancy* (1986): Chloe Webb, Gary Oldman.

its formal and thematic legacy to British national cinema was great. It bequeathed the then-radical stylistic conventions of the New Wave to a cinema stagnant with armchair narrative traditions carried over from the prewar era. And in its new concern for the aesthetics of everyday life and outspokenness about the dynamics of sex, class, and power in the postindustrial world, it gave the class-ridden, hidebound British film a vastly wider range of themes than it had ever known before. Social realism also produced a handful of important directors, like Lindsay Anderson, John Schlesinger, Tony Richardson, and Karel Reisz, and a new pool of international acting talent including young and previously unknown stars such as Albert Finney, Rita Tushingham, Rachel Roberts, Alan Bates, Tom Courtenay, Susannah York, Richard Harris, Oliver Reed, Michael Caine, David Warner, Julie Christie, Glenda Jackson, James Fox, Terence Stamp, David Hemmings, Michael York, Vanessa Redgrave, and Lynn Redgrave.

The fact that British film has rarely been a major force in world cinema is partially explained by America's domination of the English-language film market, and partially by the innate conservatism of British visual and aural culture. Satyajit Ray once said that the British are "temperamentally unsuited" to cinema, and François Truffaut claimed that the terms "cinema" and "Britain" were incompatible. As if to confirm this, the preponderance of successful British films in the later twentieth and early twenty-first century fall into a culturally conservative genre known as "heritage cinema," whose origins can be traced back to the patriotic (and, it now seems, Thatcherite) *Chariots of Fire* (1981). These are essentially period or costume dramas, which include adaptations from canonical works of national literature—in which the British are exceedingly rich—as well as historical reconstructions based on modern texts. In the former category are the works of Jane Austen (*Sense and Sensibility* [Ang Lee, 1995]; *Emma* [Douglas McGrath, 1996]; *Mansfield Park* [Patricia Rozema, 1999]), Charles Dickens (*Little Dorrit* [Christine Edzard, 1987]); the Brontës (*Wuthering Heights* [Peter Kosminsky, 1992]; *Jane Eyre* [Franco Zeffirelli, 1996]), Thomas Hardy (*Jude* [Michael Winterbottom, 1996]; *The Claim* [Winterbottom, 2001; from *The Mayor of Casterbridge*]), Henry James—by adoption (*The Portrait of a Lady* [Jane Campion, 1996]; *The Wings of the Dove* [Iain Softley, 1998]; *The Golden Bowl* [James Ivory, 2000]), Oscar Wilde (*An Ideal Husband* [Oliver Parker, 1999]; *The Importance of Being Earnest* [Oliver Parker, 2002]); Evelyn Waugh (*A Handful of Dust* [Charles Sturridge, 1988]); Virginia Woolf (*Mrs. Dalloway* [Marleen Gorris, 1997]), E. M. Forster (*A Passage to India* [David Lean, 1984]; *A Room with a View* [James Ivory, 1987]; *Where Angels Fear to Tread*, [Charles Sturridge, 1991]; *Howards End* [James Ivory, 1991]), and, above all, Shakespeare (Kenneth Branagh's *Henry V* [1989], *Much Ado about Nothing* [1993], and *Hamlet* [1996]; Adrian Noble's *A Midsummer Night's Dream* [1996]; Trevor Nunn's *Twelfth Night* [1996]; Michael Hoffman's *A Midsummer Night's Dream* [1999]; etc.). The category of historical reconstructions would include dramatized portraits of British royalty (*Lady Jane* [Trevor Nunn, 1985]; *The Madness of King George* [Nicholas Hytner, 1995]; *Mrs. Brown* [John Madden, 1997; about Queen Victoria]); adaptations from contemporary literature set in the past (*Heat and Dust* [James Ivory, 1982]; *White Mischief* [Michael Radford, 1987]; *The Remains of the Day* [James Ivory, 1993]; *Restoration* [Michael Hoffman, 1994]; *Angels & Insects* [Philip Haas, 1995]), political and literary biopics (*Gandhi* [Richard Attenborough, 1982]; *Shadowlands* [Richard Attenborough, 1993; about C. S. Lewis]; *Wilde* [Brian Gilbert, 1997], and, finally, period dramas based on original screenplays—e.g., *Another Country* (Marek Kanievska, 1984); *The Serpent's Kiss* (Philippe Rousselot, 1997); *The Governess* (Sandra Goldbacher, 1998); *Elizabeth* (Shekhar Kapur, 1998); and *Shakespeare in Love* (John Madden, 1998). Although there are exceptions (e.g., in the work of Campion, Rozema, and Gorris, above; and in Sally Potter's *Orlando* [1992], adapted from Virginia Woolf), most heritage films have conventionally structured narratives and conservative social attitudes as correlatives to their obsession with costume and decor. In their heavy reliance on *mise-en-scène*, their pictorialist camera style, and their fetishization of accurate period detail, heritage films can be best described as having a "museum aesthetic."[7] While the British seem to have invented the genre in its current form, it has an obvious precedent in the early German *Kostümfilm* (see Chapter 4), as well as in Hungarian director Alexander Korda's London Film costume spec-1930s (see Chapter 9); and it exists today in all the cinemas of Europe (very prominently, e.g., in France; see Chapter 13), where it is culturally aligned with a kind of post–Cold War retro nationalism.

Despite this conservatism, the spirit of New Cinema lives on in the work of a handful of directors who did their apprentice work under its major figures. Sometimes called "four Mikes and a Michael" (after *Four Weddings and a Funeral*, a popular film directed by one of them), Mike Figgis, Mike Leigh, Mike Hodges, Mike Newell, and Michael Radford have all made important contributions to the Anglo-American cinema. Most of them started out working in television and later found their way into film. Figgis (b. 1948) was trained as a musician, and he writes the score for most of his films. His debut feature, *Stormy Monday* (1988), was a gangster film set against the backdrop of a Newcastle jazz club, and *Internal Affairs* (1990), his American breakthrough, was an atmospheric neo-*noir* about a corrupt cop (brilliantly portrayed by Richard Gere). Although he has scored a number of commercial successes (e.g., *Leaving Las Vegas* [1995], for which Nicolas Cage won an Academy Award for Best Actor), Figgis's artistic commitment to the experimental extends throughout his career—from the mood-drenched *Liebestraum*

(1991) to his Super 16mm adaptation of Strindberg's Expressionist play *Miss Julie* (1999) to his digital video jigsaw puzzle *Time Code* (2000), in which four separate continuous story elements shot with four separate cameras run simultaneously on screen throughout the film.

Mike Leigh (b. 1943), who is often compared (invidiously, he believes) to Ken Loach, harks back to the "kitchen sink" realism of early New Cinema, although he has no specific ideological point of view. Trained in the theater, Leigh's films have tended to focus on the inherent absurdity of everyday life (e.g., *High Hopes* [1989]; *Life Is Sweet* [1991]), and his working methods valorize performance and improvisation over tightly organized scripts (although he rehearses from screenplays that he writes himself). Leigh was recognized as a major talent when *Naked* (1993), which follows the aimless wanderings of a young drifter (David Thewlis) through post-Thatcherite London, won the Best Director's Prize at Cannes and Thewlis won Best Actor. As with *Naked*, the key performances in the family melodrama *Secrets & Lies* (1996) were largely improvised, and the film won a host of international awards, most notably the Palm d'Or at Cannes and a Best Actress Award for Brenda Blethyn as a mother who must form an adult relationship with the biological daughter she had given up for adoption at birth. Leigh turned away from intimate character study in the buoyant *Topsy-Turvy* (1999), a biography of the comic-opera composers W. S. Gilbert and Arthur Sullivan, whose work was phenomenally popular with middle-class audiences in late Victorian Lon-

---

7. The term is from Andrew Higson, "Re-Presenting the National Past: Nostalgia and Pastiche in the Heritage Film," Ch. 7 in *Fires Were Started: British Cinema and Thatcherism* ed. Lester Friedman (Minneapolis: University of Minnesota Press, 1993). See also Sheldon Hall, "The Wrong Sort of Cinema: Refashioning the Heritage Film Debate," in *The British Cinema Book*, ed. Robert Murphy, 2nd ed. (London: British Film Institute, 2001); Pamela Church Gibson, "Fewer Weddings and More Funerals: Changes in the Heritage Film," Ch. 12 in *British Cinema of the 90s*, ed. Robert Murphy (London: British Film Institute, 2000); John Hill, "The Heritage Film: Issues and Debates," ch. 4 in John Hill, *British Cinema in the 1980s: Issues and Themes* (Oxford: Oxford University Press, 1999); Sarah Street, "Genres in Transition, 1970s–1990s," ch. 4 in Sarah Street, *British National Cinema* (London: Routledge, 1997); Amy Sargeant, "Making and Selling Heritage Culture," ch. 21 in Justine Ashby and Andrew Higson, *British Cinema, Past and Present* (London: Routledge, 2000); Andrew Higson, "The Heritage Film and British Cinema," ch. 15 in *Dissolving Views: Key Writings on British Cinema*, ed. Andrew Higson (London: Cassell, 1996); and John Caughie, with Kevin Rockett, *The Companion to British and Irish Cinema* (London: Cassell, 1996).

14.24 *Time code* (Mike Figgis, 2000): an experiment in digital video that pushes at the doorframes of perception.

don. Working with his team of regular collaborators—cinematographer Dick Pope, art directors Eve Stewart and John Bush, and costume designer Lindy Hemming (who won an Academy Award for the film)—from his own original screenplay, Leigh achieved a brilliant period reconstruction, complete with a staging of Gilbert and Sullivan's most famous operetta *The Mikado,* set in feudal Japan.

14.25 *Topsy-Turvy* (Mike Leigh, 1999): Jim Broadbent and Allan Corduner as the Victorian light-opera composers Gilbert and Sullivan.

Like Figgis, Mike Newell (b. 1942) started in television, producing the TV-movie *The Man in the Iron Mask* (1977) for Granada; released theatrically in the United States by Lord Grade's ITC, it attracted critical notice, and Newell was hired to direct the U.S./U.K. coproduction *The Awakening* (1980)—a big-budget horror film adapted from Bram Stoker's novel *The Jewel of the Seven Stars.* This was the beginning of a prolific career in directing features in many genres, but always with an edge of social commentary or moral probing. His most important film of the 1980s was *Dance with a Stranger* (1985), the story of the last woman to be executed in England (for murdering her upper-class lover), which contains a deft analysis of Britain's rigid caste system and the self-destructive power of obsessive love. During the 1990s, Newell became associated with romantic comedy through the success of *Enchanted April* (1992) and *Four Weddings and a Funeral* (1994), which had the dual distinction of introducing Hugh Grant (b. 1960) and becoming the most successful British film of all time, earning $244 million worldwide against a $6 million budget. Other major work by Newell includes *Donnie Brasco* (1997), a character study focusing on the divided loyalties that ensue when an undercover cop infiltrates the Mafia, and *Pushing Tin* (1999), an unusual film about the intense competition among stressed-out air-traffic controllers working the New York corridor. In addition to directing, Newell has many executive-producer credits to his name (e.g., Steven Soderbergh's *Traffic* [2000]).

Mike Hodges (b. 1932) had a career as a writer, producer, and director for BBC-TV before making his first feature *Get Carter* (1971), an ultraviolent gangster film starring Michael Caine, now considered to be one of the genre's best. (A 2000 remake directed by Stephen Kay and starring Sylvester Stallone only served to enhance the reputation of the original.) Hodges acquired a reputation for making tough genre thrillers in the 1970s (e.g., *The Terminal Man* [1974]) and then directed the campily hilarious *Flash Gordon* for Dino De Laurentiis in 1980. Scored with original rock music by Queen, this big-budget send-up of B-movie serials of the 1930s brought a colorful comic-strip aesthetic to the screen, complete with comic-book grammar and syntax, in a way that cannily anticipates later films like *Batman* (Tim Burton, 1989), *Dick Tracy* (Warren Beatty, 1990), *The Phantom* (Simon Wincer, 1996), and *Spider-Man*

14.26 *Dance with a Stranger* (Mike Newell, 1985): Miranda Richardson as Ruth Ellis, the last woman to be executed for murder in England. Fighting for her honor in the middle ground is Rupert Everett as David Blakeley, the lover she will later kill.

(Sam Raimi, 2002). Hodges continued to work in television, producing one very remarkable film, *Black Rainbow* (1989), about a phony spiritualist travelling the deep South who is suddenly visited with the real power precognition. Hodges worked intermittently during the 1990s and ended the decade strongly with *Croupier* (1998), a gloomy, morally complicated *film noir* about a writer who goes to work as a dealer in a casino and gets involved in a highly dangerous plan to rob it.

Michael Radford (b. 1950) worked as a documentary filmmaker until 1983, when he directed *Another Time, Another Place*, a drama of wartime romance set in the Scottish Highlands. He followed with an adaptation of George Orwell's *1984* (1984), which was Richard Burton's last film, and then

White Mischief (1987), based on a true story of adultery and murder among decadent British colonials in Kenya during the early years of World War II. Radford's greatest success came with *Il Postino* (*The Postman*, 1994), a film about the relationship between the exiled Chilean Nobel

14.27 *Four Weddings and a Funeral* (Mike Newell, 1994): Andie MacDowell, about to become the object of Hugh Grant's affection at wedding reception number one. This socially astute romantic comedy enjoyed worldwide popularity and became the highest-earning British film of all time.

14.28 *Get Carter* (Mike Hodges, 1971). Michael Caine (out of frame) prepares to exact vengeance on one of his brother's murderers. Originally rated "X" in the United States for violence and nudity (but later reclassified as "R"), *Get Carter* upped the ante on cynical amorality in the British gangster film.

Prize–winning poet Pablo Neruda (Philippe Noiret) and his postman (Massimo Troisi, who died of heart failure on the last day of the shoot), which takes place on a small island off the coast of Italy in the 1950s. The film, a remake of *Ardiente Paciencia* (*Burning Patience*, 1983) by the Portuguese director Antonio Skármeta, was nominated for an American Academy Award for Best Picture

in 1995, the first time that a foreign film had received that honor since Ingmar Bergman's *Cries and Whispers* in 1973 (and, like Bergman's film, *Il Postino* didn't win). Since then, Radford has made an urban crime thriller set in London (*B. Monkey* [1998]) and his first American feature, *Dancing at the Blue Iguana* (2000), which examines the lives of five exotic dancers and their attitudes toward their work.

Stephen Frears (b. 1941) came into the film industry as an assistant to Lindsay Anderson and Karel Reisz, for whom he worked until he directed his first feature, *Gumshoe* (1971), an homage to hard-boiled detective movies like *The Maltese Falcon* (John Huston [1941]) and *The Big Sleep* (Howard Hawks [1946]), containing resonances of both. In 1972 he joined BBC-TV and spent twelve years directing a series of impressive telefilms (e.g., the surreally violent *Bloody Kids* [1983]) and plays (including works by David Hare, Christopher Hampton, Tom Stoppard, and Alan Bennett) before making his next feature, *The Hit* (1984), a psychological thriller about two killers sent to Spain to murder a former associate. Then Frears directed *My Beautiful Laundrette* (1985) from a script by the Anglo-Pakistani novelist and playwright Hanif Kureishi (b. 1954), which became one of the defining docu-

14.29 *Flash Gordon* (Mike Hodges, 1980): the Nazi-esque throne room of Emperor Ming. This film set the style for using comic-book aesthetics in the adaptation of comic strips; compared to it, Richard Donner's *Superman: The Movie* (1978) looks like a documentary.

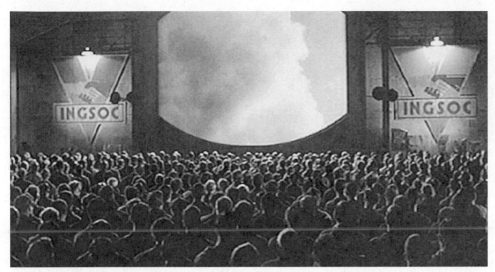

14.30 *1984* (Michael Radford, 1984): the totalitarian masses, waiting for Big Brother to appear and speak at the start of a workday.

and stardom to Day-Lewis. Next, Frears completed the long-cherished project *Prick Up Your Ears* (1987), scripted by Alan Bennett, from John Lahr's biography of murdered gay playwright Joe Orton (1933–1967), which gave Gary Oldman (b. 1958) his first starring role. Coming on the heels of these two oblique satires on British hypocrisy was a frontal assault on Maggie Thatcher's England that bordered on the polemical— *Sammy and Rosie Get Laid* (1988), also scripted by Kureishi. Then Frears was

ments of 1980s British cinema and urban life under the conservative Thatcher government. This modestly budgeted ($400,000) film, shot in 16mm and blown up to 35mm for theatrical distribution, stars Daniel Day-Lewis (b. 1957) as a racist youth from an East London slum who falls unexpectedly in love with a male Pakistani laundrette owner. An understated blend of ironic comedy and cultural politics, *My Beautiful Laundrette* was an unexpected hit, bringing critical acclaim to Frears and Kureishi (who won several awards for the screenplay) and

tapped by Hollywood to direct a big-budget version of Christopher Hampton's play *Dangerous Liaisons* (1988), based on Choderlos de Laclos's classic novel of sexual intrigue, *Les Liaisons Dangereuses* (1782). A film of uncharacteristic opulence and literate ensemble performances, *Dangerous Liaisons* won three Oscars (Screenplay, Art Direction, Costumes) and set Frears up to make *The Grifters* (1990), a down-and-dirty version of Jim Thompson's pulp thriller and his last film to find a popular audience for nearly a decade. A string of failures—*Hero*

14.31 *Dancing at the Blue Iguana* (Michael Radford, 2000): Daryl Hannah as one of five exotic dancers whose lives are examined in this partially improvised film, shot on digital video; and 14.32 *Mary Reilly* (Stephen Frears, 1996): John Malkovich as Dr. Jekyll, with Julia Roberts in the title role. This underrated adaptation of Valerie Martin's novel revises Robert Louis Stevenson's *Dr. Jekyll and Mr. Hyde* by presenting the story from a working-class woman's point of view, that of Jekyll's housekeeper.

14.33 *The House of Mirth* (Terence Davies, 2000): a New York street scene, circa 1900, partially created through CGI. Davies's adaptation of Edith Wharton's novel (he wrote the screenplay, as well as directing it) dissects the moral bankruptcy of America's Gilded Age in the story of a beautiful socialite destroyed by her own integrity.

(1992), *Mary Reilly* (1996), *The Van* (1996), *The Hi-Lo Country* (1998)—and BBC-TV movies—e.g., *The Snapper* (1993), *Liam* (1990)—was followed by the successful comedic feature *High Fidelity* (2000) and the bravura direction of a black-and-white live-TV version of the 1960s nuclear disaster novel *Fail Safe* (telecast by CBS on April 9, 2000). These last two projects demonstrated that Frears's concern with people living on the margins of society and his facility for efficient, cost-effective production strategies were still very much intact.

Terence Davies (b. 1945) is a much more personal filmmaker than the other directors discussed in this section. He began his career with three black-and-white shorts produced under a grant from the BFI that comprise an autobiographical trilogy: *Children, Madonna and Child,* and *Death and Transfiguration* together present a decidedly gloomy view of working-class family life, fraught with starkly religious imagery. In his first feature, *Distant Voices, Still Lives* (1988), also BFI-produced, Davies elaborated his earlier portrait of a dysfunctional family dominated by an abusive father, this time in color, which he used to create an ironic contrast between upbeat images of 1950s prosperity and the grim reality of his subject. The story continued in *The Long Day Closes* (1992), a series of nostalgic, impressionistic sketches of a twelve-year-old boy's coming of age in 1956 Liverpool, shot in sepia-toned color and layered with references to

movies and other popular media. The measured pacing and poetic visual style of Davies's British films were transferred to the rural American South in *The Neon Bible* (1995), another treatment of working-class family life, this time set in Georgia during World War II and adapted from a novel by John Kennedy Toole. (*The Neon Bible* was Davies's last film with cinematographer Michael Coulter [b. 1952], who was a major collaborator in creating the director's deliberately composed, painterly style; Coulter worked to similar effect with other directors in two Jane Austen adaptations, *Sense and Sensibility* [1995] and *Mansfield Park* [1998]). Davies's biggest project to date was an adaptation of Edith Wharton's novel *The House of Mirth* (2000), set in early twentieth-century New York, London, and Venice, which Davies recreated with a remarkable economy of means, including the strategic use of CGI to enhance exterior backgrounds and lighting effects. Davies is exemplary of the way in which the British Film Institute has encouraged artistic production through public funding. From small, intensely personal work, Davies has worked his way up to medium-budget, full-resource filmmaking. Furthermore, the autobiographical film of working-class family life that he pioneered—together with Ken Loach, it must be said, who preceded him—has become a British subgenre; see, e.g., such recent work as Gary Oldman's *Nil by Mouth* (1997) and Tim Roth's *The War Zone* (1999).

Neil Jordan (b. 1950) is Ireland's most prominent director. He was already a successful novelist and short-story writer when he began working as a script consultant on John Boorman's *Excalibur* (1980), which was shot on location in the Irish countryside and at the National Film Studio of Ireland at Ardmore, where Boorman was chairman of the board. Boorman subsequently founded the Motion Picture Company of Ireland to produce low-budget films, and its first production was Neil Jordan's crime thriller *Angel* (U.S. title: *Danny Boy*, 1982), which was also the first film to receive a grant from the newly established Irish Film Board (the rest of the film's production capital was provided by Channel Four Television). Jordan followed with the extraordinary *The Company of Wolves* (1984), a horrific version of "Little Red Riding Hood" adapted from an Angela Carter story that has a Freudian subtext and the atmosphere of a Grimms' fairy tale. But Jordan's breakthrough film was *Mona Lisa* (1986), directed from his own script, about the relationship between a high-class call girl and her gangland chauffer, played by Bob Hoskins (b. 1942) in a performance that brought him multiple critical awards. After a series of disappointing comedies (e.g., *High Spirits* [1988]), Jordan adapted his own coming-of-age story, "Night in Tunisia," as *The Miracle* (1991) and then made *The Crying Game* (1992), a psychological thriller that became his ticket to Hollywood when it unexpectedly became a smash hit. Owing in part to a mar-

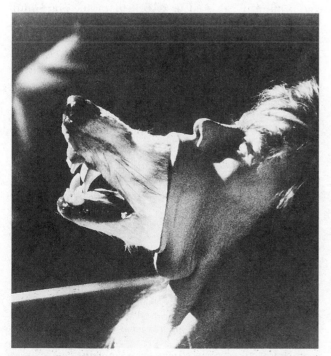

14.34 Neil Jordan's Freudian fairytale *The Company of Wolves* (1984).

keting campaign that emphasized the film's "secret" (that, unbeknownst to him, a character's girlfriend is actually a man), *The Crying Game* grossed $62.5 million worldwide and won an Oscar (for Jordan) for Best Original Screenplay. Next, Jordan was entrusted with a $50 million adaptation of Anne Rice's best-selling novel from the 1970s, *Interview with the Vampire* (1994). Saddled with two miscast stars (Tom Cruise and Brad Pitt), Jordan was still able to create a credible gothic atmosphere and mine the same vein of psychosexual horror as he did in *The Company of Wolves*, and the film was his most popular to date, earning $221 million worldwide. Jordan's next film was a biography of the Irish revolutionary hero and IRA cofounder *Michael Collins* (1996), which featured Oscar-nominated cinematography by Chris Menges (b. 1940). Based on a script that Jordan had been trying to bring to the screen for more than thirteen years, the film recreated early twentieth-century Ireland in rich detail and offered an inspired performance by Liam Neeson (b. 1952) in the title role. *Michael Collins* won the Golden Bear at Berlin, and Jordan's next film, *The Butcher Boy* (1997), won the Silver. This darkly comedic story of a teenage boy's descent into bloody-minded madness was followed by the stylish psychic thriller *In Dreams* (1999), stunningly photographed by Darius Khondji, and an adaptation of Graham Greene's World War II romance *The End of the Affair* (1999), which had been given a Hollywood treatment twenty-four years earlier by Edward Dmytryk. More recently, Jordan remade Jean-Pierre Melville's 1955 caper film *Bob le Flambeur*, originally shot in black-and-white by Henri Decae as *The Good Thief (2003)*, with a classic jazz score and expressive color cinematography by Chris Menges. Jordan is the leading industry figure on the Irish Film Board (established 1981), charged with aiding domestic production and developing the industry. Today, the Film Institute of Ireland maintains an Irish Film Center (IFC) in Dublin that houses a national film theater and film archive; in the early 1990s, an Irish Film Institute was founded as well. Other Irish filmmakers of note include writer-director Jim Sheridan (b. 1949—*My Left Foot* [1989]; *The Field* [1990]; *In the Name of the Father* [1993]; *The Boxer* [1997]); Pat O'Connor (b. 1943—*Cal* [1984]; *Fools of Fortune* [1990]; *Circle of Friends* [1995]; *Dancing at Lughnasa* [1998]); and Cathal

Black (b. 1952—*Pigs* [1984]; *Korea* [1995]; *Love and Rage* [1998]).

The independent producer Bill Cartlidge once said that the British film industry is "permanently ill, but goes into remission now and then;"[8] and the late 1990s was clearly one of those times. In 1998, British production reached its highest level in fifty years with over 130 films. Yet less than 50 percent of these found their way to cinema screens; the rest appeared on television or went directly into video release. Britain was second only to Hollywood as a center for international production. By 2001, total production costs exceeded $1 billion ($1.1 billion to be more precise), which gave Britain the third (or possibly fourth) largest industry in the world, after India, the United States, and (sometimes) France. But distribution remained heavily skewed toward Hollywood blockbusters, with five distributors tied to the majors—Fox, Buena Vista, UIP, Columbia, and Warners—controlling over 80 percent of the market. Furthermore, 75 percent of total British production ($775 million) is funded with outside money attracted by government-mandated tax incentives that permit producers to write off 100 percent of first-year costs of British films budgeted at under $24 million. This has led to what some have described as a new era of "quota quickies" (referring to the cheaply made films cranked out during the 1930s to meet the requirements of the Cinematograph Film Act of 1927—see Chapter 9)— These so-called "new age quickies" are poorly planned and executed projects that come into being mainly so that their backers can achieve tax benefits. An example would be the rash of witless gangster comedies that followed the international success of Guy Ritchie's *Lock, Stock and Two Smoking Barrels* in 1998 (e.g., Andy Hurst's *You're Dead* [1998], Edward Thomas's *Rancid Aluminum* [2000], Ray Burdis's *Love, Honor and Obey* [2000], Rob Walker's *Circus* [2000], David A. Stewart's *Honest* [2000], and Ritchie's own *Snatch* [2000], with exceptions made for Paul McGuigan's *Gangster No. 1*[2000] and Jonathan Glazer's *Sexy Beast*[2000]). On the other hand, significantly enhanced government funding (e.g., $233 million for 2000 and 2001) has made possible the rise of a thriving independent cinema, much of it Celtic in character and originating in the renaissance of national pride that accompanied the etting up of the Scottish Parliament and the Welsh National Assembly in the late 1990s. (Scotland, in fact,

has established its first purpose-built film studio in Edinburgh with the backing of Sony Pictures and Sean Connery's Fountainbridge Films; the Isle of Man intends to do the same.)[9] In April 2000, the publicly funded Film Council (FC) was formed as an umbrella organization to incorporate the British Film Institute (BFI), the British Film Commission, and all of the lottery funding previously administered by the Arts Council. Publicly funded at the level of $88 million annually, the FC has a mandate to seek coproduction deals between the government and private corporations, and to address the industry's long-standing structural problem of poor distribution.

Australia and New Zealand

AUSTRALIA

A recent and most unexpected development in English-language cinema has been the emergence of Australian film from nearly total obscurity into international prominence. Maintained by the British as a penal colony from 1788 to 1840, Australia (from the Latin *australis*, meaning "southern") existed as a British protectorate until

---

8. Bill Cartlidge, quoted in Peter Cowie, ed., *Variety International Film Guide, 2000* (Los Angeles: Silman-James, 1999), p. 305.

9. Whereas Ireland has made a consistent, if not always successful, effort to develop a national film industry and film culture since the mid-1970s, Scotland and Wales lagged behind until the late 1980s. Scotland has been the home of the Edinburgh International Film Festival since 1947, but the origins of an indigenous Scottish cinema can be traced to Bill Douglas (1937–1991), who made a semiautobiographical trilogy about his youth in a remote village in the Highlands (*My Childhood* [1972], *My Ain Folk* [1974], and *My Way Home* [1978]) and a single British feature, *Comrades* (1986), which presented in the style of dioramas and magic-lantern shows the story of "the Tolpuddle martyrs," a group of English farmworkers who formed one of the first trade unions during the 1830s and were massacred by government troops in the course of a strike. The beginnings of a commercial Scottish cinema can be seen in the films of Bill Forsyth (b. 1946), trained as a documentarist for the BBC, whose *That Sinking Feeling* (1979) was, in his own words, "the first fiction film made in Scotland by a native Scot living in Scotland." This Glasgow-based comedy about teenagers trying to sell off a load of stolen kitchen sinks was followed by a series of similarly droll comedies of Scottish regional life (*Gregory's Girl* [1980], *Local Hero* [1983], *Comfort and Joy* [1984]), which were funded in part by Goldcrest. Their success encouraged further investment in regional production by Channel Four as well as the establishment of a Scottish Film Production Fund in 1982 by the Scottish Film Council (active since the late 1970s), whose purpose was the development funding of domestic

1901, when it became a self-governing commonwealth of six federated states. It had a small film industry during the silent era and produced a handful of features after World War I that were successful with both domestic and British audiences (e.g., Raymond Longford's *The Sentimental Bloke*, 1919, and Norman Dawn's *For the Term of His Natural Life*, 1927), but the coming of sound left the country with only one major production facility (Cinesound, formerly Australasian Films) from 1932 to 1956. During World War II, Australia produced only ten features, although the numerous documentaries of the Commonwealth Film Unit claimed international attention. In the postwar period, Australia virtually ceased to have a film industry of its own but became instead a location for such British productions as *The Overlanders* (Harry Watt, 1946), *Bush Christmas* (Ralph Smart, 1947; remade as an all-Australian production by Henri Safran in 1983), and *Robbery under Arms* (Jack Lee, 1957; remade as an all-Australian production by Donald Crombie and Ken Hannam in 1985). American productions shot in Australia included *Kangaroo* (Lewis Milestone, 1952—not to be confused with Tim Burstall's adaptation of the D. H.

Lawrence novel of the same title in 1986), *On the Beach* (Stanley Kramer, 1959), and *The Sundowners* (Fred Zinnemann, 1960). As late as 1970, Australia was known to the world mainly as the exotic site of such foreign-backed features as Tony Richardson's *Ned Kelly*, Nicolas Roeg's *Walkabout*, and Ted Kotcheff's *Wake in Fright*.

But Australia underwent a profound socioeconomic transformation in the late 1960s and early 1970s, and in 1970 the federal government established the Australian Film Development Corporation (the Australian Film Commission, or AFC, after 1975) to subsidize the growth of an authentic national cinema. In 1973, the government set up the Australian Film and Television School (AFTS)—with Jerzy Toeplitz, formerly of the Polish State Film School at Łódź, as director—to train filmmakers to work in a new domestic feature industry. The government simultaneously enacted a system of lucrative tax incentives to attract foreign investment capital to Australian film production. The result was a creative explosion unprecedented in the English-language cinema. Australia produced nearly 400 films between 1970 and 1985—more than were made in all of its prior history—with

features. The Scottish Arts Council National Lottery Fund also made awards for film production, as did the Glasgow Film Fund, created in 1992, whose first grant facilitated the production in that city of Danny Boyle's (b. 1956) 1994 black comedy *Shallow Grave*. (Boyle's *Trainspotting* [1996] is often cited as a landmark in Scottish cinema because it was shot on location in Edinburgh and went on to become the second most popular film in U.K. history; but it was funded entirely by Channel Four and manages to make Edinburgh look like London, Manchester, or any other British city.) In 1997, all of these various funding agencies were integrated into a single agency called Scottish Screen, whose financial clout was such that by 1999 no fewer than seven Scottish features were released in the United Kingdom. In Wales, the introduction of Channel Four in 1982 involved the addition of a separate Welsh-language channel (Wales Sianel Pedwar Cymru, or S4C), and this created a demand for indigenous programming, which ultimately led to the establishment of the Wales Film Council in 1993. Early landmarks in Welsh feature production are Stephen Bayly's low-budget comedy *Rhosyn a Rhith/Coming Up Roses* (1987); Karl Francis's *Milwr Bychan/Boy Soldier* (1987), the first Welsh-English bilingual film given general U.K. release; Steve Gough's BFI-financed *Elenya* (1992); and Paul Turner's *Hedd Wyn* (1993), in Welsh (Cymric) with English subtitles, which was nominated for an Academy Award as Best Foreign Film. Although they were financed with outside money, two other films of Welsh origin are noteworthy here—Andrew Grieve's *On the Black Hill* (1987), adapted from a Bruce Chatwin novel covering eighty years in the lives of identical twins in a small Welsh farming community, and Chris Monger's *The Englishman Who Went up a Hill, but Came down a Mountain* (1995), a period comedy set in a Welsh village in 1917 that received

international distribution, probably because it starred Hugh Grant. (*Human Traffic* [Justin Kerrigan, 1999], which examines rave culture in Cardiff, was also distributed internationally, but, as with *Trainspotting*, its regional locale is generic.)

On Irish cinema, see Kevin Rockett, Luke Gibbons, and John Hill, *Cinema and Ireland* (Syracuse, N.Y.: Syracuse University Press, 1988); Anthony Slide, *The Cinema and Ireland* (Jefferson, N.C.: McFarland, 1988); Brian McIlroy, *World Cinema 4: Ireland* (London: Flicks, 1988); John Hill, Martin McLoone, and Paul Hainsworth, eds., *Border Crossing: Film in Ireland, Britain and Europe* (Belfast: Institute of Irish Studies/BFI, 1994); Arthur Flynn, *Irish Film: 100 Years* (Wicklow, Ire.: Kestrel, 1996); Michael Gray, *Stills, Reels, and Rushes: Ireland and the Irish in Twentieth Century Cinema* (Dublin: Ashfield, 1999); James MacKillop, *Contemporary Irish Cinema: From "The Quiet Man" to "Dancing at Lughnasa"* (Syracuse, N.Y.: Syracuse University Press, 1999); Lance Pettitt, *Screening Ireland: Film and Television Representation* (Manchester: Manchester University Press, 2000); and Martin McLoone, *Irish Film: The Emergence of a Contemporary Cinema* (London: British Film Institute, 2000).

On Scottish cinema, see Colin McArthur, ed., *Scotch Reels: Scotland in Cinema and Television* (London: British Film Institute, 1982); Eddie Dick, ed., *From Limelight to Satellite: A Scottish Film Book* (Glasgow and London: Scottish Film Council/British Film Institute, 1990); and Duncan Petrie, *Screening Scotland* (London: British Film Institute, 2000).

On Welsh cinema, see David Berry, *Wales and Cinema: The First Hundred Years* (Cardiff: University of Wales Press in cooperation with the Wales Film Council and the British Film Institute, 1994).

14.35 Australian locations enhanced Warner Bros.' production of *The Sundowners* **(Fred Zinnemann, 1960): Deborah Kerr.**

financing from the AFC and such semiofficial bodies as the New South Wales Film Corporation (by the end of the decade each of the federal states had its own funding agency). These were later (and somewhat pejoratively) called "AFC genre films" in that they were commissioned to become "cultural flagships of the nation," tending heavily toward period drama and literary adaptation that emphasized Australia's cultural history.

The first films, appearing in the early 1970s, were *The Adventures of Barry Mackenzie* (Bruce Beresford, 1972) and *Alvin Purple* (Tim Burstall, 1973). Within the next few years some extraordinary work emerged in the films of Peter Weir (b. 1944)—*Picnic at Hanging Rock*, 1975, and *The Last Wave*, 1977; Beresford (b. 1940)—*Don's Party*, 1976, and *The Getting of Wisdom*, 1977; Fred Schepisi (b. 1939)—*The Devil's Playground*, 1976, and *The Chant of Jimmy Blacksmith*, 1978; George Miller (b. 1945)—*Mad Max*, 1979; and the feature debuts of the first AFTS graduates: Phillip Noyce (b. 1950)—*Newsfront*, 1978—and Gillian Armstrong (b. 1950)—*My Brilliant Career*, 1979. Unlike the productions financed with foreign capital through the Canadian Film Development Corporation during the same period (see p. 523), these new Australian films were mandated to have indigenous

14.36 *Ned Kelly* **(Tony Richardson, 1970), a British film shot on location in Australia: Mick Jagger as the legendary nineteenth-century bandit.**

14.37 *The Chant of Jimmy Blacksmith* **(Fred Schepisi, 1978).**

casts and crews and to treat distinctly national themes, often by adapting novels and stories from the turn-of-the-century literary revival that accompanied federation. By the end of the 1970s, Australian films were being prominently featured at the Cannes International Film Festival and were competing strongly at European box offices. What made these films so appealing to non-Australian audiences was a combination of their cinematic vitality as the latest international new wave; their remarkable diversity of locations on the world's only island continent; and the clear, lambent quality of natural southern light, an asset that filmmakers exploited to capture the bright colors of the Australian land and its people, and also to compensate for a shortage of studio facilities. (On the other hand, Australian light is so pure that the industry's leading cinematographers—Russell Boyd (b. 1944), Don McAlpine (b. 1934), John Seale (b. 1942), Dean Semler (b. 1943), Peter James (b. 1947), and Geoff Burton (b. 1946)—often used diffusion filters to reduce its harshness, giving their outdoor shots a subdued, "romantic" look.)

In 1981, Australia penetrated the American market with two critical hits. The first was *Breaker Morant* (Beresford, 1980), an adaptation of a play about the actual court-martial of three Australian irregulars by the British on trumped-up atrocity charges during the Boer War. The second, *Gallipoli* (Peter Weir, 1981), was based upon another episode of British treachery in which the World War I Allied command under Winston Churchill sent some 35,000 Anzac (Australian and New Zealand Army Corps) troops to be slaughtered in a suicidal attempt to invade Turkey across the Dardanelles. The following year, the Australian industry achieved a smashing commercial success in the United States with George Miller's *Mad Max II* (1981; retitled *The Road Warrior* for distribution by Warner Bros.). But Australia's banner year was 1986, when Peter Faiman's tongue-in-cheek *"Crocodile" Dundee*, starring the popular television comic Paul Hogan, became the highest grossing Australian film *both* at home and in the United States, reversing a consistent postwar trend and earning a total of $120 million. In that same year, in order to generate more internal revenue, the federal government was able to lower the ceiling on its tax incentives for film investment by 13 percent without causing a negative impact on production, and it seemed as if Australia's experiment in creating a thriving and prestigious national cinema out

of nothing had become a resounding, certifiable, and permanent success.

Historically, however, such success has always had its price—the migration of the very best native talent to Hollywood—and the Australian experience proved no exception. By the early 1980s, many Australian directors had come to work for the American industry. Gillian Armstrong, for example, followed her Australian punk-rock musical *Starstruck* (1982) with an American-produced film, *Mrs. Soffle* (1984), based on the turn-of-the-century case of the Biddle brothers. Its commercial failure returned her to regional Australian themes, in *High Tide* (1987) and *The Last Days of Chez Nous* (1991), but she scored a solid American success with her feminist version of Louisa May Alcott's *Little Women* (1994). Armstrong returned to Australia again to make *Oscar and Lucinda* (1997), based on a Booker Prize–winning novel about two risk-oriented eccentrics who fall in love and attempt to build a church made of glass in the remote outback. *Charlotte Gray* (2001), an Anglo-American coproduction, is an adaptation of a best-selling novel about a Scottish woman who joins British intelligence during World War II in order to locate her lover, an RAF pilot who has been shot down over France.

Bruce Beresford, who came to Hollywood after *Puberty Blues* (1981) and *The Club* (1981), both adapted from Australian authors, logged a critical hit with *Tender Mercies* (1982). But his filming of the Biblical tale of *King David* (1985) was a commercial disaster, and his version of Beth Henley's play *Crimes of the Heart* (1986) was only a limited success, as was the offbeat mystery-comedy *Her Alibi* (1989). Beresford returned occasionally to Australia to direct such culturally indigenous material as *The Fringe-Dwellers* (1986), concerned with the plight of unassimilable aborigines in Queensland, and *Sydney: A Story of a City* (1999), a documentary portrait shot in the 70mm IMAX format. But in the United States, he continued to work the mainstream, sometimes quite successfully—as in *Driving Miss Daisy* (1989), based on Alfred Uhry's Pulitzer Prize–winning play about race relations in the Deep South in the early days of the civil rights movement, which won four Academy Awards, including Best Picture—and sometimes not. In fact, Beresford's career seemed to have peaked with *Driving Miss Daisy*, the critical esteem accorded *The Black Robe* (1991) notwithstanding. In fact, public rejection of this bleak, anthropologically precise re-creation of life among the

Hurons and Algonquins during the French colonization of Quebec was the beginning of a series of failed projects constructed around weak scripts—*Mister Johnson* (1991), *Rich in Love* (1993), *A Good Man in Africa* (1994), *Silent Fall* (1994), and *Last Dance* (1996) were not well received by either the critics or the public. *Paradise Road* (1997), based on the testimony of women who survived a brutal Japanese POW camp during World War II, marked a return to form; and *Double Jeopardy* (1999), a by-the-numbers thriller, was his first box-office hit in a decade. With *Bride of the Wind* (2001), Beresford seemed to have once more fulfilled the promise of his early work. This biography of Alma Shindler, wife of Gustave Mahler, who was at the same time (but serially) the lover of the architect Walter Gropius, the painter Oskar Kokoschka, and the novelist Franz Werfel, offers a magnificent re-creation of the cultural ambiance of fin-de-siècle Vienna.

Fred Schepisi has experienced similar ups and downs with his American productions: *Iceman* (1981); *Barbarosa* (1982); *Plenty* (1985), adapted from the David Hare play; *Roxanne* (1987), a contemporary comedic reworking of Edmond Rostand's *Cyrano de Bergerac*; and the highly acclaimed *A Cry in the Dark* (1988), based on Australia's infamous "Dingo dog" murder case against Lindy Chamberlain for infanticide in 1980. Genre turns like *The Russia House* (1990) and *Mr. Baseball* (1992) did little to enhance Schepisi's reputation; but *Six Degrees of Separation* (1993), adapted from John Guare's play about a charming black con man's manipulation of white liberal guilt, was a sharp, effective satire on upper middle-class social pretensions. Schepisi continued to make comedies such as *I.Q.* (1994), whose central character is Albert Einstein's niece, and *Fierce Creatures* (1997), which reunited the cast of *A Fish Called Wanda* (Charles Critchton, 1988) in a farce set in a declining London zoo. With *Last Orders* (2001), Schepisi returned to more downbeat material, adapting a novel by Graham Swift about the interactions among a group of lifelong friends on their way to scatter the cremated ashes of one of their number into the sea. (Since *The Russia House*, Schepisi has functioned as his own producer, a rarity among Hollywood directors).

Even George Miller, whose lively if overblown *Mad Max: Beyond Thunderdome* (1985) was one of the year's top-grossing films, performed equivocally in his adaptation of John Updike's *The Witches of Eastwick* (1987) and his own medical docudrama *Lorenzo's Oil* (1992). But Miller, who was trained as a physician, scored an enormous hit as the producer and cowriter of *Babe* (Chris

14.38 *Last Orders* (Fred Schepisi, 2001): three of the friends who carry Jack Dodd's ashes to the seaside town of Margate—Tom Courtenay, David Hemmings, Bob Hoskins. The film is narrated as a series of flashbacks from this event and features some of England's most accomplished actors (including the absent Michael Caine and Helen Mirren, playing Jack and his wife, Amy).

Noonan, 1995), the mock-heroic story of an Australian pig who learns to herd sheep that earned seven Oscar nominations (including Best Picture) and won, deservedly, for Best Visual Effects for its creative use of CGI. The film earned $241 million worldwide against a $30 million budget; the sequel, *Babe: Pig in the City* (1998), which Miller co-wrote, produced, and directed, was even more CGI-intensive but it lost money, returning only $18.3 million against an $80-million investment.

Phillip Noyce (b. 1950) was committed to working in Australia during the first part of his career. His major films there were the socially incisive thriller *Backroads* (1977), shot in four weeks for $25,000; *Newsfront* (1978), focusing on the competition between rival Australian and American newsreel companies in the early years of television; *Heatwave* (1982), a visually opulent *film noir* set among the power elite of Sydney; *Shadows of the Peacock* (1987), a stylish melodrama about an interracial love affair; and the inventive suspense thriller *Dead Calm* (1989), based on the Charles Williams novel partially filmed by Orson Welles between 1967 and 1969 as *The Deep* (see footnote, p. 353). With the exception of *Patriot Games* (1992) and its sequel, *Clear and Present Danger* (1994), both based on high-tech espionage thrillers by Tom Clancy, Noyce's Hollywood films have been generally disappointing (e.g., *Blind Fury* [1990]; *Sliver* [1993];

The Saint [1977]); although *The Bone Collector* (1999), a fairly standard thriller involving the hunt for a serial killer in New York City, made innovative use of CGI to seamlessly blend dramatic action shot on a soundstage in Montreal with second-unit photography of the streets of New York (see Chapter 21). Less conventionally, *The Quiet American* (2002) is an adaptation of the Graham Greene novel set in Saigon in 1952; while *Rabbit-Proof Fence* (2002), based on a novel by Doris Pilkington, deals with the adventures of three young aboriginal girls as they trek across the outback in search of their homeland.

The most consistent Australian director working in America today is Peter Weir, who is also the most internationally prominent figure to emerge from his nation's new wave. Weir's first two films were the quirky black comedies *Homedale* (1971) and *The Cars That Ate Paris* (1974), both made and distributed domestically on an ad hoc basis. But his first serious feature was *Picnic at Hanging Rock* (1975), a haunting adaptation of Joan Lindsay's novel about the mysterious disappearance of three girls and a mistress from their country boarding school during a holiday outing in the bush on St. Valentine's Day 1900. While this visually and aurally arresting film contains elements of Antonioni's *L'Avventura*, *Picnic* is finally about the dangerous energy released in the clash of alien cultures and environments—here, the disciplined bourgeois

14.39 *Rabbit-Proof Fence* **(Phillip Noyce, 2002): the three young aboriginal girls who escape from a government-run orphanage to return to their home territory 1,500 miles into the outback—Tianna Sansbury, Laura Monaghan, Everlyn Sampi.**

14.40 *Picnic at Hanging Rock* (Peter Weir, 1975): Anne Lambert.

repressiveness of Appleyard College and the seductive but menacing physicality of the strange volcanic formation known as Hanging Rock. No less spiritually harrowing is *The Last Wave* (1977), based on an original idea by

14.41 *The Last Wave* (Peter Weir, 1977): Richard Chamberlain.

Weir, in which a cataclysmic deluge is announced to a resolutely conventional Sydney corporate lawyer (Richard Chamberlain) in a series of strange premonitory dreams; as the mystery unravels, we learn that the attorney has entered the mythic "dream time" of tribal aborigines, in which he is the messianic avatar of a primal apocalypse that does, in fact, occur at the film's conclusion. In 1978 Weir wrote and directed a 16mm feature for Australian television entitled *The Plumber*, which explored the limits of rationality on a more human scale than his previous films. In it, an enigmatic handyman disrupts the lives of two repressive, hidebound academics (anthropologists, no less). *Gallipoli* (1981) was Weir's last completely Australian-funded feature. *The Year of Living Dangerously* (1982) was his first to be fully financed by an American major (MGM). This film adapts Christopher Koch's novel about the experiences of a young Australian journalist stationed in Jakarta, Indonesia, during the fall of the Sukarno government in 1965. With its $6 million budget and star performances by Sigourney Weaver and Mel Gibson, it is somewhat glossier than Weir's earlier work. But *The Year of Living Dangerously* probably renders more vividly than any non-Marxist film of its era the appalling degradation of Third World poverty and its symbiotic relationship with political violence. *Witness* (1985), shot in the United States by the Australian cinematographer John Seale (Weir's previous films had employed the Australian Russell Boyd), pits the pacifist subculture of the Amish, who maintain a seventeenth-century agrarian lifestyle, against the violent world of urban American cops. In *The Mosquito Coast* (1986), shot by Seale on location in Belize from a screenplay by Paul Schrader, Weir adapted Paul Theroux's novel of a contemporary Swiss Family Robinson as yet another fateful impingement of worlds, in which a man destroys his family and himself by attempting to live in harmony with nature on a remote Caribbean island. In 1989, Weir and Seale collaborated on *Dead Poets Society*, a lyrical evocation of youth in a New England prep school that resonates with Vigo's *Zéro de conduit* and its heirs (see p. 314), produced by Buena Vista. Weir then went on to make the romantic comedy *Green Card* (1990) and the mystically reaffirming *Fearless* (1993) for the same studio, while Seale returned to Australia to direct his first feature (*Till There Was You* [1990]). Weir's highly praised *The Truman Show* (1998) is a self-reflexive film about a man whose life, unbeknownst to him, is a twenty-four-hour-a-day reality television show enacted on a huge soundstage that contains his entire halcyon community. Its sharp commentary on the postmodern culture of voyeurism and the pervasiveness of media in our lives impelled *The Truman Show* toward box-office success, but it seems less than original when compared to predecessors like *Being There* (Hal Ashby, 1979) or even other contemporary films about life on television (e.g., *Pleasantville* [Gary Ross, 1998]).

Of the large number of excellent directors who have chosen to work largely in Australia, the most prominent are John Duigan, Tim Burstall, Donald Crombie, Carl Schultz, Simon Wincer, the Dutch expatriate Paul Cox, and Jane Campion.[1] The British-born John Duigan (b. 1949) is known for such intelligent, well-acted low-budget human dramas as *Mouth to Mouth* (1978), *Winter of Our Dreams* (1981), *One Night Stand* (1984), and *The Year My Voice Broke* (1987), all of which he wrote himself, as well as the failed musical *Dimboola* (1979), and *Far East* (1982), an inventive reworking of *Casablanca*. Before leaving Australia, Duigan wrote and directed *Flirting* (1990), a charming sequel to *The Year My Voice Broke*; *Wide Sargasso Sea* (1992), dynamically adapting Jean Rhys's gothic "prequel" to Charlotte Brontë's *Jane Eyre*; and *Sirens* (1994), a vignette from the bohemian life of the Australian erotic painter Norman Lindsay. Duigan's American work has been quite varied, ranging from biopic (*Romero* [1989]) to romantic comedy (*The Leading Man* [1996]) to melodrama (*Molly* [1999]) to psychological thriller (*Paranoid* [2000]). His most distinguished work, however, deals with people living on the fringes of society, notably the award-winning *Lawn Dogs* (1997), about a friendship that develops between a ten-year-old girl from an affluent suburban family and an alienated young man who does the neighborhood's yard work.

Involved in filmmaking since the early 1960s, Tim Burstall (b. United Kingdom, 1929) was a pioneer director of the new Australian cinema. His sex comedy *Alvin Purple* (1973) did much to establish the commercial viability of the industry, as did *Petersen* (1974), *End Play* (1975), and the period piece *Eliza Fraser* (1976). His adaptation of the John Powers play *The Last of the Knucklemen* (1979) and his World War II commando film, *Attack Force Z* (1981), were also commendable. Although his marital melodrama, *Duet for Four* (1982), misfired, Burstall's survival epic, *The Naked Country* (1986), and his D. H. Lawrence adaptation, *Kangaroo* (1986), were solid critical hits. Burstall's last feature was *Great Expectations:*

The Untold Story (1987), edited down from a five-hour Australian Broadcasting Company (ABC) miniseries; it offers a speculative account of the Dickens character Abel Magwitch and how he amassed a fortune in Australia after escaping from an English prison ship with the help of young Pip (to whom he later becomes a mysterious benefactor).

Donald Crombie (b. 1942) is considered a sensitive chronicler of underdogs. His dramatized documentaries *Caddie* (1976), about the life and death of a Sydney barmaid during the Depression, and *Cathy's Child* (1979), based on an actual case of child abduction, were both critical and commercial successes. His Fordlike saga *The Irishman* (1978) and the comic *Kitty and the Bagman* (1982) were notable for their historical reconstruction of Australian life in the 1920s. Crombie's *The Killing of Angel Street* (1981) is a telling exposé of rampant corruption in the contemporary urban-redevelopment enterprise, and his *Robbery under Arms* (co-directed with Ken Hannam, 1985) is a handsome remake of a 1957 British film. *Playing Beatie Bow* (1986) is a time-travel fantasy in the mold of Robert Zemeckis's *Back to the Future*. With the exception of an occasional feature (*Rough Diamonds* [1994]); *Selkie* [2000]), Crombie has spent the remainder of his career directing films for Australian television.

Hungarian-born Carl Schultz (b. 1939) debuted with the scenic family film *Blue Fin* (1978) and continued with the stylish comedy-drama *Good-bye Paradise*. But he produced a truly complex major work in *Careful, He Might Hear You* (1983), a marvelously ornate drama of a child custody battle fought between two sisters in Depression-era Sydney. Recently, Schultz directed the outdoor adventure film *Bullseye* (1986), a pungent adaptation of *Travelling North* (1986), David Williamson's popular stage play about retirement and old age. Schultz's first Hollywood venture (for TriStar) was *The Seventh Sign*

---

1. A significant minority of Australian filmmakers are émigrés. This is because Australia, with its total population of 19 million, contains over 4 million immigrants, including 1 million British, 300,000 Italians, 178,000 Yugoslavs, 154,000 Greeks, and 80,000 Vietnamese. All are apparently treated with great tolerance. By contrast, the country's 200,000 aborigines, an authentic Stone Age people, have not been well integrated into Australian society. During the 1960s, most of Australia's immigrants came from Europe, but by the 1970s only slightly more than half did. Today, the largest number come from Asia.

(1988), a dramatization of the coming of the Judeo-Christian apocalypse. Schultz began directing for American television and was responsible for several episodes of the *The Young Indiana Jones Chronicles* (Amblin Entertainment, 1992) and TV movies on the subject (*Young Indiana Jones and the Treasure of the Peacock's Eye* [Lucasfilm, 1995]. He also made an impressive sequel to *Born Free* (James H. Hill, 1966), produced in part by the Kenyan government, entitled *To Walk with Lions* (1999).

Simon Wincer (b. 1943), who got off to a rocky start with *Snapshot* (1979) and the intriguing but manipulative *Harlequin* (1980), produced in *Phar Lap* (1983), a superb biography of the champion Australian racehorse that died under mysterious circumstances in California in 1932. Also outstanding was his rousing cavalry adventure epic, *The Lighthorsemen* (1987), about the victorious charge of an Australian Light Horse regiment on Turkish-held Beersheba in 1917. Wincer continued occasionally to direct in Australia (e.g., *Quigley Down Under* [1990]), but he entered the American mainstream with several popular hits (*Lonesome Dove* [1989]; *Free Willy* [1994]) and, like Schultz, also directed episodes of *The Young Indiana Jones Chronicles* (1992) and such TV movies as *The Adventures of Young Indiana Jones: The Trenches of Hell* (1999). Despite a few box-office disasters (*Operation Dumbo Drop* [1995]; *The Phantom* [1996]), Wincer succeeded with Australian comic material in two collaborations with Paul Hogan (see above)—the Western *Lightning Jack* (1994) and *Crocodile Dundee in Los Angeles* (2001).

Paul Cox (b. 1940), however, is probably the most important director working in Australia today. Born in the Netherlands, Cox emigrated to Melbourne and began to make low-budget experimental films in 1965. His first features—*Illuminations* (1976) and *Inside Looking Out* (1977)—were autobiographical mood pieces with shoestring budgets, but *Kostas* (1979), about a Greek journalist in exile working as a Melbourne taxi driver, was solidly funded by the Victorian Film Corporation and proved to be Cox's breakthrough film. His next feature, *Lonely Hearts* (1982), won several international awards for its sensitive depiction of the slowly developing romance of a shy, middle-aged couple; and his visually and aurally striking *Man of Flowers* (1983) impressed many critics with its tense, Hitchcock-like rendition of an emotionally

isolated eccentric. *My First Wife* (1984) is a harrowing account of the collapse and breakup of a ten-year marriage; it was shot, like *Man of Flowers*, by the gifted cinematographer Yuri Sokol. After his sensuous documentary on Egypt, *Death and Destiny* (1985), Cox produced a clear masterpiece in *Cactus* (1986), easily the most *tactile* film made in Australia since *Picnic at Hanging Rock*. *Cactus* is about a love affair between two persons, one blind since childhood, the other threatened with blindness through an automobile accident after a lifetime of sight; it represents a complex blend of intense emotional drama, documentary technique, and abstract experimental form. Cox's *Vincent—the Life and Death of Vincent Van Gogh* (1987) is an experimental film that re-creates the artist's subjective world and his uncompromising philosophy of art. Since that time, Cox has continued to work exclusively in Australia, directing such remarkable features as *Golden Braid* (1990), adapted from a Maupassant short story about an antiquarian who becomes romantically obsessed with a lock of hair; *A Woman's Tale* (1991), focusing on the last days of a seventy-eight-year-old woman dying of lung cancer; and *The Nun and the Bandit* (1992), a film about the unintended consequences of a criminal abduction. Cox's concentration on disturbing themes continued in *Exile* (1994), about a man exiled to a desert island for stealing sheep, and *Father Damien* (also known as *Molokai*, 1999), based on the true story of a nineteenth-century priest who volunteered to work in a leper colony on the island of Molokai and contracted the disease himself. In *Innocence* (2000), Cox treats the rekindling of a passionate love affair between septuagenarians who had been lovers in their youth, cutting back and forth across forty-five years to examine how the two have, and have not, changed. Cox's versatility extends to directing comedy (*Lust and Revenge* [1996], a satire on corporate underwriting of the arts) and experimental IMAX 3-D shorts (*Four Million Houseguests*, 1997).

Jane Campion (b. 1955 in Wellington, New Zealand) is unquestionably the most interesting filmmaker to emerge from the Australian cinema in recent years. A number of her shorts—*Peel* (1982/83), *Passionless Moments* (1983/84), *A Girl's Own Story* (1983/84), and *After Hours* (1984)—received wide recognition while she was still a student at the AFTS, with *Peel* winning the Golden Palm at Cannes for the Best Short Film in

1986. Experimental in form and feminist in theme, these films focus on such subjects as familial power relationships and sexual harrassment. Campion's first feature, *Sweetie* (1989), was a black comedy about an eccentric young woman whose emotional disturbance ultimately wreaks havoc on her family, while *An Angel at My Table* (1990) is based on the harrowing autobiography of Janet Frame, a writer who was misdiagnosed as a chronic schizophrenic and institutionalized for much of her early life. Campion directed her third feature, *The Piano* (1993), from her own screenplay about an unwed mother who is sent by her family in mid-Victorian Scotland to consummate an arranged marriage with an emigrant English farmer in the wilds of coastal New Zealand. This woman has the "dark power" of willing herself mute, "speaking" mainly through the medium of music played on a massive grand piano that she brings with her against enormous odds from home. Her emotional blockage and subsequent sensual awakening in a tumultuous affair with her husband's neighbor unleash forces that nearly destroy all three parties (and do, in fact, destroy the symbol-making genius of her art). Rapturously photographed on location by Stuart Dryburgh in the Gothic mode of *Picnic at Hanging Rock*, this darkly romantic film won a number of international awards, including three American Oscars, and demonstrated the remarkable staying power of the Australian New Wave. After the phenomenal success of *The Piano*, Campion undertook an adaptation of *The Portrait of a Lady* (1996), one of Henry James's most opaque novels. As in *The Piano*, Stuart Dryburgh's cinematography maintains a level of expressivity that occasionally approaches the surreal, but in the end the story of Isabel Archer lacks the symbolic resonance of the earlier work. The same could be said of *Holy Smoke* (1999), a satiric comedy about the deprogramming of a young woman who has come under the spell of an Indian guru. The confrontation between the deprogrammer, or "exit counselor," and his charge becomes sexual, and the film ends up being about the relationship between sex and psychological power. This is also the theme of *In the Cut* (2003), Campion's adaptation of Susanna Moore's quasi-pornographic novel about a female college professor who becomes involved with a serial killer.

The Australian film industry, which owes its existence to government subsidies begun in the early 1970s, is still heavily dependent on government investment and protective legislation to survive. In 1988, the Australian Film Finance Corporation (AFFC) was created to invest in commercially viable production, while the Australian Film Commission was left to fund "cultural products" that were unlikely to return investments (although the Film Commission itself has only about $10 million a year to go around). The AFFC requires that some kind of presale agreement be in place before giving support to a film project, and this has clearly encouraged a trend toward commercialization. On the other hand, such help is crucial because of what David Stratton described in 2000 as "the overwhelming competition from Hollywood films swamping the nation's

14.42 Jane Campion's *The Piano* (1993): Holly Hunter, Anna Paquin, and the piano on a distant shore.

cinemas."[2] In other words, just as in the United Kingdom, the American majors control distribution. So even though the Australian industry currently produces 20 to 25 films a year, the Australian audience for them is hard to find. Furthermore, to take 1998 and 1999 as an example, 41 films were made with a combined budget of U.S. $72 million, but only a few had budgets over $3.5 million, and more than 16 were made for less than $600,000. This means that Australia is still the low-cost gateway to English-language production that it has been for the past twenty years, and it makes Australia a desirable place for offshore companies to produce films with outside money but largely with Australian casts and crews. Recent examples are George Miller's *Babe: Pig in the City* (1998), Alex Proyas's *Dark City* (1998), Jane Campion's *Holy Smoke* (1999), and Baz Luhrmann's *Moulin Rouge* (2001), which were all produced on location in Australia by Australian directors working with foreign investment capital under the aegis of major American distributors. This practice is good for full employment but creates disequilibrium within the industry—e.g., Luhrmann's *Moulin Rouge* budget of $60 million was ten times larger than that of any recent Australian feature, but, once local salaries were paid, all of the profits went back to Fox. Thus, the question of cultural priorities is rising once more: Australians must choose between becoming a mini-Hollywood (e.g., Australian media baron Rupert Murdoch opened Fox Studios in Sydney in 2000, where George Lucas created much of *Star Wars: Episode 2—Attack of the Clones* [2002]) or having a truly indigenous film industry whose creative direction lies in reflecting something authentically and unmistakably Australian.

NEW ZEALAND

New Zealand (population 3.8 million), Australia's small island neighbor, sought to imitate that nation's success by establishing a film commission in 1978 to encourage the development of an indigenous film industry that would enable "the world to see New Zealanders as they see themselves."[3] New Zealand, whose topography is even more spectacularly varied than Australia's, had produced twenty-seven features between 1910 and 1930, but only seventeen from 1930 to 1970, owing to American domination after the coming of sound. When Roger Donaldson's (b. Australia, 1945) futuristic political thriller

Sleeping Dogs (1977) received international distribution, the government became convinced that an indigenous industry could be formed, and it threw the support of the new commission behind that director's second feature, *Smash Palace* (1981), a tense drama of marital discord that was a great critical success and New Zealand's highest-earning film to date. At about the same time, four other domestic features appeared from new directors trained in television—*Skin Deep* (Geoff Steven, 1979), *Beyond Reasonable Doubt* (John Laing, 1980), *Pictures* (Michael Black, 1981), and *Goodbye Pork Pie* (Geoff Murphy, 1981)—which confirmed the Film Commission's success in promoting New Zealand films on New Zealand subjects. Loopholes in the New Zealand tax code during this time created investment incentives in the form of tax shelters, and this caused the exponential expansion of film production from two features in 1980, to five in 1981, six in 1982 and 1983, and fourteen in 1984, when the loopholes were closed. (Many of the tax-shelter films were coproductions—e.g., Mike Newell's *Bad Blood* [1982], produced with the United Kingdom, and Roger Donaldson's *The Bounty* [1984], produced with the United States). For the rest of the 1980s, domestic production leveled off at an average of five to six films annually, and New Zealand films began to appear regularly in competition at Cannes and other festivals. The Film Commission then gradually assumed its role as a funding agency for script development and for some production finance, as well as a sales agent for completed projects.

Throughout the 1980s, the Film Commission facilitated the work of a growing number of talented directors, several of whom would follow their Australian counterparts to Hollywood, of whom Roger Donaldson has been the most commercially successful. His American films have covered a broad range of genres—comedy (*Cocktail* [1988]; *Cadillac Man* [1990]), *film noir* thriller (*No Way Out* [1987]; *White Sands* [1992]; *The Getaway* [1994]), science fiction (*Species* [1995]), disaster film (*Dante's Peak* [1997]), docudrama (*Thirteen Days* [2000]), and espionage (*The Recruit* [2003])—and he has moved onto

---

2. David Stratton, "Australia," *Variety International Film Guide 2000* (Los Angeles: Silman-James, 2000), p. 80.

3. New Zealand Film Commission charter, quoted in Helen Martin and Sam Edwards, *New Zealand Film, 1912–1995* (New York: Oxford University Press, 1997), p. 13.

another plane entirely from the industry he helped to found in the late 1970s. After the riotous road film *Goodbye Pork Pie*, Geoff Murphy (b. Wellington, New Zealand, 1938) directed *Utu* (1983), one of foundational texts of New Zealand cinema.. This film, whose title is the Maori word for "retribution," is set in 1870 during the last of the Land Wars and concerns a fictionalized renegade uprising against colonial British rule. (The script is deliberately vague about the locations and tribes involved to avoid offending contemporary Maori sensibilities.) *Utu*'s epic scale (and its impressive box-office performance) led Murphy to other local projects (e.g., *The Quiet Earth* [1985]) and eventually to Hollywood, where he made two unsuccessful action films, the Western *Young Guns II* (1990) and the time-travel film *Freejack* (1992), before returning to New Zealand to work in television (and later as second-unit director for Peter Jackson's *The Lord of the Rings* trilogy [2001–2003]). Vincent Ward (b. Greytown, New Zealand, 1956), whose hieratic coming-of-age drama *Vigil* (1984) was the first New Zealand film to be shown in competition at Cannes, also directed the New Zealand/Australian coproduction *The*

14.44 *Vigil* (Vincent Ward, 1984), with Fiona Kay.

Navigator: A Medieval Odyssey (1988), a fantasy adventure about fourteenth-century English villagers who escape the Black Death by tunneling to the other side of the earth through an abandoned mine shaft and stumble onto twentieth-century Auckland. The international coproduction *Map of the Human Heart* (1993) was nearly as fantastic in its blending of interracial romance (Inuit and Native American), cartography, and World War II aerial combat; and it brought Ward to Hollywood, where he directed the astonishing *What Dreams May Come* (1998), whose vision of the afterlife as a "Painted World" flowing from nineteenth-century art was one of the most imaginative uses of CGI to date (see Chapter 21). Budgeted at $85 million, the film returned only $55 million, and, like Murphy, Ward eventually returned to work in New Zealand.

The year 1994 was a banner year for the new industry, witnessing the release of both Peter Jackson's *Heavenly Creatures* and Lee Tamahori's *Once Were Warriors*. The former, based on a real-life case, is about two school girls in Auckland in the 1950s who fall in love, construct an elaborate fantasy world, and then commit murder when reality intrudes. The film contains extraordinary performances, lush cinematography (by Alun Bollinger and Allen Guilford), and innovative production design and special effects to mark a true maturity of vision for New Zealand cinema. As harshly realistic as *Heavenly Creatures* is romantic, *Once Were Warriors* is about the violent,

14.43 Geoff Murphy's *Utu* (1983): Anzac Wallace as Te Wheke, leader of a late nineteenth-century Maori uprising against the British.

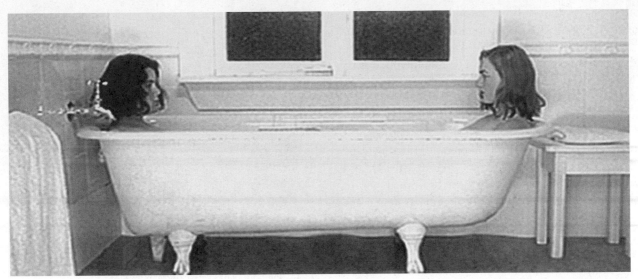

14.45 *Heavenly Creatures* (Peter Jackson, 1994): Melanie Lynskey and Kate Winslet as two schoolgirls who fall in love and play out their fantasies in the imaginary kingdom of "Borovnia," which they ultimately commit murder to sustain. Based on a true story.

degraded life of Maoris living on welfare in an Auckland slum; it unflinchingly presents scenes of brutal spousal abuse and became the highest grossing film in New Zealand history in the year of its release. (A sequel, Ian Mune's *What Becomes of the Broken Hearted* [1999], became the second most commercially successful film in New Zealand.) Half Maori himself, Tamahori (b. 1950) won international acclaim for *Once Were Warriors*, which was his debut feature, and he landed pretty quickly in

14.46 *Once Were Warriors* (Lee Tamahori, 1994): young Maoris with ancient tribal face carvings, now an emblem of the urban street gang to which they belong in contemporary Auckland. This film became the highest-grossing film in New Zealand history in the year of its release.

Hollywood. There he made the retro-*noir* mystery *Mullholland Falls* (1996); *The Edge* (1997), a unique existential adventure film written by David Mamet and set in the Alaskan wilderness (though shot, by Donald McAlpine, on location in Canada); and *Along Came a Spider* (2001), a serial-killer thriller made as a sequel to *Kiss the Girls* (Gary Fleder, 1997). Tamahori vowed to return to New Zealand to make another independent feature after completing his third Hollywood film, but MGM/UA made him an offer he couldn't refuse—the opportunity to direct the twentieth film in the James Bond series, *Die Another Day* (2002).

Before *Heavenly Creatures*, Peter Jackson (b. Wellington, New Zealand, 1961) had directed three cheerfully distasteful, in-your-face splatterfests—*Bad Taste* (1987), in which human-flesh-eating aliens come to earth to stock supplies for an off-world fast-food franchise; *Meet the Feebles* (1989), which mixes puppet animation with live action in a kind of grotesque parody of *The Muppet Show*; and *Braindead* (U.S. title: *Dead-Alive* [1992]), an imaginatively designed and executed "splatstick comedy" that carries visceral outrage to new heights and was described by one critic as "a necrophiliac's wet dream." All three of these low-budget films were produced by Jackson's own WingNut Films Ltd., with assistance from the New Zealand Film Commission; they employed elab-

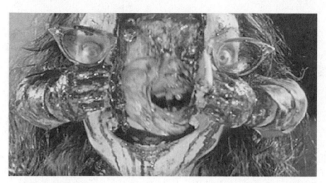

14.47 *Braindead* (U.S. title: *Dead-Alive* [Peter Jackson, 1992]): an abominable head-birth in a film that took the prosthetic representation of gore to new levels; produced with the assistance of the New Zealand Film Commission.

orate but cost-efficient special effects. After *Braindead*, Jackson and his partners founded Weta Digital Ltd., a computer-animation studio, in an old factory in Wellington, which was used to produce the visual effects for *Heavenly Creatures*. These caught the attention of Hollywood producer-director Robert Zemeckis, who hired Jackson to direct *The Frighteners* (1996), a horror-comedy financed and released by Universal Pictures but shot and postproduced in New Zealand, with digital effects supplied by Weta. (Zemeckis also used Weta to produce some of the digital effects for his 1997 science-fiction film *Contact*.) The film, which is about a supernatural private eye who solves a twenty-year-old murder mystery with the help of a posse of assorted ghosts and poltergeists, was not commercially successful in the United States, but it was recognized as "a creative landmark"[4] in computer-generated imagery (*Washington Times*) and raised New Zealand's international profile as a professional production site.[5] All of these factors figured in New Line Cinema's decision to award Jackson the contract to produce all three films in the fantasy trilogy *The Lord of the Rings*. With a budget of $270 million, the trilogy represents not only the most expensive production ever undertaken south of the equator, but a sum larger than the combined budget of every 35mm New Zealand feature ever made. (The Film Commission, which sees government funding not so much as a subsidy as an investment in the future, cannot fail to be impressed by this staggering return on the $2.5 million it invested in Jackson's first four films—this is exactly how the system is supposed to work.) The first installment in the Tolkien

epic, *The Lord of the Rings: The Fellowship of the Ring* (2001) was a huge critical and commercial windfall, returning more than three times its negative cost. Jackson did principal live-action photography on all three films at once between 2000 and 2001, with postproduction at Weta continued through the release of the second and third films, *The Two Towers* (2002) and *The Return of the King* (2003). The trilogy represents a landmark in the history of computer-generated imagery (see Chapter 21) and has made New Zealand one of the most attractive locations for production and postproduction anywhere in the world, although the industry's infrastructure is still precarious because the economy of New Zealand is so small. Furthermore, because of the country's tiny population, the New Zealand film industry depends on exports, whereas Australia, for example, is large enough to maintain a medium-sized industry on the strength of its domestic market alone (although stiff competition from American distributors makes this increasingly difficult).

Nevertheless production was booming at the turn of the century, with seven domestic features completed in 1999 and nine in 2000. American feature productions like Columbia's *Vertical Limit* (Martin Campbell, 2000) have been shot on location there, as have dozens of Indian "Bollywood" musicals and American television series like Universal TV's *Xena: Warrior Princess* and *Hercules: The Legendary Journeys*. Maori filmmakers have been work-

---

4. *Washington Times*, quoted in Martin and Edwards, p. 190.

5. Between *The Frighteners* and *The Lord of the Rings* trilogy, Jackson made *Forgotten Silver* (1996; co-directed with Costa Botes), a hilarious "mockumentary" on a fictional New Zealand director named "Colin McKenzie," who was lost until recently to film history but who, it seems, arrived at every important technical and narrative innovation in the cinema before anyone else in the world. In retelling McKenzie's supposed achievements, Jackson's film becomes a revisionist history of the cinema skewed toward New Zealand as the fount of all knowledge and a terrifically sharp satire on both the insularity of New Zealanders and the pomposity of academic film history (and documentary programs about it). To make things even funnier, when the film was shown on New Zealand television, many viewers thought it was authentic and were furious with Jackson when they learned the truth. (They have forgiven him since *The Lord of the Rings* earned more money for the nation between 2000 and 2002 than its vaunted wine industry.) To be fair to those who were duped, the emulation of PBS-style documentary form is so perfect and the simulation of eighty years of film style in the "excerpts" from McKenzie's work so authentic (thanks in no small part to Alun Bollinger's brilliant cinematography) that *Forgotten Silver* is easily mistaken on first viewing for the real thing.

ing since 1983, when *Patu!*, a feature-length documentary about the 1981 Springbok Tour protests in New Zealand, was made by Merata Mita, who also produced *Mauri* (1988), a powerful film based on Maori legend and shot mainly with a cast of Maori nonprofessional actors. These two films were, respectively, the first feature-length film and the first fiction film directed by women in New Zealand. Since that time, both Maoris and women have been active in New Zealand cinema. Barry Barclay's *Ngati* (1987), shot by a Maori crew, lays claim to being the world's first feature made by an indigenous culture living within a white majority culture,[6] and his *Te Rua* (1991) was the first Maori-European coproduction (offshore finance and locations were provided by the West Berlin state film fund). In 2001, the first full-length Maori-language feature appeared in Don Selwyn's *Te Tangata Whai Rawa o Weniti*, a version of *The Merchant of Venice*. The most prominent New Zealand woman director (aside from Jane Campion, who has been adopted by Australia) is Alison Maclean (b. Ottawa, 1958), whose first feature, the dark psychological thriller *Crush* (1992), won several international awards. More recently, she directed the independent American feature *Jesus' Son* (1999), a film about heroin addiction in the early 1970s financed by Lion's Gate. The New Zealand film that has spoken the most directly to women's issues in the past several years, however, was written and directed by a man, Gregor Nicholas (b. Auckland, 1959). *Broken English* (1996) is the story of a familial war between a reactionary Croatian immigrant living as a successful drug dealer in Auckland and his two defiant daughters, both thoroughly modern young adults; it speaks to the hybridization of New Zealand urban culture. The film became the third most popular of the 1990s with domestic audiences, after *Once Were Warriors* (1994) and its sequel, *What Becomes of the Broken Hearted* (1999), suggesting that New Zealand is very much a contemporary society in transition.

Canada

Canada is another Commonwealth nation whose cinema has experienced sudden and unexpected growth. Although Canada is one of the largest and wealthiest countries in the world, its film market was dominated until very recently by American productions, much as British

cinema had been during the 1930s. Before 1978, film production in Canada was basically a cottage industry under the tight control of the National Film Board (NFB). Founded in 1939 by British documentary producer John Grierson, the NFB coordinated all government film activities in an attempt to end Hollywood dominance and establish a national cinema that would, in Grierson's words, "interpret Canada to Canadians and the world." For this purpose, Grierson gathered about him a group of talented documentarists (Stuart Legg, Stanley Hawes, Raymond Spottiswoode, Joris Ivens, John Fernhout, and Irving Jacoby). During World War II, Canada became the world's leading producer of Allied war propaganda films (the *World in Action* series, 1942–45, and *Canada Carries On*, 1940–45), as well as other types of nonfiction film. After the war, Grierson returned to England, but the NFB continued to produce distinguished documentaries and animated shorts, as in the brilliant experimental work of Norman McLaren[7] (1914–1987). With the arrival of television, Canadian filmmakers turned increasingly to *cinéma vérité* techniques (the **cinéma-direct** movement, in fact, was founded in the early 1960s by French-Canadian filmmakers at the NFB, including Michel Brault, Pierre Perrault, and Claude Jutra, under the influence of Jean Rouch—see Chapter 13).

For all of Canada's success with documentary and animated cinema, feature filmmaking was left almost exclusively to the Americans until 1963, when the NFB produced two remarkable semidocumentaries. Don Haldane's *Drylanders* is an account of the harsh existence of a Canadian farming family during the first thirty years of the century, and Paul Perrault and Michel Brault's *Pour la suite du monde* (*So That the World Goes On/Moontrap*), about the attempt of the people of an isolated St. Lawrence River island to revive the hunting of Beluga whales. By 1964, the NFB was supporting feature production in both French (Gilles Groulx's *Le Chat dans le sac* [*The Cat in the Sack*] and English (Don Owen's *Nobody Waved Goodbye*). But Canadian feature produc-

---

6. Martin and Edwards, p. 128.

7. McLaren developed and perfected the technique of the cameraless film, originated by Len Lye (1901–1980) in 1934. He worked by painting and drawing his images directly on the celluloid, regardless of frame divisions. See Valliere T. Richard, *Norman McLaren, Manipulator of Movement: The National Film Board Years, 1947–1967* (Newark, N.J.: University Press of Delaware, 1982).

tion averaged only four films per year, and many Canadian directors (e.g., Norman Jewison, Sidney J. Furie, Arthur Hiller, Silvio Narizzano, Ted Kotcheff) and actors (Donald Sutherland, Christopher Plummer, Michael Sarrazin, Joanna Shimkus) migrated south to work in the American industry. And it was a rare Canadian feature indeed—such as Irvin Kershner's *The Luck of Ginger Coffey* (U.S.-Canada, 1964), shot on location in Montreal—that enjoyed even modest success beyond its own borders.

In an effort to reverse this trend, the Canadian Film Development Corporation (CFDC) was established by an act of Parliament in 1967 with a fund of $10 million (now a revolving annual fund of $4.5 million) to promote the national feature industry through grants and guaranteed loans. By 1972, the annual feature output had risen to twelve and included such notable French- and English-language films as Michel Brault's *Entre la mer et l'eau douce* (*Between the Sea and the Still Waters*, 1968); Gilles Carle's *Le Viol d'une jeune fille douce* (*The Rape of a Sweet Young Girl*, 1968) and *La Vraie nature de Bernadette* (*The True Nature of Bernadette*, 1972); Gilles Groulx's *Entre tu et vous* (*Between Yourselves*, 1969); Claude Jutra's *Mon oncle Antoine* (*My Uncle Antoine*, 1971) and *Kamouraska* (1973); Denys Arcand's *Réjeanne Padovani* (1972); Paul Almond's *Isabel* (1968); Don Owen's *The Ernie Game* (1968); Allan King's *Warrendale* (produced for the CBC) and *A Married Couple* (1969); Don Shebib's *Goin' down the Road* (1970) and *Between Friends* (1973); Jean Chabot's *Mon Enfance à Montréal* (*My Childhood in Montreal*, 1972); William Fruet's *Wedding in White* (1972); and Eric Till's *A Fan's Notes* (1972). In 1974, the CFDC scored an unprecedented international success with Ted Kotcheff's *The Apprenticeship of Duddy Kravitz*, which won the Golden Bear at Berlin, as well as an Oscar nomination for Best Foreign Film. Nevertheless, by 1977 less than $6 million in private funds was being invested in Canadian feature films.

But in 1978 two things occurred that radically changed the nature of the Canadian industry. The first was a policy change at the CFDC in which the seed money for Canadian feature projects was lent to producers rather than directors, increasing investment incentive within the business community. Second, and infinitely more important, the Canadian government enacted wide-ranging tax-shelter legislation which allowed a 100 percent write-off for film investment, which rapidly became the second most popular form of tax relief in the country (after oil depletion allowances). The result was a boom in the production of commercial features the likes of which few countries have experienced in modern times: $6 million were invested in Canadian feature production in 1977; over $150 million in 1979; and $300 million in 1980. At the same time, coproductions with the United States, France, Italy, and Japan, as well as domestic productions on a previously unthinkable big-budget scale, have combined to produce one of the most commercially lucrative production environments anywhere in the world today. Between 1979 and 1981, more than 150 features were shot in Canada, stretching the industry's technical capacity very thin. Among the first big winners were Ivan Reitman's *Meatballs*, with $40 million in receipts for 1979, and Bob Clark's odious *Porky's* (1981) with $100 million, which, though shot on location in Florida, became the highest grossing "Canadian" film in the industry's brief history. That the environment and the films lacked a specifically Canadian character troubled some observers, but there can be no question that the kind of filmmaking activity financed in Canada during this time represented a solid economic achievement.

Between 1977 and 1981, for example, Canada produced or coproduced all of the following films, among many others: *Why Shoot the Teacher* (Silvio Narizzano, 1977), *Who Has Seen the Wind?* (Allan King, 1977), *J. A. Martin, Photographe* (Jean Beaudin, 1977), *Outrageous* (Richard Brenner, 1977), *Skip Tracer* (Zale Dalen, 1977), *Le Soleil se lève en retard* (*The Sun Rises Late*; André Brassard, 1978), *Caro papa* (*Dear Papa*; Dino Risi, 1978), *Una giornata particolare* (*A Special Day*; Ettore Scola, 1977), *À Nous deux* (*Us Two*; Claude Lelouch, 1979), *A Man, a Woman, and a Bank* (Noel Black, 1979), *Silent Partner* (Daryl Duke, 1979), *Mourir à tue-tête* (English title: *Primal Fear*; Anne-Clair Poirier, 1979), *The Changeling* (Peter Medak, 1979), *Murder by Decree* (Bob Clark, 1979), *Agency* (George Kaczender, 1979), *Bear Island* (Don Sharp, 1980), *Out of the Blue* (Dennis Hopper, 1980), *Circle of Two* (Jules Dassin, 1980), *Atlantic City* (Louis Malle, 1980), *L'Affair Coffin* (*The Coffin Affair*; Jean-Claude Labrecque, 1980), *L'Arrache coeur* (*The Broken Heart*; Mireille Dansereau, 1980), *Les Bon débarras* (*Good Riddance*; Francis Mankiewicz, 1980), *The Lucky Star* (Max Fischer, 1980), *Fantastica* (Gilles Carle, 1980), *Keiko* (Claude Gagnon, 1980), *Shades of Silk* (Mary Stephen, 1980), *L'Homme à tout faire* (*The*

Handyman; Micheline Lanctôt, 1980), *Scanners* (David Cronenberg, 1981), *The Hounds of Notre Dame* (Zale Dalen, 1981), *Ticket to Heaven* (R. L. Thomas, 1981), *Heartaches* (Don Shebib, 1981), *Quest for Fire* (Jean-Jacques Annaud, 1981), *Threshold* (Richard Pearce, 1981), *Improper Channels* (Eric Till, 1981), *Surfacing* (Claude Jutra, 1981), and *Les Plouffe* (Gilles Carle, 1981).

With twenty-four entries at the 1980 Cannes Festival, Canada announced its intention to become a "world class" force in cinema, but in fact its success in this arena has been limited at best. Although Canada has continued to produce a number of interesting films with uniquely Canadian content—e.g., *Suzanne* (Robin Spry, 1981), *The Grey Fox* (Phillip Borsos, 1982), *Unfinished Business* (Don Owen, 1984; a sequel to *Nobody Waved Goodbye*, twenty years after), *Big Meat Eater* (Chris Windsor, 1982), *The Terry Fox Story* (Ralph Thomas, 1983), *Videodrome* (David Cronenberg, 1983),[8] *Crime Wave* (John Paizs, 1985), *My American Cousin* (Sandy Wilson, 1985), *Loyalties* (Anne Wheeler, 1986), *Dancing in the Dark* (Leon Marr, 1986), *Keeping Track* (Robin Spry, 1987), *Candy Mountain* (Robert Frank, 1987), *I've Heard the Mermaids Singing* (Patricia Rozema, 1987), *Blindside* (Paul Lynch, 1988), *Thirty-Two Short Films about Glenn Gould* (François Girard, 1993)—the majority of them are either shot out of the country with CFDC funding or use Canadian locales to represent other places entirely (par-

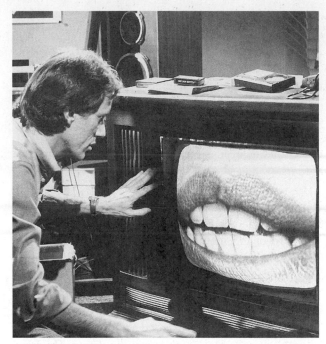

14.48 Hallucinated reception: David Cronenberg's *Videodrome* (1983): James Woods.

ticularly aggravating to Canadians in this regard are the hundreds of so-called "Stars and Stripes" films, which feature Canadian towns as cities or unidentified locations in the United States and employ mainly American actors).[9]

---

8. On the body of Cronenberg's work, see the science-fiction section of Chapter 12.

9. Other recent Canadian English-language features of note are *Alligator Shoes* (Clay Borris, 1981); *Running Brave* ("D. S. Everett," 1983); *Of Unknown Origin* (George Pan Cosmatos, 1983); *The Wars* (Robin Phillips, 1983); *Cross Country* (Paul Lynch, 1983); *Ups & Downs* (Paul Almond, 1983); *Siege* (Maura O'Connell, 1983); *Music of the Spheres* (G. Philip Jackson, 1984); *Bedroom Eyes* (William Fruet, 1984); *Bay Boy* (Daniel Petrie, 1984); *The Masculine Mystique* (John N. Smith and Giles Walker, 1984); *Low Visibility* (Patricia Gruben, 1984); *Night Magic* (Lewis Furey, 1985); *One Magic Christmas* (Phillip Borsos, 1985); *The Peanut Butter Solution* (Michael Rubbo, 1985); *Samuel Lount* (Laurence Keane, 1985); *The Adventure of Faustus Bidgood* (Michael Jones and Andy Jones, 1986); *Tramp at the Door* (Allan Kroeker, 1986); *The Vindicator* (also known as *Frankenstein '88*, Jean-Claude Lord, 1986); and *The Gate* (Tibor Takacs, 1987).

In the documentary form, ever strong in Canada, the following titles are prominent: *A Private World* (Eric Saretzky, 1981); *Being Different* (Harry Rasky, 1981); Janis Cole and Holly Dale's *P4W: Prison for Women* (1981) and *Hookers on Davie Street* (1984); *Behind the Veil* (Gloria Demes, 1984); *Abortion: Stories from the North and South* (Gail

Singer, 1985); *Dark Lullabies* (Irene Lilienheim Angelico, 1985); *Tears Are Not Enough* (John Zaritsky, 1985); *The Championship Part 3—The Final Battle* (Donald Brittain, 1986); *Prison Mother, Prison Daughter* (John Kastner, 1986); *Karsh: The Searching Eye* (Harry Rasky, 1986); *Sitting in Limbo* (John N. Smith, 1986); and *Passiflora* (Fernand Bélanger, 1986). Within the documentary field, the Canadians have finely honed the subgenre of the concert film, of which the following are examples: *Ladies and Gentlemen the Fabulous Stains* (Lou Adler, 1982); *Rumours of Glory* (Martin Lavut, 1983); *Rock & Rule* (Clive A. Smith, 1983; animated); and *We Will Rock You* (Saul Swimmer, 1983).

See Gerald Pratley, *Torn Sprockets: The Uncertain Projection of the Canadian Film* (Newark N.J.: University of Delaware Press, 1987); Robert E. Miller, "The Canadian Feature Film Conundrum: 1894–1967," in *Current Research in Film: Audiences, Economics, and Law*, Vol. 4, ed. Bruce A. Austin (Norwood, N.J.: Ablex, 1988), pp. 125–46; Manjunath Pendakur, *Canadian Dreams and American Control: The Political Economy of the Canadian Film Industry* (Detroit, Mich.: Wayne State University Press, 1988); and "The Internationalization of the Canadian Film Industry," in Austin, ed., *Current Research in Film: Audiences, Economics, and Law*, Vol. 4, pp. 147–69.

In fact, according to Maurice Yacowar, in 1982 foreign-dominated—largely American—film and video distribution companies accounted for 73 percent of Canada's gross industry revenues; and non-Canadians also earned 95 percent of all royalties, rentals, and commissions.[1] For all the abuses of the tax-shelter period, the production boom did result in the development of a cadre of skilled technical workers as well as experienced producers such as Robert Lantos, whose Alliance Communications Corporation (since 1998, Alliance Atlantis) became an important distributor of Canadian features (and the world's twelfth largest communications company, on the basis of revenues). In 1982 the government moved to reduce the film investment write-off to 50 percent, and in 1985 and 1986 the Canadian government restructured the CFDC, which had changed its name to Telefilm Canada in 1984, to encourage local production and control, and to eliminate certain tax incentives for foreign investment. In 1988, the noted Hollywood director Norman Jewison, a Canadian by birth, founded the Canadian Film Centre (CFC) in Toronto to train screenwriters, directors, cinematographers, editors, and other filmmaking personnel. Supported by both government and corporate funds, this national film school is dedicated to creating a solidly Canadian industrial infrastructure. Nevertheless, the Canadian film industry remains dominated by the American majors, who continue to control distribution and collect 80 percent of annual box-office receipts. (In 1987, however, the government established the Broadcast Fund as part of Telefilm, and it became increasingly involved in teleproduction, so that by the late 1990s, Canada had become the second largest exporter of television programming, after the United States.)

While the country at large was becoming a major center for international production, several directors with a distinctly Canadian vision emerged: David Cronenberg (b. 1943), Atom Egoyan (b. 1960), Guy Maddin (b. 1956), and Denys Arcand (b. 1941). Cronenberg made avant-garde shorts before turning to features in the 1970s, when he wrote and directed three horror films with the backing of the CFDC: *They Came from Within* (U.S. title: *Shivers* [1975]) was about phallic parasites who attack the residents of a Montreal high-rise, adding a new trope to the repertoire of splatter when one of the invaders erupts from the abdomen of its human host (a trick stolen, with great fanfare, by Ridley Scott in *Alien* four years later); in *Rabid* (1977), a woman is turned into a virulent vampire when a medical experiment misfires; and in *The Brood*, a woman is able to externalize her murderous rage as a pack of monstrous dwarfs. Like the NZFC-funded splatter films of Peter Jackson, Cronenberg's CDFC-supported work is antibourgeois and has a high quotient of gore, but it is considerably less cheerful. In fact, these early films function like allegory—they are both monster movies and meditations on social decay in the form of sexual promiscuity, child abuse, divorce, etc.—because Cronenberg's horror is a unique blend of the visceral and the cerebral, a strain that continued in his later mainstream work for American studios, such as his adaptation of Stephen King's *The Dead Zone* (1983) for Paramount and his remake of *The Fly* (1986) for Fox. But it is arguably his Canadian-produced films that achieve the most thematic coherence and distinctiveness of vision. After *Scanners* (1981), a cautionary fable about mind control complete with exploding heads, Cronenberg wrote and directed *Videodrome* (1983), whose phantasmagoric equation of television with pornography was realized in the 1990s with internet porn and tabloid TV, and then established his reputation as a serious artist with *Dead Ringers* (1988). This story of twin brothers, both celebrated gynecologists who fall in love with the same woman (a well-known movie actress), was simultaneously a study of erotic obsession, psychological codependency, and misogyny. Photographed in highly stylized color by Peter Suschitzky, who would become Cronenberg's regular director of photography, part of the film's brilliance lay in the computer-assisted split-screen effects that turned lead performer Jeremy Irons convincingly into identical twins. Following typically idiosyncratic adaptations of Beat novelist William Burroughs's *Naked Lunch* (1991) and David Henry Hwang's stage play, *M Butterfly* (1993), Cronenberg wrote and directed the controversial *Crash* (1996), which won the Special Jury Prize at Cannes. Inspired by a J. G. Ballard novel, *Crash* concerns a technosexual subculture that fetishizes injuries sustained in automobile accidents, the more extreme the better. Seeking ever more supercharged thrills, these individuals become orgasmic by staging crashes that bring them as close to death as possible in a perverse sexual act that merges their flesh with the metallic wreckage of their

1. Maurice Yacowar, "The Canadian as Ethnic Minority," *Film Quarterly* 60, 2 (Winter 1986–87): 13–19.

14.49 *Crash* (David Cronenberg, 1996): fetishized leg brace, fetishistically photographed, on James Spader (whose film character is named James Ballard, after the novelist who wrote the book on which the film is based).

artistic achievement. David Cronenberg is recognized today as a major figure in world cinema, even though he works on a relatively small scale (e.g., *Crash, eXistenZ,* and *Spider* [2002] all had budgets of around $10 million) in the context of an industry dwarfed by the might of its American neighbor, although much of his recent work has been produced by the Canadian communications giant Alliance.

Atom Egoyan, born in Cairo, Egypt (1960), to Armenian parents who immigrated to Victoria, British Columbia, became a household word among film critics with the international success of *The Sweet Hereafter* (1997), his adaptation of a Russell Banks novel about the impact of a deadly school-bus accident on survivors in a small upstate New York town (Egoyan changed the locale to western Canada). The film, produced for Alliance Communications, won a Special Grand Jury Prize at Cannes and was nominated for two Academy Awards, including "Best Director," although Egoyan had been directing low-budget independent features in Canada since *Next of Kin* in 1984. Working as his own writer, producer, and (sometimes) editor and lead actor, Egoyan began making a series of films about dysfunctional families and alienated individuals trying to connect with others—*Family Viewing* (1987), *Speaking Parts* (1989), and *The Adjuster* (1991)—in which a central theme is video voyeurism and the self-reflexivity of the filmic image. *Calendar* (1993),

cars. Although it offended many critics (and was reviled by Ted Turner, corporate owner of its own distributor, Fine Line Features), *Crash* is a sophisticated, if sometimes repellent, critique of the necrophilia inherent in late capitalism's material culture—a critique continued with a vengeance in *eXistenZ* (1999). Based on an original screenplay by Cronenberg, this film is set in a future in which much of the population spends most of its time enmeshed in "organic" virtual-reality games, and its intricate plot concerns the inventor of one such game, "eXistenZ," who together with her partner becomes trapped inside the game system. What makes this particular game so unique is that it is downloaded directly into the central nervous system and adapted to the individual user so that it is scarcely distinguishable from reality itself—with the exception of the fact that it is endlessly fascinating. Intellectually complex and philosophically speculative, *eXistenZ* makes the Warchowski brothers' *The Matrix* (1999) look like Cliff Notes, and it won the Silver Bear at Berlin for high

14.50 *eXistenZ* (David Cronenberg, 1999): Jennifer Jason Leigh and Jude Law, attached to an organic video game pod through their "bio-ports," synthetic sphincters installed at the base of their spines. The umbilical reference is entirely deliberate.

14.51 *The Sweet Hereafter* (Atom Egoyan, 1997): an idealized image of family life that appears at intervals in this somber film about the impossibility of sustaining families.

a 16mm film whose "look" was inspired by Sergei Parajanov's *The Color of Pomegranates* (1969), explores issues of Armenian identity in the story of a photographer (Egoyan) and his wife (Egoyan's actual wife, Arsinée Khanjian) who visit former Soviet Armenia to take pictures of churches to use as calendar copy. This part of the film is narrated by amateur videos that the couple has made of their trip, which the photographer watches obsessively in the wife's absence (it soon becomes clear that she has stayed in Armenia because she has fallen in love with their driver). The other part of *Calendar* is devoted to a series of identical "romantic" dinners that the photographer stages in his home for a series of women who resemble his wife as part of a perverse erotic ritual that the women are apparently paid to enact. These early films are all part of a clear path leading to *Exotica* (1994), Egoyan's first mainstream work, produced as a medium-budget project for Alliance. This film's title comes from the name of a strip club on the outskirts of Toronto that satisfies a broad range of psychosexual male fantasies; several seemingly unrelated plots revolve around the denizens of this club that seem, until the very end, like pieces of a jigsaw puzzle that refuse to fit together. Only when *Exotica* is over and the spectator can work backward through its various individual stories is their central thread clear; then we realize that the film has been about the fact that things are never what they seem because the past that might reveal their true meaning is consistently repressed by social consensus—the "loading of the dice" invoked by Leonard Cohen's title

song "Everybody Knows." Constructed in his signature mosaic style and treating themes that pervade his earlier work, *The Sweet Hereafter* is quintessential Egoyan and a film that offers persuasive testimony to the artistic vitality of Canadian cinema. It is hard to imagine a story, a filmmaker, and a production context as well matched, and, indeed, Egoyan's subsequent work has never quite equaled it. *Felicia's Journey* (1999), about the relationship that develops between a middle-aged, petty bourgeois serial killer (a kind of British Norman Bates, expertly played by Bob Hoskins) and a pregnant Irish teenager, and *Ararat* (2002), a fictionalized account of the making of a documentary on the Armenian genocide that occurred just after World War I, are both fascinating films, but neither approaches the depth of moral clarity attained by *The Sweet Hereafter*. Like Cronenberg, however, Egoyan has helped to put Canadian cinema distinctively on the map, and many of his films are now produced with the backing of Robert Lantos's Alliance Atlantis.

Guy Maddin (b. 1956) is the most experimental of Canadian directors to have achieved some mainstream recognition. He began his career making avant-garde shorts for the Winnipeg Film Group (e.g., *The Dead Father* [1986]), producing in 1988 his first feature, *Tales from the Gimli Hospital*, which he wrote, directed, shot, and edited himself, as he would continue to do through his next three films. Frequently compared to David Lynch's debut feature *Eraserhead* (1979), *Tales from the Gimli Hospital* is set during an early twentieth-century smallpox outbreak in backwoods Manitoba and is constructed as a series of fables told by two patients in the title institution. Invoking the narrative vocabulary of silent and early sound film, Maddin gives the film a stark, expressionistic look and a self-consciously archaic technical veneer. Shot like *Gimli Hospital* in luminous black-and-white, *Archangel* (1990) uses Joseph von Sternberg's *The Scarlet Empress* (1935) as the subtext for its story of

14.52 *Exotica* (Atom Egoyan, 1994): the interior of Club Exotica, where every man's fantasy can be fulfilled.

a crippled British officer stranded in the Russian Arctic during World War I, and *Careful* (1992) is shot in a style reminiscent of the German *Bergfilm* ("mountain film"), so popular in the late 1920s, although it is colored with what appears to be hand-tinting. The film is set in the remote Alpine village of Tolzbad, where all of the residents speak in whispers to avoid causing an avalanche, clearly an allegory of emotional and psychological repres-

14.53 *Tales from the Gimli Hospital* (Guy Maddin, 1988): one of many subjective sequences in a film that owes a substantial (and acknowledged) debt to German Expressionism, here evoking a similar shot in F. W. Murnau's *The Last Laugh* (1924).

sion. Among its many technical anachronisms is a hissing, popping sound track evocative of early sound films. Maddin's fourth feature *Twilight of the Ice Nymphs* (1997), his first made on less than a shoestring budget (about $1 million) with a cast of name actors (e.g., Shelley Duvall), is a bizarre love story that charts no new ground, but his six-minute short *Heart of the World* (2000), a dystopic miniepic about the end of the world as conceived by a late 1920s Soviet montage artist (e.g., Dziga Vertov), has won multiple awards. Maddin's unique appropriation of film history has been called "postmodern expressionism," and it suggests an aesthetic sensibility that is more Germanic (harking back, e.g., not only to Expressionism, but also to *Kammerspielfilm*, Universal horror, and *film noir*) than Soviet despite his experiments with Soviet-style montage. In 1995, Maddin became the youngest person ever to win a Lifetime Achievement Award at the Telluride Film Festival.

Denys Arcand (b. 1941) began his film career making documentaries for the National Film Board of Canada, including a feature-length indictment of the miserable conditions inside Quebec's textile industry, *On est au coton* (1970), which was officially banned by NFB until 1976. He also made a handful of theatrical features, such as the muckraking, anticorruption crime melodrama *Réjeanne Padovani* (1973), and directed films for television before he wrote and directed *Le Déclin de l'empire américain* (*The Decline of the American Empire*, 1986), which was a breakthrough for him in several respects. Not only did it win the International Critics Prize at Cannes and eight Genies (the Canadian equivalent of Oscars), but it was also a crossover hit in Canada, where it was seen by more English-language speakers than any previous Quebec-produced French-language film to date. (It remains the highest grossing Quebec film of all time in the international market.) *Le Déclin*, superbly photographed by Arcand's regular director of photography Guy

Dufaux (b. 1943), is constructed as a series of conversations among a group of Montreal academics, four men and four women, as they prepare for a gourmet dinner party. Discussing both their personal and professional lives, the eight individuals create a sharply etched portrait of contemporary urban life. Arcand scored another hit with his next film, *Jésus de Montréal* (1989), which won the Jury Prize at Cannes and four Genies, and, like its predecessor, was nominated for an Academy Award for Best Foreign Film. Another satirical critique of contemporary social mores, *Jésus* is about the staging of a revisionist passion play that is ultimately rejected by Church officials so that the actors become outcasts and assume their roles from the play in real life. Adapted by Brad Fraser from his own play, Arcand's *Love and Human Remains* (1993), is another dark comedy of sexual manners that examines a group of urban twentysomethings as they move through a series of meaningless relationships and couplings at the same time that a serial killer relentlessly stalks the city's women. Arcand was less successful with his docudrama on Montreal's homeless, *Joyeux calvaire* (also known as *Poverty and Other Delights* [1996]), but his mockumentary about the media manipulation involved in the discovery and creation of a new celebrity supermodel, *Stardom* (2000), was widely hailed as a shrewd autocritique of contemporary "infotainment," and it became the first Canadian film in fifty years to be selected to close the Cannes Film Festival.

Arcand is the most prominent and successful exemplar of the film movement begun in the 1970s known as *le cinéma québecois*, led by the former critic Jean-Pierre Lefebvre (b. 1941), who between 1964 and 1998 directed twenty-three features, most of them shot in 16mm or, later, on Hi-8 video. Many of these films were in the experimental, polemical style of Jean-Luc Godard (e.g., *Jusqu'au coeur* [1968]), but others were classically constructed dramatic works, such as *Les Fleurs sauvages* (*Wild Flowers* [1982]), a rural family melodrama, beautifully photographed by Guy Dufaux, that won a Special Jury Prize at Cannes. *Québecois* filmmakers who were influenced by Lefebvre include André Forcier (b. 1947), who has specialized in a kind of neorealist guerrilla cinema (*Bar Salon* [1975]; *Au clair de la lune* [1983]); Jacques Leduc (b. 1941), who moved from controversial documentaries (e.g., the banned *Cap d'espoir* [1969]) to experimental features sponsored by the Office National du Film (ONF, the Quebec unit of the NFB), such as *On*

est loin du soleil (*We're Far from the Sun* [1970]); Michel Brault (b. 1928), Canada's most influential cinematographer, who also directed features in the *cinéma vérité* style, the most important of which was *Les Ordres* (*Orders* [1974]), a docudrama about the October Crisis of 1970, when the militant separatist organization FLQ (Front de Libération du Québec) kidnapped two government ministers[2] and the Canadian government invoked the War Measures Act, giving unlimited arrest powers to the police (Brault won the Best Director Prize at Cannes for this film); and Gilles Groulx (1931–1994), an exponent of *cinéma direct* who made the satiric *Les Raquetteurs* (1958; the first short released by the ONF) with Michel Brault and directed the feature-length *Le Chat dans le sac* (1964), a Godardian study of Quebec's youth during the "Quiet Revolution"[3] that won the Grand Prix at the Festival du Cinéma Canadien, as well as the avowedly Marxist *24 Heures ou Plus . . .* (*24 Hours or More* [1971–72; released 1977]), which uses Eisensteinian intellectual montage to critique Quebec's social and economic structure and raise questions of national identity. Other Francophone directors formative of Quebec cinema are Claude Jutra (1930–1986), whose meditative *Mon oncle Antoine* (1971) is still considered one of the best Canadian films ever made, and whose nineteenth-century period piece *Kamouraska* (1973) was one of the most expensive; Gilles Carle (b. 1929), whose family melodrama *Les Plouffe* (1981) and epic romance *Maria Chapdelaine* (1983) were both adapted from influential novels; Jean-Claude Lauzon (1953–1997), whose debut feature, the violent crime drama *Un Zoo la nuit* (*Night Zoo* [1987]), swept the Genies and was followed by the hallucinatory *Léolo* (1992); Mireille Dansereau (b. 1943), whose *La Vie rêvée* (1972) was the first Quebec dramatic feature to be directed by a woman as well as a call to liberation from Quebecois machismo; and Léa Pool (b. 1950), whose early features *La Femme de l'hôtel* (*A Woman in Transit* [1984]) and *Anne Trister* (1986)

---

2. The FLQ kidnapped the visiting British trade minister James Cross and the provincial cabinet minister Pierre Laporte; Laporte was subsequently murdered by his captors.

3. The *Révolution tranquille*, or "Quiet Revolution," begun under the leadership of Premier Jean Lesage (1960–66), was Quebec's shift from a rural society dominated by the Catholic Church to an urban one whose main cohering force was the state and the movement toward independence—i.e., separation from Anglophone Canada.

ripened the feminist strain in Quebec cinema with a European art-film sensibility. The prominent position of *cinéma québecois* filmmakers within the Canadian industry was illustrated by the talent on display in *Montréal vu par* . . . (1991), an anthology of six short films made to celebrate the 350th anniversary of the city's first European settlement, which were directed by Denys Arcand, Michel Brault, Atom Egoyan, Léa Pool, Patricia Rozema, and Jacques Leduc.

Today there is a thriving Francophone film industry centered in Montreal, and the Quebec audience is intensely loyal. Nevertheless, *le cinéma québecois* com-

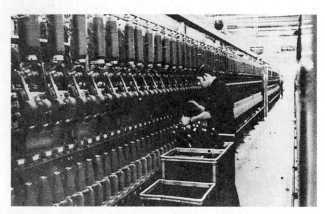

14.54 *Le cinéma quebécois: On est au coton* (Denys Arcand, 1970), a feature-length documentary about the economic oppression of Canadian textile workers by American mill-owners, made for the National Film Board and suppressed by the government.

mands less than an 8 percent share of the province's theatrical gross, with the lion's share going to American films. Ironically, many of these will have been shot on soundstages and locations in Montreal, Toronto, and Vancouver because the favorable exchange rate combined with lower wages, tax breaks, and subsidies make it approximately 35 percent cheaper for an American film to be shot in Canada than in the United States. (Canada's other attractions include a wide variety of locations, skilled film crews, and state-of-the-art postproduction facilities in the same time zones as New York and Los Angeles, all conveniently accessible by air.) The Directors Guild of America (DGA) and the Screen Actors Guild (SAG) claimed that 23,500 film jobs were lost to "runaway production" in 1998, a full 80 percent of it to Canada, which collected $2.5 billion in production costs from American film companies. The inverse corollary, no less striking, is this: in 2000, Telefilm Canada supported the production of 46 domestic features by contributing $15.4 million to their budgets of $89.2 million combined.[4] This means that the entire budget for a full year of Canadian production was equivalent to the budget of single major Hollywood-produced feature. This kind of a economic disparity is one reason the government of Quebec has threatened to amend the Quebec Cinema Act to require that all non-French films be dubbed into that language for distribution, erecting one small barrier to entry against the American majors.

---

4. Production figures are quoted from Brendan Kelly, "Canada," in *Variety International Film Guide 2001* (Los Angeles: Silman-James, 2000), p. 102.

European Renaissance: West

The Second Italian Film Renaissance

Like the American, French, and British cinemas, Italian cinema experienced a creative decline during the 1950s as the neorealist impulse died out and the studios returned to the business of producing mass entertainment. Visconti, Rossellini, and De Sica (see Chapter 11) continued to make serious films, but, as elsewhere, the industry's emphasis was on spectacle and mildly titillating sex. The 1950s was largely a period of "rosy realism" in the Italian film—a mode that might best be understood as a merging of *telefono bianco* and neorealism—and the decade witnessed the appearance of such international sex symbols as Sophia Loren, Gina Lollobrigida, and Marcello Mastroianni. But two figures were working within the domestic cinema at this time who would create the second postwar Italian film renaissance—Federico Fellini (1920–93) and Michelangelo Antonioni (b. 1912).

FEDERICO FELLINI

Formerly a newspaper cartoonist, Fellini began his film career as a scriptwriter for Rossellini (*Roma, città aperta*, 1945; *Paisà*, 1946; *Il miracolo*, 1948[1]), for Pietro Germi (*In nome della legge*, 1949; *Il cammino della speranza*, 1950), and for Alberto Lattuada (*Senza pietà*, 1948). His early films were very much in the orthodox neorealist tradition. *Luci del varietà* (*Variety Lights*, 1950), co-directed with Lattuada, provides an ironic portrait of a seedy itinerant vaudeville troupe. Fellini's first solo film, *Lo sceicco bianco*

---

1. Released in the United States in 1950 as one of three episodes in a film distributed by Joseph Burstyn as *Ways of Love* (the other episodes were Marcel Pagnol's *Jofroi* [1933] and Jean Renoir's *Une Partie de campagne* [1936; 1946]). Fellini also starred in *Il miracolo* as the tramp who is mistaken by a peasant woman for St. Joseph. See Chapter 11 for a discussion of the 1952 Supreme Court *Miracle* decision.

(*The White Sheik*, 1952), is a sardonic account of a young bride's infatuation with the hero of a *fumetto*, or popular photomagazine strip. But *I vitelloni* (*The Loafers/The Young and the Passionate*, 1953) was the first film to reveal the director's remarkable feeling for character and atmosphere. This episodic study of aimless young loafers in the seaside resort town of Rimini, where Fellini grew up, contains semiautobiographical elements, and is one of his finest achievements.

With *La strada* (*The Road*, 1954), produced by Dino De Laurentiis and Carlo Ponti,[2] Fellini made a break with neorealism to tell the story of a simpleminded peasant girl who is sold to a circus strongman for a plate of pasta. He treats her brutally and, after a series of misadventures, finally abandons her. Years later, he learns of her death and collapses in a fit of weeping. Realistic in form but essentially allegorical in content, *La strada* was attacked by leftist critics, including Zavattini (see Chapter 11), for betraying the social commitment of neorealism. But it attracted worldwide attention and won a Silver Lion, the second highest honor, at the prestigious Venice Film Festival in 1954. By the time he made *La strada*, Fellini had assembled about him the group of collaborators with whom he was to work for most of his career: his coscenarists, Ennio Flaiano and Tullio Pinelli; his director of photography, Otello Martelli; his composer, Nino Rota; and his leading lady, Giulietta Masina, who was also his wife. Fellini's next film was *Il bidone* (*The Swindle*, 1955); like *La strada*, it was realistic in style but symbolic in content. This tale of two-bit swindlers who victimize the

poor has an aura of tragedy about it and contains a number of surreal touches that adumbrate Fellini's later concern with psychology and myth. *Le notti di Cabiria* (*Nights of Cabiria*, 1956), which Fellini wrote with the Marxist poet and future director Pier Paolo Pasolini, again has Giulietta Masina as the central figure. Here she plays a plucky, indomitable Roman prostitute who is betrayed and robbed by the young man she loves but who nevertheless has the spirit to begin life anew.

After a hiatus of nearly four years, Fellini produced *La dolce vita* (1960), his first film in widescreen and a turning point in his work. This film concerns the life of a Roman journalist and press agent (Marcello Mastroianni) as he seeks sensational stories and hobnobs with the international jet set. Its superficially realistic milieu is corruption and decadence, and its visual extravagance borders on the fantastic. The film begins with a long traveling shot of a statue of Christ being flown by helicopter over the city and ends at the seashore with the capture of a monstrous dead fish. *La dolce vita* was a huge commercial success because of its sexual explicitness, but it neverthe-

---

2. De Laurentiis (b. 1919) and Ponti (b. 1912) both began their careers as producers during the neorealist period, the former with *Riso amaro* (1948), whose star, Silvana Mangano, De Laurentiis married in 1949, the latter with *Senza pietà* (1948) and *Il mulino del Po* (1949). In 1950 they formed Ponti–De Laurentiis Productions, which produced some of the most important Italian films of the decade—Rossellini's *Europa '51* (1952) and Fellini's *La strada* (1954) and *Le notti di Cabiria* (1956) among them—as well as the epic American/Italian coproduction *War and Peace* (King Vidor, 1956). The partnership was dissolved in 1957, when Ponti married Sophia Loren and began to produce films for her (*The Black Orchid* [Martin Ritt, 1958]; *That Kind of Woman* [Sidney Lumet, 1959]; *Heller in Pink Tights* [George Cukor, 1960]; *Two Women* [Vittorio De Sica, 1960]). In the 1960s, De Laurentiis turned to the production of epic spectacles, such as *Barabbas* (Richard Fleischer, 1962), *The Bible* (John Huston, 1966), and *Waterloo* (Sergei Bondarchuk, 1970), at his vast studios near Rome (also producing Visconti's *Lo straniero* [1967] and Roger Vadim's *Barbarella* [1968]). But he liquidated the property and moved to the United States in the early 1970s, where he has since produced such notable and/or infamous films as *Serpico* (Sidney Lumet, 1973), *Death Wish* (Michael Winner, 1974), *King Kong* (John Guillermin, 1976), *The Serpent's Egg* (Ingmar Bergman, 1977), and *King of the Gypsies* (Frank Pierson, 1979). During the same period, Ponti became a French citizen and produced for Godard (*Une Femme est une femme* [1961] and *Les Carabiniers* [1963]), Varda (*Cléo de cinq à sept* [1962]), Demy (*Lola* [1960]), and Chabrol (*Landru* [1962]). He also produced for David Lean (*Dr. Zhivago* [1965]), Elio Petri (*La decima vittima* [1965]), Antonioni (*Blow-Up* [1966], *Zabriskie Point* [1970], and *The Passenger* [1975]), Andy Warhol (*Andy Warhol's Frankenstein* [1974] and *Andy Warhol's Dracula* [1974], both directed by Paul Morrissey), and Ettore Scola (*Brutti, sporchi, e cattivi* [1976] and *Una giornata particolare* [1977]).

15.1 Fellini's *La Strada* (1954): Giulietta Masina, Anthony Quinn.

15.2 Christ transported by helicopter in the opening shot of Fellini's *La dolce vita* (1960). This was the last feature Fellini shot with his regular cinematographer, Otello Martelli.

less brought Fellini international recognition as a major artist and a new master of widescreen composition.

With *Otto e mezzo* (*8½*, 1963)—so named because it was his eighth-and-a-half film (the "half" having been his contributions to the anthology films *Amore in città*, 1953, and *Boccaccio '70*, 1962)—Fellini moved directly into the world of self-reflexive fantasy. In *8½*, Guido (Mastroianni), a film director who seems to represent Fellini himself, has undertaken a large-scale production but runs out of creative energy in the process. This blockage plunges him (and us) into a subconscious dreamworld of nightmares, fantasies, and flashbacks, that interpenetrate his perceptions of the present and jumble narrative logic.

When Guido finally emerges from his unconscious, he is able to accept the fact that the film he has planned will never be made (although, by this point, Fellini's is nearly complete). In *8½*'s final image, all of the major characters in the director's life and aborted film, many of whom are the same, link hands to dance around the rim of a circus ring as Guido—now a little boy—stands in the middle and directs them confidently through a megaphone. This surrealistic parable of the agony of artistic creation won many international awards; though it has been called a twentieth-century version of Dante's *Inferno*, *8½* is ultimately about the process of its own making.

In *Giulietta degli spiriti* (*Juliet of the Spirits*, 1965), his first feature in color, Fellini focused on a woman (played by Masina) who, like Guido in *8½*, collapses into a world of fantasy under the pressure of an unpleasant external reality (her husband's infidelity, the dominance of her glamorous mother and sisters) and who struggles out of it toward her own identity. Like *8½*, this basically nonnarrative film is concerned with the psychodynamics of memory, obsession, fantasy, and dream, and, like Antonioni's *Il deserto rosso* (see p. 537) the year before, it made highly expressive use of color. After contributing a characteristically haunting episode ("Toby Dammit") to the French anthology film *Histoires extraordinaires* (English title: *Spirits of the Dead*, 1968), Fellini embarked on his most ambitious project to date—*Fellini Satyricon* (1969), a flamboyant, personalized version of Petronius's epic paean to hedonism. In this lavish costume extrava-

15.3 Fellini's *Otto e mezzo* (1963), shot by Gianni De Venanzo: Marcello Mastroianni, Eddra Gale.

15.4 *Fellini Satyricon* (1969), shot by Giuseppe Rotunno.

15.5 A family gathering from Fellini's *Amarcord* (1974), also shot by Rotunno.

years ago. More directly autobiographical than *I vitelloni* and far less mannered and extravagant than its immediate predecessors, the film has been viewed by some critics as a return to Fellini's neorealist roots. It is actually a restrained and muted elegy for the director's youth that provided Fellini with a breathing space before he undertook a spectacular English-language version of Casanova's *Memoirs* (*Casanova*, 1976)—a film more controversial with the critics for its glacially sumptuous tableaux than even *Fellini Satyricon. Prova d'orchestra* (*Orchestra Rehearsal*, 1979), which uses the metaphor of a discordant symphony orchestra to comment on the dangerously chaotic state of modern democracy, has been widely praised for its cinematic beauty and intellectual depth. And the episodic *La città delle donne* (*City of Women*, 1980) offers an intelligent, if fanciful, vision of contemporary sexual warfare within the framework of its male protagonist's dreams. After a hiatus of two and a half years, Fellini returned to directing with *E la nave va* (*And the Ship Sails On*, 1983), a bizarre allegory on the nature of art (and, perhaps, the decline of the cinema) set in the context of a 1914 ocean voyage from Naples to Erimo Island, whose purpose is to scatter the ashes of a recently cremated opera diva. *Ginger e Fred* (*Ginger and Fred*, 1986) is a more conventional but equally hilarious satire on contemporary television and its cult of instant celebrity, while *Intervista* (*Federico Fellini's Interview*, 1987)

ganza based on a script by the director himself, he created a nightmarish portrait of the decadence of ancient Rome. Lacking any specific point of view or human reference, the film was felt by many critics to be purely a feast for the eye, as decadent and grotesque as its subject matter. But others maintained that Fellini had created a unique audiovisual language that transcended traditional narrative to suggest the continuity of depravity throughout human history.

I clowns (*The Clowns*, 1970) was a cinematic essay on the circus, a favorite Fellini metaphor, made on a low budget for Italian television, and it is a decidedly minor work. In *Fellini Roma* (1972), stunningly photographed by Giuseppe Rotunno, the director continued to explore his preoccupation with subjective history in an impressionistic study of Rome that combined stylized documentary with Fellini's own memories of the city as a youth. *Amarcord* (1974; the title is regional dialect for "I remember"), his next major work, is an autobiographical film about a young man growing up in the seaside town of Rimini some forty

15.6 *Intervista* (1987), shot by Tonino Delli Colli.

is an entertaining personal documentary on the director's career at Cinecittà. The last film Fellini completed before his death in 1993 was *La voce della luna* (*The Voice of the Moon*, 1990), which returns to the popular culture of his provincial youth to make a comic, if pessimistic, plea for a quieter, less technocentric world.

Deeply influenced by neorealism in the formlessness and circularity of his narratives, Fellini structured his work through the sheer force of his own personality and obsessions. To use one of his favorite images, Fellini was first and foremost a great ringmaster whose circus was the human comedy as it existed both inside and outside himself. His theme was the mystery of identity (often his own or that of the characters played by Giulietta Masina), and he learned to tap a large portion of the cinema's vast but generally unrealized potential to objectify subjective states, and vice versa. Fellini's rich frescoes and intoxicating images create a stylized world of mental fantasy in which reality is reinterpreted and made significant by the imagination of the artist. As Foster Hirsch has put it, "In his own way, [Fellini] combines the two strains that have always dominated Italian movies: the epic tradition, with its fondness for spectacle and operatic gesture, and the humanist tradition, with its deep feeling for the outcast and the oppressed."

MICHELANGELO ANTONIONI

Michelangelo Antonioni, like Fellini, began his career in film as a neorealist. The son of a wealthy Ferrara businessman, he attended the Centro Sperimentale in Rome and wrote criticism for *Cinema*, after receiving a degree in political economy from the University of Bologna. In 1942 he collaborated on the script of Rossellini's *Un pilota ritorna* and served as an assistant to Marcel Carné on *Les Visiteurs du soir*. His first films as a director were bleak and uncompromising neorealist documentary shorts like *Gente del Po* (*People of the Po*, 1943; 1947), *N.U./Nettezza urbana* (*Dustmen*, 1948), and *La villa dei mostri* (*The House of Monsters*, 1950). But Antonioni's first features broke away from neorealist conventions to examine the middle-class milieu with which he was most familiar. *Cronaca di un amore* (*Story of a Love Affair*, 1950) depicts the consequences of an affair between a wealthy housewife and a car salesman. *I vinti* (*The Vanquished*, 1952) is an episodic film that examines violence among the restless youth of postwar Europe. *La signora senza camelie*

(English title: *Camille without Camellias*, 1953) concerns the rise and fall of a young movie star. All three films deal with social displacement and alienation, major themes in Antonioni's later work.

Antonioni continued to examine middle-class malaise in his first major feature, *Le amiche* (*The Girl Friends*, 1955), based on a novel by Cesare Pavese. In this pessimistic study of the alienated bourgeois women of Turin, Antonioni announced a new style, one that abandoned traditional plotting for a series of seemingly random events and that connected his characters intimately with their environment through the long take, or sequence shot, as opposed to montage. Use of the long take in *Le amiche*, which won the Silver Lion at Venice in 1955, enabled Antonioni to render the duration of real time on the screen and to emphasize the overwhelming importance of the material environment on the interior lives of his characters—the two major components of his mature style. In *Il grido* (*The Cry*, 1957), Antonioni turned briefly from the bourgeois milieu to portray the doomed journey of a factory worker and his daughter across the desolate wasteland of the Po Valley. Here, as in *Le amiche*, Antonioni used the physical environment of his film to express the psychology of the characters. But it was with *L'Avventura* (*The Adventure*, 1959) that Antonioni achieved his first great masterpiece of *mise-en-scène*.

The first film in his brilliant trilogy about displacement and alienation in the modern world, and his first film in

15.7 *Il grido* (Michelangelo Antonioni, 1957): the aesthetics of alienation in an early collaboration with the great cinematographer Gianni Di Venanzo. Mirna Girardi, Steve Cochran.

15.8 Lost in space: Monica Vitti in *L'Avventura* (Michelangelo Antonioni, 1959), shot by Aldo Scarvada.

15.9 *La notte* (Michelangelo Antonioni, 1961): a portrait in despair, with brooding cinematography by Di Venanzo. Marcello Mastrioanni, Monica Vitti.

widescreen, *L'Avventura* concerns a yachting party of rich Italians who land on a deserted volcanic island in the Mediterranean. A young woman, Anna, quarrels with her lover, Sandro, the leader of the party, and then mysteriously disappears. Anna's best friend, Claudia (played by Monica Vitti, who starred in Antonioni's next three films), and Sandro, both of whom have been marginal figures in the film up to this point, search the island for her and can find no trace. At Claudia's instigation, they return to mainland Sicily and continue their search, but they ultimately forget the missing woman and become lovers. The lack of final resolution and the seeming aimlessness of the narrative caused *L'Avventura* to be jeered at the 1960 Cannes Festival; but it received the Jury Prize, and the impact of its revolutionary style was soon felt around the world.

For one thing, Antonioni used the sequence shot in *L'Avventura* to equate film time with **real time:** every scene in the film, whether edited or not, takes the same amount of time to occur on the screen as it would in empirical reality. He also employed widescreen deep focus to link his characters inexorably with their oppressive surroundings. Both techniques have the effect of transferring the psychological experience of the characters to the audience since both groups are required to perceive time and space in precisely the same terms, unmediated by expressive montage. Thus, we experience the long and tedious search for Anna, first on the island and later on Sicily, very much as do Sandro and Claudia— at first with interest and anticipation, then with desperation, and finally with disgust and boredom, which leads us to forget the object of the search altogether and con-

centrate on the relationship of the searchers, just as do the searchers themselves. From one moment to the next, Antonioni never permits us to know any more about the mystery of Anna's disappearance (or about the mystery of their own relationship) than do Sandro and Claudia, and when the film ends with these mysteries unresolved, we realize that the psychological "adventure" of the characters has been made our own.

Antonioni continued his trilogy on what he calls "the great emotional sickness of our era" with *La Notte* (*The Night*, 1960), a film about the growing estrangement of a successful novelist and his wife, and the alienation of both from the vacuous environment of modern industrial Milan. *L'Eclisse* (*The Eclipse*, 1962), a brilliant conclusion to the trilogy, offered Antonioni's most sustained vision of the disorder and incoherence of mod-

15.10 Madness on the floor of the Milan stock exchange in Antonioni's *L'Eclisse* (1962), also shot by Di Venanzo: Alain Delon.

15.11 *Il deserto rosso* **(Michelangelo Antonioni, 1964), shot by Carlo Di Palma: Monica Vitti, Richard Harris.**

ern existence. In Rome, two lovers conclude an affair, having "nothing left to say to each other," and the woman drifts into another affair with her mother's handsome young stockbroker. This affair, too, leads toward estrangement, and the film concludes with a seven-minute montage sequence of fifty-eight shots showing places in the city from late afternoon to nightfall where the lovers have met regularly during the course of the film but in which neither of them now appears. Their unexplained disappearance (and our mute acceptance of it) is a chilling reminder of the fragility and impermanence of personal relationships and provides the perfect coda for a trilogy whose theme is the hopelessness of love in the modern age.

In *Il deserto rosso* (*The Red Desert*, 1964), his first color film and winner of the Venice Golden Lion in 1964, Antonioni portrayed the neurotic wife of a wealthy engineer searching for meaning in the industrial wasteland of Ravenna. Her sense of personal dislocation and the chaotic impingement of industry upon nature are both heightened by Antonioni's impressionist/expressionist use of color, the first of its kind in the history of film. Great poisonous clouds of yellow smoke billow from the factories, ships pass continuously in the background through the gray mists of the harbor, and chemical dyes give a nightmarish cast to the industrial wastes and slag heaps that intrude upon the natural landscape of the town. Antonioni created a foreshortened perspective for this nightmare world by using telephoto lenses (see p. 556) in excess of 100mm to eliminate depth of field and heighten the film's abstraction.

Antonioni also used color symbolically in *Blow-Up* (1966), an abstract and mystifying film about a fashion photographer in "swinging" London who seems to have inadvertently photographed a murder in the background of some random shots he has taken of an anonymous woman in a park. As he "blows up" the telltale prints to

15.12 David Hemmings takes the crucial photograph in Antonioni's *Blow-Up* (1966), also shot by Di Palma.

greater and greater scale, objective reality becomes pure abstraction, and the film ends by suggesting that modern experience, even (or, perhaps, especially) when rendered visible on film, is not subject to interpretation and is, therefore, meaningless. *Blow-Up* was Antonioni's first film to reach a large popular audience, and its commercial success led to his filming of *Zabriskie Point* for MGM in America in 1969. Shot partly on location in Death Valley, this beautiful color film was an attempt to suggest the decadence of American society through the fantasies of the revolutionary young, but it failed due to Antonioni's misunderstanding of the American idiom and American culture. (Some critics had charged *Blow-Up* with a similar distortion of British society, but context was subordinate to concept in that particular film.) For a director to whom milieu is so crucial to meaning, a misunderstanding of this sort can be fatal.

After the commercial failure of *Zabriskie Point*, Antonioni went to China for five weeks to film a 220-minute documentary for Italian television. This poetic color film, entitled *Chung kuo/Cina* (1972), is among Antonioni's finest documentary achievements, but it was attacked by the Chinese for denigrating their revolution (which it most certainly does not). For two years after his return from China, Antonioni worked on a project entitled *Technically Sweet* (*Tecnicamente dolce*), a feature film to be shot on location in the Amazon jungles with a new color telecamera system that would permit him to experiment

still further with expressionistic color. The film's producer, Carlo Ponti, finally vetoed the project and asked Antonioni to consider filming a suspense thriller based on an original story by Mark Peploe about a man who changes his identity. The result was not a thriller at all but a despairing existential meditation on the uselessness of human individuality entitled *Professione: Reporter* (English title: *The Passenger*, 1975). Set in exotic international locations, *The Passenger* concerns a television news reporter at midlife who finds a corpse in a Moroccan hotel and assumes the identity of the dead man. This desperate bid for self-liberation ends in disaster when the dead man turns out to have been a political operative dangerously involved in a Third World guerrilla war. Filmed as a series of long takes and concluding with an elaborate seven-minute zoom-and-tracking shot in which the death of the reporter is obliquely implied rather than observed, *The Passenger* has been acclaimed as a masterpiece, although its clinical detachment from its subject verges on the inhuman. Antonioni has since adapted Jean Cocteau's *L'Aigle à deux têtes* (*The Eagle with Two Heads*) for Italian television as *Il mistero di Oberwald* (*The Mystery of Oberwald*), starring Monica Vitti, and has directed *Identificazione di una donna* (*Identification of a Woman*, 1982), a film that encapsulates a lifetime of personal themes in a more or less straightforward narrative and that won the Special Thirty-fifth Anniversary Prize at Cannes in the year of its release.

When he turned ninety in 2002, Antonioni remained one of the world's greatest living film artists. Although a cerebral hemorrhage suffered in 1985 prevented him from working for a decade, in 1995 he teamed with Wim Wenders to co-direct *Beyond the Clouds* (*Par-delà les nuages/Al di là delle nuvole*), which interweaves four different stories about the vagaries of attraction between men and women. Despite its flaws, the film shows the same numinous reverence

15.13 Postcapitalist apocalypse: from the conclusion of *Zabriskie Point* (Michelangelo Antonioni, 1969), shot by Alfio Contini.

15.14 *Beyond the Clouds* (Michelangelo Antonioni and Wim Wenders, 1995): the surfaces of reality, shot by Wenders's regular cinematographer Robby Muller and Alfio Contini.

for the surfaces of reality (brilliantly photographed by Robby Müller and Alfio Contini) that characterizes the entire body of his work. From *L'Avventura* (1959) through *Beyond the Clouds* (1995), then, Antonioni has tenaciously maintained his integrity and independence to become a poet of the modern individual's estrangement from his environment and of his tragic inability to communicate with others and with himself. His films contain little dialogue and less music, implying the virtual irrelevance of human communication, but they make brilliant use of naturalistic sound and silence to emphasize his characters' isolation in a seemingly random, if not hostile, universe. Antonioni has, by his own account, been concerned with behavior rather than story, and he lets the situations of his films grow out of the personalities and surroundings of his characters, rather than imposing situations through plot. His oblique and languorous narrative style, with its simultaneous capacity for distancing and involvement, has decisively influenced the development of the modern widescreen cinema. What he said of *L'Avventura* after its Cannes premiere speaks for all that he has done since:

> I have rid myself of much unnecessary technical baggage, eliminating all the logical narrative transitions, all those connective links between sequences where one sequence served as a springboard for the one that followed. . . . Cinema today should be tied to the truth rather than logic. . . . The rhythm of life is not made up of one steady beat; it is, instead, a rhythm that is sometimes fast, sometimes slow. . . . There are times when it appears almost static. . . . I think that through these pauses, through this attempt to adhere to a definite reality—spiritual, internal, and even moral—there springs

forth what today is more and more coming to be known as modern cinema, that is, a cinema which is not so much concerned with externals as it is with those forces that move us to act in a certain way and not in another.

OLMI, PASOLINI, AND BERTOLUCCI

While Fellini and Antonioni were becoming acknowledged masters of the international cinema during the 1960s, a second generation of postwar Italian directors was coming to prominence. Ermanno Olmi (b. 1931) was the young filmmaker most clearly in the neorealist tradition, though the slow-paced, elliptical style of his narratives brings him close to the later Antonioni. After making some forty documentaries in Milan between 1952 and 1959, Olmi established an international reputation in his narrative feature *Il posto* (*The Job/The Sound of Trumpets*, 1961). This sympathetic, insightful, and wistfully comic film concerns a young man from the provinces who takes a tedious job as a clerk with a large industrial firm in Milan. It contrasts the systematically dehumanizing nature of the job with his own naïve happiness at finding a place for himself in a complex, urbanized world. Like the films of Olmi's neorealist predecessors, *Il posto* was shot entirely on location with a cast of nonprofessional actors, and it is virtually plotless. *I fidanzati* (*The Fiancés*, 1963) confirmed Olmi's talent for the sympathetic and sophisticated treatment of the lives of ordinary working people. In it, an engaged couple is forced to separate so that the man can pursue his job in faraway Sicily, but they manage to endure and to sustain their relationship.

After an uncharacteristically pedestrian film about the life of Pope John XXIII, *E venne un uomo* (English title: *A Man Named John*, 1965), Olmi produced his finest work to date, *Un certo giorno* (*One Fine Day*, 1968). This film concerns a successful advertising executive who kills a man in an automobile accident and is forced to reexamine the course of his entire life in an attempt to make some sense of it. In the end, he is acquitted of his crime through the services of a smart lawyer and once more succumbs to bourgeois insensitivity. *I ricuperanti* (*The Scavengers*), made for Italian television, Radiotelevisione Italiana (RAI), in 1969, is about the vagrant life of battlefield scavengers in postwar Italy. But with *Durante l'estate* (*In the Summertime*, 1971), also made for RAI, Olmi moved toward romantic fantasy in the visually sumptuous tale of a forger whose rich inner life lends him dignity and significance. As always, Olmi's surface realism here is informed by a sense of the sad and absurd comedy of everyday life. His other films of the 1970s are *La circostanza* (*The Circumstance*, 1974) and *L'albero degli zoccoli* (*The Tree of Wooden Clogs*, 1978). The latter, filmed as a three-part, 180-minute television series on peasant survival in the late nineteenth century, was produced, written, directed, photographed, and edited by Olmi himself. His *Camminacammina* (1983)—which he also wrote, designed, photographed, and edited, as well as directed—is a beautiful children's film about the coming of the Magi made for Italian television. *Milano '83* (1984), a documentary on the cultural life of the city, was also funded by RAI. Olmi's theatrical feature, *Lunga vita alla Signora!* (*Long Live the Lady*, 1987), is a complex political allegory cast in the form of a gothic melodrama, while *La leggenda del santo bevitore* (*The Legend of the Holy Drinker*, 1988) is a religious parable set in 1920s Paris. During the 1990s, Olmi worked mainly on documentaries for television but in 2001 delivered *Il mestiere delle armi* (*Profession of Arms*), a feature-length historical film set in the sixteenth century and based on the circumstances surrounding the death of Giovanni de'Medici in battle, which the director intended as an antiwar parable.

The Marxist poet, novelist, and essayist Pier Paolo Pasolini (1922–1975), who had worked with Fellini on the script of *Le notti di Cabiria* (1956), made his first two films in the neorealist tradition but later rejected it in favor of what he called an "epical religious," or mythic, vision of experience. *Accattone* (*The Beggar*, 1961) and *Mamma Roma* (1962) were tough, uncompromising studies of Roman low-life. Filmed on location with mostly nonprofessional actors, they contained none of the sentimentality that sometimes marred the neorealist films of Rossellini and De Sica. The magnificent *Il vangelo secondo Matteo* (*The Gospel According to St. Matthew*, 1964) was a semidocumentary reconstruction of the life of Christ from the Annunciation to the Resurrection that implicitly examined the relationship between the Marxist dialectic and Christian myth. This stark but brilliant work, shot in *cinéma vérité* style by Tonino Delli Colli (who would become Pasolini's regular cinematographer thenceforth) with nonprofessional actors, stands today as the most dynamic version of the gospel story ever filmed.

As the 1960s progressed, Pasolini turned more and more to allegory and myth. *Uccellacci e uccellini* (English

15.15 *Il vangelo secondo Matteo* **(Pier Paolo Pasolini, 1964), shot by Tonino Delli Colli: Enrique Irazoqui, a nonprofessional actor, as Christ.**

title: *Hawks and Sparrows*, 1966) was, to use Pasolini's term, an "ideo-comic" film about the course of Italian Marxism. In *Edipo re* (*Oedipus Rex*, 1967), shot on location in Morocco, Pasolini set Sophocles' tragedy in a primitive region analogous to the unconscious mind and framed it with a contemporary Freudian prologue and epilogue in order "to project psychology onto myth." *Teorema* (*Theorem*, 1968) and *Porcile* (*Pigsty*, 1969) were both major works in Pasolini's mythico-ideological mode, establishing him as a filmmaker of great intellectual importance. *Teorema* is a mythical allegory set among the bourgeoisie that equates religious experience with sex: a bisexual, extraterrestrial Christ-figure visits an Italian middle-class family and causes it to disintegrate under the pressure of his mysterious sexual attraction. *Teorema* scandalized the Catholic Church, but its companion piece, *Porcile*, goes even further in its attack upon the religious and political hypocrisies of bourgeois culture. The film proceeds by intercutting two savage and revolting parables of capitalism—one about a band of medieval cannibals who live in the hills and eat the flesh of kidnapped travelers, the other about a wealthy contemporary West German industrialist who has made his fortune from the Holocaust and whose demented son loves intercourse with pigs. At the end of the film, the cannibals are ripped apart by wild dogs at the instigation of the local police authorities, and the German youth is eaten by his pigs.

After shooting an extraordinary version of Euripides' *Medea* (1969) in Turkey, Pasolini abandoned the surrealist satire of the 1960s to make a "trilogy of life," as he called it, by adapting three of the world's greatest works of omnibus literature: Boccaccio's *Decameron* (*Il decamerone*, 1971), Chaucer's *Canterbury Tales* (*I racconti di Canterbury*, 1972), and *A Thousand and One Nights/The Arabian Nights* (*Il fiore delle mille e una notte*, 1974), shot on location in Italy, England, and Persia, respectively. His last film was *Salò; o le centoventi di Sodoma* (English title: *The 120 Days of Sodom*, 1975), a version of de Sade's bizarre pornographic epic, which Pasolini updated and set in the Salò Republic of Italy during the last days of Fascist rule. An important theoretician of film in many published essays as well as a brilliant director, Pasolini at his best succeeded in creating an intellectual cinema in which metaphor, myth, and narrative form all subserved materialist ideology. By a grim irony, given his vision of the human race as a "pigsty," Pasolini's remarkable career was cut short in the fall of 1975, when he was murdered by a young thug who claimed that the director had made sexual advances toward him.[3]

Bernardo Bertolucci (b. 1940), Pasolini's assistant on

Accattone, has gone on to become the most significant new director to emerge from the Italian cinema of the 1960s. His film *La commare secca* (*The Grim Reaper*, 1962), made from a script by Pasolini when Bertolucci was only twenty and extremely well received at the Venice Festival, is a documentary-style investigation into the murder of a prostitute. But it was *Prima della rivoluzione* (*Before the Revolution*, 1964) that brought the young director to international attention. This visually complex and intelligent film concerns a young man's inability to break away from bourgeois values and fully commit himself to Marxist ideals. *Partner* (1968) is an uneven film, overtly derivative of Godard, about a modern intellectual who meets his double. But with his dense philosophical investigations into the roots of Fascism—*La strategia del ragno* (*The Spider's Strategy*, 1970), adapted from the Borges fiction "Theme of the Traitor and Hero," and *Il conformista* (*The Conformist*, 1970)—Bertolucci forged a complex and elliptical visual style that bordered on surrealism but was still very much his own.[4]

In *La strategia del ragno*, produced for Italian television, a young man seeks to discover the truth behind his father's death during the Fascist period. *Il conformista*, from the novel by Alberto Moravia, explores the psychology of a young man who is hired by Italian Fascists

15.16 *Salò, o le centoventi giornate di Sodoma/The 120 Days of Sodom* (Pier Paolo Pasolini, 1975), also shot by Delli Colli: the victims enter "The Circle of Obsession."

3. When he died, Pasolini was his country's most prominent Marxist intellectual. He was well on his way toward making an accommodation with the Italian Communist party, which had expelled him for scandals involving homosexuality in 1950, and rumors persist to this day that his murder was politically motivated. In addition to his work as a director, he was a prolific and highly respected author of poetry (in both standard Italian and his native Friulian dialect), fiction, and cultural criticism, as well as an important film theorist (see, e.g., his "The Cinema of Poetry" in Bill Nichols, ed., *Movies and Methods: An Anthology*, 2 vols. [Berkeley: University of California Press, 1976]). Pasolini's poetry and cultural writings are still focal points of contemporary Italian thought. See Enzo Siciliano, Pasolini, trans. John Shepley (New York: Random House, 1982); and Pier Paolo Pasolini, *Roman Nights and Other Stories*, trans. John Shepley (Marlboro, Vt.: Marlboro Press, 1986). See also Dutch documentarist Philo Bregstein's *Whoever Says the Truth Shall Die* (1984), a film biography of Pasolini that attempts to resolve the mysterious circumstances of his death, and Barth David Schwartz's now standard print biography *Pasolini Requiem* (New York: Pantheon, 1992).

4. See Robert Phillip Kolker's provocative critical study *Bernardo Bertolucci* (New York: Oxford University Press, 1985), and T. Jefferson Kline, *Bertolucci's Dream Loom: A Psychoanalytic Study of Cinema* (Amherst: University of Massachusetts Press, 1987). Bertolucci's cousin, Giovanni Bertolucci, often functions as his producer. His brother Giuseppe has collaborated with him as cowriter and is a director of some importance himself (e.g., *Segreti segreti* [*Secrets Secrets*, 1985]).

15.17 *Il conformista* (Bernardo Bertolucci, 1970): Dominique Sanda, Jean-Louis Trintignant.

15.18 **The fruits of political violence:** *Novecento* (Bernardo Bertolucci, 1976). Donald Sutherland.

to assassinate his former professor in France, and it makes a remarkable equation between sexual disorder, social decadence, and the authoritarian personality. Both films employ intricate narrative structures that move freely back and forth through time, emphasizing its relativity. *Il conformista*, Bertolucci has said, is a film not of the past but of the present, because "however the world has changed, feelings remain the same." Bertolucci's controversial *Last Tango in Paris* (*Ultimo tango a Parigi*, 1972) is less complex than *Il conformista*, but like its predecessor it employs an expressionistic color scheme and a disjointed narrative style to take us into the mind of a man deranged by grief, where sex, pain, and death have all melded. The epic *Novecento* (*1900*, 1976)[5]—reputedly the most expensive feature ever made in Italy—employs a cast of international stars to tell the stories of two families, one rich and one poor, through the first fifty years of the twentieth century in a paean to the political consciousness of the Italian agricultural classes.

Influenced by Pasolini, Godard, and the later Visconti rather than the neorealist tradition, Bertolucci is clearly a filmmaker of major importance, and he has continued to produce significant work. Although *La luna* (*Luna*, 1979), his sensuous film about an incestuous mother-son relationship, disappointed some critics, *La tragedia di un uomo ridicolo* (*The Tragedy of a Ridiculous Man*, 1981) offered a brilliant dissection of contemporary Italian political and social life in the drama of a manufacturer attempting to deal with the enigmatic kidnapping of his

son by terrorists. In 1987, Bertolucci directed a film of unique visual splendor in *The Last Emperor*, the winner of multiple international prizes, including nine American Academy Awards. This Italian-Chinese-British coproduction, a biography of Pu Yi, the last imperial ruler of China, was sumptuously photographed by Vittorio Storaro (b. 1940), cost $25 million and employed some 19,000 extras.[6] *The Sheltering Sky* (1990), a much more intimate film, was adapted from a Paul Bowles novel about a spoiled American couple who travel to North Africa in the late 1940s, seeking to rekindle their flagging romance; instead of finding exotic adventure, they wind through a

5. There are two versions of *Novecento* in current release: a 320-minute European version and a 248-minute English-language version, which was edited by Bertolucci himself at the demand of the film's producer-distributor, Paramount. In the English-language version the principal actors speak in their own voices, whereas in the European version the voices are dubbed in Italian.

6. Storaro has been Bertolucci's regular cinematographer since *La strategia del ragno* with the single exception of *La tragedia di un uomo ridicolo*, which was shot by the equally distinguished Carlo Di Palma. Storaro also contributed the vibrant color to Franco Zeffirelli's *Romeo and Juliet* (1968), the sensuous surfaces of Visconti's *Morte a Venezia* (*Death in Venice*, 1971), and the desaturated images of 1938 Rome for Ettore Scola's *Una giornata particolare* (1977), as well as many others. His work on Francis Ford Coppola's *Apocalypse Now* (1979) and Warren Beatty's *Reds* (1981) won him Academy Awards, and he won again in 1987 for *The Last Emperor*. Since then, Storaro has collaborated several times with the veteran Spanish director Carlos Saura (see below), for whose *Tango* (1998) he won a Jury Technical Prize at Cannes.

torturous route from innocence to experience, including death and sexual slavery, against Storaro's hypnotic wide-screen images of the Sahara Desert. *Little Buddha* (1993), also photographed by Storaro, is no less visually splendid. It retells the legend of Siddhartha's youth in contemporary terms when Tibetan monks believe that they have discovered a reincarnation of their mystical leader in a ten-year-old American boy living in 1990s Seattle. (Simultaneously, a film within the film dramatizes the Buddha's spiritual quest as a series of "flashbacks" inspired by the illustrations in a storybook presented to the boy by the monks.) Bertolucci returned to Italy for his next two films—specifically, to Tuscany for *Stealing Beauty* (1996), an idyll about a young woman's coming of age set against the backdrop of the lush Italian country-side, and to Rome for *Besieged* (1998), wherein a British composer falls in love with his African cleaning woman whose husband is being held as a political prisoner in their native Kenya. As always in Bertolucci's work, the cinematography was remarkable, provided in the former film by the Iranian-born director of photography Darius Khondji (b. 1955) and in the latter by the Italian camera-man Fabio Cianchetti.

OTHER ITALIAN *AUTEURS*

Other important figures in the new Italian cinema are Marco Bellocchio (b. 1939), Francesco Rosi (b. 1922), Vittorio De Seta (b. 1923), Elio Petri (1929–1982), and Gillo Pontecorvo (b. 1919). Bellocchio's savage *I pugni in tasca* (*Fist in the Pocket*) shocked Italy in 1965 with its portrait of a young epileptic who makes a rational choice to murder off the members of his diseased bourgeois family. The director's complex and outrageously funny political satire *La Cina è vicina* (*China Is Near*, 1967) launched another frontal assault on bourgeois values and shared the Venice Jury Prize in 1967 with Godard's *La Chinoise*. With *Nel nome del padre* (*In the Name of the Father*, 1971), Bellocchio offered a stylized autobiograph-ical account of life in a provincial Jesuit college in the late 1950s. Like Vigo in *Zéro de conduite* (1933) and Lindsay Anderson in *if. . . .* (1968), Bellocchio uses school as a microcosm for the oppressive, joyless, and class-ridden society that creates and sustains it. Characteristically, his fourth feature, *Marcia trionfale* (*Triumphal March*, 1976), is set in a military academy, but, as in several of Bellocchio's subsequent films (for example, *Il gabbiano*

[*The Seagull*, 1977] and *Salto nel vuoto* [*Leap into the Void*, 1979]), its formal qualities are frequently obscured by a heavy overlay of Marxist ideology. With *Gli occhi, la bocca* (*The Eyes, the Mouth*, 1982), however, Bellocchio became less critical in his analysis of bourgeois family life in a sympathetic if labyrinthine study of the effects of a favorite son's suicide on his mother and brothers. In his adaptation of Pirandello's *Enrico IV* (*Henry IV*, 1984), Bellocchio returned to the theme of his 1974 documen-tary *Matil da slegare* (*Fit to Be Tied*; co-directed with Silvano Agosti, Sandro Petraglia, and Stefano Rulli) on the sanity of those socially defined—and institutional-ized—as being mad. Here, Marcello Mastroianni gives a brilliant performance as a nobleman who is thrown from his horse on his way to a costume party—a trauma that apparently induces the delusion that he is the medieval monarch of the Holy Roman Empire and causes his fam-ily to isolate him in royal splendor in the ancestral castle for twenty years. Subsequently, Bellocchio directed *Il diavolo in corpo* (1986), an erotic, apolitical version of Raymond Radiguet's novel *La Diable au corps* (*The Devil in the Flesh*), already adapted twice before. *La visione de Sabba* (*Witches' Sabbath*, 1988) is a psychological drama about a psychiatrist whose dreams begin to merge with those of one of his most disturbed patients, while *La con-danna* (*The Conviction*, 1990) examined rape from the male perspective artfully enough to win a Silver Bear at Berlin in 1991. Much of Bellocchio's recent work involves literary adaptation. *Il sogno della farfalla* (*The Butterfly's Dream*, 1994) is a version of an existential play by Mas-simo Fagioli; *Il principe di Homburg*, (*The Prince of Homburg*, 1997) is an adaptation of Heinrich von Kleist's 1811 verse play set during the Thirty Years' War between Germany and Sweden; and *La balia* (*The Nanny*, 1999) was inspired by one of Luigi Pirandello's political novellas.

Francesco Rosi, a former assistant to both Visconti and Antonioni, came into his own with *Salvatore Giuliano* (1962), a semidocumentary account of the real-life career of a bandit and folk hero and his murder by the author-ities in postwar Sicily. Shot on location with nonprofes-sional actors, the film has an extremely elliptical narrative structure that moves back and forth in time with the facil-ity of Bertolucci's *Il conformista*. Rosi has since proven himself to be a director of great social commitment and a legitimate heir to neorealism. His *Le mani sulla città* (*Hands over the City*, 1963) is a powerful political film

15.19 *Salvatore Giuliano* (Francesco Rosi, 1962), shot by Gianni De Venanzo.

shot on location in documentary style about the corrupt relationship between real-estate development and modern city planning. *Il momento della verità* (*Moment of Truth*, 1965) is a critical analysis of the collective psychology of bullfighting. Rosi's next films were *Uomini contro* (*Men Against*, 1970), a diatribe against Italy's involvement in World War I, and *Il caso Mattei* (*The Mattei Affair*, 1972), yet another documentary reconstruction of a historical event, in this case the mysterious murder of a government official. *A proposito Lucky* (English title: *Lucky Luciano*, 1973) attempts to show the link between American and Sicilian gangsters and governments, and *Cadaveri eccellenti* (*Illustrious Corpses*, 1976), a characteristic film of political murder and intrigue, won many international prizes. In 1980 Rosi completed work on a four-hour television film (which was also released as a two-and-a-half-hour theatrical feature) based on Carlo Levi's 1945 memoir of political exile, *Cristo si è fermato a Eboli* (*Christ Stopped at Eboli*; English title: *Eboli*, 1980). This award-winning film was followed by another, *Tre fratelli* (*Three Brothers*, 1981), in which three surviving sons return to their small village home for their mother's funeral and discuss the state of contemporary

Italy. Rosi's version of Bizet's opera *Carmen* (1984) was intelligent but unspectacular, while *Cronaca di una morte annunciata* (*Chronicle of a Death Foretold*, 1987) was a stunning critical success. This adaptation of Gabriel García Márquez's fantastic novel of love and death in a sleepy Colombian river town circa 1950 was magnificently shot on location by Rosi's regular cinematographer Pasqualino De Santis[7] (1927–1996) with newly improved Super-Technirama cameras. *Dimenticare Palermo* (*To Forget Palermo*/also known as *The Palermo Connection*,) returned to the familiar terrain of political intrigue in its focus on an imaginary New York mayoral candidate framed by the Mafia. Rosi worked for nearly a decade to produce his last film, *La tregua* (*The Truce*, 1997), a somber adaptation of Primo Levi's novel about his liberation from Auschwitz and nine-month journey homeward to Turin.

The Sicilian-born director Vittorio De Seta, who writes and photographs his own films, made independent documentaries before directing *Banditi a Orgosolo* (*Bandits of Orgosolo*, 1961), a semidocumentary feature shot on location with nonactors, about a Sardinian shepherd who joins a group of revolutionary bandits. The film influenced the development of *cinéma vérité* camera styles in both Italy and France, but with the exception of *Un uomo a metà* (*Almost a Man*, 1965), the story of a young man's descent into madness that took awards at the 1966 Venice Film Festival, and the four-hour semidocumentary *Diario di un maestro* (*Diary of a Schoolmaster*, 1973), De Seta has done little significant work since.

Elio Petri began his career as a scriptwriter for Giuseppe De Santis and Carlo Lizzani during the last days of the neorealist movement, but he later developed into a subtle filmmaker with a sensuous and elliptical visual style of his own. Petri was a Marxist, and his most characteristic films are social satires cast in the form of con-

7. Director of photography for Rosi's first four films was Gianni Di Venanzo (1920–1966); De Santis apprenticed as his camera operator before becoming a director of photography himself. Di Venanzo shot some of the most important Italian films of the 1950s and 1960s, including Antonioni's *Le amiche* (1955), *Il grido* (1957), *La notte* (1961), and *L'eclisse* (1962), and Fellini's *8½* (1963) and *Giulietta degli spiriti* (1965). One of his finest achievements, however, was not an Italian film, but an international coproduction directed by Joseph Losey—*Eva* (1962)—and shot on location in Venice. Di Venanzo revolutionized lighting for black-and-white cinematography by challenging the Italian industry's classical practices, which were theater-based.

ventional genre pieces like *L'assassino* (*The Assassin*, 1961), *La decima vittima* (*The Tenth Victim*, 1965), *Un tranquillo posto di campagna* (*A Quiet Place in the Country*, 1968), and his flamboyant analysis of the contemporary fascist personality, *Indagine su un cittadino al di sopra di ogni sospetto* (*Investigation of a Citizen above Suspicion*, 1970). In the 1970s Petri became more aggressively political, in films like *La classe operaia va in paradiso* (*The Working Class Goes to Heaven*, 1972), winner of the Cannes Grand Prix; *Todo modo* (*All Roads . . .*, 1976); and *Le Buone notizie* (*Good News*, 1979).

Gillo Pontecorvo was a film journalist and an assistant to Yves Allégret before turning to narrative cinema in 1960 with *Kapo*, a semidocumentary account of a young Jewish girl in Auschwitz who collaborates with the SS. Since then, most of Pontecorvo's films have been scrupulously researched documentary reconstructions of historical events using authentic locations and nonactors. His most significant work to date is the remarkable *La battaglia di Algeri* (*The Battle of Algiers*, 1966), which employed the whole city and most of its population to reconstruct with verisimilitude the horrific events leading up to the liberation of Algeria. Financed by the Algerian government, the film won the Golden Lion at Venice in 1966. Impressive but less successful was *Queimada!* (*Burn!*, 1969), an attempt to probe the dynamics of colonial exploitation in the context of a nineteenth-century slave revolt on a Caribbean sugar plantation, and *Operation Ogro* (also known as *The Tunnel*, 1979), about the assassination of Spanish prime minister Luis Carrero Blanco by Basque terrorists in 1973. Since that time, Pontecorvo has directed several shorts (e.g., *Nostalgia di protezione* [1997]) but no features.

Finally, some note should be taken of the important role played by state-operated Italian television, RAI, in the production of major feature films. During the 1970s, distinguished directors like Fellini (*I Clowns*, 1970), Antonioni (*Chung kuo/Cina*, 1972), Bertolucci (*La strategia del ragno*, 1970), Olmi (*I recuperanti*, 1969), and Rossellini (*Socrate*, 1970) have all made films for RAI, often in collaboration with foreign television networks, as in the 1980s have Francesco Rosi, Paolo and Vittorio Taviani, and Ettore Scola. RAI also commissioned features during the 1970s from such promising young directors as Nelo Risi, Gianni Amico, Adriano Aprà, and Liliana Cavani. Private television networks—the most powerful of which were created by media baron Silvio Berlusconi—began to appear in the 1980s, and they largely usurped RAI's role in film production (see below).

Cavani (b. 1933) emerged as a filmmaker of some importance with the notoriety of *Il portiere di notte* (*The Night Porter*, 1974), a sadomasochistic love story that attempts to dissect the culture of fascism, and *Al di là del bene e del male* (*Beyond Good and Evil*, 1977), which re-creates the last, mad years of the German philosopher Friedrich Nietzsche in scatological detail. In the 1980s, Cavani's work descended to Grand Guignol (*La pelle* [*The Skin*, 1981]) and melodramatic excess (*Oltre la porta* [*Beyond the Door*, 1982]), although *Interno Berlinese* (*The Berlin Affair*, 1985), her erotic account of a suicide pact *à trois* in Nazi Germany, earned critical respect. As if to repent, Cavani's most recent films have been an episodic biography of St. Francis of Assisi (*Francesco*, 1989) and a psychological drama about the deaf learning to cope in the hearing world (*Dove siet? Io sono qui* [*Where Are You? I'm Here*, 1993]).

Other notable Italian filmmakers who entered their major productive period during the 1970s are Marco Ferreri (1928–1997), Ettore Scola (b. 1931), the Taviani brothers—Paolo (b. 1931) and Vittorio (b. 1929)—and

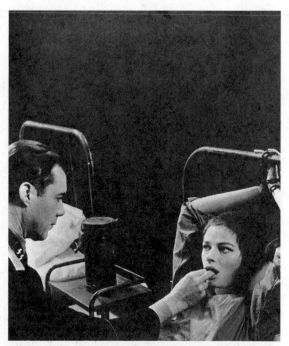

15.20 Liliana Cavani's *Il portiere di notte* (1974), shot by Alfio Contini: Dirk Bogarde, Charlotte Rampling.

Lina Wertmuller (b. 1928). Ferreri, who also worked in France and the United States, was a surrealist social critic in the mode of Buñuel whose characters often end up committing unpremeditated murder (*Dillinger e morto* [*Dillinger Is Dead*, 1968]) or self-mutilation (*La Dernière femme* [*The Last Woman*, 1977]; *Chiedo asilo* [*My Asylum*, 1979]). His most characteristic films of the decade were *La grande bouffe/La grande abbuffata* (*Blow-Out*, 1973), in which four gourmets gorge themselves and die surrounded by their own excrement and vomit, and *Bye Bye Monkey* (1979), an allegory about the extinction of the human race set in New York. *Storie di ordinaria follia* (*Tales of Ordinary Madness*, 1981), adapted from stories by poet Charles Bukowski, depicts the 1960s Los Angeles counterculture as a sleazy pit of self-destructive impulse. *Storia di Piera* (*Story of Piera*, 1983) adapts the controversial autobiography of actress Piera Degli Esposti, whose childhood was allegedly sacrificed to incestuous relationships with both of her parents. Ferreri's other films of the 1980s (*Il futuro èdonna* [*The Future Is Woman*, 1984]; *Y'a bon les blancs* [*Um, Good de White Folks*, 1988]) were not as successful, but *I Love You* (1986), about a young man who develops a fetish for a doll-like talking key-holder, showed that his anarchic spirit was nevertheless still intact, as did *La casa del sor-*

riso (*The House of Smiles* [1991]—winner of the Golden Bear at Berlin), which concerns *l'amor fou* between septuagenarians; *La carne* (*The Flesh* [1991]), in which a nightclub entertainer must cope with a perpetual erection; and *Diario di un vizio* (*Diary of a Madman* [1993], about a man who is ultimately consumed by his sexual fantasies. Ferreri's last two films read like testaments to his bizarre artistic achievement: *Faictz que vous voudras* (*Do What Thou Wilt* [1995]) is a stylized biography of the sixteenth-century satirist François Rabelais, whose epic scatological vision is close in sensibility to Ferreri's own; while *Nitrato d'argento* (*Silver Nitrate/Nitrate Base*, 1996) is a polemical compilation film that mourns the passing of the cinema as mass art.

Ettore Scola was a scriptwriter who began directing comedies in the 1960s and achieved international critical acclaim with *C'eravamo tanto amati* (*We All Loved Each Other So Much*, 1975), an ambitious film that intertwines an examination of the myriad social and economic changes Italy has undergone since the end of World War II with a history of postwar Italian cinema as it has reflected and sometimes catalyzed those changes. *C'eravamo* is dedicated to Vittorio De Sica; and *Brutti, sporchi, e cattivi* (*Dirty, Mean, and Nasty/Down and Dirty*, 1976), a parody of that director's *Miracolo a Milano* (1950), shows the urban poor to be not a happy-go-lucky, socially cohesive group, but hopelessly atomized and infected with capitalist greed. *Una giornata particolare* (*A Special Day*, 1977) recounts a chance meeting between two lonely outsiders—a weary housewife (Sophia Loren) and an antifascist homosexual journalist (Marcello Mastroianni)—on May 6, 1938, the occasion of Hitler's visit to Rome to sign the Axis alliance treaty with Mussolini. *La terrazza* (*The Terrace*, 1980) is a film of comic vignettes that gently probes the relationship between Italian society and the cinema. *Passione d'amore* (1981) meticulously adapts a late-nineteenth-century novel about a strange liaison between a dashing young officer and an unattractive spinster. Scola's reputation as an international figure was resoundingly confirmed by *La Nuit de Varennes* (1982), a comedy of ideas that brings together Casanova, Thomas Paine, and Restif de La Bretonne on June 20, 1791, the day of the abortive flight of Louis XVI and Marie-Antoinette from the Tuileries. Since that time, Scola has directed *Le Bal* (*The Ball*, 1983), an adaptation of the Théâtre du Campagnol's hit stage musical; the wistful comedy *Maccheroni* (*Macaroni*,

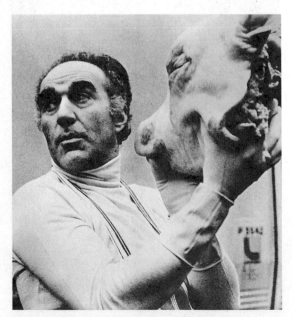

15.21 *La grande bouffe/La grande abbuffata* **(Marco Ferreri, 1973): Michel Piccoli plays with his food.**

1985); *La famiglia* (*The Family*, 1987), a chronicle of the everyday life of a middle-class Roman family between 1906 and 1986; and *Splendor* (1989) a nostalgic salute to movie going in the provinces in the immediate postwar years. Over the next decade, Scola's work continued to be remarkably eclectic, ranging from picaresque romantic comedy in a period setting (*Il viaggio di Capitan Fracassa* [*Captain Fracassa's Journey*, 1990]), to contemporary political drama (*Mario, Maria e Mario* [*Mario, Maria, and Mario*, 1993]), to Hitchcockian psychological thriller (*Romanzo di un giovane povero* [*Story of a Poor Young Man*, 1995]), to a film dramatizing the rise of anti-Semitism during the Fascist period (*Concorrenza sleale* [*Unfair Competition*, 2001]).

The Taviani brothers directed a number of openly political films during the 1960s (*Un uomo da bruciare* [*A Man for Burning*, 1962]; *I sovversivi* [*The Subversives*, 1967]), before turning to a concern with the evolution of the "decent core" of society in the 1970s. *Allonsanfan* (1974)—an Italian mispronunciation of the first two words of the French national anthem, "Allons enfants . . ."—is set in post-Napoleonic Italy, where the Jacobins fight it out with the Freemasons over the purity of revolutionary ideals. *Padre padrone* (*Father Master*, 1977), originally produced for Italian television, brought the Tavianis the Palm d'Or at Cannes, the New York Film Festival award, and international renown. This complex work, based on Gavino Ledda's autobiographical account of how he rose from the illiterate Sardinian peasantry to become a professor of linguistics, weaves fact and fiction, subjective sound and concrete image, to create a narrative that is at once emotionally satisfying and ideologically persuasive. After this stunning achievement, *Il prato* (*The Meadow*, 1979), about the social frustrations of a young Tuscan magistrate, was generally disappointing; but the Tavianis scored another triumph with *La notte di San Lorenzo* (*The Night of Shooting Stars*, 1982), which depicts the successful struggle of a small rural community to survive a massacre by the Germans in 1944, based on an actual atrocity that took place in their hometown. (The brothers' first film, *San Miniato, Iuglio '44* [*San Miniato, July 44*, 1954] was a documentary short on the same subject, produced in collaboration with Cesare Zavattini.) This film, which won a Special Jury Prize at Cannes, was written by the Tavianis and is narrated in flashback by a woman who was six years old at the time. Since then, the brothers have written and directed *Kaos* (*Chaos*, 1984),

an anthology of five episodes adapted from the novels of Pirandello, *Good Morning, Babilonia* (*Good Morning, Babylon*, 1987), an original film in which two Italian immigrant brothers impersonate master masons in order to get jobs as set designers on D. W. Griffith's epic spectacle *Intolerance* (1916), and *Il sole anche di notte* (*Night Sun*, 1990), an eighteenth-century drama of political intrigue and redemption based on Tolstoi's "Father Sergius." The Tavianis continued to examine the dynamics of family life in their native Tuscany in *Fiorile* (*Wild Flower*, 1993) and to adapt works of literature—*Le Affinità Elettive* (1996), from Goethe's novel *Elective Affinities*, and *Tu Ridi* (*You're Laughing*, 1998), from two novellas by Luigi Pirandello.

Lina Wertmuller, who became something of a cult figure in the United States during the 1970s, began her film career as an assistant to Fellini on *8½* (1963). That year she directed her first feature, a sociocomedy of Italian provincial life entitled *I basilischi* (*The Lizards*). She continued to make intelligent comic films for the domestic market until she scored her first international success with *Film d'amore e d'anarchia* (*Love and Anarchy*, 1973), an ironic examination of sex and politics in Fascist Italy, focusing on the attempts of a bungling anarchist (played by Giancarlo Giannini—a Wertmuller regular) to assassinate Mussolini. *Mimímetallurgico ferito nell'onore* (*Mimi the Metalworker/The Seduction of Mimi*, 1972) and *Tutto a posto e niente in ordine* (*Everything's in*

15.22 The Taviani brothers' *Good Morning, Babilonia* **(1987): on the Babylonian set of** *Intolerance.*

Order But Nothing Works/All Screwed Up, 1974) also deal with the situations of hopeless underdogs (both played by Giannini) pitted against the system, and both carry the connection between sex and politics one step further. The ultimate statement of that connection, however, is *Travolti da un insolito destino nell'azzurro mare d'Agosto* (*Swept Away by an Unusual Destiny in the Blue Sea of August / Swept Away*, 1974), in which a wealthy woman and a deckhand are swept away by a storm from a pleasure yacht to a desert island, where their roles as master and slave are temporarily reversed. Eventually the two fall in love, but when they return to society their old roles reassert themselves. Many feminist critics were disturbed by the film's ironic balance, but such irony is precisely Wertmuller's stock in trade as an artist. As proof, we have *Pasqualino settebellezze* (English title: *Seven Beauties*, 1976), a physically sumptuous paean to survival ethics set largely in a Nazi concentration camp where the Giannini character, an Italian army deserter, spends the duration of World War II. This complex film is by turns beautiful and repellent since we are asked to identify with a protagonist who possesses the moral sensibility of a cockroach as well as the knack of surviving like one. The moral relativism of *Seven Beauties* outraged as many liberal critics as *Swept Away* did feminists because both films seemed to endorse patriarchal fascism. Whatever their point ideologically, the last films made by Wertmuller in the 1970s—*The End of the World in Our Usual Bed in a Night Full of Rain* (1978) and *Blood Feud* (1979)—failed at the box

15.24 Lina Wertmuller's *Pasqualino settebellezze (Seven Beauties,* 1976), shot by Tonino Delli Colli: Shirley Stoler as the concentration camp commandant.

office. Wertmuller did not direct again until *Scherzo del destino in agguato deitro l'angolo come un brigante di strada* (*A Joke of Destiny Lying in Wait around the Corner Like a Robber*, 1983), a social allegory about a government minister getting locked up in his bullet proof and soundproof limousine; *Camorra* (1986), a murder mystery with social themes set in the context of Neapolitan gang wars; and *Notte d'estate con profilo Greco, occhi a mandorla e odore di basilico* (*Summer Night with Greek Profile, Almond Eyes, and Scent of Basil*, 1986), a reworking of the class- and sex-war themes of *Swept Away*, set on a Sardinian isle. Several of her more recent films—e.g., *Il decimo clandestino* (1989) and *Sabato, Domenicae Lunedì* (1990)—have not been distributed outside of Italy, but *Ciao, Professore* (1993), a tale of a dozen Neopolitan children reclaimed from their lives as truants by a straightlaced northern Italian schoolteacher, was a critical and commercial success in the United States. Since then, Wertmuller has worked more regularly, producing films of gender-based social criticism (*Ninfa plebea* [*The Nymph*, 1996]; *Francesca e Nun-*

15.23 *Swept Away* (Lina Wertmuller, 1974): Mariangela Melato, Giancarlo Giannini.

ziata [2001]), historical comedy (*Ferdinando e Carolina* [1999]), and the ironic mix of sexuality and political power that, during the 1970s, she made uniquely her own (*Metalmeccanico e parrucchiera in un turbine di sesso e di politica* [*The Worker and the Hairdresser in a Whirl of Sex and Politics*, 1996]).

The most significant development for Italian cinema in the 1980s was the emergence of a new generation of talented comedy directors whose roots reach back to the traditions of *commedia dell'arte* but whose social consciousness and filmic technique are firmly grounded in contemporary reality. This group includes Maurizio Nichetti (b. 1948), whose brilliant surrealist pantomime *Ratataplan* (the word imitates the sound of a drum roll to Italian ears) swept the awards at Venice in 1979. He followed with the equally hilarious send-up of contemporary advertising, *Ho fatto splash!* (*I Made a Splash!*, 1980), and the absurdist satires *Domani si balla* (*Tomorrow We Dance*, 1982) and *Il be e il ba* (*The Bi and the Ba*, 1986). More mainstream were *Ladri de saponette* (*The Icicle Thief*, 1989), Nichetti's combined satire of television and the art-film mystique, and *Volere volare* (*I Want to Fly*, 1991), another satire of modern media, which combines animation and live action. Nichetti appears as the main comic character in nearly all of his films, which in recent years have turned increasingly toward fantasy—e.g., *Luna e l'altra* (*Luna and Her Double*, 1996) and *Honolulu Baby* (2001). Nanni Moretti (b. 1953) began making films in Super 8, and his first hit was the 16mm *Ecce Bomba* (1978), a parody of traditional Italian film comedy that, like the work of Nichetti, owed much to American silent slapstick as well as to the satiric wit of Woody Allen and Mel Brooks. Moretti's next film, *Sogni d'oro* (*Golden Dreams*, 1981), about a Fellini-like director making a film on Freud's mother, won the Golden Lion at Venice. He continued to mine this vein of sardonic, irreverent social comedy in *Bianca*

(1984) and *La messa è finita* (*The Mass Is Over*, 1985), and *Palombella rossa* (*The Little Red Dove*, 1989)—the last two about the decay of the Catholic Church and the Italian Communist party, respectively—and, more recently, *Caro Diario* (*Dear Diary*, 1994), a film diary in three chapters. Moretti continued in the diaristic mode with *Aprile* (1998), which charts nearly three years of his life, including the pregnancy of his partner and the birth of their son in April. *La stanza del figlio* (*The Son's Room*, 2001) was Moretti's first dramatic feature in over ten years and his first deeply serious one: it concerns the reaction of a successful psychiatrist (Moretti) and his family to the accidental death of their teenage son, and, quite unexpectedly, it won the Palm d'Or at the 2001 Cannes Film Festival.

Carlo Verdone (b. 1950) has been successful with such episodic film sketches in Roman dialect as *Un sacco bello* (*Life Is Beautiful*, 1980); *White, Red, and Verdone* (1981, with the director's name replacing the *verde* of the Italian tricolored flag); *Acqua e sapone* (*Soap and Water*, 1983); *I due carabinieri* (*The Two Cops*, 1985); and many more. (In fact, Verdone wrote, directed, and starred in an average of one film a year between 1979 and 2000, making him the most prolific of all of the Italian directors discussed in this chapter.) Massimo Troisi (1953–1994), whose *Ricomincio da tre* (*I'm Starting Over from Three*) was a smash hit in 1981, made low-budget films in the Neapolitan dialect; most recently he

15.25 *Life Is Beautiful* (Roberto Benigni, 1997): father (Benigni) and son (Giorgio Cantarini) escape from a Nazi concentration camp, shot by the distinguished director of photography, Tonino Delli Colli. Some critics took exception to the idea of a comedy set during the Holocaust.

teamed with the Tuscan dialect comic Roberto Benigni to produce *Non ci resta che piangere* (*Nothing Left to Do but Cry*, 1985), *Le vie del Signore sono finite* (*The Ways of the Lord Are Finite*, 1987), a period comedy set in the early days of Fascism, and *Penasavo forse amore invece era un calesse* (1991). (Benigni's own films as a director, especially *Il piccolo diavolo* [*The Little Devil*, 1987] and his Sicilian Mafia spoof *Johnny Stecchino* [1992], were very popular with Italian audiences, but his big international breakthrough was *La vita è bella* [*Life is Beautiful*, 1997]. This comedy set in a Nazi concentration camp convinced many critics that Begnini was a serious artist, and it won several Oscars and the Jury Prize at Cannes.) Like Nichetti, Moretti, and Verdone, Troisi not only wrote and directed his films, but also played leading roles in them. A final comic filmmaker of note is the prolific Bolognese director Pupi Avati (b. 1938). Though of an older generation than the quartet discussed above, Avati came to filmmaking relatively late. He is best known for the highly original musical about Italy's fascination with American culture *Aiutami a sognere* (*Help Me to Dream*, 1981) and such offbeat light comedies as *Una gita scolastica* (*A School Outing*, 1983), *Noi tre* (*We Three*, 1984), *Festa di laurea* (*Graduation Party*, 1985), *Fratelli e sorelle* (*Brothers and Sisters*, 1993), and *Festival* (1996—a send-up of the Venice Film Festival), as well as historical reconstructions (*Magnificat*, 1993—set among ninth-century religious pilgrims; *I cavalieri che fecero l'impresa* [*The Knights of the Quest*, 2001]—set in 1272, during the Crusades). But he has also made serious contemporary dramas such as *Regalo di natale* (*Christmas Present*, 1986), *Ultimo minuto* (*Last Moment*), *The Story of Boys and Girls* (1990), and *Bix* (1991—a film about jazz pioneer Bix Beiderbecke, shot on location in the musician's hometown of Davenport, Iowa); and *Il Testimone dello Sposo* (also known as *The Best Man*, 1997), a provincial marital drama that won multiple international awards. Avati's artistic breadth is illustrated by the fact that he began his career writing and directing horror films, some of which are considered to be genre classics—e.g., *La casa dalle finestre che ridono* (*The House with the Laughing Windows*, 1976), *Macabro* (1980; script only), *Zeder/Revenge of the Dead* (1983), and more recently *L'arcano incantatore* (*The Arcane Enchanter*, 1996), based on the true story of an eighteenth-century necromancer.

THE ITALIAN EXPLOITATION FILM

Although they brought international prestige to the Italian cinema, art-film directors like Fellini and Antonioni did not sustain the industry financially during the 1960s and 1970s. No account of the Italian cinema after neo-realism would be complete without a discussion of three exploitation genres that became financial mainstays for both studios and independent producers during this period—the "peplum" epics, the "spaghetti Western," and the Italian horror film, especially the subtype known as the *giallo* and its clones. These genres were important not only in an industrial and economic sense, but—like Hollywood B-films of the 1930s and 1940s, and the youth-cult exploitation films produced by AIP during the 1950s and 1960s—they provided the training ground for many directors who later became important figures in the mainstream cinema. With roots in the Italian pre–World War I superspectacle (see Chapter 2), the peplum films (named for the short skirt worn by the protagonists, both male and female) were sword-and-sandal epics with plots inspired by classical mythology and heroes drawn from the ancient world.[8]—e.g., Hercules, Ulysses, and Spartacus, who were often played by American bodybuilders like Steve Reeves; 170 such films were produced by the Italian industry between 1957 and 1964, representing 10 percent of national production. The first was *Le fatiche di Ercole* (*The Labors of Hercules* [Pietro Francisci, 1957]), which, imported into the United States by Joseph E. Levine as *Hercules* in 1959, grossed an astonishing $18 million. This success led to the creation of multiple peplum franchises—the original *Hercules* series, 1958 to 1965; the *Maciste* series, 1959–1965; and the *Ursus* series, 1960–1962 (the latter two based on characters from the paradigmatic superspectacle *Cabiria* [1914]).

As the peplum cycle was winding down, Cinecittà began to make Westerns to fill the void left by Hollywood when it abandoned the genre to television. These films

---

8. Although most peplum epics relied on allusions to Greek mythology and Roman history, they often strayed from classical antiquity into Biblical (Sampson and Goliath occasionally appeared) and even non-Western terrain (e.g., Osvaldo Civirani's *Ercole contro i figli del sole*/ *Hercules against the Sons of the Sun* [1964] has the superhero doing battle against Aztec gods, whereas Antonio Margheriti's *Ursus il terrore dei Kirghisi* [1964] has Hercules fighting Kirghisian werewolves).

15.26 *Le fatiche di Ercole* (*The Labors of Hercules*, [Pietro Francisci, 1957]), shot by Mario Bava: American bodybuilder Steve Reeves in the title role. Picked up by American distributor Joseph E. Levine and retitled *Hercules* (1959), this film was North America's introduction to the Italian peplum genre.

by the innovative and distinguished Ennio Morricone), a Latinate cast and a Mexican setting (here represented by Spanish locations), and an emphasis on sudden and shocking violence. Leone's ironic stylization of American myths continued though two more Westerns—*C'era una volta il West* (*Once Upon a Time in the West*, 1967) and *Giù la testa* (*A Fistful of Dynamite/ Duck, You Sucker!*, 1971)— and a gangster epic—*C'era una volta in America* (*Once Upon a Time in America*, 1983)—and he is today regarded as a major figure in postwar Italian cinema.

competed head-to-head with other Euro-Westerns from the same period, especially with German-Yugoslav coproductions adapted from Karl May's adventure novels (e.g., Harald Reinl's *Der schatz im Silbersee* [*Treasure of Silver Lake*, 1962]). Cinecittà had made approximately twenty-five of them using some of the same creative personnel as were used in the peplum epics—Riccardo Freda (1909–1999), Mario Bava (1914–1980), Sergio Corbucci (1926–1990)—before Sergio Leone (1929–1989) set the standard for the genre in his "Dollars" trilogy, starring Clint Eastwood as "Man With No Name." Leone, who had directed the spectacular peplum *Il colosso di Rodi* (*The Colossus of Rhodes*, 1961) and had worked as assistant director on Robert Aldrich's *Sodom and Gomorrah* (1963), is usually credited with establishing an international market for the Italo-Western, some 400 of which were produced between 1963 and 1973, dominating Italian film exports for a decade. Leone's trilogy—*Per un pugno di dollari* (*A Fistful of Dollars*, 1964), *Per qualche dollaro in più* (*For a Few Dollars More*, 1965), and *Il buono, il brutto, il cattivo* (*The Good, the Bad, and the Ugly*, 1966)—contain all of the hallmarks of the classical spaghetti Western—baroque framings, an emphasis on duration through both the long take and montage, an electronically synthesized score (in this case,

Among the 400 plus spaghetti Westerns that imitated Leone's successful formula, there were several notable series—e.g., the more than twenty sequels to Sergio Corbucci's ultraviolent *Django* (1966), starring Franco Nero; Duccio Tessari's "Ringo" series (*Una pistola per Ringo/A Pistol for Ringo*, 1965); Gianfranco Parolini's *Sabata* (1969) series; Giuliano Carnimeo's "Sartana" series (*Sartana the Gravedigger*, 1969); and Enzo Barboni's "Trinity" series (*Lo chiamavano Trinità/They Call Me Trinity*, 1970). Some spaghetti Westerns had overtly political themes, such as Damiano Damiani's *¿Quien sabe?/A Bullet for the General* (1966) and Carlo Lizzani's *Un fiume di dollari/The Hills Run Red* (1966), and by the end of the cycle others verged on self-parody (e.g., Tonino Valerii's *Il mio nome è nessuno/My Name Is Nobody* [1973]). The Italian Western had an enormous influence on American pracitioners as diverse as Sam Peckinpah, Ralph Nelson, and Robert Altman (see Chapters 13 and 20),[9] and it raised the bar on the graphic depiction of violence in cinema generally. So, too, did the Italian horror film—especially

---

9. Spaghetti Western directors and stars were often credited under American-sounding pseudonyms to increase their U.S. market appeal— Leone was "Bob Robertson," Corbucci was "Stanley Corbett," Barboni

15.27 *A Fistful of Dollars* (Sergio Leone, 1964): Clint Eastwood ("Man With No Name") faces off against a gang of bandits in this influential spaghetti Western, itself a conscious remake of Kurosawa's *Yojimbo* (1961); stylized widescreen cinematography (here by Massimo Dallamano in Techniscope) was a Leone hallmark.

the *giallo*, which codified the psychoslasher genre and made its transgressive gore acceptable to mainstream audiences.

The Italian horror cinema came into being at the same time as the peplum epic—with few exceptions, it can be dated from the appearance of Riccardo Freda's *I vampiri* (*The Vampires/Lust of the Vampire*, 1957), a visually ornate retelling of the Elizabeth Báthory legend that tapped into the gothic roots of the genre. Inspired by Roger Corman's Poe adaptations (and, philosophically by Poe himself), Freda's cinematographer, Mario Bava, confirmed this commitment to gothic in the lyrical *La maschera del demonio* (*Mask of the Demon/Black Sunday*, 1960), which launched the career of the British-born actress Barbara Steele (b. 1937) as Italy's horror diva par excellence and contained an undercurrent of sexual pathology that would become a hallmark of the Italian horror film—a tendency readily glimpsed in Freda's necrophiliac fantasy *L'orribile segreto del Dr. Hichcock* (*The Terrible Secret of Dr. Hichcock/The Horrible Dr. Hichcock*, 1962) and its sequel, *Lo Spettro* (*The Ghost/The Spectre*, 1963), which also starred Steele, as well as Bava's own hymn to sadomasochism, *La frusta e il corpo* (*The Whip and the Body*, 1963). Gothic imagery was key to Antonio Margheriti's similarly atmospheric *Danza macabra* (English title: *Castle of Blood*, 1964) and *I lunghi capelli della morte* (*The Long Hair of Death*, 1964), as well as to Massimo Pupillo's *Cinque tombe per un medium* (English title:

Terror-Creatures from the Grave, 1965) and Mario Caiano's *Amanti d'oltretomba* (English title: *Nightmare Castle*, 1965), all four of which starred Steele. After the gothic anthology *I tre volti della paura* (*Three Faces of Fear/Black Sabbath*, 1963), Bava made the film that would steer Italian horror in a completely new direction—that of sadistic terror. *Sei donne per l'assassino* (*Six Women for the Murderer/Blood and Black Lace*, 1964), uses the flimsiest of murder-mystery plots in order to focus our attention on the act of murder itself as sado-voyeuristic spectacle. This was the fundamental impulse of the thriller genre known as the *giallo* that would come to dominate Italian horror in the 1970s, and Bava himself made many other such films (e.g., *Un hacha para la luna de miel* [*Hatchet for the Honeymoon*; 1969]; *Cinque bambole per la luna d'agosto* [*Five Dolls for an August Moon*, 1970]; *Reazione a catena/Antefatto* [English title: *A Bay of Blood* [1971]), but his last important work was a ghost story in the gothic mode—*Operazione paura* (*Operation Fear* [also known as *Kill, Baby, Kill*, 1966]—whose hallucinatory color palette and sensuously fluid camera movement demonstrated how deeply art can interfuse a low-budget form.

With the international success of a single film in 1969, Dario Argento (b. 1940) made the *giallo* his special province for a decade. (*Giallo* means "yellow" in Italian and refers to the low-grade yellow paper that detective

was "E. B. Clucher," Parolini was "Frank Kramer," Carnimeo was "Anthony Ascott," Lizzani was "Lee Beaver," and so on. This practice was adopted by Italian horror and *giallo* directors too, although here the cachet was Anglo-American (Riccardo Freda became "Robert Hampton;" Antonio Margheriti was "Anthony Dawson," etc.), presumably to cater to the large market for sadistic-terror films in Britain. (In fact, it was the success of Hammer Films' *Horror of Dracula* [Terence Fisher, 1958] in Italy, where it was released as *Dracula, il vampiro*, that inspired the Italian gothic-horror boom.)

15.28 *La maschera del demonio* (*Mask of the Demon/Black Sunday* [Mario Bava, 1960]): gothic horror icon Barbara Steele as the resurrected Asa, a high satanic priestess executed in the seventeenth century. Originally a cinematographer, Bava was a master at creating atmosphere through light and shade.

and horror novels were printed on in the 1930s and 1940s—the English-language equivalent might be "pulp," indicating a form of fiction that is cheap, lurid, and sensational but also highly efficient.) *L'uccello dale piume di cristallo* (*The Bird with the Crystal Plumage*) is a sort of ultraviolent version of *Blow-Up* in which the attempt to solve a series of slasher murders puts the protagonists in ever-greater jeopardy from the murderer. While it has some interest at the level of character and plot, the film is essentially a stripped-down machine for the delivery of sado-voyeuristic thrills. From *Il gatto a nove code* (*Cat o' Nine Tails*, 1971) and *Quattro mosche di velluto grigio* (*Four Flies on Grey Velvet*, 1971) through *Profondo Rosso* (*Deep Red*, 1975), *Suspiria* (1977), *Inferno* (1980), and *Tenebrae* (1982), Argento refined his style until he approached a level of nearly plotless, abstract horror—a visionary cinema of attractions whose stylistic hallmarks are a lurid, saturated color palette, a perpetually moving Steadicam, and increasingly bizarre special effects (e.g., *Phenomena* [1985]; *Opera* [1987]). But his early films were widely imitated, and the *giallo* became for several years an extremely popular form. Whereas most of the gothic horror films of 1960s had been shot in stylized black and white, all of the *gialli* were shot in Technicolor and Techniscope, as befits a subgenre whose most salient content was visceral horror; many also featured edgy scores by Ennio Morricone and/or his frequent collaborator Bruno Nicolai, as well as makeup effects by Carlo Rambaldi

(who would later share Oscars for *King Kong* [1976], *Alien* [1979], and *E.T.* [1982]); and some of the best were written by Ernesto Gastaldi (b. 1934), a veteran scenarist of both gothic horror and peplum films. There were over 100 *gialli* released between 1971 and 1975; some of the best were directed by Lucio Fulci (*Una lucertola con la pelle di donna* [*Lizard in a Woman's Skin*, 1971]; *Non si sevizia un paperino* [*Don't Torture a Duckling*, 1972], Riccardo Freda (*L'iguana dalla lingua di fuoco* [*The Iguana with the Tongue of Fire*, 1971], Paolo Cavara (*La tarantola dal ventre nero* [*Black Belly of the Tarantula*, 1971), Sergio Martino (*Lo strano vizio della signora Wardh* [English title: *Next!*, 1970]; *La coda dello scorpione* [*The Case of the Scorpion's Tail*, 1971]; *Tutti I colori del buio* [English title: *They're Coming to Get You*, 1972]; *I corpi presentano trace di violenza carnale* [*Torso*, 1973], Umberto Lenzi (*Oasis of Fear* [*Un posto ideale per uccidere*, 1971]; *Sette orchidee macchiate di rosso* [*Seven Blood-stained Orchids*, 1972]; *Il coltello di ghiaccio* [*Knife of Ice*, 1972]; *Spasmo* [1974], Massimo Dallamano (*Cosa avete fatto a Solange?* [*What Have They Done to Solange?*, 1971]; *La polizia chiede aiuto* (English title: *What Have They Done to Our Daughters?*, 1974]), Luciano Ercoli (*Le foto proibite di una signora per bene* [*Forbidden Photos of a Lady above Suspicion*, 1970]; *La morte cammina coni tacchi alti* [*Death Walks on High Heels*, 1971]; *La morte accarezza a mezzanotte* [English title: *Cry Out in Terror*, 1971]), Armando Crispino (*L'etrusco uccide ancora* [English title: *The Dead Are Alive*, 1972]; *Macchie solari*

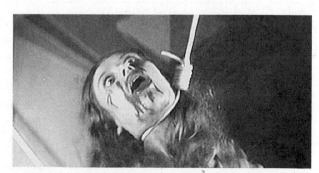

15.29 The sado-erotic *giallo* meets horror in *Suspiria* (Dario Argento, 1977), a stylized murder mystery shot in three-strip matrix Technicolor (by Luciano Tovoli) to give the film a hallucinatory intensity equal to its Goblin score

[English title: *Autopsy*, 1973]), Renato Polselli (*Delirio caldo* [*Delirium*, 1972]), and Enzo G. Castellari (*Gli Occhi freddi della paura* [English title: *Cold Eyes of Fear*, 1974]). The *giallo* peaked in 1975 but reemerged during the American slasher cycle of the early 1980s, which it had decisively influenced—e.g., John Carpenter's *Halloween* [1978] bears a striking resemblance to Argento's *Four Flies on Grey Velvet*; Sean Cunningham's *Friday the 13th* [1980] is a virtual remake of Bava's *A Bay of Blood*; and Brian De Palma's *Dressed to Kill* [1980] is so *giallo*-esque that it might have been shot at Cinecittà. In the wake of the slasher boom, Italian directors demonstrated that the *giallo* was still a viable form—Fulci produced *The New York Ripper* (1982); Mario Bava's son Lamberto directed *La casa con la scala nel buio* (English title: *A Blade in the Dark*, 1983) and *Delirium* (1987); Ruggero Deodato made *Camping del terrore* (English title: *Body Count*, 1986) and *Ragno gelido* (*Dial Help*, 1988)—but in fact, by the mid-1980s, Italian horror had already entered a new stage.

Starting with Argento's *Suspiria*, a new style of hallucinatory horror had been broached that involved heavy doses of neo-gothic fantasy and prosthetic gore. During the 1980s, the master of this style was Lucio Fulci (1927–1996), a paragon of the Italian exploitation cinema who had worked in every genre from peplum films to spaghetti Westerns and *gialli* (see above).[1] In 1979, with *Zombi 2* (U.K. title: *Zombie Flesh Eaters*; U.S. title: *Zombie*), Fulci embarked upon a series of

films described by one critic as "brutal journeys into metaphysical chaos and abject physical horror."[2] (The title of Fulci's film was chosen to capitalize on the success of George Romero's Italian-made *Dawn of the Dead*, coproduced by Dario Argento, and released in Italy in the fall of 1978 as *Zombi*.) *Zombi 2* was a resounding success, grossing $30 million internationally on an investment of about $500,000, and, together with Romero's film, it led to a wave of Italian zombie and cannibal films that concentrated on scenes of mutilation, torture, and dismemberment with savage intensity—brilliantly provided in many cases by the special-effects and makeup artist Gianetto (Gino) De Rossi (b. 1942). Under the influence of Fulci, however, Italian zombie films attained a kind of weird, if repulsive, poetry—e.g., Marino Girolami's *Zombie Holocaust* (1980) and Andrea Bianchi's *Le notti del terrore* (*Night of Terror/Burial Ground*, 1980)—whereas the 1980s cannibal films (whose lineage was older and included Gualtiero Jacopetti's and Franco Prosperi's shocking "documentary" feature *Mondo Cane* [1962], Umberto Lenzi's *Il paese del sesso selvaggio* [English title: *Deep River Savages*, 1973], and Ruggero Deodato's *Ultimo mondo cannibale* [English title: *Jungle Holocaust*, 1977]) tended toward graphic, stomach-churning realism presented from a speciously clinical "ethnographic" point of view. (Disgusting and arguably obscene, the apocalyptic carnality of several cannibal films—e.g., Deodato's *Cannibal Holocaust* [1979] and Lenzi's *Cannibal ferox* [English title: *Make Them Die Slowly*, 1981]—lent them a per-

---

1. Fulci also made erotic comedies (*All'onorevole piacciono le donne* [*The Senator Likes Women*/also known as *The Eroticist*, 1972]), adventures (*Zanna Bianca* [*White Fang*, 1972] and *Il ritorno di Zanna Bianca* [*The Return of White Fang*, 1974]), Westerns (*I Quattro dell'apocalisse* [*Four of the Apocalypse*, 1975]); crime thrillers (*Luca il contrabbandiere* [*The Smuggler*, 1980], sword-and-sorcery epics (*La conquista* [*The Conquest*, 1983]), science fiction (*I guerrieri dell'anno 2072* [*Rome, 2072—The Fighter Centurions*, 1983]), and historical melodrama (*Beatrice Cenci*, 1969).

2. Stephen Thrower, *Beyond Terror: The Films of Lucio Fulci* (Surrey, Eng.: FAB Press, 1999), p. 11. The contorted titling of *Zombi 2* came about because George Romero's *Dawn of the Dead* (1978), an American/Italian coproduction shot in Italy (the Italian producers were Dario Argento and his brother Claudio), was released in Italy as *Zombi* and was a huge hit in the fall of 1978. With Dario Argento's blessing, Fulci's film was entitled *Zombie 2*, suggesting that it was a sequel; but, since it

could not suggest this association in either the United Kingdom or the United States for legal reasons, different titles were chosen for each market. Much like the *cinéastes* of the French New Wave, Italian exploitation directors often supported each other's projects in this way. For example, Fulci's last film was to have been a collaboration with Dario Argento to remake André De Toth's *House of Wax* (1953; 3-D), itself a remake of *Mystery of the Wax Museum* (Michael Curtiz, 1933), but Fulci died before the project was realized, leaving a script that was reworked and ultimately realized by Sergio Stivaletti, Argento's longtime special-effects director, as *Maschera di cera* (*Wax Mask*) in 1997. Many Argento protégés still populate the Italian horror field—most notably Mario Bava's son Lamberto (b. 1944—*Macabro* [1980]; *Demoni* and *Demoni 2* [1985/1986]; *Delirium* [1987]) and Michele Soavi (b. 1957—*Deliria* [English title: *StageFright*, 1987]; *La Chiesa* [*The Church*, 1988]; *Dellamorte Dellamore* [English title: *Cemetary Man*, 1994]).

verse lyricism, attracting many steadfast and serious admirers as well as armies of outraged critics.) Over the next decade, Fulci made a succession of brilliant, gory horror films about the returning dead, many of them with the same team that had produced *Zombie*—screenwriter Dardano Sacchetti (with Fulci coscripting, as was his career-long practice), cinematographer Sergio Salvati, special-effects and makeup artist Gianetto De Rossi, editor Vincenzo Tomassi, composer Fabio Frizzi, and producer Fabrizio de Angelis (for Fulvia Film-Rome). The best of these—*Paura nella città dei morti viventi* (*City of the Living Dead*/also known as *Gates of Hell*, 1980), *Quella villa accanto al cimitero* (*House by the Cemetery*, 1981), and *L'Aldilà* (*The Beyond*/also known as *Seven Doors of Death*, 1981)[3]—offer delirious, dreamlike descents into hell; indeed, *The Beyond* is often described as one of the most visually beautiful horror films ever made. Fulci was an exploitation director, working almost always on a small budget, and of his 54 features several were undeniably squalid (e.g., the cynically misogynistic *Lo squartatore di New York* [*The New York Ripper*, 1982]). But his horror films had a remarkable consistency of vision and logic in creating their world of the damned. It is a place that the characters in Marco Ferreri's *La Grande Bouffe* (1973) would have no trouble recognizing, much less those of Liliana Cavani's *Il portiere di notte* (1974) or Pasolini's *Porcile* (1969) and *Salò* (1975)—or, indeed, of Visconti's *La caduta degli dei* (English language title: *The Damned*, 1969)—which is to say that, perhaps more than any

other national cinema, Italy's has bumped up against the edges of the lurid and sensational for much of its mainstream history.

The Italian industry today produces 80 to 100 films a year and is dominated by two major distributors—Vittorio Cecchi Gori[4] (Cecchi Gori Distribuzione), who is also a leading producer (e.g., of Gabriele Salvatore's award-winning digital-effects extravaganza *Denti* [*Teeth*, 2001] and Argento's neo-*giallo Nonhosonno* [*Sleepless*, 2001]), and Silvio Berlusconi (Medusa Distribuzione), the right-wing media tycoon who became Italy's prime minister in 1994. (Cecchi Gori and Berlusconi interests briefly combined into a single production-distribution venture called Penta between 1989 and 1995.) Domestic features usually account for 20 to 25 percent of the total annual gross, and it is still possible for small, independent projects to flourish (e.g., Paolo Benvenuti's *Gostanza da Libbiano* [2001], a black-and-white documentary-style account of a historic witchcraft trial during the Inquisition, based on the official transcript of the proceedings). Yet it is clear that in the twenty-first century, Italian film production, historically entrepreneurial and decentralized, will become increasingly corporatized.

Contemporary Widescreen Technologies and Styles

The French and Italian film renaissances of the 1960s paved the way for a new era of cinematic expression in the 1970s, 1980s, and 1990s, one in which narrative is no

15.30 *City of the Living Dead* (Lucio Fulci, 1980): Giovanni Lombardo Radice (also known as John Morghen) is given the Fulci treatment—extreme, prolonged, and psychologically assaultive body horror.

3. *Seven Doors of Death*, the American-release version of *The Beyond*, was recut and retitled to eliminate its most gruesome scenes, crediting Fulci as "Louis Fuller." The film was restored by Quentin Tarantino's Rolling Thunder Pictures and Grindhouse Releasing in the late 1990s; this version is available today on DVD in a pristine widescreen transfer from Anchor Bay Entertainment.

4. Vittorio was the son of company founder Mario Cecchi Gori (1920–1993), whose long career as a producer included a partnership with Dino De Laurentiis and the founding of his own studio in 1957 to produce popular comedy (*commedia all'italiana*). He was a major force in the Italian industry, producing some 170 films between 1948 and his death in 1993.

longer an end in itself, but a medium for audiovisual essays in philosophy, psychology, ideology, and social criticism—essays, that is, on the human condition. In short, the cinema has become today at the level of general practice what it has always been for its greatest individual *auteurs*, regardless of their particular aesthetic: a form of audiovisual literature. But contemporary widescreen cinema is as formally distinct from the postwar sound film as the postwar sound film was from the silent film. Aesthetically, the new cinema is one of subjective involvement and *mise-en-scène* predicated upon the widescreen sequence shot.

This is the future cinema of the "integral style" announced by André Bazin before his death in 1958. Its predecessors were early masters of the long take—Feuillade, von Stroheim, and Murnau in the silent cinema; Renoir, Rossellini, and Welles in the sound film. These *mise-en-scène auteurs* had been forced to do their pioneer work within the black-and-white rectangle of the Academy frame and were recognizably eccentric to the mainstream tradition of narrative and expressive montage. The introduction of the widescreen processes and the improvement of color film stock in the 1950s were the technological preconditions for a full-scale revolution in favor of *mise-en-scène* aesthetics, and Bazin recognized this in his last essays. But Bazin could not have foreseen two vastly significant technological developments of the 1960s: (1) the perfection and widespread use of handheld 35mm cameras, which permit continuous and spontaneous on-location shooting, and (2) refinements achieved within the optical industries using computer technology, which include improved wide-angle and telephoto lenses and ultimately produced the modern zoom lens. This latter development was especially significant since by the mid-1960s all three types of lenses were standard equipment for Western and Eastern filmmakers alike, and lens optics had become an essential component of the integral style.

The wide-angle lens is a lens of short **focal length,**[5] as low as 12.5mm, which covers a greater angle of vision than a conventional lens (the normal focal length for 35mm filmmaking is 35mm to 50mm). It is used by cinematographers to shoot relatively large subjects at short range under the kinds of physical restrictions that obtain, for example, in small rooms and in automobiles. Since the wide-angle lens works like an inverted telescope, it gives its images an exaggerated depth of field. The **tele-photo lens,** on the other hand, is a lens of great focal length, up to 500mm, and is capable of achieving a variety of long-distance, telescopic close-ups. As the optical opposite of the wide-angle lens, the telephoto produces images that have little or no depth of field. The **zoom lens,** finally, is a lens of variable focal length that can move continuously from an extreme wide-angle long shot to an extreme telephoto close-up, traversing all positions in between (optically, for example, from a focal length of 25mm to 250mm—a fairly standard zoom ratio of 10:1).[6]

The zoom lens introduced the important capacity for tracking *optically* without moving the camera. When such a lens is advanced toward its telephoto setting, the field of the image decreases radically and the camera seems to move toward its subject, and vice versa. Countless shots in Stanley Kubrick's *Barry Lyndon* (1975), for which a special 20:1 zoom lens was designed (the Cine-Pro T9 24–480mm), are structured according to this principle. Similarly, if the camera pans slightly in its telephoto setting, the effect on the screen will be that of a lateral tracking shot. An outstanding example of this latter technique occurs near the end of Arthur Penn's *Bonnie and Clyde* (1967), when the camera pans a long row of shops in slightly out-of-focus close-up before coming to rest and refocusing on C. W. Moss's father, as he betrays the two outlaws to a Texas Ranger through the window of an ice cream parlor. Visconti's *Morte a Venezia (Death in Venice,* 1971) is an excellent example of a film that consistently employs telephoto and zoom shots as substitutes for

---

5. Focal length is the distance in millimeters from the optical center of the lens (a point midway between the front and rear elements) to the emulsion surface of the film stock when the lens is sharply focused on "infinity"—that is, an extremely distant object. Focal lengths vary with the gauge of the film stock—e.g., a 25mm lens used with 16mm film gives the same results as a 50mm lens with 35mm stock.

6. A lens of variable focal length—the Taylor-Hobson 40–120mm "Varo," with a zoom ratio of 3:1—was introduced in Hollywood in 1932 and used in films intermittently through 1935. Its use can be noted, for example, in the opening scene of Rouben Mamoulian's *Love Me Tonight* (1932) and in the shipboard dance sequence in Harry Lachman's *Dante's Inferno* (1935). Cumbersome in size and shape, the "Varo" also had serious optical limitations that caused it to be abandoned. The "zoom" lens reappeared under its current name in 1955, but it was not sufficiently refined to maintain constant focus and *f*-stop (see footnote, p. 321, and Glossary) until the mid-1960s. The most striking use of the zoom lens before this time occurs in *Vertigo* (1958), where Hitchcock employed simultaneous tracking-out/zooming-in shots to convey the protagonist's acrophobia in the rooftop and staircase sequences.

15.31 Two wide-angle lens shots from *Barry Lyndon* **(Stanley Kubrick, 1975): director of photography, John Alcott. Note the great depth of field.**

15.32 An extreme wide-angle lens shot from *Barry Lyndon* **and the same subject shot from head on through a telephoto lens (actually, a zoom lens that has moved from its wide-angle position to its telephoto position, so that these two stills are the beginning and end of the same shot). Note the loss of depth of field—the "flattening out" of the image in the telephoto setting.**

tracking, as are virtually all of the films of Robert Altman. But perhaps the most stunning use of optical traveling in recent cinema occurs at the end of Ján Kadár's *Adrift* (1971; see p. 627), when the anguished and apparently deranged protagonist, who has been standing under a tree outside his house at evening, attempts to return to the house. At the beginning of the shot, the camera is behind the man with the zoom lens in its telephoto setting, so that there seems to be very little distance between either him and the house or him and the camera. But as he starts to walk toward the house, the lens begins to zoom slowly backward toward its wide-angle position, putting ever greater distance between both man and house and man and camera. As he sees his house recede before him, the man starts to run wildly toward it, and the lens zooms backward at an ever-increasing pace, paralleling his headlong flight, until

finally the runner is left optically adrift, hanging suspended in space as both camera and house recede toward infinity. This powerful image of madness and horror would have been impossible to achieve without a lens of variable focal length.

Another effect of which the zoom lens is capable is that of hovering or searching, as if the camera were trying to decide which element of a scene to focus on from moment to moment—an especially valuable device for composing mass scenes like the mess-hall sequences in Robert Altman's *M*A*S*H* (1970) or the outlaws' long walk through the teeming village of Agua Verde that precedes the final massacre in Sam Peckinpah's *The Wild Bunch* (1969). The zoom lens can also cause the camera to seem to leap backward or forward in space to isolate a significant detail in close-up without a cut. Thus, lenses of variable focal length permit a filmmaker to move back

15.33 Optical hovering in *The Wild Bunch* (Sam Peckinpah, 1969): director of photography, Lucien Ballard.

and forth—from long shot, to medium shot, to close-up—without the loss of continuity imposed by montage. It has even been suggested that Griffith would not have developed the syntax of narrative editing if zoom lenses had been available to him when he made his pioneering masterworks. This seems unlikely since editing of some sort will always be an essential component of cinematic expression and since Griffith was too innovative a genius not to have recognized the fact; but in principle, at least, the suggestion is a valid one.

Of course, the possibilities for cutting on movement have been greatly increased by the cinema's new capacity for optical traveling, and the action sequences in Peckinpah's *The Wild Bunch* and *Junior Bonner* (1971) provide fine examples of the powerful kinetic impact that cutting on optical movement can achieve (see Chapter 20). Furthermore, unique visual effects can be obtained by intercutting telephoto and zoom shots with shots made through conventional lenses, which possess greater depth of field. This is because lenses of variable focal length have a distorting characteristic that makes optical movement qualitatively different from real camera movement—that is, they destroy depth of field. As Paul Joannides has written: "Unlike a tracking shot, a zoom represents a denial of perspective. The effect is not one of moving *through* space, but of space warping toward or away from the camera." For this reason, lenses of variable focal length can in some sense be said to eliminate the third dimension and to deny the reality of space by abstracting

it. In Antonioni's *Il deserto rosso* (1964), for example, recurring telephoto close shots of the heroine depict a lone figure against an abstracted and flattened array of shapes, forms, and patterns—in reality the industrial landscape of Ravenna—that not only connects the character with her environment, but emphasizes its meaninglessness.

This expressive effect could have been achieved only by shooting the scenes through a wide-open telephoto or zoom lens, and it plainly illustrates how variable-focus lenses have become an important new aesthetic resource for contemporary filmmakers who practice the integral style. In fact, the recent refinement of lens optics, more than any technological development since the introduction of widescreen, has made possible the new cinema of subjective involvement and psychological affect—a cinema of *mise-en-scène* whose surface is often as abstractly expressionistic as it is realistic. Writing of this future cinema in 1970, Joannides noted: "The camera will . . . play a more passive role dramatically, but a more potent one visually. Rather than being placed to *construct* the scene, it will treat the scene as a formal entity. Thus observation and group composition will be more important than the dialectic of 'significant' detail which usually makes up drama. Dialogue will tend to be replaced by conversation and will be arranged differently, in set-pieces rather than by cross-

15.34 Giuliana (Monica Vitti) and her son in Antonioni's *Il deserto rosso* (1964): director of photography, Carlo Di Palma. The diminished depth perspective of the telephoto lens forces the two humans into the same plane as the abstracted industrial landscape.

15.35 A shot composed for the variable-focus lens in *The Red and the White* (Miklós Jancsó, 1967): director of photography, Tamás Somló.

cutting." By the last quarter of the twentieth century, this cinema had arrived. In fact, as French and Italian films of the era demonstrate, the world's most advanced filmmakers had for some time been composing for the lens rather than for the frame. It is wholly typical of this phenomenon that one of the most talented *auteurs* to emerge from Eastern Europe in the 1960s and 1970s, the Hungarian director Miklós Jáncsó (b. 1921— *The Round-Up* [*Szegénylengények,* 1965]; *The Red and the White* [*Csillagosok, katonák,* 1967]; *Red Psalm* [*Még kér a nép,* 1972]), characteristically made epic films of great visual complexity, some of which were composed of as few as a dozen long takes of ten minutes each (see Chapter 16).

15.36 A frame from a zoom-lens sequence shot in Jancsó's *Red Psalm* (1972): director of photography, János Kende.

Scandinavian or Nordic Cinema

INGMAR BERGMAN

The work and reputation of the Swedish director Ingmar Bergman (b. 1918) eclipsed that of all other Scandinavian filmmakers for much of the postwar era. The son of a Lutheran pastor to the royal court of Sweden, Bergman was trained in theater and opera. Between 1940 and 1944 he worked on scripts for Svensk Filmindustri, the Swedish national film trust, which was undergoing a wartime revival. He received his first screenplay credit for Alf Sjöberg's *Torment* (*Hets*, 1944), a film about a sadistic schoolmaster. Sjöberg ([1903–1980]—*The Road to Heaven* [*Himlaspelet*, 1942]; *Miss Julie* [*Fröken Julie*, 1951, adapted from Strindberg]) was a director very much in the Sjöstrom/Stiller tradition of poetic naturalism (see Chapter 4), and Bergman's earliest films reflect his influence. Between 1945 and 1955 Bergman wrote and directed thirteen somber films that explored the themes of loneliness, alienation, and the sheer difficulty of being alive, the best of which were *Thirst* (*Törst*, 1949), *Summer Interlude* (*Sommarlek*, 1951), *Monika/Summer with Monika* (*Sommaren med Monika*, 1952), and *Sawdust and Tinsel/The Naked Night* (*Gycklarnas afton*, 1953). It was during this apprenticeship that Bergman discovered a long-term collaborator, the cinematographer Gunnar Fischer (b. 1910), and built up his first stock company of distinguished performers: Max von Sydow, Gunnar Björnstrand, Ingrid Thulin, Gunnel Lindblom, Harriet Andersson, Bibi Andersson, and Eva Dahlbeck (Liv Ullmann and Erland Josephson joined him later). He also evolved his characteristic working method of first writing his films as novels and then distilling them into screenplays and, finally, audiovisual images.

It was *Smiles of a Summer Night* (*Sommarnattens leende*, 1955) that first brought Bergman to worldwide attention, although few critics recognized beneath the surface of this sophisticated farce a Swedish version of Renoir's *La Règle du jeu* (1939). In *The Seventh Seal* (*Det sjunde inseglet*, 1956), a poetic allegory of a medieval knight caught up in a losing chess match with Death, Bergman brilliantly evoked the Middle Ages and posed the first of a series of metaphysical questions about the

15.37 The Dance of Death at the conclusion of *The Seventh Seal* (Ingmar Bergman, 1956).

relationship of man to God, a theme that was to occupy him for a decade. *The Seventh Seal* established Bergman as an important artist, but *Wild Strawberries* (*Smultron-stället*, 1957), the film that followed, was clearly his greatest work of the 1950s. This beautifully lyrical film is constructed around dreams and memories as they assail the elderly Isak Borg, a distinguished professor of science (superbly played by Bergman's greatest predecessor in Swedish cinema, Victor Sjöström), who is being driven across contemporary Sweden by his daughter-in-law to receive an honorary doctorate at the University of Lund.

Borg's journey occasions a descent into the unconscious mind in which he is forced to confront all that he has been and become to his parents, his siblings, his children, and himself in the course of his life. Structurally, Bergman makes his transitions from the present to the past and back again in single shots, so that one constantly has the impression of being in both time frames simultaneously. In its broad grasp of the basic philosophical problems of existence, *Wild Strawberries* is an even more important film than *The Seventh Seal*, and it holds a high place among Bergman's masterworks.

The Magician/The Face (*Ansiktet*, 1958) tells a cryptic tale of a magic lanternist and prestidigitator (Bergman himself?) who dupes a bourgeois family (the audience?) into believing an elaborately contrived nightmare of murder and mayhem that has no substance. A stylistic tour de force, *The Magician* is somehow empty at the core. Bergman concluded his important work of the 1950s with *The Virgin Spring* (*Jungfrukällen*, 1959), a powerful film based on a thirteenth-century ballad. In it, a beautiful young girl on her way to church is brutally raped and murdered in the woods by three herdsmen, who later seek refuge at her father's fortress. He discovers their guilt and butchers them like pigs in a sequence of nearly apocalyptic violence. When the girl's body is discovered later in the woods, the father vows to build a church on the spot, and in an ironic conclusion a spring wells up miraculously from the ground, signifying divine forgiveness. This devastating film concludes on an uncharacteristic note of hope (probably because Berg-

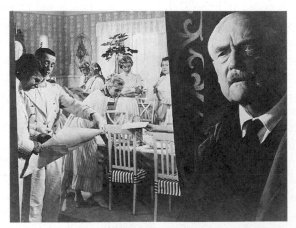

15.38 Victor Sjöström in Bergman's *Wild Strawberries* (1957).

15.39 Bergman's *The Virgin Spring* (1959): Max von Sydow.

man was adapting someone else's material), but Bergman next made an austere trilogy about the difficulty of existing in a universe wholly unredeemed by the presence of God.

Through a Glass Darkly (*Sasom i en spegel*, 1961), the first work of what might be called a "religious" trilogy, is a starkly unappealing film about a schizophrenic woman living on a remote Baltic island with her physician husband, her father, and her teenage brother. When she comes to realize that her father is keeping a clinical journal of her breakdown for the purpose of writing a novel about it, she deteriorates altogether, commits incest with her brother, and is flown off the island by helicopter. In the plotless *Winter Light/The Communicants* (*Nattsvardsgästerna*, 1961), the austerity of Bergman's relentless spiritual probing becomes almost unbearable: a widowed village pastor celebrates communion regularly but can do nothing to assuage the real spiritual suffering of his communicants because he lacks literally what the Church gives him officially—the ability to make sense of a senseless universe by mediating between man and God. Much of *Winter Light* is constructed from extreme close-ups of the characters' faces, a technique that Bergman came to use more and more as a means of suggesting psychological torment. With the third film, *The Silence* (*Tystnaden*, 1963), Bergman succeeded in creating another masterpiece. In it, two sisters come to a Central European city accompanied by the younger woman's small son. The language of the city's inhabitants and even the natural sounds on the brilliantly edited sound track are incomprehensible both to the travelers and to ourselves, and so—like most of us—they are forced to move through a meaningless world in relative isolation from their peers. Speech finally becomes irrelevant for the three travelers, as images of perverse eroticism and impending disaster come to dominate the film—visually the most striking of the trilogy. For Bergman, as for Antonioni, it seems that modern alienation has reduced human communication to a series of desperate sexual encounters that can only end in chaos.

The Silence was brilliantly photographed by Sven Nykvist (b. 1922), who had been Bergman's cinematographer since *The Virgin Spring*, the collaboration having begun when Nykvist was an assistant on *The Naked Night*. Working with Bergman from 1959 through the present, Nykvist has become one of the world's leading color cinematographers. Since the mid-1960s, Bergman and Nykvist have

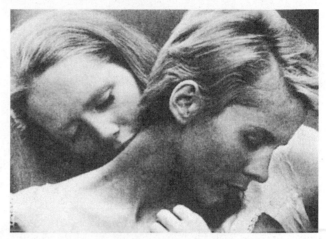

15.40 Bergman's *Persona* (1966): Liv Ullmann, Bibi Andersson.

incorporated some of the more boldly experimental techniques of the French and Italian cinemas into their work. This change in style signaled Bergman's new thematic concern with the nature of human psychology, perception, and identity, explored in the director's second great trilogy of the 1960s: *Persona* (1966), *Hour of the Wolf* (*Vargtimmen*, 1968), and *Shame* (*Skammen*, 1968).

Framed by sequences that seemingly depict the projection and photographing of the film itself, *Persona* collapses virtually every narrative convention of the cinema to suggest the illusory character of both the medium and the human personalities it seems so realistically to incarnate. The film is essentially about a transference of iden-

15.41 *Hour of the Wolf* (Ingmar Bergman, 1968).

tity between nurse and patient to the point that their two faces merge, with perfect visual logic, into one. It is also about the different levels on which film, or media in general, can be said to represent the real. But its narrative style is so elliptical, disjointed, and self-reflexive that *Persona* ultimately suggests that the cinema is no more illusory than the reality that it pretends to record.

Hour of the Wolf is a hallucinatory parable of the agonies of artistic creation, reminiscent of Fellini at his most serious best. An artist and his wife live on a remote island and are one day invited to dinner at the castle of the island's owner, where the artist is humiliated by his host. The wife later discovers her husband's secret diary, which recounts trysts with his former mistress and the strange death of a boy. The artist goes mad and returns to the castle, where he finds his former mistress lying nude on a bier. He is invited to make love to her corpse, but she awakes and kisses him, to the raucous laughter of the ghoulish castle guests, and the artist flees madly into a swamp, where he is pursued by the entire company and finally done to death by a huge bird of prey. This bizarre but visually arresting allegory of a creative artist and his wife fallen into the ever-threatening grip of madness is less successful than *Persona*. But *Shame*, the final film of the second trilogy, is an utterly unique masterpiece.

Shame is about the hopelessness of maintaining human values and relationships in a state of perpetual war (which, Bergman seems to suggest, is the state of the modern world). In a nameless country, in the midst of a long and bloody civil war on the mainland, a childless husband and wife, both artists, have chosen to live an isolated existence on a relatively secure island off the coast. Former philharmonic musicians, they attempt to remain detached from the war that rages everywhere about them but are drawn irrevocably into it when their island is invaded and they are accused by both sides of collaborating with the enemy. The woman is strong and capable, but the husband proves himself to be a coward and, finally, a murderous turncoat. War devastates the beautiful island, turning it into a landscape of hell, and the couple—hating each other—escape together in a boat of refugees that drifts aimlessly on a sea of death. As the film concludes, the woman dreams hopelessly of having a child after the war, which we know will never end. Relying on close-ups of the faces of his protagonists, Bergman created in *Shame* a terrifying parable about the

way war inevitably destroys all things valuable and human.

In *The Passion of Anna* (*En passion*, 1969), his first important color film, Bergman depicted the tense psychic interplay of four persons living on the small Swedish island of Farö, where he himself resided (also the location for *Shame* and *Hour of the Wolf*). Characteristically, it is a drama of guilt, anguish, and finally rage, in which each of the four characters is caught up in his own unique kind of spiritual martyrdom. *The Passion of Anna* is unique in that it employs the Brechtian (and Godardian) distancing device of stopping the drama at moments of highest tension and having each of the four principals step briefly out of his role to discuss with the audience the character he is playing. The film is also brilliantly photographed by Nykvist and makes expressive use of color, sound, and the telephoto lens.

After filming a 78-minute *cinéma vérité*–style documentary on his adopted home of Faeroe,[7] entitled *Faro Document* (*Fårödokument*, 1970), Bergman made a theatrical feature for the newly organized ABC Pictures Corporation. *The Touch* (*Beröringen*, 1970) probed the disintegration of a middle-class marriage through the story of a model Swedish housewife who leaves her comfortable but conventional surroundings for a life with an unstable American archaeologist. The focal point of the film is the neurotic pathology of the conventionally "normal" housewife as oppposed to the relative emotional health of the "abnormal" archaeologist. To emphasize this conflict Bergman deliberately clogged his dialogue with the platitudes and clichés that make normal social intercourse as meaningless as the foreign speech of *The Silence*. *The Touch*, Bergman's first English-language film, was not generally regarded as a success due to the miscasting of Elliott Gould in

---

7. In 1976 Bergman emigrated from Sweden to France because of harassment by the Swedish government, which claimed that he owed hundreds of thousands of dollars in income taxes and even had him arrested and incarcerated briefly. Bergman and his supporters maintain that he was driven out of the country because of his implied criticisms of Swedish society in films like *The Touch* and *Scenes from a Marriage*. (Ironically, Swedish film critics had for decades attacked Bergman for his supposed detachment from contemporary Swedish life.) The tax dispute was settled almost entirely in his favor in late 1979, and he was welcomed back to a somewhat embarrassed Sweden to begin shooting *Fanny and Alexander* in Uppsala in the fall of 1981.

the part of the archaeologist, but his next endeavor, *Cries and Whispers* (*Viskningar och rop*, 1972), was hailed as a masterpiece.

This highly stylized film about the nature of death and dying is a work of excruciating beauty in which reality, memory, and fantasy become one. Superbly photographed by Nykvist in rich autumnal hues, *Cries and Whispers* concerns the interrelationship of four women who are brought together by death in a gorgeously appointed manor house at the turn of the century. One is a spinster, dying slowly and painfully of cancer; two others are her wealthy married sisters, who have returned to their former home to attend her death; the fourth is the peasant servant, Anna, the only true "sister" of the dying woman because she can minister to her failing spirit with a warm, fleshly love. Eerie, enigmatic, and intense beyond measure, *Cries and Whispers* is constructed like a Strindberg dream play, but it is also quintessential Bergman, a brilliant distillation of his stylistic and thematic obsessions.

Bergman's next film, *Scenes from a Marriage* (*Scener ur ett äktenskap*, 1974), was originally made in six 50-minute installments for Swedish television but was cut to

15.42 Bergman's *Cries and Whispers* (1972): Ingrid Thulin, Harriet Andersson, Liv Ullmann, Lena Nyman.

2 hours and 48 minutes for theatrical release. (The six installments were shown uncut on American public television in 1977.) The theatrical version retains Bergman's original episodic structure: six scenes from a middle-class marriage spanning a decade. During this period, the relationship slowly disintegrates and ends in divorce, but the two individuals become progressively stronger in separation, and by the end of the film both are married to other people. As usual, Bergman relies heavily on the close-up to convey anguish (and also, of course, to make the film work on television), but his characteristic psychological realism is pursued with uncharacteristic verisimilitude in this film, minus fantasy, memory, and metaphor. Open-ended, slow-paced, and involving multiple dramatic climaxes, *Scenes from a Marriage* is actually structured like a soap opera but possesses a depth of feeling and intelligence usually alien to the form.

The Magic Flute (1975) is the triumphal realization of Bergman's lifelong ambition to adapt the Mozart opera about the transcendent power of love and art. Lighthearted and exuberant, the film shows a playful, sprightly side of Bergman rarely seen in the decade of the trilogies, *The Passion of Anna*, and *Cries and Whispers*. Bergman mounted the film like an eighteenth-century stage production, and his obsession with the machinery of stage illusion in *The Magic Flute* links it implicitly with both *Persona* and *The Magician*. *Face to Face* (*Ansikte mot ansikte*, 1976), about the harrowing descent of a woman psychiatrist into mental illness, and *The Serpent's Egg* (1977), a film dealing with the psychological conflicts of a Jewish circus performer in pre-Nazi Germany and shot in English in Berlin, were not critically successful. But with *Autumn Sonata* (*Herbstsonate*, 1978), an intense study of the relationship between a concert pianist and her middle-aged daughter, filmed on location in Norway, and *From the Life of the Marionettes* (1980), a searing account of psychosexual breakdown made in Germany, Bergman returned successfully to the tangled human relationships that he had illuminated so well in the past. In *Fanny and Alexander* (*Fanny och Alexander*, 1982), his most lavishly produced and accessible work and the winner of four American Academy Awards, Bergman recreated the magical world of his childhood in the university town of Uppsala in the early years of the twentieth century. Though not directly autobiographical, it is as close to a cinematic memoir as anything he ever pro-

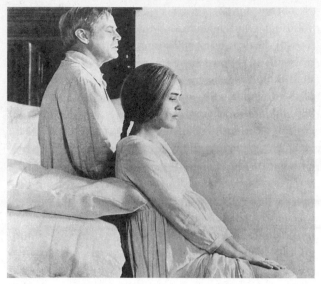

15.43 *Fanny and Alexander* (Ingmar Bergman, 1982): parents (Jan Malmsjö, Ewa Fröling) and children (Bertil Guve, Pernilla Allwin) in a collapsing marriage.

duced, and on its release Bergman declared it to be his last film. In fact, he did shoot another film for Swedish television in 16mm that was never intended for theatrical release. *After the Rehearsal* (*Efter repetitionen*, 1984) concerns the relationship between a middle-aged theater director and the actress daughter of his dead mistress, also an actress, and is essentially a one-act play for three characters. Bergman unsuccessfully tried to block the release of this telefilm when its producer, Jörn Donner, sold it to an American distributor, and he seems firm in his commitment to retire from "the world of cinema" and devote the rest of his life to the theater, which was his first love.

Bergman is an artist of vast and unusual talent, and he is clearly among the most important filmmakers in the history of Western cinema. His vision of the human condition is as gloomy as that of his great predecessors in Scandinavian cinema, the Swedes Mauritz Stiller and Victor Sjöström, and the Dane Carl-Theodor Dreyer (by whom he was profoundly influenced). His themes hark back, too, to those of the two Scandinavian giants of late nineteenth-century drama, Ibsen and Strindberg (whose works *The Stranger* and *A Dream Play* stand behind *Persona* and *Fanny and Alexander*, respectively). But his pessimistic vision is not wholly unredeemed. Despite his cosmic nihilism, Bergman is essentially a religious artist

whose films concern the fundamental questions of human existence: the meaning of suffering and pain, the inexplicability of death, the solitary nature of being, and the difficulty of locating meaning in a seemingly random and capricious universe. With the possible exception of *Persona*, Bergman has never been a great innovator in narrative form as Welles, Antonioni, or Godard have

15.44 *Fanny and Alexander* (Ingmar Bergman, 1982): Bertil Guve, Pernilla Allwin.

been, but he has been quick to assimilate the important innovations of others. His experiments have been intellectual and metaphysical rather than formal, for he has risked alienating his audiences time and again by asking difficult questions and pursuing inherently disturbing themes.

Bergman was free to follow his dark vision of experience with integrity and independence largely due to the economic structure of Svensk Filmindustri, through which he produced all but four of his forty features. Since this organization guarantees to underwrite the production and distribution costs of any approved project that does not return a domestic profit, it is fair to say that Bergman has rarely had to work under the extreme economic pressures that afflict most other filmmakers. But Bergman would surely have pursued his vision under any circumstances, no matter how difficult, because, as he has declared many times, "to make films is for me a natural necessity, a need similar to hunger and thirst." Bergman has also maintained his independence by producing his films with a remarkable economy of means: he uses small casts and crews, and he shoots in natural locations whenever possible. Gunnar Fischer and Sven Nykvist, for instance, have between them photographed virtually all of his films, and Bergman often writes his scripts with specific actors from his stock company in mind. In a very important sense, Bergman views filmmaking as an essentially collective art form. He has often compared it to the process of building a medieval cathedral, in which each artisan dedicated the maximum skill of his craft anonymously to the greater glory of God; as he has written, "Regardless of whether I believe or not, whether I am Christian or not, I would play my part in the collective building of the cathedral."

SWEDEN

The Swedish film industry itself is small, state-subsidized, and oriented largely toward the domestic market of 8.6 million people. Bergman is its sole international postwar giant, but other Swedish directors produced notable films during the same period. Arne Sucksdorff (1917–2001), for example, produced a series of unique quasi documentaries about children and animals, including *A Divided World* (*En kluven värld*, 1948), *The Great Adventure* (*Det stora äventyret*, 1953), and *My Home Is Copacabana* (*Mitt hem är Copacabana*, 1965), which won

numerous international awards. Four other key figures of the era are Bo Widerberg (1930–1997), Vilgot Sjöman (b. 1924), Jan Troell (b. 1931), and Jörn Donner (b. 1933). Widerberg's main films of the 1960s—*Raven's End* (*Kvarteret korpen*, 1964), *Elvira Madigan* (1967), *The Adalen Riots* (*Ådelen' 31*, 1969), *The Ballad of Joe Hill* (*Joe Hill*, 1971)—demonstrated the stylistic influence of Godard and a strong sense of political commitment lacking in Bergman. (Widerberg's later films were mainly genre thrillers, but *The Serpent's Way* [*Ormens väg på hälleberget*, 1986] won recognition at the 1987 Moscow Film Festival for its powerful portrayal of the exploitation of a widowed nineteenth-century tenant farmer in northern Sweden.) Vilgot Sjöman, a close friend of Bergman (and his assistant on *Winter Light*), probed subversive sexuality in his own *My Sister, My Love* (*Syskonbädd 1782*, 1966), a historical account of incest in eighteenth-century Sweden, and his *cinéma vérité* epics *I Am Curious—Yellow* (*Jag är nyfiken—gul*, 1967) and *I Am Curious—Blue* (*Jag är nyfiken—blå*, 1968), in which a young woman conducts a private opinion poll about the state of Sweden after thirty years of Social Democratic rule, finding little but complacency and casual sex. (Its graphic rendition of sex caused the film to be confiscated by U.S. Customs authorities in 1967, leading to a ground breaking legal decision in 1969 when the U.S. Supreme Court ruled in a split decision [with Justice William O. Douglas recusing himself] that its depiction of sexual intercourse was not obscene—see Chapter 20.) Sjöman's later films (e.g., *You're Lying* [*Ni ljuger*, 1969], *Linus*, 1979, *I Am Blushing* [*Jag rodnar*, 1981]) continued his critique of Swedish institutions, although several films (*Troll*, 1971; *A Handful of Love* [*En handfull kärlek*, 1974]; *Malacca*, 1987; *The Trap* [*Fallgropen*, 1989]) are more conventional dramatic features, and *Behind the Shutters* (*Bakom jalusin*, 1984) is a Vertigo-like study of sexual obsession set in North Africa. Jan Troell's *The Emigrants* [*Utvandrarna*, 1971] and its sequel, *The New Land* (*Nybyggarna*, 1972), formed an epic of resettlement that proved especially popular in the United States, where Troell came to make the similarly themed *Zandy's Bride* (1974) and an ill-fated, big-budget ($22 million; Todd-AO 35) remake of John Ford's 1937 *The Hurricane* (*Hurricane*, 1979). Returning to Sweden, Troell made the survival sagas *The Flight of the Eagle* (*Ingenjör Andrées luftfärd*, 1982) and *Land of Dreams* (*Sagolandet*, 1989), demonstrating the importance of the Swedish countryside to his work. The Finnish writer/director Jörn Donner played an important role in Swedish cinema during the 1960s: as film critic for the Stockholm paper *Dagen nyheter*, he ran a series of scathing attacks on Bergman; then he married one of Bergman's talented actresses, Harriet Andersson, and cast her in four features that he directed for Svensk Filmindustri—*A Sunday in September* (*En söndag i september*, 1963); *To Love* (*Att älska*, 1964); *Adventure Starts Here* (*Här börjar äventyret*, 1965), and *Roof-Tree* (*Tvärbalk*, 1967). In 1967, Donner returned to Finland, where he directed several striking features—*Black on White* (*Mustaa valkoisella*, 1967); *69*, 1969; *Fuck Off! Images of Finland* (*Perkele! Kuvia suomesta*, 1971)—in the manner of Godard. Another active figure during the 1960s was the former actress Mai Zetterling (1925–1994), whose *Loving Couples* (*Alskande par*, 1964), *Night Games* (*Nattlek*, 1965), *The Girls* (*Flickorna*; 1968), and *Glas* (*Doktor Glas*, 1969; produced in Denmark) helped bring Swedish cinema to the attention of the mainstream export markets.

Swedish cinema during the 1970s produced some interesting new filmmakers, including the former Bergman actress Gunnel Lindblom (b. 1931—*Paradise Place*, 1977), Christer Dahl (b. 1940—*The Score* [*Lyftet*, 1978]), and Kjell Grede (b. 1936—*Clare's Lust* [*Klara Lust*, 1972], *A Simple Melody* [*En enkel melodi*, 1974]). During the 1980s, film attendance declined sharply in Sweden due to the country's wholesale embrace of VCR technol-

ogy, and the Swedish Film Institute became increasingly active in funding production by government mandate in 1982. Important films that have appeared from Sweden in this context are Kay Pollak's *Children's Island* (*Barnens ö*, 1980) and *Love Me!* (*Alska mej!*, 1984); Gunnel Lindblom's *Sally and Freedom* (1981) and *Summer Nights on the Planet Earth* (*Sommarkväller på jorden*, 1987); Lárus Óskarsson's *The Second Dance* (*Andra dansen*, 1982); Hans Alfredson's *The Simple-Minded Professor* (*Den enfaldige mördaren*, 1982), winner of the Silver Bear at Berlin, and *False as Water* (*Falsk som vatten*, 1985); Stefan Jarl's *Nature's Revenge* (*Naturens hämnd*, 1984) and *The Threat* (*Uhkkadus*, 1985); Agneta Elers-Jarleman's *Beyond Sorrow, Beyond Pain* (*Smärtgränsen*, 1983); Jon Lindström's *The Last Summer* (*Den sista leken*, 1984); Allan Edwall's *Åke and His World* (*Åke och has värld*, 1985); Christer Dahl's *At Last!* (*Åntligen!*, 1985); Lasse Hallström's *My Life as a Dog* (*Mit liv som hund*, 1985), winner of the 1987 American Academy Award for Best Foreign Film; Mai Zetterling's *Amorosa* (1986); Suzanne Osten's (b. 1944) *The Mozart Brothers* (*Bröderna Mozart*, 1986); Kjell Grede's *Hip, Hip Hurra!* (1987).

The 1990s began propitiously with Suzanne Osten's *The Guardian Angel* (*Skyddsängeln*, 1990) winning prizes at Cannes and cinematographer Sven Nykvist's *The Ox* (*Oxen*, 1991) being nominated for an Oscar for Best Foreign Film. At the same time, *Il Capitano* (1991), Jan Troell's documentary-style account of a 1988 killing spree by two young Finns in rural Sweden, won the 1992 Silver Bear at Berlin. Any doubts about Bergman's lingering influence on Swedish cinema were dispelled, moreover, when Bille August's *The Best Intentions* (*Den goda viljan*, 1992) became the most honored film of the year. Based on a script by Bergman himself, it examines the early lives of his parents in Stockholm and Lund, 1909–18. August is a Danish-born cinematographer (b. 1948) who has directed for Svensk Filmindustri, the German producer Constantin Film (*The House of the Spirits*, 1995; *Smilla's Sense of Snow*, 1997), and American studios (e.g., Columbia—*Les Misérables*, [1998]). And *Sunday's Children* (*Söndagsbarn*, 1993) marked the directorial debut of Bergman's son Daniel (b. 1962) with yet another memoir of his father's youth in the insular province of Dalarna. After Bergman *père*, the most prominent Swedish director outside of his own country is probably Lasse Hallström (b. 1946), who has delivered several successful literary adaptations for American producers—e.g., *The*

15.45 *Black on White* (Jörn Donner, 1967).

Cider House Rules (1999), *Chocolat* (2000), and *The Shipping News* (2001), all released by Miramax. Yet Swedish cinema generally continues to be focused inward. Small-town life, for example, was the subject of the critically acclaimed *Fucking Amal* (English title: *Show Me Love*, 1998), directed by Lukas Moodysson (b. 1969), which follows the lives of two alienated teenage girls in a typically Swedish provincial city ("Amal"). Moodysson repeated this success in 2000 with *Together* (*Tillsammans*), a comedy about young people living in collectives during the 1970s, which was widely distributed abroad. In the same year, Sweden produced thirty-five new films, accounting for approximately 25 percent of the domestic box office.

FINLAND

In addition to Sweden, all of the other Nordic countries have small, state-subsidized film industries. The most prolific in the postwar era has been that of Finland, where support from the Finnish Film Foundation enables a nation of only five million people to produce an annual average of twenty films. Jörn Donner is credited with bringing the influence of Godard to Finnish cinema during the late 1960s, inspiring a brief New Wave in the literature-based Finnish cinema, exemplified in the work of such young filmmakers as Risto Jarva (1934–1977)— *Worker's Diary* (*Työmiehen päiväkirja*, 1967); *Rally* (*Bensaa suonissa*, 1970); *The Year of the Hare* (*Jäniksen vuosi*, 1977); Rauni Mollberg (b. 1929)—*Earth Is a Sinful Song* (*Maa on syntinen laulu*, 1973); *Pretty Good for a Human Being* (*Aika hyvä ihmiseksi*, 1977); *Milka*, 1980; and *The Unknown Soldier* (*Tuntematon sotilas*, 1985), a remake of Finland's most famous postwar film (the original was directed by Edvin Laine in 1955); Erkko Kivikoski (b. 1936)—*Gunshot in the Factory* (*Laukaus tehtaala*, 1973); Jaakko Pakkasvirta (b. 1934)— *Home for Christmas* (*Jouluksi kotiin*, 1975); *The Elegance of Life* (*Elämän koreus*, 1979); *Poet and Muse* (*Runoilija ja muusa*, 1979); *Sign of the Beast* (*Pedon merkki* (b. 1943), 1981); Eija-Elina Bergholm—*Poor Maria* (*Marja pieni!*, 1972); Pirjo Honkasalo (b. 1947) and Pekka Lehto (b. 1948)—*Flame Top* (*Tulipää*, 1980); Tapio Suominen—*Right On, Man!* (*Täältä tullaan, elämä*, 1980); Marrku Lehmuskallio (b. 1938)—*The Raven's Dance* (*Korpinpolska*, 1980); *Skierri—Land of the Dwarf Birch* (*Skierri—vaivaiskoivujen maa*, 1982);

Blue Mammy, 1985; *Inuksuk*, 1987; Anssi Mänttäri (b. 1941)—*The Holy Family*, 1976; *Toto*, 1982; *Regina and the Men*, 1983; *April Is the Cruelest Month*, 1983; *The Clock* (*Kello*, 1984); *Nothing but Love* (*Rakkauselokuva*, 1984); *Morena*, 1986; *The King Goes Forth to France*, 1986; *Goodbye, Farewell*, 1986; and Lauri Törhönen (b. 1947)—*Burning Angel* (*Palava enkeli*, 1984); *The Undressing* (*Riisuminen*, 1986); *Tropic of Ice*, 1987. (Donner himself returned to Stockholm in 1972, where he served as director of the Swedish Film Archive until 1975 and was named president of the Swedish Film Institute in 1978.) In the meantime, the Finns had experimented liberally with coproduction (e.g., with the United States, *Born American* [Renny Harlin, 1985]), and two major figures announced themselves in the brothers Mika and Aki Kaurismäki (b. 1955 and 1957, respectively). The Kaurismäkis each direct their own films, collaborating in scriptwriting, fund raising, and production. Both have as their theme the corruption of Finland by Swedish and American influences, but Mika is the lighter of them, creating films like *The Worthless* (*Arvottomat*, 1982), *The Clan* (*Klaani*, 1984), *Rosso* (1985), and *Helsinki-Napoli—All Night Long* (1987), which focus on contemporary urban aimlessness. Aki is definitely the more fatalistic and subtle of the two: his directorial debut was an ultramodern version of Dostoevsky's *Crime and Punishment* (*Rikos ja rangaistus*, 1983), and his "Helsinki trilogy"—*Shadows in Paradise* (*Varjoja paratiisissa*, 1986), *Ariel* (1989), and *Match Factory Girl* (*Tulitikkutehtaan tyttö*, 1990)—presents the city as a cold, unwelcoming place inhabited mainly by criminals and other sociopaths, whereas *Hamlet Gets Business* (1987), *Leningrad Cowboys Go America* (1989), and *I Hired a Contract Killer* (1990) are characterized equally by chaotic humor and parody. Recent Kaurismäki films include Mika's *L.A. without a Map* (1998), based on a novel by Richard Rayner about a young British writer's adventures in Hollywood, and Aki's *Juha* (1999), adapted from a classic nineteenth-century Finnish novel and shot silent, in black-and-white, with captioned dialogue (one of Aki's trademarks). Until 1998, Finnish cinema was dominated by Finnkino, a statewide distribution/exhibition company owned by the Union Bank of Finland; in that year, domestic films took a nosedive at the box office, and the Finnkino monopoly was challenged by the Swedish-Norwegian theater corporation Sandrews and the Danish distribution firm Scanbox, an agent for both Polygram and Miramax. At the same time, the Finnish Film Foundation joined with the four national television channels in a joint production venture that yielded a number of popular hits (e.g., Marrku Pölönen's *A Summer by the River* [*Kuningasjätkä*, 1999]; Olli Saarela's *Ambush* [*Rukajärven tie*, 1999]), which enabled domestic features to achieve a 25 percent market share in 1999, even edging out American blockbusters like *Star Wars: Episode I—The Phantom Menace*. Recent Finnish domestic hits include Aku Louhimies's hip sex comedy *The Restless* (*Levottomat*, 2000) and Auli Mantila's police-dossier thriller *The Geography of Fear* (*Pelon maantiede*, 2000).

DENMARK AND DOGME95

With a history extending back to pre–World War I dominion of Ole Olsen's Nordisk Films Kompagni A/S (see Chapter 4), and an art heritage including both Benjamin Christensen and Carl-Theodor Dreyer, Danish cinema produces ten to fifteen features a year for a population of 5.36 million. The National Film School of Denmark was founded in 1968, and during the 1970s, the market share for domestic features was 25 to 30 percent, not bad given the dominance of American distributors throughout Scandinavia. Since 1981, the industry has had the financial support of the Danish Film Institute (DFI), established in 1972 as a department of the Ministry of Cultural Affairs, and Danish directors who came to prominence under its auspices include Gabriel Axel (b. 1918—*Babette's Feast* [*Babettes gaestebud*, 1987]); Henning Carlsen (b. 1927—*Wolf at the Door* [*Oviri*, 1986]); Erik Clausen (b. 1942—*Dark Side of the Moon* [*Manden i månen*, 1986]); Helle Ryslinge (b. 1944—*Coeurs flambés* [*Falmberede hjerter*, 1986]); Søren Kragh-Jacobsen (b. 1947—*Shower of Gold* [*Guldregn*, 1988]); Bille August (b. 1948—*Pelle the Conqueror* [*Pelle erobreren*, 1987; a coproduction of the DFI and Svensk Filmindustri, and winner of the Palm d'Or, Cannes, and Academy Award for Best Foreign Film, 1988]); Jon Bang Carlsen (b. 1950—*Ophelia Comes to Town* (*Ofelia kommer til byen*, 1985]); Lars von Trier (b. 1956—*The Element of Crime* [*Forbrydelsens element*, 1984]; *Epidemic* [1987]; *Europa* [1991]); and Susanne Bier (b. 1960—*Freud Leaving Home* [*Freud flyttar hemifrån*, 1990]). By the early 1990s, aggressive competition from American films had driven the Danish market share below 20 percent, and in 1995 domestic features accounted for only 8 percent of box-office receipts, with 81 percent going to the Americans. By 1999, however, the Danish share had returned to its 1970s level (28 percent) thanks to the phenomenal success of several genre films, like Ole Bornedal's *Nightwatch* (*Nattevagten*, 1996; remade by Bornedal [b. 1959] for Disney as *Nightwatch* in 1998) and Susanne Bier's *The One and Only* (*Den eneste ene*, 1999), and to the movement known as Dogme95 ("Dogma 95").

In 1995, several young Danish directors banded together to form a production collective in response to what they considered the current decadence and artificiality of world cinema. Recognizing that they were in the midst of a technological revolution, driven by the proliferation of digital video, that would lead to "the ultimate democratization of the cinema," Lars von Trier, Thomas Vinterberg (b. 1969), Søren Kragh-Jacobsen, and Kristian Levring produced the Dogme95 Manifesto together with a set of rules called "The Vow of Chastity," which were designed to liberate the cinema from its bondage to illusionist dramaturgy and bourgeois romanticism (and, thus, auteurism). This "indisputable set of rules" was rendered as the following ten commandments:

1. Shooting must be done on location. Props and sets must not be brought in. (If a particular prop is necessary for the story, a location must be chosen where the prop is found.)
2. The sound must never be produced apart from the images or vice versa. (Music must not be used unless it occurs where the scene is being shot.)
3. The camera must be handheld. Any movement or immobility attainable in the hand is permitted. (The film must not take place where the camera is standing; shooting must take place where the film takes place.)
4. The film must be in color. Special lighting is not acceptable. (If there is too little light for exposure, the scene must be cut or a single lamp attached to the front of the camera.)
5. Optical work and filters are forbidden.
6. The film must not contain superficial action. (Murders, the use of weapons, etc. must not occur.)
7. Temporal and geographic alienation are forbidden. (That is to say, the film takes place here and now.)

8. Genre movies are not acceptable.
9. The film format must be in Academy 35mm [most often digital video transferred to film and blown up for 35mm theatrical distribution].
10. The director must not be credited.

Furthermore, the individual filmmaker had to "swear as a director to refrain from personal taste" and to make the following declaration: "I am no longer an artist. . . . My supreme goal is to force the truth out of my characters and settings. I swear to do so by all the means available and at the cost of any good taste and any aesthetic considerations."

Aimed specifically at the feature-length fiction film format (which does not mean that documentaries and short films cannot be aligned with Dogme95 precepts), these rules would have been nearly impossible to follow before the era of lightweight 35mm and digital video cameras, and even now they require considerable discipline to achieve. Their expressed intention was to return the cinema to its realist roots through a minimalist model of production, but their formal difficulty also served to impose a discipline on the production process that encouraged innovation within the confines of the rules.

Initially perceived as a marketing gimmick to boost the domestic industry, the Dogme95 movement quickly demonstrated its serious artistic purpose with three films that won international critical acclaim and did well at the box office, too—Vinterberg's *Festen* (*The Celebration*, 1998), von Trier's *Idioterne* (*The Idiots*, 1998), and Kragh-Jacobsen's *Mifunes sidste sang* (*Mifune*, 1999). *The Celebration*, which adhered very closely to the *Vow of Chastity*, won the Jury Prize at Cannes with its harrowing account of a family gathering that turns dark and ugly with the revelation of a respected father's sexual abuse of his children. *The Idiots*, in which a group of "normal" young people imitate the behavior of the mentally retarded in order to subvert the conventions of Copenhagen's bourgeoisie, is the only von Trier film made in total compliance with the Dogme95 Manifesto, although virtually all of his work—e.g. *The Kingdom* (1994), *Breaking the Waves* (1996), *Dancer in the Dark* (2000)—has been inflected by Dogme principles, and it has brought both prestige and controversy to the Danish film industry by radically deconstructing Hollywood genre codes. (Lars von Trier and producer Peter Aalbaek Jensen work through their own Zentropa Entertainment, an intricately structured amalgam of about sixty smaller companies that has become the most active production company in Denmark.) Kragh-Jacobsen's *Mifune* was another assault on bourgeois hypocrisy shot in stark Dogme style about the son of a poor farming family who aspires to Yuppiedom and lies his way through the film like the bogus samurai character played by Toshiro Mifune in Kurosawa's *The Seven Samurai* (1954).

With Kristian Levring's *The King Is Alive* (2000), in which a group of bus passengers who get stranded in the Namibian desert decide to put on a production of *King Lear* to cope with their isolation, all of the original manifesto signatories had made Dogma films, and the movement had begun to evince an international impact. Dogma certificates, affirming that productions have adhered to all ten rules as stated in the Vow of Chastity, have been issued to films made in France (*Lovers* [Jean-Marc Barr, 1999]),

15.46 *Dancer in the Dark* **(Lars von Trier, 2000), a Dogme95-like deconstruction of the Hollywood musical starring Icelandic pop singer Björk (who won the Best Actress prize at Cannes for her role) and shot on digital video.**

Korea (*Interview* [Daniel H. Byun, 2000]), Argentina (*Fuckland* [José Luis Marquès, 2000]), Sweden (*Babylon* [Vladan Zdravkovic, 2001]), Italy (*Diapason* [Antonio Domenici, 2001]), Switzerland (*Joy Ride* [Martin Rengel, 2001]), Norway (*Cabin Fever/Når nettene blir lange* [Mona J. Hoel, 2001]), Belgium (*Strass* [Vincent Lannoo, 2001]), Spain (*Once upon Another Time/Era outra vez* [Juan Pinzas, 2000]), and the United States (*Julien Donkey-Boy* [Harmony Korine, 1999]; *Camera* [Richard Martini, 2000]; *Bad Actors* [Shaun Monson, 2000]; *Reunion* [Leif Tilden, 2001]; *Converging with Angels* [Michael Sorenson, 2002]). Furthermore, the spontaneity and directness of the Dogme style has influenced established directors as diverse in their concerns as Wim Wenders (*Buena Vista Social Club*, 1999) and Agnès Varda (*The Gleaners and I*, 2000), both of whom now shoot on digital video (DV) for transfer to film. Mainstream filmmakers who have recently used Dogme-style DV for features include Mike Figgis (*Timecode* [2000]), Miguel Arteta (*Chuck & Buck* [2000]), Joel Schumacher (*Tigerland* [2000]), Wayne Wang (*The Center of the World* [2001]),

Jennifer Jason Leigh and Alan Cumming (*The Anniversary Party* [2001]), and Richard Linklater (*Waking Life* [2001]). Closer to home, Dogme directors produced a number of solid commercial hits (e.g., Lone Scherfig's *Italian for Beginners/Italiensk for begyndere* [2001] and Åke Sandgren's *Truly Human* [*Et rigtigt menneske*, 2001]) that have reinvigorated the Danish film industry. Credit for the turnaround must also go to the Danish government, which, in 1997, combined the industry's four main components into a single institution—the DFI (features), the National Film Board of Denmark (shorts and documentaries), the Danish Film Workshop (experimental films and videos), and the Danish Film Museum (the national film archive)—now operating under a single roof at the newly built Film House in Copenhagen. At the same time, the government more than tripled its level of production funding, facilitating the making of eighteen domestic features in 1998 and a record 48 percent of market share for Danish films in 2000.

NORWAY AND ICELAND

Of the other Scandinavian countries, Norway and Iceland both have small film industries. Like Denmark, Norway (population 4.5 million) has a film history extending back to the silent period, but its unique system of municipally owned theaters impeded growth until after World War II, when the government began a system of partial production subsidies based on a "tickets tax." This funding enabled a small domestic industry to thrive, considerably enhanced by the North Sea oil boom of the late 1970s and 1980s. Norway gained interna-

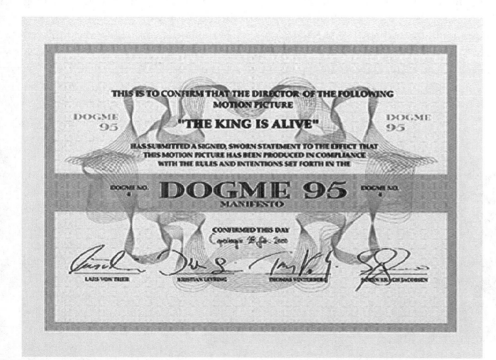

15.47 The Dogme95 Certificate issued to *The King Is Alive* (Kristian Levring, 2000) for having observed its "Vow of Chastity."

tional recognition in 1986, when director Oddvar Einarson (b. 1949) won the Silver Lion at Venice for his first feature, *X* (1986); Vibeke Løkkeberg's (b. 1945) *Skin* (*Hud*) was officially selected for Cannes' "Un Certain Regard"; and Ola Solum's (b. 1943) *Orion's Belt* (*Orions belte*) became the nation's first worldwide release. Norway's other leading directors are Lasse Glomm (b. 1944)—*Zeppelin*, 1981; *Black Crows* (*Svarte fugler*, 1984); *Northern Lights* (*Havlandet*, 1985); *Sweetwater*, 1987; Per Blom (b. 1946)—*Mother's House* (*Mors hus*, 1974); *The Woman* (*Kvinnene*, 1981); *The Ice-Palace* (*Is-slottet*, 1987); and the two leading feminist filmmakers, Anja Breien (b. 1940)—*Rape* (*Voldtekt*, 1971); *Wives* (*Hustruer*, 1975); *Witch Hunt* (*Forgøgelsen*, 1981); *Paper Bird* (*Papirfuglen*, 1984); *Wives—Ten Years After* (*Hustruer—ti år etter*, 1985)—and Vibeke Løkkeberg—*The Revelation* (*Åpenbaringen*, 1978); *The Betrayal/Kamilla* (*Løperjenten*, 1981); *Skin* (*Hud*, 1986). Notable recent coproductions are the Swedish-Soviet-Norwegian *Mio in the Land Far Away* (Ágúst Guðmundsson, 1987) and the Norwegian-Lapp epic *Pathfinder* (*Ofelas* [Nils Gaup, 1987]), the first Lapp-language feature and the second Norwegian-backed film to receive international distribution. More recently, Norway scored a worldwide hit with London-trained Erik Skoldbjaerg's (b. 1964) *Insomnia* (1998), a psychological thriller about a murder investigation in a small coastal town beyond the Arctic Circle, which was remade in 2002 by the American director Christopher Nolan (b. 1970—*Memento* [2001]). During the 1980s and 1990s, there were three sources of government production subsidy in Norway: the Foundation for Audiovisual Productions for documentaries, the national Film Institute, and the state-owned production company Norsk Film for features; at the same time, a film school was established at Lillehammer and a film museum in Oslo. Norsk Film was privatized in 2000, the same year that the industry scored a series of domestic hits with such films as Nathilde Overrein Rapp's *Lime—a Bit Green* (*Lime—litt grønn*) and Pal Sletaune's *You Really Got Me* (*Amatorene*). Finally, although Norway's 159 municipally owned cinemas are responsible for 90 percent of all ticket sales, privately owned theaters have begun to appear in and around Oslo, which is the country's only major city.

Icelandic cinema remains a cottage industry, yet that

15.48 *Insomnia* (**Erik Skoldbjaerg, 1998): Stellan Skarsgård as a guilt-ridden Swedish cop on the trail of a serial killer in northern Norway. The film was remade under the same title by Christopher Nolan in 2002, with Al Pacino as the cop and the setting changed to Alaska.**

a country of only 279,000 inhabitants supports a film industry at all is nothing short of astounding. Iceland did not begin postwar production until 1977, but its breakthrough came in 1980 when a film by Ágúst Guðmundsson (b. 1947)—*Land and Sons* (*Land og synir*)—and one by Hrafn Gunnlaugsson (b. 1948)—*Ancestral Estate* (*Óðal feðranna*)—both concerned with the tensions between rural and urban society, were noted at several international festivals. Similar attention was accorded Gudmundsson's rock musical *On Top* (*Með allt á hreinu*, 1982) and Gunnlaugsson's saga-inspired Viking epic *When the Raven Flies* (*Hrafninn flýgur*, 1984), both of which also became domestic smash hits. Other Icelandic directors are þráinn Bertelsson (b. 1944)—*Pastoral Life*, 1984; *Magnús*, 1989; Thorsteinn Johnsson (b. 1946)—*The Atomic Station* (*Atomstodin*, 1984); Fridrik Thor Fridriksson (b. 1954)—*White Whales* (*Skyttuhrnar*, 1987), *Children of Nature* (*Born natturunnar*, 1990), and *Devil's Island* (1996), a Tarentino-like crime film that beat out the American blockbuster *Independence Day* to become the top-grossing film of 1996. Fridriksson's biography of a schizophrenic Icelandic poet, *Angels of the Universe* (*Englar alheimsins*, 2000), was widely regarded as the greatest film to emerge from Iceland to date. The tiny nation produces an average of six features a year, many on digital video and all receiving some support from the government-sponsored Icelandic Film Fund. Until 1998, however, this funding was meager, which encouraged Icelandic producers to seek outside investment and coproduction deals underwritten by other European governments. The Film Fund also supports the Reykjavík Film Festival and the National Film Archive of Iceland.

Spain

LUIS BUÑUEL

For decades the Spanish cinema was associated almost exclusively with the work of Luis Buñuel (1900–1983), who was, paradoxically, the quintessential artist in exile for most of his career.[8] After making the bitter and sardonic documentary *Las Hurdes* (1932; see Chapter 9)—which was banned by the Spanish Republican government of 1933–35 as "defamatory" but later released by the Popular Front government during the civil war—Buñuel did not direct another film for fifteen years. He worked sporadically as a producer in Paris, Hollywood, and Madrid before emigrating to America in 1938 to escape fascism. Here he edited war documentaries for the Museum of Modern Art (MoMA) in New York[9] and supervised the Spanish-language versions of films for Warner Bros. and MGM. In 1947 he was given a chance to direct two popular comedies for the Mexican producer Óscar Dancigers, *Gran casino*, (*Grand Casino*, 1947) and *El gran calavera* (*The Great Madcap*, 1949), and on the strength of their commercial success he was permitted to make *Los olvidados* (*The Forgotten Ones/The Young and the Damned*, 1950), the film that restored his reputation as an important international artist.

Ostensibly a neorealist portrayal of juvenile delinquency in modern Mexico City, *Los olvidados* is actually a disturbing catalogue of man's darkest and most destructive impulses, as subversive in its way as Buñuel's earlier surrealist films. The corrupted slum youth of the city are condemned to live in a nightmarish world of violence, brutality, and degradation, not only because of the poverty imposed on them by bourgeois capitalism (whose image is ever-present in the rising skyscrapers that dominate the film's background) but also because of the wretchedness of reality itself. Images of horror abound, all recorded with documentary-like objectivity: a limbless cripple is tipped off his cart and sent sprawling on his back like a turtle, a blind man is tormented and robbed

15.49 *Los olvidados* (Luis Buñuel, 1950): Roberto Cobo (center).

by a gang of young thugs, a boy is bludgeoned to death with a rock by his companion, an old degenerate fondles the bare legs of a little girl, and finally the film's pathetic young protagonist is slashed to death and his body dumped on a garbage heap. Austerely photographed by the Mexican cinematographer Gabriel Figueroa (1907–1997), who was to work on all of Buñuel's Mexican masterpieces, *Los olvidados* achieves an almost hallucinatory quality through the relentless exposition of an external reality (not to mention a brilliant and terrifying Freudian dream sequence) that is literally hell on earth. The extraordinary quality of this film was recognized when it won Buñuel the Cannes Director's Prize in 1951. He continued to work within the Mexican commercial cinema for the next five years, producing a series of unique and expertly crafted films on low budgets and short production schedules.

Some of these films were neorealistic melodramas of sexual passion, like *Susana* (1951) and *El bruto* (*The*

---

8. This paradox is explored most thoroughly by Marsha Kinder in *Blood Cinema: The Reconstruction of National Identity in Spain* (Berkeley: University of California Press, 1993), ch. 6: "Exile and Ideological Reinscription: The Unique Case of Luis Buñuel," pp. 278–338.

9. Buñuel was forced to resign from his position at MoMA in 1943 under pressure from the State Department, which was itself under pressure from the Catholic lobby in Washington because the filmmaker had been described as an atheist and a Marxist in Dalí's *The Secret Life of Salvador Dalí* (1942). See Buñuel's autobiography, *My Last Sigh*, trans. Abigail Israel (New York: Knopf, 1983).

Brute, 1952); others were whimsical and sometimes fantastic comedies, like *Subida al cielo* (English title: *Mexican Bus Ride*, 1952) and *La ilusión viaja en tranvía* (*Illusion Travels by Streetcar*, 1954). Buñuel also made remarkable versions of two important English novels—an English-language *The Adventures of Robinson Crusoe* (1952), his first film in color, which turns Defoe on his ear to suggest the total uselessness of bourgeois civilization, and a Spanish-language *Wuthering Heights* (*Cumbres borrascosas/Abismos de pasión*, 1952), which ends with the Heathcliff character ripping open his beloved's recently interred coffin and attempting to make love to her corpse. Buñuel's most characteristic and personal films of this period, however, were *Él* (English titles: *This Strange Passion/Torment*, 1952) and *Ensayo de un crimen* (*Rehearsal for a Crime/The Criminal Life of Archibaldo de la Cruz*, 1955).

Él is a tale of pathological erotic obsession in which fantasy and reality, photographed from equally objective points of view, are constantly threatening to merge. A wealthy, repressed, middle-aged landowner, who is a pillar of society and a secret foot fetishist (a Buñuel trademark), woos and wins a beautiful girl. After the marriage, he turns his oppressive rococo villa into a hothouse of sexual neurosis, as his own impotence drives him to become insanely jealous of his perfectly innocent bride. The young woman begins to fear for her life, and one night she awakens to find her husband stealthily preparing to suture her vagina. She runs away and he goes totally mad, ultimately attempting to strangle his priest. But the

15.50 *Cumbres borrascosas* (Luis Buñuel, 1952).

Church takes him to its bosom and imprisons him in a monastery, where he becomes a monk. Years later, his former wife visits him and discovers that despite his external calm he is as lunatic as before. *Él* is among Buñuel's most savage attacks on the Catholic Church and the repressive mechanisms of bourgeois culture. It was booed from the screen at Cannes, but it was terrifically popular in Mexico, where audiences accepted it as a sympathetic study of a man driven crazy by jealousy.

Ensayo de un crimen is another film about a man in the grip of an overpowering erotic obsession. It is a black comedy—as, in some sense, are all of Buñuel's best films—but it is considerably lighter than *Él*. As a young boy, the film's hero has been told that his music box has the magical power to kill anyone he desires. The boy experiments on his governess, who is immediately shot dead by a stray bullet from a street riot, and he carries an erotic fascination with murder into adulthood. He attempts to become a sadistic murderer of young women but bungles every attempt, finally loses his obsession, and goes on to lead a normal life.

After 1955 Buñuel went to Paris, where he directed three international coproductions that are openly political in theme. As Raymond Durgnat observes, *Cela s'appelle l'aurore* (*It Is Called the Dawn*, Italy/France, 1955), *La Mort en ce jardin* (English title: *Evil Eden*, France/Mexico, 1956), and *La Fièvre mont à El Pao/Los ambiciosos* (English title: *Republic of Sin*, France/Mexico, 1959) together form a triptych that explores the morality of armed revolt against fascist dictatorships.

Buñuel returned to Mexico in 1958 to direct *Nazarín*, the masterpiece that marked the beginning of his greatest period. Based on a nineteenth-century Mexican novel set during the dictatorship of Porfirio Díaz, this film concerns the spiritual pilgrimage of a saintlike priest who makes the error of sincerely attempting to follow Christian doctrine and imitate the life of Christ. Cast out and reviled by his church, Father Nazarín journeys into the wilderness, followed by a band of protégées whose attraction for him, it turns out, is less spiritual than fleshly. Like the Biblical story of Jesus, the film has an episodic structure, and as Nazarín moves from one parabolic incident to the next, he becomes increasingly disillusioned with his mission. He is finally hunted down by police for his part in fomenting a workers' rebellion and is tossed into jail. The film ends with Nazarín chained to a wall between two thieves; but he is seemingly brought new hope when a peasant woman offers him a pomegranate. *Nazarín* was mistaken by many Catholic critics as signaling Buñuel's return to the fold, and in a fine irony the film was nearly awarded the prize of the International Catholic Cinema Office. But the point of this intentionally ambiguous film is that Nazarín, who undertakes his quest with sincerity, humility, and great moral courage, manages to achieve absolutely nothing in the course of it but his own destruction. As Buñuel said in another context, "One can be *relatively* Christian, but the absolutely pure being, the innocent, is condemned to defeat."

This attitude was given its most brilliant exposition in *Viridiana* (1961), an anti-Catholic, antifascist parable that Buñuel shot in Catholic Spain under the very noses of fascist censors, who approved the script.[1] Like *Nazarín, Viridiana* concerns a devout and saintly person whose attempts to lead a truly Christian life end in disaster for herself and everyone around her. Viridiana (the name derives from that of a little-known medieval saint), a beautiful young woman about to enter a convent, is advised by her mother superior to visit the country estate of an elderly uncle whom she barely knows. The uncle is overwhelmed by Viridiana's resemblance to his wife, who died years ago on their wedding night, and he falls madly in love with her. She gently rebuffs him, and finally (in a sequence highly reminiscent of *Él*), he has her drugged and laid out like a corpse in his wife's wedding gown. He nearly rapes her, and the next day, as Viridiana is about to flee for the convent, she learns that her uncle has hanged himself with a jump rope. Feeling herself responsible for the old man's death, she stays on to help run the estate with her uncle's illegitimate son, Jorge; and in a Nazarín-like act of contrition, she invites a group of diseased beggars from a nearby town to come live in some deserted cottages on her uncle's property. A famous montage sequence contrasts her futile efforts to save these villainous wretches through prayer with Jorge's strenuous practical endeavors to restore order to the estate. One day Viridiana and Jorge go to town on business, and the beggars break into the manor house and stage a riotous feast that Buñuel composed in grotesque parody of Leonardo da Vinci's fresco *The Last Supper*. The beggars' banquet ends in a frenzied orgy accompanied by the strains of Handel's *Messiah*, and when Jorge and Viridiana return, the girl is all but raped by a leper. This obscenity finally breaks her spiritual

15.51 The parody of *The Last Supper* in Buñuel's *Viridiana* (1961).

pride, and the final sequence of the film shows her joining Jorge and his mistress in a three-handed game of cards.

Blasphemous, ironic, and masterfully constructed, *Viridiana* is quintessential Buñuel—and all the more so for its being an outrageous practical joke on the fascist state that permitted its production. No sooner was the film released than Spanish authorities realized its subversive nature and attempted to destroy all copies. But it was too late: prints had already reached Cannes, where the film was accepted as the official Spanish entry in the festival and awarded the Palme d'Or—the first ever won by a Spanish film—to the everlasting chagrin of the Franco regime. Moreover, there was so little ambiguity about the film's anticlericalism that it was officially denounced by the Vatican as "an insult to Christianity."

If *Viridiana* truly is Buñuel's ultimate insult to Christianity, then its successor, *El ángel exterminador* (*The Exterminating Angel*, Mexico, 1962), is clearly his ultimate insult to conventional bourgeois morality. In this film, which many critics regard as Buñuel's greatest, a group of wealthy people gather at an elegant villa for a sumptuous dinner party. After the meal they retire to a drawing room, but when it is time to go home they find themselves mysteriously unable to leave the room— and, just as strangely, no one from outside can get in.

---

1. Between *Nazarín* and *Viridiana*, Buñuel made his second English-language film, *The Young One* (Mexico, 1960), a relatively light work (for Buñuel) about an American black man, unjustly accused of rape, who flees to an offshore island to escape a lynch mob and becomes dangerously entangled there with a fourteen-year-old white girl and the man who loves her.

15.52 *L'univers concentrationnaire:* the trapped bourgeoisie of Buñuel's *El ángel exterminador* (1962).

The situation, initially humorous, persists for weeks and becomes a nightmare as the drawing room is transformed into a miniature concentration camp. To eat, the inmates are forced to slaughter stray sheep that roam the villa in the aftermath of an elaborate practical joke. They cannot bathe, and they have no toilet facilities. When an old man dies and two lovers commit suicide, their corpses are stuffed into a closet for possible future use, it is darkly hinted, should the supply of sheep run out. Filthy, foul-smelling, and driven to the brink of madness by their extreme situation, the prisoners finally attempt to reconstruct the circumstances leading up to their imprisonment. Miraculously, the tactic works, and they stumble out of the villa toward an anxiously waiting public like the emaciated survivors of a death camp. The film ends in a cathedral where the survivors have come to give thanks for their salvation. After a solemn *Te Deum,* the entire congregation finds itself unable to leave the church, and a flock of sheep suddenly enters the building, while anarchic violence erupts in the streets outside. As Raymond Durgnat has suggested, "the exterminating angel" of this film is the bourgeois ethos of conformity and convention that traps the dinner guests and, finally, everyone in the culture in their social roles. In this brilliant surrealist parable, Buñuel suggests that bourgeois concepts of self are as systematically delimiting and destructive of human freedom as the Nazi death camps, and that liberation can be achieved only by thinking ourselves back to the beginning of things.

With *Le Journal d'une femme de chambre* (*Diary of a Chambermaid,* 1964; also filmed by Renoir, 1946),

Buñuel returned to France to make his most political film—and his first in widescreen. He transposed the setting of Octave Mirbeau's decadent novel of erotic obsession among the French upper classes from the turn of the century to 1928, a time when French fascism was gathering the force that would ultimately permit the collapse of the Third Republic and the Nazi Occupation. A Parisian chambermaid (Jeanne Moreau) quits her post to take a job in the manor house of a large provincial estate that proves to be a hotbed of reactionary politics and sexual pathology. Her elderly employer is a boot fetishist whose frigid married daughter is similarly obsessed with internal hygiene. The estate's gamekeeper, Joseph, a surly right-winger committed to the "moral rebirth of France," is a psychopathic sadist who likes to torture the farm animals and who rapes and murders a little girl with whom the maid has become friends. The maid suspects Joseph immediately and has an affair with him in order to gather enough evidence to avenge her little friend. She does so and finally denounces him to the police, for which she is fired. Joseph is not prosecuted, and the film ends years later in Marseilles, with the former gamekeeper, now a prosperous café owner, shouting slogans in support of a large fascist rally. Buñuel cuts to a bolt of lightning rending the sky, an unequivocal reminder that brutality will continue to triumph over decency and innocence in the coming storm of war. Buñuel's equation of fascism, decadence, and sexual perversion in *Le Journal* is perfectly made, and it brings the film close in spirit to Bertolucci's *Il conformista* (1970).

Buñuel's next film, *Simón del desierto* (*Simon of the Desert,* Mexico, 1965) is a 42-minute feature based on the temptations of St. Simon Stylites, the fifth-century anchorite who spent his life perched atop a 60-foot column in the desert, preaching and performing miracles for devout Christians who came to supplicate him. Written by the director himself and shot in Mexico in twenty-five days, the film is a jovial catalogue of Buñuelian obsessions and motifs: crowds of spectators rate Simon's miracles ("not bad"); local merchants attempt to corrupt him while local priests try to do him in; Simon lavishes equal care on restoring the chopped-off hands of a convicted thief (who immediately uses them to beat his child) and on blessing a piece of food picked from between his teeth; the Devil appears to him as a little girl in a sailor suit and as a sexy young woman unconvincingly disguised as Christ. Finally, the devil whisks him off to New York

15.53 *Simón del desierto* (Luis Buñuel, 1965): Claudio Brook as Saint Simeon Stylites, tempted by Silvia Pinal in the guise of Christ the Good Shepherd.

City on a jet-propelled coffin and leaves him sipping Coke in a discothèque crowded with teenagers doing a fashionable new dance ("the latest and the last," the Devil tells him) dubbed the "Radioactive Flesh." Subtly photographed in atonal black and white by Gabriel Figueroa and playfully pessimistic in mood, *Simón del desierto* won a special jury prize at Venice in 1965.

In 1967, at the age of sixty-seven, Buñuel returned to France to make *Belle de jour*, the film that he claimed would be his last (although he was to direct five more unequivocal masterpieces). Exquisitely photographed in color by Sacha Vierny, *Belle de jour* is another Buñuelian classic of erotic obsession: Séverine, the beautiful wife of a successful surgeon who is also a kind husband, has a secret compulsion for sexual degradation. She attempts to realize her masochistic fantasies by working afternoons in Madame Anaïs's brothel, where she is christened "Belle de jour" (a play on *belle de nuit*, a French euphemism for prostitute). Here she caters to a whole range of perversions from simple fetishism to necrophilia, and her fantasy life grows apace. For Buñuel, the old surrealist,

the brothel is a place of absolute freedom precisely because it *is* a region where fantasy interpenetrates reality. As the film progresses, it becomes increasingly difficult to distinguish Séverine's fantasies from the linear narrative, which now involves a sadistic young gangster who has fallen in love with Belle at the brothel. The gangster attempts to murder her husband and paralyzes him, we are told, for life. In an act of atonement, Séverine quits the brothel and becomes her husband's devoted nurse, until a jealous family friend tells him of her past existence as Belle de jour. At this, he first seems to die of shock and then rises from his wheelchair, miraculously cured. An empty black carriage with jingling bells, which has been associated with Séverine's fantasy world throughout the film, passes by in the park beneath the window of their fashionable apartment, and we are left to wonder whether the whole film has not been a dream or an extended fantasy in the mind of its heroine. *Belle de jour* is a hypnotically engaging film, as beautiful in its artistic intelligence as in its visually exquisite surface, and it was justly awarded the Golden Lion at the Venice Festival in 1967.

As if to contradict himself with all due haste, Buñuel turned to his next project immediately after the release of *Belle de jour*. *La Voie lactée* (*The Milky Way*, France, 1969) is a symbolic history of the Roman Catholic Church with all its heresies and schisms, told in the form of an episodic narrative about two tramps journeying from Paris to the shrine of the Apostle James at Santiago de Compostela ("St. James of the Field of Stars") in Spain. The road they follow is popularly known in Europe as "the Milky Way," but for Buñuel the term also signifies the supposedly celestial path of Christianity through the ages. Thus, in the course of their journey the tramps encounter figures from the past who either dramatize church history (for instance, an eighteenth-century Jansenist fencing with a Jesuit) or incarnate it (Christ, the Virgin Mary, the Devil). The film is less savage than impudently funny, although we are treated to the usual assortment of Buñuelian horrors: leprous blind beggars, the Marquis de Sade flogging a victim, a crucified nun, etc. Beautifully photographed in color by the veteran French cinematographer Christian Matras, *La Voie lactée* was not well received by some critics, who thought its exposition (and deflation) of Catholic theological doctrine too arcane.

About *Tristana* (1970), however, there were no doubts

at all. This French/Italian coproduction is set in the ancient Spanish city of Toledo in the 1920s and concerns a decadent aristocrat, Don Lope, who systematically corrupts and enslaves his innocent young ward, Tristana (from *triste*, sad). Tristana, for her part, attempts to resist by running away from her guardian with an artist who wishes to marry her. But she returns two years later with a crippling illness that has made it necessary for a leg to be amputated, confining her permanently to a wheelchair. Totally dependent now on Don Lope, Tristana begins to internalize his perversity, taking as her own victims the half-witted deaf mute who pushes her wheelchair, and finally Don Lope himself: the old man dies of a heart attack while she callously refuses to call a doctor. Subtly photographed by José Aguayo in autumnal hues, this film is as much about the decay of Spain as about the interrelationships of its characters. Tristana is the victim not simply of Don Lope, but of the corrupt and impotent moral code that he embodies and that was to be institutionalized by Franco (although Don Lope is himself a sort of liberal) after the civil war.

Buñuel's next film, *Le Charme discret de la bourgeoisie* (*The Discreet Charm of the Bourgeoisie*, France, 1973), is a legitimate successor to both *L'Âge d'or* (1930) and *El ángel exterminador* (1962) but exchanges their savage bite for gently mocking irony. It is a buoyant satire about the foibles and follies of the privileged class, structured as an extended dream in the mind of Don Rafael, the ambassador to France from the Latin American country of Miranda, a military dictatorship that has the highest homicide rate in the world. Don Rafael's dream, which includes the dreams of others and dreams within dreams, concerns the constantly frustrated efforts of six friends to dine together in a civilized manner. Every time the attempt is made, the dinner is interrupted by some twist of dream logic or by another dream, which will in turn be interrupted by a dream or another attempted dinner party as soon as the situation has become engaging. The film, in fact, is one long pattern of interrupted episodes, and in this sense Buñuel has created a delightful parody of the mechanisms of narrative cinema. As soon as he draws us into a story, he cuts away to another, and the charming, civilized, self-indulgent bourgeoisie never do get to eat their dinner. A couple is overcome by sexual passion and has coitus on the table; a member of the party vomits just as the meal begins; the diners suddenly discover themselves upon a stage before a live audience and

forget their lines; the whole group is arrested for being accomplices in a heroin-smuggling ring (an in-joke since Fernando Rey, who plays Don Rafael, had played the heroin kingpin in William Friedkin's *The French Connection* a year before). Other dreams are darker and concern loss of identity and death, but the good bourgeoises manage to meet most situations with composure and a kind of bemused tolerance toward the shallowness of their own existence. Buñuel himself seems uncharacteristically mellow toward the confusion of values embodied in his characters, as if a kind of serene compassion for a long-hated enemy had set in. *Le Charme discret de la bourgeoisie* is good-humored and frequently hilarious, and its technical virtuosity demonstrates Buñuel's mastery of his medium. As in many of his other films, notably *Belle de jour* and *Tristana*, Buñuel uses no musical score, which contributes to the eerie surrealism of the piece.

Le Fantôme de la liberté (*The Phantom of Liberty*, France, 1974) continues the experiments begun in *Le Charme discret* and may well be Buñuel's most stylistically revolutionary work since *Un Chien andalou* and *L'Âge d'or*. In it, the director combines virtually every known story-telling device—narrative painting, the Gothic mode, the epistolary mode, omniscient narration, the flashback, the exemplary tale, the dream sequence, and dense patterns of allusion to other films—to create an episodic narrative that is simultaneously circular and self-reflexive. As Marsha Kinder has noted, *Le Fantôme de la liberté* is about the impossibility of escaping con-

15.54 Roused from a poker game in Buñuel's *Le Fantôme de la liberté* (1974), two priests, two monks, and a nurse witness an act of sexual perversion: Paul Le Person, Milena Vukotic, Gilbert Montagné, Bernard Musson, Marcel Pérès.

vention in society, politics, and art—and, ultimately, in the process of its own narrative, however radical that narrative may appear. There is no recurrent motif to bind together the separate episodes such as the dinner party in *Le Charme discret*, only the dream logic of continuous interruption and circularity. By interweaving episodes from the past and present which constantly disappoint our narrative expectations, Buñuel has produced an authentically surrealist essay on the political violence, necrophilia, and sadism that underlie bourgeois cultural conventions and make an elusive phantom of personal freedom.

For his last film, Buñuel chose to adapt Pierre Louÿs's short novel *La Femme et le pantin* (1896), which was also the source of von Sternberg's *The Devil Is a Woman* (1935) and Duvivier's *A Woman Like Satan* (1958). *Cet obscur objet du désir* (*That Obscure Object of Desire*, 1977) is an urbane and coolly ironic film about a young Spanish girl who teases and ultimately fleeces a middle-aged French widower. Buñuel compounds the irony by having two actresses with distinctly different physical appearances play the single "object" of the title, as if to suggest the polymorphous nature of desire itself.

From *Un Chien andalou* to *Cet obscur objet du désir*, Buñuel proved himself to be the most experimental and anarchistic filmmaker in the history of the narrative cinema. He was fundamentally a brilliant satirist, comparable to Swift and Goya, who used sexual pathology as a metaphor for the distorting nature of bourgeois Christian culture. Necrophilia, sadomasochism, fetishism, cannibalism, and bestiality were for Buñuel at once both cause and effect of the mass psychosis that we call Western civilization. Like all great satirists, Buñuel was simultaneously a moralist, a humorist, and a savage social critic who hoped that by exposing the nauseating inhumanity of human beings he would somehow make us more human. Until very near the end of his career, Buñuel employed a restrained and uncomplicated visual style, which led some critics to charge him with cinematic "indifference." We should remember, however, that for most of his career Buñuel was forced either to make films for other people on their terms or to not make films at all. This often meant shooting on low budgets with production schedules as short as three or four weeks. It also meant that Buñuel could not make his first film in color until 1952 or his first film in widescreen until 1964, and it would be fair to argue that, while an artist in Bergman's

position can afford style, one in Buñuel's cannot.

But actually, of course, Buñuel's indifference to style is a style in itself. John Russell Taylor has written: "Style is for him the best and most economical way of saying a thing. . . . The highest tribute one can pay to Buñuel's direction is to say that one is hardly ever conscious of it." This is as it should be for an artist who deals so consistently in the blasphemous, sardonic, and perverse. The invisibility of Buñuel's style is the deliberate artistic strategy of a master ironist: what we see is so clearly what we get in Buñuel that we trust him not to dupe us, which enables him to dupe us every time. But he always dupes us for our own good, by forcing us to acknowledge what we really are instead of what we would like to be, and the jokes he makes at our expense are most often hilariously funny. Buñuel's ironic vision of human experience is perhaps best summed up in a statement he once made when asked if he had ever been a religious person. "I have always been an atheist," he responded, "thank God."

NEW SPANISH CINEMA

With the exception of the work of Buñuel (most of which was done outside of Spain, in any case), Spanish cinema was little known beyond its national borders until after Francisco Franco's death in 1975. Under El Caudillo, the Spanish cinema had remained state supported and paternalistic (e.g., the official film version of the Civil War, *Raza* [*Race*, 1941], was written under a pseudonym by Franco himself and directed by a relative of Falangist founder Primo de Rivera). Production was controlled by a private monopoly (CIFESA) and a government-operated newsreel service (Noticiario Cinematográfico Español, or "No-Do"). But a film school, Instituto de Investigaciones y Experiences Cinematograficas (IIEC), was founded at Madrid in 1947, and some changes began to stir there during the 1950s, beginning with an Italian film week held in May 1951. According to Marsha Kinder, this event featured a program of recent neorealist films, most of which were banned from public exhibition, that strongly influenced the work of IIEC graduates Juan Antonio Bardem (1922–2002) and Luis García Berlanga (b. 1921), shaping the future course of Spanish cinema.[2] Their collaboration the following year produced *Bienvenido, Mr. Marshall* (*Welcome, Mr. Marshall*, 1952), an

---

2. Kinder, *Blood Cinema*, p. 3.

immensely popular satire about the enrichment of a small Spanish village as a result of the Marshall Plan, which won special mention at Cannes. Working separately for the rest of the decade, the two continued to make mildly sardonic social satires—Bardem directing *Muerte de un ciclista* (*Death of a Cyclist*, 1955—International Critics Award, Cannes) and *Calle mayor* (*Main Street*, 1956—Critics Award, Venice), Berlanga producing *Calabuch* (1956) and *Los jueves, milagro* (*A Miracle Every Thursday*, 1957). Aside from their films, Bardem and Berlanga influenced the direction of Spanish cinema in their sponsorship of the Salamanca "Conversations," a national symposium on film held in the spring of 1955 that called for a more realistic approach to contemporary social ills, and their participation in UNINCI, an independent production company established in 1951 in the wake CIFESA's financial collapse.

It was UNINCI that invited Buñuel back to Spain to make *Viridiana* (1961), and the company's shooting permit was cancelled by the government when this subversive film won the Cannes Grande Prix (see above). Yet in general, the period 1962–72 was one of *apertura*, or "opening," in Spanish culture as the country itself was moved toward greater integration with Europe. In 1962, Franco's new minister of information, Manuel Fraga Iribarne, appointed an ardent *cinéphile* as director general of cinema. This was José María García Excudero, who reorganized the IIEC as the Escuela Oficial de Cinematografía (EOC, or National Film School) and liberalized the policy of state production subsidies to create the grounds for what he called the "New Spanish Cinema." This liberalization led to the production of such award-winning work as Berlanga's *El verdugo* (*The Executioner*, 1963), Miguel Picazo's *La Tía Tula* (*Aunt Tula*, 1964), Basilio Martín Patino's *Nueve cartas a Berta* (*Nine Letters to Berta*, 1965), and the first major films of Carlos Saura (b. 1932), who established himself during the 1960s as Spain's leading resident director with a series of black comedies clearly influenced by Buñuel—*La caza* (*The Hunt*, 1965); *Peppermint frappé* (1967); and *El jardín de las delicias* (*The Garden of Delights*, 1970). A political crackdown ended this period, as Franco appointed a new cabinet in 1969 and replaced Fraga with the right-wing Alfredo Sánchez Bella, who was minister of information through 1973. As a result of this shift, the National Film School was shut down in 1970 and not reopened until 1995.

A third and definitive phase of New Spanish Cinema can be distinguished in the period from 1973 through the present. When Franco's handpicked successor, Admiral Luis Carrero Blanco, was assassinated by Basque separatists in 1973, the nation's movement toward non-Falangist normalization was virtually assured. Franco's last years were the time of the time of the *dictablanda*, or "soft dictatorship," when a number of groundbreaking, politically allusive films appeared—Saura's *La prima Angélica* (*Cousin Angelica*, 1973) and *Cría cuervos* (*Raise Ravens*, 1975—Special Jury Prize, Cannes, 1976), Jaime De Armiñán's *El amor del Capitán Brando* (*The Love of Captain Brando*, 1974), Jaime Camino's *Las largas vacaciones del 36* (*The Long Vacations of '36*, 1975), Ricardo Franco's *Pascual Duarte* (1975), and José Luis Borau's *Furtivos* (*Poachers*, 1975). The most courageous of all, Víctor Erice's *El espíritu de la colmena* (*The Spirit of the Beehive*, 1973), presented a densely symbolic account of life on the loser's side in post–Civil War Spain and won several international awards. Franco, who had been seriously ill for years, died at the age of eighty-two on November 20, 1975. By the end of 1977, censorship had been abolished and the first free elections held in over forty years; a democratic constitution was approved in 1978. As Spain emerged from its Fascist darkness over the next decade, its economy became increasingly integrated with that of Europe and the world, opening new channels of film distribution for the generation of directors emerging from the EOC as well as new work by Berlanga, Bardem, Saura, and others. Berlanga returned from self-imposed exile in France to direct *La escopeta nacional* (*The National Shotgun*, 1977), a satire on the final years of the Franco dictatorship, and several popular sequels, while Bardem made such post-Franco political thrillers as *Siete dias de enero* (*Seven Days in January*, 1978), a documentary-style reconstruction of the murder of some communist lawyers by right-wing terrorists in Madrid in 1977. Vicente Aranda (b. 1926) produced *Cambio de sexo* (*Sex Change*, 1977) and Jaime De Armiñán (b. 1927) *El nido* (*The Nest*, 1980), both about the extreme repressiveness of Spanish family life, while José Luis Borau (b. 1929) made *La Sabina* (1979), a mythic evocation of sexual politics in nineteenth-century Andalusia. Similarly, it was during this period that Saura made his mark as a truly international figure, producing *Elisa, vida mía* (*Elisa, My Life*, 1977), *Los ojos vendados* (*Blindfolded Eyes*, 1978), *Mama cumple 100 años* (*Mama Turns*

15.55 *Los ojos vendados* (Carlos Saura, 1978): Geraldine Chaplin.

100, 1979), and *Deprisa, deprisa* (*Hurry, Hurry!*, 1980). Saura has since distinguished himself with his Antonio Gades dance trilogy—*Boldas de sangre* (*Blood Wedding*, 1981; adapted from Lorca's verse tragedy), *Carmen* (1983; adapted from Bizet's opera), and *El amor brujo* (*A Love Bewitched*, 1986; adapted from Manuel de Falla's ballet)—and *El Dorado* (1988), a historical epic of the conquistador Lope de Aguirre's ill-fated expedition up the Amazon in 1560 (also the subject of Werner Herzog's *Aguirre, the Wrath of God* [1972]), which became the most expensive ($8 million) film ever produced by Spain. More recently, Saura won accolades for *Ay, Carmela!* (1990), a more modest production about the fortunes of some music-hall entertainers during the Civil War reminiscent of Lubitsch's classic comedy *To Be or Not to Be* (1942).

Major attention was focused on the second generation of New Spanish filmmakers by Pilar Miró (1940–1997), originally a television director (Spanish television, RTVE, was founded in 1956) whose theatrical feature *El crimen de cuenca* (*The Cuenca Crime*, 1979) became a *cause célèbre* for critics of the limitations on freedom of expression in Spain. Based on a 1912 incident in which two members of the Civil Guard had brutally tortured an innocent peasant to extract a murder confession, the film was briefly suppressed by military authorities, and Miró herself was tried unsuccessfully for defamation. When it was finally released in 1981, *El crimen de cuenca* quickly became the highest grossing film in Spanish box-office history, and Miró was appointed director general of cinematography by the newly elected Socialist premier Felipe Gonzalez in December 1981. In this post, as Peter Besas points out, Miró adopted a policy of virtually unlimited subsidization of "quality" producers and "prestige" directors such as those described above and created the context for a true Spanish art cinema among filmmakers of her own generation.[3] These include most prominently Miró herself—*Werther* (1968; adapted from Goethe); *Beltenebros* (*Prince of Shadows*, 1991); *El pájaro de la felicidad* (*The Bird of Happiness*, 1993); Jaime Chávarri (b. 1943)—*El desencanto* (*The Disenchantment*, 1976); *A un dios desconocido* (*To an Unknown God*, 1977); *Dedicatoria* (*Dedication*, 1980); *Bearn* (*La sala de las muñecas*, 1983); *Las bicicletas son para el verano* (*Bicycles Are for Summer*, 1948); *El río de oro* (*Golden River*, 1986); Jaime Camino (b. 1936)—*La vieja memoria* (*The Old Memory*, 1977); *La campanada* (1980); *El balcon abierto* (*The Open Balcony*, 1984); *Luces y sombras* (*Light and Shadows*, 1988); *El largo invierno* (*The Long Winter*, 1992); Víctor Erice (b. 1940)—*El sur* (*The South*, 1983); *El sol de membrillo* (*The Quince Tree Sun*, 1991); Ricardo Franco (1949–1998)—*Pascual Duarte*, 1975; *Los restos del naufragio* (*The Remains of the Shipwreck*, 1978); *San Judas de la frontera* (Mexico; 1984); José Luis Garci (b. 1944)—*Solos en la madrugada* (*Alone in the Early Hours*, 1978); *Las verdes praderas* (*Green Pastures*, 1979); *El crack* (*The Crack*, 1980); *Volver a empezar* (*To Begin Again*, 1982, winner of the American Academy Award for Best Foreign Film); *El crack II* (1983); *Sesión continua* (*Double Feature*, 1984); Antonio Drove (b. 1942)—*La verdad sobre el caso Savolta* (*The Truth in the Savolta Case*, 1978); Manuel Gutiérrez Aragón (b. 1942)—*Camada negra* (*Black Brood*, 1977, winner of the Directors Prize, Berlin, 1979); *Sonámbulos* (*Sleepwalkers*, 1977); *El corazón del bosque* (*The Heart of the Forest*, 1978); *Maravillas* (*Marvels*, 1980); *Demonios en el jardín* (*Demons in the Garden*, 1982); *Feroz* (*Wild*, 1984); *La noche más hermosa* (*The Most Beautiful Night*, 1984); *La mitad del cielo* (*Half of Heaven*, 1986); *Malaventura* (*Misadventure*, 1988); José Juan Bigas Luna (b. 1946)—*Bilbao, una historia de amor* (*Bilbao, a Love Story*, 1978);

3. Peter Besas, *Behind the Spanish Lens: Spanish Cinema under Fascism and Democracy* (Denver: Arden Press, 1985), pp. 229–30.

Caniche (*Poodle*, 1979); *Renacer* (*Reborn*, USA, 1981); *Lola* (1985); *Angustia* (*Anguish*, 1987); *Las edades de Lulú* (*The Ages of Lulu*, 1991); *Jamón, Jamón* (1992); *Huevos de oro* (*Golden Balls*, 1993); Eloy de la Iglesia (b. 1944)—*Los placeres ocultos* (*Hidden Pleasures*, 1977); *El diputado* (*The Deputy*, 1978); *Navajeros* (*Knife Fighters*, 1980); *Colegas* (*Pals*, 1982); *El pico* (*The Shoot*, 1983); *El pico II* (1984); *Otra vuelta de tuerca* (*The Turn of the Screw*, 1985); Pedro Olea (b. 1938)—*La corea* (1976); *Akelarre* (*Witches Sabbath*, 1984); *El maestro de esgrima* (*The Fencing Master*, 1992); Fernando Trueba (b. 1955)—*Mientras el cuerpo aguante* (*While the Body Lasts*, 1982); *El sueño del mono loco* (*The Mad Monkey/Twisted Obsession*, 1989); *Belle époque* (1992); Agustín Villaronga (b. 1953)—*Tras el cristal* (*Behind the Glass/In a Glass Cage*, 1986); and the enormously successful Pedro Almodóvar (b. 1951)—*Laberinto de pasiones* (*Labyrinth of Passions*, 1982); *Entre tinieblas* (*In the Dark*, 1983); *¿Qué he hecho yo para merecer esto?* (*What Have I Done to Deserve This?*, 1984); *Matador* (1986); *La ley del deseo* (*The Law of Desire*, 1987); *Mujeres al borde de un ataque de nervios* (*Women on the Verge of a Nervous Breakdown*, 1988); *Atame!* (*Tie Me Up! Tie Me Down!*, 1989); *Tacones lejanos* (*High Heels*, 1991); *Kika* (1993). Almodóvar's perverse, anarchic, and wildly funny films have consistently led the list of top Spanish exports to the West since 1986, and they are paradigmatic (if not entirely typical) of the current vitality of Spanish cinema.

With a population of 39 million, post-Franco Spain was able to produce an average of 50 films a year throughout the 1980s and 80 films a year during the 1990s—an astonishingly high volume for its population—which was made possible by a well-funded industrial infrastructure. Among the sources for production finance were national and regional television networks (e.g., Sogotel, Telefónica, RTVE, Antena 3 TV) and such companies as Lolafilms, Aurum, Cartel, and Mate Productions. In fact, at the turn of the century 80 percent of Spanish film production relied on some form of cofinancing from public and private television stations in exchange for broadcast rights. Even though Spanish films command only 10 to 12 percent of the domestic box office, they have achieved a high level of quality and diversity among several generations of directors. Examples of recent popular films include Pilar Miró's *The Dog in the Manger* (*El perro del hortelano*, 1997), a comedy by sixteenth-century playwright Lope de Vega spoken in verse; first-time director Mateo Gil's high-octane thriller *Nobody Knows Anybody* (*Nadie conoce a nadie*, 1999); and Alejandro Amenábar's thriller *Thesis* (also known as *Snuff*, 1996), in which a serial killer stalks victims at the National Film School, reopened for the first time in 1995 after being closed during the right-wing crackdown of 1970. (Mainstream horror has, in fact, become a staple Spanish genre.) The recent comic works of Pedro Almodóvar—*Live Flesh* (*Carne trémula*, 1998), *All about My Mother* (*Todo sobre mi madre*, 1999), *Talk to Her* (*Hable con ella*, 2002)—continue to enjoy popularity both at home and abroad, as do the slapstick spoofs of Santiago Segura—*Torrente—The Dumb Arm of the Law* (*Torrente—el brazo tonto de la ley*, 1998); *Torrente 2: Mission in Marbella* (2001). New works by Amenábar (*Open Your Eyes* [*Abre los ojos*, 1997]; *The Others* [*Los otros*, 2001]), Julio Medem (*The Lovers of the Arctic Circle* [*Los amantes del Círculo Polar*, 1998]), Trueba (*The Girl of your Dreams* [*La Niña de tus ojos*, 1998]), J. J. Bigas Luna (*Volavérunt*, 1999), and José Luis Garci (*The Grandfather* [*El abuelo*, 1998]; *You're the One*, 2000) confirm the continuing vitality of the Spanish cinema: all of these films experienced commercial success at home, and Amenábar's stylishly Jamesian ghost story *The Others* became an international hit, grossing nearly $100 million in the American market alone. It is notable, too, that production continues apace from the classically oriented Carlos Saura—*Tango* (1998), *Goya* (also known as *Goya in Bordeaux*, 1999), and *Buñuel and King Solomon's Table* (*Buñuel y la mesa del rey Salomón*, 2001—about the relationship among Buñuel, Lorca, and Dalí)—as well

15.56 *Mujeres al borde de un ataque de nervios* (Pedro Almodóvar, 1988): Carmen Maura as Pepa, a woman on the verge of a nervous breakdown.

15.57 *Tango* (Carlos Saura, 1998): a film about a film about Argentine tango, shot on location in Buenos Aires by the distinguished Italian cinematographer Vittorio Storaro.

Guillermo del Toro (b. 1964—*The Devil's Backbone* [2001]). Both as popular entertainment and as art, the Spanish cinema remains distinctive for its dark and somewhat surrealistic cast, as appropriate to the nation's twentieth-century history.

Germany: *Das Neue Kino*

POSTWAR ORIGINS

Related to other modernist European film movements through its emphatic rejection of conventional narrative syntax and its Marxist ideological perspective, ***das neue Kino*** ("the new cinema") made West German cinema among the most exciting in the world during the 1970s and 1980s, compensating for its long postwar eclipse. After World War II, Germany was split into Western and Eastern parts, which ultimately became the Federal Republic of Germany (FRG, population 63 million) and the German Democratic Republic (GDR, population 17.5 million), until reunification in 1990. Most of the film-production equipment was under Soviet control in the Eastern zone, as were the former UFA studios at Neubabelsberg. In May 1946, all activities of these production facilities were nationalized under the Deutsche Film Aktiengesellschaft (German Film Company, or DEFA), which provided new production capital in the form of state subsidies. In the Western sector, the Americans installed the former UFA producer Erich Pommer (see Chapter 4) as film commissioner for that zone and insured, through various decartelization laws, that no centralized German film industry could emerge to compete with their own. Nevertheless, the Allies began to license individual production companies in 1946, and the years 1946 through 1948 saw the release of several notable films dealing with immediate postwar social problems in both the Eastern and Western zones, among them *Die Mörder sind unter uns* (*The Murderers Are among Us*

as from the darkly ironic newcomer Álex de la Iglesia (b. 1965)—*El día de la bestia* (*Day of the Beast*, 1995), *Perdita Durango* (also known as *Dance with the Devil*, 1997), *Die Laughing* (*Muertos de risa*, 1999), and *La comunidad* (*Common Wealth*, 2000)—and that the Spanish market has room for them both. Furthermore, such veterans as Luis García Berlanga (*París-Timbuctú*, 1999) and Vicente Aranda (*Jealousy* [*Celos*, 1999]; *Mad Love* [*Locura de amor*, 2002]) continued to work in the industry, which also attracted such foreign-born Hispanic directors as Peru's Francisco J. Lombardi (b. 1949)—*Don't Tell Anyone* [*No se lo digas a nadie*, 1998]) and Mexico's

15.58 *The Devil's Backbone* (Guillermo del Toro, 2001): a ghost story set in a boys orphanage during the Spanish Civil War, directed by a Mexican but shot on location in northern Spain.

[Wolfgang Staudte, East Germany, 1946]); *Freies Land* (*Free Land* [Milo Harbich, East Germany, 1946]); *Morituri* (Eugen York [West Germany, 1946]); *In jenen Tagen* (*In Those Days* [Helmut Käutner, West Germany, 1947]); and *Berliner Ballade* (*The Ballad of Berlin* [Robert Stemmle, West Germany, 1948]). These were known as *Trümmerfilme* ("rubble films") because of the devastated physical condition of the Germany they portrayed, and they gave some hope of a realist German film movement, similar to the one being born concurrently in Italy.[4] But as production rose to over 70 German films a year in 1949, currency reform brought the promise of prosperity to West Germany, and the films of that sector turned away from self-scrutiny toward lightweight entertainment.[5]

Economic recovery proceeded rapidly through the 1950s, and West Germany became the fifth largest producer of films in the world. Yet its increasingly escapist *Heimatfilme* ("homeland films") were directed exclusively at the domestic audience, and they compared unfavorably with the glossy Hollywood products that flowed ceaselessly into the market through American-owned distributors. (Although the Americans had prevented the re-emergence of a centralized German film industry during the Occupation, they had supported the rebuilding of the exhibition and distribution sectors. After a series of monetary crises during the 1950s, all but one of the major West German distributors, Constantin Film, had fallen into American hands.) In East Germany, the DEFA output remained relatively small and ideologically focused, attacking Nazism as the archenemy of the new socialist state.

When television and increased mobility began to change patterns of leisure activity in the late 1950s, West German film attendance fell off dramatically, just as it did in the rest of Europe and in the United States. Between 1956 and 1968, in fact, it dropped from 900 million to 192 million annually. Domestic production was badly hurt, and the West German film industry had no alternative but to appeal to the federal government for subsidies. These were granted at first in the form of guaranteed credits (Ausfallbürgschaften) but were eliminated in 1961 when the Ministry of the Interior decided to help rejuvenate German cinema by awarding production grants for feature films.

YOUNG GERMAN CINEMA

The seeds of das *neue Kino* were sown at the Oberhausen Film Festival in 1962, when twenty-six writers and filmmakers who had accepted ministry grants called for the establishment of a *junger deutscher film*, a "young German cinema," in a manifesto that concluded as follows:

> The collapse of the commercial German film industry finally removes the economic basis for a mode of filmmaking whose attitude and practice we reject. With it, the new film has a chance to come to life. The success of German shorts at international festivals demonstrates that the future of the German cinema lies with those who have shown that they speak the international language of the cinema. This new cinema needs new forms of freedom: from the conventions and habits of the established industry, from intervention by commercial partners, and finally freedom from the tutelage of other vested interests. We have specific plans for the artistic, formal and economic realization of this new German cinema. We are collectively prepared to take the economic risks. The old cinema is dead. We believe in the new.

4. Roberto Rossellini's neorealist classic *Germania, anno zero* (*Germany, Year Zero*, 1947) was shot on location in bombed-out Berlin (see p. 361).

5. In April 2002, the Film Society of Lincoln Center and the Goethe Institute sponsored a retrospective series of *Trümmerfilme* entitled "After the War, before the Wall: German Cinema, 1945–60," making the somewhat tenuous case that they represented a "golden age" of German film in that they demonstrate the rebirth of film art in Germany after the Nazis had destroyed it.

15.59 A typical *Heimatfilm: Ich denke oft an Piroschka* (*I Often Think of Piroschka*, Kurt Hoffmann, 1956): Liselotte Pulver.

Through its spokesmen, the directors Alexander Kluge and Norbert Kückelmann, the Oberhausen group successfully lobbied the West German parliament (Bundestag) for the formation in 1965 of the Young German Film Board (Kuratorium Junger Deutscher Film), an institution charged with implementing the proposals of the Oberhausen Manifesto. Specifically, drawing from the cultural budgets of the various federal states, the Kuratorium sponsored the first features of Kluge, Hans-Jürgen Pohland, and Werner Herzog, and seventeen other features, between 1965 and 1968. The Oberhausen group was also able to achieve the foundation of two professional film schools (at Munich and Berlin) and a German film archive in Berlin.

But by 1970 the successes of the "young German cinema" rang rather hollow. The passage of a film subsidies bill by the Bundestag in 1967 had established a Film Subsidies Board (Filmförderungsanstalt, or FFA) that concentrated economic power in the hands of the commercial studios and distributors, and the result was a boom in the production of quick, shoddily made features that were foisted on a dwindling audience through block booking. Most of these productions were idiotic classroom comedies and soft-core pornographic films aimed at West Germany's 2 million immigrant workers. Theater owners were forced to book them as part of package deals with distributors, whether a local audience existed for the films or not. With West German production hitting an all-time high of 121 films per year in 1969 and film attendance slipping at the rate of 1 million per year, the late 1960s and early 1970s witnessed a wave of theater closings all over the country. The drivel produced by the first three years of FFA subsidies had alienated serious filmgoers, bored the general public, and brought the West German film industry to the brink of another financial crisis. As recently as 1971 the *New York Times* could write, "The persistently dismal situation of German film art is unique; a list of new films comprises a greater proportion of trash than anywhere else."

THE NEW GERMAN CINEMA

Nevertheless, a new German cinema was about to be born from the combined efforts of the Oberhausen group and a group of somewhat younger independent filmmakers who began their careers in West German television. In 1971 this group formed the Filmverlag der Autoren

(literally, the "Authors' Film Publishing Group") as a private company to distribute on a cooperative basis the films of its members, who quickly came to include Alexander Kluge, Rainer Werner Fassbinder, Bernhard Sinkel, Peter Lilienthal, Ulli Lommel, Edgar Reitz, Hans W. Geissendörfer, Hark Bohm, Reinhard Hauff, Uwe Brandner, and Wim Wenders. (In 1985, the Filmverlag was sold to the independent producer-distributor Futura Films.) The impetus of the Oberhausen group, the resources of West German television and the Kuratorium, and a liberalized FFA grant policy[6] made possible the phenomenal rise of the New German Cinema. Although the films of the movement had only a small following in West Germany itself, they created more excitement within the international cinema than anything since the French New Wave. The young film artists whose work collectively constituted the New German Cinema were quite diverse, but they did have some distinct stylistic traits in common. Thomas Elsaesser in 1976 wrote of

an unusual degree of aesthetic closure towards formal beauty and abstraction, a refusal to be explicit on the level of argument and meaning. Sensuousness, color, and emotional luxuriance to the point of morbidity lure the viewer into accepting as valid discourse a social stance that is poignantly defensive and individualistic to a vulnerable extent. A style has evolved in the German cinema of the last five or six years that vacillates between satirical realism and symbolism of almost oppressive obliqueness, a style not unconnected with the cultural limbo affecting much of Germany's intellectual life today.

The last point is important because Germany has only just recently begun to come to terms with the nightmare of its own recent history, its *unbewältige Vergangenheit* ("unassimilated past"). The generation of young filmmakers represented by *das neue Kino* grew up in an Americanized, economically prospering Germany; they were only dimly aware of the Nazi past. Cultural historians

---

6. The FFA made about $7.5 million available for film production annually by levying a 6-cent (DM 0.15) tax on every ticket sold in West Germany's 3,000 cinema theaters. (In 1979 a new law raised the tax by 50 percent.) Only directors whose previous films had returned at least $500,000 could apply for funds, which gave the FFA a decidedly commercial bias. From 1975, $3 million annually was earmarked for worthy independent projects selected by an eleven-man committee of critics and businessmen. The committee provided up to 80 percent funding for 41 projects between 1975 and 1978.

point out that since the collapse of the "Thousand-Year Reich," the German people have suffered from a kind of collective amnesia about the "brown years" of Nazi rule, 1933–45. The shock and humiliation of defeat, the appalling devastation of the material environment, the partitioning of the country, and the collective guilt for the most terrible acts of barbarism and genocide ever committed—all conspired to rob Germany of its cultural identity by robbing it of access to its immediate past. The past was not discussed in postwar German households or dwelled upon in postwar German schools.[7] Since the early 1970s, however, when the postwar generation began demographically to displace the generation that had actually experienced Nazism, public curiosity and confusion about the past has steadily increased. Added to this is the fact that, through its lucrative postwar alliance with the United States, West Germany traded off large chunks of its cultural identity to become one of the most highly technocratized countries in the world, surpassing perhaps even Japan and the United States itself in some sectors of the gross national product. This set of circumstances produced in the postwar generation an acute sense of alienation and anomie (signs of which are apparent in Japan, the United States, and many other industrialized nations as well). Robbed of their past by the infamy of Nazism and of their future by American cultural imperialism, the filmmakers of *das neue Kino* expressed the sense of psychological and cultural dislocation described by the film critic Michael Covino as "a worldwide homesickness." Their films are unsettling and sometimes depressing, but there can be no question of their unique contribution to international cinema.

VOLKER SCHLÖNDORFF, ALEXANDER KLUGE, AND MARGARETHE VON TROTTA

Historically, the New German Cinema movement can be said to date from the release of Volker Schlöndorff's independently produced *Der junge Törless* (*Young Törless*, 1966), a psychologically detailed adaptation of Robert Musil's antimilitarist novel set in a boy's school before World War I, which won the International Critics' Prize at Cannes. Schlöndorff (b. 1939), who studied at IDHEC (Paris), had worked as an assistant to Louis Malle, Alain Resnais, and Jean-Pierre Melville before directing this feature. His next independent film[8] was *Baal* (1969), an adaptation of Bertolt Brecht's first play, which was followed by *Der plötzliche Reichtum der armen Leute von Kombach* (*The Sudden Wealth of the Poor People of Kombach*, 1971), a bizarre parody of the *Heimatfilme* tradition in which a group of nineteenth-century peasants rebel against the degradation of rural life by becoming bandits and are put to death by the state. Other notable Schlön-

---

7. In a survey of West German teenagers taken in 1970, an overwhelming majority could identify Hitler only as "the man who built the *Autobahn*." Indeed, the Bonn government expressed concern in 1978 that the lack of understanding of Nazism among West German youth could lead to a rekindling of it. As if to certify this concern, after *Holocaust* (the NBC-produced miniseries on the Nazis' extermination of the Jews) was shown on West German television in January 1979, national polls revealed that 70 percent of viewers between the ages of fourteen and nineteen felt that they had learned more about Nazism from the American television program than from all their years of studying German history.

That telecast, in fact, was the source of great emotional upheaval in West Germany and became a cultural phenomenon akin to the first broadcast of *Roots* in the United States. Initially opposed on the grounds that it would open old wounds—and denied national broadcast on the First German Network (WDR [Westdeutscher Rundfunk], Cologne)—*Holocaust* was finally aired regionally on the Third German Network (ZDF [Zweites Deutsches Fernsehen], Mainz). Over half of the adult population of the country (20 million viewers, or 48 percent of the West German audience of 61 million) saw all or part of it. Polls conducted by the Bonn government and the Marplan Institute in the months after the telecast indicated a profound and lasting effect. In one poll, 64 percent of the viewers said that they were "deeply shocked," and 21 percent had been moved to tears. The number of viewers who, after viewing the program, favored the 1944 plot to assassinate Hitler increased from 49 to 63 percent; over half of the viewers reported that they had learned something new about Nazi atrocities; 73 percent felt "very positive" about the experience of watching *Holocaust;* and over half of the adults and two-thirds of the teenagers said that they would like to see it again because the program was so informative. (*Variety,* May 23, 1979.) The miniseries was finally broadcast on the national West German network in the fall of 1982. Characteristically, the East German government refused to broadcast *Holocaust* on the grounds that its people had already been thoroughly schooled about Nazism and its crimes.

8. Two commercial features intervened: a murder mystery entitled *Mord und Totschlag* (*A Degree of Death*, 1966) and the German-Czech-American coproduction *Michael Kohlhass—der Rebell* (1969), an epic of a sixteenth-century German political rebellion based on an 1808 story by Heinrich von Kleist (the same story was filmed as *Michael Kohlhaas* in 1979 by the director Wolf Vollmar).

dorff films are *Coup de grâce* (*Der Fangschuss*, 1976), a psychological drama set among German volunteers in the Baltic States at the end of World War I, and *Nur zum Spass—nur zum Spiel, Kaleidoskop Valeska Gert* (1977), in which a famous cabaret artist, shortly before her death in 1978, reminisces about her more than sixty years in show business. In 1979 Schlöndorff's adaptation of Günter Grass's novel *The Tin Drum* (*Die Blechtrommel*) shared the Grand Prix at Cannes with the American director Francis Ford Coppola's *Apocalypse Now*, and in 1980 it won the American Academy Award for Best Foreign Film. Schlöndorff has worked frequently for the commercial studios, where he has collaborated with his wife, Margarethe von Trotta (b. 1942), the scenarist and actress, on a number of important films dealing with feminism and other social and political themes. Most notable among these have been *Strohfeuer* (*Summer Lightning/A Free Woman*, 1972), and *Die verlorene Ehre der Katharina Blum* (*The Lost Honor of Katharina Blum*, 1975; from the novel by Heinrich Böll [1917–1985]). During the 1980s, Schlöndorff produced *Die Fälschung* (*Circle of Deceit/The Forgery*, 1981), based on events in the Lebanese civil war, 1974–76, as they are experienced by a German photojournalist; *Un Amor de Swann* (*Swann in Love*, 1984), a lavish adaptation of the second part of the first volume of Proust's *À la Recherche du temps perdu* (sixteen volumes, 1913–27), shot on location in Paris and environs by Sven Nykvist; and an unusual version of Arthur Miller's *Death of a Salesman* (1985), with Dustin Hoffman as Willy Loman, produced for American television. More recently, he directed adaptations of three novels—*The Handmaid's Tale* (1990), from Margaret Atwood's novel of the same title; *Voyager* (1991), from Max Frisch's *Homo Faber*; and *Der Unhold* (*The Ogre*, 1996) from Michel Tournier's *Le Roi des Aulnes*, the latter a kind of adult fairy tale about a simpleton who becomes a recruiter for the Nazi SS youth camp at Kaltenborn; *Palmetto* (1998), an American neo-*noir*; and *Die Stille nach dem Schuss* (English title: *Legend of Rita*, 1999), about an ex–West German terrorist living in the East, were visually striking but less successful. Since 1992, Schlöndorff has been chief executive of Studio Babelsberg GmbH, the production company that now runs the former UFA / DEFA facility just outside of Berlin.

Another founder of *das neue Kino* was Alexander Kluge (b. 1932), whose *Die Artisten in der Zirkuskuppel:*

15.60 *Die Artisten in der Zirkuskuppel: ratlos* (Alexander Kluge, 1968): Hanne-lore Hoger.

ratlos (*The Artists under the Big Top: Disoriented*, 1968) provided a metaphor for the plight of the serious film artist in Germany in the Godardian parable of a young woman who inherits a circus but cannot reform its deeply embedded traditions to create a new role for it in the "media world." Kluge, a practicing lawyer, novelist, legal scholar, and social theoretician, worked as an assistant to Fritz Lang (see Chapter 4) during Lang's brief return to Germany in the late 1950s, and he is the intellectual father of New German Cinema. As spokesman for the original Oberhausen *junger deutscher Film* group, he was responsible for convincing the federal government to establish the Kuratorium and the film schools in Munich and Berlin. Kluge's style is objective, coolly rational, and satirical. His films almost always involve the precise analysis of some social problem that besets contemporary Germany, focusing on a representative protagonist (often played by his younger sister, Alexandra Kluge). Kluge's most significant films of the 1970s are *Gelegenheitsarbeit einer Sklavin* (*Part-Time Work of a Domestic Slave*, 1974), which examines the issue of women's liberation and political organizing, and *Strong Man Ferdinand* (*Der starke Ferdinand*, 1976), a satirical allegory of fascism about an industrial security guard whose paranoid quest for order results in catastrophe for everyone around him. Kluge then brought together ten other New German filmmakers and the Nobel Prize–winning novelist Heinrich Böll to produce *Deutschland im Herbst* (*Germany in Autumn*, 1978) for the Filmverlag der Autoren. Highly reminiscent of SLON's *Loin de Vietnam* (1967), this semidocumentary cooperative feature is a rumination on the events of autumn 1977, when a public official was kidnapped and murdered by terrorists, and several of the terrorists later died under mysterious circumstances in prison. Kluge, expanding his contribution to *Deutschland im Herbst*, made *Die Patriotin* (*The Patriot*, 1980), a meditation on the teaching of German history both in and out of school. In other cooperative projects, Kluge, Schlöndorff, and two younger directors produced *Der Kandidat* (*The Candidate*, 1980), an ironic documentary portrait of Franz Josef Strauss, the right-wing challenger in the 1980 West German federal elections, and *Krieg und Frieden* (*War and Peace*, 1983), an omnibus work on the nation's peace movement. Kluge himself has produced and directed the documentary *Die Macht der Gefüehle* (*The Power of Emotion*, 1983), as well as *Der Angriff der Gengenwart auf die übrige Zeit* (*The Assault of the Present upon the Rest of Time*, 1985) and *Vermischte Nachrichten* (*Odds and Ends*, 1987), the latter two composed of documentary-style vignettes about contemporary German life and attitudes.

Schlöndorff and Kluge remain important representatives of *das neue Kino*; in the late 1970s and 1980s their ranks were joined by Margarethe von Trotta as a major director in her own right with the appearance of *Das zweite Erwachen der Christa Klages* (*The Second Awakening of Christa Klage*, 1978) and *Schwestern, oder die Bilanz des Glücks* (*Sisters, or the Balance of Happiness*, 1979), both concerned in different ways with the emergence of feminist consciousness. Von Trotta's breakthrough film, however, was *Die bleierne Zeit* (*The German Sisters/Marianne and Juliane*, 1981), a film about the coming to political awareness of two siblings in the late 1960s and the radically different paths chosen by each. Based on the true story of a member of the Baader-Meinhof terrorist gang, *Die bleierne Zeit* became the second film by a woman to win the Golden Lion at Venice in thirty-nine years (the first was, ironically, Leni Riefenstahl's *Olympia*), but von Trotta was not so successful with her subsequent *Frauenfilme* ("women's films")

Heller Wahn (*Sheer Madness*, 1982), *Paura e Amore* adapted from Chekhov's play *The Three Sisters* (1988), and *L'Africana* (*The Woman from Africa*, 1990), a dismal drama about the betrayal of friendship. On the other hand, von Trotta's *Rosa Luxemburg* (1986), a biography of the revolutionary socialist leader and cofounder of the Spartacus League who was murdered by Freikorps troops in 1919, is regarded as a major work. So, too, is *Il lungo silenzió* (*The Long Silence*, 1993), a political thriller in which the widows of assassinated Italian judges rally the nation against murderous gang lords, and *Das Versprechen* (*The Promise*, 1994), a film about the reunion of lovers separated for thirty years by the Berlin Wall.

Von Trotta was the most visible West German female director of the 1980s, but there were many others, and their *Frauenfilme* made a significant impact on *das neue Kino* by establishing a kind of "female aesthetic" that initially combined autobiographical elements with stories of everyday life. The earliest such films were often melodramas in fairly conventional narrative form, but later *Frauenfilme* sometimes took the shape of experimental cultural critiques and radical polemics. Some of the most prominent women directors of this era were Heidi Genee (b. 1938)—*1 + 1 = 3* (1980); *Stachel im Fleisch* (*Thorn in the Flesh*, 1981); *Kraftprobe* (*Test of Strength*, 1982); Doris Dörrie (b. 1955)—*Mitten ins Herz* (*Straight to the Heart*, 1983); *Im innern des Wals* (*Inside the Whale*, 1985); *Männer* (*Men*, 1985); *Paradies* (*Paradise*, 1986); *Me and Him* (1989); *Happy Birthday, Türke!* (1992); Jutta Brückner (b. 1941)—*Tue Recht und scheue niemand* (*Do Right and Fear No One*, 1978); *Hungerjahre* (1980); *Ein Blick—und die Liebe bricht aus* (*One Look—and Love Begins*, 1985); Ula Stöckl (b. 1938)—*Erikas Leidenschaften* (*Erika's Passions*, 1976); *Der Schlaf der Vernunft* (*The Sleep of Reason*, 1984); Helke Sander (b. 1937), founder of the feminist film journal *Frauen und Film* (*Women and Film*) in 1974—*Der subjektive Faktor* (*The Subjective Factor*, 1981); *Die Deutschen und ihre Männer* (*The Germans and Their Men*, 1990); *Befreier und Befreite* (*Liberators Take Liberties*, 1992); Ulrike Ottinger (b. 1942)—*Bildnis einer Trinkerin* (*Ticket of No Return*, 1979); *Johanna d'Arc of Mongolia* (1988); *Countdown* (1990); Monika Treut (b. 1954)—*Verführung: die grausame Frau* (*Seduction: The Cruel Woman*, 1985); *Die Jungfrauenmaschine* (*The Virgin Machine*, 1988); *My Father Is Coming* (1991); and Helma

15.61 Monika Treut's *Verführung: die grausame Frau* (*Seduction: The Cruel Woman,* 1985): sadomasochism as liberation.

Sanders-Brahms (b. 1940)—*Deutschland, bleiche Mutter* (*Germany, Pale Mother,* 1980); *Die Berührte* (*The Touched/No Exit, No Panic,* USA [*No Mercy, No Future,* UK], 1981); *L'Avenir d'Emilie* (*The Future of Emily,* 1984); *Laputa* (1986); *Maneuvers* (1988); *Apfelbäume* (*Apple Trees,* 1992).

INTERNATIONAL STATURE: FASSBINDER, HERZOG, WENDERS, AND OTHERS

Outside of Germany itself, the work of three other film-makers garnered international acclaim for *das neue Kino* during the 1970s. They are Rainer Werner Fassbinder, Werner Herzog, and Wim Wenders.

RAINER WERNER FASSBINDER

Rainer Werner Fassbinder (1946–1982) was extremely well known and very prolific, having completed forty-seven features between 1969 and 1982. Previously an actor, a playwright, and a theater director, he became the undisputed leader of the New German Cinema. Fassbinder began shooting low-budget features while he was still directing experimental theater in Munich, using a stock company of actors and technicians who stayed with him through his later work. Many of these early films were based on scenarios improvised by Fassbinder and concerned with the untreated malaise beneath the affluent surface of contemporary West German society. His film *Katzelmacher* (1969)—the term is Bavarian slang for a foreigner from the south who is possessed of great sexual potency—is about a Greek *Gastarbeiter,* or immigrant worker (played by Fassbinder), who is lynched by a group of young toughs because he is so attractive to their girls. *Warum läuft Herr R. amok?* (*Why Does Herr R. Run Amok?,* 1969) concerns a successful technical designer who one day murders his wife, their child, and a friend, and later commits suicide at his office by hanging himself over an open toilet. In *Der amerikanische Soldat* (*The American Soldier,* 1970), an extended *hommage* to the American gangster film, a young German who has just returned to Munich from service with the American Special Forces in Vietnam is hired by three cops to commit a series of murders; all of the principals, of course, have been killed by the end of the film.

If the plots of these films sound melodramatic, it is because Fassbinder intended them to be. He had a high regard for melodrama as a popular form, as evinced by his admiration for the films of Douglas Sirk (b. Detlef Sierck, 1900–1987), the Danish-born German émigré director who settled in Hollywood during the Nazi years and became master of the widescreen melodrama in the 1950s (*Magnificent Obsession,* 1954; *All That Heaven Allows,* 1956; *Written on the Wind,* 1957; *Interlude,* 1957; *The Tarnished Angels,* 1958; *Imitation of Life,* 1959). Most of Fassbinder's films are about people who don't "make it," who have somehow failed to reap the material benefits of the German "economic miracle." For depicting the condition of these people, he saw melodrama as a form of heightened realism. He wrote: "I don't find melodrama 'unrealistic'; everyone has the desire to dramatize the things that go on around him . . . everyone has a mass of small anxieties that he tries to get around in order to avoid questioning himself; melodrama comes up hard against them. . . . The only reality that matters is in the viewer's head." Melodrama, in other words, is about real life. From this perspective, bourgeois culture despises melodrama, preferring much more repressive forms of communication (for example, the high-culture forms of classical music and art, literature, and history) whose aim is to conceal process and

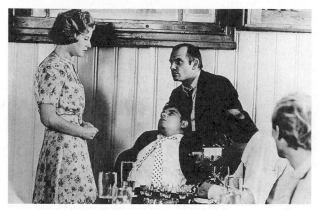

15.62 Fassbinder's *Der Händler der vier Jahreszeiten* (1971): Irm Hermann, Hans Hirschmüller, Klaus Löwitsch.

15.64 *Angst essen Seele auf* (R. W. Fassbinder, 1973): Brigitte Mira, El Hedi ben Salem.

function, and therefore to keep the bourgeoisie unaware of itself as a class in relationship to other classes. So it was as a Marxist that Fassbinder chose melodrama as his particular form, but it was as a humanist that he chose Marxism, and this is finally what he admired in Sirk: "Sirk has made the tenderest films I know; they are films of someone who loves people and doesn't despise them as we do."

The most obvious stylistic influence on Fassbinder's early films (some of which were shot in less than ten days) was Godard, but with *Der Händler der vier Jahreszeiten* (*The Merchant of Four Seasons*, 1971) he began to develop a style of his own. The melodrama, however—stripped bare of theatrics, mock-heroics, and senti-

mentality, but nearly always photographed in garish color—remained a constant in his work. In *Der Händler*, which was extremely popular with German audiences, a failed engineer enters a loveless marriage and becomes a fruit vendor. Bullied by his wife and betrayed by his friends, he grows terminally depressed and finally drinks himself to death in a bar. In *Die bitteren Tränen der Petra von Kant* (*The Bitter Tears of Petra von Kant*, 1972), the title character has an affair with a younger woman who constantly betrays her and drives her to a nervous break-

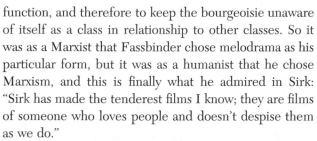

15.63 *Die bitteren Tränen der Petra von Kant* (R. W. Fassbinder, 1972): Margit Carstensen, Hanna Schygulla.

15.65 *Fontane Effi Briest* (R. W. Fassbinder, 1974): Hanna Schygulla.

down. *Wildwechsel* (*Wild Home*, 1972) deals with a sexual liaison between a fourteen-year-old girl and a nineteen-year-old boy. The boy is sent to prison for seducing a minor, and on his release the couple murders the girl's father. *Angst essen Seele auf* (*Fear Eats the Soul/Ali*, 1973), which won the International Critics' Prize at Cannes in 1974, is about the prejudice encountered by a widowed Munich charwoman when she marries a Moroccan immigrant worker some twenty years her junior. *Fontane Effi Briest* (*Effi Briest*, 1974), Fassbinder's least characteristic film, is an adaptation of a late nineteenth-century novel by Theodor Fontane about a young middle-class woman destroyed by rigid social conventions because she is believed to have committed adultery. The film was shot in austere black and white, and Fassbinder used devices such as fades to white,[9] titles, and voice-over narration to replicate the narrative strategies of nineteenth-century fiction.

In *Faustrecht der Freiheit* (*Fox and His Friends*, 1975) a young working-class homosexual (Fassbinder) wins DM 500,000 in the national lottery and is taken up by a group of corrupt bourgeois homosexuals who spend all of his money and abandon him, after which he takes an overdose of tranquilizers and dies on the floor of an ultra-modern Frankfurt subway station. In *Mutter Küsters Fahrt zum Himmel* (*Mother Küster's Trip to Heaven*, 1975), the working-class husband of a sweet little old lady goes berserk at his factory, killing himself and his foreman. The widowed Mother Küster suddenly finds herself the center of attention, as her husband's former employers, the popular press, her careerist daughter, and

15.67 Fassbinder's *Die Ehe der Maria Braun* (1979): Günter Lamprecht, Gisela Uhlen, Gottfried John, Anton Schiersner, Hanna Schygulla, Elisabeth Trissenaar.

assorted political groups attempt to use the scandal for their own ends. Ultimately, like so many of Fassbinder's protagonists, she is used shamelessly and abandoned. *Angst vor der Angst* (*Fear of Fear*, 1975) is a study of a happily married middle-class housewife who has a psychotic breakdown; the film, as Vincent Canby pointed out, dramatizes one possible end of capitalism, "when everything becomes perfect and, suddenly, nothing works." *Eine Reise ins Licht* (*Despair*, 1978), with a scenario by the British playwright Tom Stoppard, is a brilliant adaptation of Vladimir Nabokov's ironic novel about a man who tries to murder his double. Shot in Germany on a big budget ($2.5 million) and with a predominantly English cast, this film marked a departure from Fassbinder's usual, more improvisational, mode of production. But he returned to that mode in *Die Ehe der Maria Braun* (*The Marriage of Maria Braun*, 1979), a rambling

15.66 *Faustrecht der Freiheit* (R. W. Fassbinder, 1975): Fox (Fassbinder) and his friend.

9. Of these unusual fades to white instead of black, Fassbinder has commented: "According to [Siegfried] Kracauer [in *Theory of Film*], when it gets black, the audience begins to fantasize, to dream, and I wanted to make them awake. It should not function like most films through the subconscious, but through the conscious. It's . . . the first time that I know of where the audience is supposed to have its own fantasy, like reading a novel—the first normal fiction film. . . . It's like a novel that one reads where you can have your own dreams and fantasies at the same time. When you read a book, a novel, you imagine your own characters. That's just what I wanted to do in this film. I didn't want to have predetermined characters made for the audience; rather, the audience should continue the work. . . ." (Quoted in Paul Thomas, "Fassbinder: Poetry of the Inarticulate," *Film Quarterly* 30, 2 [Winter 1977–78]: 6.)

melodrama set in wartime and postwar Berlin that was a great commercial success in both Germany and America; *Die dritte Generation* (*The Third Generation*, 1979), a film about the relationships among a group of young terrorists; and *In einem Jahr mit 13 Monden* (*In a Year of 13 Moons*, 1979), a portrait of the hellish life of a contemporary transsexual. Fassbinder also contributed to *Deutschland im Herbst* (see p. 587) and adapted Alfred Döblin's classic novel of working-class life, *Berlin Alexanderplatz* (1929—first filmed in 1930 by Piel Jutzi), as a fourteen-part[1] series for German television in 1980. He completed the features *Lili Marlene* (1981), *Lola* (1981), and *Veronika Voss* (1982)—all concerned with wartime and postwar German society—before his death from a drug overdose in 1982. His last film was *Querelle* (1982), a version of Jean Genet's dark novel of homosexuality *Querelle de Brest* (1947).

Clearly, Fassbinder's is a cinema of the underdog, the exploited, and the oppressed. It is also a cinema of great formal beauty grounded in the expressive use of color, lighting, and decor (much of it accountable to the fluid cinematography of Michael Ballhaus [b. 1935], who shot fourteen of Fassbinder's films before relocating to the United States in 1980). Again, Fassbinder's comments on Sirk are instructive:

> Sirk has said: you can't make films *about* things, you can only make films *with* things, with people, with light, with flowers, with mirrors, with blood, in fact with all the fantastic things that make life worth living. Sirk has also said: a director's philosophy is his lighting and camera angles. . . .[2] Sirk's lighting is always as unnatural as possible. Shadows where there shouldn't be any make feelings plausible which one would rather have left unacknowledged. In the same way, the camera angles in *Written on the Wind* are almost always tilted, mostly from below, so that the strange things in the story happen on the screen, not just in the spectator's head. Douglas Sirk's films liberate your head.

So Fassbinder was pictorial, even painterly, but not for the sake of pictorialism, any more than he was melodramatic for the sake of creating melodrama. Of his true ends, he said this: "I don't want to create realism the way it's usually done in films. It's a collision between film and the subconscious that creates a new realism. If my films are right, then a new realism comes about in the head, which changes the social reality." Fassbinder preeminently deserved his reputation as the most exciting young director of the 1970s, as well as the most prolific, and he will probably be remembered as the most original talent to appear in the international cinema since Godard.

WERNER HERZOG

Werner Herzog (b. Werner H. Stipetic, 1942) studied literature and theater at the University of Pittsburgh and worked briefly in American television. When he returned to Germany, Herzog became a welder in order to finance his own short documentaries, of which he made four before shooting his first feature in 1967. Produced by the Kuratorium, this was *Lebenszeichen* (*Signs of Life*), the allegorical tale of a young German soldier on a Greek island during World War II who stages a one-man rebellion against the army. But it was the bizarre *Auch Zwerge haben klein angefangen* (*Even Dwarfs Started Small*, 1970), shot on location in the Canary Islands, that first brought Herzog to international attention. The film is a black, Buñuelesque fantasy, played entirely by dwarfs and midgets, about an abortive revolt staged by the inmates of a correctional institution. Its grotesque vision of human futility was matched by *Land des Schweigens und der Dunkelheit* (*Land of Silence and Darkness*, 1971), a feature-length documentary about a deaf and blind woman who attempts to liberate others similarly handicapped. Both films speak to the flawed nature of humanity itself rather than to the insufficiency of particular social institutions, and they emphasize the metaphysical, even mystical, nature of Herzog's central artistic concerns. To film *Fata Morgana* (1970), Herzog went to the Sahara Desert for what can only be described as a transcendental documentary about disintegration and alienation. The nearly hallucinatory camera style of this film, with its 360-degree pans and seemingly interminable tracking shots, is accompanied by sacred texts from Guatemalan Indian creation myths of the sixteenth century. It has no narrative line but proceeds on a poetic, visionary level to create from the material surfaces of reality images of total wreckage and decay. As Amos Vogel writes, the result is "an interior travelogue; an obsessive, hypnotic, and iconoclastic 'comment' on technology, sentimentality, and stupidity, filled with everyday objects that reveal their frightening secrets."

---

1. Thirteen segments, totaling thirteen and a half hours, plus a two-hour epilogue.

2. Compare Godard's "The dolly shot is a moral statement."

15.68 *Auch Zwerge haben klein angefangen* (Werner Herzog, 1970).

15.69 Herzog's *Aguirre, der Zorn Gottes* (1972): Klaus Kinski, Cecilia Rivera.

Aguirre, der Zorn Gottes (*Aguirre, the Wrath of God*, 1972), Herzog's most powerful film to date, was shot on location in the jungles of Brazil and Peru and was based on an actual historical incident of the sixteenth century. It concerns a detachment of Spanish conquistadors in search of El Dorado in the steaming rain forests of the Andes. The quest is suicidal from beginning to end since the Spaniards insist on dragging the clumsy accoutrements of modern civilization into the tangled wilderness with them. The film opens with the very image of futility, as about fifty conquistadors in heavy battle dress attempt to maneuver a huge cannon down a plunging forest hillside to the river valley below. What we witness in this sequence is a concrete visualization of the characteristic that dooms all "civilized" peoples: their inability to surrender their dependence on technology in situations that render technology utterly useless.[3] But the folly of the Spaniards is protracted by Aguirre, a fanatical officer strikingly portrayed by Klaus Kinski, who usurps the crown of King Philip II, declaring himself to be "the Wrath of God," and drives the group ever deeper into the jungle in his mad obsession to establish a new order of civilization at El Dorado. As the quest ensues, it

becomes increasingly pathological and ruthless until it ends in the destruction of everyone but Aguirre himself, who in the final frames stands among the dead on a drifting raft, shouting orders to the monkeys in the trees that line the river. The film, shot like most of Herzog's subsequent work by Thomas Mauch in splendidly evocative color, is a brilliant study of idealism turned to barbarism through zealotry, and the Nazi past clearly stands behind it. But so, too, does the European conquest of Africa in the late nineteenth century,[4] the American experience in

---

3. Western cultural historians used to point to the fact that the Peruvian Incas had not invented the wheel as proof that their civilization was not a highly advanced one. But it was subsequently observed that the technology of the wheel would have been inappropriate to the mountainous terrain of the Andes.

4. As elaborated, say, in Joseph Conrad's novel *Heart of Darkness* (1898), to which *Aguirre* has been aptly compared (Aguirre = Kurtz, the Amazon = the Congo, etc.). Compare *Apocalypse Now* (Francis Ford Coppola, 1979).

Vietnam, and all other historical tragedies in which high-minded aspirations have ended in a welter of murder, madness, and despair.

Herzog's next film, *Jeder für sich und Gott gegen alle* (*Every Man for Himself and God Against All/The Mystery of Kaspar Hauser*, 1974), is an equally bizarre allegory of the human condition: as the prologue announces, it was based upon an actual event and treats "the sole known case in human history in which a man was born as an adult." In 1828, a young man who has been locked in a cellar since birth, without access to memory or speech, suddenly appears in a small German town, where he is at first treated as a freak and then gradually taught to live by the systems of rational men. His acquisition of language, logic, religion, and natural philosophy plunges him into despair, and he is finally murdered by the man who had initially redeemed him from his brutish state. Reminiscent of Truffaut's *L'Enfant sauvage* (1969) in terms of theme and plot, *Kaspar Hauser* is considerably darker in its vision of the relationship between civilization and its discontents. Herzog employs a variety of unpredictable camera angles, awkward framing devices, and unusual lighting effects to transfer Kaspar's experience of perceptual disorientation to the audience. But Herzog achieves the film's most spectral and estranging effect by casting a former schizophrenic brought up in various institutions, the pseudonymous "Bruno S.," in the title role. The disaffected but strangely endearing Bruno S. also has the title role in Herzog's *Stroszek* (1977), a balladic tale of three oddly assorted losers—two street musicians and a prostitute—who become friends and set out from contemporary Berlin to find the Promised Land in the backwoods of northern Wisconsin; of course, what they discover there is something altogether different. But for all its bitter irony, the film is full of a spontaneous and sympathetic humor which, Herzog seems to suggest, may be our only conceivable means of survival.

Herz aus Glas (*Heart of Glass*, 1976) is simultaneously Herzog's most beautiful and most enigmatic film. Shot in 1976 in Wyoming, Alaska, Utah, Bavaria, Switzerland, and the Skellig Islands off the coast of Ireland, it concerns (apparently) a small medieval village whose entire economy is based upon the production of a certain "ruby glass" by its glassworks. The secret of producing this strange crystal dies with an aged glassblower, and for the rest of the film every inhabitant of the town constructs and acts out fantas-

15.70 *Jeder für sich und Gott gegen alle* (**Werner Herzog, 1974**): Bruno S.

tic hypotheses about the missing formula. A young man who is to inherit the glassworks becomes obsessed with the notion that the secret ingredient is blood, and he murders a young girl to obtain it. In the apocalypse that follows, he burns the factory to the ground, destroying all hope for the village and plunging its inhabitants into collective madness. If *Herz aus Glas* resists any concrete allegorical interpretation, it is because the film seems to be about the nature of mystery itself, in the same way that *Aguirre* is about the nature of idealism (and, possibly, of power). More than in other Herzog films, in *Herz aus Glas* the interpenetration of fantasy and reality is so thorough that we find it difficult to distinguish the two realms—perhaps because the people of the age he re-creates did not themselves make that distinction. It is in fact this magical view of reality, so alien to the contemporary world, to which Herzog would recall us. He attempted to evoke it for *Herz aus Glas* by hypnotizing its cast every day in advance of shooting. "It was a stylistic effort," he has said. "I wanted this air of the floating, fluid movements, the rigidity of a culture caught in decline and superstition, the atmosphere of prophecy. . . . My heart is very close to the Middle Ages." Herzog's *Nosferatu* (1979), a U.S.–French–West German coproduction backed by 20th Century–Fox, is a studied remake of Murnau's 1922 classic (see Chapter 4) that uses exquisite European locations and rings some interesting changes on the vampire theme. But neither it nor the more modestly produced version of Georg Büchner's 1850 play *Woyzeck* (1979) enjoyed the critical esteem accorded Herzog's earlier films.

With *Fitzcarraldo* (1982), Herzog returned (literally) to the terrain of *Aguirre* in the fact-based tale of a Peruvian rubber baron, played by Kinski, who attempts in about 1894 to build an opera house in the Amazonian jungle—a project that involves the portage of a 320-ton riverboat across a mountainous, mile-wide isthmus by five hundred Indians. The difficulties that plagued this film in production (including charges by human rights groups that Herzog had enslaved his Indian extras!) were legion and became the subject of Les Blank's fascinating documentary *Burden of Dreams* (1982). More recently, *Wo die grünen Ameisen träumen* (*Where the Green Ants Dream*, 1984), shot on location in Australia, pits aboriginals against a conglomerate that intends to violate one of their sacred places to mine uranium. The feature *Cobra verde* (*Slave Coast*, 1988) casts Kinski once again as a European afflicted with tropical madness in an account of the legendary nineteenth-century Brazilian slave trader Francisco Manoel da Silva, while in *Schrei aus Stein* (*Scream of Stone*, 1991) two climbers are locked in an insane duel to conquer a remote peak in South America. Equally typical,

Herzog's documentary *Echos aus einem Düstern Reich* (*Echoes from a Somber Empire*, 1990) is based upon the ghastly career of Jean Bokassa, the deposed dictator of the Central African Republic whose casual brutality was legend. For much of the 1990s, Herzog turned to directing opera, although he continued to produce eccentric documentaries (*Little Dieter Needs to Fly* [1997]; *Mein liebster Feind—Klaus Kinski* [*My Best Fiend*], 1999]), and in 2001 returned to features with *Invincible* (*Unbesiegbar*), based on the true story of a Polish-Jewish strongman exploited by the Nazis.

In addition to his major features, Herzog has made two extraordinary documentary shorts: *Die grosse Ekstase des Bildschnitzers Steiner* (*The Great Ecstasy of the Wood-Sculptor Steiner*, 1975), about a man so obsessed with ski jumping[5] that he constantly risks his life to break records, and *La Soufrière* (1977), a 30-minute record of what happened on Guadeloupe in 1976 when the prediction of a dire volcanic eruption caused the mass evacuation of the Caribbean island's entire population of 75,000, except for a single old peasant who refused to leave, though he was warned of certain death. Despite absolute confirmation by a team of international scientists and meteorologists, the eruption failed to materialize, and *La Soufrière* ends with Herzog peering into the depths of the smoking volcanic crater and commenting, "This, then, is a report about an inescapable catastrophe that did not take place." *La Soufrière*, at least as much as *Aguirre* and *Herz aus Glas*, epitomizes Herzog's metaphysical vision of reality. As Amos Vogel has so acutely written,

> To reveal a metaphysical element in life or art without becoming a reactionary is one of the challenges of the day: and Herzog, compulsively, and whenever possible, rubs salt into this particular, festering wound. . . . He examines the Holy Fool . . . the person considered a fool because outsider and eccentric, the one who dares more than any human should, and who is therefore—and this is why Herzog is fascinated by him—closer to possible sources of deeper truth though not necessarily capable of reaching them.

Our twentieth-century technology and rationalism have become an infallible religion to us, Herzog warns

15.71 *Woyzeck* (Werner Herzog, 1979): Klaus Kinski, Willy Semmelrogge.

---

5. As Herzog himself is obsessed—his favorite photograph of himself shows him upside down in midair, in the midst of a jump.

us, no less than sixteenth-century technology and rationalism were an infallible religion to the conquistadors in Peru. And he suggests that we, no less than Aguirre, are engaged in a self-destructive process of dragging heavy artillery into jungles where there is no one to bombard but ourselves and the monkeys. As Herzog himself remarked:

> We are surrounded by worn-out images, and we deserve new ones. Perhaps I seek certain utopian things, space for human honor and respect, landscapes not yet offended, planets that do not exist yet, dreamed landscapes. Very few people seek these images today which correspond to the time we live, pictures that can make you understand yourself, your position today, our status of civilization. I am one of the ones who try to find those images.

As if to confirm his facility for new ways of seeing, Herzog's favorite documentary is the 45-minute *Ballade vom kleinen Soldaten* (*Ballad of the Little Soldiers*, co-directed with Denis Reichle, 1984), which views the resettlement of the Miskito Indians by the Sandinista government of Nicaragua in such a way that he has been accused of being both procommunist and "an opportunistic lackey for the CIA."

WIM WENDERS

Wim Wenders (b. 1945) is the newest director of *das neue Kino* to achieve an international reputation, largely on the basis of his 1976 film *Im Lauf der Zeit* (see below), which won the International Critics' Prize at Cannes in the year of its release. While studying at the Munich Film School from 1962 to 1970, Wenders worked as a critic for cinema journals and newspapers. In 1971, after making several experimental shorts, he completed his first feature, a version of Peter Handke's novel *Die Angst des Tormanns beim Elfmeter* (*The Goalie's Anxiety at the Penalty Kick*), from a script that he had written with Handke. Ostensibly a murder mystery, *Die Angst des Tormanns* is in fact a film of psychological disintegration in which a soccer goalie goes quietly mad from the fragmentation and discontinuity of his existence. Through Ozu-like camera placement and a variety of unusual subjective shots, Wenders attempts to induce in the viewer a state of anxiety similar to that experienced by the goalie. After a liberal adaptation of Hawthorne's *The Scarlet Letter* in 1972,

Wenders made *Alice in den Städten* (*Alice in the Cities*, 1974), another film of existential questing. In it, a down-and-out young journalist and an abandoned nine-year-old girl meet in New York City and begin a search for the girl's European relatives that takes them across West Germany. The search becomes a symbol of futility and dislocation since the only clue to the whereabouts of Alice's relatives is a random, unmarked snapshot of her grandmother's house.

Covino has described Wenders's major theme as "a worldwide homesickness," the anxiety-ridden sense of psychological and geographical dislocation induced by living in the modern world. Wenders's next film, *Im Lauf der Zeit* (*In the Course of Time/As Time Goes By*; English title: *Kings of the Road*, 1976), provides his most brilliant exposition of this theme. It is a story of two men in their thirties who meet by accident on the road and begin an aimless journey across the desolate plains of northern Germany. Bruno lives in his van and survives by driving from one country town to another repairing broken movie projectors. Robert is a psycholinguist from Geneva whose wife has recently left him; he meets Bruno in the course of an absurd attempt to commit suicide by driving his Volkswagen into a shallow river. The two men tacitly agree to travel together, and the rest of the film chronicles their movement through the stark wastelands of the East–West border regions. Strikingly photographed in crisp black and white by Wenders's cinematographer, Robby Müller, *Im Lauf der Zeit* is nearly three hours long (176 minutes), but the film is so carefully and uniquely composed that we barely notice the passage of time (which, as the original title announces, is what the film is really about). Nothing much happens to Bruno and Robert in the course of time, and very little is communicated between them, but Wenders has a genius for creating cinematic metaphors for the contemporary malaise afflicting the two men. Extremely long takes and slow traveling shots, unusual camera angles and framing devices, and, above all, the manipulation of offscreen space generate in the viewer a sense of perceptual dislocation corresponding to the spiritual disorientation of Bruno and Robert. In this sense, *Im Lauf der Zeit*, like other Wenders films, is extremely self-contained: it can be said to describe itself by calling into question conventional modes of film structure.

After *Falsche Bewegung* (*The Wrong Move*, 1976),

another film about rootlessness from a script by Handke, Wenders made his first (relatively) big-budget production,[6] a version of Patricia Highsmith's novel *Ripley's Game*, entitled *Der amerikanische Freund* (*The American Friend*; original title: *Regel ohne Ausnahme* [*Rule without Exception*], 1977), which continued the theme of dislocation in the form of an international thriller. In 1980, Wenders collaborated with the late American director Nicholas Ray to produce *Lightning over Water/Nick's Movie*, a sensitive film about Ray's attempt to continue his work while dying of cancer. The following year Wenders went to work on *Hammett* (1982), based on mystery writer Dashiel Hammett's early days in San Francisco, for the American producer Francis Ford Coppola. Amid numerous delays in the scripting and shooting of this film, Wenders independently directed *Der Stand der Dinge* (*The State of Things*, 1982), a low-budget black-and-white feature on the difficulties of making an independent film. In contrast to *Hammett*, which was not particularly successful at interpreting the American experience, *Paris, Texas* (1984) is a brilliant American odyssey of self-recognition based on Sam Shepard's "Motel Chronicles" short stories, which confirmed Robby Müller as one of the world's best cinematographers. After the ruminative *Tokyo-Ga* (1985), a self-described "filmed diary" of his search for the vanished Tokyo inscribed in the films of Yasujiro Ozu (1903–1963), Wenders returned to Germany and produced a magical masterpiece in *Der Himmel über Berlin* (*The Sky over Berlin/Wings of*

15.73 *Paris, Texas* **(Wim Wenders, 1984): Harry Dean Stanton.**

Desire, 1987), a film written in collaboration with Handke about angels watching over the people of Berlin, in the tradition of *Here Comes Mr. Jordan* (Alexander Hall, 1941), *It's a Wonderful Life* (Frank Capra, 1946), and *Heaven Can Wait* (Warren Beatty, 1978). Its sequel, *In weiter Ferne, so nah!* (*Faraway, So Close!*, 1993—Special Jury Prize, Cannes), was not as well received, but the three-hour postmodern road film *Bis ans Ende der Welt* (*Until the End of the World*, 1991), shot in fifteen cities on four continents, successfully evoked Wenders's paradigmatic themes of global mystery and wandering. Wenders next made several films devoted to the art of cinema—*Lisbon Story* (1994) is about a director making a silent film in contemporary Portugal, while *Die Gebrüder Skladanowsky* (also known as *A Trick of the Light*, 1995) is about the two German brothers who developed the Bioskop projector and gave the first public performance of motion pictures at the Berlin Wintergarten on November 1, 1895), beating out the debut of the Lumière Cinématographe in Paris by nearly two months (see pp. 9–11). These films were probably inspired by Wenders's participation in the omnibus *Lumière et compagnie* (1995), in which forty international directors were

15.72 Wenders's *Der amerikanische Freund* **(1977): Dennis Hopper.**

6. $1.2 million, or more than his first six films put together.

15.74 *In weiter Ferne, so nah!* (1993), Wender's sequel to *Wings of Desire* (1987).

commissioned to make a short film using the original Cinematograph to mark the one-hundredth anniversary of motion pictures. More recently, Wenders returned to the United States to make *The End of Violence* (1997) and *The Million Dollar Hotel* (2000), both Hollywood murder mysteries set in a near future characterized by universal government surveillance. But his most successful film of the 1990s was undoubtedly *Buena Vista Social Club* (1999), a documentary about a group of aging Cuban musicians brought together by Ry Cooder to make a CD, shot on location in New York and Havana.

Unlike many of his associates in the Filmverlag, Wenders is not openly political. Yet he has said that "film language is always political: it is either exploitation or it isn't exploitation . . . not only the story that is told, but the way it is told." In this regard, Wenders claims as his masters Yasujiro Ozu and the American action director Anthony Mann, both of whom had a brilliant facility for the creation of spatial metaphors. Clearly, Wenders has a similar gift, but there is something in the austerity of his vision which is reminiscent of Bresson and Dreyer. Like his frequent collaborator Peter Handke (now a film director in his own right: *Die linkshändige Frau* [*The Left-Handed Woman*, 1978]; *Das Mal des Todes* [*The Malady of Death*, 1985]; *Die Abwesenheit* [*The Absence*, 1993]). Wenders seems to have a clear vision of the modern world's spiritual confusion and a tremendous talent for translating that confusion into the terms of his art.

HANS-JÜRGEN SYBERBERG AND OTHERS

A fourth director of international stature, one associated with *das neue Kino* but not of it, is Hans-Jürgen Syberberg (b. 1935). Originally from what was East Germany, he escaped to the West when he was seventeen, ultimately studying theater at the University of Munich. After working for several years as a director for Bavarian television, he began making low-budget features in the late 1960s and spent much of the 1970s producing his "German trilogy" of fictionalized documentaries on the irrational in Teutonic history and myth. *Ludwig: Requiem für einen jungfräulichen König* (*Ludwig: Requiem for a Virgin King*, 1972), shot in eleven days on a minuscule budget, constructs a Brechtian tour through the psyche of Ludwig II, the "mad" king of Bavaria who was Richard Wagner's patron and the primary architect, in a literal sense, of Germany's nineteenth-century romantic mythology. *Karl May* (1974) focuses on a crucial period in the life of its title character (1842–1912), an immensely popular writer of exotic/utopian fiction, most often adventure novels set on an imaginary American frontier. May's works were, astonishingly, favorites of Hitler's and Einstein's. The last film in the trilogy was preceded by *Winifred Wagner und die geschichte des hauses wahnfried von 1914–1975* (*The Confessions of Winifred Wagner*, 1975), a five-hour interview with Wagner's English-born daughter-in-law, who became the director of the Bayreuth Festival and a close friend of Hitler's during the Nazi years. The culmination of these works was *Hitler: Ein Film aus Deutschland* (*Hitler: A Film from Germany*, 1977; distributed in the United States as *Our Hitler*), shot in twenty days after four years of planning on a budget of $500,000. This seven-hour film is a complex, multifaceted attempt to answer the central, agonizing question posed by the trilogy and by twentieth-century German history: "Why Hitler?" The answer is that Hitler became "the greatest filmmaker of all time," staging National Socialism, World War II, and the Holocaust; engaging the irrationalism of the German people; and finally, fulfilling the promise of Ludwig, Wagner, and May to make Germany part of a grand, all-consuming myth. Syberberg continued his extraordinary critique of Germanic *Angst* in a four-hour-and-fifteen-minute adaptation of Wagner's last opera *Parsifal* (1982), and *Die Nacht* (*The Night*, 1985), a six-hour pastiche of music from Bach and Wagner and text from the great nineteenth-century German

15.75 *Hitler: Ein Film aus Deutschland* (Hans Jürgen Syberberg, 1977).

poets described by the director as "the swan-song of Europe."

During the late 1970s and 1980s a number of directors emerged from *das neue Kino* whose work has had less cumulative effect than that of Syberberg and his contemporaries but has nonetheless received international attention. In concert with his prison film *Die Verrohung des Franz Blum* (*The Brutalization of Franz Blum*, 1975) and its sequel, *Endstation Freiheit* (*Last Stop Freedom*, 1981), Reinhard Hauff (b. 1939) has been remarkably consistent in such features as the *Kasper Hauser*-like *Messer im Kopf* (*Knife in the Head*, 1978); *Der Mann auf der Mauer* (*The Man on the Wall*, 1982), a metaphorical tale of a man who leaps across the East-West border blockade; his documentary portrait of Indian director Mrinal Sen, *10 Tage in Calcutta* (*10 Days in Calcutta*, 1984); *Stammheim* (1986), an extraordinary account of the trial of the Baader-Meinhof gang in the Stuttgart-Stammheim prison; the witty musical *Linie 1* (*Line 1*, 1988); and the Argentine political thriller *Blauäugig* (*Blue Eyes*, 1989), Niklaus Schilling (b. 1944), functioning as his own writer, designer, and cameraman (e.g., *Rheingold*, 1978), is an auteur in the complete sense of the term. He specializes in "border films" like *Der Willi-Busch Report*

(*The Willi Busch Report*, 1979) and *Der Westen Leuggt!* (*Lite Trap*, 1982), and experimental works mixing film and video—e.g., *Zeichen und Wunder* (*Signs and Wonders*, 1982), *Die Frau ohne Körper und der Projektionist* (*The Woman without a Body and the Projectionist*, 1984), *Dormire* (1985), and *Der Atem* (*The Spirit*, 1989). Schilling's films run the gamut of genres from comedy to futuristic crime thriller, but all deal in some way with social tensions between East and West. The documentary-like features of Peter Lilienthal (b. 1929) often have a political theme, as in *Es herrscht Ruhe im Land* (*The Country Is Calm*, 1975), which evokes the Pinochet dictatorship in Chile; *David* (1978), about a young Jew struggling to survive in Nazi Germany; *Der Aufstand* (*The Insurrection*, 1980), filmed on location during the overthrow of the Somoza government in Nicaragua; *Dear Mr. Wonderful* (1982), shot on location in working-class neighborhoods in New York; *Das Autogram* (*The Autograph*, 1984), set in post-World War II Argentina; and *Das Schweigen des Dichters* (*The Silence of the Poets*, 1986), which concerns the creative struggles of a Jewish poet and was shot on location in Israel. More recently, Lilienthal made *Angesichts der Wälder* (*Facing the Forest*, 1995) in Israel, a political drama about the tensions between Palestinians and Israelis set in a forest preserve. More clearly in the art-film tradition is the work of Hans W. Geissendörfer (b. 1941), who has mounted impressive literary adaptations of Ibsen (*The Wild Duck*, 1977), Thomas Mann (*Der Zauberberg* [*The Magic Mountain*, 1982]), and Friedrich Dürrenmatt (*Jastiz*, 1993], as well as of such Patricia Highsmith thrillers as *Die gläserne Zelle* (*The Glass Cell*, 1977) and *Ediths Tagebuch* (*Edith's Diary*, 1983). Edgar Reitz (b. 1932), whose earlier work includes the television films *Stunde null* (*Zero Hour*, 1977) and *Der Schneider von Ulm* (*The Tailor from Ulm*, 1979), became world famous through a single remarkable work, the sixteen-hour *Heimat* (*Homeland*, 1984), which recounts the history of twentieth-century Germany as reflected in the lives of three families from the Rhineland village of Hunsrück; it took him over five years to complete and has been called "the fulfillment of all the hopes of the New German cinema over the past two decades," as well as a milestone in contemporary film history.[7]

The remarkably eclectic Fassbinder protégé and opera

---

7. *Variety*, September 8, 1984, p. 14.

director Werner Schroeter (b. 1945) moves with ease between the experimental under-ground—*Die Generalprobe* (*Dress Rehearsal*, 1981); *Tag der Idioten* (*Day of the Idiots*, 1982); *Der lachende Stern* (*The Laughing Star*, 1984); *De l'Argentine* (*About Argentina*, 1986); the historical epic—*Il regno di Napoli* (*The Kingdom of Naples*, 1978); contemporary social commentary—*Palermo oder Wolfsberg* (1980; winner of the Golden Bear at Berlin); and the art film—*Liebeskonzil* (*Council of Love*, 1982); *Der Rosenkönig* (*The Rose King*, 1986); *Malina* (1991). Schroeter's openly gay perspective was shared by Rosa von Praunheim (b. Holger Mischwitzky, 1942), Lothar Lambert (b. 1944), and Frank Ripploh (1949–2002), who formed the core of the so-called Berlin Underground during the 1980s. Their films tended to be both polemical and confrontational—especially von Praunheim's—and they often took the form of outrageous comedies—e.g., von Praunheim's *Armee der Liebenden, oder Revolte der Perversen* (*Army of Lovers, or Revolt of the Perverts*, 1979); *Rote Liebe* (*Red Love*, 1982); and *Ein Virus kennt keine Moral* (*A Virus Knows No Morals*, 1986); Lambert's *Tiergarten* (*Zoo*, 1980); *Die Alptraumfrau* (*The Nightmare Lady*, 1981), and *Die Liebeswüste* (*The Desert of Love*, 1986); and Ripploh's *Taxi zum Klo* (*Taxi to the Loo*, 1981) and *Taxi nach Kairo* (*Taxi to Cairo*, 1987). Members of the Berlin Underground shot their films in 16mm on extremely low budgets; the films were often written, directed, photographed, and edited by an *auteur* who was also their star. The Bavarian humorist Herbert Achternbusch (b. 1938) makes dialogue-laden low-budget comedies in the tradition of the Marx Brothers and W. C. Fields at the rate of about two a year, and he has acquired a committed following through such features as *Der Komantsche* (*The Comanche*, 1979); *Der neger Erwin* (*Black Erwin*, 1981—a send-up of the film subsidy system that produced it); *Der Depp* (*The Blockhead*, 1982); *Die Olympiasiegerin* (*The Woman Olympic Winner*, 1984); *Blaue Blumen* (*Blue Flower*, 1985); *Heilt Hitler!* (*Heal Hitler!*, 1986); *Punch Drunk* (1987); *I Know the Way to the Hofbrauhaus* (1991), and *Hades* (1995). Like the comedies of the more visually inclined Walter Bockmayer (b. 1948) and Rolf Bührmann—*Flammende Herzen* (*Flaming Hearts*, 1978), *Looping* (1981), *Salzstangen-Gefluester* (*Pretzel Whispers*, 1982), *Kiez* (*Hell's Kitchen*, 1983), and *Geierwally* (1988)—Achternbusch's are often shot in Super 8mm and blown up for exhibition to 16mm or 35mm. Far more sophisticated

intellectually and cinematically are the films of Robert van Ackeren (b. 1946), whose rigorously stylized portraits of middle-class behavior often reveal a decadent underside combining sexual perversity and emotional paralysis. Such, at least, is the force of his best work—*Belcanto* (1977), an adaptation of Heinrich Mann's last Hollywood-written novel; *Die Reinheit des Herzens* (*Purity of Heart*, 1980), *Deutschland: Privat* (*Germany: Private*, 1981); *Die flambierte Frau* (*A Woman in Flames*, 1983, see below); and *Die Venusfalle* (*The Venus Trap*, 1988)—all produced with expertise and great formal precision.

JEAN-MARIE STRAUB AND MARXIST AESTHETICS

A final figure who must be mentioned as having inspired and influenced *das neue Kino*, although his own aesthetic concerns are independent of it, is the French-born Jean-Marie Straub (b. 1933). Straub, who has lived and worked in Germany since 1958, is the patron saint of minimalist cinema—cinema that involves minimal dependence on the technical conventions of the medium as a narrative form. Specifically, this means the consistent use of direct sound, natural lighting, nonnarrative editing and camera styles, and, of course, nonactors. (Straub worked as an assistant to Robert Bresson during the 1950s[8] and was permanently influenced by his austerity of technique, especially that of *Les Dames du Bois de Boulogne* [1945].) Philosophically, Straub regards cinema as a material rather than narrative form. While narrative forms tell stories that encourage audience identification with fictitious characters and events, material forms can be said to create primary experiences for their audience rather than secondary or vicarious ones. It is the difference between being told a story about a madman or a "wild child" and being asked to participate in the experience of perceptual disorientation and disaffection that characterizes a state of madness or savagery. In a sense, it is the difference between Truffaut's *L'Enfant sauvage* (1970) and Herzog's *Kaspar Hauser* (1974), or between Dennis Hopper's *Easy Rider* (1969) and Wenders's *Im Lauf der Zeit* (1976).

---

8. During the same period, Straub also worked as an assistant to Abel Gance (*La Tour de Nesle*, 1954), Jean Renoir (*French Cancan*, 1955, and *Eléna et les hommes*, 1956), Jacques Rivette (*Le Coup de berger*, 1956) and Alexandre Astruc (*Une Vie*, 1958); see Chapters 9 and 13.

In pursuing his own vision of materialist cinema, Straub has created (in collaboration with his wife, Danièle Huillet) a number of extraordinary films whose structures of light, space, and sound approach the mathematical precision of musical composition. These include *Nicht versöhnt* (*Not Reconciled*, 1965), a series of moving tableaux derived from Heinrich Böll's novel *Billiards at Half Past Nine* (1959); *Chronik der Anna Magdalena Bach* (*The Chronicle of Anna Magdalena Bach*, 1968), a historical study whose viewpoint is that of Bach's wife; *Othon* (1970), an intentionally static, ahistorical version of Pierre Corneille's most rigidly formalized verse tragedy; *Leçons d'histoire* (*History Lessons*, 1972), a narrative analysis of the mercantile system of ancient Rome borrowed from Brecht's novel *The Business Affairs of Mr. Julius Caesar*; *Moses und Aron* (1975), a severe version of Arnold Schoenberg's modernist opera; *Fortini-Cani* (1977), the text of Franco Fortini's polemic on the Israel-Palestine conflict accompanied by contrapuntal imagery; *Klassenverhältnisse* (*Class Relations*, 1984), an uncharacteristically faithful adaptation of Kafka's posthumous novel fragment *Amerika* (1927); and *Der Tod des Empedokles* (*The Death of Empedocles*, 1987), a self-described nonfilm based on Hölderlin's 1798 verse play. Recent Straub/Huil-

15.77 Minimal/materialist cinema: the chorus in *Moses und Aron* (Jean-Marie Straub and Danièle Huillet, 1975).

let collaborations are a version of Jean Anouilh's *Antigone* (1992), a modernist rendition of Sophocles' tragedy; *Von Heute auf Morgen* (English title: *From Today until Tomorrow*, 1997), an adaptation of Schoenberg's rarely produced comic opera shot on a bare stage with a static camera; and two unusual adaptations of work by the Sicilian novelist Elio Vittorini—*Sicilia!* (1999) and *Operai, Contadini* (2001).[9] As with musical composition, Straub/Huillet's films are "about" what happens to the viewer while watching them as much as they are "about" their ostensible content. That is, in their restraint these films create a vacuum that the viewer must fill with the primary experience of his or her own life, forcing introspection rather than encouraging vicarious identification with invented characters and plots.

It is this theoretical assumption that links Straub/Huil-

15.76 Cinema as musical composition: Straub/Huillet's *Chronik der Anna Magdalena Bach* (1968).

9. There were a number of other experimental avant-garde filmmakers associated with New German Cinema in addition to Straub/Huillet. The two most important were Hellmuth Costard (1940–2000) and Harun Farocki (b. 1945). Costard, whose ten-minute short *Besonders wertvoll* (*Of Special Merit*, 1968) had scandalized the 1968 Oberhausen Festival by having as its central character a talking penis, was mainly a purveyor of experimental feature-length documentaries like *Fussball wie noch nie* (*Football as Never Before*, 1970), a hypostacized rendition of a championship soccer match; Farocki's main concern was the politics of representation in such experimental documentary features as *Etwas wird sichtbar* (*Something Becomes Evident*, 1981), on the media's distorted version of the American war in Vietnam, and *Leben: BRD* (*Life—Federal Republic of Germany*, aka *How to Live in the German Federal Republic*, 1990), a film about the German obsession with order and planning.

let with the young filmmakers of *das neue Kino*, although as individual artists they are more clearly members of the experimental avant-garde. Straub/Huillet and their followers take the Marxist position that perception is an ideological as well as a physiological phenomenon, or at least that perception is ideologically and culturally conditioned. Cinema is a communications medium whose basic signifying unit (the shot) is a discrete unit of perception: every shot, and every individual frame within a shot, offers a unique perceptual perspective on some event or object. But in the conventional narrative cinema of the Western capitalist countries, those perceptual perspectives have been ideologically appropriated to create fictions about life, and we, the audience, have been ideologically conditioned to expect and receive these fictions. From the Marxist perspective, fiction or narrative is defined as a bourgeois form designed to propagate illusions about the real nature of our society and our lives within it in order to divert our attention from the exploitation, violence, and oppression that are the necessary by-products of our economic system; the Marxists insist that our cinema (and most of our other art forms) has traditionally been a narrative medium whose purpose is the creation of illusionist spectacle that serves the ideology of the ruling class.

What the new breed of radical filmmakers attempted is the *deconstruction* of bourgeois perceptual ideology through a deconstruction of conventional cinematic language—language that has, since its inception and throughout its history (with notable exceptions during the periods of Soviet silent realism, Italian neorealism, and the French New Wave) been a bourgeois medium for the production of narrative pleasure. J. Dudley Andrew summarizes the Marxist position: "The Marxists call for a critical cinema which will 'deconstruct' itself at every moment. Instead of fabricating an illusion, this cinema will let the viewer see beneath the images and the story to the process of creation itself. . . . Every subject should be exposed for its socioeconomic underpinnings; every signification (every image and narrative relation) should expose its own work. This way we can strive toward the conscious reshaping of the world." In other words, the cinema's enslavement to a narrative code of vision has radically restricted its potential for the expression of new cultural realities. The vast range of ideas, feelings, perceptions, and experience that film is capable of communicating has barely been touched upon in the ninety-odd

years of its history as a narrative form. But radical filmmakers like Straub/Huillet and the leaders of *das neue Kino* attempted to tap that potential as never before, and it was this effort—much of it successful—that lent the quality of strangeness and mystery and otherness to their films. They were groping toward a new cinematic language with which to express the formerly inexpressible, and the process demands that the audience feel, see, and think things formerly alien to the experience of film watching.

Unfortunately, this same process can anger an audience that *wants* to be diverted by illusion rather than to struggle to acquire new codes of vision and experience. And this process of audience disaffection occurred in West Germany during the era of *das neue Kino*, just as it occurred in France during the New Wave. With a few exceptions (such as Fassbinder's *Der Händler der vier Jahreszeiten* and Wenders's *Im Lauf der Zeit*), the movement's films were not popular with German audiences, who found them obscure, depressing, and overly intellectual.[1] The largest markets were in France, Great Britain, and the United States, where many *das neue Kino* directors won festival prizes and became fashionable cult figures among the intelligentsia. It is ironic that a cinema that aspired to create a new vision of the world could not find a popular audience, while the illusionist spectacle it sought to replace enjoyed mass approval. In West Germany itself, the films with the biggest box-office receipts during the 1970s and 1980s were American superproductions like *The Godfather, Part II* (Francis Ford Coppola, 1974), *Jaws* (Steven Spielberg, 1975), *Cross of Iron* (Sam Peckinpah, 1977—shot in Germany), *Return of the Jedi* (Richard Marquand, 1983), *Ghostbusters* (Ivan Reitman, 1984), *Out of Africa* (Sydney Pollack, 1985), and *Indiana Jones and the Last Crusade* (Spielberg, 1989).[2] American

---

1. This was true for other forms as well. West Germany was concurrently the center of a European experimental avant-garde that extended from literature (Günter Grass, Jakov Lind, Peter Handke, Peter Weiss) to electronic rock (Brian Eno, Kraftwerk) and encompassed a broad spectrum of radical ideologies, sexual practices, and politics.

2. Wolfgang Petersen (b. 1941), whose early films *Die Konsequenz* (*The Consequence*, 1977) and *Schwarz und weiss wie Tage und Nächte* (*Black and White Like Day and Night*, 1978) were associated with *das neue Kino*, produced West Germany's two domestic box-office hits of the 1980s in *Das Boot* (*The Boat*, 1981) and *Die unendliche Geschichte* (*The Never-Ending Story*, 1984)—respectively, a World War II combat film

distributors remain in control of 60 to 65 percent of the German market, even after reunification, despite a continuing high level of government support for indigenous films.

Obviously, a major problem for the filmmakers of *das neue Kino* was distribution. While the Film Subsidies Board generously supported independent production of all sorts, the films of the New German cinema grew too elaborate and too numerous for the exhibition outlets available to them. During the 1970s, some *neue Kino* directors began to make films for large production companies in order to achieve blanket distribution. Fassbinder shot the $2.5 million international coproduction *Despair* (1978) for Bavaria Film; Herzog's *Nosferatu* (1979) was underwritten by Fox; Wenders's *Hammett* (1982) was finally produced for several million dollars after four years of fits and starts. During the 1980s, budgets of $3 million and more were not uncommon for period pieces like Herzog's *Fitzcarraldo* (1982) and Schlöndorff's *Un Amor de Swann* (1984); Geissendörfer's *Der Zauberberg* (1982) cost $10 million; and coproduction with the ZDF television network and with other countries became routine. As Jan Dawson remarked, "The New German Cinema [was], for the seventies [and eighties], what the *nouvelle vague* was for the sixties: a questioning of received values, an intoxicating burst of energy, a love affair with the cinema, and a love-hate relationship with Hollywood." Like the New Wave, *das neue Kino*[3] finally expired of its own aesthetic successes—so many aspiring new talents were able to direct their own films in such a short span of time that the market became glutted with them and the movement, as such, collapsed. But not before it had flourished brilliantly for two decades, changing the form of film language for many years to come.

Since 1990, the film industry of a reunited Germany has continued its struggle to survive against both American and other European distributors with unhappy results. In 1991, domestically produced films captured only 10 percent of the market, while Hollywood dominated with a 70 percent share. The privatization of the obsolete DEFA-Neubablesberg studios of the former German Democratic Republic (East Germany) did little initially to boost industry prospects. Even with heavy coproduction financing from the nation's two public television networks, ARD and ZDF, German films have been unable to recapture the 25 percent market share that most analysts consider necessary to survival, although the national success of Joseph Vilsmaier's $12.5-million antiwar epic *Stalingrad* (1993) suggested that German audiences would still rally to serious domestic films that strike a responsive chord. And, in fact, by 1997 Germany's market share had increased to 17.3 percent, thanks largely to the support of five federal state subsidy boards that, together with public and private television and the Bonn Economic Ministry, was contributing $170 million in production funds annually to the industry. In that year, Joseph Vilsmaier contributed another hit with *Comedian Harmonists* (1997), based on the true story of a phenomenally popular male vocal group that was driven into exile by Joseph Goebbels because three of its members were Jewish. One of several late-1990s films dealing with Nazi era anti-Semitism as a fact of everyday life (e.g., the lesbian love story *Aimée & Jaguar* [Max Färberböck, 1999]), this $10-million period film managed to hold its own against American blockbusters, as did Tom Tykwer's *Run Lola Run* (*Lola rennt*, 1998) the following year. This film attracted lavish praise for its technically dazzling structure in which the same action-packed trajectory (a young woman attempting to

---

set in a submarine and a fantastic children's adventure film. Petersen was subsequently successful with the American-produced science-fiction film *Enemy Mine* (1985) and the thrillers *Shattered* (1991) and *In the Line of Fire* (1993). Other domestic features that did well locally in the 1980s were Uli Edel's *Problemfilm* ("problem film") Christiane F.—*Wir Kinder vom Bahnhof Zoo* (*Christiane F.—We Children from Bahnhof Zoo*, 1981), focusing on heroin addiction among affluent Berlin teenagers, and Robert van Ackeren's *Die flambierte Frau* (*A Woman in Flames*, 1983), a coldly elegant account of a Berlin prostitute who caters to the sexual underground.

3. A celebration of *das neue Kino* and its place in German film history was created in 1995 by Edgar Reitz (*Heimat*, 1984), himself an important figure in the movement, to commemorate the centenary of motion pictures. This was *Die Nacht der regisseure* (*The Night of the Filmmakers*), a feature-length "documentary" that—via computer-generated effects and montage—brings Germany's most famous living directors together in an imaginary theater to discuss the state of the art. Appearing in the film are Leni Riefenstahl, Margarethe von Trotta, Wim Wenders, Helke Sander, Volker Schlöndorff, Edgar Reitz, Rosa von Praunheim, Hans-Jürgen Syberberg, Hans W. Geissendörfer, Reinhard Hauff, Ulrike Ottinger, Peter Lilienthal, Werner Herzog, Alexander Kluge, and former DEFA director Frank Beyer, as well as Fassbinder's regular cinematographer Michael Ballhaus and a number of performers like Hanna Schygulla indelibly associated with the New German Cinema.

raise DM 20,000 in twenty minutes to save her boyfriend's life) is repeated three times with slight variations, producing entirely different results each time. Tykwer (b. 1965) had been exploring the theme of overlapping/alternative temporal trajectories since *Winter Sleepers* (*Winterschläfer*, 1997), and he continued in this vein with the *The Princess and the Warrior* (*Der Krieger und die Kaiserin* (2000), which failed to produce similar box-office results. The big domestic hit

15.79 *Anatomie* (*Anatomy* [Stefan Ruzowitzky, 2000]) mixed medical horror with vestigial Nazism to become one of the most popular domestic features of the year. Ironically, this proto-German film was produced for a subsidiary of the American distributor Columbia Pictures.

of 2000 in fact was a homegrown horror film, Stefan Ruzowitzky's *Anatomie* (*Anatomy*), which crossed the Frankenstein story with neo-Nazis in a contemporary medical-school setting. Unlike Ruzowitsky's (b. 1961) rural Austrian allegory *The Inheritors* (*Die Siebtelbauern*, 1998), the film was extremely popular with German audiences and inspired its director to make a sequel in 2002 (*Anatomie 2*). Like Tykwer, Ruzowitzky writes his own screenplays. Another German writer-

director who scored critical and popular successes at the turn of the century is Michael Haneke (b. 1942), a Munich-born filmmaker working in Austria and other European Union venues, whose films formulated an autocritique of the media's debasement of human values. In *Funny Games* (1997), *Code Unknown* (*Code Inconnu*, 2000), and *The Piano Teacher* (*La Pianiste*, 2001; winner of three top awards at Cannes), for example, Haneke eschewed the formal austerity of his earliest films (e.g., *The Seventh Continent* [*Der 7. Kontinent*, 1989]; *Benny's Video* [1992]) to create a disturbingly explicit cinema of postmodern malaise focusing on the spectator's sadomasochistic complicity in the act of representation. With these notable exceptions, the German cinema today is dominated by light comedy and other escapist genres whose major producer-distributor is Neue Constantin Film. This reincarnation of Constantin Film, founded in 1949 and bankrupted in 1977, is managed by Bernd Eichin-

15.78 *Run Lola Run* (Tom Tykwer, 1998): Franka Potente as Lola, running to save her boyfriend Manni's life. *Lola*'s multiform temporal structure, pulsing energy, and stylistic éclat won more critical accolades for German cinema than any film since *das neue Kino*.

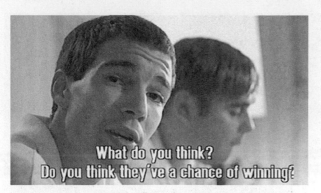

15.80 *Funny Games* **(Michael Haneke, 1997): Frank Giering and Arno Frisch as Peter and Paul, the pleasant young men "from next door" who become brutal sadists when they invade the summer home of a vacationing family. In a Brechtian address to the camera, Peter asks the audience to bet on the odds that the family will survive their visit.**

ger, who adopted a policy of competing with Hollywood products head to head in every genre from action-adventure (*Das Boot*, 1981) to teenage sex comedy (*Girls on Top*, 2001). In this climate, it seems somehow appropriate that one of the most popular German films of the new century, Ruzowitzky's *Anatomie*, was produced by a newly established subsidiary of Columbia, Deutsche Columbia Pictures Film produktion, which funnels most of its profits back to the United States through German banks in Frankfurt. (The film was in fact dubbed into English and distributed in the United States, where it earned nearly $6 million to completely recoup its negative cost of DM 8.4 million, or about $4 million; its entire German earnings were thus pure profit for Columbia.)

European Renaissance: East

All of the countries of Eastern Europe except for the former Soviet Union were occupied by the Nazis or collaborated with them during World War II, and those that had strong national film industries at the time, such as Czechoslovakia and Hungary, saw them subverted for the purpose of propaganda. When the war ended, these countries were "liberated" by the Soviet army and found themselves once again occupied by a foreign, totalitarian power. Gradually, but with much brutality, the Soviet government placed its own puppets at the heads of the Eastern European states, Stalinized the national governments, and forced the entire area into the Soviet bloc—a move formalized by the Warsaw Pact of 1955. Among the first acts of the new regimes was to nationalize the Eastern European film industries in order to use them, as the Nazis had, for the production of political propaganda. In Czechoslovakia and Poland, nationalization took place in conjunction with the establishment of state-supported film schools, repeating the pattern of the Soviet Union just after its revolution. The Czech film school, the Film and Television Faculty of the Academy of Dramatic Arts (FAMU), was founded in Prague in 1945; the Polish version, the Leon Schiller State Film School at Łódź, was established in 1948. Ultimately, each of the major Eastern European nations would have its own state-operated film school—Hungary its Academy for Dramatic and Cinematographic Art in Budapest (1947), Yugoslavia its Film Institutes in Belgrade and Zagreb (1950), Romania its Institute of Theater and Film Art (IATC, 1950) in Bucharest, and Bulgaria its Sofia Film and Television Academy (1973).[1] The thoroughness of the postwar nationalization meant that there would always be a close relationship between film and

---

1. Two former Warsaw Pact countries are omitted from this survey. The first is Albania, a small, extremely poor Balkan nation (population 3.5 million) that withdrew from the pact in 1968. Until recently, Albania was militantly closed to the West. The second is the German Democratic Republic (GDR; East Germany), treated in Chapter 15 with the Federal Republic of Germany (West Germany), with which it was reunited in 1990. Like its Warsaw Pact allies, the GDR had a thriving state-run film school, the Deutsche Hochschule für Filmkunst in Potsdam, established in 1954.

politics in Eastern Europe. Generally speaking, in times of oppression the Eastern European cinemas have been used for the purpose of political indoctrination; during periods of liberalization (Poland, 1954–63 and 1976–81; Czechoslovakia, 1963–68; Hungary, 1963 to the present), the cinema has become a vehicle for social criticism and ideological debate. For this reason, the cinema has always been one of the most important arts for the Eastern European intelligentsia, while in the West this has only very recently become true.

During the repressive postwar years from 1945 to 1953, few Eastern European countries produced significant films. Most adopted official Soviet-style "socialist realism" as decreed at the first Congress of the Soviet Writers Union in 1934 (see Chapter 5), which demanded that the everyday life of the socialist worker be glorified at the expense of all thematic analysis and formal experiment. In the Soviet Union itself this policy had succeeded in effacing the great avant-garde heritage of the 1920s, putting its creators either out of work (Vertov, Kuleshov) or under strict ideological control (Eisenstein, Pudovkin, Dovzhenko). After the war, the situation grew even worse as Andrei Zhdanov, the party boss in charge of ideological affairs, demanded rigid conformity to the style. When Stalin died in 1953, however, there was a brief period of liberalization, followed by an official policy of de-Stalinization that witnessed a distinct move away from the style of socialist realism in many Eastern European cinemas. The first to change was the cinema of Poland.

Poland

THE POLISH SCHOOL

Before World War II, the Polish cinema had been a rather modest affair. Perhaps the most significant prewar development was the founding in 1929 of the radical avant-garde film society, Society of the Devotees of the Artistic Film, or START, which included the future directors Wanda Jakubowska (1907–1998) and Aleksander Ford (1908–1980)—whose *Knights of the Teutonic Order* (*Krzyżacy*, 1960) was to become the first great Polish film epic—as well as the film historian Jerzy Toeplitz (1909–1995). During the war, the Nazis forbade

16.1 *Five Boys from Barska Street* (Aleksander Ford, 1952): Tadeusz Janczar.

domestic production, but the material base of Polish cinema was kept alive by the Polish Army Film Unit under the direction of Ford. With the establishment of the socialist state after the war, the provisional government nationalized the film industry under a single centralized authority, Film Polski, in 1945. The first postwar films were about the horrors that the country had endured during the Nazi Occupation. Of these, the best were Jakubowska's *The Last Stage* (*Ostatni etap*, 1948), a semidocumentary account of her own experiences in Auschwitz, and Ford's *Border Street* (*Ulica Graniczna*, 1948), a fictionalized version of the Warsaw Ghetto uprising of 1943. Ford's neorealistic *Five Boys from Barska Street* (*Piątka z ulicy Barskiej*, 1952), the first major Polish color film, was also notable. But in general the rigid dogma of socialist realism kept the standards of Polish film at a relatively low level until after the death of Stalin in 1953. In 1954, things began to change. At a meeting of the Polish Association of Cinema and Theater, Jerzy Toeplitz, then director of the Łódź Film School, attacked the tenets of socialist realism and called for a new national cinema. A year later, Film Polski was reorganized as a confederation of individual, self-contained production units known collectively as the United Groups of Film Producers. These mutually competitive production groups (*zespóły*)—first eight and finally ten—were each headed by a senior director and possessed considerable artistic autonomy, but until 1989 they depended exclusively on the state for production subsidies and distribution.[2] Simultaneously with the founding of the zespóły, the first generation of trained directors emerged from Łódź, and in the fall of 1956 the Polish Communist party chief, Władisław Gomułka, decreed a thorough de-Stalinization of Poland.[3] Thus the way was cleared for the Polish film movement known as the Polish School, the influence of which was international in scope from 1956 to 1963.

16.2 *The Saragossa Manuscript* **(Wojciech Has, 1965): Captain Alfonse Van Worden (Zbigniew Cybulski) contemplates a place of execution in one of the film's many intersecting narratives.**

The first major talents to rise from the Łódź Film School were Jerzy Kawalerowicz (b. 1922), Andrzej Munk (1921–1961), and Andrzej Wajda (b. 1926). Kawalerowicz was the least characteristic of the group. His first films, *A Night to Remember* (*Celuloza*, 1953) and *Under the Phrygian Star* (*Pod gwiazdą frygijską*, 1954), make up a two-part epic about the gradual radicalization of a young peasant between the wars. In *Night Train* (*Pociąg*, 1959), he turned what might have been a conventional murder mystery into an impressive parable of intolerance and mob violence. But his two most significant films are visually stylized historical dramas written by the director/writer Tadeusz Konwicki (b. 1926), that reveal a highly developed sense of compositional form. Based on the famous French case of the devils of Loudon—which also provided the raw material for Ken Russell's *The Devils* (1971)—*Mother Joan of the Angels* (*Matka Joanna od Aniołów*, 1961) is a tension-charged film about the demonic possession of a nun in a

---

2. Until 1984, these groups and their leaders were the following: "Aneks" (Grzegorz Królikiewicz), "Iluzjon" (Czesław Petelski), "Kadr" (Jerzy Kawalerowicz), "Perspektywa" (Janusz Morgenstern), "Profil" (Bohdan Poręba), "Rondo" (Wojciech Has), "Silesia" (Ernest Bryll), "Tor" (Krzysztof Zanussi), "Zodiak" (Jerzy Hoffman), "X" (Andrzej Wajda). In 1983, Wajda's Unit X was dissolved by the government for political reasons (see pp. 618–19). In 1989, the zespóły were transformed into independent studios that continued, however, to receive a measure of state support. All of the *zespóły* heads were prominent directors in the Polish industry, although many were little known outside of their own country. Wojciech Has (1925–2000), for example, head of "Rondo" (and also head of the Łódź Film School from 1990 to 1996) was famous in Poland for visually rich, psychologically complex period films such as *The Doll* (*Lalka*, 1968), a dissection of mid-nineteenth-century bourgeois hypocrisy, and *The Hourglass Sanatorium* (*Sanatorium pod klepsydra*, 1973), a stream-of-consciousness narrative set in pre–World War II Poland, constituting the childhood memories of the author Bruno Schulz. Outside of Poland, Has was known for a single, if influential, film, *The Saragossa Manuscript* (*Rękopis Znaleziony w Saragossie*, 1965), a complicated picaresque narrative with a score by avant-garde composer Krzysztof Penderecki. Originally running 182 minutes, *The Saragossa Manuscript* was cut by nearly an hour for international distribution but remained powerful enough to attract ardent admirers, including Luis Buñuel. It tells a multiply redacted story within a story within a story based on an 1813 Polish novel written in French by the historian, travel writer, and raconteur Count Jan Potocki. The only complete surviving print of the film was discovered in 1997 and restored at the Pacific Film Archive with funds provided by Martin Scorsese. This full-length 182-minute version was shown for the first time in New York in 1999, and it has since become available on DVD from Cowboy Pictures.

3. Gomułka (1905–1982), a popular Polish Workers' party leader who had been purged and imprisoned by the Stalinists in 1951, was rehabilitated in the summer of 1956 when workers' rebellions in Poznań and other cities threatened the stability of the Communist government. This led directly to the so-called Polish Spring in October of that year, during which Gomułka faced down the threat of a Soviet invasion and was

16.3 Jerzy Kawalerowicz's *Mother Joan of the Angels* (1961).

16.4 *Eroica* (Andrzej Munk, 1957): Josef Nowak.

seventeenth-century Polish convent. *Pharaoh* (*Faraon*, 1966) is an expensively produced spectacle set in the Egypt of Ramses XIII, whose underlying theme is the corrupting nature of political power. For a decade after *Pharaoh*, Kawalerowicz made only two films, Game (*Gra*, 1965) and *Maddalena* (1970), neither of which was a critical success. But he was one of the most serious and influential artists of the Polish School during the height of its power, and his first film since 1970, *Death of the President* (*Śmierć prezydenta*, 1978), displayed a newly spontaneous style in probing the 1922 assassination of Poland's first elected president. Happily, Kawalerowicz continued to make important films well into the 1980s, most notably *A Chance Meeting on the Ocean* (*Spotkanie na Atlantyku*, 1980) and *Austeria* (1983).

After graduating from Łódź, Andrzej Munk worked for several years in the documentary field and continued to do so often after he directed his first feature, *Man on the Track* (*Człowiek na torze*, 1955), which many critics believe to be his greatest finished film. Working closely with the scriptwriter Jerzy Stefan Stawiński (b. 1921), a cofounder of the Polish School, Munk completed only two other films before his death in an automobile accident in September 1961—the antiheroic war film *Eroica* (*Heroism*, 1957), which satirized the Polish national devotion to lost causes, and *Bad Luck* (*Zezowate szczęście*, 1959), an ironic look at opportunism in postwar Polish society. At the time of his death, Munk had nearly finished shooting *The Passenger* (*Pasażerka*), which would surely have been his masterpiece. In it, a former

SS guard traveling on an ocean liner is forced to relive her relationship with a young Jewish woman in Auschwitz through a series of flashbacks. In the process, we come to see the death camp from the guard's point of view as well as from the prisoner's, and an extraordinary humanistic comment is made upon the nature of guilt and suffering. The film was released in 1963 in a 62-minute version pieced together by Munk's assistant, Witold Lesiewicz, and it was hailed as a classic, giving Munk posthumous international status. Today, on the strength of four features and a score of documentaries, there can be no question that the cinema was impoverished by the loss of Munk.

Though his subject matter (unlike that of Kawalerowicz) was always Poland's present and recent past, in his ironic and antiheroic attitude Munk was outside the basically romantic vision of the Polish School as it

appointed first secretary by reformists within the party's Central Committee. Gomułka removed his conservative opposition, made some modest—mainly cosmetic—reforms (including easing the government's campaign against religion and releasing Cardinal Wyszński from jail), and in general preserved a veneer of liberalism for a few years. But as Chris Harman has observed: "Ten years after 'October,' people were receiving prison sentences for such heinous offences as tape recording satirical plays and reading forbidden books. Those who dared to express public sympathy with them were expelled from the party and later deprived of their jobs" (*Class Struggles in Eastern Europe, 1945–83*, 2nd ed. [London: Pluto Press, 1983], p. 118). In fact, in 1970 Gomułka was forced from office for the same illiberal excesses that had brought him to power in 1956.

finally evolved. Much more characteristic and formative was the work of Andrzej Wajda, the first Eastern European director whose films were widely shown in the West. The son of a Polish cavalry officer, Wajda studied painting at the Fine Arts Academy in Kraków before attending the Łódź Film School. After graduating, he assisted Aleksander Ford on *Five Boys from Barska Street*, and in 1954 he made his first feature, *A Generation (Pokolenie)*. This film, the first in a trilogy about his country's horrific experience of the war, established Wajda as a major European director and brought Polish cinema to international attention.[4] An essentially romantic film in neorealist form, *A Generation* was about a group of teenagers who become radicalized during the Occupation, join a left-wing Resistance movement, and are ultimately tracked down by the Gestapo. Wajda meant it to capture the mood and attitudes of the "lost generation" of young Poles (his own) who had come of age in the crucible of World War II. The second part of the trilogy was the unrelievedly grim *Kanał (Canal, 1956)*, adapted by Jerzy Stefan Stawiński from his own novel. The film deals with hundreds of Home Army Resistance fighters who find themselves trapped beneath the streets in the city's sewer system during the brutally suppressed Warsaw uprising of 1944. Utterly devoid of hope from the outset, they wander through a watery labyrinth of excrement and carrion while the Nazis leisurely pick them off from above with explosives and automatic weapons.

16.6 *Ashes and Diamonds* (Andrzej Wajda, 1958): Zbigniew Cybulski, Adam Pawlikowski.

Wajda's despairing vision of heroes doomed to die like sewer rats is the very prototype of the romantic fatalism that came to characterize the Polish School.

So, too, is the last and greatest film in Wajda's war trilogy, *Ashes and Diamonds (Popiół i diament, 1958)*. It depicts a few hours in the life of a young Resistance fighter, Maciek Chełmicki, on May 9, 1945, the first day after the war in Europe. Maciek has been ordered by the military commander of his nationalist underground unit to go to a provincial city and assassinate the new Communist party district secretary. He has no real political commitment to his mission, and he begins to vacillate when he discovers his victim to be only a tired and rather kindly old man. But he carries out his orders like a good soldier, is himself shot in reprisal, and dies in agony on a garbage dump, which he reaches by flailing his way through line after line of ghostly hanging laundry. The film's rich visual symbolism lends it universality of theme and should remind us that Wajda studied painting for four years before he entered the cinema. But *Ashes and Diamonds* also contains an implicit comment on some specific difficulties of a traditional society's adjustment to a revolution, and it offers Wajda's most disillusioned view of the futility of heroism in the modern world. Signifi-

16.5 *A Generation* (Andrzej Wajda, 1954): Roman Polanski (center).

4. The scripts of the film trilogy are now available in an excellent edition; see *Andrzej Wajda: Three Films* (London: Lorrimer, 1984), introduction by Bolislaw Sulik.

16.7 Maciek's death in *Ashes and Diamonds*.

cantly, the part of Maciek was the first major role of Zbigniew Cybulski (1927–1967), the brilliant and versatile young actor who became the icon of the Polish School's romantic pessimism from 1958 until his accidental death in 1967.

Wajda made two more films set in the war period and one with a contemporary context before turning to historical themes in the 1960s. *Lotna* (1959) deals with the suicidal charge of the Polish mounted cavalry against a German panzer division during the Nazi invasion of September 1938; *Samson* (1960) is the story of a Jew who attempts to escape the Warsaw Ghetto. *Innocent Sorcerers* (*Niewinni czarodzieje*, 1960), written by the future New Wave director Jerzy Skolimowski (see pp. 614–15), moved away from the wartime obsessions of the Polish School to examine the attitudes, problems, and values of the generation that succeeded Wajda's own. It is generally agreed that Wajda's historical films of the 1960s constitute a falling-off from his previous level of achievement. *A Siberian Lady Macbeth* (*Sibirska Ledi Magbet*, 1962), shot in Yugoslavia with a Yugoslav cast and crew, was an uneven, stylized melodrama set in a nineteenth-century Russian village; *Ashes* (*Popioły*, 1965) was a large-scale epic account of the Polish involvement in the Napoleonic Wars; and *Gates of Paradise* (*Bramy raju*), also shot in Yugoslavia, was an unsuccessful (and, to date, unreleased) study of the moral issues surrounding the thirteenth-century

Children's Crusade. The only totally satisfying work Wajda produced during this period was his short contribution to the French anthology film *L'Amour à vingt ans* (1962), which starred Zbigniew Cybulski as a former Resistance fighter who rescues a child from the bear pit at the Warsaw zoo.

With *Everything for Sale* (*Wszystko na sprzedaż*, 1969), however, Wajda again hit his stride and made his most personal film. Like Fellini's *8½* (1963) and Truffaut's *Day for Night* (1973), *Everything for Sale* is about a filmmaker in the process of making a film and therefore about the relationship between cinematic illusion and reality, but it is more Pirandello-like than the other works that deal with this theme. The film was inspired by the gruesome death in January 1967 of the actor Cybulski, who was run over by a train that he was attempting to board. Cybulski was not only Wajda's close personal friend and Poland's most popular star, but—like James Dean in America—he was an important cultural symbol

16.8 *Everything for Sale* (Andrzej Wajda, 1969): the film within the film. Elzbieta Czyzewska.

of a whole generation's attitude toward life; his senseless death shocked the nation. *Everything for Sale* memorializes that death and poses some disturbing questions about the morality of art: a film crew has prepared itself to shoot a scene in which an actor is to fall under a train at the Wrocław station (where Cybulski was killed), but the actor fails to arrive for the take. The crew searches for him and discovers that he has been accidentally killed. The director then makes the decision to finish the film using a stand-in, thereby committing crew members to killing their former friend and colleague on film in the same way that he has been killed in actuality. At times the reality of the film *Everything for Sale* and the film within the film overlap and merge, so that it is difficult for the viewer to distinguish between them. And this, of course, is played off against the "real" reality outside both films—the reality of Cybulski's horrible death and its impact upon the Polish film community. Ultimately, *Everything for Sale* asks the same question as that posed by the director, Ferrand (Truffaut), in *Day for Night*: "Are films [or art] more important than life?" Truffaut's answer was: "Yes, for film artists, they must be and they are"; in Wajda's case the answer is more ambivalent and more bitter.

Most of Wajda's films since 1968, except the lightweight sex comedy *Hunting Flies* (*Polowanie na muchy*, 1969), have been characterized by the kind of stylized impressionism announced in *Everything for Sale*. *Landscape after Battle* (*Krajobraz po bitwie*, 1970), *The Birch-Wood* (*Brzezina*, 1970), *Pilatus and Others* (*Pilatus und Andere*, 1972), and *Wedding* (*Wesele*, 1972) are all technically innovative, visually baroque meditations on the great themes of time, art, love, and death, without regard to historical context. But *The Promised Land* (*Ziemia obiecana*, 1976), which offers a vibrant account of the brutal industrialization of Poland by foreigners in the early twentieth century, marked a return to the political themes of the 1950s. Both *Man of Marble* (*Człowiek z marmuru*, 1977),[5] a sweeping indictment of officially fabricated postwar Polish history, and *Without Anesthesia* (*Bez znieczulenia*, 1978) concern the political corruption of the Polish news media (and both films were threatened with official censorship but eventually reached the United States intact). Wajda completed two more nonpolitical films—*The Young Girls of Wilko* (*Panny z Wilka*, 1979; a Polish-French coproduction), a

16.9 *Man of Marble* **(Andrzej Wajda, 1977).**

poetic film of love and memory set on a country estate in the period between the world wars, and *The Conductor* (*Dyrygent*, 1980), in which an internationally famous orchestra conductor (Sir John Gielgud) returns to his native Poland in pursuit of lost love and youth in the person of a former mistress's daughter. He then confronted Poland's government head-on in *Man of Iron* (*Człowiek z żelaza*, 1981), which became the standard-bearer for the new Solidarity movement (see pp. 617–21) and made Wajda himself, more than ever before, a symbol of the greatness and courage of Polish cinema. As a benefactor of such younger directors as Feliks Falk (b. 1941), Agnieszka Holland (b. 1948), and Janusz Kijowski (b. 1948) in his Production Unit "X" and as a filmmaker in his own right (*Danton*, 1982; *A Love in Germany*, 1984; *Notes of Love*, 1985), Andrzej Wajda has established himself as both the aesthetic grand mas-

---

5. Regarded by Wajda, after *Ashes and Diamonds*, as his most important film, *Man of Marble* won the International Critics' Prize at Cannes in 1978 and became the most popular film in Polish box-office history. It is formally modeled on *Citizen Kane*, the film that Wajda says inspired his career.

ter and moral conscience of Polish film. After thirty years as a director in that industry, his international stature and influence have never been higher, as was demonstrated by *A Chronicle of Amorous Incidents* (*Kronika wypadków miłosnych*, 1987), his masterful adaptation of Dostoevsky's *The Possessed* (*Les Possédés*, 1988), and *Korczak* (1990), the true story of a Jewish doctor who gave his life to protect orphaned children in the final weeks of the Warsaw Ghetto—all shot on location in Poland.

THE SECOND GENERATION

The so-called Polish School came to an end in the early 1960s when the Gomułka regime began to attack the national cinema for presenting a negative view of everyday Polish life. At the Thirteenth Party Congress in July 1964, Wajda's *Innocent Sorcerers* (1960) and Roman Polanski's *Knife in the Water* (*Nóż w wodzie*, 1962) were singled out for special abuse as examples of this tendency.

16.10 *Knife in the Water* (Roman Polanski, 1962): Jolanta Umecka, Zygmunt Malanowicz.

The Łódź Film School came under fire, too, since four-fifths of the country's forty-eight professional directors had been trained there. Thus, the generation of filmmakers that succeeded Wajda's made their first features in Poland, but as social and political conditions became increasingly repressive they left one by one to work in the West.

The two most prominent members of this generation are Roman Polanski (b. 1933) and Jerzy Skolimowski (b. 1938), both of whom attended the Łódź Film School and were decisively influenced by the French New Wave. Polanski began his career as an actor in Wajda's *A Generation* (1954), and his first films were the absurdist shorts *Two Men and a Wardrobe* (*Dwaj ludzie z szafą*, 1958), *The Fat and the Lean* (*Le Gros et le maigre*, shot in France, 1961), and *Mammals* (*Ssaki*, 1962), all of which contain dark undertones reminiscent of the plays of Samuel Beckett. Polanski's first feature—and the only one of his features shot in Poland before *The Pianist* (2002)—was *Knife in the Water*, an economical, tension-charged account of sexual rivalry among a husband, a wife, and a young stranger during a weekend sailing trip on the husband's yacht. The stranger and the wife make love aboard the boat while the husband is gone, and an electrifying sense of repressed sexual violence is sustained throughout. *Knife in the Water* (1962) achieved widespread recognition as a brilliant feature debut,[6] and Polanski subsequently made three films in England, working as he most often does from his own screenplays. *Repulsion* (1965) is a chillingly precise study of an individual's descent into madness under the pressure of sexual neurosis. In it, a beautiful young working girl, superbly played by Catherine Deneuve, is driven to murder by a combination of isolation and sexual repression. Polanski's masterful evocation of the hallucinated horror of psychosis, through both image and sound, makes *Repulsion* one of the classic studies of mental breakdown in modern cinema, comparable to Alain Jessua's *La Vie à l'envers* (*Life upside Down*, 1964; see p. 466) and Ján Kadár's *Adrift* (1971; see p. 627). *Cul-de-sac* (1966) is a strangely engaging film about an eccentric married couple on a desolate

---

6. The film also received considerable hype: *Time* magazine ran a still from the film on its cover in conjunction with an article about international cinema, and *Knife* was nominated by the Academy for its Best Foreign Film award in 1963.

16.11 Polanski's *Repulsion* (1965): Catherine Deneuve.

Northumberland island whose life is dramatically altered by the arrival of two wounded gangsters from the mainland. A combination of Pinteresque black humor and forties film noir, *Cul-de-sac* is thought by many critics to be Polanski's finest film, and it is the director's own favorite. *The Dance of the Vampires/The Fearless Vampire Killers* (1967), a stylish parody of the horror-film genre, is a much lighter affair but impressive nonetheless for its atmospheric evocation of Central Europe.

In 1968 Polanski came to the United States to direct the most popular and commercially successful of all his films, *Rosemary's Baby*, based on the novel by Ira Levin. This tale of witchcraft and Satanism was shot on location in New York City for Paramount. The tension between its muted naturalistic style and its horrific material makes the film a classic of the genre of demonic possession. It far outdistances contemporaneous manifestations like *The Exorcist* (William Friedkin, 1973) and *The Omen* (Richard Donner, 1976) in creating a sense of real evil beneath its sensationalist surface. Polanski returned to England in 1971 to do a personalized, hyperrealistic version of *Macbeth* that was generally well received but was

criticized in some quarters for excessive violence. While he was in Europe he also made the poorly distributed *Che?* (*What?*, 1972), a comic account of an American virgin's encounter with a cornucopia of sexual perversions on her first visit to Italy. Ultimately, Polanski returned to America to direct *Chinatown* (1974), an extremely successful essay in *film noir* set in Los Angeles during the 1930s. His most conventional film in terms of structure, *Chinatown* nevertheless conveys that sense of evil, menace, and sexual tension that has become the hallmark of Polanski's work. In terms of intellectual influence, it is possible to speak of surrealism and the theater of the absurd—of Kafka, Ionesco, Beckett, and Pinter. In terms of cinematic influence, Buñuel and Hitchcock clearly come to mind. But Polanski's thematic obsession with cruelty, violence, and the forces that produce them must also reflect the uniquely grim circumstances of his own life. In 1941, when he was eight years old, Polanski's parents were both sent to concentration camps—his father to Matthausen, where he managed to survive; his mother to Auschwitz, where she died—and he was forced to live a wretched existence in hiding until the end of the war. In 1969, his pregnant wife, the actress Sharon Tate, along with several of her friends, was brutally murdered and mutilated by the Charles Manson gang in one of the most repugnant crimes of the decade. More recently, Polanski himself was charged with the statutory rape of a thirteen-year-old girl in Los Angeles County and fled the country to avoid prosecution. Since then, he has completed a superb version of *Tess of the d'Urbervilles* (*Tess*, 1979), Thomas Hardy's tragic novel of innocence destroyed, in England; directed stage versions of Peter Shaffer's *Amadeus* in Warsaw (1981) and Paris (1982); and written his autobiography (*Roman*, 1984). His mock-heroic *Pirates* (1986), shot on location in Tunisia and the Seychelles, was not well received, but the perverse thriller *Frantic* (1988) returned Polanski to critical favor. *Bitter Moon* (*Lunes de fiel*, 1992) is a tale of perverse sexual rivalry in Paris that covers some of the same ground as *Knife in the Water* with a decadent, and fatal, Eurotrash twist; while *Death and the Maiden* (1992) adapts the Chilean writer Ariel Dorfman's tense play about a victim of South American political torture who, fifteen years after the crime, encounters by chance and then takes hostage one of her tormentors. *The Ninth Gate* (1999), one of several occult thrillers that appeared from Hollywood at the millennium, failed to duplicate the success of *Rosemary's Baby*; but *The Pianist*

(2002) was another story. Returning to film in Poland for the first time since *Knife in the Water*, Polanski produced a chilling study of Jewish artists struggling to survive in the Warsaw Ghetto based on the memoirs of real-life musician Władysław Szpilman (originally published in 1946 as *Death of a City*). The film was nominated for seven Academy Awards and won three, including best achievement in Directing, which Polanski was unable to accept in person because of his continuing status as a fugitive from U.S. justice. The nightmare vision of human experience set forth in Polanski's films should hardly surprise us: in his own life the director has been intimately acquainted with the nightmarish and the horrific.

Jerzy Skolimowski began his career as an actor and as coscriptwriter for Wajda's *Innocent Sorcerers* (1961). He became a student at the Łódź Film School in 1961 and the same year collaborated with Polanski on the script of *Knife in the Water*. Between matriculation and graduation in 1964, Skolimowski worked continuously on his first feature, which was released as *Identification Marks: None* (*Rysopis*, 1964). A loosely structured account of an expelled student's last ten hours of civilian life before entering the military, this film freely appropriated the stylistic devices of *cinéma vérité* and the New Wave. Like other Skolimowski protagonists (usually played by Skolimowski himself), the student is an outsider whose alienated vision of his society is implicitly critical. In *Walkover* (*Walkower*, 1965), a feature film composed of only thirty-five long takes, an amateur boxer (Skolimowski) attempts to make it in the professional ring knowing full well that he will lose—although, ironically, he does not. Skolimowski characteristically represents this attempt as a form of rebellion against the prevailing social order. *Barrier* (*Bariera*, 1966) firmly established Skolimowski as the principal spokesman for his generation as well as one of the most important Polish directors to emerge in the 1960s. Influenced by Godard, this film is an intricately stylized account of a student's mythic journey through contemporary Poland, and its surrealist *mise-en-scène* makes it Skolimowski's most bizarre and poetic work to date. After shooting the mild black comedy *Le Départ* (*The Departure*, 1967) in Brussels, Skolimowski returned to Poland to make *Hands Up!* (*Ręce do góry*, 1967), his most scathing attack yet upon the enclosure and barrenness of modern Polish society, and the film that he personally regards as his best and most mature work. Unfortunately, the film was banned by Polish authorities on its comple-

16.12 *Hands Up!* (Jerzy Skolimowski, 1967).

tion, and at this point Skolimowski—like Polanski before him—became an émigré. (*Hands Up!* was finally shown at the 1981 Gdańsk Film Festival, edited by Skolimowski and with a new prologue shot by him in Beirut and London.) He has since made films in Czechoslovakia (*Dialogue 20–40–60*, 1968), Italy (*The Adventures of Gérard*, 1970), England (*Deep End*, 1970), and West Germany (*König, Dame, Bube*, 1972—an adaptation of Vladimir Nabokov's novel *King, Queen, Knave*). Much of his non-Polish work is impressive, e.g., *The Shout* (1978), an expressionistic tale of aboriginal sorcery, sexual enslavement, and madness; it is narrated in flashback during a cricket match and makes brilliant use of Dolby sound. The film was chosen to represent Britain at Cannes in 1978 and won high praise in its general release. Similarly distinguished, Skolimowski's *Moonlighting* (1982) is a dark political fable of four Polish workers who are sent to London by "the Boss" to renovate an expensive townhouse on a poverty-line budget. When they have finally completed the job at great personal sacrifice, they find that they cannot return to Poland because martial law has been declared, and they must adapt to ruthlessly exploitative capitalism or starve. After shooting *Success Is the Best Revenge* (1984), another drama of exile set in London, Skolimowski directed, for CBS Productions, *The Lightship* (1986), a sort of metaphysical version of Hitchcock's *Lifeboat* (1944) set in the coastal waters off Virginia in 1955. He has also resumed his career as an actor in such films as Volker Schlöndorff's *Circle of Deceit* and Taylor Hackford's *White Nights* (1985). Skolimowski's most recent films are a sensuously photographed adaptation of the Ivan Turgenev short story *Torrents of Spring* (1989) and *Ferdydurke* (also known as *30 Door Key*, 1992), a comedy based on a novel by Witold Gombrowicz.

THE THIRD POLISH CINEMA

Of the third postwar generation of Polish directors, sometimes called collectively the Third Polish Cinema, the most important is Krzysztof Zanussi (b. 1939), who is today the only rival to Wajda among those filmmakers who are still regularly working in Poland. Trained as a physicist, Zanussi posits a deterministic social and biological order, while simultaneously offering the hope that human beings may somehow free themselves from it. His films tend to focus on a single contemporary problem and treat it in a highly analytic manner. In *The Structure of Crystals* (*Struktura kryształu*, 1969), for example, the focus is on the meeting of two former university classmates—one an extremely successful physicist, the other the manager of an isolated weather station. The film is a dissection of the two men's inability to communicate to one another their separate visions and values. During the 1970s, Zanussi made similarly provocative films: *Family Life* (*Życie rodzinne*, 1971); *Behind the Wall* (*Za ścianą*, 1971); *Illumination* (*Iluminacja*, 1973); *Quarterly Balance/A Woman's Decision* (*Bilans kwartalny*, 1975); *Camouflage* (*Barwy ochronne*, 1977); *Spiral* (*Spirala*, 1978); and *Night Paths* (*Wege in der Nacht*, West Germany, 1979). All use the multiple resources of cinema, drama, and language (including that

16.14 Jan Lenica's *Labyrinth* (1962).

of mathematics) to examine some aspect of contemporary Polish society and the individual's position within it. As head of Production Unit Tor, however, Zanussi became closely identified with the "cinema of moral anxiety" in the Solidarity era, and his *The Constant Factor* (*Constans*), which won the Jury Prize at Cannes in 1980, was one of its primary documents. After the imposition of martial law in 1981 (see p. 618) Zanussi became one of several directors who were forced to work outside of Poland for political reasons, although he has since returned to make such films as the controversial World War II drama *The Year of the Quiet Sun* (*Rok spokojnego słonca*, 1984), which won the Golden Lion at Venice and was given limited release at home, and *Wherever You Are* (1988), a British–Polish–West German coproduction on the same theme.

The last major Polish filmmaker who must be considered here is an internationally famous animator who has recently turned, with notable success, to the production of live-action features. Walerian Borowczyk (b. 1923) was trained as a painter and was already an established artist when he won the Polish National Prize for his graphic work in 1953. He made his first animated shorts in collaboration with Jan Lenica (1928–2001) one of the great modern innovators in the field. These films tended to be menacing surrealistic fables like *Dom* (*House*, 1958), which portrays the paranoid hallucinations of a young girl left alone overnight in her house. In 1959 Borowczyk emigrated to Paris (Lenica followed in 1963), where he produced a series of animated shorts projecting a world of absurd violence and private nightmare. Characteristic is *Renaissance* (1963), in which a number of heaped-up

16.13 Krzysztof Zanussi's *Illumination* (1973): Stanislaw Latallo as a young physicist plunged into confusion over the mysteries of life.

disintegrated objects reconstitute themselves, only to reconstitute as well the source of their original destruction—a time bomb that duly explodes at the end of the film, returning the objects to their state of chaos. In the twelve-minute *Les Jeux des anges* (*Games of Angels*, 1964), Borowczyk takes us on an abstractionized tour of a concentration camp whose transmogrified horrors rival the images of Hieronymus Bosch.[7] In some twenty-five disquieting allegorical shorts and a single feature (*Le Théâtre de M. et Mme. Kabal*, 1967) made between 1959 and 1967, Borowczyk experimented with every known form of animation to project his vision of ironic, hallucinated horror. He has painted images directly on his film stock, combined live action with animation, and regularly employed collage, pixilation, and film loops.

When he turned to short live-action films in 1966 with *Rosalie* and *Gavotte*, Borowczyk remained essentially a graphic artist with a fine sense of the cruelty of modern existence. His first live-action feature, *Goto, l'île d'amour* (*Goto, Island of Love*, 1967), was an absurdist fable of a barbaric dictatorship on a paradisiacal tropical island, full of inane brutality and arbitrary destruction. Borowczyk then became preoccupied with sexual perversity as an image of modern disorder. His *Contes immoraux* (*Immoral Tales*, 1974), a visually lush anthology film containing four separate tales of sexual perversion, became the second most popular film in France in the year of its

release. *The Story of Sin* (*Dzieje grzechu*, 1975), which Borowczyk made in his native Poland and which was the most popular domestic film of 1975, is a surrealistic allegory of an innocent young girl who is drawn down into a terrible vortex of crime, perversion, and murder. Borowczyk's most recent features are *La Bête* (*The Beast*, 1976), a parable of sexual obsession and insatiability concerning a hideous beast and a lovely maiden; *Zone de feu* (*Belt of Fire*, 1978), a comedy about the fifteenth-century mass murderer Gilles de Rais; and *Lulu* (1980), a graphic rendition of the Frank Wedekind sex tragedies of which Pabst's *Die Büchse der Pandora* (1929) remains the classic treatment. From both his live-action features and his animated films, it is clear that Borowczyk shares with many of his compatriots a fatalistic and absurdist vision of life. His work embodies a profound pessimism for the human heritage of dissolution, disorder, and decay. But pessimism is not cynicism and need not lead to despair. There is in Borowczyk's films a kind of affirmation in his utter outrage at human misery and in his sense of horror at the human stupidities that produce it. In his best work, in fact, Borowczyk has much more in common with the Buñuel of *Un Chien andalou*, *L'Âge d'or*, and *Las Hurdes* than he does with Wajda, Polanski, Skolimowski, or Zanussi, yet in the 1980s the director was reduced to making soft-core sex farces like *L'Art d'aimer* (*The Art of Love*, 1983) and *Emmanuelle 5* (1987). Nevertheless, with his four feature films of the 1970s, Borowczyk is significantly responsible for bringing the Polish cinema to a position of international prominence, as was the similar work of Andrzej Żulawski (b. 1940—*The Third Part of the Night* [*Trzecia cześć nocy*, 1971] and *The Devil* [*Diabeł*, 1972; released 1988]).

That position was temporarily weakened in the late 1960s, during the political crisis that followed the student demonstrations of March 1968. In an attempt to forestall the kind of liberalization then sweeping Czechoslovakia, the Gomułka regime tightened censorship, increased police surveillance, and purged the leadership of the entire Polish film industry. The shake-up was blatantly anti-Semitic: Aleksander Ford was forced to emigrate to Israel; Jerzy Bossak, head of the highly respected Polish documentary production unit, was fired; and Jerzy Toeplitz,

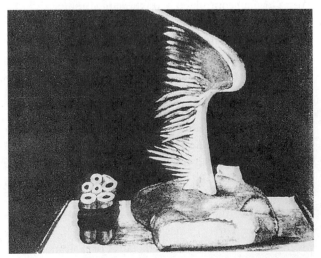

16.15 *Les Jeux des anges* (Walerian Borowczyk, 1964).

---

7. A Dutch painter (1450–1516) whose elaborate, hallucinatory depictions of the torments of the damned in Hell have made his work a landmark in the tradition of grotesque art.

director of the Łódź Film School since 1949, was summarily dismissed. In 1968, Poland produced only twenty films, most of them officially sanctioned literary adaptations, and several older films, like Wajda's *Samson* (1961), were banned. By 1971, however, Gomułka had been forced from office by the more moderate Edward Gierek, who relaxed censorship and promoted the reorganization of the state production units to give them more autonomy, which in turn enabled new talents like Zanussi to appear. But in the late 1970s, as the result of a steadily deteriorating economy, Poland was plunged into a social crisis of major proportions that ultimately led to the militant strikes of the summer of 1980 and to the formation of the free labor union movement Solidarity (*Solidarność*), 1980–81, under the leadership of Lech Wałęsa (b. 1943).

SOLIDARITY AND THE POLISH CINEMA

Like the Czech New Wave during the 1960s, Polish cinema during the 1970s played a crucial role in crystalizing public consciousness about the need for liberalization. Unlike the subtly allusive Czech films, however, the Polish films were often abrasive and directly confrontational in their social criticism. In works like Wajda's *Man of Marble* and *Without Anesthesia* and Zanussi's *Camouflage* and *The Constant Factor* (but also those of many newer directors, such as Krzysztof Kieślowski's *Camera Buff*, 1976; Janusz Kijowski's *Index*, 1977; Feliks Falk's *Top Dog*, 1978; Edward Żebrowski's *Transfiguration Hospital*, 1979; and Agnieszka Holland's *Provincial Actors*, 1980), the Poles created what they called *kino moralnego niepokoju*—a cinema of moral anxiety—whose central theme was the isolation experienced by persons of integrity in a corrupt and dishonest society. Despite low budgets and a documentary-like austerity of means, these films were immensely popular with Polish audiences (whose contempt for the hypocrisies of the state-controlled broadcast and print media was nearly universal), and the films became closely identified with the nation's yearning for greater political and social freedom.[8] Thus, when Solidarity was set up in August 1980 in Gdańsk (formerly Danzig)—the site, appropriately, of both the 1970 Lenin Shipyard strikes that helped to force Gomułka's resignation and of Poland's major film festival—not only did most Polish filmmakers support its demands for economic and political reform but nine out of ten became members,

founding their own self-governing union in September (the Cinematography Workers' Independent Trade Union, as distinct from the officially sanctioned Polish Filmmakers' Association [PFA]).

During the next sixteen months, Polish filmmakers enjoyed unprecedented creative and political freedom. Within a year, in fact, Poland had become one of the most talked-about film-producing countries in the world, and the Eighth Gdańsk Festival of Polish Films, held in August 1981, was widely recognized to be a celebration of this fact. Its centerpiece was Andrzej Wajda's docudrama on the birth of Solidarity, *Man of Iron*, a sort of sequel to *Man of Marble* and winner of the 1981 Cannes Grand Prix. Equally compelling were two actual documentaries— Andrzej Piekutowski's *Peasants '81* (*Chłopi '81*), a heroic account of the creation of Rural Solidarity, and Tomasz Pobog-Malinowski's *100 Days* (*Sto dni*), a record of the construction and dedication of the Gdańsk Martyrs' Monument at the Lenin Shipyards on December 16, 1980.[9] Like the electrifying *Workers '80* (*Robotnicy '80*, Andrzej Zajaczkowski and Andrzej Chodakowski, 1980), documenting the 1980 shipyard strikes and the negotiations that followed, these films were intended as rallying cries for Solidarity and the newly won right to strike that it briefly guaranteed. Another notable category at Gdańsk in 1981 comprised four films previously banned by government censors and publicly screened for the first time: Jerzy Skolimowski's legendary *Hands Up!* (*Ręce do góry*, 1967; edited and partially reshot by Skolimowski, 1981), Antoni

8. The standards of censorship for films in communist Poland (and, indeed, in many Eastern bloc countries) had at times been more liberal than those for television, radio, books, or newspapers, which were perceived to be more dangerously influential since they enter the home. An official censorship handbook smuggled out of Poland in 1980 revealed a curious double standard under which controversial films could be shown in theaters but not mentioned in other media. In other words, publicity for Polish films was more carefully monitored than the films themselves. See *The Black Book of Polish Censorship*, ed. Jane L. Curry (New York: Vintage, 1984).

9. The monument, consisting of three gigantic iron crosses soaring ten stories above the shipyard gate, was erected by the Polish people in one hundred days to memorialize the dozens of civilian workers massacred there by the military during the Gdańsk uprising of December 16, 1970, on the tenth anniversary of that event. Another film about this remarkable achievement is the Finnish-Polish documentary *The Memorial in Gdańsk* (Jarmo Jaaskilaenan, 1982); two other notable documentary works on the Solidarity movement in general are the New York–based filmmaker Jill Godmilow's *Far from Poland* (1984) and Henrik Byrn's Danish–West German *Solidarność—The Hope from Gdańsk* (1985).

Krauze's *The Pad* (*Meta*, made for TV, 1971; 1974), Krzysztof Kieślowski's *The Calm before the Storm* (*Spokój*, made for TV, 1976), and Janusz Kijowski's feature debut *Index* (*Indeks*, 1977). Among contemporary films at the festival were three ringing indictments of the repressive Stalinist era, Filip Bajon's *Shilly-Shally* (*Wahadelko*), Feliks Falk's *There Was Jazz* (*By Ł Jazz*), and Wojceich Marczewski's *Shivers* (*Dreszcze*—winner of the Silver Bear, Berlin, 1982). Further evidence of the stunning new vitality of Polish cinema was offered by Stanislaw Różewicz's *Lynx* (*Ryś*), Grzegorz Królikiewicz' *The Supreme Value of a Free Conscience* (*Klejnot wolnego sumienia*), Edward Żebrowski's *In Broad Daylight* (*W biały dzień*), Zanussi's *The Contract* (*Kontrakt*, made for TV), Piotr Szulkin's science-fiction allegory *The War of the Worlds— Next Century* (*Wojna swiatów-nastęne stulecie*), and Agnieszka Holland's drama of revolutionary violence, *Fever* (*Gorączka*). Appropriately, the First National Solidarity Congress ran concurrently with the Eighth Gdańsk Festival, and both concluded with a three-day program of twenty-six Solidarity-inspired documentaries entitled "A Document of Protest." Several months later, in the euphoria inspired by the new freedom, Wajda and nine other directors (Krzysztof Zanussi, Krzysztof Kieślowski, Feliks Falk, Agnieszka Holland, Filip Bajon, Janusz Zaorski, Edward Żebrowski, Wojciech Maczewski, and Tomasz Pobog-Malinowski) announced plans to hold their own festival in Warsaw in February 1982, with the expressed purpose of circumventing Film Polski and arranging coproduction with the West.

Then, suddenly, it was over. On the morning of December 13, 1981, Poland was invaded from within, as the military led by General Wojciech Jaruzelski abruptly replaced the civilian government and declared martial law with the moral and tactical support of the Soviet Union, which had its largest ally surrounded by fifty-nine armored divisions and garrisoned by four others when the coup took place. A curfew was imposed, assembly banned, travel restricted, and all telephone and telex lines cut; strikes were broken by armed force, Solidarity leaders arrested en masse, and the union itself brutally suppressed. The consequences for the film industry were immediate and grim. Undercapitalized and financially dependent by law upon the state, the Polish cinema found itself threatened with extinction through bankruptcy.[1] All of the nation's 1,180 film theaters were closed under the ban on public assembly, cutting the industry's immediate cash flow, and when the theaters reo-

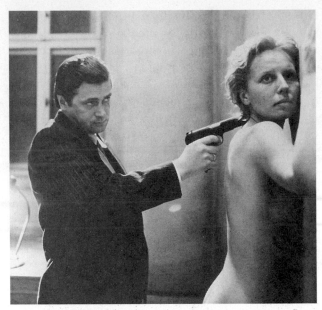

16.16 *The Interrogation* (Ryszard Bugajski, 1982; released 1990): Krystyna Janda in her award-winning role as a cabaret singer imprisoned and tortured for five years under false accusations of dissent in 1950s Warsaw.

pened two months later Polish audiences discovered a significantly changed national cinema.

Pro-party conservatives like Ewa and Czesław Petelski, Bohdan Poręba, and Ryszard Filipski had been temporarily given control of the industry to make orthodox World War II epics and historical films. The Gdańsk Festival was suppressed, and most films produced during the flowering of Solidarity were banned, many without ever having been released, including Antoni Krauze's *The Weather Forecast* (*Prognoza pogody*), Agnieszka Holland's *The Lonely Woman* (*Kobieta samotna*), Krzysztof Kieślowski's *Blind Chance* (*Przypadek*), Janusz Zaorski's *Mother of Kings* (*Matka królów*), Jerzy Domaradzki's *The Big Race* (*Wielki bieg*), Ryszard Bugajski's *The Interrogation* (*Przesluchanie*),[2] and two films seen at Gdańsk in 1981, Falk's

---

1. Despite its vitality and its size (over 30,000 workers), the Polish film industry under communism always operated on thin financial margins. Equipment came at such a premium that a director generally worked under a thirty-day production schedule and was fined for exceeding it; film stock was so scarce that directors were seldom allowed more than two takes per scene (compare Hollywood's fifteen to twenty); and actors and actresses were so underpaid that they routinely worked in several films at once in order to make a living.

2. Officially banned until 1990, The *Interrogation* became the most influential Polish film of 1985 when thousands of copies of it were dis-

There Was Jazz and Szulkin's *The War of the Worlds—Next Century*. In this climate, several of Poland's major filmmakers found it prudent to work abroad for a while—most notably Wajda, whose *Danton* (1982), a parable of counterrevolution adapted from Stanisława Przybyszewska's play *The Danton Affair*, was produced in Paris[3] and whose *A Love in Germany* (1984), adapted from a Rolf Hochhuth novel of Nazi Germany, was produced in Munich; and Zanussi, who made his biography of Pope John Paul II,[4] *From a Far Country* (1982), in Italy and produced a number of dramatic films for French and West German television between 1982 and 1984.

In May 1983, Wajda was dismissed as head of Film Unit X by Jaruzelski's minister of culture, Kazimierz Zygulski, for having made films "which have nothing in common with the cultural policy of the state." At the same time, Unit X and Zanussi's Unit Tor—those most closely associated with the "cinema of moral anxiety" and, ironically, the two units with the greatest margin of success over costs—were denounced by the Central Committee of the Polish United Workers Party (PZPR) as "oppositional, demagogic, and existential." In December 1983, Wajda resigned as chairman of the Polish Filmmakers' Association (a posi-

tion that he had held since 1978) along with the organization's entire governing board, and it seemed briefly as if the group might disintegrate, as had a number of other artists' unions under martial law. But the PFA reconstituted itself with virtually the same board as before (Krzysztof Zanussi, Kazimierz Kutz, Jerzy Kawalerowicz, Wojciech Has, Krzysztof Kieślowski, Jerzy Hoffman, Tadeusz Chmielewski, Feliks Falk, Andrzej Trzos-Rastawiecki, and Jerzy Toeplitz) and Wajda's close friend Janusz Majewski as chairman.

After 1984, when the Gdańsk Festival was reopened, a kind of uneasy truce existed between the film industry and the Jaruzelski regime. Just as many of the original strictures of martial law were lifted and most political prisoners freed, so were restrictions on the Polish cinema eased. Most of the exiled filmmakers returned,[5] including Wajda, who in 1985 directed a screen adaptation of Tadeusz Konwicki's *Notes of Love* in Warsaw—his first Polish film since *Man of Iron*. Most of the banned films from the early Solidarity era were released (some, like Wiesław Saniewski's *Custody* [*Nazdór*, 1981], with cuts), although several—e.g., Holland's *The Lonely Woman*, Bugajski's *The Interrogation*, and Kieślowski's *A Short Day's Work* (*Krótki dzień pracy*, 1982)—remained shelved until 1990. Serious films with a contemporary setting became

16.17 Wajda's *A Love in Germany* (1984), produced in Munich. Hanna Schygulla.

tributed on videocassette by the cultural underground. Because the government did not initially control the diffusion of VCRs, Poland now has more per capita than any other country in Eastern Europe, a situation that has opened a whole new sphere in the struggle to achieve a culture independent of the state and ultimately assisted in the restoration of civilian government in 1989. (While Bugajski's harrowing film of Stalinist-style police tactics was being seen all over Poland, the director himself was forced into exile in Canada; its star, the brilliant actress Krystyna Janda [b. 1952], won the Best Actress award for her performance at the Cannes Film Festival in 1990.)

3. A Polish-French coproduction, *Danton* was originally to have been shot in Poland, but Wajda moved the project to France in the wake of the Jaruzelski coup. Film Polski's response was to slash its participation to less than 10 percent, leaving French Gaumont to put up the balance of funds and the Mitterand government to provide a grant of $500,000 for postproduction. The film won France's prestigious Louis Delluc Prize for 1982, and the Onassis Foundation awarded Wajda its Athinai Prize "for his contribution to human dignity."

4. Formerly Karol Cardinal Wojtyla, a supporter of the liberalization movement and archbishop of Kraków.

5. Polanski and Skolimowski had chosen permanent exile before the events of 1980–81; Agnieszka Holland settled in France and has since directed such successful coproductions as *Angry Harvest* (1985), *To Kill a Priest* (1988), *Europa Europa* (1991), *Olivier Olivier* (1992), and *The Secret Garden* (1993).

possible once more (e.g., Kieślowski's film of the grim year 1982, *Without End* [*Bez końca*, 1985]), but in general, social criticism was out and genre films were in, especially science fiction (Maciej Wojtyszko's *The Synthesis* [*Synteza*, 1984], Piotr Szulkin's *O-Bi, O-Ba—The End of Civilization* [*O-Bi, O-Ba—Koniec cywilizacji*, 1985]), horror (Marek Piestrak's *The She-Wolf* [*Wilczyca*, 1983], Marek Nowicki's *Phantom* [*Widziadło*, 1984]), comedy (Juliusz Machulski's *Sex Mission* [*Seksmisja*, 1984], Michal Dudziewicz's *The Job* [*Fucha*, 1985]), and historical drama (Tadeusz Konwicki's *The Issa Valley* [*Dolina Issy*, 1983], Janusz Majewski's *Epitaph for Barbara Radziwill* [1983], Stanislaw Różewicz's *Mrs. Latter's Pension* [*Pensja Pani Latter*, 1984], and Filip Bajon's *The Magnate* [*Magnat*, 1987]). Perhaps the most encouraging sign was the founding of a new experimental production collective, the Irzykowski Film Studio, modeled on the Béla Balázs Studio in Hungary, from which Waldemar Dziki's shattering drama of the Holocaust, *Postcard from a Journey* (*Kartka z podróży*) emerged to international acclaim in 1984. The Film and Television School at Katowice also came forth as an important training ground for new talent, and there were indications everywhere that, despite continuing repression and internal subversion, the Polish film industry was bouncing back from its post-1981 crisis well before the restoration of a Solidarity-controlled civilian government in August 1989. Their thematic monotony notwithstanding, over thirty quality features were produced in 1985—an impressive 15 percent of which were made by first-time directors—and the Tenth Gdańsk Festival in August of that year gave ample proof of a revival, with the promise of better things to come. And, in fact, Polish films had become considerably more frank in the late 1980s, as is demonstrated by such work as Janusz Zaorski's *Lake Constance* (*Jezioro bodenskie*, 1986), Janusz Majewski's *The Deserters* (*C. K. Dezertenzy*, 1987), Feliks Falk's impressive sequel to *Top Dog*, *Hero of the Year* (*Bohater roke*, 1987), Robert Glinski's *Sunday Pranks* (*Niedzielne igraszki*, 1987), and Krzysztof Kieślowski's *Blind Chance* (*Przypadek*, 1987), *A Short Film about Love* (*Krótki film o miłości*, 1988), and *A Short Film about Killing* (*Krótki film o zabijaniu*, 1988), winner of the Best Film Prize at the first European Film Awards Festival in November 1988. (The last two are part of Kieślowski's ten-film magnum opus *Dekalog* [*The Ten Commandments*], completed in 1989.)

Simultaneously, however, Poland's ongoing economic

16.18 From *A Short Film about Killing* (1988) in Kieślowki's epic *Dekalog* (1989): murder by an individual/murder by the state.

crisis threatened to destroy its cinema from within. By the late 1980s, the level of inflation in production costs had reached 100 percent, while government grants increased by only 40 percent; from thirty-seven features in 1987, annual production fell to twenty-eight films in 1989 and twenty-two in 1990. The nation's economic situation had grown so desperate by April 1989 that the Jaruzelski regime legalized Solidarity and invited the union to participate in a partially free election in August, gambling that the Communists could hold their own. In fact, Solidarity replaced the Communists as Poland's ruling party in that election, and the new government extended relief to the film industry in October 1989 by ending the *zespóły* system and transforming the film units into independent production companies, owning for the first time everything they produced and controlling distribution and export rights. The production companies continue to receive subsidies amounting to as much as 70 percent of a given film's budget, and several state agencies have been created to assist them with script development and distribution, but the studios have been forced increasingly to concentrate on commercial productions to avoid bankruptcy. This tendency led initially to an unfortunate merger of comedy and soft-core pornography in such popular features as *The Art of Love* (*Sztuka Kochania* [Jacek Bromski, 1989]) and *Porno* (Marek Koterski, 1990), which latter became the top-grossing Polish film of 1990. Although serious films continued to be made—including Wojciech Marczewski's *Escape from the "Freedom" Cinema* (*Ucieczka z kina*

"Wolność"), Feliks Falk's *Capital, or How to Make Money in Poland* (*Kapital, czyli jak zrobić pienadze w Polsce*), and his own *Korczak*—Andrzej Wajda denounced Polish cinema at the end of 1990 as "a desert." By 1992, however, Lech Wałęsa had become president of Poland, the economy had stabilized, and annual film production had risen once more to thirty-eight features, permitting important new works by Kieślowski (*The Double Life of Veronique* [*Podwojne zycie Weronki*, 1991]; *Three Colors: Blue* [1993], *White* [1994], *Red* [1994]—a French-Polish coproduction), Zanussi (*The Silent Touch* [*Dotkniecie reki*, 1992]), and Wajda himself (*Horse Hair Ring* [*Pierscionek z orlem w kornie*, 1993]). In 1997, for the first time since Poland returned to democracy, a domestic film dominated the box office—Juliuss Machulski's comedy-thriller *Killer*, with a record-breaking 1.6 million admissions; its sequel, *Killer 2*, did nearly as well in the following year. This trend continued into 1999 with the stunning success of two (relatively) big-budget blockbusters—Jerzy Hoffman's $8.5 million *With Fire and Sword* (*Ogniem i mieczem*), the third installment of Henryk Sienkiewicz's epic trilogy set in the seventeenth century Ukraine (then part of the Polish Empire),[6] and Andrzej Wajda's $3.5 million *Pan Tadeusz* (*Colonel Tadeusz*), a family saga set during the Napoleonic wars based on the work of Polish national poet Adam Mickiewicz. Between them, these two films captured a 40-percent share of the year's box-office revenues, and they spawned many imitators, the most impressive of which was Polish School veteran Jerzy Kawalerowicz's ancient Roman spectacle *Quo Vadis* (2000), adapted from another Sienkiewicz novel. That serious, low-budget films still had a place in Poland's cinema was demonstrated by the critical success of Zanussi's *Love as a Sexually Transmitted Disease* (*Życie jako smiertelna choroba przenoszona droga plciowa*, 2001), a near-clinical account of a doctor's struggle with cancer, which won multiple international awards.

Former Czechoslovakia

THE POSTWAR PERIOD

Unlike Poland, Czechoslovakia had a distinguished cinematic tradition long before World War II. One of the major pioneers of camera technology, J. E. Purkyně (1787–1869), was from the Czech land of Bohemia. Commercial production began in Prague in 1908, six years ahead of Berlin, and the city became a major continental film capital in the period just before World War I. When the Austro-Hungarian Empire collapsed in the aftermath of that conflict, the Czechs and the Slovaks—regionally separate but culturally and linguistically similar—united to form the joint state of Czechoslovakia. By 1933 Prague (in the Czech region) had the most sophisticated production facilities in Europe, at the Barrandov studios. Between the wars, several Czech directors achieved international reputations—Karl Anton (1898–1979) for the first Czech sound film, *Tonka of the Gallows* (*Tonka šibenice*, 1930); Gustav Machatý (1901–1963), who had worked as an assistant in Hollywood to both Griffith and von Stroheim, for his *Erotikon* (1929), *From Saturday to Sunday* (*Ze soboty na neděli*, 1931), and the sensational *Ecstasy* (*Extase*, 1932), which won a prize at Venice in 1933; Martin Frič (1902–1968) for his Slovak folk epic *Jánošík* (1935); Josef Rovenský (1894–1937) for his lyrical film-poem *The River* (*Řeka*, 1934); and Otakar Vávra for *Guild of the Kutná Hora Maidens* (*Cech panen kutnohorských*, 1938), which won the Golden Lion at Venice in the year of its release. The Czech cinematographers Otto Heller (1896–1970) and Jan Stallich (1907–1973) also became internationally prominent during this period.[7] During the Occupation, domestic production slumped from forty films in 1940 to

---

6. Actually, *With Fire and Sword* was the first book in Sienkiewicz's trilogy but the third to be filmed by Hoffman; the first film was *Colonel Wolodyjowski* (*Pan Wolodyjowski*, 1969), adapted from the last book of the trilogy, while the second film, *The Deluge* (*Potop*, 1974) was adapted from the second book. A low-budget Italian version of *With Fire and Sword* (*Col ferro e col fuoco*) was directed by Fernando Cerchio in 1961.

7. In his important study *The Czechoslovak New Wave* (Berkeley: University of California Press, 1985), Peter Hames points out that many significant long-term developments for Czech cinema grew out of the avant-garde Devětsil movement of the 1930s, which included among its members the poet Vítězslav Nezval, the novelist Vladislav Vančura, and the film director Martin Frič. Nezval wrote several important film scripts, Vančura directed five films before his execution by the Nazis as part of their retaliation for the Heydrich assassination in 1942, and Frič became Czechoslovakia's most popular director when he teamed fellow Devětsil members Jiří Voskovec and Jan Werich in the comedies *Heave Ho* (*Hej rup*, 1934) and *The World Belongs to Us* (*Svět patří nám*, 1937). It was no coincidence that Werich was featured in one of the first Czech New Wave films, Vojtěch Jasný's *Cassandra Cat* (1963), or that some of the New Wave's most important works were adapted from Devětsil writers—e.g., František Vláčil's *Markéta Lazarová* (1967, from Vančura), Jiří Menzel's *Capricious Summer* (1967, from Vančura), and Jaromil Jireš's *Valérie and Her Week of Wonders* (1969, from Nezval).

16.19 *Ecstasy* (Gustav Machatý, 1932): Hedy Lamarr.

16.20 *Old Czech Legends* (Jiří Trnka, 1953).

nine in 1944, as the Nazis appropriated the Barrandov studios and greatly expanded their production capacity in order to make German-language films (in fact, toward the end of the war, the Nazis planned to transfer their entire film industry to Prague). But during the same period, certain Czech filmmakers were already formulating plans for the nationalization of the industry when the Nazis withdrew. On August 11, 1945, the Czech president, Eduard Beneš,[8] signed a nationalization decree that established a new production system with three major components: (1) a specially equipped studio for the production of puppet and animation films, (2) the organization of collective production groups for live-action features, and (3) the foundation of a state film school—the Prague Film (and Television, after 1960) Faculty of the Academy of Dramatic Arts (FAMU). In 1947, a separate Slovak production system was organized, with its own documentary and feature studios in Bratislava. Czechoslovakia thus became the second country in Eastern Europe, after the Soviet Union, to totally and permanently nationalize its film industry.

Nationalization freed producers to concentrate on serious political themes, and the first postwar Czech films dealt with the historic struggle to create a communist state. Of these, the most impressive were Jiří Weiss's (b. 1913) *Stolen Frontier* (*Uloupená hranice*, 1947), which concerned Hitler's plundering of the Czech frontier in 1938; Karel Steklý's (1903–1987) *The Strike* (*Siréna*, 1947), a film about an 1889 miners' rebellion that won the Golden Lion at Venice in the year of its release; and Otakar Vávra's *Silent Barricade* (*Němá barikáda*, 1948), whose subject was the Prague uprising against the Nazis just prior to the Red Army's "liberation" of the city. All three bore the marked influence of Italian neorealism. Of more lasting significance were the first feature-length animated puppet films of Jiří Trnka (1912–1969). His *The Czech Year* (*Špalíček*, 1947), a seven-part compilation film celebrating his country's rich folk tradition, won several festival prizes. He followed this with *Song of the Prairie* (1949), a parody of American Westerns, then with a magical adaptation of a Hans Christian Andersen fairy tale, *The Emperor's Nightingale* (*Císařův slavík*, 1948), and *The Happy Circus* (*Veselý cirkus*, 1950), a short that employed the nearly forgotten technique of animating paper cutouts. Trnka made his two greatest puppet films in the 1950s. *Old Czech Legends* (*Staré pověsti české*, 1953) was a folk epic comprising seven distinct heroic tales, and it has been justly described as both *ciné*-ballet and *ciné*-opera. *A Midsummer Night's*

---

8. Beneš's postwar democratic government lasted less than three years. In 1948, it was replaced by a communist dictatorship that became one of the most repressive in Eastern Europe, instituting mass purge trials and executions as early as 1949 that continued through 1955.

16.21 Trnka's later work: *The Hand* (1966).

16.22 *The Invention of Destruction* (Karel Zeman, 1958), adapted from the writings of Jules Verne.

Dream (*Sen noci svatojanské*, 1958) was an enchanting widescreen adaptation of the Shakespeare play that abandoned the text for mime and dance. Three years in production, this film is widely regarded as Trnka's masterpiece, but the English-language versions have, unfortunately, been dubbed with a voice-over narration and quotations from the play that run counter to the director's intentions. Karel Zeman (1910–1989), an early follower of Trnka, developed a unique style that combined graphics, live action, puppet animation, and special optical effects in four award-winning science-fiction features, including *Prehistoric Journey* (*Cesta do pravěku*, 1954) and *The Invention of Destruction* (*Vynález zkázy*, 1958), which took the Grand Prix at the Brussels World's Fair.

With the exception of the films of Trnka and Zeman, the Czech cinema in the early 1950s was one of doctrinaire socialist realism like that of the other Warsaw Pact nations, and the Czech film industry was rigidly centralized. Perhaps the most important event of the period was the formation in 1952 of the close association between the directors Elmar Klos (1910–1993) and Ján Kadár (1918–1979), which would produce two of the greatest films of what came to be called the Czech New Wave, *The Shop on Main Street and Adrift* (see p. 627). Klos and Kadár also collaborated on some of the most interesting Czech films of the 1950s, culminating in the controversial *Three Wishes* (*Tři přání*, 1958), a veiled analysis of the mechanisms of social repression. By the year of the film's release, the post-Stalinist thaw had given Czech filmmakers greater freedom to explore both contemporary and histor-ical themes, and the industry had been decentralized into five semiautonomous production groups according to the Polish model. But *Three Wishes* became the object of a neo-Stalinist attack on the industry at a conference at Banská Bystrica in 1959, and, along with several other films, it was banned until 1963. This new and unexpected wave of repression caused directors to retreat to the perennially safe subject matter of the Nazi Occupation, but this time the Czech experience of the war was used as a vehicle for contemporary social comment. Jiří Weiss's *Romeo, Juliet, and the Darkness/Sweet Light in the Dark Room* (*Romeo, Julie a tma*, 1960) tells the story of a young Jewish girl sent to her death in a concentration camp through the indifference of her neighbors. Weiss's *The Coward* (*Zbabělec*, 1961) concerns a simple teacher in rural Slovakia who heroically supports his students in the face of Nazi terrorism. Vojtěch Jasný (b. 1925), an early FAMU graduate (1950) and a forerunner of the Czech New Wave, contributed *I Survived Certain Death* (*Přežil jsem svou smrt*, 1960), which deals with the courageous struggle of a concentration-camp prisoner to keep himself alive. But the most important of the Occupation films of the early 1960s were Zbyněk Brynych's (1927–1995) *Transport from Paradise* (*Transport z ráje*, 1963), a neorealistic account of the transfer of Jews from the "model" ghetto of Terezin (Teresienstadt) to the gas chambers of Auschwitz; and Klos and Kadár's *Death Is Called Engelschen* (*Smrt si říká Engelchen*, 1963), a formally innovative indictment of war as a corruptor of vanquished and victor alike.

Another haven from the neo-Stalinist assault on Czech film was formal experimentation. Jasný led the way with *Desire* (*Touha*, 1958), a film poem on the "four seasons" of life that used the camera as a metaphorical device. The art historian František Vláčil (1924–1999)[9] followed with *The White Dove* (*Bílá holubice*, 1960), a formalist allegory of repression, isolation, and entrapment in the guise of a tale about a sick boy who captures a dove. In Bratislava, the Slovak director Štefan Uher (1930–1993), whose first feature had been the unusual children's film *Grade 9A* (*My z deviatej A*, 1961), made *Sunshine in a Net* (*Slnko v sieti*, 1962), which many historians identify as the first film of the Czech New Wave. Technically unconventional and highly stylized, *Sunshine in a Net* deals primarily with the inner lives of its characters; it was attacked by the first

secretary of the Slovak Communist party for exalting subjective vision over socialist realism. Ultimately the film was banned in Bratislava, but Czech film critics organized a special premier showing in Prague and voted overwhelmingly for its artistic merit. Also notable were several collaborations of the director Karel Kachyňa (b. 1924) and the writer Jan Procházka (1929–1971), especially *Coach to Vienna* (*Kočár do Vídně*, 1966) and *Night of the Bride* (*Noc nevěsty*, 1967), which were inflected by the "magical realism" of cinematographer Josef Illík (b. 1919). At about the same time, a major reform of the Slovak Communist party placed the liberal Alexander Dubček at its head and prepared the way for his subsequent challenge to Czech president and party secretary Antonín Novotný in January 1968 and the brief period of democratization that followed.

THE CZECH NEW WAVE

The official vindication of *Sunshine in a Net* helped to clear the path for the Czech New Wave. So, too, did the extraordinary experimental films of Věra Chytilová (b. 1929), a former draftswoman and fashion model who attended FAMU along with other future directors of the New Wave. Chytilová's medium-length graduation film, *Ceiling* (*Strop*), was distributed commercially with her second film, *A Bag of Fleas* (*Pytel blech*), in 1962, and they established her immediately as the chief formal innovator of the New Wave. Markedly influenced by French and American *cinéma vérité* techniques, both of these films were stories of young women seeking self-actualization in the closed world of Czech urban society. Chytilová's first feature, for which she also wrote the screenplay, was *Something Else/Something Different* (*O něčem jiném*, 1963), a *cinéma vérité* portrait of the lives of two quite different women, an Olympic gymnast and a frustrated housewife. With *Daisies* (*Sedmikrásky*, 1966), however, Chytilová moved

16.23 *Markéta Lazarová* **(František Vláčil, 1967).**

9. Of all the New Wave directors, Vláčil combined a concern for experimental form with a preference for historical subjects. His masterpiece is *Markéta Lazarová* (1967), a four-hour two-part adaptation of Vančura's novel of thirteenth-century Bohemia (1931). This violent and hypnotic widescreen spectacle took Vláčil four years to complete and has been compared to the epic films of Kurosawa, Eisenstein, and Griffith. To amortize the costs of its elaborate sets and costumes, Vláčil followed *Markéta* with *Valley of the Bees* (*Údolí včel*, 1967), a lesser but similarly stylized medieval film.

16.24 *Daisies* (Věra Chytilová, 1966): Jitka Čerhová, Ivana Karbanová.

embark upon an outrageous binge of destruction that ultimately destroys them as well. A bizarre and beautiful satire, *Daisies* was shot by Chytilová's husband, the brilliant cinematographer Jaroslav Kučera (b. 1929), who made free use of superimposition, collage, prismatic distortion, and expressive color to achieve dazzling visual effects for the film. It was designed and partially written by the versatile film artist Ester Krumbachová (1923–1996), a leading figure of the New Wave who has worked in close collaboration with Chytilová, Jan Němec, and Jaromil Jireš (see p. 635; see below). Openly anarchic and subversive, *Daisies* was banned until 1967, when it won considerable critical acclaim both at home and abroad. Chytilová, however, was denied state funds to continue her filmmaking, and her next film, another collaboration with Kučera and Krumbachová, was financed by a Belgian production company. Her most surrealistic film to date, *The Fruit of Paradise* (*Ovoce stromů rajských jíme*, 1969) is a complicated parable about the fantasies of women trapped in a man's world; it won several international awards. But after 1970, Chytilová, who had chosen to remain and work in her homeland despite the Soviet invasion and the overthrow of the liberal Dubček regime in 1968, was forbidden by the government to make films altogether. The ban was lifted in 1975, and she produced *The Apple Game* (*Hra o jablko*, 1976), a furiously paced satire on the inefficiency and corruption of the Czech medical profession, followed by *Prefab Story*

away from *cinéma vérité* into the realm of surrealist fantasy and produced one of the outstanding works of the Czech New Wave. The film concerns two bored and self-indulgent girls (the "daisies" of the title) who

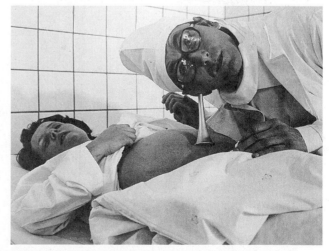

16.25 and 16.26 Chytilová's *The Apple Game* (1976): Jiří Menzel and friends.

(*Panelstory*, 1978) and *Calamity* (*Kalamita*, 1979). Whatever her future as a filmmaker, Chytilová stands today as the most influential formal innovator of the Czech New Wave.

Another young formalist of note was Jaromil Jireš (1935–2001), who worked briefly with Chytilová on the script of *Daisies*. His first feature was a stylistically dazzling portrait of contemporary Czech society entitled *The First Cry* (*Křik*, 1963). It depicted a day in the life of a television repairman making his rounds from house to house while his wife lies in the hospital in labor. Clearly influenced by the French New Wave, Jireš cut back and forth with great precision among the repairman at work in a variety of social contexts (especially in the homes of the powerful, the only Czechs who could afford to own TV sets at this time), his wife in the hospital, and their memories of their past life together to suggest the nature of the world the child will be born into. Between 1963 and 1968 Jireš made no feature films because all of his scripts were rejected by the censors. But in the Prague Spring of 1968, the brief period of democratization fostered by the Dubček regime, he was able to produce a

dark, ironic masterpiece, *The Joke* (*Žert*). Based on a contemporary novel by Milan Kundera, the film provides a savage indictment of the Stalinist system in the story of a postwar philosophy student who is unjustly expelled from school and sent to serve in one of the Czech army's notoriously brutal "black units" because he made a political joke. Stylistically restrained and harshly realistic, *The Joke* contrasts sharply with Jireš's later films. *Valerie and Her Week of Wonders* (*Valérie a týden divů*, 1969), adapted from a story by the Czech surrealist poet Vítězslav Nezval, is a beautifully photographed vampire film that alternates between the erotic and the grotesque. *And Give My Love to the Swallows* (*A pozdravují vlaštovky*, 1971) is a stylized version of the diaries of a young girl who was executed for aiding the Resistance during the Nazi Occupation, and *The Island of Silver Herons* (*Ostrov stříbrných volavek*, 1976) is a poetic meditation on honor and tradition as seen through the eyes of a young boy in a small German town at the close of World War I. (None of Jireš's more recent films have reached the West, but several have won domestic prizes.)

The films of Chytilová and Jireš signaled the beginning of the Czech New Wave, or the "Czech Film Miracle," as it has also been called. This movement was to have an impact on world cinema equivalent to that of Italian neorealism; it was political as well as artistic in that its ultimate goal was to make the Czech people collectively aware that they were participants in a system of oppression and incompetence that had brutalized them all. The success of this consciousness-raising was nearly total, and there is little doubt today that the Czech cinema of 1963–68—like the Polish "cinema of moral anxiety," 1976–81—laid much of the groundwork for liberalization.[1] It also brought the Czech film industry into a position of international prominence once again.

16.27 *The First Cry* (Jaromil Jireš, 1963).

---

1. There was this significant difference, however: the Polish agitation for reform began with the working class and acquired the widespread support of Polish intellectuals only after the birth of Solidarity, but the Czechoslovak reform movement began within the intelligentsia and extended to the working class only during the Prague spring of 1968. It is noteworthy in this regard that the Czech New Wave cinema was closely associated with concurrent experimental movements in literature and theater. In fact, at the Fourth Congress of the Czechoslovak Writers Union in 1971, Milan Kundera went so far as to describe the leading New Wave films as part of the history of Czechoslovak literature.

Though it was dominated by the youngest generation of FAMU-trained directors, the New Wave was a movement in which Czech filmmakers of all generations participated precisely because it *was* a national political phenomenon. The veterans Klos and Kadár first contributed *The Defendant* (*Obžalovaný*, 1964), an unconventional courtroom drama about a man being tried for achieving economic success within the socialist system. They then produced an internationally acclaimed masterpiece, *The Shop on Main Street* (*Obchod na korze*, 1965), which won the American Academy Award as Best Foreign Film of 1965. This film is about Tono, a carpenter in a small Slovak town, who becomes the "Aryan controller" of a button shop owned by an old Jewish woman during the early years of the Occupation. Because the woman is nearly deaf, Tono cannot explain his position to her, so for practical purposes he pretends to be her shop assistant. Initially the situation and film are gently comic, but as Tono gradually comes to pity the woman he recognizes the serious and potentially dangerous nature of his commitment. When the town's Jews are finally rounded up and deported to the death camps, he must choose between protecting the old lady and saving his own skin. He tries to conceal her but accidentally kills her in the process, after which he commits suicide. By making the tragedy of the Jews a metaphor for the multiple tragedies of modern Europe, Klos and Kadár evoked the collective responsibility of all Europeans for the existence and perpetuation of political oppression.

In 1968 Klos and Kadár began work on their greatest film, the Czech-American coproduction *Adrift/A Longing Called Anada* (*Touha zvaná Anada*, 1971), based on a novel by Lájos Zihály, from a screenplay by the Hungarian writer and future film director Imre Gyöngyössy. The shooting, in Kadár's native Slovakia, was interrupted by the Soviet-led invasion and finally completed after the interval of a year, during which Kadár came to the United States to direct *The Angel Levine* (1970), from a Bernard Malamud story. *Adrift* is an elaborately conceived parable of a man cutting himself loose from all traditional ties to his family, his culture, and his religion. Paradoxically, this liberation takes the form of madness, and its vehicle is sexual obsession. Catalyzed by his wife's apparently terminal illness, a simple, middle-aged fisherman is overwhelmingly attracted by the image of a beautiful young woman whom he may or may not have pulled from the waters of the Danube. Except for its beginning and end—which recount the same action from different points of view—the whole film takes place in the mind of its protagonist as he stands on the brink of poisoning his sick wife and interrogates himself about the mental events that have led him to this pass. Its stylistic and structural complexity, which extends to a brilliantly modulated score by František Černý, caused many American critics to dismiss *Adrift* as incomprehensible. But the film has the circular logic of a fantasy or a dream, and to try to read it as a conventional narrative is to misconceive its intentions. After *Adrift*, Klos chose to remain in Czechoslovakia, but Kadár became a permanent resident of the United States, where he was made a Fellow of the American Film Institute. Kadár directed *Lies My Father Told Me* (1975), a moving Canadian production about a Jewish boy growing up in a Montreal immigrant neighborhood, and he did some interesting work for American television (e.g., an adaptation of Stephen Crane's short story "The Blue Hotel" for PBS [1977] and the miniseries *Freedom Road* for NBC [1979]) before his death in 1979.

16.28 *The Shop on Main Street* (Jan Kadár and Elmar Klos, 1965): Ida Kamínska, Jozef Kroner.

Vojtěch Jasný, the first director of importance to emerge from FAMU, made an important contribution to the New Wave with his highly stylized fantasy *Cassandra Cat* (*Až přijde kocour*, 1963) that helped to break a number of neo-Stalinist cinematic and social conventions. This balletic fable of a magic cat whose gaze makes everyone tell the truth was a modern political morality play masquerading as a fairy tale; its technical virtuosity won it a Special Jury Prize at Cannes. But Jasný's most significant film of the New Wave came at the very end of the period. This was the wistfully lyrical *All My Countrymen* (*Všichni dobří rodáci*, 1968), a bittersweet paean to the inhabitants of a small Moravian village who had worked together with Jasný since the war to achieve the reform of their society so recently and brutally crushed by the Soviet-led invasion. (Like many other Czech filmmakers, Jasný emigrated to the United States following the invasion, returning to Prague in 1991 to direct the political documentary *Why Havel?*, with narration by Milos Forman.)

Most characteristic of the younger directors of the Czech New Wave, and ultimately the most famous, was Milos Forman (b. 1932). Forman, who was orphaned by the Nazis during the Occupation, graduated from FAMU in 1955 as a scriptwriter and worked as an assistant to both Martin Frič and Alfred Radok (1914–1976)[2] before making his first feature, *Black Peter/Peter and Pavla* (*Černý Petr*, 1963), which is generally considered to be one of the landmarks of the New Wave. Clearly influenced by Olmi's *Il posto* (1961), this was an ironic film about generational conflict shot in *cinéma vérité* fashion with nonactors and a deliberately functional camera style. A young man takes his first job as a detective in a supermarket, but he finds the work of spying on people so distasteful that it puts him at odds with his hidebound parents. The film, which won the Czech Film Critics' Prize, marked Forman's first association with his coscenarists, Ivan Passer (b. 1933) and Jaroslav Papoušek (b. 1929), and with the cinematographer Miroslav Ondříček (b. 1933), all of whom were to collaborate on his next two films. Like *Black Peter*, these were subtle behavioral studies built upon elaborated anecdotes rather than traditional plot structures, employing improvised dialogue, nonprofessional actors, and a "nonstudio" look (natural lighting, real locations, and so forth). And, like *Black Peter*, they were greeted with both popular acclaim and official disapproval. *Loves of a Blonde/A Blonde in Love*

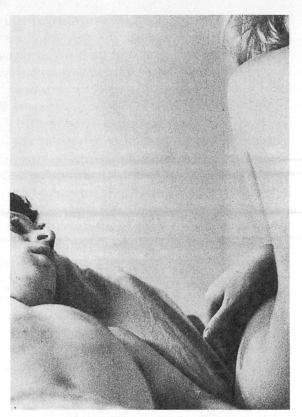

16.29 *Loves of a Blonde* (Milos Forman, 1965).

(*Lásky jedné plavovlásky*, 1965), which brought Forman to international attention, was the simple tale of a young factory girl who meets a touring piano player at a local dance and ends up going to bed with him. She later visits him in his hometown, to the acute embarrassment of the boy and his parents. The film is a sharply observed comedy of everyday life, and its superb sense of timing recalls the American screwball comedies of the 1930s. But *Loves of a Blonde* also contained an implicit criticism of the banality of modern Czech society, its bureaucratic incompetence and ideological rigidity, which did not pass unnoticed by the authorities.

---

2. Radok was already one of Prague's most distinguished stage directors when he turned his energies to the cinema as an art consultant in 1947. In 1949, he directed his first feature, *The Long Journey* (*Daleká cesta*, 1949), an expressionistic portrait of life in the Terezín ghetto, which was the first Czech film to deal with the Nazis' extermination of the Jews. (The film was later ordered withdrawn by government censors for violating the canons of socialist realism.)

The Firemen's Ball (*Hoří, má panenko*, 1967) went even further in this direction—so far that its release was temporarily blocked by President Novotný himself. The film is a satire on Czechoslovakia's most sensitive contemporary political debate: What should be the official attitude toward the Stalinist brutality of the 1950s (during the purges, 1949–55, some 190,000 victims were executed and imprisoned) and toward those still in power who perpetrated it? This issue is presented in the form of a comedy about a small town's commemorative celebration for its dying fire chief. The ball is interrupted by a fire, and the firemen return to discover that all of the food, gifts, and prizes have been stolen by the guests. Some are caught, and a great argument ensues over how the culprits should be treated. At the same time, *The Firemen's Ball* is a slice-of-life comedy satirizing the stolidly heroic socialist-realist melodramas made in the Soviet bloc countries during the 1940s and 1950s: The organizers of a pivotal beauty contest are totally disorganized, the contestants are all ugly, the narration is deflated and undramatic, and so forth. *The Firemen's Ball* opened on December 15, 1967, just two weeks before the political crisis that overthrew Novotný and brought the liberal Alexander Dubček to power. When Dubček himself was ousted following the Soviet-led invasion, Forman, like so many of his colleagues, was forced to leave the country. With Ondříček, he came to the United States, where he directed *Taking Off* (1971), a social comedy about contemporary American mores in the *cinéma vérité* style of his Czech films.

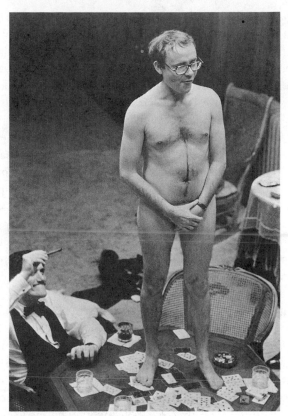

16.31 *Taking Off* (Milos Forman, 1971): Buck Henry, stoned.

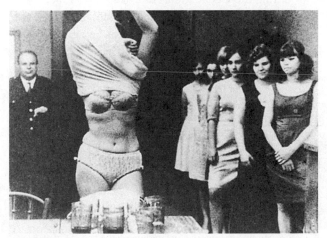

16.30 *The Firemen's Ball* (Milos Forman, 1967): the beauty contest.

After contributing *The Decathlon* to the omnibus film of the 1972 Munich Olympics, *Visions of Eight* (1973; see p. 295), Forman produced a highly acclaimed adaptation of Ken Kesey's novel *One Flew over the Cuckoo's Nest* (1975) and a dynamic film version of the Broadway musical *Hair* (1979), shot on location in New York City. Although he stands today as a mainstream commercial talent in the West, Forman has never deserted the concrete visual poetry of his early work. In his concern for the texture of the everyday, Forman seems to have been influenced by Italian neorealism (and such latter-day exponents as Olmi) and also by British Free Cinema and social realism (see Chapter 14), as practiced by Lindsay Anderson (*This Sporting Life*, 1963) and Karel Reisz (*Saturday Night and Sunday Morning*, 1960). His nearly perfect sense of comic timing has been attributed to the influences of Chaplin, Keaton, and Hawks. But there is something uniquely Czech in the experiential quality of his shooting and lighting, and in the black humor of his satire. His adaptation of E. L. Doctorow's panoramic, turn-of-the-century novel *Ragtime* (1981) confirmed Forman's status as a major figure; and in 1983, he returned triumphantly to Prague to film his sumptuous, much-heralded version of Peter Shaffer's *Amadeus* (1984), which makes brilliant use of Ondříček's widescreen color cinematography and Chris Newman's Dolby stereo sound.[3] The production reunited many former collaborators, and its technical credits read like an alumni roster of the New Wave. More recently Forman directed *Valmont* (1989), a French-American adaptation of Choderlos de Laclos's epistolary novel *Les liaisons dangereuses* (1782). Today he is a permanent resident of New York and Chair of the Columbia University Film Division, where fellow expatriate Vojtech Jasný and Bosnian director Emir Kusturica (see below) are also on the faculty.

Forman's influence upon his peers in Czechoslovak cinema was great. His coscenarists, Ivan Passer (*Intimate Lighting* [*Intimní osvětlení*, 1965]) and Jaroslav Papoušek (*The Most Beautiful Age* [*Nejkrásnější věk*, 1968]), both made plotless, anecdotal films in the manner of Forman during the New Wave. The FAMU-trained scriptwriter Pavel Juráček (1935–1989), who made the highly respected expressionistic *Josef Kilián* (*Postava k podpírání*, 1963)[4] and the apocalyptic science-fiction film *The End of August at the Hotel Ozone* (*Konec srpna v hotelu Ozón*, 1966) with Jan Schmidt (b. 1934), shot his first independent feature, *Every Young Man* (*Každý mladý muž*, 1965), in imitation of Forman. Juráček directed only one other film, *A Case for the Rookie Hangman* (*Případ pro začínajícího kata*, 1969), which was based on the third book of *Gulliver's Travels* and banned two months after its release; he emigrated to West Germany in 1978.

But the most important figure to adopt the antiheroic *cinéma vérité* style developed by Forman was Jiří Menzel (b. 1938), although all of his films of the 1960s were based on literary sources. Menzel graduated from FAMU in 1963 and spent the next two years working as an assistant to Věra Chytilová and as an actor for Evald Schorm (see below). His first motion picture as a director was a contribution to the anthology film *Pearls of the Deep* (*Perličky na dně*, 1964), based on five short stories by Bohumil Hrabal. (Schorm, Jan Němec, Chytilová, and Jireš were the other contributors, making *Pearls of the Deep* a kind of omnibus of the Czech New Wave.) Men-

16.32 *Josef Kilián* (Pavel Juráček and Jan Schmidt, 1963).

zel's first feature, *Closely Watched Trains* (*Ostře sledované vlaky*, 1966), was also adapted from Hrabal, who ultimately preferred the film to his original; it brought Menzel international fame and became the second Czech film to win an American Academy Award (as Best Foreign Film of 1966). The film is an elliptical, Formanesque study of human attitudes and behavior set in a railway town during the Occupation. An awkward youth apprentices himself to the village railroad-station guard, whose sexual exploits he much admires. After failing miserably in his first sexual encounter, the young man makes a suicide attempt. He finally succeeds at sex with a beautiful

---

3. Critically short of convertible currencies, the Czechoslovak government permitted Forman's return to earn much-needed dollars for the Barrandov studios (the facility is regularly rented to foreign production companies). He had to promise not to visit former friends among the dissidents, and the authorities agreed not to harm friends who came to visit him on the set. (Forman had also returned to Czechoslovakia in 1980.)

4. *Josef Kilián* was written under the direct influence of Franz Kafka (1883–1924), whose literary reputation as a Czech (although he wrote in German) had been rehabilitated at the Liblice symposium in May 1963.

16.33 *Closely Watched Trains* (Jiří Menzel, 1966): Václav Neckář, Jitka Bendová.

Resistance fighter and, in a dramatic assertion of virility, blows up a Nazi ammunition train; during this act, he is killed by a German train guard's machine gun. *Closely Watched Trains* is both comic and deadly serious, often simultaneously, and in this regard it epitomizes an essential characteristic of Czech New Wave cinema—its ironic and often detached intermixing of dichotomous emotional responses. The film also owes a debt to surrealism in its subversive equation of sexual and political freedom. Menzel's other notable New Wave film is *Capricious Summer* (*Rozmarné léto*, 1967), a humorous but sometimes dark fable adapted from a Vančura novel about the sexual misadventures of three middle-aged friends in a

16.34 Menzel in his film *Capricious Summer* (1967).

small fishing village; it won the Grand Prix at Karlovy Vary in 1968. Menzel's reverential parody of American musical comedy, *Crime in the Nightclub* (*Zločin v šantánu*, 1968), was immensely popular in Czechoslovakia during the months that followed the invasion, but his *Skylarks on a String* (*Skřivánci na niti*, 1969), adapted from Hrabal, was banned, and Menzel was not permitted to make another film until the unremarkable *Who Looks for Gold?* (*Kdo hledá zlaté dno?*, 1975) and the routine comedy *Seclusion Near a Forest* (*Na samotě u lesa*, 1976). Next he directed *Those Wonderful Movie Cranks* (*Báječní muži s klikou*, 1978), commemorating the seventieth anniversary of the film industry in Prague. It is a humorous and affectionate account of its beginnings in 1907, shot in the sepia tones of the era. For his next film, Menzel adapted another novel by Hrabal, *Cutting It Short* (*Postřižiny*, 1981), a lyrical comedy about life in a small provincial town just before the First World War.

The two most politically controversial and morally committed directors of the Czech New Wave were Evald Schorm (1931–1989) and Jan Němec (b. 1936). Schorm, who is often called "the conscience of the New Wave," graduated from FAMU in 1962 and made eight documentary shorts before directing his first feature, *Everyday Courage/Courage for Every Day* (*Každý den odvadhu*) in 1964. In it he eschewed both the formal experiments of Chytilová and Jireš and the *cinéma vérité* techniques of Forman, Passer, and Menzel to make a traditional dramatic film of uncompromisingly serious intent. *Everyday Courage* is the story of an idealistic Communist organizer who gradually comes to recognize that his ideals are wrong and that they have caused much human misery. The official response to this allegory of de-Stalinization was violent condemnation. When *Everyday Courage* won the Czech Film Critics' Prize in 1965, the government refused to let Schorm accept it and attempted to sabotage the film's distribution. International outcry finally forced official acceptance of *Everyday Courage*, but Schorm's next feature, *The Return of the Prodigal Son* (*Návrat ztraceného syna*, 1966), was banned outright for several months. This film, considered to be Schorm's masterpiece, is a parable of the fate of the individual in an authoritarian society. Its protagonist, Jan, is confined to a mental institution after a suicide attempt. Jan's failure to "adjust" to the existing social structure stems from his unwillingness to compromise his personal integrity, and he is hunted down by a mob that mistakes him for a rapist. Schorm's third film of contemporary social criticism, *Saddled with Five Girls* (*Pět holek na krku*, 1967), forms a kind of trilogy with *Everyday Courage* and *The Return of the Prodigal Son*. Less pessimistic than his earlier work, *Saddled* is a film of youthful love and alienation that juxtaposes its narrative with scenes from Weber's opera *Der Freischütz*. In *Pastor's End/The End of a Priest* (*Konec faráře*, 1968), Schorm and the scriptwriter Josef Škvorecký (b. 1924)—who has also worked with Menzel and other New Wave directors—collaborated on a farcical reworking of the Christ legend with pronounced political overtones. In a rural village, a sexton poses as a priest and accomplishes much good, but he is finally exposed and done to death by the repressive institutions of church and state. The release of *Pastor's End* was delayed by the authorities for a year, but it has now become generally available in the West. Schorm's next films, *The Seventh Day, the Eighth Night* (*Sedmý den, osmá noc*, 1969) and *Dogs and People* (*Psi a lidé*, 1970), were permanently banned in the spring of 1970, and Schorm was forbidden to work in the Czech film industry again. After that time, he made his living by directing operas in provincial theaters—like one of his own heroes, unwilling to compromise his moral integrity or his seriousness of purpose for the comfortable security of "fitting in." Schorm emerged from internal exile to make his final film, *Killing with Kindness* (*Lastne se nic nestalo*, 1989), a parable of suffocating mother love that is highly reminiscent of his pre-1968 work. He died of heart failure in 1989.

Like Schorm, Jan Němec is an ethically committed filmmaker concerned with the survival of individual integrity in a repressive, regimented society. But unlike Schorm, he experimented boldly with form and was on the cutting edge of the New Wave since his student days. His first feature, *Diamonds of the Night* (*Démanty noci*, 1964), was adapted by Němec and Arnošt Lustig from a novel by Lustig about two young Jews who escape from a Nazi death march. Němec turned the narrative into a nightmarish representation of the mental anguish of human beings under extreme physical and psychological stress. Documentary-like footage of the four-day hunt for the boys is intercut with images from their dreams, fantasies, and hallucinations as they become increasingly desperate. The film was a great domestic critical success and won several international awards.

Němec's next film began a brief but fruitful collaboration with the designer Ester Krumbachová and brought the wrath of officialdom down upon the heads of both. *The*

16.35 *Diamonds of the Night* (Jan Němec, 1964).

Party and the Guests/A Report on the Party and the Guests (*O slavnosti a hostech*, 1966) was a stylized, Kafkaesque allegory about the mechanisms of repression in Czech society and the most politically venomous film of the New Wave. The Host throws an elegant dinner party in a beautiful forest glade, assuring his guests throughout the evening that his only desire is to make them happy. As the party progresses, the guests assure The Host one by one that they are indeed supremely happy. Only one of them, The Guest Who Refused to Be Happy, resists being intimidated into contentment, and, significantly, he is played by the director Evald Schorm, whose *Return of the Prodigal Son* was then under a government ban. Eventually the unhappy guest discreetly slips away, and the crowd of

16.36 Němec's *The Party and the Guests* (1966), with Josef Škvorecký (wearing glasses) second from left.

remaining guests turns ugly. If a single guest refuses to join the merrymaking, it spoils the party for all, so the party takes to its feet and pursues the malcontent with dogs. This sinister parable of social conformity and political dissent was brilliantly designed by Krumbachová to achieve just the proper sense of strange beauty intermixed with menace. Many of the scenes were modeled on contemporary Czech paintings and media images, giving the film a rich subtext of visual allusion. Most of the roles were played by friends of the filmmaker's, so at yet another level of allusion the film stands as a collective political manifesto by Prague's artists and intellectuals. When President Novotný screened *The Party and the Guests*, he was outraged and is said to have remarked, "It's about the way we banned that fellow Schorm's film and then set the dogs on him, isn't it?" This time the dogs were set upon Němec and his friends. The film was banned for two full years and became the object of violent invective. Together with Chytilová's *Daisies*, it was used as an excuse for a denunciation of the entire New Wave in the Czechoslovak National Assembly in May 1967. Němec and Krumbachová, in the meantime, turned to the nonpolitical theme of sexual fantasy in the three-episode *Martyrs of Love* (*Mučedníci lásky*, 1967), which recalled the hypervisual, hallucinatory quality of *Diamonds of the Night*. When Dubček assumed power in January 1968, *The Party and the Guests* was finally released domestically, and that spring it was sent to Cannes as the official Czech entry. Němec was at work with Josef Škvorecký on a documentary about Prague when Soviet tanks entered the city on August 20–21. This film became *Oratorio for Prague* (1968), a melancholy account of the invasion which was smuggled out of Czechoslovakia for screening in the West. Němec was blacklisted immediately, and he was unable to make films from 1968 to 1974; in that year he was allowed to emigrate to France. He subsequently found work in West German television and completed *Czech Connection: Reflection of My Own Death* (1975), a 40-minute autobiographical film begun secretly in his homeland. In 1977, Němec moved to Santa Monica, California, where he remained virtually unknown. In 1989 he returned to Czechoslovakia to shoot the Ladislav Klíma adaptation noted below.

"BANNED FOREVER"

The Czech film miracle came to an abrupt end in 1968 with the Soviet-led invasion and the subsequent occupation of

the country by Warsaw Pact troops. The liberalization of Czechoslovakia—the attempt to create a "socialism with a human face"—had threatened Soviet hegemony over Eastern Europe, and so it was suppressed by force. Party Secretary Dubček and his supporters were eased from office over the next eight months, to be replaced by a Novotný-like regime under Gustav Husák that undertook the "normalization" of Czechoslovakia.[5] Films in production were halted. Many already in release were withdrawn by party censors and banned. The managing directors of both the Barrandov studios and the Koliba studios in Bratislava were fired, and the director of the state distribution organization, Czechoslovak Film, was arrested and imprisoned for "antisocialist activities." The five autonomous production groups together with the Union of Czechoslovak Film and Television Artists (FITES) were dissolved, and every Czech filmmaker discussed in this chapter, except Jireš and Uher, was blacklisted and forbidden to work in the film industry indefinitely. Kadár, Jasný, Forman, Passer, and, ultimately, Němec and Juráček left the country for good, and a whole rising generation of new talent was permanently quashed. By 1973 virtually every important film of the previous decade lay buried in a vault in the cellar of the Barrandov studios, and four of these had been labeled "banned forever"—Forman's *The Firemen's Ball*, Schorm's *The Pastor's End*, Němec's *The Party and the Guests*, and Jasný's *All My Countrymen*. It was as if the New Wave and everything it had accomplished had never existed. What might have happened had the New Wave cinema been allowed to grow and prosper—and what that growth might have meant for the development of international cinema—is impossible to say. Surely its significance would have been great. But, instead, "normalization" left a huge vacuum that the Czech film industry has been unable to fill ever since.

Very few notable films came from Prague in the 1970s, although there was recognition for the work of several Slovak directors: the films of the surrealist Juraj Jakubisko (b. 1938)—*Deserters and Nomads* (*Zbehovia a pútníci*, 1968); *Birds, Orphans, and Fools* (*Vtáčkovia, siroty a blázni*, 1969); *Build a House, Plant a Tree* (*Postav dom, zasad strom*, 1980); *The Millennial Bees* (*Tisícročná včela*, 1983); *Frau Holle* (1985)—which have been compared to those of Dovzhenko in their violent, elemental force; the

5. In December 1987, Husák in turn was replaced by Miloš Jakeš.

baroque allegories of Juraj Herz (b. 1934)—*The Cremator* (*Spalovač mrtvol*, 1968); *Kerosene Lamps* (*Petrolejové lampy*, 1971); *Morgiana* (1972); *A Day for My Love* (*Den pro mou lásku*, 1977); *Beauty and the Beast* (1972); *Bulldogs and Cherries* (*Buldoci a třešně*, 1981); *The Ferat Vampire* (*Závody se smrtí*, 1982); and Dušan Hanák's (b. 1938) lyrical Gypsy romance *Rose-Tinted Dreams* (*Růšové sny*, 1976).[6] The comedies of Oldřich Lipský (1924–1986)—*Dinner for Adele* (*Adéla ještě nevečeřela*, 1978); *Long Live Ghosts* (*Ať žijí duchové!*, 1979); *The Mysterious Castle in the Carpathians* (*Tajemství hrada v Karpatech*, 1984)—also enjoyed some international success. The years 1976–77 marked the return of several major directors and actors after years of enforced idleness, and Czech entries at the important Karlovy Vary festival gave evidence of a gradual rapprochement between the film industry and the government. Examples would be Jiří Krejčík's *The Divine Emma* (*Božská Ema*, 1979); Karel Kachyňa's *Love among the Raindrops* (*Laški mesi kapkami deště*, 1980) and *Fandy* (1983); Jaromil Jireš's *The Rabbit Case* (*Causa králík*, 1980), *Escapes Home* (*Uteky domu*, 1981), *Opera in the Vineyard* (*Opera ve vinci*, 1983), and *Partial Eclipse* (*Néupliné zatmění*, 1983); František Vláčil's *Smoke on the Potato Fields* (*Dým bramborové natě*, 1976), *Shadows of a Hot Summer Day* (*Stíny horkého leta*, 1977), *Serpent's Poison* (*Hadí jed*, 1982), and *Shepherd Boy from the Lowlands* (*Pasáček z doliny*, 1984); Štefan Uher's *Concrete Pastures* (*Pásla kone na betóne*); Jiří Menzel's Hrabal adaptation *Snowdrop Celebrations* (*Slavnŏsti sněženek*, 1984), and the documentary *Prague* (1985), co-directed with Věra Chytilová; and Chytilová's own *The Very Late Afternoon of a Faun* (*Faunovo velmi pozdní odpoledne*, 1984), her first collaboration with Ester Krumbachová since *Daisies* in 1966. Also notable were Chytilová's *Tainted Horseplay* (*Kopytem sem, kopytem tam*, 1989), the first Czech film to deal with AIDS, and the debut feature *Why?* (*Proč?* [Karel Smyczek, 1987]), which examines the phenomenon of violence among young soccer fans.

In 1989, democracy was reborn in Czechoslovakia in the wake of the Velvet Revolution of November 17–December 10—massive but mainly bloodless street demonstrations leading to the fall of the communist government and, in June 1990, to the first free elections in forty-four years.[7] In that year, dissident playwright Vaclav Havel was swept into office as president of the Czechoslovak Republic, and twenty years of state censorship were

reversed at the twenty-seventh Karlovy Vary Film Festival, July 7–19, when twenty-two formerly banned features and eleven shorts were shown to world acclaim. Seven of the features, made between the fall of 1968 and the end of 1969, had never been domestically released—Menzel's *Skylarks on a String*, Schorm's *The Seventh Day, the Eighth Night*, Karel Kachyňa's *The Ear* (*Ucho*), Zdenek Sirovy's *Funeral Rites* (*Smuteční slavost*), Drahomíra Vihanová's *A Wasted Sunday* (*Zabitá nedělě*), Ivan Balada's *Pavilion No. 6* (*Pavilón č. 6*), and the Bulgarian director Rangel Vulchanov's coproduction *Aesop* (*Ezop*). Fifteen others—including Němec's *A Report on the Party and the Guests*, Jireš's *The Joke*, Jasný's *All My Good Countrymen*, Schorm's *Everyday Courage*, Kachyňa's *Coach to Vienna* (*Kočár do Vídně*, 1966), and several blacklisted Jakubisko films (e.g., *See You in Hell, Fellows* [*Do videnia v pekle, priatelia*, 1970]—had received only limited release before being shelved. One immediate result was a bonanza of festival awards—a Silver Bear at Berlin in 1990 for the Slovak director Dušan Hanák's *I Love, You Love* (*Ja milujem, ty milujěs*), shelved since 1980, multiple prizes for his long-banned short *Pictures of the Old World* (*Obrazy starého sveta*, 1972), and a Golden Bear at Berlin in 1991 for Menzel's *Skylarks on a String*.

At the end of 1990 the Central Management of Czechoslovak Film, which had controlled all film production and distribution in the nation, was disbanded. A number of independent, joint-stock film companies (e.g., Bonton, Microfilm, and Cinepont) were formed immediately with foreign capital, but none of the Czech or Slovak features produced that year could even amortize their costs, as domestic audiences favored American imports and film attendance generally declined. In 1991, the Barrandov studios, still government-owned, reduced its workforce by half and managed to complete only sixteen features, compared with an average of twenty-five during the communist era. With state production grants running at 30 percent of budget or less, some began to question whether

---

6. Only one of these features, Jakubisko's *Deserters and Nomads*, has been seen in the West; as Peter Hames points out, Slovak films traditionally received little active support from Czechoslovak Filmexport, which regarded them as "regional" items (*The Czechoslovak New Wave*).

7. These events were chronicled only months later in the first film production of the new regime, the feature-length documentary *The Velvet Revolution* (Jiří Strěcha and Peter Slavík, 1990).

the Czechoslovak film industry could survive in the context of its small (15.6 million) and increasingly competitive domestic market. Milos Forman, Miroslav Ondříček, and others argued strongly for the privatization of Barrandov (effected in 1993), and there was agreement on all sides that the sheer number of domestic productions would have to decline. Amid this uncertainty, however, there was great hope: Jan Němec returned to Prague for the first time since 1974 to direct *In the Light of the King's Love* (*V žáru královské lásky*, 1990), a controversial adaptation of a macabre novella by the "cursed" writer and philosopher Ladislav Klíma (1878–1928); Jan Schmidt directed *Lenin, Mother, and the Lord* (*Vracenky*, 1991), a period piece about a young boy coming of age under Stalinism; Jiří Menzel, named in 1991 both Head of Production at FAMU and Committee Chair of the Karlovy Vary Fest, delivered film versions of Vaclav Havel's *The Beggars Opera* (1991) and Josef Škvorecký's *The Engineer of Human Souls* (1993), as well as *The Life and Extraordinary Adventures of Private Choukin* (1994), based on a mid-1960s Russian dissident novel; and new work was forthcoming from the Slovak masters Dušan Hanák (*Private Lives* [*Sukromne životy*, 1989/1991]) and Juraj Jakubisko (*It Is Better to Be Rich and Handsome Than Poor and Ugly*, 1992). Among the rising generation, there were two outstanding debuts in the work of Irena Pavlásková (*Time of the Servants*, 1991) and Jan Svěrák (*Elementary School* [*Obecná škola*, 1992]), which latter was nominated for an American Academy Award. Despite the shock to the system administered by its rapid conversion to capitalism, the Czechoslovak film industry faced an artistically promising, if financially uncertain, future.

In the summer of 1992, however, Czechs and Slovaks voted in national elections to abandon the federal state and form separate, independent republics. The Velvet Revolution, it was said, had led to a "velvet divorce." Havel resigned as president (he remained president of the new Czech Republic), and, on December 31, 1992, the country that had created the Czechoslovak film miracle officially ceased to exist. Since that time, the Czech and Slovak cinemas have gone their separate ways. The Czech industry has remained in a fairly healthy state, producing around twenty films annually, but Slovakia has made only a handful each year (e.g., Václav Vorlíček's fairy tale for children *King of Falcons* [*Sokoliar Tomás*, 2000] and Martin Sulík's period satire *Little Country* [*Krajinka*, 2000]), part of which is accountable to its small size (5.4 million people).

The Czechs, on the other hand, number 10.2 million and have experienced a number of international successes—e.g., Jan Svěrák's *Kolya* (1996), which won many festival prizes plus an Oscar for Best Foreign Film, and Jan Hrebejk's *Divided We Fall* (*Musíme si pomáhat*, 2000), which was an Academy-award nominee as well. Furthermore, veterans of the film miracle have continued to produce new work—e.g., Jaromil Jireš's cerebral science-fiction film *Double Role* (*Dvojrole*, 1999), Vojtěch Jasný's nostalgic tale of Moravian rural life *Which Side Eden?* (*Návrat ztraceného ráje*, 2000), and the ever-radical Věra Chytilová's *Traps, Traps, Little Traps* (*Pasti, pasti, pasticky*, 1998) and *Banned from Paradise* (*Vyhnání z ráje*, 2001), both protofeminist attacks on consumer society. Such films tend to be critical rather than popular successes, but domestic productions still have a national audience; in 1999, e.g., Jan Hrebejk's comedy about the Prague Spring, *Cosy Dens* (*Pelisky*), became the top box-office attraction and broke all-time attendance records in early 2000 with over 1 million admissions. In general, however, Czech films only rarely return their costs through theatrical distribution; as in other parts of Europe, state-supported national television (Czech TV) coproduces most Czech features in exchange for broadcast rights. Whatever their separate fates, the Czech Republic and Slovakia share one of the richest and oldest film cultures in the world. It can never be forgotten that during the Prague Spring a country with a population of less than 16 million, inhabiting a land mass no larger than the state of Tennessee, was able to produce over three hundred films that had a radical impact on

16.37 *Divided We Fall* (Jan Hrebejk, 2000): Boleslav Polivka as Josef, the proud new father of another man's child. This comedy of moral courage during the Nazi Occupation of Prague harked back to best films of the Czech New Wave.

its own sociopolitical structure and simultaneously changed the shape of international cinema.

Hungary

THREE REVOLUTIONS

Like Czechoslovakia, Hungary has had a long and distinguished cinematic tradition. The Hungarians, in fact, seem to have identified film as an art form before any other nationality in the world, including the French. From the beginning, they emphasized the literary and intellectual aspects of film, and most films were adapted from classical Hungarian novels and plays. For this reason, famous authors and actors from the legitimate stage had none of the qualms about working in film that afflicted their counterparts in the West. In 1912 the radical writer Sándor Korda[8] (who later worked in Britain as the producer-director Alexander Korda) founded *Pesti mozi* ("Pest[9] cinema"), the first Hungarian film journal, and by 1920 it had been joined by sixteen others. A strong tradition of advanced film theory was founded in the teens by the philosophers Jenö Török and Cecil Bognár, and passed on to Béla Balázs (pronounced "Ballázh"; 1884–1949), whose *Der Film—Werden und Wesen einer neuen Kunst*[1] became greatly influential. As in France, film attracted the avant garde—between 1923 and 1928 the painter László Moholy-Nagy (1895–1946), for example, conducted numerous experiments with film's ability to transform space and light. Hungary also had the first nationalized film industry in history. Béla Kun's socialist revolution of March 1919 declared Hungary a "Red Republic of Councils," and the cinema was nationalized in April of that year—four months before Lenin nationalized the Soviet industry. This adventure lasted only until the rightest counter-revolution of Admiral Miklós Horthy, who installed himself as regent in August, but thirty-one films were produced in the interim. Hungary's first important director was Mihály Kertész (1888–1962), who studied filmmaking at Denmark's Nordisk studios, directed a number of films in Germany in the 1920s, and settled in the United States, where he worked for Warner Bros. as Michael Curtiz. Other important figures were Pál Fejös (1898–1963) and Endre Tóth (1912–2002); also known as André De Toth), both of whom ultimately emigrated to America, with Fejös returning to Hungary in 1931 to make his internationally celebrated *Spring Shower* (*Tavaszi zápor*, 1932).

In 1920 the Horthy regime restored film production to the private sector, and during the 1920s and 1930s the Hungarian industry became commercialized along American lines. Most films of the period were made on an assembly-line basis in imitation of Hollywood; and after the conversion to sound in 1930, musicals like István Székely's *The Rákóczi March* (*Rákóczi-induló*, 1933) and Béla Gaál's *The Dream Car* (*Meseautó*, 1934) became extremely popular. Serious films appeared in the work of Fejös and in the Austrian director George Hoellering's *Hortobágy* (1935), a starkly realistic account of contemporary peasant life shot on location on the *puszta*, the great Hungarian plain. When World War II broke out, the Horthy government, which was allied with the Germans, took control of the industry through the National Film Committee and permitted it to produce only conformist entertainment and propaganda films. A notable exception was István Szőts's (b. 1912) anticapitalist *People on the Alps* (*Emberek a havason*, 1942), shot on location in the mountains of Transylvania, which won a prize at Venice in the year of its release and was hailed by the Italian journal *Cinema* as a model for neorealism. Unsure of the country's stability, the Nazis seized Hungary in March 1944, deposed Horthy, and set up their own government. The Soviet Union invaded in late 1944, and Hungary concluded an armistice with the Allies in January 1945. Almost immediately, the Academy for Dramatic and Cinematographic Art was founded, and hundreds of Soviet and American films were shown in Hungary for the first time. The most significant Hungarian film of this period was the privately produced *Somewhere in Europe* (*Valahol Európában*, 1947), a humanitarian fantasy about the reclamation of war orphans, written by Béla Balázs and directed by Géza von Radványi (1907–1986). When a Communist government came to power early in 1948, the Hungarian film industry was nationalized for the second time. The first state-subsidized films, such as Frigyes Bán's (1902–1969) revolutionary peasant melodrama *The Soil under Your Feet*

---

8. Hungarian names are given here with the surname last, although in Hungary the convention is the reverse.

9. The present city of Budapest was formed in 1873 by the union of Buda and Óbuda, on the right bank of the Danube River, with Pest (pronounced "Pesht") on the left bank. Even today, many Hungarians refer to "Buda" or to "Pest" rather than to "Budapest," depending on which side of the river they live.

1. The Balázs work was published in 1948 in Berlin; in English it appeared as *Theory of the Film: Character and Growth of a New Art*, trans. Edith Bone (London: Dobson, 1952; New York: Dover, 1970).

(*Talpalatnyi föld*, 1948), were quite promising, but the political climate deteriorated rapidly under Stalinism, and the period 1949–53 was one of stolid socialist realism.

The death of Stalin in 1953 and the subsequent replacement of Mátyás Rákosi as the Hungarian premier by Imre Nagy marked the beginning of the nation's New Course, a brief era of liberalization. This period was one of high achievement for Hungarian cinema. It witnessed the emergence of a new generation of directors: Zoltán Fábri (1917–1994)—*Fourteen Lives in Danger* (*Életjel*, 1954), *Merry-Go-Round* (*Körhinta*, 1955), the anti-Stalinist parable *Professor Hannibal* (*Hannibál, tanár úr*, 1956; banned 1957); Károly Makk (b. 1925)—*Liliomfi* (1954); János Herskó (b. 1926)—*Under the City* (*A város alatt*, 1954); and Félix Máriássy (1919–1976)—*Spring in Budapest* (*Budapesti tavász*, 1955); *A Glass of Beer* (*Egy pikoló világos*, 1955). Many of these filmmakers are still active in the Hungarian cinema today.[2] Their films expressed the increasingly liberal sentiments of the Hungarian workers and their yearning for a true social democracy. On October 23, 1956, this yearning began to manifest itself in demonstrations, street fighting, and, finally, armed violence in Budapest. As revolution spread swiftly throughout Hungary, workers' councils took control of most government functions, and on November 1, Nagy declared his intention to withdraw from the Warsaw Pact. Three days later the Soviet Union intervened—as it would do in Czechoslovakia in 1968 (but with considerably less brutality)—with 200,000 troops and 3,000 tanks under air cover. Over 25,000 Hungarian citizens died in the systematic tank bombardment of cities and industrial centers. Imre Nagy and about 2,000 of his supporters were arrested and ultimately executed. Another 10,000 persons were deported to Soviet labor camps, an undetermined number were imprisoned for years without trial, and 200,000 fled into exile. The revolution was crushed, but the moderate János Kádár was installed as premier; he gradually embarked upon a realistic course of liberalization and economic growth (fostered by the New Economic Mechanism, or NEM, which injected free-market elements into the predominantly socialized system) that left Hungary substantially freer and more stable financially than any of its Warsaw Pact neighbors.

The effect of the revolt—branded in party dogma as a "counterrevolution" until 1989—upon Hungarian cinema was to arrest its development. The films of 1954–56 had been notable primarily for their content, rather than for the kind of formal innovations that liberalization would produce in Poland and Czechoslovakia. In the matter of style and structure, Hungarian film was still essentially realist (or, at most, neorealist) when the revolution was put down. Afterward, it could evolve in neither form nor content until Kádár's steady process of liberalization had been realized. The films of 1957–61, therefore, were unremarkable. But between 1958 and 1961, the experimental Béla Balázs Studio was founded and put on a sound financial basis in order to give graduates of the state-operated Academy for Dramatic and Cinematographic Art in Budapest an opportunity to make their first films. The year 1961 saw the release of the studio's first batch of shorts and the reappearance of political themes in the work of Fábri (*Two Half-Times in Hell* [*Két félidő a pokolban*]) and Makk (*The Fanatics* [*Megszállottak*]). In 1962, Kádár unexpectedly declared a general amnesty, and the stage was set for a major resurgence of Hungarian cinema. The two figures of signal importance to this renaissance were András Kovács and Miklós Jancsó.

ANDRÁS KOVÁCS

András Kovács (pronounced "Kovach"; b. 1925) attended the Budapest Academy and made several features before undertaking a two-year period of study in Paris. There, Kovács fell under the influence of *cinéma vérité*, whose techniques he employed in *Difficult People* (*Nehéz emberek*, 1964) upon his return to Hungary. This film examines the true cases of five Hungarian inventors whose work had been opposed or ignored through bureaucratic stupidity. *Difficult People* sparked a debate throughout the country since it was the first time since 1955 that contemporary reality had been so directly confronted on the screen. Kovács's next film, *Cold Days* (*Hideg napok*, 1966), was a visually engaging account of the massacre of some three thousand Jews and Serbs in the town of Novi Sad (now part of the Serbian portion of the Yugoslav Federation) by Hungarian troops in January 1942. The event is narrated in flashback by four participants who are in prison awaiting trial for the atrocity some years later. This film, too, provoked debate—this time about the collective nature of responsibility in both the national present and the national past. *Cold Days* appeared at several international festivals and attracted world attention to the new

---

2. The contributions of both Fábri and Makk, for example, have been remarkably consistent to date and have helped to build an international audience for Hungarian cinema.

Hungarian cinema. In *Walls* (*Falak*, 1968) and *Relay Race* (*Staféta*, 1970), Kovács continued to probe the contradictions of contemporary Hungarian society with a degree of artistic freedom unprecedented in any other country in Eastern Europe. *Blindfold* (*Bekötött szemmel*, 1974) is close to *Cold Days* in its sober, black-and-white reconstruction of an actual incident from World War II—that of a priest brought before a military tribunal for having caused the "miracle" that saves a condemned soldier from execution; while *Labyrinth* (*Labirintus*, 1976) follows Truffaut, Wajda, and Fellini in creating a self-reflexive film about the process of filmmaking itself. Kovács returned to politics in *The Stud Farm* (*Ménesgazda*, 1978), a tale of political terror set during the first nervous months of the new Stalinist regime in 1950 and his first film in color, and *A Sunday in October* (*Októberi vasárnap*, 1980), a historical reconstruction of Admiral Horthy's secret attempt to abandon the Axis and negotiate a separate peace with the Soviet Union on October 15, 1944, near the end of World War II. Recent Kovács films include the romantic dramas *Temporary Paradise* (*Ideiglenes paradicsom*, 1981) and *An Afternoon Affair* (*Szeretők*, 1984); *The Red Countess* (*Vörös grófnő*, 1985), a richly mounted two-part biography of Count Mihály Károlyi and his wife, who were major political figures at the time of World War I and the socialist revolution of 1919 (Károlyi was, in fact, president of the short-lived First Republic of 1918); and *Rear Guard* (*Valahol Magyarországon*, 1988), a documentary-style drama about grass-roots party politics.

MIKLÓS JANCSÓ

The first major film of Miklós Jancsó (pronounced "Yahn-cho"; b. 1921), *Cantata* (*Oldás és kötés*, 1962), is also considered to be the first film of the Hungarian New Wave. Jancsó had studied law (in which he holds a doctorate), ethnography, and art history before he entered the Budapest Academy, from which he graduated in 1950. For eight years he made newsreels and documentaries that were fairly conventional in both form and content, as was his first feature, *The Bells Have Gone to Rome* (*A harangok Rómába mentek*, 1958). But *Cantata*, written by his perennial collaborator, Gyula Hernádi, and shot in eleven days, revealed a striking talent for visual composition and psychological analysis. Photographed in the neutralized style of Antonioni, it concerns a young physician educated during the Stalin era who has risen to a favorable position within the socialist hierarchy and effectively isolated him-

self from the larger realities of Hungarian society. Returning after many years to the village of his birth, he is forced to confront his peasant origins in the person of his aged father and ultimately comes to realize his moral complicity in a system that, while offering him personal advancement, has ruined the lives of many others. It was *My Way Home* (*Így jöttem*, 1964), however, that announced the style for which Jancsó would become famous—one based upon extended long takes sustained by rhythmic tracking movements of the camera and optical traveling through the zoom lens. The film is about a sixteen-year-old Hungarian conscript who has deserted the army and is attempting to make his way home across the western frontier during the last chaotic days of World War II. His life is threatened successively by Hungarian partisans, renegade Cossacks, the retreating Hungarian Fascists, and the advancing Red Army. He is finally captured by the latter and assigned to help a badly wounded Soviet soldier of about his own age tend some cows. Mutually distrustful at first, the two gradually become friends; and when the Russian dies of his wounds, the Hungarian sets off homeward again in his uniform, across the same landscape of murderously contending factions as before. *My Way Home* offers a pessimistic view of a hostile universe in a structure of great formal beauty—traits strikingly present in Jancsó's next film.

The Round-Up/The Hopeless Ones (*Szegénylegények*, 1965), which brought Jancsó to international prominence when it was shown at Cannes in 1966, is a chilling account of a historical incident that occurred in 1868 and the first of many Jancsó films about great events from the Hungarian past. Under the commission of Count Gedeon Ráday, the political police of the Austro-Hungarian monarchy attempt to unmask Sándor Rózsa, the chief of a rebel army group during the 1848 Revolution, which was led by Lájos Kossuth,[3] who is now operating as a local *betyár*, or bandit.

---

3. In 1848, as part of the revolutionary agitation then shaking all of Europe, Kossuth (1802–1994) formed a government that declared his nation independent of Austria and of Hapsburg rule. The Austrians and their Russian allies succeeded in crushing the rebellion the following year, and Hungary again came under Hapsburg rule. But over the next two decades, Hapsburg power waned, and in 1867 Emperor Franz Josef I of Austria agreed to give Hungary equal status with Austria in the Austro-Hungarian Empire, or Dual Monarchy, which lasted until Hungary became a republic after World War I. The events in Jancsó's film took place as part of a combined Austro-Hungarian attempt to quell continuing political unrest and banditry on the Great Plain in the Dual Monarchy's first year. (In Hungary during the Cold War, the national obsession with the 1848 Revolution became a covert channel for anti-Soviet feelings since the Russians participated in the revolt's suppression.)

16.38 Openness and closure in Jancsó's *The Round-Up* (1965).

The police round up several hundred peasants, herds-men, and suspected outlaws—some of them former com-rades-in-arms of Rózsa's, but most of them innocent civilians—putting them in a prison stockade on the great Hungarian plain (*puszta*), where they employ sophisti-cated modern means of interrogation, torture, and polit-ical terror to force the inmates into mutual betrayal. A film of stark beauty and terrific force, *The Round-Up* introduced many of Jancsó's mature personal symbols and stylistic obsessions: the use of nudity to signify humil-iation; the totally impersonal depiction of cruelty and vio-lence; the menacing image of incessantly circling horsemen on the empty spaces of the plain; the balletic choreography of the camera and groups of actors within the frame; the replacement of characterization through dialogue with bureaucratic jargon, slogans, and songs; and a densely interwoven music track combining folk and classical melodies with incidental sound. The film also demonstrated that Jancsó was an absolute master of the new aesthetics, whose cinematic structures are depend-ent upon widescreen composition, the long take, and the zoom lens. *The Round-Up* was shot by the cinematogra-pher Tamás Somló (b. 1929), who worked with Jancsó on his next film as well.

Jancsó continued his bold stylistic experiments in a series of films whose symbolic subject was Hungary's past but whose real theme was Hungary's present and future. All were characterized by the abstract, mytho-graphic, and sometimes theatrical quality visible in *The Round-Up*, but they tended to extend these modes to the very limits of coherence. *The Red and the White* (*Csillagosok, katonák*, 1967) was concerned with Hun-garians fighting in the Red Army in 1918 during the civil

war in Russia. It employed sustained lateral tracking and widescreen composition brilliantly to visualize the con-stantly shifting balance of power between two great armies massed against one another in empty space. *Silence and Cry* (*Csend és kiáltás*, 1968) was set in 1919 just after the fall of the Red Republic of Councils, at the time of the White Terror, when police were hunting down and punishing anyone suspected of radical sympa-thies. Like *The Round-Up*, it is a film about degradation, torture, alienation, and betrayal. *Silence and Cry* was also Jancsó's first film with the cinematographer János Kende (b. 1941), who has been his almost constant col-laborator ever since. *The Confrontation* (*Fényes szelek*, 1969), Jancsó's first film in color, dealt with student dis-turbances in 1947 (procommunist students picketing, heckling, and bullying to force the closure of Catholic

16.39 Symbolic use of nudity in Jancsó's *The Red and the White* (1967).

schools), but it had obvious reference to contemporary student unrest. Yet it was the director's most stylized film to date, a virtual ballet for camera and sound track in which every gesture had ritual significance.

In *Winter Wind* (*Téli sirokkó*, 1969), a film composed of only thirteen shots, some as long as 10 minutes, a group of Croatian nationalists are being trained to assassinate King Alexander of Yugoslavia on the Hungarian-Yugoslav border. Again, Jancsó's theme is the destructive effects of political terror on the individual will. In *Agnus Dei* (*Égi bárány*, 1970), set like *Silence and Cry* during the defeat of the Republic of Councils, Jancsó went further than ever before in the direction of symbolic abstraction. This beautiful color film is essentially a celebration of the revolutionary spirit; in it, all dialogue takes the form of quotations from the Bible or from national songs. With *Red Psalm* (*Még kér a nép*, 1972), Jancsó produced his masterpiece. Composed of fewer than thirty shots, this film is a stunning symbolic analysis of the revolutionary process, its psychological and social preconditions, and its ultimate, necessary failure. For 80 minutes, camera and lens move incessantly, circling and encircling the choric participants in the drama—historically, an abortive agrarian socialist rebellion in the late nineteenth century. Music and sound, color, focus—virtually every element in the film—work in concert to make *Red Psalm* a film of nearly perfect formal beauty, great humanity, and awesome cinematic power. Jancsó won the Golden Palm at Cannes for its direction in 1972. Jancsó's twelve-shot *Elektreia* (*Szerelmem, Elektra*, 1974) extended his abstractionist vision into the realm of Greek myth, but not without his characteristic political subtext: the film is adapted from a play by László Gyurkó that uses the Electra legend as an allegory of the Stalinist period to explore the morality of making reprisals against a tyrant's henchmen after his death.

After the Italian-Yugoslavian coproduction *Private Vices and Public Virtues* (*Vizi privati, pubbliche virtù*, 1976), loosely based on the Mayerling affair that had scandalized the Austro-Hungarian court in the last days of the empire, Jancsó returned to his national heritage and began work on an ambitious trilogy intended to represent Hungarian history from the turn of the century through World War II. Only two parts have so far been completed: *Hungarian Rhapsody* (*Magyar rapszódia*, 1979) and *Allegro Barbaro* (1979), which were shown as *Hungarian Rhapsody, Parts I* and *II* at Cannes in 1979, when Jancsó was awarded the Special Jury Prize for the entire body of his work. The films symbolically reconstruct the life of a single young man, István Zsdányi, based on the historical figure of Endre Bajcsy-Zsilinszky, who incarnated much of twentieth-century Hungarian politics. Bajcsy-Zsilinszky was the son of a minor aristocrat, who began his career as a counterrevolutionary terrorist under Horthy, became a leader of the radical peasant party during the 1930s, and was executed by the Nazis in 1944 as the head of the Hungarian Resistance. Together the films represent the consummation of Jancsó's mature style (*Allegro Barbaro*, for example, is a masterpiece of widescreen choreography for camera containing only twenty-two shots), and afterward he began to experiment with drama on a more intimate scale. *The Tyrant's Heart, or Boccaccio in Hungary* (*A zsarnok szíve, avagy Boccaccio Magyarországon*, 1981), for example, is a Hamlet-like parable of royal intrigue con-

16.40 The aesthetics of widescreen space: Jancsó's *The Red and the White* (1967) and *Red Psalm* (1972).

fined to a fifteenth-century Hungarian palace and shot entirely in the studio. *L'Aube* (*Dawn*, 1986)[4]—a French-Israeli coproduction made for television and Jancsó's first color feature shot without János Kende—takes place in a single room in the course of one night in 1947 as Israeli freedom fighters debate the morality of killing a British hostage. Jancsó has also made two successful feature-length documentaries—*Music* (*Muzsika*, 1984), a striking portrait of Budapest, and *Omega, Omega* (1985), a record of a 1982 rock concert—as well as *Faustus, Faustus, Faustus* (1985), the widely hailed nine-part adaptation of László Gyurkó's controversial novel on the past fifty years of Hungarian history entitled *The Blessed Descent to Hell of Dr. Faustus* (*Faustus Doktar boldogságos pokoljorása*), for national television. In 1987, Jancsó returned to theatrical feature-filmmaking with *Season of Monsters* (*Szörnyek évadja*), a surrealistic tale of contemporary suicide splendidly photographed by János Kende. More recently, Jancsó directed *Jesus Christ's Horoscope* (*Jézus Krisztus horoszkópja*, 1989), a visually and aurally brilliant work—his most thematically challenging in years, though many thought it self-indulgent. Not so Jancsó's next two films, which demonstrated the durability of his signature style of long takes, female nudity, mass groupings, and song. *God Walks Backwards* (*Isten hátrafelé megy*, 1991) is a self-reflexive allegory set in a deserted police academy shortly after the withdrawal of Soviet troops in 1989, where rival Hungarian groups feud among themselves until the Russians return to annihilate them all. *The Blue Danube Waltz* (*Kék Duna keringö*, 1992), a sharply observed satire on the political environment of post-Soviet Hungary, is similarly framed by Jancsó's stylistic trademarks and revolves around a political assassination in a posh Budapest hotel.

It has often been said of Jancsó that all of his films seem to be one and the same. But this criticism against consistency of vision might apply equally to Bergman, Antonioni, Ozu, and many other masters of contemporary cinema. The mysterious, mythopoeic qualities of Jancsó's images and structures, his symbolic use of song and ritual to embody his themes of human submission and domination, his seeming closeness to the earth, all remind one of Dovzhenko—but a Dovzhenko who has consciously and willfully rejected montage. Jancsó's mastery of widescreen composition and the extended long take alone would assure him a permanent place in the history of film. But Jancsó has always used this technical mastery to make films of hallucinatory beauty, profound feeling, and great intellectual depth. And it is this, above all else, that makes him one of the great artists of the modern cinema, as well as Hungary's greatest national film poet.

GAÁL, SZABÓ, AND MÉSZÁROS

Three other Hungarian filmmakers who have achieved international distinction within the past two decades are István Gaál (b. 1933), István Szabó (b. 1938), and Márta Mészáros (b. 1931). Gaál graduated from the Academy for Dramatic and Cinematographic Art in 1959 and studied for two years on an Italian State Scholarship at the Centro Sperimentale in Rome before returning to Budapest to join the experimental Béla Balázs Studio as one of its founding directors. There he made a series of shorts (for example, *Tisza—Autumn Sketch* [*Tisza—őszi vázlatok*, 1963]) before venturing the semiautobiographical trilogy, *Current* (*Sodrásban*, 1964), *The Green Years* (*Zöldár*, 1965), and *Baptism* (*Keresztelö*, 1967), which focuses on a recurring theme in new Hungarian cinema—the situation of the intellectual who comes from peasant origins, and the radical division between town and country in contemporary Hungary. *The Falcons* (*Magasiskola*, 1970), widely regarded as Gaál's masterpiece, is set on the Great Plain in a falconry camp that becomes a paradigm for Hungarian fascism and its retreat into the feudal past. This brilliant study of the authoritarian mentality, which took a prize at Cannes, creates a kind of concrete poetry in its Jancsó-like camera movement, relentlessly dynamic editing, and stunning manipulations of color and sound. *Dead Landscape* (*Holt vidék*, 1971), inspired by the actual case of the deserted village of Gyürüfü, is an investigation of the ways in which people interact with their environment—here, three who have chosen to stay on in a small, decaying rural village after the rest of the population has moved away. At first, the lack of community seems a challenge to them, but it leads with mounting horror to loneliness, alienation, and psychological disintegration for all three. Though he now works slowly (having made only three theatrical features since 1971—*Legato* [1977], *Buffer Zone* [*Cserepek*, 1981], and a version of Gluck's opera *Orpheus and Eurydice* [*Orfeus és Eurydike*, 1985]), Gaál is very much a personal *auteur*

---

4. The film adapts the second novel in Elie Wiesel's Holocaust trilogy, consisting of *Night*, *Dawn*, and *The Accident*.

16.41 Istán Gaál's *Dead Landscape* (1971).

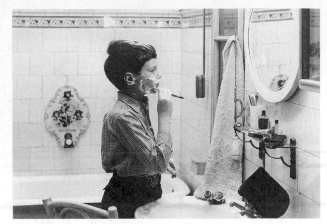

16.42 *Father* (István Szabó, 1966): Dániel Erdélyi.

who has written all of his own scripts and edited all of his own films. He also has always worked with the same composer, András Szöllősy, one of Hungary's most prominent modernists. In addition, Gaál often functions as his own art director and sometimes collaborates on the camera work (as was the case in *The Falcons*).

István Szabó (pronounced "Shahbow") graduated from the Budapest Academy in 1961 and immediately joined the Béla Balázs Studio, where he directed two acclaimed shorts, *Variations on a Theme* (*Variációk egy témára*, 1961) and *You* (*Te*, 1963), the last of which has become a minor classic and the most-awarded short in Hungarian film history. His first feature, *The Age of Daydreaming* (*Álmodozások kora*, 1964), follows the fortunes of five newly graduated engineers as they set out to conquer the world in the optimistic 1960s, and it bears the marked influence of the French New Wave, especially Truffaut, to whom it contains several explicit *hommages*. *Father* (*Apa*, 1966), a more tightly constructed and ambitious film, concerns a young man's attempts to come to terms with his dead father's reputation as a partisan hero of World War II in the context of his own involvement with the 1956 revolution. In its concern with the impingement of the past on the present and future, *Father* is closer in theme to Resnais than to Truffaut, and Szabó's next two films actually employ many of Resnais's editing techniques: flashbacks cued by association, the repetition of significant scenes

with slight variations, the steady integration of past and present through montage. These techniques characterize both *Love Film* (*Szerelmesfilm*, 1970), which focuses on a single couple separated by the events of 1956 who now seek reunion, and *25 Fireman's Street* (*Tüzoltó utca 25*, 1973), a stylistically and structurally difficult film about the "dreams" experienced by an old house in Budapest on the eve of its demolition. *Budapest Tales* (*Budapesti mesék*, 1976) is a picaresque work that provides an allegory of the Hungarian postwar condition as a group of survivors organize to push an abandoned streetcar from the outskirts of the city into Budapest. *Confidence* (*Bizalom*, 1979) is a restrained film shot in beautifully muted color by Lajos Koltai; it depicts a man and a woman living together in a Budapest suburb under false identities in the closing days of World War II; they begin in distrust but end as lovers.

With the Hungarian–West German coproduction *Mephisto* (1981), Szabó achieved his first great international success and reached a watershed in his career. Freely adapted by the director and Péter Dobai from Klaus Mann's 1936 novel (which itself was based on the career of the famous German actor Gustaf Gründgens, who married Mann's sister), this uncharacteristically dark film chronicles the Machiavellian climb to fame of the provincial actor Hendrik Höfgen (Klaus Maria Brandauer) during the Nazi era. From playing with a left-wing theater troupe in Hamburg in 1929, he rises to the directorship of Berlin's National Theater by 1936 through a series of personal betrayals and artistic compromises that make him a

16.43 *Love Film* (István Szabó, 1970).

favorite of the Nazi elite. At the pinnacle of his good fortune, however, Hendrik is forced to realize that he has made a truly Faustian bargain with the Nazis, who now own his soul. Distinguished by its superb performances, rich period detail, and Lajos Koltai's multitextured cinematography, *Mephisto* won many international awards, including the Cannes Jury Prize for Best Screenplay, the International Film Press Federation (FIPRESCI) Prize for Best Picture, and the American Academy Award for Best Foreign Film (all 1982). Szabó's next endeavor reunited the *Mephisto* team (Dobai, Koltai, Brandauer, and the producer Manfred Durniok) to create the Hungarian–West German–Austrian coproduction *Colonel Redl* (*Redl Ezredes/Oberst Redl*, 1985), based on the life of Alfred Redl, who was head of the Austro-Hungarian political police near the outbreak of World War I. An open homosexual, Redl was accused of being a Russian agent as well and was forced to commit suicide to smooth over his political and sexual indiscretions. Another dark study of the ravages of ambition and obsession, *Colonel Redl* stands as Szabó's most complex and impressively mounted film to date, and it took the Jury Prize at Cannes. *Hanussen* (1988)—similarly scripted by Szabó, shot by Koltai, and starring Brandauer—is also based on a real character, in this case a psychic who briefly became the darling of the National Socialists between the wars and was later murdered by them. After the unsuccessful English-language production *Meeting Venus* (1991), in which an opera company's troubled efforts to stage Wagner's *Tannhäuser* in Paris become a metaphor for contemporary Europe, Szabó returned to Hungary to make *Sweet Emma, Darling*

16.44 *Mephisto* (István Szabó, 1981): Klaus Maria Brandauer behind the mask.

16.45 Szabó's *Colonel Redl* (1985): Klaus Maria Brandauer in the title role.

Bobe—Sketches, Nudes (*Édes Emma, drága Böbe—vázlotok, aktok*, 1992), a highly structured, novelistic account of *anomie* in post-Soviet Hungary that follows the lives of two country girls working as teachers in contemporary Budapest. Unlike Jancsó, who often improvises while on location from a basic outline of dialogue and action, Szabó works from a meticulously detailed—and almost always original—shooting script of his own device (*Mephisto* is his only film to date to be adapted from the work of another). This scrupulous preplanning has meant that each of his films has engaged Szabó for at least two years, but once in production, he seems capable of adapting to whatever circumstances are dictated by the shoot.

Márta Mészáros (pronounced "Messarowsh") was born in Budapest in 1931 but grew up in the Soviet Union where her leftist father, the noted sculptor László Mészáros, was forced to emigrate in 1936 (and where he later died in prison during the Stalinist purges). She attended the VGIK in Moscow on scholarship and worked briefly in the Romanian industry after graduating in 1956. In 1959 she returned to Budapest where she made some thirty documentary shorts before directing her first feature, *The Girl* (*Eltávozott nap*, 1968), which announced both the style and theme of her later features—a documentary-like flatness of presentation combined with a deep and abiding concern for the situation of women and children within contemporary Hungarian society. Like *The Girl*, in which a young woman raised in a state orphanage searches for her biological parents, most of Mészáros's films involve an independent woman who finds herself faced with making an important decision on her own, and they tend to be both intimate and open-ended. In *Binding Sentiments* (*A "holdudvar*," 1969), for example, an alcoholic[5] mother and her son's fiancée play a cat-and-mouse game at a hillside villa overlooking Lake Balaton; and *Don't Cry, Pretty Girls* (*Szép lányok, ne sírjatok*, 1970) recounts a romance between a city-bred musician and a country girl at a youth hostel. After the documentary feature *Women at the Spinnery/At the Lörinc Spinnery* (*A Lörinci fonóban*, 1971), Mészáros made *Riddance/Free Breath* (*Szabad lélegzet*, 1973), which focuses on the struggles of a factory girl and her student lover to maintain their relationship against the prejudicial demands of his parents. *Adoption* (*Örökbefogadás*, 1975), winner of the Grand Prix at Berlin, is widely regarded as Mészáros's most aesthetically and psychologically satisfying feature to date. It concerns a middle-aged woman who wants to have a child by her married lover. She

befriends a young girl from a nearby community house, "adopts" her spiritually, and helps her toward marriage with her boyfriend. For this film, Mészáros adopted a fluid visual style to chart the changing emotional relationships between the two women.

In *Nine Months* (*Kilenc hónap*, 1976), winner of the FIPRESCI Prize at Cannes and Mészáros's first film in color, a factory woman with a child has an affair with a company engineer and becomes pregnant, but neither can compromise his or her individuality sufficiently to form a relationship; and the woman leaves him to bear her second child alone (Lili Monori, the Mészáros regular who played this part, was pregnant at the time, and the birth of her child was photographed for inclusion in the film). *Two of Them* (*Ők ketten*, 1977) deals with a cross-generational relationship similar to that of *Adoption*. Mari, the middle-aged director of a hostel for working women, is trapped in a dead marriage in an industrial town. Juli is a factory girl saddled with an alcoholic husband. The two women form a meaningful but troubled friendship in a world in which there are clearly no easy answers for either gender. In *Just Like at Home* (*Olyan, mint otthon*, 1978), whose strangely lyrical beauty owes much to the cinematography of Lajos Koltai, Mészáros shifts focus to study the male psyche from a female perspective in the haunting story of the relationship that develops between an alienated intellectual and a ten-year-old girl. With *The Heiresses/The Heritage* (*Örökség*, 1980), a French-Hungarian coproduction, she produced a period film that mirrored her contemporary themes. During the rise of Nazism and World War II, a wealthy but sterile woman persuades a Jew to have a child by her husband in order to inherit her father's estate. The husband eventually falls in love with the surrogate wife, and his real wife responds by having the husband arrested for violating the Nuremberg Laws and the Jewish woman deported to Auschwitz. *Mother and Daughter/Anna* (*Anna és leánya*, 1981), Mészáros's second French-Hungarian film, concerns a middle-aged woman hunting in contemporary Budapest and Paris for her long-lost daughter, who disappeared in the wake of the 1956 uprising. More recently, *Land of Miracles* (*Délibábok országa*, 1983) is a version of Gogol's *The Inspector General*. *Diary for My Children* (*Napló gyermekeimnek*, 1984) is a small-

---

5. Hungary has inordinately high rates of alcoholism, suicide, and divorce.

16.46 *Just Like at Home* (Márta Mészáros, 1978): Zsuzsa Czinkóczi, Jan Nowicki.

scale but intensely personal autobiographical work about a young girl's coming of age during the grimmest years of Stalinism, 1947–53, that won the Special Jury Prize at Cannes.[6] Its sequel, *Diary for My Loves* (*Napló szerelmeimnek*, 1987), continues her story from 1949 through the fateful year of 1956. Mészáros next made *Bye Bye, Red Riding Hood* (*Piroska és a farkas*, 1989), adapting the classic German fairy tale as a children's film with feminist overtones, and she completed her *Diary* trilogy in 1990 with *Diary for My Father and Mother* (*Napló apámnak, anyámnak*), a complex representation of the 1956 uprising and the terror that followed. More recently, she wrote and directed *Fetus* (*Foetus*, 1994), a powerful feature about a wealthy woman's overwhelming desire for a child that won several major festival awards, and *The Seventh Room* (*Siódmy pokój*, 1994), produced for Poland's Studio Tor. All of Mészáros's films since 1982 have been photographed by her former stepson Miklós ("Nyika") Jancsó, Jr. (she was married to Miklós Jancsó from 1960 to 1973). On one level, Mészáros bears witness to Hungarian society from a consciously female perspective to confront issues usually ignored by Eastern European (and most other) cinema: the subjugation of women in a patriarchal system, the dissolution of traditional family structures, the plight of children raised without parental affection or control. But on another level, as Derek Elley has observed, her theme is the search by all people "for human warmth and companionship in a present-day, industrialized society,"[7] and she

has created a body of work that shows remarkable stylistic consistency in pursuing it.

OTHER HUNGARIAN DIRECTORS

Other Hungarian directors who have recently attracted world attention are Sándor Sára (b. 1933), Pál Gábor (1932–1987), Péter Bacsó (b. 1928), Ferenc Kósa (b. 1937), Imre Gyöngyössy (1930–1994), Pál Sándor (b. 1939), Zsolt Kézdi-Kovács (b. 1936), Judit Elek (b. 1937), Lívia Gyarmathy (b. 1932), István Dárday (b. 1940), János Rózsa (b. 1937), Ferenc Kardos (1937–1999), Zoltán Huszárik (1931–1981), Pál Zolnay (1928–1995), Gábor Bódy (1947–1985), and Péter Gothár (b. 1945). Sára, primarily a photographer and cameraman (for example, for Gaál's *Current*, Szabó's *Father* and 25 *Fireman's Street*, Zoltán Huszárik's *Sindbad*, and all but one of Ferenc Kósa's features), directed the famous Béla Balázs Studio short *Gypsies* (*Cigányok*, 1963) before making a successful feature debut in *The Upthrown Stone* (*Feldobott kő*, 1968), which deals with the disillusionment of an idealistic intellectual under the dictatorial Rákosi government in the early 1950s; in the end we learn that he has actually made the film we are watching in order to expose that regime's brutality. In the dark satire *Pheasant Tomorrow* (*Holnap lesz fácán*, 1974) a contemporary holiday camp for young people becomes a microcosm of totalitarian society as a middle-aged "Leader" and his friends take control of the establishment and set up a miniature authoritarian state. *Eighty Hussars* (*80 Huszár*, 1978) makes a parable of a true episode from the 1848 revolution: a squadron of hussars deserts the Imperial Army for home in order to fight with the rebels, but only a handful of the men make it back, rendering their heroic gesture futile. In *The Teachers*

6. Shot in black and white, *Diary* had originally included footage from the ludicrously stolid Soviet socialist-realist films of the period, but Mészáros agreed to substitute clips from Hungarian films so as not to irritate the Russians. Her comment on this matter illustrates the rather modest (by Eastern bloc standards) state of film censorship in Hungary at the time: "The same point is made and I did not think this was a great compromise for me. If I insisted on the Soviet footage there would have been a conflict, and I didn't want that" (quoted in William Wolf, "Blue Danube Diary," *Film Comment* 10, 3 [May–June 1984], p. 4).

7. Derek Elley quoted in "Márta Mészáros," *World Film Directors*, vol. II: 1945–1985, ed. John Wakeman (New York: H. W. Wilson, 1988), p. 682. See also Catherine Portuges's excellent critical study *Screen Memories: The Hungarian Cinema of Márta Mészáros* (Bloomington: Indiana University Press, 1993).

16.47 Sándor Sára's *Eighty Hussars* (1978).

(*Néptanitók*, 1982) Sára took his camera to a reunion of the class of 1930 at the University of Pécs, where sixteen men talk of why they chose to become teachers, what the choice has meant to their lives, and how it involved them in the multiple upheavals of twentieth-century Hungarian history. *On the Crossroad* (*Keresztuton*, 1987) is a similarly engaging documentary about the experience of an expatriate Hungarian peasant communist caught murderously between borders during World War II, while *Bábolna* (1986–88) is an ambitious attempt to trace the history of Hungary from 1945 to the mid-1980s through a series of six feature-length documentaries on the fate of the cooperative farm Bábolna. Sára returned to dramatic features in 1988 with *A Thorn under the Fingernail* (*Tüske a köröm alatt*), a rural melodrama directly critical of party corruption.

The features of Pál Gábor, whose debut *Forbidden Ground* (*Tiltott terület*) was the Hungarian entry at Venice in 1969, often take a documentary approach to the problems of modern life. *Horizon* (*Horizont*, 1970), for example, deals with the phenomenon of industrial alienation in a manner similar to that of British New Cinema (see Reisz's *Saturday Night and Sunday Morning*, 1960), a fact Gábor acknowledges by having his protagonist's antiestablishment rebellion sparked by watching Lindsay Anderson's *if . . . (1968) several times. Journey with Jacob* (*Utazás Jakabbal*, 1972) has two young men knocking about together among the small towns and villages of Hungary in their mindless jobs as fire-equipment inspectors, and it bears the influence of such American "road"

films as *Easy Rider* (Dennis Hopper, 1969). *Epidemic* (1976) is an uncharacteristic historical film set during the "cholera rebellion" that rocked northern Hungary in 1831, the first great peasant uprising since the 1500s. Gábor's most successful and widely distributed feature to date is *Angi Vera* (1978), set in 1948 as the Stalinists were asserting their control over the party machinery. The film's youthful heroine, Vera Angi,[8] touchingly portrayed by Veronika Papp, shows early "political consciousness" (that is, Communist leanings) by denouncing her former boss and is sent to a three-month training camp for aspiring party leaders. There, she has an affair with her married teacher István, which she later confesses out of political expediency, ruining him but advancing herself a step further up the party ladder. Written by Gábor and subtly photographed by the brilliant Lajos Koltai, *Angi Vera* is a deeply felt film: Vera's motivations are always ambiguous, at the very least, and her betrayal of István out of party loyalty has a tragic sincerity about it and a resonance for her future life that she can only vaguely understand. More recently, Gábor directed *Wasted Lives* (*Kettévált mennyezet*, 1982)—which is set during the shifting thaw of 1953–55 and also deals with the human consequences of a regime totally committed to politics— and *The Long Ride* (*Hosszú vágta*, 1985), a Hungarian-U.S. coproduction about a peasant boy who helps a downed American flyer escape from the Great Plain into Yugoslavia during World War II. His last film was *The Bride Was Radiant* (*A menyasszony gyönyörüvolt/La sposa era bellissima*, 1987), an ebullient tale of sexual initiation set in Sicily and coproduced with Italy. Gábor died of a heart attack in October 1987, while participating in a forum on Hungarian film in Rome.

Péter Bacsó's work consists mainly of comedies with a sharp satirical edge. *Outbreak* (*Kitörés*, 1970) concerns a disgruntled factory worker who protests his working conditions, a local housing shortage, and other indignities, only to lose his girlfriend and his job for his pains. In *Present Indicative* (*Jelenidő*, 1971) a conscientious factory boss tries to instill his workers with a sense of pride in their jobs to no avail, and in *The Last Chance* (*Harmadik nekifutás*, 1973) a manager improbably decides to take responsibility for his plant's shortcomings and demotes himself to the

---

8. In Hungarian, as mentioned previously, last names precede first names.

16.48 *Angi Vera* (Pál Gábor, 1978): Veronika Papp, Tamás Dunai.

ranks of the workers, who naturally regard him as a madman. In the mid-1970s Bacsó continued to follow his satirical bent in contemporary comedies like *Don't Pull My Beard!* (*Ereszd el a szakállamat!*, 1975) and the absurdist thriller *Alarm Shot* (*Riasztólövés*, 1976), but 1977 saw the release of his bristling satire of the Stalinist show trials, *The Witness* (*A tanú*), made in 1968 but suppressed due to the Warsaw Pact invasion of Czechoslovakia in that year (and not released abroad until 1981). Bacsó's *Electric Shock* (*Áramütés*, 1979) illuminates a contemporary brother-sister relationship, while *Let's Talk about Love* (*Ki beszél itt szerelemröl!?*, 1979) is a light satire on political opportunism. His film *The Man Who Went Up in Smoke* (*A svéd, akinek nyoma veszett*, 1981) was a Hungarian-Swedish coproduction based on a Maj Sjöwall–Per Wahlöö *policier*. In *The Day before Yesterday* (*Tegnapelött*, 1982), strikingly shot in color by János Zsombolyai (b. 1939), Bacsó returned to the period of *The Witness* with a film reminiscent of *Angi Vera* in its tale of a young woman whose revolutionary idealism turns to gall and wormwood when she gives false testimony against her lover; *Oh, Bloody Life!* (*Te rongyos élet . . . !*, 1984) treats the same kind of predicament in the same period, only here a popular young singing star is denounced as a "class enemy" (because she was

once briefly married to an aristocrat) and she is sent to a rural labor camp in an isolated farming village. Bacsó returned triumphantly to black comedy with *What's the Time, Mr. Clock?* (*Hány az óra, Vekker Uro?*, 1985), set in the picturesque little village of Koszeg in 1944, where a popular Jewish watchmaker falls afoul of the invading Nazis but manages to save himself through his gift for split-second timing. *Banana Skin Waltz* (*Banánhéjkeringö*, 1987) is a tragicomedy about greed and corruption within contemporary Hungarian society, while *Titánia, Titánia* (1989) is a savage satire on the excesses of the Ceausescu dictatorship in neighboring Romania. More recently, Bacsó directed the Hungarian-German-Swiss coproduction *Stalin's Fiancée* (*Sztálin menyasszonya*, 1991), a black comedy set in a Ukrainian village during collectivization. For the past two decades, Péter Bacsó has been one of Hungary's most prolific directors, and he has remained remarkably consistent in his absurdist portrayal of horrendous events from recent history. His shooting style is documentary-like and involves great attention to the details of everyday life. Whenever possible he works with nonactors in real locations, although he has also earned a reputation for his ability to evoke strong ensemble performances from professionals.

Ferenc Kósa graduated from the Budapest Academy in 1963 and completed his first feature in 1965, but its release was delayed for political reasons until 1967, when it was justly awarded the Grand Prix at Cannes. The result of years of documentary research, *Ten Thousand Suns* (*Tízezer nap*) traces the life of the peasant-born communist István Széles in flashback through all of the social changes that have overtaken Hungary in the thirty years from his birth through the 1956 revolution. (The title refers both to the ten thousand days of its time frame and to István's vision of a new Utopia when he would see "ten thousand suns" bursting into flames above the sea.) In effect, the film is a complex meditation on whether the benefits brought to Hungary by communism (industrialization, urbanization, positive growth) can ever justify the brutal means used to achieve them. But it is also a richly poetic visual experience that has been compared to the work of Dovzhenko in its lyricism and of Eisenstein in its treatment of mass movement on the screen. Brilliantly photographed in widescreen black and white by Sándor Sára, *Ten Thousand Suns* was a landmark for the new Hungarian cinema both in terms of its political integrity and its striking compositional effects. *Judgment* (*Ítélet*, 1970) was a Romanian-

Yugoslavian coproduction concerning a peasant uprising in 1514, and it was not well received critically; but *Beyond Time* (*Nincs idö*, 1972) proved a worthy successor to *Ten Thousand Suns*, and it was similarly controversial (though not suppressed). Set in a Hungarian prison in 1929, this intentionally baroque film charts the attempts of a weak but well-meaning governor to prevent a hunger strike among political prisoners, mainly communists; he fails in the end, and his job is turned over to the ruthless chief warden, a personification of the authoritarian mentality. In *Snowfall* (*Hószakadás*, 1974), a young soldier sets out across Transylvania with his peasant grandmother in search of his parents, who disappeared in the closing days of World War II. *Portrait of a Champion* (*Küldetés*, 1977), a great popular success with domestic audiences, provides a series of documentary interviews with a former Hungarian Olympic athlete who, in espousing meritocracy, is openly critical of the prevailing social system. *The Match* (*A mérkőzés*, 1981) is set during the tense summer of 1956 and, like Gábor's *Angi Vera* and Bacsó's *The Day after Yesterday*, is concerned with the acceptable limits of political expediency. In a provincial town, the police chief is also manager of the local soccer club; enraged over a miscall that costs his team a game, he kills the referee in a locker-

16.50 *Beyond Time* (Ferenc Kósa, 1972).

room brawl and hastily conceals the crime. When a journalist attempts to investigate the cover-up, his family is threatened, he is arrested, and the district party boss whitewashes the whole affair. In *Guernica* (1982), the first Kósa film not shot by Sára, a young woman who works at a brick factory becomes obsessed with the prospect of nuclear war after watching some television programs on the East-West arms race. She eventually falls in love with an artist who has been moved by seeing Picasso's *Guernica* to devote his life to creating a gigantic sculpture representing the horrors of war in the granite hillside where his pacifist father was killed during World War II; the woman finally journeys to Spain to see the famous painting for herself, and the sculptor is murdered by her jealous boyfriend in her absence. Superbly photographed by Lajos Koltai, *Guernica* introduced a strain of hopelessness into Kósa's work that has remained ever since. His two-part historical drama *The Other Person* (*A másik ember*, 1988) provided yet another impressive display of visual imagination and ideological praxis in two stories of a father's and a son's separate encounters with fascism—the father's as a soldier during World War II and the son's as a student insurgent during the 1956 revolution, with each part filmed magnificently in a style appropriate to its theme.

Imre Gyöngyössy, scriptwriter for Gaál's *The Green Years*, Kósa's *Ten Thousand Suns*, and the Czechoslovak film *Adrift* (Jan Kadár, 1971), made his debut as a director

16.49 Ferenc Kósa's *Snowfall* (1974).

with *Palm Sunday* (*Virágvasárnap*, 1969). Clearly influenced by Jancsó in its stylization of historical events, the film presents the violent demise of the Red Republic of Councils in 1919 as a kind of passion play in which the supporters of the revolution are collectively crucified. In *Legend about the Death and Resurrection of Two Young Men* (*Meztelen vagy*, 1971), Gyöngyössy created an intensely poetic film that works on both the literal level of narrative and the metaphorical level of ritual, symbol, and myth. A young Gypsy returns with a friend to his native settlement determined to help his people rise above their poverty and squalor; but they turn against him, ultimately cutting out his tongue and drowning the friend in a vat of concrete. *Legend* is both an authentic documentary record of Gypsy life and an attempt to re-create that life in the form of myth. As such, it is distinguished by its sophisticated, if ambiguous, montage structure (constantly cutting forward to its own climax, for example, and providing the narrative with three separate conclusions) and the sensual, dreamlike cinematography of János Kende. *Sons of Fire* (*Szarvassá vált fiúk*, 1974), loosely based on the "Stag Boy" legend, concerns the attempted escape of a group of communists from a Hungarian prison at the end of World War II. Once again, Gyöngyössy's provocative associative editing produced a complex, multileveled film that concludes with a *tour de force* montage sequence as the escapees are relentlessly hunted down and killed by local landowners amid scenes of natural plentitude and splendor. The director's subsequent credits include numerous austere documentaries such as *A Quite Ordinary Life* (*Két elhatározás*, 1977), and the features *Expectations* (*Várakozók*, 1975), set in a large family mansion during the siege of Budapest, and *Glimpses of Life* (*Töredék az életről*, 1982), concerning long-concealed tensions in a village to which a successful middle-aged woman returns to celebrate an award at work. Gyöngyössy's most distinguished and commercially successful achievement to date has been the Hungarian–West German coproduction *The Revolt of Job* (*Jób lázadása*, 1983), which he co-directed with Barna Kabay (b. 1949), his assistant since the mid-1970s, from a screenplay by the directors and Katalin Petényi (Gyöngyössy's wife). Perhaps the most accessible of his features, this autobiographical work concerns an elderly Jewish couple—Jób and Roza—who adopt a seven-year-old Christian boy, Lackó, in order to pass on their property and knowledge to him before the Holocaust consumes them.[9] Set in an east Hungarian village in 1943 and 1944, the film re-creates the whole tapestry of Jewish life in a rural community through Lackó's eyes. From his child's perspective, the ominous portents of war and genocide are merely distant thunder until the village world is shattered by the coming of the Nazis. Shot in beautiful autumnal hues by Gábor Szabó, *The Revolt of Job* is finally a celebration of human dignity and courage in the face of impossible odds, as is *That Ye Inherit/In Memory of 450,000 Hungarian Peasant Jews* (*Add tudtul fiadnak*, 1985), a Hungarian–West German television documentary produced by the team of Gyöngyössy, Kabay, and Petényi on the same subject. Made to commemorate the fortieth anniversary of the German defeat in World War II, this film has been praised as the best documentary ever made about the survivors of the Nazi camps. More recently the Gyöngyössy-Kabay-Petényi group completed the Hungarian–West German–Canadian–British coproduction *Yerma*, an adaptation of a moody García Lorca play filmed on location by Szabó in Andalusia, and *Exiles* (*Számüzöttek*, 1992) a semidocumentary feature examining the plight of the present-day Volga German homeless.

Pál Sándor's first films, *Clowns on the Wall* (*Bohóc a falon*, 1967) and *Sarah, My Dear* (*Sárika drágám*, 1971), were French New Wave–influenced works—full of mock *cinéma vérité* interviews and trick photography—about generational conflict within contemporary Hungarian society. But *Football in the Good Old Days* (*Régi idők focija*, 1973) brilliantly combines technical experimentation with serious intentions in its tale of a Chaplinesque soccer manager attempting to field a winning team in Budapest in 1924. Deliberately imitative of American slapstick comedy, which was at the height of its vogue in 1924, the film boasts detailed period reconstruction and is ever mindful of the political tensions seething just beneath the surface of everyday Hungarian life in the wake of 1919 and the counterrevolutionary terror. In *A Strange Role* (*Herkulesfürdői emlék*, 1977) a young Communist boy, disguised as a girl, literally finds asylum in a sanatorium for women after the fall of the Red Republic

---

9. The Holocaust came late to Hungary—not until April 1944, after the Nazis had seized control of the Hungarian government. Aware that time was running out for them, the SS overlords streamlined the Hungarian extermination program, so that 565,000 of the country's 825,000 registered Jews perished within the eight months before January 1945, when Hungary concluded an armistice with the Allies. Hungarian deportation and killing operations were under the direct command of Adolf Eichmann.

of Councils. This moody and melancholic film, distributed in the United States as *Improperly Dressed*, won the Silver Bear at Berlin in 1978. *Deliver Us from Evil* (*Szabadíts meg a gonosztól*, 1979) successfully blends pantomimic humor with a haunting evocation of Budapest in its final stages of wartime exhaustion in December 1944: the theft of a coat from a dancing-school cloakroom sends its attendant on a labyrinthine tour of the bombed-out city and its inhabitants in an effort to retrieve the stolen article. *Ham Actors* (*Ripacsok*, 1981) is a sort of madcap tragicomedy about the seamy side of contemporary show business that harks back stylistically to *Football in the Good Old Days*. Like *Deliver Us*, it is a character-rich fable, subtly photographed by Elemér Ragályi (b. 1939) in luminous Eastmancolor. More recently, Sándor has directed *Daniel Takes a Train* (*Szerencsés Dániel*, 1983—International Critics' Prize, Cannes), a controlled tale of two friends caught up in the stampede to leave Budapest in 1956, and *Just a Movie* (*Csak egy mozi*, 1985), a Truffaut-like film about a film director who finds himself stumped for creative ideas (and a purpose in life) in the midst of shooting a version of *Swan Lake*. Both films contain the Sándor trademarks of whimsy, bizarre characterization, and the stylized camera work and lighting of Ragályi. But *Miss Arizona* (1988) is a more serious affair—a romantic melodrama spanning the turbulent years 1920–45 and focusing on the fate of Hungary's middle-class Jews.

Zsolt Kézdi-Kovács graduated from the Budapest Academy and spent several years as an assistant to Jancsó before making his feature debut with *Temperate Zone* (*Mérsékelt égöv*, 1970), a chamber piece in which three contemporary characters try to come to terms with their respective Stalinist pasts in a series of complicated sequence shots. But it was the extraordinarily beautiful and quite different *Romanticism* (*Romantika*, 1972) that attracted international attention to his work. Set during the Enlightenment, this film concerns a young Hungarian nobleman who rejects his father's "civilized" material values for the philosophical ideal of the noble savage and ends as a kind of wild child, roaming the forests first with a band of local outlaws and finally with a pack of stags. Shot as a series of sustained long takes with zoom and telescopic lenses by János Kende, *Romanticism* bears the marked influence of Jancsó and has the visually rhapsodic quality of his greatest work. *When Joseph Returns* (*Ha megjön József*, 1976) is a probing psychodrama about the relationship that develops between the mother and the wife of a man during his long absence in the merchant marine, and *The Good Neighbor* (*A kedves szomszéd*, 1979) is a similar kind of film about the relationship between a man and his neighbors in an old tenement block. After the somewhat desultory *The Right to Hope* (*A remény joga*, 1982), dealing with a twelve-year-old boy's attempt to reconcile his estranged parents, Kézdi-Kovács staged a magnificent return to form with *Forbidden Relations* (*Visszaesők*, 1983). Based on the transcripts of a true case, the film gives a sensitive account of an incestuous affair that develops between a sister and her half brother in a small rural village, and it is distinguished by its sensuous re-creation of country life and by János Kende's richly textured photography. Kézdi-Kovács and Kende also collaborated on the contemporary drama of divorce *The Absentee* (*A rejtőzködő*, 1985) and *Cry and Cry Again* (*Kiáltás és kiáltás*, 1988), a love story set in the terror-filled postrevolutionary years. More recently Kézdi-Kovács directed *After All* (*És mégis*, 1991), a complex collage of newsreel footage and contemporary narrative examining the past fifty years of Hungarian history.

Judit Elek, another Academy graduate from the banner year 1961, made numerous documentaries before directing her first feature, *The Lady from Constantinople* (*Sziget a szárazföldön*) in 1969. This closely observed portrait of an aging widow who must exchange apartments in Budapest was widely admired for its emotional authenticity and its resonant evocation of the old lady's lost world of memories, memorabilia, and faded dreams. Elek's next two films, *A Hungarian Village* (*Istenmezején*, 1974) and *A Simple Story* (*Egyszerű történet*, 1975), were politically engaged semidocumentaries on the quite different lives of two young girls working in the same contemporary mining town over a period of several years. Using nonprofessional actors, *cinéma vérité*–style interviews, and elaborate montage, she demonstrates the generational conflicts between tradition and modernity lingering on just beneath the surface of the new social order as well as the rootlessness of life in the new industrial towns. During the 1980s, Elek made *Maybe Tomorrow* (*Majd holnap*, 1980), an unadorned story of two married lovers who can never quite bring themselves to make a permanent commitment to one another and leave their respective spouses, and *Maria's Day* (*Mária nap*, 1984), a Chekhovian account of the Szendrey family's reunion at a country house in September 1866 to celebrate the eldest daughter's name day.

This woman had once been married to the revolutionary poet Sándor Petőfi, who was killed during the 1848 revolution, and the film charts the various political and familial tensions proceeding from this circumstance—tensions that still are experienced by Hungarian society as a whole. More recently, Elek directed *Memoirs of a River* (*Tutajosok*, 1991), a historical drama based on an outbreak of anti-Semitism in Austro-Hungary in the 1880s.

Another woman director who uses *cinéma vérité* techniques to deal with the social milieu of contemporary Hungary is Lívia Gyarmathy. Trained as a chemical engineer, Gyarmathy's first feature, *Do You Know Sunday—Monday?* (*Ismeri a szandi mandit?*, 1968), was a sardonic, Formanesque comedy about worker alienation in a large chemical plant. She continued in this vein with *Stop the Music* (*Álljon meg a menet*, 1973), a collage of vignettes of blue-collar life. In the 1980s, she made *Koportos* (1980), an adaptation of József Balázs's novel about an impoverished Gypsy who returns to his village in an attempt to provide a decent burial for his bride, *Every Wednesday* (*Minden szerdán*, 1980), a film about the friendship that grows between an alienated teenager and a philosophical old man, and *Coexistence* (*Együttélés*, 1983), a portrait of a German-Hungarian community seen from the perspective of a couple's mixed marriage. *Now It's My Turn, Now It's Yours* (*Egy kicsit en . . . egy kicsit te . . .*, 1985) is a *cinéma vérité*–style comedy of the domestic tensions among three generations of a family living together in a Budapest apartment, while *Blind Endeavor* (*Vakvilágban*, 1986) weaves together two separate stories of the frustrations of everyday life. More recently Gyarmathy has co-directed three documentary features with Géza Böszörményi—*The Poet György Faludy* (*Faludy György, költö*, 1988), *Recsk 1950–53: The Story of a Secret Forced Labour Camp* (*Recsk 1950–53: Egy titkos kényszermunkatábor története*, 1989), and *Where Tyranny Prevails* (*Hol zsarnokság van*, 1989).

In 1974, another 1961 Academy graduate, István Dárday, pioneered a new genre mixing documentary and fiction in *Holiday in Britain* (*Jutalomutazás*). This satire concerns a peasant boy who wins a musical competition to travel with a government-sponsored youth group to Britain. His mother refuses to let him go, fearing that he will be "changed" by the experience (much as Hungarian rural life has been changed by collectivization), which puts her into direct conflict with the socialist bureaucracy. Shot on location with nonactors improvising from their own real-life roles, *Holiday* is a very funny film but also a markedly serious one in delineating the conflict betweeen a centuries-old peasant mentality and the attitudes of a modern bureaucratic state. Inspired by Dárday's success, the Béla Balázs Studio conducted a yearlong series of experiments on new ways of integrating the forms of documentary and feature films. The result was the genre of the "film-novel" (literally, *filmregény*, also known as "docudrama," "fiction-documentary," and "documentary play"), a kind of sociographic documentary as epitomized by Dárday's *Film Novel—Three Sisters* (*Filmregény—Három nővér*, 1979). This four-and-one-half-hour feature follows the lives of three sisters between the ages of twenty and thirty over a period of two years in contemporary Budapest to provide an authentic portrait of Hungarian society today. Nonactors were cast in roles corresponding to those they play in real life and were then directed to flesh out fictional personalities according to a tightly constructed narrative line (written by Dárday and Györgyi Szalai), which is devised so as to encourage improvisation. This so-called "factional" technique was employed with similar success in the second Dárday-Szalai collaboration, *Point of Departure/Metamorphosis* (*Átváltozás*, 1984). Cut down from eight hours to two hours and thirty-five minutes, this film focuses entirely on the interaction among family members and friends within a two-story suburban home. Dárday's 215-minute *The Documentator* (*A dokumentátor*, 1989) is a semidocumentary examination of the impact of Western-style media on Hungarians' social values and their daily lives. As a mode of analyzing contemporary social problems, the film-novel genre has become extremely popular with Hungarian audiences, and a new production group (Tarsulas)[1] has been established to devote all of its activity to the form.

János Rózsa and Ferenc Kardos, who began their careers by co-directing the Truffaut-inspired film about schoolchildren, *Grimace* (*Gyerekbetegségek*), in 1965, have both made important individual contributions to the new Hungarian cinema. Rózsa's *Dreaming Youth* (*Álmodó ifjúság*, 1974) was based on an autobiographical novel by the great Hungarian film theorist Béla Balázs, while his *Spider Football* (*Pókfoci*, 1976) uses academic infighting at a newly opened technical school as a metaphor for Hun-

---

1. Mozgókép Innovációs Társulás—literally, "Motion Picture Innovation Union."

garian politics. *The Trumpeter* (*A trombitás*, 1979) is a violent but visually poetic epic about an anti-Hapsburg rebellion in the early seventeenth century, seductively photographed by Elemér Ragályi. Rózsa made two films of contemporary life: *Sunday Daughters* (*Vasárnapi szűlők*, 1980), set in a girls' reformatory, and *Mascot* (*Kabala*, 1982), about a brother and sister's futile struggle to reconcile their divorced parents. Next he turned to the highly successful *Witches' Sabbath* (*Boszorkányszombat*, 1984), a lavish fantasy in which all of the famous fairy-tale characters—Little Red Riding Hood, Snow White and the Seven Dwarfs, Cinderella, and so forth—gather together to celebrate the awakening of Sleeping Beauty after her hundred-year slumber. Rózsa returned to contemporary problems in *Love, Mother* (*Csók, Anyu*, 1987), a film about middle-class family disintegration that focuses on the children and their neglect by their fast-track parents. More recently Rózsa has directed *The Little Alien* (*Ismeretlen ismerős*, 1989), a sentimental account of the relationship between a little boy and a lonely woman, and *Brats* (*Félálom* [literally "Half-Asleep"], 1992), a realistic film about a gang of rural adolescents on a rampage in Budapest. Kardos's *Petőfi '73* (1973) was a stylized reconstruction of the 1848 revolution in which the heroes of that revolt (among them, the poet Sándor Petőfi) are portrayed by contemporary young people dressed in jeans and T-shirts. His *Unruly Haiduks* (*Hajdúk*, 1974) concerns a cattle drive by Hungarian patriots during the seventeenth-century uprising also depicted in Rózsa's *The Trumpeter*; it features the magnificent cinematography of János Kende and ends with the Jancsó-like massacre of the peasants and their mercenaries (*haiduks*)[2] by the Austrian army. *The Accent* (*Ékezet*, 1977), by contrast, deals with a civil servant who attempts the hopeless task of bringing "cultural education" to a small factory town. After the relative failure of the contemporary *Once One* (*Egyszeregy*, 1979) and a long hiatus, Kardos returned to strength with the audaciously operatic *Heavenly Hosts* (*Mennyei seregek*, 1984). Set in 1664, when Hapsburg forces were driving the Turks from Hungary, this film concerns the effects on a small community of rescuing a wounded angel, and it is interpenetrated with the elemental symbolism of fire, smoke, light, and water, all heightened by the celestial cinematography of Lajos Koltai and by György Selmeczy's otherworldly score. Decidedly more mundane, Kardos's *Truants* (*Iskolakerülők*, 1989) is a drama set in a boarding school for wayward boys.

Zoltán Huszárik, an eminent graphic artist and painter, entered the Budapest Academy in 1948 and was forced to leave for political reasons three years later. Through the intervention of Károly Makk, he was able to return in 1954, and he finally graduated with the "Béla Balázs generation" in 1961. All of Huszárik's films are extensions of his personal artistic vision that at the same time draw heavily on the native tradition of aestheticism in the fine arts. His internationally famous short, *Elegy* (*Elégia*, 1965), uses the life cycle of the horses of the Great Plain—the oldest of Magyar[3] cultural symbols—to create a lyrical meditation on life and death; and Huszárik's first feature, *Sindbad* (*Szindbád*, 1971), became one of the most highly praised Hungarian films of the decade. Sumptuously photographed by Sándor Sára, it presents the reveries, memories, and dreams of an aging sensualist in *fin de siècle* Budapest in images of astounding formal beauty. What begins as a hedonist's tour through the decadent splendors of the national capital gradually becomes a meditation on the transience of experience itself and the passing away of all things. Huszárik made only one other film before his death in 1981, and it was every bit as visionary as *Sindbad*. *Csontváry* (1980) contains dual narratives of the life of the turn-of-the-century "primitive" painter for whom the film is named and of a stage actor breaking down under the strain of playing Csontváry in the present. Huszárik and cinematographer Péter Jankura present both stories as a series of dazzling *tableaux* of light and color in an attempt to examine the sources of human creativity.

Several other Hungarian directors deserve mention here because at least one of their films has made a singular contribution to world cinema. Pál Zolnay's *Photography* (*Fotográfia*) caused a sensation in 1974 with its documentary account of two photographers who travel about the country soliciting orders for family photographs and inad-

---

2. The *haiduk*, or heroic bandit, is a figure of mythical signficance in the Hungarian and Balkan cinemas, with many of the attributes of the gunfighter in Hollywood Westerns and the *ronin* in Japanese samurai films. Especially in Balkan films, the *haiduk* is romanticized for his patriotic resistance to the Turks during the period of the Ottoman occupation, and in former Yugoslavia, Romania, and Bulgaria the *haiduk* film has become a distinct popular genre.

3. Although a number of other ethnic groups live in contemporary Hungary (including, for example, Gypsies and Romanians), Magyars make up about 95 percent of the population. They are descended from the Magyar tribesmen who migrated to Hungary from the east in the late ninth century and who evolved the present-day Hungarian language (whose official designation is "Magyar").

vertently uncover a long-concealed pair of murders. Shot in *cinéma vérité* style by Elemér Ragályi, *Photography*'s power derives in no small part from Zolnay's actual discovery of the crime (an elderly couple having years ago killed their two daughters) in the process of making the film and his use of photographic evidence from the production to prove it. Zolany's *Embryos* (*Embriok*, 1986) is an equally successful dramatized documentary about a thirty-three-year-old obstetrician/gynecologist's tortured decision to have an abortion. In 1981, Gábor Bódy, one of the founders of the experimental Studio K3 of the Béla Balázs Studio and director of the award-winning short *American Fragment* (1976), delivered the elaborately stylized *Narcissus and Psyche* (*Nárcisz és Psyché*). Based on Sándor Weöres's classic novel-in-verse, it transfers the ancient Greek myth to nineteenth-century Central Europe, where Psyche becomes a revolutionary poetess and Narcissus an epicene dramatist. The film is presented as a series of richly staged widescreen *tableaux* with voice-over narration to simulate novelistic form, and it won wide acclaim for both Bódy and the Hungarian cinema. Péter Gothár's *Time Stands Still* (*Megáll az idő*, 1982), on the other hand, deals very specifically with the recent Hungarian past and also with the experience of an entire generation whose members were teenagers in the early 1960s. (The title refers to both a Hungarian hit song of the era and to the moment of the 1956 revolution.) The film is about coming of age in the grim shadow of the failed uprising, when Hungarian society was being gradually reconstructed along Western lines. Even as the young men and women of this period begin to experience American rock and roll (which makes up most of the sound track), liberated sex, and Coca-Cola, the past weighs heavily upon them. The two young heroes are discriminated against because their father is an exiled freedom fighter; teachers appear and disappear at school according to the prevailing political climate; and there are strange unspoken tensions among neighbors who have betrayed other neighbors in the aftermath of the revolt. Charged with a nervous energy reminiscent of Truffaut's *Les Quatre cents coups* (1959) and Malle's *Le Souffle au coeur* (1971), *Time Stands Still* focuses consistently on its adolescent protagonists; but their passage from youthful rebellion to social assimilation has obvious reference to the journey of the whole national body politic since 1956. In the background of their story, we witness Hungary growing progressively more affluent with every passing year, and when the film ends it is hard

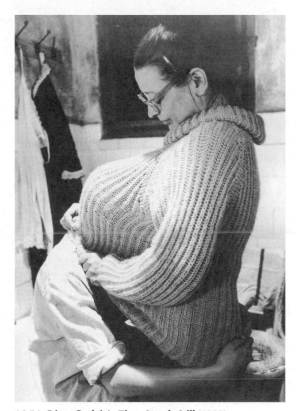

16.51 Péter Gothár's *Time Stands Still* (1982).

not to feel that these young people have been induced to "grow up"—in the same way that their parents' aspirations for freedom have been bought off—by the state with consumer goods. Like so many recent Hungarian films, *Time Stands Still* is notable for its subtle visual texture as well as for its intelligence and vitality of spirit. Lajos Koltai's cinematography achieves a strikingly expressive range of color (and black and white for the pretitle sequence in which we see the father defect in the last hours of fighting), and Gothár uses slow motion, dissolves, and freeze frames with both discretion and dramatic effect. Unfortunately, Gothár's subsequent films—*Time* (*Idő van*, 1985) and *Just Like America* (1987)—have not been able to equal his debut feature, although *Melodrama: Love and Freedom* (*Melodráma: Szabadság és szerelem*, 1991), in its mixture of historical incident (the 1968 Warsaw Pact invasion of Czechoslovakia) and wry comedy, comes close, as does *The Section* (*Részleg*, 1995), a Communist-era romance set in the Carpathians.

As the preceding account should make clear, the Hungarian cinema is one of the most politically acute and sensuously beautiful in the world today. Before the collapse of Communism, it produced only twenty to twenty-five features per year on an average budget of $300,000 per film, but it was the only cinema in Eastern Europe to have *consistently* maintained an international standing since its inception, and especially since World War II. Even today, scholastic standards for admission to the Academy of Dramatic and Cinematographic Art in Budapest are as rigorous as those of an American medical school—by the late 1980s, for example, there were twenty-seven applicants for every position—and it is militantly craft-oriented. All prospective directors are required first to study screenwriting and cinematography, and the industry itself is notoriously exclusive. (Between 1978 and 1983, Hungary's 121 theatrical features were directed by only 70 persons.) Before 1990, as in other Eastern European countries, the state film monopoly, Mafilm, was divided into five semi-autonomous production groups (including the Béla Balázs Studio) that turned out documentaries, animated shorts, children's films, film-novels, and regular features, which were marketed through the state distribution agency, Hungarofilm. Hungary also has the only Eastmancolor processing plant in the former Eastern bloc, and in the late 1980s it had begun an aggressive campaign of coproduction with the West.

In May 1988, Károly Grósz replaced the aged János Kádár as party secretary and began reforms that paved the way for democracy from the top down. The following year, the events of 1956 were officially declared a "popular uprising" rather than a "counterrevolution"; Imre Nagy was rehabilitated, his body exhumed from an unmarked grave and publicly reburied with honor. The Communist party dissolved itself in October, and by the end of the year, Hungary finally had gained its freedom. In 1990, however, Hungary experienced a severe financial crisis resulting from its early embrace of *nyilvánosság*, the Magyar equivalent of *glasnost*. (Socialist Hungary had introduced market principles into its economy as early as the 1970s, producing a so-called "goulash communism" which by 1989 had badly failed.) At that time, Hungary had the highest per capita national debt of any Eastern European country, and inflation was running at 27 percent, hitting 35 to 40 percent by mid-1991. Mafilm director Zsolt Kézdi-Kovács calculated that the annual film production budget for 1990, frozen for the past two years, had lost 30 percent of its value in real terms. There was

near panic in the industry as distribution was opened to the U.S. majors and Hungarian audiences—never particularly enamored of their national cinema's exquisite refinement—flocked to see American blockbusters. The industry came to a virtual standstill in early 1990, and rumors abounded that the Mafilm studio complex was about to be sold to the French.

Following the first noncommunist elections in March 1990, the new government mandated the privatization of state-run enterprises and the introduction of foreign investment. By the summer of 1991, however, in the midst of its transition to market capitalism, the government had also created a structure for the continued flow of state funds into the film industry—the Motion Picture Foundation of Hungary (Magyar Mozgókép Alapítvány). This institution is run by industry representatives through a series of advisory boards, and it is charged with funding individual projects on the basis of artistic merit, with 60 percent reserved for projects submitted by the major Mafilm studios and 40 percent for individuals and other companies. (The latter provision is an effort to encourage foreign investment in the numerous small production companies that have sprung up since the end of Communism.) The Motion Picture Foundation seems to ensure the continued existence of Hungary's cinema, if not its restoration to full strength. In 1991, for example, only fourteen Hungarian-produced features were released. Yet despite its recent economic afflictions, decades of political repression, and its relatively small size (population 10 million; land mass 35,919 square miles)—Hungary has evolved an extraordinarily sophisticated national film culture, requiring, for example, four years of academic film study in all of its public high schools. Moreover, there have traditionally been fewer constraints on filmmakers (and artists generally) in Hungary than in any other country in Eastern Europe, in part because the Hungarians were committed to a policy of gradual liberalization since the failure of their premature rebellion in 1956. The nation's turn toward democracy since the fall of 1989 guarantees its artists ever greater freedom. It is wholly indicative of the Hungarian cinema's resilience that one of its most remarkable films of the decade was produced in that worst year (1989–90) of its postwar history—Ildikó Enyedi's feature debut *My 20th Century (Az én XX. század)*, an astonishing, fabulistic display of the century's technological promise and ideological failure, whose keen stylistic mastery won it the 1989 Camera d'Or at Cannes. Seed money from

16.52 *My 20th Century* (Ildikó Enyedi, 1989).

spanning the most critical decades of modern Hungarian history, coproduced with Austria, Canada, and Germany. Veterans like Jancsó (e.g., *The Lord's Lantern in Budapest* [*Nekem lámpást adott kezembe az Úr Pesten,* 1999]) and Mészáros (*Little Vilma: The Last Diary* [*Kisvilma—az utolsó napló,* 2000], a prequel to her *Diary* trilogy) continued to produce interesting, if unpopular, work. But the chief provocateur of the Hungarian cinema during the 1990s was Béla Tarr (b. 1955), whose slow, visually stylized black-and-white sequence shots imparted a haunting, Wellesian beauty to grim psychological dramas like *Damnation* (*Kárhozat,* 1988), *Werckmeister Harmonies* (*Werckmeister harmóniák,* 2000), and above all his masterpiece, *Satan's Tango* (*Sátántangó,* 1994), a seven-hour epic of bleakness and apocalyptic despair judged by many critics to be the last great film of the twentieth century. Beginning as a straight social realist in the mode of Ken Loach and the style of John Cassavetes (e.g., *Family Nest* [*Családi tüzfészek,* 1979]; *The Outsider* [*Szabadgyalog,* 1981]; *Prefab People* [*Panelkapcsolat,* 1982]), by the mid-1990s Tarr had evolved a unique and expressive cinematic voice, working closely with cinematographer Gábor Medvigy and cowriter László Kraznahorkai (who also wrote the source novels for *Satan's Tango* and *Werckmeister*) in a way that only rich artistic traditions of the Hungarian cinema could make possible. As the director Imre Gyön-

the state-funded Motion Picture Foundation of Hungary and coproduction subsidies from state television (Magyar Televisio) have facilitated an output of around twenty features a year, but the Hungarian cinema is still very much art-film oriented. Comedies are the exception, with Péter Tímár's retro 1960s musical *Dollybirds* (*Csinibaba*), and Péter Bacsó's contemporary satire *Gulls and Gangsters* (*Balekok és banditák*) both becoming box-office hits in 1997. Other 1990s films enjoying a measure of commercial success were Károly Makk's period drama *The Gambler* (1997), a British-Dutch-Hungarian coproduction that combined incidents from the life of Fyodor Dostoevsky with scenes from his novella of the same title, and István Szabó's *Sunshine* (1999), a Jewish family saga

16.53 *Sunshine* (Istvan Szabo, 1999): a Stalinist choral concert and party rally, occurring shortly after the Communist takeover of Hungary—one of several troubled eras in twentieth-century Hungary represented in the film.

gyössy once said so pointedly of his nation: "We are a small country . . . and we have a very, very difficult language and a very closed culture. Cinema has become for us a kind of international language, to open the doors and to make a dialogue between different cultures, sometimes different continents."

Former Yugoslavia

The Yugoslavs in effect had no national film industry until after World War II, and their cinema did not attract attention abroad until fifteen years thereafter, when the Zagreb school of animation began piling up international awards. With the exception of Poland, no country in Eastern Europe suffered more wartime devastation than Yugoslavia, which had been created at the end of World War I out of six separate republics made up of six Slavic nationalities—the Bosnia Muslims, the Croatians, the Macedonians, the Montenegrins, the Serbs, and the Slovenes.[4] Officially named the "Kingdom of the Serbs, Croats, and Slovenes," the country was founded on December 1, 1918, as a constitutional monarchy to be ruled by Alexander I of Serbia; but King Alexander abolished the constitution in 1929 and ruled as a dictator, changing the country's name to Yugoslavia, which means "land of the South Slavs." Alexander was assassinated by Croatian nationalists in 1934 (the subject of Jancsó's *Winter Wind* [1969]—see p. 640), but his policies were continued by his cousin Prince Paul, acting as regent for the eleven-year-old Peter II. When Paul attempted to ally Yugoslavia with the Axis on March 25, 1941, he was deposed by a military coup that briefly installed Peter II as monarch. The Nazis invaded on April 6 and forced an unconditional surrender within eleven days, after which Yugoslavia was dismembered and divided among the bordering Axis states. Resistance was quickly organized by two separate groups, the Chetniks, led by Colonel (later General) Draža Mihajlović and loyal to the government-in-exile of Peter II, and the communist Partisans, led by Marshal Tito. Cooperating at first, the two groups ended by fighting each other and the brutal Croatian Ustashis (Praetorian Guard) to the death in a savage civil war in which the Partisans, liberally assisted by the Allies, were victorious over all factions. Politically, they won the widespread support of the people and proclaimed Yugoslavia a federal "People's Republic"—modeled on the USSR—

in November 1945, with Tito as party secretary and president. In 1948, Tito broke with Stalin over Yugoslavian self-determination, and the country was expelled from the Cominform (an alliance of communist countries) in June. Tito then turned to the United States and other Western nations for aid; and even though Yugoslavia resumed relations with the Soviet Union in 1955, it developed in the interim an economic system based on worker self-management and regional autonomy quite different from the planned central economies of the rest of the Eastern bloc (it also remained nonaligned in the Cold War, identifying itself, at Tito's behest, with the Third World in international politics). The complexity of Yugoslavia's so-called socialist market economy mirrored the diversity of a state of 24 million people comprising six republics (Slovenia, Croatia, Bosnia and Herzegovina, Serbia, Montenegro, and Macedonia) and two autonomous provinces (Vojvodina and Kosovo), with three official languages (Serbo-Croatian, Slovenian, and Macedonian), three major religions (Eastern Orthodox, Roman Catholic, and Muslim), and two alphabets (Cyrillic, based on Greek, which is generally used by the Serbs as well as by the Bulgarians and the Russians; and Latin, supplemented with diacritical marks, used in Eastern Europe by the Croatians, the Poles, and the Czechs—as well as by the author of this book).

The Yugoslav resistance against the Nazis plus a civil war, known collectively as the National War of Liberation, left 1.9 million of the country's 16 million people dead and its economic infrastructure nearly destroyed. When Belgrade was liberated by the Red Army and the Yugoslav Partisans in October 1944, the country had virtually no material base for film production or distribution, and most of its five hundred theaters were badly damaged by war.

PARTISAN CINEMA AND NATIONALIST REALISM

The new communist government led by former Partisan commander and marshal of Yugoslavia, Josip Broz, known

---

4. The country that calls itself Yugoslavia (or the "Yugoslav Federation") today is made up only of Serbia and Montenegro. It was expelled from the United Nations in September 1992 for waging aggressive war against Croatia and Bosnia-Herzegovina as "part of a systematic campaign toward . . . the creation of an ethnically 'pure' [Serbian] state."

as Tito (1892–1980), quickly established a federal Committee for Cinematography, which in turn established regional committees in each of the six republics. The committee also began construction of a new studio complex, Film City (*Filmski grad*), at Košŭtnak on the outskirts of Belgrade, founded a state film school (the Faculty of Dramatic Arts) at Belgrade, with separate technical institutes at Belgrade and Zagreb, and established the monthly journal *Film* as a forum for criticism, polemics, and theoretical debate. By 1951, in spite of the economic dislocations that followed Tito's dramatic break with Stalin and Yugoslavia's expulsion from the Cominform in June 1948, centrally administered subsidies from the State Film Fund had increased over ten times and the country had produced thirteen features. Most of these were patriotic Partisan war epics,[5] such as Vjekoslav Afríc's *Slavica* (1947, Yugoslavia's first dramatic feature) and France Štiglic's *On Their Own Ground* (*Na svojij zemlji*, 1948), or dramas of socialist reconstruction like Vladimir Pogačić's *Story of a Factory* (*Priča o fabrici*, 1949), and they all followed the principles of "nationalist realism," Yugoslavia's more moderate variant of Zhdanovian socialist realism. (A notable exception was Radoš Novaković's *Sofka* (1948), adapted from the classic nineteenth-century Serbian novel *Impure Blood* [*Nečista krv*] by Borisav Stanković.) During this same period, however, Yugoslavia produced over five hundred compilation films, documentary shorts, and newsreel segments (known collectively as *kinokronika*) that graphically documented horrors of the National War of Liberation and early socialist efforts to rebuild the country. Finally, by 1951, central studios were in operation in all six of the republics, and the number of Yugoslav theaters had nearly doubled to some 920 (as had domestic ticket sales, from 31,520,000 in 1946 to 67,926,000 by the end of 1950).

On June 27, 1950, the National Assembly passed the "Basic Law on the Management of State Economic Enterprises and Higher Economic Associations by the Work Collectives," more commonly known as the law on workers' self-management, which, as Daniel J. Goulding points out, became the second founding myth of the postwar Yugoslav state (after the National War of Liberation). This legislation introduced Tito's unique concept of a socialist market economy, in which ownership was neither solely private nor public, but rather administered for the state through a trusteeship of autonomous workers' councils. For the fledgling film industry, this meant the dis-

solution of the Committee for Cinematography and the formation of the Union of Film Workers of Yugoslavia (Savez filmskih radnika Jugoslavije), whose production groups were theoretically free to raise their own funds through distribution contracts, leasing and rental fees, coproduction royalties, and the like, just as in the West. In practice, however, the industry was too underdeveloped for these arrangements, and the new system did not get off the ground until the passage of the Basic Law of Film in 1956, which replaced state subsidies with a tax on film admission tickets (17 to 20 percent), the lion's share of which went to finance new production. This mode of self-finance (*samofinansiranja*) enabled the rate of domestic production to rise from six films per year through 1954 to fourteen films annually from 1957 through 1960. During the same period, admissions for domestic films more than tripled, and for foreign films (mainly American, owing to Tito's temporary break with Moscow) doubled. Furthermore, nineteen coproductions had been undertaken by the end of the decade, many of them with Western countries,[6] including Helmut Käutner's *The Last Bridge* (*Die letzte Brücke*, 1954), Giuseppe

---

5. Partisan films are popular not only in Yugoslavia, where the term designates an actual political faction during the National War of Liberation, but all over the Balkans and in the Soviet Union, where they are sometimes referred to by English-speaking critics as "Easterns" (i.e., eastern Westerns). They tell action-packed stories of heroic resistance to fascism during World War II, usually focusing on a small band of young guerrilla fighters operating out of isolated areas in the countryside. American critics, unfamiliar with this genre, failed to notice that John Milius's *Red Dawn* (1985) was a domestic version of the Eastern European Partisan film in almost every detail, including its reactionary politics.

6. Like southern California, Yugoslavia boasted a richly varied topography and was long a favored site for foreign production and coproduction (one of the reasons, in fact, that the country was so long in developing an authentic national cinema). Within the space of 98,766 square miles—approximately the size of Wyoming—there were the alpine regions of Slovenia; the wooded farmlands of south Serbia; the plains of the Vojvodina; the beautiful Adriatic coastline of Croatia; and, in Macedonia, areas reminiscent of the Pacific Northwest. Furthermore, as in other Eastern European countries, professional salaries and shooting costs were low by Western standards. Well-known "Western" films shot in Yugoslavia in whole or in part include J. Lee Thompson's *The Guns of Navarone* (1961), Orson Welles's *The Trial* (1962), Brian G. Hutton's *Kelly's Heroes* (1971), Norman Jewison's *Fiddler on the Roof* (1971), Sam Peckinpah's *Cross of Iron* (1977), Volker Schlöndorff's *The Tin Drum* (1979), Alan J. Pakula's *Sophie's Choice* (1982), Brian G. Hutton's *High Road to China* (1983), Rudy De Luca's *Transylvania 6–5000* (1985), and Jim Kaufman's *Race for the Bomb* (1987); also the "American" telefilms *Mussolini* (1985), *Guts and Glory* (1985), *Winds of War* (1985), *Wallenberg* (1986), *Escape from Sobibor* (1987), and *War and Remembrance* (1987).

De Santis's *A One-Year Trip* (*Cesta duga godinu dana*, 1958), Gillo Pontecorvo's *The Great Blue Road* (*Veliki plavi put*, 1958), and Claude Autant-Lara's *Thou Shalt Not Kill* (*Tu ne tueras point*, 1961).

For Yugoslav film itself, the 1950s witnessed a move away from nationalist realism and an expansion in the range of subject matter and genres. There were successful comedies, such as the Czech émigré director František Čap's *Vesna* (1953), and the debut of Yugoslavia's first woman director, Soja Jovanović (1922–2002), with *Father Círa and Father Spira* (*Pop Círa i pop Spira*, 1957), the country's first color feature and winner of the first prize at the Pula Festival (inaugurated in 1953 to showcase all new Yugoslav features). Literary-historical films—like Fedor Hanžeković's (1913–1997) version of Simo Matavulj's 1892 story *Monk Brne's Pupil* (*Bakonja Fra Brne*, 1951) and his adaptation of Slavko Kolar's play *Master of One's Own Body* (*Svoga tela gospodar*, 1956)—were also popular, as were the action-adventure films of the Serbian director Živorad Mitrović (b. 1921)—*Echelon of Dr. M* (*Ešalon Doktora M*, 1955), and *Captain Leši* (*Kapetan Leši*, 1960)—and the children's films of the Slovenian Jože Gale (b. 1913)—*Kekec* (1951—first prize in its category, Venice, 1952)—and the Croatian Branko Bauer (1921–2002)—*Grey Seagull* (*Sinji galeb*, 1953) and *Millions on an Island* (*Milioni na otoku*, 1955). Yugoslavia's revolutionary past was by no means ignored, but it began to be treated with a new realism in such Partisan films as Radoš Novaković's (1915–1979) *The Sun Is Far Away* (*Daleko je sunce*, 1953), Vladimir Pogačić's (1919–1999) *Big and Small* (*Veliki i mali*, 1956) and *Alone* (*Sam*, 1959), and the Serbian director Stole Janković's (1925–1987) two-part *Partisan Stories* (*Partizanske priče*, 1960). Two films of Ustashi-occupied Zagreb—Branko Bauer's (1921–2002) *Don't Turn Around, My Son* (*Ne okreći se, sine*, 1956) and the Slovenian France Štiglic's (1919–1993) *The Ninth Circle* (*Deveti krug*, 1960)—also tapped the realistic vein, while Pogačić's anthology film *On Saturday Evening* (*Subotom uveče*, 1957) dealt in similar fashion with contemporary life. The direct influence of Italian neorealism was perceptible in the work of the Montenegrin Veljko Bulajić (b. 1928)—*Train without a Schedule* (*Vlak bez voznog reda*, 1959); *City in Ferment* (*Uzavreli grad*, 1961)—who had studied at the Centro Sperimentale with Zavattini and worked as an assistant to De Santis.

In the late 1950s and early 1960s, a movement toward formal experimentation began to coalesce around several institutions outside of the mainstream feature cinema. One was the specialized animation studio Zagreb Film, founded in 1953, where the Croatian writer-director Vatroslav Mimica (b. 1923) and the Montenegrin Dušan Vukotić (1927–1998) pioneered an abstract, whimsical style that won international acclaim for the Yugoslavian cinema in such films as the former's *Alone* (*Samac*—Festival Prize, Venice, 1958) and the latter's *Ersatz* (*Surogat*—American Academy Award, 1961;[7] the first ever for a foreign animated film). Another realm of modernist experimentation was that of the documentary and short film, with "schools" centered in Belgrade, Zagreb, and Sarajevo, where future feature directors like Puriša Djordjević (b. 1924) and Aleksander Petrović (1929–1994) were trained. Finally, there was a strong Yugoslav amateur film movement organized by the country's leading film theorist Dušan Stojanović around the Belgrade ("Beograd") kino klub. It was in this context that future leaders of the *novi film* movement (also called *novi val*, or "new wave"), such as Dušan Makavejev (b. 1932), Živojin Pavlović (1933–1998), and Boštjan Hladnik (b. 1929), made their first shorts.

NOVI FILM

In the 1960s, the Yugoslav cinema experienced a further decentralization of its production activities as studios were established in the two autonomous regions of Vojvodina and Kosovo, and it entered into its most richly creative

---

7. As Mira and Antonín J. Liehm point out (*The Most Important Art: Eastern European Film after 1945* [Berkeley: University of California Press, 1977], p. 250), the development of children's and animated films was the great success story of the nationalization of the Eastern European cinemas in the 1950s. Having no relationship with contemporary social and political realities, these kinds of films enjoyed a special creative mandate even in the worst years of Stalinism. In addition to the work of the Zagreb school, one thinks in this connection of the films of Jan Lenica (1928–2001) and Walerian Borowczyk (b. 1923) in Poland, the puppet films of Jiří Trnka (1912–1969) and the animated features of Karel Zeman (1910–1989) in Czechoslovakia, the cartoons of the Hungarians Attila Dargay (b. 1927) and Marcell Jankovics (b. 1941), and the work of Todor Dinov (b. 1919) in Bulgaria, Ion Popescu-Gopo (1923–1989) in Romania, and Alexander Ptushko (1900–1973) in the Soviet Union—all of whom are discussed in the text. See Ronald Holloway, *Z Is for Zagreb* (South Brunswick, N.J.: Barnes, 1972); Ralph Stephenson, *The Animated Film* (New York: Barnes, 1973); and Bruno Edera, *Full Length Animated Feature Films* (New York: Hastings House, 1977).

period. The annual rate of production in 1961 was thirty-three features, double that of the previous decade, and in the years 1967 to 1969 it reached its zenith, averaging thirty-five features each year. Many of these were made under the rubric of *novi film* ("new film," or "open film"), an avant-garde movement closely associated with the wider agitation toward the democratization of Yugoslav society known as the Second Yugoslav Revolution.[8] Though *novi film* lacked a specific set of aesthetic principles, its advocates had as their goals (1) the liberation of the filmmaking process from bureaucratic constraints and ideological dogma, (2) the promotion of experiments with film as an audiovisual language along the lines of the French and Czech new waves, and (3) the use of film to examine contemporary themes (*savremene teme*)—when necessary, from a critical perspective. Innovative in terms of means, *novi film* conceived of its practice firmly within the context of a Marxist-Leninist state and was not intent upon political subversion. But officials of the League of Communists of Yugoslavia (LCY), the country's ruling (and only) party, initially saw things in a different light.

In the vanguard of *novi film* were Aleksander Petrović's *Two* (*Dvoje*, 1961) and Boštjan Hladnik's *A Dance in the Rain* (*Ples v dežju*, 1961), both of which dispensed with conventional narrative structure in favor of visual metaphor and dealt pessimistically with contemporary themes. Their second films—Petrović's *Days* (*Dani*, 1963) and Hladnik's *Sand Castle* (*Peščani grad*, 1962)—followed these trends even further and were banned from official showing at the 1963 Pula Festival. At the same time, *The City* (*Grad*, 1963), the second film of the Belgrade *kino klub* associates Živojin Pavlović, Kokan Rakonjac, and Marko Babac, was seized and impounded in Sarajevo for portraying "a meaningless view of life . . . reduced to physical, senseless lust" and for presenting "a Yugoslav town in such a negative light that it raises the question whether it is worthwhile to live there." The famous Belgrade painter Miča Popović (1923–1996) was forced to re-edit his darkly brilliant first feature, *Man from the Oak Forest* (*Čovek iz hrastove šume*, 1963), because it made a Chetnik shepherd its major protagonist and gave him a credible psychology; while *The Return* (*Povratak*, 1963), Živojin Pavlović's first independent feature, was shelved until 1966 for showing the indifference of Yugoslav society to the plight of a former convict.

But the tide began to turn at the 1965 Pula Festival, where Petrović's third film, *Three* (Tri), won first prize,

Puriša Djordjević inaugurated his surrealist tetralogy on the Partisan war and its aftermath with *Girl* (*Devojka*), Dušan Makavejev made his feature debut with *Man Is Not a Bird* (*Čovek nije tica*), and Rakonjac's Horn (*Klakson*) and Pavlović's *The Enemy* (*Neprijatelj*) were both well received. As if to confirm *novi film*'s ascendency, July 1966 witnessed the triumph of the League of Communists' most liberal wing, when the conservative Aleksander Ranković—founder and chief of the State Security Service (OZNA),[9] party secretary, and chosen successor to Tito—was forced from office for attempting a political coup.

At its height, *novi film* activity was centered in the country's two largest production sites, Belgrade and Zagreb. At Belgrade, Petrović followed *Three*, his multi-episode revaluation of the sacrosanct War of National Liberation, with *I Even Met Happy Gypsies* (*Skupljači perja*, 1967), an unromanticized portrait of Gypsy life in the Vojvodina region filmed with nonactors and an authentic multilingual sound track (of Serbo-Croatian, Romany, and Slovak), which shared the Grand Prix at Cannes.[1] His *It Rains in My Village* (*Biče skoro propast sveta*, 1969) was a collage of motifs inspired by Dostoevsky's *The Possessed*, a contemporary news story, and the Soviet invasion of Czechoslovakia; while *The Master and Margarita* (*Majstor i Margarita*, 1972) is an ambitious adaptation of the Russian Mikhail Bulgakov's fantastic anti-Stalinist novel, which also implicitly attacks reactionism within the LCY. Pavlović's most important "new films" were often dark and brutally naturalistic: *Awakening of the Rats* (*Budjenje pacova*, 1966) is an account of degradation among slum-dwellers in contemporary Belgrade; *When I Am Pale and Dead* (*Kad budem mrtav i beo*, 1967) is a bitter comedy

---

8. As should be obvious by this point, all of the Eastern European countries experienced changes in the period from 1961 to 1967 as the Stalinist system disintegrated and individual states began to introduce economic and political reforms that redefined their relationship with the Soviet Union. The changes in Yugoslavia were nearly extreme enough to warrant the term *revolution* since the party's liberal wing took control in 1966 and turned Yugoslavia into the Eastern bloc's most market-oriented country in less than five years.

9. An acronym for *Odeljenje za zaštitu norodna*, "Department for the Protection of the People," organized as the VDBA by Ranković in 1944 and fundamentally Stalinist in character.

1. Western awareness of *novi film* was high, even extending to the United States, where *Three* and *I Even Met Happy Gypsies* were both nominated for Academy Awards in 1967.

16.54 *When I Am Pale and Dead* (Živojin Pavlović, 1967).

tures, love, and sex, Makavejev inaugurated experiments in free association that culminated in the remarkable cinematic essay *WR—The Mysteries of the Organism* (*WR— Misterije organizma*, 1971). In between, he made the remarkable montage piece *Innocence Unprotected* (*Nevinost bez zaštite*, 1968), which juxtaposes excerpts from the first Serbian "all-talking" film, made clandestinely by circus strongman Dragoljub Aleksić during the Nazi occupation in 1942, with documentary footage from the period, animation, and interviews with members of the original production crew. *WR*, clearly influenced by the work of Věra Chytilová in Czechoslovakia (see pp. 624–26), is a surrealist collage that applies the radical theories of the Austrian psychoanalyst Wilhelm Reich (1897–1957) critically to both capitalist decadence and socialist authoritarianism. Like Reich, Makavejev ultimately equates social and sexual repression. The film won several international awards, including the Luis Buñuel Prize at Cannes, but it was banned in Yugoslavia and eventually forced Makavejev's emigration to the West.

about a pop musician, the human detritus of forced industrialization; *The Ambush* (*Zaseda*, 1969), which was banned shortly after release, was a deeply controversial film set in a Serbian village during the worst postwar excesses of OZNA; and *The Red Wheat* (*Rdeče klasje*, 1971) concerned the failures of postwar collectivization of agriculture. During this same period in Belgrade, Puriša Djordjević completed his stylized tetralogy on the War of Liberation and its aftermath with *Dream* (*San*, 1966), *Morning* (*Jutro*, 1967—Grand Prix, Venice), and *Noon* (*Podne*, 1968).

But the most widely acclaimed director to emerge from the Belgrade *novi film* group by far was the Serbian Dušan Makavejev, who might best be described as an avant-garde satirist of great intellect. The forms of his films are experimental, and their subject is sexual and social repression, which he sees as intimately related phenomena. *Man Is Not a Bird* (*Čovek nije tica*, 1966) is a satirical romantic comedy set against the backdrop of an east Serbian copper mine that evokes the dehumanization of the socialist worker through regimentation. In *An Affair of the Heart, or The Tragedy of the Switchboard Operator* (*Ljubavni slučaj ili tragedija službenice PTT*, 1967), a film about the relationship between social struc-

16.55 Dušan Makavejev's *WR—The Mysteries of the Organism* (1971): Milena Dravić.

In Zagreb the most important *novi film* figure was the former animator Vatroslav Mimica, whose films of the era include the abstractionist *Prometheus from Vishevica Island* (*Promentej sa otoka Viševice*, 1964), *Monday or Tuesday* (*Ponedeljak ili utorak*, 1966), *The Event* (*Dogadjaj*, 1969), and *The Adoptee* (*Hranjenik*, 1971). Mimica's most powerful "new film," however, was the radically experimental *Kaja, I'll Kill You* (*Kaja, ubit ću te*, 1967), which uses the Italian occupation of a Dalmatian coastal town during World War II to examine the psychopathology of fascism. Another Zagreb-based filmmaker, the documentarist Krsto Papić (b. 1933), won international acclaim for his feature *Handcuffs* (*Lisice*, 1970) on the brutal and random purging of Stalinists (uncharacteristically portrayed as victims) in a small Croatian village just after Yugoslavia's expulsion from the Cominform in the summer of 1948; and the musician-turned-scriptwriter Zvonimir Berković (b. 1928) made an impressive feature debut with *Rondo* (1966), a portrait of a love triangle cinematically structured on the variations of a Mozart piece. By the end of the decade, in fact, the influence of *novi film* had reached well beyond Belgrade and Zagreb to the provinces. At the newly established Neoplanta Film at Novi Sad, for example, Želimir Žilnik (b. 1942) made the archetypal "new film" in his debut feature *Early Works* (*Rani radovi*, 1969), a radically Godardian reflection on Marx's own Early Works, which won the Golden Bear at Berlin but was banned from domestic distribution. (Želnik's sequel, *Das Kapital*, 1971, has never seen the light of day.) At Bosnia Film in Sarajevo, the documentarist Bato Čengić (b. 1933) followed his controversial antiwar film *Little Soldiers* (*Mali vojnici*, 1968) with the ideological satires *The Role of My Family in the World Revolution* (*Uloga moje porodice u svetskoj revoluciji*, 1971) and *Scenes from the Life of a Shock Worker* (*Slike iz života udarnika*, 1972), the latter focused on the political absurdities and human tragedies of Yugoslavia's postwar industrialization campaign. And in Slovenia, at Ljubljana, the film critic and former Godard assistant Matjaž Klopčič (b. 1934) directed *On Wings of Paper* (*Na papirnatih avionih*, 1967), a film about the transience of contemporary media and modern love.

Between 1969 and 1972, however, political events conspired to turn the tide against *novi film*. The June 1968 student demonstrations in Belgrade had alarmed Yugoslav authorities, and the Warsaw Pact invasion of Czechoslovakia in August had chastened them. More

16.56 *WR:* Makavejev arranging Dravić's severed head(s).

frightening yet, the Croatian nationalist movement erupted into antigovernment terrorism in 1971, when Tito was seventy-nine and still without a chosen successor. These circumstances pushed the League of Communists to the right once more and resulted in a purge of nonorthodox Marxists. Makavejev was expelled from the party and forced into exile in Paris; Petrović was dismissed from his faculty position at the film academy for "extreme political negligence" and also emigrated to France; Pavlović was similarly dismissed but reinstated without rank the following year. The term "new film" was officially replaced with "black film" (after a polemical essay by Vladimír Jovičić entitled "The Black Wave in Our Film" in *Borba*, the central daily of the LCY, in 1969) to condemn the movement's socially negative qualities, and ideologically unconventional films, such as Pavlović's *The Ambush* and Žilnik's *Early Works*, were once again seized and banned or drastically recut. The Twentieth National Pula Festival in 1973 told the tale: the awards were dominated by Stipe *Delić's Sutjeska*, a three-hour widescreen Partisan epic harking back to the days of nationalist realism that starred Richard Burton as Marshal Tito.

The "black film" counteroffensive was led by centrists rather than reactionaries and was in no way as brutal as, for example, the purge of the Czech New Wave following the Prague Spring. Nevertheless, the Yugoslav film industry was damaged by the crisis, and the period from 1973 to 1977 experienced the lowest annual rates of production since the early 1960s, averaging fewer than eighteen films per year. Amid a generally listless return to the time-honored genres of the heroic Partisan film, action-adventure, and light comedy, there were beacons of hope in Krsto Papić's *A Village Performance of Hamlet* (*Predstava Hamleta a selu Mrduša Donja*, 1973), adapted from Ivo Brešan's pungently satirical play; Pavlović's *The Flight of a Dead Bird* (*Let mrtve ptice*, 1974), a tale of rural decay filmed in northeast Slovenia; and Djordjević's *Pavle Pavlović* (1975), a satire on bureaucratic corruption that was banned from the Pula Festival even though Tito publicly defended it.

THE "PRAGUE GROUP"

Yugoslavian cinema did not make a real comeback until the late 1970s and early 1980s, when a new course was charted by five young directors known as the "Prague Group" because they had all studied at FAMU in the years of the "black film" counterattack. As the Yugoslav heirs of Forman, Menzel, Passer, and Chytilová, the members of the Prague Group practiced a kind of absurdist social satire, without the confrontational politics of their *novi film* predecessors. They also formed the kind of close collaborative relationship among themselves and other young Yugoslav filmmakers that once characterized the French New Wave, and won large domestic audiences and many international awards.

The members of the original Prague Group were the directors Goran Paskaljević (b. 1947), Goran Marković (b. 1946), Lordan Zafranović (b. 1944), Rajko Grlić (b. 1947), and Srđjan Karanović (b. 1945), as well as the cinematographers Živko Zalar (b. 1948), Vilko Filač (b. 1950), and Miodrag Popović (1923–1996). Paskaljević's most critically successful and popular films have been *The Beach Guard in Winter* (*Čuvar plaže u zimskom periodu*, 1976); *The Dog Who Liked Trains* (*Pas koji je voleo vozove*, 1978); *The Days Are Passing* (*Zemaljski dani teku*, 1979); and *Special Treatment* (*Poseban tretman*, 1980). More recently, his *Deceptive Summer of '68* (*Varljivo leto*, 1984) provides a deftly comic treatment of a Yugoslav student's sexual initiation by a young Czech girl in the latter days of Alexander Dubček's Prague Spring. The film, an *hommage* to FAMU, is deliberately evocative of both Forman's *Black Peter* (1963) and Menzel's *Closely Watched Trains* (1966). *Guardian Angel* (*Andjeo čuvar*, 1987; written and produced by the director), on

the other hand, is a horrifying documentary-style exposé of the traffic in Gypsy children between Yugoslavia and Italy, where they are exploited as virtual slaves. Marković is best known for his fast-paced comedies about contemporary Yugoslav youth in such films as *Special Education* (*Specijalno vaspitanje*, 1977—First Prize, Mannheim Festival), *National Class up to 26 Feet* (*Nacionalna klasa do 785 cm*, 1979), and *Teachers, Teachers* (*Majstori, majstori*, 1981), all bearing the marked influence of the Czech New Wave. His *Variola Vera* (1982—First Prize, Valencia Festiva) is a dark satire about the incompetence of medical and public-health officials during an outbreak of the fatal strain of smallpox named in the title, while *Taiwan Canasta* (*Tajvanska kanasta*, 1985) is an ironic comedy about an aging hippie unable to find a place in a society that, he feels, has betrayed his youthful idealism. *Déja Vu* (*Već Viđeno*), winner of the Pula Festival's 1987 Grand Prix, is a stylish psychological thriller in the Hitchcock mode.

Lordan Zafranović is the most visionary filmmaker of the Prague Group, as demonstrated by his *Occupation in Twenty-six Scenes* (*Okupacija u 26 slika*, 1978—First Prize, Pula Festival). This poetic re-creation of the Italian occupation of the ancient coastal city of Dubrovnik

16.57 *Occupation in Twenty-six Scenes* (Lordan Zafranović, 1978).

evokes the graciousness of prewar bourgeois life as well as the brutal smashing of that order by the Fascists and their bestial Ustashi collaborators. Zafranović's next film, which also won a Pula First Prize, was similarly concerned with the effects of the war on his native Dalmatian coast and appeared to be the second work in a trilogy on the subject: *Fall of Italy* (*Pad Italije*, 1981; English title: *Island Chronicle*) is a stylized and often grimly beautiful account of Partisan fighting and Italian reprisals on a small Adriatic island. *Evening Bells* (*Večernja zvona*, 1986) is an adaptation of Mirko Kovač's prize-winning novel of the crucible of Yugoslavia's civil war; Zafranović won the director's award at Pula for it in the year of its release. Rajko Grlić's *Bravo Maestro* (1978), on the other hand, has a contemporary setting and comments caustically on the rise of an ambitious young composer who manages to subvert the self-management system of the musical establishment by manipulating personal connections (*veze*), as so many Yugoslavs of the time learned to do. His next film, *The Melody Haunts My Revery* (*Samo jednom se ljubi*, 1981), whose English title translates a phrase from Hoagy Carmichael's popular 1940s song "Stardust," also has a political theme. It depicts the psychological disintegration of a dedicated young socialist leader under the pressures of Stalinism in a small Croatian village just after the war. No less philosophical, Grlić's *The Jaws of Life* (*U raljama života*, 1984) is a bittersweet comedy about the symbiotic relationship between a middle-aged woman filmmaker and the fictitious heroine of a television series she is directing. *Three's Happiness* (*Za sreću je pótrebno troje*, 1986), constructed around three overlapping love triangles, is also a witty comedy that won the Golden Palm at Valencia in 1986. More recently, Grlić directed the British-Yugoslav coproduction *The Summer of White Roses* (1989) about the delayed impact of World War II on an idyllic lakeside resort.

Srđjan Karanović is an important collaborator of Grlić's (the former FAMU classmates having reciprocated on each other's screenplays six times to date) and is a major Yugoslav director in his own right. His *The Scent of Wild Flowers* (*Miris poljskog cveća*, 1978), which shared the International Critics' Prize at Cannes, is a subtly ironic portrayal of an aging, world-famous actor who tries vainly to find some personal respite from the media's ravenous appetite for publicity, scandal, and "news." Considerably more dense and sober, *Petra's Wreath* (*Petrijin venac*, 1980—Director's Prize, Pula) is about the traumatized lifetime odyssey of an illiterate peasant before, during, and after the war, based on the experiences of a real woman. With *Something in Between* (*Nešto izmedju*, 1983), which took first prizes at both the Pula and Valencia festivals, Karanović proved himself to be the leading intellectual filmmaker of his generation. Shot in English, with locations in New York, Belgrade, Dubrovnik, and Istanbul, this sophisticated comedy is on its surface about the whirlwind competition between two Yugoslav men, one a respected surgeon and the other a charming rogue, for the affections of an American female journalist on a six-week Eastern tour; on another level, however, the film is a social commentary on the contradictions inherent in Yugoslav daily life and the country's unique position "in between" East and West. More recently, Karanović has made *Caught in the Throat* (*Jagode u grlu*, 1985), a self-referential film about a reunion of the cast and crew of a thirteen-part serial he directed for Yugoslav television in 1974, and *Still Lacking a Good Title* (*Za sada bez dobrog naslova*, 1988), a multilevel satire about a TV crew attempting to document a contemporary Yugoslav-Albanian border incident, which intricately mixes film and video footage.

Closely associated with the Prague Group are the directors Miloš Radivojević (b. 1939), Bogdan Žižić (b. 1934), Slobodan Šijan (b. 1946), and Emir Kusturica (b. 1954). Radivojević's work tends toward the experimental and often deals with mental breakdown. His most significant films constitute an informal trilogy on the frustration of revolutionary idealism among the young: in *Breakdown* (*Kvar*, 1979) a successful television journalist comes apart when he realizes the false value system in which his career and his social life have become enmeshed; *Dreams, Life, and Death of Filip Filipović* (*Snovi, život, smrt Filipa Filipovića*, 1980) takes us into the mind of the first secretary of the Yugoslav Communist party, who was killed in Stalin's purges in Russia in 1938, as he writes his memoirs while awaiting execution; and *Living Like the Rest of Us* (*Živeti kao svet normalan*, 1982) is a sharp satire on the elitist pretensions of contemporary students at the Belgrade Academy of Music when confronted with a working-class idealist as classmate. With *Una, My Love* (1986), Radivojević captured worldwide attention in a wildly erotic film about a sultry female student employed by the state to seduce her journalism professor and pump him for enough information to send him to jail. All of Radivojević's films

16.58 *Who's That Singing over There?* (Slobodan Šijan, 1980).

are remarkably patterned in formal terms; *Filip Filipović*, for example, mixes archival period footage with distorted wide-angle images of the title character's reveries. Bogdan Žižić's reputation rests on two films with a single theme: the plight of exploited Yugoslav "guest workers" (*Gastarbeiter*—immigrant blue-collar and service workers) in West Germany. *Don't Lean Out of the Window* (*Ne naginji se kroz prozor*, 1977) is a fictional documentary on the wretched demimonde of the provincial Gastarbeiter in Frankfurt, which won the Pula first prize; while *Early Snowfall in Munich* (*Rani snijeg u Münchenu*, 1984) portrays the cultural confusion of *Gastarbeiter* who have worked outside of Yugoslavia for so long that their sense of identity is divided between their native and their adoptive countries.

Slobodan Šijan has become internationally famous for his black comedies of Serbian manners. *Who's That Singing over There?* (*Ko to tamo peva?*, 1980) is an episodic account of a twenty-four-hour bus ride across the back roads of Serbia that delivers its passengers to Belgrade at the precise moment of the Nazi blitzkrieg on April 6, 1941, killing all aboard but two Gypsies, whose songs have connected the narrative. This film won prizes at Pula and Rotterdam, as well as France's coveted Georges Sadoul Award for best debut film by a foreign director. Šijan followed his success with *The Marathon Family* (*Maratonci trče počasni krug*, 1982), which deals in Formanesque fashion with a five-generation family of undertakers in the

early 1930s who must fight a gang war to maintain their ascendancy. More recently Šijan has produced *How I Was Systematically Destroyed by an Idiot* (*Kako sam sistematiski uništen od idiota*, 1983), a political satire about an aging revolutionary who becomes self-destructively involved in the 1968 student uprising at the University of Belgrade, and *Strangler vs. Strangler* (*Davitelja protiv davitelja*, 1984), a sophisticated *hommage* to Hitchcock's *Psycho* (1960), replete with allusions to other classics of the horror genre.

But, ironically, the rising star of Yugoslav cinema in the mid-1980s was the Bosnian director Emir Kusturica, whose award-winning films *Do You Remember Dolly Bell?* (*Sjećaš li se Dolly Bell?*, 1981) and *When Father Was Away on Business* (*Otac na službenom putu*, 1985) brought new prominence to Sarajevo as a production center. As a recent graduate of FAMU (1978), where he studied under Jiři Menzel, Kusturica worked in collaboration with the Bosnian poet Abdulah Sidran as screenwriter and the FAMU-trained Vilko Filač as cinematographer to mine a vein of ironic, even tragicomic, reminiscence from his region's recent past. *Dolly Bell*, which won the Golden Lion at Venice, for example, is an anecdotal story of a young boy's coming of age in a patriarchal Muslim family on the outskirts of Sarajevo in the early 1960s; while *Father*, which won the Golden Palm Award at Cannes, assumes the perspective of an even younger child in the period 1947–52, when Tito had broken with Stalin and countless innocent Yugoslavs experienced arbitrary denunciation and imprisonment, in a Stalinist-style purge

16.59 *When Father Was Away on Business* (Emir Kusturica, 1985).

directed *against* suspected Stalinists. Like other films by members of the Prague Group and their associates discussed above, Kusturica's have been both critically successful and enormously popular with audiences at home and abroad (*Father*, for example, having done a brisk business in the United States and been nominated for an Academy Award for Best Foreign Film). Kusturica's *Time of the Gypsies* (*Dom za vesanje*, 1989), however, is much less mainstream than his earlier work in its poetic evocation of Gypsy life and its occasionally experimental structure.

At the same time that the Prague Group and its followers were breathing new life into Yugoslav cinema and gaining great popularity with the domestic audience, many veterans of the *novi film* movement were forgiven their heresies and reintegrated with the mainstream industry. Among those who have returned are Puriša Djordjević (*Eight Kilos of Happiness* [*Osam kila sreće*, 1980]), Živojin Pavlović (*See You in the Next War* [*Nasvidenji u. naslednji vojni*, 1980]; *Body Scent* [*Zadah*, 1983]; *On the Road to Katanga* [*Na puta za Katangu*, 1987]), Vatroslav Mimica (*The Falcon* [*Banović Strahinja*, 1981]), Krsto Papić (*The Secret of Nikola Tesla* [*Tajna Nikole Tesle*, 1980]), Želimir Žilnik (*The Second Generation* [*Druga generacija*, 1983]; *Beautiful Women Walking About Town* [*Lijepe zene prolaze kroz grad*, 1986]), Bato Čengić (*Heads or Tails* [*Pismo-Glava*, 1983]), and Zvonimir Berković (*Love Letters with Intent* [*Ljubavna pisma s predumišljajem*, 1985]). Boštjan Hladnik returned indirectly through the 1983 release of his long-shelved *Masquerade* (*Maskarada*, 1971), and Aleksander Petrović, who devotes himself now mainly to directing live theater, reappeared briefly to collaborate with Mimica on the screenplay for *The Falcon* (1981).

Of the major *novi film* directors, only Dušan Makavejev has not participated actively in his country's cinema since the "black film" counteroffensive of the early 1970s; all of his subsequent films were made abroad, until 1988. *Sweet Movie* (1974), for example, was shot on location in the United States and Western Europe. Like *WR*, it uses the strategies of free association and, more especially, the manipulation of alternately attractive and repellent images to counterpose American commodity fetishism with the decadence of the Marxist ideal. Although it acquired a reputation for scandal, the film was a critical and commercial failure, and Makavejev has had difficulty funding his productions ever since. One effect has been to push him in the direction of more conventional nar-

16.60 Makavejev's *Sweet Movie* (1974).

rative form, as the Swedish-British coproduction *Montenegro/Pigs and Pearls* (1981) demonstrates. Shot with English dialogue, the film concerns an American-born Swedish housewife (Susan Anspach), neglected by her businessman husband, who escapes into a world of anarchistic sexual pleasure at the Zanzibar, an underground club for transplanted Montenegrins in Stockholm. This linear plot contrasts sharply with an elaborate montage structure featuring graphic close-ups of sexual activity and nudity in motion, plus Makavejev's characteristic psychoanalytic equation of violence, sex, blood, and death. Similarly, the Australian-financed *Coca-Cola Kid* (1985), a decade in preparation and two years in production, mixes eroticism and social satire with a more or less conventional plot: a corporate troubleshooter is sent from Atlanta to a remote part of Australia to discover why Coca-Cola sales have dried up and finds that a local land baron has enforced his own soft-drink monopoly on the populace. The ensuing feud between the parties counterposes American and Australian attitudes toward everything from politics to sex (always equated in Makavejev, of course) and ends in a merger. Makavejev was an invited guest at the Pula Festival in 1982, and in 1988 he made his first film in Yugoslavia in twenty years, although it was produced by the American-based Cannon Group. Shot on location in the beautiful Slovenian village of Skofja Loka and adapted from a story by Zola, *Manifesto* (1988) is a comedy of political intrigue set in an unnamed Central European country in 1920, and like all of Makavejev's work, it is ultimately about the relationship between sex and revolution. More typical, *Gorilla Bathes at Noon* (1992; a German-Yugoslav coproduction) is a hilarious satire of Marxist-Leninism set in November 1989 in Berlin that uses footage from the Stalinist epic *The Fall of Berlin* (Mikheil Chiaureli, 1949) to comment on the dismantling of East German Communism.

Lacking the distinguished national traditions of Poland, Czechoslovakia, and Hungary, the Yugoslav cinema was spontaneously generated in the postwar era to become over the next several decades one of the most unusual in all of Eastern Europe. Not a little of its success was owed the vision of Josip Tito, who not only echoed Lenin on the importance of film for socialist society, saying, "Film is one of the most influential means of modern communication and its social, moral, and educational role is, therefore, great," but was himself an avid film buff who saw every feature film made in his country in his lifetime. His death on April 5, 1980, was mourned very specifically as a loss for Yugoslav cinema as well as for the country at large. It was Tito's vision that gave Yugoslavia its unique concept of worker self-management, which meant for the film industry a level of autonomy and competition among its twenty-seven production companies that by the late 1980s very nearly resembled the American system.[2] Unlike Poland, Czechoslovakia, and Hungary before 1990, where state subsidies guaranteed the careers of critically successful filmmakers even when the box office didn't, Yugoslavia generated the lion's share of its film financing from the domestic audience. So it was a sign of great promise that the films of the Prague Group and its associates managed to outdistance first-run American films at the Yugoslav box office in every year from 1978 to 1988. In the years of their release, in fact, Karanović's *Something in Between* (1983) and Kusturica's *When Father Was Away on Business* (1985) outsold their nearest American competitors in the urban centers by three to one. At the same time, Yugoslavia Film—the national association of Yugoslav producers, distributors, and exhibitors—was making plans to mount an aggressive marketing campaign to ensure widespread distribution of its films to the West. As the decade closed, the world anticipated both superb entertainment and critical distinction from the Yugoslav cinema for years to come.

When the Soviet union collapsed in 1991, it seemed briefly possible that Yugoslavia might follow Poland, Hungary, and Czechoslovakia toward liberal democracy, but

Slobodan Milošević, the communist president of Serbia, began at once to exploit the paranoid nationalism of the country's most populous and powerful republic and agitate for the creation of an ethnically "pure" Serbian state. Meanwhile, Slovenia (population 2 million) and Croatia (population 4.5 million), and then Bosnia-Herzegovina (population 3.9 million) and Macedonia (population 2 million), elected noncommunist democratic coalition governments, and in June 1991, Slovenia, with no significant minority population, and Croatia, whose population includes many Serbians, declared their independence. (Montenegro remained allied with Serbia in what is now called the Yugoslav Federation, or "Greater Serbia;" population 10.6 million.) At this point Milošević, who controlled the army from the Yugoslav capital in Belgrade (also the capital of Serbia), ordered his "federal" troops to invade them both under the guise of preserving the union. Slovenia forced a Serbian withdrawal in less than two weeks, but the Croats and Serbs fought on savagely for six months until approximately one-fourth of Croatia was annexed to "Greater Serbia" and many of its towns destroyed. Milošević then turned his attention to Bosnia, also home to a large Serbian population, which declared independence in March 1992, authorizing the creation of a Serb republic there under Radovan Karadžić and assisting its paramilitary forces in the merciless artillery bombardment of Sarajevo. At the same time, Croatian forces turned on their former Muslim allies and joined with the Serbs to carve up Bosnian territory for themselves. By the end of 1993, Bosnia had been virtually partitioned, with Serbian forces occupying two-thirds of the country outside of Sarajevo and the Croatians controlling the rest, and what had become by then the second Yugoslav civil war—complete with "ethnic cleansing" and other world-class atrocities—was in full swing. The formation of a Muslim-Croatian federation in March 1994 under UN and American diplomatic pressure, however, gave Bosnia renewed hope of survival.

The Yugoslav cinema fell apart like Yugoslavia itself. First, there was separatism, then war. The first signs of

---

2. An important difference, of course, was that salaries (and, therefore, production costs) were very low by American standards, with maximums ranging from $2,000 for writing a screenplay to $10,000 for directing a film.

trouble came with a serious decline in production from thirty-six films in 1988 to twenty-five in 1989. At the same time, however, nearly all of the forty "black films" shelved during the late 1960s and 1970s were rehabilitated and directors like Žilnik, Petrović, and Čengić given a chance to work again in their native industry. Notable Yugoslav films in that year were Goran Marković's *Collecting Point* (*Sabirni centar*), Želimir Žilnik's *How the Steel Was Wrought*, Veljko Bulajić's *The Donator* (*Donator*), and Rajko Grlić's *That Summer of White Roses* (*Davolji raj*), the first two from Belgrade and the latter from Zagreb. By 1990, however, the production systems of the six republics had begun to pull apart and falter: the Serbian system, which had regularly accounted for half of the annual Yugoslav output (fifteen to eighteen of thirty-five), announced that in the future it would produce only six to eight films per year; Croatia's Jadran Film committed itself exclusively to foreign coproduction, making only a single film for domestic distribution; and Bosnia, after producing its last features in Ademir Kenović's *Kuduz* (1989) *and A Festival Day in Sarajevo* (*Praznik u Sarajevu*, 1990), began stocking its theaters with television features transferred to film.

Signs of impending civil strife loomed when Croatian director Rajko Grlić was attacked by his compatriots for making *Caruga* (*Charuga*, 1991), on the subject of a Serbian bandit-hero, and Serbian director Srđjan Karanović was denied a share of Croatian funding for *Virginia* (*Virgina*, 1991), a grim tale of peasant life in nineteenth-century Serbia that became the last film produced in a united Yugoslavia. In that same year, Goran Paskaljević removed his *Time of Miracles* (*Vreme čudam*, 1990) from the thirty-seventh annual Pula Festival because one of his Serbian crew members was allegedly assaulted by Croatian thugs (the town of Pula is in Croatia). In 1991, the thirty-eighth Pula Festival was canceled for political reasons, and by 1992 Pula was no longer a Yugoslav film festival at all but an exclusively Croatian one, showcasing eight Croat features, of which Krsto Papić's *Story from Croatia* (*Prica iz Hrvatske*, 1992) took most of the awards. At the same time, Serbian cinema, its state film bureaucracy recently supplemented by a handful of private producer-distributors, continued to produce interesting work for a domestic market nearly ruined by wartime inflation and UN economic sanctions. (In 1992, the UN recognized Slovenia, Croatia, and Bosnia-Herzegovina as indepen-

16.61 *Tito and Me* **(Goran Markovic, 1992): Vesna Trivalic as the Instructor, counseling Young Communists on the equality of the six Yugoslav republics. His resemblance to Stalin is entirely deliberate.**

dent states and expelled the Yugoslav Federation, simultaneously imposing tough sanctions.) In 1992, for example, Goran Marković made the iconoclastic *Tito and Me* (*Tito i ja*) and Živojin Pavlović adapted Dostoevsky's *The Eternal Husband* as *The Deserter* (*Dezerter*), updating and shooting it on location in the ruined town of Vukovar, but many 1993 projects remain uncompleted.

With markets split and/or physically destroyed and the former national audience divided against itself in civil war, the Yugoslav cinema, like Yugoslavia itself, has ceased to exist. In its forty-five-year history, it produced 904 feature films, nearly half of which (426) were Serbian, but 186 of which were true interrepublican coproductions made possible by the extraordinary creative and financial context of the unified Yugoslav film industry. Maja Vujovic has linked the destruction of Yugoslav cinema with the pathology of state censorship under Tito: "The same paranoia that sought to lobotomise Yugoslavian cinema . . . generated a savage national chauvinism off-screen and thus destroyed the delicate device it had governed: a multi-national, multi-religious, cosmopolitan Yugoslavia."[3] In this context, Bosnian director Emir Kusturica's *Underground* (1995), a French-German-Hungarian coproduction that won the 1995 Cannes Grand Prix, can be seen as a eulogy for the Yugoslav cinema's fragmentary remains as well as for the nation itself. In fact, much of

3. Maja Vujovic, "Yugoslavia," *Variety International Film Guide 1993*, ed. Peter Cowie (Hollywood: Samuel French Trade, 1993), p. 423.

this epic black comedy of Yugoslavia from 1941 to 1992 revolves around the production of a socialist-realist–style film glorifying a legendary hero of the Partisan war ("Blacky") who was in fact a common criminal; the mendacity of the film within the film suggests that the whole Yugoslav state has been built upon a lie; and in a visionary reprise at *Underground*'s conclusion, all of its main characters (most of them long dead) come together at an outdoor wedding feast on the banks of the Danube to sing a song celebrating Yugoslav unity, when the land mass they occupy begins to break up and its fragments float away separately into the river. Similarly, Srđan Dragojević's (b. 1963) *Pretty Village, Pretty Flame* (*Lepa sela lepo gore*, 1996), which presents a startling view of the Bosnian war from the Serbian perspective, is dedicated "To the Cinema of a Country that No Longer Exists," acknowledging the crucial role that the course of the one had in the shaping of the other. The extreme black humor of this film carried over into *Wounds* (*Rane*, 1998), Dragojević's cynical account of juvenile delinquents in the Belgrade criminal underworld, and Goran Paskaljević's *The Powder Keg* (*Bure baruta*, 1999), a series of violent vignettes set in various war zones just before the implementation of the Dayton peace accords.

The war in Kosovo and NATO bombing of Belgrade in March 1999 seriously inhibited the Serbian film industry (one of the primary targets was RTS—Radio Television of Serbia—whose offices and transmitters were destroyed, killing sixteen employees), and the first features to appear after the war were set during the NATO raids and shot on digital video—Milutin Petrović's *The Land of Truth, Love,and Freedom* (*Zemlja istine, ljubavi slobode*, 2000), the title referring ironically to life under Milosěvić, and Darko Bajić's *War Live* (*Rat uzivo*, 2002), about a film crew operating in Belgrade during the attacks. The Croatian industry makes about six films a year, all of them coproduced with HRT (Hvratsk Televizija, or Croatian Television). Since the death of president Franjo Tudjman in December 1999 and the ouster of his Croatian Democratic party from power in 2000, there has been a liberalization of media policy, among whose fruits are Vinko Brešan's *Marshal Tito's Spirit* (2001), a comic fantasy about the appearance of the ghost of Tito on a small Dalmatian island, and Rajko Grlić's *Croatia 2000* (2001), a documentary portrait of the nation on the eve the election that changed its course. In Bosnia, cinema has more or less disappeared. Not only was its material base in Sarejevo destroyed by years of shelling, but also the breakup of Yugoslavia left its filmmakers without access to equipment rental and laboratory facilities in Belgrade and Zagreb. A large-scale epic on the Bosnian war by Partisan film veteran Veljko Bulajić (see above) has been sidetracked several times since the Dayton accords by ethnic politics (Bulajić is a Montenegrin residing in Croatia), but in 2001 Bosnian writer/director Danis Tanović produced there, with French backing, his grim antiwar satire *No Man's Land*, and the film won an Academy Award for Best Foreign Film, at least giving the *idea* of a Bosnian cinema a much-needed shot in the arm.

16.62 *Pretty Village, Pretty Flame* **(Srdjan Dragojevic, 1996): Bosnian Serb militiaman Milan (Dragan Bjelogrlic) about to mow down a former Muslim neighbor as part of a war that plunged its soldiers into genocidal barbarism without restraint.**

16.63 *No Man's Land* (Danis Tanovic, 2001): feckless UN troops in Bosnia, unable, in this film, to keep even one Serb and one Bosnian soldier from killing each other.

Bulgaria

Some fifty-five feature films were produced in Bulgaria in the thirty-five years before Boris Borozanov's *Kalin the Eagle* (*Kalin Orelat*, 1950) appeared as the first fiction film of the recently nationalized film industry. Most of these films—such as Vassil Gendov's *Bai Ganiu* (1922), Nikolai Larin's *Under the Old Sky* (*Pod staroto nebe*, 1922), Peter Stojchev's *Land* (*Zemia*, 1930) and *Song of the Mountains* (*Planinska pesen*, 1934), Alexander Vazov's *Cairn* (*Gramada*, 1936), and Josip Novak's *Strahil the Voivoda* (*Strahil voivoda*, 1938)—were based on the rich literature of the Bulgarian National Revival, which had occurred in the nineteenth century and reached its pinnacle with the country's liberation from nearly five hundred years of Turkish rule in 1876. Also notable were the films of Boris Grezhov—especially *Maiden Rock* (*Momina skala*, 1923), *After the Fire over Russia* (*Sled Pozhara v Russia*, 1929), and *Graves without Crosses* (*Beskrastini grobove*, 1931), the last a controversial elegy for the victims of the White Terror of 1923 and Bulgaria's first sound film—as well as the weekly newsreels of the Bulgarsko Dělo company, founded 1939, the organization that would later give birth to the anti-Fascist Resistance.

Bulgaria entered World War II on the side of the Germans in 1941 but, when defeated by the Soviet Union on September 10, 1944, became one of that country's staunchest allies. The Bulgarians and the Russians have always been close, owing to their shared Orthodox religion and Byzantine cultural heritage; furthermore, Russia helped to liberate Bulgaria from the Turks by joining its war of independence against the Ottoman Empire in 1876—an act precipitating the Russo-Turkish War of 1877–78. A People's Republic was established following World War II on September 15, 1946, and the film industry was nationalized in 1948. As noted above, the first official feature film of the new state was *Kalin the Eagle*, a wedding of traditional Bulgarian patriotism and Zhdanovian socialist realism in which an exiled *haiduk* turned freedom fighter returns to his homeland after the expulsion of the Turkish overlords to find his people newly oppressed by foreign capitalists. The second and more important film, *Alarm* (*Trevoga*, 1951), was the first feature of the well-known cinematographer and documentarist Zahari Zhandov (1911–1998). Scripted by Anzhel Wagenstein (b. 1922), a recent graduate of the Moscow State Film School (VGIK), this film was a semidocumentary story of the division of political loyalties within a single Bulgarian family during the last days of World War II.

Zhandov and Wagenstein also collaborated on *Septembrists* (*Septemvriytsi*, 1954), a historically researched account of the 1923 uprising against the monarchy that generated the White Terror. Other landmarks of the era were Dako Dakovski's (1919–1962) *Under the Yoke* (*Pod igoto*, 1952), an ambitious adaptation of a classic novel by the Bulgarian national poet Ivan Vazov that is set just before the 1876 rebellion; Todor Dinov's (b. 1919) *Brave Marko* (1953; released 1955), the first cartoon from the newly reorganized animation and puppet studio in Sofia; and the Russian director Sergei Vasiliev's *The Heroes at Shipka Pass* (*Geriote na Shipka*, 1955), a coproduction with the Soviet Union depicting a heroic battle of the Russo-Turkish War. By 1957, the new Bulgarian film industry had produced a total of twenty-six features, no small accomplishment for an enterprise that began in 1950 with (by Zahari Zhandov's account) two or three Arriflex cameras, antiquated sound equipment, and few laboratories or theaters.

A major turning point for Bulgarian cinema was Rangel Vulchanov's (b. 1928) *On a Small Island* (*Na malkiia ostrov*, 1958), scripted by the poet Valeri Petrov (b. 1920) and shot in thirty days by Dimo Kolarov (1924–1997) on the Black Sea island of Saint Anastasia. Set just after the September 1923 uprising, when the island was used as a prison camp for suspected rebels, the film describes the doomed escape attempt of four individuals—a fisherman, a student, a carpenter, and a doctor—who represent a cross section of Bulgarian society and become in the film's stylization a metaphor for the destiny of the country as an independent state. The production team for *Island*—Vulchanov, Petrov, Kolarov, and the composer Simeon Pironkov (1927–2000)—made two more features to form a trilogy epitomizing the style of "poetic realism" then entering the Bulgarian cinema. This movement had affinities with French poetic realism and Italian neorealism but was more formally experimental than either of them, as demonstrated by *First Lesson* (*Parvi urok*, 1960), a tragic tale of young love set during the Resistance, and *Sun and Shadow* (*Slansteto i syankata*, 1962), which won a number of international awards. *Sun and Shadow* is an abstract statement on the cultural paranoia induced by living under the constant threat of a nuclear war between East and West. Another important film of the era was the German Democratic Republic–Bulgarian coproduction *Stars* (*Zvezdi/Sterne*, 1959), directed by the East German Konrad Wolf (1925–1982) with the assis-

16.64 *We Were Young* **(Binka Zheliazkova, 1961).**

tance of Vulchanov and written by Wagenstein, Wolf's former VGIK classmate. This extraordinary film about a love that grows between a German soldier and a Jewish girl during a transport to Auschwitz won the Special Jury Prize at Cannes in the year of its release and called world attention to the dynamic potential of Bulgarian cinema, as did Binka Zheliazkova's (b. 1923) *We Were Young* (*A biiahme mladi*, 1961), scripted by her husband Hristo Ganev (b. 1924).[4] Like Vulchanov a graduate of the Sofia Academy of Dramatic Art,[5] Zheliazkova was the first woman director in Bulgaria, and her feature debut was a lyrical story of love among Sofia Resistance fighters composed in the style of modern Bulgarian pictorial art.

Though it won a Gold Medal at the Moscow Festival, *We Were Young* was criticized at home, and Zheliazkova didn't make another film for six years. Vulchanov, whose *Sun and Shadow* had also been attacked in Bulgaria (for "abstract humanism"), next carried poetic realism into the

---

4. An earlier Zheliazkova-Ganev collaboration, *Partisans/Life Flows Quietly By* (*Partizani / Zhivostat si teche tiho*, 1958), was officially suppressed due to its controversial subject of political careerism among former Partisan heroes. It was shelved until 1990, remaining a rare, though hardly unique, instance of state censorship of the Bulgarian film industry since the thaw of the late 1960s.

5. The Academy of Dramatic Art in Sofia maintained a small film department in one of its wings as the only domestic source of professional training until the establishment of the Sofia Film and Television Academy (VITIS) in 1973.

realm of *film noir* in two complicated psychological thrillers, *The Inspector and the Night* (*Inspektorat i noshta*, 1963) and *The She-Wolf* (*Valchitsata*, 1965), both admired at Cannes. Vulchanov then journeyed to North Africa to make the documentary *Between Two Shores* (*Mezhdu dva briaga*, 1967), and he settled briefly in Czechoslovakia, where he made three films, the Czechoslovakian-Bulgarian historical tract *Aesop* (*Ezop*, 1968; released 1970) among them, before returning to Bulgaria in 1970. The pinnacle of Bulgarian poetic realism was reached in the directorial debut of the cinematographer Vulo Radev (1923–2001), *The Peach Thief* (*Kradetsut na praskovi*, 1964), a romantic story about a love triangle among a Bulgarian officer, his wife, and a Serbian POW set in the ancient fortress city of Turnovo during World War I and distinguished by its lush visual imagery. Radev practiced the same lyrical style in *Tsar and General* (*Tsar i general*, 1966), Bulgaria's first widescreen historical epic, which presents the conflict between King Boris III and General Zaimov, who heroically attempted to prevent the country's entry into World War II on the side of the Axis.

Zheliazkova returned to directing with the extraordinary *The Attached Balloon* (*Privarzaniat balon*, 1966; released 1967), adapted by Zheliazkova and the brilliant satirist Iordan Radichkov from his own novella. Like its source, the film is an absurdist fantasy about a military

dirigible that drifts into the vicinity of an isolated peasant village during World War II. The villagers see the balloon as a magical source of escape from their wretched daily lives and attempt to fly away in it, only to discover that it is tethered as firmly to the earth as they themselves are. Full of black humor and sardonic allusions to Stalinism, the film was released a year late and then quietly shelved, although it was transformed into a successful stage play entitled *Attempt to Fly* (after Radichkov's original) a decade later and presented at the Bulgarian Drama and Theater Festival in Sofia to great acclaim in 1979.

The cultural thaw that made such turnabouts possible occurred in Bulgaria much later than in other Eastern bloc countries, where its beginnings can generally be said to date from Khrushchev's "de-Stalinization" speech to the Twentieth Soviet Communist Party Congress in February 1956. That year in Bulgaria, by contrast, Stalinist premier Vulko Chervenkov lost his title to one of his own lieutenants (Anton Iugov) and was made minister of culture, from which position he became the scourge of the intelligentsia and continued to control the government. His chief opponent, the more moderate Todor Zhivkov, had to bide his time as first secretary of the Communist party of Bulgaria until he was able to become premier himself in 1962, purge Chervenkov, and move cautiously, like Khrushchev, toward a policy of gradual reform. Even so, the new president of the Bulgarian Writers' Union proclaimed as late as 1964 the validity of Zhdanovian socialist realism, and it was not until the late 1960s that signs of a real cultural thaw began to emerge in such films as Grisha Ostrovski and Todor Stoianov's *Sidetrack* (*Otklonenie*, 1967), Metodi Andonov's *The White Room* (*Bialata staia*, 1968), Georgi Stoianov's *Birds and Greyhounds* (*Ptitsi i hratki*, 1969), and Todor Dinov and Hristo Hristov's *Iconostasis* (*Ikonostasat*, 1969).

Ostrovski (b. 1918) and Stoianov's (1930–1999)[6] *Sidetrack*, scripted by the poet Blaga Dimitrova, received international attention as the first Bulgarian film to deal openly with the Stalinist past. It is constructed as a series of Resnais-like flashbacks triggered by a chance meeting between two former lovers and party comrades, although

16.65 *The Peach Thief* **(Vulo Radev, 1964).**

6. Among its other distinctions, *Sidetrack* was the first feature of its codirectors—Ostrovski was a gifted state director at the Sofia Satirical Theater and Stoianov a veteran cinematographer (for example, *The Peach Thief*). Despite the film's success, Ostrovski never worked in the cinema again, and Stoianov returned to directing only sporadically.

16.66 *Sidetrack* (Grisha Ostrovski and Todor Stoianov, 1967): Nevena Koka-nova.

16.68 *Iconostasis:* Dimitar Tashev.

its ultimate stylistic allegiance is to Antonioni. Andonov's (1932–1974) *The White Room* focuses on the dilemma of a nondogmatic scientist during the same era. Georgi Stoianov (b. 1936, Moscow), a 1964 graduate of the Institut des Hautes Études Cinématographiques (IDHEC) in Paris, founded by Marcel L'Herbier in 1943 (see Chapter 13), used elements of lyricism and grotesque black humor in *Birds and Greyhounds* to treat the subject of a group of young Partisans on trial for their lives in a small Bulgarian village during World War II. The high-water mark of Bulgarian cinema of the late 1960s, however, was *Iconostasis*,[7] directed in 1969 by the distinguished animator Todor Dinov (b. 1919) and by Hristo Hristov (b. 1926), recently graduated from the VGIK. Set at the height of the Bulgarian National Revival, near the end of the Turkish occupa-

tion, this national epic has its literary source in Dimitar Talev's novel *The Iron Candlestick* (published 1952), but it also bears the obvious influences of Tarkovski's *Andrei Rublev* (1966) and Parajanov's *Shadows of Forgotten Ancestors* (1964). Filmed by Atanas Tasev in widescreen in austere black-and-white,[8] *Iconostasis* recounts the life, dreams, and visions of a late nineteenth-century iconostasis wood-carver who draws upon the depth and breadth of the national folk culture for his inspiration.

The year of the release of *Iconostasis* marked the twenty-third anniversary of the Bulgarian People's Republic (BPR). Within that period its cinema had produced 160 features, 1,003 documentaries, 1,164 popular science films, and 144 cartoons. The number of theaters had increased exponentially from 165 in 1944 to 2,900,

16.67 *Iconostasis* (Todor Dinov and Hristo Hristov, 1969).

7. An iconostasis is the elaborately decorated screen dividing the sanctuary from the laity in Eastern Orthodox churches. For Bulgarians especially, the iconostasis has deep ritual and cultural significance.

8. Color did not become general in Bulgarian cinema until 1973.

while total attendance had leaped from 13 million to over 100 million per year. The annual production rate had risen to 14 features and 200 shorts. As if to accelerate this progress, in 1971 a new general director was appointed for the Bulgarian State Cinematography Corporation in the person of Pavel Pisarev, who reorganized it into three independent production units (Haemus, Mladost [Youth], and Sredets, 1973–74, with a fourth, Suvremenik [Contemporary], added in 1978–79) and saw to the establishment of a Film and Television Academy in Sofia (VITIS) in 1973. In 1972 Vulchanov was named Honored Artist of the BPR, and Zheliazkova was permitted to make her first film in six years with *The Last Word* (*Poslednata duma*, 1973), a story of six women in a death cell awaiting execution for activities in the anti-Fascist Resistance. Obviously, things were poised for change.

The next breakthrough was the stunning box-office success of Metodi Andonov's *The Goat Horn* (*Kozijat rog*, 1972), which was seen by over 3 million Bulgarians in the year of its release. This revenge tragedy, adapted by Nikolai Haitov from his own short story, was set in the seventeenth century, when *haiduks* conducted a kind of guerrilla warfare against the occupying Turks. Nationalism was also a key element in Hristo Hristov's *Hammer or Anvil* (*Nakovalnia ili chuk*, 1972), a large-scale Soviet–East German–Bulgarian epic on the infamous Leipzig trial of Georgi Dmitrov, the Bulgarian patriot accused of setting the Reichstag fire in 1933. Other significant works of 1972 were Liudmil Kirkov's (1933–1995) satire on provincial life, *A Boy Becomes a Man* (*Momcheto si otiva*), the first of a two-part series scripted by the humorist

Georgi Mishev (the second is *Don't Go Away* [*Ne si otivai*, 1976]); Georgi Stoianov's omnibus science-fiction film (Bulgaria's first), *The Third Planet from the Sun* (*Treta sled slantseto*); and Liudmil Staikov's (b. 1937) feature debut, *Affection* (*Obich*), a film about the generation gap that probed the surface of contemporary Bulgarian society and won a Gold Medal at the Moscow Festival in 1973. But by far the most significant film to proceed from the reorganization was Hristov's *The Last Summer* (*Posledno liato*), completed in 1972 but not released until 1974. Adapted by Iordan Radichkov from his novel of the same title, it concerns the fate of a peasant who refuses to leave his home when his valley is evacuated for submersion as part of an industrial dam project. Widely admired as an avatar of Bulgarian surrealism, the film employs stream-of-consciousness techniques and fantasy sequences to evoke both the protagonist's private crisis and the submersion of traditional village life by the tide of modern progress.

In 1973, a new generation of filmmakers announced itself to the world in the first major work of Ivan Terziev (b. 1934), Eduard Zahariev (1938–1996), and Georgi Djulgerov (b. 1943). Terziev's *Men without Work* (*Mazhe bez rabota*) inaugurated a series of films about the ethical problems of workers and productivity in a socialist economy, of which Terziev's own *Strong Water* (*Silna voda*, 1975) and Todor Andreikov's (1933–1997) *Sunday Games* (*Nedelnite machove*, 1975) were the most immediate successors. Zahariev's *Hare Census* (*Prebroiavane na divite zaitsi*), written in collaboration with Georgi Mishev,

16.69 *The Goat Horn* (Metodi Andonov, 1972).

16.70 *Hare Census* (Eduard Zahariev, 1973).

achieved a milestone for Bulgarian cinema in its absurdist satire of socialist bureaucracy: it recounts the story of an official statistician who is inexplicably sent to survey the number of hares near a small village, and it won several international awards. In *And the Day Came* (*I doide deniat*), Georgi Djulgerov inverted the standard formula for the "Eastern" (for Eastern Europeans, a Hollywood-style Western with a Resistance setting) to show Partisan warfare as it had really been—unheroic, inglorious, and tragically wasteful of the members of the "lost generation" who had waged it.

In 1974 and 1975, another problem endemic to Bulgarian society—and that of other Eastern European countries since World War II—became the subject of important films. This was the rapid migration of peasants from villages to towns and the radical changes imposed by urbanization on traditional ways of life. Hristov's *A Tree without Roots* (*Darvo bez koren*, 1974), Kirkov's *Peasant on a Bicycle* (*Selianinat s koleloto*, 1974), and Asen Shopov's *Eternal Times* (*Vechni vremena*, 1975) were all "migration films," but the most successful internationally was Zahariev and Mishev's *Villa Zone* (*Vilna zona*, 1975), a biting satire on the new urban class and its materialist values in the tale of a socially ambitious couple from the country trying to improve their status by giving a garden party. The actor and animator Ivan Andonov's

16.71 *Villa Zone* **(Eduard Zahariev and Georgi Mishev, 1975).**

(b. 1934) debut, *Fairy Dance* (*Samodivsko horo*, 1976), also written by Mishev, treated similar themes in its send-up of the art world and provincial consumerism. The other important films of 1976 dealt with historical subjects (for example, Borislav Sharaliev's (1922–2002) *The Apostles* [*Apostolite*], commemorating the rebels who led the April 1876 uprising against the Turks; Liudmil Staikov's *Amendment to the Defense-of-State Act* [*Dopalnenie kam Zakona za zashtita*], a reconstruction of the terrorist bombing of Sofia's Holy Sunday Cathedral during a state funeral in 1925, written by Anzhel Wagenstein) or were *auteur* films (Hristov's metaphysical science-fiction parable *Cyclops* [*Tsiklopat*], which he also wrote and designed,[9] and Georgi Stoianov's *A Cricket in the Ear* [*Shturets v uhoto*], a sort of Bulgarian *Waiting for Godot*).

It was during the 1977–78 season that Bulgarian cinema achieved an international profile that rivaled that of its Eastern-bloc neighbors. Eight films that won major festival awards appeared in this time frame, announcing a new artistic maturity for Bulgarian film. In its story of a conman during the Stalinist era, Georgi Djulgerov's *Advantage* (*Avantazh*, 1977), scripted by Djulgerov and photographed by Radoslav Spassov, contained more information about national political history than any Bulgarian film ever made. It compares favorably with Pál Gábor's *Angi Vera* and took the Silver Bear for Direction at Berlin in 1978. Eduard Zahariev's *Manly Times* (*Muzhki vremena*, 1977), a Gold Medal–winner at Teheran, was adapted by Nikolai Haitov from an ancient legend and brilliantly shot by Radoslav Spassov on location in the Rhodope Mountains. It tells the story of a peasant girl kidnapped for a rich suitor by a *haiduk*; she falls in love with her abductor during the course of their arduous journey across the mountains—with tragic results. Binka Zheliazkova's *The Swimming Pool* (*Basseinat*, 1977) was her first collaboration with her husband, the screenwriter Hristo Ganev, since *We Were Young* in 1961, and it won a Gold Medal at Moscow for its Proustian story of memories from the Stalinist past called up by a gathering of former friends and comrades around a luxurious swimming pool. Also reunited was the team of Vulchanov and Petrov (formerly of *Sun and Shadow*, 1962) for *With Love and Ten-*

---

9. Hristov frequently writes his own screenplays, designs his own sets, and directs his films as complete artistic units.

16.72 *Advantage* (Georgi Djulgerov, 1977).

derness (*S liubov i nezhnost*, 1978), a sophisticated study of a sculptor living in self-imposed exile on an island in the Black Sea.

Other important films were Ivan Nitchev's (b. 1940) *Stars in Her Hair, Tears in Her Eyes* (*Zvezdi v kosite, salzi v ochite*, 1977), an affectionate and historically accurate account of an itinerant theater troupe at the height of the Bulgarian National Revival during the late nineteenth century, which was written by Anzhel Wagenstein and took a prize at the Anitalia Festival; and Georgi Stoianov's *Pantelei* (1978), a satire reminiscent of Pinter (or Chaplin) about a political innocent who loses his identification papers and is drawn into the murderous Partisan uprising of 1944—on both sides. Liudmil Kirkov's *Matriarch* (*Matriarhat*, 1977), scripted by Georgi Mishev, deals with a village collective inhabited exclusively by women whose men have been forced to seek industrial work in distant towns. (This increasingly common social problem was also the subject of *Agronomists*, made the same year by the distinguished documentarist Hristo Kovachev [1929–1997], which won the Golden Dove at Leipzig in 1978.) Stefan Dimitrov's (1933–1990) *Hark to the Cock!* (*Chui petela!*, 1978) treats a similar theme in its portrait of old people in an abandoned village, while Ivan Andonov's *The Roof* (*Pokriv*, 1978) is a bittersweet love story that also analyzes the booming black market in ille-

gally procured construction materials. The season was capped by Georgi Djulgerov's *Swap* (*Trampa*, 1978), a structurally complex drama about an eminent writer's return to the provincial town whose collectivization he had covered for Radio Sofia during the postwar years; the journey triggers flashbacks to the Bulgarian Stalinist past and his own participation in it, using actual newsreel footage from the era. Finally, Kiran Kolarov (b. 1946), one of the first graduates of VITIS and a student of Hristov and Djulgerov, made a striking debut in *Status—Orderly* (*Sluzhebno polozhenie—ordinarets*, 1978), an ironic portrait of the lives of peasant military orderlies and their decadent officers in the royal barracks at the turn of the century.

As Bulgaria moved toward a jubilant celebration of its thirteen-hundredth anniversary as a nation (681–1981), the film industry was commissioned by the authorities of the State Cinematography Corporation to produce four superspectacles commemorating great events from the national past—Zahari Zhandov's *Master of Boiana* (*Boianskiiat maistor*, 1981), Liudmil Staikov's *Khan Asparukh* (1981), Georgi Stoianov's *Constantine the Philosopher* (*Konstantin Filosof*, 1983), and Borislav Sharaliev's *Boris the First* (*Boris Purvi*, 1984). Georgi Djulgerov's *Measure for Measure* (*Mera spored mera*, 1981), a three-part epic of the Macedonian struggle for liberation from the Ottoman Turks, was also produced for the celebration, as was Nikola Korabov's (b. 1928) documentary on the career of Bulgaria's world-famous operatic basso, *Nikolai Ghiaurov—50* (1980). But while these films were in production, Bulgarian cinema continued to garner world attention in Rangel Vulchanov's *The Unknown Soldier's Patent Leather Shoes* (*Lachenite obuvko na neznaniia voin*, 1979), Hristo Hristov's *Barrier* (*Barierata*, 1979) and *The Truck* (*Kamionat*, 1980), Liudmil Staikov's *Illusion* (*Ilyuziya*, 1980), and Binka Zheliazkova's *The Big Night Bath* (*Goliamoto noshino kupane*, 1980).

The Unknown Soldier's Patent Leather Shoes, which opened the London Festival in the year of its release and won the Grand Prix at New Delhi in 1981, was based on a 1963 script by Vulchanov and had been fifteen years in the planning. Cast with nonprofessionals in the leading roles, lyrically photographed by Radoslav Spassov, and narrated by the director himself, it evokes the lost village culture of the era between the wars through a series of childhood memories, and many critics regard it as one of the most

16.73 *The Unknown Soldier's Patent Leather Shoes* (Rangel Vulchanov, 1979).

beautiful Bulgarian films ever made. Hristov's *Barrier* is a psychological fantasy about a composer on the brink of a nervous breakdown who encounters a clairvoyant *anima* sprite and is taught "how to fly." The film, which ends with the protagonist's death "in flight," won first prize at the Moscow Festival in 1979, and its Chagall-like *mise-en-scène* brought cinematographer Atanas Tasev to international prominence. The following year, the same team produced *The Truck* (whose Bulgarian title, *Kamionat,* literally means "burden bearer"), a film about the tortuous journey of four companions through the mountains in the depths of winter to return the body of a dead comrade to his village for burial. Inspired by Clouzot's *The Wages of Fear* (1953), *The Truck* has all of that film's explosive tension, but it also provides a sharp metaphor for a society in the throes of profound social change, and it won the Grand Prix at Karlovy Vary in the year of its release. Staikov's *Illusion*—winner of the same prize in 1980—was an abstract philosophical "prequel" to his *Amendment to the Defense-of-State Act* (1976), set during the September uprising of 1923 which, when crushed, precipitated the two-year White Terror under the Fascist regime of Premier Alexander Tsankov. Filmed as a succession of poetic images, some contextually related and others posing questions on the nature of social responsibility and revolutionary praxis, *Illusion* requires a knowledge of Bulgarian history for full comprehension but is visually and aurally absorbing in the same fashion as *Barrier*. Zheliazkova's *The Big Night Bath*, chosen to represent Bulgaria at Cannes, is an existential

parable about a group of artists and bored vacationers at a Black Sea resort who, after an episode of night bathing, become involved in an ancient Thracian game.[1] As with *Illusion*, complete appreciation of the film is enhanced by a knowledge of Bulgaria's rich cultural heritage and its status as an archaeological treasure trove, but the themes of social responsibility and the burden of history become clear enough as the game proceeds from joke to deadly ritual and finally death for one of the players.

In the spring of 1981, the first of the superspectacles commissioned to celebrate the thirteen-hundredth anniversary of Bulgaria's founding as a state appeared in Zhandov's *Master of Boiana*, a fictionalized biography of the anonymous painter who did the world-famous egg-tempera frescoes at the Boiana Church on the outskirts of Sofia in 1259, a full half-century before Giotto introduced naturalism into religious painting in the West at the dawn of the Italian Renaissance. The film features vast sets duplicating the medieval village of Boiana and its church, which had recently been declared a cultural monument under UNESCO protection. The second celebration film to be released in 1981 was Staikov's monumental national epic *Khan Asparukh*, which depicts the mass migration of the Proto-Bulgars from the steppes of Central Asia to the Danube region between A.D. 679 and 681. This was an event in Bulgarian history comparable to the Norman invasion of the British Isles in 1066 since it resulted in the foundation of the Bulgarian state and its national culture. Running six hours and released as three separate features, *Khan Asparukh* took over a year to complete and employed some 50,000 extras from the Bulgarian army for its battle scenes. Part I, *Phanagoria*, is set on the plains of Azovian Great Bulgaria in what is now Kazakhstan, from which the title character (a relative of Attila the Hun) sets out to lead his people to a new homeland following the death of his father, Khan Kubrat, and the division of his kingdom. Part II, *Migration*, tells the story of

---

1. The Thracians were an Indo-European people who occupied the Balkan peninsula from approximately 3000 B.C. until it became part of the Roman Empire during the *Pax Romana*, 17 B.C.–A.D. 180. Racially, the Thracians were absorbed by the Slavs, who in turn bred with the Proto-Bulgars to become the Bulgarians. The Thracians, whom some historians credit with founding the music, mythology, and philosophy of ancient Greece, are thus the oldest identifiable ancestors of the Bulgarian people—who are justly proud of this heritage. A Thracian art exhibit, a collection of one thousand gold and silver artifacts from the third and fourth centuries, toured the world's museums as part of Bulgaria's thirteen-hundredth anniversary celebration.

the Bulgarian horde's two-decade trek westward across the Dnieper and the Danube to its friendly encounter with the Slavic tribes of the fertile Danube delta. Part III, *Land Forever*, recounts Asparukh's supreme accomplishment in his victory over the Byzantine army of Constantine IV Pogonatus in A.D. 680 against 10-to-1 odds and the subsequent foundation of the Bulgarian state in partnership with the Slavs. Sumptuously costumed and superbly photographed by Boris Ianakiev in widescreen Technovision and Eastmancolor, *Khan Asparukh* was seen by 11 million people in its first six months of release, creating a national—and perhaps even a world—per capita attendance record since the population of Bulgaria is only about 9 million. (A 95-minute English-language version produced for a Warner Bros. release abroad as *681 A.D.: The Glory of Khan*, 1984, was truncated beyond the point of comprehension.) Staikov followed this trilogy in 1988 with *Time of Violence (Vreme razdelno)*, a dazzling CinemaScope epic of the forced Islamization of a Bulgarian valley in the Rhodope Mountains in the seventeenth century. This four-and-one-half-hour film was released domestically as two films and set new box-office records in its very first month, but a seamlessly edited 160-minute version was shown to wide acclaim at Cannes.

The last commissioned film to be completed in 1981 was Djulgerov's *Measure for Measure*, a three-part chronicle of Macedonia's struggle for liberation from the Ottoman Turks from 1878 to 1912, based on historical records and eyewitness accounts of survivors. Beautifully photographed in color by Radoslav Spassov and employing Macedonian dialect throughout, this five-hour[2] spectacle synthesizes the history of the troubled region into a dynamic blend of fact, metaphor, symbol, and myth. Part I deals with the origination of the "Macedonian question" (which still disturbs geopolitical relations among former Yugoslavia, Bulgaria, and Greece today), when Bulgaria was liberated from the Turks in 1876 but the western part of its former empire, known as Macedonia, remained under Ottoman control. The period from 1878 to 1903 was one of awakening national identity for Macedonia, culminating in the bloody Ilinden Day uprising of August 2, 1903. Part II deals with the revolution that followed and the brutal counterinsurgency tactics of the Turkish army, from 1903 to 1906. Part III covers the years 1906 to 1912, when the revolutionaries finally succeeded by aligning themselves with the Young Turks in their own revolt against the Ottoman Empire.[3]

The last two of the great historical epics produced to celebrate Bulgaria's thirteen-hundredth anniversary were completed in 1983 and 1984, respectively. Georgi Stoianov's three-part *Constantine the Philosopher* tells the story of Cyril (Constantine) and Methodius, the ninth-century brother-saints who, as missionaries from the Greek Christian Church in Constantinople to the Moravian Slavs, devised the Cyrillic alphabet still used in Eastern Orthodox countries today and who prepared their disciples for the conversion of the Bulgarians, A.D. 864–65. Borislav Sharaliev's *Boris the First*, an epic in two parts (*The Conversion to Christianity* and *Discourse on Letters*), scripted by Anzhel Wagenstein, deals with that conversion itself and with its impact upon Bulgarian history. King Boris ascended the throne in 852 and was converted in 864; he ruled for thirty-seven years, until 889, and was ultimately succeeded by his son Simeon, who heralded the "Golden Age" of the First Bulgarian Empire. By choosing the Christianity of Constantinople over that of Rome and by elevating Simeon, Boris set the course of the Eastern Orthodox Church in Bulgaria for the next thousand years. (Sharaliev's spectacle won the Golden Rose at the 1984 Varna Festival of Bulgarian Feature Films.) Taken together, these five films, commissioned to celebrate Bulgaria's thirteenth centennial, chronicle the history of the Bulgarian people from their first migration from the Central Asian steppes through early Christianity to the cataclysmic events of the twentieth century.[4] It would be difficult to find a comparable body of work in the history of Eastern European or indeed any other cinema, although Hungary's fascination with its own national past provides an obvious parallel.

---

2. A shortened three-hour "festival version" is available.

3. In a tragic coda to its long war of liberation, Macedonia was simultaneously claimed by Serbia, Greece, and Bulgaria, resulting in the First (1912) and Second (1913) Balkan Wars and ultimately igniting World War I.

4. The critical blanks in this chain were filled by two other films produced in conjunction with the anniversary, Borislav Sharaliev's *The Thrust (Udaret*, 1982) and Vladislav Ikonomov's *The Day of the Rulers (Deniat na vladetelite*, 1985). The former is a two-part chronicle of events in Sofia from August 26 to September 9, 1944, the date marking the liberation of the city by Soviet troops and the moment of victory for the communist revolution. The latter, also in two parts, used sets left over from the major anniversary epics to recount the crucial years of A.D. 803–14, the reign of Khan Krum, who defeated the armies of the Byzantine emperor Nicephorus I at Vurbishki Pass in 811 and expanded Bulgarian territory at the expense of the Greeks.

Since the anniversary celebration of 1981, New Bulgarian Cinema, as it is now known to international critics, has continued to grow and prosper, producing major contributions with, in 1981, Ianko Iankov's *The Queen of Turnovo* (*Turnovskaia tsaritsa*) and Ivan Pavlov's debut, *Mass Miracle* (*Massovo chudo*); in 1982, Hristo Hristov's *A Woman at Thirty-three* (*Edna Zhena na trideset i tri*), Eduard Zahariev's *Elegy* (*Elegiia*), the distinguished Spanish director Juan Antonio Bardem's version of the Leipzig trial, *The Warning* (*Preduprezhdenieto*; coproduced with the GDR), and Ivan Andonov's *White Magic* (*Biala magiia*), which can be favorably compared with the work of Parajanov; in 1983, Rangel Vulchanov's *Last Wishes* (*Posledni zhelania*), the TV director Veselin Branev's *Hotel Central* (*Hotel Tsentral*), Ivanka Grybcheva's *The Golden River* (*Zlatnata reka*), Nikola Korabov's *Destiny* (*Orissia*), Liudmil Kirkov's *Balance* (*Ravnovesie*; his third collaboration with the scriptwriter Stanislav Stratiev and winner of the Silver Prize at Moscow), and Nikolai Volev's tribute to Balkan silent comedy at its best in *King for a Day* (*Gospodin za edin den*); in 1984, Kiran Kolarov's *Case No. 205/1913* (*Delo No. 205/1913*) and Hristov's *Question Time* (*Subesednik po zhelanie*); and in 1985, Hristov's *Reference* (*Herakteristika*). More recently, Nikolai Volev's *All for Love* (*Da obichash na inat*, 1986) and *Margarit and Margarita* (1988) have explored official corruption, Rangel Vulchanov's *Where Do We Go from Here?* (*A sega nakude?*, 1988) and Georgi Dyulgerov's musical *Acadamus* (*Akatamus*, 1988) have

both used staged events at the Sofia Drama Academy as metaphors for the state of contemporary Bulgarian society, and Ivan Nitchev's *Ivan and Alexandra* (*Ivan i Aleksandra*, 1989) demonstrates the influence of glasnost by recounting the horrifying use of children to denounce their parents during the Stalinist fifties.

Before 1990, Bulgaria made approximately 25 theatrical features and 25 features for television per year, in addition to 25 animated films and over 200 shorts and documentaries—an astounding rate for an industry that averaged only one feature per year as late as 1953. All of these were produced under the authority of the Bulgarian State Cinematography Corporation (BCC), which had five separate components: the Boiana Feature Film Studio,[5] a vast production complex, or film city, located at the foot of Mt. Vitosha on the outskirts of Sofia; the Sofia Animation Film Studio, made world famous by the award-winning work of Todor Dinov during the 1960s;[6] the Vreme Popular Science and Documentary Film Studio; the Film Laboratory, which currently has facilities for processing Eastmancolor, Sovcolor, Fujicolor, and Orwocolor (which still makes Bulgaria an attractive site for foreign coproduction); and Bulgariafilm, the industry's foreign trade, cultural exchange, and public-relations branch, which among its other functions, distributed a large number of feature, documentary, and animated films to Western television and video companies.[7] Bulgarian filmmakers—formerly trained abroad (usually at the VGIK or another Eastern-bloc academy) or at the

---

5. Until 1983, Boiana was made up of four production collectives, according to the Polish model. A filmmaker could join any group, which in turn had the right to final approval of story concepts and scenarios. In 1983, to increase the efficiency of the system, the four groups were disbanded and all feature production placed under the double management of industry veterans Zako Heskija and Liudmil Kirkov. Despite its highly centralized and hierarchical character, the Bulgarian film industry as a whole enjoyed considerable autonomy from the government under communism, a situation enhanced by the elimination of subsidies in 1968.

6. Dinov developed what has come to be known as the "Bulgarian Animation School," whose hallmark is the philosophical parable in pen and ink (for example, *The Story of the Pinetree Branch*, 1960; *Duet*, 1961; *The Lightning Rod*, 1962; *Jealousy*, 1963; *The Apple*, 1963; *The Daisy*, 1965). Dinov's major protégés are Donio Donev (b. 1929—*Three Fools*, 1970; *The Clever Village*, 1972; *Three Foolish Hunters*, 1972; *De Facto*, 1973; *The Three Fools and the Cow*, 1974; *The Musical Tree*, 1976; and

Causa Perduta, 1977) and Stoian Dukov (b. 1931—*Houses Are Forts*, 1967; *Mini*, 1971; *En Passant*, 1975; *A Musical Story*, 1976; and *February*, 1977). But Ivan Andonov (for example, *The Shooting Range*, 1964; and *Trouble*, 1967) and Ivan Vesselinov (*Tightrope Walker*, 1969; *The Devil in the Church*, 1969; and *The Heirs*, 1970) have also won many festival prizes. Recently, Sofia began the production of its first animated features in Rumen Petkov's *Treasure Planet* (*Planeta na sukrovishtata*, 1983), a science-fiction version of Robert Louis Stevenson's *Treasure Island*, and Donio Donev's *We Called Them Montagues and Capulets* (*Narekohme gi Monteki i Kapuleti*, 1985), loosely based on Shakespeare's *Romeo* and *Juliet*.

7. For example, Iankov's *The Queen of Turnovo* (1981) was recently shown by TVS in England, Zhandov's *Master of Boiana* (1981) was broadcast by Irish Television, and TF1 and Antenne 2 in France and Swiss Television all regularly feature Bulgarian animation. Moreover, Bulgarian features are widely available on videocassette in the Scandinavian countries and Spain.

small film department within the Academy of Dramatic Art in Sofia—since 1973 have been able to attend the Sofia Film and Television Academy (VITIS), which offers integrated degree programs in both cinema and theater. (Bulgarian cinema has always felt at home with its sister arts, with, for example, approximately 50 percent of its titles adapted from the national literature.) The Bulgarian film archive is one of the most sophisticated in the world, and attendance at the country's 3,600 theaters is among the highest in all of Europe—and, it should be noted, essential to the survival of the industry since the government eliminated direct production subsidies in 1968. Additionally, the Black Sea resort town of Varna was, until recently, the home of three major festivals—the National Feature Film Festival (October), the World Animated Film Festival (October), and the International Festival of Red Cross and Health Films (June)—each held every other year. All of this activity is quite remarkable for a country that barely had a cinema at all until the late 1950s, but with the fall of Todor Zhivkov's communist regime in November 1989, it came to an abrupt halt.

In 1990, the Bulgarian economy collapsed in the face of political upheaval and a staggering national debt; simultaneously, Bulgaria lost the Soviet Union as its primary trading partner and export market. The Boiana Film Studio, once the busiest on the Balkan peninsula, was forced to cut its staff from 1,220 to 340, and not a single Bulgarian film project was initiated that year (and only one—Docho Bodjakov's anticommunist *The Well* [1990]—was finally completed and released). In 1991, however, free elections were held, and the film industry was overhauled through the creation of the National Film Center (NFC) by an act of parliament. This agency is responsible for the allocation of state subsidies on the basis of artistic merit (as high as 80 percent for features) and for encouraging private investment. As a result of the NFC's efforts, Bulgaria was able to host four international coproductions in 1992, including Rangel Vulchanov's *Catastrophic Tenderness/Love Summer of a Bird* (*Lyubovta e nemirna ptitsa*), and to produce a handful of domestic works—e.g., Georgi Djulgerov's *The Camp*, an ironic study of a Young Communist work brigade, and Ivan Pavlov's philosophical fable *Walks with an Angel*. By 1993, there was speculation that both Boiana and the Vreme documentary studio, now completely autonomous, would become joint-stock companies partially owned by foreign investors. Since Boiana alone requires ten to fifteen annual in-house productions to

remain solvent, foreign investment is clearly a key factor for the Bulgarian industry's revival. To date, however, that investment has not been forthcoming, and what little production there is has been funded by the Television Films Production Center created by Bulgarian National Television in 1998. This entity and a modest state-subsidy program (no more than 25 percent of budget) have helped to fund a bare trickle of new films, most notably Ivan Nitchev's *After the End of the World* (*Sled kraja na sveta*, 1998), about the dissolution of ethnic tolerance that came with the imposition of Communism; Nickolai Volev's *Emergency* (1999), an award-winning documentary on the state of medical services in Sofia; and Iglika Triffonova's debut future *Letter to America* (2001), in which a young intellectual returns to Bulgaria from America to console a dying friend. Despite the relative slippage in production, Bulgaria continues to host several international festivals (in Sofia, Varna, and Plovdiv). As to the future, it is well to remember that the Bulgarians in just three decades created out of the most primitive and archaic film industry in all of Eastern Europe (excepting, of course, Albania) a national cinema that was less cosmopolitan, perhaps, but every bit as rich as that of Czechoslovakia or Hungary. The odds are that they will do it again, especially in the reform democratic conditions that have existed since the mid-1990s.

Romania

The Romanian film industry was initially more advanced than the Bulgarian by virtue of having its own film school, the Institute of Theater and Film Art (IATC), established in 1950, and an elaborate set of studios (completed in 1956) at Buftea, just outside of Bucharest. Romania produced about fifty full-length features even before World War II, many of them documentaries and travelogues funded by the Cinematographic Service of the National Tourism Office, established in 1936. After 1941, when the Cinematographic Service was transformed into the National Cinematographic Office (ONC), private production all but disappeared as a casualty of war. ONC dominated feature production until it, too, collapsed in 1943 after the failure of a joint filmmaking venture with the Italian government (CineRomIt). Nationalization of the industry began in 1948 with even less of a material base than that which existed in Yugoslavia, and the process was slowed by the Romanian Communist party's close dependence upon the Soviet Union and its occupying forces. The Romanian Communist party had a scant record of wartime resistance and was never part of a popular political movement, as were the Communist parties in Yugoslavia and Poland. (Traditionally anti-Russian, Romania had allied itself closely with the Nazis under the leadership of the Fascist premier, Ion Antonescu, 1940–45.) The Communist party was propped up by the presence of occupying Red Army troops from 1944 through 1958, during which time the USSR directed the Romanian economy through the creation of Soviet-Romanian corporations (SOVROM) and set its foreign policy. From the beginning of the 1960s onward, the Romanians moved away from the Soviets, contracted economic and political relationships with the West, and became the only Warsaw Pact nation to maintain friendly relations with the People's Republic of China.[8] But despite the adoption of a constitution calling for its complete independence in 1965, Romania remained in practical terms very much part of the Soviet-dominated Eastern bloc until the bloc's dissolution in 1989.

The first Romanian postwar films were rural dramas like Paul Călinescu's (1902–2000) *The Valley Resounds* (*Rașună valea*, 1949) and Dinu Negreanu's (b. 1919) two-part chronicle of peasant life, *The Bugler's Grandsons* (*Nepoții gornistului*, 1953) and *The Sun Rises* (*Răsare soarele*, 1954), constructed along strict Zhdanovian lines. There were also comedies adapting the farces of the world-famous Romanian playwright Ion Luca Caragiale (1852–1912), such as Jean Georgescu's *Chain of Weakness* (*Lanțul slăbiciunilor*), *The Visit* (*Vizita*), and *Romanian Farmer* (*Arendașul român*), all 1952. But it wasn't until Premier Gheorghe Gheorghiu-Dei, drawing his inspiration from Tito, led a successful movement to break away from the Soviet Union and its policies in the early 1960s that a truly national cinema began to emerge in the work of the first generation of IATC graduates, including Mircea Drăgan (b. 1932)—*Thirst* (*Setea*, 1960; the first Romanian widescreen film); *Lupeni 29* (1962); *Golgotha* (*Golgota*, 1967); Liviu Ciulei (b. 1923)—*The Danube Waves* (*Valurile Dunării*, 1959); *The Forest of the Hanged* (*Pădurea spinzuratilor*, 1965; winner of the Best Director Prize at Cannes in that year); and Mircea Mureșan (b. 1930)—*Blazing Winter* (*Răscoala*, 1965). During this same period the work of Ion Popescu-Gopo (1923–1989)—*A Short History* (*Scurtă istorie*, 1957; Palme d'Or, Cannes); *The Seven Arts*

(*Sapte arte*, 1958); *Homo Sapiens* (1960); *Hello! Hello!* (*Allo! Allo!*, 1962); *Sancta Simplicitas* (1968)—made Romania one of the world centers for animated film; since 1966, in fact, the International Festival of Animated Film has been held every second year in Mamaia (alternating with Annecy, France).[9]

As part of the new "Romanization of Romanian Culture"—which included the dropping of compulsory Russian from the public-school curriculum and the elevation of such Romanian émigré artists as the sculptor Constantin Brancuși (1876–1957) and the playwright Eugène Ionesco (1912–1994), both naturalized French citizens—Romanian filmmakers turned to the national historical tradition. They produced epics like Sergiu Nicolaescu's (b. 1930) *The Dacians* (*Dacii*, 1966) and *Michael the Brave* (*Mihai viteazul*, 1971; an Oscar nominee), as well as the films of the swashbuckling "haiduk" cycle of Dinu Cocea (b. 1929). These latter works—*The Haiduks* (*Haiducii*, 1965), *The Revenge of the Haiduks* (*Răzbunarea haiducilor*, 1968), *The Haiduks of Captain Anghel* (*Haiducii lui Șaptecai*, 1970), and others—translate the plots and techniques of Hollywood Westerns into romantic tales of *haiduks*, patriotic Romanian brigands doing battle with corrupt foreign overlords in the Carpathians. By 1965, the year in which Nicolae Ceausescu (1918–1989) succeeded Gheorghiu-Dei as first secretary of the Romanian Communist party, the country's film industry was in full swing, producing 15 to 18 features annually plus approximately 25 animated cartoons and about 100 newsreels.

It was in this context that the first authentically Romanian *auteur* films appeared in the work of Lucian Pintilie (b. 1933), whose *Sunday at Six* (*Duminica lă ora 6*, 1965) and *Reconstruction* (*Reconstituirea*, 1969) both won an international following. The former was a Resnais-like evocation of an incident from the Resistance, skillfully directed and shot, and completely lacking in dogma, while the latter was a controversial allegory of social irresponsibility whose release was delayed for a year by Romaniafilm officials charging "evidence of Western influence." *Recon-*

---

8. Romania was also the only Warsaw Pact country to maintain diplomatic relations with Israel after the Six Days' War in 1967 and to oppose the invasion of Czechoslovakia in 1968.

9. After producing the antiwar fantasy *Stolen Bomb* (*S a furat o bombă*, 1961), Popescu-Gopo turned to making features combining animation and live action, usually in the fairy-tale or science-fiction genres.

16.74 *Reconstruction* (Lucian Pintilie, 1969).

struction was in fact a profoundly Romanian film, focused on the perennial national traits of indifference to the fate of others and dereliction of duty, both encouraged by the consumption of enormous quantities of alcohol. It recounts the "reconstruction" of a crime by its original participants for an incompetent rural judge, all of whom couldn't care less about the event or its consequences. Strongly colored by Czech-inspired black humor, the film ends with a second and more serious crime being committed in the process of the reconstruction. Several of Pintilie's contemporaries, for example, Gheorghe Vitanidis (b. 1929)—*A Woman for One Season* (*O femeie pentru un anotimp*, 1969)—and Nicolae Breban (b. 1934)—*Sick Animals* (*Animale bolnave*, 1971)—also made films of social criticism during this era, and for a while it seemed as if there might be a Romanian cultural breakthrough of the sort experienced concurrently (however briefly) in Poland, Czechoslovakia, Hungary, and Yugoslavia. This hope appeared to be crushed in the spring of 1971, when Ceausescu, then president and self-proclaimed *conducatore* ("leader"), absorbed in the formation of a Stalinlike cult of personality, delivered a speech sharply critical of liberalizing tendencies among Romanian intelligentsia and creative artists. But in fact Ceausescu's attack was so stringent as to generate a strong wave of dissent, which resulted in an accommodation between Romanian politics and Romanian culture later in the year.

This left the way clear for the third generation of postwar Romanian filmmakers—"the Class of the 1970s," as it is called, since most of its members started working after the turn of the decade—to deal with themes that were formerly taboo in an atmosphere of increased tolerance for formal experimentation. Mircea Daneliuc (b. 1943) is the most prominent filmmaker of this generation, if not of all Romanian directors today, and he is followed closely by Dan Pița (b. 1938), Mircea Veroiu (1941–1998), and Alexandru Tatos (1937–1990). Daneliuc illuminated the generally dull landscape of the mid-1970s with *The Race/Long Drive* (*Cursa*, 1975), centering on the 24-hour odyssey of two truck drivers and a pretty hitchhiker, and *Special Issue* (*Ediție speciala*, 1978), a historical police thriller set in the context of the Romanian Fascist "Green Shirt" movement of the 1930s and 1940s. The following year his *Microphone Test* (*Proba de microfon*, 1980) won enormous popular success and was nationally rated among the ten best Romanian films ever made. It employs *cinéma vérité* techniques to describe the hectic, if dispassionate, life of a TV news cameraman who tends to see reality in the terms of a filmic montage and who ultimately has a stormy romance with one of his interview subjects. The same kind of formal innovation characterizes *The Cruise* (*Croaziera*, 1981), in which a large group of workers from various companies and factories are treated to a weeklong outing on the Danube for their exceptional service to the state. The film becomes a parable of generational conflict in contemporary Romania, as the cruise's organizers and the younger cruisers lock horns over moral, political, and sexual attitudes. *Fox-Hunting* (*Vînetoarea de vulpi*, 1981), adapted by Dinu Săraru from his best-selling novel *Some Peasants* (*Niște țrani*), is Daneliuc's most controversial work to date. It uses flashbacks, flashforwards, and multiple points of view to tell the story of a group of peasants in the postwar years who stubbornly refuse to cede their land to the state, while party officials argue with them just as stubbornly for the historical necessity of collectivization. More recently, Daneliuc has attempted to create a metaphor for Romanian history itself in *Glissando* (1984), adapted from a short story by Cezar Petrescu (the term *glissando* denotes the rapid sliding up and down a musical scale). Set in the 1930s, this film follows the descent of a dissipated bourgeois intellectual into obsession and madness, and it concludes with a sustained Dantesque fantasy sequence that affirms the capacity for human dignity even in the grips of the most horrendous spiritual oppression. Despite several festival awards, *Glissando* proved offensive to the Romanian censors, and Daneliuc was prevented from making another film until *Jacob* (*Iacob*, 1988). This film skirted politics in its complicated parable of a gold miner and his family in Transylvania in the 1930s who are brutalized by an unspecified economic system, which might equally well be capitalism or communism. Like Daneliuc's other prerevolutionary films, *Jacob* won unanimous praise abroad and box-office success at home; and after the fall of Ceausescu, Daneliuc would continue to probe the Romanian conscience in films of extraordinary beauty (see below).

The best-known Romanian filmmaker after Daneliuc is Dan Pița, who directed two award-winning medium-length features with Mircea Veroiu about Carpathian peasant life—*The Stone Wedding* (*Nunta de piatra*, 1973) and its sequel, *Lust for Gold* (*Duhul aurului*, 1974)—before switching to contemporary issues in *Philip the Kind* (*Filip cel bun*, 1974), a realistic portrait of a young man's search for moral identity in the midst of rampant social change. He followed with a brilliant adaptation of the classic Romanian novel *Summer Tale* (*Tănase scatiu*, 1977) by Duilui Zamfirescu. Photographed in luxurious sequence shots by Călin Ghibu, this beautiful and elliptical film centers on the *fin de siècle* power struggle between the aristocracy and the bourgeoisie and is—from atmosphere, through music, to decor—highly reminiscent of late Visconti. Pița next scored a smashing box-office success with his hilarious Romanian Western, *The Prophet, Gold, and the Transylvanians* (*Profetul, aurul, şi Ardelenii*, 1979), centering on a Transylvanian peasant family relocated in the trigger-happy American West of the 1800s. But he turned deeply serious, even metaphysical, in *Contest/Orientation Course* (*Concurs*, 1983; FIPRESCI Prize, New Delhi), the story of a group of alienated people running an obstacle course through the wilderness. In the manner of Tarkovsky's *Stalker* (1979), the film becomes a dense parable about the failure of collectivity through indifference and is widely regarded as one of the most profound Romanian films ever made. *Chained Justice* (*Dreptate în lanțuri*, 1985; Special Jury Prize and Press Prize, Santarem) won similar praise in its tale of the real-life Pantelimon, a latter-day *haiduk* who fought against the oligarchy's police state circa 1910. More recently, Pița directed the highly stylized *Pas in Doi* (*Paso doble*, 1986), in which a rather conventional love triangle becomes a vehicle for some incisive criticism of contemporary Romanian society.

After co-directing *The Stone Wedding* and *Lust for Gold* with Dan Pița, Mircea Veroiu achieved a masterpiece in his adaptation of Ioan Slavici's classic novel *Mara*, as *Beyond the Bridge* (*Dincolo de pod*, 1977). Set in a small town in Transylvania on the eve of the 1848 revolution, this film tells a romantic love story in modern psychological terms, and its virtuoso photography by constant Veroiu collaborator Călin Ghibu evokes the past in allusions to famous Flemish and other northern European Renaissance paintings. Veroiu followed with *Mînia* (*Chronicle of the Barefoot Emperors*, 1978), an epic film based on the tragic peasant uprising of 1907 when over 11,000 rebels were shot down by the Romanian Army of King Carol I (also the subject of Mureşan's *Blazing Winter*). Recent Veroiu films include *To Die from Love of Life* (*Să mori rănit din dragoste de viață*, 1984), a sophisticated rendition of communist resistance to the Fascist "Green Shirts" in 1934, replete with stylish allusions to 1930s' cinema, and *Adela* (1985), a sumptuously produced Chekhovian love story, set on a country estate in the lazy summer of 1899, which won the Gran Premio at San Remo.

Alexandru Tatos brought into the Romanian cinema a rich intellectual background from the theater. He dealt initially with contemporary themes in such films as *Red Apples* (*Mere rossi*, 1977) and *The Wandering* (*Rătăcire*, 1978). The former is a realistic exploration of a recently graduated surgeon in a rural hospital, while the latter concerns a young Romanian girl, attracted by the market economy's glittering prizes, who marries an ambitious West German but finds herself unable to adapt to the culture of mass consumption. *The House in the Fields* (*Casa dintre cîmpuri*, 1980; originally made for television) tells the story of an idealistic agronomist who must battle corrupt and dishonest bureaucrats in the village where he is sent to work. But Tatos's most poetic film was *Anastasia Passed By/Gently Was Anastasia Passing* (*Duios Anastasia trecea*, 1980), adapted by Dumitru Radu Popescu, one of the leading figures of contemporary Romania literature, from his own novella. It is a version of Sophocles' *Antigone*, set in a Nazi-occupied Danubian village, where a young schoolteacher defies a German edict not to bury a Serbian partisan at the cost of her life. Tatos followed *Anastasia* with *Sequence* (*Secvente*, 1983), his most experimental film to date, which offers three original "short stories" in film about the relationship among cinematic illusion, history, and the quotidian real. More recently, Tatos has resumed his partnership with D. R. Popescu to produce *Forest Fruit* (*Fructe de padure*, 1984), a melancholy portrait of a seventeen-year-old country girl seduced and abandoned by her lover, which manages to become a lyrical testament to human dignity. Tatos also directed *Gathering Clouds* (*Intunercare*, 1988), which was featured with six other works at a Romanian Film Week held by the American Film Institute at the Kennedy Center, Washington, D.C., in 1989.

From a virtually nonexistent material base in the late 1940s, Romanian cinema in the 1980s grew into one of the more viable in Eastern Europe. In the early 1970s, the film industry was decentralized and the production of feature films split into five groups, according to the Polish model. Between 1978 and 1989, these groups produced an average of 30 features annually, with a high of 36 in 1984. (Furthermore, from 1971 through 1989 the Romanian TV Film Studio, under the leadership of Victoria Marinescu, produced or coproduced with the film industry 15 serials, 40 long- and medium-length features, 30 cartoons, and 562 medium and short documentaries or musicals, all in color.)[1] Under communism, the Romanian industry was more completely self-financed than any in the Eastern bloc, and domestic box-office success was crucial to its survival. In a still developing country of 22.3 million people, it is no small accomplishment that between 1979 and the 1989 revolution over one-third of all admissions in the nation's 634 theaters were for domestic films of an often high aesthetic and intellectual caliber.

The violent overthrow of the Ceausescu dictatorship in December 1989 placed the country in the hands of the National Salvation Front (FSN), whose leader, Ion Iliescu, was elected president in 1990. Iliescu attempted to move Romania toward a free-market economy but left the authoritarian communist infrastructure, including the dreaded *securitate* (secret police), partially intact. When students and intellectuals staged a 53-day anticommunist street demonstration in Bucharest's University Square from April 23 to June 15, 1990, they were savagely attacked and routed by "coal miners" called in from the provinces and coached by *securitate* agents. Iliescu denied any complicity in the rampage, but Stere Gulea's feature-length compilation documentary *University Square* (1991), produced by Lucian Pintilie with funds from the Ministry of Culture, makes it clear that the government orchestrated the whole thing. Despite frantic attempts to suppress it, this film set a record for documentary attendance in Romania (where it provoked further rioting) and won sev-

eral international awards; and Stere Gulea was subsequently named head of the Institute of Theater and Film and, later still, director of the National Film Office.

The situation of *University Square* was symptomatic of the widening rift between the FSN government and Romanian filmmakers. Shortly after the revolution, the General Assembly created the National Cinema Center to facilitate the transition from state monopoly to private industry, but it functioned so poorly that a general strike of film workers was called in early summer 1991 to protest it. At that point, the government cut off subsidies, which had reached subsistence level in any case thanks to rampant inflation. (Ceausescu's megalomaniacal scheme to rebuild Romania through "systematization" had left the nation nearly bankrupt.) Still, foreign capital has recently enabled the production of a handful of important Romanian features. These include Lucian Pintilie's *The Oak* (1991), a satire about Romania under Ceausescu; Stere Gulea's *Fox Hunter* (1992), a study of the psychology of a *securitate* agent and his wife; Mircea Daneliuc's antiauthoritarian parables *The Eleventh Commandment* (1992) and *The Conjugal Bed* (1993), set during World War II and 1992, respectively; and Dan Piţa's *Hotel de Luxe* (1993; Silver Lion, Venice), a gloomy meditation on dictatorship. American companies, such as Full Moon Entertainment, have also set up in post-Ceausescu Romania to cash in on its relatively low production costs. More recently, Castel Film, with four fully equipped soundstages, became the largest full-service private studio in Romania; although it mainly caters to American and French companies, it stimulates the industry indirectly by employing local talent. In 1997, the government created the National Cinematographic Office (Oficiul National al Cinematografiei, or ONC) to replace the old National Cinema Center and help to

---

1. Collaboration between the film and television industries in Romania was stronger than in any other Eastern European country and resulted in some distinguished achievements. *August in Flames* (*August in flăcări*, 1974), for example, was a thirteen-part series directed by Dan Piţa, Alexandru Tatos, and Doru Năstase on the anti-Fascist uprising of August 23, 1944, which opened the floodgates of the revolution; *Independence War* (*Razboiul Independentei*, 1976–77), a colorful eight-part period piece directed by Sergiu Nicolaescu, celebrated the centenary of the Romanian war of liberation against Turkey; while *Lights and Shadows* (*Lumini şi umbre*, 1981–82) was an ambitious thirty-three-part series on the activities of the communist underground during World War II, directed by Andrei Blaier, Mihai Constantinescu, and Mircea Mureşan, which was awarded the Prize of the Romanian Filmmakers Association.

reform the industry along free-market lines. The ONC finances projects up to 50 percent of budget on a competitive basis and has recently helped to produce such work as Mircea Veroiu's last film *The Women in Red* (*Femeia în rosu* (1997), about the Romanian émigré who became John Dillinger's mistress and turned him in to the FBI; Dan Piţa's *The Man of the Day* (*Omul zilei*, 1998), a hard-edged look at contemporary Romanian politics; Sergiu Nicolaescu's First World War drama *Deadly Triangle* (*Triunghiul mortii* (1999); and Lucian Pintilie's dark studies in the psychology of authoritarian repression *Last Stop Paradise* (*Terminus Paradis*, 1998), winner of the Silver Lion at Venice, and *L'après-midi d'un tortionnaire* (*The Afternoon of a Torturer*, 2001). And yet it remains true that the same Romanian industry that before the 1989 revolution produced 25 to 30 features annually—most of them for domestic consumption—today produces only 2 or 3 a year, although these tend to be high-profile works by known *auteurs* destined for exhibition on the festival circuit.

Other Balkan Countries

Two other Balkan countries that have evolving film industries are Turkey (population 67.3 million) and Greece (population 10.6 million). The Turkish industry is large but erratic and geared mainly toward the production of domestic exploitation films. For example, 128 features were produced in 1978 and 195 in 1979, but only 70 in 1980 and 1981. This is because the industry is heavily dependent on the vicissitudes of the inflation-ridden national economy and, since the army seized control of the government in 1980, on political whim as well. Although the military junta was succeeded by the "reformist" rule of a right-wing/conservative coalition in 1991, political censorship is still practiced today. Mainstream commercial cinema is closely associated with "Yeş-ilçam," the street in Istanbul where most film companies had their offices during the 1950s and 1960s when production reached historic heights of 200 to 300 features per year, and the term has somewhat negative connotations. (*Yeşilçam* literally means "green pine," or, metaphorically, "Hollywood.") Nevertheless, Turkey has produced several filmmakers of great talent and at least one of legendary prominence since World War II.

During the relatively liberal 1960s, a movement was born known as Young Turkish Cinema, or the National Cinema, which centered around the actor-writer Yilmaz Güney (1937–1984), who had become a matinee idol early in the decade. Güney began directing from his own scripts in the late 1960s, and in the early 1970s he produced a significant body of politically motivated work through his own company, Güney-Filmcilik, focused on the everyday poverty and oppression of his people—*Hope* (*Umut*, 1970), *The Fugitives* (*Kaçaklar*, 1971), *The Wrongdoers* (*Vurguncular*, 1971), *Tomorrow Is the Final Day* (*Yarin son gundur*, 1971), *The Hopeless Ones* (*Umutsuzlar*, 1971), *Pain* (*Aci*, 1971), *Elegy* (*Agit*, 1971), and *The Father* (*Baba*, 1971). The ironically titled *Hope* was banned by the Turkish government, which also forbade the film's entry in the Cannes Film Festival. A smuggled print of it was shown there in 1971, however, and attracted some attention. In 1972, in the midst of shooting *The Poor Ones* (*Zavallilar*, completed 1975), set in the underbelly of Istanbul, Güney was arrested, charged with harboring fugitive anarchists, and imprisoned without trial for twenty-six months. Released in 1974 under a general amnesty for political prisoners, Güney jumped immediately into producing *The Friend* (*Arkadas*, 1974), *Anxiety* (*Endise*, 1974), and completing *The Poor Ones* before being imprisoned again on trumped-up charges of murdering a right-wing judge (the initial sentence was twenty-four years of hard labor, later commuted to eighteen). In jail—owing to his popularity as an actor-director—Güney was permitted to screen films and continue to write scripts, which were directed by associates on the outside; these included *The Herd* (*Sürü* [directed by Zeki Ökten, 1978]), *The Enemy* (*Dusman* [Zeki Ökten, 1979]), and his extraordinary masterpiece *Yol* (Serif Gören, 1982). This film, whose title literally means "the way," was shot by Gören but edited by Güney in France after his 1981 escape from Toptasi prison. It traces the fortunes of five men on one-week's leave from prison as they traverse the country from west to east and is a relentless, unflinching indictment of Turkey's patriarchal system of values. *Yol* shared the Golden Palm at Cannes in 1982 with Costa-Gavras's *Missing*, and Güney directed one last film—*Le Mur* (*The Wall*, France, 1983), based on a brutally suppressed prison revolt that occurred in Ankara in 1976—before dying of stomach cancer in Paris in 1984. At this writing, Güney's films are still officially banned by the Turkish government.

16.75 *Yol* (Serif Gören, 1982).

Güney's co-directors, the so-called "middle generation," have since become important figures in Turkish cinema—Ökten (b. 1941), for example, with *The Wrestler* (*Pehlivan*, 1985), *The Voice* (*Ses*, 1987), and *The Queen World* (*Düttürü Dünya*, 1989), and Gören with *Remedy* (*Derman*, 1984), *Germany, Bitter Land* (*Almanya, aci vatan*, 1985), *The Escape* (*Firar*, 1985), *The Frogs* (*Kurbagalar*, 1986), *Blood* (*Kan*, 1986), and *One Weird Movie* (1990). Güney's teacher, the veteran director Atif Yilmaz (b. 1925), has also produced significant films in the 1980s and 1990s (for example, *Her Name Is Vasfiye* [*Adi Vasfiye*, 1986]; *The Mill* [*Degirmen*, 1987]; *My Dreams, My Love, and You* [*Hayallerim, askim ve sen*, 1988]; *My Friend the Devil* [*Arkadasim Seytan*, 1989]; *A Dead Sea* [*Ölü bir deniz*, 1990]; *Barter Bride* [*Berdel*, 1991]; *Walking after Midnight* [1992]). Güney's former assistant, Ali Özgentürk (b. 1945), has made *Horse, My Horse* (*At*, 1982), *The Guard* (*Bekci*, 1985), *Water Also Burns* (1987), and *Naked* (1992); and his former composer, Ömer Zülfü Livanel: made *Iron Earth, Copper Sky* (*Yer demir, gok bakir*) in 1987. Other Turkish filmmakers of note are Erden Kiral (b. 1942—*On the Fertile Land* [*Bereketli topraklar uzerince*, 1980]; *Dilan* [1987]; *Hunting Time* [*Av zamani*, 1988]; *The Blue Exile* [1992]); Yusuf Kurçenli (b. 1947—*Blackout Nights*, 1990); and Ömer Kavur (b. 1944), widely held to be the most European-style director in the country (*A Brokenhearted Love Story*

[*Kirik bir ask hikayesi*, 1983]; *The Desperate Road* [*Amansiz yol*, 1986]; *Motherland Hotel* [*Anayurt oteli*, 1987]; *Night Journey* [*Gece Yolculugu*, 1988]; *Secret Face* [*Gizli yüz*, 1991]).

In 1989, Turkish cinema entered a period of crisis as inflation reached 70 percent and a sudden television boom tripled the number of available national channels. Domestic film attendance plummeted, and a substantial number of theaters closed. From 100 domestic features in 1988, annual output declined to fewer than 50 in 1989, stabilizing at about 60´in 1991. Many production companies folded, and those remaining downsized to accommodate both a shrinking domestic market and the loss of a major export market in the Soviet Union. Nevertheless, Turkey still possesses a very active film industry and film culture. In 1993, for instance, 6 million spectators accounted for 30 million theater admissions, the national Antalya Film Festival celebrated its twenty-ninth anniversary, and the twelfth Istanbul International Film Festival presented approximately 120 films from all over the world to an audience of 150,000 people. By the mid-1990s, however, Turkish production had fallen to just 20 films per year, with an occasional sleeper like Yavuz Turgul's *The Bandit* (*Eskiya*, 1997), the simple story of a Kurdish outlaw who is captured and betrayed by a friend, doing record business. Another unanticipated blockbuster was Mustafa Altioklar's *Cholera Street* (*Agir roman*, 1998), adapted from a novel of Istanbul Gypsy life. Several directors from the "middle generation" of the 1970s and 1980s made comebacks during this time—e.g., Ali Özgentürk delivered *The Letter* (*Metktup*, 1999), about a man researching the death of his father, a political prisoner killed in the custody of the police; Zeki Ökten produced the old-fashioned love story *Goodbye* (*Güle, güle*, 2000); Atif Yilmaz directed *After the Fall* (*Eylül firtinasi*, 2000), about the lives of left-wing intellectuals after a 1980's military coup; and Ömer Kavur turned in *House of the Angels* (*Melekler evi*, 2001), a political thriller based on a real-life political-corruption scandal. The younger generation of Turkish filmgoers, however, seems essentially uninterested in politics: it made an all-time box-office hit out of Yilmaz Erdogan's *Vizontele* (*Television, 2001*), a nostalgic comedy about the introduction of television in a small rural village in the 1970s, while the young female director Yesim Ustaoglu's *Journey to the Sun* (*Günese yolculuk*, 2000), winner of multiple international awards, was rejected for its treatment of a politically volatile theme—the friendship between a young Turkish boy and a Kurdish boy in Turkey.

Because Greece was involved in a bloody civil war between communist and loyalist factions for four years beyond the end of World War II, the film industry did not really revive itself until the 1950s when the output fluctuated between 15 and 30 features per year, many of them broad *farsocomedies*, or so-called *foustanelas*, patriotic action films named after the traditional Greek male kilt. In 1951 the Lycourgos Stavrakos Film School was established in Athens, and most Greek filmmakers of the 1950s and 1960s received some training there. Serious films, such as Grigoris Grigoriou's (b. 1919) *Bitter Bread* (*Picro psoume*, 1951) and Stelios Tatasopoulos's *Black Earth* (*Mavri yee*, 1952), were heavily influenced by Italian neorealism, but Michael Cacoyannis's (b. 1922) *Stella* (1956), a film about a tavern singer played by Melina Mercouri, combined social criticism with Hollywood-style sex appeal to attract international attention at Cannes. During the 1960s commercial cinema boomed as Greece became the site for such coproductions as *Never on Sunday* (Jules Dassin, 1960), *The Guns of Navarone* (J. Lee Thompson, 1961), and *Zorba the Greek* (Cacoyannis, 1965); and the domestic production rate reached nearly 100 films per year, most of them blatantly commercial. With government backing, Thessaloníki became the home of a major domestic festival; and Greek performers like Mercouri, Irene Papas, and Georges Foundas and Greek composers like Manos Hadjidakis and Mikis Theodorakis gained international reputations.

But a truly national film culture did not emerge until after the colonels' coup of April 21, 1967, when the junta's attempts to stifle social change produced a cinema far more radical than anything Greece had experienced to date. Its founder and leader was Theodoros Angelopoulos (b. 1935), whose first features, *Reconstruction* (*Anaparastassi*, 1970) and *Days of '36* (*Mere toy*, 1972), were both fairly direct critiques of the social system. But of Angelopoulos's later works, *Traveling Players* (*Thiassos*, 1975) is a formally complicated, multilayered tapestry of scenes tracing the performances of an itinerant theater troupe as it wanders the provinces during the crucial years of modern Greek history, 1939–50, while *The Hunters* (*I kynigi*, 1977) is a densely symbolic meditation on the civil war that consolidates the director's mature style

of achronological narrative and extremely long, Jancsó-like takes, faintly resolved by cinematographer Giorgos Arvanitis. During the 1980s Angelopoulos produced a series of demanding, impressive, and, ultimately, mysterious, films—*Alexander the Great* (*O Megalexandros*, 1980; Golden Lion, Venice), *Voyage to Cythera* (*Taxidi sta Kithira*, 1984; Best Screenplay, Cannes), *The Beekeeper* (*O melissokomos*, 1986); *Landscape in the Mist* (*Topio stin omihli*, 1988; Silver Lion, Venice), and *The Suspended Step of the Stork* (*To meteoro vima tou pelargou*, 1990)—that placed him among the ranks of such world-class directors as Tarkovsky, Mizoguchi, and Ozu. After Jancsó, however, the director Angelopoulos most closely resembles is Antonioni both for his slow, deliberately paced sequence shots and the fundamental modernism of his themes. This was most apparent in two films of the 1990s that brought great prestige to Greek cinema—*Ulysses' Gaze* (*To vlemma tou Odyssea*, 1995), which won the Grand Jury Prize at Cannes, and *Eternity and a Day* (*Mia eoniotita ke mia mera*, 1998), which won the Cannes Palm d'Or for Best Film—both of them spellbinding works about metaphysical journeys and the relationship among memory, history, and time in a uniquely Balkan setting.

Angelopoulos's films inspired a generation of directors whose work in creating the New Greek Cinema began in earnest after the military dictatorship of George Papadopoulos ended in 1973, and flourished with the election

16.76 *Ulysses' Gaze* (Theodoros Angelopoulos, 1995): the head from a huge disassembled statue of Lenin being crane-lifted into a river barge, one of many mysterious images in the film, strikingly photographed by Angelopoulos's regular cinematographer Giorgos Arvanitis.

of socialist Andreas Papandreou as prime minister in 1981. Papandreou appointed exiled dissident Melina Mercouri (1923–1994) to the post of Minister of Culture with the mission to reinvigorate the government-funded Greek Film Center (GFC), which she successfully did until the fall of Papandreou's government in 1988. During her eight years in office, Mercouri progressively increased the GFC's budget and engineered the passage of a comprehensive cinema law in 1986 that guaranteed a tax rebate to exhibitors who would agree to program a certain number of domestic features. During this period the GFC's participation in feature production rose as high as 60 percent, and by 1989 it had become the only steady source of funding for domestic projects. When the Papandreou government fell in the wake of a financial scandal in 1988, production declined sharply. But the passage of a new cinema law in 1989, combined with the newly formed conservative government's recommitment to the GFC in 1990, suggested that Greek cinema would survive an annual inflation rate of 17 percent, as well as the more recent threat posed by satellite broadcasting and VCRs. As a sign of the industry's relative good health, the thirty-two-year-old Thessaloníki Film Festival became an international event for the first time in 1992.

Among the more prominent figures in New Greek Cinema, directors who often write as well as produce their own films and who still practice today are Nikos Panayotopoulos (b. 1941)—*The Colors of Iris* (*Ta chromata tis iridos*, 1974); *The Idlers of the Fertile Valley* (1978); *The Woman Who Dreamed* (*I Yineka pou evlepe ta onira*, 1988); Pantelis Voulgaris (b. 1940)—*The Engagement of Anna* (*To proxento tis Annas*, 1972); *Great Love Song* (*O megalos erotikos*, 1973); *Happy Day* (1976); *Eleftherios Venizelos, 1910–1927* (1980); *Stone Years* (*Petrina chronia*, 1985); *Striker with the No. 9* (1988); *Quiet Days in August* (1990); Pavlos Tassios (b. 1942)—*Yes, But* (*Nai men all*, 1972); *Special Request* (*Parangelia*, 1980); *Stigma* (1984); *Knock-Out* (1986); Nikos Koundouros (b. 1926)—*Young Aphrodites* (*Mikres Afrodites*, 1963); *1922* (1978; released 1981); *Bordello* (1985); *Byron: Ballad of a Daemon* (1992); Frieda Liappa—*The Roads of Love Are Night Roads* (*I dromi tis agape ine nykterini*, 1981); *A Quiet Death* (*Enas isichos thanatos*, 1986); Tonia Marketaki (b. 1942)—*The Price of Love* (*I timi tis agape*, 1984); Nikos Nikolaidis (b. 1939)—*Sweet Bunch* (*Glykia symmoria*, 1983); *Morning Patrol* (*Proini peripolis*, 1987); *Singapore Sling* (1990); Yorgos

Katakouzinos—*Angel* (*Anguelos*, 1982); *Absences* (*Apoussies*, 1987); Dimos Avdeliodis (b. 1952)—*The Tree We Were Hurting* (*To dendro pou pligoname*, 1986); Tassos Psarras (b. 1950)—*The Reason Why* (1974); *May* (1976); *Caravan Palace* (*Caravan sarai*, 1986); Nikos Papatakis (b. 1918)—*Les Abysses* (1963); *The Photograph* (*I photographia*, 1986); Costas Vrettakos—*The Children of the Swallow* (*Ta pedia tis chelidonas*, 1987); and Tassos Boulmetis—*The Dream Factory* (*Viotechnia oniron*, 1990). Although Greek films face stiff competition from television networks and American films, which consistently have an 80 percent share of the local market, the industry continues to produce about 15 films a year with combined funding from the Greek Film Center, foreign investors, and private television stations. Successful features are often domestic comedies like Thanasis Papathanasiou's *Safe Sex* (2000) and Olga Malea's *Risotto* (2001), both of which broke box-office records. But there is still room for such art-house fare as Michael Cacoyannis's adaptation of Chekhov's *The Cherry Orchard* (*Varya*, 1999) and Dimos Avdeliodis's *The Four Seasons of the Law* (*I earini synaxis ton agrofylakon*, 1999), a film about the politics of village life on the island of Chios circa 1960.

As Lenin predicted in 1917, film for Eastern Europeans became "the most important art." It helped to support their revolutions and to transform their societies. And it managed to attain for itself a sophistication of form unparalleled in any other part of the world. The reasons are many, but two stand out clearly. Culturally, the countries of Eastern Europe have always had an affinity for the kind of sensuous thinking that produces great films and creates new cinematic languages. Their apprehension of art forms has historically been at once abstract and concretely structural. It is no coincidence that the same milieu that produced Franz Kafka, Karel Capek, Eugène Ionesco, and Stanislaw Lem also produced Věra Chytilová, Jan Němec, and Miklós Jancsó, for all of these artists fuse romanticism and cynicism into a strong sense of existential absurdity. Secondly, the countries of Eastern Europe have been plundered, colonized, occupied, and otherwise oppressed for most of their histories. In periods of great social and political oppression, art often provides the only means of self-expression a culture can attain. And film art—"the most important art"—traditionally served this function in Eastern Europe. As proof, one has only to note the correlation between periods of political turbulence and great achievement in Eastern European film: Poland, 1954–63, for example; Czechoslovakia, 1963–68; and, most recently, the Soviet Union, 1985–91. When the Berlin Wall came down in 1989 and the USSR disbanded in 1991, communism in this part of the world unraveled. But the euphoria that greeted the coming of freedom to the former Warsaw Pact nations and Soviet republics was soon followed by the sober realization that, separately, their economies and their relatively small populations could not support the surplus production of their industries—especially their film industries. Under communism, filmmaking, distribution, and exhibition had been privileged activities, heavily protected from foreign competition and subsidized by the state. Under capitalism, it looked as if Eastern Europe's "most important art" might soon become its least—in the sense that film is no longer an instrument of ideology, policy, or national expression, but just another commodity to be traded on the open market.

The Former Soviet Union, 1945-Present

The Soviet Union, whose political and military presence loomed so large over the other countries discussed in the previous chapter until its dissolution in 1991, also produced some remarkably distinguished cinema after World War II. But before this could occur, the country went through a period of Stalinist repression even darker than that experienced by its satellites. During the war itself, the film industry had been evacuated to Central Asia, with the largest studios (Mosfilm, Lenfilm) and the VGIK relocated to Alma-Ata in Kazakhstan. Here were produced such morale-boosting wartime films as Sergei and Georgi Vasiliev's *The Defense of Tsaritsyn* (*Oborona Tsaritsyna*, 1942) and *The Front* (*Front*, 1943), Friedrich Ermler's *She Defends the Motherland* (*Ona zash-chishchaet rodinu*, 1943; distributed in the United States as *No Greater Love*), Sergei Gerasimov's *Great Land* (*Bol'shaia zemlia*, 1944), and, most prominently, Eisenstein's *Ivan the Terrible, Part I* (1945) and *Part II* (1946). Regional studios in other Central Asian cities (Tashkent, Ashkhabad, Stalinabad) and the Caucasus (Tbilisi, Baku, and Erevan) assumed new importance in the production of features at this time (see below), while documentary cameramen at the front gathered footage for such Moscow-produced compilation films as L. V. Varlamov and I. P. Kopalin's *The Defeat of the German Armies Outside Moscow* (*Razgom nemetskikh voisk pod Moskvoi*, 1942; aka *Moscow Strikes Back*) and Alexander Dovzhenko's *Battle for Our Soviet Ukraine* (*Bitva za nashu radiansku Ukrainu*, 1943). Although the mission of the Soviet cinema during the war was overtly propagandist, its films were more realistic than any others made under Stalin before or after. Indeed, as the historian Peter Kenez has remarked, the war years constituted "a small oasis of freedom in the film history of the Stalinist years."[1]

---

1. Peter Kenez, *Cinema and Soviet Society*, 1917–1953 (New York: Cambridge University Press, 1992), p. 204.

Stalinist Cinema

From 1934 onward the supreme arbiter of socialist realism had been Andrei A. Zhdanov (1896–1948), secretary of the Central Committee of the Communist Party of the Soviet Union (CPSU) and Stalin's chief lieutenant in the Politburo. (Zhdanov is credited today, in fact, with creating many of the ideological components of Stalinism.) As party boss in charge of ideological affairs, Zhdanov's mission was to correct "aberrant" tendencies in Soviet art, especially as represented in the cinema by the avantgarde heritage of Vertov, Kuleshov, Eisenstein, Pudovkin, and Dovzhenko, which he set out systematically to discredit and destroy. In 1946, as part of a national crusade to "reestablish ideological conformity in the arts" (which had necessarily been relaxed during the war), Zhdanov embarked upon a course that nearly destroyed the Soviet film industry as a functioning entity. First came a dramatic decree from the Central Committee banning four current films—Leonid Lukov's *A Great Life, Part II* (*Bolshaia zhizń*; recut and rereleased 1958), Grigori Kozintsev and Leonid Trauberg's *Plain People* (*Prostie liudi*; recut and rereleased 1956), Eisenstein's *Ivan the Terrible, Part II* (rereleased 1958), and Pudovkin's *Admiral Nakhimov* (reshot and rereleased 1947)—and sharply warning the industry to reform itself. Then a thinly veiled campaign of anti-Semitism was unleashed against "rootless cosmopolitanism" and "foreign influences" in the arts, followed by personal attacks on individual filmmakers, like Trauberg, in *Pravda*.[2]

In the wake of such intimidation, only a handful of films were produced between 1948 and 1952, and the Central Committee demanded that two themes be portrayed in all of them: (1) that the CPSU was the motive force in all Soviet activities, foreign and domestic, and (2) that Stalin was personally involved in all decisions of consequence for the USSR, past and present. This latter dictate resulted in a virtual genre of what were called "artistic documentaries" (we would now call them "docudramas")—pseudohistorical epics deifying Stalin as the greatest ideologist, economic planner, and military strategist in recorded history (though a kindly, avuncular man of the people withal). Stalin had been heroically portrayed in Soviet films many times before (for example, in Mikhail Romm's *Lenin in October* [*Lenin v oktiabre*, 1937] and *Lenin in 1918* [*Lenin v 1918 godu*, 1939]; in

the Vasilievs' *Defense of Tsaritsyn* [*Oborona Tsaritsyna*, 1941]; and, in passing, as early as Eisenstein's *October* [1928]), but these new films almost literally proposed Stalin as a god.

They combined documentary footage with fictional scenes to portray a charismatic Stalin (usually played by Mikhail Gelovani, a handsome look-alike who made a career of the part) carrying forth Lenin's putative mandate to develop the Soviet economy through a series of five-year plans (Mikhail Chiaureli's *The Vow* [*Kliatva*, 1946]), personally directing brilliant military offensives (Igor Savchenko's *The Third Blow* [*Tretii udar*, 1948] and Chiaureli's *The Fall of Berlin* [*Padenie Berlina*, 1949; released 1950]), defending the sacred Russian soil (Vladimir Petrov's *The Battle of Stalingrad* [*Stalingradskaia bitva*, 1949]), and crushing an anti-Bolshevik rebellion in Leningrad (Chiaureli's *The Unforgettable Year 1919* [*Nezabyvaemyi 1919-yi god*, 1951; released 1952]).[3] As André Bazin wrote in "The Stalin Myth in Soviet Cinema" (1950), Stalin becomes in these films "History incarnate . . . omniscient, infallible, irresistible. . . ." It was a strange detour for a revolutionary cinema founded on the rejection of conventional narrative and individual heroes.

The "artistic documentaries" (most of which, with perfectly paranoid circularity, received the Stalin Prize for Artistic Merit) were in fact part of a larger propaganda effort to establish Stalin as a mythic figure in Soviet pol-

---

2. Legal discrimination against the Jews—widely practiced in tsarist Russia—was officially prohibited by the Bolsheviks in setting up their new regime, but de facto discrimination persisted, especially in the professions. As an institution born of the October Revolution and closely identified with it, the Soviet cinema attracted many Jewish persons who had experienced discrimination in other fields. For this very reason, the film industry became a vulnerable target for Stalinist anti-Semitism in the general arsenal of state terrorism, 1927–53. When Zhdanov died under mysterious circumstances in August 1948, for example, his death was attributed to a conspiracy of prominent Moscow physicians—most of them Jewish—aimed at the destruction of the Soviet leadership. Publicly identified in December 1952 as the Doctors' Plot, the conspiracy was declared a fake immediately after Stalin's death four months later. By this point, however, the terror engendered by charges of a plot had brought the film industry to a standstill. The talented scenarist Yevgeni Gabrilovich (1899–1993) was one of several film workers blacklisted during this period; for his account of it, see his "Inquisition in the Other Eden," *Film Comment* 5, 1 (1968): 22–27.

3. Since Stalin's death and fall from grace, some of these films have been re-edited to eliminate or minimize his role in them—much as he had demanded the elimination of Trotski's part in *October*. See Alexander Sesonske, "Re-editing History: *Lenin in October*, Then and Now," *Sight and Sound* 53, 1 (Winter 1983/84): 56–58.

itics and culture that was undertaken in the last terror-filled years of his reign. To ensure this priority, the party in 1951 decreed that the film industry should produce "only masterpieces," to be directed only by "acknowledged masters of the art." The result was that by 1952 annual output had fallen to a record low of five features,[4] and no new graduates could be admitted to the industry from the VGIK (Soviet film workers later referred to this period as "the time of few films" or "*malokartinie*").

Cinema during the Khrushchev Thaw

Stalin's death on March 5, 1953, caused an immediate loosening of ideological criteria, and 1954 witnessed the production of forty Soviet features. But it was not until Nikita Khrushchev (1894–1971) became first secretary of the Central Committee and denounced Stalin's brutal despotism in his famous "secret speech" before the Twentieth Party Congress in February 1956 that the de-Stalinization process began in earnest. Khrushchev's charges against his former boss ranged from self-glorification to political mass murder, and he roundly indicted Stalin's promulgation of a "cult of personality" through the film. More striking still, perhaps, was his assertion that Stalin had lost touch with the reality of his country as he rose to power and that he eventually knew it only through the pseudorealistic film images mandated by his own cultural bureaucracy, which, when he did not like the images, he caused to be ruthlessly purged. In fact, Khrushchev declared that Stalin had not set foot in a village since 1928, adding:

> He knew the country and agriculture only from films. And these films had dressed up and beautified the existing situation. . . . Many films so pictured *kolkhoz* life that the tables were bending from the weight of turkeys and geese. Evidently, Stalin thought it was actually so.

It is important to understand, however, that although Stalin was officially discredited, Zhdanov was not, and socialist realism as a doctrine was not then and never was officially rescinded (although it was unanimously rejected by a vote of the Filmmakers Union in June 1990, shortly before the collapse of the Soviet state). It was simply interpreted with greater moderation than previously.

The Khrushchev regime's more flexible attitude toward the arts (initially, at least) produced a thaw in the Soviet film industry that started dramatically in 1956. In that year new films began to appear from recent graduates of the VGIK for the first time since the 1930s,[5] many of which had contemporary themes. Among them were Grigori Chukhrai's (1921–2001) *The Forty-first* (*Sorok pervyi*), Stanislav Rostotski's (1922–2001) *The Land and the People* (*Zemlia i liudi*), Samson Samsonov's (1921–2002) *The Grasshopper* (*Poprygunia*—from a Chekhov story), the Georgian director Marlen Khutsiev (b. 1925) and Felix Mironer's (1927–1980) *Spring on Zarechnaia Street* (*Vesna na Zarechnoi ulitse*), Eldar Ryazanov's (b. 1927) musical comedy *Carnival Night* (*Karnavalnaia noch*), Vasili Ordynski's (1923–1985) *A Man Is Born* (*Chelovek rodilsia*), Alexander Alov (1923–1983) and Vladimir Naumov's (b. 1927) *Pavel Korchagin* (based on Nikolai Ostrovski's *How Steel Was Tempered*), Lev Kulijanov (1924–2002) and Iakov Segel's (1923–1995) *This Is How It Began* (*Eto nachinaloś tak*), and the first non-Russian postwar film, *Magdana's Little Donkey* (*Lurdzha*

---

4. By comparison, in 1951 the United States had produced 432 films; India, 250; and Japan, 215. Average annual output of the Soviet Union from 1956–91 was around 100 films. (See S. V. Utechin, *A Concise Encyclopaedia of Russia* [New York: Dutton, 1964], p. 111.) One type of Soviet film that saw a rise in production in the early 1950s was the recorded stage play. Stalin considered himself a connoisseur of the theater but had grown increasingly fearful of appearing in public in his latter years. Accordingly, he ordered that favorite performances be filmed for "posterity" so that he could watch them privately in the Kremlin. Over twenty plays were transcribed at his mandate in the first two months of 1953 alone.

5. Ironically, the artistic integrity of the Soviet cinema had been well preserved at the VGIK even during the worst years of the cult of personality owing to the Stalinist practice of compulsorily retiring "formalist" directors from the industry to the classroom during purges. Thus, Kuleshov had taught introductory courses from 1944 until his death in 1970; Eisenstein had designed the professional directing curriculum—the first of its kind in the world—between 1932 and 1935 and held the director's Chair from 1939 until his death in 1948; and Pudovkin, Dovzhenko, Tisse, Kozintsev, and Iutkevich had all held lectureships at the institute during the worst years of Stalin's regime. During the early years of the thaw, it was revealed that these and other VGIK teachers had kept the experimental impetus of the 1920s alive for their students by cultivating a distinction between "production films" (orthodox films for public distribution) and "diploma films" (stylistically advanced films made within the institute that were required to demonstrate a working knowledge of contemporary innovations such as Italian neorealism). In this way, the old guard at the VGIK was able to infuse the rising generation of Soviet directors with a cinematically vital tradition during "the time of few films" so they were able to do significant work of their own during the thaw.

17.1 *Othello* (Sergei Iutkevich, 1956).

Magdany), by the Georgian directors Tengis Abuladze (1924–1994) and Rezo Chkheidze (b. 1926). Veteran directors were also productive in the early thaw—Sergei Iutkevich with *Othello* (1956), the first Soviet Shakespearean adaptation, and *Stories about Lenin* (*Rasskazy o Lenine*, 1957); Mark Donskoi with a remake of Pudovkin's *Mother* (*Mat*, 1956); Alexander Ptushko (1900–1973) with the first Soviet widescreen feature, the puppet-animation fairy tale *Ilia Muromets* (1957); and, most prominently, Mikhail Kalatozov with *The Cranes Are Flying* (*Letiat zhuravli*, 1957).

When the latter won the Grand Prix at Cannes in 1958, it announced to the world that some sort of revival was taking place within the Soviet cinema. Just over a year before, however, Soviet tanks had brutally crushed the

17.2 *The Cranes Are Flying* (Mikhail Kalatozov, 1957).

Hungarian revolution, and this had produced a chilling effect on domestic culture. For a while, the safest subjects for films became literary adaptations, and the late 1950s witnessed a glut of them, especially among directors of an older generation—for example, Sergei Gerasimov's (1907–1985) three-part version of Mikhail Sholokhov's *And Quiet Flows the Don* (*Tikhii Don*, 1957); Ivan Pyriev's (1901–1968) adaptations of Dostoevsky's *The Idiot* (*Idiot*, 1958) and *White Nights* (*Belye nochi*, 1959); Donskoi's Gorki adaptation, *Foma Gordeev* (1959); Vladimir Petrov's (1896–1965) version of Turgenev's *On the Eve* (*Nakanune*, 1959); the actor Alexei Batalov's (b. 1928) adaptation of Gogol's *The Overcoat* (*Shinel*, 1959—actually a remake of the Kozintsev and Trauberg 1926 version, but this time done in the Moscow Art Theater's naturalistic style); and Iosif Heifitz's (1905–1995) adaptations from Chekhov, *The Lady with the Little Dog* (*Dama s sobachkoi*, 1960) and *In the Town of S* (*V gorode "S,"* 1966). Also notable in this category are the actor-director Sergei Bondarchuk's (1920–1994) version of *Fate of a Man* (*Sudba cheloveka*, 1959), adapted from Mikhail Sholokhov, and the four-part epic *War and Peace* (*Voina i mir*, 1965–67), adapted from Tolstoi; and Kozintsev's distinguished adaptations of *Don Quixote* (1956), *Hamlet* (1964), and *King Lear* (*Korol Lir*, 1972).

Yet Khrushchev was not Stalin, and advances in the industry continued to be made under his regime: by 1958 the annual output had reached 115 features, of which one-third were in color (introduced to the Soviets in 1950); in 1959 the Moscow International Film Festival was inaugurated on a regular biennial basis; and, most significant perhaps, production was either renewed or begun on a full-time basis in all of the non-Russian republics in the period 1955–65. Furthermore, the bolder Soviet filmmakers continued to test the waters of social comment during this time with such works as Kulijanov and Segel's *The House I Live In* (*Dom v kotorom ia zhivu*, 1957); Chkheidze's *Our Courtyard* (*Nash dvor*, 1957) and *Father of a Soldier* (*Otets soldata*, 1964); Chukhrai's internationally acclaimed *Ballad of a Soldier* (*Ballada o soldate*, 1958)—a prizewinner at Cannes and San Francisco—and *Clear Skies* (*Chistoe nebo*, 1961); Kalatozov and Sergei Urusevski's (1908–1974) *The Letter That Wasn't Sent* (*Neopravlennoe pismo*, 1960) and *I Am Cuba* (*Ia Kuba*, 1964), a fantastic two-and-one-half hour propaganda epic scripted by Evgeny Yevtushenko that was released in the United States in 1995;[6] Yuli Raizman's *If This Is Love* (*A esli eto liubov*, 1961); Mikhail Romm's philosophical feature *Nine Days in a Year* (*Deviat dnei odnogo goda*, 1962) and remarkable compilation documentary *Ordinary Fascism* (*Obyknovennyi fashizm*, 1965);[7] Elem Klimov's first feature, *Welcome, but Unauthorized Persons Not Allowed* (*Dobro požalovat, ili postoronnim vhod vosprěščën*, 1964), an antiauthoritarian satire in the guise of a youth film; and, most strikingly, Marlen Khutsiev's *Lenin's Guard* (also known as *Ilich Square* [*Zastava Ilicha*], produced 1962), which provoked a storm of official outrage and had to be reshot as *I'm Twenty* (*Mne dvadsat let*, released 1964) over the next eighteen months.

In December 1962, Khrushchev announced that liberalism in the arts had gone too far, and he issued a stinging indictment of Soviet modernist painting on the occasion of the exhibition *Thirty Years of Pictorial Art* in Moscow. This was followed by party-line attacks on *Nine Days in a Year* and *The Letter That Wasn't Sent*, making it clear that the basic tenets of socialist realism hadn't changed a bit. Caution immediately became the industry watchword, although remarkable debuts continued to be made—for example, by the Georgian directors Georgi Danelia (b. 1930; *I Walk about Moscow* [*Ia shagaiu po Moskve*, 1963]) and Eldar Shengelaia (b. 1933; *White Caravan* [*Belyi karavan*, 1963]) and by the actor-director Vasili Shukshin (1929–1974; *There Was a Lad* [*Zhivet takoi pareń*, 1964]).

In October 1964, Khrushchev was removed from office by a conspiracy among his deputies, and a diumvirate was installed consisting of Leonid Brezhnev (1906–1982) and Alexei N. Kosygin (1904–1980) as first secretary of the Central Committee and chairman of the Council of Ministers, respectively. (Brezhnev became general secretary in 1966, and ultimately he superseded all of his comrades to become supreme leader of the country, a position he held until his death.) There followed a period of uncertainty and indecision for the arts that ended abruptly with the Warsaw Pact occupation of Czechoslovakia in August 1968 and a renewed domestic campaign against the liberalization of Soviet culture in 1969. Appropriately, however, the brief period of the Khrushchev thaw ended with the production of one of the most extraordinary and beautiful films ever made: Sergei Parajanov's *Shadows of Forgotten Ancestors* (*Teni zabytykh predkov*, 1964).

17.3 *Shadows of Forgotten Ancestors* (Sergei Parajanov, 1964).

Sergei Parajanov and *Shadows of Forgotten Ancestors*

There was little in Parajanov's (1924–1990) early career to announce the remarkable sensibility displayed in *Shadows*. Born Sarkis Paradjanian (his name was later transliterated and "Russified") to Armenian parents in the Georgian capital of Tbilisi, he studied at the Kiev Conservatory of Music during World War II and then attended the VGIK, where his major professor was the Ukrainian director Igor Savchenko (1906–1951), who had studied under Dovzhenko, and where he was also tutored extensively by Lev Kuleshov and by Dovzhenko himself.

---

6. A dazzling realization of the concept of Eisenstein's Mexican project of 1930–32. See Steven P. Hill, "Soviet Cinema Today," *Film Quarterly* 20, 4 (Summer 1967): 33–52.

7. Mikhail Romm (1901–1971) was one of the most influential teachers at the VGIK since it was founded by Lev Kuleshov in 1919. His career spanned the entire history of Soviet cinema, centering around Stalinist socialist realism—of which his *Lenin in October* (1937) and *Lenin in 1918* (1939) are the most impressive works. He made effective anti-German films during World War II (e.g., *Girl No. 217* [*Celovek No. 217*, 1944; shot in Uzbekistan]) and anti-American ones during the Cold War (*The Russian Question* [*Russkij vopros*, 1950]), but in 1962 he renounced most of his earlier work and urged his students to look toward documentary realism for their inspiration, as in his latter years he did himself. Among Romm's protégés are Elem Klimov, Sergei Soloviev, Gleb Panfilov, and Grigori Chukhrai (d. 2001), as well as Vasili Shukshin (d. 1974), Andrei Tarkovsky (d. 1986), Andrei Konchalovski, Georgi Danelia, Tengiz Abuladze (d. 1994), Nikita Mikhalkov, and Vadim Abdrashitov. Clearly, much of the character of postwar Soviet cinema was shaped in Romm's VGIK workshops.

17.4 *Shadows of Forgotten Ancestors.*

Parajanov graduated from the Directing Department in 1951 and was assigned to the Dovzhenko Kiev Studio, where he made five Ukrainian-language films for regional consumption—all of them indifferent, by his own account—before undertaking the project that became *Shadows of Forgotten Ancestors.* Adapted by Parajanov and Ivan Chendei from a prerevolutionary novelette by the distinguished Ukrainian writer Mykhailo Kotsyubynsky to celebrate the centennial of his birth, the film retells an ancient Carpathian folk legend of universal resonance. Deep in the Carpathian Mountains, at the westernmost reach of the Ukraine, a young man (Ivan) and a young woman (Marichka) become lovers despite a blood feud between their families. Marichka accidentally drowns one night searching for Ivan, and after a long period of bereavement, he marries another (Palagna). But Ivan is persistently haunted by the image of his first love and eventually chooses to join her in death.

Like the legends of Tristan and Isolde and Romeo and Juliet, *Shadows* offers a relatively familiar and uncomplicated tale of undying love that has variants in cultures all over the world. But in the telling of the tale, Parajanov created a vision of human experience so radical and unique as to subvert all authority. To say that *Shadows* violates every narrative code and representational system known to the cinema is an understatement—at times, in fact, the film seems intent upon deconstructing the very process of representation itself. The relationship between narrative logic and cinematic space—between point of view inside and outside of the frame—is so consistently undermined that most critics on first viewing literally cannot describe what they've seen. Adjectives frequently

used to characterize *Shadows* are "hallucinatory," "intoxicating," and "delirious"—terms that imply, however positively, confusion and incoherence. But the camera and editing techniques that elicit such comments are all part of Parajanov's deliberate aesthetic strategy to interrogate a whole set of historically evolved assumptions about the nature of cinematic space and the relationship between the spectator and the screen.

Parajanov proceeds by means of perceptual dislocation so that it becomes impossible at any given moment to imagine a stable time-space continuum for the dramatic action. Often, for example, the viewer will be invited by conventional stylistic means to share a point of view that is suddenly ruptured by camera movement or some other disjunction in spatial logic; spaces that appear to be contiguous in one shot sequence are revealed to be miles apart in the next; surfaces that seem to be two-dimensional at the beginning of a shot will become richly textured in process by focal manipulation. Sometimes a shot will begin with a camera angle that encourages the viewer to misconstrue narrative space, as when a wall is momentarily made to resemble the surface of a roof. At other times, the camera assumes perspectives and executes maneuvers that appear to be *physically*, as well as dramatically, impossible: the camera looks down from the top of a falling tree several hundred feet tall; it looks up through a pool with no optical distortion as Ivan drinks from its surface; it whirls 360 degrees on its axis for nearly a full minute, dissolving focus and color to abstraction; it turns corners and swoops down embankments with inhuman celerity. Finally, Parajanov and his cinematographer Iuri Ilyenko (b. 1936)[8] use a variety of lenses, including

---

8. Ilyenko is today regarded as the leading figure in Ukrainian cinema. He studied cinematography at the VGIK, graduating in 1961, and he worked as a director of photography at Yaltafilm studios before moving to the Dovzhenko Film studios in Kiev in 1963. He made his first feature as a director there in 1965, *A Spring for the Thirsty* (*Rodnik dlia zhazhdushchikh*), but it was shelved for formalist excess. Ilyenko directed many subsequent films at Dovzhenko—notably *On the Eve of Ivan Kupala Day* (*Noch' nakanune Ivana Kupaly*, 1968), *White Bird with a Black Spot* (*Belaya ptitsa s chernoi otmetinoi*, 1971), *The Feast of Roast Potatoes* (*Prazdnik pecenoi kartoski*, 1977), *A Patch of Unmown Flowers* (*Poloska neskosennych dikih cvetov*, 1979), *The Forest Song: Mavka* (*Lesnaia pesnia: Mavka*, 1981), *The Legend of Princess Olga* (*Legenda o knjagine Ol'ge*, 1983), *Straw Bells* (*Solomennye kolokola*, 1987), and *Swan Lake—the Zone* (*Lebedinoe ozero*, 1990; from a story by Parajanov)—often serving as cowriter and cinematographer. He is also a much-exhibited painter, and his films are best known for their striking visual quality.

telephoto zoom and 180-degree wide angle, or "fish-eye," to warp the film's scenographic space to the outer limits of narrative comprehension—but never quite beyond it. The point of these techniques is not to confuse the spectator, but to prevent the kind of comfortable, familiar, and logically continuous representational space associated with traditional narrative form. The reason is simply that the film posits a world that is neither comfortable, familiar, nor logically continuous, for *Shadows* exists most fully not in the realm of narrative, but in the worlds of myth and the unconscious. It is above all else a deeply psychological film, rich in both Freudian and Jungian[9] imagery, and one whose sophistication makes the Pavlovian tactics of Eisenstein's montage seem almost primitive by comparison.

Shadows' psychological subtlety extends to its use of sound and color. It has been frequently noted that the film has an operatic, pageantlike quality; and Parajanov uses a complex variety of music—from atonal electronics, to lush orchestral romanticism, to hieratic religious chants, to vocal and instrumental folk music—to create leitmotifs for the film's various psychological atmospheres. Similarly, Parajanov employs color in a psychologically provocative way, having developed for *Shadows* what he called a "dramaturgy of color." When Ivan and Marichka are first drawn together as children, for example, the prevailing color is the white of the snow, corresponding to their innocence; the green of spring dominates their young love; monochrome and sepia tones are used to drain the world of color during the period of Ivan's grieving; but color returns riotously, if briefly, after he meets Palagna; as that relationship turns barren, the film is dominated by autumnal hues; monochrome returns during Ivan's death delirium; and at the moment of his death the natural universe is painted in surreal shades of red and blue. The ultimate effect of both the sound track and the color system, like that of the film's optical distortions and dislocations, is to destabilize the spectator perceptually, and therefore psychologically, in order to present a tale that operates at the level not of narrative but of myth, a tale that is an archetype of life itself: youth passes from innocence to experience to solitude and death in a recurring cycle, eons upon eons (as in Dovzhenko's *Earth*, the only Soviet film that bears even remote comparison to *Shadows*). This is the "shadow" of "forgotten ancestors": the archetypal pattern that outlasts and transcends individual identity.

When *Shadows of Forgotten Ancestors* appeared in the West in 1965, it was immediately recognized that the Soviet cinema had acquired a new genius on the order of Eisenstein and Dovzhenko. The film won sixteen foreign festival awards and was released in the United States and Europe to wide critical acclaim. Rarely since the triumph of *Potemkin*, in fact, had a Soviet motion picture enjoyed such international esteem. But at home the cultural situation had already begun to take its next nasty turn—*Shadows* was variously accused of "formalism" and "Ukrainian nationalism," and it was deliberately underbooked in domestic theaters by officials of Goskino (see Chapter 5). Parajanov found himself personally attacked by the party secretary for "Ideological Problems," and when invitations to other countries began to pour in as the film's reputation spread, he was consistently denied permission to travel abroad. During the next ten years, Parajanov went on to write ten complete scenarios based on classical Russian literature and folk epics—all of which he was refused permission to shoot by Soviet authorities. He did make one more film—a visionary life of the Armenian poet Arutin Sayadyan (1712–1795) entitled *The Color of Pomegranates (Sayat nova)*—which was banned on its release in 1969 and finally given limited distribution in a version "re-edited" by Sergei Iutkevitch in the early 1970s (it was first seen in the United States at the 1980 New York Film Festival). Another project, *Kiev Frescoes (Kievskie freski)*, was approved but aborted after the first edited rushes were screened—the same kind of ritual humiliation accorded Eisenstein by the Stalinists during the production of *Bezhin Meadows (Bezhin lug, 1935)*. Then, while he was working on an adaptation of some fairy tales of Hans Christian Andersen for Soviet television in January 1974, Parajanov was arrested on a variety of specious charges and sentenced to six years at hard labor in the Gulag. An international petition campaign motivated the Soviets to release him in late 1977,[1] but he was not allowed to work in the film industry again until 1984, when he was exonerated and assigned to Georgia's

---

9. The very title *Shadows of Forgotten Ancestors* resonates with Jung's "archtypes of the collective unconscious," and the film on one level is about experiences common to all humanity since the race evolved— love, despair, solitude, death. (American prints of the film also bear the title *Wild Horses of Fire*, added by its Chicago distributor in 1966.)

1. According to Richard Grenier, the campaign's success was due largely to the relentless lobbying of Lily Brik (Maiakovski's former mis-

Gruziafilm Studios. Parajanov's first film there, *The Legend of Suram Fortress* (*Legenda Suramskoi kreposti*, 1985), co-directed with Dodo (David) Abashidze, was a return to the mythopoetic mode of *Shadows* that showed his remarkable cinematic sensibilities to be still very much intact, as did *Arabesques on Themes from Pirosmani* (*Arabeski na temu Pirosmani*, 1986), a documentary short on the work of the famous Georgian "primitive" painter. Similarly, *Asik Kerib* (Gruziafilm, 1988), a folklore-based adaptation of a Lermontov tale shot on location in Georgia, Armenia, and Azerbaijan, abounds in the ritualized *tableaux* and magical invention of Parajanov's earlier work. He died July 21, 1990, in Yerevan, Armenia, of cancer.

17.5 Andrei Tarkovski's *Andrei Rublev* (1966): Anatoli Solonitsyn in the title role.

Cinema under Brezhnev

What happened to Parajanov during the Brezhnev years was extreme. More typical was the plight of Andrei Tarkovsky (1932–1986), the second major figure to emerge from the postwar Soviet cinema during the 1960s. Son of the acclaimed Russian poet Arseni Tarkovsky, Andrei studied at the VGIK under Mikhail Romm and had already won first prize at the New York Student Film Festival for his diploma project, *Steamroller and Violin* (*Katok i skripka*, co-directed with Andrei Mikhalkov Konchalovski) when he graduated in 1960. His first feature, *Ivan's Childhood* (aka *My Name Is Ivan*), which began his long collaborations with cinematographer Vadim Yusov and composer Viacheslav Ovchinnikov, won the Golden Lion at Venice in 1962. In content, this story of a heroic young orphan who becomes a frontline spy for the Soviet army during World War II follows the traditional pattern. But in terms of form, *Ivan's Childhood* approaches the avant-garde in its surreal rendition of the horrors of war; and Tarkovsky's next film, *Andrei Rublev* (1966), from a script by Konchalovski, produced an official scandal. The title character is a historical figure, the Russian Orthodox monk who brought the art of religious icon painting to its zenith in the fifteenth century. Tarkovsky used Rublev's life, reconstructed in loosely connected episodes, to symbolize the conflict between Russian barbarism and idealism. The film was banned in the Soviet Union on the grounds that it gave an inaccurate (that is, negative) account of medieval Russian history, although an edited version won the International Critics' Award at Cannes in 1969, and *Rublev* was ultimately

given limited domestic release in a version further re-edited and cut by forty minutes.[2]

Tarkovsky's third feature was the metaphysical science-fiction film *Solaris* (1971), adapted from a novel by the Polish writer Stanislaw Lem, which he conceived as a response to Kubrick's *2001* (1968); it won the Special Jury Prize at Cannes in 1972 and was uncontroversial at home. (*Solaris* was, however, cut by thirty-five minutes by its American distributor in 1976 and not restored to its original 167-minute length until 1990.) But his autobiographical *A Mirror* (*Zerkalo*, 1974), reminiscent of Fellini's *Amarcord*, was much criticized for its labyrinthine structure and parabolic style; it was not suppressed, but neither was it offered for export until 1980. After directing an acclaimed stage version of *Hamlet* in Moscow in 1976, Tarkovsky made *Stalker* (1979), a complex allegory of decay shot in Estonia and interpreted by many European critics as an indictment of the Soviet government's

tress, over eighty at the time) and the French communist leader Louis Aragon (Brik's brother-in-law), who interceded personally with Leonid Brezhnev ("A Soviet 'New Wave'?" *Commentary* [July 1981], pp. 62–67). Parajanov celebrated his freedom in a 7-minute short documenting his return to his family home in old Tbilisi in 1979. Alternately titled *Return to Life* and *Le signe du temps*, the film was produced with the assistance of the Armenfilm documentary studio and shown at Cannes in 1980. See Alan Stanbrook, "The Return of Paradjanov," *Sight & Sound* 55, 4 (Autumn 1986): 257–61; Anne Williamson, "Prisoner: The Essential Paradjanov," *Film Comment* 25, 3 (May–June, 1989): 57–63; and Patrick Cazals, *Serguei Paradjanov* (Paris: Cahiers du Cinema, 1993).

2. Tarkovsky's original 185-minute version is now available in the United States from Kino Films International, as is the restored *Solaris*.

17.6 *Solaris* (Andrei Tarkovski, 1971): a communication from the Solaric Ocean.

17.7 *Solaris* (Andrei Tarkovski, 1971).

repression of intellectual freedom. In this gloomy film, a writer and a scientist are led by "the Stalker" on a journey through a wastelandlike "Zone" to a "Room" where all wishes may be fulfilled, but they fail in their quest through lack of will. By this point, Tarkovsky had acquired an international reputation as the Soviet Union's most unorthodox filmmaker, and he soon became one of the few Soviet directors in many years to work outside of the country with official sanction.

In 1982, Tarkovsky began shooting *Nostalghia* (*Nostalgiia*, 1983) in Italy for Gaumont and RAI, with Soviet cooperation. Scripted by Tonino Guerra, a frequent collaborator of Fellini, Antonioni, and Francesco Rosi, *Nostalghia* portrays the memories, dreams, and waking experience of a Russian professor of architecture who has come to Italy for the first time, accompanied by a female interpreter who is a Botticelli-like beauty. It is perhaps Tarkovsky's most mysterious and inaccessible film, but it was a great success at Cannes in 1983, where it shared a specially created Best Direction award with Robert Bresson's *L'Argent* and also received the International Critics' Award. Largely on the strength of such prestige, Tarkovsky continued working outside of the Soviet Union, in 1983 directing Mussorgsky's opera *Boris Godunov* for the London stage and in 1985 completing the international coproduction *The Sacrifice* (*Zhertoprinoshenie*, 1986) in

17.8 Tarkovski's *Nostalghia* (1983).

Sweden. Shot on location by the great cinematographer Sven Nykvist, this visionary work concerns the spiritual response of a small group of people on an isolated Baltic island to an imminent nuclear holocaust, and it won multiple international awards, including five at Cannes alone. Since *Andrei Rublev*, Tarkovsky had won his creative freedom by remaining politically ambiguous, yet to many Western observers even his films made abroad bore the marks of careful, covert Soviet censorship. Fittingly, *The Sacrifice* showed no signs of reticence in providing a compendium of Tarkovsky's lifelong themes and symbols. It was his last film; he died of lung cancer in Paris in December 1986.

A middle path is suggested by the work of Andrei Mikhalkov Konchalovski. Konchalovski was born in 1937, a member of the Soviet artistic elite. His grandfather and great-grandfather were both famous painters; his mother and father were well-known writers (the latter having served as president of the Writers Union and written the words to the national anthem); and his brother is the talented actor-director Nikita Mikhalkov (b. 1945).[3] Kon-

chalovski's first film as a director, *The First Teacher* (*Pervii uchitel*, 1965), was a revisionist account of the conflict between revolutionary idealism and tradition in the Kirghiz mountains in the wake of October 1917, and it raised some eyebrows in official circles. But his second film, *Asya's Happiness* (*Asino schaste*, 1966), was so critical of the poverty and backwardness of Soviet collective farms that it was damned and banned until 1987. (The public "damning" of films by party critics began in 1965, when Alov and Naumov's version of Dostoevsky's *Bad Joke* [*Skvernyi anekdot*] was pilloried; the practice continued for several years.) So Konchalovski prudently turned to the classics with subtle adaptations of Turgenev's *A Nest of Gentlefolk* (*Dvorianskoe gnezdo*, 1969) and Chekhov's *Uncle Vania* (*Diadia Vania*, 1970). Then he wrote some scripts for regional studios and directed the safely conformist modern musical romance *In Love* (*Vliublonnye*, 1974), before making the monumental *Siberiad/Sibiriana* (*Sibiriada*, 1979), which traces the histories of two Siberian families over a period of three generations from the revolution to modern times. Widely regarded as the Soviet Union's greatest postwar epic, *Siberiad* was both a popular success at home and winner of the Special Jury Prize at Cannes in the year of its release.

17.9 *The Sacrifice* (1986): Tarkovski's testament.

3. Mikhalkov is an important director who occupies an ambiguous position in late Soviet film history. A film actor in the early 1960s, he studied with Mikhail Romm at the VGIK, 1966–71, and directed his first feature, *At Home among Strangers, A Stranger at Home* (*Svoi sredi chuzhikh, chuzhoi sredi svoikh*), in 1975. This was a parody of an Italian "spaghetti Western" set during the Civil War between the Reds and the Whites that followed the 1917 Revolution. *A Slave of Love* (*Raba liubvi*, 1976), another genre parody set in the same era, is about the production of a silent melodrama, while *Unfinished Piece for a Player Piano* (*Neokonchennaia piesa dla mekhanícheslogo pianino*, 1979), *Oblomov* (1980; adapted from the 1859 novel by Ivan Goncharov), *Kinfolk* (*Rodnia*, 1982), *Without Witnesses* (*Bez svidetelei*, 1983), *Dark Eyes* (*Oci cernye*, 1987; a Soviet-Italian coproduction adapted from several Chekhov stories), *Hitchhiking* (1990; a Soviet-Swiss-Italian coproduction), *Urga* (English title: *Close to Eden*, 1992) have demonstrated a talent for psychological introspection and intimate drama detached from the world of ideology and politics. This aestheticism, combined with the privileged position of Mikhalkov's family in Soviet society, buffered him against persecution during the worst of the pre-glasnost years and created resentment among his colleagues in the Film Workers Union, from whose secretariat he was removed during the 1986 shake-up (see p. 725). Nevertheless, Mikhalkov has become one of Russia's most internationally prominent directors; he is a complete *auteur* who usually cowrites and acts in his films, as amply demonstrated in *Burnt by the Sun* (1994), which depicts the destruction of an upper-class family by Stalinism in the summer of 1936 and won the 1994 American Academy Award for Best Foreign Film.

In 1980, Soviet authorities allowed Konchalovski to emigrate to the United States (with the very rare option of returning in the government's good graces), where he has made the downbeat, noncommercial *Maria's Lovers* (1983; released 1985) and *Runaway Train* (1985; screenplay by Akira Kurosawa) for the Cannon Group, which latter became a box-office and critical hit. More recently, he has directed an adaptation of Tom Kempinski's play *Duet for One* (1986), a wild tale of survival in the backcountry Louisiana swamps ironically entitled *Shy People* (1987), the postmodern road film *Homer & Eddie* (1990), and *The Inner Circle* (1991), a film about life under Stalin as seen through the eyes of his lowly projectionist, which was based on a true story and shot on location in Moscow.

The various fates of Parajanov, Tarkovsky, and Konchalovski notwithstanding, most Soviet directors remained at home in the post-Khrushchev era and adapted to the policy articulated by the new head of the State Committee on Cinematography, Fillip Ermash,[4] in his 1972 Resolution of the Central Committee of the CPSU:

> There are too many grey, formless works in which contemporary and historical themes are worked in a superficial manner, not finding any reflection of a fundamental social change taking place in Soviet society. . . . Persistent thematic planning will make possible the creation of films which will center on the positive hero of our time—man, for whom the struggle for the embodiment of the Communist ideal becomes the personal aim of his existence.

Clearly reminiscent of socialist realism, this new "pedagogic line," in fact, permitted greater technical innovation and complexity of expression. Typically, it was from the cinemas of the non-Russian republics, where a concentration on regional themes was tolerated and even encouraged, that some of the most extraordinary talent emerged in the 1970s and 1980s.

Cinema of the Non-Russian Republics

Historically, the Soviet industry was structured around national studios in each of the fifteen autonomous republics, as well as five other studios specializing in the production of children's and youth films, documentary films, educational films, industrial films, and animated features. Filmmakers were trained in their speciality at the VGIK in Moscow[5] and then sent out to work in one of the twenty regional or specialized studios, which by the early 1990s averaged a total of 150 theatrical features, plus 80 to 90 telefilms, per year. Despite the strong central control of Goskino, the State Committee on Cinematography in Moscow, and the economic dominance of the Russian studios Mosfilm and Lenfilm, each of the national studios produced a cinema with its own ethnic, cultural, and linguistic traditions. Overdubbed in Russian, films from all

17.10 *The Inner Circle* **(Andrei Konchalovski, 1991): Tom Hulce with bust of Stalin.**

4. Ermash replaced Alexei Romanov, who had been the chairman of Goskino since it was resurrected as the state film trust in 1963.

5. The VGIK, or State Film Institute, founded 1919, was the world's largest film school. In addition to training students from nearly forty foreign countries, it provided the core of artistic personnel for the Soviet film and television industries through professional instruction in seven separate departments—directing, cinematography, acting, scriptwriting, film criticism and history, set design, and economics and organization. After completing a five-year course of training and writing a thesis, graduates were assigned to a specific studio in Russia or the non-Russian republics, from which there was typically little mobility. (Several former republics have their own film academies—most notably Georgia, whose industry predated that of the Soviet Union.) Today the VGIK is struggling to survive, sustained by a combination of public and private funds, but its equipment is old and broken, and market forces subvert its mission.

fifteen republics were distributed to cinemas throughout the Soviet Union. (Even Russian films were [and are] overdubbed, since postsynchronization of dialogue was the standard production practice throughout the USSR.) Conventionally, the cinemas of the fifteen republics were grouped into five categories in terms of both geographical criteria and production/support structures. The strongest, oldest, and most prominent of these categories was Slavic cinema—that of Russia (emanating from the Mosfilm [Moscow] and Lenfilm [Leningrad] studios), Belorussia (from Belarusfilm [Minsk]), and Ukraine (from the Dovzhenko Kiev Studio and the Odessafilm and Yaltafilm studios)—which accounted for about one-half of overall annual production and will be considered later in this chapter. Baltic cinema (from Lithuanian Film Studio [Vilnius], Riga Film Studio [Latvia], and Tallinfilm [Estonia]) and Moldavian cinema (from Moldova-Film [Kishinev]) both took their first steps in the postwar era and are culturally and linguistically distinct from one another and from the cinemas of the other republics; they were together responsible for about one-eighth of annual Soviet production. Transcaucasian cinema (from Gruziafilm [Tbilisi], Armenfilm [Yerevan], and Azerbaijanfilm [Baku]), representing distinct cultures that exist in close proximity, and Central Asian cinema (from Uzbekfilm [Tashkent], Kazakhfilm [Alma-Ata], Kirghizfilm [Bishkek, formerly Frunze], Tadjikfilm [Dushanbe], and Turkmenfilm [Ashkhabad]), which shares a collective heritage of Islam, accounted together for approximately one-fourth of the industry's yearly output. (The remaining one-eighth came from such specialized studios as the Moscow-based Gorki Film Studio [children's/youth films] and Soiuzmultfilm [animation]).

Baltic Cinema

LITHUANIA

Of the Baltic cinemas, that of Lithuania (population 3.7 million) is the most prominent. The Lithuanian Film Studio was founded in 1949 but did not produce distinctive work until the 1960s, when Vitautas Zalakiavicius (1930–1996) made *The Chronicle of One Day* (1964) and *Nobody Wanted to Die* (*Nikto ne khotel umirat*, 1965), the latter a politically charged and violent tale of

guerrilla warfare between the KGB and anticommunist partisans after World War II. (The Soviets annexed Lithuania, Latvia, and Estonia in 1940, and the Nazis occupied all three from 1941 to 1944, after which they were recaptured by the USSR. In both Lithuania and Latvia, nationalist guerrillas who had resisted the Nazis fought on against the Soviets in struggles that lasted until 1952 and 1948, respectively, and produced many casualties.) This same decade witnessed the poetic children's films of Arunas Zhebrunas (b. 1931—*The Girl and the Echo* [*Devushka i ekho*, 1965]; *The Little Prince*, 1967) and the literary adaptations of Raymondas Vabalas (b. 1937—*Stairs to the Sky* [*Lesnitsa v nebo*, 1966]) and former cinematographer Algirdas Araminas (b. 1931—*When I Was Young* [*Kogda byl malenkim*, 1969]). During the Brezhnev years, Lithuanian cinema turned to traditional genres—e.g., Vabalas's detective film *Near the Boundary* (1973) and Zhebrunas's musical *The Devil's Bride* (1974)—as well as to the adaptation for Soviet central television of works by such Western authors as Jack London, Theodore Dreiser, and G. K. Chesterton (this apparently owing to the Western "look" of Lithuania's countryside and actors).

In the 1980s, however, the poetically stylized work of Algimantas Puipa (b. 1951) began to appear, and his *A Woman and Her Four Men* (*Zhenshchina i chetvero ee muzhchin*, 1983) won acclaim at several international festivals. This adaptation of a nineteenth-century Danish novel relocated to the Lithuanian coast pits a family of peasant fishermen against an extreme physical and political environment representing the contemporary situation in the Soviet Union. In the era of glasnost, the new "openness" promoted by Mikhail Gorbachev after his succession to the party Secretariat in 1985 (see p. 725), Puipa's films grew increasingly direct in their nationalism and experimental in form—*Eternal Light* (*Vechnoye siyaniye*, 1987) is a grim rural romance set in 1956, during the height of Sovietization, while *Fish Day* (*Zuvies diena*, 1990) is a portrait of a self-obsessed artist living at the fringes of communal life. *Ticket to Taj Mahal* (*Biletas iki Taj Mahal*, 1991; produced by the Katarsis Film Cooperative, Kazakhstan) is Puipa's most complex work to date, a blending of historical reconstruction and fantasy set during the postwar partisan struggle with the Soviets, which suggests that the only way to escape some forms of political oppression is in our dreams.

The appearance of films with overt anti-Soviet content coincided with Lithuania's declaration of independence on March 11, 1990. (Latvia and Estonia declared their independence in August 1991, a week after the aborted coup in Moscow.) Jonas Vaitkus's *Awakening* (*Probuzhdeniye*, 1990) was adapted from an agitational stage play about the fate of individuals caught up in the political terror following the Soviet annexation in 1940. Similar in theme is *The Children from Hotel "America"* (Raimundas Banionis, 1990), based on a true incident that occurred in 1972 in Kaunas, Lithuania's historical capital, when some teenagers tried to re-create a Woodstock-style rock festival and were brutalized by the KGB. But perhaps the most disturbing film to come from Lithuania in recent years is the haunting documentary *Homecoming* (Petrus Abukevicius, 1990), recounting the secret deportation and genocide of nearly one-quarter of Lithuania's population in Stalin's Gulag concentration camps, 1940–41 and 1944, and the survivors' retrieval of their loved ones' remains at the expense of the Soviet state, a policy introduced by Gorbachev during the period of glasnost preceding the dissolution of the USSR. After liberation, Lithuania had to struggle to keep its film industry alive. Among other problems, it did not have access to the various European film funds because it was not a member of the European Community. Furthermore, the founding generation of its national cinema, represented by the humanist director and playwright Vitautas Zalakiavicius, had all died off by the late 1990s, leaving a rising generation that was more intensely poetic and formally experimental. The most prominent middle-generation figure, Algimantas Puipa, continued to produce mainstream narratives—e.g., *A Wolf-Teeth Necklace* (*Vilko dantu karoliai*, 1997) and *Elze of the Sands* (*Elze is gilijos*, 1999)—while younger directors like Sharunas Bartas (b. 1964) and Valdas Navasaitis made radically stylized works like *The House* (*A casa*, 1997) and *The Courtyard* (*Kiemas*, 1999). (Bartas is a true *auteur* who writes, directs, shoots, acts in, and composes the scores for all of his films.) Following the lean year of 1998, when no Lithuanian films were released, the government created a fund that guarantees finance for three features annually, in addition to ten documentary shorts and an hour's worth of animation. In 2001, Lithuania joined with Latvia and Estonia to create a joint distribution venture called Baltic Films.

LATVIA

The film industries of Latvia (population 2.4 million) and Estonia (population 1.4 million) are considerably smaller than Lithuania's but significant nonetheless. Under Soviet domination, Latvia's Riga Film Studio produced ten to twelve features a year and was well known for its detective films, children's films, and documentaries. In fact, it was the glasnost-era documentary *Is It Easy to Be Young?* (*Legko li byt molodym?*, Juris Podnieks, 1987) that first focused world attention on the plight of the Baltic nations under Soviet rule. In *cinéma vérité* fashion, the film follows a variety of Latvian young people over a two-year period as they seek to give some shape and direction to their lives within the rigid constraints of the communist system, and it became the model for a number of disillusioned Soviet youth films of the late 1980s. Stylistically expressive and technically inventive, *Is It Easy to Be Young?* ultimately conveys a sense of hopelessness and futility, especially with regard to the poisonous effect of the Afghan war on Soviet youth and society generally (one of the few clear choices open to young men in the late Soviet era was to join the army and go to Afghanistan—many of the youths at the film's conclusion are shown to have become disabled veterans of that war).[6] Since 1990, Latvia's production system has been restructured under the umbrella of the Latvian Film Corporation, which includes three feature studios, a documentary and animation studio, and a production services plant. Annual output has been halved, but the country's leading directors, such as Jañis Streičs (b. 1936—*To Remember or to Forget* [*Pomnit ili zabyt*, 1982]; *Other People's Passions* [*Svesas kaislibas*, 1986]; *The Child of Man* [*Cilveka berns*, 1992]) and Gunaris Piesis (b. 1931—*In the Shadow of Death* [*Naves ena*, 1981]; *Spriditus*, 1991; *Maija and Paija*, 1993), continue to win international

6. The Afghan War began with a Soviet invasion in 1979 in the wake of an Islamic coup. (Afghanistan has common borders with the then-Soviet republics of Turkmenistan, Uzbekistan, and Tadjikistan, and it had been in the Soviet/Russian sphere of influence since the early nineteenth century.) The Soviets set up a puppet government in Kabul but met with fierce resistance from the Mujahadeen (Islamic freedom fighters), who waged a guerrilla war against them that killed 13,000 Soviet troops before a phased withdrawal was implemented in 1988–89. Militarily and politically fruitless, the Afghan War was the USSR's Vietnam, producing a widespread dissatisfaction at home that ultimately contributed to the dissolution of the Soviet state.

awards. Not long after the Soviet Union collapsed, the Latvian government created the National Film Center— a state body like the film institutes of the Scandinavian countries, designed both to promote film culture and stimulate production. A decision was made to support four feature projects a year, and the center has been fairly successful at keeping to this goal. As in Lithuania, a new generation of directors has emerged whose ties to the old Soviet system and its repressive history are tenuous at best. Young *auteurs* include several who studied film-making abroad, notably Anna Viduleja, whose *The Colour of Lead* (*Svina krasa*, 1999) explores the life of the early twentieth-century Latvian painter Georgs Eliass, and Una Celma (b. 1960), whose *The Curse of Gravitation* (*Gravitacijas lasts*, 1999) and *Follow Me* (*Seko man*, 2000) both compare Latvian and Swedish cultural perceptions. By 1999, the Latvian film industry had pretty fully adapted to the new market economy, and veteran Jānis Streičs reappeared after a six-year hiatus to score a national hit with the contemporary fairy tale *The Mill of Destiny* followed by *The Mystery of the Old Parish House* (2000). Currently, the state underwrites about 37 percent of the industry's overhead, with the rest coming from private investment; and the Latvian cinema has shown itself to be surprisingly healthy despite its small audience base.

ESTONIA

Estonia's Tallinfilm Studio produced an average of five films annually, most of which were less Soviet in sensibility than Nordic. (Culturally and linguistically, the Estonians are much closer to the Finns than to either the Russians or their Baltic neighbors.) For example, the work of Kaljo Kiisk (b. 1925—*Madness* [*Hullumeelsus*, 1968]; *Nipernaadi* [*Toomis Nipernaadi*, 1983]) is reminiscent of Bergman's, and the films of Leida Laius (*Ukuaru*, 1973; *Keep Smiling* [*Naerata ometi*, 1985]; *Games for School Children* [*Igry dija detej skolnogo vozrasta*, 1987; co-directed with Arvo Iho]; *The Stolen Meeting* [*Ukradennoye svidaniye*, 1989]) are comparable in theme to those of such Norwegian feminist directors as Anja Breien (see Chapter 15). During the 1980s, a number of Estonian features won festival awards (e.g., Olav Neuland's *Nest in the Wind* [*Gnezdo na vetru*, 1980]) and, during the glasnost era, became increasingly critical of Soviet-style socialism in such films as Peeter

Simm's (b. 1953) *Ideal Landscape* (*Ideaalmaastik*, 1986) and Arvo Iho's *The Observer* (*Vaatleja*, 1987). By 1990, Estonian cinema had become directly confrontational, with Jüri Sillart's *The Awakening* (*Aratus*), a film about the KGB's mass deportation of Estonian citizens to the Gulag in 1949, and Peeter Simm's *The Man Who Never Was* (*Inimene keda polnud*), a black comedy of the German/Russian occupation, becoming the year's most popular features. Independence brought industry restructuring in that Tallinfilm became a 50 percent state-owned joint stock company and two private companies— Freyja Film and Arcadia—entered the market, but annual production has remained stable throughout the transition, producing a remarkable number of films relative to Estonia's tiny population of 1.4 million. A recent example is *Darkness in Tallinn* (*Tallinn pimeduses*, 1993), a patriotic thriller directed by Ilkka Järvilatura and coproduced with Finland, Sweden, and the United States. In 1997, the Estonian Film Foundation was established as a Scandinavian-type institution to promote film development, production, and distribution. Its first act was to liquidate Tallinfilm and use the proceeds to build a new cinema center with screening facilities, edit suites, and laboratories to serve the nation's sixty-five (yes, sixty-five) small production companies, most of which are devoted to teleproduction. The state provides about 50 percent of all production funding (minimum budgets per feature are about $350,000), and recent films include Hardi Volmer's (b. 1957) *All My Lenins* (*Minu Leninid*, 1999), a fantasy in which a real-life Estonian secret agent helps the German government establish a school for Lenin impersonators in pre–World War I Europe, and veteran Peeter Simm's contemporary romantic comedy *Good Hands* (*Head Käed/Labas Rokas*, 2001), an Estonian-Latvian coproduction that was a hit in both countries. Arvo Iho's mythopoetic *The Heart of the Bear* (*Karu süda*, 2001), coproduced with Russia, Germany, and the Czech Republic, proved similarly successful in foreign markets. Although it is smaller than many American cities, Estonia remains a viable film-producing nation, accounting for an average of three features per year.

MOLDAVIA (MOLDOVA)

Moldavian cinema enjoyed some prominence in the 1960s and 1970s, but its achievements were of a distinctly national character, embodying local customs, everyday rituals, and the traditional arts. Moldavia, or Moldova, was originally part of Romania, and Romanian is still its primary language, making the region ethnically and culturally distinct from its Soviet neighbors. Nevertheless, Moldova-Film Studio was founded in 1957 and produced its first feature in *Chieftain Kodr* (Mikhail Kalik, Boris Rytsarev, and Olga Ulitskaya, 1958), an epic about a national folk hero, and almost immediately two major figures emerged—Mikhail Kalik (b. 1927), whose richly colored *Man Follows the Sun* (*Chelovek idet za solntsem*, 1961) provided a quite startling leap into the avant-garde, and Vadim Derbenev (b. 1934), Kalik's cinematographer, whose *Journey into April* (*Puteshestviye v aprel*, 1963) and *The Last Month of Autumn* (*Posledniy mesiats oseni*, 1965) continued in this same poetic vein. All three of these latter films won international festival awards, providing encouragement for such younger Moldavian filmmakers as Vadim Lysenko (b. 1932) and Valerju Gaziu (b. 1938), who co-directed the postwar peasant chronicle *Bitter Grains* (1967), and Emil Lotianu (b. 1936), whose *The Red Glades* (*Krasnye poliany*, 1966) offered a nearly ethnographic account of the folk culture of shepherds in the Bessarabian mountains. Perhaps the most extraordinary film to come out of Moldavia during this brief groundswell of national expression was Lotianu's *The Leutary* (*Leutary*, 1971), which concerns the adventures of a legendary tribe of Bessarabian gypsies devoted to the practice of music. Virtuoso musicians and singers all, the Leutary were ill treated at home, so they traveled Europe for centuries, performing for whomever would receive them. Loteanu conceived and executed the film like a musical composition, blending original Leutary songs with variations by leading contemporary musicians to create a stunning, multitenored display of Moldavian folk art. As the Brezhnev regime grew increasingly hostile to "ethnic nationalism," however, the brilliance was drained out of Moldova-Film. Kalik, for example, was allowed to emigrate to Israel in the early 1970s, and Lotianu was co-opted by Mosfilm, for whom he directed the colorful *Gypsies Take Off for the Sky* (*Tabor uhodit v nebo*, 1976), a distinguished, if gloomy, version of Chekhov's *The Shooting Party* (*Moi laskovyi i nezhnii zver'*, 1979), the international biopic *Anna Pavlova* (coproduced with Britain, 1984), and similar large-scale projects in the 1980s. At this writing, moreover, the political turmoil and civil strife that have afflicted Moldavia (population 4.4 million) since the collapse of the Soviet Union make the future of its cinema unclear.

Transcaucasian Cinema[7]

GEORGIA

Of all the cinemas of the former Soviet republics, that of Georgia (population 5 million) is the oldest and most sophisticated, preceding the Bolshevik Revolution by at least ten years. Its first feature, *Berikaoba-Keenoba* (Aleksandre Tsutsunava [1881–1955]), was made in 1909, and its first full-length documentary, *The Travels of Akaki Tsereteli in Racha and Lechkhumi* (Vasil Amashukeli [1886–1977]), appeared in 1912. By the eve of World War I, there were twenty-nine movie theaters in Georgia, and the first national production company was at work making *Kristine* (Tsutsunava, 1916), a realistic social drama based on a Georgian novel, starring famous performers from the Georgian stage. (The cinema's tradition of collaborating with Tbilisi's Rustaveli Theater Institute, which now has its own film department, continues to this day.) In 1921, the Soviet regime was established in Georgia, and Goskinprom Gruzia, the state film company, was established at Tbilisi the following year. Appropriately, one of its first productions was Ivan Perestiani's (1870–1959) *The Little Red Devils* (1923), a revolutionary "Western" about three young people fighting with the Red cavalry during the civil war (1918–20), which was highly influential of the Soviet industry as a whole.

The period 1924 to 1937 is known as the "silver age" of Georgian cinema because it witnessed the greatest work of its first generation of professional directors—e.g., Perestiani's *Three Lives* (1924), lavishly praised by Anatoli Lunacharski as a landmark in Soviet cinema; Kote Marjanishvili's black comedy *Samanishvili's Stepmother* (1927), adapted by Nikolai Shengelaia (1901–1943) from a popular nineteenth-century play; Kote Mikaberidze's

---

7. The Georgian and Armenian languages have their own alphabets and are written in a unique script; Azerbaijani (Azeri) is a Turkic language written, like Russian, in Cyrillic. No attempt is made here to render the transliterated Russian-language titles of Transcaucasian films, unless they had wide currency by those titles in the USSR.

(1896–1973) expressionistic satire *My Grandmother* (1929); Mikhail Kalatozov's extraordinary documentary *Salt for Svanetia* (*Sol Svanetii*, 1930); Shengelaia's twin masterworks *Eliso* (1928) and *The Twenty-six Commissars* (1932; shot in Baku, Azerbaijan); Siko (Semion) Dolidze's (1903–1983) *The Last Crusaders* (1934), an ethnographic analysis of a small Khevsurian tribe; Davit Rondeli's (1904–1976) wry critique of fin de siècle nobility, *Lost Paradise* (1937); and Mikhail Chiaureli's (1894–1974) *Arsena* (1937), a socialist-realist account of an early nineteenth-century peasant revolt. The most influential of these were the Shengelaia films—*Eliso*, recounting an incident in which a tsarist decree attempted to evict an entire Caucasian mountain village and give its land to the Cossacks, and *The Twenty-six Commissars*, based on events that took place in Baku, Azerbaijan, during the civil war. Admired by both Eisenstein and Pudovkin, these films established Shengelaia as the founder of Georgia's most important film family[8] and, with other films of the "silver age," moved the Russian Formalist poet/critic Viktor Shklovsky to remark that Soviet cinema began not in Moscow, but Tbilisi.

During World War II only a handful of films were made, among them Chiaureli's nationalist epic *Georgi Saakadze* (1942–43), and after the war—as elsewhere in the Soviet Union and its client states—Zhdanovian socialist realism held sway in such "artistic documentaries" as Chiaureli's *The Vow* (1946) and *The Fall of Berlin* (1949). From 1938 to 1952, Goskinprom Gruzia was renamed Tbilisi Studios, and after 1953 it adopted its current configuration as the Georgian Film Studio, or Gruziafilm. Modern Georgian cinema is considered to have begun with the release of Tengiz Abuladze and Rezo Chkheidze's[9] *Magdana's Little Donkey* (*Lurdzha Magdany*, 1956) on the cusp of the Khrushchev thaw. Its directors were part of the second generation of Georgian filmmakers, many of whom had graduated from the VGIK but went on to revive the best tradition of Georgian cinema of the 1920s and 1930s—including, most prominently, Abuladze (1924–1994), Georgi (b. 1937) and Eldar Shengelaia (b. 1933), Otar Iosseliani (b. 1934), and Lana Gogoberidze (b. 1928). (Other Georgian filmmakers, however, such as Mikhail Kalatozov [1903–1973] and Georgi Danelia [b. 1930], were co-opted by Mosfilm during the same period.)

Though Abuladze's best work—*Grandma, Iliko, Illarion, and I* (1962), *The Prayer* (1967), *The Tree of Desire*

17.11 *Repentence* (Tengiz Abuladze, 1984): the first Soviet film to confront Stalinist terror.

(1976)—is based on Georgian literature, he became internationally famous for *Repentence* (1984), a parable about a ruthless Georgian dictator ("Varlam Aravidze," or "no one") that was the first Soviet film to deal unflinchingly, if indirectly, with the murderous legacy of Stalin. This film, which was originally made for Georgian television and was briefly shelved under the regime of Gorbachev's immediate predecessor, Konstantin Chernenko, received national Soviet distribution in 1985 thanks largely to lobbying by Eduard Shevardnadze, then secretary of the Georgian Communist party. In its open confrontation of the Stalin Terror and its absolute resistance to censorship, *Repentence* marked a crucial turning point

---

8. Georgian cinema has traditionally been organized around intermarried extended families. Typically, the father (or, less often, mother) will be a leading director and the children actors/actresses, cinematographers, or other sorts of production artists. Older established families include the Shengelaia, Chiaureli, Dolidze, Managadze, and Kalatozishvili; younger ones are the Gogoberidze, Kobakhidze, and Iosseliani.

9. Chkheidze made several notable films after *Magdana*—e.g., *Our Courtyard* (*Nash dvor*, 1956), *Father of a Soldier* (*Otets soldata*, 1964), *Saplings* (*Sazhentsy*, 1973), and *Your Son, the Earth!* (1981), the latter an avatar of glasnost—but has been most notable for his committed leadership of the Georgian Film Studio (Gruziafilm) since 1973.

in Soviet film history and became a public icon of glasnost.

Georgi and Eldar Shengelaia, the sons of Nikolai Shengelaia (who died in an automobile accident in 1943) and the famous actress Nato Vachnadze (who died in an airplance crash in 1953) were unquestionably the most influential Georgian filmmakers of the 1960s and 1970s. Georgi's short feature *Alaverdoba*, made while he was still at the VGIK in 1962 but unreleased until 1966, is an extraordinary essay on the corruption of Georgian folk culture by modernity set during a religious festival at an ancient cathedral in the Alazani Mountains. *Pirosmani* (1969), his visionary biography of the primitivist painter Niko Pirosmanishvili (1862–1918), became a landmark of new Georgian cinema by reaffirming it as an index of national identity. Often compared to Tarkovsky's *Andrei Rublev* (1966), Shengelaia's film conveys the color, texture, and formal composition of the painter's work, as well as his sense of the magical harmony between art and life. In his subsequent work—*Melodies of the Veri Quarter* (1973), the first Georgian musical; his documentary on winemaking *Come to the Valley of the Grapes* (1976); *Journey of a Young Composer* (1983), a dramatic feature set in tzarist Georgia circa 1908; and *Khareba and Gogia* (1988), a period piece about a gang of Caucasian bandits—Georgi extended his scrutiny of the Georgian character to other national pastimes. Meanwhile, his brother, Eldar, worked the fantastic vein of Georgian humor in *White Caravan* (1963), a parable about the generation gap set among Khevsurian shepherds, and *Samanishvili's Stepmother* (1977), a modern-day version of the play his

father had first adapted as a screenwriter in 1927. Eldar's satiric sensibility occasionally brought him into conflict with the Soviet authorities. His phantasmagoric *Screwballs* (also known as *The Eccentrics*, 1973), for example, became the catalyst for an attack by Moscow critics on Georgian cinema as "elitist," and *The Blue Mountains*, or *An Improbable Tale* (1983), a whimsical allegory of the crumbling away of Georgian national values under socialism, was nearly banned.

The films of Otar Iosseliani provoked a similar response, and several were, in fact, either shelved or banned. Both a professional musician and painter before he turned to filmmaking, Iosseliani studied at the VGIK under Dovzhenko, and his first film, *April* (*Aprel*, 1961; also known as *Stories about Things*), was attacked by the censors and withdrawn from general release. An apolitical fable about how human relationships are destroyed by the possession of material objects, the film apparently offended in its spirituality, and Iosseliani did not make another film until the documentary *Cast Iron* (*Chugun*, 1964), shot with a hidden camera at the Rustavi Metal Works, Georgia, and clearly influenced by Georgi Shengelaia's *Alaverdoba*. Iosseliani's next film, *When Leaves Fall* (*Listopad*, 1967), was a dramatic feature similarly shot in documentary style. Set in contemporary Tbilisi, it concerns the disillusionment of an idealistic young man who takes a job at a state wine distillery and learns the corruption of Soviet industry from the inside. Heavily edited for distribution, *When Leaves Fall* was succeeded by *There Lived a Singing Blackbird* (*Zhil pevchiy drozd*, 1970) and *Pastorale* (1976), both of which were shelved for their "subjectivity," and Iosseliani emigrated to Paris, having acquired an international reputation on the festival circuit with all three films.[1] Here he has produced several highly regarded, plotless films, which are rich both in their documentary-like observation of human nature and their cinematic poetry—*Les Favoris de la lune* (*Favorites/Minions of the Moon*, 1984—Golden Lion, Venice, 1984), set in a residential district of Paris over the period of about one hundred years, and *Et la lumière fut* (*Let There Be Light*, 1989), an allegory of paradise lost in a matriarchal African village.

Lana Gogoberidze was the first Soviet director to focus

17.12 *Pirosmani* **(Georgi Shengelaia, 1969).**

---

1. *When Leaves Fall* won the Critics' Prize at Cannes in 1968; *There Was a Singing Blackbird* won the Directors' Fortnight at Cannes in 1974; and *Pastorale* won the Critics' Prize at Berlin in 1981.

on women's issues since the 1920s, and her first feature, *Under One Sky* (1961), was adapted from an anthology of novellas about women in different periods of Georgian history. She worked on similar themes throughout the 1960s (e.g., *I See the Sun* [1965], about the women of a Georgian village during World War II), producing her best work in the late 1970s and 1980s—*Some Interviews on Personal Questions* (*Neskolko interviu po lichnym voprosam*, 1979), *The Day Is Longer Than the Night* (*Den' dlinnee nochi*, 1984), and *Whirl of Life* (*Full Circle/Whirlpool* [*Krugovorot*, 1987]), winner of the best director's award at the 1987 Tokyo Film Festival. Gogoberidze's style is exemplified by *Some Interviews*, a multilayered film about a female journalist interviewing people, like herself, whose lives have been traumatized by the Stalin Terror.[2]

The work of the third generation of Georgian directors, most of them trained by the Faculty of Cinema established in 1975 at the Tbilisi State Theatrical Institute, began to appear during the 1980s. Prominent were Irakli Kvirikadze's (b. 1939) *The Swimmer* (*Plovets*, 1981), a period film that satirized the Stalinist cult of the hero prematurely and was shown only in a severely edited version until glasnost, and his wife Nana Djordjadze's (b. 1948) *Robinsoniad, or My English Grandfather* (*Robinzonada, ili moi angliskii dedushka*, 1987)—scripted by Kvirikadze and winner of the 1987 Cannes Golden Camera award—a satire about a British engineer who comes to a remote Georgian village during the 1920s to build a link in the London–New Delhi telegraph line and falls desperately in love with the sister of a local party boss. Other leading filmmakers of the third generation include Aleksandre Rekhviashvili (b. 1938—*Georgian Chronicle of the Nineteenth Century* [*Gruzinskaia Khronika XIX veka*, 1979]; *The Step* [*Stupen'*, 1986]), Levan Zakareishvili (b. 1953—*The Father* [1984]; *The Theme* [*Temo*, 1988]), Nodar Managadze (b. 1943, son of second-generation director Shota Managadze—*Spring Passes*, 1984; *Eh, Maestro!*, 1987), Vakhtang (Tato) Kotetshvili (b. 1959—*Anemia*, 1987), Gogita Chkonia (b. 1950—*Father, Son, and the Wind*, 1988), and Aleko Tsabadze (b. 1956—*The Spot* [*Pyatno*, 1985]; *Night Dance*, 1991). Georgian cinema was further enriched during the 1980s by the posting of Armenian director Sergei Parajanov to Gruziafilm, for which he directed his last two films.

The situation of Georgian cinema in the 1990s was, as usual, inextricably entwined with national politics. In March 1991, Georgians voted overwhelmingly to declare their independence from the Soviet Union, and elected Zviad K. Gamsakhurdia as their president the following month. Gamsakhurdia quickly assumed dictatorial powers and, with virtually all filmmakers opposed to him, restructured Gruziafilm into twelve separate production units with financing negotiable only through his office. This sent shock waves through the industry but had a less immediate effect on production than did the civil war that broke out over Christmas 1991, wrecking Tbilisi and forcing the Gamsakhurdia government to flee. In February 1992, a coalition of democrats and rebel warlords invited Eduard Shevardnadze—former Georgian Communist party chief, former Soviet foreign minister, and the world's most famous living Georgian—to save the nation. Meanwhile, Gamsakhurdia established a stronghold in Sukhumi in western Georgia, formed an alliance with the Abkhazian rebels and renegade Russian Army troops of that region, and resumed the civil war. Shevardnadze, serving as president of an independent but considerably weakened Republic of Georgia, preserved order until September 1993, when the Abkhazian separatists prevailed over his own army and took control of western Georgia. Gamsakhurdia's rebels now threatened Tbilisi, and Shevardnadze was forced to strike a deal for protection with Russian president Boris Yeltsin and join the Commonwealth of Independent States. By 1994, Russian troops were supplying Georgia's army and protecting its railways and ports, as in former times; and the Georgian film industry was able to crank back up again after a hiatus of nearly two years (albeit in a context in which industrial production generally had shrunk by 40 to 70 percent). By the end of that year, work was completed on Georgi Shengelaia's adaptation of Tolstoi's Caucasian short story *Khadzhi Murat*; Eldar Shengelaia's satire on the pre-glasnost film bureaucracy, *The Dog Rose*; and Lana Gogoberidze's *Waltz in Petchora*, a dramatization of incidents from the 1937 Stalinist crackdown. Between 1995 and 1999, only a handful of films were produced by Georgiafilm (e.g., Nana Djordjadze's Oscar-nominated *A*

---

2. Other leading figures of the second generation of Georgian directors are Mikhail Kobakhidze (b. 1939—*The Wedding* [*Svadba*, 1964]; *The Umbrella* [*Zontik*, 1967]; *The Musicians* [1969]), whose short fiction fims have won numerous international awards, and Shota Managadze (1901–1977), whose *Ballad of Khevsur* (1965) remains one of the great epics of Georgian folk culture extending into modern times.

Chef in Love [*Les Mille et une recettes du cuisinier amoureux*, 1996]), and Georgian cinema stayed alive through the offices of independent production companies like Sameda and Debiujti, and investment capital from France, Germany, Russia, the United Kingdom, and Denmark. New work appeared in 2000 that won numerous festival awards and announced a renewed vitality for Georgian film. Nana Djordjadze's coming-of-age comedy *27 Missing Kisses* (2000), Kakhaber Kakabidze's urban melodrama *The Lake* (2000), Georgi Shengelaia's *Georgian Grapes* (part of the European omnibus film *3 Erotic Tales* [2000]), Otar Iosseliani's French-produced comedy of manners *Farewell, Home Sweet Home* [*Adieu, plancher des vaches*, 1999) and Dito Tsintsadze's *Lost Killers* (*Dakarguli mkvlelebi*, 2000), set among alienated illegal immigrants in Mannheim, Germany, all won international awards. The 2001–2 season saw the release of six new Georgian features, most notably Nodar Managadze's philosophical parable *Angels Fly Over* (*Angelozebis gadaprena*), Goderdzi Chokheli's historical fantasy *Chained Knights* (*Midjachvuli raindebi*), and Mikhail Kalatozishvili's metaphysical adventure *Mysteries* (*Misteriebi*), which won further festival recognition. (Kalatozishvili is the grandson of Mikhail Kalatozov [*The Cranes are Flying*, etc.].) Yet this is clearly a comedown for an industry that produced an average of fourteen features a year during the Soviet era, more than sixty of whose highly trained directors cannot find work today. Because the size of its domestic market is so small (there are only six movie theaters in the entire city of Tbilisi), the preservation of Georgia's uniquely diverse national film culture will increasingly depend on Western export markets cultivated through competition in international festivals.

ARMENIA

The first Armenian feature was *The Tragedy of Turkish Armenia* (also known as *Under the Kurds*, 1915), written, directed, and photographed by A. Minervin. In 1922, Armenia joined the Soviet Union, and its cinema was nationalized as Gosfotokino, then Armenkino, with studios in the capital city of Yerevan. The first feature-length documentary, *Soviet Armenia* (1924), appeared at the same time. Armenian silent cinema was dominated by the work of Amo Bek-Nazarov (1891–1965),[3] whose historical drama *Namus* (1925) and slapstick *Shor and Shorshor* (1927) set the national standard for realism and comedy,

respectively. Bek-Nazarov's other silent films include *Zareh* (1926), a melodrama about life in a Kurdish tribe under the tsars, and *Khas-Push*, a documentary on the exploitation of the people of Iran (then Persia) by British trading companies at the turn of the century. The late silent period was enriched by the return to Armenkino of Amasi Martirosyan (1897–1971) and Patvakan Barkhudaryan (1898–1948), both of whom had apprenticed as directors with Goskinprom Gruzia, Tbilisi. Martirosyan's satire *The Mexican Diplomats* (co-directed with Levon Kalantar, 1931) and Barkhudaryan's *Kikos* (1933) made a star of the great Armenian comic Hambartsum Khachanyan.

Sound came late to Armenia—its last silent feature was Martirosyan's village tragedy *Gikor* (1934—remade in 1982 by Sergei Israelyan), adapted from a literary classic, and its first sound film Bek-Nazarov's *Pepo* (1935), a period drama on the theme of social justice with a score by composer Aram Khachaturian. Like the rest of the Soviet Union, Armenia experienced a grim period of Stalinist repression during the 1930s and 1940s, when only a handful of films could be made. Hewing to the Zhdanovian socialist-realist line, Armenkino (renamed Yerevan Studio, 1938) produced Bek-Nazarov's *Zanguezour* (1938), a "historical-revolutionary" account of Sovietization, and *David-Bek* (1944), an epic of resistance to an eighteenth-century invasion designed to mobilize the Armenian people against the Nazis in a manner similar to *Giorgi Saakadze* (Chiaureli) in Georgia, *Alexander Nevski* (Eisenstein) in Russia, and *Shchors* (Dovzhenko) in Ukraine. A postwar revival did not occur until Yerevan Studio, renamed Armenfilm in 1957 to emphasize its national distinctness, attracted a new generation of directors who made films about Armenian daily life—Frunze Dovlatyan (1927–1997—*Hello, It's Me!*, 1965); Armand Manaryan (b. 1929—*Tzhvzhik*, 1961; *Karine*, 1967,

---

3. Armenian by birth, Bek-Nazarov was instrumental in the development of all three Transcaucasion cinemas. In the early 1920s, he made films in Tbilisi (e.g., *In the Pillory*, 1924) and, as an administrator at Goskinprom-Gruzia, took an active role in expanding Georgian distribution and exhibition outlets throughout the Soviet Union. Once the Armenia cinema was established, Bek-Nazarov devoted his creative energies to it for the next thirty years, but in the late 1920s he also made two important features for the fledging Azerbaijanfilm in Baku (see below), at the end of his career working briefly in Tadjikistan. When he died in 1965, the Armenfilm Studios in Yerevan were officially renamed for him.

Armenia's first musical comedy); and Henrik Malyan (1925–1988—*The Triangle*, 1967; *We Are Our Mountains*, 1969). At the same time, the work of two other Armenian directors—Sergei Parajanov (1924–1990) and Ardavazd (Arthur) Peleshyan (b. 1938)—was coming to international attention.

Although he worked the first part of his career for Ukrainian studios and the last for Gruziafilm, it is clear today that Parajanov's art was deeply and irrevocably Armenian in character. Nowhere is this more apparent than in *Sayat-Nova* (also known as *The Color of Pomegranates*), the single, astonishing feature he made for Armenfilm in 1969. Conceived as an extraordinarily complex series of *tableaux* representing the life and work of the visionary eighteenth-century poet Arutin Sayadyan, the film was shelved by Soviet authorities until 1973, when it was released in a drastically re-edited version supervised by Sergei Yutkevich. In 1992, *Sayat-Nova* became available in the "director's cut" originally submitted to Soviet censors in 1969, and an even fuller version is known to exist today only in the Armenfilm archives. Peleshyan, who was a close personal friend of Parajanov, began making documentaries while a student at the VGIK, including *The Beginning* (*Nachalo*, 1967), an emotionally charged compilation film on the October Revolution. This ten-minute short replaced narrative commentary with a complicated audio-visual structure based on what Peleshyan would later call "distance montage." Over the next twenty years, he went on to produce at Armenfilm a body of work very similar in structure to polyphonic music, where linear and horizontal progressions interact. Elaborately theorized in his 1988 book *My Cinema* (*Moye Kino*), Peleshyan's practice of "distance montage" appears to best advantage in a series of short, intense black-and-white films—*We* (*Menk*, 1969; 30 minutes), *Inhabitants* (*Obitateli*, 1970; 10 minutes), *The Seasons of the Year* (*Tarva Yeghanaknere*, 1975; 30 minutes), and *Our Century* (*Mer Dare*, 1982/91; 30 minutes)—which are only recently starting to be seen in the West.

In 1971, the Telefilm Studios of Armenia were established in Yerevan by the State Television and Radio Committee and became a key factor in production financing (e.g., much of Peleshyan's later work). The decade also witnessed major films by Malyan (*The Father*, 1972; *Nahapet*, 1977) and Dovlatyan (*Chronicle of the Days of Yerevan*, 1972; *Birth*, 1977) as well as new work by Bagrat

Hovhannisyan (1929–1990—*The Green Raisin*, 1973; *Autumn Sun*, 1977) and Edmond Keossayan (b. 1936—*The Gentlemen*, 1972), who went on to become a leading director at Mosfilm. During the glasnost era, a new generation of Armenian filmmakers focused on stylistic experimentation. Inspired by the examples of Parajanov and Peleshyan, respectively, Suren Babayan (b. 1950) directed *The Thirteenth Apostle* (1988) and *Blood* (1990), while documentarist Harutiun Khachatryan (b. 1955) produced *Kond* (1988), *The White City* (1988), and *Return to the Promised Land* (1991). Armenian animation reached its height during this same period in the award-winning work of Robert Sahakyants (b. 1950—*The Lesson*, 1987; *The Button*, 1989; *Everything's Fine, Madam Marquise*, 1991), Lyudmilla Sahakyants (b. 1950—*Rock Salt*, 1988; *The Interpretation of Dreams*, 1989), and Stepan Galstyan (b. 1951—*The Corridor*, 1989).

Even before the collapse of the Soviet Union, the terrible earthquake of December 7, 1988, and ethnic warfare with Azerbaijan for control of Nagorno-Karabakh[4] injected elements of raw tragedy into Armenian cinema, evident in the dark documentaries of Ruben Gevorkiants (b. 1945—*Requiem*, 1989; *Ashkharums*, 1989), Robert Sahakyant's collage piece *For You, Armenia* (1990), Frunze Dovlatyan's *Nostalgia* (1990), and David Safarian's (b. 1952) *Paradise Lost* (1991). These and similar films concern the catastrophes of the nation's recent past, beginning with the genocidal massacre of more than 1 million Armenians between 1915 and 1918 by the Ottoman Turks. Since 1992, the Republic of Armenia has been an independent state, and Armenfilm's monopoly has been challenged by a whole series of "cooperative" or private producers. In the mid 1990s, the economic situation of Armenia became grim—since the winter of 1993, its crucial lifelines to the outside world had been cut off, first by an Azerbaijani blockade and then by unrest in neighboring Georgia. Electricity could be generated only a few hours each day, and Yerevan was lit at night by candlelight. In the short term, then, any resurgence of Armenian cinema depended on the activity of numerous Armenian filmmakers living outside of the country. (Only one-third of all Armenians make up the

---

4. The death toll from the earthquake was estimated at 25,000 and the war in Karabakh had taken at least 4,000 lives by the time of the cease fire in 1994.

17.13–17.17 Images from the life and poetry of Arutiun Sayadian in Parajanov's astounding *The Color of Pomegranates* (1969; released uncut 1992). 17.13 The poet as a youth. 17.14–17 The adult poet and his Muse.

republic's population of 3.5 million; the rest are dispersed throughout the globe.) These include, remarkably, Don Askarian (b. 1949—*Komitas*, 1988) in Germany, Atom Egoyan (b. 1960—*Family Viewing*, 1987; *Speaking Parts*, 1989; *Calendar*, 1992; *Erotica*, 1995) in Canada, Michael Hagopian (b. 1913—*The Forgotten Genocide*, 1977; *Strangers in the Promised Land*, 1984; *Ararat Beckons*, 1990; *The Armenian Genocide*, 1991), Theodore Bogosian (b. 1951—*An Armenian Journey*, 1988), Ara Madzounian (b. 1953—*The Pink Elephant*, 1988; *The Land of Open Graves*, 1990), and Nigol Bezjian (b. 1955—*Chickpeas*, 1992) in the United States, Per-Åke Holmquist and Suzanne Khardalian (b. 1947 and 1956, respectively—*Back to Ararat*, 1988) in Sweden, Yervant Gianikian (b. 1942—*Uomini, anni, vita*, 1990) in Italy, and Henri Verneuil (1920–2002—*Mayrig: 588 rue du Paradis*, 1991) and Jacques Kébadian (b. 1941—*Memoires arméniennes*, 1993) in France. Immediately following the Soviet period, 1991–93, Armenian production doubled, and there was talk of a "New Armenian Cinema"; but investment capital dried up quickly during the general financial crisis of 1994–95, and most of the newly created studios failed. By 1996, it was clear that only state intervention could save the cinema, and to that end its main studios—Hayfilm Hayk, and Yerevan—would remain under state control for several years past the turn of the century. The most promising new director to emerge from post-Soviet Armenia is Edgar Baghdasaryan, whose early feature *Outflow/The Black Wall* (*Hosk/Sev Pat*, 1997) won some festival notices; his independently produced, full-length documentary *Aratta—the Land of Holy Rituals* (*Aratta—srpazan tserery erkir*, 2000) commemorated the arrival and spread of Christianity to mark the 1,700th anniversary of its adoption as the Armenian state religion. Appropriately, Baghdasaryan's next film, the Armenian-French coproduction *Mariam* (2001), was a parable about a modern-day Virgin Mary. Other notable post-Soviet films are Harutiun Khachatryan's *Documentalist* (*Vaveragrogh*, 1997; released 1999), about a director shooting a film on Yerevan; Armen Dovlatian's mystically inflected crime drama *Dreams* (1998); Suren Babayan's *Crazy Angel* (*Khent hreshtak*, 2000), which takes place on the set of a Biblical film adapted from Pär Lagerkvist's novel *Barabbas*; Albert S. Mkrtchyan's *A Happy Bus* (also known as *Melody of a Destroyed City/Kandvats kaghaki meghedy*, 2001), set in the aftermath of the 1988 earthquake that

devastated Yerevan; and Tigran Xmalian's *Pierlequin* (2001), based on the life of Leonid Engibarov, a great Armenian clown and poet. At a significantly reduced Armenfilm, Ardavazd Peleshyan continued to make feature-length documentaries—e.g., *An Armenian World*, coproduced by the Armenian Ministry of Culture and France's Centre National du Cinéma. As Armenia approached the tenth anniversary of its independence from the former Soviet Union, it could count thirty feature films to its credit between 1991 and 2001, a remarkable achievement for this small nation, which is so depleted of natural resources that it was forced to ration water and electricity for much of the decade. Contributing to the general improvement in studio conditions, however, was the fact that Iranian and Western filmmakers have been using Armenia as a production base because of its spectacular scenery.

AZERBAIJAN

Prerevolutionary cinema in Azerbaijan was dominated by Boris Svetlov, whose national epic *In the Realm of Oil and Millions* (1916)[5] and *Arshin mal-alan* (1917), adapted from popular theater, were the first Azerbaijani features. After the Bolshevik Revolution, the cinema was nationalized and directed toward the production of such "documentaries" as *One Year of Power in Soviet Azerbaijan* (1921) and *In the Name of God* (Abas-Mirza Sharif-Zade, 1925), a propaganda film directed against Islam. Sharif-Zade (1892–1937) also directed the popular *Haji-Kara* (1929), a version of a classical comedy by Mirza Akhundov. During the 1930s, Azerbaijanfilm hosted directors from other republics, who came to its studios in Baku to take advantage of regional scenery and culture—Amo Bek-Nazarov of Armenia (*House on a Volcano and Sevil*, both 1929), Nikolai Shengelaia of Georgia (*The Twenty-six Commissars*, 1932), Boris Barnet of Russia (*The Bluest of Seas*, 1936—the first Soviet color film), and Viktor Turin of Ukraine (*Baku People*, 1938), among others. During the World War II era, Samed Mardanov directed the obligatory socialist-realist epic, *Countrymen* (1940),

---

5. The economy of Azerbaijan (population 7.7 million) is almost totally dependent on oil production—the name itself means "land of flames" in reference to a history of spontaneous combustion in its rich oil fields. Unlike its Christian neighbors Georgia and Armenia, Azerbaijan is predominantly Muslim.

and the first postwar film was a remake of *Archin mal-alan* (1945) by Rza Takhmasib (1894–?) and Nikolai Leshchenko. This latter began a cycle of remakes that has characterized the Azerbaijani cinema since the war—e.g., *The Twenty-six Commissars of Baku*[6] (1965), directed by Azhder Ibragimov (b. 1919); yet another *Archin mal-alan* (1965), directed by T. Tagi-Zade; *Sevil*, directed by Vladimir Gorikker (b. 1925)—testifying to its relative lack of strength among the other Transcaucasian film cultures. Nevertheless, four Azerbaijani directors have achieved reputations beyond their regional borders in films that stand apart from the mainstream: Gasan Seidbejli (b. 1920—*The Telephonist*, 1962; *I Remember You, Master*, 1969; *The Price of Happiness*, 1976), Tofik Tagi-Zade (b. 1919—*Encounter*, 1955; *Distant Shores*, 1958; *My Seven Sons*, 1970; *By the Light of Dying Fires*, 1976), Rasim Odzagov (b. 1933—*The Interrogation*, 1979; *Before the Closed Door*, 1981; *The Park*, 1983; *Another Life*, 1987; *Temple of Air*, 1989); and Eldar Kuliev (b. 1941—*In a Southern City*, 1969; *Babek*, 1979; *Nizami*, 1982; *A Legend of Silver Lake*, 1984; *A Scoundrel*, 1988). Also, Vaghif Mustafayev (b. 1954) attracted critical attention with his glasnost-era black-market satire *The Villain* (1989), the first postwar domestic feature shot in the Azerbaijan language (Azeri) rather than in Russian. After proclaiming independence in 1991, Azerbaijan broke completely with Moscow, and the government began a modest subsidy program to encourage independent production of films. The first Azerbaijani feature made under this new system was Ayaz Salayev's (b. 1960) somewhat hermetic allegory on life and art, *The Bat* (1995).

Central Asian Cinema[7]

UZBEKISTAN

Uzbekistan (population 25.5 million) has the oldest and largest of all the Central Asian national cinemas. The first films were shown in the capital of Tashkent in 1897, and a major production company—the Russo-Bukhar company, Bukhkino—was founded there in 1924, after the Uzbeks joined the Soviet Union. The state-run Uzbekgoskino studio was established the following year under the direction of Nabi Ganiev (1904–1952) and immediately released two Russian-directed anti-Islamic features, *The Muslim Woman* (Dmitri Bassalygo, 1925) and *The*

Minaret of Death (V. Viskovski, 1925).[8] Most Uzbek silents were documentaries and popular science films, and the first sound film, Aleksandr Usoltsev-Graf's *The Vow* (1937), was a socialist-realist epic of collectivization. During World War II, several central Russian studios were evacuated to Tashkent, and Uzbekgoskino became home to the likes of Leonid Lukov (*Alexander Parkhomenko*, 1942; *Two Soldiers*, 1943), Iakov Protazanov (*Nasreddin in Bukhara*, 1943), and Mikhail Romm (*Girl No. 217*, 1944). In the 1950s, historical and biographical films, such as Kamil Jarmatov's (1903–1978) *Avicenna* (1957), were the order of the day until a new generation of Central Asian filmmakers graduated from the VGIK and were dispersed to their respective national studios in the 1960s, where they quickly became a dominant force. In 1969, for example, four of the six features produced by the Uzbek studios (renamed Uzbekfilm in 1961) were made by just such young directors.

Chief among these was Elior Ishmukhamedov (b. 1942), whose first feature, *Tenderness* (1966), attracted attention at several international festivals for its stylistic originality. This multi-episode film was written by Odelsha Agishev and photographed by Dilshat Fatkhullin, both VGIK graduates, who continued to work with the director for much of his early career. The same team worked to produce the coming-of-age film *In Love* (1969) and *Meetings and Partings* (1973), about the plight of Uzbek *gastarbeiters*, or "guest workers," in West Germany. When Ishmukhamedov's next film, *The Birds of*

---

6. The "twenty-six commissars" were Bolshevik officials abducted from Baku by counterrevolutionaries and killed in the desert near Kransnovdsk, Turkmenistan, in 1918. They became the subject of a major Soviet cult; there is an official Twenty-six Commissars Museum in Baku, and monuments to them are scattered throughout the former USSR.

7. The Uzbek, Kazakh, Kirghiz, and Turkmen languages belong to the Turkic family; Tadjik is an Iranian language, very close to Persian. All were written in the Arabic alphabet until the Russification effort replaced it with Cyrillic in the 1940s. Central Asian film titles are therefore given in English, without Russian-language transliteration.

8. It was Soviet policy in Central Asia to stifle Muslim unity and custom, which it connected with the murderous (and very nearly successful) Basmachi revolt in the Ferghana Valley region, 1918–24. The cultural and religious identification of most Central Asians with Islam was, historically, the thorniest "nationalities" problem the USSR had to face. At the time of its dissolution, there were 60 million Muslims living in and around Soviet Central Asia—more than in any other country except Indonesia, Pakistan, India, and Bangladesh. See Michael Rywkin, *Moscow's Muslim Challenge: Soviet Central Asia*, rev. ed. (Armonk, N.Y.: M. E. Sharpe, 1990).

Our Hopes (1977), was shelved for being implicitly critical of Soviet society, he was encouraged to make a historical spectacle. The resulting *The Youth of a Genius* (1983) is an epic costume film that re-creates the youth of the great medieval philosopher Avicenna (980–1037) in ancient Bukhara in remarkably precise detail. But *Farewell Green Summer* (1985), a love story that spans the history of modern Uzbekistan from Stalin to Gorbachev, alludes quite specifically to the official corruption then strangling the republic, setting the stage for Ishmukhamedov's 1989 signature work, *The Shock*. Based on an actual incident from the Brezhnev era, this conspiracy thriller concerns an investigative reporter who attempts to expose the leaders of a mafia syndicate that is manipulating the Uzbek cotton industry for illegal profit; in the process, he discovers that the crime ring operates at the highest levels of the Uzbek power structure and is killed for his trouble. *The Shock* became a Soviet box-office hit in 1989 and was praised by Gorbachev himself as "new thinking in cinema, very representative of *perestroika*."[9] At last report, Ishmukhamedov was working on another historical epic, a film about the Great Silk Route that once wove through the legendary cities of Bukhara, Khiva, and Samarkand.

Another prominent Uzbek director is Ali Khamraev (b. 1937), whose *White, White Storks* (1966), scripted by Agishev and photographed by Fatkhullin, attracted considerable attention for its portrayal of a Muslim country woman who elects to leave her husband for her lover. His *Dilorom* (1969) was the first Uzbek film-opera, based on classical poems of Alisher Navoi recounting the doomed love of a slave girl for a court painter. Most of Khamraev's subsequent work has dealt with the liberation of Uzbek women from Muslim cultural oppression (*Without Fear*, 1971; *Tryptych*, 1978; *The Garden of Desire*, 1988) or historical events (*The Bodyguard*, 1980; *Hot Summer in Kabul*, 1983; *Red Arrow*, 1986), although he has also made several symbolic dramas, among them *Bo Ba Bu* (1998). He recently completed *Tamerlane*, an international coproduction being shot under the auspices of Uzbekfilm. Other notable Uzbek filmmakers are Shukhrat Abbasov (b. 1931—*Tashkent, City of Bread*, 1967; *Little Man in a Big War*, 1989[1]), Ravil Batyrov (b. 1931—*We'll Be Waiting for You Lad*, 1972; scripted by A. Konchalovski), Melo Absalov (*The Daughter-in-Law's Rebellion*, 1984; *Granny General*, 1986), Djanka Faiziyev (*Who Are You?*, 1990; *Kammi*, 1992), and Farid Davletshin, whose remarkable feature *Kiep's Last Journey* (1990), based on a modernist novel evoking centuries-old folk customs, was the first film shot and released in the Uzbek language. (The Soviet

17.18 *Farewell Green Summer* **(Elior Ishmukhamedov, 1985).**

9. During Stalin's last years, Soviet central planners decided to turn Uzbekistan into the world's largest cotton plantation by diverting water from the Aral Sea to irrigate its deserts. By the 1970s, the Aral—once the world's fourth largest lake—had lost 75 percent of its volume, and the entire Central Asian watershed was destroyed. Cotton production, successful at first, began to decline because the state-run farms did not practice crop rotation. As the exhausted Uzbek soil afforded less and less cotton, Moscow raised quotas; and the farms responded by dumping tons of fertilizers onto the land (with the result that Uzbekistan today has one of the highest rates of toxic chemical pollution—and the defective birth rates that go with it—of any country on earth). Still there was not enough cotton, so a criminal conspiracy among Communist party officials, Uzbek political leaders, state farm operators, and local gangsters evolved to falsify production statistics and shipment records. This conspiracy became the first target of Gorbachev's anticorruption campaign when glasnost was declared in 1986.

1. Like many popular Uzbek films of the 1980s, this one concerns national involvement in the long and fruitless Afghan War, 1979–89. Nearly a quarter of the 13,000 Soviet soldiers who died in that war were native Uzbeks.

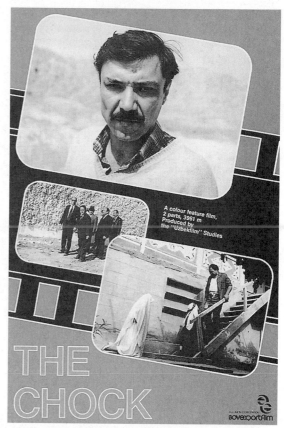

17.19 and 17.20 Old and new in Uzbek cinema: posters for *Farewell Green Summer* (1985) and *The Shock* (1989), appealing respectively to nostalgia for the past and the new sensibility of glasnost.

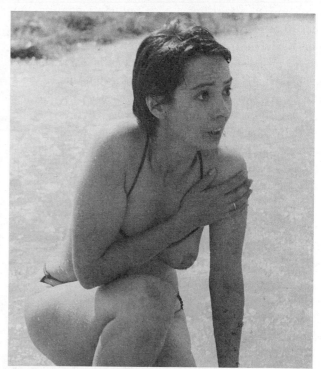

17.23 *Kiep's Last Journey* **(Farid Davletshin, 1990): the first film shot and released in Uzbek.**

in 1937 and the evacuation thereto of Mosfilm and Lenfilm after the German invasion of June 1941 (see Chapter 9). For the duration of World War II, Alma-Ata (the name means "Father of Apples") became the film capital of the Soviet Union, producing more than three-fourths of its features from 1942 through 1945. It was here, less than 150 miles west of the Chinese border, that Eisenstein shot *Ivan the Terrible, Part I* (1945) and *Part II* (1946), and that Iuli Raizman (*Mashenka*, 1942), Boris Barnet (*A Priceless Head*, 1942), Leonid and Ilia Trauberg (*The Actress*, 1943), Georgi and Sergei Vasiliev (*The Front*, 1944), and Pudovkin (*In the Name of the Fatherland*, 1943) produced their most important wartime work. The postwar years were marked by the first adaptation from Kazakh literature (*The Songs of Abaij* [Efim Aron, 1945], from the novel by Muhtar Auezov) and the first Kazakh film in color (*Djamboul* [Efim Dzigan, 1952]). At this point, Kazakhfilm settled into a steady rhythm of producing several features and four to five documentary shorts per year, attracting modest attention here and there for works by such traditional directors as Abdulla Karsakbayev (b. 1926—*My Name Is Kozha*, 1964; *Journey into Childhood*, 1970) and Shaken Ajmanov (1914–1970—*Land of Ancestors*, 1966; *End of the Ataman*, 1970).

Recently, however, Alma-Ata has become, in *Variety*'s term, "the Hollywood of Central Asia"[2] for several reasons. Kazakhstan (population 16.7 million) is geographically the largest former Soviet republic after Russia, and it is a prime target for Western development capital owing to both its size and wealth of natural resources, including oil. At the same time, Kazakhstan has experienced a remarkable surge of cinematic talent known alternately as the "Wild Kazakh boys" or the "Kazakh New Wave." This phenomenon was engendered in 1984, when a special five-year program to train filmmakers for the Kazakhfilm Studios was begun at the VGIK under the direction of avant-garde auteur Sergei Soloviev (*The White Pigeon*, 1986; *Assa*, 1988; *Black Rose Stands for Sorrow, Red Rose Stands for Love*, 1989, etc.—see below) and theater director Anatoly Vasiliev. Even before they graduated,

practice had been to dub films from all of the republics into Russian for national distribution, repressing the most fundamental form of nationalist expression.) Since the collapse of the USSR, Uzbekfilm has been the home of several international coproductions; it has a staff of over 1,000 and in the early 1990s was producing 12 to 14 features per year, about half of which were telefilms, as well as about 50 shorts. A market crisis in 1995–96 caused major retrenchment. The government partnered with private interests to create Uzbek Kino, a joint production-distribution entity that by the turn of the century was releasing about 6 domestic features annually.

KAZAKHSTAN

Viktor Turin's documentary feature on the building of the Turkistan-Siberian railway, *Turksib* (see p. 166), was filmed in Kazakhstan in 1929, as was the first indigenous short, *The Arrival of the First Train at Alma-Ata*. But Kazakh cinema didn't really begin until the creation of the Alma-Ata documentary film studios in that capital city

---

2. Deborah Young, "Alma-Ata—the Hollywood of Central Asia," *Variety*, June 9, 1991, p. 46.

four of the program's ten students[3] had made their first
feature films—including, most explosively, Rachid Nugmanov's (b. 1954) *The Needle*, (*Igla*, 1988) which became
first a Soviet, then an international box-office hit in 1989.
This stylish, hypnotic thriller features the late Leningrad
rock star Viktor Tsoi as a young man who fights to smash
a local drug ring, and its success inspired three other
Soloviev students to produce offbeat, low-budget features
in 1989—Serik Aprimov's (b. 1960) *The Last Stop*
(*Qijan*), Alexander Baranov (b. 1955) and Bakhyt Kili-
baev's (b. 1958) *The Three* (*Troye*), and Abai Karpikov's
(b. 1955) *Little Fish in Love* (*Vliublennaya rybka*)—all
of which received international distribution. When Nugmanov was elected first secretary of the Kazakh Filmmakers Union in April 1989, it was clear to all that major
changes were afoot. The following year saw the completion of two important projects—Ardak Amirkulov's (b.
1955) three-hour epic *The Fall of Otrar* (*Gibel Otrara*,
1991), which uses the siege of a Kazakh city destroyed by
Genghis Khan in the thirteenth century as an allegory for
Russia's social/political climate on the eve of Hitler's invasion in 1941; and Yermak Shinarbaev's (b. 1953) *Revenge*
(*Mesti*, 1990), a philosophical meditation on violence in
seven chapters based on ancient Korean legends and shot
on location in Kazakhstan and Sakhalin Island. Other

**17.25 Russian poster for *The Needle*, fetishizing Viktor Tsoi and
promoting its "youth market" appeal.**

important New Wave figures are Bakhit Karakulov (*The
Sorcerers* [*Razluchnitsy*, 1991], Amir Karakulov (b.
1965—*Woman between Two Brothers*, 1990), and Talgat
Temenov (b. 1954—*Wolf Cub among People* [*Volchonok
sredni lyudi*, 1989]; *Running Target* [*Byegushaya michen*,
1991]). Nugmanov's much anticipated second feature,
The Wild East: or The Last Soviet Film (*Diki vostok*,
1992), was in production when the USSR collapsed.
Beautifully shot in the mountains of Kirghizia by Nugmanov's brother Murat, it is a wildly eclectic parody of
Western and Soviet genres that provides an ironic epitaph
for what had been one of the world's greatest cinemas.

Kazakhfilm had the fourth largest studio in the USSR
and what is currently the largest production facility in

**17.24 *The Needle* (Rachid Nugmanov, 1988): Kazakhfilm's first
box-office hit.**

3. Five directors, two cinematographers, two art directors, and one
screenwriter, headed by the Kazakh film critic Murat Adezov, who came
to constitute Kazakhfilm's "Alem" (Universe) production unit. While
they were Soloviev's students, the group worked collectively to produce
Wild Pigeon (*Cuzaja belaja i rajabo*) at Kazakhfilm in 1986, which ultimately won the Special Jury Prize at Cannes.

Central Asia, employing over 1,200 people, but it badly needs new facilities and equipment. Soviet policy heavily favored allocation of funds to Mosfilm and Lenfilm over regional studios and was notably ungenerous to the cinemas of the nation's southern rim. Even during the 1990s, Kazakh filmmakers experienced shortages of film stock, an inability to record sound during shooting, and a dearth of postproduction equipment. Despite these obstacles, Kazakhfilm maintained an average output of 4 theatrical features and 4 telefilms, plus 5 to 6 feature documentaries, 50 documentary shorts, and 5 animated cartoons a year for much of the decade. More promising still, in the first rush of freedom that followed the collapse of the Soviet empire, over 30 independent production companies were operating in Kazkhstan, the largest of which, Katharsis, financed nearly 50 films with international capital in Kazakhstan after its inception in 1987, including such distinguished works as Algimantas Puipa's 1991 *Ticket to Taj Mahal* (see p. 700). Yet, by 1995, the boom was over; many private studios went out of business, while a few were kept afloat by state financing. In 1996, Kazakhstan, which has about 30 highly trained directors, released only 9 features, all of them backed by the state through the newly created National Production Center (NPC), with average budgets of about $500,000. (One of the surviving independents was Caravan, which coproduced Sergei Bodrov's very successful *Prisoner of the Mountains* [1996] with Russia; another is Kazakh Film Studios [KFS], which produces popular genre films like the jingoistic *Paratroopers* [*Desant*; Lelia Oranysheva, 2000]). Subsequent examples of films with state funding include Abai Karpikov's *The Tender One Will Win* (*Tot kto nezehneye*, 1997), a mystery about two lovers who run up against the local mafia while hunting for buried treasure; Ardak Amirkulov's *Abai* (1998), an epic about the life of a great Kazakh poet; the Kazakh-Kirghiz period film *The Last Love of Genghis Khan* (Bakhit Karakulov, 1998); Darezhan Omirbayev's *Killer* (*Tuer à gages*, 1998), a Kazakh-French crime drama that won a Jury Prize at Cannes; Serik Aprimov's lyrical coming-of-age film *Three Brothers* (*Tri brata*, 2000); and the historical epic *Sardar* (2002), a Kazakh-Chinese coproduction about a famous military leader, from a script by Andrei Tarkovsky. Like most recent Kazakh films, these productions were cofinanced with foreign capital, attracted through a variety of government tax incentives, and distributed abroad.

17.26 *Killer* (Darezhan Omirbayev, 1998): Talgat Assetov in the title role of a young man in contemporary Alma-Ata who is forced to commit a murder for the Mafia to obtain release from a personal debt.

KIRGHIZIA (KYRGYZSTAN)

Studios were founded in Kirghizia's capital of Frunze (now Bishkek) in 1942, but there was no development until well after World War II. In 1963, the Russian director Larisa Shepitko came to Kirghizfilm to shoot *Heat*, an adaptation of a story by the famous Kirghiz novelist Chingiz Aitmatov (b. 1928), who was the studio's artistic director at the time and later first secretary of the Kirghiz Filmmakers' Union, a position he held for over twenty years.[4] This film employed (as sound engineer and leading player, respectively) two men who were to join the first ranks of Kirghiz cinema, Tolomush Okeyev (1935–2001) and Bolotbek Shamshiev (b. 1941).

Okeyev graduated from the Leningrad Institute of Cinema Engineers (LIKI) in 1958 and then went on to study screenwriting and direction at Goskino. His first film, *These Are the Horses* (1965), was a documentary short about the life cycle of horses. (The Kirghizians are nomadic horsemen whose language had no alphabet until 1922; Okeyev himself was born in a tent on the steppes.) Other early films were semidocumentaries like the feature *Worship of Fire* (1972), which re-created the life of

---

4. Other Aitmatov stories became the bases for Andrei Konchalovski's *The First Teacher*, shot at Kirghizfilm in 1965, and Irina Poplavskaya's *Djamila*, coproduced by Mosfilm and Kirghizfilm in 1968. Most of Kirghiz director Bolotbek Shamshiev's features have been adapted from Aitmatov novels and plays (see below), as have films from other Central Asian republics (e.g., Turkmenistan's *Mankurts* [Hodjakuli Narliev, 1990]).

17.27 Larisa Shepitko's seminal Kirghizfilm production *Heat* (1963).

the republic's first woman communist, Urkui Salieva, who was murdered by Muslim reactionaries during the collectivization of the 1930s. Okeyev's first dramatic feature, *The Sky of Our Childhood* (1967), became one of the seminal works of Kirghiz cinema in its dramatization of the effect of the passing away of traditional nomadic culture during the 1920s. Deeply psychological, *Sky* was followed by *Heritage* (1970), presented as a dialogue between an old man on the verge of death and his wife, *The Savage One* (1974), a mythical fable about a boy's friendship with a wolf, and *The Red Apple* (1975), adapted from a contemporary Aitmatov novel. Okeyev's masterpiece, however, is *The Descendant of the Snow Leopard* (1985), based on the oral epic of the Kirghiz culture hero Koshoshash. Shot on location in the majestic Tien Shan Mountains, this film recounts the struggle of Koshoshash to save his people from enemies natural and human, ultimately at the expense of his own life, and Okeyev endows it with legendary grandeur appropriate to its cyclic, balladic structure. More recently Okeyev has directed the Kirghiz-Syrian coproduction *Mirages of Love* (1987), which portrays the Oriental Renaissance in Khiva and Bukhara under Tamerlane, and the multinational epic *Genghis Khan* (Kirghizia/Italy/China, 1993).

Bolotbek (Bolot) Shamshiev is a VGIK graduate, and his diploma film, the documentary short *Manaschi* (also known as *Bards of Manas*, 1965), won the first prize at the Oberhausen Festival in 1966. His second short, *The Herdsman* (1966), also won several international awards, but it was his first feature, *Gunshot at the Mountain Pass* (also known as *A Shot on the Karash Pass*, 1967), that established his reputation for historical re-creation and thrilling scenes of mass action. This account of the life of a horse thief in prerevolutionary times was followed by *The Curse* (also known as *Red Poppies of Issyk-Kul*, 1971), an adventure film about the Kirghiz heroin trade in the 1920s. Many of Shamshiev's subsequent films— *The White Ship* (1975), *Among the People* (1978), *Early Cranes* (1979), *The Wolf Pit* (1982), and *Snipers* (1985)— have been adaptations from Chingiz Aitmatov cowritten by himself. Shamshiev also directed Kirghizia's first glasnost-era production, *The Ascent of Fujiyama* (1988), an elaborate allegory of the republic under communism set in the context of a May Day celebration during the Brezhnev era and adapted from a controversial Aitmatov play first produced in 1973.

Kirghizfilm boasts a handful of other directors—e.g., Melis Ubykeyev (b. 1935), whose *White Mountains* (1964) re-creates Kirghizia during the civil war, and Bakhit Karakulov, whose *Cry of a Bird of Passage* (1991) is based on an account, by Aitmatov, of a Red Army deserter—but it is the smallest of Central Asian studios. As of 1990, it owned only one Western-made camera and had only a single soundstage. The irony of the film industry of this small nation (population 4.8 million)—officially renamed Kyrgyzstan in 1992—is that it possesses the spectacular scenery and cinematic talent to sustain international coproductions like *Genghis Khan* (Ken Annakin, 1991), with its 56 weeks of shooting, 20,000 extras, and 3,000 horses. (The Kirghiz partner in *Genghis Khan* was Future, a private production company owned by Tolomush Okeyev.) Among the handful of Kirghiz features that have appeared since independence, the most prominent is *Beshkempir: The Adopted Son* (Aktan Abdykalykov, 1998), a collaboration between Kirghizfilm and France's Noe Productions. A simple coming-of-age tale, shot by cinematographer Hassan Kidiraliev in stark black and white with occasional explosions of color, *Beshkempir* resonates with the clash between modernity and Kirzghizia's still preindustrial society. A similar conflict appears in *The Stars' Caravan* (Arto Halonen, 2000), a Belgium-

17.28 *Beshkempir: The Adopted Son* (Aktan Abdykalykov, 1998): Beshkempir (Mirlan Abdykalykov) and friends sitting in front of a mud-walled building in their rural Kirghizian village.

produced documentary about an itinerant projection-ist who brings movies to the far-flung reaches of the Kirghiz highlands—a tradition since early Soviet times: on foot and horseback.

TADJIKISTAN

Tadjik-kino (later Tadjikfilm) was founded in 1930 and produced only a handful of films before the 1980s (e.g., Kamil Yarmatov's [d. 1978] *Emigrant*, 1934; Boris Kimjagarov's [1920–1979] epic cycle on the Persian legend of Rostám—*The Tale of Rostám*, 1971, and *Rostám and Sohráb*, 1972—and other mythic figures from Firdousi's epic poem *Shâhnâme*), but with glasnost and perestroika a variety of genres and styles emerged to forge a link with the long-repressed Tadjik past. Fundamental to contemporary Tadjik cinema is the work of Davlat Khudonazarov (b. 1944), who is one of the leading figures in the noncommunist opposition movement and the current chair of the CIS (Commonwealth of Independent States) Union of Cinematographers. (As such, Khudonazarov now lives and works in Moscow.) His best-known features, *First Spring of Youth* (1982) and *The Ringing Streams in Melting Snow* (1982), present a lyrical vision of life in the Pamir Mountains, while *Ustod* (*Master*, 1988) uses archival material to portray the life of the revolutionary national poet Abulkosim Lakhurty and the world through which he moved. Among Khudonazarov's followers are the documentarists Margarita Kasymova (b. 1938—*Shout*, 1988; *White Road*, 1989), Safarbek Soliev (*In the Name of Akumramzada*, 1989), Pulat Akhmatov

17.29 Davlat Khudonazarov directing the Tadjikfilm production *First Spring of Youth* (1982).

(*First Hand*, 1988), and Gennadij Artikov (*Stalinabad 1937*, 1989), all of whom delve into the ethnographic contexts of recent Tadjik history, and the much-lauded Bako Sadykov (b. 1941), whose "all-animal" VGIK diploma film *Adonis XIV* was banned in 1977 but went on to win multiple international awards when it was finally released ten years later. The political satire of *Adonis* was carried over into Sadykov's *The Whirlwind* (1989), which was featured in "Un Certain Regard" at Cannes, and *Blessed Bukhara* (1991), a synoptic, magical history of the city from ancient times through its mafia-dominated present. Like Valery Akhadov's (b. 1945) *The Look* (1988), Mariam Yusupova's *Time of Yellow Grass* (1991), and Bakhtiar Khudonazarov's *Brothers* (1991) and *Kosh ba Kosh* (1993—Silver Lion, Venice), *Blessed Bukhara* won several international awards and is part of a minor "new wave" in Tadjik cinema. This is an amazing phenomenon because, after the collapse of the Soviet Union, state funding and centralized control were scrapped, and the fate of Tadjik cinema was tied to coproduction among independent companies,

17.31 Narliev's *Mankurts* (1990): a scathing indictment of totalitarian terror.

17.30 *Daughter-in-Law* (Hodjakuli Narliev, 1972).

of which there were originally about ten. All told, Tadjikistan (population 6.7 million) produced six to seven films annually in all categories in the early 1990s, and its capital, Dushanbe, became the sight of an annual festival of films from Turkey, Iran, Afghanistan, and India until a ferocious civil war between Islamic fundamentalists and the secular (and still Communist-dominated) government forced its closing. This war, which began shortly after independence in 1991 and was concluded by a peace accord in 1997, sapped the Tadjik economy and brought filmmaking activities to a halt. In the early twenty-first century, with the lowest per capita gross domestic product in the former Soviet Union, Tadjikistan has lost its national cinema.

TURKMENISTAN

Turkmen cinema, institutionalized as Turkmenfilm in 1961, was established in the capital, Ashkhabad, in 1926. Among its first films was Yuli Raizman's *The Earth Thirsts* (1930), a documentary feature about the building of a canal through the desert produced for Vostok-kino, which became one of the first Soviet sound films when narration and music were added in 1931. With that exception, few films of note were produced in Turkmenistan until the

1960s, when VGIK-trained directors like Bulat Mansurov (b. 1937) and Hodjakuli Narliev (b. 1937) began their work in the industry. Mansurov's first film, *The Competition* (1963)—which was also the first feature made by a native Turkmenian—is about the perennial war between the Turkmen tribes and the Iranian Kurds, and it was shot by Narliev. Their next collaboration, *Quenching the Thirst* (1967), based on a Russian novel, concerns the digging of a modern-day canal in the Kara-Kum Desert, but *The Slave-Girl* (1970) is generally regarded as their finest work. Carefully attuned to the complexities of the nation's recent past, this brilliantly stylized color and widescreen film concerns the explosive intersection of ancient Turkmen and Persian cultures with European revolutionary ideals. Narliev became an important director in his own right with *Daughter-in-Law*. (1972), the story of a Turkmenian woman's courage and endurance in waiting for her husband to return from World War II, which won the Special Jury Prize at the Locarno International Festival in 1972. Most of Narliev's subsequent films—e.g., *When a Woman Saddles a Horse* (1973), *None Dare Say* (1976), *Djamal* (1980)—are similarly focused on the role of women in Muslim society. *Mankurts*, (also known as *Wings of Memory*, 1990), however, is an allegory of totalitarian regimes adapted from Chin-

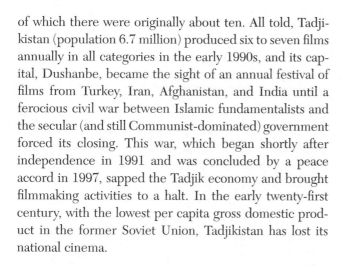

17.32 Turkmenfilm's children's classic *To Bring Up a Man* (Usman Saparov, 1982).

giz Aitmatov's novel *The Day Lasts Longer Than a Hundred Years*. This powerful film, the last completed at Turkmenfilm Studios, is about an ancient tribe that captures warriors from other tribes and subjects them to prolonged torture, destroying their memories and their wills. Like the citizens of a totalitarian state, the victims become docile slaves (*mankurts*), with no sense of the past or expectations for the future.

The Turkmen cinema, like most in Central Asia, is technologically impoverished but creatively and spiritually rich. It has, for example, a very fine tradition of making feature films for and about children, some of which rank among the best Turkmen films ever produced—Usman Saparov's (b. 1938) *To Bring Up a Man* (1982), for example, and Khalmamed Kakabaev's (b. 1939) *When My Father Comes Back* (1982) and *The Son* (1989). The government of Turkmenistan, still Communist-dominated, mandated in 1992 that all films be made in the Turkmen language; it also committed itself to subsidizing five "art films" per year (the average annual output under Soviet rule). As the smallest Central Asian republic, however, Turkmenistan (population approximately 4.7 million) has a difficult time supporting a national cinema without foreign investment, of which there has so far

been relatively little. Speaking to this issue, Narliev remarked, "for several years we should work for technology, then money,"[5] which may, in fact, provide a practical solution to the problem facing the second poorest of the former Soviet states.

Soviet Russian Cinema

Among the Russian studios of the pre-glasnost era (and the Ukrainian and Belorussian, too), the byword was *entertainment*. As Anna Lawton points out, under the leadership of Fillip Ermash from 1972 to 1986, the Soviet film industry was encouraged to produce "commercial" films that catered to public tastes and increased box-office profits for the Soviet government.[6] This policy led to the proliferation of mediocre genre films during the 1970s, but in the 1980s a trend was revived from the late silent era in the form of the *bytovoy*, or "slice of life," film—anything from comedy to melodrama that provided a slightly satiric perspective on contemporary society. Beginning in 1980 with Georgi Danelia's *Autumn Marathon*, Eldar Riazanov's *Garage*, and Vladimir Menshov's *Moscow Does Not Believe in Tears* (which unaccountably won the American Academy Award for Best Foreign Film in that year), the *bytovoy* film became the 1980s' genre of choice among the Soviet mass audience, no doubt in part because it provided a forum for veiled social criticism in a society that officially permitted none. Many *bitovoy* were risqué romantic comedies, like Pyotr Todorovski's *The Beloved Woman of Mechanic Gavrilov* (also known as *Gavrilov's Woman* [*Liubimaia zenshchinia mekhanika Gavrilova*, 1982]), but others focused on such formerly forbidden subjects as the black market (Ryazanov's *Train Station for Two* [*Voksal dlia dvoikh*, 1983]; Vladimir Bortko's *The Blonde around the Corner* [*Blondinka za uglom*, 1984]) and other aspects of the underground economy (Viktor Tregubovich's *A Rogue's Saga* [*Prokhindiada*, 1984]; Alla Surikova's *Sincerely Yours . . . [Ish-*

5. Quoted in Forrest S. Ciesol, "The Many Hollywoods of Central Asia," *World Monitor*, February 1990, p. 70. I am indebted to Ciesol for much of the specific information on Tadjik and Turkmen cinema contained in this section, as well as on Central Asian cinema generally, since he is the foremost English-speaking authority on the subject.

6. Anna Lawton, *Kinoglasnost: Soviet Cinema in Our Time* (Cambridge, Eng.: Cambridge University Press, 1992), p. 9.

krenne vash . . . , 1985]; Vitaly Melnikov's *One of a Kind* (*Unikum*, 1985]). To prevent official censure, filmmakers added fantastic plot elements to their *bytovoy* films so that their films could be characterized as "social fiction" (*sotsial'naia fantastika*), analogous to "science fiction" (*nauchnaia fantastika*). Until the dawning of glasnost, however, *bytovoy* remained escapist fare for a closed society, and many topics—such as criticism of the party, the depiction of dissidents, and the representation of emigration—were taboo under any circumstance.

Other Soviet film types indirectly expressive of dissent in this era were the so-called "chamber films," dealing with disillusionment in personal lives (e.g., Yuli Raizman's *Private Life* [*Chastnaia zhizn'*, 1983] and *Time of Desires* [*Vremia zhelanii*, 1984], Pyotr Todorovski's *A Wartime Romance* [*Voenno-polevoi roman*, 1984], and Konstantin Khudiakov's *Success* [*Uspekh*, 1984]), and films on the newly articulated problems of juvenile delinquency and troubled youth (e.g., Aida Manasarova's *Look Back* [*Oglianis!*, 1984], Rolan Bykov's *Scarecrow* [*Chuchelo*, 1984], and Dinara Asanova's *Tough Kids* [*Patsany*, 1984] and *Dear, Dearest, Beloved . . .* [*Milyi, dorogoi, liubimyi, edinstvennyi . . .*, 1984]). Also obliquely critical of the system were the works of director Vadim Abdrashitov and screenwriter Alexander Mindadze, a Ukrainian and a Georgian, respectively, working at Mosfilm and protégés of Yuli Raizman (1903–1994). In films like *The Turning Point* (*Povorot*, 1979), *Fox Hunt* (*Okhata na lis*, 1980), *The Train Stopped* (*Ostanovilsia poezd*, 1982), and *Parade of the Planets* (*Parad planet*, 1984), Abdrashitov and Mindadze practiced a kind of "socialist surrealism," valorizing old-fashioned virtues of heroism, duty, and honor in a society that no longer sustained them. Their use of a coded "Aesopian language" of allusion, evocation, and allegory was typical of many Soviet and Eastern European filmmakers during the last years of ideological censorship.[7]

Most of the films described above emanated from Mosfilm in Moscow, the largest and best equipped of the Russian studios.[8] Other socially committed films were produced by Vasili Shukshin (1929–1974) at the smallest, Gorki Film Studio, also in Moscow. Shukshin was a talented actor, writer, and director who made all of his features at Gorki (e.g., *Strange People* [*Strannye liudi*, 1970]; *Shop Crumbs* [*Pechki-lavochki*, 1973]) except for his last, *The Red Snowball Tree* (*Kalina krasnaia*, 1974); this film was briefly shelved for its sympathetic depiction

of an ex-convict's return to society and its satiric treatment of bureaucracy, but it became on release one of the most popular Soviet films of the 1970s. At mid-decade, the Lenfilm studio in Leningrad (now St. Petersburg), Russia's second largest, also emerged as an important source of reform-minded cinema in the work of Gleb Panfilov (b. 1934), Alexei German (b. 1938), and Dinara Asanova (1942–1985). This so-called "Leningrad school" was characterized by a stylistically restrained approach to complex human problems, often using black-and-white cinematography. Panfilov, for example, made three Lenfilm features focusing on the inner strength of women, each starring his wife, the gifted actress Inna Churikova— *No Path through the Flames* (*V ogne broda net*, 1968), *Debut* (*Nachalo*, 1970), and *May I Have the Floor?* (*Proshu slova?*, 1973; banned until 1976)—before going to Mosfilm to make *Theme* (*Tema*) in 1979. This latter film deals with the self-doubts of an officially acclaimed Soviet playwright and was banned for seven years as a threat to the prevailing cultural bureaucracy. Panfilov's *Valentina* (1981) continued the theme of women's integrity and spiritual wisdom, as did his two adaptations from Maxim Gorki—*Vassa* (1983) and *Mother* (*Mat*, 1990), the fifth version of the novel made famous by Pudovkin's film of 1926.[9] All three of Alexei German's films were either marginally released or shelved during the pre-glasnost years. *Trial on the Road* (*Proverka na dorogakh*, 1971; released 1986), *Twenty Days without War* (*Dvadtsat' dnei bez*

7. Old-line directors still active during this period included Grigori Chukrai (*Life Is Fine* [*Zhizn prekrasna*, 1980]); Iosif Heifitz (*Married for the First Time* [*Vpervye zamuzhem*, 1980] and *Asya* [1982; adapted from Turgenev]); Alexander Zarkhi (*Chicherin*, 1986); Andrei Khrzhanovski (*A Pushkin Trilogy* [1985; animated]); Sergei Iutkevich (*Lenin in Paris* [*Lenin v. Parizhie*, 1981]); Sergei Bondarchuk (*Red Bells* [*Krasnye kolkola*, in two parts, 1982; 1983] and *Boris Godunov* [1986; adapted from Pushkin's epic poem]); Alexander Alov and Vladimir Naumov (*River Bank* [*Berg*, 1984]); and Sergei Gerasimov, who wrote, directed, and played the lead in *Lev Tolstoi* (1984), his final film.

8. Before the collapse of the Soviet Union in 1991, Mosfilm had 4,000 workers and 11 production units making approximately 50 features and 50 telefilms per year. Lenfilm had 2,600 workers and 8 production units making 15 to 20 films and as many telefilms per year. Gorki had 5 production units and made about 20 theatrical features per year. In 1994, Mosfilm was forced to reduce its staff by 75 percent; its future and that of the other Russian studios at present is unclear.

9. The other three were Alexander Razumni's 1920 version, which hasn't survived, Leonid Lukov's 1941 version, and Mark Donskoi's 1956 version, which is very much in the party-line socialist-realist mode of representation pioneered in literature by Gorki himself.

voiny, 1976), and *My Friend Ivan Lapshin* (*Moi drug Ivan Lapshin*, 1983; released 1986) comprise an authentically revisionist trilogy of the 1930s and 1940s that could not be seen whole until 1986. German's fourth film was not completed until the Soviet Union had passed into history. Many years in production, *Khrustalyov, mashinu!* (*Khrustalyov, My Car!* 1998) is a black comedy about a physician caught up in the specious "Doctor's Plot" dragnet of the early 1950s who ends up tending the dying Stalin. Dinara Asanova, who died just as perestroika began, completed eight films in her brief career—many, like those noted above, on the subject of adolescents in crisis. A native of Kirghizia, Asanova studied at the VGIK under Mikhail Romm and was influenced by his documentary-like style. In such films as *Woodpeckers Don't Get Headaches* (*Ne bolit golova u diatla*, 1975), *The Restricted Key* (*Kliuch bez prava peredachi*, 1977), and *The Wife Has Left* (*Zhena ushla*, 1980), she relied on improvisation and nonactors to create a sense of immediacy in her work.

Several other women directors have played important roles in the liberation of Soviet cinema in the past few decades, most notably Larisa Shepitko (1938–1979) and Kira Muratova (b. 1934). Shepitko was Ukrainian by birth, and she studied under Dovzhenko at the VGIK. Her diploma film, *Heat* (*Znoi*, 1963), was shot on location in the Kirghizian steppes and created a sensation among Moscow critics, but her second feature, *Wings* (*Krillia*, 1966), provoked considerable controversy in its depiction of a decorated female fighter pilot who cannot adjust to postwar life. In 1967 Shepitko contributed to a four-part anthology film entitled *The Beginning of an Unknown Era* (*Nachalo nevedomogo veka*), which was commissioned by Goskino to celebrate the fiftieth anniversary of the Bolshevik Revolution but then suppressed. Her episode, *Homeland of Electricity* (*Rodina electrichestva*), together with another by Andrei Smirnov called *Angel*, was finally released in 1987; in it, Shepitko suggests a remarkable, Dovzhenko-esque equation between rural electrification and spiritual enlightenment. As her films became increasingly religious and inflected with the iconography of the Orthodox Church, Shepitko's problems with the censors grew. Her last completed work, *The Ascent* (*Voskhozhenie*, 1977—Golden Bear, Berlin), was an account of World War II POWs, collaborators, and deserters that challenged the official Soviet mythology of the "Great Patriotic War" by infusing it with imagery from

17.33 Shepitko's *Farewell* (1980; released 1983), as completed by Elem Klimov.

the Passion of Christ. When Shepitko died in an automobile accident in 1979, she was in the process of shooting *Farewell* (*Proschchan'e*), the extraordinary film completed by her husband, Elem Klimov, in 1980[1] and released in 1983. Simultaneously a fugue on ecological tragedy (a village is flooded by the government to create a reservoir) and a dirge for biological extinction, *Farewell* confirmed for many critics that death had become a presence in her work long before she actually encountered it.

Born in what is now Moldavia, Kira Muratova studied direction under Sergei Gerasimov at the VGIK, where she graduated in 1962, and was posted to the Odessa Film Studio in Ukraine. Her diploma film *By the Steep Ravine* (*U krutogo jara*, 1961) and her first feature *Our Honest Bread* (*Nas cestny hleb*, 1962) were both co-directed with Alexander Muratov, her ex-husband, who now works at the Dovzhenko Kiev Film Studio. Her first solo film, *Brief Encounters* (*Korotkie vstrechi*, 1967; released 1987), scripted by the feminist writer Natalya Ryazantseva, portrays a love triangle among a government housing administrator (Muratova herself), an itinerant geologist (played by the late dissident poet/folksinger Vladimir Vysotsky), and a village girl (Nina Ruslanova) who becomes Muratova's maid. Shot in grainy black and white and experimentally structured, *Brief Encounters* offered a less-than-flattering version of daily life in the Worker's

---

1. Klimov simultaneously made the moving documentary *Larisa* (1980) to commemorate her life and death.

Paradise and was effectively banned until the time of perestroika. *Long Farewells* (*Dolgie provody*, 1971; released 1987), another experimental collage of family relationships (here, an aging mother and her teenage son) set against the backdrop of Odessa, was also banned, and Muratova did not direct again until Lenfilm invited her to make *Getting to Know the Big, Wide World* (*Poznavaia belyi svet*, 1979), a comedy about the love life of construction workers. This film, Muratova's first in color, was shelved and her Odessafilm production *Among the Grey Stones* (*Sredi serykh kamnei*, 1983; released 1988) so badly recut that she had her name removed from the credits. After perestroika, Muratova's works were rehabilitated, and she was herself able to direct *Change of Fortune* (*Peremena uchasti*, 1987), adapted from a Somerset Maugham story, and *The Asthenic Syndrome* (*Astenicheskii sindrom*, 1990), a montage of vignettes of contemporary Soviet life revealing universal "asthenia" (exhaustion) as well as social disorder and urban decay. Since the rediscovery and recuperation of her singular talent (which includes writing most of her own scripts) in the late 1980s, Kira Muratova has been regarded as one of the most important film artists working in the former Soviet Union. During the 1990s, she made a series of absurdist comedies set in Ukraine, where she lives—*The Sentimental Policeman* (*Chuvstvitelny militsioner*, 1992), *Little Passions* (*Uvlecheniya*, 1994), *Three Stories* (*Tri istorii*, 1997)—and turned to savage satire in the new century (e.g., *Second Class Citizens* [*Vtorostepyenniye lyudi*] 2001; *Chekhov's Motifs* [*Chekovskie motivy*], 2002).

Similarly iconoclastic was the work of Elem Klimov (b. 1933), probably the Soviet cinema's single most important figure in its historic transition from state control to creative freedom. Klimov worked as an aviation engineer and, then, as a foreign correspondent for Soviet radio and television before attending the VGIK, 1959–64. His diploma film was *Welcome, but Unauthorized Persons Not Allowed* (*Dobro požalovat', ili postoronnim vhod vospreščën*, 1964), a satire on bureaucracy and regimentation at a Young Pioneers summer camp that established his early grotesque style. In a hilarious example of life imitating art, Khrushchev had the film briefly banned because of a physical resemblance between himself and the protagonist's grandmother. Klimov's next feature was another satire, *Adventures of a Dentist* (*Pohoždenija zubnogo vrača*, 1965), a clear allegory of the plight of the

Soviet artist in its tale of a professionally brilliant dentist forced into teaching because his colleagues can't stand the competition. After the genre parody *Sport, Sport, Sport* (1971), an inventive collage of dramatic sequences, documentary footage, and interviews, Klimov completed Mikhail Romm's final film, *And I Still Believe* (*I vse-taki ja verju . . .*), with Marlen Khutsiev in 1974, and then embarked on his most controversial project—*Agoniia*, or *Rasputin*. Commissioned to celebrate the sixtieth anniversary of the Bolshevik Revolution, this film is a remarkable assemblage of newsreel footage, old photographs, and staged *tableaux* that re-creates the last days of the imperial Russian court. Klimov sutures the narrative with voice-over historical commentary and uses transitions from black and white to color (and back again) both between and within shots to suggest the surreality of the Romanovs' situation. But *Agoniia* was shelved in 1975 because it portrayed Rasputin and Tsar Nicholas II sympathetically and, worse, made no mention of Lenin or the Bolsheviks. It was recut and released for the Moscow Film Festival in 1981 but not distributed in its original form until 1985 (although a nearly complete version was sold abroad by Sovexport and won the FIPRESCI Prize at Venice in 1982). Despite these difficulties, on the very eve of glasnost, Klimov made his greatest film, *Come and See* (*Idi i smotri*, 1985), perhaps the most apocalyptic work of postwar Soviet cinema.

One of many war films commissioned by Goskino to commemorate the fortieth anniversary of victory over Hitler, *Come and See* quickly established itself as definitive, winning both the Grand Prix at the 1985 Moscow International Festival and immense, awestruck popularity with Soviet audiences. Its title derived from the Revelations of St. John, *Come and See* is based on an account[2] of the Nazis' destruction of the Belorussian village of Khatyn, one of 628 such villages razed by the Germans in their invasion of the USSR's western flank in 1943. Through the eyes of Florya, who joins the Belorussian partisans as a young boy and is transformed into a wizened wreck by war, we are taken on a relentless 142-minute journey toward the center of a horror so profound that the film itself is actually rendered speechless. (By the time Flyora witnesses the burning of Khatyn [here called

---

2. "The Story of Khatyn," by the Belorussian writer Ales Adamovich, who also wrote the screenplay.

17.34 Multilingual poster for Klimov's apocalyptic *Come and See* (1985).

"Perekhody"] at midfilm, he—and we—can no longer hear distinct sounds because his eardrums have been ruptured by an aerial bombardment.) The destruction of the village and murder of its inhabitants is one of the great mass scenes in contemporary cinema; it achieves such an extraordinary level of intensity in its montage of swooping Steadicam shots and shattering images of atrocity, visual and aural, that we are left with a nearly physical sense of devastation. Indeed, Klimov's depiction of brutality is so visceral as to approach the surreal, and in some ways *Come and See* is as stylistically experimental as the work of Tarkovsky or Parajanov. Near the end of the film, for example, Flyor pumps bullets into a portrait of Hitler lying in a puddle while newsreel footage of his rise to power runs backward on screen, regressing finally to a photograph of an infant Hitler in his mother's arms—which the boy cannot bring himself to shoot. By suggesting that history can run backward and, implicitly, that it

can be reclaimed, Klimov is speaking to his own time and place with a radical if allusive flourish. Yet the film ends on a positive note, the partisans marching silently into the woods to the chords of Mozart's *Requiem* after having ambushed the SS unit that burned the village and Klimov's camera tilting to the sky. Thus *Come and See* is almost perfectly balanced on the cusp of glasnost, affirming some of the most cherished myths of the Soviet state about the "Great Patriotic War" at the same time that it subverts official codes of representation. It should come as no surprise that Klimov was elected first secretary/president of the Film Workers Union in the year following its release and pressed the fight for artistic freedom within the Soviet film industry to its logical conclusion.

Glasnost, Perestroika, and the Collapse of the Soviet Union

During the 1970s and 1980s, filmgoing became an extremely popular activity in the Soviet Union. The average feature was seen by 17 million people, tickets cost $1 or less, and there were permanent theaters everywhere (5,257 of them in 1987). Even the country's most popular television show, *Film Panorama* (*Kinopanorama*), hosted by director Eldar Riazanov and drawing 140 million viewers per week, was about the movies. At this time, there were 20 studios throughout the USSR producing an average of 150 theatrical features per year, plus 80 to 90 telefilms. As discussed above, each director, cinematographer, scriptwriter, set designer, and producer was required to graduate from the VGIK[3] or its equivalent (such as the Leningrad Institute of Theater, Music, and Cinematography) and then assigned to a specific studio in Russia or the non-Russian republics. Until 1987, scripts were subject to prior approval by the studio leadership, and films were rated by a national censorship commission after production; those not approved—like Tarkovsky's *Andrei Rublev* or Klimov's *Agoniia*—were either shelved or remade until they were acceptable to the censors.

With the succession of Mikhail Gorbachev (b. 1931)

---

3. Two other institutions of note were Sovexportfilm (established in 1937), the state monopoly in charge of exporting Soviet films and importing foreign ones (and thus the liaison to all international festivals),

to the Soviet leadership in 1985, however, a more liberal policy was advanced by Goskino officials.[4] Several formerly banned films were released and offered for export for the first time, for example; and the much persecuted director Sergei Parajanov was rehabilitated and allowed to work again (indeed, Gorbachev chose as his first foreign minister Eduard Shevardnadze, who as party secretary of Georgia was an outspoken supporter of such "difficult" directors as Parajanov and Otar Iosseliani). Coproduction with Western countries was encouraged (for example, NBC's eight-hour mini-series *Peter the Great* [Marvin J. Chomsky and Lawrence Schiller, 1986] was shot on location in the Soviet Union), as was foreign-location shooting of Soviet films (such as Tarkovsky's *The Sacrifice* [1986], produced in Sweden with British, Swedish, and Soviet capital). The Gorbachev regime even ended the freeze on VCRs imposed under Brezhnev in the late 1970s, enabling Soviet citizens to see on cassette foreign films that were officially banned from public exhibition (Wajda's *Man of Iron* [1981] and Forman's *Amadeus* [1984], for instance, were extremely popular on video).

These were welcome changes, but they were thought to be largely cosmetic until 1986, which marked a major turning point for Soviet cinema. In that year, Gorbachev announced a serious bid to change the nature of Soviet society through a new glasnost ("openness") and perestroika ("restructuring"), and the Film Workers Union responded in May by ousting two-thirds of its leadership and replacing old-guard president Lev Kulijanov with the dynamic Elem Klimov, whose films were among the most shelved of any contemporary *cinéaste*. In December the conservative Brezhnev-era bureaucrat Fillip Ermash was replaced as head of Goskino, the state film committee, by the liberal Alexander Kamshalov; and all studios acquired the right to plan their own yearly production schedules and to move toward self-financing. Finally, calls to abolish the long-standing system of postproduction censorship met with success in 1987 when twenty-five shelved features were officially released in their homeland for the first time, many at the Moscow Film Festival for that year. These included the full version of Marlen Khutsiev's recut *I'm Twenty* (1963), Iuri Ilyenko's *A Fountain for the Thirsty* (*Rodnik dlia zhazhdushchikh*, 1965), Konchalovski's *Asya's Happiness* (1966), Alexander Askoldov's *The Commissar* (*Komissar*, 1966), Larisa Shepitko's *Homeland of Electricity* and Andrei Smirnov's

Angel (the only surviving elements of the four-part anthology *The Beginning of an Unknown Era* [*Nachalo nevedomogo veka*, 1967]), Alexei Germans's *Trial on the Road* (*Proverka na dorogakh*, 1971) and *My Friend Ivan Lapshin* (*Moi drug Ivan Lapshin*, 1983), Alexander Sokurov's *A Lonely Man's Voice* (*Odinokii golos cheloveka*, 1978), Gleb Panfilov's *Theme* (*Tema*, 1979; winner of the Berlin Golden Bear, 1987), Klimov's own *Agoniia* (1975) and *Farewell* (1981), and Tengiz Abuladze's hallucinatory satire *Repentence* (*Pokaianie*, 1984), the first Soviet film to be openly critical of Stalin. In addition to permitting the release of suppressed films, glasnost encouraged the production of such outspoken and/or stylistically innovative new Russian features as Konstantin Lopushansky's (b. 1947) postnuclear *Letters from a Dead Man* (*Pis'ma mertvogo cheloveka*, 1986) and *Visitor to a Museum* (*Posetitel muzeja*, 1989), Valeri Ogorodnikov's *Burglar* (*Vzlomshik*, 1987). Vadim Abdrashitov's *Plumbum, or a Dangerous Game* (*Pliumbrum, ili opasnaia igra*, 1987) and *The Servant* (*Sluga*, 1988), Roman Balayan's (b. 1941) *Lady Macbeth of the Mtsensk District* (*Ledi Makbet Mtsenskogo uezda*, 1989), Karen Shakhnazarov's (b. 1952) *Zero City* (*Gorad zero*, 1989) and *The Assassin of the Tsar* (*Careubijca*, 1991; USSR/UK), Vitaly Kanevsky's (b. 1935) *Freeze, Die, Come to Life* (1989), as well as the work of such new directors as the Ukrainian Mikhail Belikov (b. 1940—*How Young We Were Then* [*Kak molodi mi byli*, 1986]), the Georgians Nana Djordjadze (b. 1948—*Robinsoniad; or, My English Grandfather* [*Robinzoniada, ili moi angliiskii dedushka*, 1986; winner of the 1987 Golden Camera award at Cannes]) and Timar Babluani (b. 1948—*The Sparrow's Flight* [*Perelet voro-*

---

and Gosfilmofond (established in 1948), the state film archive housing over 50,000 titles. The average Soviet feature cost about $600,000 to produce, with budgets scarcely ever rising above $1 million. As in other Eastern European countries, both filmmakers and performers were modestly paid by Western standards, although Soviet directors were eligible to receive bonuses based on the quality of their completed productions, as determined by the national censorship commission mentioned above.

4. Neither of Gorbachev's immediate predecessors—Yuri Andropov (1914–1984), who replaced Leonid Brezhnev as secretary general of the Central Committee of the CPSU when he died in November 1982, or Konstantin U. Chernenko (1911–1985), who replaced Andropov when he died in February 1984—was in power long enough to have had much effect on the Soviet film industry, although a thaw of sorts was expected under Andropov, and Chernenko publicly called for a return to the rigid principles of socialist realism.

biev, 1987]), and the documentaries *Trumpet Solo* (*Solo truby* [Alexander Ivankin, 1986]), *Risk-2* (Dmitri Barshchevski and Natalya Violina, 1988), Arkady Ruderman's *Theater in the Times of Perestroika and Glasnost* (*Teatr vremen perestroiki i glasnosti*, 1988), and *More Light* (Marina Babak [*Bol'she sveta!*, 1988]), an enthusiastic attempt to fill in some of the blank pages of Soviet history.

More pitched toward mass taste were glasnost-era blockbusters ("*boeviki*") like Alla Surikova's (b. 1940) *The Man from the Boulevard des Capucines* (*Chelovek s Bul'vara Kaputsinov*, 1987), Iuri Kara's (b. 1954) *Kings of Crime* (*Vory v zakone*, 1988), and Pyotr Todorovski's (b. 1925) *Integirl* (*Interdevochka*, 1989), each of which sold over 40 million tickets in their year of release. Also popular were the so-called *chernukha*, or films "painted black," that characterized the late 1980s—Valeri Ogorodnikov's (b. 1951) *Burglar* (*Vzlomshchik*, 1987), Vasili Pichul's (b. 1961) *Little Vera* (*Malen'kaia Vera*, 1988— the first Soviet film to contain graphic sex scenes), Olga Narutskaya's *The Husband and Daughter of Tamara Alexandrovna* (*Much i doch' Tamary Aleksandrovy*, 1989), Vladimir Prokhorov and Alexander Alexandrov's *Assuage My Sorrow* (*Utoli moia pechali*, 1989), and Pavel Lounguine's *Taxi Blues* (*Taksi-bliuz*, 1990—winner of the Best Director prize at Cannes and one of few "black" films to be distributed in the United States). The *chernukha* focused morbidly on the collapse of Soviet society, often exploiting lurid aspects of sex, violence, and drug abuse in the name of frankness.

Aesthetically, however, the glasnost era was dominated by formerly "difficult" directors. At Mosfilm studio Sergei Soloviev (b. 1944), the muse and mentor of the Kazakh New Wave at the VGIK (see p. 714), made the carnivalesque *The White Pigeon* (1986), the extraordinary pop-rock thriller *Assa* (1988), the farce of "comic decay" entitled *Black Rose Stands for Sorrow, Red Rose Stands for Love* (1989), and *The House under the Starry Sky* (*Dom pod zvezdynm nebom*, 1991) to form what he calls a "*perestroika* trilogy" entitled "Three Songs of the Motherland"—an ironic allusion to Vertov's ruined early sound epic *Three Songs of Lenin* (1934). In the post-Soviet era, Soloviev became more mainstream in such films as the coming-of-age comedy *Tender Age* (*Nezhnyi vozrast*, 2001), written by and starring his son Dmitri. At Lenfilm studio Alexander Sokurov (b. 1951), considered to be the artistic and spiritual heir of Tarkovsky, finished his *Mournful Indifference* (*Skorbnoe beschuvstvie*, 1983;

completed 1987), based on Bernard Shaw's *Heartbreak House*, and embarked on a series of philosophical features (*Days of the Eclipse* [*Dni zatmeniia*, 1988]; *Save and Protect* [*Spasi i sokhrani*, 1989; loosely based on Flaubert's *Madame Bovary*]; and *The Second Circle* [*Krug vtoroj*, 1990]) and documentaries (*Moscow Elegy* [*Moskovskaia elegiia*, 1988]; *Soviet Elegy* [*Sovetskaia elegiia*, 1989]; *St. Petersburg Elegy* [*Peterburgskaia elegiia*, 1989]; *Leningrad Retrospective* [*Leningradskaia retrospektiva*, 1990]; *Spiritual Voices* [*Dukhovnye golosa*, 1995]) unlike anything seen before on Soviet screens. With the remarkable

17.35 and 17.36 Still and poster: Alexander Sokurov's Lenfilm production *Days of the Eclipse* (1988).

Mother and Son (*Mat i syn*, 1997), Sokurov reached a new artistic plateau in a visually and aurally evocative work about the relationship between a dying woman and her son on the last day of her life. The special filters and lenses used in this film to create refracted planes of light appeared again in the controversial *Moloch* (*Molokh*, 1999), which probes the deeply conflicted psyches of Hitler and Eva Braun at a crucial moment in their relationship in 1942. Sokurov produced *Moloch* as the first film in a trilogy on the psychology of twentieth-century political power, whose second installment was *Taurus* (*Telets*, 2001), in which Stalin visits and manipulates the dying Lenin, although neither character is mentioned by name. In 2002, Sokurov won praise for the technical brilliance of his *Russian Ark* (*Russkij Kovcheg*) a 96-minute exploration of the Hermitage Museum in St. Petersburg shot in a single take with a specially designed digital video camera. Lenfilm also produced the remarkable first works of Iuri Mamin (b. 1946), a former student of Eldar Riazanov, whose fantastic trilogy *Neptune Festival* (*Prazdnik Neptuna*, 1986), *Fountain* (*Fontan*, 1988), and *Sideburns* (*Bakenbardy*, 1990) represents a significant contribution to the Russian tradition of grotesque comedy as practiced by nineteenth-century writer Nikolai Gogol (e.g., *The Inspector General*, 1837; *Dead Souls*, 1842). An interesting development has been the recent emergence of a new Russian avant-garde known as "parallel cinema." Initially an underground "alternative culture" movement like Soviet rock, parallel cinema now has its own journal

17.37 *Mother and Son* **(Alexander Sokurov, 1997): Gudrun Geyer as Mother and Alexei Ananishnov as Son, shot through one of the special refracting lenses that Sokurov and cinematographer Alexei Fyodorov used throughout the film.**

(*Cine-Phantom*) and two distinct subgroups, the Moscow and Leningrad schools. In Moscow, the Aleinikov brothers, Gleb (b. 1966) and Igor (1962–1994), and their followers critiqued official cinematic icons in work like *Tractors* (*Traktora,* 1987) and *Postpolitical Cinema* (*Postpoliticheskoe kino,* 1988), while the Leningraders Evgeny Yufit (b. 1961—*Suicide Boars* [*Vepri suitsida,* 1988]), Evgeny Kondratev (*Lena's Men* [*Leniny mushciny,* 1989]), and others evolved the irreverent style of "necrorealism," which used necrophilic images and themes to comment on the moribund nature of the body politic, suggesting that the Soviet Union had become by the end of the decade nothing but an animated corpse.

And, of course, the necrorealists were right: the Soviet state was already dead—a condition signaled in June 1990, when the Congress of the Filmmakers Union unanimously voted to reject adherence to the laws of socialist realism—and the state ended in collapse in December 1991. All over the country, glasnost and perestroika had brought with them agitation for increased political freedom—especially in the non-Russian republics, where, in the late 1980s, demonstrations had erupted in violence. In 1989–90, the example of Eastern Europe and the dissolution of the Warsaw Pact encouraged the Baltic republics to break away; Lithuania declared independence in March 1990 but suspended the declaration in the face of a Soviet economic blockade. Mass demonstrations followed in Vilnius and other Baltic cities, and Gorbachev unsuccessfully ordered Red Army troops to suppress them, angering both Kremlin hardliners and liberals. In August of 1991, reactionary elements within the Politburo attempted to stage an anti-Gorbachev coup that ended in failure but made it clear to all that the USSR could not continue to function as a unified nation. One by one, the republics declared their independence and intention to secede from the state, and in December 1991, the USSR was officially dissolved and replaced by the loosely confederated Commonwealth of Independent States (CIS).

The impact on the former Soviet film industry was fragmentation as each of the republics became separate countries with their own national studios and domestic markets. What they lost, of course, was centralized state funding and the vast multinational market that had been the USSR. They also lost access to the systematic training that the VGIK—one of the world's greatest film schools—had provided to their aspiring filmmakers, free of charge.

The deleterious effect on the cinemas of the non-Russian republics has been described earlier in this chapter. In the Russian republic (population 146.5 million), the potentially huge market for Russian-language films made the transition to privatization somewhat easier at first. As early as 1988, joint venture companies like Primodessa (with 50 percent German ownership) and International Cinema Co. (ICC) were coproducing films with Russian studios, and the future looked good. But as time wore on, the traumas of Russia's transition to capitalism practically brought the domestic film industry to a standstill. Rampant inflation pushed production costs through the roof, while ticket prices went up and attendance dropped radically—problems compounded by a flood of American B-films and widespread video piracy. In 1994, its seventieth year of operation, Mosfilm reduced the size of its staff from 4,000 to 1,000 and predicted an annual output of only 12 films instead of its usual 50. Worse, the VGIK was struggling to survive, its equipment old and broken and its students demoralized at their slim prospects for employment. And since these conditions were sympomatic of structural weaknesses in the Russian economy and society as a whole, the real question was not whether Russian cinema could survive them, but whether the nation could continue to exist at all in its present form.

Obviously, the answer for both cinema and state was affirmative. (In fact at the very height of the crisis, three post-Soviet films were nominated in three successive years for the American Academy Award for Best Foreign Film—Nikita Mikhalkov's (b. 1945) *Burnt by the Sun* [*Utomlyonnye solntsem*, 1994]; Sergei Bodrov's (b. 1948) *Prisoner of the Mountains* [*Kavkazsky plennik*, 1996]; and Pavel Chukhrai's (b. 1946) *The Thief* [*Vor*, 1997]—the first of which won for 1994.) But first, the Hollywood model of producing many films in a free-market environment had to be abandoned for a European (and,

more specifically, French) model of protecting the domestic industry through government mandate. After 1996, the worst year in post-Soviet film history, when fewer than 30 features were completed, government investment in production increased from 6 percent in 1992 to 90 percent; but by 1998 it had leveled off at 25 percent. In 1999, Vladimir Putin, Russia's newly elected president, abolished Goskino, the Russian Ministry of Film since the 1930s, and transferred its functions to the Ministry of Culture, raising fears that government subsidies would be reduced even further, but in fact by the beginning of 2001, 30 of the 50 features completed since the changeover had received at least partial state funding. The distribution sector also grew stronger as part of an attempt to reach a 30 percent domestic market share, again using the French system as a model. These successes have enabled veterans like Eldar Ryazanov (*Old Hags* [*Starye klyachi*, 2000]) and Georgi Danelia (*Fortune* [*Fortuna*, 2000]), both masters of Soviet comedy, to work again. Directors associated with the glasnost era also returned—e.g., Konstantin Lopushansky (the apocalyptic *Turn of the Century* [*Konets veka*, 2001]), Vadim Abdrashitov (*Time of the Dancer* [*Vremya tantsora*, 1998]), Karen Shakhnazarov (*Poisons, or the World History of Poisoning* [*Yady, ili vsemirnaya istoriya otravlenij*, 2001]), Vasili Pichul (*The Sky with Diamonds* (*Nebo v almazakh*, 1999), and Pavel Lounguine (*The Wed-

17.38 *The Thief* (Pavel Chukhrai, 1997): Misha Philipchuk in the title role, caught in the act, in one of several Russian films nominated for American Academy Awards for Best Foreign Film during the 1990s.

ding [*Svadba*, 2000]; *Tycoon* [*Oligarkh*, 2002])—as did leading necrorealist Evgeny Yufit (*Silver Heads* [*Serebryanyye*, 1998]). There was even support for several big-budget (by Russian standards, where average features cost around $1 million) costume films: Nikita Mikhalkov's *The Barber of Siberia* (*Sibirskiy tsyryulnik*, 1999), an epic romance set in late nineteenth-century Russia, and Gleb Panfilov's *The Romanovs: An Imperial Family* (*Romanovy: ventsenosnaya semya*, 2000), cowritten with his son Ivan and his wife, Inna Churikova. The most promising new talent was Alexei Balabanov (b. 1959), whose two low-budget gangster films *The Brother* (*Brat*, 1997) and *The Brother 2* (*Brat 2*, 2000) were ultraviolent black comedies in the Quentin Tarantino mode, but whose haunting, sepia-toned *Of Freaks and Men* (*Pro urodov i lyudej*, 1998) makes an unusual equation between social corruption and the production of deviant pornography through the new medium of motion pictures in turn-of-the-century St. Petersburg. Similarly notable was the work of Aleksandr Rogozhkin (b. 1950), whose two satires, *Peculiarities of the National Hunt* (*Osobennosti natsionalnoj okhoty*, 1995) and *Peculiarities of National Fishing* (Osobennosti nat-

17.39 *Of Freaks and Men* (Alexei Balabanov, 1998): a film whose sepia-toned images evoke a past redolent of decay, suggesting that the cinema, both literally and figuratively, was born a pornographic medium.

sionalnoj rybalki, 1998), proved popular at home, while his antiwar comedy *Cuckoo* (*Kukushka*, 2000), set in Finland near the end of Worl War II, won several international prizes. *Of Freaks and Men*, *Brother 2*, and *Cuckoo* were all produced by CTB Film Company, a semiprivate studio established in late 1990s St. Petersburg.

Wind from the East: Japan, India, and China

Japan

THE EARLY YEARS

The Japanese cinema, like most other aspects of Japanese culture, evolved in nearly total isolation from the West until the end of World War II. The Edison Kinetograph was introduced into Japan as early as 1896, and movies almost immediately became a popular cultural form. But Japanese cinema went through a much longer "primitive" period than the cinemas of the West (roughly from 1896 to 1926) because of the persistence of an older, more venerable cultural form: the *kabuki* theater. Ironically, it was *kabuki* that had stimulated Eisenstein in elaborating his radically innovative theory of montage.

Kabuki is a highly stylized and somewhat overwrought dramatic form deriving from the feudal Tokugawa period (1603–1868), and because of its perennial popularity in Japan, the earliest Japanese fiction films were versions of famous *kabuki* plays (there exist some 350 of them). As Japanese cinema grew into a large-scale domestic industry in the first two decades of the twentieth century, the stylized conventions of *kabuki* became the mainstream conventions of Japanese narrative film. This prohibited the kind of formal experimentation then going on in the West in the work of Griffith, Eisenstein, Feuillade, and Murnau, but allowed Japanese cinema to develop along its own path.

Two conventions of *kabuki* are especially unusual relative to Western films. First, all female roles until well into the 1920s were played by professional female impersonators known as *onnagata* or *oyama*, which worked against even the simplest sort of photographic realism. Second, and much more formative in the development of Japanese cinema, was the convention of the *benshi*—an actor who stands at the side of the stage (or screen, in the case of films) and narrates the action for the audience. In the earliest Japanese films, the *benshi* provided both voices for the characters and commentary on

18.1 *A Page of Madness* (Teinosuke Kinugasa, 1926): Masuo Inoue.

the action. After 1912, the *benshi* concentrated exclusively on dialogue in response to an influx of foreign films using intertitles, a practice quickly imitated by domestic producers. By 1920, however, the *benshi* had returned to the practice of mixing description/commentary with spoken dialogue—sometimes read from intertitles, sometimes interpolated from the action itself. As Donald Kirihara has pointed out, the effect on film form was immense: "[T]he presence of the *benshi* was a fact that filmmakers could assume during production, allowing them to make films with ambiguous spatial and temporal transitions or undermotivated plots with the knowledge that the *benshi* would be present to provide whatever narrative coherence was lacking." In short, the presence of a human, *verbal* narrator permitted Japanese *cinematic* narrative to remain relatively diffuse.

In September 1923, an earthquake leveled large portions of Tokyo and neighboring Yokohama, including many film studios and theaters.[1] After the quake, the industry, like much of urban Japan, had to be rebuilt from scratch, and one result, as Donald Richie points out, was a new division of production: historical films (**jidai-geki**) were henceforth made in Kyoto, where studios and ancient buildings were still standing; and contemporary films (**gendai-geki**) were made in Tokyo, where modern Western-style buildings had either survived the quake or were subsequently built to replace those that hadn't.[2] There was, in addition, a turning away from the past and an increased receptivity to modern ideas, especially those

from the West. The *oyama* rapidly disappeared, and Japanese films adopted nonnative styles, such as the newly discovered Western modes of naturalism (in Minoru Murata's[3] *The Street Juggler* [*Machi no tejinashi*, 1924]) and Expressionism (in Teinosuke Kinugasa's *A Page of Madness* [*Kurutta ippeiji*, 1926] and *Crossways* [*Jujiro*, 1928]). The *benshi*, however, many of whom had become stars in their own right, would remain a potent force in Japanese cinema until well after the introduction of sound. In 1927, there were 6,818 *benshi*, including only 180 women, who were licensed to practice throughout the Japanese Empire. Though their stranglehold on the industry was eventually broken by reorganization, there were still 1,295 of them—mostly unemployed—in 1940. Nevertheless, the coming of sound insured that directors could finally become the major creative force in Japanese film, as they already were in most countries of the West.

By 1925, the *kabuki*-oriented cinema had been replaced by a new director's cinema, consciously divided into two large genres, or types, that persist to this day: the *jidai-geki*, or period film set before 1868 (the year marking the beginning of the Meiji Restoration and the abolition of feudal Japan), and the *gendai-geki*, or film of contemporary life. Both genres are obviously very broad, and each has come to contain a large number of subtypes. Currently, for example, the *jidai-geki* encompasses the *chanbara*, or sword-fight film,[4] which focuses on the figure of the masterless *samurai* ("warrior"), or *ronin*; the historical romance; and the ghost film. The *gendai-geki* includes such disparate types as the lower-middle-class comedy-drama (*shomin-geki*); the "children's film," in which the inanities and corruptions of the adult world are satirized by presenting them from a child's point of view; and the *yakuza-eiga*, or modern gangster film. The years 1926 to 1932 saw the appearance of the first major

---

1. The great Kanto earthquake struck at noon on September 1, 1923, with shocks so violent that the seismographs at the Central Weather Bureau broke trying to record them. In the five ensuing tidal waves, 140,000 people were killed and 64 percent of standing structures in the two-city area were destroyed.

2. Donald Richie, *A Hundred Years of Japanese Film: A Concise History, with a Selective Guide to Videos and DVDs* (New York: Kodansha, 2001), p. 44.

3. Japanese names in this chapter are mostly given in the Western style, with the surname last.

4. For the Japanese the term *chanbara* is onomatopoeic since it imitates the sound of two swords clashing together, as "*chan-chan, bara-bara.*"

works of Japanese cinema in the beautiful period films of Teinosuke Kinugasa (1896–1982) and Kenji Mizoguchi (see pp. 743–45), and in the *shomin-geki* of Yasujiro Shimazu (1897–1945), Heinosuke Gosho (1902–1981), Mikio Naruse (1905–1969), and—above all—Yasujiro Ozu (see pp. 745–47). In careers that extended well into the postwar period, both Mizoguchi and Ozu became masters of the classical Japanese film (which followed the primitive period, from roughly 1926 until the 1950s); the third master was Akira Kurosawa (see pp. 736–43), whose career did not begin until the middle years of World War II, or the "Pacific War," as it is known to the Japanese.

SOUND

Sound entered the cinema in Japan more gradually and smoothly than it did in the countries of the West, because it was less of a novelty for both audiences and filmmakers. Japanese movies had always "talked" through the mediation of the *benshi*, and far from retarding the formal development of Japanese cinema (as it had for a brief period in the West), the coming of synchronously recorded sound actually accelerated it by permanently liberating films from subservience to a live narrator. The first successful talkie, Gosho's comic *shomin-geki The Neighbor's Wife and Mine* (*Madamu to nyobo*, 1931), ranked very high in

formal achievement among early sound films generally. But the addition of sound was a leisurely process in Japan. In 1932 only 45 feature-length sound films were produced out of a total of 400, and silent features continued to be made until 1937 (the most important Japanese film of 1932, for example, was Ozu's silent "children's comedy" *I Was Born, but . . .* [*Umarete wa mita keredo*]). Other changes were swifter and ultimately more significant.

One important consequence of the reorganization was the complete monopolization of the Japanese film industry by three, and later five, major production companies, called *zaibatsu* ("conglomerates"), through the Japan Motion Picture Producers' Association (founded 1925) in a pattern remarkably similar to the American studio system. As in the American system, each of the three Japanese studios during the 1930s (Nikkatsu, founded 1914; Shochiku, founded 1920; and Toho, founded 1932) had been formed by the ruthless absorption of smaller companies. And, as in the American system, they existed solely for the purpose of producing films for mass consumption through a highly efficient, rigidly structured production process. With some modification, this system still operates in Japan today, and until the economic recession of the late 1970s it was the most productive in the world, averaging over 400 features a year.

One aspect of the Japanese studio system that differed from the American, however—and that differs to this day as part of an ingrained cultural pattern—was the hierarchical master-pupil (*sempai–kohai*, or "senior–junior") relationship between directors and their assistants. Aspir-

18.2 Shochiku's *The Neighbor's Wife and Mine* (Heinosuke Gosho, 1931), Japan's first commercially successful talkie: Satoko Date, Atsushi Watanabe, Tokuji Kobayashi.

18.3 *I Was Born, but . . .* (Yasujiro Ozu, 1932): Hideo Sugawara, Tokkan Kozo.

ing young filmmakers had to apprentice themselves to older, more experienced directors and literally prove their worth (that is, their ability to turn a profit for the studio) before being permitted to direct on their own. Thus, Yasujiro Shimazu, who founded the *shomin-geki* in the early 1920s, himself had been taught by the first-generation Shochiku director Kaoru Osanai, and in the course of his own long career trained ten younger directors, including the now prominent Keisuke Kinoshita (1912–1998), Masaki Kobayashi (1916–1996), and Kaneto Shindo (b. 1912). Another unique aspect of the Japanese studio system is the paternalistic relationship between the director and the entire cast and crew of a film. It seems clear that both the apprenticeship system and the familial organization of production recapitulate an element deeply rooted in Japanese society, which may be best described as feudalistic.

The Meiji Restoration of 1868–1912 provided a brief respite of enlightenment after seven hundred years of feudal culture. In 1868, the fifteen-year-old Emperor Meiji (the word means "Enlightened Rule") abolished the *shogunate*, the military dictatorship that had ruled Japan in the legitimate emperor's stead since 1192 and had been controlled by the Tokugawa clan since 1603, and outlawed the *samurai*, who had supported it.[5] But these centuries-old feudal institutions did not disappear. Instead, the *samurai* translated themselves into a modern form and emerged in the late 1920s as the general staff and officer corps of a powerful military establishment. By the end of 1931, they had virtually reasserted their control of the government. As sound came to the Japanese cinema in the early 1930s, militarism, patriotism, and xenophobia pervaded every segment of Japanese society. These factors led first to Japan's war of aggression against China in 1937 and ultimately to its catastrophic confrontation with the United States.

As ultranationalism gripped Japan, a new film genre appeared opposing it—the left-wing "tendency film" (*keiko-eiga*) that, whether in period or contemporary guise, was devoted to criticism of the established social order. The founder of the tendency film was Daisuke Ito (1898–1981), whose violently realistic *jidai-geki* of the late 1920s—*Servant* (*Gero*, 1927), *Diary of Chuji's Travels* (*Chuji tabinikki*, 1927–28), *Ooka's Trial* (*Ooka seidan*, 1928), and the famous *Man-Slashing, Horse-Piercing Sword* (*Zanjin zamba ken*, 1930)—all attacked the feudalism of the Tokugawa period. Most tendency films,

however, were *shomin-geki* that dealt with contemporary social problems and availed themselves of the heightened realism made possible by sound. The most important were Kinugasa's *Before Dawn* (*Reimei izen*, 1931); Shimazu's *O-Koto and Sasuke* (*O-Koto to Sasuke*, 1935); Gosho's *Everything That Lives* (*Ikitoshi ikerumono*, 1936); Shiro Toyoda's *Young People* (*Wakai hito*, 1937); Tomu Uchida's *The Naked Town* (*Hadaki no machi*, 1937); Ozu's first sound film, *The Only Son* (*Hitori musuko*, 1936); and Mizoguchi's two masterpieces, thought to be the greatest of Japanese prewar sound films, *Osaka Elegy* (*Naniwa ereji*, 1936) and *Sisters of the Gion* (*Gion no shimai*, 1936).

WAR

In response to the tendency film and other dissident elements in the culture, the government, through its Ministry of Propaganda, imposed a system of state censorship, the severity of which increased as the 1930s wore on. In 1937, to the horror of the progressive filmmakers grouped around Mizoguchi and Ozu, Sadao Yamanaka's (1907–1938) humanistic film of life in the Tokugawa era, *Humanity and Paper Balloons* (*Ninjo kami-fusen*, 1937), was suppressed and its young director ordered to the Chinese front, where he was killed shortly after arriving. In addition to censoring what it did not like, the Ministry of Propaganda began to actively involve itself in production, demanding war films that showed Japanese military prowess in battle. Ironically, the first two films commissioned by the ministry—Tomotaka Tasaka's *Five Scouts* (*Go-nin no sekkohei*, 1938) and *Mud and Soldiers* (*Tsuchi to heitai*, 1939)—were profoundly humanistic accounts of men in battle that compare favorably with the great prewar pacifist films of the West, G. W. Pabst's *Westfront 1918* (1930) and Lewis Milestone's *All Quiet on the Western Front* (1930). Kimisaburo Yoshimura's (1911–2000) highly regarded *The Story of Tank Commander Nishizumi* (*Nish-*

---

5. The Emperor Meiji (1852–1912) was succeeded by his son Prince Yoshihito (1879–1926), whose reign, known as the Taishō era, extended from 1912 to 1926. Because Yoshihito was afflicted with a disabling illness, his own son, Crown Prince Hirohito (1901–1989), was appointed regent (*Sesshō*) in 1921. Hirohito became emperor himself in 1926, inaugurating the Shōwa Era, which lasted until his death in 1989, when the Crown Prince Akihito (b. 1933) ascended the throne and the Heisei Era began. During the 1930s, the military frequently invoked the terms "the imperial way" (*Kodo*) and "the Shōwa Restoration" to suggest that Hirohito approved of their warlike plans, which often he did not.

izumi senshacho-den, 1940) was equally humane and individualistic in its outlook. It was almost as though Japanese directors had carried the banner of social realism into the war itself.

After the attack on Pearl Harbor in December 1941, the Japanese government issued strict guidelines and established quotas for the production of films on specific national policy themes (*kokusaku-eiga*). Then, following the example of Goebbels in Nazi Germany, Japanese government officials consolidated the ten existing studios into two large corporations under the Office of Public Information to ensure that the guidelines would be adhered to. The result was a wave of conventional war propaganda films, both narrative and documentary, with titles like *Flaming Sky* (*Moyuru ozora*, Yutaka Abe, 1941), *The Suicide Troops of the Watch Tower* (*Boro no kesshitai*, Tadashi Imai, 1942), *The War at Sea from Hawaii to Malaya* (*Hawai-Marei oki kaisen*, Kajiro Yamamoto, 1942), and *Generals, Staff, and Soldiers* (*Shogun to sambo to hei*, Tetsu Taguchi, 1943). Since little battle footage was available from the Pacific at this point in the war, these films made remarkably sophisticated use of special effects and models to replicate battle action—a practice that became common in such films as the war progressed and that helps to explain the high quality of special effects in some of the better postwar Japanese science-fiction films.

As the war grew more intense, virtually all genres, including the "children's" film (*Chocolate and Soldiers* [*Chokoreto to heitai*, Také Sado, 1942]) and the middle-class comedy-drama (*The Daily Battle* [*Nichijo no tatakai*, Yasujiro Shimazu, 1944]), were pressed into the service of national policy. Some directors, like Ozu (*The Brothers and Sisters of the Toda Family* [*Toda-ke no kyodai*, 1941]) and Gosho (*New Snow* [*Shinsetsu*, 1942]), protested the war by more or less ignoring it. Others, like Mizoguchi— *The Story of the Late Chrysanthemums* (*Zangiku monogatari*, 1939) and *Woman of Osaka* (*Naniwa onna*, 1940)—and Hiroshi Inagaki (1905–1980)—*The Rikisha Man/The Life of Matsu the Untamed* (*Muho Matsu no issho*, 1943)—avoided militaristic themes by turning to the *Meiji-mono* (historical dramas set in the enlightened Meiji era), but both were forced by the government to make *jidai-geki* set in the feudal Tokugawa period as well (Mizoguchi's *The 47 Loyal Ronin, Part I and Part II* [*Genroku chushingura*, 1941–42] and Inagaki's *Musashi Miyamoto* (1940) and *The Last Days of Edo* [*Edo saigo no hi*, 1941]).[6] Akira Kurosawa began his career as a director with a *Meiji-mono* about the founder of judo, *The Judo Story* (*Sanshiro sugata*, 1943), which the Ministry of Propaganda liked so much (for the wrong reasons) that it sponsored a sequel, *The Judo Story, Part II* (*Zoku sanshiro sugata*, 1945).

OCCUPATION

When World War II ended on August 14, 1945, much of Japan lay in ruins. The massive firebombing of its sixty

18.4 Expert model work and special effects were used to simulate live battle action in *The War at Sea from Hawaii to Malaya* (Kajiro Yamamoto, 1942).

6. Inagaki's black-and-white *Musashi Miyamoto* (1940) was based on Eiji Yoshikawa's sprawling novel by the same title, which in turn was based on a real-life figure who rose from the peasantry to become a master swordsman in the service of Lord Tadotoshi Hosokawa in seventeenth-century Edo. (Mizoguchi also adapted Yoshikawa's novel during World War II, in a 1944 production by the same title for Shochiku; the story was vastly popular and became the basis for no less than twenty-two features.) After the Occupation, Inagaki remade the film as an epic *chanbara* trilogy in color: *Samurai I: Miyamoto Musashi* (1954), *Samurai II: Ichijoji no ketto* (1955), and *Samurai III: Ketto ganryujima* (1956). Produced by Toho, these films proved very popular in the West, with *Samurai I* winning an Oscar for Best Foreign Film of 1954. Inagaki justly earned a reputation for sweeping historical spectacle, as is clearly on display in such later works as *Chushingura* (also known as *The Loyal 47 Ronin* [1962]) and *Samurai Banners* (*Furin kazan* [1969]), which have been favorably compared with *The Birth of a Nation* (1914) and *Gone with the Wind* (1939). The Chushingura legend, based on historical events from the Edo period at the end of the nineteenth century, is a perennially popular one and has been adapted as a feature film at least thirteen times, most prominently by Inagaki and Mizoguchi, whose own *The Loyal 47 Ronin* (*Genroku chushingura*) was produced as a two-part "national policy" film in 1941–42.

major cities from March through June 1945 and the dropping of atomic bombs on Hiroshima and Nagasaki had resulted in some 900,000 casualties and the nearly total paralysis of civilian life. On the morning of August 15, when Emperor Hirohito broadcast to his subjects the news that the war had ended and that Japan had lost, there was widespread disbelief. Never in their history had the Japanese people been defeated or the nation occupied, and so the circumstances of the American Occupation, 1945–52, were utterly unique.

The Occupation forces were led by General Douglas MacArthur, whose title, Supreme Commander for the Allied Powers, lent his administration the acronym SCAP. SCAP's primary objective was the "democratization" of Japan; to this end it imposed strict censorship through its Civil Information and Education Section (CIE). Nearly half of Japan's movie theaters had been destroyed by Allied bombing (there were only 845 in operation in October 1945), but most of the studios remained intact, and films continued to be produced. With the officially published vow that "Japan will never in the future disturb the peace of the world," CIE demanded that these films do nothing to glorify feudalism, imperialism, or militarism—which necessarily eliminated the whole genre of *jidai-geki* and encouraged the production of *Meiji-mono* and films of contemporary life. Of the 554 wartime and postwar films confiscated by SCAP, 225 were banned on the grounds that they promoted antidemocratic tendencies, and many of them were destroyed.[7]

Between 1946 and 1950, when the Allies began to ease their powers of occupation, the Japanese could hardly have been said to control their own film industry. In an attempt at demonopolization, SCAP broke up the huge wartime *zaibatsu* in 1946 (they regrouped into five, later six, major corporations as soon as the Occupation ended—Nikkatsu, Shochiku, Toho, Toei, Shintoho, and Daiei). SCAP also attempted to ferret out war criminals within the industry, and CIE dictated the subject matter of Japanese films. These phenomena were significant but short-lived; of more lasting consequence was the influx of American films into Japan for the first time since the beginning of the war—a time when domestic production was at a very low ebb (only 67 indigenous films were released in 1946; the figure for 1927 had been over 700). The influence of Frank Capra, John Ford, Howard Hawks, and Orson Welles upon the first postwar generation of Japanese directors was comparable to their influence upon

18.5 Akira Kurosawa's postwar detective film *Stray Dog* (1949): Toshiro Mifune, Takashi Shimura.

the *cinéastes* of the French New Wave. In any case, many Japanese studios during the Occupation found it politic to copy American styles and themes. The only domestic themes thoroughly endorsed by SCAP were those dealing with the new social freedoms made possible by democracy, especially the emancipation of women. Mizoguchi, Kinugasa, Kinoshita, Kurosawa, Gosho, Yoshimura, and Ozu all made fine films on this subject. During the Occupation, Akira Kurosawa (1910–1998) made four films for Toho—*The Men Who Tread on the Tiger's Tail* (*Tora no o wo fumu otoko tachi*, 1945), *No Regrets for Our Youth* (*Waga seishun ni kuinashi*, 1946), *Drunken Angel* (*Yoidore tenshi*, 1948), and *Stray Dog* (*Nora inu*, 1949)—which established him as one of the great postwar directors. But it was not until his *Rashomon* (1950), produced for Daie, unexpectedly won the Golden Lion at the Venice International Film Festival in 1951 that the real postwar renaissance of Japanese cinema began.

RASHOMON, KUROSAWA, AND THE POSTWAR RENAISSANCE

Rashomon, based on two short stories by Ryunosuke Akutagawa (1892–1927), is a film about the relativity of truth in which four conflicting versions of the same event are offered by four equally credible (or equally incredible)

---

7. The definitive English-language work on Occupation cinema is Kyoko Hirano's *Mr. Smith Goes to Tokyo: Japanese Cinema under the American Occupation, 1945–1952* (Washington, D.C.: Smithsonian Institution Press, 1992).

18.6 *Rashomon* (Akira Kurosawa, 1950): the bandit (Toshiro Mifune), the husband (Masayuki Mori), the wife (Machiko Kyo).

narrators. In twelfth-century Japan, three men take cover from a rainstorm under the crumbling Rashomon gate of the ancient capital, Kyoto. Two of them, a woodcutter and a priest, have just come from police headquarters, and they tell the third a strange tale that becomes the main portion of the film in flashback. The woodcutter explains how he had found the body of a nobleman in the woods; the man had been stabbed to death, but the weapon was missing. The priest says that he had encountered this same nobleman traveling with his wife on the road shortly before the murder.

While the woodcutter and the priest were at police headquarters, where both had come to give evidence, the police captured a bandit (played by Toshiro Mifune [1920–1997]—a brilliant actor and Kurosawa's constant collaborator) who confessed to killing the man and who gave the following account: The bandit was asleep in the woods when the nobleman passed by with his beautiful wife. Consumed with desire for her, he tricked the husband, tied him to a tree, and raped the wife. Afterward the woman forced the two men into a duel in which the husband was killed. Next, the wife was brought to police headquarters, where she gave her version of the truth. As she told the story, the bandit had left after the rape, and her husband then spurned her for being so easily dishonored. She had fainted from grief and awakened to find a dagger in her husband's breast. The priest and the woodcutter then inform the stranger that a third version was offered by the spirit of the dead husband, speaking through the lips of a medium. He testified that after the rape his wife had begged the bandit to kill her husband

and carry her away. The bandit refused; the wife ran off into the woods; and her husband committed suicide with the dagger, which he felt someone remove from his body after his death. Finally, the woodcutter admits to the priest and the stranger that he had actually witnessed the whole sequence of events from a hiding place in the forest: "There was no dagger in that man's breast," he says. "He was killed by a sword thrust." The woodcutter's story is that both men were cowards and had to be goaded into the duel by the shrewish woman. In the event, he says, the bandit killed the husband almost by accident, and the woman ran off into the woods. But this "objective" account of things is called into question when the stranger accuses the woodcutter of having stolen the missing dagger.

Thus all four versions of the truth are shown to be relative to the perspectives and self-serving intentions of the individual participants. Even the woodcutter's detached account suggests the possibility of distortion. Kurosawa implies that reality or truth does not exist independent of human consciousness, identity, and perception. It is small wonder, then, that Alain Resnais claimed *Rashomon* as the inspiration for his own film about the enigmatic nature of reality, *L'Année dernière à Marienbad* (1961; see Chapter 13).

Cinematically, *Rashomon* is a masterpiece, and its release marked the emergence of Kurosawa as a major international figure. Each of the four tales has a unique style appropriate to the character of its teller, but the film as a whole is characterized by the many complicated tracking shots executed by cinematographer Kazuo Miyagawa (1908–1999), superbly paced editing, and thematically significant composition of the frame in depth. The camera seems to be almost constantly in motion, much of it violent, and Kurosawa uses many subjective shots to represent "reality" from the perspective of the individual narrators. Ironically, the Japanese had been somewhat reluctant to enter *Rashomon* in the Venice Festival, thinking that foreigners would misunderstand it. They were as amazed as they were pleased when the film won the Golden Lion, but their industry was quick to capitalize on its success. From 1951 through the present, the Japanese have consistently submitted entries to international film festivals, and they have achieved recognition and respect for their cinema all over the world. Between 1951 and 1965, as vast new export markets opened in the West and as Japanese films won prizes in festival after festival, Japanese cinema experienced a renaissance unprecedented in the history of any national cinema. Established figures like Mizoguchi and Ozu produced their greatest work during this period, and relatively new figures like Kurosawa, Shindo, Ichikawa, and Kobayashi all made films that stand among the classics of the international cinema.

Kurosawa became the most famous Japanese director in the West perhaps because his films are more Western in construction than those of his peers. He followed *Rashomon* with an adaptation of Dostoevsky's *The Idiot* (*Hakuchi*, 1951) for Shochiku and the brilliant *shomin-geki Ikiru* (*Living/To Live*, 1952), a fatalistic yet ultimately affirmative account of the last months of a minor bureaucrat dying of cancer. *Ikiru* was made for Toho, which would produce and/or distribute all of Kurosawa's films but one from 1952 to 1991. In 1954 Kurosawa produced the epic *jidai-geki, Seven Samurai* (*Shichinin no samurai*), which many critics regard as his greatest work. Over eighteen months in production, this spectacular and deeply humanistic film tells the story of a small village that hires seven unemployed *samurai* to defend it against bandit raids in sixteenth-century Japan, an era in which the *samurai* as a class were rapidly dying out (in fact, the bandits are themselves unemployed samurai). As an epic, *Seven Samurai* clearly ranks with the greatest films of Griffith and Eisenstein, and cinematically it is a stunning achievement. As several critics have pointed out, the entire film is a tapestry of motion. Complicated tracking shots compete with equally elaborate and fast-paced editing to create a prevailing tempo that is like that of war punctuated by ever shorter intervals of peace. For the

18.8 The *samurai* enter the village.

battle between bandits and *samurai* that concludes the film, Kurosawa created a montage sequence that rivals the massacre on the Odessa steps in *Potemkin* in its combination of rapid tracking shots and telephoto close-ups of the action at various decelerated camera speeds. *Seven Samurai* was honored on a global scale, received the Kinema Jumpo award in Japan, the Silver Lion at Venice, and the Academy Award for Best Foreign Film in the United States. It was remade by John Sturges as *The Magnificent Seven* (1960), with its setting transposed to the American West, and it stands firmly behind the theme

18.7 *Seven Samurai* (Akira Kurosawa, 1954): Toshiro Mifune, Yoshio Inaba, Takashi Shimura, Ko Kimura, Daisuke Kato, Seiji Miyaguchi, Minoru Chiaki.

18.9 The three peasants who had been sent to hire the *samurai* return to find the villagers terrified of their guests.

18.10 A lyrical interlude between a village girl and the youngest *samurai:* Keiko Tsushima, Ko Kimura.

18.12 In the attack, one of their number is killed and many of the bandits escape.

and style of Sam Peckinpah's classic anti-Western *The Wild Bunch* (1969; see Chapter 20).

Kurosawa's other masterpiece of the 1950s was a brilliant adaptation of Shakespeare's *Macbeth* as a *jidai-geki* set in medieval Japan. Despite the cultural transposition, *Throne of Blood/Cobweb Castle* (*Kumonosujo*, 1957) is perhaps the greatest version of Shakespeare on film. The supernatural element of the drama was enhanced by the sparing use of ritualized conventions from classical *noh* plays[8] and by the exteriors shot in the misty forests around Mount Fuji. Like *Seven Samurai*, *Throne of Blood* concludes with an elaborate montage sequence in which the

18.13 The remaining bandits launch an all-out attack on the village.

18.11 Without waiting to be attacked, the *samurai* storm the bandits' river fortress and burn it to the ground.

8. Developed in medieval Japan, *noh* is a form of ritualized drama that treats mythic, historical, or literary themes. Whereas the more popular *kabuki* theater tends toward extravagance and relates events that are in the process of occurring, *noh* theater, for which about 250 plays exist, is more refined intellectually and always deals with events that occurred in the past. Its settings and gestures are symbolic, and its language is formal and highly allusive. Much use is made of mime and masks. Though *Throne of Blood* is his only film to employ *noh* elements throughout, many of Kurosawa's films use *noh* choruses (*The Men Who Tread on the Tiger's Tail*), music (*Seven Samurai*), and plot structure (*The Hidden Fortress*).

18.14 In the final battle in the rain, all of the bandits are killed, but only three *samurai* survive. (Note the flattening of perspective produced by the telephoto lens.) On the following day, the *samurai* prepare to leave: "We've lost again . . . the farmers are the winners. Not us."

18.15 Masterful widescreen composition in Kurosawa's *The Hidden Fortress* (1958) and *Yojimbo* (1961). Compare the American and Italian-American Westerns of the same period (see Chapter 12).

Macbeth figure, Lord Washizu (Toshiro Mifune), is immolated by a hail of arrows.

In *Seven Samurai* and *Throne of Blood*, Kurosawa succeeded in elevating the *jidai-geki* from a simple action genre to an art form. After another literary adaptation, of Maxim Gorki's play *The Lower Depths* (*Donzoko*, 1957), he made three superb *chanbara*—*The Hidden Fortress* (*Kakushi toride no san-akunin*, 1958), *Yojimbo* (*The Bodyguard*, 1961), and *Sanjuro* (*Tsubaki sanjuro*, 1962). Though these films lack the thematic depth of his earlier *jidai-geki*, they are masterworks of widescreen composition and rival their predecessors in visual richness.

In 1960, Kurosawa was put in charge of his own production unit at Toho and given complete control of it. Kurosawa Production's first effort was *The Bad Sleep Well* (*Warui yatsu hodo yoku nemuru*, 1960), a film about corporate versus social responsibility in the form of a murder mystery. It was followed by *Yojimbo; Sanjuro; High and Low* (*Tengoku to jigoku*, 1963), a strikingly formalized film of kidnapping and detection, loosely based on a novel

18.16 The famous "explosion of blood" from the final sword-fight in Kurosawa's *Sanjuro* (1962): Toshiro Mifune, Tatsuya Nakadai.

by Ed McBain (Evan Hunter), which contains some of the most thematically complex widescreen framings of Kurosawa's career; and *Red Beard* (*Aka hige*, 1965), the story of a young doctor's education in late-Tokugawa Japan. Although *Red Beard* was one of his most successful films financially, it was five years before Kurosawa pro-

18.17 *High and Low* (Akira Kurosawa, 1963): the police—Ko Kimura (driving), Takeshi Kato, Kenjiro Ishiyama (facing camera), Tatsuya Nakadai—stalk the kidnapper.

duced another. In the interim, he wrote the screenplay for *Runaway Train*, based on a *Life* magazine article about an actual train accident in upstate New York, and contracted with 20th Century–Fox to shoot it in Rochester as his first color film. But bad weather on location forced cancellation of the project (it was eventually realized by Russian émigré director Andrei Mikhalkov Konchalovski for Cannon Films in 1985). Kurosawa was then invited by Fox to coproduce and direct the Japanese sequences of the Pearl Harbor battle epic *Tora! Tora! Tora!* (Richard Fleischer, 1970; see Chapter 21), an experience that ended bitterly for both parties in January 1969 when the director's footage was rejected and Fox terminated his contract. From this point, Kurosawa Production was not active again until *Dreams* in 1990.

Returning to Japan, Kurosawa organized an artists' collective consisting of himself, Keisuke Kinoshita,

Masaki Kobayashi, and Kon Ichikawa, which was called Yonki no kai, or "the Four Musketeers." The group's first and only production was Kurosawa's next film, the low-budget *Dodes'ka-den* (1970), based on a collection of short stories entitled *A Town without Seasons* by Shugoro Yamamoto, who was also the source for *Sanjiro* and *Red Beard*. This unstructured narrative about the lives of the very poor in a Tokyo slum was Kurosawa's first film in color (albeit Eastmancolor), but it failed at the box office, another first for the director, and spelled the end of Yonki no kai. Apparently despondent over this loss, in December 1971 Kurosawa attempted suicide by cutting his wrists (a logical and culturally acceptable act for a Japanese who perceives the possibilities of his or her life to be exhausted). Fortunately he survived, and in 1976, after six years of silence, Kurosawa gave the cinema another masterpiece—*Dersu Uzala*, a Soviet-Japanese coproduction shot in 70mm with six-track sound. Set in the forests of eastern Siberia at the turn of the century, it is a portrait of the friendship between an aging hunter of the Goldi tribe and a young Russian surveyor. By 1977 the film, which was distributed by Mosfilm, had won the Grand Prize at the Moscow Festival and an Academy Award in America. In 1980 Kurosawa completed *Kagemusha* (*Shadow Warrior*), a tragic *jidai-geki* set during the sixteenth-century civil wars; this film was cowinner of the Grand Prix at Cannes in the year of its release, but, as great as it was, *Kagemusha* was in many ways simply a test run for Kurosawa's masterpiece, *Ran* (literally, *Chaos*), in 1985. This $10 million Japanese-French coproduction—the most

18.18 A telephoto shot from *Kagemusha*'s climactic battle (Akira Kurosawa, 1980).

18.19 Kurosawa's *Ran* (1985).

more conscious of Western styles of filmmaking than any of his Japanese peers and always claimed a great stylistic debt to John Ford (American cinema's recent debt to Kurosawa has been noted; in 1991 he received an Academy Award for lifetime achievement). Kurosawa was a professional student of Western painting before he entered the cinema, but it would be a mistake to assume that the Western "look" of his films betokens Western values. Sometimes mistakenly identified by Western critics as a humanist, he was, in fact, a fatalist, or at least an existentialist, in subtle but thoroughly Japanese terms. His vision of human experience was firmly rooted in the value system of feudal Japan. Zen Buddhism, the *samurai* code of *bushido* ("the way of the warrior"—loyalty and self-sacrifice), and the master-pupil relationship are all-important ethical components of his films. Because of his great universality of spirit, we can recognize ourselves in Kurosawa, but we would do well to remember that Kurosawa also shared many sympathies with Yukio Mishima (1925–1970), the famous anti-intellectual novelist and right-wing militant who staged a raid on the Tokyo headquarters of the nation's "peacekeeping" forces on November 25, 1970, and committed a spectacular act of *seppuku*, or *hara-kiri*, there to protest the decadence of contemporary Japan and the declining role of feudalism in its culture.[9]

KENJI MIZOGUCHI

More clearly Oriental in form than the work of Kurosawa is that of Kenji Mizoguchi (1898–1956), a director whose career spanned thirty-four years and encompassed 90 feature films. Like Kurosawa, Mizoguchi studied Western painting as a student, but his themes and visual style were purely Japanese. He began his career as an actor for the Nikkatsu studio and became a director there in 1922. Appearing from a variety of studios, Mizoguchi's first

expensive film ever made in Japan—was the culmination of a life's work: a stylized, epic version of *King Lear* set in the context of the same clan wars as those portrayed in *Kagemusha*. *Ran* was internationally recognized as the director's most brilliant, profound, and magisterial film. In 1987 Kurosawa announced his intention to retire from directing, as if after *Ran* there was little left to say, but in 1990 he produced the eight-part fantasy anthology *Dreams* (*Yume*) and in 1991 the contemplative *Rhapsody in August* (*Hachigatsu no kyoshikyoku*), a rumination on the atomic bombing of Nagasaki at the end of World War II. For his thirtieth and final feature, Kurosawa directed *Not Yet* (*Madadayo*, 1993), a rambling account of the writer Hyakken Uchida and his protégés. As a testament, he left a completed screenplay based on a story about a masterless *samurai*, or *ronin*, by Shugoro Yamamoto entitled *Ame Agaru* (*After the Rain*, 1999); this was made into a Kurosawa-style film by Takashi Koizumi, starring as the *ronin* Shiro Mifune (the son of Kurosawa's lifelong collaborator Toshiro Mifune, who had died the year before him).

Kurosawa was unquestionably a giant of the international cinema. Like Bergman and Antonioni, he was the true *auteur* of his films—he set up his own shots, did his own editing, and wrote his own scripts. He was probably

9. Mishima, who also directed films and acted in them, was the subject of a highly stylized, expressionistic film biography by Paul Schrader. Based on an assortment of the writer's semiautobiographical works, it was entitled *Mishima: A Life in Four Chapters* (1985). The film was barred from the 1985 Tokyo Festival and never distributed in Japan. Other Mishima adaptations are Kon Ichikawa's *Conflagration* (*Enjo*, 1958), adapted from the novel *Temple of the Golden Pavilion* (*Kinkaku-ji*, 1956); Senkichi Taniguchi's *The Sound of Waves* (*Shiosai*, 1959), based on the 1956 novel; and the British-produced *The Sailor Who Fell from Grace with the Sea* (John Lewis Carlino, 1976), based on the novel *Gogo no eiko*, 1983.

films were mainly thrillers and melodramas adapted from popular literature (such as *Harbor in the Fog* [*Kiri no minato*, 1923]), but in 1925 he began to make films dealing with the impact of urbanization on Japanese life (*Tokyo March* [*Tokyo koshin-kyoku*, 1929]; *Metropolitan Symphony* [*Tokai kokyogaku*, 1929]). Few of his silent films have survived, but those that do reveal an almost painterly evocation of atmosphere and mood. After a politically committed film about the urban working class, *Nevertheless, They Go On* (*Shikamo karera wa yuku*, 1931), Mizoguchi turned increasingly to period films to avoid government censorship. Yet his two greatest films of the 1930s, *Osaka Elegy* (*Naniwa ereji*, 1936—banned in 1940) and *Sisters of the Gion* (*Gion no shimai*, 1936), both have contemporary settings and announce Mizoguchi's major thematic concern: the position of women within the social order and the redemptive power of their love. The films also contain Mizoguchi's first consistent use of the technique that would become the hallmark of his later films—the extended long take composed in depth for a static camera. Critics have compared *Osaka Elegy* and *Sisters of the Gion* with Jean Renoir's prewar films (see Chapter 9) in terms of both their humanism and their *mise-en-scène*. Like Renoir, Mizoguchi constantly sought ways to portray internal states through external means, and he felt that in the long take he had discovered what he called "the most precise and specific expression for intense psychological moments." Diagonal composition leading the eye outward toward the world beyond the frame, fluid and thematically significant moving camera shots, luminous photography (often by Kazuo Miyagawa), and minimal cutting are other characteristics of Mizoguchi's mature style, which link him with the *mise-en-scène* tradition of the West.

During the war, Mizoguchi was forced to make a certain number of government-policy films, although he was able to confine them to *jidai-geki* like *The Loyal 47 Ronin, Part I* and *Part II* (*Genroku chushingura*, 1941–42). After the surrender, he continued to examine the condition of Japanese women in films like *Women of the Night* (*Yoru no onnatachi*, 1948), which concerns prostitution during the Occupation. But in the last six years of his life, with the Occupation ended, Mizoguchi produced his greatest masterpieces, nearly all of them for Daiei. In rapid succession he shot five films that many critics regard as among the most beautiful and haunting ever made. *The*

18.20 *The Life of Oharu* **(Kenji Mizoguchi, 1952): Kinuyo Tanaka, prone, in the title role.**

Life of Oharu (*Saikaku ichidai onna*, 1952), winner of the International Director's Prize at the 1952 Venice Film Festival, is a humane critique of feudalism centered around the degraded life of a prostitute in seventeenth-century Kyoto. *Ugetsu* (*Ugetsu monogatari*, 1953), which won the Silver Lion at Venice in 1953, is set during the feudal wars of the sixteenth century. Two ambitious young men leave their wives to seek wealth and glory. In the course of a long and picaresque pilgrimage, they both come to realize that nothing they have gained on their journey is worth the love of the women they have cast away. Simultaneously realistic, allegorical, and supernatural, *Ugetsu* is the most stylistically perfect of all Mizoguchi's works, and to some critics it is the greatest Japanese film ever made. *Gion Festival Music* (*Gion bayashi*, 1953) is a highly successful remake of *Sisters of the Gion*; but with *Sansho the Bailiff* (*Sansho dayu*, 1954), set in the

18.21 *Mise-en-scène* aesthetics in Mizoguchi's *Ugetsu* (1953): luminous photography, diagonal composition, the long take. Machiko Kyo, Masayuki Mori.

eleventh century, and *The Crucified Lovers/A Story from Chikamatsu* (*Chikamatsu monogatari*, 1954), set in the seventeenth century, Mizoguchi continued his concentrated scrutiny of the feudal social system and its impact upon women, although neither film was the equal of *The Life of Oharu or Ugetsu*. *The Empress Yang Kwei Fei* (*Yokihi*, 1955) and *New Tales of the Taira Clan* (*Shin heike monogatari*, 1955) were Mizoguchi's only films in color, and although both are decidedly "popular" in their content, they show a marvelously expressive sense of the medium. Characteristically, the last film Mizoguchi completed before his death in 1956 was *Street of Shame* (*Akasen chitai*, 1956), a fictionalized account of the lives of Tokyo prostitutes.

Mizoguchi is popularly perceived in the West, which has seen only about a tenth of his total opus, as a maker of period films. Indeed, as Kurosawa remarked when the elder director died, "Now that Mizoguchi is gone, there are very few directors left who can see the past clearly and realistically." But when Mizoguchi looked at the past, it was always as a mirror for the present. His lifelong critique of feudalism, his sympathetic concern for the social and psychological condition of women, and his simple humanism in the face of a callous world are the thematic bridges uniting his period and his contemporary films. Furthermore, his absolute mastery of decor, the long take, and the moving camera make Mizoguchi one of the great *mise-en-scène* directors of the international

cinema, a rival of Murnau, Ophüls, and Welles, to name only his contemporaries. Nevertheless, his nearly transcendental visual style finally makes Mizoguchi unique in the history of film. As the French New Wave director Jacques Rivette said of him, "Mizoguchi, alone, imposes a feeling of a unique world and language, is answerable only to himself."

YASUJIRO OZU

The Japanese director whose work most expresses traditional Japanese values is undeniably Yasujiro Ozu (1903–1963); for that reason, he was the last of the three great masters of Japanese cinema to be discovered by the West. As a boy in Tokyo, Ozu spent much of his time in movie houses, entranced by Italian spectacles like *Quo vadis?* (1913) and by American comedy, melodrama, and romance (he particularly admired Lubitsch and Griffith). After briefly attending Waseda University, he became a scriptwriter at the Shochiku studio, where he was to work for the rest of his life. Here he soon became an assistant director under the tutelage of Tadamoto Okubo, a specialist in light comedies known as *nansensu-mono*, or "nonsense films," and by 1927 Ozu had directed his first feature, a *jidai-geki* entitled *The Sword of Penitence* (*Zange no yaiba*). This film was unremarkable except for the fact that it was written by Kogo Noda, who was to become Ozu's lifelong collaborator and friend.

For a time Ozu specialized in nonsense films in the manner of Okubo, but he soon turned his attention to the more serious genre of *shomin-geki*, social comedies that concentrate on the daily lives and interpersonal relationships of the members of lower-middle-class families. Ozu seems to have chosen this genre because he found in the routine lives of these people—in their necessary ability to cope with hardship—a "sympathetic sadness" at the harshness of the natural order that ultimately enables one to transcend it. In Western culture, the lower middle class has not often been a traditional subject for art but rather, at best, for soap opera and low comedy. In Japan, however, the simple lifestyle necessarily practiced by the people of this class is highly regarded as the most authentic, valid, and human way to live, unencumbered as it is by false values, pretensions, and distortions. As Barbara Wolf has put it, "After all, what could possibly be so real as to be born, make a living, bring forth a new generation and

18.22 Left: Ozu's *Late Spring* (1949): Chishu Ryu, Setsuko Hara, Haruko Sugimura. Right: Ozu's *Tokyo Story* (1953): Chishu Ryu, Chieko Higashiyama. Note the low-angle horizontal composition, here and throughout the Ozu stills, as if the camera were a person seated on a *tatami* (mat). Note also the reliance on offscreen space.

then die?" Of Ozu's 54 films, nearly all deal with the life cycles and life crises of lower-middle-class family members, but beyond this they are about the impact of modernization and modernity on traditional Japanese culture. Often using the same actors, Ozu's films are, in a sense, all parts of one film that the director was driven to remake throughout his career.[1] Even the titles seem barely distinguishable from one another: *I Graduated, but . . .* (*Daigaku wa deta keredo*, 1929), *Life of an Office Worker* (*Kaishain seikatsu*, 1930), *I Flunked, but . . .* (*Rakudai wa shita keredo*, 1930), *The Chorus of Tokyo* (*Tokyo no gassho*, 1931), *I Was Born, but . . .* (*Umarete wa mita keredo*, 1932), *The Story of Floating Weeds* (*Ukigusa monogatari*, 1934), *Tokyo's a Nice Place* (*Tokyo yoi toko*, 1935), *College Is a Nice Place* (*Daigaku yoi toko*, 1936), *The Only Son* (*Hitori musuko*, 1936), *There Was a Father* (*Chichi ariki*, 1942), *Late Spring* (*Banshun*, 1949), *Early Summer* (*Bakushu*, 1951), *The Flavor of Green Tea over Rice* (*O-chazuke no aji*, 1952), *Tokyo Story* (*Tokyo monogatari*, 1953), *Early Spring* (*Soshun*, 1956), *Tokyo Twilight* (*Tokyo boshoku*, 1957), *Equinox Flower* (*Higanbana*, 1958), *Good Morning* (*Ohayo*, 1959), *Floating Weeds* (*Ukigusa*, 1959), *Late Autumn* (*Akibiyori*, 1960), *The End of Summer* (*Kohayagawa-ke no aki*, 1961), *An Autumn Afternoon* (*Samma no aji*, 1962).

To these films of people living restrained and minimal lives, Ozu brought a restrained and minimal cinematic

18.23 Yasujiro Ozu shooting a scene for *The Flavor of Green Tea over Rice* (1952). Note the low-angle, eye-level perspective.

style. Most of the films he made from 1936 on take place within the confines of a typical Japanese home. His camera is often motionless, and it frequently assumes the low-

1. In the fall of 1982, the Japan Society of New York sponsored the first American retrospective of Ozu's extant work, including many films never before seen in the United States. Today, Ozu's work has become a paragon of "art cinema" in American critical discourse, as publications as diverse as David Bordwell's *Ozu and the Poetics of Cinema* (Princeton: Princeton University Press, 1988) and Mindy Aloffe's "How American Intellectuals Learned to Love Ozu" (*New York Times*, Sunday, April 3, 1994: 13–17H) attest.

18.24 "Empty scenes" from the opening sequence of *Early Spring* (Yasujiro Ozu, 1956).

angle position of a person seated on a *tatami*, mat, whose eye level is about 3 feet above the floor, as if it were a guest or visitor in the household. Its attitude is one of calmness, quiescence, and repose. The composition of the frame is inevitably horizontal, and the editing style is spare, with no fades or dissolves but straight cuts only, and with little concern for traditionally fluid continuity. In fact, the characteristic Ozu film is composed of a series of static long takes in which the dialogue, always written by Ozu in close collaboration with Noda, sustains the drama. Sometimes, however, moments of stillness and stasis in which there are no human beings at all occur in Ozu's films. These are Ozu's famed "empty scenes" or "still lifes," and they are extremely important both to his aesthetic and to the international cinema at large.

It often happens in an Ozu film that the characters

leave a room to eat or go to the bathroom or to bed, while the camera remains behind in its stationary position to record for a while the empty space that the actors have created by their departure. This preoccupation corresponds to a concept in Zen aesthetics known as *mu*, which, technically, designates the empty space between the flowers in the Japanese art of flower arrangement, but which more generally refers to the Zen doctrine that the spaces between the materials used to create a work of art are an integral part of the work. Will Peterson has put it this way: "The blank sheet of paper is perceived only as paper, and remains as paper. Only by filling the paper does it become empty." So Ozu's "still lifes," which appear in each of his major films, are an integral part of his transcendental vision of reality. But they are also of great importance to the formal evolution of narrative film. Through his use of the empty scene, Ozu became one of the first directors in the history of film to create **offscreen space.**

OFFSCREEN SPACE

There are two ways of conceptualizing the cinema screen. In one, the outer edges of the screen become a framing device for the visual composition centered within it, like the frame of a painting or a still photograph. In this model, the reality of the film is contained entirely *within* the screen, and the edges of the screen are borders separating the film's reality from the categorically "real" reality outside. This way of regarding the screen and the method of composition it demands has, with a few notable exceptions (in the work of von Stroheim, Murnau, Renoir, Welles, Hitchcock, and Rossellini), dominated the narrative cinema of the West until relatively recently—perhaps the last forty years. In the other mode of conceptualizing cinematic space, first formally articulated by André Bazin, the screen is conceived as a window on the world whose frame, if moved to the right or to the left or up or down, would reveal more of the same spatial reality contained within the screen. Of course, the screen must contain most of the action most of the time, so this offscreen space must be revealed by camera movement (as in the lateral tracking shots of the films Godard made after 1968) or, more provocatively, by what can be termed off-center or noncentered framing. In this technique, the film frame is made to contain only part of the significant action, or sometimes, as in Ozu, no action at all.

Figure 18.25 below shows two consecutive noncentered shots from Ozu's *Floating Weeds* (1959), which help to illustrate the concept. In traditional or centered framing, the force of the image is, in Bazin's terms, *centripetal*: the image is composed so that our eyes are drawn inward toward the vanishing point at the center of the frame. In antitraditional or off-center framing, the force of the image is *centrifugal*: our eyes are thrown out upon the world beyond the frame, a process that suggests the essential reality of that world. Centered framing has the effect of denying the reality of the world beyond the frame by isolating it from us; off-center framing has the effect of affirming the reality of the world beyond the frame by constantly calling our attention to it. In short, centered framing creates an illusion about the structure of reality that off-center framing seeks to destroy. Thus, the latter is an inherently more realistic technique in terms of the way we actually perceive reality. For this reason, off-center framing is increasingly favored by young Marxist directors on the Continent and in the Third World since it promises to deconstruct what is for them an essentially deceptive, illusionist way of looking at the world and one's position in it.

Ozu's use of offscreen space was somewhat differently motivated. Many Ozu films exploit offscreen space by means of empty scenes in which the motionless camera trains its attention for some time on dramatically insignificant objects—a vase on a nightstand, a ticking wall clock, an empty hallway—which, because they are themselves meaningless in terms of narrative and theme, draw our attention to the fact that they are surrounded by spaces containing meaningful objects and people offscreen. By showing us *nothing*, these shots draw our attention to the surrounding *something* in the same way—but much more emphatically—that off-center framing makes us aware of the world beyond the frame instead of denying its existence by isolating it from us. It is generally true that the longer the screen remains empty, the more our attention is drawn to offscreen as opposed to on-screen space, and Ozu was among the first directors anywhere to realize this. Another way that Ozu uses offscreen space is by training his stationary camera on some significant action while significant action is also in progress offscreen. This could be suggested by offscreen dialogue or naturalistic sound effects or, as in many of Ozu's later films, by having the action oscillate between offscreen and on-screen space. In *The End of Summer* (1960), for example, the static camera trains on a mother ironing a dress in full shot while her son and her father play catch, moving in and out of the frame at random as the game grows increasingly noisy and wild.

Yet, for all this, Yasujiro Ozu was an extremely conservative director. He did not make his first sound film until 1936 or his first color film until 1958, and he never used

18.25 Offscreen space can be created in front of the screen (and thus behind the camera) as well as beyond its linear borders. For example, classical Hollywood framing conceives an imaginary axis that positions the camera within a 180-degree semicircle vis-à-vis the action, cutting the viewer off from the 180 degrees of filmic space behind it. Antitraditional framing often conceives filmic space as a full circle, breaking the imaginary axis of action and creating a totally new spatial paradigm. In the shot-reverse-shot sequence above, the same actor's feet extend into the frame first from the left and then from the right, making it clear that the camera has turned 180 degrees on its axis (Ozu's *Floating Weeds* [1959]).

widescreen. His films employed only the most fundamental of stylistic devices—basically those that had been available since before 1914. Ozu's simplicity of style derives from the fact that his art is essentially religious in nature. It is an art predicated on the Zen Buddhist reverence for the mystery of the everyday. As Donald Richie has pointed out, it assumes that it is only through the mundane and the common that the transcendent can be expressed, and like much religious art, it is primitive in terms of technique. From this elementary base, however, Ozu made films of great emotional sophistication and subtlety, and he ranks today as one of the great *auteurs* of international cinema. From 1936 until his death in 1963 he kept the writing, casting, shooting, and editing of his films tightly under his control, building up his own repertory company of trusted performers and technicians. Although he was quintessentially Japanese, Ozu, like Shakespeare and Tolstoi, had a single universal subject: human nature. And in the course of his long career he became, as he was recently voted by the British Film Institute, "one of the greatest artists of the twentieth century in any medium and in any country."

The generation of Kurosawa, Mizoguchi, and Ozu also included Teinosuke Kinugasa (1896–1982), whose beautifully photographed *jidai-geki Gate of Hell* (*Jigokumon*, 1953), is considered one of the finest color films ever made,[2] and Keisuke Kinoshita (1912–1998), whose humanistic *Twenty-four Eyes* (*Nijushi no hitomi*, 1954) traces the course of Japanese fascism from 1927 to 1946 through the eyes of a young schoolteacher and her pupils. Although he directed propaganda films for the government during the war, Tadashi Imai (1912–1991) became a politically committed critic of vestigial feudalism and a prolific exponent of neorealism. His three-part *Muddy Waters* (*Nigori*, 1953), for example, is an exposé of political and social repression during the "liberal" Meiji Restoration.[3]

THE SECOND POSTWAR GENERATION

The second generation of the postwar renaissance came to prominence in the 1950s and 1960s and comprised primarily Masaki Kobayashi (1916–1996), Kon Ichikawa (b. 1915), and Kaneto Shindo (b. 1912). The works of Kobayashi and Ichikawa are probably better known in the West than those of Shindo. Kobayashi was trained in phi-

18.26 Masaki Kobayashi's *Hara kiri* (1962): Akira Ishihama.

losophy at Waseda University, and his early films dealt mainly with social and political problems in a realistic vein. His first masterpiece was *Human Condition III* (*Ningen no joken III*, 1959–61), a nine-and-one-half-hour antiwar epic depicting Japan's occupation and rape of Manchuria, 1943–45. Released in three parts, this humanistic but grimly realistic widescreen film tells the story of a young pacifist forced into the war and ultimately destroyed by it. Kobayashi's next important films were graphically violent *jidai-geki*—*Hara kiri* (*Seppuku*, 1962) and *Rebellion* (*Joi-uchi*, 1967), both of which used the

---

2. It is impossible, however, to experience *Gate of Hell* in its original form due to severe color fading of the negative. For more on this problem, see Chapter 12.

3. Though Kinugasa retired in the late 1960s and died in 1982, Kinoshita and Imai both continued working into the 1980s, the latter directing *The Proper Way* (*Kosakade gokko*, 1980) and *Tower of Lilies* (*Himeyuri no to*, 1982; a remake of his own 1953 film), and the former having produced *Children of Nagasaki/These Children Survive Me* (*Kono ko wo nokoshite*, 1983) and *Big Joys, Small Sorrows* (*Shin yorokobimo kanashimimo ikutoshitsuki*, 1986).

situation of an individual's doomed revolt against the authoritarian social system of the Tokugawa period to make serious comments on the survival of feudalism in modern technological Japan. In the uncharacteristic but strikingly beautiful film *Kwaidan* (*Kaidan*, 1964), Kobayashi made carefully controlled use of the widescreen format and expressive color to tell four haunting ghost stories adapted from the writings of Lafcadio Hearn (1850–1904), an American author who became a Japanese citizen. One of the tales, "Hoichi the Earless" ("Minimachi Hoichi"), draws heavily on elements of the *noh* play. Among Kobayashi's works from the 1970s are the period gangster film *Inn of Evil* (*Inochi bo ni furo*, 1971) and the thirteen-part television series *Kaseki* (1975), a sensitive account of an elderly business executive who discovers that he is dying of cancer and must reassess his life. In the 1990s, he directed the intensely tactile erotic melodrama *Glowing Autumn* (*Moeru aki*, 1981); the Ozu-like domestic tragedy *Fate of a Family* (*Shokutaku no nai ie*, 1985), which treats the deeply ingrained cultural concept of shame in the context of a son who dishonors (and accordingly ruins) his family by becoming a terrorist; and the two-part, 265-minute documentary *The Tokyo Trial* (*Tokyo saiban*, 1985), an extraordinary account of the war-crimes trials held by the Allies from 1946 to 1948 of twenty-eight top Japanese officials charged with conspiracy and aggression in World War II.

Kon Ichikawa is widely acknowledged in the West as one of the Japanese cinema's most brilliant stylists. He began his career as an animator, but his first important film was *The Burmese Harp* (*Biruma no tategoto*, 1956), a lyrical epic about a Japanese soldier whose guilt at his complicity in the collective horrors of war drives him to become a saintly Buddhist monk; like all of his major work through 1965, this was scripted by his wife, Natto Wada (1920–1983). Ichikawa's other great pacifist film, *Fires on the Plain* (*Nobi*, 1959), is set during the last days of the Japanese occupation of the Philippines, when the remnants of the decimated Japanese army turned to murder and cannibalism in order to survive and face their final battle with "honor." The film offers a nightmarish vision of an inferno that goes far beyond its implicit social criticism of the feudal code of *bushido*. *Conflagration* (*Enjo*, 1958), adapted from a novel by Yukio Mishima, is a richly textured widescreen film that tells the true story of a young Buddhist novitiate who burns down the Tem-

ple of the Golden Pavilion at Kyoto in disgust at the worldly corruption that surrounds him. Other Ichikawa films admired in the West include *Odd Obsession/The Key* (*Japanese title: Kagi*, 1959), a disturbing tale of an elderly man's sexual perversion, based on a darkly comic novel by Junichiro Tanizaki (and twice remade in Japan, with increasingly graphic sex scenes); *Alone in the Pacific* (*Taiheiyo hitoribochi*, 1963), based on the true story of a young man who sailed the Pacific from Osaka to San Francisco in three months; and the monumental documentary *Tokyo Olympiad* (1965), which compares favorably with Leni Riefenstahl's *Olympia* (1936). Less well known are Ichikawa's ambiguous critiques of Japanese family life, *Bonchi* (1960), *Younger Brother* (*Ototo*, 1960), and *Ten Dark Women* (*Kuroi junin no onna*, 1961), and the remarkable *An Actor's Revenge* (*Yukinojo henge*, 1963), the third screen version of Otokichi Mikami's story of an *onnagata* who sets out to avenge his father's death in 1836 Edo, which Donald Richie called one of the most visually ravishing films ever to come from Japan.[4] In 1973, Ichikawa produced *The Wanderers* (*Matatabi*), generically a nineteenth-century *chanbara*, which many critics saw as the consummation of his career to date in its combination of savage irony, technical mastery, and lush compositional beauty. After directing a series of overplotted potboilers for producer Haruki Kadokawa (e.g., *The Inugami Family* [*Inugami-ke no ichizoku*, 1976]; *The Devil's Bouncing Ball Song* [*Akuma no temari-uta*, 1977]; *Island of Horror* [*Gokumonto*, 1977]; *Queen Bee* [*Jobachi*, 1978]; *House of Hanging* [*Byoinzaka no kubikukuri no ie*, 1979]), Ichikawa returned to his former high standards. *Lonely Hearts* (*Kofuku*, 1982) is an adaptation of an Ed McBain crime thriller, shot by Ichikawa's regular cinematographer Kazuo Hasegawa (1908–1984) in a filtering process midway between black and white and color, while *The Makioka Sisters* (*Sasame yuki*, 1983) is a poignant family epic set in the 1920s, based on the classic novel by Junichiro Tanizaki and arguably the director's most important film since the 1960s. *Ohan* (1984), an old-fashioned domestic melodrama set in the same era, is, like all of Ichikawa's best work, notable for its rhapsodic use of color and widescreen. Equally resplendent in visual terms is *Princess from the Moon* (*Taketori monogatari*,

---

4. Donald Richie, *Japanese Cinema: An Introduction* (New York: Oxford University Press, 1990), pp. 59–60.

18.27 Kon Ichikawa's *The Makioka Sisters* (1983): Keiko Kishi, Yoshiko Sakuma, Sayuri Yoshinaga, Yuko Kotegawa, Juzo Itami.

1987), based on a ninth-century legend about a magical moon woman who is temporarily stranded on earth, and *Actress* (*Eiga joyu*, 1987), a fascinating biography of Japan's great female movie star Kinuyo Tanaka (1910–1977), whose career spanned most of Japanese film history. In 1985, Ichikawa remade *The Burmese Harp* in color and CinemaScope, and it quite properly became a domestic box-office hit in the year of the fortieth anniversary of the Hiroshima-Nagasaki holocaust. Remarkably, Ichikawa continued directing into his eighties, producing for Toho a remake of *Chushingura* (Hiroshi Inagaki, 1962) entitled *47 Ronin* (*Shijushichinin no shikaku*, (1994) to celebrate the one-hundredth anniversary of the invention of the cinema, and *Dora-heita* (1999), an old-fashioned *samurai* film about a new magistrate who is sent to root out corruption in a lawless town, from a script written by Ichikawa, Kurosawa, Kinoshita, and Kobayashi in their collective configuration as Yonki no kai in 1969–70 (see above).

Kaneto Shindo began as a scriptwriter for Kurosawa, Ichikawa, and others. His status as a film artist is less secure than that of either Kobayashi or Ichikawa, but he has made a number of important films since the war. Shindo worked as an assistant to Mizoguchi on *The Life of Oharu* and *Ugetsu*,[5] and in 1952 he made his first major

film, *Children of Hiroshima* (*Genbaku no ko*), a stylized semidocumentary about the atomic holocaust and its effects upon the Japanese people. Shindo's reputation in the West rests on the international success of another semidocumentary, *The Island* (Japanese title: *Naked Island* [*Hadaka no shima*, 1961]), which concerns the struggle of a peasant farming family to survive on a barren Pacific atoll. The film is poetic in the manner of Robert Flaherty's work—some consider it self-consciously beautiful—but it has obvious authenticity as a representation of human experience, which stems from the fact that it is largely autobiographical. Another Shindo film that is known outside of Japan is the folkloristic *jidai-geki Onibaba* (1964), which concerns a mother and daughter who survive the civil wars of the sixteenth century by killing wounded *samurai* and selling their armor for rice. This strange and brutal film blends gorgeous widescreen photography with sickening violence and graphic sex, and it never achieves the poetic quality Shindo apparently sought for it. *Kuroneko* (1968), a horrific ghost story, forms a pendant with *Onibaba*, and Shindo produced a final *jidai-geki* in *The Solitary Travels of Chikuzan* (*Chikuzan hitori tabi*, 1977), a film about the life of a wandering blind *shamisen* musician. Although some of his work has tended toward the sensational and melodramatic, Shindo is a prolific scriptwriter and remains a figure of importance in his nation's cinema. A notable Shindo film from the 1980s is *The Horizon* (*Chiheisen*, 1984), a chronicle of a Japanese woman who is fashioned after his own sister. She comes to San Francisco as the purchased bride of a Japanese farmer in 1920, raises a family, undergoes internment in an American concentration camp during World War II, and is ultimately reassimilated into American society after the war. During the 1990s, Shindo made the erotic drama *Bokuto kidan* (also known as *The Strange Story of Oyuki* [1993]), about a writer who searches for the perfect woman in the Ginza and Yoshiwara brothels of Tokyo; *Gogo no Yuigon-jo* (also known as *A Last Note* [1995]), which deals with a suicide pact between an elderly man and his wife; and *Sanmon yakusha* (also known as *By Player*, 2000), a biopic of the hard-drinking, womanizing character actor Taiji Tonoyama (1915–1989), which was completed when Shindo

---

5. In 1979, Shindo produced and directed *Mizoguchi Kenji*, a documentary about the director's life and work.

was eighty-eight years old, making him the world's second oldest practicing director (Portuguese filmmaker Manoel de Oliveira, who was born in 1908 and still working in 2002, was the oldest).

The popular work of the director Inoshiro (or Ishiro) Honda (1911–1993), whose *Godzilla* (*Gojira*, 1954) started a fifty-year cycle of formulaic monster films, has demonstrated to the world the Japanese facility for special effects. Almost all of Honda's science-fiction films are parabolic: the monster is unleashed through the careless explosion of an atomic bomb, and after wreaking havoc on the urban centers of the nation, it is finally destroyed by Japanese scientists. Working closely with special-effects director Eiji Tsuburaya (1901–1970), Honda made dozens of such films for Toho during the 1950s and 1960s, gearing them increasingly toward children as the cycle progressed. Some characteristic Honda titles, in translation, are *Rodan* (1956), *The Mysterians* (1957), *Mothra* (1961), *Varan the Unbelievable* (1962), *King Kong vs. Godzilla* (1962), *Godzilla versus Mothra* (1964), *Ghidrah, the Three-Headed Monster* (1965), *Atragon* (1966), *The War of the Gargantuas* (1966), *Destroy All Monsters* (1968), and *Godzilla's Revenge* (1969). Other studios attempted to imitate the Honda/Toho monster formula with varying degrees of success. Daiei did it best with its eighteen-film "Gamara" series (directed mainly by Noriyaki Yuasa), starting with *Daikaiju Gamera* in 1965, which was released in the United States as *Gammera, the Invincible* (1966). (Most Japanese monster films of this era

were prepared in English-language versions that featured dubbed sound tracks and downscale American actors in specially shot scenes and cutaways, leaving the impression that they were American-made). Nikkatsu's entry was the worst. *Gappa, the Triphibian Monsters* (also known as *Monster from a Prehistoric Planet*, 1967) was so bad that it did not even inspire a sequel. After dying out in the early 1970s, Godzilla, Mothra, and Gamera were all revived in the 1990s and given a whole new range of special effects through computer-generated imagery (see Chapter 21).

THE JAPANESE NEW WAVE

The third postwar generation of Japanese filmmakers emerged during the late 1960s and the 1970s to form a kind of radical New Wave (*nuberu bagu*). Many of them worked initially for the studios (Shinoda, Yoshida, and Oshima, for example, worked for Shochiku) and for this reason did much of their early work in some form of CinemaScope, to which the studios had converted wholesale by 1960 in order to combat the threat of television. But ultimately, most of them moved away from the studios to form their own independent production companies. Some characteristic directors are Hiroshi Teshigahara (1927–2001), Susumu Hani (b. 1928), Masahiro Shinoda (b. 1931), Yasuzo Masumura (1924–1986), Yoshishige Yoshida (b. 1933), Seijun Suzuki (b. 1923), Koji Wakamatsu (b. 1936), Shohei Imamura (b. 1926), and Nagisa Oshima (b. 1932).

Teshigahara is an avant-garde abstractionist whose international reputation rests upon a single film, *Woman in the Dunes* (*Suna no onna*, 1964), adapted by Kobo Abé from his own novel and produced for less than $100,000. Among the premier works of the Japanese New Wave, this film—which won the Cannes Special Jury Prize for the year of its release—is a complex allegory in which a young scientist becomes trapped in an isolated sand pit through the mysterious powers of a woman who apparently is condemned to shovel away the sand interminably by hand. Teshigahara continued his existential probing in *The Face of Another* (*Tanin no kao* [1966]), in which a wealthy businessman is facially disfigured in a laboratory fire and has a lifelike mask made for him by a famous plastic surgeon; over time the mask begins to warp his identity, changing all of his relationships and finally driving him mad. After feature-length documentaries on American army deserters in Tokyo during the Vietnam

18.28 Toho's *Godzilla* (Inoshiro Honda, 1954) and other Japanese monster films relied on a proficiency with models and special effects acquired in the production of domestic propaganda films during World War II.

18.29 *Woman in the Dunes* (Hiroshi Teshigahara, 1964): Kyoko Kishada, Eiji Okada.

War (*Summer Soldiers* [1972]) and on the architectural/sculptural work of Catalan artist Antonio Gaudí (1984), Teshigahara returned to drama in *Rikyu* (1989), a meditative work about the sixteenth-century Buddhist priest who mastered the art of the tea ceremony and came into conflict with Hideyoshi Toyotomi, Japan's most powerful warlord. *The Princess Goh* (*Goh-hime* [1992]) is a sequel that focuses on the activities of Oribe Furuta, Rikyu's protégé, who is appointed tea master by Toyotomi after Rikyu has committed suicide at the lord's command. In addition to his filmmaking activities, Teshigahara is headmaster at the famous Sogestsu school of flower arranging.

Susumu Hani began his career by making documentaries, which helped to shape his later *cinéma vérité* style. Most of Hani's feature films are shot on location with nonactors, and they typically treat the problems of the postwar generation—specifically, the problems of living in a once traditional culture disintegrating under the pressures of rapid social change. Hani has also made films about what it means to be Japanese in foreign lands—for example, the semidocumentary *Bwana Toshi* (Kenya, 1965) and *Bride of the Andes* (*Andesu no hanayome*, Peru, 1966). According to many critics, Hani's best and most characteristic film is *Inferno of First Love* (*Hatsukoi jigoku-hen*, 1968), in which two teenagers attempt through physical love to cope with the social chaos that surrounds them, only to be destroyed. In 1978 Hani's former wife,

Sachiko Hidari (1930–2001), one of Japan's finest actresses and the star of most of Hani's films, directed her own first feature, *The Far Road* (*Toi ippono michi*), which concerns the day-to-day life of an aging railroad worker, his wife, and his family. Hani himself subsequently made *A Tale of Africa* (*Afurika monogatari*, 1981), a symbolic drama about three people caught up alone in the wilds of Kenya.

Masahiro Shinoda is a New Wave director similarly committed to the younger generation's struggle against society, but unlike Hani, he is a supreme stylist whose sense of pictorial composition compares favorably with that of the "classical" directors of the 1950s (and, in fact, he had worked as Ozu's assistant on *Tokyo Twilight*, 1957). He has made films on every major aspect of his country's history as well as on contemporary life. Like the films of his peers, Shinoda's tend to be violent and nihilistic, but they are also ethically committed and formally precise. Working at Shochiku during the New Wave, Shinoda produced significant films across a broad range of genres, from youth films (*Youth in Fury* [*Kawaita mizummi*, 1960]) to *yakuza-eiga* (*Pale Flower* [*Kawaita hana*, 1963]), *chanbara* (*Assassination* [*Ansatsu*, 1964]), melodrama (*With Beauty and Sorrow* [*Utsukushisa to kanashimi to* [1965]), action-adventure (*Punishment Island* [*Shokei no shima*, 1966]), modernist *bunraku* adaptation (*Double Suicide/The Love Suicide at Amijima* [*Shinju ten no amijima*, 1969]; see caption for figure 18.30), historical comedy (*Buraikan* [also known as *The Scandalous Adventures of Buraikan* [1970]), historical tragedy (*Hanre Goze Orin* [*Banished Orin*, 1977]), and mythological fantasy (*Demon Pond* [*Yashagaike*, 1979]).

In the 1980s, Shinoda produced two major mainstream works, both beautifully photographed by Kazuo Miyagawa, the foremost Japanese cinematographer of his day (*Rashomon*, *Ugetsu*, etc.). *MacArthur's Children* (*Setouchi shonen yakudan*, 1984) treats the trauma of Japan's defeat in World War II and its seven-year occupation by the American army as experienced in the microcosm of a rural island. *Gonza the Spearman* (*Yari no gonza*, 1986), a classical, if bloody, adaptation of an early eighteenth-century play by Chikamatsu in the *bunraku* puppet-theater tradition,[6] tells the story of a *samurai*

6. In *bunraku* puppet theater, developed during the Tokugawa period (1603–1868), white-faced dolls, expressionless except for mobile eyelids, are manipulated by as many as three black-robed, masked, but fully visible puppeteers (*kuroko*); the musical narrative (*joruri*) is chanted by

18.30 The highly stylized *Double Suicide* (Masahiro Shinoda, 1969): Shima Iwashita, Kichiemon Nakamura. Shinoda's fatalism is perfectly embodied in this adaptation of a famous Chikamatsu *bunraku* play, which also entered the *kabuki* canon, by his mixing of the traditional puppets and human actors through match cutting until they become interchangeable. The *kuroko* (stagehands or puppeteers dressed in black) represent instruments of destiny for both groups, and the film's deliberate theatricality is balanced by Shinoda's brilliant manipulation of the Academy frame, slightly cropped in this still.

trilogy, begun in *MacArthur's Children*, about life in postwar Japan; and *Fukuro no shiro* (also known as *Owls' Castle* [1999]) is a satirical *jidai-geki* about a ninja sent to assassinate the powerful warlord Hideyoshi Toyotomi in 1591, after he has consolidated his power over most of Japan.

Another New Wave director of note is Yasuzo Masumura, who studied filmmaking on a scholarship at the Centro Sperimentale in Rome from 1949 to 1953 and worked briefly as an assistant to Ozu at Shochiku and to Mizoguchi at Daiei before directing his first feature in 1958, a brilliant satire on Japanese advertising called *Battleships and Toys* (*Kyojin to gangu*, 1958), shot in anamorphic Daieiscope by Hiroshi Murai.[7] Masumura went on to make a broad range of features, all characterized by eye-popping visuals and stylized editing tropes. Among the most significant are the satirical *yakuza-eiga Afraid to Die* (*Karakkazi yaro*, 1960), which stars iconic novelist Yukio Mishima in a rare screen appearance as a young gangster who would rather stay in prison than re-enter the underworld; *Hoodlum Soldier* (*Heitai yakuza*, 1965), which inaugurated a nine-film series about a *yakuza* drafted into the army during World War II and sent to fight at the Russian Front; *Red Angel* (*Akai tenshi*, 1966), a bloody antiwar film set in a field hospital during Japan's 1939 invasion of China; *Moju* (*Warehouse* [also known as *Blind Beast*], 1969), a bizarre tale of a blind sculptor who kidnaps an artist's model and imprisons her in his studio, coercing her into a demented sadomasochistic universe where sight is replaced by touch and accelerated by pain; and *Double Suicide of Sonezaki* (*Sonezaki shinju*, 1978), set in 1703 during a period of great cultural upheaval— like the late 1960s—when mercantile values of getting and spending were replacing the *samurai* code of honor as a societal norm. After a fifty-seven-film career, includ-

trapped in the coils of his own implacable code of honor; it won the Silver Bear at Berlin in the year of its release. Both of these films starred the popular Japanese rock singer Hiromi Go (b. 1956), for whom Shinoda filmed the phenomenally successful 45-minute music video *Allusion* in 1985. More recently, Shinoda swept the Japanese Academy Awards with *Childhood Days* (*Shonen jidai*, 1991), a film about the deep cultural conflict between private emotion and public duty. *Sharaku* is a period film that speculates on the life of the mysterious *ukiyo-e* (woodblock print) artist named in the title, who produced about 150 portraits of famous Kabuki performers during the 1790s, before he disappeared from sight. *Setouchi munraito serenade* (also known as *Moonlight Serenade* [1997]) is the second film in the *Setouchi*

---

a reciter (*gidayu*) to the accompaniment of instruments. Many *bunraku* plays revolved around the theme of *shinju*, or lovers' suicide, motivated by the tension between *giri* (duty) and *ninjo* (human desires). Monzaemon Chikamatsu (1653–1725) was the greatest literary master of the form, and his work forms the basis of many significant Japanese films (e.g., Mizoguchi's *The Crucified Lovers* [*Chikamatsu monogatari*, 1954]). *The Love Suicides at Sonezaki*, first filmed by Yasuzo Masumura in 1977, was filmed again in 1982 by Midori Kurisaki as an actual *bunraku* play, photographed by Kazuo Miyagawa.

7. Hiroshi Murai was an important director of photography during the late 1950s and 1960s, when he worked most notably with action director Kihachi Okamoto (b. 1923) on such *chanbara* classics as *Samurai Assassin* (1965) and *The Sword of Doom* (*Daibosatsu toge*, 1967).

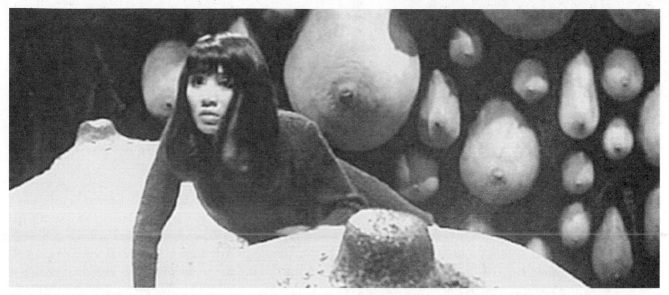

18.31 *Blind Beast* (Yasuzo Masumura, 1969): Mako Midori as Aki, the kidnapped model, feeling her way through the "breast" section of the blind sculptor's warehouse gallery. Among the extraordinary sets for this film were two gigantic reclining female torsos, on which much of the action was played. The film was shot in Daieiscope by Setsuo Kobayashi.

ing copious works of exploitation, Masumura died of a cerebral hemorrhage in November 1986.

Even more significant, however, is Yoshishige Yoshida— *Farewell to the Summer Light* (*Saraba natsu no hikari*, 1968), and the important avant-garde trilogy about twentieth-century radicalism *Eros + Massacre* (*Eros + gyakusatsu*, 1969), which focuses on both the Taishō-era anarchist Sakae Osugi and his female lovers (who were murdered by the military police [*kempeitai*] in the aftermath of the 1923 Kanto earthquake) and their contemporary student counterparts. Yoshida's films of the 1970s include *Heroic Purgatory* (*Rengoku eroica*, 1970), a densely symbolic analysis of student activism during the 1950s; and *Coup d'État* (Japanese title: *Martial Law* [*Kaigenrei*, 1973]), an elliptical biography of Ikki Kita, whose writings inspired the abortive coup d'état of February 26, 1936, in which 1,400 young right-wing officers and troops briefly seized control of Tokyo and murdered a number of prominent civilian officials (and were in turn, along with Kita, executed by the military police when the rebellion was suppressed three days later; Mishima's short feature *The Rite of Love and Death* [*Yukoku*, 1965] graphically depicts a young officer's ritual act of *seppuku* on the heels of this uprising). Yoshida did not make another feature for thirteen years, when *A Promise* (*Ningen no*

yakusoku, 1986), a film that seemed to plead for euthanasia, appeared at Cannes. This was followed by *Arishigoaka* (1988), an adaptation of Emily Brontë's *Wuthering Heights*.

Seijun Suzuki, a comedy and action-film director for Nikkatsu, produced a number of youth films (*seishuneiga*), such as *Kanto Wanderer* (*Kanto mushuku*, 1963), *Our Blood Won't Allow It* (*Oretachi no chi ga yuru sanai*, 1964), and *Tokyo Drifter* (*Tokyo nagaremono*, 1966), that contained New Wave themes, but his major contributions to the movement were *Elegy to Violence/The Born Fighter* (*Kenka ereiji*, 1966), scripted by Kaneto Shindo, about a fighting youth from the provinces who becomes ensnared in the politics of the 1936 attempted coup d'état; and *Branded to Kill* (*Koroshi no rakuin*, 1967), a *yakuza* film (see below) whose labyrinthine plot and elliptical narrative structure confused audiences and contributed to Suzuki's firing by Nikkatsu. After this, Suzuki became a prolific director of "pink" films (see below), although his two beautifully decadent ghost films *Zigeunerweisen* (1980) and *Heat Shimmer Theater* (*Kageroza*, 1981), both independently produced, were critically acclaimed in the early 1980s.

At the same time, the former Nikkatsu contract director and Marxist radical Koji Wakamatsu made a successful bid to raise the pink film to the level of New Wave abstraction with his *Secret Act inside Walls* (*Kabe no naka himegoto*, 1965), for which he was fired from Nikkatsu, and his low-budget, independently produced *The Embryo Hunts in Secret* (*Taiji ga mitsuryo suru toki*, 1966) and *Violated Angels/Violated Women in White* (*Okasareta byakuri*, 1967), which was inspired by the mass murder of nine nurses in Chicago in 1964. Wakamatsu also produced the bizarre *Go, Go Second Time Virgin* (*Yuke, yuke nidome no shojo*, 1969)—whose point of reference is the Tate-LaBianca murders committed by the Manson gang in the same year—and the revolutionary fantasy *The Ecstasy of Angels* (*Tenshi no kokotsu*, 1972). Wakamatsu directed an average of four 35mm features a year in the decade between 1964 and 1975 (most for his own thinly capitalized production company, Wakamatsu Productions), an output on a par with the 16mm/digital-video directors of the "new New Wave." Some of these were *jitsuro*—lurid but supposedly true accounts of sex crimes—yet all contain elements of style and theme that link them with the underground/avant-garde. He continued to make about a film a year in the 1980s and 1990s, turning from more conventional soft-core porn (*Pool without Water* [*Mizu no nai puuru*, 1982]) to hardboiled *yakuza-eiga* like *Ready to Shoot* (*Ware ni utsu yoi ari* [1990]) and *End of Our Own Real* (*Asu naki machikado* [1997]).

Another outstanding director of the New Wave is Shohei Imamura—*Pigs and Battleships* (*Buta to gunkan*, 1961); *Intentions of Murder/Unholy Desire* (*Akai satsui*, 1964); *The Insect Woman* (*Nippon konchuki*, 1964); *The Pornographer* (*Jinruigaku nyumon*, 1966); *A Man Vanishes* (*Ningen johatsu*, 1967); *The Profound Desire of the Gods/Kuragejima: Tales from a Southern Island* (*Kamkgami no fukaki yokubo*, 1968); *History of Postwar Japan as Told by a Bar Hostess* (*Nippon sengo-shi: Madamu Omboro no seikatsu*, 1970). The first four films, all photographed in high-contrast black and white by Shinsaku Himeda, deal, respectively, with the *yakuza* subculture living off the detritus of the American fleet in the Japanese port city of Yokusuka circa 1960; a housewife who becomes the willing victim and finally the accomplice of a rapist; a poor woman who achieves enormous success through prostitution in postwar Japan (her corruption clearly symbolizes that of her country during the same era); and a mild-mannered businessman who produces pornographic films to support his middle-class and classically Oedipal family. Characterized by a mixture of fiction and the documentary-like incrementation of sociological detail, and by a boldly experimental use of the anamorphic widescreen frame, Imamura's New Wave films have about them a kind of anthropological precision that prepared audiences for such essays in classical anthropology as *A Man Vanishes* and *The Profound Desire of the Gods*, the latter a narrative analysis of an incestuous family on a primitive southern island (the mythic origin of the story is an incestuous relationship between brother and sister gods).

A former assistant to Ozu, Imamura completely rejected his mentor's restrained camera style and worked mainly in documentary television during the 1970s (e.g., *History of Postwar Japan as Told by a Bar Hostess* [1970]; *The Making of a Prostitute* [*Karayuki-san*, 1975]), but emerged at the end of the decade as a truly major figure with *Vengeance Is Mine* (*Fukushu suruwa wareniari*, 1979). A relentless, semidocumentary account of an actual 78-day murder spree, the film refuses to judge either society, the criminal, or his victims. *Eijanaika* (1980) is a drama about the culture shock involved in the opening of Japan to the West after two hundred years of self-imposed isolation (the title—which means "Why Not?" or "What the Hell?"—derives from the rallying cry of the bloody anarchist riots of 1867, which explode at the film's conclusion). Imamura's *The Ballad of Narayama* (*Narayamabushi-ko*, 1983), based on a story by Shichiro Fukazawa about a people in a remote section of Japan who traditionally take their aged to a high mountaintop to die, won the Golden Palm at Cannes in the year of its release (a 1958 version by Keisuke Kinoshita

18.32 Shohei Imamura's *The Ballad of Narayama* (1983).

had adapted the narrative as if it were a *kabuki* play). And his work *The Pimp* (*Zegen*, 1987), which links the rising fortunes of a pimp with the success of Japan's military adventures in creating the Greater Southeast Asia Coprosperity Sphere prior to World War II, was also critically acclaimed. Imamura's own production company also helped to make Japan's most controversial film since the New Wave—*The Emperor's Naked Army Marches On* (*Hara Yuki yukite shingun* [Kazuo Hara, 1987]), a two-hour documentary portrait of Kenzo Okuzaki, an aging veteran who demands that Emperor Hirohito apologize publicly to the Japanese people for causing the horrors of World War II. More recently, Imamura has produced a restrained adaptation of Masuji Ibuse's novel on the atomic bombing of Hiroshima, *Black Rain* (*Kuroi ame*, 1989), which won the Technical Prize at Cannes. With *The Eel* (*Unagi*, 1997) Imamura won his second Palm d'Or at Cannes for a character study of crime, punishment, and redemption as they affect a white-collar worker who stabs his unfaithful wife and her lover to death in a fit of rage; after eight years in prison he is paroled to a Buddhist priest in a small village where he opens a barbershop, talks incessantly to his pet eel, and gradually reconnects with humanity. The meditative quality of *The Eel* extended to *Dr. Akagi* (*Kanzo sensei*, 1998), about a doctor researching a cure for hepatitis in a POW camp near the end of World War II, and to *Warm Water under a Red Bridge* (*Akai hashi no shita no nurui mizu*, 2001), which takes place in a small seaside town in which a man near the end of his social tether meets a woman with preternatural sexual powers.

But by far the most influential filmmaker of the Japanese New Wave is Nagisa Oshima, a militantly radical intellectual who was trained at Kyoto University in political history and law. He joined the Shochiku studios as a scriptwriter in 1955 and began directing there in 1959. Among his earliest work is *Cruel Story of Youth* (*Seishun zankoku monogatari*, 1960), a virtual paradigm of the New Wave in its expressive use of color and widescreen composition to embody youthful rebellion through sex and violence. When one of Oshima's Shochiku films, *Night and Fog in Japan* (*Nihon no yoru to kiri*, 1960), was withdrawn for political reasons, he left the studio to form his own production company, Sozosha (Creation), which is still in operation. Much of his early work was in the genre of the *yakuza-eiga*, or contemporary gangster film. It tended to be violent, sexually explicit, and politi-

18.33 New Wave paradigm: Nagisa Oshima's *Cruel Story of Youth* (1960).

cally radical in that Oshima's criminals were figures in open revolt against modern Japanese society. The malaise of this society was to become Oshima's overriding theme, making him the first major postwar director to concentrate solely on the problems of being Japanese in the present. Appropriately, Oshima rejected his culture's cinematic past as well as its historical one, so that even his earliest films reveal the influence of the French New Wave rather than that of his great Japanese predecessors. The use of handheld cameras, *cinéma vérité* shooting techniques, and on-location sound recording is typical of Oshima's early work, although all of his films since 1960 have been made in widescreen and color. By the late 1960s Oshima had moved away from narrative, and the influence of Godard and the Yugoslav avant-gardist Dušan Makavejev became apparent in his blending of fantasy and reality and in his use of printed chapter titles, voice-over narration, extreme long shots, and audience-alienation effects. As the Japanese critic Hideo Osabe puts it, the films of Oshima have become "provocations directed at the spectators." Like Godard's, Oshima's films are audiovisual polemics designed to generate in the audience indignation and rebellion at the state of contemporary society.

Japanese society is one in which massive industrialization, urbanization, and technocratization have accelerated social change and caused the disintegration of traditional (and, in Japan's case, centuries-old) values without offering anything in their place. As Oshima sees it in films like *Death by Hanging* (*Koshikei*, 1969), *The Diary of a Shinjuku Thief* (*Shinjuku dorobo nikki*, 1969), *Boy* (*Shonen*, 1969), *The Man Who Left His Will on Film* (*Tokyo senso*

18.34 *The Man Who Left His Will on Film* (Nagisa Oshima, 1970).

sengo hiwa, 1970), and *The Ceremony* (*Gishiki*, 1972), the Japanese family structure so dear to Ozu has degenerated into a series of empty rituals; the giant corporations have destroyed the physical and psychological environment of the entire country; Japan's cities are sinks of pollution, overcrowding, and violent crime. In response, the Japanese state has become feudal once more—authoritarian, imperialistic, racist, and politically repressive. For Oshima, then, Japan is in the midst of a nightmare of social disorder that increasingly courts a rebirth of fascism. His films are works of aggressive, often violent, social protest. Frequently, the graphic, even pornographic, depiction of sex becomes a vehicle for his radical indictment of modern, technocratized Japan, as vividly demonstrated in his films of the late 1970s, *In the Realm of the Senses/Empire of the Senses* (*Ai no corrida*, 1976) and *In the Realm of Passion/Empire of Passion* (*Ai no borei*, 1978). *In the Realm of the Senses*, for example, is based on the true story

of a former geisha, Abe Sada, who sexually mutilated her lover during the 1930s; and it contains scenes of full frontal nudity and genital exposure explicitly forbidden by Japanese censorship laws.[8] (For this reason, the film's negative could not be processed in Japanese labs, and even as late as 2002 it could not be officially shown in Japan in unexpurgated form.) Ultimately, ideas are more important to Oshima than visual surfaces, and he is frequently accused of having no consistent style. But critics often confuse inconsistency with versatility, and there can be no question that Oshima the social critic is also a great film artist and one of the foremost innovators of the international cinema—a reputation confirmed in the 1980s by *Merry Christmas, Mr. Lawrence* (1983), depicting the tragic results of cultural ambivalence between East and West in a Japanese prisoner-of-war camp on Java during World War II, and *Max, mon amour* (*Max, My Love*, 1986), a Buñuelian satire shot in Paris by Raoul Coutard about a British diplomat's wife who has an affair with a chimpanzee. After a hiatus of thirteen years, during which he directed a handful of documentaries (e.g., *100 Years of Japanese Cinema*, 1995), Oshima returned to feature filmmaking in 2000 with *Taboo* (*Gohatto*), a transgressive and subversive tale of homoerotic longing among the Shinsengumi *samurai* at the end of the shogunate in 1865 Kyoto.

JAPANESE FILMMAKING AFTER THE NEW WAVE

Of the post–New Wave generation, several filmmakers have already achieved international profiles, including Yoshimitsu Morita (b. 1950), Kohei Oguri (b. 1945), Mitsuo Yanagimachi (b. 1944), Shinji Somai (1948–2001), Ishii Sogo (b. Toshihiro Ishii, 1957), Juzo Itami (1933–1997), Takeshi Kitano (b. 1947), and Kiyoshi Kurosawa (b. 1955). Morita became popular for cheaply made,

---

8. Notoriously hypocritical, these laws have generally allowed perverse displays of sexual brutality and torture as well as most forms of nudity—short of genital exposure or depiction of pubic hair. Film censorship in Japan is the province of Eirin (where *ei* is short for "film," and *rin* for "ethics"), or the Eiga rinri kanri inkai (Administration Commission of the Motion Picture Code of Ethics), originally formed by the six major studios in 1949. Censorship can take the form of banning, editing, or the optical distortion of offending images (i.e., fogging). The story of Abe Sada has been told in at least two other films: Noboru Tanaka's *Nikku roman porno* masterpiece *The True Story of Abe Sada* (*Jitsuroku Abe Sada*, 1975) and Nobuhiko Obayashi's *Sada* (1998).

breezy comedies such as *Something Like That* (*No yona-mono*, 1981) and *Boys and Girls* (*Boizu & gaaruzo*, 1982), but achieved his first major critical acclaim for *The Family Game* (*Kazoku gemu*, 1983)—a hilarious satire on contemporary Japanese family life and Ozu-style "home drama" films, as well as on the nation's educational system. Morita followed with *And Then* (*Sorekara*, 1986), an uncharacteristically serious adaptation of a period novel set in 1909. Since then, he has made films in a wide variety of genres—family melodrama (*The Hours of Wedlock* [*Uhoho tankentai*, 1987]), social and political satire (*All for Business's Sake* [*Sorobanzuku*, 1987]; *Bakayaroo!—Watakushi, Okotteimasu* [*You Bloody Fool!—I'm Angry*, 1988]), romantic comedy (*Last Christmas* [*Mirai no omiode*, 1992]; *Haru* [1996]), romantic tragedy (*Lost Paradise* [*Shitsurakuen*, 1997]), psychological mystery-thriller (*Keiho* [*39 keiho dai sanjukyu jo*, 1998]), horror (*Kuroi ie* [*The Black House*, 1999]), and comic fantasy (*Colorful* [2000]). Even though Morita's work has entered the mainstream, it is still stylistically challenging.

Kohei Oguri achieved something of a coup when his first feature, *Muddy River* (*Doro no kawa*, 1981), was produced and distributed privately before being picked up by Toei and winning numerous Japanese awards as well as an Oscar nomination and the silver prize at Moscow. This unsentimental black-and-white film depicts the friendship between two little boys of the underclass in 1956 Osaka, and it harks back in both form and content to the postwar humanism of Mizoguchi and Ozu. Four years in production, Oguri's second feature, *For Kayako* (*Kayako no tameni*, 1985), is a visually exquisite, formally stylized story set in 1957 of a love affair between a Korean man (Koreans are notoriously subjected to racial discrimination in Japan) and a Japanese woman. *Sting of Death* (*Shi no toge*, 1990), a study of the trauma of postwar alienation on a young married couple, won both the Grand Prix du Jury and the FIPRESCI critics award at Cannes in the year of its release, bringing Oguri's work to international prominence. Oguri made only one other film during the 1990s, *Sleeping Man* (*Nemuru otoko*, 1996), which is constructed as a series of intricately interwoven stories and memories surrounding the inhabitants of an idyllic region in the mountains of Japan, gorgeously photographed by Osamu Maruike.

The focus of Mitsuo Yanagimachi's work to date has been the way in which rapid technological modernization has alienated the Japanese from nature, a major theme in a society that still practices a form of pantheism, which is associated with the religion of Shinto. His *A Nineteen Year Old's Map* (*Jukyusai no chizu*, 1979) concerns a deracinated student who wages displaced guerrilla warfare against urban chaos through his paper route, while *Farewell to the Land* (*Saraba itoshiki daichi*, 1982) is about a disaffected truck driver who descends to drug abuse and murder in reaction to the sterile industrial landscape that surrounds him. But Yanagimachi received worldwide recognition for *Fire Festival* (*Himatsuri*, 1985), based on an actual mass murder that occurred in 1980 in the Kumano region of southern Japan. There, in an area sacred to Shinto, where gods are believed to occupy both the mountains and the sea, land developers are attempting to build a tourist resort and marine park; the protagonist, a forty-year-old woodcutter and avid Shintoist, attempts to fight modernization of the region and, failing that, commits the ultimate self-declarative act by killing his family and himself with a shotgun. Since *Fire Festival*, Yanagimachi has turned his attention to the Chinese. *Shadow of China* (1991), shot on location by Toyomichi Kurita (*Cookie's Fortune* [1999]; *Gohatto* [1999]), is about a student dissident who escapes the mainland to Hong Kong and becomes a powerful businessman. In *About Love, Tokyo* (*Ai ni tsuite, Tokyo*, 1992), an oppressed Chinese student studying in Tokyo runs afoul of a *yakuza* boss; and *The Wandering Peddlers* (*Tabisuru pao-jiang-hu*, 1995) is a Japanese-Taiwanese coproduction about a family of itinerant Chinese snake-oil peddlers and their attempts to survive in the modern world.

Shinji Somai was an assistant director under the old studio system at Nikkatsu, where he worked on *roman pornos* before making his first features, which were fast-paced teen comedies (e.g., *The Hip Couple* [*Tonda kappuru*, 1980]; *School Uniforms and Machine Guns* [*Serafuku to kikanju*, 1981]; *P. P. Rider* [*Shonben rider*, 1983]). Somai's first serious film was *The Big Catch* (*Gyoei no mure*, 1983), a documentary-style account of the life and work of an uncompromising Pacific-coast tuna fisherman that employs extremely long takes. But his *Typhoon Club* (*Taifu kurubu*, 1984) brought him instant success when it shared the prize for the Young Cinema competition at the Tokyo International Festival for that year with Péter Gothár's *Time Stands Still* and Ali Özgentürk's *Horse, My Horse*. Characterized, like his earlier film, by magnificently revealing sequence shots,

Typhoon Club concerns four junior-high-school students who are stranded inside their school building by a seasonal storm that becomes for each of them a major rite of passage. Somai made eight more films before his early death, some of them shot very quickly (*Love Hotel* [1985] reportedly in ten days) on interconnected sets built on soundstages (e.g., *Stepchildren/Snowflakes* [*Yuki no dansho—jonetsu*, 1985]), but all of them relying on extended takes and disruptive tracking shots in lieu of narrative montage. The most impressive are *Moving* (*Ohikkoshi*, 1993), about a young woman's coming of age as she simultaneously comes to terms with her parent's divorce, which was favorably noticed at Cannes; and *Wait and See* (*Ah haru*, 1998), in which a vagrant poses as a long-lost patriarch and wins a bourgeois family's heart; this film won the International Critics prize at the 1999 Berlin Festival.

Ishii Sogo has parallel careers making films and directing rock videos and commercials. He produced several chaotic gang-war fantasies—*Crazy Thunder Road* (*Kuruizaki Thunder Road*, 1980); *Burst City* (*Bakuretsu toshi*, 1981)—before scoring both commercially and critically with *The Crazy Family* (*Gyakufunsha-kazou* [literally, "*Back-Jet Family*," 1987]), a ferocious satire on contemporary Japanese consumerism. Sogo next directed a pair of technically brilliant crime thrillers—*Angel Dust* (*Enjeru dasuto*, 1994) involves a series of subway murders solved by a psychiatrist, whereas *Labyrinth of Dreams* (*Yume no ginga*, 1997) is about a Tokyo bus conductor who falls in love with a serial killer. Science fiction (*August in the Water* [*Mizu no naka no hachigatsu*, 1995]) and a twelfth-century folk legend (*Gojoe senki*, 2000) required a more conventional approach of the director, but in *Electric Dragon 80,000 V* (2001) Sogo returned to his cyberpunk roots in a hyperkinetic action film about the rivalry between two young men in Tokyo who have been endowed with the power to command high-voltage electricity.

Certainly the best known of the post–New Wave directors is Juzo Itami, a former actor who directed his first film at the age of fifty—the black comedy *The Funeral* (*Ososhiki*, 1984), which won a Japanese Academy Award for Best Picture and numerous festival prizes for its mordantly hilarious depiction of how the rising middle class handles one of its culture's most elaborate, expensive, and important social rituals. Itami, who also wrote and produced his own work, continued in this vein with *Tampopo* (1986), a comic film about sex, food, and eating, and *A Taxing Woman* (*Marusa no onna*, 1987), a satire on the intricacies of the Japanese tax system. More recently, Itami directed the comedies *The Gangster's Moll* (*Minbo-no onna*, 1992) and *The Last Dance* (*Daibyonin*, 1993), the former dealing with a *yakuza* extortion ring and the latter with the vagaries of contemporary hospitalization based on Itami's own experience (Itami's face and neck were slashed by *yakuza* thugs in retaliation for the critique of *Minbo-no onna*). Itami's last films were increasingly autobiographical—e.g., *The Last Dance* (*Daibyonin*, 1993), highly reminiscent of Kurosawa's *Ikiru*, is about a middle-aged film director and actor who is dying of stomach cancer while having an affair with his leading lady; *Marutai no onna* (1997) is a satire about an actress (played by Nobuko Miyamoto, Itami's

18.35 *Angel Dust* (Ishii Sogo [Toshishiro Ishii], 1994): Kaho Minami starring as Setsuko Suma, a police psychiatrist and homicide investigator who believes that mysterious serial killings on the Tokyo subway are the work of a religious cult "reprogrammer."

18.36 Juzo Itami's *Tampopo* (1986): Ken Watanabe, Ryutaro Otomo.

18.37 *Boiling Point* (Takeshi Kitano, 1990): Takeshi Kitano (credited as "Beat" Takeshi) as a renegade gangster paying off his debt to the Mob with a submachine gun concealed inside a bouquet of tropical flowers.

wife and the star of all of his films) who identifies the murderer of a lawyer investigating members of a terroristic doomsday cult (modeled on the Aum Shinnkyo sect responsible for releasing deadly nerve gas in the Tokyo subway in 1995) and becomes the target of their vengeance, which takes the form of exposing her secret love affair to the tabloid press. Itami committed suicide in late 1997, apparently to avoid a similar kind of exposure.

Takeshi Kitano (b. 1947) is another actor who turned to writing and directing in mid-career. Popularly known as "Beat" Takeshi (owing to the fact that he was one of "The Two Beats" in a popular comedy duo in the early 1970s), Kitano began directing with *Violent Cop* (Japanese title: *Sono otoko, kyobo hi tsuki* [*Warning: This Man Is Wild*, 1989]), a brutal gangster film that he took over from *yakuza* veteran Kinji Fukasaku (see below) and turned into an oddly meditative work. *Violent Cop*, in fact, inaugurated a style and a theme that Kitano would extend through a number of similar works—*Boiling Point* (*3–4x jugatsu* [1990]), *Sonatine* (1993), *Fireworks* (Japanese title: *Hana-bi* [1997]; winner of the Golden Lion at the Venice Festival), and *Brother* (2000; coproduced with the United Kingdom)—in which he also starred. Although Kitano has worked in other genres (e.g., the coming-of-age film *Kids Return* [1996]), his signature films are crime melodramas in which savage violence is randomly juxtaposed with scenes of Zenlike calm sustained through restrained dialogue and a minimalist camera style. As the star of these films, Kitano has created an antiheroic persona, whether criminal or cop, who is so inured to violence that he experiences it with a weariness bordering on ennui. Kitano's impassivity combines with deadpan humor and mordant wit to produce films that are fundamentally morality plays, despite their copious bloodletting. Intricately structured yet compositionally severe—at times even static—they suggest the sensibility of Ozu negotiating the world of Quentin Tarantino.

For better or worse, most of the above-named post–New Wave directors produced their work for major studios or for newly formed independent companies like Tanaka Promotions and Kinema Tokyo (both of which went out of business in 1993). Even Takeshi Kitano's first four films were produced by Shochiku until he formed his own production company after *Sonatine*. During the 1990s, however, a so-called "new Japanese New Wave" arose that circumvented the major studios and distributors to make features on budgets ranging from $100,000 to $1 million, often for distribution to the V-Cine (direct to video) market as well as to theaters. These new directors effectively set up shop for themselves and in the process achieved an unprecedented degree of artistic freedom, even to the point of establishing their own film schools (e.g., Eiga Bi Gakko, founded by producer Kenzo Horikoshi in Tokyo in 1998). Whereas the mainstream is currently dominated by foreign (mainly American) product and *anime,* the new New Wave distribution network is dominated by low-budget thrillers made by directors who typically produce three to five features a year, shooting on 16mm and digital video as well as 35mm. The most prominent among them is writer/director Kiyoshi Kuro-sawa (b. 1955; no relation to Akira Kurosawa), who studied film at Rikkyo University under the noted theoretician Shigehiko Hasumi and began his career as a Super 8 avant-garde experimentalist. After making several 16mm genre films that showed the influence of Godard (including the philosophical *pinku* comedy *The Excitement of the Do-Re-Me-Fa Girl* [*Do-re-me-fa musume no chi wa sawaju*, 1985), Kurosawa scored a critical and commercial hit with *Cure* (*Kyua*, 1997), a moody, supernatural police thriller that poses questions about the nature of postmodern identity. While continuing to make *films noir* on 16mm for video release (e.g., *The Revenge—A Scar That Never Fades* [1997]), Kurosawa turned his attention increasingly to 35mm allegorical techno-horror in features like *Charisma* (*Karisuma* [1999]), *Seance* (*Korei* [2000]), and *Kaïo* (*Pulse*, 2001). In the latter, for example, a series of mysterious disappearances leads to the revelation that computer users all over the world are being absorbed progressively into the internet through a series of "forbidden rooms," which function as portals between the world of the living and the dead.

Philosophically inflected horror that begins as graphic exploitation and takes an unexpectedly subtle metaphysical twist has, in fact, become the métier of the "new New Wave," in the same way that the *pinku-eiga* was the industry entrée for New Wave directors like Wakamatsu and Masumura (although porn and ultraviolent *yakuza* fare remain popular exploitation genres in Japan). Some key players here are actor-director Shinya Tsukamoto (b. 1960), whose 16mm *Tetsuo: The Iron Man* (1989) and its higher-budget sequel *Tetsuo II: Body Hammer* (1992) achieved a level of urban paranoia and body horror worthy of David Cronenberg. Working not only as star and director but also as his own cinematographer and editor, Tsukamoto continued his look at the modern urban nightmare in *Tokyo Fist* (1995) and *Bullet Ballet* (1998), as well as in the Kubrickian gothic thriller *Gemini* (Japanese title: *Soseiji* [*The Twins*, 1999]). The same pervasive sense of doom pervades the *Evil Dead Trap* films of Toshiharu Ikeda (*Shiryo no wana* [1988] and *Shiryo no wana: Chigireta ai no satsujin* [1993]). These two films, together with the second film in the series *Shiryo no wana 2: Hideki* (Izo Hashimoto, 1991), were written by Takashi Ishii (b. 1946), who is most famous for directing films in Nikkatsu's "Angel Guts" series, a cycle of surrealistic rape-revenge thrillers based on Takashi's own adult *manga* of the same

18.38 *Tetsuo: The Iron Man* (Shinya Tsukamoto, 1989): Tomoroh Taguchi as the salaryman who undergoes a metamorphosis when he begins to exfoliate chunks of scrap metal from every part of his body, becoming in the process a kind of postindustrial hybrid of man and machine.

title originally published in 1973 (e.g., *Tenshi no harawata: Akai memai* [1988]; *Tenshi no harawata; akai senko* [1994]);[9] he is also responsible for the violent gangster epics *Gonin* (1995) and *Kuro no tenshi, vols. 1 and 2* [*Black Angel 1* and *2*, 1997, 1999), and for the erotic thriller *Freeze Me* (2000). Other notable "new New Wave" Japanese horror films are *Organ* (1996), about a ring of human organ thieves, directed by the former actress and cinematographer Kei Fujiwara, the films in Katsuya Matsumura's controversial *All Night Long* rape-revenge series (*Ooru naito rongu* [1992]; *Ooru naito rongu 2: Sanji* [1995]; and *Ooru naito rongu 3: Saishuu-sho* [1996]), and the films in Hideo Nakata's *Ring* series (*Ring* [*Ringu*, 1998]; *Ring 2* [1999]), whose phenomenal popularity gave rise to a Hollywood-style franchise of multiple sequels and prequels.[1] *Ring*'s conceit of a murderous spirit residing in videotape that kills all who watch it was deliberately evocative of the videotaped torture murders in the *Evil Dead*

---

9. There are nine entries in the "Angel Guts" series produced by Nikkatsu between 1978 and 1995, all of which were based on characters created by Takashi Ishii. Ishii directed only the last three in the series; others were directed by Toshiharu Ikeda, Noboru Tanaka, and several lesser lights.

1. It also gave rise to a $45-million Hollywood remake, *The Ring* (Gore Verbinski, 2002), that grossed $129 million in the United States alone; the film had erlier been remade in Korea as *Ring* (Dong-bin Kim, 1999).

18.39 *Ringu* (Hideo Nakata, 1998): an image of horror from one of the most popular horror films ever made in Japan, which generated several domestic sequels and a television series as well as Korean and American remakes.

derous innkeepers and the zombies they create through their murders. After directing a series of brooding *yakuza* films (*Helpless* [1996], *Two Punks* [*Tsumetai chi*, 1997], *Wild Life* [1997], Shinji Aoyama (b. 1964) made *EM/ Embalming* (1999), a horror film about a ring of illicit body-parts dealers that seems intent upon deconstructing the conventions of the genre, as if to comment on the current tendency in Japanese cinema. One of the new New Wave's leading lights, Aoyama won the International Critics Award at Cannes for *Eureka* in 2000. This starkly lyrical examination of the aftermath of a terroristic bus hijacking in rural Kyushi and its impact upon the survivors runs nearly four hours and was shot in black-and-white CinemaScope by the gifted director of photography Masaki Tamura, recalling the sweeping widescreen compositions of second postwar-generation directors like Kobayashi and Shindo. Hirozaku Kore-Eda (b. 1962) was trained in documentary production, and his first dramatic feature, *Maboroshi no hikari* (*Illusory Light*), won multiple awards at the 1995 Venice International Film Festival. This restrained but deeply moving account of a young woman's coming to terms with her husband's apparent suicide was shot on location on the rugged Noto peninsula by Masao Nakabori, and many critics compared it stylistically to the work of Ozu and the Taiwanese master Huo Hsiao-hsien. Kore-Eda infused *After Life* (also known as *Wonderful Life* [*Wandafuru raifu*, 1998]) with the same transcendental sensibility, but with a documentary twist: in the five months before production, he sent teams of assistants out all over Japan to capture on video the "best memories" of some 500 elderly people, who he then used to cast the film, a fantasy in which twenty-two of the newly

Trap films. So, in a different way was *Audition* (*Odishon* [1999]) by the frenetically prolific New Waver Takashi Miike (b. 1960), who directed twenty-four features and television miniseries between 1999 and 2002. This anti-traditional narrative of a romantic relationship that descends abruptly into a horrendously sadistic nightmare shocked Western audiences at the same time it picked up numerous festival awards and critical accolades; for Japanese audiences, *Audition* had the additional frisson of reversing the traditional sex roles of its sadoerotic encounters. Other remarkable Miike works include the ultraviolent *yakuza* films *Fudoh: The New Generation* (*Gokudo sengokushi: Fudo* [1996]), *Dead or Alive 2* (2000), and *City of Lost Souls* (*Hyoryuu-gai* [2000]), as well as *The Happiness of the Katakuris* (*Katakuri-ke no kofuku* [2001]), a musical comedy populated by a family of mur-

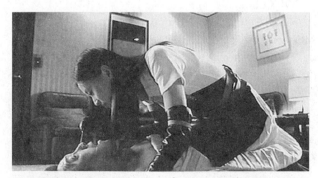

18.40 *Audition* (Takashi Miike, 1999): Ryo Ishibashi, as Aoyama, about to have an eyeball acupunctured by his bride-to-be (Eihi Shiina, as Asami).

18.41 *Maborosh no hikarii* (Hirozaku Kore-Eda, 1995): an Ozu-like composition from a film about the emotional burden of the past and the "sympathetic sadness" of everyday life.

dead at a way station between life and death are asked to re-create a favorite memory to carry with them into the afterlife. The staff at the way station turns these memories into films, and *After Life* becomes a complex meditation on the subjective construction of memory and on the role of the cinema in preserving it. In *Distance* (2001), yet another meditation on death, time, and memory, Kore-Eda explored the relationship among four people from different walks of life united in a common bond of grief— all have lost relatives who were members of an Aum Shinn-rikyo–like cult responsible for a terror attack on the Tokyo water supply. Other noteworthy new directors associated with the cutting edge in Japanese cinema are Nobuhiro Suwa (b. 1960—*M/Other* [1999]; *H Story* [2001]), Junji Sakamoto (b. 1954—*Face* [*Kao*, 2000]); Hisayasu Sato (b. 1959—*Splatter: Naked Blood* [*Megyaku: Akuma no yoro-kobi*, 1996]); Shunji Iwai (b. 1963—*Love Letter* [1995]; *Swallowtail* [1996]; *All about Lily Chou-Chou* [2001]); Rokuro Mochizuki (b. 1957—*Onibi: The Fire Within* [1997]; *A Yakuza in Love* [Japanese title: *Koi gokudo*, 1997]); Atsushi Muroga (*Score* [1995]; *Junk* [Japanese title: *Shiryour gari*, 1999]); and Higuchinsky (b. Akihiro Higuchi, 1969—*Uzumaki* [*Whirpool/Spiral*, 2000]).

DECLINE OF THE STUDIOS

The rise of independent production and the New Wave was a consequence of the economic decline of the Japanese studio system. Multiple-channel color television (*terebi*) was introduced in Japan in 1960, and ever since that time there has been a steady drop in film attendance (from 1 billion admissions in 1960, for example, to 150 million in 1980), accelerated by the rise of home video, paralleling the experience of the West. The studios had begun their long, slow decline as early as 1961, when Shintoho went bankrupt; it was followed by Daiei in 1971, the same year that Nikkatsu, Japan's oldest studio, turned exclusively to the production of soft-core pornography, known as *roman porno* (also, "eroduction," or "pink film" [*pinku-eiga*]—see below). The remaining three studios— Toei, Toho, and Shochiku—turned increasingly to the production of exploitative genre films.

The mid-1960s, in fact, saw the rise of two new domestic exploitation genres that together came to constitute the industry mainstay for the next twenty years. The first was the *yakuza-eiga*, or contemporary gangster film, which was pioneered by Toei but quickly became a staple genre, replacing the *samurai* film in popularity among Japanese audiences. The *yakuza* is in fact a kind of latter-day *samurai*, an outlaw swordsman in the urban jungle who nevertheless lives by a traditional code; this character type possesses considerable symbolic appeal for audiences whose traditional values have been eroded by a repressive technocracy. Moreover, *yakuza* films are invariably brutal and bloody, and their sensational violence clearly provide audiences with a socially acceptable channel for their hostility and aggression—much of it directed toward society itself. In 1974, some one hundred *yakuza* films were produced by the Japanese studios, which constituted more than a third of the industry's output for that year.

The second exploitation genre to sweep Japan, the "eroduction," or "pink film" (*pinku-eiga*), was a feature-length sex film with a high content of sadism. (Censorship in any form was illegal in Japan from 1966 to 1972, when these films were popularized.) The first such film produced by a major studio was Shochiku's *Daydream* (*Haku-jitsumu*, 1964), directed by Tetsuji Takechi, which presented its sadistic sex scenes as part of a hallucination experienced by a young man under anesthesia in a dentist's chair. Takechi then made the far more controversial *Kuroi yuki* (*Black Snow*, 1965) for Nikkatsu, which used violent, nude rape scenes as a vehicle for anti-Americanism (the rapists are GIs) and was prosecuted, unsuccessfully, for obscenity. This was the beginning of a close association between political commentary and erotic representation in the work of the Japanese New Wave (e.g., Wakamatsu's *Violated Angels* [1967]; Imamura's *The Pornographers* [1966]; Hani's *Inferno of First Love* [1968]), Shindo's *Heatwave Island* [*Kagerou*, 1969], Yoshida's *Eros + Massacre* [1969], Oshima's *Empire of the Senses* [1976], etc.); and it marked a change in direction for Nikkatsu, which would soon turn its attention entirely to the production of "artistic" pink films, which it marketed as *roman porno* ("romantic pornography").[2] Starting with Shogoro Nishimura's *Apartment Wife: Affair in the Afternoon* (*Danchizuma hirusagari no joji*) in 1971, Nikkatsu made hundreds of

---

2. In October 1971, with competition from television and Hollywood at an all-time high, Nikkatsu announced that it would abandon its signature action genres in order to concentrate on upscale *pinku-eiga*, which it branded *Nikku roman porno* ("Nikkatsu romance pornogra-

18.42 *Female Convict Scorpion* (Shunya Ito, 1972): exploitation as art in Toei's "pinky violence" product line; Meiko Kaji is "Scorpion" in the second of six films based on a popular adult *manga* series.

such films, using in-house production teams guided by young contract directors, many of whom would become important mainstream figures after their apprentice work in *roman porno* (very much as young talent rose from exploitation genres like horror, science fiction, and biker films in the West—e.g., the youth programmers produced by Roger Corman's unit during the 1950s and early 1960s at AIP). Other studios followed Nikkatsu's lead—Toei, for example, offering its so-called "pinky violence" line (e.g., Shunya Ito's *Female Convict Scorpion* [*Joshu sasori*, 1972] trilogy), which subdivided product into the *shigeki rosen* ("sensational line"), *ijoseiai rosen* ("abnormal line"), and *harenchi rosen* ("shameless line")—and by the mid-1970s, the Japanese film industry was producing more pink films than any other kind.

In fact, between 1965 and 1975 the Japanese film industry devoted over 50 percent of its total output to *yakuza-eiga* and eroductions, producing some 1,600 of these popular genre films in a single decade. The *yakuza* film remained a staple theatrical genre well into the 1990s—as practiced, e.g., by Takeshi Kitano (*Sonatine* [1993]), Rokuro Mochizuki (*Another Lonely Hitman* [*Shin kanashiki hittoman*, 1995]), Sadao Nakajima (*Gokudo no onnatachi: kejime* [*Gang Wives: Decision*, 1998]),

Kinji Fukasaku (*Omocha* [also known as *The Geisha House*, 1999]), Ikuo Sekimoto (*Zankyo* [also known as *Remains of Chivalry*, 1999]), and others—but, as with sexploitation and adult hardcore films in the West, the pink film was rendered obsolete in the 1980s by home video recording, in which the Japanese took an early and commanding lead (the Sony Corporation having

phy"), and from 1971 to 1982, when competition from the adult video industry forced another change of direction, the studio produced little else. Nikkatsu was thus the first and only major studio in the history of the cinema to devote itself exclusively to the production of self-proclaimed pornography (although, since Japanese cultural and legal standards forbade the depiction of full frontal nudity or genitalia, "erotica" is probably a better English-language description of *roman porno* than "pornography"; the first Japanese mainstream film to show full frontal nudity was Toshiharu Ikeda's *Kagi* [1997], the fourth version of Junichiro Tanizaki's novel *The Key*). Nikkatsu offered a full pink product line, with such subgenres as "Best SM" and "Violent Pink" for specialized tastes. At least two Nikkatsu *roman porno* directors became important figures during this time—Noboru Tanaka (1937–1991), who refined the technique of the self-reflexively voyeuristic camera in films like *A Woman Called Sada Abe* (Japanese title: *Jitsuroku Abe Sada* [1975], from the same source as Oshima's *In the Realm of the Senses* [1975]), and Tatsumi Kumashiro (1927–1995), whose award-winning *Woman with Red Hair* (*Akai kami no onna* [1979]) is considered to be the best *Nikku roman porno* film the studio ever produced.

invented the VCR and dominated its international diffusion). As pornographic "AV" ("adult video") rose, Nikkatsu saw its own fortunes decline so that it was forced to declare bankruptcy in 1993. But the sadoerotic component in Japanese cinema remained strong in pornographic animated features (*hentai anime*) that adapt *ero-manga* comics like *Urotsukidoji* (also known as *Legend of the Overfiend* [Hideki Takayama, 1987]) and *La Blue Girl* (Raizo Kitakawa and Kan Fukumoto, 1992), both based on the work of popular *manga*[3] artist Toshio Maeda.

The box-office success of Fox's *Star Wars* (George Lucas, 1977) and Columbia's *Close Encounters of the Third Kind* (Steven Spielberg, 1977) in Japan led to a glut of cheaply produced imitations, such as Toho's *War in Space* (*Wakusei daisenso* [Jun Fukuda, 1977]) and Toei's *Message from Space* (*Uchu kara no messeji* [Kinji Fukasaku, 1978]), which recycled the creaky special-effects techniques of 1950s monster films to the credit of neither. By the mid-1980s, Japan had become the single largest export market for the major American producer-distributors, with Columbia's *Ghostbusters* (Ivan Reitman, 1984) and Warners' *Gremlins* (Joe Dante, 1984) challenging the all-time box-office record set there by Universal's *E.T.: The Extra-Terrestrial* (Steven Spielberg) in 1982. Since then, the American market share has hovered at around 60 percent, and Japanese production levels have fallen from a high of 547 features in 1960 to 249 in 1998, of which only 65 were released by the remaining "Big Three" studios—Toho, Shochiku, and Toei. Moreover, in 1996 film attendance hit a historic low, falling below 120 million annual admissions for the first time.

Of the Big Three, during the 1980s and 1990s, Toho successfully revived its *Godzilla* franchise, scoring hits with *Godzilla 1985* (1984) and *Godzilla vs. Biollante* (1989), and releasing a new Godzilla picture for each New Year's holiday season from 1991 to 1995, ending the series with *Godzilla vs. Destoroyah*, after which the studio sold the international rights to the character to Tristar Pictures, producer of Roland Emmerich's CGI-intensive Hollywood version, *Godzilla* (1998). (Toho retained the domestic rights, however, and produced *Godzilla 2000* in 1999, when it became clear that Japanese audiences preferred the original.) Toho was also distributor for the independently produced comedies of Juzo Itami (see above) and the animated features of Hayao Miyazaki (e.g., *My Neigh-*

bor Totoro [*Tonari no Totoro*, 1989]; *Kiki's Delivery Service* [*Majo no takkyubin*, 1989]), who had founded the Studio Ghibli animation house with his frequent collaborator Isao Takahata (*Grave of the Fireflies* [*Hotaru no haka*, 1988]), in 1985. Often called "the Walt Disney of Japan," Miyazaki enjoyed both artistic and commercial success, culminating in his eco-fable *Princess Mononoke* (*Mononoke Hime*, 1997), which combined hand-drawn foreground animation with computer-generated backgrounds; it grossed $150 million domestically to break Japan's all-time box-office record, previously established by Spielberg's *E.T.: The Extra-Terrestrial* in 1982 (a distinction it subsequently shared with James Cameron's *Titanic* [1997], which edged *Princess Mononoke* out to become first later in the year). Shochiku was not so lucky with its signature franchise, the comic *Tora-san* series, which had starred TV comedian Kiyoshi Atsumi as a simple wandering peddler in 48 consecutive features. When Kyoshi died in 1996, there was no legitimate successor, and several attempted spin-offs failed, so that the studio faced restructuring when the century turned; in 2000, Shochiku was forced to sell its long-term base, Ofuna Studios near Tokyo, in order to cut costs. Toei, whose signature genre had been the *yakuza-eiga* (particularly the subgenre known as *ninkyo-eiga*, or "chivalry films") for more than thirty years, began releasing *yakuza* films straight to video as V-Cine ("video films") or OVs ("original videos") and relying on animation produced for television as its mainstay. It was particularly successful with the

---

3. *Manga* was originally a name given to a type of woodblock print meaning "irresponsible pictures." Going back to the seventeenth century, *makura-e* ("pillow pictures"), *ukiyo-e* ("pictures of the floating world"), *muzan-e* ("atrocity pictures"), and *shunga* (erotic "spring pictures") could all be categorized as *manga*. The modern sense of *manga* as comic book or graphic novel arose during the Occupation, when American comics flooded Japan and their popularity fueled a domestic production boom. Comic books, cheap to produce, distribute, and buy, were a perfect medium of entertainment/communication for Japan's decimated economy. Cinematic techniques, adapted from the American comic-book practice of sequential paneling, were rapidly adopted because they increased the speed of consumption and expanded the market. Conversely, this use of cinematic codes facilitates the adaptation of *manga* as films since they read like storyboards in continuity form. In the years following the Occupation, reading *manga* became one of the most popular forms of entertainment in Japan, offering everything from children's fairy tales to adult graphic novels (*gekiga*). Today, over 40 percent of all books and magazines sold in Japan are *manga*, an average annual consumption rate of 15 titles for every man, woman, and child in the country.

Dragon Ball (begun 1986), *Sailor Moon* (begun 1992), and *Neon Genesis Evangelion* series (begun 1995), all of which were released in some form theatrically and gained a huge following among *anime otaku* (avid fans).

Nevertheless, the Japanese film industry throughout the 1990s remained surprisingly strong. Despite an ongoing economic crisis, Japanese films continued to hold about a 32 percent domestic market share and support a healthy export market (witness, e.g., the international commercial

18.43 *Ghost in the Shell* **(Mamoru Oshii, 1995): a Tokyo street scene from Oshii's realistic animated techno-thriller, adapted from a** *manga* **by Masamune Shirow.**

success of Masayuki Suo's romantic comedy *Shall We Dance?* [1995]). In the early years of the twenty-first century, in fact, Japanese cinema enjoyed a wave of international popularity unprecedented since its postwar golden age, grounded not in live action film, but in *anime* (pronounced "ah-nee-may"), which by some accounts constitutes 60 percent of total annual production.[4] A Japanese coinage of the English "animation" (and sometimes popularly called "Japanimation"), *anime* combines elements of the Japanese pictorial tradition—silkscreen paintings, woodblock prints, *manga*—with American genre styles and character design. Although animation lies outside the original scope of this book, it has come to assume a new importance, thanks to the rise of computer graphics, which cannot be ignored. (Indeed, the whole of Chapter 21, "Hollywood Enters the Digital Domain," is about the type of computer animation that produces CGI.) Much *anime* is adapted from *manga* (Japanese comic books), but beyond that it can take many generic forms, from Disney-style family entertainment to sadoerotic pornography of the most perverse and violent kind. Its place in the history of narrative film has been assured by a number of *anime* features that approach or exceed their live-action counterparts in subtlety and sophistication of form—e.g., Katsuhiro Otomo's seminal tapestry of analog and digital animation *Akira* (1988),

Mamoru Oshii's futuristic action films *Patlabor* (1990) and *Ghost in the Shell* (*Kokaku kidotai*, 1995), Satoshi Kon's psychological thriller *Perfect Blue* (1997), HayaoMiyazaki's mythopoeic epic *Princess Mononoke* (1997), Hiroyuki Kitakubo's all-digital *Blood: The Last Vampire* (2000), and Rintaro's *Metropolis* (2001) based on Osamu Tezuka's 1949 *manga*, itself inspired by Fritz Lang's 1927 film—all evince a structural complexity, visual density, and richness of theme that gives them a legitimate place within the history of Japanese narrative film.

Looking back on that history, especially after World War II and the Occupation, it is hard not to notice that in general Japanese cinema is extremely violent. Even in the hands of classical first-generation directors like Akira Kurosawa, two of the nation's most popular mainstream genres—the *chanbara* and the *yakuza-eiga*—offered up graphic depictions of dismemberment, evisceration, and gore at least a decade before these displays became acceptable in the West. Then, too, of the second postwar generation and everything after, it is hard not to draw the conclusion reached by Olaf Moller

---

4. In the year 2000, e.g., there were over 2,000 *anime* titles licensed for U.S. video release.

of directors who have emerged since the 1980s: "Almost every notable recent mainstream filmmaker . . . started out in sex films, either directing (Mochizuki), screenwriting (Sakamoto, Takeshi Ishii, Aoyama), or assistant directing (like the late Somai)."[5] There is no precedent for this in the West—one could argue (speciously) for the greatness of a Russ Meyer or a Radley Metzger, but American and European directors who have emerged from soft-core pornography hardly constitute the backbone of their respective mainstream industries. But in Japan they do, in part at least because a disproportionate number of Japanese films are pornographic. According to *Wired* magazine, the Japanese adult-entertainment industry in the early twenty-first century produced more than 5,000 X-rated films a year, most of them on video.[6] So pornography is a good and available place for new directors to learn their craft and make their mark. Within the 35mm industry, the typical *pinku-eiga* is about an hour long, is budgeted at around $35,000, and takes five days to shoot with a skeletal crew—very much like the Hollywood B-film or Roger Corman drive-in quickie. This much is clear, but the question of why there is such a voluminous demand for pornography— and why so much of it has a perverse, sadomasochistic, and/or excessively violent cast—is one whose answer lies buried deep inside the cultural history of Japan. Because Japan experienced the greatest economic miracle of the postwar world, its relationship to that history is problematic: in exchange for its astonishing transformation from broken nation into economic powerhouse, it forfeited many things of cultural and spiritual value, and it remains deeply conflicted by this loss. During the postwar period 1951 to 1968, more than 400 Japanese films won prizes at foreign film festivals, yet, as Westerners, we should not assume that even now we know a great deal about Japan or its cinema. As Tadao Sato wrote of such directors as Yoshimitsu Morita, Kohei Oguri, Mitsuo Yanagimachi, and Shinji Somai: "[They] have the ability to depict the subtle uneasiness that underlies Japan's superficial stability. They capture clearly the various contradictions: the confidence and fear, the timidity and pride, the traditional values that were upset in social revolution that followed World War II, and the simultaneous questioning of modernization and Westernization. Their achievement lies in highlighting the deeper meanings of this confusion."

India

Because television did not exist as a mass medium in India until very recently, cinema is still the most popular form of entertainment. In the mid-1990s, the estimated weekly audience was 100 million for a population of nearly 900 million people,[7] and since 1971 India has been the largest film-producing nation in the world, accounting for fully one-fourth of the total global output each year. Its film industry—the country's tenth largest—is centered in Bombay, or "Bollywood" (for Hindi-language films, which account for about 25 percent of the total), with substantial production facilities in Calcutta (for Bengali-language films) and Madras (for Tamil, Kannada, and Telugu films). India produces between 800 and 900 features annually in more than 16 different languages. But 90 percent of these films are rigidly conventionalized musicals[8] and mythological romances made for consumption by a largely uneducated and impoverished domestic audience. (Significant export markets for Indian films also

---

5. Olaf Moller, "Shameless," *Film Comment* 38, 1 (January/February, 2002): 45.

6. "Ichiban: 10 Reasons Why the Sun Still Rises in the East," *Wired* (September 2001): 125.

7. As compared, e.g., with Japan's 1988 population of 126 million, the former USSR's of 285 million, and the United States' of 256 million. (India's population is exceeded only by that of mainland China, which in 1993 was 1.18 billion.) Introduced experimentally in 1959, Indian television was initially the province of the ruling elite, with less than one receiver available for every 700 people, until the government of Prime Minister Indira Gandhi ordered an extension of coverage to 70 percent of the population through the massive setting up of relay transmitters in 1984. Except for instructional programming brought to about one-fifth of the country's villages by direct satellite, however, Indian television remained urban-oriented and consumerist—which is to say, basically irrelevant to the vast majority of Indians. There were still only 3 million sets in use as the population approached 800 million in the late 1980s, but that number jumped to 30 million in the early 1990s, augmented by 10 million VCRs, and 4 million homes linked by cable to satellite dishes, ultimately yielding 90 million viewers per week. Today, the Indian cinema must compete not only with Doordarshan, the state-controlled television network, but with CNN, STAR-TV, ATN (Asian Television Network), and—almost unbelievably—MTV Europe.

8. The songs are not sung, but lip-synchronized by the stars of the films. The actual singers—professional voice doublers, known as "playback singers"—often become stars in their own right by recording songs from current films and marketing the disks with their pictures on the jackets. The composers also sell records on the strength of their names, often recording their own songs.

exist in Indonesia, Malaysia, and the United Kingdom, with smaller ones in Central Asia, the Middle East, and North Africa; these markets are sustained largely by an expatriate Indian population that numbered 15 million in 2000.) The formula has been described as "a star, six songs, and three dances"—usually about three hours long and in garish color. The Indian film industry is dominated today by a star system similar to that of Hollywood's early years, and the cinematic quality of the star vehicles matters less to Indian audiences than their value as spectacle—and those audiences are huge, accounting for more than 6 billion theater admissions per year. Despite these conditions, India has managed to produce some filmmakers of extraordinary talent in the past few decades and, in Satyajit Ray, at least one contemporary director of major international stature.

The current structure of the mainstream Indian commercial film industry—the only major industry in the world to develop under colonial rule—was engendered by the coming of sound. The audience for Indian silent cinema had consisted of hundreds of thousands of Indians, Burmese, and Ceylonese, who spoke many different tongues. But with sound, production was initially forced to fragment into regional language groups, of which, within India alone, there were no fewer than twenty-six, fifteen of them official ones. Even the majority Hindi-speaking market of 140 million people had at least three separate dialects. Under these conditions, the first talking feature, the Hindi music drama *Alam Ara* (*Beauty of the World* [Ardeshir Irani, 1931]), might well have plunged the industry into chaos. But instead the film was a huge success—as indeed were all early Indian sound films—heralding an unprecedented boom. The reason was grounded deep in Indian culture: sound permitted a revival of the vastly popular folk-music drama of the nineteenth century (itself based on centuries-old religious myths), which had been, literally, "all-talking, all-singing, all-dancing." (The Urdu Parsi theater of the 1930s played a pivotal role in this revival, wedding Indian content to the stage techniques of nineteenth-century British melodrama; many early Indian sound films were adapted from the theater's repertoire of "mythological" plays, and many Parsi theater performers migrated to the cinema.) Between 1931 and 1932, the resurgence of this form on the screen played an enormous role in winning widespread acceptance for the Indian sound film despite language barriers. Although

most Indian sound films were produced for domestic consumption and seemed to exist mainly as an excuse for musical performance and representation (as they still are and do), the Indian film industry nevertheless became a powerful entity during the transition to sound: from producing 28 films in 1931—23 of which were in Hindi, 3 in Bengali, and 1 each in Tamil and Telugu—it was producing 233 in 1935 in 10 different languages.

As in the United States, the rapid diffusion of sound in India helped to consolidate a studio system that was already in place. But World War II saw the steady rise of independent production, initially as a means of laundering black-market money. By the war's end, most of the major studios were bankrupt, and the vast majority of production was carried out on an ad hoc basis until the distributor-financiers reconsolidated in the mid-1960s. After national independence was granted in 1947 and Pakistan[9] was partitioned off in 1948, however, the film industry came under increasing government supervision through the promulgation of official censorship codes, and independent production became the order of the day. With the arrival of color in the industry, there was an

---

9. As a consequence of independence from British rule, Pakistan (meaning "Land of the Pure") was created in 1948 by partitioning off the Muslim regions of northern India into East and West Pakistan. (East Pakistan was comprised of the former province of East Bengal; West Pakistan of Sindh, Punjab, Baluchistan, the Northwest Frontier province.) The idea was to prevent violence between Muslims and the overwhelmingly Hindu population of India by creating a separate Muslim state; but in fact, the Partition displaced 12 million people, about 1 million of whom died in attendant religious violence—a subject that was largely suppressed in Indian cinema until after 1971, when the Pakistani Civil War resulted in independence for East Pakistan, which became the new state of Bangladesh with a population of 100 million people (131.2 million in 2002). The nation that remained as the Islamic Republic of Pakistan is the second largest Muslim country in the world (after Indonesia), with a 2002 population of 144.6 million; and it has a domestic film industry centered in Lahore ("Lollywood") that produces about 80 Urdu-language features a year, virtually all of which are negligible. Pakistani filmmakers blame the deplorable state of their industry on India, starting with the Partition, when Hindus stripped the studios of equipment and removed it to Bombay. Yet, even though their theatrical presentation is severely restricted by government protectionism and religious censorship, Indian films are hugely popular in Pakistan, where they sustain a vast underground market in smuggled videocassettes. Lollywood's best-known director is Jamil Dehlavi, whose allegorical *The Blood of Hussain* (1980) won praise at several international festivals although it was banned in Pakistan under the regime of General Zia-ul-Haq, 1977–88; in 1998, Dehlavi produced *Jinnah*, an interesting biopic of Pakistan's founding father Mohammed Ali Jinnah (1876–1948) that starred Christopher Lee in the title role.

enormous boom in costume films and "mythologicals," both perfectly suited to the new technology in the "Hindustani" cinema (i.e., Bollywood films made in *filmi Hindustani*, a colloquial blend of Hindi and Urdu that is spoken all over northern and western India). Because so many films of this era were financed as one-shot deals backed by a major star, directors experienced a considerable degree of artistic freedom. One such star was Raj Kapoor (1924–1988), who became a producer-director himself during this period, and while the bulk of his work was romantic and popular, he also made films of social comment, or "socials," in the 1950s, including *The Vagabond* (*Awaara*, 1951; a smash hit in the Soviet Union in 1954); *Boot Polish* (1954); and *Mr. 420* (*Shri 420*, 1955). So, too, did his contemporary Bimal Roy (1909–1966)— *Two Acres of Land* (*Do bigha zameen*, 1953; a prizewinner at Cannes and at Karlovy Vary); *Madhumati* (1958); and *The Jew* (*Yahudi*, 1958). Other interesting filmmakers of the 1950s were Guru Dutt (1925–1964— *Mr. and Mrs. 55*, 1955; *Eternal Thirst* [*Pyaasa*, 1957]; *Paper Flowers* [*Kaagaz ke phool*, 1959; India's first widescreen film]) and Mehboob Khan (1907–1964), whose epic *Mother India* (*Bharat Mata*, 1957) is widely regarded as the Indian *Gone with the Wind* (although it is in fact a remake of his earlier *Aurat* [*Woman*, 1940]).

The Golden Age of "Hindustani" film was roughly

18.45 *Mother India* (Mehboob Khan, 1957): Nargis as the suffering mother in a mythopoeic film about self-sacrifice for the collective good (a remake of Mehboob's own 1940 *Woman*). The influence of Soviet-style socialist realism is again apparent.

18.44 *Awaara* (Raj Kapoor, 1951): maidens cavorting in the fields in a typical song-and-dance number from a "Hindustani" classic. In addition to its landmark success in India, this Oedipal melodrama was phenomenally popular in the Soviet Union when it was distributed there in 1954, perhaps because of its borrowings from the style of socialist realism.

from 1940 to 1960, but Bollywood became an international phenomenon over the next few decades, producing multigeneric hits like *Sholay* (*Flames* [Ramesh Sippy, 1975]), a 204-minute Hollywood-influenced "curry Western" that played nonstop domestically for nearly five years and became India's most profitable film to date. Like most Bollywood films, *Sholay*, though ostensibly an action film, was full of carnivalesque song-and-dance routines because there is no popular Hindi cinema without music (indeed, in many ways the Indian film industry and music industry are one). Another immensely popular "curry Western" was *God Is My Witness* (*Khuda gawah* [Mukul S. Anand, 1992]); since its mythic plot involves a romantic liaison in premodern Afghanistan that can only be consummated through gangland violence in contemporary India, the film mixes several action genres with epic spectacle and lavish musical production numbers, including a pitched battle between hundreds of singing, saber-wielding Afghan horsemen. When Hollywood films began to erode India's domestic market after the phenomenal success of blockbusters like *Jurassic Park* (Steven Spielberg, 1993) and *Titantic* (James Cameron, 1997), Bollywood's musicals became increasingly Westernized—e.g., *Dil to pagal hai* (*The Heart Is Crazy/Somewhere, Someone Waits for You* [Yash Chopra, 1997]), whose college scenes were patterned after the popular American television series *Beverly Hills 90210*, and *Kuch*

kuch hota hai (*Something Happens* [Karan Johar, 1998]), which was modeled on Nora Ephron's hit romantic comedy *Sleepless in Seattle* (1993). Yet the formulaic structure of these films, as well as their spirit, remained unmistakably Indian. By the end of the century, the Bollywood musical form was being widely imitated in the West, providing a major source of inspiration for everything from music videos to postmodern musical features like Baz Luhrmann's *Moulin Rouge!* (2001). But during the 1950s and 1960s, while Bollywood was still a local enterprise, a filmmaker of singular talent and vision was claiming international attention for the Indian cinema, and that was Satyajit Ray (1921–1992).

SATYAJIT RAY

As a young man, Ray studied painting with the Bengali poet Rabindranath Tagore (1861–1941)[1] and then worked for a while for the Calcutta branch of a British advertising agency as an illustrator. In 1947 he founded the Calcutta Film Society with his coworker Chidananda Das Gupta (later a film critic), and its membership came to include many young Bengali intellectuals who would later become filmmakers, including Ritwik Ghatak and Mrinal Sen. Ray's job took him to London for six months in 1950; there he saw Vittorio De Sica's *Ladri di biciclette* (1948) and was tremendously impressed by the film and by the style of Italian neorealism. On his return to Calcutta, he met Jean Renoir and was able to observe him filming *The River* (1951). After many practical difficulties, Ray made his first film, a visualization of the first part of a long novel by the Bengali writer Bibhutibhushan Banerjee entitled *The Song of the Road* (*Pather panchali*, 1955), which, to the astonishment of nearly everyone, won the Jury Prize at Cannes in 1956 in addition to becoming a box-office hit in Bengal. Ray followed with two more films, *The Unvanquished* (*Aparajito*, 1957) and *The World of Apu* (*Apur sansar*, 1958), which together completed his adaptation of the novel and form the *Apu* trilogy—a sensitive, humanistic story of the growth of a young Bengali boy from childhood to maturity. Ray's style was neorealistic in its simplicity and directness, and he made brilliant use of classical Indian music with a sound track composed and played by Ravi Shankar (Ray composed his own scores thereafter). He acquired a large international following in the 1960s based on his films *The Music Room* (*Jalsaghar*, 1958; released 1963); *The Goddess* (*Devi*,

18.46 Family members in *Pather panchali* (Satyajit Ray, 1955): Karuna Bannerjee, Runki Banerjee, Subir Bannerjee.

1960); *Two Daughters* (*Teen kanya*, 1961); *The Big City* (*Mahanagar*, 1963); *The Lonely Wife* (*Charulata*, 1964; adapted from a novel by Tagore); and *Days and Nights in the Forest* (*Aranyer din ratri*, 1970)—all of them studied accounts of some telling aspect of Bengali life.

Because his focus fell so frequently on personal relationships and the small intimacies of everyday life, Ray was sometimes accused of ignoring India's pressingly serious problems of poverty, official corruption, and religious intolerance. In the 1970s, however, he produced more politically conscious films such as *The Adversary* (*Pratidwandi*, 1971), which deals with unemployment among middle-class youth; *Distant Thunder* (*Ashani sanket*, 1973), a depiction of the effects of famine on Bengal during World War II; *The Chess Players* (*Shatranj ke khilari*, 1978; Ray's first film in Urdu rather than Bengali), set during the British annexation of India's last independent princely state in 1856; and *The Middleman* (*Jana aranya*, 1979), a bitter satire about the Calcutta business world. During the 1980s Ray wrote, directed, and scored the 50-minute telefilm *Deliverance* (*Sadgati*, 1982), a stark depiction of the brutalities of the Hindu caste system adapted from a story by Munshi Premchand; the full-length theatrical feature *The Home and the World* (*Ghare*

---

1. India's only writer to win a Nobel Prize (1913), Tagore founded the liberal-humanist Hindu reform movement known as Brahmo, which became closely associated with the politics of nationalist leader Jawaharlal Nehru (1889–1964) later in the century.

baire, 1984), based on a novel by Tagore set in 1905, when the British viceroy Lord Curzon deliberately provoked antagonism between the Hindus and Muslims of Bengal to consolidate his rule; and an adaptation of Ibsen's socially conscious melodrama *An Enemy of the People* (*Ganashatru*, 1989). Before his death in 1992, Ray directed two more films—*Family Reunion* (*Sakha prasakha*, 1990), an Indo-French production about three generations of a Biharian family gathered at the ancestral home in 1900, and *The Visitor* (*Agantuk*, 1991), in which a long-lost uncle returns to a family in contemporary Calcutta after a thirty-five-year sojourn among native South Americans. Just a month before his death from a long illness in April 1992, Ray received an American Academy award for lifetime achievement. At the time, he was working on *The Broken Journey* (*Jargoran*), a film about a young physician's futile attempts to bring modern medical practice to a backward Bengali village, which was completed by his son Sandip Ray in 1993. Whatever his status as a social critic, Ray was a genuine artist who made the Indian cinema worthy of serious attention for the first time in its history. Furthermore, as the last representative of the Bengali cultural renaissance founded by Tagore, he was held in remarkably high regard by his fellow Hindus: the day of Ray's funeral was declared a state holiday, and his last rites in Calcutta were attended by over 1 million people.

PARALLEL CINEMA

Ray's *Apu* trilogy also created the split in Indian cinema between commercial entertainment and art that persists to this day, and it generated great enthusiasm among other Bengali filmmakers, notably Ritwik Ghatak (1925–1976) and Mrinal Sen (b. 1923).[2] A radical Marxist intellectual, Ghatak made only eight films, the best known of which is *Pathetic Fallacy* (*Ajantrik*, 1958), a popular fable about a rural cabbie's love for his aging taxi. But Ghatak's true genius lay in the creation of an authentic alternative cinema. In his semiautobiographical trilogy on East Pakistani refugees—*The Cloud-Capped Star* (*Meghe dhaka tara*, 1960), *E-Flat* (*Komal ghandhar*, 1961), and *River of Gold* (*Subarnarekha*, 1965)—brutal directness belies the rich mythic subtext. His masterpiece, *Reason, Debate and a Tale* (*Jukti takko aar gappo*, 1974), is an autobiographical account of an alcoholic intellectual who must come to terms with the decay of his own revolutionary idealism.

Sen was much more prolific, making films throughout the 1950s and 1960s (e.g., *The End of Night* [*Raat-bhor*, 1953] and *The Wedding Day* [*Baishay sravan*, 1960]), but his breakthrough film was *Bhuvan Shome* (*Mr. Shome*, 1969), which is generally considered to mark the beginning of New Indian Cinema, or "parallel cinema" (parallel, i.e., to the mainstream commercial industry). Inspired by the French *nouvelle vague*, specifically Truffaut's *Jules et Jim* (1961), *Bhuvan Shome* tells the story of a petty-minded railway official on holiday who is humbled and then liberated by an uninhibited village girl, and it was financed by a small unsecured loan from the Indian Film Finance Corporation (FFC, restructured in 1980 as the National Film Development Corporation, or NFDC).

This agency had been founded by the government in 1960 as part of a constellation of institutions designed to enhance the quality of domestic films (the others were the Film Institute of India in Poona, established in 1961 to train aspiring directors, and the National Film Archive, founded in 1964), but until *Bhuvan Shome* it had only supported the work of established figures, like Ray. The critical and commercial success of Sen's film opened the FFC's doors to unknown directors of small- to medium-

---

2. Another young filmmaker influenced by Ray during this period was the American independent James Ivory (b. 1928), who had come to India with producer Ismail Merchant (b. 1936) to make *The Householder* (1963), based on a novel by Ruth Prawer Jhabvala, a German-Polish writer educated in England and married to an Indian. The film was shot by Ray's cameraman Subrata Mitra and edited (uncredited) by Ray himself, who continued to advise Ivory through the rest of his Indian sojourn. Ultimately, Merchant Ivory Productions made four more features in India based on Jhabvala scripts—*Shakespeare Wallah* (1965), *The Guru* (1969), *Bombay Talkie* (1970), and *Savages* (1972), all of them to some degree comedies of manners—before Ivory came to the United States to direct *The Wild Party* (1975) for AIP. After this critical and commercial failure, Ivory returned to his collaboration with Merchant and Jhabvala, independently producing *Autobiography of a Princess* (1975), *Roseland* (1977), *Hullabaloo over Georgie and Bonnie's Pictures* (1978), *The Europeans* (1979; from the novel by Henry James), *Jane Austen in Manhattan* (1980), *Quartet* (1981; adapted from an autobiographical novel by Jean Rhys), and *Heat and Dust* (1983; adapted by Jhabvala from her own award-winning novel). It was these latter films that pointed Merchant Ivory Productions in the spectacularly successful direction it would take in the later 1980s and 1990s—that of the superbly crafted, high-culture literary adaptation. From *The Bostonians* (1984), through *A Room with a View* (1986), *Maurice* (1987), and *Howards End* (1992), to *The Remains of the Day* (1993), Merchant Ivory has played the *Masterpiece Theatre* end of the Anglo-American market like a finely tuned instrument, producing some remarkable works of cinema in the bargain and not overlooking "colonial" literature (Ivory having been thoroughly Anglicized once he moved abroad) in films like *Slaves of New York* (1989) and *Mr. and Mrs. Bridge* (1990).

18.47 *The Cloud-Capped Star* (Ritwik Ghatak, 1960): the first film in Ghatak's trilogy about East Pakistani refugees.

budget features. Over the next decade about 55 such films were produced under its auspices, including such extraordinary first works as Basu Chatterjee's *The Whole Sky* (*Sara akaash*, 1969), Awtar Krishna Kaul's *27 Down* (1973), and M. S. Sathyu's Urdu-language saga *Scorching Wind* (*Garam hawa*, 1973). Kaul died in a drowning accident on the day his film won the Best Hindi Feature award, but Chatterjee (*Tuberoses* [*Rajinigandha*, 1974]; *Just a Trifle* [*Choti si baat*, 1975]; *The Love Thief* [*Chitchor*, 1976]; *Sweet and Sour* [*Khatta meetha*, 1977]; *Mischief* [*Dillagi*, 1979]; etc.) and Sathyu (*The Legendary Outlaw* [*Kenneshwara rama*, 1977]; *The Restless Corpse* [*Chitegu chinte*, 1979]; *The Famine* [*Bara*, 1980]; etc.) both established careers as prolific directors within the Bengali industry.

Sen followed his success with the formally experimental *Interview* (1971) and *Calcutta '71* (1972); clearly influenced by Godard, these works mix third-person narrative with direct address to the audience. Next Sen produced a series of films—*The Guerrilla Fighter* (*Padatik*, 1973), *The Royal Hunt* (*Mrigaya*, 1976), *The Village Story/The Outsiders* (*Oka oorie katha*, 1977), *Man with the Axe*

(*Parasuram*, 1978), and *In Search of Famine* (*Aakaler sandhane*, 1980)—that deal with the exploitation of the urban and the rural poor by multinational corporations, the British raj, Indian businessmen, and bourgeois leftist filmmakers, respectively. In the late 1970s and 1980s, Sen began a critique of middle-class hypocrisy in such films as *Quiet Rolls the Dawn* (*Ek din pratidin*, 1979), *Kaleidoscope* (*Chaalchitra*, 1981), *The Case Is Closed* (*Kharji*, 1982), *The Ruins* (*Khandaar*, 1983), and *Their Own Faces* (*Tasveer apni apni*, 1985). With the Indian-French-Belgian-Swiss coproduction *Genesis* (1986), a richly beautiful parable of the cyclical rise, decline, and fall of the human race, Sen achieved an international reputation that has been sustained through his most recent work, such as *The Confined* (*Antareen*, 1993).

REGIONAL CINEMAS

In the late 1960s, the nonstar parallel-cinema movement was basically Hindi (or "Hindustani")-speaking and centered in Bombay, but during the 1970s, regional industries in the southwest—especially Karnatka and Kerala—began to subsidize independent production, resulting in a "southern new wave." In Karnatka, a state of over 40 million inhabitants, whose Kannada-language industry is centered in Bangalor, Pattabhi Rama Reddy (b. 1919) began the revival with *Funeral Rites* (*Samskara*, 1970), a film about the influence of Brahmins on village life, and it was sustained by his protégés Girish Karnad (b. 1938) in *The Forest* (*Kaadu*, 1973), a brilliant film about two feuding villages as seen through a child's eyes, and B. V. Karanth (b. 1929) in *Choma's Drum* (*Chomana dudi*, 1975), a chronicle of Harijan family life in the 1920s. Equally impressive are Karanth and Karnad's *The Cow-*

Dust Hour (*Godhuli*, 1977); Girish Kasaravalli's (b. 1949) *The Ritual* (*Ghatashraddha*, 1977), *The Siege* (*Akramana*, 1979), *The Three Paths* (*Mooru darigalu*, 1980), and *Tabara's Tale* (*Tabarana kathe*, 1986); and Karnad's *Once upon a Time* (*Ondanondu kalladalli*, 1979), a lavish homage to Kurosawa that revitalizes a long-forgotten native martial-arts tradition, and *Festival* (*Utsav*, 1984), an erotic comedy based on a fourth-century Sanskrit play. In neighboring Kerala, India's most densely populated and literate state, where Malayalam is the principal language, the first major work was Adoor Gopalakrishnan's (b. 1941) *One's Own Choice* (*Swayamvharam*, 1972), a film about the grim consequences of a young couple's flaunting social convention. He followed this with the politically resonant *Ascent* (*Kodiyettam*, 1977), *The Rat Trap* (*Elippathayam*, 1981), and *Face to Face* (*Mukhamukham*, 1984), the latter a portrait of a disillusioned Keralese Communist labor hero. More recently, Gopalakrishnan has contributed to India's quality cinema with *The Walls* (*Mathilukal*, 1990), an award-winning film based on V. M. Basheer's account of his life in prison dur-

ing the freedom struggle of the early 1940s, and *The Servile* (*Vidheyan*, 1993), a psychological drama about the domination of a weak Keralese by his Karnatakan landlord. Gopalakrishnan's *Man of the Story* (*Kathapurushan*, 1996) was voted "Best Film" in India's National Film Awards, providing an elliptical political history lesson in its autobiographical account of the failure of Marxian socialist movements in postwar Kerala. Other notable Keralese directors are M. T. Vasudevan Nair (b. 1934—*Blessed Offering* [*Nirmalayan*, 1973]) and Govindan Aravindan (1935–1991), known for such lyrically poetic works as *Throne of Capricorn* (*Uttarayanam*, 1974), *Golden Sita* (*Kanchana sita*, 1977), *The Tent* (*Thampu*, 1978), *The Bogeyman* (*Kummatty*, 1979), *Stephen* (*Esthappan*, 1980), *Twilight* (*Pokkuveyil*, 1981), *Chidambaram* (1986), and *There Was a Village/Somewhere* (*Oridathu*, 1987).

Two former students of Ghatak, Mani Kaul (b. 1944) and Kumar Shahani (b. 1940), both graduates of the Poona Film Institute, carried on their teacher's tradition of uncompromising Marxist praxis. Mani Kaul produced such Bressonian exercises as *Daily Bread* (*Uski roti*, 1969); *In Two Minds* (*Duvidha*, 1973); *Rising from the Surface* (*Satah se uthata aadmi*, 1981); *Dhrupad* (1982; a documentary about a medieval form of Indian classical music); *Mind of Clay* (*Mati manas*, 1985), and, more recently, *Siddheshwari* (1990), a biography of the acclaimed classical singer, and *The Servant's Shirt* (*Naukar ki kameez*, 1999), an allegory about the Indian class system that won an award at the Rotterdam Film Festival. Shahani made the epic narratives *Mirror of Illusion* (*Maya darpan*, 1972), *Wages and Profits/Vibrations* (*Tarang*, 1984), *Khayal gatha* (1989; a documentary produced by the government of Madhya Pradesh on the history of a musical genre), and *Kasba* (1991), a family crime drama adapted from Anton Chekhov's novella *In the Valley*.

The most commercially successful director of the parallel cinema, however, is indisputably Shyam Benegal (b. 1934), whose feature debut *The Seedling* (*Ankur*, 1974) provided a model for much of the new cinema that followed. This stylistically polished film depicts the exploitation that underlies the landlord-serf relationship in a narrative that is at once realistic and dramatically satisfying. Benegal followed with *Night's End* (*Nishant*, 1975); *The Churning* (*Manthan*, 1976); and *The Boon* (*Anugraham*, 1977), which underscore the link between entrenched feudal power and the sexual exploitation of women. He then delivered a sweeping and highly suc-

18.48 Adoor Gopalakrishnan's *The Rat Trap* (1981).

cessful historical epic of the 1857 Sepoy rebellion in *The Obsession* (*Junoon*, 1978), and he moved even closer to the tastes of the popular audience with such spectacles as *The Machine Age* (*Kalyug*, 1981), *The Market Place* (*Mandi*, 1983), and *Past, Present, and Future* (*Trikal*, 1986). But Benegal's social commitment is still apparent in his two feature-length documentaries of 1985, *Pandit Nehru* and *Satyajit Ray*, and in such theatrical features as *The Essence* (*Susman*, 1987), about corruption in the hand-loom industry in his native Telugu-speaking state of Andhra Pradesh. In the 1990s, Benegal continued to produce important work. *The Seventh Horse of the Sun* (*Suraj ka satvan ghoda*, 1992), involving three separate stories told over a two-night period by a young bachelor, is an experiment in creating a fabric of interwoven narratives, whereas *Mammo* (1994) is a smaller, more personal film about a middle-aged woman from Pakistan who comes to live in the home of her sister in Bombay; there she develops a friendship with the sister's twelve-year-old grandson and experiences a broad range of anti-Pakistani prejudice, highlighting the cultural, political, and religious differences between the two countries. With *The Making of the Mahatma* (1996), Benegal returned to the realm of social comment in a 150-minute biopic of Mohandas K. Gandhi's political awakening during his years in South Africa and his growing commitment to the policy of passive resistance. Based on a true story, *Sardari Begum* (1997) similarly used the biopic genre to explore the political realm as a newspaper reporter investigates the death of a popular singer during a riot between Hindus and Muslims. More recently, Benegal's *Conflict* (*Samar*, 2000) was selected as "Best Film" in the Forty-sixth National Film Awards competition; it offers an analysis of India's caste system in the story of a dispute over the installation of a village water pump, which self-reflexively becomes the subject of a documentary on the caste system by some Bombay filmmakers who inadvertently plunge the village into violence. Most of Benegal's films are produced or coproduced by the NFDC.

During the 1980s, several young Marxist directors became prominent in Bengali parallel cinema, especially Goutam Ghose (b. 1950—*The Occupation* [*Dakhal*, 1982], *The Crossing* [*Paar*, 1984], *Meeting a Milestone* [1990—on the distinguished instrumentalist Bismillah Khan], *Boatman of the River Padma* [*Padma nadir majhi*, 1992], *Kite* [*Patang*, 1993]), *The Doll* [*Gudia*, 1997; Hindi-language], and *Ray: Life and Work of Satyajit Ray*

[1999]); Aparna Sen (b. 1945—*36 Chowringhee Lane*, 1982, *Paroma*, 1986, and *Sati* [*Suttee*, 1989]); and Buddhadev Dasgupta (b. 1944—*Civil War* [*Grihayuddha*, 1982], *The Return* [*Phera*, 1988], and *The Red Door* [*Lal darja*, 1997]). But many observers feel that India may in fact be moving toward a so-called "middle cinema," patterned more or less on the work of Benegal—i.e., films whose political and social concerns are not at odds with audience accessibility and even entertainment. This tendency can be seen in the political thrillers of Benegal's former cameraman Govind Nihalani (b. 1940—*Cry of the Wounded* [*Aakrosh*, 1981], *Half Truth* [*Ardh satya*, 1983], *Blood of Brothers* [*Aaghat*, 1986], and *Times of Betrayal* [*Droh kaal*, 1995]) and the dramatic work of Ramesh Sharma (*New Delhi Times*, 1986) and Jahnu Barua (b. 1952—*The Catastrophe* [*Halodhia choraye baodhan khai*, 1988], *It's a Long Way to the Sea* [*Hkhagoroloi bohu door*, 1995], and *Kuhkhal* [1998]); the fast-paced comedies of Kundan Shah (b. 1947—*Let It Pass, Boys* [*Jaane bhi do yaaro*, 1983]) and Saeed Mirza (b. 1943—*The Court Summons Joshi* [*Mohan Joshi hazirho!* 1984]); the eclectic work of Ketan Mehta (b. 1952—*A Folk Tale* [*Bhavni bhavai*, 1981], *Festival of Fire* [*Holi*, 1985], *Spices* [*Mirch masala*, 1987], and *Maya Memsaab* [1992], an adaptation of Flaubert's *Madame Bovary*); and the feminist films of Aruna Raje (b. 1946—*Liberation* [*Rihaee*, 1992]), one of India's few women directors. During the 1990s the political stability of India—always rocky—became increasingly tenuous. The assassination of Rajiv Gandhi in May 1991 while he was campaigning for re-election as prime minister (a post he had held from 1984 to 1989, in the wake of his mother Indira's assassination) brought to an end the Nehru-Gandhi dynasty that had ruled India for most of its forty-four years of independence to date.

Since that time, the Hindu nationalist Bharatiya Janata (or Indian People's) party has replaced the Congress party in India's ruling coalition, and India and Pakistan have both acquired nuclear arsenals, threatening regional and global peace in their confrontation over the disputed province of Kashmir. India itself has experienced massive waves of religious violence between its 820 million Hindus and 130 million Muslims (such as the riots that took place in the western province of Gujarat in February and March of 2002), as well as several sharp devaluations of its currency (the rupee) that have seriously impaired the workings of the film industry. From a high of 938 films in 1994, annual production has declined year by year almost ever since; and about 85 percent of Indian films now fail at the box office, while demand for Hollywood product by the domestic audience grows. The involvement of organized crime in film finance (about 5 percent of the total) and a wave of murder and extortion chilled the industry in the late 1990s. Nevertheless, in 1999 Columbia TriStar ventured successfully into Hindi film distribution and exhibition; and Indian digital-effects studios are flush with work on projects from all over the world (e.g., Madras-based Pentafour produced Trimark's *Sinbad: Beyond the Veil of Mists* [Alan Jacobs and Evan C. Ricks, 2000], which was the first animated feature made using the 3-D Animated Motion Capture process; and CGI software companies like Discreet Logic, Inc., and Alias/Wavefront have established large Bombay offices; see Chapter 21). Furthermore, a number of Indian films at the turn of the century broke domestic box-office records and subsequently became international hits as well—e.g., *From the Heart* (*Dil Se* [Mani Rathnam, 1998]); *The Terrorist* (Santosh Sivan, 1998); *Land Tax* (*Lagaan* [Ashutosh Gowariker, 2001]—only the second Bollywood film to be nominated for an Academy Award for Best Foreign Film); and *Monsoon Wedding* (Mira Nair, 2001; Golden Lion at Venice). Finally, several Indian-born directors have made their mark on world cinema by operating in a global context—e.g., Shekhar Kapur (b. 1945), the success of whose *Bandit Queen* (1994) led him to England to produce the much-lauded historical biopic *Elizabeth* (1998),[3] and Deepa Mehta (b. 1950), the Toronto-based feminist whose

18.50 *Monsoon Wedding* **(Mira Nair, 2001). The traditional and the modern meet—and sometimes clash—in this comedy of manners surrounding a large wedding celebration in contemporary Delhi.**

18.51 *Bandit Queen* **(Shekhar Kapur, 1994): Seema Biswas as Phoolan Devi, a real-life character who revolted against the land-based caste system in central India during the late 1970s and became a national folk hero. This combined action and social-consciousness film brought fame to its director, who went on to do prestigious work in the United Kingdom (***Elizabeth*** [1998];** ***The Four Feathers*** [2002]).**

18.49 *The Terrorist* **(Santoshi Sivan, 1998): Ayesha Dharker as the title character, Malli, contemplating her mission to assassinate an Indian politician. This was the debut feature of Santosh Sivan, a distinguished cinematographer who functions as his own director of photography when he directs.**

controversial trilogy of the elements—*Fire* (1996), *Earth* (1998), and *Water* (2003)—was shot on location in India and treats various deeply repressed elements of its history and culture.

---

3. Kapur's British films are in fact very Indian in their postcolonial perspective—e.g., his adaptation of A. E. W. Mason's 1929 novel *The Four Feathers* (2002), set in England and the Sudan during the revolt of the Mahdi in 1884. Whereas the novel and its four previous film versions were sweeping colonial adventure epics, Kapur reshaped the narrative as an unmistakable anticolonial, anti-British polemic.

China

Motion pictures were introduced in China by European and American entrepreneurs at the same time as in the West, and the Chinese immediately loved them, calling them *ying she*, or "shadow play." The first indigenous films appeared in 1905, and by 1910 an industry began to form, centered in Shanghai and with outposts in other coastal cities. Sound was introduced in 1929 and gradually gained widespread acceptance. At the same time, the Chinese Communist party established the Film Group (*Dianying zu*), whose members infiltrated several major studios during the 1930s and produced leftist-liberal films of high artistic caliber. Often based on works of May Fourth[4] literature, these films tended to be socially conscious melodramas with an anti-Japanese slant, such as *Spring Silkworms* (*Chuncan* [Cheng Bugao, 1933]), *The Goddess* (*Shennu* [Wu Yonggang, 1934; silent]), *The Highway* (*Dalu* [Sun Yu, 1934]), *Street Angel* (*Malu tianshi* [Mu-jih Yuan, 1937]), and *Crossroads* (*Shizi jietoŭ* [Shen Xiling, 1937]). But the Japanese invasion of 1937 and the occupation of Shanghai forced the Chinese film industry to move south into the British Crown Colony of Hong Kong, where a large outpost was established, and into Southeast Asia. When production resumed on the mainland in 1945, the focus was mainly on the traumas of the war and occupation (known in China as the "War of Resistance to Japan") in such epics as *Spring River Flows East* (*Yijiang chunshui xiang dong liu* [Cai Chusheng and Zheng Junli, 1947]) and *Eighty Thousand Miles of Clouds and the Moon* (*Ba ianli lu yun he yue* [Shi Dongshan, 1947]). Meanwhile a civil war raged between Chiang Kai-shek's Nationalists and the Communist forces of Mao Zedong (1893–1976); when the latter won in 1949, he proclaimed the mainland as the People's Republic of China (PRC) and Chiang's government fled to Taiwan, which was subsequently proclaimed the Republic of China (ROC) and ruled for the next forty years by Chiang's Kuomintang party (KMT). Afterward, Chinese cinema, though unified by a single cultural heritage, developed in mainland China (People's Republic), Hong Kong, and Taiwan along separate paths.

THE PEOPLE'S REPUBLIC OF CHINA

In the People's Republic, the period from 1949 to 1966 was one of nationalization and collectivization. The film industry was placed under the minister of culture, and the government undertook to build ten major studios in each of the country's largest cities and to modernize the Northeast Film Studio in Changchun, a holdover from the Japanese invasion. Up to 1956 hundreds of socialist-realist films that celebrated the revolution and the glories of life in the new socialist state were produced. The so-called "hundred flowers" movement of 1957 invited constructive criticism of the Communist party and briefly permitted the production of such mildly dissident films as Lü Ban's *Before the New Director Arrives* (*Xin juzhang daolai zhi qian*, 1956) and literary adaptations like Chen Xihe's *Family* (*Jia*, 1956).

This period was followed by a politically repressive "Anti-Rightist" movement and the launching in 1958 of the "Great Leap Forward" (China's second five-year plan, the first having been undertaken from 1953 to 1957). The Great Leap Forward was designed to increase national economic output, and from 1958 to 1959 the film industry was able to double production to 229 features and animated shorts, most of them—like Zhao Ming's *Loving the Factory as One's Home* (*Ai chang ru jia*, 1958) and Lu Ren's *Steel Man and Iron Horse* (*Gangren tiema*, 1958)—devoted to Great Leap themes. Between 1959 and 1964, however, the film industry was less subject to politicization, if not to ideology, and directors found themselves able to produce such stylistically interesting work as Zheng Junli's *Lin Zexu* (1959), based on Chinese poetry, and Xie Jin's *The Red Detachment of Women* (*Hongse niangzijun*, 1961). The early 1960s witnessed the adaptation of a number of classic operas—Su Li's *Third Sister Liu* (*Liu sanjie*, 1960), Cui Wei's *Wild Boar Forest* (*Yezhe lin*, 1962), and Cen Fan's *Dream of the Red Chamber* (*Honglou meng*, 1962; itself adapted from a famous novel)—as well as novels, like Xie Tieli's *Early Spring in February* (*Zaochun eryue*, 1963, which had previously been forbidden as a "bourgeois" form). Also produced were such comedies of contemporary life as Xie Jin's *Fat Li, Young Li, and Old Li* (*Da Li, xiao Li, he lao Li*, 1962) and Yen Gong's *Satisfied or Not* (*Manyi bu manyi*, 1963).

---

4. The allocation of former German-held Chinese territory to Japan by the Treaty of Versailles caused urban protests all over China on May 4, 1919, and that date gave its name to a progressive intellectual and social movement centered in Shanghai that rejected traditional values in favor of Westernized, reformist (but not necessarily Marxist) ideas. Before 1949, many Chinese writers and filmmakers shared May Fourth's cultural conviction.

Three films of particular note made during this era were Lu Jen's popular comedy *Li Shuangshuang* (1962); Xie Jin's *Two Stage Sisters* (*Wutai jiemei*, 1965), a sensitive account of the relationship between two talented opera singers; and the two-part animated feature *Uproar in Heaven* (*Da nao tian gong* [Wan Laiming, 1961; 1964]).

In 1966 Mao unexpectedly swung his support to the ultraradicals within the Chinese Communist party, bringing on the ten-year reign of terror known as the Cultural Revolution, during which every social and economic institution in the country was disrupted and many were destroyed. The impact on the film industry was enormous, as filmmakers, like most other Chinese professionals, were driven into the countryside for "re-education" by the peasants. Feature production ground to a halt between 1967 and 1969, and was resumed in 1970 largely by amateurs working in a single, newly synthesized genre—*Geming Yangbanxi*, or "revolutionary model operas." This form, typified by Xie Tieli's *Taking Tiger Mountain by Strategy* (*Zhiqu Weihushan*, 1970), Cheng Yin's *The Red Lantern* (*Hongdeng ji*, 1970), and Pan Wenzhan and Fu Jie's *The Red Detachment of Women* (*Hongse niangzijun*, 1971—a remake of Xie Jin's 1961 narrative feature) was characterized by melodramatic

18.52 *Battle Song of Taching* **(Sun Yung Ping, 1966), one of the last films released before the Cultural Revolution.**

plots, stylized dances, acrobatics, and grandiose orchestral finales to create a kind of *circus maximus* of the revolution.[5] They gave mainland Chinese cinema an unwarranted reputation for egregiousness from which it suffered until very recently. Professional filmmakers gradually returned from the re-education camps between 1973 and 1976, but political conditions still were such that few films of quality could be made.

Party Chairman Mao and Premier Zhou Enlai both died in 1976, and a power struggle ensued between a group of moderates led by Hua Guofeng and Mao's widow, Jiang Qing. Hua won and briefly succeeded Mao and Zhou, while Jiang Qing and three of her followers (called the "Gang of Four")—now revealed as the real power behind the Cultural Revolution—were tried and imprisoned for treason. Hua was himself replaced by Deng Xiaoping (1904–1997) in 1978, ushering in a period of moderation and relative liberalization for mainland China that ended abruptly with the Tiananmen Square massacre of Sunday, June 4, 1989, and the crackdown that followed. Political conditions have since moderated, thanks to world economic incentives (like being chosen to host the 2008 Olympic Games) and China's embrace of mixed-market capitalism, but the government remains authoritarian, and serious human-rights abuses still exist. After Mao's death, the state distribution enterprise, the China Film Corporation, eliminated full subvention of production and required each of the country's twenty-two (now sixteen) official studios to do its own financial planning and balance its own budget. Yet subsidies continued for distribution and exhibition until 1993, when market forces were allowed to take over, and production came to depend more directly on audience demand (although films were still subject to precensorship by the Chinese Film Bureau, a gatekeeping division of the Ministry of Broadcast). For a brief period, however, neither politics nor popular taste determined what films were made in China, and an "exploratory" film movement surfaced that was both formally experimental and ideologically unbound. In

---

5. These filmed versions of revolutionary Peking operas and ballets were intended by Jiang Qing as models (*yangban*) for China's 3,000 performing stage groups. They emphasized the key elements of the Cultural Revolution—struggle, criticism, and rehabilitation—and valorized proletarian representation over the "decadent" content of traditional Peking opera. Interestingly, the singing and acting styles of the traditional form were retained because they served to conceal the individuality of the performers.

China, it was commonly referred to as the New Wave or "art wave" cinema because it appropriated techniques of modernist film movements like the French New Wave and blended them with those of classical Chinese landscape painting; it was closely associated with a group of film-makers known as the "Fifth Generation," so named to acknowledge their place in the history of Chinese cinema.

The Chinese divide their filmmakers into generations: first, the pioneers; second, those who developed socialist realism in the 1930s and 1940s; the third comprises those who were unable to study film formally because of the war and occupation but who entered the industry shortly after the liberation; and the fourth is the generation that studied film before the Cultural Revolution but couldn't enter the industry until the Cultural Revolution had ended. The state film school, the Beijing Film Academy, reopened in 1978, after having been shut down since 1966 by the Cultural Revolution. In 1981 the academy graduated 2,100 students from the fourth generation in acting, directing, cinematography, sound recording, and graphic arts. The fifth generation of filmmakers comprises those who graduated from the academy between 1982 and 1989; the sixth generation is comprised of post-Tiananmen graduates. Because of their training, the fourth and fifth generations are sometimes grouped together as the "academic school." This fifth generation of Chinese filmmakers coalesced with the new, more market-oriented production context to produce a new kind of mainland cinema, much of it devoted initially to the trauma of individuals, regardless of class, during the Cultural Revolution. For example, Yang Yanjin and Deng Yimin's *Troubled Laughter* (*Ku'naoren de xiao*, 1979), Xie Jin's *Legend of Tianyun Mountain* (*Tianyunshan chuanqi*, 1980), and Wu Yigong's *Evening Rain* (*Bashan yeyu*, 1980) all were sympathetic to the plight of intellectuals, and Wang Qimin and Sun Yu's *At Middle Age* (*Ren daozhong nian*, 1982) and Wu Tianming's *River without Buoys* (*Meiyou hangbiao de heliu*, 1983) and *Life* (*Ren sheng*, 1984) concern the suffering of professionals and intellectuals alike. Contemporary, even naturalistic, social commentary was also apparent in films like Chiang Liang's *Yamaha Fish Stall* (*Yamaha yu dang*, 1984) and *Juvenile Delinquents* (*Shaonian fan*, 1985) and Lu Xiaoya's *Girl in Red* (*Hongye shaonu*, 1985), as well as Yan Xueshu's *Wild Mountains* (*Yeshan*, 1986), an ironic comedy on provincial wife-swapping. Huangjian Zhong's *A Dead Man Visits the Living* (*Yigesizhe dui shengzhe de fang wen*, 1988) on the other hand, is social criticism in the form of a fantasy in which the spirit of a man murdered during a robbery returns from the dead to impugn the incompetent bureaucratic and social systems that permitted the crime. Zheng Junzhao's *One and Eight* (*Yige he bage*, 1984; released, 1987), generally considered to be the first film of the New Wave, tells a grim story of criminals freed by the Red Army to fight the invading Japanese in 1939; despite its highly restrained style, the film was implicitly critical of Communist ideals, and its release was delayed until certain scenes were reshot and re-edited.

But perhaps the most exciting figures to emerge in recent mainland cinema are Chen Kaige (b. 1952), Zhang Yimou (b. 1951), and Tian Zhuangzhuang (b. 1952), all of whom were in the first class to graduate from the Beijing Film Academy since the Cultural Revolution. Chen's first feature, *Yellow Earth* (*Huang tudi*, 1984), marked a critical and commercial breakthrough for Chinese film on the international distribution circuit. It was an extraordinarily poetic rendition of the folk culture of the Yellow River plateau circa 1939, filmed in the flat, impressionistic style of the southern school of landscape painting

18.53 Chen Kaige's *Yellow Earth* (1984).

and the patterned, primary colors of Chinese New Year prints, followed by *The Big Parade* (*Dayue bing*, 1985) and *King of the Children* (*Haizi wang*, 1988), the former about military life in contemporary China and the latter about the mistakes of the Cultural Revolution. In the 1990s Chen has directed *Life on a String* (*Bian zou bian chang*, 1991), a German-British-Chinese coproduction about a blind traveling musician and his young blind apprentice, shot on location in remote Shanxi Province, and *Farewell My Concubine* (*Bawang bie ji*, 1993— Palme d'Or, Cannes, with Jane Campion's *The Piano*), a sensuously ravishing film that charts the course of a love triangle among two male Peking opera stars and a female prostitute over forty years of Chinese history, from the 1920s to the Cultural Revolution. (*Concubine* was banned and unbanned twice in China in 1993, as the government campaigned to host the Olympic Games in the year 2000, and was ultimately released in censored form.) Nevertheless, *Concubine* was an international hit, and it brought renewed prestige to the Chinese film industry. Chen's *Temptress Moon* (*Feng yue*, 1996) reunited the cast of *Concubine* in a similarly themed saga of a wealthy family ravaged by opium addiction in the latter years of the imperial era, circa 1911. The film is rich in period detail and features opulent cinematography by the Australian cameraman Christopher Doyle, a close collaborator of several Chinese directors, including Wong Kar-wai (Hong Kong) and Edward Yang (Taiwan), but it was also controversial in China for its unblinking depiction of drug use and sexual degradation. Lavishly budg-

eted (by Chinese standards) at $15 million, *The Emperor and the Assassin* (*Jing ke ci qin wang*, 1999) was a sweeping historical epic about Ying Zheng, the ruler who unified China, and was considerably more commercial than Chen's earlier projects. (Ying Zheng was also the subject of Zhou Xiaowen's *The Emperor's Shadow* [*Qin song*, 1996], another historical epic reputed to have been the most expensive film made in China to that point.)

Zhang Yimou was cinematographer for Zhang's *One and Eight* and Chen's *Yellow Earth* and *The Big Parade*, and his debut feature was the strikingly shot *Red Sorghum* (*Hong gaoliang*, 1988), which won the Golden Bear at Berlin and became a commercial success in the United States. This sumptuous widescreen film employs the entire arsenal of anamorphic and zoom-lens aesthetics to evoke northern village life in the 1930s, first as light comedy and finally as a horrendous tapestry of atrocities committed by the invading Japanese. Zhang's commercial hijack thriller *Code Name "Cougar"* (*Daihao "Meizhoubao,"* 1989) was a domestic box-office hit, underwriting the visual splendor of his subsequent works. *Ju dou* (1990; produced by Japan's Tokuma Communications) and *Raise the Red Lantern* (*Da hong denglong gao gua*, 1991; produced by Taiwan's ERA International) are both set in the pre-Communist 1920s and deal with the theme of feudalism and the struggle for women's rights in rural settings (both were also initially banned in China), and they continued Zhang's painterly, pictorialist style. *The Story of Qiu Ju* (*Qiu Ju da guansi*, 1992) offered a change of pace in its quasidocumentary comedy of contemporary village life, shot on location in Super 16mm (but blown up to 35mm for theatrical distribution), and it won the

18.54 *King of the Children* (Chen Kaige, 1988).

18.55 Zhang Yimou's *Red Sorghum* (1988): Gong Li.

Golden Lion at Venice. *To Live* (*Huozhe*, 1994) chronicles the fortunes of a single family from World War II through the Cultural Revolution and is implicitly critical of the government; it won numerous international awards, including the Cannes Grand Prix, but was censured in China, and Zhang was not permitted to work for two years. He returned with *Shanghai Triad* (*Yao a yao yao dao wai po jia*, 1995), a gangster film set in the 1930s and his final film with Gong Li (b. 1965), the brilliant young actress who had been his leading lady since *Red Sorghum* and became an icon of Fifth Generation cinema (having starred also in such Chen Kaige films as *Farewell My Concubine*). After another atypical film, the fast-paced *cinéma vérité*–style comedy *Keep Cool* (*You hua hao hao shuo*, 1997), Zhang produced two distinguished visions of contemporary China: *Not One Less* (*Yi ge dou bu neng shao*, 1999), which won another Golden Lion at Venice, and the beautiful family saga *The Road Home* (*Wode fuquin muqin*, 2000), which won the Silver Bear at Berlin. Recently he has directed the contemporary urban comedy *Happy Times* (*Xingfu shiguang*, 2000) and also directed opera in Italy (e.g., Puccini's *Turandot* in 1997) and ballet in Beijing (an adaptation of his own *Raise the Red Lantern* in 2001).

Tian Zhuangzhuang's career began with an ethnographic study of Mongolian peasant life entitled *On the Hunting Ground* (*Lie changzha sha*, 1985) and proceeded to *Horse Thief* (*Daoma zei*, 1986), a film shot on location in Tibet about the relationship between tribal rights and Buddhist religion. Predictably, the film was heavily cut by Chinese censors. Tian then turned to patently commercial projects for several years (e.g., *Rock 'n' Roll Kids* [*Yaogun qingnian*, 1988]) before directing *The Blue Kite* (*Lan fengzheng*, 1993), a muted film about the impact of early Communist rule on the daily life of a Beijing family from 1953 to 1967, banned in China despite winning awards at both the Cannes and Tokyo International festivals. Following *The Blue Kite*, Tian was prohibited from working in film for several years, and he has directed only one film since, a finely crafted remake of the 1949 period melodrama *Springtime in a Small Town* (*Xiao cheng zhi chun*, 2002). But he has been active in producing films of the rising Sixth Generation of directors who graduated from the Beijing Film Academy in 1989 and 1990 (e.g., Lu Xuechang's *Zhanga Chengren* [1998]).

Like those described above, virtually all serious Chinese films are adapted from published literary work because cinema in China is understood and taught as a form of literature. Yet as China's economic reforms took hold in the mid-1990s and consumption became the driving force of economic growth, Chinese filmmakers found it increasingly necessary to appeal to popular tastes. Mainland films were suddenly in the position of needing to earn money at the domestic box office in order to justify their studio's shrinking subsidies from the state,[6] and so nearly all of the new films have an element of mass appeal, including the common use of widescreen and Technicolor (the People's Republic operates the only extant Technicolor dye-transfer printing plant in the world, although it does not have first-rate editing facilities and most postproduction work is done elsewhere, usually in Japan). Work by rising talents from the Sixth Generation, most of whom were in their thirties as the century turned, has been notably more commercial than that of their Fifth Generation counterparts—e.g., Zhang Yang's *Spicy Love Soup* (*Aiqing mala tang*, 1998) and *Shower* (*Xizao*, 2000); Zhang Yuan's *Seventeen Years* (*Guo nian hui jia*, 2000); Wang Xiaoshuai's *So Close to Paradise* (*Biandan, guniang*, 1998) and *Beijing Bicycle* (*Shiqisuide danche*, 2001; coproduced with Taiwan and France); and Lou Ye's *Suzhou River* (*Suzhou he*, 2000). Annual attendance, once averaging 3 billion admissions per year at some 5,000 theaters, has been declining since the mid-1980s, due both to the popularity of television (which has achieved 90 percent penetration in the cities) and to the increasing affluence of China's urban populations, for whom the movies are now just one of many leisure-time distractions. There is increasing competition from foreign films, which the China Film Corporation is empowered to import in an amount equivalent to one-third of the industry's annual domestic feature output, which averaged about 120 for most of the 1980s and 1990s. Since the late

---

6. Extramural funding is another option (such as that for Zhang's most recent films, above), which accounts for a considerable amount of coproduction with Hong Kong (e.g., Chang Hsin-yen's *Shaolin Temple* [*Shao-lin si*, 1982] and its sequels, Ann Hui's *Boat People* [*Tou bun no hoi*, 1982] and her two-part *Romance of Book and Sword* [*Shu jian en chou lu* 1988]); with Japan (Junya Sato's *The Unfinished Chess Match* [*Yu pan mei you xia wan de qi*, 1983] and *The Go Masters*, 1983); and with the West (NBC's Italian-produced miniseries *Marco Polo* [Giuliano Montald, 1983], Bertolucci's *The Last Emperor* [1986], and the first feature-length Chinese-American coproduction, Peter Wang's *The Great Wall Is a Great Wall* [1986]).

18.56 *Beijing Bicycle* (Wang Xiaoshuai, 2001): Cui Lin as Gui, newly arrived in the big city from the provinces. In this variant of De Sica's neorealist classic *Ladri di biciclette* (1948), Gui finds work as a bicycle messenger, but his bike is stolen, and he spends the rest of the film trying to get it back.

1990s, the major American distributors have attempted to gain an even larger share of China's domestic market, leveraging their efforts through Washington's support for China's entry into the World Trade Organization. But the Chinese government continues to protect the film industry through subsidies, and, until 1998, it denied foreign distributors direct control of rental income. In fact, until Jack Valenti of the Motion Picture Association of America (MPAA) negotiated a new quota system, the only way a foreign distributor could show a film in China was to sell it outright to the China Film Corporation. Today, profits from American films are split 50–50 between the Film Corporation and the Hollywood majors, but distribution and marketing are left exclusively to the Chinese.

HONG KONG

In postwar Hong Kong, a British crown colony at the time, production was carried on throughout the 1950s by a variety of small- to medium-sized companies that nevertheless managed to produce between 150 and 170 films per year in such popular genres as the family melodrama and the Cantonese-dialect swordplay (*wu xia*) and martial-arts (*kung fu*) films. During the 1960s these were replaced by comedies, urban musicals, and Mandarin-dialect swordplay films, characterized by greater violence and montage-style editing. At the same time, the Shaw Brothers Studio emerged as a vertically integrated major, with production facilities, laboratories, and dubbing studios in Hong Kong, and exhibition chains in Hong Kong, Singapore, and Malaysia. Shaw Brothers specialized in Mandarin swordplay films, turning out as many as 50 a year and giving birth to several major directorial talents: Li Han-hsiang (1926–1996), who made *Magnificent Concubine* (*Yang guifei*, 1961), *Empress Wu* (*Wu hou*, 1960), and *The Happiest Moment* (*Yi le ye*, 1973); and King Hu (1931–1997), whose "Inn Trilogy" (*Come Drink with Me* [*Dazui xia*, 1966], *Dragon Inn* [*Longmen kezhan*, 1967], and *The Fate of Lee Khan* [*Ying-ch'un qizhi feng-bo*, 1973]) combined the styles of Peking opera and classical Chinese painting to elevate the swordplay genre to the level of art. Hu continued to inject the genre with philosophical mysticism in his "Buddhist Trilogy," produced outside of the Shaw system—*A Touch of Zen* (*Xia nu*,

18.57 *Suzhou River* (Lou Ye, 2000): Zhou Xun as the nightclub performer Meimei, one of two characters she plays in this Sixth Generation take on Hitchcock's *Vertigo* (1958).

18.58 King Hu's swordplay classic *A Touch of Zen* (1971).

1971), *Raining in the Mountain* (*Kong shanling yu*, 1979), and *Legend of the Mountain* (*Shanzhong chuanqi*, 1979)—the first of which won a prize for technique at Cannes in 1975. With the commercial success of such widescreen color sword epics in the mid- to late-1960s, Shaw Brothers was able to dominate the markets of Taiwan, Singapore, Malaysia, and Thailand.

In 1970, Raymond Chow, head of advertising and publicity at Shaw Brothers since 1958, broke away to form his own studio with partner Leonard Ho: the now-legendary Golden Harvest, which experienced its first great success in the early 1970s with three Mandarin *kung fu* films starring Bruce Lee (1940–1973)—*The Big Boss/* also known as *Fists of Fury* (*Tang shan da xiong* [Lo Wei, 1971]), *The Chinese Connection/*also known as *Fist of Fury* (*Jing wu men* [Lo Wei, 1972]), and *Way of the Dragon/*also known as *Return of the Dragon* (*Meng long guojiang* [Bruce Lee, 1973]); but this bonanza ended with Lee's sudden death of a brain aneurysm at the age of thirty-two shortly after he had completed *Enter the Dragon* (Robert Clouse, 1973) for Warner Bros., produced in association with Raymond Chow and shot on location in Hong Kong (and, as of 2002, *still* Hong Kong's highest-grossing film in the United States in constant-dollar terms). *Kung fu* films in general, and Lee's in particular, had a significant impact on the American market during the early 1970s, when they became a popular exploitation genre. Their primary appeal was their skillfully shot and edited fight sequences, which were performed by authentic martial-arts masters according to centuries-old disciplines of self-defense, some of them extending back to the Ming dynasty. These disciplines were integral to the expressive gymnastic style of Peking opera, in which many *kung fu* film performers and fight directors had been classically trained. Just as Hollywood dance musicals used separate directors of choreography for production numbers, *kung fu* movies usually employed separate martial-arts directors for fights; and these second-unit directors were often assisted themselves by specially trained "fight choreographers."[7] (Certain fight techniques —*kung fu* translates literally as "technique" or "skill"— became associated with particular stars, nationalities, or character types—*hapkido* [turning an attacker's energy against himself] with Angela Mao, who was promoted by Golden Harvest as a female Bruce Lee; *jeet kune do* ["fist-intercepting way"] and *wing chun kung fu* ["lightning fast" close-range fighting] with Bruce Lee; *judo* [from

jujitsu—a backup technique used by *samurai* against taller opponents] with the Japanese, usually the villains in Hong Kong martial-arts films; *tae kwon do* ["hand and foot fighting"] with the Korean police and militia; and *karate* ["empty hand" boxing] with villains of every sort.)[8] Hong Kong fight sequences were traditionally shot in short segments in order to save time and preserve the coherence of the actual fight, as opposed to the Hollywood practice of "master shot/coverage"—i.e., taking a single master shot of all the principal elements in a scene and then shooting close-ups and medium shots to "cover" the scene from different angles. This "segment shooting" style, in which action is choreographed and shot progressively rather than built up from "coverage," is one of the chief differences between Hollywood and Hong Kong modes of production.

After Lee's death, Golden Harvest turned to social satires starring and directed by popular variety show host Michael Hui (b. 1942—*Teppanyaki* [1984]; *Chocolate Inspector* [*Shen tan zhu gu li*, 1986]) and to Keatonesque *kung fu* action-comedies with Jackie Chan and Sammo Hung (see below). Both Shaw Brothers and Golden Harvest continued to mass-produce cheap genre films during much of the 1970s; approximately thirty smaller competitors produced even cheaper clones.

In 1977, Hong Kong became the site of an annual domestic and international film festival that was held each April, bringing a new measure of respect to the local industry. Television also became widespread and popular at this time, and Hong Kong's three TV stations all produced their own programming for the local market in their own studios. Television thus became an important training ground for young directors, writers, and producers, who introduced significant cross-fertilization to filmmaking when the first generation of television production personnel began working in cinema during the late 1970s and the 1980s. The members of this group—most of whom were educated in the West—included Tsui Hark (b. 1951), Ann Hui (b. 1947), Yim Ho (b. 1952), Ronny Yu (b. 1950), Patrick Tam (Tan Jiaming), Allen Fong (b. 1947), Stanley Kwan (b. 1957), and Wong Kar-wai (b. 1958); and they were cohesive in that they all demon-

---

7. Stuart M. Kaminsky, *American Film Genres*, 2nd ed. (Chicago: Nelson-Hall, 1985), p. 73; Mark A. Reid, *Redefining Black Film* (Berkeley: University of California Press, 1993), p. 35.

8. Kaminsky, p. 73; Reid, p. 35.

strated a sophisticated grasp of film form as well as a commitment to representing the reality of contemporary Hong Kong, even if that were done in metaphoric fashion. Their first features—Tsui Hark's *The Butterfly Murders* (*Die bian*, 1979) and *We Are Going to Eat You* (*Diyu wu men*, 1980); Yim Ho's *The Happenings* (*Ye che*, 1980); Ann Hui's *The Secret* (*Feng jie*, 1979), *The Spooky Bunch* (*Zhuang dao zheng*, 1980), and *Boat People* (*Tou bun nohoi*, 1982); Patrick Tam's *Love Massacre* (*Ai sha*, 1981) and *The Nomad* (*Lie huo qing chun*, 1982); and Allen Fong's *Father and Son* (*Fuzhi qing*, 1981) and *Ah Ying* (*Banbian ren*, 1983)—all used innovative techniques and new visual styles as a means of personal expression very much like their European counterparts. Furthermore, because they had been trained in teleproduction, the new filmmakers were skilled at working efficiently on tight schedules within modest budgets (which included the early and imaginative use of cost-effective CGI; see Chapter 21); and they were practiced at shooting on location with light, flexible equipment. Finally, their television-honed audience awareness and their urban sensibility ensured that the city of Hong Kong would become a major character in their features.

During the 1980s, these young television-trained directors combined with others like John Woo (b. 1946), Ringo Lam (b. 1954), Sammo Hung (b. 1952), Peter Chan (b. 1962), Wong Jing (b. 1955), Clara Law (b. 1957), and Jackie Chan (b. 1954), who were already working inside the film industry, to form the Hong Kong New Wave. Together they brought Hong Kong cinema to international prominence in very short order, making films across a range of genres but focusing most intensely on urban crime thrillers, action comedies, and martial-arts fantasy and swordplay films. Heavily influenced by American directors like Sam Peckinpah, the crime films offered a unique blend of melodrama and balletic ultra-violence that came to be known as "heroic bloodshed." Hong Kong's film industry was operating at full capacity throughout the 1980s, producing upward of 160 films a year, not just for its movie-addicted population of 6.2 million people, but for large export markets from Singapore to Seoul. Until recently, Hong Kong was one of the few industrialized nations outside the United States that controlled its own market so that year by year domestic films dominated the box office; and in 1992 (its biggest revenue year ever, with $160 million in grosses), it briefly became the third largest producer of films in the world, after India

and the United States. But things began to change rapidly after 1993, when Universal's *Jurassic Park* became the first foreign film to lead in domestic box-office revenues since the 1960s. In this same year, it became clear that the pirate VCD (video compact disc) market was seriously eroding industry profits, cutting theater admissions by as much as 40 percent and forcing some theater chains out of business. The involvement of organized crime in production finance (through secret gangs known as triads) had long been a given, but in the mid-1990s the triads swung their investment support to the far more lucrative enterprise of VCD piracy, delivering a double blow to the film industry. By 1998, it was possible to buy illegal VCD copies of most new and soon-to-be-released Hong Kong films openly in stores or street stalls for U.S. $2, less than half the price of a movie ticket; at the same time, non–Hong Kong films began to outgross local product for the first time since 1980. Production figures quickly told the tale: from making 160 films in 1994, the industry turned out 140 in 1995 and just 100 in 1996. Moreover, an increasingly large proportion of these (e.g., 47 percent of the total for 1998 and 1999) were Category III films—adults-only exploitation films featuring graphic sex and/or sadistic violence and restricted to those eighteen years of age and older.[9] Exacerbating the slump was the East Asian financial crisis, which began in Thailand in 1997 and was regionwide by 1998, undercutting key Hong

---

9. As the percentage suggests, Category III films are far from being a marginal element in Hong Kong cinema. In any given year since the early 1990s, when their production began to boom, they have constituted at least a 25 percent share of the market. Category III films tend to be either conventional genre films freighted with extreme content or borderline pornography emphasizing perverted sex (e.g., *Naked Killer* [*Chiklo gouyeung*; Clarence Fok Yiu-leung, 1992]; *Sex and Zen* [*Rou pu tuan zhi tou qing bao jian*; Michael Mak, 1992]) or ghastly crime (e.g., *The Untold Story*/also known as *Bunman* [*Ba Xian fan dian zhi ren rou cha shao bao* [Herman Yau, 1992]; *Dr. Lamb* [*Gao yang yi sheng*; Danny Lee, 1992]; *Red to Kill* [*Ruo sha*; Billy Tang, 1994]). Since 1987, all films released in Hong Kong have been classified by the Hong Kong Television and Entertainment Licensing Authority (TELA) according to a three-tiered system: in Category I are films intended for all audiences; in Category II are films "not suitable for children"; and in Category III are films restricted to those 18 or older. In 1994, Category II was subdivided into IIA ("not suitable for children") and IIB ("not suitable for children or young persons"—i.e., teenagers). See Darrell W. Davis and Yeh Yeuh-yu, "Warning! Category III," *Film Quarterly* 54, 4 (Summer 2001): 12–26, and Julian Stinger, "Category 3: Sex and Violence in Postmodern Hong Kong," in Christopher Sharrett, ed., *Mythologies of Violence in Postmodern Media* (Detroit: Wayne State University Press, 1999), pp. 361–79.

Kong export markets. Production budgets for mainstream films dwindled from the neighborhood of several million U.S. dollars to U.S. $200,000 or U.S. $300,000, and production activity became frenetic in an effort to cut costs, with directors shooting as many as three films simultaneously (one each in the morning, afternoon, and evening) and stars like Chow Yun-fat and Andy Lau sometimes appearing in twelve to fourteen films a year. In 1999, the Shaw Brothers sold its valuable film library—over 700 titles, representing much of the industry's postwar history—to a Taipei cable company, and Golden Harvest moved toward liquidating its production arm altogether (although, as of 2002, it remained an important producer).

Complicating the situation politically was the fact that in 1984 the British colonial rulers of Hong Kong pledged to cede the entire territory to the People's Republic of China in July 1997, creating an unprecedented migration of people and capital from the Crown Colony and causing a slump in its normally expansive economy. The Tiananmen Square massacre of June 1989 did little to reverse this trend; but once the handover had actually taken place, it became clear that the PRC intended to continue its march toward capitalism and that south China would in fact provide a vast new market for Hong Kong's products. Dire predictions of a film-industry collapse proved unfounded as the nation's political economy stabilized, and Hong Kong transformed itself into a diversified talent base for the region—a kind of "Hollywood East"—as well as the main engine of Chinese-language film production, whose epicenters were Beijing, Shanghai, Taipei, and Singapore. Among other attractions, Hong Kong had acquired a world-class CGI studio, Central Digital Pictures, which had demonstrated its prowess by creating 550 digital effects for the Golden Harvest fantasy adventure *The Storm Riders* (*Feng yun xiong ba tian xia* [Andrew Lau, 1998]), an international hit that helped restore market credibility to the industry. The success of a second CGI extravaganza from Central Digital/Golden Harvest, *A Man Called Hero* (*Zhong hua ying xiong* [Andrew Lau, 1999]), made it clear that Hong Kong had become an important site for digital postproduction (see Chapter 21). By 2000, Hong Kong production was booming again and, with 144 features, had returned to preslump levels. Tellingly, much new production capital came from internet companies, who see the downloadable digital marketplace as the future of film.

A number of Hong Kong filmmakers have achieved world-class reputations since emerging from the New Wave of the 1980s, among them John Woo, Tsui Hark, Ringo Lam, Sammo Hung, Jackie Chan, Ann Hui, Ronny Yu, Stanley Kwan, and Wong Kar-wai. John Woo (born Wu Yu Sen, 1946) had worked as an assistant on martial-arts films at Shaw Brothers before directing a series of comedies starring the popular Ricky Hui during the 1970s. His breakthrough feature, however, was *A Better Tomorrow* (*Ying huang boon sik* [1986]), which was characterized by marital-arts film expert Rick Baker when he first saw it as a film of "heroic bloodshed," coining the term that has been attached to Hong Kong gunplay films ever since. Woo's poetic fusion of the Chinese martial-arts tradition with the conventions of Western action films effectively created a new genre, whose ore he continued to mine through a superior sequel (*A Better Tomorrow II* [1987]) and such operatic gangster sagas as *The Killer* (*Die xue shuang xiong* [1989]), *Once a Thief* (*Zong heng si hai* [1990]), *Bullet in the Head* (*Die xue jie tou* [1990]), and *Hard-boiled* (*Lashou shentan* [1992]), all starring Hong Kong romantic icon Chow Yun-fat (b. 1955), which drew their inspiration from such existential action direc-

18.59 Hong Kong gunplay in overdrive: John Woo's *The Killer* (1989): Chow Yun-Fat, Danny Lee.

18.60 *The Killer* (John Woo, 1989). At the film's conclusion, Danny Lee and Chow Yun-fat blast their way out a church baement in an apocalypse of "heroic bloodshed" worthy of Peckinpah's *The Wild Bunch* (1969).

(2000) as a dazzling tribute to Hong Kong's cinema of pure acceleration, full of complicated wire-work stunts and rapid-fire editing, with an admittedly cartoonish plot. Although it failed to generate the blockbuster earnings of the original, *M:i-2* grossed an impressive $225 million domestically and earned Woo a place in Hollywood's big-budget action-director hierarchy (which includes the likes of Renny Harlin, John McTiernan, Tony Scott, and Wolfgang Petersen). In this context, his *Windtalkers* (2002) was a major disappointment in retelling its true story of Navajo Indian "code

tors as Jean-Pierre Melville, Sam Peckinpah, and Sergio Leone, and which influenced in turn a younger generation of American directors led by Quentin Tarantino (*Reservoir Dogs* [1992]; *Pulp Fiction* [1994]), Robert Rodriguez (*El Mariachi* [1992]; *Desperado* [1995]), and Sam Raimi (*A Simple Plan* [1998]). *The Killer* was the first "heroic bloodshed" film to be distributed in the United States, and its popular success brought Woo contracts to direct *Hard Target* (1993), a Jean-Claude Van Damme vehicle, for Universal, and the bigger-budget *Broken Arrow* (1996), starring John Travolta, for Fox—both of them exciting, if predictable, Hollywood action films. But with Buena Vista's *Face/Off* (1997), Woo brought both the letter and spirit of Hong Kong–style heroic bloodshed into the American cinema. This intricate, obsessive thriller, which involves (literal) identity transference between a maniacal killer and the vengeful FBI agent who is stalking him, contained the director's signature ultraviolence rendered through balletic slow motion, as well as the homoerotic subtext that had characterized his best Hong Kong action films. After *Face/Off* became one of the top-grossing films of the year ($112 million domestic), Woo took the challenge of delivering a successful sequel to Paramount's vastly popular *Mission: Impossible* (Brian De Palma, 1996). Working with a $125 million budget—one of the highest for an American film to date—Woo crafted *M:i-2*

talkers" in the Pacific theater during World War II. Woo remains in Hollywood today, together with his producer Terence Chang and the gifted actor Chow Yun-fat, although several other Hong Kong filmmakers who immigrated to the United States around the time of the handover have since returned east (e.g., Ringo Lam, Stanley Tong, and Peter Chan). In addition to directing, he has also worked as an executive producer on such Hong Kong–oriented films as *The Replacement Killers* (Antoine Fuqua, 1998) and *The Big Hit* (Kirk Wong, 1998).

Tsui Hark (pronounced "Choy Hok") is also a producer as well as director and, since the 1980s, has been a major force in the development of Hong Kong cinema. Born Xu Wen Guang in Vietnam in 1951, Hark attended the University of Texas and worked as a documentary filmmaker in New York City before returning to Hong Kong in 1977 to work as a television producer and then as a founding figure of New Wave cinema. During this time, his most important work as a director was Golden Harvest's *Zu: Warriors of the Magic Mountains* (*Shu shan* [1983]), a sword-and-sorcery epic reminiscent of *Star Wars* for which he imported four American special-effects experts, introducing optical effects to Hong Kong cinema. Dissatisfied with local studio practice, Tsui and his wife, Nansun Shi, founded their own company in 1984, Film Workshop, which went on to become one of

18.61 *Once upon a Time in China* (Tsui Hark, 1991): Jet Li as Master Wong Fei-hung, the nineteenth-century physician, good Samaritan, and martial artist who became a Chinese folk hero for resisting the cultural imperalism of the West. The film inspired three sequels, two of them written and directed by Hark.

the most successful small studios in Hong Kong; and in 1986, Tsui founded Cinefex Workshop, Hong Kong's first full-service special-effects house, which would sustain hundreds of domestic fantasy and swordplay films over the next few decades. Hark's next achievement was *Peking Opera Blues* (*Do ma daan* [1986]), a comedy-drama about three women from different walks of life during the Chinese revolution of 1913 whose flamboyant style of "controlled chaos" (Tsui) and generic hybridity made it a hit on the Western art-house circuit, calling unprecedented international attention to Hong Kong's New Wave cinema. In that same year, Tsui produced John Woo's *A Better Tomorrow* and directed *A Chinese Ghost Story* (*Sinnui yauman* [1991], an atmospheric and colorful supernatural love story that proved popular and engendered two numbered sequels in 1990 and 1991, both directed by Hark, as well as numerous imitations, the best of which was Ronny Yu's *The Bride with the White Hair* (*Bai fa mo nu zhuan* [1993]). (Multiple sequels, cycles, and series spun off from popular films were typical of Hong Kong's high-energy cinema during this period, their formulaic nature facilitating speedy, cost-effective production—as one distributor put it, "The sequels come out almost before the original movie.")[1] After directing a prequel to John Woo's *A Better Tomor-*

row series (*A Better Tomorrow III* [1989]), Tsui turned his attention to the legendary nineteenth-century martial artist, Confucian scholar, and physician Wong Fei-hung, creating a three-part epic—*Once upon a Time in China* (*Wong Fei-hung ji yi* [1991; 1992; 1993])—devoted to Master Wong's heroic exploits in defending his downtrodden people from European imperialism. (A fourth installment was written by Hark and directed by Sammo Hung in 1997; see below.) The series was a smash hit domestically and made a star of Jet Li (b. 1963), the young *kung fu* veteran who played Wong Fei-hung. Another impressive group of films produced by Tsui Hark was the martial-arts adventure series that was begun with *Swordsman* (*Xiao ao jiang hu* [1990]) and continued through *East Is Red: Swordsman III* (*Dung fong bat baai 2: fung wan joi hei* [1993]). Set in the Ming dynasty (1368–1644), these fantastic *wu xia* films were written and produced by Tsui but directed by others (King Hu, Ching Sui-tung), yet the Hark imprimatur is unmistakable, as it was in *The Blade* (*Dao* [1996]), Hark's gory adaptation of Chang Cheh's 1967 martial-arts classic

1. Wouter Barendrecht of Fortissimo Film Sales, quoted in "A Touch of Realism," *Asiaweek*, July 20, 2001, p. 38.

One-Armed Swordsman (*Dubi dao*), which many consider to be the high-water mark of 1990s swordplay. But Tsui's talents as a director continued to extend across a broad range of genres, including mythological fantasy (*Green Snake* [*Ching se*, 1993]), melodrama (*The Lovers* [*Leung juk*, 1994]), slapstick *kung fu* (*Chinese Feast* [*Jin yu man tang*, 1995]), and espionage thriller (*Double Team* [1997]; *Knock Off* [1998]). Like many of his compatriots, Tsui left Hong Kong briefly for Hollywood in the mid-1990s but returned in 2000 to direct the gangster film *Time and Tide* (*Seunlau ngaklau*) and to begin work on a sequel to his 1983 fantasy adventures *Zu: Warriors* entitled *The Legend of Zu* (*Shu shan zheng zhuan* [2001]), this time with digital, rather than optical, effects.

Two other action directors with close ties to Woo and Hark are Ringo Lam (b. 1954) and Sammo Hung (b. 1952). Lam studied film at York University in Toronto and returned to Hong Kong to work in the industry in the early 1980s. His breakthrough film was *City on Fire* (*Long hu feng yun* [1987]), a gritty crime thriller starring Chow Yun-fat as a disaffected undercover cop who infiltrates a gang of thieves. *City on Fire* became the model for Tarantino's *Reservoir Dogs* (1992) and a kind of emblem for the realistic Hong Kong gangster film in general. Lam reprised its plot through a series of similarly entitled films (*Prison on Fire* [*Gaam yuk fung wan*, 1987]; *Prison on Fire II* [*Tao fan*, 1991]; *School on Fire* [*Xue xiao feng yun*, 1988]), arriving finally at the brutal and graphically violent *Full Contact* (*Xia dao Gao Fei* [1992]), a revenge thriller that also starred Chow Yun-fat. Like Woo, Lam came to Hollywood to direct a martial-arts action thriller starring Jean-Claude Van Damme; but the result (Columbia/Sony's *Maximum Risk* [1996]) was considerably less happy, and Lam returned to Hong Kong in 1997. Here he made a series of high-octane thrillers— *Full Alert* (*Ko dou gai bei* [1997]), *Suspect* (*Jidu zhongfan* [1998]), and *Victim* (*Mu lu xiong guang* [1999])—that restored his status as one of Hong Kong's greatest action directors. Sammo Hung (b. Sammo Hung Kam-bo) was originally part of a popular comedy team with Jackie Chan and Yuen Biao. (All three were childhood friends who had trained together in acrobatics at Sifu Yu Jim Yuen's famous Peking Opera School in Hong Kong. They were part of a popular group of child entertainers from the school known as the "Seven Little Fortunes," and their early life there was the subject of the 1988 Hong Kong film *Painted Faces* [*Qi qiao fu*, 1988], directed by Alex

Law, in which Sammo played the role of Master Yu.) Sammo Hung mainly worked in film as an actor and occasional producer (e.g., *Mr. Vampire* [*Geung si sin sang*; Ricky Lau, 1986]) until he directed a series of successful action films in genres ranging from realistic combat (*Eastern Condors* [*Dung fong tuk ying*, 1986]), to slapstick *kung fu* (*Shanghai Express*/also known as *Millionaire's Express* [*Foo gwai lit che*, 1986]; *Dragons Forever* [*Fei lung maang jeung*, 1987]), to period swordplay (*Moon Warriors* [*Zhan shen chuan shuo*, 1993]; *Blade of Fury* [*Yat do king sing*, 1993]; *Once upon a Time in China IV* [*Wong Fei-hung chi saiwik hung si*, 1997]). Sammo Hung often stars in his films and provides his own consistently inventive fight choreography.

Although Jackie Chan (b. Chan Kong Sang, 1954) is best known to Western audiences as an astonishingly inventive practitioner of physical comedy, he is also a brilliant writer, producer, and director of his own work. From his rigorous training in martial arts and acrobatics at Master Yu's Peking Opera School, he moved into cinema in his teens, and his original film persona—oddly, it now seems—was modeled on Bruce Lee. But it was his talent for comic martial artistry that connected with the audience in early Golden Harvest films like *Drunken Master* (*Zui quan* [Yuen Woo-ping, 1978]) and *Dragon Lord* (*Long xiao ye* [Jackie Chan, 1982]), and his work in non-stop action comedies like *Project A* (*'A' gai waak* [Jackie Chan, 1983]), *Wheels on Meals* (*Kwai tsan tseh* [Sammo Hung, 1984]), *Police Story* (*Ging chaat goo si* [Jackie Chan, 1985]), and *The Armour of God*/also known as *Operation Condor 2* (*Longxiong hudi* [Jackie Chan,

18.62 *The Armour of God* (also known as *Operation Condor 2* [Jackie Chan, 1986]): Chan practicing the intensely physical brand of humor that made him an international star.

1986]), and *Operation Condor*/also known as *Armour of God II* (*Feiying gaiwak* [Jackie Chan, 1990]) soon made Chan a pan-Asian superstar. Especially notable in these films were his Keatonesque trajectory stunts, which clearly placed him in physical danger during the shoot and which several times caused him life-threatening injury. (Since *Dragon Lord* in 1982, this element of his popularity has been highlighted in signature outtakes during the closing credits that show botched stunts and resultant injuries.) Chan did not acquire a large American following until the U.S. release of *Rumble in the Bronx* (1995), which starred him as a visiting Hong Kong cop pitted against a New York street gang. This film, like the excellent *Supercop* (1992) and *First Strike*/also known as *Police Story 4* (1993), was directed by Stanley Tong (b. 1960), one of Hong Kong's pre-handover Hollywood émigrés, and it was terrifically successful in its own terms, returning $32 million on its modest $7.5 million investment. After this, all of Chan's films made money in the United States, and the American-produced *Rush Hour* (1998), directed by Brett Ratner for New Line Cinema, became a genuine blockbuster, grossing $141 million against its $35 million investment and breathing new life into the action-comedy genre more or less depleted in recent years by the four-part *Lethal Weapon* franchise. *Rush Hour 2* (Brett Ratner, 2000) was even more successful, and Chan finally achieved the kind of stardom in the American cinema that he had enjoyed in the rest of the world for decades, giving him an international currency that few comics have enjoyed since the days of Chaplin, Keaton, and Lloyd.

By contrast, there are several Hong Kong New Wave directors notable for their seriousness and generic unconventionality: Ann Hui, Stanley Kwan, and Wong Kar-wai. Ann Hui (b. Manchuria, 1947) began working for the government television network RTHK in 1978, where she made the first two parts of her "Vietnam trilogy," "Boy from Vietnam" (1978) and "The Story of Woo Viet" (1981), which was completed by the feature *Boat People* (*Tou bun no hoi* [1982]). Although she has occasionally directed conventional genre films—e.g., her psychological thriller *The Secret* (*Feng jie* [1979]) and her comic ghost story *The Spooky Bunch* (*Zhuang dao zheng* [1980]—her work tends to be more personal than that of her peers. Thus, *Starry Is the Night* (*Gam ye sing gwong chaan laan* [1988]) and *Song of Exile* (*Ketu qiuhen* [1990]) are both autobiographical accounts of past relationships. The domestic dramas *My American Grandson* (*Shanghai jiaqi* [1990]) and

Summer Snow (*Xiatian de xue* [1994]) offer carefully nuanced portraits of Chinese family life. Other Hui films adapt the work of Hong Kong/Shanghai novelist Eileen Chang—*Love in a Fallen City* (*Qing cheng zhi lian* [1984]) and *Eighteen Springs* (*Boon sang yuen* [1997]). Even her period action film *The Romance of Book and Sword* (*Shu jian en chou lu* [1987]), which recounts a folk legend about an attempt by the secret Red Flower Society to restore the Han Empire, adopts her distinctive style of uncoded flashbacks and voice-over narration.

Another director who eschews commercialism is Stanley Kwan (b. 1957), who apprenticed as an assistant director under Ann Hui in both television and features in the early 1980s. Like Hui, he has devoted much of his work to exploring the condition of women in modern China, from his early melodramas *Women* (*Nu ren xin* [1985]) and *Love unto Waste* (*Deiha tsing* [1986]), through *Full Moon in New York* (*Ren zai Niu Yue* [1989]), in which women from the PRC, Hong Kong, and Taiwan form a friendship abroad, to his biopic of Ruan Ling-yu (*The Actress*/also known as *Centre Stage* [*Yuen Ling-yuk*, 1992]), a hugely popular silent-film star who committed suicide at the age of twenty-five in 1935 as the result of a scandal. But Kwan's most famous New Wave film—and one that became emblematic of the aesthetic aspirations of the movement as a whole—was *Rouge* (*Yin ji kau* [1987]), an atmospheric supernatural melodrama about the ghost of a high-class call girl who has committed suicide in the 1930s and finds herself transported to a 1987 Hong Kong that is much obsessed with its past (a result of the recently announced handover, at this point ten years hence). By constructing a double storyline, Kwan was able to contrast the two Hong Kongs point by point and create a sense of the impenetrable barrier between past and present at a time when the city was faced with an uncertain future. Explorations of sexual desire and gender roles have characterized Kwan's more recent work and underlined his stylistic affinity with the avant-garde lyricism of his contemporary, Wong Kar-wai. *Red Rose, White Rose* (*Hong meigui, bai meigui* [1994]), adapted from an Eileen Chang short story, and *Hold You Tight* (*Yue kuai le, yue duo luo* [1997]) are both about individuals caught up in the crosscurrents of passion, while *Yang ± Yin: Gender in Chinese Cinema* (1996) is a British Film Institute–sponsored documentary about issues of transgender representation. *Lan Yu* (2001), based on an anonymous novel published on the internet in 1997, blends a homosexual love story with the events leading up to the Tiananmen Square massacre of 1989. The film was shot on location in Beijing—clandestinely, for obvious reasons.

Wong Kar-wai (b. Shanghai, 1958) is the Hong Kong director with the highest artistic reputation and, after John Woo, the most internationally prominent. After working as a production assistant in serial television and scriptwriting for soap operas, he directed his first feature, the realistic gangster film *As Tears Go By* (*Wong gok ka moon* [1988]), apparently inspired by Martin Scorsese's *Mean Streets* (1973). For *Days of Being Wild* (*A Fei jing juen* [1991]), Wong assembled a cast of stellar performers (Leslie Cheung, Maggie Cheung, Andy Lau) and created a film of youthful alienation and unrequited love that swept the Hong Kong Film Awards. It was *Ashes of Time* (*Dung che sai duk* [1994]), however, that announced his full maturity as an artist. Two years in production at a cost of $40 million (astronomical for a Hong Kong film), *Ashes* is an Antonioni-esque meditation on time and memory cast in the form of a martial-arts epic. The award-winning cinematography by Christopher Doyle (b. Sydney, Australia, 1952), who would work with Wong consistently from *Days of Being Wild* through *In the Mood for Love* (*Hua yang nian hua* [2000]), established a new standard in dreamlike lyricism. (Doyle, who won the 1994 Best Cinematography Award at Venice for *Ashes of Time*, is also the regular cinematographer for Stanley Kwan, which explains some of the textural similarity between the work of the two directors.) *Chungking Express* (*Chong qing sen lin* [1994]), which was shot during production delays on *Ashes of Time*, demonstrated that Wong's postmodern sensibility was perfectly suited to capturing the uncertain mood of Hong Kong in the years just prior to the handover. The film contains two unrelated stories of policemen and the women they love, revolving around the lonely urban lifestyles and chance encounters of its four alienated characters. (In the United States, *Chungking Express* was distributed with something close to missionary zeal by Quentin Tarantino's Rolling Thunder Pictures, suggesting the growing importance of Hong Kong styles to cutting-edge American cinema and confirming Tarantino's own artistic debt.) The international art-house success of *Chungking Express* led to a widespread imitation of Wong's style of free-form camera movement, step-printed slow motion, and voice-over interior monologues in other Hong Kong, Taiwanese, and mainland Chinese films, sometimes by way of parody but more often as an *homage* to the artistic prestige Wong was bringing to a cinema generally perceived to be relentlessly and unabashedly commercial. (Good examples of Wong's influence on Sixth Generation Chinese directors are Wang Xiaoshuai's *So Close to Paradise* [1998] and Lou Ye's *Suzhou River* [2000].) *Fallen Angels* (*Duo luo tian shi* [1995]) continued Wong's mood-drenched romanticization of anomie in a disjointed series of episodes that follow various characters on their personal odysseys through nighttime Hong Kong. Their stories seem less important somehow than the palpable urban element through which they move, confirming what the director told an interviewer in 2001: "I sometimes treat space as a main character in my films."[2] *Happy Together* (*Cheun gwong tsa sit* [1997]) seemed to some critics like a change of pace, but in fact this story of the doomed relationship of two gay lovers from Hong Kong in Buenos Aires is cut from the same cloth as its predecessors: it is about estrangement and disconnectedness as the very stuff of modern life, and Christopher Doyle's dazzling cinematography creates a level of romantic imagery that redeems the self-destructive impulses of its characters. *In the Mood for Love* (2000) is probably the most widely admired film to emerge from the Hong Kong cinema in

18.63 *In the Mood for Love* (Wong Kar-wai, 2000). Like ships passing in the night, these two neighbors (Maggie Cheung and Tony Leung Chiu-wai) come to realize that their respective spouses are lovers and finally fall in love themselves. The film's mood of reverie and romantic longing is sustained through lush, award-winning cinematography by Christopher Doyle and Mark Li Ping-bin.

---

2. Wong Kar-wai, quoted in Leslie Camhi, "Getting His Tale of Love Found in a City Long Lost," *The New York Times*, January 28, 2001, p. AR 26.

a decade. Set in 1962 among the exiled Shanghaiese community in Hong Kong, it concerns two young couples living in a cramped apartment block. The husband in one couple and the wife in the other gradually come to realize that their spouses (never shown unobscured in the film) are having an affair, and, in the slow process of coming to terms with this knowledge, they fall in love. The film manages to be intensely erotic and sensual, even though the principals rarely touch, thanks in large part to Doyle's multiple-award-winning cinematography (Technical Grand Prize, Cannes; National Society of Film Critics Award; New York Film Critics Award, all for 2000), which evokes a vanished time and place with rare beauty. (Ironically, Doyle was replaced by the less visually flamboyant Mark Li Ping-bin, Hou Hsiao-hsien's regular director of photography midway through principal photography.) Most of *In the Mood for Love* was shot in Bangkok, to re-create the look and feel of 1960s Hong Kong, with one or two Hong Kong locations (these had already been built over by the time of the film's release, so quickly does the city reinvent itself). Working as always from a story idea without a finished script, Wong infused *In the Mood for Love* with a combination of nostalgia and postmodern hipness that has become his stock in trade. In a way, his project all along has been to create a memory for a city that wants to deny it has one—a "city on fire" that, like its cinema, has become a kind of self-consuming artifact. As Stephen Teo suggests, *In the Mood for Love* is an emblem for the slow recovery of the Hong Kong film industry from its near-fatal slump. Likewise, it perfectly encapsulates Hong Kong's post-1997 sensibility "because it reverberates with muted nostalgia for Hong Kong's golden age, while making a statement about the people of Hong Kong's propensity for overcoming adversity and withstanding loss."[3]

TAIWAN (REPUBLIC OF CHINA)

From 1947 through 1987, the island nation of Taiwan—which mainland China threatens militarily and still claims as its own—was ruled by Chiang Kai-shek's authoritarian Kuomintang (KMT) government under martial law, and all media were subject to political censorship. For this reason, its film industry developed slowly and was long dominated by that of Hong Kong, although with 21.9 million people Taiwan has nearly four times Hong Kong's population. During the 1960s, the government-owned Central Motion Picture Corporation (CMPC) attempted to boost feature production through a system of direct funding and loans. This maneuver helped Li Han-hsiang (1926–1996; see above), a director of costume films at Shaw Brothers, to found the Grand Motion Picture Company in Taipei in 1963. Here were made films like *The Love Eterne* (*Liang Shan bo yu Zhu Yingtai* [1963]) and *Four Moods* (*Hsi nou ai lueh* [1970]) that helped to lay the groundwork for an indigenous Taiwanese feature cinema. Another Shaw Brothers transplant, Hu Chin-chuan (1931–1997), founded International Motion Picture Studio in Taipei at about the same time and introduced swordplay (*wu xia*) films to Taiwan (e.g., his own *Dragon Inn* [*Lung men ke zhan*, 1966]). Such local filmmakers as there were tended to focus mainly on the problems of rural communities, but as the island rapidly industrialized and its people became more affluent during the 1970s, wave after wave of locally produced martial-arts films (mainly Mandarin-dialect) and slick youth-oriented melodramas (mostly Taiwanese-dialect) appeared in a market formerly given over to Shaw Brothers' productions. For example, over half (327) of the 609 features produced in Taiwan between 1972 and 1974 were swordplay or *kung fu* genre films. In the early 1980s, however, a new generation of filmmakers, most of whom had studied abroad and had a clearer sense of their cultural identity, entered the industry. Assisted by the CMPC (which by this time controlled theaters as well as production finance) and by a liberalization of government censorship that came with the end of martial law in 1987, they created a distinctive "New Cinema," or "New Wave" (*hsin-jui*), in low- to medium-budget films that dealt with day-to-day reality in Taiwan but were often stylistically experimental.

The major figures of New Taiwan Cinema are Edward Yang (Yang De-chang; b. 1947) and Hou Hsiao-hsien (b. 1947). Yang's first feature, *That Day on the Beach* (*Haitan de yitian*, 1983), showed the influence of European modernism, especially the work of Antonioni, in its depiction of contemporary urban alienation. Similarly, in *Tapei Story* (*Qingmei zhuma*, 1985) a materially successful husband and wife unexpectedly find their relationship falling apart in the rapidly changing capital city, while *The Ter-*

---

3. Stephen Teo, "Hong Kong Journal," *Film Comment* 36, 6 (November/December, 2000): 13.

18.64 Edward Yang's *Taipei Story* (1985).

rorizer (*Kongbu fenzi*, 1987) concerns an estranged office worker who murders his wife and her lover in a fit of anomie. In the early 1990s, Yang directed the four-hour *A Brighter Summer Day* (*Guling jie shaonian sha ren shijian*, 1991), generally considered to be his masterpiece. This sprawling film offers a precision-honed reconstruction of an actual Taipei street murder at the same time that it provides a detailed account of its dislocated 1960s social context. It was followed by the contemporary urban satire *A Confucian Confusion* (*Duli shidai*, 1994), in which the attitudes of the Taipei nouveau riche are given complex scrutiny. With the comic action thriller *Mahjong* (*Majiang*, 1996), Yang briefly took a more commercial turn, but *Yi yi* (also known as *A One and a Two . . .*, 2000), with its episodic narrative of a middle-class family thrown into crisis through a series a random incidents, exhibits both the novelistic sweep and metaphoric exploration of Taiwanese cultural identity that characterize his greatest work; and it deservedly won the 2000 Palm d'Or at Cannes for Best Direction.

The work of Hou Hsiao-hsien is more traditional and nostalgic, reaching back to a preindustrial Chinese culture and family life. Nearly all of his films to date—e.g., *The Boys from Fengkuei* (*Fengkuei lai te jen*, 1983), *A Summer at Grandpa's* (*Dongdong de jiaqi*, 1984); *Dust in the Wind* (*Lianlian feng chen*, 1987); *Daughter of the Nile* (*Niluohe nuer*, 1987)—are about the disorienting, often disintegrating impact of city life on people newly arrived from rural towns. Some take the form of family chronicles—*A Time to Live and a Time to Die* (*Tongnien wangshi*, 1985) depicts three generations of Chinese villagers as they adapt and survive migration to modernizing Taiwan, while Hou's magnum opus *City of Sadness* (*Beiqing chengshi*, 1989) focused on the fate of a Taiwanese family during the island's transfer from Japanese to Chinese hands, from 1945 to 1949, and the setting up of Chiang Kai-shek's repressive Nationalist government. *City of Sadness* won the Golden Lion at Venice and came to form the first part of a loose trilogy on the history of postwar Taiwan. The second installment, *The Puppetmaster* (*Hsi-meng jen-sheng*, 1993), was shot on location in the mainland province of Fujan. This biography of veteran puppeteer Li T'ien-lu takes place between 1908 and 1945, when the province was under Japanese rule, and it collapses narrative and documentary form by having the real Li narrating and commenting on the dramatization of events from his life. *Good Men, Good Women* (*Hao nan hao nu*, 1995), the trilogy's final entry, deals with Taiwan during the early 1950s, when Chiang Kai-shek launched an anti-Communist terror campaign against his own people. Throughout the trilogy, as in all of his work, Hou uses long takes, offscreen space, and Ozu-like "empty scenes" to create a meditative quality that resonates with his evocation of history, but *Good Men, Good Women* signaled a new attention to moving camera shots that was brought to fruition in *Flowers of Shanghai* (*Hai shang hua*, 1998), a coproduction with Japan's Shochiku studio. This uncharacteristic period drama, set in the brothels of nineteenth-century Shanghai, was filmed with a continuously moving camera by Hou's frequent collaborator Mark Li Ping-bin, with sequence shots linked together by slow fades to black. *Goodbye South, Goodbye* (*Nanguo zaijan, nanguo*, 1996) and *Millennium Mambo* (*Qianxi manbo*, 2001) both employ this newly mobile camera to examine the rootlessness and decadence of contemporary Taiwanese life. Because of the intellectual difficulty and challenging artistic complexity of his work, Hou Hsiao-hsien has never been a popular filmmaker either at home or abroad. But

18.65 *Good Men, Good Women* (Hou Hsiao-hsien, 1995): left-wing political refugees returning to Taiwan from the mainland after World War II, soon to be victims of Chiang Kai-shek's anti-Communist "White Terror," instigated by American counterintelligence.

among international critics, he is regarded as one of the world's greatest living directors for his mastery of style and for his principled critique of modernity on both an existential and a cultural level.

In the late 1980s, the Taiwanese Government Information Office (GIO) set up a system to encourage local production by making cash awards for scripts. The chief beneficiaries of this Guidance Fund for Domestically Produced Films, known as the *fudao jin* (subsidy) system, were the so-called "second wave" of the New Taiwan Cinema led by Ang Lee and Tsai Ming-liang. Ang Lee (b. Taiwan, 1954), who studied film at NYU, made his feature debut with the intergenerational comedy *Pushing Hands* (*Tui shou*, 1992), which was about cultural conflict in a Taiwanese family living in New York. Many of Ang Lee's subsequent work would deal with similar themes—e.g., his breakthrough film *The Wedding Banquet* (1993), a romantic comedy in which a gay Taiwanese immigrant in New York stages a heterosexual wedding for the benefit of his traditionally conservative parents, who insist on coming from China to attend the ceremony; and *Eat Drink Man Woman* (*Yinshi nan nu*, 1994), another look at an intrafamilial generation gap, shot on location in Taiwan and revolving around the psychological and social meanings of food in a traditional culture. Even Ang's most thoroughly Westernized films—his Jane Austin

adaptation *Sense and Sensibility* (1995), his version of Rick Moody's novel of suburban anomie *The Ice Storm* (1997), and his literal, generic Western *Ride with the Devil* (1999)—are about societies and/or social groups whose future is as uncertain and tenuous as that of Taiwan because they have lived through periods of rapid social change. Moreover, Ang Lee was clearly reclaiming his Chinese heritage in *Crouching Tiger, Hidden Dragon* (2000), a wonderfully realized "magical action" or "flying swordsman" adventure epic of the sort that Hong Kong directors had been turning out for decades (e.g., King Hu's *A Touch of Zen* [1969]; Tsui Hark's *Zu: Warriors* [1983]; Ching Siu-tung's *The East Is Red* [1992]; Andrew Lau's *The Storm Riders* [1998]); and it had the additional cachet of fight choreography by Yuen Woo-ping, who had performed the same service for the Wachowski brothers' popular *The Matrix* (another film highly derivative of Hong Kong action genres) the year before.

18.66 *Eat Drink Man Woman* (Ang Lee, 1994). Widowed master chef Chu (Sihung Lung) prepares a groaning board of traditional Chinese delicacies for his three daughters (Yu-wen Wang, Chien-lien Wu, and Kuei-mei Yang) every Sunday, which their slender figures and fast-track urban lifestyles can barely accommodate.

Crouching Tiger caused a sensation in the West; it was nominated for fourteen Academy Awards and received four—for Best Foreign Film, Best Cinematography (Peter Pau), Best Art Direction (Tim Yip), and Best Score (Tan Dun)—and won many other honors (e.g., Best Director from the British Academy, the Directors Guild of America, and the Golden Globes). But *Crouching Tiger* bombed in all three Chinese markets because audiences there had seen it all before (and, many felt, had seen it better). As to wild speculation about an Asian invasion of Hollywood in trade-press articles with titles like "The Irresistible Rise of Asian Cinema" and "It's Raining Tigers and Dragons in the Land of Film," there *had* been an invasion, but it was the other way around.

In 1999, under pressure from the United States, Taiwan lifted the import quotas that had protected its domestic industry for decades, and in the following year production dropped to just 16 features, which upon release shared among themselves less than 1 percent of annual box-office revenues. This makes the GIO subsidies, which have a ceiling of U.S. $330,000 per title, crucial to the continued existence of Taiwanese cinema; and, indeed, more than half of all domestic films receive some government funding. Since the minimum feature budget is approximately $530,000, however, filmmakers can usually start production without considering the local market at all, which explains how a national cinema with only one functioning studio (the CMPC, which also owns theaters) and massive competition from abroad can sustain an artist like Tsai Ming-liang (b. Malaysia, 1957). Produced by the GIO and the CMPC, Tsai's austere study of nihilistic Taipei youth, *Rebels of the Neon God* (*Ch'ing shaonien na cha*, 1992) reminded critics of Antonioni in its disposition of real time, and it won multiple international awards. Composed of very long takes, virtually without dialogue, *Vive l'Amour* (*Aiqing wansui*, 1994) revolves around anonymous couplings in a vacant Taipei apartment; it evoked comparisons with the work of Bresson and Ozu, and it won the Golden Lion at Venice. The last film in what became a vague trilogy on the soulessness of modern Taipei, *The River* (*He liu*, 1997) extends the stories of some of the characters from *Rebels of the Neon God* as they have formed dysfunctional families. Tsai's more recent films reveal a turn toward the absurdist avant-

garde. *The Hole* (*Dong*, 1998), for example, is a grim tale of urban bleakness in the near future whose alienated characters express their feelings in lip-synched production numbers from 1950s Hong Kong musicals, calling to mind the work of screenwriter Dennis Potter (*Pennies from Heaven* [Piers Haggard, 1978]) or Danish director Lars von Trier (*Dancer in the Dark* [2000]), whereas *What Time Is It There?* (*Ni neibian jidian*, 2001) concerns several characters who become obsessed with the idea that the differential between time zones conceals a hidden dimension. The absurdist note in Tsai's work can be thought to resonate with the situation of Taiwan itself, whose national and cultural identity has been called constantly into question for the past one hundred years. Brutally occupied by the Japanese from 1895 to 1945, ruled by the repressive Kuomintang from 1947 to 1988, treated as a nation-state and heavily armed by the United States (which is its largest trading partner, followed by Japan) during the Cold War, but regarded by much of the world (including the United Nations and, officially at least, the United States) as belonging to mainland China, which stands ready to go to war if its claim on the island is materially disputed, Taiwan's geopolitical existence is tinged with absurdity. Add to this the social dislocations produced by the rapid industrialization and urbanization of a centuries-old agrarian economy (metropolitan Taipei contains 7.7 million people, over one-third of the country's population), and Taiwan's cinema of postmodern absurdity begins to make a lot of sense.

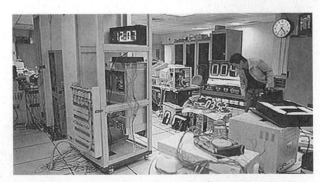

18.67 *What Time Is It There?* (Tsai Ming-liang, 2001): Lee Kang-sheng as a watch salesman obsessed with time in a dramatic feature inflected by the postmodern avant-garde and suggesting the historical rootlessness of the Taiwanese people.

Third World Cinema

Vital national film cultures have gradually developed in the nations of Latin America, Africa, the Middle East, and the Pacific Rim, collectively known as the Third World[1] in the past thirty-five years. By the mid-1970s, Third World cinema was widely recognized as one of the most important and innovative movements in contemporary filmmaking, as significant historically as were Italian neorealism and the French New Wave. The term covers a wide range of films produced on three continents, in countries most of which have long histories of exploitation and colonial oppression by Western powers. Only now are these countries emerging from centuries of underdevelopment, and their struggle to do so has produced one of the most exciting creative impulses in cinema today.

Despite the ethnic and political diversity of Third World countries, their cinemas tend to have several common characteristics that identify them as parts of a coherent international movement. First, Third World filmmakers conceive of cinema not as an entertainment commodity produced to make a profit, but as a compelling means of mass

---

1. The term also includes India and the PRC, as discussed in the previous chapter. Historically, the concept of a Third World is a post–World War II phenomenon in which the "developing nations"—most of them formerly colonies of various European countries—were counterposed to the "free world" of the Western democracies dominated by the United States, and to the "socialist world" of the Communist countries dominated by the Soviet Union. Geopolitically, the postwar world came to be divided into developed countries with market economies (the United States; Canada; Western Europe, including Scandinavia; Japan; Australia; New Zealand; and, less clearly, Israel and South Africa), countries with centrally planned economies (the Soviet Union, Eastern Europe, the People's Republic of China, Mongolia, North Korea, and Vietnam), and developing countries with mixed or market economies (i.e., Latin America, the rest of Asia, Africa, and the Middle East). This latter group came to be called the "Third World" after the Bandung Conference of nonaligned nations in 1955. Economically, the developed countries account for one-fifth of the world's population and consume about 60 percent of the gross domestic product; and the Third World, which accounts for half of the world's land mass and half of its population, consumes around 12 percent of the gross product. In other words, the countries of the Third World are bound together by a level of poverty barely conceivable to the majority of inhabitants of the rest of the world.

persuasion, cultural consolidation, and consciousness raising. Second, Third World filmmakers often, but not always, operate from an independent production base outside of their countries' established (and usually Western-dominated) film industries. For this reason, Third World cinema is distinguished by its use of unconventional production modes, including collective production, secret or "underground" production, on-location shooting of guerrilla warfare, and non-Western extranational funding. Finally—and most important from an aesthetic standpoint—Third World cinema rejects the conventional narrative syntax of Hollywood and other Western film industries in an effort to extend the limits of film structure and provide audiences with new ways of seeing their sociopolitical reality. The ultimate goal of this process is the reclamation of authentic forms of national cultural expression long obscured by imposed foreign values. As the militant Argentine filmmakers Fernando Solanas and Octavio Getino—*La hora de los hornos* (*The Hour of the Furnaces*, 1968)—put it, theirs is a "third cinema" that goes beyond conventional Hollywood narrative ("first cinema") or the auteurist cinema of personal expression ("second cinema"). The practitioners of this third cinema mean to counter

> a cinema of characters with a cinema of themes, one of individuals with one of the masses, one of *auteurs* with one of operative groups, a cinema of neocolonial misinformation with a cinema of information, one of escape with one that recaptures the truth, a cinema of passivity with one of aggression. To an institutionalized cinema, it counterposes a guerrilla cinema; to movies as shows or spectacles, it counterposes a film act or action; to a cinema of destruction, one that is both destructive and constructive; to a cinema made for and by the old kind of human beings, it counterposes a cinema *fit for a new kind of human being, for what each one of us has the possibility of becoming* [original emphasis].

Latin America

Historically, the Latin American film industries have been dominated by large U.S.-based producer-distributors. In 1984, for example, American corporations controlled the largest shares of the film markets in all Latin American countries except Cuba, whose market is closed, and Brazil, which for the first time in history achieved a 50 per-

cent share of its own market through the successful creation of a state-controlled monopoly. Typically, a Latin American country will harbor a strong and tightly knit group of American-based distribution companies that market major American and European productions in uneven competition with a handful of local distributors who market local productions and some minor European and American product. The Americans are organized as branches of the U.S. Motion Picture Export Association (MPEA), and in general they function to oppose all forms of state protectionism for the local industries, including the placing of ceilings on the price of theater tickets, and any measures that would restrict the outward flow of foreign (i.e., American) currency. Furthermore, as Jorge Schnitman points out, the United States has always had the largest domestic film market in the capitalist world, a market where investments in production can be completely amortized before a film is sent abroad.[2] This has meant that American films in foreign markets had only to recover local distribution costs before realizing a profit, while local films had to recover both production and distribution costs in the same market, with little hope of export.

Film as an entertainment commodity appeared in Latin America shortly after the first commercial projection by the Lumières in Paris in December 1895. There were projections in Brazil in July 1896 and in Argentina in September, and even though film appeared much later in some of the smaller countries (in Bolivia, e.g., in 1909), exhibition facilities in general developed rapidly throughout Latin America—at first, as in the United States, mainly for working-class audiences. Latin American markets existed initially for both European and American films, but during World War I, the region was forced to rely exclusively on American products, and by 1916 American silent features dominated Latin American screens. At the same time (and about a decade after the United States), the Latin American distribution system changed from one of outright sale of prints to exhibitors to the leasing of prints to them for a percentage of the gross receipts, which favored the policy of American companies to establish their own local distributorships. By the early 1920s, the Latin American audience had expanded to

---

2. Jorge A. Schnitman, *Film Industries in Latin America: Dependency and Development* (Norwood, N.J.: Ablex, 1984), p. 22.

include the middle and upper-middle class, and U.S. companies dominated distribution to the virtual exclusion of local and European competitors. American dominion remained unchanged even after the coming of sound, which in other parts of the world generally increased the muscle of local industries by creating a language barrier against the Hollywood product. Simply put, dependency on America had rendered the Latin American industries incapable of supplying their own markets—collectively estimated in 1920 to include 100 million people—even after the advent of sound created a demand for Spanish-language films. So Hollywood happily filled the gap by converting its studios to the production of features in Spanish and Portuguese, and, later, by dubbing its own productions into the local languages. By 1935, for example, over 76 percent of the 504 feature films distributed in Argentina were brokered by American companies; and in Mexico three years later 80 percent of all films in release were American-made. The outbreak of war in Europe intensified the situation because it drastically decreased Hollywood's foreign-film revenues. As explained elsewhere, Germany and the countries it occupied banned American films outright; other countries, like Britain and Australia, needed foreign exchange so badly that they imposed rigorous currency restrictions of their own. In fact, continental Europe, where the American majors had done over 25 percent of their international business in 1936, had practically vanished as a market by 1940, when the only business conducted there by American film companies was with neutral Switzerland and Sweden.

By 1941, only Central and South America remained major importers of American films, persuading Hollywood to recolonize its neighbors with a vengeance. The State Department aided the cause by creating the Office of the Coordinator of Inter-American Affairs (CIAA) in October 1940, whose objective was to promote the Good Neighbor Policy and combat pro-Axis sentiment in Latin America. The CIAA's Motion Picture Division was put under the directorship of John Hay Whitney, whose first goal was to eliminate unflattering Latin American stereotypes and misinformation from Hollywood features and to encourage the production of films employing authentic Latin stars. In short order, the war years would witness reverential biographies of nineteenth-century Mexican President Benito Juárez and continental liberator Simón Bolívar, as well as films with contemporary settings that

differentiated, for the first time in American films, among various Latin American locales. Some examples of CIAA-influenced films are *Down Argentine Way* (Irving Cummings, 1940), *Week-End in Havana* (Walter Lang, 1941), *That Night in Rio* (Irving Cummings, 1941), and so on. There were also Latin American musical cycles from both RKO (e.g., *Too Many Girls* [George Abbott, 1940]; *They Met in Argentina* [Leslie Goodwins, 1941]; *Pan-Americana* [John H. Auer, 1945]) and 20th Century–Fox (e.g., *The Gang's All Here* [Busby Berkeley, 1943]). Finally, planeloads of Latin talent were imported into Hollywood during this era, acquainting American audiences with such performers as Lupe Velez, Carmen Miranda, Desi Arnaz, and Cesar Romero, to name but a few. Whitney's second initiative was more overtly political and involved the neutralization of propaganda flowing into Argentina, Brazil, and Chile from Axis wire services, features, and documentaries. To this end, he created the Newsreel Section, and by 1943 the CIAA had shipped more than 200 pro-American newsreels for free distribution in Latin American theaters. By the war's end, the United States' conquest of the Latin American film markets was as total as its geopolitical victory over the Axis. And, as Jorge Schnitman observes: "Although the U.S. film industry underwent remarkable transformations dur-

19.1 Busby Berkeley's CIAA-influenced musical *The Gang's All Here* (1943): Carmen Miranda in "The Lady in the Tutti Frutti Hat" production number.

ing the 1930–1980 period, for all practical purposes the problem of its overwhelming presence in Latin America remained throughout that period [with the obvious exception of Cuba after 1959], and only decreased somewhat whenever Latin American governments implemented consistent protectionist policies or when specific markets lost their appeal due to unfavorable exchange rates and similar problems."[3] Only three countries followed the protectionist path with any consistency—Argentina, Mexico, and Brazil—and of these only Mexico and Brazil have achieved even semiautonomy in their own markets.

MEXICO

The less successful of the two has been Mexico, which attempted to model its industry on that of the United States and which, at its extraordinary best, could produce films like Buñuel's *Los olvidados* (1950; winner of the Best Direction prize at Cannes, 1951). At its worst, it churned out hundreds of low-budget quickies—known locally as *churros*, a popular fried-dough confection of little nutritional value—the staple product of the 1960s and beyond. The Mexican cinema's "golden age" occurred during the 1940s, which began with the establishment in 1942 of the Banco Cinematográfico, a credit-granting agency for producers backed by the central government. By 1945, Mexico was producing a record 80 to 90 films a year, compared to Argentina's and Spain's 50 to 60, and an oligarchic, star-based studio system was being consolidated along American lines. It was during this decade that the collaboration of the director Emilio "El Indio" Fernández (1904–1986) and cinematographer Gabriel Figueroa (1907–1997)—e.g., *Flor silvestre* (*Wild Flower*, 1943—grand prize, Locarno, 1946); *María Candelaria* (1943—grand prize, Cannes, 1946); and *Río escondido* (*Hidden River*, 1947)—became world famous, as did the work of the brilliant comic actor Cantinflas (Mario Moreno), and, less spectacularly, the working-class melodramas of Alejandro Galindo—*Campeón sin corona* (*Champion without a Crown*, 1945)—and Ismael Rodriguez—*Nosotros los pobres* (*We Poor Folks*, 1947). During the 1950s and early 1960s, locally popular genres were the ranch comedy (*comedia ranchera*) and the cabaret melodrama, while international attention was claimed by the Mexican films of Buñuel (see Chapter 15) and, to a lesser degree, those of his Spanish-born scriptwriter Luis

Alcoriza—*Los jóvenes* (*The Young Ones*, 1960); *Tiburoneros* (*Shark Fishermen*, 1962); *Tarahumara* (1964). By the early 1960s, however, the golden age was over. Production fell from an all-time high of 136 features in 1958 to a record low of 71 in 1961, and a wave of cheaply produced *churros* overwhelmed the industry.

In 1963, however, the country's first film school, Centro Universitario de Estudios Cinematográficos (CUEC), was established in Mexico City, and by the late 1960s it was graduating young directors who turned for the first time to independent production in films that openly challenged the repressive regime of President Gustavo Díaz Ordaz. This generation included the Chilean-born Alejandro Jodorowsky, Jorge Fons, Felipe Cazals, Marcela Fernández Violante, Arturo Ripstein, Ariel Zúñiga, and Jaime Humberto Hermosillo, as well as Paul Leduc and Sergio Olhovich, both trained abroad. From 1970 to 1976, the new filmmakers benefited from the pro-left policies of President Luis Echeverría Álvarez, who encouraged them to make films of social criticism and revolutionary zeal that would at the same time upgrade the quality of Mexican cinema. To this end Echeverría virtually nationalized the film industry and placed the administration of the Banco Cinematográfico in the hands of his brother Rodolfo. As a result, the 1970s witnessed an extraordinary flourishing of Mexican film in such works as Jodorowsky's fabled cult classic *El Topo* (1970); Olhovich's *Muñeca reina* (1971); Leduc's *Reed: México insurgente* (*Reed: Insurgent Mexico*, 1971) and *Etnocidio: Notas sobre el Mezquital* (*Ethnocide: Notes on the Mezquital*, 1976); Fons's *Fé, esperanza, y caridad* (*Faith, Hope, and Charity*, 1974) and *Los albañiles* (*The Brick Layers*, 1975); Cazals's *Canoa* (1975), *El apando* (*Solitary Confinement*, 1975), and *Las Poquianchis* (1976); Violante's *De todos modos Juan te llamas* (English-language title: *The General's Daughter*, 1975); Ripstein's *El castillo de la pureza* (*The Castle of Purity*, 1972), *El lugar sin límites* (*The Place without Limits*, 1977), and *Cadena perpetua* (*Life Term*, 1978); Zúñiga's *Anacrusa* (1978); and Hermosillo's "Aguascalientes trilogy"—*La pasión según Berenice* (*The Passion According to Berenice*, 1975), *Matinée* (1976), and *Las apariencias engañan* (*Deceitful Appearances*, 1977)—and his *Naufragio* (*Shipwreck*, 1977) and *María de mi corazón* (*My Dearest Maria*, 1979). But this renais-

---

3. Schnitman, p. 26.

19.2 *El Topo* (*The Mole*, 1970). Chilean-born Alejandro Jodorowsky's violent, hallucinatory Western about an outlaw in quest of sainthood became a counterculture classic when it was distributed in the United States at the behest of Beatle John Lennon.

sance did not survive the administration of President José López Portillo, 1976–82, who put his sister Margarita in charge of the film industry.

In a disastrous attempt to return production to the private sector, she dissolved the Banco Cinematográfico and drove many of the independent artists fostered by Echeverría out of filmmaking altogether. At the same time, a fire in 1982 totally destroyed the Cineteca Nacional, Mexico's national film archive and the most important cinematheque in Latin America. In addition, Mexico— the world's third largest debtor nation, with a population of 97.4 million—began to experience one of the worst financial crises in its history. The establishment of the Mexican Film Institute (IMCINE) by the administration of President Miguel de la Madrid Hurtado in 1983 could do little to aid the film industry financially (although it ultimately became the home of a second national film school), and it returned to the production of privately financed *churro*-like genre films—chiefly soft-core bordello comedies, gritty urban-crime films, and borderline thrillers—at the rate of about 75 features per year. Still, this period saw the production of much interesting work, including Zúñiga's *Uno entre muchos* (*One of Many*, 1981) and *El diablo y la dama* (*The Devil and the Lady*, 1983); Violante's *Misterio* (*Mystery*, 1983); Leduc's *Frida* (1983) and *¿Cómo ves?* (*Waddya Think?*, 1987); Ripstein's *La seducción* (*The Seduction*, 1980), *El otro* (*The Other*, 1984), *El imperio de la fortuna* (*The Realm of Fortune*, 1986), and *Mentiras piadosas* (*White Lies*, 1988); Hermosillo's *El corazón de la noche* (*The Heart of the Night*, 1983), *Doña Herlinda y su hijo* (*Dona Herlinda and Her Son*, 1985), and *Clandestino destino* (*Clandestine Destiny*, 1987); Cazals's *Bajo la metralla* (*At Gunpoint*, 1982) and *El tres de copas* (*Three of Hearts*, 1987); Olhovich's *Esperanza* (*Hope*, 1988); and the work of such recent film-school graduates as documentarists Carlos Cruz and Carlos Mendoza—the rural trilogy *Chapopote* (1979), *El Chahuistle* (1980), and *Charrotitlan* (1982); Juan Antonio de la Riva—*Vidas errantes* (*Wandering Lives*, 1984) and *Obdulia* (1986); and Busi Cortés—*El secreto de Romelia* (*Romelia's Secret*, 1988). The election of President Carlos Salinas de Gortari caused a brief production boom in 1988, as annual output reached 112 features—the highest volume since the 1950s—most shot in four weeks with an

19.3 *El lugar sin limites* (*The Place without Limits*, also known as *Hell without Limits* [Arturo Ripstein, 1977]). The influence of Buñuel (for whom Ripstein was an assistant on *El Ángel exterminador* in 1962) is clear in this film about a transvestite flamenco dancer who runs a small-town whorehouse with his daughter.

19.4 *Frida* (1983), Paul Leduc's evocation of the iconoclastic life and art of modernist painter Frida Kahlo: Ofelia Medina.

average budget of $200,000 per film. But the government's subsequent withdrawal of state support for production, combined with the steady shrinking of both domestic and international markets for Mexican features, caused an industry crisis in the 1990s, when annual production plummeted below the levels of the 1930s (34 features in 1991, 41 in 1992, etc.)—a situation not remedied by the government of President Ernesto Zedillo, elected in 1994. Ironically, the need to secure outside financing has brought to fruition a number of critically acclaimed independent projects by industry veterans—e.g., Fons's *Rojo amanecer* (*Red Dawn*, 1990—the first film about the Tlatelolco student massacre of October 2, 1968), Ripstein's *La mujer del puerto* (*The Woman of the Port*, 1991), Hermosilla's *La tarea* (*Homework*, 1991), and de la Riva's *Pueblo de madera* (*Lumber Town*, 1992)—and such relative newcomers as Alfonso Arau, whose *Como agua para chocolate* (*Like Water for Chocolate*, 1992) became an art-house hit in the United States, and two new women directors, Dana Rotberg (*Ángel de fuego* [*Angel of Fire*, 1992]) and María Novaro (*Danzón*, 1992). Yet for the entire decade of the 1990s, the annual output was only 8 or 9 films, of which IMCINE produced about half, leaving the lion's share of the domestic market to imports (with a 74 percent share of ticket sales to Hollywood product). Increasingly, Mexican films are shot on DV (digital video) and transferred to 35mm—e.g., recent award-winning work by Arturo Ripstein (*That's Life* [*Así es la vida*, 2000]) and Alejandro González Iñárritu's *Amores Perros* (*Love's a Bitch*, 2000).

Two Mexican directors have established international reputations for their work both inside and outside of the domestic industry. Guillermo del Toro (b. 1964) began by directing horror films (e.g., the Mexican vampire film *Cronos* [1993]; the Hollywood mutant-bug movie *Mimic* [1997]), then produced in Spain *The Devil's Backbone* (*El espinazo del Diablo*, 2001), a sophisticated ghost story with a political subtext, before turning out the big-budget American franchise sequel *Blade II* (2002). Alfonso Cuarón (b. 1961) began working in Mexican television, directed the children's classic *A Little Princess* (1995) and a modernized version of Dickens's *Great Expectations* (1998) in Hollywood, before returning to Mexico to make the sexually

19.5 *El Imperio de la fortuna* (*The Realm of Fortune* [Arturo Ripstein, 1986]). Cockfighting and gambling in the realm of Buñuel.

graphic coming-of-age film *Y tu mamá también* (*And Your Mother Too*, 2001), whose hemispheric success won Cuarón a contract to direct the third *Harry Potter* film, *Harry Potter and the Prisoner of Azkaban* (2003).

BRAZIL

Brazil has been more successful than Mexico in developing its own film industry. The country (population approximately 176 million) initially adopted a Hollywood-style studio system but finally rejected it in favor of independent production. Despite an early attempt from 1908 to 1911 to organize a vertically integrated monopoly of national entrepreneurs, by 1924 the preponderance of films in the Brazilian market were from Hollywood, paralleling the situation in the rest of Latin America. Of 1,422 films presented for censorship that year, 1,268, or 86 percent, came from the United States. But in 1932, President Getúlio Vargas established the precedent of screen quotas for local film production. From that time until Vargas's death by suicide in 1954,[4] the model of state-directed, capitalist development of the national industry prevailed, although it hardly provided a serious threat to American hegemony. The most successful national genre during this period was a hybrid of musical revue and popular comedy called the *chanchada* (loosely translated as "cultural trash"), featuring comic performers from the radio and the Brazilian equivalent of cabaret. After Vargas's death, there was a decade of indecision during which continuing economic crises and a succession of weak governments raised the promise of radical social change, and it was in this context that Brazilian *cinema novo* ("new cinema") was born.

19.6 *Como agua para chocolate* (*Like Water for Chocolate* [Alfonso Arau, 1992]). A film about sexual attraction and the magical power of cooking, shot by the brilliant Mexican cinematographer Emmanuel Lubezki, *Like Water for Chocolate* became one of the highest grossing foreign films in the American market to date.

19.7 *Amores Perros* (also known as *Love's a Bitch* [Alejandro González Inuarritu, 2000]). Three interlocking stories about abuses of loyalty and affection at several different levels of Mexican society.

19.8 *Y tu mama tambien* (*And Your Mother Too* [Alfonso Cuarón, 2001]). This sexually explcit road-trip movie, also shot by Emmanuel Lubezki, enjoyed both critical and commercial success in the U.S. market.

---

4. Vargas ruled as a dictator from 1930 until 1945, when he was deposed by the military. Elected president again under a new constitution in 1950, he was forced from office by another coup in 1954, after which he killed himself.

Cinema novo sought new approaches to the realities of underdevelopment, poverty, and exploitation that had gone unacknowledged in Brazilian films to date. Drawing on new links with the working class and a new focus on native folklore and tradition, *cinema novo* filmmakers modeled their practice on the improvisatory techniques of the Italian neorealists (e.g., the use of nonactors and location shooting) and the production strategies of the French New Wave (i.e., creative financing and low-budget, sometimes collective, production). As part of their Marxist ideology, these directors decried the colonization of Brazilian cinema by Hollywood and subverted classical narrative codes in their own work wherever possible. The clear leader of the movement was Glauber Rocha (1938–1981), whose films and theoretical writings laid the foundation for a new Latin American cinema—one that would acknowledge the political and social realities of a land half of whose people were unemployed and half of whom were illiterate. Appropriately, Rocha's major work corresponds to each of the three recognized stages of *cinema novo*. The films of the first phase, 1960–64, drew on the history of proletarian revolt and were distinguished by radical optimism; to this period belong Rocha's *Deus e o diabo na terra do sol* (*Black God, White Devil*, 1964); Ruy Guerra's (b. 1931) *Os fuzis* (*The Guns*, 1964); and Nelson Pereira dos Santos's (b. 1928) *Vidas secas* (*Barren Lives*, 1963); all three works were focused in various ways on peasant life in the *sertao*, Brazil's drought-ridden, impov-

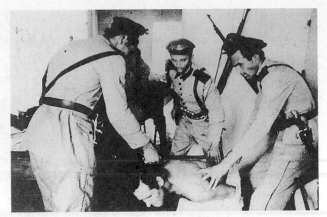

19.10 Political violence in *Vidas secas* (Nelson Pereira dos Santos, 1963).

erished northeastern plain. Also belonging to this first phase was Carlos Diegues's (b. 1940) *Ganga Zumba* (1963), a historical account of a successful slave revolt on a seventeenth-century surgarcane plantation. These films and their counterparts were extraordinarily successful on the international festival circuit, five of them winning major awards in 1962, when they represented 20 percent of the Brazilian industry's total output.

The second stage, 1964–68, marked a period of reassessment and, ultimately, disillusionment as the civilian government was overthrown by a military coup and the forms of democracy all but disappeared. This was the time of Paulo Cesar Saraceni's *O desafio* (*The Challenge*, 1966) and Rocha's *Terra en transe* (*Land in Anguish*, 1967), whose protagonists are urban intellectuals consumed with self-doubt. In the movement's final, and in many ways its richest phase, 1968–72, corresponding to the imposition of a repressive military dictatorship by the Fifth Institutional Act, *cinema novo* filmmakers turned heavily to symbolism to circumvent military censorship. According to Randal Johnson and Robert Stam, this stage came to be known as the "cannibal-tropicalist" phase[5] because so many of its films were cast in the form of

19.9 A peasant turned *cangaceiro* (rebel-bandit) in *Deus e o diabo na terra do sol* (Glauber Rocha, 1964), the first *cinema novo* feature to be widely seen outside Brazil.

5. Randal Johnson and Robert Stam, *Brazilian Cinema* (Rutherford, N.J.: Fairleigh Dickinson University Press, 1982; repr. Austin: University of Texas Press, 1988), p. 37. *Cinema novo* filmmakers borrowed the cannibal metaphor from the Brazilian modernist writers of the 1920s (e.g., Mario de Andrade, 1893–1945), who had used it to critique a world in which political, economic, and social relationships were fundamentally cannibalistic.

immediate result was a wave of *pornochanchadas*, soft-core erotic comedies popular mainly with local audiences, but the eventual result of Embrafilme's mandate was the state-led vertical integration of the Brazilian industry. Distinguished *cinema novo* directors like Carlos Diegues and Nelson Pereira dos Santos returned at the virtual invitation of the government to enter mainstream production. Over the next fifteen years, the Brazilian industry produced at least a dozen international hits, most of them based on indigenous folklore, history, or literature, including Diegues's *Xica da Silva* (1976), Brazil's first worldwide box-office success, and *Bye Bye Brazil* (1980); Bruno Barreto's (b. 1955) *Dona Flor e seus dois maridos* (*Dona Flor and Her Two Husbands*, 1976), which was so popular that it prompted the inferior 20th Century–Fox

19.11 Glauber Rocha's *Terra en transe* (1967).

19.12 *Xica da Silva* (Carlos Diegues, 1976): Zezé Motta in the title role.

mythological allegories—like Rocha's *Antonio das Mortes* (1968) and Guerra's *Os deuses e os mortos* (*The Gods and the Dead*, 1969)—or anthropological documents—like Pereira dos Santos's *Como era gostoso meu frances* (*How Tasty Was My Little Frenchman*, 1970)—or gaudily grotesque celebrations of Brazil as a tropical paradise—like the work of Joaquim Pedro de Andrade (1932–1988— *Macunaíma*, 1969) and, in part at least, Diegues's *Os herdeiros* (*The Heirs*, 1969).

Despite their repressiveness, however, the military regimes of the 1960s did attempt to support the expansion of Brazilian film production, creating the National Film Institute in 1966 and the state film trust Embrafilme in 1969. Strict sexual censorship was partially rescinded in the early 1970s, although ideological censorship prevailed until the restoration of democracy in 1985. The

19.13 *Bye Bye Brazil* (Carlos Diegues, 1980): Betty Faria as "Salome the Rumba Queen."

19.14 Hector Babenco's *Pixote* (1981): Fernando Ramos Da Silva, Marília Pêra.

Santos's *Na Estrada da vida* (*Road of Life*, 1980) and *Jubaibá* (1986); Tizuka Yamasaki's (b. 1949) *Gaijin* (1980), *Parahyba, mulher macho* (1982), and *Patriamada* (1986); Suzana Amaral's (b. 1932) *A hora da estrela* (*The Hour of the Star*, 1985); Sérgio Rezende's *O homem da capa preta* (*The Man with the Black Cape*, 1986); Lauro Escorel Filho's *Sonho sem fim* (*Endless Dream*, 1986); Chico Botelho's (1948–1991) *Cidade oculta* (*Hidden City*, 1986); Caetano Veloso's (b. 1942) *Cinema falado* (*Talking Pictures*, 1986); Diegues's *Quilombo* (1984) and *Um trem para as estrelas* (*A Train for the Stars*, 1987); Bruno Barreto's *Romance da Empregada* (*The Story of Fausta*, 1988); Paulo Cesar Saraceni's (b. 1933) *Natal da portela* (*One-Armed Natal*, 1988); and Hirszman's *Imagens do inconsciente* (*Pictures from the Unconscious*, 1988).

By 1985, when democracy was restored and the country elected its first civilian president since 1964, Embrafilme had not only captured foreign attention for Brazilian cinema but also an unprecedented 50 percent share of its own market. From producing only 12 films in 1963, Brazil had become the sixth largest film producer in the world, with an average output of 100 features per year since 1983. It seemed to be a triumph of capitalist initiative combined with state protectionism and politically committed talent. Unfortunately, the new government of José Sarney inherited from its predecessors an annual inflation rate of 800 percent and a staggering burden of foreign debt. As a result, Embrafilme production in the late 1980s fell off by 30 to 40 percent, and rigor-

remake *Kiss Me Goodbye* (Robert Mulligan, 1982); Leon Hirszman's (1938–1987) *Eles não usam black-tie* (*They Don't Wear Black Tie*, 1981); Pereira dos Santos's *Tenda dos milagres* (*Tent of Miracles*, 1977) and *Memórias do cárcere* (*Memories of Prison*, 1984), based on the memoirs of Graciliano Ramos, a political prisoner of the Vargas dictatorship and the author of *Vidas secas*, the source of the director's first film; Argentine-born Hector Babenco's (b. 1946) *Pixote* (1981; winner of the New York Critics award for Best Foreign Film) and *O beijo da mulher aranha* (*Kiss of the Spider Woman*, 1985); and Ruy Guerra's *Eréndira* (1983), *Ópera do Malandro* (*Malandro*, 1986), and *Fábula de la bella palomera* (*Fable of the Beautiful Pigeon Fancier*, 1988), all based on the work of Gabriel García Márquez. Other recent Brazilian films of note are Ana Carolina's (b. 1943) *Mar de rosas* (*Sea of Roses*, 1977) and *Das tripas coração* (*Bending over Backwards*, 1980); Rocha's controversial last work *A idade da terra* (*The Age of the Earth*, 1980); Carlos Alberto Prates Correia's (b. 1941) *Cabaret Mineiro* (*Cabaret in Minas*, 1980) and *Noites de sertão* (*Sertão Nights*, 1984); Pereira dos

19.15 *Central Station* (Walter Salles, Jr., 1998). Documentary and neorealist influences abound in this story of an impoverished, abandoned boy trying to locate his natural father.

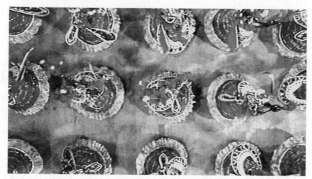

19.16 *Orfeu* (Carlos Diegues, 1999). An aerial shot of Carnival dancers from a version of the Orpheus and Euridice myth set in a Rio de Janeiro slum.

ous new protectionist legislation was enacted. A wave of domestically produced pornographic films, both soft-and hard-core, came to dominate the industry, although many films of international caliber continued to be made. In 1990, however, the Sarney government withdrew all funds from Embrafilme, and Hector Babenco declared at Cannes that the Brazilian cinema was dead. Over the next few years, Brazil experienced a rapid spiral of deflation, and the film industry ground to a near standstill, with only 6 features completed in 1992. In that year, Sarney and his cabinet were impeached for financial malfeasance and replaced by the government of President Itamar Franco, which took steps to revive the national cinema with subsidies from Brazil's central bank. In subsequent years, the government was successful in stimulating domestic production with tax breaks for companies investing in films; but—with a handful of exceptions, like Walter Salles, Jr.'s (b. 1956) internationally hailed *Central Station* (*Central do Brasil*, 1998)— Brazilian films did not play well in the local theatrical market, which, not incidentally, is the ninth largest in the world. In 1999, however, the Brazilian media conglomerate Globo created Globofilmes, many of whose productions have been based on popular television shows, but which has also invested in art films such as Carlos Diegues's *Orfeu* (1999), a retelling of the Orpheus and Euridice myth based on the same play (Vinícius de Moraes's *Orfeu da Conceicaol*) that inspired Marcel Camus's 1959 *Black Orpheus*. Since Globofilmes entered the picture, the Brazilian industry has averaged about 35 films a year.

ARGENTINA

Argentine cinema existed under various forms of state protectionism together with a rigorous system of pre- and postproduction censorship from the coming of sound until 1984. After the fall of the Perónist government in 1955, controls were relaxed and the studio system collapsed, but after 1957 new restrictions on imports were imposed, and domestic production was resumed on a film-by-film basis. It was at this time that the Argentine director Leopoldo Torre Nilsson (1924–1978) emerged as an international figure. The son of a Swedish mother and the Argentine director Leopoldo Torres Ríos (1899–1960), Torre Nilsson's first independent production was an adaptation of a short story by Jorge Luis Borges, *Días de odio*, in 1954. The four films that brought him to the attention of European critics— *La casa del ángel* (*The House of the Angel*, 1957), *La caída* (*The Fall*, 1959), *La mano en la trampa* (*The Hand in the Trap*, 1961), and *Sententa veces siete* (*Seventy Times Seven* [also known as *The Female*], 1962)— were all adapted, from her own writings, by his wife and frequent collaborator, Beatriz Guido (1924–1988). Among Torre Nilsson's later successes were *La Maffia* (*The Mafia*, 1972), *Los siete locos* (*The Seven Madmen*, 1973), and *Boquitas pintadas* (*Painted Lips*, 1974), a scathing criticism of the Argentine middle classes. Like Buñuel, with whom he is often compared, Torre Nilsson deals with the hypocrisy and repressiveness of the bourgeoisie. A near contemporary of Torre Nilsson is Fernando Birri (b. 1925), founder of the Documentary

19.17 *Setenta veces siete* (*Seventy Times Seven*, also known as *The Female* [Leopoldo Torre Nilsson, 1962]). Torre Nilsson's tumultuous film about a facially scarred woman who falls in love with an outlaw, scripted by his wife Beatriz Guido.

19.18 Fernando Birri's *Tire dié* (1958), the paradigm for Latin American social documentary.

were Fernando Ayala (1920–1997)—*El jefe* (*The Boss*, 1958); *El candidato* (*The Candidate*, 1959); Lautaro Murúa (1927–1995)—*Shunko* (1960); *Alias Gardelito* (also known as *Little Gardel*, 1961); Manuel Antin (b. 1926)—*La cifra impar* (*The Odd Number*, 1961; adapted by Julio Cortázar from his own story); and Leonardo Favio (b. 1938)—*Crónica de un niño solo* (*Chronicle of a Boy Alone*, 1965); *El romance del Aniceto y la Francisca . . .* (*The Romance of Aniceto and Francisca . . .*, 1966). The influence of Brazilian *cinema novo* revealed itself in the birth of the Cine Liberación group in the late 1960s in response to both the doldrums of the Argentine commercial industry and the social upheavals of the era. Cine Liberación's most famous production was the three-part agitprop documentary *La hora de los hornos* (*The Hour of the Furnaces*, 1968), directed by the group's founders, Fernando Solanas (b. 1936) and Octavio Getino (b. 1935). This film combines newsreel and documentary footage with dramatic re-enactments and printed slogans in a rapid-fire montage that is distinctly revolutionary (and nonrational) in its appeal. It is a classic example of "third cinema" in that its primary value is neither as entertainment nor art, but rather as an agent of ideological praxis. Other work by members of Cine Liberación or influenced by it are Hugo Santiago's (b. 1939) *Invasión* (*Invasion*, 1968), adapted from a premonitory Borges story about a civil war in Buenos Aires; Gerardo Vallejo's (b. 1942) *El camino hacia la muerte del viejo Reales* (*The Road towards Death of the Old Reales*, 1969), a study of the

Film School of Santa Fe (La Escuela Documental de Santa Fe) at Argentina's National University of the Littoral in 1956 and a pioneer of what was to become the New Latin American Cinema movement. Birri, who studied at Rome's Centro Sperimentale, produced with his own students one of Latin America's first social documentaries in *Tire dié* (*Throw a Dime*, 1958), a short about the degrading poverty of Buenos Aires' slums, as well as the neorealistic feature *Los inundados* (*Flood Victims/Flooded Out*, 1962), a prizewinner at Venice in 1962. Living in exile since 1964, Birri has helped materially to develop the cinemas of Cuba, Mexico, and Venezuela, and in 1986 was named director of the newly established School of Film and Television (La Escuela de Cine y Televisión) in the suburbs of Havana.

In the early 1960s there was some interesting activity among a group of young filmmakers who called themselves the "1960 generation" and practiced a European-style new cinema (*nuevo cine*). Most notable among them

19.19 *La hora de los hornos* (Fernando Solanas and Octavio Getino, 1968): agitational cinema.

exploitation of rural laborers; and Héctor Olivera's (b. 1931) *La Patagonia rebelde* (*Rebellion in Patagonia*, 1974; Silver Bear, Berlin), based on an actual massacre by the army of southern Argentine farmhands at the behest of powerful British landowners during the 1920s. Another important contemporary figure was Raúl de la Torre (b. 1938), whose thoughtful character studies of women—*Juan Lamaglia y señora* (*Juan Lamaglia and His Wife*, 1969), *Crónica de una señora* (*Story of a Lady*, 1971), *Heroína* (*Heroine*, 1972), and *Sola* (*Alone*, 1976)— won critical acclaim for their intelligence and style, and are still a mainstay of Argentine cinema (for example, *El Color escondido* [*Hidden Color*, 1988]).

In 1973 Juan Perón returned to Argentina from exile in Spain and was elected president; when he died a year later, his wife, Isabel, replaced him until she was removed by a military coup in 1976. The country then was plunged into an economic and political crisis of major proportion; inflation reached 100 percent, and the film industry was virtually paralyzed. Only one director of note emerged during this period: Adolfo Aristarain (b. 1943), whose compelling *films noir*—*La parte del león* (*The Lion's Share*, 1978), *Tiempo de revancha* (*Time for Revenge*, 1981), and *Últimos días de la víctima* (*The Last Days of the Victim*, 1982)—had submerged social themes. By 1982, domestic production had fallen to an all-time low of 18 films per year, and under pressure from filmmakers the military government empowered the National Film Institute (INC, founded 1955) to make production loan guarantees and named director Manuel Antin as its head. Then came the disastrous Malvinas/Falkland Islands war with Britain in 1982, the collapse of the Argentine dictatorship, and the restoration of democracy under President Raúl Alfonsín. Censorship was eliminated, and exiled filmmakers returned from abroad. There followed a great wave of films examining the recent past, especially the fate of the 15,000 to 30,000 *desaparecidos*[6] ("the disappeared") during the *guerra sucia* ("dirty war") of terror, torture, and murder conducted from 1976 to 1983 by the generals against suspected subversives. Into this category fall Héctor Olivera's *No habrá más penas ni olvido* (*Funny, Dirty Little War*, 1983—Silver Bear, Berlin); Fernando Ayala's *Pasajeros de una pesadilla* (*Passengers of a Nightmare*, 1984); Alejandro Doria's (b. 1936) *Darse cuenta* (*Becoming Aware*, 1984); Luis Puenzo's (b. 1946) Oscar-winning *La historia oficial* (*The Official Story*, 1985); and Carlos Lemos's (c. 1912–1988) *Los dueños del silencio* (*The Owners of Silence*, 1987). Other films deal

19.20 *La Patagonia rebelde* (Héctor Olivera, 1974).

with problems of exile—Fernando Solanas's *Tangos—el exilio de Gardel* (*Tangos—the Exile of Gardel*, 1985—Golden Lion, Venice) and *Sud* (*South*, 1988); Juan José Jusid's (b. 1941) *Made in Argentina* (1987)—and with repression and terror in Argentine history—Manuel Antin's *La invitación* (*The Invitation*, 1982); Jusid's *Asesinato en el senado de la nación* (*Murder at the National Senate*, 1984); María Luisa Bemberg's (1992–1995) *Camila* (1984) and *Miss Mary* (1986); and Raúl de la Torre's *Pobre mariposa* (*Poor Butterfly*, 1986). Recent manipulations of the Argentine economy by foreigners are considered in Ayala's *Plata dulce* (*Easy Money*, 1982), *El arreglo* (*The Deal*, 1983), and *El año del conejo* (*The Year of the Rabbit*, 1987). There have also been outstanding documentaries, such as Rodolfo Kuhn's (1934–1987) *Todo es ausencia* (*Only Emptiness Remains*, 1983); and Susana Muñoz and Lourdes Portillo's *Las madres* (*The Mothers of the Plaza de Mayo*, 1986), both on the politically organized mothers of the *desaparecidos*; Miguel Pérez's two-part history of Argentina, 1930–84, *La república perdida* (*The Lost Republic*, 1983) and *La república perdida II* (1986); and nonpolitical works by such talented new directors as Jorge Polaco (*Diapasón*, 1986), Teo Kofman (*Perros de la noche* [*Dogs of the Night*, 1986]), Eliseo Subielà (*Hombre mirando al sudeste* [*Man Facing Southeast*, 1986]), and Alejandro Agresti (*El hom-*

---

6. The 1988 population of Argentina was approximately 30 million.

bre que ganó la razón [*The Man Who Gained Reason,* 1986]) and *El amor es una mujer gorda* ([*Love Is a Fat Woman,* 1987]).

In 1989, the newly elected government of President Carlos Menem undertook a series of tough economic reforms designed to reduce public spending and privatize inefficiently run national industries. With wholesale subsidies effectively eliminated, the Argentine cinema came briefly to a halt in 1991; but a new tax levied on video rentals has helped to provide production funds for recent films from Subiela (*Últimas imágenes del naufragio* [*Last Images of the Shipwreck,* 1990]; *El lado oscuro del corazón* [*The Dark Side of the Heart,* 1992]), Bemberg (*Yo, la peor de todas* [*I, The Worst of It,* 1990]; *De eso no se habla* [*I Don't Want to Talk about It,* 1993]), Aristarain (*Un lugar en el mundo* [*A Place in the World,* 1992]), Solanas (*El viaje* [*The Voyage,* 1992]), and Raúl de la Torre (*Funes, un gran amor* [*Funes: A Great Love,* 1993]). All of these films, furthermore, were box-office hits in Argentina, whose domestic audience of 37 million seemed to find theatrical features attractive again after a five-year hiatus in full-scale production. By the early years of the twenty-first century, despite continuing economic and social crises, Argentine cinema was once again growing, due both to a dramatic expansion in the exhibition sector and the rise of independent distributors. At that time, the domestic industry was producing an average of 35 features a year.

BOLIVIA, PERU, AND CHILE

The Andean countries of Bolivia (population 8.4 million), Peru (7.9 million), and Chile (15.5 million) all experienced brief surges within their small domestic industries in the late 1960s. Following the example of Brazilian *cinema novo,* Bolivia's Jorge Sanjinés (b. 1937) and the Grupo Ukamau (a filmmaking collective named for *Ukamau* [1966], Sanjinés's award-winning first feature on Indian peasant life) produced the controversial *Yawar mallku* (*Blood of the Condor,* 1969), which became the most popular domestic feature made to date. Shot in neorealist fashion, the film shows the native Quechuan Indians being methodically wiped out through an involuntary sterilization program administered by the American "Progress Corps"; and it was ultimately responsible for the Peace Corps' expulsion from the country. *El Coraje del pueblo* (*The Courage of the People*), about a 1967 mas-

19.21 Quechuan Indians exploited by the "Progress Corps" in *Yawar mallku* (Jorge Sanjinés and the Grupo Ukamau, 1969).

sacre of striking miners and their families by the army, was Sanjinés first film in color and was produced for Italian television in 1971.[7] In the same year, Bolivia experienced the right-wing coup that brought Colonel Hugo Bánzer Suárez to power. Sanjinés and several members of Grupo Ukamau sought asylum first in Peru, where they made *El enemigo principal* (*The Principal Enemy,* 1974), and then Ecuador, where they produced *¡Fuera de aquí!* (*Out of Here!,* 1977). Meanwhile, Sanjinés's cinematographer, Antonio Eguino, remained in Bolivia with the rest of the group and directed two successful features during the 1970s—*Pueblo chico* (*Small Town,* 1974) and *Chuquiago* (1977), the latter a four-part analysis of the social structure of La Paz that became the biggest box-office hit in the nation's history. With another change of government in 1979, Sanjinés returned to Bolivia and produced *Las banderas del amanecer* (*The Banners of Dawn,* 1983), a feature-length documentary recording the nation's history from 1979 through 1983. In 1984, Eguino also directed a film—*Amargo mar* (*Bitter Sea*), a fictionalized account of Chile's invasion of Bolivia in 1879, coproduced with Cuba, but few films have been made in the country since, owing to a 60 percent decrease in attendance—the

---

7. To justify the massacre, the army accused the miners, who were not insurrectionists but who had publicly declared their sympathies with the antigovernment guerrillas led by Che Guevara in the south, of fomenting revolution. Guevara himself was killed by the Bolivian army shortly thereafter.

result of the diffusion of television between 1985 and 1987. Nevertheless, the nation has both an active film institute, Instituto Cinematográfico Boliviano (ICB, founded 1953), and the necessary technical equipment to resume production when economic circumstances permit. An important event for contemporary Bolivian cinema was the international and domestic success of Sanjinés's *La nación clandestina* (*The Hidden Nation*, 1989), an allegory of recent Bolivian history in the form of a fabulous quest.

In Peru, which had produced little but government-sponsored newsreels (*actualidades*) and the ethnographic features of the so-called Cuzco school (e.g., Eulogio Nishiyama, Luis Figueroa, and César Villanueva's *Kukuli* [1960] and *Jarawi* [1965]), there was little theatrical film-making activity until the work of Armando Robles Godoy, especially *La muralla verde* (*The Green Wall*, 1970), was recognized both at home and abroad. In 1972, the government passed legislation designed to encourage national film production, and independent companies began to form throughout the 1970s and 1980s to make both documentaries and commercial features. Especially notable in the latter category is the work of Francisco José Lombardi (b. 1949), whose *Muerte al amanecer* (*Death at Dawn*, 1977), *Maruja en el infierno* (*Maruja in Hell*, 1983), *La ciudad y los perros* (*The City and the Dogs*, 1985; adapted from the first novel of Mario Vargas Llosa), and *La boca del lobo* (*The Wolf's Den*, 1988) have all received international attention. Also well known are Jorge Reyes's (b. 1938) neorealistic account of Peru's first labor organizer, *La familia Orozco* (*The Orozco Family*, 1982), and Federico García Hurtado's trilogy of Peruvian-Cuban coproductions dealing with political events from the country's past—*Melgar, poeta insurgente* (1982); *Tupac Amaru* (1983), based on a late eighteenth-century Inca rebellion against Spanish rule; and *El socio de Dios* (*The Partner of God*, 1986). Another recent coproduction (with Cuba, West Germany's ZDF, and England's Channel Four) is *Malabrigo* (1986), Alberto Durant's atmospheric evocation of corruption in a small fishing port. The future of the small Peruvian industry, like that of the democratic government of center-left president Alan García, was much in doubt in the late 1980s, when an escalating civil war between the army and the Maoist guerrillas of the Sendero Luminoso, the "Shining Path," movement threatened to tear the country apart. Inflation

had reached a devastating 1 million percent when Alberto Fujimori was elected president in 1990. By 1993, Fujimori had reduced that figure to 35 percent and partially contained the Sendero movement at the price of seizing dictatorial power for himself. His government eliminated all state subsidies for the film industry, but individual careers continued to prosper—especially that of Francisco Lombardi, whose *Caídos del cielo* (*Fallen from the Sky*, 1990) won the Montreal World Film Festival, and Federico García Hurtado, whose *La lengua de los zorros* (*The Language of Foxes*, 1992) creates a rich tapestry of Andean mythology to foreground and explicate the guerrilla war but went unreleased until 1998. In 1996 and 1997, no Peruvian features were produced, despite subsidies for three features awarded by the Consejo Nacional de Cinematografía (CONACINE), the government office that supports film production through an annual script competition. It was actually the Peruvian-Spanish coproduction *Don't Tell Anyone* (*No se lo digas a nadie*, 1998), directed by Francisco J. Lombardi, that revived domestic production; and the following year, Lombardi's Peruvian-Venezuelan coproduction *Pantaleón and the Visitors* (2000), adapted from Mario Vargas Llosa's novel *Pantaleon y las visitadoras*, became a local blockbuster, knocking *Star Wars: Episode I* (1999) into second place. Meanwhile, CONACINE has begun to act as broker for finance capital at home and abroad.

From its earliest years through 1960, the Chilean film industry produced fewer than 160 films, half of them before the coming of sound. Yet the government had experimented with a national production company (Chile Films) in the 1940s, and in the 1950s and 1960s supported the development of university-based programs in both filmmaking and critical studies—e.g., the Film Institute of the Catholic University, founded 1955, and the Experimental Film Center of the University of Chile, founded 1957. The country also had a distinguished tradition of political documentary film production, especially in the work of Sergio Bravo—*Mimbre* (*Wicker*, 1957), *Trilla* (*Threshing*, 1958), *La marcha al carbón* (*Coal March*, 1963), *Las banderas del pueblo* (*The Banners of the People*, 1964)—which was influenced by that of Joris Ivens. With the election of Salvador Allende Gossens's socialist coalition ("Popular Unity") government in 1970, there was an explosion of cinematic expression as Miguel Littin (b. 1942), whose debut feature *El chacal de Nahueltoro* (*The Jackal of Nahueltoro*, 1969) had rad-icalized Chilean audiences the year before, was named to head the nation's film industry. The Allende regime was overthrown by a bloody CIA-backed coup in 1973, but its three years in power marked the most creative era in Chilean film history. This brief period witnessed the pro-duction of such extraordinary documentaries as *Vencer-emos* (*We Shall Win*, Pedro Chaskel and Héctor Ríos, 1970), *Compañero Presidente* (Miguel Littin, 1971), *No es hora de llorar* (*No Time for Tears*, Pedro Chaskel and Luis Alberto Sanz, 1971), *El primer año* (*The First Year*, Patricio Guzmán, 1971), *La respuesta de octobre* (*The Answer to October*, Guzmán and the *Primer Año* group, 1972), and *Abastecimiento* (*Stocking Up*, Raoul Ruiz, 1973). Also produced were such features as Helvio Soto's *Voto + fusil* (*The Vote and the Gun*, 1970) and *Meta-morfosis de un jefe de la policía política* (*Metamorphosis of a Political Police Chief*, 1973); Raoul Ruiz's *Nadie dijo nada* (*No One Said a Thing*, 1971); Aldo Francia's (b. 1923) *Ya no basta con rezar* (*Praying Is No Longer Enough*, 1971); and Littin's *La tierra prometida* (*The Promised Land*, 1973, unreleased in Chile).

After General Pinochet's junta seized control of the government, murdering Allende and many of his follow-ers (see, e.g., Constantin Costa-Gavras's film *Missing* [1982]), most Popular Unity filmmakers went into exile—Littin to Mexico; Ruiz, Soto, and Guzmán and his *Primer Año* group to France—where they continued their polit-ical project. Guzmán's group produced *La batalla de Chile* (*The Battle of Chile*, 1975–79) in Paris and later

Cuba (where it was edited at ICAIC [see pp. 814–15] with the assistance of Julio García Espinosa) as well as a remarkable three-part documentary on the final year of the Allende presidency—*La insurrección de la burguesía* (*The Insurrection of the Bourgeoisie*, 1975), *El golpe de estado* (*The Coup d'État*, 1977), and *El poder popular* (*Popular Power*, 1979)—with the help of French docu-mentarist Chris Marker. Marker also produced with the Chilean refugees his own account of the Allende years, the two-and-one-half-hour *La Spirale* (1975). Now living in Cuba, Guzmán (b. 1941) has since directed the Cuban-Venezuelan coproduction *La rosa de los vientos* (*The Rose of the Winds*, 1985), a poetic meditation on the survival of Latin American identity despite five hundred years of cultural colonization, and *En el nombre de Dios* (*In the Name of God*, 1987), a documentary for Spanish televi-sion about the role of the Roman Catholic Church in Chile in the years following the coup. Helvio Soto (1930–2001) directed only two features in exile—*Llueve sobre Santiago* (*It's Raining on Santiago*, 1976) and *La triple muerte del tercer personaje* (*The Triple Death of the Third Character*, 1979). But Raoul Ruiz (b. 1941) has become one of the world's most prolific and experimental direc-tors. His *Diálogo de exilados* (*Dialogue of Exiles*, 1974) harks back ideologically to his radical first feature *Tres triste tigres* (*Three Sad Tigers*, 1968), but Ruiz has since become increasingly metaphysical in such films as *La Vocation suspendue* (*The Suspended Vocation*, 1977), *L'Hypothèse du tableau volé* (*Hypothesis of a Stolen Painting*, 1978), *Las tres coronas del marinero* (*The Sailor's Three Crowns*, 1982), *La Ville de pirate* (*City of Pirates*, 1983), *La Présence réelle* (*The Real Presence*, 1983), and *Mémoire des apparences* (*Memories of Appear-ances*, 1986), to name but a few of the more than fifty films he has made after leaving Chile. Working mainly on commission in Portugal and France, Ruiz also directed documentaries, video essays, and children's films, all informed by his vaguely surrealist sensibility and all shot at lightning speed, until his return to Chile in 1990.

In Mexico, Miguel Littin produced *Actas de Marusia* (*Letters from Marusia*, 1976), which draws a historical parallel between a 1907 massacre of Chilean mineworkers and the 1973 coup d'etat. He also made *Viva el Presi-dente*, also known as *El recurso del método* (*The Dis-course on Method*, 1978) and *La viuda de Montiel* (*Montiel's Widow*, 1980), before directing *Alsino y el cón-dor* (*Alsino and the Condor*, 1983) for Nicaragua's film

19.22 *La tierra prometida* (Miguel Littin, 1973).

19.23 *It's Raining on Santiago* (*Llueve sobre Santiago* [Helvio Soto, 1976]). A semidocumentary re-creation of the CIA-backed coup that overthrew the popularly elected government of Salvador's Allende Gossens on September 11, 1973. Here, students and faculty come under attack by tanks that have rolled onto the campus of Santiago University.

smuggled out of the country for distribution abroad—the Cine-Oio collective's *Chile, no invoco tu nombre in vano* (*Chile, I Do Not Call Your Name in Vain*, 1984), Juan Andres Racz's *Dulce patria* (*Sweet Country*, 1986), and Gaston Ancelovici's *Memorias de una guerra cotidiana* (*Images of an Everyday War*, 1986)—and such features as Pablo Perelman's *Imagen latente* (*Latent Image*, 1987), a film about the Chilean disappeared edited in Canada and not released in Chile until 1991. In October 1988, the Pinochet regime was unexpectedly defeated in a national referendum, and the following year witnessed

institute, INCINE, and Cuba's ICAIC, but he never again achieved the stylistic complexity of his early work. In 1985, Littin returned secretly to Chile and spent six weeks incognito filming the Cuban-produced television documentary *Acta general de Chile* (*General Document on Chile*, 1986), a moving four-hour condemnation of the Pinochet dictatorship.

Early in the 1980s many exiled filmmakers were able to return to Chile. They found an economy wrecked by the junta, barely able to finance a handful of cheaply made films each year, most of them shot in 16mm and blown up to 35mm. Examples are Sergio Bravo's first feature *No eran nadie* (*They Were Nobody*, 1981), shot in the archipelago of Chile for $115,000; Christián Sánchez's *Los deseos concebidos* (*Conceived Desires*, 1982), made for $70,000; Alejo Álvarez's *Cómo aman los Chilenos* (*How Chileans Love*, 1984), made for $100,000; Luis R. Vera's *Hechos consumados* (*An Accomplished Fact*, 1985) shot in Santiago for $60,000; Cristián Lorca's *Nemesio* (1986) made for $50,000; and so on. In fact, between 1977 and 1990 only thirty-odd films and videos were produced in Chile, and these were shot under very difficult conditions. To this total should be added a number of militant anti-Pinochet documentaries made in Chile but

nessed the first presidential/parliamentary election in two decades. During the 1990s, the government of President Patricio Aylwin Ozocar worked cautiously to restore democracy under the military's watchful eye, as film production officially resumed and the Viña del Mar festival was reopened in 1990 to greet a whole generation of exiled Chilean filmmakers, most notably Miguel Littin and Raoul Ruiz. Ruiz took this opportunity to re-edit his unreleased feature *Palomita blanca* (*White Dove*), which had been in postproduction when the military took over at Chile Films in 1973. Based on a bestselling novel by Enrique Lafourcade, the film is an elliptical love story set against the turbulent Allende elections of 1970, and it became a national box-office hit when released in 1992. Other recent Chilean films are Ricardo Larrain's *La frontera* (1991), the story of a teacher condemned to internal exile by the junta that won the 1992 Silver Bear at Berlin, and Pablo Perelman's *Achipiélago* (1993), a political allegory of modern Chile selected for the Critics' Week at Cannes. These and similar films demonstrate that Latin America's most politically and aesthetically vibrant film culture of the 1970s has survived its seventeen-year exile. But its economic survival cannot be ensured without a successful structure of state subsidies; this may be forthcoming from the recently formed joint-stock company Cine Chile (1993), an organization of twenty-eight Chilean directors and producers underwritten by Banco del Estado.

After several lean years in the mid-1990s, Chilean cinema bounced back toward the end of the decade due to the exponential spread of multiplex theaters and the consolidation of several government agencies dedicated to stimulating domestic production. The landmark year was 1999, when a Chilean feature—Cristián Galaz's *The Sentimental Teaser* (*El chocotero sentimental*), based on a popular talk-radio show—broke box-office records to become the most successful domestic film of all time.

VENEZUELA, COLOMBIA, AND CENTRAL AMERICA

During the late 1960s oil-rich Venezuela experienced a surge in documentary production with such works as Jesús Enrique Guédes's *La ciudad que nos ve* (*The City Which Sees Us*, 1967) and Carlos Rebolledo's *Pozo muerto* (*Dead Well*, 1968), and in 1973 the government embarked upon a program of developing a national cinema by guaranteeing production subsidies and regulating the distribution of foreign product. From 1975 to 1980, the state subsidized the production of nearly thirty films, including Mauricio Wallerstein's (b. 1945) *La empresa perdona un momento de locura* (*The Company Excuses a Moment of Insanity*, 1977), Román Chalbaud's (b. 1931) *Sagrado y obsenco* (*Sacred and Obscene*, 1975) and *El pez que fuma* (*The Smoking Fish*, 1977), Carlos Rebolledo's (b. 1932) *Alias, el rey del Joropo* (*Alias the Joropo King*, 1978), and Iván Feo (b. 1947) and Antonio Llerandi's *País portátil* (*Portable Country*, 1978), the latter Venezuela's biggest box-office hit to date. *Variety* proclaimed Venezuela's the fastest-growing film industry in Latin America, which, in fact, it was. Various factors—including a sharp drop in world oil prices between 1982 and 1991, when the Gulf War drove them up again—have since weakened government support for the film industry, but it is still producing a large number of well-made films, considering Venezuela's population of only 24.2 million. During the 1980s these have most prominently included Thaelman Urgelles's *La boda* (*The Wedding*, 1982); Diego Rísquez's *Bolívar* (1982), *Orinoko—neuvo mundo* (1984), and *América, terra incógnita* (*America, Unknown Land*, 1988); Antonio Llerandi's *Adiós Miami*

(*Bye, Bye, Miami*, 1983); Freddy Siso's *Diles que no me maten* (*Tell Them Not to Kill Me*, 1984); Dominique Cassuto de Bonet/Salvador Bonet's *Tiznao* (1984); José Novoa's *Agonía* (*Agony*, 1985); Fina Torres's *Oriane* (*Oriana*, 1985); Olegario Barrera's *Pequeña revancha* (*Little Revenge*, 1985); Román Chalbaud's *Manon* (1986) and *La oveja negra* (*The Black Sheep*, 1987); and the Venezuelan-Colombian coproductions *De mujer a mujer* (*Woman to Woman* [Mauricio Wallerstein, 1987]) and *Profundo* (*Deep* [Antonio Llerandi, 1989]). In the early 1990s, Venezuela experienced severe economic belt-tightening under the presidency of Carlos Andrés Pérez, leading to large-scale rioting and an attempted military coup in February 1992. The election of Ramón José Velásquez in 1993 produced a return to order, and the budget of Venezuela's film development agency, Fondo de Fomento Cinematografico (FONCINE), was quintupled in the period of relative prosperity that followed, enabling it to support such work as Olegario Barrera's *End of the Round* (*Fin de round*), Marilda Vera's *Señora Bolero*, and Fernando Venturini's feature-length documentary *Zoo* (all 1993). In contrast to most Latin American countries, Venezuelan audiences have always supported their cinema, which has won over 100 international prizes since FONCINE's founding in 1982. In 1993 the functions of FONCINE were shifted to the Autonomous National Center for Cinematography (CNAC), which became the main source of production funding for domestic films for the next six years. Between 1993 and 1999, CNAC helped to produce about 35 Venezuelan features; but when the new president Hugo Chávez took office in February 1999, he cut the agency's budget by 60 percent. Among other things, this put on hold the production of *Bolívar*, a large-scale big-budget biopic of Simón Bolívar (1783–1830), the liberator of Venezuela, Colombia, Ecuador, Peru, Bolivia, and Panama. It also forced Venezuelan filmmakers to look to coproduction deals with other Spanish-speaking countries in order to stay in business. Despite the lull in production, however, Venezuela continues to rank fourth in Latin American annual production, behind Argentina, Brazil, and Mexico.

Neighboring Colombia (population 41.4 million) also produced a number of interesting documentaries in the late 1960s, especially Jorge Silva and Marta Rodríguez's *Chircales* (*Brickmakers*, 1968), Carlos Álvarez's *Asalto*

(*Assault*, 1968), and Julia Álvarez's *Un día yo pregunté* (*One Day I Asked*, 1969). In 1971 the government attempted to protect its small industry by requiring the exhibition of Colombian shorts at all first-run domestic theaters and mandating an admission-ticket surcharge to be rebated to producers. This had the effect of stimulating the production of shorts to the level of nearly 100 per year by 1975, and in 1978 the government attempted to promote feature production by setting up a national film production company, Compañía de Fomento Cinematografico (FOCINE). Since that time, Colombia has seen the production of such theatrical films as Dunav Kuzmanich's semidocumentary *Canaguaro* (1981); Luis Ospina's *Pura sangre* (*Pure Blood*, 1983); Lisandro Duque Naranjo's *El escarabajo* (*The Bicycle Racer*, 1983) and *Visa U.S.A.* (1986; a Colombian-Cuban coproduction); Francisco Norden's *Cóndores no entierran todos los días* (*Condors Don't Die Every Day*, 1984); Carlos Mayolo's *Carne de tu carne* (*Flesh of Your Flesh*, 1984) and *La mansión de Araucaima* (*The Araucaima Mansion*, 1986); Leopoldo Pinzón's *Pisingana* (*Hopscotch*, 1985); Jorge Alí Triana's Colombian-Cuban coproduction *Tiempo de morir* (*A Time to Die*, 1985; based on an original screenplay by Gabriel García Márquez); Carlos Palau's *A la salida nos vemos* (*See You after School*, 1986); Pepe Sánchez's *San Antonito* (*Little Saint Anthony*, 1986); and Manuel Franco Posse's *La recompensa* (*The Reward*, 1988). When the Colombian government declared open war on the drug cartels in 1989 as a result of the assassination of presidential candidate Luis Carlos Galán, the film industry was among the first to suffer since the subsequent wave of "narco-terrorism" reduced box-office receipts by as much as 30 percent. Only four films were produced in the 1990–91 season, and in 1992 FOCINE was dissolved by federal decree. Among its last productions were Víctor Gaviria's *Rodrigo D.—No Futuro* (1990; shot in 1986), a *cinéma vérité* feature about the street kids of Medellín, and Sergio Cabrera's *La Estrategia del caracol* (*The Snail's Strategy* [1992; shot 1989]), a comedy about political corruption in Bogotá. Recent Colombian films have understandably been focused on the social and political problems resulting from terrorism and a virtual civil war among the government, leftist guerrillas, and drug cartels. For example, Víctor Gaviria's *La Vendedora de rosas* (*The Rose Seller*, 1998) and Lisandro Duque Naranjo's *Los niños invisibles* (*The Invisible Children*, 2001) are both about the lives of urban street kids;

19.24 Ramiro Meneses in *Rodrigo D.—No Futuro* (Víctor Gaviria, 1986; released 1990), shot in the slums of Medellín with nine nonprofessional actors, six of whom were dead of street violence before the film's release.

whereas Jorge Alí Triana's *Bolívar soy yo* (*Bolivar Is Me*, 2001) is a satire about a delusional actor who is cast as Simón Bolívar in a TV miniseries and ultimately assumes the Liberator's mission to unify Latin America, only to be manipulated by corrupt local politicians.

The Central American countries of Nicaragua (population 5.0 million) and El Salvador (population 6.3 million) both were sites of revolutionary filmmaking activity in the 1980s despite the fact that neither is economically capable of producing more than a few films each year. The Nicaraguan Film Institute—Instituto Nicaraguense de

Cine, or INCINE—was established by the Sandinista government shortly after the Somoza dictatorship was overthrown in 1979. Though its resources were extremely limited, INCINE played host to numerous documentaries produced by filmmakers from other countries—the Finnish director Victoria Schultz's *Women in Arms* (1980), the Brazilian Helena Solberg's *Nicaragua: From the Ashes* (1981), the West German/Chilean Tercer Cine Collective's *Women in Nicaragua: The Second Revolution* (1983), the Australian David Bradbury's *Nicaragua—No Pasarán* (1984), the Americans Susan Meiselas's *Living at Risk: The Story of a Nicaraguan Family* (1985) and Anita Clearfield's *Vacation Nicaragua* (1986). In addition, there have been such ambitious features as Peter Lilienthal's *The Insurrection* (1980); *Alsino y el Cóndor* (*Alsino and the Condor* [Miguel Littin, 1983]), a Nicaraguan–Cuban–Mexican–Costa Rican coproduction about the friendship between an American military adviser and a peasant boy; the U.S.-backed *Walker* (Alex Cox, 1987), dealing with an American adventurer who installed himself as president of Nicaragua in 1855; and Nicaragua's first domestic theatrical release *Mujeres de la frontera* (*Women of the Frontier*, Ivan Arguello, 1987), coproduced with Cuba. Subsequent Nicaraguan-Cuban features, like *El espectro de la guerra* (*The Ghost of War*, Ramiro Lacayo Deshón, 1988), have dealt mainly with the vagaries of the Contra war. In 1990, national elections removed the Sandinistas from power, and the new government threw the country open to market forces. Since Nicaragua has traditionally been the area's strongest film market, this meant fierce competition for INCINE from foreign distributors, most notably the American majors.

Guerrilla cinema activities are even more tenuous in neighboring El Salvador, where revolutionary collectives like the Radio Venceremos film group have produced such documentaries as *La decisión de vencer* (*Decisions to Win*, 1981) and *Tiempo de audacia* (*A Time of Daring*, 1983), both filmed on the front lines of the guerrilla war. There have also been such Salvadoran-U.S. coproductions as Glenn Silber and Teté Vasconcellos's Oscar-winning *El Salvador: Another Vietnam* (1981) and Frank Christopher's *In the Name of the People* (1985), both documentaries, and Oliver Stone's controversial feature *Salvador* (1986).

Other Central American countries producing militant cinema are Costa Rica (Valeria Sarmiento's *Un hombre, cuando es un hombre* [*A Man, When He Is a Man*, 1985])

and Guatemala (Gregory Nava's PBS-financed *El Norte* [*The North*, 1983]; Pamela Yates and Thomas Sigel's *When the Mountains Tremble* [1985]). The relative pacification of these regions during the 1990s caused a decline in such revolutionary cinema, although Honduras was able to release its first feature in 2001, Juan Carlos Fanconi's Nicaraguan-financed *Almas de la media noche*, a chilling film about life after death based on regional Lenca legends.

Cuba and the New Latin American Cinema

A small colonial film industry in Cuba before 1959 produced approximately 150 features in its sixty-year history. Many were Mexican-Cuban coproductions, like Emilio Fernández's *La rosa blanca* (*The White Rose*, 1953), and yet prerevolutionary Cuba had the highest film-attendance rates of any Latin American country. A foretaste of the future was provided in 1955, when Tomás Gutiérrez Alea (1928–1996) and Julio García Espinosa (b. 1926), both of whom had studied at Rome's Centro Sperimentale in the early 1950s and would become major figures in Cuban cinema after the revolution, produced the neorealistic *El mégano* (*The Charcoal Worker*), an indictment of peasant exploitation under the corrupt regime of President Fulgencio Batista. These same directors were the leading lights of Cine Rebelde, the rebel army's film unit, which produced two documentary shorts—*Esta tierra nuestra* (*This Is Our Land*, Gutiérrez Alea) and *La vivienda* (*Housing*, Espinosa)—for the National Board of Culture in 1959 before the unit became part of the revolutionary government's national film institute—Instituto, Cubano del Arte e Industria Cinematográficos, or ICAIC.

Like other revolutionary leaders before him, Fidel Castro understood the potential of motion pictures as a medium for mass education and persuasion—especially among a poor and largely illiterate populace—and, according to Alfredo Guevara, the founding director of ICAIC, the development of an indigenous film industry was in fact a major priority of the new government, second only to the national literacy campaign of 1960–61. ICAIC was created on March 24, 1959—only three months after the overthrow of Batista—by an act of law declaring cinema to be a national art and mandating the "re-education" of the Cuban people through its "fount of revolutionary inspiration, of culture, and of information."[8] On that day, the Cuban film industry consisted of a few offices, some old 35mm equipment, a black-and-white laboratory, and a small group of people with virtually no filmmaking experience beyond the limited forays of Gutiérrez Alea and Espinosa. As the screenwriter Manuel Pereira has said, the Cuban cinema was born "without original sin."[9] Over the next twenty-four years, however, ICAIC managed to produce 112 features (both documentary and theatrical), approximately 900 documentary shorts, and over 1,300 weekly newsreels.[1]

The first films were brilliant, controversial documentaries—most prominently those of Santiago Álvarez (1919–1998)—e.g., *Hanoi martes 13* (*Hanoi, Tuesday the 13th*, 1967); *LBJ* (1968); *79 primaveras* (*79 Springtimes*, 1969)—which experimented in early Soviet fashion with every known variety of montage. Then in the late 1960s and early 1970s came fiction features like Gutiérrez Alea's *La muerte de un burócrata* (*Death of a Bureaucrat*, 1966) and *Memorias del subdesarrollo* (*Memories of Underdevelopment*, 1968); Humberto Solás's (b. 1941) *Lucía* (1968); and Manuel Octavio Gómez's (1934–1988) *La primera carga al machete* (*The First Charge of the Machete*, 1969), all of which mixed documentary and narrative technique in startlingly innovative ways and claimed international attention for the new Cuban cinema. *Memorias*, for example, is a collage evoking the prerevolutionary consciousness of the intellectual bourgeoisie set against the backdrop of the missile crisis of 1962, and *La primera carga* assumes the imaginary per-

19.26 Gutiérrez Alea's *Memorias del subdesarrollo* (1968): prerevolutionary consciousness. Sergio Corrieri.

spective of a news crew covering the 1868 war of independence. Perhaps the most formally original of all, *Lucía* tells the stories of three women by that name in three crucial periods in Cuban history, each in a filmic style that evokes its era. It provides a critique of Cuban society both before and after the revolution through an analysis of the changing roles of women. During the 1970s, epic-scale documentary features—García Espinosa's *Tercer mundo, tercera guerra mundial* (*Third World, Third World War*, 1970), Pastor Vega's (b. 1940) *¡Viva la república!* (*Long Live the Republic!*, 1972), and Álvarez's *Abril de Vietnam en el año del gato* (*April in Vietnam in the Year of the Cat*, 1975)—began to appear, astonishing international audiences with their sophistication and stylistic versatility.

At the same time, ICAIC was educating its domestic audience by taking *cine-mobiles*—trucks, wagons, and even boats equipped with projection gear and revolutionary films, as well as films such as those of Charlie Chaplin—to the provinces, in the manner of the Bolshevik "agit-trains" of the 1920s (see Octavio Cortázar's [b. 1935] award-winning short *Por primera vez* [*For the First Time*, 1967]). Later, a full-scale film-education program for

19.25 The dark comedy *La muerte de un burócrata* (Tomás Guitiérrez Alea, 1966), which the director dedicated to Laurel and Hardy, among others: Salvador Wood, Silvia Planas.

8. Quoted in Dennis West, "Cuba: Cuban Cinema before the Revolution and After," in *World Cinema since 1945*, ed. William Luhr (New York: Ungar, 1987), p. 141.

9. Quoted in Pat Aufderheide, "Red Harvest," *American Film* 9, 5 (March 1984): 29.

1. Figures cited by Julianne Burton, "Film and Revolution in Cuba: The First Twenty-five Years," in *Jump Cut: Hollywood, Politics and Counter-Cinema*, ed. Peter Steven (New York: Praeger, 1985), p. 345.

19.27–19.29 Scenes from the three parts of _Lucía_ (Humberto Solás, 1969): Raquel Revuelta, Eslinda Nuñez, Adela Legra.

Cuba's 11 million people was established. When fully institutionalized, this program involved the dissemination of ICAIC's own periodical _Cine cubano_, which features interviews, essays, and production information on Cuban and other Latin American cinema; mass screenings at the Cinemateca de Cuba for approximately 100,000 spectators per week; and two national television programs devoted to film education. (In the most popular, _24 por secondo_ [_Twenty-four Frames a Second_], the host described current films, showed clips from them, and discussed their history and structure.) As Cuba's audience grew ever more sophisticated, so too did its already exciting cinema.[2] The 1970s witnessed an explosion of genres and styles in such work as the black director Sergio Giral's (b. 1937) _El otro Francisco_ (_The Other Francisco_, 1975), a complex experimental film that attempts a Marxist critique of the bourgeois liberalism underlying Cuba's first antislavery novel, Anselmo Suárez y Romero's _Francisco_ (1839); Gutiérrez Alea's _La última cena_ (_The Last Supper_, 1976), which uses the historical context of a late eighteenth-century slave rebellion to fashion a hieratic confrontation between Christian and Afro-Cuban culture, and the same director's _Los sobrevivientes_ (_The Survivors_, 1978), a darkly comic allegory of the bourgeoisie's descent from "civilization" through slaveholding to barbarism and finally cannibalism; and Sara Gómez's (1943–1974) _De cierta manera_ (_One Way or Another_, 1974; released 1977), which interfuses a traditional Hollywood-style narrative about young lovers from different socio-ethnic backgrounds with _cinéma vérité_ and agitational techniques to expose the vestiges of neocolonial racism and sexism still facing Cuba's new order. The same theme is developed in the more conventionally structured _Retrato de Teresa_ (_Portrait of Teresa_, 1979), Pastor Vega's first theatrical feature, which shows the persistence of machismo and the double standard facing working women in Cuban daily life. One of the most formally innovative films of the era was Manuel Octavio Gómez's _Una mujer, un hombre, una ciudad_ (_A Woman, a Man, a City_, 1978), whose structure in many ways resembles

---

2. As Gutiérrez Alea has said of this film-education project, "Filmmakers can't move faster than the audience. That's what happened to Godard. His analytical cinema attracted me, but the public didn't get it. You have to include in your considerations what the known cinematic language is." (Quoted in Pat Aufderheide, "Red Harvest," 31.)

19.30 *La primera carga al machete* (Manuel Octavio Gómez, 1969).

tious failure. His subsequent work included the Cuban-Spanish coproduction *Cecilia* (1981; based on a novel by Cirilo Villaverde), an allegorical film of political intrigue among slaveholders in nineteenth-century Havana; *Amada* (1983), a stylized melodrama about a bourgeois wife who falls in love with an anarchist in 1914; and *Un hombre de éxito* (*A Successful Man*, 1986), a chronicle tracing the very different lives of two Havana brothers from 1932 through the Cuban Revolution. The decade also witnessed the first dramatic feature of

Citizen Kane, although Gómez's next film, *El señor presidente* (*Mr. President*, 1983), was a more or less conventional adaptation of Miguel Ángel Asturias's novel of life under the Guatemalan dictatorship.

The 1980s marked the return to prominence of Humberto Solás, whose feature-length epic *La Cantata de Chile* (1975) had been widely regarded as an ambi-

Santiago Álvarez, *Los refugiados de la cueva del muerto* (*The Fugitives of Dead Man's Cave*, 1983), a historical reconstruction of a guerrilla assault on the Moncada army barracks in 1953; and *Patakín!* (*Fable!* [Manuel Octavio Gómez, 1984]), a tongue-in-cheek Hollywood-style musical about contemporary life in the Workers' Paradise. Also of note were Gutiérrez Alea's *Hasta cierto punto* (*Up to a Certain Point*, 1983), an attempt to renew the dialogue begun by Sara Gómez's *De cierta manera* at the level of

19.31 Gutiérrez Alea's *La última cena* (1976): the count (Nelson Villagra) with one of the twelve slaves he has invited to his "last supper."

19.32 *De cierta manera* (Sara Gómez, 1974), a critique of racism and sexism in contemporary Cuba.

the professional artist; Pastor Vega's *Habanera* (1984), an atypical European-style film of midlife crisis among Cuba's intellectual professionals; Juan Carlos Tabío's (b. 1943) *Se permuta* (1985), adapted from his own comic play about Cuba's housing shortage; Juan Padrón's (b. 1947) bawdy animated feature *Vampiros en la Habana* (*Vampires in Havana*, 1985); and two works by newcomer Jésus Díaz (1941–2002), *Polvo rojo* (*Red Dust*, 1981), an epic of postrevolutionary reconstruction, and *Lejanía* (*Distance*, 1985), a film about the irreconcilable differences between Cuban and American society. Ironically, Díaz's younger brother, Rolando (b. 1947), has developed a flair for American-style commercial comedy in such films as *Los pájaros a la escopeta* (*Birds Will Fly*, 1984) and *En tres y dos* (*Full Count*, 1985). The 1980s ended eclectically in Cuba, with a literate historical romance, Gutiérrez Alea's *Cartas del parque* (*Letters from the Park*, 1988); an agitational account of prerevolutionary terrorism, Fernando Pérez's (b. 1944) *Clandestinos* (*Living Dangerously*, 1988); a colorful adaptation from Gabriel García Márquez, Fernando Birri's *Un señor muy viejo con unas alas enormes* (*A Very Old Man with Enormous Wings*, 1988); and a raucous contemporary satire, Juan Carlos Tabío's *Plaff!* (1989), which lampoons all things Cuban, from the socialist bureaucracy to Santería.

In terms of production ICAIC operates as a collective in which there is—amazingly—no government oversight and directors are free to choose their own subjects and write their own scripts. In the mid-1990s, the Cuban cinema continued to evolve on course, but the U.S. trade embargo and the country's endemic poverty made creative improvisation within the industry a way of life. There was, for example, a chronic shortage of raw film stock. Moreover, U.S. disapproval had a negative impact on international sales, and many distributors wouldn't buy Cuban films for fear of boycotts by American producers. Furthermore, the United States froze all profits from Cuban bookings within its borders so that only a handful of Cuban films are known to American audiences, and Unifilm, ICAIC's main American distributor, was driven into bankruptcy in the early 1980s by the squeeze. (In the early 1990s, the embargo was eased to allow for limited payment for "cultural goods" between both countries; it was reimposed in 1994.) Yet, in a short span of time, Cuban cinema and Cuban spectators came a long way, and they provided enormous inspiration, not to men-

tion valuable production and postproduction assistance, to militant film movements all over the hemisphere. The Festival of New Latin American Cinema held annually in Havana became an event of international importance following its inception in 1979 and, during the 1980s, was widely considered to be the most important Spanish-language festival in the world, surpassing both Barcelona and Madrid in attendance and market share. At the conclusion of the 1986 festival, Fidel Castro announced the creation of the New Latin American Cinema Foundation in Havana, under the direction of Nobel Prize–winning novelist Gabriel García Márquez, and the establishment of the International Film and Television School (La Escuela de Cine y Televisión), commonly known as "the School of the Three Worlds," just outside Havana, in San Antonio de las Baños (the location of Gutiérrez Alea's *Los sobrevivientes*), under the direction of Argentine documentarist Fernando Birri, a pioneer of the New Latin American Cinema movement. The foundation's major goals were the creation of an "information bank" on Latin American cinema and the lobbying of local governments for economic support of the movement. The film school replaced Cuba's existing apprenticeship system and also trained film-and videomakers from Africa, Asia, and the rest of Latin America to work, as its charter proclaims, "for the growing and effective solidarity of Latin American filmmakers within a framework of dignity, social justice, and the preservation of the cultural heritage of the Latin American peoples."[3]

All of this changed in the early 1990s, as the collapse of communism in Eastern Europe and the Soviet Union forced Cuba into an era of extreme cultural and economic isolation, leaving it with no allies but China and North Korea. Cuban cinema entered a period of sharp decline: from its highwater mark of 8 to 10 features and 40 to 45 shorts annually, production fell off to 2 or 3 films per year. Both the International Film School and the Festival of New Latin American Cinema experienced budget crises, and in 1992 ICAIC was merged with the film department of the armed forces to ensure its survival. A handful of revolutionary films continued to appear in the period 1991–93—e.g., Sergio Giral's murky evocation of Afro-

---

3. Quoted in Dennis West, "A Film School for the Third World," *Cineaste* 15, 3 (1987): 37.

Cuban mythology *María Antonia* (1991) and Humberto Solás's French-Cuban-Spanish-Russian coproduction *El siglo de las luces* (*Explosion in a Cathedral*, 1993)—but most films exhibited in Cuba at this time were locally produced genre fare or ideological tracts from North Korea. As the financial situation worsened, political repression grew—in 1992, Daniel Díaz Torres's (b. 1948) *Alicia en el pueblo de maravillas* (*Alice in Wonderland*), a mildly critical satire of contemporary Cuban life, was banned as "counterrevolutionary" after playing to record crowds for four days in Havana; and Gutiérrez Alea's *Fresa y chocolate* (*Strawberry and Chocolate*, 1993), with its open sympathy for Cuba's gays, received only limited distribution. Several other films were banned outright that year, and a number of Cuban filmmakers (Jésus Díaz, Sergio Giral, etc.) went into exile in other Latin American countries. In either desperation or defiance, Castro declared that Cuba, with its now 11.2 million people, is the "last bastion of Marxist-Leninist purity" on earth. But as fuel shortages caused the government to close theaters and dim the lights at ICAIC, it seems clear that Cuba's revolutionary cinema, if not its revolution, came full circle to its beginnings with no cinema at all.

Thanks in part to investment by European and Canadian companies in the tourism and mining industries, Cuban cinema started to grow again in the late 1990s, and a Cuban film appeared at Havana's Twentieth Festival of New Latin American Cinema in December 1998 for the first time in several years. This was Fernando Pérez's poetic meditation on day-to-day existence in contemporary Cuba, *Life Is to Whistle* (*La vida es silbar*), and it won the top award, signaling a revival of Cuban cinema. In that same year, ICAIC was put under new leadership (with newcomer Omar Gonzales replacing Castro confidant Alfredo Guevara), and a number of coproduction deals were struck with Spain. Veteran filmmakers produced new work—e.g., Pastor Vega's *The Prophecies of Amanda* (*Las Profecías de Amanda*, 2000), Juan Carlos Tabío's *The Waiting List* (*Lista de espera*, 2000), and Humberto Solas's *Miel para Oshún* (2000). The latter was the first Cuban feature shot on digital video, and ICAIC is aggressively promoting digital technology as a means of expanding feature production without outside money and its influences—e.g., Juan Padrón's animated digital feature *Vampires in Havana II* (*Vampiros de la Habana II*) was produced entirely with ICAIC funds. (Here, as elsewhere, Cuba is a leader—first, as the only Latin American country to have developed its own animation industry and, second, as the first to convert to 3-D digital imagery.)

Africa

NORTH AFRICA

As Clyde Taylor points out, over fifty African nations have gained independence since World War II—most of them since 1960—and yet the African film market is small by Western standards. It can logically be divided between North African and sub-Saharan cinema.

In the north, the most prominent film-producing country is Algeria, whose film industry was nationalized shortly after the nation won its independence in a savage war of liberation with France that lasted from 1954 to 1962. Algeria's first films concerned that struggle and were collectively known as *cinéma mudjahad*—"freedom-fighter cinema." Several of these films, such as Ahmed Rachedi's (b. 1938) *L'Aube des damnés* (*Dawn of the Damned*, 1965) and Mohammed Lakhdar-Hamina's (b. 1934) *Le Vent des Aurés* (*The Wind of Aurés*, 1966; winner of the Cannes Camera d'or), were of superior quality, but it was not until the *cinéma djidid* ("new cinema") movement of the 1970s that Algeria established an authentic and sophisticated (albeit state-controlled) alternative cinema, especially in the work of Ali Ghalem— *Mektoub* (1970); Mohamed Bouamari (b. 1941)—*Le Charbonnier* (*The Coal-Miner*, 1973); Mohamed Slimane Riad (b. 1932)—*Ryah el janoub* (*The South Wind*, 1975); and Mohammed Lakhdar-Hamina—*Chronique des années de braise* (*Chronicle of the Years of Embers*, 1975), an epic film about a family's coming to revolutionary consciousness in the crucial period from 1939 to 1954, which won the Grand Prix at Cannes. More recently, Ali Ghalem has returned with *Maraa le ibni* (*A Wife for My Son*, 1983), and Ahmed Rachedi with *Tahounet al sayed Fabre* (*Mr. Fabre's Mill*, 1986), while Lakhdar-Hamina has directed the French-Algerian coproduction *La Dernière image* (*The Last Image*, 1986). Algeria, whose population is approximately 32.2 million, produced about 5 or 6 features and 60 to 80 shorts a year until the early 1990s, and it has also coproduced films with Italy (Gillo Pontecorvo's

19.33 *Chronique des années de braise* (Mohammed Lakhdar-Hamina, 1975): reflections on the Algerian war of liberation. Leila Shenna (right).

La battaglia di Algeri [*The Battle of Algiers*, 1966]) and Egypt (Youssef Chahine's *al-Asfour* [*The Sparrow*, 1973]). Moreover, there are a number of native Algerian filmmakers who live and work in France, including Mehdi Charef—*Le thé au harem d'Archimède* (*Tea in the Harem*, 1985), *Miss Mona* (1987), *Camomille* (1988); and Merzak Allouache—*Un Amour à Paris* (*A Romance in Paris*, 1987). Starting in 1992, the government of Algeria was faced with a militant Islamic insurgency that continued into the new century and at times approached the dimensions of a civil war. Filmmaking became extremely difficult amid the violence and terror unleashed by these hostilities, and nearly impossible after the abrupt shutting down of the main government funding agencies for cinema in 1997 and 1998. Algeria's state-subsidized cinema had been provisionally privatized in 1993 and was now cut off from government funds altogether. Although a handful of films have since been made in the formerly banned Berber language of the mountains—e.g., Abderrahmane Bouguermouh's *The Forgotten Hillside* (*La colline oubliée*, 1992; 1997) and Azzeddine Meddour's *Baya's Mountain* (*La montagne de Baya*, 1998)—most Algerian directors now live and work abroad.

Neighboring francophone Tunisia (population 9.8 million), which has been host of the Carthage Film Festival since 1966, has a small government-supported industry that has coproduced such notable features as *Dhil al-Ardh* (*Shadow of the Earth*, Taieb Louhichi, 1982; with

France); *La Ballade de Mamlouk* (*The Ballad of Mamlouk*, Abdelhafidh Bouassida, 1982; with Czechoslovakia); and two documentaries of Férid Boughedir—*Caméra d'Afrique: 20 Years of African Cinema* (1983) and *Caméra Arabe: The Young Arab Cinema* (1987), both with France. In 1986, an all-Tunisian production, Nouri Bouzid's *Rih al saad* (*Man of Ashes*) won the golden prize at the twenty-second Taormina Film Festival in Sicily, and its companion-piece *Sfayah min dhahab* (*The Golden Horseshoes*, 1989) was an official jury selection three years later at Cannes. Bouzid's third long feature, *Bezness* (*Business*, 1991), about a male prostitute who caters to female tourists, and Nacer Khemir's mystical fantasy *Tawk al hamama al mafkoud* (*The Missing Collar of the Pigeon*, 1991) both won various festival awards, while Férid Boughedir's intimate coming-of-age comedy *Halfaween, asfoor al satah* (*Halfaween, the Bird of the Roofs*), also known as *Halfaouine—l'enfant des terrasses* (*Halfaouine—Boy of the Terraces*, 1990), broke all Tunisian box-office records in 1991. Tunisia produces only two or three films a year, usually coproductions with France or Morocco. Among the more interesting developments for Tunisian cinema in the past decade has been the emergence of two of North Africa's only women filmmakers—Kalthoum Bornaz (b. 1945—*Keswa, al-Khayt al-Dhai* [*Keswa: The Lost Thread*, 1997]) and IDHEC-trained former editor Moufida Tlatli (b. 1947—*Samt el Qusur* [*Silences of the Palace*, 1994]; *La saison des hommes* [*The Season of Men*, 2000]).

19.34 *Man of Ashes* (*Rih al saad* [Nouri Bouzid, 1986]). A film about the sexual insecurities of a young man (Imed Maalal) on the eve of his wedding in a male-dominated but secularized Muslim society. Here, a Western-style bachelor party.

Morocco (population 31.1 million), the other country of the Maghreb (liberally, "the sunset"—that region of northern Africa that extends most prominently into the Mediterranean and includes Algeria, Tunisia, and Morocco), made only about 20 features in the years from independence in 1956 to 1980, but these films were notably more experimental than those of Algeria and Tunisia, perhaps because of Morocco's relatively high cultural level and active *ciné-club* tradition. The success of such films as Latif Lahlou's *Soleil de printemps* (*Spring Sun*, 1970), Souheil Ben-Barka's (b. 1942) *Les Mille et une mains* (*The Thousand and One Hands*, 1972), Moumen Smihi's (b. 1945) *El chergui* (*The Violent Silence*, 1975), and Ahmed El Maanouni's (b. 1944) *Alyam! Alyam!* (*Oh the Days! Oh the Days!*, 1978) created the grounds for a system of government support through the Centre Cinematographique Marocaine (CCM). Between 1980 and 1984, 30 new films were produced under its auspices; prominent among them were *Le Coiffeur du quartier des pauvres* (*The Neighborhood Barber*, Mohamed Reggab, 1982), *Amok* (Souheil Ben-Barka, 1983), *Cauchemar* (*Nightmare*, Ahmed Yasfine, 1984), and *Zeft* (*Concrete*, Tayeb Saddiki, 1984). Among recent Moroccan films notable for their formal stylization are Moumen Smihi's *44 ou les Récits de la nuit* (*44 or Tales of the Night*, 1985), Mohamed Aboulouakar's *Hadda* (1986), and Najib Sefraoui's *Chams* (1986). Morocco has the most successful system of state funding in all of North Africa, making it the region's leading producer, with 40 features during the 1990s. Some of its directors, like Souheil Ben-Barka, who was trained at the Centro Sperimentale in Italy and worked as an assistant director to Pier Paolo Pasolini during the 1960s, have international ambitions. In fact, Ben-Barka, who has been director general of the CCM since the late 1980s, made two big-budget epics with international casts during the 1990s—*Les cavaliers de la gloire* (*Horsemen of Glory*, 1993) and *L'ombre du pharaon* (*Shadow of the Pharoah*, 1996). Other Moroccan filmmakers aim more exclusively at the local market—e.g., Łódź-trained Abdelkader Lagtaa (b. 1948), whose gritty *Un amour à Casablanca* (*A Love Affair in Casablanca*, 1991) was the nation's first domestic blockbuster; and Farida Ben Lyazid (b. 1948), a rare female writer-director who makes socially insightful comedies like *Keïd ensa* (*Women's Wiles*, 1996). In the early years of the twenty-first century, Morocco's industry grew increasingly robust,

releasing on average 10 features annually and bringing home numerous festival awards.

Egypt (population 70.7 million) is the other North African country with a sizable film industry, although it is by and large relentlessly commercial and star-oriented. (For example, actor Omar Sharif [b. 1932] was a product of the Egyptian star system.) Centered in a huge Cairo studio complex called "Cinema Town," Egyptian cinema has long dominated the Arab world, with its potential audience of 300 million, and is the third most prolific in the world at large, after those of the United States and India. Recently Egypt has turned out 70 to 80 features annually, until the early 1990s, with significant state support. Its filmmakers are capable of producing such complex individual films as Shadi Abdes-Salam's (b. 1930) *Al-momia* (*The Night of Counting the Years*, 1969), and it has a director of international standing in Youssef Chahine (b. 1926), whose major works have been *Bab el-hadid* (*Cairo Station*, 1958), *al-Ard* (*The Land*, 1969), *The Sparrow* (an Algerian coproduction noted above), and *El Yom el sades* (*The Sixth Day*, 1986), a melodrama set during the 1947 cholera epidemic. Equally powerful is Chahine's autobiographical trilogy—*Iskandarija . . . Lih?* (*Alexandria . . . Why?*, 1978), *Hadduta misrija* (*An Egyptian Story*, 1982), and *Iskandarija, kaman waka-man* (*Alexandria, Again and Forever*, 1990)—which is also a social history of modern Egypt. Other Egyptian directors of note are veterans Salah Abouseif—*El*

19.35 Mohsen Mohiedine in *Alexandria . . . Why?* (1978), the first film in Youssef Chahine's autobiographical trilogy.

bedaya (*Satan's Empire/The Beginning*, 1986); Kamal El Sheikh—*El-taous* (*The Peacock*, 1982); *Kaher el zaman* (*Conqueror of Time*, 1986); and the relative new-comer Mohamed Khan (b. 1942), most of whose films are shot on location in the streets of Cairo—*El harrif* (*Street Player*, 1983); *Awdat mowatin* (*Return of a Citizen*, 1986); *Zawgat ragol mohim* (*Wife of an Important Man*, 1987); the feminist *Ahlam Hind wa Camilia* (*Dreams of Hind and Camelia*, 1989); and the uncharacteristically mythlike *Al ghaarkana* (1992). Developments in the 1980s included a marked relaxation in government censorship and the emergence of several women directors, most of them graduates of the Egyptian Film Institute, who make films on feminist themes—among them Asmaa El-Bakri (*Beggars and Proud Ones*, 1991) and Inas el-Degheidy (*Lady Killers*, 1992)—as well as the surrealistic visual stylist Daoud Abdel Sayed (*The Search for Sayed Marzouk* [*El bahths an al-Sayed Marzouk*, 1991]; *Kit Kat*, 1992). In the early 1990s, Egyptian cinema experienced a crisis that resulted in steeply declining levels of production—18 features in 1994, 25 in 1995, 22 in 1996, 16 in 1997, 20 in 1998—the lowest numbers in fifty years. The reasons were twofold: in the short term, the Gulf War in 1991 halted Egypt's distribution to many of its Arab neighbors; in the long term, satellite television and other forms of electronic entertainment began to cut heavily into its domestic market. Furthermore, state-run television, in the form of the Egyptian Radio and Television Union (ERTU), began to compete head to head with the film industry by going into production and releasing its tele-films both theatrically and on the air. Ultimately, Egypt's film producers were able to partner with ERTU, and by the late 1990s yearly production had begun to rise again. At the same time, two large companies—Sho'aa (Cultural Media) and Egyptian Renaissance—started a theater-building boom in Alexandria and Cairo. As a result, for the first time in history, the nine top-grossing films of 1999 were domestic productions (although 85 percent of them were comedies). Veterans like Youssef Chahine produced new work (*Al-Akhar* [*The Other*, 1999]; *Silence . . . on tourne* [*Quiet, We're Rolling*, 2001]), and a new generation of directors emerged with debut features—e.g., Ahmad Atef's *Omar Alfeen* (*Omar 2000* [2001]); Mohamed Amin's *Film Thakafy* (*Cultural Movie* [2001]); and Khaled Youssef's *Al Asifa* (*Desert Storm* [2001]).

SUB-SAHARAN AFRICA

The most important film-producing country in sub-Saharan Africa, and also one of the first, is Senegal (population 9.9 million), largely owing to the work of one director, Ousmane Sembene (b. 1923), who studied filmmaking in Moscow with Mark Donskoi and is also a distinguished writer of short stories and novels as well as of his own screenplays. Sembene made all of his films outside of the French Ministry of Cooperation program, which assisted production in its former sub-Saharan colonies from 1962 to 1980. Most historians identify his 20-minute short *Borom Sarret* (1963), which won a prize at the International Festival of Tours, as the first indigenous black African film. Sembene followed this realistic account of a day in the life of an impoverished Dakar cartman with his 60-minute *La Noire de . . .* (*Black Girl*, 1966; adapted from his own story). Arguably the first sub-Saharan feature and one of the first significant anti-colonial documents of Africa, *La Noire de . . .* describes a young black woman who loses her cultural identity as a maid in service to a French family. *Mandabi* (*The Money Order*, 1968), Sembene's first full-length color feature, was shot in both French and Wolof, a language spoken by 90 percent of the Senegalese people. A muted social satire about the humiliating ordeal of an illiterate Dakar workingman trying to cash a check sent to him by his nephew in Paris, it took prizes at international festivals in Tashkent, New York, and Atlanta, and became the first Senegalese feature to be distributed commercially in its home country. His *Emitai* (1971) mixes epic and documentary aspirations in its rendition of a confrontation between a group of Diola villagers and French troops sent to requisition their harvest during World War II. The film, whose title means "god of thunder" in Diola, was shot almost entirely in that language and concludes with the brutal massacre of the villagers. Although it won major awards at Moscow and Tashkent, *Emitai* could not be distributed in Senegal because of pressure from the French government, which has maintained close economic and cultural ties with its former colony since independence was granted in 1959. Sembene's next film, *Xala* (1974), was adapted from a short novel he published in French the same year. Its title, usually translated as *The Curse*, actually means "impotence" in Wolof, and the film is a ferocious satire on the black bourgeoisie of the new Senegalese republic. Its protagonist is a corrupt bureau-

19.36 *Xala* (Ousmane Sembene, 1974): a government official (Thierno Leye) caught between neocolonialism and the ancient curse of impotence.

Faat Kiné, a domestic drama about a female Senegalese gas-station operator that he dedicated to the "everyday heroism of African women." Another important Senegalese filmmaker is Djibril Diop Mambéty (1945–1998), whose *Touki Bouki* (1973) is widely regarded as Africa's first avant-garde film and whose *Hyenas* (1992) is adapted from Dürrenmatt's absurdist play *The Visit*. Near the end of his life, Mambéty, who wrote his own screenplays, was working on a series of short films collectively entitled "Tales of Ordinary People," of which he completed only *Le franc* (1994) and *La petite vendeuse de soleil* (*The Little Girl Who Sold the Sun*, 1999). Other Senegalese filmmakers are Mahama Johnson Traoré (b. 1942)—*Reou-takh* (*The Big City*, 1971) and *Njangaan* (1974); Safi Faye (b. 1943), the first sub-Saharan African woman to make a feature—*Kaddu-beykat* (*Letter from a Village*, 1976), *Fad'jal* (*Grandfather*, 1979), *Ambassades nourricières* (*Culinary Embassies*, 1980), and *Mossane* (1996); Ben Diogaye Beye—*Seye seyeti* (*One Man, Many Women*, 1980); Ababakar Samb-Makharam (1934–1987)—

crat who is stricken by impotence on the night of wedding his third wife and must exorcise the curse by resorting to a degrading primitive ritual. Sembene then made *Ceddo* (1977), which he adapted from his own novel and produced himself with the profits from *Xala* and a government-sponsored loan. It collapses several centuries of colonial African history into the events of several days in the exemplary tale of an Islamic imam (spiritual teacher) who dethrones a village king and imposes his religion on the people. The imam ultimately is killed by the *ceddo* ("outsiders" in Wolof), who reject his claims. Richly stylized and highly controversial in a country that is 80 percent Muslim, *Ceddo* was banned by the Senegalese government for eight years. In the meantime, Sembene pursued his career as a writer and planned his projected magnum opus—a six-hour epic on the life of Samori Toure, the nineteenth-century West African nationalist who resisted French and British imperialism. While seeking funding for *Samori*, Sembene directed (with Thierno Faty Sow) the Senegalese-Tunisian-Algerian coproduction *Camp de Thiaroye* (*Camp Thiaroye*, 1988). This powerful anticolonial film is based upon an actual massacre ordered by the French army against black veterans returning to Senegal from World War II. In 1992 Sembene made *Guelwaar*, about a historical confrontation between Muslims and Christians at the funeral of the anticolonial freedom fighter named in the title; and in 2000, at the age of seventy-seven, Sembene produced

19.37 *Touki-Bouki* (Djibril Diop Mambéty, 1973).

Kodou (1971) and *Jom* (1981); Paulin Soumanou Vieyra (1925–1987), a former documentarist whose collaborative short *Afrique sur Seine* (*Africa on the Seine*, 1955) is sometimes described as the foundation stone of African cinema—*En Résidence surveillée* (*Under House Arrest*, 1982); and the Vietnamese documentarist Trinh T. Minh-ha, who worked in Africa during the 1980s—*Réassemblage* (1982); *Naked Spaces* (1985). Between 1968 and 1983, Senegal produced 26 features, most of them with the assistance of the French Ministry of Cooperation and the government-backed SNPC (Societé nouvelle de promotion cinématographique). When this agency was dismantled in the midst of an economic crisis in 1989, the Senegalese industry was privatized and, after a brief hiatus, surged forward again with the work of such third-generation directors as Moussa Touré (*Toubab-Bi*, 1991) and short-film specialist Mansour Sora Wade (*Taal pexx*, 1991; *Aida Souka*, 1992; *Piticumi*, 1992).

Other sub-Saharan film-producing countries are Mali (population 11.3 million), Burkina Faso (formerly Upper Volta—population 12.6 million), the Ivory Coast (population 16.8 million), Ghana (population 20.2 million), Nigeria (population 129.9 million), and Angola (population 10.6 million). Mali has two filmmakers whose work is becoming known in the West, both of whom produce, like Sembene, outside the system of French assistance available to most of France's former colonies. They are Souleymane Cissé (b. 1940), trained in Moscow—*Den muso* (*The Girl*, 1975); *Baara* (*The Porter*, 1978); *Finye* (*The Wind*, 1982); *Yeelen* (*Brightness*, 1987); *Waati* (1995); and Cheick Oumar Sissoko (b. 1945), whose *Nyamanton* (*The Garbage Boys*, 1986), *Finzan* (*A Dance for the Heroes*, 1989), *Guimba* (*Guimba the Tyrant*, 1995), and *La Genèse* (*Genesis*, 1999) attracted considerable international attention. Cissé's films are open-ended and mythic, depending on Malian oral tradition and inviting audience interaction, whereas Sissoko's are more typically Western in structure and tend toward social satire. Another Malian director of note is Adama Drabo, whose *Ta Dona* (*Fire!*, 1991) has been hailed as one of Africa's first environmental features and whose fantastic comedy *Taafé fanga* (*Skirt Power*, 1997) is based on a Dogon oral legend. In Burkina Faso (Upper Volta) the work of Gaston Kaboré (b. 1952)—*Wend Kuuni* (*God's Gift*, 1982) and *Buud yam* (1997), a sequel to *Wend Kuuni*; *Zan Boko* (1988); *Rabi* (1991); *Madame Hado* (1992); of Kollo Sanou—*Paweogo* (*The Emigrant*, 1983); of Paul Zoumbara—*Jours de tourmentes* (*Days of*

19.38 *Finye* (**Souleymane Cissé, 1982**): village boys study for a high-school exam in Mali.

19.39 *Yeleen* (*Brightness*, **1987**): ritual magic in Souleymane Cissé's adaptation of a thirteenth-century Bambaran oral epic.

Torment, 1983); and of Idrissa Ouedraogo (b. 1954)—*Poko* (1981); *Yam daabo* (*The Choice*, 1986—FIPRESCI Prize, Cannes); *Yaaba* (*Grandmother*, 1989);[4] *Tilai* (1990—Prix de Jury, Cannes); *Samba Traoré* (1992—Sil-

---

4. The subject of a rare 1990 documentary, *Parlons Grandmère*, by Ouedraogo's friend, the Senegalese director Djibril Diop Mambéty.

19.40 and 19.41 *Zan Boko* (Gaston Kaboré, 1988), a film about the impact of urbanization on traditional African culture. The title means "the place where the placenta is buried" and evokes the waning continuity between the present and past in Burkino Faso's village life.

ver Bear, Berlin)—has all received marked attention. Ouedraogo's films are often family dramas whose appeal reaches beyond national borders, and some of his more recent work was filmed on locations outside of Burkina Faso—e.g., *Le cri du couer* (*The Heart's Cry*, 1994) in Paris, and *Kini & Adams* (1997) in South Africa. The nation's capital, Ouagadougou, is the home of the Pan-African Federation of Filmmakers (FEPACI) and has been host to the annual Pan-African Film Festival (Festival Panafricain du Cinéma de Ouagadougou, or FESPACO) since 1969. From the Ivory Coast have come such recent independent features as Fadika Kramo-Lanciné's *Djeli* (*The Girot*, 1981), Désiré Ecaré's *Visages de femmes* (*Faces of Women*, 1985), and Roger Gnoan M'Bala's *Ablakon* (1985) and *Bouka* (1988). And from anglophone Ghana there have come Kwaw Ansah's *Love Brewed in the African Pot* (1980), King Ampaw's *Kukurantumi—The Road to Accra* (1983) and *Nana Akoto* (1985), and Kwate Nee-Owoo and Kwesi Owusu's *Ouaga* (1988), a documentary on the work of FESPACO. In Nigeria, IDHEC-trained Ola Balogun (b. 1945) has produced ten anglophone features since 1972, including *Cry Freedom!* (1981), *Money Power* (1982), and *A deusa negra* (*Black Goddess*, 1983). But Nigeria also has a large popular film industry centered in the Surulere district of Lagos that, since the late 1990s, has been producing about 400 features a year, most of them shot on digital video in several days for under $15,000. These films (known locally as "home videos") have become as popular as those from Hollywood and "Bollywood" with Africa's English-speaking audiences and have had a broad influence on Africa's popular culture. By 2002, the Nigerian industry was generating revenues of about $45 million and had developed its own star system as well as a burgeoning bootleg market.[5] Lusophone (Portuguese-speaking) Angola established a film institute in 1977, two years after liberation from Portugal, and has produced a major director in Ruy Duarte de Carvalho (b. 1941)—*Faz la coragem, camarada!* (*Courage, Comrade!*, 1977); *Nelisita* (1983); *Le Message des Îles* (1989). There are also occasional Lusophone films from Guinea-Bissau (Flora Gomes's *Mortu nega*, [1988] and *Po di sangui* [*Tree of Blood*, 1998]); and Mozambique (Mario Henrique Borgneth's *Frontières sanglantes* [*Borders of Blood*, 1987]); as well as francophone films from Cameroon (Bassek Ba Kobhio's *Sango malo* [*The Village Teacher*, 1991]; Jean-Pierre Bekolo's *Quartier Mozart* [1992] and *Aristotle's Plot* [1996]; Jean-Marie Téno's *Afrique, je te plumerai* [*Africa, I Will Fleece You*, 1992] and *Clando* [1996]); the Democratic Republic of the Congo, formerly Zaire, (Mweze Ngangura and Benoît

5. Norimitsu Onishi, "Step Aside, L.A. and Bombay, for Nollywood," *New York Times*, September 16, 2002: A1, A8.

19.42 *Quartier Mozart* (Jean-Pierre Bekolo, 1992): forty-eight hours in the urban slums of Yaounde, Cameroon.

Lamy's *La Vie est belle* [*Life Is Rosy*, 1987]); and the eastern island of Madagascar (César Paes's *Angano . . . Angano . . .* [*Tales from Madagascar*, 1989]).[6]

Also significant is the work of several African film-makers living abroad. Especially notable is the Mauritanian Med Hondo (b. 1936), whose *Soleil O* (*O Sun*, 1970), after a song sung by African slaves transported to the West Indies, *Les Bicots-nègres, vos voisins* (*The Negroes, Your Neighbors*, 1973), and *West Indies* (1979)[7] are vigorous indictments of slavery, racism, and the neocolonial mentality. For *Sarraounia* (1986), Med Hondo returned to Africa (Burkina Faso) to direct an epic account of a tribal queen's victory over French expeditionary forces in central Africa in 1898–99. More recently, Hondo directed two political thrillers set in Paris—*Lumière noire* (*Black Light*, 1994) and *Watani, un monde sans mal* (*Watani: A World without Evil*, 1998). Other exiles are the UCLA-trained Ethiopian Haile Gerima (b. 1946), whose monumental docudrama *Mirt sost shi amit* (*Harvest: 3,000 Years*, 1975) was shot on location in Ethiopia on the eve of the revolution there, and whose feature *Sankofa* (1993) re-creates the slave era at Ghana's Cape Coast castle in the same way that his documentary *Adwa* (1999) reconstructs the legendary Ethiopian victory over Italy in 1896; and Sarah Maldoror (b. Sarah Ducades, 1929), a French resident of Guadeloupe parentage, trained in Moscow, whose tense film of the Angolan liberation struggle, *Sambizanga* (1973), was shot secretly in the Democratic Republic of the Congo during the actual revolution there and won many international awards.

---

6. Omitted from this list is South Africa (population 43.6 million), whose industry produced approximately 50 films per year between 1980 and 1990, thanks to a generous system of tax incentives and government subsidies. Most of these, however, were cheap commercial productions made for the benefit of the ruling white majority. Exceptions existed in the trilogy of filmscripts by the distinguished playwright Athol Fugard (b. 1932)—*Boesman and Lena* (1974), *The Guest,* (1977) and *Marigolds in August* (1980), all directed by Ross Devenish; the adaptations of eleven Nadine Gordimer (b. 1923) stories made by various film crews for West German television; and such occasional, courageous independent features as *Last Grave at Dimbaza* (Nana Mahomo, 1975). An important South African filmmaker in exile is documentarist Lionel Ngakane (b. 1928), whose feature-length *Vukani* (*Awake*, 1964), *Jemima and Johnny* (1975), *Once upon a Time* (1975), and *Nelson Mandela* (1985) have all been made abroad. (Ngakane returned to South Africa in 1993 and became the FEPACI regional secretary.) As South Africa moved uneasily toward majority rule in the late 1980s, such controversial films as Oliver Schmitz's *Mapantsula* (1990), the story of a contemporary township gangster, and Darrell Roodt's trilogy about rural racial conflicts—*A Place for Weeping* (1987), *The Stick* (1988), and *Jobman*

(1989)—were made but often went undistributed. Quality mainstream productions of the 1990s include Gray Hofmeyr's *Lambarene* (1991), a life of Albert Schweitzer; Mane Van Rensburg's *The Fourth Reich* (1990), a historical account of Afrikaaner nationalism during World War II, and the biracial comedy *Taxi to Soweto* (1991); and a very successful adaptation of Athol Fugard's play *The Road to Mecca* (Peter Goldsmid and Athol Fugard, 1992). The transition to majority rule in 1994 produced anticipated financial and cultural turmoil within the film industry that took some time to overcome. The first post-apartheid feature by a black South African was Ramadan Suleman's *Fools* (1997), a slice-of-life drama about the disillusionment of a political idealist in December 1989, just before ANC leader Nelson Mandela was released from prison.

7. In the West Indies themselves, films have been produced in Jamaica (population 2.6 million)—e.g., the cult classic *The Harder They Come* (Perry Henzell, 1973); *Countryman* (Dickie Jobson, 1982); *Cool Runnings* (Robert Mugge, 1983; released 1986); *Diggers* (Roman J. Foster, 1986); plus Brian Saint-Juste's *Children of Babylon* and *Smile Orange*; and Martinique—*Sugar Cane Alley/Street of Black Shacks* (*Rue cases nègres*, 1983), directed by Euzhan Palcy.

19.43 *Harvest: 3,000 Years* **(1975), Haile Gerima's explosive indictment of Third World exploitation: Melaku Makonen.**

The Middle East

Excluding Egypt, which is treated with the North African nations, above, the only major film-producing countries in the Middle East are Iran and Israel. However, several Arab states made interesting contributions to world cinema during the 1980s and 1990s. Lebanon (population 3.7 million), which once had the best studios and laboratories in the Arab world and is still making films despite twenty years of civil war, produced Rafiq Hadjar's *Explosion* (*Al-infigar*, 1983), Heiny Srour's *Leila and the Wolves* (*Leila wal dhiab*, 1984), Jean Khalil Chamoun's *Wild Flowers: Women from South Lebanon* (1985), Jocelyn Saab's *Sugar of Love* (*Gazl el banat*, 1985) Samir Habchi's *The Tornado* (*El-Aasar*, 1992), Jean-Claude Codsi's *The Time Has Come* (*Ana al-Awan*, 1994), and Ziad Doueiri's *West Beirut* (1998). Syria (population 17.1 million), whose films are funded through the National Film Organization (NFO), made *Dreams of the City* (*Ahlam al madina* [Mohamed Malas, 1984]), *The Sun on a Hazy Day* (Mohamed Chanin, 1986), *The Stars of Midday* (*Nujum al-Nahar* [Usama Muhammad, 1989]), *Nights of the Jackal* (*Layali ibn awa* [Abdellatif Abdelhamid, 1989]), and *The Extras* (*al-Kombars* [Nabil Maleh, 1992]), while Libya (population 5.4 million) produced *Shrapnel* (*Alshazhia* [Mohamed Abdul Salam, 1987]), and the Sudan (population 30.0 million) made *Tajoog* (Gadalla Gubara [1984]) and *Paradise Slum* (*Deim dar el-naemi* [Cornelia Schlede, 1986]). Iraq (population 24.0

million) has produced films since 1945, and its cinema was formerly controlled through the Ba'thist General Organization for Film and Theater. It produced its first epic in 1980, the $15 million *al-Gaadisiyya*, directed by the Egyptian Salah Abouseif, based on a historical episode from A.D. 636 in which outnumbered Arab forces repulsed an army of invading infidels. Like most Iraqi films made during its bloody war with Iran, 1980–88 (e.g., Mohamed Shukri Jameel's *Clashing Loyalties* [*Al-mas ala al-kubra*, 1983]; Mohamed Moumir Fanari's *The Lover* [*Al asheke*, 1986]; Sahib Haddad's *Flaming Borders* [*Al-hudud al multahiba*, 1986]), this one is redolent with militant nationalism. After the Gulf War of 1991, Iraqi cinema temporarily ceased to function and has produced nothing for export since.

IRAN

From the coming of sound through the revolution of 1979, the media of Iran (population 66.6 million)—like those of Latin America—were dominated by the United States through the powerful lobby of the Motion Picture Export Association and, after 1960, the Television Program Export Association. A domestic feature-film industry, therefore, developed in Iran along America-oriented, escapist lines; between 1931 and the revolution, Iran produced over 1,100 motion pictures. Between 1966 and 1976, a progressive national film movement came into being as foreign-trained directors such as Fereydoun Rahnema (*Siavash in Persepolis* [*Siavash-e-takhte ajmshid*, 1965]), Davoud Molapoor (*Madam Ahoo's Husband*, 1966), and Assoud Kimaee (*Gheysar*, 1966) made their first features. Various film festivals—particularly the Tehran International Festival, inaugurated in 1972—were established with the support of the Ministry of Art and Culture to showcase the new work. The breakthrough film for this Iranian New Wave or New Cinema (*cinema motefavet*) was Dariush Mehrjui's (b. 1939) second feature *The Cow* (*Gaav*, 1969). This starkly realistic account of peasant life adapted from a short story by the leftist writer Gholam-Hossein Saedi was banned in Iran for more than a year but won prizes at the Chicago and Venice festivals in 1971. It was immediately followed by such other independently produced features as Bahram Beizai's (b. 1938) *Downpour* (*Ragbar*, 1972), Arbi Ovanesian's *The Spring* (1971), Naser Taghvai's *Tranquility in the Presence of Others* (*Aramesh deir hozu-re digaran*,

1969) and *Sadegh the Kurd* (*Sadeq Kordeh*, 1972), Hajir Daryush's *Bita* (1972), and Mehrjui's *The Postman* (*Postchi*, 1970; released 1972). In 1974 the New Wave directors created a film cooperative known as the Progressive Filmmakers' Union (PFU; Kanun-e Sinemagaran-e Pishro), which produced Sohrab Shahid Saless's *Still Life* (*Tabi at-e-bijan*, 1974), Mehrjui's *The Cycle* (*Dayerh-e-mina*, 1974; one of the few Iranian films at the time to be distributed in the United States, in 1979), and Parviz Kimiavi's *Stone Garden* (*Bagh-e-sanghi*, 1975, winner of the Silver Bear at Berlin in 1976). In that year, Iran released 80 films, exceeding the production of both Egypt and Turkey and including Beizai's allegorical *The Stranger and the Fog* (*Gharibeh va meh*, 1975) and Bahman Farmanara's (b. 1942) *Prince Ehtejab* (*Shazdeh Ehtejab*, 1974), a visually stunning adaptation of a contemporary Persian novel about a despotic pre-Pahlavi ruler. (Farmanara's film won the Grand Prix at the Tehran Film Festival and became a milestone in Iranian cinema.) But an economic squeeze encouraged by American distributors brought a halt to independent production in Iran, and during 1977 and 1978 few features or documentaries of any worth were released.

In 1979 Shah Mohammed Reza Pahlavi, Iran's ruler since 1941, was overthrown by the Islamic Revolution of

19.44 Bahman Farmanara's political allegory *Tall Shadows of the Wind* (*Sayeha-ye Boland-e Bad*, 1978) was shown in the Director's Fortnight at Cannes and later banned.

Ayatollah Ruhollah Khomeini. The Khomeini government imposed strict theocratic (that is, Muslim fundamentalist) censorship, and many filmmakers fled the country (Saless, e.g., went to West Germany, Mehrjui to Paris); by 1983, only 40 films had been made in the four years since the revolution and 23 of these had been banned. In that same year, however, the government sponsored the creation of the Farabi Cinema Foundation, a quasi-independent organization whose mission was to increase the quality and quantity of Iranian films. (Khomeini was not opposed to film as such, but rather to the way it had been used by the Pahlavi regime to create false values—i.e., secularized Western ones. As he rather famously put it, "We are not against cinema; we are against prostitution.") Farabi restricted imports and helped to fund domestic production through a combination of low-interest loans and subsidies. In 1984 annual production rose from 23 to 57 films, and by 1991 Iran was producing 70 films a year to approximate its prerevolutionary high of 90 in 1972. Congruent with the Farabi Foundation's success, Islamic censors became more tolerant (although much was still taboo and, in order to be granted exhibition licenses, projects had to be approved by the Ministry of Culture and Islamic Guidance [MCIG] in four separate stages of development and completion), and many former New Wave directors—e.g., Mehrjui (*The Tenants* [*Ejarehneshina*, 1987]; *Shirak*, 1989); Taghvai (*Captain Khorshid* [*Nakhoda Khorshid*, 1987]—returned to Iran. At the same time, Farabi helped to recruit and train a new generation of filmmakers such as Amir Naderi (b. 1946—*The Runner* [*Davandeh*, 1985]; *Water, Wind, Dust* [*Aab, baad, khaak*, 1987]); Mohsen Makhmalbaf (see below); Masud Kimiai (b. 1941—*Blade and Silk* [*Tiq va abrisham*, 1986; released with 45 minutes cut]; *Snake's Fang* [*Dandan-e-mar*, 1989]; *The Sergeant* [*Goruban*, 1991]; *Wolf Tracks* [*Radd-e pay-e-gorg*, 1993]); Ebrahim Forouzesh (*The Key* [*Kelid*, 1986; screenplay and editing by Abbas Kiarostami]); and Kianoush Ayari (b. 1951—*Beyond the Flames* [*Ansu-ye atash*, 1987])—whose works often deal candidly with social and political problems despite censorship limitations. There were even a handful of women directors exploring feminist themes—e.g., Puran Derakhsandeh (b. 1951—*Mute Contact* [*Rabeteh*, 1986]; *Little Bird of Happiness* [*Parandeh-ye kouschak-e khoshbakhti*, 1988]; *Lost Time* [*Zaman as dast rafteh*, 1991]); Rakhshan Bani Etemad (b. 1954—*Off the Limits* [*Kharej az mahdudeh*, 1987]; *Canary Yellow* [*Zard-e qan-*

ari, 1989]; *Nargess* [1991]; *The Blue-Veiled* (*Rusari abi*, 1994]; *The May Lady* [*Banu-ye Ordibehesht*, 1997]); and Tahmineh Milani (b. 1960—*Children of Divorce* [*Bach-ehha-ye talaq*, 1989]; *Kakadu* [1994; released and banned]; *Two Women* [*Do zan*, 1999]—a considerably daring practice within the context of patriarchal Islamic fundamentalism.[8] By the end of the 1980s, the financial and technical infrastructures were in place for Iran to once again achieve a high level of annual production, which currently averages about 50 features per year.

It was in the 1990s, however, that the Iranian cinema became what officials at the 1992 Toronto International Film Festival called "one of the pre-eminent national cinemas in the world today."[9] This has in part to do with the Iranian industry's more or less definitive division of product between commercial projects ("populist cinema") and what are self-consciously labeled art films ("art cinema")—subsidized productions not dependent on box-office success for their directors' continued creative health, although, like Abbas Kiarostami's *Through the Olive Trees* (1994) and Mohsen Makhmalbaf's *Gabbeh* (1996), they have sometimes proved quite popular with local audiences. This art-film aesthetic is part of the Farabi Cinema Foundation's continuing commitment to the promotion of "superior Iranian films," not so much to export the Islamic revolution as to establish Iran's cultural prominence on the world stage. Although art films constitute no more than 15 percent of the total national product, this effort has been overwhelmingly successful—from placing Iranian films in international festivals 44 times in 1988, the number rose to 744 placements in 1995, with an attendant rise in the number of prizes from 2 in 1988 to 41 in 1995. Furthermore, the election of the relatively moderate Mohammad Khatami as president in 1997 and his subsequent appointment of filmmaker Seifollah Dad as deputy minister of cinema led to a liberalization of the Supervision and Evaluation Department and ultimately to the elimination of state script approval. This brought to the industry a new degree of legal freedom, permitting filmmakers to deal with certain social issues for the first time since the revolution. At the same time, Dad issued exhibition licenses to a number of films previously banned for their "unacceptable" content, such as Davoud Mir Bagheri's *The Snowman* (1994) and Mohamad Reza Honarmand's *The Visit* (1994), which became unexpected box-office hits in the 1998–99 season. Dad's ultimate goal, only partially realized, was to privatize the industry and turn control of production and exhibition over to the filmmakers via film trade guilds. Dad also created the National Film Organization with the purpose of promoting foreign investment and increasing annual production from 56 films in 2000–01 to 109 by 2004–05, and expanding the exhibition sector from its 2000–01 capacity of 210,000 screens to 360,000 during the same period, effectively doubling the size of the domestic market to absorb accelerated production.

Among prerevolutionary directors, Dariush Mehrjui directed *Hamoon* (1990), a Felliniesque comedy of modern marriage, and *The Lady* (*Baanoo*, 1992), a version of Buñuel's *Viridiana* (1961). Merhjui continued in this adaptive vein with *Sara* (1994), a version of Ibsen's *A Doll's House*, and *Pari* (1995), an unacknowledged rendition of J. D. Salinger's *Franny and Zooey*. Merhjui's *The Pear Tree* (*Derkht-e golabi* [1998] is a coming-of-age drama set in post–World War II Tehran. Bahram Beizai (b. 1938) and Parviz Kimiavi (b. 1939) are two other prerevolutionary writers/directors who continued working in the 1990s. Beizai is particularly admired for the antiwar children's film *Bashu, the Little Stranger* (1985; released 1989); *Maybe Some Other Time* (*Shayad vaqti digar*, 1988), about a TV commentator who suspects his wife of adultery but discovers a deeper truth; and the mystical allegory *Travellers* (*Mosaferan*, 1992). Kimiavi, on the other hand, didn't really enlarge upon his stylistic experiments of the 1970s (e.g., *The Mongols* [*Mongholha*, 1973]; *Stone Garden* [*Baghé Sangui*, 1975]) until he made *Iran Is My Homeland* (*Sarzamin-e Man Iran Ast*, 1998), which reaches toward a melding of Iranian cinematic and literary traditions. Other art-cinema directors who received international recognition during the 1990s were Majid Majidi (b. 1959—*The Children of Heaven* [*Bachehaye aseman*, 1997]; *The Color of Paradise* [*Rang-e Khoda*, 1999], Jafar Panahi (b. 1960—*The White Balloon* [*Badkonake sefid*, 1995]; *The Mirror* [*Ayneh*, 1997]), Ebrahim Hatamikia (b. 1961—*The Green Ashes* [*Khak-*

---

8. The fate of the magnetic Iranian actress Susan Taslimi is a case in point: she was hounded out of the country in 1988 for screen appearances—often in the films of Bahram Beizai—that suggested too much strength of character and showed too much hair (in the words of one censor, Ms. Taslimi's hair "created electricity").

9. Quoted in Hamid Naficy, "Iranian Cinema," in *Companion Encyclopedia to Middle Eastern and North African Film*, ed. Oliver Leaman (New York: Routledge, 2001), p. 175.

19.45 *The Color of Paradise* (*Rang-e Khoda* [Majid Majidi, 1999]): Mohsen Ramezani, Salime Feizi. A visually, aurally, and tactilely stunning look at the world of a blind eight-year-old boy.

estar-e sabz, 1994]; *The Glass Agency* [*Ajance shunhei*, 1998]) and Abolfazl Jalili (b. 1957—*Dance of Dust* [*Raqs-e-khak*, 1992]; *A True Story* [*Yek dastan-e vaghe'i*, 1995]).

But the most important postrevolutionary figure is unquestionably Abbas Kiarostami (b. 1940), who writes the screenplays for most of his own features, as well as executing their production design and editing. Although he made a handful of shorts and features before 1979, virtually all of Kiarostami's major work was done from the mid-1980s through the present, most of it produced for the Center for the Intellectual Development of Children and Young Adults, whose film division he founded in 1970. Known for his minimalist, self-reflexive style, involving the use of extended long takes and scant dialogue, Kiarostami's cinema has been called "interventionist" and "interactive" because it tends to put its viewers in a position that blurs the distinction between life and art, between documentary and fiction. The film that established Kiarostami's reputation with Western critics was *Where Is the Friend's Home?* (*Khane-ye doust kodjast?* 1987), a deceptively simple story in which a grade-school student goes on an Odyssean quest to return his classmate's misplaced notebook. The paradigm of reflexivity was central to his next film *Close-up* (*Nema-ye nazdik*, 1989), which was based upon a true story: an unemployed bus passenger convinces a fellow traveler that he is the famous Iranian filmmaker Mohsen Makh-

malbaf (see below) and that he is going to make a docudrama starring members of her family. The family subsequently sues him for fraud, and Kiarostami appears as himself to direct a film about the court proceedings, which he restages using the "real" participants, with a different ending. This play on the narrow distinction between reality and fiction similarly informs *Life, and Nothing More* (also known as *And Life Goes On* [*Zendegi va digar hich*, 1991]), in which Kiarostami and his son set out to find his two performers from *Where Is the Friend's Home?*, whose village has been destroyed in an earthquake. When he arrives in the region, he hires two local quake survivors to play him and his son, who then go on to find the two boys, also played by actors. The devastation caused by the earthquake is real, and the circumstances of Kiarostami's quest only

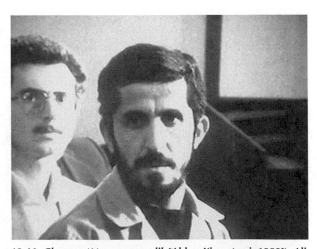

19.46 *Close-up* (*Nema-ye nazdik* [Abbas Kiarostami, 1989]): Ali Sazian, as himself, on trial for impersonating the famous Iranian director Mohsen Makhmalbaf, in a docudrama about the affair produced, reflexively, by Kiarostami within the film we are watching.

slightly fictionalized, so that once again the cleavage between film and reality is never quite clear. The third film in what is now known as Kiarostami's "Northern Iran" or "Earthquake" trilogy was *Through the Olive Trees* (*Zire darakhtan zaitun*, 1993). Here a director, played by Kiarostami, casts a film about the recent quake with quake victims, whose personal lives become so intertwined with their roles that he has to rewrite the film in order to straighten out their lives. The reflexive element in these three films is so apparently natural and understated that it never seems like a stylistic fetish; similarly, the empathy with which Kiarostami approaches the human suffering in them is unmistakable. These tendencies reached their apex in *Taste of Cherry* (*T'am e guilass*, 1997), which was banned by the Iranian government until it won the 1997 Cannes Palm d'Or. In this film, a middle-aged man wishing to kill himself searches for someone courageous or venal enough (because he is offering a large sum of money) to break Islamic law by assisting him. We never learn why he wants to die or whether he, in fact, succeeds in his quest; and the film's conclusion suggests that whole affair has been staged as part of a movie anyway. Among its other qualities, *Taste of Cherry* forces the audience to interrogate conventional assumptions about death, life, and the ultimate meaning of living. *The Wind Will Carry Us* (*Bad ma ra khahad bord*, 1999) pushes this interrogative process to another level—that of conventional cinema's narrative codes. In this film,

19.47 Taste of Cherry (*T'am e guilass* [Abbas Kiarostami, 1997]): Kiarostami and his crew (apparently) shooting the film we have just been watching about a man trying to find someone to violate Islamic law and assist him in committing suicide. Banned in Iran until it became co-recipient of the 1997 Cannes Palm d'Or.

which won the Golden Lion at Venice in 1999, a group of four professionals from Tehran visit a remote village in northern Kurdistan in search of something unspecified that is never found. Instead, the film digresses into the small events of the villagers' everyday lives, filmed with a static camera, and finally goes nowhere in a narrative sense, making its audience keenly aware of the passive nature of spectatorship. The terms that are generally used by Western critics to describe Kiarostami's cinema are "meditative," "serene," "hypnotic," and, above all, "humanistic." But, as Ali Mohammadi and Eric Egan have pointed out, it is humanism within an Islamic fundamentalist context, where God is the agency of all human action, and it is, therefore, a kind of revolutionary challenge to a government whose legitimacy is grounded in Islamic principles—humanism as a form of political dissent.[1] What is remarkable is the degree of latitude that Kiarostami has achieved for his art by bringing international prestige to his people.

Practicing on the same plane as Kiarostomi, although less well known in the West, is the remarkably prolific Mohsen Makhmalbaf (b. 1957), who was once a member of an underground Islamist group and jailed for five years by the Pahlavi government, from 1974 to 1979. Released in the wake of the revolution, Makhmalbaf became a propagandist for the Islamist utopia promised by the new state. Between 1982 and 1985, which might be called his "Islamic period," Makhmalbaf contributed four films to the state-sponsored "Official Cinema" that directly advocated new government policies. Then he made a trilogy focusing on social problems—*Peddler* (*Dastforoush*, 1987), *The Cyclist* (*Bysikelran*, 1988), and *Marriage of the Blessed* (*Arousi-ye khouban*, 1989)—still working within an Islamic political framework but without specific reference to Islamist ideology, before he turned to several Kiarostami-like ruminations on film form and film ontology—*Once upon a Time, Cinema* (*Ruzi, Ruzagari, Cinema*, 1992), *The Actor* (*Honarpisheh*, 1993), and *Salaam Cinema* (1995)—although Makhmalbaf favors a rapid editing style rather than the long take. More recently, Makhmalbaf—who has always written his own screenplays and often does his own cutting—has begun to formulate a poetics of art and culture, still centering

1. Ali Mohammadi and Eric Egan, "Cinema and Iran: Culture and Politics in the Islamic Republic," *Asian Cinema* 12, 1 (Spring/Summer 2001): 20.

19.48 *The Wind Will Carry Us* (*Bad ma ra khahad bord* [Abbas Kiarostami, 1999]). A film that goes nowhere (but won the Golden Lion at Venice in 1999).

around film, in such self-reflexive works as *Gabbeh* (1996, whose title refers to a type of quiltlike carpet made by the Ghashgani tribe of southern Iran and whose rich tapestry of colors owes much to the work of Sergei Parajanov, especially *The Color of Pomegranates* (*Sayat nova* [1969]). Similarly, *Moment of Innocence* (*Nun va goldun*, 1996), coproduced with France, presents a convoluted, *Rashomon*-like narrative that has Makhmalbaf—as himself—directing a film about an event from his own earlier life as an Islamic revolutionary from the perspective of several different participants. More recently, Makhmalbaf has been hailed for two other Iranian-French coproductions set in neighboring Islamic lands—civil-war-torn Tadjikistan (*Silence* [*Sokhout*, 1997]) and the formerly Taliban-controlled Afghanistan (*Kandahar* [2001]). A byproduct of this latter work, the documentary *The Afghan Alphabet* (*Alefbay-e Afghan*, 2002), set in an Iranian refugee camp for Afghan children, joins the ranks of other philosophical nonfiction films produced by Iranian feature directors like Mehrjui, Beizai, Kimiavi, and Kiarostami. Sounding very much like Kiarostami, in fact, Makhmalbaf has said that "life is larger than politics" and that the "best approach to save humanity is through going back to the beauty and poetry of everyday life."[2] Makhmalbaf's daughter, Samira Makhmalbaf (b. 1980), is also a director of note, having produced *The Apple* (*Sib*, 1998)

and *Blackboards* (*Takhte siah*, 2000), both simple stories about relationships between children and adults in postrevolutionary Iran. Her film *At Five in the Afternoon* (*Panj e asr*, 2003), about a young Afghan woman who attempts to break free of the Taliban by running for president, won the Jury Prize at Cannes and, like her other work, is reminiscent of Italian neorealism in form and theme.

In fact, neorealism is frequently invoked to describe films of the new Iranian cinema—in part because the stories they tell (except in the self-consciously reflexive art cinema) tend to be deceptively simple and in part because so many of them are shot on location out of doors. This is a function of their relatively low budgets as well as of culturally specific factors such as the rules of *hejab* (veiling and modesty), which require the wearing of *chadors* (overscarfs) and *burkas* (full-body overgarments) by female performers, coverings that make more "realistic" sense in scenes shot out of doors. The fact that postrevolutionary Iranian cinema is ideologically based is another feature it shares with neorealism; and even though the ideologies are different, the end result is often the same—films that deal with the everyday lives of ordinary people and their attempts to create order and meaning in their worlds. Finally, both cinemas emerged during the final stages of a devastating war—in Italy, of course, World War II, and in Iran, the Iran-Iraq War of 1980–88, which produced heavy losses on both sides (600,000 Iranians died, 400,000 Iraqis) and cost a total of $1.2 billion. Unlike neorealism, however, the Iranian cinema must walk a tightrope between vital artistic/social expression and the moral demands of a fundamentalist Islamic state. Thirty percent of all Iranian films are government-made, another 35 percent are pro-

---

2. Makhamalbaf, quoted in Mohammadi and Egan, p. 24.

duced by the state-sponsored Farabi Foundation, and only 35 percent are privately funded, Cinema Minister Dad's liberalization efforts notwithstanding. This means that postrevolutionary Iranian film—which has been called "one of the most exciting in the world today"[3]—still cannot show women with uncovered hair, or women singing and dancing; neither can it in any way challenge the legitimacy of the Islamic republic or the rule of Muslim clerics.

ISRAEL

The state of Israel (population 6.1 million) was not founded until 1948, but a Hebrew cinema had existed in Palestine at least since the silent documentaries of Yaakov Ben Dov (1882–1968). Trained as a professional photographer, Ben Dov brought motion-picture cameras to the Holy Land and formed his own production company in Jerusalem—First Palestinian Film Society, called "Menorah"—to make Zionist-oriented features about the British liberation of Palestine from the Turks (*Judea Liberated*, 1917; *The Land of Israel Liberated*, 1919–20) and the impact of the Balfour Declaration (*Return to Zion*, 1920–21; *The New Jewish Palestine*, 1921). Later Ben Dov films concerned the Jewish settlement of Palestine (*Palestine Awakening*, 1923), the construction of the Hebrew University of Jerusalem (*The Sons Build*, 1925), and Hebrew-language education (*Young Palestine*, 1926). His six-reel feature *Springtime in Palestine* (1928), which was edited and scored at the UFA studios in Berlin for distribution to fifty-six countries worldwide, was financed by the Palestine Foundation Fund and the Jewish National Fund to promote Zionist recruitment.[4] Ben Dov ended his filmmaking career as associate cinematographer for the American production *My People's Dream* (A. J. Bloome, 1933), a musical documentary set in Palestine featuring the famous cantor Josele Rosenblatt, released in Hebrew, English, and Yiddish. (On the popularity of Yiddish cantorial films in the United States, see Chapter 8, pp. 253–55.)

Ben Dov was succeeded by two other pioneering producers, Natan Axelrod and Baruch Agadati. Axelrod worked at the Moledet (Homeland) company, founded in 1927 at Tel Aviv to produce weekly Zionist newsreels, and in 1933 produced the first silent Hebrew feature, *Oded the Wanderer* (*Oded haNoded*, 1933; directed by

Chaim Halachmi); he then established the Carmel Film Company, which produced weekly Zionist newsreels (*Yoman Carmel*) until well into the 1950s. Agadati turned out occasional newsreels (*Yoman Aga*) between 1931 and 1934, when he produced *This Is the Land* (*Zot hi ha'Aretz*), a semidocumentary history of Jewish settlement with recorded narration and dialogue. At about the same time, the sound documentary *The Land of Promise* (Judah Leman, 1935), a propaganda epic lauding Zionist achievement in Palestine, was produced by the Keren Hayesod in collaboration with Louis De Rochemont, and distributed internationally in English, German, Hebrew, Yiddish, French, and Polish.[5] Another notable Hebrew film made before 1948 was the sound feature *Sabra* (*Tzabar*, 1933), which depicts a struggle over water rights between Jewish immigrants and Arab villagers. Directed by the Polish filmmaker Aleksander Ford at the invitation of impresario Ze'ev Markovitz, *Sabra* was cut by British censors to remove its scenes of ethnic conflict and rereleased as *The Pioneers* (*HeKhalutzim*); it was restored and shown intact for the first time at a film festival in Haifa in 1954.

After the creation of the state of Israel in 1948, two major studios were founded—Geva (1950) and Herzliya (1951)—mainly for the production of documentaries and information films by the government. To this point, the country's industry had been documentary-based; but from the mid-1940s to the mid-1950s, partly as an attempt to move in a more feature-oriented direction, many documentaries acquired plots and characters. In 1954, the Knesset passed the Encouragement of Israel Film Law, which provided financial aid in the form of tax subsidies to both foreign and domestic producers, resulting in such

---

3. Richard Pena, program director of the Film Society of the Lincoln Center, New York, quoted in Judith Miller, "Movies of Iran Struggle for Acceptance," *New York Times*, Sunday, July 19, 1992: H9;14.

4. Hillel Tryster, senior researcher at the Steven Spielberg Jewish Film Archive in Jerusalem, points out that the Jewish National Fund (JNF) and the Palestine Foundation Fund were the financial parents of almost all filmmaking in the country, even after 1948. In earliest times, the JNF provided logistical assistance to private filmmakers from abroad, including amateurs, in exchange for on-screen coverage. "Participation by the institutions," he writes, "remained an indispensible budget item later on even for private, commercial filmmakers." (Tryster to author, private correspondence, 10/23/94.)

5. See Hillel Tryster, "Anatomy of an Epic Film," *Jerusalem Post Magazine*, October 30, 1992, pp. 16–18.

"heroic-nationalist" epics as *Hill 24 Doesn't Answer* (*Giv'a 24 eina ona* [Thorold Dickinson, 1955]), *Pillar of Fire* (*Amud haEsh* [Larry Frisch, 1959]), *They Were Ten* (*Hem hayu asara* [Baruch Dienar, 1961]), and *Rebels against the Light* (*Mordei ha'Or* [Alexander Ramati, 1964; distributed abroad as *Sands of Beer Sheba*])—all of them about crucial Arab-Israeli conflicts in Zionist history. These and such Hollywood-originated productions as *The Juggler* (Edward Dmytryk, 1953), *Exodus* (Otto Preminger, 1960), *Judith* (Daniel Mann, 1965), and *Cast a Giant Shadow* (Melville Shavelson, 1966) gave local filmmakers valuable technical experience, but it really wasn't until the wave of prosperity that followed the 1967 Arab-Israeli war that sufficient money, talent, and equipment came together to found a viable national industry centered in Tel Aviv. Israeli television was inaugurated at that time (1968), providing work for filmmakers at all levels, and in 1969 the government established the Israeli Film Center to attract foreign investment. By the early 1970s, annual production had reached 20 features, quadrupling the rate of a decade before.

It was in this context that producer-director Menahem Golan (b. 1929) joined forces with his cousin Yoram Globus (b. 1941) to form the fantastically successful Golan-Globus Productions, whose combination of low-budget local films and international coproductions enabled it to acquire New York–based Cannon Films in 1979 and become a major force in the industry for the ten next years.[6] The 1970s also witnessed the rise of the *bourekas* film as the dominant genre within the Israeli industry, many of them produced by Golan-Globus. Named for a type of Near Eastern pastry, these extremely popular films were ethnic comedies and melodramas about Israel's central social problem—the tensions between the lower-class Mizrakhi (native Sephardic Jews and those who had immigrated from Arab countries during the 1950s) and the middle-class Ashkenazi (educated Central and Eastern European Jews, many of them Holocaust survivors, who had become the nation's leadership class).[7] Initiated in the 1960s by Ephraim Kishon (*Sallah Shabati*, 1964) and Menahem Golan (*Fortuna*, 1966), the *bourekas* became a mainstream genre during the 1970s in the work of Boaz Davidson—*Charlie and a Half* (*Charlie veKhetzi*, 1974), *Billiards* (*Snuker*, 1975), *Tzan'ani Family* (*Mishpakhat Tzan'ani*, 1976)—who coined the term. Davidson also turned the genre toward a youth-oriented, soft-core market with the Golan-produced *Lemon Pop-*

19.49 *Nashim*, also known as *Nasheem* (*Women* [Moshe Mizrahi, 1997]). A romantic drama set among the community of Sephardic Jews in the Old City of Jerusalem near the end of the nineteenth century.

sicle (*Eskimo limon*, 1979), which adapted the *bourekas* formula to the erotic adventures of high-school students à la George Lucas's *American Graffiti* (1973) and inspired many successful sequels.

The 1970s also saw the establishment of the first Israeli film schools, the Israel Film Institute, and a number of municipal cinematheques, but the government was concerned about the increasing commercialization of the industry and in 1979 created the Fund for the Promotion of Quality Films to help finance independent projects such as those favored by "Kayitz," the transliterated acronym for "Young Israeli Cinema." This movement produced low-budget, open-ended films focusing on the psychological situations of individuals within the larger

---

6. In 1987, Cannon was bought by the Italian media mogul Giancarlo Paretti and renamed Pathé Communications Corp. In 1990, Paretti bought MGM/UA to form MGM-Pathé Communications, of which Globus was briefly president.

7. Films about the richness of Sephardic culture were also made— Moshe Mizrahi's *I Love You Rosa* (*Ani ohev otach Rosa*, 1972) portrays traditional Sephardic family life in late nineteenth-century Jerusalem, while his *The House on Chelouche Street* (*Ha'bait be'rechov Chelouche*, 1974) revealed the seeds of discrimination against Oriental Jews at the foundation of the Israeli state. (In 1978 Mizrahi became the first Israeli director to receive an American Academy Award when his French production *Madame Rosa* [*La vie devant soi*, 1977] won as Best Foreign Film.) Mizrahi (b. Egypt, 1931) made films about the Sephardic community well into the 1990s—e.g., *Women* (*Nasheem*, 1996), which like *I Love You Rosa* is set in late nineteenth-century Jerusalem.

society—e.g., Uri Zohar's trilogy, *Peeping Toms* (*Metzit-zim*, 1972), *Big Eyes* (*Einaim gdolot*, 1974), and *Save the Lifeguard* (*Hatsilu et ha'matzil*, 1976)—an examination of the post-1967 war's "lost generation"; Avraham Heff-ner's deconstruction of the Israeli national stereotype *Where Is Daniel Vax?* (*Le'An Ne'elam Daniel Vax?*, 1973), Dan Wolman's post-Holocaust odysseys *My Michael* (*Michael sheli*, 1975) and *Hide and Seek* (*Machvoim*, 1980); and Daniel Wachsmann's low-budget epic of root-lessness in 1960s Tel Aviv *Transit* (1980). During the 1980s, many Kayitz directors turned to political themes, especially after Israel's 1982 incursion into Lebanon, often focusing on the Palestinian dimension of the Arab-Israeli conflict. In such "Palestinian Wave" films as Wachsmann's *Hamsin*[8] (1982—winner of the Israeli Oscar for Best Film and the Israel Prize for the Arts), Yehuda (Judd) Ne'eman's *Fellow Travelers* (*Magash haKessef*; literally *The Silver Platter*, 1983), Uri Barbash's *Beyond the Walls* (1983—Critic's Prize, Venice), Nissim Dayan's *A Very Narrow Bridge* (*Gesher Tzar Me'od*, 1985), and Shimon Dotan's *The Smile of the Lamb* (*Khiukh haGdi*, 1986—Israeli Oscar for Best Film), the occupation of the West Bank and Gaza is treated ambi-valently and Palestinians are sympathetically portrayed. (Implicitly critical of the Israeli establishment, many "Pal-estinian Wave" films were nevertheless produced with government assistance and should not be confused with

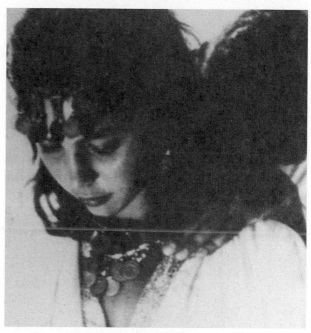

19.51 *Wedding in Galilee* (Michel Khleifi, 1987), an Israeli Palestinian film that won the **FIPRESCI prize at Cannes.**

the award-winning work of the Israeli Palestinian director Michel Khleifi—e.g., *Fertile Memory* [*La Mémoire fer-tile*, 1980], *Wedding in Galilee* [*Urs al-Jalil*, 1987—FIPRESCI prize, Cannes], and *Canticle of the Stones* [*Naslid al-hajjar*, 1990]—which interweaves the history of Palestinian dispossession with contemporary themes and was financed by foreign capital and the Palestinian Liberation Organization [PLO].)

During the 1990s, the Israeli cinema experienced an economic crisis resulting from high inflation and its small domestic market (203 theaters; 11 million tickets sold, only 10 percent for Israeli films). Production slumped to a record low of five features in 1991, but financial aid from the Fund for the Promotion of Quality Israeli Films helped it to return to normal levels by mid-decade. Iron-ically, the fund has supported the bitterly ironic work of the Israeli Palestinian filmmaker Elia Suleiman (b. 1960—*Chronicle of a Disappearance* [*Waqa'i' ikhtifa'*, 1996]) at the same time that it has turned down projects by one of the Israeli cinema's best-known figures, the documentar-ist-turned-feature-director Amos Gitai (b. 1950), whose

19.50 Uri Barabash's award-winning Israeli prison film *Beyond the Walls* **(1983—Critics Prize, Venice Film Festival).**

8. Released in the United States as *Heat Wave*, the untranslated title refers to a hot desert wind that blows across the Middle East.

19.52 *Kadosh* (*Sacred* [Amos Gitai, 1999]). A Jerusalem street scene from the last film in Gitai's trilogy of contemporary Israeli life (the others are *Devarim* [*Things*, 1995], set in Tel Aviv, and *Yom Yom* [*Day after Day*, 1998], set in Haifa).

Kadosh [1999] and *Kippur* [2000] were both critical of Israeli institutions—Orthodox codes of sexual conduct and the Yom Kippur War, respectively. In the late 1990s, government film subsidies were cut in half, but the parliament passed a Cinema Law in 2000 whereby half the taxes levied on all commercial broadcasters in the nation will be allocated to underwriting the cinema, both as production capital and as subsidies for archives, festivals, and film schools. As the closest ally of the United States in the Middle East, Israel has a special relationship with Hollywood. In addition to widespread American distribution, Israeli cinema receives the support of American film personalities like Goldie Hawn, who helped to build the Tel Aviv Cinematheque in 1989, and Steven Spielberg, who funded the Jewish Film Archive at the Hebrew University, Jerusalem, in 1991.

The Pacific Rim

Third World cinemas of the Pacific rim are those of Thailand, Vietnam, Indonesia, Malaysia, North and South Korea, and the Philippines. The Thai industry is star-and genre-based, and until the late 1970s produced nearly 200 films a year for its proportionately large population (currently 62.3 million). But in the 1980s, television, video, and American imports drained off the domestic audience, and for the last two decades of the twentieth century Thai production shrank to an exponential 12 films annually. Even so, the work of a handful of serious directors shone through—e.g., Permphol Cheuriaroon (*Red Bamboo* [*Pai Daeng*, 1979]), Suchart Vuthivichai (*The Last Dewdrop*, 1978), Suwat Sichue (*Khun-Sa the Opium Emperor*, 1982), Vichit Kounavudhi (*Mountain People* [*Khon poo khao*, 1982]), Cherd Songsri (*Puen-Paeng*, 1983), Euthana Mukdasanit (*Butterfly and Flowers*, 1985), and Chart Kopjitti (*House*, 1987). Despite the Southeast Asian currency crisis (which actually began with the collapse of several Thai banks), Thai cinema began to rebound in the late 1990s, thanks to the phenomenal success of a handful of films by Nonzee Nimibutr, a former director of television commercials—especially his gangster melodrama *2499 Antapan krong muang* (also known as *Dang Bireley and the Young Gangsters*, 1997) and his splashy retelling of a traditional Thai ghost story, *Nang Nak* (*Mrs. Nak*, 1999). Nimibutr's *film noir Jan Dara* (2001), involving lesbian passions in the 1930s, failed to connect with Thai audiences, who found it to be both too demanding and too daring, although they made a gigantic sleeper hit out of Youngyoot Thongkonthun's *Iron Ladies* (*Sa tree lex*, 2000), based on the true story of a transvestite volleyball team that won the national championship in 1996. In 2000, Prince Chatrichalerm Yukol's 190-minute historical spectacle *Suriyothai*, the story of a sixteenth-century queen who fought at her husband's side to repel a Burmese invasion, also achieved local blockbuster status, as did Tanit Jitnukul's epic *Bangrajan* (2001), about Siamese villagers who sabotaged a Burmese occupation force in 1765, and Bhandit Rittakol's *The Moonhunter* (2002), which dramatizes the student protests that led to the downfall of Thailand's military dictatorship in October 1973. Thai films also began to appear at international festivals—e.g., Wisit Sasanatieng's *Tears of the Black Tiger* (*Fa talai jone*, 2000), a parody of low-budget "Thai Westerns" from the 1950s and 1960s, which played in Un Certain Regard at Cannes, as did Apichatpong Weerasethakul's *Blissfully Yours* (2001) a year later. Nevertheless, as in the other nations of Southeast Asia, "globalization" has meant the domination of Hollywood films at the box office, where they account for about 80 percent of annual revenue.

Neighboring Vietnam (population 81.0 million) has a small industry with studios located in Hanoi and Ho Chi Minh City (formerly Saigon), and all films are produced with the assistance of the Ministry of Culture, according to the former Soviet model. Even in this context, however, a handful of interesting films have appeared—e.g., Nguyen Ngoc Trung's *Orange-Colored Bells* (*Hoi duiong*

19.53 *Nang Nak* (*Mrs. Nak* [Nonzee Nimibutr, 1999]). A traditional Thai ghost story about a village possessed by spirits of the dead, set in the 1860s.

mau da cam, 1984), Dang Nhat Minh's *October Won't Return* (*Bao gio cho den thang muoi*, 1984), and Ho Quong Minh's *Karma* (1986), produced in Vietnam with Swiss backing.

With a population of 232 million, 12.3 million living in Jakarta alone, Indonesia produced about 70 features per year until the mid-1990s, most of them imitations of American action films. As in Thailand, there are a handful of serious directors—e.g., Ami Priyono, known for his lavish period films (*Roro Mendut*, 1985) and comedies (*Dearest* [*Yang*, 1985]); the prolific Teguh Karya, whose work has been lauded at several international festivals (e.g., *Under the Mosquito Net* [*Dibalik kelambu*, 1983]; *Bitter Coffee* [*Secangkir kopi pahit*, 1986]; *Mementos* [*Doea tanda mata*, 1986]; *Mother* [*Ibunda*, 1987]); and the brothers Slamet Djarot Rahardjo (*The Moon and the Sun* [*Rembulan dan Matahari*, 1980]; *White Is Her Heart, Red Are Her Lips* [*Seputih Hatinya Semerah Birirnya*, 1981]; *Ponirah for Justice* [*Ponirah Terpidana*, 1983]; *My Sky, My Home* [*Langitku, rumahku*, 1990]) and Eros Djarot Rahardjo (*A Woman of Courage* [*Tjoet Nja Dhien*, 1988]). In 1997 and 1998, Indonesia was hit with simultaneous political and economic crises. Amid charges of massive corruption, President Suharto ended his thirty-two-year regime by resigning in May 1998, and he was provisionally replaced by his vice president, Jusuf Habi-

bie; at the same time, the Southeast Asian monetary crisis, begun in Thailand in mid-1997, hit the Indonesian economy hard, producing widespread social unrest. Film production, which had already leveled off to about 30 features annually, dropped even further as producers found themselves unable to raise production capital or even pay laboratories for film processing and printing. It took one veteran director, the previously mentioned Slamet Rahardjo, three years to produce *Telegram* (2000), even though it was based on a popular Indonesian novel and coproduced with a French company that provided 30 percent of its $500,000 budget. Yet the new government attempted to help the film industry by revoking the tax on domestic box-office receipts and rescinding the previous policy of script censorship, and annual production has begun to creep gradually upward again from its low point in 1998, when only 8 Indonesian features were made. A new generation of filmmakers has graduated from the Faculty of Film and Television (FFTV) of the Jakarta Institute of Arts (IKJ)—Indonesia's only film school—and started to work in the industry, and several major new works have appeared that reflect the new climate of reform by addressing formerly taboo political and social issues—e.g., Garin Nugroho's (b. 1961) *Unconcealed Poetry* (*Puisi tak terkuburkan*, 2000) explores the execution of a celebrated poet (and hundreds of other innocent prisoners) in Aceh, North Sumatra, by the forces of General Sukarno in the wake of the attempted coup of 1965; and Slamet Rahardjo's *Marsinah* (2001) recounts the true story of a female labor leader who was murdered for her protest activities at a factory. Futhermore, new women directors are exploring themes like mother-daughter relationships (Nan T. Achnas's *Whispering Sands* [*Pasir berbisik*, 2001]) and interracial marriage (Nia Di Nata's *Woman* [*Ca-bau-kan*, 2001]) for the first time in Indonesian cinema.

Malaysian cinema, which inherited an old-style studio system from the 1930s, was virtually monopolized by Shaw Brothers until the Nation Film Development Corporation (FINAS) was established in 1981 to upgrade the aesthetic quality of domestic cinema and film culture generally among its population of 22.7 million. Since that time a number of young independent directors have emerged—Jins Shamsuddin, whose politically themed *Bukit kepong* (1982) broke domestic box-office records, Jamil Sulong (*No Harvest but a Thorn* [*Ranjau sepanjang jalan*, 1985]), Rahim Razali (*Death of a Patriot* [*Matinya seorang patriot*, 1985], and Stephen Teo (*To Go on a Journey* [*Bejalai*, 1987]). In the 1990s, the Malaysian government began to promote the concept of a Multimedia Super Corridor (MSC) that would spread southward from the capital of Kuala Lumpur to cover an area of 270 square miles and become the keystone in its bid to turn the nation into the Silicon Valley of Southeast Asia by 2020. Included in the plan was the construction of a $60-million high-tech Entertainment Village (E-Village) in the new government headquarters at Cyberjaya, with studios for digital production, a color-processing laboratory, and a theme park. A new digital postproduction facility was also planned for the MSC as a joint venture of Malaysia and Hollywood. (The first Malaysian film to use integral computer-generated imagery [CGI] was Othman Hafsham's *Fool's Treasure* [1998].) As in Indonesia, the monetary crisis that swept Southeast Asia in mid-1997 had devastating short-term effects on the Malaysian economy, with the cost of goods and services rising by 50 percent, and the entertainment industry was among the hardest hit—e.g., all but two films released in 1998 lost money. But by 2000, the Central Bank of Malaysia predicted an economic growth rate of 5 percent, and there was an attendant growth in film production. Furthermore, to stimulate the industry the government Information Ministry provided a $26.3 million grant to fund up to 12 films annually at the rate of $500,000 each, to be administered by the FINAS. At the end of 2000, over 100 international companies had joined the MSC venture, including Microsoft and Siemens, AG, and it promised a state-of-the-art environment for the development and production of multimedia products. The first phase of the E-Village at Cyberjaya, the "Studio Precinct," was completed in 2001; it contains eight digitally equipped soundstages, one of which, at nine stories, is the tallest in

world—linking it iconically to the Petronas Twin Towers in Kuala Lumpur, which is the world's tallest building. One of the Malaysian industry's goals is to attract foreign production to its new facilities, as it did near the turn of the century with Fox's *Entrapment* (Jon Amiel, 1999) and *Anna and the King* (Andy Tennant, 1999). Another is to gear up its own production engines, which it did by producing a number of big box-office hits in the 2001–02 season–Aziz M. Osman's large-scale war film *Lt. Adnan* (2001), Yusof Haslam's police melodrama *Special Force: The Movie* (*Gerak Khas: The Movie*, 2001), and S. Mohan's martial-arts epic *The Deadly Disciples* (2002). (About half of Malaysian films are made in English.)

The industry of South Korea (Republic of Korea, population 48.3 million) currently produces about 60 features per year and has a history going back to the 1920s, much of it quite distinguished if little known outside the country. During the 1960s, in fact, South Korea became one of the largest film producers in the world, averaging 200 annually for much of the decade; but it experienced a severe slump following the mass diffusion of television in 1969. By late 1970s, Korean films had begun to appear on the international festival circuit, and in the 1980s, despite some of the strictest censorship laws in any noncommunist nation, a so-called "cinema of quality" emerged that featured subject matter from the country's ancient mystic culture and some of the best cinematography and lighting available in Asia. Until recently, Korean cinema was all but ignored in the West, due in large part to its inaccessibility. As David James has pointed out, there are no surviving prints of any Korean film made before 1943, although about 240 films were produced during the Japanese colonial period, 1910–45,[9] and the earliest of these were made by Japanese companies since the first films from Korean distributors did not appear until 1923. After 1937, most were Japanese-language films since Korean was outlawed as a public language from the late 1930s until the end of World War II. (The first Korean sound film was *Ch'unhyang chon* [*The Tale of Chunhyang*], directed by Yi Myongu in 1935; it was based on a thirteenth-century folktale, itself derived from an ancient shamanistic ritual, redacted as *p'ansori*—

---

9. David E. James and Kyung Hyun Kim, *Im Kwon-taek: The Making of a Korean National Cinema* (Detroit: Wayne State University Press, 2002), p. 20.

a traditional performance art in which a story is told by singing, chanting, and gesticulatory dancing.)[1] Korea was liberated from the Japanese on August 16, 1945, but there immediately followed an American military occupation of the southern part of the peninsula and a Soviet occupation of the north above the 38th parallel. South Korea was proclaimed the Republic of Korea in 1948, with its capital at Seoul. A communist government was established in North Korea, styled the Democratic People's Republic of Korea, with its capital at Pyongyang. When North Korea invaded South Korea on June 25, 1950, a civil war ensued that became the Korean War when UN forces led by the United States intervened on the side of South Korea and communist China supported the North. The war ended in a stalemate three years later, leaving 3 million dead on both sides. The North has remained in communist hands ever since, while the South experienced a succession of harsh military dictatorships from 1961 to 1992, tacitly sanctioned by the continuing presence of about 40,000 combat-ready American troops (who were still in place as of 2003).

The film industry of South Korea, which had traditionally been located in the Ch'ungmuro district of Seoul, moved to the port city of Pusan during the war (as did the seat of government itself). It returned to Ch'ungmuro after 1953 to find its equipment and facilities wrecked by the war, but the government of the first Korean president, Syngman Rhee, attempted to stimulate the industry at that time by exempting it from taxes. This policy worked effectively to increase production year by year, resulting in at least one solid box-office hit in 1955 (yet another adaptation of *The Tale of Chunhyang*, directed by Yi Kyahwan), and by the end of the decade annual production was approaching 100 films. But these were tightly controlled by government censorship. When student protests forced the resignation of Rhee in 1960, there was a brief period of artistic freedom, but censorship was reimposed in the wake of a coup d'etat that toppled the civilian government in 1961 and put General Park Chung Hee in power as president. During the 1960s and 1970s, films were subject to precensorship by the aggressively anticommunist military authorities, but they were also produced in great number. From 1968 to 1971, the industry made over 200 features per year, with a high of 229 in 1969, for both domestic and large export markets, mainly in Hong Kong. (In the 1980s and 1990s, this trend was

reversed, with South Korea becoming a major export market for Hong Kong, importing as many as 80 Hong Kong features a year; this produced a market glut, followed by a decline in popularity for Hong Kong product.) In 1973, the Park government promulgated a new Motion Picture Law that institutionalized a licensing system based on two separate censorship reviews, one before production and the other before release, to ensure that films adhered closely to the state ideology of economic Darwinism and anticommunism. (The Korean Motion Picture Promotion Corporation [KMPC] was formed at the same time to shore up the production sector; it remained a major force in the industry until it was replaced in 1999 by the Korean Film Commission [KOFIC].) Quotas were set on foreign imports, but the rigidity of the censorship process forced all but the largest production companies out of business and drove down the annual output to 101 films by 1977. Aggravating this general industry decline was the shrinkage of the national audience due to competing forms of entertainment, especially television: from about 170 million throughout the 1960s, the film audience shrank to 44 million in 1981.

On October 26, 1979, President Park was assassinated by his own CIA chief, and General Chun Doo Hwan staged a military coup shortly thereafter. Chun's administration encouraged international recognition for the Korean film industry as a way of building the nation's image abroad. It encouraged the subtitling of prints for submission to foreign festivals, underwrote directors' travel to those events, and provided cash incentives for filmmakers receiving international awards. The results were impressive: during the 1980s, South Korean films picked up awards at Venice, Moscow, Montreal, Locarno, Tokyo, and Berlin. South Korea needed the help because, with the Cold War winding down, the United States terminated South Korea's status as a "most favored nation," and in 1988 Hollywood began to flood its domestic market with American product. In that same year, Chun was replaced by his chosen successor, General Roh Tae Woo, who accelerated South Korea's now expansive economic growth and established diplomatic relations for the first

---

1. *P'ansori* was popular in eighteenth- and nineteenth-century Korea. Many Korean folk legends are preserved as *p'ansori*, which is a fundamental source for several genres of Korean film, in the same way that Kabuki theater was for japanese film.

time with communist nations like the USSR and China. His successes led directly to South Korea's successful hosting of the 1988 Olympic Games and to the election in 1992 of its first twentieth-century civilian government, that of President Kim Young Sam (1992–96), which was followed by that of President Kim Dae Jung (1997–2001). Although censorship was lifted from most other media in the late 1980s and early 1990s, it took another five years for the Supreme Court of South Korea to rule that motion-picture censorship was unconstitutional in 1996. Still, there was a relaxation of film oversight throughout the 1980s, and the new South Korean constitution of February 1988 specified "the right to artistic freedom" for all citizens.

It was during the liberalizing 1980s that the phenomenon now known as "New Korean Cinema" or the Korean New Wave was born. For the first time since the 1950s, filmmakers were able to choose their own subjects, and there was a new realism with regard to contemporary social issues. There had been a similar movement during the 1970s, when a group of directors led by Yi Chang Ho and calling themselves *yongsang sedae*—"the image generation"—had attempted to incorporate European art-film techniques into their work, but it was suppressed and Yi was forced into retirement. The new movement combined art-film aesthetics with social commitment in films that ultimately examined what it meant to be Korean. Notable directors of the decade were Kim Soo-Yong (b. 1929—*Gat-Mah-Eul*, 1980; *Late Autumn* [*Man Chu*, 1983]); Chung Jin-Won (b. 1938—*Shall the Cuckoo Sing at Night?* [*Pocukido bame un-nka*, 1983]; *The Noble-woman* [*Janyo-nok*, 1985]); Lee Doo-Yong (b. 1942—*Pee-Mak* [*House of Death*, 1982]; *The Wheel* [*Yoinchanhoksa: mulleya mulleya*, 1984]; *First Son* [*Jangnam*, 1985]; *Pong* [*The Mulberry Tree*, 1986]; *Eunuch*, 1986); Lee Chang-Ho (*Fool's Manifesto* [*Pabo sunon*, 1983]; *The Entertainer* [*Er woo dong*, 1986]); Bae Chang-Ho (*Deep Blue Night* [*Gipgo pureun bam*, 1985]; *Hwang Chinee*, 1986; *Sweet Days of Youth*, 1987); and Myeong-Jung Ha (*The Blazing Sun* [*Deng-Pyot*, 1985]). By and large, these first New Wave filmmakers were oblique in their critique of Korean society and avoided the specifically political.

In the 1990s, however, the gloves came off, and two figures in particular stood out for their caustic view of recent Korean history—Jang Sun-Woo (b. 1952) and Park Kwang-su (b. 1955). Jang is known for a combination of political engagement and stylistic experiment that have

brought comparison with Ozu and Godard. His early films ran the gamut from social satire (*Seoul Jesus*, 1986) to redacted Buddhist sutras (*Hwa Om-Kyong*, 1993), but his most characteristic work is *A Petal* (*Kotyip*, 1996), which combines documentary and staged footage to tell the story of a traumatized survivor of the notorious Kwangju massacre of 1980, in which hundreds of antigovernment protestors were slaughtered by army troops at the order of President Chun Doo Hwan (later sentenced to death for the crime). Jang experimented with this docudrama form in other films, including *Bad Movie* (*Napun Yeunghwa*, 1997), a *cinéma vérité*-style account of Seoul street kids, featuring drug abuse and prostitution, that mixes 35mm with digital video, and the controversial *Lies* (*Gojitmal*, 1999), an adaptation of a famous banned novel by Jang Jung-Il about an obsessive sadomasochistic relationship between a middle-aged sculptor and a teenage girl. (Jang is the subject of a 2001 feature-length documentary by Tony Rayns entitled *The Jang Sun-Woo Variations*.) Park began by making slice-of-life social comedies (*Chilsu and Mansu* [*Chilsu oa Mansu*, 1988]; *They, Like Us* [*Keduldo urichurum*, 1991]) but graduated to more serious themes in *To the Starry Island* (*Geu seome gago shibda*, 1993]), which makes a case for Korean reunification in a story of repressed hostilities from the nation's war-torn past returning to poison social relationships in the present on a small island. In *A Single Spark* (*Jeon tae-il*, 1996), Park used documentary-like footage to tell the story of a 1970s student radical (Jeon) whose self-immolation in protest of brutal factory conditions catalyzed the Korean labor move-

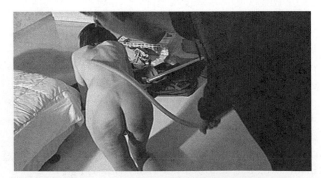

19.54 *Lies* (*Gojitmal* [Jang Sun-Woo, 1999]). Based on a banned novel, this film depicts an obsessive, sadomasochistic relationship between a thirty-eight-year-old sculptor (Lee Sang Hyun) and an eighteen-year-old girl (Kim Tae Yeon).

ment. *The Uprising* (*Lee jae-sueui nan*, 1999) is likewise based on a historical event—in this case the bloody revolt of Chejuan islanders against French Catholic missionaries and the government, which attempted to tax them to fund their conversion to Christianity in 1901. Other committed filmmakers of the 1990s are Byun Young-Joo, whose moving documentary *Murmuring* (1996; released recut, in the United States as *Habitual Sadness: Korean Comfort Women Today*) examined the plight of six aged "comfort women" who were commandeered as girls to service Japanese Imperial Army troops during World War II,[2] and Hong Sang-soo (b. 1960), whose *The Day a Pig Fell into the Well* (*Daijiga Umule Pajinnal*, 1996) is a dark, picaresque comedy of contemporary urban morals, implicitly critical of Korea's nascent consumerism—a theme it shares with Park Chul-Soo's horror film *301/302* (1995), though the métier of the latter is cannibalism and the former is adultery. Support from the Korean Film Commission combined with rapidly accelerating foreign sales (to both Southeast Asia and, increasingly, Europe) and a strong local market (with an average 35 percent share for domestic product) have made the South Korean film industry one of the world's strongest—as confirmed by the performance of record-setting national blockbusters like Kang Je-gyu's espionage thriller *Shiri* (1999) and Park Chan-wook's *Joint Security Area* (*Gongdong gyeongbi guyeok JSA*, 2000), an action-oriented mystery about the murder of two North Korean soldiers on the DMZ.

Participating in the New Korean Cinema but not *of* it is Im Kwon-taek (b. 1936), South Korea's only world-class

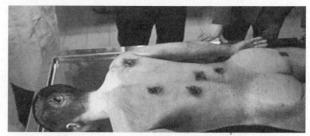

19.56 *Joint Security Area* (*Gondong gyeongbi guyeok JSA* [Park Chan-wook, 2000]). Another commercially successful, action-oriented thriller from Korea, but one with a distinctly serious antiwar edge.

director. With over 100 titles to his credit, Im has participated actively in every stage of post–World War II Korean cinema and is in many ways its most paradigmatic figure. He began working in the industry as an assistant director in the late 1950s and made his first feature, *Dumanganga Jal itgeola* (also known as *Farewell to the Duman River*), in 1962. For the next ten years, he directed formulaic genre films, mainly crime and swordfighting programmers, turning to more serious dramatic work in the 1970s—e.g., *The Deserted Widow* (*Jabcho*, 1973) and *Geneaolgy* (*Chopko*, 1978). His international breakthrough came with *Mandala* (1981), which won the Grand Prix at the Hawaii Film Festival and was invited to compete at Berlin. This film, about the crisis of faith of a Buddhist monk, was constructed of beautifully composed long takes and has been compared to the best work of Tarkovsky and Angelopoulos, although it is also steeped in Korean traditional culture. After it was discovered by the West, Im's work became increasingly intense and increasingly honored; many of his 1980s films won festival prizes: *Daughter of the Flames* (*Pul-ui tal*, 1983) and *Adada* (1989), dramas about the persistence of shamanism and feudalism, respectively, won awards at Montreal; *Gilsottum* (1986), a film about dismembered families reuniting across the 38th parallel, at Berlin; *The Contract Mother* (*Sibaji*, 1987), about the centuries-old Korean practice of surrogate childbearing, at Venice; and the religious drama *Come, Come, Come Upward* (*Aje, aje bara, aje*, 1989), at Moscow (as the first South Korean film ever

19.55 *Shiri* (*Swiri* [Kang Je-gyu, 1999]). American-style action fueled this blockbuster about North Korean espionage and helped it to become one of the most popular Korean films of the decade.

2. The sentiments of Koreans about their treatment by the Japanese may be gauged by the fact that there was a total ban on Japanese movies, popular music, and public performances from 1945 to 1998.

allowed to compete there). His art-film image notwithstanding, Im continued to direct occasional mass-market genre films—e.g., the violent period gangster melodramas *Son of the General* (*Chang-gun ui Adeul*, 1990) and its two sequels (1991; 1992). In addition to this successful franchise, Im broke box-office records in 1993 with *Sopyonje*, a melodramatic account of a traditional *p'ansori* singer who attempts to extend his art into the post–Korean War era, based on a best-selling novel by Lee Chung-Joon. With *The Taebaek Mountains* (*Taebaek Sanmaek*, 1995), adapted from an epic novel by Cho Jeong-lae, Im contributed to the new political discourse on modern Korean history—here with a nearly allegorical drama about the struggle to control a small southwestern village on the eve of the Korean War. More recently, Im has again addressed traditional culture: *Festival* (*Ch'ukji*, 1997), also based on a Lee Chung-Joon novel, is a part-documentary and part-fictional account of the funeral celebration of an eighty-seven-year-old matriarch, whereas *Downfall* (also known as *Chang, the Prostitute* [*Nonun kyejip, ch'ang*, 1997]) is an old-fashioned melodrama, made from an original screenplay, in which a hardened prostitute falls in love with a client, destroying her business and ruining her life. In one of his most critically admired works so far, Im contributed *Chunhyang* (2000) to the burgeoning cinematic literature on the thirteenth-

19.58 *Chunghyang* (Im Kwon-taek, 2000). Inside the film, however, the narration shows considerable daring in melding its traditional subject matter with contemporary modes of presentation, suggesting how rapidly public taste is changing in Korea.

century Chunhyang legend, subject of the first existing text of *p'ansori*. (There have been at least 15 film versions to date, including the second Korean silent film and the first Korean talkie—see above.) Im's film is framed by a *p'ansori* recital of the tale in a theater so that the screen images are narrated by the chanting *p'ansori* artist; and shots of the *p'ansori* audience reacting to his performance are used to confirm our own responses to the film. *Chunhyang* is a remarkably effective experiment in translating a traditional performance art into the language of film, and the stunning color cinematography by Jung Il-sung makes it a feast for the eye as well as the ear. Although he is frequently compared to Kenji Mizoguchi (for his use of the long take and his appropriation of abused women as vehicles for social criticism) and to Abbas Kiarostami (for his sometimes self-reflexive humanism), the director whom Im Kwon-taek most resembles is probably John Ford—a filmmaker who encapsulates an entire industrial system (the classical Hollywood cinema) and

19.57 *Chunhyang* (Im Kwon-taek, 2000). This fifteenth film version of the thirteenth-century legend is narrated by a traditional *p'ansori* artist, who chants, sings, and performs elements of the story before a live audience.

worked a lifetime within its fairly rigid confines, but who nevertheless managed to achieve a cinema of technical perfection, vision, and virtually religious grace.

North Korean film history began in 1945 when Kim Il Sung proclaimed the Democratic People's Republic. It initially concentrated on the production of documentaries and, especially during the Korean War of 1950–53, propaganda. A feature cinema began to develop slowly during the 1960s and 1970s, and in 1987 the first international North Korean film festival was held at Pyongyang, home of the state University of Cinematography since 1953. The most important directors practicing in North Korea (population 22.2 million) today are Rim Chang Bom (*Thaw* [*Pomnaiui nunsogi*, 1986; winner of the main prize at the twenty-fifth Karlovy Vary Festival]) and Yun Riyong Gyu (the widescreen historical epic *Talmae and Pomdari*, 1987). In 1986 the country's best-known director, Shin Sang-ok, and his actress wife, missing since the late 1970s, surfaced in Vienna and asked for American political asylum.

The film industry of the Philippines (population 84.5 million) was large, exploitative, and studio-based until the 1960s. Most films at the time were shot in Tagalog (which helped to consolidate it as the national language), and they tended to be cheap knockoffs of Hollywood and European genre product—e.g., bloody Tagalog Westerns in the Italian vein—or low-budget sex films called *bombas*.[3] Characteristic of the Philippine industry in the 1960s and 1970s was producer-director Eddie Romero (b. 1924), who incorporated Hemisphere Pictures to crank out B-grade action films (e.g., *The Raiders of Leyte Gulf* [1963]) and horror films (e.g., *The Mad Doctor of Blood Island* [1969]) for international release, mainly to American exploitation venues. (Romero ultimately partnered with American International Pictures to produce such classic grindhouse fodder as *Big Doll House* [1971] and *Black Mama, White Mama* [1973] before turning to more serious films about modern Philippine history and society like *The Eagle* [*Aguila*, 1980] and *Ganito kami noon, paano rayo ngayon* [*This Is the Way We Live*, 1981].)

Then the system began to collapse, and its major stars established their own production companies, churning out a decade's worth of *bakya*, or films for low-brow tastes. During the 1970s, however, several Philippine directors garnered international profiles and earned new respect for the domestic industry, most prominently, Lino Brocka

19.59 *Macho Dancer* (Lino Brocka, 1988). Prostitution, drug trafficking, and police corruption punctuate the seamy side of Manila life in this Filipino *film noir*.

(1940–1991), whose *Manila in the Claws of Neon Signs* (*Maynila samga kuko ng liwanag*, 1975) is thought to be the most important Filipino film of the decade, and whose *Insiang* (1976) captured attention at Cannes in 1978. Brocka's success started a Philippine new wave, in which the collaboration of stylistically experimental directors with adventurous young writers produced such work as the French-trained Ishmael Bernal's *Speck in the Water* (*Nunal sa tubig*, 1976), and Mike De Leon's *Itim* (1976). When Brocka's *Jaguar* (1980) became the first Filipino film ever to compete at Cannes and Bernal's *City after Dark* (1980) the first Filipino film to succeed in the international marketplace, then First Lady Imelda Marcos organized the Manila International Film Festival, which ran for two years, in 1982 and 1983. In that short period, the Philippine new wave gained an international reputation in the continuing work of Brocka (*Lamentations* [*Dung-aw*, 1981]; *Bona*, 1981; *P.X.*, 1982; *My Country* [*Bayan ko*, 1984]; *Macho Dancer*, 1988; *Les Insoumis* [*Fight for Us*, 1989]), Bernal (*Himala*, 1983; *Affair* [*Relasyon*, 1985]); De Leon (*In the Twinkling of an Eye* [*Kisapmata*, 1981]; *Batch '81*, 1982), and a newly respectable Eddie Romero (*This Is the Way We Live* [*Ganito kami noon, paano rayo ngayon*, 1981]; *Desire* [1983]), as well as the work of such relative newcomers as Kidlat Tahimik

---

3. Lee Server, *Asian Pop Cinema: Bombay to Tokyo* (San Francisco: Chronicle, 1999), p. 102.

(*The Perfumed Nightmare*, 1979; *Turumba*, 1983), Laurice Guillen (*Salome*, 1981), Peque Gallaga (*Gold, Silver, Death* [*Oro, plata, mata*, 1983]), and Marilou Díaz-Abaya (*Moral*, 1983; *Of the Flesh* [*Karnal*, 1984]). During the 1980s, the Philippines ranked among the top ten filmmaking nations in the world, with three large companies (Seiko, Regal, and Viva) and a handful of smaller ones producing approximately 150 features per year. President Marcos was overthrown in February 1986; the new government of Corazon Aquino chose to retain Marcos's strict policies of censorship without adopting his enthusiasm for the arts, and the "New Filipino Cinema" languished. When Lino Brocka was killed in an automobile crash in 1991, the Philippine cinema lost its leading director and its most eloquent social critic. Under the regime of President Fidel V. Ramos, an Aquino protégé elected in 1992, the industry returned to the production of low-budget popular entertainment at the rate of about 130 features annually, rising as high as 204 in 1997.

Remarkably, perhaps, film culture is deeply ingrained in Philippine society and politics. Movie stars have for many years occupied top political posts, and in 1997 the popular movie actor Joseph Estrada was elected president. During his short term in office, Estrada encouraged the flowering of a creative and experimental cinema by installing a liberal political ally at the head of the censorious Movie and Television Review and Classification Board (MTRCB). When Estrada was ousted in the wake of a corruption scandal in 2000, he was replaced by Vice President Gloria Macapagal-Arroyo, herself the daughter of a past president. She supported the industry through tax relief but was conservative in terms of film content, cracking down on works like Jose Javier Reyes's controversial *Live Show* (2001). This *cinéma vérité*–style film about impoverished men and women in Manila who perform live sex acts for pay was both a critique of Philippine society and of the preponderance of *bombas* in Philippine cinema, which remains in the early years of the twenty-first century an industry fundamentally devoted to exploitation and pulp fiction.

Hollywood, 1965–1995

In the 1960s, for the first time in its history, Hollywood fell behind the rest of the world—aesthetically, commercially, and even technologically, the latter due to the conservatism of its unions. Its decline resulted from the American industry's obstinate refusal to face a single fact: that the composition of the weekly American film audience was changing as rapidly as the culture itself. (The long-term effects of the Paramount decrees were another factor since the majors could no longer control exhibition.) Between the mid-1950s and the mid-1960s, that audience shifted from a predominantly middle-aged, modestly educated, middle- to lower-class group to a younger, better-educated, more affluent, and predominantly middle-class group. The new audience in America, as all over the world, was formed by the postwar generation's coming of age. It was smaller than the previous audience, and its values were different. By the early 1960s, the old audience had begun to stay home and watch television, venturing out occasionally for some spectacular family entertainment but generally staying away from movie theaters. As the size of audiences decreased, admission prices rose well above the rate of general inflation,[1] which had the effect of further decreasing the demand for the traditional Hollywood product. Yet the industry continued to make films according to the stylistic conventions of the 1940s and 1950s, as if its old constituency still existed when only vestiges of it did.

The principal change in filmmaking during this period was the cost of production, which by 1966 averaged $3 million per film due to both monetary inflation and the industry's own extravagant search for a winning box-office formula. The new audience was not interested in seeing these films any more than was the old one because as long as American cinema simply duplicated the popular entertainment function of television on a larger scale, neither audience particularly needed it. By 1962, Hollywood's yearly

---

1. Between 1956 and 1972, when the general cost of living in the United States rose 53.9 percent, theater admission prices rose 160 percent.

box-office receipts had fallen to their lowest level in history—$900 million, or one-half of the immediate postwar figure. The studios were in serious financial trouble, which grew worse as they made increasingly desperate attempts to recapture the old audience with spectacular flops like 20th Century–Fox's *Cleopatra* (1963). In 1965, the unprecedented success of Fox's *The Sound of Music*, which grossed more than $135 million nationwide, rekindled false hope in the spectacle formula, but a succession of stunning failures, such as 20th Century–Fox's *Doctor Dolittle* (Richard Fleischer, 1967), *Star!* (Robert Wise, 1968), *Hello, Dolly!* (Gene Kelly, 1969), and *Tora! Tora! Tora!* (Richard Fleischer, Toshio Masuda, and Kinji Fukasaku, 1970), and Paramount's *Paint Your Wagon* (Joshua Logan, 1969), *Darling Lili* (Blake Edwards, 1970), and *The Molly Maquires* (Martin Ritt, 1970), pushed the industry to the brink of catastrophe by the early 1970s.

As Hollywood's financial troubles worsened throughout the 1960s, several commercial forces coalesced to bring the new American audience into the theaters. For one thing, the French and Italian New Waves had demonstrated to producers all over the world that "art" films could make money—especially if they were shot rapidly on low budgets by young directors who were willing to work

20.2 First-class disaster: Julie Andrews and Rock Hudson in Paramount's World War II espionage spoof *Darling Lili* (Blake Edwards, 1970); produced for $22 million, it earned $3.3 million for a then-record loss of $18.7 million.

for less money than older, more established ones. This realization had two profound consequences for the American cinema. In the first place, there was an increased tolerance for independent production of the type being practiced in Europe by Godard, Truffaut, Antonioni, Fellini, and others. By the mid-1960s, independent producers like Roger Corman of New World Films were able to sponsor young directors like Francis Ford Coppola (b. 1939) and George Lucas (b. 1944), who were making their first features. Independent producer-directors like Stanley Kubrick (1928–1999) and Arthur Penn (b. 1922) found themselves for the first time able to control the financing of their own films and to achieve an unprecedented degree of creative freedom. In the second place, the major studios, who were turning increasingly to television production to save themselves from financial ruin,[2] became the willing distributors of these independent productions—a thing they would never have considered several years before—because distribution provided them with a badly needed source of revenue. The majors also became large-

20.1 Twentieth Century flop: *Tora! Tora! Tora!* (Richard Fleischer, Toshio Masuda, Kinji Fukasaku, 1970), produced for $25 million, returned $14.5 million in domestic rentals for a loss of $10.5 million. A shot from one of many Oscar-winning special-effects sequences (see Chapter 21).

2. By the 1970s, 50 percent of the approximately 25,000 jobs in Hollywood were in television production and distribution, and 90 percent of all prime-time programming was shot on film.

20.3–20.4 New directors from television demonstrate the influence of *cinéma vérité* and the French New Wave.

20.3 *Seven Days in May* (John Frankenheimer, 1964): demonstrators clash in front of the White House

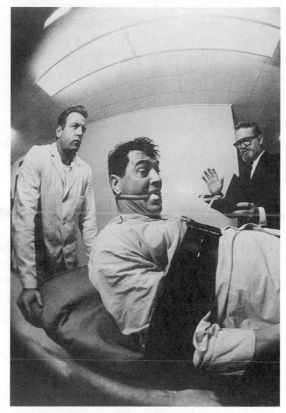

20.4 *Seconds* (John Frankenheimer, 1966): Rock Hudson on the brink of deconstruction; cinematography by James Wong Howe.

scale domestic distributors of foreign films, whose circulation in the United States they had successfully managed to limit when they were powerful monopolies. By the mid-1960s, the work of Fellini, Antonioni, Bergman, and Buñuel, as well as that of French New Wave directors—which had previously been available in this country only in specialized "art houses" in major urban centers, if at all—suddenly began to appear regularly in first-run theaters all over America. By the 1970s, foreign films were as readily available as American ones, not just in cities but even in many small towns.[3]

As the rigid structure of the studio system began to crumble, new talent entered the film industry in the late 1950s and early 1960s and, between 1960 and 1966, a number of young directors from television began to make theatrical films. These included Irvin Kershner (b. 1923)—*The Hoodlum Priest*, 1961; *The Luck of Ginger Coffey*, 1964; *A Fine Madness*, 1966; John Frankenheimer (1930–2002)—*The Manchurian Candidate*, 1962; *Seven Days in May*, 1964; *The Train*, 1965; *Seconds*, 1966; Sidney Lumet (b. 1924)—*12 Angry Men*, 1957; *Long Day's Journey into Night*, 1962; *Fail-Safe*, 1964; *The Hill*, 1965; *The Pawnbroker*, 1965; *The Group*, 1966; Arthur Penn (b. 1922)—*The Miracle Worker*, 1962; *Mickey One*, 1965; *The Chase*, 1966; and Sam Peckinpah (1925–1984)—*Ride the High

Country, 1962; *Major Dundee*, 1965. New cinematographers from the East Coast also entered the film industry, including Conrad Hall (1926–2003), Haskell Wexler (b. 1926), William Fraker (b. 1923), and the Hungarian émigrés László Kovács (b. 1933) and Vilmos Zsigmond (b. 1930). As these new filmmakers, working with ever-increasing creative freedom and mobility, assimilated the French and Italian innovations, a new kind of American cinema was born for a new American audience.

This audience was composed of the first generation in history that had grown up with the visually, if not intellec-

---

3. The availability of foreign films in this country, however, has decreased in the past three decades owing to several international recessions and the constantly rising domestic costs of advertising, distribution, and dubbing.

tually, stimulating medium of television. Through hours of watching television as children and teenagers, its members knew the language of cinema implicitly, and when film-makers like Frankenheimer, Lumet, Penn, and Peckinpah began to move out of the studios in the mid-to late 1960s and to employ the New Wave techniques of the French and Italian cinemas for the first time on the American screen, this young audience liked what it saw. A phenomenal increase in the number and quality of college and university film study courses simultaneously enabled many members of the new audience to *understand* what they saw as well as to enjoy it.[4] It is important to realize that the values of the new audience, like its lifestyles, were radically different from those of the old. For better or worse, it had a generally permissive attitude toward such former cultural taboos as the explicit representation of sex, violence, and death. Thus, when censorship was completely abolished and replaced by a ratings system in October 1968, the content of American cinema, as well as its form, was revolutionized to permit the depiction of virtually everything under the sun, including graphic sex and violent death. That this liberalization opened the mainstream cinema to exploitation is inarguable, but it was necessary before the American film could achieve full maturity of content. It is difficult, for example, to imagine a director like Robert Altman (*Nashville*, 1975; *Three Women*, 1977) working at his best during the 1970s in the moral climate that produced *The Sound of Music* in 1965.

The New American Cinema

THE IMPACT OF *BONNIE AND CLYDE*

A new American cinema and a new American film audience announced themselves emphatically with the release in 1967 of Arthur Penn's *Bonnie and Clyde*. This film, which was universally attacked by the critics when it opened in August, had by November become the most popular film of the year.[5] It would subsequently receive ten Academy Award nominations and win two awards (Best Cinematography: Burnett Guffey; Best Supporting Actress: Estelle Parsons), win the New York Film Critics' Award for Best Script (David Newman and Robert Benton), and be named the Best Film of 1967 by many of the critics who had originally panned it. Most triumphant of all, perhaps, *Bonnie and Clyde* is the only film ever to

20.5–20.6 Romantic revolutionaries: a touched-up publicity shot and an unretouched still from *Bonnie and Clyde* (Arthur Penn, 1967): Faye Dunaway, Warren Beatty.

have forced the public retraction of a critical opinion by *Time* magazine, which dismissed the film in a summer issue and, in its issue of December 8, 1967, ran a long cover story on its virtues. Indeed, the phenomenal success of *Bonnie and Clyde* caused many retractions on the part of veteran film critics, who, on first viewing, had mistaken it for a conventional, if gratuitously bloody, gangster

---

4. As the number of film-studies courses continues to increase in the United States, more and more of the country's educated citizens are achieving a state of what could be called cinema or media literacy (Charles Eidsvik's useful term is "cineliteracy"—see his *Cineliteracy: Film Among the Arts* [New York: Viking, 1978]). By 1981, the American Film Institute's *Guide to College Courses in Film and Television* listed nearly 8,000 courses in film and television at over 600 American colleges and universities, and the number of schools that offer programs leading to a degree in one subject or both has continued to grow.

5. The film was so popular at the time of its release that its protagonists became cult figures. Double-breasted suits and fedora hats of the type worn by Clyde were all the rage in men's clothing, and Bonnie's 1930s hemlines temporarily banished the miniskirt from the world of women's fashion. You could even buy transparent decals with which to simulate bullet holes on the windshield of your car in imitation of a famous shot from the film.

film. *Bonnie and Clyde* was in fact a sophisticated blend of comedy, violence, romance, and—symbolically, at least—politics that borrowed freely from the techniques of the French New Wave (it was originally to have been directed by Truffaut and then Godard) and that perfectly captured the rebellious spirit of the times.

Based on the real-life career of Bonnie Parker and Clyde Barrow, the film tells the story of two young and attractive small-time criminals (Warren Beatty and Faye Dunaway) from the Midwest who during the Depression fall in love, go on a spree of robberies and killings, and become national folk heroes in the process. Their targets are not the common people, but the avaricious banks and the armies of police that protect them—in other words, "the system." Bonnie and Clyde were thus prototypes of the antiestablishment heroes who have come to dominate so many American films since, and they resonated per-

fectly with the revolutionary tenor of the late 1960s. ("They're young! They're in love! And they kill people!" the advertising copy proclaimed.) By midfilm the lovers are clearly doomed, but nothing could prepare audiences in 1967 for the apocalyptic violence of the ending, in which Bonnie and Clyde are ambushed after a romantic interlude and their bodies ripped apart by machine-gun slugs in a protracted ballet of agony and death. Penn shot this conclusion with four cameras running at different speeds and with different lenses, and intercut the footage into a complex montage sequence that gives the deaths a mythic, legendary quality: Bonnie and Clyde are not simply killed; they are destroyed. Even today the sequence has an almost unbearable intensity because our dramatic identification with the characters is so complete. In the social climate of the times, however, the new American audience identified with Bonnie and Clyde less as dramatic

20.7 A new aesthetic of violence: shots from the montage sequence that concludes *Bonnie and Clyde.* **By intercutting footage of the death scene from several separate cameras equipped with different lenses and running at different speeds, Penn and his collaborators created an unprecedented (though now widely imitated) effect.**

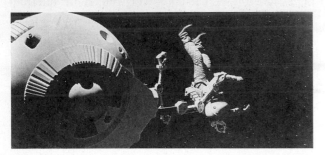

20.8–20.10 *2001: A Space Odyssey* (Stanley Kubrick, 1968). A space station transformed from a prehistoric bone; the discovery of the monolith on the moon; deep space.

characters than as types of romantic revolutionaries. And the tense, nervous texture of the film, with its unpredictable shifts in mood and its graphic, sensual depiction of violent death, was as revolutionary in 1967 as were its protagonists. The form of *Bonnie and Clyde* has been imitated so many times by hundreds of "criminal couple" and "road" pictures since 1967[6] that it is hard for contemporary audiences to comprehend the originality of the film when it was released. But in 1967 it was clearly subversive in both form and content, and the angry critical debate it caused in the United States was, in many ways, less about a pair of 1930s gangsters than about the morality of violent dissent against an oppressive social order.

2001: A SPACE ODYSSEY

Another film that caught the imagination of a generation in the late 1960s was Stanley Kubrick's *2001: A Space Odyssey* (1968). Produced at a cost of $10.5 million over a period of two and a half years, *2001* offered a mythic vision of the relationship between humanity and technology at a time when that relationship had crucial bearing on the future of American society and of the entire Western world. Like its Greek namesake, the film has an epic structure. In Section I, we watch a tribe of prehistoric ape-men learn how to use bones as instruments of destruction (our first technology being weaponry, preceding even language) shortly after they have encountered an enormous monolithic slab in the middle of the desert.

Later, one ape-man crushes the skull of a rival with a bone and tosses the weapon jubilantly into the air, where it rotates in slow motion until an associative cut transforms it into the axis of a gigantic space station (actually a weapons platform) several million years later. In Section II, a shuttle is launched from this station carrying scientists who have discovered a similar monolith buried beneath the surface of the moon; it is emitting a radio signal in the direction of the planet Jupiter. Section III opens eighteen months later with a huge phallic spacecraft gliding toward Jupiter in empty space. Inside are a team of astronauts and a brand-new HAL 9000[7] talking computer, which guides the ship and controls all of its vital functions.

---

6. In addition to relentlessly juvenile drive-in fare like *Dirty Mary Crazy Larry* (John Hough, 1974) and *aloha, bobby and rose* (Floyd Mutrux, 1975), the "criminal couple" format has produced such interesting films as Sam Peckinpah's *The Getaway* (1972; remade under the same title by Roger Donaldson, 1994), Robert Altman's *Thieves Like Us* (1974), Terrence Malick's *Badlands* (1974), Steven Spielberg's *Sugarland Express* (1974), Ted Kotcheff's *Fun with Dick and Jane* (1977), Jim McBride's *Breathless* (1983; a remake of Godard's 1959 film), Emilio Estevez's *Wisdom* (1986), Ridley Scott's *Thelma & Louise* (1991), Tamra Davis's *Gun Crazy* (1992; a loose remake of Joseph H. Lewis's 1950 *Gun Crazy*), Tony Scott's *True Romance* (1993), and Oliver Stone's *Natural Born Killers* (1994). Bonnie and Clyde also had distinguished forebears in Fritz Lang's *You Only Live Once* (1937), Nicholas Ray's *They Live by Night* (1948), and Joseph H. Lewis's *Gun Crazy* (1950).

7. "HAL" is an acronym derived from the terms for two systems of problem solving used in mathematics, computer science, and artificial intelligence—heuristic and algorithmic.

The mission of this probe is unclear, but it is apparently to track the radio signal.

HAL, who seems more highly evolved in emotional terms than any of the humans, suffers a paranoid breakdown when he makes a miscalculation, and he sets about killing all of his human shipmates in the belief that they are botching the mission and intend to disconnect him. He succeeds in terminating the life functions of three hibernating astronauts and in marooning another in deep space, but the lone human survivor destroys HAL as a thinking entity by disconnecting his memory bank, while HAL tries desperately to talk him out of it. As we witness the computer regress to its basic language programs and finally expire, we feel a disturbing sympathy for it—disturbing because we have been encouraged to feel so little for the coolly disaffected humans of this future world. Alone aboard the drifting spacecraft now, the final astronaut is drawn toward Jupiter and, abandoning ship in a pod, encounters a third monolith floating through space. Suddenly he is sucked into another dimension, where he experiences a hallucinatory trip through time and space in which all perceptual relationships are blurred. Arriving as an older man in a conventional, completely white bedroom suite furnished in Louis XVI style, the astronaut ages to decrepitude before our eyes and is reborn in the film's final frames as the luminous, embryonic Star-Child—a new order of intelligence, beyond ape, man, and machine, moving through space toward the earth from which it began its evolution millions of years before.

Enigmatic, mystical, and profoundly sensuous, *2001* resists concrete logical interpretation because in a real sense its medium *is* its message. As Kubrick himself has pointed out, the film is "essentially a nonverbal experience. . . . It attempts to communicate more to the subconscious and to the feelings than it does to the intellect." Indeed, less than half of the film contains dialogue; the rest alternates between a brilliantly scored combination of classical and avant-garde electronic music and the silence of deep space. *2001* also broke new ground in photographic special effects (supervised by Douglas Trumbull and Con Pederson), particularly in the technique of **front projection,**[8] which it is credited with perfecting. It was shot by Geoffrey Unsworth (1914–1978) in Super Panavision for presentation in Cinerama in both 35mm and 70mm formats. Immensely popular in 1968, the film has a large cult following even today and is constantly revived. It has been

---

8. A more effective alternative to rear projection (see Glossary), in which action is shot against a glass-beaded reflective screen. The background image is projected onto this screen by means of a small semi-silvered mirror, which both transmits and reflects light, lying along the same axis as the camera lens. Since this puts the projector and the camera in the same optical position, the camera does not record the shadows cast on the screen from the projection by actors and sets. Extremely bright studio lighting is used to drown out the background image as projected on actors and set. The process requires half the studio space of rear projection and is more convincing on-screen.

The special effects for *2001* took eighteen months to produce and cost $6.5 million, over 60 percent of the film's entire budget; they have never been equaled in verisimilitude, although the special effects of *Star Wars* and subsequent films have gone beyond them in scope. (The fullest account of how the *2001* effects were accomplished is contained in John Brosnan, *Movie Magic: The Story of Special Effects in the Cinema* [New York: St. Martin's, 1974], pp. 218–29.) The space-travel sequences in *Star Wars*, like those in 2001, were made through a process known as traveling matte photography, in which models of spaceships and other miniatures are manipulated for the camera in front of a blue screen that leaves the background of the shot unexposed. The background is then superimposed—or "matted in"—in the printing process via double exposure. Any number of images can be layered in this way on the same piece of film, but the matching of them must be absolutely precise. Traveling matte shots were torturously difficult and time-consuming before the intervention of computers. The process was so expensive, in fact, that the use of 20 or 30 traveling mattes, even in a spectacular production like *2001*, was considered extreme. The innovation wrought by *Star Wars*, which used 365 traveling matte special effects, was a computerized motion-control system designed by effects director John Dykstra and patented as Dykstraflex. The heart of the system is a motorized camera mount, governed by multitrack magnetic tape, which permits the camera to pan, tilt, roll, and perform 8 feet of vertical and 42 feet of horizontal tracking movement. Operators can "program" their cameras through complicated plotted motions one frame at a time, and the whole sequence can be repeated precisely by numeric control, making traveling matte work cost-effective for the first time. Since the development of Dykstraflex, numerous refinements in motion-control systems have taken place (e.g., Walt Disney Productions' automated camera-effects system, or ACES, which used computer automation to control the movement of both camera *and* model, and the same studio's Matte-Scan, first used in the abysmal *The Black Hole* [Gary Nelson, 1979], which permits the integration of matte paintings with live scenes in which the camera is moving). But the most remarkable interaction between electronics and special effects in recent years has been the advent of computer-generated imagery, or CGI, in which scenes are digitalized and printed directly onto the film stock without the intervention of photography. The first film to employ CGI at any length was Disney's *Tron* (Steven Lisberger, 1982), for which Digital Productions, Inc., created approximately 5 minutes of completely digitalized high-resolution imagery with a $6.5 million Ramtek Cray-1 computer. For *The Last Starfighter*, Digital Productions leased Ramtek's $10.5 billion supercomputer, the Cray X-MP, to generate 230 scenes or about 27 of its 100 minutes, making it the first feature film in history to simulate *all* of its special effects. Although the simulation cost $4.9 million of *Starfighter's* $14 million budget, the film's producers (Lorimar) figured that it had been completed in one-third the time and at half the expense of traditional effects (see Chapter 21).

ranked by the critic Fred Silva with *The Birth of a Nation* and *Citizen Kane* as an American landmark film—that is, a film that describes "a critical, unsettled area of American life"—in this case, the emptiness of technology in the form of a film that is itself a technological wonderment. From any perspective, *2001* is that most rare of cinematic achievements: a big-budget, nonnarrative spectacle of enormous technical sophistication that nevertheless makes an original and personal artistic statement about the human condition.[9]

THE WILD BUNCH: "ZAPPING THE CONG"[1]

The years 1968 and 1969, perhaps the darkest in American history since the Civil War, witnessed some of the most original American films since the late 1940s. Like *Bonnie and Clyde*, many of them were aimed at the new youthful audience and were either covertly or overtly concerned with the political hysteria that had gripped the nation over the war in Vietnam. If *Bonnie and Clyde* was about the type of romantic rebel who would fight the military-industrial complex to end the war and usher in the greening of America, Sam Peckinpah's *The Wild Bunch* (1969) was about America's mercenary presence in Vietnam itself. In this film, which opens with the bloody massacre of an entire Texas town in the course of a payroll robbery, a gang of aging outlaws led by Pike Bishop (William Holden) finds itself increasingly confined by the closing of the American frontier and, pursued by bounty hunters, crosses the border into Mexico

in search of greener pastures. The year is 1914, and the Mexican Civil War is in full swing, but the members of the Wild Bunch aren't looking for a cause, only some action. (As one of them comments after they have crossed the Rio Grande, "Just more of Texas, as far as I'm concerned.") The group falls in with Mapache, a brutish general who is leading federal troops in the fight against Pancho Villa and the insurgents. Brilliantly played by the Mexican director Emilio Fernández, Mapache is a sadistic thug who murders and tortures indiscriminately. His military base in the village of Agua Verde is a corrupt, barely competent dictatorship propped up by powerful foreign governments (in this case Germany and her allies) and their sophisticated weapons technology. The Bunch agrees to rob an American munitions train near the border for Mapache, who then attempts to seize the arms without paying for them. The gang outwits him, but Mapache captures one of their number—a Mexican Indian who has collaborated with the rebels—and tortures him to death before their eyes. In disgust, Pike and his men confront Mapache and kill him. The film ends in a sustained bloodbath as the outlaws seize the *federales'* machine gun and blast Agua Verde to pieces, all of them dying in the process.

The spectacular massacres that open and close *The Wild Bunch* are filmed in the style of the final ambush of *Bonnie and Clyde*, with a variety of lenses and different cameras running at different speeds, usually decelerated to depict the moment of death. With the death scene from Penn's film, they are among the most complex, kinetic, and shocking montage sequences in postwar

20.11 Mercenaries as mythic heroes: *The Wild Bunch* (Sam Peckinpah, 1969). Ernest Borgnine, William Holden, Warren Oates. (Note the expertly balanced composition.)

9. Kubrick's best films have always been both technically and intellectually a decade ahead of their time. His classic antiwar statement *Paths of Glory* (1957), set in a French army unit during World War I, relentlessly exposed the type of military stupidity and callousness that would lead us into Vietnam. *Dr. Strangelove, or How I Learned to Stop Worrying and Love the Bomb* (1963) is an unsparing black comedy about the inevitability of nuclear holocaust, produced amid the optimism of the New Frontier. And *A Clockwork Orange* (1971) projected a vision of the alienated, drug-ridden, ultraviolent future incarnated by "punk" culture in the late 1970s and 1980s. *The Shining* (1980) is less the conventional horror film it was initially thought to be than an account of America's long-concealed history of domestic violence and child abuse, while *Full Metal Jacket* (1987) suggests that the country itself is a sort of distopic Disneyland in which the Vietnam War became one of the more elaborate rides. *Eyes Wide Shut* (1999) is a horror film about sex in the twilight of the American empire.

1. A common slang phrase from the period that referred to the indiscriminate killing of Vietnamese, usually with automatic weapons fired at a distance.

20.12 Radical destruction: a shot from the massacre that concludes *The Wild Bunch.* **Ernest Borgnine, William Holden.**

American cinema, and they are balletically choreographed in a manner reminiscent of the battle scenes from Kurosawa's *Seven Samurai*. The film is also a stunning piece of widescreen composition from beginning to end, skillfully photographed by Lucien Ballard (1908–1988) in Panavision. Nevertheless, critics of the period were outraged at the extent and ferocity of the bloodshed. The final massacre has about it a sort of mad, orgasmic ecstasy as the slaughter grows more and more intense until it reaches Eisensteinian (or Buñuelian) proportions: we see more people die than could possibly fill the small village; we see the same people die over and over again. Furthermore, the victims of this "heroic" violence are principally civilians caught in the crossfire. But a year before the revelation of the My Lai massacre, the outraged critics could not know that they were watching a mythic allegory of American intervention in Vietnam.[2]

As with *Bonnie and Clyde*, the violence of *The Wild Bunch was* revolutionary, *was* excessive for its time—a thing difficult to see today, when slow-motion bloodletting has passed from innovation to convention to cliché. Nevertheless, Penn and Peckinpah were committed filmmakers during the time of the war. Like their counterparts in the *film noir* movement of the late 1940s (see Chapter 11), they were interested in exposing their audience to certain dark realities of contemporary American life that the audience had itself largely chosen to ignore. Their films introduced conventions for the depiction of violence and carnage that others exploited ad nauseam in the 1970s and beyond. But both directors insisted for the first time in American cinema that the human body is

made of real flesh and blood; that arterial blood spurts rather than drips demurely; that bullet wounds leave not trim little pinpricks but big, gaping holes; and, in general, that violence has painful, unpretty, humanly destructive consequences. By bringing the American film closer to reality in its depiction of what high-powered modern weaponry can do to the human body, Penn and Peckinpah had overturned decades of polite filmic convention that the body has the resilience of rubber and that death is simply a state of terminal sleep. This was important new knowledge for the citizens of a nation whose government was waging a savage war of annihilation in Southeast Asia by remote control.[3]

END OF A DREAM

In the years 1968 and 1969 the violence of our lives erupted onto our screens. The veteran cinematographer Haskell Wexler's *Medium Cool* (1969) was literally *about* media representations of violence in an America divided against itself by the war. Its main character is an alienated news cameraman who learns in the course of the film how

---

2. In 1969, the original release print of *The Wild Bunch* was said to have had more individual shots than any color film ever made—a claim difficult to substantiate today since the film was withdrawn by Warner Bros. after its debut and rereleased in several different versions, none of them as long or elaborate as Peckinpah had intended. For example, Warners cut an entire series of flashbacks establishing the prior relationship between Pike and his pursuer, Deke Thornton, which is crucial to the film's themes of honor and betrayal. Also cut was an elaborate sequence in which Mapache's troops are routed at a provincial railroad station by Villa's, which adds depth to the general's characterization and opens up the plot. During 1969, *The Wild Bunch* was shown in alternate versions of 190, 148, 145, 143, and 135 minutes. Only the 145- and 135-minute versions are available in 16mm today, although Warner Bros. still owns the master print and may someday restore it for public exhibition. In 1985, Warners released a 145-minute restored version on videocassette; in 1995, it rereleased this version theatrically in both 35mm and 70mm with six-track Dolby Stereo Digital sound.

3. What *Bonnie and Clyde* and *The Wild Bunch* did for violence, *The Graduate* (Mike Nichols, 1967), *I Am Curious—Yellow* (Vilgot Sjöman, 1967; U.S. release, 1969), *Midnight Cowboy* (John Schlesinger, 1969), and *Carnal Knowledge* (Nichols, 1971) did for sex. All four films were enormously popular with the youth market of the period, and all four dealt explicitly with human sexuality in ways unthinkable only a few years before. *The Graduate* concerned a sexual liaison between a recent college graduate and a middle-aged woman (his girlfriend's mother). *I Am Curious—Yellow*, which was confiscated by U.S. Customs authorities in 1967 but released by federal circuit court order in 1969 and later found by the U.S. Supreme Court to fall "within the ambit of intellectual effort that the First Amendment was designed to protect," contained male and female frontal nudity and simulated copulation. *Midnight Cowboy*, a fine dramatic feature that became the first X-rated film to

20.13 The illusion of freedom: *Easy Rider* (Dennis Hopper, 1969).
Dennis Hopper, Peter Fonda, Jack Nicholson.

20.14 *Alice's Restaurant* (1969), Arthur Penn's requiem for the counterculture: Arlo Guthrie waits in line to take his Army induction physical.

easily the "detachment" of the media blends into distortion. As if to comment on itself, *Medium Cool* was shot in *cinéma vérité* fashion with a climax staged against the very real backdrop of the police riots at the 1968 Democratic National Convention in Chicago. *Easy Rider* (Dennis Hopper, 1969) also dealt openly with the violence and paranoia of an ideologically divided nation, although like other movies of the period it was praised for its radical social perspective far beyond its value as a film. In it, two hippies score a big drug deal and set off from California to Florida on their motorcycles "in search of America." But, as the ad copy read, they "couldn't find it anywhere." Treated with unmitigated contempt because of their appearance everywhere they go, the bikers are finally gunned down on a southern highway by some angry rednecks. A modestly competent synthesis of *Bonnie and Clyde* and the grade-B biker film scored with good contemporary rock, *Easy Rider* shrewdly exploited the paranoia of a generation that felt itself at war with a hostile and increasingly belligerent establishment, and it became the box-office phenomenon of the decade. Produced for $375,000, it grossed $50 million and convinced old-guard Hollywood that a vast new youth market was ready to be tapped.

This conviction led to a spate of low-budget "youth culture" movies about protest, drugs, and the generation gap. *Getting Straight* (Richard Rush, 1970), *The Strawberry Statement* (Stuart Hagmann, 1970), *Move!* (Stuart Rosenberg, 1970), *Joe* (John G. Avildsen, 1970), *Little Fauss and Big Halsey* (Sidney J. Furie, 1970), and *Cisco Pike* (Bill L. Norton, 1971) were probably the best of this type, while most were so bad that they couldn't even be sold to television after their theatrical release. Perhaps

win an Academy Award, dealt allusively with homosexual prostitution; while *Carnal Knowledge*, incisively scripted by Jules Feiffer, offered a candid analysis of the sexual—and sexist—obsessions of two male friends from college through middle age. These four films and inferior imitations opened the floodgates for the graphic representation of sex on American screens in the 1970s, making possible everything from *Deep Throat* (Gerard Damiano, 1972) to *Last Tango in Paris* (Bernardo Bertolucci, 1972).

Black film was also born as a mainstream enterprise in the late 1960s, with films like Robert Downey's bitter satire *Putney Swope* (1969), Gordon Parks's *The Learning Tree* (1969), Melvin Van Peebles's *Sweet Sweetback's Baadasssss Song* (1970), and Ossie Davis's *Cotton Comes to Harlem* (1970). The loosening up and subsequent disappearance from the American cinema of taboos about racial mixing on screen (and of *some* racial stereotypes)—probably stronger than those against sex and violence put together—produced the black exploitation, or "blaxploitation," films of the 1970s (*Shaft* [Gordon Parks, 1971]); *Super Fly* [Gordon Parks, Jr., 1972]; *Hit Man* [George Armitage, 1972]); *Slaughter* [Jack Starrett, 1972]; *Trouble Man* [Ivan Dixon, 1972]; *Coffy* [Jack Hill, 1973]; *Black Caesar* [Larry Cohen, 1973]; *Blacula* [William Crain, 1972]), parodied so astutely in Keenan Ivory Wayans's *I'm Gonna Git You Sucka* (1988), and such interesting features as *Sounder* (Martin Ritt, 1972); *Black Girl* (Ossie Davis, 1972); *Lady Sings the Blues* (Sidney J. Furie, 1973); *Ganja & Hess* (Bill Gunn, 1973); *Claudine* (John Berry, 1974); *The Bingo Long Traveling All-Stars & Motor Kings* (John Badham, 1977); and *Stony Island* (Andrew Davis, 1978). (See the sections on AIP and New World Pictures in Chapter 12.)

20.15 *Woodstock* (Michael Wadleigh, 1970).

20.16 *Gimme Shelter* (Albert and David Maysles, 1971).

the only youth-oriented dramatic feature of the era to achieve any real distinction—and this on a standard production budget—was Arthur Penn's extraordinary *Alice's Restaurant* (1969), a nearly plotless film about the failed idealism of the protest movement. There was, however, a good deal of vitality in another form calculated to appeal exclusively to the youth market: the rock documentary.[4] While films like *Monterey Pop* (D. A. Pennebaker, 1969) and *Mad Dogs & Englishmen* (Pierre Adidge, 1971) did a fine job of re-creating the experience of a live rock concert for a movie audience, Michael Wadleigh's *Woodstock* (1970) and, especially, Albert and David Maysles's *Gimme Shelter* (1971) attempted to make serious statements about the nature of rock music by approaching their respective concerts as social metaphors.

The "youth-cult" bubble of 1969–70 was soon to burst as the youth movement itself became increasingly disoriented and confused, and Hollywood returned to more conventional modes of production. With so many important films like *Bonnie and Clyde, The Wild Bunch, 2001,* and *Medium Cool* clustered around the years 1967–69, it had seemed for a time that America was headed for a major cinematic (and social) renaissance. But neither came to pass. Significantly, not one of the directors mentioned above, with the clear exception of Stanley Kubrick, has since made a film that truly equals in stature his contribution to the late-1960s groundswell. Arthur Penn's *Little Big Man* (1970), *Night Moves* (1975), *The Missouri Breaks* (1976), and *Four Friends* (1981) are all serious, intelligent, and cinematically sophisticated films, but they do not compare in originality and vitality with *Bonnie and Clyde*. Peckinpah's genius for depicting mass slaughter moved from self-plagiarism (*Straw Dogs,* 1971) to self-parody (*The Getaway,* 1972; *The Killer Elite,* 1975; *Con-*

voy, 1978) in the 1970s, although he continued to make interesting films (*Junior Bonner,* 1972; *Pat Garrett and Billy the Kid,* 1973; *Bring Me the Head of Alfredo Garcia,* 1974; *Cross of Iron,* 1977; *The Osterman Weekend,* 1983)—when he could find the work—until he died in 1984. Even Kubrick, whose reputation as a major figure is assured, never produced a film to rival *2001* in historical importance, although some critics feel that his lavish attempt to recreate the structures of the nineteenth-century novel in *Barry Lyndon* (1975; from the novel by Thackeray) comes close. His epic of domestic horror, *The Shining* (1980), adapted from Stephen King, did little to alter the balance of critical opinion, although *Full Metal Jacket* (1987) is clearly the definitive statement of why we were in Vietnam and his last film, *Eyes Wide Shut* (1999), is a lasting testament to the inability of men and women to communicate at any level. Haskell Wexler has worked mainly as a cinematographer since 1968, collaborating as director with Saul Landau on *Interview with President Allende* (1971) and *Report on Torture in Brazil* (1971), and with Emile de Antonio on *Underground* (1976), but finally returning to features with the hard-hitting *Latino* (1985), set in war-torn Nicaragua, and *Bus Rider's Union* (2000), a *cinéma vérité* documentary about the decline of Los Angeles's public-transit system. Dennis Hopper, whose success as a filmmaker was purely circumstantial in the first place, completed six features as a director after

---

4. The rock concert film, or "rockumentary," is today a recognized genre around the world with roots in *Don't Look Back* (1967), D. A. Pennebaker's *cinéma direct* account of Bob Dylan's 1965 English tour, and such brilliant contemporary manifestations as *The Last Waltz* (Martin Scorsese, 1979—The Band) and *Stop Making Sense* (Jonathan Demme, 1984—Talking Heads).

20.17–20.19 Penn after *Alice*:

20.17 *Little Big Man* (1970), an antiwar anti-Western adapted from Thomas Berger's picaresque novel: Dustin Hoffman in the title role.

20.19 *The Missouri Breaks* (1976), the Western as folkloric grotesque: Randy Quaid, Jack Nicholson.

20.18 *Night Moves* (1975), a Watergate-era *film noir* of multiple betrayals: Gene Hackman, Jennifer Warren.

thing about the political and intellectual ferment of the late 1960s that produced, however briefly, a period of great creativity in the American cinema and contributed to the sweeping away of time-honored conventions of both form and content. It was comparable in kind, if not in degree, to the Czech renaissance that preceded the Soviet invasion of 1968. The hope of liberalization released a surge of creative energy, whose influence continued to be felt long after the hope was crushed.

20.20–20.23 Peckinpah in the seventies:

20.20 *Straw Dogs* (1971): Ken Hutchison, Dustin Hoffman, and Del Henney with Susan George (foreground).

Easy Rider—The Last Movie (1971), *Out of the Blue* (1980), *Colors* (1988), *Backtrack* (1989; rereleased 1991); *The Hot Spot* (1990), *Chasers* (1994)—but none approaches the vitality of his first film; and he is best known today as a character actor. There was clearly some-

20.21 *Pat Garrett and Billy the Kid* (1973): James Coburn, Kris Kristofferson.

20.22 *Cross of Iron* (1977): World War II from the German point of view.

20.23 *Convoy* (1978): poetry into parody.

Hollywood in the Seventies and Eighties

INFLATION AND CONGLOMERATION

The enormous popular success in 1970 of two conventional formula films, *Love Story* (Arthur Hiller) and *Airport* (George Seaton), restored Hollywood's faith in the big-budget, mass-appeal feature, and the 1970s witnessed an inflation in the production costs of American films unparalleled in the industry's history. It was a decade of ever-bigger hits—*The Poseidon Adventure* (Ronald Neame, 1972); *The Godfather* (Francis Ford Coppola, 1972); *The Exorcist* (William Friedkin, 1973); *The Sting* (George Roy Hill, 1973); *The Towering Inferno* (John Guillermin, 1974); *Jaws* (Steven Spielberg, 1975); *Star Wars* (George Lucas, 1977); *Saturday Night Fever* (John Badham, 1977); *Grease* (Randal Kleiser, 1978); *Superman* (Richard Donner, 1978)—and ever-bigger flops—*Jesus Christ Superstar* (Norman Jewison, 1973); *Lucky Lady* (Stanely Donen, 1975); *The Hindenburg* (Robert

Wise, 1975); *Gable and Lombard* (Sidney J. Furie, 1976); *Sorcerer* (William Friedkin, 1977); *The Wiz* (Sidney Lumet, 1978); *1941* (Steven Spielberg, 1979). Between 1972 and 1977 the average production budget (or "negative cost") for a single film increased by 178 percent, or nearly four times the general rate of inflation. By the end of 1979, average production costs were nearly double the 1977 figure, having reached the staggering sum of $8.9 million per feature. Profits rose accordingly only if the film was a huge success,[5] so the financial risks of production were substantially multiplied. This caused a trend

---

5. A Hollywood rule of thumb equates a film's breaking even with returning two-and-a-half times its "negative cost" (literally, all costs required to produce the final cut of the master negative, excluding the costs of promotion, distribution, and exhibition). This break-even figure allows for advertising, studio overhead, and distribution prints (which cost about $1,000 apiece). Therefore, a low- to medium-budget film

20.24–20.26 Seventies mega-hits:

20.24 The dark side of American business: *The Godfather*
(Francis Ford Coppola, 1972). Robert Duvall, Marlon Brando.

20.26 High-tech fairy tale: *Star Wars* **(George Lucas, 1977).
Darth Vader (David Prowse) and Ben (Obi-Wan) Kenobi (Alec
Guinness).**

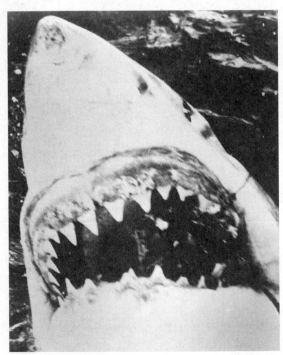

20.25 Primal fear of mutilation: *Jaws* **(Steven Spielberg,
1975). The great white shark.**

By 1975 it was not unusual for a single production
company like Paramount or 20th Century–Fox to have
all of its capital tied up in 5 or 6 films annually, every one
a potential blockbuster with an average budget of $4 mil-
lion to $7 million (compare this figure with MGM's aver-
age of 42 features per year during the 1930s). In 1977 at
least one company (Columbia) had all of its capital,
reportedly $20 million, invested in a single film (*Close
Encounters of the Third Kind*, which it cost another $9
million in leveraged funds to advertise), and production
budgets of $15 million to $20 million became common
in the 1980s. Francis Ford Coppola's *Apocalypse Now*
(1979) and Robert Wise's *Star Trek* (1979) topped the list
at $40 million and $42 million, respectively. The combined production costs of *Superman, Parts I* and *II* (Richard Donner, 1978; Richard Lester, 1980) are estimated
to have been more than $60 million. The profits reaped
by a success like *Jaws* or *Star Wars* could be immense,[6]

toward the production of fewer and fewer films with
every year that passed until the end of the decade, plus
a steady increase in the amount spent on advertising and
marketing campaigns designed to ensure the films' success, these expenditures often rising as high as twice the
production costs.

($750,000 to $3 million in the mid-1970s) was once regarded as a success if it returned four times its negative cost. This calculation went
haywire in the late 1970s, with big-budget features like *Star Wars*
recouping as much as two hundred times their initial investment. The
gross that returns to the producer-distributor—which determines all
profits—represents what remains after the exhibitors have taken their
cut. According to *Variety* for October 22, 1980, the average production
cost per feature rose to $10 million, with another $6 million in average
marketing costs—this, exclusive of another $24 million per feature in
national distribution costs. In 1980, in other words, the average American film had to earn $40 million simply to return its investment. By
1988, these figures had doubled.

6. As of January 1, 1993, *Jaws* had grossed $216 million and *Star Wars*
$323 million in the domestic market alone, making them the tenth and

but a single big-budget flop could threaten the solvency of an entire studio. This condition clearly inhibited the creative freedom of people working within the industry, especially since it became common practice for producers, directors, writers, and stars to receive a percentage of the net and/or gross profits of their films as well as a smaller fixed salary, or fee-for-service. It also created a hit-or-miss mentality among film executives who, as Leo Janos writes, were "trapped between the need to reap huge, ever-increasing profits and the absence of any body of professional knowledge or skill that can guarantee a hit."[7] In this volatile fiscal environment, it was almost impossible for a new writer or director to be given a chance to work on an even modestly expensive—$7 million to $10 million—film. The fact that in 1978 there were approximately 3,000 filmmakers competing to make about 70 major films provides an index of the limitations this situation placed upon contemporary American cinema.

Exacerbating these constraints is the fact that during the financial and social turbulence of the 1960s most of the established Hollywood studios allowed themselves to be absorbed by huge conglomerates. Universal was acquired in 1962 by Music Corporation of America (MCA, Inc.); Paramount in 1966 by Gulf & Western Industries (whose holdings at the time included firms supplying natural resources, agricultural products, and financial services); United Artists in 1967 by Transamerica Corporation; Warner Bros. (later reincorporated as Warner Communications, Inc., or WCI) in 1969 by the vastly diversified Kinney Services; and MGM in 1970 by the Las Vegas financier Kirk Kerkorian, who liquidated much of the studio's real estate at a huge profit, which he reinvested in resort hotels. (MGM re-emerged as a major force in the motion-picture industry in 1981, when Kerkorian bought United Artists from Transamerica in the wake of the *Heaven's Gate* disaster, forming MGM/UA Entertainment in 1983.) For most of these conglomerates, film and television production initially accounted for only a small percentage of their annual revenues. In 1977, for example, the entire "Leisure Time" division of Gulf & Western—which then owned several publishing companies and major sports franchises in addition to Paramount—accounted for less than 11 percent of total corporate income. But as Anthony Hoffman, entertainment analyst for the investment firm of Bache Halsey Stuart Shields, remarked at the time: "One thing that is obvious about this industry, and what has attracted the conglomerates to it in the first place, is that if you take

any recent four- or five-year period, and you match total investment in production costs with pre-tax profits, it is not unusual to come up with average rates of return of 40 to 50 percent. . . . No other industry has that rate of return, particularly one that has such a low asset base."

Given this compelling reason for conglomeration, only 20th Century–Fox, Columbia Pictures Industries, and the family-owned Walt Disney Productions, together with its wholly owned distributor, Buena Vista, remained in the control of veteran film-industry management at the end of the 1970s.[8] But, continuing this trend, Fox was purchased in 1981 by the Denver oil millionaire Marvin Davis, who sold it to the international newspaper baron Rupert Murdoch in 1985; the following year Murdoch merged the studio with the Metromedia Television group to form Fox, Inc. and its subsidiary Fox Broadcasting Company. Today, Fox is an important part of News Corporation (News Corp.), Murdoch's powerful global media cartel. Columbia was acquired in 1982 by the Coca-Cola Company as part of its entertainment division, and in 1985 Turner Broadcasting Systems (TBS) bought MGM/UA from Kirk Kerkorian in order to acquire MGM's vast film library (over 3,300 titles, which include both the RKO and the pre-1949 Warners libraries) for its superstations. Turner then resold MGM/UA to Kerkorian and in 1986 sold the MGM Culver City studio and laboratory facilities to Lorimar-Telepictures. (In 1993 Turner

---

third top-grossing films of all time (and Fox estimated that over $500 million worth of *Star Wars* toys were sold between the film's opening on May 25, 1977, and January 1, 1980). The films were produced for $8 million and $10 million, respectively. Some idea of what this means financially to the filmmakers is provided by the fact that Richard Zanuck, the producer of *Jaws*, has made more money from his share of that film's profits than his father, the veteran producer Darryl F. Zanuck, made in his entire career.

7. More and more, however, production companies are resorting to the sophisticated demographic and psychographic techniques of contemporary market research to discover what the public wants to see and then to "pre-sell" it.

8. Even before they were purchased by larger interests, both Columbia and Fox were rapidly diversifying. In 1977, Columbia drew 46 percent of its income from feature-film production and the rest from television production and recording industry and broadcasting activities. During the same period, 20th Century–Fox earned 63 percent of its annual income from film production and the rest from similarly diversified acquisitions, including Coca-Cola Bottling Midwest and Aspen Skiing Corporation. In 1979, profits from *Star Wars* enabled Fox to acquire for $72 million the Pebble Beach Corporation, which owns several fashionable resorts and golf courses on the Monterey peninsula.

formed his own production company, Turner Pictures, and bought both Castle Rock Entertainment and New Line Cinema.)

Another convulsion of merger mania took place at the decade's end, when in 1990 MGM/UA was taken over by Pathé Communications Corporation (formerly Cannon Entertainment—see p. 834), an Italian media conglomerate headed by Giancarlo Paretti, who appointed the Israeli-born producer Yoram Globus as president. As MGM-Pathé Communications, the new company went through several abrupt changes in management, including the ousting of Paretti in 1991, and was acquired in 1992 by the French bank Crédit Lyonnais; the name Metro-Goldwyn-Mayer, Inc., was then restored, while UA remained moribund, but the company's financial future remained uncertain until it was sold back to Kirk Kerkorian's Trancinda Corporation in 1995. In 2001, MGM reanimated UA as a specialty film division and moved its headquarters to New York. In 1989 Warner Communications acquired Lorimar and merged with Time, Inc., owner of HBO, Cinemax, and many other holdings, to form Time Warner, Inc.—the world's largest communications company, which became even larger when it merged with America Online (AOL), the world's biggest internet service provider, to become Time Warner–AOL in 2000. Columbia merged with TriStar to become Columbia Pictures Entertainment in 1987, which was then acquired by Japan's Sony Corporation in 1989 and renamed as Sony Pictures Entertainment in 1991 (Columbia and TriStar function as self-contained producer-distributors under the Sony umbrella). In 1990 MCA, Inc., and with it Universal Pictures, was purchased by Japan's Matsushita Electrical Industrial Corporation; and Gulf & Western spun off its financial-services unit to become Paramount Communications, Inc. in order to concentrate exclusively on its media holdings, which included Paramount Pictures, broadcast stations and cable systems, and publishers like Simon & Schuster. In 1994 Paramount merged with Viacom (owner of MTV, Nickelodeon, and Showtime/The Movie Channel) to become one of the world's leading producer-distributors of filmed entertainment, cable programming, and published information. In 1995, Matsushita sold 80 percent of MCA to the Canadian conglomerate Seagram Co., which had also acquired a 15 percent share in Time Warner in 1993; and the Walt Disney Company acquired Capital Cities/ABC Inc. to become the largest entertainment and distribution company in the country. In 1994 a new major, Dreamworks SKG, was founded by Steven Spielberg, Jeffrey Katzenberg, and David Geffen with the intention of becoming "the digital studio of the 21st century"—a promise it has largely fulfilled (see Chapter 21); Dreamworks handles its own US theatrical distribution and releases internationally through Universal/MCA (a function of Spielberg's long-term relationship with the older studio).

The upheavals and mergers of the 1970s and 1980s changed the American film industry in fundamental ways. From 1975 on, the majors began to curtail production, deliberately limiting the supply of motion pictures, and cast their fates with a handful of calculated blockbusters. They learned that a *Godfather* (1972), a *Jaws* (1975) or a *Star Wars* (1977)—with domestic rentals (i.e., returns to distributors)[9] of $86.3 million, $129.5 million, and $193.5 million, respectively—could carry a company for years; and marketing, a secondary consideration during the studio era, when the majors controlled exhibition, became an essential component of the blockbuster strategy. Average negative costs rose more than 500 percent during the 1970s, and by the end of the decade it often cost more to sell a film than to produce it. No longer the primary suppliers of motion pictures, the majors became financiers and distributors of films produced by others through ad hoc, agent-packaged deals. By the end of the decade, the majors once again dominated domestic and international markets, including the new medium of video and new "franchise" concepts like *Star Wars, Superman*, and *Alien*, whose life could extend through multiple sequels and product licenses. (Home-video license fees, non-existent in 1969, accounted for less than $9 million before

---

9. Gross receipts are the total amount of money a film takes in at the box office; rentals are the percentage of the gross that the exhibitor pays to the distributor to rent the film, excluding his own percentage under the terms of the licensing agreement (normally 30 to 45 percent on a sliding scale, but as little as 10 percent for blockbusters), taxes, and theater operating expenses known as the "house nut." During the 1970s, total film rental represented 30 to 50 percent of the gross, and the average today is less than 50 percent of the gross. Grosses are the best index of a film's popularity, while rentals are a more significant gauge of its profitability to the producer-distributor. (In two oft-quoted examples, *The Sound of Music* [1965] grossed $135 million but returned "only" $80 million in rentals; *Easy Rider* [1960] grossed $50 million and returned $19 million. However, *Easy Rider* was much more profitable than *The Sound of Music* in relative terms since its rentals represented more than 50 times its negative cost of $375,000, whereas *The Sound of Music*'s were slightly less than ten times its negative cost of $8.2 million).

the resolution of *Universal v. Sony/Betamax*[1] in October 1979, but by 1985 the sale of movies on videocassette would be worth $4.55 billion, exclusive of rentals.) In fact, 1980—the watershed year of conglomeration—was the most lucrative year in industry history before 1987, and new producer-distributor organizations like Orion (1978), the Ladd Company (1979), and Tri-Star (1982) sprang up on either side of it. But it is also true that during the 1970s, fewer than 80 major films were produced each year out of an average total output of 160 (compared with a record 538 in 1937 and 513 in 1988 [many of these, however, for direct release to video]), and there arose serious questions about the creative vitality of the American cinema.

NEW FILMMAKERS OF THE SEVENTIES AND EIGHTIES

Yet some critics have claimed that Hollywood—far from declining in creativity—actually experienced a renaissance of creative talent in the 1970s as a result of the many young directors then working in the industry who were professionally trained at American film schools. Most new directors of the 1960s—Penn, Peckinpah, Irvin Kershner, John Frankenheimer, Sidney Lumet—had been trained in the medium of television, and the modes of teleproduction that they knew best emphasized economy, flexibility, and speed. As with the *cinéastes* of the French New Wave, some of their best films bore the mark of spontaneous improvisation. Many new directors of the 1970s and 1980s, on the other hand, had studied film history, aesthetics, and production as formal academic subjects in university graduate-school programs. Francis Ford Coppola (b. 1939) and the screenwriter/director Paul Schrader (b. 1946) went to film school at UCLA; George Lucas (b. 1944) and the screenwriter/director John Milius (b. 1944) graduated from the University of Southern California; Martin Scorsese (b. 1942) and Brian De Palma (b. 1940) attended New York University; Steven Spielberg (b. 1946) studied film and dramatic arts at California State; others, like Peter Bogdanovich (b. 1939) and William Friedkin (b. 1935), had been documentarists and critics before making their first features. This highly specialized training produced a generation of American filmmakers whose visual and technical sophistication was immense but whose films were sometimes so painstakingly calculated for effect as to lack spontaneity.

Coppola, for example, is unquestionably a major American filmmaker; the first two films in his epic trilogy of organized crime in the United States, *The Godfather* (1972) and *The Godfather, Part II* (1974), are among the most significant American films of the decade. But there is something about *The Conversation* (1974), like De Palma's *Blow Out* (1981), that makes it all too obviously a remake of Antonioni's *Blow-Up* (1966) in audio electronics terms. George Lucas's *Star Wars* (1977) is important historically because of its unprecedented use of computer technology to generate special photographic and auditory effects,[2] but it is also a film intensely manipulative of its audience's perception. There is no room for interpretation or speculation in *Star Wars*: everyone who sees it has more or less the same experience. The same might be said of Steven Spielberg's *Jaws* (1975) and *Close Encounters of the Third Kind* (1977), both technically polished, but so calculated in terms of effect that they have all the predictability of a Big Mac hamburger. Scorsese's *Mean Streets* (1973) is a strikingly original independent feature; but *Taxi Driver* (1976) exploits the paranoid alienation it pretends to examine; and *New York, New York* (1977), a meticulously studied effort to re-create the musicals of the Big Band era, seems more like a scholarly article than a feature film. Finally, Brian De Palma, who directed some of the most stylish and effective horror thrillers of the period (*Sisters*, 1973; *Phantom of the Paradise*, 1974; *Obsession*, 1975; *Carrie*, 1976; *The Fury*, 1978), admits that he approaches film from a scientific point of view and says that he tends to equate filmmaking with "building machines." All of these extremely talented

---

1. Sony introduced the first consumer-grade half-inch videocassette recorder (VCR), the Betamax SL-7300, into the American market in 1976, which was followed several months later by JVC's competing VHS format. Sony initially promoted the Betamax as a "time-shifting" technology, enabling the recording of TV programs for subsequent playback; but the majors, led by Disney and Universal, filed suit against Sony for copyright infringement in November 1976, charging that the Betamax primarily enabled illicit copying of broadcast movies. By the time the case was decided for the defendants in October 1979, U.S. sales of VCRs has passed the 1 million mark, and most of the majors had laid plans to license movies for sale on prerecorded cassettes in order to profit from their own defeat. Furthermore, at the same time, the Beta format was being supplanted in the consumer market by VHS, whose resolution was lower and, therefore, less threatening to Hollywood's theatrical sales.

2. *Star Wars* was the first widely released film to be both recorded and exhibited in Dolby stereo optical sound (Dolby SR). (See the footnote on page 865.)

20.27–20.28 Francis Ford Coppola:

20.29–20.32 Martin Scorsese, from realism to academism:

20.27 *The Godfather, Part II* (Francis Ford Coppola, 1974): Robert De Niro as the young Vito Corleone in Sicily.

20.29 *Mean Streets* (1973).

20.28 *Apocalypse Now* (1979): Marlowe's patrol boat reaches the remote jungle outpost of Colonel Kurtz.

20.30 *New York, New York* (1977): Robert De Niro, Liza Minnelli.

film-school–trained directors have produced works of distinction—some of near genius. Yet even in their best work—say, Coppola's *Apocalypse Now* (1979), Scorsese's *Raging Bull* (1980), De Palma's *Dressed to Kill* (1980), or, more recently, Coppola's *Bram Stoker's Dracula* (1992), Scorsese's *Cape Fear* (1991), and De Palma's *Carlito's Way* (1993)—there is at times an almost academic preoccupation with cinematic effect and audience response. Furthermore, the unevenness that has characterized their careers from the beginning continued into the 1990s, producing both respectable failures like Coppola's *The Godfather, Part III* (1990) and unmitigated dis-

asters like De Palma's *The Bonfire of the Vanities* (1990), as well as works of mind-numbing aesthetic refinement like Scorsese's *The Age of Innocence* (1993). More recently, they have lapsed into repetition and self-parody: De Palma's *Snake Eyes* (1998) exists almost exclusively to display its 10-minute opening sequence shot and *Mission to Mars* (2000) is a showcase of bravura special-effects shots without a coherent theme; Scorsese's *Casino* (1995)

20.31 *Cape Fear* (1991): Robert De Niro as Max Cady.

20.33 *Phantom of the Paradise* (Brian De Palma, 1974): William Finley in a rock version of the gothic classic.

20.32 *The Age of Innocence* (1993): Michelle Pfeiffer, Michael Gough, Alexis Smith, Kevin Sanders.

20.34 Sissy Spacek as the telekinetic teenager in *Carrie* (Brian De Palma, 1976).

is an extension of *Goodfellas* (1990), and his *Bringing Out the Dead* (1999) is an unwatchable variant of *After Hours* (1985); and after the terribly unfunny Robin Williams comedy *Jack* (1996), Coppola functioned mainly as an executive producer, whose only creative work was literally a rehash of his last important film, *Apocalypse Now Redux* (2001). Their attitude toward their profession was nicely described by Vincent Canby in the 1970s when he wrote of "major contemporary American filmmakers who, more and more, tend to put films together with such deliberation you might think that instead of making movies they were building arks to save mankind." The apotheosis of this phenomenon in the 1990s was clearly Steven Spielberg's *Schindler's List* (1993), in which the technical brilliance wasted on sophomoric entertainments like *Indiana Jones and the Temple of Doom* (1984) and *Hook* (1991) was finally turned to a truly serious purpose—but in a no less calculated manner than it was in his *Jurassic Park*, produced the same year. By focusing on the worst act of genocide in human history to date, Spielberg indemnified the appeal of his project in a thoroughly legitimate way, and its success brought him the cultural prestige that had eluded him for decades. Moreover, the universal accolades for his holocaust epic effectively concealed the fact that since 1945 hundreds of less spectacular but no less serious films had been made on the subject in the United States, Europe, and the Soviet Union, creating the popular impression that *Schindler's List* had originated one of the cinema's most sober genres. Spielberg's *The Lost World: Jurassic Park* (1997) and *Saving Private Ryan* (1998) seemed to confirm his reputation for adolescent fantasy and adult sentimentality, respectively (although *Private Ryan* contained an astonishingly violent rendition of the Normandy beachhead landing, as powerful as the clearing of the Warsaw Ghetto sequence in *Schindler's List*). But *A.I.: Artificial Intelligence* (2001) and *Minority Report* (2002) were riskier ventures altogether—the former adapted from a screen treatment by Stanley Kubrick about a robot boy who acquires human feeling, and the latter adapted from a distopic science-fiction thriller by Philip K. Dick dealing with precognition and mind control in 2054.

Perhaps the most important filmmaker working within the American commercial system during the 1970s—as his own producer, through Lion's Gate Films, from 1971 to 1981—was Robert Altman (b. 1925). Altman came to film from television, where he directed episodes of *Alfred Hitchcock Presents, Combat!, Bonanza*, and *Bus Stop*. His first major feature was *M*A*S*H* (1970), an iconoclastic comedy set in a mobile army surgical hospital during the Korean War, which became the basis for the popular television series. The film is characterized by a subversive combination of humor and gore, and it makes effective use of the wide-angle Panavision compositions and overlapping dialogue for which Altman has become justly famous. While *M*A*S*H* had a tough, absurdist edge and set new standards for the melding of cruelty, violence, and humor, it never pretended to be more than a hip service comedy. *Brewster McCloud* (1970), on the other hand, is a deliberate venture into social satire and Altman's personal favorite among his films. It concerns a young man who is preparing for a bird flight in the Houston Astrodome under the tutelage of a bird-woman mentor named Louise. McCloud must avoid sex, which binds him to earth, and must kill a number of reactionary characters in order to realize his dream of total freedom through flight, an equation perfectly made by Altman through subjective aerial photography. Some critics thought the film eccentric nonsense, but Andrew Sarris was closer to the mark when he called it "the first American film to apply an appropriate tone and style to the absurdist follies of our times."

20.35 *Close Encounters of the Third Kind* (Steven Spielberg, 1977): one of Douglas Trumbull's predigital special effects; cinematography by Vilmos Zsigmond.

20.36 The "last supper" for Painless the dentist in *M*A*S*H*. (Robert Altman, 1970): Carl Gottlieb, David Arkin, Tom Skerritt, John Schuck (Painless), Donald Sutherland (Hawkeye), and Elliott Gould (Trapper John).

McCabe & Mrs. Miller (1971), Altman's next film, has become increasingly interesting in light of his later work. Beautifully photographed on location in British Columbia by Vilmos Zsigmond, who "flashed" the negative stock to give the film a tinted, old-fashioned look,[3] it is about a small-time gambler and (by his own account) gunfighter near the turn of the century who founds the town of Presbyterian Church. With the aid of an enterprising brothel madam, he helps the town grow and prosper until representatives of a large mining conglomerate approach him and attempt to buy him out. Always something of a buffoon beneath his self-confident exterior, McCabe actually believes in the free-enterprise system, and he refuses to sell his interest in the town. Naturally, agents are sent to kill him, and after a seriocomic gun battle he is shot to death in the snow. The film ends with a slow zoom into the constricted pupil of Mrs. Miller as she lies in bed stoned on opium after the murder, suggesting an option that many Americans have chosen in order to avoid confronting the brutality of our economic system.

After *Images* (1972), an experimental feature that attempted rather unsuccessfully to probe the mind of a schizophrenic, Altman made his most cinematically elegant film, an updated version of Raymond Chandler's fifties detective novel *The Long Goodbye* (1973). Shot by Zsigmond on location in Los Angeles and Malibu, the film is less a detective story than a sardonic comment on contemporary American narcissism drenched in the languid and decadent atmosphere of southern California. Philip Marlowe, an unsuccessful private detective, helps a friend who is accused of murdering his wife and defends him staunchly, only to discover that the friend actually committed the crime and has used Marlowe shamelessly

to avoid detection. Marlowe, whose throwaway line throughout the film has been "It's OK with me," is finally backed up against something that's not OK, not even in the modern Babylon of Los Angeles, and he tracks his friend to his hideaway in Mexico and shoots him. *The Long Goodbye* was Altman's most visually elaborate film before *3 Women* (1977), and it makes striking thematic use of Zsigmond's wide-angle and telephoto zoom shots.

Thieves Like Us (1974), Altman's entry in the *Bonnie and Clyde* category, is adapted from the same novel as Nicholas Ray's *They Live by Night* (1949). It deals with three prison escapees during the Depression who set out on a spree of bank robbing, become notorious, and are finally killed by the police. *California Split* (1974), Altman's first film to use the proprietary Lion's Gate eight-track wireless sound system, is an episodic story about compulsive gambling set in Las Vegas which, like *Thieves Like Us*, is ultimately about American rootlessness. But it was in *Nashville* (1975) that Altman made his most telling comment on the nature of American society.

Nearly three hours long[4] and recorded in Lion's Gate eight-track stereo, with individually controlled wireless microphones on seven of the principal players plus one track for background noise (all using the Dolby noise-reduction [NR] system),[5] *Nashville* is set in the present and has no plot in the traditional sense. It concerns the lives of twenty-four separate characters in the five-day period preceding a rally to be given at the city's Par-

20.37 From the final frames of *The Long Goodbye* (Robert Altman, 1973): Marlowe (Elliott Gould) does a soft-shoe down a dusty Mexican road as the soundtrack plays "Hooray for Hollywood."

3. "Flashing" or "fogging" was used by a number of innovative cinematographers during the 1970s to achieve this effect. It involved exposing the negative briefly to white light in a printer before or after exposure in the camera, which produces a speed increase as well as desaturates the color. Zsigmond used the process to achieve the same effect for Michael Cimino's *Heaven's Gate* (1980). Other notable uses of flashing during this era occur in Conrad Hall's cinematography for *Butch Cassidy and the Sundance Kid* (George Roy Hill, 1969) and Haskell Wexler's for *Bound for Glory* (Hal Ashby, 1976), both period films.

4. Various rough cuts of *Nashville* ran between 6 and 8 hours. A 4-hour version was released theatrically, withdrawn, and pared to 161 minutes. There were plans to show the 8-hour version as a miniseries on television, but as of 1990 only a heavily edited theatrical print had been aired (on *The ABC Sunday Night Movie*). *Nashville* is available on videocassette, as are most of the works discussed in this book.

5. Dolby NR, which reduces background noise and increases frequency response, was the forerunner of dolby stereo optical sound. It was developed by Ray Dolby in the Dolby Laboratories during the 1960s for use in the recording industry and was later applied to the movies. Dolby stereo optical was innovated in the early 1970s as a way of bringing stereo sound to theaters that did not have expensive stereo magnetic equipment—which was the vast majority of them—by squeezing left

thenon for the "Replacement party" presidential candidate, Hal Philip Walker (whose ironic campaign slogan is "New Roots for the Nation"). The characters all come from different walks of life, but they have one thing in common: all are seeking either to become or to remain celebrities in the world of country music and, by extension, of American mass-mediated culture at large. Their individual lives coalesce at the political rally that concludes the film, where a young assassin who has come there to kill Walker kills one of the celebrities instead. As Pauline Kael has remarked, *Nashville* is "a country-and-Western musical; a documentary essay on Nashville and American life; a meditation on the love affair between performers and audiences; and an Altman party." But *Nashville* is also a film about the ways in which our national entertainment media and our national politics— all but indistinguishable from one another—work constantly to distract us from the massive inequalities of our society and the violence of our recent national past. Altman finds many American virtues to admire, but the most important theme of *Nashville* is how quickly we forget and gloss over such things as the terrible public violence of the 1960s and the human consequences of the war in Vietnam. Its most urgent comment is that we Americans, in our blind pursuit of success and our compulsive need for social change, are leading unexamined lives.

Nashville was Altman's bicentennial birthday present to the United States. Such was the high-risk mentality of Hollywood in the 1970s that though the film returned $9.3 million,[6] it nonetheless was deemed a commercial failure. But Altman continued to produce original and

20.38 *Nashville* **(Robert Altman, 1975): Barbara Harris as Albuquerque.**

sophisticated films. *Buffalo Bill and the Indians* (1976) is, like *Nashville*, an attack on the hypocrisy and exploitativeness of American "show biz" as reflected in the way in which the title character sustains his own popular myth in his dealings with Chief Sitting Bull. From this completely plotless film, Altman moved confidently into the realm of dreams with *3 Women* (1977), which deals with the nature of the female psyche in surrealistic terms. The film begins as a social satire with a strong subtext of mythic imagery and becomes progressively more allusive

and right channel tracks into the space on the film strip normally occupied by the monaural optical track. Thus, an unconverted projector could run a stereo optical track and still generate a mono-compatible signal, but a theater that chose to convert its projectors for the relatively modest price of $5,000 would get two-channel stereo, with a third channel, synthesized by a "Dolby Cinema Processor" from the left and right track signals, sent to the center speaker. (Most 35mm theaters at the time deployed three speakers behind the screen—left, right, and center—all fed by a single-channel monaural track.) This system, Dolby SR, produced multitrack stereo sound that was virtually indistinguishable from four-track stereo magnetic sound and brought high-fidelity stereo within the reach of most exhibitors for the first time. Going a step further, Dolby developed a way of adding information to the optical track at the mixing stage via "stereo matrix" circuitry that encoded it onto the two-track signal; the matrix was then decoded by the Dolby Cinema Processor to create a fourth channel that could be sent to speakers positioned around the auditorium's side and back walls to "surround" the audience with sound. Thus was born Dolby surround sound, which

got its first serious workout on the sound track for George Lucas's *Star Wars* (1977), specially designed to demonstrate the dynamic range of the new system. The general release prints for this film were Dolby-encoded stereo optical with a surround track, making *Star Wars* the first film to be both recorded and released in four-channel Dolby stereo. Research by Twentieth Century–Fox indicated that Dolby-equipped theaters significantly outgrossed non-Dolby ones on the film's initial release, and by the end of 1977 nearly 200 theaters had converted to Dolby, and five of the season's biggest releases carried Dolby tracks. Another 800 theaters were equipped by the end of 1978, and by 1985 virtually every American film was released in Dolby format, which became standard industry practice until the advent of digital sound tracks in the 1990s, also pioneered by Dolby (although Dolby SRD had to share the market with several other proprietary systems, notably Sony's Dynamic Digital Sound [SDDS] and Universal's Digital Theater Sound [DTS]—see Chapter 21).

6. The remarkably low production cost was $2.2 million.

and mysterious until it transforms itself completely in the concluding sequences, which are surely among the most unusual in contemporary American cinema.

From the irreverent humor of *M*°*A*°*S*°*H* to the film dreaming of *3 Women*, Robert Altman proved himself to be one of the most innovative American filmmakers of the past thirty years. But near the end of this period he stumbled badly with *A Wedding* (1978), *Quintet* (1979), and *A Perfect Couple* (1979). He then made two highly original films—the political satire *H.E.A.L.T.H.* (1980) and the musical *Popeye* (1980), starring Robin Williams in the title role—both of which were savagely panned by the critics. At this point, Altman turned to theater, filming Ed Graczyk's *Come Back to the Five and Dime, Jimmy Dean, Jimmy Dean* (1982) in Super 16mm; David Rabe's *Streamers* (1983) in 35mm; and both *Secret Honor* (a one-man show featuring the ravings of a post resignation Richard M. Nixon, made while Altman was a visiting professor at the University of Michigan in 1984) and Marsha Norman's *The Laundromat* (1985) in video for HBO. Toward the end of the decade, Altman filmed theatrical adaptations of Sam Shepard's *Fool for Love* (1986) and Christopher Durang's *Beyond Therapy* (1987), and shot a series of unique political docudramas for HBO entitled *Tanner '88*, which followed an imaginary candidate for the Democratic presidential nomination (played by Michael Murphy) from month to month as the actual 1988 primaries were taking place. He also worked again for television, adapting Herman Wouk's 1953 play *The Caine Mutiny Court-Martial*[7] for CBS in 1988 and directing for European broadcast a four-hour miniseries on the relationship between Vincent van Gogh and his brother, which he recut for theatrical release as *Vincent & Theo* (1990).

Critically admired, Altman's 1980s films[8] seemed to have lost touch with the mass audience, but in 1992 he returned to mainstream box-office success quite unexpectedly with *The Player*. Scripted by Michael Tolkin from his own novel, this dark satire of contemporary Hollywood concerns a studio executive who murders a writer and gets away with it—a paradigm for the workings of the studio system ad infinitum. The film is a directorial tour de force, crammed full of hilarious star cameos and inside jokes, but it succeeds mainly in Altman's exquisitely precise sense of the moral corruption at the film industry's core. *Short Cuts* (1993) extends the metaphor to southern California (and, by extension, the nation) at large. Adapted by Altman from the short stories of Raymond Carver, it is a sort of *Nashville*

for the 1990s—a 189-minute mosaic of critical moments in the lives of six Los Angeles couples and assorted others, culminating in an earthquake (a "typical" American catastrophe, like the earlier film's political assassination). Altman charts the intersecting courses of these multiple characters—who are all alternately venal, predatory, weak, irresponsible, and entirely human—to create a panorama of life in the 1990s, when the amoral cynicism of the bad guys in *The Long Goodbye* had become a kind of lingua franca for the American middle class. Closer in spirit to *H.E.A.L.T.H* than *Nashville*, *Ready to Wear* (*Prêt-a-porter*, 1994), featuring an ensemble of thirty-one players, is a documentary-like extravaganza that satirizes the world of high fashion. Altman made his share of potboilers during the 1990s, including the period crime drama *Kansas City* (1996) and the neo-*noir* thriller *The Gingerbread Man* (1998) from an original script by novelist John Grisham; neither film was particularly distinguished although each had elements of interest (the latter, e.g., was shot on location in Savannah by Chen Kaige's regular cinematographer, Changwei Gu). Two quirky comedies—*Cookie's Fortune* (1999) and *Dr. T & the Women* (2000)—also failed with both audiences and critics. But *Gosford Park* (2001) demonstrated Altman's amazing resilience in an elegant and witty murder mystery that dissects the British class system circa 1932. With equal devotion to period detail, astute social observation, and brilliant ensemble playing, this film comes close in both spirit and execution to Renoir's *La Règle de jeu* (1939), and it stands among Altman's finest achievements.

Like many of his European counterparts during the 1970s, Altman progressively abandoned conventional narrative to develop his own highly personal style. Certain hallmarks make an Altman film of the era easy to identify: the overlapping dialogue and experimental use of sound; the sardonic humor; the visual lushness and density based on an uncommonly perceptive use of the wide-angle and telephoto zoom lenses; the intriguingly unusual faces of his repertory company (Shelley Duvall, Michael Murphy,

---

7. This play was adapted by Wouk from his own best-selling Pulitzer Prize-winning novel, *The Caine Mutiny* (1951), which was itself filmed by Edward Dmytryk in 1954.

8. These include several short telefilms (e.g., *The Dumb Waiter* and *The Room*, both 1987), the "Les Boréades" segment of the omnibus opera film *Aria* (1988), and the feature *O.C. and Stiggs* (1983; released 1987), which Altman also produced.

20.39 *Gosford Park* (Robert Altman, 2001). Part of Altman's brilliant ensemble cast, assembled in the drawing room before dinner.

Bert Remsen, etc.). It is argued that style sometimes takes precedence over substance in these films, but it seems more accurate to suggest that in works like *3 Women*, style and substance have finally become indistinguishable. In the 1970s, Altman saw us with our raw nerves exposed at a time in American history when the conflicting demands of community and individual freedom were never more extreme, and he became an epic poet of that conflict. But in the 1980s, he was out of step, making *H.E.A.L.T.H.* rather than *Terms of Endearment* (James L. Brooks, 1983), *Popeye* rather than *E.T.* (Steven Spielberg, 1982), and maintaining consistently that movies are for adults as well as teenagers. After a brief detour into theater, Altman re-emerged in the 1990s with his aesthetic and moral vision fully intact to produce *The Player* and *Short Cuts*, two of his most challenging essays in social criticism, and he began the new century with one of his most aesthetically satisfying films to date in *Gosford Park*. Problems of artistic consistency (and they do exist) notwithstanding, Altman throughout his career has made the most intellectually honest films about the American experience of any director since Orson Welles. During the Reagan-Bush years, when intellectual integrity went out of fashion (not that it has necessarily returned), he briefly found himself without an audience. Unlike Welles, however, Altman typically works with more economy and discipline than his contemporaries, and his strong comeback in the 1990s has already fulfilled Gary Arnold's prediction of 1976: that by the time

he retires, Altman will be the only American filmmaker of his generation with as many major films to his credit as the directors who worked in Hollywood during its Golden Age.

THE AMERICAN FILM INDUSTRY IN THE AGE OF "KIDPIX"

The 1980s began with the single largest financial disaster ever to hit a major studio when Michael Cimino's $40 million adult Western, *Heaven's Gate* (1980), was withdrawn

20.40 Michael Cimino's ruinous *Heaven's Gate* (1980): Christopher Walken.

from distribution immediately following its release, amid critics' charges of incomprehensibility. Actually one of the decade's better films, this three-hour-and-forty-minute epic about the destruction of America's frontier due to ruthless capitalism nevertheless went down to perdition itself, taking United Artists as a corporate entity with it. In this context, it was probably inevitable that an industry which during the 1970s had enjoyed some of the greatest profits in its history from films targeted for children (*Star Wars*, 1977; *Close Encounters of the Third Kind*, 1977; *Superman*, 1978) and teenagers (*Saturday Night Fever*, 1977; *Grease*, 1978) would turn nearly wholesale to such productions in the wake of *Heaven's Gate*. Furthermore, the industry was now being run by corporate attorneys and accountants who lacked the experience of industry veterans, and who tended to rely on vehicles with proven track records (thus, to date, three *Rambos*, five *Star Wars*, four *Jaws*, five *Rockys*, and at least two of almost everything else) and on the viscerally sensational (that is, films containing graphic sex, violence, or, preferably, both combined).

An alarming manifestation of sex and violence was the flood of "psycho-slasher" films that glutted the domestic market in the wake of John Carpenter's ultrasuccessful *Halloween* (1978), an artful low-budget chiller that grossed $50 million on a $400,000 investment. The formula—confirmed by the record-breaking profits of the oafishly directed *Friday the 13th* (Sean S. Cunningham, 1980)—involves the serial murder of teenagers by a ruthless, unstoppable psychotic, with plenty of gratuitous sex and mayhem, and with realistic gore provided by high-tech makeup and special-effects artists like Dick Smith, Rob Bottin, and Tom Savini, who became stars in their own right. There were precedents for psycho-killer violence in Hitchcock's *Psycho* (1960) and Tobe Hooper's *The Texas Chainsaw Massacre* (1974), and the exploitation of gore had existed at the periphery of the industry for decades (for example, in the "splatter" movies of Herschell Gordon Lewis—*Blood Feast*, 1963; *Two Thousand Maniacs!*, 1964; *Color Me Blood Red*, 1964; and others). But slasher films took it fully into the R-rated mainstream in literally hundreds of *Halloween/Friday the 13th* spin-offs like *The Toolbox Murders* (Dennis Donnelly, 1979), *Driller Killer* (Abel Ferrara, 1979), *Prom Night* (Paul Lynch, 1980), *Terror Train* (Roger Spottiswoode, 1980), *Final Exam* (Jimmy Huston, 1981) *Hell Night* (Tom DeSimone, 1981), *Graduation Day* (Herb Freed, 1981),

20.41 Ur-slasher: *The Texas Chainsaw Massacre* (Tobe Hooper, 1974).

My Bloody Valentine (George Mihalka, 1981), *New Year's Evil* (Emmett Alston, 1981), *Deadly Blessing* (Wes Craven, 1981), *The Burning* (Tony Maylam, 1981), *Happy Birthday to Me* (J. Lee Thompson, 1981), *Night School* (Ken Hughes, 1981), *The Slumber Party Massacre* (Amy Jones, 1982), *Visiting Hours* (Jean-Claude Lord, 1982), *The Evil Dead* (Sam Raimi, 1983), *A Nightmare on Elm Street* (Wes Craven, 1984), and, of course, the interminable sequels and imitations. In fact, *Variety* reported 25 slashers among the 50 top-grossing films of 1981, a year in which slashers accounted for nearly 60 percent of all domestic releases. The wave of popularity peaked shortly thereafter, but slasher films remained a regular feature of the annual production schedule, and their porno-violent chic became obligatory for many mainstream horror films such as *Poltergeist* (Tobe Hooper, 1982), *The Hunger* (Tony Scott, 1983), *Fright Night* (Tom Holland, 1985), *Poltergeist II* (Brian Gibson, 1986); *The Serpent and the Rainbow* (Wes Craven, 1987), and *Pet Sematary* (Mary Lambert, 1989); for some science-fiction films, like *Aliens* (James Cameron, 1986), *RoboCop* (Paul Verhoeven, 1987), and *Total Recall* (Paul Verhoeven, 1990); and for many thrillers, such as *Body Double* (Brian De Palma, 1984), *Jagged Edge* (Richard Marquand, 1985), *Psycho III* (Anthony Perkins, 1986), *Angel Heart* (Alan Parker, 1987), *The Believers* (John Schlesinger, 1987), and *Blue Steel* (Kathryn Bigelow, 1989). Their grim social implications notwithstanding, slashers became an important staple of the home-video and **cable television** markets,

20.42 and 20.43 Porno-violent SF. *RoboCop* (Paul Verhoeven, 1987): Peter Weller; *Total Recall* (Paul Verhoeven, 1990): Arnold Schwarzenegger and mutant (growing out of Marshall Bell).

owing to the sheer number in which they were (and still are) produced. By the 1990s, their gore-drenched sensationalism had become a staple of tabloid television shows like *Hard Copy* and pervaded crime reporting on television news.

On a lighter note, science fiction/fantasy—which ran the gamut from Steven Spielberg's then-all-time box-office champ *E.T.: The Extra-Terrestrial* (1982) and its close second *Ghostbusters* (Ivan Reitman, 1984) and *Gremlins* (Joe Dante, 1984), to Lucasfilm's $35 million

fiasco *Howard the Duck* (William Huyck, 1986)—was pervasively present in the 1980s. So, too, was adventure/fantasy, in the vein of Spielberg's *Raiders of the Lost Ark* (1981), *Indiana Jones and the Temple of Doom* (1984), and *Indiana Jones and the Last Crusade* (1989), as well as in the sword-and-sorcery genre, popularized by *Dragonslayer* (Matthew Robbins, 1981), *Conan the Barbarian* (John Milius, 1982), *The Sword and the Sorcerer* (Albert Pyun, 1982), *Krull* (Peter Yates, 1983), *The Dark Crystal* (Jim Henson, 1983), *The BeastMaster* (Don Coscarelli, 1983), *Ladyhawke* (Richard Donner, 1985), and *Willow* (Ron Howard, 1988), a type that owed its appeal to the role-playing board game "Dungeons and Dragons." Most of these films were rated PG and relied heavily on action and special effects to attract an audience that cut across broad demographic groups. However, through a variety of tools, ranging from television to tie-ins, they were marketed mainly to young people. So, too, were the so-called "teenpix," a category of films created to exploit the PG-13 rating when it was instituted in 1984. This form had clear antecedents both during the 1980s (for example, *Little Darlings* [Ronald F. Maxwell, 1980]; *Fast Times at Ridgemont High* [Amy Heckerling, 1982]; *Valley Girl* [Martha Coolidge, 1983]) and in previous decades (for example, AIP's "Beach Blanket" cycle—see Chapter 12). Inspired by the financial success of the R-rated *Risky Business* (Paul Brickman) in 1983, filmmakers produced a glut of teen and preteen comedies with sexual/social themes over the next several years. Many were as forgettable as *Revenge of the Nerds* (Jeff Kanew, 1984), *Fraternity Vacation* (James Frawley, 1985), *Mischief* (Mel Damski, 1985), and *Better Off Dead* ("Savage" Steve Holland, 1985), but others were visually innovative, like *Tuff Turf* (Fritz Kiersch, 1985; shot by Willy Kurant, Godard's cinematographer on *Masculin féminin*) and *St. Elmo's Fire* (Joel Schumacher, 1985), or thought-provoking, like *The Flamingo Kid* (Garry Marshall, 1984), *The Karate Kid* (John G. Avildsen, 1984), and *Just One of the Guys* (Lisa Gottlieb, 1985). The master of intelligent teenpix in the 1980s was producer-director John Hughes (b.1950), whose *Sixteen Candles* (1984), *The Breakfast Club* (1985), *Weird Science* (1985), *Pretty in Pink* (directed by Howard Deutch, 1986), *Ferris Bueller's Day Off* (1986), and *Some Kind of Wonderful* (directed by Deutch, 1987) all show a fine grasp of the social anxieties created by the rigid class stratifications of American high schools. Indeed, so lucrative was the teen market in the mid-1980s that films like

20.44 Teenage wasteland: John Hughes's *The Breakfast Club* (1985). Molly Ringwald, Anthony Michael Hall, Emilio Estevez, Ally Sheedy, Judd Nelson.

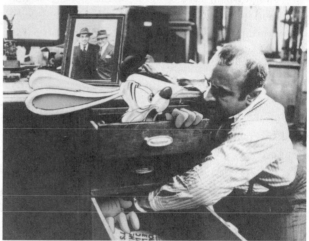

The Last Starfighter (Nick Castle, 1984) and *Back to the Future* (Robert Zemeckis, 1985), which combined teen comedy with other genres (in both cases, science fiction), became instant hits. Perhaps the apex (or nadir) of age regression was reached in this era by *Pee Wee's Big Adventure* (Tim Burton, 1985)—an admittedly hilarious, even brilliant, film—in which the infantile title character has a series of picaresque misadventures while searching for his stolen bicycle. Appropriately, the box-office smash of 1988 ($81.2 million in rentals) was Robert Zemeckis's *Who Framed Roger Rabbit*, a technically dazzling blend of live action and animation that was fundamentally a feature-length cartoon.

20.45 *Who Framed Roger Rabbit* (Robert Zemeckis, 1988): 'Toontown star Roger Rabbit linked to Bob Hoskins (see also Chapter 21).

THE EFFECTS OF VIDEO

While teenagers and their younger siblings were driving American box-office receipts toward an all-time high of $4.3 billion in 1987, their parents were at home watching the same movies on what used to be called television, for during the 1980s the fortunes of Hollywood were being affected by new technologies of video delivery and imaging as never before. Cable networks, direct broadcast satellites, and half-inch videocassettes provided unprecedented new means of motion-picture distribution. In addition, **computer-generated graphics** provided new means of production, especially in the realm of special effects, forecasting the arrival of a fully automated "electronic cinema." Some studios, like Columbia and Universal, devoted the majority of their schedules to the production of telefilm for the commercial networks, while

nearly all the studios began to presell their theatrical features for cable and videocassette distribution. Indeed, TriStar, one of the industry's major producer/distributors, currently owned by Sony Pictures Entertainment, began as a joint venture of CBS, Columbia Pictures, and Time, Inc.'s premium cable service, Home Box Office (HBO). And HBO and Showtime both function as producer/distributors themselves by directly financing feature films and entertainment specials for transmission by cable. Starting in 1985, independent film producers released more motion pictures than the major studios for the first time since the early decades of this century, so voracious had the cable and home-video markets become. In 1987, combined video rentals and sales totaled an astounding $7.2

billion ($4.4 billion in rentals; $2.8 billion in sales), or nearly twice that year's record-breaking income from theatrical rentals.

In terms of theatrical filmmaking, this penetration of video during the 1980s meant a step toward the demise of the normative 35mm feature, as producers sought properties, on the one hand, with video or "televisual" characteristics that would play well on the small screen or, on the other, that would draw audiences into the theaters with the promise of spectacular 70mm photography and multitrack Dolby sound. In the former category were such music-video–style films as *Flashdance* (Adrian Lyne, 1983), *Footloose* (Herbert Ross, 1984), *Streets of Fire* (Walter Hill, 1984), and *Dirty Dancing* (Emile Ardolino, 1987), all of which also cashed in on the teenpix phenomenon; and in the latter category were films like *Amadeus* (Milos Foreman, 1984), *Runaway Train* (Andrei Konchalovski, 1985), *The Color Purple* (Steven Spielberg, 1985), *Aliens* (James Cameron, 1986), *The Untouchables* (Brian De Palma, 1987), *Empire of the Sun* (Steven Spielberg, 1987), and *The Last Emperor* (Bernardo Bertolucci, 1987), whose maximum effect derives from visual and aural spectacle. Films like *Top Gun* (Tony Scott, 1986), structured as a feature-length music video but full of breathtaking aerial cinematography that can only be fully appreciated on a wide screen, managed to have it both ways—which is probably why it has to date earned over $177 million to become the fortieth highest-grossing American film in history to date. *Top Gun* also had the canniness to be a military film at a time when that long-buried genre was coming back into fashion.

20.47 *Top Gun* (Tony Scott, 1986): mixing music video, jingoism, and beefcake. Val Kilmer and Tom Cruise in the foreground, Rick Rossovich and Anthony Edwards to the rear.

Repressed culturally by ambivalent feelings about the Vietnam War and commercially by the middling box-office performance of such earlier Vietnam-themed films as *Go Tell the Spartans* (Ted Post, 1978), *Coming Home* (Hal Ashby, 1978), *Apocalypse Now* (Francis Ford Coppola, 1979),[9] the war film re-emerged like an exploding land mine when Oliver Stone's *Platoon* hit the screen in 1986. *Platoon* went on to become one of the highest-grossing American films of all times (twenty-sixth, in fact, in *Variety*'s 1988 survey, and still fifty-second in 1993). It was followed in rapid succession by a spate of Vietnam films of varying quality and political bias but obvious sincerity—*Gardens of Stone* (Francis Ford Coppola, 1987), *Hamburger Hill* (John Irvin, 1987), *Full Metal Jacket* (Stanley Kubrick, 1987), *Bat∗21* (Peter Markle, 1988), *Good Morning, Vietnam* (Barry Levinson, 1988), *Off Limits* (Christopher Crowe, 1988), the HBO-produced *War Stories* (1987) and *Dear America: Letters Home from Vietnam* (1988), *84 Charlie Mopic* (Patrick Duncan, 1989), and Brian De Palma's horrific *Casualties of War* (1989). Some other military films seemed less sincere, however, (like *Top Gun*, for example) as the studios responded to the patriotic climate of the Reagan years by producing their most jingoistic works since the Korean War. There were films that endorsed the myth of political betrayal in Vietnam—*Uncommon Valor* (Ted Kotcheff, 1983); *Rambo: First Blood, Part II* (George Pan Cosma-

20.46 *Aliens* (James Cameron, 1986): Sigourney Weaver and Carrie Henn in the egg chamber. Note the similarity with the shot in still 12.28 from *Them!* (Gordon Douglas, 1954).

---

9. Michael Cimino's *The Deer Hunter* (1979) was a smash hit in 1979, but it wasn't really about Vietnam, as any veteran will testify.

20.48 *Full Metal Jacket* (Stanley Kubrick, 1987).

20.49 New *film noir: Angel Heart* (Alan Parker, 1987): Mickey Rourke.

tos, 1985); *The Hanoi Hilton* (Lionel Chetwynd, 1987); that exploited fear of a Soviet invasion—*Invasion U.S.A.* (Joseph Zito, 1985); *Red Dawn* (John Milius, 1985); and that glorified military vigilantism—*Born American* (Renny Harlin, 1986); *Iron Eagle* (Sidney J. Furie, 1986).

Perhaps because there was so little recognizably adult fare in the theaters, films with a "literary" quality, many of them British-made, were also popular in the American market during the 1980s, as is typical of a period of political reaction—e.g., *Chariots of Fire* (Hugh Hudson, 1981); *Gandhi* (Richard Attenborough, 1982); *A Passage to India* (David Lean, 1984); *A Room with a View* (James Ivory, 1985); *Out of Africa* (Sydney Pollack, 1985). Another adult genre that appeared in the second half of the decade was *film noir*. More generally characteristic of moral confusion than a specific political condition, this film type had its first 1980s venue in the steamy and very nearly perfect *Body Heat* (1981), written and directed by Lawrence Kasdan, who would soon give America its first feature-length yuppie music video in *The Big Chill* (1983). After a lull of several years, *film noir* came back into its own as "neo-*noir*" in such well-made and intelligent films as *Black Widow* (Bob Rafelson, 1986), *Angel Heart* (Alan Parker, 1987), *Manhunter* (Michael Mann, 1986), *No Way Out* (Roger Donaldson, 1987), *Best Seller* (John Flynn, 1987), *Fatal Attraction* (Adrian Lyne, 1987), *Someone to Watch over Me* (Ridley Scott, 1987), *The Big Easy* (Jim McBride, 1987), *Into the Fire* (Graeme Campbell, 1987), *House of Games* (David Mamet, 1987), *Frantic* (Roman Polanski, 1988), *Masquerade* (Bob Swaim,

1988), *D.O.A.* (Rocky Morton, 1988), *True Believer* (Joseph Ruben, 1989), and *Sea of Love* (Harold Becker, 1989). This trend toward textbook reworkings of the dark 1940s genre continued strongly in the 1990s, when neo-noir became a major form of American film practice for first-time directors and veterans alike. Among the best entries of the early decade were 1990's *After Dark My Sweet* (James Foley) and *The Grifters* (Stephen Frears),

20.50 *Manhunter* (Michael Mann, 1986): William L. Petersen.

both based on Jim Thompson novels, *Bad Influence* (Curtis Hanson), *Internal Affairs* (Mike Figgis), *Kill Me Again* (John Dahl), *Impulse* (Sondra Locke), *The Hot Spot* (Dennis Hopper), *Rush* (Lili Fini Zanuck), *Narrow Margin* (Peter Hyams; a remake of Richard Fleischer's 1952 original), and *Miami Blues* (George Armitage); 1991's *Cape Fear* (Martin Scorsese; a remake of J. Lee Thompson's 1962 original), *Dead Again* (Kenneth Branagh), *Delusion* (Carl Colpaert), *A Kiss before Dying* (James Dearden), *Liebestraum* (Mike Figgis), *Mortal Thoughts* (Alan Rudolph), *Shattered* (Wolfgang Petersen); 1992's *Basic Instinct* (Paul Verhoeven), *Final Analysis* (Phil Joanou), *Night and the City* (Irwin Winkler; a remake of Jules Dassin's 1950 original), *One False Move* (Carl Franklin), *Bad Lieutenant* (Abel Ferrara), and *Reservoir Dogs* (Quentin Tarantino); 1993's *Red Rock West* (John Dahl), *Kalifornia* (Dominic Sena), *The Last Seduction* (John Dahl), *True Romance* (Tony Scott), and *Flesh and Bone* (Steve Kloves); and 1994's *Romeo Is Bleeding* (Peter Medak), *Pulp Fiction* (Quentin Tarantino), and *Trial by Jury* (Heywood Gould).

Another phenomenon of the 1980s was the relative strength of independent production, briefly resurgent under the new regime of video delivery. Some of the most unusual and interesting work the American cinema had seen for many years appeared from small companies like Circle Films, Hemdale, Island Pictures, New Line Cinema, Cinecom, and Miramax—e.g., Susan Seidelman's (b. 1952) *Smithereens* (1982) and *Desperately Seeking Susan* (1985); Victor Nuñez's (b. 1945) *A Flash of Green* (1984); Joel Coen's (b. 1954) *Blood Simple* (1984) and *Raising Arizona* (1987); Jim Jarmusch's (b. 1953) *Stranger Than Paradise* (1984), *Down by Law* (1986), and *Mystery Train* (1989); James Foley's *At Close Range* (1986); Oliver Stone's (b. 1946) *Salvador* (1986); Tim Hunter's *River's Edge* (1987); John Sayles's (b. 1950) *Matewan* (1987) and *Eight Men Out* (1988); and Steven Soderbergh's (b. 1963) *sex, lies, and videotape* (1989; Grand Prix, Cannes). Most of these films were too original to have been made in the studio era and too eccentric for the mass-market economies of the 1980s. Most of their directors remained independent into the 1990s—Sayles (*City of Hope*, 1991; *Passion Fish*, 1992; *The Secret of Roan Inish*, 1995), Jarmusch (*Night on Earth*, 1991), Soderbergh (*Kafka*, 1991; *King of the Hill*, 1993), and Nuñez (*Ruby in Paradise*, 1993), for example. Others entered the mainstream and

20.51 and 20.52 Nineties neo-*noir*: Paul Verhoeven's *Basic Instinct* (1992): Sharon Stone, Michael Douglas; Quentin Tarantino's *Reservoir Dogs* (1992): Harvey Keitel (standing).

began working for majors, as was the case with Susan Seidelman (*She Devil*, 1990) and Joel Coen and his producer-writer brother, Ethan (*Miller's Crossing*, 1990; *Barton Fink*, 1991; *The Hudsucker Proxy*, 1993). And yet another went on to become the most audaciously brilliant American filmmaker of the 1990s, as well as one of the industry's most influential writer-directors.

This was Oliver Stone, whose work has been both

20.53 *Down by Law* (Jim Jarmusch, 1986): John Lurie, Tom Waits, Roberto Benigni.

20.55 *Sex, lies, and videotape* (Steven Soderbergh, 1989): Andie MacDowell.

20.54 *Raising Arizona* (Joel and Ethan Coen, 1987): Holly Hunter, Nicolas Cage.

notoriously controversial and strikingly eclectic since the appearance of *Salvador* in the midst of the conservative Reagan era.[1] Based on the real-life experiences of journalist Richard Boyle, 1980–81, and deeply critical of American support for El Salvador's right-wing government, it was followed immediately by the grippingly realistic combat film *Platoon* (1986), which won four Academy Awards (for Best Picture, Director, Film Editing [Claire Simpson-Crozier], and Sound) and catalyzed the revisionist Vietnam cycle noted above. *Wall Street* (1987) was no less stridently topical in its focus on the destructive greed of an Ivan Boesky–like arbitrager, and neither was *Talk Radio* (1988), which conflated Eric Bogosian's one-act play of the title with elements from

the real-life murder of talk-show host Alan Berg. *Born on the Fourth of July* (1989) recurred to the cultural trauma of Vietnam in its account of a gung-ho Marine recruit who returns from the war paralyzed from the waist down and, after a torturous period of readjustment, becomes an antiwar activist. Based on the autobiography of Ron Kovic, this film powerfully evoked the divisiveness of Vietnam and won Academy Awards for Best Direction and Editing (Joe Hutshing and David Brenner). After what many critics felt to be a self-indulgent, if penetrating, portrait of late-1960s rock and drug culture in *The Doors* (1991), Stone produced in *JFK* (1991) one of the most dynamically controversial films in recent American history. Compared by David Ansen in his *Newsweek* review (12/23/91) to *The Birth of a Nation* (1915), *JFK* mixes documentary, pseudodocumentary, and theatrical footage to create a "counter myth" to the Warren Commission Report on the assassination of President Kennedy on November 22, 1963. Because it takes the widely discredited 1967 conspiracy investigation of New Orleans D.A. Jim Garrison as its vehicle, many critics accused the

---

1. Before 1986, Stone had written and directed the thriller *Seizure* (1974) and the horror film *The Hand* (1981); he had also written the screenplays for *Midnight Express* (Alan Parker, 1978), *Conan the Barbarian* (John Milius, 1982), *Scarface* (Brian De Palma, 1983), and *Year of the Dragon* (Michael Cimino, 1985), among others.

20.56 *Born on the Fourth of July* (Oliver Stone, 1989): Tom Cruise as Ron Kovic.

20.57 Oliver Stone's *JFK* (1991): Jim Garrison (Kevin Costner) and his chief investigator (Jay O. Sanders) attempt to re-enact Oswald's alleged assassination of the president.

film of attempting to rewrite history. But, in addition to some certifiably paranoid speculation, Stone puts more *accurate* information about the assassination and its aftermath on screen in 189 minutes than most contemporary audiences would have encountered in their lifetimes— and does so in such riveting, bravura fashion that few audiences could fail to attend. Nominated for all the major Academy Awards, *JFK* won Oscars for veteran Stone collaborators Robert Richardson (Cinematography) and Joe Hutshing and Pietro Scalia (Editing), and it stimulated a national debate about the veracity of the Warren Report and access to its sealed records, which led Congress to pass the JFK Assassination Records Collection Act of 1992 calling for the disclosure of virtually all of the government's files. Stone's next film, *Heaven & Earth* (1993), was based on the memoirs of Le Ly Haslip, a young Vietnamese peasant woman whose life was changed utterly by the war. In portraying Le Ly's odyssey from her shattered childhood through her difficult marriage to an American soldier and her adjustment to American life, Stone completed his Vietnam trilogy "through the looking-glass," i.e., by showing the war from the perspective of its victims, as well as from its front line and home front.

Perhaps because of the media firestorm that greeted *JFK* and the accusations that he had used his own medium to twist the truth, Stone chose to make his next film a scathing indictment of media manipulation. At one level, *Natural Born Killers* (1994) is an ultraviolent, hell-bent-for-leather "criminal couple" movie that has the raw feel of an exploitation film (which, on this level, it most certainly is). At another level, it is about the violent media images that surround and engulf us, working their way into our psyches until they have become a crucial part of our mental lives, producing a national psychosis that creates both couples like the film's and audiences like ourselves. As the young lovers, Mickey and Mallory, go on a killing spree across New Mexico, genre elements from the *Gun Crazy/Bonnie and Clyde/Badlands* mode converge with slasher-style gore and a tradition of animated mayhem that extends from Saturday morning cartoons through Japanimation to create a collage of the many ways violence is imaged in our culture. Catapulted to stardom by the media, Mickey and

20.58 *Natural Born Killers* **(Oliver Stone, 1994): Mickey (Woody Harrelson) and Mallory (Juliette Lewis) getting back theirs.**

Mallory are captured and imprisoned for the murders of forty-eight "innocent" people, but when a true-crime TV journalist attempts a live-feed interview with Mickey on Superbowl Sunday, an apocalyptic prison riot ensues. This event, playing on stereotypes from countless prison films and shot in the heroic-absurd mode of Peckinpah's *The Wild Bunch*, manipulates sound and image to put the audience on the side of the killers, who finally escape to freedom and, presumably, some future domestic bliss after killing another fifty-odd people on live TV, including the paradigmatic TV journalist. Stylistically, *Natural Born Killers* picks up where *JFK* left off. The narrative, if it can be called that, is filmed by Robert Richardson in a variety of stocks (35mm color, black and white, Super 8, and video) at different speeds, and integrated with a wide variety of animated/electronic effects; in terms of editing (Hank Corwin/Brian Berdan), it alternates between the style of a music video and live TV, and there is not a continuity cut in the entire film. Stone creates a rhythm of violence that is frenetic from the start but rises to a fever pitch during the riot, and he keeps upping the ante on what is acceptable to watch until we are deeply implicated in the most prurient forms of voyeurism that media can pander to, because *Natural Born Killers* is ultimately about Stone's manipulation of us as we watch it. *Nixon* (1995) was a less successful

extension of the political subtext of *JFK*, structured (somewhat egregiously) like *Citizen Kane* (1941), that managed to capture some of the thirty-seventh president's manifold contradictions (such as his combination of political astuteness with rampant paranoia) and offered a chilling vision of the White House under siege in the waning days of the Watergate scandal. (Furthermore, Anthony Hopkins was astonishingly effective in the title role, considering that he neither looked nor sounded like Nixon.) Although his cinematic revision of 1960s history may have ended with *JFK*, in films like *Natural Born Killers*—and, to a lesser extent, *Nixon*—Oliver Stone was still making late 1960s–style movies whose defining mark was their challenge to think seriously about social issues and to stir people up about them as never before.[2] Much of Stone's work since has been self-indulgent (*U Turn* [1997]) or inflated (*Any Given Sunday* [1999]), but between 1986 and 1995 he produced enduring works of social criticism that only one mainstream American filmmaker has rivaled—and that is Michael Mann (b. 1943), whose *The Insider* (1999) and *Ali* (2001), while more subtly inflected than Stone's films, cut no less close to the bone in representing the effects of unbridled corporate power and racism on our social fabric.

Near the end of this period, as the Internet became a growth industry and the era of digital production dawned, the American majors began to realize that someday soon their movies would be distributed online or downloaded into digital displays by satellite. They wanted to introduce one more generation of "software" into the consumer market before this happened, and at an ad hoc committee meeting held in Hollywood in 1994 they agreed that the new format should take the form of a compact disc (CD), but with greater storage capacity and faster access speed. At that time, electronics manufacturers were developing two competing formats for movies on CD that used a new generation of video compression technology known as MPEG-2: Toshiba/Matsushita's SuperDisc (SD) and Philips/Sony's MultiMedia CD (MMCD). Both formats were demonstrated in Hollywood in 1995, and in September of that year Sony formed a consortium with nine

---

2. Stone also produces films—*Blue Steel* (Kathryn Bigelow, 1989), *Reversal of Fortune* (Barbet Schroeder, 1990), *Iron Maze* (Hiroaki Yoshida, 1991), *Zebrahead* (Anthony Drazan, 1992), *South Central* (Steve Anderson, 1992), *The Joy Luck Club* (Wayne Wang, 1993), and most of his own—as well as television (*Wild Palms,* 1993).

20.59 *The Insider* (Michael Mann, 1999): Russell Crowe (center frame) as Dr. Jeffrey Wigand, the former tobacco company chemist who blew the whistle on industry collusion to poison its customers with tar and nicotine.

other companies to create a single, unified standard for what came to be known as the Digital Video Disc (later, in some markets, "Digital Versatile Disc"), or DVD. In addition to Sony, the DVD consortium was comprised of Hitachi, JVC, Matsushita, Mitsubishi, Philips, Pioneer, Thomson, Time Warner, and Toshiba; in 1997, as the DVD Forum, it came to include IBM, the Industrial Technology Research Institute of Taiwan, Intel Corporation, LG Electronics, NEC Corporation, Samsung Electronics, and Sharp Corporation—in other words, the world's largest manufacturers of electronic and digital equipment. (One of their goals was to avoid repeating the costly compatibility war between Betamax and VHS tape formats that had plagued the early years of the VCR.) In December 1995, the Hollywood majors committed to the single standard format known as DVD; in 1996, the first set of specifications for DVD-ROM and DVD-Video were published, and the first DVD players were sold in Tokyo. The format's U.S. launch was in 1997, with a full launch in Europe in 1998. No consumer electronic product in history had enjoyed such widespread international collaboration across multiple industries in the development stage as DVD, and none in history experienced such a rapid and explosive diffusion after it was launched. By the first years of the twenty-first century, DVD had successfully challenged VHS tape as the principle mode

of viewing movies in the home, taking a 50 percent share of the $14-billion-a-year home-rental market and 65 percent of the $12.4 billion video-sales market in 2002, and it stood poised to become a major revenue stream in Hollywood's international system of staggered theatrical release. (This is facilitated by region coding, which prevents DVDs released in any one of eight Hollywood-defined world markets from playing on machines manufactured for use in the others. A kind of digital "run-zone-clearance system," region code management helps the industry to maintain the exclusivity of international distribution rights and keeps current films from entering foreign markets before their theatrical release, demonstrating that Hollywood's historic impulse toward monopoly control is still very much intact.)

For much of the 1980s and 1990s, a new film's domestic release typically accounted for one-fifth of its total revenue, with two-fifths coming from home entertainment, and the rest from foreign and ancillary sales. Since the advent of DVD, the home-entertainment portion has come to account for more than half of a film's total revenue. As Martin W. Greenwald, president of Image Entertainment (one of the largest DVD producers in the United States) puts it with only modest hyperbole: "The initial release of the motion picture in movie theaters is becoming, to a large extent, little more than a preview trailer for the subsequent purchase of the DVD."[3] The downside of DVD for Hollywood was its potential for creating perfect digital copies. (One of the main reasons that the majors had backed VHS over the Beta format was its comparative lack of resolution in copy generation.) To prevent piracy, the studios forced the adoption of a data encryption and authentication standard for DVD called the Content Scrambling System (CSS) that prevented copying video files directly from the disc, but it was not long before the CSS algorithm was decoded and posted on the Internet. The industry's search for an unbreakable Digital Copy Protection System (DCPS) or some other way to disable digital copying (like requiring hardware manufacturers to inhibit it) has become its Grail quest of the new century, second only to preventing the spread of "runaway" production—the phenomenon of U.S. filmmakers moving their productions wholesale to Canada (or, less frequently, Mexico) where they can hire skilled crews and state-of-the-art studios, laboratories, and postproduction facilities for 10 to 15 percent less than in Hollywood, owing to a combination of favorable exchange rates, foreign subsidies, and less expensive labor. On a $150 million project like *Terminator 3* (Jonathan Mostow, 2003), this can result in a significant savings. The concern is that, as film budgets continue to soar, runaway production—which by some estimates is already costing the American industry $1 billion a year in lost wages—will become built into the system.

3. Martin W. Greenwald, quoted in Rick Lyman, "Revolt in the Den: DVD Has the VCR Headed to the Attic," *New York Times*, September 26, 2002: A1; A13.

Hollywood Enters the Digital Domain

The challenge which digital media poses to cinema extends far beyond the issue of narrative. Digital media redefines the very identity of cinema.

—LEV MANOVICH, "WHAT IS DIGITAL CINEMA?"

We have [in *The Lord of the Rings* trilogy] full battles where we have 10,000 Orcs and 10,000 Gondorian soldiers running toward each other, clashing in battle. Orcs stabbing Gondorians, Gondorians stabbing Orcs, they're falling down, they're dying. But the cool part is they all do it by themselves.

—JIM RYGIEL, VFX SUPERVISOR, *THE LORD OF THE RINGS* TRILOGY

Since the mid-1990s, digital-imaging technology has transformed the making of feature films in the industrialized West, and it will soon transform their distribution and exhibition as well on a global scale. There is hardly an aspect of film production that has not been changed by digital imaging, some of it spectacularly obvious but much of it invisible to all but the industry professionals who design and use it. Film is an **analog** medium: it creates images by recording the light bouncing off of objects in empirical reality onto a photosensitive chemical surface (the emulsion-coated negative stock), focused by a lens. As light is converted into film, the quality of the images varies with the quality of the light, the emulsion, and the lens; and, as in all analog media, this process of transference involves some degradation, or loss of information between the original and the master copy. When the master copy is duplicated further to produce other copies, a process known in film as "print generation," even more information is lost. In digital image recording, however, light is not converted into another medium, but into a series of binary numbers, an abstraction that has no physical relationship to the original. The result is a **digital file** that can be used to reconstruct the original image or be manipulated by a computer through mathematical formulas to create a new one. (Digital

21.1 *The Lord of the Rings: The Fellowship of the Ring* (Peter Jackson, 2001). Orcs fighting Gondorians on the dark plain of Gogoroth in the prologue to the film.

imaging cannot completely reconstruct an image, however; it can only give an approximation at the resolution, or frequency, of the sample.) In either case, the image is manufactured through the digital interpretation of numbers, and this information can be copied or transferred endlessly, through digital means, without degradation. In effect, each digital copy is not a replica of the original but its clone. Thus, digital imaging technology, whose ultimate filmic manifestation is CGI, offers the filmmaker complete control over the image without any additional loss of quality, limited only (and it's a big "only") by computer memory, or digital storage space.

CGI, the acronym for **computer-generated imagery** (also computer graphic imagery), stands for the entire field of digital effects—from the manipulation of a film's color palette in postproduction to the creation of 3-D objects and characters entirely in the digital realm without the intervention of photography. Fundamentally, CGI is a form of computer animation that produces images frame by frame from thousands of discrete digital parts, or pixels, each of which the computer calculates and precisely positions to create a "virtual" reality, whether it be color that didn't exist in the original medium (as in the practice of "colorizing" black-and-white films from the studio era for video) or some illusory three-dimensional world (e.g., ancient Rome in Ridley

Scott's *Gladiator* [2000]); Middle Earth in Peter Jackson's *The Lord of the Rings: The Fellowship of the Ring* [2001]). The first computer-generated images appeared sparingly in films during the late 1970s and early 1980s, becoming more common in the late 1980s and early 1990s as computing power increased and costs went proportionally down. During this period, CGI was used primarily for special effects, but filmmakers soon realized that it could be used in more mundane ways to achieve production economies by creating synthetic sets and props (e.g., the hook in Steven Spielberg's *Hook* [1991]), erasing unwanted elements in principal photography (e.g., "flying wires" in martial-arts sequences), simulating weather and atmospheric conditions (adding rain, snow, and clouds; replacing skies), and multiplying small groups of extras into large crowds. By the mid-1990s, as increasingly sophisticated **animation software** became available, CGI had become an important feature of nearly all films that relied on special effects, and such films—especially those in the science-fiction and disaster genres—had become an industry mainstay. At the same time, CGI-induced production economies grew more complex in their ability to create lighting effects like day for night, to enhance lens optics (rendering digital zoom and "split diopter" shots), and to provide a variety of traditionally cost-intensive physical effects (e.g., digital pyrotechnics) and stunts (e.g., doubling stars, or their faces, with digital replacements; setting dangerous stunts in completely digital environments) in a safe and cost-efficient manner.

Origins of Computer Animation, 1962–1988

CGI was first used in the late 1950s in the aerospace industry to create high-resolution images for flight simulators (the Boeing Corporation coining the acronym in 1960 to describe their air-traffic-control displays) and for a variety of other industrial applications throughout the 1960s. In 1962, as part of his dissertation research at MIT, Ivan Sutherland authored a computer program called Sketchpad that allowed him to animate three-dimensional images by drawing lines directly onto a cathode ray tube (CRT) with a "light-pen." Sutherland joined with Dr. David Evans to found the first department of computer graphics at the University of Utah in 1964, and they subsequently formed their own company, Evans & Sutherland (E&S), which in 1969 unveiled LDS-1 (Line Drawing System-1), the first computer-assisted design (CAD) workstation for the production of **wireframes,** the line-based polygonal drawings that provide the foundation of all three-dimensional computer animation. At about the same time, another computer animation company, the Mathematical Applications Group, Inc. (MAGI) developed a process called "ray tracing" to simulate reflections, refractions, and shadows in three-dimensional models with a degree of optical precision that approached that of photography. Ray-tracing technology provided a giant step toward the kind of **photorealistic** animation that would transform the cinema in the 1990s, but it required large amounts of computer time and memory. Thus, when CGI first entered features, it was as a means of representing the two-dimensional operations of spaceship instrumentation and computer displays in science-fiction films like *2001: A Space Odyssey* (Stanley Kubrick, 1968), *The Andromeda Strain* (Robert Wise, 1970), *Silent Running* (Douglas Trumbull, 1971), and *Westworld* (Michael Critchton, 1973).[1] For much of the 1970s, it was broadcasters rather than filmmakers who maximized the potential of computer graphics, incorporating them into flying network logos and spot commercials, where the attention they attracted was most profitable.

21.2 *2001: A Space Odyssey* (Stanley Kubrick, 1968), an early use of computer graphics to represent the two-dimensional imagery of spacecraft instrumentation.

The film debut of **three-dimensional computer animation** came in *Futureworld* (Richard T. Heffron, 1976), for which American International Pictures contracted Dr. Edwin Catmull, head of the New York Institute of Technology's computer graphics lab, to design a wireframe hand for display on a monitor screen within the film. Critics and audiences barely noticed this computer-generated hand, but it attracted the attention of George Lucas, who would hire Catmull, following the phenomenal success of *Star Wars* (1977), to head his newly created Lucasfilm Computer Development Division in 1978. This was an early component of Industrial Light & Magic (ILM), the special-effects house that Lucas had established in Van Nuys in 1975 to provide effects for *Star Wars*, which, although it pioneered the use of computerized motion control in the Dykstraflex system (see Chapter 12), did not use CGI as such. However, after its move to Marin County in the Bay area in 1980, ILM soon provided the first extensive sequence of photorealistic computer animation to appear on screen—the "Genesis effect" in *Star Trek II: The Wrath of Khan* (Nicholas Meyer, 1982), wherein a dead planet is transformed by a missile blast into a vibrant, edenic place in about 60 seconds. Using software designed by Catmull, the sequence involved the creation of the first **digital matte painting** and new computer-graphics algorithms to generate fire, mountains, and shoreline from fractal equations.

---

1. Michael Critchton's *Looker* (1981) is about a company that makes full-body digital replications of women for use in television commercials, but the images themselves were achieved by means of traditional cel animation. The holographic body armor in David Lynch's *Dune* (1984) was probably the first considered attempt to simulate the human form with CGI.

In the same year, Walt Disney Productions, which had used CGI to simulate the black hole in *The Black Hole* (Gary Nelson, 1979), produced *Tron* (Steven Lisberger), now regarded as a breakthrough in computer animation. This film, a fantasy about a man who enters his own computer program, combined live action with computer-generated scenes, of which there were 235, totaling over 15 minutes. *Tron* thus contained more CGI than any previous film, and Disney bid the work out to four of the top computer-graphics studios of the day, all coordinated by MAGI, which set up a transcontinental computer link to transfer data between New York and California during production. With a negative cost of $17 million, *Tron* was Disney's second most expensive film (*The Black Hole*, at $18.5 million, was first), and, although it turned a profit, it was not the watershed in digital production that Disney had hoped, and Hollywood's ardor toward CGI cooled for the rest of the decade. But it inspired a younger generation of computer graphic artists and could not impede the progress of Digital Productions, a new company formed in 1982, which staked its claim through the $10.5 million purchase of a Cray X-MP, the most powerful, high-speed computer for graphics generation then available. This "supercomputer" was immediately contracted to produce 27 minutes of deep-space sequences—some 230 separate scenes—for Lorimar's *The Last Starfighter* (Nick Castle, 1984), making it the first feature film in history to simulate *all* of its special effects. Although the simulation cost $4.9 million of the film's $14 million budget, the producers figured that its digital effects had been completed in one-third the time and at half the expense of traditional effects. Despite such economies, *The Last Starfighter* barely broke even at the box office, but it had signaled an important principle—that CGI could not only be used to create photorealistic simulations cost-effectively, but that it could do so *more* efficiently and *less* expensively than the same scenes played out in real time. (At one level, the industry immediately grasped the film's significance: cinematographers Gary Demos and John Whitney, Jr. won a 1984 Scientific and Technical award from the Academy for "the practical simulation of motion picture photography by means of computer-generated images." In retrospect, what made the simulation imperfect was its very perfection—it took filmmakers nearly another decade to realize that optical imperfections like **motion blur** had to be programmed into their computer simulations in order to replicate the look of real-time photography.)

Meanwhile at ILM, Ed Catmull's computer division had developed the Pixar, a high-resolution computer specifically designed for graphics, the first such machine dedicated exclusively to CGI. Under the direction of **visual-effects (VFX) supervisor** Dennis Muren (b. 1946), ILM used it to create CGI sequences for two other films: the three-dimensional holograph of Endor Moon and the Death Star in *Star Wars: Episode VI—The Return of the Jedi* (Richard Marquand, 1983), and the sword-wielding stained-glass knight who emerges from a chapel window to chase a priest in *Young Sherlock Holmes* (Barry Levinson, 1985). For the latter film, an electronic paint station was used to create the knight in the computer, where it was animated three-dimensionally and given its final appearance. The stained-glass knight thus became the feature film's first **computer-generated character**—a direct antecedent of all the dinosaurs, giant insects, ogres, and Orcs to follow (not to mention the "synthespians" in films like *Shrek* [Andrew Adamson, 2001] and *Final Fantasy: The Spirits Within* [Hironobu Saka-

21.3 *Tron* (Steven Lisberger, 1982), the first film to combine computer-generated imagery with live action in extended scenes.

21.4 *The Last Starfighter* (Nick Castle, 1984). Digital Productions simulated all of the film's special effects in a state-of-the-art Cray X-MP computer to save on costs, but the animation retained a cartoon-like quality because it failed to compensate for optical phenomena like motion blur.

compositing CGI. By the late 1980s, ILM, in collaboration with Kodak, had built a digital laser scanner capable of resolutions of up to 4,000 pixels per line per frame. (In 1994, the ILM / Kodak scanner won the Scientific and Technical Achievement Award from the Academy of Motion Picture Arts and Sciences.)

The next advances in CGI involved the technology of **morphing,** the process whereby one image is gradually transformed into another. ILM was once again the industry leader here, although in 1986 Lucas had spun off Catmull's Computer Development Division and sold his controlling interest in it to Steve Jobs of Apple Computers. (Renamed Pixar, after Catmull's computer, the company would become the world's first digital-animation studio and the producer of *Toy Story* [John Lasseter, 1995], the first feature made completely with CGI.) The morphs for *Willow* (Ron Howard, 1988), wherein a sorceress is transformed from a goat into an ostrich and then successively into a turtle, a tiger, and finally a human, were accomplished by digitizing images of an actress, a real tiger, and several animal puppets and merging them progressively in the computer. The transformation sequence was then scanned directly onto film and composited with live action in an optical printer. The metamorphosis software, known as the "morphing system," permitted the manipulation of images not only frame by frame but pixel by pixel, and it was authored by Doug Smythe, who in 1992 won a technical achievement award from the Academy for creating the morph computer-software program. (An earlier version that simply changed an image's shape had been used to assist the transformation of one man's face into another in Joe Dante's 1987 film *Innerspace*, whose effects were also supervised by Dennis Muren.) This same software was used a year later to create the "Donovan's Destruction" sequence in *Indiana Jones and the Last Crusade* (Steven Spielberg, 1989), in which a Nazi-sympathizing industrialist drinks from the Holy Grail, then ages rapidly and

guchi, 2001]). At this point, standard practice would have been to capture the animated figure by filming it directly off of the computer screen for compositing with live action in an optical printer, which involved some natural degradation of the digital image since the transfer process itself (cinematography) was analog. Muren, however, conceived the idea of using a laser recorder to scan the knight directly onto the film stock, a digital transfer that preserved the digital integrity and high resolution of the image. The process was so successful that **laser scanning** has since become the primary means of outputting and

21.5 *Final Fantasy: The Spirits Within* (Hironobu Sakaguchi, 2001). The face of the future? Dr. Aki Ross, one of the "synthespians" that populate this photorealistic animated feature based on a popular video game. Some observers believe that digitally synthesized performers like Aki will dominate the cinema of the twenty-first century, but that remains to be seen. For the time being, human audiences seem prejudiced toward their own species.

21.6 *Willow* (Ron Howard, 1988). A tiger is transformed into a human, an illusion created through an early application of morphing software at ILM.

disintegrates on screen. As in *Willow*, the various stages of decomposition were represented by models whose images were scanned into the computer and merged, but they were also digitally composited there before being scanned back out to film, thus creating the first all-digital composite. The practices of morphing and **digital compositing** are common today, and in fact commercial software for both is available that will run on a desktop computer; but in the late 1980s they were still very difficult to accomplish. Although the Pixar computers of the era were capable of manipulating 80 million **polygons**—the basic building blocks of CGI—it took 16 hours to scan and store 1 minute of film and 720 floppy disks (about 1 gigabyte) to store a 2-hour feature.

Industrial Light & Magic

FROM *THE ABYSS* TO *DEATH BECOMES HER*

The evolution of digital effects in the cinema was at this point greatly accelerated by two films contracted out to ILM, both written and directed by James Cameron. For *The Abyss* (1989), produced by 20th Century–Fox, Cameron had conceived an irregularly shaped, organic-looking "psuedopod" that communicated by forming the faces of characters in the film. The creature was supposed to be made entirely of water, a virtually transparent substance that both reflects and refracts light and is not easy to simulate. Cameron had explored several options for creating the pseudopod through traditional means, including stop-motion animation and hydraulics, before he was sold on 3-D animation by Dennis Muren at ILM. In what would be their biggest CGI project to date, Muren's team created a 75-second sequence of 27 shots on powerful new workstations purchased from Silicon Graphics. (Although the pseudopod was created digitally, it was composited with live-action elements optically—large-scale digital compositing awaited the advent of the CCD scanner described below.) In addition to improved morphing software and programs for realistic water creation, ILM's *Abyss* team introduced the **digital set**—a completely malleable digital environment within which the animator can control such variables as lighting, camera position and movement, and the movement of objects on the set. (Borrowing from the techniques of traditional animation, software developers began to release programs between 1989 and 1991—e.g., Macromedia Director [1989], Adobe Photoshop [1990], QuickTime [1991]—that facilitated 3-D modeling within the context of digital sets.)[2] Unlike earlier digital effects—with the possible exception of the "Genesis effect" in *Star Trek II*—the pseudopod sequence was central to the narrative of *The Abyss* and received much critical attention. The film won the 1989 Academy Award for Best Visual Effects and provided a major boost to the computer-graphics department at ILM, where it was seen as the culmination of all the division's work since 1978; it also demonstrated to the industry at large that CGI had reached the point where it could provide credible photorealistic effects integrated with live action in cost-effective ways.

ILM's digital effects for Cameron's *Terminator 2: Judgment Day* (Carolco Pictures, 1991), also supervised by Dennis Muren, took morphing to the next level with

---

2. None of these programs, all very different, is an actual 3-D program, but all three generally made 3-D modeling easier in their varied ways. (James True to author, 8 / 13 / 02.)

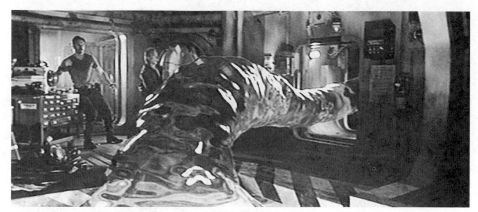

21.7 *The Abyss* **(James Cameron, 1989). The now-famous "psuedopod" was created digitally on a "digital set" at ILM but composited with live-action scenes optically. The film won the 1989 Academy Award for Best Visual Effects.**

ical. Magnetic systems track variations in a moving object or person's magnetic field via transmitters, whose signals are then used to calculate the position of the object in space. Using one or more video cameras, optical motion trackers rely on finding markers embedded at key points on the object or person. Mechanical systems use linkages like potentiometers to measure the relative position of the object or person in movement. All three methods result in digital information that can be used to construct and animate wireframe skeletons; but at the time of *Terminator 2*, only a small part of the human form could be recorded in a single scan so that the motion of various body parts had to be captured separately and then assembled into a whole body image. (Present-day motion-capture systems can not only capture a moving body in its entirety, but allow it to be viewed from virtually any angle for rotation during post-production, which facilitates the process of 3-D animation.)

the T-1000 cyborg, the first computer-generated character realistically modeled on the three-dimensional human form. In the film, the T-1000 is composed of liquid chrome that can morph into any shape, and the ILM team created him by drawing grid lines on a live actor's body and scanning them into the computer as the actor moved in order to create a digital skeleton, or wireframe. Known as **motion capture,** this process was initially developed for the medical industry to analyze the dynamics of physical injuries and was later adapted to the needs of film and video-game production. There are three types of motion-capture systems: magnetic, optical, and mechan-

Once the wireframe of the T-1000 was built, ILM artists gave it photorealistic features like shading, color, and texture—a process known in computer graphics as **rendering.** Using a new software program called Body Sock, they gave the figure musculature and a smooth, continuous surface. As conceived by Cameron, this surface was metallic, but it could not have been otherwise since the software did not yet exist to give it the textures of human skin and hair. To generate the 44 T-1000 shots required by the script, ILM purchased 35 high-powered workstations from Silicon Graphics and increased its

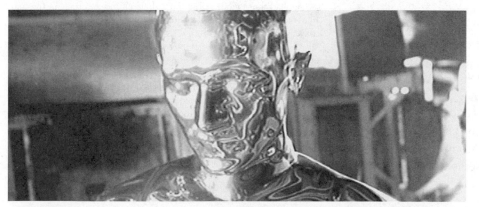

21.8 *Terminator 2: Judgement Day* **(James Cameron, 1991). The T-1000 morphs from liquid chrome into human form. ILM introduced the CCD Digital Input Scanner for work on this film so that all of its forty-four digital-effects shots could be composited in the digital realm.** *Terminator 2* **won the 1991 Oscar for Best Visual Effects as well as three other technical awards.**

computer-graphics staff from 8 to more than 40 people. To handle the huge volume of digital work (100 elements and nearly 8,000 frames of CGI), ILM used a new type of scanner—the Trilinear Multispectral High Resolution CCD (Charge Coupled Device) Digital Input Scanner—which had been in development since 1988 and was first used at the end of *Die Hard 2: Die Harder* (Renny Harlin, 1990) to digitally blend the matte painting of the Dulles Airport runway with live action. This machine could scan a film frame at ten times the speed of earlier scanners (between 20 and 30 seconds per frame), and it could scan in and digitize all types of 35mm film, including standard four-perforation 35mm, eight-perforation VistaVision (widely used for optical compositing since *Star Wars*),[3] original negatives, interpositives, and positive print film. The CCD scanner also output a high-resolution image ready for intercutting with production footage, so that all of *Terminator 2*'s digital-effects shots could be digitally composited without recourse to an optical scanner (although the film's other effects shots were still composited optically). The **CCD input scanner** was revolutionary because it enabled effects artists to enter their material into the digital realm, manipulate it digitally there, and then exit with high-resolution images for printing. Before it, there had been no standard and reliable input scanner for feature-film production; and most digitally created elements were being optically composited. By 1994, the CCD scanner had made the optical printer nearly obsolete.[4] Together with digital-software toolboxes and output systems, it ensured that images could be created, animated, and composited within an entirely digital environment.

Industry response to *Terminator 2* was overwhelmingly positive (as was the public's, which made it the highest earning film of 1991 with $122.5 million in domestic grosses), and the film won four technical Academy Awards, including Best Visual Effects. Suddenly, everybody wanted to "go digital," and new effects houses began to appear all over the country. Universal Pictures bankrolled the next major advance in CGI when the CCD scanner was used to produce 45 of 140 visual-effects shots in *Death Becomes Her* (1992), some as long as 1 minute in duration. For this film, director Robert Zemeckis (b. 1952) teamed up with ILM effects supervisor Ken Ralston (b. 1955) to meet the difficult challenge of realistically simulating human skin and anatomy in the digital realm. Like James Cameron, Zemeckis had consistently

21.9 *Death Becomes Her* (Robert Zemeckis, 1992). At the end of the film, Meryl Streep and Goldie Hawn literally fall apart, an illusion facilitated by morphing software designed to interface with Dick Smith's makeup effects and credibly simulate human skin. The film won the 1992 Academy Award for Best Visual Effects.

been on the cutting edge in his use of special effects. He had collaborated with Ralston on the effects-intensive *Back to the Future* (1985) and its two sequels (*Back to the Future II* [1989] and *Back to the Future III* [1990]), which pioneered the use of digital **wire removal** for its flying sequences. (Wire-removal software enables artists

---

3. When Lucas was preplanning the FX for *Star Wars* in the early days at ILM, he was looking for a film format that could withstand the degrading effects of print generation in the complex optical compositing process he envisioned, and he hit upon VistaVision. Although it had been defunct as a production format since the early 1960s (see Chapter 12), horizontal-feed VistaVision exposed a film frame twice the normal size (which had thus eight perforations—four on top and four on the bottom—rather than the standard four), so that when printed down optically to four-perforation 35mm it would have twice the resolution and stand up well in multiple-print generation. Better still, because it was commercially obsolete, VistaVision cameras and optical printers were available and cheap. VistaVision worked so well as a medium for optical compositing on the *Star Wars* project that it became an industry standard. The CCD scanner eliminated the necessity of large-format film since there is no print-generation deficit in digital compositing.

4. Optical compositing is still used in some special-effects work today, largely to save on costs since digital compositing remains considerably more expensive, although the savings that CGI can bring to production costs more often than not compensate for the difference. The first film to use electronic compositing in postproduction was Disney's *Honey, I Blew Up the Kid* (Randal Kleiser, 1992), a sequel to *Honey, I Shrunk the Kids* (Joe Johnston, 1989), which used Adobe After Effects software to add animation to live action in 210 shots through video equipment. Many of these involved imagery that did not suffer from video's low resolution relative to film, such as electrical shimmer and halo effects.

to manipulate the pixels of digitized shots so that wire rigs, harnesses, cranes, and cables can be colored over and melded into surrounding backgrounds; separate software adds simulated film grain so that the digital image will match the photographic one.) Zemeckis and Ralston had won the 1988 Academy Award for the visual effects in *Who Framed Roger Rabbit*, whose combination of animation with live action represented the pinnacle of optical compositing (and also its last important use—the next feature to blend live action with animation was *Space Jam* [Joe Pytka, 1996], whose cartoon characters were computer-animated and digitally composited with live actors). Their visual-effects work on *Death Becomes Her* introduced a wide range of software that had not been available for *Terminator 2* just the year before, and according to digital artist Doug Smythe the film became a "kind of guinea pig" for programs that would be used for *Jurassic Park* in 1993. Because *Death Becomes Her* contains multiple sequences involving maimed and contorted bodies, new morphing software was developed that could combine CGI with makeup effects (by Dick Smith) and **animatronic puppetry.** This included a painting and digital **rotoscoping** program called ColorBurst, a digital bluescreen matte program (designed by Smythe) known as C-Bal, and a refined version of MM2, a digital **pin-blocking** program for aligning and interlocking all the elements of a composited shot so that a director can move his camera without compensating for computer graphics. (Rotoscoping isolates an object frame by frame by tracing around its edges to create a silhouette, which can then be replaced by another image in postproduction; digital pin-blocking software had first been used at ILM for compositing bluescreen and wirework in Steven Spielberg's *Hook* [1991]). *Death Becomes Her* also innovated a program that synchronized the camera's frames-per-second (fps) speed with its shutter aperture so that effects sequences could be filmed at variable speeds continuously. Overall, the film marked an exponential leap forward in organic simulation, an achievement recognized when it received the 1992 Academy Award for Best Visual Effects.

THE IMPACT OF *JURASSIC PARK*, 1993–1996

Steven Spielberg's *Jurassic Park* (Universal Pictures, 1993) is well known as a landmark film in the history of CGI for its use of computer-generated dinosaurs. But Spielberg had originally intended to use full-scale animatronic puppets, provided by Stan Winston (b. 1946), creator of the alien queen in *Aliens* (James Cameron, 1986), and animated via Phil Tippett's proprietary **Go-Motion system,** which used computer-controlled rods to move objects in real time; the only CGI was to involve two shots of a stampeding gallimimus herd, provided by ILM. Dennis Muren, however, convinced the director that it would be possible to create photorealistic digital dinosaurs for the entire film. Winston's animatronic creatures would still be used for some shots, and Tippett (b. 1951) was retained to work with ILM on their animation. The goal was to create three-dimensional, full-bodied dinosaurs that would look like real animals rather than "movie monsters" for digital compositing with live action.

21.10 *Jurassic Park* **(Steven Spielberg, 1993). A watershed for the CGI-driven cinema of the latter 1990s, this film featured a seamless blending of 3-D computer graphics, animatronics, and live action, facilitated through innovations like ILM's Digital Input Device.**

To expedite this work, ILM set up a fiber-optic video and audio link between its Marin County facility, the Tippett studio across the Bay in Berkeley, and Spielberg's Amblin Entertainment in Los Angeles, and the team ultimately produced 52 CGI shots for the film. (During postproduction, Spielberg was in Kraków, Poland, on location for *Schindler's List*, and the fiber-optic link was extended to him there by satellite, its pathway protected by digital encryption.) Since Tippett, whose studio produced 15 of these (those representing the T-rex attack on two cars and their occupants, and those of the two raptors hunting children in the conference center's kitchen), found it awkward to use the computer keyboard and mouse, he invented the **Digital Input Device** (DID, also known as the "Dinosaur Input Device"), essentially a blending of stop-motion and computer-animation technologies, to facilitate the **modeling** and animation of the dinosaurs. (The DID consisted of an **armature** [a model or puppet with articulated joints] with electronic sensors at the pivot points that could create a wireframe model in the computer when put through a series of stop-motion maneuvers. Its most advanced use came in Tippett's creation of the giant alien bugs in *Starship Troopers* [1997]). The other 37 CGI shots (the gallimimus stampede, the concluding battle between the T-rex and the raptors, and several leaf-eating brachiosaurs) were created at ILM, using three newly evolved software programs that represented significant advances in the achievement of photorealism: (1) ViewPaint—new texture-mapping software that allowed artists to paint the surface of a dinosaur as if it were a real 3-D sculpture by enabling them to rotate the wireframe during the painting process; (2) Enveloping—ILM proprietary software that worked with Body Sock to give computer-generated dinosaur flesh the appearance of actually moving against muscle and bone; and (3) Softimage—a commercial package for 3-D character animation that included **inverse kinematics,** the ability to link one movement with another or others as in life (e.g., parts of a leg or arm could be made to work together—the thigh moving with the knee, or the wrist with forearm and elbow) and made it possible to precisely match computer-generated virtual camera movements with those actually made on the set (a process called **"match moving"**—see below). During the last stages of the process, artists painted corrections directly on the finalized composite using Photoshop or Parallax's Matador software. Then, ILM **technical directors** (TDs)

21.11 *Baby's Day Out* (Patrick Read Johnson, 1994). The baby in question is inserted into a 3-D cityscape of downtown Chicago by digitally compositing his bluescreen image with digitized photographs of the buildings.

added motion blur to every shot to make it look like the product of real-time cinematography. As TD George Murphy put it: "We spent a lot of time adding defects that real-location photographers work so hard to get rid of, such as added film grain for a more organic and natural look."[5] They even added "camera bounce" to the T-rex sequences, as if the cinematographer were responding to the creature's shattering footfalls. (Murphy: "Even just the slightest move helps give the impression that there's a real person behind the camera")[6] The finished product so seamlessly blended computer graphics, animatronics, and live-action photography that even today it is difficult to determine which is which.

If *Terminator 2* had created digital fever in the film industry, *Jurassic Park* caused a revolution. Phil Tippett, who would be one of its leaders, put it this way: "When I saw *T2*, I felt like the tide was pulling at my calves, but it wasn't until those first T-rex tests on *Jurassic Park* that I saw the tidal wave on the horizon."[7] Dennis Muren was even more succinct: as filmmakers, he said, "computer graphics is now the most potent tool we have." The fact that *Jurassic Park* became, based on international grosses exceeding $1 billion, the most popular film in history to

5. George Murphy, quoted in Mark Cotta Vaz and Patricia Rose Duignan, *Industrial Light & Magic: Into the Digital Realm* (New York: Ballantine, 1996), p. 227.

6. Vaz and Duignan, pp. 227–28.

7. Phil Tippett, quoted in Vaz and Duignan, p. 231.

date offered ringing confirmation of this perspective. From being an embellishment to science-fiction and action films ten years before, CGI had become the driving force of the American cinema. In a clear case of putting the cart before the horse, for the rest of the decade big-budget projects would be valorized in Hollywood for the amount of CGI they could be made to contain. The years 1993 to 2001 became a novelty period for a new kind of cinema, and in the same way that "talkies" dominated the early sound era and epic spectacle characterized the early years of widescreen, so, too, did a cinema of digital legerdemain dominate the early years of photorealistic CGI. It was cinema that said brazenly to its audience, "I am showing you the impossible and fantastic, not because it has merit or meaning, but simply because I *can.*"

Films of 1994 that showcased advances in CGI technology were *The Flintstones* (Brian Levant), *Baby's Day Out* (Patrick Read Johnson), *Radioland Murders* (Mel Smith), *Stargate* (Roland Emmerich), *Forrest Gump* (Robert Zemeckis), and *The Mask* (Chuck Russell). Universal's *The Flintstones*, produced by Spielberg's Amblin Entertainment, featured the first computer-generated character (Kitty, the saber-toothed tiger) with realistic hair or fur—a much more difficult element for computer graphics to create than skin, which is generated as a two-dimensional form whose only gradient is texture. Hair, on the other hand, is three-dimensional and directional but not uniformly so; and the direction of each hair has to be individually determined. Fur added the element of thickness, and, in the end, several different types of software—for modeling, animating, painting, and rendering—had to be modified to conform with the hair-generating program to create realistic fur for Kitty. This is no small point since detailed photorealistic humans could not be created without an accurate rendition of hair. Fox's *Baby's Day Out* was notable for setting more than 50 percent of its shots in a computer-generated photorealistic city whose 3-D buildings were composited with actors, models, and traffic extracted from a bluescreen process. The film, in which a baby escapes from kidnappers and has a series of hair-raising adventures in downtown Chicago, was so convincing that protests were filed against the filmmakers for recklessly endangering the life of a child performer. (This mode of production would become increasingly common as the decade drew to a close: e.g., the Beijing exterior locations for Jon Avnet's *Red Corner* (1997) were provided by photographs digitized, rendered three-dimensional, and composited with live-action foot-

21.12 and 21.13 *Stargate* (Roland Emmerich, 1994). In shots like this one (top), crowds and buildings were multiplied digitally to save on production costs. The stargate (bottom) convulses backward, a completely digital creation.

21.14 *Forrest Gump* (Robert Zemeckis, 1994). Gump meets JFK in an effect achieved with ILM's Sabre System.

age shot in Hollywood; and nearly all of the dramatic scenes in Phillip Noyce's serial-killer thriller *The Bone Collector* (2000), set in the streets of Manhattan, were shot on a bluescreen soundstage in Montreal to save on production costs and then digitally composited with second-unit location footage shot in New York; see below.) Lucasfilm's *Radioland Murders*, set in a 1930s-style network radio station, used ILM's new Sabre System interactive compositing and editing suite to process over 100 shots of virtual sets at costs more closely approaching those of teleproduction than feature film.

Another 1994 film important for its use of CGI to cut production costs was Roland Emmerich's *Stargate*, produced by Carolco, which used computer graphics supplied by Emmerich's own company, Centropolis Effects LLC, to multiply the size of its cities by replicating and/or reversing images of a relatively small number of miniatures; crowds of extras were multiplied the same way.

21.15 *The Mask* (Chuck Russell, 1994). Jim Carrey's facial contortions in this fantasy, created by ILM's Sabre System, were a big step toward the creation of a completely computer-generated character.

Visual-effects supervisor Kit West collaborated closely with digital artist Jeffrey A. Okun to create the film's most elaborate effect, the stargate itself, which pulls humans into an ancient time warp in a flash of light and color. Although it contained nearly 300 effects shots, *Stargate* demonstrated a remarkable economy of means, impressing industry leaders when it returned $70 million on a relatively modest investment of $50 million, and it helped to put Emmerich's company Centropolis Film Productions and its special-effects facility on the Hollywood map.

Meanwhile at ILM, the **Sabre System** was used to composite about 30 percent of the shots in Paramount's *Forrest Gump*. Named for the power of the light sabres of the Jedi knights in the *Star Wars* films, this was a highly flexible "open architecture" system that could accept a wide range of software and perform many different compositing functions, from digital matte painting through editing and image processing. For *Forrest Gump*, it was used to create the opening sequence of a white feather drifting slowly down from the sky and onto Gump's shoe by digitally blending together 25 different bluescreen shots of real feathers. Sabre was also was used to replicate crowds (e.g., the Washington, D.C., antiwar rally) and sets (the University of Alabama football stadium) and also to remove the legs of an amputee (Gary Sinise's character, Lt. Dan Taylor). But its most salient use was to provide shots of Gump interacting with various historical figures like John F. Kennedy, Lyndon Johnson, and Richard Nixon by manipulating documentary footage and digitally enhancing it. With those exceptions, most of the digital effects in *Forrest Gump* were invisible, whereas those in New Line Cinema's *The Mask* were egregiously notable. Based on a Dark Horse comic-book character and meant to evoke the madcap style of 1940s Warner Bros. animation (e.g., Tex Avery's "Bugs Bunny") in photorealistic fashion, this film took CGI one step closer to digital character creation in its simulation of actor Jim Carrey's facial and bodily contortions while wearing a magically transformational mask. The distortions and embellishments of Carrey's digitally scanned face in ILM's Sabre System were the prototype of the first completely computer-generated character, Casper the Friendly Ghost.

Basically a three-dimensional cartoon, Amblin Entertainment's *Casper* (Brad Silberling, 1995) required an ILM team of 30 animators to create over 400 separate shots of continuous CGI, many of them more than a minute long (or over 1,700 frames). Amblin had originally conceived the ghosts in *Casper* as mechanical puppets, but this clumsy idea was soon abandoned for a computer-graphics solution. The main challenge was to credibly represent the two-dimensional ghosts of the original cartoon as three-dimensional characters for compositing with live action. The process of creation was exemplary: the ghosts began as 10-inch **maquettes,** or sculpted clay figures, which were scanned into the Sabre computer for conversion into skeletal wireframes. These, in turn, were used to construct and animate the characters, whose facial expressions and dialogue-synchronized lip movements were created by new motion-capture software. (The issue of the ghosts' performances was critical since it depended on the yet untested ability of contemporary animation software to represent emotion; and to work on this problem a fiber-optic video/audio link was set up between ILM and *Casper*'s Los Angeles production unit, similar to that established for the production of *Jurassic Park*.) For compositing the ghosts with live action, ILM artists employed **animatics** (see below) to place the ghosts during live-action shooting. These are, effectively, moving storyboards comprised of rough drawings or computer-generated stick figures that are composited with video recordings of live-action scenes to give both actors and digital artists a map for the positioning of the characters and other CGI in the final composite. (For George Lucas's 1999 *Star Wars: Episode I—The Phantom Menace*, e.g., animatics were used to previsualize every shot.) Although it was a critical failure (but popular nonetheless), *Casper* was nearly a year in postproduction and represented an exponential leap over *Jurassic Park* in terms of character design—its computer-generated ghosts were on-screen for 40 of the film's 100 minutes, whereas Spielberg's dinosaurs had occupied less than 7 minutes of screen time. The ghosts also talked and had facial expressions that could be described as photorealistic within the context of the cartoonlike world they inhabit in the film.

Even greater leaps came in the same year with Tristar's *Jumanji* and Universal's *Dragonheart*. Directed by former ILM effects supervisor Joe Johnston, who had won a visual-effects Oscar for his work on Steven Spielberg's *Raiders of the Lost Ark* (1981), *Jumanji* involved the digital creation of numerous photorealistic animals for the first time. These included lions, elephants, a rhinoceros, pelicans, monkeys, and bats that inhabit the jungle of a magic board game and are transported to a small New England town. As with *The Flintstones*, the biggest problem lay in capturing the look of organic materials, espe-

21.16 *Jumanji* (Joe Johnston, 1995). This stampede near the end of the film was created through "flocking" software that gave each animal an individually variable run cycle.

cially the soft textures of features, fur, and hair. The hair-generating software created for that film was customized so that each hair could be individually modeled in the computer to adjust its color, length, thickness, and density, and also to recoil during body movement. There was also the necessity for creating two mass animal scenes—a stampede and a grand finale in which all of the animals swirl into a vortex, which returns them to the game. These were accomplished through new, improved **"flocking" software** that controls the individual movements of animals in a group relative to one another. Thus, in the stampede, the course of the whole group was charted frame by frame, but each of the 60 stampeding animals was given an individually variable run cycle. *Dragonheart*, directed by Rob Cohen, is important in the history of CGI for its innovation of new software called Caricature, or Cari, which permits the animation of a fully rendered figure rather than its wireframe, enabling artists

21.17 *Dragonheart* (Rob Cohen, 1996). Draco the Dragon was animated via Caricature software (or Cari) developed at ILM by Cary Phillips. It was a completely digital creation, especially notable for its complicated facial expressions, and four times more detailed than *Jurassic Park*'s T-Rex.

to envision the way their images will look on-screen as they create them. Developed by ILM effects artist Cary Phillips, Cari also facilitated more complicated facial expressions and movement, with the result that *Dragonheart*'s central computer-generated character, Draco, a talking dragon, was four times more detailed than *Jurassic Park*'s T-rex and became, excluding the three-dimensional cartoon characters of *Casper* and the fully animated *Toy Story* (John Lasseter, 1995), the cinema's first completely photorealistic digital creature.

Digital Domain and *Titanic*

From the foregoing account, it should be clear that the centrality of ILM in the development of CGI is indisputable. But there were other important contributors—Digital Domain, for example, the special-effects house founded by James Cameron, Stan Winston, and Scott Ross in the successful wake of *Terminator 2*. In addition to providing CGI for Cameron's *True Lies* (1994) and *Titanic* (1997), Digital Domain did the effects work for Paramount's *Interview with the Vampire* (Neil Jordan, 1994), which involved a seamless blending of digital effects with animatronics, and Universal's *Apollo 13* (Ron Howard, 1995), which included a complicated 42-element launch-and-explosion sequence involving computer-generated gases and debris, and won an Academy Award for it in the process. The company would also supply CGI for Universal's *Dante's Peak* (Roger Donaldson, 1997), whose computer-generated lava effects represented a marked improvement over those of *Congo* (Frank Mar-

shall, 1995) in terms of color consistency and precise interaction with other scenic elements. (*Congo*'s lava, in fact, was created from a liquid material called methocel, with color and glow added in postproduction by computer graphics. Another film with extensive lava effects, Mick Jackson's *Volcano* [1997], did not use CGI at all, but methocel dyed red with ultraviolet-sensitive paint, which was lit from below by ultraviolet lights to make it glow.) Unquestionably, however, Digital Domain's most impressive achievement of the decade was its visual-effects work for *Titanic*, for which it won yet another Oscar. *Titanic* employed a combination of traditional effects and CGI to simulate disaster on an epic scale. A full-scale 44-foot model of the ship was constructed for filming with motion-control cameras for compositing with computer-generated water, fog, smoke, passengers, and other elements; and

21.18 and 21.19 *Titanic* (James Cameron, 1997). One thousand computer-generated stuntmen, provided by Digital Domain through a process called "roto-capture," peopled the decks of the *Titanic* as it sank; in some shots, the ship itself was all digital. *Titanic* swept the 1997 Academy Awards, winning in nearly every major category, including Best Visual Effects.

some of the ship's interiors were created from miniatures, with actors digitally composited into them. But the most innovative use of digital technology involved the creation of computer-generated stuntmen for the film's disaster sequences. During the sinking, for example, as the ship tilts end to end into the water, over 1,000 falling figures were created via CGI, modeled on real stunt falls by means of a process called "roto capture," in which the motion-captured falls were scanned into a computer and used as templates for the animation of computer-generated mannequins. Similarly, scenes of crowds or of people strolling on deck were created through capturing and digitizing approximately 30 extras in real motion, then using it to animate computer-generated characters, sometimes as many as 500 per scene. All told, there were over 100 such shots in *Titanic,* some of which involved digital **face replacement** and/or the mixing of live and computer-generated characters. A computer-generated ship was used to facilitate placement of these elements, to previsualize camera movement, and to stand in for missing sections of live-action sets. (The CGI ship also appeared in three overhead shots of the Titanic at sea). Because it contained over 450 visual-effects shots, the film underwent elaborate compositing in postproduction, and although Digital Domain provided the vast majority of the these, thirteen other companies worked at various points on the film, whose negative cost was reputedly in excess of $200 million. *Titanic* went on to become the most commercially successful film in the history of the cinema, earning $601 million in the North American market alone.

Particle Animation, 1996–1997: *Twister, Independence Day,* and *Starship Troopers*

While Cameron's film was in production, a disaster film of a different sort made a seminal contribution to the development of photorealistic CGI. Warner Bros.' *Twister* (1996) was directed by Jan de Bont, a former cinematographer who had made an impressive debut in 1994 with the adrenaline-pumping chase film *Speed* (20th Century–Fox, 1994). Preproduction planning called for *Twister*'s tornadoes to be computer-generated at ILM; and the design team, led by Habib Zargarpour, had orig-

inated a new type of **particle-animation software** for the task, which played a major role not just in de Bont's film, but in several contemporaneous landmarks in CGI, including Roland Emmerich's *Independence Day* (20th Century–Fox, 1996) and Paul Verhoeven's *Starship Troopers* (Touchstone Pictures, 1997). Particle systems are a form of modeling known as **procedural description** in which objects simulate the processes of natural growth, including elements of randomness, recursion, and accident. Typically, particle systems will employ small points in 3-D space that are programmed with growth attributes and specific behavioral trajectories. Particle animation software—first used extensively to simulate submarine wakes, torpedo trails, and floating plankton in Paramount's *The Hunt for Red October* (John McTiernan, 1990)—creates automated instructions for controlling the movement of large numbers of objects that cannot be animated individually in a cost-effective way. Since, in *Independence Day,* whose visual effects won a 1996 Oscar for VFX supervisor Douglas Smith (not to be confused with morphing pioneer Doug Smythe at ILM), the massive dogfights between alien spaceships and F-18s contained hundreds of aircraft, to animate them individually would have been practically impossible. Instead, computer engineers programmed each type of craft with specific behavioral norms: spaceships and F-18s were given different speeds and weapons, different objectives and capabilities, so that they would react automatically when they came within each others' range. In effect, the spacecraft and aircraft were programmed to fight a virtual battle; when a craft was hit by weapons fire, the computer replaced its image with that of an explosion (no mean feat—*Independence Day* used 340 digital composites to create these and other effects). Particle animation is a variant of this procedure, dealing with vast numbers of objects too numerous to animate in any other way. The ILM software designed for *Twister* could not only isolate and animate individual particles within a larger whole, but could also program random patterns of chaos into the mix. The film ultimately contained 135 tornado and hailstorm shots generated by this software, as well as numerous digital mattes painted to change the look of the sky. Digital manipulation was also performed on the landscape to keep the field crops at regular heights over the course of filming and to replace a tanker-truck model destroyed by pyrotechnical effects for one spectacular, in-your-face shot of the truck careening toward the (virtual) camera lens.

21.20 and 21.21 *Twister* (Jan de Bont, 1996). ILM used particle-animation software to randomize elements of the 135 digitally created tornado and hailstorm shots in the film (top). Yet, despite the sophisticated procedural animation of its storms, some of the film's other effects were as cartoonish as those of *The Last Starfighter*. Here a tanker truck careens into the lens of a virtual camera, looking much like a panel in a comic strip (bottom).

21.22 *Independence Day* (Roland Emmerich, 1996). A frame from the concluding dogfight between alien spaceships and F18s, created through particle-animation software that programmed hundreds of individual aircraft to fight a virtual battle. The film won the 1996 Oscar for Best Visual Effects.

Particle-animation software was similarly crucial to the production of *Starship Troopers*, which made several new advances on the digital frontier. The film is based on Robert A. Heinlein's 1959 novel about a war between earth and a race of gigantic intelligent bugs, and it features hundreds of shots of the insect armies swarming en masse during battle sequences. The bugs were created by Phil Tippett, the genius behind Go-Motion and many other innovations in animatronics, who, working with 100 other digital artists at his Tippett Studios, designed six different insect types, all but one of which began life as drawings and sculpted maquettes. The exception was the tanker bug, which was created entirely in the digital domain. Animation of individual bugs was accomplished either by digital artists or through the application of an improved DID (Digital Input Device—see *Jurassic Park*, above), and Dynamation software was used to animate the swarms. (The term *Dynamation*, a conflation of "Dynamic Animation," was coined by special-effects pioneer Ray Harryhausen in the 1960s to designate his process of three-dimensional stop-motion animation; the name was later borrowed for proprietary particle-animation software developed by Alias|Wavefront and Silicon Graphics, Inc. (SGI) in the

21.23 and 21.24 *Starship Troopers* (Paul Verhoeven, 1997). **Giant arachnids swarming on the surface of Tango Urilla, achieved through Dynamation particle-animation software at the Tippett Studios (top); Dynamation generated multiple dots to represent each bug, which were then replaced with 3-D digital insects animated against 3-D background plates of the physical terrain, a process that required 25 to 30 hours of work per frame. A frame from the destruction of the tanker bug by nuclear hand grenade (bottom). The sequence combined live action, model shots, and CGI, but the explosion itself was completely computer-generated.**

task hat ultimately required 25 to 30 hours of work per frame, so that a 10-second shot could take as long as 300 hours to render completely. *Starship Troopers* also featured computer-generated humans both to multiply crowds and troop movements and to represent soldiers attacked and dismembered by bugs. In many such sequences, live action and model work were seamlessly cut together with CGI. One the most complicated effects in the film, for example, involved the destruction of a tanker bug with a nuclear hand grenade; it called for protagonist Casper Van Dien to jump on the beetle's back, gouge a hole in its shell, and drop the explosive into it. Part of the scene was constructed through close shots of live action on a model shell, but long and medium shots were computer-generated, as was the explosion. Most of *Starship Troopers'* space battles were executed in miniature by 270 artists under the direction of Scott F. Anderson at Sony Pictures Imageworks (SPI)[8] and composited with computer-generated spacescapes, which began as traditional 2-D matte paintings before being digitized in three dimensions and computer-enhanced with a cloudlike nebulae. In one particu-

mid-1990s.) Dynamation generated multiple dots to represent the swarming bugs, each with its own radius, direction, and speed, which were instructed to respond to variations in the live-action terrain and in their own movements relative to each other (so that, for example, they wouldn't run into rocks in compositing or into other bugs). The dots were digitally replaced with 3-D insects and animated against 3-D background plates of the setting, a

8. Sony Pictures Imageworks (SPI), a division of Sony Pictures Entertainment, was founded in 1992 by former ILM-er Ken Ralston (b. 1955). In addition to *Starship Troopers*, SPI provided visual effects for *Contact* (1997), *Godzilla* (1998), and *Star Trek: Insurrection* (1998), among many others.

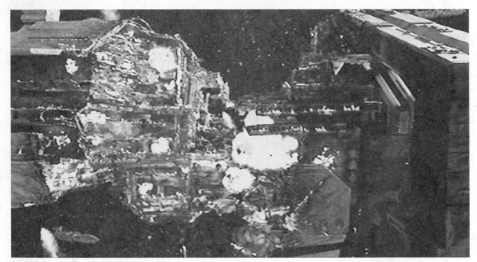

21.25 and 21.26 *Starship Troopers* (1997). The battle cruiser *Rodger Young* and a frame from its breaking apart—a sequence combining model and miniature work with live action and CGI in 125 separate layers of imagery. Most of the film's space battles were executed at Sony Pictures Imageworks.

larly complex series of shots provided by Boss Film Studios[9] the battle cruiser *Rodger Young* is hit by a computer-generated plasma burst and splits in two. The combination of model and miniature work with live action and CGI in this sequence made it one of the most heavily composited to date, involving 125 separate layers of imagery whose interaction required extensive previsualization. In addition to Tippett Studio, SPI, and Boss, ILM, Visual Concept Engineering (VCE), Compound Eye, and Banned from the Ranch Entertainment (BFTRE)[1] also contributed to the 550-plus special-effects shots of *Starship Troopers*, and it became one the most effects-intensive films in history, spending by some accounts as much as 50 percent of its $110 million negative cost to produce them. (By contrast, Spielberg's *The Lost World: Jurassic Park*, made the same year, cost $73 million and had fewer than 200 effects shots.) Another precedent-setting

---

9. Boss Film Studios was founded by Richard Edlund (b. 1940) in 1983, after leaving ILM, where he shared the Best Visual Effects Oscar with Dennis Muren, Ken Ralston, and Phil Tippett for *Return of the Jedi* (he was also part of ILM teams recognized by the Academy for *Raiders of the Lost Ark* [1981] and *The Empire Strikes Back* [1980]). Among other films, Boss provided special effects for *Ghostbusters* (Ivan Reitman, 1984), *2010* (1984), *Aliens*[3] (David Fincher, 1992), *Batman Returns* (1992), *Cliffhanger* (1993), *Waterworld* (1995), *Species* (Roger Donaldson, 1995), *Multiplicity* (1996), and *Air Force One* (1997), as well as *Starship Troopers* (1997) and *The Parent Trap* (1998), before going out of business in 1997. Although its work was nominated for seven Academy Awards and it was briefly one of the most successful effects houses in the industry, Boss fell victim to the increased capacity and rapidly dropping price of desktop computers, which made its large investments in mainframe computers obsolete.

1. BFTRE was founded by Casey Cannon 1995 to accommodate unconventional creativity in the field of digital effects. The "ranch" is Skywalker Ranch, George Lucas's headquarters in Novato, California, from which several of the company's original partners had been "banned" (fired) for violating ILM company policy. BFTRE specializes in digital compositing, wire removal, morphing, and 3-D animation; and it also creates computer-screen displays for movies, known as "burn-ins" (which it provided for *Starship Troopers*, together with the FedNet broadcast sequences). Its current president is Van Ling, who was James Cameron's visual-effects liaison for *The Abyss* and *Terminator 2*.

feature of *Starship Troopers* was its confluence of digital and live-action direction, wherein Verhoeven directed the live actors on locations and sets during the six months of principal photography, while Tippett choreographed the digital bugs and Anderson managed the spaceships during the year of postproduction. Although Verhoeven and his three visual-effects supervisors (Tippett, Scott F. Anderson at SPI, and Scott Squires at ILM) worked in close collaboration with each other and with director of photography (DP) Jost Vacano, each had to perform his creative tasks in separate locations and production contexts.[2]

Twister and *Starship Troopers* are watersheds in the history of CGI and the new kind of cinema it facilitates. In the other CGI landmarks discussed above, the special-effects sequences could have been accomplished by conventional means, and, indeed, most were originally planned that way (e.g., animatronics were envisioned for *Jurassic Park*, mechanical puppets for *Casper*, etc.). In many cases, similar films had already been made using such effects: stop-motion dinosaurs and other prehistoric creatures had roamed the earth from *The Lost World* (Harry O. Hoyt, 1925) through *King Kong* (Merian C. Cooper and Ernest B. Schoedsack, 1933) to *The Land That Time Forgot* (Kevin Connor, 1975); the Titanic had gone down before (in *Titanic* [Jean Negulesco, 1953] and *A Night to Remember* [Roy Ward Baker, 1958]), as had ships of more recent vintage (*The Last Voyage* [Andrew L. Stone, 1960]; *The Poseidon Adventure* [Ronald Neame, 1972]); and actors had appeared in films with historical personages as if in newsreels or home movies (Charles Foster Kane with Teddy Roosevelt, Mussolini, and Hitler in *Citizen Kane* [Orson Welles, 1941]; Zelig with a variety of famous people in *Zelig* [Woody Allen, 1983]). Characters like *Dragonheart*'s Draco had been attempted before, most notably in *Dragonslayer* (Matthew Robbins, 1981), with its Go-Motion dragon puppets, and *The NeverEnding Story* (Wolfgang Petersen, 1984), whose Falkor the "luckdragon" was also an animatronic puppet. But *Twister* and *Starship Troopers* could not have been made without CGI, and digital-effects planning was present at the moment of their conception. In a quite literal sense, both films are *about* their effects—*Twister*'s funnel-shaped cyclones and *Starship Troopers*' armies of giant insects—neither of which could have been credibly produced through traditional effects (FX) technology. (The difference between them, of course, is that whereas the FX phenomena of *Twister* exist in nature but could not be practically controlled for filming, the FX phenomena of *Starship Troopers* do not. Digital technology seems to work best when it gives concrete form to the imagined impossible rather than attempts to replicate the real. The critical response to Wolfgang Petersen's *The Perfect Storm* in 2000, for example, indicated that digital weather effects are still somewhat problematic.) Interestingly, though, the classical cinema remains the paradigm for this new work: e.g., Phil Tippett claimed *Zulu* (Cy Endfield, 1964) and *The Charge of the Light Brigade* (Tony Richardson, 1968) as his models for the bug attack on the Foreign Legion-like fort at Whiskey Outpost in *Starship Troopers*, and countless World War II combat films stand behind it as a whole, as do the populist propaganda epics of Frank Capra's *Why We Fight* series (1942–44).

A New "New Hollywood," 1997–1998

As digital effects became an integral part of the motion-picture industry during the late 1990s, whole new crafts sprang up around the need for live-action and digital directors to work in separate spheres—animatics, for example, which is essentially the practice of creating moving storyboards. In animatics, computer-generated stick figures or line drawings representing special effects are composited with live-action footage and/or other elements to show how the effects will work in the final cut of the film. The first animatic to schematize an entire sequence, as opposed to a single shot, was created by David Dozoretz (b. 1971) at ILM for the 7-minute helicopter-train chase sequence that concludes Brian De Palma's *Mission Impossible* (Paramount, 1996)—a sequence in which every shot is a visual effect, including a computer-generated train running on real rails, a com-

---

2. Like Cameron, Verhoeven had some early history with CGI. His ultraviolent adaptation of Philip K. Dick's *Total Recall* (Tristar, 1990) features a computer-generated skeleton that breaks through the glass of an X-ray machine, shatters the image, and becomes a three-dimensional human (a stunt double). The CGI was provided by Metrolight and Dream Quest Images, but matching the movements of the computer-generated skeleton and the live-action stuntman had to be done by hand in the absence of match-modeling software.

puter-generated MD520 helicopter, and a completely digital "Chunnel" environment into which the actors were composited at the climax. This complicated sequence was shot almost precisely as projected, and animatics have since become an important part of the preproduction process and not for effects sequences alone: in 1999, George Lucas employed Dozoretz to previsualize every shot of *Star Wars: Episode I—The Phantom Menace* with a 3-D animation program that established the placement of objects and characters on the set as well as camera positions and movements. Recorded on digital videotape, these animatics were played back on the set before shooting so that the cast and crew could anticipate the dynamics of each scene. Three-D **previsualization,** or "previs," through aniamatics has become a normative part of preproduction for films that employ extensive digital effects, and there are several companies that specialize in it, including Dozoretz's own Persistence of Vision (POV) and Pixel Liberation Front (PLF), founded by Colin Green, who was responsible for previsualizing the futuristic twenty-second–century cityscapes of *Judge Dredd* (Danny Cannon, 1995) and the elaborate miniature sequences of *Starship Troopers*. Another new craft that emerged with the rise of CGI was match moving, whereby the movement of the **virtual camera** is synched with that of the live-action camera and computer-animated figures are correctly positioned within the live-action frame. (A virtual camera is implied in all 3-D animation; its "lens" is the point toward which all lines of perspective in the computer-generated image converge. Like real cameras, virtual ones can track, pan, tilt, and zoom; unlike real ones they can go anywhere the human imagination is capable of taking them.) In effect, the process of match moving more or less inverts that of animatics in that it seeks to represent the live-action components of a production for combination with CGI: the match mover models all of the characters and objects in the live-action environment as wireframes and lays them over live-action background plates as the first step in the postproduction integration of digital and real-time elements. The level of match moving for any given film depends on the complexity of the production. For some, one or two match movers will do; but for an effects-laden work like Spielberg's *The Lost World: Jurassic Park* (1997), as many as eight might be required.

In the same way that new CGI-related crafts emerged in the late-1990s film industry, many full-service effects and animation facilities became more focused on creating specific varieties of CGI. Rhythm & Hues, for example, was a studio that specialized in creating digital mouth movements such as those of the talking farm animals that propelled *Babe* (1995) toward the 1995 Academy Award for Best Visual Effects. That film employed over 500 live animals and approximately 100 animatronic ones, some of which were given digital mouth movements via 3-D animation. In fact, *Babe* had 132 computer-generated shots, as compared to 150 animatronic shots, a ratio more or less inverted in the sequel *Babe: Pig in the City* (1998), which also generated 3-D animals for stunt work and used motion-capture data to program the movement of animatronic animals. Rhythm & Hues employed 2-D rather than 3-D animation to create most of the animal mouth movements in *Dr. Dolittle* (1998), and it similarly brought its expertise to *Mouse Hunt* (1997), for which new software was devised to create digital mice and animate a swarm of moths. Richard Edlund's Boss Film Studios developed a new digital compositing system specifically for use in *Multiplicity* (1996), in which Michael Keaton plays himself and his four clones. It enabled filmmakers to view digital video of scenes moments after filming and facilitated the interaction between Keaton and the composited clones. This system was improved and used the following year for *The Nutty Professor* (1997), in which Eddie Murphy plays six characters seated

21.27 *Babe* (Chris Noonan, 1995). Many of the farm animals in this film were given 3-D digital mouth movement by Rhythm & Hues, a company specializing in such effects. *Babe* won the 1995 Academy Award for Best Visual Effects.

21.28 *Multiplicity* (Harold Ramis, 1996). Interaction between Michael Keaton and his clones was facilitated by a new digital compositing system developed by Boss Film Studios that helped to track the movements of multiply duplicated characters from shot to shot.

together at a dinner table in an extended single take, and then for *The Parent Trap* (1998), in which identical twins, both played by Lindsay Lohan, attempt to reunite their divorced parents. Other, usually smaller, special-effects houses focus almost exclusively on certain categories or tasks. For example, Persistence of Vision and Pixel Liberation Front (see above) specialize in previsualization, House of Moves concentrates on motion capture, Matte World Digital and Compound Eye exist primarily to create digital mattes and 3-D composites, and The Computer Film Company (CFC) focuses on the jobs of digital compositing, paint work, and wire removal, and, together with BFTRE, on 2-D computer-monitor "burn-ins," which are matted into screens left blank in live-action filming (e.g., CFC provided over 120 burn-ins for the interior spaceship scenes of *Event Horizon* [Paul Anderson, 1997]; see below).

The wonder years for CGI in Hollywood were 1997 and 1998. In addition to *Titanic* and *Starship Troopers*, landmark films of 1997 included Universal's *The Lost World: Jurassic Park*; Gaumont's *The Fifth Element*; Warner Bros.' *Batman & Robin, Contact,* and *Mars Attacks!* (1996); Columbia's *Men in Black* ; and Fox's *Alien: Resurrection* and *The X Files* (1998). Of these, *The Lost World*, Spielberg's sequel to *Jurassic Park*, was especially important for its advances in **procedural animation,** used to create a group of stampeding dinosaurs, and for its refinement of Cari software to provide not facial expressions as in *Dragonheart*, but realistic muscle reflexes and breathing motions for the dinosaurs. (These refinements were important to the live-action version of

New Line Cinema's *Spawn* [Mark A. Z. Dippé, 1997], whose title character was animated by Cari and new **muscle-enveloping software** at ILM under the direction of Habib Zargarpour.) Because the computer-generated shots in *The Lost World* are longer and have more camera movement and live-action interface, post-production required nearly ten months as opposed to seven for *Jurassic Park* and three times as many technical personnel; furthermore, whereas *Jurassic Park* had only 50 3-D shots, *The Lost World* had 91 3-D shots and another 100 2-D digital effects involving wire removal, sky replacement, color correction, and other refinements. (ILM's Dennis Muren was visual-effect supervisor for both films.) Luc Besson's *The Fifth Element*, with effects supplied by Digital Domain, made elaborate use of digital matte paintings to extend its cityscapes and in several cases combined upward of 82 separate effects elements within a single shot; furthermore, all but a handful of its 225 effects shots were previsualized by computer. The *Batman* series had been an innovator in digital effects from its second installment, *Batman Returns* (Tim Burton, 1992), when the transformation of the Batmobile from normal car to supervehicle was accomplished through computer graphics. By the time of the third film, *Batman Forever* (Joel Schumacher, 1995), an all-digital Batman was being used for stunts, and for *Batman & Robin* (Joel Schumacher, 1997) CGI was used to previsualize camera movement by running a virtual camera through wireframe models of the sets as well as to plot the trajectories of miniature vehicles around miniature buildings and to extend the sets both horizontally and vertically.[3] CGI was also used to previsualize the alien transport machine in *Contact* and did the job so convincingly that director Robert Zemeckis decided to use the computer-generated image rather than build the miniature it was intended to model. For Tim Burton's *Mars Attacks!*, Cary Phillips refined the **Cari software** tool he had created at ILM in 1996 for *Dragonheart* so that it could animate up to 20 computer-generated characters at once, a major advance in CGI software since it radically reduced postproduction time (for example, the

---

3. The *Batman* series showed a progressive reliance on CGI as digital effects multiplied from film to film and eventually eclipsed optical effects: the progression in the number of effects shots from the first *Batman* film in 1989 through the last in 1997 was 100, to 115, to 250, to 400.

21.29 *The Fifth Element* (Luc Besson, 1997). The canyon of skyscrapers that Leeloo (Milla Jovovich) plunges through is comprised of digital matte paintings created at Digital Domain.

film's 440 CGI shots were created in less than eight months, an unthinkable timetable just several years before). Cari was also used to give facial expressions to the alien character Mikey in *Men in Black*, a film whose popularity was based in large part on its inventive use of CGI to represent the existence of grotesque shape-shifting aliens among us; its contributions were recognized when it won the 1997 Oscar for Best Visual Effects. *Alien: Resurrection* (Jean-Pierre Jeunet) relied so heavily on computer-graphics for its 205 visual-effects shots that it cost 50 percent more than any previous *Alien* film ($70 million) and became the first film in the franchise to lose money, effectively ending it; some sequences, such as when the full-bodied aliens swim underwater, dispensed with animatronics altogether and were completely computer-generated. *The X Files* (Rob Bowman) was important for its sophisticated, but cost-effective, digital extension of 48 live-action sets, using 3-D computer graphics and 2-D matte paintings. The CGI roster for 1997 would not be complete without mentioning George Lucas's three *Star Wars* "Special Edition" reissues. Dissatisfied with certain predigital creature and animation effects in *Star Wars* (1977), *The Empire Strikes Back* (1980), and *Return of the Jedi* (1983), Lucas re-released the trilogy with computer-generated enhancement, substituting digital for analog imagery and adding about 5 minutes to the running time, all at a cost of approximately

$10 million (which also included color restoration and remastering the sound tracks for 5.1 digital playback). Although several of the digital extravaganzas of 1997 lost money (*The Fifth Element*, *Mars Attacks!*, *Alien: Resurrection*, and—unaccountably—*Starship Troopers*), most made a good profit and three entered the ranks of highest-grossing films of all time—*Titanic* ($601 million), *Men in Black* ($250 million) and *The Lost World: Jurassic Park* ($229 million), where they remain today (as numbers 1, 20, and 27, respectively). Not insignificantly, the reissued *Star Wars* became the fourth highest-grossing film of 1997 with $138 million and—more to the point—set the public up for Lucas's 1999 *Star Wars: Episode I—The Phantom Menace*, 70 percent of whose shots contained CGI.

The most unique film of 1998 from a CGI perspective was Roland Emmerich's *Godzilla* (Sony/Tristar), produced by the director's Centropolis Film Productions at a cost of $125 million, which, unlike previous films with computer-generated creatures (e.g., *Jurassic Park*, *Dragonheart*, and *The Lost World*), did not supplement them extensively with animatronics. In the entire film, there were only 24 shots involving animatronic puppets, most of them head shots of Godzilla and its offspring, and the rest of the 155 Godzilla shots were entirely CGI, as were many others. There were a total of 587 digital effects in the film, provided by Centropolis Effects LLC, and in several scenes virtually everything on screen was digital. Great expectations and heavy marketing by Sony Pictures Entertainment did not produce the expected blockbuster, and the film returned a modest $136 million, suggesting that the public was becoming glutted on its now steady diet of digital effects. Further proof of this was provided by another 1998 film involving a large amount of digital work, New Line Cinema's *Lost in Space* (Stephen Hopkins), whose effects were the first CGI created by Jim Henson's Creature Shop

21.30 *Godzilla* (Roland Emmerich, 1998). All but 24 of the 179 creature shots in this film were produced through CGI, making Godzilla and its offspring the first (nearly) all-digital monsters.

(although ten other London FX houses ultimately worked on the film, too). This film, based on a popular television series from the mid-1960s, contained 750 digital composites, and most of its sets and miniatures were enhanced by computer graphics. Furthermore, the central creature was a computer-generated, ape-like alien that had over 300 vectors of facial movement. Despite its then-lavish budget of $125 million, its audience-friendly "Space Family Robinson" theme, and numerous awards for technical achievement, *Lost in Space* barely broke even at the box office. The worst FX disaster of 1998, however, was another science-fiction film, *Sphere* (Barry Levinson), set 2,000 feet underwater where U.S. government scientists are sent to investigate a submerged alien spacecraft. On the basis of extensive previsualization by effects supervisor Jeffrey A. Okun (effects coordinator for 1984's digital vanguard *The Last Starfighter*) and Carlos Arguello of Cinesite Hollywood, a company that made its mark in the industry by designing **water-simulation software** for *Waterworld* (Kevin Reynolds, 1995), and later the flood-disaster film *Hard Rain* (Mikael Salomon, 1998), Warners decided that *Sphere* was too expensive to make as planned, so they shut production down while it was reconceptualized. (Levinson used the interval to quickly shoot *Wag the Dog* for New Line Cinema, a political satire that became one of the most profitable films of the year.) Rerigged, *Sphere* relied heavily on CGI to simulate its underwater environment as well as to provide key elements in sequences like the initial submarine descent and a mass attack by jellyfish, economies that

enabled the film to be brought in for $80 million. But nothing could save it from its broken-backed structure and clumsy script, and it returned less than half of its negative cost at the box office to become one of 1998's biggest commercial failures. (Among *Sphere*'s many problems were its close resemblance to another science fiction/horror film that had bombed at the box office just six months earlier—Paramount's *Event Horizon*, which similarly combined conventional special effects with CGI.) For the more practically budgeted *Small Soldiers* (Joe Dante), Dream Works SKG's child-oriented fantasy about a war between misprogrammed toy soldiers, ILM developed new scanning and software tools to match computer-generated characters with their animatronic counterparts. Grossing $54 million against a negative cost of $40 million, the film suffered from its market positioning since its humor was actually more appealing to adults than to children. Disney's $49 million *Mighty Joe Young* (Ron Underwood—nominally produced by RKO, which owned the original copyright) was also targeted for young audiences and experienced a similar fate. A remake of Ernest B. Schoedsack's 1949 classic (itself a kind of sequel to *King Kong*), *Mighty Joe Young*'s digital effects were provided by Disney-owned Dream Quest Images,[4]

---

4. Dream Quest Images, currently owned by Walt Disney Productions, is a full-service effects and animation facility in Simi Valley. It has contributed notable work to *Flubber* (1997), *Mighty Joe Young* (1998), *Armageddon* (1998), and *Mission to Mars* (2000), and helped *Total Recall* (1990) to win a Special Achievement Academy Award for its visual effects.

which designed new **hair-simulation software** and new software to animate the giant ape's face and create realistic musculature, but the film failed with the public, grossing just $50.6 million to barely break even. (Dream Quest's hair-simulation program combined the geometric approach of ILM's software for *Jumanji* [Joe Johnston, 1995], which created an individual geometry for each hair, with Digital Domain's volumetric approach for *The Island of Dr. Moreau* [John Frankenheimer, 1996], which added full patches of hair at the rendering stage).

Although it seemed clear by the summer of 1998 that the mass appeal of CGI was fading, Disney was considerably more successful with Touchstone Pictures' disaster epic *Armageddon*, directed by Michael Bay. Produced at the record-breaking cost of $174 million (the film was budgeted at $139 million and went $35 million over-budget), it posits an asteroid the size of Texas on a deadly collision course with Earth and had spectacular digital and pyrotechnic effects produced by Digital Domain and 14 other effects companies, including Dream Quest Images, Blue Sky|VIFX, The Computer Film Company, and Cinesite Hollywood. One of its most elaborate set pieces involved the destruction of Paris, which was accomplished by creating a real explosion in a southern California rock quarry and compositing it with three-dimensional aerial photographs of the city, a computer-generated asteroid, and props (e.g., mock-ups of gargoyles) blown out of an air cannon in front of a bluescreen, a total of 50 separate elements. Another major stint of CGI occurs at the film's beginning, when an early, eons-old collision between an asteroid and Earth is depicted in a manner intentionally evocative of the "Genesis effect" sequence in *Star Trek II: The Wrath of Khan* (1982). The limitations of its genres notwithstanding, *Armageddon* succeeds as an action-adventure/science-fiction–disaster film on almost every level, but it had the misfortune to be released in mid-summer, after Dream Works' similarly plotted *Deep Impact* (Mimi Leder) had dominated the post–Memorial Day box office for weeks and after the public's enthusiasm for computer-generated effects had clearly waned. Thus, despite an expensive promotion campaign, *Armageddon* was a major disappointment for Disney, even though its $202 million take made it the highest-grossing film of 1998, inching out Dream Works' *Saving Private Ryan* by a hair. (Spielberg's old-fashioned combat film featured 40 digitally enhanced shots provided by ILM, most of them appearing in the D-day landing sequence at Omaha

21.31 and 21.32 *Armageddon* **(Michael Bay, 1998). In an all-digital shot from the beginning of the film (top), the Chrysler Building is decapitated by an asteroid. A frame from the destruction of Paris (bottom), digitally composited from footage of a real explosion, 3-D aerial photographs of the city, and CGI.**

Beach; these included computer-generated characters in landing craft, a computer-generated jeep, digital bullet hits and tracer fire, and digital matte paintings of hundreds of battleships massed in the English Channel. Spielberg told *American Cinematographer* that to have staged this sequence with real ships etc. would have cost $85 million— $10 million more than the film's entire budget: "With a few $100,000 digital effects," he said, "I was able to save millions.")[5]

The Digital Manipulation of Color: *What Dreams May Come, Pleasantville,* and Beyond

Two other films of 1998 pointed CGI in a different—and subtler—direction than character creation and action-oriented effects. PolyGram Filmed Entertainment's *What Dreams May Come* (see color insert), based on a novel by Richard Matheson and directed by Vincent Ward, took the original step of designing backgrounds to look like oil paintings on canvas. It is about an afterlife journey undertaken by a man (Robin Williams) who is killed in a car accident at the outset of the film and whose wife commits suicide out of grief. To save her from hell, he must leave heaven and retrieve her from the underworld in a mythic quest that resonates back to classical antiquity. The "painted world" of paradise is modeled on the work of such painters as Monet, van Gogh, and nineteenth-century German romanticists like Caspar David Friedrich, while hell is modeled on the colorless engravings of nineteenth-century French artist Gustave Doré, famous for his illustrations of Dante's *Divine Comedy*. The look of the Painted World was achieved through the application of new image-based animation software that could attach brush strokes to scenic elements to make them appear painted. For example, photographic images of real settings could be scanned into the computer and layered with brush strokes based on the styles of real painters. The brush strokes could be wet or dry, and they could be animated to appear three-dimensional. In postproduction, live-action footage of the actors was matched and composited with the painted backgrounds using a

new laser-based tracking system called Lidar. Many of the shots contained 120 to 150 different layers, and it took 30 computer animators at Digital Domain and Pacific Ocean Post (POP) nine months to put together the film's 250,000 separate elements in an unprecedented melding of CGI and painting. Vincent Ward justifiably claimed that *What Dreams May Come* "breaks new ground perceptually by combining a sense of wet viscous oil painting with moving image photography"; and Robin Williams captured another aspect of the film's uniqueness when he remarked that he was "fascinated by the idea of using computer technology to create something other than an explosion or a raptor."[6]

New Line Cinema's *Pleasantville* (see color insert), directed by Gary Ross, is about two teenagers from the late 1990s who suddenly find themselves transported into the sanitized and lobotomized world of a 1950s-style TV sitcom ("Pleasantville"). To convey the unreality and colorlessness of this world, the filmmakers used new **color-correction technology** to turn color-film images into black and white (a transition that is also medium-specific since television images during the 1950s were broadcast in black and white); as the teenagers gradually begin to humanize "Pleasantville," color comes to it selectively and literally, as color returns selectively to the black-and-white portion of the film. (Director Ross and DP John Lindley briefly considered shooting in black and white and adding color in postproduction rather than the other way around, but they realized that resolution would suffer since modern color stocks record much sharper images than black-and-white.) In standard color-correction technology, film images are scanned into a computer, digitally changed to black and white (or vice versa), and then scanned back out onto film, a process that normally takes 10 to 30 seconds per frame, depending on image content. To perform the high-volume work of scanning approximately 100 minutes (some 163,000 frames) of a 120-minute film, *Pleasantville* producers used the Philips Spirit DataCine at Cinesite Digital Imaging in Los Angeles, a new kind of **telecine** device developed in Europe that transfers film to digital files and digital files to video-

---

5. Steven Spielberg, quoted in *American Cinematographer* 79, 12 (December 1998): 62.

6. Vincent Ward and Robin Williams, quoted in a brochure for the DVD edition of *What Dreams May Come* (PolyGram Video, 1998), pp. 7 and 4.

tape at 2,000 lines of resolution for editing at the speed of 4 frames per second (2K resolution is the minimum standard for the conversion of film images to digital video without significant loss of definition; 4K is ideal but impractical in terms of contemporary digital storage capacities). The filmmakers incorporated their own company, Pleasantville Effects, to supervise **color timing** during the conversion of the original negative into data files and contracted out the other effects, primarily to The Computer Film Company (digital compositing and paint work) and Compound Eye (digital matte paintings). Two years later, DP Roger Deakins would use the same DataCine technology at Cinesite to desaturate and fine-tune the color palette of the Coen brothers' *O Brother, Where Art Thou?* (Buena Vista, 2000; see color insert), shot on location in Mississippi, both to give it a period look and to compensate for the intensity of greens in the lushly forested shooting environment (the same problem that had led DP Vilmos Zsigmond to the stark and desaturated look of *Deliverance* in 1971; see color insert). After considering several proprietary bleach-bypass processes, Deakins and the Coens decided to use the same **digital intermediate process** as *Pleasantville* because it allowed them to manipulate the film's color selectively. In color-correction procedures, as in so many other areas of filmmaking, digitization has led to increased artistic control.

Digital manipulation of color in motion pictures began on a large scale in 1985, when Ted Turner set out to "colorize" studio-era black-and-white films that he had acquired during his brief ownership of MGM/UA (over 3,300 titles in the MGM library—which included not only MGM, but also RKO and pre-1949 Warner Bros.). Several companies at the time—e.g., Color Systems Technology in Los Angeles and Colorization, Inc., in Toronto—specialized in digitizing black-and-white films and coloring them frame by frame for distribution on television and videocassette. The practice was controversial at the time because, among other things, it skewed the intentions of the original filmmakers and distorted film history. (Turner even vowed to colorize *Citizen Kane* and probably would have done so had not a clause in Orson Welles's orginal RKO contract prevented him.) But **colorization** also created excitement among filmmakers about the artistic possibilities of selectively manipulating color, and by the mid-1990s they had begun to experiment with a variety of ways to exercise this new form of control over the film image, including, of course, the dig-

ital intermediate process described above, but also several types of **silver-retention** and **bleach-bypass** processes done in the lab. Although these latter processes are photochemical rather than digital, they represent attempts to imitate, in an optical environment, the creative license of computer graphics and are worth noting here. Modern color film stocks are **low-grain, high-contrast,** and color-saturated, qualities that work together to produce sharp, clean images. But directors and cinematographers frequently want more grain and less saturation to achieve a certain effect or to correct for prevailing qualities of light and/or color inherent in certain kinds of locations (as in the example of *O Brother, Where Art Thou?*, above).

Color negative stock consists of three layers, each of which is sensitive to one of the primary colors of the spectrum—red, green, and blue. Developing color negatives is a multistep process that involves sending the film through three separate chemical baths, the first of which develops the **latent images** as black and white or **silver halide** on all three layers. The next step is **dye coupling,** in which each of the three layers is infused with color, which is copresent with the black-and-white, silver-halide images. The third step is bleaching, whereby the silver halide is washed away, leaving a fully developed color negative. Silver-retention, bleach-bypass (or skip-bleach), and proprietary processes like Technicolor's ENR all either skip or degrade the bleaching process, which has the effect of increasing contrast and grain, desaturating the color, and producing blacker blacks.[7] (Since, under normal conditions, the bleach is used to eliminate all of the excess chemicals and the silver halide from the negative, bypassing or skipping the bleaching stage retains the silver and produces a thicker, darker negative.) This was the look that director David Fincher and his DP, Darius Khondji, wanted for their dark murder mystery *Seven* ([also known as *Se7en*] New Line Cinema, 1995; see color insert), which was processed using a Deluxe silver-retention process called Color Contrast Enhancement (CCE); this same process was chosen by Tim Burton and DP Emmanuel Lubezki for the horror-fantasy *Sleepy Hollow* (Paramount, 1999; see color

---

7. The French lab Éclair's equivalent of Technicolor's ENR is NEC (Noir en Couleur), which translates as "Black-and-White in Color," a perfect way to describe the look produced by bleach-bypass and silver-retention processes.

insert) to give it the combined ambience of a Hammer horror film and Mario Bava's *Black Sunday* (1960). For the science-fiction thriller *Pitch Black* (USA Films, 2000; see color insert), director David Twohy and DP David Eggby employed a skip-bleach process on the original camera negative of exteriors shot in the Australian desert to represent the washed-out quality of daylight on a planet with three suns. (Twohy consciously chose the bleach-bypass method in lieu of digitizing to stay within his $23 million budget; he modified the process to "crunch down" his blacks by underexposing his film, limiting filtration, and ordering high printer lights in the lab in order to print through the dense negative. Because CG artists need the cleanest possible elements to work with, the VFX team, led by Peter Chiang at Double Negative, Ltd., used normally developed Kodak EXR-50D Film 5245 for the effects plates and faded them digitally after compositing to match the live-action exterior footage.) Similarly, Steven Soderbergh and DP Peter Andrews used bleach-bypass to give the Mexican sequences of *Traffic* (USA Films, 2000; see color insert) a harsh, **desaturated** look, as did Janusz Kaminski (himself an award-winning DP) and DP Mauro Fiore to create the stark imagery of their theological horror film *Lost Souls* (New Line Cinema, 2000). A different approach to color manipulation was taken by director Josef Rusnak and DP Wedigo von Schultzendorff in *The Thirteenth Floor* (Columbia Pictures, 1999; see color insert), much of which takes place within the confines of an elaborate virtual-reality game set in Los Angeles circa 1937, brilliantly re-created by compositing surviving architecture with CGI from Centropolis Effects LLC. To give the Los Angeles sequences the look of an old postcard, the film was shot on color stock and the negative processed to create both color and black-and-white **interpositives;** in the final printing process, a percentage of each was extracted and combined (after some experiment) in a ratio of 60 percent color to 40 percent black and white, producing an image with the appropriate retro color palette.

The major CGI event of 1999 was 20th Century–Fox's release of George Lucas's *Star Wars* prequel *Star Wars: Episode I—The Phantom Menace*, which contained more than 60 computer-generated characters (including a major one, Jar Jar Binks, who appeared in about 350 shots) and roughly 2,200 visual effects produced at ILM. Approximately 70 percent of the film was composited

21.33 *Star Wars: Episode I—The Phantom Menace* (George Lucas, 1999). The all-digital Jar Jar Binks in conversation with Obi-Wan Kenobi (Ewan McGregor) and Qui-Gon Jinn (Liam Neeson). This film was completely previsualized with computer-generated animatics and contained CGI in 70 percent of its shots.

with CGI, and 100 percent of it was previsualized with animatics (see above), making *The Phantom Menace* a film that could not have come into being without computer graphics. (Furthermore, on Lucas's initiative, the film was given a filmless digital presentation at selected theaters, marking the first such exhibition of a feature film in the United States, and its excellent image quality foretold a bright future for digital projection systems generally.) It cost $115 million to produce and grossed $432 million domestically to become the third highest-earning film of all time, demonstrating definitively (and, by this point, needlessly) that the future of motion pictures was digital. Another popular release of 1999, Stephen Sommers's *The Mummy* (MCA/Universal) confirmed the cinema's new direction. For this film, ILM developed new software to create a simulacrum of a partially decayed living corpse whose body movement was made realistic through automated **animation "chains"**—linkages that

21.34 *The Mummy* (Stephen Sommers, 1999). The decaying corpse of the mummy was brought to life at ILM by automated animation chains that synchronized the movements of his body parts and organs; Cari software was used to animate the mummy's face.

allow for synchronicity of motion among skin, muscles, bones, and organs when these are visible on screen. Advanced Cari software, originally designed for *Dragonheart*, was used to animate the mummy's face, and particle-animation software was combined with new **shading software** to create a massive sandstorm in the desert near the film's conclusion. Similarly complicated was the hailstorm sequence in Cairo, some of whose shots com-

21.35 *The Matrix* (Andy and Larry Wachowski, 1999). "Flow-Mo," or "bullet-time" photography, was used to digitally manipulate the speed of moving objects and bodies in this film.

prised upward of 100 separate elements, bringing the sequence close to the destruction of the ship *Rodger Young* in *Starship Troopers* in complexity. Though it was not as wildly successful as *The Phantom Menace*, *The Mummy* took the industry by surprise when it returned $155 million on its $76 million cost; *The Mummy Returns*, a sequel with the same personnel, released in 2001, was more successful yet, returning $202 million on an investment of $98 million. Another influential film of 1999 was the Wachowski brothers' *The Matrix* (Warner Bros.), whose eye-catching martial-arts effects were heavily assisted by computer graphics, especially the technique called "Flow-Mo," or **"bullet time" photography,** which makes it possible for filmmakers to change the speed of moving objects in progress. In this process, an actual movement is filmed and scanned into a computer to create a wireframe of the person or object from which its trajectory is mapped. Then a battery of still cameras is placed along this path, and the movement is photographed again as a series of sequential stills. These are scanned into the computer, which arranges them in the manner of a film strip so that they can be digitally manipulated to reproduce the movement at varying speeds—a return to the practice of Eadweard Muybridge in the digital age. These and other computer-graphic techniques (such as new shading tool work that created lightning-like gun blasts and cascading matrix codes) lent a unique look to *The Matrix*, whose balletic martial-arts and gun battles were already passé in the Hong Kong cinema from which they were lifted by the Wachowskskis very nearly intact; the film was another sleeper, however, grossing $171 mil-

lion against a negative cost of $63 million. Columbia Pictures' *Stuart Little* (Rob Minkoff), an adaptation and updating of E. B. White's whimsical children's classic about the adventures of a white mouse who is adopted by a human family in Manhattan, made a significant contribution to photorealistic character generation in the same year as *The Matrix*. The character of Stuart was an all-digital creation whose most difficult component was computer-generated fur, a problem for computer graphics artists since the medium began. For Stuart, much of whose hair would be seen in close-up, software engineer Armin Bruderlin at Sony Pictures Imageworks developed a fur-generation program that worked by modeling a select number of control hairs that were multiplied into hundreds of thousands of hairs through interpolation;

21.36 *Stuart Little* (Rob Minkoff, 1999). Computer graphics artists at Sony Pictures Imageworks developed a realistic fur-generation program for Stuart, an all-digital character who would often appear in close-up.

then nearly 30 layers of **texture mapping** determined such characteristics as density, color, and sheen. (In addition to SPI, *Stuart* effects were provided by Centropolis and Rhythm & Hues, which collaborated to produce several all-digital talking cats.) Several other films of 1999 were notable for their CGI (and not much else), including *The Haunting* (DreamWorks SKG), Jan de Bont's truly awful remake of Robert Wise's poetic psychological horror film of 1963, which nevertheless had some wonderfully imaginative effects by the Tippett Studio (Phil Tippett was the film's VFX supervisor); *Wild, Wild West* (Warner Bros.), Barry Sonnenfeld's failed attempt to trump *Men in Black* with a comedy-Western based on a popular 1960s TV series (which features some extravagantly diabolical machines provided by ILM); and Peter Hyam's *End of Days* (MCA/Universal), in which Arnold Schwarzenegger saves the world from Satan, accompanied by spectacularly infernal effects from Centropolis and Rhythm & Hues. On the other hand, David Fincher's highly original *Fight Club* featured CGI from many sources, from a credit sequence that starts deep inside the cellular structure of the human brain, through an airline disaster in which a small plane collides with a jetliner, to a nearly all-digital finale in which a whole cityscape of skyscrapers is imploded one after another by explosions (FX primarily by Digital Domain; Blue Sky; BUF, Inc.; Gray Matter; and Toybox).

A New Aesthetic for a New Century

MARTIAN CHRONICLES

Disney's Touchstone Picture's *Mission to Mars* (Brian De Palma, 2000) was the first film since Kubrick's *2001: A Space Odyssey* in 1968 to attempt a realistic and credible representation of the future of manned space flight through state-of-the-art special effects. It concerns a NASA team sent to rescue fellow astronauts who have established the first base camp on Mars and who have suddenly lost radio contact with Earth; when the rescue mission lands on Mars (minus their ship which has imploded in a meteor shower), they encounter a cosmic metaphysical mystery. Disney had selected its in-house company Dream Quest to do the special effects, but

when Warner Bros. announced a rival Mars project (*Red Planet*—see below), the studio accelerated production and split the work with ILM. With the generous collaboration of NASA, De Palma and production designer Ed Verreaux used official projections of near-future space exploration to design the film's look and give it a level of verisimilitude approaching that of Ron Howard's *Apollo 13* (1995). This demanded a technically precise representation of NASA spaceships and space stations as well as a scientifically accurate re-creation of the red planet's surface environment, a process that involved the use of 3-D digital matte paintings and the color correction of backgrounds to create a red-orange palette, which became known as "Mars imaging." One of the more spectacular surface effects near the beginning of the film involved a massive sandstorm provided by Dream Quest proprietary "Hookah" software, a **fluid dynamic simulator** that also does rendering (Tippett Studio animators were called in to help with this "vortex" sequence because of their experience with particle, or procedural, animation from *Starship Troopers*). Later, the rescue team discovers a huge alien artifact in the shape of a humanoid face, which was generated by computer at ILM. The deep-space sequences are among the most elaborately composited since those in *Starship Troopers*, and the entire film has just fewer than 400 effects shots, many of them digital. For example, establishing shots of the orbital space station and the Mars recovery ship launched from it in the first part of the film are computer-generated elements composited with earth imagery photographed by NASA; but the interior of the rescue vehicle is introduced via one of De Palma's signature tracking shots, which moves seamlessly from a point in space far beyond the computer-generated ship into a close live-action shot of two crew members inside the command module, passing (apparently) through a flight deck window while executing several 360-degree pirouettes. Similarly, in the film's 10-minute climactic sequence on Mars, produced by ILM, the rescuers enter the giant face and discover an enormous white room, then a holographic planetarium representing the solar system, and then the holographic simulacrum of a Martian hovering above them. This alien being reveals that life on Mars was destroyed eons ago by striking meteors but that Mars preserved its species by seeding other planets—Earth among them—with its DNA in order to ensure the survival of its genetic code. Then, in an aston-

21.37 and 21.38 *Mission to Mars* **(Brian De Palma, 2000). A sandstorm on the planet's surface (top) becomes a dangerously swirling vortex rendered via Dream Quest's "Hookah" software, a fluid dynamic simulator, with the assistance of veteran particle animators at the Tippett Studios. Fish morph into lizards (bottom), leaving the water for dry land, in the computer-generated evolution sequence near the end of the film.**

always difficult for CGI because they recede to infinity—were created by "Stella," the starfield generator designed by Sean Jenkins for *Armageddon* two years before (see above). As a narrative, *Mission to Mars* clearly shows signs of Disney's haste to rush it into theaters before *Red Planet*; but as a piece of computer-graphics engineering, it approaches the achievement of *Starship Troopers* in complexity, if not depth.

Red Planet, made without the cooperation of NASA (which objected to its negative portrayal of one of the astronauts as a murderous coward), was a troubled production whose principle effects, supervised by Jeffrey A. Okun, were farmed out to eight companies. (The use of many effects houses is common on a medium-to-big-budget production, but one or two companies usually provide the principle effects

ishing sequence, we witness the whole of evolution as an ascending series of creatures morphing progressively from paramecium to human, each one of which was modeled entirely in the computer and contained the complex geometry of the whole. At the film's conclusion, most of the crew leaves the interior, but one remains and is taken aboard a Martian spaceship in the form of a cylindrical tube that rises up out of the floor; finally, the mountainlike face disintegrates, its debris serving as fuel for the launch of the ship into the starfields above. Most of this 10-minute sequence was created digitally at ILM, with the actors shot against a black background for compositing in postproduction. Custom software was written to collapse the computer model of the face and make it swirl up into a vortex; the starfields of the final shots—

and the others do detail and finishing work, which appears in the end credits as "Additional Visual Effects.") The results, however, were impressive, ranging from an exciting zero-gravity fire aboard the spaceship *Mars 1* (computer-generated by Hammerhead Productions), through a highly credible all-digital military robot ("AMEE," computer-generated and animated by Cinesite), to vast swarms of extraterrestrial insects called "nematodes" (created digitally by Rhythm & Hues). Location exteriors, shot in the Australian and Jordanian deserts, were given a uniform reddish-orange hue by filtration in principal photography (devised by DP Peter Suschitzky) and meticulous color-correction at Digital FilmWorks. Despite their elaborately executed effects, neither Mars film was a popular success. Nor was

Supernova, directed by Walter Hill (under the pseudo-nym of "Thomas Lee"),[8] a production compromised, tellingly enough, by a battle over its special effects (the film's producers wanted to use Hammerhead, which they partially owned, but the distributor, MGM, awarded the main contract to Digital Domain, which created much of its full-resolution space imagery). Interestingly, all three of the 2000 science-fiction films discussed above had roughly similar budgets ($90 million for *Mission to Mars*; $75 million for *Red Planet*; $60 million for *Supernova*), and all lost money. (In fact, the only future-gazing CGI-specific film to turn a profit in 2000 was Warner Bros.' *Space Cowboys*, directed by Clint Eastwood, whose $90 million return on its $65 million budget was probably the result of star appeal rather than its ILM-created special effects.) In the year 2000, it seemed that audiences had turned away from the computer-generated future world toward a disaster-prone present and a distant, glorious past.

BREAD AND CIRCUSES

Since the 1970s, rising production costs had virtually eliminated the period epic as a genre. Sweeping spectacles like MGM's *Ben-Hur* (William Wyler, 1959) and Universal International's *Spartacus* (Stanley Kubrick, 1960) that had been shot on location with vast crowds of extras were unthinkable at a time when the average production cost per class-A feature had risen to $75 million, as it had by 1999. (As it was, 20th Century–Fox's $40 million *Cleopatra* [Joseph L. Mankiewicz] had nearly bankrupted the studio in 1963.) The last historical epic as such produced by a major studio was probably Warner Bros.' *Barry Lyndon* (Stanley Kubrick, 1975), whose $11 million cost had raised eyebrows when the film failed at the box office; but when Michael Cimino's sprawling $44 million Western *Heaven's Gate* (1980) earned less than $2 million and forced the sale of United Artists by Transamerica to MGM, historical films became anathema in the industry for the next two decades. By the end of the century, however, CGI offered a new way to mount historical spectacles without having to resort to elaborate sets, extensive location shooting, and/or multitudes of extras.

Digital effects were part of Ridley Scott's original plans for *Gladiator* (DreamWorks SKG, 2000) from the moment of conception. To achieve a look inspired by nineteenth-century British and French Romantic painters (especially the work of Jean-Léon Gérôme) and such monumental German films as Fritz Lang's *Metropolis* (1926) and Leni Riefenstahl's *Triumph of the Will* (1936), Scott employed production designer Arthur Max (*G.I. Jane; Seven*) and decided to go with a single effects house, Mill Film Ltd., a British company that had worked with him on *G.I. Jane* (1997) and had done the bulk of the digital effects for *Babe: Pig in the City* (George Miller, 1998). In over 100 digital-effects shots, Mill would create digital matte paintings of ancient Rome, multiply human figures for crowd scenes, and help create battle sequences too dangerous to shoot as live action. For example, for the opening battle sequence between the Roman army and German barbarians (set in Germania, but actually shot in Surrey, outside of London), Mill created sweeping views of the opposing forces by **tiling** together still photographic plates of limited numbers of costumed extras representing just a small fraction of the actual numbers involved. (Tiling is the process of creating patterns based on the repetition of a single rectangular **image map,** such as a digitized photograph.) In this way, Scott was able to use about 1,500 soldiers to represent 10,000. Furthermore, a major component of this battle involved the Romans' shooting flaming arrows and flinging flaming pitch pots from catapults at the Germans, both quite dangerous in live-action terms. To accomplish the effect, real arrows and pitch pots were fired into the air toward safe areas, and the pinnacles of their arcs became the starting points for digital trajectory extensions, complete with computer-generated smoke trails. Other digital effects involved the construction of partial and, in some cases, entire buildings. In the midsection of the film, the former Roman general Maximus (Russell Crowe, now a slave) is turned into a gladiator and fights in a provincial arena in Roman-occupied Morocco; and digital vultures dominate the landscape here, created through flocking software to avoid laborious hand ani-

---

8. Hill petitioned the Directors Guild of America (DGA) to have his name removed from the credits after MGM recut the film to make it less philosophical. Ironically, the re-editing was supervised by Francis Ford Coppola, once the apostle of artistic freedom in Hollywood. The film's original editor, Freeman Davies, also had his name removed from the credits.

to the structure and masses of spectators: specifically, 27,000 extras were created for the Colosseum crowd by procedural animation, as were digital chariots and gladiators in long shot. The much-remarked aerial shot of the Colosseum, taken as if from a blimp at a contemporary sporting event, was also digitally created. Rome itself evolved in postproduction as a combination of digital matte painting, digitized photographs, and computer graphic models. On Scott's initiative, some of the Roman exterior shots were made deliberately evocative of *Metropolis* and *Triumph of the Will*: for example, a mass scene in which Commodus reviews his troops resembles a Nazi party rally, complete with standards and regalia. According to visual-effects supervisor John Nelson, the scale and grouping reference for this scene was the Riefenstahl film, and the footage was desaturated in the color-correction process so that it would resemble old newsreels. These are just a few of the digital enhancements in a film that was as CGI-based as any of the science-fiction or fantasy films examined thus far.[9]

21.39 *Gladiator* (Ridley Scott, 2000). The interior of the Roman Colosseum (top): the first level is a 52-foot-tall set built in Malta, while the middle and upper decks are CGI produced at Mill Films Ltd., London, which also created masses of spectators through procedural animation.
21.40 and 21.41 *Gladiator* (2000). Two frames (bottom) from the spectacular aerial pass over the Colosseum, as if shot from a blimp, completely simulated through CGI.

mation. The Roman Colosseum, seen later in the film, was a partial, 52-foot-tall set built in Malta and completed via CGI, which added a complete middle and upper deck

9. Another of *Gladiator*'s digital effects was born of necessity: when Oliver Reed, in the role of the gladiatorial entrepreneur, Proximo, died before the completion of principal photography, his image was extracted from his completed scenes and "dropped in" to the backgrounds where his presence was required (none of which were dialogue scenes).

Because *Gladiator* was made on an extremely tight production schedule, numerous laborsaving devices were adopted in postproduction to accomplish its effects quickly and efficiently (e.g., the use of tiling and procedural animation to generate crowds). One of the most innovative expediencies involved the use of WAM!-NET's compressed digital-video–delivery service, which allowed the transfer of huge CGI data files back and forth from Mill Film in London to its American outpost in Los Angeles and ultimately to *Gladiator*'s online edit suite in Hollywood. This enabled the British and American units to take advantage of the time difference to maximize their work day so that visual-effects production for *Gladiator* could go on literally around the clock. Ridley Scott's ability to marshal such resources places him, with Paul Verhoeven, Roland Emmerich, Wolfgang Petersen, and Michael Bay, in the first rank of practitioners of a new aesthetic—one that demands the full integration of CGI and live action at the preproduction stage, carries production forth on both of those levels simultaneously, and performs a creative synthesis of the two in postproduction, which now assumes a role equal in importance to production in the filmmaking process. This is not, by any means, to exclude the originators of the form—James Cameron, Robert Zemeckis, Steven Spielberg, and George Lucas (whose Industrial Light & Magic looms so large in this account)—nor to sideline the occasionally brilliant contributor such as Vincent Ward, Brian De Palma, Baz Luhrmann, and Peter Jackson. Nor is it to say that the first-named directors always—or even primarily—make important films. It is simply to say that they now look to CGI as a fundamental building block of their work—not as a "special" effect, but as a normative one; not as an enhancement or refinement, but as the very stuff of the medium.

To make a film like *Gladiator* without CGI could easily have tripled its cost.[1] In any event, its budget of $103 million was amortized within three weeks of release in May 2000, and it eventually grossed $188 million. It was in some sense a serious film as well as a successful one—serious enough, at least, to be nominated for twelve Academy Awards and receive four, including Best Picture, Best Actor (Crowe), Best Visual Effects (John Nelson and his VFX team at Mill), and Best Costume Design (Janty Yates). No one would argue that *Gladiator* is a masterpiece, but, like *Mission to Mars*, it is an aesthetically pleasing genre film that made expert use of CGI to

achieve production economies and, at the same time, to offer its audience a high level of representational credibility. The same could be said for Roland Emmerich's *The Patriot* (Columbia Pictures, 2000), one of a handful of American films set during the Revolutionary War. Shot on location in and around Charleston, South Carolina, which was historically retrofitted via miniatures and 3-D matte paintings, the film contained 150 visual-effects shots provided by Emmerich's own Centropolis Effects LLC under the supervision of Stuart Robertson. Fully 70 percent of these involved battle scenes enhanced by thousands of computer-generated soldiers; the other 30 percent involved extending locations via digital matte paintings and model work. "Soldier replication" became a major focus at Centropolis, where a decision was made early on that the figures should be no more than an inch high within the frame (about 100 feet from the camera in scale—i.e., a medium long shot), avoiding the necessity of photorealistic hair and cloth simulation or facial animation. After extensive experiments in motion capture and modeling, Centropolis ended up with eight models that would stand in as background soldiers, each with a different body type, and four interchangeable faces. Irregularities were programmed into their movements through proprietary **randomization software** called the "soldier placement instancing tool," which, together with digital color and lighting correction, helped them to be matched with live action in the production plates. In some cases, a **2-D cloning** technique could be used to

---

1. In fact, a film like *Gladiator* had been made once before, without benefit of CGI and at about twice the cost. Anthony Mann's *The Fall of the Roman Empire* (1964), produced by Samuel Bronston and distributed by Paramount, was one the last great spectacles of the widescreen-blockbuster era. Produced at a cost of $19 million (about $200 million, adjusted for inflation), the film had a cast of international stars and thousands of extras; it was shot on location in Spain (to save money, actually, by circumventing the Hollywood unions), had elaborate three-dimensional sets representing ancient Rome, battles and chariot races staged in real time, and so on. (Studio publicity traded on this extravagance, hailing the film's 27 full-scale structures, 350 individual statues, 8 victory columns, 1,000 hand-sculpted bas-reliefs, etc., as comprising the biggest and most expensive Roman set ever built.) It was also shot in Ultra Panavision 70, the widest 65mm negative process of its time (whereas *Gladiator* was shot in far less expensive Super 35). Like *Gladiator*, *The Fall of the Roman Empire* tells the story of the death of Marcus Aurelius in Germania and the rise of Commodus as emperor, as well as recounting the bitter rivalry between Commodus and a Roman general (a former friend). Unlike *Gladiator*, however, it was a box-office flop and helped to extinguish the classical epic as a viable commercial form.

21.42 *The Patriot* (Roland Emmerich, 2000). In this Revolutionary War epic, randomization software at Centropolis Effects LLC helped to individualize the movement of computer-generated soldiers. Some battle scenes featured up to 8,000 soldiers, only about 200 of whom were real.

larger scale, Jean-Jacques Annaud gave a credible rendition of bombed-out, wartorn Stalingrad, circa 1943, in *Enemy at the Gates* (2001) through a handful of GGI cityscapes provided by London's Double Negative.

MILLENNIAL VISIONS

For Wolfgang Petersen's *The Perfect Storm* (Warner Bros., 2000), the challenge was to come up with a credible computer-generated rendition of a storm at sea, historically

fill in areas too close to the camera for the computer-generated soldiers. In this process, live-action extras would be extracted (or "stolen") from one take and scanned into another. Ultimately, wide-angle shots of *The Patriot*'s biggest battle sequences would feature up to 8,000 soldiers, perhaps 200 of which were real costumed actors (troop numbers that the filmmakers knew were far too high for historical accuracy but highly satisfying as spectacle). Released, like Emmerich's *Independence Day*, during the week of July 4 to capitalize on its theme, *The Patriot* barely returned its $110 million negative cost (about 25 percent of which went to compensate its star, Mel Gibson), but it is an impressive technical achievement nonetheless. Recent period films have used CGI more modestly—*The House of Mirth* (Terence Davies, 2000; see Figure 14.33), e.g., which uses CGI in several scenes to re-create the exterior look of turn-of-the-century New York; and *A Knight's Tale* (Brian Helgeland, 2001), which re-creates precincts of fourteenth-century Rouen, Paris, and London, as well as jousting-tournament crowds, with CGI from Mill Film. On a

one of Hollywood's least convincing areas of representation. The assignment was given to visual-effects supervisor Stefen Fangmeier and special-effects supervisor John Frazier at ILM, the same team that had produced the tornadoes of *Twister* in 1996. The difference between the two films, however, indicated how rapidly the state of CGI had advanced in just four years: whereas in *Twister* the tornadoes were computer-generated elements to be integrated into a live-action environment, in *The Perfect Storm*, the human characters and their boats were integrated into the total environment of a computer-generated storm. To accomplish this unprecedented task,

21.43 *Enemy at the Gates* (Jean-Jacques Annaud, 2001). Stalingrad under German attack, created digitally by London's Double Negative, in one of many recent historical films made cost-effective through CGI.

21.44 *A Perfect Storm* (Wolfgang Petersen, 2000). A live-action boat inserted into a computer-generated storm at sea, whose level of detail was high: swelling "bottom water" was created through procedural physical simulation; misty "top water" via particle systems.

a crew of digital artists was assembled at ILM almost as large as the one used for *The Phantom Menace*, and they produced 250 3-D shots, about 30 percent of which involved surrounding the live-action boat with a digital ocean. The other 70 percent were all computer-generated shots of boats on water and rescue helicopters, often with computer-generated and digital human clones. (There were also 135 2-D shots, 30 of which were sky replacements.) Development of software tools to create the storm began 18 months before the film's projected release. Procedural physical simulation was used to produce hundreds and hundreds of swells in the so-called "bottom water," while layer upon layer of particle systems generated the choppy, misty surface of the "top water." In the end, the storm's level of detail was extremely high, requiring months and months to render and producing huge digital files. For example, one foam-crested 70-foot wave was estimated to have a particle count of 4 billion per frame. Like *Twister*, *The Perfect Storm* was a huge popular success, earning $327 million worldwide, as was another disaster/adventure film of 2000, Columbia's *Vertical Limit* (Martin Campbell), a film whose silliness was matched only by the extraordinary effectiveness of its digitally composited climbing sequences, avalanches, and snowstorms. Most of *Vertical Limit*'s digital effects were provided by the newly formed Anohana, a company committed to providing big effects with the smallest number of personnel (and, therefore, lower costs); with the exception of finishing work by Digiscope and Peerless Camera, Anohana produced virtually all of the 400 CGI shots employed in the film.

Other CGI-intensive films released in 2000 and 2001 demonstrated just how widespread the use of digital effects had become. They range from action-oriented science fiction (*Virus* [John Bruno, 1999]; *Deep Blue Sea* [Renny Harlin, 1999]; *The 6th Day* [Roger Spottiswoode, 2000]; *Ghosts of Mars* [John Carpenter, 2001]); to comic science fiction/fantasy (*Galaxy Quest* [Dean Parisot, 1999]; *Monkeybone* [Henry Selick, 2001]; *Evolution* [Ivan Reitman, 2001]; to meditative science fiction (*A.I.: Artificial Intelligence* [Steven Spielberg, 2001]); to action-adventure (*Mission Impossible II* [John Woo, 2000]; *Driven* [Renny Harlin, 2001]); to combat films (*Enemy at the Gates* [Jean-Jacques Annaud, 2001]; *Pearl Harbor* [Michael Bay, 2001]); to high-budget horror (*The Cell* [Tarsem Singh, 2000]; *Hollow Man* [Paul Verhoeven, 2000]; *The Mummy Returns* [Stephen Sommers, 2001], upscale remakes of low-budget horror (contemporary versions of William Castle's *House on Haunted Hill* [William Malone, 1999] and *13 Ghosts* [Steve Beck, 2001]), and horror comedy (*Lake Placid* [Steve Miner, 1999]); to franchised sequels (*Jurassic Park III* [Joe Johnston, 2001]) and remakes (*Planet of the Apes* [Tim Burton, 2001]); to comic-book and cartoon adaptations (*X-Men 1.5* [Bryan Singer, 2000]; *How the Grinch Stole Christmas* [Ron Howard, 2000]); to family comedy (*102 Dalmatians* [Kevin Lima, 2000]; *Cats & Dogs* [Lawrence Guterman, 2001]); to feature versions of video games (*Dungeons & Dragons* [Courtney Solomon, 2000]; *Lara Croft: Tomb Raider* [Simon West, 2001]); to photorealistic digital animation (*Dinosaur* [Eric Leighton, 2000]; *Shrek* [Andrew Adamson, 2001]; *Final Fantasy: The Spirits Within* [Hironubu Sakaguchi, 2001]); to musicals (*Moulin Rouge* [Baz Luhrmann, 2001]); to epic fantasy (*The Lord of the Rings: The Fellowship of the Ring* [Peter Jackson, 2001]). The cost of run-of-the-mill CGI has dropped so low that even exploitation producers can afford to use it. In 1997, the popularity of Wolfgang Petersen's $85-million *Air Force One* (Columbia Pictures), for which Boss Film and Cinesite produced highly realistic computer-generated flight sequences, led to a series of cheaper imitations, initially the respectable medium-budget *Turbulence* (Robert Butler, 1997), but descending rapidly through *Turbulence 2: Fear of Flying* (David Mackay, 2000), *Turbulence 3: Heavy Metal* (Jorge Montesi, 2001), and *Submerged* (2000), directed by one "Ed Raymond," a pseudonym for the ubiquitous B-filmmaker Fred Olen Ray. (Jetliners in flight are particularly easy for digital artists to model because of their aerodynamically "perfect" contours; even location-specific class-A features like Mike Newell's *Pushing Tin* [1999] or John Boorman's *The Tailor of Panama* [2000] resort to computer-generated planes, which can be cheaper to come by than stock footage.) Similarly, Columbia's $35-million *Anaconda* (Luis Llosa) grossed twice its negative costs in 1997, propelled by the novelty of a computer-generated title character that swallowed actors whole. Over the next few years, there was a proliferation of digital reptiles in films whose budgets seemed skewed toward the production of a single, monstrous CGI effect—*Komodo* (Michael Lantieri, 1999), *Reptilian* (Hyung-rae Shim, 1999), *King Cobra* (David Hillenbrand, 1999), *Python* (Richard Clabaugh, 2000), *Crocodile* (Tobe Hooper, 2000), *Raptor* (Jim Wynorski, 2001), *Venomous* ("Ed Raymond," 2001), and so on. In fact, low- to medium-budget horror films were among the first to use CGI as a means of containing costs. Hollywood Pictures' *An American Werewolf in Paris* (Anthony Waller, 1997) was an innovator here as an independent low-budget ($22 million) production, giving Santa Barbara Studios its first character animation assignment—to create 50 shots worth of 7-foot-tall, 700-pound digital werewolves that could walk on two legs or all fours and appear in close-ups as well as long and medium shots. As usual, the biggest difficulty for the artists was computer-generated fur, and they finally opted to eschew the volumetric approach of Digital Domain in *The Island of Dr. Moreau* the year before (see above) and create individual geometry for every single hair, which numbered over 360,000 per werewolf model. For the viewer, however, the biggest problem in the fin-

21.46 *Deep Rising* (Stephen Sommers, 1998). CGI enters low-budget horror: computer-generated splatter issuing from the tentacles of a computer-generated sea monster.

ished product is the werewolves' apparent lack of volume (which is also, of course, an *actual* lack of volume). All images in the cinema are two-dimensional representations of three-dimensional space—the screen is flat although the scenographic space it represents exists in the round—but characters and objects within that scenographic space displace volume relative to each other and to their surroundings. Computer-generated characters cannot displace volume because they have none, so the illusion of displacement has to be created through lighting and shading at the rendering stage, a time-consuming and expensive process. This lack of volumetric displacement can often be detected in the digital effects of low- to medium-budget American genre films of the 1990s—horror films like *Phantoms* (Joe Chappelle, 1989) and *Deep Rising* (Stephen Sommers, 1998), where the monsters are entirely generated by computer; it can also be seen in many Hong Kong genre films of the same period, where low-resolution CGI was often the cheapest and easiest way to render sets and locations on a tight production schedule (e.g., Tsui Hark's *Shanghai Grand* [1996]; Gordon Chan's *Armageddon* [1997]; Ronny Yu's *The Phantom Lover*, 1997]).

Low-end use of CGI to achieve production economies is now common in the American industry, where it is used for stunt wire and harness removal, sky enhancement and replacement, color and lighting correction from shot to shot, and correction of a multitude of other production errors and/or omissions. These procedures are not cheap, but they are usually priced below retakes and other means of correction. For example, Ang Lee used sky replacement and digital rain for several sequences in his modestly budgeted ($16.5 million) Jane Austen adapta-

21.45 *An American Werewolf in Paris* (Anthony Waller, 1997). The cartoon-like quality of this film's all-digital werewolves illustrates a lack of volumetric displacement common to computer-generated characters when (usually for reasons of budget) they are not carefully rendered.

21.47 *Red Corner* **(John Avnet, 1997). Digitized 3-D photographs of Beijing were composited with live traffic at a California location to create this street scene at the beginning of the film.**

very credible backdrop for the opening sequence of Jon Avnet's political thriller *Red Corner* (1997) at a time when shooting on location there would have been impossible, even if there had been a budget for it (which there wasn't). The same technique was used to place two teenage girls on the grounds of Richard Nixon's White House in the $13-million comedy *Dick* (Andrew Fleming, 1999). In like fashion, Stephan Elliott shot most of his psychological thriller *Eye of the Beholder* (1999), budgeted at $15 million, in Montreal, Canada, and morphed American landmarks, shot over a three-week period after principal photography was completed, into the Canadian landscape in postproduction. In the $25 million independent feature *Elizabeth* (1998)-director Shekhar Kapur created the queen's coronation sequence by digitally multiplying a small crowd of spectators into a multitude and compositing it into the digitally enhanced nave of a real cathedral, a practice increasingly common in low- to medium-budget films since it saves on the cost of extras, costumes, and the logistics of a real location shoot. Occasionally, CGI will be used to create the total environment of a film, as in Phillip Noyce's police procedural *The Bone Collector* (1999), which was shot primarily on a blue-screen stage in Montreal and composited with second-unit photography of the streets of Manhattan, where the drama supposedly takes place. (This film also contains an astonishing "virtual" snap-zoom from a murder on a

tion *Sense and Sensibility* (1995) to cope with the vagaries of shooting on location in English weather. More recently, when Rob Cohen made his $15 million *The Skulls* (2000) on location at the University of Toronto (whose buildings he altered to resemble those of Yale through strategic application of CGI), he was able to shoot most of his scenes day for night, correcting color and adding blue-black shadows in postproduction. In another example, Roman Polankski and DP Darius Khondji were shooting a scene for their neo-gothic horror film *The Ninth Gate* (1999) inside a Paris café when they inadvertently photographed some passersby gawking through the window; rather than throw out the shot, Polanski was able to remove this unwanted element in digital postproduction by replacing the real background with a 3-D photograph of an empty street and to avoid overextending his tight $38 million budget. Similarly, director Jean-Pierre Jeunet erased graffiti from walls and cars from busy Parisian streets to create a sweeter, less cluttered environment for *Amélie* (2001). In a variant of this practice, digitized 3-D still photographs of Beijing provided a

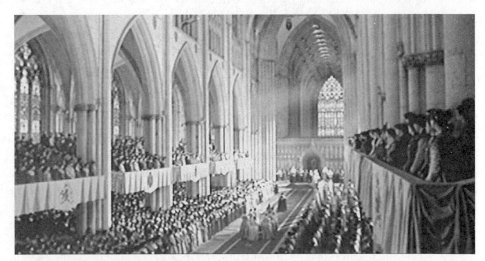

21.48 *Elizabeth* **(Shekhar Kapur, 1998). The queen's coronation in Westminster Abbey was created by compositing a digitally multiplied crowd into a digitally enhanced 3-D photograph of the real thing.**

21.49 *The Bone Collector* (Phillip Noyce, 1999). The cop (Angelina Jolie) trying to stop a train in this thriller is not really standing in front of it. Her actions were shot on a bluescreen stage in Montreal and digitally composited with a train shot by a second unit on location in New York. About 80 percent of the film was put together this way.

Hackford's like-minded *The Devil's Advocate* [1997]). (Digital pyrotechnics are often accompanied by digital lens distortion to make it appear as if they were filmed through the heatwave produced by real fire.) Following the same logic, the producers of *Dracula 2000* (Patrick Lussier, 2000) decided to create a casket full of leeches digitally in order to save on valuable production time rather than deal with the notoriously cranky American Society for the Prevention of Cruelty to Animals (ASPCA), which monitors all Hollywood productions employing animals and insects and demands an individual accounting of them at the end of each shooting day.

crowded New York street into a sixth-floor hospital room at least three blocks away, which is not only unreal under the circumstances of production but optically impossible, then as now.) CGI can also add photorealistic components to a scene that might be too expensive, difficult, or dangerous to achieve in real time and space. This can be something as simple as adding a bullet hole to a door in order to maintain continuity, as in Neil LaBute's *Nurse Betty* (2000), or as crucial as the doomed school bus that motivates Atom Egoyan's *The Sweet Hereafter* (1997) as it sinks into the ice in long shot. In 2000, Roger Donaldson employed computer-generated submarines in a computer-generated sea to represent underwater military activity in the Cuban-blockade sequence of *Thirteen Days* (whose mixture of black-and-white and color footage was supplied by colorization software at Cinesite); and in 2002, Tom Shadyac used CGI in the supernatural thriller *Dragonfly* to create a thematically important waterfall in the middle of a rain forest (supposedly in Venezuela but actually Hawaii) where there wasn't one. To save on both insurance costs and logistics, weapons fire is frequently computer generated so that no firearms need be discharged on the set. Similarly, as digital artists have become expert at rendering fire and flame, computer-generated pyrotechnics have increasingly replaced, or been combined with, real pyrotechnics so that costly sets (and lives) will not be touched by flames. Polanski's *The Ninth Gate* offers another example here—about 80 percent of the flames in this satanic thriller are CGI (as were the flames and infernal animated bas-relief of Taylor

The State of the Art, circa 2002: *Moulin Rouge* and *The Lord of the Rings: The Fellowship of the Ring*

Whereas Baz Luhrmann's *Romeo + Juliette* (20th Century–Fox, 1996) had been filmed mainly on location and used CGI sparingly for sky replacement and set extensions, Luhrmann and DP Don McAlpine shot most of *Moulin Rouge* (Fox, 2001) on a soundstage where they could control lighting and choreography, and relied on digital effects to create exterior views of Paris and the Montmartre cabaret of the title as well as to enhance production numbers; its more than 300 effects shots were provided mainly by Animal Logic, Asylum VFX, and Digital Filmworks. Luhrmann wanted his effects to evoke the flamboyant theatricality of fin de siècle Paris, whose visual currency was Art Nouveau, and the look of early filmmakers like the Lumières and Georges Méliès, who were practicing in Paris at the time. The former yielded what VFX supervisor Chris Godfrey called "the postcard effect," whereby computer-generated 2-D images would morph into 3-D images and then live action; the early-cinema look was produced in postproduction by lowering contrast, tinting the image in various tones of sepia, and adding grain, splice marks, and flicker. Fifteen scenes, many of them elaborately stylized musical performances, would blend live-action with elaborate motion-control model photography and 3-D CGI. David Dozoretz's Per-

21.50 and 21.51 *Moulin Rouge* (Baz Luhrmann, 2001). A frame that occurs near the end of the 3-mile track over Paris: as the virtual camera sweeps toward the Montmarte gate (top), 2-D images yield to 3-D ones and finally live action via "the postcard effect" (bottom).

the high technology of early twenty-first-century Hollywood was exceeded only by Peter Jackson's creation of an entire mythographic world in his first installment of *The Lord of the Rings* trilogy, *The Fellowship of the Ring* (New Line Cinema, 2001).

All three *Lord of the Rings* films were shot on location in New Zealand simultaneously, and the numbers alone are staggering: 350 studio and location sets; 15,000 pieces of clothing; 10,000 facial appliances; 1,800 suits of body prosthetics and 1,800 Hobbit feet; at least 1,500 digital-effects shots; and a budget estimated at about $270 million spread over three films. To provide the effects, Jackson assembled an international team of visual-effects artists to work under the auspices of his own effects company, Weta Workshop, directed by VFX supervisor Jim Rygiel, and Three Foot

sistence of Vision (POV) company was called in to previsualize these scenes with animatics because they involved complicated virtual camera moves. For example, the film's opening shot involves a 3-mile wide-angle track across Paris with the camera finally diving into a street that leads to the gates of Montmartre and then flying up through the hero's garret window (intended by Luhrmann as an allusion to the fluid subjective tracking shots of the hero's arrival in the big city in Murnau's 1927 *Sunrise*).[2] Later, another shot reverses this movement as the camera snaps back from the interior of the garret into a wide-angle view of the city, then darts into a computer-generated version of the train station Gare du Nord, rendered via "the postcard effect" with added radiosity to heighten its hyperreal feel. Lurhmann's unique blend of the bohemian sensibility of turn-of-the-century Paris and

Six (the height of a Hobbit), a production company set up by New Line Cinema specifically for the *Lord of the Rings* project. The effects produced by this team (and some contracted out to Digital Domain in Hollywood) mix live action, miniature shots, motion-control camerawork, digital matte painting, digitally enhanced miniatures, and completely digital environments. From the outset, Jackson strove to avoid the "perfection" associated with CGI and create a Middle Earth that might have been shot on real locations. To this end, he avoided the trend toward blending 3-D computer-generated environments with digital matte paintings so clearly present in *Moulin*

2. "15 Minutes with *Moulin Rouge* Director Baz Luhrmann," *Sound & Vision* (May 2002): 98.

21.52 and 21.53 *The Lord of the Rings: The Fellowship of the Ring* (Peter Jackson, 2001). Orcs fighting Gondorians on the dark plain of Gogoroth in the prologue to the film (top), orchestrated by a procedural animation program called "Massive" that gave each figure in the battle enough artificial intelligence to act (within well-defined parameters) on his own. Rivendell (bottom), a composite of real New Zealand locations, models and miniatures, and CGI.

they will move and act. As VFX supervisor Rygiel explains it: "They can see if the thing that's in front of them is an Orc or a Gondorian. If it's a [fellow] Orc and they're catching up to it, they run around it. If it's a Gondorian, they go into battle with it.... And if an Orc is running behind a hill the Gondorian will change his direction and head for the Orc that's running behind the hill. So they'll literally [seek] each other out."[3] *The Fellowship of the Ring* contained about 450 visual-effects shots ranging from digital face replacement, through compositing miniatures with live-action and digital characters, to the Massive all-digital battle sequence described above. The negative was digitally graded at a purpose-built facility by Peter Doyle and PostHouse AG, a digital-timing and visual-effects house in Germany. Software,

Rouge and created much of Middle Earth photographically, with only a few characters, such as Gollum and the Balrog, generated entirely in the digital realm. For *The Lord of the Rings: The Fellowship of the Ring*, a software program called Massive was developed by Stephen Regelous that took the concept of procedural animation to a new level. Simply put, this program uses motion capture to create behavior cycles that can be multiplied into elaborate battle sequences involving tens of thousands of Orcs and Gondorians. The complex library of movements that Massive provides for each type of figure is actually an order of artificial intelligence in which programmers build the "brains" of Orcs or Gondorians by giving them modules of vision and hearing as well as physical descriptors such as height, weight, and speed to instruct how

custom-designed by the Hungarian company Colorfront, enabled DP Andrew Lesnie to manipulate subtle areas of the color spectrum, from the lavender-blues of Lothlorien to the magenta-pinks of Rivendell, as well as to increase contrast, burn out highlights, blacken blacks, and cause Elvish skin tones to radiate a warm glow without affecting surrounding elements. As Peter Jackson remarked to *American Cinematographer*: "Digital grading allows you to apply a remarkable layer of creativity to the film after you've shot it. Andrew [Lesnie] and I didn't want anything to feel artificial; we wanted to make the film feel like a "real fairy tale" [by giving it] a slightly fan-

3. Jim Rygiel, quoted in *Box Office* (November 2001): 41.

tastic feel, while also making it feel real."[4] A fusion of the fantastic and the real is exactly what they have achieved: armies of artificially intelligent Orcs fighting armies of artificially intelligent Gondorians on their own recognizance while digital animators stand idly by can hardly be described in any other way. (The real-world equivalent of this may be the U.S. Air Force's JDAM [Joint Direct Attack Munition] "smart" bomb, which uses encrypted data pulses from the Global Positioning Satellite [GPS] network to determine its destination within three-dimensional space to an accuracy of less than 1 meter.)

21.54 *From Here to Eternity* (Fred Zinnemann, 1953). The Pearl Harbor attack recreated through documentary footage of the real thing.

Digital Technology and the Future of Cinema: Three Pearl Harbors, 1953–2001

Only twelve years separate the animation of the watery pseudopod in James Cameron's *The Abyss* (1989), arguably the first computer-generated character of any real complexity to appear in a feature film, and the artificially intelligent (or stupid) Orcs and Gondorians fighting to the death—*on their own*—on the dark plain of Gogoroth in Peter Jackson's *Lord of the Rings: The Fellowship of the Ring* (2001). Using a desktop computer and commercial software, it is now possible for any one of us to achieve in a relatively short amount of time what it took a team of ILM animators months to accomplish in 1989. Can there be any doubt that twelve years from now, at the very least, we will have at our fingertips the capabilities that allowed Peter Jackson's 200 digital artists at Three Foot Six to send those not-so-ignorant armies off to clash by night in the fields of Mordor? Every generation thinks that it stands at the pinnacle of its civilization's technologies of representation, and no less do we. So it is instructive to conclude this book by looking back at the way films from three different American eras configured then–state-of-the-art filmmaking technologies to represent a seismic event in American history.

From Here to Eternity (Fred Zinnemann, 1953), *Tora! Tora! Tora!* (Richard Fleischer, 1970), and *Pearl Harbor* (Michael Bay, 2001) all attempt to re-create the Japanese attack on Pearl Harbor on December 7, 1941, as their dramatic and cinematic climax; and each was made at a crucial point in the history of the American cinema. *From Here to Eternity* was released in the year that the majors sold off the last of their theater chains, as ordered by the Consent Decrees of 1948, marking the end of their oligopolistic control of the industry. *Tora! Tora! Tora!* appeared in the midst of the worst financial crisis that the American industry had faced since the Great Depression, a time when most of the studios had been absorbed into larger corporations, many of them conglomerates whose major revenue streams lay elsewhere. And *Pearl Harbor* appeared at a major crux in the history of both the industry and the nation: on the one hand, it marked a radical shift in the nature of production that involved the total integration of computer graphics with live-action filming; on the other—although we wouldn't know it until three months after its Memorial Day 2001 release—it was the last time that the events at Pearl Harbor could ever again be taken to refer only to themselves. It is perhaps ironic that the ultimate representation of these events in *Pearl Harbor* should involve a technology whose systematic binary logic is fundamentally ahistorical. Whereas computer-graphics technology gave Michael Bay unprecedented access to images virtually unbound by material reality, earlier representations of the attack on Pearl

---

4. Peter Jackson, quoted in *American Cinematographer* 82, 12 (December 2001): 59.

21.55 *Tora! Tora! Tora!* (Richard Fleischer, Toshio Masuda, and Kinji Fukasku, 1970). Pearl Harbor re-enacted via special effects using scale models in real time.

Tora! is a very different kind of film that attempts to tell the story of Pearl Harbor as a colorful, widescreen battle epic from both the Japanese and American points of view. To this end, 20th Century–Fox hired Akira Kurosawa to write the script and direct the Japanese episodes at the Toei studio in Kyoto, but he left the project after only two weeks of shooting and was replaced by Toshio Masuda and Kinji Fukasaku. The American portion of *Tora! Tora! Tora!* was shot on loca-

Harbor had been hampered by the physical limitations of scale and, like most other depictions of World War II battle action, had to rely primarily on mock-ups and miniatures to depict the raid and its aftermath. *From Here to Eternity*, based on a best-selling novel by James Jones, was shot on location in Hawaii by DP Burnett Guffey over a 41-day period at a negative cost of $1.65 million, very little of which went toward the production of its special effects. Yet the film was extremely popular, grossing $18 million to become the tenth highest-earning film of the 1950s; it was also nominated for thirteen Academy Awards and won eight—including Best Picture, Best Director, Best Screenplay, Best Cinematography (Black-and-White), Best Sound, and Best Editing—tying the record previously held by *Gone with the Wind*. The attack itself occupies only a few minutes of screen time at the film's conclusion and is a skillfully edited patchwork of live-action footage (mainly of troops at an army base being strafed by Japanese Zeros and firing back), miniatures of exploding battleships, and documentary footage of the actual event, all perfectly matched to the 1:33 Academy frame. Although it marked the first time that the Pearl Harbor attack was depicted as part of an American feature film, *From Here to Eternity* staged the event primarily as a means of plot resolution since (as in the novel) it ends in the death of a major character. The film is distinctive yet highly typical of the late studio era in its emphasis on character and story, and its relegation of special effects to a minor role in the production.[5]

Based on several works of popular history, *Tora! Tora!*

tion in Hawaii, where principal photography was completed in 13 weeks over 68 shooting days, starting on March 4, 1969. So elaborate were its special effects that the film took over 16 months in editing and postproduction before its September 1970 release, providing an early paradigm for the dynamic new relationship between production and postproduction that would come to characterize the cinema of CGI some thirty years later. Of the film's 144 minutes, 28 depict the attack itself, much of it with full-scale three-dimensional models in real time. For example, the sets for the Japanese aircraft carriers *Agaki* and *Nagato* were the largest ever constructed in the Japanese industry (the latter was 660-feet long and 10 stories high); and in Hawaii, a full-scale model of half of the USS *Arizona* was built on three oceangoing barges, engineered with a collapsible mast in order to replicate documentary images of the real ship as it listed and sank. According to director Richard Fleischer, all of the live-action sequences of the attack were covered by five Panavision cameras (under the supervision of DP Charles F.

---

5. Between *From Here to Eternity* in 1953 and *Tora! Tora! Tora!* in 1970, there was another, highly selective rendition of the attack on Pearl Harbor—Otto Preminger's *In Harm's Way* (1965), which was based on a novel by Wendell Mayes and shot in Panavision anamorphic (black and white) by DP Loyal Griggs. The attack sequence runs approximately 6 minutes and occurs about 12 minutes into the film; shown in real time, it consists mainly of a destroyer escort leaving the harbor as explosions representing bombs are detonated in the water surrounding it. No destruction of ships is depicted on screen, but we do see, in real time, an inland barracks building exploded and a car run off a cliff as a result of the attack.

21.56 *Pearl Harbor* (Michael Bay, 2001). The Pearl Harbor attack, fully digitized (top). A frame from the film's signature shot, a Japanese bomb falling toward the USS *Arizona* anchored far below, shot from the bomb's perspective. The effect was achieved by tiling together stills extracted from aerial background plates to create a synthetic trajectory for a virtual camera. Everything else in the sequence—the bomb, the smoke, the planes, the ships, and the people on them—was also computer-generated.

21.57 and 21.58 *Pearl Harbor* (2001). Two frames (bottom) from the destruction of the USS *Arizona* once the bomb has hit and penetrated its deck. The computer-generated ship swells and buckles just before it explodes in an inferno of fire and black petroleum smoke, provided by newly designed particle simulation software.

Wheeler) and required the precise coordination of stunt-men, stunt pilots, planes, ships, and explosives. Especially difficult and dangerous was the Zero attack on Wheeler Airfield, which involved blowing up numerous planes on the ground and a Japanese kamikaze plane crashing full-scale into a hanger, photographed by remote control from inside the building. Miniature work for the film was shot with high-speed cameras at the Fox ranch in Malibu by an in-house FX team under the supervision of L. B. Abbott and A. D. Flowers, who won an Academy Award for their effort. These elements were combined with live action through front projection, a new mechanical effects process introduced by Stanley Kubrick for the "Dawn of Time" sequences of *2001* in 1968. (In it, processed background elements are projected on to a screen behind the actors, whose direct alignment with the camera conceals their shadow, while that part of the projected image falling on the actors is concealed by lighting. In addition to enhancing image clarity and luminance, front projection enables a director to see an effects sequence in next-day rushes rather than having to wait a week for optical composites to be processed in the lab.) Like the CGI films discussed above, much of *Tora! Tora!*

Tora!'s $25-million budget was dedicated to its special effects (the USS *Arizona* set alone cost $1 million), and it was said at the time that Fox had spent more money on the re-enactment of the Pearl Harbor attack than the Japanese had spent to mount it in the first place, which, given the low Japanese casualty rate on December 7, 1941 (and adjusting for inflation), was probably true. The film's producers constructed an international blockbuster, but *Tora! Tora! Tora!* failed to strike a responsive chord in the audience and became one of the signal flops of the period, earning less than $15 million.

Disney chairman Michael Eisner and producer Jerry Bruckheimer also had an international blockbuster in mind when they enlisted Michael Bay in early 1999 to direct *Pearl Harbor* from a script by Randall Wallace (*Braveheart* [1995]; *We Were Soldiers* [2002]). Mindful of Bay's $35 million cost overrun on *Armageddon*, Eisner took the unusual step of vetting the project through Disney's strategic planning committee, a body responsible for corporate fiscal policy, which fixed the budget at $145 million; another $10 million was subsequently cut during the film's production, which Bay reputedly quit several times in protest. To save on costs, the principal actors and crew as well as Bruckheimer and Bay deferred their up-front salaries against box-office profits, which wouldn't appear until the Touchstone Pictures release had earned $400 million worldwide (amortizing its negative cost, plus distribution and marketing fees).[6] Thus, *Pearl Harbor* was paradigmatic of late twentieth-century Hollywood deal-making, in which the "green-lighting" of big-budget productions depends on negotiated corporate decisions calculated to reduce risk in an increasingly volatile marketplace. It was similarly typical in its use of CGI to contain costs and maintain economies of scale.

The apex of the film's narrative arc is the attack, which extends for 45 minutes from the pre-attack sequence, as the Japanese air fleet flies in across Oahu, through the attack itself, alternating between battle action in the harbor, at a hospital, and on various airfields, to the aftermath hours later where Admiral Kimmel surveys the damage to the harbor in a launch. With liberal Pentagon cooperation (the U.S. Navy, e.g., provided visuals of period ships and aircraft as well as a real aircraft carrier to re-create the Dolittle raid on Tokyo at the film's conclusion), this sequence was realized through an elaborate integration of full-scale, live-action special effects supervised by John Frazier and scale-enhancing CGI created

at ILM under the direction of Eric Brevig. Of nearly 300 visual-effects shots contracted out to the firm, two-thirds represented the events of the attack, which Bay had divided into those that could be rendered live and those that demanded CGI prior to shooting on location in Hawaii. Among other things, computer graphics were dictated by a scarcity of period planes and ships. For example, the production had only 9 Japanese aircraft, including the last surviving Zero, with which to represent the fleet of 186 actually involved in the attack; similarly, although a few real period ships—cruisers and destroyers—were available for filming, none of the surviving battleships could be used as sets: they were either relegated to museum status or, like the USS *Missouri*, anchored in the wrong position (once the film crew arrived in Hawaii, however, Bay was able to negotiate the use of 17 ships from the navy's inactive or "mothball" fleet on which to simulate explosions during the attack). Once it became clear that computer-generated planes and ships would be used rather than full-scale models, Bay began to pre-visualize the attack sequence through animatics produced by Dream Quest (which merged with Disney's own computer-animation division to become The Secret Lab during *Pearl Harbor*'s production). This process enabled Bay to design his shots by trial and error on virtual sets before committing to actual shooting, a practice that saved both time and money. Because the director demanded historical accuracy in reconstructing the attack, Bruckheimer's office conducted extensive archival research involving news footage and photographs as well as interviews with survivors that materially influenced the design of the shots. Over 100 final animatics of the attack provided a detailed visual reference for the sequence, complete with 3-D animation, accurate lighting and color effects, particle animation of explosions, and aerodynamically accurate planes and animated pilot figures inside of them. Using this schema, Bay and DP John Schwartzman spent six weeks in Hawaii shooting backgrounds and other live-action elements; then they moved on to complete principal photography in three more places: to studio and backlot locations in Hollywood for dialogue scenes, to the Fox Studios Baja tank, where large-scale harbor action (such as the sinking of the USS *Oklahoma*)

---

6. John Horn, "The Road to Pearl Harbor," *Newsweek* (May 14, 2001): 49.

was shot, and finally to Houston for action scenes staged aboard the real battleship USS *Texas* and the aircraft carrier *Lexington* anchored at Corpus Christi. For the film's numerous aerial sequences, a specialized cinematographer (David Nowell) was employed, who, in addition to motion-picture plates shot from a helicopter, produced some of his live-action Hawaiian backgrounds through the process of tiling together still photographs. (Tiling is the procedural repetition of an image or single rectangular image map multiple times along the vertical and/or horizontal axes.) This process had the advantage of flexibility over aerial plates shot from a fixed camera since virtual camera movements can be created at random in a tiled environment. In both cases, post–World War II buildings, memorials, and other modern-day features of the harbor were digitally removed.

For the first aerial view of Pearl Harbor, an establishing shot of navy nurses being ferried to their new station on Oahu, battleship row and all harbor activity except the movement of the ferry were computer-generated. The creation of the eight highly detailed digital battleships visible in this shot and used continuously throughout the attack (the *Arizona, Nevada, Oklahoma, West Virginia, California, Tennessee, Maryland*, and the supply ship *Vestal*) was a major challenge for ILM, whose key issue proved to be lighting. The standard practice for lighting digital models at this time was to add virtual lights individually based on location or photographic reference. But given the complexity and length of the shots in which the computer-generated ships were to appear, as well as their proximity to the virtual camera, it soon became clear that another approach was necessary. Radiosity, in which light bounces interactively off each surface of the model, required too much rendering to be cost-effective, so ILM developed a way to precalculate approximate radiosity and then reuse it from shot to shot. This was done by creating reflection maps through a new ray-tracing technology that accounted for shadow-causing light occlusions and then integrating them into the surface maps of the models. This new way of creating ambient light, which ILM dubbed the "global illumination lighting technique," also proved essential to the creation of ultrarealistic planes. Bay insisted that these be extremely detailed and accurate to the rivet since they would be flying side by side with real planes; furthermore, when the digital planes were blown up or shot down with anti-aircraft fire, their mechanical insides were extruded in photorealistic

fashion. The use of digital planes and battleships during the attack made it easier to credibly integrate computer-generated characters into them, circumventing the repetitive labor of tracking and compositing digital people into a live-action model or miniature, as was the practice in *Titanic* (see above). As Eric Brevig pointed out, this achieved an economy of effort that enabled his visual-effects team to spend more time on photorealistic rendering of characters once they had been inserted into the digital model.[7]

Other important CGI involved in the attack sequence required the creation of synthetic explosions, fire, and smoke on a scale never attempted before. Using photographs of the actual Pearl Harbor event as a reference, the volume of black smoke created by burning diesel fuel was particularly problematic. It could only be created sparingly in real terms on location because its toxicity violated U.S. environmental laws, and existing particle simulators were not capable of creating realistic digital smoke on a large scale. But using the IMAX film *Fires of Kuwait* (David Douglas, 1992) as a visual reference, ILM conferred with the team that had developed the dynamic simulations for *The Perfect Storm*'s storms at sea and designed new simulation software to create the vast expanses of billowing smoke that proceeds from the stricken ships and planes of *Pearl Harbor*. Similar resources were devoted to the creation of digital flames, tracer fire, and bullet hits, and to the creation of turbulence in the placid water of the Baja tank.

Three major set pieces of the harbor assault involved extensive use of CGI. The first was the film's signature shot and the highlight of its trailer, in which a camera appears to follow a Japanese bomb as it falls toward the USS *Arizona*, anchored below. ILM originally attempted to capture the movement with an aerial background plate into which a CGI bomb and ships would be composited, but Bay felt that the camera moved too slowly. So ILM tiled together stills from the background to create a synthetic environment through which a virtual camera could drop at the desired rate to accompany a digital bomb as it hurtled through a digital sky, full of digital planes and smoke, toward the digital ships, people, and water below. Thus, the bomb drop became 100 percent CGI, and virtual-camera wobble was introduced to avoid the too per-

---

7. Eric Brevig, quoted in *Cinefex* 86 (July 2001): 75.

fect look of a shot that could never have been made in real time.

The second CGI-intensive shot of the harbor attack shows the destruction of the *Arizona* after the bomb has penetrated the deck and explodes in the munitions hold. Although the historical footage of the battleship blowing up isn't very dramatic, Bay wanted the explosion to become the centerpiece of the film by giving it great symbolic force. Eric Brevig put it this way: "Battleships are so big that they actually stress when they blow up, so we [decided we] wanted to see this 600-foot metal ship 'flex' briefly before the explosion ripped through its skin. That's something we could only do with CG."[8] To achieve this effect, ILM digital artists custom-built a computer-generated *Arizona* so that they could make the deck buckle and the hull begin to rip apart at the seams as the explosion came blasting out. Animators used a dynamic-simulation tool to create the buckling and subsequent disintegration of the ship, while another simulator replicated the percussive effect of the explosion on the surface of the harbor. The *Arizona* explosion was one of *Pearl Harbor*'s most complicated shots, begun on the first day of postproduction and finished only weeks before the final negative cut.

The film's third major computer-graphics sequence simulated the final event of the harbor attack—the torpedoing, 180-degree roll, and capsizing of the *Oklahoma*, which involved the compositing of a large number of disparate elements: computer-generated battleship exteriors; live-action shots on a gimbaled, 150-foot full-scale deck set in the Baja tank; hundreds of digital characters—many appearing very close to the virtual camera—in 64 different performance states (and requiring the development of a "sailor management" interface to coordinate their actions); as well as computer-generated water, explosions, and smoke. This elaborate capsizing sequence is followed by a wide-angle crane shot of Pacific Fleet commander Admiral Kimmel surveying the damage from a launch, in which only the overturned *Oklahoma* set and the launch are real (the burning ships, the billowing smoke, the sailors in the water, and the numerous rescue craft were all computer-generated, as was the matte painting of the horizon). The punitive Dolittle raid that concluded *Pearl Harbor*, like the earlier RAF Spitfire–German Messerschmitt dogfights over the English Channel, featured a combination of real and digital aircraft perfectly matched against a tiled background plate in aerial sequences too dangerous or difficult to be performed by live actors.

Clearly, the representation of the Pearl Harbor attack in *Pearl Harbor* is light years removed from its sketchy rendition in *From Here to Eternity* (although, ironically, the earlier representation was comprised largely of documentary footage of the event itself). But it would be wrong to see the movement from the 1953 film to its 2001 counterpart as simply a progression in the technology of special effects. It actually represents a shift in the direction of a new film aesthetic in which postproduction acquires a status equal to production and cinema is no longer exclusively the art of the moving photographic image. In a 1997 essay entitled "What Is Digital Cinema?," Lev Manovich extrapolates from the field of computer-generated special effects five basic principles of this new aesthetic.[9] First, the ability to generate photorealistic images directly in the computer displaces live-action photography as the *only* basic material from which film is constructed. Second, once live-action footage is digitized, it loses its privileged one-to-one relationship with reality, becoming just another set of pixels that the computer can sort and alter as it does computer-generated pixels. Third, digitization enables film to achieve a degree of plasticity formerly possible only in painting or animation, so that it becomes not an end in itself, but raw material for further manipulation through compositing, morphing, cloning, etc. Fourth, the computer collapses the distinction between editing and special effects, both practically and conceptually, since reordering a sequence of images in time (editing) and compositing them together in space (special effects) involves the same digital operation—the algorithmic manipulation of pixels, or, generically, "image processing." Fifth, working in the digital domain eliminates the distinction between creation and modification so endemic to film-based media (in photography, shooting versus lab work; in film, production versus postproduction). In this new aesthetic, in fact, cinema becomes, according to Manovich, "a particular case of animation which uses live action footage as one of its many ele-

---

8. Eric Brevig, quoted in *American Cinematographer* 82, 8 (August 2001): 73.

9. Lev Manovich, "What Is Digital Cinema?" *BLIMP* 37 (1997): 38.

ments. . . . In short, production becomes just the first stage of post-production."[1]

If, in fact, the cinema can no longer be clearly distinguished from animation, then movies like *Pearl Harbor* cannot be judged by the same standards as *From Here to Eternity* or *Tora! Tora! Tora!* or, indeed, most of the narrative films described in this book. I am not suggesting that CGI-intensive films be exempt from the laws of coherent narrative, but rather that we also give them credit for being the truly brilliant works of animation that they sometimes are. For example, *Pearl Harbor* is not very successful as a narrative (although it is hardly less so than most of Hollywood's World War II–era melodramas and combat films), but its 45-minute attack sequence is surely one of the most astonishing works of three-dimensional computer animation ever rendered, and as a representation of epic modern battle action it simply has no peer. It is easy to imagine that Griffith and Eisenstein would have readily availed themselves of CGI to enhance the scale of their very different forms of spectacle; and it is difficult to imagine that Welles and Hitchcock would *not* have done so since both directed heavily composited films well before computer graphics evolved. *Citizen Kane* (1941), for example, contains more optically composited shots than any film made before *Who Framed Roger Rabbit* (1988)—over 50 percent, according to Robert Carringer in *The Making of "Citizen Kane"*[2]—and *The Birds* (1963) is literally a tapestry of traveling matte shots, some containing as many as 30 separate elements. What CGI promises is a new kind of cinema, described by *Dragonheart* (1996) director Rob Cohen as "the blending of something that's imaginary with something that's really there,"[3] and a new canon of realism, defined by Lev Manovich as the creation of "something which is intended to look exactly as if it could have happened, although it really could not."[4] If CGI really is a new beginning, perhaps we should look at the films of its first decade in the same way that we look at those discussed in the first three chapters of this book, when narrative cinema was being shaped and codified. We do not valorize *Cabiria*, *The Birth of a Nation*, or *Intolerance* for their intellectual or conceptual content, much less *A Trip to the Moon*, *The Great Train Robbery*, or *The Lonely Villa*. We prize them, rather, for meeting difficult challenges of narrative expression and coherence at a time when the medium itself was new. Once these problems were solved and the solutions formalized, successive generations of filmmakers (aesthetic rather than chronological)—e.g., Murnau, Lang, Eisenstein, Pudovkin, Hitchcock, Renoir, and Welles—were free to infuse the medium with their unique vision and make the cinema the most important art form of the twentieth century. In works like *Moulin Rouge* and *The Lord of the Rings: The Fellowship of the Ring*, we can see intimations of the next generation of digital cinema and of CGI's potential to transform the narrative language of film into an even more powerful medium than it was during its first one hundred years.[5]

---

1. Manovich, p. 33.

2. Robert L. Carringer, *The Making of "Citizen Kane"* (Berkeley: University of California Press, 1985), p. 99.

3. Rob Cohen, quoted in Paula Parisi, "The New Hollywood: Silicon Stars," *Wired* (December 1995): 202.

4. Manovich, p. 33.

5. Digital technology has impacted other areas of production, distribution, and exhibition exclusive of CGI. Much feature-film editing, for example, is now done on nonlinear systems like the Avid Film Composer, Montage III, LightWorks, and D/Vision Pro. In the realm of audio, digital technology has achieved full frequency response, allowing sound engineers to move action convincingly offscreen and to strategically isolate musical themes and instruments, as well as dialogue and Foley effects, on discrete tracks. As digital sound design assumes an ever more important role in the production process, more than 50,000 theaters worldwide have equipped themselves with one of three digital playback systems—Dolby's SRD, Sony's SDDS, and Universal's DTS. Theatrical exhibition of features via satellite downlink and digital projection is already a reality in some urban venues. And theaters themselves may become obsolete when the delivery of digital multimedia (high-definition video, sound, graphics, and text) into the home becomes widely available, as is predicted for 2010. Finally, feature films in digital-video form are regularly distributed on the internet as MPEG-2 (VCD) and MPEG-3 (DVD) files, much to the chagrin of Hollywood, which wants computer manufacturers to disable the technology that makes such file sharing possible.

Glossary

Academy aperture   The **frame** size established by the Academy of Motion Picture Arts and Sciences to standardize the sound film in 1932. It indicates an **aspect ratio** of 4:3, or 1.33:1. See **widescreen.**

accelerated montage   A sequence made up of **shots** of increasingly shorter lengths that creates a psychological atmosphere of excitement and tension. See **montage; parallel action.**

accelerated motion   See **fast motion.**

aerial shot   A shot from above, usually made from a plane, helicopter, or crane. See **crane shot.**

"agit-Guignol"   Eisenstein's term for agitational effects involving shocking violence; derived from the Grand Guignol, a theater in Paris (1897–1962) that specialized in realistic depiction of murder and torture.

analog   Describes any process that attempts to mimic the waveforms of an original signal, such as radio frequencies or video signals. Unlike digital information, analog data are continuously variable, without discrete steps or quantization.

anamorphic lens   A **lens** that squeezes a wide image to fit the dimensions of a standard 35mm film **frame.** In projection, an anamorphic lens on the projector reverses the process and redistributes the wide image on the **screen.** See **widescreen.**

animatics   Animated storyboards comprised of rough drawings or **computer-generated characters** that are composited with video recording or live-action **scenes** to give both actors and digital artists a guide for the positioning of characters and other **CGI** in the final composite.

animation   All techniques that make inanimate objects move on the **screen,** such as drawing directly on the film, individually photographing animation cells, and photographing the objects one **frame** at a time while adjusting their position between frames. See **pixillation; stop-motion photography.**

animation "chains"   In **computer graphics,** linkages that allow for synchronicity among linked objects. See **inverse kinematics.**

animation software   A computer program designed for creating and animating three-dimensional graphics. Popular examples include Maya and Houdini.

animatronic puppetry   Electronic mechanical puppetry—controlled by hand, remote, cable, or computer—used for a live-action shoot.

arc light   The source of high-energy illumination on the movie **set** and in the projector; the principle source of film lighting during the 1920s and for three-strip Technicolor. It is produced by an electric current that arcs across the gap between two pieces of carbon (the direct-current carbon arc) or, more recently, by a mercury arc between tungsten electrodes sealed in a glass bulb (the alternating-current arc or HMI—"Hydrargyum Medium Arc-Length Iodide"—globe).

armature   The skeletal framework of a **stop-motion** puppet or model with articulated joints.

Arriflex   A light, portable camera first used in the late 1950s; it was essential to the mobile, **handheld** photography of the **New Wave** and to most contemporary **cinematography. Mitchell cameras,** however, are the industry's workhorses.

art director   The person responsible for set design and graphics.

art houses   Small theaters that sprang up in the major cities of the United States during the 1950s to show "art films" (foreign films with intellectual and aesthetic aspirations) as opposed to "commercial films" (all American films except for occasional experimental productions like *Citizen Kane*)—a distinction that can no longer be made.

aspect ratio   The ratio of the width to the height of the cinematic image, or **frame.** The **Academy aperture,** standard through 1952, was 1.33:1. Contemporary **widescreen** ratios vary, but the most common are **1.66:1** in Europe and 1.85:1 in the United States. Anamorphic processes such as **CinemaScope** can range from 2.00:1 to 2.55:1. See **widescreen.**

associative editing   The cutting together of **shots** to establish their metaphorical, or symbolic—as opposed to their **narrative**—relationship. The prehistoric bone that becomes a futuristic space station in Kubrick's *2001* (1968) is a prime example. See **match cut.**

asynchronous sound   (also called **contrapuntal sound**) Sound that does not proceed directly from the film image. See **synchronous sound.**

audion   Lee de Forest's vacuum tube, which first permitted amplification of audio signals for large audiences.

auteur   A director or other creative intelligence with a recognizable and distinctive style who is considered the prime "author" of a film. See **politique des auteurs.**

backlighting   Lighting directed at the camera from behind the subject, thus silhouetting the subject. See **key light.**

back lots   Large tracts of open land owned by the studios and used to simulate various locations.

back projection   See **rear projection.**

B-films   (also B-features, B-pictures) Films that were made cheaply and quickly. They were used to fill the bottom half of a double bill when double **features** were standard.

biopic   A biographical film, especially the kind produced by Warner Bros. in the 1930s and 1940s.

bleach-bypass process   A color-film developing technique that skips most or all of the bleaching process, retaining the **silver halide** on the **negative**; this increases contrast and grain, desaturates the color, and produces black blacks in the print image.

blimp   An awkward soundproofing cover for the camera first used in the early years of sound. Most cameras today are constructed with their own internal soundproofing.

block booking   The practice whereby distributors forced exhibitors to rent a production company's films in large groups, or "blocks," tied to several desirable titles in advance of production. Initiated by Adolph Zukor in 1916, block booking became fundamental to the studio-system monopoly and was ruled illegal by the U.S. Supreme Court in 1948 as part of the Paramount decrees. Elements of block booking persist in the practice of blind bidding for films in the preproduction stage, a source of constant complaint among contemporary exhibitors.

blockbuster   A film that is enormously popular or one that was so costly to make that it must be enormously successful to make a profit. The first blockbusters were probably Italian superspectacles like *Cabiria* (Giovanni Pastrone, 1913), followed by the Griffith epics *The Birth of a Nation* (1915) and *Intolerance* (1916). During the 1920s, films like *The Thief of Bagdad* (Raoul Walsh, 1924) and *Ben-Hur* (Fred Niblo, 1926) were conceived and marketed as blockbusters, as was David O. Selznick's *Gone with the Wind* (Victor Fleming, 1939) in the sound era. In the 1950s and 1960s, the epic-scale **widescreen** blockbuster (e.g., Cecil B. DeMille's *The Ten Commandments*, 1956) became a veritable **genre.** More recent examples include the record-breaking *Jaws* (Steven Spielberg, 1975), *Star Wars* (George Lucas, 1977), *Raiders of the Lost Ark* (Spielberg, 1981), and, of course, Warner Bros.' paradigmatic *Batman* (Tim Burton, 1989).

bluescreen photography   A **special-effects** process that involves shooting live action, models, or miniatures in front of a bright blue **screen,** leaving the background of the **shot** unexposed. This produces footage that can later be composited with other elements such as traveling mattes into the primary film. See **matte shot.**

boom   A mobile arm that suspends the **microphone** above the actors and outside of the **frame.**

broadcast   The transmission of an electromagnetic signal over a widely dispersed area.

"bullet-time" photography   (also called "Flow-Mo") A technique that enables filmmakers to change the speed of moving objects in progress. First, an actual movement is filmed and scanned into a computer to create a **wireframe** of the person or object from which its trajectory is mapped. Then a battery of still cameras is placed along this path, and the movement is photographed again as a series of sequential **stills.** These are scanned into the computer, which arranges them in the manner of a film strip so that they can be digitally manipulated to reproduce the movement at varying speeds.

cable television   The transmission of television signals via wire instead of broadcast radio waves. Although it was originally developed to permit television transmission to special geographical areas, it has become a popular alternative to broadcast television.

Cahiers du cinéma   Paris-based film journal founded by André Bazin and Jacques Doniol-Valcroze in 1951 that featured important articles by future directors of the French **New Wave.** It is still being published.

calligraphism   A term adopted by the **neorealist** director and critic Giuseppe De Santis to designate a style of interwar Italian filmmaking devoted to the formally meticulous adaptation of late nineteenth- and early twentieth-century fiction; the neorealists associated it with the decadence of the Fascist cinema.

camera angle   The perspective that the camera takes on the subject being shot. Low angle, high angle, or tilt angle are the three most common.

camera-stylo   (literally, "camera pen") A phrase first used by Alexandre Astruc in 1948 to suggest that cinema could be as multidimensional and personal as the older literary arts.

Cari software   (or Caricature software) **Animation software** that permits the creation of a fully rendered figured rather than its **wireframe,** enabling artists to envision the way their images will look on-screen as they create them. Developed by Industrial Light & Magic effects artist Cary Phillips for *Dragonheart* (Rob Cohen, 1996), Cari software also facilitates more complicated facial expressions and movements, as evident in the film's talking dragon, Draco. Phillips updated Cari later that year for Tim Burton's *Mars Attacks!* in order to allow for the creation of up to twenty **computer-generated characters** at once, radically reducing postproduction time.

CCD (charge-coupled device) input scanner   A device used for scanning film images into digital form. The CCD input scanner uses a light-sensitive semiconductor chip (a charge-coupled device) to capture the image. When the charge-coupled device is struck by light, the color and brightness information is converted into digital information.

CGI   Standard abbreviation for "computer-generated imagery." See **digital effects.**

chanbara   A Japanese sword-fight film.

chiaroscuro   The artistic technique of arranging light and dark elements in pictorial composition.

cinéaste   An artistically committed filmmaker.

Cinecittà   The largest Italian studio complex; it is located in Rome.

cinema direct   Since the early 1960s, the predominant **documentary** style in the United States. It is similar to (or, some argue, the same as) *cinéma vérité* in that it uses light, mobile equipment; but it stringently avoids narration or participation on the part of the filmmaker.

cinema novo   (literally, "new cinema") Politically committed Brazilian cinema of the 1960s.

CinemaScope   The trade name used by 20th Century–Fox for its anamorphic **widescreen** process. The word is frequently used today to refer to all anamorphic processes.

Cinémathèque Française   Established by Henri Langlois and Georges Franju in Paris in 1936, it is reputed to have the world's largest film library. By making older classics available to the public, it is also said to have influenced the style and themes of French films in the 1950s and 1960s.

Cinématographe   The camera-projector-printer invented by the Lumière brothers in 1895.

cinematographer   The **director of photography (DP)** or **lighting cameraman** (British), who is responsible for the camera technique and the lighting of a film in production.

cinematography   Motion-picture photography.

cinéma vérité   (literally, "cinema truth," the French translation of Vertov's *Kino-pravda*) As originally used in postwar France, the term described a particular kind of cinema that utilized lightweight equipment, small crews, and direct interviews. The term is now used more casually to refer to any documentary technique. See **cinema direct** and **documentary.**

cinéphile   A person who loves cinema.

Cinerama   A **widescreen** process invented by Fred Waller that requires three electronically synchronized cameras; it was first used in the 1952 film *This Is Cinerama* and was abandoned in 1962 in favor of an anamorphic process marketed under the same name.

close-up   In its precise meaning, a **shot** of a human subject's face or other object alone; more generally, any close shot.

color-correction technology   Computer technology used to modify the color, degree of contrast, highlights, or shadows of video, film, or digital images.

colorization   Any practice by which black-and-white films are modified to include color.

color timing   The color balance of an image or **scene,** or any process used to color-correct or balance an image or **scene,** so that color **continuity** is maintained throughout the film.

compilation film   A film whose **shots, scenes,** and **sequences** come from other films, often archival **newsreel** footage. *The Fall of the Romanov Dynasty* (Esther Shub, 1927) is an early example.

computer-generated character   A film character that is completely computer-generated. Computer-generated characters are often integrated into live-action **scenes** (such as the withered Gollum of Peter Jackson's *The Lord of the Rings* trilogy [2001–2003]), as well as made to star in **CGI** environments (such as the "synthespians" of Andrew Adamson's *Shrek* [2001] and Hironobu Sakaguchi's *Final Fantasy: The Spirits Within* [2001]).

computer graphics   Electronically generated **animation,** used since the late 1970s to provide credit **sequences** (*Superman*, 1978) and **special effects** (*Star Wars*, 1977) for theatrical films. It is also used in television commercials and for network logos.

Constructivism   A movement in the theater arts closely related to **Futurism.** It advocated the use of modern architectural and/or mechanical **set** designs to express three-dimensionality.

continuity The final editing structure of a completed film; also, arranging events by editing as if they had occurred continuously when, in fact, they were shot out of **sequence.**

continuity editing Editing **shots** together imperceptibly so that the action of a **sequence** appears to be continuous. See **off-screen space** and **180-degree system.**

contract director A director who works on projects from contract to contract rather than on an annual salary, as was common under the studio system.

contrapuntal sound Sound used in counterpoint, or contrast, to the image.

crane shot A **shot** taken from a mobile-crane device. See **aerial shot.**

credits The list of the writers, actors, technical personnel, and production staff of a film.

crosscutting Juxtaposing **shots** from two or more **sequences,** actions, or stories to suggest **parallel action,** as D. W. Griffith did in *Intolerance* (1916).

cutting Moving from one image or **shot** to another by editing.

day for night The technique used to shoot night **scenes** during the day. The necessary effect is created by stopping down the **lens** aperture or by using special lens filters.

deep focus A technique that exploits **depth of field** to render subjects near the camera **lens** and far away with equal clarity and permits the composition of the image in depth. Orson Welles's *Citizen Kane* (1941) is one of the earliest and most famous films to use deep-focus **shots** as a basic structural element.

definition A term used to describe the facility of **film stock** to articulate the separate elements of an image. See **resolution.**

depth of field The varying range of distances from the camera at which an object remains in sharp **focus.**

desaturated Describes color-film images that are dull, washed out, and gray.

diaphragm (also iris diaphragm) A louvered disk, located midway between the front and rear elements of a **lens,** with an opening (the *aperture*) that can be made smaller or larger to regulate the amount of light that passes through the lens. See **f-stop.**

digital compositing The process of digitally combining multiple-source images (such as live-action components, model shots, cloud and sky effects, digitally painted artwork, or computer-generated images) to produce an integrated result.

digital effects Effects created directly by the use of computer imaging, so that the actual image is generated and/or manipulated by computer software. Also known as **CGI** (computer-generated imagery).

digital file The series of binary numbers converted from the original light signal during digital image recording and then stored on disk. A digital file can be used to reconstruct the original image or can be manipulated by a computer through mathematical formulas to create a new one.

Digital Input Device (DID) (also known as the "Dinosaur Input Device") Developed by Craig Hayes and Phil Tippett to assist **stop-motion** model animators in creating computer **animation** for Steven Spielberg's *Jurassic Park* (1993), the DID is a metal puppet **armature** with electronic sensors at its pivot points that can generate a digital **wireframe** model in the computer when put through a series of maneuvers.

digital intermediate process The process by which a film **negative** is converted into digital files in order to undergo digital manipulation (such as **color timing** or the addition of computer-generated effects) before being converted back into film.

digital matte painting The use of computer paint programs to create **photorealistic** matte paintings (hand-painted images that are intended to be integrated with live-action footage) directly inside the computer, as opposed to traditional matte painting, which is accomplished outside the computer.

digital set Literally, a digital **"set"**—a completely malleable digital environment within which computer animators can control such variables as lighting, camera position and movement, and the movement of objects.

director of photography (DP) See **cinematographer.**

direct sound Sound that is recorded simultaneously with the image. With modern developments such as portable tape recorders and soundproofed cameras, direct sound has become common.

dissolve (frequently called a "lap dissolve") A transitional or expressive device that superimposes a **fade-out** over a **fade-in**, so that one image seems to overlap with another.

documentary Coined by John Grierson in the 1920s to describe formally structured nonfiction films like those of Robert Flaherty, the term has come to mean any film that is not entirely fictional.

Dolby A system (named for its inventor, Ray Dolby) for audio recording and playback that reduces background noise and improves frequency response, adding 2½ octaves to the range. In motion-picture exhibition, it can be used to produce multitrack **stereophonic sound** optically or magnetically—an advantage, since most exhibitors still use the less expensive optical playback equipment. Dolby was first used theatrically in rock-concert **documentaries** and rock musicals (e.g., Ken Russell's *Tommy*, 1975). Francis Ford Coppola (*The Conversation*, 1974) and Robert Altman (*Nashville*, 1975) were the first directors to use it for strictly aesthetic ends, and *Star Wars* (1977) was the first widely released film recorded in Dolby throughout. Since 1977, Dolby has played an increasingly important role in films, innovating both surround sound (an extra channel that feeds rear and/or side speakers to envelop audiences with the sound field) and digital theater sound (Dolby Stereo Digital).

DP   Standard abbreviation for **director of photography.**

dubbing   The recording and **postsynchronization** of a dialogue or **sound effects** track—for example, foreign-language dubbing.

dye coupling   Describes the process whereby the globules of dye in the different **emulsion** layers are coupled to silver grains and their dyes are released during development of those grains.

editor   The person who supervises the splicing or **cutting** together of the **shots** of a film into their final structure.

electronic compositing   The manipulation of film images in digital postproduction, using nonlinear editing systems to retouch **shots,** composite synthetic images, or integrate separate photographic elements into one.

emulsion   A thin, light-sensitive coating of chemicals covering the base of the **film stock.**

emulsion speed   A measure of a **film stock**'s sensitivity to light. According to a scale established by the American Standards Association (ASA), the faster emulsion speeds are more sensitive to light and have a higher ASA number.

establishing shot   A **shot,** usually a **long shot,** that orients the audience in a film **narrative** by providing visual information (such as location) for the **scene** that follows.

exploitation film   A negative term for a film aimed at a particular audience and designed to succeed commercially by appealing to specific psychological traits in that audience.

exposure   The amount of light allowed to strike the surface of a film. Film can be underexposed to create dark, murky images, or overexposed to create lighter ones.

Expressionism   An artistic (including cinematic) style that seeks to express the artist's or **auteur**'s private vision, emotional state, or subjective responses to objective reality. *Das Kabinett des Doktor Caligari* (1920) is an early Expressionist film.

extreme long shot   A **shot** made from a considerable distance, sometimes as far away as a quarter of a mile. It provides a panoramic view of a location without camera movement. See **long shot** and **full shot.**

face replacement: In **computer graphic** imaging, the substitution of one actor's face for another's. This technique is most often used to replace the face of a stunt double with that of the actor whose stunts they are performing.

fade-in   A technique for beginning a **scene** whereby an image gradually appears on a blackened **screen,** finally brightening into full visibility.

fade-out   The opposite of **fade-in.**

fast motion   Action filmed at less than 24 **frames** per second (standard sound-film speed), so that when the processed film is projected at normal speed the action appears accelerated. Most silent films were shot at close to 16 frames per second, and so they display unintentional fast motion when projected at sound speed, as they frequently are today.

feature   The main film in a program of several films, or any film over 4 reels (approximately 45 minutes) in length. Standard theatrical feature length is 90 to 120 minutes. See **short.**

fill light   A secondary light that illuminates the subject from the side or that lights areas not lit by the **key light.**

film clip   A short section of a film cut out of context, usually for the purpose of reviewing or previewing. Also used in making a **compilation** film.

film d'art   A movement in French cinema, started around 1908, that attempted to produce exact records of stage productions (minus, of course, the sound); it featured renowned dramatic personalities such as Sarah Bernhardt.

film gauge   The width of **film stock,** measured in millimeters (mm): standard commercial film is 35mm, although 16mm is becoming more common; 70mm film produced from 65mm **negative** stock is often used for epic productions; 16mm is standard for most other films; Super 8mm is still basically the province of amateurs, and 8mm is now obsolete.

film noir   (literally, "black film") A French term for a film set in a sordid urban atmosphere that deals with dark passions and violent crimes. Many American thrillers of the late 1940s and late 1980s were of this type.

filmography   A listing of films, their directors, and their dates; similar to what a bibliography is to books.

film plane   The front surface of the film as it lies in the camera or projector gate (i.e., the film aperture).

film stock   The basic material of film, made of cellulose triacetate and coated with photographic **emulsions.**

filter   A plate of glass, plastic, or gelatin that alters the quality of light passing through a **lens.**

final cut   A film in its completed form. See **rough cut.**

first run   The distribution of a new film to a limited number of showcase theaters. On its second run the film is usually distributed to a large number of theaters in less exclusive locations.

fish-eye lens   A radically distorting **wide-angle lens** with an angle of view that approaches 180 degrees.

flashback   A **shot, scene, sequence,** or (sometimes) major part of a film inserted into the narrative present in order to recapitulate the narrative past.

flash forward   Like a **flashback,** a **shot, scene,** or

sequence outside the narrative present but projected into the narrative future.

"flocking" software   **Animation software** that aids in the simulation of the motion of a large number of creatures in herding or schooling patterns by controlling each individual movement or animal in a group in relation to one another.

fluid dynamic simulator   **Animation software** that renders volume in the representation of fluid turbulence.

focal length   The distance in millimeters from the optical center of the lens (a point midway between the front and rear elements) to the **emulsion** surface of the **film stock** when the lens is sharply focused on "infinity"—i.e., an extremely distant object. Short lenses are called **wide-angle lenses,** while long lenses are called **telephoto lenses.**

focus   The clarity and sharpness of an image, limited to a certain range of distance from the camera. See **deep focus** and **shallow focus.**

focus plane   The plane at which the **lens** forms an image when focused on a given **scene,** measured as the distance from the **film plane.** See **depth of field.**

Foley effects   Live **sound effects** produced by performers known as "Foley artists," after Universal Pictures film editor Jack Foley, who created the first studio for such effects in the 1950s. Foley artists—also known as "Foley walkers" since the most common sound effect is footsteps—are often trained dancers because they have a good sense of timing.

Formalism   The elevation of form over content. Formalism posits that meaning is a function of the strictly formal features of a discourse and not the content or the referent of the content.

frame   The smallest compositional unit of film structure, the frame is the individual photographic image both in projection and on the film strip. The term also designates the boundaries of the image as an anchor for composition.

Free Cinema   An important **documentary**-style film movement in Britain started by Lindsay Anderson, Karel Reisz, and Tony Richardson in the mid-1950s.

freeze frame   A **shot** that replicates a **still** photograph. The effect is achieved by printing a single **frame** many times in succession.

front projection   An alternative to **rear projection.** While live action is filmed against a reflective backdrop, another image is projected on the backdrop by means of mirrors lying along the same axis as the camera lens. The lighting and reflective backdrop prevent shadows.

f-stop   The setting on a **lens** that indicates the diameter of the aperture (e.g., f-1, f-1.4, f-2, f-2.8, f-4, f-5.6, f-8, f-11, f-16, f-22, f-32, f-45, f-64). The size of the aperture determines how much light the lens will transmit to the **emulsion** surface of the film and therefore determines the visual quality of the image imprinted on the **negative** stock. The larger the f-number, the smaller the aperture and the greater the **depth of field.** See **diaphragm.**

full shot   A **shot** that includes the subject's entire body and often a three-fourths view of the **set.** A type of **medium long shot.**

Futurism   A revolutionary movement in the arts, closely allied with **Constructivism,** that glorified power, speed, technology, and the machine age at the expense of more traditional cultural forms. It had a natural affinity for the cinema and its mechanized apparatus.

gaffer   The chief electrician and supervisor of all lighting on a **set.**

gendai-geki   One of two major Japanese film **genres,** the *gendai-geki* deals with stories of contemporary life. A popular subtype is the *shomin-geki*, or comedy of middle-class and lower-middle-class family life. See *jidai-geki.*

genre   A category used to classify a film in terms of certain general patterns of form and content, such as the Western, the horror film, or the gangster film.

glass shot   A **special-effects** technique in which sections of a **scene** are painted on a glass plate, which is then mounted in front of the camera for integration with live action.

Go-Motion system   An **animation** technique, developed by Phil Tippett, which uses computer-controlled rods to move puppets or objects during filmmaking. Unlike **stop-motion** animation, Go-Motion achieves **motion blur** because the model is moving during the exposure of each frame.

grip   The person who rigs up equipment, such as lights and props, and makes certain they function properly.

gross   The total amount of money a film makes in rental and ticket receipts before deducting costs. The word is also used as a verb.

hair-simulation software   **Animation software** that allows animators to render realistic-looking hair digitally.

handheld shot   A type of **shot** made possible by portable, single-operator cameras. See **Arriflex.**

high-contrast   Describes color **film stock** that produces sharply distinguished hues.

high key   A lighting setup in which the **key light** is particularly bright.

highlighting   The use of extremely concentrated or fine light beams to accentuate certain parts of the subject.

holography   A modern photographic technique that uses **laser** beams to replicate three-dimensionality.

image map   Two-dimensional images such as painted images, photographs, or patterns for use in computer-**animation** processes such as **texture mapping** or **tilting.**

intercutting   See **crosscutting.**

internegatives   The **negative** duplicates used to make release prints in order to protect the original negative from damage and wear.

interpositives (short for *intermediate positives*) **Positive** prints created from original **negatives** and used to make **internegatives.**

intertitles Printed titles that appear within the main body of a film to convey dialogue and other **narrative** information. Intertitles are common in (but not essential to) the silent cinema.

inverse kinematics A computer **animation** technique for easily simulating character movement. This approach links one body movement to another in a chainlike manner whereas one joint follows the movement of the joint below it. Thus, when an animated character's foot is moved forward to simulate a step, the leg moves accordingly, the hip shifts, the spine alters position, and the head and arms assume the pose of a walking character. See **animation "chains."**

iris shot A **shot** in which a circular, **lens**-masking device contracts or expands to isolate or reveal an area of the **frame** for symbolic or **narrative** visual effect.

jidai-geki One of two major Japanese film **genres**, the *jidai-geki* is a period film set before the Meiji Restoration of 1868. All *samurai* films are *jidai-geki*.

jump cut A **cut** that is made in the midst of a continuous **shot**, or a mismatched cut between shots (the opposite of a **match cut**'s apparent seamlessness). Jump cuts create discontinuity in filmic time and space, and draw attention to the medium itself, as opposed to its content.

key light The main light on a set, normally placed at a 45-degree angle to the camera-subject axis, mixed in a contrast ratio with fill light, depending on the desired effect. See **fill light** and **backlighting.**

key lighting In **high-key** lighting, the **scene** is almost entirely lit by the **key light;** in low-key lighting, little of the scene's illumination is provided by the key light.

Kinetograph The first viable motion-picture camera, invented in 1889 by W. K. L. Dickson for the Thomas Edison Laboratories. See **Cinématographe; Kinetoscope.**

Kinetophone Edison's unsynchronized sound-film system (never successfully marketed).

Kinetoscope Invented before the projector, this was Edison's peep-show device in which short, primitive moving pictures could be seen.

kino-glaz (Literally, "kino-eye") An early *cinéma vérité* approach to film aesthetics conceived by Dziga Vertov in the 1920s and best typified by his film *The Man with a Movie Camera* (1929).

lap dissolve See **dissolve.**

laser (acronym for "Light Amplification by Stimulated Emission of Radiation") Developed in 1960, lasers project concentrated beams of light whose different rays are coherent. Owing to its peculiar properties, laser light is a central factor in **holography.**

laser scanning The use of a **laser** recorder to scan film images into digital images, computer-generated images onto **film stock,** or models into three-dimensional **computer graphics.**

latent images The invisible images that are created when light hits the **emulsion** on photographic film or paper. The latent images become visible during the developing process.

Latham loop In early projection systems, a set of sprockets that looped the film to keep it from breaking as a result of its own inertia.

lens The optical device used in cameras and projectors to focus light rays by refraction.

lighting cameraman The British term for **cinematographer.**

linkage V. I. Pudovkin's description of **montage,** to which Sergei Eisenstein took exception.

location shooting Any shooting not done inside a studio or on the studio's **back lots.**

long shot A **shot** that generally includes the whole figure of its subjects and a good deal of background. See **full shot, medium long shot,** and **extreme long** shot.

long take A single unbroken **shot,** moving or stationary, that describes a complex action that might otherwise be represented through **montage.** It is essential to *mise-en-scène* aesthetics. See **sequence shot.**

low-grain Describes **film stock** that exhibits very little film grain (the **silver-halide** crystals that capture the image when exposed to light) when projected. Low-grain stock aids in producing crisp, clear images.

maquettes Small-scale practical models used to visualize the three-dimensional shape of **animatronic puppets** or scanned into a computer to create **wireframes.** Maquettes can also simply serve as an artist's reference when **rendering** a CGI object.

mask A covering of some type placed before the camera **lens** to block off part of the photographed image. A mask can also refer to an aperture plate inserted behind a projector lens in order to obtain a desired **aspect ratio.** See **matte shot.**

master shot A **shot,** usually a **long** or **full** one, that establishes the spatial relationships among characters and objects within a dramatic **scene** before it is broken into closer, more discrete shots through editing.

match cut A cut in which two different **shots** are linked together by visual and/or aural **continuity.** See **associative editing.**

match moving The process by which computer-generated

camera movements and settings are correctly integrated into live-action photography.

matte shot A **shot** that is partially opaque in the frame area so that it can be printed together with another frame, masking unwanted content and allowing for the addition of another **scene** on a reverse matte. In a *traveling matte shot* the contours of the opaque areas can be varied from **frame** to frame.

medium close-up A **shot** distanced midway between a **close-up** and a **medium shot;** e.g., a human subject's face and torso from the chest up.

medium long shot A **shot** distanced between a **medium shot** and a **long shot,** usually showing a subject's entire figure (a **full shot**) or three-fourths of it from the knee up (a so-called *"plan americain"*).

medium shot A **shot** distanced midway between a **close-up** and a **full shot;** e.g., a human subject from the waist up.

microphone A piece of electronic equipment that picks up sound waves and converts them into electrical signals for amplification.

microphotography Photographing or filming done through a microscope; also called photomicrography.

minimal cinema A particularly stark, simplified kind of **realism** involving as little **narrative** manipulation as possible, associated with the films of Carl-Theodor Dreyer, Robert Bresson, and, most recently, Jean-Marie Straub.

mirror shot A **shot** taken in a mirror, or a type of **glass shot.**

mise-en-scène (literally, "putting in the scene") A term that describes the action, lighting, decor, and other elements within the **shot** itself, as opposed to the effects created by **cutting. Realists** generally prefer the process of *mise-en-scène* to the more manipulative techniques of **montage.**

Mitchell camera The standard Hollywood studio camera of the 1930s, 1940s, and 1950s, introduced in 1921 to compete with the Bell & Howell 2709 (the industry standard from about 1920 until the introduction of sound), and still heavily used today. According to *David Samuelson's "Hands-on" Manual for Cinematographers* (Oxford, Eng.: Focal Press, 1994), the Mitchell workhorse models NC, BNC, and BNCR will "never wear out" (pp. 4–13).

mix Optically, a **dissolve.** Aurally, the combination of several different **sound tracks,** such as dialogue and music.

mixing The work of the general sound editor, who refines, balances, and combines different **sound tracks.**

modeling In **computer graphics,** the process of digitally creating three-dimensional objects, environments, and **scenes.**

model shot A **shot** that uses miniatures instead of real locations, especially useful in disaster or science-fiction films.

mogul (originally, "powerful conqueror") The word today designates the heads of the Hollywood studios in their heyday.

monogatari (Japanese for "story" or "narrative") The word appears in many Japanese film titles.

montage Its simplest meaning is "**cutting.**" Sergei Eisenstein, however, developed an elaborate theory of montage based on the idea that contiguous **shots** relate to each other in a way that generates concepts not materially present in the content of the shots themselves. (Montage can also refer to the presentation of a great deal of **narrative** information through editing in a short period of time.)

morphing The **digital effects** process whereby one image is gradually transformed into another.

motion blur The blurred visual effect that occurs when the object being recorded is moving faster than the **shutter** speed of the camera. To re-create accurately the perceptual appearance of high-speed motion, this effect must be added to **computer graphics** using three-dimensional motion-blur simulation software during **rendering** or two-dimensional motion-blur simulation software after the image is rendered.

motion capture The process whereby the precise movements of an actor or a moving object are recorded, then converted into digital information that can be used to construct and animate **wireframe** skeletons. There are three types of motion-capture systems: magnetic (which track variations in a moving object or person's magnetic field via transmitters whose signals are then used to calculate the position of the object in space), optical (which rely on finding markers embedded at key points on the object or person with one or more video cameras), and mechanical (which use linkages like potentiometers to measure the relative position of the object or person in movement).

muscle-enveloping software **Animation software** developed by Industrial Light & Magic to allow animators to make computer-generated muscles move realistically with a creature's skeletal system.

narrative A story with a beginning, a middle, and an end (though—to paraphrase Godard—not necessarily in that order).

narrative film A film whose structure follows a story line of some sort. The mainstream of film history from the medium's birth through the present has been **narrative.**

naturalism A concept in literature and film that assumes that the lives of the characters are biologically, sociologically, or psychologically determined. Von Stroheim's *Greed* (1924) is a classic example of naturalism in film. (Frank

Norris's *McTeague* [1899], the novel on which the film is based, is a classic of naturalism in fiction.)

negative Film that inversely records the light and dark areas of a photographed **scene. Positive** prints are produced from negatives.

negative cost The cost of producing a film, exclusive of advertising, studio overhead, and distribution prints.

neorealism A post–World War II movement in filmmaking associated primarily with the films of Roberto Rossellini, Luchino Visconti, and Vittorio De Sica in Italy. It was characterized by leftist political sympathies, **location shooting**, and the use of nonprofessional actors.

neue Kino, das Literally, "the new cinema" of West Germany since 1968.

newsreel Filmed news reports shown along with the main feature in American theaters in the 1930s, 1940s, and 1950s; eclipsed by television news.

New Wave (*nouvelle vague*) (literally, "new wave") Originally a school of French filmmakers who, in the 1950s, started their careers as critics for *Cahiers du cinéma*. The year 1959 can be said to mark the beginning of this movement since it was the release date of Truffaut's *Les Quatre cents coups,* Godard's *À bout de souffle,* and Resnais's *Hiroshima, mon amour.* The phrase is also used to describe any new group of directors in any country whose approach to filmmaking is radically different from that of the established tradition, as in the Czech New Wave.

nickelodeon The first permanent movie theaters, converted from storefronts. From *nickel* (the price of admission) plus *odeon* (Greek for "theater").

offscreen space The implied filmic space beyond the borders of the film **frame** at any given moment in projection. In conventional modes of representation (e.g., classical Hollywood **narrative**), offscreen space is treated as "dead," giving the borders the status of a compositional framing device beyond which filmic reality ceases to exist. Antitraditional modes of representation (e.g., in the films of Ozu or in contemporary materialist cinema) attempt to suggest the continuity of offscreen and on-screen space, giving the borders the status of a window frame beyond which there is more filmic reality. Offscreen space can also be created in front of the screen, as well as beyond its borders, if the camera traverses the 180-degree axis of action established by traditional practice and shoots what is, in effect, "behind" it.

180-degree system The method of filming action that ensures **continuity** in the spatial relationships between objects on-screen. The camera must stay on one side of an imaginary 180-degree line, or axis of action, that runs through the center of the **set,** or from one side of the **frame** to the other.

optical effects Effects created using special cameras,

optical printers, animation, rotoscoping, or motion-control devices that cannot be done in front of the camera. Unlike **digital effects,** all of them involve some manipulation of the photographic process itself.

optical printer The machine that performs many postproduction optical processes such as **dissolves,** color balancing, and some **special effects.** Film prints are duplicated in a contact printer.

orthochromatic stock A kind of black-and-white **film stock** that reacts particularly to the blue and green areas of the color spectrum rather than the red; widely replaced by **panchromatic stock** after 1926, but still used for special applications.

outtake A **take** that is not included in the final print of the film.

pan Any pivotal movement of the camera around an imaginary vertical axis running through it; from "panorama." See **roll; swish pan; tilt shot.**

Panavision The anamorphic process most commonly used today; it replaced **CinemaScope** in the early 1960s. Super Panavision (originally called Panavision 70) uses 70mm **film stock** to produce a 65mm **negative** without squeezing the image. Ultra Panavision produces a 65mm negative anamorphically compressed in filming by a ratio of 1.25:1. The process now referred to as Panavision 70 is an optical printing method that allows 70mm **release prints** to be blown up from 35mm negatives, either anamorphic or spherical. Panavision is also the trade name of a widely used camera based on the design of the **Mitchell.**

panchromatic stock Black-and-white **film stock** that is sensitive to all the colors of the spectrum, from red to blue, but is less capable of achieving great **depth of field** than the **orthochromatic** stock it replaced in 1927. The introduction of **widescreen** processes in the 1950s greatly enhanced panchromatic depth of field.

parallel action A **narrative** strategy that **crosscuts** between two or more separate actions in order to create the illusion that they are occurring simultaneously. See **accelerated montage.**

particle-animation software **Animation software** that generates automated instructions for reproducing the natural, random movement of large numbers of objects that cannot be animated individually in a cost-effective way. First used to simulate submarine wakes, torpedo trails, and floating plankton in John McTiernan's *The Hunt for Red October* (1990), particle-animation software is often utilized to create smoke, fire, flocks of birds, tornadoes, and other types of natural phenomena.

persistence of vision The physiological foundation of the cinema: an image remains on the retina of the eye for a short period of time after it disappears from the actual field of vision; when a successive image replaces it immediately, as on a moving strip of film, the illusion of continuous motion is produced.

photorealistic   Resembling photography in its attention to precise visual detail.

pin blocking   The process of aligning and interlocking all the elements of a digitally composited **shot** so that the director can move his or her camera without having to compensate for **computer graphics.**

pixillation   A technique used for animating models by photographing them one **frame** at a time (as in *King Kong*, 1933). The technique can also be applied so that the illusion of continuous motion is disrupted. This effect is achieved either by **stop-motion photography** or by culling out particular frames from the **negative** of the film stock, as in work of Canadian filmmaker Norman McLaren (1914–1987).

politique des auteurs   (literally, "authors' policy") The idea that a single person, most often the director, has the sole aesthetic responsibility for a film's form and content. François Truffaut first postulated the idea in his article "*Une certaine tendance du cinéma français,*" which appeared in the January 1954 issue of **Cahiers du cinéma.** Other prominent exponents of this theory of film have been André Bazin in France and Andrew Sarris in the United States.

polygons   Planar surfaces comprised of at least three edges and three points. Polygons are the basic building blocks of the complicated **wireframes** used to create **computer graphic** images.

positive   A print in which the light values of the film correspond to those of the **scene** recorded. Produced from a **negative.**

postsynchronization   **Synchronization** of sound and image after the film has been shot—an important step forward in the liberation of the early sound-film camera from its glass-paneled booth. Also called **dubbing.**

previsualization   Any method that aids the filmmaker in configuring how a **scene** will look before it is shot. In modern **special-effects** filmmaking, previsualization in the form of **animatics** is regularly used during prepoduction to plan intricate special-effects **sequences.**

procedural animation   A computer **animation** technique that generates motion through an algorithm or rule-based computer language. Forms of procedural animation, such as **particle animation,** simulate the processes of natural growth and movement (including elements of randomness, recursion, and accident) and are used to re-create natural phenomena such as plant growth, tornadoes, and tidal waves.

procedural description   See **procedural animation.**

process shot   See **special effects.**

rack focus   A **shallow-focus** technique that forcibly directs the vision of the spectator from one subject to another. The **focus** is pulled and changed to shift the **focus plane.**

randomization software   A software application used to add irregularities to otherwise uniform computer-generated arrangements, such as to vary the motion within **particle animation.**

ratings   A system of film classification based on the amount of violence, sex, or "adult" language in a film. The British Board of Censors has three categories: U (universal); A (adult); and X (prohibited to children). The Motion Picture Association of America has five categories: G (general); PG (parental guidance suggested); PG-13 (parental guidance for children under thirteen); R (restricted to persons under seventeen unless accompanied by an adult); and NC-17 (prohibited to persons under seventeen).

reaction shot   A **shot** that cuts away from the central action to show a character's reaction to it.

realism   In cinema, realism describes a type of filming in which fidelity to the nature of the subject itself is more important than the director's attitude toward it. As opposed to **Expressionism,** there is usually a minimum of **montage** and **special effects.** See **Formalism; minimal cinema; neorealism.**

real time   The actual time it would take for an event to occur in reality, outside of filmic time. In the works of modernist directors like Antonioni and Jancsó, real time and filmic time often coincide for long **sequences,** although not usually over the entire length of the film. In rare instances, however (Robert Wise's *The Set-Up,* 1949; Agnès Varda's *Cleo de 5 à 7,* 1962), real time and filmic time coincide precisely.

rear projection   A technique in which a **scene** is projected onto a translucent **screen** located behind the actors so that it appears that they are in a specific location.

reel   The casing and holder for the film or tape. The feed-reel supplies the film, and the take-up reel rewinds it. A 35mm reel holds up to 1,000 feet; a 16mm reel, 400 feet. At sound speed (24 **frames** per second), a full 35mm reel runs about 10 minutes; at silent speed (approximately 16 frames per second), between 14 and 16 minutes.

release print   The final print used for screening and distribution.

rendering   The process by which **photorealistic** features—shading, color, texture, etc.—are digitally added to three-dimensional **wireframe** skeletons.

resolution   The ability of a camera **lens** to define images in sharp detail.

reverse-angle shot   A **shot** taken at a 180-degree angle from the preceding shot—in practice rarely used. Instead, filmmakers have adopted shot/reverse-shot editing in which the angle separating the two perspectives is usually between 120 degrees and 160 degrees. Two-party dialogue **sequences** are usually constructed through shot/reverse-shot editing in a manner the French call *"champ-contra-champ"*—(visual) field against field.

reverse motion   Shooting a subject so that the action runs backward—achieved by turning the camera upside down (so long as the film is double-**sprocketed**), then turning the processed film end over end, or by running it backward through an **optical printer.**

roll   The rotation of the camera around the imaginary axis that runs through the **lens** to the subject, called the "lens axis."

rotoscoping   The technique of isolating an object **frame** by frame by tracing around its edges to create a silhouette, which can then be replaced by another image during post-production.

rough cut   The first completed version of a film prepared by the **editor.** General polishing and the finer points of timing and **continuity** are accomplished later.

rushes   (also *dailies*). In production, the sound and image prints of each day's shooting, rapidly processed overnight so that filmmakers can evaluate the previous day's work before shooting begins again in the morning.

Sabre System   Developed by Industrial Light & Magic, a highly flexible "open architecture" **digital-effects** system that can accept a wide range of software and perform many different compositing functions from **digital matte painting** through editing and image processing.

scenario   Either a part or the whole of a screenplay.

scene   A vague term that describes a unit of narration. In film, it may consist of a series of shots or of a single sequence that was shot in one location. See **sequence; shot**.

Schüfftan process   A process-photography technique that combines **mirror shots** and **model shots** to create a composite image. It was invented by the UFA **cinematographer** Eugen Schüfftan (later Eugene Schuftan) and was first used on a large scale by Fritz Lang to create the futuristic vistas of *Metropolis* (1926).

Scope   An abbreviation for **CinemaScope** or any other anamorphic process.

score   The musical **sound track** for a film. The word is also used as a verb.

screen   As a noun, the specially treated surface on which a film is projected; as a verb, the act of projecting or watching a film.

screenplay   The script of a film. It may be no more than a rough outline that the director fills in, or it may be detailed, complete with dialogue, **continuity,** and camera move-

ments, as were most Hollywood studio scripts of the 1930s and 1940s.

screwball comedy   A type of comedy popular in American films of the 1930s; characterized by frantic action and a great deal of verbal wit. The focal point of the plot is usually a couple in a bizarre predicament, as in Capra's *It Happened One Night* (1934) and Hawks's *Bringing Up Baby* (1938).

second unit   In an elaborate production, a supplementary film crew that photographs routine **scenes** not shot by the first unit. Background and establishing shots, for instance, are usually shot by the second unit.

sequence   A unit of film structure made up of one or more **scenes** or **shots** that combine to form a larger unit.

sequence shot   A **long take** that usually requires sophisticated camera movement. Sometimes called by the French term *plan-séquence*.

set   The location where a **scene** is shot, often constructed on a **soundstage.**

setup   The position of the camera, lights, sound equipment, actors, etc., for any given **shot**. The number of different setups that a film requires can be an important economic factor.

shading software   A software application that aids in the realistic **rendering** of **computer graphics** by taking into account the surface characteristics of the object being rendered as well as the number, intensity, and location of light sources in the **scene,** and then tinting the image accordingly.

shallow focus   A technique that deliberately uses a shallow **depth of field** in order to direct the viewer's perception along a shallow focus plane. See **deep focus; rack focus.**

short   A film whose running time is less than 30 minutes.

shot   A continuously exposed, unedited piece of film of any length: the basic signifying unit of film structure. The average shot length (ASL) and the number of shots vary with every film.

shutter   The mechanism that opens and closes to admit and obstruct light from individual film **frames** as they are moved into position for **exposure** in the camera and projection in the projector.

silver halide   The individual crystals on **film stock** that capture the image when exposed to light.

silver retention   Color-film developing techniques that retain or redevelop **silver halide** on the **negative,** increasing contrast and grain, **desaturating** the color, and producing blacker blacks in the print image.

slapstick   A type of comedy that relies on acrobatic physical gags and exaggerated pantomine rather than on verbal humor. It was, obviously, the dominant comic form during the silent era.

slow motion   The camera is overcranked to film action at a speed faster than 24 frames per second. When the film is later projected at normal speed, the action appears much slower on the **screen** than it would in reality.

socialist realism   The aesthetic doctrine promulgated in the Soviet Union in the late 1920s that insisted that all art be rendered intelligible to the masses and subserve the purposes of the state. It had little to do with either socialism or realism.

soft focus   By means of **lens** filters, special lenses, or even petroleum jelly smeared directly on a normal lens, the **definition** of a subject is blurred or softened, producing a dreamy or romantic effect (and, often, making an actor or actress appear younger).

sound effects   All sounds that are neither dialogue nor music.

soundstage   A specially designed soundproof building in which **sets** are constructed for filming.

sound track   There are two basic types of sound track in use today: optical and magnetic. Optical sound tracks encode information on a photographic light band that widens, narrows, or varies in density on the edge of the film strip. Magnetic sound tracks encode information electromagnetically on specially treated surfaces.

special effects   A term used to describe a range of synthetic processes used to enhance or manipulate the filmic image. They include **optical effects,** such as **front projection, model shots, rear projection,** etc.; mechanical or physical effects, such as explosions, fires, fog, flying and falling objects or people, etc.; makeup effects, such as animatronics, the use of blood bags and prosthetics, etc.; and **digital effects.**

split screen   Two or more images contained within a single **frame** that do not overlap. Abel Gance used the technique extensively in *Napoléon* (1927).

sprockets   The evenly spaced holes on the edge of the film strip that allow it to be moved forward mechanically; also, the wheeled gears that engage these holes in the camera and projector.

stereophonic sound   The use of two or more high-fidelity speakers and **sound tracks** to approximate the actual dimensionality of hearing with two ears.

still   A photograph that re-creates a **scene** from a film for publicity purposes, or a single-**frame** enlargement from a film that looks like a photograph.

stock footage   Film borrowed from a collection or library that consists of standard, often-used **shots** such as of World War II combat or street crowds in New York City.

stop-motion photography   A technique used for trick photography and **special effects** in which one **frame** is exposed at a time so that the subject can be adjusted between frames; reputedly discovered by Georges Méliès. See **pixillation.**

subjective camera   A technique that causes the viewer to observe events from the perspective of a character in the film, either empirically or psychologically.

subtitle   A printed title superimposed over the images, usually at the bottom of the **frame,** to translate foreign dialogue, etc.

surrealism   A movement in painting, film, and literature that aims to depict the workings of the subconscious by combining incongruous imagery or presenting a situation in dream-like, irrational terms; more generally, surrealism may suggest any fantastic style of representation.

swish pan   A **pan** that moves from one **scene** to another so quickly that the intervening content is blurred.

synchronization   (also known as "sync") The use of mechanical or electronic timing devices to keep sound and image in a precise relationship to each other.

synchronous sound   Sound whose source is made clear by the image **track.** See **asynchronous sound; contrapuntal sound.**

take   A director shoots one or more takes of each **shot** in a given setup, only one of which appears in the final version of the film.

technical director (TD)   Individual responsible for the direction of the technical components of a **digital-effects shot,** including models, **animation, match moving,** and **rotoscoping.**

telecine   A device used to rapidly convert film into a video format.

telephoto lens   A **lens** with a long **focal length** that functions like a telescope to magnify distant objects. Because its angle of view is very narrow, it flattens the depth perspective.

television   A system for the broadcast transmission of moving images and sound to home receivers, invented in the 1930s but not available for mass marketing until after World War II. Since that time, television has usurped the cinema as America's dominant mass medium of audiovisual communication to the point that Hollywood is kept alive today less by theatrical filmmaking than by the production of tele-film. The word *television* derives from the Greek for "seeing at a distance."

texture mapping   The process by which a 2-D image is applied to a 3-D image (like gift wrapping a box).

theatrical distribution   The distribution of films through normal commercial agencies and theaters.

theatrical film   A film made primarily for viewing in a motion-picture theater rather than for television or some other specialized delivery system.

Third World cinema   A type of militant cinema now being produced in the countries of Latin America, Africa, and Asia. It is generally Marxist in ideology.

three-dimensional computer animation The creation of three-dimensional figures within the computer.

tiling In computer **animation,** the technique of creating patterns by procedurally repeating a single image (such as a digital photograph) multiple times—a process similar to creating a tiled ceramic surface. For example, to generate sweeping views of the Germanic forces of *Gladiator* (Ridley Scott, 2000), **digital effects** animators tiled together **still** photographic plates of a limited number of costumed extras representing just a small fraction of the actual numbers involved.

tilt shot A **shot** made by turning the camera up and down so that it rotates on an axis running horizontally through the camera head. See **pan; roll.**

time-lapse photography Used primarily as a scientific tool to photograph natural phenomena that occur too slowly for normal observation, it is a kind of extreme **fast-motion** shooting that compresses real time by photographing a subject at a rate (for example) of one **frame** every 30 seconds. The opposite type of time-lapse photography would rapidly expose film to capture movement that occurs too quickly to be seen by the naked eye.

track A single recording channel on a **sound track** that can be **mixed** with others and modified to create a variety of effects.

tracking shot A single continuous **shot** made on the ground with a moving camera; also known as a *traveling shot.* **Aerial shots** and **crane shots** are also continuous.

tungsten incandescent light The main source of "soft" or low-intensity illumination on the movie **set;** the principle source of film lighting during the early sound period owing to its relative silence. Like household lighting, it is produced within a bulb when a tungsten filament is made incandescent by electric current. In contemporary incandescent film lighting, ordinary glass bulbs have been replaced by quartz halogen globes.

2-D cloning The process by which an image is copied from one position or **shot** and scanned into another. This technique is often utilized in **wire removal** to clone the image from either side of an unsightly apparatus and then to use the copied image to fill in over the wire's pixels.

two-reeler A film running about 30 minutes, the standard length of silent comedies.

typage A theory of casting actors and actresses that was used by Eisenstein: instead of professionals with individual characteristics, he sought "types" and representative characters.

undercrank To run a camera at a speed of less than 24 **frames** per second. When the film is projected at normal speed, the subject appears in **fast motion.** See **slow motion.**

VCR Abbreviation for "videocassette recorder" or "videocassette recording." See **videocassette.**

VHS Abbreviation for "video home system." Any video system or combination of systems designed for home use, including **VCRs, videodisc players,** video games, and home computers with video display. More specifically, VHS is the technical designation for a popular ½-inch **videotape** format (RCA, Panasonic, JVC, etc.) which competed on the consumer market with the Beta format (Sony, Zenith, Toshiba, etc.) until it won the day in the mid-1980s. Since that time, only Sony (which invented the Beta format) has continued to manufacture Beta equipment, although many video professionals consider it to be technologically superior to VHS.

videocassette A sealed two-reel system of ¾-inch or ½-inch **videotape** generally used for private recording and viewing.

videodisc A system for home-video playback of prerecorded discs. Audiovisual information is encoded on plastic discs by a **laser** beam for decoding by a corresponding laser beam on the playback unit.

videotape Magnetic tape for recording video images and sound; manufactured in 2-inch (professional), ¾-inch, ½-inch, and 8mm ¼-inch (amateur) formats.

virtual camera Implied in all three-dimensional computer **animation,** the virtual camera's "**lens**" is the point toward which all the lines of perspective in the computer-generated image converge. Like real cameras, virtual cameras can **track, pan, tilt,** and **zoom,** yet with more freedom of placement.

VistaVision A nonanamorphic **widescreen** process developed by Paramount to compete with Fox's CinemaScope in 1954. It ran 35mm **film stock** through the camera horizontally rather than vertically to produce a double-**frame** image twice as wide as the conventional 35mm frame. The **positive** print could be projected horizontally with special equipment to cast a huge image on the screen, or it could be reduced anamorphically for standard vertical 35mm projection. Because the process is very expensive, VistaVision since 1961 has been used only for **special effects.**

visual-effects (VFX) supervisor The person in charge of the technical and creative aspects of **special-effects** production, including computer-generated imaging, **blue-screen** and greenscreen **photography,** and the use of miniatures.

voice-over A voice track laid over the other **tracks** in a film's sound **mix** to comment upon or narrate the action on **screen.**

VTR   Abbreviation for "videotape recorder" or "videotape recording," reel-to-reel or cassette.

water-simulation software   Pioneered by Cinesite Hollywood for *Waterworld* (Kevin Reynolds, 1995) **animation software** that allows animators to simulate water digitally, complete with realistic details that include foam, crests, splashes, and color changes.

wide-angle lens   A **lens** whose broad angle of view increases the illusion of depth but distorts the linear dimensions of the image. See **fish-eye lens; telephoto lens.**

widescreen   Sometimes reserved to describe any flat (i.e., nonprocessed) film format with an **aspect ratio** of 1.66:1 (European standard) or 1.85:1 (American standard), the term "widescreen" may also refer broadly to any format that gives a **screen** image wider than the Academy ratio of 1.33:1, whether processed or not. Most widescreen processes are anamorphic, but some employ wide-gauge film (**Panavision 70, Todd-AO**) or multiple camera processes (**Cinerama**).

wild recording   Recording sound (usually to be used later as **sound effects**) independently of the visuals.

wild shooting   Shooting a film without simultaneously recording the **sound track.**

wild sound   See **wild recording.**

wipe   An optical process whereby one image appears to wipe the preceding image off the **screen**—a common transitional device in the 1930s. See **dissolve; fade-out.**

wireframes   The line-based **polygonal** drawings—created from scratch or by using scanned physical structures as a guide—that provide the foundation of all three-dimensional computer **animation.** Wireframes, which have no surface details, are given **photorealistic** features during **rendering.**

wire removal   The use of **digital** painting or **compositing** techniques to eliminate cables, rigs, or harnesses that were used to execute stunts or **special effects** during filmmaking.

zoom   A variable-**focus lens** (one capable of focal lengths ranging from **wide-angle** to **telephoto**), often used to create optical motion without **tracking** the camera. Also used to describe a **shot** made with such a lens.

Selective Bibliography

David A. Cook and Aubry D'Arminio

CHAPTER 1. ORIGINS

Abel, Richard, ed. *Silent Film*. New Brunswick, N.J.: Rutgers University Press, 1996.

———. *The Red Rooster Scare: Making Cinema American, 1900–1910*. Berkeley: University of California Press, 1999.

Abel, Richard, and Rick Altman, eds. *The Sounds of Early Cinema*. Bloomington: Indiana University Press, 2001.

Acker, Ally. *Reel Women: Pioneers of the Cinema, 1896 to the Present*. New York: Continuum, 1991.

Allen, Jeanne Thomas. "Copyright and Early Theater, Vaudeville, and Film Competition." *Journal of the University Film Association*, 31, no. 2 (Spring 1979): 5–11. Repr. in Fell, ed., *Film before Griffith*, pp. 176–85.

Allen, Robert C. *Vaudeville and Film, 1895–1915: A Study in Media Interaction*, Ph.D. diss., University of Iowa, 1977. Repr. New York: Arno, 1980.

———. "Contra the Chaser Theory." *Wide Angle* 3, no. 1 (1979): 4–11. Repr. in Fell, ed., *Film before Griffith*, pp. 105–15.

———. "Motion Picture Exhibition in Manhattan, 1906–1912: Beyond the Nickelodeon." *Cinema Journal* 18, no. 2 (Spring 1979): 2–15. Repr. in Kindem, ed., *The American Movie Industry*, pp. 12–24, and in Fell, ed., *Film before Griffith*, pp. 162–75.

———. "Vitascope/Cinématograph: Initial Patterns of American Film Practice." *Journal of the University Film Association* 31, no. 2 (Spring 1979): 13–18. Repr. in Kindem, ed., *The American Movie Industry*, pp. 3–11, and in Fell, ed., *Film before Griffith*, pp. 144–52.

———. "Looking at 'Another Look at the Chaser Theory.'" *Studies in Visual Communication* 10, no. 4 (Fall 1984): 44–50.

Allen, Robert C., and Douglas Gomery. *Film History: Theory and Practice*. New York: McGraw-Hill, 1985.

Amengual, Barthélemy. "*The Life of an American Fireman* et la naissance du montage." *Cahiers de la cinémathèque* 17 (Christmas 1975): 23–27.

Anderson, Joseph, and Barbara Anderson. "Motion Perception in Motion Pictures." In de Lauretis and Health, *The Cinematic Apparatus*, pp. 76–95.

Anderson, Joseph, and Barbara Fisher. "The Myth of Persistence of Vision." *Journal of the University Film Association* 30, no. 4 (Fall 1978): 3–8.

Armour, Robert A. "Effects of Censorship Pressure on the New York Nickelodeon Market, 1907–1909." *Film History* 4, no. 2 (1990): 113–21.

Aronson, Michael G. "The Wrong Kind of Nickel Madness: Pricing Problems for Pittsburgh's Nickelodeons." *Cinema Journal* 42, no. 1 (Fall 2002): 71–96.

Auerback, Jonathan. "McKinley at Home: How Early American Cinema Made News." *American Quarterly* 51, no. 4 (1999): 797–832.

Aumont, Jacques. "Lumière Revisited." *Film History* 8, no. 4 (1996): 416–30.

Azlant, Edward. "Screenwriting for the Early Silent Film: Forgotten Pioneers, 1897–1911." *Film History* 9, no. 3 (1997): 228–56.

Bachman, Gregg, and Thomas J. Slater, eds. *American Silent Film: Discovering Marginalized Voices*. Carbondale: Southern Illinois University Press, 2002.

Balio, Tino, ed. *The American Film Industry*. Rev. ed. Madison: University of Wisconsin Press, 1985.

Barnes, John. *The Beginnings of the Cinema in England*. London: David & Charles; New York: Barnes & Noble, 1976. Repr. as *The Beginnings of the Cinema in England: 1894–1901*, vol. 1: *1894–1896*. Rev. enl. ed. Ed. Richard Maltby. Exeter: University of Exeter Press, 1998.

———. *The Pioneers of the British Film, 1898: The Rise of the Photoplay*. London: Bishop's Gate, 1983. Repr. as *The Beginnings of the Cinema in England: 1894–1901*, vol. 3: *1898*. Exeter: University of Exeter Press, 1996.

———. *The Rise of the Cinema in Great Britain: Jubilee Year 1897*. London: Bishop's Gate, 1983. Repr. as *The Beginnings of the Cinema in England: 1894–1901*, vol. 2: *1897*. Exeter: University of Exeter Press, 1996.

———. *Filming the Boer War*. London: Bishop's Gate, 1992. Repr. as *The Beginnings of the Cinema in England: 1894–1901*, vol. 4: *1899*. Exeter: University of Exeter Press, 1996.

———. *The Beginnings of Cinema in England, 1894–1901*, vol. 5: *1900*. Exeter: University of Exeter Press, 1997.

Barnouw, Erik. *The Magician and the Cinema*. New York: Oxford University Press, 1981.

Barr, Charles. "Before *Blackmail*: Silent British Cinema." In Murphy, ed., *The British Cinema Book*, pp. 1–19.

Batchen, Geoffrey. *Burning with Desire: The Conception of Photography*. Cambridge, Mass.: MIT Press, 1997.

Benjamin, Walter. "A Short History of Photography." *Screen* 13, no. 1 (Spring 1972): 5–26.

Bottomore, Stephen. "Shots in the Dark: The Real Origins of Film Editing." *Sight and Sound* 57, no. 3 (Summer 1988): 200–204.

Bowers, Q. David. *Nickelodeon Theaters and Their Music*. Vestal, N.Y.: Vestal, 1986.

Bowser, Eileen. "The Brighton Project: An Introduction." *Quarterly Review of Film Studies* 4, no. 4 (1979): 509–38.

———, ed. *The Merrit Crawford Papers*. Frederick, Md.: University Publications of America, 1987. Microfilm.

Braun, Marta. *Picturing Time: The Work of Etienne-Jules Marey*. Chicago: University of Chicago Press, 1992.

Brewster, Ben. "A Scene at the Movies." *Screen* 23, no. 2 (July–August 1982): 4–15.

Brosnan, John. *Movie Magic: The Story of Special Effects in the Cinema*. Rev. ed. London: Abacus, 1976.

Brown, Richard, and Barry Anthony. *A Victorian Film Enterprise: The History of the British Mutoscope and Biograph Company, 1897–1915*. Trowbridge, Eng.: Flicks, 1999.

Brownlow, Kevin. "Silent Film: What Was the Right Speed?" *Sight and Sound* 49, no. 3 (Summer 1980): 164–67.

Burch, Noël. "Porter, or Ambivalence." *Screen* 19, no. 4 (Winter 1978–79): 91–105.

———. "Narrative/Diegesis—Thresholds, Limit." *Screen* 23, no. 2 (July–August 1982): 16–33.

———. *Life to Those Shadows*. Trans. and ed. Ben Brewster. Berkeley: University of California Press, 1990.

Burton, Alan, and Laraine Porter, eds. *Crossing the Pond: Anglo-American Film Relations before 1930*. Trowbridge, Eng.: Flicks, 2002.

Cahn, Iris. "The Changing Landscape of Modernity: Early Film and America's 'Great Picture' Tradition." *Wide Angle* 18, no. 3 (July 1996): 85–100.

Ceram, C. W. *Archaeology of the Cinema*. London: Thames & Hudson, 1965.

Chanon, Michael. *The Dream That Kicks: The Prehistory and Early Years of Cinema in Britain*. London: Routledge & Kegan Paul, 1980.

Charney, Leo. *Empty Moments: Cinema, Modernity, and Drift*. Durham, N.C.: Duke University Press, 1998.

Charney, Leo, and Vanessa R. Schwartz, eds. *Cinema and the Invention of Modern Life*. Berkeley: University of California Press, 1995.

Cherchi Usai, Paolo. "Origins and Survival." In Nowell-Smith, ed., *The Oxford History of World Cinema*, 6–13.

———. *Silent Cinema: An Introduction*. Trans. Emma Sansone Rittle. Rev. and exp. ed. London: British Film Institute, 2000.

"A Chronology of Cinema: 1889–1896." Special issue of *Film History* 7, no. 2 (1995).

"Cinema Pioneers." Special issue of *Film History* 10, no. 1 (1998).

Coe, Brian. *Muybridge and the Chronophotographers*. London: Museum of the Moving Image, 1992. Exhibition catalog.

Conot, Robert. *A Streak of Luck: The Life and Legend of Thomas Alva Edison*. New York: Seaview, 1979.

Cook, Olive. *Movement in Two Dimensions*. London: Hutchinson, 1963.

Corkin, Stanley. *Realism and the Birth of the Modern United States*. Athens: University of Georgia Press, 1996.

Cosandey, Roland. " 'Sensational Films—Ascent of the Alps by Motor Car: Mutoscope and Biograph in Switzerland, 1903." *Historical Journal of Film, Radio and Television* 15, no. 4 (1995): 475–93.

Couperie, Pierre, et al. *A History of the Comic Strip*. Trans. Eileen B. Hennessy. New York: Crown, 1968.

Dagognet, François. *Étienne-Jules Marey: A Passion for the Trace*. Trans. Robert Galena with Jeanine Herman. Cambridge, Mass.: MIT Press, 1992.

Darrah, William C. *The World of Stereographs*. Gettysburg, Pa.: Darrah, 1977.

de Lauretis, Teresa, and Stephen Heath. *The Cinematic Apparatus*. London: Macmillan, 1981.

Deutelbaum, Marshall. "Structural Patterning in the Lumière Films." *Wide Angle* 3, no. 1 (Spring 1979): 28–37.

Dickson, W. K. L. *The Biograph in Battle: Its Story in the South African War Related with Personal Experiences*. London: Unwin, 1901. Repr. Trowbridge, Eng.: Flicks, 1995.

Dickson, W. K. L., and Antonia Dickson. *History of the Kinetograph, Kinetoscope, and Kinetophonograph*. New York: Bunn, 1895. Repr. New York: Arno, 1970.

Doane, Mary Ann. "Temporality, Storage, Legibility: Freud, Marey, and the Cinema." *Critical Inquiry* 22, no. 2 (Winter 1996): 313–43.

"Early Cinema." Special issue of *Persistence of Vision* 9 (1991).

"Early Cinema." Special issue of *Film History* 11, no. 3 (1999).

"Early Cinema Audiences." Special issue of *Iris* 11 (Summer 1990).

Edison Catalogue. New York, 1904.

Elsaesser, Thomas, and Adam Barker, eds. *Early Cinema: Space-Frame-Narrative*. London: British Film Institute, 1990.

Everdell, William R. *The First Moderns: Profiles in the Origins of Twentieth-Century Thought*. Chicago: University of Chicago Press, 1997.

Ezra, Elizabeth. *Georges Méliès: The Birth of the Auteur*. Manchester, Eng.: Manchester University Press; New York: St. Martin's, 2000.

Fell, John L. *Film and the Narrative Tradition*. Norman: University of Oklahoma Press, 1975.

———. "Motive, Mischief and Melodrama: The State of Film Narrative in 1907." *Film Quarterly* 33, no. 3 (Spring 1980): 30–37. Repr. in Fell, ed., *Film before Griffith*, pp. 272–83.

———. "Before the Nickelodeon." *Film Quarterly* 36, no. 4 (Summer 1983): 21–25.

———, ed. *Film before Griffith*. Berkeley: University of California Press, 1983.

Fielding, Raymond. *The Technique of Special Effects Cinematography*. 3rd ed. New York: Hastings House, 1972.

Fischer, Lucy. "The Lady Vanishes: Women, Magic and the Movies." *Film Quarterly* 33, no. 1 (Fall 1979): 30–40. Repr. in Fell, ed., *Film before Griffith*, pp. 339–54.

Frampton, Hollis. "Stan and Jane Brakhage, Talking." *Artforum* 11, no. 5 (January 1973): 72–79. Interview with Stan and Jane Brakhage.

Fullerton, John, ed. *Celebrating 1895: The Centenary of Cinema*. London: Libbey, 1998.

Fullerton, John, and Astrid Söderbergh-Widding, eds. *Moving Images: From Edison to the Webcam*. Sydney: Libbey, 2000.

Gaines, Jane M. *Fire and Desire: Mixed-Race Movies in the Silent Era*. Chicago: University of Chicago Press, 2001.

Gartenberg, Jon. "Vitagraph before Griffith: Forging Ahead in the Nickelodeon Era." *Studies in Visual Communication* 10, no. 4 (Fall 1984): 7–23.

Gaudreault, André. "Detours in Film Narrative: The Development of Cutting." *Cinema Journal* 19, no. 1 (Fall 1979): 39–59.

———. "Temporality and Narrativity in Early Cinema, 1895–1908." In Fell, ed., *Film before Griffith*, pp. 311–29.

———. "Theatricality, Narrativity, and 'Trickality': Reevaluating the Cinema of Georges Méliès." Trans. Paul Attallah. *Journal of Popular Film and Television* 15, no. 3 (Fall 1987): 110–19.

Gernsheim, Helmut. *The History of Photography*. New York: Oxford University Press, 1955.

Geuens, Jean-Pierre. "Morning Light: A Study of the Visual Signifiers between 1895 and 1915." *Spectator* 7, no. 1 (Fall 1986): 7–9.

Gregory, R. L. *Eye and Brain: The Psychology of Seeing*. 2nd ed., New York: McGraw-Hill, 1973.

Gubern, Roman. "David Wark Griffith et l'articulation cinématographique." *Cahiers de la cinémathèque* 17 (Christmas 1975): 7–21.

Gunning, Tom. "Le Style non-continu du cinéma des premiers temps (1900–1906)." *Cahiers de la cinémathèque* 29 (Winter 1979): 24–34.

———. "An Unseen Energy Swallows Space: The Space in Early Film and Its Relation to American Avant-Garde." In Fell, ed., *Film before Griffith*, pp. 355–66.

———. "The Cinema of Attraction: Early Film, Its Spectator and the Avant-Garde." *Wide Angle* 8, nos. 3 and 4 (Autumn–Winter 1986): 63–77.

———. "In Your Face: Physiognomy, Photography, and the Gnostic Mission of Early Film." *Modernism/Modernity* 4, no. 1 (1997): 1–29.

Hammond, Paul. *Marvelous Méliès*. London: Gordon Fraser Gallery, 1974.

Harding, Colin, and Simon Popple, eds. *In the Kingdom of Shadows: A Companion to the Early Cinema*. Madison, N.J.: Fairleigh Dickinson University Press, 1996.

Hark, Ina Rae, ed. *Exhibition: The Film Reader*. London: Routledge, 2002.

Hecht, Hermann. *Pre-Cinema History: An Encyclopedia and Annotated Bibliography of the Moving Image before 1896*. Ed. Ann Hecht. London: Bowker Saur, 1993.

Hendricks, Gordon. *The Edison Motion Picture Myth*. Berkeley: University of California Press, 1961. Repr. in Hendricks, ed., *Origins of the American Film*.

———. *Beginnings of the Biograph*. New York: Hendricks, 1964. Repr. in Hendricks, ed., *Origins of the American Film*.

———. *Eadweard Muybridge: The Father of Motion Pictures*. New York: Grossman, 1965.

———. *The Kinetoscope*. New York: Hendricks, 1966. Repr. in Hendricks, ed., *Origins of the American Film*.

———. *Origins of the American Film*. New York: Arno, 1972.

Hepworth, Cecil. *Came the Dawn: Memories of a Film Pioneer*. London: Phoenix House, 1961.

Herbert, Stephen, and Luke McKernan, eds. *Who's Who of Victorian Cinema*. London: British Film Institute, 1996.

Herzog, Charlotte. "The Movie Palace and the Theatrical Source of Its Architectural Style." *Cinema Journal* 20, no. 1 (Spring 1981): 15–37.

———. "The Archaeology of Cinema Architecture: The Origins of the Movie Theater." *Quarterly Review of Film Studies* 9, no. 1 (Winter 1984): 11–32.

Higashi, Sumiko; Robert C. Allen; and Ben Singer. "Dialogue: Manhattan's Nickelodeons." *Cinema Journal* 35, no. 3 (1996): 72–128.

Higson, Andrew, ed. *Young and Innocent?: The Cinema in Britain, 1896–1930*. Exeter: University of Exeter Press, 2002.

Hiller, John. "Film History for the Public: The First National Movie Machine Collection." *Film History* 11, no. 3 (1999): 371–86.

Hollyman, Burns. "Alexander Black's Picture Plays: 1893–1894." *Cinema Journal* 16, no. 2 (Spring 1977): 26–33.

Holman, Roger, ed. *Cinema 1900–1906: An Analytical Study by the National Film Archive and the International Federation of Film Archives*. Brussels: Fédération Internationale des Archives du Film, 1982.

Horak, Jan-Christopher. "The Magic Lanterne Moves: Early Cinema Reappraised." *Film Reader 6: Investigations in Film History and Technology* (1985): 93–101.

Jacobs, Lewis. *The Rise of the American Film*. Rev. ed. New York: Teachers College Press, 1968.

Josephson, Matthew. *Edison*. London: Eyre and Spottiswoode, 1961; New York: McGraw-Hill, 1963.

———. *Edison: A Biography*. New York: Wiley, 1992.

Jowett, Garth S. "The First Motion Picture Audiences." *Journal of Popular Film* 3, no. 1 (Winter 1974): 39–54. Repr. in Fell, ed., *Film before Griffith*, pp. 196–206.

Kattell, Alan D. "The Evolution of Amateur Motion Picture Equipment 1895–1965." *Journal of Film and Video* 38, nos. 3–4 (Summer–Fall 1986): 47–57.

Kelkres, Gene G. "A Forgotten First: The Armat-Jenkins Partnership and the Atlanta Projection." *Quarterly Review of Film Studies* 9, no. 1 (Winter 1984): 45–58.

Kerr, Paul. "Re-Inventing the Cinema." *Screen* 21, no. 4 (Winter 1980): 80–84.

Kindem, Gorham, ed. *The American Movie Industry: The Business of Motion Pictures*. Carbondale: Southern Illinois University Press, 1982.

Kirby, Lynne. *Parallel Tracks: The Railroad and Silent Cinema*. Durham, N.C.: Duke University Press, 1997.

Kovács, Katherine Singer. "Georges Méliès and the Féerie." *Cinema Journal* 16, no. 1 (Fall 1976): 1–13.

Lacassin, Francis. "The Comic Strip and Film Language." Trans. and supp. notes by David Kunzle. *Film Quarterly* 26, no. 1 (Fall 1972): 11–23.

Lanzoni, Rémi Fournier. *French Cinema: From Its Beginning to the Present*. New York: Continuum, 2002.

Lederman, Susan J., and Bill Nichols. "Flicker and Motion in Film." In Nichols, ed., *Ideology and the Image*, pp. 293–301.

Leyda, Jay, et al. *Before Hollywood: Turn-of-the-Century American Film*. New York: Hudson Hills Press/American Federation of Arts, 1987.

Lindstrom, J. A. " 'Almost Worse than the Restrictive Measures': Chicago Reformers and the Nickelodeons." *Cinema Journal* 39, no. 1 (1999): 90–112.

Low, Rachael, with Roger Manvell. *The History of the British Film, 1896–1906*. London: Allen & Unwin, 1948. Repr. with a new introduction by Jeffrey Richards. London: Routledge, 1997.

Lumière, Auguste, and Louis Lumière. *Letters*. Ed. and annot. Jacques Rittaud-Hutinet with Yvelise Dentzer. Trans. Pierre Hodgson. London: Faber & Faber, 1995.

McCay, Winsor. *Little Nemo*. New York: Nostalgia, 1972.

MacDonnell, Kevin. *Eadweard Muybridge*. Boston: Little, Brown, 1972.

Macgowan, Kenneth. *Behind the Screen*. New York: Delacorte, 1965.

McInroy, Patrick. "The American Méliès." *Sight and Sound* 48, no. 4 (Autumn 1979): 250–54.

Mannoni, Laurent. *Étienne-Jules Marey, la mémoire de l'oeil*. Milan: Mazzotta; Paris: Cinémathèque française, 1999.

———. *The Great Art of Light and Shadow: Archaeology of the Cinema*. Trans. and ed. Richard Crangle. Exeter: University of Exeter Press, 2001.

Mannoni, Laurent; Donata Pesenti Campagnoni; and David Robinson. *Incunabula of the Motion Picture, 1420–1896*. London: British Film Institute, 1996.

Marey, E. J. *E. J. Marey, 1830–1904: La Photographie du mouvement*. Paris: Musée National d'Art Moderne, 1977.

May, Larry. *Screening Out the Past: The Birth of Mass Culture and the Motion Picture Industry*. New York: Oxford University Press, 1980.

Méliès, Georges. *Mes Mémoires*. Originally published in the Italian journal *Cinema* (Rome, 1938). Repr. in Bessy, Maurice, and G. M. Lo Duca. *Georges Méliès, mage*. 2nd ed. Paris: Pauvert, 1961.

Merritt, Russell. "Nickelodeon Theaters: Building an Audience for the Movies." *Wide Angle* 1, no. 1 (1979): 4–9. Repr. in Balio, ed., *The American Film Industry*, pp. 59–70.

Millard, Andre. *Edison and the Business of Innovation*. Baltimore: Johns Hopkins University Press, 1990.

Motion Picture Catalogues by American Producers and Distributors, 1894–1908. Thomas A. Edison Papers Series. Frederick, Md.: University Publications of America, 1987. Six microfilm reels and guide.

"Movies before Cinema Part I." Special issue of *Wide Angle* 18, no. 2 (April 1996).

"Movies before Cinema Part II." Special issue of *Wide Angle* 18, no. 3 (July 1996).

Mullins, Patrick. "Ethnic Cinema in the Nickelodeon Era in New York City: Commerce, Assimilation, and Cultural Identity." *Film History* 12, no. 1 (2000): 115–29.

Münsterberg, Hugo. *The Photoplay: A Psychological Study*. New York: Appleton, 1916. Repr. as *The Film: A Psychological Study*. New York: Dover, 1970.

Murphy, Robert, ed. *The British Cinema Book*. 2nd ed. London: British Film Institute, 2001.

Musser, Charles. "The Early Cinema of Edwin Porter." *Cinema Journal* 19, no. 1 (Fall 1979): 1–38.

———. "Another Look at the Chaser Theory." *Studies in Visual Communication* 10 no. 4 (Fall 1984): 24–44.

———. "Musser's Reply to Allen." *Studies in Visual Communication* 10, no. 4 (Fall 1984): 51–52.

———. "The Nickelodeon Era Begins: Establishing the Framework for Hollywood's Mode of Representation." *Framework* 22/23 (Autumn 1984): 4–11.

———. "Toward a History of Screen Practice." *Quarterly Review of Film Studies* 9, no. 1 (Winter 1984): 60–69.

———. "The Cinema of Edwin S. Porter." Ph.D. diss., New York University, 1985.

———. *The Emergence of Cinema: The American Screen to 1907. History of the American Cinema*. Vol 1. New York: Scribner's, 1990.

———. *Before the Nickelodeon: Edwin S. Porter and the Edison Manufacturing Company*. Berkeley: University of California Press, 1991.

———. "Rethinking Early Cinema: Cinema of Attractions and Narrativity." *Yale Journal of Criticism* 7, no. 2 (Fall 1994): 203–32.

———. *Thomas A. Edison and His Kinetographic Motion Pictures*. New Brunswick, N.J.: Friends of Edison National Historic Site/Rutgers University Press, 1995.

———. "Nationalism and the Beginnings of Cinema: The Lumière Cinématographe in the US, 1896–1897." *Historical Journal of Film, Radio and Television* 19, no. 2 (June 1999): 149–76.

Muybridge, Eadweard. *Muybridge's Complete Human and Animal Locomotion: All 781 Plates from the 1887 "Animal Locomotion."* 3 vols. New York: Dover, 1979.

Nichols, Bill, ed. *Ideology and the Image*. Bloomington: Indiana University Press, 1981.

Nowell-Smith, Geoffrey, ed. *The Oxford History of World Cinema*. Oxford: Oxford University Press, 1996.

Olsson, Jan. "Hollywood's First Spectators: Notes on Ethnic Nickelodeon Audiences in Los Angeles." *Aztlán* 26, no. 1 (Spring 2001): 181–95.

Pearson, Roberta. "The Filmmaker as a Scholar and Entertainer: An Interview with Charles Musser." *Cineaste* 13, no. 3 (1984): 22–24.

———. "Early Cinema." In Nowell-Smith, ed., *The Oxford History of World Cinema*, pp. 13–23.

Petro, Patrice, ed. *Fugitive Images: From Photography to Video*. Bloomington: Indiana University Press, 1995.

Phillips, Ray. *Edison's Kinetoscope and Its Films: A History to 1896*. Westport, Conn.: Greenwood, 1997.

Prodger, Phillip. *Time Stands Still: Muybridge and the Instantaneous Photography Movement*. New York: Iris & B. Gerald Cantor Center for Visual Arts at Stanford University/Oxford University Press, 2002. With an essay by Tom Gunning.

Ramsaye, Terry. *A Million and One Nights: A History of the Motion Picture*. New York: Simon & Schuster, 1926; 1964.

Rawlence, Christopher. *The Missing Reel: The Untold Story of the Lost Inventor of Moving Pictures*. New York: Atheneum, 1990.

Robinson, David. *Music of Shadows: The Use of Musical Accompaniment with Silent Pictures, 1896–1936*. Pordenone, Italy: Le Giornate del cinema muto, 1990. Exhibition catalog.

———. *Georges Méliès: Father of Film Fantasy*. London: Museum of the Moving Image, 1993.

———. *From Peep Show to Palace: The Birth of the American Film*. New York: Columbia University Press/Library of Congress, Washington, D.C., 1996.

Rock, Irving. *An Introduction to Perception*. New York: Macmillan, 1975.

Rossell, Deac. *Living Pictures: The Origins of the Movies*. Albany: State University of New York Press, 1998.

Ryall, Tom. *Britain and the American Cinema*. London: Sage, 2001.

Sadoul, Georges. *Histoire du cinéma mondial des origines à nos jours*. 8th ed. Paris: Flammarion, 1949.

———. *Louis Lumière*. Paris: Seghers, 1964.

Salt, Barry. "Film Form, 1900–1906." *Sight and Sound* 47, no. 3 (Summer 1978): 148–53.

———. "The Early Development of Film Form." In Fell, ed., *Film before Griffith*, pp. 284–98.

———. *Film Style and Technology: History and Analysis*. 2nd ed. London: Starword, 1992.

Sander, David. "Shooting for the Moon: Méliès, Verne, Welles, and the Imperial Satire." *Extrapolation* 39, no. 1 (Spring 1998): 5–25.

Sanderson, Richard A. *A Historical Study of the Development of American Motion Picture Content and Techniques Prior to 1904*. New York: Arno, 1977.

Singer, Ben. "Manhattan Nickelodeons: New Data on Audiences and Exhibitors." *Cinema Journal* 35, no. 3 (1995): 5–35.

Sklar, Robert, and Charles Musser. *Resisting Images: Essays on Cinema and History*. Philadelphia: Temple University Press, 1990.

Slide, Anthony. *Early American Cinema*. New rev. ed. Metuchen, N.J.: Scarecrow, 1995.

Sopocy, Martin. "A Narrated Cinema: The Pioneer Story Films of James A. Williamson." *Cinema Journal* 28, no. 1 (Fall 1978): 1–20.

———. "French and British Influences on Porter's *American Fireman*." *Film History* 1, no. 2 (1987): 137–48.

———. *James Williamson: Studies and Documents of a Pioneer of the Film Narrative*. London: Associated University Press, 1998.

Spehr, Paul C. *The Movies Begin: Making Movies in New Jersey, 1887–1920*. Newark, N.J.: Newark Museum, 1977.

Spiegel, Alan J. *Fiction and the Camera Eye*. Charlottesville: University of Virginia Press, 1976.

Star Film Catalogue. New York and Paris, 1903. 80pp.

Sutherland, Allan T. "The Yorkshire Pioneers." In Fell, ed., *Film before Griffith*, pp. 92–98.

Toulet, Emmanuelle. *Cinematographe, invention du siècle*. Paris: Découvertes Gallimard, 1988.

Toulmin, Vanessa. "Telling the Tale: The Story of the Fairground Bioscope Shows and the Showmen Who Operated Them." *Film History* 6, no. 2 (Summer 1994): 219–37.

Uricchio, William, and Roberta E. Pearson. "Constructing the Audience: Competing Discourses of Morality and Rationalization during the Nickelodeon Period." *Iris* 17 (1994): 43–54.

Vardac, Nicholas. *Stage to Screen*. Cambridge, Mass.: Harvard University Press, 1949.

Vaughan, Dai. "Let There Be Lumière." *Sight and Sound* 50, no. 2 (Spring 1981): 126–27.

Waller, Gregory A., ed. *Moviegoing in America: A Sourcebook in the History of Film Exhibition*. Malden, Mass.: Blackwell, 2002.

Weiss, Ken. *To the Rescue: How Immigrants Saved the American Film Industry 1896–1912*. San Francisco: Austin & Winfield, 1997.

Wenden, D. J. *The Birth of the Movies*. New York: Dutton, 1974.

Whissel, Kristen. "Uncle Tom, Goldilocks, and Rough Riders:

Early Cinema's Encounter with Empire." *Screen* 40, no. 4 (Winter 1999): 384–404.

Williams, Alan. "The Lumière Organization and Documentary Realism." In Fell, ed., *Film before Griffith*, pp. 153–61.

Media

Burch, Noël. *Correction Please, or How We Got into Pictures*. Great Britain, Arts Council of Great Britain, 1979. 52 min./col./16mm.

———. *What Do Those Old Films Mean?* UK/France, Channel Four/FR3/PI Productions, 1985. 6 × 30 min.

Herbst, Helmut. *Der Film Pionier Guido Seeber*. West Germany, Stiftung Deutsche Kinemathek Berlin, 1971. 59 min./col./16mm.

Musser, Charles. *Before the Nickelodeon: The Early Cinema of Edwin S. Porter*. USA, A Film for Thought Production, 1982.

Nekes, Werner. *Film before Film*. West Germany, Werner Nekes Film, 1985/86. 83 min./col./16mm.

Schmitt, Franz, supervisor. *La Voie Lumière (The Lumière Approach)*. France, French State Film Archive in Bois d'Arcy, 1983.

———, supervisor. *Méliès et ses contemporains*. France, French State Film Archive in Bois d'Arcy, 1983.

CHAPTER 2. INTERNATIONAL EXPANSION, 1907–1918

Abel, Richard. *The Ciné Goes to Town: French Cinema, 1896–1914*. Berkeley: University of California Press, 1994.

———, ed. *Silent Film*. New Brunswick, N.J.: Rutgers University Press, 1996.

Acker, Ally. *Reel Women: Pioneers of the Cinema, 1896 to the Present*. New York: Continuum, 1991.

Altomara, Rita Ecke. *Hollywood on the Palisades: A Filmography of Silent Features Made in Fort Lee, New Jersey, 1903–1927*. New York: Garland, 1983.

Bachman, Gregg, and Thomas J. Slater, eds. *American Silent Film: Discovering Marginalized Voices*. Carbondale: Southern Illinois University Press, 2002.

Balio, Tino, ed. *The American Film Industry*. Rev. ed. Madison: University of Wisconsin Press, 1985.

Balshoffer, Fred J., and Arthur C. Miller. *One Reel a Week*. Berkeley: University of California Press, 1967.

Barbas, Samantha. *Movie Crazy: Fans, Stars, and the Cult of Celebrity*. New York: Palgrave, 2001.

Bean, Jennifer M. "Technologies of Early Stardom and the Extraordinary Body." *Camera Obscura* 16, no. 3 (2001): 9–57.

Bean, Jennifer M., and Diane Negra, eds. *A Feminist Reader in Early Cinema*. Durham, N.C.: Duke University Press, 2002.

Benjamin, Walter. *Illuminations*. Ed. Hannah Arendt. Trans. Harry Zohn. New York: Harcourt Brace & World, 1968.

———. "The Work of Art in the Age of Mechanical Reproduction." In Benjamin, *Illuminations*, pp. 219–53. in Repr. Mast, Cohen, and Braudy, *Film Theory and Criticism*, pp. 665–81.

Bernhardt, Sarah, with Victoria Tietze Larson. *My Double Life: The Memoirs of Sarah Bernhardt*. Albany: State University of New York Press, 1999.

Bertetto, Paolo, and Gianni Rondolino, eds. *"Cabiria" e il suo tempo*. Milan: Editrice Il Castoro; Turin: Museo Nazionale del Cinema, 1998.

Blaché, Alice Guy. *The Memoirs of Alice Guy Blaché*. Trans. Roberta and Simone Blaché. Ed. Anthony Slide. Metuchen, N.J.: Scarecrow, 1986.

Bordwell, David. "La Nouvelle Mission de Feuillade; or, What Was Mise en Scène?" *Velvet Light Trap* 37 (Spring 1996): 10–29.

Bowser, Eileen. *The Transformation of the Cinema: 1907–1915*. Vol. 2 of *History of the American Cinema*. New York: Scribner's, 1990.

Brewster, Ben, and Lea Jacobs. *Theatre to Cinema: Stage Pictorialism and the Early Feature Film*. Oxford: Oxford University Press, 1997.

Brown, Kelly R. *Florence Lawrence, The Biograph Girl: America's First Movie Star*. Jefferson, N.C.: McFarland, 1999.

Burrows, Jon. *Legitimate Cinema: Theatre Stars in Silent British Film, 1908–1918*. Exeter: University of Exeter Press, 2003.

Callahan, Vicki. "The Innovators 1910–1920: Louis Feuillade—Detailing the Impossible." *Sight and Sound* 9, no. 4 (April 1999): 28–32.

Campani, Ermelinda M. "*Cabiria*, the *Novel of Fire*, and the Making of Cinema/History." *Stanford Humanities Review* 7, no. 2 (Winter 1999): 166–79.

Cherchi Usai, Paolo. "Italy: Spectacle and Melodrama." In Nowell-Smith ed., *The Oxford History of World Cinema*, pp. 123–30.

Chiti, Roberto. *Dizionario de registi del cinema muto italiano*. Rome: Museo Internazionale del Cinema e dello Spettacolo, 1997.

"Cinema in 1913." Special issue of *Griffithiana* 50 (May 1994).

Crafton, Donald. *Before Mickey: The Animated Film, 1898–1928*. Cambridge, Mass.: MIT Press, 1982.

———. *Emile Cohl, Caricature, and Film*. Princeton, N.J.: Princeton University Press, 1990.

———. "Tricks and Animation." In Nowell-Smith, ed., *The Oxford History of World Cinema*, pp. 71–78.

Dalle Vacche, Angela. "Goddesses of Modernity: Part Goddesses and Part Emancipated New Women, the Female Movie Stars of Italy's Silent Era Were Fascinating, Enigmatic Icons." *Film Comment* 36, no. 5 (September–October 2000): 44–48.

deCordova, Richard. *Picture Personalities: The Emergence of the Star System in America*. Urbana: University of Illinois Press, 1990, 2001.

"Early Italian Cinema." Special issue of *Film History* 12, no. 3 (2000).

Eckhardt, Joseph P. *The King of the Movies: Film Pioneer Siegmund Lubin*. Cranbury, N.J.: Fairleigh Dickinson University Press, 1998.

"1895–1910: Les Pionniers du cinéma Français." Special issue of *L'Avant scène cinéma* 3, no. 334 (November 1984).

Everson, William K. *American Silent Film*. New York: Oxford University Press, 1978.

"Exhibition." Special issue of *Film History* 6, no. 2 (1994).

Fell, John L. *Film and the Narrative Tradition*. Norman: University of Oklahoma Press, 1974.

"Female Stardom and Early Film History." Special issue of *Camera Obscura* 16, no. 3 (2001).

"Feuillade and the French Serial." Special issue of *Velvet Light Trap* 37 (Spring 1996).

French, Philip. *The Movie Moguls*. London: Weidenfeld & Nicholson, 1969.

Fuller, Kathryn Helgesen. "You Can Have the Strand in Your Own Town: The Marginalization of Smalltown Film Exhibition in the Silent Era." *Film History* 6, no. 2 (Summer 1994): 166–77.

Garçon, François. *Gaumont: A Century of French Cinema*. Trans. Bruce Alderman and Jonathan Dickinson. New York: Abrams, 1994.

Gifford, Denis. *American Animated Films: The Silent Era, 1897–1929*. Jefferson, N.C.: McFarland, 1990.

Gillet, John. "Scandinavian Panorama." *Sight and Sound* 56, no. 1 (Winter 1986/87): 50–51.

Gomery, Douglas. "The Picture Palace: Economic Sense or Nonsense?" *Quarterly Review of Film Studies* 3, no. 1 (Winter 1978): 23–26.

———. "The Movies Become Big Business: Public Theaters and the Chain-Store Strategy." *Cinema Journal* 28, no. 2 (Spring 1979): 26–40. Repr. in Kindem, ed., *The American Movie Industry*, pp. 104–16.

———. "U.S. Film Exhibition: The Formation of a Big Business." In Balio, ed., *The American Film Industry*, pp. 218–28.

Grieveson, Lee. " 'A Kind of Recreative School for the Whole Family': Making Cinema Respectable, 1907–1909." *Screen* 42, no. 1 (Spring 2001): 64–76.

Hark, Ina Rae, ed. *Exhibition: The Film Reader*. London: Routledge, 2002.

Hayward, Susan. "A History of French Cinema: 1895–1991: Pioneering Film-Makers (Guy, Dulac, Varda) and Their Heritage." *Paragraph* 15, no. 1 (March 1992): 19–37.

Holmes, Sean P. "The Hollywood Star System and the Regulation of Actor's Labour, 1916–1934." *Film History* 12, no. 1 (2000): 97–114.

Horne, Jennifer. "Nostalgia and Non-Fiction in Edison's 1917 Conquest Program." *Historical Journal of Film, Radio and Television* 22, no. 3 (2002): 316–31.

Hurt, James. *Focus on Film and Theatre*. Englewood Cliffs, N.J.: Prentice-Hall, 1974.

"International Cinema of the 1910s." Special issue of *Film History* 9, no. 4 (1997).

Jacobs, Lewis. *The Rise of the American Film*. New York: Harcourt, Brace, 1939. Repr. New York: Teachers College Press, 1968.

Jarratt, Vernon. *The Italian Cinema*. London: Falcon, 1951.

Keil, Charlie. "Advertising Independence: Industrial Performance and Advertising Strategies of the Independent Movement, 1909–1910." *Film History* 5, no. 4 (1993): 472–88.

———. *Early American Cinema in Transition: Story, Style, and Filmmaking 1907–1913*. Madison: University of Wisconsin Press, 2001.

Kindem, Gorham, ed. *The American Movie Industry: The Business of Motion Pictures*. Carbondale: Southern Illinois University Press, 1982.

Knight, Arthur. *The Liveliest Art*. Rev. ed. New York: Mentor, 1978.

Lacassin, Francis. *Louis Feuillade*. Paris: Seghers, 1964.

Lindsay, Vachel. *The Art of the Moving Picture*. New York: Macmillan, 1915. Repr. New York: Liveright, 1970.

Macgowan, Kenneth. *The Living Stage*. Englewood Cliffs, N.J.: Prentice-Hall, 1955.

———. *Behind the Screen: The History and Techniques of the Motion Picture*. New York: Dell, 1965.

McMahan, Alison. *Alice Guy Blaché: Lost Visionary of the Cinema*. New York: Continuum, 2002.

Magliozzi, Ronald S., ed. *Treasures from the Film Archives: A Catalogue of Short Silent Films Held by FIAF Archives*. Metuchen, N.J.: Scarecrow, 1988.

Mast, Gerald; Marshall Cohen; and Leo Braudy. *Film Theory and Criticism*. 5th ed. New York: Oxford University Press, 1999.

Münsterberg, Hugo. *The Photoplay: A Psychological Study*. New York: Appleton, 1916. Repr. as *The Film: A Psychological Study*. New York: Dover, 1970.

Musser, Charles, with Carol Nelson. *High-Class Moving Pictures: Lyman H. Howe and the Forgotten Era of Traveling Exhibition, 1880–1920*. Princeton, N.J.: Princeton University Press, 1991.

Naylor, David. *Great American Movie Theatres: A National Trust Guide*. Washington, D.C.: Preservation, 1987.

Neergaard, Ebbe. *The Story of Danish Film*. Trans. Elsa Guess. Copenhagen: Danish Institute, 1962.

Nowell-Smith, Geoffrey, ed. *The Oxford History of World Cinema*. Oxford: Oxford University Press, 1996.

Pathé, Charles. *De Pathé frères à Pathé cinéma*. Lyon: Société d'études, recherches et documentation cinématographiques, 1970.

Pearson, Roberta. "Transitional Cinema." In Nowell-Smith, ed., *The Oxford History of World Cinema*, pp. 23–43.

Potamianos, George. "Movies at the Margins: The Distribution of Films to Theaters in Small Town America, 1895–1919." In Bachman and Slater, eds., *American Silent Film*, pp. 9–26.

Pratt, George. *Spellbound in Darkness: A History of the Silent Film*. Rev. ed. Greenwich, Conn.: New York Graphic Society, 1973.

Pryluck, Calvin. "The Itinerant Movie Show and the Development of the Film Industry." *Journal of the University Film and Video Association* 36, no. 4 (Fall 1983): 11–22.

Puttnam, David, with Neil Watson. *Movies and Money*. New York: Knopf, 1998. Published in the United Kingdom as *The Undeclared War: The Struggle for Control of the World's Film Industry*. London: HarperCollins, 1997.

Quinn, Michael. "Paramount and Early Feature Distribution: 1914–1921." *Film History* 11, no. 1 (1999): 98–113.

———. "Distribution, the Transient Audience, and the Transition to the Feature Film." *Cinema Journal* 40, no. 2 (2001): 35–56.

Robinson, David. *The History of World Cinema*. New York: Stein & Day, 1973; 2nd ed., 1981.

———. "The Italian Comedy." *Sight and Sound* 55, no. 2 (Spring 1986): 105–12.

———. "Rise and Fall of the Clowns: The Golden Age of French Comedy, 1907–1914." *Sight and Sound* 56, no. 3 (Summer 1987): 198–203.

Rondi, Gian Luigi. *Italian Cinema Today*. London: Denis Dobson, 1966.

Rosenbloom, Nancy J. "Between Reform and Regulation: The Struggle over Film Censorship in Progressive America, 1909–1922." *Film History* 1, no. 4 (1987): 307–25.

Sadoul, Georges. *The French Film*. London: Falcon, 1953.

Shull, Michael Slade. *Radicalism in American Silent Films, 1909–1929: A Filmography and History*. Jefferson, N.C.: McFarland, 2000.

Sinclair, Upton. *Upton Sinclair Presents William Fox*. Los Angeles: Upton Sinclair, 1933.

Singer, Ben. *Melodrama and Modernity: Early Sensational Cinema and Its Contexts*. New York: Columbia University Press, 2001.

Slide, Anthony. *Early American Cinema*. Cranbury, N.J.: Barnes, 1969.

———. *Aspects of American Film History Prior to 1920*. Metuchen, N.J.: Scarecrow, 1978.

———. *Early Women Directors*. New York: Da Capo, 1984.

Sorlin, Pierre. *Italian National Cinema 1896–1996*. London: Routledge, 1996.

Spadoni, Robert. "The Figure Seen from the Rear, Vitagraph, and the Development of Shot/Reverse Shot." *Film History* 11, no. 3 (1999): 319–41.

Spehr, Paul C. *The Movies Begin: Making Movies in New Jersey, 1887–1920*. Newark, N.J.: Newark Museum, 1977.

Staiger, Janet. *Bad Women: Regulating Sexuality in Early Cinema*. Minneapolis: University of Minnesota Press, 1995.

Stamp, Shelley. *Movie-Struck Girls: Women and Motion Picture Culture after the Nickelodeon*. Princeton, N.J.: Princeton University Press, 2000.

Stokes, Melvyn, and Richard Maltby, eds. *American Movie Audiences: From the Turn of the Century to the Early Sound Era*. London: British Film Institute, 1999.

Tariol, Marcel, ed. *Louis Delluc*. Paris: Seghers, 1965.

Thompson, Kristin. *Exporting Entertainment: America and the World Film Market, 1907–1934*. London: British Film Institute, 1985.

United States of America v. Motion Picture Patents Company and Others (1914). Repr. in *Film History* 1, no. 3 (1987).

Uricchio, William, and Roberta E. Pearson. *Reframing Culture: The Case of the Vitagraph Quality Films*. Princeton, N.J.: Princeton University Press, 1993.

Valentine, Maggie. *The Show Starts on the Sidewalk: An Architectural History of the Movie Theatre, Starring S. Charles Lee*. New Haven, Conn.: Yale University Press, 1994.

Vasey, Ruth. "The World-Wide Spread of Cinema." In Nowell-Smith, ed., *The Oxford History of World Cinema*, pp. 53–62.

Vincendeau, Ginette. *Stars and Stardom in French Cinema*. London: British Film Institute, 1996.

Walker, Alexander. *Stardom: The Hollywood Phenomenon*. New York: Stein & Day, 1970.

Williams, Alan. *Republic of Images: A History of French Filmmaking*. Cambridge, Mass.: Harvard University Press, 1992.

Woal, Linda. "When a Dime Could Buy a Dream: Siegmund Lubin and the Birth of Motion Picture Exhibition." *Film History* 6, no. 2 (Summer 1994): 152–65.

Zierold, Norman. *The Moguls*. New York: Coward-McCann, 1969.

Media

Phillipe, Pierre. *Mille et une Marguerites (A Thousand and One Daisies)*. 1988.

CHAPTER 3. D. W. GRIFFITH AND THE DEVELOPMENT OF NARRATIVE FORM

Abel, Richard, and Rick Altman, eds. *The Sounds of Early Cinema*. Bloomington: Indiana University Press, 2001.

Aitken, Roy E. *"The Birth of a Nation."* Middleburg, Va.: Delinger, 1965.

Allen, Michael. *Family Secrets: The Feature Films of D. W. Griffith*. London: British Film Institute, 1999.

Altman, Rich. *"The Lonely Villa* and Griffith's Paradigmatic Style." *Quarterly Review of Film Studies* 6, no. 2 (Spring 1981): 123–34.

Andrew, Dudley. *"Broken Blossoms:* The Art and Eros of a Perverse Text." *Quarterly Review of Film Studies* 6, no. 1 (Winter 1981): 81–90.

Barnouw, Erik. "The Sintzenich Diaries." *Quarterly Journal of the Library of Congress* 37, nos. 3–4 (Summer–Fall 1980): 310–31.

Barry, Iris. *D. W. Griffith, American Film Master*. New York: Museum of Modern Art, 1940. Repr. ed. Eileen Bowser. New York: Garland, 1985.

Belton, John, ed. *Movies and Mass Culture*. New Brunswick, N.J.: Rutgers University Press, 1996.

Bernardi, Daniel, ed. *The Birth of Whiteness: Race and the Emergence of U.S. Cinema*. New Brunswick, N.J.: Rutgers University Press, 1996.

Bernstein, Matthew, ed. *Controlling Hollywood: Censorship and Regulation in the Studio Era*. New Brunswick, N.J.: Rutgers University Press, 1999.

Bitzer, G. W. *Billy Bitzer: His Story*. New York: Farrar, Straus & Giroux, 1973.

Bordwell, David, and Kristin Thompson. "Toward a Scientific Film History?" *Quarterly Review of Film Studies* 10, no. 3 (Summer 1985): 224–37.

———. *Film Art: An Introduction*. 6th ed. New York: McGraw-Hill, 2001.

Bordwell, David; Kristin Thompson; and Janet Staiger. *The Classical Hollywood Cinema: Film Style and Mode of Production to 1960*. New York: Columbia University Press, 1985.

Bowser, Eileen. "The Reconstitution of *A Corner in Wheat.*" *Cinema Journal* 15, no. 2 (Spring 1976): 42–55.

———. "Addendum to the Reconstitution of *A Corner in Wheat.*" *Cinema Journal* 19, no. 1 (Fall 1979): 101–102.

———. "Griffith's Film Career before *The Adventures of Dollie.*" *Quarterly Review of Film Studies* 6, no. 1 (Winter 1981): 1–9.

Brown, Karl. *Adventures with D. W. Griffith*. New York: Farrar, Straus & Giroux, 1973.

Browne, Nick, ed. *Refiguring American Film Genres: History and Theory*. Berkeley: University of California, 1998.

Bush, Gregory W. "Like 'a Drop of Water in the Stream of Life': Moving Images of Mass Man from Griffith to Vidor." *Journal of American Studies* 25, no. 2 (August 1991): 213–34.

Butters, Gerald R. *Black Manhood on the Silent Screen*. Lawrence: University Press of Kansas, 2002.

Cadbury, William. "Theme, Felt Life and the Last-Minute Rescue in Griffith after *Intolerance*." *Film Quarterly* 28, no. 1 (Fall 1974): 39–48.

Carnes, Mark C., ed. *Past Imperfect: History According to the Movies*. New York: Holt, 1996.

Carter, Everett. "Cultural History Written with Lightning: The Significance of *The Birth of a Nation*." In Silva, ed., *Focus on "The Birth of a Nation,"* pp. 133–43.

Chadwick, Bruce. *The Reel Civil War: Mythmaking in American Film*. New York: Knopf, 2001.

Charney, Mark. " 'Picturizing' History: The Assassination of Lincoln in D. W. Griffith's *The Birth of a Nation*." *South Carolina Review* 22, no. 2 (Spring 1990): 58–62.

Cherchi Usai, Paolo, ed. *The Griffith Project*, Vol. I: *Films Produced in 1907–1908*. London: British Film Institute, 1999.

———, ed. *The Griffith Project*. Vol. II: *Films Produced in January–June 1909*. London: British Film Institute, 1999.

———, ed. *The Griffith Project*. Vol. III: *Films Produced in July–December 1909*. London: British Film Institute, 2000.

———, ed. *The Griffith Project*. Vol. IV: *Griffith at the Biograph Company in 1910*. London: British Film Institute, 2000.

———, ed. *The Griffith Project*. Vol. V: *Films Produced in 1911*. London: British Film Institute, 2002.

———, ed. *The Griffith Project*. Vol. VI: *Films Produced in 1912*. London: British Film Institute, 2003.

Cook, Pam, ed. *The Cinema Book*. London: British Film Institute, 1985.

Corkin, Stanley. *Realism and the Birth of the Modern United States: Cinema, Literature, and Culture*. Athens: University of Georgia Press, 1996.

Corrigan, Timothy. *Film and Literature: An Introduction and Reader*. Upper Saddle River, N.J.: Prentice-Hall, 1999.

Cripps, Thomas. *Slow Fade to Black: The Negro in American Film, 1900–1942*. New York: Oxford University Press, 1977.

D. W. Griffith Papers 1897–1954. Frederick, Md.: University Publications of America, 1982. Microfilm.

de Grazia, Edward, and Roger K. Newman, eds. *Banned Films: Movies, Censors and the First Amendment*. New York: Bowker, 1982.

Deutelbaum, A. Marshall. "Reassessing *The Birth of a Nation*." Unpub. paper presented at *"The Birth of a Nation" and 1915*. Society for Cinema Studies, 1976.

Dixon, Thomas E., Jr. *Southern Horizons: The Autobiography of Thomas Dixon*. Alexandria, Va.: IWV, 1984.

Dorr, John. "The Griffith Tradition." *Film Comment* 10, no. 2 (March–April 1974): 48–54.

Drew, William M. *D. W. Griffith's "Intolerance": Its Genesis and Its Vision*. Jefferson, N.C.: McFarland, 1968.

Dyer, Richard. "Into the Light: The Whiteness of the South in *The Birth of a Nation*." In *Dixie Debates:* King and Taylor, eds., *Perspectives on Southern Culture*, pp. 165–76.

Eisenstein, Sergei. *The Film Form*. Trans. and ed. Jay Leyda. Repr. New York: Harcourt Brace Jovanovich, 1969.

Färber, Helmut. "Shot-by-Shot Analysis of D. W. Griffith's *A Corner in Wheat*." Special issue of *Griffithiana* 20, no. 59 (May 1997).

Fell, John L. *A History of Films*. New York: Holt, Rinehart, & Winston, 1979.

———, ed. *Film before Griffith*. Berkeley: University of California Press, 1983.

Fleener, Nickie. "Answering Film with Film: The Hampton Epilogue, a Positive Alternative to the Negative Black Stereotypes Presented in *The Birth of a Nation*." *Journal of Popular Film and Television* 7, no. 4 (Summer 1980): 400–25.

Flitterman-Lewis, Sandy. "The Blossom and the Bole: Narrative and Visual Spectacle in Early Film Melodrama." *Cinema Journal* 33, no. 3 (1994): 3–15.

Foner, Eric. *Reconstruction: America's Unfinished Revolution, 1863–1877*. New York: Harper & Row, 1988.

Gaines, Jane M. "Birthing Nations." In Hjort and MacKenzie, eds., *Cinema and Nation*, pp. 298–316.

———. *Fire and Desire: Mixed-Race Movies in the Silent Era*. Chicago: University of Chicago Press, 2001.

Gaines, Jane M., and Neil Lerner. "The Orchestration of Affect: The Motif of Barbarism in Breil's *The Birth of a Nation* Score." In Abel and Altman, eds., *The Sounds of Early Cinema*, pp. 252–68.

Gartenberg, Jon. "Camera Movement in Edison and Biograph Films 1900–1906." *Cinema Journal* 19, no. 2 (Spring 1980): 1–16.

Geduld, Harry M., ed. *Focus on D. W. Griffith*. Englewood Cliffs, N.J.: Prentice-Hall, 1971.

Gerster, Carole J. "Narrative Form Transformed from *The Clansman* to *The Birth of a Nation*." *West Virginia University Philological Papers* 45 (1999): 10–19.

Graham, Cooper C.; Steven Higgins; Elaine Mancini; and João Luiz Viera. *D. W. Griffith and Biograph Company*. Metuchen, N.J.: Scarecrow, 1985.

Green, Ronald J. "Micheaux v. Griffith." Trans. Andrea Filippi. *Griffithiana* 20, nos. 60–61 (October 1997): 32–49.

Griffith, D. W. *The Man Who Invented Hollywood: The Auto-*

biography of D. W. Griffith. Ed. James Hart. Louisville, Ky.: Touchstone, 1972.

Griffith, Linda Arvidson. *When Movies Were Young.* Repr. New York: Dover, 1969.

Gunning, Tom. "Weaving a Narrative: Style and Economic Background in Griffith's Biograph Films." *Quarterly Review of Film Studies* 6, no. 1 (Winter 1981): 11–12.

———. "Rebirth of a Movie." *American Film* 10, no. 1 (October 1984): 18–19, 93.

———. "D. W. Griffith and the *Narrator-System:* Narrative Structure and Industry Organization in Biograph Films, 1908–1909." Ph.D. diss., New York University, 1986.

———. *D. W. Griffith and the Origins of the American Narrative Film: The Early Years at Biograph.* Urbana: University of Illinois Press, 1991.

Hansen, Miriam. "Universal Language and Democratic Culture: Myths of Origin in Early American Cinema." In Meindl, Horlacher, and Christadler, eds., *Myth and Enlightenment in American Literature*, pp. 321–51.

———. "Rätsel der Mütterlichkeit: Studie zum Wiegenmotiv in D. W. Griffith's *Intolerance.*" Trans. Nele Löw-Beer. *Frauen und Film* 41 (December 1986): 32–48.

———. *Babel and Babylon: Spectatorship in American Silent Cinema.* Cambridge, Mass.: Harvard University Press, 1988.

———. "The Hieroglyph and the Whore: D. W. Griffith's *Intolerance.*" *South Atlantic Quarterly* 88, no. 2 (Spring 1989): 361–92.

———. "Griffith's Real *Intolerance.*" *Film Comment* 25, no. 5 (September–October 1989): 28–29.

Hansen, Miriam, and Martin Christadler. "David Wark Griffiths *Intolerance* (1916): Zum Verhältnis von Film un Geschichte in der Progressive Era." *Amerikastudien/American Studies* 21, no. 1 (1976): 7–37.

Hanson, Bernard. "D. W. Griffith: Some Sources." *Art Bulletin* 54 (December 1972): 493–515.

Henderson, Robert M. *D. W. Griffith: The Years at Biograph.* New York: Noonday, 1970.

———. *D. W. Griffith: His Life and Work.* New York: Oxford University Press, 1972.

Hjort, Mette, and Scott MacKenzie, eds. *Cinema and Nation.* London: Routledge, 2000.

Hood, James. W. "Tennyson, D. W. Griffith, and Victorian Pneumatography." *VIJ: Victorians Institute Journal* 25 (1997): 59–76.

Huff, Theodore. *A Shot Analysis of D. W. Griffith's "The Birth of a Nation."* New York: Museum of Modern Art Film Library, 1961.

———. *"Intolerance"—The Film by David Wark Griffith: Shot-by-Shot Analysis.* New York: Museum of Modern Art, 1966.

Jacobs, Lewis. *The Rise of the American Film.* New York: Harcourt Brace, 1939. Repr. New York: Teachers College Press, 1968.

Jampolski, Mikhail. *The Memory of Tiresias: Intertextuality and Film.* Trans. Harsha Ram. Berkeley: University of California Press, 1998.

Jay, Gregory S. " 'White Man's Book No Good': D. W. Griffith and the American Indian," *Cinema Journal* 39, no. 4 (2000): 3–26.

Jesionowski, Joyce E. *Thinking in Pictures: Dramatic Structure in D. W. Griffith's Biograph Films.* Berkeley: University of California Press, 1987.

Jewitt, Garth S. " 'A Capacity for Evil': The 1915 Supreme Court *Mutual* Decision." In Bernstein, ed., *Controlling Hollywood*, pp. 16–40.

Johnson, William. "Early Griffith: A Wider View." *Film Quarterly* 29, no. 3 (Spring 1976): 2–13.

Kaplan, Amy. "The Birth of an Empire." *PMLA: Publications of the Modern Language Association of America* 114, no. 5 (October 1995): 1068–76.

Kawin, Bruce F. *Mindscreen: Bergman, Godard, and First-Person Film.* Princeton, N.J.: Princeton University Press, 1978.

Keil, Charles. "Transition through Tension: Stylistic Diversity in the Late Griffith Biographs." *Cinema Journal* 28, no. 3 (Spring 1989): 22–40.

Keply, Vance, Jr. "Griffith's *Broken Blossoms* and the Problem of Historical Specificity." *Quarterly Review of Film Studies* 3, no. 1 (Winter 1978): 37–48.

King, Richard H., and Helen Taylor, eds. *Dixie Debates: Perspectives on Southern Culture.* New York: New York University Press, 1996.

Knight, Arthur. *The Liveliest Art.* Rev. ed. New York: Mentor, 1978.

Koshy, Susan. "American Nationhood as Eugenic Romance." *Differences: A Journal of Feminist Cultural Studies* 12, no. 1 (Spring 2001): 50–78.

Koszarski, Richard, ed. *The Rivals of D. W. Griffith: Alternate Auteurs 1913–1918.* Minneapolis: Walker Art Center, November–December 1976. Exhibition catalog.

Kuhn, Annette. "The History of Narrative Codes." In Cook, ed., *The Cinema Book*, pp. 208–11.

Lang, Robert, ed. *"The Birth of a Nation." D. W. Griffith, Director.* Rutgers Films in Print. New Brunswick, N.J.: Rutgers University Press, 1994.

Leab, Daniel J. *"The Birth of a Nation* as a Public Event." Unpub. paper presented at *"The Birth of a Nation" and 1915* (Society for Cinema Studies, 1976).

Lehman, Peter, ed. *Close Viewings: An Anthology of New Film Criticism.* Tallahassee: Florida State University Press, 1990.

Lennig, Arthur. "The Birth of *Way Down East.*" *Quarterly Review of Film Studies* 6, no. 1 (Winter 1981): 105–116.

Lindsay, Vachel. *The Art of the Moving Picture.* New York: Macmillan, 1915. Repr. New York: Liveright, 1970.

Litwack, Leon F. "The Birth of a Nation." In Carnes, ed., *Past Imperfect*, pp. 136–41.

Louvish, Simon. "Burning Crosses." *Sight and Sound* 10, no. 9 (September 2000): 12–13.

MacCann, Richard Dyer. *The Silent Screen.* Lanham, Md.: Scarecrow, 1997.

McHugh, Kathleen Anne. *American Domesticity: From How-to Manual to Hollywood Melodrama.* New York: Oxford University Press, 1999.

May, Lary. "Apocalyptic Cinema: D. W. Griffith and the Aesthetics of Reform." In Belton, ed., *Movies and Mass Culture*, pp. 25–58.

Meindle, Dieter; Friedrich W. Horlacher; with Martin Christadler. *Myth and Enlightenment in American Literature: In Honor of Hans-Joachim Lang.* Erlangen Forschungen, series A. vol. 38. Erlangen, W. Ger.: University of Erlangen–Nürnberg, 1985.

Merritt, Russell. "On First Looking into Griffith's Babylon: A Reading of a Publicity Still." *Wide Angle* 1, no. 2 (Spring 1979): 12–21.

———. "Rescued from a Perilous Nest: D. W. Griffith's Escape from Theatre into Film." *Cinema Journal* 21, no. 1 (Fall 1981): 2–30.

———. "D. W. Griffith Directs the Great War: The Making of *Hearts of the World.*" *Quarterly Review of Film Studies* 6, no. 1 (Winter 1981): 45–65.

———. "D. W. Griffith's *The Birth of a Nation:* Going after Little Sister." In Lehman, ed., *Close Viewings*, pp. 215–37.

Münsterberg, Hugo. *The Photoplay: A Psychological Study.* New York: Appleton, 1916. Repr. as *The Film: A Psychological Study.* New York: Dover, 1970.

Noble, Peter. "The Negro in *The Birth of a Nation.*" In Silva, ed., *Focus on "The Birth of a Nation,"* p. 131.

O'Dell, Paul. *Griffith and the Rise of Hollywood.* Cranbury, N.J.: Barnes, 1970.

Painter, Nell Irvin. *Standing at Armageddon: The United States, 1877–1919.* New York: Norton, 1987.

Pearson, Roberta. *Eloquent Gestures: The Transformation of Performance Style in the Griffith Biograph Films.* Berkeley: University of California Press, 1992.

Petric, Vlada. "Griffith's *The Avenging Conscience:* An Early Dream Film." *Film Criticism* 6, no. 2 (Winter 1982): 5–27.

Pitts, Michael. *Hollywood and American History.* Jefferson, N.C.: McFarland 1984.

Ray, Robert B. *A Certain Tendency of the Hollywood Cinema, 1930–1980.* Princeton, N.J.: Princeton University Press, 1985.

Reeves, Nicholas. *Official British Film Propaganda during the First World War.* London: Wolfeboro, 1986.

Robinson, Cedric J. "In the Year 1915: D. W. Griffith and the Whitening of America." *Social Identities* 3, no. 2. (June 1997): 161–92.

Sadoul, Georges. *Dictionary of Films.* Trans. and ed. Peter Morris. Berkeley: University of California Press, 1972.

Salt, Barry. *Film Style and Technology: History and Analysis.* 2nd ed. London: Starword, 1992.

———. "*Der Arzt des Schlosses.*" *Sight and Sound* 54, no. 4 (Autumn 1985): 284–85.

Sarris, Andrew. "About Faces." *American Film* 4, no. 8 (June 1979): 54–61.

Schickel, Richard. *D. W. Griffith: An American Life.* New York: Simon & Schuster, 1984.

Silva, Fred, ed. *Focus on "The Birth of a Nation."* Englewood Cliffs, N.J.: Prentice-Hall, 1971.

Simcovitch, Maxim. "The Impact of Griffith's *Birth of a Nation* on the Modern Ku Klux Klan." *Journal of Popular Film* 1, no. 1 (Winter 1972): 45–54.

Simmon, Scott. *The Films of D. W. Griffith.* Cambridge, Eng.: Cambridge University Press, 1993.

Slide, Anthony. *The Big V: A History of the Vitagraph Company.* Rev. ed. Metuchen, N.J.: Scarecrow, 1987.

Sloan, Kay. *The Loud Silents: Origins of the Social Problem Film.* Urbana: University of Illinois Press, 1988.

Spehr, Paul C. "Filmmaking at the American Mutoscope and Biograph Company 1900–1906." *Quarterly Journal of the Library of Congress* 37, nos. 3–4 (Summer–Fall 1980): 413–21.

Staiger, Janet. "The Politics of Film Canons." *Cinema Journal* 24, no. 3 (Spring 1985): 4–23.

———. *Interpreting Films: Studies in the Historical Reception of American Cinema.* Princeton, N.J.: Princeton University Press, 1992.

Taylor, Clyde. "The Re-Birth of the Aesthetic in Cinema." *Wide Angle* 13, nos. 3–4 (1991): 12–30.

Thomas, Emory M. *The American "War and Peace."* Englewood Cliffs, N.J.: Prentice-Hall, 1973.

Tsivian, Yuri. "Homeless Images: D. W. Griffith in the Eye of Soviet Filmmakers." Trans. Andrea Filippi. *Griffithiana* 20, nos. 60–61 (October 1997): 50–75.

Tucker, Jean E. "Voices from the Silents." *Quarterly Journal of the Library of Congress* 37, nos. 3–4 (Summer–Fall 1980): 387–412.

Vineburg, Steve. "The Restored *Way Down East.*" *Film Quarterly* 39, no. 3 (Spring 1986): 54–57.

Wagenknecht, Edward, and Anthony Slide. *The Films of D. W. Griffith.* New York: Crown, 1975.

Wasko, Janet. "D. W. Griffith and the Banks." *Journal of the University Film Association* 30, no. 1 (Winter 1978): 15–20.

———. *Movies and Money: Financing the American Film Industry*. Norwood, N.J.: Ablex, 1982.

Williams, Linda. "Melodrama Revised." In Browne, ed., *Refiguring American Film Genres*, pp. 42–88.

Williams, Martin. *Griffith: First Artist of the Movies*. New York: Oxford University Press, 1980.

Wilson, Woodrow. *A History of the American People*. 5 vols. New York: Harper, 1902.

Media

Brownlow, Kevin, and David Gill. *D. W. Griffith: Father of Film*. A Co-Production of Thames TV/Amercian Masters Series, 1993.

Burns, Ken. *The Civil War*. A Film by Ken Burns in Nine Parts. Florentine Films, WETA. Originally broadcast by PBS, Fall 1989.

CHAPTER 4. GERMAN CINEMA OF THE WEIMAR PERIOD, 1919–1929

Amengual, Barthélemy. *G. W. Pabst*. Paris: Seghers, 1966.

Andrew, James Dudley, with Sally Shafto, eds. *The Image in Dispute: Art and Cinema in the Age of Photography*. Austin: University of Texas Press, 1997.

Atwell, Lee. *G. W. Pabst*. Boston: Twayne, 1977.

Austin, Bruce A., ed. *Current Research in Film: Audiences, Economics, and Law*. Vol. 1. Norwood, N.J.: Ablex, 1985.

Bacher, Lutz. *The Mobile Mise-en-Scène*. New York: Arno, 1978.

Balàzs, Béla. *The Visible Man, or Film Culture*. Halle, Ger.: Deutsch-Österreichische Verlag, 1924.

Baxter, John. *The Hollywood Exiles*. New York: Taplinger, 1967.

Béranger, Jean. *La Grand aventure du cinéma suédois*. Paris: Losfeld, 1960.

Bergfelder, Tim; Deniz Göktürk; and Erica Carter, eds. *The German Cinema Book*. London: British Film Institute, 2003.

Bernstein, Matthew. "Visual Style and Spatial Articulations in *Berlin, Symphony of a City* (1927)." *Journal of Film and Video* 36, no. 4 (Fall 1984): 5–12.

Bessel, Richard. *Germany after the First World War*. Oxford: Clavendon, 1993.

Bogdanovich, Peter. *Fritz Lang in America*. New York: Praeger, 1967.

Bordwell, David. *Narration in the Fiction Film*. Madison: University of Wisconsin Press, 1985.

Branigan, Edward. *Point of View in the Cinema: A Theory of Narration and Subjectivity in Classical Film*. New York and Berlin: Mouton, 1984.

———. "Point of View in the Fiction Film." *Wide Angle* 8,

nos. 3–4 (1986): 4–7. Special issue on "Narrative/Non-Narrative."

Bronner, Stephen Eric, and Douglas Kellner, eds. *Passion and Rebellion: The Expressionist Heritage*. New York: Universe, 1983.

Brooks, Louise. *Lulu in Hollywood*. Exp. ed. Minneapolis: University of Minnesota Press, 2000.

Brownlow, Kevin. *The War, the West and the Wilderness*. New York: Knopf, 1979.

Bucher, Felix. *Germany: An Illustrated Guide*. Screen Series. London: Zwemmer, 1971.

Budd, Michael. "Retrospective Narration in Film: Rereading *The Cabinet of Dr. Caligari*." *Film Criticism* 4 (Fall 1979): 35–43.

———. "*The Cabinet of Dr. Caligari*: The Conditions of Reception." *Cine-Tracts* 3 (Winter 1981): 41–49.

———. "The National Board of Review and the Early Art Cinema in New York: *The Cabinet of Dr. Caligari* as Affirmative Culture." *Cinema Journal* 26, no. 1 (Fall 1986): 3–18.

———. "*The Cabinet of Dr. Caligari*: Production, Reception, History." In Lehman, ed., *Close Viewings*, pp. 333–52.

———. ed. "*The Cabinet of Dr. Caligari*": *Texts, Contexts, Histories*. New Brunswick, N.J.: Rutgers University Press, 1990.

Calhoon, Kenneth Scott, ed. *Peripheral Visions: The Hidden Stages of Weimar Cinema*. Detroit: Wayne State University Press, 2001.

Cherchi Usai, Paolo. "The Scandinavian Style." In Nowell-Smith, ed., *The Oxford History of World Cinema*, pp. 151–59.

Cherchi Usai, Paolo, and Lorenzo Codelli, eds. *Before Caligari: German Cinema, 1895–1920*. Pordenone, Italy: Biblioteca dell'Immagine, 1990.

Coates, Paul. *The Gorgon's Gaze: German Cinema, Expressionism, and the Image of Horror*. Cambridge, Eng.: Cambridge University Press, 1991.

Cowie, Peter. *Sweden*. Rev. ed. Screen Series. 2 vols. Cranbury, N.J.: Barnes, 1969.

———. *Finnish Cinema*. Cranbury, N.J.: Barnes, 1977.

Drum, Jean, and Dale D. Drum. *My Only Great Passion: The Life and Films of Carl Th. Dreyer*. Lanham, Md.: Scarecrow, 2000.

Dyer, Richard, and Ginette Vincendeau, eds. *Popular European Cinema*. New York: Routledge, 1992.

Ehrenburg, Ilya. *Men, Years—Life*. Vol. 3. London: McGibbon & Kee, 1963.

Eisner, Lotte H. *The Haunted Screen: German Expressionism and the Influence of Max Reinhardt*. Trans. Richard Greaves. Berkeley: University of California Press, 1969.

———. *Murnau*. Berkeley: University of California Press, 1973.

————. *Fritz Lang*. New York: Oxford University Press, 1977.

Elsaesser, Thomas. "Germany: The Weimar Years." In Nowell-Smith, ed., *The Oxford History of World Cinema*, pp. 136–51.

————. *Metropolis*. London: British Film Institute, 2000.

————. *Weimar Cinema and After: Germany's Historical Imaginary*. London: Routledge, 2000.

Elsaesser, Thomas, with Michael Wedel, eds. *A Second Life: German Cinema's First Decades*. Amsterdam, the Neth.: Amsterdam University Press, 1996.

————, eds. *The BFI Companion to German Cinema*. London: British Film Institute, 1999.

Eyman, Scott. *Ernst Lubitsch: Laughter in Paradise*. Baltimore: Johns Hopkins University Press, 2000.

Feldman, Gerald D. *The Great Disorder: Politics, Economics, and Society in the German Inflation, 1914–1924*. New York: Oxford University Press, 1994.

Forslund, Bengt. *Victor Sjöström: His Life and Work*. Trans. Peter Cowie. New York: New York Zoetrope, 1988.

Fullerton, John. "AB Svenska Biografteatern: Aspects of Production." In Austin, ed., *Current Research in Film*, pp. 165–80.

Fullerton, John, and Jan Olsson, eds. *Nordic Explorations: Film before 1930*. Sydney: Libbey, 1999.

Gandart, Gero, ed. *Der Film der Weimarer Republik: Ein Handbuch der zeitgenossischen Kritik*. Berlin: de Gruyter, 1993.

Gillett, John. "Munich's Cleaned Pictures." *Sight and Sound* 47, no. 1 (Winter 1977–78): 37–39.

Ginsberg, Terri, and Kirsten Moana Thompson, eds. *Perspectives on German Cinema*. New York: Hall, 1996.

Grant, Barry Keith, ed. *Fritz Lang: Interviews*. Jackson: University Press of Mississippi, 2003.

Gunning, Tom. *The Films of Fritz Lang: Allegories of Vision and Modernity*. London: British Film Institute, 2000.

Hake, Sabine. *Passions and Deceptions: The Early Films of Ernst Lubitsch*. Princeton, N.J.: Princeton University Press, 1992.

————. *The Cinema's Third Machine: Writing on Film in Germany, 1907–1933*. Lincoln: University of Nebraska Press, 1993.

————. "Faces of Weimar Germany." In Andrew and Shafto, eds., *The Image in Dispute*, pp. 117–47.

————. *German National Cinema*. London: Routledge, 2002.

Haller, Robert A., ed. *Fritz Lang 2000*. New York: Anthology Film Archives, 2000.

Hardt, Ursula. *From Caligari to California: Eric Pommer's Life in the International Film Wars*. Providence, R.I.: Berghahn, 1996.

Hardy, Forsyth. *Scandinavian Film*. London: Falcon, 1952.

Heilbut, Anthony. *Exiled in Paradise: German Refugee Artists and Intellectuals in America from the 1930s to the Present*. New York: Viking, 1983.

Hensley, Wayne E. "The Contribution of F. W. Murnau's *Nosferatu* to the Evolution of Dracula." *Literature/Film Quarterly* 30, no. 1 (2002): 59–64.

Idestam-Almquist, Bengt. *Victor Sjöström*. *Anthologie du Cinéma*, 10. Paris: L'Avant-scène du cinéma, 1965. Supplement to *L'Avant-scène du cinéma*.

Jackman, Jarrell C., and Carla M. Borden, eds. *The Muses Flee Hitler: Cultural Transfer and Adaptation, 1930–1945*. Washington, D.C.: Smithsonian Institution Press, 1983.

Jacobs, Lewis. *The Rise of the American Film*. New York: Harcourt Brace, 1939. Repr., New York: Teachers College Press, 1968.

Jacobsen, Wolfgang. *G. W. Pabst*. Berlin: Argon, 1997.

Jensen, Paul M. *The Cinema of Fritz Lang*. Cranbury, N.J.: Barnes, 1969.

Josef Fenneker, 1895–1956: Cinema Posters from the Weimar Republic. Munich: Goethe-Institut, 1990.

Jung, Uli. "Local Views: A Blind Spot in the Historiography of Early German Cinema." *Historical Journal of Film, Radio and Television* 22, no. 3 (2002): 253–73.

Jung, Uli, and Walter Schatzberg. *Beyond Caligari: The Films of Robert Wiene*. New York: Berghahn, 1999.

Kaes, Anton; Martin Jay; and Edward Dimendberg. *The Weimar Republic Sourcebook*. Berkeley: University of California Press, 1994.

Kawin, Bruce F. *Mindscreen: Bergman, Godard, and First-Person Film*. Princeton, N.J.: Princeton University Press, 1978.

————. "An Outline of Film Voices." *Film Quarterly* 38, no. 2 (Winter 1984–85): 38–46.

Kniesche, Thomas W., and Stephen Brockman, eds. *Dancing on the Volcano: Essays on the Culture of the Weimar Republic*. Columbia, S.C.: Camden House, 1994.

Knight, Arthur. *The Liveliest Art*. Rev. ed. New York: Mentor, 1978.

Kobal, John. *Great Film Stills of the German Silent Era: 125 Stills from the Stiftung Deutsche Kinemathek*. Mineola, N.Y.: Dover, 1981.

Koller, Michael, and Clare Stewart, eds. *Fritz Lang: Traps for the Mind and Eye*. Melbourne: Melbourne Cinémathèque/Goethe Institute, 1998.

Koller, Michael; Clare Stewart; and Stuart Lord, eds. *Trouble in Paradise: The Films of Ernst Lubitsch*. Melbourne: Melbourne Cinémathèque, 1997.

Kracauer, Siegfried. *From Caligari to Hitler: A Psychological Study of the German Film*. Princeton, N.J.: Princeton University Press, 1947.

———. *The Mass Ornament: Weimar Essays*. Trans. and ed. Thomas Y. Levin. Cambridge, Mass.: Harvard University Press, 1995.

Kreimeier, Klaus. *The Ufa Story: A History of Germany's Greatest Film Company, 1918–1945*. Trans. Robert and Rita Kimber. New York: Hill & Wang, 1996.

Kwiaikoski, Aleksander. *Swedish Film Classics: A Pictorial Survey of Twenty-five Films from 1913 to 1957*. New York: Dover, 1983.

Lehman, Peter, ed. *Close Viewings: An Anthology of New Film Criticism*. Tallahassee: Florida State University Press, 1990.

Levin, David J. *Richard Wagner, Fritz Lang, and the Nibelungen: The Dramaturgy of Disavowal*. Princeton, N.J.: Princeton University Press, 1998.

McCormick, Richard W. *Gender and Sexuality in Weimar Modernity: Film, Literature, and "New Objectivity."* New York: Palgrave, 2002.

McGilligan, Patrick. *Fritz Lang: The Nature of the Beast*. New York: St. Martin's, 1997.

Mänz, Peter, and Christian Maryška, eds. *Ufa Film Posters, 1918–1943*. Heidelberg: Umschau Braus, 1998.

Mayne, Judith. "Dracula in the Twilight: Murnau's *Nosferatu* (1992)." In Rentschler, ed., *German Film and Literature*, pp. 25–39.

Milne, Tom. *The Cinema of Carl Dreyer*. Cranbury, N.J.: Barnes, 1971.

Minden, Michael, and Holger Bachmann, eds. *Fritz Lang's "Metropolis": Cinematic Visions of Technology and Fear*. Rochester, N.Y.: Camden House, 2000.

Mottram, Ron. *The Danish Cinema before Dreyer*. Metuchen, N.J.: Scarecrow, 1988.

Mühl-Benninghaus, Wolfgang. "German Film Censorship during World War I." *Film History* 9, no. 1 (1997): 71–94.

Murray, Bruce A. *Film and the German Left in the Weimar Republic*. Austin: University of Texas Press, 1990.

Murray, Bruce A., and Christopher Wickham, eds. *Framing the Past: The Historiography of German Cinema and Television*. Carbondale: University of Southern Illinois Press, 1992.

Neergaard, Ebbe. *The Story of Danish Film*. Trans. Elsa Gress. Copenhagen: Danish Institute, 1962.

Nowell-Smith, Geoffrey, ed. *The Oxford History of World Cinema*. Oxford: Oxford University Press, 1996.

Paris, Barry. *Louise Brooks: A Biography*. Minneapolis: University of Minnesota Press, 2000.

Paris, Michael. *The First World War and Popular Cinema: 1914 to the Present*. New Brunswick, N.J.: Rutgers University Press, 2000.

Pattison, Barry. *The Seal of Dracula*. New York: Bonanza, 1975.

Pensel, Hans. *Seastrom and Stiller in Hollywood*. New York: Vantage, 1969.

Petley, Julian. *Capital and Culture: German Cinema 1933–45*. London: British Film Institute, 1979.

Petrie, Graham. *Hollywood Destinies: European Directors in America, 1922–1931*. London: Methuen, 1985.

Petro, Patrice. *Joyless Streets: Women and Melodramatic Representation in Weimar Germany*. Princeton, N.J.: Princeton University Press, 1989.

———. *Aftershocks of the New: Feminism and Film History*. New Brunswick, N.J.: Rutgers University Press, 2002.

Phillips, M. S. "The Nazi Control of the German Film Industry." *Journal of European Studies* 1, no. 1 (1971): 37–68.

Pirie, David. *The Vampire Cinema*. London: Tantivy, 1977.

"Point of View." Special section of *Film Reader 4: Point of View/Metahistory of Films* (1979): 105–236.

Pratt, David B. " 'Fit Food for Madhouse Inmates'; The Box Office Reception of the German Invasion of 1921." *Griffithiana* 16, nos. 48/49 (October 1993): 96–157.

Rentschler, Eric, ed. *German Film and Literature: Adaptations and Transformations*. New York and London: Methuen, 1986.

———. ed. *The Films of G. W. Pabst: An Extraterritorial Cinema*. New Brunswick, N.J.: Rutgers University Press, 1990.

Rhode, Eric. *A History of the Cinema from Its Origins to 1970*. New York: Hill & Wang, 1976.

Rickels, Laurence. "The Demonization of the Home Front: War Neurosis and Weimar Cinema." In Kniesche and Brockman, eds. *Dancing on the Volcano*, pp. 181–93.

Robinson, David. *Das Cabinet des Dr. Caligari*. London: British Film Institute, 1997.

Roters, Eberhard, et al. *Berlin 1910–1933*. Trans. Marguerite Mounier. New York: Rizzoli, 1982.

Rotha, Paul. *The Film till Now*. London: Jonathan Cape, 1930.

Rother, Rainer, and Susan Anna Gunther. "The Experience of the First World War and the German Film." In Paris, ed., *The First World War and Popular Cinema*, pp. 217–46.

Salt, Barry. *Film Style and Technology: History and Analysis*. London: Starword, 1983; 2nd ed. 1992.

Sanford, John. "Chaos and Control in the Weimar Film." *German Life and Letters* 48, no. 3 (July 1995): 311–23.

Saunders, Thomas J. *Hollywood in Berlin: American Cinema and Weimar Germany*. Berkeley: University of California Press, 1994.

Schlüpmann, Heide. "The First German Art Film: Rye's *The Student of Prague* (1913)." In Rentschler, ed., *German Film and Literature*, pp. 9–24.

———. "Early German Cinema: Melodrama: Social Drama." In Dyer and Vincendeau, eds., *Popular European Cinema*, pp. 206–19.

Schürman, Ernst. *German Film Directors in Hollywood: Film*

Emigration from Germany and Austria. San Francisco: Goethe Institutes of North America, 1978. Exhibition catalog.

Silberman, Mark. *German Cinema: Texts in Context.* Detroit: Wayne State University Press, 1995.

———. "What Is German in the German Cinema?" *Film History* 8, no. 3 (1996): 297–315.

Silver, Alain, and James Ursini. *The Vampire Film.* South Brunswick, N.J.: Barnes, 1975.

Skoller, Donald, ed. *Dreyer in Double Reflection.* New York: Dutton, 1973. Translation of Dreyer's *Om Filmen.*

Smith, David Calvert. *The German Filmography, 1895–1949.* Jefferson, N.C.: McFarland, 2000.

Taylor, John Russell. *Strangers in Paradise: The Hollywood Émigrés, 1933–1950.* New York: Holt, Rinehart, & Winston, 1983.

Thompson, Kristin. *Exporting Entertainment: America in the World Film Market, 1907–1934.* London: British Film Institute, 1985.

Tomasulo, Frank. "*Cabinet of Dr. Caligari*: History/Psychoanalysis/Cinema." *On Film* 11 (Summer 1983): 2–7.

Turim, Maureen. *Flashbacks in Film: Memory and History.* New York: Routledge, 1989.

Vlasov, Eduard. "Overcoming the Threshold: Bakhtin, Eisenstein, and the Cinema of German Expressionism." *Canadian Review of Comparative Literature/Revue Canadienne de Littérature Comparée* 23, no. 3 (September 1996): 659–78.

von Ankum, Katherina, ed. *Women in the Metropolis: Gender and Modernity in Weimar Culture.* Berkeley: University of California Press, 1997.

Wager, Jans B. *Dangerous Dames: Women and Representation in the Weimar Street Film and Film Noir.* Athens: Ohio State University Press, 1999.

Waller, Gregory A. *The Living and the Undead: From Stoker's Dracula to Romero's Dawn of the Dead.* Urbana: University of Illinois Press, 1986.

Waltje, Jörg. "Filming Dracula: Vampires, Genre, and Cinematography." *Journal of Dracula Studies* 2 (2000): 24–33.

"Weimar Film Theory." Special issue of *New German Critique* 40 (Winter 1987).

Welsh, Tricia. "Foreign Exchange: German Expressionism and Its Legacy." *Cinema Journal* 38, no. 4 (Summer 1999): 98–102.

Wilson, George M. *Narration in Light: Studies in Cinematic Point of View.* Baltimore: Johns Hopkins University Press, 1986.

Wollenberg, Hans H. *Fifty Years of German Film.* Ed. Roger Manvell. London: Falcon, 1948. Repr., New York: Arno, 1972.

CHAPTER 5. SOVIET SILENT CINEMA AND THE THEORY OF MONTAGE, 1917–1931

Abel, Richard, ed. *Silent Film.* New Brunswick, N.J.: Rutgers University Press, 1996.

Aumont, Jacques. *Montage Eisenstein.* Trans. Lee Hildreth, Constance Penley, and Andrew Ross. Bloomington: Indiana University Press, 1987.

Barna, Yon. *Eisenstein.* Trans. Lisa Hunter. Bloomington: Indiana University Press, 1973; Boston: Little, Brown, 1973.

Barry, Iris. *D. W. Griffith: American Film Master.* New York: Museum of Modern Art, 1940.

Bazin, André. "The Evolution of the Language of the Cinema." In André Bazin, *What Is Cinema?* I, pp. 23–40.

———. *What Is Cinema?* Selected and trans. Hugh Gray. 2 vols. Berkeley: University of California Press, 1967, 1971.

Beller, Jonathan. "Dziga Vertov and the Film of Money." *Boundary 2* 26, no. 3 (1999): 151–99.

Bergen, Ronald. *Sergei Eisenstein: A Life in Conflict.* Woodstock, N.Y.: Overlook, 1999.

Billington, James H. *The Face of Russia: Anguish, Aspiration, and Achievement in Russian Culture.* New York: TV Books, 1998. Companion book to the PBS series of the same title.

Bordwell, David. "Dziga Vertov: An Introduction." *Film Comment* 8, no. 1 (Spring 1972): 38–45.

———. *The Cinema of Eisenstein.* Cambridge, Mass.: Harvard University Press, 1993.

Braun, Edward. *The Theater of Meyerhold: Revolutions on the Modern Stage.* New York: Drama Book Specialists, 1979.

Bulgakowa, Oksana. *Sergei Eisenstein: A Biography.* Trans. Anne Dwyer. Berlin: Potemkin, 2001.

Burns, Paul E. "Cultural Revolution, Collectivization, and Soviet Cinema: Eisenstein's *Old and New* and Dovzhenko's *Earth.*" *Film and History* 11, no. 4 (December 1981): 84–105.

Charney, Leo. *Empty Moments: Cinema, Modernity, and Drift.* Durham, N.C.: Duke University Press, 1998.

Cherchi, Paolo, et al., eds. *Silent Witnesses: Russian Films, 1880–1919.* London: British Film Institute, 1989.

Conquest, Robert. *The Harvest of Sorrow: Soviet Collectivization and the Terror Famine.* New York: Oxford University Press, 1986.

Constantine, Mildred, and Alan Fern. *Revolutionary Soviet Film Posters.* Baltimore: Johns Hopkins University Press, 1974.

de Jonge, Alex. *Stalin and the Shaping of the Soviet Union.* New York: Morrow, 1986.

de Zegher, M. Catherine, ed. *The Body of the Line: Eisenstein's Drawings.* New York: Drawing Center, 2000. Exhibition catalog.

Dickinson, Thorold. *Soviet Cinema.* London: Falcon, 1948.

Dovzhenko, Alexander. *Alexander Dovzhenko: The Poet as Filmmaker*. Trans. and ed. Marco Carynnyk. Cambridge, Mass.: MIT Press, 1973.

Drobashenko, Sergei. "Soviet Documentary Film, 1917–1940." In Pronay and Spring, eds., *Propaganda, Politics and Film, 1918–1945*, pp. 249–69.

Eisenstein, Sergei. *The Film Sense*. Trans. and ed. Jay Leyda. New York: Harcourt Brace Jovanovich, 1942, 1974.

———. *The Film Form*. Trans. and ed. Jay Leyda. New York: Meridian, 1949. Repr., New York: Harcourt Brace Jovanovich, 1977.

———. "The Cinematographic Principle and the Ideogram." Repr. as "The Collision of Ideas." In MacCann, ed., *Film: A Montage of Theories*, pp. 34–37.

———. *Notes of a Film Director*. Trans. X. Danko. Rev. ed. New York: Dover, 1970.

———. *Immoral Memories*. Trans. Herbert Marshall. Boston: Houghton Mifflin, 1983.

———. *S. M. Eisenstein: Selected Works*. Vol. II: *Towards a Theory of Montage*. Ed. Richard Taylor and Michael Glenny. Trans. Richard Taylor. 2nd ed. London: British Film Institute, 1991.

———. *S. M. Eisenstein: Selected Works*. Vol. IV: *Beyond the Stars: The Memoirs of Sergei Eisenstein*. Ed. and trans. Richard Taylor. London: British Film Institute, 1996.

———. *The Eisenstein Reader*. Ed. Richard Taylor. Trans. Richard Taylor and William Powell. London: British Film Institute, 1998.

Feldman, Seth. *The Evolution of Style in the Early Work of Dziga Vertov*. New York: Arno, 1977.

———. " 'Cinema Weekly' and 'Cinema Truth': Dziga Vertov and the Leninist Film Proportion." In Waugh, ed., *"Show Us Life,"* pp. 3–20.

———. " 'Peace between Man and Machine': Dziga Vertov's *The Man with a Movie Camera*." In Grant and Sloniowski, eds., *Documenting the Documentary*, pp. 40–54.

Fischer, Lucy. "*Enthusiasm*: From Kino-Eye to Radio Eye." *Film Quarterly* 31, no. 2 (Winter 1977–78): 25–35. Repr. in Weis and Belton, eds., *Film Sound*, pp. 247–64.

Fowler, Catherine, ed. *The European Cinema Reader*. London: Routledge, 2002.

Gillespie, David. *Early Soviet Cinema: Innovation, Ideology, and Propaganda*. London: Wallflower, 2001.

Goodwin, James. *Eisenstein, Cinema, and History*. Urbana: University of Illinois Press, 1993.

Grant, Barry Keith, and Jeannette Sloniowski, eds. *Documenting the Documentary: Close Readings of Documentary Film and Video*. Detroit: Wayne State University Press, 1998.

Hill, Stephen. "Kuleshov—Prophet without Honor?" *Film Culture* 44 (1967): 1–41.

———. "The Strange Case of the Vanishing Epigraphs." In Marshall, ed., *Battleship Potemkin*, pp. 74–86.

Hough, Richard. *The Potemkin Mutiny*. Englewood Cliffs, N.J.: Prentice-Hall, 1960.

Influence of Silent Soviet Cinema on World Cinema, The. Proceedings of the International Federation of Film Archives Symposium. Varna, Bulgaria, June 29–July 2, 1977.

Jacobs, Lewis. *The Rise of the American Film*. New York: Harcourt Brace, 1939. Repr. New York: Teachers College Press, 1968.

Kenez, Peter. *Cinema and Soviet Society, 1917–1953*. Cambridge: Cambridge University Press, 1992. Repr. as *Cinema and Soviet Society from the Revolution to the Death of Stalin*. New York: Tauris, 2001.

———. *Cinema and Soviet Society from the Revolution to the Death of Stalin*. New York: Tauris, 2001.

Kepley, Vance, Jr. "*Intolerance* and the Soviets: A Historical Investigation." *Wide Angle* 3, no. 1 (Spring 1979): 22–27.

———. "Pudovkin and the Classical Hollywood Tradition." *Wide Angle* 7, no. 3 (Fall 1985): 53–61.

———. "The Origins of Soviet Cinema: A Study of Industry Development." *Quarterly Review of Film Studies* 10, no. 1 (Winter 1985): 22–38.

———. *In the Service of the State: The Cinema of Alexander Dovzhenko*. Madison: University of Wisconsin Press, 1986.

———. "Building a National Cinema: Soviet Film Education, 1918–1934." *Wide Angle* 9, no. 3 (Summer 1987): 4–20.

———. "Cinema and Everyday Life: Soviet Worker Clubs of the 1920s." In Sklar and Musser, eds., *Resisting Images*, pp. 108–25.

———. " 'Cinefication': Soviet Film Exhibition in the 1920s." *Film History* 6, no. 2 (Summer 1994): 262–77.

———. "Eisenstein and Soviet Cinema." In Lehman, ed., *Defining Cinema*, pp. 37–55.

———. "Ukrainian Pastoral." *Film Comment* 38, no. 3 (May–June 2002): 58–61. Profile of Alexander Dovzhenko.

Kepley, Vance, Jr., and Betty Kepley. "Foreign Films on Soviet Screens, 1922–1931." *Quarterly Review of Film Studies* 4, no. 4 (Fall 1979): 429–42.

Kernig, Claus Dieter, ed. *Marxism, Communism, and Western Society*. 8 vols. New York: Herder & Herder, 1973.

Knight, Arthur. *The Liveliest Art*. Rev. ed. New York: Mentor, 1978.

Kuleshov, Lev. *Kuleshov on Film*. Trans. and ed. Ron Levaco. Berkeley: University of California Press, 1974.

Laing, Dave, ed. *Marxist Theories of Art*. Atlantic Highlands, N.J.: Harvester, 1978.

Large, Gerry. "Lev Kuleshov and the Metrical-Spatial Web: Postmodern Body Training in Space and Time." *Theatre Topics* 10, no. 1 (March 2000): 65–75.

LaValley, Albert J., and Barry P. Scherr, eds. *Eisenstein at 100.* New Brunswick, N.J.: Rutgers University Press, 2001.

Leach, Robert; Victor Borovsky; and Andy Davies, eds. *A History of Russian Theatre.* Cambridge, Eng.: Cambridge University Press, 1999.

Lefebvre, Martin. "Eisenstein, Rhetoric and Imaginicity: Towards a Revolutionary Memoria." *Screen* 41, 4 (Winter 2000): 349–68.

Lehman, Peter, ed. *Defining Cinema.* New Brunswick, N.J.: Rutgers University Press, 1997.

Levaco, Ron. "Kuleshov." *Sight and Sound* 40, no. 2 (Spring 1971): 86–91, 109.

Leyda, Jay. *Kino: A History of the Russian and Soviet Cinema.* 3rd ed. Princeton, N.J.: Princeton University Press, 1983.

Liber, George O. *Alexander Dovzhenko: A Life in Soviet Film.* Berkeley: University of California Press, 2003.

MacCann, Richard Dyer, ed. *Film: A Montage of Theories.* New York: Dutton, 1966.

McReynolds, Louise, and Joan Neuberger, eds. *Imitations of Life: Two Centuries of Melodrama in Russia.* Durham, N.C.: Duke University Press, 2002.

Malevich, Kazimir. "Painterly Laws and the Problems of Cinema." Trans. Cathy Young. In Tupitsyn, ed., *Malevich and Film,* pp. 147–59.

Marshall, Herbert, ed. *Battleship Potemkin: The Greatest Film Ever Made.* New York: Avon, 1978.

Mayer, David. *Eisenstein's "Potemkin."* New York: Grossman, 1972. Shot-by-shot analysis.

Mayne, Judith. *Kino and the Woman Question: Feminism and Soviet Silent Film.* Columbus: Ohio State University Press, 1989.

Meyerhold, Vsevolod. *Meyerhold on the Theater.* Ed. Edward Braun. London: Hill & Wang, 1969.

Moussinac, Léon. *Sergei Eisenstein.* Trans. D. Sandy Petrey. New York: Crown, 1970.

Musser, Charles. "Work, Ideology, and the Little Tramp." In Sklar and Musser, eds., *Resisting Images,* pp. 36–67.

Nizhnii, Vladimir. *Lessons with Eisenstein.* Trans. Ivor Montagu. London: Allen & Unwin, 1952; New York: Hill & Wang, 1962.

Nowell-Smith, Geoffrey, ed. *The Oxford History of World Cinema.* Oxford: Oxford University Press, 1996.

Petríc, Vlada. "Dziga Vertov as Theorist." *Cinema Journal* 18, no. 1 (Fall 1978): 29–44.

———. "Esther Shub: Cinema Is My Life." *Quarterly Review of Film Studies* 3, no. 4 (Fall 1978): 429–48.

———. "Esther Shub's Unrealized Project." *Quarterly Review of Film Studies* 3, no. 4 (Fall 1978): 449–56.

———. "The Difficult Years of Dziga Vertov: Excerpts from His Diaries." *Quarterly Review of Film Studies* 7, no. 1 (Winter 1982): 7–21.

———. "Esther Shub: Film as Historical Discourse." In Waugh, ed., *"Show Us Life,"* pp. 21–46.

———. *Constructivism in Film, the Man with the Movie Camera—A Cinematic Analysis.* Cambridge: Cambridge University Press, 1987.

———. "Vertov's Cinematic Transposition of Reality." In Warren, ed., *Beyond Document,* pp. 271–94.

Prince, Stephen, and Wayne E. Hensley. "The Kuleshov Effect: Recreating the Classic Experiment." *Cinema Journal* 2 (Winter 1992): 59–75.

Pronay, Nicholas, and D. W. Spring, eds. *Propaganda, Politics and Film, 1918–1945.* London: Macmillan, 1982.

Pudovkin, V. I. *Film Technique and Film Acting.* Trans. Ivor Montagu. Enl. ed. London: Newnes, 1933. Repr., New York: Grove, 1970.

———. "Foreword" to *The Art of Cinema.* Repr. in Kuleshov, *Kuleshov on Film,* p. 41.

Reeves, Nicholas. *The Power of Film Propaganda: Myth or Reality?* London: Cassell, 1999.

Roberts, Graham. *Forward Soviet! History and Non-Fiction Film in the USSR.* London: Tauris, 1999.

———. *The Man with the Movie Camera.* London: Tauris, 2000.

Robinson, David. "Evgeni Bauer and the Cinema of Nikolai II." *Sight and Sound* 59, no. 1 (Winter 1989–90): 51–55.

Rosenthal, Alan, ed. *Why Docudrama? Fact-Fiction on Film and T.V.* Carbondale: Southern Illinois University Press, 1999.

Sadoul, Georges. *Dziga Vertov.* Paris: Éditions Champ Libre, 1971.

———. *Dictionary of Film Makers.* Trans. and ed. Peter Morris. Berkeley: University of California Press, 1972.

———. *Dictionary of Films.* Trans. and ed. Peter Morris. Berkeley: University of California Press, 1972.

Salt, Barry. *Film Style and Technology: History and Analysis.* 2nd ed. London: Starword, 1992.

Sargeant, Amy. *Vsevolod Pudovkin: Classic Films of the Soviet Avant-Garde.* New York: Tauris, 2000.

Schnitzer, Jean, ed. *Cinema in Revolution.* New York: Hill & Wang, 1973.

Schnitzer, Jean, and Luda Schnitzer. *Alexandre Dovjenko.* Paris: Éditions Universitaires, 1966.

Selden, Daniel L. "Vision and Violence: The Rhetoric of Potemkin." *Quarterly Review of Film Studies* 7, no. 4 (Fall 1982): 308–29.

Seton, Marie. *Sergei M. Eisenstein.* New York: Wyn, 1953.

Seydor, Paul. "Eisenstein's Aesthetic: A Dissenting View." *Sight and Sound* 43, no. 1 (Winter 1973–74): 38–43.

Shlapentokh, Dmitry, and Vladimir Shlapentokh. *Soviet Cinematography, 1918–1991: Ideological Conflict and Social Reality.* New York: de Gruyter, 1993.

Sklar, Robert, and Charles Musser, eds. *Resisting Images.* Philadelphia: Temple University Press, 1990.

"Soviet Film." Special issue of *Cinema Journal* 17, no. 1 (Fall 1977).

Swallow, Norman. *Eisenstein: A Documentary Portrait.* London: Allen & Unwin, 1976; New York: Dutton, 1977.

———. "Alexandrov." *Sight and Sound* 48, no. 4 (Autumn 1979): 246–49.

Taylor, Richard. *The Politics of the Soviet Cinema, 1917–1929.* Cambridge, Eng. Cambridge University Press, 1979.

———. "A 'Cinema for the Millions': Soviet Socialist Realism and the Problem of Film Comedy." *Journal of Contemporary History* 18 (1983): 439–61.

———, ed. *Film Propaganda: Soviet Russia and Nazi Germany.* 2nd rev. ed. London: Tauris, 1998.

———. *Battleship Potemkin.* London: Tauris, 1999.

———. *October.* London: British Film Institute, 2002.

Taylor, Richard, and Ian Christie, eds. *The Film Factory: Russian and Soviet Cinema in Documents, 1896–1939.* London: Routledge & Kegan Paul, 1988.

———, ed. *Inside the Film Factory: New Approaches to Russian and Soviet Cinema.* London: Routledge, 1994.

Taylor, Richard; Nancy Wood; Julian Graffy; and Dina Iordanova, eds. *The BFI Companion to Eastern European and Russian Cinema.* London: British Film Institute, 2000.

Thompson, Kristin; Yuri Tsivian; and Ekaterina Khokhlova. "The Rediscovery of a Kuleshov Experiment: A Dossier." *Film History* 8, no. 3 (1996): 357–67.

Tsivian, Yuri. *Early Cinema in Russia and Its Cultural Reception.* Trans. Alan Bodger. London: Routledge, 1994.

———. "The Rorschach Test for Culture: On Some Parallels between Early Film Reception in Russia and the United States." *Yale Journal of Criticism* 7, no. 2 (Fall 1994): 177–88.

———. "Pre-Revolutionary Russia." In Nowell-Smith, ed., *The Oxford History of World Cinema*, pp. 159–62.

———. "The Wise and Wicked Game: Re-Editing and Soviet Film Culture of the 1920s." *Film History* 8, no. 3 (1996): 327–43.

Tupitsyn, Margarita; Kazimir Malevich; and Victor Tupitsyn. *Malevich and Film.* New Haven, Conn.: Yale University Press, 2002.

Turvey, Malcolm. "Can the Camera See?: Mimesis in *Man with a Movie Camera.*" *October* 89 (Summer 1999): 25–50.

Vertov, Dziga. *Kino Eye: The Writings of Dziga Vertov.* Trans. Kevin O'Brien. ed. Annette Michelson. Berkeley: University of California Press, 1984.

Warren, Charles, ed. *Beyond Document: Essays on Nonfiction Film.* Hanover, N.H.: University Press of New England, 1996.

Waugh, Thomas, ed. *"Show Us Life.": Toward a History and Aesthetics of the Committed Documentary.* Metuchen, N.J.: Scarecrow, 1984.

Weis, Elisabeth, and John Belton, eds. *Film Sound: Theory and Practice.* New York: Columbia University Press, 1985.

Wendon, D. J. "Battleship Potemkin: Film and Reality." In Rosenthal, ed., *Why Docudrama?*, pp. 236–59.

Widdis, Emma. *Visions of a New Land: Soviet Film from the Revolution to the Second World War.* New Haven, Conn.: Yale University Press, 2003.

Withall, Keith. *The Battleship Potemkin: Director Sergei Eisenstein.* New York: Longman, 2000.

Wollen, Peter. *Signs and Meaning in the Cinema.* 2nd ed. Bloomington: Indiana University Press, 1972.

Youngblood, Denise J. *Soviet Cinema in the Silent Era, 1918–1935.* Repr. Austin: University of Texas Press, 1991.

———. *Movies of the Masses: Popular Cinema and Soviet Society in the 1920s.* Cambridge, Eng.: Cambridge University Press, 1992.

———. *The Magic Mirror: Moviemaking in Russia 1908–1918.* Madison: University of Wisconsin Press, 1999.

Media

The Harvest of Sorrow: Soviet Collectivization and the Terror Famine. (Oct. 1986, PBS) Robert Conquest. Documentary film.

Hawkins, Jim. *Thank You, Comrades.* BBC Documentary Film, 1978.

CHAPTER 6. HOLLYWOOD IN THE TWENTIES

Acker, Ally. *Reel Women: Pioneers of the Cinema, 1896 to the Present.* New York: Continuum, 1991.

Anderson, Mark Lynn. "Shooting Star: Understanding Wallace Reid and His Public." In McLean and Cook, eds., *Headline Hollywood*, pp. 83–106.

Asplund, Una. *Chaplin's Films.* Trans. Paul Britten Austin. London: David & Charles, 1971.

Austin, Bruce A., ed. *Current Research in Film.* Vol. 2. Norwood, N.J.: Ablex, 1986.

Bachman, Gregg, and Thomas J. Slater, eds. *American Silent Film: Discovering Marginalized Voices.* Carbondale: Southern Illinois University Press, 2002.

Balio, Tino. "Stars in Business: The Founding of United Artists." In Balio, ed., *The American Film Industry*, pp. 153–72.

———, ed. *The American Film Industry.* Rev. ed. Madison: University of Wisconsin Press, 1985.

Barr, Charles. *Laurel and Hardy.* Berkeley: University of California Press, 1968.

Barsam, Richard. *The Vision of Robert Flaherty: The Artist as*

Myth and Filmmaker. Bloomington: Indiana University Press, 1988.

Basinger, Jeanine. *Silent Stars*. New York: Knopf, 1999.

Bazin, André. "The Evolution of the Language of Cinema." In Bazin, *What Is Cinema?*, I, pp. 23–40.

———. *What Is Cinema?* Selected and trans. Hugh Gray. 2 vols. Berkeley: University of California Press, 1967.

Bean, Jennifer M., and Diane Negra, eds. *A Feminist Reader in Early Cinema*. Durham, N.C.: Duke University Press, 2002.

Beauchamp, Cari. *Without Lying Down: Frances Marion and the Powerful Women of Early Hollywood*. New York: Scribner's, 1997.

"Before Screwball." Special issue of *Film History* 13, no. 4 (2001).

Benayoun, Robert. *The Look of Buster Keaton*. Trans. and ed. Randall Conrad. New York: St. Martin's, 1983.

Bengtson, John. *Silent Echoes: Discovering Early Hollywood through the Films of Buster Keaton*. Santa Monica, Calif.: Santa Monica Press: 2000.

Bernardi, Daniel, ed. *The Birth of Whiteness: Race and the Emergence of U.S. Cinema*. New Brunswick, N.J.: Rutgers University Press, 1996.

Bernstein, Matthew, ed. *Controlling Hollywood: Censorship and Regulation in the Studio Era*. New Brunswick, N.J.: Rutgers University Press, 1999.

Blesh, Rudi. *Keaton*. New York: Macmillan, 1996.

Bordwell, David; Kristin Thompson; and Janet Staiger. *The Classical Hollywood Cinema: Film Style and Mode of Production to 1960*. New York: Columbia University Press, 1985.

Braff, Richard E. *The Universal Silents: A Filmography of the Universal Motion Picture Manufacturing Company, 1912–1929*. Jefferson, N.C.: McFarland, 1999.

Brownlow, Kevin. *The Parade's Gone By*. New York: Knopf, 1968.

Brownlow, Kevin, and John Kobal. *Hollywood: The Pioneers*. New York: Knopf, 1979.

Byron, Stuart. *Movie Comedy*. New York: Grossman, 1977.

Calder-Marshall, Arthur. *The Innocent Eye*. New York: Museum of Modern Art, 1970.

Card, James. *Seductive Cinema: The Art of the Silent Film*. Minneapolis: University of Minnesota Press, 1998.

Carey, Gary. *Lost Films*. New York: Museum of Modern Art, 1970.

Carringer, Robert, and Barry Sabath. *Ernst Lubitsch: A Guide to References and Resources*. Boston: Hall, 1978.

Carter, Gaylord Beach. *The Million Dollar Life of Gaylord Carter*. Ed. and comp. Nancy Grimley Carleton. Oakland, Calif.: Paramount Theatre of the Arts, 1995.

Chaplin, Charles. *My Autobiography*. New York: Pocket, 1966.

"Chaplin and Sound." Special issue of *Journal of the University Film Association* 31, no. 1 (Winter 1979).

"Chaplin: Twelve Essays." Special issue of *Film Comment* 8, no. 3 (September–October 1972).

Cohen, Paula Marantz. *Silent Film and the Triumph of the American Myth*. Oxford: Oxford University Press, 2001.

Cooke, Alistair. *Douglas Fairbanks: The Making of a Screen Character*. New York: Macmillan, 1940.

Couvares, Francis G. "Hollywood, Main Street, and the Church: Trying to Censor the Movies before the Production Code." *American Quarterly* 44, no. 4 (December 1992): 584–616.

Curtis, Thomas Quinn. *Von Stroheim*. New York: Farrar, Straus & Giroux, 1971.

Dale, Alan. *Comedy Is a Man in Trouble: Slapstick in American Movies*. Minneapolis: University of Minnesota Press, 2002.

Dardis, Tom. *Keaton: The Man Who Wouldn't Lie Down*. New York: Scribner's, 1979.

———. *Harold Lloyd: The Man on the Clock*. New York: Viking, 1983.

———. *Buster Keaton: The Man Who Wouldn't Lie Down*. Minneapolis: University of Minnesota Press, 2002.

Dobi, Steve. "Restoring *Nanook of the North*." *Film Library Quarterly (FLQ)* 10 (1984): 16–18.

Durgnat, Raymond. *The Crazy Mirror*. New York: Horizon, 1969.

Dwyer, Ruth Anne. *Malcolm St. Clair: His Films, 1915–1948*. Lanham, Md.: Scarecrow, 1997.

"Early Women Stars." Special issue of *Camera Obscura* 16, no. 1 (2001).

Edmonds, Andy. *Frame Up!: The Shocking Scandal That Destroyed Hollywood's Biggest Comedy Star, Roscoe "Fatty" Arbuckle*. New York: Avon, 1991.

Eyman, Scott. *Ernst Lubitsch: Laughter in Paradise*. Baltimore: Johns Hopkins University Press, 2000.

"Female Stardom and Early Film History." Special issue of *Camera Obscura* 16, no. 3 (2001).

Gardner, Jared. "Covered Wagons and Decalogues: Paramount's Myths of Origins." *Yale Journal of Criticism* 13, no. 2 (Fall 2000): 361–89.

Finler, Joel. *Stroheim*. Berkeley: University of California Press, 1968.

Geduld, Harry M. *Chaplinania*. 3 vols. Bloomington: Indiana University Press, 1987–89.

Gifford, Denis. *Chaplin*. Garden City, N.Y.: Doubleday, 1974.

Giroux, Robert. *A Deed of Death: The Story behind the Unsolved Murder of Hollywood Director William Desmond Taylor*. New York: Knopf, 1990.

Golden, Eve. *Golden Images: Forty-one Essays on Silent Film Stars*. Jefferson, N.C.: McFarland, 2001.

Gomery, Douglas. "Hollywood, the National Recovery Administration, and the Question of Monopoly Power." *Journal of the University Film Association* 31, no. 2 (Spring 1979): 47–52. Repr. with commentary, in Kindem, ed., *The American Movie Industry*, pp. 205–14.

———. "Rethinking American Film History: The Depression Decade and Monopoly Control." *Film and History* 10, no. 2 (May 1980): 32–38.

———. ed. *The Will Hays Papers, Part I: December 1921–March 1929*. Frederick, Md.: University Publications of America, 1987. Microfilm with printed guide, 43 reels.

———. "The Hollywood Studio System." In Nowell-Smith, ed., *The Oxford History of World Cinema*, pp. 43–53.

Gunning, Tom. "Thomas H. Ince, American Filmmaker." *Domitor Bulletin* 1, no. 2 (December 1986). Publication of Domitor: An International Association to Promote the Study of Early Cinema.

Hake, Sabine. *Passions and Deceptions: The Early Films of Ernst Lubitsch*. Princeton, N.J.: Princeton University Press, 1992.

Hall, Ben. *The Golden Age of the Movie Palace*. New York: Clarkson Potter, 1961.

Halsey, Stewart & Company. "The Motion Picture Industry as a Basis for Bond Financing." In Balio, ed., *The American Film Industry*, pp. 195–217.

Hampton, Benjamin. *A History of the American Film Industry*. New York: Covicin, 1931. Repr., New York: Dover, 1970.

Herndon, Booton. *Mary Pickford and Douglas Fairbanks*. New York: Norton, 1977.

Henry, Nora. *Ethics and Social Criticism in the Hollywood Films of Erich von Stroheim, Ernst Lubitsch, and Billy Wilder*. Westport, Conn.: Praeger, 2000.

Higashi, Sumiko. *Cecil B. DeMille and American Culture: The Silent Era*. Berkeley: University of California Press, 1994.

Horowitz, David A. "An Alliance of Convenience: Independent Exhibitors and Purity Crusaders Battle Hollywood, 1920–1940." *Historian* 59, no. 3 (Spring 1997): 553–72.

Hounshell, David A. *From the American System to Mass Production*. Baltimore: Johns Hopkins University Press, 1984.

Karnick, Kristine B., and Henry Jenkins, eds. *Classical Hollywood Comedy*. New York: Routledge, 1995.

Keaton, Eleanor, and Jeffrey Vance. *Buster Keaton Remembered*. New York: Abrams, 2001.

Kerr, Walter. *The Silent Clowns*. New York: Knopf, 1975.

Kindem, Gorham, ed. *The American Movie Industry: The Business of Motion Pictures*. Carbondale: Southern Illinois University Press, 1982.

Kirkpatrick, Sidney D. *A Cast of Killers*. New York: Dutton, 1986.

Knight, Arthur. *The Liveliest Art: A Panoramic History of the Movies*. Rev. ed. New York: Macmillan, 1978.

Koszarski, Richard. *The Man You Loved to Hate: Erich von Stroheim and Hollywood*. New York: Oxford University Press, 1983.

———. *An Evening's Entertainment: The Age of the Silent Feature Picture, 1915–1928*. Vol. 3 of *History of the American Cinema*. New York: Scribner's, 1990.

———. " 'Addio, maestro . . .': Von Stroheim e Griffith/'So Long, Master . . .': Stroheim, Griffith and the Griffith Studio." *Griffithiana* 24, no. 71 (2001): 44–81.

Kramer, Peter. "A Slapstick Comedian at the Crossroads: Buster Keaton, the Theater, and the Movies in 1916/17." *Theatre History Studies* 17 (1997): 133–46.

———. " 'Clean, Dependable Slapstick': Comic Violence and the Emergence of Classical Hollywood Cinema." In Slocum, ed., *Violence and American Cinema*, pp. 104–16.

Krutnick, Frank, ed. *Hollywood Comedians: the Film Reader*. London: Routledge, 2003.

Langer, Mark J. "*Tabu:* The Making of a Film." *Cinema Journal* 24, no. 3 (Spring 1985): 43–64.

Lebel, J. P. *Buster Keaton*. Cranbury, N.J.: Barnes, 1967.

Lloyd, Harold. *An American Comedy*. New York: Dover, 1971.

Louvish, Simon. *Stan and Ollie, the Roots of Comedy: The Double Life of Laurel and Hardy*. New York: St. Martin's, 2002.

Lyons, Timothy J. *The Silent Partner: The History of the American Film Manufacturing Company, 1910–1921*. New York: Arno, 1974.

McCabe, John. *Laurel and Hardy*. New York: Dutton, 1975.

McCaffrey, Donald W., ed. *Focus on Chaplin*. Engelwood Cliffs, N.J.: Prentice-Hall, 1971.

MacCann, Richard Dyer, ed. *The Silent Comedians*. Metuchen, N.J.: Scarecrow, 1993.

———. *The Silent Screen*. Metuchen, N.J.: Scarecrow, 1997.

MacGillivray, Scott. *Laurel and Hardy: From the Forties Forward*. Lanham, Md.: Vestal, 1998.

McLean, Adrienne L., and David A. Cook, eds. *Headline Hollywood: A Century of Film Scandal*. New Brunswick, N.J.: Rutgers University Press, 2001.

Maltby, Richard Dyer. "To Prevent the Prevalent Type of Book: Censorship and Adaptation in Hollywood, 1924–1934." *American Quarterly* 44, no. 4 (December 1992): 554–83.

Maltin, Leonard. "Silent Film Buffs Stalk and Find a Missing Tramp." *Smithsonian* 18, no. 4 (July 1986): 46–58.

Mast, Gerald. *The Comic Mind: Comedy and the Movies*. 2nd ed. Chicago: University of Chicago Press, 1979.

Merritt, Russell, and J.B. Kaufman. *Walt in Wonderland: The Silent Films of Walt Disney*. Pordenone, Italy: Le Giornate del cinema muto, 1993. Distributed by Johns Hopkins University Press.

Millar, Gavin. "The Unknown Chaplin." *Sight and Sound* 52, no. 2 (Spring 1983): 98–99.

Mitry, Jean. "Thomas H. Ince: His Esthetic, His Films, His Legacy." Trans. Martin Sopocy with Paul Attallah. *Cinema Journal* 22, no. 2 (Winter 1983): 2–25.

Moews, Daniel. *Keaton: The Silent Features Close Up*. Berkeley: University of California Press, 1977.

"Monographic Issue on Frank Borzage." Special issue of *Griffithiana* 15, no. 46 (December 1992).

Montgomery, John. *Comedy Films*. London: Allen & Unwin, 1986.

Murphy, William T. *Robert Flaherty: A Guide to References and Resources*. Boston: Hall, 1978.

Nelson, Richard Alan. "Before Laurel: Oliver Hardy and the Vim Comedy Company, a Studio Biography." In Austin, ed., *Current Research in Film*; II, pp. 136–55.

Nowell-Smith, Geoffrey, ed. *The Oxford History of World Cinema*. Oxford: Oxford University Press, 1996.

Oderman, Stuart. *Roscoe "Fatty" Arbuckle: A Biography of the Silent Film Comedian, 1887–1933*. Jefferson, N.C.: McFarland, 1994.

Petrie, Graham. "Fejos." *Sight and Sound* 47, no. 3 (Summer 1978): 175–77.

———. "Paul Fejos in America." *Film Quarterly* 32, no. 2 (Winter 1978–79): 28–37.

———. *Hollywood Destinies: European Directors in America, 1922–1931*. London: Routledge & Kegan Paul, 1985.

Potamianos, George. "Movie Mad: Audiences and Censorship in a California Town, 1916–1936." *Velvet Light Trap* 42 (Fall 1998): 62–75.

"Rewriting the American 1920s." Special issue of *Wide Angle* 13, no. 1 (January 1991).

Rheuban, Joyce. *Harry Langdon: The Comedian as Metteur-en-Scène*. Rutherford, N.J.: Associated University Presses, 1983.

Robinson, David. *Hollywood in the Twenties*. Cranbury, N.J.: Barnes, 1968.

———. *Buster Keaton*. Bloomington: Indiana University Press, 1969.

———. *Hollywood in the Twenties*. New York: Paperback Library, 1970.

———. *Chaplin: The Mirror of Opinion*. Bloomington: Indiana University Press, 1984.

———. *Chaplin: His Life and Art*. New York: McGraw-Hill, 1985.

Rosenbaum, Jonathan. *Greed*. London: British Film Institute, 1993.

Ross, Steven J. *Working-Class Hollywood: Silent Film and the Shaping of Class in America*. Princeton, N.J.: Princeton University Press, 1998.

Rotha, Paul. *Robert Flaherty: A Biography*. Ed. Jay Ruby. Philadelphia: University of Pennsylvania Press, 1983.

Rubinstein, E. *Filmguide to "The General."* Bloomington: Indiana University Press, 1973.

Ruby, Jay, and Larry Gross, eds. "A Reevaluation of Robert J. Flaherty, Photographer and Filmmaker." *Studies in Visual Communication* 6, no. 2 (Summer 1980): 2–4.

Sadoul, Georges. *Dictionary of Films*. Trans. and ed. Peter Morris. Berkeley: University of California Press, 1972.

Sanders, Judith, and Daniel Lieberfeld. "Dreaming in Pictures: The Childhood Origins of Buster Keaton's Creativity." *Film Quarterly* 47, no. 4 (Summer 1994): 14–28.

Schickel, Richard, and Douglas Fairbanks, Jr. *The Fairbanks Album*. Boston: New York Graphic Society, 1975.

Sennett, Mack. *King of Comedy*. Garden City, N.Y.: Doubleday, 1954.

Shull, Michael Slade. *Radicalism in American Silent Films, 1909–1929: A Filmography and History*. Jefferson, N.C.: McFarland, 2000.

Silver, Charles. "Chaplin Redux." *American Film* 9, no. 10 (September 1984): 20–23, 72.

Sinclair, Upton. *Upton Sinclair Presents William Fox*. Los Angeles: Upton Sinclair, 1933.

Slide, Anthony. *Silent Players: A Biographical and Autobiographical Study of 100 Silent Film Actors and Actresses*. Lexington: University Press of Kentucky, 2002.

Slocum, David, ed. *Violence and American Cinema*. London: Routledge, 2000.

Smith, Julian. *Chaplin*. Boston: Twayne, 1984.

Staiger, Janet. "Dividing Labor for Production Control: Thomas Ince and the Rise of the Studio System." *Cinema Journal* 18, no. 2 (Spring 1979): 16–25.

———. "Mass Produced Photoplays: Economic and Signifying Practices in the First Years of Hollywood." *Wide Angle* 4, no. 3 (Fall 1982): 12–27.

———. "The Handmaiden of Villainy: Methods and Problems in Studying the Historical Reception of a Film." *Wide Angle* 8, no. 1 (Winter 1986): 19–27.

Stempel, Tom. "The Sennett Screenplays." *Sight and Sound* 55, no. 1 (Winter 1985–86): 58–60.

Stoloff, Sam. "Fatty Arbuckle and the Black Sox: The Paranoid Style of American Popular Culture, 1919–1922." In McLean and Cook, eds., *Headline Hollywood: A Century of Film Scandal*, pp. 52–82.

Thomson, David. *Movie Man*. New York: Stein & Day, 1967.

Tibbetts, John C. "*Coquette:* Mary Pickford Finds a Voice." *Films in Review* 48, nos. 1–2 (January 1997): 61–66.

Trahair, Lisa. "Short-Circuiting the Dialectic: Narrative and Slapstick in the Cinema of Buster Keaton." *Narrative* 10, no. 3 (2002): 307–25.

Tyler, Parker. *Chaplin, Last of the Clowns*. New York: Horizon, 1972.

Vance, Jeffrey, and Suzanne Lloyd. *Harold Lloyd: Master Comedian.* New York: Abrams, 2002.

Vasey, Ruth. *The World According to Hollywood, 1918–1939.* Madison: University of Wisconsin Press, 1997.

———. "Beyond Sex and Violence: 'Industry Policy' and the Regulation of Hollywood Movies, 1922–1939." In Bernstein, ed., *Controlling Hollywood,* pp. 102–29.

Villecco, Tony. *Silent Stars Speak: Interviews with Twelve Cinema Pioneers.* Jefferson, N.C.: McFarland, 2001.

Wallace, David. *Lost Hollywood.* New York: St. Martin's, 2001.

Wasko, Janet. *Movies and Money: Financing the American Film Industry.* Norwood, N.J.: Ablex, 1982.

Wead, George. *The Film Career of Buster Keaton.* Boston: Hall, 1977.

Weinberg, Herman G. *The Lubitsch Touch.* New York: Dutton, 1971.

———. *The Complete "Greed."* New York: Dutton, 1972.

———. *Stroheim: A Pictorial Record of His Nine Films.* New York: Dover, 1975.

Weissman, Stephen M. "Charlie Chaplin's Film Heroines." *Film History* 8, no. 4 (1996): 439–45.

Whitney, Simon N. "Anti-Trust Policies and the Motion Picture Industry." In Kindem, ed., *The American Movie Industry,* pp. 161–201.

Young, Robert, Jr. *Roscoe "Fatty" Arbuckle: A Bio-Bibliography.* Westport, Conn.: Greenwood, 1994.

Media

Brownlow, Kevin, and David Gill. *The Unknown Chaplin.* Thames Television Documentary, 1985.

———. *The Unknown Keaton.* Thames Television Documentary, 1989.

The Man You Loved to Hate. Directed by Patrick Montgomery, written by Richard Koszarski. Film Profiles, Inc., 1978; Kino on Video, 1990.

CHAPTER 7. THE COMING OF SOUND AND COLOR, 1926–1935

Altman, Rick, ed. *Sound Theory/Sound Practice.* AFI Film Reader Series. New York: Routledge, 1992.

Barnouw, Erik. *Tube of Plenty.* 2nd rev. ed. New York: Oxford University Press, 1990.

Bergman, Andrew. *We're in the Money: Depression America and Its Films.* New York: New York University Press, 1971.

Bordwell, David; Kristin Thompson; and Janet Staiger. *The Classical Hollywood Cinema: Film Style and Mode of Production to 1960.* New York: Columbia University Press, 1985.

Cameron, Evan W., ed. *Sound and the Cinema: The Coming of Sound to American Film.* Pleasantville, N.Y.: Redgrave, 1980.

Chion, Michel. *Audio-Vision: Sound on Screen.* Trans. and ed. Claudia Gorbman. New York: Columbia University Press, 1994.

Clair, René. "The Art of Sound." Repr. in McCann, ed., *Film,* pp. 38–40.

"Colour Film." Special issue of *Film History* 12, no. 4 (2000).

Crafton, Donald. *The Talkies: American Cinema's Transition to Sound, 1926–1931.* Vol. 4 of *History of the American Cinema.* New York: Scribner's, 1997.

Dibbets, Karel. "The Introduction of Sound." In Nowell-Smith, ed., *The Oxford History of World Cinema,* pp. 211–19.

Eisenstein, Sergei, Vsevelod Pudovkin, and Grigori Alexandrov. "Sound and Image." Repr. in Moussinac. *Sergei Eisenstein:* 154–56.

Eyeman, Scott. *The Speed of Sound: Hollywood and the Talkie Revolution.* New York: Simon & Schuster, 1997.

Fischer, Lucy. "René Clair, *Le Million,* and the Coming of Sound." *Cinema Journal* 16, no. 2 (Spring 1977): 34–50.

———. "*Applause*: The Visual and Acoustic Landscapes." In Cameron, ed., *Sound and the Cinema,* pp. 182–210.

Fountain, Leatrice Gilbert, and John R. Maxim. *Dark Star.* New York: St. Martin's, 1985.

Geduld, Harry M. *The Birth of the Talkies: From Edison to Jolson.* Bloomington: Indiana University Press, 1975.

Gitt, Robert, and Richard Dayton. "Restoring *Becky Sharp.*" *American Cinematographer* 65, no. 10 (November 1984): 99–106.

"Global Experiments in Early Synchronous Sound." Special issue of *Film History* 11, no. 4 (1999).

Gomery, Douglas. "Economic Struggle and Hollywood Imperialism: Europe Converts to Sound." *Yale French Studies* 60 (1960): 80–93.

———. "Tri-Ergon, Tobis-Klangfilm, and the Coming of Sound." *Cinema Journal* 16, no. 1 (Fall 1976): 51–61.

———. "The Warner-Vitaphone Peril: The American Film Industry Reacts to the Innovation of Sound." *Journal of the University Film Association* 28, no. 1 (Winter 1976): 11–19. Repr. in Kindem, ed., *The American Movie Industry,* pp. 119–35.

———. "The Growth of Movie Monopolies: The Case of Balaban and Katz." *Wide Angle* 3, no. 1 (Spring 1979): 54–62.

———. "Hollywood Converts to Sound: Chaos or Order?" In Cameron, ed., *Sound and the Cinema,* pp. 24–37.

———. "Movie-Going during Hollywood's Golden Age." *North Dakota Quarterly* 51, no. 3 (Summer 1983): 36–45.

———. "The Coming of Sound: Technological Change in the

American Film Industry." In Weis and Belton eds., *Film Sound*, pp. 5–24.

Griffith, Richard. *The Movies*. Rev. ed. New York: Simon & Schuster, 1970.

Haines, Richard W. *Technicolor Movies: The History of Dye Transfer Printing*. Jefferson, N.C.: McFarland, 1993.

Higgins, Scott. "Technology and Aesthetics: Technicolor Cinematography and Design in the Late 1930s." *Film History* 11, no. 1 (1999): 55–76.

Hoffman, Charles. *Sounds for Silents*. New York: Museum of Modern Art, 1970.

Jacobs, Lewis. *The Movies as Medium*. New York: Farrar, Straus & Giroux, 1970.

Jenkins, Henry. *What Made Pistachio Nuts? Early Sound Comedy and the Vaudeville Aesthetic*. New York: Columbia University Press, 1992.

Kalmus, Herbert T., with Eleanore King Kalmus. *Mr. Technicolor*. Absecon, N.J.: MagicImage, 1993.

Kindem, Gorham. *The American Movie Industry: The Business of Motion Pictures*. Carbondale: Southern Illinois University Press, 1982.

———. "The Demise of Kinemacolor." In Kindem, ed., *The American Movie Industry*, pp. 136–45.

———. "Hollywood's Conversion to Color." In Kindem, ed., *The American Movie Industry*, pp. 146–58.

Klingender, F. D., and Stuart Legg. *Money behind the Screen: A Report Prepared on Behalf of the Screen Council*. London: Lawrence & Wishart, 1937.

Knight, Arthur. *The Liveliest Art*. Rev. ed. New York: Mentor, 1978.

Lastra, James. *Sound Technology and the American Cinema: Perception, Representation, Modernity*. New York: Columbia University Press, 2000.

Lewis, John R. "J. T. Tykociner: A Forgotten Figure in the Development of Sound." *Journal of the University Film Association* 33, no. 3 (Summer 1981): 33–40.

McCann, Richard Dyer, ed. *Film: A Montage of Theories*. New York: Dutton, 1966.

Macgowan, Kenneth. *Behind the Screen: The History and Techniques of the Motion Picture*. New York: Dell, 1985.

Marks, Martin Miller. *Music and the Silent Film: Contexts and Case Studies, 1895–1924*. New York: Oxford University Press, 1997.

Mottram, Ron. "American Sound Films, 1926–1930." In Weis and Belton, eds., *Film Sound*, pp. 221–31.

Moussinac, Léon. *Sergei Eisenstein*. Trans. D. S. Petry. New York: Crown, 1970.

Neale, Steve. *Cinema and Technology: Image, Sound, Colour*. Bloomington: Indiana University Press, 1985.

Neupert, Richard. "A Studio Built of Bricks: Disney and

Technicolor." *Film Reader 6: Investigations in Film History and Technology* (1985): 33–40.

Nowell-Smith, Geoffrey, ed. *The Oxford History of World Cinema*. Oxford: Oxford University Press, 1996.

Pudovkin, V. I. *Film Technique and Film Acting*. Trans. Ivor Montagu. London: Gollancz, 1929. Enl. ed. London: George Newnes, 1993.

Rosten, Leo C. *Hollywood: The Movie Colony, the Movie Makers*. New York: Harcourt Brace, 1941.

Rotha, Paul. *The Film till Now*. New York: Funk & Wagnalls, 1950.

Ryan, Roderick T. *A History of Motion Picture Color Technology*. New York: Focal, 1978.

Salt, Barry. "Film Style and Technology in the Thirties." *Film Quarterly* 30, no. 1 (Fall 1976): 19–32. Repr. in part as "Film Style and Technologies in the Thirties: Sound." In Weis and Belton, ed., *Film Sound*, pp. 37–43.

Salt, Barry. *Film Style and Technology: History and Analysis*. 2nd ed. London: Starword, 1992.

Sinclair, Upton. *Upton Sinclair Presents William Fox*. Los Angeles: Upton Sinclair, 1933.

Thorp, M. F. *America at the Movies*. New Haven, Conn.: Yale University Press, 1939.

Thrasher, Frederic. *Okay for Sound*. New York: Duell, Sloan & Pierce, 1964.

Van Wert, William F. "Intertitles." *Sight and Sound* 49, no. 2 (Spring 1980): 98–105.

Walker, Alexander. *The Shattered Silents: How the Talkies Came to Stay*. London: Elm Tree, 1978.

Wasko, Janet. *Movies and Money*. Norwood, N.J.: Ablex, 1982.

Weis, Elizabeth, and John Belton, eds. *Film Sound: Theory and Practice*. New York: Columbia University Press, 1985.

Media

Aux Sources des couleurs, de son et de l'animation (The Beginnings of Color, Sound and Animation). Film documentary prepared by Franz Schmitt. French State Film Archives in Bois D'Arcy, 1983.

CHAPTER 8. THE SOUND FILM AND THE AMERICAN STUDIO SYSTEM

Adair, Gene. *Alfred Hitchcock: Filming Our Fears*. New York: Oxford University Press, 2002.

Albrecht, Donald. *Designing Dreams: Modern Architecture in the Movies*. New York: Harper & Row/Museum of Modern Art, 1988.

Allen, Frederick Lewis. *Only Yesterday*. New York: Harper, 1940.

Allen, Richard, and S. Ishii Gonzalès, eds. *Alfred Hitchcock: Centenary Essays*. London: British Film Institute, 1999.

Altman, Rick. *The American Film Musical*. Bloomington: Indiana University Press, 1987.

Anderegg, Michael A. *William Wyler*. Boston: Twayne, 1979.

Arendt, Hannah. *Eichman in Jerusalem*. New York: Meridian, 1963.

Auiler, Dan. *Vertigo: The Making of a Hitchcock Classic*. New York: St. Martin's, 1998.

Auiler, Dan. *Hitchcock's Notebooks: An Authorized and Illustrated Look inside the Creative Mind of Alfred Hitchcock*. New York: Avon, 1999.

Balio, Tino. *United Artists*. Madison: University of Wisconsin Press, 1976.

———. *Grand Design: Hollywood as a Modern Business Enterprise, 1930–1939*. Vol. 5 of *History of the American Cinema*. New York: Scribner's, 1993.

Barr, Charles. "*Blackmail*: Sight and Sound." *Sight and Sound* 52, no. 2 (Spring 1983): 122–26.

———. *English Hitchcock*. Moffat, Scot.: Cameron & Hollis, 1999.

Barrios, Richard. *A Song in the Dark: The Birth of the Musical Film*. Oxford: Oxford University Press, 1995.

Barsacq, Léon. *Caligari's Cabinet and Other Grand Illusions: A History of Film Design*. Rev. and ed. Elliot Stein. New York: New American Library, 1978.

Basinger, Jeanine. *A Woman's View: How Hollywood Spoke to Women, 1930–1960*. New York: Knopf, 1993.

Baxter, John. *Hollywood in the Thirties*. Cranbury, N.J.: Barnes, 1968.

———. *The Cinema of John Ford*. London: Tantivy, 1971.

———. *The Cinema of Josef von Sternberg*. New York: Barnes, 1971.

———. "The Birth of *Venus*." *Wide Angle* 10, no. 1 (Winter 1988): 4–15.

Behlmer, Rudy, ed. *Memo from David O. Selznik*. New York: Viking, 1972.

Benchley, Nathaniel. *Bogart*. Boston: Little, Brown, 1975.

Berg, A. Scott. *Goldwyn: A Biography*. New York: Knopf, 1989.

Bernardi, Daniel, ed. *Classic Hollywood, Classic Whiteness*. Minneapolis: University of Minnesota Press, 2001.

Bernds, Edward. *Mr. Bernds Goes to Hollywood: My Early Life and Career in Sound Recording at Columbia with Frank Capra and Others*. Lanham, Md.: Scarecrow, 1999.

Bernstein, Matthew. "Hollywood's 'Arty Cinema': John Ford's *The Long Voyage Home*." *Wide Angle* 10, no. 1 (Winter 1988): 30–45.

———. *Walter Wanger, Hollywood Independent*. Berkeley: University of California Press, 1994.

Black, Gregory D. *Hollywood Censored: Morality, Codes, Catholics, and the Movies*. Cambridge, Eng.: Cambridge University Press, 1994.

Bogdanovich, Peter. *John Ford*. Berkeley: University of California Press, 1968.

———. *Who the Devil Made It: Conversations with Legendary Film Directors*. New York: Knopf, 1997.

Bogle, Donald. " 'B' . . . for Black." *Film Comment* 21, no. 5 (September–October 1985): 31–34.

———. *Toms, Coons, Mulattoes, Mammies and Bucks: An Interpretive History of Blacks in American Films*. New exp. ed. New York: Continuum, 1990.

Bona, Damien, and Mason Wiley. *Inside Oscar: An Unofficial History of the Academy Awards*. Ed. Gail MacColl. 10th anniversary ed. New York: Ballantine, 1996.

Bordwell, David; Kristin Thompson; and Janet Staiger. *The Classical Hollywood Cinema: Film Style and Mode of Production to 1960*. New York: Columbia University Press, 1985.

Bowser, Pearl, and Louise Spence. *Writing Himself into History: Oscar Micheaux, His Silent Films, and His Audiences*. New Brunswick, N.J.: Rutgers University Press, 2000.

Brill, Leslie. *The Hitchcock Romance: Love and Irony in Hitchcock's Films*. Princeton, N.J.: Princeton University Press, 1988.

Brown, Geoff. "Preston Sturges, Inventor." *Sight and Sound* 55, no. 4 (Autumn 1986): 272–77.

Brown, Royal S. "Hermann, Hitchcock, and the Music of the Irrational." *Cinema Journal* 21, no. 2 (Spring 1982): 14–49.

Buscombe, Edward. "Painting the Legend: Frederic Remington and the Western." *Cinema Journal* 23, no. 4 (Summer 1984): 12–27.

———. *Stagecoach*. London: British Film Institute, 1992.

Butters, Gerald R. *Black Manhood on the Silent Screen*. Lawrence: University Press of Kansas, 2002.

Byrge, Duane, and Robert Milton Miller. *A Critical Study of the Screwball Comedy Film*. Ann Arbor, Mich.: UMI Research Press, 1989.

Canham, Kingsley; Clive Denton; John Belton; et al. *The Hollywood Professionals*, Vols. 1–4. New York: Barnes, 1974–78.

Capra, Frank. *The Name above the Title*. New York: Bantam, 1971.

Cavell, Stanley. *Pursuits of Happiness: The Hollywood Comedy of Remarriage*. Cambridge, Mass.: Harvard University Press, 1981.

Ceplair, Larry. *A Great Lady: A Life of the Screenwriter Sonya Levien*. Lanham, Md.: Scarecrow, 1996.

CinémAction. *Dossier: Le Cinéma noir américain*. Ed. Mark Reid, Janine Euvard, Francis Bordat, and Raphael Bassan. Paris: Cerf, 1988.

Ciraulo, Dina. "Narrative Style in Oscar Micheaux's *within Our Gates*." *Wide Angle* 20, no. 4 (1998): 75–91.

Cohan, Steve, ed. *Hollywood Musicals: The Film Reader.* London: Routledge, 2002.

Cormack, Mike. *Ideology and Cinematography in Hollywood, 1930–1939.* New York: St. Martin's, 1994.

Cripps, Thomas. *Slow Fade to Black: The Negro in American Film, 1900–1942.* New York: Oxford University Press, 1977, 1993.

———. *Making Movies Black: The Hollywood Message Movie from World War II to the Civil Rights Era.* New York: Oxford University Press, 1993.

———. *Hollywood's High Noon: Moviemaking and Society before Television.* Baltimore: Johns Hopkins University Press, 1997.

Croce, Arlene. *The Fred Astaire and Ginger Rogers Book.* New York: Vintage, 1977.

Cross, Robin. *B Movies.* New York: St. Martin's, 1981.

Curtis, James. *Between Flops: A Biography of Preston Sturges.* New York: Harcourt Brace, 1982.

Custen, George F. *Twentieth Century's Fox: Darryl F. Zanuck and the Culture of Hollywood.* New York: Basic, 1997.

Cywinski, Ray. *Preston Sturges: A Guide to References and Resources.* Boston: Hall, 1984.

Danly, Linda, ed. *Hugo Friedhofer, the Best Years of His Life: A Hollywood Master of Music for the Movies.* Lanham, Md.: Scarecrow, 1999.

Davis, Ronald L. *John Ford: Hollywood's Old Master.* Norman: University of Oklahoma Press, 1995.

Deutelbaum, Marshall, and Leland Pogue, eds. *A Hitchcock Reader.* Ames: Iowa State University Press, 1986.

Diawara, Manthia, ed. *Black American Cinema.* AFI Film Readers Series. New York: Routledge, 1993.

Dick, Bernard F. *The Merchant Prince of Poverty Row: Harry Cohn of Columbia Pictures.* Lexington: University Press of Kentucky, 1993.

———. *City of Dreams: The Making and Remaking of Universal Pictures.* Lexington: University Press of Kentucky, 1997.

———. *Engulfed: The Death of Paramount Pictures and the Birth of Corporate Hollywood.* Lexington: University Press of Kentucky, 2001.

Dickos, Andrew. *Intrepid Laughter: Preston Sturges and the Movies.* Metuchen, N.J.: Scarecrow, 1985.

Dixon, Wheeler. *The "B" Directors: A Biographical Dictionary.* Metuchen, N.J.: Scarecrow, 1985.

———. *Producers Releasing Corporation: A Comprehensive Filmography and History.* Jefferson, N.C.: McFarland, 1986.

Durgnat, Raymond. *The Strange Case of Alfred Hitchcock.* Cambridge, Mass.: MIT Press, 1974.

———. *A Long Hard Look at "Psycho."* London: British Film Institute, 2002.

Eames, John D. *The MGM Story: The Complete Story of Fifty Roaring Years.* New York: Crown, 1964.

Erens, Patricia. *The Jew in American Cinema.* Bloomington: Indiana University Press, 1984.

Fernett, Gene. *Poverty Row.* Satellite Beach, Fla.: Coral Reef, 1973.

———. *American Film Studios: An Historical Encyclopedia.* Jefferson, N.C.: McFarland, 1988.

Feuer, Jane. *The Hollywood Musical.* 2nd ed. Bloomington: Indiana University Press, 1993.

Fielding, Raymond. *The March of Time.* New York: Oxford University Press, 1978.

Finch, Christopher. *The Art of Walt Disney.* New York: Abrams, 1975.

Findler, Joel W. *Hitchcock in Hollywood.* New York: Continuum, 1992.

Ford, Dan. *Pappy: The Life of John Ford.* Englewood Cliffs, N.J.: Prentice-Hall, 1979.

French, Warren. *Filmguide to "The Grapes of Wrath."* Bloomington: Indiana University Press, 1973.

Friedman, Lester D. *Hollywood's Image of the Jew.* New York: Ungar, 1982.

Gabler, Neal. *An Empire of Their Own: How the Jews Invented Hollywood.* New York: Crown, 1988.

Gaines, Jane M. *Fire and Desire: Mixed-Race Movies in the Silent Era.* Chicago: University of Chicago Press, 2001.

Gallagher, Tag. *John Ford: The Man and His Films.* Berkeley: University of California Press, 1986.

Garncarz, Joseph. "German Hitchcock." Trans. Annemone Ligensa. *Hitchcock Annual* (2000–1): 73–79.

Gehring, Wes D. *Screwball Comedy: A Genre of Madcap Romance.* Westport, Conn.: Greenwood, 1986.

Girgus, Sam B. *Hollywood Renaissance: The Cinema of Democracy in the Time of Ford, Capra, and Kazan.* Cambridge, Eng.: Cambridge University Press, 1998.

Glancy, Mark. *The 39 Steps.* London: Tauris, 2002.

Glatner, Richard, ed. *Frank Capra.* Ann Arbor: University of Michigan Press, 1975.

Goldberg, Judith N. *Laughter through Tears: The Yiddish Cinema.* Rutherford, N.J.: Fairleigh Dickinson University Press, 1983.

Goldman, Eric A. *Visions, Images, and Dreams: Yiddish Film Past and Present.* Ann Arbor, Mich.: UMI Research Press, 1983.

Gomery, Douglas. *The Hollywood Studio System.* New York: St. Martin's 1986.

Gottlieb, Sidney, ed. *Hitchcock on Hitchcock: Selected Writings and Interviews.* London: Faber & Faber, 1995.

———. "Early Hitchcock: The German Influence." *Hitchcock Annual* (1999–2000): 100–130.

————, ed. *Alfred Hitchcock: Interviews*. Jackson: University Press of Mississippi, 2003.

Gottlieb, Sidney, and Christopher Bookhouse, eds. *Framing Hitchcock: Selected Essays from the Hitchcock Annual*. Detroit: Wayne State University Press, 2002.

Griffin, Sean. "The Gang's All Here: Generic versus racial Integration in the 1940s Musical." *Cinema Journal* 42, no. 1 (Fall 2002): 21–45.

Grupenhoff, Richard. "The Rediscovery of Oscar Micheaux: Black Film Pioneer." *Journal of Film and Video* 40, no. 1 (Winter 1988): 40–48.

Halliwell, Leslie. *Mountain of Dreams: The Golden Years of Paramount Pictures*. New York: Stonehill, 1976.

Hambley, John, and Patrick Downing. "Fifty Years of Art Direction." In *The Art of Hollywood*. London: Victoria & Albert Museum, 1979. Thames Television program guide.

Harris, Robert A. *The Films of Alfred Hitchcock*. Rev. ed. New York: Citadel, 2002.

Harvey, James. *Romantic Comedy in Hollywood, from Lubitsch to Sturges*. New York: Knopf, 1987.

Haver, Ronald. "A Star Is Born Again." *American Film* 8, no. 9 (July–August 1983): 28–33, 59.

————. "Trail Blazing." *American Film* 11, no 7 (May 1986): 17–19.

Haydock, Ron. *Deerstalker! Holmes and Watson on the Screen*. Metuchen, N.J.: Scarecrow, 1978.

Henderson, Brian. "Sturges at Work." *Film Quarterly* 39, no. 2 (Winter 1985–86): 16–28.

Higham, Charles. *Hollywood Cameramen*. Bloomington: Indiana University Press, 1970.

————. *Warner Brothers: A History of the Studio*. New York: Scribner's, 1975.

Hillier, Jim, and Peter Wollen. *Howard Hawks: American Artist*. London: British Film Institute, 1997.

Hirschhorn, Clive. *The Warner Brothers Story*. New York: Crown, 1979.

"Hitchcock/Bellour." Special issue of *Camera Obscura* 3–4 (1979).

Hoberman, J. *Bridge of Light: Yiddish Film between Two Worlds*. New York: Museum of Modern Art/Schocken, 1991.

hooks, bell. *Black Looks: Race and Representation*. Boston: South End Press, 1992.

Hurst, Richard Maurice. *Republic Studios: Between Poverty Row and the Majors*. Metuchen, N.J.: Scarecrow, 1979.

Izod, John. *Hollywood and the Box Office, 1895–1986*. New York: Columbia University Press, 1988.

Jacobs, Diane. *Christmas in July: The Life and Art of Preston Sturges*. Berkeley: University of California Press, 1992.

Jacobs, Lea. *The Wages of Sin: Censorship and the Fallen Woman Film, 1928–1942*. Madison: University of Wisconsin Press, 1991.

Jacobs, Lea, and Richard de Cordova. "Spectacle and Narrative Theory." *Quarterly Review of Film Studies* 7, no. 4 (Fall 1982): 293–307.

Jacobs, Lewis. *The Rise of the American Film*. New York: Harcourt Brace, 1939. Repr. New York: Teachers College Press, 1968.

Jones, G. William. *Black Cinema Treasures: Lost and Found*. Denton: University of North Texas Press, 1991, 1997.

Kapsis, Robert E. *Hitchcock: The Making of a Reputation*. Chicago: University of Chicago Press, 1992.

Karnick, Kristine Brunovska, and Henry Jenkins, eds. *Classical Hollywood Comedy*. AFI Film Readers Series. New York: Routledge, 1994 (dated 1995).

Kawin, Bruce. *Faulkner and Film*. New York: Ungar, 1977.

————. Introduction to *To Have and Have Not* by Jules Furthman et al. Warner Bros. Screenplay Series. Madison: University of Wisconsin Press, 1980.

Kehr, Dave. "Hitch's Riddle." *Film Comment* 20, no. 3 (May–June 1984): 9–18.

Kempton, Murray. *Part of Our Time: Some Monuments and Ruins of the Thirties*. New York: Simon & Schuster, 1955.

Kisch, John, and Edward Mapp. *A Separate Cinema: Fifty Years of Black-Cast Posters*. New York: Farrar, Straus & Giroux, 1992.

Klingender, F. D., and Stuart Legg. *Money behind the Screen*. London: Lawrence & Wishart, 1937.

Knight, Arthur. *Disintegrating the Musical: Black Performance and American Musical Film*. Durham, N.C.: Duke University Press, 2002.

Koppes, Clayton R., and Gregory D. Black. *Hollywood Goes to War*. New York: Free Press, 1987.

Koszarski, Richard. *Hollywood Directors, 1914–1940*. New York: Oxford University Press, 1976.

Krohn, Bill. "Kings of the B's." *Film Comment* 19, no. 4 (July–August 1983): 60–64.

Lambert, Gavin. *On Cukor*. New York: Capricorn, 1973.

Lasky, Betty. *RKO: The Biggest Little Major of Them All*. Englewood Cliffs, N.J.: Prentice-Hall, 1984.

LaValley, Albert, ed. *Focus on Hitchcock*. Englewood Cliffs, N.J.: Prentice-Hall, 1972.

Leff, Leonard J. *Hitchcock and Selznick: The Rich and Strange Collaboration of Alfred Hitchcock and David O. Selznick in Hollywood*. New York: Weidenfeld & Nicholson, 1987.

Leff, Leonard J., and Jerold L. Simmons. *The Dame in the Kimono: Hollywood, Censorship, and the Production Code from the 1920s to the 1960s*. New York: Grove Weidenfeld, 1990.

Levy, Emanuel. *And the Winner Is . . . : The History and Politics of the Oscar Awards*. New York: Ungar, 1987.

———. *George Cukor, Master of Elegance*. New York: Morrow, 1994.

Leyda, Julia. "Black-Audience Westerns and the Politics of Cultural Identification in the 1930s." *Cinema Journal* 42, no. 1 (Fall 2002): 46–70.

Liebman, Roy. *From Silents to Sound: A Biographical Encyclopedia of Performers Who Made the Transition to Talking Pictures*. Jefferson, N.C.: McFarland, 1998.

Long, Robert Emmet, ed. *George Cukor: Interviews*. Jackson: University Press of Mississippi, 2001.

Lourie, Eugene. *My Work in Films*. New York: Harcourt Brace, 1985.

Lupack, Barbara Tepa. *Literary Adaptations in Black American Cinema: From Micheaux to Morrison*. Rochester: University of Rochester Press, 2002.

MacAdams, William. *Ben Hecht: The Man behind the Legend*. New York: Scribner's, 1990.

McBride, Joseph, ed. *Focus on Howard Hawks*. Englewood Cliffs, N.J.: Prentice-Hall, 1972.

McBride, Joseph, and Michael Wilmington. *John Ford*. New York: Da Capo, 1975.

McCarthy, Todd. "Phantom Hawks." *Film Comment* 18, no. 5 (September–October 1982): 63–76.

———. *Howard Hawks: The Grey Fox of Hollywood*. New York: Grove, 1997.

McCarthy, Todd, and Charles Flynn, eds. *Kings of the B's: Working within the Hollywood System*. New York: Dutton, 1975.

McCarty, John, and Brian Kelleher. *Alfred Hitchcock Presents: An Illustrated Guide to the Ten Year Television Career of the Master of Suspense*. New York: St. Martin's, 1985.

McDonald, Paul. *The Star System: Hollywood's Production of Popular Identities*. London: Wallflower, 2000.

Madsen, Axel. *William Wyler*. New York: Crowell, 1973.

Maltby, Richard. "The Genesis of the Production Code." *Quarterly Review of Film and Video* 15, no. 4 (March 1995): 5–63.

———. "The Spectacle of Criminality." In Slocum, ed., *Violence and American Cinema*, pp. 118–52.

Mandelbaum, Howard, and Eric Myers. *Screen Deco: A Celebration of High Style in Hollywood*. New York: St. Martin's, 1985.

Marx, Arthur. *Goldwyn*. New York: Norton, 1976.

Marx, Samuel. *Mayer and Thalberg*. New York: Random House, 1975.

Mast, Gerald. *Howard Hawks, Storyteller*. New York: Oxford University Press, 1982.

———. Introduction to *Bringing up Baby*. Ed. Gerald Mast.

Rutgers Films in Print, vol. 10. New Brunswick, N.J.: Rutgers University Press, 1988.

Mast, Gerald; Marshall Cohen; and Leo Braudy, eds. *Film Theory and Criticism*. 5th ed. New York: Oxford University Press, 1999.

Maurice, Alice. "Cinema at Its Source: Synchronizing Race and Sound in the Early Talkies." *Camera Obscura* 17, no. 1 (2002): 31–71.

Mayne, Judith. *Directed by Dorothy Arzner*. Bloomington: Indiana University Press, 1994.

Miller, Don. *"B" Movies*. New York: Curtis, 1973.

Milne, Tom. *Rouben Mamoulian*. London: Thames & Hudson, 1969.

Modleski, Tania. *The Women Who Knew Too Much: Hitchcock and Feminist Theory*. New York: Methuen, 1988.

Moley, Raymond. *The Hays Office*. Indianapolis: Bobbs-Merrill, 1945.

Moorhead, Caroline. *Sidney Bernstein, a Biography*. London: Jonathan Cape, 1984.

Morris, Christopher D. *The Hanging Figure: On Suspense and the Films of Alfred Hitchcock*. Westport, Conn.: Greenwood, 2002.

Mulvey, Laura. "Visual Pleasure and Narrative Cinema." *Screen* 16, no. 3 (1975): 6–18. Repr. in Mast, Cohen, and Braudy, eds., *Film Theory and Criticism*, pp. 746–57.

Munby, Jonathan. *Screening the Gangster from "Little Caesar" to "Touch of Evil."* Chicago: University of Chicago Press, 1999.

Musser, Charles; Pearl Bowser; and Jane Gaines, eds. *Oscar Micheaux and His Circle: African-American Filmmaking and Race Cinema of the Silent Era*. Bloomington: Indiana University Press, 2001.

Naremore, James. *Filmguide to "Psycho."* Bloomington: Indiana University Press, 1973.

Nevins, Francis M. *Joseph H. Lewis: Overview, Interview, and Filmography*. Lanham, Md.: Scarecrow, 1998.

Nichols, Bill, ed. *Movies and Methods*. Vol. 2. Berkeley: University of California Press, 1985.

Nochimson, Martha P. *Screen Couple Chemistry: The Power of 2*. Austin: University of Texas Press, 2002.

Null, Gary. *Black Hollywood: The Black Performer in Motion Pictures*. New York: Citadel, 1975, 1990.

O'Connor, John E. "A Reaffirmation of American Ideas: *Drums along the Mohawk* (1939)." In O'Connor and Jackson, eds., *American History/American Film*, pp. 97–120.

O'Connor, John E., and Martin A. Jackson, eds. *American History/American Film: Interpreting the Hollywood Image*. New exp. ed. New York: Ungar, 1988.

Parish, James R. *The Golden Era: The MGM Stock Company*. New Rochelle, N.Y.: Arlington House, 1974.

————. *The Great Gangster Pictures*. Metuchen, N.J.: Scarecrow, 1976.

Paul, William. *Ernst Lubitsch's American Comedy*. New York: Columbia University Press, 1983.

Peary, Gerald, and Jenny Lefcourt, eds. *John Ford: Interviews*. Jackson: University Press of Mississippi, 2001.

Perlman, William. *The Movies on Trial*. New York: Macmillan, 1936.

Perry, George. *The Films of Alfred Hitchcock*. New York: Dutton, 1965.

Pitts, Michael R. *Poverty Row Studios, 1929–1940: An Illustrated History of 53 Independent Film Companies, with a Filmography for Each*. Jefferson, N.C.: McFarland, 1997.

Pohle, Robert W., and Douglas C. Hart. *Sherlock Holmes on the Screen: The Motion Picture Adventures of the World's Most Popular Detective*. South Brunswick, N.J.: Barnes, 1977.

Register, Charlene. "Lynched, Assaulted, and Intimidated: Oscar Micheaux's Most Controversial Films." *Popular Culture Review* 5, no. 1 (February 1994): 47–55.

Reid, Mark A. *Redefining Black Film*. Berkeley: University of California Press, 1993.

Richards, Jeffrey. *Visions of Yesterday*. London: Routledge, 1973.

Robinson, David. *Hollywood in the Twenties*. Cranbury, N.J.: Barnes, 1968.

————. *The History of World Cinema*. 2nd ed. New York: Stein & Day, 1981.

Roddick, Nick. *A New Deal in Entertainment: Warner Brothers in the 1930s*. London: British Film Institute, 1983.

Rohmer, Eric, and Claude Chabrol. *Hitchcock: The First Forty-four Films*. Trans. and ed. Stanly Hochman. New York: Ungar, 1979.

Rosow, Eugene. *Born to Lose: The Gangster Film in America*. New York: Oxford University Press, 1978.

Rothman, William. *Hitchcock—the Murderous Gaze*. Cambridge, Mass.: Harvard University Press, 1982.

Rubenstein, Elliot. "The Home Fries: Aspects of Sturges' Wartime Comedy." *Quarterly Review of Film Studies* 7, no. 2 (Spring 1982): 131–41.

Rubin, Martin. *Showstoppers: Busby Berkeley and the Tradition of Spectacle*. New York: Columbia University Press, 1994.

Ryall, Tom. *Alfred Hitchcock and the British Cinema*. Urbana: University of Illinois Press, 1986.

————. *Blackmail*. London: British Film Institute, 1993.

Sadoul, Georges. *Dictionary of Film Makers*. Trans. and ed. Peter Morris. Berkeley: University of California Press, 1972.

Sampson, Henry T. *Blacks in Black and White: A Source Book on Black Films*. 2nd ed. Metuchen, N.J.: Scarecrow, 1995.

Sarris, Andrew. *The Films of Josef von Sternberg*. New York: Museum of Modern Art, 1966.

————. *The American Cinema*. New York: Dutton, 1968.

————. *The John Ford Movie Mystery*. Bloomington: Indiana University Press, 1975.

————. "The Importance of Winning Oscar." *Film Comment* 15, no. 2 (March–April 1979): 53–56.

————. *"You Ain't Heard Nothin' Yet": The American Talking Film—History and Memory, 1927–1949*. New York: Oxford University Press, 1998.

Schatz, Thomas. *The Genius of the System: Hollywood Filmmaking in the Studio Era*. New York: Pantheon, 1988.

————. " 'A Triumph of Bitchery': Warner Bros., Bette Davis and *Jezebel*." *Wide Angle* 10, no. 1 (Winter 1988): 16–29.

————. *Boom to Bust: American Cinema in the 40s*. Vol. 6 of *History of the American Cinema*. New York: Scribner's, 1997.

Schikel, Richard. *The Disney Version*. New York: Simon & Schuster, 1968.

Seale, Paul. " 'A Host of Others': Poverty Row and the Coming of Sound." *Wide Angle* 13, no. 1 (January 1991): 72–98.

Sennett, Robert S. *Setting the Scene: The Great Hollywood Art Directors*. New York: Abrams, 1994.

Sennett, Ted. *Warner Brothers Presents*. New Rochelle, N.Y.: Arlington House, 1971.

Shindler, Colin. *Hollywood Goes to War: Films and American Society, 1939–1952*. London: Routledge & Keegan Paul, 1979.

————. *Hollywood in Crisis: Cinema and American Society, 1929–1939*. London: Routledge, 1996.

Sinclair, Andrew. *John Ford*. New York: Dial/James Wade, 1979.

Sklar, Robert. *Movie-Made America: A Cultural History of the American Movies*. Rev. ed. New York: Vintage, 1994.

Sklar, Robert, and Vito Zagarrio, eds. *Frank Capra: Authorship and the Studio System*. Philadelphia: Temple University Press, 1998.

Slocum, J. David, ed. *Violence and American Cinema*. London: Routledge, 2000.

Spergel, Mark. *Reinventing Reality: The Art and Life of Rouben Mamoulian*. Metuchen, N.J.: Scarecrow, 1993.

Spoto, Donald. *The Art of Alfred Hitchcock: Fifty Years of His Motion Pictures*. New York: Hopkinson & Blake, 1976.

————. *The Dark Side of Genius: The Life of Alfred Hitchcock*. Boston: Little, Brown, 1983.

————. *Madcap: The Life of Preston Sturges*. Boston: Little, Brown, 1990.

Staiger, Janet, ed. *The Studio System*. New Brunswick, N.J.: Rutgers University Press, 1995.

Steinbrunner, Chris, and Norman Michaels. *The Films of Sherlock Holmes*. Secaucus, N.J.: Citadel, 1978.

Stempel, Tom. *Framework: A History of Screenwriting in the American Film*. New York: Continuum, 1988.

Sternberg, Josef von. *Fun in a Chinese Laundry*. London: Secker & Warburg, 1965.

Studlar, Gaylyn. "Masochism and the Perverse Pleasures of the Cinema." *Quarterly Review of Film Studies* 9, no. 4 (Fall 1984): 267–82. Repr. in Nichols, ed., *Movies and Methods*, vol. 2, pp. 602–21, and in Mast, Cohen, and Braudy, eds., *Film Theory and Criticism*, pp. 773–90.

———. "Visual Pleasure and the Masochistic Aesthetic." *Journal of Film and Video* 37, no. 2 (Spring 1985): 5–26.

———. *In the Realm of Pleasure: Von Sternberg, Dietrich, and the Masochistic Aesthetic*. Urbana: University of Illinois Press, 1988.

Sturges, Preston. *Five Screenplays by Preston Sturges*. Ed. Brian Henderson. Berkeley: University of California Press, 1985.

Suid, Lawrence Howard. Introduction to *Air Force* by Dudley Nichols et al. Warner Bros. Screenplay Series. Madison: University of Wisconsin Press, 1983.

Sussex, Elizabeth. "The Fate of F3080." *Sight and Sound* 53, no. 2 (Spring 1984): 92–97.

Taves, Brian. *The Romance of Adventure: The Genre of Historical Adventure Movies*. Jackson: University Press of Mississippi, 1993.

Taylor, John Russell. *Hitch: The Life and Times of Alfred Hitchcock*. New York: Pantheon, 1978.

Thomas, Bob. *Walt Disney*. New York: Simon & Schuster, 1976.

Thomas, Tony. *The Busby Berkeley Book*. Greenwich, Conn.: New York Graphic Society, 1969.

———. *Howard Hughes in Hollywood*. Secaucus, N.J.: Citadel, 1985.

Thomas, Tony, and Aubrey Solomon. *The Films of 20th Century–Fox: A Pictorial History*. Secaucus, N.J.: Citadel, 1979.

Thomson, David. *Movie Man*. New York: Stein & Day, 1967.

———. "The Big Hitch." *Film Comment* 15, no. 2 (March–April 1979): 26–29.

———. *Showman: The Life of David O. Selznick*. New York: Knopf, 1992.

Truffaut, François, with Helen G. Scott. *Hitchcock*. Rev. ed. New York: Simon & Schuster, 1984.

Tuska, Jon, ed. *Close-Up: The Contract Director*. Metuchen, N.J.: Scarecrow, 1976.

———, ed. *Close-Up: The Hollywood Director*. Metuchen, N.J.: Scarecrow, 1978.

———. *The Vanishing Legion: A History of Mascot Pictures, 1927–1935*. Jefferson, N.C.: McFarland, 1982.

Vasey, Ruth. *The World According to Hollywood, 1918–1939*. Madison: University of Wisconsin Press, 1997.

Vered, Karen Orr, "White and Black in Black and White:

Management of Race and Sexuality in the Coupling of Child-Star Shirley Temple and Bill Robinson." *Velvet Light Trap* 39 (Spring 1997): 52–65.

Vidor, King. *On Film Making*. New York: David McKay, 1972.

Wallace, David. *Lost Hollywood*. New York: St. Martin's, 2001.

Warshow, Robert. "The Gangster as Tragic Hero." In Warshow, *The Immediate Experience*, pp. 127–33.

———. *The Immediate Experience: Movies, Comics, Theatre and Other Aspects of Popular Culture*. Garden City, N.Y.: Doubleday, 1962. Enl. ed., Cambridge, Mass.: Harvard University Press, 2001.

Weinberg, Herman G. *Josef von Sternberg*. New York: Dutton, 1967.

Willis, Donald C. *The Films of Frank Capra*. Metuchen, N.J.: Scarecrow, 1974.

———. *The Films of Howard Hawks*. Metuchen, N.J.: Scarecrow, 1975.

Wollstein, Hans J. *Vixens, Floozies, and Molls: Twenty-eight Actresses of Late 1920s and 1930s Hollywood*. Jefferson, N.C.: McFarland, 1999.

———. *Howard Hawks*. Garden City, N.Y.: Doubleday, 1968.

Wood, Robin. *Hitchcock's Films*. Cranbury, N.J.: Barnes, 1969.

———. "Fear of Spying." *American Film* 7, no. 1 (November 1983): 28–35.

Yacowar, Maurice. *Hitchcock's British Films*. Hamden, Conn.: Archon, 1977.

Media

Cram, Bestor, and Pearl Bowser. *Midnight Ramble: Oscar Michaux and the Story of Race Movies*. USA, A Northern Lights Production for *The American Experience*, 1984.

Karel, Russ. *Almonds and Raisins*. England, A Book Productions and Willowgold Production, London, 1984. Yiddish cinema.

Kochenrath, Hans Peter. *Das Jiddische Kino*. West Germany, ZDF, Cologne, 1983. Yiddish cinema.

CHAPTER 9. EUROPE IN THE THIRTIES

Abel, Richard. "Charge and Counter-Charge: Coherence and Incoherence in Gance's *Napoleon*." *Film Quarterly* 35, no. 3 (Spring 1982): 2–14.

———. "Abel Gance's Other Neglected Masterwork: *La Roue* (1922–23)." *Cinema Journal* 22, no. 3 (Winter 1983): 26–41.

———. *French Cinema: The First Wave, 1915–1929*. Princeton, N.J.: Princeton University Press, 1984.

———. *French Film Theory and Criticism*. 2 vols. Princeton, N.J.: Princeton University Press, 1993.

Aitken, Ian, *Film and Reform: John Grierson and the Documentary Film Movement*. London: Routledge, 1990.

———, ed. *The Documentary Film Movement: An Anthology.* Edinburgh: Edinburgh University Press, 1998.

———. *Alberto Cavalcanti: Realism, Surrealism and National Cinemas.* Trowbridge, Eng.: Flicks, 2001.

———. "The British Documentary Film Movement." In Murphy, ed., *The British Cinema Book*, pp. 61–67.

———. *European Film Theory and Cinema.* Edinburgh: Edinburgh University Press, 2001.

Aldgate, Anthony, and Jeffrey Richards. *Best of British: Cinema and Society from 1930 to the Present.* Rev. ed. London: Tauris, 1999.

Andrew, J. Dudley. "Sound in France: The Origins of a Native School." *Yale French Studies: Cinema/Sound* 60 (1980): 94–114. Repr. in Bandy, ed., *Rediscovering French Film*, pp. 57–65.

———. "Poetic Realism." In Bandy, ed., *Rediscovering French Film*, pp. 115–19.

———. *Mists of Regret: Culture and Sensibility in Classic French Film.* Princeton, N.J.: Princeton University Press, 1995.

Ashby, Justine, and Andrew Higson, eds. *British Cinema, Past and Present.* London: Routledge, 2000.

Babitsky, Paul, and John Rimberg. *The Soviet Film Industry.* New York: Praeger, 1955.

Backemeyer, Silvia, ed. *The Silent Screen: German Film Posters from the Central Saint Martins Museum & Study Collection.* London: Central Saint Martins College of Art & Design, 1999.

Baillieu, Bill and John Goodchild. *The British Film Business.* West Sussex, Eng. Wiley, 2002.

Balcon, Michael. *Twenty Years of British Film.* London: Falcon, 1947.

Balter, L. "*Alexander Nevsky.*" *Film Culture* 70–71 (1983): 43–87.

Bamford, Kenton. *Distorted Images: British National Identity and Film in the 1920s.* London: Tauris, 1999.

Bandy, Mary Lea, ed. *Rediscovering French Film.* New York: Museum of Modern Art, 1983.

Barkhausen, Hans. "Footnote to the History of Riefenstahl's *Olympia.*" *Film Quarterly* 28, no. 1 (Fall 1974): 8–12.

Barsacq, Léon. *Caligari's Cabinet and Other Grand Illusions: A History of Film Design.* New York: New American Library, 1976, 1978.

Baxter, John. *The Hollywood Exiles.* New York: Taplinger, 1976. European émigrés in Hollywood.

Bazin, André. *Jean Renoir.* Trans. W. W. Halsey II and William H. Simon. Ed. François Truffaut. New York: Simon & Schuster, 1973.

Bergfelder, Tim; Deniz Göktürk; and Erica Carter, eds. *The German Cinema Book.* London: British Film Institute, 2003.

Bernstein, Matthew. "Fritz Lang, Incorporated." *Velvet Light Trap* 22 (1986): 33–52.

Berry, David. *Wales and Cinema: The First Hundred Years.* Cardiff: University of Wales Press/Wales Film Council/British Film Institute, 1994.

Biggers, Jeff. "*Que Viva Mexico!*: The Folly of Upton Sinclair and Sergei Eisenstein." *Brick* 65–66 (Fall 2000): 142–52.

Birkos, Alexander S. *Soviet Cinema: Directors and Films.* Hamden, Conn.: Archon, 1976.

Blakeway, Claire. *Jacques Prévert: Popular French Theater and Cinema.* Rutherford, N.J.: Associated University Presses, 1990.

Borde, Raymond. " 'The Golden Age': French Cinema of the '30's." In Bandy, ed., *Rediscovering French Film*, pp. 67–81.

Bordwell, David. *Filmguide to "La Passion de Jeanne d'Arc."* Bloomington: Indiana University Press, 1973.

———. *The Films of Carl-Theodor Dreyer.* Berkeley: University of California Press, 1981.

Bourne, Stephen. *Brief Encounters: Lesbians and Gays in British Cinema, 1930–1977.* London: Cassell, 1996.

———. *Black in the British Frame: Black People in British Film and Television, 1896–1996.* London: Cassell, 1998.

Braudy, Leo. *Jean Renoir.* Garden City, N.Y.: Doubleday, 1972.

Brown, Geoff, and Laurence Kardish. *Michael Balcon: The Pursuit of British Cinema.* New York: Museum of Modern Art, 1984.

Brownlow, Kevin. *The Parade's Gone By.* New York: Knopf, 1967, 1968.

———. "Abel Gance's Epic *Napoleon* Returns from Exile." *American Film* 6, no. 1 (January–February 1981): 28–31, 68–72.

———. *Napoleon: Abel Gance's Classic Film.* New York: Knopf, 1983.

———. "The Glory That Was France." *Sight and Sound* 56, no. 3 (Summer 1987): 204–9.

Bruno, Giuliana. *Streetwalking on a Ruined Map: Cultural Theory and the City Films of Elvira Notari.* Princeton, N.J.: Princeton University Press, 1993.

Buchsbaum, Jonathan. "Vote for the Front Populaire! Vote Commiste! *La Vie est à nous.*" *Quarterly Review of Film Studies* 10, no. 3 (Summer 1985): 184–212.

———. "Toward Victory: Left Film in France, 1930–35." *Cinema Journal* 25, no. 3 (Spring 1986): 25–52.

———. *Cinema Engagé: Film in the Popular Front.* Urbana: University of Illinois Press, 1988.

———. "Left Political Filmmaking in the West: The Interwar years." In Sklar and Musser, eds., *Resisting Images*, pp. 126–48.

Burrows, Elaine; Janet Moat; David Sharp; and Linda Wood,

eds. *The British Cinema Source Book: BFI Viewing Copies and Library Materials*. London: British Film Institute, 1995.

Burrows, Jon. "Big Studio Production in the Pre-Quota Years." In Murphy, ed., *The British Cinema Book*, pp. 20–27.

Christie, Ian, and David Elliott, eds. *Eisenstein at Ninety*. Oxford: Museum of Modern Art, 1988.

Cook, Pamela, ed. *Gainsborough Pictures*. London: Cassell, 1997.

Crisp, Colin. *The Classic French Cinema, 1930–1960*. Bloomington: Indiana University Press, 1993.

Crisp, Colin. *Genre, Myth, and Convention in the French Cinema, 1929–1939*. Bloomington: Indiana University Press, 2002.

Culbert, David, ed. *"Triumph of the Will": A Documentary History*. Frederick, Md.: University Publications of America, 1987.

Curran, James, and Vincent Porter, eds. *British Cinema History*. Totowa, N.J.: Barnes & Noble, 1983.

Dacre, Richard. "Traditions of British Comedy." In Murphy, ed., *The British Cinema Book*, pp. 233–40.

Dickinson, Margaret, and Sarah Street. *Cinema and State: The Film Industry and the Government, 1927–1984*. London: British Film Institute, 1985.

Dimendberg, Edward. "From Berlin to Bunker Hill: Urban Space, Late Modernity and Film Noir in Fritz Lang's and Joseph Losey's *M*" *Wide Angle* 19, no. 4 (1997): 63–93.

Dixon, Wheeler Winston, ed. *Re-Viewing British Cinema, 1900–1992: Essays and Interviews*. Albany: State University of New York Press, 1994.

Downing, Taylor. *Olympia*. London: British Film Institute, 1992.

Drew, William M. "Abel Gance: Prometheus Bound." *Take One* 6, no. 8 (July 1978): 30–32, 45.

Drum, Jean, and Dale D. Drum. *My Only Great Passion: The Life and Films of Carl Th. Dreyer*. Lanham, Md.: Scarecrow, 2000.

Durgnat, Raymond. *Jean Renoir*. Berkeley: University of California Press, 1975.

Dyer, Richard, and Ginette Vincendeau. *Popular European Cinema*. London: Routledge, 1992.

Eaton, Katherine Bliss, ed. *Enemies of the People: The Destruction of the Soviet Literary, Theater, and Film Arts in the 1930s*. Evanston: Northwestern University Press, 2002.

Eisenstein, Sergei. *Immoral Memories: An Autobiography*. Trans. Herbert Marshall. Boston: Houghton Mifflin, 1983.

———. *Nonindifferent Nature*. Trans. Herbert Marshall. Cambridge, Eng.: Cambridge University Press, 1987.

———. *S. M. Eisenstein: Selected Works*. Vol. I: *Writings*

1922–1934. Trans. and ed. Richard Taylor. London: British Film Institute, 1988.

———. *S. M. Eisenstein: Selected Works*. Vol. III: *Writings, 1934–1947*. Trans. and ed. Richard Taylor. London: British Film Institute, 1996.

Eisner, Lotte. *Fritz Lang*. London: Secker & Warburg, 1976.

Ellis, Jack C. "Changing of the Guard: From the Grierson Documentary to Free Cinema," *Quarterly Review of Film Studies* 7, no. 1 (Winter 1982): 23–35.

———. "The Final Years of British Documentary as the Grierson Movement." *Journal of Film and Video* 34 (Fall 1984): 41–48.

———. *John Grierson: Life, Contributions, Influence*. Carbondale: Southern Illinois University Press, 2000.

Elsaesser, Thomas. *Weimar Cinema and After: Germany's Historical Imaginary*. London: Routledge, 2000.

Elsaesser, Thomas, with Michael Wedel, eds. *The BFI Companion to German Cinema*. London: British Film Institute, 1999.

Etlin, Richard A., ed. *Art, Culture, and Media under the Third Reich*. Chicago: University of Chicago Press, 2002.

Everson, William K. "The Many Lives of '*Napoleon*.'" *Film Comment* 17, no. 1 (January–February, 1981): 21–23.

Ezra, Elizabeth and Sue Harris. *France in Focus: Film and National Identity*. Oxford: Berg, 2000.

Falk, Quentin. *The Golden Gong: Fifty Years of the Rank Organisation, Its Films and Its Stars*. London: Columbus, 1987.

Faulkner, Christopher. *Jean Renoir: A Guide to References and Resources*. Boston: Hall, 1979.

———. *The Social Cinema of Jean Renoir*. Princeton, N.J.: Princeton University Press, 1986.

Fischer, Lucy. "Dr. Mabuse and Mr. Lang." *Wide Angle* 3, no. 3 (Fall 1979): 18–26.

Flitterman-Lewis, Sandy. *To Desire Differently: Feminism and the French Cinema*. Urbana: University of Illinois Press, 1990. Repr., New York: Columbia University Press, 1996.

Fox, Jo. *Filming Women in the Third Reich*. Oxford: Berg, 2000.

Fraigneau, André. *Cocteau on the Film*. Trans. Vera Traill. New York: Roy, 1954. Repr., New York: Dover, 1972.

"Fritz Lang." In *New York World Telegram* (June 11, 1941). Quoted in Kracauer, Siegfried. *From Caligari to Hitler*. Princeton, N.J.: Princeton University Press, 1947.

Furhammer, Leif, and Folke Isaksson. *Politics and Film*. Trans. Kersti French. New York: Praeger, 1971.

Geduld, Harry M., and Ronald Gottesman, eds. *The Making and Unmaking of "Que Viva México!"* Bloomington: Indiana University Press, 1970.

Gilliatt, Penelope. *Jean Renoir: Essays, Conversations, Reviews*. New York: McGraw-Hill, 1975.

Gilson, René. *Jean Cocteau*. New York: Crown, 1974.

Ginsberg, Terri, and Kirsten Moana Thompson, eds. *Perspectives on German Cinema*. New York: Hall, 1996.

Gomery, Douglas. "Economic Struggle and Hollywood Imperialism: Europe Converts to Sound." *Yale French Studies: Cinema/Sound* 60 (1980): 80–93. Repr. in Weiss and Belton, eds., *Film Sound*, pp. 25–43.

Gough-Yates, Kevin. "Exiles and British Cinema." In Murphy, ed., *The British Cinema Book*, pp. 170–76.

Graham, Cooper C. *Leni Riefenstahl and Olympia*. Metuchen, N.J.: Scarecrow, 1986, 2001.

Grant, Barry Keith, and Jeannette Sloniowski, eds. *Documenting the Documentary: Close Readings of Documentary Film and Video*. Detroit: Wayne State University Press, 1998.

Gunning, Tom. *The Films of Fritz Lang: Allegories of Vision and Modernity*. London: British Film Institute, 2000.

Hagener, Malte, and Jan Hans, eds. *Als die Filme singen Lernten: Innovation und Tradition im Musikfilm 1928–1938*. Munich: edition text + kritik, 1999.

Hake, Sabine. *German National Cinema*. New York: Routledge, 2002.

———. *Popular Cinema in the Third Reich*. Austin: University of Texas Press, 2002.

Harper, Sue. *Picturing the Past: The Rise and Fall of the British Costume Film*. London: British Film Institute, 1994.

———. "From Wholesome Girls to Difficult Dowagers: Actresses in 1930s British Cinema." In Ashby and Higson, eds., *British Cinema, Past and Present*, pp. 137–51.

Harpole, *Charles H. Gradients of Depth in the Cinema Image*. New York: Arno, 1978.

———. "Ideological and Technological Determinism in Deep-Space Cinema Images." *Film Quarterly* 33, no. 3 (Spring 1980): 11–21.

Hayward, Susan. *French National Cinema*. London: Routledge, 1993.

Hayward, Susan, and Ginette Vincendeau, eds. *French Film: Texts and Contexts*. 2nd ed. London: Routledge, 2000.

Higson, Andrew, ed. *Dissolving Views. Key Writings on British Cinema*. London: Cassell, 1996.

Higson, Andrew, and Richard Maltby, eds. *"Film Europe" and "Film America": Cinema, Commerce and Cultural Exchange, 1920–1939*. Exeter: University of Exeter Press, 1999.

Hinton, David B. *The Films of Leni Riefenstahl*. Metuchen, N.J.: Scarecrow, 1978.

Hoffmann, Hilmar. *The Triumph of Propaganda: Film and National Socialism, 1933–1945*. Trans. John A. Broadwin and V. R. Berghahn. Providence, R.I.: Berghahn, 1996.

Hogenkamp, Bert. *Deadly Parallels: Film and the Left in Britain, 1929–1939*. London: Lawrence & Wishart, 1986.

Hughes, Alex, and James S. Williams, eds. *Gender and French Cinema*. Oxford: Berg, 2001.

Hull, David Stewart. *Film in the Third Reich*. Berkeley: University of California Press, 1969.

Humphries, Reynold. *Fritz Lang: Genre and Representation in His American Films*. Baltimore: Johns Hopkins University Press, 1989.

Infield, Glenn B. *Leni Riefenstahl: The Fallen Film Goddess*. New York: Crowell, 1976.

Insdorf, Annette. "Maurice Jaubert and François Truffaut: Musical Continuities from *L'Atalante* to *L'Histoire d'Adèle H.*" *Yale French Studies: Cinema/Sound* (1980): 204–218.

Ivens, Joris. *The Camera and I*. New York: International, 1969.

Jarvie, Ian. *Hollywood's Overseas Campaign: The North Atlantic Movie Trade, 1920–1950*. Cambridge, Eng.: Cambridge University Press, 1992.

Jaubert, Maurice. "Music in the Film." In Bandy, ed., *Rediscovering French Film*, pp. 89–90.

Jenkins, Stephen, ed. *Fritz Lang: The Image and the Look*. London: British Film Institute, 1981.

Kaes, Anton. *M*. London: British Film Institute, 2000.

Karetnikova, Inga. "Eisenstein's Mexican Drawings: Communicators of Cinematic Ideas." *LAMP* (1985): 5–11.

Kaup, Bert Hogem. *Deadly Parallels: Film and the Left in Britain, 1929–39*. London: Lawrence & Wishart, 1987.

Kay, Karyn, and Gerald Peary. *Women and the Cinema*. New York: Dutton, 1977.

Kepley, Vance, Jr. "The First Perestroika: Soviet Cinema under the First Five-Year Plan." *Cinema Journal* 35, no. 4 (Summer 1996): 31–53.

King, Norman. *Abel Gance: A Politics of Spectacle*. London: British Film Institute, 1984.

Koepnick, Lutz. *The Dark Mirror: German Cinema between Hitler and Hollywood*. Berkeley: University of California Press, 2002.

Kuenzli, Rudolf E., ed.: *Dada and Surrealist Film*. New York: Willis, Locker & Owens, 1987.

Kulik, Karol. *Alexander Korda*. London: Allen, 1975.

Landy, Marcia. *British Genres: Cinema and Society, 1930–1960*. Princeton, N.J.: Princeton University Press, 1991.

———. *The Folklore of Consensus: Theatricality in the Italian Cinema, 1930–1943*. Albany: State University of New York Press, 1998.

———. *Italian Film*. New York: Cambridge University Press, 2000.

Lanzoni, Rémi Fournier. *French Cinema: From Its Beginning to the Present*. New York: Continuum, 2002.

Lawder, Standish D. *The Cubist Cinema*. New York: New York University Press, 1969.

Leiser, Erwin. *Nazi Cinema*. New York: Macmillan, 1974.

Leprohon, Pierre. *Jean Renoir*. Trans. Brigid Elson. New York: Crown, 1971.

Leyda, Jay, and Zina Voynow. *Eisenstein at Work*. New York: Pantheon/Museum of Modern Art, 1982.

Lourie, Eugene. *My Work Is Films*. New York: Harcourt Brace, 1985.

Low, Rachael. *The History of the British Film, 1929–1939: Documentary and Educational Films of the 1930s*. The History of British Film, vol. 5. London: Allen & Unwin, 1979.

———. *The History of the British Film, 1929–1939: Films of Comment and Persuasion of the 1930s*. The History of British Film, vol. 6. London: Allen & Unwin, 1979.

———. *The History of the British Film, 1929–1939: Film Making in 1930s Britain*. The History of British Film, vol. 7. London: Allen & Unwin, 1985.

Lowry, Edward. *The Filmology Movement and Film Study in France*. Ann Arbor, Mich.: UMI Research Press, 1985.

McCreary, Eugene C. "Louis Delluc, Film Theorist, Critic, and Prophet." *Cinema Journal* 16, no. 1 (Fall 1976): 14–35.

Macnab, Geoffrey. *J. Arthur Rank and the British Film Industry*. London: Routledge, 1993.

MacPherson, Don, ed. *Traditions of Independence: British Cinema in the Thirties*. London: British Film Institute, 1980.

Mancini, Elaine. *Struggles of the Italian Film Industry during Fascism, 1930–1935*. Ann Arbor, Mich.: UMI Research Press, 1985.

Mancini, Marc. "Prévert: Poetry in Motion Pictures." *Film Comment* 17, no. 6 (November–December 1981): 24–37.

Merritt, Russell. "Recharging *Alexander Nevsky:* Tracking the Eisenstein-Prokofiev War Horse." *Film Quarterly* 48, no. 2 (Winter 1994–95): 34–47.

Miles, Peter, and Malcolm Smith. *Cinema, Literature and Society: Elite and Mass Culture in Interwar Britain*. London: Croom Helm, 1987.

Minney, R. J. *The Films of Anthony Asquith*. South Brunswick, N.J.: Barnes, 1976.

Minton, David B. *The Films of Leni Riefenstahl*. Metuchen, N.J.: Scarecrow, 1978.

Mitchell, Greg. "The Greatest Movie Never Made." *American Film* 8, no. 4 (January–February, 1983): 53–85.

Moeller, Felix. *The Film Minister: Goebbels and the Cinema in the Third Reich*. Trans. Michael Robinson. Stuttgart: Edition Axel Menges, 2000.

Montagu, Ivor. *With Eisenstein in Hollywood: A Chapter of Autobiography*. New York: International, 1967.

Murphy, Robert, ed. *The British Cinema Book*. 2nd ed. London: British Film Institute, 2001.

———. "Postscript: A Short History of British Cinema." In Murphy, ed., *The British Cinema Book*, pp. 310–17.

Napper, Lawrence. "A Despicable Tradition?: Quota-Quickies in the 1930s." In Murphy, ed., *The British Cinema Book*, pp. 46–52.

Nesbitt, Anne. "Inanimations: *Snow White* and *Ivan the Terrible*." *Film Quarterly* 50, no. 4 (Summer 1997): 20–31.

Ogle, Patrick. "Technological Influences upon the Development of Deep Focus Photography in the United States." *Screen* 13, no. 1 (Spring 1972), 45–72.

O'Shaughnessy, Martin. *Jean Renoir*. Manchester, Eng.: Manchester University Press, 2000.

Ott, Frederick W. *The Films of Fritz Lang*. Secaucus, N.J.: Citadel, 1979.

Out of the Dark: Crime, Mystery, and Suspense in the German Cinema, 1915–1990. Conceived and comp. Willi Johanns. Munich: Goethe-Institute Film Department, 1992. Exhibition catalogue.

Pappas, Peter. "The Superimposition of Vision: Napoleon and the Meaning of Fascist Art." *Cineaste* 11, 2 (1981), 4–13.

Perry, George. *The Great British Picture Show*. New York: Hill & Wang, 1974.

Petley, Julian. *Capital and Culture: German Cinema, 1933–45*. London: British Film Institute, 1979.

Petrie, Duncan, ed. *Cinema and the Realms of Enchantment: Lectures, Seminars, and Essays*. London: British Film Institute, 1993.

Petro, Patrice. "Nazi Cinema at the Intersection of the Classical and the Popular." *New German Critique* 74 (Spring/Summer 1998): 41–55.

Plummer, Thomas G., et al., eds. *Film and Politics in the Weimar Republic*. New York: Holmes & Meier, 1982.

"Politics and the Cinema of Jean Renoir." Special issue of *Persistence of Vision* 12–13 (1996).

Porter, Vincent. "Methodism versus the Market-place: The Rank Organisation and British Cinema." In Murphy, ed., *The British Cinema Book*, pp. 85–92.

Prokofiev, Sergei. *Selected Letters of Sergei Prokofiev*. Ed. and trans. Harlow Robinson. Boston: Northeastern University Press, 1998.

Puttnam, David, with Neil Watson. *The Undeclared War: The Struggle for Control of the World's Film Industry*. London: HarperCollins, 1997. Published in the United States as *Movies and Money*. New York: Knopf, 1998.

Quinlan, David. *British Sound Films: The Studio Years, 1928–1959*. London: Batsford, 1984.

Reeves, Nicholas. *The Power of Film Propaganda: Myth or Reality?* London: Cassell, 1999.

" '*La Règle du jeu.*' " Special issue of *Quarterly Review of Film Studies* 7, no. 3 (Summer 1982).

Reich, Jacqueline, and Piero Garofalo, eds. *Re-Viewing Fascism: Italian Cinema, 1922–1943*. Bloomington: Indiana University Press, 2002.

Reimer, Robert C., ed. *Cultural History through a National*

Socialist Lens: Essays on the Cinema of Nazi Germany.
Rochester, N.Y.: Camden House, 2000.

Renoir, Jean. *My Life and My Films*. Trans. Norman Denny.
New York: Atheneum, 1974.

Rentschler, Eric, ed. *The Films of G. W. Pabst: An Extraterritorial Cinema*. New Brunswick, N.J.: Rutgers University
Press, 1990.

———. *The Ministry of Illusion: Nazi Feature Films and
Their Afterlife*. Cambridge, Mass.: Harvard University
Press, 1995.

Richards, Jeffrey. *Visions of Yesterday*. London: Routledge &
Kegan Paul, 1973.

———. *The Age of the Dream Palace: Cinema and Society in
Britain, 1930–1939*. London: Routledge & Kegan Paul,
1984.

———, ed. *The Unknown 1930s: An Alternative History of
the British Cinema, 1929–1939*. London: Tauris, 1998.

Riefenstahl, Leni. *Leni Riefenstahl: A Memoir*. New York: St.
Martin's, 1993.

Romani, Cinzia. *Tainted Goddesses: Female Film Stars of the
Third Reich*. Trans. Robert Connolly. New York: Sarpendon,
1992.

Rother, Rainer. *Leni Riefenstahl: The Seduction of Genius*.
Trans. Martin H. Bott. London: Continuum, 2002.

Rutherford, Ward. *Hitler's Propaganda Machine*. London:
Bison, 1978.

Ryall, Tom. *Britain and the American Cinema*. London: Sage,
2001.

———. "A British Studio System: The Associated British Picture Corporation and the Gaumont-British Picture Corporation in the 1930s." In Murphy, ed., *The British Cinema
Book*, pp.35–41.

Sadoul, George. *The French Film*. London: Falcon, 1953.

Salles Gomes, P. E. *Jean Vigo*. Berkeley: University of California Press, 1971.

Schulte-Sasse, Linda. *Entertaining the Third Reich: Illusions
of Wholeness in Nazi Cinema*. Durham, N.C.: Duke University Press, 1996.

Sedgwick, John. *Popular Filmgoing in 1930s Britain: A Choice
of Pleasures*. Exeter: University of Exeter Press, 2000.

Sellar, Maurice, et al. *Best of British: A Celebration of Rank
Film Classics*. London: Sphere, 1987.

Sesonske, Alexander. *Jean Renoir: The French Films, 1924–
1939*. Cambridge, Mass.: Harvard University Press, 1980.

———. "Discovering America: Jean Renoir, 1941." *Sight and
Sound* 50, no. 4 (Autumn 1981): 256–61.

———. "À la Recherche du Temps Perdu." *Quarterly Review
of Film Studies* 10, no. 3 (Summer 1985): 261–65.

Shafer, Stephen C. *British Popular Films, 1929–1939: The
Cinema of Reassurance*. London: Routledge, 1997.

Sklar, Robert, and Charles Musser, eds. *Resisting Images:*

Essays on Cinema and History. Philadelphia: Temple University Press, 1990.

Slide, Anthony. *Banned in the USA: British Film in the United
States and Their Censorship, 1933–1960*. London: Tauris,
1998.

Smith, David Calvert. *The German Filmography 1895–1949*.
Jefferson, N.C.: McFarland, 2000.

Smith, John M. *Jean Vigo*. New York: Praeger, 1972.

Sorlin, Pierre. *Italian National Cinema 1896–1996*. London:
Routledge, 1996.

Strebel, Elizabeth Grottle. "Renoir and the Popular Front."
Sight and Sound 49, no. 1 (Winter 1979–80): 36–41.

Street, Sarah. *British National Cinema*. London: Routledge,
1997.

———. "Stepping Westward: The Distribution of British Feature Films in America, and the Case of *The Private Life of
Henry VIII*." In Ashby and Higson eds., *British Cinema,
Past and Present*, pp. 51–62.

———. "British Film and the National Interest 1927–1939."
In Murphy, ed., *The British Cinema Book*, pp. 29–34.

———. *Transatlantic Crossings: British Feature Films in the
USA*. London: Continuum, 2002.

Surow, Catherine A. "Maurice Jaubert: Poet of Music." In
Bandy, ed., *Rediscovering French Film*, pp. 87–88.

Sussex, Elizabeth. *The Rise and Fall of the British Documentary*. Berkeley: University of California Press, 1976.

Sutton, David. *A Chorus of Raspberries: British Film Comedy, 1929–1939*. Exeter: University of Exeter Press,
2000.

Swann, Paul. *The British Documentary Film Movement 1926–
1946*. Cambridge: Cambridge University Press, 1989.

Taschen, Angelika. *Leni Riefenstahl: Five Lives*. Cologne:
Taschen, 2000.

Taylor, Richard. *Film Propaganda: Soviet Russia and Nazi
Germany*. 2nd rev. ed. London: Tauris, 1998.

Thompson, Kristin. *Eisentein's "Ivan the Terrible": A Neoformalist Analysis*. Princeton, N.J.: Princeton University Press,
1981.

Tifft, Stephen. "Theater in the Round: The Politics of Space
in the Films of Jean Renoir." *Theater Journal* 39, no. 3
(October 1987): 328–46.

Tomasulo, Frank P. "The Mass Psychology of Fascist Cinema:
Leni Riefenstahl's *Triumph of the Will*." In Grant and Sloniowski, eds., *Documenting the Documentary*, pp. 99–118.

Traubner, Richard. "The Sound and the Führer." *Film Comment* 14, no. 4 (July–August 1978): 17–23.

Tsivian, Yuri. *Ivan the Terrible*. London: British Film Institute,
2001.

Turk, Edward Baron. "The Birth of *Children of Paradise*."
American Film 4, no. 9 (July–August 1979): 42–49.

———. *Child of Paradise: Marcel Carné and the Golden Age*

of French Cinema. Cambridge, Mass.: Harvard University Press, 1989.

Wakelin, Michael. *J. Arthur Rank—the Man behind the Gong*. Oxford: Lion, 1996.

Warren, Patricia. *British Film Studios: An Illustrated History*. London: Batsford, 2001.

Weiss, Elizabeth, and John Belton, eds. *Film Sound: Theory and Practice*. New York: Columbia University Press, 1985.

Welch, David, ed. *Nazi Propaganda*. London: Croom Helm, 1983.

———. *Propaganda and the German Cinema, 1933–1945*. Oxford: Oxford University Press, 1983.

Welles, Orson. *Los Angeles Times* (February 18, 1979). Eulogy for Renoir.

Welsch, James, and Steven Kramer. *Abel Gance*. Boston: Twayne, 1978.

Werner, Gösta. "Fritz Lang and Goebbels: Myth and Facts." *Film Quarterly* 43, no. 3 (Spring 1990): 24–27.

Widdis, Emma. "Borders: The Aesthetic of Conquest in Soviet Cinema of the 1930s." *Journal of European Studies* 30, no. 4 (December 2000): 401–11.

Williams, Alan. *Republic of Images: A History of French Film-making*. Cambridge, Mass.: Harvard University Press, 1992.

Winston, Brian. *Claiming the Real: The Grierson Documentary and Its Legitimations*. London: British Film Institute, 1995.

Witte, Karsten. "The Indivisible Legacy of Nazi Cinema." *New German Critique* 74 (Spring/Summer 1998): 23–30.

Wollen, Peter. *Signs and Meaning in the Cinema*. 3rd ed. Bloomington: Indiana University Press, 1972.

Wollenberg, Hans H. *Fifty Years of German Film*. London: Falcon, 1947. Repr., New York: Arno, 1972.

Zagarrio, Vito. "Ideology Elsewhere: Contradictory Models of Italian Fascist Cinema." In Sklar and Musser, eds., *Resisting Images*, pp. 149–72.

CHAPTER 10. ORSON WELLES AND THE MODERN SOUND FILM

Adams, Jeffrey. "Orson Welles's *The Trial*: Film Noir and the Kafkaesque." *College Literature* 29, no. 3 (Summer 2002): 140–57.

Altman, Rick. "Deep-Focus Sound: *Citizen Kane* and the Radio Aesthetic." *Quarterly Review of Film and Video* 15, no. 3 (December 1994): 1–33.

Anderegg, Michael. *Orson Welles, Shakespeare, and Popular Culture*. New York: Columbia University Press, 1999.

Anderegg, Michael. "Welles/Shakespeare/Film: An Overview." In Naremore, ed., *Film Adaptation*, pp. 154–71.

Andrew, J. Dudley. "Echoes of Art: The Distant Sounds of Orson Welles," 152–71. In *Film in the Aura of Art*. Princeton, N.J.: Princeton University Press, 1984.

Bates, Robin, and Scott Bates. "Fiery Speech in a World of Shadows: Rosebud's Impact on Early Audiences." *Cinema Journal* 26, no. 2 (Winter 1987): 3–26.

Bazin, André. *Orson Welles: A Critical View*. Trans. Jonathan Rosenbaum. New York: Harper & Row, 1978.

Belton, John. "A New Map of the Labyrinth: The Unretouched *Touch of Evil*." *Movietone News* 47 (January 21, 1976): 1–9, and 48 (February 29, 1976).

Berg, Chuck, and Thomas L. Erskine. *The Encyclopedia of Orson Welles: From "Citizen Kane" to "Othello."* New York: Facts on File, 2002.

Bogdanovich, Peter. "The Kane Mutiny." *Esquire* (October 1972): 99–105, 180–90.

Brady, Frank. "The Lost Film of Orson Welles." *American Film* 4, no. 2 (November 1978): 63–69.

———. *Citizen Welles: A Biography of Orson Welles*. New York: Scribner's, 1989.

Callow, Simon. *Orson Welles: The Road to Xanadu*. London: Jonathan Cape, 1995.

Cameron, Evan William. "Citizen Kane: The Influence of Radio Drama on Cinematic Design." In Cameron, ed., *Sound and Cinema*, pp. 202–16.

———, ed. *Sound and Cinema: The Coming of Sound to American Film*. Pleasantville, N.Y.: Redgrave, 1980.

Cardullo, Bert. *Indelible Images: New Perspectives on Classic Films*. Lanham, Md.: University Press of America, 1987.

Cardullo, Bert. "The Real Fascination of *Citizen Kane*." In Cardullo, *Indelible Images*, pp. 179–99.

Carringer, Robert L. "The Scripts of *Citizen Kane*." *Critical Inquiry* 5, no. 2 (Winter 1978): 369–400.

———. *The Making of "Citizen Kane."* Berkeley: University of California Press, 1985.

———. *The Magnificent Ambersons: A Reconstruction*. Berkeley: University of California Press, 1993.

Chatman, Seymour. "2½ Film Versions of *Heart of Darkness*." In Moore, ed., *Conrad on Film*, pp. 207–23.

Combs, Richard. "Burning Masterworks from *Kane* to *F for Fake*." *Film Comment* 30, no. 1 (January–February 1994): 50–59.

Comito, Terry, ed. *"Touch of Evil."* Rutger's Films in Print Series. New Brunswick, N.J.: Rutgers University Press, 1985.

Cowie, Peter. *A Ribbon of Dreams*. Cranbury, N.J.: Barnes, 1973.

Donnelly, K. J., ed. *Film Music: Critical Approaches*. New York: Continuum, 2001.

Estrin, Mark W., ed. *Orson Welles: Interviews*. Jackson: University Press of Mississippi, 2002.

Fitzsimmons, Lorna. *"The Magnificent Ambersons*: Unmasking the Code." *Literature/Film Quarterly* 28, no. 4 (2000): 293–302.

France, Richard. *The Theatre of Orson Welles*. Lewisburg, Pa.: Bucknell University Press, 1977.

———, ed. *Orson Welles on Shakespeare: The WPA and Mercury Theatre Playscripts*. Westport, Conn.: Greenwood, 1990.

Goldfarb, Phyllis. "Orson Welles's Use of Sound." In Gottesman, ed., *Focus on Orson Welles*, pp. 85–94.

Gottesman, Ronald, ed. *Focus on "Citizen Kane."* Englewood Cliffs, N.J.: Prentice-Hall, 1971.

———, ed. *Focus on Orson Welles*. Englewood Cliffs, N.J.: Prentice-Hall, 1976.

———, ed. *Perspectives on Citizen Kane*. New York: Hall, 1996.

Hamann, G. D., ed. *Marion Davies in the 30s*. Hollywood: Filming Today, 1996.

Higham, Charles. *The Films of Orson Welles*. Berkeley: University of California Press, 1970.

———. *Orson Welles: The Rise and Fall of an American Genius*. New York: St. Martin's, 1985.

Hill, John, and Pamela Church Gibson, eds. *The Oxford Guide to Film Studies*. Oxford: Oxford University Press, 1998.

Jackson, Russell, ed. *Shakespeare on Film*. Cambridge: Cambridge University Press, 2000.

Jarvie, Ian. "*Citizen Kane* and the Essence of a Person." In Jarvie, *Philosophy of the Film*, pp. 267–94.

———. *Philosophy of the Film: Epistemology, Ontology, Aesthetics*. New York: Routledge & Kegan Paul, 1987.

Johnson, William. "*F for Fake*." *Film Quarterly* (Summer 1976). Review.

Kael, Pauline. "Rising Kane." *New Yorker* (February 20 and 27, 1971).

———, ed. *The Citizen Kane Book*. Boston: Little, Brown, 1971.

Kalinak, Kathryn. "The Text of Music: A Study of *The Magnificent Ambersons*." *Cinema Journal* 27, no. 4 (Summer 1988): 45–63.

Kau, Edvin. "Great Beginnings—and Endings: Made by Orson Welles." *p.o.v.* 2 (December 1996): 77–94.

Koch, Howard. *The Panic Broadcast*. Boston: Little, Brown, 1970.

Leff, Leonard J. "Reading *Kane*." *Film Quarterly* 39, no. 1 (Fall 1985): 10–21.

McBride, Joseph. *Orson Welles*. New York: Viking, 1972.

Martin, Adrian. "An Abandoned Mine: Notes on Orson Welles' Radio Work." *Senses of Cinema: An Online Film Journal Devoted to the Serious and Eclectic Discussion of Cinema* 18 (January–February 2000): http://www.sensesof cinema.com.

Mason, Pamela. "Orson Welles and Filmed Shakespeare." In Jackson, ed., *Shakespeare on Film*, pp. 183–98.

Mintz, Penny. "Orson Welles's Use of Sound." In Weis and Belton, eds., *Film Sound*, pp. 289–97.

Moore, Gene M., ed. *Conrad on Film*. Cambridge, Eng.: Cambridge University Press, 1997.

Naremore, James. *The Magic World of Orson Welles*. New York: Oxford University Press, 1978.

———, ed. *Orson Welles: A Guide to References and Resources*. Boston: Hall, 1980.

———, ed. *Film Adaptation*. New Brunswick, N.J.: Rutgers University Press, 2000.

Perkins, V. F. *The Magnificent Ambersons*. London: British Film Institute, 1999.

Pizzitola, Louis. *Hearst over Hollywood: Power, Passion, and Propaganda in the Movies*. New York: Columbia University Press, 2002.

Rosar, William H. "The Dies Irae in *Citizen Kane*: Musical Hermeneutics Applied to Film Music." In Donnelly, ed., *Film Music*, pp. 103–16.

Rosenbaum, Jonathan, ed. *This Is Orson Welles: Orson Welles and Peter Bogdanovich*. New York: HarperCollins, 1992. Interviews.

Rosenbaum, Jonathan; Leonard Leff; and Robin Bates. "Dialogue: Jonathan Rosenbaum, Leonard Leff, and Robin Bates on Viewer Response to *Citizen Kane*." *Cinema Journal* 26, no. 4 (Summer 1987): 60–66.

Rosenbaum, Jonathan, and Henry Sheehan. "Welles, Lost and Found." *Film Comment* 28, no. 1 (January–February 1992): 50–59.

Rothwell, Kenneth S. "Orson Welles: Shakespeare for the Art Houses." *Cineaste* 24, no. 1 (1998): 28–33. Repr. in Rothwell, *A History of Shakespeare on Screen*, pp. 72–94.

———. *A History of Shakespeare on Screen: A Century of Film and Television*. Cambridge: Cambridge University Press, 2001.

Sarris, Andrew. "The Great Kane Controversy." *World* (January 16, 1973).

Spadoni, Robert. "The Seeing Ear: The Presence of Radio in Orson Welles' *Heart of Darkness*." In Moore, ed., *Conrad on Film*, pp. 78–92.

Taylor, John Russell. *Orson Welles: A Celebration*. New York: Applause, 1999.

Thieme, Claudia. *"F for Fake," and the Growth in Complexity of Orson Welles' Documentary Form*. Frankfurt-am-Main: Lang, 1997.

Thomson, David. *Rosebud: The Story of Orson Welles*. New York: Knopf, 1996.

Weis, Elisabeth, and John Belton, eds. *Film Sound: Theory and Practice*. New York: Columbia University Press, 1985.

Williams, Dan. *Citizen Kane: Director, Orson Welles*. New York: Longman, 2000.

Wollen, Peter. "Foreign Relations: Welles and *Touch of Evil.*" *Sight and Sound* 6, no. 10 (October 1996): 21–23.

Wollen, Peter. "Citizen Kane." In Hill and Gibson, eds., *The Oxford Guide to Film Studies*, pp. 26–29.

CHAPTER 11. WARTIME AND POSTWAR CINEMA: ITALY AND THE UNITED STATES, 1940–1951

Agee, James. *Agee on Film.* Vol. 1: *Reviews and Comments.* Vol. 2: *Five Film Scripts.* Boston: Beacon, 1958.

Agel, Henri. *Romance américaine.* Paris: Cerf, 1963.

Alloway, Lawrence. *Violent America: The Movies, 1946–1964.* New York: Museum of Modern Art, 1965.

Alton, John. *Painting with Light.* New York: Macmillan, 1950.

Armes, Roy. *Patterns of Realism: A Study of Italian Neo-Realist Cinema.* London: Tantivy, 1971.

Arthur, Paul. "L.A. as Scene of the Crime," *Film Comment* 32, no. 4 (July–August 1996): 20–27.

Arthur, Paul. "Murder's Tongue: Identity, Death, and the City in Film Noir." In Slocum, ed., *Violence and American Cinema*, pp. 154–75.

Bacon, Henry. *Visconti: Explorations of Beauty and Decay.* Cambridge, Eng.: Cambridge University Press, 1998.

Baker, M. Joyce. *Images of Women in Film: The War Years, 1941–1945.* Ann Arbor, Mich.: UMI Research Press, 1980.

Baron, Cynthia. "As Red as a Burlesque Queen's Garters: Cold War Politics and the Actors' Lab in Hollywood." In McLean and Cook, eds., *Headline Hollywood: A Century of Film Scandal*, pp. 143–62.

Basinger, Jeanine. *The World War II Combat Film: Anatomy of a Genre.* New York: Columbia University Press, 1986.

———. *A Woman's View: How Hollywood Spoke to Women, 1930–1960.* New York: Knopf, 1993.

Bazin, André. *What Is Cinema?* 2 vols. Selected and trans. Hugh Gray. Berkeley: University of California Press, 1967, 1971.

Bernardini, Aldo, and Jean A. Gili, eds. *Cesare Zavattini.* Paris: Éditions du Centro Pompidous, 1990.

Biberman, Herbert. *"Salt of the Earth": The Story of a Film.* Boston: Beacon, 1965.

Birdwell, Michael E. *Celluloid Soldiers: Warner Bros.'s Campaign against Nazism.* New York: New York University Press, 1999.

Bloom, John Morton. *V Was for Victory.* New York: Harcourt Brace, 1976.

Bogart, Humphrey. "I'm No Communist." *Photoplay* (March 1948).

Bohn, Thomas W. *An Historical and Descriptive Analysis of the "Why We Fight" Series.* New York: Arno, 1977.

Bondanella, Peter. *The Films of Roberto Rossellini.* Cambridge, Eng.: Cambridge University Press, 1993.

———. *Italian Cinema: From Neo-Realism to the Present.* 3rd ed. New York: Continuum, 2001.

Borde, Raymond, and Étienne Chaumeton. "The Sources of Film Noir." Trans. Bill Horrigan. *Film Reader* 3 (1978): 58–66.

Browne, Nick, ed. *Refiguring American Film Genres: History and Theory.* Berkeley: University of California Press, 1998.

Brunette, Peter. "Rossellini and Cinematic Realism." *Cinema Journal* 25, no. 1 (Fall 1985): 34–49.

———. *Roberto Rossellini.* New York: Oxford University Press, 1987.

Buhle, Paul, and Dave Wagner. *A Very Dangerous Citizen: Abraham Lincoln Polonsky and the Hollywood Left.* Berkeley: University of California Press, 2001.

———. *Radical Hollywood: The Untold Story behind America's Favorite Movies.* New York: New Press, 2002.

Butler, Terence. "Polonsky and Kazan: HUAC and the Violation of Personality." *Sight and Sound* 57, no. 4 (Autumn 1988): 262–67.

Byars, Jackie. *All That Hollywood Allows: Re-Reading Gender in 1950s Melodrama.* Chapel Hill: University of North Carolina Press, 1991.

Calvocoressi, Peter. *Total War.* New York: Random House, 1972.

Cameron, Ian, ed. *The Book of Film Noir.* New York: Continuum, 1993.

Campbell, Russell. *Cinema Strikes Back: Radical Filmmaking in the United States, 1930–1942.* Ann Arbor, Mich.: UMI Research Press, 1982.

Cardullo, Bert. *What Is Neorealism? A Critical English-Language Bibliography of Italian Cinematic Neorealism.* Lanham, Md.: University Press of America, 1992.

Caute, David. *The Great Fear: The Anti-Communist Purge under Truman and Eisenhower.* New York: Simon & Schuster, 1978.

Celant, Germano, ed. *The Italian Metamorphosis, 1943–1968.* New York: Guggenheim Museum, 1994. Also available on CD-ROM.

Celli, Carlo. "The Legacy of Mario Camerini in Vittorio De Sica's *The Bicycle Thief* (1948)." *Cinema Journal* 40, no. 4 (Summer 2001): 3–17.

Ceplair, Larry, and Steven Englund. *The Inquisition in Hollywood: Politics in the Film Community, 1930–1960.* Garden City, N.Y.: Doubleday, 1980. Repr. Berkeley: University of California Press, 1983.

Chase, Donald. "Anna Magnani—Hers Was the Face of Italian Neorealism, and Her Excellence Made Her the Prisoner of 'Truth' Even to Her Admirers: It's High Time to

Rediscover the Actress." *Film Comment* 29, no. 6 (November 1993): 42–47.

Christopher, Nicholas. *Somewhere in the Night: Film Noir and the American City*. New York: Free Press, 1997.

Cogley, John. *Report on Blacklisting*. 2 vols. New York: Fund for the Republic, 1956.

Conant, Michael. *Antitrust in the Motion Picture Industry*. Berkeley: University of California Press, 1960.

Conley, Tom. "Stages of Film Noir." *Theater Journal* 39, no. 3 (October 1987): 347–63.

Copjec, Joan, ed. *Shades of Noir: A Reader*. London: Verso, 1993.

Corkin, Stanley. "Cowboys and Free Markets: Post–World War II Westerns and U.S. Hegemony." *Cinema Journal* 39, no. 3 (2000): 66–91.

Costello, John. *Virtue under Fire: How World War II Changed Our Social and Sexual Attitudes*. Boston: Little, Brown, 1986.

Cowen, Tyler. "The Great Twentieth Century Foreign-Aid Hoax." *Reason* 17, no. 11 (April 1986): 37–41.

Culbert, David, ed. *Information Control and Propaganda: Records at the Office of War Information*. Frederick, Md.: University Publications of America, 1988.

Curle, Howard, and Stephen Snyder, eds. *Vittorio De Sica: Contemporary Perspectives*. Toronto: University of Toronto Press, 2000.

Damico, James. "*Film Noir:* A Modest Proposal." *Film Reader* 3 (1978): 48–57.

de Giusti, Luciano. *I Film di Luchino Visconti*. Rome: Gremese, 1985.

Demming, Barbara. *Running Away from Myself: A Dream Portrait of America Drawn from the Films of the Forties*. New York: Grossman, 1969.

Dick, Bernard F. *The Star-Spangled Screen: The American World War II Film*. Lexington: University Press of Kentucky, 1985.

Dickos, Andrew. *Street with No Name: A History of the Classic American Film Noir*. Lexington: University Press of Kentucky, 2002.

Doane, Mary Anne. "The 'Woman's Film': Possession and Address." Doane, Mellencamp, and Williams, eds., In *Re-vision*.

———. *The Desire to Desire: The Woman's Film of the 1940s*. Bloomington: Indiana University Press, 1987.

———. *Femmes Fatales: Feminism, Film Theory, Psychoanalysis*. London: Routledge, 1991.

Doane, Mary Anne; Patricia Mellencamp; and Linda Williams, eds. *Re-vision: Essays in Feminist Film Criticism*. Frederick, Md.: University Publications of America/American Film Institute, 1984.

Doherty, Thomas. *Projections of War: Hollywood, American Culture, and World War II*. New York: Columbia University Press, 1993.

———. "An Elusive Factoid: World War II Motivation at Warner Bros.?" *Film and History* 27, nos. 1–4 (1997): 120–23.

Durgnat, Raymond. "Paint It Black: The Family Tree of Film Noir." *Cinema* (August 1976): 49–56.

Fielding, Raymond. *The March of Time, 1935–1951*. New York: Oxford University Press, 1978.

Fischer, Lucy. "Two-Faced Women: The 'Double' in Women's Melodrama of the 1940's." *Cinema Journal* 23, no. 1 (Fall 1983): 24–43.

Forgacs, David. *Rome Open City*. London: British Film Institute, 2000.

Forgacs, David; Geoffrey Nowell-Smith; and Sarah Lutton, eds. *Roberto Rossellini: Magician of the Real*. Berkeley: University of California Press, 2001.

Friedrich, Otto. *City of Nets: A Portrait of Hollywood in the 1940s*. New York: Harper & Row, 1986.

Fyne, Robert. *The Hollywood Propaganda of World War II*. Metuchen, N.J.: Scarecrow, 1995.

Gallagher, Tag. *The Adventures of Roberto Rossellini: His Life and Films*. New York: Da Capo, 1998.

Glancy, H. Mark. *When Hollywood Loved Britain: The Hollywood "British" Film, 1939–1945*. Manchester, Eng.: Manchester University Press, 1999.

Gomery, Douglas. "Failed Opportunities: The Integration of the U.S. Motion Picture and Television Industries." *Quarterly Review of Film Studies* 9, no. 3 (Summer 1984): 219–28.

———. "The Coming of Television and the 'Lost' Motion Picture Audience." *Journal of Film and Video* 37, no. 3 (Summer 1985): 5–11.

———. "Theater Television: The Missing Link of Technological Change in the U.S. Motion Picture Industry." *Velvet Light Trap* 21 (Summer 1985): 54–61.

Guarner, José Luis. *Rossellini*. New York: Praeger, 1970.

Guback, Thomas. "The Evolution of the Motion Picture Theater Business in the 1980s." *Journal of Communications* 37, no. 2 (Spring 1987): 60–77.

Handel, Leo A. *Hollywood Looks at Its Audience: A Report of Film Audience Research*. Urbana: University of Illinois Press, 1950.

Hastings, Max. "Time Marches On!" *Sight and Sound* 54, no. 4 (Autumn 1985): 274–77.

Hay, James. *Popular Film Culture in Fascist Italy: The Passing of the Rex*. Bloomington: Indiana University Press, 1987.

Hendershot, Cynthia. *Anti-Communism and Popular Culture in Mid-Century America*. Jefferson, N.C.: McFarland, 2003.

Higham, Charles, and Joel Greenberg. *Hollywood in the Forties*. London: Tantivy, 1968.

Hirsch, Foster. *The Dark Side of the Screen: Film Noir*. San Diego: Barnes, 1981. Repr. New York: Da Capo, 2001.

Houston, Penelope. *The Contemporary Cinema*. Rev. ed. Baltimore, Md.: Penguin, 1971.

Hovald, Patrice G. *Le Néo-réalisme italien et ses créateurs*. Paris: Cerf, 1959.

Huaco, George A. *The Sociology of Film Art*. New York: Basic, 1965.

"Italian Neorealism." Ed. Luciana Bohne. Special issue of *Film Criticism* 3, no. 2 (Winter 1979).

Jacobs, Lea. "The Paramount Case and the Role of the Distributor." *Journal of the University Film and Video Association* 35, no. 1 (Winter 1983): 44–49.

Jacobs, Lewis. "World War II and the American Film." *Cinema Journal* 7, no. 2 (Winter 1967–68): 153–77. Repr. in McClure, ed., *The Movies: An American Idiom*, pp. 153–77.

James, David E., and Rick Berg, eds. *The Hidden Foundation: Cinema and the Question of Class*. Minneapolis: University of Minnesota Press, 1996.

Johanns, Willi. *Out of the Dark: Crime, Mystery, and Suspense in the German Cinema, 1915–1990*. Munich: Goethe-Institut Film Department, 1992.

Jones, Dorothy B. "Communism and the Movies: A Study of Film Content." In Cogley, *Report on Blacklisting*, vol. 1, pp. 196–233.

Jones, Ken D., and Arthur F. McClure. *Hollywood at War*. Cranbury, N.J.: Barnes, 1973.

Kagan, Norman. *The War Film*. New York: Pyramid, 1974.

Kane, Kathryn. *Visions of War: Hollywood Combat Films of World War II*. Ann Arbor, Mich.: UMI Research Press, 1982.

Kaplan, E. Ann. *Women in Film Noir*. London: British Film Institute, 1980.

Karimi, A. M. *Toward a Definition of the American Film Noir*. New York: Arno, 1976.

Kazan, Elia. *A Life*. New York: Knopf, 1988.

Kemp, Philip. "From the Nightmare Factory: HUAC and the Politics of Noir." *Sight and Sound* 55, no. 4 (Autumn 1986): 266–71.

Kerr, Paul. "My Name Is Joseph H. Lewis." *Screen* 24, nos. 4–5 (July–October 1983): 48–66.

———. "Out of What Past? Notes on the B Film Noir." In Kerr, ed., *The Hollywood Film Industry*, pp. 220–44.

———, ed. *The Hollywood Film Industry*. London: British Film Institute, 1986.

Kopper, Clayton R., and Gregory D. Black. *Hollywood Goes to War*. New York: Free Press, 1987.

Kozloff, Sarah. *Invisible Storytellers: Voice-Over Narration in American Fiction Film*. Berkeley: University of California Press, 1988.

Krutnik, Frank. *In a Lonely Street: Film Noir, Genre, and Masculinity*. London: Routledge, 1991.

Landy, Marcia. *Italian Film*. New York: Cambridge University Press, 2000.

Lawson, John Howard. *Film: The Creative Process*. New York: Hill & Wang, 1967.

Leprohon, Pierre. *The Italian Cinema*. Trans. Roger Greaves and Oliver Stallybrass. New York: Praeger, 1972.

Lewis, Jon. *Hollywood v. Hard Core: How the Struggle over Censorship Saved the Modern Film Industry*. New York: New York University Press, 2000.

Liehm, Mira. *Passion and Defiance: Italian Film from 1942 to the Present*. Berkeley: University of California Press, 1984.

Lyons, Arthur. *Death on the Cheap: The Lost B Movies of Film Noir*. New York: Da Capo, 2000.

Lyons, Donald. "Visconti's Magnificent Obsession." *Film Comment* 15, no. 2 (March–April 1979): 9–13.

McAdams, Frank. *The American War Film: History and Hollywood*. Westport, Conn.: Praeger, 2002.

MacCann, Richard Dyer. *The People's Films: A Political History of U.S. Government Motion Pictures*. New York: Hastings House, 1973.

McClure, Arthur, ed. *The Movies: An American Idiom*. Rutherford, N.J.: Fairleigh Dickinson University Press, 1971.

McGilligan, Pat. "Tender Comrades." *Film Comment* 23, no. 6 (November–December 1987): 38–48.

McLean, Adrienne L., and David A. Cook, eds. *Headline Hollywood: A Century of Film Scandal*. New Brunswick, N.J.: Rutgers University Press, 2001.

Mai, Stefano, and Enrico Lancia. *Italian Movie Goddesses: Over Eighty of the Greatest Women in the Italian Cinema*. Trans. Lenor Rosemberg. Rome: Gremese, 1997.

Maltby, Richard. "*Film Noir*: The Politics of the Maladjusted Text." *Journal of American Studies* 18, no. 1 (1984): 12–16.

Manvell, Roger. *Films and the Second World War*. Cranbury, N.J.: Barnes, 1974.

Marcus, Millicent. *Italian Film in the Light of Neorealism*. Princeton, N.J.: Princeton University Press, 1986.

Mariani, John. "Let's Not Be Beastly to the Nazis." *Film Comment* 15, no. 1 (January–February 1979): 49–53.

Maxfield, James F. *The Fatal Woman: Sources of Male Anxiety in American Film Noir, 1941–1991*. Madison, N.J.: Fairleigh Dickinson University Press, 1996.

Mee, Charles L., Jr. *The Marshall Plan: The Launching of the Pax Americana*. New York: Simon & Schuster, 1985.

Miller, Tom. "*Salt of the Earth* Revisited." *Cineaste* 13, no. 3 (1984): 30–36.

Mitchell, Tony. "The Construction and Reception of Anna

Magnani in Italy and the English-Speaking World, 1945–1988." *Film Criticism* 14, no. 1 (Fall 1989): 2–21.

Modleski, Tania. *Loving with a Vengeance: Mass-Produced Fantasies for Women.* Hamden, Conn.: Archon, 1982.

———. "Never to Be Thirty-six Years Old: Rebecca as Female Oedipal Drama." *Wide Angle* 5, no. 1 (1982): 34–41.

———. "Time and Desire in the Woman's Film." *Cinema Journal* 23, no. 3 (Spring 1984): 19–30.

Morella, Joe; Edward Z. Epstein; and John Griggs. *The Films of World War Two.* Secaucus, N.J.: Citadel, 1973.

Muller, Eddie. *Dark City: The Lost World of Film Noir.* New York: St. Martin's, 1998.

———. *Dark City Dames: The Wicked Women of Film Noir.* New York: Regan, 2001.

Munby, Jonathan. *Screening the Gangster from "Little Caesar" to "Touch of Evil."* Chicago: University of Chicago Press, 1999.

Myers, James M. *The Bureau of Motion Pictures and Its Influence on Film Content during World War II.* Lewiston: Mellen, 1998.

Naremore, James. *More Than Night: Film Noir and Its Contexts.* Berkeley: University of California Press, 1998.

Navasky, Victor. *Naming Names.* New York: Viking, 1980.

Nowell-Smith, Geoffrey. *Luchino Visconti.* Garden City, N.Y.: Doubleday, 1968.

Nowell-Smith, Geoffrey, with James Hay and Gianni Volpi. *The Companion to Italian Cinema.* London: Cassell/British Film Institute, 1996.

Nowell-Smith, Geoffrey, and Steven Ricci, eds. *Hollywood and Europe: Economics, Culture, and National Identity 1945–1995.* London: British Film Institute, 1998.

Oliver, Kelly, and Benigno Trigo. *Noir Anxiety.* Minneapolis: University of Minnesota Press, 2002.

Ottoson, Robert. *A Reference Guide to Film Noir.* Metuchen, N.J.: Scarecrow, 1981.

Overbey, David, ed. and trans. *Springtime in Italy: A Reader in Neo-Realism.* Hamden, Conn.: Archon, 1979.

Palmer, R. Barton, ed. *Perspectives on Film Noir.* New York: Hall, 1996.

Perry, Ted. "The Road to Neo-Realism." *Film Comment* 14, no. 6 (November–December 1978): 13–15.

Place, J. A., and L. S. Peterson. "Some Visual Motifs of Film Noir." *Film Comment* 10, no. 1 (January–February 1974): 30–31.

Polan, Dana. "College Course File: *Film Noir.*" *Journal of Film and Video* 37 (Spring 1985): 75–83.

Polan, Dana. *Power and Paranoia: History, Narrative, and the American Cinema, 1940–50.* New York: Columbia University Press, 1986.

Pye, Michael, and Lina Miles. *The Movie Brats: How the Film Generation Took Over Hollywood.* New York: Holt, Rinehart, & Winston, 1979.

Reeves, Nicholas. *The Power of Film Propaganda: Myth or Reality?* London: Cassell, 1999.

Reich, Jacqueline, and Piero Garofalo, eds. *Re-Viewing Fascism: Italian Cinema, 1922–1943.* Bloomington: Indiana University Press, 2002.

Renov, Michael. *Hollywood's Wartime Women: A Cultural Perspective.* Ann Arbor, Mich.: UMI Research Press, 1987.

Richardson, Carl. *Autopsy: An Element of Realism in Film Noir.* Metuchen, N.J.: Scarecrow, 1992.

Robinson, Edward G. (and George Sokolsky). "How the Reds Made a Sucker Out of Me." *American Legion Magazine* (October 1952).

Rocchio, Vincent F. *Cinema of Anxiety: A Psychoanalysis of Italian Neorealism.* Austin: University of Texas Press, 1999.

Rodowick, David. "The Filmic Transaction: On the Openings of Film Noirs." *Velvet Light Trap* 20 (Summer 1983): 2–9.

Rohdie, Sam. "Capitalism and Realism in the Italian Cinema: An Examination of Film in the Fascist Period." *Screen* 24, nos. 4–5 (July–October 1983): 37–46.

Rondolino, Gianni. "Italian Propaganda Films: 1940–1943." In Short, ed., *Film and Radio Propaganda in World War II,* pp. 230–44.

Rosenfelt, Deborah Silverton. Commentary on *Salt of the Earth* by Michael Wilson. Old Westbury, N.Y.: Feminist, 1978.

———. "Ideology and Structure in *Salt of the Earth.*" *Jump Cut* 30 (December 1979).

Rossellini, Roberto. *My Method: Writings and Interviews.* Ed. Adriano Aprà. Trans. Annapaola Cancogni. New York: Marsilio, 1995.

Sarris, Andrew. *The American Cinema: Directors and Directions, 1929–1968.* New York: Dutton, 1968.

Sarris, Andrew. *"You Ain't Heard Nothin' Yet:" The American Talking Film—History and Memory, 1927–1949.* New York: Oxford University Press, 1998.

Schatz, Thomas. *Boom and Bust: American Cinema in the 1940s.* History of the American Cinema, Vol. 6. New York: Scribner's, 1997.

Schrader, Paul. "Notes on *Film Noir.*" *Film Comment* 8, no. 1 (Spring 1972).

Schwartz, Nancy Lynn. *The Hollywood Writer's Way.* New York: Knopf, 1982.

Schwartz, Ronald. *Noir, Now and Then: Film Noir Originals and Remakes, 1944–1999.* Westport, Conn.: Greenwood, 2001.

Selby, Spencer. *Dark City: The Film Noir.* Jefferson, N.C.: McFarland, 1984.

Sesti, Mario. *Tutto il Cinema di Pietro Germi*. Milan: Baldini & Castoldi, 1997.

Servadio, Gaia. *Luchino Visconti: A Biography*. New York: Watts, 1983.

Shindler, Colin. *Hollywood Goes to War: Films and American Society, 1939–52*. London: Routledge & Kegan Paul, 1979.

Short, K. R. M., ed. *Film and Radio Propaganda in World War II*. Knoxville: University of Tennessee Press, 1983.

Siegel, Joel E. *Val Lewton: The Reality of Terror*. New York: Viking, 1973.

Silver, Alain, and James Ursini, eds. *Film Noir Reader*. New York: Limelight, 1996.

———, eds. *Film Noir Reader 2*. New York: Limelight, 1999.

Silver, Alain; James Ursini; and Robert Porfirio, eds. *Film Noir Reader 3: Interviews with Filmmakers of the Classic Noir Period*. New York: Limelight, 2001.

Silver, Alain, and Elizabeth Ward, eds. *Film Noir: An Encyclopedic Reference to the American Style*. Rev. exp. ed. Woodstock, N.Y.: Overlook, 1992.

Sitney, P. Adams. *Vital Crises in Italian Cinema: Iconography, Stylistics, Politics*. Austin: University of Texas Press, 1999.

Slide, Anthony. *Actors on Red Alert: Career Interviews with Five Actors and Actresses Affected by the Blacklist*. Lanham, Md.: Scarecrow, 1999.

Slocum, David J., ed. *Violence and American Cinema*. London: Routledge, 2000.

Smith, Murray. "*Film Noir*, the Female Gothic, and 'Deception.'" *Wide Angle* 10, no. 1 (Winter 1988): 62–75.

Smoodin, Eric. "Motion Pictures and Television, 1930–1945: A Pre-History of the Relations between the Two Media." *Journal of the University Film and Video Association* 34, no. 3 (Summer 1982): 3–8.

Smoodin, Eric L., and Ann Martin, eds. *Hollywood Quarterly: Film Culture in Postwar America, 1945–1957*. Berkeley: University of California Press, 2002.

Sorlin, Pierre. *Italian National Cinema 1896–1996*. London: Routledge, 1996.

Stirling, Monica. *A Screen of Time: A Study of Luchino Visconti*. New York: Harcourt Brace Jovanovich, 1979.

Suid, Lawrence H. *Guts and Glory: Great American War Movies*. Reading, Mass.: Addison-Wesley, 1978.

Telotte, J. P. "Film Noir and the Dangers of Discourse." *Quarterly Review of Film Studies* 9, no. 2 (Spring 1984): 102–12.

———. *Dreams of Darkness: Fantasy and the Films of Val Lewton*. Urbana: University of Illinois Press, 1985.

———. "Film Noir and the Double Indemnity of Discourse." *Genre* 18, no. 1 (Spring 1985): 57–73.

———. "Siodmak's Phantom Women and Noir Narrative." *Film Criticism* 11, no. 3 (Spring 1987): 1–10.

Trainor, Richard. "Major Powers." *Sight and Sound* 57, no. 1 (Winter 1987/88): 27–30.

Trumbo, Dalton. *The Time of the Toad: A Study of Inquisition in America and Two Related Pamphlets*. New York: Harper & Row, 1972.

Tuska, Jon. *Dark Cinema: American Film Noir in Cultural Perspective*. Westport, Conn.: Greenwood, 1984.

Vitti, Antonio. *Giuseppe De Santis and Postwar Italian Cinema*. Toronto: University of Toronto Press, 1996.

Vorhaus, Bernard. *Saved from Oblivion: An Autobiography*. Lanham, Md: Scarecrow, 2000.

Wager, Jans B. *Dangerous Dames: Women and Representation in the Weimar Street Film and Film Noir*. Athens: Ohio State University Press, 1999.

Waldman, Diane. "'At Last I Can Tell It to Someone!': Feminine Point of View and Subjectivity in the Gothic Romance Film of the 1940's." *Cinema Journal* 23, no. 2 (Winter 1983): 29–40.

Walsh, Andrea S. *The Women's Film and Female Experience, 1940–1950*. New York: Praeger, 1984.

Warshow, Robert. *The Immediate Experience*. Garden City, N.Y.: Doubleday, 1962. Repr. Epilogue Stanley Cavell. Foreword Sherry Abel. Cambridge, Mass.: Harvard University Press, 2002.

Weinberg, Gerhard L. *A World at Arms: A Global History of World War II*. Cambridge, Eng.: Cambridge University Press, 1994.

Wetta, Frank J., and Stephen J. Curley. *Celluloid Wars: A Gude to Film and the American Experience of War*. New York: Greenwood, 1992.

Wilinsky, Barbara. *Sure Seaters: The Emergence of Art House Cinema*. Minneapolis: University of Minnesota Press, 2001.

Williams, Carol Traynor. *The Dream beside Me: The Movies and the Children of the Forties*. Rutherford, N.J.: Fairleigh Dickinson University Press, 1980.

Woll, Allen L. *The Hollywood Musical Goes to War*. Chicago: Nelson-Hall, 1983.

"World War II in Film." Special issue of *Film and History* 27, nos. 1–4 (1997).

Zavattini, Cesare. *Sequences from a Cinematic Life*. Trans. William Weaver. Englewood Cliffs, N.J.: Prentice-Hall, 1970.

Zavattini, Cesare. "Some Ideas on the Cinema." In Curle and Snyder, eds., *Vittorio De Sica*, pp. 50–61.

CHAPTER 12. HOLLYWOOD, 1952–1965

"American Widescreen." Special issue of *Velvet Light Trap* 21 (Summer 1985).

Anderson, Christopher. *Hollywood TV: The Studio System in the Fifties*. Austin: University of Texas Press, 1994.

Andrew, J. Dudley. *André Bazin*. New York: Oxford University Press, 1978.

———. "The Postwar Struggle for Color. *Cinema Journal* 18, no. 2 (Spring 1979): 41–52. Repr. in de Lauretis and Heath, eds., *The Cinematic Apparatus*, pp. 61–75.

Arick, Michael. "In Stereo: The Sound of Money!" *Sight and Sound* 57, no. 1 (Winter 1987/88): 35–42.

Baer, William, ed. *Elia Kazan: Interviews*. Jackson: University Press of Mississippi, 2000.

Balio, Tino. "When Is an Independent Producer Independent? The Case of United Artists after 1948." *Velvet Light Trap* 22 (1986): 55–64.

———. *United Artists: The Company That Changed the Film Industry*. Madison: University of Wisconsin Press, 1987.

———, ed. *Hollywood in the Age of Television*. Boston: Unwin Hyman, 1990.

Barr, Charles. "Cinemascope: Before and After." *Film Quarterly* 16, no. 4 (1963): 4–24.

Basinger, Jeanine. *A Woman's View: How Hollywood Spoke to Women, 1930–1960*. New York: Knopf, 1993.

Battcock, Gregory, ed. *The New American Cinema*. New York: Dutton, 1967.

Baxter, John. *Science Fiction in the Cinema*. New York: Paperback Library, 1970.

———. *Hollywood in the Sixties*. New York: Macmillan, 1972.

Bazin, André. *What Is Cinema?* 2 vols. Selected and trans. Hugh Gray. Berkeley: University of California Press, 1967, 1971.

Beck, Philip. "Technology as Commodity and Representation: Cinema Stereo in the Fifties." *Wide Angle* 7, no. 3 (Summer 1986): 62–73.

Belton, John. "Pan and Scan Scandals." *Perfect Vision* 1, no. 3 (Indian Summer 1987): 40–49.

———. "The Shape of Money." *Sight and Sound* 57, no. 1 (Winter 1987/88): 44–47.

———. "The Age of Cinerama: A New Era in the Cinema." *Perfect Vision* 1, no. 4 (Spring/Summer 1988): 78–90.

———. "CinemaScope and Historical Methodology." *Cinema Journal* 28, no. 1 (Fall 1988): 22–44.

———. *Widescreen Cinema*. Cambridge, Mass.: Harvard University Press, 1992.

Berliner, Todd. "Hollywood Movie Dialogue and the 'Real Realism' of John Cassavetes."*Film Quarterly* 52, no. 3 (Spring 1999): 2–16.

Bernardi, Daniel, ed. *Classic Hollywood, Classic Whiteness*. Minneapolis: University of Minnesota Press, 2001.

Bernstein, Matthew, ed. *Controlling Hollywood: Censorship and Regulation in the Studio Era*. New Brunswick, N.J.: Rutgers University Press, 1999.

Biskind, Peter. *Seeing Is Believing*. New York: Pantheon, 1983.

Bogdanovich, Peter. *Who the Devil Made It: Conversations with Legendary Film Directors*. New York: Knopf, 1997.

Branigan, Edward. "Color and Cinema: Problems in the Writing of History." *Film Reader 4: Point of View/Metahistory of Film* (1979): 16–33.

Brill, Lesley. *John Huston's Filmmaking*. New York: Cambridge University Press, 1997.

Brosnan, John. *The Horror People*. New York: St. Martin's, 1976.

———. *Future Tense: The Cinema of Science Fiction*. New York: St. Martin's, 1978.

Butler, Ivan. *Horror in the Cinema*. New York: Barnes, 1970.

Byars, Jackie. *All That Hollywood Allows: Re-Reading Gender in 1950s Melodrama*. Chapel Hill: University of North Carolina Press, 1991.

Carney, Ray. *The Films of John Cassavetes: Pragmatism, Modernism, and the Movies*. Cambridge, Eng.: Cambridge University Press, 1994.

———. *John Cassavetes: The Adventure of Insecurity*. 2nd ed. Walpole, Mass.: Company C, 2000.

———, ed. *Cassavetes on Cassavetes*. London: Faber & Faber, 2001.

Carney, Raymond. *American Dreaming: The Films of John Cassavetes and the American Experience*. Berkeley: University of California Press, 1985.

Carr, Robert E., and R. M. Hayes. *Wide Screen Movies: A History and Filmography of Wide Gauge Filmmaking*. Jefferson, N.C.: McFarland, 1988.

Carroll, Noel. *The Philosophy of Horror: Paradoxes of the Heart*. New York: Routledge, 1990.

Casper, Joseph A. *Vincente Minnelli and the Film Musical*. London: Yoseloff, 1977.

Chandler, Charlotte. *Nobody's Perfect: Billy Wilder, a Personal Biography*. New York: Simon & Schuster, 2002.

Charity, Tom. *John Cassavetes: Lifeworks*. London: Omnibus, 2001.

Chute, David. "The New World of Roger Corman." *Film Comment* 18, no. 2 (March–April 1982): 27–32.

Ciment, Michel. *Kazan on Kazan*. New York: Viking, 1973.

Clarens, Carlos. *An Illustrated History of the Horror Film*. New York: Capricorn, 1967.

Coe, Brian. *The History of Movie Photography*. London: Ash & Grant, 1981.

Cohan, Steve. *Masked Men: Masculinity and Movies in the Fifties*. Bloomington: Indiana University Press, 1997.

Cohen, Allen, and Harry Lawton. *John Huston: A Guide to References and Resources*. New York: Hall, 1997.

Crowe, Cameron. *Conversations with Wilder*. New York: Knopf, 1999.

Cumbow, Robert C. *Once upon a Time: The Films of Sergio Leone*. Metuchen, N.J.: Scarecrow, 1987.

De Franco, J. Phillip, ed. *The Movie World of Roger Corman*. New York: Chelsea House, 1979.

de Lauretis, Teresa, and Stephen Heath, eds. *The Cinematic Apparatus*. New York: St. Martin's, 1980.

Derry, Charles. *Dark Dreams: A Psychological History of the Modern Horror Film*. New York: Barnes, 1977.

Doherty, Thomas. "Hollywood Agit-Prop: The Anti-Communist Cycle, 1948–1954." *Journal of Film and Video* 40, no. 4 (Fall 1988): 15–27.

———. *Teenagers and Teenpics: The Juvenalization of American Movies in the 1950s*. Boston: Unwin, 1988.

Dowdy, Andrew. *The Films of the Fifties: The American State of Mind*. New York: Morrow, 1975.

Edelson, Edward. *Visions of Tomorrow: Great Science Fiction from the Movies*. Garden City, N.Y.: Doubleday, 1975.

Eisenschitz, Bernard. *Nicholas Ray: An American Journey*. Trans. Tom Milne. London: Faber & Faber, 1996.

Everson, William K. *Classics of the Horror Film*. Secaucus, N.J.: Citadel, 1974.

———. *Living in Fear: A History of Horror in the Mass Media*. New York: Scribner's, 1975.

Eyles, Allen; Robert Adkinson; and Nicholas Fry, eds. *The House of Horror: The Complete Story of Hammer Films*. London: Lorrimer, 1973, 1984.

Frank, Alan. *The Science Fiction and Fantasy Film Handbook*. Totowa, N.J.: Barnes & Noble, 1983.

Frayling, Christopher. *Spaghetti Westerns: Cowboys and Europeans from Karl May to Sergio Leone*. London: Routledge & Kegan Paul, 1981.

French, Philip et al. *The Films of Jean-Luc Godard*. London: Studio Vista, 1967.

Fried, Richard M. *Nightmare in Red: The McCarthy Era in Perspective*. New York: Oxford University Press, 1990.

Fry, Roy, and Pamela Fourzon. *The Saga of Special Effects*. Englewood Cliffs, N.J.: Prentice-Hall, 1977.

Fuller, Samuel; Christa Lang Fuller; and Jerome Henry Rudes. *A Third Face: My Tale of Writing, Fighting, and Filmmaking*. New York: Knopf, 2002.

Garnham, Nicholas. *Samuel Fuller*. New York: Viking, 1971.

George-Warren, Holly. *How Hollywood Invented the Wild West: Featuring the Real West, Campfire Melodies, Matinee Idols, Four Legged Friends, Cowgirls and Lone Guns*. Pleasantville, N.Y.: Reader's Digest, 2002.

Girgus, Sam B. *Hollywood Renaissance: The Cinema of Democracy in the Time of Ford, Capra, and Kazan*. Cambridge, Eng.: Cambridge University Press, 1998.

Gow, Gordon. *Hollywood in the Fifties*. London: Zwemmer, 1971.

Grant, Barry Keith, ed. *Planks of Reason: Essays on the Horror Film*. Metuchen, N.J.: Scarecrow, 1984.

Grey, Rudolph. *Nightmare of Ecstasy: The Life and Art of Edward D. Wood, Jr.* Los Angeles, Calif.: Feral House, 1994.

Halliday, Jon. *Sirk on Sirk*. New York: Viking, 1972.

Halliwell, Leslie. *The Dead That Walk*. London: Grafton, 1986.

Hardy, Phil. *Samuel Fuller*. New York: Praeger, 1970.

———, ed. *Science Fiction*. New York: Morrow, 1984.

Harryhausen, Ray. *Film Fantasy Scrapbook*. 2nd ed., rev. New York: Barnes, 1974.

Harvey, Stephen. *Movie Love in the Fifties*. New York: Knopf, 2001.

Haver, Ron. "The Saga of Stereo in the Movies." *Perfect Vision* 1, no. 1 (Winter 1986/7): 64–73.

———. "The Saga of Stereo in the Movies: Part II." *Perfect Vision* 1, no. 3 (Summer 1987): 51–71.

Hayes, R. M. *3-D Movies: A History and Filmography of Stereoscopic Cinema*. Jefferson, N.C.: McFarland, 1989.

Hendershot, Cynthia. *Anti-Communism and Popular Culture in Mid-Century America*. Jefferson, N.C.: McFarland, 2003.

Henry, Nora. *Ethics and Social Criticism in the Hollywood Films of Erich von Stroheim, Ernst Lubitsch, and Billy Wilder*. Westport, Conn.: Praeger, 2000.

Hickman, Gail Morgan. *The Films of George Pal*. New York: Barnes, 1977.

Horton, Robert, ed. *Billy Wilder: Interviews*. Jackson: University Press of Mississippi, 2002.

Huss, Roy, and T. J. Ross, eds. *Focus on the Horror Film*. Englewood Cliffs, N.J.: Prentice-Hall, 1972.

Ih, Charles S. "Holographic Process for Color Motion Picture Preservation." *Society of Motion Picture and Television Engineers Journal* 87, no. 2 (December 1978).

Johnson, William. *Focus on the Science Fiction Film*. Englewood Cliffs, N.J.: Prentice-Hall, 1972.

Kanfer, Stephan. *A Journal of the Plague Years*. New York: Atheneum, 1973. Witchhunts and blacklisting.

Kindem, Gorham A. "Hollywood's Conversion to Color: The Technological, Economic, and Aesthetic Factors." *Journal of the University Film Association* 31, no. 2 (Spring 1979): 29–36. Repr. in Kindem, ed., *The American Movie Industry*, pp. 146–58.

———, ed. *The American Movie Industry: The Business of Motion Pictures*. Carbondale: Southern Illinois University Press, 1982.

Kinnard, Roy. *Beasts and Behemoths: Prehistoric Creatures in the Movies*. Metuchen, N.J.: Scarecrow, 1988.

Knight, Arthur. *The Liveliest Art: A Panoramic History of the Movies*. Rev. ed. New York: Mentor, 1978.

Kreidl, John Francis. *Nicholas Ray*. Boston: Twayne, 1977.

Langman, Larry, and David Ebner. *Encyclopedia of American Spy Films*. New York: Garland, 1990.

Lee, Walt, ed. *Reference Guide to Fantastic Films: Science Fiction, Fantasy, and Horror*. 3 vols. Los Angeles: Chelsea-Lee, 1972–74.

Lewis, Jon. *The Road to Romance and Ruin: Teen Films and Youth Culture*. New York: Routledge, 1992.

Limbacher, James L. *Four Aspects of the Film*. New York: Brussell & Brussell, 1969.

Lipton, Lenny. *Foundations of the Stereoscopic Cinema: A Study in Depth*. New York: Van Nostrand Reinhold, 1982.

Long, Robert Emmet, ed. *John Huston: Interviews*. Jackson: University Press of Mississippi, 2001.

Lourie, Eugene. *My Work Is Films*. New York: Harcourt Brace, 1985.

Lucanio, Patrick. *Them or Us: Archetypal Interpretations of Fifties Alien Invasion Films*. Bloomington: Indiana University Press, 1988.

———. *With Fire and Sword: Italian Spectacles on American Screens, 1958–1968*. Metuchen, N.J.: Scarecrow, 1995.

McGee, Mark Thomas. *Fast and Furious: The Story of American International Pictures*. Jefferson, N.C.: McFarland, 1984.

Madsen, Axel. *Billy Wilder*. Bloomington: Indiana University Press, 1969.

Manvell, Roger. *New Cinema in the U.S.A.* New York: Dutton, 1968.

Marshall, Bill, and Robyn Stilwell, eds. *Musicals: Hollywood and Beyond*. Exeter, Eng.: Intellect, 2000.

Mast, Gerald. *Can't Help Singin': The American Musical on Stage and Screen*. Woodstock, N.Y.: Overlook, 1987.

Menville, Douglas. *A Historical and Critical Survey of the Science Fiction Film*. New York: Arno, 1975.

Menville, Douglas, and R. Reginald. *Things to Come: An Illustrated History of the Science Fiction Film*. New York: Times Books, 1977.

———. *Futurevisions: The New Golden Age of the Science Fiction Film*. San Bernardino, Calif.: Borgo, 1985.

Miller, Gabriel. *The Films of Martin Ritt: Fanfare for the Common Man*. Jackson: University Press of Mississippi, 2000.

———, ed. *Martin Ritt: Interviews*. Jackson: University Press of Mississippi, 2003.

Mitchell, Lee Clark. "Violence in the Film Western." In Slocum, ed., *Violence and American Cinema*, pp. 176–91.

Morgan, Hall, and Dan Symmes. *Amazing 3-D*. Boston: Little, Brown, 1982.

Morris, Gary. *Roger Corman*. Boston: Twayne, 1985.

Munby, Jonathan. *Screening the Gangster from "Little Caesar" to "Touch of Evil."* Chicago: University of Chicago Press, 1999.

Naha, Ed. *The Films of Roger Corman: Brilliance on a Budget*. New York: Arno, 1982.

Naremore, James. *The Films of Vincente Minnelli*. Cambridge, Eng.: Cambridge University Press, 1993.

Neale, Stephen. *Cinema and Technology: Image, Sound, Colour*. Bloomington: Indiana University Press, 1985.

Neve, Brian. *Film and Politics in America: A Social Tradition*. London: Routledge, 1992.

Nolletti, Arthur, Jr., ed. *The Films of Fred Zinnemann: Critical Perspectives*. Albany: State University of New York Press, 1999.

Noriega, Chon. "Godzilla and the Japanese Nightmare: When Them! Is Us." *Cinema Journal* 27, no. 1 (Fall 1987): 47–62.

O'Connell, Bill. "Fade Out." *Film Comment* 15, no. 5 (September–October 1979): 11–18.

Ottoson, Robert. *American International Pictures: A Filmography*. New York: Garland, 1985.

Parish, James Robert, and Michael R. Pitts. *The Great Spy Pictures*. Metuchen, N.J.: Scarecrow, 1974.

———. *The Great Science Fiction Pictures*. Metuchen, N.J.: Scarecrow, 1977.

———. *The Great Spy Pictures II*. Metuchen, N.J. Scarecrow, 1986.

Perry, Danny, ed. *Omni's Screen Flights/Screen Fantasies: The Future According to Science Fiction*. Garden City, N.Y.: Doubleday, 1984.

Pirie, David. *A Heritage of Horror: The English Gothic Cinema 1946–1972*. London: Gordon Fraser, 1973.

Pratley, Gerald. *The Cinema of John Frankenheimer*. Cranbury, N.J.: Barnes, 1969.

———. *The Cinema of Otto Preminger*. Cranbury, N.J.: Barnes, 1971.

———. *The Cinema of John Huston*. Cranbury, N.J.: Barnes, 1977.

Prawer, S.S. *Caligari's Children: The Film as a Tale of Terror*. New York: Oxford University Press, 1980.

Ramonet, Ignacio. "Italian Westerns as Political Parables." *Cineaste* 15, no. 1 (1986): 30–35.

Reeves, Hazard. "This Is Cinerama." *Film History* 11, no. 1 (1999): 85–97.

Robinson, David. *The History of World Cinema*. New York: Stein & Day, 1973.

Rogin, Michael. *Ronald Reagan, the Movie and Other Episodes in Political Demonology*. Berkeley: University of California Press, 1987.

Ross, Lillian. *Picture*. New York: Avon, 1952. On the filming of John Huston's *Red Badge of Courage*.

Roven, Jeff. *A Pictorial History of Science Fiction Films.* Secaucus, N.J.: Citadel, 1975.

———. *S-F 2: A Pictorial History of Science Fiction Films from "Rollerball" to "Return of the Jedi."* Secaucus, N.J.: Citadel, 1984.

Sarris, Andrew. *The American Cinema: Directors and Directions, 1929–1968.* New York: Dutton, 1968.

Sayre, Nora. *Running Time: Films of the Cold War.* New York: Dial, 1982.

Schumach, Murray. *The Face on the Cutting Room Floor.* New York: Morrow, 1964.

"Science Fiction and Sexual Difference." Special issue of *Camera Obscura* 15 (1988).

Seidman, Steve. *The Film Career of Billy Wilder.* Boston: Hall, 1977.

Shapiro, Jerome E. *Atomic Bomb Cinema: The Apocalyptic Imagination on Film.* London: Routledge, 2002.

Sikov, Ed. *Laughing Hysterically: American Screen Comedy of the 1950s.* New York: Columbia University Press, 1994.

———. *Sunset Boulevard: The Life and Times of Billy Wilder.* New York: Hyperion, 1998.

Silverman, Stephen M. *Dancing on the Ceiling: Stanley Donen and His Movies.* New York: Knopf, 1996.

Sinyard, Neil, and Adrian Turner. *Journey down Sunset Boulevard: The Films of Billy Wilder.* London: BCW, 1980.

Slocum, David J., ed. *Violence and American Cinema.* London: Routledge, 2000.

Slusser, George, and Eric C. Rabkin, eds. *Shadows of the Magic Lamp: Fantasy and Science Fiction in Film.* Carbondale: Southern Illinois University Press, 1985.

Smoodin, Eric L., and Ann Martin, eds. *Hollywood Quarterly: Film Culture in Postwar America, 1945–1957.* Berkeley: University of California Press, 2002.

Sobchak, Vivian. *Screening Space: The American Science Fiction Film.* 2nd ed. New York: Ungar, 1987.

Spehr, Paul C. "Fading, Fading, Faded: The Color Film Crisis." *American Film* 5 (November 1979): 56–61.

Stern, Michael. *Douglas Sirk.* Boston: Twayne, 1979.

Sterritt, David. *Mad to Be Saved: The Beats, the '50s, and Film.* Carbondale: Southern Illinois University Press, 1998.

Strickland, A. W., and Forrest J. Ackerman. *A Reference Guide to American Science Fiction Films.* Bloomington, Ind.: T.I.S., 1981.

Tavernier, Bertrand. "The Ethical Romantic: Delmer Daves Was a Progressive Republican, a Passionate Craftsman, and a Maker of Exquisitely Enlightened Genre Films." *Film Comment* 39, no. 1 (January–February 2003): 42–49.

"3-D." Special issue of *American Cinematographer* 64, no. 7 (July 1983).

Twitchell, James B. *Dreadful Pleasures: An Anatomy of Modern Horror.* New York: Oxford, 1985.

Walker, Alexander. *Stardom.* New York: Stein & Day, 1970.

Waller, Gregory A., ed. *American Horrors: Essays on the Modern American Horror Film.* Urbana: University of Illinois Press, 1988.

Warren, Bill. *Keep Watching the Skies: American Science Fiction Movies of the Fifties.* 2 vols. Jefferson, N.C.: McFarland, 1982, 1986.

Weaver, Tom. *Interviews with B Science Fiction and Horror Movie Makers: Writers, Producers, Directors, Actors, Moguls, and Makeup.* Jefferson, N.C.: McFarland, 1988.

"The Western." Special issue of *Film Criticism* 20, no. 3 (1996).

"Wide Screen Formats: Their Future." Special issue of *American Cinematographer* 71, no. 3 (March 1990).

Willemen, Paul, and David Will, ed. *Roger Corman: The Millennic Vision.* Edinburgh, Scot.: Edinburgh Film Festival '70, 1970.

Willis, Donald. *Horror and Science Fiction Films: A Checklist.* Metuchen, N.J.: Scarecrow, 1972.

———. *Horror and Science Fiction Films II.* Metuchen, N.J.: Scarecrow, 1982.

———, ed. *Variety's Complete Science Fiction Reviews.* New York: Garland, 1985.

Winston, Brian. "A Whole Technology of Dyeing." *Daedalus* (Fall 1985): 105–23.

Wysotsky, Michael Z. *Wide-Screen Cinema and Stereophonic Sound.* New York: Hastings House, 1971.

Young, Jeff. *Kazan—the Master Director Discusses His Films: Interviews with Elia Kazan.* New York: Newmarket, 1999.

Yudkoff, Alvin. *Gene Kelly: A Life of Dance and Dreams.* New York: Back Stage, 1999.

Zolotow, Maurice. *Billy Wilder in Hollywood.* New York: Putnam, 1977.

CHAPTER 13. THE FRENCH NEW WAVE AND ITS NATIVE CONTEXT

Affron, Mirella Jona. "Bresson and Pascal: Rhetorical Affinities." *Quarterly Review of Film Studies* 10, no. 2 (Spring 1985): 118–34.

Allen, Don. *Truffaut.* New York: Viking, 1974.

Allen, Don. *Finally Truffaut.* New York: Beaufort, 1985.

Almendros, Nestor. *A Man with a Camera.* Trans. Rachel Phillips Belash. New York: Farrar, Straus & Giroux, 1984.

Anderson, Melissa. "The Modest Gesture of the Filmmaker: An Interview with Agnès Varda." *Cineaste* 24, no. 4 (Fall 2001): 24–27.

"André Bazin." Special issue of *Wide Angle* 9, no. 4 (1985).

Andrew, J. Dudley. "Bazin before *Cahiers.*" *Cineaste* 12, no. 1 (1962): 11–15.

———. *André Bazin*. New York: Oxford University Press, 1978.

Armes, Roy. *The Cinema of Alain Resnais*. Cranbury, N.J.: Barnes, 1968.

———. *French Cinema since 1946*. 2nd enl. ed. 2 vols. Cranbury, N.J.: Barnes, 1970.

———. *French Film*. New York: Dutton, 1970.

———. *French Cinema*. New York: Oxford University Press, 1985.

———. "A Cinema of Continuity: French Film Making during the Fourth Republic." *Cinefocus* 4 (1996): 25–33.

Atack, Margaret. *May '68 in French Fiction and Film: Rethinking Society, Rethinking Representation*. Oxford: Oxford University Press, 1999.

Austin, Bruce A., ed. *Current Research in Film: Audiences, Economics, and Law* 2 (Norwood, N.J., Ablex, 1986). Periodical; ceased publication with vol. 5.

———, ed. *Current Research in Film: Audiences, Economics, and Law* 4 (Norwood, N.J., Ablex, 1988). Periodical; ceased publication with vol. 5.

Austin, Guy. *Contemporary French Cinema: An Introduction*. Manchester, Eng.: Manchester University Press, 1996.

———. *Claude Chabrol*. Manchester, Eng.: Manchester University Press, 1999.

Bazin, André. "Three Forgotten French Filmmakers: André Cayatte, Georges Rouquier, and Roger Leenhardt." Trans. Bert Cardullo. *Cinema Journal* 42, no. 1 (Fall 2002) 3–20.

Bellos, David. *Jacques Tati: His Life and Art*. London: Harvill, 2001.

Bessy, Maurice, and Raymond Chirat. *Histoire du cinéma français: Encyclopédie des films 1940–1950*. Paris: Pygmalion/Watelet, 1994.

Biggs, Melissa E. *French Films, 1945–1993: A Critical Filmography of the 400 Most Important Releases*. Jefferson, N.C.: McFarland, 1996.

Bíró, Yvette, and Catherine Portuges. "Caryatids of Time: Temporality in the Cinema of Agnès Varda." *Performing Arts Journal* 19, no. 3 (September 1997): 1–10.

Braudy, Leo, ed. *Focus on "Shoot the Piano Player."* Englewood Cliffs, N.J.: Prentice-Hall, 1972.

Bresson, Robert. *Notes on the Cinematographer*. Trans. Jonathan Griffin. London: Quartet, 1986.

Brown, Nick, ed. *Cahiers du Cinéma, 1969–72: The Politics of Representation*. Cambridge, Mass.: Harvard University Press, 1990.

Brown, Royal S., ed. *Focus on Godard*. Englewood Cliffs, N.J.: Prentice-Hall, 1972.

Brunette, Peter. "But Nothing Happened: The Everyday in French Postwar Cinema." In Gumpert, ed., *The Art of the Everyday*, pp. 72–92.

Brunette, Peter, and Gerald Peary. "A Child of the New Wave: An Interview with Benoît Jacquot." *Cineaste* 25, no. 3 (2000): 23–27.

Buss, Robin. *French Film Noir*. London: Boyars, 1994.

Cameron, Ian, ed. *The Films of Jean-Luc Godard*. New York: Praeger, 1969.

———. ed. *The Films of Robert Bresson*. New York: Praeger, 1969.

———. ed. *Claude Chabrol*. New York: Praeger, 1970.

Chabrol, Claude, and Eric Rohmer. *Hitchcock: The First Forty-Four Years*. Trans. Stanley Hochman. New York: Ungar, 1979.

Chang, Chris. "Escape from New York." *Film Comment* 33, no. 4 (1997): 56–61. Profile of Luc Besson, with an emphasis on his film *The Fifth Element* (1997).

Chion, Michel. *The Films of Jacques Tati*. Trans. Michel Chion and Antonio D'Alfonso. 2nd ed. Tonawanda, N.Y.: Guernica, 2002.

Ciment, Michel. "The Poetry of Precision." *American Film* 9, no. 1 (October 1983): 70–73.

Collet, Jean. *Jean-Luc Godard*. New York: Crown, 1968.

Collington, Tara L. "History Is Not Just a Thing of the Past: The Chronotropic Transpositions of *La Reine Margot*." *Lit: Literature Interpretation Theory* 13, no. 2 (April–June 2002): 97–116.

Colombat, André Pierre. *The Holocaust in French Film*. Metuchen, N.J.: Scarecrow, 1993.

Conley, Tom. "Revamping *Irma:* Immodest Reflections on French Cinema and Globalization." *Sites* 4, no. 2 (Fall 2000): 417–33.

Cooper, Caroline M. "Humour and Gender in French New Wave Cinema." In Parkin, ed., *French Humour*, pp. 201–21.

Cousins, Russell. "The Heritage Film and Cultural Politics: *Germinal* (Berri, 1993)." In Powrie, ed., *French Cinema in the 1990s*, pp. 25–36.

Crisp, C. G. *François Truffaut*. New York: Praeger, 1972.

———. *Eric Rohmer: Realist and Moralist*. Bloomington: Indiana University Press, 1988.

Crisp, Colin. *The Classic French Cinema, 1930–1960*. Bloomington: Indiana University Press, 1993.

Cubitt, Sean. "*Delicatessen:* Eco-Apocalypse in the New French Science Fiction Cinema." In Sardar and Cubitt, eds., *Aliens R Us*, pp. 18–33.

Danan, Martine. "From the 'Prenational' to a 'Postnational' French Cinema." *Film History* 8, no. 1 (1996): 72–83. Repr. in Fowler, ed., *The European Cinema Reader*, pp. 232–45.

de Baecque, Antoine, and Serge Toubiana. *Truffaut: A Biography*. Trans. Catherine Temerson. New York: Knopf, 1999.

Dine, Philip. *Images of the Algerian War: French Fiction and Film, 1954–1992*. Oxford: Clarendon, 1994.

Dixon, Wheeler Winston. *The Films of Jean-Luc Godard*. Albany: State University of New York Press, 1997.

Douchet, Jean; Cedric Anger; and Robert Bonnonno. *French New Wave*. Trans. Robert Bonnonno. New York: Hazan/ Distributed Art Publishers, 1999.

Drake, Chris. "Desire Is Violence." *Sight and Sound* 10, no. 7 (July 2000): 16–18. Interview with Claire Denis.

Durgnat, Raymond. *Franju*. London: Studio Vista, 1967.

Durham, Carolyn A. *Double Takes: Culture and Gender in French Films and Their American Remakes*. Hanover, N.H.: University Press of New England, 1998.

Elsaesser, Thomas. "Rivette and the End of Cinema." *Sight and Sound* 1, no. 12 (1992): 20–23.

Erickson, John; Lynn A. Higgens; Dalton Krauss; and Steven Ungar, eds. *Gender and French Film since the New Wave/ Questions de "gender" dans le cinéma français depuis la Nouvelle Vague*. Lexington: University Press of Kentucky, 2002.

Erickson, Steve. "Making a Connection between the Cinema, Politics, and Real Life: An Interview with Olivier Assayas." *Cineaste* 22, no. 4 (1997): 6–9.

Ezra, Elizabeth, and Sue Harris. *France in Focus: Film and National Identity*. Oxford: Berg, 2000.

Finney, Angus. *The State of European Cinema: A New Dose of Reality*. London: Cassell, 1996.

Forbes, Jill. *The Cinema in France: After the New Wave*. Bloomington: Indiana University Press, 1992.

Fowler, Catherine, ed. *The European Cinema Reader*. London: Routledge, 2002.

French, Philip, ed. *Malle on Malle*. London: Faber & Faber, 1993.

Giannetti, Louis D. *Godard and Others*. London: Tantivy, 1975.

Godard, Jean-Luc. *Godard on Godard*. Ed. Jean Narboni and Tom Milne. New York: Viking, 1972.

Godard, Jean-Luc; Emmanuel Burdeau; and Charles Tesson. *The Future(s) of Film: Interview with Jean-Luc Godard*. London: Gachnang & Springer, 2002.

"The Godard Dossier." Special section of *Screen* 40, no. 3 (Autumn 1999): 304–47.

Graham, Peter, ed. *The New Wave*. Garden City, N.Y.: Doubleday, 1968.

Greene, Naomi. *Landscapes of Loss: The National Past in Postwar French Cinema*. Princeton, N.J.: Princeton University Press, 1999.

Gumpert, Lynn, ed. *The Art of the Everyday: The Quotidian in Postwar French Culture*. New York: New York University Press, 1997.

Hanlon, Linda. *Fragments: Bresson's Film Style*. Rutherford, N.J.: Fairleigh Dickinson University Press, 1986.

Harcourt, Peter. "Alain Resnais." *Film Comment* 9, no. 6 (November–December 1973): 47.

Harris, Geoffrey, T., ed. *On Translating French Literature and Film*. Amsterdam: Rodopi, 1996.

Harvey, Sylvia. *May '68 and Film Culture*. London: British Film Institute, 1978.

Hay, Stephen. *Bernard Tavernier: The Film-Maker of Lyon*. London: Tauris, 2000.

Hayward, Susan. "A History of French Cinema: 1895–1991: Pioneering Film-Makers (Guy, Dulac, Varda) and Their Heritage." *Paragraph* 15, no. 1 (March 1992): 19–37.

———. *French National Cinema*. London: Routledge, 1993.

———. *Luc Besson*. Manchester, Eng.: Manchester University Press, 1998.

Hayward, Susan, and Ginette Vincendeau, eds. *French Film: Texts and Contexts*. 2nd ed. London: Routledge, 2000.

Higgins, Lynn A. *New Novel, New Wave, New Politics: Fiction and the Representation of History in Postwar France*. Lincoln: University of Nebraska Press, 1996.

Hillier, Jim, ed. *Cahiers du Cinéma, the 1950s—Neo-Realism, Hollywood, New Wave*. Cambridge, Mass.: Harvard University Press, 1985.

———, ed. *Cahiers du Cinéma, the 1960s: New Wave, New Cinema, Reevaluating Hollywood*. Cambridge, Mass.: Harvard University Press, 1986.

Hoffmann, Stanley. Introduction to *The Sorrow and the Pity* by Marcel Ophüls. New York: Grove, 1972. Screenplay.

Hogue, Peter. "Melville: The Elective Affinities." *Film Comment* 23, no. 6 (November–December, 1996): 17–22.

Holmes, Diana, and Robert Ingram. *François Truffaut*. Manchester, Eng.: Manchester University Press, 1998.

Howe, Susan. "Sorting Facts, or, Nineteen Ways of Looking at Marker." In Warren, ed., *Beyond Document*, pp. 295–343.

Hughes, Alex, and Keith Reader, eds. *Encyclopedia of Contemporary French Culture*. London: Routledge, 1998.

Hughes, Alex, and James S. Williams, eds. *Gender and French Cinema*. New York: Berg, 2002.

Ilott, Terry. *Budgets and Markets: A Study of the Budgeting of European Films*. London: Routledge, 1996.

Insdorf, Annette. *François Truffaut*. New York: Morrow, 1979.

Jameson, Richard T. "Wild Child, Movie Master." *Film Comment* 21, no. 1 (January–February 1985): 34–41.

"Jean-Luc Godard: Histoire(s) du cinéma (1988–1998)." Special section of *Screen* 40, no. 3 (Autumn 1999): 304–47.

Johnston, Sheila. "Death Every Day." *Sight and Sound* 11, no. 4 (April 2001): 12–13. Interview with François Ozon.

Kael, Pauline. *Deeper into Movies*. Boston: Little, Brown, 1973.

Kawin, Bruce F. *Faulkner and Film*. New York: Ungar, 1977.

———. *Mindscreen: Bergman, Godard, and First-Person Film*. Princeton, N.J.: Princeton University Press, 1978.

Kehr, Dave. "*Cahiers* Back in the Day." *Film Comment* 37, no. 5 (September–October 2001): 31–36.

Lanzoni, Rémi Fournier. *French Cinema: From Its Beginning to the Present*. New York: Continuum, 2002.

Lellis, George. *Bertolt Brecht, Cahiers du Cinéma, and Contemporary Film Theory*. Ann Arbor, Mich.: UMI Research Press, 1982.

Lipkin, Steve. "The New Wave and the Post-War Film Economy." In Austin, ed., *Current Research in Film* 2: 156–85.

MacBean, James Roy. "Godard and the Dziga Vertov Group: Film and Dialectics." *Film Quarterly* 26, no. 1 (Fall 1972): 30–43.

———. *Film and Revolution*. Bloomington: Indiana University Press, 1975.

MacCabe, Colin. *Jean-Luc Godard: A Portrait of the Artist at Seventy*. London: Bloomsbury, 2003.

Marie, Michel. *The French New Wave: An Artistic School*. Trans. Richard John Neupert. Malden, Mass.: Blackwell, 2003.

Marker, Chris. *Le Fond de l'aire est rouge: Scènes de la Troisième Guerre mondiale, 1967–1977*. Paris: Maspero, 1978.

Martin, Marcel. *France: Screen Guide*. New York: Barnes, 1971.

Mast, Gerald; Marshall Cohen; and Leo Braudy, eds. *Film Theory and Criticism*. 5th ed. New York: Oxford University Press, 1999.

Mazdon, Lucy. *Encore Hollywood: Remaking French Cinema*. London: British Film Institute, 2000.

———, ed. *France on Film: Reflections on Popular French Cinema*. London: Wallflower, 2001.

Milne, Tom. "Angels and Ministers." *Sight and Sound* 56, no. 4 (Autumn 1987): 285–87.

Moeller, Hans-Bernhard. "Brecht and 'Epic' Film Medium: The Cineaste Playwright/Film Theoretician and His Influence." *Wide Angle* 3, no. 4 (Winter 1980): 4–11.

Monaco, James. *The New Wave: Truffaut, Godard, Chabrol, Rohmer, Rivette*. New York: Oxford University Press, 1976.

———. *Alain Resnais*. New York: Oxford University Press, 1979.

Mosley, Philip. *Split Screen: Belgian Cinema and Cultural Identity*. Albany: State University of New York Press, 2001.

Mouton, Janice. "From Feminine Masquerade to Flâneuse: Agnès Varda's *Cléo in the City*." *Cinema Journal* 40, no. 2 (2001): 3–16.

Mussman, Toby, ed. *Jean-Luc Godard*. New York: Dutton, 1968.

Myrent, Glenn, and Georges P. Langlois. *Henri Langlois, First Citizen of Cinema*. Trans. Lisa Nesselson. New York: Twayne, 1995.

Neupert, Richard John. *A History of the French New Wave Cinema*. Madison: University of Wisconsin Press, 2002.

Nichols, Bill, ed. *Movies and Methods*. Vol. 1. Berkeley: University of California Press, 1976.

Nogueira, Rui. *Melville*. New York: Viking, 1971.

Nowell-Smith, Geoffrey. "Paris Match: Godard and *Cahiers*." *Sight and Sound* 11, no. 6 (June 2001): 18–21.

Parkin, John, ed. *French Humour*. Amsterdam: Rodopi, 1999.

Petrie, Graham. *The Cinema of François Truffaut*. Cranbury, N.J.: Barnes, 1970.

Porton, Richard. "Elusive *Intimacy:* An Interview with Patrice Chéreau." *Cineaste* 27, no. 1 (2001): 16–19.

Powrie, Phil. *French Cinema in the 1980s: Nostalgia and the Crisis of Masculinity*. Oxford: Clarendon, 1997.

———, ed. *French Cinema in the 1990s: Continuity and Difference*. Oxford: Oxford University Press, 1999.

———. "Heritage, History, and 'New Realism': French Cinema in the 1990s." In Powrie, ed., *French Cinema in the 1990s*, pp. 1–21.

———. *Jean-Jacques Beineix*. Manchester, Eng.: Manchester University Press, 2001.

Prédal, René. *Le Cinéma Français depuis 1945*. Paris: Nathan, 1991.

Puttnam, David, with Neil Watson. *Movies and Money*. New York: Knopf, 1998. Published in the United Kingdom as *The Undeclared War: The Struggle for Control of the World's Film Industry*. London: HarperCollins, 1997.

Quandt, James, ed. *Robert Bresson*. Toronto: Cinémathèque Ontario, 1998.

Raskin, Richard. "Five Explanations for the Jump Cuts in Godard's *Breathless*." *p.o.v.* 6 (December 1998): 141–53.

Reader, Keith. *Robert Bresson*. Manchester, Eng.: Manchester University Press, 2000.

Reisz, Karel, and Gavin Millar. *The Technique of Film Editing*. 2nd enl. ed. New York: Hastings House, 1968.

Rohmer, Eric. *Le Goût de la beauté*. Paris: Éditions de l'Étoile, 1985.

Rosenbaum, Jonathan. *Rivette: Texts and Interviews*. London: British Film Institute, 1977.

Roud, Richard. *Jean-Luc Godard*. Bloomington: Indiana University Press, 1969.

Salama-Carr, Myriam, ed. *On Translating French Literature and Film II*. Amsterdam: Rodopi, 2000.

Sardar, Ziauddin, and Sean Cubitt, eds. *Aliens R Us: The Other in Science Fiction Cinema*. London: Pluto, 2002.

Sarris, Andrew. "Max Ophüls: An Introduction by Andrew Sarris." *Film Comment* 7, no. 2 (Summer 1971): 57.

———. "Notes on the Auteur Theory in 1962." In Mast, Cohen, and Braudy, eds., *Film Theory and Criticism*, pp. 585–88.

Sellier, Geneviève, and Dawn Cornelio. "Masculinity and Politics in New Wave Cinema." *Sites* 4, no. 2 (Fall 2000): 471–87.

Serceau, Michel. *Erich Rohmer: Les jeux de l'amour, du hazard et du discours*. Paris: Cerf, 2000.

Sherzer, Dina, ed. *Cinema, Colonialism, Postcolonialism: Perspectives from the French and Francophone World*. Austin: University of Texas Press, 1996.

Siegel, Marc. "Clichés of Unity: History and Memory in Postwar French Film." *Paroles Gelés: UCLA French Studies* 16, no. 2 (1998): 57–64.

Silverman, Kaja. "The Author as Receiver." *October* 96 (Spring 2001): 17–34.

Silverman, Kaja, and Harun Farocki. *Speaking about Godard*. New York: New York University Press, 1998.

Smith, Alison. *Agnès Varda*. Manchester, Eng.: Manchester University Press, 1998.

Steeples, Shelia, and Allen Katona. "Beyond the New Wave: Four Perspectives on French Cinema." *Film Quarterly* 49, no. 4 (Summer 1996): 2–15.

Sterritt, David, ed. *Jean-Luc Godard: Interviews*. Jackson: University Press of Mississippi, 1998.

———. *The Films of Jean-Luc Godard: Seeing the Invisible*. Cambridge, Eng.: Cambridge University Press, 1999.

Tarr, Carrie, with Brigitte Rollet. *Cinema and the Second Sex: Women's Filmmaking in France in the 1980s and 1990s*. New York: Continuum, 2001.

Temple, Michael, and James S. Williams, eds. *The Cinema Alone: Essays on the Work of Jean-Luc Godard, 1985–2000*. Amsterdam, the Neth.: Amsterdam University Press, 2000.

Truffaut, François. *The Films in My Life*. Trans. Leonard Mayhew. New York: Simon & Schuster, 1978.

Truffaut, François, with Helen G. Scott. *Hitchcock*. Rev. ed. New York: Simon & Schuster, 1984.

Tsakiridou, Cornelia, ed. "Reviewing *Orpheus*: Essays on the Cinema and Art of Jean Cocteau." *Bucknell Review* 41, no. 1 (Lewisburg, Pa.: Bucknell University Press, 1997).

Van Wert, William F. *The Film Career of Alain Robbe-Grillet*. Boston: Hall, 1977.

———. "Chris Marker: The SLON Films." *Film Quarterly* 32, no. 3 (Spring 1979): 38–46.

Vincendeau, Ginette. *The Companion to French Cinema*. London: British Film Institute, 1996.

———. *Stars and Stardom in French Cinema*. London: Continuum, 2000.

———, ed. *Film/Literature/Heritage: A Sight and Sound Reader*. London: British Film Institute, 2001.

Ward, John. *Alain Resnais; or, The Theme of Time*. Garden City, N.Y.: Doubleday, 1968.

Warehime, Marja. "Mixing Genres, May '68 and the Ghosts of History: Louis Malle Rewrites the *Rules of the Game*." *Historical Reflections/Réflexions Historiques* 24, no. 2 (Summer 1998): 179–203.

Warren, Charles, ed. *Beyond Document: Essays on Nonfiction Film*. Hanover, N.H.: University Press of New England, 1996.

White, Susan M. *The Cinema of Max Ophüls: Magisterial Vision and the Figure of Woman*. New York: Columbia University Press, 1995.

Willemen, Paul, ed. *Ophüls*. London: British Film Institute, 1978.

Williams, Alan. *Republic of Images: A History of French Filmmaking*. Cambridge, Mass.: Harvard University Press, 1992.

Wills, David, ed. *Jean-Luc Godard's "Pierrot le fou."* Cambridge, Eng.: Cambridge University Press, 2000.

Wilson, Emma. *French Cinema since 1950: Personal Histories*. London: Duckworth, 1999.

Wood, Robin, and Michael Walker. *Claude Chabrol*. New York: Praeger, 1970.

Zants, Emily. *Creative Encounters with French Films*. 2nd rev. ed. Lewiston, N.Y.: Mellen, 2000.

CHAPTER 14. NEW CINEMAS IN BRITAIN AND THE ENGLISH-SPEAKING COMMONWEALTH

Aitken, Ian. *Alberto Cavalcanti: Realism, Surrealism and National Cinemas*. Trowbridge, Eng.: Flicks, 2001.

Aldgate, Anthony. *Censorship and the Permissive Society: British Cinema and Theatre, 1955–1965*. Oxford: Clarendon, 1995.

Aldgate, Anthony, and Jeffrey Richards. *Britain Can Take It: British Cinema and the Second World War*. 2nd ed. Edinburgh: Edinburgh University Press, 1994.

———. *Best of British: Cinema and Society from 1930 to the Present*. Rev. ed. London: Tauris, 1999.

Allon, Yoram; Del Cullen; and Hannah Patterson, eds. *The Wallflower Critical Guide to Contemporary British and Irish Directors*. London: Wallflower, 2000.

Andrew, Dudley. "The Theater of Irish Cinema." *Yale Journal of Criticism* 15, no. 1 (Spring 2002): 23–58.

Armatage, Kay; Kass Banning; Brenda Longfellow; and Janine Marchessault, eds. *Gendering the Nation: Canadian Women's Cinema*. Toronto: University of Toronto Press, 1999.

Armes, Roy. *A Critical History of British Cinema*. New York: New York University Press, 1978.

Arnold, Kevin, and Onyekachi Wambu. *A Fuller Picture: The Commercial Impact of Six British Films with Black Themes in the 1990s*. London: British Film Institute, 1999.

Ashby, Justine, and Andrew Higson, eds. *British Cinema, Past and Present*. London: Routledge, 2000.

Auty, Martyn, and Nick Roddick, eds. *British Cinema Now*. London: British Film Institute, 1985.

Badder, David. "Powell and Pressburger: The War Years." *Sight and Sound* 28, no. 1 (Winter 1978–79): 8–13.

Baillieu, Bill, and John Goodchild. *The British Film Business.* West Sussex, Eng.: Wiley, 2002.

Bank, Mirra. "Mike Leigh." *Films in Review* 48, nos. 1–2 (January–February 1997): 29–34.

Baron, Cynthia. "Films by Tracey Moffatt: Reclaiming First Australian's Rights, Celebrating Women's Rights." *Women's Studies Quarterly* 30, nos. 1–2 (Spring/Summer 2002): 151–77.

Barr, Charles. *Ealing Studios.* London: Cameron & Taylor, 1977.

———, ed. *All Our Yesterdays: Ninety Years of British Cinema.* London: British Film Institute, 1986.

Barton, Ruth. "From History to Heritage: Some Recent Developments in Irish Cinema." *The Irish Review* 21 (Autumn–Winter 1997): 41–56.

Baxter, John. *The Australian Cinema.* Sydney: Pacific, 1970.

———. *An Appalling Talent: Ken Russell.* London: Michael Joseph, 1973.

Beard, William, and Jerry White, eds. *North of Everything: English-Canadian Cinema since 1980.* Edmonton, Can.: University of Alberta Press, 2002.

Beilby, Peter, and Ross Lansell, eds. *Australian Motion Picture Yearbook 1983.* Melbourne: 4 Seasons/Cinema Papers, 1983.

Berrington, Hugh, ed. *Britain in the Nineties: The Politics of Paradox.* London: Cass, 1998.

Berry, Chris. "Not Necessarily the Sum of Us: Australian Not-So-Queer Cinema." *Metro* 101 (Spring 1995): 12–16.

Berry, David. *Wales and Cinema: The First Hundred Years.* Cardiff: University of Wales Press, 1994.

Betts, Ernest. *The Film Business: A History of British Cinema 1896–1972.* London: Allen & Unwin, 1973.

Bliss, Michael. *Dreams within a Dream: The Films of Peter Weir.* Carbondale: Southern Illinois University Press, 2000.

Blonski, Annette; Barbara Creed; and Freda Freiberg, eds. *Don't Shoot Darling!: Women's Independent Filmmaking in Australia.* Richmond, Australia: Greenhouse, 1987.

Blythe, Martin. *Naming the Other: Images of the Maori in New Zealand Film and Television.* Metuchen, N.J.: Scarecrow, 1995.

Boot, Andy. *Fragments of Fear: An Illustrated History of British Horror Films.* Rev. and upd. ed. London: Creation, 2000.

Bourne, Stephen. *Brief Encounters: Lesbians and Gays in British Cinema, 1930–1977.* London: Cassell, 1996.

———. *Black in the British Frame: Black People in British Film and Television, 1896–1996.* London: Cassell, 1998.

Brand, Simon. *The Australian Film Book: 1930–Today.* Sydney: Dreamweaver, 1985.

"British Cinema 1900–1975." Ed. Wheeler Winston Dixon. Special double issue of *Film Criticism* 16, nos. 1–2 (Fall/Winter 1991–92).

Brooks, Xan. *Choose Life: Ewan McGregor and the British Film Revival.* London: Chameleon, 1998.

Brown, Geoff. "Paradise Found and Lost: The Course of British Realism." In Murphy, ed., *The British Cinema Book,* pp. 248–55.

Brown, John. "A Suitable Job for a Scot." *Sight and Sound* 52, no. 3 (Summer 1983): 157–63.

Brown, John. "Land beyond Brigadoon." *Sight and Sound* 53, no. 1 (Winter 1983/84): 40–46.

Brownlow, Kevin. *David Lean.* New York: St. Martin's, 1996.

Bruce, David. *Scotland the Movie.* Edinburgh: Polygon, 1996.

Burns-Bisogno, Louisa. *Censoring Irish Nationalism: The British, Irish, and American Suppression of Republican Images in Film and Television.* Jefferson, N.C.: McFarland, 1997.

Burrows, Elaine; Janet Moat; David Sharp; and Linda Wood, eds. *The British Cinema Source Book: BFI Viewing Copies and Library Materials.* London: British Film Institute, 1995.

Burton, Alan; Tim O'Sullivan; and Paul Wells, eds. *The Family Way: The Boulting Brothers and British Film Culture.* Trowbridge, Eng.: Flicks, 1999.

———, eds. *Liberal Directions: Basil Dearden and Postwar British Film Culture.* Trowbridge, Eng.: Flicks, 1999.

Butler, Ivan. *Cinema in Britain.* London: Tantivy, 1969.

"Canadian Cinema." Special issue of *Post Script* 15, no. 1 (Fall 1995).

Caputo, Raffaele, and Geoff Burton, eds. *Second Take: Australian Film-Makers Talk.* St. Leonards, N.S.W., Australia: Allen & Unwin, 1999.

Carney, Ray, and Leonard Quart. *The Films of Mike Leigh: Embracing the World.* Cambridge, Eng.: Cambridge University Press, 2000.

Carruthers, Ashley. "Substantial Ways of Reading Cultural Difference in the Mainstream Australian Media." *Media Information Australia* 77 (August 1995): 86–93.

Caughie, John, with Kevin Rockett, eds. *The Companion to British and Irish Cinema.* London: Cassell, 1996.

Caute, David. *Joseph Losey: A Revenge on Life.* London: Faber & Faber, 1994.

Chapman, James. *The British at War: Cinema, State and Propaganda, 1939–1945.* London: Tauris, 1998.

———. "Cinema, Propaganda, and National Identity: British Film and the Second World War." In Ashby and Higson, eds., *British Cinema, Past and Present,* pp. 193–206.

Chibnall, Steve. "Travels in Ladland: The British Gangster

Film Cycle 1998–2001." In Murphy, ed., *The British Cinema Book*, pp. 281–91.

Chibnall, Steve, and Robert Murphy, eds. *British Crime Cinema*. British Popular Cinema series. London: Routledge, 1999.

Chibnall, Steve, and Julian Petley, eds. *British Horror Cinema*. British Popular Cinema series. London: Routledge, 2002.

Christie, Ian, ed. *Powell, Pressburger, and Others*. London: British Film Institute, 1978.

———. *Arrows of Desire: The Films of Michael Powell and Emeric Pressburger*. London: Waterstone, 1985.

———. "Michael Powell (1905–90)." *Film Comment* 26, no. 3 (May–June 1990): 26–43.

———, ed. *Gilliam on Gilliam*. London: Faber & Faber, 1999.

Churchman, Geoffrey B.; Stephen Cain; and Patrick Hudson, eds. *Celluloid Dreams: A Century of Film in New Zealand*. Wellington, N.Z.: IPL, 1997.

Clark, Al. *The Lavender Bus: How a Hit Movie Was Made and Sold*. Sydney: Currency, 1999.

Coencas, Joseph. "British Film Renaissance." *Millimeter* 8, no. 5 (June 1980): 118–23.

Collins, Felicity. *The Films of Gillian Armstrong*. St. Kilda, Vic.: Australian Teachers of Media, 1999.

Conrich, Ian. "Traditions of the British Horror Film." In Murphy, ed., *The British Cinema Book*, pp. 226–31.

"Contemporary British Cinema." Special supplement to *Cineaste* 26, no. 4 (2001): 30–67.

"Contemporary Irish Cinema." Special supplement to *Cineaste* 24, nos. 2–3 (1999): 23–76.

Cook, Pam. *Fashioning the Nation: Costume and Identity in British Cinema*. London: British Film Institute, 1996.

Coombs, Felicity, and Suzanne Gemmell. *Piano Lessons: Approaches to "The Piano."* Sydney: Libbey, 1999.

Coulombe, Michel, and Marcel Jean, eds. *Le Dictionnaire du cinéma québécois*. Montreal: Boréal, 1999.

Coveney, Michael. *The World According to Mike Leigh*. London: HarperCollins, 1996.

Cowie, Peter, ed. *Variety International Film Guide 2001*. Los Angeles: Silman-James, 2001.

Cowie, Peter; Derek Elley; and Daniel Rosenthal, eds. *Variety International Film Guide 2000*. Los Angeles: Silman-James, 2000.

Coyle, Rebecca, ed. *Screen Scores: Studies in Contemporary Australian Film Music*. Sydney: Australian Film, Television and Radio School, 1998.

Craven, Ian, ed. *Australian Cinema in the 1990s*. London: Cass, 2001.

———. "Australian Cinema towards the Millennium." In Craven, ed., *Australian Cinema in the 1990s*, pp. 1–14.

Cunningham, Stuart, and Graeme Turner, eds. *The Media in Australia: Industries, Texts, Audiences*. 2nd ed. Sydney: Allen & Unwin, 1997.

Curtis, Rosemary, and Cathy Gray. *Get the Picture: Essential Data on Australian Film, Television, Video and the New Media*. 6th Edition. Sydney: Australian Film Commission, 1998.

Dale, Martin. *The Movie Game: The Film Industry in Britain, Europe and America*. London: Cassell, 1997.

Dawson, Jonathan, and Bruce Molloy, eds. *Queensland Images in Film and Television*. Brisbane: University of Queensland Press, 1990.

Dennis, Jonathan, and Jan Bieringa, eds. *Film in Aotearoa New Zealand*. 2nd ed. Wellington, N.Z.: Victoria University Press, 1996.

Dermody, Susan, and Elizabeth Jacka. *Anatomy of a Film Industry*. Vol. 1 of *The Screening of Australia*. Sydney: Currency, 1987.

———, eds. *The Imaginary Industry: Australian Film in the Late '80s*. North Ryde, N.S.W., Australia: Australian Film, Television, and Radio School, 1988.

———. *Anatomy of a National Cinema*. Vol. 2 of *The Screening of Australia*. Sydney: Currency, 1988.

Dick, Eddie. *From Limelight to Satellite: A Scottish Film Book*. Edinburgh: Scottish Film Council/British Film Institute, 1990.

Dickinson, Margaret, ed. *Rogue Reels: Oppositional Filmmaking in Britain 1945–90*. London: British Film Institute, 1999.

Dickinson, Margaret, and Sarah Street. *Cinema and State: The Film Industry and the Government, 1927–1984*. London: British Film Institute, 1985.

Donnelly, K. J. *Pop Music in British Cinema: A Chronicle*. London: British Film Institute, 2002.

Donohoe, Joseph I., ed. *Essays on Quebec Cinema*. East Lansing: Michigan State University Press, 1991.

Dorland, Michael. *So Close to the State/s: The Emergence of Canadian Feature Film Policy*. Toronto: University of Toronto Press, 1998.

Drazin, Charles. *The Finest Years: British Cinema of the 1940s*. London: Deutsch, 1998.

Durgnat, Raymond. *A Mirror for England: British Movies from Austerity to Affluence*. New York: Praeger, 1971.

———. "The Ploughman's (Just) Desserts." *American Film* (November 1985): 48–54, 80.

Ehrenstein, David. "Out of the Wilderness—an Interview with Sally Potter." *Film Quarterly* 47, no. 1 (Fall 1993): 2–7.

Elder, Bruce R. *Image and Identity: Reflections on Canadian Film and Culture*. Waterloo, Ont.: Wilfred Laurier University Press, 1989.

Elliott, Bridget, and Anthony Purdy. *Peter Greenaway: Architecture and Allegory*. Chichester, Eng.: Academy, 1997.

Feldman, Seth, and Joyce Nelson, eds. *Canadian Film Reader*. Toronto: Peter Martin Associates, 1977.

Fenton, Harvey, ed. *Flesh and Blood Compendium*. Guildford, Eng.: FAB, 2003.

Fenton, Harvey, and David Flint, eds. *Ten Years of Terror: British Horror Films of the 70s*. Guildford, Eng.: FAB, 2001.

Finney, Angus. *The Egos Have Landed: The Rise and Fall of Palace Pictures*. London: Heinemann, 1996.

———. *The State of European Cinema: A New Dose of Reality*. London: Cassell, 1996.

Flynn, Arthur. *Irish Film: 100 Years*. Wickelow, Ire.: Kestrel, 1996.

Fowler, Catherine, ed. *The European Cinema Reader*. London: Routledge, 2002.

French, Lisa. "Patterns of Production and Policy: The Australian Film Industry in the 1990s." In Craven, ed., *Australian Cinema in the 1990s*, pp. 15–36.

Friedman, Lester, ed. *Fires Were Started: British Cinema and Thatcherism*. Minneapolis: University of Minnesota Press, 1993.

Frow, John, and Meaghan Morris, eds. *Australian Cultural Studies: A Reader*. St. Leonards, N.S.W.: Allen & Unwin, 1994.

Fuller, Graham. "Right Villains—Supergrasses, Spivs, and Razorboys: A Short History of British Crime Movies, Including *Chicago Joe* and *The Krays*." *Film Comment* 26, no. 5 (September–October 1990): 47–52.

———. ed. *Loach on Loach*. London: Faber & Faber, 1999.

Gale, Steven H. *Sharp Cut: Harold Pinter's Screenplays and the Artistic Process*. Lexington: University Press of Kentucky, 2003.

Gasher, Mike. *Hollywood North: The Feature Film Industry in British Columbia*. Vancouver: University of British Columbia Press, 2002.

"Genre and British Cinema." Special issue of *Journal of Popular British Cinema* 1 (1998).

Geraghty, Christine. *British Cinema in the Fifties: Gender, Genre and the "New Look."* London: Routledge, 2000.

Gibson, Pamela Church. "Fewer Weddings and More Funerals: Changes in the Heritage Film." In Murphy, ed., *British Cinema of the 90s*, pp. 115–24.

Gifford, Denis. *British Cinema*. Cranbury, N.J.: Barnes, 1968.

Gittings, Christopher E. *Canadian National Cinema: Ideology, Difference, and Representation*. New York: Routledge, 2002.

Gledhill, Christine, and Gillian Swanson, eds. *Nationalising Femininity: Culture, Sexuality and British Cinema in the Second World War*. Manchester, Eng.: Manchester University Press, 1996.

Gomez, Joseph A. *Peter Watkins*. Boston: Twayne, 1979.

Grant, Barry Keith. *A Cultural Assault: The New Zealand Films of Peter Jackson*. Nottingham: Kakapo/Nottingham Trent University Centre for Asia Pacific Studies, 1999.

Gras, Vernon, and Marguerite Gras, eds. *Peter Greenaway: Interviews*. Jackson: University Press of Mississippi, 2000.

Gray, Michael. *Stills, Reels, and Rushes: Ireland and the Irish in 20th Century Cinema*. Dublin: Blackhall, 1999.

"Green Screen." Special supplement to *Fortnight* 379 (June 1999).

Grunberg, Serge. "Australia, from the Desert to Hollywood." *Metro* 100 (Summer 1994): 27–31.

Hacker, Jonathan, and David Price. *Take Ten: Contemporary British Film Directors*. New York: Oxford University Press, 1991.

Hall, Sheldon. "The Wrong Sort of Cinema: Refashioning the Heritage Film Debate." In Murphy, ed., *The British Cinema Book*, pp. 191–99.

Haltof, Marek. *Peter Weir*. New York: Twayne, 1996.

Handling, Piers. *The Films of Don Shebib*. Ottawa, Ont.: Canadian Film Institute, 1978.

Harcourt, Peter. "Imaginary Images: An Examination of Atom Egoyan's Films." *Film Quarterly* 48, no. 3 (Spring 1995): 2–13. Repr. in Orr and Taxidou, eds., *Post-War Cinema and Modernity*, pp. 410–21.

Harper, Sue. *Picturing the Past: The Rise and Fall of the British Costume Film*. London: British Film Institute, 1994.

———. "Bonnie Prince Charlie Revisited: British Costume Film in the 1950s." In Murphy, ed., *The British Cinema Book*, pp. 127–34.

———. *Women in British Cinema: Mad, Bad and Dangerous to Know*. London: Continuum, 2000.

Harper, Sue, and Vincent Porter. "Moved to Tears: Weeping in the Cinema in Postwar Britain." *Screen* 37, no. 2 (Summer 1996): 152–73.

———. "Cinema Audience Tastes in 1950s Britain." *Journal of Popular British Cinema* 2 (1999): 66–82.

Haynes, Roslynn. *Seeking the Centre: The Australian Desert in Literature, Art and Film*. Cambridge, Eng.: Cambridge University Press, 1998.

Hearn, Marcus, and Alan Barnes. *The Hammer Story*. London: Titan, 1997.

Hedling, Erik. *Lindsay Anderson: Maverick Filmmaker*. London: Cassell, 1998.

———. "Lindsay Anderson and the Development of British Art Cinema." In Murphy, ed., *The British Cinema Book*, pp. 241–47.

Higson, Andrew. "Space, Place, Spectacle: Landscape and

Townscape in the 'Kitchen Sink' Film." *Screen* 25, nos. 4–5 (July–October 1984): 2–21.

———, ed. "Re-presenting the National Past: Nostalgia and Pastiche in the Heritage Film." In Friedman, ed., *Fires Were Started*, pp. 109–29.

———. *Waving the Flag: Constructing a National Cinema in Britain*. Oxford: Clarendon, 1995.

———, ed. *Dissolving Views: Key Writings on British Cinema*. London: Cassell, 1996.

———. "The Heritage Film and British Cinema." In Higson, ed., *Dissolving Views*, pp. 232–48.

———, ed. *English Heritage, English Cinema: Costume Drama since 1980*. Oxford: Oxford University Press, 2002.

Hill, John. *Sex, Class and Realism: British Cinema 1956–1963*. London: British Film Institute, 1986.

———. "British Film Policy." In Moran, ed., *Film Policy: International, National and Regional Perspectives*, pp. 101–13.

———. " 'Every Fuckin' Choice Stinks': Ken Loach." *Sight and Sound* 8, no. 11 (November 1998): 18–21.

———. *British Cinema in the 1980s: Issues and Themes*. Oxford: Oxford University Press, 1999.

———. "The Heritage Film: Issues and Debates." In Hill, *British Cinema in the 1980s*, pp. 73–98.

———. "Failure and Utopianism: Representations of the Working Class in British Cinema of the 1990s." In Murphy, ed., *British Cinema of the 90s*, pp. 178–87.

———. "From the New Wave to 'Brit-grit': Continuity and Difference in Working-Class Realism." In Ashby and Higson, eds., *British Cinema, Past and Present*, pp. 249–60.

Hill, John, and Pamela Church Gibson, eds. *World Cinema: Critical Approaches*. Oxford: Oxford University Press, 2000.

Hill, John, and Martin McLoone, eds. *Big Picture, Small Screen: The Relations between Film and Television*. Luton, Eng.: University of Luton Press, 1996.

Hill, John; Martin McLoone; and Paul Hainsworth, eds. *Border Crossing: Film in Ireland, Britain, and Europe*. Belfast: Institute of Irish Studies/British Film Institute, 1994.

Houston, Beverle, and Marsha Kinder. "The Losey-Pinter Collaboration." *Film Quarterly* 32, no. 1 (Fall 1978): 17–30.

Hudgins, Christopher C. "Inside Out: Filmic Technique and the Creation of Consciousness in Harold Pinter's *Old Times*." *Genre* 13, no. 3 (Fall 1980): 355–76.

Hughes, Robert. *The Fatal Shore: The Epic of Australia's Founding*. New York: Knopf, 1987.

Hunt, Leon. *British Low Culture: From Safari Suits to Sexploitation*. London: Routledge, 1998.

Hunt, Martin. "The Poetry of the Ordinary: Terence Davies and the Social Art Cinema." *Screen* 40, no. 1 (Spring 1999): 1–16.

Hunter, I. Q., ed. *British Science Fiction Cinema*. London: Routledge, 1999.

Hunter, Jack, ed. *House of Horrors: The Complete Hammer Films Story*. 2nd rev. ed. London: Creation, 1996.

Huss, Roy, ed. *Focus on "Blow-Up."* Englewood Cliffs, N.J.: Prentice-Hall, 1971.

Hutchings, Peter. *Hammer and Beyond: The British Horror Film*. Manchester, Eng.: Manchester University Press, 1993.

———. "Beyond the New Wave: Realism in British Cinema, 1959–1963." In Murphy, ed., *The British Cinema Book*, pp. 146–52.

Ilott, Terry. *Budgets and Markets: A Study of the Budgeting of European Films*. London: Routledge, 1996.

Izod, John. *The Films of Nicolas Roeg: Myth and Mind*. London: Macmillan, 1992.

Jacka, Elizabeth. "Australian Cinema." In Hill and Gibson, eds., *World Cinema*, pp. 132–38.

James, Nick. "They Think It's All Over: British Cinema's US Surrender." In Murphy, ed., *The British Cinema Book*, pp. 301–9.

Jarman, Derek. *Kicking the Pricks*. Woodstock, N.Y.: Overlook, 1997.

Jennings, Karen. *Sites of Difference: Cinematic Representations of Aboriginality and Gender*. South Melbourne: Australian Film Institute Research and Information Centre, 1993.

Jennings, Mary-Lou, ed. *Humphrey Jennings: Film-maker, Painter, Poet*. London: British Film Institute, 1982.

Johnson, Lucy, and Graham Jones, eds. *Talking Pictures: Interviews with Contemporary British Film-makers*. London: British Film Institute, 1997.

Johnson, Tom, and Deborah Del Vecchio. *Hammer Films: An Exhaustive Filmography*. Jefferson, N.C.: McFarland, 1996.

Jones, Ross. *Cut! Protection of Australia's Film and Television Industries*. St. Leonards, N.S.W., Australia: Centre for Independent Studies, 1991.

Kelly, Brendan. "Canada." In Cowie, ed., *Variety International Film Guide 2001*, pp. 101–6.

Kemp, Philip. *Lethal Innocence—the Cinema of Alexander Mackendrick*. London: Methuen, 1991.

Kennedy, Harlan. "The British Are Coming." *Film Comment* 16, no. 3 (May–June 1980): 57–60.

———. "The Brits Have Gone Nuts." *Film Comment* 21, no. 4 (July–August 1985): 51–55.

———. "Whither Britain?" *Film Comment* 12, no. 1 (February 1987): 50–51.

———. "The New Wizards of Oz." *Film Comment* 25, no. 5 (September–October, 1989): 73–77.

———. "A Modest Magician." *American Film* 15, no. 10 (July 1990): 32–37.

———. "How They Won the War: British Cinema and World

War Two." *Film Comment* 32, no. 5 (September–October 1996): 24–34.

———. "Kiltspotting: Highland Reels." *Film Comment* 32, no. 4 (July–August 1996): 28–33.

Kennedy, Harlan, and Nigel Andrews. "Peerless Powell." *Film Comment* 15, no. 3 (May–June 1979): 49–55.

Krelman, Martin. *This Is Where We Came In: The Career and Character of Canadian Film*. Toronto: McClelland & Stewart, 1978.

Kulik, Karol. *Alexander Korda*. London: Allen, 1975.

Kuna, Franz, and Graeme Turner, eds. *Studying Australian Culture: An Introductory Reader*. Hamburg: Kovac, 1994.

Lambert, Gavin. *Mainly about Lindsay Anderson*. New York: Knopf, 2000.

Landy, Marcia. *British Genres: Cinema and Society, 1930–1960*. Princeton, N.J.: Princeton University Press, 1991.

Lant, Antonia, *Blackout: Reinventing Women for Wartime British Cinema*. Princeton, N.J.: Princeton University Press, 1991.

Lanza, Joseph. *Fragile Geometry: The Films, Philosophy, and Misadventures of Nicolas Roeg*. New York: PAJ, 1989.

Larson, Randall D. *Music from the House of Hammer: Music in the Hammer Horror Films 1950–1980*. Lanham, Md.: Scarecrow, 1996.

Lazar, David, and H. S. Chawla, eds. *Michael Powell: Interviews*. Jackson: University Press of Mississippi, 2003.

Leahy, James. *The Cinema of Joseph Losey*. Cranbury, N.J.: Barnes, 1967.

Leigh, Jacob. *The Cinema of Ken Loach: Art in the Service of the People*. London: Wallflower, 2002.

Lewis, Glenn. *Australian Movies and the American Dream*. New York: Praeger, 1987.

"Lindsay Anderson." Special issue of *Cambridge University Film Quarterly* 1 (Winter 2002).

Lippard, Chris, ed. *By Angels Driven: The Films of Derek Jarman*. Westport, Conn.: Greenwood, 1996.

Loiselle, André. "Subtly Subversive or Simply Stupid: Notes on Popular Quebec Cinema." *Post Script* 18, no. 2 (Winter 1999): 75–83.

Lowenstein, Adam. "Under-the-Skin-Horrors: Social Realism and Classlessness in *Peeping Tom* and the British New Wave." In Ashby and Higson, eds., *British Cinema, Past and Present*, pp. 221–32.

Lyons, Robert J. *Michelangelo Antonioni's Neo-Realism*. New York: Arno, 1976.

McArthur, Colin, ed. *Scotch Reels: Scotland in Cinema and Television*. London: British Film Institute, 1982.

McCabe, Bob. *Dark Knights and Holy Fools: The Art and Films of Terry Gilliam*. London: Orion Media, 1999.

McCarthy, Greg. "Caught between Empires: Ambivalence in Australian Films." *Critical Arts* 15, nos. 1–2 (2001): 154–73.

Macdonald, Kevin. *Emeric Pressburger: The Life and Death of a Screenwriter*. London: Faber & Faber, 1994.

MacDonald, Scott. "Interview with Sally Potter." *Camera Obscura* 35 (May 1995): 187–220.

McFarlane, Brian. *Australian Cinema 1970–1985*. London: Secker & Warburg, 1987.

———. *Sixty Voices: Celebrities Recall the Golden Age of British Cinema*. London: British Film Institute, 1992.

———. *An Autobiography of British Cinema by the Actors and Filmmakers Who Made It*. London: Methuen, 1997.

———. "The More Things Change . . . British Cinema in the 90s." In Murphy, ed., *The British Cinema Book*, pp. 273–80.

McFarlane, Brian, and Geoff Mayer. *New Australian Cinema: Sources and Parallels in American and British Cinema*. Cambridge, Eng.: Cambridge University Press, 1992.

McFarlane, Brian; Geoff Mayer; and Ina Bertrand, eds. *The Oxford Companion to Australian Film*. South Melbourne: Oxford University Press, 1999.

McIlroy, Brian. *World Cinema 4: Ireland*. Trowbridge, Eng.: Flicks, 1988.

———. *Shooting to Kill: Filmmaking and the "Troubles" in Northern Ireland*. Trowbridge, Eng.: Flicks, 1999.

McIntyre, Steve. "New Images of Scotland." *Screen* 25, no. 1 (January–February 1984): 53–59.

MacKenzie, S. P. *British War Films, 1939–1945: The Cinema and the Services*. London: Hambledon & London, 2001.

MacKenzie, Scott. *Screening Québec: Québécois Moving Images, National Identity and the Public Sphere*. Manchester, Eng.: Manchester University Press, 2003.

MacKillop, James, ed. *Contemporary Irish Cinema: From "The Quiet Man" to "Dancing at Lughnasa."* Syracuse, N.Y.: Syracuse University Press, 1999.

McKnight, George, ed. *Agent of Challenge and Defiance: The Films of Ken Loach*. Westport, Conn.: Greenwood, 1997.

McLoone, Martin. *Irish Film: The Emergence of a Contemporary Cinema*. London: British Film Institute, 2000.

———. "Internal Decolonisation?: British Cinema in the Celtic Fringe." In Murphy, ed., *The British Cinema Book*, pp. 184–90.

Macnab, Geoffrey. *Searching for Stars: Stardom and Screen Acting in British Cinema*. London: Cassell, 2000.

Magder, Ted. *Canada's Hollywood: The Canadian State and Feature Films*. Toronto: University of Toronto Press, 1993.

Malcomson, Scott L. "Modernism Comes to the Cabbage Patch: Bill Forsyth and the 'Scottish Cinema.' " *Film Quarterly* 38, no. 3 (Spring 1985): 16–21.

Manvell, Roger. *New Cinema in Britain*. New York: Dutton, 1968.

Marshall, Bill. *Quebec National Cinema*. Montreal: McGill-Queen's University Press, 2001.

Martin, Adrian. "Ghost . . . of a National Cinema." *Cinema Papers* (April 1994): 14–15.

———. *Phantasms: The Dreams and Desires at the Heart of Our Popular Cinema*. Melbourne: McPhee Gribble, 1994.

Martin, Helen, and Sam Edwards. *New Zealand Film, 1912–1996*. New York: Oxford University Press, 1997.

Mathews, Sue. *35mm Dreams: Conversations with Five Directors about the Australian Film Revival*. New York: Penguin, 1984.

Mazierska, Ewa, and Laura Rascaroli. *From Moscow to Madrid: European Cities, Postmodern Cinema*. London: Tauris, 2002.

Meikle, Denis, with Christopher T. Koetting. *A History of Horrors: The Rise and Fall of the House of Hammer*. Lanham, Md.: Scarecrow, 1996.

Michie, Alastair. "Scotland: Strategies of Centralisation." In Barr, ed., *All Our Yesterdays*, pp. 252–71.

Milne, Tom, ed. *Losey on Losey*. Garden City, N.Y. Doubleday, 1968.

Minney, R. J. *The Films of Anthony Asquith*. South Brunswick, N.J.: Barnes, 1976.

Monk, Claire. "The British 'Heritage Film' and Its Critics." *Critical Survey* 7, no. 2 (1995): 116–24.

———. "Heritage Films and Gendered Spectatorship," *Close Up: The Electronic Journal of British Cinema* 1, no. 1 (1997).

———. "Heritage Films and the British Cinema Audience in the 1990s." *Journal of Popular British Cinema* 2 (1999): 22–38.

———. "Underbelly UK: The 1990s Underclass Film, Masculinity and the Ideologies of 'New' Britain." In Ashby and Higson, eds., *British Cinema, Past and Present*, pp. 274–87.

Monk, Claire, and Amy Sargeant, eds. *British Historical Cinema: The History, Heritage, and Costume Film (British Popular Cinema)*. London: British Film Institute, 2002.

Monks, Robert. *Cinema Ireland: A Database of Irish Films and Filmmakers, 1896–1996*. Dublin: National Library of Ireland, 1996.

Monopolies and Mergers Commission. *Report on the Supply of Films for Exhibition in Cinemas in the UK*. London: Monopolies and Mergers Commission, 1995.

Moor, Andrew. "No Place Like Home: Powell, Pressburger, Utopia." In Murphy, ed., *The British Cinema Book*, pp. 109–15.

Moran, Albert, ed. *Film Policy: An Australian Reader*. Queensland, Australia: Institute for Cultural Policy Studies, Faculty of Humanities, Griffith University, 1994.

———, ed. *Film Policy: International, National and Regional Perspectives*. London: Routledge, 1996.

Molloy, Simon, and Barry Burgan. *The Economics of Film and Television in Australia*. Sydney: Australian Film Commission, 1993.

Morris, Peter. *Embattled Shadows: A History of Canadian Cinema, 1895–1939*. Montreal: McGill-Queen's University Press, 1978, 1992.

Movshovitz, Howie, ed. *Mike Leigh Interviews*. Jackson: University Press of Mississippi, 2000.

Muecke, Stephen. *Textual Spaces: Aboriginality and Cultural Studies*. Sydney: University of New South Wales Press, 1992.

Muir, Anne Ross. "The British Film Industry: Dead or Alive?" *Cineaste* 12, no. 3 (1983): 12–15.

Murphy, Robert. *Realism and Tinsel: Cinema and Society in Britain 1939–1949*. London: Routledge, 1992.

———. *Sixties British Cinema*. London: British Film Institute, 1992.

———. "A Revenger's Tragedy—*Get Carter*." In Chibnall and Murphy, eds., *British Crime Cinema*, pp. 123–33.

———. *British Cinema and the Second World War*. London: Continuum, 2000.

———, ed. *British Cinema of the 90s*. London: British Film Institute, 2000.

———, ed. *The British Cinema Book*. 2nd ed. London: British Film Institute, 2001.

———. "Postscript: A Short History of British Cinema." In Murphy, ed., *The British Cinema Book*, pp. 310–17.

Murray, Scott, ed. *The New Australian Cinema*. Melbourne: Nelson, 1980.

———, ed. *Australian Film, 1978–1992: A Survey of Theatrical Features*. South Melbourne: Oxford University Press/Austalian Film Commission/Cinema Papers, 1993.

———, ed. *Australian Cinema*. Sydney: Allen & Unwin/Australian Film Commission, 1994.

Neaverson, Bob. *The Beatles Movies*. London: Cassell, 1997.

Nowell-Smith, Geoffrey, and Stephen Ricci, eds. *Hollywood and Europe: Economics, Culture and National Identity 1945–1995*. London: British Film Institute, 1998.

Oliver, James. *English with English Subtitles: The Films of Ken Loach*. Suffolk, Eng.: ScreenPress, 2003.

O'Pray, Michael. *Derek Jarman: Dreams of England*. London: British Film Institute, 1996.

———, ed. *The British Avant-Garde Film, 1926–1995: An Anthology of Writings*. Luton, Eng.: University of Luton Press, 1997.

O'Regan, Tom. *Australian National Cinema*. London: Routledge, 1996.

Orr, John. "The Art of National Identity: Peter Greenaway

and Derek Jarman." In Ashby and Higson, eds., *British Cinema, Past and Present*, pp. 327–38.

Orr, John, and Olga Taxidou, eds. *Post-War Cinema and Modernity: A Film Reader*. Edinburgh: Edinburgh University Press, 2000.

Pallister, Janis L. *The Cinema of Québec: Masters in Their Own House*. Madison, N.J.: Fairleigh Dickinson University Press, 1995.

Park, James. *Learning to Dream: The New British Cinema*. London: Faber & Faber 1984.

———. *British Cinema: The Light That Failed*. London: Batsford, 1990.

Pascoe, David. *Peter Greenaway: Museums and Moving Images*. London: Reaktion, 1997.

Peake, Tony. *Derek Jarman: A Biography*. Woodstock, N.Y.: Overlook, 2000.

Pendakur, Manjunath. *Canadian Dreams and American Control: The Political Economy of the Canadian Film Industry*. Detroit: Wayne State University Press, 1990.

Petrie, Duncan. *New Questions of British Cinema*. London: British Film Institute, 1992.

———. *The British Cinematographer*. London: British Film Institute, 1996.

———. *Screening Scotland*. London: British Film Institute, 2000.

Petrie, Duncan, with Nick Pettigrew. *Inside Stories: Diaries of British Film-makers at Work*. London: British Film Institute, 1996.

Pettitt, Lance. *Screening Ireland: Film and Television Representation*. Manchester, Eng.: University of Manchester Press, 2000.

Pike, Andrew, and Ross Cooper. *Australian Film 1900–1977: A Guide to Feature Film Production*. South Melbourne: Oxford University Press/Australian Film Institute, 1979.

Polan, Dana. *Jane Campion*. London: British Film Institute, 2001.

Porter, Vincent. *On Cinema*. London: Pluto, 1985.

Posner, Michael. *Canadian Dreams: The Making and Marketing of Independent Films*. Vancouver: Douglas & McIntyre, 1993.

Powell, Michael. *A Life in the Movies*. London: Heinemann, 1986.

———. *Million-Dollar Movie: Life in the Movies*. Vol. 2. London: Heinemann, 1992.

Pulleine, Tim. "A Song and Dance at the Local: Thoughts on Ealing." In Murphy, ed., *The British Cinema Book*, pp. 79–84.

Pym, John. *Film on Four, 1981–1992: A Survey*. London: British Film Institute, 1992.

———. *Merchant Ivory's English Landscapes: Room, Views, and Anglo-Saxon Attitudes*. New York: Abrams, 1995.

Quinlan, David. *British Sound Films: The Studio Years, 1928–1959*. London: Batsford, 1984.

Ramiel, Aline. "Censorship: Cross-Media Cutting in 1950s–1960s Britain." *Canadian Review of Comparative Literature* 23, no. 2 (1996): 547–60.

Rattigan, Neil. *Images of Australia: 100 Films of the New Australian Cinema*. Dallas: Southern Methodist University Press, 1991.

———. *This Is England: British Film and the People's War, 1939–1945*. Madison, N.J.: Fairleigh Dickinson University Press, 2001.

Rayner, Jonathan. *The Films of Peter Weir*. London: Cassell, 1998.

———. *Contemporary Australian Cinema: An Introduction*. Manchester, Eng.: University of Manchester Press, 2000.

Reade, Eric. *Australian Silent Films*. Melbourne: Lansdowne, 1970.

———. *History and Heartburn: The Saga of Australian Film, 1896–1978*. Sydney: Harper & Row, 1979.

Rees, A. L. *A History of Experimental Film and Video: From the Canonical Avant-Garde to Contemporary British Practice*. London: British Film Institute, 1999.

Reeves, Nicholas. *The Power of Film Propaganda: Myth or Reality?* London: Cassell, 1999.

Reid, Mary Anne. *Long Shots to Favourites: Australian Cinema Successes in the 90s*. Sydney: Australian Film Commission, 1999.

Rich, Ruby. "The Very Model of a Modern Minor Industry." *American Film* (May 1983): 47–64.

Richards, Jeffrey. *Films and British National Identity: From Dickens to Dad's Army*. Manchester, Eng.: Manchester University Press, 1997.

Rigby, Jonathan. *English Gothic: A Century of Horror Cinema*. 2nd ed. London: Reynolds & Yearn, 2002.

Robinson, David. *The History of World Cinema*. 2nd ed. New York: Stein & Day, 1981.

Robson, Jocelyn, and Beverley Zalcock. *Girls' Own Stories: Australian and New Zealand Women's Films*. London: Scarlet, 1997.

Rockett, Kevin, ed. *The Irish Filmography: Fiction Films, 1896–1996*. Dublin: Red Mountain Press, 1996.

Rockett, Kevin; Luke Gibbons; and John Hill. *Cinema and Ireland*. Syracuse, N.Y.: Syracuse University Press, 1988.

Rodenberg, Hans-Peter. "Bridging the Abyss: Neil Jordan, the Irishman in British Hollywood." *Journal for the Study of British Cultures* 5, no. 2 (1998): 155–70.

Romney, Jonathan. "London Journal: On New Trends and Emerging Talents in Current British Cinema." *Film Comment* 37, no. 1 (January–February 2001): 11–13.

Ryall, Tom. *Britain and the American Cinema*. London: Sage, 2001.

Sabine, James, ed. *A Century of Australian Cinema*. Port Melbourne, Vic., Australia: Heinemann Australia, 1995.

Sachs, Bruce, and Russell Wall. *Greasepaint and Gore: The Hammer Monsters of Roy Ashton*. Sheffield, Eng.: Tomahawk, 1998.

Salwolke, Scott. *The Films of Michael Powell and the Archers*. Lanham, Md.: Scarecrow, 1997.

Sammon, Paul M. *Ridley Scott*. New York: Thunder's Mouth, 1999. Includes *Variety* reviews of Scott's films from 1977 to 1997.

Sargeant, Amy. "Making and Selling Heritage Culture: Style and Authenticity in Historical Fictions on Film and Television." In Ashby and Higson, eds., *British Cinema, Past and Present*, pp. 301–15.

Scheckels, Theodore F. *Celluloid Heroes Down Under: Australian Film, 1970–2000*. Westport, Conn.: Praeger, 2002.

Schwartz, Richard A. *The Films of Ridley Scott*. Westport, Conn.: Praeger, 2001.

Shary, Timothy. "Video as Accessible Artifact and Artificial Access: The Early Films of Atom Egoyan." *Film Criticism* 19, no. 3 (1995): 2–29.

Shaw, Tony. *British Cinema and the Cold War: The State, Propaganda and Consensus*. London: Tauris, 2001.

Shepard, Deborah. *Reframing Women: A History of New Zealand Film*. Auckland: HarperCollins New Zealand, 2000.

Shiach, Don. *The Films of Peter Weir: Visions of Alternative Realities*. London: Letts, 1993.

Shirley, Graham, and Brian Adams. *Australian Cinema: The First Eighty Years*. Sydney: Angus & Robertson, 1983.

Sinyard, Neil. *The Films of Richard Lester*. London: Croom Helm, 1985.

———. *Jack Clayton*. Manchester, Eng.: Manchester University Press, 2000.

Slavin, John. "The Films of Jane Campion." *Metro* 95 (Spring 1993): 28–30.

Slide, Anthony. *The Cinema and Ireland*. Jefferson, N.C.: McFarland, 1988.

———. *Banned in the USA: British Film in the United States and Their Censorship, 1933–1960*. London: Tauris, 1998.

Smith, Chris. *Creative Britain*. London: Faber & Faber, 1998.

Soderbergh, Steven, and Richard Lester. *Getting Away with It: Or: The Further Adventures of the Luckiest Bastard You Ever Saw*. London: Faber & Faber, 2000.

Stein, Eliott. " 'A Very Tender Film, a Very Nice One': Michael Powell's *Peeping Tom*." *Film Comment* 15, no. 5 (September–October 1979): 57–59.

Stratton, David. *The Last New Wave: The Australian Film Revival*. Sydney: Angus & Robertson, 1980.

———. *The Avocado Plantation: Boom and Bust in the Australian Film Industry*. Sydney: Pan Macmillan, 1990.

———. "Australia." In Cowie, Elley, and Rosenthal, eds., *Variety International Film Guide 2000*, pp. 80–88.

Straw, Will. "Canadian Cinema." In Hill and Gibson, eds., *World Cinema*, pp. 139–42.

Street, Sarah. *British National Cinema*. London: Routledge, 1997.

———. "Genres in Transition, 1970s–1990s." In Street, *British National Cinema*, pp. 92–113.

———. *British Cinema in Documents*. London: Routledge, 2000.

———. *Transatlantic Crossings: British Feature Films in the USA*. London: Continuum, 2002.

Sussex, Elizabeth. *Lindsay Anderson*. New York: Praeger, 1970.

Swann, Paul. *The Hollywood Feature Film in Postwar Britain*. New York: St. Martin's, 1987.

———. "The British Culture Industries and the Mythology of the American Market: Cultural Policy and Cultural Exports in the 1940s and 1990s." *Cinema Journal* 39, no. 4 (2000): 27–42.

Taylor, John Russell. *Directors and Directions: Cinema for the Seventies*. New York: Hill & Wang, 1975.

———. "Michael Powell: Myths and Supermen." *Sight and Sound* 47, no. 4 (Autumn 1978): 226–29.

Thomson, David. "Listen to Britain." *Film Comment* 22, no. 3 (April 1986): 56–63.

Threadgill, Derek. *Shepperton Studios: An Independent View*. London: British Film Institute, 1994.

Thumim, Janet. "The 'Popular,' Cash and Culture in the Post-War British Cinema Industry." *Screen* 32, no. 3 (Autumn 1991): 245–85. Repr. in Fowler, ed., *The European Cinema Reader*, pp. 194–211.

Todd, Peter. "The British Film Industry in the 1990s." In Murphy, ed., *British Cinema of the 90s*, pp. 17–26.

Turner, Graeme. *National Fictions: Literature, Film and the Construction of Australian Narrative*. 2nd ed. St. Leonards, N.S.W., Australia: Allen & Unwin, 1993.

———, ed. *Nation, Culture, Text: Australian Cultural and Media Studies*. London: Routledge, 1993.

———. *Making It National: Nationalism and Australian Popular Culture*. St. Leonards, N.S.W., Australia: Allen & Unwin, 1994.

Veroneau, Pierre, ed. *The Canadian Cinemas*. Ottawa, Ont.: Canadian Film Institute, 1979.

Vincendeau, Ginette, ed. *Film/Literature/Heritage: A Sight and Sound Reader*. London: British Film Institute, 2001.

Walker, Alexander. *Hollywood, U.K.* New York: Stein & Day, 1974.

Walker, John. *The Once and Future Film: British Cinema in the Seventies and Eighties*. London: Methuen, 1985.

Warren, Patricia. *British Film Studios: An Illustrated History*. London: Batsford, 1995.

Watson, Neil. "Hollywood UK." In Murphy, ed., *British Cinema of the 90s*, pp. 80–87.

Wexman, Virginia Wright, ed. *Jane Campion: Interviews*. Jackson: University Press of Mississippi, 1999.

White, David. *Australian Movies to the World: The International Success of Australian Films since 1970*. Melbourne: Fontana, 1984.

White, Jerry. "To Act It to Be: Identity in Recent Quebec Cinema." *Cineaction* 45 (1996): 18–26.

Williams, Tony. *Structures of Desire: British Cinema, 1939–1955*. Albany: State University of New York Press, 2000.

Wood, Robin. *The Wings of the Dove: Henry James in the 1990s*. London: British Film Institute, 1999.

Woods, Alan. *Being Naked, Playing Dead: The Art of Peter Greenaway*. Manchester, Eng.: Manchester University Press, 1996.

Wright, Bruce Lanier. *Nightwalkers: Gothic Horror Movies—the Modern Era*. Dallas: Taylor, 1995.

Wyver, John. "The English Channel 4." *American Film* (July/August 1986): 46–49.

Yule, Andrew. *Richard Lester and the Beatles: A Complete Biography of the Man Who Directed "A Hard Day's Night" and "Help."* New York: Primus, 1995.

CHAPTER 15. EUROPEAN RENAISSANCE: WEST

Alegre, Sergi, et al., eds. *El Cine en Cataluña: una aproximación histórica*. Barcelona: PPU, 1993.

Allan, Seán, and John Standford, eds. *DEFA: East German Cinema, 1946–1992*. New York: Berghahn, 1999.

Allinson, Mark. *A Spanish Labyrinth: The Films of Pedro Almodóvar*. London: Tauris, 2001.

Alter, Nora M. *Projecting History: German Non-Fiction Cinema 1967–2000*. Ann Arbor: University of Michigan Press, 2002.

Alvares, Rosa, and Belén, Frías. *Vicente Aranda, Victoria Abril: el cine como pasión*. Valladolid, Spain: 36 Semana Internacional de Cine, 1991.

Angulo, Jesús; Carlos F. Heredero; and José Luis Rebordinos, eds. *Un cineasta llamado Pedro Olea*. San Sebastián, Spain: Filmoteca Vasca, 1993.

Aranda, Francisco. *Luis Buñuel*. London: Secker & Warburg, 1969.

Armes, Roy. *The Ambiguous Image: Narrative Style in Modern European Cinema*. Bloomington: Indiana University Press, 1976.

Arocena, Carmen. *Víctor Erice*. Madrid: Ediciones Cátedra, 1996.

Arrowsmith, William. *Antonioni: The Poet of Images*. Ed. Ted Perry. New York: Oxford University Press, 1995.

Bachman, Gideon. "The Man on the Volcano: A Portrait of Werner Herzog." *Film Quarterly* 31, no. 3 (Fall 1977): 2–10.

———. "A Guest in My Own Dreams: An Interview with Federico Fellini." *Film Quarterly* 47, no. 3 (1994): 2–15.

Balmain, Colette. "Mario Bava's *The Evil Eye*: Realism and the Italian Horror Film." *Postscript* 21, no. 3 (Summer 2002): 20–31.

Belton, John. "The Bionic Eye: Zoom Esthetics." *Cineaste* 10, no. 1 (Winter 1980–81): 20–27.

Belton, John, and Lyle Tector. "The Bionic Eye: The Aesthetics of the Zoom." *Film Comment* 16, no. 5 (September–October 1980): 11–17. This article was edited and rewritten by *Film Comment*'s editorial staff (bylined collectively as "Lyle Tector") without Belton's permission. The original, which is more scholarly and theory-specific, appears as "The Bionic Eye: Zoom Esthetics" (see entry above).

Bergman, Ingmar. *The Magic Lantern: An Autobiography*. London: Hamilton, 1988.

Bergfelder, Tim; Deniz Göktürk; and Erica Carter, eds. *The German Cinema Book*. London: British Film Institute, 2003.

Bergom-Larsson, Maria. *Swedish Film: Ingmar Bergman and Society*. Cranbury, N.J.: Barnes, 1979.

Besas, Peter. *Behind the Spanish Lens: Spanish Cinema under Fascism and Democracy*. Denver: Arden, 1985.

Betti, Liliana. *Fellini: An Intimate Portrait*. Boston: Little, Brown, 1979.

Björkman, Stig; Torsten Manns; and Jonas Sima. *Bergman on Bergman: Interviews with Ingmar Bergman*. Trans. Paul Britten Austin. New York: Simon & Schuster, 1973.

Black, Andy, ed. *Necronomicon: Book One*. London: Creation, 1993.

Blackwell, Marilyn Johns. *Gender and Representation in the Films of Ingmar Bergman*. Columbia, S.C.: Camden House, 1997.

Blank, Les, and James Bogan, eds. *"Burden of Dreams": Screenplay, Journals, Reviews, Photographs*. Berkeley, Calif.: North Atlantic, 1984.

Bondanella, Peter. *The Cinema of Federico Fellini*. Princeton, N.J.: Princeton University Press, 1992.

———. "Beyond Neorealism: Calvino, Fellini and Fantasy." *Michigan Romance Studies* 16 (1996): 103–20.

Bondebjerg, Ib. "Between War and Welfare: Danish Documentary Films in the 1950s." *Aura* 2, no. 31 (1996): 30–56.

Bordwell, David, and Noël Carroll, eds. *Post-Theory: Reconstructing Film Studies*. Madison: University of Wisconsin Press, 1996.

Bromley, Roger. *From "Alice" to "Buena Vista": The Films of Wim Wenders*. Westport, Conn.: Praeger, 2001.

Brunetta, Gian Piero. *Cent'anni di cinema italiano*. Rome: Laterza, 1991.

Brunette, Peter. *The Films of Michelangelo Antonioni*. Cambridge, Eng.: Cambridge University Press, 1998.

Buache, Freddy. *The Cinema of Luis Buñuel*. Cranbury, N.J.: Barnes, 1973.

Buñuel, Luis. *My Last Sigh*. Trans. Abigail Israel. New York: Knopf, 1983.

Burdick, Charles; Hans-Adolf Jacobsen; and Winfried Kudszus, eds. *Contemporary Germany: Politics and Culture*. Boulder: Westview, 1984.

Burke, Frank. *Fellini's Films: From Postwar to Postmodern*. New York: Twayne, 1996.

Burke, Frank, and Marguerite K. Waller, eds. *Federico Fellini: Contemporary Perspectives*. Toronto: University of Toronto Press, 2002.

Byg, Barton. "What Might Have Been: DEFA Films of the Past and the Future of German Film." *Cineaste* 17, no. 4 (1990): 9–15.

Cameron, Ian, *Antonioni*. London: Studio Vista, 1969.

Caparrós-Lera, J. M., and Rafael de España. *The Spanish Cinema: An Historical Approach*. Barcelona: Centro des Investigaciones Film-Historica, 1987.

Celant, Germano, ed. *The Italian Metamorphosis, 1943–1968*. New York: Guggenheim Museum, 1994. Also available on CD-ROM.

Celli, Carlo. *The Divine Comic: The Cinema of Roberto Benigni*. Lanham, Md.: Scarecrow, 2001.

Chandler, Charlotte, *I, Fellini*. New York: Random House, 1995.

Chatman, Seymour. *Antonioni; or, The Surface of the World*. Berkeley: University of California Press, 1985.

Christensen, Ove. "Authentic Illusions—the Aesthetics of Dogma 95." *p.o.v.* 10 (December 2000): 111–12.

Coates, Paul. *The Gorgon's Gaze: German Cinema, Expressionism, and the Image of Horror*. Cambridge, Eng.: Cambridge University Press, 1991.

Cohen, Hubert I. *Ingmar Bergman: The Art of Confession*. New York: Twayne, 1993.

Collins, Richard, and Vincent Porter. *WDR and the Arbeiterfilm: Fassbinder, Ziewer, and Others*. London: British Film Institute, 1981.

Colmeiro, José, et al., eds. *Spain Today: Essays on Literature, Culture, Society*. Hanover, N.H.: Dartmouth College, Department of Spanish and Portuguese, 1995.

Conboy, Martin. "The Discourse of Location: Realigning the Popular in German Cinema." *European Journal of Communication* 14, no. 3 (September 1999): 353–77.

Conrich, Ian, and Estella Tincknell. "Film Purity, the Neo-Bazinian Ideal, and Humanism in Dogma 95." *p.o.v.* 10 (December 2000): 171–80.

Cook, Roger F., and Gerd Gemünden, eds. *The Cinema of Wim Wenders: Image, Narrative, and the Postmodern Condition*. Detroit: Wayne State University Press, 1997.

Corrigan, Timothy. *New German Cinema: The Displaced Image*. Austin: University of Texas Press, 1983.

———. "Cinematic Snuff: German Friends and Narrative Murders." *Cinema Journal* 14, no. 2 (Winter 1985): 9–18.

———, ed. *The Films of Werner Herzog: Between Mirage and History*. New York: Methuen, 1986.

———. *A Cinema without Walls: Movies and Culture after Vietnam*. London: Routledge, 1991.

Covino, Michael. "A Worldwide Homesickness: The Films of Wim Wenders." *Film Quarterly* 30, no. 2 (Winter 1977–78): 9–19.

Cowie, Peter. *Finnish Cinema*. London: Tantivy, 1976.

———. *Dutch Cinema: An Illustrated History*. London: Tantivy, 1979.

———. *Scandinavian Cinema: A Survey of Films and Filmmakers in Denmark, Finland, Iceland, Norway, and Sweden*. London: Tantivy, 1992.

Cozzi, Luigi. *Dario Argento: il suo cinema, i suoi personaggi, I suoi miti*. Rome: Fanucci, 1991.

Crowdus, Gary. "Investigating the Relationship between Causes and Effects: An Interview with Francesco Rosi." *Cineaste* 20, no. 4 (1994): 26–27. Repr. in Crowdus and Georgakas, eds., *The Cineaste Interviews* 2, pp. 155–59.

———. "Francesco Rosi: Italy's Postmodern Neorealist." *Cineaste* 20, no. 4 (1995): 19–25.

———. "The Lack of Historical Memory: An Interview with Gianni Amelio." *Cineaste* 28, no. 1 (2002): 14–18.

Crowdus, Gary, and Dan Georgakas. "The Audience Should Not Be Just Passive Spectators: An Interview with Francesco Rosi." *Cineaste* 7, no. 1 (Fall 1975): 2–8.

———, eds. *The Cineaste Interviews 2: On the Art and Politics of the Cinema*. Chicago: Lake View, 2002.

Crowdus, Gary, and Richard Porton. "Beyond Neorealism: Preserving a Cinema of Social Conscience—an Interview with Gianni Amelio." *Cineaste* 21, no. 4 (1995): 6–13.

———. "Coming to Terms with the German Past: An Interview with Volker Schlöndorff." *Cineaste* 26, no. 2 (2001): 18–23.

Csiscery, George Paul. "Ballad of the Little Soldier: Werner Herzog in a Political Hall of Mirrors." *Film Quarterly* 39, no. 2 (Winter 1985–86): 7–15.

Cuccu, Lorenzo. *The Cinema of Paolo and Vittorio Taviani: Nature, Culture, and History Revealed by Two Tuscan Masters*. Rome: Gremese, 2001.

Cumbow, Robert C. *Once upon a Time: The Films of Sergio Leone*. Metuchen, N.J.: Scarecrow, 1987.

Davidson, John E. *Deterritorializing the New German Cinema*. Minneapolis: University of Minnesota Press, 1999.

Dawson, Jan. *Wim Wenders*. New York: New York Zoetrope, 1976.

———. "A Labyrinth of Subsidies: The Origins of the New German Cinema." *Sight and Sound* 50, no. 2 (Winter 1980–81): 14–20.

De Bernardinis, Flavio. *Nanni Moretti*. Rome: Il Castro, 1993.

De España, Rafael. *Directory of Spanish and Portuguese Film-Makers and Films*. Westport, Conn.: Greenwood, 1994.

De Fornari, Oreste. *Sergio Leone: The Great Italian Dream of Legendary America*. New York: Gremese International, 1997.

Degli-Esposti, Cristina. "Recent Italian Cinema: Maniera and Cinematic Theft." *Canadian Journal of Italian Studies* 20 (1997): 19–36.

Dellamorte, Daniel, and Tobias Petterson. *Violent Italy*. Sweden: PM Förlag, 2002.

Delmar, Rosalind. *Joris Ivens: 50 Years of Film-making*. London: British Film Institute, 1979.

De Stefano, George. "Post-Franco Frankness." *Film Comment* (June 1986): 58–60.

Deveney, Thomas G. *Cain on Screen: Contemporary Spanish Cinema*. Metuchen, N.J.: Scarecrow, 1993.

———. *Contemporary Spanish Film from Fiction*. Lanham, Md.: Scarecrow, 1999.

Di Carlo, Carlo. *Michelangelo Antonioni*. Rome: Bianco e Nero, 1964.

DiMatteo, Robert. "Who Framed Maurizio Nichetti?" *Film Comment* 26, no. 5 (September–October 1990): 53–57.

D'Lugo, Marvin. "Catalan Cinema: Historical Experience and Cinematic Practice." *Quarterly Review of Film and Video* 13, nos. 1–3 (1991): 131–47. Repr. in Fowler, ed., *The European Cinema Reader*, pp. 163–73.

———. *The Films of Carlos Saura: The Practice of Seeing*. Princeton, N.J.: Princeton University Press, 1991.

——— *Guide to the Cinema of Spain*. Westport, Conn.: Greenwood, 1997.

———, ed. "Spanish Cinema." Special issue of *Post Script* 21, no. 2 (Winter–Spring 2002).

Dyer, Richard, and Ginette Vincendeau, eds. *Popular European Cinema*. London: Routledge, 1992.

Edwards, Gwynne. *Indecent Exposures: Buñuel, Saura, Erice and Almodóvar*. London: Boyars, 1995.

Ehrenstein, David. "Your Own Reality: An Interview with Paolo and Vittorio Taviani." *Film Quarterly* 47, no. 4 (Summer 1994): 2–6.

Ehrlich, Linda C., ed. *An Open Window: The Cinema of Victor Erice*. Lanham, Md.: Scarecrow, 2000.

Eidsvik, Charles. "The State as Movie Mogul." *Film Comment* 15, no. 2 (March–April 1979): 60–66.

———. "Behind the Crest of the Wave: An Overview of the New German Cinema." *Literature/Film Quarterly* 7, no. 3 (Summer 1979): 167–81.

Eleftheriotis, Dimitris. *Popular Cinemas of Europe: Studies of Texts, Contexts and Frameworks*. New York: Continuum, 2001.

Elsaesser, Thomas. "Murder, Merger, Suicide." In Raynes, ed., *Fassbinder*, pp. 37–53.

———. *New German Cinema: A History*. New Brunswick, N.J.: Rutgers University Press, 1989.

———. *Fassbinder's Germany: History, Identity, Subject*. Amsterdam, the Neth.: Amsterdam University Press, 1996.

———. *Weimar Cinema and After: Germany's Historical Imaginary*. New York: Routledge, 2000.

Elsaesser, Thomas, with Michael Wedel, eds. *The BFI Companion to German Cinema*. London: British Film Institute, 1999.

———. "Defining DEFA's Historical Imaginary: The Films of Konrad Wolf." *New German Critique* 82 (Winter 2001): 3–24.

Engberg, Marguerite. *Danish Films through the Years: A Survey of Films, Directors, Cinemas, Companies, etc. in Denmark, 1896–1989*. Copenhagen: Danish Film Institute, 1990.

Evans, Peter William, ed. *Spanish Cinema: The Auteurist Tradition*. Oxford: Oxford University Press, 1999.

Fassbinder, Rainer Werner. *The Marriage of Maria Braun*. Ed. Joyce Rheuban. New Brunswick, N.J.: Rutgers University Press, 1986. Screenplay.

———. *The Anarchy of the Imagination: Interviews, Essays, Notes*. Ed. Michael Töteberg and Leo A. Lensing. Trans. Krishna Winston. Baltimore: Johns Hopkins University Press, 1992.

Fehrenbach, Heide. *Cinema in Democratizing Germany: Reconstructing National Identity after Hitler*. Chapel Hill: University of North Carolina Press, 1995.

Feinstein, Howard. "Francesco Rossi: Interviewed by Howard Feinstein." *Film Comment* 31, no. 3 (January 1995): 64.

Feinstein, Joshua. *The Triumph of the Ordinary: Depictions of Daily Life in the East German Cinema, 1949–1989*. Chapel Hill: University of North Carolina Press, 2002.

Fellini, Federico. *Fellini on Fellini*. Trans. Isabel Quigley. New York: Delacorte, 1976.

Fenton, Harvey; Julian Grainger; and Gian Luca Castoldi. *Cannibal Holocaust and the Savage Cinema of Ruggero Deodato*. Guildford, Eng.: FAB, 1999.

Fernández, Emilio C. García. *Historia Ilustrada del Cine Español*. Barcelona: Planeta, 1985.

Ferrucci, Riccardo, ed. *Paolo and Vittorio Taviani: Poetry of the Italian Landscape*. Rome: Gremese, 1995.

Fiddian, Robin W., and Peter W. Evans. *Challenges to Authority: Fiction and Film in Contemporary Spain*. London: Tamesis, 1988.

Finney, Angus. *The State of European Cinema: A New Dose of Reality*. London: Cassell, 1996.

Fisher, Jaimey. "Who's Watching the Rubble-Kids? Youth, Pedagogy, and Politics in Early DEFA Films." *New German Critique* 82 (Winter 2001): 91–125.

Fisher, William. "Germany: A Neverending Story." *Sight and Sound* 54, no. 3 (Summer 1985): 174–79.

———. "Aki Kaurismäki Goes Business." *Sight and Sound* 58, no. 4 (Autumn 1989): 252–55.

Foix-Molina, Vincente. *New Cinema in Spain*. London: British Film Institute, 1977.

Fowler, Catherine, ed. *The European Cinema Reader*. London: Routledge, 2002.

Franklin, James. *New German Cinema: From Overhausen to Hamburg*. Boston: Twayne, 1983.

Frayling, Christopher. *Spaghetti Westerns: Cowboys and Europeans from Karl May to Sergio Leone*. Rev. ed. London: Tauris, 1998.

———. *Sergio Leone: Something to Do with Death*. London: Faber and Faber, 2000.

Frieden, Sandra, et al. *Gender and German Cinema: Feminist Interventions*. 2 vols. Providence, R.I.: Berg, 1993.

Fullerton, John, ed. "Nordic Cinema." Special issue of *Film History* 13, no. 1 (2001).

Fullerton, John, and Jan Olsson, eds. *Nordic Explorations: Film before 1930*. Sydney: Libbey, 1999.

Gallant, Chris, ed. *The Art of Darkness: The Cinema of Dario Argento*. Guildford, Eng.: FAB, 2000.

Geist, Kathe. *The Cinema of Wim Wenders: From Paris, France to "Paris, Texas."* Ann Arbor, Mich.: UMI Research Press, 1988.

Gelder, Ken, ed. *The Horror Reader*. London: Routledge, 2000.

Gemünden, Gerd. *Framed Visions: Popular Culture, Americanization, and the Contemporary German and Austrian Imagination*. Ann Arbor: University of Michigan Press, 1999.

———. "Between Karl May and Karl Marx: The DEFA 'Indianerfilm' (1965–1983)." *New German Critique* 82 (Winter 2001): 25–38.

Gérard, Fabien S.; T. Jefferson Kline; and Bruce Sklarew, eds. *Bernardo Bertolucci: Interviews*. Jackson: University Press of Mississippi, 2000.

Geuens, Jean-Pierre. "Dogma 95: A Manifesto for Our Times." *Quarterly Review of Film and Video* 18, no. 2 (April 2001): 191–202.

Gieri, Manuela. *Contemporary Italian Filmmaking: Strategies of Subversion—Pirandello, Fellini, Scola, and the Directors of the New Generation*. Toronto: University of Toronto Press, 1995.

Gili, Jean, ed. *Italian Filmmakers—Self-Portraits: A Selection of Interviews*. Trans. Sandra E. Tokunga. Rome: Gremese, 1998.

———, ed. *Nanni Moretti*. Rome: Gremese, 2001.

Ginsberg, Terri, and Kirsten Moana Thompson, eds. *Perspectives on German Cinema*. New York: Hall, 1996.

Golden, Christpher, ed. *CUT! Horror Writers on Horror Film*. New York: Berkley, 1992.

Gómez Rufo, Antonio. *Berlanga, contra el poder y la gloria*. Madrid: Temas de Hoy, 1990.

Goulding, Daniel J., ed. *Post New Wave Cinema in the Soviet Union and Eastern Europe*. Bloomington: Indiana University Press, 1989.

Graf, Alexander. *The Cinema of Wim Wenders: The Celluloid Highway*. London: Wallflower, 2002.

Graham, Helen, and Jo Labanyi, eds. *Spanish Cultural Studies: An Introduction*. Oxford: Oxford University Press, 1995.

Grassi, Raffaella. *Territori di fuga: Il cinema di Gabriele Salvatores*. Alessandria: Falsopiano, 1997.

Greene, Naomi. *Pier Paolo Pasolini: Cinema as Heresy*. Princeton, N.J.: Princeton University Press, 1990.

Griffiths, Keith M., ed. *The Brechtian Aspect of Radical Cinema: Essays by Martin Walsh*. London: British Film Institute, 1981.

Guback, Thomas. "Shaping the Film Business in Postwar Germany: The Role of the U.S. Film Industry and the U.S. State." In Kerr, ed., *The Hollywood Film Industry*, pp. 245–75.

Guins, Ray. "Tortured Looks: Dario Argento and Visual Displeasure." In Black, ed., *Necronomicon*, pp. 141–53.

Gundle, Stephen. "Hollywood Glamour and Mass Consumption in Postwar Italy." *Journal of Cold War Studies* 4, no. 3 (2002): 95–118.

Hake, Sabine. *German National Cinema*. New York: Routledge, 2002.

Halle, Randall, and Margaret McCarthy, eds. *Light Motives: German Popular Cinema in Perspective*. Detroit: Wayne State University Press, 2003.

Harcourt, Peter. *Six European Directors*. New York: Penguin, 1974.

Hayman, Ronald. *Fassbinder: Filmmaker*. New York: Simon & Schuster, 1984.

Helt, Richard C., and Marie E. Helt. *West German Cinema since 1945: A Reference Handbook*. Metuchen, N.J.: Scarecrow, 1987.

———. *West German Cinema, 1985–1990: A Reference Handbook*. Metuchen, N.J.: Scarecrow, 1992.

Heredero, Carlos F. *José Luis Borau: teoría y práctica de un cineasta*. Madrid: Instituto de la Cinematografía y las Artes Audiovisuales, 1990.

———. *Las huellas del tiempo: cine español, 1951–1961*.

Valencia: Archivo de la Filmoteca de la Generalitat Valenciana, 1993.

———. *El lenguaje de la luz: entrevistas con directores de fotografía del cine español*. Madrid: Festival de Cine de Alcalá de Henares, 1994.

Higginbottom, Virginia. *Spanish Film under Franco*. Austin: University of Texas Press, 1988.

Hillier, Jim. *Cinema in Finland: An Introduction*. London: British Film Institute, 1975.

Hirsch, Foster. "*Amarcord*." *Film Quarterly* 1, no. 29 (Fall 1975): 50. Review.

Hjort, Mette. "Danish Cinema and the Politics of Recognition." In Bordwell and Carroll, eds., *Post-Theory*, pp. 520–32.

———. "Themes of a Nation." In Hjort and Mackenzie, eds., *Cinema and Nation*, pp. 103–17.

Hjort, Mette, and Ib Bondebjerg. *The Danish Directors: Dialogues on a Contemporary National Cinema*. Trans. Mette Hjort. Bristol: Intellect, 2001.

Hjort, Mette, and Scott Mackenzie, eds. *Cinema and Nation*. London: Routledge, 2000.

———, eds. *Purity and Provocation: Dogme 95*. London: British Film Institute, 2000.

Hoerschelmann, Olaf. " 'Memoria Dextera Est': Film and Public Memory in Postwar Germany." *Cinema Journal* 40, no. 2 (2001): 78–97.

Holmes, Diana, and Alison Smith, eds. *100 Years of European Cinema: Entertainment or Ideology?* Manchester, Eng.: Manchester University Press, 2000.

Hopewell, John. *Out of the Past: Spanish Cinema after Franco*. London: British Film Institute, 1986.

Howarth, Troy. *The Haunted World of Mario Bava*. London: Fab, 2002.

Hunt, Leon. "A (Sadistic) Night at the *Opera:* Notes on the Italian Horror Film." In Gelder, ed., *The Horror Reader*, pp. 324–35.

Huss, Roy, ed. *Focus on "Blow-Up."* Englewood Cliffs, N.J.: Prentice-Hall, 1971.

Iden, Peter et al. *Fassbinder*. Trans. Ruth McCormick. New York: Tanam, 1981.

Ilott, Terry. *Budgets and Markets: A Study of the Budgeting of European Films*. London: Routledge, 1996.

Insdorf, Annette. "Spain Also Rises." *Film Comment* 16, no. 4 (July–August 1980): 13–17.

"Italian Cinema." Special issue of *Canadian/American Journal of Italian Studies* 20 (1997).

Joannides, Paul. "The Aesthetics of the Zoom Lens." *Sight and Sound* 40, no. 1 (Winter 1970–71): 40–42.

Johanns, Willi, ed. *Out of the Dark: Crime, Mystery and Suspense in the German Cinema, 1915–1990—A Film-Retrospective and Exhibition Catalogue*. Munich: Goethe-Institut Film Department, 1992.

Johnston, Sheila. "The Author as Public Institution: The 'New' Cinema in the Federal Republic of Germany." *Screen Education* 32–33 (1979–80): 67–78. Repr. in Fowler, ed., *The European Cinema Reader*, pp. 121–31.

Jordan, Barry, and Rikki Morgan-Tamosunas. *Contemporary Spanish Cinema*. Manchester, Eng.: Manchester University Press, 1998.

Katz, Robert. *Love Is Colder Than Death: The Life and Times of Rainer Werner Fassbinder*. New York: Random House, 1987.

Kelly, Richard. *The Name of This Book Is "Dogma 95."* London: Faber & Faber, 2000.

Kerr, Paul, ed. *The Hollywood Film Industry: A Reader*. New York: Routledge & Kegan Paul, 1986.

Kezich, Tullio. *Giulietta Masina*. Bologna: Cappelli, 1991.

Kinder, Marsha. "The Tyranny of Convention in *The Phantom of Liberty*." *Film Quarterly* 28, no. 4 (Summer 1975): 20.

———. "Carlos Saura: The Political Development of Individual Consciousness." *Film Quarterly* 32, no. 3 (Spring 1979): 14–25.

———. "The Children of Franco in the New Spanish Cinema." *Quarterly Review of Film Studies* 8, no. 2 (Spring 1983): 57–76.

———. "José Luis Borau *On the Line* of the National/International Interface in Post-Franco Cinema." *Film Quarterly* 40, no. 2 (Winter 1986–87): 35–48.

———. "Pleasure and the New Spanish Cinema: A Conversation with Pedro Almodóvar." *Film Quarterly* 41, no. 1 (Fall 1987): 33–44.

———. *Spanish Cinema: The Politics of Family and Gender*. Los Angeles: Spanish Ministry of Culture/University of Southern California School of Cinema and Television, 1989.

———. *Blood Cinema: The Reconstruction of National Identity in Spain*. Berkeley: University of California Press, 1993.

———, ed. *Refiguring Spain: Cinema, Media, Representation*. Durham, N.C.: Duke University Press, 1997.

Kino: German Film 1–56 (1980–94). A quarterly journal from Berlin, edited by Dorothea and Ronald Holloway.

Klawans, Stuart. "Illustrious Rosi." *Film Comment* 31, no. 1 (January 1995): 60–63, 65.

Kline, T. Jefferson. *Bertolucci's Dream Loom: A Psychoanalytic Study of Cinema*. Amherst: University of Massachusetts Press, 1987.

Knight, Julia. *Women and the New German Cinema*. London: Verso, 1992.

Koepnick, Lutz Peter. "Consuming the Other: Identity, Alterity, and Contemporary German Cinema." *Camera Obscura* 15, no. 2 (2000): 41–73.

Kolker, Robert Phillip. *Bernardo Bertolucci*. Oxford: Oxford University Press, 1985.

Kolker, Robert Phillip, and Peter Beicken. *The Films of Wim*

Wenders: Cinema as Vision and Desire. Cambridge, Eng.: Cambridge University Press, 1993.

Kolstrup, Søren. "The Press and Dogma 95." *p.o.v.* 10 (December 2000): 123–36.

Kosta, Barbara. *Recasting Autobiography: Women's Counter-fictions in Contemporary German Literature and Film*. Ithaca, N.Y.: Cornell University Press, 1994.

Kovacs, Katherine S. "Demarginalizing Spanish Film." *Quarterly Review of Film and Video* 11, no. 4 (1990): 73–82.

Kuzniar, Alice A. *The Queer German Cinema*. Stanford, Calif.: Stanford University Press, 2000.

Lagny, Michele. "Popular Taste: The Peplum." In Dyer and Vincendeau, eds., *Popular European Cinema*, pp. 163–80.

Landy, Marcia. *Italian Film*. Cambridge, Eng.: Cambridge University Press, 2000.

Leonhard, Sigrun D. "Testing the Borders: East German Film between Individualism and Social Commitment." In Goulding, ed., *Post New Wave Cinema in the Soviet Union and Eastern Europe*, pp. 51–101.

Leprohon, Pierre. *Michelangelo Antonioni*. New York: Simon & Schuster, 1963.

Liehm, Mira, and Antonin J. Liehm. *The Most Important Art: Eastern European Film after 1945*. Berkeley: University of California Press, 1977.

Linville, Susan E. *Feminism, Film, Fascism: Women's Autobiographical Film in Postwar Germany*. Austin: University of Texas Press, 1998.

Long, Robert Emmet. *Ingmar Bergman: Film and Stage*. New York: Abrams, 1994.

Luhr, William, ed. *World Cinema since 1945*. New York: Ungar, 1987.

Lumholdt, Jan, ed. *Lars von Trier: Interviews*. Jackson: University Press of Mississippi, 2003.

Lutze, Peter C. *Alexander Kluge: The Last Modernist*. Detroit: Wayne State University Press, 1998.

Lyons, Robert J. *Michelangelo Antonioni's Neo-Realism*. New York: Arno, 1976.

McCallum, Lawrence. *Italian Horror Films of the 1960s: A Critical Catalog of 62 Chillers*. Jefferson, N.C.: McFarland, 1995.

McCourt, James. "*The Innocent:* Visconti's Last Fresco." *Film Comment* 15, no. 2 (March–April 1979): 14–16.

McDonagh, Maitland. *Broken Mirrors/Broken Minds: The Dark Dreams of Dario Argento*. Secaucus, N.J.: Carol, 1994.

McIlroy, Brian. *World Cinema 2: Sweden*. London: Flicks, 1986.

Majer O'Sickey, Ingeborg, and Ingeborg von Zadow, eds. *Triangulated Visions: Women in Recent German Cinema*. Albany: State University of New York Press, 1998.

Manvell, Roger. *New Cinema in Europe*. New York: Dutton, 1966.

———. *The German Cinema*. London: Dent, 1971.

Marcus, Millicent. *Italian Film in the Light of Neorealism*. Princeton, N.J.: Princeton University Press, 1986.

———. *Filmmaking by the Book: Italian Cinema and Literary Adaptation*. Baltimore: Johns Hopkins University Press, 1993.

———. "*Caro Diario* and the Cinematic Body of Nanni Moretti." *Italica* 73, no. 2 (Summer 1996): 233–47.

———. *After Fellini: National Cinema in the Postmodern Age*. Baltimore: Johns Hopkins University Press, 2002.

Marrone, Gaetana. *The Gaze and the Labyrinth: The Cinema of Liliana Cavani*. Princeton, N.J.: Princeton University Press, 2000.

Martí-Olivella, Jaume. "Toward a New Transcultural Dialogue in Spanish Film." In José Colmeiro et al., eds., *Spain Today*, pp. 46–66.

Masi, Stefano. *Roberto Benigni*. Rome: Gremese, 1999.

Masi, Stefano, and Enrico Lancia. *Italian Movie Goddesses: Over 80 of the Greatest Women in Italian Cinema*. Trans. Lenor Rosemberg. Rome: Gremese, 1997.

Mazierska, Ewa, and Laura Rascaroli. *From Moscow to Madrid: European Cities, Postmodern Cinema*. London: Tauris, 2002.

Mellen, Joan, ed. *The World of Luis Buñuel: Essays in Criticism*. New York: Oxford University Press, 1978.

Mendik, Xavier. "Detection and Transgression: The Investigative Drive of the Giallo." In Black, ed., *Necronomicon*, pp. 35–54.

Mensh, Elaine, and Harry Mensh. *Behind the Scenes in Two Worlds*. New York: International, 1978.

Meurer, Hans Joachim. *Cinema and National Identity in a Divided Germany, 1979–1989: The Split Screen*. Lewiston, N.Y.: Mellen, 2000.

Moeller, Hans-Bernhard. "New German Cinema and Its Precarious Subsidy and Finance System." *Quarterly Review of Film Studies* 5, no. 2 (Spring 1980): 157–68.

Molina-Foix, Vicente. *New Cinema in Spain*. London: British Film Institute, 1977.

Moore, Kevin Z. "Eclipsing the Commonplace: The Logic of Alienation in Antonioni." *Film Quarterly* 48, no. 4 (1995): 22–34.

Murray, Bruce A., and Christopher J. Wickham. *Framing the Past: The Historiography of German Cinema and Television*. Carbondale: Southern Illinois University Press, 1992.

Murray, Edward. *Fellini the Artist*. New York: Ungar, 1976.

Naughton, Leone. *That Was the Wild East: Film Culture, Unification, and the 'New' Germany*. Ann Arbor: University of Michigan Press, 2002.

"New German Cinema." Special issue of *Persistence of Vision* 2 (Fall 1985).

"New Landscapes in Contemporary Italian Cinema." Special issue of *Annali d'Italianistica* 17 (1999).

Newman, Kim. "Thirty Years in Another Town: The History of Italian Exploitation I. *Monthly Film Bulletin* 624 (1986): 20–24.

———. "Thirty Years in Another Town: The History of Italian Exploitation II. *Monthly Film Bulletin* 625 (1986): 51–55.

———. "Thirty Years in Another Town: The History of Italian Exploitation III. *Monthly Film Bulletin* 626 (1986): 88–91.

"New Spanish and Portugese Cinema." Special issue of *Journal of the University Film and Video Association* 35, no. 2 (Summer 1983).

"New Spanish Cinema." Special issue of *Quarterly Review of Film Studies* 8, no. 2 (Spring 1983).

Nichols, Bill, ed. *Movies and Methods*. Vol. 1. Berkeley: University of California Press, 1976.

Nowell-Smith, Geoffrey. *L'Avventura*. London: British Film Institute, 1998.

Nowell-Smith, Geoffrey; James Hay; and Gianni Volpi. *The Companion to Italian Cinema*. London: Cassell/British Film Institute, 1996.

Nowell-Smith, Geoffrey, and Stephen Ricci, eds. *Hollywood and Europe: Economics, Culture, and National Identity 1945–1995*. London: British Film Institute, 1998.

Orto, Nuccio. *Maurizio Nichetti: Un comico, un autore*. Chieti, Italy: Métis, 1990.

Osmond, Jonathan. *German Reunification: A Reference Guide and Commentary*. London: Longman, 1992.

Palmerini, Luca M., and Gaetano Mistretta. *Spaghetti Nightmares: Italian Fantasy-Horrors as Seen through the Eyes of Their Protagonists*. Ed. Margo Winick. Trans. Gilliam M. A. Kirkpatrick. Key West, Fla.: Fantasma, 1996.

Pasolini, Pier Paolo. "The Cinema of Poetry." In Nichols, ed., *Movies and Methods*, vol. 1, pp. 542–58.

———. *Roman Nights and Other Stories*. Trans. John Shepley. Marlboro, Vt.: Marlboro, 1986.

Peitsch, Helmut; Charles Burdett; and Claire Gorrara, eds. *European Memories of the Second World War*. New York: Berghahn, 1999.

Pérez Millán, Juan Antonio. *Pilar Miró: Directora de cine*. Valladolid, Spain: Semana internacional de Cine, 1992.

Perry, Ted. *Filmguide to "8½"*. Bloomington: Indiana University Press, 1975.

Pflaum, Hans Günther. *Germany on Film: Theme and Content in the Cinema of the Federal Republic of Germany*. Ed. Robert Picht. Trans. Richard C. Helt and Roland Richter. Detroit: Wayne State University Press, 1990.

Pflaum, Hans Günther, and Hans Helmut Prizler. *Cinema in the Federal Republic of Germany: The New German Film, Origins and Present Situation—a Handbook*. Trans. Timothy Nevill. Bonn: Inter Nationes, 1983.

Phillips, Klaus, ed. *New German Filmmakers: From Oberhausen through the 1970s*. New York: Ungar, 1984.

Pistoia, Marco. *Maurizio Nichetti*. Milan: Il Castoro, 1997.

Porcelli, Tina. *Lars von Trier e Dogma*. Milan: Il Castoro, 2001.

Porton, Richard, and Lee Ellickson. "Comedy, Communism, and Pastry: An Interview with Nanni Moretti." *Cineaste* 21, nos. 1–2 (1995): 11–15.

Prono, Franco. *Bernardo Bertolucci: "Il conformista."* Turin: Lindau, 1998.

Puttnam, David, with Neil Watson. *Movies and Money*. New York: Knopf, 1998. Published in the United Kingdom as *The Undeclared War: The Struggle for Control of the World's Film Industry*. London: HarperCollins, 1997.

Qvist, Per Olov, and Peter von Bagh. *Guide to the Cinema of Sweden and Finland*. Westport, Conn.: Greenwood, 2000.

"Rainer Werner Fassbinder." Special issue of *October* 21 (Summer 1982).

Ranucci, Georgette, and Stefanella Ughi, eds. *Carlo Verdone*. Rome: Audino, 1994.

Raskin, Richard. "An Interview with Daniel Kothenschulte on Dogma 95." *p.o.v.* 10 (December 2000): 181–90.

Raynes, Tony, ed. *Fassbinder*. 2nd ed. London: British Film Institute, 1979. Oberhausen Manifesto.

Reich, Jacqueline, and Piero Garofalo, eds. *Re-Viewing Fascism: Italian Cinema, 1922–1943*. Bloomington: Indiana University Press, 2002.

Rentschler, Eric. *West German Film in the Course of Time: Reflections on the Twenty Years since Oberhausen*. Bedford Hills, N.Y.: Redgrave, 1984.

———, ed. *German Film and Literature: Adaptations and Transformations*. New York: Methuen, 1986.

Repetto, Monica, and Carlo Tagliabue, eds. *La vita è bella? Il cinema italiano alla fine degli anni novanta e il suo pubblico*. Milan: Il Castoro, 2000.

Restivo, Angelo. *The Cinema of Economic Miracles: Visuality and Modernization in the Italian Art Film*. Durham, N.C.: Duke University Press, 2002.

Riemer, Willy, ed. *After Postmodernism: Austrian Literature and Film in Transition*. Riverside, Calif.: Ariadne, 2000.

Rhodie, Sam. *Antonioni*. London: British Film Institute, 1990.

———. *Fellini Lexicon*. London: British Film Institute, 1995.

———. *The Passion of Pier Paolo Pasolini*. London: British Film Institute, 1995.

Roman, Shari. *Digital Babylon: Hollywood, Indiewood & Dogme 95*. Los Angeles: IFILM, 2001.

Rosenthal, Stuart. *The Cinema of Frederico Fellini*. Cranbury, N.J.: Barnes, 1976.

Roth, Lane. *Film Semiotics, Metz, and Leone's Trilogy*. New York: Garland, 1983.

Roud, Richard. *Straub*. New York: Viking, 1972.

Rumble, Patrick A., and Bart Testa, eds. *Pier Paolo Pasolini: Contemporary Perspectives*. Toronto: University of Toronto Press, 1994.

Salachas, Gilbert. *Federico Fellini*. New York: Crown, 1969.

Sandford, John. *The New German Cinema*. New York: Da Capo, 1980.

Scherpe, Klaus R. "Alexander Kluge: Germany—an Experience of Worlds and Images." In Peitsch, Burdett, and Gorrara, eds., *European Memories of the Second World War*, pp. 175–84.

Schubin, Mark. "Lenses: The Depth of the Field." *Videography* (February 1986): 39–44.

Schürer, Ernst; Manfred Keune; and Philip Jenkins, eds. *The Berlin Wall: Representations and Perspectives*. New York: Lang, 1996.

Schwartz, David Barth. *Pasolini Requiem*. New York: Pantheon, 1992.

Schwartz, Ronald. *Spanish Film Directors (1950–1985): 21 Profiles*. Metuchen, N.J.: Scarecrow, 1986.

———. *The Great Spanish Films: 1950–1990*. Metuchen, N.J.: Scarecrow, 1991.

Shandley, Robert R. *Rubble Films: German Cinema in the Shadow of the Third Reich*. Philadelphia: Temple University Press, 2001.

Shattuc, Jane. *Television, Tabloids, and Tears: Fassbinder and Popular Culture*. Minneapolis: University of Minnesota Press, 1995.

Siciliano, Enzo. *Pasolini*. Trans. John Shepley. New York: Random House, 1982.

Silberman, Mark. "Remembering History: The Filmmaker Konrad Wolf." *New German Critique* 49 (Winter 1990): 163–87.

———. *German Cinema: Texts in Context*. Detroit: Wayne State University Press, 1995.

———. "What Is German in the German Cinema?" *Film History* 8, no. 3 (1996): 297–315.

Simon, John. *Ingmar Bergman Directs*. New York: Harcourt Brace Jovanovich, 1972.

Sitney, P. Adams. *Vital Crises in Italian Cinema: Iconography, Stylistics, Politics*. Austin: University of Texas Press, 1995.

Sklarew, Bruce. "Returning to My Low Budget Roots: An Interview with Bernardo Bertolucci." *Cineaste* 24, no. 4 (1999): 16–19.

Sklarew, Bruce H., et al., eds. *Bertolucci's "The Last Emperor": Multiple Takes*. Detroit: Wayne State University Press, 1998.

Slater, Jay. *Eaten Alive!: Italian Cannibal and Zombie Movies*. London: Plexus, 2002.

Smith, Paul Julian. *Laws of Desire: Questions of Homosexuality in Spanish Writing and Film 1960–1990*. Oxford: Oxford University Press, 1992.

———. *Desire Unlimited: The Cinema of Pedro Almodóvar*. London: Verso, 1994.

———. *Vision Machines: Cinema, Literature, and Sexuality in Spain and Cuba 1983–1993*. London: Verso, 1996.

Soila, Tytti; Astrid Söderberg-Widding; and Gunnar Iverson. *Nordic National Cinemas*. London: Routledge, 1998.

Sorlin, Pierre. *Italian National Cinema 1896–1996*. London: Routledge, 1996.

Stack, Oswald, ed. *Pasolini on Pasolini*. Bloomington: Indiana University Press, 1969.

Staig, Laurence, and Tony Williams. *Italian Western: The Opera of Violence*. London: Lorrimer, 1975.

Stanbrook, Alan. "Hard Times for Portuguese Cinema." *Sight and Sound* 58, no. 2 (Spring 1989): 118–21.

Steene, Brigitta. *Ingmar Bergman*. New York: Twayne, 1968.

———, ed. *Focus on "The Seventh Seal."* Englewood Cliffs, N.J.: Prentice-Hall, 1972.

Stevenson, Jack. *Lars von Trier*. London: British Film Institute, 2002.

Stone, Rob. *Spanish Cinema*. Harlow, Eng.: Pearson Education, 2001.

Strauss, Frederic, ed. *Almodóvar on Almodóvar*. Trans. Yves Baignères. London: Faber & Faber, 1996.

Strout, Andrea. "West Germany's Film Miracle." *American Film* 5, no. 7 (May 1980): 37–39.

Talens, Jenaro, and Santos Zunzunegui Diez, eds. *Modes of Representation in Spanish Cinema*. Minneapolis: University of Minnesota Press, 1998.

Tatò, Francesco, ed. *The Stuff Dreams Are Made Of: The Films of Marcello Mastroianni*. Rome: Marchesi Garfiche, 1998.

Taylor, Elayne. "Dancing in Denmark: Elayne Taylor Talks with Lars von Trier." *Creative Screenwriting* 8, no. 1 (January–February 2001): 32–35.

Testa, Carlo, ed. *Poet of Civic Courage: The Films of Francesco Rosi*. Westport, Conn.: Greenwood, 1996.

Thomas, Paul. "Fassbinder: Poetry of the Inarticulate." *Film Quarterly* 30, no. 2 (Winter 1976–77): 2–17.

Thomsen, Bodil Marie. "Idiocy, Foolishness, and Spastic Jesting." *p.o.v.* 10 (December 2000): 47–60. Analysis of Dogme '95.

Thrower, Stephen. *Beyond Terror: The Films of Lucio Fulci*. Guildford, Eng.: FAB, 1999.

Tohill, Cathal, and Pete Tombs. *Immoral Tales*. New York: St. Martin's, 1994.

Tonetti, Claretta Micheletti. *Bernardo Bertolucci: The Cinema of Ambiguity*. New York: Twayne, 1995.

Torres, Augusto M. *Diccionario del cine español*. Madrid: Espasa Calpe, 1994.

Triana-Toribio, Núria. *Spanish National Cinema*. London: Routledge, 2003.

van Scheers, Rob. *Paul Verhoeven*. Trans. Aletta Stevens. London: Faber & Faber, 1997.

Vernon, Kathleen M., and Barbara Morris, eds. *Post-Franco,*

Postmodern: The Films of Pedro Almodóvar. Westport, Conn.: Greenwood, 1995.

Viano, Maurizio. "*Life Is Beautiful:* Reception, Allegory, and Holocaust Laughter." *Film Quarterly* 53, no. 1 (Fall 1999): 26–34.

Vincendeau, Ginette, ed. *Encyclopedia of European Cinema.* New York: Facts on File, 1995.

Vogel, Amos. "Herzog in Berlin." *Film Comment* 13, no. 5 (September–October 1978): 37–38.

von Trier, Lars. "Open Film City." In Hjort and Bondebjerg, *The Danish Directors,* pp. 224–27.

Wagstaff, Christopher. "A Forkful of Westerns: Industry, Audiences and the Italian Western." In Dyer and Vincendeau, eds., *Popular European Cinema,* pp. 245–62.

Weinrichter, Antonio. *La línea del vientre: el cine de Bigas Luna.* Gijón, Spain: Festival de Cine de Gijón, 1992.

Weisser, Thomas. *Spaghetti Westerns—the Good, the Bad, and the Violent: A Comprehensive, Illustrated Filmography of 558 Eurowesterns and Their Personnel, 1961–1977.* Jefferson, N.C.: McFarland, 1992.

Wenders, Wim. *My Time with Antonioni: The Diary of an Extraordinary Experience.* Trans. Michael Hoffman. London: Faber & Faber, 2000.

———. *Once: Pictures and Stories.* Trans. Marion Kagerer. London: Schirmer, 2001.

———. *On Film: Essays and Conversations.* London: Faber & Faber, 2001.

"West German Film in the 1970s." Special issue of *Quarterly Review of Film Studies* 5, no. 2 (Spring 1980).

Willem, Linda M., ed. *Carlos Saura: Interviews.* Jackson: University Press of Mississippi, 2003.

Willemen, Paul, ed. *Pier Paolo Pasolini.* London: British Film Institute, 1977.

Williams, Phillip. "The New Spanish Cinema." *Moviemaker* 48, no. 9 (Fall 2002): 18–22.

Winter, Douglas E. "Opera of Violence: The Films of Dario Argento." In Golden, ed., *CUT!*

Wolfram, Manfred K. "Film in the Federal Republic of Germany." In Burdick, Jacobsen, and Kudszus, eds., *Contemporary Germany,* pp. 371–94.

Wood, Robin. *Ingmar Bergman.* New York: Praeger, 1969.

Wright, Rochelle. *The Visible Wall: Jews and Other Ethnic Outsiders in Swedish Film.* Carbondale: Southern Illinois University Press, 1998.

Wyke, Maria. *Projecting the Past: Ancient Rome, Cinema and History.* New York: Routledge, 1997.

Young, Deborah. "Me, Myself, and Italy." *Film Comment* 38, no. 1 (January–February 2002): 56–61. Profile of Nanni Moretti.

Young, Vernon. *Cinema Borealis: Ingmar Bergman and the Swedish Ethos.* New York: Avon, 1971.

CHAPTER 16. EUROPEAN RENAISSANCE: EAST

Arthur, Paul. "Escape from Freedom: The Films of Dušan Makavejev." *Cineaste* 27, no. 1 (2001): 11–15.

Atkinson, Michael. "Trouble Every Day: From Amour Fou to Primal Scream: Inside the Movie Madhouse of Andrzej Żulawski." *Film Comment* 39, no. 1 (January–February 2003): 38–41.

Balski, Grzegorz, ed. *Directory of Eastern European Film-Makers and Films 1945–1991.* Westport, Conn.: Greenwood, 1992.

Banaszkiewicz, Wladyslaw, et al. *Contemporary Polish Cinematography.* Warsaw: Polonia, 1962.

Bell, John D., ed. *Bulgaria in Transition.* Boulder: Westview, 1998.

Bickley, Daniel. "Socialism and Humanism: The Contemporary Hungarian Cinema." *Cineaste* 9, no. 2 (Winter 1978–79): 30–35.

Bogdan, Henry. *From Warsaw to Sofia: A History of Eastern Europe.* Ed. Istvan Fehervary. Trans. Jeanie P. Fleming. Santa Fe, N.M.: Pro Libertate, 1989.

Boorsma, Peter B.; Annemoon van Hemel; and Niki van der Wielen, eds. *Privatization and Culture: Experiences in the Arts, Heritage and Cultural Industries in Europe.* Boston: Kluwer, 1998.

Bren, Frank. *Poland.* World Cinema Series. Vol. 1. London: Flicks, 1986.

Brinker-Gabler, Gisela, and Sidonie Smith. *Writing New Identities: Gender, Nation, and Immigration in Contemporary Europe.* Minneapolis: University of Minnesota Press, 1997.

Brown, J. F. *Hopes and Shadows: Eastern Europe after Communism.* Durham, N.C.: Duke University Press, 1994.

Broz, Jaroslav. *The Path of Fame of the Czechoslovak Film: A Short Outline of Its History.* Prague: Českaslovenský filmový ustav, 1967.

Burns, Bryan. *World Cinema: Hungary.* Madison, N.J.: Fairleigh Dickinson University Press, 1996.

Butler, Ivan. *The Cinema of Roman Polanski.* Cranbury, N.J.: Barnes, 1970.

Campan, Véronique. *Dix brèves histoires d'image: Le Décalogue de Krzysztof Kieślowski.* Paris: Presses de la Sorbonne nouvelle, 1993.

Coates, Paul. *The Story of the Lost Reflection: The Alienation of the Image in Western and Polish Cinema.* London: Verso, 1985.

Coates, Paul. ed. *Lucid Dreams: The Films of Krzysztof Kieślowski.* Trowbridge, Eng.: Flicks, 1999.

Coates, Paul. "Shifting Borders: Konwicki, Zanussi and the Ideology of 'East-Central Europe.'" *Canadian Slavonic Papers* 42, nos. 1–2 (2000): 87–98.

Crnkovic, Gordana P. "Interview with Agnieszka Holland." *Film Quarterly* 52, no. 2 (1998–99): 2–9.

Curry, Jane L., ed. *The Black Book of Polish Censorship*. New York: Random House, 1983.

Dakovic, Nevena. "Mother, Myth, and Cinema: Recent Yugoslav Cinema." *Film Criticism* 21, no. 2 (Winter 1996–97): 40–50.

Donia, Robert J., and John V. A. Fine, Jr. *Bosnia and Herzegovina: A Tradition Betrayed*. New York: Columbia University Press, 1994.

Durgnat, Raymond. *W. R.: Mysteries of the Organism*. London: British Film Institute, 1999.

Dyer, Richard, and Ginette Vincendeau, eds. *Popular European Cinema*. London: Routledge, 1992.

"East European Film." Supplement to *Cineaste* 19, no. 4 (March 1993): 43–64.

Edera, Bruno. *Full Length Animated Feature Films*. Ed. John Halas. New York: Focal, 1977.

Eidsvik, Charles. "The Comedy of Futility in Eastern Europe." In Horton, ed., *Comedy/Cinema/Theory*, pp. 91–95.

Eleftheriotis, Dimitris. *Popular Cinemas of Europe: Studies of Texts, Contexts and Frameworks*. New York: Continuum, 2001.

Estève, Michel. *Miklós Jancsó*. Paris: Lettres Moderne, 1975.

———, ed. *Theo Angelopoulos*. Études Cinematographiques, nos. 142–145. Paris: Lettres Modernes/Minard, 1991.

Estève, Michel, and Yvette Biró. *Études Cinématographiques: Krzysztof Kieślowski*. Paris: Lettres Modernes, 1994.

Fainaru, Dan, ed. *Theo Angelopoulos: Interviews*. Jackson: University Press of Mississippi, 2001.

Falkowska, Janina. " 'The Political' in the Films of Andrzej Wajda and Krzysztof Kieślowski." *Cinema Journal* 34, no. 2 (1995): 37–50.

———. *The Political Films of Andrzej Wajda: Dialogism in "Man of Marble," "Man of Iron," and "Danton."* Providence, R. I.: Berghahn, 1996.

Forman, Milos, and Jan Novák. *Turnaround: A Memoir*. New York: Villard, 1994.

Fuksiewicz, Jacek. *Film and Television in Poland*. Warsaw: Interpress, 1976.

Gálik, Mihály. "Who Laughs Last: Film and Broadcasting in Hungary." In Boorsma, van Hemel, and van der Wielen, eds., *Privatization and Culture*, pp. 131–141.

Garbowski, Christopher. *Krzysztof Kieślowski's Decalogue Series: The Problem of the Protagonists and Their Self-Transcendance [sic]*. Boulder: East European Monographs, 1996.

Gati, Charles. *The Bloc That Failed: Soviet-East European Relations in Transition*. Bloomington: Indiana University Press, 1990.

Glenny, Misha. *The Fall of Yugoslavia: The Third Balkan War*. New York: Penguin, 1992.

Gocic, Goran. *Notes from the "Underground": The Cinema of Emir Kusturica*. London: Wallflower, 2001.

Goulding, Daniel J., ed. *Post New Wave Cinema in the Soviet Union and Eastern Europe*. Bloomington: Indiana University Press, 1989.

———, ed. "Yugoslav Film in the Post-Tito Era." In Goulding, ed. *Post New Wave Cinema in the Soviet Union and Eastern Europe*, pp. 248–84.

———, ed. *Five Filmmakers: Tarkovsky, Forman, Polanski, Szabo, Makavejev*. Bloomington: Indiana University Press, 1994.

———. "East Central European Cinema: Two Defining Moments." In Hill and Gibson, eds., *The Oxford Guide to Film Studies*, pp. 471–77.

———. *Liberated Cinema: The Yugoslav Experience*. Rev. ed. Bloomington: Indiana University Press, 2003.

Haltof, Marek. "A Fistful of Dollars: Polish Cinema after the 1989 Freedom Shock." *Film Quarterly* 48, no. 3 (1995): 15–25.

———. *Polish National Cinema*. New York: Berghahn, 2002.

Hames, Peter. *The Czechoslovak New Wave*. Berkeley: University of California Press, 1985.

———. "Czechoslovakia: After the Spring." In Goulding, ed., *Post New Wave Cinema in the Soviet Union and Eastern Europe*, pp. 102–42.

Harman, Chris. *Class Struggles in Eastern Europe, 1945–83*. London: Pluto, 1983.

Hess, Franklin L. "Sound of the Nation: Rethinking the History of Early Greek Film Production." *Journal of Modern Greek Studies* 18, no. 1 (May 2000): 13–36.

Hibbin, Nina. *Eastern Europe: An Illustrated Guide*. Screen Series. Cranbury, N.J.: Barnes, 1969.

Hill, John, and Pamela Church Gibson, eds. *The Oxford Guide to Film Studies*. Oxford: Oxford University Press, 1998.

Hoberman, J. "Budapest's Business." *Film Comment* 22 (May–June 1986): 68–71.

Holloway, Ronald. *Z Is for Zagreb*. Cranbury, N.J.: Barnes, 1972.

———. *The Bulgarian Cinema*. Rutherford, N.J.: Associated University Presses, 1986.

———. "Bulgaria: The Cinema of Poetics." In Goulding, ed., *Post New Wave Cinema in the Soviet Union and Eastern Europe*, pp. 215–47.

Holmes, Diana, and Alison Smith, eds. *100 Years of European Cinema: Entertainment or Ideology?* Manchester, Eng.: Manchester University Press, 2000.

Horton, Andrew. "Satire and Sympathy: A New Wave of Yugoslavian Filmmakers." *Cineaste* 11, no. 2 (1981): 18–22.

——. "The New Serbo-Creationism." *American Film* 11, no. 4 (January–February 1986): 24–30.

——. "The Rise and Fall of the Yugoslav Partisan Film," *Film Criticism* 12, no. 3 (Winter 1987–88): 18–27.

——, ed. *Comedy/Cinema/Theory*. Berkeley: University of California Press, 1991.

——, ed. "The Mouse Who Wanted to F——k a Cow: Cinematic Carnival Laughter in Dušan Makavejev's Films." In Horton, ed., *Comedy/Cinema/Theory*, pp. 222–39.

——. " 'Only Crooks Can Get Ahead': Post-Yugoslav Cinema/TV/Video in the 1990s." In Ramet and Adamovich, eds., *Beyond Yugoslavia*, pp. 413–41

——. *The Films of Theo Angelopoulos: A Cinema of Contemplation*. Princeton, N.J.: Princeton University Press, 1999.

Insdorf, Annette. *Double Lives, Second Chances: The Cinema of Krzysztof Kieślowski*. New York: Miramax/Hyperion, 1999.

Iordanova, Dina. "Conceptualizing the Balkans in Film." *Slavic Review* 55, no. 1 (Winter 1996): 223–54.

——. "Women in New Balkan Cinema: Surviving on the Margins." *Film Criticism* 21, no. 2 (Winter 1996–97): 24–40.

——. "Balkan Film Representations since 1989: The Quest for Admissibility." *Historical Journal of Film, Radio and Television* 18, no. 2 (1998): 263–80.

——. "Balkans Revisited." *Canadian Slavonic Papers* 33, nos. 3–4 (1998): 479–89.

——. "Canaries and Birds of Prey: The New Season of Bulgarian Cinema." In Bell, ed., *Bulgaria in Transition*, pp. 255–81.

——. "Kusturica's *Underground* (1995): Historical Allegory or Propaganda." *Historical Journal of Film, Radio, and Television* 19, no. 1 (1998): 69–86.

——. "College Course File: Eastern European Cinema." *Journal of Film and Video* 51, no. 1 (Spring 1999): 56–57.

——. "East Europe's Cinema Industries since 1989: Financing Structure and Studios." *Javnost/The Public* 6, no. 2 (1999): 45–60.

——. "The Cinema of the Dispersed Yugoslavs: Diasporas in the Making." *Cineaction* 52 (2000): 69–72.

——. *Cinema of Flames: Balkan Film, Culture, and the Media*. London: British Film Institute, 2001.

——. *Emir Kusturica*. London: British Film Institute, 2002.

Jaehne, Karen. "István Szabó: Dreams of Memories." *Film Quarterly* 32, no. 1 (Fall 1978): 30–41.

Kieślowski, Krzysztof, and Krzysztof Piesiewicz. *Decalogue: The Ten Commandments*. Trans. Danusia Stok. London: Faber & Faber, 1998.

——. *Three Colors Trilogy: Blue, White, Red*. Trans. Danusia Stok. London: Faber & Faber, 1998.

Klawans, Stuart. "Life Is Beautiful." *Film Comment* 38, no. 1 (January–February 2002): 48–49. Profile of Andrzej Monk.

Koliodimos, Dimitris. *The Greek Filmography, 1914–1996*. Jefferson, N.C.: McFarland, 1999.

Kurzewski, Stanislaw. *Contemporary Polish Cinema*. London: Wischhusen, 1980.

Langdon, Dewey. *Outline of Czechoslovakian Cinema*. London: Informatics, 1971.

Laqueur, Walter. *Europe in Our Time: A History 1945–1992*. New York: Viking, 1992.

Leaming, Barbara. *Polanski, a Biography: The Filmmaker as Voyeur*. New York: Simon & Schuster, 1981.

Liehm, Antonín J. *Closely Watched Films: The Czechoslovak Experience*. White Plains, N.Y.: International Arts & Sciences, 1974.

——. "Franz Kafka in Eastern Europe." *Telos* 23 (Summer 1975): 72–86.

——. *The Milos Forman Stories*. White Plains, N.Y.: International Arts & Sciences, 1975.

Liehm, Mira, and Antonín J. Liehm. *The Most Important Art: Eastern European Film after 1945*. Berkeley: University of California Press, 1977.

Magas, Branka. *The Destruction of Yugoslavia: Tracking the Break-up, 1980–92*. London: Verso, 1993.

Mazierska, Ewa. "Non-Jewish Jews, Good Poles, and Historical Truth in the Films of Andrzej Wajda." *Historical Journal of Film, Radio and Television* 20, no. 2 (2000): 213–26.

Mazierska, Ewa, and Laura Rascaroli. *From Moscow to Madrid: European Cities, Postmodern Cinema*. London: Tauris, 2002.

Michalek, Boleslaw. *The Cinema of Andrzej Wajda*. Trans. Edward Rothert. Cranbury, N.J.: Barnes, 1973.

Michalek, Boleslaw, and Frank Turaj, dirs. and eds. *Le Cinéma Polonais*. Cinéma/Pluriel series. Paris: Centre Georges Pompidou, 1992.

——. *The Modern Cinema of Poland*. Bloomington: Indiana University Press, 1988.

Miczka, Tadeusz. "Cinema under Political Pressure: A Brief Outline of Authorial Roles in Polish Post-War Feature-Film 1945–1995." *Kinema* 4 (1995): 32–48.

Mojzes, Paul. *Yugoslavian Inferno: Ethnoreligious Warfare in the Balkans*. New York: Continuum, 1994.

Murri, Serafino. *Krzysztof Kieślowski*. Milan: Il Castoro, 1997.

Nemeskürty, István. *Word and Image: History of the Hungarian Cinema*. Trans. Zsuzsanna Horn and Fred Macnicol. 2nd ed., enl. Budapest: Corvina, 1974.

O'Grady, Gerald, ed. *Makavejev Fixtionary; The Films of Dušan Makavejev*. New York: American Museum of the Moving Image/Film and the Public, 1995.

Pangon, Gerárd, and Jean Luc Douin. *Andrzej Wajda*. Paris: Mille et une nuits, 1997.

Passek, Jean-Loup, et al., dirs. and eds. *Le Cinéma Hongrois*. Cinema/Pluriel series. Paris: Centre Georges Pompidou, 1979.

Passek, Jean-Loup, et al., dirs. and eds. *Le Cinéma Yougoslave*. Cinema/Pluriel series. Paris: Centre Georges Pompidou, 1986.

Paul, David W., ed. *Politics, Art and Commitment in the East European Cinema*. London: Macmillan, 1983.

———. "The Esthetics of Courage: The Political Climate for the Cinema in Poland and Hungary." *Cineaste* 14, no. 4 (1986): 16–22.

———. "Hungary: The Magyar on the Bridge." In Goulding, ed., *Post New Wave Cinema in the Soviet Union and Eastern Europe*, pp. 172–214.

Petrie, Graham. *History Must Answer to Man: The Contemporary Hungarian Cinema*. London: Tantivy, 1979.

Petrie, Graham, and Ruth Dwyer. *Before the Wall Came Down: Soviet and East European Filmmakers Working in the West*. Lanham, Md.: University Press of America, 1990.

Portuges, Catherine. "Border Crossings: Recent Trends in East and Central European Cinema." *Slavic Review* 51, no. 3 (Fall 1992): 531–35.

———. *Screen Memories: The Hungarian Cinema of Márta Mészáros*. Bloomington: Indiana University Press, 1993.

———. "Hidden Subjects, Secret Identities: Figuring Jews, Gypsies, and Gender in 1990s Cinema of Eastern Europe." In Brinker-Gabler and Smith, eds., *Writing New Identities*, pp. 196–215.

Purš, Jirí. *Obrysy vývoje ceskoslovenské znárodnené kinematografie, 1945–1980*. Prague: Československý filmový ústav, 1985.

Ramet, Sabrina Petra, and Ljubisa S. Adamovich, eds. *Beyond Yugoslavia: Politics, Economics, and Culture in a Shattered Community*. Boulder: Westview, 1995.

Siegel, Joshua. *The Lodz Film School of Poland: 50 Years*. New York: Museum of Modern Art, 1998. Exhibition catalog.

Skwara, Anita. "Film Stars Do Not Shine in the Sky over Poland: The Absence of Popular Cinema in Poland." In Dyer and Vincendeau, eds., *Popular European Cinema*, pp. 220–31.

Škvorecký, Josef. *All the Bright Young Men and Women: A Personal History of the Czech Cinema*. Toronto: Martin, 1971.

Slater, Thomas J. *Handbook of Soviet and East European Films and Filmmakers*. Westport, Conn.: Greenwood, 1992.

Sobanski, Oskar. *Polish Feature Films: A Reference Guide, 1945–1985*. West Cornwall, Conn.: Locust Hill, 1987.

Sosnowski, Alexandra. "Polish Cinema Today: A New Order in the Production, Distribution, and Exhibition of Film." *Polish Review* 40, no. 1 (1995): 315–29.

———. "Cinema in Transition: The Polish Film Today." *Journal of Popular Film and Television* 24, no. 1 (1996): 10–16.

Stankiewicz, Marketa Goetz. "The Theater of the Absurd in Czechoslovakia." *Survey* 21 (Winter–Spring 1975): 85–100.

Stassinopoulou, Maria A. "Creating Distraction after Destruction: Representations of the Military in Greek Film." *Journal of Modern Greek Studies* 18, no. 1 (May 2000): 37–52.

Stoil, Michael J. *Cinema beyond the Danube: The Camera and Politics*. Metuchen, N.J.: Scarecrow, 1974.

———. *Balkan Cinema: Evolution after the Revolution*. Ann Arbor, Mich.: UMI Research Press, 1982.

Stok, Danusia, ed. and trans. *Kieślowski on Kieślowski*. London: Faber & Faber, 1993.

Stoyanovich, Ivan, et al. *The Bulgarian Cinema Today*. Sofia: Sofia Press, 1981.

Tarkovsky, Andrei. *Time within Time: The Diaries 1970–1986*. Trans. Kitty Hunter-Blair. London: Faber & Faber, 1994.

Tarkovsky, Andrei. *Collected Screenplays*. Trans. William Powell and Natasha Synessios. London: Faber & Faber, 1999.

Taylor, Richard; Nancy Wood; Julian Graffy; and Dina Iordanova, eds. *The BFI Companion to Eastern European and Russian Cinema*. London: British Film Institute, 2000.

Terziev, Yanko. "Bulgarian Cinema: Landscape after the Battle." *Bulgarian Quarterly* 1 (1992): 48–60.

Turaj, Frank. "Poland: The Cinema of Moral Concern." In Goulding, ed., *Post New Wave Cinema in the Soviet Union and Eastern Europe*, pp. 143–71.

Vogel, Amos. *Film as a Subversive Art*. New York: Random House, 1974.

Wajda, Andrzej. "Andrzej Wajda's Censored Speech." *Cineaste* 13, no. 3 (1984): 12–13.

———. *Andrzej Wajda: Three Films*. London: Lorrimer, 1984.

———. *Double Vision: My Life in Film*. Trans. Rose Medina. New York: Holt, 1989.

Weschler, Lawrence. "Poland's Banned Films." *Cineaste* 13, no. 3 (1984): 11.

Whyte, Alistair. *New Cinema in Eastern Europe*. New York: Dutton, 1971.

Woodhead, Christine. *Turkish Cinema: An Introduction*. London: Centre for Near and Middle Eastern Studies, University of London, 1989.

Žalman, Jan. *Films and Film-Makers in Czechoslovakia*. Prague: Orbis, 1968.

Zizek, Slavoj. *The Fright of Real Tears: Krzysztof Kieślowski between Theory and Post-Theory*. London: British Film Institute, 2001.

Zsuffa, Joseph. *Béla Balázs: The Man and the Artist*. Berkeley: University of California Press, 1987.

CHAPTER 17. THE FORMER SOVIET UNION, 1945–PRESENT

Akiner, Shirin. *Islamic Peoples of the Soviet Union*. London: Kegan Paul, 1983.

Atwood, Lynne, ed. *Red Women on the Silver Screen: Soviet Women and Cinema from the Beginning to the End of the Communist Era*. London: Pandora, 1993.

Avrutin, Lily. "The Soldier, the Girl, and the Dragon: Battles of Meanings in Post-Soviet Cinematic Space." *Cinema Journal* 38, no. 2 (1999): 72–97.

Balski, Grzegorz, ed. *Directory of Eastern European Film-Makers and Films 1945–1991*. Westport, Conn.: Greenwood, 1992.

Bazin, André. "The Stalin Myth in Soviet Cinema." In Nichols, ed., *Movies and Methods*, vol. 2, pp. 29–40.

Berry, Ellen, and Anesa Miller-Pogacar, eds. *Re-Entering the Sign: Articulating New Russian Culture*. Ann Arbor: University of Michigan Press, 1995.

Beumers, Birgit, ed. *Russia on Reels: The Russian Idea in Post-Soviet Cinema*. London: Tauris, 1999.

———. *Burnt by the Sun*. London: Tauris, 2000.

———. "Myth-Making and Myth-Taking: Lost Ideals and the War in Contemporary Russian Cinema." *Canadian Slavonic Papers/Revue Canadienne des Slavistes* 42, nos. 1–2 (March–June 2000): 171–89.

Birkos, Alexander S. *Soviet Cinema: Directors and Films*. Hamden, Conn.: Archon, 1976.

Blankoff-Scarr, Goldie. "Tengiz Abuladze and the Flowering of Georgian Film Art." *Central Asian Survey* 8, no. 3 (1989): 61–86.

———. "The Seventh Art in Georgia: Political, Cultural, and Axiological Aspects." *Revue des Pays de l'Est* ½ (1991): 123–53.

Bordwell, David. *The Cinema of Eisenstein*. Cambridge, Mass.: Harvard University Press, 1993.

Brashinsky, Michael, and Andrew Horton, eds. *Russian Critics on the Cinema of Glasnost*. Cambridge, Eng.: Cambridge University Press, 1994.

Bryld, Mett, and Erik Kulavig, eds. *Soviet Civilization between Past and Present*. Odense, Den.: Odense University Press, 1998.

Cazals, Patrick. *Serguie Paradjanov*. Paris: Éditions de l'Étoile/Cahiers du Cinéma, 1993.

Chambers, John Whiteclay, II, and David Colbert. *World War II: Film and History*. New York: Oxford University Press, 1996.

Christensen, Julie. "Fathers and Sons at the Georgian Film Studio." *Wide Angle* 12, no. 4 (October 1990): 49–60.

Christie, Ian. "Shukshin: Holidays for the Soul." *Sight and Sound* 55, no. 4 (Autumn 1986): 261–63.

———. "Back in the USSR." *Film Comment* 36, no. 6 (November–December 2000): 39–42.

Christie, Ian, and David Elliott, eds. *Eisenstein at Ninety*. Oxford: Museum of Modern Art, 1988.

Ciesol, Forrest. "Kazakhastan Wave." *Sight and Sound* 59, no. 1 (Winter 1989–90): 51–55, 56–58.

———. "The Many Hollywoods of Central Asia." *World Monitor* (February 1990): 66–70.

Condee, Nancy, ed. *Soviet Hieroglyphics: Visual Culture in Late Twentieth-Century Russia*. Bloomington: Indiana University Press, 1995.

"Contemporary Soviet Cinema." Ed. Vance Kepley. Special issue of *Wide Angle* 12, no. 4 (October 1990).

Critchlow, James. *Nationalism in Uzbekistan: A Soviet Republic's Road to Sovereignty*. Boulder: Westview, 1991.

Dempsey, Michael. "Lost Harmony: Tarkovsky's *The Mirror* and *The Stalker*." *Film Quarterly* 35, no. 1 (Fall 1981): 12–17.

Dmytryshyn, Basil. *USSR: A Concise History*. 4th ed. New York: Scribner's, 1984.

Dolmatovskaya, Galina, and Irina Shilova. *Who's Who in the Soviet Cinema: Seventy Different Portraits*. Trans. Galina Dolmatovskaya. Moscow: Progress, 1979.

Elley, Derek. "Light in the Caucacus: Georgian Cinema." *Films and Filming* 23, no. 5 (February 1977): 16–21.

Estève, Michel, ed. *Andrei Tarkovsky*. Études Cinématographiques, nos. 135–138. Paris: Lettres Modernes, 1983.

Faraday, George. *Revolt of the Filmmakers: The Struggle for Artistic Autonomy and the Fall of the Soviet Film Industry*. University Park: Pennsylvania State University Press, 2000.

Fisher, William. "Gorbachev's Cinema." *Sight and Sound* 56, no, 4 (Autumn 1987): 243–49.

Fitzpatrick, Shelia. *The Cultural Front: Power and Culture in Revolutionary Russia*. Ithaca, N.Y.: Cornell University Press, 1992.

Flake, Carol. "Stranger in a Strange Land." *American Film* 11, no. 3 (December 1985): 40–46.

Forman, Milos, and Jan Novak. *Turnaround: A Memoir*. New York: Villard, 1994.

Fowler, Catherine, ed. *The European Cinema Reader*. London: Routledge, 2002.

Frierman, William, ed. *Soviet Central Asia: The Failed Transformation*. Boulder: Westview, 1991.

Galetski, Kirill. "The Foundation of Film Art: An Interview with Alexander Sokurov." *Cineaste* 26, no. 3 (Summer 2001): 4–9.

Galichenko, Nicholas. *Glasnost: Soviet Cinema Responds*. Ed. Robert Allington. Austin: University of Texas Press, 1991.

Geyer, Georgie Anne. *Waiting for Winter to End: An Extraordinary Journey through Soviet Central Asia*. Washington, D.C.: Brassey's, 1994.

Gillespie, David. "Identity and the Past in Recent Russian

Cinema." In Fowler, ed., *The European Cinema Reader*, pp. 143–52.

Gillespie, David C. *Russian Cinema*. Harlow, Eng.: Longman, 2002.

Givens, John. *Prodigal Son: Vasilii Shukshin in Soviet Russian Culture*. Evanston, Ill.: Northwestern University Press, 2000.

Golovsky, Val S., with John Rimberg. *Behind the Soviet Screen: The Motion-Picture Industry in the USSR 1972–1982*. Trans. Steven Hill. Ann Arbor, Mich.: Ardis, 1986.

Goodwin, James. *Eisenstein, Cinema, and History*. Urbana, Ill.: University of Chicago Press, 1993.

Goulding, Daniel J., ed. *Post New Wave Cinema in the Soviet Union and Eastern Europe*. Bloomington: Indiana University Press, 1989.

———, ed. *Five Filmmakers: Tarkovsky, Forman, Polanski, Szabo, Makavejev*. Bloomington: Indiana University Press, 1994.

Green, Peter. "Andrei Tarkovsky (1932–1986): Apocalypse and Sacrifice." *Sight and Sound* 56, no. 2 (Spring 1987): 108–119.

———. *Andrei Tarkovsky: The Winding Quest*. London: Macmillan, 1993.

Grenier, Richard. "A Soviet 'New Wave'?" *Commentary* (July 1981): 62–67.

Hill, Steven P. "Soviet Cinema Today." *Film Quarterly* 20, no. 4 (Summer 1967): 33–53.

Hiro, Dilip. *Between Marx and Muhammed: The Changing Face of Central Asia*. London: HarperCollins, 1994.

Holmes, Diana, and Alison Smith, eds. *100 Years of European Cinema: Entertainment or Ideology?* Manchester, Eng.: Manchester University Press, 2000.

Horton, Andrew, ed. *Inside Soviet Film Satire: Laughter with a Lash*. Cambridge, Eng.: Cambridge University Press, 1993.

Horton, Andrew, and Michael Brashinsky. *The Zero Hour: Glasnost and Soviet Cinema in Transition*. Princeton, N.J.: Princeton University Press, 1992.

Jaehne, Karen. "Rehabilitating the Superfluous Man: Films in the Life of Nikita Mikhalkov." *Film Quarterly* 34, no. 4 (Summer 1981): 14–21.

Johnson, Vida T., and Graham Petrie. *The Films of Andrei Tarkovsky: A Visual Fugue*. Bloomington: Indiana University Press, 1994.

Kaplan, Robert. *Balkan Ghosts: A Journey through History*. New York: St. Martin's, 1993.

Katz, Zev, ed. *Handbook of Major Soviet Nationalities*. New York: Free Press, 1975.

Kelly, Catriona, and David Shepard, eds. *Russian Cultural Studies: An Introduction*. Oxford: Oxford University Press, 1998.

Kenez, Peter. *Cinema and Soviet Society, 1917–1953*. Cambridge: Cambridge University Press, 1992.

Kepley, Vance, Jr. "The Origins of Soviet Cinema: A Study in Industry Development," *Quarterly Review of Film Studies* 10, no. 1 (Winter 1985): 22–38.

———. "Building a National Cinema: Soviet Film Education, 1918–1934," *Wide Angle* 9, no. 3 (1987): 4–20.

Khrushchev, Nikita. "De-Stalinization Speech, February 24–25, 1956." In Dmytryshyn, *USSR*, p. 563.

Kozintsev, Grigori. *King Lear, the Space of Tragedy: The Diary of a Film Director*. Trans. Mary Mackintosh. Berkeley: University of California Press, 1977.

———. *The Age and Its Conscience*. Moscow: BPSK, 1981.

Lawton, Anna. "Towards a New Openness in Soviet Cinema, 1976–1987." In Goulding, ed., *Post New Wave Cinema in the Soviet Union and Eastern Europe*, pp. 1–50.

———. *Kinoglasnost: Soviet Cinema in Our Time*. Cambridge, Eng.: Cambridge University Press, 1992.

———, ed. *The Red Screen: Politics, Society, Art in Soviet Cinema*. London: Routledge, 1992.

Le Fanu, Mark. *The Cinema of Andrei Tarkovsky*. London: British Film Institute, 1987.

Lewis, Robert A. *Geographic Perspectives on Soviet Central Asia*. London: Routledge, 1992.

Liehm, Mira, and Antonín J. Liehm. *The Most Important Art: Eastern European Film after 1945*. Berkeley: University of California Press, 1977.

McReynolds, Louise, and Joan Neuberger, eds. *Imitations of Life: Two Centuries of Melodrama in Russia*. Durham, N.C.: Duke University Press, 2002.

Manz, Beatrice F., ed. *Central Asia in Historical Perspective*. Boulder: Westview, 1994.

Mazierska, Ewa, and Laura Rascaroli. *From Moscow to Madrid: European Cities, Postmodern Cinema*. London: Tauris, 2002.

Menashe, Louis. "Glasnost in the Soviet Cinema." *Cineaste* 16, nos. 1–2 (1987–88): 28–33.

———. "Buttons, Buttons, Who's Got the Workers?: A Note on the (Missing) Working Class in Late- and Post-Soviet Russian Cinema." *International Labor and Working-Class History* 59, no. 1 (2001): 52–59.

———. "Moscow Believes in Tears: The Problems (and Promise?) of Russian Cinema in the Transition Period." *Cineaste* 26, no. 2 (Summer 2001): 10–17.

Mickiewicz, Ellen Propper. *Media and the Russian Public*. New York: Praeger, 1981.

Mitchell, Tony. "Andrei Tarkovsky and *Nostalgia*." *Film Criticism* 8, no. 3 (Spring 1984): 2–11.

Nahaylo, Bohan, and Victor Swoboda. *Soviet Disunion: A History of the Nationality Problem in the USSR*. New York: Free Press, 1990.

Nichols, Bill, ed. *Movies and Methods*. Vol. 2. Berkeley: University of California Press, 1985.

Prajanov. "Shadows of Forgotten Ancestors." *Film Comment* 5, no. 1 (Fall 1968): 38–48.

Passek, Jean-Loup, et al., dirs. and eds. *Le Cinéma Russe et Sovietique*. Cinema/Pluriel series. Paris: Centre Georges Pompidou, 1981.

Petric, Vlada. "Tarkovski's Dream Imagery." *Film Quarterly* 43, no. 2 (Winter 1989–90): 28–34.

Petrie, Graham, and Ruth Dwyer. *Before the Wall Came Down: Soviet and East European Filmmakers Working in the West*. Lanham, Md.: University Press of America, 1990.

Plakhov, Andrei. "Soviet Cinema in the Nineties." *Sight and Sound* 58 (Spring 1990): 23–24.

Radvanyi, Jean, et al., dirs. and eds. *Le Cinéma Armenien*. Cinema/Pluriel series. Paris: Centre Georges Pompidou, 1993.

———, dirs. and eds. *Le Cinéma d'Aisle Centrale*. Cinema/Pluriel series. Paris: Centre Georges Pompidou, 1991.

———, dirs. and eds. *Le Cinéma Georgien*. Cinema/Pluriel series. Paris: Centre Georges Pompidou, 1989.

Rashid, Ahmed. *The Resurgence of Central Asia: Islam or Nationalism?* London: Zed, 1994.

Remnick, David. *Lenin's Tomb: The Last Days of the Soviet Empire*. New York: Random House, 1993.

Roberts, Graham. "Look Who's Talking: The Politics of Representation and the Representation of Politics in Two Early Films by Kira Muratova." *Elementa* 3 (1997): 309–23.

Robinson, David. "Evgeni Bauer and the Cinema of Nikolai II." *Sight and Sound* 59, no. 1 (Winter 1989–90): 51–55.

Rosenbaum, Jonathan. "Inner Space: Exploring Tarkovski's *Solaris*." *Film Comment* 26, no. 4 (July–August 1990): 57–62.

Rosenberg, Karen. "Shepitko." *Sight and Sound* 56, no. 2 (Spring 1987): 119–22.

Rywkin, Michael. *Moscow's Muslim Challenge: Soviet Central Asia*. Rev. ed. Armonk, N.Y.: Sharpe, 1990.

Shalin, Dmitri N., ed. *Russian Culture at the Crossroads*. Boulder: Westview, 1996.

Shlapentokh, Dmitry, and Vladimir Shlapentokh. *Soviet Cinematography, 1918–1991: Ideological Conflict and Social Reality*. New York: de Gruyter, 1993.

Slater, Thomas J. *Handbook of Soviet and East European Films and Filmmakers*. Westport, Conn.: Greenwood, 1992.

Smith, Michael G. "Cinema for the 'Soviet East': National Fact and Revolutionary Fiction in Early Azerbaijani Film." *Slavic Review* 56, no. 4 (Winter 1997): 645–78.

Stanbrook, Alan. "The Return of Paradjanov." *Sight and Sound* 55, no. 4 (Autumn 1986): 257–61.

Suny, Ronald Grigor. *The Making of the Georgian Nation*. Bloomington: Indiana University Press, 1990.

———. *Looking toward Ararat: Armenia in Modern History*. Bloomington: Indiana University Press, 1993.

Tarkovsky, Andrei. *Sculpting in Time: Reflections on the Cinema*. Trans. Kitty Hunter-Blair. Austin: University of Texas Press, 1989.

Taubman, Jane A. "The Cinema of Kira Muratova." *Russian Review* 52, no. 3 (1993): 367–81.

Taylor, Richard, and Ian Christie, eds. *The Film Factory: Russian and Soviet Cinema in Documents*. Cambridge, Mass.: Harvard University Press, 1988.

———, eds. *Inside the Film Factory: New Approaches to Russian and Soviet Cinema*. London: Routledge, 1991.

Taylor, Richard, and Derek Spring, eds. *Stalinism and Soviet Cinema*. London: Routledge, 1993.

Taylor, Richard; Nancy Wood; Julian Graffy; and Dina Iordanova, eds. *The BFI Companion to Eastern European and Russian Cinema*. London: British Film Institute, 2000.

USSR State Cinema Committee. *Soviet Cinema*. Moscow: Planeta, 1979.

Utechin, S. V. *Everyman's Concise Encyclopedia of Russia*. New York: Dutton, 1964.

Vorontsov, Yuri, and Igor Rachuk. *The Phenomenon of Soviet Cinema*. Trans. Doris Bradbury. Moscow: Progress, 1980.

Voskeritchian, Taline. "A Poet of Montage: Ardavazt Peleshian." *Armenian International Magazine* (November 1991): 45–46.

———. "The Other Museum of Yerevan." *Armenian International Magazine* (January 1993): 34–37.

Vronskaya, Jeanne. *Young Soviet Film-Makers*. London: Allen & Unwin, 1972.

Williamson, Anne. "Prisoner: The Essential Paradjanov." *Film Comment* 25, no. 3 (May–June 1989): 57–63.

Willis, Don. "A Singing Blackbird and Georgian Cinema." *Film Quarterly* 31, no. 3 (Spring 1978): 11–15.

Woll, Josephine. *Real Images: Soviet Cinema and the Thaw*. London: Tauris, 2000.

Yefimov, Eduard. *Vasily Shukshin*. Trans. Avril Pyman. Moscow: Raduga, 1986. Contains "Articles" by Shukshin.

Youngblood, Denise J. *Soviet Cinema in the Silent Era, 1918–1935*. Austin: University of Texas Press, 1980, 1991.

Zankar, Anil. "Beauty Is the Symbol of Truth: An Interview with Andrei Tarkovsky." *New Quest* 116 (March–April 1996): 99–102.

Zorkaya, Neya. *The Illustrated History of Soviet Cinema*. New York: Hippocrene, 1989.

CHAPTER 18. WIND FROM THE EAST: JAPAN, INDIA, AND CHINA

Agnihotri, Ram Awatar. *Film Stars in Indian Politics*. New Delhi: Commonwealth, 1998.

Anderson, Joseph L. "Spoken Silents in the Japanese Cinema: Essay on the Necessity of Katsuben." *Journal of Film and Video* 40, no. 1 (Winter 1988): 13–33.

Anderson, Joseph L., and Donald Richie. *The Japanese Film: Art and Industry*. Rutland, Vt.: Tuttle, 1959.

"Asian Cinema History Today." Special issue. *Film History* 7, no. 1 (1995).

"Asian Film." Special issue of *Wide Angle* 11, no. 3 (1989).

Baker, Rick, and Toby Russell. *The Essential Guide to Hong Kong Movies*. Ed. Lisa Tilston. London: Eastern Heroes, 1994.

Banerjee, Shampa, and Anil Srivastava. *One Hundred Indian Feature Films: An Annotated Filmography*. New York: Garland, 1988.

Banker, Ashok. *Bollywood*. Harpenden, Eng.: Pocket Essentials, 2001.

Barnouw, Erik, and Subramanyam Krishnaswamy. *Indian Film*. New York: Columbia University Press, 1963, 1980.

Beasley, W. G. *The Modern History of Japan*. New York: Praeger, 1963.

Bedetti, Simone, and Massimo Mazzoni. *La Hollywood d'Oriente: Il cinema di Hong Kong dalle origini a John Woo*. Bologna: PuntoZero, 1996.

Bernardi, Joan. *Writing in Light: The Silent Scenario and the Japanese Pure Film Movement*. Detroit: Wayne State University Press, 2001.

Berry, Chris. "Chinese Cinema: A New Synthesis." In Gauhar, ed., *Third World Affairs 1985*, pp. 412–18.

———. "Chinese Urban Cinema: Hyper-realism versus Absurdism." *East-West Film Journal* 3, no. 1 (December 1988): 76–96.

———, ed. *Perspectives on Chinese Cinema*. London: British Film Institute, 1991.

———. "Race: Chinese Film and the Politics of Nationalism." *Cinema Journal* 31, no. 2 (Winter 1992): 45–58.

———. "If China Can Say No, Can China Make Movies? or, Do Movies Make China?: Rethinking National Cinema and National Agency." *Boundary 2* 25, no. 3 (Fall 1998): 129–50.

Binford, Mira Reym. "The New Cinema of India." *Quarterly Review of Film Studies* 8, no. 4 (Fall 1983): 47–67.

Bock, Audi. *Japanese Film Directors*. New York: Kodansha, 1978.

"Bollywood Rising." Special section of *Film Comment* 38, no. 3 (May–June 2002): 35–57.

Bordwell, David. "Our Dream-Cinema: Western Historiography and the Japanese Film." In *Film Reader 4: Point of View/Metahistory of Film* (1979): 45–62.

———. *Ozu and the Poetics of Cinema*. Princeton, N.J.: Princeton University Press, 1988.

———. *Planet Hong Kong: Popular Cinema and the Art of Entertainment*. Cambridge, Mass.: Harvard University Press, 2000.

———. "Transcultural Spaces: Toward a Poetics of Chinese Film." *Post Script* 20, nos. 2–3 (Winter–Summer 2001): 9–24.

Browne, Nick, et al., eds. *New Chinese Cinemas: Forms, Identities, Politics*. Cambridge, Eng.: Cambridge University Press, 1994.

Burch, Noël. *Theory of Film Practice*. Trans. Helen R. Lane. New York: Praeger, 1973.

———. *To the Distant Observer: Form and Meaning in Japanese Cinema*. Rev. and ed. Annette Michelson. Berkeley: University of California Press, 1979.

Camhi, Leslie. "Getting His Tale of Love Found in a City Long Lost." *New York Times* (January 28, 2001): AR 26.

Castillon, Pierre Le. *Le Cinéma japonais: Notes et études documentaires*. nos. 4. 158–4.159. Paris: Documentation Française, 1975.

Chabria, Suresh, ed. *Light of Asia: Indian Silent Cinema, 1912–1934*. New Delhi: Wiley, 1994.

Chakravarty, Sumita S. *National Identity in Popular Indian Cinema, 1947–1987*. Austin: University of Texas Press, 1993.

Chan, Jackie, with Jeff Yang. *I Am Jackie Chan: My Life in Action*. New York: Ballantine, 1998.

Chatterjee, Gayatri. *Mother India*. London: British Film Institute, 2002.

Chen, Kuan-Hsing. "Taiwanese New Cinema." In Hill and Gibson, eds., *World Cinema*, pp. 173–77.

Chen, Xiaoming. "The Mysterious Other: Postpolitics in Chinese Film." *Boundary 2* 24, no. 3 (Fall 1997): 123–41.

Cheuk, Pak-Tong. "The Beginning of the Hong Kong New Wave: The Interactive Relationship between Television and the Film Industry." *Post Script* 19, no. 1 (Fall 1999): 10–27.

"Chinese Film." Ed. George S. Semsel and Xia Hong. Special issue of *Wide Angle* 11, no. 2 (1989).

Chow, Rey. *Primitive Passions: Visuality, Sexuality, Ethnography, and Contemporary Chinese Cinema*. New York: Columbia University Press, 1995.

———. "Sentimental Returns: On the Uses of the Everyday in the Recent Films of Zhang Yimou and Wong Kar-Wai." *New Literary History* 33, no. 4 (2002): 639–54.

Chu, Blanche. "The Ambivalence of History: Nostalgia Films Understood in the Post-Colonial Context." *Hong Kong Cultural Studies Bulletin* 8–9 (Spring/Summer 1998): 41–54.

Chunovic, Louis. *Bruce Lee: The Tao of the Dragon Warrior*. New York: St. Martin's Griffin, 1996. Published in the United Kingdom as *The Unseen Bruce Lee*. London: Titan, 1996.

Chute, David, ed. "Midsection: Made in Hong Kong." *Film Comment* 24, no. 3 (May–June 1988): 33–56.

Ciecko, Anne T. "Transnational Action: John Wood, Hong Kong, Hollywood." In Lu, ed., *Transnational Chinese Cinema*, pp. 221–38.

Clark, Paul. *Chinese Cinema: Culture and Politics since 1949*. Cambridge, Eng.: Cambridge University Press, 1987.

———. "Ethnic Minorities in Chinese Films." *East-West Film Journal* 1, no. 2 (June 1987): 15–31.

———. "Reinventing China: The Fifth-Generation Filmmakers." *Modern Chinese Literature* 5, no. 1 (Spring 1989): 121–36.

Cooper, Darius. *The Cinema of Satyajit Ray: Between Tradition and Modernity*. Cambridge, Eng.: Cambridge University Press, 2000.

Cortazzi, Sir Hugh. *Modern Japan: A Concise Survey*. London: Macmillan, 1993.

Curtin, Michael. "Industry on Fire: The Culture Economy of Hong Kong Media." *Post Script* 19, no. 1 (Fall 1999): 28–51.

Da Cunha, Uma. *Indian Film, '78/'79*. New Delhi: Rampal, 1979.

Dai, Jinhua. "Invisible Women: Contemporary Chinese Cinema and Women's Film." Trans. by Mayfair Yang. *Positions* 3, no. 1 (Spring 1995): 255–80.

Dannen, Fredric, and Barry Long. *Hong Kong Babylon: An Insider's Guide to the Hollywood of the East*. London: Faber & Faber, 1997.

Dariotis, Wei Ming, and Eileen Fung. "Breaking the Soy Sauce Jar: Diasporas and Displacement in the Films of Ang Lee." In Lu, ed., *Transnational Chinese Cinema*, pp. 187–220.

Das, Santi, ed. *Satyajit Ray: An Intimate Master*. New Delhi: Allied, 1998.

Das Gupta, Chidananda. *The Cinema of Satyajit Ray*. New Delhi: Vikas, 1980.

———. "New Directions in Indian Cinema." *Film Quarterly* 34, no. 1 (Fall 1980): 32–41.

———. "A Passage from India." *American Film* 11, no. 1 (October 1985): 33–38.

———. "Seeing and Believing, Science and Mythology: Notes on the 'Mythological' Genre." *Film Quarterly* 42, no. 4 (Summer 1989): 12–18.

Datta, Sangeeta. *Shyam Benegal*. London: British Film Institute, 2003.

Davis, Darrell William. *Picturing Japaneseness: Monumental Style, National Identity, Japanese Film*. New York: Columbia University Press, 1996.

Davis, Darrell William, and Yeh Yeuh-yu. "Warning! Category II." *Film Quarterly* 54, no. 4 (Summer 2001): 12–26.

Derné, Steve. *Movies, Masculinity, and Modernity: An Ethnography of Men's Filmgoing in India*. Westport, Conn: Greenwood, 2000.

Desser, David. *Eros plus Massacre: An Introduction to the Japanese New Wave Cinema*. Bloomington: Indiana University Press, 1988.

Dickey, Sara. "Accommodation and Resistance: Expression of Working-Class Values through Tamil Cinema." *Wide Angle* 11, no. 3 (1989): 26–32.

———. *Cinema and the Urban Poor in South India*. Cambridge, Eng.: Cambridge University Press, 1993.

Dissanayake, Wimal. "Self and Modernization in Malayam Cinema." *East-West Film Journal* 1, no. 2 (June 1987): 74–90.

———. "Questions of Female Subjectivity and Patriarchy: A Reading of Three Indian Women Film Directors." *East-West Film Journal* 3, no. 2 (June 1989): 60–77.

———, ed. *Melodrama and Asian Cinema*. New York: Cambridge University Press, 1993.

———. *Colonialism and Nationalism in Asian Cinema*. Bloomington: Indiana University Press, 1994.

———. "Asian Cinema and the American Cultural Imaginary." *Theory, Culture & Society* 13, no. 4 (1996): 102–22.

Donald, Stephanie. "Landscape and Agency: *Yellow Earth* and the Demon Lover." *Theory, Culture & Society* 14, no. 1 (1997): 97–112.

———. "Symptoms of Alienation: The Female Body in Recent Chinese Film." *Continuum* 12, no. 1 (1998): 91–103.

———. *Public Secrets, Public Spaces: Cinema and Civility in China*. Lanham, Md.: Rowman & Littlefield, 2000.

Dwyer, Rachel. *Yash Chopra*. London: British Film Institute, 2002.

Dwyer, Rachel, and Divia Patel. *Cinema India: The Visual Culture of Hindi Film*. New Brunswick, N.J.: Rutgers University Press, 2002.

Dym, Jeffrey A. "Benshi and the Introduction of Motion Pictures to Japan." *Monumenta Nipponica* 55, no.4 (Winter 2000): 509–36.

Eder, Klaus, and Deac Rossell, eds. *New Chinese Cinema*. London: National Film Theatre, 1993.

Ehrlich, Linda C., and David Desser. *Cinematic Landscapes: Observations on the Visual Arts of China and Japan*. Austin: University of Texas Press, 1994.

Ellis, John. "Electric Shadows in Italy." *Screen* 23, no. 2 (July–August 1982): 79–83.

Erens, Patricia Brett. "The Film Work of Ann Hui." In Fu and Desser, eds., *The Cinema of Hong Kong*, pp. 176–95.

Farquhar, Mary Ann. "The 'Hidden' Gender in *Yellow Earth*." *Screen* 33, no. 2 (Summer 1992): 154–64.

Fields, Simon, and Tony Rayns, eds. *Branded to Thrill: The Delirious Cinema of Suzuki Seijun*. London: Institute of Contemporary Arts, 1994.

Fong, Suzie Young-Sau. "The Voice of Feminine Madness in Zhang Yimou's *Raise the Red Lantern*." *Asian Cinema* 7, no. 1 (1995): 12–23.

Fonoroff, Paul. *Silver Light: A Pictorial History of Hong Kong Cinema, 1920–1970*. Hong Kong: Joint, 1997.

———. *At the Hong Kong Movies: 600 Reviews from 1988 till the Handover*. Hong Kong: Film Biweekly, 1998.

Fore, Steve. "Golden Harvest Films and the Hong Kong Movie Industry in the Realm of Globalization." *Velvet Light Trap* 34 (1994): 40–58.

———. "Introduction: Hong Kong Movies, Critical Time Warps, and Shapes of Things to Come." *Post Script* 19, no. 1 (Fall 1999): 2–9.

Fu, Poshek. "The Ambiguity of Entertainment: Chinese Cinema in Japanese Occupied Shanghai, 1942 to 1945." *Cinema Journal* 37, no. 1 (Fall 1997): 66–84.

Fu, Poshek, and David Desser. "Chronology of Hong Kong Cinema." In Fu and Desser, eds., *The Cinema of Hong Kong*, pp. 13–16.

———, eds. *The Cinema of Hong Kong: History, Arts, Identity.* New York: Cambridge University Press, 2000.

Galbraith, Stuart, IV. *The Japanese Filmography: A Complete Reference to 209 Filmmakers and Over 1250 Films Released in the U.S., 1900 through 1994.* Jefferson, N.C.: McFarland, 1996.

———. *The Emperor and the Wolf: The Lives and Films of Akira Kurosawa and Toshiro Mifune.* London: Faber & Faber, 2002.

Ganguly, Suranjan. *Satyajit Ray: In Search of the Modern.* Lanham, Md.: Scarecrow, 2000.

Gateward, Francis K., ed. *Zhang Yimou: Interviews.* Jackson: University Press of Mississippi, 2001.

Gauhar, Raana, ed. *Third World Affairs 1985.* London: Third World Foundation, 1986.

Gaul, Lou. *The Fist That Shook the World: The Cinema of Bruce Lee.* Baltimore: Midnight Marquee, 1997.

Gazdar, Mushtaq. *Pakistan Cinema, 1947–1997.* New York: Oxford University Press, 1997.

Geist, Kathe. "Yasujiro Ozu: Notes on a Retrospective." *Film Quarterly* 37, no. 1 (Fall 1983): 2–9.

———. "Narrative Style in Ozu's Silent Films." *Film Quarterly* 40, no. 2 (Winter 1986–87): 28–35.

———. "The Role of Marriage in the Films of Yasujiro Ozu." *East-West Film Journal* 4, no. 1 (December 1989): 44–52.

Gentry, Clyde, III. *Jackie Chan: Inside the Dragon.* Dallas: Taylor, 1997.

Gladney, Dru C. "Tian Zhuangzhuang, the Fifth Generation, and Minorities Film in China." *Public Culture* 8, no. 1 (Fall 1995): 161–75.

Glaessner, Verina. *Kung Fu: Cinema of Vengeance.* New York: Bounty, 1974.

Gokulsing, K. Moti, and Wimal Dissanayake. *Indian Popular Cinema: A Narrative of Cultural Change.* Staffordshire, Eng.: Trenham, 1998.

Goodwin, James. *Akira Kurosawa and Intertextual Cinema.* Baltimore: Johns Hopkins University Press, 1994.

———, ed. *Perspectives on Akira Kurosawa.* Perspectives on Film Series. New York: Hall, 1994.

Gopalan, Lalitha. *Cinema of Interruptions: Action Genres in Contemporary Indian Cinema.* London: British Film Institute, 2002.

Haggard, Stephen. "Indian Film Posters." *Sight and Sound* 57, no. 1 (Winter 1987–88): 62–63.

Hall, Kenneth E. *John Woo: The Films.* Jefferson, N.C.: McFarland, 1999.

Hammond, Stefan. *Hollywood East: Hong Kong Movies and the People Who Made Them.* New York: Contemporary, 2000.

Hammond, Stefan, and Mike Wilkins. *Sex and Zen and a Bullet in the Head: The Essential Guide to Hong Kong's Mind-Bending Films.* New York: Simon & Schuster, 1996.

Hansen, Jeremy, and Alexandra A. Seno. "A Touch of Realism." *Asiaweek* 27, no. 28 (July 20, 2001): 30–36.

Heath, Stephen, and Patricia Mellencamp, eds. *Cinema and Language.* American Film Institute Monograph Series. Frederick, Md.: University Publications of America, 1983.

Heider, Carl G. *Indonesian Cinema: National Culture on Screen.* Honolulu: University of Hawaii Press, 1991.

High, Peter B. "The Dawn of Cinema in Japan." *Journal of Contemporary History* 19 (1984): 23–57.

Hill, John, and Pamela Church Gibson, eds. *World Cinema: Critical Approaches.* Oxford: Oxford University Press, 2000.

Hirano, Kyoko. "The Japanese Tragedy: Film Censorship and the American Occupation." In Sklar and Musser, eds., *Resisting Images*, pp. 200–24.

———. *Mr. Smith Goes to Tokyo: Japanese Cinema under the American Occupation, 1945–52.* Washington, D.C.: Smithsonian Institution Press, 1992.

Hitchcock, Peter. "The Aesthetics of Alienation, or China's 'Fifth Generation.' " *Cultural Studies* 6, no. 1 (1992): 116–41.

Holland, Gray, et al. "Ichiban: 10 Reasons Why the Sun Still Rises in the East." *Wired* 9, no. 9 (September 2001): 120–25.

Hong, Junhao. "The Evolution of China's War Movie in Five Decades: Factors Contributing to Changes, Limits, and Implications." *Asian Cinema* 10, no. 1 (Fall 1998): 93–106.

Hong Kong Film Archive, ed. *50 Years of the Hong Kong Film Production and Distribution Industries: An Exhibition.* Hong Kong: Urban Council, 1997.

Hood, John W. *The Essential Mystery: Major Filmmakers of Indian Art Cinema.* London: Samgan, 2000.

Houston, Penelope. *The Contemporary Cinema.* Rev. ed. Baltimore, Md.: Penguin, 1971.

Howkins, John. *Mass Communication in China.* New York: Longman, 1982.

"Indian Cinema." Ed. Mira Reym Binford. Special issue of *Quarterly Review of Film and Video* 11, no. 3 (1989).

Ing, David. "Love at Last Site: Waiting for Oedipus in Stanley Kwan's *Rouge*." *Camera Obscura* 32 (1993–94): 75–101.

Iwazaki, Akira. *Kenji Mizoguchi.* Paris: L'Avant Scène du Cinéma, 1967. Supplement to no. 75.

Jaehne, Karen. "*Boat People:* An Interview with Ann Hui." *Cineaste* 13, no. 2 (1984): 16–19.

"Japanese Cinema." Ed. Peter Lehman. Special issue of *Journal of Film and Video* 39, no. 1 (Winter 1987).

"Japanese Cinema." Special issue of *Wide Angle* 1, no. 4 (1977).

Jarvie, I. C. *Window on Hong Kong: A Sociological Study of the Hong Kong Film Industry and Its Audience*. Hong Kong: University of Hong Kong, 1977.

Joshi, Lalit Mohan, ed. *Bollywood: Popular Indian Cinema*. London: Dakini, 2002.

Kabir, Nasreen Munni. *Bollywood: The Indian Cinema Story*. London: Channel 4, 2001.

Kaige, Chen. "Breaking the Circle: The Cinema and Cultural Change in China." *Cineaste* 17, no. 3 (1990): 28–31.

Kaminsky, Stuart M. *American Film Genres*. 2nd ed. Chicago: Nelson-Hall, 1985.

Kaplan, E. Ann. "Melodrama/Subjectivity/Ideology: Western Melodrama Theories and Their Relevance to Recent Chinese Cinema." *East-West Film Journal* 5, no. 1 (1991): 6–27.

———. "Reading Formations and Chen Kaige's *Farewell My Concubine*." In Lu, ed., *Transnational Chinese Cinema*, pp. 265–76.

Kasza, Gregory J. *The State and the Mass Media in Japan, 1918–1945*. Berkeley: University of California Press, 1988.

Kaul, Gautam. *Cinema and the Indian Freedom Struggle: Covering the Subcontinent*. New Delhi: Sterling, 1998.

Kazmi, Fareed. *The Politics of India's Conventional Cinema: Imaging a Universe, Subverting a Multiverse*. New Delhi: Sage, 1999.

Kazmi, Nikhat. *The Dream Merchants of Bollywood*. New Delhi: UBS, 1998.

Keeler, Ward. *Javanese Shadow Puppets*. Singapore: Oxford University Press, 1992.

Kehr, Dave. "The Last Rising Sun." *Film Comment* 19, no. 5 (September–October 1983): 31.

Kellner, Douglas. "New Taiwan Cinema in the 80s." *Jump Cut* 42 (1998): 90–93.

Kennedy, Harlan. "Boat People." *Film Comment* 19, no. 5 (September–October, 1983): 41–46.

Kirahara, Donald. *Patterns of Time: Mizoguchi and the 1930s*. Madison: University of Wisconsin Press, 1992.

Komatsu, Hiroshi. "Japan: Before the Great Kanto Earthquake." In Nowell-Smith, ed., *The Oxford History of World Cinema*, pp. 177–82.

———. "The Lumière Cinématographe and the Production of the Cinema in Japan in the Earliest Period." *Film History* 8, no. 4 (1996): 431–38.

Komatsu, Hiroshi, and Charles Musser. "Benshi Search." *Wide Angle* 19, no. 2 (1987): 72–90.

Kong, Haili. "Symbolism through Zhang Yimou's Subversive Lens in His Early Films." *Asian Cinema* 8, no. 2 (1996–97): 98–115.

Kraicer, Shelly, and Lisa Roosen-Runge. "Edward Yang: A Taiwanese Independent Filmmaker in Conversation." *Cineaction* 47 (September 1998): 48–55.

Kuoshu, Harry H. *Lightness of Being in China: Adaptation and Discursive Figuration in Cinema and Theater*. New York: Lang, 1999.

Larson, Wendy. "The Concubine and the Figure of History: Chen Kaige's *Farewell My Concubine*." In Lu, ed., *Transnational Chinese Cinema*, pp. 331–46.

Lau, Jenny Kwok Wah. "Towards a Cultural Understanding of Cinema: A Comparison of Contemporary Films from the People's Republic of China and Hong Kong." *Wide Angle* 11, no. 3 (1989): 42–49.

———. "*Farewell My Concubine:* History, Melodrama, and Ideology in Contemporary Pan-Chinese Cinema." *Film Quarterly* 49, no. 1 (Fall 1995): 16–27.

———. "Besides Fists and Blood: Hong Kong Comedy and Its Master of the Eighties." *Cinema Journal* 37, no. 2 (Winter 1998): 18–34. Repr. as "Besides Fists and Blood: Michael Hui and Cantonese Comedy." In Fu and Desser, eds., *The Cinema of Hong Kong*, pp. 158–75.

———, ed. *Multiple Modernities: Cinema and Popular Media in Transcultural East Asia*. Philadelphia: Temple University Press, 2002.

Lau, Shing-hon, ed. *A Study of the Hong Kong Swordplay Film (1945–1980)*. Rev. ed. Hong Kong: Hong Kong International Film Festival/Urban Council, 1996.

Law, Kar, ed. *Cinema of Two Cities: Hong Kong–Shanghai*. Hong Kong: Hong Kong International Film Festival/Urban Council, 1994.

———, ed. *Early Images of Hong Kong and China*. Hong Kong: Hong Kong International Film Festival/Urban Council, 1995.

———, ed. *The Restless Breed: Cantonese Stars of the Sixties*. Hong Kong: Hong Kong International Film Festival/Urban Council, 1996.

———, ed. *Fifty Years of Electric Shadows*. Hong Kong: Hong Kong International Film Festival/Urban Council, 1997.

———, ed. *Hong Kong Cinema in the Eighties*. Rev. ed. Hong Kong: Hong Kong International Film Festival/Urban Council, 1997.

———, ed. *The Hong Kong New Wave: Twenty Years After*. Hong Kong: Hong Kong International Film Festival/Urban Council, 1999.

Lee, Joann. "Zhang Yimou's *Raise the Red Lantern:* Contextual Analysis of Film through a Confucian/Feminist Matrix." *Asian Cinema* 8, no. 1 (1996): 120–27.

Lee, Linda. *The Bruce Lee Story*. Los Angeles: Ohara, 1989.

Le Fanu, Mark. "To Love Is to Suffer: Reflections on the Later Films of Heinosuke Gosho." *Sight and Sound* 55, no. 3 (Summer 1986): 198–202.

Lent, John, A. "Asian Cinema: A Selected International Bibliography." *Journal of Film and Video* 36, no. 3 (Summer 1984): 75–84.

———. *The Asian Film Industry*. Austin: University of Texas Press, 1990.

Levi, Antonia. *Samurai from Outer Space: Understanding Japanese Animation*. Chicago: Open Court, 1996.

Lewinsky, Marianne, and Peter Delpeut, eds. *Producer of Directors: Kido Shiro*. Amsterdam: Nederlands Filmmuseum, 1995.

Leyda, Jay. *Dianying: Electric Shadows: An Account of Films and the Film Audience in China*. Rev. ed. Cambridge, Mass.: MIT Press, 1979.

Li, Cheuk-to, ed. *A Study of Hong Kong Cinema in the Seventies (1970–1979)*. Hong Kong: Hong Kong International Film Festival/Urban Council, 1984.

———, ed. *The Traditions of Hong-Kong Comedy*. Hong Kong: Hong Kong International Film Festival/Urban Council, 1985.

———, ed. *Phantoms of Hong Kong Cinema*. Hong Kong: Hong Kong International Film Festival/Urban Council, 1989.

———, ed. *Cantonese Melodrama (1950–1969)*. Rev. ed. Hong Kong: Hong Kong International Film Festival/Urban Council, 1997.

———, ed. *Changes in Hong Kong Society through Cinema*. Rev. ed. Hong Kong: Hong Kong International Film Festival/Urban Council, 1997.

———, ed. *The China Factor in the Hong Kong Cinema*. Rev. ed. Hong Kong: Hong Kong International Film Festival/Urban Council, 1997.

Li, Suyuan, and Hu Jubin. *Chinese Silent Film History*. Ed. Wang Rui. Rev. Wang Rui and Tabetha Miller. Trans. Wang Rui et al. Beijing: China Film Press, 1997.

Little, John R., ed. *Words of the Dragon: Interviews, 1958–1973*. Bruce Lee Library, Vol. 1. Boston: Tuttle, 1997.

———, ed. *Letters of the Dragon: Correspondence, 1958–1973*. Bruce Lee Library, Vol. 5. Boston: Tuttle, 1998.

Little, John R., and Curtis F. Wong, eds. *Jackie Chan*. Chicago: Contemporary, 1999.

Logan, Bay. *Hong Kong Action Cinema*. Woodstock, N.Y.: Overlook, 1996.

Lopate, Phillip. "A Taste for Naruse." *Film Quarterly* 39, no. 4 (Summer 1986): 11–21.

———. "Odd Man Out: Interview with Tian Zhuangzhuang." *Film Comment* 30, no. 4 (1994): 6–64.

Lu, Sheldon Hsiao-peng. "National Cinema, Cultural Critique, Transnational Capital: The Films of Zhang Yimou." In Lu, ed., *Transnational Chinese Cinema*, pp. 106–38.

———, ed. *Transnational Chinese Cinema: Identity, Nationhood, Gender*. Honolulu: University of Hawaii Press, 1997.

Luhr, William, ed. *World Cinema since 1945*. New York: Ungar, 1987.

McDonald, Keiko I. *Cinema East: A Critical Study of Major Japanese Films*. Rutherford, N.J.: Fairleigh Dickinson University Press, 1983.

———. "Family, Education, and Postmodern Society: Yoshimitsu Morita's *The Family Game*." *East-West Film Journal* 4, no. 1 (December 1989): 53–68.

———. *Japanese Classical Theater in Films*. Rutherford, N.J.: Fairleigh Dickinson University Press, 1994.

———. *From Book to Screen: Modern Japanese Literature in Film*. Armonk, N.Y.: Sharpe, 2000.

MacDougall, Bonnie S., ed. *Popular Chinese Literature and Performing Arts in the People's Republic of China, 1949–1979*. Berkeley: University of California Press, 1984.

———. *The Yellow Earth: A Film by Chen Kaige, with a Complete Translation of the Filmscript*. Hong Kong: Chinese University Press, 1991.

The Making of Martial Arts Movies—As Told by Filmmakers and Stars. Hong Kong: Provisional Urban Council, 1999.

Malcolm, Derek. "Mrinal Sen." *Sight and Sound* 50, no. 4 (Autumn 1981): 263–65.

———. "Tiger: The Films of Ritwik Ghatak." *Sight and Sound* 51, no. 3 (Autumn 1982): 184–87.

———. "India's Middle Cinema." *Sight and Sound* 55, no. 3 (Summer 1986): 172–74.

Malcomson, Scott L. "Mitsuo Yanagimachi." *Film Criticism* 8, no. 1 (Fall 1983): 12–19.

Marion, Donald. *The Chinese Filmography: The 2444 Feature Films Produced by Studios in the People's Republic of China from 1949 through 1995*. Jefferson, N.C.: McFarland, 1997.

Mellen, Joan. *Voices from the Japanese Cinema*. New York: Liveright, 1975.

———. *The Waves at Genji's Door*. New York: Pantheon, 1976.

———. *Seven Samurai*. London: British Film Institute, 2002.

Meyers, Richard; Amy Harlib III; and Karen Palmer. *Martial Arts Movies: From Bruce Lee to the Ninjas*. Secaucus, N.J.: Citadel, 1985.

Mishra, Vijay. *Bollywood Cinema: Temples of Desire*. New York: Routledge, 2001.

Moller, Olaf. "Shameless." *Film Comment* 38, no. 1 (January–February 2002): 45.

Mujun, Shao. "Chinese Film amidst the Tide of Reform." *East-West Film Journal* 1, no. 1 (December 1986): 59–68.

Nandy, Ashis, ed. *The Secret Politics of Our Desires: Innocence, Culpability and Indian Popular Cinema. London: Zed, 1999.

Narkewar, Sanjit, ed. Directory of Indian Film-Makers and Films. Westport, Conn.: Greenwood, 1994.

"New Japanese Cinema." Special supplement to Film Comment 38, no. 1 (January–February 2002): 35–46.

Newitz, Annalee. "Magical Girls and Atomic Bomb Sperm: Japanese Animation in America." Film Quarterly 49, no. 1 (Fall 1995): 2–15.

Ning, Ma. "Satisfied or Not: Desire and Discourse in the Chinese Comedy of the 1960s." East-West Film Journal 2, no. 1 (December 1987): 32–49.

———. "Symbolic Representation and Symbolic Violence: Chinese Family Melodrama of the Early 1980s." East-West Film Journal 4, no. 1 (December 1989).

———. "Leftist Chinese Cinema of the Thirties." Cineaste 17, no. 3 (1990): 28–31.

———. "New Chinese Cinema: A Critical Account of the Fifth Generation." Cineaste 17, no. 3 (1990):32–35.

Nolletti, Arthur, Jr., and David Desser, eds. Reframing Japanese Cinema: Authorship, Genre, History. Bloomington: Indiana University Press, 1992.

Nornes, Abé Mark, and Fukushima Yukio, eds. The Japan/America Film Wars: World War II Propaganda and Its Cultural Contexts. Chur, Switz.: Harwood Academic, 1994.

Nowell-Smith, Geoffrey, ed. The Oxford History of World Cinema. Oxford, Eng.: Oxford University Press, 1996.

Nyce, Ben. Satyajit Ray: A Study of His Films. New York: Praeger, 1988.

Ortolani, Benito. The Japanese Theatre: From Shamanistic Ritual to Contemporary Pluralism. Rev. ed. Princeton, N.J.: Princeton University Press, 1995.

Ozu, Yashujiro. Carnets: 1933–1963. Trans. Josiane Pinon-Kawataké. Paris: Éditions Alive, 1996.

Palmer, Bill; Karen Palmer; and Richard Meyers. Encyclopedia of Martial Arts Movies. Metuchen, N.J.: Scarecrow, 1995.

"The People's Republic of China." Ed. Gina Marchetti. Special section of Jump Cut 24 (1989): 85–121.

Pezzotta, Alberto. Tutto il cinema di Hong Kong: Stili, caratteri, autori. Milan: Baldini & Castoldi, 1999.

Pfleiderer, Beatrix, and Lothar Lutze. The Hindi Film: Agent and Re-Agent of Cultural Change. New Delhi: Manohar, 1985.

Pinsky, Mark L. "A Small Leap Forward." American Film 9, no. 6 (April 1984): 52–54.

Prasad, M. Madhava. Ideology of the Hindi Film: A Historical Construction. Delhi: Oxford University Press, 2001.

Pratt, David R. " 'We Must Make the Government Tremble': Political Filmmaking in the South Indian State of Tamil Nadu." Velvet Light Trap 34 (Fall 1994): 10–39.

Prince, Stephen. The Warrior's Camera: The Cinema of Akira Kurosawa. Princeton, N.J.: Princeton University Press, 1991.

Pym, John. The Wandering Company: Twenty-one Years of Merchant Ivory Films. London and New York: British Film Institute/Museum of Modern Art, 1983.

Rajadhyaksha, Ashish. Encyclopedia of Indian Cinema. Bloomington: Indiana University Press, 1994.

Rajadhyaksha, Ashish, and Paul Willemen. Encyclopedia of Indian Cinema. Rev. ed. London: British Film Institute, 1999.

Ramachandran, T. M., ed. 70 Years of Indian Cinema. Bombay: CINEMA India-International, 1985.

Rangoonwalla, Firoze. A Pictorial History of Indian Cinema. London: Hamlyn, 1979.

Rao, Maithili. "Looking beyond Bollywood, Maithili Rao Surveys Current Indian Cinema in the Age of Hindi Nationalism." Film Comment 39, no. 1 (January–February 2003): 12–13.

Ray, Satyajit. Our Films, Their Films. Bombay: Orient Longman, 1976.

———. Satyajit Ray's Art. New Delhi: Clarion, 1980.

Rayns, Tony. "Chinese Changes." Sight and Sound 54, no. 1 (Winter 1984–85): 24–29.

———. "The Position of Women in New Chinese Cinema." East-West Film Journal 1, no. 2 (June 1987): 32–44.

———. "Lonesome Tonight: Edward Yang's Extraordinary Epic A Brighter Summer Day." Sight and Sound (incorporating Monthly Film Bulletin) 3, no. 3 (March 1993): 14–17.

———. "Loosening the Knot: On Set with Zhang Yimou." Sight and Sound (incorporating Monthly Film Bulletin) 4, no. 5 (May 1994): 14–18.

Reid, Craig D. "Fighting without Fighting: Film Action Fight Choreography." Film Quarterly 47, no. 2 (1993–94): 30–35.

———. "Interview with Tsui Hark." Film Quarterly 48, no. 3 (1995): 34–41.

Reuben, Bunny. Mehoob, India's DeMille: The First Biography. New Delhi: Indus, 1999.

Reynaud, Bérénice. Nouvelles Chines, nouveaux cinemas. Paris: Cahiers du cinéma, 1999.

Richie, Donald. The Films of Akira Kurosawa. Berkeley: University of California Press, 1965.

———. The Japanese Movie. Tokyo: Kodansha, 1966.

———. Japanese Cinema. Garden City, N.Y.: Anchor, 1971.

———. Focus on "Rashomon." Englewood Cliffs, N.J.: Prentice-Hall, 1972.

———. Ozu. Berkeley: University of California Press, 1974.

———. "Viewing Japanese Film: Some Considerations." East-West Film Journal 1, no. 1 (December 1986): 23–35.

———. The Films of Akira Kurosawa. 3rd ed. Berkeley: University of California, 1998.

———. *A Hundred Years of Japanese Film: A Concise History, with a Selective Guide to Videos and DVDs*. New York: Kodansha, 2001.

Roberge, Gaston. *Communication, Cinema, Development: From Morosity to Hope*. New Delhi: Manohar, 1998.

Robinson, Andrew. *Satyajit Ray: The Inner Eye*. Berkeley: University of California Press, 1992.

Rovin, Jeff, and Kathy Tracy. *The Essential Jackie Chan Sourcebook*. New York: Pocket, 1997.

Russell, Catherine. "Men with Swords and Men with Suits: The Cinema of Akira Kurosawa." *Cineaste* 28, no. 1 (Winter 2001): 4–13.

Sakamura, Ken, and Hasuji Shigehiko, eds. *From behind the Camera: A New Look at the World of Director Yasujiro Ozu*. Tokyo: University of Tokyo, 1998.

Sandell, Jillian. "Reinventing Masculinity: The Spectacle of Male Intimacy in the Films of John Woo." *Film Quarterly* 49, no. 4 (1996): 23–34.

Sato, Tadao. "The Art of Yasujiro Ozu." *Wide Angle* 1, no. 4 (1977): 44–48.

———. "Rising Sons." *American Film* 11, no. 3 (December 1985): 58–62, 78.

Schilling, Mark. *The Encyclopedia of Japanese Pop Culture*. New York: Weatherhill, 1997.

———. *Contemporary Japanese Film*. New York: Weatherhill, 1999.

Schrader, Paul. *Transcendental Style in Film: Ozu, Bresson, Dreyer*. Berkeley: University of California Press, 1972.

Semsel, George S., ed. *Chinese Film: The State of the Art in the People's Republic*. New York: Praeger, 1987.

Semsel, George S.; Xia Hong; and Hon Jianping, eds. *Chinese Film Theory: A Guide to the New Era*. New York: Praeger, 1990.

Semsel, George S.; Chen Xihe; and Xia Hong, eds. *Film in Contemporary China: Critical Debates, 1979–1989*. Westport, Conn.: Praeger, 1993.

Server, Lee. *Asian Pop Cinema: Bombay to Tokyo*. San Francisco: Chronicle, 1999.

Seton, Marie. *Portrait of a Director: Satyajit Ray*. Bloomington: Indiana University Press, 1971.

Sharrett, Christopher, ed. *Mythologies of Violence in Postmodern Media*. Detroit: Wayne State University Press, 1999.

Shoesmith, Brian. *Indian Cinema*. Cambridge, Eng.: Cambridge University Press, 2003.

Shu Kei, ed. *Cantonese Cinema Retrospective (1960–1969)*. Rev. ed. Hong Kong: Hong Kong International Film Festival/Urban Council, 1996.

Sibergeld, Jerome. *China into Film: Frames of Reference in Contemporary Chinese Cinema*. London: Reaktion, 1999.

Silver, Alain. *The Samurai Film*. Cranbury, N.J.: Barnes, 1977.

Sipe, Jeffrey. "Death and Taxes: A Profile of Juzo Itami." *Sight and Sound* 58, no. 3 (summer 1989): 186–89.

Sklar, Robert, and Charles Musser, eds. *Resisting Images: Essays on Cinema and History*. Philadelphia: Temple University Press, 1990.

Somaaya, Bhawana. *Salaam Bollywood: The Pain and the Passion*. South Godston: Spantech & Lancer, 2000.

"Southeast Asian Cinema." Ed. Wimal Dissanayake. Special issue of *East-West Journal* 6, no. 2 (July 1992).

Stanbrook, Alan. "The Flowers in China's Courtyard." *Sight and Sound* 56, no. 3 (Summer 1987): 67–72.

———. "Tokyo's New Satirists." *Sight and Sound* 57, no. 1 (Winter 1987–88): 54–57.

———. "The Worlds of Hou Hsiao-Hsien." *Sight and Sound* 59, no. 2 (Spring 1990): 120–24.

Standish, Isolde. *Myth and Masculinity in the Japanese Cinema: Towards a Political Reading of the "Tragic Hero."* Richmond: Curzon, 2000.

Stein, Elliot. "Bangalore, Mon Amour: A Voyage to India." *Film Comment* 16, no. 3 (May–June 1980): 61–71.

———. "Film India." *Film Comment* 17, no. 4 (July–August 1981): 60–65.

———. "India, Inc." *Film Comment* 18, no. 4 (July–August 1982): 69–75.

———. "The Other India." *Film Comment* 19, no. 3 (June 1983): 28–32.

Stephens, Chuck. "Time Pieces: Wong Kar-Wai and the Persistence of Memory." *Film Comment* 32, no. 1 (1996): 12–18.

Stokes, Lisa Odham, and Michael Hoover. *City on Fire: Hong Kong Cinema*. London: Verso, 1999.

Stringer, Julian. " 'Your Tender Smiles Give Me Strength': Paradigms of Masculinity in John Woo's *A Better Tomorrow* and *The Killer*." *Screen* 38, no. 1 (1997): 25–41.

———. "Category 3: Sex and Violence in Postmodern Hong Kong." In Sharrett, ed., *Mythologies of Violence in Postmodern Media*, pp. 361–79.

Sutton, Donald S. "History, Ritual, and the Films of Zhang Yimou." *East-West Film Journal* 8, no. 2 (July 1994): 31–46.

Svensson, Arne. *Japan: An Illustrated Guide*. Cranbury, N.J.: Barnes, 1971.

Tam, Kwok-kan, and Wimal Dissanayake. *New Chinese Cinema*. New York: Oxford University Press, 1998.

Tan, See Kam. "Hong Kong Cinema: Double Marginalization and Cultural Resistance." *Southeast Asian Journal of Social Science* 22 (1994): 53–71.

———. "Chinese Diasporic Imaginations in Hong Kong Films: Sinicist Belligerence and Melancholia." *Screen* 42, no. 1 (Spring 2001): 1–20.

Tang, Xiaobing, and Stephen Snyder, eds. *In Pursuit of Contemporary East Asian Culture*. Boulder: Westview, 1996.

Teo, Stephen. *Hong Kong Cinema: The Extra Dimensions*. London: British Film Institute, 1997.

———. "Hong Kong Journal." *Film Comment* 36, no. 6 (November–December 2000): 11–13.

Thoraval, Yves. *The Cinemas of India*. London: Macmillan, 2000.

Tiedeman, Arthur E., ed. *An Introduction to Japanese Civilization*. New York: Columbia University Press, 1974.

Torgovnik, Jonathan. *Bollywood Dreams: An Exploration of the Motion Picture Industry and Its Culture in India*. New York: Phaidon, 2003.

"Tribute to Zhang Yimou, A." Special issue of *Cinemaya* 30 (Autumn 1995).

Tsui, Curtis. "Subjective Culture and History: The Ethnographic Cinema of Wong Kar-Wai." *Asian Cinema* 7, no. 2 (1995): 93–124.

Turim, Maureen. *The Films of Oshima Nagisa: Images of a Japanese Iconoclast*. Berkeley: University of California Press, 1998.

Valicha, Kishore. *The Moving Image: A Study of Indian Cinema*. Bombay: Orient Longman, 1988.

Varley, H. Paul. *Samurai*. New York: Delacorte, 1970.

Vasuder, Aruna. *Liberty and License in the Indian Cinema*. New Delhi: Vikas, 1978.

———. *The New Indian Cinema*. Delhi: Macmillan India, 1986.

Vasuder, Aruna, and Phillipe Lenglet, eds. *Indian Cinema Superbazaar*. New Delhi: Vikas, 1983.

Vasudevan, Ravi S., ed. *Making Meaning in Indian Cinema*. Delhi: Oxford University Press, 2000.

———. "National Pasts and Futures: Indian Cinema." *Screen* 41, no. 1 (Spring 2000): 119–25.

Virdi, Jyotika. *The Cinematic Imagination: Indian Popular Films as Social History*. New Brunswick, N.J.: Rutgers University Press, 2003.

Wang, Ban. "Trauma and History in Chinese Film: Reading *The Blue Kite* against Melodrama." *Modern Chinese Literature and Culture* 11, no. 1 (Spring 1999): 125–55.

Washburn, Dennis, and Carole Cavanaugh, eds. *Word and Image in Japanese Cinema*. Cambridge, Eng.: Cambridge University Press, 2001.

Weisser, Thomas. *Asian Trash Cinema: The Book*. Houston: Asian Trash Cinema/European Trash Cinema, 1994.

———. *Asian Trash Cinema: The Book (Part 2)*. Miami: Vital, 1996.

———. *Asian Cult Cinema*. New York: Boulevard, 1997.

Weisser, Thomas, and Yuko Mihara Weisser. *Japanese Cinema: The Essential Handbook*. 4th rev. ed. Miami: Vital/Asian Cult Cinema, 1998.

———. *Japanese Cinema Encyclopedia: The Horror, Fantasy, and Sci-Fi Films*. 2nd ed. Miami: Vital/Asian Cult Cinema, 1998.

———. *Japanese Cinema Encyclopedia: The Sex Films*. Miami: Vital/Asian Cult Cinema Publications, 1998.

Widmer, Ellen, and David Der-wei Wang, eds. *From May Fourth to June Fourth: Fiction and Film in Twentieth Century China*. Cambridge, Mass.: Harvard University Press, 1993.

Williams, Tony. "From Hong Kong to Hollywood: John Woo and His Discontents." *Cineaction* 42 (1997): 40–46.

———. "Space, Place, and Spectacle: The Crisis Cinema of John Woo," *Cinema Journal* 36, no. 2 (1997): 67–84. Repr. in Fu and Desser, eds., *The Cinema of Hong Kong*, pp. 137–57.

Witterstaetter, Renée. *Dying for Action: The Life and Films of Jackie Chan*. New York: Warner, 1997.

Wolf, Barbara. *The Japanese Film*. Mt. Vernon, N.Y.: Audio Brandon, 1976.

Wood, Miles. *Cine East: Hong Kong Cinema through the Looking Glass*. Guildford, Eng.: FAB, 1998.

Wood, Robin. *The Apu Trilogy*. New York: Praeger, 1971.

Yamane, Sadao. "Tokyo Journal: Sadao Yamane on the 'Post-Postwar' Generation of Japanese Filmmakers." *Film Comment* 38, no. 1 (January–February 2002): 10–11.

Yang, Mayfair Mei-hui, ed. *Spaces of Their Own: Women's Public Sphere in Transnational China*. Minneapolis: University of Minnesota Press, 1999.

Yau, Esther. "China." In Luhr, ed., *World Cinema since 1945*, pp. 116–39.

———. "*Yellow Earth*: Western Analysis and a Non-Western Text." *Film Quarterly* 61, no. 2 (Winter 1987–88): 22–33.

———. "International Fantasy and the 'New Chinese Cinema.'" *Quarterly Review of Film and Video* 14, no. 3 (1993): 95–107. Special issue edited by Marcia Butzel and Ana M. Lopez.

———, ed. *At Full Speed: Hong Kong Cinema in a Borderless World*. Minneapolis: University of Minnesota Press, 2001.

Yeh, Wen-hsin, ed. *Cross Cultural Readings of Chineseness: Narratives, Images and Interpretations of the 1990s*. Berkeley: Institute of East Asian Studies, University of California, 2000.

Yeh, Yueh-yu. "A Life of Its Own: Musical Discourse in Wong Kar-Wai's Films." *Post Script* 19, no. 1 (Fall 1999): 120–36.

Yip, June. "Constructing a Nation: Taiwanese History and the Films of Hou Hsiao-hsien." In Lu, ed., *Transnational Chinese Cinema*, pp. 139–68.

Yoshimoto, Mitsuhiro. *Kurosawa: Film Studies and Japanese Cinema*. Durham, N.C.: Duke University Press, 2000.

Zha, Jianying. "Chen Kaige and the Shadows of the Revolution." *Sight and Sound* (incorporating *Monthly Film Bulletin*) 4, no. 2 (February 1994): 28–36.

Zhang, Yingjin. "From 'Minority Film' to 'Minority Discourse': Questions of Nationhood and Ethnicity in Chinese Cinema." In Lu, ed., *Transnational Chinese Cinema*, pp. 81–104.

———, ed. *Cinema and Urban Culture in Shanghai, 1922–1943*. Stanford, Calif.: Stanford University Press, 1999.

———. *Screening China: Critical Interventions, Cinematic*

Reconfigurations, and the Transnational Imaginary in Contemporary Chinese Cinema. Ann Arbor: Center for Chinese Studies, University of Michigan, 2002.

Zhang, Yingjin, and Zhiwei Xiao. *Encyclopedia of Chinese Film*. Ed. Yingjin Zhan. Additional contributions Ru-shou Robert Chen et al. New York: Routledge, 1998.

Zhang, Zhen. "The 'Shanghai Factor' in Hong Kong Cinema: A Tale of Two Cities in Historical Perspectives." *Asian Cinema* 10, no. 1 (Fall 1998): 146–59.

CHAPTER 19. THIRD WORLD CINEMA

Adelman, Alan, ed. *A Guide to Cuban Cinema*. Latin American Monograph and Document Series 4. Pittsburgh: Center for Latin American Studies, University of Pittsburgh, 1981.

"African and Black Diaspora Film/Video." Special section of *Jump Cut: A Review of Contemporary Media* 36 (May 1991): 43–126.

"African Cinema." Special issue of *Critical Arts* 7, nos. 1–2 (1993).

"African Cinema." Special issue of *Research in African Literatures* 26, no. 3 (Fall 1995).

"African Cinema." Special section of *Sight and Sound* 5, no. 9 (September 1995): 30–39.

"African Film." Special section of *Jump Cut: A Review of Contemporary Media* 31 (1986): 44–50.

Akrami, Jamsheed. "The Blighted Spring: Iranian Cinema and Politics in the 1970s." In Downing, ed., *Film and Politics in the Third World*, pp. 131–44.

Akudinobi, Jude G. "Nationalism, African Cinema, and Frames of Scrutiny." *Research in African Literatures* 32, no. 3 (Fall 2001): 123–42.

Anyidoho, Kofi, and James Gibbs, eds. *FonTomFrom: Contemporary Ghanaian Literature, Theatre, and Film*. Amsterdam: Rodopi, 2000.

Arab Cinema and Culture: Round Table Conferences under the Auspices . . . of the UNESCO Beirut, October 1963. Beirut: Arab Film & Television Centre, 1965.

"Arab Image in American Film and Television, The" Supplement to *Cineaste* 17, no. 1 (1989).

Arasoughly, Alia, ed. and trans. *Screens of Life: Critical Film Writing from the Arab World*. St.-Hyacinthe, Quebec: World Heritage, 1996.

Armbrust, Walter. "Islamists in Egyptian Cinema." *American Anthropologist* 104, no. 3 (September 2002): 922–31.

Armes, Roy. *Third World Film Making and the West*. Berkeley: University of California Press, 1987.

Asfour, Nana. "The Politics of Arab Cinema: Middle Eastern Filmmakers Face Up to Their Reality." *Cineaste* 26, no. 1 (2000): 46–48.

Association des Trois Mondes, L'. *Dictionaire du cinéma africain*. Vol. 1. Paris: Karthala, 1991.

Atkinson, Michael. "Ousmane Sembene: We Are No Longer in the Era of Prophets." *Film Comment* 29, no. 4 (July–August 1993): 63–69.

Aufderheide, Pat. "Will Success Spoil Brazilian Cinema?" *American Film* 8, no. 5 (March 1983): 65–70.

———. "El Salvador: Bringing the War Home." *American Film* 8, no. 8 (June 1983): 50–54.

———. "Red Harvest." *American Film* 9, no. 5 (March 1984): 28–34.

———. "On Castro's Convertible." *Film Comment* 21, no. 3 (May–June 1985): 49–52.

———. "Awake, Argentine." *Film Comment* 22, no. 2 (March–April 1986): 51–55.

———. "Se Permuta." *Film Quarterly* 39, no. 3 (Spring 1986): 59–60.

Bachy, Victor. *Le Cinéma au Gabon*. Collection Cinemedia: Cinémas d'Afrique Noire. Brussels: L'Organisation Catholique Internationale du Cinéma, 1986.

Bakari, Imruh, and Mbye B. Cham, eds. *African Experiences of Cinema*. London: British Film Institute, 1995.

Balderston, Daniel, and Donna J. Guy, ed. *Sex and Sexuality in Latin America*. New York: New York University Press, 1997.

Balogun, Françoise. *The Cinema in Nigeria*. Enugu, Anambra State, Nigeria: Delta of Nigeria, 1987.

Barlet, Olivier. *African Cinemas: Decolonizing the Gaze*. Trans. Chris Turner. London: Zed, 2000.

Barnard, Tim, ed. *Argentine Cinema*. Toronto: Nightwood, 1986.

Barné, Scot. "Early Thai Cinema and Filmmaking: 1897–1922." *Film History* 11, no. 3 (1999): 308–18.

Bedoya, Ricardo. *100 Años de Cine en el Peru: Una Historia Critica*. Lima: Universidad de Lima, Instituto de Cooperacion Iberoamericana, 1992.

Benamou, Catherine. "Redefining Documentary in the Revolution: An Interview with Paolo Martin of the El Salvador Film and Television Unit." *Cineaste* 17, no. 3 (1990): 11–17.

Ben-Shaul, Nitzan S. *Mythical Expressions of Siege in Israeli Films*. Studies in Art and Religious Interpretation, Vol. 17. Lewiston, N.Y.: Mellen, 1997.

Berg, Charles Ramírez. *Cinema of Solitude: A Critical Study of Mexican Film, 1967–1983*. Austin: University of Texas Press, 1992.

———. *Latino Images in Film: Stereotypes, Subversion, and Resistance*. Austin: University of Texas Press, 2002.

Bernard, Tim. "After the Military: Film in the Southern Cone Today." *Review: Latin American Literature and Arts* 46 (1992): 29–36.

Bernard, Tim, and Peter Rist, ed. *South American Cinema: A Critical Filmography, 1915–1994*. New York: Garland, 1996.

Bertelsen, Eve. "Radical Cheek: Film Theory and the Common Viewer." *South African Theatre Journal* 5, no. 1 (1991): 5–23.

Bhabha, Homi K. "The Other Question: The Stereotype and Colonial Discourse." *Screen* 24, no. 6 (November–December 1983): 18–36.

Blignaut, Johan, and Martin Botha, eds. *Movies, Moguls, Mavericks: South African Cinema 1979–1991*. Cape Town: Showdata, 1992.

Boni-Claverie, Isabelle. "When Gazelles Fly: An Inventory of Cinema." *Revue Noire* 28 (March–May 1998): 58–61.

Botha, Martin, and Adri van Aswegen. *Images of South Africa: The Rise of the Alternative Film*. Pretoria: Human Sciences Research Council, 1992.

"Brazil—Post Cinema Novo." Special issue of *Framework* 28 (1985).

Burton, Julianne. "The Camera as a 'Gun': Two Decades of Film Culture and Resistance in Latin America." *Latin American Perspectives* 5, no. 1 (Winter 1978): 49–76.

———. "Portrait of Teresa." *Film Quarterly* 34, no. 3 (Spring 1981): 51–58.

———. "Theory and Practice of Film and Popular Culture in Cuba: A Conversation with Julio García Espinosa." *Quarterly Review of Film Studies* 7, no. 4 (Fall 1982): 341–51.

———. *The New Latin American Cinema: An Annotated Bibliography, 1960–1980*. New York: Smyrna, 1983.

———. "Film and Revolution in Cuba: The First Twenty-five Years." In Steven, ed., *Jump Cut*, pp. 344–59.

———, ed. *Cinema and Social Change in Latin America: Conversations with Filmmakers*. Austin: University of Texas Press, 1986.

———. "Latin America: On the Periphery of the Periphery." In Luhr, ed., *World Cinema since 1945*, pp. 424–46.

———, ed. *The Social Documentary in Latin America*. Pittsburgh: University of Pittsburgh Press, 1990.

Carbone, Giancarlo, ed. *El Cine en el Peru, 1950–1972: Testimonios*. Lima: Universidad de Lima, 1993.

Cham, Mbye-Baboucar. "Art and Ideology in the Work of Sembene Ousmane and Haile Gerima." *Presence Africaine: Revue Culturelle du Monde Noir/Cultural Review of the Negro World* 129, no. 1 (1984): 79–91.

———. "Film Production in West Africa: 1979–81." In Downing, ed., *Film and Politics in the Third World*, pp. 13–29.

Cham, Mbye-Baboucar, and Claire Andrade-Watkins, eds. *Blackframes: Critical Perspectives on Black Independent Cinema*. Cambridge, Mass.: MIT Press, 1988.

Cham, Mbye-Baboucar, and Anne Mungai. "African Women and Cinema: A Conversation with Anne Mungai." *Research in African Literatures* 23, no. 3 (Fall 1994): 93–104.

Chanan, Michael, ed. *Chilean Cinema*. London: British Film Institute, 1976.

———. *The Cuban Image: Cinema and Cultural Politics in Cuba*. London: British Film Institute, 1985.

Cheshire, Godfrey. "Where Iranian Cinema Is." *Film Comment* 29, no. 2 (March–April 1993): 38–43.

Christie, Ian. "Raúl Ruiz and the House of Culture." *Sight and Sound* (Spring 1987): 96–100.

Cleveland, William L. *A History of the Modern Middle East*. Boulder: Westview, 1994.

Collinge, Jo-Anne. "Under Fire." *American Film* 11, no. 2 (November 1985): 30–36.

Cooper, Carol. "Central America: The Domino Next Door." *Film Comment* 22, no. 3 (May–June 1986): 39–42.

Cowie, Peter, ed. *Variety International Film Guide 1993*. Hollywood: Samuel French, 1993.

Crowdus, Gary. "Up to a Point: An Interview with Tomás Gutiérrez Alea and Mirta Ibarra." *Cineaste* 14, no. 2 (1985): 26–30.

———. "South African Filmmaking in Exile: An Interview with Lionel Ngakane." *Cineaste* 15, no. 2 (1986): 16–17.

"Culture in the Age of Mass Media." Special issue of *Latin American Perspectives* 16, 5 (Winter 1978).

Cyr, Helen W. *A Filmography of the Third World: An Annotated List of 16mm Films*. Metuchen, N.J.: Scarecrow, 1976.

———. *A Filmography of the Third World, 1976–1983: An Annotated List of 16mm Films*. Metuchen, N.J.: Scarecrow, 1985.

Dabashi, Hamid. *Close-Up: Iranian Cinema, Past, Present, and Future*. London: Verso, 2001.

David, Joel. *The National Pastime: Contemporary Philippine Cinema*. Pasig, Metro Manila: Anvil, 1990.

———. *Fields of Vision: Critical Applications in Recent Philippine Cinema*. Manila: Ateneo de Manila University Press, 1995.

———. *Wages of Cinema: Film in Philippine Perspective*. Diliman, Quezon City: University of the Philippines Press, 1998.

Davis, Peter. *In Darkest Hollywood: Exploring the Jungles of Cinema's South Africa*. Randburg, South Africa: Raven, 1996.

Dear, Michael, and Gustavo Leclerc. "Tijuana Desenmascarada," *Wide Angle* 20, no. 3 (1998): 211–21.

Del Mundo, Clodualdo. *Native Resistance: Philippine Cinema and Colonialism, 1898–1941*. Manila: De La Salle University Press, 1998.

Diawara, Manthia. "Sub-Saharan African Film Production: Technological Paternalism." *Jump Cut: A Review of Contemporary Media* 32 (1987): 61–65.

———. "Popular Culture and Oral Traditions in African Films." *Film Quarterly* 41, no. 3 (Spring 1988): 6–14.

———, ed. *Black Cinema*. London: Routledge, 1990.

———. *African Cinema: Politics and Culture.* Bloomington: Indiana University Press, 1992.

———. "Whose African Cinema Is It Anyway?" *Sight and Sound* (incorporating *Monthly Film Bulletin*) 3, no. 2 (February 1993): 24–25.

———. "New York and Ouagadougou: The Homes of African Cinema." *Sight and Sound* (incorporating *Monthly Film Bulletin*) 3, no. 11 (November 1993): 24–25.

Diawara, Manthia, and Elizabeth Robinson. "New Perspectives in African Cinema: An Interview with Cheick Oumar Sissoko." *Film Quarterly* 41, no. 2 (Winter 1987–88): 43–48.

Dissanyake, Wimal, ed. *Colonialism and Nationalism in Asian Cinema.* Bloomington: Indiana University Press, 1994.

Douglas, María Eulalia. *Diccionario de cineastas Cubanos, 1959–1987.* Mérida, Venezuela: Universidad de los Andes, 1989.

Downing, John D. H., ed. *Film and Politics in the Third World.* New York: Praeger, 1987.

———. "Post Tricolor African Cinema: Toward a Richer Vision." In Sherzer, ed., *Cinema, Colonialism, Postcolonialism,* pp. 188–228.

Dratch, Howard, and Barbara Margolis. "Film and Revolution in Nicaragua: An Interview with INCINE Filmmakers." *Cineaste* 15, no. 3 (1987): 27–31.

Ehrenstein, David. "Raúl Ruiz at the Holiday Inn." *Film Quarterly* 40, no. 1 (Fall 1986): 1–7.

Ekwuazi, Hyginus. *Film in Nigeria.* 2nd ed. Jos: Nigerian Film Corporation, 1991.

Ekwuazi, Hyginus, and Yakubi Abdullahi Nasidi, eds. *Operative Principles of the Film Industry: Towards a Film Policy for Nigeria.* Jos: Nigerian Film Corporation, 1992.

Eyoh, Dickson. "Social Realist Cinema and Representations of Power in African Nationalist Discourse." *Research in African Literatures* 29, nos. 2 (Summer 1998): 112–27.

Falcoff, Mark. *Modern Chile 1979–1989: A Critical History.* New Brunswick, N.J.: Transaction, 1989.

Falicov, Tarmar L. "Argentina's Blockbuster Movies and the Politics of Culture under Neoliberalism, 1989–1998." *Media, Culture, and Society* 22 (May 2000): 327–42.

———. "Film Production in Argentina under Democracy, 1983–1989: *The Official Story* (*La historia oficial*) as an International Film." *Southern Quarterly* 29, no. 4 (Summer 2001): 123–34.

———. "Film Policy under MERCOSUR: The Case of Uruguay." *Canadian Film Journal of Communication* 27, no. 1 (2002): 33–46.

Fawal, Ibrahim. *Youssef Chahine.* London: British Film Institute, 2001.

Fisher, William. "Ouagadougou." *Sight and Sound* 58, no. 3 (Summer 1989): 170–73.

Foster, David William. *Contemporary Argentine Cinema.* Columbia: University of Missouri Press, 1992.

———. *Gender and Society in Contemporary Brazilian Cinema.* Austin: University of Texas Press, 1999.

———. *Mexico City in Contemporary Mexican Cinema.* Austin: University of Texas Press, 2002.

Foster, Gwendolyn Audrey. *Women Filmmakers of the African and Asian Diaspora: Decolonizing the Gaze, Locating Subjectivity.* Carbondale: Southern Illinois University Press, 1997.

Fox, Elizabeth, and Silvio Waisbord, eds. *Latin Politics, Global Media.* Austin: University of Texas Press, 2002.

Fregoso, Rosa Linda, ed. *Lourdes Portillo: "The Devil Never Sleeps" and Other Films.* Austin: University of Texas Press, 2001.

Friedman, Régine Mihal. "Between Silence and Abjection: The Film Medium and the Israeli War Widow." *Film Historia* 3, nos. 1–2 (1993): 79–89.

Fusco, Coco. "Flipped Out in Nicaragua: An Interview with Alex Cox." *Cineaste* 16, no. 3 (1988): 12–16.

Gabriel, Teshome H. *Third Cinema in the Third World: The Aesthetics of Liberation.* Ann Arbor, Mich.: UMI Research Press, 1982.

———. "Toward a Critical Theory of Third World Films." In Martin, ed., *Cinemas of the Black Diaspora,* pp. 70–90.

Gadjigo, Samba. "Africa through African Eyes." *Research in African Literatures* 23, no. 4 (Winter 1992): 97–105.

Gadjigo, Samba, et al., eds. *Ousmane Sembene: Dialogues with Critics and Writers.* Amherst: University of Massachusetts Press, 1993.

García Márquez, Gabriel. *Clandestine in Chile: The Adventures of Miguel Littín.* Trans. Asa Zatz. New York: Holt, 1987.

García Tsao, Leonardo. "Mexico Tinderbox." *Film Comment* (May–June 1985): 36–38.

Georgakas, Dan, and Lenny Rubenstein, eds. *The Cineaste Interviews: On the Art and Politics of the Cinema.* Chicago: Lake View, 1983.

Gertz, Nurith. *Motion Fiction, Israeli Fiction in Film.* Tel Aviv: University of Israel, 1993.

———. *Myths in Israeli Culture: Captives of a Dream.* London: Vallentine Mitchell, 2000.

Givanni, June. "Dream Aloud: Interview with John Akomfrah, the Ghanaian-British Director, on the Exhilaration of African Cinemas." *Sight and Sound* 5, no. 9 (September 1995): 37–39.

———, ed. *Symbolic Narratives/African Cinema: Audiences, Theory, and the Moving Image.* London: British Film Institute, 2000.

Gray, John. *Blacks in Film and Television: A Pan-African Bibliography of Films, Filmmakers, and Performers.* Bibliographies and Indexes in Afro-American and African Studies, No. 27. New York: Greenwood, 1990.

Gross, Ya'ackov. 75 *Years of Hebrew Film.* Jerusalem: Israel Postal Authority, 1992.

Gutiérrez Alea, Tomás. "I Wasn't Always a Filmmaker." *Cineaste* 14, no. 1 (1985): 36–38.

Halachmi, Joseph. *No Matter What—Studies in the History of the Jewish Film in Israel.* Jerusalem: Steven Spielberg/Jewish Film Archive, 1995.

Harrow, Kenneth W., ed. *With Open Eyes: Women and African Cinema.* Amsterdam: Rodopi, 1997.

———, ed. *African Cinema: Postcolonial and Feminist Readings.* Trenton, N.J.: African World Press, 1999.

Harrow, Kenneth W.; Maureen N. Eke; and Emmanuel Yewah, eds. *African Images: Recent Studies and Text in Cinema.* Trenton, N.J.: Africa World Press, 2000.

Haynes, Jonathan. "Returning to the African Village." *Jump Cut: A Review of Contemporary Media* 40 (March 1996): 62–66.

———. "Nigerian Cinema: Structural Adjustments." *Research in African Literatures* 26, no. 3 (Fall 1998): 97–119.

———, ed. *Nigerian Video Films.* Athens: Ohio University Center for International Studies, 2000.

Hees, Edwin. *The National Film Board of South Africa: A Short History.* Stellenbosch, South Africa: University of Stellenbosch, 1991.

Hershfield, Joanne. *Mexican Cinema/Mexican Women, 1940–1950.* Tuscan: University of Arizona Press, 1996.

Hershfield, Joanne, and David R. Maciel, eds. *Mexico's Cinema: A Century of Film and Filmmakers.* Wilmington, Del.: Scholarly Resources, 1999.

Hess, John, and C. Davies. "Debate: No mas Habermas, or . . . Rethinking Cuban Cinema in the 1990s." *Screen* 4, no. 2 (Summer 1999): 193–207.

Hildago, Narciso J. "On Cuban Film: A Brief History in Four Easy Lessons." Trans. Edward Santos Townsend. *Hopscotch* 2, no. 4 (2001): 108–15.

Hill, John, and Pamela Church Gibson, eds. *World Cinema: Critical Approaches.* Oxford: Oxford University Press, 2000.

Hintz, Eugenio, et al. *Historia y filmografía del cine Uruguayo.* Montevideo: Ediciones de la Plaza, 1988.

Hourani, Albert. *A History of the Arab Peoples.* Cambridge, Mass.: Belknap, 1991.

Howard, Steve. "A Cinema of Transformation: The Films of Haile Gerima." *Cineaste* 14, no. 1 (1985): 28–29, 30.

Issa, Rose, and Sheila Whitaker, eds. *Life and Art: The New Iranian Cinema.* Rev. ed. London: National Film Theatre, 1999.

Issari, M. Ali. *Cinema in Iran, 1900–1979.* Metuchen, N.J.: Scarecrow, 1989.

James, David E., and Kyung Nyun Kim, eds. *Im Kwon-Taek:*

The Making of a Korean National Cinema. Detroit: Wayne State University Press, 2002.

Johnson, Randal. *Cinema Novo × Five: Masters of Contemporary Brazilian Film.* Austin: University of Texas Press, 1984.

———. *The Film Industry in Brazil: Culture and the State.* Pittsburgh: University of Pittsburgh Press, 1987.

Johnson, Randal, and Robert Stam. *Brazilian Cinema.* Rutherford, N.J.: Fairleigh Dickinson University Press, 1982. Rev. ed. New York: Columbia University Press, 1995.

Kernan, Margot. "Cuban Cinema: Tomás Guitiérrez Alea." *Film Quarterly* 29, no. 2 (Winter 1975–76): 45–52.

Khan, Mohamed. *An Introduction to Egyptian Cinema.* London: Informatics, 1969.

Kim, Kyung Hyun. "Post-Trauma and Historical Remembrance in Recent South Korean Cinema: Reading Park Kwang-su's *A Single Spark* (1995) and Chang Son-u's *A Petal* (1996)." *Cinema Journal* 41, no. 4 (2002): 95–115.

King, John. *Magical Reels: A History of Cinema in Latin America.* London: Verso, 1990.

King, John; Ana M. Lopez; and Manuel Alvarado, eds. *Mediating Two Worlds: Cinematic Encounters in the Americas.* London: British Film Institute, 1993.

King, John; Sheila Whitaker; and Rosa Bosch. *An Argentine Passion: María Luisa Bemberg and Her Films.* London: Verso, 2000.

Kolbowski, Silvia. "Out of Cold Blood: New Argentine Cinema." *Afterimage* 14, no. 1 (Summer 1986): 5–7.

Kronish, Amy. *World Cinema: Israel.* Madison, N.J.: Fairleigh Dickinson University Press, 1996.

Kronish, Amy; Edith Falk; and Paula Weiman-Kelman, eds. *The Nathan Axelrod Collection,* Vol. 1. Trowbridge, Eng.: Flicks, 1994.

Landy, Marcia. "Political Allegory and 'Engaged Cinema': Sembene's *Xala*." *Cinema Journal* 23, no. 3 (Spring 1984): 31–46.

"Latin American Film." Special section of *Jump Cut: A Review of Contemporary Media* 30 (1984): 44–62.

Lau, Jenny Kwok Wah, ed. *Multiple Modernities: Cinema and Popular Media in Transcultural East Asia.* Philadelphia: Temple University Press, 2002.

Leaman, Oliver, ed. *Companion Encyclopedia to Middle Eastern and North African Film.* London: Routledge, 2001.

Lee, Hyangjin. *Contemporary Korean Cinema: Identity, Culture, and Politics.* Manchester, Eng.: Manchester University Press, 2001.

Lee, Young-Il. *The History of Korean Cinema: Main Current of Korean Cinema.* Trans. by Richard Lynn Greever. Seoul: Motion Picture Promotion Corporation, 1988.

Lent, John A. "Lousy Films Had to Come First." *Asian Cinema* 7, no. 2 (Winter 1995): 86–92.

Lesage, Julia. "For Our Urgent Use: Films on Central America." *Jump Cut: A Review of Contemporary Media* 27 (1982): Repr. in Steven, ed., *Jump Cut*, pp. 375–89.

Lopez, Ana M. "The Melodrama in Latin America: Films, Telenovelas, and the Currency of a Popular Form." *Wide Angle* 7, no. 3 (1956): 5–13.

———. "Towards a 'Third' and 'Imperfect' Cinema: A Theoretical and Historical Study of Filmmaking in Latin America." Ph.D. diss., University of Iowa, 1986.

———. "An 'Other' History: The New Latin American Cinema." In Sklar and Musser, eds., *Resisting Images*, pp. 308–330.

———. "The 'Other' Island: Cuban Cinema in Exile." *Jump Cut: A Review of Contemporary Media* 38 (1993): 51–59.

———. "Early Cinema and Modernity in Latin America." *Cinema Journal* 40, no. 1 (2000): 48–78.

Loshitzky, Yosefa. *Identity Politics on the Isreali Screen*. Austin: University of Texas Press, 2001.

Luhr, William, ed. *World Cinema since 1945*. New York: Ungar, 1987.

Macbean, James Roy. *Film and Revolution*. Bloomington: Indiana University Press, 1975.

———. "A Dialogue with Tomás Gutiérrez Alea on the Dialectics of *Hasta cierta punta*." *Film Quarterly* 38, no. 3 (Spring 1985): 22–29.

Maghsoudlou, Bahman. *Iranian Cinema*. New York: Hagop Kevorkian Center for Near Eastern Studies, New York University, 1987.

Malkmus, Lizbeth. "The 'New' Egyptian Cinema: Adopting Genre Conventions to a Changing Society." *Cineaste* 16, no. 3 (1988): 30–33.

Malkmus, Lizbeth, and Roy Armes. *Arab and African Film Making*. London: Zed, 1991.

Mangin, Geoffrey. *Filming Emerging Africa: A Pioneer Cinematographer's Scrapbook from the 1940s to the 1960s—New Colour Systems, New Film-makers, New Audiences, New Developments in Southern Africa*. Cape Town: Mangin, 1998.

Marranghello, Daniel. *El cine en Costa Rica 1903–1920*. San José, Costa Rica: Jiménez y Tanzi, 1988.

———. *Cine y Censura en Costa Rica*. San José, Costa Rica: Ediciones Cultura Cinematográfica, 1989.

Martin, Michael T., ed. *Cinemas of the Black Diaspora: Diversity, Dependence, and Oppositionality*. Detroit: Wayne State University Press, 1995.

———, ed. *New Latin American Cinema*. Vol. 1: *Theory, Practices, and Transcontinental Articulations*. Detroit: Wayne State University Press, 1997.

———, ed. *New Latin American Cinema*. Vol. 2: *Studies of National Cinemas*. Detroit: Wayne State University Press, 1997.

Mathews, Louis. "Hollywood Invades Nicaragua." *Mother Jones* 12, no. 9 (December 1987): 28–33.

Mermin, Elizabeth. "Window on Whose Reality?: The Emerging Industry of Senegalese Cinema." *Research in African Literatures* 26, no. 3 (Fall 1995): 120–33.

Meyer, Birgit. "Popular Ghanaian Cinema and 'African Heritage.'" *Africa Today* 46, no. 2 (Spring 1999): 93–114.

Mgbejume, Onyero. *Film in Nigeria: Development, Problems, and Promise*. African Media Monography Series, No. 7. Nairobi: African Council on Communication Education, 1989.

Mohammadi, Ali, and Eric Egan. "Cinema and Iran: Culture and Politics in the Islamic Republic." *Asian Cinema* (Spring–Summer 2001): 14–28.

Moorman, Marissa. "Of Westerns, Women and War: Re-Situating Angolan Cinema and the Nation." *Research in African Literatures* 32, no. 3 (Fall 2001): 103–22.

Mora, Carl J. *Mexican Cinema: Reflections of a Society, 1896–1980*. Berkeley: University of California Press, 1982.

Motavalli, John. "Exiles." *Film Comment* 19, no. 4 (July–August 1983): 56–59.

Murphy, Caryle. "Iran's Islamic Revolution." *Washington Post National Weekly Edition* (June 1–7, 1992): 10–11.

Murphy, David. "Africans Filming Africa: Questioning Theories of an Authentic African Cinema." *Journal of African Cultural Studies* 13, no. 2 (December 2000): 239–49.

Myerson, Michael, ed. *Memories of Underdevelopment: The Revolutionary Films of Cuba*. New York: Grossman, 1973.

Nacify, Hamid. "Iranian Feature Film: A Brief Critical History." *Quarterly Review of Film Studies* 4, no. 4 (Fall 1979): 443–64.

———. *Iran Media Index*. Westport, Conn.: Greenwood, 1984.

———. "Theorizing 'Third-World' Film Spectatorship." *Wide Angle* 18, no. 4 (1996): 3–26.

———. "Iranian Cinema." In Leaman, ed., *Companion Encyclopedia to Middle Eastern and North African Film*, pp. 133–222.

Nayeri, Farah. "Iranian Cinema: What Happened in Between." *Sight and Sound* (incorporating *Monthly Film Bulletin*) 3, no. 12 (December 1993): 26–28.

Niang, Sada, and Sambo Gadjigo. "Interview with Ousmane Sembene." *Research in African Literatures* 26, no. 3 (Fall 1995): 174–78.

Noriega, Chon A., ed. *Visible Nations: Latin American Cinema and Video*. Minneapolis: University of Minnesota Press, 2000.

Noriega, Chon A., and Ana M. López, eds. *The Ethnic Eye: Latino Media Arts*. Minneapolis: University of Minnesota Press, 1996.

Noriega, Chon A., and Steven Ricci. *The Mexican Cinema Project*. Los Angeles: UCLA Film and Television Archive, 1994.

Okome, Onookome, and Jonathan Haynes. *Cinema and Social Change in West Africa*. Jos.: Nigerian Film Corporation: 1995.

Onishi, Norimitsu. "Step Aside, L.A. and Bombay, for Nollywood." *New York Times* (September 16, 2002): A1, A8.

Oshana, Maryann. *Women of Color: A Filmography of Minority and Third World Women*. New York: Garland, 1985.

Osiel, Mark. "Bye Bye Boredom: Brazilian Cinema Comes of Age." *Cineaste* 24, no. 1 (1985): 30–35.

Park, Seung Hyun. "Film Censorship and Political Legitimation in South Korea, 1887–1992." *Cinema Journal* 42, no. 1 (Fall 2002): 120–38.

Pearson, Lyle. "Four Years of North African Film." *Film Quarterly* 26, no. 4 (Summer 1973): 18–26.

Petty, Shelia, ed. *A Call to Action: The Films of Ousmane Sembene*. Contributions to the Study of Popular Culture, No. 60. Westport, Conn.: Greenwood, 1996.

———. "The Archeology of Origin: Translational Visions of Africa in a Borderless Cinema." *African Studies Review* 42, no. 2 (September 1999): 73–86.

Pfaff, Françoise. *The Cinema of Ousmane Sembene: A Pioneer of African Film*. Westport, Conn.: Greenwood, 1984.

———. *Twenty-five Black African Filmmakers: A Critical Study, with Filmography and Bio-Bibliography*. Westport, Conn.: Greenwood, 1988.

———. "Conversation with Ghanaian Filmmaker Kwaw Ansah." *Research in African Literatures* 26, no. 3 (Fall 1995): 186–93.

Pick, Zuzana M. "A Special Section on Chilean Cinema." *Cinétracts* 3, no. 1 (Winter 1980): 17–28.

———. "Chilean Cinema: Ten Years of Exile: 1973–1983." *Jump Cut: A Review of Contemporary Media* 32 (1987): 66–70.

———. *The New Latin American Cinema: A Continental Project*. Austin: University of Texas Press, 1993.

Pierce, Robert N. *Keeping the Flame: Media and Government in Latin America*. New York: Hastings House, 1979.

Pilcher, Jeffrey M. *Cantinflas and the Chaos of Mexican Modernity*. Wilmington, Del.: Scholarly Resources, 2001.

Pines, Jim, and Paul Willemen, eds. *Questions of Third Cinema*. London: British Film Institute, 1989.

Ranucci, Karen, and Julie Feldman, eds. *A Guide to Latin American, Caribbean, and U.S. Latino-Made Film and Video*. Lanham, Md.: Scarecrow, 1998.

Raskin, Elissa J. *Women Filmmakers in Mexico: The Country of Which We Dream*. Austin: University of Texas Press, 2001.

Rayns, Tony. "Korea's New Wavers." *Sight and Sound* 4, no. 11 (November 1994): 22–25.

Raz, Yousef. "Broken Skin: Male Fantasies, Male Anxieties, and the Representation of the "Feminine" Male Body in Isreali Cinema." *Cinematheque* 97 (March–April 1998): 20–25.

Reid, Mark A. "Producing African Cinema in Paris: Interview with Andree Davanture." *Jump Cut: A Review of Contemporary Media* 36 (1991): 47–51.

Reyes, Luis, and Peter Rubie. *Hispanics in Hollywood: An Encyclopedia of Film and Television*. New York: Garland, 1994.

Reyes Nevares, Beatriz. *The Mexican Cinema: Interviews with Thirteen Directors*. Albuquerque: University of New Mexico Press, 1976.

Richard, Alfred Charles, Jr. *The Hispanic Image on the Silver Screen: An Interpretive Filmography from Silents into Sound, 1898–1935*. Westport, Conn.: Greenwood, 1992.

———. *Censorship and Hollywood's Hispanic Image: An Interpretive Filmography, 1936–1955*. Westport, Conn.: Greenwood, 1993.

———. *Contemporary Hollywood's Negative Hispanic Image: An Interpretive Filmography, 1956–1993*. Westport, Conn.: Greenwood, 1994.

Rosenthal, Alan. "*When the Mountains Tremble:* An Interview with Pamela Yates." *Film Quarterly* 39, no. 1 (Fall 1985): 2–10.

Russell, Sharon A. *Guide to African Cinema*. Westport, Conn.: Greenwood, 1998.

Ryan, Susan. "Behind Rebel Lines: Filmmaking in Revolutionary El Salvador." *Cineaste* 14, no. 1 (1985): 16–21.

Safford, Tony, and William Triplett. "Haile Gerima: Radical Departures to a New Black Cinema." *Journal of the University and Television Association* 35, no. 2 (Spring 1983): 59–65.

Salmane, Hala; Simon Hartog; and David Wilson. *Algerian Cinema*. London: British Film Institute, 1976.

Sánchez H., José. *The Art and Politics of Bolivian Cinema*. Lanham, Md.: Scarecrow, 1999.

Sanjinés, Jorge, and the Ukamau Group. *Theory and Practice of a Cinema with the People*. Trans. Richard Schaaf. Willimantic, Conn.: Curbstone, 1989.

Sauvage, Pierre. "Cine Cubano." *Film Comment* 8, no. 1 (Spring 1972): 24–31.

Schmidt, Nancy. *Sub-Saharan African Films and Filmmakers: An Annotated Bibliography*. London: Zell, 1988.

———. *Sub-Saharan African Films and Filmmakers, 1987–1992: An Annotated Bibliography*. London: Zell, 1994.

Schnitman, Jorge A. *Film Industries in Latin America: Dependency and Development*. Norwood, N.J.: Ablex, 1984.

Schwartz, Ronald. *Latin American Films, 1932–1994: A Critical Filmography*. Jefferson, N.C.: McFarland, 1997.

Server, Lee. *Asian Pop Cinema: Bombay to Tokyo*. San Francisco: Chronicle, 1999.

Shafik, Viola. *Arab Cinema: History and Cultural Identity*. Cairo: American University in Cairo Press, 1998.

Sherzer, Dan, ed. *Cinema, Colonialism, Postcolonialism: Perspectives from the French and Francophone World*. Austin: University of Texas Press, 1996.

Shiran, Shaul. *Israeli Cinema: Facts, Plots, Directors, Opinions*. Jerusalem: Kinneret, 1994.

Shiri, Keith, ed. *Directory of African Film-Makers and Films*. Westport, Conn.: Greenwood, 1992.

Shohat, Ella. "Anomalies of the National: Representing Israel/Palestine." *Wide Angle* 11, no. 3 (1989): 33–41.

———. *Israeli Cinema: East/West and the Politics of Representation*. Austin: University of Texas Press, 1989.

———. "Master Narrative/Counter Readings: The Politics of Israeli Cinema." In Sklar and Musser, eds., *Resisting Images*, pp. 251–78.

Skidmore, Thomas E., and Peter H. Smith. *Modern Latin America*. 2nd ed. New York: Oxford University Press, 1989.

Sklar, Robert. "Anarchic Visions." *Film Comment* 36, no. 3 (May–June 2000): 40–43. Profile of Djibril Diop Mambéty.

———. "The Politics of Pure Emotion: An Interview with Tran Anh Hung." *Cineaste* 26, no. 4 (Fall 2001): 69–70.

Sklar, Robert, and Charles Musser, eds. *Resisting Images: Essays on Cinema and History*. Philadelphia: Temple University Press, 1990.

Slavin, David Henry. *Colonial Cinema and Imperial France, 1919–1939: White Blind Spots, Male Fantasies, Settler Myths*. Baltimore: John Hopkins University Press, 2001.

Spaas, Lieve. *The Francophone Film: A Struggle for Identity*. Manchester, Eng.: Manchester University Press, 2000.

Spence, Louise, and Robert Stam. "Colonization, Racism and Representation." *Screen* 24, no. 2 (March–April 1983): 2–20.

Stam, Robert. "Slow Fade to Afro: The Black Presence in Brazilian Cinema." *Film Quarterly* 36, no. 2 (Winter 1982–83): 16–32.

———. *Tropical Multiculturalism: A Comparative History of Race in Brazilian Cinema and Culture*. Durham, N.C.: Duke University Press, 1997.

Stam, Robert, and Ismail Xavier. "Recent Brazilian Cinema: Allegory/Metacinema/Carnival." *Film Quarterly* 41, no. 3 (Spring 1988): 15–30.

———. "Transformation of National Allegory: Brazilian Cinema from Dictatorship to Redemocratization." In Sklar and Musser, eds. *Resisting Images*, pp. 279–307.

Stein, Elliott. "Don Hermosillo and the Sun." *Film Comment* (June 1986):53–57.

Steven, Peter, ed. *Jump Cut: Hollywood, Politics and Counter Cinema*. New York: Praeger, 1985.

Stevens, Donald F. *Based on a True Story: Latin American History at the Movies*. Wilmington, Del.: Scholarly Resources, 1997.

Stock, Ann Marie, ed. *Framing Latin American Cinema: Contemporary Critical Perspectives*. Minneapolis: University of Minnesota Press, 1997.

Stollery, Martin. "Masculinities, Generations, and Cultural Transformation in Contemporary Tunisian Cinema." *Screen* 42, no. 1 (Spring 2001): 49–63.

Stone, Judy. "On the Edge." *American Film* 10, no. 1 (October 1984): 68–71, 80.

Tang, Xiaobing, and Stephen Snyder, ed. *In Pursuit of Contemporary East Asian Culture*. Boulder: Westview, 1996.

Tapper, Richard, ed. *New Iranian Cinema: Politics, Representation and Identity*. London: Tauris, 2002.

Taylor, Anna Marie. "Lucia." *Film Quarterly* 27, no. 2 (Winter 1974–75): 53–58.

Taylor, Clyde. "Africa: The Last Cinema." In Luhr, ed., *World Cinema since 1945*, pp. 1–21.

Thompson, Currie K. "Remaking Buenos Aires: Argentine Film from *Tango* to *Kilometro 111*." *Post Script* 21, no. 1 (Fall 2001): 24–30.

Tomaselli, Keyan G. "The Teaching of Film and Television Production in a Third World Context: The Case of South Africa." *Journal of the University Film and Video Association* 34, no. 4 (Fall 1982): 3–12.

———. "Racism in South African Cinema," *Cineaste* 13, no. 1 (1983): 12–15.

———. *The Cinema of Apartheid: Class and Race in South African Cinema*. New York: Smyrna, 1988.

Tomaselli, Keyan G.; Arnold Shepperson; and Maureen Eke. "Towards a Theory of Orality in African Cinema." *Research in African Literatures* 26, no. 3 (Fall 1995): 18–35.

Trelles Plazaola, Luis. *South American Cinema: Dictionary of Film Makers*. Trans. Yudit de Ferdinandy. Río Piedras: Editorial de la Universidad de Puerto Rico, 1989.

Treviño, Jesús Salvador. "The New Mexican Cinema." *Film Quarterly* 32, no. 3 (Spring 1979): 26–37.

Tryster, Hillel. *Israel before Israel: Silent Cinema in the Holy Land*. Ed. Asher Weil. Jerusalem: Steven Spielberg/Jewish Film Archive, 1995.

———. "*The Land of Promise* (1935): A Case Study in Zionist Film Propaganda." *Historical Journal of Film, Radio and Television* 15, no. 2 (1995): 187–217.

Turner, Graeme. *Film as Social Practice*. New York: Routledge, 1988.

20 Años de cine Cubano. Havana: Ministerio de Cultura, Centro de Información Cinematográfica, 1983.

Ukadike, N. (Nwachukwu) Frank. "Anglophone African Media." *Jump Cut: A Review of Contemporary Media* 36 (1991): 74–80.

———. *Black African Cinema*. Berkeley: University of California Press, 1994.

———. *Questioning African Cinema: Conversations with Filmmakers*. Minneapolis: University of Minnesota Press, 2002.

Ungar, Sanford J. *Africa: The People and the Politics of an Emerging Continent*. New York: Simon & Schuster, 1985.

Usabel, Gaizka S. de. *The High Noon of American Films in Latin America*. Ann Arbor, Mich.: UMI Research Press, 1982.

van der Heide, William. *Malaysian Cinema, Asian Film*. Amsterdam, the Neth.: Amsterdam University Press, 2002.

Vogel, Amos. *Film as a Subversive Art*. New York: Random House, 1974.

Wayne, Mike. *Political Film: The Dialectics of Third Cinema*. London: Pluto, 2001.

West, Dennis. "Revolution in Central America: A Survey of Recent Documentaries." *Cineaste* 12, no. 1 (1982): 18–23.

———. "Revolution in Central America: A Survey of New Documentaries." *Cineaste* 14, no. 3 (1986): 14–21.

———. "Cuba: Cuban Cinema before the Revolution and After." In Luhr, ed., *World Cinema since 1945*, pp. 140–53.

———. "A Film School for the Third World." *Cineaste* 15, no. 3 (1987): 37, 57.

West, Dennis, and Joan M. West. "Alice in a Cuban Wonderland: An Interview with Daniel Díaz Torres." *Cineaste* 20, no. 1 (1993): 24–27.

———. "Conversation with Marta Rodríguez." *Jump Cut: A Review of Contemporary Media* 38 (1993): 39–44, 19.

———. "*Strawberry Chocolate*, Ice Cream and Tolerance: Interviews with Tomás Gutiérrez Alea and Juan Carlos Tabío." *Cineaste* 21, nos. 1–2 (1995): 16–20.

Yakir, Dan. "Eye on Zion." *Film Comment* 19, no. 3 (June 1983): 60–63.

———. "Braziliant." *Film Comment* 20, no. 3 (May–June 1984): 56–59.

———. "Israel's Black Box." *Film Comment* 24, no. 4 (July–August 1988): 69–70.

Yearwood, Gladstone L., ed. *Black Cinema Aesthetics. Issues in Independent Black Filmmaking*. Athens: Center for Afro-American Studies, Ohio University, 1982.

Young, Deborah. "Dossier: Iranian Cinema Now." In Cowie, ed., *Variety International Film Guide 1993*, pp. 27–50.

Zacks, Stephen A. "The Theoretical Construction of African Cinema." *Research in African Literatures* 26, no. 3 (Fall 1995): 6–17.

Media

Akrami, Jamsheed. *Dreams Betrayed: A Study of Political Cinema in Iran, 1969–1979*. 1985. 118 min.

Chanan, Michael. *New Cinema of Latin America*. Part 1: *Cinema of the Humble*; Part 2: *The Long Road*. Coproduced with ICAIC, INCINE, Dpto. de Cine, ULA (Venezuela), GECU (Panama), Zafra AC (Mexico), and Tatu Films, Ltda. (Brazil); a Cinema Guild, New York, release, 1986. Part 1: 83 min.; Part 2: 85 min.

Gross, Yakov. *Yakov Ben Dov: Father of the Hebrew Film*. Israel, Steven Spielberg Jewish Film Archive; Hebrew University, Mt. Scopus, Jerusalem, 1993.

"Internal Exile" program. Third World Newsreel. Films and videos from Chile.

CHAPTER 20. HOLLYWOOD, 1965–1995

Acker, Ally. *Reel Women: Pioneers of the Cinema, 1896 to the Present*. New York: Continuum, 1993.

Agel, Jerome. *The Making of "2001."* New York: Signet, 1970.

Allen, Michael. *Contemporary US Cinema*. New York: Longman, 2003.

Allon, Yoram; Del Cullen; and Hannah Paterson, eds. *The Wallflower Critical Guide to Contemporary North American Directors*. London: Wallflower, 2000.

Andrew, J. Dudley. *The Major Film Theories*. New York: Oxford University Press, 1976.

Austin, Bruce A., ed. *Current Research in Film: Audiences, Economics and Law*. Vol. 3. Norwood, N.J.: Ablex, 1987.

Bach, Steven. *Final Cut: Art, Money, and Ego in the Making of "Heaven's Gate," the Film That Sank United Artists*. Rev. ed. New York: Newmarket, 1999.

Baker, Christopher W. *How Did They Do It?: Computer Illusion in Film and TV*. Indianapolis: Alpha, 1994.

Barnes, Alan, and Marcus Hearn. *Tarantino A to Zed: The Films of Quentin Tarantino*. 2nd rev. ed. London: Batsford, 1999.

Bart, Peter. *Fade Out: The Calamitous Final Days of MGM*. New York: Morrow, 1990.

———. *The Gross: The Hits, the Flops—the Summer That Ate Hollywood*. New York: St. Martin's, 1999.

———. *Who Killed Hollywood? And Put the Tarnish on Tinseltown*. Los Angeles: Renaissance, 1999.

Bauer, Tassilo, ed. *Special Effects and Stunts Guide*. 2nd ed. Los Angeles: Lone Eagle, 1993.

Baughman, James L. *The Republic of Mass Culture: Journalism, Filmmaking, and Broadcasting in America since 1941*. Baltimore: Johns Hopkins University Press, 1992.

Bernstein, Jonathan. *Pretty in Pink: The Golden Age of Teenage Movies*. New York: St. Martin's, 1997.

Bernstein, Matthew, ed. *Controlling Hollywood: Censorship*

and Regulation in the Studio Era. New Brunswick, N.J.: Rutgers University Press, 1999.

Biskind, Peter. *Easy Riders, Raging Bulls: How the Sex-Drugs-and-Rock-'n'-Roll Generation Saved Hollywood.* New York: Simon & Schuster, 1998.

Bliss, Michael. *Justified Lives: Morality and Narrative in the Films of Sam Peckinpah.* Carbondale: Southern Illinois University Press, 1991.

———. *Doing It Right: The Best Criticism on Sam Peckinpah's "The Wild Bunch."* Carbondale: Southern Illinois University Press, 1994.

Bodroghkozy, Aniko. "Reel Revolutionaries: An Examination of Hollywood's Cycle of 1960s Youth Rebellion Films." *Cinema Journal* 41, no. 3 (Spring 2002): 38–58.

Bona, Damien. *Inside Oscar 2.* New York: Ballantine, 2002.

Bordwell, David. "Intensified Continuity: Visual Style in Contemporary American Film." *Film Quarterly* 55, no. 3 (Spring 2002): 16–28.

Bouzereau, Laurent. *Ultraviolent Movies: From Sam Peckinpah to Quentin Tarantino.* Rev. and upd. ed. New York: Citadel, 2000.

Brode, Douglas. *The Films of the Eighties.* Secaucus, N.J.: Carol, 1990.

Brosnan, John. *Movie Magic: The Story of Special Effects in the Cinema.* New York: St. Martin's, 1974.

Browne, Nick, ed. *Refiguring American Film Genres: History and Theory.* Berkeley: University of California Press, 1998.

Cagin, Seth, and Philip Dray. *Born to Be Wild: Hollywood and the Sixties Generation.* Boca Raton: Coyote, 1994.

Cameron, Ian, et al. *Second Wave.* New York: Praeger, 1970.

Carson, Diane, ed. *John Sayles: Interviews.* Jackson: University Press of Mississippi, 1999.

Cawelti, John G., ed. *Focus on "Bonnie and Clyde."* Englewood Cliffs, N.J.: Prentice-Hall, 1972.

Chown, Jeffrey. *Hollywood Auteur: Francis Coppola.* New York: Praeger, 1988.

Ciment, Michel. *Kubrick.* Trans. Gilbert Adair. New York: Holt, Rinehart, & Winston, 1982.

Clarke, Arthur C. *Lost Worlds of "2001."* New York: Signet, 1972.

Cook, David A. "American Horror: *The Shining.*" *Literature/Film Quarterly* 12, no. 1 (Spring–Summer 1984): 1–4.

———. "*The Wild Bunch* Fifteen Years After." *North Dakota Quarterly* 51, no. 3 (Summer 1984): 123–30.

———. "*The Wild Bunch.*" In Thomas, ed., *International Dictionary of Films and Filmmakers,* vol. 1, pp. 979–80.

———. *Lost Illusions: American Cinema in the Shadow of Watergate and Vietnam, 1970–1979.* Vol. 9 of *History of the American Cinema.* New York: Scribner's, 2000.

Corbett, Kevin J. "The Big Picture: Theatrical Moviegoing, Digital Television, and beyond the Substitution Effect." *Cinema Journal* 20, no. 2 (2001): 17–32.

Corliss, Richard. "We Lost It at the Movies: The Generation That Grew Up on *The Graduate,* Took Over Hollywood—and Went into Plastics." *Film Comment* 16, no. 1 (January–February 1980): 34–38.

Cowie, Peter. *Coppola.* London: Deutsch, 1989.

Davies, Philip John, and Paul Wells, eds. *American Film and Politics from Reagan to Bush, Jr.* Manchester, Eng.: Manchester University Press, 2002.

Dawson, Jeff. *Quentin Tarantino: The Cinema of Cool.* New York: Applause, 1995.

Dick, Bernard F. *Columbia Pictures: Portrait of a Studio.* Lexington: University Press of Kentucky, 1992.

Dixon, Wheeler Winston, ed. *Film Genre 2000.* Albany: State University of New York Press, 2000.

Dominick, Joseph R. "Film Economics and Film Content: 1964–1983." In Austin, ed., *Current Research in Film,* vol. 3, pp. 136–53.

Eidsvik, Charles. *Cineliteracy: Film among the Arts.* New York: Random House, 1978.

Evans, Robert. *The Kid Stays in the Picture.* New York: Hyperion, 1994.

Falsetto, Mario. *Stanley Kubrick: A Narrative and Stylistic Analysis.* New York: Praeger, 1994.

Farber, Stephen, and Marc Green. *Outrageous Conduct: Art, Ego, and the Twilight Zone Case.* New York: Arbor House/Morrow, 1988.

Fine, Marshall. *Bloody Sam: The Life and Films of Sam Peckinpah.* New York: Fine, 1991.

Fleming, Charles. *High Concept: Don Simpson and the Hollywood Culture of Excess.* New York: Doubleday, 1998.

Friedman, Lawrence S. *The Cinema of Martin Scorsese.* New York: Continuum, 1999.

Fuchs, Cynthia, ed. *Spike Lee: Interviews.* Jackson: University Press of Mississippi, 2002.

Gateward, Frances, and Murray Pomerance, eds. *Sugar, Spice, and Everything Nice: Cinemas of Girlhood.* Detroit: Wayne State University Press, 2002.

Geduld, Carolyn. *Filmguide to "2001: A Space Odyssey."* Bloomington: Indiana University Press, 1973.

Geirland, John, and Eva Sonesh Kedar. *Digital Babylon: How the Geeks, the Suits, and the Ponytails Fought to Bring Hollywood to the Internet.* New York: Arcade, 1999.

Gross, Lynne S., and Larry Ward. *Electronic Moviemaking.* 4th ed. Belmont, Calif.: Wadsworth, 2000.

Grover, Ron. *The Disney Touch: How a Daring Management Team Revived an Entertainment Empire.* Homewood, Ill.: Business One Irwin, 1991.

Hark, Ina Rae, ed. *Exhibition, the Film Reader.* London: Routledge, 2001.

Haward, Philip, and Tana Wollen, eds. *Future Visions: New Technologies of the Screen*. London: British Film Institute, 1993.

Hertzberg, Ludvig, ed. *Jim Jarmusch: Interviews*. Jackson: University Press of Mississippi, 2001.

Hillier, Jim. *The New Hollywood*. London: Studio Vista, 1992.

———, ed. *American Independent Cinema: A Sight and Sound Reader*. London: British Film Institute, 2001.

Hirsch, Foster. *Detours and Lost Highways: A Map of Neo-Noir*. New York: Limelight, 1999.

Hoberman, J., and Jonathan Rosenbaum. *Midnight Movies*. New York: Harper & Row, 1983.

Horsley, Jake. *The Blood Poets: A Cinema of Savagery 1959–1999*, Vol. 1: *American Chaos from "Touch of Evil" to the "Terminator."* Lanham, Md.: Scarecrow, 1999.

———. *The Blood Poets: A Cinema of Savagery 1959–1999*, Vol. 2: *Millennial Blues from "Apocalypse Now" to "The Matrix."* Lanham, Md.: Scarecrow, 1999.

Houston, Penelope. *The Contemporary Cinema*. Rev. ed. Baltimore: Penguin, 1971.

Hubbard, Jaimie. *Public Screening: The Battle for Cineplex Odeon*. Toronto: Lest & Orpen Dennys, 1990.

Jacobs, Diane. *Hollywood Renaissance*. Cranbury, N.J.: Barnes, 1977.

Jeffords, Susan. *Hard Bodies: Hollywood Masculinity in the Reagan Era*. New Brunswick, N.J.: Rutgers University Press, 1994.

Johnson, Robert K. *Francis Ford Coppola*. Boston: Twayne, 1977.

Kagan, Norman. *American Skeptic: Robert Altman's Genre-Commentary Films*. Ann Arbor, Mich.: Pierian, 1982.

———. *The Cinema of Stanley Kubrick*. New exp. ed. New York: Continuum, 1989.

Karp, Alan. *The Films of Robert Altman*. Metuchen, N.J.: Scarecrow, 1981.

Kast, Judith. *Robert Altman: American Innovator*. New York: Popular Library, 1978.

Kaufman, Andy, ed. *Steven Soderbergh: Interviews*. Jackson: University Press of Mississippi, 2002.

Kerr, Paul, ed. *The Hollywood Film Industry*. London: British Film Institute, 1986.

King, Geoff. *Spectacular Narratives: Hollywood in the Age of the Blockbuster*. London: Tauris, 2000.

Kipen, David M., ed. *Film Producers, Studios, Agents and Casting Directors Guide*. 4th ed. Los Angeles: Lone Eagle, 1994.

Kline, Sally, ed. *George Lucas: Interviews*. Jackson: University Press of Mississippi, 1999.

Knapp, Laurence F., ed. *Brian De Palma: Interviews*. University Press of Mississippi, 2003.

Kolker, Robert Phillip. *A Cinema of Loneliness: Penn,* *Kubrick, Coppola, Scorsese, Altman*. 3rd ed. New York: Oxford University Press, 2000.

Koszarski, Richard, ed. *Hollywood Directors, 1941–1976*. New York: Oxford University Press, 1977.

Kramer, Peter. *The Big Picture: Hollywood Cinema from "Star Wars" to "Titanic."* London: British Film Institute, 2000.

Krutnick, Frank, ed. *Hollywood Comedians, the Film Reader*. London: Routledge, 2003.

Lanning, Michael Lee. *Vietnam at the Movies*. New York: Fawcett Columbine, 1994.

Lardner, James. *Fast Forward: Hollywood, the Japanese, and the VCR Wars*. New York: Norton, 1987.

Leitch, Thomas. "The World According to Teenpix." *Literature and Film Quarterly* 20, no. 1 (January 1992): 43–48.

Lev, Peter. *American Films of the '70s: Conflicting Visions*. Austin: University of Texas Press, 2000.

Levine, Josh. *The Coen Brothers: The Story of Two American Filmmakers*. Toronto: ECW, 2000.

Lewis, Jon. *Whom God Wishes to Destroy: Francis Ford Coppola and Hollywood*. Durham, N.C.: Duke University Press, 1995.

———, ed. *The New American Cinema*. Durham, N.C.: Duke University Press, 1998.

———. *Hollywood v. Hard Core: How the Struggle over Censorship Saved the Modern Film Industry*. New York: New York University Press, 2000.

———, ed. *The End of Cinema as We Know It: American Films in the Nineties*. New York: New York University Press, 2001.

LoBrutto, Vincent. *Selected Takes: Film Editors on Editing*. New York: Praeger, 1991.

———. *By Design: Interviews with Film Production Designers*. New York: Praeger, 1992.

Luhr, William, ed. *World Cinema since 1945*. New York: Ungar, 1987.

Lyman, Rick. "Revolt in the Den: DVD Has the VCR Headed to the Attic." *New York Times* (September 26, 2002): A1, A3.

McCarty, John. *Splatter Movies: Breaking the Last Taboo*. Albany, N.Y.: FantaCo, 1981.

———. *Psychos: Eighty Years of Mad Movies, Maniacs, and Murderous Deeds*. New York: St. Martin's, 1986.

———. *The Modern Horror Film: 50 Contemporary Classics*. New York: Citadel, 1990.

McClintock, David M. *Indecent Exposure: A True Story of Hollywood and Wall Street*. New York: Morrow, 1982.

McGilligan, Patrick. *Robert Altman: Jumping off the Cliff: A Biography of the Great American Director*. New York: St. Martin's, 1989.

McKinney, Doug. *Sam Peckinpah*. Boston: Twayne, 1979.

Madsen, Axel. *The New Hollywood*. New York: Crowell, 1975.

Martin, Richard. *Mean Streets and Raging Bulls: The Legacy of Film Noir in Contemporary Cinema*. Lanham, Md.: Scarecrow, 1997.

Miller, Toby; Nitin Govil; John McMurria; and Richard Maxwell, eds. *Global Hollywood*. London: British Film Institute, 2001.

Monaco, James. *American Film Now: The People, the Power, the Money, the Movies*. New York: Oxford University Press, 1979.

Monaco, Paul. *The Sixties, 1960–1969: History of the American Cinema*. Vol. 8. New York: Scribner's, 2001.

Mottram, James. *The Coen Brothers: The Life of the Mind*. Dulles, Va.: Brassey's, 2000.

Musun, Chris. *The Marketing of Motion Pictures*. Los Angeles: Musun, 1969.

Neale, Steve, ed. *Genre and Contemporary Hollywood*. London: British Film Institute, 2002.

Neale, Steve, and Murray Smith, eds. *Contemporary Hollywood Cinema*. London: Routledge, 1998.

Nelson, Thomas Allen. *Kubrick: Inside a Film Artist's Maze*. Bloomington: Indiana University Press, 1982.

Newman, Kim. *Nightmare Movies: A Critical Guide to Contemporary Horror Films*. New York: Harmony, 1988.

———, ed. *Science Fiction/Horror: A Sight and Sound Reader*. London: British Film Institute, 2002.

Notbohm, Brent, and Lester D. Friedman, eds. *Steven Spielberg: Interviews*. Jackson: University Press of Mississippi, 2000.

"Oliver Stone as Cinematic Historian: Part 1." Special issue of *Film and History* 28, nos. 1–2 (1998).

"Oliver Stone as Cinematic Historian: Part 2." Special issue of *Film and History* 28, nos. 3–4 (1998).

Palmer, William J. *The Films of the Eighties: A Social History*. Carbondale: Southern Illinois University Press, 1993.

Paul, William. "Hollywood Harakiri." *Film Comment* 13, no. 2 (March–April 1977): 40–43, 56–62.

———. *Laughing Screaming: Modern Hollywood Horror and Comedy*. New York: Columbia University Press, 1994.

Peary, Gerald, ed. *Quentin Tarantino: Interviews*. Jackson: University Press of Mississippi, 1998.

Perren, Alisa. "Sex, Lies and Marketing: Miramax and the Development of the Quality Indie Blockbuster." *Film Quarterly* 55, no. 2 (2001): 30–38.

Phillips, Gene D. *Stanley Kubrick: Interviews*. Jackson: University Press of Mississippi, 2001.

Pierson, John. *Spike, Mike, Slackers and Dykes: A Guided Tour across a Decade of American Independent Cinema*. New York: Miramax/Hyperion, 1995.

Plecki, Gerard. *Robert Altman*. Boston: Twayne, 1985.

Prince, Stephen. *Savage Cinema: Sam Peckinpah and the Rise of Ultraviolent Movies*. Austin: University of Texas Press, 1998.

———. "Graphic Violence in the Cinema: Origins, Aesthetic Design, and Social Effects." In Prince, ed., *Screening Violence*, pp. 1–44.

———. *A New Pot of Gold: Hollywood under the Electronic Rainbow, 1980–1989*. Vol. 10 of *History of the American Cinema*. New York: Scribner's, 2000.

———, ed. *Screening Violence*. New Brunswick, N.J.: Rutgers University Press, 2000.

Prindle, David F. *Risky Business: The Political Economy of Hollywood*. Boulder: Westview, 1993.

Pye, Michael, and Lina Miles. *The Movie Brats: How the Film Generation Took Over Hollywood*. New York: Holt, Rinehart, & Winston, 1979.

Quart, Barbara Koenig. *Women Directors: The Emergence of a New Cinema*. Westport, Conn.: Praeger, 1988.

Quart, Leonard, and Albert Auster. *American Film and Society since 1945*. 2nd ed., rev. and exp. Leonard Quart. New York: Praeger, 1991.

Quirke, Antonia. *Jaws*. London: British Film Institute, 2002.

Reynolds, Christopher. *Hollywood Power Stats*. Valley Village, Calif.: Cineview, 1993.

Roberts, Kenneth H., and Win Sharples, Jr. *A Primer for Film-Making*. New York: Pegasus, 1971.

Rowe, John Carlos, and Rick Berg. *The Vietnam War and American Culture*. New York: Columbia University Press, 1991.

Russell, Carolyn R. *The Films of Joel and Ethan Coen*. Jefferson, N.C.: McFarland, 2001.

Sadoul, Georges. *Dictionary of Films*. Trans. and ed. Peter Morris. Berkeley: University of California Press, 1972.

Samuelson, David. *David Samuelson's "Hands-On" Manual for Cinematographers*. London: Focal, 1994.

Sanello, Frank. *Spielberg: The Man, the Movies, the Mythology*. Dallas: Taylor, 1996.

Sarris, Andrew. "After *The Graduate*." *American Film* 3, no. 9 (July–August 1978): 32–37.

Self, Robert T. *Robert Altman's Subliminal Reality*. Minneapolis: University of Minnesota Press, 2002.

Seydor, Paul. *Peckinpah: The Western Films*. Urbana: University of Illinois Press, 1980.

———. *Peckinpah: The Western Films: Reconsideration*. Urbana: University of Illinois Press, 1999.

Shary, Timothy. *Generation Multiplex: The Image of Youth in Contemporary American Cinema*. Austin: University of Texas Press, 2002.

Silet, Charles L. P., ed. *Oliver Stone: Interviews*. Jackson: University Press of Mississippi, 2001.

Silva, Fred, et al., eds. *Film Literature Index*. Vols. 1–5: 1973–77. New York: Bowker, 1975–79.

Silverman, Stephen M. *The Fox That Got Away: The Last Days of the Zanuck Dynasty at Twentieth Century–Fox*. Secaucus, N.J.: Lyle Stewart, 1988.

Simonet, Thomas. "Market Research: Beyond the Fanny of the Cohn." *Film Comment* 16, no. 1 (January–February 1980): 66–69.

———. "Conglomerates and Content: Remakes, Sequels, and Series in the New Hollywood." In Austin, ed., *Current Research in Film*, 3: pp. 154–62.

Singer, Michael. *Film Directors: A Complete Guide*. 10th internat. ed. Los Angeles: Lone Eagle, 1993.

Sklar, Robert. *Movie-Made America: A Cultural History of the American Movies*. Rev. upd. ed. New York: Vintage, 1994.

Slocum, J. David, ed. *Violence and American Cinema*. London: Routledge, 2000.

Smith, Julian. *Looking Away: Hollywood and Vietnam*. New York: Scribner's, 1975.

Soderbergh, Steven, and Richard Lester. *Getting Away with It; Or, The Further Adventures of the Luckiest Bastard You Ever Saw*. London: Faber & Faber, 2000.

"Sound and Cinema." Special issue of *Film Journal International* 100, no. 9 (October 1997).

Stern, Lesley. *The Scorsese Connection*. London: British Film Institute, 1996.

Sterritt, David, ed. *Robert Altman: Interviews*. Jackson: University Press of Mississippi, 2000.

Steven, Peter, ed. *Jump Cut: Hollywood, Politics and Counter Cinema*. New York: Praeger, 1985.

Stockly, Ed, ed. *Cinematographers, Production Designers, Costume Designers, and Film Editors*. 4th ed. Los Angeles: Lone Eagle, 1993.

Stringer, Julian, ed. *Movie Blockbusters*. London: Routledge, 2003.

Telotte, J. P. *The Cult Film Experience: Beyond All Reason*. Austin: University of Texas Press, 1991.

Thomas, Nicholas, ed. *The International Dictionary of Films and Filmmakers*. Vol. 1. *Films*. 2nd ed. Chicago: St. James, 1990.

Thompson, David, and Ian Christie, ed. *Scorsese on Scorsese*. London: Faber & Faber, 1996.

Toeplitz, Jerzy. *Hollywood and After: The Changing Face of Movies in America*. Trans. Boleslaw Sulik. Chicago: Regnery, 1974.

Turan, Kenneth. *Sundance to Sarajevo: Film Festivals and the World They Made*. Berkeley: University of California Press, 2002.

Valenti, Jack. "Statement by Jack Valenti, MPAA President, before the National Commission on the Causes and Prevention of Violence." In Prince, ed., *Screening Violence*, pp. 62–75. Statement issued by Jack Valenti on December 19, 1968, on the 1966 Production Code and *Bonnie and Clyde*.

Wake, Sandra, ed. *The "Bonnie and Clyde" Book*. London: Lorrimer, 1972.

Walker, Alexander. *Stanley Kubrick Directs*. New York: Harcourt Brace Jovanovich, 1971.

Waller, Gregory. *American Horrors: Essays on the Modern American Horror Films*. Urbana: University of Illinois Press, 1987.

Walsh, Michael. "National Cinema, National Imaginary." *Film History* 8, no. 1 (Spring 1996): 5–17.

Wasko, Janet. *Hollywood in the Information Age*. Austin: University of Texas Press, 1995.

Wasser, Frederick. *Veni, Vidi, Video: The Hollywood Empire and the VCR*. Austin: University of Texas Press, 2002.

Weddle, David. *"If They Move . . . Kill 'Em!": The Life and Times of Sam Peckinpah*. New York: Grove, 1994.

Wexman, Virginia Wright, and Gretchen Bisplinghoff. *Robert Altman: A Guide to Reference and Research*. Boston: Hall, 1984.

White, Armond. "Kidpix." *Film Comment* 21, no. 4 (August 1985): 9–16.

Wood, Aylish. *Technoscience in Contemporary American Film*. Manchester, Eng.: Manchester University Press, 2002.

Wood, Robin. *Arthur Penn*. New York: Praeger, 1969.

Woods, Paul, ed. *Joel & Ethan Coen: Blood Siblings*. London: Plexus, 2000.

Wyatt, Justin. *High Concept: Movies and Marketing in Hollywood*. Austin: University of Texas Press, 1994.

Yule, Andrew. *Fast Fade: David Puttnam, Columbia Pictures, and the Battle for Hollywood*. New York: Delacorte, 1989.

Zucker, Joel S. *Arthur Penn: A Guide to References and Resources*. Boston: Hall, 1980.

CHAPTER 21. HOLLYWOOD ENTERS THE DIGITAL DOMAIN

Aberly, Rachel. *The Making of "Godzilla."* New York: HarperPrism, 1998.

Baker, Christopher W. *How Did They Do It?: Computer Illusion in Film and TV*. Indianapolis: Alpha, 1994.

Baker, Robin. "Computer Technology and Special Effects in Contemporary Cinema." In Hayward and Wollen, eds., *Future Visions*, pp. 31–45.

Barclay, Steven. *The Motion Picture Image: From Film to Digital*. Boston: Focal, 2000.

Beachman, Frank. "Digital Post Begets Digital Field Recording." *American Cinematographer* 75, no. 9 (September 1994): 77–78.

Billups, Scott. "The Power of Plug-Ins." *Moviemaker* 48, no. 9 (Fall 2002): 56–58.

Bizony, Piers. *Digital Domain: The Leading Edge of Visual Effects*. New York: Billboard, 2001.

Boal, Iain A. "In the Tracks of *Jurassic Park*: Phil Tippett Interviewed by Iain A. Boal." In Brook and Boal, eds., *Resisting the Virtual Life*, pp. 253–62.

Bouzereau, Laurent, and Jody Duncan. *"Star Wars": The Making of "Episode I: The Phantom Menace."* New York: Ballantine, 1999.

Brawn, David. *"The Lord of the Rings: The Two Towers":* *Creatures.* Boston: Houghton Mifflin, 2002.

Bresman, Jonathan. *The Art of "Star Wars, Episode I: The Phantom Menace."* New York: Del Rey, 1999.

Brinkmann, Ron. *The Art and Science of Digital Compositing.* San Diego: Morgan Kaufmann, 1999.

Brook, James, and Iain A. Boal, eds. *Resisting the Virtual Life: The Culture and Politics of Information.* San Francisco: City Lights, 1995.

Buckland, Warren. "Between Science Fact and Science Fiction: Spielberg's Digital Dinosaurs, Possible Worlds and the New Aesthetic Realism." *Screen* 40, no. 2 (1999): 177–92.

Bukatman, Scott. *Matters of Gravity: Special Effects and Supermen in the Twentieth Century.* Durham, N.C.: Duke University Press, 2003.

Bulluck, Vic, and Valerie Hoffman. *The Art of "The Empire Strikes Back."* Ed. Deborah Call. New York: Ballantine, 1997.

Cameron, James. "Effects Scene: Technology and Magic." *Cinefex* 51 (August 1992): 5–7.

Carringer, Robert L. *The Making of "Citizen Kane."* Berkeley: University of California Press, 1985.

Conner, Doug. "Morphing Brings Computer-Generated Images to Life. Software Smoothly Transforms One Image to Another." *EDN* 38, no. 26 (December 23, 1993): 66–68.

Cooper, Gary. *The Art of Digital Filmmaking.* London: Allworth, 2002.

Craig, J. R. "Establishing New Boundaries for Special Effects: Robert Zemeckis's *Contact* and Computer-Generated Imagery." *Journal of Popular Film and Television* 28, no. 4 (2001): 158–65.

Creed, Barbara. "The Cyberstar: Digital Pleasures and the End of the Unconscious." *Screen* 41, no. 1 (2000): 79–86.

Crisafulli, Chuck. "The Mask." *Cinefantastique* 25, no. 4 (August 1994): 8–11.

Crogan, Patrick. "Things Analog and Digital." *Senses of Cinema: An Online Film Journal Devoted to the Serious and Eclectic Discussion of Cinema* 5 (April 2000): http://www.sensesofcinema.com.

Cubitt, Sean. *Digital Aesthetics.* London: Sage, 1998.

———. "Le réel, c'est l'impossible: The Sublime Time of Special Effects." *Screen* 4, no. 2 (Summer 1999): 123–30.

———. "Phalke, Méliès, and Special Effects Today." *Wide Angle* 21, no. 1 (1999): 115–30.

Daly, James, ed. "Hollywood 2.0 Special Report: The People Who Are Reinventing Entertainment." *Wired* 5, no. 11 (November 1997): 200–15.

Darley, Andrew. "From Abstraction to Simulation: Notes on the History of Computer Imaging." In Hayward, ed., *Culture, Technology and Creativity in the Late Twentieth Century,* pp. 39–64.

———. *Visual Digital Culture: Surface Play and Spectacle in New Media Genres.* London: Routledge, 2000.

de Leeuw, Ben. *Digital Cinematography.* Boston: AP Professional, 1997.

"Digital Image, Digital Cinema." Special supplement of *Leonardo* (1990).

"Digitality and the Memory of Cinema." Special issue of *Wide Angle* 21, no. 1 (1999).

Dixon, Wheeler Winston. "The Digital Domain: Some Preliminary Notes on Image Mesh and Manipulation in Hyperreal Cinema/Video." *Film Criticism* 20, nos. 1–2 (Fall 1995–Winter 1996): 55–66.

Doherty, Thomas. "*The Abyss:* James Cameron's Magnum Opus, a Mature Work, Splendid to Behold." *Cinefantastique* 20, no. 3 (January 1990): 32–34.

———. "*Jurassic Park:* Steven Spielberg Launches the Unfolding of a Whole New Communications Revolution." *Cinefantastique* 24, no. 5 (December 1993): 52–58.

Dooley, Michael. "Memoirs of a Digital Man; or, Inside ILM." *Print* 46, no. 3 (May–June 1992): 74–83.

Dormer, Peter, ed. *The Culture of Craft: Status and Future.* Manchester, Eng.: Manchester University Press, 1997.

Druckrey, Timothy, ed. *Electronic Culture: Technology and Visual Representation.* New York: Aperture, 1996.

Duncan, Jody. *The Making of "The Lost World."* New York: Ballantine, 1997.

———. "Movie War." *Cinefex* 86 (July 2001): 64–95.

Duncan, Jody, and Don Shay. *The Making of "Jurassic Park."* New York: Ballantine, 1993.

Eby, Douglas. "*MIB* The Aliens: Rubber vs. CGI." *Cinefantastique* 29, no. 1 (July 1997): 23–25.

Elsaesser, Thomas, and Kay Hoffman, eds. *Cinema Futures: Cain, Abel or Cable?* Amersterdam, the Neth.: Amsterdam University Press, 1998.

Everett, Anna, and John T. Caldwell, eds. *New Media: Theories and Practices of Digitextuality.* London: Routledge, 2003.

Faden, Eric S. "The Cyberfilm: Hollywood and Computer Technology." *Strategies* 14, no. 1 (2001): 77–90.

Fangmeier, Stefan. "Designing Digital Tornados—How the Artists and Designers at Industrial Light & Magic Overcame the Many Challenges They Encountered When Creating *Twister*'s Tornados." *Computer Graphics World* 19, no. 8 (1996): 58–62.

Feeney, Ray; Chuck Spaulding; and Kevin Mullican. "The Visual Effects Industry Needs a New Production Model: Why *Titanic* is the *2001* of Our Time." *Millimeter* 26, no. 11 (November 1998): 65–71.

Fischer, Dennis K. "The Last Starfighter." *Cinefantastique* 15, no. 1 (January 1985): 24–36.

———. "The Making of *The Matrix*." *Cinefantastique* 31, no. 5 (May 1999): 16–18.

French, Lawrence. "*Toy Story:* Disney and Pixar Launch First CGI Animated Feature." *Cinefantastique* 26–27, no. 6 (October 1995): 8–9, 125.

"FX, CGI, and the Question of Spectacle." Special issue of *Screen* 40, no. 2 (1999).

Goldman, Michael. "Expanding the *X-Files: X-Files* Film Uses Pyro, Prosthetics, Models, and CGI. *Millimeter* 26, no. 7 (July 1998): 75–80.

Goulekas, Karen E. *Visual Effects in a Digital World: A Comprehensive Glossary of over 7,000 Visual Effects Terms*. San Diego: Morgan Kaufmann, 2001.

Gross, Edward, with Mark A. Altman et al. *The Making of the Trek Films*. London: Boxtree, 1995.

Grossman, Wendy. "Taking Effect: IL&M Is the Award Winning Company that Pioneered Special Cinematic Effects Using Computer Algorithms. Wendy M. Grossman Heard Its Chief Animator Talk about His Methods and a Future 'Generation' of Digital Actors." *Personal Computer World* 16, no. 3 (March 1993): 324–28.

Hayward, Philip, ed. *Culture, Technology, and Creativity in the Late Twentieth Century*. London: Libbey, 1990.

Hayward, Philip, and Tana Wollen, eds. *Future Visions: New Technologies of the Screen*. London: British Film Institute, 1993.

Heard, Christopher. *Dreaming Aloud: The Life and Films of James Cameron*. Toronto: Doubleday Canada, 1997.

Hess, John, and Patricia R. Zimmermann. "Transnational Digital Imaginaries." *Wide Angle* 21, no. 1 (1999): 149–67.

Hollander, Judd, and Sue Feinberg. "Men in Black." *Cinefantastique* 29, no. 1 (July 1997): 16–31.

Horn, John. "The Road to Pearl Harbor." *Newsweek* 137, no. 20 (May 14, 2001): 44–51.

Hurley, James. "Titanic Allegories: The Blockbuster as Art Film." *Strategies: Journal of Theory, Culture and Politics* 14, no. 1 (2001): 91–120.

Jacob, Oren. "Pixar: Computer Graphics Story—a Personal Overview of Computer Animation in the Movies." *Computer Graphics* 31, no. 1 (February 1997): 26–28.

Jones, Karen R. "*Mars Attacks!*" *The Art of the Movie*. New York: Ballantine, 1996.

Kelly, Doug. *Digital Compositing in Depth*. Scotsdale, Ariz: Coriolis, 2000.

Kelly, Kevin, and Paula Parisi. "Beyond *Star Wars*." *Wired* 5, no. 2 (February 1997): 160–66, 210–17.

Kent, Steven, ed. *The Making of "Final Fantasy: The Spirits Within."* Indianapolis: Brady, 2001.

Kerlow, Isaac Victor. *The Art of 3-D: Computer Animation and Imaging*. 2nd ed. New York: Wiley, 2000.

Krebs, Joseph. "15 Minutes with *Moulin Rouge* Director Baz Luhrmann." *Sound and Vision* 17, no. 98 (May 2002): 17, 98.

Laing, Gordon. "The State of the Art: The Making of CGI Movies." *Personal Computer World* 24, no. 11 (November 2001): 168–74.

Lamm, Spencer, ed. *The Art of "The Matrix."* New York: Newmarket, 2000.

Landau, Diana, ed. *"The Gladiator": The Making of the Ridley Scott Epic*. New York: Newmarket, 2000.

Lasseter, John, and Steve Daly. *"Toy Story": The Art and Making of the Animated Film*. New York: Hyperion, 1995.

Luhrmann, Baz; Sue Adler; and Miro Bilbrough. *"Moulin Rouge": The Splendid Illustrated Book That Charts the Journey of Baz Luhrmann's Motion Picture*. New York: Newmarket, 2001.

Lunenfeld, Peter, ed. *The Digital Dialectic: New Essays on New Media*. Cambridge, Mass.: MIT Press, 1999.

Luther, Arch C. *Principles of Digital Audio and Video*. Boston: Artech House, 1997.

Lyons, Mike. "*ID4* Visual Effects: Supervisors Doug Smith and Volker Engel on Fashioning Alien Armageddon." *Cinefantastique* 27, nos. 11–12 (July 1996): 14–15.

McClean, Shilo T. *So What's This All about Then?: A Non-User's Guide to Digital Effects in Filmmaking*. North Ryde, N.S.W., Australia: Australian Film, Television and Radio School, 1998.

Magid, Ron. "The Director Surfaces: Up from the Abyss." *Cinefantastique* 20, no. 5 (May 1990): 32–33.

———. "Blood on the Beach." *American Cinematographer* 79, no. 12 (December 1998): 56–66.

———. "Effects Jedi." *American Cinematographer* 80, no. 9 (September 1999): 78–81.

———. "Virtual Realities." *American Cinematographer* 80, no. 9 (September 1999): 82–83.

———. "Earning Their Wings: Crack Aerial Cameramen Take Flight for *Pearl Harbor*." *American Cinematographer* 82, no. 5 (May 2001): 50–57.

———. "Allied Powers." *American Cinematographer* 82, no. 8 (August 2001): 68–74.

———. "Lord of the Realm." *American Cinematographer* 82, no. 12 (December 2001): 52–59.

Manovich, Lev. "What Is Digital Cinema?" *Blimp* 37 (1997): 29–38. Repr. in Lunenfeld, ed., *The Digital Dialectic*, pp. 172–96.

———. *The Language of New Media*. Cambridge, Mass.: MIT Press, 2001.

Marchese, Francis T., ed. *Understanding Images: Finding Meaning in Digital Imagery*. Santa Clara, Calif.: TELOS, 1995.

Masson, Terrence. *CG 101: A Computer Graphics Industry Reference*. Indianapolis: New Riders, 1999.

Monaco, James. *The Dictionary of New Media: The New Digital World—Video, Audio, Print, DVD, Home Theatre, Satellite, Digital Photography, Wireless, Super CD, Internet.* New York: Harbor Electronic, 2000.

Moszkowicz, Julia. "To Infinity and Beyond: Assessing the Technological Imperative in Computer Animation." *Screen* 43, no. 3 (Autumn 2002): 293–314.

Murdock, Andrew, and Rachel Aberly. *The Making of "Alien Resurrection."* New York: HarperPrism, 1997.

Myerson, Jeremy. "Tornadoes, T-Squares and Technology: Can Computing Be a Craft?" In Dormer, ed., *The Culture of Craft,* pp. 176–86.

Nathan, Ian. "It Is a Dark Time for the Rebellion." *Lord of the Rings Collectors' Edition* of *Empire* 163 (January 2003): 101–37.

Ndalianis, Angela. "The Frenzy of the Visible: Spectacle and Motion in the Era of the Digital." *Senses of Cinema: An Online Film Journal Devoted to the Serious and Eclectic Discussion of Cinema* 3 (February 2000): http://www.sensesofcinema.com.

———. "Special Effects, Morphing Magic, and the Nineties' Cinema of Attractions." In Sobchack, ed., *Meta-Morphing,* pp. 251–71.

Netzley, Patricia D. *Encyclopedia of Movie Special Effects.* New York: Checkmark, 2001.

Ohanian, Thomas A., and Michael E. Phillips. *Digital Filmmaking: The Changing Art and Craft of Making Motion Pictures.* 2nd ed. Boston: Focal, 2000.

Ostrover, Lisa. "Step by Step: Monkey Business—Monkey See, ILM Do: How Industrial Light & Magic Built *Jumanji's* Rampaging CGI Primates." *Millimeter* 24, no. 2 (February 1, 1996): 92–93.

Parisi, Paula. "The New Hollywood Silicon Stars." *Wired* 3, no. 12 (December 1995): 142–45, 202–10.

———. "Cameron Angle: *The Abyss, Terminator 2, True Lies*—James Cameron's Films Are the Milestones by Which We Measure the Development of the Silicon Cinema. Paula Parisi Talks with Him about What Comes Next." *Wired* 4, no. 4 (1996): 130–35, 175–79.

———. *"Titanic" and the Making of James Cameron: The Inside Story of the Three Year Adventure That Rewrote Motion Picture History.* London: Orion, 1998.

Persons, Dan. "*Casper:* Amblin Owns Memorial Day with Another CGI Blast from '50s Animation Past." *Cinefantastique* 26, no. 4 (June 1995): 14–15, 61.

———. "*Starship Troopers:* Sony Imageworks, Taking the Troopers to Outer Space." *Cinefantastique* 28, no. 8 (December 1997): 24–25, 60.

Pierson, Michele. "CGI Effects in Hollywood Science-Fiction Cinema 1989–1995: The Wonder Years." *Screen* 40, no. 2 (1999): 158–76. Repr. in Pierson, *Special Effects,* pp. 93–136.

———. "No Longer State-of-the-Art: Crafting a Future for CGI." *Wide Angle* 21, no. 1 (2001): 29–47. Repr. in Pierson, *Special Effects,* pp. 137–58.

———. *Special Effects: Still in Search of Wonder.* New York: Columbia University Press, 2002.

Prince, Stephen. "True Lies: Perceptual Realism, Digital Images, and Film Theory." *Film Quarterly* 49, no. 3 (Spring 1996): 27–37.

Probst, Christopher. "One Nation under Siege: *Pearl Harbor* Revisits the Infamous Day." *American Cinematographer* 82, no. 5 (May 2001): 36–49.

Prokop, Tim. "*Stargate:* CGI Effects." *Cinefantastique* 26, no. 3 (April 1995): 50–51.

Rickitt, Richard. *Special Effects: The History and Technique.* New York: Billboard, 2000.

Robertson, Barbara. "Dinosaur Magic." *Computer Graphics World* 16, no. 9 (September 1993): 44–52.

———. "Real Troopers: As the 218 Shots in *Starship Troopers* Will Attest, Tippet Studio Has Completed Its Transition from Traditional Stop-Motion Animation to CG." *Computer Graphics World* 20, no. 9 (September 1997): 26–29, 33–34.

———. "Right on Track: Commercial 3D Camera-Tracking Software Is Helping Animators Deal with the Complexities of Merging 3D Animation into Live-Action Footage." *Computer Graphics World* 21, no. 5 (1998): 54–58.

———. "War Effort: Digital Planes, Ships, Smoke, and Sailors Crafted at ILM Help Create Realistic WWII Battle Scenes in the Movie *Pearl Harbor.*" *Computer Graphics World* 24, no. 6 (2001): 22–29.

———. "*The Fellowship of the Ring*—More Than a Little Digital Wizardry Was Required to Bring J. R. R. Tolkien's Fantastical Saga to the Silver Screen." *Computer Graphics World* 24, no. 12 (2001): 18–24.

Robley, Les Paul. "CGI on a Shoestring Budget." *American Cinematographer* 75, no. 7 (July 1994): 70–76.

———. "CGI on a Shoestring Budget, Part II." *American Cinematographer* 75, no. 9 (September 1994): 70–76.

———. "CGI on a Shoestring, Part III." *American Cinematographer* 75, no. 11 (November 1994): 26–32.

———. "Low-Budget Magic." *Cinefantastique* 26, no. 4 (June 1995): 40–42, 61.

Rogers, Pauline B. *The Art of Visual Effects: Interviews on the Tools of the Trade.* Boston: Focal, 1999.

Rogin, Michael. *"Independence Day"; Or, How I Learned to Stop Worrying and Love the Enola Gay.* London: British Film Institute, 1998.

Ryfle, Steve. "A Tale of Two Godzillas." *Cinefantastique* 30, no. 2 (June 1998): 13, 61.

Sammon, Paul M. *The Making of "Starship Troopers."* New York: Boulevard, 1997.

———. "Bug Bytes." *Cinefex* 73 (March 1998): 66–91.

Sandler, Kevin S., and Gaylyn Studler, eds. *"Titanic": Anatomy of a Blockbuster.* New Brunswick, N.J.: Rutgers University Press, 1999.

Shay, Don. "Thirty Minutes with the Godfather of Digital Cinema." *Cinefex* 65 (March 1996): 58–67.

Sibley, Brian. *"The Lord of the Rings" Official Movie Guide.* Boston: Houghton Mifflin, 2001.

———. *"The Lord of the Rings": The Making of the Movie Trilogy.* Boston: Houghton Mifflin, 2002.

Smith, Thomas G. *Industrial Light and Magic: The Art of Special Effects.* New York: Ballantine, 1986.

Sobchack, Vivian, ed. *Meta-Morphing: Visual Transformation and the Culture of Quick-Change.* Minneapolis: University of Minnesota Press, 2000.

Spielmann, Yvonne. "Aesthetic Features in Digital Imaging: Collage and Morph." *Wide Angle* 21, no. 1 (January 1999): 131–48.

———. "Expanding Film into Digital Media." *Screen* 40, no. 2 (1999): 131–45.

Starship Troopers Official Movie Magazine. New York: Starlog Communications International, 1997.

Stecker-Orel, Elinor. *Special Effects Photography Handbook.* Buffalo, N.Y.: Amherst Media, 1998.

Street, Rita. *Computer Animation: A Whole New World.* Rockport, Mass.: Rockport, 1998.

Telotte, J. P. "Verhoeven, Virilio, and 'Cinematic Derealization.'" *Film Quarterly* 53, no. 2 (Winter 1999–2000): 30–38.

———. "Heinlen, Verhoeven, and the Problem of the Real: *Starship Troopers.*" *Literature/Film Quarterly* 29, no. 3 (2001): 196–202.

Titleman, Carol, ed. *The Art of "Star Wars Episode IV: A New Hope."* New York: Ballantine, 1997.

———. *The Art of "Star Wars Episode VI: Return of the Jedi."* New York: Ballantine, 1997. Includes the complete script by Lawrence Kasdan and George Lucas.

Titleman, Carol; Deborah Call; Valerie Hoffman; and Vic Bullock. *The Art of "Star Wars Episode V: The Empire Strikes Back."* New York: Ballantine, 1996.

Turim, Maureen. "Artisanal Prefigurations of the Digital: Animating Realities, College Effect and Theories of Image Manipulation." *Wide Angle* 21, no. 1 (January 1999): 48–62.

Vaz, Mark Cotta. *Visions of "Armageddon."* New York: Hyperion, 1998.

———. *The Art of "Star Wars Episode II: Attack of the Clones."* New York: Del Ray, 2002. Includes the complete script by George Lucas and Jonat Hales.

Vaz, Mark Cotta, and Craig Barron. *The Invisible Art: The Legends of Movie Matte Painting.* San Francisco: Chronicle, 2002.

Vaz, Mark Cotta, and Patricia Rose Duignan. *Industrial Light & Magic: Into the Digital Realm.* New York: Ballantine, 1996.

Vaz, Mark Cotta, and Shinji Hata. *From "Star Wars" to "Indiana Jones": The Best of the Lucasfilm Archives.* San Francisco: Chronicle, 1994.

Vincenzi, Lisa. "*Star Wars* Revisited: A Facelift for Jabba the Hutt." *Millimeter* 25, no. 2 (February 1997): 74–75.

"Virtual Reality: Venus Return or Vanishing Point." Special issue of *Leonardo* 27, no. 4 (1994).

"Visfx." Special supplement to *Millimeter* 26, no. 9 (September 1998).

Vitaris, Paul. "X-File: Computer Graphics." *Cinefantastique* 26–27, no. 6 (October 1995): 71–72.

Weisher, Peter. *Blue Sky: The Art of Computer Animation Featuring Ice Age and Bunny.* New York: Abrams, 2002.

Wheeler, Paul, *Digital Cinematography.* Boston: Focal, 2001.

Wolff, Ellen. "Animation Attacks!: The Aliens in *Mars Attacks!* Are a Lot Less *ET* Than CGI." *Millimeter* 25, no. 2 (February 1997): 73–74.

———. "*Small Soldiers*, Big Action: ILM's Animation Is No Small Feat." *Millimeter* 26, no. 9 (September 1998): 72–73.

Wright, Steve. *Digital Compositing for Film and Video.* Boston: Focal, 2002.

THEORY AND AESTHETICS

Affron, Charles. *Star Acting.* New York: Dutton, 1977.

———. *Cinema and Sentiment.* Chicago: University of Chicago Press, 1982.

Affron, Charles, and Mirella Jona Affron. *Sets in Motion: Art Direction and Film Narrative.* New Brunswick, N.J.: Rutgers University Press, 1995.

Agee, James. *Agee on Film: Reviews and Comments.* Boston: Beacon, 1964.

Agel, Henri. *Le Cinéma et le sacré.* Paris: Cerf, 1961.

———. *Poétique du cinéma: Manifeste essentialiste.* Paris: Éditions du Signe, 1973.

———. *Le Cinéma, ses diverses méthodes d'enseignement.* Fribourg, Switz.: Éditions Universitaires, 1978.

Aitken, Ian. *European Film Theory and Cinema: A Critical Introduction.* Edinburgh: Edinburgh University Press, 2001.

Allen, Jeanne. "The Film Viewer as Consumer." *Quarterly Review of Film Studies* 5, no. 4 (Fall 1980): 481–99.

Allen, Richard. *Projecting Illusion: Film, Film Theory and the Impression of Reality.* Cambridge, Eng.: Cambridge University Press, 1994.

Allen, Richard, and Murray Smith, eds. *Film Theory and Philosophy*. Oxford: Oxford University Press, 1999.

Allen, Robert C., and Douglas Gomery. *Film History: Theory and Practice*. New York: McGraw-Hill, 1985.

Alpert, Hollis. *The Dreams and the Dreamers*. New York: Macmillan, 1962.

Althusser, Louis. *Lenin and Philosophy, and Other Essays*. Trans. Ben Brewster. London: New Left, 1971.

Altman, Rick. *The American Film Musical*. Bloomington: Indiana University Press, 1987.

———. "Dickens, Griffith, and Film Theory Today." *South Atlantic Quarterly* 88, no. 2 (Spring 1989): 321–59.

———. ed. *Sound Theory/Sound Practice*. New York: Routledge, 1992.

———. *Film/Genre*. London: British Film Institute, 1999.

Amengual, Barthélemy. *Clefs pour le cinéma*. Paris: Seghers, 1971.

"American Widescreen." Special issue of *Velvet Light Trap* 21 (Summer 1985).

Anderson, Perry. *Origins of Postmodernity*. New York: Verso, 1998.

Andrew, J. Dudley. *The Major Film Theories*. New York: Oxford University Press, 1976.

———. *André Bazin*. New York: Oxford University Press, 1978.

———. *Concepts in Film Theory*. New York: Oxford University Press, 1984.

Andrew, J. Dudley, with Sally Shafto, eds. *The Image in Dispute: Art and Cinema in the Age of Photography*. Austin: University of Texas Press, 1997.

Ang, Ien. *Living Room Wars: Rethinking Media Audiences for a Postmodern World*. London: Routledge, 1996.

Aristarco, Guido. *Storia delle teoriche del film*. Turin: Einaudi, 1951.

Armes, Roy. *Film and Reality*. New York: Penguin, 1974.

Arnheim, Rudolf. *Art and Visual Perception: A Psychology of the Creative Eye*. Berkeley: University of California Press, 1954.

———. *Film As Art*. Berkeley: University of California Press, 1957.

———. *Visual Thinking*. Berkeley: University of California Press, 1969.

———. *Film Essays and Criticism*. Comp. Helmut H. Diederichs. Trans. Brenda Benthien. Madison: University of Wisconsin Press, 1997.

Aumont, Jacques. *Montage Eisenstein*. Bloomington: Indiana University Press, 1986.

———. *The Image*. Trans. Claire Pajackowska. London: British Film Institute, 1997.

Aumont, Jacques; Alain Bergala; Michel Marie; and Marc Vernet. *Aesthetics of Film*. Trans. Richard Neupert. Austin: University of Texas Press, 1992.

Aumont, Jacques, and Jean-Louis Leutrat, eds. *La Théorie du film: Colloque de Lyon*. Paris: Albatros, 1980.

Aumont, Jacques, and Michel Marie. *L'Analyse du film*. Paris: Nathan, 1986.

"Auteurism Revisited." Special issue of *Film History* 7, no. 4 (1995).

Ayfre, Amédée. *Le Cinéma et sa vérité*. Paris: Cerf, 1964.

———. *Conversion aux images?* Paris: Cerf, 1964.

———. *Cinéma et mystère*. Paris: Cerf, 1969.

Baird, Robert. " 'The Startle Effect.': Implications for Spectator Cognition and Media Theory." *Film Quarterly* 53, no. 3 (Spring 2000): 13–24.

Bakhtin, Mikhail. *Rabelais and His World*. Trans. Helene Iswolsky. Cambridge, Mass.: MIT Press, 1968.

———. *The Dialogic Imagination: Four Essays*. Ed. Michael Holquist. Trans. Caryl Emerson and Michael Holquist. Austin: University of Texas Press, 1981.

Balázs, Béla. *Theory of the Film: Character and Growth of a New Art*. Trans. Edith Bone. New York: Roy, 1953. Repr. New York: Dover, 1970.

Barker, Martin, with Thomas Austin. *From Antz to Titanic: Reinventing Film Analysis*. London: Pluto, 2000.

Barker, Martin, and Julian Petley, eds. *Ill Effects: The Media/Violence Debate*. 2nd ed. London: Routledge, 2001.

Barr, Charles. "Cinemascope: Before and After." *Film Quarterly* 16, no. 4 (Summer 1963): 4–24.

Barthes, Roland. *Elements of Semiology*. Trans. Annette Laversy and Colin Smith. New York: Hill & Wang, 1967.

———. *Mythologies*. Ed. and trans. Annette Laversy. New York: Hill & Wang, 1972.

———. *S/Z*. Trans. Richard Miller. New York: Hill & Wang, 1974.

———. *The Pleasure of the Text*. Trans. Richard Miller. New York: Hill & Wang, 1975.

———. *Image, Music, Text*. Trans. Stephen Heath. New York: Hill & Wang, 1977.

Bataille, Robert. *Grammaire cinématographique*. Paris: Lefort, 1947.

Battcock, Gregory, ed. *The New American Cinema*. New York: Dutton, 1967.

Baudry, Jean-Louis. "The Apparatus: Metapsychological Approaches to the Impression of Reality in the Cinema." Trans. Jean Andrews and Bertrand Augst. In Rosen, ed., *Narrative, Apparatus, Ideology*, pp. 299–318.

———. "Ideological Effects of the Basic Cinematographic Apparatus." Trans. Alan Williams. In Rosen, ed., *Narrative, Apparatus, Ideology*, pp. 286–98.

Bazelon, Irwin. *Knowing the Score: Notes on Film Music*. New York: Van Nostrand Reinhold, 1972.

Bazin, André. *What Is Cinema?* 2 vols. Selected and trans.

Hugh Gray. Berkeley: University of California Press, 1967, 1971.

Bell-Metereau, Rebecca. *Hollywood Androgyny*. 2nd ed. New York: Columbia University Press, 1993.

Bellour, Raymond. *L'Analyse du film*. Paris: Albatros, 1979.

———. "To Alternate/to Narrate." *Australian Journal of Film Theory* 15/16 (1983): 35–56.

———. *L'Entre-images: Photo, cinéma, vidéo*. Paris: La Différence, 1990.

Belton, John. *Widescreen Cinema*. Cambridge, Mass.: Harvard University Press, 1992.

———, ed. *Movies and Mass Culture*. New Brunswick, N.J.: Rutgers University Press, 1995.

Benjamin, Walter. *Illuminations*. Ed. Hannah Arendt. New York: Harcourt Brace, 1968.

Benveniste, Emile. *Problèmes de linguistique générale*. 2 vols. Paris: Gallimard, 1966.

Berenstein, Rhona. J. *Attack of the Leading Ladies: Gender, Sexuality, and Spectatorship in Classic Horror Cinema*. New York: Columbia University Press, 1996.

Bergala, Alain. *Initiation à la sémiologie du récit en images*. Paris: Cahiers de l'Audiovisuel, 1978.

Bergman, Andrew. *We're in the Money: Depression America and Its Films*. New York: New York University Press, 1971.

Bergstrom, Janet, and Mary Ann Doane. "The Female Spectator: Contexts and Directions." *Camera Obscura* 20–21 (1990): 5–27.

Bernstein, Matthew, and Gaylyn Studlar, eds. *Visions of the East: Orientalism in Film*. New Brunswick, N.J.: Rutgers University Press, 1997.

Berthomieu, André. *Essai de grammaire cinématographique*. Paris: La Nouvelle Édition, 1946.

Bingham, Dennis. *Acting Male: Masculinities in the Films of James Stewart, Jack Nicholson, and Clint Eastwood*. New Brunswick, N.J.: Rutgers University Press, 1994.

Bluestone, George. *Novels into Film*. Baltimore: Johns Hopkins University Press, 1957. Repr. Berkeley: University of California Press, 1966.

Bobker, Lee R. *Elements of Film*. New York: Harcourt Brace, 1969.

Bolter, Jay David, and Richard Grusin. *Remediation: Understanding New Media*. Cambridge, Mass.: MIT Press, 1999.

Bondebjerg, Ib. "Public Discourse/Private Fascination: Hybridization in 'True-Life-Story' Genres." *Media, Culture and Society* 18, no. 1 (1996): 27–45.

———, ed. *Moving Images, Culture and the Mind*. Luton, Eng.: University of Luton Press, 2000.

Bonitzer, Pascal. *Le Regard et la voix: Essais sur le cinéma*. Paris: Union Générale d'Éditions, 1976.

Bordwell, David. "Textual Analysis, Etc." *Enclitic* 5, nos. 2–6, no. 1 (Fall 1981–Spring 1982): 125–36.

———. "Jump Cuts and Blind Spots." *Wide Angle* 6, no. 1 (1984): 4–11.

———. *Narration in the Fiction Film*. Madison: University of Wisconsin Press, 1985.

———. *Making Meaning: Inference and Rhetoric in the Interpretation of Cinema*. Cambridge, Mass.: Harvard University Press, 1989.

———. *On the History of Film Style*. Cambridge, Mass.: Harvard University Press, 1997.

Bordwell, David, and Noël Carroll, eds. *Post-Theory: Reconstructing Film Studies*. Madison: University of Wisconsin Press, 1996.

Bordwell, David, and Kristin Thompson. *Film Art: An Introduction*. 6th ed. New York: McGraw-Hill, 2001.

Brakhage, Stan. *Film Biographies*. Berkeley, Calif.: Turtle Island, 1977.

Branigan, Edward. *Point of View in the Cinema: A Theory of Narration and Subjectivity in Classical Film*. New York: Mouton, 1984.

———. *Narrative Comprehension and Film*. New York: Routledge, 1992.

Braudy, Leo. *The World in a Frame*. 2nd ed. Chicago: University of Chicago Press, 1984.

———. *Native Informant: Essays on Film, Fiction and Popular Culture*. New York: Oxford University Press, 1991.

Brennan, Teresa, and Martin Jay, eds. *Vision in Context: Historical and Contemporary Perspectives on Sight*. New York: Routledge, 1996.

Bresson, Robert. *Notes on Cinematography*. Trans. Jonathan Griffin. New York: Urizen, 1975.

Brooker, Peter. *Cultural Theory: A Glossary*. London: Arnold, 1999.

———. *Modernity and Metropolis: Writing, Film, and Urban Formations*. New York: Palgrave, 2002.

Brooker, Peter, and Will Brooker, eds. *Postmodern Afterimages: A Reader in Film, Television, and Video*. London: Arnold, 1997.

Brown, Royal S. *Overtones and Undertones: Reading Film Music*. Berkeley: University of California Press, 1994.

Browne, Nick. *The Rhetoric of Film Narrative*. Ann Arbor, Mich.: UMI Research Press, 1982.

———, ed. *Refiguring American Film Genres: History and Theory*. Berkeley: University of California Press, 1998.

Brunette, Peter, and David Wills. *Screen/Play: Derrida and Film Theory*. Princeton, N.J.: Princeton University Press, 1989.

Bruzzi, Stella. *Undressing Cinema: Clothing and Identity in the Movies*. London: Routledge, 1997.

Bryson, Norman; Michael Ann Holly; and Keith Moxey, eds. *Visual Culture: Images and Interpretations*. Hanover, N.H.:

University Press of New England/Wesleyan University Press, 1994.

Buckland, Warren, ed. *The Film Spectator: From Sign to Mind*. Amsterdam, the Neth.: Amsterdam University Press, 1995.

Bukatman, Scott. *Terminal Identity: The Virtual Subject in Postmodern Science Fiction*. Durham, N.C.: Duke University Press, 1993.

Burch, Noël. *The Theory of Film Practice*. Trans. Helen R. Lane. New York: Praeger, 1973.

———. "Narrative/Diegesis-Threshold, Limits." *Screen* 23, no. 2 (July–August 1982): 16–33.

———. "Passion, poursuite." *Communications* 38 (1983): 30–50.

———. "Un mode de représentation primitif?" *Iris* 2, no. 1 (1984): 112–23.

———. "Primitivism and the Avant-Gardes: A Dialectical Approach." In Rosen, ed., *Narrative, Apparatus, Ideology*, pp. 483–505.

———. *Life to Those Shadows*. London: British Film Institute, 1990.

Burch, Noël, and Jorge Dana. "Propositions." *Afterimage* 5 (Spring 1974): 40–67.

Burnett, Ron, ed. *Explorations in Film Theory: Selected Essays from Ciné-tracts*. Bloomington: Indiana University Press, 1991.

Buscombe, Edward, ed. *Film Reader 4: Point of View/Metahistory of Film* (1979).

Butler, Jeremy G., ed. *Star Texts: Image and Performance in Film and Television*. Detroit: Wayne State University Press, 1995.

Butler, Judith P. *Bodies That Matter: On the Discursive Limits of "Sex."* New York: Routledge, 1993.

Cahiers du cinéma. "John Ford's Young Mr. Lincoln." *Screen* 13, no. 3 (Autumn 1972): 5–94.

Cameron, Ian, ed. *Movie Reader*. New York: Praeger, 1972.

Carroll, Noël. "Address to the Heathens." *October* 23 (Winter 1982): 89–163.

———. *Mystifying Movies: Fads and Fallacies in Contemporary Film Theory*. New York: Columbia University Press, 1988.

———. *Philosophical Problems of Classical Film Theory*. Princeton, N.J.: Princeton University Press, 1988.

———. *Theorizing the Moving Image*. Cambridge: Cambridge University Press, 1996.

———. *A Philosophy of Mass Art*. Oxford: Clarendon, 1998.

Carson, Diane; Linda Dittmar; and Janice Welsch, eds. *Multiple Voices in Feminist Film Criticism*. Minneapolis: University of Minnesota Press, 1994.

Cartmell, Deborah, et al, eds. *Trash Aesthetics: Popular Culture and Its Audience*. London: Pluto, 1997.

Casebier, Allan. *Film and Phenomenology: Toward a Realist Theory of Cinematic Representation*. New York: Cambridge University Press, 1991.

Caughie, John, ed. *Theories on Authorship*. BFI Series. London: Routledge & Kegan Paul, 1981.

Caughie, John, and Annette Kuhn, eds. *The Sexual Subject: A Screen Reader on Sexuality*. London: Routledge, 1992.

Cavell, Stanley. *The World Viewed: Reflections on the Ontology of Film*. Enl. ed. Cambridge, Mass.: Harvard University Press, 1979.

Cawelti, John. *The Six-Gun Mystique*. Bowling Green, Ohio: Bowling Green Popular Press, 1971.

———. *Adventure, Mystery and Romance: Formula Stories as Art and Popular Culture*. Chicago: University of Chicago Press, 1976.

Charney, Leo. *Empty Moments: Cinema, Modernity, and Drift*. Durham, N.C.: Duke University Press, 1998.

Chatman, Seymour. *Story and Discourse: Narrative Structures in Fiction and Film*. Ithaca, N.Y.: Cornell University Press, 1978.

———. *Coming to Terms: The Rhetoric of Narrative in Fiction and Film*. Ithaca, N.Y.: Cornell University Press, 1990.

Cherchi Usai, Paolo, ed. *Vitagraph Co. of America: Il cinema prima di Hollywood*. Pordenone, Italy: Studio Tesi, 1987.

Chion, Michel. *Audio-Vision: Sound on Screen*. Ed. and trans. Claudia Gorbman. New York: Columbia University Press, 1994.

———. *The Voice in Cinema*. Ed. and trans. Claudia Gorbman. New York: Columbia University Press, 1999.

Chisolm, Ann. "Missing Persons and Bodies of Evidence." *Camera Obscura* 15, no. 1 (2000): 122–61.

"Cinéma militant, Le." Special issue of *Cinéma d'aujourd'hui* (March–April 1976).

Clair, René. *Reflections on the Cinema*. Trans. Vera Traill. London: Kimber, 1953.

Cleto, Fabio, ed. *Camp: Queer Aesthetics and the Performing Subject—a Reader*. Ann Arbor: University of Michigan Press, 1999.

Clover, Carol J. *Men, Women, and Chain Saws: Gender in the Modern Horror Film*. Princeton, N.J.: Princeton University Press, 1992.

Cocteau, Jean. *The Art of Cinema*. Ed. André Bernard and Claude Gauteur. Trans. Robin Buss. London: Boyars, 1992.

Cohan, Steven, and Ina Rae Hark, eds. *Screening the Male: Exploring Masculinities in the Hollywood Cinema*. New York: Routledge, 1993.

Cohen, Keith. "On the Spot, in the Raw: Impressionism and the Cinema." *Film Reader 3* (1978): 150–68.

———. *Film and Fiction: The Dynamics of Exchange*. New Haven, Conn.: Yale University Press, 1979.

Cohen-Séat, Gilbert. *Essai sur les principes d'une philosophie du cinéma*. Paris: Presses Universitaires de France, 1958.

———. *Problèmes du cinéma et de l'information visuelle*. Paris: Presses Universitaires de France, 1961.

Collet, Jean; Michel Marie; Daniel Percheron; Jean-Paul Simon; and March Vernet. *Lectures du film*. Paris: Albatros, 1980.

Collins, Jim; Hilary Radner; and Ava Preacher Collins. *Film Theory Goes to the Movies: Cultural Analysis of Contemporary Film*. AFI Film Readers. New York: Routledge, 1993.

Comolli, Jean Louis. "Technique and Ideology: Camera, Perspective, Depth of Field." *Film Reader 2* (1977): 128–40. Repr. in Nichols, ed., *Movies and Methods* 2: 40–57.

Conley, Tom. *Film Heiroglyphics: Ruptures in Classical Cinema*. Minneapolis: University of Minnesota Press, 1990.

Cook, David A. "Some Structural Approaches to Cinema: A Survey of Models." *Cinema Journal* 14 (Spring 1975): 41–54. Repr. in MacCann and Ellis, eds., *Cinema Examined*, pp. 269–282.

Cook, Pamela, ed. *The Cinema Book*. London: British Film Institute, 1985.

Cook, Pamela, and Philip Dodd, eds. *Women and Film: A Sight and Sound Reader*. Philadelphia: Temple University Press, 1993.

Corrigan, Timothy. *Film and Literature: An Introduction and Reader*. Upper Saddle River, N.J.: Prentice-Hall, 1999.

Cowie, Elizabeth. *Representing the Woman: Cinema and Psychoanalysis*. Minneapolis: University of Minnesota Press, 1997.

Crary, Jonathan. *Techniques of the Observer: On Visions and Modernity in the Nineteenth Century*. Cambridge, Mass.: MIT Press, 1990.

———. *Suspensions of Perception: Attention, Spectacle, and Modern Culture*. Cambridge, Mass.: MIT Press, 1999.

Creed, Barbara. *The Monstrous-Feminine: Film, Feminism, Psychoanalysis*. London: Routledge, 1993.

Creekmur, Corey K., and Alexander Doty, eds. *Out in Culture: Gay, Lesbian, and Queer Essays on Popular Culture*. Durham, N.C.: Duke University Press, 1995.

Cresswell, Tim, and Deborah Dizon, eds. *Engaging Film: Geographies of Mobility and Identity*. Lanham, Md.: Rowman & Littlefield, 2002.

Curtis, David. *Experimental Cinema*. New York: Universal, 1971.

Dalle Vacche, Angela. *Cinema and Painting: How Art Is Used in Film*. Austin: University of Texas Press, 1996.

———, ed. *The Visual Turn: Classical Film Theory and Art History*. New Brunswick, N.J.: Rutgers University Press, 2003.

Dayan, Daniel. "The Tutor-Code of Classical Cinema." *Film Quarterly* 28, no. 1 (Fall 1974): 22–31.

Debord, Guy. *Society of the Spectacle*. Detroit: Black & Red, 1977.

deCordova, Richard. "The Emergence of the Star System in America." *Wide Angle* 6, no. 4 (1985): 4–13.

deCordova, Richard. *Picture Personalities: The Emergence of the Star System in America, 1907–1922*. Urbana: University of Illinois Press, 1990.

de Lauretis, Teresa. *Alice Doesn't: Feminism, Semiotics, Cinema*. Bloomington: Indiana University Press, 1984.

———. *Technologies of Gender*. Bloomington: Indiana University Press, 1987.

De Lauretis, Teresa, and Stephen Heath, eds. *The Cinematic Apparatus*. New York: St. Martin's, 1980.

Deleuze, Gilles. *Cinema*. Trans. Hugh Tomlinson and Barbara Holderjam. 2 vols. Minneapolis: University of Minnesota Press, 1986–89.

Delluc, Louis. *Cinéma et Cie: Confidences d'un spectateur*. Paris: Grasset, 1919.

Denzin, Norman K. *Images of Postmodern Society: Social Theory and Contemporary Cinema*. London: Sage, 1991.

———. *The Cinematic Society: The Voyeur's Gaze*. London: Sage, 1995.

Derrida, Jacques. *Of Grammatology*. Trans. Gayatri Chakravorty Spivak. Baltimore: Johns Hopkins University Press, 1976.

———. *Writing and Difference*. Chicago: University of Chicago Press, 1978.

———. *Dissemination*. Trans. Barbara Johnson. Chicago: University of Chicago Press, 1981.

Deutelbaum, Marshall A., ed. *"Image": On the Art and Evolution of the Film*. New York: Dover, 1979.

Dickinson, Kay, ed. *Movie Music, the Film Reader*. London: Routledge, 2003.

Dickinson, Roger; Olga Linné; and Ramaswami Harindranath, eds. *Approaches to Audiences: A Reader*. London: Arnold, 1998.

"Digitality and the Memory of Cinema." Special issue of *Wide Angle* 21, no. 1 (1999).

Dixon, Wheeler Winston. *The Transparency Spectacle: Meditations on the Moving Image*. Albany: State University of New York Press, 1998.

Doane, Mary Ann. "The Voice in the Cinema: The Articulation of Body and Space." *Yale French Studies* 60 (1980): 33–50.

———. "Film and the Masquerade: Theorizing the Female Spectator." *Screen* 23 (1982): 74–87. Repr. in Mast, Cohen, and Braudy, eds., *Film Theory and Criticism*, pp. 758–72.

———. "The Moving Image." *Wide Angle* 7, nos. 1–2 (1985): 42–58.

———. *The Desire to Desire: The Woman's Film of the 1940s*. Bloomington: Indiana University Press, 1987.

————. *Femmes Fatales: Feminism, Film Theory, Psychoanalysis*. New York: Routledge, 1991.

Doane, Mary Anne; Patricia Mellencamp; and Linda Williams, eds. *Re-Vision: Essays in Feminist Film Criticism*. Frederick, Md.: University Publications of America/American Film Institute, 1984.

Donald, James, ed. *Psychoanalysis and Cultural Theory: Thresholds*. London: Macmillan, 1990.

Doty, Alexander. *Making Things Perfectly Queer: Interpreting Mass Culture*. Minneapolis: University of Minnesota Press, 1993.

————. *Flaming Classics: Queering the Film Cannon*. New York: Routledge, 2000.

Durgnat, Raymond. *Films and Feelings*. Cambridge, Mass.: MIT Press, 1967.

Dyer, Richard. *Stars*. London: British Film Institute, 1979.

————. *Gays and Film*. New York: New York Zoetrope, 1984.

————. *Heavenly Bodies: Film Stars and Society*. Basinstoke, Eng.: Macmillan, 1986.

————. *Now You See It: Studies on Lesbian and Gay Film*. London and New York: Routledge, 1990, 2003.

————. *White*. London: Routledge, 1997.

————. *The Culture of Queers*. London: Routledge, 2002.

————. *The Matter of Images: Essays on Representations*. 2nd ed. London: Routledge, 2002.

————. *Only Entertainment*. 2nd ed. New York: Routledge, 2002.

Eco, Umberto. *The Semiotic Threshhold*. The Hague: Mouton, 1973.

————. *A Theory of Semiotics*. Bloomington: University of Indiana Press, 1976.

————. *Travels in Hyper Reality: Essays*. Trans. William Weaver. San Diego: Harcourt Brace Jovanovich, 1986.

Erlich, Victor. *Russian Formalism: History, Doctrine*. 3rd ed. New Haven, Conn.: Yale University Press, 1981.

Eikhenbaum, Boris. *The Poetics of Cinema*. Trans. Richard Taylor. Russian Poetics in Translation 9. Oxford: RPT, 1982.

Eisenstein, Sergei. *The Film Sense*. Ed. and trans. Jay Leyda. New York: Harcourt Brace & World, 1942.

————. *The Film Form*. Ed. and trans. Jay Leyda. New York: Harcourt Brace & World, 1949.

————. *Film Essays and a Lecture*. Ed. and trans. Jay Leyda. New York: Praeger, 1970.

————. *Notes of a Film Director*. Translated X. Danko. Rev. ed. New York: Dover, 1970.

————. *The Non-Indifferent Nature*. Trans. Herbert Marshall. Cambridge, Eng.: Cambridge University Press, 1987.

————. *The Eisenstein Reader*. Ed. Richard Taylor. Trans. Richard Taylor and William Powell. London: British Film Institute, 1998.

Ellis, John. *Visible Fictions*. London: Routledge & Kegan Paul, 1982.

Elsaesser, Thomas, and Warren Buckland. *Studying Contemporary American Film: A Guide to Movie Analysis*. New York: Oxford University Press, 2002.

Epstein, Jean. *Bonjour, cinéma*. Paris: Éditions de la Sirène, 1921.

————. *Écrits sur le cinéma, 1921–1953*. 2 vols. Paris: Seghers, 1974.

Erens, Patricia, ed. *Issues in Feminist Film Criticism*. Bloomington: Indiana University Press, 1990.

Ewen, Elizabeth. "City Light: Immigrant Women and the Rise of the Movies." Supplement to *Signs* 4, no. 3 (Spring 1980): 45–65.

Farber, Manny. *Negative Space*. New York: Praeger, 1971.

Faure, Elie. *The Art of Cineplastics*. Trans. Walter Pach. Boston: Four Seas, 1923.

Fawell, John. "The Musicality of the Filmscript." *Literature/Film Quarterly* 17, no. 1 (1989): 44–49.

Fell, John L. *Film and the Narrative Tradition*. Norman: University of Oklahoma Press, 1974.

————, ed. *Film before Griffith*. Berkeley: University of California Press, 1983.

Fellemen, Susan. "Dirty Pictures, Mud Lust, and Abject Desire: Myths of Origin and the Cinematic Object." *Film Quarterly* 55, no. 1 (Fall 2001): 27–40. A discussion of the representation of art and artists in film.

Ferguson, Otis. *The Film Criticism of Otis Ferguson*. Ed. Robert Wilson. Philadelphia: Temple University Press, 1971.

Feuer, Jane. *The Hollywood Musical*. 2nd ed. Bloomington: Indiana University Press, 1993.

"Film and Psychoanalysis." Special issue of *Persistence of Vision* 10 (1993).

"Film and Semiotics." Special issue of *Quarterly Review of Film Studies*. 2, no. 1 (Winter 1977).

"Film Genres." Special issue of *Journal of Film and Video* 43, nos. 1–2 (1996).

"Film Music." Special issue of *Cinema Journal* 17, no. 2 (Spring 1978).

Fischer, Lucy. "The Lady Vanishes: Women, Magic and the Movies." *Film Quarterly* 33, no. 1 (Fall 1979): 30–40.

————. *Shot/Countershot: Film Tradition and Women's Cinema*. Princeton, N.J.: Princeton University Press, 1989.

Flaxman, Gregory, ed. *The Brain Is the Screen: Deleuze and the Philosophy of Cinema*. Minneapolis: University of Minnesota Press, 2000.

Fleishman, Avrom. *Narrated Film: Storytelling Situations in Cinema History*. Baltimore: Johns Hopkins University Press, 1992.

Flichy, Patrice. *Les Industries de l'imaginaire: Pour une analyse économique des media*. Grenoble, France: Presses Universitaires de Grenoble, 1980.

Flinn, Caryl. *Strains of Utopia: Gender, Nostalgia and Hollywood Film Music*. Princeton, N.J.: Princeton University Press, 1992.

Freeland, Cynthia A., and Thomas E. Wartenberg, eds. *Philosophy and Film*. New York: Routledge, 1995.

Foucault, Michel. *The Order of Things: An Archaeology of the Human Sciences*. New York: Random House, 1970.

———. *The Archaeology of Knowledge*. Trans. A. M. Sheridan Smith. New York: Harper & Row, 1971.

———. *Discipline and Punish: The Birth of the Prison*. Trans. Alan Sheridan. New York: Random House, 1977.

———. *The History of Sexuality*, Vol. 1: *An Introduction*. Trans. Robert Hurley. New York: Random House, 1978.

Francastel, Pierre. *Art et technique*. Paris: Études de Sociologie de l'Art, 1970.

Fredericksen, Donald L. *The Aesthetic of Isolation in Film Theory: Hugo Münsterberg*. New York: Arno, 1977.

Freidburg, Anne. *Window Shopping: Cinema and the Postmodern*. Berkeley: University of California Press, 1993.

Freud, Sigmund. *Beyond the Pleasure Principle*. In Freud, *Standard Edition*, vol. 18.

———. *Civilization and Its Discontents*. In Freud, *Standard Edition*, vol. 21.

———. *The Ego and the Id*. In Freud, *Standard Edition,* vol. 19.

———. *Fetishism*. In Freud, *Standard Edition*, vol. 21.

———. *The Interpretation of Dreams*. In Freud, *Standard Edition*, vols. 4 and 5.

———. *The Standard Edition of the Complete Psychological Works of Sigmund Freud*. Ed. and trans. James Strachey. 24 vols. New York: Norton, 1976.

———. *Studies on Hysteria*. In Freud, *Standard Edition*, vol. 2.

———. *Three Essays on the Theory of Sexuality*. In Freud, *Standard Edition,* vol. 7.

———. *Totem and Taboo*. In Freud, *Standard Edition*, vol. 13.

Gaines, Jane, and Charlotte Herzog, eds. *Fabrications: Costume and the Female Body*. AFI Film Readers. New York: Routledge, 1990.

Gaudreault, André. "Detours in Film Narrative: Cross Cutting." *Cinema Journal* 19, no. 1 (Fall 1979): 39–59.

———. "Temporality and Narrativity in Early Cinema." In Holman, ed., *Cinema 1900–1906*, pp. 201–18.

———. "Narration et monstration au cinéma." *Hors cadre* 2 (April 1984): 87–98.

———, ed. *Ce que je vois de mon ciné: La représentation du regard dans le cinéma des premiers temps*. Paris: Méridiens Klincksieck, 1988.

———. *Du Littéraire au filmique: Système du récit*. Paris: Méridiens Klincksieck, 1988.

———. "Un spectacle monstratif à narration assistée," In Gaudrealt, *Du Littéraire au filmique*, pp. 159–70.

Gauthier, Guy. *Initiation à la sémiologie de l'image*. Paris: Cahiers de l'Audiovisuel, 1979.

———. *Vingt leçons sur l'image et le sens*. Paris: Edilig, 1982.

Geduld, Harry M., ed. *Filmmakers on Filmmaking*. Bloomington: Indiana University Press, 1967.

———, ed. *Authors on Film*. Bloomington: Indiana University Press, 1972.

Genette, Gérard. *Figures II*. Paris: Éditions du Seuil, 1969.

———. *Narrative Discourse: An Essay in Method*. Ithaca, N.Y.: Cornell University Press, 1980.

Gerstner, David A., and Janet Staiger, eds. *Authorship and Film*. New York: Routledge, 2003.

Gessner, Robert. *The Moving Image: A Guide to Cinematic Literacy*. New York: Dutton, 1970.

Geuns, Jean-Pierre. *Film Production Theory*. Albany: State University of New York Press, 2000.

Giannetti, Louis. *Understanding Movies*. 6th ed. Englewood Cliffs, N.J.: Prentice-Hall, 1993.

Gibson, Pamela Church, and Roma Gibson, eds. *Dirty Looks: Women, Pornography, Power*. Bloomington: Indiana University Press, 1993.

Gidal, Peter, ed. *Structural Film Anthology*. London: British Film Institute, 1976.

Gledhill, Christine. *Home Is Where the Heart Is*. London: British Film Institute, 1987.

———, ed. *Stardom: Industry of Desire*. London: Routledge, 1991.

Godard, Jean-Luc. *Godard on Godard*. Ed. Tom Milne. New York: Viking, 1972.

Gombrich, E. H. *Art and Illusion*. Princeton, N.J.: Princeton University Press, 1972.

Gorbman, Claudia. *Unheard Melodies: Narrative Film Music*. London: British Film Institute, 1987.

Grant, Barry Keith, ed. *Film Genre Reader*. Austin: University of Texas Press, 1986.

———, ed. *Film Genre Reader II*. Austin: University of Texas Press, 1995.

Grant, Barry Keith, and Jeannette Sloniowski, eds. *Documenting the Documentary: Close Readings of Documentary Film and Video*. Detroit: Wayne State University Press, 1998.

Green, Eileen, and Alison Adam, eds. *Virtual Gender: Technology, Consumption, and Identity*. London: Routledge, 2001.

Greenberg, Harvey Roy. *Screen Memories: Hollywood Cinema*

on the Psychoanalytic Couch. New York: Columbia University Press, 1993.

Griemas, Algirdas Julien, and Joseph Courtés. *Sémiotique: Dictionnaire raisonné de la théorie du langage.* Paris: Hachette, 1986.

Grierson, John. *Grierson on Documentary.* Ed. Forsyth Hardy. New York: Harcourt Brace, 1947.

Grindon, Leger. *Shadows on the Past: Studies in the Historical Fiction Film.* Philadelphia: Temple University Press, 1994.

Grodal, Torben. *Moving Pictures: A New Theory of Film Genres, Feelings, and Cognition.* Oxford: Clarendon, 1999.

Gross, Larry P. *Up from Invisibility: Lesbians, Gay Men, and the Media in America.* New York: Columbia University Press, 2002.

Guibbert, Pierre, ed. *Les Premiers Ans du cinéma français.* Perpignan, France: Institut Jean Vigo, 1985.

Gunning, Tom. "The Non-Continuous Style of Early Film 1900–1906." In Holman, ed., *Cinema 1900–1906,* pp. 219–30.

———. "An Unseen Energy Swallows Space: The Space in Early Film and Its Relation to American Avant-Garde Film." In Fell, ed., *Film before Griffith,* pp. 355–66.

———. "Non-Continuity, Continuity, Discontinuity: A Theory of Genres in Early Film." *Iris* 2, no. 1 (1984): 101–112.

———. "The Cinema of Attraction: Early Film, Its Spectator and the Avant-Garde." *Wide Angle* 8, nos. 3–4 (Fall 1986): 63–70.

———. "Vitagraph Film and the Cinema of Narrative Integration." In Cherchi Usai, ed., *Vitagraph Co. of America,* pp. 225–40.

———. "What I Saw from the Rear Window of the Hôtel des Folies-Dramatiques, or the Story Point of View Films Told." In Gaudreault, ed., *Ce que je vois de mon ciné,* pp. 33–44.

Hansen, Miriam. "Early Silent Cinema: Whose Public Sphere?" *New German Critique* 29 (Spring/Summer 1983): 147–84.

———. "Reinventing the Nickelodeon: Notes on Kluge and Early Cinema." *October* 46 (Fall 1988): 179–98.

———. "The Hieroglyph and the Whore: D. W. Griffith's *Intolerance.*" *South Atlantic Quarterly* 88, no. 2 (Spring 1989): 361–92.

———. *Babel and Babylon: Spectatorship in American Silent Film.* Cambridge, Mass.: Harvard University Press, 1991.

Harries, Dan, ed. *The New Media Book.* London: British Film Institute, 2002.

Harrington, John. *The Rhetoric of Film.* New York: Holt, Rinehart, & Winston, 1973.

Harvey, David. *The Condition of Postmodernity: An Enquiry into the Origins of Cultural Change.* Oxford: Blackwell, 1989.

Harvey, Sylvia. *May '68 and Film Culture.* BFI Series. New York: New York Zoetrope, 1980.

Haskell, Molly. *From Reverence to Rape: The Treatment of Women in the Movies.* Baltimore, Md.: Penguin, 1974.

Hauser, Arnold. *The Social History of Art,* Vol. 4: *Naturalism, Impressionism, the Film Age.* New York: Vintage, 1960.

Hayward, Susan. *Cinema Studies: The Key Concepts.* 2nd ed. London: Routledge, 2000.

Heath, Stephen. *Questions of Cinema.* Bloomington: Indiana University Press, 1981.

———. "Le Père Noël." *October* 26 (1983): 63–115.

Heath, Stephen, and Patricia Mellencamp, eds. *Cinema and Language.* Frederick, Md.: University Publications of America, 1983.

Henderson, Brian. *A Critique of Film Theory.* New York: Dutton, 1980.

Hill, John, and Pamela Church Gibson, eds. *The Oxford Guide to Film Studies.* Oxford, Eng.: Oxford University Press, 1998.

———, eds. *Film Studies: Critical Approaches.* Oxford, Eng.: Oxford University Press, 2000.

"Hitchcock/Bellour." Special issue of *Camera Obscura* 3–4 (1979).

Hjelmslev, Louis. *Prolegomena to a Theory of Language.* Trans. Francis J. Whitfield. Baltimore, Md.: Waverly, 1953.

———. *Essais linguistiques.* Copenhagen: Nordisk Sprog-og Kulturforlag, 1959.

Hjort, Mette, and Scott Mackenzie, eds. *Cinema and Nation.* London: Routledge, 2000.

Hollows, Joanne, and Mark Jancovich, eds. *Approaches to Popular Film.* Manchester, Eng.: Manchester University Press, 1995.

Holman, Roger, ed. *Cinema 1900–1906: An Analytical Study by the National Film Archive and the International Federation of Film Archives.* Brussels: Fédération Internationale des Archives du Film, 1982.

Holmlund, Chris. *Impossible Bodies: Femininity and Masculinity at the Movies.* London: Routledge, 2002.

Horton, Andrew S., ed. *Comedy/Cinema/Theory.* Berkeley: University of California Press, 1991.

Houston, Beverle, ed., "Feminist and Ideological Criticism." Special issue of *Quarterly Review of Film Studies,* 3, no. 4 (Fall 1978).

Houston, Beverle, and Marsha Kinder. *Self and Cinema.* Pleasantville, N.Y.: Redgrave, 1980.

Humm, Maggie. *Feminism and Film.* Bloomington: Indiana University Press, 1997.

Huss, Roy, and Norman Silverstein. *The Film Experience: Elements of Motion Picture Art.* New York: Delta, 1968.

"Interdisciplinary Approaches to Study." Special issue of *Quarterly Review of Film Studies* 1, no. 2 (Summer 1976).

"Interpretation, Inc.: Issues in Contemporary Film Studies." Special issue of *Film Criticism* 17, nos. 2–3 (1993).

Jackson, Earl, Jr. *Strategies of Deviance: Studies in Gay Male Representation*. Bloomington: Indiana University Press, 1995.

Jacobs, Lewis, ed. *Introduction to the Art of Movies*. New York: Farrar, Straus & Giroux, 1960.

———. *The Movies as Medium*. New York: Farrar, Straus & Giroux, 1970.

James, David, and Rick Berg, eds. *The Hidden Foundation: Cinema and the Question of Class*. Minneapolis: University of Minnesota Press, 1996.

Jameson, Fredric. *The Prison-House of Language: A Critical Account of Structuralism and Russian Formalism*. Princeton, N.J.: Princeton University Press, 1972.

———. *The Political Unconscious: Narrative as a Socially Symbolic Act*. Ithaca, NY: Cornell University Press, 1982.

———. *The Geopolitical Aesthetic: Cinema and Space in the World System*. Bloomington: Indiana University Press, 1992.

———. *The Cultural Turn: Selected Writings on the Postmodern, 1983–1998*. London: Verso, 1998.

Jampolski, Mikhail. " 'Totaler' Film und 'Montage' Film." *Kunst und Literatur* 5 (September–October 1983): 661–72.

———. "Les experiences de Kulechov et la nouvelle anthropologie de l'acteur." *Iris* 4, no. 1 (1986): 25–48.

———. *The Memory of Tiresias: Intertextuality and Film*. Trans. Harsha Ram. Berkeley: University of California Press, 1998.

Jancovich, Mark. "Cult Fictions: Cult Movies, Subcultural Capital, and the Production of Cultural Distinctions." *Cultural Studies* 16, no. 2 (2002): 306–22.

Jancovich, Mark; Lucy Faire; and Sarah Stubbings. *The Place of the Audience: Cultural Geographies of Film Consumption*. London: British Film Institute, 2003.

Jarvie, I. C. *Movies and Society*. New York: Basic, 1970.

Jenks, Chris, ed. *Visual Culture*. London: Routledge, 1995.

Joe, Jeongwon, and Rose Teresa, eds. *Between Opera and Cinema*. New York: Routledge, 2002.

Johnson, Lincoln. *Film: Space, Time, Light and Sound*. New York: Holt, Rinehart, & Winston, 1974.

Jost, François, and Dominique Chateau. *Nouveau cinéma, nouvelle sémiologie: Essai d'analyse des films d'Alain Robbe-Grillet*. Paris: Union Générale d'Éditions, 1979.

Jowett, Garth. *Film: The Democratic Art*. Boston: Little, Brown, 1976.

Jowett, Garth, and James M. Linton. *Movies as Mass Communication*. Beverly Hills, Calif.: Sage, 1980.

Kabir, Shameen. *Daughters of Desire: Lesbian Representations in Film*. London: Cassell, 1997.

Kael, Pauline. *I Lost It at the Movies*. Boston: Little, Brown, 1965.

Kalinak, Kathryn. *Settling the Score: Music and the Classic Hollywood Film*. Madison: University of Wisconsin Press, 1992.

Kaminsky, Stuart M. *American Film Genres: Approaches to a Critical Theory of Popular Film*. Dayton, Ohio: Pflaum, 1974.

Kaplan, E. Ann, ed. *Women in Film Noir*. BFI Series. New York: New York Zoetrope, 1980.

———. *Women and Film: Both Sides of the Camera*. New York: Methuen, 1983.

———, ed. *Psychoanalysis and Cinema*. New York: Routledge, 1990.

———. *Looking for the Other: Feminism, Film and the Imperial Gaze*. London: Routledge, 1997.

Kaufmann, Stanley, with B. Henstell. *American Film Criticism*. New York: Liveright, 1972.

Kawin, Bruce F. *Mindscreen: Bergman, Godard and First-Person Film*. Princeton, N.J.: Princeton University Press, 1978.

Kay, Karyn, and Gerald Peary. *Women and the Cinema*. New York: Dutton, 1977.

Kellner, Douglas. *Media Culture: Cultural Studies, Identity and Politics between the Modern and the Postmodern*. New York: Routledge, 1995.

Kerr, Paul. "Re-inventing the Cinema." *Screen* 21, no. 4 (1980–81): 80–84.

Kinder, Marsha, and Beverle Houston. *Close Up: A Critical Perspective on Film*. New York: Harcourt Brace Jovanovich, 1972.

King, Norman. "The Sound of Silents." *Screen* 25, no. 3 (May–June 1984): 2–15.

Kirihara, Donald. "A Reconsideration of the Institution of the Benshi." *Film Reader 6: Investigations in Film History and Technology* (1985): 41–53.

Kitses, Jim. *Horizons West*. Bloomington: Indiana University Press, 1970.

Kozloff, Sarah. *Overhearing Film Dialogue*. Berkeley: University of California Press, 2000.

Kracauer, Siegfried. *From Caligari to Hitler: A Psychological Study of the German Film*. Princeton, N.J.: Princeton University Press, 1947.

———. *Theory of Film: The Redemption of Physical Reality*. New York: Oxford University Press, 1960.

———. *The Mass Ornament: Weimar Essays*. Ed. and trans. Thomas Y. Levin. Cambridge, Mass: Harvard University Press, 1995.

Kress, Gunther, and Theo van Leeuwen. *Reading Images:*

The Grammar of Visual Design. London: Routledge, 1996.

Kuhn, Annette. "History of Narrative Codes." In Cook, ed., *The Cinema Book*, pp. 208–11.

———. *Women's Pictures: Feminism and Cinema.* 2nd ed. London: Verso, 1994.

Kuleshov, Lev. *Kuleshov on Film.* Ed. and trans. Ronald Levaco. Berkeley: University of California Press, 1975.

Kuntzel, Thierry. "The Film-Work." *Enclitic* 2, no. 1 (1973): 38–61.

———. "The Film-Work 2." *Camera Obscura* 5 (1980): 7–68.

Lacan, Jacques. *The Four Fundamental Concepts of Psychoanalysis.* Ed. Jacques-Alain Miller. Trans. Alan Sheridan. New York: Norton, 1976.

———. *Écrits: A Selection.* New York: Norton, 1977.

Landry, Marcia, ed. *Imitations of Life: A Reader on Film and Television Melodrama.* Detroit: Wayne State University Press, 1991.

Langdale, Allan, ed. *Hugo Münsterberg on Film. The Photoplay—a Psychological Study and Other Writings.* New York: Routledge, 2002.

Langer, Susanne K. *Feeling and Form.* New York: Scribner's, 1953.

Lant, Antonia. *Blackout: Reinventing Women for Wartime British Cinema.* Princeton, N.J.: Princeton University Press, 1991.

Lawder, Standish D. *The Cubist Cinema.* New York: New York University Press, 1975.

Lawson, John Howard. *Film: The Creative Process.* New York: Hill & Wang, 1964.

Lebeau, Vicky. *Psychoanalysis and Cinema: The Play of Shadows.* London: Wallflower, 2002.

Lebel, Jean-Patrick. *Cinéma et idéologie.* Paris: Éditions Sociales, 1971.

Lehman, Peter. *Masculinity: Bodies, Movies, Culture.* New York: Routledge, 2001.

Lemon, Lee T., and Marion J. Reis. *Russian Formalist Criticism: Four Essays.* Lincoln: University of Nebraska Press, 1965.

Lévi-Strauss, Claude. "Structural Analysis in Linguistics and in Anthropology." In Lévi-Strauss, *Structural Anthropology*, pp. 31–54.

———. *Structural Anthropology.* Trans. Claire Jacobson and Brooke Grundfest Schoeph. New York: Basic Books, 1963, 2000.

———. *The Raw and the Cooked.* Trans. John Weightman and Doreen Weightman. New York: Harper & Row, 1969.

———. *Structural Anthropology.* Vol. 2. Trans. Monique Layton. Chicago: University of Chicago Press, 1976.

Lindgren, Ernest. *The Art of the Film.* Rev. ed. London: Allen & Unwin, 1963.

Lindsay, Vachel. *The Art of the Moving Picture.* New York: Macmillan, 1915. Repr. New York: Liveright, 1970.

Lorentz, Pare. *Lorentz on Film.* New York: Harcourt Brace Jovanovich, 1975.

Lotman, Jurij. *Semiotics of the Cinema.* Trans. Mark E. Suino. Ann Arbor: University of Michigan Press, 1976.

Lovell, Terry. *Pictures of Reality: Aesthetics, Politics, Pleasure.* BFI Series. New York: New York Zoetrope, 1980.

Lyotard, Jean-François. *The Postmodern Condition: A Report on Knowledge.* Trans. Geoff Bennington and Brian Massumi. Minneapolis: University of Minnesota Press, 1984.

Macbean, James Roy. *Film and Revolution.* Bloomington: Indiana University Press, 1975.

MacCabe, Colin. *Tracking the Signifier: Theoretical Essays.* Minneapolis: University of Minnesota Press, 1985.

MacCann, Richard Dyer, ed. *Film: A Montage of Theories.* New York: Dutton, 1966.

MacCann, Richard Dyer, and Jack C. Ellis, eds. *Cinema Examined.* New York: Dutton, 1982.

McConnell, Frank. *Storytelling and Mythmaking: Images from Film and Literature.* New York: Oxford University Press, 1970.

MacDonald, Scott. *Avant-Garde Film: Motion Studies.* New York: Cambridge University Press, 1993.

———. *The Garden in the Machine: A Field Guide to Independent Films about Place.* Berkeley: University of California Press, 2001.

MacDougall, David. *Transcultural Cinema.* Ed. Lucien Taylor. Princeton, N.J.: Princeton University Press, 1998.

Manvell, Roger. *Film.* Harmondsworth, Eng.: Penguin, 1950.

———. *Shakespeare and the Film.* New York: Praeger, 1971.

Marinetti, Filippo T. *Selected Writings.* Trans. Arthur A. Coppotelli and R. W. Flint. New York: Noonday, 1972.

Martin, Marcel. *Le Langage cinématographique.* Paris: Cerf, 1955.

Martinet, André. *Elements of General Linguistics.* Trans. Elisabeth Palmer. London: Faber & Faber, 1960.

Mast, Gerald. *Film/Cinema/Movie: A Theory of Experience.* New York: Harper & Row, 1977.

———. *The Comic Mind: Comedy and the Movies.* 2nd ed. Chicago: Chicago University Press, 1979.

Mast, Gerald; Marshall Cohen; and Leo Braudy, eds. *Film Theory and Criticism.* 5th ed. New York: Oxford University Press, 1999.

Matthews, J. H. *Surrealism and Film.* Ann Arbor: University of Michigan Press, 1971.

Mayne, Judith. "Immigrants and Spectators." *Wide Angle* 5, no. 2 (1982): 32–41.

———. "Der primitive Erzähler." *Frauen und Film* 41 (1986): 4–16.

————. *The Woman at the Keyhole: Feminism and Women's Cinema.* Bloomington: Indiana University Press, 1990.

————. *Cinema and Spectatorship.* London: Routledge, 1993.

Mekas, Jonas. *Movie Journal: Rise of the New American Cinema: 1969–1971.* New York: Macmillan, 1972.

Mellen, Joan. *Women and Their Sexuality in the New Film.* New York: Horizon, 1974.

————. *Big Bad Wolves: Masculinity in American Films.* New York: Pantheon, 1978.

Mellencamp, Patricia. *Indiscretions: Avant-Garde Film, Video, and Feminism.* Bloomington: Indiana University Press, 1990.

————. *A Fine Romance: Five Ages of Film Feminism.* Philadelphia: Temple University Press, 1995.

Merleau-Ponty, Maurice. "The Film and the New Psychology." In Merleau-Ponty, *Sense and Non-sense*, 48–59.

————. *Sense and Non-Sense.* Trans. Hubert L. Dreyfus and Patricia Allen Dreyfus. Evanston, Ill.: Northwestern University Press, 1964.

Messaris, Paul. *Visual Literacy: Image, Mind, and Reality.* Boulder, Col.: Westview 1994.

Metz, Christian. *Film Language: A Semiotics of the Cinema.* Trans. Michael Taylor. New York: Oxford University Press, 1974.

————. *Language and Cinema.* Trans. Donna Jean Umiker-Sebeok. The Hague: Mouton, 1974.

————. *The Imaginary Signifier: Psychoanalysis and the Cinema.* Trans. Celia Britton et al. Bloomington: Indiana University Press, 1982.

Meyerhold, Vsevelod. *Meyerhold on Theater.* Ed. and trans. Edward Braun. London: Methuen, 1969.

Miller, Toby. *The Well-Tempered Self: Citizenship, Culture, and the Postmodern Subject.* Baltimore: Johns Hopkins University Press, 1993.

————. *Technologies of Truth: Cultural Citizenship and the Popular Media.* Minneapolis: University of Minnesota, 1998.

Miller, Toby, and Robert Stam, eds. *Film Theory: A Companion.* Oxford: Blackwell, 1999.

Mirzoeff, Nicholas, ed. *Visual Culture Reader.* London: Routledge, 1998.

Mitry, Jean. *Esthétique et psychologie du cinéma.* 2 vols. Paris: Éditions Universitaires, 1963–65.

————. *Semiotics and the Analysis of Film.* Trans. Christopher King. Bloomington: Indiana University Press, 2000.

Modleski, Tania. *Loving with a Vengeance: Mass-Produced Fantasies for Women.* London: Methuen, 1984.

————. *Studies in Entertainment: Critical Approaches to Mass Culture.* Bloomington: Indiana University Press, 1986.

————. *Feminism without Women: Culture and Criticism in a "Postfeminist" Age.* New York: Routledge, 1991.

Moholy-Nagy, László. *Vision in Motion.* Chicago: Theobald, 1947.

Monaco, James. *How to Read a Film: The Art, Technology, Language, History and Theory of Film and Media.* Rev. ed. New York: Oxford University Press, 1981.

Montagu, Ivor. *Film World.* Baltimore, Md.: Penguin, 1964.

Morin, Edgar. *Le Cinéma; ou, L'homme imaginaire: Essai d'anthropologie sociologique.* Paris: Minuit, 1956.

————. *The Stars.* Trans. Richard Howard. New York: Grove, 1960.

Morse, Margaret. *Virtualities: Television, Media Art and Cyber-Cultures.* Bloomington: Indiana University Press, 1998.

Mulvey, Laura. "Visual Pleasure and Narrative Cinema." *Screen* 16 (Autumn 1975): 6–18. Repr. in Mast, Cohen, and Braudy, eds., *Film Theory and Criticism*, pp. 746–57.

————. *Visual and Other Pleasures.* Bloomington: Indiana University Press, 1989.

Münsterberg, Hugo. *The Photoplay: A Psychological Study.* New York: Appleton, 1916. Repr. as *The Film: A Psychological Study.* New York: Dover, 1970.

Murray, Janet H. *Hamlet on the Holodeck: The Future of Narrative in Cyberspace.* Cambridge, Mass.: MIT Press, 1997.

Naficy, Hamid, ed. *Home, Exile, Homeland: Film, Media, and the Politics of Place.* New York: Routledge, 1998.

Naremore, James. *Acting in the Cinema.* Berkeley: University of California Press, 1988.

Naremore, James, and Patrick Brantlinger, eds. *Modernity and Mass Culture.* Bloomington: Indiana University Press, 1991.

Neale, Steve. *Genre.* London: British Film Institute, 1980.

————. *Cinema and Technology: Image, Sound, Color.* Bloomington: Indiana University Press, 1985.

Neupert, Richard. *The End: Narration and Closure in the Cinema.* Detroit: Wayne State University Press, 1995.

"The New Auteurism." Special issue of *Film Criticism* 19, no. 3 (1995).

Newcomb, Horace, ed. *Television: The Critical View.* 3rd ed. New York: Oxford University Press, 1982.

"New Masculinities." Special issue of *Velvet Light Trap* 38 (Fall 1996).

Nichols, Bill, ed. *Movies and Methods.* 2 vols. Berkeley: University of California Press, 1977, 1985.

————. *Ideology and Image.* Bloomington: Indiana University Press, 1981.

————. "Global Image Consumption in the Age of Late Capitalism." *East-West Film Journal* 8, no. 1 (January 1994): 68–85.

Nicoll, Allardyce. *Film and Theatre.* New York: Crowell, 1937.

Nilsen, Vladimir. *Cinema as Graphic Art.* New York: Hill & Wang, 1973.

Olson, Elder. *The Theory of Comedy*. Bloomington: Indiana University Press, 1968.

Orr, John, and Olga Taxidou, eds. *Post-War Cinema and Modernity: A Film Reader*. New York: New York University Press, 2001.

Paech, Joachim. *Literatur und Film*. Stuttgart: Metzler, 1988.

Panofsky, Erwin. *Studies in Iconology*. Oxford: Oxford University Press, 1939.

Peirce, Charles Sanders. *Collected Papers*. Ed. Charles Hartshorne and Paul Weiss. 8 vols. Cambridge, Mass.: Harvard University Press, 1931–58.

Penley, Constance. *Feminism and Film Theory*. New York: Routledge, 1988.

Penley, Constance, and Andrew Ross, eds. *Technoculture*. Minneapolis: University of Minnesota Press, 1991.

Penley, Constance, and Sharon Willis, eds. *Male Trouble*. Minneapolis: University of Minnesota Press, 1993.

Penz, François, and Maureen Thomas, eds. *Cinema and Architecture: Méliès, Mallet-Stevens, Multimedia*. London: British Film Institute, 1997.

Petro, Patrice, ed. *Fugitive Images: From Photography to Video*. Bloomington: Indiana University Press, 1995.

———. *Aftershocks of New: Feminism and Film History*. New Brunswick, N.J.: Rutgers University Press, 2002.

Perkins, V. F. *Film as Film: Understanding and Judging Movies*. New York: Penguin, 1972.

"Philosophy and Film." Special issue of *Journal of Value Inquiry* 29, no. 4 (1995).

"Philosophy of Film History, The." Special issue of *Film History* 6, no. 1 (1994).

Pietropaolo, Laura, and Ada Testaferri, eds. *Feminisms in the Cinema*. Bloomington: Indiana University Press, 1995.

Pilling, Jayne, ed. *A Reader in Animation Studies*. London: Libbey, 1997.

Polan, Dana. *The Political Language of Film and the Avant-Garde*. Ann Arbor, Mich.: UMI Research Press, 1985.

———. *Power and Paranoia: History, Narrative and the American Cinema*. New York: Columbia University Press, 1986.

"Pour une théorie de l'histoire du cinéma." Special issue of *Iris* 2, no. 2 (1984).

Prendergast, Roy M. *Film Music: A Neglected Art*. New York: Norton, 1977.

Prince, Stephen. "The Discourse of Pictures: Iconicity and Film Studies." *Film Quarterly* 47, no. 1 (Fall 1993): 16–28.

"Psychoanalysis and Cinema." Special issue of *Journal of Popular Film and Television* 18, no. 1 (1990).

"Psychoanalysis and Film." Special issue of *Journal of Film and Video* 46, no. 2 (1994).

Pudovkin, V. F. *Film Technique and Film Acting*. Trans. Ivor Montagu. London: Gollancz, 1929. Repr. New York: Grove, 1970.

Rabaté, Jean-Michel, ed. *Writing the Image after Roland Barthes*. Philadelphia: University of Pennsylvania Press, 1997.

Ray, Robert B. *How a Film Theory Got Lost and Other Mysteries in Cultural Studies*. Bloomington: Indiana University Press, 2001.

Real, Michael R. *Exploring Media Culture: A Guide*. Thousand Oaks, Calif.: Sage, 1996.

Reiser, Martin, and Andrea Zapp, eds. *New Screen Media: Cinema/Art/Narrative*. London: British Film Institute, 2002.

Renan, Sheldon. *An Introduction to the American Underground Film*. New York: Dutton, 1967.

Renov, Michael. *Theorizing Documentary*. New York: Routledge, 1993.

Rhodie, Sam. *Promised Lands: Cinema, Geography, Modernism*. London: British Film Institute, 2001.

Richter, Hans. "The Film as an Original Art Form." *Film Culture* 1, no. 1 (January 1955).

Robertson, Pamela. *Guilty Pleasures: Feminist Camp from Mae West to Madonna*. Durham, N.C.: Duke University Press, 1996.

Rodowick, D. N. *The Difficulty of Difference: Psychoanalysis, Sexual Difference and Film Theory*. New York: Routledge, 1991.

Romney, Jonathan, and Adrian Wootton. *Celluloid Jukebox: Popular Music and the Movies since the 50s*. London: British Film Institute, 1995.

Rosen, Philip, ed. *Narrative, Apparatus, Ideology: A Film Theory Reader*. New York: Columbia University Press, 1986.

Rosenbaum, Jonathan. *Movies as Politics*. Berkeley: University of California Press, 1997.

Rosenblum, Ralph, and Robert Karen. *When the Shooting Stops . . . the Cutting Begins*. New York: Viking, 1979.

Rosenstone, Robert A., ed. *Revisioning History: Film and the Construction of a New Past*. Princeton, N.J.: Princeton University Press, 1995.

———. *Visions of the Past: The Challenge of Film to Our Idea of History*. Cambridge, Mass.: Harvard University Press, 1995.

Rotha, Payl; Road Sinclair; and Richard Griffith. *Documentary Film*. London: Faber & Faber, 1966.

Rothman, William. *Hitchcock: The Murderous Gaze*. Cambridge, Mass.: Harvard University Press, 1982.

Rowe, Kathleen. *The Unruly Woman: Gender and Genres of Laughter*. Austin: University of Texas Press, 1995.

Rushing, Janice Hocker, and Thomas S. Frentz. *Projecting the*

Shadow: The Cyborg Hero in American Film. Chicago: University of Chicago Press, 1995.

Russo, Vito. *The Celluloid Closet: Homosexuality in the Movies*. New York: Harper & Row, 1981.

Said, Edward. *Orientalism*. New York: Vintage, 1979.

Salt, Barry. "The Space Next Door." In Guibbert, ed., *Les Premiers Ans du cinéma français*, pp. 198–203.

Sarris, Andrew. *The American Cinema: Directors and Directions 1929–1968*. New York: Dutton, 1969.

———. "Notes on the *Auteur* Theory in 1970." *Film Comment* 6, no. 3 (Fall 1970): 6–9.

———. "Film Criticism in the Seventies." *Film Comment* 14, no. 1 (January 1978): 9–11.

———. "Notes on the *Auteur* Theory in 1962." In Mast, Cohen, and Braudy, eds., *Film Theory and Criticism*, pp. 585–88.

Saussure, Ferdinand de. *Course in General Linguistics*. Trans. Wade Baskin. New York: McGraw-Hill, 1966.

Schatz, Thomas. *Hollywood Genres: Formulas, Filmmaking, and the Studio System*. New York: Random House, 1981.

Sconce, Jeffrey. " 'Trashing' the Academy: Taste, Excess, and Emerging Politics of Cinematic Style." *Screen* 36, no. 4 (Winter 1995): 371–93.

Seldes, Gilbert. *The Great Audience*. New York: Viking, 1950.

"Sex and Sexuality." Special issue of *Journal of Popular Film and Television* 22, no. 4 (1995).

Shaviro, Steven. *The Cinematic Body*. Minneapolis: University of Minnesota Press, 1993.

Shklovsky, Victor. "Poetry and Prose in Cinema." In Eikhenbaum, ed., *The Poetics of Cinema*.

Shohat, Ella. *Talking Visions: Multicultural Feminism in a Transnational Age*. Cambridge, Mass.: MIT Press, 1999.

Silverman, Kaja. *The Subject of Semiotics*. New York: Oxford University Press, 1983.

———. *The Acoustic Mirror: The Female Voice in Psychoanalysis and Cinema*. Bloomington: Indiana University Press, 1988.

———. *Male Subjectivity at the Margins*. New York: Routledge, 1992.

———. *The Threshold of the Visible World*. New York: Routledge, 1995.

Sitney, P. Adams. *The Film Culture Reader*. New York: Praeger, 1970.

———. *The Essential Cinema*. New York: New York University Press, 1975.

———, ed. *The Avant-Garde Film: A Reader of Theory and Criticism*. New York: New York University Press, 1978.

———. *Visionary Film: The American Avant-Garde*. Rev. ed. New York: Oxford University Press, 1979.

Sklar, Robert. *Movie-Made America: A Cultural History of the American Movies*. Rev. upd. ed. New York: Vintage, 1994.

Smelik, Anneke. *And the Mirror Cracked: Feminist Cinema and Film Theory*. Basingtoke, Eng.: Palgrave, 2001.

Smith, Murray. *Engaging Characters: Fiction, Emotion, and the Cinema*. Oxford: Clarendon, 1995.

Solanas, Fernando, and Octavio Getino. "Towards a Third Cinema." *Cineaste* 4, no. 3 (1970): 1–10.

Sontag, Susan. *Against Interpretation*. New York: Farrar, Straus & Giroux, 1966.

———. *Styles of Radical Will*. New York: Farrar, Straus & Giroux, 1966.

———. *On Photography*. New York: Farrar, Straus & Giroux, 1977.

Sopocy, Martin. "The Theatrical Frame." In Guibbert, ed., *Les Premiers Ans du cinéma français*, pp. 190–97.

Spottiswoode, Raymond. *A Grammar of the Film*. Berkeley: University of California Press, 1950.

———. *Film and Its Techniques*. Berkeley: University of California Press, 1951, 1965.

Stacey, Jackie. *Star Gazing: Hollywood Cinema and Female Spectatorship*. London: Routledge, 1994.

Staiger, Janet. "Seeing Stars." *Velvet Light Trap* 20 (1983): 10–14.

———. "The Eyes Are Really the Focus: Photoplay Acting and Film Form and Style." *Wide Angle* 6, no. 4 (1985): 14–23.

———. *Interpreting Films: Studies in the Historical Reception of American Cinema*. Princeton, N.J.: Princeton University Press, 1992.

Stam, Robert. *Subversive Pleasures: Bakhtin, Cultural Criticism, and Film*. Baltimore: Johns Hopkins University Press, 1989.

Stam, Robert; Robert Burgoyne; and Sandy Flitterman-Lewis. *New Vocabularies in Film Semiotics, Structuralism, Post-Structuralism and Beyond*. London: Routledge, 1992.

Stam, Robert, and Toby Miller, eds. *Film and Theory: An Anthology*. Oxford: Blackwell, 2000.

Stephenson, Ralph, *The Animated Film*. Cranbury, N.J.: Barnes, 1973.

Stephenson, Ralph, and J. R. Debrix. *The Cinema as Art*. New York: Penguin, 1965.

Stewart, Garrett. *Between Film and Screen: Modernism's Photo Synthesis*. Chicago: University of Chicago Press, 1999.

Stokes, Melvyn, and Richard Maltby, eds. *Identifying Hollywood's Audiences: Cultural Identity and the Movies*. London: British Film Institute, 1999.

———, eds. *Hollywood Spectatorship: Changing Perceptions of Cinema Audiences*. London: British Film Institute, 2001.

Stoneman, Ron. "Perspective Correction: Early Film to the Avant-Garde." *Afterimage* 8–9 (Spring 1981): 50–63.

Storey, John, ed. *What Is Cultural Studies?: A Reader*. London: Arnold, 1996.

Straayer, Chris. *Deviant Eyes, Deviant Bodies: Sexual Re-Orientations in Film and Video*. New York: Columbia University Press, 1996.

Street, Sarah. *Costume and Cinema: Dress Codes in Popular Film*. London: Wallflower, 2002.

Studlar, Gaylyn. "Masochism and the Perverse Pleasures of Cinema." *Quarterly Review of Film Studies* 9, no. 4 (1985): 5–26.

———. *In the Realm of Pleasure: Von Sternberg, Deitrich, and the Masochistic Aesthetic*. Urbana: University of Illinois Press, 1988.

———. *This Mad Masquerade: Stardom and Masculinity in the Jazz Age*. New York: Columbia University Press, 1996.

"Style in Cinema." Special issue of *Style* 32, no. 3 (1998).

Talbot, Daniel, ed. *Film: An Anthology*. Berkeley: University of California Press, 1967.

Tan, Ed S. *Emotion and the Structure of Narrative Film: Film as an Emotion Machine*. Mahwah, N.J.: Erlbaum, 1996.

Tarkovsky, Andrei. *Sculpting in Time: Reflections on the Cinema*. Trans. Kitty Hunter-Blair. New York: Knopf, 1987.

Tasker, Yvonne. *Spectacular Bodies: Gender, Genre, and the Action Cinema*. New York: Routledge, 1993.

Taylor, Clyde. *The Mask of Art: Breaking the Aesthetic Contract in Film and Literature*. Bloomington: Indiana University Press, 1998.

Taylor, John Russell. *Cinema Eye, Cinema Ear*. New York: Hill & Wang, 1964.

Thompson, Kristin. *Eisenstein's "Ivan the Terrible": A Neoformalist Analysis*. Princeton, N.J.: Princeton University Press, 1987.

———. *Breaking the Glass Armor: Neoformalist Film Analysis*. Princeton, N.J.: Princeton University Press, 1988.

Thomson, David. *Movie Man*. New York: Stein & Day, 1967.

Thornham, Sue, ed. *Feminist Film Theory: A Reader*. New York: New York University Press, 1999.

Thornham, Sue, and Paul Morris, eds. *Media Studies: A Reader*. 2nd ed. New York: New York University Press, 2000.

Tinkom, Matthew. *Working Like a Homosexual: Camp, Capital, and Cinema*. Durham, N.C.: Duke University Press, 2002.

Tinkom, Matthew, and Amy Villarejo, eds. *Keyframes: Popular Cinema and Cultural Studies*. London: Routledge, 2002.

Todd, Janet, ed. *Women and Film*. New York: Holmes & Meier, 1988.

Todorov, Tsvetan. *The Poetics of Prose*. Trans. Richard Howard. Ithaca, N.Y.: Cornell University Press, 1977.

Tsivian, Yuri. "Notes historiques en marge de l'expérience de Koulechov." *Iris* 4, no. 1 (1986): 49–59.

Tudor, Andrew. *Theories of Film*. New York: Viking, 1973.

Turim, Maureen. "Designs of Motion: A Correlation between Early Serial Photography and the Avant-Garde." *Enclitic* 7, no. 2 (Fall 1983): 44–54.

Tyler, Parker. *Hollywood Hallucination*. New York: Simon & Schuster, 1944, 1970.

———. *Magic and Myth in the Movies*. New York: Holt, 1947. Repr. New York: Grove, 1970.

———. *The Three Faces of the Film*. New York: Yoseloff, 1960.

———. *Underground Film*. New York: Grove, 1969.

———. *Sex, Psyche, etcetera in the Film*. New York: Penguin, 1971.

———. *The Shadow of an Airplane Climbs the Empire State Building: A World Theory of Film*. Garden City, N.Y.: Doubleday, 1973.

Vertov, Dziga. *Kino-Eye: The Writings of Dziga Vertov*. Trans. Kevin O'Brien, Berkeley: University of California Press, 1984.

Vescio, Bryan. "Reading in the Dark: Cognitivism, Film Theory, and Radical Interpretation." *Style* 35, no. 4 (Winter 2001): 572–91.

Vogel, Amos. *Film as a Subversive Art*. New York: Random House, 1974.

Walker, Janet. *Couching Resistance: Women, Film, and Psychoanalytic Psychiatry*. Minneapolis: University of Minnesota Press, 1993.

Walsh, Martin. *The Brechtian Aspect of Radical Cinema*. London: British Film Institute, 1981.

Warshow, Robert. *The Immediate Experience*. Garden City, N.Y.: Doubleday, 1962. Repr. Cambridge, Mass.: Harvard University Press, 2002.

Waugh, Thomas. *Hard to Imagine: Gay Male Eroticism in Photography and Film from Their Beginnings to Stonewall*. New York: Columbia University Press, 1996.

Wees, William C. *Light Moving in Time: Studies in Visual Aesthetics of Avant-Garde Film*. Berkeley: University of California Press, 1991.

Weis, Elizabeth, and John Belton, eds. *Film Sound: Theory and Practice*. New York: Columbia University Press, 1985.

Wells, Paul. *Animation: Genre and Authorship*. London: Wallflower, 2002.

Wexman, Virginia Wright, ed. *Film and Authorship*. New Brunswick, N.J.: Rutgers University Press, 2003.

Willemen, Paul. *Looks and Frictions: Essays in Cultural Studies and Film Theory*. Bloomington: Indiana University Press, 1994.

Williams, Alan, ed. *Film and Nationalism*. New Brunswick, N.J.: Rutgers University Press, 2002.

Williams, Christopher, ed. *Realism and the Cinema: A Reader*. London: Routledge & Kegan Paul, 1980.

Williams, Linda. *Figures of Desire: A Theory and Analysis of Surrealist Film*. Urbana: University of Illinois Press, 1981.

————. "Film Body: An Implantation of Perversions." *Cinétracts* 12 (Winter 1981): 19–35.

————. *Hard Core: Power, Pleasure, and the "Frenzy of the Visible."* Berkeley: University of California Press, 1989.

————, ed. *Viewing Positions: Ways of Seeing Film*. New Brunswick, N.J.: Rutgers University Press, 1994.

Wilson, George. *Narration in Light: Studies in Cinematic Point of View*. Baltimore: Johns Hopkins University Press, 1986.

Wilson, Rob, and Wimal Dissanayake, eds. *Global/Local: Cultural Production and the Transnational Imaginary*. Durham, N.C.: Duke University Press, 1996.

Wilton, Tamsin, ed. *Immortal Invisible: Lesbians and the Moving Image*. London: Routledge, 1995.

Wolfenstein, Martha, and Nathan Leites. *Movies, a Psychological Study*. Glencoe, Ill.: Free Press, 1950.

Wollen, Peter. *Signs and Meaning in the Cinema*. 2nd ed. New York: Viking, 1972.

Wollenberg, H. H. *Anatomy of Film*. London: Marsland, 1947.

Wood, Michael. *America at the Movies*. 2nd ed. New York: Columbia University Press, 1990.

Wood, Robin. *Personal Views*. London: Gordon Fraser, 1976.

————. *Hollywood from Vietnam to Reagan*. New York: Columbia University Press, 1986.

Wyborny, Klaus. "Random Notes on the Conventional Narrative Film." *Afterimage* 8–9 (Spring 1981): 112–32.

Yearwood, Gladstone. *Black Film as a Signifying Practice: Cinema, Narration and the African American Aesthetic Tradition*. Trenton, N.J.: Africa World Press, 2000.

Young, Lola. *Fear of the Dark: "Race," Gender, and Sexuality in the Cinema*. London: Routledge, 1996.

Young, Vernon. *On Film*. New York: Quadrangle, 1973.

Youngblood, Gene. *Expanded Cinema*. New York: Dutton, 1970.

Zizek, Slavoj. *Looking Awry: An Introduction to Jacques Lacan through Popular Culture*. Cambridge, Mass.: MIT Press, 1991.

————, ed. *Everything You Always Wanted to Know about Lacan But Were Afraid to Ask Hitchcock*. London: Verso, 1992.

————. *Enjoy Your Symptom!: Jacques Lacan in Hollywood and Out*. New York: Routledge, 1993.

————, ed. *Cogito and the Unconscious*. Durham, N.C.: Duke University Press, 1998.

————. *The Fright of Real Tears: Krzysztof Kieślowski between Theory and Post-Theory*. London: British Film Institute, 2001.

Index